ST. JAMES GUIDE TO

YOUNG ADULT
Writers

St. James Guide to Writers Series
(formerly Twentieth-Century Writers Series)

St. James Guide to Children's Writers
St. James Guide to Crime & Mystery Writers
St. James Guide to Fantasy Writers
St. James Guide to Horror, Ghost & Gothic Writers
St. James Guide to Science Fiction Writers
St. James Guide to Young Adult Writers

Twentieth-Century Romance & Historical Writers
Twentieth-Century Western Writers

ST. JAMES GUIDE TO

YOUNG ADULT
Writers

SECOND EDITION

WITH A PREFACE BY
RICHARD PECK

EDITORS
TOM PENDERGAST
&
SARA PENDERGAST

ST. JAMES PRESS

AN IMPRINT OF GALE

DETROIT • LONDON

Tom Pendergast & Sara Pendergast, *Editors*

Laura Standley Berger and David Collins, *Project Coordinators*

Joann Cerrito, Nicolet V. Elert, Miranda Ferrara,
Kristin Hart, Margaret Mazurkiewicz, Michael J. Tyrkus,
St. James Press Staff

Peter M. Gareffa, *Managing Editor, St. James Press*

Mary Beth Trimper, *Production Director*
Deborah Milliken, *Production Assistant*

Cynthia Baldwin, *Product Design Manager*
Pamela Galbreath, *MacIntosh Artist*

The paper used in this publication meets the minimum
requirements of American National Standard for Information Sciences—
Permanence Paper for Printed Library Materials, ANSI Z39.48-1984.

This book is printed on recycled paper that meets Environmental Protection Agency Standards.

ISBN 1-55862-368-x

Printed in the United States of America
Published simultaneously in the United Kingdom

St. James Press is an imprint of Gale

10 9 8 7 6 5 4 3 2 1

CONTENTS

PREFACE

Young Adult Books: Writing for People We Never Were

by Richard Peck

Because my favorite readers are young, I write with my feet. Here at the desk I'm growing older every minute; out there, young readers remain the same age, and the gulf widens. Thanks to thriving Author-in-the-School programs I travel sixty thousand miles every year for author programs in libraries and the occasional bookstore and for school visits arranged by teachers and school librarians. I go to schools and libraries to tell young readers about the books I've written because they don't read reviews. I go, too, to learn what my next book will be about. Being young now is nothing I ever experienced. I can't imagine what it would be like to grow up without two parents; I needed both of mine. I can't imagine attending a school where the chief authority figure is another child. And if I'd been allowed out on a school night as early as the age of sixteen, I don't want to know where I might have gone. We don't write what we know. We write what we can find out. And we don't write about what happened to us. We write for people we never were. A book for teen and pre-teen readers had better never be the autobiography of the author; it had far better be the biography of the person the reader would like to be.

All fiction is based on research, on taking notes and taking note. A new book of mine was inspired by a school librarian's invitation. It was a rural consolidated school, and I looked forward to the visit as I see very few farm kids. Most of my invitations come from large public school systems in sprawling suburbs. Standing out in open country, the school looked promising. All the students came by bus, and I was watching from the library window when they arrived. Off the bus tumbled every urban problem I'd ever seen. These couldn't be farm kids. I asked the librarian who they were.

She said they were children sent by their parents or the welfare establishment to live with extended family, mostly grandparents.

"How many?" I asked as the buses kept drawing up.

"Eighty percent of the school," she said. "But for them, we'd be closed now."

Here was evidence of a vast internal migration in this country as the children of misfiring parents--the youth generation of the 1970s--are now looking for new homes. But just as I stumble upon this blinding revelation, I learn there's a website on the subject, and a national magazine called *Grandparenting*.

Finally, I had to write a novel about this phenomenon sweeping the generation of my readers, and their schools. The novel is *Strays Like Us,* about a girl brought by a case worker to her great-aunt, a childless, elderly woman with problems of her own. It's the story too of the boy next door, come to live with his grandparents because the parents of both these seventh-graders have been consumed by two of the catastrophes stalking this decade. It didn't happen to me, this novel, and I couldn't have imagined it.

I write in awe of what being young is today, of the choices I never had to make. One of the choices now is whether or not to be literate. Now that literacy has become a school elective, we find we don't write for YAs. We write for PLs--the pubescent literate. There is a literature for them now that recognizes them, offering companionship and alternatives, a literature far harder for them to deny than the adult readings of the traditional curriculum. Robert Cormier's *The Chocolate War,* for example, retells William Golding's *The Lord of the Flies.* Golding's novel is too easy; it's about little British schoolboys on a distant, mythic island. *The Chocolate War* is set in the school the young reader is presently attending.

The Chocolate War is the pivotal book in all Young Adult fiction for its portrayal of the peer group leader the young set up over themselves when adult authority, at home and school, fails them. All novels are about private life, and our novels explore a generation of young people in all classes of society who are creating a mysteriously self-referential world increasingly remote from even the nearest adult. Adolescence is no longer the preparation for adulthood it once was, and now there are books to raise questions about the present and the future in the minds of the most thoughtful young.

It's a revolutionary literature born in the revolutionary late 1960s. Our beginnings are generally traced to two books, each pointing in a direction we were to take. S. E. Hinton's *The Outsiders* is about a gang as surrogate family. Because it portrays a caring family freed of parents, the world of young readers made it an enduring bestseller. The other is Judy Blume's *Are You There, God? It's Me, Margaret,* arguably the first successful attempt in human history to give honest aid and comfort to girls embarking upon the physical and emotional ordeal of puberty. A generation later Judy Blume still takes heat from book-burning mothers because she is making contact with their daughters just as they are losing it.

These two novels--one treating puberty, the other adolescence, one about girls, the other about boys--alerted publishers to a vast and untapped generation of readers for whom coming of age could no longer be trivialized. They were soon followed by Paul Zindel's *The Pigman,* a quiet story about a girl, a boy, and an old man, that asks some necessary questions about personal responsibility, questions parents ought to have asked.

In 1975 *The Chocolate War* went through three paperback printings, and we were off and running. The end of that decade saw Chris Crutcher's first novel, *Running Loose.* It's about a high school football player whose senior-year epiphany is that he's being packaged like meat for the political convenience of a racist, power-drunk coach. It followed Robin Brancato's *Winning,* a story about a boy who must enter manhood flat on his back, paralyzed for life by a football injury. Any body of books that questions the power of the coaching staff and the premature stardom of the jock is a literature of serious intent, meant to give voices to young people who dare not question the power elites ruling their own lives.

YA novels receive an exaggerated press for the serious, even grim issues some explore. To many people--many teachers-- who have never read them, all YA books are journalistic treatments of contemporary sociology, designed to exploit and titillate. But in fact our books approach the young from every direction fiction takes: science fiction and fantasy and time travel, from Madeleine L'Engle's *A Swiftly Tilting Planet* to William Sleator's *House of Stairs* and the legendry of Rosemary Sutcliff and Jane Yolen. There's historical fiction, from Avi's *The True Confessions of Charlotte Doyle* to Graham Salisbury's *Under the Blood-Red Sun.* There is the suspense of Joan Lowery Nixon and Lois Duncan and John Rowe Townsend, not to omit Annette Curtis Klause's vampires. We have comedy. We have tragedy. Like conscientious, hard-pressed teachers, we circle the young, hoping to win them to reading. And like the teachers of the modern age, our lesson plans must entertain first before they can do anything else.

What passes largely unremarked is that our novels, like most novels, are family stories, or the search for family. The central quest of American adolescence is the impossible dream of replacing your family with your friends, and now the search for the elusive parent as we address the children of our first readers.

Newbery-winner Sharon Creech's *Walk Two Moons* follows a girl's search for a missing mother. Even issue-driven novels are told in the context of family. M.E. Kerr's brilliant *Night Kites* is about the effect of AIDS upon a loving suburban family that does not believe that bad things happen to good people. The beautifully crafted novels of Sue Ellen Bridgers, Pam Conrad, and Rita Williams-Garcia lyrically celebrate family and provide elders and grandparents too often missing in the readers' own suburban settings.

Now in the second generation of YA books, a signal fact of life is the rise of censorship. Are we asking for trouble with such a book as Jacqueline Woodson's *I Hadn't Meant to Tell You,* on the taboo topic of incest? In fact none of our subjects is safe now from the attack of increasingly well-funded and organized groups--and from the parent acting all alone who can often bring a school to its knees.

Lowry's dystopian *The Giver* is a big target now, largely because it is widely assigned in the classroom. But so is Katherine Paterson's Newbery winner, *Bridge to Terabithia,* because the young character in the story copes with personal grief without the consolation of being a Christian. No topic is safe from censors looking for scapegoats for their own failures as parents or from groups programmed to take political control of school boards.

What are these books that have generated so much heat and light? For all their variety, each is the story of a step--one step a young character takes nearer maturity, and usually all alone because nobody ever grows up in a group. We dare never leave our characters on the last page where we found them on the first.

They are all the biographies of survivors, now that coming of age is creating so many casualties. And these books have to be far better crafted than adult novels. We don't allow ourselves five-hundred pages, and we can't resort to pornography to mask weak writing or to keep the pacing peppy. Some of the best fiction of the last quarter century is in our pages, none better conceived than Will Hobbs's *Downriver*. It's a story narrated by a self-delusive girl sent to a camp for the fashionably disturbed teenaged children of wealthy families. There, a group of them who call themselves "hoods in the woods" run away to shoot the Grand Canyon rapids of the Colorado River without a map, a permit, or an adult. Their journey downriver becomes adolescence itself, and they fall immediately under the authority of their least stable member.

The Young Adult novel reaches readers in late childhood and the early teens, just the age at which we have lost most people to reading, even in far better days than these. It's an inescapably American form. After all, the first real American novel was about an at-risk, attention-deficit-disordered, sociologically-challenged boy who is no longer quite a child if he ever was one. He's a boy whose single parent is a homeless substance abuser. He's a boy named Huckleberry Finn.

EDITOR'S NOTE

The *St. James Guide to Young Adult Writers* is a new edition of *Twentieth-Century Young Adult Writers*. The book continues to be a comprehensive source of information on the authors read and enjoyed by young adults, providing biographical, bibliographical, and critical information on almost 500 authors of fiction, poetry, and drama for young adults published in the English language. Authors whose works have been published in translation and selected authors of nonfiction works are also included.

Entries include a biography, a complete list of published works, and a signed critical essay. Critical essays were written especially for this book by professors of English and young adult literature, librarians, teachers, book reviewers, critics, and other individuals knowledgeable in the field. All living authors were encouraged to submit a personal comment on their books for young adults.

For the purpose of determining inclusion, "young adult" has been defined as readers between the ages of eleven and nineteen. In addition to writers traditionally identified as "young adult" authors, such as Robert Cormier, S. E. Hinton, and Paul Zindel, users will also find authors of works written primarily for an older audience but often read by young adults, such as Ken Kesey, Terry McMillan, and Alice Walker. Authors of adult works of science fiction, fantasy, and horror popular with young adults, including Michael Crichton, Stephen King, and Anne Rice, are also listed. In addition, authors of classic works studied in middle schools and high schools are featured, including Maya Angelou, Aldous Huxley, and John Steinbeck. A handful of authors whose works were published prior to the twentieth century, such as Jack London and Mark Twain, are also included due to their continuing literary significance and appeal to young adult readers.

Every effort has been made to identify those titles an author has written specifically for the young adult audience or which are appropriate for that audience; however, the inclusion of nontraditional young adult authors makes the categorization of bibliographical listings a challenging one, especially when an author writes for several age groups. If an author writes for several age groups, the publications are listed under separate, identifying rubrics. If a book could possibly be placed under two separate rubrics, such as both young adult and adult, every effort has been made to place the book under the rubric with which it is most often associated. Authors who write only works primarily intended for an older audience, but which appeal to young adults, however, have their works listed under "Publications."

The *St. James Guide to Children's Writers* is a companion volume to this guide. It contains similar information on more than 700 authors of children's literature. Some authors of young adult literature, who write primarily for younger children, are featured in the *St. James Guide to Children's Writers*.

ADVISERS

Margaret Bush
Michael Cart
Catherine Clancy
Kenneth L. Donelson
Donald R. Gallo

David H. Jenkinson
Donald J. Kenney
Cathi Dunn MacRae
Alleen Pace Nilsen
Maurice Saxby

CONTRIBUTORS

Hugh Agee
Janice M. Alberghene
Janice Antczak
Marilyn Apseloff
Judith Atkinson
Keith Barker
Henry J. Baron
Craig W. Barrow
Melanie Belviso
Linda Benson
Sharon Clontz Bernstein
Susan P. Bloom
Patricia L. Bradley
Bill Buchanan
Dennis Butts
Michael Cart
Rosemary Chance
Edgar L. Chapman
Joel Chaston
Cathy Chauvette
Ruth K.J. Cline
Carol Jones Collins
Anne Drolett Creany
Hillary S. Crew
Hazel K. Davis
Madison J. Davis
Lesa Dill
Robert Dingley
Ruth E. Dishnow
Rosanne Donahue
Ken Donelson
Carol Doxey
William Ryland Drennan
Charles R. Duke

Eileen Dunlop
Audrey Eaglen
Edna Earl Edwards
Barbara Elleman
Laurie Ann Eno
Bonnie O. Ericson
Mary D. Esselman
Gwyneth Evans
Ron Evans
Jack Forman
Maggie Freeman
Lawrence B. Fuller
Linda Garrett
Lois Rauch Gibson
Virginia L. Gleason
Karen J. Gould
John Gough
M. Jean Greenlaw
Marlene San Miguel Groner
Laurie Schwartz Guttenberg
Lyman B. Hagen
Dennis Hamley
Jane Anne Hannigan
Diane Hebley
Terry Heller
Linnea Hendrickson
James E. Higgins
Elbert R. Hill
Patricia Hill
Maryclare O'Donnell Himmel
Martha Hixon
Peter Hollindale
Caroline C. Hunt
Sylvia Patterson Iskander

David H. Jenkinson
Judith Gero John
Deidre Johnson
Susanne L. Johnston
Patrick Jones
Joan F. Kaywell
Hugh T. Keenan
Donald J. Kenney
Cosette Kies
Lee Kingman
Judson Knight
Fiona Lafferty
Keith Lawrence
Anne Lazim
Kate Lentz
Parish Lentz
Teri S. Lesesne
Leon Lewis
Myra Cohn Livingston
Mary Lowe-Evans
Hollis Lowery Moore
Mary Lystad
Alexandra MacLennan
Cathi Dunn MacRae
Alf Mappin
Janelle Mathis
Fred McEwen
Caroline S. McKinney
Cathryn M. Mercier
Etta Miller
Joseph R. Millichap
Christian H. Moe
Kareo Ferris Morgan
Gerald W. Morton
Charmaine Allmon Mosby
Mattie J. Mosley
John Murray
Claudia Nelson
Harold Nelson
Linda Newbery
Agnes Nieuwenhuizen
Alleen Pace Nilsen
Michael J. O'Neal
Jill Paton Walsh
Lissa Paul
Jenny Pausacker
Kit Pearson
Pat Pflieger
Kathy Piehl
Reba Pinney
Elizabeth A. Poe

Catherine Price
Robert Protherough
Nicholas Ranson
Sheila Ray
Arthea J.S. Reed
John Reiss
Susan Rich
Garyn G. Roberts
Linda Ross
Leonie Margaret Rutherford
Walker Rutledge
Rebecca Saulsbury
Maurice Saxby
Elizabeth D. Schafer
Gary D. Schmidt
Richard D. Seiter
Pamela L. Shelton
Carolyn Shute
Karen Patricia Smith
Mary Snyder
Albert F. Spencer
John D. Stahl
Susan B. Steffel
Madeleine B. Stern
Michael Stone
Robbie W. Strickland
Tracy J. Sukraw
Zena Sutherland
Gwen Athene Tarbox
Jennifer Taylor
Gillian Thomas
Divna Todorovich
John Rowe Townsend
Felicity Trotman
Margaret M. Tye
Jan Tyler
Michael J. Tyrkus
Suzanne M. Valentic
Kay E. Vandergrift
Karen E. Walsh
Marcia Welsh
Donna R. White
Kerry White
Frank Whitehead
Winifred Whitehead
Angela Wigan
Linda Wilson
Louise J. Winters
Lisa A. Wroble
Jessica Yates
Laura M. Zaidman

ST. JAMES GUIDE TO

YOUNG ADULT
Writers

LIST OF ENTRANTS

Richard Adams
C. S. Adler
Arnold Adoff
Joan Aiken
Vivien Alcock
Louisa May Alcott
James Aldridge
Lloyd Alexander
Margaret Anderson
V. C. Andrews
Judie Angell
Maya Angelou
Anonymous
Piers Anthony
Jennifer Armstrong
William H. Armstrong
Brent Ashabranner
Sandy Asher
Bernard Ashley
Isaac Asimov
Margaret Atwood
Avi

Alice Bach
Allan Baillie
Thomas Baird
James Baldwin
T.A. Barron
Marion Dane Bauer
Nina Bawden
Peter S. Beagle
Patricia Beatty
Harry Behn
William Bell
Nathaniel Benchley
Jay Bennett
Ernesto Bethancourt
Richard Blessing
Francesca Lia Block
Joan W. Blos
Judy Blume
Janet Bode
Janine Boissard
Nancy Bond
Frank Bonham
Malcolm Bosse
L. M. Boston
Ray Bradbury
Karleen Bradford
Marion Zimmer Bradley
Robin F. Brancato
Robbie Branscum
Sue Ellen Bridgers
Bruce Brooks
Martha Brooks
Terry Brooks
Eve Bunting

Robert J. Burch
Anthony Burgess
Olive Ann Burns
Edgar Rice Burroughs
Hester Burton
Octavia E. Butler
Betsy Byars

Michael Cadnum
Patricia Calvert
Eleanor Cameron
Philip Caputo
Orson Scott Card
Alden R. Carter
Sylvia Cassedy
Rebecca Caudill
Betty Cavanna
Aidan Chambers
C. J. Cherryh
Grace Chetwin
Alice Childress
Agatha Christie
John Christopher
Lesley Choyce
Marchette Chute
Sandra Cisneros
Patricia Clapp
Mary Higgins Clark
Arthur C. Clarke
Eldridge Cleaver
Vera and Bill Cleaver
Bruce Clements
Elizabeth Coatsworth
Judith Ortiz Cofer
Brock Cole
Christopher and James Lincoln Collier
Hila Colman
Ellen Conford
Jane Leslie Conly
Pam Conrad
Caroline B. Cooney
Susan Cooper
Robert Cormier
Sharon Creech
Gary Crew
Linda Crew
Michael Crichton
Gillian Cross
Kevin Crossley-Holland
Chris Crutcher
Christopher Paul Curtis
Karen Cushman
Richie Tankersley Cusick

Roald Dahl
Maureen Daly
Edwidge Danticat

Paula Danziger
Jenny Davis
Terry Davis
Julie Reece Deaver
Charles de Lint
Carl Deuker
Farrukh Dhondy
Peter Dickinson
Eilis Dillon
Berlie Doherty
John Donovan
Michael Anthony Dorris
Arthur Conan Doyle
Brian Doyle
Sharon Draper
Diane Duane
Ursula Dubosarsky
Tessa Duder
Lois Duncan
Eileen Dunlop

David Eddings
Clyde Edgerton
Amy Ehrlich
Sarah Ellis
Ralph Ellison
Sylvia Engdahl
Jeannette Hyde Eyerly

Walter Farley
Nancy Farmer
Penelope Farmer
Howard Fast
Tom Feelings
Jean Ferris
Nicholas Fisk
Paul Fleischman
Ian Fleming
June Foley
Esther Forbes
James D. Forman
Paula Fox
Anne Frank
Russell Freedman
Paul French
Simon French
Jean Fritz
Monica Furlong

Ernest J. Gaines
Jane Gardam
Nancy Garden
Leon Garfield
Alan Garner
Eve Garnett
Jean Craighead George
Adèle Geras
William Gibson
Nikki Giovanni
Fred Gipson
Mel Glenn
William Golding

Nadine Gordimer
Lorenz Graham
Cynthia D. Grant
Joanne Greenberg
Bette Greene
Sheila Greenwald
Rosa Guy

Ann Halam
Barbara Hall
Lynn Hall
Marilyn Halvorson
Virginia Hamilton
Cynthia Harnett
Sonya Hartnett
James S. Haskins
Esther Hautzig
Ann Head
Robert A. Heinlein
Joseph Heller
Nat. Hentoff
Frank Herbert
Patricia Hermes
James Herriot
Karen Hesse
Douglas Hill
Tony Hillerman
S. E. Hinton
Minfong Ho
Will Hobbs
Linda Holeman
Anne Holm
Felice Holman
H. M. Hoover
James A. Houston
Janni Howker
Linda Hoy
Dean Hughes
Langston Hughes
Monica Hughes
Ted Hughes
Irene Hunt
Kristin Hunter
Mollie Hunter
Zora Neale Hurston
Johanna Hurwitz
Aldous Huxley

Hadley Irwin

Brian Jacques
Paul B. Janeczko
Catherine Jinks
Annabel and Edgar Johnson
Julie Johnston
Allan Frewin Jones
Diana Wynne Jones
June Jordan
Norton Juster

Josephine Kamm
Welwyn Katz

Harold Keith
Victor Kelleher
Carol Kendall
M. E. Kerr
Ken Kesey
Jamaica Kincaid
Stephen King
David Klass
Sheila Solomon Klass
Annette Curtis Klause
Norma Klein
Robin Klein
John Knowles
R. R. Knudson
Ron Koertge
E. L. Konigsburg
Dean R. Koontz
William Kotzwinkle
Trudy Krisher
Paul Kropp
Joseph Krumgold

Mercedes R. Lackey
Jane Langton
Kathryn Lasky
Jean Lee Latham
Louise Lawrence
Harper Lee
Mildred Lee
Tanith Lee
Robert Leeson
Ursula K. Le Guin
Madeleine L'Engle
Julius Lester
Steven Levenkron
Sonia Levitin
Myron Levoy
C. S. Lewis
Elizabeth Foreman Lewis
Kenneth Lillington
Joan Lingard
Robert Lipsyte
Jean Little
Alison Lohans
Jack London
Lois Lowry
Katie Letcher Lyle
Chris Lynch

R. A. Macavoy
Michelle Magorian
Margaret Mahy
Kevin Major
Jan Mark
John Marsden
Victor Martinez
Bobbie Ann Mason
Carol Matas
Mark Mathabane
Sharon Bell Mathis
William Mayne
Harry Mazer

Norma Fox Mazer
Anne McCaffrey
Geraldine McCaughrean
Carson McCullers
Eloise Jarvis McGraw
Vonda N. McIntyre
Patricia A. McKillip
Robin McKinley
Terry McMillan
Florence Crannell Means
Cornelia Lynde Meigs
O.R. Melling
Milton Meltzer
Eve Merriam
David Metzenthen
Carolyn Meyer
Gloria D. Miklowitz
Betty Miles
Frances A. Miller
Jim Wayne Miller
Margaret Mitchell
Louise Moeri
Nicholasa Mohr
James Moloney
N. Scott Momaday
Kyoko Mori
Michael Morpurgo
Toni Morrison
Farley Mowat
Jess Mowry
Patricia Moyes
Shirley Rousseau Murphy
Walter Dean Myers

Beverley Naidoo
Lensey Namioka
Donna Jo Napoli
Phyllis Reynolds Naylor
Jan Needle
Theresa Nelson
John Neufeld
Emily Cheney Neville
Garth Nix
Joan Lowery Nixon
Han Nolan
Sterling North
Andre Norton
Christine Nöstlinger

Robert C. O'Brien
Scott O'Dell
Jean Davies Okimoto
Zibby Oneal
Judith O'Neill
Doris Orgel
Uri Orlev
George Orwell

Ruth Park
Francine Pascal
Katherine Paterson
Jill Paton Walsh

Gary Paulsen
Kit Pearson
Richard Peck
Robert Newton Peck
P. J. Petersen
K. M. Peyton
Joan Phipson
Meredith Ann Pierce
Tamora Pierce
Christopher Pike
Daniel Manus Pinkwater
Sylvia Plath
Chaim Potok
Randy Powell
Philip Pullman
Howard Pyle

Marsha Qualey

Ayn Rand
Ellen Raskin
Marjorie Kinnan Rawlings
Chap Reaver
Lynne Reid Banks
Johanna Reiss
Anne Rice
Conrad Richter
Hans Peter Richter
Ann Rinaldi
Willo Davis Roberts
Keith Robertson
Spider Robinson
Barbara Rogasky
Margaret I. Rostkowski
Gillian Rubinstein
Lois F. Ruby
Cynthia Rylant

Marilyn Sachs
J. D. Salinger
Graham Salisbury
R. A. Salvatore
Pamela Sargent
Harriet May Savitz
Sandra Scoppettone
Ouida Sebestyen
Ian Serraillier
Pamela Service
Ntozake Shange
Zoa Sherburne
Barbara Shoup
Norman Silver
Upton Sinclair
Marilyn Singer
William Sleator
Jan. Slepian
Doris Buchanan Smith
Zilpha Keatley Snyder
Gary Soto
Ivan Southall
Muriel Spark
Elizabeth George Speare

Eleanor Spence
Art Spiegelman
Jerry Spinelli
Suzanne Fisher Staples
John Steinbeck
Robert Louis Stevenson
Mary Stewart
R. L. Stine
Mary Stolz
Todd Strasser
Rosemary Sutcliff
Glendon Swarthout
Robert Swindells

Amy Tan
Eleanora E. Tate
Mildred D. Taylor
Theodore Taylor
Stephen N. Tchudi
Frances Temple
Colin Thiele
Joyce Carol Thomas
Rob Thomas
J. R. R. Tolkien
John Rowe Townsend
Sue Townsend
Geoffrey Trease
Don Trembath
Dalton Trumbo
John R. Tunis
Mark Twain
Anne Tyler

Jean Ure

Joan D. Vinge
Elizabeth Gray Vining
Cynthia Voigt
Kurt Vonnegut, Jr.
Ida Vos

Amelia Elizabeth Walden
Alice Walker
Rich Wallace
Mildred Pitts Walter
Walter Wangerin, Jr.
Maureen Crane Wartski
Sally Watson
William Weaver
Margaret Weis
H. G. Wells
Rosemary Wells
Barbara Wersba
Jessamyn West
Robert Westall
Ellen E. White
Robb White
T. H. White
Phyllis A. Whitney
Diana Wieler
Elie Wiesel
Brenda Wilkinson

Barbara Willard
Margaret Willey
Tad Williams
Rita Williams-Garcia
Budge Wilson
Terri Windling
Patricia Windsor
Maia Wojciechowska
Virginia Euwer Wolff
Hilma Wolitzer
Jacqueline Woodson
Patricia C. Wrede
Richard Wright
Patricia Wrightson

Elizabeth Yates
Laurence Yep
Jane Yolen

Jane Breskin Zalben
Paul Zindel

A

ADAMS, Richard (George)

Nationality: British. **Born:** Newbury, Berkshire, England, 9 May 1920. **Education:** Bradfield College, Berkshire, 1933-38; Worcester College, Oxford, 1938-39, 1946-48, B.A. in modern history 1948, M.A. 1953. **Military Service:** Served in the British Army, 1940-46. **Family:** Married Barbara Elizabeth Acland in 1949; two daughters. **Career:** Worked in Ministry of Housing and Local Government, London, 1948-68; assistant secretary, Department of the Environment, London, 1968-74; full-time writer, since 1974; writer-in-residence, University of Florida, Gainesville, 1975, and Hollins College, Virginia, 1976; president, Royal Society for the Prevention of Cruelty to Animals, 1980-82 (resigned); Independent Conservative parliamentary candidate for Spelthorne, 1983. **Awards:** Carnegie Medal, 1972, and Guardian award, 1973, both for *Watership Down*; fellow, Royal Society of Literature, 1975; California Young Readers' Association award, 1977. **Agent:** David Higham Associates Ltd., 5-8 Lower John St., London W1R 4HA. **Address:** 26 Church Street, Whitchurch, Hampshire RG28 7AR, England.

PUBLICATIONS FOR YOUNG ADULTS

Fiction

Watership Down. London, Collings, 1972; New York, Macmillan, 1974.
Shardik. London, Allen Lane-Collings, 1974; New York, Simon & Schuster, 1975.
The Plague Dogs, illustrated by A. Wainwright. London, Allen Lane-Collings, 1977; New York, Knopf, 1978.
The Bureaucats, illustrated by Robin Jacques. Viking Kestrel, 1985.
Traveller. New York, Knopf, 1988; London, Hutchinson, 1989.
Tales from Watership Down. London, Hutchinson, and New York, Knopf, 1996.

Poetry

The Tyger Voyage, illustrated by Nicola Bayley. London, Cape, and New York, Knopf, 1976.
The Adventures and Brave Deeds of the Ship's Cat on the Spanish Maine: Together with the Most Lamentable Losse of the Alcestis and Triumphant Firing of the Port of Chagres, illustrated by Alan Aldridge and Harry Willock. New York, Knopf, 1977.

Other

Nature through the Seasons, with Max Hooper, illustrated by David Goddard and Adrian Williams. London, Kestrel, and New York, Simon & Schuster, 1975.
Nature Day and Night, with Max Hooper, illustrated by David Goddard and Stephen Lee. London, Kestrel, and New York, Viking, 1978.
The Watership Down Film Picture Book. London, Allen Lane, and New York, Macmillan, 1978.

The Iron Wolf and Other Stories (folktales), illustrated by Yvonne Gilbert and Jennifer Campbell. London, Allen Lane, 1980; as *The Unbroken Web,* New York, Crown, 1980.
Editor, *Grimm's Fairy Tales,* illustrated by Pauline Ellison. London, Routledge, 1981.
Editor, *Richard Adams's Favorite Animal Stories,* illustrated by Beverly Butcher. London, Octopus, 1981.
Editor, *The Best of Ernest Thompson Seton.* London, Fontana, 1982.

PUBLICATIONS FOR ADULTS

Novels

The Girl in a Swing. London, Allen Lane, and New York, Knopf, 1980.
Maia. London, Viking, 1984; New York, Knopf, 1985.

Poetry

The Legend of Te Tuna. Los Angeles, Sylvester and Orphanos, 1982; London, Sidgwick and Jackson, 1986.

Other

Voyage through the Antarctic, with Ronald Lockley. London, Allen Lane, 1982; New York, Viking, 1986.
A Nature Diary. London, Viking, 1985; New York, Viking, 1986.
The Day Gone By. An Autobiography. London, Hutchinson, 1990; New York, Knopf, 1991.
Editor and contributor, *Occasional Poets: An Anthology.* London, Viking, 1986.

*

Media Adaptations: *Watership Down* (animated film), Avco-Embassy, 1978; *The Plague Dogs* (film), 1982; *The Girl in a Swing* (film), 1989.

Critical Studies: Entry in *Children's Literature Review,* Vol. 20, Detroit, Gale, 1990.

*   *   *

Richard Adams is probably best known for his classic novel *Watership Down,* marketed for juveniles in England and for adults in America. He composed the book on a long car trip to amuse his two daughters, who insisted that he write the tale down. After Adams spent two years completing the novel, it was rejected by four publishers and three agents. Since Adams wished to present his daughters with a published version, he was pondering publishing the book himself when he read of a small publisher who had just reissued an animal fantasy. Rex Collins accepted *Watership Down* for a limited printing of 2,000 copies. Reprinted later by Penguin, the novel was a surprising financial success.

Watership Down tells of the exploits of a group of rabbits who seek a new home when their old one is leveled by developers who plan to gas all animal life. Even though older readers are tempted to read the novel as allegory or fable, Adams comments that it is merely a story about rabbits and as such can be enjoyed by a younger readership. In addition to being a novel of tremendous imagination, describing a civilization with its own language, politics, history, and mythology, *Watership Down* is a well-crafted novel in the traditional sense with cliff-hanging chapter endings, excellent controlled tone, and a vast array of character types.

Adams's second novel, *Shardik,* is set in a mythical country and time. Shardik is a giant bear, respected and worshipped by the inhabitants of the country. Allison Lurie of the *New York Review of Books* views the novel as an ecological allegory of how humans choose and follow their gods. Belief causes cruel and destructive acts, as well as novel ones. The language of the novel is descriptive. It shows Adams's love of similes. Some critiques believe it to be a colorless facsimile of an epic: grim, obsessed with virginity, and full of the weakly supernatural.

The third novel by Adams, *The Plague Dogs,* is a return to the anthropomorphic use of animals. This novel is about two dogs who escape from an experimental laboratory in the English Lake District. The novel is criticized as being too literarily self-conscious and replete with tantrums, puns, parody, and, perhaps worst of all, bitter contempt. Even when being praised, the novel is viewed by most as savage satire.

The Girl on a Swing relates the meeting and marriage of Alan Desland and the mysterious German woman, Kaethe. It is both supernatural and erotic, and may be viewed as both too mature and too intense for younger readers.

Maia is a tale of adventure and romance set in the Berklan Empire, a magical land. It deals with the life and adventures of a beautiful girl sold into slavery. Although degraded, the girl survives and becomes a heroine to her people. The novel has been praised as delightful and full of suspense.

Adams's sixth novel is called *Traveller.* The hero of this book is General Robert E. Lee's horse. Seen through the horse's eyes, the events of the Civil War are recounted. Once again a wise animal laments the follies of humans, especially their tendency to kill one another. The novel is composed as a conversation between Traveller and his stablemate, a cat named Tom. Amidst the horse's tales of the agony of defeat and the sweetness of victory is a tribute to Robert E. Lee.

A giant among contemporary English writers of fantasy, Adams will be remembered not only for his originality, epic scope, and masterful storytelling skills, but for his faith that youth and children will understand and appreciate the values inherent in his timeless stories.

—Lesa Dill

ADLER, C(arole) S(chwerdtfeger)

Nationality: American. **Born:** Rockaway Beach, Long Island, New York, 23 February 1932. **Education:** Hunter College (now the City University of New York), B.A. (cum laude) 1953; Russell Sage College, Troy, New York, M.S. 1964. **Family:** Married Arnold R. Adler in 1952; three sons, one deceased. **Career:** Advertising assistant, Worthington Corp., Harrison, New Jersey, 1952-54; English teacher, Niskayuna Middle Schools, New York, New York, 1967-77; writer, since 1977. **Awards:** Golden Kite award from Society of Children's Book Writers, and "Book of the Year" citation from Child Study Association, both 1979, and William Allen White children's book award, 1982, all for *The Magic of the Glits;* "Best Young Adult Book of the Year" citation, American Library Association, 1983, for *The Shell Lady's Daughter;* children's book award from Child Study Children's Book Committee, Bank St. College of Education, 1985, for *With Westie and the Tin Man;* "Children's Choice" citation from International Reading Association and Children's Book Council, 1979, for *The Magic of the Glits,* 1987, for *Split Sisters,* and 1991, for *One Sister Too Many* and *Ghost Brother.* **Address:** 7041 N. Cathedral Rock Pl, Tucson, Arizona 85718-1303, U.S.A.

PUBLICATIONS FOR YOUNG ADULTS

Fiction

The Magic of the Glits, illustrated by Ati Forberg. New York, Macmillan, 1979.
The Silver Coach. New York, Coward, 1979.
In Our House Scott Is My Brother. New York, Macmillan, 1980.
Shelter on Blue Barns Road. New York, Macmillan, 1981.
The Cat that Was Left Behind. New York, Clarion Books, 1981.
Down by the River. New York, Coward, 1981.
Footsteps on the Stairs. New York, Delacorte, 1982.
Some Other Summer (sequel to *The Magic of the Glits).* New York, Macmillan, 1982.
The Evidence that Wasn't There. New York, Clarion Books, 1982.
The Once in a While Hero. New York, Coward, 1982.
Binding Ties. New York, Delacorte, 1983.
Get Lost, Little Brother. New York, Clarion Books, 1983.
Roadside Valentine. New York, Macmillan, 1983.
The Shell Lady's Daughter. New York, Coward, 1983.
Fly Free. New York, Coward, 1984.
Good-bye, Pink Pig. New York, Putnam, 1985.
Shadows on Little Reef Bay. New York, Clarion Books, 1985.
With Westie and the Tin Man. New York, Macmillan, 1985.
Split Sisters, illustrated by Mike Wimmer. New York, Macmillan, 1986.
Kiss the Clown. New York, Clarion Books, 1986.
If You Need Me. New York, Macmillan, 1987.
Carly's Buck. New York, Clarion Books, 1987.
Eddie's Blue-Winged Dragon. New York, Putnam, 1988.
Always and Forever Friends. New York, Clarion Books, 1988.
One Sister Too Many (sequel to *Split Sisters).* New York, Macmillan, 1989.
The Lump in the Middle. New York, Clarion Books, 1989.
Ghost Brother. New York, Clarion Books, 1990.
Help, Pink Pig! (sequel to *Good-Bye, Pink Pig).* New York, Putnam, 1990.
Mismatched Summer. New York, Putnam, 1991.
A Tribe for Lexi. New York, Macmillan, 1991.
Tuna Fish Thanksgiving. New York, Clarion Books, 1992.
Daddy's Climbing Tree. New York, Clarion Books, 1993.
Willie, the Frog Prince. New York, Clarion Books, 1994.
That Horse Whiskey. New York, Clarion Books, 1994.

Courtyard Cat. New York, Clarion Books, 1995.
Youn Hee and Me. San Diego, Harcourt Brace, 1995.
What's to Be Scared of Suki? New York, Clarion Books, 1996.
Her Blue Straw Hat. San Diego, Harcourt Brace, 1997.
More than a Horse. New York, Clarion Books, 1997.
Not Just a Summer Crush. New York, Clarion Books, 1998.

*

Media Adaptations: *Get Lost, Little Brother* (cassette), Talking Books, 1983.

Biography: Entry in *Sixth Book of Junior Authors,* New York, H.W. Wilson, 1989; essay in *Authors and Artists for Young Adults,* Volume 4, Gale, 1990; essay in *Something About the Author Autobiography Series,* Volume 15, Detroit, Gale, 1993; essay in *Speaking for Ourselves, Too* compiled and edited by Donald R. Gallo, Urbana, Illinois, National Council of Teachers of English, 1993.

Critical Studies: Entry in *Contemporary Literary Criticism,* Volume 35, Detroit, Gale, 1985.

C. S. Adler comments:

I'm not one of those adventuresome writers who take to sea on a blank page without first charting their courses. Before I sit down to that emptiness, which is now for me a computer screen, I know who my characters are and have probably done a written portrait of the main ones. I know the theme of the story I'm going to tell and I've sketched out a plot in a sequence of events that will each become a chapter. I know my destination before I start telling myself the story in the first draft of the book, but that doesn't mean there's no adventure for me in the telling. There are minor characters and incidents that surprise me, quirks of my characters that are revealed to me by what they suddenly say or do, bits of interesting dialogue that can't possibly have come from my head.

Each of the five or six drafts I go through before I subject my book to the keen eye of an editor has some challenge and pleasure in accomplishment for me. I just plain like writing—all aspects of it. Although, something I like even better is reading a wonderful book some other author has written.

*   *   *

A sensitive, sympathetic writer, skillfully dealing with problems facing adolescents, C. S. Adler ranks high on the list of young adult writers. She has received many awards and honors, including Best Young Adult Book of the Year citation in 1983 from the American Library Association for *The Shell Lady's Daughter,* besides recognition for her books for younger readers.

Adler's award-winning *The Magic of the Glits,* Junior Literary Guild selection *The Silver Coach,* along with *Good-bye, Pink Pig* and *Help, Pink Pig!,* weave a little magic throughout endearing, entertaining stories. The Glits are magical, sparkling creatures with the capability of granting wishes and filling humans with fuzzy joy. The Glits make the summer bearable for twelve-year-old Jeremy with his broken leg and Lynette who has recently lost her mother and has been pushed off on Jeremy and his family because her stepfather doesn't know how to cope with her. In *The Silver Coach,* Grandma Wallace has a small silver coach that shimmers and grows big enough to take twelve-year-old Chris and younger sister Jackie places far away to escape the trauma of their parents' divorce. A pink quartz pig figurine is the magical means of helping Amanda escape to an imaginary world in the pink pig stories where she battles dangers, but wins even in the real world with help from the pink pig. Sometimes young people need imagination and magic to help deal with reality, and these stories fulfill that need while conveying love, caring, sharing and growing, and learning to face problems of divorce, death, and other obstacles while growing up in the real world.

In *Some Other Summer,* a sequel to *The Magic of the Glits,* Jeremy comes to the ranch where Lynette is living with her Uncle Josh who has adopted her. Lynette is going on thirteen and Jeremy is going on eighteen, and Lynette finds she has a crush on Jeremy. Unfortunately, her feelings are not returned because Lynette's pretty cousin has captured his eye. But Lynette learns that she is still an important part of Jeremy's life as well as that of her uncle, and she faces reality.

In *Carly's Buck,* Carly Alinsky goes to stay with her aunt and uncle in the Adirondack Mountains of upstate New York after her mother dies of cancer, and she decides she doesn't want to stay with her seemingly uncaring father. When Carly decides to protect a family of deer just before the hunting season, her favorite buck is accidentally shot and killed by a neighbor boy's father. It is difficult for Carly to realize that everyone makes mistakes, including herself, and that she is just as guilty as her father of not showing enough love and affection in their lives. This is a warm, loving story of a young girl coming to grips with reality and with herself, learning to face her shortcomings and vowing to do something about them. Young adults will learn from this book, while enjoying a light romance.

With Westie and the Tin Man portrays fifteen-year-old Greg Wightman, just released from a juvenile detention center after spending a year there for shoplifting. He goes home to two recovering alcoholics, his mother and her business partner, Manny. Greg becomes friends with Annabelle Waks, an honest, responsible young girl who is having problems of her own at home with a mother and father talking of divorce. Greg learns, like recovering alcoholics, that he must stop lying to himself as well as to others, stop rationalizing and denying things that make him look bad, and stop feeling guilty about the past. Adler has written an informative book about AA and recovering alcoholics, but has used this information to show that the AA concepts can be applied to the problems of an adolescent recovering from a history of shoplifting and a stint in a correctional facility. An enlightening book, young adults will gain from the information to influence their own lives.

Split Sisters and *One Sister Too Many* are about sisters Case and Jen living in Connecticut with a mother and stepfather who split up and then get back together. Then an unexpected member arrives in the form of a screaming, howling baby girl who keeps the family on edge with her squalling. A babysitter is hired to help, but the babysitter turns out to have mental problems and kidnaps the baby. Once more the family is faced with a crisis, but sticks together and faces it head-on. With Case's help and sharp insight, the baby is found, and once more the family is happy. Spell-binding books that keep the reader's nose glued to the tension-filled pages, the books are highly recommended for young adults, especially those with family problems.

In *Mismatched Summer* two seventh-grade girls, totally different from each other, are forced to spend a summer together, but after exuberant, fun-loving Mikale causes shy, orderly Meg the devastating embarrassment of losing her pants in the middle of a Fourth of July parade, the girls work out their differences. They learn to blend together, growing and learning by allowing a bit of each to rub off on the other during their sandpaper-like summer. A treat for young adults, the book is warm and humorous, delightfully realistic.

Thirteen-year-old Kelsey Morris and her family are uprooted from their home when Mr. Morris loses his job in *The Lump in the Middle*. Kelsey, a middle child, is blamed for everything that goes wrong and feels neglected, awkward, and unwanted. With the help of her friend Gabe whose father is dying of cancer, Kelsy learns that life would be easier for her if she tried harder to get along with others, particularly her own family. This is a thought-provoking story that middle children especially will enjoy.

Adler writes about many problems facing young people, including terminal illnesses, death, alcoholism, being left out, having parents that seem uncaring and unfeeling, and on and on. She handles these problems in a warm and positive manner, showing that young people are capable of facing these problems and becoming stronger because of them.

—Carol Doxey

————

AFFABEE, Eric. *See* **STINE, R(obert) L(awrence).**

————

AIKEN, Joan (Delano)

Nationality: British. **Born:** Rye, Sussex, 4 September 1924. **Education:** Wychwood School, Oxford, 1936-40. **Family:** Married 1) Ronald George Brown in 1945 (died 1955), one son and one daughter; 2) Julius Goldstein in 1976. **Career:** Worked for the BBC, 1942-43; information officer, then librarian, United Nations Information Centre, London, 1943-49; sub-editor and features editor, *Argosy*, London, 1955-60; copywriter, J. Walter Thompson, London, 1960-61. **Awards:** *Guardian* award, and runner-up for Carnegie award, 1969, both for *The Whispering Mountain*; Mystery Writers of America Edgar Allan Poe award, 1972, for *Night Fall*. **Agent:** A.M. Heath, 40-42 William IV Street, London WC2N 4DD. **Address:** The Hermitage, East Street, Petworth, West Sussex GU28 0AB, England.

PUBLICATIONS FOR YOUNG ADULTS

Fiction

All You've Ever Wanted and Other Stories, illustrated by Pat Marriott. London, Cape, 1953.
More Than You Bargained For and Other Stories, illustrated by Pat Marriott. London, Cape, 1955; New York, Abelard Schuman, 1957.
The Kingdom and the Cave, illustrated by Dick Hart. London, Abelard Schuman, 1960; New York, Doubleday, 1974.
The Wolves of Willoughby Chase, illustrated by Pat Marriott. London, Cape, 1962; New York, Doubleday, 1963.
Black Hearts in Battersea, illustrated by Robin Jacques. New York, Doubleday, 1964; London, Cape, 1965.
Nightbirds on Nantucket, illustrated by Pat Marriott. London, Cape, and New York, Doubleday, 1966.
The Whispering Mountain. London, Cape, 1968; New York, Doubleday, 1969.
A Necklace of Raindrops and Other Stories, illustrated by Jan Pienkowski. London, Cape, and New York, Doubleday, 1968.
Armitage, Armitage, Fly Away Home, illustrated by Betty Fraser. New York, Doubleday, 1968.
A Small Pinch of Weather and Other Stories, illustrated by Pat Marriott. London, Cape, 1969.
Night Fall. London, Macmillan, 1969; New York, Holt Rinehart, 1971.
Smoke from Cromwell's Time and Other Stories. New York, Doubleday, 1970.
The Green Flash and Other Tales of Horror, Suspense, and Fantasy. New York, Holt Rinehart, 1971.
The Cuckoo Tree, illustrated by Pat Marriott. London, Cape, and New York, Doubleday, 1971.
All and More, illustrated by Pat Marriott. London, Cape, 1971.
A Harp of Fishbones and Other Stories, illustrated by Pat Marriott. London, Cape, 1972.
Arabel's Raven, illustrated by Quentin Blake. London, BBC Publications, 1972; New York, Doubleday, 1974.
The Escaped Black Mamba, illustrated by Quentin Blake. London. BBC Publications, 1973.
All But a Few. London, Penguin, 1974.
The Bread Bin, illustrated by Quentin Blake. London, BBC Publications, 1974.
Midnight Is a Place. London, Cape, and New York, Viking Press, 1974.
Not What You Expected: A Collection of Short Stories. New York, Doubleday, 1974.
Mortimer's Tie, illustrated by Quentin Blake. London, BBC Publications, 1976.
A Bundle of Nerves: Stories of Horror, Suspense, and Fantasy. London, Gollancz, 1976.
The Faithless Lollybird and Other Stories, illustrated by Pat Marriott. London, Cape, 1977; New York, Doubleday, 1978.
The Far Forests: Tales of Romance, Fantasy, and Suspense. New York, Viking Press, 1977.
Go Saddle the Sea, illustrated by Pat Marriott. New York, Doubleday, 1977; London, Cape, 1978.

Tale of a One-Way Street and Other Stories, illustrated by Jan Pienkowski. London, Cape, 1978; New York, Doubleday, 1979.

Mice and Mendelson, music by John Sebastian Brown, illustrated by Babette Cole. London, Cape, 1978.

Mortimer and the Sword Excalibur, illustrated by Quentin Blake. London, BBC Publications, 1979.

The Spiral Stair, illustrated by Quentin Blake. London, BBC Publications, 1979.

A Touch of Chill: Stories of Horror, Suspense, and Fantasy. London, Gollancz, 1979; New York, Delacorte Press, 1980.

Arabel and Mortimer (includes *Mortimer's Tie, The Spiral Stair, Mortimer and the Sword Excalibur),* illustrated by Quentin Blake. London, Cape, 1980; New York, Doubleday, 1981.

The Shadow Guests. London, Cape, and New York, Delacorte Press, 1980.

Mortimer's Portrait on Glass, illustrated by Quentin Blake. London, Hodder and Stoughton, 1981.

The Stolen Lake, illustrated by Pat Marriott. London, Cape, and New York, Delacorte Press, 1981.

The Mystery of Mr. Jones's Disappearing Taxi, illustrated by Quentin Blake. London, Hodder and Stoughton, 1982.

A Whisper in the Night: Stories of Horror, Suspense, and Fantasy. London, Gollancz, 1982; New York, Delacorte Press, 1984.

Mortimer's Cross, illustrated by Quentin Blake. London, Cape, 1983; New York, Harper, 1984.

Bridle the Wind, illustrated by Pat Marriott. London, Cape, and New York, Delacorte Press, 1983.

The Kitchen Warriors, illustrated by Jo Worth. London, BBC Publications, 1983.

Up the Chimney Down (stories), illustrated by Pat Marriott. London, Cape, and New York, Harper, 1984.

Fog Hounds Wind Cat, Sea Mice. London, Macmillan, 1984.

Mortimer Says Nothing and Other Stories, illustrated by Quentin Blake. London, Cape, 1985; New York, Harper, 1987.

The Last Slice of Rainbow and Other Stories, illustrated by Margaret Walty. London, Cape, 1985; New York, Harper, 1988.

Dido and Pa, illustrated by Pat Marriott. London, Cape, and New York, Delacorte Press, 1986.

Past Eight O'Clock: Goodnight Stories, illustrated by Jan Pienkowski. London, Cape, 1986.

A Goose on Your Grave. London, Gollancz, 1987.

The Moon's Revenge, illustrated by Alan Lee. London, Cape, and New York, Knopf, 1987.

The Teeth of the Gale, illustrated by Pat Marriott. London, Cape, and New York, Harper, 1988.

The Erl King's Daughter, illustrated by Paul Warren. London, Heinemann, 1988.

Voices. London, Hippo, 1988.

Give Yourself a Fright: Thirteen Tales of the Supernatural. New York, Delacorte Press, 1989.

A Fit of Shivers: Tales for Late at Night. London, Gollancz, 1990; New York, Delacorte, 1992.

A Foot in the Grave. London, Cape, 1990.

The Haunting of Lamb House. London, Gollancz, 1991.

Is. London, Cape, 1992; as *Is Underground,* New York, Delacorte, 1993.

The Shoemaker's Boy. New York, Childrens, 1994.

Creepy Company: Ten Tales of Terror. New York, Dell, 1995.

Cold Shoulder Road. New York, Delacorte, 1996.

The Cockatrice Boys. New York, Tor, 1996.

The Jewel Seed. London, Hodder and Stoughton, 1997.

Moon Cake. London, Hodder and Stoughton, 1998.

Plays

Winterthing, music by John Sebastian Brown, illustrated by Arvis Stewart (produced Albany, New York, 1977). New York, Holt Rinehart, 1972; included in *Winterthing, and The Mooncusser's Daughter,* 1973.

Winterthing, and The Mooncusser's Daughter, music by John Sebastian Brown. London, Cape, 1973; *The Mooncusser's Daughter* published separately, New York, Viking Press, 1974.

The Dark Streets of Kimballs Green (television play). 1976.

The Apple of Trouble (television play). 1977.

Midnight Is a Place (television serial), from her own story. 1977.

Street, music by John Sebastian Brown, illustrated by Arvis Stewart (produced London, 1977). New York, Viking Press, 1978.

Armitage, Armitage, Fly Away Home (television play), from her own story. 1978.

The Rose of Puddle Fratrum (television play). 1978.

Moon Mill (produced London, 1982).

Black Hearts in Battersea (television play; BBC-TV). 1996.

Poetry

The Skin Spinners, illustrated by Ken Rinciari. New York, Viking Press, 1976.

Other

Reteller, *The Kingdom under the Sea and Other Stories,* illustrated by Jan Pienkowski. London, Cape, 1971

Translator, *The Angel Inn,* by Contessa de Ségur, illustrated by Pat Marriott. London, Cape, 1976; Owings Mills, Maryland, Stemmer House, 1978.

PUBLICATIONS FOR ADULTS

Novels

The Silence of Herondale. New York, Doubleday, 1964; London, Gollancz, 1965.

The Fortune Hunters. New York, Doubleday, 1965.

Trouble with Product X. London, Gollancz, 1966; as *Beware of the Bouquet,* New York, Doubleday, 1966.

Hate Begins at Home. London, Gollancz, 1967; as *Dark Interval,* New York, Doubleday, 1967.

The Ribs of Death. London, Gollancz, 1967; as *The Crystal Crow,* New York, Doubleday, 1968.

The Embroidered Sunset. London, Gollancz, and New York, Doubleday, 1970.

Died on a Rainy Sunday. London, Gollancz, and New York, Holt Rinehart, 1972.

The Butterfly Picnic. London, Gollancz, 1972; as *A Cluster of Separate Sparks,* New York, Doubleday, 1972.

Voices in an Empty House. London, Gollancz, and New York, Doubleday, 1975.

Castle Barebane. London, Gollancz, and New York, Viking Press, 1976.

Last Movement. London, Gollancz, and New York, Doubleday, 1977.

The Five-Minute Marriage. London, Gollancz, 1977; New York, Doubleday, 1978.

The Smile of the Stranger. London, Gollancz, and New York, Doubleday, 1978.

The Lightning Tree. London, Gollancz, 1980; as *The Weeping Ash,* New York, Doubleday, 1980.

The Young Lady from Paris. London, Gollancz, 1982; as *The Girl from Paris,* New York, Doubleday, 1982.

Foul Matter. London, Gollancz, and New York, Doubleday, 1983.

Mansfield Revisited. London, Gollancz, 1984; New York, Doubleday, 1985.

Deception. London, Gollancz, 1987; as *If I Were You,* New York, Doubleday, 1987.

Blackground. London, Gollancz, and New York, Doubleday, 1989.

Jane Fairfax. London, Gollancz, 1990; New York, St. Martin's 1991.

Morningquest. London, Gollanz, and New York, St. Martin's, 1992.

Eliza's Daughter. London, Gollanz, and New York, St. Martin's, 1994.

Emma Watson. London, Gollanz, and New York, St. Martin's, 1996.

The Youngest Miss Ward. London, Gollanz, and New York, St. Martin's, 1998.

Short Stories

The Windscreen Weepers and Other Tales of Horror and Suspense. London, Gollancz, 1969.

Other

The Way to Write for Children. London, Elm Tree, 1982; New York, St. Martin's Press, 1983.

Contributor, *Sixteen: Short Stories by Outstanding Writers for Young Adults,* edited by Donald R. Gallo. New York, Dell, 1984.

*

Media Adaptations: *Midnight Is a Place* (television series), Southern Television, 1977; *Armitage, Armitage, Fly Away Home* (television play), BBC, 1978; *The Wolves of Willoughby Chase* (cassette), Caedmon, 1978; *A Necklace of Raindrops and Other Stories* (cassette), Caedmon, 1978; *Apple of Discord* (play), BBC-TV; *The Rose of Puddle Fratrum* (play), BBC-TV.

Biography: Essay in *Something about the Author Autobiography Series,* Volume 1, Detroit, Gale, 1986; entry in *Authors and Artists for Young Adults,* Volume 1, Detroit, Gale, 1989; essay in *Speaking for Ourselves: Autobiographical Sketches by Notable Authors of Books for Young Adults,* Volume 1, compiled and edited by Donald R. Gallo, National Council of Teachers of English, 1990.

Critical Studies: Entry in *Children's Literature Review,* Volume 1, Detroit, Gale, 1976; Volume 19, 1990; entry in *Contemporary Literary Criticism,* Volume 35, Detroit, Gale, 1985.

*   *   *

Joan Aiken's prolific writings showcase her marvelous imagination, spiced with wit and wisdom. Her stories for young adults are rich in bizarre situations and startling surprises. Ghosts, monsters, witches, and demons are often found in both her novels and short stories.

Many of Aiken's stories combine elements of historical fiction and gothic romance and quite a few are set in Aiken's own fictitious nineteenth-century England, where a Stuart king reigns over a country beset by constant threats, including wild wolves which not only roam the countryside but close in on London. This setting appears in such novels as *The Wolves of Willoughby Chase, Black Hearts in Battersea, The Cuckoo Tree, The Stolen Lake,* and *Dido and Pa.*

The Wolves of Willoughby Chase, is a Victorian melodrama that pits good against evil and provides a just and happy ending. Young Bonnie and her cousin Sylvia are left in the care of a wicked governess when Bonnie's sick mother and her wealthy father have to go on a long, recuperative cruise. The great English country estate, Willoughby Chase, seems like a warm and safe stronghold for Bonnie and Sylvia. But as soon as the parents leave, the two girls are terrorized by wolves outside and their evil governess within. It is the young Simon, who lives in a cave near the estate, who assists them throughout each misadventure.

Twenty years later Aiken still writes in this historical vein. In *Dido and Pa* Simon appears as the sixth Duke of Battersea. He is joined by another recurring character in Aiken's stories, Dido Twite, a forthright, tough young lady, resourceful in adversity and intolerant of evil. In this book Dido is placed in the midst of a dastardly Hanoverian conspiracy, which involves skullduggery all around.

Armitage, Armitage, Fly Away Home is a funny fantasy that begins with Mr. and Mrs. Armitage honeymooning at the beach, where Mrs. Armitage finds a wishing stone. She wishes for two children who will never be bored, who will have lots of interesting and unusual experiences and her wishes come true with the births of Mark and Harriet.

Aiken has written a number of suspenseful short stories. They are filled with all manner of supernatural beings as well as natural beings with unconventional behaviors. *A Fit of Shivers: Tales for Late at Night* contains ten such stories. In "Number Four, Bowstring Lane" a TV personality, Marcus Fantail, buys a country retirement home and orders up a ghost for company, to disastrous consequences. In "An L-Shaped Grave" the artist Luna Knox knocks off the art critic of a bad review with a full-size pair of elk's antlers. And in "Something" a ninety-year-old grandfather, lying cold in his bier, has one last nightmare and falls out of his box onto the stone church floor.

Joan Aiken is a wonderful storyteller. Her characters, even the ghoulies and ghosties, are great fun and have amazing adventures. The reader who finishes one Aiken book will look for more, to see what further surprises lie ahead.

—Mary Lystad

ALCOCK, Vivien (Dolores)

Nationality: British. **Born:** Worthing, Sussex, 23 September 1924. **Education:** Devizes High School, Wiltshire; Ruskin School of Art, Oxford, 1940-42. **Military Service:** Served as an ambulance driver in the Auxiliary Territorial Service, 1942-46. **Family:**

Married Leon Garfield in 1948 (died 1996); one adopted daughter. **Career:** Artist, Gestetner Ltd., London, 1947-53; secretary, Whittington Hospital, London, 1953-58. **Awards:** *Travellers by Night* was named to the *Horn Book* Honor List and named ALA notable book of the year, both 1985; *The Cuckoo Sister* was named ALA notable book of the year, 1986; *The Monster Garden* was named *Voice of Youth Advocate* best science fiction/fantasy book and ALA notable book of the year, both 1988. **Agent:** John Johnson Ltd., 45-47 Clerkenwell Green, London EC1R 0HT. **Address:** 59 Wood Lane, London N6 5UD, England.

Publications for Young Adults

Fiction

The Haunting of Cassie Palmer. London, Methuen, 1980; New York, Delacorte, 1982.

The Stonewalkers. London, Methuen, 1981; New York, Delacorte, 1983.

The Sylvia Game. London, Methuen, 1982; New York, Delacorte, 1984.

Travellers by Night. London, Methuen, 1983; New York, Delacorte, 1985.

Ghostly Companions, illustrated by Jane Lydbury. London, Methuen, 1984; New York, Delacorte, 1987.

The Cuckoo Sister. London, Methuen, and New York, Delacorte, 1985.

Wait and See, illustrated by Jill Bennett. London, Deutsch, 1986.

The Mysterious Mr. Ross. London, Methuen, and New York, Delacorte, 1987.

The Monster Garden. London, Methuen, and New York, Delacorte, 1988.

The Trial of Anna Cotman. London, Methuen, 1989; London, Delacorte, 1990.

A Kind of Thief. London, Methuen, 1991; New York, Delacorte, 1992.

Singer to the Sea God. London, Methuen, 1992; New York, Delacorte, 1993.

The Red-Eared Ghosts. Boston, Houghton Mifflin, 1997; as *Time Wreck,* London, Methuen, 1997.

Publications for Children

Wait and See, illustrated by Jill Bennett. London, Deutsch, 1986.

The Thing in the Woods, illustrated by Sally Holmes. London, Hamish Hamilton, 1989.

The Dancing Bush, illustrated by Honey de Lacey. London, Hamish Hamilton, 1991.

Othergran, illustrated by Elaine Mills. London, Methuen, 1993.

The Wrecker, illustrated by Kate Aldous. London, Hamish Hamilton, 1994.

The Face at the Window. London, Methuen, 1994.

Best Stories for Seven-year-olds. London, Hodder, 1995.

The Silver Egg, illustrated by Ivan Bates. London, Walker, 1997.

*

Media Adaptations: *The Sylvia Game* (television movie), BBC-TV, 1983; *The Haunting of Cassie Palmer* (television series), Television South, 1984; *Travellers by Night* (television movie), BBC-TV, 1984; (television series), Television South, 1985; *Frankie's Monster* (later published by Heinemann as *The Play of the Monster Garden,* adapted by Diane Samuels), 1992.

Biography: Double interview with Leon Garfield in *Publishers Weekly,* 30 September 1988,; entry in *Authors and Artists for Young Adults,* Volume 8, Detroit, Gale, 1992; entry in *Speaking for Ourselves, Too,* compiled and edited by Donald R. Gallo, National Council of Teachers of English, 1993.

Critical Studies: Entry in *Children's Literature Review,* Volume 26, Detroit, Gale, 1992; entry in *Something about the Author,* Volume 76, Detroit, Gale, 1994.

*   *   *

Vivien Alcock's books, whether for young adults or for younger children, explore boundaries: between childhood and adolescence, between reality and imagination, between natural and supernatural, between good and evil. Her prolific output falls into three main periods: an early one emphasizing the question of reality, an early middle period in which more realistic mysteries and family relationships come to the fore, and a late group in which ethical and social issues predominate. In her most recent books, Alcock again focuses on the supernatural.

The Haunting of Cassie Palmer, Alcock's first novel, introduces many of the author's major themes: reality versus imagination, parent-child conflict, and ethical dilemmas. Does Cassie, seventh child of a seventh child, have the "gift" to deal with the spirit world more successfully than her mother, a fraudulent medium whose failures force the family to move whenever she is exposed? Is Deverill, the dark shadowy figure Cassie meets in a cemetery, really a ghost—or a figment of her early adolescent mind? Cassie's sympathy and imagination bring a happy ending for both; ironically, it is her success in bringing peace to Deverill's troubled spirit that enables Cassie to grow beyond her mother's spiritualism and prepare for a healing career in the ordinary world. More melodramatic than *The Haunting of Cassie Palmer,* Alcock's second novel for young adults, *The Stonewalkers,* presents the boundaries of reality differently: Poppy Brown and two of her friends realize that some local statues have come to life, but no one believes them. An exciting chase scene and a long captivity in a cave with the dangerous statues mark high points in this book, a favorite with young readers. Other themes from Alcock's first novel recur: again, the main character's difficult relationship with her mother is shown capable of improvement through love; again, the implications of dishonesty (in this case, telling lies) are explored.

After these successful forays into the supernatural, Alcock turned toward a more direct focus on family and values. *The Sylvia Game* presents another irresponsible parent, a painter whose daughter Emily suspects him of complicity in a forgery scheme. Emily's remarkable resemblance to a portrait by Renoir involves her in an odd friendship with two very different boys: Oliver, heir to the Mallerton estates, and the illegitimate, colorful Kevin. For all three, loyalty to an imperfect parent collides with the demands of honor. Although the parents in this novel do not change as much as those in the earlier ones, Oliver and Emily come to accept their fathers as people. The examination of class differences is both accurate and unsentimental. In *The Cuckoo Sister,* a stolen child returns years later—but is she really Emma, kidnapped years ago as a baby, or an imposter? Personality problems, class differences, and the lingering possibility of fraud combine to create tension and uncertainty in Kate's comfortable Hampstead family before the question of

Emma's true identity is cleared up. Several Alcock novels of the 1980s aim at a slightly younger adolescent readership, such as the charming quest story *Travellers by Night,* with its brother and sister seeking refuge for a circus elephant, and the Carnegie Medal nominee, *The Monster Garden. Travellers by Night* has few real moral issues (no reader wants to see the elephant sent to slaughter) and, although *The Monster Garden* raises the issue of responsible laboratory experimentation with genetic materials, it concentrates on the fate of the charming Monnie more than on the ethical problems involved in his creation.

Turning away from supernatural and adventure themes in 1989-90, Alcock's books became darker in mood. *The Trial of Anna Cotman* pits a lonely girl against a secret society whose rituals both fascinate and degrade her. Alcock deftly contrasts the colorful costumes, imaginative hierarchy, and compelling ceremonies of the group to Anna's drab surroundings. Her stand against the group's corruption occurs naturally and inevitably, rather than as the result of any simplistic decision or fearless heroics. That she prevails almost by chance, and then only with adult help, is a suitable ending to this somber and convincing tale of group psychology. *A Kind of Thief* reverts to the trials of an early adolescent with a socially unacceptable parent. Unlike the deceptive parents of Cassie Palmer and Emily Dodd, even more unlike the largely absent parents in many of Alcock's other young adult books, this story examines the effects of having a father who is actually in jail. The predictable breakup of Elinor's step family, which might have formed the climax of a less skilled writer's plot, occurs near the beginning. Though victims, Ellie's young stepmother and Ellie herself do not always behave well; indeed, the efforts to rescue and preserve her father's hidden suitcase make her into "a kind of thief," as culpable in her own way as he is. All the characters in *A Kind of Thief* are flawed, from the young stepmother Sophia to elderly Mrs. Carter, the children's great aunt; yet nearly all are resourceful and capable of sometimes surprising generosity. The slow realization of human strength and human weakness leads Ellie finally to accept herself as she is and to accept her family also.

In her most recent works, Alcock has returned to the supernatural: first to the world of mythology, in *Singer to the Sea God,* which uses the myth of Perseus as the basis for a quest story, then in *The Red-Eared Ghosts,* as time travel story. Like *A Kind of Thief,* both books end in recognition and acceptance.

—Caroline C. Hunt

ALCOTT, Louisa May

Nationality: American. **Born:** Germantown, Philadelphia, Pennsylvania, 29 November 1832. Daughter of the philosopher Armos Bronson Alcott; grew up in Boston, and Concord, Massachusetts. **Education:** Schooled at home by her father, with instruction from Thoreau, Emerson, and Theodore Parker. **Career:** Began to write for publication (author of novels, short stories, and poems), 1848; also worked as a teacher, seamstress, and domestic servant; army nurse at the Union Hospital, Georgetown, Washington, D.C., during the Civil War, 1862-63; editor of the children's magazine *Merry's Museum,* 1867. **Died:** 6 March 1888.

Fiction

The Rose Family: A Fairy Tale. Boston, James Redpath, 1864.
Moods. A.K. Loring, 1865.
Nelly's Hospital. U.S. Sanitary Commission, 1865.
The Mysterious Key, and What It Opened. Boston, Elliott, Thomes & Talbot, 1867.
Aunt Kipp. A. K. Loring, 1868.
Kitty's Class Day. A. K. Loring, 1868.
Little Women or, Meg, Jo, Beth and Amy, two volumes, Boston, Roberts Brothers, 1868-69; volume 2 republished as *Little Women Wedded,* London, Low, 1872, as *Little Women Married,* London, Routledge, 1873; as *Nice Wives,* London, Weldon, 1875; both volumes republished as *Little Women and Good Wives,* London, Nisbet, 1895.
Psyche's Art. A. K. Loring, 1868.
An Old-Fashioned Girl. Boston, Roberts Brothers, 1870.
Will's Wonder Book. Boston, Horace B. Fuller, 1870; as *Louisa's Wonder Book: An Unknown Alcott Juvenile,* edited by Madeleine B. Stern, Mount Pleasant, Central Michigan University/ Clark Historical Library, 1975.
Little Men: Life at Plumfield with Jo's Boys. Boston, Roberts Brothers, 1871.
Work: A Story of Experience. Boston, Roberts Brothers, 1873.
Eight Cousins; or, The Aunt-Hill. Boston, Roberts Brothers, 1875.
Rose in Bloom: A Sequel to "Eight Cousins." Boston, Roberts Brothers, 1876.
A Modern Mephistopheles (published anonymously). Boston, Roberts Brothers, 1877.
Under the Lilacs. Boston, Roberts Brothers, 1878.
Meadow Blossoms. New York, Crowell, 1879.
Sparkles for Bright Eyes. New York, Crowell, 1879.
Water Cresses. New York, Crowell, 1879.
Jack and Jill: A Village Story. Boston, Roberts Brothers, 1880.
Jo's Boys, and How They Turned Out: A Sequel to "Little Men." Boston, Roberts Brothers, 1886.
A Garland for Girls. Boston, Roberts Brothers, 1887.
An Old-fashioned Thanksgiving, illustrated by Holly Johnson. Philadelphia, Lippincott, 1974.
Trudel's Siege, art by Stan Skardinski. New York, McGraw-Hill, 1976.
Diana and Persis, edited by Sarah Elbert. Salem, New Hamshire, Ayer Company, 1978.
The Faded Banners: A Treasury of Nineteenth Century Civil War Fiction, edited by Eric Soloman. New York, Promontory Press, 1986.

Short Stories

Flower Fables. Boston, George W. Briggs, 1855.
On Picket Duty, and Other Tales. Boston, James Redpath, 1864.
Louisa M. Alcott's Proverb Stories (contains *Kitty's Class Day, Aunt Kipp,* and *Psyche's Art*), A. K. Loring, 1868.
Morning-Glories, and Other Stories. Boston, Horace B. Fuller, 1868.
Hospital Sketches [and] Camp and Fireside Stories. Boston, Roberts Brothers, 1869.

Aunt Jo's Scrap-Bag. Boston, Roberts Brothers, Volume 1, 1872, Volume 2, 1872, Volume 3, 1874, Volume 4, 1878, Volume 5, 1879, Volume 6, 1882.

Something to Do (contains *Proverb Stories*). London, Ward, Lock & Tyler, 1873.

Silver Pitchers [and] Independence, a Centennial Love Story. Boston, Roberts Brothers, 1876.

Spinning-Wheel Stories. Boston, Roberts Brothers, 1884.

Lulu's Library. Boston, Roberts Brothers, Volume 1: *A Christmas Dream,* 1886, Volume 2: *The Frost King,* 1887, Volume 3: *Recollections,* 1889.

A Modern Mephistopheles [and] A Whisper in the Dark. Boston, Roberts Brothers, 1889.

Comic Tragedies Written by "Jo" and "Meg" and Acted by the Little Women. Boston, Roberts Brothers, 1893.

A Round Dozen: Stories, edited by Anne Thaxter Eaton. New York, Viking, 1963.

Glimpses of Louisa: A Centennial Sampling of the Best Short Stories by Louisa May Alcott, edited by Cornelia Meigs. Boston, Little, Brown, 1968.

Behind a Mask: The Unknown Thrillers of Louisa May Alcott, edited by Madeleine B. Stern. New York, Morrow, 1975.

Plots and Counterplots: More Unknown Thrillers of Louisa May Alcott, edited by Madeleine B. Stern. (As A.M. Barnard), Boston, Thomes and Talbot, c. 1870; New York, Morrow, 1976.

The Hidden Louisa May Alcott: A Collection of her Unknown Thrillers, edited by Madeleine Stern. New York, Avenel Books, 1984.

The Works of Louisa May Alcott, 1832-1888. Kent, Connecticut, Reprint Services Corp., 1987.

Alternative Alcott, edited by Elaine Showalter. New Brunswick, New Jersey, Rutgers University Press, 1988.

A Double Life: Newly Discovered Thrillers of Louisa May Alcott, edited by Madeleine B. Stern. Boston, Little, Brown, 1988.

Freaks of Genius: Unknown Thrillers of Louisa May Alcott. edited by Daniel Shealy, Madeleine B. Stern, and Joel Myerson. New York, Greenwood Press, 1991.

Louisa May Alcott's Fairy Tales and Fantasy Stories, edited by Daniel Shealy. Knoxville, University of Tennessee Press, 1992.

Nonfiction

Hospital Sketches. Boston, James Redpath, 1863.

Louisa May Alcott: Her Life, Letters and Journals, edited by Ednah D. Cheney. Boston, Roberts Brothers, 1889.

Transcendental Wild Oats and Excerpts from the Fruitlands Diary, illustrated by J. Streeter Fowke. Harvard, Massachusetts, Harvard Common Press, 1975.

The Selected Letters of Louisa May Alcott, edited by Joel Myerson. Boston, Little, Brown, 1987.

*

Media Adaptations: *Little Women* (film), Famous Players, Lasky Corp., 1919; *Little Women* (play), RKO, 1933; *Little Women* (film), Metro-Goldwyn-Mayer, 1949; *Little Men* (film), Mascott, 1934; *Little Men* (film), RKO, 1940; and *An Old-Fashioned Girl* (film), Pathe Industries, 1949; several recordings of Alcott's work have also been made.

Manuscript Collection: Family papers at Houghton Library, Harvard University, Cambridge, Massachusetts.

Biography: Entry in *Dictionary of Literary Biography,* Detroit, Gale, Volume 1: *The American Renaissance in New England,* edited by Joel Myerson, 1978, Volume 42: *American Writers for Children before 1900,* edited by Glenn E. Estes, 1985, and Volume 79: *American Magazine Journalists, 1850-1900,* edited by Sam G. Riley, 1989.

Bibliography: *Louisa May Alcott: The Children's Friend* by Ednah D. Cheney, Sandusky, Ohio, Prang, 1888; *Louisa May Alcott: Her Life, Letters and Journals,* edited by Ednah D. Cheney, Boston, Roberts Brothers, 1889; *The Story of the Author of "Little Women": Invincible Louisa* by Cornelia Meigs, New York, Little, Brown, 1933; *Louisa May Alcott* by Katharine S. Anthony, New York, Knopf, 1938; *Louisa May Alcott* by Madeleine B. Stern, Norman, University of Oklahoma Press, 1950. *We Alcotts: The Story of Louisa May Alcott's Family as Seen through the Eyes of "Marmee," Mother of Little Women* by Aileen Fisher and Olive Rabe, New York, Atheneum, 1968.

Critical Study: Entry in *Children's Literature Review,* Volume 1, Detroit, Gale, 1976.

*   *   *

In 1868 when, at the request of Thomas Niles of Roberts Brothers, Louisa May Alcott sat down to write a household story for girls, the domestic novel as evolved by Susan Warner, Maria Cummins, Ann Stephens, and Mrs. E.D.E.N. Southworth consisted of commonplace episodes worked into a trite plot involving pious and insipid characters. Bronson Alcott's opinion of juvenile literature, recorded in his diary for 1839, had, in the generation that followed, been given no cause for alteration. In 1868 it was still true that the "literature of childhood" had not been written. If such extraordinary moral tales as *The Wide, Wide World,* the Rollo books, the Lucy books, and the first of the Elsie books became unbearable, there was compensation for a youthful reader only in grave-and-horror stories, Hawthorne's legendary tales, or "Peter Parley's" edifying descriptions of natural wonders.

The times were ripe for Alcott and she was well equipped to fill the gap in domestic literature. With the publication of *Little Women* (1868-69) she created a domestic novel for young people destined to influence writers in that genre for generations to come. Responding to her publisher's request, she drew her characters from those of her own sisters, her scenes from the New England where she had grown up, and many of her episodes from those she and her family had experienced. In all this she was something of a pioneer, adapting her autobiography to the creation of a juvenile novel and achieving a realistic but wholesome picture of family life with which young readers could readily identify.

The literary influence of Bunyan and Dickens, Carlyle and Hawthorne, Emerson, Theodore Parker, and Thoreau can be traced in her work, but primarily she drew upon autobiographical sources for her plot and her characters, finding in her family and neighbors the groundwork for her three-dimensional characters. Her perceptively drawn adolescents, the Marches, modeled upon her sisters and herself, were not merely lifelike but alive. Her episodes, from the opening selection of a Christmas gift to the plays in the barn, from Jo March's literary career to Beth's death, were thoroughly believable for they had been lived. The Alcott humor which induced a chuckle at a homely phrase was appreciated by children. The Alcott poverty was sentimentalized; the eccentric Alcott father was an adumbrated shadow; yet, for all the glossing over, the core of the domestic drama was apparent. Reported simply and directly in a style that obeyed her injunction "Never use a long word, when a short one will do as well," the narrative embodied the simple facts and persons of a family and so filled a gap in the literature of childhood. Alcott had unlatched the door to one house, and "all find it is their own house which they enter." Twentieth-century writers for young people who aim at credibility and verisimilitude in their reconstructions of contemporary family life are all, in one way or another, indebted to Alcott.

By the time she created *Little Women* she had served a long apprenticeship and was already a professional writer. She had edited a juvenile monthly, *Merry's Museum,* and produced several books aimed at a juvenile readership: her first published book, *Flower Fables,* "legends of faery land"; *The Rose Family: A Fairy Tale;* and *Morning-Glories and Other Stories,* readable short stories in which autobiographical details were combined with nature lore and moral tidbits.

Alcott had also written in a variety of genres for a wide range of adult readers, weaving stories of sweetness and light, dramatic narratives of strong-minded women and poor lost creatures, realistic episodes of the Civil War, and blood-and-thunder thrillers of revenge and passion whose leading character was usually a vindictive and manipulating heroine. From the exigencies of serialization for magazines she had developed the skills of the cliffhanger and the page-turner. Her first full-length novel, *Moods* (1865), was a narrative of stormy passion and violence, death and intellectual love in which she attempted to apply Emerson's remark: "life is a train of moods like a string of beads." Off and on, she had worked at her autobiographical and feminist novel *Success,* subsequently renamed *Work: A Story of Experience.* By 1868, Alcott had run a gamut of literary experimentation from stories of virtue rewarded to stories of vice unpunished. She had attempted tales of escape and realism and stirred her literary ingredients in a witch's cauldron before she kindled the fire in a family hearth.

With few exceptions—notably *A Modern Mephistopheles* (1877) in which she reverted to the sensational themes of her earlier blood-and-thunders—Alcott clung to that family hearth during the remainder of her career. Between 1868 when Part One of *Little Women* appeared and 1888 when she died, she produced in her so-called *Little Women Series* a string of wholesome domestic narratives more or less autobiographical in origin, simple and direct in style, perceptive in the characterization of adolescents. *An Old-Fashioned Girl, Little Men, Eight Cousins, Rose in Bloom, Under the Lilacs, Jack and Jill,* and *Jo's Boys* are all in a sense sequels to *Little Women* though none of them quite rises to its level. *An Old-Fashioned Girl* is a domestic drama in reverse, exposing the fashionable absurdities of the Shaw home by contrast with Polly, the wholesome representative of domesticity. The Campbell clan of *Eight Cousins* exalts the family hearth again. In *Jack and Jill* the author enlarges upon the theme of domesticity, describing the home life of a New England village rather than of a single family.

Despite her experimentation with a diversity of literary techniques, despite the fact that she was a complex writer drawn to a variety of themes, Alcott has inevitably achieved fame as the author of a single masterpiece. Thanks to its psychological perceptions, its realistic characterizations, and its honest domesticity, *Little Women* has become an embodiment of the American home at its best. Consciously or unconsciously all subsequent writers who have attempted the domestic novel for young people have felt its influence, for in *Little Women* the local has been transmuted into the universal and the incidents of family life have been translated to the domain of literature.

Today not only *Little Women* but the entire Alcott oeuvre are being subjected to critical re-evaluation. For this the reprinting of her previously unknown thrillers (written in secret during the 1860s and published anonymously or pseudonymously) is largely responsible. Their themes (mind control and madness, hashish experimentation and opium addiction, mesmerism, and a powerful feminism) are leading critics to re-examine the simplistic interpretation of "America's best-loved author of juveniles."

—Madeleine B. Stern

———

ALDON, Adair. *See* **MEIGS, Cornelia Lynde.**

———

ALDRICH, Ann. *See* **KERR, M.E.**

———

ALDRIDGE, (Harold Edward) James

Nationality: Australian. **Born:** White Hills, Victoria, 10 July 1918. **Education:** Swan Hill High School. **Family:** Married Dina Mitchnik in 1942; two sons. **Career:** Free-lance writer; office boy and file clerk, 1934-37, reporter, 1937-38, both for Melbourne *Herald;* reporter, Melbourne *Sun,* 1937-38; writer, London *Daily Sketch* and *Sunday Dispatch,* 1939; European and Middle East war correspondent, Australian Newspaper Service and North American Newspaper Alliance (in Finland, Norway, Greece, the Middle East, and the Soviet Union), 1939-44; Tehran correspondent, *Time* and *Life,* 1944. **Awards:** Rhys Memorial prize, 1945; World Peace Council gold medal; International Organization of Journalist prize, 1967; Lenin Memorial Peace prize, 1972; Australian Children's Book Council Book of the Year award, 1985; *Guardian* award, for children's book, 1987. **Agent:** Curtis Brown, 28/29 Haymarket, London SW1Y 4SP, England. **Address:** 21 Kersley St., London SW11, England.

PUBLICATIONS FOR YOUNG ADULTS

Fiction

The Flying 19. London, Hamish Hamilton, 1966.
The Marvellous Mongolian. Boston, Little, Brown, and London, Macmillan, 1974.
The Broken Saddle. London, MacRae, 1982; New York, Watts, 1983.
The True Story of Lilli Stubeck. South Yarra, Victoria, Hyland House, 1984; London, Penguin, 1986.
The True Story of Spit MacPhee. Victoria, Ringwood, and London, Viking Kestrel, 1986.
The True Story of Lola Mackeller. Victoria, Ringwood, and New York, Viking, 1992.

PUBLICATIONS FOR ADULTS

Novels

Signed with Their Honour. London, Joseph, and Boston, Little, Brown, 1942.
The Sea Eagle. London, Joseph, and Boston, Little, Brown, 1944.
Of Many Men. London, Joseph, and Boston, Little, Brown, 1946.
The Diplomat. London, Lane, 1949; Boston, Little, Brown, 1950.
The Hunter. London, Lane, 1950; Boston, Little, Brown, 1951.
Heroes of the Empty View. London, Lane, and New York, Knopf, 1954.
I Wish He Would Not Die. London, Bodley Head, 1957; New York, Doubleday, 1958.
The Last Exile. London, Hamish Hamilton, and New York, Doubleday, 1961.
A Captive in the Land. London, Hamish Hamilton, 1962; New York, Doubleday, 1963.
My Brother Tom. London, Hamish Hamilton, 1966; as *My Brother Tom: A Love Story,* Boston, Little, Brown, 1967.
The Statesman's Game. London, Hamish Hamilton, and New York, 1966.
A Sporting Proposition. London, Joseph, and Boston, Little, Brown, 1973; as *Ride a Wild Pony,* London, Penguin, 1976.
Mockery in Arms. London, Joseph, 1974; Boston, Little, Brown, 1975.
The Untouchable Juli. London, Joseph, 1975; Boston, Little, Brown, 1976.
One Last Glimpse. London, Joseph, and Boston, Little, Brown, 1977.
Flying. London, Pan, 1979.
Goodbye Un-America. London, Joseph, and Boston, Little, Brown, 1979.

Short Stories

Gold and Sand. London, Bodley Head, 1960.

Plays

The 49th State (produced London, 1947).
One Last Glimpse (produced Prague, 1981).
Also author of scripts for *Robin Hood* series.

Other

Undersea Hunting for Inexperienced Englishmen. London, Allen & Unwin, 1955.
Cairo: Biography of a City. Boston, Little, Brown, 1969; London, Macmillan, 1970.
Living Egypt, photographs by Paul Strand. London, MacGibbon and Kee, and New York, Horizon Press, 1969.
Contributor, *Winter's Tales 15,* edited by A.D. Maclean. London, Macmillan, 1969; New York, St. Martin's, 1970.

*   *   *

James Aldridge began his career as a journalist reporting from the front lines during the Second World War. While working as a war correspondent he published two novels about the war, *Signed with Their Honour* and *The Sea Eagle,* and following their success gave up journalism to become a full-time writer, publishing many successful novels for adults—*The Diplomat* published in 1950 was translated into twenty-five languages and was a best-seller in Russia.

In 1966 Aldridge turned from these novels with international settings to writing young adult books situated in Australia. "I can't escape Australia, and I don't want to," he once remarked. He published seven novels set in the town of St. Helen, fictional counterpart of Swan Hill, a town he was born near and which he had left as a young man of nineteen. St. Helen, like Swan Hill, is situated on the banks of the Murray River, a river that is to Australians what the Mississippi is to Americans. Aldridge himself associates the two rivers when one of his characters talks about an idyllic "adventuresome Tom Sawyerian sort of boyhood on our lazy Murray River which had steamboats, floods, good fishing, hunting and the sort of adventure that lasted as a faint and unbelievable nostalgia for the rest of my life."

My Brother Tom, the first of the St. Helen novels, tells the love story of Tom Quayle and Peggy MacGibbon against the background of the Depression and the coming threat of the Second World War. Their fathers are archenemies and the couple have to cope with the prejudice of a small town divided by religious bigotry.

The True Story of Lilli Stubeck tells the story of Lilli, daughter of an itinerant family who sell her to a wealthy spinster for twenty-five pounds. The story concerns Lilli's determination to remain true to her own nature. *The True Story of Spit MacPhee* is another story of a tough individual who becomes the subject of a legal tussle between two couples when his grandfather becomes too old to care for him. Again there is religious division—Catholic versus Protestant—and the individual is pitted against a well-meaning town and the law. Paramount in the story is the question of what is best for the individual.

Aldridge's most recent novel is another of his "true" stories, *The True Story of Lola Mackellar.* Like Spit MacPhee and Lilli Stubeck who arrive in St. Helen with incomplete backgrounds, Lola Mackellar (real name Lorelei), arrives from a foster home in Melbourne. This story, like other St. Helen novels, centres upon the question of identity; why does the wealthy landowning family bring Lola to the town but settle her with a poorer family like an outcast? When Lola's twin from Germany arrives, the question of identity becomes all important and the subtext of the novel raises issues about Australia's European heritage and the development of a national culture.

St. Helen itself has an important character of its own in these books. As individuals the townspeople are basically kind but collectively they are intolerant. One issue that plays an important role in the novels is the damaging effect of gossip. The novels take place in Australia in the 1930s and the town is divided by different levels of social self-interest. The social rules are written by the shopkeepers; the lawyers, doctors, and chemists are its decorative gentry, while the sheep farmers along the plains are the aristocracy, no less feudal for their easy link with the town. Middle-class mentality and morality prevail. In this situation, where materialism and money are emphasised, the fear of justice operating for the rich becomes a threat, but the principle of equality before the law always succeeds.

The novel *Ride a Wild Pony* (originally published as *A Sporting Proposition*) tells the story of thirteen-year-old Scott Pirie, a poor but fiercely independent spirit whose Welsh pony, Taff, is an extension of himself. As one character puts it, the horses "know they are the centre of attention and obviously enjoy it." Conflict develops when Scott loses the pony and believes it has come into the possession of the wealthy but crippled daughter of a rich landowner. The whole town becomes involved in the struggle for the pony's ownership and Aldridge offers no neat solution to the problem. The right to equality before the law is an important theme for the St. Helen novels and has its place here. *Ride a Wild Pony* was made into a Disney film in the late seventies, and this story along with Aldridge's *The Broken Saddle* and *The Marvellous Mongolian* are considered among the finest horse stories written by an Australian.

Through his novels Aldridge seeks to answer age-old questions that have concerned humanity since Plato and Aristotle: how people ought to live in communities and how best to organise their political and social life. Aldridge is concerned with the betterment of life through the search for moral and religious understandings. The St. Helen novels take up these questions no less than his adult books, and because the prose is so concentrated with meaning in his young adult books, the points are effectively made. The characters are urged to overcome "the impoverishments of their generation," "the bigotry of dead morals," and "the violence of violent systems." Aldridge invites us to align with those characters of his who strive at "the frontiers of hope."

—Michael Stone

ALEXANDER, Lloyd (Chudley)

Nationality: American. **Born:** Philadelphia, Pennsylvania, 30 January 1924. **Education:** West Chester State College and Lafayette College, Pennsylvania, 1942-43; the Sorbonne, Paris, 1946. **Family:** Married Janine Denni in 1946; one daughter. **Career:** Since 1946, writer and translator. Author-in-residence, schools in Springfield, Pennsylvania, 1967-68, and Temple University, 1970-74. Cartoonist, layout artist, advertising copywriter, and editor of industrial magazine, 1947-70. Since 1970 director, Carpenter Lane Chamber Music Society, Philadelphia; since 1973 member of the Editorial Advisory Board, *Cricket* magazine, Peru, Illinois. **Military Service:** Served in the U.S. Army Combat Intelligence and

Counter-Intelligence corps, 1942-46: Staff Sergeant. **Awards:** Isaac Siegel Memorial Juvenile award, 1959, for *Border Hawk: August Bondi;* ALA notable book citation, 1964, for *The Book of Three;* Newbery Honor Book, 1965, for *The Black Cauldron;* "Best Books" citations, *School Library Journal,* 1967, for *Taran Wanderer,* 1971, for *The King's Fountain,* and 1982, for *Westmark;* citation from American Institute of Graphic Arts Children's Books, 1967- 68, for *The Truthful Harp;* "Children's Book of the Year" citation, Child Study Association of America, 1968, for *The High King,* 1971, for *The King's Fountain,* 1973, for *The Cat Who Wished to Be A Man,* 1974, for *The Foundling and Other Tales of Prydain,* 1975, for *The Wizard in the Tree,* 1982, for *The Kestrel,* and 1985, for *The Black Cauldron* and *Time Cat;* Newbery Medal, National Book award nomination, both 1969, both for *The High King;* "Best Books of the Year" citation, Library of Congress, 1970, and National Book Award, 1971, both for *The Marvelous Misadventures of Sebastian;* Drexel award, 1972 and 1976, for outstanding contributions to literature for children; *Boston Globe-Horn Book* award, 1973, for *The Cat Who Wished to Be a Man;* "Outstanding Books of the Year" citation, *New York Times,* 1973, for *The Foundling and Other Tales of Prydain;* Laura Ingalls Wilder award nomination, 1975; CRABbery award, Oxon Hill Branch of Prince George's County Library (Maryland), 1979, National Book award nomination, 1979, Silver Pencil award, 1981, and Austrian Children's Book award, 1984, all for *The First Two Lives of Lukas-Kasha;* American Book Award nomination, 1980, for *The High King,* and 1982, for *The Wizard in the Tree;* ALA "Best Books for Young Adults" citation, 1981, for *Westmark,* 1982, for *The Kestrel,* and 1984, for *The Beggar Queen;* American Book award, 1982, for *Westmark;* Parents' Choice award, 1982, for *The Kestrel,* 1984, for *The Beggar Queen,* and 1986, for *The Illyrian Adventure;* Golden Cat award, Sjoestrands Foerlag (Sweden), 1984, for excellence in children's literature; Regina Medal, Catholic Library Association, 1986; Church and Synagogue Library Association award, 1987; Field award, Pennsylvania Library Association, 1987, for *The Illyrian Adventure;* Lifetime Achievement award, Pennsylvania Center for The Book in Philadelphia, 1991; "Best Book" Citations from *Booklist, School Library Journal,* and Parents' Choice award, all 1991, all for *The Remarkable Journey of Prince Jen;* Parents' Choice award, *Parenting* award, both 1992, both for *The Fortune-Tellers;* *Boston Globe-Horn Book* award for *The Fortune-Tellers,* 1993. **Agent:** Brandt & Brandt, 1501 Broadway, New York, New York 10036. **Address:** 1005 Drexel Ave., Drexel Hill, Pennsylvania 19026, U.S.A.

PUBLICATIONS FOR YOUNG ADULTS

Fiction

The Marvelous Misadventures of Sebastian. New York, Dutton, 1970.
The First Two Lives of Lukas-Kasha. New York, Dutton, 1978.
The Remarkable Journey of Prince Jen. New York, Dutton, 1991.
The Iron Ring. New York, Dutton, 1997.

Prydain series:

The Book of Three. New York, Holt Rinehart, 1964; London, Heinemann, 1966.
The Black Cauldron. New York, Holt Rinehart, 1965; London, Heinemann, 1967.

The Castle of Llyr. New York, Holt Rinehart, 1966; London, Heinemann, 1968.

Taran Wanderer. New York, Holt Rinehart, 1967; London, Fontana, 1979.

The High King. New York, Holt Rinehart, 1968; London, Fontana, 1979.

The Westmark Trilogy:

Westmark. New York, Dutton, 1981.
The Kestrel. New York, Dutton, 1982.
The Beggar Queen. New York, Dutton, 1984.

The Vesper Holly Adventures:

The Illyrian Adventure. New York, Dutton, 1986.
The El Dorado Adventure. New York, Dutton, 1987.
The Drackenberg Adventure. New York, Dutton, 1988.
The Jedera Adventure. New York, Dutton, 1989.
The Philadelphia Adventure. New York, Dutton, 1990.

Biographies

Border Hawk: August Bondi, illustrated by Bernard Krigstein. New York, Farrar, Straus, 1958.

The Flagship Hope: Aaron Lopez, illustrated by Bernard Krigstein. Philadelphia, Jewish Publication Society, 1960.

PUBLICATIONS FOR CHILDREN

Fiction

Time Cat: The Remarkable Journeys of Jason and Gareth, illustrated by Bill Sokol. New York, Holt Rinehart, 1963; as *Nine Lives,* London, Cassell, 1963.

Coll and His White Pig, illustrated by Evaline Ness. New York, Holt Rinehart, 1965.

The Truthful Harp, illustrated by Evaline Ness. New York, Holt Rinehart, 1967.

The King's Fountain, illustrated by Ezra Jack Keats. New York, Dutton, 1971.

The Four Donkeys, illustrated by Lester Abrams. New York, Holt Rinehart, 1972; Kingswood, Surrey, World's Work, 1974.

The Foundling and Other Tales of Prydain, illustrated by Margot Zemach. New York, Holt Rinehart, 1973.

The Cat Who Wished to Be a Man. New York, Dutton, 1973.

The Wizard in the Tree, illustrated by Laszlo Kubinyi. New York, Dutton, 1975.

The Town Cats and Other Tales, illustrated by Laszlo Kubinyi. New York, Dutton, 1977.

The Fortune-Tellers, illustrated by Trina Schart Hyman. New York, Dutton, 1992.

PUBLICATIONS FOR ADULTS

And Let the Credit Go (novel). New York, Crowell, 1955.
My Five Tigers. New York, Crowell, and London, Cassell, 1956.
Janine Is French. New York, Crowell, 1958; London, Cassell, 1960.
My Love Affair with Music. New York, Crowell, 1960; London, Cassell, 1961.
Park Avenue Vet, with Dr. Louis Camuti. New York, Holt Rinehart, and London, Deutsch, 1962.

Fifty Years in the Doghouse. New York, Putnam, 1963; as *Send for Ryan!,* London, W. H. Allen, 1965.

My Cats and Me: The Story of an Understanding. Philadelphia, Running Press, 1989.

Translator from the French

The Wall and Other Stories, by Jean-Paul Sartre. New York, New Directions, 1948; as *Intimacy and Other Stories,* London, Peter Nevill, 1949.

Nausea, by Jean-Paul Sartre. New York, New Directions, 1949; as *The Diary of Antoine Roquentin,* London, Lehmann, 1949.

Selected Writings, by Paul Eluard. New York, New Directions, 1951; as *Uninterrupted Poetry: Selected Writings,* New York, New Directions, 1975.

The Sea Rose, by Paul Vialar. London and New York, Neville Spearman, 1951.

Contributor

Horn Book Reflections on Children's Books and Reading, edited by Elinor Whitney Field. Boston, Horn Book, 1969.

Cricket's Choice. Chicago, Open Court, 1974.

Celebrating Children's Books, edited by Betsy Hearne and Marilyn Kaye. New York, Lothrop, 1981.

Innocence and Experience, edited by Barbara Harrison and Gregory Macguire. New York, Lothrop, 1987.

The Voice of the Narrator in Children's Literature, edited by Charlotte F. Otten and Gary D. Schmidt. Westport, Connecticut, Greenwood, 1989.

The Big Book for Peace, edited by Ann Durell and Margaret Sachs. New York, Dutton, 1990.

The Cat on My Shoulder, edited by Lisa Angowski. Stamford, Connecticut, 1993.

The Zena Sutherland Lectures, 1983-1992, edited by Betsy Hearne. New York, Clarion, 1993.

*

Media Adaptations: Stage versions of *The Cat Who Wished to Be a Man* and *The Wizard in the Tree.* produced in Japan; television serial version of *The Marvelous Misadventures of Sebastian.* produced in Japan; *The Black Cauldron* (film based on the Prydain novels), Walt Disney Productions, 1985.

Biography: Entry in *Third Book of Junior Authors,* New York, H.W. Wilson, 1972; entry in *Dictionary of Literary Biography,* Volume 52, Detroit, Gale, 1986; essay in *Authors and Artists for Young Adults,* Volume 1, Detroit, Gale, 1989; essay in *Speaking for Ourselves: Autobiographical Sketches by Notable Authors of Books for Young Adults,* Volume 1, compiled and edited by Donald R. Gallo, National Council of Teachers of English, 1990; *Lloyd Alexander* by Jill P. May, Boston, Twayne, 1991.

Bibliography: *Lloyd Alexander, Evangeline Walton Ensley, Kenneth Morris: A Primary and Secondary Bibliography* by Kenneth J. Zahorski, Boston, Hall, 1981; *Lloyd Alexander: A Bio-Bibliography* by James S. Jacobs and Michael O. Tunnell, Westport, Connecticut, Greenwood, 1991.

Critical Studies: *Children's Literature Review,* Detroit, Gale, Volume 1, 1976, Volume 5, 1983; *A Tribute to Lloyd Alexander* by Myra Cohn Livingston, Philadelphia, Drexel Institute, 1976; *Lloyd Alexander: A Critical Biography* by James S. Jacobs, unpublished dissertation, University of Georgia, 1978; *Contemporary Literary Criticism,* Detroit, Gale, Volume 35, 1985; *The Prydain Companion* by Michael O. Tunnell, Westport, Connecticut, Greenwood, 1989.

Lloyd Alexander comments:

Although most of my books have been in the form of fantasy, I have always hoped to use this genre in a most personal way, to express my warm feelings and attitudes toward the real world and the real people in it. Writing realism or fantasy, my concerns are the same: how we learn to be genuine human beings.

*   *   *

The adjective that best describes Lloyd Alexander's work is "American." Whether he is writing about legendary Welsh sorcerers, turn-of-the-century adventurers, or ancient Chinese princes, Alexander's themes and outlook are clearly American. His favorite plot involves freeing an oppressed society and reordering it along democratic principles. During this democratization, Alexander's feisty young heroines and heroes grow up as their youthful idealism becomes tempered by a sometimes grim reality.

Alexander's most noted works are the five volumes of "The Chronicles of Prydain"—*The Book of Three, The Black Cauldron, The Castle of Llyr, Taran Wanderer,* and *The High King.* Although the characters and plots are inspired by Welsh legends, American values permeate the books. The orphaned Taran, whose family background remains a mystery, becomes high king of Prydain in a medieval version of the "any boy can be President" myth, and the self-ruled Free Commots are held up as the ideal democratic society. After many magical adventures and epic battles between good and evil, magic itself must depart Prydain so that a new human order can be established. "The Chronicles of Prydain" not only established Alexander's reputation as a fantasy writer, but they also reinvented American fantasy, bringing the genre critical respect as a serious dramatic form and setting high standards for other fantasy writers as well. This series represents Alexander at his best and highlights his gift for blending humor with high fantasy or other dramatic forms.

The "Westmark" trilogy displays a darker approach to Alexander's main themes of growing up and democratizing society. Political issues come to the fore as a printer's apprentice joins a rebellion against a tyrannical ruler in *Westmark,* the first volume of the series. *The Kestrel* and *The Beggar Queen* continue to raise issues about war, freedom of speech, and the right of self-government. Alexander makes no clear division between good and evil; moral choices are ambiguous, and characters must live with the often difficult consequences of their decisions. At the end of the series the young queen—an enlightened monarch—abdicates her throne in favor of a democratic government. Although Westmark and its neighbors are invented countries, this is not technically a fantasy series; indeed, the first volume is more of a picaresque adventure tale. Altogether, however, the three books are serious novels that explore painful questions of conscience for which there are no easy answers.

The "Vesper Holly" books comprise a much more light hearted series. Set at the turn of the century, these stories recount the adventures of a young lady from Philadelphia and her adoring, slightly stuffy guardian as they pursue their scientific interests to obscure corners of the world. Beginning with *The Illyrian Adventure* and continuing through *The El Dorado Adventure, The Drackenberg Adventure, The Jedera Adventure,* and *The Philadelphia Adventure,* Vesper and Brinnie use their American ingenuity and democratic principles to foil villains, join uprisings, uncover lost treasures, and restore stability in a number of imaginary countries. The series boasts a fast-paced vitality reminiscent of the best Victorian adventures; it's as if Sherlock Holmes and Dr. Watson were racing Captain Nemo to King Solomon's mines. These books represent a departure for Alexander: there are no lessons in growing up, no heavy political issues, and nothing serious to interfere with the humor and adventure.

Aside from these three series, Alexander has written a number of independent novels and biographies for young readers. His two biographies are *Border Hawk: August Bondi* and *Flagship Hope: Aaron Lopez.* Most of his other works are fantasies that rework his favorite themes. *Time Cat,* Alexander's first fantasy, follows the adventures of a cat and his boy as they travel through time to nine different countries. Another feline fantasy, *The Cat Who Wished to Be a Man,* is as light hearted as the "Vesper Holly" tales. Lionel, the cat of the title, convinces his master—a wizard—to transform him into a man so that he may see how humans live. Most of the action takes place in a small town ruled by a despotic mayor. Although Alexander paints on a smaller canvas in this book, he still employs his favorite themes: Lionel matures as he becomes more human, and the tyrannical mayor is overthrown by the democratic town council.

Three other fantasies deal with young men who grow up through travel and adventure, saving various kingdoms from tyranny along the way. The adventure in *The First Two Lives of Lukas-Kasha* takes place in the main character's mind, but when his fantasy adventure casts him as a king, his goal for his country is to make the monarchy obsolete. Similarly, the young musician in *The Marvelous Misadventures of Sebastian* helps a princess free her country from a ruthless regent, and the book concludes with the princess planning to convert her monarchy into a democracy. *The Remarkable Journey of Prince Jen* tells a similar story of ancient China. In this case, however, the hero is the highborn character and the heroine is the commoner—a reversal of Alexander's usual pattern. Totally isolated in the royal palace, Prince Jen has no idea what life is like in his country. A quest to find a mythical kingdom brings him and his companions face to face with the greed, petty tyranny, poverty, and despair that is crippling their country. Like other Alexander heroes, Jen must learn harsh lessons before he is fit to rule himself, let alone his people, but eventually he and his friends succeed in establishing a fair and equitable monarchy.

Although his underlying themes are serious and complex political issues, Alexander invariably leavens them with humor, thus making them more palatable. He is a master at creating memorable characters with a comic twist. But above all, he is a Philadelphian, and everything he writes reflects the values of the cradle of liberty.

—Donna R. White

ALLEN, Betsy. *See* CAVANNA, Betty.

ANDERSON, Margaret Jean

Nationality: American. **Born:** Gorebridge, Scotland, 24 December 1931; immigrated to Canada, 1955, and to the United States, 1963. **Education:** University of Edinburgh, B.Sc. (honors) 1953. **Family:** Married Norman H. Anderson in 1956; one son and three daughters. **Career:** Statistician, East Malling Research Station, Kent, England, 1953-1955; entomologist, Canada Department of Agriculture, Summerland, British Columbia, 1955-1956; statistician, Oregon State University, Corvallis, 1956-1957; writer, since 1957. **Awards:** Writing award, Canadian Entomological Society, 1973; Outstanding Science Book for Children selection, National Science Teachers Association and Children's Book Council, 1974, for *Exploring the Insect World,* and 1994, for *Charles Darwin: Naturalist,* and 1996, for *Isaac Newton: The Greatest Scientist of All Time; New York Times Book Review* outstanding book of the year, 1975, for *To Nowhere and Back;* Dorothy Canfield Fisher Award nominee, 1978, for *Searching for Shona,* 1978; Charlie May Simon Award, 1993, for *The Ghost Inside the Monitor;* Smithsonian notable book, 1997, for *Children of Summer: Henri Fabre's Insects.* **Address:** 3325 NW 60th Street, Corvallis, Oregon 97330-3102, U.S.A. **E-mail Address:** mja@pcak.org.

PUBLICATIONS FOR YOUNG ADULTS

Fiction

To Nowhere and Back. New York, Knopf, 1975.
In the Keep of Time. New York, Knopf, 1977.
Searching for Shona. New York, Knopf, 1978.
In the Circle of Time. New York, Knopf, 1979.
The Journey of the Shadow Bairns. New York, Knopf, 1980.
The Brain on Quartz Mountain, illustrated by Charles Robinson. New York, Knopf, 1982.
Light in the Mountain. New York, Knopf, 1982.
The Mists of Time. New York, Knopf, 1984.
The Druid's Gift. New York, Knopf, 1989.
The Ghost Inside the Monitor. New York, Knopf, 1990.

Non-Fiction

Exploring the Insect World. New York, McGraw-Hill, 1974.
Exploring City Trees, and the Need for Urban Forests. New York, McGraw-Hill, 1976.
Food Chains: The Unending Cycle. Hillside, New Jersey, Enslow Publishers, 1991.

Charles Darwin, Naturalist. Hillside, New Jersey, Enslow Publishers, 1994.
With Nancy Field and Karen Stephenson, *Ancient Forests: Discovering Nature,* illustrated by Sharon Torvik. Middleton, Wisconsin, Dog-Eared Publications, 1995.
Bizarre Insects. Hillside, New Jersey, Enslow Publishers, 1996.
Isaac Newton: The Greatest Scientist of All Time. Hillside, New Jersey, Enslow Publishers, 1996.
Carl Linnaeus, Prince of Botany/Father of Classification. Hillside, New Jersey, Enslow Publishers, 1997.
Children of Summer: Henri Fabre's Insects, illustrations by Marie Le Glatin Keis. New York, Farrar, Straus and Giroux, 1997.
With Nancy Field and Karen Stephenson, *Leapfrogging through Wetlands,* illustrated by Michael Maydak. Middleton, Wisconsin, Dog-Eared Publishers, 1998.

Contributor of nature articles to *Ranger Rick's Nature Magazine, Nature and Science, Insect-World Digest,* and *Instructor;* contributor to *Medley,* compiled by William K. Durr, Vivian O. Windley, and Anne A. McCourt, Boston, Houghton Mifflin, 1976, and *Ranger Rick's Surprise Book,* Washington, D.C., National Wildlife Federation, 1979.

*

Critical Studies: "Gather, Ye Witches and Warlock" by Alix Nelson, in *New York Times,* 4 May 1975, 26; review of *To Nowhere and Back,* in *Horn Book* (Boston), August 1975, 379; review of *In The Keep of Time,* in *Bulletin of the Center for Children's Books* (Chicago), July-August 1977, 169; review of *Searching for Shona* by Karla Kuskin, in *New York Times,* 26 November 1978, sec. 7, 100; entry in *Something About the Author,* Detroit, Gale, Vol. 27, 1982, 26-27; *Something About the Author Autobiography Series,* Detroit, Gale, Vol. 8, 1989, 17-31.

Margaret Anderson comments:

With the publication of *Bizarre Insects* (1996) and *Children of Summer: Henri Fabre's Insects* (1997), my writing seems to have gone full circle tying in to my first book *Exploring the Insect World* (1974). In between I wrote ten novels, mostly time-travel and historical fiction, and then I turned to writing biographies for Enslow's Great Minds of Science Series and two Nature Discovery Books on old-growth forests and wetlands. Although these titles sound very diverse they all reflect my two main interests—history and the care of our environment. And these two interests aren't unrelated. Studying history and where we've come from helps us see where we are heading. The people who have gone before us laid the foundation for most of today's triumphs and many of our problems. In the same way, our present-day discoveries and decisions affect the future.

Describing my career as a circle sounds a bit final. I'm hoping it's a spiral! At present I'm finishing up another biography for Enslow—*Scientists of the Ancient World,* which I'm co-authoring with my daughter Karen Stephenson. I plan to do another Nature Discovery book and the may go back to fiction again now that I have grandchildren asking for more!

*   *   *

Identity is the prevalent theme in Margaret J. Anderson's fiction. In her fiction and her nonfiction, characters discover who they are and learn about the environment in which they live. Anderson's time slip fantasies, many of which are set in Scotland, enable protagonists to experience different places, cultures, and eras and escape their restrictive lives. Through their time travel, many of her characters reexamine their preconceived ideas and become more accepting of themselves and their families and friends. These stories often have a scientific element and are highlighted by suspense and adventure.

Elizabeth, an American child living in England while her father pursues research, is lonely in *To Nowhere and Back.* In the village of Dorset, she watches children play around an English cottage. Touching a girl named Ann, Elizabeth magically enters her body and becomes a part of a nineteenth-century English peasant family. She experiences poverty and burdens but also finds acceptance and love. Angry that she cannot attend school like the boys, she realizes how fortunate she is in the twentieth century to have opportunities and choices. She values her access to food, school, and medical care and alters her perceptions of history and herself.

Supernatural time warps are the subject of Anderson's "Circle of Time" trilogy, which includes *In the Keep of Time, In the Circle of Time,* and *The Mists of Time.* In these books, Anderson stresses the importance of the past to the present and how decisions in the present create the future. She transports twentieth-century Scottish children to the fifteenth and twenty-second centuries through Smailholm Tower, an abandoned border keep. The first group of time travelers are four London children, Elinor, Andrew, Ian, and Ollie, who are staying in the countryside with their Aunt Grace while their parents are in France. The aunt provides them a key to the tower, and they magically travel to 1460 Scotland where Ollie becomes a child known as Mae. When the children return to the twentieth century, Mae refuses to resume her identity as Ollie, and the children have to teach her twentieth-century ways while disguising her change from their aunt. They decide to go through the tower again and arrive in the twenty-second century where they meet Vianah, an elderly woman, who helps to restore Ollie in time for a reunion with the children's parents.

In the Circle of Time sends two more children ahead in time to the year 2179. Robert Guthrie and Jennifer Crandall decide to look for missing stones in the Circle of Time for different reasons. Robert has heard his grandfather's stories about the stones moving toward the sea, and Jennifer is intrigued by archeology. Both have unhappy home lives. Robert wants to be an artist, but his father thinks he should run the family farm, especially since his older brother Duncan disappeared. Jennifer's mother is unhappy with rural life and is critical of everything, including her daughter. While debating superstition versus fact, the children are transported to another time. They encounter Kartan, who has heard Vianah's tales about meeting children from the past. Kartan's people believe in peace and simplicity and are fearful of the Barbaric Ones who threaten to conquer them. Robert and Kartan travel to the twentieth century, where Robert reconciles with his brother, parents, and himself, and Kartan gains wisdom about the past that created his people. In the third novel, *The Mists of Time,* Anderson focuses on Lara Avara, who lives in 2179. She has the "sight" which allows her to contact people in other times. When the Barbaric Ones enslave many of her people, she seeks Robert and Jennifer to help her. This book revolves around Anderson's themes of identity and trust. She portrays technology as a negative factor in society while emphasizing the value of preserving natural resources. The place where Kartan, Lara Avara, and Vianah live seems utopian and a symbol of good mitigating evil through non-violence.

Anderson continued her examination of these themes in two other books. *The Druid's Gift* is set on the remote St. Kilda Islands off the Scottish coast. Villagers rely on native seabirds for food and are peaceful, like the people of the trilogy. Their technology is simple and functional. Anderson combines history, legend, and fantasy to narrate Caitlin's time slips into other eras. Confused about her identity, Caitlin is aware that she is unusual and gradually realizes that she may be partially Druid. Caitlin embraces truth as the only way to conquer her fears and accept herself. Rana, a physically crippled girl, undergoes a similar spiritual transformation in *Light in the Mountain.* Saved from being a volcanic sacrifice to Atua Ahi, the God of Fire, Rana becomes the high priestess of her ancient Maori tribe. Manipulated by the treacherous Matakana, who wants to be chief, Rana leaves her parents and home to find the Land of the Long White Cloud where she is nurtured by the wise, elderly woman Hekura. Rana and her successor Ngaio choose to seek the truth and achieve love and peace for their community.

Anderson's focus on the discovery of one's identity is best represented in *Searching for Shona.* Orphans Marjorie Malcolm-Scott and Shona McInnes exchange identities and destinations at an Edinburgh train station in September 1939. Marjorie had been raised by a wealthy uncle and was supposed to travel to Canada during World War II, and Shona had grown up in an orphanage and was supposed to be evacuated to a rural Scottish town. Anderson focuses on Marjorie's six years posing as Shona, during which she unravels the mystery of who Shona was based on an oil painting in Shona's suitcase and serendipitous discoveries at the Clairmont House. As Shona, Marjorie carefully saves all the information she finds, planning to meet the real Shona after the war and resume her identity. Shona has other plans for the future, however, and Marjorie realizes that "She had found herself at last. And she liked what she had found."

Elspeth MacDonald also discovers who she is in *The Journey of the Shadow Bairns.* When her parents die in 1903, Elspeth is determined not to be separated from her four-year-old brother Robbie. She decides to emigrate to a Canadian settlement, using tickets her father had already bought for the family. Embarking on an uncertain journey from her Glasgow tenement, she cuts all ties to her past. Elspeth relies on her intelligence and intuition to secure passage on trains and ships and avoid scrutiny so that she and Robbie remain together. She creates the game "shadow bairns" to keep Robbie hidden from authorities. Anderson skillfully creates suspense when the children are separated during their final days of travel. Elspeth perseveres and finds Robbie while also learning to trust herself and new friends. She is brave and responsible but able to adjust and accept others' points of view, hinting at her future maturation and leadership within the community.

Anderson creates similar autonomous characters in *The Brain on Quartz Mountain* and *The Ghost Inside the Monitor.* In *The Brain on Quartz Mountain,* Dave accompanies his parents to a research center where he reads to a chicken brain as part of an experiment. The brain helps him win the Brain Scan contest sponsored by a radio station but he ultimately relies on himself in a final quiz. Sarah uses her computer skills and her ingenuity to solve a time travel mystery in *The Ghost Inside the Monitor.* Anderson's non-fiction also examines identity, whether that of a famous scientist or the characteristics of insects or plants. Her books about insects discuss the essential roles insects have in ecology. She urges readers to explore their environment and provides activities to aid comprehension of insect behavior. Her books about forests also stress understanding nature and explore the different viewpoints humans have toward the environment. Anderson urges readers to reconsider any preconceptions they might have about nature and to value natural resources. Her primary purpose is to interest people in science.

Anderson's biographies promote access to science by focusing on the humanity of each man. She shows how their personal lives and situations affected their development as scientists, often threatening their intellectual growth. For example, Sir Isaac Newton's mother pressured him to become a farmer instead of a scholar, Charles Darwin's father wanted him to become a doctor, and Carl Linnaeus was considered a poor student. Newton struggled with contemporary scientists and often delayed publishing his theories; Darwin also was deliberate with publicizing his ideas. Anderson uses her biographies to correct myths and explain complex ideas. She includes experiments, chronologies, glossaries, and maps to enhance her text. Illustrations of scientific instruments and places important to each scientist's life are included. In her effort to inspire readers, she resorts to dramatizing some details while other aspects are minimized. Her notes, however, suggest more comprehensive, scholarly sources.

Anderson blends fiction and non-fiction, past and present, in her exquisite example of literary non-fiction, *Children of Summer: Henri Fabre's Insects.* Based on the writings of Jean Henri Fabre, Anderson presents information about insects through the experiences of Fabre's ten-year-old son Paul. Supplemented with an index and glossary, her text explores such eccentricities as eating grubs and describes such familiar sights as moths hovering around lights. She explains insect behavior and corrects misconceptions in an inspiring manner that teaches without being overly didactic. This quality makes Anderson's work, both fiction and non-fiction, appealing to readers and offers a timeless approach in the literary search for identity and purpose.

—Elizabeth D. Schafer

ANDREWS, V(irginia C(leo)

Nationality: American. **Born:** Portsmouth, Virginia. **Education:** Educated in Portsmouth, Virginia. **Career:** Writer. Formerly worked as a fashion illustrator, commercial artist, portrait artist, and gallery exhibitor. **Died:** 19 December 1986.

PUBLICATIONS

Novels

Flowers in the Attic. New York, Pocket Books, 1979.
Petals on the Wind. New York, Simon and Schuster, 1980.
If There Be Thorns. New York, Simon and Schuster, 1981.
My Sweet Audrina. New York, Poseidon Press, 1982.
Seeds of Yesterday. New York, Poseidon Press, 1984.
Heaven. New York, Poseidon Press, 1985.
Dark Angel. New York, Poseidon Press, 1986.
Garden of Shadows. New York, Pocket Books, 1987.

Fallen Hearts. New York, Pocket Books, 1988.
Gates of Paradise. New York, Pocket Books, 1989.
Dawn. New York, Pocket Books, 1990.
Web of Dreams. Boston, G.K. Hall, 1990.
Secrets of the Morning. Boston, G.K. Hall, 1991.
Jardin Sombrio. La Costa Press, 1992.
Midnight Whispers. New York, Pocket Books, 1992.
Twilight's Child. Boston, G.K. Hall, 1992.
Darkest Hour. New York, Pocket Books, 1993.

*

Media Adaptations: *Flowers in the Attic* (film), Fries Entertainment-New World Pictures, 1987.

Biography: Essay in *Authors and Artists for Young Adults,* Volume 4, Detroit, Gale, 1990.

*   *   *

V.C. Andrews wrote several, extremely popular Gothic novels and was reported as one of the fastest-selling authors in America. Her works were originally published in paperback by Pocket Books and were especially popular with adolescents.

Flowers in the Attic, published in 1979, is the story of the four Dollanganger children who are locked in the attic by their mother and tortured by their grandmother. These four beautiful children are the product of an incestuous union. Their imprisonment occurs because their mother fears that she will be excluded from their fundamentalist grandfather's will if he learns of their existence. The children create their own world and turn to each other for love. *Flowers in the Attic* was originally a 290,000-word story called *The Obsessed.* Pared down to ninety-eight pages, the book was very ''reserved.'' Editors encouraged Andrews to write more from her imagination, so she began to tackle difficult subjects many had neglected. *Flowers in the Attic* was adapted into a movie in 1987 and filmed by Fries Entertainment—New World Pictures.

The lives of the Dollanganger children and their revenge continued in the next two novels—*Petals on the Wind* and *If There Be Thorns. Flowers in the Attic* was so popular that when readers found a sequel was forthcoming, demand became so great that Pocket Books advanced the publication date by several months. *Petals on the Wind* was so successful that it not only appeared on the best-seller list for nineteen weeks but also pulled *Flowers in the Attic* back on to the list for a time. Shocking and entrancing, *Petals on the Wind* continues *Flowers in the Attic*'s themes and may tax credibility. The last novel of the trilogy, *If There Be Thorns,* was also incredibly popular, reaching the number two slot only two weeks after its release. The ''Dollanganger'' series then continued with *Seeds of Yesterday* and *Garden of Shadows.*

The themes of the books—misogyny, rape, incest, and revenge—are touchy subjects to some readers and have provoked a degree of outrage. Adolescent girls still constitute a large portion of their readership. Some critics have called Andrews' plots unbelievable. A few critics, however, have praised her ability to captivate an audience with absorbing narrative and realistic point of view.

My Sweet Audrina was published in 1982. It relates the strange life of Audrina Adare who has been protected from the world by her parents. She has no sense of time or memory of the past. She is the second daughter of that name. The first was a beloved girl who died mysteriously at age nine. As the second Audrina grows up and falls in love, she is plagued by a jealous cousin and haunted by the memory of her dead older sister and her father's possessiveness. When she is grown, she confronts her father and learns of the intricate web of lies that protects her from a terrible truth.

Andrews' other novels continue with her themes of darkness and secrets. *Garden of Shadows* was published in 1987 after Andrews' death. This novel takes place before *Flowers in the Attic* and tells the story of forbidden passions and dreadful secrets. Its main character is Olivia, whose happiness becomes tainted when a jealous obsession threatens her two boys and beautiful girl, and the wicked curse of the Dollanganger family begins.

V.C. Andrews' "Casteel" series includes *Heaven, Dark Angel, Fallen Hearts, Gates of Paradise,* and *Web of Dreams.* After her death, Andrews' family chose a writer to complete her stories, beginning with her final books in the "Casteel" series. Much controversy has arisen from this ploy to keep a "dead" author writing other best-sellers.

Dawn, published in 1990, is solely the work of Andrew Neiderman. It tells the story of Dawn Longchamp and her brother, Jimmy, who have grown up in poverty. They are allowed to attend an exclusive private school because their father is a janitor there. When Dawn's mother dies, she discovers she was kidnapped at birth from a wealthy family. Humiliated and scorned, Dawn tries to find Jimmy and to rid herself of the awful lies that have changed their lives.

More novels in the "Dawn" series are promised. The Andrews family wrote the following in a letter prefaced to *Dawn:* "When Virginia became seriously ill while writing the 'Casteel' series, she began to work even harder, hoping to finish as many stories as possible so that her fans could one day share them. Just before she died we promised ourselves that we would take all of these wonderful stories and make them available to her readers."

—Lesa Dill

ANGELL, Judie

Has also written as Fran Arrick and Maggie Twohill. **Nationality:** American. **Born:** New York City, 10 July 1937. **Education:** Syracuse University, Syracuse, New York, B.S. 1959. **Family:** Married Philip Gaberman 20 December 1964; two sons. **Career:** Elementary school teacher, Brooklyn, New York, 1959-62; associate editor, New York City metropolitan edition of *TV Guide,* 1962-63; writer, WNDT-TV (now WNET-TV), New York City, from 1963; also worked as a switchboard operator and a waitress. **Awards:** Ethical Culture School Book Award, 1977, for *In Summertime It's Tuffy,* and 1979, for *A Word from Our Sponsor or, My Friend Alfred*; Best Books for Young Adults citation, American Library Association, 1978, for *Steffie Can't Come Out to Play,* 1980, for *Tunnel Vision,* 1983, for *God's Radar,* and 1985, for *One-Way to Ansonia.*

PUBLICATIONS FOR YOUNG ADULTS

Novels as Judie Angell

In Summertime It's Tuffy. New York, Bradbury Press, 1977.
Ronnie and Rosey. New York, Bradbury Press, 1977.
Tina Gogo. New York, Bradbury Press, 1978.
Secret Selves. New York, Bradbury Press, 1979.
A Word from Our Sponsor; or, My Friend Alfred. New York, Bradbury Press, 1979.
Dear Lola; or, How to Build Your Own Family: A Tale. New York, Bradbury Press, 1980.
What's Best for You. New York, Bradbury Press, 1981.
The Buffalo Nickel Blues Band. New York, Bradbury Press, 1982.
First, the Good News. New York, Bradbury Press, 1983.
Suds, a New Daytime Drama/Brought to You by Judie Angell. New York, Bradbury Press, 1983.
A Home Is to Share—and Share—and Share—. New York, Bradbury Press, 1984.
One-Way to Ansonia. New York, Bradbury Press, 1985.
The Weird Disappearance of Jordan Hall. New York, Orchard Books, 1987.
What's Best for You. New York, Collier, 1990.
Don't Rent My Room! New York, Bantam Books, 1990.
Leave the Cooking to Me. New York, Bantam Books, 1990.
Yours Truly. New York, Orchard Books, 1993.
The Case of the Burning Building; and, the Case of the Ruby Ring: The Adventures of Shirley Holmes (movie novelization). New York, Bantam Doubleday, 1999.

Novels as Fran Arrick

Steffie Can't Come Out to Play. New York City, Bradbury Press, 1978.
Tunnel Vision. New York City, Bradbury Press, 1980.
Chernowitz! New York City, Bradbury Press, 1981.
God's Radar. New York City, Bradbury Press, 1983.
Nice Girl from a Good Home. New York City, Bradbury Press, 1984.
Where'd You Get the Gun, Billy? New York City, Bantam Books, 1991.
What You Don't Know Can Kill You. New York City, Bantam Books, 1992.

Novels as Maggie Twohill

Who Has the Lucky Duck in Class 4-B? New York City, Bradbury Press, 1984.
Jeeter, Mason and the Magic Headset. New York City, Bradbury Press, 1985.
Bigmouth. New York City, Bradbury Press, 1986.
Valentine Frankenstein. New York City, Bradbury Press, 1991.
Superbowl Upset. New York City, Bradbury Press, 1991.

*

Media Adaptations: *Dear Lola; or, How to Build Your Own Family: A Tale* (videotape as *The Beniker Gang*), Scholastic, 1984; *Ronnie and Rosey* (audiocassette, Young Adult Cliffhangers Series), Listening Library, 1985.

Autobiography: *Speaking for Ourselves: Autobiographical Sketches by Notable Authors of Books for Young Adults,* edited by Donald R. Gallo, Urbana, Illinois, National Council of Teachers of English, 1990.

*   *   *

Judie Angell once identified the emotions of her own childhood as her most important source of inspiration: "I take a lot of those feelings, hug them, wrap them carefully in some words, and present them in a book with an invisible card that says, maybe this'll help a little—make you laugh—make you feel you're not alone."

As a child in New York City Angell loved to listen to music. While enjoying jazz, pop, and classical recordings she would use a crayon to write stories about a girl who saves animals from danger. In the 1950s she became a baseball fan, and the dark, moody atmosphere of music by composers such as Grieg and Tchaikovsky helped her draw pictures of the defeats of her favorite team, the Brooklyn Dodgers. In her teens she wrote in her diary while listening to music, finding that the music lent a rhythm to her entries. Angell's abiding interest in music—even her husband, Philip Gaberman, is a pop and jazz musician—was a source of inspiration in such novels as *The Buffalo Nickel Blues Band.*

Angell launched her career as a writer in 1977 with *In Summertime It's Tuffy.* Based on the author's experiences as both a camper and a counselor at summer camps, this novel is typical of those the author published under her real name by blending comedy with serious examination of the feelings and insights of adolescents. At the center of the novel is a witty eleven-year-old, Betsy, whose nickname is Tuffy. Her camp bunkmates include one who is obsessed with her weight, another who is irritatingly neat, and a third who thinks of little but boys and clothes. Between swimming, crafts, and other common camp activities, Tuffy becomes friends with Iris, whose wealthy parents pack her off to camp so they can travel. Iris takes an interest in black magic, hoping to use it to get her parents to spend more time with her. In the meantime Tuffy and her peers have to contend with "Uncle Otto," the camp's sometimes cruel head counselor.

Several of the author's Judie Angell books stand out for readers and reviewers. In *Dear Lola; or, How to Build Your Own Family: A Tale,* a group of adolescents escape from an orphanage to form their own family—with the aid of a syndicated advice columnist known to the public as Lola. *One-Way to Ansonia* is based on the life of Angell's grandmother. It tells the story of Rose, a teenage Jewish immigrant who arrives in the United States in the 1800s and finds her own path in life despite the prejudices of her family and community. At the center of *Leave the Cooking to Me* is a fifteen-year-old girl who, without the knowledge of her disapproving mother, finds independence by forming her own catering company. In *Yours Truly* a girl from a broken family loses contact with her father and tries to find someone to love. In all of these books the author gives honest and compassionate treatment to the emotional issues adolescents contend with in their relationships with friends and family.

The novels the author published under the name Fran Arrick are more somber in their mood and examine some of the issues older teenagers face in contemporary life: prostitution, suicide, AIDS, and violence. *Tunnel Vision,* for example, begins with the suicide of a talented fifteen-year-old and, through the use of flashbacks, explores the reactions to it of relatives and friends. *Nice Girl from a Good Home* looks at the devastating effects of sudden unemployment on a previously well-off family. In *Where'd You Get the Gun, Billy?* a town's peace is destroyed when a high school student shoots and kills his girlfriend. In *What You Don't Know Can Kill You* an eighteen-year-old girl faces hostility and prejudice when she contracts HIV, the virus that causes AIDS, from a boyfriend who has been unfaithful to her.

Under the pseudonym Maggie Twohill, the author also wrote several lighthearted books for middle-school readers. But despite the differences in tone and subject matter in the Angell, Arrick, and Twohill novels, the author applies to all her work a talent for exploring the feelings of resilient, likable characters who find unusual, creative ways to cope with changes in their lives as they grow up. By telling many of these stories through first-person narrators, she allows readers to encounter directly their thoughts and perceptions as they negotiate the difficult path from adolescence to adulthood.

—Michael J. O'Neal

ANGELOU, Maya

Pseudonym for Marguerita Annie Johnson. **Nationality:** American. **Born:** St. Louis, Missouri, 4 April 1928. **Education:** Attended schools in Arkansas and California; studied music privately, dance with Martha Graham, Pearl Primus, and Ann Halprin, and drama with Frank Silvera and Gene Frankel. **Family:** Married 1) Tosh Angelou in 1950 (divorced); 2) Paul Du Feu in 1973 (divorced 1981), one son. **Career:** Author, poet, playwright, educator, actress, dancer, and singer. Appeared in *Porgy and Bess* on twenty-two nation tour sponsored by the U.S. Department of State, 1954-55; appeared in Off-Broadway plays, *Calypso Heatwave,* 1957, and Jean Genet's *The Blacks,* 1960; with Godfrey Cambridge wrote, produced, and performed in *Cabaret for Freedom,* Off-Broadway, 1960; associate editor, *Arab Observer,* Cairo, 1961-62; assistant administrator, School of Music and Drama, University of Ghana Institute of African Studies, Legon and Accra, 1963-66; freelance writer for *Ghanaian Times* and Ghanaian Broadcasting Corporation, both Accra, 1963-65; appeared in *Mother Courage* at University of Ghana, 1964; feature editor, *African Review,* Accra, 1964-66; appeared in *Meda* in Hollywood, 1966; lecturer, University of California, Los Angeles, 1966; made Broadway debut in *Look Away,* 1973; writer-in-residence or visiting professor, University of Kansas, Lawrence, 1970, Wake Forest University, Winston-Salem, North Carolina, 1974, Wichita State University, Kansas, 1974, and California State University, Sacramento, 1974; director, *Moon on a Rainbow Shawl* by Errol John, London, 1988; Reynolds Professor, Wake Forest University, since 1981. Also television host and interviewer, and composer. Writer for Oprah Winfrey television series *Brewster Place.* Northern coordinator, Southern Christian Leadership Conference, 1959-60; member, American Revolution Bicentennial Council, 1975-76; member of the advisory board, Women's Prison Association; member of the board of trustees, American Film Institute, since 1975. Read poem, "On the Pulse of Morning," at President Clinton's inaugural ceremony in 1993. **Awards:** National Book Award nomination, 1970, for *I Know Why the Caged Bird Sings*; Yale University fellowship, 1970; Pulitzer Prize nomination, 1972, for *Just Give Me a Cool Drink of Water 'fore I Diiie*; Tony Award nomination, 1973, for performance in *Look Away*; Rockefeller grant, 1975; named Woman of the Year in Communications by *Ladies Home Journal,* 1976; Matrix Award in the field of books, Women in Communication, Inc., 1983; Distinguished Woman of North Carolina, 1992; Grammy Award, Best Spoken Word or Non-Traditional Album, for recording of "On the Pulse of Morning," 1993; named UNICEF National Ambassador, 1996; honorary degrees: Smith College, Northampton, Massachusetts, 1975; Mills College, Oakland, California, 1975; Lawrence University, Appleton, Wisconsin, 1976. **Agent:** Lordly and Dame Inc., 51 Church Street, Boston, Massachusetts 02116. **Address:** Department of Humanities, Wake Forest University, Reynolds Station, Winston-Salem, North Carolina 27109, U.S.A.

PUBLICATIONS

Novels

I Know Why the Caged Bird Sings. New York, Random House, 1970; London, Virago Press, 1984.
Gather Together in My Name. New York, Random House, 1974; London, Virago Press, 1985.
Singin' and Swingin' and Gettin' Merry Like Christmas. New York, Random House, 1976; London, Virago Press, 1985.
The Heart of a Woman. New York, Random House, 1981; London, Virago Press, 1986.
All God's Children Need Traveling Shoes. New York, Random House, 1986; London, Virago Press, 1987.
Wouldn't Take Nothing for My Journey Now. New York, Random House, 1993.

Poetry

Just Give Me a Cool Drink of Water 'fore I Diiie. New York, Random House, 1971; London, Virago Press, 1988.
Oh Pray My Wings Are Gonna Fit Me Well. New York, Random House, 1975.
Poems: Maya Angelou. New York, Bantam, 1981.
Shaker, Why Don't You Sing? New York, Random House, 1983.
Now Sheba Sings the Song, illustrated by Tom Feelings. New York, Dial Press, and London, Virago Press, 1987.
I Shall Not Be Moved. New York, Random House, 1990.
On the Pulse of Morning. New York, Random House, 1993.
Soul Looks Back in Wonder. New York, Dial, 1993.
The Complete Collected Poems of Maya Angelou. New York, Random House, 1994.
Phenomenal Woman: Four Poems Celebrating Women. New York, Random House, 1994.
A Brave and Startling Truth. New York, Random House, 1995.
Even the Stars Look Lonesome. New York, Random House, 1997.
Contributor of poetry, *Poetic Justice* (film). 1993.

Plays

With Godfrey Cambridge, *Cabaret for Freedom* (revue; produced New York, 1960).
The Least of These (produced Los Angeles, 1966).
Ajax (from the play by Sophocles; produced Los Angeles, 1974).

Georgia, Georgia (screenplay). Independent-Cinerama, 1972.
All Day Long (screenplay; also director). American Film Institute, 1974.
And Still I Rise (also director; produced in Oakland, California, 1976). New York, Random House, 1978; London, Virago Press, 1986.
With John Berry, *Sister, Sister* (television play). National Broadcasting Co., Inc., 1982.
With Alistair Beaton, *King* (lyrics), book by Lonne Elder III, music by Richard Blackford (produced London, 1990).

Recordings: *Miss Calypso,* Liberty Records, 1957; *The Poetry of Maya Angelou,* GWP Records, 1969; *An Evening with Maya Angelou,* Pacific Tape Library, 1975.

PUBLICATIONS FOR CHILDREN

Mrs. Flowers: A Moment of Friendship, illustrations by Etienne Delessert. Minneapolis, Redpath Press, 1986.
Life Doesn't Frighten Me, paintings by Jean-Michel Basquiat, edited by Sara Jane Boyers. New York, Stewart, Tabori & Chang, 1993.
My Painted House, My Friendly Chicken, and Me, photographs by Margaret Courtney-Clarke, designed by Alexander Isley Design. New York, C. Potter, 1994.
Kofi and His Magic, photographs by Margaret Courtney-Clarke, designed by Alexander Isley Design. New York, Clarkson Potter, 1996.

*

Media Adaptations: *Black, Blues, Black* (documentary), National Educational Television, 1968; *Assignment America* (documentary), 1975; *The Legacy* (documentary), 1976; *The Inheritors* (documentary), 1976; *I Know Why the Caged Bird Sings* (audio cassette with filmstrip and teacher's guide), Center for Literary Review, 1978, abridged version read by Angelou, New York, Random House, 1986; *I Know Why the Caged Bird Sings* (television movie), Columbia Broadcasting System, Inc., 1979; *Women in Business,* University of Wisconsin, 1981; *And Still I Rise* (television special), Public Broadcasting Service, 1985; *Making Magic in the World,* New Dimensions, 1988; *Trying to Make It Home* (documentary; *Byline* series), 1988; *Maya Angelou's America: A Journey of the Heart* (documentary; also host).

Biography: Entry in *Dictionary of Literary Biography,* Volume 38, Detroit, Gale, 1985; *Maya Angelou: Woman of Words, Deeds, and Dreams* by Stuart A. Kallen, Edina, Minnesota, Abdo & Daughters, 1993; *Maya Angelou* by Miles Shapiro, New York, Chelsea House, 1994; *Meet Maya Angelou* by Valerie Spain, New York, Random House, 1994; *Maya Angelou: More than a Poet* by Elaine S. Lisandrelli, Springfield, New Jersey, Enslow, 1996; *Maya Angelou: Journey of the Heart* by Jayne Pettit, New York, Lodestar, 1996.

Manuscript Collections: Wake Forest University, Winston-Salem, North Carolina.

Critical Studies: Entry in *Contemporary Literary Criticism,* Detroit, Gale, Volume 12, 1980, Volume 35, 1985; *Conversations with Maya Angelou* edited by Jeffrey M. Elliot, University, University of Mississippi, and London, Virago Press, 1989; *Order Out of Chaos: The Autobiographical Works of Maya Angelou* by Dolly A. McPherson, New York, P. Lang, 1990; *Heart of a Woman, Mind of a Writer, and Soul of a Poet: A Critical Analysis of the Writings of Maya Angelou* by Lyman B. Hagen, Lanham, Maryland, University Press of America, 1996; *Readings on Maya Angelou* edited by Mary E. Williams, San Diego, Greenhaven, 1997; *Understanding ''I Know Why the Caged Bird Sings'': A Student Casebook to Issues, Sources, and Historical Documents* by Joanne Megna-Wallace, Westport, Connecticut, Greenwood Press, 1998.

*   *   *

Maya Angelou has called herself ''the only serious writer who has chosen the autobiographical form to carry her work, her expression.'' In her five autobiographies, and also in her poetry, she dramatizes both the pleasure and the plight of a young black female in America.

The sequential books written by Angelou tell not just what has happened to her, but the effect upon her of these happenings. She relates things she has learned, how she has grown, and how she has moved along the trail of self-discovery. Her stories seem to tell themselves, and from them emerge the exposition of her themes. Angelou's dedication to personal growth and self-evaluation comes up repeatedly, and she continually modifies her ideas about black/white relationships over time. Despite early environmental conditioning, she eventually realizes—as did her friend Malcolm X—that not all whites are evil. Three familiar themes of black autobiography are found in both Angelou's prose and her poetry: repeated triumphs over obstacles, a search for identity, and the value of literacy and learning.

Angelou examines her childhood and responds to its problems by creating a persona. She has said she ''invented'' herself because she was tired of society inventing her, of distorting her personality, of turning a stereotype into reality, of bestowing upon her a label she rejected.

The biographical facts of Angelou's early life in Stamps, Arkansas in the 1930s—where she lived from the age of three to thirteen with Grandmother ''Momma'' Henderson after the divorce of her parents—are interwoven in her first autobiography, the highly successful and immensely popular *I Know Why the Caged Bird Sings* (1970). This book contains a series of anecdotes linked together by a theme of displacement: ''If growing up is painful for the Southern Black girl,'' she writes, ''being aware of her displacement is the rust on the razor that threatens the throat. It is an unnecessary insult.'' *Caged Bird* takes Angelou through high school graduation and the birth of her son. It includes most of the general elements of childhood autobiographies. A lack of self-esteem and a sense of insignificance show when Angelou says she is ''Awful'' because she wears hand-me-down clothes, and is a ''too-big Negro girl, with nappy black hair, broad feet and a space between her teeth that would hold a number-two pencil.'' Rejection is a factor related to the mostly absent mother and to the father, who is never depicted as affectionate. Being black in a segregated society, Angelou sees herself as dependent, ineffective, and small. She has to rely on the kindness of others—mainly her grandmother.

Angelou's four subsequent autobiographies proceed chronologically. The second volume, *Gather Together in My Name* (1974), covers her life as a teenaged mother, her introduction to drugs and illicit activities, and the basics of economic survival, and her young adult years as a show business personality are the focus of *Singin' and Swingin' and Gettin' Merry Like Christmas* (1976). Most of the latter tells about her adventures while on a *Porgy and Bess* tour for the U.S. State Department. Her life as an activist embroiled in social causes reflects a maturing Angelou in *The Heart of a Woman* (1981); and *All God's Children Need Traveling Shoes* (1986) relates her experiences as an expatriate in Ghana.

Much of Angelou's work is accessible to young readers, and she often speaks from the voice of a youthful protagonist. The persona of *Life Doesn't Frighten Me* (1993) issues a litany of things that she doesn't fear—though clearly she struggles with such fear, or she wouldn't need to declaim with such vigor. The book brings together Angelou's verse with paintings by the Haitian artist Jean-Michel Basquiat, a startling combination all the more successful in light of the fact that Basquiat's primitive images were not composed specifically for the book. A sense of the return to traditional African ways of life imbues *My Painted House, My Friendly Chicken, and Me* (1994), in which Thandi introduces the reader to her people, the Ndebele of Zimbabwe. Again, the book uses a strong visual counterpoint, in this case the geometric wall-paintings of the Ndebele themselves, to bring out the power of Angelou's straightforward prose.

Maya Angelou's stories are aptly called testimonials. She ''testifies'' not only for herself but also for her community. She writes about what she knows, and the universals embodied in her work serve to underscore her frequently expressed thesis: that as people, we are more alike than unalike.

—Lyman B. Hagen, updated by Judson Knight

ANONYMOUS (*Go Ask Alice*)

In 1971 a book for young adult readers was published and became an immediate success. Today, more than two decades later, *Go Ask Alice* is still going strong, with some three million copies in print, seventy-seven printings at this writing, translation into sixteen languages, and a made-for-TV movie based on it that still shows up regularly on late-night video. Many people who have expertise or interest in YA books, however, believe that *Alice's* greatest success is that it probably is one of the biggest hoaxes in publishing history.

When Prentice-Hall published the book, the author was listed as ''Anonymous,'' ostensibly to protect the identity of the fifteen-year-old drug addict whose diary it was. The original diary, P-H claimed, was hidden in a secure place and would not be released to anyone even though the girl was supposed to have died of an overdose, either accidental or intentional, only a few weeks after the last entry in her diary. A few years later, however, P-H ran an ad in *Publishers Weekly* describing their fall 1977 list of titles for young readers. One of the titles was *Voices,* and the annotation mentioned that its author, Beatrice Sparks, was ''the *author* [italics mine] of *Go Ask Alice.''* Curious, a number of librarians asked P-H how this could be, since the Epilogue to *Alice* clearly stated that the diarist had died of an overdose six years earlier. No response was forthcoming, but when the book finally appeared, its jacket stated that it was "from Beatrice Sparks . . . the author who brought you *Go Ask Alice.*" A year later, another Sparks title appeared, *Jay's Journal,* and this one also claimed to be "edited by Beatrice Sparks, who brought you . . . *Alice.*"

Needless to say, YA literature mavens were puzzled. One of these people, Alleen Pace Nilsen of Arizona State University, was puzzled enough to seek Sparks out and interview her about *Alice;* the interview, entitled "The House that Alice Built," appeared in the October 1979 issue of *School Library Journal* and a fascinating interview it was—and still is. Suffice it to say that after it appeared in *SLJ* very few people believed that *Alice* was a teenager's true tale.

The discussion above is given to illustrate how controversial *Go Ask Alice* is and has been, while at the same time a whole generation of young readers has bought it hook, line, and sinker, believing that they are reading a true story about someone very much like themselves. This goes a long way toward proving just how foolish the old saw about how you can't really fool the young is, because they are and always have been fooled by this book. And it is a dreadful book in almost every way. Not a line rings true as the word of a young person, but instead is blatantly the work of an adult trying mightily to sound like a kid but unable to do it. And there is a great deal of extremely clumsy swearing; anyone who knows young people knows that they know how to use cuss words very realistically and appropriately. Finally, the book is as didactic as any nineteenth-century religious tract; Sparks bludgeons the reader on nearly every page with pietistic preaching. A few passages from the book should illustrate these criticisms:

Oh to be stoned, to have someone tie me off and give me a shot of anything. I've heard paregoric is great. Oh hell, I wish I had enough anything to end the whole shitty mess.

July 27
Dear Diary,
I truly must have lost my mind or at least control of it, for I have just tried to pray. I wanted to ask God to help me but I could utter only words, dark, useless words which fell on the floor beside me and rolled off into the corners and underneath the bed. I tried. I really tried to remember what I should say after "Now I lay me down to sleep," but they are only words, useless, artificial, heavy words which have no meaning and no powers. They are like the ravings of the idiotic spewing woman who is now part of my inmate family. Verbal rantings, useless, groping, unimportant, with no power and no glory. Sometimes I think death is the only way out of this room.

If there were still doubts in anyone's mind about whether *Alice* was fact or fiction after Nilsen's damning interview in *SLJ* and the profound shallowness and phoniness of the book itself, they were surely dissolved by Sparks's next two books. Both purported to be true stories of real young people, told in their own words; each is as clumsy, shallow, phony, and didactic as *Alice,* with, if such is possible, a writing style that is simply unbelievably bad. *Voices* is supposed to be the stories of four teenagers who fall victim to some awful conditions of modern life. Mary, a bored sophomore in high

school, takes up with Dawn, "a clear-eyed quiet smiling girl," who inspires Mary to run off with her and join a cult called Heaven House presided over by the stereotypical guru, Sky, who soon sends Mary out to panhandle in the big city. At one point, Mary is rhapsodizing in her mind about her new life, which is "too wonderful, too special, too yummy" for words. A half dozen lines later she is "flipping the bird" at "a couple of cute dudes in a convertible." She is finally rescued (near death from starvation) from the satanic Sky, but not before the reader has been subjected to about eighty pages of totally unbelievable as well as totally bad prose.

Mark, whose story is subtitled "the lure of suicide," begins his turgid account with this statement: "As I think about the whole a-hole concept of life, I wonder if it's worth the hassle. Man, what a grind, what a hassle." Four lines later, he is telling about an incident when he was a little kid: "Like the time we made our Christmas home movie [and] the dad-gummed donkey we borrow-ed from someone wouldn't go." No teenager in the twentieth century has used the expression "dad-gummed" and probably their grandparents haven't either. Millie gets into what Sparks calls "the homosexual alternative" but what Millie calls "the Lizzie set," when Mrs. Stephens, Millie's typing teacher, takes an interest in her. In Millie's words, "Now that I'm an 'into it' person. I can't believe the time and patience she took to turn me on. Actually she softened me up for over three months before she finally laid it to me. Man, when I want someone, I want them now! I don't want to fool around. I guess you know most gays are real single shots, picking up numbers in gas station rest rooms and stuff, but her. I dunno . . . I guess it was the big conquest bit or something" (Author's note: Millie is thirteen at this time.) Millie is finally sent to a private girls' school, which of course is a hotbed of young "Lizzies." Jane, the last speaker in the book, pays "the price of peer pressure," which in her case means getting "hooked on sex." At one point she describes her life: "Once I went home with Marty, whose Mother (sic) worked. He was only twelve years old and I raped him—actually raped him! Can you believe that of a girl from a nice family like mine?" Mercifully, Jane's entire story takes only ten and one half pages to tell, because it's even sillier than the three which preceded it.

Two years after *Voices,* Sparks's final book was published. Called *Jay's Journal,* the book's cover says it is "The haunting diary of a sixteen-year-old in the world of witchcraft" This is another of her "true" stories, given to her in the form of a journal/diary such as the one Alice kept. Jay is her usual unhappy teenager, lonely and anxious until he enters "the eerie and dangerous world of the occult . . . a weird world of levitation and psychic forces, 'wangas' or feathered voodoo charms, auras and black presences, and grisly mystic rites like the Bootan ritual of cattle mutilation and baptism by blood." The book is pure Sparks; full of florid prose, outdated slang, teenage *angst,* and a message with a capital M— voodoo will get you just like drugs and cults and Lizzies and suicide and peer pressure, as it got Jay, who committed suicide. To no one's surprise except perhaps Sparks and her publisher, even the Library of Congress came to its senses with *Voices* and *Jay's Journal* and catalogued them as fiction (as which they later recatalogued *Alice* as well). Mercifully, both books have long been out of print, even though *Alice* goes on and on and on fooling the vulnerable young—and that's the real tragedy of *Go Ask Alice.*

—Audrey Eaglen

ANTHONY, Piers (Piers Anthony Dillingham Jacob)

Pseudonym: Also writes as Robert Piers (a joint pseudonym). **Nationality:** American. **Born:** Oxford, England, 6 August 1934; became United States citizen, 1958. **Education:** Goddard College, Plainfield, Vermont, B.A. 1956; University of South Florida, Tampa, teaching certificate 1964. **Military Service:** Served in the United States Army, 1957-59. **Family:** Married Carol Marble in 1956; two daughters. **Career:** Technical writer, Electronic Communications Inc., St. Petersburg, Florida, 1959-62; English teacher, Admiral Farragut Academy, St. Petersburg, 1965-66; freelance writer, from 1966. **Awards:** British Fantasy award, 1977, for *A Spell for Chameleon.* **Address:** P. O. Box 2289, Inverness, Florida 34451-2289, U.S.A.

PUBLICATIONS FOR YOUNG ADULTS

Novels

Omnivore. New York, Ballantine, 1968; London, Faber, 1969.
Sos the Rope. New York, Pyramid, 1968; London, Faber, 1970.
The Ring, with Robert E. Margroff. New York, Ace, 1968; London, Macdonald, 1969.
The E.S.P. Worm, with Robert E. Margroff. New York, Paperback Library, 1970.
Orn. New York, Avon, 1971; London, Corgi, 1977.
Prostho Plus. London, Gollancz, 1971; n.p., Berkley, 1973.
Var the Stick. London, Faber, 1972; New York, Bantam, 1973.
Rings of Ice. New York, Avon, 1974; London, Millington, 1975.
Triple Détente. New York, DAW, 1974; London, Sphere, 1975.
Neq the Sword. London, Corgi, 1975.
But What of Earth?, with Robert Coulson. Toronto, Laser, 1976; revised edition, New York, Tor, 1989.
Ox. New York, Avon, 1976; London, Corgi, 1977.
Steppe. London, Millington, 1976; New York, Tor, 1985.
Cluster. New York, Avon, 1977; London, Millington, 1978; as *Vicinity Cluster,* London, Panther, 1979.
Hasan. San Bernardino, California, Borgo Press, 1977.
A Spell for Chameleon. New York, Ballantine, 1977; London, Macdonald, 1984.
Chaining the Lady. New York, Avon, and London, Millington, 1978.
Kirlian Quest. New York, Avon, and London, Millington, 1978.
Castle Roogna. New York, Ballantine, 1979; London, Macdonald, 1984.
The Pretender, with Frances Hall. San Bernardino, California, Borgo Press, 1979.
The Source of Magic. New York, Ballantine, 1979; London, Macdonald, 1984.
God of Tarot. New York, Jove, 1979.
Faith of Tarot. New York, Berkley, 1980.
Vision of Tarot. New York, Berkley, 1980.
Split Infinity. New York, Ballantine, 1980; London, Granada, 1983.
Thousandstar. New York, Avon, 1980; London, Panther, 1984.
Blue Adept. New York, Ballantine, 1981; London, Granada, 1983.
Mute. New York, Avon, 1981; London, New English Library, 1984.
Centaur Aisle. New York, Ballantine, 1982; London, Macdonald, 1984.
Juxtaposition. New York, Ballantine, 1982.
Ogre, Ogre. New York, Ballantine, 1982; London, Futura, 1984.

Viscous Circle. New York, Avon, 1982; London, Panther, 1984.
Dragon on a Pedestal. New York, Ballantine, 1983; London, Futura, 1984.
Night Mare. New York, Ballantine, 1983; London, Futura, 1984.
Bearing an Hourglass. New York, Ballantine, and London, Severn House, 1984.
On a Pale Horse. New York, Ballantine, 1984; London, Panther, 1985.
Crewel Lye: A Caustic Yarn. New York, Ballantine, 1985; London, Futura, 1986.
With a Tangled Skein. New York, Ballantine, 1985; London, Panther, 1986.
Golem in the Gears. New York, Ballantine, and London, Futura, 1986.
Of Man and Mantra: A Trilogy (includes *Omnivore, Orn,* and *Ox*). London, Corgi, 1986.
Shade of the Tree. New York, St. Martin's, 1986; London, Grafton, 1987.
Wielding a Red Sword. New York, Ballantine, 1986; London, Grafton, 1987.
Being a Green Mother. New York, Ballantine, 1987; London, Grafton, 1988.
Dragon's Gold, with Robert E. Margroff. New York, Tor, 1987.
Out of Phaze. New York, Putnam, 1987; London, New English Library, 1989.
Tarot (includes *God of Tarot, Vision of Tarot,* and *Faith of Tarot*). New York, Ace, and London, Grafton, 1987.
Vale of the Vole. New York, Avon, 1987; London, New English Library, 1988.
Heaven Cent. New York, Avon, 1988; London, New English Library, 1989.
For Love of Evil. New York, Morrow, 1988; London, Grafton, 1989.
Robot Adept. New York, Putnam, 1988; London, New English Library, 1989.
Serpent's Silver, with Robert E. Margroff. New York, Tor, 1988.
Man from Mundania. New York, Avon, 1989; London, New English Library, 1990.
Unicorn Point. New York, Putnam, 1989; London, New English Library, 1990.
And Eternity. New York, Morrow, and London, Severn House, 1990.
Balook. Lancaster, Pennsylvania, Underwood Miller, 1990.
Chimaera's Copper, with Robert E. Margroff. New York, Tor, 1990.
Hard Sell. Houston, Texas, Tafford, 1990.
Isle of View. New York, Morrow, 1990.
Orc's Opal, with Robert E. Margroff. New York, Tor, 1990.
Phaze Doubt. New York, Putnam, 1990.
Through the Ice (completion of work by Robert Kornwise). Lancaster, Pennsylvania, Underwood Miller, 1990.
MerCycle, illustrated by Ron Lindham and Val Lindham. Houston, Texas, Tafford, 1991.
Question Quest. New York, Morrow, 1991.
Virtual Mode. New York, Putnam, 1991.
The Caterpillar's Question, with Philip Jose Farmer. New York, Ace, 1992.
The Color of Her Panties. New York, Morrow, 1992.
Fractal Mode. New York, Putnam, 1992.
Mouvar's Magic, with Robert E. Margroff. New York, Tor, 1992.
Demons Don't Dream. New York, Tor, 1993.
If I Pay Thee Not in Gold, with Mercedes Lackey. Riverdale, New York, Baen, 1993.
Killobyte. New York, Putnam, 1993.

Letters to Jenny. New York, Tor, 1993.
Isle of Woman. New York, Tor, 1993.

Other

Race against Time (for children). New York, Hawthorn, 1973.
Battle Circle (includes *Sos the Rope, Var the Stick,* and *Neq the Sword*). New York, Avon, 1978; London, Corgi, 1984.
The Magic of Xanth. New York, Doubleday, 1981.
Double Exposure (includes *Split Infinity, Blue Adept,* and *Juxtaposition*). New York, Doubleday, 1982.
Bio of an Ogre: The Autobiography of Piers Anthony to Age 50. New York, Ace, 1988.
Pier Anthony's Visual Guide to Xanth, with Jody Lynn Nye, illustrated by Todd Cameron Hamilton and James Clouse. New York, Avon, 1989.
Alien Plot (collection). New York, Doherty, 1992.
Chaos Mode. New York, Putnam, 1993.
Happy Thyme. England, New England Library, 1993.
Tales from the Great Turtle (anthology). New York, Tor, 1994.
Shames of Man. New York, Tor, 1994.
Geis of the Gargoyle. New York, Tor, 1995.
Roc and a Hard Place. New York, Tor, 1995.
Yon Ill Wind. New York, Tor, 1996.
Hope of Earth. New York, Tor, 1997.
Faun & Games. New York, Tor, 1997.
Spider Legs, with Clifford Pickover. New York, Tor, 1998.
Quest for the Fallen Star, with James Richey and Alan Riggs. New York, Tor, 1998.
Zombie Lover. New York, Tor, 1998.

Contributor, *Science against Man,* edited by Anthony Cheetham. New York, Avon, 1970.
Contributor, *Nova One: An Anthology of Original Science Fiction,* edited by Harry Harrison. New York, Delacorte Press, 1970.
Contributor, *Again, Dangerous Visions,* edited by Harlan Ellison. New York, Doubleday, 1972.
Contributor, *Generation,* edited by David Gerrold. New York, Dell, 1972.
Contributor, *The Berkley Showcase,* edited by Victoria Schochet and John Silbersack. New York, 1981.
Editor, with Barry N. Malzberg, Martin H. Greenberg, and Charles G. Waugh, *Uncollected Stars.* New York, Avon, 1986.

PUBLICATIONS FOR ADULTS

Novels

Chthon. New York, Ballantine, 1967; London, Macdonald, 1970.
Macroscope. New York, Avon, 1969; London, Sphere, 1972.
Kiai!, with Roberto Fuentes. New York, Berkley, 1974.
Mistress of Death, with Roberto Fuentes. New York, Berkley, 1974.
The Bamboo Bloodbath, with Roberto Fuentes. New York, Berkley, 1975.
Ninja's Revenge, with Roberto Fuentes. New York, Berkley, 1975.
Phthor. New York, Berkley, 1975; London, Panther, 1978.
Amazon Slaughter, with Roberto Fuentes. New York, Berkley, 1976.
Refugee. New York, Avon, 1983.
Mercenary. New York, Avon, 1984.

Bio of a Space Tyrant. Boston, Gregg Press, 1985.
Executive. New York, Avon, 1985.
Politician. New York, Avon, 1985.
Ghost. New York, Tor, 1986.
Statesman. New York, Avon, 1986.
Pornucopia. Houston, Texas, Tafford, 1989.
Total Recall. New York, Morrow, 1989; London, Legend, 1990.
Dead Morn, with Roberto Fuentes. Houston, Texas, Tafford, 1990.
Firefly. New York, Morrow, 1990.
Tatham Mound. New York, Morrow, 1991.
Volk (Internet novel; www.Pulpless.com and www.Xlibris.com). 1996.
With Alfred Tella, *The Willing Spirit.* New York, Tor, 1996.

Other

Anthonology (collection). New York, Tor, 1985; London, Grafton, 1986.

Also contributor, with Robert Margroff, under joint pseudonym Robert Piers, of a short story to *Adam Bedside Reader.* Also contributor of short stories to science fiction periodicals, including *Analog, Fantastic, Worlds of If, Worlds of Tomorrow, Amazing, Magazine of Fantasy and Science Fiction,* and *Pandora.*

*

Biography: Entry in *Dictionary of Literary Biography,* Volume 8, Detroit, Gale, 1981.

Manuscript Collections: Syracuse University, New York; University of South Florida, Florida.

Critical Studies: *Piers Anthony* by Michael R. Collings, Mercer Island, Washington, Starmont House, 1983; entry in *Contemporary Literary Criticism,* Volume 35, Detroit, Gale, 1985.

Piers Anthony comments:

I did not set out to write for young adults, but when I got into fantasy, the young adopted me, helping to make me a bestseller, and thereafter I wrote increasingly for them. Raising two daughters gave me perspective, because I became hyper-aware of whatever age they were, from infancy through college, and this helped me relate. Also, when I mentioned a suicidally depressive fourteen year old female correspondent in an Author's Note, others of that persuasion wrote to me, so that I gained an unanticipated education. I never was a teen girl, but I do have half a notion what depression is, and I take it seriously, so I relate well. Finally I used what I had learned to make a character of that type, Colene in *Virtual Mode,* and thereafter had confirmation from girls (and a few boys) that I had gotten it right. Some of these young folk have fully adult problems, and there is nothing trivial about their depression. I hope to show about twenty of their evocative, sometimes savage, sometimes shocking poems in the sequel to my autobiography, *How Precious Was that While,* which has not yet been published. Thus I have found that there is no clear line between juvenile and adult status, emotionally; youth is not necessarily a time of innocence, unfortunately.

* * *

Known as a prolific and controversial writer of fantasy and science fiction for young adults, Piers Anthony himself suggests that his works are merely entertaining and relaxing. Even though his plots may sound familiar, Anthony is capable of making the ordinary extraordinary with his unique plot twists and unusual phrasings.

Among the myriad novels to his credit are several series. The first novel to be published, *Chthon,* was a Nebula and Hugo Award nominee. It has a sequel called *Phthor.* Both novels share Anthony's characteristic motifs and organization. They contain a mixture of classical myth and legend, modern psychoanalysis, more traditional literary themes, and folk tales. *Chthon* tells of Anton Five and his fellow prisoners in the garnet mines inside the planet Chthon. *Phthor* continues with the tale of Arlo, Anton's son, and concludes with a major conflict between mineral and organic intelligence. While Anton's imprisonment is symbolic of humanity's status today, his escape foreshadows hope for mankind.

In the "Omnivore" series (*Omnivore, Orn, Ox*), three space explorers from Earth—Veg, Cal, and Aquilon—explore alternate worlds. Through their adventures, the human race is assessed to its detriment as Anthony examines man's role in the natural world. The "Battle Circle" trilogy (*Sos the Rope, Var the Stick, Neq the Sword*) takes place after the devastation of nuclear war has reduced America to barbaric nomads and an underground of technological experts who have survived. *Macroscope,* considered Anthony's best work by some critics, features a mechanical device that enables man to penetrate the mysteries of the universe and the human consciousness so that humanity loses significance in relation to the universe, even as an individual might lose meaning versus mass society.

The Tarot novels—originally *God of Tarot, Vision of Tarot,* and *Faith of Tarot* —again question humanity, this time in the form of questioning the beliefs of the individual. Brother Paul of the secular Holy Order of Vision investigates odd tarot animations that may imply the existence of a deity and at the same time makes discoveries of his own.

The "Apprentice Adept" novels (*Split Infinity, Blue Adept, Juxtaposition, Out of Phaze, Robot Adept, Unicorn Point, Phaze Doubt*) attempt to combine fantasy and science fiction. Science fiction is sprinkled with magic and the natural in *Out of Phaze.* The world of Phaze is contrasted to Proton. The former is magical but still natural, while the latter is scientific and ecologically controlled.

The "Magic of Xanth" series (*A Spell for Chameleon, The Source of Magic, Castle Roogna, Centaur Aisle, Ogre, Ogre, Night Mare, Dragon on a Pedestal, Crewel Lye: A Caustic Yarn, Golem in the Gears, Vale of the Vole, Heaven Cent, Man from Mundania*), the most popular of Anthony's writings, is light-hearted and pun-filled. Xanth is a fairy-tale peninsula populated by dragons, ogres, centaurs, and nymphs. These episodic novels, filled with references to classical myths, reflect Anthony's environmental concerns. Some readers, however, are troubled by their over-reliance on word play and by their use of sexist humor.

The "Bio of a Space Tyrant" series (*Refugee, Mercenary, Politician, Executive, Statesman*) and the "Incarnations of Immortality" series (*On a Pale Horse, Bearing an Hourglass, With a Tangled Skein, Wielding a Red Sword, Being a Green Mother, For Love of Evil,* and *And Eternity*) comprise Anthony's "serious" phase and express his views on society. In "Incarnations,"

personifications of Death, Time, Space, War, and Nature battle Satan. The "Bio" novels show the rise to power of a space refugee on the planet Jupiter.

Anthony's prodigious output includes a number of individual novels of science fiction and fantasy, a collection of short stories *Anthology,* an autobiography entitled *Bio of an Ogre,* and *Race against Time,* specifically marketed as juvenile fiction. While entertaining his readers with his inventive word play, numerous literary allusions, apt symbolism, humorous satire, and wild adventures, Anthony effectively conveys his personal convictions about man's responsibilities in and to the universe.

—Lesa Dill

ARMSTRONG, Jennifer

Has also written as Julia Winfield. **Nationality:** American. **Born:** Waltham, Massachusetts, 12 May 1961. **Education:** Smith College, Northampton, Massachusetts, B.A. 1983. **Career:** Assistant editor, Cloverdale Press, New York City; free-lance writer, since 1985. Girl Scout leader, 1987-89; Smith College recruiter, since 1990; board president, Literacy Volunteers of Saratoga, 1991-93; leader of writing workshops; puppy raiser for Guiding Eyes for the Blind. **Awards:** Best Book Award, American Library Association, Golden Kite Honor Book Award, Society of Children's Book Writers and Illustrators, and American Library Association (ALA) Notable Children's Book citation, all 1992, all for *Steal Away;* American Library Association (ALA) Notable Children's Book citation, 1992, for *Hugh Can Do,* and 1994, for *Chin Yu Min and the Ginger Cat.* **Agent:** Susan Cohen, Writer's House, 21 West 26th Street, New York, New York 10010, U.S.A.

PUBLICATIONS FOR YOUNG ADULTS

Fiction as Julia Winfield

Only Make-Believe. New York, Bantam, 1987.
On Dangerous Ground. New York, Bantam, 1989.
Partners in Crime. New York, Bantam, 1989.
Private Eyes. New York, Bantam, 1989.
Tug of Hearts. New York, Bantam, 1989.

Fiction

Steal Away. New York, Orchard Books, 1992.
Ann of the Wild Rose Inn. New York, Bantam, 1994.
Bridie of the Wild Rose Inn. New York, Bantam, 1994.
Claire of the Wild Rose Inn. New York, Bantam, 1994.
Emily of the Wild Rose Inn. New York, Bantam, 1994.
Grace of the Wild Rose Inn. New York, Bantam, 1994.
Laura of the Wild Rose Inn. New York, Bantam, 1994.
Black-Eyed Susan. New York, Crown, 1995.
The Dreams of Mairhe Mehan. New York, Knopf, 1996.
Mary Mehan Awake. New York, Knopf, 1997.

PUBLICATIONS FOR CHILDREN

The Puppy Project. New York, Bantam, 1990.

Too Many Pets. New York, Bantam, 1990.

Hillary to the Rescue. New York, Bantam, 1990.

That Champion Chimp. New York, Bantam, 1990.

Hugh Can Do, illustrated by Kimberly Bulcken Root. New York, Crown, 1992.

Chin Yu Min and the Ginger Cat, illustrated by Mary GrandPre. New York, Crown, 1993.

That Terrible Baby, illustrated by Susan Meddaugh. New York, Tambourine Books, 1994.

Little Salt Lick and the Sun King, illustrated by Jon Goodell. New York, Crown, 1994.

Wan Hu Is in the Stars, illustrated by Barry Root. New York, Tambourine Books, 1995.

King Crow, illustrated by Eric Rohmann. New York, Crown, 1995.

The Snowball, illustrated by Jean Pidgeon. New York, Random House, 1996.

Patrick Doyle Is Full of Blarney, illustrated by Krista Brauckmann-Towns. New York, Random House, 1996.

Sunshine, Moonshine. illustrated by Lucia Washburn. New York, Random House, 1997.

Foolish Gretel, illustrated by Donna Diamond. New York, Knopf, 1997.

The Whittler's Tale, illustrated by Valery Vasiliev. New York, Tambourine Books, 1994.

Pockets, illustrated by Mary GrandPre. New York, Crown, 1998.

Nonfiction

Shipwreck at the Bottom of the World. New York, Crown, 1998.

*

Critical Studies: Review of *Steal Away* by Jeanette Lambert, in *The Book Report* (Worthington, Ohio), November/December 1992, 41; entry in *Something About the Author,* Detroit, Gale, Vol. 77, 1994, 5-8; "The Young Adult Perplex: Reading Teenagers Enjoy" by Cathi Dunn MacRae, in *Wilson Library Bulletin* (Bronx, New York), May 1994, 100-101; "A Kaleidoscope of Perspectives in Children's Literature About Slavery and the American Civil War" by Maria A. Perez-Stable, in *The Social Studies* (Washington, D.C.), January/February 1996; review of *Black-Eyed Susan* by Elizabeth S. Watson, in *Horn Book* (Boston), March/April 1996, 193-194; review of *The Dreams of Mairhe Mehan* in *The Book Report* (Worthington, Ohio), January/February 1997, 33; review of *Mary Mehan Awake* by Marie Wright, in *School Library Journal* (New York), January 1998, 108.

Jennifer Armstrong comments:

When my father was a small boy, he would play beneath the ironing bozrd while my grandmother, who was a high school English teacher, recited Shakespeare to make the chore of ironing more pleasant. This image, the child beneath the ironing board, the mother reciting from *Hamlet* and *Measure for Measure,* is one I used in a novel of mine, *Black-Eyed Susan.* I admit I took it from my father, as I have taken many things from both my father and my mother.

Of course, it is an author's job to take things, ingredients, ideas, images, and use them and make meaning with them. Although I would not have defined the work of an author this way when I was in first grade, I still knew—way back then—that I was going to be one.

*   *   *

"This is the forest primeval. The murmuring pines and the hemlocks. . ." recites thirteen-year-old Susannah McKnight, as she embarks on her run-away journey from her uncle's house in Virginia back to her home in Vermont, in Jennifer Armstrong's first book for young adults, *Steal Away.* "Steal away! Steal away to freedom!" sings Susannah's thirteen-year-old companion, Bethlehem Reid, who is fleeing from her life as Susannah's uncle's slave. Although the girls have different personal motives and vastly different stakes in the outcome of their perilous voyage, they are equally determined to see it through, and see it through they do. Their story, told here forty-one years later by the grown women they have become and transcribed by Susannah's thirteen-year-old granddaughter Mary and Bethlehem's thirteen-year-old student Free, is a rare and moving tale of slavery and freedom, of courage and determination, and, most of all, of true friendship that transcends the bounds of color and class, distance and time.

Jennifer Armstrong's next young adult novel, *Black-Eyed Susan,* written for slightly younger readers, is set in the Dakota Territory in the days of prairie schooners and pioneers. Like her homesteader father, ten-year old Susie, the narrator, loves the wide-open spaces, the endless miles of prairie grass. But her mother is lonesome for her old home, her family and friends in Ohio. On the day the novel takes place, Susie leads her depressed mother to the front porch and envisions a wonderful transformation: "We shared the view again, seeing how the land lay about us and fell in swells and rises, the movement of the wind visible in the movement of the grass. I imagined my mother diving into the inland sea at Lake Huron and swimming down in the darkness, swimming west until she pulled herself up out of the depths into the bright sky of the Dakotas, rising up and sparkling like crystal. I imagined her turning with a smile, smiling at me and holding out her hand and saying, 'Good morning, Black-Eyed Susan.'" Readers who liked Patricia MacLachlan's *Sarah, Plain and Tall* (New York, Harper, 1985) will like this book, too.

"Were these my dreams? Were these then my brother's dreams? Was I my dreams?," asks Mairhe Mehan at the opening of *The Dreams of Mairhe Mehan:*

"I'll tell you what happened to Mike in the night, of the three sounds of sorrow, of Lincoln's hornpipe, of my Da. I was Mairhe Mehan, and these were my dreams . . . . Or perhaps they never were dreams at all. Their province is the edge of things, as it was mine: in the doorway, on the threshold, in the twilight, between one world and another. So who can say if they happened or no? They're true enough, that I swear. They're woven tight and strong as any story is woven, thread following thread, the patterns emerging, the knots broken, the stitches dropped and reclaimed, the loose ends left or tied, the way we weave our own lives. They are stories. I'll tell them."

Mairhe (pronounced "Moira") lives with her brother Mike and her father in the Irish slum of Swampoodle in Washington, D.C. After Mike enlists in the Union Army, Mairhe's father suffers a mental collapse and is taken in by the parish, leaving Mairhe to make it on her own. The proprietors of Shinny's saloon, where she works, take her in in their upstairs apartment. All alone, Mairhe is desperate to get her brother Mike back home and away from the mortal danger of the battlefield. She saves all her tips (her wages pay for her room and board) and makes yards and yards of lace to earn enough money to pay for Mike's discharge. In her desperation, Mairhe turns to a large kindly man with "wild, white hair" she runs into when he is on an errand in Swampoodle. It is Walt Whitman. The poet befriends her, helps her try to get information on Mike and his whereabouts, and urges her to help the sick and dying soldiers.

Mary Mehan Awake continues Mairhe's (now Mary) story. Mike has died in battle, Mary has followed Whitman's advice by helping nurse the soldiers, and she has come to the brink of mental and physical collapse herself. Her friend "The Good Gray Poet" again intercedes, and gets her a job with a naturalist, Jasper Dorsett, and his wife Diana on their peaceful country estate in upstate New York. At first, Mary cannot get the sound of the soldiers' screaming out of her ears, the sight of their bleeding, mutilated bodies out of her eyes, or the raw emotion of dealing with life and death day after day out of her heart. With the Dorsett's gentle help—and with the companionship of their gardener, Henry, who lost his hearing in the shock of battle—she slowly comes back to life. In her January 1998 review of the book for *School Library Journal*, Marie Wright described this beautifully lyrical book as a "wonderful story about love, dreams, and renewal."

Graduates of the Pleasant Company's "American Girls" series of historical fiction who have reached their teen years will love Armstrong's "Wild Rose Inn" series. Beginning with *Bridie of the Wild Rose Inn* (set in the Massachusetts Bay Colony in 1695), the series follows the lives of generations of teenage girls who have lived in the Marblehead, Massachusetts, inn over the years: Ann (1774), Emily (1858), Laura (1898), Claire (1928) and Grace (1944). Lively characterization and vivid historical detail and language help make history come alive. Moreover, as Cathi Dunn MacRae wrote in her May 1994 *Wilson Library Bulletin* column on "Reading Teenagers Enjoy": "Despite youths' fixation with the moment, some young adults wonder how life was for those before.... The span of the Wild Rose series allows readers to connect America's unfolding with the fortunes of one family, watching one town grow and change, building anticipation for future volumes."

—Marcia Welsh

ARMSTRONG, William H(oward)

Nationality: American. **Born:** Lexington, Virginia, 14 September 1914. **Education:** Hampden-Sydney College, A.B. (cum laude) 1936; graduate study at University of Virginia, Charlottesville, 1937-38. **Family:** Married Martha Stone Street Williams in 1943 (died, 1953); two sons, one daughter. **Career:** History teacher, Virginia Episcopal School, 1939-44; history master, Kent School, Kent, Connecticut, beginning 1945; farmer, writer, real estate

agent. **Awards:** National School Bell Award of National Association of School Administrators, 1963, for distinguished service in the interpretation of education; Lewis Carroll Book Shelf Award, 1970; John Newbery Medal from American Library Association, 1970, Mark Twain Award from Missouri Association of School Librarians, 1972, and Nene Award from Hawaii Association of School Librarians and Hawaii Library Association, all for *Sounder;* Academy Award nomination for the media adaptation of *Sounder,* 1972; Jewish-Christian Brotherhood award, 1972; Sue Hefley Award, 1976; D. Litt.: Hampden-Sydney College, 1986. **Address:** Kimadee Hill, Kent, Connecticut 06757, U.S.A.

PUBLICATIONS FOR YOUNG ADULTS

Fiction

Sounder, illustrated by James Barkley. New York, Harper, 1969; London, Gollancz, 1971.
Sour Land, illustrated by David B. Armstrong. New York, Harper, 1971; illustrated by Chris Molan, London, Penguin, 1993.
The MacLeod Place, illustrated by Eros Keith. New York, Coward, 1972.
The Mills of God, illustrated David B. Armstrong. New York, Doubleday, 1973.
JoAnna's Miracle. Nashville, Broadman, 1978.
The Tale of Tawny and Dingo, illustrated by Charles Mikolaycak. New York, Harper, 1979.

Other

Tools of Thinking: A Self-Help Workbook for Students in Grades 5-9 Woodbury, New York, Barron's, 1968; as *Word Power in 5 Easy Lessons: A Simplified Approach to Excellence in Grammar, Punctuation, Sentence Structure, Spelling and Penmanship,* 1969.
Barefoot in the Grass: The Story of Grandma Moses. New York, Doubleday, 1970.
Hadassah: Esther the Orphan Queen, illustrated by Barbara Byfield. New York, Doubleday, 1972.
My Animals, illustrated by Mirko Hanak. New York, Doubleday, 1973.
The Education of Abraham Lincoln, illustrated by William Plummer. New York, Coward, 1974.
Adapter, with Hana Doskocilova, *Animal Tales,* illustrated by Mirko Hanak, translated from the Czechoslovakian by Eve Merriam. New York, Doubleday, 1970.

PUBLICATIONS FOR ADULTS

Other

Study Is Hard Work. New York, Harper, 1956.
Through Troubled Waters, New York, Harper, 1957.
Peoples of the Ancient World, with Joseph W. Swain. New York, Harper, 1959.
87 Ways to Help Your Child in School. Great Neck, New York, Barron's, 1961.
Study Tapes. Woodbury, New York, Barron's. 1975.
Study Tips: How to Improve Your Study Habits and Improve Your Grades. Woodbury, New York, Barron's, 1976; revised edition, as *Study Tactics,* 1983.

*

Media Adaptations: *Sounder* (film), Twentieth Century-Fox, 1972.

Biography: Entry in *More Books by More People* by Lee Bennett Hopkins, Citation, 1974; essay in *Something about the Author Autobiography Series,* Volume 7, Detroit, Gale, 1988, pp. 1-16.

Manuscript Collections: Kerlan Collection, University of Minnesota.

Critical Studies: Entry in *Children's Literature Review,* Volume 1, Detroit, Gale, 1976.

*   *   *

William Armstrong was for over thirty years a high school history teacher. His perspective of the past, his interest in social change, and his deep concern for individuals are reflected in both the biographical and the fictional books he writes. Armstrong has written about ancient times in *The MacLeod Place,* and about great Americans in *The Education of Abraham Lincoln* and *Barefoot in the Grass* (the life of Grandma Moses). But it is his writings about the twentieth century—its social values and institutions, its social problems—that are particularly compelling and for which he is best known.

His most successful book is the novel *Sounder,* which reflects two developments in mid-twentieth-century American literature for children: a willingness to look at the presence and the pain of racial and ethnic injustices in society and a willingness to look at adolescent development—at the growing up process, including the joys and the hurts that accompany transition from childhood to adulthood.

Sounder is one of the few books of mid-century focused on black adolescents in the South. Armstrong tells us that *Sounder* is the black man's story, told to him by an elderly teacher who ran the one-room black school several miles from Armstrong's childhood home in Virginia. This man worked for Armstrong's father after school and in the summer, and attended Armstrong's white church because there was seldom a preacher for the church in his black district. In the evening the teacher told the Armstrong children stories from Aesop, the Old Testament, and Homer. One night at the table after he had told the story of Argus, the faithful dog of Odysseus, he told the story of Sounder, a faithful coon dog. This story was not from Aesop, the Old Testament, or Homer, but from his own history.

Sounder describes the rural South at the turn of the century, a society caught up in a web of ignorance, prejudice, and great poverty. The focus is on one nameless black family: its isolation from society but its love for one another, its lack of opportunity and its determination, despair, and hope. It begins with the father, the coon dog, and the oldest child (a boy) going hunting. Later the father, a sharecropper, steals food for his hungry family and is imprisoned in a terrible criminal justice system. The mother then toils alone, with determination and skill, to provide for her children. The boy does as much as he can for the family. He does something else as well; he goes to school. He walks for miles and miles to find an education.

The father comes home to die after being seriously wounded in a dynamite blast in the prison quarry—one side of his body crushed under an avalanche of limestone. The old dog Sounder, crushed in spirit, also dies. But the boy returns to school and learns to read. His teacher helps him, through a discussion of literature, to understand that love does not die but continues for whoever has known it.

In *Sounder* Armstrong engages the reader in a history of brave and caring people who do not cry out against the wrongs meted them, but who continue in whatever way they are able, to survive with dignity and rightness. The book with stunning clarity points out the devastating consequences of racial discrimination to members of minority and majority groups.

Armstrong has received many book awards, including the John Newbery Medal and the Mark Twain award for *Sounder. Sounder* was the basis of a compelling movie of that name, produced by Twentieth Century Fox in 1972. Armstrong has also received awards for distinguished service in education, including the National School Bell Award.

Armstrong writes about complicated characters and cultures in a careful, deliberate style, elegant in its simplicity and honesty. His stories are for adolescents, but adults are welcome to read them for they offer extraordinarily moving pictures of people and their changing places in the world. They extol human resilience and raise questions of human responsibility.

—Mary Lystad

———

ARRICK, Fran. *See* **ANGELL, Judie.**

———

ASHABRANNER, Brent (Kenneth)

Nationality: American. **Born:** Shawnee, Oklahoma, 3 November 1921. **Education:** Oklahoma State University, B.S. 1948, M.A. 1951; additional study at University of Michigan, Ann Arbor, 1955, and Boston University, Massachusetts, and Oxford University, 1959-60. **Military Service:** Served in the U.S. Navy, 1942-45. **Family:** Married Martha White in 1941; two daughters. **Career:** Oklahoma State University, Stillwater, instructor in English, 1952-55; Ministry of Education, Technical Cooperation Administration, Addis Ababa, Ethiopia, educational materials adviser, 1955-57; International Cooperation Administration, Tripoli, Libya, chief of Education Materials Development Division, 1957-59; Agency for International Development, Lagos, Nigeria, education program officer, 1960-61; Peace Corps, Washington, DC, acting director of program in Nigeria, 1961-62, deputy director of program in India, 1962-64, director of program in India, 1964-66, director of Office of Training, 1966-67, deputy director of Peace Corps, 1967-69; Harvard University, Center for Studies in Education and Development, Cambridge, Massachusetts, research associate, 1969-70; Pathfinder Fund, Boston, Massachusetts, director of Near East-South Asia Population Program, 1970-71; director of project development for World Population International Assistance Division, Planned Parenthood, 1971-72; Ford Foundation, New York City, associate representative and population program officer, 1972-80, deputy representative to Philippines, 1972-75, deputy representative to Indonesia, 1975-80; writer, since 1980. **Awards:** National Civil Service League career service award, 1968; Notable Children's Trade Book in the Field of Social Studies, 1982, and Carter G. Woodson Book Award, National Council for the Social Studies, 1983, both for *Morning Star, Black Sun: The Northern Cheyenne Indians and America's Energy Crisis;* Notable Children's Trade Book in the Field of Social Studies, American Library Association (ALA) Notable Book, and Books for the Teen Age, New York Public Library, all 1983, all for *The New Americans: Changing Patterns in U.S. Immigration;* Notable Children's Trade Book in the Field of Social Studies, 1984, ALA Best Book for Young Adults, 1984, and Carter G. Woodson Book Award, 1985, all for *To Live in Two Worlds: American Indian Youth Today;* Notable Children's Book in the Field of Social Studies and ALA Notable Book, both 1984, both for *Gavriel and Jemal: Two Boys of Jerusalem;* ALA Notable Book, 1985, *Boston Horn-Globe* Honor Book, 1986, and Carter G. Woodson Book Award, 1986, all for *Dark Harvest: Migrant Farmworkers in America;* ALA Notable Book and *School Library Journal* Best Book of the Year, both 1986, both for *Children of the Maya: A Guatemalan Indian Odyssey;* Notable Children's Trade Book in the Field of Social Studies, *School Library Journal* Best Book of the Year, ALA Notable Book, and Christopher Award, all 1987, all for *Into a Strange Land: Unaccompanied Refugee Youth in America;* Notable Children's Trade Book in the Field of Social Studies, 1987, for *The Vanishing Border: A Photographic Journey along Our Frontier with Mexico;* ALA Notable Book and ALA Best Book for Young Adults, both 1988, both for *Always to Remember: The Story of the Vietnam Veterans Memorial; Born to the Land: An American Portrait, Counting America: The Story of the United States Census, People Who Make a Difference,* and *The Times of My Life: A Memoir* were named Books for the Teen Age by New York Public Library. **Address:** 15 Spring W., Williamsburg, Virginia 23188, U.S.A.

PUBLICATIONS FOR YOUNG ADULTS

Fiction

The Lion's Whiskers, with Russell Davis. Boston, Little, Brown, 1959.
Ten Thousand Desert Swords, with Russell Davis. Boston, Little, Brown, 1960.
The Choctaw Code, with Russell Davis. New York, McGraw, 1961.
Strangers in Africa, with Russell Davis. New York, McGraw, 1963.

Nonfiction

Point Four Assignment: Stories from the Records of Those Who Work in Foreign Fields for the Mutual Security of Free Nations, with Russell Davis. Boston, Little, Brown, 1959.
Chief Joseph: War Chief of the Nez Perce, with Russell Davis. New York, McGraw, 1962.
Land in the Sun: The Story of West Africa, with Russell Davis. Boston, Little, Brown, 1963.

Morning Star, Black Sun: The Northern Cheyenne Indians and America's Energy Crisis, photographs by Paul Conklin. New York, Dodd, 1982.
The New Americans: Changing Patterns in U.S. Immigration, photographs by Paul Conklin. New York, Dodd, 1983.
To Live in Two Worlds: American Indian Youth Today, photographs by Paul Conklin. New York, Dodd, 1984.
Gavriel and Jemal: Two Boys of Jerusalem, photographs by Paul Conklin. New York, Dodd, 1984.
Dark Harvest: Migrant Farmworkers in America, photographs by Paul Conklin. New York, Dodd, 1985.
Children of the Maya: A Guatemalan Indian Odyssey. photographs by Paul Conklin. New York, Dodd, 1986.
Into a Strange Land: Unaccompanied Refugee Youth in America, with Melissa Ashabranner. New York, Dodd, 1987.
The Vanishing Border: A Photographic Journey along Our Frontier with Mexico, photographs by Paul Conklin. New York, Dodd, 1987.
Always to Remember: The Story of the Vietnam Veterans Memorial, photographs by Jennifer Ashabranner. New York, Dodd, 1988.
Born to the Land: An American Portrait, photographs by Paul Conklin. New York, Putnam, 1989.
I'm in the Zoo, Too!, illustrated by Janet Stevens. New York, Cobblehill Books, 1989.
Counting America: The Story of the United States Census, with Melissa Ashabranner. New York, Putnam, 1989.
People Who Make a Difference, photographs by Paul Conklin. New York, Cobblehill Books, 1989.
A Grateful Nation: The Story of Arlington National Cemetery, photographs by Jennifer Ashabranner. New York, Putnam, 1990.
The Times of My Life: A Memoir. New York, Dutton, 1990.
Crazy about German Shepherds, photographs by Jennifer Ashabranner. New York, Dutton, 1990.
An Ancient Heritage: The Arab-American Minority, photographs by Paul Conklin. New York, Harper, 1991.
Land of Yesterday, Land of Tomorrow: Discovering Chinese Central Asia, photographs by Paul Conklin. New York, Dutton, 1992.
A Memorial for Mr. Lincoln, photographs by Jennifer Ashabranner. New York, Putnam, 1992.
Still a Nation of Immigrants, photographs by Jennifer Ashabranner. New York. Dutton, 1993.
A New Frontier: The Peace Corps in Eastern Europe, photographs by Paul Conklin. New York, Dutton, 1994.

Other

A First Course in College English (textbook), with Judson Milburn and Cecil B. Williams. Boston, Houghton, 1962.
A Moment in History: The First Ten Years of the Peace Corps. New York, Doubleday, 1971.
Editor, *The Stakes Are High.* New York, Bantam, 1954.

*

Biography: Entry in *Sixth Book of Junior Authors and Illustrators,* New York, H.W. Wilson, 1989; essay in *Authors and Artists for Young Adults,* Volume 6, Detroit, Gale, 1991; essay in *Something about the Author Autobiography Series,* Volume 14, Detroit, Gale, 1992.

Critical Studies: Entry in *Children's Literature Review,* Volume 28, Detroit, Gale, 1992.

Brent Ashabranner comments:

Much of my nonfiction is about immigrants, refugees, Native Americans, and young adults in crisis. No matter what ethnic minority or disadvantaged social group my books may deal with, I have one overriding hope for each of them that the people I write about will emerge as human beings who have lives that are real and valuable and who have a right to strive for decent lives.

*   *   *

A personal and professional commitment to furthering cross cultural awareness and understanding characterizes the informational books of Brent Ashabranner. By combining timely social issues with individual life experience through case studies, anecdotes, and interviews, Ashabranner draws compelling portraits of adversity and triumph, of difference and commonality, of conflict and resolution. A common theme throughout much of Ashabranner's work concerns the power of the individual's commitment to effect change. The author evokes images of real-life role models confronting difficult social and cultural issues while maintaining and strengthening the bonds of the land, the home, and the family. Ashabranner's award winning books address many of the fundamental social issues of our times, providing the reader with both factual information and personal narrative.

Drawing upon his own extensive experience of living and working outside of the United States, Ashabranner incorporates various journalistic techniques into his work. Documented historical information and factual data temper personal memoirs and interviews. His lucid writing style and attention to detail reflect his commitment to effective communication and scholarly research. The tone of much of Ashabranner's work reflects his extensive professional experience working with diverse societies and his intense personal respect for these cultures. His talent for letting his subjects speak for themselves provides readers with a human voice to associate the larger societal issues at hand with. In using this voice, Ashabranner builds a bridge from simple awareness to more complex reactions of empathy and understanding. Black and white photographs of many of his featured subjects and of diverse locales and situations expand the text and amplify the human element so pervasive in Ashabranner's work. These essential elements all contribute to the work's effectiveness, both in factual and in aesthetic terms.

Ashabranner's first young adult effort, *Morning Star Black Sun: The Northern Cheyenne Indians and America's Energy Crisis,* combines cultural, social, and historical perspectives with questions of ethical rights and responsibilities. Ashabranner draws parallels between the past history of government relations with the Montana tribe and the present need to mine coal for energy production. The conflicts between the northern Cheyenne people, government agencies, and the power and oil companies reflect the fundamental desire of the tribe to control their land and maintain their ancient heritage in the face of complicated modern problems involving financial and environmental concerns.

The struggle to reach the United States and then establish a productive, healthy life characterizes many of the personal histories presented in *The New Americans: Changing Patterns of U.S. Immigration.* In tracing the early history of immigration, Ashabranner establishes a factual base for further investigation of immigration patterns and the discussion of issues of diverse peoples. Their desire for freedom and safety and need for education and training are common themes explored. *Into a Strange Land: Unaccompanied Refugee Youth in America* also addresses the complex issues of refugees in American life by examining the linguistic, cultural, historical, and societal dilemmas facing young people caught up in political turmoil. The book describes the plight of youth who are faced with making a new life, alone, in an alien environment. Despite the emotional reactions, cultural differences, and humanitarian concerns, Ashabranner manages to effectively convey the hope, courage, and determination of the protagonists.

The tabulation and interpretation of census data is explored in a collaborative effort with Melissa Ashabranner, *Counting America: The Story of the United States Census.* The Ashabranner's offer a history of the census, a look at its use in business, education, and government, and a review of the complicated procedures involved in gathering, compiling, and interpreting demographic data. Inclusion of reproductions and archival photographs of early history and techniques gives a real sense of the effects of technology on data collection.

The acclaimed *Always to Remember: The Story of the Vietnam Veterans Memorial* captures the spirit and resolve of the veterans and others involved in the monument's planning, design, and construction. Ashabranner effectively draws parallels between the sense of continuing controversy and divisiveness surrounding the memorial's design and the conduct of the Vietnam War. The themes of conflict and resolution resonate throughout the work, from the perseverance of Jan Scruggs, the activist behind the Vietnam Veterans Memorial Fund, to the determination of Maya Lin, the designer of the memorial, to the simple and eloquent statements of the visitors to the monument. An interview with the curator of the mementos left behind at the memorial provides insight into the depth of feeling expressed by the Memorial's visitors.

In *A Grateful Nation: The Story of Arlington National Cemetery,* Ashabranner considers "the forces of reconciliation." Complemented with photographs by Jennifer Ashabranner and by historical artifacts, the book traces the history and administration of the grounds, and details the exacting military ceremonies which honor the interred. Another historical work set in the nation's capitol is *A Memorial for Mr. Lincoln,* which also features the photographs of Jennifer Ashabranner. A brief treatment of Lincoln's presidency and his contributions leads to a discussion of the search for a fitting tribute to the man. Ashabranner effectively portrays the motives and visions of the memorial's designers and craftsmen and carefully details the exacting work required for its production. The dedication and subsequent influence of the monument as a focal point for events such as the 1963 "March on Washington" serve as fitting reminders of the symbolic importance of the memorial in American history.

Conflict and resolution are again present in the biographical sketches of *Gavriel and Jemal: Two Boys of Jerusalem.* Both the content and the structure of the work emphasize the shared history and traditions of the two protagonists. By moving back and forth between the households of the Palestinian youth and his Jewish counterpart, Ashabranner presents the parallels which characterize life in the Middle East. The love of family, the devotion to religious beliefs and rituals, the significance of traditional education, and the concern for the future are graphically expressed by Ashabranner's facile text and through the dynamic photographs of Paul Conklin. Ashabranner's style, once again, provides an effective framework which allows the reader to reach conclusions about the future of the conflict through the lives and feelings of two young men. A related book, *An Ancient Heritage: The Arab American Minority* chronicles the lives and influence of Arab Americans as a cultural, artistic, and economic force. It offers a positive view of the history of immigration patterns and the subsequent assimilation of Arab peoples into American culture.

Several of Ashabranner's books address the conflict of tradition and life in the modern world. In *To Live in Two Worlds: American Indian Youth Today,* the personal stories of the young men and women featured reflect the struggle to establish a meaningful place in modern society while retaining the essential knowledge and traditions of the past. Through interviews, personal histories, and statistics, the author's portrait of Native American life balances the sense of traditional tribal pride with the reality of unemployment, poverty, and lack of educational opportunity. A view of farm and family life in New Mexico is found in Ashabranner's *Born to the Land: An American Portrait.* Concentrating on ranching families, the author describes the problems of working the land, the effects of the environment, and the need for a strong sense of family and community. The importance of community highlights a shortcoming of this work, which gives too little emphasis on the contributions of the local Hispanics in the overall development of the region. *The Vanishing Border: A Photographic Journey Along Our Frontier with Mexico* provides an additional perspective on life near the U.S.-Mexican border, dealing primarily with immigration and work related issues.

A starker view of family life is presented in the 1986 publication *Children of the Maya: A Guatemalan Indian Odyssey,* which traces the flight of Mayan Indians from violence and death in their own country to a new life in rural Florida. The examples of the desperate living conditions in their homeland and in the refugee camps serve as a powerful testament to the plight of the Mayas. Conklin's black and white photographs provide the essential human face to personalize both the suffering and the perseverance of the subjects featured. Another title dealing with the lives of migrant workers is *Dark Harvest: Migrant Farmworkers in America.* In this book, Ashabranner chronicles the typical lack of educational, housing, and health facilities, and the enormous desire of many workers to break the cycle of poverty and isolation. Community efforts to improve opportunities and living conditions by organizing workers serve as examples of how change can occur. Paul Conklin's photographic contributions focus particular attention to the role of the entire family, even young children, in the field work.

People Who Make a Difference exemplifies Ashabranner's talent for social commentary and emphasis on the power of the individual. This title describes, in a series of brief biographical sketches and interviews, the efforts of individuals who have dedicated themselves to service, working in a variety of settings and attacking problems with unique and innovative solutions. Their human voices resound with resolve, patience, and persistence. Photographs of each subject add an additional personal dimension to this powerful and up-beat work.

Ashabranner has also written an illustrated autobiography, *The Times of My Life: A Memoir.* In which Ashabranner gives a personal account of his early life during the Depression, his military service, his subsequent careers in government and as an author. His work in the Peace Corps and the civil rights movement verify his lifelong interest in humanitarian concerns and establish his credentials as an author who offers young people a unique and valuable perspective on some of the most volatile and complicated issues of our times. Through history and personal anecdotes, Ashabranner downplays his accomplishments with the specific intention of focusing the reader on the overriding themes of his life—those of the need for genuine compassion for and service to humanity. This work exemplifies both the writing style and the personal commitment which make Ashabranner's a unique and valuable human voice in the world of informational books for young people.

—Mary Snyder

ASHER, Sandy

Also writes as Sandra Fenichel Asher. **Nationality:** American. **Born:** Philadelphia, Pennsylvania, 16 October 1942. **Education:** University of Pennsylvania, 1960-62; Indiana University, B.A. 1964; graduate study at University of Connecticut, Storrs, Connecticut, 1973; Drury College, Springfield, Missouri, elementary education certificate, 1974. **Family:** Married Harvey Asher in 1965; one daughter and one son. **Career:** Novelist and playwright. WFIU-Radio, Bloomington, Indiana, scriptwriter, 1963-64; Ball Associates (advertising agency), Philadelphia, Pennsylvania, copywriter, 1964; *Spectator,* Bloomington, Indiana, drama critic, 1966-67; instructor in creative writing, 1978-85, writer in residence, since 1985, Drury College, Springfield, Missouri. Instructor, Institute of Children's Literature, 1986-96. Instructor in creative writing for children's summer programs, Summerscape, 1981-82, and Artworks, 1982. Frequent guest speaker at conferences, workshops, and schools. **Awards:** Award of excellence from Festival of Missouri Women in the Arts, 1974, for *Come Join the Circus*; National Endowment for the Arts fellowship, 1978, for *God and a Woman;* first prize in one-act play contest from Little Theatre of Alexandria, 1983, and Street Players Theatre, 1989, for *The Grand Canyon;* first prize from Children's Musical Theater of Mobile contest and Dubuque Fine Arts Players contest, both 1984, both for *East of the Sun/West of the Moon;* Mark Twain Award nomination, 1984, for *Just Like Jenny;* University of Iowa Outstanding Books for Young Adults List and Child Study Association Best Books List, both 1985, both for *Missing Pieces; Little Old Ladies in Tennis Shoes* was named best new play of the season by Maxwell Anderson Playwriting Series, 1985-86, and was a finalist for the 1988 Ellis Memorial Award, Theatre Americana; *God and a Woman* won Center Stage New Horizons contest in 1986, Mercyhurst College National Playwrights Showcase, 1986-87, and the Unpublished Play Project of the American Alliance for Theatre in Education, 1987-88; *Things Are Seldom What They Seem* was nominated for Iowa Teen Award and Young Hoosier Award, both 1986-87; IUPUI/Bonderman Awards, Children's Theatre Symposium, for *Prince Alexis and the Silver Saucer,* 1987, *A Woman Called Truth,* 1989, and *The Wolf and Its Shadows,* 1995; *Dancing with Strangers* won playwriting contests sponsored by TADA!, 1991, and Choate Rosemary Hall, 1993; Joseph Campbell Memorial Fund Award from the Open Eye, 1991-92, for *A Woman Called*

Truth; New Play Festival Award from the Actors' Guild of Lexington, Inc., 1992, for *Sunday, Sunday; Once, In the Time of Trolls* won a playwriting contest sponsored by East Central College in Union, Missouri, 1993; Outstanding Play for Young Audiences citation, U.S. Center of the International Association of Theatres for Children and Young People, 1993, and Kennedy Center's New Vision/New Voices Forum choice, 1995, for *A Woman Called Truth.* **Agent:** Harold Ober Associates, Inc., 425 Madison Ave., New York, New York 10017, U.S.A.

PUBLICATIONS FOR YOUNG ADULTS

Novels as Sandy Asher

Summer Begins. Elsevier-Nelson, 1980; as *Summer Smith Begins,* New York, Bantam, 1986.

Daughters of the Law. New York, Beaufort Books, 1980; as *Friends and Sisters,* London, Gollancz, 1982.

Just Like Jenny. New York, Delacorte, 1982; London, Gollancz, 1985.

Things Are Seldom What They Seem. New York; Delacorte, 1983; London, Gollancz, 1985.

Missing Pieces. New York, Delacorte, 1984.

Teddy Teabury's Fabulous Fact. New York, Dell, 1985.

Everything Is Not Enough. New York, Delacorte, 1987; London, Macmillan, 1987; as *Sunnyboy und Aschenputtel,* Bergisch Gladbach, Bastei-Verlag, 1990.

Teddy Teabury's Peanutty Problems. New York, Dell, 1987.

Out of Here: A Senior Class Yearbook. New York, Dutton/Lodestar, 1993.

"Ballet One" Series

Best Friends Get Better. New York, Scholastic, 1989.
Mary-in-the-Middle. New York, Scholastic, 1990.
Pat's Promise. New York, Scholastic, 1990.
Can David Do It? New York, Scholastic, 1991.

Plays as Sandra Fenichel Asher

Come Join the Circus (one-act; first produced Springfield, Missouri, 1973).

Afterthoughts in Eden (one-act; first produced Los Angeles, 1975).

The Ballad of Two Who Flew (one-act), *Plays,y* March, 1976.

How I Nearly Changed the World, but Didn't (one-act; first produced Springfield, Missouri, 1977).

Witling and the Stone Princess, Plays, 1979.

The Insulting Princess (one-act; first produced Interlochen, Michigan, 1979), Orem, Utah, Encore Performance Publishing, 1988.

Food Is Love (one-act; first produced Springfield, Missouri, 1979).

The Mermaid's Tale (one-act; first produced Interlochen, Michigan, 1979), Orem, Utah, Encore Performance Publishing, 1988.

Dover's Domain, Denver, Colorado, Pioneer Drama Service, 1980.

The Golden Cow of Chelm (one-act), *Plays,y* 1980.

Sunday, Sunday (two-act; first produced Lafayette, Indiana, 1981). Woodstock, Illinois, Dramatic Publishing Company, 1994.

The Grand Canyon (one-act; first produced Alexandria, Virginia, 1983).

Little Old Ladies in Tennis Shoes (two-act; first produced Philadelphia, Pennsylvania, 1985), Woodstock, Illinois, Dramatic Publishing Co., 1989.

East of the Sun/West of the Moon (one-act; first produced Mobile, Alabama, 1985).

God and a Woman (two-act; first produced Erie, Pennsylvania, 1987).

Prince Alexis and the Silver Saucer (one-act; first produced Springfield, Missouri, 1987).

A Song of Sixpence (one-act), Orem, Utah, Encore Performance Publishing Co., 1988.

A Woman Called Truth (one-act; first produced Houston, Texas, 1989), Woodstock, Illinois, Dramatic Publishing Co., 1989.

The Wise Men of Chelm (one-act; first produced Louisville, Kentucky, 1991), Woodstock, Illinois, Dramatic Publishing Co., 1992.

All on a Saturday Morning (one act; first produced Columbia, Missouri, 1992).

Blind Dating (one-act; first produced New York, 1992).

Perfect (one-act; first produced New York, 1992).

Dancing with Strangers (three one-acts; first produced Wallingford, Connecticut, 1993). Woodstock, Illinois, Dramatic Publishing Company, 1994.

Where Do You Get Your Ideas? (adapted for stage from book of same title; first produced Chester, New Jersey, 1993).

Once, in the Time of Trolls (one-act; first produced in Lawrence, Kansas, 1995). Woodstock, Illinois, Dramatic Publishing Company, 1995.

Across the Plains: The Journey of the Palace Wagon Family (one-act; first produced in Kansas City, Missouri). Woodstock, Illinois, Dramatic Publishing Company, 1997.

Emma (two-act; first produced in Springfield, Missouri). Woodstock, Illinois, Dramatic Publishing Company, 1997.

Other

The Great American Peanut Book (as Sandra Fenichel Asher), illustrated by Jo Anne Metsch Bonnell. New York, Tempo, 1977.

Where Do You Get Your Ideas? Helping Young Writers Begin, illustrated by Susan Hellard. New York, Walker and Co., 1987.

Wild Words! How to Train Them to Tell Stories, illustrated by Dennis Kendrick. New York, Walker and Co., 1989.

Editor, *But That's Another Story* (short stories and interviews with authors), New York, Walker and Co., 1996.

PUBLICATIONS FOR CHILDREN

Fiction

Princess Bee and the Royal Good-night Story (picture book), illustrated by Cat Bowman Smith. Niles, Illinois, A. Whitman, 1990.

Contributor of plays to anthologies, including *Center Stage,* Harper, 1990. Contributor of stories and articles to books, including

Visions, edited by Donald Gallo, Delacorte/Dell, 1987; *Writers in the Classroom,* edited by Ruth Nathan, Christopher-Gordon, 1991; *Performing the Text: Reading, Writing, and Teaching the Young Adult Novel,* edited by Virginia Monseau and Gary Salvner, Heinemann-Boynton/Cook, 1992; *Authors' Perspectives: Turning Teenagers into Readers and Writers,* edited by Donald Gallo, Heinemann-Boynton/Cook, 1992. Contributor of stories and articles to magazines, including *The Alan Review, The Journal of Reading,y Spark!,* and *Theater for Young Audiences Today.*

*

Biography: Entry in *Dictionary of Literary Biography Yearbook: 1983* by Judith S. Baughman, Detroit, Gale, 1984; essay in *Speaking for Ourselves: Autobiographical Sketches by Notable Authors of Books for Young Adults,* Volume 1, compiled and edited by Donald R. Gallo, National Council of Teachers of English, 1990; essay in *Something about the Author Autobiography Series* by Sandy Asher, Detroit, Gale, Volume 13, 1991.

Sandy Asher comments:

I've centered my work on "nice kids"—the ones who rarely give a teacher a minute's trouble, who would never confront a police officer except to ask directions, who might never attract the attention of social workers, sociologists, journalists, and so on. I'm not talking about saints here, just decent young people who are trying to figure out how to lead productive, meaningful lives.

Like the characters in my books, these young adults learn to deal with grief, loneliness, fear, jealousy, anger, frustration, confusion, love—and the lack of it because nice kids must, and nice kids do. And they need and deserve books that cheer them on, that encourage them to go with their own best instincts, and that assure them there is a cure for adolescence: equal parts of time, understanding, and laughter.

*   *   *

Sandy Asher has the ability to climb inside the heads of her characters and see the world from their points of view. Her writing style of showing, not telling, makes her stories come alive and the characters and their relationships convincing.

Preteens and young teens face change and stress as they strive toward maturity, and Asher, reflecting on some of her experiences from her own early years, skillfully portrays realistic characters dealing with and handling such challenges as they approach and struggle through their teenage years, ranking her as very popular with young adult readers.

Just Like Jenny, a story with a ballet theme, but more importantly portraying a struggle of two young dancers maintaining a true friendship regardless of competition and differences of abilities, proves that true friendship can survive during a difficult period of maturing and changing. The book also provides authentic knowledge of ballet, of the fatiguing, demanding work required, leaving little time for extracurricular activities.

Asher's vivid, precise descriptions, strong nouns and verbs, clear sensory details, and specifics rather than generalizations are tools she uses in all her books. *Things Are Seldom What They Seem* grabs the reader's attention and holds it as tension and suspense fill the entire book. Debbie's sister, Maggie, is enamored with her handsome high school drama coach, to the point where she doesn't realize the effect he is having upon her.

Debbie's friend Karen joins the drama club, and she, like Maggie, changes, spending all her spare time with the "wonderful" Mr. Carraway. Debbie feels left out, but she also feels something is terribly wrong. With the help of her friend Murray, Debbie discovers that Mr. Carraway has been making sexual advances toward his students, including Debbie's sister, Maggie. Sexual abuse is a tough subject to write about and is an ugly topic, but Ms. Asher deals with it head-on in a bold yet sensitive way, showing that young people can handle such predicaments with or without support from adults.

Everything Is Not Enough is a good example of change and growing up. Michael, seventeen years old, with everything he could possibly want including money, popularity, and a great future, decides that this is what his parents want for him and not what he himself wants. While spending the summer by the sea, Michael goes to work at the Jolly Mackerel, a local restaurant, working hard as a busboy for minimum wage and enduring the cold shoulder and sarcasm from co-workers and local residents, but proving that he can be what he wants to be. Linda, a local girl also working at the Jolly Mackerel, determined to save enough money to move to New York where she can begin a career in fashion design, wants nothing to stand in the way of her future, and that includes Michael. But the two of them are drawn together when Linda's friend Traci is beaten and abused by her boyfriend. Dealing with a tragic social issue, violence against women, Asher skillfully and realistically presents the problem, creating a spine-tingling story, portraying young people courageously facing the real world with their eyes wide open.

A story in a lighter vein, *Summer Begins,* also published in paperback as *Summer Smith Begins,* portrays a young girl, Summer Smith, who detests making waves and prefers to keep a low profile. An editorial she writes for the school newspaper, however, sets off unexpected fireworks. Summer finds herself in the middle of an uproar centering on the annual Christmas program, a boring tradition that is the same every year. Summer's editorial suggests the program include ALL religious traditions, and not just Christian as in the past. A heartwarming story about a sensitive young girl striving to overcome her shyness and standing up for what she believes, it is also about coping with a frustrated mother going through menopause. The writer, without the reader even being aware of it, delivers her message that young people can overcome damaging peer pressure as well as adult bigotry.

Ideas for writing stories, poems, and plays may be found in Asher's *Where Do You Get Your Ideas? Helping Young Writers Begin.* According to this instructive book, ideas are found everywhere, and, when found, should be written in a journal to be used when needed. Also in the book are over two dozen views from other authors that briefly describe how they, too, get their ideas for stories. The budding author is encouraged, and many practical suggestions are provided for writers young and old.

Missing Pieces deals with many losses of loved ones. Heather loses her brother when he gets married, her father when he dies, her mother when she withdraws after the death of her husband, and her boyfriend when he runs away. The girl overcomes a lack of communication as well as the feeling of overwhelming loneliness and deals effectively with family problems and self-preservation. Asher's sympathetic story of grief and conflict once again proves her competence and popularity.

With numerous awards and honors for her many plays and novels, Sandy Asher ranks high in the field of writers for young adults, skillfully portraying characters who deal realistically with problems facing young people as they strive toward maturity, ever changing, growing, and learning as they go.

—Carol Doxey

ASHLEY, Bernard

Nationality: British. **Born:** London, 2 April 1935. **Education:** Roan School, Blackheath, London, and Sir Joseph Williamson's School, Rochester, Kent, 1947-53; Trent Park College of Education, 1955-57, Cert. Ed. 1957; Cambridge Institute of Education, 1970-71, associate diploma in primary education, 1971. **Military Service:** Served in the Royal Air Force, 1953-55; became senior aircraftman. **Family:** Married Iris Holbrook in 1958; three sons. **Career:** Teacher, Kent Educational Committee, Gravesend, 1957-65; headteacher, Hertfordshire Educational Committee, Hertford Heath, 1965-71, Hartley Junior School, Newham, London, 1971-76, and Charlton Manor Junior School, London, 1971-95. **Awards:** Other award, Children's Rights Workshop, 1976, for *The Trouble with Donovan Croft*; Carnegie Medal commendation, 1979, for *A Kind of Wild Justice,* and 1987, for *Running Scared*; Royal Television Society Award for best children's entertainment, 1993, for *Dodgem*. **Address:** 128 Heathwood Gardens, London SE7 8ER, England.

PUBLICATIONS FOR YOUNG ADULTS

Fiction

The Trouble with Donovan Croft, illustrated by Fermin Rocker. London, Oxford University Press, 1974.
Terry on the Fence, illustrated by Charles Keeping. London, Oxford University Press, 1975; New York, Phillips, 1977.
All My Men. London, Oxford University Press, 1977; New York, Phillips, 1978.
A Kind of Wild Justice, illustrated by Charles Keeping. London, Oxford University Press, 1978; New York, Phillips, 1979.
Break in the Sun, illustrated by Charles Keeping. London, Oxford University Press, and New York, Phillips, 1980.
Dodgem. London, MacRae, 1981; New York, Watts, 1982.
High Pavement Blues. London, MacRae, and New York, Watts, 1983.
Janey. London, MacRae, 1985.
Running Scared. London, MacRae, 1986.
Bad Blood. London, MacRae, 1988.
The Country Boy (novelization of his own television series). London, MacRae, 1989.
Seeing Off Uncle Jack. London, Viking, 1991.

Johnnie's Blitz. London, Viking, 1995.
City Limits—Stitch-Up. London, Orchard, 1997.
City Limits—The Scam. London, Orchard, 1997.
City Limits—Framed. London, Orchard, 1997.
City Limits—Mean Street. London, Orchard, 1997.
Roller Madonnas. London, A. & C. Black, 1997.
Tiger Without Teeth. London, Orchard, 1998.

Plays

Running Scared (television play; from his own story), 1986.
The Old Woman Who Lived in a Cola Can (music by David Smith; produced on tour, 1988).
The Country Boy (television series), 1989.
The Secret of Theodore Brown (produced 1989).
Dodgem (television play), 1992.
With Chris Ashley, *3-7-11* (television play), 1994.

Other

The Men and the Boats: Britain's Life-Boat Service. London, Allman, 1968.
Weather Men. London, Allman, 1970; revised edition, 1974.

Editor, *The Puffin Book of School Stories.* London, Puffin, 1993.

PUBLICATIONS FOR CHILDREN

Dinner Ladies Don't Count, illustrated by Janet Duchesne. London, MacRae, and New York, Watts, 1981.
I'm Trying to Tell You, illustrated by Lyn Jones. London, Kestrel Books, 1981.
Linda's Lie, illustrated by Janet Duchesne. London, MacRae, and New York, Watts, 1982.
Your Guess Is as Good as Mine, illustrated by Steven Cain. London, MacRae, and New York, Watts, 1983.
A Bit of Give and Take, illustrated by Trevor Stubley. London, Hamish Hamilton, 1984.
Clipper Street Stories (*Calling for Sam, Taller Than Before, Down and Out, The Royal Visit, All I Ever Ask . . . , Sally Cinderella*), illustrated by Jane Cope. London, Orchard, 6 vols., 1987-89.
The Dockside School Stories (*Boat Girl, The Ghost of Dockside School, Getting In, The Caretaker's Car*). London, MacRae, 4 vols., 1990.
Cleversticks, illustrated by Derek Brazell. New York, Crown, 1992.
I Forgot! said Troy, illustrated by Derek Brazell. London, Viking, 1996.
A Present for Paul. London, HarperCollins, 1996.
Justin and the Demon Drop-kick, illustrated by Nick Ward. London, Viking, 1997.
Flash. London, Orchard, 1998.

Readers

Don't Run Away, illustrated by Ray Whittaker. London, Allman, 1965.
Wall of Death, illustrated by Ray Whittaker. London, Allman, 1966.

The Big Escape, illustrated by James Hunt. London, Allman, 1967.
Space Shot, illustrated by Laszlo Acs. London, Allman, 1967.

*

Critical Studies: Entry in *Children's Literature Review,* Volume 4, Detroit, Gale, 1984.

Bernard Ashley comments:

Some writers say they write for themselves, some for their children or grandchildren, some for the child they used to be. I suppose I write for a combination of all three, but I'm also writing for *change* (of attitude to certain people and concepts), and for readers I might draw into a story if I pace it right and give it enough excitement. I'm aware that I also write for the pleasure of another centimetre of shelf space, and for the approval of the parents, teachers, librarians and publishers I respect and who I want to respect me. It's complicated and it's all-encompassing. I haven't mentioned money. Well, that's good to receive, it pays for the odd vacation, but I've never depended on it (as a full time teacher for thirty-eight years, nor now in retirement from education).

I once said on a poster: "For me writing brings many pleasures: the one pleasing phrase I might manage at the end of a busy day, the fat and final manuscript under my hand, the printed product and the knowledge that every reader will combine with me to make a new book out of every copy. There is an enormous sense of privilege in anyone spending a few hours with me in a book. It's like giving a party—without the washing up! And, like a party, it's all for entertainment: but if there should be something left to think about the next morning then that's a bonus for which I'm grateful." I still go along with that.

In Britain there's a danger that my sort of writing—urban, gritty, with a sense of place and something below the surface—will wither out of print because the High Street booksellers want quick turnovers of fast-selling series titles (which people often collect rather than read). New authors with fresh voices find it hard to get a start in the cash impoverished areas of state education and public libraries, which used to support emerging talent. I hope times will change. Meanwhile, I'll defiantly continue to plough my furrow till I run out of field.

*   *   *

Bernard Ashley first came to attention as the author of books for young children, drawing heavily on his own background and on extensive experience as a classroom teacher. He has continued to write stories about troubling situations with which young children can identify, like *Linda's Lie* and *I Forgot, said Troy.* His particular interest in children with learning difficulties and working as headmaster in multicultural primary schools led to *The Trouble with Donovan Croft.* This was hailed as one of the first British books to give a central role to a black child, a West Indian boy who becomes mute when separated from his parents to be fostered with a white family. It introduced a number of the elements that were to become common in Ashley's later writing: a young person isolated and misunderstood by adults, an awareness of the roots of social conflict, and convincing presentation of young people's behaviour and language in urban, multi-ethnic settings.

In the eighties, Ashley turned increasingly to writing for adolescents, beginning in 1978 a sequence of tough stories of contemporary life, combining features of the thriller with those of books exploring social issues. The young protagonists, like Donovan, have problems (they include a grubby non-reader and a bed-wetter) and lead secret, dangerous lives. Ronnie in *A Kind of Wild Justice* exists dangerously on the fringe of violent crime, Kevin has to guard the family's market stall against takeover in *High Pavement Blues,* and the title character in *Janey* acts as a look-out for thieves. Conventional relationships between parent and child are frequently reversed; the young people have to take on the active, caring role. In *Dodgem,* Simon struggles to care for his father who was paralysed in the car crash that killed his mother. Kevin tries to look after his mother and to bring back his father, who deserted them both. Ritchie in *Bad Blood* busies himself in the attempt to get the transplant that may save his father's life. Largely ignored by the adult world, these young people have to grow up quickly. They struggle to reconcile the conflicting demands made on them by the different worlds in which they exist: home and school, black and white communities, criminal groups and law enforcers. A repeated theme is the experience of a character uprooted from one environment to be plunged into another. It may simply be a change to a different kind of school (as in *All My Men*), or the more dramatic changes of Patsy in *Break in the Sun,* escaping with a bargeload of amateur actors, or Simon being hidden in a travelling fair in *Dodgem.*

Ashley is an excellent, uncondescending story-teller. In the later novels he cuts cinematically from scene to scene, the descriptions are vivid and convincing, and the dialogue is appropriate to the characters, racy and immediate (but therefore inevitably dating in places). The titles and themes are frequently symbolic but at a level appropriate to young readers. Simon describes himself as a dodgem, "bashed into from all angles"; the "bad blood" refers to heredity and to fraternal antipathy as well as to leukemia. The novels are moral without undue moralising, but the lessons we can draw are not cut and dried. Few characters are shown as straightforwardly good or bad and they rarely understand the whole truth of the situations in which they are involved. Issues are seen as complex and ambiguous. For this reason, some readers have been unhappy about Ashley's realism. Figures of authority (like the social services in *Dodgem*) are not always presented sympathetically, and sexual relationships are presented frankly. However, without much sense of contrivance, the books do convey clear moral positives. The central characters move through painful experiences towards greater understanding of themselves and of the world. For example, the stories about a black London family in *Seeing Off Uncle Jack* describe significant shifts in Winny Stone, the character through whose eyes they are told. In the first story she discovers while making funeral arrangements that there was more to her blind old Uncle Jack than she had imagined, and in *The Princess Watch* she comes to realize that family loyalty is more important than her personal pride, and learns to keep silent about knowledge she has acquired. At the end of the book, "she was old enough to know that everything wasn't just the way it looked." Much of this learning in the novels comes about through young people's significant contacts with others who are very different from themselves. Paul learns from Lorraine, Ronnie from the Pakistani girl Margit, and Janey from the elderly Mrs. Woodcroft.

These qualities of moral complexity, social confusion and personal development are shown clearly in novels like *Running Scared* and *Johnnie's Blitz.* The first of these, based on Ashley's BBC television series for young people, centres on the relationship between a London schoolgirl, Paula Prescott, and her best friend Narinder, a member of a Sikh family settled in England for some years. They live in an area where crime is common, and Paula's cabbie grandfather is the innocent witness of a robbery that goes wrong. Paula's cousin Brian is one of the local gang extorting protection money from local Asians, and under this pressure Narinder's father thinks of taking his family back to India. Paula discovers that her grandfather died leaving a clue to the whereabouts of a vital piece of evidence and the girls work together, ultimately finding it in a Sikh temple. She then faces a difficult choice: to be responsible for sending her cousin to prison or to condone evil. There is an effective and plausible climax to the book, which combines an exciting plot and strong characters with moral seriousness that is not over-didactic.

Further moral dilemmas are posed in *Johnnie's Blitz,* set in the East End of London during the bombing of World War II. Johnnie Stubbs goes on the run from the approved school where he has been sent unjustly for stealing a gold watch, once the property of his father, now missing in action. Johnnie seeks security in the scrapyard of Grandad Stubbs, which has become a haven for a colourful group of other characters living on the fringes of society. The novel gives a vivid description of huddling in air-raid shelters during the bombing, attempts at rescue and distraught victims scrabbling through the wreckage that had once been homes. One of these survivors is a toddler called Shirley, who runs into the night after a bomb has hit her house to try to find her mother. Johnnie rescues Shirley, but is confronted by a difficult decision: if he helps her to return to her parents, he risks capture.

It can be seen that Ashley's novels are not for passive readers. They demand that we interpret events, assess characters, and judge motives much as we do in real life. It is not surprising that they have proved so popular both for use in school and with young people who are choosing books that will relate to their own situations and problems of identity.

—Robert Protherough

ASIMOV, Isaac

Pseudonyms: George E. Dale; Dr. A; Paul French. **Nationality:** American. **Born:** Petrovichi, U.S.S.R., 2 January 1920; immigrated to the United States in 1923; became citizen 1928. **Education:** Columbia University, New York, B.S. 1939, M.A. 1941, Ph.D. in chemistry 1948. **Military Service:** Served in the United States Army, 1945-46. **Family:** Married 1) Gertrude Blugerman in 1942 (divorced 1973), one son and one daughter; 2) Janet Opal Jeppson in 1973. **Career:** Writer; instructor, 1949-51, assistant professor, 1951-55, associate professor, 1955-79, and since 1979 professor of biochemistry, Boston University School of Medicine, Boston,

Massachusetts. Worked as a civilian chemist at U.S. Navy Air Experimental Station, Philadelphia, 1942-45. **Awards:** Edison Foundation National Mass Media award, 1958; Blakeslee award for nonfiction, 1960; special Hugo award for distinguished contributions to the field, 1963, for science articles in the *Magazine of Fantasy and Science Fiction,* special Hugo award for best all-time science fiction series, 1966, for *Foundation, Foundation and Empire,* and *Second Foundation,* Hugo award for best novel, 1973, for *The Gods Themselves,* and 1983, for *Foundation's Edge,* Hugo award for best short story, 1977, for ''The Bicentennial Man,'' Hugo award, 1983, all from World Science Fiction Conventions; World Science Fiction Convention citation, 1963; American Chemical Society James T. Grady award, 1965; American Association for the Advancement of Science-Westinghouse award for science writing, 1967; Nebula award, Science Fiction Writers of America, 1973, for *The Gods Themselves,* and 1977, for ''The Bicentennial Man''; Glenn Seabord award, International Platform Association, 1979; *Locus* award, for non-fiction, 1981, for fiction, 1983; Washington *Post* Children's Book Guild award, for non-fiction, 1985; ''Nightfall'' was chosen the best science fiction story of all time in a Science Fiction Writers of America poll. Guest of Honor, Thirteenth World Science Fiction Convention, 1955. **Died:** 6 April 1992.

PUBLICATIONS FOR YOUNG ADULTS

Nonfiction

Building Blocks of the Universe. New York, Abelard Schuman, 1957; London, Abelard Schuman, 1958; revised edition, 1961, 1974.

Breakthroughs in Science, illustrated by Karoly and Szanto. Boston, Houghton Mifflin, 1960.

Satellites in Outer Space, illustrated by John Polgreen. New York, Random House, 1960; revised edition, 1964, 1973.

The Kite That Won the Revolution. Boston, Houghton Mifflin, 1963.

The Moon, illustrated by Alex Ebel. Chicago, Follett, 1967; London, University of London Press, 1969.

To the Ends of the Universe. New York, Walker, 1967; revised edition, 1976.

Mars, illustrated by Herb Herrick. Chicago, Follett, 1967; London, University of London Press, 1971.

Stars, illustrated by Herb Herrick, diagrams by Mike Gordon. Chicago, Follett, 1968.

Galaxies, illustrated by Alex Ebel and Denny McMains. Chicago, Follett, 1968; London, University of London Press, 1971.

ABC's of Space. New York, Walker, 1969; as *Space Dictionary,* New York, Scholastic, 1970.

Great Ideas of Science, illustrated by Lee Ames. Boston, Houghton Mifflin, 1969.

The ABC's of the Ocean. New York, Walker, 1970.

The Heavenly Host, illustrated by Bernard Colonna. New York, Walker, 1975; London, Penguin, 1978.

Light, photography by Allen Carr. Chicago, Follett, 1970.

What Makes the Sun Shine?, illustrated by Marc Brown. Boston, Little Brown, 1971.

ABC's of the Earth. New York, Walker, 1971.

ABC's of Ecology. New York, Walker, 1972.

Ginn Science Program. Boston, Ginn, 5 vols., 1972-73.

Comets and Meteors, illustrated by Raul Mina Mora. Chicago, Follett, 1972.

The Sun, illustrated by Alex Ebel. Chicago, Follett, 1972.

Jupiter, the Largest Planet. New York, Lothrop, 1973; revised edition, 1976.

Please Explain, illustrated by Michael McCurdy. Boston, Houghton Mifflin, 1973; London, Abelard Schuman, 1975.

Earth: Our Crowded Spaceship. New York, Day, and London, Abelard Schuman, 1974.

The Solar System, illustrated by David Cunnigham. Chicago, Follett, 1975.

Alpha Centauri, the Nearest Star. New York, Lothrop, 1976.

Mars, the Red Planet. New York, Lothrop, 1977.

Saturn and Beyond, diagrams by Giulio Maestro. New York, Lothrop, 1979.

Venus: Near Neighbor of the Sun, diagrams by Yukio Kondo. New York, Lothrop, 1981.

Beginnings: The Story of Origins—Of Mankind, Life, the Earth, the Universe. New York, Walker, 1987.

Franchise. Mankato, Minnesota, Creative Education, 1988.

All the Troubles of World. Mankato, Minnesota, Creative Education, 1988.

Little Treasury of Dinosaurs, illustrated by Christopher Santoro. New York, Crown, 1989.

Think about Space: Where Have We Been and Where Are We Going, with Frank White. New York, Walker, 1989.

Isaac Asimov's Pioneers of Science and Explorations (Christopher Columbus: Navigator to the New World; Ferdinand Magellan: Opening the Door to World Exploration; Henry Hudson: Arctic Explorer and North American Adventurer). Milwaukee, Stevens, 1991.

PUBLICATIONS FOR CHILDREN

Fiction

The Key Word and Other Mysteries, illustrated by Rod Burke. New York, Walker, 1977.

Norby, the Mixed-Up Robot, with Janet Asimov. New York, Walker, 1983; London, Methuen, 1984.

Norby's Other Secret, with Janet Asimov. New York, Walker, 1984; London, Methuen, 1985.

Norby and the Invaders, with Janet Asimov. New York, Walker, 1985.

Norby and the Lost Princess, with Janet Asimov. New York, Walker, 1985.

The Norby Chronicles (includes *Norby, the Mixed-Up Robot* and *Norby's Other Secret),* with Janet Asimov. New York, Ace, 1986.

Norby and the Queen's Necklace, New York, Walker, 1986.

Norby: Robot for Hire (includes *Norby and the Lost Princess* and *Norby and the Invaders),* with Janet Asimov. New York, Ace, 1987.

Norby Finds a Villain, with Janet Asimov. New York, Walker, 1987.

Norby through Time and Space (includes *Norby and the Queen's Necklace* and *Norby Finds a Villain),* with Janet Asimov. New York, Ace, 1988.

All the Troubles of the World, illustrated by David Shannon. Mankato, Minnesota, Creative Education, 1989.

Franchise, illustrated by David Shannon. Mankato, Minnesota, Creative Education, 1989.

Norby Down to Earth, with Janet Asimov. New York, Walker, 1989.

Norby and Yobo's Great Adventure, with Janet Asimov. New York, Walker, 1989.

Robbie, illustrated by David Shannon. Mankato, Minnesota, Creative Education, 1989.

Sally, illustrated by David Shannon. Mankato, Minnesota, Creative Education, 1989.

Norby and the Oldest Dragon, with Janet Asimov. New York, Walker, 1990.

Norby and the Court Jester, with Janet Asimov. New York, Walker, 1991.

Fiction as Paul French

David Starr, Space Ranger. New York, Doubleday, 1952; Kingswood, Surrey, World's Work, 1953; as Isaac Asimov, Boston, Twayne, 1978.

Lucky Starr and the Pirates of the Asteroids. New York, Doubleday, 1953; Kingswood, Surrey, World's Work, 1954; as Isaac Asimov, Boston, Twayne, 1978.

Lucky Starr and the Oceans of Venus. New York, Doubleday, 1954; as *The Oceans of Venus* (as Isaac Asimov), London, New English Library, 1973; as Isaac Asimov, Boston, Twayne, 1978.

Lucky Starr and the Big Sun of Mercury. New York, Doubleday, 1956; as *The Big Sun of Mercury* (as Isaac Asimov), London, New English Library, 1974; as Isaac Asimov, Boston, Twayne, 1978.

Lucky Starr and the Moons of Jupiter. New York, Doubleday, 1957; as *The Moons of Jupiter* (as Isaac Asimov), London, New English Library, 1974; as Isaac Asimov, Boston, Twayne, 1978.

Lucky Starr and the Rings of Saturn. New York, Doubleday, 1958; as *The Rings of Saturn* (as Isaac Asimov), London, New English Library, 1974; as Isaac Asimov, Boston, Twayne, 1978.

Poetry

Isaac Asimov's Limericks for Children, illustrated by Wally Neibart. New York, Caedmon, 1984.

Nonfiction

Twentieth Century Discovery. New York, Doubleday, and London, Macdonald, 1969.

The Best New Thing, illustrated by Symeon Shimin. Cleveland, World, 1971.

How Did We Find Out about Dinosaurs [the Earth Is Round, Electricity, Vitamins, Germs, Comets, Energy, Atoms, Nuclear Power, Numbers, Outer Space, Earthquakes, Black Holes, Our Human Roots, Antarctica, Coal, Solar Power, Volcanoes, Life in the Deep Sea, Our Genes, the Universe, Computers, Robots, the Atmosphere, DNA, the Speed of Light, Blood, Sunshine, the Brain, Super Conductivity, Microwaves, Photosynthesis], illustrated by David Wool and others. New York, Walker, 32 vols., 1973-89; 6 vols. published London, White Lion, 1975-76; 1

vol., published London, Pan, 1980; 7 vols. published (as *How We Found Out. . .* series), London, Longman, 1982.

I, Rabbi. New York, Walker, 1976.

Animals of the Bible. New York, Doubleday, 1978.

Those Amazing Electronic Thinking Machines! New York, Watts, 1983.

Editor, with Martin H. Greenberg and Charles G. Waugh, *Young Mutants, Extraterrestrials, Ghosts, Monsters, Star Travelers, Witches and Warlocks.* New York, Harper, 6 vols., 1984-87.

Bare Bones: Dinosaur, with David Hawcock. New York, Holt, 1986; London, Methuen, 1987.

Ask Isaac Asimov (What Is a Shooting Star?; What Is an Eclipse?; Why Do Stars Twinkle?; Why Does the Moon Change Shape?; Why Do We Have Different Seasons?; What Causes Acid Rain?; Is Our Planet Warming Up?; Why Are Whales Vanishing?; Why Are Some Beaches Oily?; Why Is the Air Dirty?; Where Does Garbage Go?; Why Does Litter Cause Problems?; Why Are Rain Forests Vanishing?; What's Happening to the Ozone Layer?; Why Are Animals Endangered?; How Is Paper Made?; What Happens When I Flush the Toilet?; How Does a TV Work?; How Do Airplanes Fly?; How Do Big Ships Float?), some titles written with Elizabeth Kaplan. Milwaukee, Stevens, vols., 1991-93.

How Did We Find Out About Pluto?, illustrated by Erika Kors. New York, Walker, 1991.

Other

An Isaac Asimov Double: "Space Ranger" and "Pirates of the Asteroids." London, New English Library, 1972.

A Second Isaac Asimov Double: "The Big Sun of Mercury" and "The Oceans of Venus." London, New English Library, 1973.

The Third Isaac Asimov Double. London, New English Library/ Times Mirror, 1973.

Editor, with Martin H. Greenberg and Charles G. Waugh, *Science Fiction Shorts* series (includes *After the End, Thinking Machines, Travels Through Time, Wild Inventions, Mad Scientists, Mutants, Tomorrow's TV, Earth Invaded, Bug Awful, Children of the Future, The Immortals, Time Warps),* illustrated by various artists. Milwaukee, Raintree, 12 vols., 1981-84.

PUBLICATIONS FOR ADULTS

Novels

Pebble In the Sky. New York, Doubleday, 1950; London, Corgi, 1958.

The Stars, Like Dust. New York, Doubleday, 1951; London, Panther, 1958; abridged edition, as *The Rebellious Stars,* New York, Ace, 1954.

Foundation. New York, Gnome Press, 1951; London, Weidenfeld and Nicolson, 1953; abridged edition, as *The Thousand-Year Plan,* New York, Ace, 1955.

Foundation and Empire. New York, Gnome Press, 1952; London, Panther, 1962; as *The Man Who Upset the Universe,* New York, Ace, 1955.

The Currents of Space. New York, Doubleday, 1952; London, Boardman, 1955.

Second Foundation. New York, Gnome Press, 1953.

The Caves of Steel. New York, Doubleday, and London, Boardman, 1954.

The End of Eternity. New York, Doubleday, 1955; London, Panther, 1958.

The Naked Sun. New York, Doubleday, 1957; London, Joseph, 1958.

The Robot Novels (includes *The Caves of Steel* and *The Naked Sun*). New York, Doubleday, 1957.

The Death Dealers. New York, Avon, 1958; as *A Whiff of Death,* New York, Walker, and London, Gollancz, 1968.

Triangle: "The Currents of Space," "Pebble In the Sky," and "The Stars, Like Dust." New York, Doubleday, 1961; as *An Isaac Asimov Second Omnibus,* London, Sidgwick and Jackson, 1969.

The Foundation Trilogy: Three Classics of Science Fiction (includes *Foundation, Foundation and Empire,* and *Second Foundation*). New York, Doubleday, 1963; as *An Isaac Asimov Omnibus,* London, Sidgwick and Jackson, 1966.

Fantastic Voyage (novelization of screenplay). Boston, Houghton Mifflin, and London, Dobson, 1966.

The Gods Themselves. New York, Doubleday, and London, Gollancz, 1972.

Murder at the ABA: A Puzzle in Four Days and Sixty Scenes. New York, Doubleday, 1976; as *Authorized Murder: A Puzzle in Four Days and Sixty Scenes,* London, Gollancz, 1976.

The Collected Fiction of Isaac Asimov: The Far Ends of Time and Earth (includes *Pebble in the Sky, Earth Is Room Enough,* and *The End of Eternity*). New York, Doubleday, 1979.

The Collected Fiction of Isaac Asimov: Prisoners of the Stars (includes *The Stars, Like Dust, The Martian Way and Other Stories,* and *The Currents of Space*). New York, Doubleday, 1979.

Foundation's Edge. New York, Doubleday, 1982; London, Granada, 1983.

The Robots of Dawn. New York, Doubleday, 1983; London, Granada, 1984.

Robots and Empire. New York, Doubleday, and London, Granada, 1985.

Foundation and Earth. New York, Doubleday, and London, Grafton, 1986.

Fantastic Voyage II: Destination Brain. New York, Doubleday, and London, Grafton, 1987.

Azazel. New York, Doubleday, 1988; London, Doubleday, 1989.

Prelude to Foundation, illustrated by Vincent DiFate. New York, Doubleday, and London, Grafton, 1988.

Nemesis. New York, Doubleday, and London, Doubleday, 1989.

Invasions. New York, New American Library, 1990.

Nightfall, with Robert Silverberg. New York, Doubleday, and London, Gollancz, 1990.

Forward the Foundation. New York, Doubleday, 1993.

Short Stories

I, Robot. New York, Gnome Press, 1950; London, Grayson, 1952.

The Martian Way and Other Stories. New York, Doubleday, 1955; London, Dobson, 1964.

Earth Is Room Enough: Science Fiction Tales of Our Own Planet. New York, Doubleday, 1957; London, Panther, 1960.

Nine Tomorrows: Tales of the Near Future. New York, Doubleday, 1959; London, Dobson, 1963.

The Rest of the Robots. New York, Doubleday, 1964; as *Eight Stories from the Rest of the Robots,* San Diego, California, Pyramid, 1966; London, Dobson, 1967.

Through a Glass Clearly. London, New English Library, 1967.

Asimov's Mysteries. New York, Doubleday, and London, Rapp and Whiting, 1968.

Nightfall and Other Stories. New York, Doubleday, 1969; as *Nightfall One* and *Nightfall Two,* London, Panther, 1969; as *Nightfall: Twenty SF Stories,* London, Rapp and Whiting, 1971.

The Early Asimov: Or, Eleven Years of Trying. New York, Doubleday, 1972; London, Gollancz, 1973.

The Best of Isaac Asimov (1939-1972), edited by Angus Wells. London, Sidgwick and Jackson, 1973; New York, Doubleday, 1974.

Have You Seen These? Cambridge, Massachusetts, NESFA Press, 1974.

Tales of the Black Widowers. New York, Doubleday, 1974; London, Gollancz, 1975.

Buy Jupiter and Other Stories. New York, Doubleday, 1975; London, Gollancz, 1976.

The Dream, Benjamin's Dream, Benjamin's Bicentennial Blast: Three Short Stories. Privately printed, 1976.

The Bicentennial Man and Other Stories. New York, Doubleday, 1976; London, Gollancz, 1977.

More Tales of the Black Widowers. New York, Doubleday, 1976; London, Gollancz, 1977.

Good Taste, illustrated by Brent Garrett. Topeka, Kansas, Apocalypse Press, 1977.

Casebook of the Black Widowers. New York, Doubleday, and London, Gollancz, 1980.

Three by Asimov. New York, Targ, 1981.

The Complete Robot. New York, Doubleday, and London, Granada, 1982.

The Union Club Mysteries. New York, Doubleday, 1983; London, Granada, 1984.

The Winds of Change and Other Stories. New York, Doubleday, and London, Granada, 1983.

Banquets of the Black Widowers. New York, Doubleday, 1984; London, Gollancz, 1985.

The Disappearing Man and Other Mysteries, illustrated by Yoshi Miyake. New York, Walker, 1985.

The Edge of Tomorrow. New York, Tor, 1985.

The Best Science Fiction of Isaac Asimov. New York, Doubleday, 1986; London, Grafton, 1987.

The Alternative Asimovs. New York, Doubleday, 1986.

The Best Mysteries of Isaac Asimov. New York, Doubleday, 1986; London, Grafton, 1987.

Robot Dreams, edited by Bryon Preiss, illustrated by Ralph McQuarrie. New York, Berkley, 1986; London, Gollancz, 1987.

The Asimov Chronicles: Fifty Years of Isaac Asimov, edited by Martin H. Greenberg. New York, Dark Harvest, 1989.

Isaac Asimov: The Complete Stories. New York, Doubleday, 1990.

Puzzles of the Black Widowers. New York, Doubleday, 1990.

Robot Visions, illustrated by Ralph McQuarrie. New York, New American Library, and London, Gollancz, 1990.

The Asimov Chronicles. New York, Ace, 3 vols., 1990.

The Asimov Chronicles. New York, Dell, 1991.

Poetry

Lecherous Limericks, illustrated by Julien Dedman. New York, Walker, 1975; London, Corgi, 1977.

More Lecherous Limericks, illustrated by Julien Dedman. New York, Walker, 1976.

Still More Lecherous Limericks, illustrated by Mel Brofman. New York, Walker, 1977.

Asimov's Sherlockian Limericks. Yonkers, New York, New Mysterious Press, 1978.

Limericks Too Gross, with John Ciardi. New York, Norton, 1978.

A Grossery of Limericks, with John Ciardi. New York, Norton, 1981.

Nonfiction

Biochemistry and Human Metabolism, with Burnham Walker and William C. Boyd. Baltimore, Williams and Wilkins, 1952; revised edition, 1954, 1957; London, Ballière Tindall and Cox, 1955.

The Chemicals of Life: Enzymes, Vitamins, Hormones. New York, Abelard Schuman, 1954; London, Bell, 1956.

Races and Peoples, with William C. Boyd. New York, Abelard Schuman, 1955; London, Abelard Schuman, 1958.

Chemistry and Human Health, with Burnham Walker and Mary K. Nicholas. New York, McGraw Hill, 1956.

Inside the Atom, illustrated by John Bradford. New York and London, Abelard Schuman, 1956; revised edition, Abelard Schuman, 1958, 1961, 1966, 1974.

Only a Trillion. New York and London, Abelard Schuman, 1957; as *Marvels of Science: Essays of Fact and Fancy on Life, Its Environment, Its Possibilities,* New York, Collier, 1962.

The World of Carbon. New York and London, Abelard Schuman, 1958; revised edition, New York, Collier, 1962.

The World of Nitrogen. New York and London, Abelard Schuman, 1958; revised edition, New York, Collier, 1962.

The Clock We Live On. New York and London, Abelard Schuman, 1959; revised edition, New York, Collier, 1962, Abelard Schuman, 1965.

The Living River. New York and London, Abelard Schuman, 1959; revised edition, as *The Bloodstream: River of Life,* New York, Collier, 1961.

Realm of Numbers, diagrams by Robert Belmore. Boston, Houghton Mifflin, 1959; London, Gollancz, 1963.

Words of Science and the History behind Them, illustrated by William Barss. Boston, Houghton Mifflin, 1959; London, Harrap, 1974.

The Double Planet, illustrated by John Bradford. New York, Abelard Schuman, 1960; London, Abelard Schuman, 1962; revised edition, 1966.

The Intelligent Man's Guide to Science. New York, Basic Books, 2 vols., 1960; published separately as *The Intelligent Man's Guide to the Physical Sciences* and *The Intelligent Man's Guide to the Biological Sciences,* New York, Pocket Books, 1964; revised edition as *The New Intelligent Man's Guide to Science,* 1 vol., New York, Basic Books, 1965; London, Nelson, 1967; as *Asimov's Guide to Science,* New York, Basic Books, 1972; London, Penguin, 2 vols., as *Asimov's New Guide to Science,* New York, Basic Books, 1984.

The Kingdom of the Sun. New York and London, Abelard Schuman, 1960; revised edition, New York, Collier, 1962; Abelard Schuman, 1963.

Realm of Measure, diagrams by Robert Belmore. Boston, Houghton Mifflin, 1960.

The Wellsprings of Life. New York and London, Abelard Schuman, 1960.

Realm of Algebra, diagrams by Robert Belmore. Boston, Houghton Mifflin, 1961; London, Gollancz, 1964.

Life and Energy. New York, Doubleday, 1962; London, Dobson, 1963.

Fact and Fancy New York, Doubleday, 1962; London, Dobson, 1963.

The Search for the Elements. New York, Basic Books, 1962.

The Genetic Code. New York, Orion Press, 1963; London, Murray, 1964.

The Human Body: Its Structure and Operation, illustrated by Anthony Ravielli. Boston, Houghton Mifflin, 1963; London, Nelson, 1965.

View from a Height. New York, Doubleday, 1963; London, Dobson, 1964.

The Human Brain: Its Capacities and Functions. Boston, Houghton Mifflin, 1964; London, Nelson, 1965.

A Short History of Biology. Garden City, New York, Natural History Press, 1964; London, Nelson, 1965.

Quick and Easy Math. Boston, Houghton Mifflin, 1964; London, Whiting and Wheaton, 1967.

Adding a Dimension: Seventeen Essays on the History of Science. New York, Doubleday, 1964; London, Dobson, 1966.

Planets for Man, with Stephen H. Dole. New York, Random House, 1964.

Asimov's Biographical Encyclopedia of Science and Technology. New York, Doubleday, 1964; London, Allen and Unwin, 1966; revised edition, New York, Doubleday, 1972, 1982; London, Pan, 1975.

The Greeks: A Great Adventure. Boston, Houghton Mifflin, 1965.

A Short History of Chemistry, illustrated by Robert Yaffe. New York, Doubleday, 1965; London, Heinemann, 1972.

Of Time and Space and Other Things. New York, Doubleday, 1965; London, Dobson, 1967.

An Easy Introduction to the Slide Rule, diagrams by William Barss. Boston, Houghton Mifflin, 1965; London, Whiting and Wheaton, 1967.

The Noble Gasses. New York, Basic Books, 1966.

The Neutrino: Ghost Particle of the Atom. New York, Doubleday, and London, Dobson, 1966.

The Roman Republic. Boston, Houghton Mifflin, 1966.

Understanding Physics. New York, Walker, 3 vols., 1966; London, Allen and Unwin, 3 vols., 1967; as *The History of Physics,* New York, Walker, 1 vol., 1984.

The Genetic Effects of Radiation, with Theodosius Dobzhansky. Washington, D.C., Atomic Energy Commission, 1966.

The Universe: From Flat Earth to Quasar. New York, Walker, 1966; London, Penguin, 1967; revised edition, New York, Walker, and London, Penguin, 1971; revised edition, as *The Universe: From Flat Earth to Black Holes—and Beyond,* New York, Walker, 1980, London, Penguin, 1983..

From Earth to Heaven: Seventeen Essays on Science. New York, Doubleday, 1966.

The Egyptians. Boston, Houghton Mifflin, 1967.

Environments Out There. New York, Abelard Schuman, 1967; London, Abelard Schuman, 1968.

From Earth to Heaven: Seventeen Essays on Science. New York, Doubleday, 1967; London, Dobson, 1968.

Is Anyone There? (essays). New York, Doubleday, 1967; London, Rapp and Whiting, 1968.

The Roman Empire. Boston, Houghton Mifflin, 1967.

The Dark Ages. Boston, Houghton Mifflin, 1968.

The Near East: Ten Thousand Years of History. Boston, Houghton Mifflin, 1968.

Photosynthesis. New York, Basic Books, 1968; London, Allen and Unwin, 1970.

Science, Numbers and I: Essays on Science. New York, Doubleday, 1968; London, Rapp and Whiting, 1969.

Words from History, illustrated by William Barss. Boston, Houghton Mifflin, 1968.

The Shaping of England. Boston, Houghton Mifflin, 1969.

Constantinople: The Forgotten Empire. Boston, Houghton Mifflin, 1970.

The Land of Canaan. Boston, Houghton Mifflin, 1970.

To the Solar System and Back. New York, Doubleday, 1970.

The Space Dictionary. New York, Starline, 1971.

The Stars in Their Courses. New York, Doubleday, 1971; London, White Lion, 1974.

The Left Hand of the Electron (essays). New York, Doubleday, 1972; London, White Lion, 1975.

Electricity and Man. Washington, D.C., Atomic Energy Commission, 1972.

The Shaping of France. Boston, Houghton Mifflin, 1972.

Worlds within Worlds: The Story of Nuclear Energy. Washington, D.C., Atomic Energy Commission, 3 vols., 1972.

Physical Science Today. Del Mar, California, CRM, 1973.

The Shaping of North America from Earliest Times to 1763. Boston, Houghton Mifflin, 1973; London, Dobson, 1975.

Today and Tomorrow and. . . New York, Doubleday, 1973; London, Abelard Schuman, 1974; as *Towards Tomorrow,* London, Hodder and Stoughton, 1977.

The Tragedy of the Moon (essays). New York, Doubleday, 1973; London, Abelard Schuman, 1974.

Asimov on Astronomy New York, Doubleday, and London, Macdonald, 1974.

Asimov on Chemistry (essays). New York, Doubleday, 1974; London, Macdonald and Jane's, 1975.

The Birth of the United States, 1763-1816. Boston, Houghton Mifflin, 1974.

Our World in Space, illustrated by Robert McCall. Greenwich, Connecticut, New York Graphic Society, and Cambridge, Patrick Stephens, 1974.

Birth and Death of the Universe. New York, Walker, 1975.

Of Matters Great and Small. New York, Doubleday, 1975.

Our Federal Union: The United States from 1816 to 1865. Boston, Houghton Mifflin, and London, Dobson, 1975.

Science Past—Science Future. New York, Doubleday, 1975.

Eyes on the Universe: A History of the Telescope. Boston, Houghton Mifflin, 1975; London, Deutsch, 1976.

The Ends of the Earth: The Polar Regions of the World, illustrated by Bob Hines. New York, Weybright and Talley, 1975.

Asimov on Physics (essays). New York, Doubleday, 1976.

The Planet that Wasn't (essays). New York, Doubleday, 1976; London, Sphere, 1977.

Asimov on Numbers. (essays). New York, Doubleday, 1977.

The Beginning and the End (essays). New York, Doubleday, 1977.

The Collapsing Universe: The Story of Black Holes. New York, Walker, and London, Hutchinson, 1977.

The Golden Door: The United States from 1865 to 1918. Boston, Houghton Mifflin, and London, Dobson, 1977.

Quasar, Quasar, Burning Bright (essays). New York, Doubleday, 1978.

Life and Time. New York, Doubleday, 1978.

The Road to Infinity (essays). New York, Doubleday, 1979.

A Choice of Catastrophes: The Disasters that Threaten Our World. New York, Simon and Schuster, 1979; London, Hutchinson, 1980.

Visions of the Universe, paintings by Kazuaki Iwasaki. Montrose, California, Cosmos Store, 1981.

The Sun Shines Bright (essays). New York, Doubleday, 1981; London, Granada, 1983.

Exploring the Earth and the Cosmos: The Growth and Future of Human Knowledge. New York, Crown, 1982; London, Allen Lane, 1983.

Counting the Eons. New York, Doubleday, 1983; London, Granada, 1984.

The Roving Mind. Buffalo, Prometheus, 1983.

The Measure of the Universe, illustrated by Roger Jones. New York, Harper, 1983.

Isaac Asimov on the Human Body and the Human Brain (includes *The Human Body: Its Structure and Operation* and *The Human Brain: Its Capacities and Functions*). Bonanza Books, 1984.

X Stands for Unknown. New York, Doubleday, 1984; London, Granada, 1985.

The Exploding Suns: The Secrets of the Supernovas, illustrated by D.F. Bach. New York, Dutton, and London, Joseph, 1985.

Asimov's Guide to Halley's Comet. New York, Walker, 1985.

Robots: Machines in Man's Image, with Karen Frenkel. New York, Harmony, 1985.

Robots: Where the Machine Ends and Life Begin, with Karen Frenkel. New York, Crown, 1985.

The Subatomic Monster: Essays on Science. New York, Doubleday, 1985; London, Grafton, 1986.

The Dangers of Intelligence and Other Science Essays. Boston, Houghton Mifflin, 1986.

Future Days: A Nineteenth-Century Vision of the Year 2000, illustrated by Jean Marc Côté. New York, Holt, and London, Virgin, 1986.

Isaac Asimov's Wonderful Worldwide Science Bazaar: Seventy-Two Up-to-Date Reports on the State of Everything from Inside the Atom to Outside the Universe. Boston, Houghton Mifflin, 1986.

As Far as Human Eye Could See (essays). New York, Doubleday, 1987; London, Grafton, 1988.

The Relativity of Wrong: Essays on the Solar System and Beyond. New York, Doubleday, 1988; Oxford, Oxford University Press, 1989.

Asimov on Science: A Thirty Year Retrospective. New York, Doubleday, 1989.

Asimov's Chronology of Science and Technology: How Science Has Shaped the World and How the World Has Affected Science from 4,000,000 B.C. to the Present. New York, Harper, 1989.

The Secret of the Universe. New York, Doubleday, 1989.

The Tyrannosaurus Prescription and One Hundred Other Essays. New York, Prometheus, 1989.

The March of the Millennia: A Key to Looking at History, with Frank White. New York, Walker, 1990.

The Next Millennium. New York, Walker, 1990.

Out of the Everywhere (essays). New York, Doubleday, 1990.

Asimov's Chronology of the World. New York, Harper, 1991.

Asimov's Guide to Earth and Space. New York, Random House, 1991.

Atom: Journey across the Subatomic Cosmos, illustrated by D.F. Bach. New York, Dutton, 1991.

Frontiers: New Discoveries about Man and His Planet, Outer Space, and the Universe. New York, Dutton, 1991.

Our Angry Earth. with Frederick Pohl. New York, Tor, 1991.

Frontiers II: More Recent Discoveries about Life, Earth, Space, and the Universe, with Janet Asimov. New York, Dutton, 1993.

The Future in Space, with Robert Giraud. Milwaukee, Stevens, 1993.

Other

Contributor, *Science Fiction Terror Tales by Isaac Asimov and Others,* edited by Groff Conklin. New York, Gnome Press, 1955.

Words from the Myths, illustrated by William Barss. Boston, Houghton Mifflin, 1961; London, Faber, 1963.

Words in Genesis, illustrated by William Barss. Boston, Houghton Mifflin, 1962.

Words on the Map. Boston, Houghton Mifflin, 1962.

Words from Exodus. Boston, Houghton Mifflin, 1963.

Asimov's Guide to the Bible: The Old Testament, The New Testament. New York, Doubleday, 2 vols., 1968-69.

Opus 100 (selection). Boston, Houghton Mifflin, 1969.

Asimov's Guide to Shakespeare: The Greek, Roman, and Italian Plays; The English Plays, illustrated by Rafael Palacios. New York, Doubleday, 2 vols., 1970.

Unseen World (teleplay). ABC-TV, 1970.

Isaac Asimov's Treasury of Humor: A Lifetime Collection of Favorite Jokes, Anecdotes, and Limericks with Copious Notes on How to Tell Them and Why. Boston, Houghton Mifflin, 1971; London, Vallentine Mitchell, 1972.

The History of Science Fiction from 1938 to the Present (filmscript), with James Gunn. Extramural Independent Study Center, University of Kansas, 1971.

The Sensuous Dirty Old Man (as Dr. A.). New York, Walker, 1971.

Contributor, *The Do-It-Yourself Bestseller,* edited by Tom Silberkleit and Jerry Biederman. New York, Doubleday, 1982.

More Words of Science, illustrated by William Barss. Boston, Houghton Mifflin, 1972.

Contributor, *Possible Tomorrows by Isaac Asimov and Others,* edited by Groff Conklin. London, Sidgwick and Jackson, 1972.

The Story of Ruth. New York, Doubleday, 1972.

Asimov's Annotated "Don Juan," illustrated by Milton Glaser. New York, Doubleday. 1972.

Asimov's Annotated "Paradise Lost." New York, Doubleday, 1974.

Familiar Poems Annotated. New York, Doubleday, 1977.

Opus 200 (selection). Boston, Houghton Mifflin, 1979.

In Memory Yet Green: The Autobiography of Isaac Asimov, 1920-1954. New York, Doubleday, 1979.

Extraterrestrial Civilizations. New York, Crown, 1979; London, Robson, 1980.

Isaac Asimov's Book of Facts. New York, Grosset and Dunlap, 1979; London, Hodder and Stoughton, 1980; abridged edition (for children), as *Would You Believe?* and *More. . .Would You Believe?,* illustrated by Sam Sirdofsky Haffner and Pat Schories. New York, Grosset and Dunlap, 2 vols., 1981-82.

In Joy Still Felt: The Autobiography of Isaac Asimov, 1954-1978. New York, Doubleday, 1980.

The Annotated "Gulliver's Travels." New York, Potter. 1980.

Opus (includes *Opus 100* and *Opus 200*). London, Deutsch, 1980.

In the Beginning: Science Faces God in the Book of Genesis. New York, Crown, and London, New English Library, 1981.

Asimov on Science Fiction. New York, Doubleday, 1981; London, Granada, 1983.

Change! Seventy-One Glimpses of the Future. Boston, Houghton Mifflin, 1981.

Isaac Asimov Presents Superquiz, with Ken Fisher. New York, Dembner, 1982.

Isaac Asimov Presents Superquiz 2, with Ken Fisher. New York, Dembner, 1983.

Isaac Asimov's Aliens and Outworlders, edited by Shawna McCarthy. New York, Dial, 1983.

Isaac Asimov's Space of Her Own, edited by Shawna McCarthy. New York, Dial, 1983.

The Robot Collection (includes *The Caves of Steel, The Naked Sun,* and *The Complete Robot*). New York, Doubleday. 1983.

Opus 300. Boston, Houghton Mifflin, 1984; London, Hale, 1985.

The Impact of Science on Society, with James Burke and Jules Bergman. Washington D.C., National Aeronautics and Space Administration, 1985.

Isaac Asimov's Fantasy!, edited by Shawna McCarthy. New York, Dial, 1985.

The Alternate Asimovs. New York, Doubleday, 1986.

Isaac Asimov. New York, Octopus Books, 1986.

Other Worlds of Isaac Asimov, edited by Martin H. Greenberg. Avenel, 1986.

Past, Present, and Future (essays). Buffalo, New York, Prometheus, 1987.

How to Enjoy Writing: A Book of Aid and Comfort, with Janet Asimov, illustrated by Sidney Harris. New York, Walker, 1987.

Asimov's Annotated Gilbert and Sullivan. New York, Doubleday, 1988.

Library of the Universe (Did Comets Kill the Dinosaurs; The Asteroids; Ancient Astronomy; Is There Life On Other Planets?; Jupiter, the Spotted Giant; Mercury, the Quick Planet; Our Milky and Other Galaxies; How Was the Universe Born?; Saturn, the Ringed Beauty; The Space Spotter's Guide; Unidentified Flying Objects; Earth, Our Home Base; The Birth and Death of the Stars; Science Fiction, Science Fact; Space Garbage; Astronomy Today; Comets and Meteors; Mythology of the Universe; Pluto, A Double Planet?; Colonizing the Planets and Stars; Neptune, The Farthest Giant; Piloted Space Flights; Projects in Astronomy; Our Solar System; Uranus: The Sideways Planet; Astronomy Today; Quasars, Pulsars, and Black Holes; Venus, A Shrouded Mystery; The World's Space Programs). Milwaukee, Stevens, 24 vols., 1988-90.

Asimov's Galaxy: Reflections on Science Fiction. New York, Doubleday, 1989.

Foundation's Friends: Stories in Honor of Isaac Asimov, edited by Martin H. Greenberg. New York, T. Doherty Associates, 1989.

The Ugly Little Boy/The Widget, the Wadget, and Boff, with Theodore Sturgeon. New York, Tor, 1989.

Isaac Asimov Laughs Again. New York, Harper, 1991.

Contributor, *The John W. Campbell Letters with Isaac Asimov and A.E. van Vogt.* A.C. Projects, 1991.

The Ugly Little Boy, with Robert Silverberg. New York, Doubleday, 1992.

Editor

Isaac Asimov Presents the Golden Years of Science Fiction, with Martin H. Greenberg. New York, Crown, 1939.

Isaac Asimov Presents the Golden Years of Science Fiction: Twenty-Eight Stories and Novellas, with Martin H. Greenberg. New York, Bonanza, 1941.

Isaac Asimov Presents the Golden Years of Science Fiction: Twenty Stories and Novellas, with Martin H. Greenberg. New York, Crown, 1943.

Isaac Asimov Presents the Golden Years of Science Fiction: Twenty-Six Stories and Novellas, with Martin H. Greenberg. New York, Crown, 1945.

Isaac Asimov Presents the Golden Years of Science Fiction: Thirty-Three Stories and Novellas, with Martin H. Greenberg. New York, Crown, 1947.

Soviet Science Fiction and *More Soviet Science Fiction.* New York, Collier, 2 vols., 1962.

The Hugo Winners 1-4. New York, Doubleday, 4 vols., 1962-85; *Volume 1* and *Volume 3,* London, Dobson, 2 vols., 1963-67; *Volume 2,* London, Sphere, 1973.

Fifty Short Science Fiction Tales, with Groff Conklin. New York, Collier, 1963.

Four Futures: Four Original Novellas of Science Fiction. New York, Hawthorn, 1971.

Tomorrow's Children: Eighteen Tales of Fantasy and Science Fiction, illustrated by Emanuel Schongut. New York, Doubleday, 1966; London, Futura, 1974.

Where Do We Go from Here? New York, Doubleday, 1971; London, Joseph, 1973.

Nebula Award Stories 8. New York, Harper, and London, Gollancz, 1973.

Before the Golden Age: A Science Fiction Anthology of the 1930's. New York, Doubleday, and London, Robson, 1974.

100 Great Science Fiction Short-Short Stories, with Martin H. Greenberg and Joseph D. Olander. New York, Doubleday, and London, Robson, 1978.

The Science Fictional Solar System, with Martin H. Greenberg and Charles G. Waugh. New York, Harper, 1979; London, Sidgwick and Jackson, 1980.

The Thirteen Crime of Science Fiction, with Martin H. Greenberg and Charles G. Waugh. New York, Doubleday, 1979.

The Great SF Stories 1-20, with Martin H. Greenberg. New York, DAW, 1979-90.

Microcosmic Tales: 100 Wondrous Science Fiction Short-Short Stories, with Martin H. Greenberg and Joseph D. Olander. New York, Taplinger, 1980.

Space Mail 1, with Martin H. Greenberg and Joseph D. Olander. New York, Fawcett, 1980.

The Future in Question, with Martin H. Greenberg and Joseph D. Olander. New York, Fawcett, 1980.

Who Done It?, with Alice Laurance. Boston, Houghton Mifflin, 1980.

The Seven Deadly Sins of Science Fiction, edited by Martin H. Greenberg and Charles G. Waugh. New York, Fawcett, 1980.

Miniature Mysteries: 100 Malicious Little Mystery Stories, with Martin H. Greenberg and Joseph D. Olander. New York, Taplinger, 1981.

Fantastic Creature. New York, Watts, 1981.

The Best Science Fiction [Fantasy, Horror and Supernatural] of the 19th Century. New York, Beaufort, 3 vols., 1981-83; *Science Fiction,* London, Gollancz, 1983; *Fantasy and Horror and Supernatural,* London, Robson, 2 vols., 1985, all with Martin H. Greenberg and Charles G. Waugh.

Asimov's Marvels of Science Fiction. London, Hale, 1981.

The Twelve Crimes of Christmas, with Carol-Lynn Rössell Waugh and Martin H. Greenberg. New York, New York, Avon, 1981.

The Seven Cardinal Virtues of Science Fiction, with Charles G. Waugh and Martin H. Greenberg. New York, Fawcett, 1981.

TV: 2000, with Martin H. Greenberg and Charles G. Waugh. New York, Fawcett, 1982.

Last Man on Earth, with Martin H. Greenberg and Charles G. Waugh. New York, Fawcett, 1982.

Tantalizing Locked Room Mysteries, with Charles G. Waugh and Martin H. Greenberg. New York, Walker, 1982.

Space Mail 2, with Martin H. Greenberg and Charles G. Waugh. New York, Fawcett, 1982.

Laughing Space: Funny Science Fiction, with J.O. Jeppson. Boston, Houghton Mifflin, and London, Robson, 1982.

Speculations, with Alice Laurance. Boston, Houghton Mifflin, 1982.

Science Fiction from A to Z: A Dictionary of the Great Themes of Science Fiction, with Charles G. Waugh and Martin H. Greenberg. Boston, Houghton Mifflin, 1982.

Flying Saucers, with Martin H. Greenberg and Charles G. Waugh. New York, Fawcett, 1982.

Dragon Tales, with Martin H. Greenberg and Charles G. Waugh. New York, Fawcett, 1982.

Asimov's Worlds of Science Fiction. London, Hale, 1982.

Hallucination Orbit: Psychology in Science Fiction, with Martin H. Greenberg and Charles G. Waugh. New York, Farrar Straus, 1983.

Magical Worlds of Fantasy series (*Wizards, Witches*). New York, New American Library, 2 vols., 1983-84; 1 vol. edition, New York, Bonanza, 1985.

Caught in the Organ Draft: Biology in Science Fiction, with Martin H. Greenberg and Charles G. Waugh. New York, Farrar Straus, 1983.

The Big Apple Mysteries. New York, Avon, 1983.

The Science Fiction Weight-Loss Book, with George R. Martin and Martin H. Greenberg. New York, Crown, 1983.

Starships, with Martin H. Greenberg and Charles G. Waugh. New York, Ballantine, 1983.

Asimov's Wonders of the World. London, Hale, 1983.

Creations: The Quest for Origins in Story and Science, with Martin H. Greenberg and George Zebrowski. New York, Crown, 1983; London, Harrap, 1984.

Computer Crimes and Capers, with Martin H. Greenberg and Charles G. Waugh. Chicago, Academy, 1983; London, Viking, 1985.

Thirteen Horrors of Halloween. Avon, 1983.

Machines That Think, Patricia S. Warrick and Martin H. Greenberg. New York, Holt Rinehart, and London, Allen Lane, 1984.

100 Great Fantasy Short-Short Stories, with Terry Carr and Martin H. Greenberg. New York, Doubleday, and London, Robson, 1984.

The Great Science Fiction Firsts, with Charles G. Waugh and Martin H. Greenberg. New York, Beaufort, 1984; London, Robson, 1985.

Murder on the Menu, with others. New York, Avon, 1984.

Sherlock Holmes Through Time and Space, with Martin H. Greenberg and Charles G. Waugh. New York, Bluejay, 1984; London, Severn House, 1985.

Isaac Asimov's Wonderful World of Science Fiction 2: The Science Fictional Olympics, with Martin H. Greenberg. New York, New American Library, 1984.

Election Day 2084: A Science Fiction Anthology on the Politics of the Future, with Martin H. Greenberg. Buffalo, New York, Prometheus, 1984.

Baker's Dozen: Thirteen Short Fantasy Novels, with Martin H. Greenberg and Charles G. Waugh. New York, Greenwich House, 1984.

Amazing Stories: Sixty Years of the Best Science Fiction, with Martin H. Greenberg and Charles G. Waugh. Lake Geneva, Wisconsin, TRS, 1985.

Living in the Future, illustrated by Lynn Williams. New York, Beaufort, 1985.

Great Science Fiction Stories by the World's Great Scientists, with Martin H. Greenberg and Charles G. Waugh. New York, Fine, 1985.

Giants, with Martin H. Greenberg and Charles G. Waugh. New York, New American Library, 1985.

Comets, with Martin H. Greenberg and Charles G. Waugh. New American Library, 1986.

Mythical Beasties, with Martin H. Greenberg and Charles G. Waugh. New York, New American Library, 1986; as *Mythic Beasts,* London, Robinson, 1988.

The Mammoth Book of Short Fantasy Novels. London, Robinson, 1986.

The Mammoth Book of Short Science Fiction Novels. London, Robinson, 1986.

The Dark Void. London, Severn House, 1987.

Beyond the Stars. London, Severn House, 1987.

Hound Dunnit, with Carol-Lynn Rössell Waugh and Martin H. Greenberg. New York, Carroll and Graf, 1987; London, Robson, 1988.

Cosmic Knight, with Martin H. Greenberg and Charles G. Waugh. London, Robinson, 1987.

The Best Crime Stories of the 19th Century, with Martin H. Greenberg and Charles G. Waugh. New York, Dembner, 1988; London, Robson, 1989.

Isaac Asimov's Book of Science and Nature Quotations, with Jason A. Shulman. New York, Weidenfeld and Nicolson, 1988.

Ghosts, with Martin H. Greenberg and Charles G. Waugh. London, Collins, 1988.

The Best Detective Stories of the 19th Century, with Martin H. Greenberg and Charles G. Waugh. New York, Dembner, 1988.

The Mammoth Book of Classic Science Fiction: Short Novels of the 1930's, with Martin H. Greenberg and Charles G. Waugh. New York, Carroll and Graf, and London, Robinson, 1988.

Monsters, with Martin H. Greenberg and Charles G. Waugh. New York, New American Library, 1988; London, Robinson, 1989.

The Mammoth Book of Golden Age Science Fiction: Short Novels of the 1940's, with Martin H. Greenberg and Charles G. Waugh. New York, Carroll and Graf, and London, Robinson, 1989.

Curses, with Martin H. Greenberg and Charles G. Waugh. New York, New American Library, 1989.

Senior Sleuths, with Martin H. Greenberg and Carol-Lynn Rossel Waugh. Boston, G.K. Hall, 1989.

Tales of the Occult, with Martin H. Greenberg and Charles G. Waugh. Buffalo, New York, Prometheus, 1989.

Robots, with Martin H. Greenberg and Charles G. Waugh. London, Robinson, 1989.

The New Hugo Winners, with Martin H. Greenberg. New York, Wynwood Press, 1989.

Visions of Fantasy: Tales from the Masters, with Martin H. Greenberg, illustrated by Larry Elmore. New York, Doubleday, 1989.

The Mammoth Book of Vintage Science Fiction: Short Novels of the 1950's, with Martin H. Greenberg and Charles G. Waugh. New York, Carroll and Graf, and London, Robinson, 1990.

Cosmic Critiques: How and Why Ten Science Fiction Stories Work, with Martin H. Greenberg. Cincinnati, Writer's Digest, 1990.

*

Media Adaptations: *Foundation: The Psychohistorians* (recording of selected chapters of *Foundation* read by William Shatner, Caedmon, 1976; *The Mayors* (recording of Asimov reading *Foundation),* Caedmon, 1977; *The Ugly Little Boy* (film), Learning Corporation of America, 1977; *Nightfall* (film), MGM/UA, 1988.

Biography: Entry in *Dictionary of Literary Biography,* Volume 8, Detroit, Gale, 1981.

Bibliography: *Isaac Asimov: A Checklist of Works Published in the United States March 1939-May 1972* by Marjorie M. Miller, Kent, Ohio, Kent State University Press, 1972; in *In Joy Still Felt,* 1980.

Manuscript Collection: Mugar Memorial Library, Boston University.

Critical Study: *Asimov Analyzed* by Neil Goble, Baltimore, Mirage Press, 1972; entry in *Contemporary Literary Criticism,* Volume 1, Detroit, Gale, 1973; Volume 3, 1975; Volume 9, 1978; Volume 19, 1981; Volume 26, 1983; *Isaac Asimov Talks: An Interview* (recording), Writer's Voice, 1974; *The Science Fiction of Isaac Asimov* by Joseph F. Patrouch, Jr., New York, Doubleday, 1974, London, Panther, 1976; *Isaac Asimov* edited by Joseph D. Olander and Martin H. Greenberg, New York, Taplinger, and Edinburgh, Harris, 1977; *Asimov: The Foundations of His Science Fiction* by George Edgar Slusser, San Bernardino, California, Borgo Press, 1980; *Isaac Asimov: The Foundations of Science Fiction* by James Gunn, New York and Oxford, Oxford University Press, 1982; *Isaac Asimov* by Jean Fiedler and Jim Mele, New York, Ungar, 1982; entry in *Children's Literature Review,* Volume 12, Detroit, Gale, 1987.

*   *   *

Isaac Asimov is the extraordinarily prolific writer of a prodigious number of works including science fiction, science fact, mystery, history, short stories, guides to the Bible and Shakespeare, and discussions of myth, humor, poems, limericks, as well as annotations of literary works. His wide-ranging interests, scholarship, and productivity should serve as inspiration to his readers.

Among Asimov's credits are several types of books for young readers and several other works written for adults but also suited for older juvenile readers. His science fiction for juveniles include a series of novels originally published under the pseudonym of Paul French and subsequently represented under Asimov's name. These are entitled *David Starr, Space Ranger* (1952); *Lucky Starr and the*

Pirates of the Asteroids (1953); *Lucky Starr and the Oceans of Venus* (1954); *Lucky Starr and the Big Sun of Mercury* (1956), published under Asimov's name as *The Big Sun of Mercury* in 1974 and later under Asimov's name under original title in 1978; *Lucky Starr and the Moons of Jupiter* (1957); and *Lucky Starr and the Rings of Saturn* (1958).

David Starr, Space Ranger and the other novels listed are "space operas." In these novels, good prevails over evil, science always wins out over ignorance, and earthlings win over those from other parts of the galaxy. These books contain constant action, imaginative gadgetry, and brisk narrative. Not surprising considering Asimov's training as a scientist is that his novels are filled with prose passages explaining space phenomena and giving information about the galaxy. All of the sequels to *David Starr, Space Ranger* present a mystery that David and the readers must solve.

David Starr, who was later called Lucky, is an interesting character. He has brains, courage, and athletic ability. He is also modest. Bigman Jones is David's devoted companion; he is a small Martian who offers comic relief. The villains are sufficiently villainous.

The David Starr novels, written when the military rivalry with the U.S.S.R. was at its height, frequently flaunt the democratic ideal and present villains as evil would-be dictators. The reissued novels allows Asimov to report new scientific findings that have relevance to the works.

Other science fiction works for young people are *The Best New Thing* (1971), The *Heavenly Host* (1975) and the Norby novels: *Norby, the Mixed up Robot* (1983); *Norby and the Lost Princess* (1985); *Norby and the Invaders* (1985); *Norby and the Queen's Necklace* (1986); *Norby Finds a Villain* (1987); *Norby Down to Earth* (1989); and *Norby and the Oldest Dragon* (1990). The Norby novels are written with Asimov's wife Janet O. Jeppson as coauthor. *Franchise, All the Troubles of the World, Sally,* and *Robbie* were all published in 1989 by creative education.

Several of Asimov's titles for adults have been widely read by a younger audience. These most notably include the Foundation Trilogy published from 1951 to 1953. The trilogy consists of three books of stories — *Foundation, Foundation and Empire,* and *Second Foundation.* These novels compose a history of the future loosely based on the events in the fall of the Roman Empire. Beyond that, the novels provide a powerful commentary on the nature of history. In the novels, the Roman Empire is the Galactic Empire. A new science called psychohistory allows people to predict what will happen in the future. This situation allows a venue for exploring historical trends, the conflict of determinism and free will, and the ability of one person or a group to control others and ultimately history. These are certainly adult subjects. Forty years after the original trilogy, in the 1980s, Asimov added a new volume, Foundation's Edge. He also linked the Foundation stories with his robot novels in *The Robots of Dawn, Robots and Empire, Foundation and Earth,* and *Prelude to Foundation.*

The novels are—in form—space operas, primarily adventure stories set in the future. As such, their appeal is wide. They have galaxy-spanning federations, fast ships that travel at above light-speed, and atomic weaponry. The Foundation triumphs on the planet Terminus. Foundation is an island of scientific knowledge— an expressed wish perhaps for reason to triumph over the irrational.

Asimov's nonfiction works for young readers are as impressive as his fiction. He wrote a number of books on astronomy: *Building Blocks of the Universe, Satellites in Outer Space, The Moon, To the*

Ends of the Universe, Mars, Stars, Galaxies and many more. In addition to astronomy topics, Asimov wrote about various aspects of science in general in *Breakthroughs in Science, Great Ideas of Science, Ginn Science Program, Please Explain,* and *Little Treasury of Dinosaurs.* All of these works are somewhat dated in their information, but are nonetheless classics of a sort. Asimov also wrote several histories, one of which was specifically designed for juveniles entitled *The Kite that Won the Revolution.*

Isaac Asimov's creativity and intelligence in presenting information both fiction and nonfiction will guarantee his place as one of the masters of science fiction.

—Lesa Dill

ATWOOD, Margaret (Eleanor)

Nationality: Canadian. **Born:** Ottawa, Ontario, Canada, 18 November 1939. **Education:** Victoria College, University of Toronto, B.A. 1961; Radcliffe College, Cambridge, Massachusetts, A.M. 1962; Harvard University, Cambridge, Massachusetts, graduate study, 1962-63, and 1965-67. **Family:** Married 1) James Polk (divorced); 2) Graeme Gibson, one daughter. **Career:** Lecturer in English, University of British Columbia, Vancouver, 1964-65; Instructor in English, Sir George Williams University, Montreal, Quebec, 1967-68; teacher of creative writing, University of Alberta, Edmonton, 1969-70; Assistant Professor of English, York University, Toronto, Ontario, 1971-72; Editor and member of board of directors, House of Anansi Press, Toronto, 1971-73. Writer-in-residence, University of Toronto, Toronto, 1972-73, University of Alabama, Tuscaloosa, 1985, Macquarie University, North Ryde, New South Wales, 1987, and Trinity University, San Antonio, Texas, 1989; Berg Visiting Professor of English, New York University, New York, 1986. President, Writers Union of Canada, 1981-82, and PEN Canadian Centre, 1984-86. **Awards:** E.J. Pratt medal, 1961, for *Double Persephone;* President's medal, University of Western Ontario, 1965; YWCA Women of Distinction award, 1966; Governor General's award, 1966, for *The Circle Game,* and 1986, for *The Handmaid's Tale;* first prize in Canadian Centennial Commission Poetry Competition, 1967; Union Prize, *Poetry,* 1969; Bess Hoskins Prize, *Poetry,* 1969 and 1974; City of Toronto award, 1976, 1989; Canadian Booksellers' Association award, 1977; Periodical Distributors of Canada Short Fiction award, 1977; St. Lawrence award for fiction, 1978; Radcliffe medal, 1980; *Life before Man* named notable book of 1980 by the American Library Association; Molson award, 1981; Guggenheim fellowship, 1981; International Writer's Prize, Welsh Arts Council, 1982; Book of the Year award, Periodical Distributors of Canada and the Foundation for the Advancement of Canadian Letters, 1983; Ida Nudel Humanitarian award, 1986; Toronto Arts award for writing and editing, 1986; *Los Angeles Times* Book award, 1986, for *The Handmaid's Tale;* named Woman of the Year, *Ms.* magazine, 1986; Arthur C. Clarke award, 1987; Commonwealth Literature Prize, 1987; Council for the Advancement and Support of Education silver medal, 1987; Humanist of the Year award, 1987; National Magazine award, for journalism, 1988; Harvard University Centennial medal, 1990; named *Chatelaine* magazine's Woman of the Year. D.Litt.: Trent University, Peterborough,

Ontario, 1973; Concordia University, Montreal, 1980; Smith College, Northampton, Massachusetts, 1982; University of Toronto, 1983; Mount Holyoke College, South Hadley, Massachusetts, 1985; University of Waterloo, Ontario, 1985; University of Guelph, Ontario, 1985; Victoria College, 1987; LL.D.: Queen's University, Kingston, Ontario, 1974. Companion, Order of Canada, 1981. Fellow, Royal Society of Canada, 1987; Honorary Member, American Academy of Arts and Sciences, 1988; Giller Prize, 1996, for *Alias Grace;* Canadian Booksellers' Association Author of the Year award, 1997. **Address:** c/o Oxford University Press, 70 Wynford Drive, Don Mills, Ontario M3C 1J9, Canada; c/o M&S, 481 University Avenue, suite 900, Toronto, Ontario, Canada M5G 2E9.

PUBLICATIONS

Novels

The Edible Woman. Toronto, McClelland and Stewart, and London, Deutsch, 1969; Boston, Little Brown, 1970.
Surfacing. Toronto, McClelland and Stewart, 1972; London, Deutsch, and New York, Simon and Schuster 1973.
Lady Oracle. Toronto, McClelland and Stewart, and New York, Simon and Schuster, 1976; London, Deutsch, 1977.
Life Before Man. Toronto, McClelland and Stewart, 1979; New York, Simon and Schuster, and London, Cape, 1980.
Bodily Harm. Toronto, McClelland and Stewart, 1981; New York, Simon and Schuster, and London, Cape, 1982.
Cat's Eye. Toronto, McClelland and Stewart, 1985; New York, Doubleday, and London, Bloomsbury, 1989.
The Handmaid's Tale. Toronto, McClelland and Stewart, 1985; Boston, Houghton Mifflin, and London, Cape, 1986.
The Robber Bride. Toronto, McClelland and Stewart, and New York, Doubleday, 1993.
Alias Grace. Toronto, McClelland and Stewart, New York, Doubleday, and London, Bloomsbury, 1996.

Short Stories

Dancing Girls and Other Stories. Toronto, McClelland and Stewart, 1977; New York, Simon and Schuster, and London, Cape, 1982.
Encounters with the Element Man. Concord, New Hampshire, Ewert, 1982.
Bluebeard's Egg and Other Stories. Toronto, McClelland and Stewart, 1983; Boston, Houghton Mifflin, 1986; London, Cape, 1987..
Murder in the Dark: Short Fictions and Prose Poems. Toronto, Coach House Press, 1983; London, Cape, 1984.
Unearthing Suite. Toronto, Grand Union Press, 1983.
Hurricane Hazel and Other Stories. Helsinki, Eurographica, 1986.
Wilderness Tips. Hampton, New Hampshire, Chivers, 1991.
Good Bones. Toronto, Coach House Press, 1992.

Poetry

Double Persephone. Toronto, Hawkshead Press, 1961.
The Circle Game (single poem). Bloomfield Hills, Michigan, Cranbrook Academy of Art, 1964; revised edition, Contact Press, 1966.

Kaleidoscopes Baroque: A Poem. Bloomfield Hills, Michigan, Cranbrook Academy of Art, 1965.

Talismans for Children. Bloomfield Hills, Michigan, Cranbrook Academy of Art, 1965.

Expeditions. Bloomfield Hills, Michigan, Cranbrook Academy of Art, 1966.

Speeches for Doctor Frankenstein. Bloomfield Hills, Michigan, Cranbrook Academy of Art, 1966.

The Animals in That Country. Toronto, Oxford University Press, 1968; Boston, Little Brown, 1969.

Who Was in the Garden. Santa Barbara, California, Unicorn, 1969.

Five Modern Canadian Poets, with others, edited by Eli Mandel. Toronto, Holt Rinehart, 1970.

The Journals of Susanna Moodie. Toronto, Oxford University Press, 1970.

Oratorio for Sasquatch, Man and Two Androids: Poems for Voices. Toronto, Canadian Broadcasting Corporation, 1970.

Procedures for Underground. Toronto, Oxford University Press, and Boston, Little Brown, 1970.

Power Politics. Toronto, Anansi, 1971; New York, Harper, 1973.

You Are Happy. Toronto, Oxford University Press, and New York, Harper, 1974.

Selected Poems, 1965-1975. Toronto, Oxford University Press, 1976; New York, Simon and Schuster, 1978.

Marsh Hawk. Toronto, Dreadnaught, 1977.

Two-Headed Poems. Toronto, Oxford University Press, 1978; New York, Simon and Schuster, 1981.

Notes Toward a Poem That Can Never Be Written. Toronto, Salamander Press, 1981.

True Stories. Toronto, Oxford University Press, 1981; New York, Simon and Schuster, and London, Cape, 1982.

Snake Poems. Toronto, Salamander Press, 1983.

Interlunar. Toronto, Oxford University Press, 1984; London, Cape, 1988.

Selected Poems II: Poems Selected and New, 1976-1986. Toronto, Oxford University Press, 1986; Boston, Houghton Mifflin, 1987.

Selected Poems 1966-1984. Toronto, Oxford University Press, 1990.

Poems 1965-1975. London, Virago Press, 1991.

Plays

Radio Plays: *The Trumpets of Summer,* CBC, 1964.

Television Plays: *The Servant Girl,* CBC-TV, 1974; *Snowbird,* CBC-TV, 1981; *Heaven on Earth,* with Peter Pearson, CBC-TV, 1986.

Other

Survival: A Thematic Guide to Canadian Literature. Toronto, Anansi, 1972.

Contributor, *The Canadian Imagination: Dimensions of a Literary Culture.* Cambridge, Massachusetts, Harvard University Press, 1977.

Days of the Rebels, 1815-1840. Toronto, Natural Science of Canada, 1977.

Up in the Tree (for children). Toronto, McClelland and Stewart, 1978.

Contributor, *To See Our World,* by Catherine M. Young. GLC Publishers, 1979; New York, Morrow, 1980.

Anna's Pet (for children), with Joyce Barkhouse, illustrated by Ann Blades. Toronto, Lorimer, 1980.

Second Words: Selected Critical Prose. Toronto, Anansi, 1982; Boston, Beacon Press, 1984.

Editor, *The New Oxford Book of Canadian Verse in English.* Toronto, New York, and Oxford, Oxford University Press, 1982.

Editor, with Robert Weaver, *The Oxford Book of Canadian Short Stories in English.* Toronto, Oxford, and New York, Oxford University Press, 1986.

Editor, *The Canlit Foodbook: From Pen to Palate: A Collection of Tasty Literary Fare.* Toronto, Totem, 1987.

Editor, with Shannon Ravenel. *The Best American Short Stories, 1989.* Boston, Houghton Mifflin, 1989.

Margaret Atwood: Conversations, edited by Earl G. Ingersoll. Princeton, New Jersey, Ontario Review Press, 1990.

For the Birds (for children). Toronto, Douglas and McIntyre, 1990.

Family Cooking Celebration: Kitchen Discoveries for All Ages!, with Victory Crealock. Seattle, Washington, Pepper Mill, 1991.

Contributor to anthologies, including *Women on Women,* 1978 and to periodicals, including *Atlantic, Poetry, Kayak, New Yorker, Harper's, New York Times Book Review, Saturday Night, Tamarack Review, Canadian Forum,* and other publications.

*

Media Adaptations: *The Poetry and Voice of Margaret Atwood* (recording), Caedmon, 1977; *The Handmaid's Tale* (film), Cinecom Entertainment Group, 1990; *Margaret Atwood Reads from A Handmaid's Tale,* Caedmon.

Biography: *Margaret Atwood* by Jerome H. Rosenberg, Boston, Twayne, 1984; Entry in *Dictionary of Literary Biography,* Volume 53, Detroit, Gale, 1986; *Margaret Atwood* by Barbara Hill Rigney, London, Macmillan, 1987.

Bibliography: "Margaret Atwood: An Annotated Bibliography" (prose and poetry) by Alan J. Horne, in *The Annotated Bibliography of Canada's Major Authors 1-2* edited by Robert Lecker and Jack David, Downsview, Ontario, ECW Press, 2 vols., 1929-80.

Manuscript Collections: Fisher Library, University of Toronto.

Critical Studies: Entry in *Contemporary Literary Criticism,* Volume 2, Detroit, Gale, 1974; Volume 3, 1975; Volume 4, 1975; Volume 8, 1978; Volume 13, 1980; Volume 15, 1980; Volume 25, 1983; Volume 44, 1987; *Margaret Atwood: A Symposium* edited by Linda Sandler, Victoria, British Columbia, University of Victoria, 1977; *A Violent Duality* by Sherrill E. Grace, Montreal, Véhicule Press, 1979, and *Margaret Atwood: Language, Text, and System* edited by Grace and Lorraine Weir, Vancouver, University of British Columbia Press, 1983; *The Art of Margaret Atwood: Essays in Criticism* edited by Arnold E. Davidson and Cathy N. Davidson, Toronto, Anansi, 1981; *Margaret Atwood: A Feminist Poet* by Frank Davey, Vancouver, Talonbooks, 1984; *Margaret Atwood: Reflection and Reality* by Beatrice Mendez-Egle, Edinburg, Texas, Pan American University, 1987; *Critical Essays on Margaret Atwood* edited by Judith McCombs, Boston, Hall, 1988; *Margaret Atwood: Vision and Forms* edited by Kathryn van Spanckeren and Jan Garden Castro, Carbondale, Southern Illinois University Press, 1988.

*   *   *

Margaret Atwood is best known for the Canadian nationalism and feminism that characterize her works. As controversial as she is versatile, however, she modifies both her national pride and her feminist sensibilities with a questioning attitude that often seems to subvert the very principles she sets out to establish.

In both her poetry collections and novels, Atwood's brand of feminism is one that views women as being generally double-minded about their status as daughters, mothers, wives. Realizing the inferiority with which society has endowed these positions, most women are willing to accept their inferior status in return for certain apparent goods, such as financial security, physical protection, and freedom from hard labor. In order to assure themselves of such goods, women learn to play the games men design for them and conspire in creating the male lovers/masters who rule them. They also learn to betray other women in the process. These themes, with variations, provide the energy for Atwood's most famous novel and one that will appeal to young adults, *The Handmaid's Tale.*

In the short time since its publication in 1985, *The Handmaid's Tale* has become a modern classic. Difficult to classify, it has been discussed as a futuristic fantasy, a cautionary tale, and a feminist tract. Indeed it is all three and more, for the dystopia that the narrator describes is a theocratic, patriarchal, nightmare world created by men, with the help of women, which proves to be equally restrictive for both sexes.

Although the narrator is thirty-three years old at the time the events of the novel occur (sometime near the turn of the twentieth century), she moves us into her past so that we begin to realize that the current sterile police state is the "fault" of myriad special interest groups including even her mother's feminist activist organization. We also realize that women as well as men are willing to subordinate and betray one another for some perceived personal gain.

In spite of the conspiracy theory of female inferiority that underpins this novel, however, Atwood makes clear that men *do* hold the power that ultimately determines the quality of life. Thus she holds men more responsible for the depressing state of affairs in the fictional country of Gilead (formerly the United States) than women. An environment made toxic by the irresponsible use of chemicals has led to a dangerous level of male and female sterility (although *male* sterility is never openly admitted). The few women who are known to be fertile are rounded up and indoctrinated as Handmaids, women who will be impersonally impregnated by "Commanders" whose barren wives passively participate in the "Ceremony" of impregnation. The narrator is one of the Handmaids, and, like others of her class, she bears the name of the Commander to whom she is temporarily assigned. She is therefore known to us simply as Offred (Of Fred), a detail that vividly dramatizes a longstanding fact of our culture: that women derive their roles, their self-respect, even their identities, from the men who master them.

Young adults quickly become engaged in the philosophical issues raised in this novel. Because Atwood does not present a simplistic view of innocent females unwillingly victimized by men, young readers are alerted to the fact that the plight of women is a very complicated issue, inextricably bound with the plight of men and of the environment. Atwood adeptly reveals the multiplicity of forces that work toward controlling gender roles in our

culture. The Bible, fairy tales (The Wives are dressed in the colors of the Blessed Virgin Mary; the Handmaids are dressed like Little Red Riding Hood), popular songs, classical literature, trendy crusades, even computer technology all can be made to pressure women's and men's behavior in ways considered to be appropriate to their gender, class, and role.

At the conclusion of the novel we learn that what we have taken to be the journal or diary of our heroine is a transcription of tapes that were discovered in the twenty-second century in a metal footlocker by a team of researchers who specialize in "Gileadean Studies." The tapes are being discussed at a typical academic conference. In spite of the fact that women are conspicuous at this conference, the very familiarity of its format suggests that conventions haven't changed as much as one might have hoped in two hundred years. The sense of familiarity conveyed by the proceedings of the conference is consistent with the déjà vu we experience throughout the novel. Attitudes about women and their roles seem to keep repeating themselves. In spite of all the technological advancements of two thousand years, it seems, women will be imprisoned by their biology if they conspire with men to be so.

—Mary Lowe-Evans

AVI (Avi Wortis)

Nationality: American. **Born:** New York City, 23 December 1937. **Education:** Elisabeth Irwin High School, New York; University of Wisconsin, Madison, B.A. in history 1959, M.A. in drama 1962; Columbia University, New York, M.S. in library science 1964. **Family:** Married 1) Joan Gabriner in 1963 (divorced), two sons; 2) Coppélia Kahn (divorced), one son. **Career:** Staff member, Lincoln Center Library of the Performing Arts Theatre Collection, New York, 1962-70, and Lambeth Public Library, London, 1968; Assistant Professor and humanities librarian, Trenton State College, New Jersey, 1970-86. Fulltime writer, from 1986. Regular reviewer, *Library Journal* and *School Library Journal,* both New York, 1965-73. **Awards:** New York Public Library grant, 1969; One of the Best Books of the Year citation, British Book Council, 1973, for *Snail Tale;* New Jersey Council on the Arts grant, 1974, 1976, 1978; Mystery Writers of America Special award, 1975, for *No More Magic,* 1979, for *Emily Upham's Revenge,* and 1983, for *Shadrach's Crossing,* and nominated for Best Juvenile Mystery of the Year, 1990, for *The Man Who Was Poe;* Christopher award, 1980, for *Encounter at Easton;* Children's Choice award, International Reading Association (IRA), 1980, for *Man from the Sky,* and 1988, for *Romeo and Juliet, Together (and Alive) at Last;* Authors award, for *Shadrach's Crossing,* 1983; *School Library Journal,* best books of the year citations, 1980, for *Night Journeys,* 1987, *Wolf Rider,* and 1990, *The True Confessions of Charlotte Doyle,* 1991, *Nothing But the Truth,* 1992, "*Who Was That Masked Man, Anyway?*", 1995, *Poppy;* American Library Association, best books for young adults citations, 1984, for *The Fighting Ground,* 1986, for *Wolf Rider,* 1993, for *Blue Heron,* and 1997, for *Beyond the Western Sea,* and notable book citation, 1990, for *The True Confessions of Charlotte Doyle,* 1991, for *Nothing But the Truth,* 1993, for "*Who Was that Masked Man, Anyway?*", 1995, for *The Barn,* 1996, for *Poppy;* Scott O'Dell award for historical fiction, *Bulletin of the Center for Children's Books,*

1984, for *The Fighting Ground*; Library of Congress, best books of the year citations, 1989, for *Something Upstairs*, and 1990, *The Man Who Was Poe*, 1992, *Nothing But the Truth*; Virginia Young Readers' award, 1990, for *Wolf Rider*; John Newbery honor award, from American Library Association, *Horn Book-Boston Globe* award, and Golden Kite award, from Society of Children's Book Authors, *Booklist's* Editors' Choice, IRA Children's Choice award, Child Study Association's one of the best books of 1990, all 1990, Judy Lopez Memorial award, 1991, all for *The True Confessions of Charlotte Doyle*; One of the Best Books of the Year, Banks St. Teachers College, 1991, for *Windcatcher*; Rhode Island award, 1991, Volunteer State award, 1991-92, Florida Sunshine award, 1992, California Young Readers award, 1993, all for *Something Upstairs*; Newbery honor award, 1992, *Boston Globe-Horn Book* Honor award, 1992, Best book citation, 1991, *Publishers Weekly,* 1991, *Hornbook,* 1992, New York Public Library, 1992, Banks St. Teachers College, notable book citation, 1991, National Council of Social Studies/Children's Book Council, 1992, Children's Trade Book in the Language Arts, *Horn Book* Fanfare award, 1992, New York State Readers award, 1994, Arizona Young Readers award, 1994, Garden State Teen award, 1995, all for *Nothing but the Truth*; One of the Best Children's Books of the Year, *Publishers Weekly,* 1993, for *City of Light, City of Dark*; Bank Street Children's Books of the Year, 1994, for *The Bird, The Frog, and the Light*; *Booklist* Editor's Choice, 1994, New York Public Library Best books of the Year, 1994, Voice of Youth Advocates' Outstanding Book, 1994, Bank Street Children's Books of the Year, 1994, IRA Teacher's Choice, 1995, for *The Barn*; New York Public Library Best Books of the Year, 1995, *Booklist* Best Books of the Year, 1995, *Horn Book-Boston Globe* Best Fiction award, 1996, for *Poppy*; New York Public Library Best Books of the Year, 1996, *Booklist* Best Books of the Year, 1996, *Booklinks* Best Books of the Year, 1996, Bulletin of the Center for Children's Books Blue Ribbon, 1997, and notable book citation, National Council of Social Studies/Children's Book Council, 1997, for *Beyond the Western Sea*; Pick of the Lists, IRA, 1997, for *Finding Providence*. **Address:** 589 S. York Street, Denver, Colorado, 80209, U.S.A. **Web Site:** www.avi-writer.com.

PUBLICATIONS FOR YOUNG ADULTS

Fiction

Captain Grey. New York, Pantheon, 1977.
Emily Upham's Revenge, illustrated by Paul O. Zelinsky. New York, Pantheon, 1978.
Night Journeys. New York, Pantheon, 1979.
Encounter at Easton. New York, Pantheon, 1980.
The History of Helpless Harry, illustrated by Paul O. Zelinsky. New York, Pantheon, 1980.
A Place Called Ugly. New York, Pantheon, 1981.
Sometimes I Think I Hear My Name. New York, Pantheon, 1982.
Shadrach's Crossing. New York, Pantheon, 1983.
Devil's Race. New York, Lippincott, 1984.
The Fighting Ground. New York, Lippincott, 1984.
Bright Shadow. New York, Bradbury Press, 1985.
Wolf Rider. New York, Bradbury Press, 1986.
Something Upstairs: A Tale of Ghosts. New York, Orchard, 1988.
The Man Who Was Poe. New York, Orchard, 1989.
The True Confessions of Charlotte Doyle. New York, Orchard, 1990.

Nothing But the Truth. New York, Orchard, 1991.
Blue Heron. New York, Bradbury, 1992.
"Who Was That Masked Man, Anyway?" New York, Orchard, 1992.
Punch with Judy. New York, Bradbury, 1993.
City of Light, City of Dark. New York, Orchard, 1993.
The Barn. New York, Orchard, 1994.
The Bird, The Frog, and the Light. New York, Orchard, 1994.
Poppy. New York, Orchard, 1995.
Tom, Babette & Simon. New York, Bradbury, 1995.
Beyond the Western Sea. New York, Orchard, 1996.
Finding Providence. New York, HarperCollins, 1997.
Keep Your Eye on Amanda. New York, Avon, 1998.
Perloo the Bold. New York, Scholastic, 1998.
Poppy & Rye. New York, Avon, 1998.

PUBLICATIONS FOR CHILDREN

Fiction

Things That Sometimes Happen (stories), illustrated by Jodi Robbin. New York, Doubleday, 1970.
Snail Tale, illustrated by Tom Kindron. New York, Pantheon, 1972; London, Hutchinson, 1973.
No More Magic. New York, Pantheon, 1975.
Man from the Sky, illustrated by David Wiesner. New York, Knopf, 1980.
Who Stole the Wizard of Oz?, illustrated by Derek James. New York, Knopf, 1981.
S.O.R. Losers. New York, Bradbury Press, 1984.
Romeo and Juliet, Together (and Alive!) at Last. New York, Orchard, 1987.
Windcatcher. New York, Bradbury, 1991.
What Do Fish Have to Do with Anything?, New York, Candlewick, 1997.
Abigail and Tom Go to School. New York, HarperCollins, 1998.

*

Media Adaptations: *Blue Heron, Something Upstairs, The True Confessions of Charlotte Doyle, "Who Was that Masked Man, Anyway?", Wolf Rider, The Man Who Was Poe, The Barn, Smuggler's Island, Poppy,* (all recordings), Recorded Books; *The Fighting Ground* (recording), Listening Library; *Emily Upham's Revenge, Shadrach's Crossing, Something Upstairs, The Fighting Ground,* and *The True Confessions of Charlotte Doyle, Nothing But the Truth,* were produced on radio programs "Read to Me", Maine Public Radio, and "Books Aloud," WWON-Rhode Island; *Something Upstairs* (play; performed Louisville (KY) Children Theatre, 1997), *Nothing But the Truth* adapted for the stage by Ronn Smith, New York, Avon, 1997.

Biography: Essay in *Speaking for Ourselves: Autobiographical Sketches by Notable Authors of Books for Young Adults,* Vol. 1, compiled and edited by Donald R. Gallo, National Council of Teachers of English, 1990.

*   *   *

Avi books for young people are often acclaimed for the wide variety of genres he covers, from historical fiction to contemporary realism. His best works are historical novels in which he creates a vivid sense of colonial America and captures the consciousness of young people coming of age. His success with this genre is evident—he has received two prominent awards for his work in this genre: *The Fighting Ground* won the Scott O'Dell Award for Historical Fiction in 1985, and he received a Newbery Honor as well as the 1991 *Boston Globe-Horn Book* Award for fiction for his historical fiction novel *The True Confessions of Charlotte Doyle.*

In *The Fighting Ground,* which takes place during the Revolutionary War, thirteen-year-old Jonathan is a self-doubting young man who lives on a farm near Trenton, New Jersey, with his parents and younger siblings. The entire novel takes place in the course of twenty-four hours. As the novel begins, Jonathan dreams of cannons, flags, drums, parades, and fighting the British, just as his elder brother and father do. He runs off to fight, joining a handful of Patriots under a domineering corporal. Once he finds himself caught up in battle, Jonathan begins to question why he is there and who the real enemy is. The themes of growth and war are timeless—Jonathan begins as a boy full of dreams of exciting battles and anticipation of heroic deeds; his experiences of the true horrors of war and death cause him to grow and mature as a man.

In *The True Confessions of Charlotte Doyle,* thirteen-year-old Charlotte begins as a docile, proper, mid-nineteenth-century school girl. By novel's end, she is a weather-cured sailor who agilely climbs masts and has survived more than a hurricane aboard the *Seahawk.* The story is told in first-person; the reader boards the *Seahawk* as Charlotte does, and sees, hears, and feels all that she experiences aboard ship. In the preface to the novel, which is called "An Important Warning," young Charlotte writes, "Not every thirteen-year-old girl is accused of murder, brought to trial, and found guilty. But I was just such a girl, and my story is worth relating even if it did happen years ago. Be warned, however, this is no "Story of a Bad Boy," no "What Katy Did." If strong ideas and action offend you, read no more. Find another companion to share your idle hours. For my part I intend to tell the truth as I lived it."

From the novel's riveting beginning to its surprise ending, *The True Confessions of Charlotte Doyle* is destined to be a favorite of young readers. Avi has included an appendix, with a sketched picture of the *Seahawk,* including illustrations of the brig, the bowspit, deck, and mainmast; he also includes a list of ship times and bells. These additions make the story even more appealing and realistic to young readers.

Sometimes I Think I Hear My Name covers one week in the life of thirteen-year-old Conrad. He is portrayed as an adolescent victim of the adult world. Conrad lives with Aunt Lu and Uncle Carl, two kind but overly sensitive relatives with whom he has lived since his parents divorced when he was nine. Since the divorce, Conrad's parents have made little effort to maintain their relationship with their son, leaving Conrad confused and disappointed. In an attempt to ease his disappointment, his aunt and uncle plan a surprise trip to England over Conrad's spring vacation. While in New York to pick up plane tickets for the trip, Conrad meets Nancy, with whom he shares many of the same adolescent fears and dreams, and they quickly establish a close relationship. With Nancy's help, he tries to locate his parents, with whom he has had little contact since they divorced. After finding his parents, it becomes clear to Conrad that they have little interest in assuming a parental relationship with him. Conrad comes to realize that his life with his aunt and uncle in St. Louis is not so bad after all. Avi treats the serious issues dealt with in this novel with a touch of humor, and writes about adolescent experiences with great sensitivity, which is why his works are so appealing to young people.

Avi once noted, "a good children's book is a book of promises. Promises are meant to be kept." Avi keeps his promises, giving young people characters they can relate to and stories that hold their interest.

—Robbie W. Strickland

———

AXTON, David. *See* **KOONTZ, Dean R.**

———

B

BACH, Alice (Hendricks)

Nationality: American. **Born:** New York City, 6 April 1942.
Education: Barnard College, New York, B.A. 1963. **Career:**
Assistant editor, Random House, New York, 1964-66; associate
editor, Harper and Row Publishers Incorporated, New York, 1966-
69; senior editor of books for young readers, Dial Press, New York,
1969-71; consultant, Bedford-Stuyvesant Writers Workshop,
1973-76. Adjunct professor of creative writing, School for Continuing Education, New York University, 1977-79. **Awards:** *New
York Times* cited *Mollie Make-Believe* as one of the best books of
the year, 1974; MacDowell Colony fellowship, 1976, 1977; American Library Association Notable Book award, 1980, for *Waiting
for Johnny Miracle.*

PUBLICATIONS FOR YOUNG ADULTS

Novels

They'll Never Make a Movie Starring Me. New York, Harp-
  er, 1973.
Mollie Make-Believe. New York, Harper, 1974.
The Meat in the Sandwich. New York, Harper, 1975.
A Father Every Few Years. New York, Harper, 1977.
Waiting for Johnny Miracle. New York, Harper, 1980.
The Grouter Connection. New York, Bantam, 1983
When the Sky Began to Roar. Boston, Houghton Mifflin, 1984.
He Will Not Walk With Me. New York, Delacorte, 1985.
Double Bucky Shanghai. New York, Dell, 1987.
Parrot Woman. New York, Dell, 1987.
Ragwars. New York, Dell, 1987.
The Bully of Library Place. New York, Dell, 1988.

PUBLICATIONS FOR CHILDREN

Fiction

Translator, *How Artists Work: An Introduction to Techniques of
  Art,* by Pierre Belves and Francois Mathey. Rochester, New
  York, Lion Press, 1968.
The Day After Christmas, illustrated by Mary Chalmers. New
  York, Harper, 1975.
The Smartest Bear and His Brother Oliver, illustrated by Steven
  Kellogg. New York, Harper, 1975.
The Most Delicious Camping Trip Ever, illustrated by Steven
  Kellogg. New York, Harper, 1976.
Grouchy Uncle Otto, illustrated by Steven Kellogg. New York,
  Harper, 1977.
Millicent the Magnificent, illustrated by Steven Kellogg. New
  York, Harper, 1978.
Warren Weasle's Worse than Measles, illustrated by Hilary Knight.
  New York, Harper, 1980.

Moses' Ark: Stories from the Bible, with J. Cheryl Exum, illustrat-
  ed by Leo Dillon and Diane Dillon. New York, Delacorte, 1989.
Miriam's Well: Stories About Women in the Bible, with J. Cheryl
  Exum, illustrated by Leo Dillon and Diane Dillon. New York,
  Delacorte, 1991.

PUBLICATIONS FOR ADULTS

Editor, *Ad Feminam.* Union Seminary Quarterly Review, 1989.
Editor, *The Pleasure of Her Text: Feminist Readings of Biblical
  and Historical Text.* Philadelphia, Trinity, 1990.
Women, Seduction, and Betrayal in Biblical Narrative. Cambridge
  and New York, Cambridge University Press, 1997.
Women, Seduction, and Betrayal in Biblical Narrative. Cambridge,
  and New York, Cambridge University Press, 1997.
Editor, *Women in the Hebrew Bible.* New York, Routledge, 1998.

*   *   *

One of the common criticisms of young adult novels is that so
many of them are so-called problem books—that is, they are one-
dimensional, focusing only on issues or problems to the exclusion
of other literary elements such as characterization or theme development. One outspoken critic of young adult problem novels is
Alice Bach, also the author of more than twenty books for children
and young adults. In an entry in *Something about the Author,* Bach
wrote, "I believe it is critical for writers of children's books to be
honest about the hardships as well as the joys of life, and never to
provide easy answers to questions about abandonment, hurt, rejection, love, betrayal, seduction, winning, losing, etc., that all people,
children and adults, feel. So many of today's supposed 'realistic
novels' for young adults are realistic in setting and then supply
meretricious reassurance about the genuine puzzlements of life."

It seems appropriate to examine Bach's writing for young adults
in the light of her own literary standards. It can certainly be argued
that a number of her novels fall within the problem novel category.
For example *Waiting for Johnny Miracle* is a story about a teenage
girl with cancer, and *A Father Every Few Years* deals with the
effect of desertion on a younger boy. According to Jack Forman,
who reviewed Bach's novel *When the Sky Began to Roar* in the
January/February 1985 issue of *Horn Book,* one criterion of
whether or not young adult fiction transcends the common definition of problem novel is whether or not the main characters "know
that there are consequences to their actions affecting other people
and that there is a price paid for their mistakes—even if they learn
the right lessons."

Applying this standard to Bach's own writing yields mixed
results. In the two novels which have received the most critical
acclaim, she has skillfully woven complex relationships among her
characters. In *Waiting for Johnny Miracle,* she turns an unflinching
eye on a children's cancer ward based on her own experience as a
volunteer at a cancer-treatment facility. Becky and Theo are
seventeen-year-old twin sisters whose typical high school world is
shattered when Becky is diagnosed with bone cancer.

The fact that they are twins provides Bach with a rich opportunity to explore the closest kind of relationship under an unusual amount of strain. Theo experiences jealousy because Becky is the focus of her parents' attention and energy; guilt because she is jealous and because she is healthy; and rejection because Becky feels more comfortable discussing her illness with the other cancer patients instead of confiding in Theo. Becky, on the other hand, experiences fear and uncertainty due to the illness; rejection and betrayal because her boyfriend cannot deal with her illness; and alienation from her classmates because her world has changed suddenly and completely. Bach does not take the easy route; her characters in this novel, including the parents and other siblings, do not always display courage. They get tired, they snap at one another, they suffer.

In *Mollie Make-Believe,* another well received novel, Mollie Fields, an upper-middle-class teenager, suffers severe guilt pangs when she spends time with Jaimie, a young man she has met, instead of staying at her ill grandmother's bedside. Once again, there are no miraculous cures for removing the guilt, only gradual insights, acceptance, and partial resolution. Her remaining novels are not as successful in terms of character development, and it can be said of at least one, *A Father Every Few Years,* that it matches the definition of the stereotypical problem novel in which problems eclipse all other literary elements.

In recent years, Bach has earned a doctorate at Union Theological Seminary and now teaches religious studies at Stanford University. Using her expertise in this field, she has turned her writing talents toward two nonfiction books for intermediate grades and above: *Moses' Ark: Stories from the Bible* and *Miriam's Well: Stories about Women in the Bible.* Together with coauthor J. Cheryl Exum and illustrators Leo and Diane Dillon, Bach has creatively woven together historical, literary, archeological, and anecdotal evidence to recreate biblical stories. These handsome books are a blend of impeccable scholarship—apparent in the notes at the end of each story—and vigorous prose, appealing to a wide audience.

—Linda J. Wilson

BACH, Bellamy. *See* **WINDLING, Terri.**

BACHMAN, Richard. *See* **KING, Stephen (Edwin).**

BAILLIE, Allan

Nationality: Scottish. **Born:** Prestwick, Scotland, 29 January 1943. **Education:** University of Melbourne, 1962-63. **Family:** Married Agnes Chow in 1972; one daughter and one son. **Career:**

Reporter/sub-editor, *Sun News—Pictroial,* Melbourne, Australia, 1961-64; sub-editor, *Middlesex Advertiser,* London, 1966-67, Australian Associated Press, Sydney, 1968-69, *Sunday Telegraph,* Sydney, 1970-73, *Daily Telegraph,* Sydney, 1973-74, ABC, Sydney, 1974-78, Women's Weekly, Sydney, 1978-80, *Sun, Sun-Herlad,* Sydney, 1980-87; Australian Broadcasting Commission, Sydney, 1973-77; fulltime freelance writer, 1969, and from 1987. **Awards:** Kathleen Fidler award from the National Book League, 1982, short list for Children's Book Council of Australia's Book of the Year, 1985, short list for Adelaide Festival, 1986, American Bookseller's pick of the lists, 1992, for *Adrift*; Arts Council Special Grant, 1984, for *Eagle Island*; short list for Guardian award, 1986, highly commended for CBCA Book of Year, 1986, American Bookseller's pick of the lists, 1992, CBC's Notable Children's Trade Book in Social Studies, 1992, Bank Street Children's Book of the Year, 1992, nominated for Utah Children's Book Award, 1993, for *Little Brother*; Arts Council Special Purpose Grant, 1983, short list for Guardian award, 1987, short list for CBCA Book of Year, 1987, selected for White Ravens of IYL in Munich, 1987, International Board on Books for Young People (IBBY) Honour Diploma, 1988, for *Riverman*; CBCA Picture Book of Year, 1989, short list for Alan Marshall award, 1989, for *Drac and the Gremlin*; short list for CBCA Book of Year, 1989, short list in NSW State Literary awards, 1989, for *Megan's Star*; Children's Book of Year exhibition, 1990, for *Hero*; Arts Council A Fellowship, 1988, short list for Guardian award, 1992, short list for Adelaide Festival, Multicultural Children's Book award, 1992, short list in NSW State Literary awards, 1992, commended in TDK Aust Audio Book awards, 1993, short list in Children's Peace Literature award, 1993, German Academy for Children's Literature's Book of Month, 1993, for *China Coin*; American Bookseller's pick of the lists, 1994, short list for CBCA Picture Book of Year, 1995, for *Rebel!*; Vic Premier's awards: Alan Marshall Diabetes Prize for children's literature, 1995, fellowship from Australia Council, 1996, for *Songman*; short list for CBCA picture book of Year, 1997, short list for NSW premier's literary awards, 1997, *DragonQuest*; short list for NSW premier's literary awards, 1997, *Secrets of Walden Rising*. **Address:** 197 Riverview Road, Clareville, New South Wales 2107, Australia.

PUBLICATIONS FOR YOUNG ADULTS

Fiction

Adrift. Blackie and Son, 1983.
Little Brother. Blackie and Son, 1985.
Riverman. Blackie and Son, 1986.
Eagle Island. Blackie and Son, 1987.
Creature. Melbourne, Australia, Nelson, 1987.
Drac and the Gremlin, illustrated by Jane Tanner. Melbourne, Australia, Nelson, 1989.
Mates. Omnibus, 1989.
Megan's Star. Blackie and Son, 1990.
Bawshou Rescues the Sun: A Han Folktale, with Chun-Chan Yeh, illustrated by Michelle Powell. New York, Scholastic, 1991.
Hero. Blackie and Son, 1991.
Little Monster, illustrated by David Cox. Omnibus, 1991.
The Boss, illustrated by Fiona O'Beirne. New York, Scholastic, 1992.
The China Coin. Blackie and Son, 1992.

The Bad Guys, illustrated by David Cox. New York, Scholastic, 1993.
Magician. Blackie and Son, 1993.
Rebel!, illustrated by Di Wu. Ticknor & Fields, 1994.
Songman. Blacki and Son, 1994.
Dream Catcher. Omnibus, 1995.
Old Magic, illustrated by Di Wu. Random, 1996.
DragonQuest, illustrated by Wayne Harris. Scholastic, 1996.
Secrets of Walden Rising. Viking, 1996.
Last Shot. Omnibus, 1997.
The Excuse, illustrated by Ned Culic. Puffin, 1997.
Star Navigator, illustrated by Wayne Harris. ABC, 1997.
Wreck! Puffin, 1997.
With Jonathon Bentley, *Archie: The Good Bad Wolf.* Random, 1998.

Other

Mask Maker (adult fiction). London, Macmillan, 1975.

Work represented in anthologies, including *Under Twenty-Five, Transition,* and *Bad Deeds Gang.* Contributor to magazines, including *Child Life, Pursuit, School,* and *Meanjin.*

*

Biography: *The Story Makers* by Margaret Dunkle, N.p., OUP, 1986; *Creature: Allan Baillie,* author series, Methuen, 1987; *How Writers Write* by Pamela Lloyd, N.p., Methuen, 1987; *Children's Authors and Illustrators* by Walter McVitty, N.p., Heinemann, 1990; *No Kidding* by Agnes Niewenhuizen, N.p., Sun, 1991; *Authors and Illustrators Scrapbook,* N.p., Omnibus, 1991; *Something about the Author; Autobiography Series,* Vol. 21, Detroit, Gale, 1995.

*   *   *

Allan Baillie's most significant works for the young adult reader demonstrate the fact that he graduated from journalism into writing books for child readers.

These books are characterised by their plots being centred around some significant element, either political (*The China Coin*—the 1989 events in Tiananmen Square) or natural disaster (*Hero*—the Sydney floods of 1986). The settings of these events are strongly realised through the author's actual experience of them—on-site reporting, as it were. In some novels, such as *The China Coin,* the author has actually experienced the event itself as well as explored the setting. It would appear that these two elements, event and setting, together with the author's involvement with either or both of them, are the dominant features of these particular novels.

Using the events as the backgrounds for the novels, Baillie presents within the structure of an adventure story the maturation of his particular characters, generally at the climactic moment of the base events. However, frequently it is the events themselves which carry more significance and it would seem that the author is propelled more by the desire to explore these fully and to make readers aware of their significance.

After a novel for younger readers, *Adrift,* which won him the 1983 Kathleen Fidler award, thus guaranteeing the manuscript would go into print and setting him on the road to this particular form of authorship, Baillie wrote *Little Brother.* The plot concerns a Kampuchean boy whose parents have been killed in the war. He now travels alone searching for his older brother.

Basically the plot is one of the adventure quest, Mang overcoming one obstacle after another as he travels throughout war-torn Kampuchea. The simple structure allows the author to expose the dreadful hardships experienced by people as the war raged about them. While the story carries a certain sense of melodrama and a rather too pat, though probably necessary (considering its audience) happy ending, Mang is one of the more memorable of the Baillie characters. His hope and indefatigable determination that his brother is still alive and will be found, and his ability to somehow still remain childishly unblemished from all that happens to him give him a humanity that extends the writer's compassion for his subject to the reader.

This is also one of Baillie's more popular reads. He has managed to balance nicely the mix of explanation of events, description of the environment and narrative so that the reader does not feel unnecessarily held up.

Some of the later novels, though they show a demonstrably greater writing skill, also move much slower, the narrative waiting for the author to tell all he knows about the setting and the "real" events. Such a novel is *Riverman,* the one that followed *Little Brother.*

Riverman, an excellent novel, was shortlisted for both the Australian Children's Book of the Year award and the Guardian Children's Fiction award and won the IBBY Honour Diploma (Australia). No doubt influenced by the battle raging in Tasmania by conservationists to preserve the wilderness around the Franklin River which the government was proposing to dam, *Riverman* is set partly on the wild Franklin River itself.

Baillie, relating events of 1912 though wanting to connect them to the current conservationist struggle, adopted the symbol of a huge Huon pine, using its long life to link the past with the present. Structurally the story is set within the confines of a prologue and epilogue in the present day wherein Great Uncle Tim tries to show young Brian the importance of the pine and the forest. The story proper is in two sections, the first relating the story of a Tasmanian mining disaster in 1912 and the effect it had upon twelve-year-old Tim, the second section telling of his life with the rivermen on the Franklin River and of how he comes to know the great Huon pine which is so significant to the narrative.

Baillie has a splendid prose, especially when he describes the things he knows at first hand: "But the creaking increased and became a savage squeal as the wood at the heart of the trunk was slowly torn apart. A cloud passed over the tree, then the tip followed the cloud and overtook it. The tree cracked, rolled a little on its stump and crashed down into the forest. It splintered a tall blackwood tree, snapped the stump of a young celery-top pine six feet from the ground, and brought a shriek from a few birds." Occasionally though, there are sections wherein the desire to tell produces a slightly didactic feel, especially in some of the direct speech. However, all in all, this is a particularly fine novel, setting the coming of age of a young boy against the almost ageless trees of the Tasmanian wilderness.

Eagle Island, while having a real setting on an island on the Great Barrier Reef, is not based on any real event and somehow lacks the emotional power which human conflicts obviously stir the author's passions to relate. However, as a straight adventure story of a boy outwitting a pair of crooks it works well.

Hero, based upon floods in an outer suburb of Sydney and giving an excellent depiction of such a disaster in action, focuses the reader's attention on three children: Darcy, a rebellious boy who in a mad fling steals a trail bike; Pam, a new girl to the district and somewhat critical of anyone who has not her wealthy status; and Barney, a serious-minded farmer. During the events of the story the three children come together in a highly exciting climax which tests the mettle of them all. The story leaves us with the question of which one of them is the hero, for the title is singular. Heroism and what constitutes it is featured in Baillie's novels, for his characters are those of the ordinary person caught up in the extraordinary.

In 1987 Baillie was part of a five-person team to visit China on invitation from the government to talk on children's literature. He was intrigued enough to return to learn more about the country, and, of course, to search out material for a book. While he was there he was in Beijing at the time of the Tiananmen Square uprising. This was to form the basis for *The China Coin.* It is a totally absorbing long read and supplies much background to present-day China and its people while relating the story of a part Chinese, part Australian girl searching out her Chinese family and her own identity through a broken coin. The writing is at times dense, with so much background information having to be supplied, but it is a fascinating read. Again it is in quest mode, as the search for the mystery of the coin leads the protagonists to Beijing at the time of the uprising.

Two other books for young adults are fantasy: *Megan's Star* and *Magician.* Both being set in the future, they must necessarily not have event bases though Baillie quite clearly shows events of the future as the results of happenings today. *Megan's Star* contains quite magical moments of mind star travel, unique in children's literature.

Allan Baillie is a significant and important writer for young adults. His particular method of taking events and setting adventure narratives within them gives his YA readers a sense of the values of humanity in today's world, wherein individuals must come to grips with a sense of themselves against the larger problems of survival in a sometimes difficult modern world.

—Alf Mappin

BAIRD, Thomas (P.)

Nationality: American. **Born:** Omaha, Nebraska, 22 April 1923. **Education:** Princeton University, B.A. 1945, M.F.A. 1950. **Military Service:** United States Naval Reserve, 1943-46. **Career:** Instructor in art history, Princeton University, Princeton, New Jersey, 1949-51, 1952-53; lecturer in art history, Frick Collection, New York, New York, 1954-57; member of curatorial staff, National Gallery of Art, Washington, D.C., 1957-60; associate director, Dumbarton Oaks, Washington, D.C., 1967-70; associate professor of art history, 1970-79, professor of art history, 1979-89, Trinity College, Hartford, Connecticut; writer, 1962-1990. **Died:** 28 March 1990.

PUBLICATIONS FOR YOUNG ADULTS

Fiction

Finding Fever. New York, Harper & Row, 1982.
Walk Out a Brother. New York, Harper & Row, 1983.
Where Time Ends. New York, Harper & Row, 1988.
Smart Rats. New York, Harper & Row, 1990.

PUBLICATIONS FOR ADULTS

Fiction

Triumphal Entry. New York, Harcourt, 1962.
The Old Masters. New York, Harcourt, 1963.
Sheba's Landing. New York, Harcourt, 1964.
Nice Try. New York, Harcourt, 1965.
Finding Out. New York, Harcourt, 1967.
People Who Pull You Down. New York, Harcourt, 1970.
Losing People. New York, Harcourt, 1974.
The Way to the Old Sailor's Home. New York, Harper & Row, 1977.
Poor Millie. New York, Harper & Row, 1982.
Villa Aphrodite. New York, St. Martin's Press, 1984.

*

Biography: Entry in *Something About the Author,* Detroit, Gale Research, Vol. 39, 1985, Vol. 64, 1991.

*   *   *

Thomas Baird's four novels for young adults are fine examples of genre fiction. Baird's work in mystery and science fiction incorporate compelling use of genre conventions with believable characters involved in strong relationships with others. This combination results in books with strong appeal for young adult readers.

Baird's first young adult novel, *Finding Fever,* combines the familiar elements of boy detective, a dog, and mysterious adventure, but moves beyond the usual. Baird has Benny O'Brien tell of his attempt to find his sister's dog Fever in first person. This point of view goes beyond descriptive narrative and exposes Benny's ambiguous feelings about this adventure. He does not like Fever, who nips, but will search for him as a favor to Polly. Ben is joined in his search by Robert Striller, or Strill, who displays a strong sense of concern about the missing dog. Strill is no friend of Ben's, and the relationship between the two boys becomes a major focus in the novel. Ben, while not a weakling, consistently follows Strill's orders, even when it conflicts with his better judgment. The novel becomes more than a search for Polly's lost dog when the boys uncover a dognapping ring, but their efforts are too late to save Fever. Ben must deal with the rich boy's intimidation, confront the legacy of his father's death, and complete this rite of passage. Ben's strength is tested when he learns that Strill lost a beloved dog to the dognappers and has joined the search to seek his own form of revenge. Baird brings the boys to the point of violence as a crucible which tests their relationship and themselves. They pass the test, ready to move on to new horizons, but not before Ben tries to help Polly heal by giving her a new puppy.

Baird returns to his themes of relationships and dealing with the death of a father in his second novel, *Walk Out a Brother*. Another first person account, the novel tells the story of Don Rennie, who resents his older brother Keith. His father and brother shared a closeness that made Don an outsider in his own family, and now Keith has been named his guardian. Don takes a backpacking trip in the Wyoming wilderness to sort out his feelings. Baird makes the novel almost a primer on camping and fishing as the outdoor adventure becomes a primary focus of the work. Still, Baird continues his focus on relationships as the two brothers must come to terms with their father's death and what that means to them as brothers. The third component of the novel, the murder mystery, brings the brothers together. Don must deal with the mysterious stranger he meets on the trail; and when he realizes that this stranger is responsible for a man's death, his own life is threatened. His own brush with death allows him to reconcile with Keith and find a new direction for his life. Baird again uses his theme of confronting death in order to grow up, find one's own way, and develop sustaining relationships. His combination mystery and coming of age stories speak directly to young adult readers.

Baird's foray into science fiction enlarged and strengthened his position as an author for young adults. While his mysteries rely on conventional adventure and personal growth, Baird's science fiction contains a speculative streak that challenges the reader to consider issues confronting the world. In his science fiction, Baird's young adult protagonists must move beyond personal angst and cope with disasters of global proportion.

Where Time Ends begins like *Walk Out a Brother* with a wilderness camping trip. Best friends Doug and Loop hear a strange sound one night while camping in the Adirondacks, a sound "so soft, distant, quick, he didn't really hear it, not even its ending." Also camping in the area are Ernie and her brother Orin. They are alone, their friends having left them behind after hearing reports of the outbreak of war. The soft sounds in the night, it turns out, were the detonation of rockets containing biological weapons launched at the United States by the Soviet Union. Doug and Loop's and Ernie and Orin's paths cross as they converge on a cottage on Kroll Lake. Their odyssey soon turns strange and dangerous with no phones, no electricity, threatening people, and crows everywhere. One by one, as the gas spreads toward the mountains, the campers sicken and die and time ends "[w]herever you are when it happens." Only the crows and the deer still come to the lake. Baird creates a believable picture of the end of civilization, and his adolescent protagonists face their fate with courage and dignity. The chilling novel contrasts the beauty and serenity of the Adirondack wilderness with man-made chaos and disaster and provides much for young adult readers to ponder.

Baird's last novel, *Smart Rats,* continues his concern with ecological disaster. This science fiction work posits a dystopian vision of the future extrapolated from our own problems with toxic waste and pollution. Baird dedicates the novel to "the passenger pigeon, the great blue whale, the mountain gorilla, the rain forests of the Amazon . . . and all the other species and places that mankind has destroyed or is destroying." Baird's fictional world cannot support its human population: food is rationed, the ozone layer is shrinking, nuclear contamination is spreading, and smart rats attack people. When the ruling Council decides to limit each household to one child, seventeen-year-old Laddie Grayson must leave his

family. He and hundreds of other boys, including many of his friends, are gathered at a relocation center and many are thrown into the sea to drown. But Laddie escapes and is driven to desperate measures by his determination to survive. He kills his younger sister before she can betray the family and he joins the oppressive system to fight it from within. He hopes to avenge his drowned friends and change the world. Laddie becomes a symbol for rebellious young heroes, and young adult readers will identify with him as he deals with personal and world crises.

Baird's novels grow in their power to provoke and challenge readers. Each of the four novels provides heroic adolescent characters who must confront themselves and their society, deal with violence in themselves and others, and come to terms with adulthood more quickly than might be expected. The strong, atmospheric images of Baird's work, whether in the wilderness or the ex-city of New York, give a sense of a place apart where adventure can and does happen.

—Janice Antczak

BALDWIN, Margaret. *See* **WEIS, Margaret.**

BANKS, Lynne Reid

Nationality: British. **Born:** London, 31 July 1929. **Education:** Schools in Canada; Italia Conti Stage School, London, 1946; Royal Academy of Dramatic Art, London, 1947-49. **Family:** Married Chaim Stephenson in 1965; three sons. **Career:** Actress in British repertory companies, 1949-54; freelance journalist, London, England, 1954-55; interviewer, reporter, and scriptwriter, Independent Television News, London, 1955-62; English teacher, Kibbutz Yasur School and Na'aman High School, Israel, 1963-71; writer, since 1971. Lecturer and volunteer teacher of English, Tanzania, Zimbabwe, India, Nepal, Navajoland, United States. **Awards:** Yorkshire Arts Literary award, 1977, and Best Books for Young Adults award, American Library Association, 1977, both for *Dark Quartet*; West Australian Young Readers' Book award, Library Association of Australia, 1980, for *My Darling Villain*; Outstanding Books of the Year award, *New York Times,* 1981, Young Reader's Choice award, Pacific Northwest Library Association, 1984, California Young Readers Medal, California Reading Association, 1985, Children's Books of the Year award, Child Study Association, 1986, Young Readers of Virginia award, 1988, Arizona Young Readers' award, 1988, and Rebecca Caudill Young Reader's Books award, Illinois Association for Media in Education, 1988, all for *The Indian in the Cupboard*; Parents' Choice award for Literature, Parents' Choice Foundation, 1986, Notable Books award, *New York Times,* 1986, Children's Books of the Year award, 1987, and Indian Paintbrush award, Wyoming Library Association, 1989, all for *The Return of the Indian*; Silver award in the Smarties Prize and Sheffield Children's Book award, 1997, both for *Harry the Poisonous Centipede.* **Agent:** Sheila Watson, Watson, Little Ltd., Capo di Monte, Windmill Road, London NW3 6RJ, England.

PUBLICATIONS FOR YOUNG ADULTS

Fiction

One More River. London, Vallentine Mitchell, and New York, Simon & Schuster, 1973; revised edition, New York, Morrow, 1992.

Sarah and After: The Matriarchs. London, Bodley Head, and as *Sarah and After: Five Women Who Founded a Nation,* New York, Doubleday, 1975.

My Darling Villain. London, Bodley Head, and New York, Harper, 1977.

The Writing on the Wall. London, Chatto & Windus, 1981; New York, Harper, 1982.

Melusine: A Mystery. London, Hamish Hamilton, 1988, New York, Harper, 1989.

The Mystery of the Cupboard, illustrated by Tom Newsom. New York, Morrow, 1993.

Broken Bridge. New York, Morrow, 1994; London, Hamish Hamilton/Penguin, 1995.

Nonfiction

Letters to My Israeli Sons: The Story of Jewish Survival. London, W.H. Allen, 1979; New York, Watts, 1980.

PUBLICATIONS FOR CHILDREN

Fiction

The Adventures of King Midas, illustrated by George Him. London, Dent, 1976; illustrated by Joseph A. Smith, New York, Morrow, 1992.

The Farthest-Away Mountain, illustrated by Victor Ambrus. London, Abelard Schuman, 1976; New York, Doubleday, 1977.

I, Houdini: The Autobiography of a Self-Educated Hamster, illustrated by Terry Riley. London, Dent, 1978; New York, Doubleday, 1988.

The Indian in the Cupboard, illustrated by Robin Jacques. London, Dent, 1980; New York, Doubleday, 1981.

Maura's Angel, illustrated by Robin Jacques. London, Dent, 1984; New York, Avon Books, 1997.

The Fairy Rebel, illustrated by William Geldart. London, Dent, 1985; New York, Doubleday, 1988.

The Return of the Indian, illustrated by William Geldart. London, Dent, and New York, Doubleday, 1987.

The Secret of the Indian. London, Collins, 1988; New York, Doubleday, 1989.

The Magic Hare, illustrated by Barry Moser. New York, Morrow, 1993.

Harry the Poisonous Centipede, illustrated by Tony Ross. London, HarperCollins, 1996; New York, Avon Books, 1997.

Angela and Diabola. London, HarperCollins, 1997; New York, Avon Books, 1997.

Key to the Indian. London, HarperCollins, 1998; New York, Avon Books, 1998.

Plays

It Never Rains (televised 1954; produced Keighley, Yorkshire, 1954). London, Deane, 1954.

Miss Pringle Plays Portia, with Victor Maddern. London, Deane, 1955.

All in a Row. London, Deane, 1956.

The Killer Dies Twice. London, Deane, 1956.

Already It's Tomorrow (televised 1962). London, Samuel French, 1962.

The Unborn (produced London, 1962).

The Gift (produced London, 1965).

The Travels of Yoshi and the Tea Kettle (produced by Polka Children's Theatre, London, 1991); Nelson, 1994.

Radio Plays: *The Stowaway* (produced by BBC, 1967); *Lame Duck* (produced by BBC, 1978); *Purely from Principal* (produced by BBC, 1984; author starred).

Television Plays: *The Wednesday Caller* (produced by BBC, 1963); *The Last Word on Julie* (produced by ATV, 1964); *The Eye of the Beholder* (*She* series, produced by ITV, 1977).

PUBLICATIONS FOR ADULTS

Novels

The L-Shaped Room. London, Chatto & Windus, 1960; New York, Simon & Schuster, 1961.

An End to Running. London, Chatto & Windus, as *House of Hope,* New York, Simon & Schuster, 1962.

Children at the Gate. London, Chatto & Windus, and New York, Simon & Schuster, 1968.

The Backward Shadow. London, Chatto & Windus, and New York, Simon & Schuster, 1970.

Two Is Lonely. London, Chatto & Windus, and New York, Simon & Schuster, 1974.

Dark Quartet: The Story of the Brontës. London, Weidenfeld & Nicholson, 1976; New York, Delacorte, 1977.

Path to the Silent Country: Charlotte Brontë's Years of Fame. London, Weidenfeld & Nicholson, 1977; New York, Delacorte Press, 1978.

Defy the Wilderness. London, Chatto & Windus, 1981.

The Warning Bell. London, Hamish Hamilton, 1984; New York, St. Martin's Press, 1987.

Casualties. London, Hamish Hamilton, 1986; New York, St. Martin's Press, 1987.

Fair Exchange. London, Piatkus Books, 1998.

Other

The Kibbutz: Some Personal Reflections (address). London, Anglo-Israel Association, 1972.

Torn Country: An Oral History of the Israeli War of Independence. New York, Watts, 1982.

*

Media Adaptations: *The L-Shaped Room* (movie starring Leslie Caron), Davis-Royal Films, 1962; *Indian in the Cupboard,* Imagine, 1996.

Biography: Entry in *Sixth Book of Junior Authors,* New York, Wilson, 1989, pp. 22-24.

Manuscript Collections: Boston University.

Critical Studies: Entry in *Contemporary Literary Criticism,* Volume 23, Detroit, Gale, 1983, pp. 40-43.

*   *   *

Lynne Reid Banks is a versatile writer who casts a wide net, and her novels for young adults are a varied haul strung together with the common thread of history, which she winds and bends through most of her work in a way that reveals its recursive nature and presence in modern life. Whether writing fantasy stories, modern adolescent problem novels, or historical fiction, Banks demonstrates a real understanding of the common questions, struggles and complicated feelings that young adults have and treats these honestly and with humor when appropriate. And while some of her novels are weakened by a heavy authorial presence that doesn't allow characters' actions to establish motives and clunky agendas that aren't believably integrated into plots, Banks's books, on the whole, continue to appeal to young readers because of their diverse and relevant themes and the way they present universal coming-of-age struggles through strong, likeable characters.

In *One More River,* her first novel for young adults, rewritten in 1992 and made more immediate and approachable than the original 1973 version, Banks presents the classic adolescent themes of rebellion and self-discovery in the context of both political and historical events. Set in 1967, *One More River* is the story of fourteen-year-old Lesley who is forced to leave behind a comfortable and carefree life in Canada when her family emigrates to a kibbutz in Israel because her father believes they have lost touch with their Jewish heritage. The eruption of the Six Day War between the Israelis and Arabs brings the novel to its climax, and Banks personalizes the historic confrontation through a clandestine acquaintance Lesley makes with an Arab boy who lives just across the Jordan River. Lesley's newly developed sense of self is thus tested by ''the mysteries of war and peace, friends and enemies, love and hatred,'' conflicts which remain a part of today's world. These themes are developed further in *Broken Bridge,* Banks's sequel to *One More River,* which perceptively discusses the violence perpetrated by *both* sides. Banks's writes with a keen awareness of the good as well as the questionable and of compassion as well as hatred. *Broken Bridge* and *One More River* discuss the failure of the established Jewish settlers not only towards the Palestinians but also towards the newer Russian Jewish immigrants who were finding it hard to gain acceptance. Both stories provoke thought about the changing circumstances in Israel, as well as the racial, religious, and national prejudices everywhere.

Rebellion and self-discovery themes also mark Banks's other adolescent problem novels. *My Darling Villain* takes a look at class consciousness in British society through the eyes of middle-class Kate, who falls into troubled first love with working-class Mark. *The Writing on the Wall* is about Tracy's rebellion against school and family rules as she takes off on a bicycle trip through Holland with several friends and, with the help of her punked-out boyfriend Kev, becomes involved in more than she can handle. These books follow the same formula: slow exposition of a girl's growing attachment to a boyfriend that her parents find unsuitable brought to an eye-opening climax by a surprising—but not too surprising—disaster, such as a motorbike accident or a brush with the law. Although this self-discovery process is predictable, the characters themselves are not. Banks consistently creates very real young people with unique personalities. She lets her protagonists make their own mistakes and face the consequences, rather than having them learn from friends who get into trouble or parents who step in with the answers. The large social agendas Banks sets out to tackle in the adolescent problem novels—like cultural identity or class prejudice—take a back seat to more immediate and appealing curiosities like falling in love, first sexual encounters, drug and alcohol experimentation, and trying on identities in search of one that fits.

The predictability that characterizes Banks's adolescent problem novels gives way in her fantasy fiction, where she loosens her grip and really lets her stories fly. These are some of her most skillful and engrossing novels, in which she demonstrates an unusual ability for weaving the supernatural into daily life in a way that makes the unbelievable somehow believable. Most of these are geared toward younger readers, and perhaps most notable is the very popular *The Indian in the Cupboard* and its sequels, in which Banks makes real the world of play as miniature plastic historical figures are magically brought to life by a boy in modern-day England. *Melusine,* however, is for young adult readers and is less about magic than it is the mysteries of identities and relationships. Roger, while vacationing in rural France with his family, befriends and becomes fascinated by a chateau owner's elusive daughter Melusine and the secrets—some of them sinister—hidden within the chateau. He happens upon a scene between the girl and her father that indicates sexual abuse and goes on to experience still stranger events which connect Melusine to ''a shadowy mythological figure'' of the same name who was believed to be a woman by day and a snake by night.

Banks pulls off this fantastic plot by grounding it, first, in the ordinary details of family life, particularly the familiar and often funny banter and spats which are inevitably the result of the forced closeness of a family vacation, and second, in genuine, many-faceted relationships. In this book, Banks overcomes the problems of many of her earlier novels by working out her characters' conflicts through their own mind work and outward actions and not through narrative. She presents the issue of abuse not as her own agenda superimposed onto the lives of her characters but rather as a part of the story's reality. The suspenseful and imaginative use of supernatural elements enhances this reality and makes *Melusine* a compelling place in which to consider the complexities of both healthy and unhealthy relationships.

Historical fiction rounds out the varied body of Banks's work. *Sarah and After* is a sensitive re-creation of the lives of Sarah, Hagar, Rebecca, Leah, Rachel, and Dinah, the Hebrew matriarchs whose stories have always been told in a skimpy and perfunctory manner in most biblical interpretations. *Dark Quartet,* though somewhat scholarly in presentation, brings to life Emily, Charlotte, Anne, and Branwell Brontë, revealing the development of intertwined brilliance in the context of their isolated, harsh upbringing and the creative games of their childhood. *Letters to My Israeli Sons* is a nonfiction historical account of Jewish survival from biblical times up to Israel's war with the Arabs in 1967. Written so that young people, like her own three sons, might understand something of the Jewish nation's historical struggle to maintain cultural and religious identity without a homeland, *Letters to My Israeli Sons* provides insightful background to current, ongoing conflict in the Middle East.

—Tracy J. Sukraw, updated by Winifred Whitehead

BARRON, Tom A

Nationality: American. **Born:** Colorado, 26 March 1952. **Education:** Princeton University, B.A.; attended Oxford University as a Rhodes Scholar. **Family:** Married Currie Cabot; five children. **Career:** Owned a small business, New York City; writer, since the 1980s. **Awards:** America Library Association Best Book for Young Adults and Colorado Book Award Finalist, both 1997, for *The Lost Years of Merlin.* **Address:** 545 Pearl Street, Boulder, Colorado 80302, U.S.A.

PUBLICATIONS FOR YOUNG ADULTS

Fantasy

Heartlight. New York, Philomel, 1990.
The Ancient One. New York, Philomel, 1992.
The Merlin Effect. New York, Philomel, 1994.
The Lost Years of Merlin. New York, Philomel, 1996.
The Seven Songs of Merlin. New York, Philomel, 1997.
The Fires of Merlin. New York, Philomel, 1998.

Other

To Walk in the Wilderness. New York, Westcliffe, 1993.
Rocky Mountain National Park: A 100 Year Perspective. New York, Westcliffe, 1995.

*

Critical Studies: "Flying Starts: New Faces of 1990," in *Publisher's Weekly,* 21 December 1990, 13-18; "Daddy, Is It True?" by T. A. Barron, in *Signal,* Summer 1995, 19-21; "Author!, Author!, Author!: T. A. Barron: Glowing like a Crystal," in *School Library Media Activities Monthly,* Vol. 11, No. 10, 1995, 38-50; "Where Fantasy Flies: An Interview with T. A. Barron" by Kylene Beers, in *Emergency Librarian,* Vol. 24, No. 4, 1997, 61-63; "The Remarkable Metaphor of Merlin" by T. A. Barron, in *Book Links,* edited by Judy O'Malley, American Library Association, January 1998.

*   *   *

Tom Barron's artfully-constructed novels transcend genre. While considered fantasy, his books also contain elements of realistic fiction, historical fiction, informational texts, and folklore. Praised by other science fiction/fantasy authors such as Madeline L'Engle, Lloyd Alexander, and Natalie Babbit, Barron is recognized for blending sophisticated concepts and contemporary themes with fantasy in deeply moving, imaginative stories.

Besides his formal education, Barron has explored the hiking trails of Scotland and backpacked across Asia. He headed a business in New York City but, after struggling to find time to write, decided to return to Colorado, where as a child he grew up surrounded by mountains, fields, and impressive skies. Barron's deep respect for nature, which he feels provides inspirational and uplifting experiences, is woven throughout his stories.

Barron maintains that the fantasy writer must create a believable world before the reader will experience personal connections to his work. In an interview with Kylene Beers, he stated: "If a writer does a good job in creating a secondary world that looks and feels and smells true, then that writer has the opportunity, distance and the perspective to make any changes in that reality that lets readers step back and view themselves through the fantasy mirror." Barron believes that the reader must be able to perceive the world of the fantasy through all of their senses in order to accept the deeper truths about themselves and their connections to humanity. Besides the reader's sensory acceptance of a fantasy world as real, Barron feels there are two other levels of truth: a highly emotional level that results in empathy with the characters; and a spiritual level that requires the author to find a way to touch the fundamental experiences of being alive, yearnings, searchings, agonies, and joys.

Barron's first book, *Heartlight,* is about a 12-year-old girl named Kate who, with her astrophysicist grandfather, travels to a distant star in search of the relationship between the nature of light and the nature of the human soul. Amidst the adventure and fantasy, Barron used Kate to explore the mysterious places within individuals' souls. Though his initial intent was not to create a trilogy, Barron's efforts to know and understand the character of Kate led to two more books. In *The Ancient One,* Kate, who with her aunt was involved in a struggle to save a spiritually and ecologically valuable redwood forest, travels back 500 years in time by way of an old tree. This book has been described by Lloyd Alexander as "a combination of ancient strength and modern vision; on an epic scale and on a human scale." Native American imagery, traditions, and beliefs are interwoven with contemporary themes involving ecological conflicts, connections, and communication among people of all cultures and eras. *The Merlin Effect* mixes environmental issues, scientific research, oceanography, and Arthurian legends as Kate helps her father search for a Spanish galleon which is thought to hold the magical horn of Merlin. She finds the horn amidst bizarre creatures and enemies when she is sucked into a giant whirlpool. These bizarre occurrences allow Kate to discover her power to choose and to create.

While the Kate's adventures and insights differ from book to book, they have several commonalities. Each book explores an adult-child relationship and each has an intriguing situation and place. Each involves difficult choices and explores complex ideas, pulling on the emotional threads that Barron says tie life together. Each book asks a question and explores connections among people, cultures, and other forms of life: What is the significant meaning of one individual's life? What are the powerful connections that unite man with other cultures and times? What is the power of creation?

After writing *The Merlin Effect,* Barron was intrigued with what he did and did not discover about the life of this legendary wizard. He decided to write an original trilogy covering the period in Merlin's life for which there is no account. *The Lost Years of Merlin* begins a trilogy in which Barron not only created an enthralling description of mythical lands, creatures, and quests, but, in the words of Madeline L'Engle, began "an extraordinary journey of mind, body, and spirit—both for Merlin and our-selves.'' Amidst the legendary lore of good and evil creatures, readers are invited on a metaphorical journey to discover their individual powers. *The Seven Songs of Merlin* and *The Fires of Merlin* continue the richly imaginative adventure. Merlin contin-ues his quest to discover the power of his own magic, to attain wisdom to understand its source, and to further experience the ability to see with his heart.

Regarding his writing, Barron says he does not write for any specific age group, but rather for ''children of all ages,'' telling a gripping story that he would like to read. As a result, Barron's audiences are quite diverse in age, color, gender, and background culture. Barron feels his own physical and spiritual experiences make his books powerfully alive, and he often plans experiences for himself to better understand the contexts of his stories. In the end, Barron hopes that his books will ''speak truthfully to human experience . . . [and] bring to life some of our most basic yearnings and hopes and fears.''

—Janelle B. Mathis

———

BARTHOLOMEW, Jean. *See* **BEATTY, Patricia.**

———

BAUER, Marion Dane

Nationality: American. **Born:** Oglesby, Illinois, 20 November 1938. **Education:** La Salle-Peru-Oglesby Junior College, 1956-58, and University of Missouri, 1958-59; University of Oklahoma, B.A. 1962. **Family:** Married Ronald Bauer in 1959 (divorced), one daughter and one son. **Career:** Writer. High school teacher, Waukesha, Wisconsin, 1962-64; Hennepin Technical Center, Minneapolis, Minnesota, instructor in creative writing for adult education program, 1975-78; instructor, University of Minnesota Continuing Education for Women, 1978-85, Institute for Child-ren's Literature, 1982-85, and The Loft, since 1987. **Awards:** American Library Association Notable Book Award, 1976, and Japanese Library Association Award, both for *Shelter from the Wind;* Golden Kite Honor Book Award, Society of Children's Book Writers, 1979, for *Foster Child;* Jane Addams Peace Asso-ciation Award, 1984, for *Rain of Fire;* Notable Children's Book Award, American Library Association, and Best Books list, *School Library Journal,* both 1986, both for *On My Honor;* Newbery Honor Book Award and British Children's Book Award runner-up, both 1987, both for *On My Honor;* Notable Children's Book Award, ALA, 1992, for *What's Your Story? A Young Person's Guide to Writing Fiction.* **Address:** 8861 Basswood Rd., Eden Prairie, Minnesota 55344, U.S.A.

PUBLICATIONS FOR YOUNG ADULTS

Fiction

Shelter from the Wind. New York, Clarion, 1976.
Foster Child. New York, Clarion, 1977.
Tangled Butterfly. New York, Clarion, 1980.
Rain of Fire. New York, Clarion, 1983.
Like Mother, Like Daughter. New York, Clarion, 1985.
On My Honor. New York, Clarion, 1986.
Touch the Moon. New York, Clarion, 1987.
A Dream of Queens and Castles. New York, Clarion, 1990.
Face to Face. New York, Clarion, 1991.
Ghost Eye. New York, Scholastic, 1992.
A Taste of Smoke. New York, Clarion, 1993.
A Question of Trust. New York, Scholastic, 1994.

Nonfiction

What's Your Story?: A Young Person's Guide to Writing Fiction. New York, Clarion, 1992.
A Writer's Story: From Life to Fiction. New York, Clarion, 1995.
Our Stories: A Fiction Workshop for Young Authors. New York, Clarion, 1996.
Editor, *Am I Blue? Coming out from the Silence.* New York, HarperCollins, forthcoming.

PUBLICATIONS FOR CHILDREN

Fiction

Alison's Wings. New York, Hyperion, 1996.
Alison's Fierce and Ugly Halloween. New York, Hyperion, 1997.
Alison's Puppy. New York, Hyperion, 1997.
If You Were Born a Kitten. New York, Simon & Schuster, 1997.
Turtle Dreams. New York, Holiday House, 1997.
When I Go Camping with Grandma (picture book). Mahwah, New Jersey, BridgeWater Books, forthcoming.

*

Media Adaptations: *Rodeo Red and the Runaway* (television movie based on *Shelter from the Wind*); *On My Honor* (videocas-sette), Random House.

Biography: Essay in *Something about the Author Autobiography Series,* Detroit, Gale, Volume 9, 1990; essay in *Speaking for Ourselves, Too,* compiled and edited by Donald R. Gallo, National Council of Teachers of English, 1993.

Marion Dane Bauer comments:

In the last few years I have been extending the range of my work, writing for younger children even to the point of producing my first picture book text. However, the most solid place my stories still emerge from are the transitional years, twelve and thirteen. The passage from childhood into the world of the young adult *feels* important to me—fraught with terror, and trembling with expecta-tion. Both the terror and the expectation remain part of my reality. They are an energy, even a passion I can tap into at will.

There are times when I find myself wishing that I could write stories that are lighter, that people would refer to as "heartwarming." I do have, after all, a warm heart. And a sense of humor, too, though my stories rarely show it. (One of my favorite reviews refers to the "brisk humor" in *Ghost Eye*.) But growing up was, for me, a solemn undertaking, even a perilous one, and it is those feelings I return to when I look out at the world through twelve- and thirteen-year-old eyes ... along with an absolutely determined hope. My most cherished dream is that emerging young adults who find their way to my stories will discover comfort in the midst of their own solemnity, reassurance in their own peril. And most important of all, I pray that they will be reaffirmed in their own determined hope.

*   *   *

Marion Dane Bauer is best known for her portrayal of the harsh realities that frequently accompany growing up in contemporary society. Her characters, who are convincingly drawn, often must make tough moral choices.

In *On My Honor* Joel is afraid to go to the rock bluffs with his friend Tony but he is more afraid of Tony's taunts of cowardice. So, his first choice is to ask his father for permission to go, feeling confident that his dad will refuse. To Joel's dismay his father assents. On the bike ride, Tony goads Joel into a swim in the river. Feeling resentful and angry, Joel is the one to make a dare—a race to the sandbar. A superior swimmer, Joel wins and looks for Tony but he has disappeared. Gradually, Joel comes to the horrifying realization that Tony has drowned. Overcome by shock, disbelief, and guilt, Joel returns home and goes to his room as if nothing had happened. His father, who accepts some of the blame for the tragedy, is finally able to coax the story from Joel.

This is not a story about loss, but one of moral choices, reaction to tragedy, and responsibility for actions. The characters in this story are realistic. Everyone knows an impulsive child like Tony who likes to live on the edge. Usually, they don't get hurt. Joel's feelings of impotence and anger are also understandable. The fear of being called a coward is powerful and leads young people to unpleasant choices—either behave in a way that causes anxiety or endure ridicule. Joel's father is a recognizable figure. He is a cautious parent who failed to read his son's apprehensions and who suffers, with his son, as a result of the tragedy. It is refreshing to find a supportive, caring parent in contemporary realistic fiction. They are a vanishing breed.

Another sympathetic parent can be found in *Like Mother, Like Daughter*. Leslie is revolted by her mother's laid-back Aquarian approach to life; she is a rescuer of strays. As an alternative role-model, Leslie selects the new journalism advisor at school who is bright, tough, and assertive. The advisor encourages Leslie to report the results of her survey of student attitudes toward faculty in the school paper. Leslie derives a certain pleasure in getting revenge on a senior faculty member who resigns in the wake of her report. As the consequences of her actions become apparent, Leslie seeks the support of the journalism advisor, only to find that she has disappeared and that she is a fraud. A supportive mother helps Leslie make the appropriate decisions.

The mother-daughter interaction in this book is as realistic as Leslie's attraction to someone who is her mother's polar opposite. The conflict and resolution are also realistic and again Bauer has

drawn attention to the morality of choices and responsibility for actions. She also illuminates how easily people can be persuaded to follow their baser instincts.

In *Rain of Fire* taunts of cowardice are leveled at Steve's brother Matthew, who has seen the horrors of Hiroshima and has returned home withdrawn and espousing antiwar sentiments. Defense of his brother's honor leads Steve into an escalating conflict with Ray, his brother's accuser. In a dramatic climax to the conflict, Steve takes Ray captive and plants an explosive nearby. He reconsiders his actions, attempts to kick away the explosive and is injured. While in the hospital Steve becomes closer to his brother as he gains understanding of Matthew's opposition to war. Although Bauer realistically portrays Steve's conflicting feelings of loyalty to his brother and frustration with his behavior, she is heavy-handed with her antiwar message.

In *Shelter from the Wind*, Bauer portrays a girl who feels unwelcome in her father's home when her stepmother becomes pregnant. She runs away in an attempt to find her own alcoholic mother but stumbles into the desert cabin of Ella, who shelters her. When Ella is hurt, Stacy must help Ella's beautiful shepherd dog whelp her pups. The birth is graphic but more so is Stacy's drowning of the abnormal puppy. The need for that bit of realism is unclear. Stacy's petulance is a recognizable trait of adolescence. Ella's reminiscences about her departed husband and lost children, however, tell a story that is less appropriate for young adult readers.

As a writer of realistic fiction, Bauer is at her best when the story lets the reader draw conclusions rather than preaching them. Overall, her books are inviting. She provides memorable characters who are involved in rapidly unfolding plots which deal with serious issues. Bauer illuminates the difficult choices with all their attendant consequences which may lie ahead for young adults. She also provides a view of problem-solving approaches which may enable them to navigate more successfully the treacherous waters of contemporary adolescent life.

—Anne Drolett Creany

BAWDEN, Nina Mary

Nationality: British. **Born:** Nina Mary Mabey in London, England, 19 January 1925. **Education:** Ilford County High School; Somerville College, Oxford, B.A. 1946, M.A. 1951; Salzburg Seminar in American Studies, 1960. **Family:** Married 1) H.W. Bawden in 1946, two sons (one deceased); 2) the broadcast executive Austen Steven Kark in 1954, one daughter. **Career:** Writer, since 1952. Assistant, Town and Country Planning Associates, 1946-47; Justice of the Peace, Surrey, 1968-76. Regular reviewer, *Daily Telegraph,* London. Member, PEN Executive Committee, 1968-71; President, Society of Women Writers and Journalists; Fellow, Royal Society of Literature. **Awards:** Carnegie commendation, 1973, for *Carrie's War; Guardian* award for children's fiction, 1975, for *The Peppermint Pig; Yorkshire Post* Novel of the Year award, 1977, for *Afternoon of a Good Woman;* Parents' Choice citation, 1982, and Edgar Allan Poe award nomination, 1983, both for *Kept in the Dark;* Parents' Choice citation, 1985, for *The Finding;* Booker Prize nomination, 1987, for *Circles of Deceit;* Phoenix award, 1993, for *Carrie's War.* **Address:** 22

Noel Rd., London N1 8HA, England; 19, Kapodistriou, Nauplion 21100, Greece.

PUBLICATIONS FOR YOUNG ADULTS

Fiction

Devil by the Sea. London, Collins, 1957; Philadelphia, Lippincott, 1959; abridged edition (for children), London, Gollancz, and Lippincott, 1976.

The Secret Passage. London, Gollancz, 1963; as *The House of Secrets,* Philadelphia, Lippincott, 1964.

On the Run. London, Gollancz, 1964; as *Three on the Run,* Philadelphia, Lippincott, 1965.

A Little Love, a Little Learning. London, Longmans, 1965; New York, Harper, 1966.

The White Horse Gang. London, Gollancz, and Philadelphia, Lippincott, 1966.

The Witch's Daughter. London, Gollancz, and Philadelphia, Lippincott, 1966.

A Handful of Thieves. London, Gollancz, and Philadelphia, Lippincott, 1967.

The Runaway Summer. London, Gollancz, and Philadelphia, Lippincott, 1969.

Squib, illustrated by Shirley Hughes. London, Gollancz, 1971; illustrated by Hank Blaustein, Philadelphia, Lippincott, 1971.

Carrie's War. London, Gollancz, and Philadelphia, Lippincott, 1973.

The Peppermint Pig. London, Gollancz, and Philadelphia, Lippincott, 1975.

Rebel on a Rock. London, Gollancz, and Philadelphia, Lippincott, 1978.

The Robbers. London, Gollancz, and New York, Lothrop, 1979.

Kept in the Dark. London, Gollancz, and New York, Lothrop, 1982.

The Finding. London, Gollancz, and New York, Lothrop, 1985.

Princess Alice. London, Deutsch, 1985.

Keeping Henry. London, Gollancz, 1988; as *Henry,* New York, Lothrop, 1988.

The Outside Child. London, Gollancz, and New York, Lothrop, 1989.

Humbug. New York, Clarion, 1992.

The Real Plato Jones. New York, Clarion, 1993.

Granny the Pag. London, Penguin and New York, Clarion, 1995.

Other

Adapter, *William Tell,* illustrated by Pascale Allamand. London, Cape, and New York, Lothrop, 1981.

St. Francis of Assisi. London, Cape, and New York, Lothrop, 1983.

In My Own Time: Almost An Autobiography. New York, Clarion, 1995.

PUBLICATIONS FOR ADULTS

Novels

Who Calls the Tune. London, Collins, 1953; as *Eyes of Green,* New York, Morrow, 1953.

The Odd Flamingo. London, Collins, 1954.

Change Here for Babylon. London, Collins, 1955.

The Solitary Child. London, Collins, 1956; New York, Lancer, 1966.

Just Like a Lady. London, Longmans, 1960; as *Glass Slippers Always Pinch,* Philadelphia, Lippincott, 1960.

In Honour Bound. London, Longmans, 1961.

Tortoise by Candlelight. London, Longmans, and New York, Harper, 1963.

Under the Skin. London, Longmans, and New York, Harper, 1964.

A Woman of My Age. London, Longmans, and New York, Harper, 1967.

The Grain of Truth. London, Longmans, and New York, Harper, 1968.

The Birds on the Trees. London, Longmans, and New York, Harper, 1970.

Anna Apparent. London, Longmans, and New York, Harper, 1972.

George beneath a Paper Moon. London, Allen Lane, and New York, Harper, 1974; as *On the Edge,* London, Sphere, 1985.

Afternoon of a Good Woman. London, Macmillan, and New York, Harper, 1976.

Familiar Passions. London, Macmillan, and New York, Morrow, 1979.

Walking Naked. London, Macmillan, and New York, St. Martin's, 1981.

The Ice House. New York, St. Martin's, 1983.

Circles of Deceit. London, Macmillan, and New York, St. Martin's, 1987.

Family Money. London, Gollancz, and New York, St. Martin's Press, 1991.

A Nice Change. London, Little, Brown, 1997.

*

Media Adaptations: Many of Bawden's children's stories have been adapted for television in Great Britain. A four-part adaptation of *Carrie's War* was shown on American Public Broadcasting in May, 1981; an adaptation of *The Finding* was broadcast in 1990 as part of the Public Broadcasting System's "Wonderworks" series.

Critical Studies: Entry in *Dictionary of Literary Biography,* Volume 14: *British Novelists since 1960,* Detroit, Gale, 1983, pp. 77-86; entry in *Children's Literature Review,* Volume 2, Detroit, Gale, 1976.

Papers: Masterial relating to *The Peppermint Pig,* de Drummond Collection, University of Southern Mississippi.

Nina Bawden comments:

Writers write for themselves and others like themselves—for kindred spirits of whatever age. When I began to write novels, it did not occur to me to write for children—by children I mean anyone who is not quite grown-up. Or, indeed, that I could. I thought—in so far as I did think about it—that children's writers were likely to be specialists of one sort or another.

I had children of my own. I told them the kind of stories my grandmother had told me; blood thirsty tales, like the story of the old woman who had had her finger chopped off at the butcher's when she was buying half a leg of lamb. That is the story that opens *The Peppermint Pig,* but at the time I told it to my boys I had no notion of writing it down. They had listened eagerly. Well, I thought, all children will listen to their mother.

I wrote my first book for younger readers by chance. I had just finished by seventh novel. We were moving house. "Why not write a children's book." My husband said. "It won't take you so long."

It took a year. And no one wanted to publish it. It was "unsuitable for children." The mother died at the beginning. The children were unhappy. One of the characters was old and mad. "I told you so" I said. "Children's books are about rabbits wearing funny clothes."

Finally, in 1963, *The Secret Passage* (called *The House of Secrets* in America) was published and sold well. Young people wrote to me. What interested them was what I had hoped would interest them. Not the plot, although they seemed to find it exciting, but the emotions of the child characters. "I didn't know," my readers wrote, "that other people felt like that."

This is the true magic of fiction. To meet someone in a book who shares your feelings, especially if they are shameful ones like jealousy or anger, is a comfort at any age. And for children it is particularly important to be reassured, told that they are not alone. I wanted to write solid, grown-up novels for children; books that treated them seriously, respecting their opinions and acknowledging the turbulent strength of their feelings—grief and hate as well as love and joy. *Carrie's War* (1973) is my own wartime story of separation and loss that depends on a sequence of real events for its excitement. And when the young heroine of *The Outside Child* (1989) uses her detective powers it is to unravel the real life mystery of her father's second family.

For thirty years I have written an adult book one year, a novel for children the next. To my mind, they are all part of a coded autobiography; the jottings that make up a life. One leads to the other and because of the difference between the child and the adult point of view, themes often overlap. And sometimes I am not sure at the beginning on which side a book will fall. *The Peppermint Pig* (1975) could have been a novel about family life at the turn of the century. *The Real Plato Jones,* (1993) which is about a conflict of loyalties in wartime Greece and its repercussions fifty years later, could have been, with a slight shift of emphasis, a novel for adults.

It seemed to me when I was young that to be a child was to be trapped in a humiliating disguise. I feel much the same now I am old. I have no theories about writing for one age group or another. Once I begin a book, write the first sentence, all I care about is doing the best I can for this particular story.

* * *

Nina Bawden is one of the very few writers for young people who will admit to making a conscious adjustment to writing for children. Perhaps because she also writes for adults she is singularly free from the temptation to write for adults on the children's list. Plot summaries of Bawden's early work might seem like run-of-the-mill escapism. The jewel thieves in *The Witch's Daughter,* the children-catch-villains theme of *A Handful of Thieves,* the Prime Minister's son saved from political kidnapping in *On the Run,* are typical examples. But Bawden is a subtle writer, who plays her themes with a difference. In *The Witch's Daughter* one of the children is blind; the Prime Minister's son in *On the Run* comes not from Ruritania but modern Africa; another of Bawden's runaways is an illegal Pakistani immigrant. Bawden's characters may have improbable adventures, but they never think, feel or say unchildlike or improbable things. Their preoccupations, their relationships

with the adults around them, their faults as well as their innocence and courage are entirely realistic and believable. This is childhood seen with particular clarity. There is also a very distinctive tone to Bawden's sympathy—a particular tenderness for children having a rough time, and for not very likeable children. Mary in *The Runaway Summer* is a good example. Lonely and miserable because her parents are getting divorced, she is beastly to her kind aunt, and even steals, and yet we never lose sympathy with her.

It is this element in Bawden's work that flowers in *Squib,* the story of a grossly neglected child. There are brilliant insights in this book which overlie the awful knowledge that Squib has been shackled in a laundry basket—especially the pathetic muddle of half-baked fears—and simply confuse the children about what is real and what is not, so that they hardly know if they are playing or rescuing a real victim. However there is also a good deal of the apparatus of adventure that had been so strong an element in Bawden's work so far—a burning tower, a disastrous raid on Squib's caravan, and on to a happy ending that involves bringing in the adults to get things right. The emotional tone of this uncomplicated complication sits rather uneasily with the real subject of *Squib*—the compassion and fear of a young girl, the courage of a young boy, and the suffering of Squib himself.

With the appearance of *Carrie's War,* it became clear Squib had been a transitional book. Carrie and her brother are evacuees in a Welsh village with a narrow, bigoted shopkeeper and his kindly, browbeaten sister. They would be miserable without the friendship of other villagers, especially Hepzibah, who feeds them love, food and stories. Once more the plot concerns the precarious hold on reality of an imaginative child. Convinced by Hepzibah's tales Carrie comes to believe that she has committed a dreadful crime, and she carries the load of grief and guilt with her into adult life. Only when she brings her own children back with her to the village can the truth emerge and all be made well again. In this book we have dispensed with the drama of external situations—there are no crooks, no villains, but Carrie's own guilty fears. In a notable shift of feeling, Carrie reaches a glimpse of sympathy and understanding even for the horrible tyrant Mr. Evans. This is a profound and affectionate book.

In *The Peppermint Pig,* the mature, subtle, and fundamentally sunny atmosphere of *Carrie's War* is brought to a peak of achievement. *The Peppermint Pig* is about the sojourn in a country village of an Edwardian family whose father has gone abroad to seek his fortune. But the true subject is the painful relationship of happiness, hope and the inexorable passing of time. These themes are delicately explored in the relationship of the children to their changed circumstances, the absence of their father, and the growth, flourishing and death of Johnny, the pet pig. All the while the book, with consummate skill, plays on the difference of scale in the life of children and adults, bringing the two perspectives into brilliant direct contrast only on the last page. *The Peppermint Pig* is a small masterpiece.

Since *The Peppermint Pig* Bawden has to some extent resumed her earlier style, though not without differences. In *Rebel on a Rock* Carrie and her family visit a foreign country (a thinly disguised Greece) in which a dictator is in power and a revolution is simmering into readiness. In *The Robbers,* a boy brought up with all the appurtenances of privilege makes friends with a boy deprived of all material wealth but rich in affection. Trying to help the poorer boy's family, they get into trouble, and the law takes a different view of them because of their different social class. In both these books there is a return to a simpler texture and characters of instant credibility, having child-sized adventures. But unlike Bawden's earlier books is the seriousness of the backgrounds—political revolution played against family loyalty, or the unfairness of justice—and the consequent large import of childish escapades. A sad, implied comment is made on children's adventure stories; this is what would really happen if children intervened in revolutions, or tried to restore the family fortunes.

With *Kept in the Dark,* Bawden returns to a subject explored earlier in *Devil by the Sea,* published originally for adults, and then republished for younger readers in a changed climate of opinion. The subject is the helplessness of young people if the adults around them are not both beneficent and competent. The children in *Kept in the Dark* are being looked after by grandparents who are themselves being preyed upon by a half-uncle who bullies and threatens with seeming impunity. The children's terror and confusion are strongly conveyed; locked in the child's viewpoint, the book conveys only partly the nature of the villain's badness, and his adult victims' weakness.

The Finding neatly inverts the typical Bawden statement of relations between adults and young people, which has gradually emerged as her quintessential theme. The fantasy of adults—the machinations of a lethally awful grandmother, and the scheming of incompetent crooks—gets Alex, an adopted foundling, into trouble. Only his sister's childish understanding of his inner world can provide the means to find him. Once again a thriller plot is combined with satisfying characterisation to provide Bawden's typical balance of readability and depth.

Keeping Henry is a new departure. It is not so much fiction as very lightly fictionalised recollection, in which the author appears as herself, in her own family, telling us the true story of Henry, the family's pet squirrel, which they kept on a Welsh farm where they spent part of the war. The story has the shapeliness and accessibility of Bawden's true fiction. Additionally it is fascinating to see the origins in the author's childhood experience of the material of both *Carrie's War* and *The Peppermint Pig,* each of which is illuminated by *Keeping Henry,* and each of which in turn throws light on the later book. *The Outside Child* is based, like *Keeping Henry,* on an autobiographical recollection, this time one of considerable mystery and force. Jane is brought up by aunts while her father, a seaman, comes and goes on his ship. Visiting him she sees a picture of his other family, her secret brother and sister. Filled with love and yearning for them she is reduced to childish spying, abetted by her friend. At the heart of the story is the selfishness and silliness of an emotional adult; the ending can only be cautiously happy.

Bawden's 1992 work for young readers, *Humbug,* continues the exploration of the relationship of young people and adults—a theme which in Bawden's hands is inexhaustible. When her grandmother is taken suddenly into hospital, Cora is parted from her brother and sister and taken care of by a neighbour, finding herself at the mercy of a repulsive child, Angelica, and her smug, self-deceiving grown-up. Angelica is Bawden's first wholly unlikeable child, but she is fearfully convincing. The terrifying gulf that opens below Cora's feet, as her grandfather forgives her with knowing understanding for a theft she did not commit, has likewise a nightmare plausibility.

Bawden can now command the gripping readability of her early work without resorting to anything but wholly credible psychological drama. Balancing the different views of young people and adults, whose relations have been gradually emerging over her whole career as a central subject of her writing on both adult and children's lists, she never unfairly prefers an adult view, and deeply ingrained in this story is the sense of what kind of moral benchmark it is for adults to have the care of children.

From *The Secret Passage* to *The Outside Child* there is a very large development and flowering of Bawden's talent; it can still be said of her that more than any other contemporary writer for the young she understands and respects the youth of her readers as well as that of her characters.

—Jill Paton Walsh, updated by Alexandra MacLennan

BEAGLE, Peter S(oyer)

Nationality: American. **Born:** New York City, 20 April 1939. **Education:** University of Pittsburgh, B.A. 1959; Stanford University, 1960-61. **Family:** Married 1) Enid Elaine Nordeen in 1964 (divorced 1980); 2) Padma Hejmadi in 1988, two daughters and one son. **Career:** Writer. **Awards:** Wallace Stegner Writing Fellowship, 1960-61; Guggenheim Foundation award, 1972-73; NEA Grant, 1977-78; Guest of Honor, Seventh World Fantasy Convention, 1981. **Address:** 2135 Humboldt Ave., Davis, California 95616, U.S.A.

PUBLICATIONS

Fiction

A Fine and Private Place. New York, Viking, 1960.
The Last Unicorn. New York, Viking, 1968, as *The Last Unicorn: A Fantastic Tale,* London, Bodley Head, 1968.
Lila the Werewolf. Santa Barbara, California, Capra Press, 1974; revised edition, Santa Barbara, California, Capra Press, 1976.
The Fantasy Worlds of Peter S. Beagle. New York, Viking, 1978.
The Folk of the Air. New York, Del Rey, 1987.
The Innkeeper's Song. New York, Roc, 1993.
With Pat Derby, *In the Presence of Elephants,* photographs by Genaro Molina. Santa Barbara, Capra Press, 1995.
The Unicorn Sonata, illustrated by Robert Rodriguez. Atlanta, Turner, 1996.
Giant Bones. New York, Roc, 1997.

Plays

Screenplays: *The Zoo,* Columbia Broadcasting System, 1973; *The Dove,* with Adam Kennedy, E.M.I., 1974; *The Greatest Thing That Almost Happened,* Fries, 1977; *The Lord of the Rings, Part One,* with Chris Conkling, United Artists, 1978; *The Last Unicorn,* Marble Arch/Rankin-Bass, 1982.

Nonfiction

I See by My Outfit. New York, Viking, 1965.
Author of introduction, *The Tolkien Reader,* by J.R.R. Tolkien. Boston, Houghton Mifflin, 1966.
The California Feeling, illustrated by Michael Bry and Ansel Adams. New York, Doubleday, 1969.
American Denim: A New Folks Art. Abrams/Warner, 1975.

The Lady and Her Tiger, with Pat Derby. New York, Dutton, 1976.
Author of foreword, *Adventures of Yemima, and Other Stories,* by Abraham Soyer, translated by Rebecca Beagle and Rebecca Soyer. New York, Viking, 1979.
Author of foreword, *The Best of Avram Davidson,* by Avram Davidson. New York, Doubleday, 1979.
The Garden of Earthly Delights. New York, Viking, 1981.

Other

Contributor, *Prize Stories: The O. Henry Awards,* edited by Williams Abrahams and Richard Poirier. New York, Dutton, 1965.
Contributor, *New Worlds of Fantasy,* edited by Terry Carr. New York, Ace, 1967.
Contributor, *New Worlds of Fantasy 3,* edited by Terry Carr. New York, Ace, 1971.
Contributor, *Phantasmagoria,* edited by Jane Mobley. Homer, Arkansas, Anchor, 1977.
Contributor, *The Fantastic Imagination: An Anthology of High Fantasy,* edited by Robert H. Boyer and Kenneth J. Zahorski. New York, Dell, 1978.
Contributor, *Dark Imaginings: A Collection of Gothic Fantasy,* edited by Robert H. Boyer and Kenneth J. Zahorski. New York, Dell, 1978.
Editor, with Janet Berliner, *Peter S. Beagle's Immortal Unicorn.* New York, HarperPrism, 1995.

*

Biography: Entry in *Dictionary of Literary Biography Yearbook,* Detroit, Gale, 1980; *Peter S. Beagle* by Kenneth J. Zahorski, Mercer Island, Washington, Starmont House, 1988.

Critical Studies: Entry in *Contemporary Literary Criticism,* Volume 7, Detroit, Gale, 1977; *Science Fiction and Fantasy Literature* by R. Reginald, Volume 2, Detroit, Gale, 1979; ''The Fantasy Worlds of Peter Beagle'' by Ina Rae Hark, in *Survey of Modern Fantasy Literature* edited by Frank N. Magill, Englewood Cliffs, New Jersey, Salem Press, 1983.

*   *   *

Peter S. Beagle is a well-respected writer of fantasy with a relatively small body of work. His works notably include a novella, novels, and several screenplays. Though a common theme in his work is the sometimes blurry distinction between people living and dead, he treats the subject with humor. Much of his work holds appeal for young adult fans of fantasy and the supernatural.

Beagle's first novel, published in 1960, was *A Fine and Private Place.* This story is set in a Bronx cemetery and is about a bankrupt fifty-three-year-old druggist named Jonathan Rebeck. Rebeck becomes disenchanted by the commercialism of his neighborhood and moves to an isolated mausoleum. There he meets a middle-aged widow who visits her dead husband, two young ghosts, and a talking raven who steals food for him from a local deli. The plot becomes more than an account of Rebeck's mundane life of chess games and long walks with the appearance of Mrs. Gertrude Klapper and the supernatural couple, Michael Morgan and Laura Durand. The latter meet as ghosts in the cemetery, fall in love, and

try to find a way to avoid drifting into oblivion. Rebeck becomes involved in the lovers' dilemma and seeks to resolve it with the support of Mrs. Klapper. The novel examines the distinctions between the living and the not living and finds them far from being clear-cut. The theme is not so much life after death as death in life. *A Fine and Private Place* was well-received because of its memorable characters, delightful humor, and significant allegorical truth. Beagle's style was praised as beautiful, confident, and charming—quite a feat since Beagle was only nineteen when he wrote the novel.

Beagle's second novel, *The Last Unicorn,* was heralded by *Fantasy Literature* as belonging to a list of the ten best in modern fantasy. The story is about the world's last surviving unicorn and her adventures in searching for others like her. She is helped in the quest by Schmendrick the Magician. Schmendrick is an inept wizard who usually cannot perform the simplest of tricks effectively, but every now and then is capable of the greatest of magic. The last unicorn is also aided by a peasant woman called Molly Grue, who finds true wonder and delight in the unicorn. The three set off in search of the lost unicorns and discover a wasteland ruled by King Haggard. The king has imprisoned the unicorns and has them under the guard of the Red Bull, a terrifying animal that frightens the unicorns and causes them to forget who and what they are. At the end of the novel, the unicorns are freed and the wasteland is transformed into a thriving community again. Like *A Fine and Private Place, The Last Unicorn* concerns death in life. King Haggard has captured the unicorns in an attempt to hold onto beauty and to possess it completely. The theme of the wasteland and its rebirth is potently retold with a degree of absurdity that makes it both a parody of traditional romantic fantasy and a reestablishment of the genre. The novel is also filled with literary allusions and contemporary colloquialisms. *The Last Unicorn* was made into an animated movie in 1982.

Lila the Werewolf and ''Come, Lady Death'' are examples of Beagle's short fiction. *Lila the Werewolf,* originally published as ''Farrell and Lila the Werewolf,'' is about a young man who discovers that his lover is transformed into a werewolf with every full moon. Its linking of lycanthropy and sexuality is unique. ''Come, Lady Death'' is a short story about a society lady of eighteenth-century London. She invites Death to a party to liven up her boring existence. Beagle apparently wrote this last story in college to please Frank O'Connor, his professor, who hated fantasy.

The Folk of the Air was published in 1987, and was the winner of the Mythopoeic Fantasy Award. It concerns Farrell's return to Avincenna, California, after some years away. He finds his old friend Ben living with Sia, an older woman who is wild and magical. Ben has become involved in a group, the League for Archaic Pleasures, known to playact medieval chivalry. However, it is revealed that the group members are not merely playacting; instead they *are* the medieval characters that they portray. Sia's house contains rooms that appear and disappear, and Sia herself possesses power that she can exert at her will. While attending a League meeting, Farrell and his girlfriend Julie watch as the young witch Aiffe conjures up Nicholas Bonner, who had been sent into limbo five centuries earlier. Bonner and Aiffe cause much chaos and attempt to defeat Sia, as Farrell comes to realize that only Sia can stand against the power of Bonner and Aiffe to protect the world from their evil.

Though he is primarily recognized as an accomplished writer of fantasy, Peter Beagle's other credits include several screenplays, such as "The Dove" with Adam Kennedy in 1974 for E.M.I., and "The Lord of the Rings, Part One" with Chris Conkling in 1978 for United Artists. Beagle also did the screenplay for "The Last Unicorn" animated film for Marble Arch/Rankin-Bass.

—Lesa Dill

BEATTY, Patricia

Has also written as Jean Bartholomew. **Nationality:** American. **Born:** Portland, Oregon, 26 August 1922. **Education:** Reed College, B. A. in History and Literature 1944; University of Idaho, 1947-50; University of Washington, Seattle, 1951. **Family:** Married 1) John Louis Beatty in 1950 (died 1975), one daughter; 2) Carl G. Uhr in 1977. **Career:** English and history teacher, Coeur d'Alene, Idaho, 1947-50; librarian, Wilmington, Delaware, 1952-53, and Riverside, California, 1953-56; creative writing teacher, University of California at Riverside, 1967-68, and University of California at Los Angeles, 1968-69. **Awards:** Commonwealth Club of California Silver Medal for best juvenile by California author for *Campion Towers,* 1965; *Horn Book* honor book for *A Donkey for a King,* 1966; Southern California Council on Children's and Young People's Literature Medal for best fiction of the year for *The Royal Dirk,* 1967; Society of Children's Book Writer's Golden Kite Award honor book for *Red Rock over the River,* 1973; Southern California Council on Children's and Young People's Literature award for distinguished body of work, 1974; Woman of the Year award, American Association of University Women, 1975; Southern California Council on Children's and Young People's Literature award, for comprehensive contribution of lasting value to the field of children's literature, 1976; Junior Literary Guild selection for *By Crumbs, It's Mine!,* 1976, and for *I Want My Sunday Stranger,* 1977; Riverside-Magnolia Center Business and Professional Women's Club Woman of the Year award, 1977; Western Writers of America honor book for *Wait for Me, Watch for Me, Eula Bee,* 1978; Junior Literary Guild selection for *Lacy Makes a Match,* 1979; Jane Addams Children's Book award honor book for *Lupita Manana,* 1982; Southern California Council on Children's and Young People's Literature award, for distinguished work of fiction for *Jonathan Down Under,* 1983; Western Writers of America award, 1984 and 1987; Scott O'Dell award, for historical fiction, for *Charley Skedaddle,* 1987. **Died:** Riverside, California, 9 July 1991.

PUBLICATIONS FOR YOUNG ADULTS

Fiction

Indian Canoemaker. Caldwell, Idaho, Caxton, 1960.
Bonanza Girl. New York, Morrow, 1962.
With John Louis Beatty, *At the Seven Stars.* New York, Macmillan, 1963.
The Nickel Plated Beauty. New York, Morrow, 1964.
With John Louis Beatty, *Campion Towers.* New York, Morrow, 1965.
Squaw Dog. New York, Morrow, 1965.
With John Louis Beatty, *The Royal Dirk.* New York, Morrow, 1966.
The Queen's Own Grove. New York, Morrow, 1966.

With John Louis Beatty, *A Donkey for the King.* New York, Macmillan, 1966.
The Lady from Blackhawk. New York, McGraw, 1967.
With John Louis Beatty, *The Queen's Wizard.* New York, Macmillan, 1967.
Me, California Perkins. New York, Morrow, 1968.
With John Louis Beatty, *Witch Dog.* New York, Morrow, 1968.
Station Four. Chicago, Science Research Associates, 1969.
With John Louis Beatty, *Pirate Royal.* New York, Macmillan, 1969.
Blue Stars Watching. New York, Morrow, 1969.
The Sea Pair. New York, Morrow, 1970.
Hail Columbia. New York, Morrow, 1970.
With John Louis Beatty, *King's Knight's Pawn.* New York, Morrow, 1971.
A Long Way to Whiskey Creek. New York, Morrow, 1971.
With John Louis Beatty, *Holdfast.* New York, Morrow, 1972.
O the Red Rose Tree. New York, Morrow, 1972.
The Bad Bell of San Salvador. New York, Morrow, 1973.
Red Rock over the River. New York, Morrow, 1973.
With John Louis Beatty, *Master Rosalind.* New York, Morrow, 1974.
How Many Miles to Sundown. New York, Morrow, 1974.
With John Louis Beatty, *Who Comes to King's Mountain?.* New York, Morrow, 1975.
Rufus, Red Rufus. New York, Morrow, 1975.
By Crumbs, It's Mine!. New York, 1976.
Something to Shout About. New York, Morrow, 1976.
Billy Bedamned, Long Gone By. New York, Morrow, 1977.
I Want My Sunday Stranger!. New York, Morrow, 1977.
Just Some Weeds from the Wilderness. New York, Morrow, 1978.
Wait for Me, Watch for Me, Eula Bee. New York, Morrow, 1978.
Lacy Makes a Match. New York, Morrow, 1979
The Staffordshire Terrier. New York, Morrow, 1979.
That's One Ornery Orphan. New York, Morrow, 1980.
Lupita Manana. New York, Morrow, 1981.
Eight Mules from Monterey. New York, Morrow, 1982.
Jonathan Down Under. New York, Morrow, 1982.
Melinda Takes a Hand. New York, Morrow, 1983.
Turn Homeward, Hannalee. New York, Morrow, 1984.
The Coach That Never Came. New York, Morrow, 1985.
Behave Yourself, Bethany Brant. New York, Morrow, 1986.
Charley Skedaddle. New York, Morrow, 1987.
Be Ever Hopeful, Hannalee. New York, Morrow, 1988.
Sarah and Me and the Lady from the Sea. New York, Morrow, 1989.
With Phillip Robbins, *Eben Tyne, Powdermonkey.* New York, Morrow, 1990.
Jayhawker. New York, Morrow, 1991.
Who Comes with Cannons?. New York, Morrow, 1992.

PUBLICATIONS FOR ADULTS

The Englishman's Mistress (As Jean Bartholomew). New York, Dell, 1974.

*

Biography: "Patricia Beatty" in *A Critical History of Children's Literature* edited by Cornelia Miegs, New York, N.p., 1969; "John

Beatty January 24, 1922— and Patricia Beatty August 26, 1922— " in *Third Book of Junior Authors* edited by Doris De Montreville and Donna Hill, New York, H. W. Wilson, 1972, 33-35; "Patricia (Robbins) Beatty 1922-1991" in *Something about the Author*, Detroit, Gale, Vol. 1, 1971, 21-22, Vol. 30, 1983, 48-53, Vol. 73, 1993, 16-19; "Patricia (Robbins) Beatty" in *Contemporary Authors* edited by Jeff Chapman and John D. Jorgensen, Vol. 55, Detroit, Gale, 1997, 42-45.

Critical Studies: *The Bulletin of the Center for Children's Books,* Vol. 35, No. 7, March 1982, 121; *The Bulletin of the Center for Children's Books,* Vol. 36, No. 7, March 1983, 121; "Master Rosalind" by C. D. Akerley *in Beacham's Guide to Literature for Young Adults* (Washington, D. C.), Vol. 2, 1990, 859-864; "Be Ever Hopeful, Hannalee" by Kirk Beetz in *Beacham's Guide to Literature for Young Adults* (Washington, D. C.), Vol. 6, 1994, 2788-2796; "Turn Homeward, Hannalee" by Kirk Beetz in *Beacham's Guide to Literature for Young Adults* (Washington, D. C.), Vol. 8, 1994, 4183 -419 1; "Who Comes with Cannons?" by Kirk Beetz *in Beacham's Guide to Literature for Young Adults* (Washington, D. C.), Vol. 8, 1994, 4289-4298.

*   *   *

Patricia Beatty's many historical novels make the past come alive and convey a sense of time and place. Her extraordinary attention to accuracy and detail make her readers aware of how life was lived during a particular period. The author's comprehensive research into the customs, dress, and language of the times in which her books are set is evident. Authentic information and real people are carefully interwoven throughout her writing and are documented in extensive endnotes. Meticulous backgrounds that instill understanding and appreciation of history are Beatty's primary strength; but her strong sense of humor is her second. Lively, amicable characters; lighthearted, amusing episodes; and fast-paced, tall tales charm young adolescent readers who include her novels among their favorites.

Though she and her husband, John Louis Beatty, co-authored an award-winning series set in 18th century England, Patricia Beatty's novels portray 19th century America. The majority of her fifty books for young people take place during frontier times in the American West. Several others are set in the South during the Civil War and *Jonathan Down Under* depicts the mining camps of the 1849 gold rush in Australia. Even in her one novel with a contemporary setting, *The Coach That Never Came,* the plot involves the actual mysterious disappearance of a stagecoach in 1873 Colorado. Whatever the setting, Beatty paints an impressive picture with rich descriptions of the landscape, conditions, inhabitants, and events.

The author uses history and humor as catalysts for her major themes: intercultural understanding, feminism, and anti-war. The importance of intercultural understanding was sparked early in Beatty's life by her interest and empathy for Native American customs and history. Because of her father's responsibilities as a Coast Guard Commander, her family lived among various tribes on Indian reservations in the northwestern United States. She was adopted by the Quillayute Indians and her first book, *Indian Canoemaker,* recounts the culture of this tribe prior to the white man's move West. Other cultures are featured in *Lupita Manana,* which earned her an award for promoting world community, and

Jonathan Down Under, which provides a good deal of information about Australian history and the Aborigines, including some Aboriginal language. The author also promotes multiculturalism through friendships between her characters: Paul Braun and Jay Jenkins, a Ute Indian, in *The Coach That Never Came*; Jonathan Cole and Prince Billy, an Aborigine, in *Jonathan Down Under*; Charley Quinn and Jerusha Bent, a mountain woman, in *Charley Skedaddle*; Melinda and her Jewish townsfolk in *Melinda Takes a Hand.*

Feminism is a theme that spans the thirty years of Patricia Beatty's writing career. The author first broached feminism in 1962 with *Bonanza Girl;* but *Hail Columbia,* published in 1970, is considered one of the first feminist books written especially for girls. Her books with feminist themes contain plenty of action. The heroines are courageous, self-reliant girls who act on their own to handle challenges in their lives. Though *By Crumbs, It's Mine!* and *Lacy Makes a Match* received favorable reviews, some have been dubbed Beatty's "lighter" novels because of unbelievable plots, stereotyped lessons learned, pat conversation, or predictable characterization. Other "light" stories in which she portrays liberated girls include *How Many Miles to Sundown*; *Melinda Takes a Hand*; *Behave Yourself, Bethany Brant*; and *That's One Ornery Orphan.*

The American Civil War is featured in Patricia Beatty's more serious novels and is the backdrop for the anti-war theme dominating her latter works. Her most substantial writing is found in her books that speak out against war and slavery, though some of these books have been described as having sketch characterization, contrived action, and conspicuous historical information. One thought to be her best is *Charley Skedaddle,* a rite-of-passage story about a Union drummer boy who deserts during a terrifying battle. *I Want My Sunday Stranger* and *Jayhawker* also received critical acclaim. The former is a suspenseful narrative of a young Mormon boy accompanying a photographer to the battlefields. *Jayhawker,* another coming-of-age story, is about a young abolitionist. Hannalee Reed is the adventurous protagonist of *Turn Homeward, Hannalee,* which chronicles General Sherman's march to the sea, and its sequel *Be Ever Hopeful, Hannalee,* which presents a picture of post-Civil War Atlanta and the effects of the war on ordinary people. *Who Comes with Cannons?* features the Underground Railroad as seen through the eyes of a strong young Quaker named Truth Hopkins.

Narratives in Patricia Beatty's historical fiction alternate between first and third person. Her use of colorful idioms help frame the period and characters. Most of the author's characters are similar: bright, courageous, lovable, and determined to carry on in the face of tragedy. They gain self-confidence and learn survival skills. They are strong, independent persons in their own right. Some are credible and sympathetic; others are not. Reviewers have most often named Beatty's characterization as her weak point. *The Bulletin of the Center for Children's Books* described her characters as having "so heavy an overlay of golly-gee-grit that they seem caricatures rather than people" and stated that Beatty used the character "as a vehicle for the material about the setting rather than to use the setting as a background for a story line." This supports what is most evident about her writing. The author's intention is to broaden the reader's understanding and appreciation of history in various times and places, not to probe characters or relationships.

Patricia Beatty brings history to life. Her research lends authenticity to her fiction which is full of fascinating historical details.

She helps younger readers distinguish the fact from the fiction of her novels by providing extensive endnotes. The author's ability to infuse reality with humor gives readers amusing, never dull stories to enjoy. Her settings are vivid; her protagonists are charming; her storylines are entertaining. However, Paramount in Patricia Beatty's many historical novels is her desire to transmit her love of history to her readers.

—Catherine Price

BEHN, Harry

Pseudonyms: Giles Behn. **Nationality:** American. **Born:** Prescott, Arizona, 24 September 1898. **Education:** Stanford University, California, 1918; Harvard University, Cambridge, Massachusetts, B.S. 1922. **Family:** Married Alice Lawrence in 1925; one daughter and two sons. Scenario writer, Metro-Goldwyn-Mayer, Twentieth Century-Fox, and Universal studios, Hollywood, 1925-35; Professor of Creative Writing, University of Arizona, Tucson, 1938-47. Founding director, Phoenix Little Theatre, 1922-23; vice president, Tucson Regional Plan, 1940-47; founding editor, *Arizona Quarterly,* Tucson, 1942-47; founder and manager of radio bureau, 1938-47; founder, University of Arizona Press, 1960. **Awards:** Fellowship for graduate study in Sweden, 1923-24, Graphic Arts awards for book design of *The Little Hill, All Kinds of Time,* and *The Painted Cave; All Kinds of Time* is one of thirty classics selected by New York Public Library and *Life;* honor award of Boys' Clubs of America for *Omen of the Birds;* award of merit of Claremont Graduate College for *Cricket Songs.* George G. Stone Center for Children's Books award, 1965. **Died:** 6 September 1973.

PUBLICATIONS FOR YOUNG ADULTS

Fiction

The Faraway Lurs, illustrated by the author. Cleveland, World, 1963; as *The Distant Lurs,* London, Gollancz, 1965.

Poetry (illustrated by the author)

The Little Hill: Poems and Pictures. New York, Harcourt Brace, 1949.
All Kinds of Time. New York, Harcourt Brace, 1950.
Windy Morning: Poems and Pictures. New York, Harcourt Brace, 1953.
The House beyond the Meadow. New York, Pantheon, 1955.
The Wizard in the Well: Poems and Pictures. New York, Harcourt Brace, 1956.
The Golden Hive: Poems and Pictures. New York, Harcourt Brace, 1966.
What a Beautiful Noise, illustrated by Harold Berson. New York, World, 1970.
Crickets and Bullfrogs and Whispers of Thunder, edited by Lee Bennett Hopkins. New York, Harcourt Brace, 1984.
Trees, illustrated by James Endicott. New York, Holt, 1992.

Other

Translator, *Cricket Songs* [and *More Cricket Songs*]: *Japanese Haiku.* New York, Harcourt Brace, 2 vols., 1964-71.

PUBLICATIONS FOR CHILDREN

Fiction

The Painted Cave, illustrated by the author. New York, Harcourt Brace, 1957.
Timmy's Search, illustrated by Barbara Cooney. Greenwich, Connecticut, Seabury Press, 1958.
The Two Uncles of Pablo, illustrated by Mel Silverman. New York, Harcourt Brace, 1959; London, Macmillan, 1960.
Roderick, illustrated by Mel Silverman. New York, Harcourt Brace, 1961.
Omen of the Birds, illustrated by the author. Cleveland, World, 1964; London, Gollancz, 1965.

PUBLICATIONS FOR ADULTS

Plays

Screenplays: *The Big Parade,* 1925; *Proud Flesh,* with Agnes Christine Johnson, 1925; *La Bohème,* with Ray Doyle, 1926; *The Crowd,* with King Vidor and John V.A. Weaver, 1928; *The Racket,* with Del Andrews, 1928; *Frozen River,* 1929; *The Sin Sister,* with Andrew Bennison, 1929; *Hell's Angels,* with Howard Estabrook, 1930.

Poetry

Siesta. Phoenix, Golden Bough Press, 1931.
The Grand Canyon (as Giles Behn). Privately printed, 1935.
Sombra. Copenhagen, Christreu, 1961.

Other

Translator, *The Duino Elegies* by Rainer Maria Rilke. Mount Vernon, New York, Peter Pauper Press, 1957.
Translator, with Peter Beilenson, *Haiku Harvest.* Mount Vernon, New York, Peter Pauper Press, 1962.
Chrysalis: Concerning Children and Poetry. New York, Harcourt Brace, 1968.

*

Manuscript Collections: Kerlan Collection, University of Minnesota, Minneapolis; University of Oregon Library, Eugene.

*   *   *

It is a fascinating and far-flung legacy which Harry Behn has left to the young reader and to those interested in literature for children, characterized, perhaps, by his own words, "Innocence is hardly more than a willingness to wonder." How unusual it is to think of Behn as a man of innocence—born in Arizona when it was still a territory, educated at Harvard, and world-traveled! And yet it is the right phrase, for his willingness to wonder and wander, his enthusiasms, and curiosity moved within a changing world which he persisted in viewing, most often, through the eyes of the innocent.

His books, ranging from the child's poetic voice of *Windy Morning* through stories and novels and further poetry as well as translation of haiku, carry a thread of transcendentalism; it is the Indian Earth-Mother, the gods of the Sun People, the god Aplu, the rising of the sun, the "almost imperceptible experience of wonder, removed from knowledge." "When a child," he wrote in *Chrysalis,* "sees his first butterfly and becomes himself a flying flower, such innocence has in it more reality than any however heroic whiz around the planet." So it was that the language of a bug, a chicken, a crow, a storm, rain, or train could spellbind him into poem or prose-making.

Like Walter de la Mare, he found elves and wizards, fairies and magical beings of whom to write; like Robert Louis Stevenson he became the child speaking in "Swing Song" or "Pirates." Yet his was an American heritage, rooted in world history. *All Kinds of Time* clearly expressed that "Seconds are bugs / minutes are children / hours are people / days are postmen / weeks are Sunday School / months are / north / south / east / west / and in between / seasons are / wild flowers / tame flowers / golden leaves / and snow / years are / Santa Claus / centuries are / George / Washington / and forever is God." This and the poems within his other books of poetry for children are those of an American child and his particular wonder: "Tell me, tell me everything! / What makes it Winter / And then Spring?" he asks through the child in "Curiosity." Yet, the series of questions of the poem end with his own continuing questions, "Tell me! or don't even grown-ups know?" This search, therefore, led him on; it was not unusual that because of his love for seasons and simplicity he should turn to the translation of Japanese haiku, that he should examine the life of a crow in *Roderick,* or Dawn Boy, the Indian, in *The Painted Cave;* that his mother's childhood in Denmark should inspire him to write *The Faraway Lurs* or that his questioning of the correlation between Etruscan and American civilization spun itself out in *Omen of the Birds.*

Poetry, he wrote, "must be presented with careful incompleteness of information." Incompletion thus sustains curiosity; information is not a *raison d'être* for the poet, and "willingness to wonder" is Harry Behn's unique contribution to children's literature.

—Myra Cohn Livingston

BELL, William

Nationality: Canadian. **Born:** William Edwin Bell in Toronto, Ontario, 27 October 1945. **Education:** New Toronto Secondary School, 1959-64; University of Toronto, B.A. (Honors) 1968; University of Toronto, M.A. 1969; University of Toronto, B.Ed. 1970; Ontario Institute for Studies in Education, M.Ed. 1984. **Family:** Married Ting-xing Ye; one daughter and two sons. **Career:** High school teacher of writing and literature, Orillia and Barrie, Ontario, since 1970; English teacher, Harbin, China, 1982-83, and Beijing, China, 1985-86. **Awards:** Ruth Schwartz Children's Book Award, 1991; Manitoba Young Reader's Choice Award, 1992; Ontario School Librarians Association Award, 1992; Belgium Youth Book Award, 1992. **Address:** c/o Doubleday Canada,

105 Bond St., Toronto, Ontario M5B 1Y3, Canada. **E-mail Address:** willbell@barint.on.ca.

PUBLICATIONS FOR YOUNG ADULTS

Crabbe. Toronto, Stoddart Kids Books, 1986; as *Crabbe's Journey,* Boston, Little Brown, 1987.
Metal Head. Toronto, Prentice Hall, 1987.
The Cripples' Club. Toronto, Stoddart Kids Books, 1988; as *Absolutely Invincible,* Toronto, General, 1991.
Death Wind. Toronto, Prentice Hall, 1989.
Five Days of the Ghost. Toronto, Stoddart Kids Books, 1989.
Forbidden City. Toronto, Doubleday Canada, and New York, Bantam, 1990.
Invincible. Toronto, General, 1991.
No Signature. Toronto, Doubleday Canada, 1992.
Speak to the Earth. Toronto, Doubleday Canada, 1994.
Zack. Toronto, Doubleday Canada, and New York, Simon and Schuster, 1998.

PUBLICATIONS FOR CHILDREN

The Golden Disk, illustrated by Don Kilby. Toronto, Doubleday Canada, 1995.
River My Friend, illustrated by Ken Campbell. Victoria and Seattle, Orca, 1996.

*

William Bell comments:

There was a funny movie made some years ago called "Throw Momma from the Train"—a catchy title if there ever was one. The character played by Billy Crystal is a writer who is "blocked"; he hasn't penned a word in a long time. By the end of the story, owing to certain dramatic experiences involving the Danny DeVito character and his deeply obnoxious mother, the writer has become "unblocked." Relieved and happy, he sits down at a desk with an old typewriter, to the left of which is a foot-high pile of blank paper. Crystal rolls a sheet into the typewriter and begins to pound away merrily on the keys. As time passes, the pile of paper diminishes while a corresponding stack of neatly typed sheets rises to the right of the typewriter. At last, Billy Crystal types THE END, slips the final piece of paper from the machine, adds it to the stack, puts the whole lot into an envelope and mails it to his publisher. The book is done.

I have met many people who think that writing goes like that—smoothly, almost effortlessly and without fault. I have never met a writer (or heard of one, or read one) who didn't describe writing as frustrating, arduous, frightening, messy, painful and fraught with revision. On the contrary, we can all point to manuscripts, every page of which shows a blizzard of slashes, underlines, over-writes, arrows and other untidy ministrations. We can usually remember how many drafts each of our books consumed. (*No Signature* took eight, *Zack* took around six, *Forbidden City*?—don't ask.) The thing of it is, creative endeavour in general is almost always messy, full of false starts, changes of mind, restarts and, we hope, improvements. Writing in particular is messy, a continuous and desperate battle against mediocrity and imperfection; and every "finished" novel or drama, poem or screenplay isn't finished at all, because there's always the feeling it can be made better.

I've talked to many, many students in many places and most of them assume that their writing process is somehow different from mine. But when you think about it, how could it be? All right, granted, much of the time students are working on projects that their teachers have assigned. But even so, once a writer (student or published) begins a piece, the process is pretty much the same. When you're writing, you're a writer, whether your work is assigned in school or assigned by that nagging little voice in your mind that some people call the creative imagination. And a writer is a struggler, searching for just the right word or image, cutting out extraneous terms or phrases (or, heaven help us, chapters), revising and polishing.

It's hard work, but listen. A sculptor starts with a lump of clay, a pile of sheet metal, a block of granite. A painter has colours and canvas or panel or glass. Think what we start with: nothing. Making something out of nothing is always worth it.

*   *   *

In the main, William Bell's central characters have been adolescent males involved in some aspect of self-discovery, a discovery which is usually related to their developing value structures. Told via journal entries, *Crabbe* is the story of 18-year-old Franklin Crabbe, the only child of wealthy, controlling parents. A brilliant honour student with an alcohol problem, Crabbe determines that his life cannot continue in its present direction with everything being parentally determined. The urban Crabbe decides to run away to an Ontario wilderness area, but his canoeing inexperience nearly causes his death. Rescued by a beautiful woman, Mary Pallas, Crabbe discovers that she, too, is fleeing something, though what she won't reveal. A summer spent with the bush-wise Mary teaches Crabbe both wilderness and home survival skills. Mary's accidental death precedes Crabbe's re-entry into civilization, where he begins to build new relationships with his parents.

The Cripples' Club's membership consists of four mid-teen members: Hook, Amie, and Heather, who are respectively paraplegic, blind, and deaf. The unofficial club's fourth member is George Ma, the book's narrator, who has significant memory loss due to the traumatic events he experienced while escaping from his war-torn Asian country. Though the quartet bands together to deal with the negative reactions from some fellow students, their biggest "enemy" is their own lessened sense of self worth. Much of the book's actions centre around the group's discovering George's real identity and helping him to confront and find meaning in his terror-filled "Dream." *The Cripples' Club* has been reissued with the more politically correct title, *Absolutely Invincible*.

The book least like Bell's other work is *Five Days of The Ghost*. While Bell normally roots his young adult novels in real world situations, *Five Days of the Ghost* contains a strong fantasy element. During summer vacation prior to ninth grade, Karen Stone is persuaded by her older brother, John, to visit an old Indian graveyard. There, the pair encounter the 150-year-old ghost of Chief Copegog, who, because of "somethin' I did wrong when I was still 'live," has to pay by leading "the new dead peoples to the spirit world." What initially appears to be a straightforward ghost story deepens with the information that Karen's twin bother had been accidentally killed two summers before and Karen had not dealt with her grief.

Having taught English at Beijing's Foreign Affairs College in 1985-86, Bell followed the 1989 student demonstrations in Beijing with an intimate knowledge of the city and its people, and his rage over the Tiananmen Square massacre led to his writing *Forbidden City*. The narrator, who recounts the story via a dated journal, is Alex Jackson, 17, whose interest in military history finds expression in his recreating battles with lead soldiers. When Alex's TV cameraman father is asked to cover Gorbachev's China visit, he persuades Alex to join him by offering Alex the chance to see the terra cotta army unearthed at an emperor's burial site. In China, Alex-the-tourist becomes Alex-the-observer and then Alex-the-participant as happenings before and after the massacre unfold. Alex discovers that military reality is much different than simply moving toy soldiers about or viewing earthenware soldiers.

Via a teen's search for his father, Bell movingly explores the many faces of loneliness in *No Signature*. Steve "Wick" Chandler, 17, was only seven when his father seemingly walked out of his life. Though Wick periodically received postcards, they contained only "DAD" and Wick's mailing address, both rubber stamped. Feeling somehow "guilty," the child Wick "punished" himself by destroying cherished objects connected with his father, and, thereafter, the cards ceased. Now, a decade later, another rubber stamped postcard arrives, and Wick determines to discover why his father left. Surprisingly, his mother arranges for her ex-husband to drive Wick to a wrestling tournament, and, during the week-long trip, Wick learns why the postcards bore no signature: his father is illiterate, a fact he successfully hid from his wife for years. Her discovery of his illiteracy, however, gave her the power to drive him from a failing marriage and the son he loved. To provide readers with the necessary antecedent information, Bell incorporates Wick's memories via numerous "REPLAY" sections. A subplot involving Wick's discovery that his best friend, Hawk, is gay allows Bell to utilize Wick's alienated response to Hawk's homosexuality as the means for causing Wick to identify with his father's illiteracy-caused isolation. Appropriately, Bell does not provide a "happy-ever-after" ending but, instead, leaves Wick still sorting out his emotional responses to these "new" people.

A portion from the Bible's Book of Job 12:8—"Speak to the earth, and it shall teach thee"—expresses the ecological theme of the novel *Speak to the Earth*. Bryan Troupe, 15, lives with his widowed mother, Iris, and her younger brother, Jimmy, in Nootka Harbour, a Vancouver Island fishing village. When Mackenzie Forest Industries (MFI), a multi-national company, receives a government license to clear-cut two-thirds of nearby Orca Sound, one of the world's last remaining untouched stands of temperate rainforest, the Troupes become a house divided. Conservationist Iris chairs the SOS (Save Orca Sound) Committee while Jimmy, a life-long logger, takes a job with MFI and later becomes local head of SAVE, an organization ostensibly representing average individuals whose livelihoods are dependant upon forestry. Bryan, initially indifferent to the entire issue, tries to remain neutral; however, his mother's "embarrassing" public actions cause Bryan so much discomfiture that he attempts, unsuccessfully, to persuade her to abandon her cause. Exacerbating Bryan's situation is the fact that his mother's behaviours have led his girlfriend's MFI-connected parents to forbid her from seeing him. A succession of events involving MFI "dirty tricks" ultimately causes Bryan to reevaluate his stance and to adopt a very public posture. Though a pro-logging position is not strongly represented, the book's array of minor and major characters does present readers with numerous facets of this most complicated issue.

Bell also authored two hi-lo titles, one for "Series Canada" and the other for "Series 2000." The former, *Metal Head*, deals with the tensions existing between two school "social" groupings. Circumstances place leather-wearing Donnie, a Metal Head, in close contact with some "Preps," and his experiences cause him to reexamine his assessments of both groups of people. *Death Wind*, an action-adventure story, focuses on high schooler Allie, whose poor relationship with her parents is positively altered by events which follow a tornado's striking their community.

—Dave Jenkinson

BENCHLEY, Nathaniel (Goddard)

Nationality: American. **Born:** Newton, Massachusetts, 13 November 1915. **Education:** Phillips Exeter Academy, Exeter, New Hampshire, 1931-34; Harvard University, Cambridge, Massachusetts, 1934-38, S.B. 1938. **Military Service:** Served in the United States Naval Reserve, 1941-45. **Family:** Married Marjorie Bradford in 1939; two sons. **Career:** City reporter, New York *Herald Tribune*, 1939-41; assistant entertainment editor, *Newsweek*, New York, 1946-47. **Awards:** Western Writers of America Spur award, 1973, for *Only Earth and Sky Last Forever*; *Bright Candles* was named an ALA notable book, 1974. **Died:** 14 December 1981.

PUBLICATIONS FOR YOUNG ADULTS

Fiction

Gone and Back. New York, Harper, 1970.
Only Earth and Sky Last Forever. New York, Harper, 1972.
Bright Candles. New York, Harper, 1974; London, Deutsch, 1976.
Beyond the Mists. New York, Harper, 1975.
A Necessary End. New York, Harper, 1976; London, Deutsch, 1978.

PUBLICATIONS FOR CHILDREN

Fiction

Red Fox and His Canoe, illustrated by Arnold Lobel. New York, Harper, 1964; Kingswood, Surrey, World's Work, 1969.
Oscar Otter, illustrated by Arnold Lobel. New York, Harper, 1966; Kingswood, Surrey, World's Work, 1967.
The Strange Disappearance of Arthur Cluck, illustrated by Arnold Lobel. New York, Harper, 1967; Kingswood, Surrey, World's Work, 1968.
A Ghost Named Fred, illustrated by Ben Shecter. New York, Harper, 1968; Kingswood, Surrey, World's Work, 1969.
Sam the Minuteman, illustrated by Arnold Lobel. New York, Harper, 1969; Kingswood, Surrey, World's Work, 1976.

The Several Tricks of Edgar Dolphin, illustrated by Mamoru Funai. New York, Harper, and Kingswood, Surrey, World's Work, 1970.
The Flying Lesson of Gerald Pelican, illustrated by Mamoru Funai. New York, Harper, 1970.
Feldman Fieldmouse, illustrated by Hilary Knight. New York, Harper, 1971; London, Abelard Schuman, 1975.
Small Wolf, illustrated by Joan Sandin. New York, Harper, 1972; Kingswood, Surrey, World's Work, 1973.
The Magic Sled, illustrated by Mel Furukawa. New York, Harper, 1972; as *The Magic Sledge,* London, Deutsch, 1974.
The Deep Dives of Stanley Whale, illustrated by Mischa Richter. New York, Harper, 1973; Kingswood, Surrey, World's Work, 1976.
Snorri and the Strangers, illustrated by Don Bolognese. New York, Harper, 1976; Kingswood, Surrey, World's Work, 1978.
George, the Drummer Boy, illustrated by Don Bolognese. New York, Harper, 1977; Kingswood, Surrey, World's Work, 1978.
Kilroy and the Gull, illustrated by John Schoenherr. New York, Harper, 1977; London, Abelard Schuman, 1979.
Running Owl, the Hunter, illustrated by Mamoru Funai. New York, Harper, 1979.
Demo and the Dolphin, illustrated by Stephen Gammell. New York, Harper, 1981.
Snip, illustrated by Irene Trivas. New York, Doubleday, 1981.
Walter, the Homing Pigeon, illustrated by Whitney Darrow, Jr. New York, Harper, 1981.

Other

Sinbad the Sailor, illustrated by Tom O'Sullivan. New York, Random House, 1960; London, Muller, 1964.

PUBLICATIONS FOR ADULTS

Novels

Side Street. New York, Harcourt Brace, 1950.
One to Grow On. New York, McGraw Hill, 1958.
Sail a Crooked Ship. New York, McGraw Hill, 1960; London, Hutchinson, 1961.
The Off-Islanders. New York, McGraw Hill, 1961; London, Hutchinson, 1962; as *The Russians Are Coming! The Russians Are Coming!* New York, Popular Library, 1966.
Catch a Falling Spy. New York, McGraw Hill, and London, Hutchinson, 1963.
A Winter's Tale. New York, McGraw Hill, and London, Hutchinson, 1964.
The Visitors. New York, McGraw Hill, 1964; London, Hutchinson, 1965.
A Firm Word or Two. New York, McGraw Hill, 1965.
The Monument. New York, McGraw Hill, and London, Hutchinson, 1966.
Welcome to Xanadu. New York, Atheneum, and London, Hutchinson, 1968.
The Wake of Icarus. New York, Atheneum, 1969.
Lassiter's Folly. New York, Atheneum, 1971.
The Hunter's Moon. Boston, Little Brown, 1972.
Portrait of a Scoundrel. New York, Doubleday, 1979.
Sweet Anarchy. New York, Doubleday, 1979.
All Over Again. New York, Doubleday, 1981.
Speakeasy. New York, Doubleday, 1982.

Plays

The Frogs of Spring, adaptation of his novel *Side Street* (produced New York, 1953). New York, French, 1954.

Screenplay: *The Great American Pastime,* 1956.

Other

Robert Benchley: A Biography. New York, McGraw Hill, 1955; London, Cassell, 1956.
Editor, *The Benchley Roundup* (writings by Robert Benchley). New York, Harper, 1954; London, Cassell, 1956.
Humphrey Bogart. Boston, Little Brown, and London, Hutchinson, 1975.

*

Media Adaptations: *Sail a Crooked Ship* (film), Columbia, 1961; *The Russians Are Coming, the Russians Are Coming* (film adaptation of *The Off-Islanders),* United Artists, 1966; *The Spirit Is Willing* (film adaptation of *The Visitors),* Paramount, 1966.

Manuscript Collection: Mugar Memorial Library, Boston University.

*   *   *

An author of books for adults who for the last seventeen years of his life turned to writing for youth, Nathaniel Benchley produced a range of fiction for young children to teenagers. Often reflecting an interest in history or nature, his stories characteristically introduce animal or child protagonists who yearn to do grown-up deeds and undertake adventures that either caution them to wait for adulthood or thrust them faster into its early stages.

Believing in the need for the teenage novel to bridge the gap between children and adult fiction, Benchley in the 1970s produced five young-adult, historical novels all characterized by strong story-telling, detailed research, and interesting characters. Set in the nineteenth century, the award-winning *Gone and Back* compellingly chronicles young Obed Taylor's growth toward maturity and slow recognition of his father as a born loser as his family treks west from Nantucket to the Oklahoma Land Rush without striking success. Benchley skillfully integrates an authentic historical setting and a mature theme with Obed's experiences. In the superbly written *Only Earth and Sky Last Forever,* a nineteenth-century Cheyenne boy named Dark Elk, seeing the humiliation suffered by Agency Indians and wanting to prove himself a warrior, joins Crazy Horse in leading forays against the white man and fighting at Little Big Horn. Peopled with convincingly historical as well as fictional characters, the story vividly portrays the Indians' last struggle for survival. *Bright Candles* tells a fast-paced and well-researched story highlighting the Danish resistance during the Nazi regime through the figure of an adolescent boy who joins the Underground. Based on the eleventh-century sagas, the richly detailed and exciting *Beyond the Mists*

centers on a Danish youth disenchanted with warring on murderous Viking raids who survives a shipwreck as a merchant seaman to join up with Leif Eriksson on a journey to North America. Plumbing his wartime Navy experience, Benchley writes a perceptive account of service aboard a World War II subchaser in training and Pacific combat in *A Necessary End.*

Not surprisingly, five of the author's fourteen adult novels hold appropriate appeal for the sixteen- to nineteen-year-old reader. The *Off-Islanders* (source of the screenplay *The Russians Are Coming! The Russians Are Coming!), Sail a Crooked Ship,* and *The Wake of the Icarus* are maritime adventures with a strong seasoning of melodrama, wry humor, and farce. *The Visitors* focuses on domestic issues, telling the story of the parents and son who occupy an old, reputedly haunted, house on the Atlantic coast where they encounter its ghosts and manage to exorcise them after several well-plotted comic complications. In *Welcome to Xanadu,* a bored, sixteen-year-old, New Mexico farmer's daughter is abducted and briefly held hostage by an erudite, mental-institution escapee who, during her captivity, teaches her to think and learn more about her life. The story is effectively suspenseful and not without humor.

Benchley produced a number of successful picture books and two works that appeal to the youngest of young adult readers: *Kilroy and the Gull,* about a restless captured orca who learns to communicate with humans once he escapes to sea, and *Demo and the Dolphin,* about a dolphin in ancient Greece who carries a boy seeking advice to Delphi, where both receive ambiguous advice but a better grasp of the mystical past.

Benchley once described an effective children's book as one which does not talk down to readers, offers humor and suspense, and, he added, ''You need a page-turner.'' His overall canon admirably reflects these qualities, and upon his death in 1981, Benchley left a rich legacy indeed to young-adult fiction.

—Christian H. Moe

BENNETT, Jay

Nationality: American. **Born:** New York, 24 December 1912. **Education:** New York University. **Family:** Married Sally Stern in 1937; two sons. **Military Service:** Served as English features writer and editor, Office of War Information, 1942-45. **Career:** Writer and lecturer. Has worked as a farmhand, factory worker, lifeguard, mailman, salesman, and senior editor of an encyclopedia. **Awards:** Edgar Allan Poe award from Mystery Writers of America for best juvenile mystery novel, 1974, for *The Long Black Coat,* and 1975, for *The Dangling Witness.* **Address:** 64 Greensward Lane, Cherry Hill, New Jersey 08002, U.S.A.

PUBLICATIONS FOR YOUNG ADULTS

Fiction

Deathman, Do Not Follow Me. New York, Meredith Press, 1968.
The Deadly Gift. New York, Meredith Press, 1969.
The Killing Tree. New York, Franklin Watts, 1972.

Masks: A Love Story. New York, Franklin Watts, 1972.
The Long Black Coat. New York, Delacorte, 1973.
The Dangling Witness. New York, Delacorte, 1974.
Shadows Offstage. New York, Nelson, 1974.
Say Hello to the Hit Man. New York, Delacorte, 1976.
The Birthday Murder. New York, Delacorte, 1977.
The Pigeon. New York, Methuen, 1980.
The Executioner. New York, Avon, 1982.
Slowly, Slowly, I Raised the Gun. New York, Avon, 1983.
I Never Said I Loved You. New York, Avon, 1984.
The Death Ticket. New York, Avon, 1985.
To Be a Killer. New York, Scholastic, 1985.
The Skeleton Man. New York, Franklin Watts, 1986.
The Haunted One. New York, Fawcett, 1989.
The Dark Corridor. New York, Fawcett, 1990.
Sing Me a Death Song. New York, Franklin Watts, 1990.
Coverup. New York, Franklin Watts, 1991.
Skinhead. New York, Franklin Watts, 1991.
The Hooded Man. New York, Fawcett, 1992.
Death Grip. New York, Fawcett, 1993.

PUBLICATIONS FOR ADULTS

Fiction

Catacombs. New York, Abelard-Schuman, 1959.
Death Is a Silent Room. New York, Abelard-Schuman, 1965.
Murder Money. New York, Fawcett, 1963.

Plays

No Hiding Place (produced New York, 1949).
Lions after Slumber (produced London, 1951).

Also author of radio scripts, including *Miracle before Christmas* and *The Wind and Stars Are Witness;* author of television scripts for *Alfred Hitchcock Presents, Crime Syndicated, Wide, Wide World, Cameo Theater,* and *Monodrama Theatre.*

*

Biography: Essay in *Something about the Author Autobiography Series,* Volume 4, Detroit, Gale, 1987; essay in *Speaking for Ourselves: Autobiographical Sketches by Notable Authors of Books for Young Adults,* Volume 1, compiled and edited by Donald R. Gallo, National Council of Teachers of English, 1990.

Critical Studies: Entry in *Contemporary Literary Criticism,* Volume 35, Detroit, Gale, 1985.

*   *   *

Jay Bennett is a recognized master of mystery and suspense novels for young adult readers. He has twice won the Mystery

Writers of America Edgar Allan Poe award for best juvenile mystery for *The Long Black Coat* and *The Dangling Witness.*

He is respected for his craft as a writer, especially his gift for creating and sustaining a mysterious atmosphere in which violence threatens the characters. His protagonists are frequently "outsiders." The "loner" character appeals to young adult readers, who often identify with that aspect of the character's personality. Yet Bennett's outsiders find through the course of the novels that it is difficult to survive alone, and it is this discovery that becomes the thematic framework for his stories.

Bennett's style tends to be an economical one. His writing is clear and simple, again appealing to many young readers; but his concise prose is rich in meaning and fully expressive. He once described himself as a "poetic realist" and this phrase truly characterizes his work. He holds himself to high standards of writing for young people, creating stories that entertain and enlighten.

Bennett has written more than twenty novels for YA readers, the majority of them suspenseful thrillers with serious themes. Two recent novels clearly show the strength of Bennett's use of theme. In *Coverup: A Novel,* the issues of teenage drinking and the homeless combine to provide the chilling effect, when the hero Brad cannot remember what happened the night before when he had been drinking with his friend Alden, the judge's son. Alden and his father try to convince Brad that nothing happened to cause his nagging feeling of an awful event occurring when Alden drove them home. When Brad meets and tries to help Ellen search for her homeless father, he learns the terrible truth about the ability of those in power to cover up scandal, even death by auto. The truth emerges when Alden's mother turns in her son and husband, and justice (another favorite Bennett theme) is served.

White supremacy becomes the catalyst for suspense in *Skinhead.* Jonathan Atwood is summoned to the deathbed of a man, three thousand miles away in Seattle. Jonathan is the grandson of a millionaire and through him has access to power. His trip to Seattle brings him an anonymous death threat linked to the man whose death summoned him West. He meets Jenny in the airport while waiting for his flight back to New York. She knows him and the dead man, Alfred Kaplan. He decides to stay in Seattle, but Skinheads are watching his movements. Kaplan had been writing a book on the white supremacists. The Skinheads saw it as a threat and now Jonathan is one, too, and his life is in danger. Jonathan must confront the violence of the Skinheads, his true paternity, and his wealthy grandfather's bigotry to come to terms with his own sense of self and justice.

Bennett's earlier award-winning novels are more typically thrillers. In *The Long Black Coat,* Phil Brant is caught in the shadow of his older brother Vinnie's death. Vinnie had been part of a bank robbery, pulled before he left to serve in Vietnam. Vinnie's two accomplices menace Phil because they think he knows about the location of the stash. The secret lies in a cashmere coat and Vinnie who is alive and well after all.

The second Edgar winner, *The Dangling Witness,* uses murder as its core event. Matthew Garth, an usher at a movie theater, is the only witness to a murder. Matt is fearful of going to the police and of the killer who knows he knows, and of the Syndicate that may want his silence or his death. Matt's fear of violence, his own guilt over the death of a fellow football player, and his troubled relationship with his father make him an easy prey for the killer. Detective Anderson and Julie Leonard, the murder victim's sister, help Matt find his way through this moral crisis.

Another earlier novel, *The Deadly Gift,* combines suspense and another moral dilemma. John-Tom Dawes's father is a Mohawk high-steel worker in New York City. One rainy night, John-Tom picks up a briefcase left behind by a man waiting for a bus. The briefcase holds ten thousand dollars. It could be money for college. Does it now belong to him or does it belong to an underworld figure who wants it back under the threat of death? John-Tom abhors violence, even the violence in a game of football, but the money draws him more and more into it.

Murder and international terrorism in New York City provide the components of the thriller *The Pigeon.* Brian Cawley is the pigeon lured to his girlfriend's apartment where he finds her dead. A well-timed phone call's rough voice tells him he's been set up and the police are on the way. With the help of a former teacher, Brian tries to find the killers. His search leads him into a terrorist net of Neo-Nazis whose plans include bombing the Staten Island ferry. The novel explores a major Bennett theme of rejecting violence as a means to an end.

Other books combine murder with contemporary issues. *The Dark Corridor* grapples with an epidemic of teenage suicide. When Alicia Kent is reported as the latest suicide her boyfriend Kerry Lanson does not believe it. If it wasn't suicide, was Alicia a murder victim? In *Sing Me a Death Song,* Jason Feldman races against time to prove that his mother was framed for a murder. He has only days before her scheduled execution to prove her innocence. Again the young protagonists of these novels are looking for justice and an antidote to violence in the world.

In addition to the works of mystery, Bennett has published two YA romance novels: *Masks: A Love Story* and *I Never Said I Loved You. Masks* is a story of the interracial romance between Jennifer, a white teenager, and Peter Yeng, the son of a Chinese doctor. The story explores family dynamics and the parent's rejections of the young couple's relationship. *I Never Said I Loved You* explores another troubled relationship. Peter, an overachieving Princeton freshman with his eye on the family law firm, falls in love with unconventional, idealistic Alice. This mismatched pair seems to be the attraction of opposites, but their divergent views of life cannot be reconciled and the relationship is doomed.

Whether writing mystery or romance, Jay Bennett creates novels that young readers respond to. He understands and presents their concerns and provides thrills in crisp dialogue and prose that attracts even reluctant readers.

—Janice Antczak

BETHANCOURT, T. Ernesto

Pseudonym for Tom Paisley. **Nationality:** American. **Born:** Thomas E. Passailaigue in Brooklyn, New York, 2 October 1932; name changed to Tom Paisley. **Education:** Attended City College of the City University of New York. **Family:** Married Nancy Yasue Soyeshima in 1970; two children. **Military Service:** Served in the U.S. Navy during the Korean War, 1950-53. **Career:** Writer, singer, musician, composer, lyricist, actor, and critic; biographer of recording artists, RCA Records and CBS Records (both New York City), 1969-76; staff lyricist, Notable Music, 1970-71; contributing editor to *Stereo Review* and *High Fidelity*; has held various

other odd jobs, including a stint during the 1950s as an undercover claims investigator for the New York office of Lloyd's of London. **Awards:** American Society of Composers, Authors and Publishers Popular Division Award, 1970-71, for *Cities*; named "Kentucky Colonel" by governor of Kentucky, 1976; National Council on Social Studies Children's Book Council notable children's book, 1978, and American Library Association (ALA) Best of the Best citation, both for *Tune in Yesterday*; University of California at Irvine "Author of the Year Award," 1978; Excellence in a Series award, Southern California Council on Literature for Children and Young People, 1983, for "Doris Fein" series; Central Missouri State University Distinguished Body of Work award, 1984; Children's Choice Award, for *Nightmare Town.* **Address:** P.O. Box 787, Alta Loma, California 91701, U.S.A.

PUBLICATIONS FOR YOUNG ADULTS

Fiction

New York City Too Far from Tampa Blues. New York, Holiday House, 1975.
The Dog Days of Arthur Cane. New York, Holiday House, 1976.
Tune in Yesterday. New York, Holiday House, 1978.
Dr. Doom, Superstar. New York, Holiday House, 1978.
Nightmare Town. New York, Holiday House, 1979.
Doris Fein, Superspy. New York, Holiday House, 1980.
Doris Fein, Quartz Boyar. New York, Holiday House, 1980.
Where the Deer and the Cantaloupe Play. San Diego, California, Oak Tree Publications, 1981.
Doris Fein, The Mad Samurai. New York, Holiday House, 1981.
Doris Fein—Phantom of the Casino. New York, Holiday House, 1981.
Doris Fein, Murder Is No Joke. New York, Holiday House, 1982.
Doris Fein, Deadly Aphrodite. New York, Holiday House, 1983.
T.H.U.M.B.B. New York, Holiday House, 1983.
Doris Fein, Dead Heat at Long Beach. New York, Holiday House, 1983.
The Tomorrow Connection. New York, Holiday House, 1984.
The Great Computer Dating Caper. New York, Crown, 1984.
Doris Fein, Legacy of Terror. New York, Holiday House, 1984.
The Me Inside of Me. New York, Lerner Publications, 1985.

Other

Lyricist and librettist, *Cities* (play; produced Off-Broadway, 1971).
Lyricist, *Music,* 3 Vols. Silver Burdett, 1973-75.
That's Together (television script). WTTW-TV (Chicago), 1974.
The New Americans (television script). KCET-TV (Los Angeles), 1981.

Also author of several collections of short stories for the General Learning Corporation; author of lesson in television series "Skills Essential to Learning," Agency for Instructional Television, 1979; author of "Easy to Read" adaptations of classics, all published by Pittman Fearon Publishing, including *Dr. Jekyll and Mr. Hyde, The Time Machine, Frankenstein, The Three Musketeers,* and *The Last of the Mohicans.*

*

Media Adaptations: *New York City Too Far from Tampa Blues* (teleplay), NBC, 1979; *The Dog Days of Arthur Cane* (teleplay), ABC, 1984.

Critical Studies: *Speaking for Ourselves: Autobiographical Sketches by Notable Authors of Books for Young Adults,* edited by Donald R. Gallo, Urbana, Illinois, National Council of Teachers of English, 1990, 19-21; *Literature for Today's Young Adults* by Aileen Pace Nilsen and Kenneth L. Donelson, 4th ed., New York, HarperCollins, 1993, 197; *Something About the Author,* Vol. 78, Detroit, Gale, 1994, 147-53.

*   *   *

T. Ernesto Bethancourt began his career as Tom Paisley (his legally changed name), a performer/songwriter of social and political satire. He learned blues guitar from legendary blues man Josh White, played at some of the same clubs and coffee houses as Bob Dylan, and performed for two presidents of the United States. He wrote his first book in 1974—the year his first daughter was born—as a memoir of his childhood and youth for her to read one day. An editor at Holiday House saw him writing it, convinced him to rework the book as a novel for young adults, published it, and "T. Ernesto Bethancourt" (a combination of his father's middle name and an old family name from his mother's side) was born.

Tom—the hero of *New York City Too Far from Tampa Blues*—was happy living in Florida: "We had a neat house there. There were two tall pine trees in the back. We had a swing made out of rope and a car tire." His dad, "Pancho," was an ice man—"a great job"—who delivered ice in his Ford truck to people with ice boxes instead of refrigerators. But with more and more people buying electric refrigerators, Pancho found himself out of a job. When Pancho announces that they'll be moving to New York City, Tom and his sisters are not happy. Dolores, the youngest, cries about their chickens—she's given them all names—which they can't bring with them. Audrey, the oldest, cries about missing her graduation. Pat goes off alone, "like she always does when things get heavy." Tom splits over to his Uncle Jack's house across the road. Uncle Jack is playing his guitar and singing. He asks Tom what's wrong. "We're moving to New York City." Uncle Jack offers Tom a beer, though he "knows I'm too little to drink beer," and they talk about it. "I told him that I'd miss my main man, Pete, and maybe going out on the ice truck to the *fincas* when there was no school. But mostly, I said that I was going to hang loose and see what New York was like. Then I said something I don't even know why I said it. 'Mostly, I'm gonna miss you and Tootsie and Aunt Margie. I can talk to you. Pancho's always so busy and uptight. And I guess now I'm never gonna learn guitar. I don't know, Uncle Jack. . .'" Uncle Jack gets a funny look on his face and then does the "wildest" thing: "He put down his guitar and reached over and grabbed me and kissed me, real fast, real rough." Uncle Jack explains to Tom that living in New York isn't going to be easy, there aren't any quiet places to go, and that he's going to have to bring his own quiet place with him. "So, I got you somethin'." He goes back into the house and comes back with a guitar, the most beautiful guitar Tom's ever seen.

Living in Brooklyn isn't easy. It's dirty and noisy, rough and tough. Tom must deal with gangs and street-corner hoodlums who call him "spic" and try to pick fights. Then Tom meets Aurelio, a tough Italian kid. They spar, and when Aurelio finds that Tom won't give in, they become friends. Aurelio's older brother Tony plays in a band and teaches Tom more about playing the guitar, and soon Tom and Aurelio are making big money singing and playing—as "The Griffin Brothers"—at a local Irish bar. Tony's band gets an agent, and when the agent hears the boys play a song they wrote themselves, "New York City Too Far from Tampa Blues," he arranges for them to record it. The boys' music teacher hears about the song too, gets them into the prestigious High School of Music and Art, and has them perform at their junior high graduation! Part autobiography and part fantasy, this is quite a story.

Arthur Cane—of *The Dog Days of Arthur Cane*—lives in a comfortable Long Island suburb. But when he laughs at a visiting African student's native beliefs—"a bunch of crap . . . superstition"—he suddenly finds himself transformed into a dog! Now, being a dog isn't easy, especially when you've grown up as a human who can use his hands, walk on two feet, and talk. In fact, being a dog is a big adjustment. To escape the local dogcatcher, Arthur jumps onto the back of a pickup truck headed, he discovers, for New York City. There, he is befriended by Tyree, a blind, black street musician whom he in turn helps cross the busy city streets. Arthur digs the Greenwich Village music scene, and he comes to love Tyree, but he's happy and greatly relieved when the curse—and his life as a dog—are finally over.

When the young heroes of Bethancourt's *Tune in Yesterday* encounter a ghost in their local cemetery who claims to hold the key to the Gate of the Past, they eagerly choose their own transformation—a transformation in time from the 1970s to 1942. Richie Gilroy, who is white, and his "main man" Matty Owen, who is black, play bass and percussion in their Branford, Long Island, high school's three bands. They love music, especially the music of the big band era, and they love old cars, so they can't wait to get into the city and see their favorite bands—and cars!—in action. But life in another time isn't so easy, either. For one thing, it's not easy to be a young black man in mid-town Manhattan. Nor is it easy when Richie falls for a young black woman he meets in the line at the Paramount, where for fifty cents the boys will see a first-run movie and the Glenn Miller Band live. But it's downright scary when the boys overhear a plot by German spies and then are chased by them and the New York City police! And it's even scarier when they must admit to each other that they're really not sure how to get back "home" to the 1970s. What a long, strange trip it is!

Plump and plucky, brash and brassy Doris Fein provides a perfect transition from Nancy Drew to Sue Grafton's Kinsey Millhone. A minor character in *Dr. Doom, Superstar,* Doris comes into her own in *Doris Fein, Superspy,* where a post-high school graduation trip from her home in California to visit her aunt and uncle in New York City leads to her involvement in international espionage—as well as her meeting a handsome Japanese-American New York City policeman, Carl Suzuki. Her adventures continue in a series of fast-paced intrigues: *Doris Fein, Quartz Boyar,* where Doris is talked into acting as a courier for the top-secret intelligence agency she became involved with in *Doris Fein, Superspy*; *Doris Fein—Phantom of the Casino,* where Doris—and the visiting Suzuki—solve a mystery on Santa Catarina Island off the California coast; and *Doris Fein, Dead Heat at Long Beach,* in which Doris has inherited a fortune from an eccentric millionaire and bought a custom sports car, only to become involved in more international intrigue at the race track where she's learning to drive her new car properly.

In his fast-paced novels for young adults, Bethancourt has written of minorities—Hispanics, blacks, Japanese-Americans—with understanding and humor. His style is hip and casual, and should grab the most reluctant reader.

—Marcia Welsh

BLACKLIN, Malcolm. *See* **CHAMBERS, Aidan.**

BLESSING, Richard Allen

Nationality: American. **Born:** Bradford, Pennsylvania, 11 September 1939. **Education:** Hamilton College, Clinton, New York, A.B. 1961; Tulane University, New Orleans, Louisiana, M.A. 1963, Ph.D. 1967. **Family:** Married Lisa Boepple in 1964; one son. **Career:** Instructor in English, Louisiana State University, New Orleans, 1964-68; assistant professor of English, Heidelberg College, Tiffin, Ohio, 1968-70; assistant professor of English, 1970-73, associate professor, since 1973, University of Washington, Seattle. **Awards:** Guggenheim fellow, 1972. **Address:** 4810 88th Pl. S.E., Mercer Island, Washington 98040, U.S.A.

PUBLICATIONS FOR YOUNG ADULTS

A Passing Season (novel). New York, Little, Brown, 1982.

PUBLICATIONS FOR ADULTS

Poetry

A Closed Book: Poems. Seattle, University of Washington Press, 1981.
Poems & Stories. Port Townsend, Washington, Dragon Gate, 1983.

Nonfiction

Wallace Stevens' "Whole Harmonium." Syracuse, New York, Syracuse University Press, 1970.
Theodore Roethke's Dynamic Vision. Bloomington, Indiana University Press, 1974.

*

Critical Studies: Entry in *Contemporary Authors,* Detroit, Gale, 1975, Vol. 53-56, 51-52; review of *A Passing Season* by Sidney Offit, in *New York Times Book Review* (New York), 7 November 1982, 43-44.

*   *   *

Richard Blessing lettered in football at high school in Bradford, Pennsylvania, and was a star quarterback in college. He went on to get a doctorate in English and become an English professor and published poet and critic. But his small-town Pennsylvania childhood and the drama and excitement of his football days remained in his blood, and, combined with his poet's eye and critic's skill, he has created a compelling novel for young adults, *A Passing Season.*

Craig Warren has been raised on football. His father wanted to be a football player in high school—"to be somebody"—but at a hundred and thirty pounds, he was laughed at by the other players, his nose was broken on the first day of practice, and the coach suggested trying cross-country or yell-leading. Then his mother died, he dropped out to help raise his younger brothers, and got a job at the local refinery where he's worked ever since. The day Craig was born, he brought a real football to the hospital, and from the time he was three or four, he took him to every Oiltown Owls home game: "So he could see it, see what it might be like to be somebody."

But it's not just Mr. Warren who's obsessed with football. It's all the other hard-working fathers who live for the Friday night games. It's Joe Hugo, "Funny" Phelps, "Quick" Keller and the other "downtown quarterbacks," former Owls players who meet on Saturday mornings in front of the Oiltown Hotel "to compare the players of the night before with the heroes of other nights and other years." It's nearly all of Oiltown High School, where banners shouting "GO OWLS—BEAT STEELERS" deck the hallways the first week of school. Oiltown is a football town.

And Craig loves football. He can run. He can throw. But once he gets on the field, he's all thumbs and weak knees, so he's only the Owls' reserve quarterback. Craig loves English class, too, especially some of the quotes that Mr. Craft writes on the blackboard for daydreaming students to ponder. An Owl can't like poetry, though, so Craig tries to keep his interest under wraps. He even surprises himself when he raises his hand to comment on Ernest Hemingway's "The Short Happy Life of Francis Macomber": "It's like if Macomber is afraid of the big thing—death—and he has always been afraid of it, same as most everybody is, then he's got to be scared of everything. His wife, other people, making mistakes. It's, well, consistent." He stops short when halfback Johnny Zale bursts out with laughter, and from then on his Owl classmates call him "Artsy-Craftsy."

The season continues. Craig does no better on the field. Some games he doesn't even play. In frustration, he unofficially "quits" the team; no one notices. Finally the Owls find themselves set to compete with the Brackenridge Bisons and their star player "Iron Mike" Michelonis for the state championship. Coach Muldoon has a brilliant idea to help his team get over Michelonis' reputation for indomitability: he makes up a fake Bison jersey, complete with Michelonis' dreaded number "44", and has Craig Warren play "Iron Mike" on the Owls' scout team during the week's practice. All of a sudden—like the quote on Mr. Craft's board from Saul Bellow's *Henderson the Rain King,* the story of a middle-aged

Connecticut millionaire who finds himself rain king in an African village and becomes transformed by a wonderful leap of imagination into a real rain king—Craig is transformed into a star quarterback himself! The transformation is so real that Coach Muldoon decides to start Warren in the final game.

On the day of the game Coach Muldoon gathers his players in the locker room:

> "No rah-rah. No win it for good old Oiltown High or for the Gipper or for Muldoon's wife and kids. . . . No, this is for yourselves. Tonight is for yourselves. You grow up in this town and you wait maybe fifteen, sixteen years to be in this room, to be Owls. If you're lucky, you play maybe twenty nights like this. Then you're out, and most of you don't play football anymore. You come to the games, and there's the band, and the people cheer, and maybe a few remember you, but it's over. What you have to remember is what you did on a few nights like this one. A football game doesn't last very long. Football doesn't last very long. Out of every game, the ball's actually in play maybe seven or eight minutes. The rest is huddles and lining up. . . . You're a good team, maybe the best I ever had. You have that seven or eight minutes to be everything you can be. Don't come back in here when it's over with anything you saved up, any little piece of courage or effort you didn't give. . . . Well, let's go see who's the number one team in this state."

On the field, Craig plays his very best, plays better than his best, saves nothing up. Time is suspended. Space opens up. It's just he against Michelonis, and he's been inside Michelonis' head for the whole week. The two young men confront each other as equals, and by the time the game's over, they are: VISITORS 21, OWLS 21. Michelonis has met his match. The season's over. And Craig Warren has been all he could be.

In *A Passing Season,* Richard Blessing has indeed composed what Sidney Offit described in review of the book for the *New York Times Book Review* as a "richly textured tale that captures the mood of the season and the continuity of the game."

—Marcia Welsh

BLOCK, Francesca Lia

Nationality: American. **Born:** Hollywood, California, 3 December 1962. **Education:** University of California, Berkeley (Phi Beta Kappa), B.A. 1986. **Career:** Cataloger, Ankrum Gallery, Los Angeles, 1989; instructor of writing workshops, Berkeley and Los Angeles, 1989; contributor of articles and short stories to *Berkeley Fiction Review, Los Angeles Times Book Review, New York Times Book Review,* and *Spin*; contributor of poetry to *Artline* (UCLA), *Berkeley Poetry Review,* and *Westwind* (UCLA); writer. **Awards:** University of California, Berkeley, short fiction award, 1986; Emily Chamberlin Cook Poetry Award, University of California Los Angeles, 1986; American Library Association (ALA) Best Books for Young Adults citations, 1989, 1992, 1993, 1995; Book of the Year shortlist, ALA, 1989; *Booklist* Book Award, 1989; Recommended Book for Reluctant Young Readers, 1989, 1990, 1992, 1993, 1994, 1995, 1996; Best Books citation, *School Library Journal,* 1991; Best Books citation, *New York Times,* 1992; Best Books citation, *Publisher's Weekly,* 1992; ALA Gay, Lesbian & Bisexual Book Award, 1995; ALA Gay and Lesbian Task Force Book Award nomination, 1996. **Agent:** Lydia Wills Artists Agency, 230 W. 55th St., Ste. 29D, New York, New York 10019, U.S.A.

PUBLICATIONS FOR YOUNG ADULTS

Fiction

Weetzie Bat. New York, Harper, 1989.
Witch Baby. New York, Harper, 1990.
Cherokee Bat and the Goat Guys. New York, Harper, 1991.
Missing Angel Juan. New York, HarperCollins, 1993.
The Hanged Man. New York, Harper, 1994.
Baby Be-Bop. New York, Harper, 1995.
Girl Goddess #9: Nine Stories. New York, HarperCollins, 1996.
Dangerous Angels: The Weetzie Bat Books. New York, HarperCollins, 1998.
I Was a Teenage Fairy. New York, HarperCollins, 1998.

Contributor of short stories to anthologies, including *Am I Blue?,* edited by Marion Dane Bauer, 1994; *When I Was Your Age,* edited by Amy Ehrlich, 1994; and *Soft Tar,* a benefit for a global children's organization, 1994.

Poetry

Moon Harvest, illustrated by Irving Block. Los Angeles, Santa Susana Press, 1978.
Season of Green, illustrated by Irving Block. Los Angeles, Santa Susana Press, 1979.

Other

Author of screenplays for *Cherokee Bat and the Goat Guys, Girl Goddess #9: Nine Stories,* and *Violet.*

PUBLICATIONS FOR ADULTS

Ecstasia. New York, ROC, 1993.
Primavera. New York, ROC, 1994.

*

Media Adaptations: *Cherokee Bat and the Goat Guys* and *Baby Be-Bop* (sound recordings), Talking Books; *Weetzie Bat* and *Missing Angel Juan* adapted for the stage by Ann Bayd and Julia Neary; *Witch Baby* adapted for the screen by Julia Hickson.

Biography: Essay in *Speaking for Ourselves, Too* compiled and edited by Donald R. Gallo, National Council of Teachers of

English, 1993; ''Francesca Lia Block,'' in *Something about the Author Autobiography Series,* Vol. 21, Detroit, Gale, 1996.

Critical Studies: ''People Are Talking About . . . Francesca Lia Block'' by Patrick Jones, in *Horn Book Magazine* (Boston), November-December 1992, 697-701, and January-February 1993, 57-63; review of *Ecstasia,* in *Library Journal,* 15 May 1993, 100; ''The Hanged Man,'' in *The Bulletin of the Center for Children's Books,* Vol. 48, September 1994, 6.

*   *   *

Francesca Lia Block has established a unique place for herself in the young adult genre. Setting her stories against the backdrop of Los Angeles punk subculture, she speaks frankly to teens about sex and sexuality in the age of AIDS, alternative families, drugs, and the pain of growing up in the nineties. In the midst of such turmoil, however, Block's quirky and endearing characters triumph and manage to find love and an unquenchable desire to survive. Indeed, her mission is to help teens, ''gay, straight, fabulous, literal,'' to accept themselves and gain acceptance from others for who they are. It should come as no surprise, then, that Block's greatest strength is her ability to connect with her readers on a profoundly personal level, writing in a style once described as ''slam-slam-bang, punk-inspired, pup-culture-driven, sentimental-tone prose poetry.'' As she once said, ''When I write a book it is a very personal experience, like writing a love letter or a message to a friend.'' Peopled with a diverse cast of characters ranging from Weetzie Bat, a punk princess in pink, to her lover, My Secret Angel Lover Man, and her best friend Dirk and his boyfriend, to their common offspring, Witch Baby and Cherokee, Block's *Weetzie Bat* series (with five titles to date) is no less than a stunning, postmodern fairy tale that offers hope and encouragement to her equally diverse young adult readers.

Block's first book, *Weetzie Bat,* is a magical fable, a tender love story, and an affirmation of the power of family—a somewhat different kind of family, perhaps, but a warm and caring one that nurtures and protects its members. It tells the story of Weetzie Bat, a young Hollywood punkgirl with a flattop who longs for security and affection (neither of which she receives from her dysfunctional, booze-ridden parents), and her gay friend Dirk, the school hunk, who sports a ''shoe-polish black Mohawk'' and drives a ''slinkster-cool red '55 Pontiac.'' They set up house together with their respective lovers, My Secret Agent Lover Man and Duck, a blond surfer, and Weetzie's pet, Slinkster Dog. The four form a loving, extended family, raising two children together: Cherokee Bat, the daughter of Dirk, Duck, and Weetzie; and Witch Baby, My Secret Agent Lover Man's daughter from a previous affair, who is left on their doorstep by the child's mother. Together, they face the hardships of modern living that threaten their familial bond and loyalty, but triumph nevertheless, saved by the power of their love for each other: ''I don't know about happily ever after,'' Weetzie concludes, ''but I know about happily.''

Witch Baby, the second novel in the Bat family saga, chronicles the story of the child abandoned on the doorstep. A child who has always felt that she is an ''almost-member'' of the family, and unable to understand her place in the world, Witch Baby's anguish and desperation finds release when she sets out to find her birth mother, her identity, and an answer to her one, burning question: ''What time are we upon and where do I belong?'' Ironically, when she finally meets her mother, Witch Baby realizes that her home has always been with the people who love her—Weetzie and the rest who chose to make her one of them many years before.

The next two installments to the *Weetzie Bat* series, *Cherokee Bat and the Goat Guys* and *Missing Angel Juan* depict the darker and more dangerous side of the Los Angeles subculture, plunging the reader into a world of drugs and rock-and-roll. *Cherokee Bat* follows Witch Baby and Cherokee when they are left behind with Coyote, a Native-American friend to Weetzie, as the adults venture off on a filming expedition in South America. Under Coyote's direction, they join with Raphael Chong Jah-Love and Angel Juan Perez to form a rock band, the Goat Guys. An instant hit, the band's success is dependent upon powerful tribal gifts that Coyote gives them. The group's initial euphoria quickly dissipates as its members descend ''into the bacchanalian hell of the nightclub scene with tequila and cocaine, skull lamps and lingerie-clad groupies drenched in cow's blood.'' Cherokee comes close to committing suicide and the others perilously close to self-destruction as well. Only when Coyote returns to take back his totems are they redeemed and able to acquire remorse and wisdom as a result of their harrowing rite of passage.

Missing Angel Juan continues the story of Witch Baby's journey to wholeness. By the end of *Cherokee Bat and the Goat Guys* the members of the band have paired off, Cherokee with Raphael and Witch Baby with Angel Juan. At the beginning of *Missing Angel Juan,* Witch Baby decides to follow Angel to New York. Her ensuing search to find him is alternately dreamlike and truly nightmarish as she combs New York from Harlem to the meatpacking district. While all of Block's novels contain elements of the supernatural and magical, she pulls out all the stops in this one, and the book is significantly weaker for it; much of the plot turns on coincidence that is simply unbelievable, and magic—both helpful and malevolent—does not make it any less so. The fairy tale quality of the magic that Block used so charmingly in her earlier books seems heavy-handed and depressing in *Missing Angel Juan.*

With the exception of *Weetzie Bat, Baby Be-Bop* is Block's most moving, painful, and celebratory installment of the series. Block revisits Dirk MacDonald, who readers first met in *Weetzie Bat,* and tells the story of his life before he meets Weetzie. The novel's opening sentence, ''Dirk had known it since he could remember,'' is the coming-out statement that enables the unconventional coming-of-age tale of how Dirk becomes Baby Be-Bop. Just sixteen, Dirk must confront the difficulties that his homosexuality brings to his life in a homophobic society. Block poignantly traces Dirk's journey from self-loathing to self-acceptance. With help from a magic lantern and his grandmother, Dirk comes to realize that ''Any love that is love is right'' and gains the courage to face others' hostility.

In the few years that she has been writing books for young adults, Francesca Lia Block has established herself as a major talent. Her books have been honored as Young Adult Best Books by the American Library Association and have been lauded by most critics and reviewers for her unique voice and transcendent themes. Block has become, as one critic put it in *Horn Book,* ''a brilliant addition to the canon of respected young adult authors.''

—Audrey Eaglen, updated by Rebecca R. Saulsbury

BLOS, Joan W(insor)

Nationality: American. **Born:** New York City, New York, 9 December 1928. **Education:** Vassar College, Poughkeepsie, New York, B.A. 1949; City College (now of the City University of New York), M.A. 1956. **Family:** Married Peter Blos, Jr., in 1953; one son (deceased), one daughter. **Career:** Research assistant, Jewish Board of Guardians, New York City, 1949-50; assistant teacher of psychology, City College (now of the City University of New York), New York City, 1950-51; research assistant, Yale University, Child Study Center, New Haven, Connecticut, 1951-53; associate editor in publications division, Bank Street College of Education, New York City, 1959-66, instructor in teacher education division, 1960-70, research assistant and specialist in children's literature, Department of Psychiatry, 1970-73, lecturer for School of Education, 1973-80, University of Michigan, Ann Arbor; writer and lecturer, 1980—. Volunteer reviewer of children's books for the Connecticut Association of Mental Health and chairperson of Children's Book Committee, 1954-56; member of editorial board, *Children's Literature in Education*, London, 1973-77, U.S. editor, 1976-81. **Awards:** John Newbery Medal from American Library Association, and American Book Award for children's hardcover fiction, both 1980, both for *A Gathering of Days: A New England Girl's Journal, 1830-32; A Gathering of Days* was also chosen as one of the Best Books of the Year by *School Library Journal* and as an Ambassador Book by the English-Speaking Union. **Agent:** Curtis Brown Ltd., 10 Astor Place, New York, New York 10003, U.S.A.

PUBLICATIONS FOR YOUNG ADULTS

Fiction

A Gathering of Days: A New England Girl's Journal, 1830-32 (historical fiction). New York, Scribner, 1979.
Brothers of the Heart: A Story of the Old Northwest, 1837-38 (historical fiction). New York, Scribner, 1985.
Brooklyn Doesn't Rhyme. New York, Scribner, 1994.

Nonfiction

The Heroine of the Titanic: A Tale Both True and Otherwise of the Life of Molly Brown, illustrated by Tennessee Dixon. New York, Morrow, 1991.

PUBLICATIONS FOR CHILDREN

Picture Books

Joe Finds a Way, with Betty Miles, illustrated by Lee Ames. Syracuse, L. W. Singer, 1967.
"It's Spring," She Said, illustrated by Julie Maas. New York, Knopf, 1968.
Just Think!, with Betty Miles, illustrated by Pat Grant Porter. New York, Knopf, 1971.
Martin's Hats, illustrated by Marc Simont. New York, Morrow, 1984.

Old Henry, illustrated by Stephen Gammell. New York, Morrow, 1987.
The Grandpa Days, illustrated by Emily Arnold McCully. New York, Simon & Schuster, 1989.
Lottie's Circus, illustrated by Irene Trivas. New York, Morrow, 1989.
One Very Best Valentine's Day, illustrated by Emily Arnold McCully. New York, Simon and Schuster, 1990.
A Seed, a Flower, a Minute, an Hour: A First Book of Transformations, illustrated by Hans Poppel. New York, Simon and Schuster, 1992.
Editor, *The Days Before Now,* by Margaret Wise Brown, illustrated by Thomas B. Allen. New York, Simon and Schuster, 1994.
The Hungry Little Boy, illustrated by Dena Schutzer. New York, Simon & Schuster, 1995.
Nellie Bly's Monkey: His Remarkable Story in His Own Words, illustrated by Catherine Stock. New York, Morrow Junior Books, 1996.
Bedtime, illustrated by Stephen Lambert. New York, Simon & Schuster, 1998.

Other

In the City (reader), illustrated by Dan Dickas. New York, Macmillan, 1964.
With Betty Miles, *People Read* (reader), illustrated by Dan Dickas. New York, Macmillan, 1964.

*

Media Adaptations: *Old Henry* (cassette), National Library Service for the Blind and Physically Handicapped, 1987; *A Gathering of Days: A New England Girl's Journal, 1830-32* (unabridged cassette), Random House.

Biography: Essay in *Something about the Author Autobiography Series,* Volume 11, Detroit, Gale, 1991.

Manuscript Collections: Kerlan Collection, University of Minnesota.

Critical Studies: Entry in *Children's Literature Review,* Vol. 18, Detroit, Gale, 1989.

Joan Blos comments:

Words, for me, have always been important. It is said that I spoke at an early age and well before I entered school my father and mother were writing down the "poems" I spoke to them. "First in town it thunders and glitters," begins one surviving example. It rises to the question: "What will you do when the storm is out, and it is beginning to rain?" Observation and question continue to be the basis of what I write.

"Writing begins in caring," I say to the children when asked to speak in schools. By that I mean that writing begins with concern for the world, the events and the people therein. I believe that this world of ours matters and that our small lives count. Writing also means caring about the words which are set down on paper. It's a struggle for me and I wouldn't call it enjoyable. Once I told an interviewer that, although I don't like writing, I *love* having written. That's what keeps me going back—back to the pads and the pens and the pencils, the typewriter, and the wastebaskets (two!) which are under my desk. I think it's important for others to know that writing isn't something you do because you find it easy. Most of the time I'm grateful if I can do it at all. Beyond the caring for words, and one's world, writing has to do with caring for those for whom you write. I suppose that's why I write for children and am happy to hear from them. I like to think of my books, my works, as ways of saying things, to children, for whom I deeply care. However hard I find this work of writing, I would not, do not, want ever to give it up! I hope I get better and better at writing; I know that there is nothing that I would rather do.

*   *   *

Joan W. Blos's first novel for older children, *A Gathering of Days: A New England Girl's Journal, 1830-32,* won numerous awards, among them the Newbery Medal and the American Book Award. It is a well-crafted book of historical fiction with a protagonist, Catherine Hall, who is as vividly alive as any of her readers. Catherine's human qualities are revealed early as she wishes "that my hair were curly, as Matty's is, and our mother's." She delights in visiting the Shipmans, their nearest neighbors, but wishes that she could reciprocate with splendid dinners on special occasions (since her mother died years before the journal begins, that is not possible). Here is a real child, loving, usually obedient, but full of fun, too. Having taken great pride in assuming many of her mother's duties, Catherine resents her new stepmother who appears with little warning about halfway through the book, constantly referring to her as "she" or "her" in the journal. On the wedding day, Catherine writes, "On this day, in Boston, they married. I will not call her Mother." Her stepbrother, Daniel, later comes up with a compromise, "Mammann," as Catherine gradually adjusts. In contrast, she dearly loves her friend Cassie, whose death is a terrible blow. Eventually matters sort themselves out as Catherine comes to terms with herself and with those around her. She accepts both Cassie's death and her stepmother; as she prepares to set off on a trip at the end of the journal, she has matured considerably from the girl who first began it.

Blos's other historical novel, *Brothers of the Heart: A Story of the Old Northwest, 1837-38,* has a male protagonist. The tale, set in Michigan, is told through flashback using devices such as letters and journal and diary entries. These fictionalized accounts give the reader a strong sense of verisimilitude; the book rings true, for Blos has also captured the speech cadences and language of the period. Through friendships and relatives several of the characters are linked to Catherine Hall, from *A Gathering of Days,* so that readers can gain a sense of continuity.

The sharp characterization of the first historical fiction novel continues in *Brothers of the Heart* as Shem Perkins, born lame, attempts to make his own way after an unfortunate scene with his upset father. After running away from home, he receives gainful employment and is sent on a dangerous expedition which almost costs him his life but which ensures his maturity and builds his self-confidence, enabling him to return to his family and to the girl he

will eventually marry. The reader also learns of another culture as Shem takes in the aged Ottowan Indian, Mary Goodhue, learning from her and tending to her until her death. Through her he discovers his own strengths and makes the realization that he and Mary's long-dead Indian husband were truly brothers of the heart.

The richness of the novel lies in the presentation of the growth of the Michigan region along with the development of characters and insight into the feelings of crippled Shem and the attitudes of others about him. The language, with its rhythms and lilt of earlier times, is remarkably spare, not replete with full-blown descriptions, yet giving the reader a strong sense of place and characterization. Blos has accomplished the fine feat of balancing history with universal human experience, uniting the book's past with the reader's present.

—Marilyn F. Apseloff

BLUE, Zachary. *See* STINE, R(obert) L(awrence).

BLUME, Judy

Nationality: American. **Born:** Judy Sussman, in Elizabeth, New Jersey, 12 February 1938. **Education:** New York University, B.S. in education 1960. **Family:** Married 1) John M. Blume in 1959 (divorced 1975); one daughter and one son; 2) Thomas A. Kitchens in 1976 (divorced); 3) George Cooper in 1987, one stepdaughter. **Career:** Writer of juvenile and adult fiction. Founder, KIDS Fund, 1981. **Awards:** *New York Times* best books for children list, 1970, Nene Award, 1975, Young Hoosier Book Award, 1976, and North Dakota Children's Choice Award, 1979, all for *Are You There God? It's Me, Margaret*; Charlie May Swann Children's Book Award, 1972, Young Readers Choice Award, Pacific Northwest Library Association, and Sequoyah Children's Book Award of Oklahoma, both 1975, Massachusetts Children's Book Award, Georgia Children's Book Award, and South Carolina Children's Book Award, all 1977, Rhode Island Library Association Award, 1978, North Dakota Children's Choice Award, and West Australian Young Readers' Book Award, both 1980, United States Army in Europe Kinderbuch Award, and Great Stone Face Award, New Hampshire Library Council, both 1981, all for *Tales of a Fourth Grade Nothing*; Arizona Young Readers Award, and Young Readers Choice Award, Pacific Northwest Library Association, both 1977, and North Dakota Children's Choice Award, 1983, all for *Blubber*; South Carolina Children's Book Award, 1978, for *Otherwise Known as Sheila the Great*; Texas Bluebonnet List, 1980, Michigan Young Reader's Award, and International Reading Association Children's Choice Award, both 1981, First Buckeye

Children's Book Award, Nene Award, Sue Hefley Book Award, Louisiana Association of School Libraries, United States Army in Europe Kinderbuch Award, West Australian Young Readers' Book Award, North Dakota Children's Choice Award, Colorado Children's Book Award, Georgia Children's Book Award, Tennessee Children's Choice Book Award, and Utah Children's Book Award, all 1982, Northern Territory Young Readers' Book Award, Young Readers Choice Award, Pacific Northwest Library Association, Garden State Children's Book Award, Iowa Children's Choice Award, Arizona Young Readers' Award, California Young Readers' Medal, and Young Hoosier Book Award, all 1983, all for *Superfudge*; American Book Award nomination, Dorothy Canfield Fisher Children's Book Award, Buckeye Children's Book Award, and California Young Readers Medal, all 1983, all for *Tiger Eyes*; Golden Archer Award, 1974; Today's Woman Award, 1981; Eleanor Roosevelt Humanitarian Award, Favorite Author—Children's Choice Award, Milner Award, and Jeremiah Ludington Memorial Award, all 1983; Carl Sandburg Freedom to Read Award, Chicago Public Library, 1984; Civil Liberties Award, Atlanta American Civil Liberties Union, and John Rock Award, Center for Population Options, Los Angeles, both 1986; D.H.L., Kean College, Union, New Jersey, 1987; South Australian Youth Media Award for Best Author, South Australian Association for Media Education, 1988; Margaret A. Ewards award for lifetime achievement, American Library Association, 1996; Distinguished Alumna Award, New York University, 1996. **Agent:** Harold Ober Associates, Inc., 425 Madison Ave., New York, New York 10017, U.S.A.

PUBLICATIONS FOR YOUNG ADULTS

Fiction

The One in the Middle Is the Green Kangaroo, illustrated by Lois Axeman. Chicago, Reilly and Lee, 1969; revised edition with new illustrations, Scarsdale, New York, Bradbury Press, 1991.
Iggie's House. Englewood Cliffs, New Jersey, Bradbury Press, 1970; London, Heinemann, 1981.
Are You There God? It's Me, Margaret. Englewood Cliffs, New Jersey, Bradbury Press, 1970; London, Gollancz, 1978.
Freckle Juice, illustrated by Sonia O. Lisker. New York, Four Winds Press, 1971; London, Heinemann, 1984.
Then Again, Maybe I Won't. Scarsdale, New York, Bradbury Press, 1971; London, Heinemann, 1979.
It's Not the End of the World. Scarsdale, New York, Bradbury Press, 1972; London, Heinemann, 1979.
Tales of a Fourth Grade Nothing, illustrated by Roy Doty. New York, Dutton, 1972; London, Bodley Head, 1979.
Otherwise Known as Sheila the Great. New York, Dutton, 1972; London, Bodley Head, 1979.
Deenie. Scarsdale, New York, Bradbury Press, 1973; London, Heinemann, 1980.
Blubber. Scarsdale, New York, Bradbury Press, 1974; London, Heinemann, 1980.
Forever. Scarsdale, New York, Bradbury Press, 1975; London, Gollancz, 1976.
Starring Sally J. Freedman As Herself. Scarsdale, New York, Bradbury Press, 1977; London, Heinemann, 1983.

Superfudge. New York, Dutton, and London, Bodley Head, 1980.
Tiger Eyes. Scarsdale, New York, Bradbury Press, 1981; London, Heinemann, 1982.
The Pain and the Great One, illustrated by Irene Trivas. Scarsdale, New York, Bradbury Press, 1984; London, Heinemann, 1985.
Just As Long As We're Together. New York, Orchard, and London, Heinemann, 1987.
Fudge-a-Mania. New York, Dutton, 1990.
Here's to You, Rachel Robinson. New York, Orchard, 1993.

Other

The Judy Blume Diary: The Place to Put Your Own Feelings. New York, Dell, 1981.

PUBLICATIONS FOR ADULTS

Novels

Wifey. New York, Putnam, 1978; London, Macmillan, 1979.
Smart Women. New York, Putnam, 1983; London, Sphere, 1984.
Summer Sisters. New York, Delacorte, 1998.

Other

Letters to Judy: What Your Kids Wish They Could Tell You. New York, Putnam, and London, Heinemann, 1986.
The Judy Blume Memory Book. New York, Dell, 1988.

Producer with Lawrence Blume, *Otherwise Known As Sheila the Great,* Barr Films, 1988.

*

Media Adaptations: *Forever* (television movie), CBS-TV, 1978; *Tales of a Fourth-Grade Nothing* (filmstrip), Pied Piper Productions, 1980; *Otherwise Known as Shelia the Great* (filmstrip), Pied Piper Productions, 1981; *Superfudge* (filmstrip), Pied Piper Productions, 1984. *Freckle Juice* (film), Barr Films, 1987; *Otherwise Known as Sheila the Great* (film), Barr Films, 1988.

Biography: *Judy Blume* (video) Temple University Department of Educational Media, 1974; *Children's Author Judy Blume* (video) NBC News/Films, Inc. 1980; *Judy Blume's Story* by Betsy Lee, Minneapolis, Minnesota, Dillon Press, 1981; entry in *Dictionary of Literary Biography,* Volume 52, Detroit, Gale, 1986; essay in *Speaking for Ourselves: Autobiographical Sketches by Notable Authors of Books for Young Adults,* Volume 1, compiled and edited by Donald R. Gallo, National Council of Teachers of English, 1990.

Manuscript Collections: Kerlan Collection, University of Minnesota, Minneapolis.

Critical Studies: Entry in *Children's Literature Review,* Detroit, Gale, Volume 2, 1976, Volume 15, 1988; entry in *Contemporary Literary Criticism,* Detroit, Gale, Volume 12, 1980, Volume 30, 1984; *The Pied Pipers* by Emma Fisher and Justin Wintle, Paddington Press, 1975; *Breakthrough: Women in Writing* by Diana Gleasner, New York, Walker, 1980; *Judy Blume's Story* by Betsey Lee, New

York, Dillon Press, 1981; *Presenting Judy Blume* by Maryann Weidt, Boston, Twayne, 1989.

*   *   *

Until the mid-1960s, fiction for young people could be characterized for the most part as predictable and simplistic; very little appeared that might disturb the reader unduly, and a tidy, happy ending was mandatory. Characters were often one-dimensional, and plots ranged from simple to silly. In 1967, however, a teen novel was published that forever destroyed the spoken and unspoken taboos defining junior fiction. S.E. Hinton's *The Outsiders,* a powerful story of class struggle in an Oklahoma high school, was iconoclastic in its gritty realism, its believable, doomed characters, and its uncompromising honesty. The book opened doors previously closed to teenage readers and, in effect, permitted a new generation of writers to tackle the real issues that concerned teenagers with honesty and realism.

It remained for another author to extend that frankness and realism into the world of literature for the younger adolescent, the eleven- and twelve-year-old on the brink, as it were, of full-blown teenage angst. By 1970 this author, Judy Blume, had published two children's books. The first was a pleasant but conventional picture book about a middle child who feels ignored by parents and siblings until he becomes a hit in a school play. The second, *Iggie's House,* was a somewhat didactic piece of junior fiction which dealt with the impact of a black family moving into a previously all-white suburban neighborhood. Reviewers were lukewarm about the book primarily because of the weakness of its characterization, its predictable plot, and some dreadful dialogue. This reception made Blume decide to write a more honest novel about the early adolescent experience based on her own vivid memories of what it was like to be an eleven-year-old girl going through this culture's rites of passage. In the process, Blume managed to ignore publishing taboos and strictures perhaps even more than Hinton had done a few years before, while at the same time penning a work that became one of the great success stories in the history of children's book publishing.

In 1970 *Are You There God? It's Me, Margaret* was published, but this time critical response was anything but lukewarm. Reviewers either loved it or hated it, but what was more important was the response of young readers to eleven-year-old Margaret's wistful longings for religion, her period, breasts, and the first bra, all dished up with large dollops of the easy, good humor that would become characteristic of many of Blume's later books. Preteen girls loved the book and wrote letters by the hundreds to tell its author just how closely they identified with Margaret and shared a sense of cozy familiarity with her dilemmas. But it was only when the book appeared in paperback in 1974 that the hundreds of letters became thousands, all of them from readers who saw themselves and their lives reflected perfectly in Margaret's story.

Response to the book clearly reveals Blume's greatest gift as a writer for young people: her ability to share her own vividly remembered childhood experiences in ways that the reader can both understand and identify with easily and completely. At the same time, Blume does not write down to her readers; she is uncompromising in the frankness of her topics and her refusal to be less than honest in her writing. As a result young people write to

Blume as one twelve-year-old did: "You are writing about me. I feel like you know all my secrets."

Her confidence in her success as a writer established with *Are You There God?,* Blume entered a highly prolific period. *Then Again, Maybe I Won't* is the story of thirteen-year-old Tony Miglion's attempts to cope with his upwardly mobile family as well as his burgeoning sexuality. The effects of divorce on a bewildered preteen girl is the subject of *It's Not the End of the World,* while *Deenie* is the story of a seventh-grader plagued by a mother who is determined that Deenie will become a model until the girl's diagnosis of scoliosis interferes with her plans. Children's cruelty toward one another is the subject of *Blubber,* a story of a fat girl, a born victim, who becomes the target of her entire class's ridicule and persecution with nearly disastrous results. In *Forever,* the joys and the disappointments of first love are shown through the story of Michael and Katherine; more importantly, however, the joys and disappointments of one's first sexual experiences are described clearly and explicitly, in a way that even preteens can understand. For this reason alone, *Forever* has made Blume the most censored children's author in the United States for several years running.

In 1981 the book that many critics felt was Blume's finest appeared. *Tiger Eyes* is the story of one family's struggle to overcome the shock and horror of a father's violent, unexpected death. Davey, the young protagonist, must not only deal with the loss of her parent, but with her mother's inability to accept what has happened and the well-meant if bumbling efforts of other relatives attempting to help. *Tiger Eyes* is notable for the strength of Blume's characterizations, often faulted by critics, and its complexities of plot and theme. Blume's latest novel, *Just as Long as We're Together,* is a return to the world of adolescent girls, much like an updated version of *Are You There God?*

In her thirty years as a writer Blume has achieved a pinnacle of success that few others have. Receiving the Margaret A. Edwards award from the American Library Association in 1996 was indeed warranted for her lifetime achievement and committment to children's literature. She is the most widely read author of contemporary young people's fiction in the world, and her books have sold tens of millions of copies, been translated into Spanish and other languages, and made into movies, filmstrips, and the "Fudge" books were made into a Saturday morning television series. She still receives up to two thousand letters a month from young readers; the most poignant of these have been collected in a book called *Letters to Judy.* Anyone who has any doubt about Blume's rapport with her readers might profit from a look at this book.

Blume has achieved her success as a result of several factors. Her almost total recall of how it felt to be young makes her books speak directly to her readers. She tends to take the side of the child in struggles between parents and children, yet she also takes the side of the underdog when in the struggle among peers that all children share in the process of growing up. She is forthright and frank as no writer for young people had dared to be before she appeared on the scene. At the same time, her own sense of humor and her sense of what makes young readers laugh has softened some of her messages and made them palatable. Her books certainly have been controversial, but their acceptance by the young has been universal. Blume continues to breach old barriers and blaze new trails, an achievement of which few contemporary authors of books for any age group can boast.

—Audrey Eagle, updated by Lisa A. Wroble

BODE, Janet

Nationality: American. **Born:** Penn Yan, New York, 14 July 1943.
Education: University of Maryland, B.A. 1965; graduate study at
Michigan State University, and Bowie State College. **Career:**
Writer, since 1975. Has worked in Germany, Mexico, and the
United States as a personnel specialist, program director, commu-
nity organizer, public relations director, and teacher. **Awards:**
Outstanding Social Studies Book by the National Council for
Social Studies and the Children's Book Council, 1979, and New
York Public Library's Book for the Teen Age selection, 1980, both
for *Rape;* American Library Association's Best Books for Young
Adults, and Notable Children's Trade Book in the Field of Social
Studies from the National Council for Social Studies and the
Children's Book Council, both 1980, and New York Public Li-
brary's Book for the Teen Age selection, 1981 and 1982, all for
Kids Having Kids. **Address:** c/o Franklin Watts, Sherman Turn-
pike, Danbury, Connecticut 06813, U.S.A.

PUBLICATIONS FOR YOUNG ADULTS

Nonfiction

Kids' School Lunch Bag. Washington, D.C., Children's Founda-
tion, 1972.
View from Another Closet: Exploring Bisexuality in Women. New
York, Hawthorn, 1976.
*Fighting Back: How to Cope with the Medical, Emotional and
Legal Consequences of Rape.* New York, Macmillan, 1978.
Kids Having Kids: The Unwed Teenage Parent. New York, F.
Watts, 1980.
*Rape: Preventing It, Coping with the Legal, Medical and Emotion-
al Aftermath.* New York, F. Watts, 1980.
Different Worlds: Interracial and Cross-Cultural Dating. New
York, F. Watts, 1989.
New Kids on the Block: Oral Histories of Immigrant Teens. New
York, F. Watts, 1989.
Real-Life Rape. New York, F. Watts, 1990.
The Voices of Rape. New York, F. Watts, 1990, revised, 1998.
Beating the Odds: Stories of Unexpected Achievers, drawings by
Stan Mack. New York, F. Watts, 1991.
Truce: Ending the Sibling War. New York, F. Watts, 1991.
Kids Still Having Kids: People Talk about Teen Pregnancy, art by
Stan Mack. New York, F. Watts, 1992.
Compiler, *Death Is Hard to Live With: Teenagers and How They
Cope with Death.* New York, Delacorte, 1993.
With Stan Mack, *Heartbreak and Roses: Real Life Stories of
Troubled Love.* New York : Delacorte Press, 1994.
Trust & Betrayal: Real Life Stories of Friends and Enemies. New
York, Delacorte Press, 1995.
Hard time: A Real Life Look at Juvenile Crime and Violence. New
York, Delacorte Press, 1996.
*Food Fight: A Guide to Eating Disorders for Preteens and Their
Parents.* New York, Simon & Schuster, 1997.

*   *   *

Janet Bode lets young adults speak for themselves. Bode's
interviews with teens are interspersed with analysis, advice, and
comments from professionals; they cover issues of immediate
importance to teens and topics that reflect the crises of society.
Bode speaks frequently to young adults, teachers, and librarians
and declares, "Students are my best resource." In her talks and in
her books, Bode provides her telephone number and address
encouraging teens to contact her to talk about problems and to share
their stories. Bode uses the young adults' own words as much as
possible and the discussions throughout Bode's books have an
honest ring that create immediate connections with readers. Expert
interviews which sometimes follow teen's stories are never preachy
or arrogant but provide information and differing viewpoints, and
offer practical suggestions for help.

Kids Having Kids: The Unwed Teenage Parent chronicles the
health risks associated with teen pregnancy and birth control,
describes options, and through each teen's story introduces the
reader to the sudden responsibilities and difficulties of the parenting role. Kimberly says, "My life came to a screeching halt when I
got pregnant and had Brandy. It's an enormous amount of responsibility that no seventeen-year-old should have."

Case histories of five interracial dating couples are recorded in
Different Worlds: Interracial and Cross-Cultural Dating. The
added pressures of society's raised eyebrows are described humorously and poignantly by teens impatient with status quos. The
stories included acknowledge the transcience of most teen relationships—four of five couples interviewed end their relationship—
but the hurt and sense of the injustices experienced lingers.

The anguish of being separated from familiar worlds and
families ties together the interviews of teen immigrants from
diverse countries in *New Kids on the Block: Oral Histories of
Immigrant Teens.* Bode introduces each teen's story with an
introductory paragraph about the youth's country of origin, but
each teen tells his or her own story of flight, often in miserable
conditions, to a land of hope for a better life. Varied cultural
backgrounds, and individual personalities meld into a common
goal—fitting in as an American teen. Abdul, age seventeen,
escaped Afghanistan with his family and after six years as a refugee
in several countries, finally made America his home. "I hated this
place. I didn't have any friends. . . . Now I'm seventeen and the
American kids don't always know that I'm a foreigner. They tease
less. I found out that if you act the way they do, say the same things
they say, do the things they do, they will be calm. So I try not to act
strange to them. I wear t-shirts and stone-washed jeans and aviator
glasses. My hair looks like their hair."

Beating the Odds: Stories of Unexpected Achievers explores the
lives of eleven adolescents who are succeeding in the face of
seemingly insurmountable odds. These young people tell how they
deal with abusive parents, drug addiction, physical disabilities,
parental suicides, and incarceration. Professional information provided by psychiatrists, probation officers, and health care workers
focuses on the importance of setting goals and ways to make
positive life changes. No rosy scenarios are painted, but a feeling of
faith in the individual's abilities to triumph over pain is prevalent.

Bode is particularly adept at exploring many sides of the
complex issues teens suggest she investigate. In *The Voices of Rape*
the author interviews teens who have been raped; teens who have
raped someone; and police, prosecutors, judges, defense attorneys,
and hospital staff involved in rape cases, as well as rape crisis

counselors and psychologists. Bode tackles date rape, stranger rape, and males who have been raped. The facts Bode presents are staggering: one out of every four women experience sexual intercourse for the first time through rape. But, as in Bode's other nonfiction works, the theme of survival and practical strategies for recovery and assistance provide hope and a sense of being in control for teen readers. Bode urges her readers to action: "Today you could make it your goal to break through what remains of the silence about sexual assault. You could choose to be the generation that deals directly and honestly with the issue, the generation that does far more than make things a little easier for rape survivors who decide to report."

Bode's abilities to communicate honestly with young adults and to provide information and help in a way that teens find palatable make her books a valuable tool for teens, parents, teachers, and librarians. Bode's works also provide snapshots and insights into some of society's most pressing issues and impart a sense of certainty that today's teens will find solutions to many of the ills they have inherited.

—Hollis Lowery-Moore

BOISSARD, Janine

Nationality: French. **Born:** Paris, France, 18 December 1932. **Family:** Married Michael Oriano in 1954; two daughters and two sons. **Career:** Freelance writer. **Awards:** *A Matter of Feeling* was selected one of New York Public Library's Books for the Teen Age, 1981, 1982; Palmes Academiques, for her young adult books. **Address:** 9 rue de Villersexel, Paris 75007, France.

PUBLICATIONS FOR YOUNG ADULTS

Fiction

L'esprit de famille. Paris, Fayard, 1977; as *A Matter of Feeling,* translated by Elizabeth Walter, Boston, Little, Brown, 1980.
L'Avenir de Bernadette ("Bernadette's Future"). Paris, Fayard, 1978.
Claire et le bonheur. Paris, Fayard, 1979; as *Christmas Lessons,* translated by Mary Feeney, Boston, Little, Brown, 1984; as *A Question of Happiness,* New York, Ballantine, 1985.
Une femme neuve. Paris, Fayard, 1980; as *A New Woman,* translated by Mary Feeney, Boston, Little, Brown, 1982.
Moi, Pauline! Paris, Fayard, 1981; as *A Time to Choose,* translated by Mary Feeney, Boston, Little, Brown, 1985.
Les miroirs de l'ombre ("The Looking-Glass of Shadows"). Paris, Fayard, 1982.
Cecile, la poison (also published as *Cecile et son amour*). Paris, Fayard, 1984; as *Cecile: A Novel,* translated by Mary Feeney, Boston, Little, Brown, 1988.
Un femme reconciliee. Paris, Fayard, 1986; as *A Different Woman,* translated by Mary Feeney, Boston, Little, Brown, 1988.
Belle grand-mere. Paris, Fayard, 1994.
Bolero. Paris, Fayard, 1995.

Une femme en blanc. Paris, R. Laffont, 1996.
Bebe couple. Paris, Fayard, 1997.

Other

L'esprit de famille ("Family Spirit"; television series). Paris, Fayard, 1977.
Rendez-vous avec mon fils ("A Date with My Son"). Paris, Fayard, 1981.
Vous verrez—, vous m'aimerez ("You'll See, You'll Love Me"). Paris, Plon, 1987.
Croisiere. Paris, Fayard, 1988.
Les pommes d'or. Paris, Fayard, 1988.

*

Janine Boissard comments:

I always knew that I would be a writer. I don't believe that I decided to be one—it was inevitable, genetic. I am a "popular" writer, meaning one who, in simple and accessible language, speaks of reading herself, of life's joys and pains. But also one which offers to her public the possibility of dreams, of escape, without which one does not live well. A popular novel reveals at one time "us" and a projection of us.

I try to make known in my books that substantive life of which Severine speaks in *Une femme reconciliee*—to help the most people possible to find themselves, to give them hope.

Style is something different from good writing, other than the simple organization of words and the choice of those words. It is an invisible thread woven by each writer, which makes the phrase vibrate, gives to it its rhythm and secret music. That thread, for me, comes directly from the soul, from its instinct, and it is that which gives life to characters, settings, and dialogue. One does not invent a style. One has it—one is it.

*   *   *

Janine Boissard writes about love—the heaving, impetuous love that sends young heroines out into winter streets barefoot, that makes them think the street lamps have been lit just for them. But her love stories are also about families—the bonds between husbands and wives, parents and children, sisters and sisters—and the self-love that results from the struggle of coming to know one's true character through first time experiences. Originally published in France, Boissard's series of novels about the Moreau family—Dr. Charles and Mathilde, portrayed as real people with desires and disappointments of their own, and their four daughters Claire ("the Princess") Bernadette (the horsewoman), Pauline (a hopeful writer and the narrator of the first three novels), and Cecile ("the Pest")—are a rich mix of spirited family conversations and descriptions of French food, changing seasons, and ordinary things made meaningful through careful observation. Readers are likely to find the French way of life as depicted by Boissard appealing: the Moreau daughters live passionately and freely, hold strong opinions, and speak frankly about politics, religion, ethics, sex and birth control, and women's roles in families and society. The narrative style is a mixture of reflective reporting and personal confession, and the novels collectively read like one long story. As with most any series, the reader who follows the family through each book is made to feel with every reference to past events like she is in on their secrets.

Like nineteenth-century novels that have at their heart great houses that become like characters, these are built around La Marette, the family house along the Oise River in a village near Paris. One of Boissard's strongest accomplishments in these novels is the sense of place she creates at La Marette that has as much to do with the family that lives there as it does the structure itself. The Moreau sisters are friends, rivals, and mentors to each other, and the comforts represented by La Marette are both help and hindrance in varying degrees to them. Each finds adventure, independence, and adversity away from La Marette; each returns to it for celebration, refuge, and comfort. Through La Marette, Boissard successfully raises home and family above their explicit, practical functions in the lives of her characters and joins them into one idea. She draws life as a series of choices, and home and family life as the process of preparation for choice making. Family members become like rooms with mirrors reflecting consequences of choices already made and windows with a view to the future.

While the life of these novels comes from the life of La Marette and the palpable energy between family members, much of their plots are devoted to romance. In fact, they contain everything one might ridiculously imagine about French affairs: moody artists and worldly doctors wooing inexperienced young women during trysts in garrets, cafes, and mountain inns—with plenty of crepes and wine thrown in for good measure. In *A Matter of Feeling*, seventeen-year-old Pauline has her first love affair with Pierre, a forty-year-old painter of troubled seascapes. In *Christmas Lessons*, Pauline spends the holiday with her lively extended family in Burgundy, where all try to come to grips with unwed Claire's pregnancy. In *A Time to Choose*, Pauline breaks the home ties to follow her own path as a writer and pursues a famous author, whom she finally snags after running away to a Brittany island. *Cecile*, narrated by the youngest Moreau as she reaches young adulthood, ties up many of the loose ends of the now grown sisters' lives and brings the series to a forward-looking close as the family deals with the death of Dr. Moreau and recognizes the foundation that a shared past gives them in developing adult relationships with one another. It is perhaps most notable of the series because Cecile is the most interesting member of the Moreau family. By bringing her out of the background and into full life, the book speaks with a fresh voice about personal and family transition. Cecile, who has spent a lonely childhood befriending imaginary saints and real juvenile delinquents who meet untimely deaths, dives into nursing school and finds first love with an angelic, "Save the Children" doctor.

Boissard takes an easy route with her romances, providing fantasy escapes rather than first love encounters that square realistically with most young readers' experiences. If not believable, these affairs do at least capture with accuracy and feeling the intense highs and lows that a person in love might experience. And all the naivete, self-importance, rebellion, and idealism of youth is here. Boissard catches these things and uses them to color the larger self-discovery process that is a familiar theme in young adult fiction, all the while bringing it home to La Marette, where the garden gate has been left open, the walnuts are ready for shelling, and where, as Pauline says in *A Matter of Feeling:* ". . .you are gently greeted by

the scent of polished wood, baked apples, and the heavy velvet from which curtains used to be made. And there are sounds, too—the everyday sounds of a happy house."

—Tracy J. Sukraw

———

BOLTON, Evelyn. *See* BUNTING, (Anne) Eve(lyn).

———

BOND, Nancy

Nationality: American. **Born:** Bethesda, Maryland, 8 January 1945. **Education:** Mount Holyoke College, B.A. 1966; College of Librarianship, Aberystwyth, Dyfed, Wales, Dip.Lib., 1972. **Career:** Correspondent in sales department, Houghton Mifflin, publishers, Boston, 1966-67; head of overseas sales publicity, Tutorial Books, Oxford University Press, London, England, 1967-68; Assistant Children's Librarian, Lincoln Public Library, Massachusetts, 1969-71; Head Librarian, Levi Heywood Memorial Library, Gardner, Massachusetts, 1973-75; administrative assistant, Massachuetts Audubon Society, Lincoln, 1976-77. Since 1979, Instructor in Children's Literature, Simmons College, Boston; since 1980, salesperson, Barrow Book Store, Concord. Director, Mount Holyoke Alumnae *Quarterly,* 1979-82. **Awards:** Newbery honor, *Boston Globe—Horn Book* honor, International Reading Association and the Welsh Arts Council, all 1976, for *A String in the Harp; Boston Globe—Horn Book* honor, 1981, for *The Voyage Begun.* **Address:** 109 Valley Rd., Concord, MA 01742, U.S.A.

PUBLICATIONS FOR YOUNG ADULTS

Fiction

Country of Broken Stone. New York, Atheneum, 1980.
The Voyage Begun. New York, Atheneum, 1981.
A Place to Come Back To. New York, Macmillan, 1984.
Another Shore. New York, Macmillan, 1988.
Truth to Tell. New York, Macmillan, 1994.
the Love of Friends. New York, McElderry and Simon & Schuster, 1997.

PUBLICATIONS FOR CHILDREN

Fiction

A String in the Harp. Atheneum, 1976.
The Best of Enemies. Atheneum, 1978.

*

Biography: Entry in *Fifth Book of Junior Authors & Illustrators,* New York, H.W. Wilson, 1983; essay in *Something about the Author Autobiography Series,* Volume 13, Detroit, Gale, 1992; essay in *Speaking for Ourselves, Too* compiled and edited by Donald R. Gallo, National Council of Teachers of English, 1993.

Critical Studies: Entry in *Children's Literature Review,* Volume 11, Detroit, Gale, 1986.

Nancy Bond comments:

Fiction has a unique power to connect us to people we would otherwise never meet—not only the characters in stories, but the writers who create them. Stories can make us think about ourselves, the world we share, and how it looks through someone else's eyes; they can make us feel less lonely, help us to put feelings into words and identify them. When I began to write stories I discovered that writing is a way of finding out about myself—what I think about things that matter to me, like the way families and friendships work, the responsibilities involved in loving, the challenges of accepting change, the different ways people have of solving the same problem.

*   *   *

Coping with life's changing patterns is ever constant, often difficult, and frequently, for children, especially traumatic. In her six novels to date Nancy Bond explores this nebulous theme through a variety of stories, each with different settings, individualized plots, and highly distinctive characters.

In *A String in the Harp* Bond uses the change theme as scaffolding around which she builds a strong, powerful story about a family's struggles to rebuild their lives after the mother dies in a car accident. David, the father, takes his children to Wales where they gradually learn, after many false starts and tattered feelings, to be a family again. This adjustment to a life without their mother, to each other as separate identities, and to a new and foreign place is skillfully molded into an intriguing and diverting story. Adding further dimension is a carefully threaded, gripping fantasy about the Welsh bard Taliesin's harp key, lost in the sixth century and returned, under strange and fantastical circumstances, by twelve-year-old Peter. This harp key supplies a pivotal point in the family's coming together and is Bond's means of melding her story into a cohesive whole.

The Best of Enemies uses a similar theme but one handled much differently. Charlotte, who has enjoyed being the youngest child in a close, loving Massachusetts family, finds herself facing numerous changes: her mother has gone back to work, her sister has become involved with her own problems, one of her brothers has married, and her ''special brother'' is pursuing his own life, leaving her behind. Unwillingly she is drawn into a community scuffle, played out against the annual Patriot's Day festivity, but through this involvement Charlotte is able to face and accept the changing patterns of life. Once more Bond's theme becomes the structural beam while the plot is the brick work that holds it all together. In *A Place to Come Back To* Bond returns to the characters and setting of *The Best of Enemies.* Charlotte, now fifteen, once more finds her inner world in turmoil as her interest in Oliver heightens, and she finds she needs to make decisions she is not sure she is ready for.

Set along Hadrian's Wall in England, *Country of Broken Stone* describes how Valerie and Edward's marriage forces adjustment on their newly combined families. Penelope, the protagonist, comfortable in the old, quiet, and organized life, finds the large, noisy group and her responsibilities as stepsister disquieting. Into this Bond introduces another troubling element—Ran, a local boy who arouses Penelope's curiosity and interest but whose upbringing, beliefs, and background are entirely alien to her own. Local legends with foreboding undertones, continued problems at Valerie's archaeological dig, and a frightening brushfire highlight the suspense and broaden the impact of the family dynamics, eventually testing Penelope's feelings for her entire family and Ran as well.

The Voyage Begun explores the theme of people's reaction to change, this time on several levels. Eleven-year-old Mickey, a rebellious, feisty girl, fights against change within herself as she comes to care first for a crotchety old boatbuilder and later for sixteen-year-old Paul who befriends her. Their struggle to help the old man after his home and boat are destroyed by vandals is set in a futuristic time on Cape Cod, when the world is quickly running out of energy, a crisis Bond uses to strengthen her theme as she subtly depicts the various characters reacting to their changing environment.

Another Shore is set in the reconstructed village of Louisbourg, Nova Scotia. Using time travel as a vehicle, Bond propels eighteen-year-old Lynn back to 1744. Time becomes the plot's antagonist as Lynn, unable to return to the twentieth century, struggles to cope in an entirely different world.

All of these books are peopled with finely etched characters whose problems, sensitivities, joys, and successes are so succinctly defined that readers easily become involved in their lives. However, such definitive portrayals, plus the author's penchant for highly detailed descriptions, create exceptionally long books for the child reader and bring Bond her greatest criticism.

At the same time this length allows the author to distinctively place her story, thoroughly probe feelings, develop intricate, multilevelled plots, and give a depth not often found in children's books. Although some paring could be accomplished without tempering the effect, the cross-generational friendship found in *The Best of Enemies* and *The Voyage Begun* and the mixing of people from different backgrounds in *A String in the Harp* and *Country of Broken Stone* are successful partly because of this slow and careful building. Readers who take the time will come away with echoes of well-turned phrases and vivid scenes and will have found rich, imaginative tales to long remember.

—Barbara Elleman

BONHAM, Frank

Nationality: American. **Born:** Los Angeles, California, 25 February 1914. **Education:** Glendale Junior College, California. **Military Service:** Served in U.S. Army, 1942-43. **Family:** Married Gloria Bailey in 1938; three sons. **Career:** Self-employed writer. Ghostwriter of western stories for Ed Earl Repp during the late 1930s; contributor of approximately five hundred short stories, novels, and novelettes to magazines, including *Saturday Evening Post* serials, short stories to *McCall's, American,* and to mystery and western magazines; former director, CRASH Inc. (Community Resources And Self-Help). **Awards:** Mystery Writers of America

Edgar Allan Poe Award runner-up, 1964, for *Honor Bound,* 1967, for *The Mystery of the Red Tide,* 1969, for *Mystery of the Fat Cat;* a notable book citation by the American Library Association, and George C. Stone Center for Children's Book Award, 1967, for *Durango Street;* Woodward Park School Annual Book Award, 1971, for *Viva Chicano;* Southern California Council on Literature for Children and Young People prize for a "notable body of work," 1980. **Died:** 17 December 1989.

PUBLICATIONS FOR YOUNG ADULTS

Fiction

Burma Rifles: A Story of Merrill's Marauders. New York, Crowell, 1960.
War beneath the Sea. New York, Crowell, 1962.
Deepwater Challenge. New York, Crowell, 1963.
Honor Bound. New York, Crowell, 1963.
The Loud, Resounding Sea. New York, Crowell, 1963.
Speedway Contender. New York, Crowell, 1964.
Durango Street. New York, Dutton, 1965.
The Mystery of the Red Tide, illustrated by Brinton Turkle. New York, Dutton, 1966.
Mystery in Little Tokyo, illustrated by Kazue Mizumura. New York, Dutton, 1966.
The Ghost Front. New York, Dutton, 1968.
Mystery of the Fat Cat, illustrated by Alvin Smith. New York, Dutton, 1968.
The Nitty Gritty, illustrated by Alvin Smith. New York, Dutton, 1968.
The Vagabundos. New York, Dutton, 1969.
Viva Chicano. New York, Dutton, 1970.
Chief. New York, Dutton, 1971.
Cool Cat. New York, Dutton, 1971.
The Friends of the Loony Lake Monster. New York, Dutton, 1972.
Hey, Big Spender! New York, Dutton, 1972.
A Dream of Ghosts. New York, Dutton, 1973.
The Golden Bees of Tulami. New York, Dutton, 1974.
The Missing Persons League. New York, Dutton, 1975.
The Rascals from Haskell's Gym. New York, Dutton, 1977.
Devilhorn. New York, Dutton, 1978.
The Forever Formula. New York, Dutton, 1979.
Gimme an H, Gimme an E, Gimme an L, Gimme a P. New York, Scribner, 1980.
Premonitions. New York, Holt, Rinehart, 1984.

Plays

Television Series: *Wells Fargo, Restless Gun, Shotgun Slade,* and *Death Valley Days.*

PUBLICATIONS FOR ADULTS

Novels

Lost Stage Valley. New York, Simon and Schuster, 1948; Kingswood, Surrey, World's Work, 1950.
Bold Passage. New York, Simon and Schuster, 1950; London, Hodder and Stoughton, 1951.
Blood on the Land. New York, Ballantine, 1952; London, Muller, 1955.

Snaketrack. New York, Simon and Schuster, 1952; as *The Outcast of Crooked River,* London, Hodder and Stoughton, 1953.
The Feud at Spanish Ford. New York, Ballantine, 1954.
Night Raid. New York, Ballantine, 1954.
Rawhide Guns. New York, Popular Library, 1955; as *Border Guns,* London, Muller, 1956.
Defiance Mountain. New York, Popular Library, 1956; London, Consul, 1962.
Hardrock. New York, Ballantine, 1958; London, Muller, 1960.
Tough Country. New York, Dell, and London, Muller, 1958.
Last Stage West. New York, Dell, and London, Muller, 1959.
The Sound of Gunfire. New York, Dell, 1959; London, Consul, 1960.
One for Sleep. New York, Fawcett, 1960; London, Muller, 1961.
The Skin Game. New York, Fawcett, 1962; London, Muller, 1963.
Trago. . . . New York, Dell, 1962.
By Her Own Hand. Derby, Connecticut, Monarch, 1963.
Cast a Long Shadow. New York, Simon and Schuster, 1964.
Logan's Choice. New York, Fawcett, 1964.
Break for the Border. New York, Berkley, 1980.
Fort Hogan. New York, Berkley Publishing, 1980.
The Eye of the Hunter. New York, Evans, 1989.
That Bloody Bozeman Trail-Stagecoach West. New York, Tor, 1990.

Short Stories

The Wild Breed. New York, Lion, 1955.
The Best Western Stories of Frank Bonham, edited by Bill Pronzini. Athens, Swallow Press/Ohio University Press, 1989.

*

Biography: Essay in *Something about the Author Autobiography Series,* Volume 3, Detroit, Gale, 1972; entry in *Authors and Artists for Young Adults,* Volume 1, Detroit, Gale, 1989.

Manuscript Collection: Kerlan Collection, University of Minnesota, Minneapolis.

Critical Study: Entry in *Contemporary Literary Criticism,* Volume 12, Detroit, Gale, 1980.

*　　*　　*

In 1965, the riots in the Watts section of Los Angeles left that area of the city in blackened ruins, reminding many people of the burned-out, bombed cities of World War II Europe. That same year, *Durango Street,* a ground-breaking young adult novel by Frank Bonham, was published. Rufus Henry, the black teenage protagonist, typified many of the youths and youth gangs existing in Los Angeles at the time of the 1965 riots. Rufus is a self-assured teenager who is paroled from a juvenile detention camp and immediately gets involved in an urban ghetto gang, the Moors. As the most clever and resourceful member, he quickly becomes the gang leader. The conflicts between the Moors and a rival gang, the Gassers, results in violence. However, a young black social worker attempts to direct the gang rivalry and activities into more constructive competition.

Much like *The Outsiders* by S.E. Hinton, another landmark young adult novel published two years later, *Durango Street* was not the typical young adult novel. Writing about a black teenager growing up and living in a ghetto was not the usual setting or model character that teenagers normally read about in the young adult books available in the early '60s. Bonham was, in part, responsible for introducing social realism into young adult fiction. Prior to this, there was very little realistic fiction being written for young adults. Most young adult books depicted the family-oriented teenager dealing with a problem or self-identity crisis. Conflicts in the earlier novels revolved around dating, cars, and teenage social life. Invariably, the main character was aided and supported by understanding middle-class parents living in a middle-class setting, and the resolution of the novel usually was a positive, happy one for the main teenage character. Rufus Henry in *Durango Street* does not fit this mold at all. He has grown up in a fatherless home, with a hardworking mother overwhelmed by the demands of parenting a teenage son. He has no father figure to turn to for guidance, and as a member of an underprivileged minority, he sees little hope for a promising future.

Like many of his novels, Bonham relied on field research to write *Durango Street,* attending the meetings of street gangs and meetings between social workers and the parents of gang members. He also visited a detention camp to observe the day-to-day life of incarcerated youths. Thus, the novel accurately depicts people and their problems in an urban slum setting that most teenagers had never before encountered in their reading. Bonham deals with the subject and characters sympathetically. He does not condemn Rufus for his actions but shows a black teenager who has the potential of escaping from poverty by developing his talents as an athlete and leader. The reader sees Rufus making the decision to complete high school and to aspire to attend college.

Bonham's earlier books for young adults were adventure tales. *Burma Rifles: A Story of Merrill's Marauders* was based on a story told to him by a police sergeant in Little Tokyo, Los Angeles. Bonham pursued the story about Japanese-American men imprisoned in an internment camp who were recruited to fight behind the enemy lines in Burma. Other adventure tales followed, including *War beneath the Sea* and *Speedway Contender,* to name a few. After the publication of *Durango Street,* he began writing mysteries aimed at a young audience—*Mystery of the Red Tide, Mystery in Little Tokyo, The Ghost Front,* and *Mystery of the Fat Cat.*

In looking at the books Bonham has written for young adults, one is struck by the many different subjects and topics he has covered—gangs, teenage suicide, auto racing, missing persons, jungle warfare. He has commented that he is a do-gooder in his books for young people. In dealing with such subjects as delinquency, he hoped his books would have a positive effect on teenager readers with personal problems. His last novel, *Gimme an H, Gimme an E, Gimme an L, Gimme a P,* published in 1980, deals with teen suicide. In writing the novel, Bonham noted that suicide is the principal cause of death among young adults, and that he hoped the novel would come to the attention of young readers with emotional problems who may have contemplated or were contemplating suicide.

Although Bonham has chosen to write about subjects that are not pleasant, his social consciousness throughout his novels is evident. He writes about significant social problems and treats them with authenticity. His background research—talking with students and counselors, exploring settings, be it an urban slum or prison—makes his novels believable to his audience. While he may be didactic, he does it with such subtlety that his young adult audience can accept it.

—Donald J. Kenney

BOSSE, Malcolm Joseph

Nationality: American. **Born:** Detroit, Michigan, 6 May 1926. **Education:** Yale University, B.A., 1950; University of Michigan, M.A., 1956; New York University, Ph.D., 1969. **Military Service:** United States Navy, 1950-54; served in United States Army and United States Merchant Marines. **Family:** Married Laura Mack (second marriage); two sons (one from previous marriage). **Career:** Editorial writer, *Barron's Financial Weekly,* New York City, 1950-52; free-lance writer, 1957-66; novelist, since 1959; professor of English, City College of the City University of New York, New York City, 1969-91; lecturer in India, Bangladesh, Burma, Thailand, Malaysia, Singapore, Taiwan, China, Hong Kong, Japan, and Fiji Islands. **Awards:** Masefield Award, Yale University, 1949; Avery and Jule Hopwood Awards, University of Michigan, 1956; *Saturday Review of Literature*'s best novels of the year citation, 1960; University Scholar Award, New York University, 1969; Newberry Library Fellowship, 1970; Edgar Allan Poe nomination for best first mystery, 1974; Edgar Allan Poe nomination for best mystery of the year, 1975; Society of the Dictionary of International Biography certificate of merit, 1976; National Endowment for the Arts creative writing fellowship, 1977-1978; Fulbright-Hays lectureship grants for India, 1978 and 1979, and for Indonesia, 1987; American Library Association Notable Book citation, 1979, 1981, 1982; Library of Congress best books of the year citation, 1980; Dorothy Canfield Fisher Award nomination, 1981; German Television ZDF Schulerexpress Preis der Leseratten, 1984; Dutch Children's Book Prize, 1984; Prix du livre pour la jeunesse de la fondation de France, 1986; Prix Lecture-Jeuness 1987; National Council of Social Studies Teachers notable book in the field of social studies citation, 1981 and 1982; Deutscher Jugendliteraturpreis nomination, 1983, award, 1984; Austrian Ministry of Education and Arts Honor List of Book Awards, 1982; American Book Award nomination, 1982; Parent's Choice Award, 1982 and 1994; Omar Award, 1982. **Address:** 1407 E. Madison #30, Seattle, Washington 98122, U.S.A.

PUBLICATIONS FOR YOUNG ADULTS

The Seventy-nine Squares. New York, Crowell, 1979.
Cave Beyond Time. New York, Crowell, 1980.
Ganesh. New York, Crowell, 1981; as *Ordinary Magic,* Sunburst, 1993.
The Barracuda Gang. New York, Crowell, 1983.
Captives of Time. New York, Delacorte, 1987.
Deep Dream of the Rain Forest. New York, Farrar, Straus, & Giroux, 1993.
The Examination. New York, Farrar, Straus, & Giroux, 1994.
Tusk and Stone. Arden, North Carolina, Front Street Press, 1996.

PUBLICATIONS FOR ADULTS

The Journey of Tao Kim Nam. New York, Doubleday, 1959.
The Incident at Naha. New York, Simon and Schuster, 1972.
The Man Who Loved Zoos. New York, Putnam, 1974.
The Warlord. New York, Simon and Schuster, 1983.
Fire in Heaven. New York, Simon and Schuster, 1986.
Stranger at the Gate. New York, Simon and Schuster, 1989.
Mister Touch. New York, Ticknor and Fields, 1991.
The Vast Memory of Love. New York, Ticknor and Fields, 1992.

*

Critical Studies: Entry in *Speaking for Ourselves, Too,* compiled and edited by Donald R. Gallo, Urbana, Illinois, National Council of Teachers of English, 1993, 21-22; review of *The Examination,* in *Kirkus Reviews,* August 15, 1994, 1121; review of *Tusk and Stone* by Debbie Carton in *Booklist,* Vol. 92, No.7, 1995, 616; "Malcolm Bosse," in *World Authors, 1985-1990,* edited by Vineta Colby, New York, H. W. Wilson, 1995; entry in *Something about the Author,* edited by Kevin S. Hile, Vol. 84, Detroit, Gale Research, 1996.

Malcolm Bosse comments:

I think the author of books for young people must face this kind of reader:

1. Someone who demands clarity of expression—no vague sentences that lead nowhere except back to the author's ego.

2. Someone without a political agenda.

3. Someone whose imagination ranges far and wide—probably beyond that of the author.

4. Someone who will go in a book to the strangest places and listen to a character even if he is weird.

5. Someone who demands honesty in writing.

Tough to write for such a reader.

*   *   *

Malcolm Bosse is recognized in the literary world as a powerful writer for both adults and young people. The stories he tells and his significant insights into the cultures he describes are the result of his travels, which began after high school when he joined the merchant marines. His six years of military service, which included significant travels in Asia, provided subject matter and personal experiences for his novels. His academic work in American studies—sociology, economics, and history—and research and teaching at the university level provided the refinement for Bosse's already existing desire to write. Bosse reveals a complexity of insights into characters, historical eras, geographical and social realms, and universal themes explained within the contexts of diverse cultures. His views are shared with his readers through a masterful weaving of setting, plot design, and characters true to their cultural heritage. Bosse's powerful writing has been described by reviewers as sensitive, classic, and richly textured. Of his own writing, Bosse said in *World Authors, 1985-1990:* "Throughout my life I have maintained a romantic belief in the power of the imagination. Life traps many of us, but the imagination, as an instrument of change and escape, enables us to break out

into the larger world of possibilities. I think this is especially true for the lonely and the disaffected who can find a way through art, literature, and music to make their lives definitely better."

For young readers, the books of Malcolm Bosse offer examples of literary excellence in creating detailed realistic settings, believable characters, and complex plots that enrich both the reading and writing experiences of students. Bosse described the literary quality of his young adult books by comparing them to his works for adults in *Speaking for Ourselves, Too:* "The vocabulary I use is essentially the same for both, the plots are similarly intricate, the characters equally complicated. I don't believe in concessions to young readers in matters of style and difficulty of content. Some of the books I most fondly remember reading as a kid were beyond me in some ways, but the stretch it took to understand them contributed to their impact and lasting impression."

Bosse's books are quite diverse in setting, both in geography and era. Prehistoric America, fourteenth-century Europe, China in the 1920s, and modern India are but a few "worlds" on the continuum of time and place that he has opened for readers of his books. Yet they share the common element of a young protagonist in search of deeper meanings of life. His first book for young adults, *The Seventy-nine Squares,* began his contributions to this field with a story set in an American community. Eric, the main character, is fourteen and on probation for vandalism. He befriends an old man whom he later discovers is an ex-convict who was convicted of killing his wife. With limited time to live due to cancer, Mr. Beck is living with his daughter in whose garden he invites Eric to embark on a project—studying each of seventy-nine squares that make up the garden. As Eric learns to "see" nature's community within each square, a compelling story is told as the town's people try to drive Mr. Beck away and Eric's old gang decides to reclaim their now distant member. Critics have praised the lessons in friendship, loyalty, understanding and forgiveness within the story, and the book has won numerous national and international awards.

Bosse's second book, *Cave Beyond Time,* mixes fact and legend as the main character travels in time to prehistoric America. In *Ganesh,* young Jeffrey, who has been born and raised for fourteen years in India, becomes an orphan and must live in the Midwest of America with an aunt. As would be expected, the culture in which Jeffrey has been raised is not well accepted in his new community. However, when Jeffrey's understandings of the resistance theories of the *Satyagraha* become the vehicle that helps save the community from an unwanted planned highway, he gains acceptance.

Captives of Time is set in medieval Europe. Two children set out to find their uncle after their parents are killed. One of them, the head-strong female protagonist, has a vision—to build a clock tower she and her uncle designed—and the story focuses on overcoming the obstacles in her way. Bosse was again praised by critics for not condescendingly telling a story but bringing to life this era. *Deep Dream of the Rain Forest* finds another orphaned young person involved in adventure. Joining his uncle with the British government at Borneo, fifteen-year old Harry is taken deep into the jungles by a young Iban tribal member who is seeking the meaning of a dream. Together with a young girl, outcast because of a foot deformity, the three journey deep into the jungles. While they survive the rain forest's dangers, each becomes a stronger individual as they learn to value each other. In *The Examination,* two young brothers set out across Ming Dynasty China as one pursues the path of a Confucian scholar accompanied by his loyal but worldly brother. This vivid work of historical fiction has been described by Kirkus review as "a graphic picture of 16th century China—its violence, ceremony, scholarship, and strict class order—in this stimulating and timeless story."

Tusk and Stone recreates the world of seventh-century India as a young Brahman and his sister leave their parents to travel with a caravan to Kashi to begin formal studies. After the caravan is attacked and Arjun's sister is captured, his compelling adventure unfolds as he is also captured, sold into an army where he becomes an elephant driver of great renown, and later uses his talent as a master stonecutter of religious sculptures. In *Booklist*, Debbie Carton called *Tusk and Stone* a "deeply spiritual novel that challenges the readers to contemplate large issues—fate, God, and one's place in the world. It is also an exciting story, a seamless blend of fiction and history that skillfully incorporates the complex social, political, and religious structures of ancient India. Arjun's struggle to make sense of the random disasters of his life will speak eloquently to teens seeking their own raison d'etre."

As readers are drawn into distant cultures and eras, they easily identify with Bosse's strong-willed, adventuresome young protagonists. By not sacrificing rich literary style and content, Bosse's novels provide entertainment and experiences for learning social studies in authentic contexts as well as the opportunities to understand other cultures and perspectives.

—Janelle B. Mathis

BOSTON, L(ucy) M(aria Wood)

Nationality: British. **Born:** Southport, Lancashire, England, 10 December 1892. **Education:** Downs School, Seaford, Sussex; Somerville College, Oxford. **Family:** Married in 1917 (marriage dissolved 1935); one son. **Career:** Author of children's books. Briefly trained as a nurse before going to France to treat the wounded during the First World War; indulged herself in the cultural arts while traveling through Europe, 1935-39; began a personal restoration project of a manor house at Hemingford Grey, which later served as a background for her books; started her literary career at the age of sixty-two. **Awards:** Carnegie (commended), 1954, and Lewis Carroll Shelf Award, 1969, for *The Children of Green Knowe,* which was also named an ALA Notable Book; Carnegie (commended), 1958, for *The Chimneys of Green Knowe;* Carnegie Medal, 1961, for *A Stranger at Green Knowe,* which was also named an ALA Notable Book; *The River at Green Knowe* was named an ALA Notable Book; Spring Book Festival Awards (middle honor), 1967, for *The Sea Egg.* **Died:** 25 May 1990.

PUBLICATIONS FOR YOUNG ADULTS

Fiction

The Children of Green Knowe, illustrated by son, Peter Boston. London, Faber, 1954; New York, Harcourt, 1955.
The Chimneys of Green Knowe, illustrated by P. Boston. London, Faber, 1958; as *Treasure of Green Knowe,* New York, Harcourt, 1958.
The River at Green Knowe, illustrated by P. Boston. London, Faber, and New York, Harcourt, 1959.

A Stranger at Green Knowe, illustrated by P. Boston. London, Faber, and New York, Harcourt, 1961.
An Enemy at Green Knowe, illustrated by P. Boston. London, Faber, and New York, Harcourt, 1964.
The Stones of Green Knowe, illustrated by P. Boston. London, Bodley Head, and New York, Atheneum, 1976.

PUBLICATIONS FOR CHILDREN

Fiction

The Castle of Yew, illustrated by Margery Gill. London, Bodley Head, and New York, Harcourt, 1965.
The Sea Egg, illustrated by P. Boston. London, Faber, and New York, Harcourt, 1967.
The House that Grew, illustrated by Caroline Hemming. London, Faber, 1969.
Nothing Said, illustrated by P. Boston. London, Faber, and New York, Harcourt, 1971.
The Guardians of the House, illustrated by P. Boston. London, Bodley Head, 1974; New York, Atheneum, 1975.
The Fossil Snake, illustrated by P. Boston. London, Bodley Head, 1975; New York, Atheneum, 1976.

PUBLICATIONS FOR ADULTS

Fiction

Yew Hall. London, Faber, 1954.
Persephone. London, Collins, 1969; as *Strongholds,* New York, Harcourt, 1969.

Plays

The Horned Man; or, Whom Will You Send to Fetch Her Away? London, Faber, 1970.

Nonfiction

Memory in a House (autobiography). London, Bodley Head, 1973; New York, Macmillan, 1974.
Perverse and Foolish: A Memoir of Childhood and Youth. London, Bodley Head, and New York, Atheneum, 1979.

*

Biography: Entry in *Third Book of Junior Authors,* New York, H.W. Wilson, 1972.

Critical Study: *Lucy Boston* by Jasper A. Rose, London, Bodley Head, 1965, New York, Walck, 1966; entry in *Children's Literature Review,* Volume 3, Detroit, Gale, 1978.

*   *   *

Lucy Boston lived an exceptionally long and active life, and she was creative in many spheres. Her achievements include a dazzling collection of masterpiece patchwork quilts and a garden of great beauty and subtlety. She did not begin to write until she was sixty.

In 1937 she bought the Manor House at Hemingford Grey and restored it. Her deep and abiding attachment to the house lit a long fuse, which later turned her into a writer in whose every work (*The Sea Egg* is the sole exception) the house appears, fictionalized as "Green Knowe." Her love of the house and its setting shines clear.

According to her own account in *Memory in a House,* Faber would have published *The Children of Green Knowe* on their adult list, alongside *Yew Hall,* her first adult novel, had Boston not wished it to be illustrated. Thus as if by accident she found her true vocation, for it was as a children's writer that she attained a worldwide reputation. In addition to an adult novel and some fine poetry, she wrote twelve children's books, moving across the past and present of her house, peopling it and giving "a local habitation and a name" to the anonymous past generations who lived there. It is worth noticing that in this enterprise, love of the house is matched by love of children; it was their company she called up to fill the void of the past.

Jasper Rose's monograph on Lucy Boston's work (Bodley Head, 1965) is at some pains to distinguish her from other children's writers, but the truth is more interesting: together with William Mayne and Philippa Pearce, who both began to publish for children at about the same time, Lucy Boston's "Green Knowe" books caught a wave. Lucy at sixty was fully in touch with the spirit of the times, and was one of a galaxy of talented writers, exploring and mapping the possibilities of children's books as fully serious literature.

Three aspects of Lucy Boston's writing made her quintessentially a children's writer. First, the limpid clarity and simplicity of her prose which made thought of subtlety and delicacy easily accessible. Second, her total lack of condescension to young readers. "I do not know how anyone can judge of what they write, unless they are writing for themselves," she has said (*Memory in a House.*) Third, it came naturally to her as a writer to take up her stand on the large ground which adults and children have in common.

Time, change, memory—the mutability of people, and the continuity of talismanic objects were among her recurring themes. Other writers have worked with those, but she has never had her equal at evoking the physical sensations of the fleeting moment— at awakening a rapt attention to the mercurial beauties of the natural world. Speaking to the Children's Book Circle in 1968, Lucy Boston said:

> I would like to remind adults of joy, now obsolete, and I would like to encourage children to use and trust their senses for themselves at first hand—their ears, eyes and noses, their fingers and soles of their feet, their skins and their breathing, their muscular joy and rhythms and heartbeats, their instinctive loves and pity and awe of the unknown. . . .

These words illuminate clearly what it was about children which so attracted her to writing about and for them. In the startling vividness with which tactile and sensory experience is observed and set down—in the sea-rough pebble with "a drag like a kitten's tongue," the cat's eyes that "had a vertical black slit that was like the gap between curtains," or the golden goblet made from a foil sweet paper—the experiences of the fictional children display the undimmed sharpness of the author's perceptions, the reverie of a childhood lived on into late old age.

The first of the sequence, *The Children of Green Knowe,* sets the framework of all the books. Alone in winter, visiting his grandmother, Tolly plays hide-and-seek with children who have lived there in the past. They are not ghosts, but presences. Of all the crowd of children past and present who people the books, it is Susan the blind girl, heroine of *The Chimneys of Green Knowe,* who really stands out; Lucy Boston's talent is peculiarly apt for conveying the world of a child who lacking one sense has the other senses honed razor sharp, who being a girl with an insensitive and conventional mother must struggle for any independence, any life of her own.

For besides the beauty of the natural world, at its pinnacle in her beloved house and garden, one other thing fired Lucy Boston's imagination to incandescence. That was her indignant sympathy for all subordinates, for all whose personality is assailed, whom the world is trying to pressure into being other than what they are. The majority of such embattled selves are and have always been children, though the finest example in the whole of her work is the magnificent tour de force with which she identifies with Hanno, the captive gorilla in *A Stranger at Green Knowe,* the most serious and the best of the books.

Atmosphere rather than plot is Lucy Boston's forte. The plots would be conventional or whimsical if not transformed by the intensity with which everything is imagined. It would be possible to suggest that all the children in all the books are really one child, and that child is as much a projection of the author as the eccentric and kindly Mrs. Oldknowe, the owner of the fictional house and grandmother and friend to the children, past and present. But one can only be grateful for the potent and lyrical talent which has enabled Lucy Boston to make a gift to her readers of her haunted and extraordinary house, her evocative garden, and her joyful, enhanced awareness of the natural world.

—Jill Paton Walsh

BRADBURY, Ray (Douglas)

Pseudonyms: D.R. Banat, Leonard Douglas, William Elliott, Douglas Spaulding, Leonard Spaulding, Brett Sterling. **Nationality:** American. **Born:** Waukegan, Illinois, 22 August 1920. **Education:** Los Angeles High School, graduated 1938. **Family:** Married Marguerite Susan McClure in 1947; four daughters. **Career:** Newsboy in Los Angeles, California, 1940-43. Since 1943, full-time writer. President, Science-Fantasy Writers of America, 1951-53; member of the Board of Directors, Screen Writers Guild of America, 1957-61. **Awards:** O. Henry prize, 1947, for short story "Homecoming," 1948, for short story "Powerhouse"; Best Author of 1949 in Science Fiction and Fantasy from the National Fantasy Fan Federation; Benjamin Franklin award for best story of 1953-54 in an American magazine, for "Sun and Shadow" in *The Reporter;* American Academy award, 1954; Commonwealth Club of California gold medal, 1954, for *Fahrenheit 451;* award from National Institute of Arts and Letters, 1954, for contribution to American literature; *New York Times* Best Illustrated Books of the Year, 1955, and Boys' Clubs of America Junior Book award, 1956, both for *Switch on the Night;* Golden Eagle award for screenwriting, 1957; Academy award nomination, 1963, for "Icarus Montgolfier Wright"; Mrs. Ann Radcliffe award, Count Dracula Society, 1965, 1971; Aviation and Space Writers award, 1968, for "An Impatient Gulliver above Our Roots," in *Life,* and 1979, for ABC-television documentary, "Infinite Space Beyond Apollo"; "Mars Is Heaven!" was selected for the Science Fiction Hall of Fame by the Science Fiction Writers of America, 1970; Valentine Davies award from the Writers Guild of America, West, 1974, for work in cinema; Life Achievement award from the World Fantasy Convention, 1977; Balrog award for best poet, 1979; Gandalf award, 1980; George Foster Peabody award from the University of Georgia, Emmy nomination from the Academy of Television Arts and Sciences, and American Film Festival Blue Ribbon award, all 1982, all for "The Electric Grandmother"; Jules Verne award, 1984; Body of Work award, PEN, 1985; Home Box Office Ace award for Writing a Dramatic Series, 1985, for *Ray Bradbury Theater;* Nebula Grand Master, 1988; Bram Stoker Life achievement award, 1989; D. Litt.: Whittier College, California, 1979. **Agent:** Don Congdon, Harold Matson Company, 276 Fifth Avenue, New York, New York 10010, U.S.A. **Address:** 10265 Cheviot Drive, Los Angeles, California 90064, U.S.A.

PUBLICATIONS

Novels

The Martian Chronicles. New York, Doubleday, 1950; as *The Silver Locusts,* London, Hart Davis, 1951.
Fahrenheit 451. New York, Ballantine, 1953; London, Hart Davis, 1954; 40th anniversary edition, with a foreword by Bradbury, New York, Simon & Schuster, 1993; with a new foreword by Bradbury, Thorndike, Maine, G.K. Hall, 1997.
Dandelion Wine. New York, Doubleday, and London, Hart Davis, 1957.
Something Wicked This Way Comes. New York, Simon and Schuster, 1962; London, Hart Davis, 1963.
Death Is a Lonely Business. New York, Knopf, 1985; London, Grafton, 1986.
The Dragon, illustrations by Ken Snyder. Round Top, New York, B. Munster, 1988.
A Graveyard for Lunatics: Another Tale of Two Cities. New York, Knopf, and London, Grafton, 1990.
Green Shadows, White Whale, illustrated by Edward Sorel. New York, Knopf, 1992.
Quicker than the Eye. New York, Avon Books, 1996.
Driving Blind. New York, Avon Books, 1997.

Short Stories

Dark Carnival. Sauk City, Wisconsin, Arkham House, 1947; abridged edition, London, Hamish Hamilton, 1948; abridged edition, as *The Small Assassin,* London, New English Library, 1962.
The Illustrated Man. New York, Doubleday, 1951; revised edition, London, Hart Davis, 1952.
The Golden Apples of the Sun. New York, Doubleday, 1953; revised edition, London, Hart Davis, 1953.
The October Country. New York, Ballantine, 1955; London, Hart Davis, 1956; with new introduction by the author, New York, Ballantine Books, 1996.
A Medicine for Melancholy. New York, Doubleday, 1959; revised edition, as *The Day It Rained Forever,* London, Hart Davis, 1959.
The Ghoul Keepers. Ontario, Canada, Pyramid Books, 1961.

The Machineries of Joy. New York, Simon and Schuster, and London, Hart Davis, 1964.
The Autumn People (comic adaptation). New York, Ballantine, 1965.
The Vintage Bradbury. New York, Random House, 1965.
Tomorrow Midnight (comic adaptation). New York, Ballantine, 1966.
Twice Twenty-Two (selection). New York, Doubleday, 1966.
Bloch and Bradbury: Ten Masterpieces of Science Fiction, with Robert Bloch. New York, Tower, 1969; as *Fever Dreams and Other Fantasies,* London, Sphere, 1970.
I Sing the Body Electric! New York, Knopf, 1969; London, Hart Davis, 1970.
Whispers from Beyond, with Robert Bloch. New York, Peacock Press, 1972.
Ray Bradbury: Selected Stories, edited by Anthony Adams. London, Harrap, 1975.
The Best of Bradbury. New York, Bantam, 1976.
Long after Midnight. New York, Knopf, 1976; London, Hart Davis MacGibbon, 1977.
The Aqueduct. Glendale, California, Squires, 1979.
To Sing Strange Songs. Exeter, Devon, Wheaton, 1979.
The Last Circus, and The Electrocution. Northridge, California, Lord John Press, 1980.
The Stories of Ray Bradbury. New York, Knopf, and London, Granada, 1980.
Dinosaur Tales. New York, Bantam, 1983.
A Memory of Murder. New York, Dell, 1984.
The Toynbee Convector. New York, Knopf, 1988; London, Grafton, 1989.
Contributor, *Urban Horrors: Stories,* edited by William F. Nolan and Martin H. Greenberg, illustrated by Robert W. Lavoie. Arlington Heights, Illinois, Dark Harvest, 1990.
The Ray Bradbury Chronicles (comic book adaptation). New York, Bantam Books, 1992-93.

Plays

The Meadow, in *Best One-Act Plays of 1947-48,* edited by Margaret Mayorga (produced Hollywood, 1960). New York, Dodd, Mead, 1948.
Way in the Middle of the Air (produced Hollywood, 1962).
The Anthem Sprinters and Other Antics (produced Beverly Hills, 1967; Los Angeles, 1968). New York, Dial Press, 1963.
To the Chicago Abyss (produced Los Angeles, 1964). Included in *The Wonderful Ice-Cream Suit and Other Plays,* 1972; Woodstock, Illinois, Dramatic Publishing Company, 1988.
The World of Ray Bradbury (produced Los Angeles, 1964; New York, 1965).
The Wonderful Ice-Cream Suit (produced Los Angeles, 1965; New York, 1987). Included in *The Wonderful Ice-Cream Suit and Other Plays,* 1972.
The Day It Rained Forever, music by Bill Whitefield (produced Edinburgh, 1988). New York, French, 1966.
Leviathan 99 (radio play). British Broadcasting Corporation, 1966; (produced Los Angeles, 1972).
The Pedestrian. New York, French, 1966.
Dandelion Wine, adaptation of his own story, music by Billy Goldenberg (produced New York, 1967). Woodstock, Illinois, Dramatic Publishing, 1988.
Any Friend of Nicholas Nickleby's Is a Friend of Mine (produced Hollywood, 1968).

Christus Apollo, music by Jerry Goldsmith (produced Los Angeles, 1969).

The Wonderful Ice-Cream Suit and Other Plays (includes *The Veldt* and *To the Chicago Abyss).* New York, Bantam, 1972; as *The Wonderful Ice-Cream Suit and Other Plays for Today, Tomorrow, and Beyond Tomorrow,* London, Hart Davis, 1973.

Madrigals for the Space Age, music by Lalo Schifrin (produced Los Angeles, 1976). Associated Music Publishers, 1972.

Pillar of Fire (produced Fullerton, California, 1973). Included in *Pillar of Fire and Other Plays,* 1975.

The Foghorn (produced New York, 1977). Included in *Pillar of Fire and Other Plays,* 1975.

Pillar of Fire and Other Plays for Today, Tomorrow, and Beyond Tomorrow (includes *Kaleidoscope, Pillar of Fire,* and *The Foghorn).* New York, Bantam, 1975.

That Ghost, That Bride of Time: Excerpts from a Play-in-Progress. Glendale, California, Squires, 1976.

The Martian Chronicles, adaptation of his own stories (produced Los Angeles, 1977).

Fahrenheit 451, adaptation of his own novel (produced Los Angeles, 1979).

The Veldt (produced London, 1980). Included in *The Wonderful Ice-Cream Suit and Other Plays,* 1972; Woodstock, Illinois, Dramatic Publishing, 1988.

Forever and the Earth (radio play). Athens, Ohio, Croissant, 1984.

A Device Out of Time. Woodstock, Illinois, Dramatic Publishing, 1986.

The Flying Machine. Woodstock, Illinois, Dramatic Publishing, 1986.

Falling Upward (produced Los Angeles, 1988).

Screenplays

With David Schwartz, *It Came from Outer Space.* Universal, 1952.

The Beast from 20,000 Fathoms. Warner Bros., 1953.

With John Huston, *Moby Dick.* Warner Bros., 1956.

With George Clayton Johnston, *Icarus Montgolfier Wright.* Format Films, 1961.

With Edwin Booth, *Picasso Summer* (as Douglas Spaulding). Warner Bros./Seven Arts, 1972.

Something Wicked This Way Comes. Walt Disney, 1983.

Television Plays

Shopping for Death, 1956, *Design for Loving,* 1958, *Special Delivery,* 1959, *The Faith of Aaron Menefee,* 1962, and *The Life Work of Juan Diaz* (all Alfred Hitchcock Presents series).

The Marked Bullet (*Jane Wyman's Fireside Theatre* series). 1956.

The Gift (*Steve Canyon* series). 1958.

The Tunnel to Yesterday (Trouble Shooters series). 1960.

I Sing the Body Electric! (*The Twilight Zone* series). 1962.

The Jail (*Alcoa Premiere* series). 1962.

The Groom (*Curiosity Shop* series). 1971.

Walking on Air. 1987.

The Coffin (from his own story). 1988.

Also author of forty-two scripts for *Ray Bradbury Television Theatre,* USA Cable Network, 1985-90.

Poetry

Old Ahab's Friend, and Friend to Noah, Speaks His Piece: A Celebration. Glendale, California, Squires, 1971.

When Elephants Last in the Dooryard Bloomed: Celebrations for Almost Any Day in the Year. New York, Knopf, 1973; London, Hart Davis MacGibbon, 1975.

That Son of Richard III: A Birth Announcement. Privately printed, 1974.

Man Dead? Then God Is Slain! Northridge, California State University, 1977.

Where Robot Mice and Robot Men Run Round in Robot Towns: New Poems, Both Light and Dark. New York, Knopf, 1977; London, Hart Davis MacGibbon, 1979.

The Bike Repairman. Northridge, California, Lord John Press, 1978.

Twin Hieroglyphs That Swim the River Dust. Northridge, California, Lord John Press, 1978.

The Author Considers His Resources. Northridge, California, Lord John Press, 1979.

This Attic Where the Meadow Greens. Northridge, California, Lord John Press, 1980.

The Ghosts of Forever, illustrated by Aldo Sessa. New York, Rizzoli, 1981.

The Haunted Computer and the Android Pope. New York, Knopf, and London, Granada, 1981.

Then Is All Love? It Is, It Is! Orange County Book Society, 1981.

The Complete Poems of Ray Bradbury. New York, Ballantine, 1982.

America. Northridge, California, Lord John Press, 1983.

The Love Affair. Northridge, California, Lord John Press, 1983.

To Ireland. Northridge, California, Lord John Press, 1983.

Forever and the Earth. Athens, Ohio, Croissant, 1984.

The Last Good Kiss, illustrated by Hans Burkhardt. Northridge, California State University, 1984.

Long after Ecclesiates. Goldstein Press, 1985.

Death Has Lost Its Charm for Me. Northridge, California, Lord John Press, 1987.

A Climate of Palettes. Northridge, California, Lord John Press, 1988.

With Cat for Comforter, illustrated by Louise Reinoehl Max. Salt Lake City, Gibbs Smith, 1997.

Dogs Think That Every Day Is Christmas, illustrated by Louise Reinoehl Max. Salt Lake City, Gibbs Smith, 1997.

Other

Editor, *Timeless Stories for Today and Tomorrow.* New York, Bantam, 1952.

Switch on the Night (for children). New York, Pantheon, and London, Hart Davis, 1955; pictures by Leo and Diane Dillon, New York, Knopf, 1993.

Editor, *The Circus of Dr. Lao and Other Improbable Stories.* New York, Bantam, 1956.

R Is for Rocket (for children). New York, Doubleday, 1962; London, Hart Davis, 1968.

S Is for Space (for children). New York, Doubleday, 1966; London, Hart Davis, 1968.

Teacher's Guide: Science Fiction, with Lewy Olfson. New York, Bantam, 1968.

Contributor, *Three to the Highest Power: Bradbury, Oliver, Sturgeon,* edited by William F. Nolan. New York, Avon, 1968.

The Halloween Tree (for children), illustrated by Joseph Mugnaini. New York, Knopf, 1972; London, Hart Davis MacGibbon, 1973.

Mars and the Mind of Man, with Bruce Murray, Arthur C. Clarke, Walter Sullivan, and Carl Sagan. New York, Harper, 1973.

Zen and the Art of Writing, and The Joy of Writing. Santa Barbara, California, Capra Press, 1973.

The Mummies of Guanajuato, photographs by Archie Lieberman. New York, Abrams, 1978.

Beyond 1984: Remembrance of Things Future. New York, Targ, 1979.

Los Angeles, photographs by West Light. Port Washington, New York, Skyline Press, 1984.

The Art of Playboy. New York, van der Marck Editions, 1985.

Orange County, photographs by Bill Ross and others. Port Washington, New York, Skyline Press, 1985.

The April Witch (for children), with Gary Kelley. Mankato, Minnesota, Creative Education, 1987.

Fever Dream (for children), illustrated by Darrel Anderson. New York, St. Martin's, 1987.

The Foghorn (for children), illustrated by Gary Kelley. Mankato, Minnesota, Creative Education, 1987.

The Other Foot (for children), with Gary Kelley. Mankato, Minnesota, Creative Education, 1987.

The Veldt (for children), with Gary Kelley. Mankato, Minnesota, Creative Education, 1987.

Zen in the Art of Writing. Santa Barbara, California, Capra Press, 1990.

The Smile. Mankato, Minnesota, Creative Education, 1991.

Yestermorrow: Obvious Answers to Impossible Futures (essays). Santa Barbara, California, Capra Press, 1991.

Editor, *A Day in the Life of Hollywood.* San Francisco, Collins, 1992.

*

Media Adaptations: *Fahrenheit 451* (film), Universal, 1966; *The Illustrated Man* (film), Warner Bros., 1969; *The Screaming Woman* (television movie), 1972; *The Foghorn* (filmstrip and cassette), Listening Library, 1975; *Frost and Fire* (filmstrip and cassette), Listening Library, 1975; *The Illustrated Man* (filmstrip and cassette), Listening Library, 1975; *A Sound of Thunder* (filmstrip and cassette), Listening Library, 1975; *There Will Come Soft Rains* (filmstrip and cassette), Listening Library, 1975; *Usher II* (filmstrip and cassette), Listening Library, 1975; *The Veldt* (filmstrip and cassette), Listening Library, 1975; *Bradbury Reads Bradbury* (recording), Listening Library, 1976; *Fahrenheit 451* (filmstrip and cassette), Listening Library, 1976; *The Illustrated Man* (cassette), Caedmon, 1976; *The Martian Chronicles* (cassette), Caedmon, 1976; *Murderer* (television movie), Boston, WGBH-TV, 1976; *The Veldt* (videocassette), Barr, 1979; *The Martian Chronicles* (television mini-series), NBC-TV, 1980; *The Small Assassin* (cassette), Caedmon, 1981; *All Summer in a Day* (videocassette), Learning Corp., 1982; *The Electric Grandmother* (television movie, based on *I Sing the Body Electric,* co-authored by Bradbury), NBC-TV, 1982; *Quest* (videocassette), Pyramid, 1983; *Forever and the Earth* (radio drama), Croissant, 1984; *Fantastic Tales of Ray Bradbury* (cassette), Listening Library, 1986; *Zukunftsmusik* (opera, by Georgia Holof and David Mettere, based on *Fahrenheit 451*), produced Fort Wayne, Indiana, 1988; *The Visitor* (videocassette), AIMS Media, 1989. Videocassettes based on short stories by Bradbury, produced by Atlantis Films and distributed by Beacon

Films include: *And So Died Riabouchinska, Coffin, The Emissary, The Fruit at the Bottom of the Bowl, Gotcha, The Man Upstairs, On the Orient North, Punishment without Crime, Skeleton, The Small Assassin, There Was an Old Woman,* and *Tyrannosaurus Rex.*

Biography: *The Ray Bradbury Companion: A Life and Career History, Photolog, and Comprehensive Checklist of Writings* (includes bibliography) by William F. Nolan, Detroit, Gale, 1975; entry in *Dictionary of Literary Biography,* Detroit, Gale, Volume 2, 1978; Volume 8, 1981; *Ray Bradbury* by Wayne L. Johnson, New York, Ungar, 1980; *Ray Bradbury* by David Morgen, Boston, Massachusetts, Twayne, 1986.

Bibliography: *Ray Bradbury,* edited by Joseph D. Olander and Martin H. Greenberg, New York, Taplinger, and Edinburgh, Harris, 1980.

Critical Studies: Introduction by Gilbert Highet to *The Vintage Bradbury,* 1965; entry in *Contemporary Literary Criticism,* Detroit, Gale, Vol. 1, 1973, Vol. 3, 1975, Vol. 10, 1979, Vol. 15, 1980, Vol. 42, 1987; *The Drama of Ray Bradbury* by Ben F. Indick, Baltimore, T-K Graphics, 1977; *The Bradbury Chronicles* by George Edgar Slusser, San Bernardino, California, Borgo Press, 1977; *Ray Bradbury and the Poetics of Reverie: Fantasy, Science Fiction, and the Reader* by William F. Toupence, Ann Arbor, UMI Research Press, 1984; *Ray Bradbury, Dramatist* by Ben P. Indick, 1989.

*   *   *

When asked how he would liked to be remembered by future generations, Ray Bradbury once replied "as a magician of ideas and words." Indeed, Bradbury is such a magician, and he is one of the twentieth century's most important storytellers and allegorists. An author who writes from personal experience and cultural inheritance, who relies on the history of ideas and free word association, and who threw his first million words away, Bradbury has proven himself a warlock of words and a teller of universal tales that incorporate myths, beliefs, themes, rituals, and character types that define both American and world cultures.

Bradbury's short stories, novels, stage plays, screen plays, poems, and radio plays appeal to all ages, and his dexterity with issues of youth and age, and coming-of-age, make his writing significant and meaningful to a wide-ranging public. He has always drawn heavily from his personal experience, making autobiography the largest overriding thematic element of his work. Bradbury is a visionary who is sensitive to the emotions and idiosyncrasies and wonders that comprise the human experience. If at times the logic of his stories is suspect, his ability to solve the human equation makes these logistical errors insignificant.

Bradbury's first professional sale, entitled "Pendulum," was co-authored with Henry Hasse and appeared in the November 1941 issue of *Super Science Stories.* Bradbury, however, had had a variety of short stories published in science fiction and fantasy fanzines as early as January 1938. By the mid-1940s, Bradbury was regularly appearing in several "pulp" magazines.

Some of his early contributions to *Weird Tales* and other such periodicals were the beginnings of his first major story type and thematic device: these were stories of the "Dark Carnival." In these tales, Bradbury used the travelling carnival as a metaphor for life. His first published book, a collection of "Dark Carnival" stories, weird tales, and others, was published in 1947 and reappeared in 1955 as *The October Country.* By 1962, several of the themes and ideas from the "Dark Carnival" stories were adapted, synthesized, and expanded into the novel *Something Wicked This Way Comes.* Ultimately, four Bradbury short-story collections have been framed by the "Dark Carnival" mythos. Between and beyond *Dark Carnival* and *The October Country,* there were *The Illustrated Man* and *The Small Assassin.* Bradbury published a second "Dark Carnival" novel, *Death Is a Lonely Business,* in 1985.

The genres and related story types that Ray Bradbury has created and contributed to since those early "pulp" days are numerous. A representative list includes the "Dark Carnival" stories, gothic tales, weird tales, dark fantasy, weird menace, detective fiction, and science fiction. Bradbury not only writes genre fiction, he crosses between genres, and even ignores such categorization all together. For example, *Fahrenheit 451* and *Dandelion Wine* fall neatly into no specific genres. *Fahrenheit 451* is a futuristic novel dependent neither on science fiction, fact, nor horror fiction for its ultimate message. It is influenced by George Orwell's *1984* but is uniquely Bradbury. Its author claims that like Orwell's novel, *Fahrenheit 451* was designed to prevent a potential future, not predict one. *Dandelion Wine* likewise is a beautiful, brilliant novel, but really does not fit any one specific genre classification.

The subjects and social issues addressed in the fiction of Ray Bradbury are some of the most poignant and profound of the human experience. Here are found detailed discussions of religions of various sorts, youth, age, death and dying, nature and the environment, life and living, family and friends, race, gender, love, sex, eros, the rural community, a variety of geographical locales, and much more. The episodic novel *The Martian Chronicles* is best appreciated as an environmental allegory. In the 1940s and early 1950s, Bradbury was writing intelligent, insightful stories about ethnicity, race relations. and gender long before such stories became fashionable. Stories like "The Big Black and White Game" and "The Other Foot" told more about racial harmony than many things before or since; stories like "I'll Not Look for Wine" and "Cora and the Great Wide World" featured women with great stamina and independence and individual identity.

This only begins to survey Bradbury's prose. It should be noted that Bradbury's best novels are episodic (i.e. they are a carefully woven series of short stories). In terms of poetry, Bradbury has published four major volumes. These include: *When Elephants Last in the Dooryard Bloomed, Where Robot Mice and Robot Men Run Round in Robot Towns, The Haunted Computer and the Android Pope,* and *The Complete Poems of Ray Bradbury.* In addition, Bradbury has written stage plays and motion picture screenplays. In the 1950s, Bradbury stories were adapted for several comic-book series. From the late 1980s through 1990, Bradbury himself adapted his stories for "The Ray Bradbury Theater" television series.

Ray Bradbury's more recent short-story collection, *The Toynbee Convector,* is as fine a collection as he has ever done and his recent novel (again episodic in organization), the fictionalized autobiography *Green Shadows, White Whale,* is considered one of his finest. The novel recounts Bradbury's experiences with famed movie director and mogul John Huston, and the making of the movie

Moby Dick (which Bradbury scripted) in the mid-1950s. Like Mark Twain, Ray Bradbury's appeal is universal; it transcends all generations and is timeless. Many young adults will not only find the author's works quite realistic, but will rank him as among the best storytellers of science fiction and fantasy.

—Garyn G. Roberts

BRADFORD, Karleen

Nationality: Canadian. **Born:** Karleen Scott in Toronto, Ontario, 16 December 1936. **Education:** Northlands, Buenos Aires, Argentina, 1951-55; University of Toronto, 1955-59, B.A. 1959. **Family:** Married James C. Bradford in 1959; one daughter and two sons. **Career:** Social Worker, West Toronto YWCA, 1959-62; writer, since 1963. **Awards:** Commcept Award, 1979; Max and Greta Ebel Memorial Award for Children's Writing, 1990; Canadian Library Association Young Adult Canadian Book Award, 1993. **Address:** R.R. #2, Owen Sound, Ontario, N4K 5N4, Canada. **Website:** http://www.makersgallery.com/bradford. **E-mail Address:** karleen@log.on.ca.

PUBLICATIONS FOR YOUNG ADULTS

Fiction

The Nine Days Queen. Toronto, Scholastic Canada Ltd., 1986.
Windward Island. Toronto, Kids Can Press, 1989.
There Will Be Wolves. Toronto, HarperCollins, 1992.
Thirteenth Child. Toronto, HarperCollins, 1994.
Shadows on a Sword. Toronto, HarperCollins, 1996.
Dragonfire. Toronto, HarperCollins, 1997.

PUBLICATIONS FOR CHILDREN

A Year for Growing. Toronto, Scholastic Canada Ltd., 1977; as
    Wrong Again, Robbie, Toronto, Scholastic Canada Ltd., 1983.
The Other Elizabeth. Toronto, Gage, 1982.
I Wish There Were Unicorns. Toronto, Gage, 1983.
The Stone in the Meadow. Toronto, Gage, 1984.
The Haunting at Cliff House. Toronto, Scholastic Canada Ltd., 1985.
Write Now! Toronto, Scholastic Canada Ltd., 1988.
Animal Heroes. Toronto, Scholastic Canada Ltd., 1995.
More Animal Heroes. Toronto, Scholastic Canada Ltd., 1996.

*

Karleen Bradford comments:

"Why do you write for kids?" I've been asked—many times. Once my daughter answered for me: "Because her own mind never grew up." It's true. I still remember what it was like to be young and experiencing things—good and bad—for the first time, and that's what I write about.

"When are you going to write a 'real' book?" is another question that I often hear. Well, books for children and young adults are real. They're about as real as you can get and as important.

There's a big plus in writing for young people. I visit schools and libraries all the time and read with children, do workshops with them. That keeps me young and keeps me writing.

*   *   *

Karleen Bradford writes in a number of genres for young adults—historical fiction, realistic fiction, and fantasy—but she is likely best known for her historical fiction. *The Nine Days Queen* is the story of Lady Jane Grey, the adolescent who became the pawn in Tudor politics following the death of Edward VI of England. Scheming Protestant politicians tried to usurp the rightful heir to the throne, Mary Tudor, by making Lady Jane Grey, the deceased king's cousin, the new monarch. After a reign of just nine days the coup failed, and "Queen" Jane was imprisoned and then, at the age of 16, beheaded. Bradford's writing breathes life into a character who, for many adolescents, may have previously just been an answer on a history test.

There Will Be Wolves, winner of the Young Adult Canadian Book Award and the first of a projected quartet of "crusade" books, features Ursula, the motherless daughter of an apothecary. Determined to be a great healer, Ursula is accused by jealous neighbours of witchcraft and sentenced to death. The teen's sentence will be commuted, however, if she joins her father, now a nobleman's personal healer, on the People's Crusade which, in 1096, set off from Cologne to liberate the holy city of Jerusalem from the Turks. As Bradford retraces the disastrous Crusade's route, she reveals the contradictory behaviours of the 20,000 crusaders who, while motivated by high religious ideals, behaved in the most base fashion.

A companion volume, *Shadows on a Sword,* introduces an entirely new set of individuals who are participants in the First Crusade (1096-1099) to liberate Jerusalem. The book's central character is a freshly minted knight, 17-year-old Theobald who, prior to going into battle, envisages war to be glorious; however, after finally liberating Jerusalem following three years of bloody conflict, a much changed Theo is ready to leave his twisted, notched sword "propped in the shadows." Bradford provides a strong supporting cast. Emma, a feisty young woman who chaffs that women cannot go to war, disguises herself as a boy, becoming both Theo's groom and romantic interest. In contrast to Theo, another young knight, Amalric, finds the adrenalin rush of battle addictive and peace suffocatingly boring. As in *There Will Be Wolves,* Bradford's superb use of language creates wonderful word pictures of the expedition and the campaigns.

Bradford has also written two contemporary problem novels. *Windward Island,* an island off Nova Scotia, is home to lifelong teen friends, Loren and Caleb. In addition to the normal stresses associated with adolescence, the boys must cope with external forces over which they seemingly have no control. The last students to graduate from their island school, the boys face the uncertainties of high school on the mainland in the fall. Because of a depleted fishery, people are deserting Windward Island for employment elsewhere, and developers plan to transform the island into a resort. Further, Loren's father will retire when the island's lighthouse is automated. Additional strain is added to the boys' friendship when Torontonian April arrives. Set against the background of inevitable change, both internal and external, Bradford's handling of the teens' relationships and their loss of heritage is most convincing.

Thirteenth Child has a pair of storylines involving Kate Halston, age 15. One deals with Kate's relationship with Mike Bridges, 16, who attempted to rob the Halston's rural Ontario gas station/snack bar. Instead of giving Mike money, Kate supplied him with a sandwich and directions to a local job. Though Kate and Mike develop a friendship, when a number of local businesses are robbed, Kate, despite her emotional attraction to Mike, cannot rule him out as a suspect. Mike's sudden disappearance, coupled with the discovery of a local girl's body, cause Kate to assume the worst. Up to the final chapter, Bradford cleverly disguises the true killer's identity. The book's other story thread revolves about Kate's deteriorating home life. Kate's father, Steve, had turned to alcohol as a way of coping with losing the family's savings. During alcohol-fuelled arguments, he physically abuses his wife, Angie, but only when Steve hits Kate does Angie finally lay charges. At the book's conclusion, there remains hope that the family might be able to come together.

With *Dragonfire,* Bradford returned to fantasy, a genre she had utilized in her books for children. Whereas her juvenile titles had largely been of the time slip variety, in *Dragonfire* she tackles high fantasy. While the book contains all the requisite ingredients of high fantasy, it lacks the form's usual protracted length, a factor which makes *Dragonfire* an excellent introduction to the genre. Saved from death at birth by his Protector and spirited to the temporary safety of another world, Dahl, now almost 17 and the rightful King of Taun, is brought back to his land to wrest control, seemingly singlehandedly, from the evil Usurper who has reduced Taun's people to slaves. Dahl, a most reluctant and doubt-filled hero, is joined on his quest by Catryn Ethelrue, a young woman from his exile period, who accidentally gets "carried" into Taun. As required by the genre, Dahl receives assistance from a variety of "magical" figures, including the aforementioned Protector, a shape-shifter; a trio of Elders, who equip Dahl with his father's sword; a horse, Dragonfire, which sprouts wings and helps him defeat a fire-breathing dragon; and the Sele, short, human-like creatures who serve as Dahl's guides. High fantasy demands that the hero confront evil in a climactic, winner-take-all battle, and Bradford provides the necessary conflict, but with a surprise twist. Though the various plot threads are tied up at *Dragonfire*'s conclusion, the uncertain futures of the central characters suggest that the book is likely the first of a trilogy.

—Dave Jenkinson

BRADLEY, Marion Zimmer

Pseudonyms: Lee Chapman, John Dexter, Miriam Gardner, Valerie Graves, Morgan Ives, and Elfrida Rivers. **Nationality:** American. **Born:** Albany, New York, 3 June 1930. **Education:** New York State College for Teachers, 1946-48; Hardin-Simmons University, Abilene, Texas. B.A. in English, Spanish, Psychology 1964; University of California, Berkeley. **Family:** Married 1) Robert A. Bradley in 1949 (divorced 1964); one son; 2) Walter Henry Breen in 1964 (divorced 1990); one son and one daughter. **Career:** Editor, *Marion Zimmer Bradley's Fantasy Magazine,* since 1988. Singer and writer. **Awards:** Invisible Little Man award, 1977; Leigh Brackett Memorial Sense of Wonder award, 1978, for *The Forbidden Tower; Locus* award, 1984, for best fantasy novel, for *The Mists of Avalon.* **Agent:** Scovil Chichak Galen Literary Agency, 381 Park Avenue South, New York, New York 10016, U.S.A.

PUBLICATIONS FOR YOUNG ADULTS

Fiction

The Door Through Space. New York, Ace, 1961; London, Arrow, 1979.

Seven from the Stars. New York, Ace, 1962.

Falcons of Narabedla. New York, Ace, 1964.

The Brass Dragon. New York, Ace, 1969; London, Methuen, 1978.

Hunters of the Red Moon. New York, DAW, 1973; London, Arrow, 1979.

Endless Voyage. New York, Ace, 1975; revised edition, as *Endless Universe,* 1979.

The Ruins of Isis. Norfolk, Virginia, Donning, 1978; London, Arrow, 1980.

The Survivors, with Paul Edwin Zimmer. New York, DAW, 1979; London, Arrow, 1985.

The House between the Worlds. New York, Doubleday, 1980.

Survey Ship. New York, Ace, 1980.

Web of Light. Norfolk, Virginia, Donning, 1982.

The Mists of Avalon. New York, Knopf, and London, Joseph, 1983.

The Inheritor. New York, Tor, 1984.

Web of Darkness. New York, Pocket Books, 1984; Glasgow, Drew, 1985.

Night's Daughter. New York, Ballantine, and London, Inner Circle, 1985.

Warrior Woman. New York, DAW, 1985; London, Arrow, 1987.

The Fall of Atlantis (contains *Web of Light* and *Web of Darkness*). Riverdale, New York, Baen Books, 1987.

The Forest House. New York, Viking, 1994.

Ghostlight. New York, Tor, 1995.

Tiger Burning Bright, with Andre Norton and Mercedes Lackey. New York, Morrow, 1995.

Glenraven, with Holly Lisle. Riverdale, New York, Baen, 1996.

Witchlight. New York, Tor, 1996.

The Gratitude of Kings. New York, ROC, 1997.

Gravelight. New York, Tor, 1997.

Lady of Avalon. New York, Viking, 1997.

In the Rift, with Holly Lisle. Riverdale, New York, Baen, 1998.

"Darkover" series:

The Sword of Aldones [and] *The Planet Savers.* New York, Ace, 1962; London, Arrow, 2 vols., 1979.

The Bloody Sun. New York, Ace, 1964; London, Arrow, 1978.

Star of Danger. New York, Ace, 1965; London, Arrow, 1978.

The Winds of Darkover. New York, Ace, 1970; London, Arrow, 1978.

The World Wreckers. New York, Ace, 1971; London, Arrow, 1979.

Darkover Landfall. New York, DAW, 1972; London, Arrow, 1978.

The Spell Sword. New York, DAW, 1974; London, Arrow, 1978.

The Heritage of Hastur. New York, DAW, 1975; London, Arrow, 1979.

The Shattered Chain. New York, DAW, 1976; London, Arrow, 1978.

The Forbidden Tower. New York, DAW, 1977; London, Prior, 1979.

Stormqueen. New York, DAW, 1978; London, Arrow, 1980.

Two to Conquer. New York, DAW, 1980; London, Arrow, 1982.

Sharra's Exile. New York, DAW, 1981; London, Arrow, 1983.

Children of Hastur (includes *The Heritage of Hastur* and *Sharra's Exile*). New York, Doubleday, 1981.

Hawkmistress. New York, DAW, 1982; London, Arrow, 1985.

Oath of the Renunciates (includes *The Shattered Chain* and *Thendara House*). New York, Doubleday, 1983.

Thendara House. New York, DAW, 1983; London, Arrow, 1985.

City of Sorcery. New York, DAW, 1984; London, Arrow, 1986.

The Heirs of Hammerfell. New York, DAW, 1989.

Rediscovery, with Mercedes Lackey. New York, DAW, 1993.

Darkover. New York, DAW, 1993.

Exile's Song: A Novel of Darkover. New York, DAW, 1996.

Short Stories

The Dark Intruder and Other Stories. New York, Ace, 1964.

The Jewel of Arwen. Baltimore, T-K Graphics, 1974.

The Parting of Arwen. Baltimore, T-K Graphics, 1974.

Lythande, with Vonda McIntyre. New York, DAW, 1986.

The Best of Marion Zimmer Bradley, edited by Martin H. Greenberg. New York, DAW, 1988.

Jamie & Other Stories: The Best of Marion Zimmer Bradley. Illinois, Academy Chicago Publishers, 1993.

PUBLICATIONS FOR CHILDREN

Fiction

The Colors of Space. Derby, Connecticut, Monarch, 1963.

PUBLICATIONS FOR ADULTS

Novels

Castle Terror. New York, Lancer, 1965.

Souvenir of Monique. New York, Ace, 1967.

Bluebeard's Daughter. New York, Lancer, 1968.

Dark Satanic. New York, Berkley, 1972.

In the Steps of the Master (novelization of TV play). New York, Grosset and Dunlap, 1973.

Can Ellen Be Saved? (novelization of TV play). New York, Grosset & Dunlap, 1975.

Drums of Darkness. New York, Ballantine, 1976.

The Catch Trap. New York, Ballantine, 1979; London, Sphere, 1986.

The Firebrand. New York, Simon & Schuster, 1987; London, Joseph, 1988.

Black Trillium, with Julian May and Andre Norton. New York, Doubleday, 1990; London, Grafton, 1991.

Lady of the Trillium. New York, Bantam, 1995.

Other

The Rivendell Suite. Privately printed, 1969.

A Complete Cumulative Checklist of Lesbian, Variant, and Homosexual Fiction. Privately printed, 1960.

Translator, *El Villano en su Ricon,* by Lope de Vega. Privately printed, 1971.

Men, Halflings, and Hero-Worship. Baltimore, T-K Graphics, 1973.

The Necessity for Beauty: Robert W. Chambers and the Romantic Tradition. Baltimore, T-K Graphics, 1974.

Contributor, *Essays Lovecraftian,* edited by Darrell Schweitzer. Baltimore, T-K Graphics, 1976.

Experiment Perilous: Three Essays in Science Fiction, with Alfred Bester and Norman Spinrad. Brooklyn, New York, Algol Press, 1976.

Editor and contributor, *Legends of Hastur and Cassilda.* Thendara House Publications, 1979.

Editor, *The Keeper's Price.* New York, DAW, 1980.

Editor and contributor, *Tales of the Free Amazons.* Thendara House Publications, 1980.

Editor, *Sword of Chaos.* New York, DAW, 1982.

Editor, *Greyhaven.* New York, DAW, 1983.

Editor, *Sword and Sorceress 1-10.* New York, DAW, 1984-93; vols. 1-5 published London, Headline, 1988-93.

Editor, *Free Amazons of Darkover.* New York, DAW, 1985.

Editor, *Other Side of the Mirror.* New York, DAW, 1987.

Editor, *Red Sun of Darkover.* New York, DAW, 1987.

Editor, *Four Moons of Darkover.* New York, DAW, 1988.

Editor, *Domains of Darkover.* New York, DAW, 1990.

Editor, *Leroni of Darkover.* New York, DAW, 1991.

Editor, *Renunciates of Darkover.* New York, DAW, 1991.

Editor, *Towers of Darkover.* New York, DAW, 1993.

*

Bibliography: *Leigh Brackett, Marion Zimmer Bradley Anne McCaffrey: A Primary and Secondary Bibliography* by Rosemarie Arbur, Boston, Hall, 1982.

Biography: Entry in *Dictionary of Literary Biograpy,* Volume 8: *Twentieth-Century American Science Fiction Writers,* Detroit, Gale, 1981.

Manuscript Collections: Boston University.

Critical Studies: *The Gemini Problem: A Study in Darkover* by Walter Breen, Baltimore, T-K Graphics, 1975; *The Darkover Dilemma: Problems of the Darkover Series* by S. Wise, Baltimore, T-K Graphics, 1976.

*   *   *

As long as inheritance is both desirable and frightful, and adolescence is a terrifying time of crisis and loss of control, the work of Marion Zimmer Bradley will have appeal for young adults. This prolific author often deals with these themes in her novels, particularly the "Darkover" series. Although her work is uneven, it is frequently powerful. The treatment of feminist themes makes her science fiction especially appealing to young women, but strong male characters make it universally accessible.

The "Darkover" novels have proven so popular that other writers, some former fans, have been eager to carry on the series while Bradley has moved on. Part of the appeal has surely been the creation of a world in which the most frightening aspects of the teen years are embodied in such a graphic style. The Darkovians are both blessed and cursed by "laran," a talent which bestows psychic gifts. At adolescence, the onset of power is accompanied by horrifying, uncontrolled manifestations of the talented child's future abilities. Fires, storms, and death are the result of this psychic mayhem before older members of society teach the newly talented to control their talents and emotions. Those without "laran" may feel themselves to be outcast by society, lacking in some essential element of a complete person, or simply at the mercy of those who manifest talent. Terran visitors to the planet create other tensions—should Darkovian society embrace the technology of the outsiders? Will they be at the mercy of their guests if they do so, or will the Terrans deny them technological advantages in order to control the balance of power? In addition, the inheritance of the gift of laran, which is a genetic trait, adds other complications. Breeding for laran has led to both undesirable mutations and a society which is harshly repressive to women. Questions of both feminine independence and male-female relationships are explored against this background.

Most recently, Bradley has become interested in the reinterpretation of myth and legend from the female or even feminist point of view. Her first work in this vein, *The Mists of Avalon* is undoubtedly her masterpiece. It is a brilliantly reimagined treatment of the Arthurian legend told from the perspectives of the various women involved, notably Arthur's sister Morgaine. Seen from this vantage, the Matter of Britain becomes the conflict between the old religion of the Goddess and the new Christian belief—a conflict that is mirrored in the land and the people, most especially in the relationships between men and women. Both the prose style and the character development are sustained to a degree rarely reached in her other work. Her descriptions of the British landscape, both as lovingly and reverently seen by Morgaine and as fearfully perceived by Gwenhyfar, are powerful evocations. She effectively captures individual and recognizable voices for Igraine, Viviane, Morgaine, and Gwenhyfar, and uses them to skillfully portray the changing philosophical and emotional climate. The male characters, although not the focus of this retelling, have believable and complex motivations. Perhaps the most triumphant success of the novel is the remarkable degree to which these stock characters, trapped in their foreordained fates, have been given independent spirit and free will. Despite these virtues, *The Mists of Avalon* is a less successful book for young adults. This is at least due in part to the fact that the narrative voice is largely given over to adult characters. Their concerns are the concerns of adulthood: aging and self-realization, relationships with children, preservation of culture and society. These are notoriously unimportant concerns to the teenaged audience. However, the novel will be a valuable reading experience for the mature reader and is likely to be one that can be returned to in later years with pleasure.

The Firebrand attempts the same kind of reimagining with the Trojan War. Again, the female characters are the focus of attention, with Kassandra providing the major viewpoint. For whatever reason, whether a failure of the modern reader to find this myth as compelling as the Arthurian legend, or the author's lack of conviction, this novel fails to create the vital tension that made *Mists* so compelling. Both the characters and the plot fail to take on the spark of life.

Bradley wrote *Black Trillium* in collaboration with Andre Norton and Julian May. Although the premise is promising—three heroines undertake a quest, each according to her abilities—the novel fails to come together satisfactorily. The characters never find their own voices, and somehow the plot threads do not converge smoothly. Despite these flaws, the presence of the names of three of science fiction's grande dames on the cover (all with a strong appeal to young adults) is sure to make this a viable title for years.

—Cathy Chauvette

BRANCATO, Robin F(idler)

Nationality: American. **Born:** Reading, Pennsylvania, 19 March 1936. **Education:** University of Pennsylvania, B.A. 1958; City College of the City University of New York, M.A. 1976. **Family:** Married John J. Brancato in 1960; two sons. **Career:** Copy editor, John Wiley & Sons, New York City, 1959-61; teacher of English, journalism, and creative writing, Hackensack High School, Hackensack, New Jersey, 1967-79, 1985, part-time teacher, 1979-84; currently teaching in Teaneck, New Jersey. Writer in residence, Kean College of New Jersey, c. 1985. **Awards:** American Library Association Best Book award, 1977, for *Winning,* 1980, for *Come Alive at 505,* and 1982, for *Sweet Bells Jangled out of Tune.*

PUBLICATIONS FOR YOUNG ADULTS

Fiction

Don't Sit under the Apple Tree. New York, Knopf, 1975.
Something Left to Lose. New York, Knopf, 1976.
Winning. New York, Knopf, 1977.
Blinded by the Light. New York, Knopf, 1978.
Come Alive at 505. New York, Knopf, 1980.
Sweet Bells Jangled out of Tune. New York, Knopf, 1980.
Facing Up. New York, Knopf, 1984.
Uneasy Money. New York, Knopf, 1986.

Also contributor of short stories to *Sixteen,* edited by Donald R. Gallo, Dell, 1984, and *Connections,* edited by Donald R. Gallo, Dell, 1989; contributor of one-act play to *Centerstage,* edited by Donald R. Gallo, HarperCollins, 1990.

*

Media Adaptations: *Blinded by the Light* (television "Movie of the Week"), Columbia Broadcasting System (CBS), December 1980.

Biography: Entry in *Speaking for Ourselves: Autobiographical Sketches by Notable Authors of Books for Young Adults* edited and compiled by Donald R. Gallo, National Council of Teachers of English, 1990; essay in *Something about the Author Autobiography Series,* Volume 9, Detroit, Gale, 1990; essay in *Authors and Artists for Young Adults,* Volume 9, Detroit, Gale, 1992.

Critical Studies: *Contemporary Literary Criticism,* Volume 35, Detroit, Gale, 1985.

*   *   *

Brancato's first two novels, which are set in Pennsylvania where the author grew up, have young female protagonists and explore some of her remembered childhood experiences. In *Don't Sit under the Apple Tree,* twelve-year-old tomboy Mary Ellis Carpenter faces a changing relationship with her closest friend, a boy named Jules, and suffers pangs of an unrelenting conscience. Set in 1945, the war permeates this novel, particularly when the friends hear that Jules' brother has been killed. Mary Ellis also learns an important lesson from her grandmother: that it is okay to enjoy life after a loved one passes away. Reviewers praised the novel for its humor and sensitivity.

Something Left to Lose fictionalizes the events leading up to Brancato's move away from her childhood home. The novel explores the bonds between Jane Ann, Rebbie, and Lydia—three ninth-grade friends with distinct personalities and problems. Overweight Rebbie resents her mother's alcoholism and strikes out by taking risks and pulling pranks. However, she also relies on her horoscope, an indication that she is looking for outside guidance. Jane Ann, the main character, is torn between following Rebbie's adventurous leadership or holding to the standards of her more stable family. Lydia seems to be the perfect daughter. Their friendship is tested several times—when Rebbie's father dies of a heart attack, and when Jane Ann must move away after her father is promoted—but the girls vow to remain friends. Critics praised the novel for showing that every adolescent faces difficult problems in his or her own way.

Other Brancato novels deal with hard-hitting, contemporary issues and are based on the author's observations and research. In *Winning,* Gary Madden, a high school senior and former football star, learns to cope with paralysis after an injury. He moves from contemplating suicide to accepting his condition through the help of his English teacher, who is grieving over the recent loss of her husband. Brancato was inspired to write the novel when her sons began playing football. It involved meticulous research into medical rehabilitation. Reviewers praised the novel for raising a difficult issue without becoming overly sentimental.

Facing Up details the overwhelming guilt junior Dave Jacoby feels over the death of Jep, his best friend. After Jep discovers that Dave has dated Jep's girl behind his back, Dave unintentionally wrecks the car they are in and Jep dies. Though he is ruled blameless in the accident, Dave cannot forgive himself. He withdraws, flees, and briefly contemplates suicide, but finally realizes, with the help of friends, that the memories will haunt him but that he can cope. This effort was less favorably received than other Brancato novels.

Sweet Bells Jangled out of Tune builds young readers' empathy for the plight of the homeless. Fifteen-year-old Ellen Dohrmann learns to accept responsibility for her once beautiful, wealthy grandmother Eva, who gave her pleasant childhood memories. Now senile, Eva wears an old fur cape in the summer; collects items from garbage and tips left on restaurant tables; and lives in a dilapidated fire hazard. Ellen realizes that her grandmother suffers from a treatable psychological problem and intervenes, but later feels guilty over her difficult decision—tricking Eva to sign herself into a psychiatric ward. The novel was widely praised by critics for its honest portrayal of the problems faced by street people.

Based on extensive research including a first-hand visit to a religious cult, *Blinded by the Light* reveals Brancato's concern about the brainwashing of cult followers. Gail Brower, a college freshman, tries to rescue her brother Jim from the Light of the World (L.O.W.) cult. When she visits him, however, she is never left alone, is caught up in the chants, and is almost sucked into the cult. Her friend Doug rescues her just in time, but her brother remains a member. Readers can gain insight into cults, their leaders, and techniques used to recruit and retain followers. Brancato's work gained much attention because of its timely subject matter and was adapted for television.

Two later Brancato novels deal with less traumatic problems. *Come Alive at 505* reflects Brancato's interest in radio and the idea that boys, as well as girls, fall in love. Denny, the protagonist, explores his interest in being a disc jockey and must decide whether to work or go to college. Critics predicted the book would particularly appeal to media-crazed teens. In *Uneasy Money*, eighteen-year-old Mike Bronti does what others only dream about: he wins two million dollars in a lottery. Mike spends recklessly until his allotment for the first year is almost gone. At that point he and a friend go through all the letters asking for money and decide to help a woman needing a wheelchair. Though relatively lighthearted, the book places an adolescent into a situation where he must learn to handle a difficult challenge.

Brancato is also the author of short fiction dealing with adolescents and their problems. Her short story "Fourth of July" provides a test of values as Chuck, whose friend has stolen money from him, resists a strong impulse to get full revenge. In her short story "White Chocolate," Wally, the son of mixed races, feels anger and clashes with his English teacher. "The War of Words," a one-act play, pits two groups, the Notes and the Grunts, against each other. The Notes use rhyming language and look down on the Grunts. As a test, the two groups have a poetry contest; the audience serves as a judge. This work reflects Brancato's background as a teacher and seems designed for a class.

Brancato's works offer young adults a chance to gain vicarious experiences while identifying with real problems. Rather than protecting young readers from adversity, Brancato teaches them about their own capacity for dealing with difficult issues. Her works often raise questions—but intentionally do not always provide answers—in order to encourage readers to think for themselves. However, her fiction also offers hope and shows the value of friendship.

—Edna Earl Edwards

BRANSCUM, Robbie

Nationality: American. **Born:** Big Flat, Arkansas, 17 June 1937. **Family:** Married 1) Duane Branscum in 1952 (divorced 1969); 2) Lesli J. Carrico in 1975 (divorced), one daughter. **Awards:** Friends of American Writers Award, 1977, for *Toby, Granny and George;* outstanding book of the year citations, *New York Times,* 1977, for

The Saving of P.S., 1978, for *To the Tune of a Hickory Stick,* and 1982, for *The Murder of Hound Dog Bates: A Novel;* "Best of the Best 1966-1978," *School Library Journal,* 1979, for *Johnny May;* Edgar Allan Poe Award, 1983, for *The Murder of Hound Dog Bates: A Novel.* **Died:** 1997.

PUBLICATIONS FOR YOUNG ADULTS

Fiction

Me and Jim Luke. Garden City, Doubleday, 1971.
Johnny May. Garden City, Doubleday, 1975.
The Three Wars of Billy Joe Treat. New York, McGraw, 1975.
Toby, Granny, and George, illustrated by Glen Rounds. Garden City, Doubleday, 1976.
The Saving of P.S. Garden City, Doubleday, 1977.
Three Buckets of Daylight. New York, Lothrop, 1978.
To the Tune of a Hickory Stick. Garden City, Doubleday, 1978.
The Ugliest Boy, illustrated by Michael Eagle. New York, Lothrop, 1978.
For Love of Jody, illustrated by Allen Davis. New York, Lothrop, 1979.
Toby Alone. Garden City, Doubleday, 1979.
Toby and Johnny Joe. Garden City, Doubleday, 1979.
The Murder of Hound Dog Bates: A Novel. New York, Viking, 1982.
Cheater and Flitter Dick: A Novel. New York, Viking, 1983.
Spud Tackett and the Angel of Doom. New York, Viking, 1983.
The Adventures of Johnny May, illustrated by Deborah Howland. New York, Harper, 1984.
The Girl. New York, Harper, 1986.
Johnny May Grows Up, illustrated by Bob Marstall. New York, Harper, 1987.
Cameo Rose. Cambridge, Massachusetts, Harper, 1989.
Old Blue Tilley. New York, Macmillan, 1991.

*

Biography: Essay in *Speaking for Ourselves: Autobiographical Sketches by Notable Authors of Books for Young Adults,* Vol. 1, compiled and edited by Donald R. Gallo, National Council of Teachers of English, 1990; essay in *Something about the Author Autobiographical Series,* Vol. 17, Detroit, Gale, 1994.

Robbie Branscum comments:

I think like a lot of writers, I write about young adults for adults to read also.

I know about the world of young adults because I live in it and understand them, I know where they are coming from and they know I know it, even though I write about a way of life that's no longer here.

Maybe the world I write about is gone, but young adults and children are the same. I don't write or talk down to them, I give them credit for knowing a lot of things I don't. I think my love for them shows in my books and I also have many adult fans—my oldest one is ninety-eight and is a school teacher from Arkansas.

I write laying flat on the floor with my dog Toby for company. I write about how things were when I was growing up and hope my young friends enjoy reading it as much as I do writing it. The hardest book I have ever written is *The Girl,* about child abuse and from the letters I received from young fans, I found I was far from alone, it's very sad but true.

I hope to bring a moment of joy to my young friends.
God bless them all.

*　　*　　*

Robbie Branscum writes novels that weave intricate patterns of love and hope, good and evil, pain and poverty, and faith and fellowship deep in the Arkansas hills where she grew up. Her success as an author is rooted in her fascination with words, her love of books and people, and her ability to translate the experiences of her youth into stories that speak vividly and candidly to her readers. She cannot recall a time when she could not read, and she remembers reading voraciously from the three crates of books that were in the one-room school she attended for seven years. Through her writing, she strives to give her readers the pleasures she found in books as she was growing up.

Branscum was four when her father died, and her mother left Robbie and her siblings with their grandparents on their small farm while she went to the city to earn a living. Both the joys and the adversities of Branscum's early years resonate in the inherent drama of her protagonists in such books as *Johnny May, Toby, Granny, and George, Three Buckets of Daylight, The Murder of Hound Dog Bates,* and *The Girl* who, left with other relatives by an absent mother, struggle to survive and to find confirmation and identity. The relatives may be grandparents, aunts, or uncles, and the circumstances can vary widely. For example, both Johnny May and Toby (her granny had named her October, her birth month) find love and happiness as they mature in the sequels to those initial novels. In stark contrast is the plight of "the girl" who, by never being named, becomes a symbolic victim of greed and abuse.

Child abuse is a significant plot element in *Toby, Granny, and George,* but its impact in *The Girl* makes this study of physical and psychological intimidation one of Branscum's strongest examples of realistic fiction. The girl's great-grandmother, Granny, nurtures the children as they dream of escaping their oppressive environment as soon as their mother returns. After Granny dies, the girl's brother Gene rescues her from their lecherous uncle's assault and forces him to leave the farm. When their mother does return, it is not to take the children away but to announce that she has married again and that they have a new half sister and brother. When their mother leaves, Gene reassures the distraught girl that, as Granny had said, it won't be long before they are grown up and free. Mystery and intrigue are familiar ingredients in Branscum's fiction. In her first novel, *Me and Jim Luke,* Sammy John and Jim Luke discover a body in a hollow tree one night while possum hunting, which leads them on an adventure that involves the Ku Klux Klan. While this opening is based on her grandfather's account of finding a dead revenuer, the fast-paced adventure that follows is the product of Branscum's rich imagination. Branscum's mysteries are often laced with a measure of humor, as in *The Murder of Hound Dog Bates* wherein Sassafras Bates is convinced that one of his guardian aunts has poisoned his dog and sets out to prove it, unaware of where his detective work will take him. In *Toby, Granny, and George* the mysterious drownings of Minnie

Lou Jackson and Deacon Treat in the church's baptizing hole give Toby great concern for Preacher Davis, who is suspect in both cases. With Granny's help, Toby not only discovers the truth about these deaths but also learns who her mother is.

A baptizing hole figures also in *Three Buckets of Daylight,* but here it is the ghostly old house in a dark hollow that commands the attention of Jackie Lee and Jimmy Jay as they discover a link between a local moonshining operation and the three witchy Blackgrove sisters, one of whom puts a curse on the boys. Jackie Lee pines for his mother, but his grandparents remind him that times are hard and that his mother is a long way off. His insecurity dissipates when he is liberated from the curse and freed of unknown fear. In *The Adventures of Johnny May* Johnny May, who is convinced she has witnessed a murder in the woods, learns that things are not always what they seem and that she and her grandparents are free to experience a joyous Christmas. In *Cameo Rose* Branscum's protagonist lives with her grandfather who is the local sheriff (her parents were killed in a car wreck), and when a man is murdered Cameo sets out to find the murderer, not realizing that she and her grandpa would be threatened also. Cameo Rose, like Johnny May and Toby, is resourceful and independent as she unravels the mysterious events.

Ministers play significant roles in many of Branscum's novels. Preacher Davis in the Toby series is a special ally to Granny in the neighborhood controversies, and his moral leadership is especially important to Toby. In a rare plot switch in *The Saving of P.S.,* Priscilla Sue lives with her widowed minister father who courts and marries a widow who has recently moved to town. Loyal to her mother's memory, P.S. runs away with their smelly old dog Brimstone. Her odyssey helps her put things into perspective so she can return home and accept her father's newfound happiness. Branscum portrays a negative side of religion in *Spud Tackett and the Angel of Doom* when during World War II a strange preacher comes to town with a scheme of salvation that Spud's grandma knows is pure fraud and declares it openly to thwart this false angel's plan. However, in *Old Blue Tilley,* set on the eve of World War II, young Hambone paints an engaging portrait of the circuit rider he has lived with since his parents died. Reminiscent of Preacher Davis in the Toby series, Blue Tilley is a strong man who lives his faith and is willing to fight for values important to his flock and to a teenage boy struggling to put his own life into perspective.

Branscum's novels of rural life in Arkansas are rich in the language, customs, and lore of the hill country Branscum knows so well. The dialect of her characters and their patterns of behavior frame a way of life that is unique for most of today's young adult readers who would benefit from reading of varying lifestyles. In her rural settings, animals such as Toby's hound dog George, Priscilla Sue's old dog Brimstone in *The Saving of P.S.,* and Cheater's pet rooster Flitter Dick in *Cheater and Flitter Dick,* add a special dimension to Branscum's stories.

Without question Robbie Branscum is a gifted storyteller whose narratives present authentic characters in unique settings. Her protagonists move toward independence and fulfillment in an atmosphere where individualism is strong but so are families and community. It is not surprising that Branscum's novels are beginning to draw the attention of filmmakers and that she is gaining a new audience in Great Britain where her books are now beginning to be published.

—Hugh Agee

BRIDGERS, Sue Ellen

Nationality: American. **Born:** Greenville, North Carolina, 20 September 1942. **Education:** East Carolina University, Greenville, 1960-63; Western Carolina University, Cullowhee, North Carolina, 1974-76, B.A. (summa cum laude) 1976. **Family:** Married Ben Oshel Bridgers in 1963; two daughters and one son. **Career:** Since 1970, writer. **Awards:** Breadloaf Writers' Conference fellowship, 1976; American Library Association (ALA) Best Books for Young Adults citation and *New York Times* Outstanding Children's Books list, both 1976, for *Home Before Dark; Boston Globe-Horn Book* Award for fiction, Christopher Award, American Book Award nominee, ALA Best Books for Young Adults citation, and *New York Times* Outstanding Books list, all 1979, all for *All Together Now;* ALA Best Books for Young Adults citation, 1985, for *Sara Will;* ALAN Award, Assembly on Literature for Adolescents of the National Council of Teachers of English, 1985, for outstanding contributions to young adult literature; ALA Best Books for Young Adults citation and Parent's Choice Gold Award, both 1987, both for *Permanent Connections;* Ragin-Rubin Award, 1992; WorldFest Film Festival award for best original screenplay, 1997, for *Paradise Falls.* **Address:** 628 Savannah Drive, Sylva, North Carolina 28779, U.S.A. **Office:** Box 248, Sylva, North Carolina 28779, U.S.A.

PUBLICATIONS FOR YOUNG ADULTS

Fiction

Home Before Dark (originally appeared in *Redbook,* July, 1976) New York, Knopf, 1976.
All Together Now. New York, Knopf, 1979.
Notes for Another Life. New York, Knopf, 1981.
Sara Will. New York, Harper, 1985.
Permanent Connections. New York, Harper, 1987.
Keeping Christina. New York, HarperCollins, 1993.
All We Know of Heaven. Wilmington, North Carolina, Banks Channel, 1996.

PUBLICATIONS FOR ADULTS

Fiction

"The World That Winter," in *Crucible,* Spring 1971, 39-41.
"All Summer Dying," in *Carolina Quarterly,* Spring 1972, 14-22.
"Time and Love," in *Cairn,* Spring 1975.
"The Beginning of Something," in *Visions,* edited by Don Gallo. New York, Dell, 1987.
"Life's a Beach," in *Connections,* edited by Don Gallo, New York, Dell, 1990.
"Lost and Found," in *Twelve Christmas Stories by North Carolina Writers.* Asheboro, North Carolina, 1997.

Non-Fiction

"My Life in Fiction," in *ALAN Review* (Athens, Georgia), Vol. 18, No. 1, Fall 1990, 2-5.
"Writing for My Life," in *ALAN Review* (Athens, Georgia), Vol. 23, No. 1, Fall 1995, 2-7.

Screenplay

With Sean Bridgers, *Paradise Falls,* 1997.

Recordings

"Sue Ellen Bridgers Talks about Writing" (videocassette). Raleigh, North Carolina, North Carolina State University, 1992.
"A Conversation with Sue Ellen Bridgers" (videocassette). Radford, Virginia, Radford University Telecommunications Bureau, 1994.

*

Manuscript Collection: Hunter Library, Western Carolina University, Cullowhee, North Carolina.

Biography: Essay in *Something about the Author: Autobiography Series,* Vol. 1, Gale, 1986; *Presenting Sue Ellen Bridgers* by Ted Hipple, Boston, Twayne, 1990; essay in *Speaking for Ourselves: Autobiographical Sketches by Notable Authors of Books for Young Adults,* Vol. 1, compiled and edited by Donald R. Gallo, National Council of Teachers of English, 1990; essay in *Contemporary Authors New Revision Series,* Volume 36, Gale, 1992; "Presenting Sue Ellen Bridgers," in *Twayne's Women Authors on CD-Rom,* Boston, Twayne, 1995; entry in *The 100 Most Popular Young Adult Authors* by Bernard A. Drew, Libraries Unlimited, 1996; entry in *Something about the Author,* Volume 90, Gale, 1997.

Critical Studies: Review of *All Together Now* by Katherine M. Flanagan, in *Horn Book,* April 1979, 197-198; review of *Notes for Another Life,* in *Bulletin of the Center for Children's Books,* October 1981, 23-24; *Teacher's Guides to Young Adult Novels,* New York, Bantam, 1983; review of *Permanent Connections,* in *Kliatt,* May 1988, 2; *Sue Ellen Bridgers' Southern Literature for Young Adults* by Pamela Sissi Carroll, Auburn, Alabama, Auburn University Press, 1989; "Music in the Young Adult Novels of Sue Ellen Bridgers" by Martha Andrews, in *ALAN Review,* Vol. 18, No. 1, Fall 1990, 14-16; "Southern Literature for Young Adults: The Novels of Sue Ellen Bridgers" by Pamela Sissi Carroll, in *ALAN Review,* Vol. 18, No. 1, Fall 1990, 10-13; *Using Young Adult Literature to Motivate Reluctant Readers; or What Do You Do When They Haven't Read Their Assignment,* conference paper presented to National Council of Teachers of English, Seattle, Washington, November 1991; *Redemption in the Novels of Sue Ellen Bridgers* by Anna M. Allred, M.A. thesis, East Tennessee State University, 1993; review of *Keeping Christina* by Hazel Rochman, in *Booklist,* July, 1993, 1957; "Rural America Singing—*Permanent Connections* by Sue Ellen Bridgers" by Eleanor Parks Gaunder, in *English Journal,* Vol. 82, No. 8, December 1993, 75; "The 'Different Truth' for Women in Sue Ellen Bridgers' *Permanent Connections,*" in *ALAN Review,* Vol. 21, No. 3, Spring 1994, 53-55; *Family Relationships in Selected Young Adult Novels by Cynthia Voigt and Sue Ellen Bridgers* by Janet Claire Rahamut, Ph.D. dissertation, University of Tennessee, Knoxville, 1995; review of *All We Know of Heaven* by Karen Simonetti, in *Booklist,* Vol. 93, No. 3, 1 October 1996, 321; review of *All We Know of Heaven* by Amy Boaz, in *New York Times Book Review,* 10 November 1996, sec. VII, 56; review of *All We Know of Heaven* by Nancy Pearl, in *Library Journal,* Vol. 121, No. 20, December 1996, 141.

Sue Ellen Bridgers comments:

Growing up in the rural South, a world steeped in the tradition of storytelling, I came to writing at a young age. The Bible stories, fairy tales, and family legends I heard showed me that, through stories, I could find meaning in the events around me. My early stories were mostly about children and the elderly, age groups that continue to interest me.

*   *   *

Sue Ellen Bridgers' novels for young adults have won much critical acclaim and popular acceptance by their intended audience. Although some critics have commented that her protagonists sometimes seem too mature for their years, part of the stories' appeal for young adults is their portrayal of capable characters the reader's age or slightly older who handle problems better than the reader could do. Strengths of Bridgers' novels include their clear sense of place (typically her native North Carolina), their perceptive examination of relationships among kin and community, and their lack of sentimentality. To create stories, she draws on her rural Appalachian background and her experiences with strong but nurturing grandmothers, a supportive extended family, and a father who battled mental illness.

In *Home Before Dark,* 14-year-old Stella initially lacks a stable home because her parents are migrant farm workers, continually traveling between jobs and often living in their car. When they return to her father's home town and get their first house, one owned by a relative, Stella is thrilled: "Because the room was bare, it seemed very large to her. In her mind, it was an empty, dusty world of filtered light waiting for her to clean it up and fill it with her whole life . . . she turned and, looking back at where she'd been, saw how good living there could be." But after her mother's death and her father's remarriage, Stella has to move from this home. She feels dispossessed in the new wife Maggie's house, until she realizes home is more than four walls—it's family. She also faces conflicts regarding her mother's death, boyfriends and other growing-up dilemmas, not all of which are resolved in this sad but optimistic book.

In *All Together Now,* 11-year-old Casey reluctantly spends a summer with her grandparents. To win the approval of Dwayne, a 33-year-old mentally-challenged man who doesn't like girls, she pretends to be a boy. When Dwayne's brother tries to have him institutionalized, Casey joins the whole town in working to prevent it, illustrating the importance of community effort. Katherine M. Flanagan comments in *Horn Book* that "the book is exceptional not only in its superb writing and skillful portrayal of human relationships, but also for its depiction of a small southern town."

Notes for Another Life's two protagonists, Wren and Kevin, live with their grandparents because of their father's mental illness and their mother's pursuit of a career in Atlanta, about six hours away. Their feeling of abandonment by their parents, one of the book's major concerns, intensifies when they learn their mother will take a new job in Chicago, much farther away. Wren must also deal with problems in romantic relationships, Kevin with self-pity and worry about following his father into mental illness, culminating in the boy's suicide attempt. *Notes for Another Life* is a moving, compellingly written story which ends without easy solutions to problems. A reviewer in *Bulletin of the Center for Children's Books* states that it "is most impressive . . . in the perceptively

drawn characters and in the intricacy and pain and love in their interrelationships."

In *Permanent Connections,* 17-year-old Rob Dickson hates having to travel with his father from New Jersey to North Carolina to see a hospitalized uncle. He becomes angrier yet at having to stay with his elderly grandfather and his agoraphobic aunt while the uncle recuperates. An explosive argument with his grandfather and the ensuing threat to the grandfather's life lead Rob to finally recognize the importance of family. A reviewer in *Kliatt* says, "Fine characterization, realistic situations, and wonderful descriptions throughout make this one of Bridgers' best works."

At the beginning of *Keeping Christina,* Annie Gerhardt is leading a comfortable, sheltered life with a loving family, friends, and an almost implausibly sensitive boyfriend. But her world is shattered after she befriends a new student at Whitney High, Christina Moore, who though apparently much like Annie and her other friends seems intriguingly different. Annie's self-sacrifice in helping Christina resolve a problem is repaid by this new "friend's" manipulating her and controlling her life. The character of Christina is a complex one, part vulnerable, part devious, and at novel's end still something of a mystery.

All We Know of Heaven, set late in the Great Depression, concerns a teenaged couple, both from troubled childhoods, who meet and marry. Bethany's mother had died young, and because her alcoholic father is unfit to raise her Bethany lives with her Aunt Charlotte. She meets Joel when he returns from military school—where he'd been sent because of his temper and violent acts—and goes to work in a slaughterhouse. But even after the birth of their baby, Caroline, Joel continues his violent ways, eventually killing both himself and Caroline. Told in short chapters by multiple narrators, including Joel, Bethany, her aunt and his mother, the story contains Bridgers' usual themes of family and the land. Although Nancy Pearl, in a review in *Library Journal,* calls it "a simplistic morality tale" with "sketchy character development and lackluster writing," other reviewers praise it highly. Amy Boaz in the *New York Times* says, "though the reader knows very well what's coming after the exultation of the wedding and the birth of the young couple's baby, when the hard work of day-to-day existence begins the destruction of their life together is no less shattering." And Karen Simonetti in *Booklist* says, "this unsettling tragedy soothes the reader with the potential of an individual's inner strength to endure and survive pain."

Whether set during the Depression, more modern times, or somewhere in between, Bridgers' novels get high marks for superb writing and deft characterization, particularly of their strong female characters. Bridgers' people ascribe to the Southern ideals of hard work, respect for tradition and family heritage, and the importance of strong kinship ties, with major conflicts occurring when such ties are loosened or severed. These universal themes and her clear, often conversational style make these outstanding books for young readers.

—Elbert R. Hill

BROOKS, Bruce

Nationality: American. **Born:** Richmond, Virginia, 23 September 1950. **Education:** University of North Carolina, Chapel Hill, B.A.

1972; University of Iowa, M.F.A. 1980. **Family:** Married Penelope Winslow in 1978; two sons. **Career:** Writer. Also worked as a letterpress printer, a newspaper reporter, a magazine reporter, and a teacher. **Awards:** *The Moves Make the Man* was named a best book of 1984 by *School Library Journal,* a notable children's book by the American Library Association (ALA), and a notable book of the year by the *New York Times,* 1984, and received a *Boston Globe-Horn Book* Award and Newbery Honor from the ALA, both 1985; *Midnight Hour Encores* was named a best book of 1986 by *School Library Journal,* a best book for young adults in 1986 by the ALA, a *Horn Book* Fanfare Honor List book in 1987, a teacher's choice by the National Council of Teachers of English in 1987, a young adult choice by the International Reading Association in 1988, and an ALA/*Booklist* best of the 1980s book for young adults; *No Kidding* was named a best book for young adults by the ALA, an ALA/*Booklist* young adult editor's choice, a best book by *School Library Journal,* and a notable children's trade book in social studies; *Everywhere* was named a notable children's book by the ALA and a best book by *School Library Journal; On the Wing* was an ALA Best Book for Young Adults, 1990; *Predator!* was an ALA Best Book for Young Adults, 1992; John Burroughs award, 1992, for *Nature By Design; What Hearts* was a Newbery Honor Book, an ALA Notable Children's Book, an ALA Best Book for Young Adults, and a Horn Book Fanfare book, all 1993. **Address:** 11208 Legato Way, Silver Spring, Maryland 20901, U.S.A.

PUBLICATIONS FOR YOUNG ADULTS

Fiction

The Moves Make the Man. New York, Harper, 1984.
Midnight Hour Encores. New York, Harper, 1986.
No Kidding. New York, Harper, 1989.
What Hearts. New York, HarperCollins, 1992.
Asylum for Nightface. New York, Laura Geringer Book, 1996.
Cody. New York, HarperCollins, 1997.
Woodsie. New York, HarperCollins, 1997.
Zip. New York, HarperCollins, 1997.
Boot. New York, HarperTrophy, 1998.
Prince. New York, HarperCollins, 1998.
Shark. New York, HarperCollins, 1998.

Nonfiction

On the Wing: The Life of Birds from Feathers to Flight. New York, Scribner, 1989.
Predator! New York, Farrar, Straus, 1991.
Nature by Design. New York, Farrar, Straus, 1991.
Making Sense: Animal Perception and Communication. New York, Farrar, Straus, 1993.
Editor, *The Red Wasteland: A Personal Selection of Writings about Nature for Young Readers.* New York, Holt, 1998.

PUBLICATIONS FOR CHILDREN

Fiction

Everywhere. New York, Harper, 1990.
Each a Piece, illustrated by Elena Pavlov. New York, HarperCollins, 1996.

Nonfiction

Boys Will Be. New York, Holt, 1993.
Those Who Love the Game, with Glenn Rivers. New York, Holt, 1994.
NBA by the Numbers. New York, Scholastic, 1997.

*

Biography: Essay in *Speaking for Ourselves: Autobiographical Sketches by Notable Authors of Books for Young Adults,* Vol. 1, compiled and edited by Donald R. Gallo, National Council of Teachers of English, 1990.

*   *   *

The publication of his much-acclaimed first novel, the 1985 Newbery Honor book *The Moves Make the Man,* established Bruce Brooks as a commanding new presence in the world of books for young readers. As one critic put it, "Armed with talent and technique [he] strode into the world of children's and young adult fiction as if on stilts."

Yet, as one of his own characters observes, "Talent and technique [alone] could not create power." What makes Brooks such a powerful writer are not only his talent and technique, but his matchless ability to create highly intelligent, complex characters invested with strong, idiosyncratic voices and his success in developing his ambitious, yet subtly stated themes. Three themes are typical: a fascination with process—analyzing and understanding how things work, whether sports, music, or the human heart in order to capture their essential truth; the characters' need to manipulate that truth and other people; and a closely reasoned examination—without violating the works' fictional form—of the sometimes symbiotic, occasionally dialectical relationship of lies and truth, of emotion and thought, of intellect and love.

These themes are ambitious considerations for the sometimes fragile framework of young-adult literature, and with these, Brooks, more than most writers of his generation, has tested and expanded the parameters of the genre, perhaps because he respects the intelligence of his "hardworking readers who are ready to be inspired," perhaps because in his writing he refuses to be confined by traditional limitations, perhaps because he recognizes the potential power of literature to enrich and expand lives.

Brooks also loves a challenge. In his first two books, *The Moves Make the Man* and *Midnight Hour,* he wrote, respectively, in the first-person voices of Jerome Foxworth, a thirteen-year-old African-American living in the recently desegregated South, and of Sibilance Spooner, a sixteen-year-old white musical prodigy, one of the finest cellists in the world. At the same time, he integrated considerable expository material about basketball and music into his narratives. That the narrators' voices are authentic in their believable verisimilitude and that the integration of exposition and fiction is seamless speak for Brooks's skill as a writer.

In his third book, *No Kidding,* he dared to distance his challenging material from the reader by writing in the more remote third person and setting the story in a bleakly dystopian future world where 69 percent of the adults are alcoholics. His fourth book, *Everywhere,* a novella, is a marvel of subtle economy, which, though marketed for a mid-range audience, reveals large and haunting truths for all ages about the healing power of love.

What Hearts, another Newbery Honor title, is a departure in form, a collection of four interrelated short stories in which the reader follows the maturation of a boy named Asa. Like Jerome and Sibilance, Asa is preternaturally intelligent. He has been forced into an unnatural adult maturity by the circumstances of a mother's illness and has, at best, an uneasy relationship with a domineering, unsympathetic stepfather.

In these characters, Brooks shows his great sympathy for young people who are outsiders, whether by virtue of their intelligence or domestic or societal circumstances. Almost all of his characters come from broken homes, and many of them are further challenged by a parent's mental illness or alcoholism. Given this context, it is no wonder that control or manipulation of the truth and other people is a consistent theme—from Brooks's first book, in which Bix Rivers resolutely refuses to learn the fake-out, duplicitous moves of basketball, to the last, in which Asa invents a reality of dramatic baseball games. To lie may be to control the truth or other people's perception of it, to bring some order to a chaotic personal world, or simply to survive, but in extreme cases it is also, as Bix understands, to invite the alternate reality of madness, which is an exercise in ultimate solitude.

For Brooks and his characters, redemption sometimes can be found in the giving up of control, as in the case of Sam, perhaps Brooks's most controlling character. In his self-imposed maturity, Sam betrays his essential adolescent self but finally finds that self when his mother practices her own deception, and Sam is released to say poignantly to her, "Can I be myself. . .can I just be your boy?" More often, though, redemption is found in a character's discovery of love, which, in its sweet simplicity, is the perfect complement to the complex intellectuality that defines so many of Brooks's characters. To give expression to words of love is, for Brooks, not only an exercise in honesty, but an act of completion, a rejection of isolation, which is most obviously manifested in Asa, but also in Sibilance and her discovery of her love for her father, and certainly in the case of the healing love of the young narrator for his grandfather in *Everywhere.*

Bruce Brooks is that rarity in the world of books for young readers—a novelist of ideas. But he is also a rare stylist whose writer's razzle always dazzles thanks to his uncanny ear for voice and his gift for powerful imagery and unforgettable simile and metaphor. Ultimately, though, it is his own luminous intelligence which brings light to the sometimes dark complexities of who we humans are and why we behave as we do. He understands the workings of the human heart and demonstrates in his memorable works of fiction how it can challenge the intellect to develop subtle and inventive strategies for survival.

—Michael Cart

BROOKS, Martha

Nationality: Canadian. **Born:** Martha Ruth Paine in Winnipeg, Manitoba, 15 July 1944. **Education:** St. Michael's Academy, Brandon, Manitoba, 1962. **Family:** Married Brian Brooks in 1967; one daughter. **Career:** Has worked as a model, secretary, mentor to young writers, and jazz singer. **Awards:** Vicky Metcalf Short Story

Award, 1989, *School Library Journal* Best Book of the Year, and *Boston Globe/Horn Book* Honor Book, 1991, all for *Paradise Cafe and Other Stories*; Chalmers Best Canadian Children's Play, 1991, for *Andrew's Tree*; Best Book for Young Adults, American Library Association and runner up for the Canadian Library Association Book of the Year for Children Award, for *Two Moons in August*; *Hungry Mind Review* Children's Books of Distinction Award for Young Adults, shortlisted for the Mr. Christie Award, *School Library Journal* Best Book of the Year, and Best Book for Young Adults, and Best Books for the Reluctant Young Adult Reader, New York Public Library's 1995 Books for the Teen Age, and IBBY honor book, 1996, all for *Traveling on into the Light*; Best Book of the Year, ALA, 1997, and Ruth Schwartz Award, both for *Bone Dance*; CLA Young Adult Canadian Book of the Year, 1998. **Address:** #58, 361 Westwood Dr., Winnipeg, Manitoba R3K 1G4, Canada.

PUBLICATIONS FOR YOUNG ADULTS

Paradise Cafe & Other Stories. Saskatoon, Saskatchewan, Thistledown Press, and Boston, Joy Street/Little Brown, 1988.
Two Moons in August. Toronto, Groundwood, and Boston, Joy Street/Little Brown, 1991.
Traveling on into the Light and Other Stories. Toronto, Groundwood, and New York, Orchard Books, 1994.
Bone Dance. Toronto, Groundwood, and New York, Orchard Books, 1997.

Other

A Hill for Looking (children's fiction). Winnipeg, Queenston House, 1982.
With Sandra Birdsell and David Gillies, *A Prairie Boy's Winter* (play; produced across Canada).
MoonLight Sonata (play; produced Winnipeg, Prairie Theater Exchange), 1994.
With Maureen Hunter, *I Met a Bully on the Hill* (play; produced across Canada). Winnipeg, Scirocco Drama, 1995.
Andrew's Tree (play; produced across Canada). Winnipeg, Scirocco Drama, 1996.

*

Martha Brooks comments:

I still "think" faster with a pencil in my hand, so I hand write most of the rewrites before putting them onto the computer. I am left handed. This frees my right hand to work the second story window of our town house in accordance with the season. For instance, in spring, I quickly shut it so that our Manx cat, Merlin, will not escape down the cedar tree and eat the neighbor's birds. In the summer, the screens go back on, and if I happen to be working at night when he *can* go out, he's always on the wrong side of the screen. In the fall and the winter, of course, the neighbors don't care, so Merlin comes and goes as he pleases through the office window. Over the past few years he has grown from his late teens into full adulthood. He was there as my novel *Bone Dance* progressed, through many many writing drafts, from uncharted new land to a detailed country that was finally embroidered with light.

* * *

Paradise Cafe and Other Stories is a significant title in Canadian Young Adult literature for its 1988 publication signalled a rebirth of the short story collection as a legitimate vehicle for adolescents' recreational reading. Nominated for the Governor General's Literary Award for Children's Literature, the collection consists of 14 stories. While none of the stories exceeds 10 pages, each packs an emotional wallop. Featuring adolescent protagonists who range in age from 12 to 15, the stories all involve the joys and pains of love of one kind or another. For example, in "Dying for Love," Arlis is humiliated when her love is not reciprocated by the handsomest boy in class. Deirdre plays matchmaker in "The Crystal Stars Have Just Begun to Shine" as she attempts to get her father to date the check-out clerk at the local grocery store. Another type of love is movingly explored in "A Boy and His Dog," which was awarded the Vicky Metcalf Short Story Award by the Canadian Authors Association. Ever since Buddy was an infant, his dog Alphonse had been one of the few stable elements in the family's nomadic life, but now a trip to the vet reveals to a 14-year-old Buddy that his beloved pet and companion has cancer.

Switching to the novel form, Brooks then wrote *Two Moons in August,* which was also nominated for a Governor General's Literary Award. The story, set in rural Manitoba during the hot, lazy summer days of 1959, finds Sidonie dreading her sixteenth birthday for the date will also mark the first anniversary of her mother's death. Still struggling with unresolved grief, Sidonie has been emotionally abandoned by her father, a doctor in the local TB sanatorium, who has chosen to deal with his personal sadness ny immersing himself in his work. The return from college of Sidonie's older sister, Roberta, does not improve the family's emotional climate for Roberta grows increasingly resentful about seemingly being left in charge. When Kieran, the next-door-neighbour's son arrives, Sidonie begins her first romance, which serves as a catalyst for sorting through her emotions.

Turning again to short stories, Brooks next work was *Travelling on into the Light and Other Stories,* which consists of 10 stories and a novella, "Moonlight Sonata," the latter dealing with the healing power of memory. The stories are longer than those found in *Paradise Cafe,* in part because the adolescent characters are dealing with more complicated problems which take longer to resolve. Readers who may have wondered what happened to *Two Moons in August*'s Sidonie will be delighted by the final three linked stories which begin a year after the novel's conclusion and are each spaced a year apart. "Sunday at Sidonie's" is told from Kieran's point of view while "All the Stars in the Universe" and "A Wedding" are related from Sidonie's perspective.

Brooks' second YA novel, *Bone Dance,* possesses a remarkable and engaging Yin-Yang quality. Divided into two parts, the work features two late-teen protagonists who ultimately come together to form a unified whole. Alexandria—a.k.a. Alex—Sinclair, 17, lives with her Dene mother in Winnipeg, Manitoba, while Lonny LaFrenière, 18, resides with his Métis stepfather, Pop, in the province's Lacs des Placottes Valley Hills. What will eventually unite Alex and Lonny is a piece of unspoiled lake property which had been in Lonny's family since the days of the first LaFrenière, a Métis trapper and buffalo hunter. To finance Lonny's future education, Pop had recently sold his cherished land to Earl McKay, Alex's nomadic, drunken father who had deserted his wife following Alex's birth. In 17 years, Earl's sole contact with Alex had been a half-dozen brief letters, but now his death has surprisingly brought her ownership of the land. When a bitter Alex reluctantly visits the property she meets Lonny, whose memories of this land are tinged by guilt for he believes his childhood act of digging up and "disturbing" bones at Medicine Bluff, a Dene burial ground, had "killed" his mother.

Although Brooks utilizes the third person in *Bone Dance,* she varies the narrator's perspective throughout the book's two divisions. In the opening section, "The Spirits," readers come to know Alex and Lonny through their separate histories. The pace quickens in "The Legacy" as short chapters flip back and forth between Alex and Lonny as they "connect" and finally exorcise their demons. A crossover title, *Bone Dance* will find readers both amongst high school students and adults.

—Dave Jenkinson

BROOKS, Terry

Nationality: American. **Born:** Sterling, Illinois, 8 January 1944. **Education:** Hamilton College, Clinton, New York, B.A. 1966; Washington and Lee University, Lexington, Virginia, LL.B. 1969. **Family:** Married Judine Elaine Alba in 1987; one daughter and one son from a previous marriage. **Career:** Partner, Besse, Frye, Arnold, Brooks and Miller, Attorneys at Law, Sterling Illinois, 1969-86; writer, 1977—. **Awards:** *The Elfstones of Shannara* was selected one of American Library Association's Best Young Adult Books, and one of *School Library Journal*'s Best Books for Young Adults, both 1982; *Magic Kingdom for Sale—Sold* was selected one of *School Library Journal*'s Best Books for Young Adults, 1986. **Address:** c/o Ballantine/Del Rey, 201 East 50th Street, New York, New York 10022, U.S.A.

PUBLICATIONS FOR YOUNG ADULTS

Novels

The Sword of Shannara, illustrated by the Brothers Hildebrandt. New York, Ballantine, 1977.
The Elfstones of Shannara, illustrated by Darrell K. Sweet. New York, Ballantine, 1982.
The Wishsong of Shannara, illustrated by Darrell K. Sweet. New York, Ballantine, 1985.
Magic Kingdom for Sale—Sold. New York, Ballantine, 1986.
The Black Unicorn. New York, Ballantine, 1987.
Wizard at Large. New York, Ballantine, 1988.
The Scions of Shannara. New York, Ballantine, 1990.
The Druid of Shannara. New York, Ballantine, 1991.
The Elf Queen of Shannara. New York, Ballantine, 1992.
Hook (based on screenplay by Jim V. Hart and Malia Scotch Marmo). New York, Fawcett Columbine, 1992.
The Talismans of Shannara. New York, Ballantine, 1993.
The Tangle Box. New York, Ballantine, 1994.
Witches Brew. New York, Ballantine, 1995.
The First King of Shannara. New York, Ballantine, 1996.
Running with the Demon. New York, Ballantine, 1997.

Other

Contributor, *Once Upon a Time: A Treasury of Modern Fairy Tales,* edited by Lester Del Rey and Risa Kessler. New York, Ballantine, 1991.
Contributor, *Masters of Fantasy.* New York, Galihad, 1992.

*

Media Adaptations: *The Sword of Shannara* (cassette), Caedmon, 1986; *Running with the Demon* (cassette) Random House Audiobooks, 1997.

*   *   *

The publication of Terry Brooks's first novel *The Sword of Shannara* in 1977 brought fantasy novels into the literary mainstream. Until *Shannara* no fantasy writer except J. R. R. Tolkien had made such an impression on the general public. Brooks's novel opened up the market for fantasy writers. The author creates a fascinating picture of a post-nuclear world where magic has succeeded science as the operational force. Brooks's ''Shannara'' series portrays a land under the influence of spells and sorceries. In some cases humanity has mutated into new races, called after the ancient legends: dwarves, trolls, and gnomes. Some of these new races are well-intentioned, and some are not. Humankind exists in the shadow of evil.

There is hope, however. The last of the magic-working druids stalks the land, combatting evil wherever he finds it. Allanon constantly seeks out the young people of a single family, the Ohmsfords, and deviously attempts to use them to fulfill the needs of the country as he perceives them. The family is distantly related to the elven royal house of Shannara, and some of its members possess innate powers beyond those of their fellows. The druid works to bring out those latent talents, and in doing so brings the young people to a new maturity. The druid also encourages respect for the land and environmental concerns.

The first three books, *The Sword of Shannara, The Elfstones of Shannara,* and *The Wishsong of Shannara,* are all individual adventures. The concluding four volumes, *The Scions of Shannara, The Druid of Shannara, The Elf Queen of Shannara,* and *The Talismans of Shannara,* make up a single quest involving several members of the Ohmsford family.

Brooks's writing is strongest when dealing with problems that relate to present concerns. The first novel, with its chapters on warring elves and wraiths contrasted with one young man's search for a talisman to use against the evil, is very reminiscent of Tolkien's work. With the second book, *The Elfstones of Shannara,* Brooks moves away from the established pattern and breaks new ground. *Elfstones* is a very environmental novel, the focus of concern being the magical tree, the Ellcrys, which protects the lands from the ancient demons. The tree is old and dying and a complex ritual is required to restore it. The protagonist, Wil Ohmsford, is recruited by the druid Allanon to keep Amberle, the elven maiden responsible for the ritual, safe until she has completed her mission. Amberle is unsure of herself, and Wil needs to keeps assuring both himself and the girl of the importance of their quest.

The druid Allanon is both a strength and a weakness in Brooks's works. His reticence keeps the plots moving along smoothly, but one feels, along with the heroes, that the druid could have been more forthcoming with his knowledge. The constant revelation that Allanon knew everything all the time grows wearisome. The character is so shrouded in mystery that the occasional glimpses of humanity he shows are almost out of place. Most of the other major characters are extremely well done, giving the reader friends to agonize over and cry for. The women are generally portrayed more sympathetically; the witches in *Elfstones* are both menacing and pathetic, and Amberle is an exceptionally endearing character.

Brooks's third novel, *The Wishsong of Shannara,* was the first to have a female protagonist. Brin Ohmsford shares the limelight with her brother Jair, but it is her power that is ultimately tested and her decision that affects the outcome of the plot. Brin is the focus of the story in a way that no female character had been in fantasy literature before. Brooks does not use another woman in a leading role until the third book of the most current Shannara saga.

Wren Ohmsford is a highly intriguing character. Raised by the Gypsy-like Rovers of the Westland, she is highly skeptical of the druid's claims that she alone can bring back the elves from their self-imposed exile. Her journey to the volcanic island where the elves are hiding has the potential to be one of the best in the series. Unfortunately it fails. Wren's journey is riddled with gloom. Almost every one of the companions she attracts meets a hideous doom. She is deceived by her most constant companion and forced to face unpleasant truths about everything she believes. This does not make her a better person, only more resigned to the will of fate.

The First King of Shannara tells the story of what came before *The Sword of Shannara,* the first title in the saga. It is Bremen's tale, of how he found himself an outcast among the Druids for continuing to study Magic instead of devoting himself to the Old Sciences as the other Druids did. It is also the story of how Allanon came to learn the Magic from Bremen and receive for safe-keeping the black elfstone. Though fans longed to hear the history behind the saga of Shannara, it serves well to read at the end of the other books since parts encapsulate the history in a running list of names and trades and future towns. It is, however, a fitting conclusion to the saga that has captivated readers of all ages and set the standard for contemporary fantasy writing.

Though he is most well-known for his Shannara series, Brooks has also created another realm called Landover, which blends humor with the usual battle between good and evil. *Running with the Demon* demonstrates his skill as a storyteller in yet another area. In this novel he brings this struggle closer to home in a world similar to our own. In the town of Hopewell, on a planet like Earth but possessing elements of magic that few people can see, a demon has targeted the town as his tool in taking over the world.

Brooks's fantasy fiction appeals to young adult readers because his heroes and heroines struggle to grow, understand their world, and accept their destiny. At the same time they are catapulted into dangerous adventures in which their success is crucial to the continued existence of their world. The reader is immersed in the adventure as the main characters wonder how they will make any difference for the future, despair in their tasks, think of giving up, and find the determination to continue on. The reader finds encouragement for his own struggles and relief that the future of our world is not dependent on the success of such a ''quest.''

—Louise J. Winters, updated by Lisa A. Wroble

_____

BUNTING, A.E. *See* **BUNTING, (Anne) Eve(lyn).**

_____

BUNTING, (Anne) Eve(lyn)

Pseudonyms: Evelyn Bolton; A.E. Bunting. **Nationality:** American. **Born:** Maghera, County Derry, Ireland, 19 December 1928; emigrated to the United States, 1958; became citizen, 1967. **Education:** Methodist College, Belfast, 1936-45; Queen's University, Belfast, 1945-47; Pasadena City College, c. 1959. **Family:** Married Edward Bunting in 1951; one daughter and two sons. **Career:** Freelance writer, mainly for young people, 1969—. Teacher of writing, University of California, Los Angeles, 1978, 1979, and at writer's conferences. **Awards:** Society of Children's Book Writers Golden Kite award, Outstanding Science Trade Book for Children from the National Science Teachers Association and the Children's Book Council, Notable Children's Trade Book in the Field of Social Studies from the National Council for Social Studies and the Children's Book Council, and Child Study Association of America's Children's Books of the Year, all 1976, all for *One More Flight; The Big Red Barn,* 1979, *Goose Dinner* and *The Waiting Game,* 1981, *The Valentine Bears,* 1986, and *The Mother's Day Mice* and *Sixth Grade Sleepover,* 1987, were all named Child Study Association of America's Children's Books of the Year; *Winter's Coming* was named one of the *New York Times* Top Ten Books, 1977; Notable Work of Fiction from the Southern California Council on Literature for Children and Young People, 1977, for *Ghost of Summer;* Classroom Choice from Scholastic Paperbacks, 1978, for *Skateboards: How to Make Them, How to Ride Them; If I Asked You, Would You Stay?* was selected one of American Library Association's Best Books for Young Adults, 1984; PEN Special Achievement award, 1984, for her contribution to children's literature; Nene award from the Hawaii Association of School Librarians and the Hawaii Library Association, 1987, for *Karen Kepplewhite Is the World's Best Kisser; The Mother's Day Mice,* 1986, and *The Wednesday Surprise,* 1989, were selected as *School Library Journal*'s Best Books of the Year; Southern California Council on Literature for Children and Young People award for Excellence in a Series, 1986, for ''Lippincott Page Turners'' series; Parents' Choice from the Parents' Choice Foundation, and one of *School Library Journal*'s Best Books of the year, both 1987, both for *Ghost's Hour, Spook's Hour;* Parents' Choice award from the Parents' Choice Foundation, 1988, for *The Mother's Day Mice;* Virginia Young Readers award, 1988-89, California Young Readers Medal, 1989, and South Carolina Young Adult Book award, 1988-89, all for *Face at the Edge of the World;* Surrey School Book of the Year award, 1989, for *Sixth Grade Sleepover;* Notable Children's Trade Book, Southern California Council on Literature for Children and Young People award for Outstanding Work of Fiction for Young Adults, 1989, Sequoyah Children's Book award from the Oklahoma Library Association, 1990, and California Young Reader's Medal, 1992, all for *A Sudden Silence;* Children's Book Council Children's Choice award, 1989, for *Seaworld Book*

of Sharks; Sequoyah Children's Book award from the Oklahoma Library Association, Mark Twain award from the State of Missouri, and Sunshine State Young Readers award, all 1989, all for *Sixth Grade Sleepover;* Southern California Council on Literature for Children and Young People award for Outstanding Work of Fiction for Young Adults, 1990, for *The Wall;* Soaring Eagle award, 1990, for *Someone Is Hiding on Alcatraz Island;* South Carolina Book award, Mystery Writers of America Edgar Allan Poe nomination, 1991, and Nebraska Golden Sower award, 1992, all for *Is Anybody There?;* Jane Addams Honor award, 1990, for *The Wednesday Surprise;* Distinguished Body of Work Award, Southern California Council on Literature for Children and Young People, 1993; Western Writers of America Storyteller Award for *Dandelions,* 1995; Regina Medal For Her Distinguished Contribution to Children's Literature, Catholic Library Association, 1997.

PUBLICATIONS FOR YOUNG ADULTS

Fiction

A Gift for Lonny, illustrated by Robert Quackenbush. Lexington, Massachusetts, Ginn, 1973.

Box, Fox, Ox and the Peacock, illustrated by Leslie Morrill. Lexington, Massachusetts, Ginn, 1974.

The Once-a-Year Day, illustrated by W.T. Mars. Chicago, Children's Press, 1974.

We Need a Bigger Zoo!, illustrated by Bob Barner. Lexington, Massachusetts, Ginn, 1974.

The Wild One. New York, Scholastic, 1974.

Barney the Beard, illustrated by Imero Gobbato. New York, Parents Magazine Press, 1975; London, Warne, 1978.

The Dinosaur Machines (The Day of the Dinosaurs, Death of a Dinosaur, The Dinosaur Trap, Escape from Tyrannosaurus), illustrated by Judith Leo. St. Paul, Minnesota, EMC Corp., 4 vols., 1975.

No Such Things. . . ? (The Creature of Cranberry Cove, The Demon, The Ghost, The Tongue of the Ocean), illustrated by Scott Earle. St. Paul, Minnesota, EMC Corp., 4 vols., 1976.

Josefina Finds the Prince, illustrated by Jan Palmer. Champaign, Illinois, Garrard, 1976.

Blacksmith at Blueridge, photographs by Peter Fine. New York, Scholastic, 1976.

Skateboard Saturday, photographs by Richard Hutchings. New York, Scholastic, 1976.

One More Flight, illustrated by Diane de Groat. New York and London, Warne, 1976.

The Skateboard Four, illustrated by Phil Kantz. Chicago, Whitman, 1976.

Winter's Coming, illustrated by Howard Knotts. New York, Harcourt Brace, 1977.

The Big Cheese, illustrated by Sal Murdocca. New York, Macmillan, 1977; London, Macmillan, 1980.

Cop Camp, photographs by Richard Hutchings. New York, Scholastic, 1977.

Ghost of Summer. New York, Warne, 1977.

Creative Science Fiction (The Day of the Earthlings, The Followers, The Island of One, The Mask, The Mirror Planet, The Robot People, The Space People, The Undersea People), illustrated by Don Hendricks. Mankato, Minnesota, Creative Education, 8 vols., 1978.

Creative Romance (*Fifteen, For Always, The Girl in the Painting, Just Like Everyone Else, Maggie the Freak, Nobody Knows But Me, Oh, Rick!, A Part of the Dream, Survival Camp!, Two Different Girls*), illustrated by Robert Gadbois. Mankato, Minnesota, Creative Education, 10 vols., 1978.

The Big Find, photographs by Richard Hutchings. Mankato, Minnesota, Creative Education, 1978.

Magic and the Night River, illustrated by Allen Say. New York, Harper, 1978.

Going Against Cool Calvin, illustrated by Don Brautigan. New York, Scholastic, 1978.

The Haunting of Kildoran Abbey. New York, Warne, 1978; London, Warne, 1979.

The Big Red Barn, illustrated by Howard Knotts. New York, Harcourt Brace, 1979.

The Cloverdale Switch. New York, Lippincott, 1979; as *Strange Things Happen in the Woods,* New York, Archway, 1984.

Yesterday's Island, illustrated by Stephen Gammell. New York, Warne, 1979.

Mr. Pride's Umbrella, illustrated by Maggie Ling. London, Warne, 1980.

The Robot Birthday, illustrated by Marie DeJohn. New York, Dutton, 1980.

Demetrius and the Golden Goblet, illustrated by Michael Hague. New York, Harcourt Brace, 1980.

Terrible Things, illustrated by Stephen Gammell. New York, Harper, 1980; as *Terrible Things: An Allegory of the Holocaust,* Jewish Publication Society, 1989.

St. Patrick's Day in the Morning, illustrated by Jan Brett. Boston, Houghton Mifflin, 1980.

Blackbird Singing, illustrated by Stephen Gammell. New York, Macmillan, 1980.

The Empty Window, illustrated by Judy Clifford. New York, Warne, 1980.

The Skate Patrol, illustrated by Don Madden. Chicago, Whitman, 1980.

Goose Dinner, illustrated by Howard Knotts. New York, Harcourt Brace, 1981.

Jane Martin and the Case of the Ice Cream Dog. Champaign, Illinois, Garrard, 1981.

Rosie and Mr. William Star. Boston, Houghton Mifflin, 1981.

The Skate Patrol Rides Again, illustrated by Don Madden. Chicago, Whitman, 1981.

The Spook Birds, illustrated by Blanche Sims. Chicago, Whitman, 1981.

The Waiting Game. New York, Lippincott, 1981.

The Ghosts of Departure Point. New York, Lippincott, 1982.

The Happy Funeral, illustrated by Vo-Dinh Mai. New York, Harper, 1982.

The Skate Patrol and the Mystery Writer, illustrated by Don Madden. Chicago, Whitman, 1982.

The Traveling Men of Ballycoo, illustrated by Kaethe Zemach. New York, Harcourt Brace, 1983.

The Valentine Bears, illustrated by Jan Brett. New York, Clarion, 1983.

Karen Kepplewhite Is the World's Best Kisser. New York, Clarion, 1983.

Clancy's Coat, illustrated by Lorinda Bryan Cauley. New York, Warne, 1984.

The Ghost Behind Me. New York, Archway, 1984.

If I Asked You, Would You Stay? New York, Lippincott, 1984.

Jane Martin, Dog Detective, illustrated by Amy Schwartz. New York, Harcourt Brace, 1984.

The Man Who Could Call Down Owls, illustrated by Charles Mikolaycak. New York, Macmillan, 1984.

Monkey in the Middle, illustrated by Lynn Munsinger. New York, Harcourt Brace, 1984.

Someone Is Hiding on Alcatraz Island. New York, Clarion, 1984; London, Fontana, 1986.

Surrogate Sister. New York, Lippincott, 1984; London, Hodder and Stoughton, 1985; as *Mother, How Could You!,* New York, Simon and Schuster, 1986.

Face at the Edge of the World. New York, Clarion, 1985; London, Fontana, 1987.

The Haunting of Safekeep. New York, Lippincott, 1985.

Janet Hamm Needs a Date for the Dance. New York, Clarion, 1986.

The Mother's Day Mice, illustrated by Jan Brett. New York, Clarion, 1986.

Sixth-Grade Sleepover. San Diego, Harcourt Brace, 1986.

Ghost's Hour, Spook's Hour, illustrated by Donald Carrick. New York, Clarion, 1987.

Will You Be My POSSLQ? San Diego, Harcourt Brace, 1987.

Happy Birthday, Dear Duck, illustrated by Jan Brett. New York, Clarion, 1988.

How Many Days to America? A Thanksgiving Story, illustrated by Beth Peck. New York, Clarion, 1988.

Is Anybody There? New York, Lippincott, 1988.

A Sudden Silence. San Diego, Harcourt Brace, 1988.

The Ghost Children. New York, Clarion, 1989.

No Nap, illustrated by Susan Meddaugh. New York, Clarion, 1989.

The Wednesday Surprise, illustrated by Donald Carrick. New York, Clarion, 1989.

The Wall, illustrated by Ronald Himler. Boston, Houghton Mifflin, 1990.

Such Nice Kids. Boston, Houghton Mifflin, 1990.

Our Sixth-Grade Sugar Babies. New York, Harper, 1990.

In the Haunted House, illustrated by Susan Meddaugh. Boston, Houghton Mifflin, 1990.

Fly Away Home, illustrated by Ronald Himler. Boston, Houghton Mifflin, 1991.

The Hideout. San Diego, Harcourt Brace, 1991.

Jumping the Nail. San Diego, Harcourt Brace, 1991.

Night Tree, illustrated by Ted Rand. San Diego, Harcourt Brace, 1991.

A Perfect Father's Day, illustrated by Susan Meddaugh. Boston, Houghton Mifflin, 1991.

Sharing Susan. New York, Harper, 1991.

A Turkey for Thanksgiving, illustrated by Diane de Groat. Boston, Houghton Mifflin, 1991.

The Bicycle Man, illustrated by Thomas B. Allen. San Diego, Harcourt Brace, 1992.

Coffin on a Case. New York, Harper, 1992.

Day Before Christmas. Boston, Houghton Mifflin, 1992.

Our Teacher's Having a Baby. Boston, Houghton Mifflin, 1992.

Summer Wheels, illustrated by Thomas B. Allen. San Diego, Harcourt Brace, 1992.

Red Fox Running, illustrated by Wendell Minor. New York, Clarion, 1993.

Someday a Tree, illustrated by Ronald Himler. Boston, Houghton Mifflin, 1993.

Flower Garden, illustrated by Kathryn Hewitt. San Diego, Harcourt Brace, 1994.

Night of the Gargoyles, illustrated by David Wiesner. New York, Clarion Books, 1994.

The In-Between Days, illustrated by Alexander Pertzoff. New York, HarperCollins, 1994.

Sunshine Home, illustrated by Diane De Groat, New York, Clarion, 1994.

Smoky Night, illustrated by David Diaz. San Diego, Harcourt Brace, 1994.

Nasty Stinky Sneakers. New York, HarperCollins, 1994.

A Day's Work, illustrated by Ronald Himler. New York, Clarion Books, 1994.

Cheyenne Again, illustrated by Irving Toddy, New York, Clarion Books, 1995.

Spying on Miss Muller. New York, Clarion Books, 1995.

Dandelions, illustrated by Greg Shed. San Diego, Harcourt Brace, 1995.

Once Upon a Time, photographs by John Pezaris. Katonah, New York, R.C. Owen Publishers, 1995.

Going Home, illustrated by David Diaz. New York, HarperCollins, 1996.

SOS Titanic. San Diego, Harcourt Brace, 1996.

Secret Place, illustrated by Ted Rand. New York, Clarion Books, 1996.

The Blue and the Gray, illustrated by Ned Bittinger. New York, Scholastic, 1996.

Train to Somewhere, illustrated by Ronald Himler. New York, Clarion Books, 1996.

Market Day, pictures by Holly Berry. New York, HarperCollins, 1996.

I Don't Want to Go to Camp, illustrated by Maryann Cocca-Leffler. Honesdale, PA, Boyds Mills Press, 1996.

Sunflower House, illustrated by Kathryn Hewitt. San Diego, Harcourt Brace, 1996.

The Pumpkin Fair, illustrated by Eileen Christelow. New York, Clarion Books, 1997.

I Am the Mummy Heb-Nefert, illustrated by David Christiana. San Diego, Harcourt Brace, 1997.

Trouble on the T-Ball Team, illustrated by Irene Trivas. New York, Clarion Books, 1997.

December, illustrated by David Diaz. San Diego, Harcourt Brace, 1997.

On Call Back Mountain, illustrated by Barry Moser. New York, Blue Sky Press, 1997.

Some Frog!, illustrated by Scott Medlock. San Diego, Harcourt Brace, 1997.

Moonstick, The Seasons of the Sioux, paintings by John Sandford. New York, HarperCollins, 1997.

Your Move, illustrated by James Ransome. San Diego, Harcourt Brace, 1997.

Twinnies, illustrated by Nancy Carpenter. San Diego, Harcourt Brace, 1997.

So Far From the Sea, illustrated by Chris Soentpiet. New York, Clarion Books, 1998.

The Day the Whale Came, illustrated by Scott Menchin. San Diego, Harcourt Brace, 1998.

Ducky, illustrated by David Wisniewski. New York, Clarion Books, 1998.

Fiction as Evelyn Bolton (illustrated by John Keely)

Stable of Fear. Mankato, Minnesota, Creative Education, 1974.

Lady's Girl. Mankato, Minnesota, Creative Education, 1974.

Goodbye Charlie. Mankato, Minnesota, Creative Education, 1974.

Ride When You're Ready. Mankato, Minnesota, Creative Education, 1974.

The Wild Horses. Mankato, Minnesota, Creative Education, 1974.

Dream Dancer. Mankato, Minnesota, Creative Education, 1974.

Fiction as A.E. Bunting

Pitcher to Center Field, illustrated by Len Freas. Chicago, Children's Press, 1974.

Surfing Country, illustrated by Dale King. Chicago, Children's Press, 1974.

High Tide for Labrador, illustrated by Bernard Garbutt. Chicago, Children's Press, 1975.

Springboard to Summer, illustrated by Rob Sprattler. Chicago, Children's Press, 1975.

Poetry

Scary, Scary Halloween, illustrated by Jan Brett. New York, Clarion, 1986.

Other

The Two Giants (Irish folktale), illustrated by Eric von Schmidt. Lexington, Massachusetts, Ginn, 1972.

Say It Fast (tongue twisters), illustrated by True Kelley. Lexington, Massachusetts, Ginn, 1974.

Skateboards: How to Make Them, How to Ride Them, with Glenn Bunting. New York, Harvey House, 1977.

The Sea World Book of Sharks, photographs by Flip Nicklin. San Diego, Sea World, 1979.

The Sea World Book of Whales. New York, Harcourt Brace, 1980.

The Giant Squid. New York, Messner, 1981.

The Great White Shark. New York, Messner, 1982.

Also author of stories for basal readers published by several educational houses, including Heath, Laidlaw Brothers, Lyons and Carnahan, Scott, Foresman, Bowmar Educational, Scholastic, and Rand McNally. Contributor to anthologies, including *Cricket's Choice,* 1975, and *Scribner's Anthology for Young People.* Contributor of adult and juvenile stories to periodicals, including *Jack and Jill* and *Cricket.*

*

Media Adaptations: *How Many Days to America?* (film), Coronet/MTI Film and Video, 1991; *A Desperate Exit* (television movie adaptation of *A Face at the Edge of the World*); *The Wall* (segment on *Reading Rainbow*).

Biography: Entry in *Authors and Artists for Young Adults,* Volume 5, Detroit, Gale, 1990; essay in *Speaking for Ourselves: Autobiographical Sketches by Notable Authors of Books for Young Adults,* Volume 1, compiled and edited by Donald R. Gallo, National Council of Teachers of English, 1990;

Manuscript Collections: Kerlan Collection, University of Minnesota, Minneapolis.

Critical Studies: Entry in *Children's Literature Review,* Volume 28, Detroit, Gale, 1992; entry in *Children's Books and Their Creators,* Boston, Houghton Mifflin, 1995.

Eve Bunting comments:

There used to be Shanachies in the Ireland of long ago. The Shanachie was the storyteller who went from house to house telling his tales of ghosts and fairies, of old Irish heroes and battles still to be won. Maybe I'm a bit of a Shanachie myself, telling my stories to anyone who'll listen.

I like to write for every child. For every age, for every interest. That is why I have such a variety of books—from pre-school, through the middle grades and beyond. The young adult novels I write border on the true adult novel, but I enjoy keeping my protagonists in their upper teens, where lives are new and filled with challenge, where nothing is impossible.

One of my greatest joys is writing picture books. I have discovered the pleasures of telling a story of happiness or sorrow in a few simple words. I like to write picture books that make young people ponder, that encourage them to ask questions. "Why did that happen, Mom? Could it happen again? Can't we help? What can we do?" One child wrote to tell me that one of my books had won the *Heal the World* award at her school. It is among the most cherished honors I have ever received, and the plaque hangs proudly above my desk.

*   *   *

Eve Bunting is one of a few talented authors who can produce everything from picture books to sensitive, suspenseful books for young adults. She is an accomplished mystery writer, as evidenced by her "Lippincott Page Turners" series and mysteries set in her native Ireland. Combining an innate gift for storytelling with a keen eye for spotting trends, Bunting is often at the forefront of the young-adult genre with topical books exploring themes like alcoholism, racism, teenage prostitution, and sexual abuse. Bunting claims to gather 90 percent of her story ideas from current events; shrewd assessment of her audience has made Bunting a very popular and marketable author.

Believing it is "dishonest to write a novel about characters free from any problems of a serious nature," Bunting explores the ways in which her characters are affected by crises both within themselves and in others. She has had varying degrees of success integrating the problem aspect of her novels within the context of the story.

A Sudden Silence is a moving portrayal of the destruction caused by alcohol abuse. When Jesse's brother is killed by a hit-and-run driver, Jesse struggles with grief coupled with guilt over his helplessness at preventing the accident. He also experiences conflicting emotions about his feelings for his brother's girlfriend, Chloe. As the two teens join forces to find the person responsible for Bry's death, a tentative friendship forms. The relationship between Chloe and Jesse is well drawn; it stands alone on its own merits while exposing the universality of alcohol abuse by depicting the social and economic differences between the two families. When Jesse discovers that Chloe's mother was responsible for his

brother's death, there is no easy resolution. Bunting resists the convenience of a happy ending.

Surrogate Sister offers an interesting slant on a very modern issue, surrogate motherhood. By presenting the matter from a sibling's point of view, Bunting poses thought-provoking questions regarding this sensitive topic. When Cassie's widowed mother, despite Cassie's objections, agrees to become a surrogate mother for a childless couple, Cassie is faced with the insensitivity of her classmates and her own confusion about the morality of her mother's decision. While the issue is presented in a straightforward and compassionate manner, Bunting tries too hard to link together disparate elements of the story, namely, Cassie's concern over her blossoming sexual relationship with a college student and her friend's pregnancy. Cassie experiences an understandable curiosity about the childless couple, but the ease with which she locates them diminishes the effect of her feelings. Most importantly, in terms of characterization, one wonders if Cassie's warm and affectionate mother would have persisted with the surrogate pregnancy in light of Cassie's extreme hostility and strong opposition.

Certain themes run throughout Bunting's books; one suspects that these issues are of fundamental concern to her. There is a self-consciousness that is, at times, disconcerting. The parents in Bunting's books are often nonconformists, yet there is always a prevailing sense of morality. In *Surrogate Sister,* for instance, Cassie decides against a sexual relationship with her boyfriend.

And in *Would You Be My POSSLQ?,* the heroine is a spunky college freshman who embarks on an alternative living arrangement with a Person of the Opposite Sex Sharing Living Quarters. Although Jamie has been raised in a strict Catholic family and has witnessed the heartache caused by her sister's decision to bear a child out of wedlock, she agrees to share her apartment with Kyle on a purely platonic level. Jamie, attracted to Kyle, does not rely on her innate good sense and bases her decision on rather flimsy financial reasons. Therefore, her subsequent decision to separate so that a romantic relationship can develop is not believable. Jamie's emotional recovery from cancer, however, adds a special element to the story. Her relationships with terminal cancer patients are honest, straightforward, and extremely touching. There is also a nice thematic juxtaposition among Jamie's and her sisters' situations: Phoebe, pregnant again, is marrying her boyfriend; Tig, at fourteen, is being pressured for a more physical relationship with her boyfriend; Jamie is trying to sort out her complicated feelings about Kyle and her own mortality.

Bunting portrays the negative consequences of peer pressure in *Jumping the Nail.* The "Nail" is a dangerous cliff, off-limits even to anyone brave enough to attempt a jump into the deep water below. Scooter, the class bad boy, decides to make the leap. He convinces his unstable girlfriend, Elisa, to join him, leading her into a downward spiral that ends in suicide. Dru and Mike are the couple who try, unsuccessfully, to stop the madness that follows. The story is somewhat superficial, especially in its treatment of the serious topics of teen depression and suicide. Elisa's illness is treated far too frivolously for it to be the motivation for the chain of events that occurs.

Perhaps one of Bunting's most successful books is *If I Asked You, Would You Stay?,* an unusual story about two runaways who forge an uneasy alliance that leads to love. While Crow and Valentine are fully realized characters, Crow lacks the intensity that is crucial to the story's success. With notable exceptions—Crow and Jesse—Bunting experiences a problem with realistic characterization in her male heroes. They are idealized, invariably sensitive, and understanding, not prone to typical teen attitudes and behavior.

Bunting is a prolific author, and produced 30 books in less than four years during the mid- to late 1990s. Among these were *Secret Place,* whose young narrator finds a duck and her ducklings hidden in an unusual urban setting. A wise grownup counsels him to be careful and not share the location of his secret place with many others, since "some people might want to take the secret place and change it." It is a valuable environmental lesson, driven home by the protagonist's own education, as the book progresses, in the varieties of wildlife. Less critically acclaimed was *The Blue and the Gray,* the story of two boys, one black and one white, whose families live near a Civil War battle site. The tale progresses in two time periods, alternating between the present day and 1862, but in spite of the powerful concept and the poetic language, the story seems predictable, and not as strong as Bunting's usual offerings.

In an evaluation of Eve Bunting, Eric Kimmel states, "She writes too often from her head rather than her gut, raising sensitive issues but pulling away from the risks that go along with them." If Bunting were less concerned with conveying her message—and therefore loosened the restraints, took some risks, and allowed her characters the freedom to tell their own stories—she would achieve the level of high-quality writing of which she is surely capable.

—Maryclare O'Donnell Himmel, updated by Judson Knight

BURCH, Robert J(oseph)

Nationality: American. **Born:** Inman, Georgia, 26 June 1925. **Education:** University of Georgia, Athens, B.A. in agriculture 1949; Hunter College, New York, 1955. **Military Service:** Served in the United States Army, in New Guinea and Australia, 1943-46. **Career:** Worked in a commercial greenhouse, 1950; civil servant, United States Army Ordinance Depot, Atlanta, 1951-53, and in Japan, 1953-55; office worker, 1953-55; Muir & Company Advertising, New York, 1956-59, and Walter E. Heller & Company, New York, 1959-62; writer, since 1959. **Awards:** Fellowship in juvenile literature, Bread Loaf Writers' Conference, 1960; children's book award from Child Study Association of America and Jane Addams Children's Book award, both 1967, for *Queenie Peavy;* Georgia Children's Book award, 1969, for *Skinny,* 1971, for *Queenie Peavy,* and 1974, for *Doodle and the Go-Cart;* George S. Stone Center for Children's Books award, 1974; Phoenix award from the Children's Literature Association, 1986, for *Queenie Peavy.* **Address:** 2021 Forest Dr., Fayetteville, Georgia 30214, U.S.A.

PUBLICATIONS FOR YOUNG ADULTS

Fiction

Tyler, Wilkin, and Skee, illustrated by Don Sibley. New York, Viking, 1963.
Skinny, illustrated by Don Sibley. New York, Viking, 1964; illustrated by Ian Ribbons, London, Methuen, 1965.

D. J.'s Worst Enemy, illustrated by Emil Weiss. New York, Viking, 1965.
Queenie Peavy, illustrated by Jerry Lazare. New York, Viking, 1966.
Simon and the Game of Chance, illustrated by Fermin Rocker. New York, Viking, 1970.
Doodle and the Go-Cart, illustrated by Alan Tiegreen. New York, Viking, 1972.
Hut School and the Wartime Home-Front Heroes, illustrated by Ronald Himler. New York, Viking, 1974; as *Home-Front,* New York, Viking, 1992.
Two That Were Tough, illustrated by Richard Cuffari. New York, Viking, 1976.
The Whitman Kick. New York, Dutton, 1977.
Wilkin's Ghost, illustrated by Lloyd Bloom. New York, Viking, 1978.
Ida Early Comes over the Mountain. New York, Viking, 1980.
Christmas with Ida Early, illustrated by Gail Owens. New York, Viking, 1983.
King Kong and Other Poets. New York, Viking, 1986.
Homefront Heroes, illustrated by Ronald Himler. New York, Puffin Books, 1992.

PUBLICATIONS FOR CHILDREN

Fiction

The Traveling Bird, illustrated by Susanne Suba. New York, McDowell, Obolensky, 1959.
A Funny Place to Live, illustrated by W. R. Lohse. New York, Viking, 1962.
Renfroe's Christmas, illustrated by Rocco Negri. New York, Viking, 1968.
Joey's Cat, illustrated by Don Freeman. New York, Viking, 1969.
The Hunting Trip, illustrated by Susanne Suba. New York, Scribners, 1971.
The Jolly Witch, illustrated by Leigh Grant. New York, Dutton, 1975.

PUBLICATIONS FOR ADULTS

Other

Translator, *A Jungle in the Wheat Field,* by Egon Mathieson. New York, McDowell, Obolensky, 1960.
A Peircean Reduction Thesis: The Foundations of Topological Logic. Lubbock, Texas Tech University Press, 1991.

*

Media Adaptations: *Ida Early Comes over the Mountain* (as "The Incredible Ida Early," television movie), National Broadcasting Corporation (NBC), 1987.

Biography: Entry in *Dictionary of Literary Biography,* Volume 52: *American Writers for Children since 1960: Fiction,* Detroit, Gale, 1986.

Manuscript Collections: University of Georgia, Athens.

*   *   *

As the author of nineteen books for children and young adults, Robert Burch writes with sensitivity and compassion about the rural Georgia landscape and people he knows so well. Despite traveling widely before becoming interested in writing at the age of thirty while living in New York, Burch has been content to draw on the experiences of his childhood and youth for the substance of his narratives. He has mastered his craft well, and his strong sense of place and his ability to develop strong characters enrich his fiction. Growth and change permeate his stories, whether it is Alan Ponder's coming to terms with the personal upheavals of his senior year in high school in *The Whitman Kick* or the elderly Mr. Hilton's coping with the perceived loss of freedom and independence he faces in *Two That Were Tough* as his daughter presses him to leave his home and the old grist mill he has operated for years to move to Atlanta to live with her.

While Burch has written four picture books, his novels have been his most effective vehicle for speaking to his readers. As a boy in a rural community during the Depression, Burch learned that being happy and enjoying life were not dependent upon material possessions, and this is a strong theme in many of his books, most notably in *Tyler, Wilkin, and Skee* and *Doodle and the Go-Cart*. In *Skinny,* readers meet a boy who longs to be adopted by Miss Bessie who operates the local hotel and who has taken him in after his father dies. Even though Skinny is not adopted and must go to an orphanage, readers come away feeling that Skinny's good qualities and resourcefulness will carry him far, and that he will come back to visit Miss Bessie at the hotel.

Queenie Peavy, a character study of a thirteen-year-old girl whose father is in prison, was Burch's first female protagonist and his first venture into contemporary realistic fiction. Queenie, a tomboy who chews tobacco and throws rocks with deadly accuracy, is frequently in trouble as she struggles with a negative self-image. She wants to believe that when her father is released from prison, he will be a changed person. This is not the case, and Burch avoids a sentimental ending as Queenie accepts the fact that her father is not a good person and that she can lead a rewarding life by building on her strengths.

Whether set in the Depression or in more contemporary times, Burch's novels remain faithful to small town life. *Tyler, Wilkin, and Skee,* the story of a year in the life of three brothers living on a farm during the Depression, offers a touching picture of family life and underscores the importance of school and church in the social fabric of a community. *Hut School and the Wartime Home-Front Heroes* and *The Whitman Kick* reflect the impact of World War II on the people in small towns. A more familiar form of change is evident for contemporary readers of *King Kong and Other Poets,* where the transformation of a community through encroaching urbanization serves as a backdrop to the changes going on in the lives of young people in this story of the power of friendship in healing the pain of loneliness and loss. Through a poetry contest, Marilyn, a shy newcomer from California whose mother has died, learns that she, too, can fit in and be accepted by her peers. The unusual title comes from the fact that the students want the security of pseudonyms before they engage in class poetry writing and sharing. Poetry also plays a significant role in *The Whitman Kick*.

Burch's most memorable character may be Ida Early who, in *Ida Early Comes over the Mountain,* arrives unexpectedly to care for the four Sutton children after their mother dies. With her tall tales and antics, she helps the children overcome their grief and find joy in life again. Ida Early's appeal—one reviewer calls Ida "a mountain Mary Poppins" while another extends the image by saying that "she makes Mary Poppins look like Elsie Dinsmore"—lies in her raucous humor which results in an unconventional and unforgettable Christmas tableau. Before his second Ida Early book, Burch had never given much thought to sequels, although he had used the middle brother of *Tyler, Wilkin, and Skee* in *Wilkin's Ghost* and Renfroe, the younger brother in *D. J.'s Worst Enemy,* as the central character of *Renfroe's Christmas.* Burch admits he had Ida as a babysitter in an early draft of *Simon and the Game of Chance,* a story that deals with a large family in which the mother suffers from mental illness, but he removed her because her strong personality was a distraction. Ida has been featured in *The Incredible Ida Early,* a television film.

To think of Burch as a regional writer would be misleading as his universal themes and unique characters have earned him an international readership with Danish editions of *Skinny, Tyler, Wilkin, and Skee,* and *D. J.'s Worst Enemy*; German editions of *Queenie Peavy* and *Ida Early Comes Over the Mountain*; and a Japanese edition of *Queenie Peavy.* Burch's work has won numerous awards, including in 1986 the Children's Literature Association's Phoenix Award which honored *Queenie Peavy* as a work of enduring literary merit.

Burch is comfortably settled in his Georgia home on land that once belonged to his grandfather, watching new businesses and new people arrive in his childhood community. Yet his childhood memories of adults telling stories on the front porch continue to feed his fertile imagination as he works on a new Ida Early story and processes thoughts of other narratives still to be written.

—William Agee

BURGESS, Anthony

Pseudonym for John Anthony Burgess Wilson. **Other Pseudonyms:** Joseph Kell. **Nationality:** British. **Born:** Manchester, Lancashire, 25 February 1917. **Education:** Xaverian College, Manchester; Manchester University, B.A. (honours) in English 1940. **Military Service:** Served in the British Army Education Corps, 1940-46; sergeant-major. **Family:** Married 1) Llewela Isherwood Jones in 1942 (died 1968); 2) Liliana Macellari in 1968, one son. **Career:** Lecturer, Extra-Mural Department, Birmingham University, 1946-48; education officer and lecturer, Central Advisory Council for Adult Education in the Forces, 1946-48; lecturer in phonetics, Ministry of Education, 1948-50; English master, Banbury Grammar School, Oxfordshire, 1950-54; senior lecturer in English, Malayan Teachers Training College, Khata Baru, 1954-57; English language specialist, Department of Education, Brunei, Borneo, 1958-59; writer-in-residence, University of North Carolina, Chapel Hill, 1969-70; professor, Columbia University, New York, 1970-71; visiting fellow, Princeton University, New Jersey, 1970-71; distinguished professor, City University of New York, 1972-73; literary adviser, Guthrie Theatre, Minneapolis, 1972-75. Also composer. **Awards:** Fellow, Royal Society of Literature, 1969; National Arts Club award, 1973; Prix du Meilleur Livre Etranger, 1981, for *Earthly Powers;* D.Litt., Manchester University, 1982; Commandeur de Mérite Cultural (Monaco), 1986; Commandeur des Arts et des Lettres (France), 1986; *Sunday*

Times Mont Blanc award, 1987. **Address:** 44 rue Grimaldi, MC 98000, Monaco.

PUBLICATIONS

Novels

A Time for a Tiger. London, Heinemann, 1956.

The Enemy in the Blanket. London, Heinemann, 1958.

Beds in the East. London, Heinemann, 1959.

The Doctor Is Sick. London, Heinemann, and New York, Norton, 1960.

The Right to an Answer. London, Heinemann, 1960; New York, Norton, 1961.

Devil of a State. London, Heinemann, 1961; New York, Norton, 1962.

The Worm and the Ring. London, Heinemann, 1961; revised edition, 1970.

A Clockwork Orange. London, Heinemann, 1962; New York, Norton, 1963.

The Wanting Seed. London, Heinemann, 1962; New York, Norton, 1963.

Honey for the Bears. London, Heinemann, 1963; New York, Norton, 1964.

The Eve of Saint Venus. London, Sidgwick and Jackson, 1964; New York, Norton, 1967.

The Malayan Trilogy (includes *Time for a Tiger, The Enemy in the Blanket, Beds in the East*). London, Heinemann, 1964; as *The Long Day Wanes,* New York, Norton, 1965.

Nothing Like the Sun: A Story of Shakespeare's Love-Life, London, Heinemann, and New York, Norton, 1964.

A Vision of Battlements, illustrated by Edward Pagram. London, Sidgwick and Jackson, 1965; New York, Norton, 1966.

Tremor of Intent. London, Heinemann, and New York, Norton, 1966.

Enderby (includes *Inside Mr. Enderby* and *Enderby Outside;* also see below). New York, Norton, 1968.

Enderby Outside. London, Heinemann, 1968.

MF. London, Cape, and New York, Knopf, 1971.

The Clockwork Testament: or, Enderby's End. London, Hart Davis MacGibbon, 1974; New York, Knopf, 1975.

Napoleon Symphony. London, Cape, and New York, Knopf, 1974.

Beard's Roman Women, photos by David Robinson. New York, McGraw Hill, 1976; London, Hutchinson, 1977.

Abba Abba. London, Faber, and Boston, Little Brown, 1977.

1985. London, Hutchinson, and Boston, Little Brown, 1978.

Man of Nazareth. New York, McGraw Hill, 1979; London, Magnum, 1980.

Earthly Powers. London, Hutchinson, and New York, Simon and Schuster, 1980.

The End of the World News. London, Hutchinson, 1982; New York, McGraw Hill, 1983.

Enderby (includes *Inside Mr. Enderby, Enderby Outside, The Clockwork Testament*). London, Penguin, 1982.

Enderby's Dark Lady; or, No End to Enderby. London, Hutchinson, and New York, McGraw Hill, 1984.

The Kingdom of the Wicked. London, Hutchinson, and New York, Arbor House, 1985.

The Pianoplayers. London, Hutchinson, and New York, Arbor House, 1986.

Any Old Iron. London, Hutchinson, and New York, Random House, 1989.

The Long Day Wanes: A Malayan Trilogy. New York, W.W. Norton, 1992.

A Dead Man in Deptford. London, Hutchinson, 1993; New York, Carroll & Graf Publishers, 1995.

Byrne: A Novel. London, Hutchinson, 1995; New York, Carroll & Graf Publishers, 1997.

Novels as Joseph Kell

One Hand Clapping. London, Davies, 1961; as Anthony Burgess, New York, Knopf, 1972.

Inside Mr. Enderby. London, Heinemann, 1963.

Short Stories

Will and Testament: A Fragment of Biography, illustrated by Joe Tilson. Verona, Italy, Plain Wrapper Press, 1977.

The Devil's Mode and Other Stories. London, Hutchinson, and New York, Random House, 1989.

Plays

Cyrano de Bergerac, adaptation of the play by Rostand (produced Minneapolis, 1971). New York, Knopf, 1971; musical version, as *Cyrano,* music by Michael Lewis, lyrics by Burgess (produced New York, 1972).

Oedipus the King, adaptation of play by Sophocles (produced Minneapolis, 1972; Southampton, Hampshire, 1979). Minneapolis, University of Minnesota Press, 1972; London, Oxford University Press, 1973.

Moses   The Lawgiver (television play), with others, 1975.

Jesus of Nazareth (television play), with others, 1977.

A Kind of Failure (television documentary; *Writers and Places* series), 1981.

The Cavalier of the Rose (story adaptation), in *Deer Rosenkavalier,* libretto by Hofmannsthal, music by Richard Strauss. Boston, Little Brown, 1982; London, Joseph, 1983.

A.D. (television play), 1985.

The Childhood of Christ (television play), music by Berlioz, 1985.

Blooms of Dublin, music by Burgess, adaptation of the novel *Ulysses* by James Joyce (radio play 1982; broadcast 1983). London, Hutchinson, 1986.

Cyrano de Bergerac (not same as 1971 version), adaptation of the play by Rostand (produced London, 1983). London, Hutchinson, 1985.

Oberon Old and New (includes original libretto by James Robinson Planché), music by Carl Maria von Weber. London, Hutchinson, 1985.

Carmen, adaptation of the libretto by Henri Meilhac and Ludovic Halévy, music by George Bizet (produced London, 1986). London, Hutchinson, 1986.

A Clockwork Orange, music by Burgess, adaptation of his own novel. London, Hutchinson, 1987.

A Clockwork Orange 2004 (produced London, 1990).

A Meeting in Valladolid (radio play). 1991.

Screenplay: special languages for *Quest for Fire,* 1981.

Poetry

Moses: A Narrative. London, Dempsey and Squires, and New York, Stonehill, 1976.
A Christmas Recipe, illustrated by Fulvio Testa. Verona, Italy, Plain Wrapper Press, 1977.

Other

Translator, with Llewela Burgess, *The New Aristocrats,* by Michel de Saint-Pierre. London, Gollancz, 1962; Boston, Houghton Mifflin, 1963.
Translator, with Llewela Burgess, *The Olive Trees of Justice,* by Jean Pelegri. London, Sidgwick and Jackson, 1962.
The Novel Today. London, Longman, 1963.
Here Comes Everybody: An Introduction to James Joyce for the Ordinary Reader. London, Faber, 1965; revised edition, London, Hamlyn, 1982; as *Re Joyce,* New York, Norton, 1965.
Translator, *The Man Who Robbed Poor Boxes,* by Jean Servin. London, Gollancz, 1965.
Editor, *The Coaching Days of England 1750-1850.* London, Elek, and New York, Time-Life, 1966.
Editor, *A Journal of the Plague Year,* by Daniel Defoe. London, Penguin, 1966.
Editor, *A Shorter Finnegans Wake* by James Joyce. London, Faber, and New York, Viking Press, 1966.
Editor, with Francis Haskell, *The Age of the Grand Tour.* London, Elek, and New York, Crown, 1967.
The Novel Now: A Student's Guide to Contemporary Fiction. London, Faber, and New York, Norton, 1967; revised edition, Faber, 1971.
Urgent Copy: Literary Studies. London, Cape, and New York, Norton, 1968.
Editor, *Malaysian Stories,* by W. Somerset Maugham. Singapore, Heinemann, 1969.
Shakespeare. London, Cape, and New York, Knopf, 1970.
Joysprick: An Introduction to the Language of James Joyce. London, Deutsch, 1973; New York, Harcourt Brace, 1975.
Obscenity and the Arts (lecture). Valletta, Malta Library Association, 1973.
New York, with editors of Time-Life books, photos by Dan Budnik. New York, Time-Life, 1976.
Ernest Hemingway and His World. London, Thames and Hudson, and New York, Scribner, 1978.
On Going to Bed. London, Deutsch, and New York, Abbeville, 1982.
This Man and Music. London, Hutchinson, 1982; New York, McGraw Hill, 1983.
Ninety-Nine Novels: The Best in English since 1939: A Personal Choice. London, Allison and Busby, and New York, Summit, 1984.
Flame into Being: The Life and Work of D.H. Lawrence. London, Heinemann, and New York, Arbor House, 1985.
Homage to QWERT YUIOP: Selected Journalism 1978-1985. London, Hutchinson, 1986; as *But Do Blondes Prefer Gentlemen?,* New York, McGraw Hill, 1986.
Little Wilson and Big God, Being the First Part of the Confessions of Anthony Burgess. New York, Weidenfeld and Nicolson, 1986; London, Heinemann, 1987.
They Wrote in English. London, Hutchinson, 1988.

You've Had Your Time: Being the Second Part of the Confessions of Anthony Burgess. London, Heinemann, and New York, Weidenfeld, 1990.
On Mozart: A Paean for Wolfgang. Boston, Houghton Mifflin, 1991.
A Mouthful of Air: Languages, Languages—Especially English. New York, Morrow, 1992.
Translator, *Cyrano de Bergerac* by Edmund Rostand. New York, Applause, 1996.

Other as John Burgess Wilson

English Literature: A Survey for Students. London, Longman, 1958.
Language Made Plain. London, English Universities Press, 1964; New York, Crowell, 1965; revised edition, London, Fontana, 1975.

PUBLICATIONS FOR CHILDREN

Fiction

A Long Trip to Teatime, illustrated by Fulvio Testa. London, Dempsey and Squires, and New York, Stonehill, 1976.
The Land Where Ice Cream Grows, illustrated by Fulvio Testa. London, Benn, and New York, Doubleday, 1979.

*

Media Adaptations: *A Clockwork Orange* (film, directed by Stanley Kubrick), Warner Brothers, 1971; *A Clockwork Orange* (cassette), Caedmon, 1973; *Anthony Burgess Reads from "The Eve of Saint Venus" and "Nothing Like the Sun"* (cassette), Caedmon, 1974; *Anthony Burgess Reads from "A Clockwork Orange" and "Enderby"* (cassette), Spoken Arts, 1974.

Biography: *Anthony Burgess* by A.A. DeVitis, New York, Twayne, 1972; entry in *Dictionary of Literary Biography,* Volume 14, Detroit, Gale, 1983.

Bibliography: *Anthony Burgess: A Bibliography* by Jeutonne Brewer, Metuchen, New Jersey, Scarecrow Press, 1980; *Anthony Burgess: An Annotated Bibliography and Reference Guide* by Paul Boytinck, New York, Garland, 1985.

Manuscript Collections: Mills Memorial Library, Hamilton, Ontario.

Critical Studies: in *The Red Hot Vacuum* by Theodore Solotaroff, New York, Atheneum, 1970; *Shakespeare's Lives* by Samuel Schoenbaum, Oxford, Clarendon Press, 1970; *Anthony Burgess* by Carol M. Dix, London, Longman, 1971; *The Consolations of Ambiguity: An Essay on the Novels of Anthony Burgess* by Robert K. Morris, Columbia, University of Missouri Press, 1971; entry in *Contemporary Literary Criticism,* Volume 1, Detroit, Gale, 1973; Volume 2, 1974; Volume 4, 1975; Volume 5, 1976; Volume 8, 1978; Volume 10, 1979; Volume 13, 1980; Volume 15, 1980; Volume 22, 1982; Volume 40, 1986; *The Clockwork Universe of Anthony Burgess* by Richard Mathews, San Bernardino, California, Borgo Press, 1978; *Anthony Burgess: The Artist as Novelist* by

Geoffrey Aggeler, Tuscaloosa, University of Alabama Press, 1979, and *Critical Essays on Anthony Burgess* edited by Aggeler, Boston, Hall, 1986; *Anthony Burgess* by Samuel Coale, New York, Ungar, 1981; *Anthony Burgess: A Study in Character* by Martina Ghosh-Schellhorn, Frankfurt, Germany, Lang, 1986.

*   *   *

Anthony Burgess has written prolifically since the 1950s. His output includes a novel trilogy set in Malay; another group of three novels featuring Enderby, an off-beat poet; two critical examinations of James Joyce; and a biography of Shakespeare. Another novel, *Earthly Powers,* provides an eccentric, comprehensive view of twentieth-century culture. He has composed numerous orchestral works, screenplays, television scripts and reviews, and continues to produce acerbic commentary on current events in London and Dublin newspapers. Yet, for many, Burgess's reputation stands on the notoriety of one novel, *A Clockwork Orange,* and its 1971 film version produced and directed by Stanley Kubrick. Certainly, *A Clockwork Orange* is the work by which young adults know Anthony Burgess best.

If there ever was a literary work that demands thorough, open discussion, *A Clockwork Orange* is that work. Typically it rivets the attention of its readers even as it repels them by its violence, iconoclasm, and neologistic "slanguage." Like many of Burgess's works, *A Clockwork Orange* bears the marks of his private fixations: a love of music; a fascination with languages; an approach-avoidance attitude toward the doctrines of Roman Catholicism; the painful memory of a violent assault on his wife by thieves that caused her to miscarry while he was away serving in the military during World War II.

Aside from these personal preoccupations, the novel addresses some deeply troubling social phenomena of the mid-twentieth century including the epidemic growth of teenage gangs throughout the Western world and the universal application of B. F. Skinner's behavior modification techniques in prisons, asylums, and psychiatric clinics. In 1961, Burgess had directly observed the *stilyaqi,* gangs of young thugs, in Leningrad. Throughout the late '50s and early '60s, he had followed in the press the horrifying antics of their London counterparts, "The Teddy Boys." As for Skinner, his influential studies, *The Behavior of Organisms* and *Verbal Behavior,* as well as his novel *Walden II* all suggest remedies for antisocial behavior (such as that of teenage gangs), but make little attempt to understand the cognitive functions and complex learning patterns underlying such behaviors. More troubling for Burgess was the failure of Skinner's behavior modification strategies to recognize the importance of free will (a primary tenet of Catholic theology) in a properly functioning human being. *A Clockwork Orange* registers Burgess's deeply felt conflict about the need to control violence while at the same time respecting the freedom of the individual to choose goodness over evil.

The medium for carrying Burgess's message is Alex, a teenaged gang leader whose very name implies his function. "Alex" might be translated as either "without law" or "without word." In some sense, Alex is without either. He recognizes no law beyond his personal pleasure in inflicting pain on innocent victims and experiencing the high that drugs and classical music alike provide him. Not even the consensus will of his gang of thugs merits his loyalty, nor does he respect or speak the legal language or "word" of his

society. What he does speak is *Nadsat,* the Russian equivalent of "teeth." *Nadsat,* Burgess's own creation, intermingles Russian words (transliterated into English) with British and American slang, sometimes combining terms in the two languages and placing them in a syntactic arrangement uncommon in either language. The effect is startling, a violation of our received idea of communication:

> Our pockets were full of deng, so there was no real need from the point of view of crasting any more pretty polly to tolchock some old veck in an alley and viddy him swim in his blood while we counted the takings and divided by four, nor to do the ultra violent on some shivering starry grey-haired ptitsa in a shop and go smecking off with the till's guts. But, as they say, money isn't everything.

Besides his inspired use of *Nadsat,* Burgess also employs more traditional literary techniques to make his problematic argument about the necessity for allowing fully realized human beings to choose from an unlimited range of behaviors. In several cases he overlaps or superimposes an evil element on an apparently good one so that we are led to conclude that the two extremes are aspects of a single human nature. For example, Alex's foil is F. Alexander, an author whose wife Alex unmercifully beats and rapes. F. Alexander's book, titled *A Clockwork Orange,* concerns the immorality of turning a juicy, sensuous organic being (an orange) into a machine (a clockwork). After Alex has been imprisoned for two years and transformed by behavior modification techniques (which are as psychologically violent as the physical brutality Alex had perpetrated on his innocent victims) into a "good" boy, he finds his way, as if by instinct, back to F. Alexander's cottage (which, significantly, bears the name HOME). Not recognizing Alex as his wife's assailant, F. Alexander invites Alex (who has just been brutally beaten himself by his former gangmate now turned policeman) into his home. There Alex discovers a copy of *A Clockwork Orange* on the spine of which is printed his host's name: "F. Alexander. Good Boy, I thought, he is another Alex. Then I leafed through, standing in his pyjamas and bare nogas. . .and I could not viddy what the book was about."

The conflation of Alex with F. Alexander and F. Alexander with Anthony Burgess works to impress on the reader the notion that we all share a common fallen nature as well as the potential to overcome that nature with good. This theme is reinforced by other coincidences of contraries and recurring symbols in the novel. For example, Ludwig van Beethoven, whose music incites Alex in his unreformed state to violent fantasies, seems related, in more than name only, to the "Ludivico technique" that is used to cure Alex of his brutal tendencies. Furthermore, Alex's frequent address to his readers, "Oh, my brothers," implies the readers' collusion in Alex's violent projects; and the recurring milk imagery in the novel suggests a common source of nourishment, one that carries both good and evil tendencies for all of humankind.

Although the original London edition of *A Clockwork Orange* includes a final chapter that anticipates a future for Alex wherein he *chooses* a law-abiding (if not truly good) life, the American version ends with Alex reverting to his natural, evil self. The reader is left to wrestle with the implications of such evil for society. While the American edition does not provide the hopeful ending that some readers might long for, it does provide a helpful afterword and (unauthorized) glossary by critic Stanley Edgar Hyman. It is particularly appropriate that this novel have an afterword for it is too disturbing, too provoking to be left unanswered.

—Mary Lowe-Evans

BURNS, Olive Ann

Pseudonyms: Amy Larkin. **Nationality:** American. **Born:** Banks County, Georgia, 17 July 1924. **Education:** Mercer University, 1942-44; University of North Carolina at Chapel Hill, A.B. 1946. **Family:** Married Andrew H. Sparks in 1956; one daughter and one son. **Career:** Writer and free-lance journalist. Staff writer for the *Coca-Cola Bottler* and the *Laundryman's Guide,* in Atlanta, Georgia, 1946-47; *Atlanta Journal and Constitution,* Georgia, staff writer for the Sunday magazine, 1947-57; author of local newspaper advice column "Ask Amy," under pseudonym Amy Larkin, 1960-67; contributor of articles to *Atlanta Weekly.* **Awards:** *Cold Sassy Tree* was included in the annual lists of recommended selections for young adults by the New York Public Library, American Library Association, *School Library Journal,* and *Booklist,* all 1985. **Died:** 4 July 1990.

PUBLICATIONS

Fiction

Cold Sassy Tree. New York, Ticknor and Fields, 1984.
Leaving Cold Sassy: The Unfinished Sequel to Cold Sassy Tree. New York, Ticknor and Fields, 1992.

Nonfiction

Down Home Southern Cooking. New York, Doubleday, 1987.

*

Media Adaptations: *Cold Sassy Tree* (cassette), Books on Tape; abridged version, Bantam Audio; *Cold Sassy Tree* (television movie), Turner Broadcasting, 1989.

*   *   *

It took Olive Ann Burns ten years to write *Cold Sassy Tree,* and it took only a few months more for it to become one of the most talked about and highly-acclaimed books in the country. Will Tweedy, the fourteen-year-old narrator of the book, has been compared to Huck Finn and Holden Caulfield. Burns herself has been compared to Southern writers Eudora Welty and Alice Walker. Burns has a wonderful ear for dialogue, which makes Will, Grandpa Blakeslee, and Grandpa Blakeslee's second wife, Miss Love, so alive and so likable.

While this book was written as an adult novel—the central character is Grandpa Blakeslee, fifty-nine years old, three weeks a widower—it has proven to be widely popular with young adults. The story begins with Grandpa Blakeslee's sudden elopement with Miss Love, and chronicles family happenings of the next year. The time is 1906 and the place is Cold Sassy, Georgia. It is filled with marvelous and funny stories of Cold Sassy, a small, pious town, which after Grandpa's death—"over his dead body"—is renamed Progressive City. The book recounts, with humor and compassion, birth and death, ordinary daily chores and extraordinary family and community celebrations. Most of all, the book celebrates life.

Focused on adult behaviors, the book shows and accepts human nature, warts and all. It is never didactic, as are many young adult novels dealing with social problems that must be resolved in present-day socially acceptable ways. The book offers a perspective on life that is time and place specific; but as we laugh about these specifics, we must smile at the specifics of our own time and place.

Before writing *Cold Sassy Tree,* Burns had collected family stories from her own parents, taking the stories down in their own words, exactly as they were told, and adding her own recollections as well as those of other family members. She wanted to preserve their voices for her own two children and she ended up with two typewritten volumes, along with letters, photographs, and other memorabilia. "Details matter," she told her editor, and she paid attention to details. Grandpa Blakeslee is modeled after her own grandfather, and Will Tweedy after her father, who was also fourteen years old in 1906.

Following the great reception of *Cold Sassy Tree,* Burns began a sequel, which she titled "Time, Dirt, and Money." She worked on this book for almost five years, while battling recurrences of cancer, but she died before it was finished. Her publisher combined this unfinished sequel with a remembrance of the author by her editor, Katrina Kenison, and titled it *Leaving Cold Sassy.* The sequel begins ten years later; Will Tweedy is twenty-five years old, about to fall in love with his wife-to-be and trying to adjust to changes in Progressive City. The story was to be a portrait of this marriage. The unfinished sequel ends though before the marriage takes place; it is less than a fourth of the length of *Cold Sassy Tree.* It has some of the same sparkling dialogue, but the central characters—Will and his beloved Sanna—are less compelling than whiskey-snorting, outspoken, cantankerous Grandpa Blakeslee.

Leaving Cold Sassy is worthwhile reading for several reasons. It shows an author's work in progress. Burns rewrote and rewrote *Cold Sassy Tree* and the difference between it and the sequel clearly shows the difference between finished and unfinished writing. Kenison provides in her reminiscence valuable details on how Burns practiced her craft, which is fascinating to those who enjoy good literature as well as to those who wish to write good literature. Kenison's discussion of Burns' methods of collecting family history is also useful to those who wish to embark on their own family history but don't know how to begin. After reading *Leaving Cold Sassy* though, the reader is likely to leave Progressive City and return to Cold Sassy itself. For the scandalous turns in Cold Sassy, Georgia, are so exuberant and so touching and so funny that you will wish you could have lived there yourself.

—Mary Lystad

BURROUGHS, Edgar Rice

Pseudonyms: Normal Bean; John Tyler McCulloch. **Nationality:** American. **Born:** Chicago, Illinois, 1 September 1875. **Education:**

Harvard School, Chicago, 1888-91; Phillips Academy, Andover, Massachusetts, 1891-92; Michigan Military Academy, Orchard Lake, 1892-95. **Military Service:** Served in the United States 7th Cavalry, 1896-97; Illinois Reserve Militia, 1918-19. **Family:** Married 1) Emma Centennia Hulbert in 1900 (divorced 1934), two sons and one daughter; 2) Florence Dearholt in 1935 (divorced 1942). **Career:** Writer, 1912-50. Instructor and assistant commandant, Michigan Military Academy, Orchard Lake, Michigan, 1895-96; owner of a stationery store, Pocatello, Idaho, 1898; associated with American Battery Company, Chicago, Illinois, 1899-1903; associated with Sweetser-Burroughs Mining Company in Idaho, 1903-04; railroad policeman, Oregon Short Line Railroad Company, Salt Lake City, Utah, 1904; manager of stenographic department, Sears, Roebuck and Company, Chicago, 1906-08; partner, Burroughs and Dentzer (advertising agency), Chicago, 1908-09; office manager, Physicians Co-Operative Association, Chicago, 1909; partner, State-Burroughs Company (sales firm), Chicago, 1910-11; worked for Champlain Yardley Company, stationers, Chicago, 1910-11; manager, System Service Bureau, Chicago, 1912-13; mayor, Malibu Beach, California, 1933; United Press war correspondent in the Pacific during Second World War. Founder of Edgar Rice Burroughs, Inc. (publishing house), 1913, Burroughs-Tarzan Enterprises, 1934-39, and Burroughs-Tarzan Pictures, 1934-37; columnist (''Laugh It Off''), *Honolulu Advertiser,* 1941-42, 1945. **Died:** 19 March 1950.

PUBLICATIONS

Novels

Tarzan of the Apes. Chicago, McClurg, 1914; London, Methuen, 1917.
The Return of Tarzan. Chicago, McClurg, 1915; London, Methuen, 1918.
The Beasts of Tarzan. Chicago, McClurg, 1916; London, Methuen, 1918.
A Princess of Mars. Chicago, McClurg, 1917; London, Methuen, 1919.
The Son of Tarzan. Chicago, McClurg, 1917; London, Methuen, 1919.
The Gods of Mars. Chicago, McClurg, 1918; London, Methuen, 1920.
Out of Time's Abyss. London, Tandem, 1918.
Tarzan and the Jewels of Opar. Chicago, McClurg, 1918; London, Methuen, 1919.
The Warlord of Mars. Chicago, McClurg, 1919; London, Methuen, 1920.
Thuvia, Maid of Mars. Chicago, McClurg, 1920; London, Methuen, 1921.
Tarzan the Terrible. Chicago, McClurg, and London, Methuen, 1921.
The Chessmen of Mars. Chicago, McClurg, 1922; London, Methuen, 1923.
At the Earth's Core. Chicago, McClurg, 1922; London, Methuen, 1923.
The Girl from Hollywood. New York, Macaulay, 1923; London, Methuen, 1924.
Pellucidar. Chicago, McClurg, 1923; London, Methuen, 1924.
Tarzan and the Golden Lion. Chicago, McClurg, 1923; London, Methuen, 1924.
Tarzan and the Ant Men. Chicago, McClurg, 1924; London, Methuen, 1925.
The Bandit of Hell's Bend. Chicago, McClurg, 1925; London, Methuen, 1926.
The Tarzan Twins (for children). Joliet, Illinois, Volland, 1927; London, Collins, 1930.

The Outlaw of Torn. Chicago, McClurg, and London, Methuen, 1927.
The War Chief. Chicago, McClurg, 1927.
The Master Mind of Mars. Chicago, McClurg, 1928; London, Methuen, 1939.
Tarzan, Lord of the Jungle. Chicago, McClurg, and London, Cassell, 1928.
The Monster Men. Chicago, McClurg, 1929.
Tarzan and the Lost Empire. New York, Metropolitan, 1929; London, Cassell, 1931.
Tanar of Pellucidar. New York, Metropolitan, 1930; London, Methuen, 1939.
Tarzan at the Earth's Core. New York, Metropolitan, 1930; London, Methuen, 1938.
A Fighting Man of Mars. New York, Metropolitan, 1931; London, Lane, 1932.
Tarzan the Invincible. Tarzana, California, Burroughs, 1931; London, Lane, 1933.
Tarzan the Triumphant. Tarzana, California, Burroughs, 1931; London, Lane, 1933.
Jungle Girl. Tarzana, California, Burroughs, 1932; London, Odhams Press; as *The Land of Hidden Men,* New York, Ace Books, 1963.
Apache Devil. Tarzana, California, Burroughs, 1933.
Tarzan and the City of Gold. Tarzana, California, Burroughs, 1933; London, Lane, 1936.
Pirates of Venus. Tarzana, California, Burroughs, 1934; London, Lane, 1935.
Tarzan and the Lion-Men. Tarzana, California, Burroughs, 1934; London, W.H. Allen, 1950.
Lost on Venus. Tarzana, California, Burroughs, 1935; London, Methuen, 1937.
Tarzan and the Leopard Men. Tarzana, California, Burroughs, 1935; London, Lane, 1936.
Swords of Mars. Tarzana, California, Burroughs, 1936; London, New English Library, 1966.
Tarzan's Quest. Tarzana, California, Burroughs, 1936; London, Methuen, 1938.
Tarzan and the Tarzan Twins, with Jad-Bal-Ja, the Golden Lion (for children). Racine, Wisconsin, Whitman Publishing, 1936.
Back to the Stone Age. Tarzana, California, Burroughs, 1937.
The Oakdale Affair: The Rider. Tarzana, California, Burroughs, 1937.
The Lad and the Lion. Tarzana, California, Burroughs, 1938.
Tarzan and the Forbidden City, illustrated by John Coleman Burroughs. Tarzana, California, Burroughs, 1938; London, W.H. Allen, 1950.
Carson of Venus. Tarzana, California, Burroughs, 1939; London, Goulden, 1950.
The Deputy Sheriff of Comanche County. Tarzana, California, Burroughs, 1940.
Synthetic Men of Mars. Tarzana, California, Burroughs, 1940; London, Methuen, 1941.
Land of Terror. Tarzana, California, Burroughs, 1944.
Escape on Venus. Tarzana, California, Burroughs, 1946; London, New English Library, 1966.
Tarzan and the Foreign Legion. Tarzana, California, Burroughs, 1947; London, W.H. Allen, 1949.
The People That Time Forgot. New York, Ace Books, 1963.
Beyond the Farthest Star. New York, Ace Books, 1964.
Tarzan and the Madman. New York, Canaveral Press, 1964; London, New English Library, 1966.

The Girl from Farris's. Kansas City, Missouri, House of Greystoke, 1965.

The Efficiency Expert. Kansas City, Missouri, House of Greystoke, 1966.

I Am a Barbarian. Tarzana, California, Burroughs, 1967.

Pirate Blood (as John Tyler McCulloch). New York, Ace Books, 1970.

Short Stories

Jungle Tales of Tarzan. Chicago, McClurg, and London, Methuen, 1919.

Tarzan the Untamed. Chicago, McClurg, and London, Methuen, 1920.

The Mucker. Chicago, McClurg, 1921; as *The Mucker* and *The Man without a Soul,* London, Methuen, 2 vols., 1921-22.

The Land That Time Forgot. Chicago, McClurg, 1924; London, Methuen, 1925.

The Cave Girl. Chicago, McClurg, 1925; London, Methuen, 1927.

The Eternal Lover. Chicago, McClurg, 1925; London, Methuen, 1927; as *The Eternal Savage,* New York, Ace Books, 1963.

The Mad King. Chicago, McClurg, 1926.

The Moon Maid. Chicago, McClurg, 1926; London, Stacey, 1972; abridged edition, as *The Moon Men,* New York, Canaveral Press, 1962; augmented edition, London, Tandem, 1975.

Tarzan the Magnificent. Tarzana, California, Burroughs, 1939; London, Methuen, 1940.

Llana of Gathol. Tarzana, California, Burroughs, 1948; London, New English Library, 1967.

Beyond Thirty. Privately printed, 1955; as *The Lost Continent,* New York, Ace Books, 1963.

The Man-Eater. Privately printed, 1955.

Savage Pelludicar. New York, Canaveral Press, 1963.

John Carter of Mars. New York, Canaveral Press, 1964.

Tales of Three Planets. New York, Canaveral Press, 1964.

Tarzan and the Castaways. New York, Canaveral Press, 1964; London, New English Library, 1966.

The Wizard of Venus. New York, Ace Books, 1970.

Other

Official Guide of the Tarzan Clans of America. Privately printed, 1939.

*

Biography: Entry in *Dictionary of Literary Biography,* Volume 8: *Twentieth Century American Science Fiction Writers,* Detroit, Gale, 1981.

Critical Studies: *Edgar Rice Burroughs: Master of Adventure* by Richard A. Lupoff, New York, Canaveral Press, 1965, revised edition, New York, Ace, 1968; *Tarzan Alive: A Definitive Biography of Lord Greystoke* by Philip José Farmer, New York, Doubleday, 1972, London, Panther, 1974; *Burroughs' Science Fiction* by Robert R. Kudlay and Joan Leiby, Geneseo, New York, School of Library and Information Science, 1973; *Edgar Rice Burroughs: The Man Who Created Tarzan* (includes bibliography) by Irwin Porges, Provo, Utah, Brigham Young University Press, 1975, London, New English Library, 1976; *A Guide to Barsoom* by John Flint Roy, New York, Ballantine, 1976; *The Burroughs Bestiary: An Encyclopaedia of Monsters and Imaginary Beings Created by Edgar Rice Burroughs* by David Day, London, New English Library, 1978; *Tarzan and Tradition: Classical Myth in Popular Literature* by Erling B. Holtsmark, Westport, Connecticut, Greenwood Press, 1981.

*   *   *

Edgar Rice Burroughs, best known as the creator of Tarzan, was a prolific author of vigorous adventure novels set in primitive lands, on other planets, and in the interior of the earth. His fiction often contains surprisingly deft satire and unexpected speculation about evolutionary mutations. As a result, his work, though frequently dismissed as immature, has been credited with stimulating the popularity of science fiction and adventure fantasy in the first half of the twentieth century.

Despite the worldwide appeal of his Tarzan character, Burroughs's Tarzan books, though often read by many young people, were for many years less familiar to the public than the long series of Tarzan films. As a result, misconceptions about Burroughs's work persist. Yet these novels, while carelessly written, are usually superior to the films. Indeed, the first Johnny Weissmuller Tarzan movie (1932) was well acted, but only the recent *Greystoke: The Legend of Tarzan, Lord of the Apes* (1983) comes close to capturing the essence of Burroughs's vision. But his science fiction series have always enjoyed a loyal following; they remain primarily appealing to those who enjoy adolescent adventure. Nevertheless, despite hasty writing and slapdash plotting, the prolific Burroughs should be recognized as a myth-making, popular novelist with a natural talent for storytelling.

Somewhat like L. Frank Baum, the creator of Oz, and later science fiction master Robert Heinlein, Burroughs turned to writing in middle age after a mediocre business career during which he had traveled widely around the United States, especially in the raw territory of the West. Yet after a tentative beginning, he enjoyed a quick success and a long career notable for a sensible professionalism during which he continued several popular series and wrote a number of interesting individual works such as *The Moon Maid* (1926).

His first professional sale was *Under the Moons of Mars,* serialized in 1912 and introducing Burroughs's popular invincible hero John Carter, who is transported to Mars apparently by astral projection, following a battle with Apaches in Arizona. This novel, published in book form as *A Princess of Mars,* described Carter's period of captivity with green warriors, his meeting with the beautiful princess Dejah Thoris of the empire of Helium, and their subsequent escape and return to her home. Two sequels, *The Gods of Mars* and *The Warlord of Mars,* continued the saga of John Carter and established this Virginia gentleman as the "greatest swordsman of two worlds." Although Burroughs's conception of a modern Mars dominated by unending wars and haunted by memories of an ancient civilized past has been traced to the influence of forgotten authors like the English adventure novelist Edwin L. Arnold, Burroughs showed originality in exploiting this setting for a series of heroic adventures.

In later years, Burroughs continued the saga of his romanticized Mars, with the descendants of John Carter and Dejah Thoris experiencing adventures among the sandy wastes and ruined cities of this imagined planet of adventure. In *The Master Mind of Mars,* Burroughs introduced a secondary hero, Ulysses Paxton, while developing satire on repressive institutional religions—always a favorite target of the author in the Tarzan novels and other books. In one of the most fast-paced and vigorous action adventures of the series, *A Fighting Man of Mars*, the hero's role is given to Hadron of Hastor, a protégé of John Carter. Plucky young princesses are permitted to star in *Thuvia, Maid of Mars* and *Llana of Gathol* which features the granddaughter of Carter. The "Martian" series eventually reached eleven books, and its popularity remains second only to the Tarzan books.

Burroughs's famous series was the Tarzan saga, describing the fortunes of John Clayton, Lord Greystoke, whose aristocratic parents are abandoned on the west coast of Africa and who, after being orphaned and raised as an ape, grows into a leader of the simian tribe and a superhuman hero. The story of Tarzan's progress to manhood in *Tarzan of the Apes* remains a compelling one despite Burroughs's extremely limited understanding of science. In essence, Burroughs's tale is a myth of the victory of heredity and talent over the constraints of a hostile environment. The narrative of Tarzan's emerging intelligence, mastery of his environment, and his discovery of his true identity—an event resulting from his involvement with the victims set ashore from another mutiny—contains a fascinating appeal for readers interested in the development of human intelligence. Although Burroughs was obviously indebted to Rudyard Kipling's story of Mowgli in his "Jungle Books," Burroughs produced a distinctly American variation on Kipling's theme.

Burroughs followed *Tarzan of the Apes* with many other Tarzan novels; the series eventually reached twenty-four entries. In *The Return of Tarzan*, Tarzan leaves civilization to return to Africa, where he becomes the chieftain of a tribe of black warriors and discovers a source of wealth in Opar, a colony established by survivors of the fall of Atlantis. However, Tarzan does not succumb to the love of La, the white-skinned queen of Opar; instead, the establishment of his identity as the true Lord Greystoke and the death of his cousin Cecil Clayton, the fiance of Jane Porter, free him to marry Jane, the American woman who is his first love.

Most of Burroughs's adventure novels depict the importance of a primitive environment to act as a stimulus and a challenge for his heroes and heroines. This return to primitivism provides the theme of *The Son of Tarzan*, one of the best novels in the Tarzan series wherein Tarzan's son gains heroic stature after being kidnapped and abandoned in Africa. Another imaginative novel in the series is *Tarzan the Terrible*, in which Burroughs draws on his inventiveness to imagine an entire lost continent or land mass in the central African jungle, complete with a dehumanizing religion which is as usual the subject of Burroughs's satire. A satirical tone also underlies *Tarzan and the Ant Men*, which Richard Lupoff, one of Burroughs's better critics, regards as one of the best Tarzan novels.

However, too many of the later Tarzan books become involved with the lost race motif of H. Rider Haggard's novels, a theme usually embodied in pairs of lost and feuding cities which have flourished in hidden valleys cut off from civilization. Late in the series, Tarzan gains immortality through an African shaman's secret formula, and his enduring quest for heroic adventure finally takes him into the jungles of Indonesia during World War II in *Tarzan and the Foreign Legion*. But in his waning years, Burroughs tended to grow tired of his invincible hero.

Early in his career, Burroughs also began an adventure saga set in a primitive world called Pellucidar located inside the earth (an idea which had been used by Jules Verne and other authors). However, after a couple of vigorous early books involving the explorer David Innes, this series quickly lost momentum (except for *Tarzan at the Earth's Core*, when the indomitable lord of the jungle is taken to Pellucidar in an effort to breathe fresh life into the series).

A fourth adventure series set on Venus was inaugurated in the thirties. Unlike Burroughs's more famous adventure series, this group of stories employs a hero, Carson Napier, who though resourceful and athletic has many limitations. Although the Venus novels blend romance and comedy and contain some of Burroughs's most imaginative depictions of alien societies, only five books in the series were completed and the final two were connected groups of pulp novelettes. Though the Venus saga continues to entertain readers, it never gained the popularity of the Tarzan and Martian series.

In addition to his four major adventure series, Burroughs also wrote a number of other imaginative novels, mostly composed in the period 1912-1932, which have interested readers of science fiction and outdoors. Generally, these books celebrate Burroughs's fascination with primitivism as an influence that produces heroic qualities. In *The Cave Girl*, a weak and sheltered Boston aristocrat develops into a manly warrior after being abandoned on a rugged Pacific island and falling in love with the lovely island princess. A similar process of rediscovering primitive strengths and emotions takes place for Victoria Custer, a proper American woman in *The Eternal Savage*, when she falls in love with a warrior from a stone age milieu.

The thematic interest in some of the other novels is more speculative. *The Moon Maid* and its sequel *The Moon Men* satirize a world dominated by a communist horde called the Kalkars, but their oppressive forces are finally routed by the Red Hawk, a nomadic war leader who is the final descendant of a line of heroes who have battled the Kalkars. *The Land That Time Forgot* and its sequels offer adventure on a primitive "lost continent" (probably suggested by Arthur Conan Doyle's *The Lost World*), but the violent action is supplemented by evolutionary speculation. Another unusual novel, *The Monster Men*, apparently influenced by H. G. Wells's *The Island of Dr. Moreau*, features a mad scientist defeated by a primitive warrior who is one of his creations. Finally, a late novella, *Beyond the Farthest Star*, is unusual in the Burroughs canon because it uses a science-fiction setting to depict the brutality and futility of war.

Burroughs's worlds of primitive adventure contain several elements which are "politically correct" by the standards of the nineties. The magnificent bond of Waziri warriors who often aid Tarzan are an admirable tribute to African blacks. Moreover, Burroughs published two Western novels about a white Apache, *The War Chief* and *Apache Devil* by drawing on his experiences in the Seventh Cavalry. These two novels are similar to Zane Grey's *The Vanishing American* and Max Brand's "Cheyenne" novels in showing a surprising sympathy for Native Americans. As for Burroughs's depiction of women, only the most extreme feminists might find fault with the courage and resourcefulness of the last of Burroughs's heroines, such as Nadara the cave girl, and Dejah Thoris, the princess of Mars.

To be sure, Burroughs's fiction is often crudely written and seldom offers a complex view of human character. But Burroughs remains a widely read author of durable adventure fiction set in a variety of primitive worlds.

—Edgar L. Chapman

BURTON, Hester (Wood-Hill)

Nationality: British. **Born:** Beccles, Suffolk, England, 6 December 1913. **Education:** Headington School, Oxford University, 1932-36, B.A. (honours) in English 1936. **Family:** Married Reginald W.B. Burton in 1937; three daughters. **Career:** Writer of historical novels for children and biographer. Part-time grammar school teacher; assistant editor, Oxford Junior Encyclopedia, London, 1956-61; examiner in public examination. **Awards:** Carnegie Medal, 1963, and Honorable Mention in the New York *Herald Tribune* Children's Spring Book Festival, 1964, for *Time of Trial;* runner up for Carnegie Medal, c. 1962, for *Castors Away!;* Boston *Globe-Horn Book* award, 1971. **Address:** Mill House, Kidlington, Oxford, England.

PUBLICATIONS FOR YOUNG ADULTS

Fiction

The Great Gale, illustrated by Joan Kiddell-Monroe. London, Oxford University Press, 1960; as *The Flood at Reedsmere,* illustrated by Robin Jacques, Cleveland, World, 1968.
Castors Away!, illustrated by Victor Ambrus. London, Oxford University Press, 1962; Cleveland, World, 1963.
Time of Trial, illustrated by Victor Ambrus. London, Oxford University Press, 1963: Cleveland, World, 1964.
No Beat of Drum, illustrated by Victor Ambrus. London, Oxford University Press, 1966; Cleveland, World, 1967.
In Spite of All Terror, illustrated by Victor Ambrus. London, Oxford University Press, 1968; New York, World, 1969.
Otmoor for Ever!, illustrated by Gareth Floyd. London, Hamish Hamilton, 1968.
Thomas, illustrated by Victor Ambrus. London, Oxford University Press, 1969; as *Beyond the Weir Bridge,* New York, Crowell, 1970.
Through the Fire, illustrated by Gareth Floyd. London, Hamish Hamilton, 1969.
The Henchmans at Home, illustrated by Victor Ambrus. London, Oxford University Press, 1970; New York, Crowell, 1972.
The Rebel, illustrated by Victor Ambrus. London, Oxford University Press, 1971; New York, Crowell, 1972.
Riders of the Storm, illustrated by Victor Ambrus. London, Oxford University Press, 1972; New York, Crowell, 1973.
Kate Rider, illustrated by Victor Ambrus. London, Oxford University Press, 1974; as *Kate Ryder,* New York, Crowell, 1975.
To Ravensrigg, illustrated by Victor Ambrus. London, Oxford University Press, 1976; New York, Crowell, 1977.
A Grenville Goes to Sea, illustrated by Colin McNaughton. London, Heinemann, 1977.
Tim at the Fur Fort, illustrated by Victor Ambrus. London, Hamish Hamilton, 1977.
When the Beacons Blazed, illustrated by Victor Ambrus. London, Hamish Hamilton, 1978.
Five August Days, illustrated by Trevor Ridley. London, Oxford University Press, 1981.

Plays

The Great Gale (radio play; adaptation of her own story). 1961.
Castors Away! (television play; adaptation of her own story). 1968.

Other

Editor, *A Book of Modern Stories.* London, Oxford University Press, 1959.
Editor, *Her First Ball: Short Stories,* illustrated by Susan Einzig. London, Oxford University Press, 1959.
A Seaman at the Time of Trafalgar, illustrated by Victor Ambrus. London, Oxford University Press, 1963.

PUBLICATIONS FOR ADULTS

Other

Barbara Bodichon, 1827-1891. London, Murray, 1949.
Editor, *Coleridge and the Wordsworths.* London, Oxford University Press, 1953.
Editor, *Tennyson.* London, Oxford University Press, 1954.

*

Biography: Essay in *Something about the Author Autobiography Series,* Vol. 8, Detroit, Gale, 1989, pp. 51-64.

Critical Studies: Entry in *Children's Literature Review,* Vol. 1, Detroit, Gale, 1976.

*   *   *

Towards the end of *The Great Gale* when the flooded East Anglian village of Reedsmere has been visited both by the Queen and by the Minister of Housing, Mr. Macmillan, Mary whispers to her friend Myrtle: "I shall never forget today. . . . Today we were part of history." Later after hearing on the radio the full extent of the havoc wrought by the gale she has a different thought. "Perhaps, after all, it was not an exciting, but a solemn and dreadful thing to be part of history." This duality of response on the part of individuals caught up in a national crisis is very characteristic of Hester Burton's novels, whether they are set in the 17th, 18th, 19th, or 20th centuries; it is not for nothing that one of her most highly praised books is called *Time of Trial* (though in this case the "time" is 1801, and the "trial" is in one sense that of the heroine's radical book-seller father accused of sedition). Burton has modestly acknowledged a tendency to "find refuge" in history because the present age is becoming increasingly difficult to understand, whereas the past, in so far as historians have selected and interpreted the evidence, is easier to see in perspective. Moreover she has confessed that she is inclined to choose an historical event or theme because it echoes something she has experienced in her own life. One can see, for instance, that *Castors Away!,* with its vivid and at times harrowing account of the autumn of the Battle of Trafalgar has its parallel in some events of the Second World War, while *No Beat of Drum,* with its portrayal of the harsh poverty of the English farm-labourers in 1829 to 1831, mirrors to a certain extent the divisive class-conflicts of the 1930s. Yet in fact her most successful novel of all is the one which is derived most directly from lived experience. *In Spite of All Terror* evokes for us with a wonderful visual concreteness the outbreak of war in 1939, the evacuation of an East London school to the remoteness of the Oxfordshire countryside, the trauma of Dunkirk, the excitement of the Battle of Britain, and the anguish of the bombing of London in the autumn of 1940. It is moreover the most compulsively readable of her novels, its characterisation remains convincing while covering an extremely varied range of social classes, and it has in Liz Hawtin a protagonist who is at the same time the most believable and the most engaging of all Burton's heroines.

Even in this novel Burton supplemented her own recollections with the use of books, as well as other people's memories. Her more strictly historical novels have all been thoroughly and intelligently researched, using contemporary documents and diaries as well as modern scholarship, so that they recreate for us with powerful authenticity both the atmosphere and the detailed ways of life of her chosen period. (In keeping with the spirit of her self-acknowledged selectivity she has made herself particularly at home in the period of the French Revolution and the Napoleonic Wars—*The Rebel, Riders of the Storm, Time of Trial,* and *Castors Away!*—and also in the period of the English Civil War—*Thomas* and *Kate Rider.*) In general her stories move at a brisk pace and are well supplied with incident; for the young adolescent reader their appeal is probably enhanced by a disposition to include, and even to work for, moments of strong feeling and uninhibited emotional release. An attractive example of her historical work at its best is *No Beat of Drum* in which the action moves from the impoverished countryside of southern England to the penal settlements of Van Diemen's Land. One cannot fault the generosity of the author's sympathy with the exploited and starving labourers, and she shows understanding of the "Captain Swing" riots even though she does not condone them. The portrayal of life in Tasmania is as vividly detailed as that of life in Hampshire, and one's only reservation about the latter part of the book is that the plot relies rather too much on coincidence.

The "excitement" of "being part of history" has always been strongly present in Burton's fiction, but in some of her later work the "solemn and dreadful" aspects have come more to the fore. Thus even in the relatively early *Castors Away!* the more barbarous features of the naval warfare of the time were rendered with an unflinching realism which makes some parts of the book strong meat for juvenile stomachs. A few years later in *Thomas* Burton seemed to have lost contact temporarily with her young readership by a too remorseless insistence on the hardships, miseries, and frustrations of her three protagonists; indeed her description of the Great Plague of London makes harrowing reading for an adult. Unfortunately, her next two novels, *The Rebel* and *Riders of the Storm,* were weakened by uncharacteristic elements of contrivance. However, in *Kate Rider* she returned fully to form, with a story about a girl growing up in the early years of the Civil War. *To Ravensrigg,* set in the late 18th century, recounts how an adolescent girl confronts the discovery of her own unsuspected illegitimacy and is helped to trace her true origins by a group of Quaker anti-slave-trade campaigners, one of whom falls in love with her; more than usually romantic in its story-line, it makes an absorbing and moving tale. Burton's most recent novel, *Five August Days,* is her sole venture into the strictly contemporary. The local East Anglian detail is as vivid as ever, and though plot and characterisation show rather less of her own individual distinction, they still make compulsive reading for eleven- to twelve-year-olds of either sex.

In addition to her full-length novels Burton has also published in *The Henchmans at Home* a collection of six related stories about a country doctor's family in Victorian England which contains some of her most appealing work.

—Frank Whitehead

BUTLER, Octavia E(stelle)

Nationality: American. **Born:** Pasadena, California, 22 June 1947. **Education:** Pasadena City College, 1965-68, A.A. 1968; California State University, 1969. **Career:** Since 1970, free-lance writer. **Awards:** Hugo award, World Science Fiction Convention, 1984, for short story "Speech Sounds"; Hugo award, Nebula award, Science Fiction Writers of America, Locus award from *Locus* magazine, and award for best novelette from *Science Fiction Chronicle Reader,* all 1985, all for novelette "Bloodchild"; Nebula award nomination, 1987, for novelette "The Evening and the Morning and the Night." **Address:** P.O. Box 40671, Pasadena, California 91114, U.S.A.

PUBLICATIONS

Science Fiction

Kindred. New York, Doubleday, 1979; London, Women's Press, 1988; Boston, Beacon Press, 1988.
The Evening and the Morning and the Night. Eugene, Oregon, Pulphouse, 1991.
Parable of the Sower. New York, Four Walls Eight Windows, 1993.
Bloodchild and Other Stories. New York, Four Walls Eight Windows, 1995.

"Patternmaster" series

Patternmaster. New York, Doubleday, 1976; London, Sphere, 1978.
Mind of My Mind. New York, Doubleday, 1977; London, Sidgwick & Jackson, 1978.
Survivor. New York, Doubleday, and London, Sidgwick & Jackson, 1978.
Wild Seed. New York, Doubleday, and London, Sidgwick & Jackson, 1980; New York, Warner, 1988.
Clay's Ark. New York, St. Martin's, 1984.

"Xenogenesis" series:

Dawn. New York, Warner, and London, Gollancz, 1987.
Adulthood Rites. New York, Warner, and London, Gollancz, 1988.
Imago. New York, Warner, and London, Gollancz, 1989.

*

Biography: Entry in *Dictionary of Literary Biography,* Volume 33: *Afro-American Fiction Writers after 1955,* Detroit, Gale, 1984.

Critical Studies: Entry in *Contemporary Literary Criticism,* Volume 38, Detroit, Gale, 1986; *Suzy Charnas, Joan Vinge, and Octavia Butler* by Richard Law, with others, San Bernardino, California, Borgo Press, 1986.

*   *   *

Octavia Butler, winner of both the Hugo and Nebula awards, writes about power, its use and abuse, and how it affects those who wield it. As a science fiction writer, she creates alternate worlds where people are bred for their psionic powers as in the Patternist series or, as in the "Xenogenesis" trilogy, a post-holocaust Earth where survivors must deal with alien visitors who are genetic "traders." Her situations pit characters against racial, gender, and sexual conflicts and the violence—personal and global—that often results. Murder, child abuse, rape, suicide, ecological disasters, and war reveal the horrific elements wrought by the misapplication of political and technological power. Butler's works are widely popular with young adult readers of science fiction.

Patternmaster, Butler's first novel, begins her exploration of these themes that run through four more books: *Wildseed, Mind of My Mind, Clay's Ark,* and *Survivor.* The psionic Patternists can, through a Patternmaster, link their minds and control mutes, humans without psionic powers, and battle Clayarks, humans mutated by an extraterrestrial disease who prey on mutes and Patternists. *Clay's Ark,* Butler's darkest, most violent novel, reveals how a surviving astronaut unwillingly spreads an extraterrestrial virus that causes the mutation the Patternists and mutes call Clayarks.

Butler, the only African-American woman publishing in science fiction, pointedly develops slave-master relationships to show how the Patternists' power allows them to "program" and often abuse mutes. In *Patternmaster*'s world of the distant future, psionic power, not race or gender, determines superiority, but the often coercive selective breeding practiced to produce superior powers harks back to the treatment of slaves on American plantations. Although such programs clearly dehumanize the people involved, ethical questions are implied rather than directly addressed in the series. Here, though, as in other of Butler's work, she makes clear that coercive relationships warp the powerful even as they debilitate the powerless.

Mind of My Mind, set in contemporary California, develops a bit of "Patternmaster" history to show how Doro, the four-thousand-year-old Founder, sees Mary, the daughter of one of his many bodies, as the culmination of one of his breeding programs. A greater success than he had counted on, she becomes the first Patternmaster by killing her father, an act with mythic resonances that establishes the violent means of succession to the position of Patternmaster. If Mary had turned out to be yet another failed experiment, Doro would simply have killed her, as he has killed untold numbers of other failures. His disregard for human life disturbs Emma, the shape-shifting healer who is his female counterpart. Their story is told in *Wildseed,* where Doro, wandering Africa as a slave trader in the 1600s, is drawn to a power he does not recognize as one his projects. He finds Anyanwu, the Emma in *Patternmaster.* Anyanwu/Emma as the life-giving, life-protecting earthmother contrasts and conflicts with the manipulative, destructive Doro. Their struggle to co-exist results in an uneasy, often violent balance of their attributes.

Survivor picks up the saga some years after *Clay's Ark.* A group of mute Missionaries, a religious sect dedicated to preserving and spreading the unmutated "God-image of humankind" by colonizing other planets, demonstrates exactly the kind of prejudice and closemindedness that undermines relationships between individuals and cultures. Only the protagonist, Alanna, comes to respect the planet's native Tehkohn and love their leader. Otherwise, the colonists embrace segregation and effectively cut themselves off from cultural growth and enrichment. Butler extends the use of alien contact as a metaphor for change through *Dawn, Adulthood Rites,* and *Imago,* the trilogy gathered in "Xenogenesis."

The "Xenogenesis" trilogy shows humans having committed the ultimate global violence of nuclear war. The alien Oankali, a species which procures new genetic material by crossbreeding with other species, enter the picture in time to rescue several hundred survivors from the ruined planet. Among the rescued is the remarkable Lilith Iyapo who becomes both midwife and mother to the race the Oankali would create. Humans, the communal Oankali learn, are plagued by the combined drives of intelligence and hierarchy which forestall peaceful co-existence. Violence will always underlie and define the human condition, unless the hierarchical element is bred out. This process presents a challenge even for the ooloi, the third sex of the Oankali who are responsible for mixing the genetic materials of parents to produce desired characteristics in the offspring. As in the "Patternmaster" series, the technique involves no technology—the ooloi manipulate DNA and RNA within their own bodies. Nor are ethical questions directly addressed, though many humans reject the Oankali "gift" because, like the Missionaries, they believe change will destroy rather than improve the human race.

Bloodchild (which first appeared in *Isaac Asimov's Science Fiction Magazine,* June 1984), the novelette for which Butler won the Hugo and Nebula awards, fits the patterns of violence and metamorphosis evident in her other work. Here, though, Terrans are kept and bred in preserves by the Tlic, aliens who must incubate their eggs in host bodies and find that initial implantation in human bodies produces the strongest offspring. The twist is that love of a sort exists between the Tlic and their selected humans, which seems an ironic commentary on the complexities of the paternalistic master-slave relationship. Butler's earlier novel *Kindred* opened up some of these master/slave connections, but in a different vein. Butler uses the convention of time travel to show how Dana, a twentieth-century African-American woman, finds herself enslaved to Rufus, her white nineteenth-century great-great-grandfather. Dana must rescue him from life-threatening situations so he can live to father her great-grandmother. The physical and mental brutality Dana experiences as she is literally whipped into servitude provides a unique and clear lesson on how both the powerful and the powerless are ill-served in such unbalanced situations.

Although Butler's strongest, most positive characters are females, she rarely focuses on gender or race as issues except as an historical point, as when Dana finds being a black woman hampers her in the nineteenth-century South. On the whole, her outlook seems dark—humankind is incapable of the communal effort demanded for the survival of the species. The possibility of the necessary qualities glimmers only in the kindness of individual characters. In *Patternmaster,* Teray's power is tempered with compassion for mutes and even Clayarks. Anyanwu/Emma in *Mind of My Mind* and *Wild Seed* eases the lives of as many of Doro's offspring as she possibly can. Rye, the protagonist of the Nebula Award-winning short story "Speech Sounds" (in *Isaac Asimov's Science Fiction Magazine,* December 1983), witnesses horror after horror in a world sundered by a virus that destroys the language center in the brains of most humans. Rye and others who can still read or talk are not only suspect but often killed. Even so, the kindness and compassion of a stranger who saves her from a crowd regenerates those qualities in Rye. Such individual kindness provides the basis for the hope offered by Octavia Butler's powerful works.

—Linda G. Benson

BYARS, Betsy

Nationality: American. **Born:** Betsy Cromer in Charlotte, North Carolina, 7 August 1928. **Education:** Furman University, Greenville, South Carolina, 1946-48; Queens College, Charlotte, 1948-50, B.A. in English 1950. **Family:** Married Edward Ford Byars in 1950; three daughters and one son. **Awards:** America's Book of the Year selection, Child Study Association, 1968, for *The Midnight Fox,* 1969, for *Trouble River,* 1970, for *The Summer of the Swans,* 1972, for *The House of Wings,* 1973, for *The Winged Colt of Casa Mia* and *The 18th Emergency,* 1974, for *After the Goat Man,* 1975, for *The Lace Snail,* 1976, for *The TV Kid,* and 1980, for *The Night Swimmers;* Lewis Carroll Shelf award, 1970, for *The Midnight Fox;* Newbery Medal, 1971, for *The Summer of the Swans;* Best Books for Spring selection, *School Library Journal,* 1971, for *Go and Hush the Baby;* Book List, *Library Journal,* 1972, for *House of Wings;* National Book award finalist, 1973, for *House of Wings; New York Times* Outstanding Book of the Year, 1973, for *The Winged Colt of Casa Mia* and *The 18th Emergency,* 1979, for *Good-bye Chicken Little,* and 1982, for *The Two-Thousand-Pound Goldfish;* Book List, *School Library Journal,* 1974, for *After the Goat Man;* Dorothy Canfield Fisher Memorial Book award, Vermont Congress of Parents and Teachers, 1975, for *The 18th Emergency;* Woodward Park School Annual Book award, 1977, Child Study Children's Book award, Child Study Children's Book Committee at Bank Street College of Education, 1977, Hans Christian Andersen Honor List for Promoting Concern for the Disadvantaged and Handicapped, 1979, Georgia Children's Book award, 1979, Charlie May Simon Book award, Arkansas Elementary School Council, 1980, Surrey School Book of the Year award, Surrey School Librarians of Surrey, British Columbia, 1980, Mark Twain award, Missouri Association of School Librarians, 1980, William Allen White Children's Book award, Emporia State University, 1980, Young Reader Medal, California Reading Association, 1980, Nene award runner up, 1981 and 1983, and Golden Archer award, Department of Library Science of the University of Wisconsin—Oskosh, 1982, all for *The Pinballs;* Best Book of the Year, *School Library Journal,* 1980, and American Book award for Children's Fiction (hardcover), 1981, both for *The Night Swimmers;* Notable Children's Book, *School Library Journal,* 1981, Children's Choice, International Reading Association, 1982, Tennessee Children's Choice Book award, Tennessee Library Association, 1983, Sequoyah Children's Book award, 1984, all for *The Cybil War;* Parents' Choice award for literature, Parents' Choice Foundation, 1982, Best Children's Books, *School Library Journal,* 1982, CRABbery award, Oxon Hill Branch of Prince George's County Library, 1983, Mark Twain award, 1985, all for *The Animal, the Vegetable, and John D. Jones;* Notable Book of the Year, *New York Times,* 1982, for *The Two-Thousand-Pound Goldfish;* Regina Medal, Catholic Library Association, 1987; Carlie May Simon award, 1987, for *The Computer Nut;* South Carolina Children's Book award, and Maryland Children's Book award, both 1988, both for *Cracker Jackson.* **Address:** 4 Riverpoint, Clemson, South Carolina 29631, U.S.A.

PUBLICATIONS FOR YOUNG ADULTS

Fiction

The Midnight Fox, illustrated by Ann Grifalconi. New York, Viking, 1968; London, Faber, 1970.
Trouble River, illustrated by Rocco Negri. New York, Viking, 1969.
The Summer of the Swans, illustrated by Ted CoConis. New York, Viking, 1970; London, Hippo, 1980.
The House of Wings, illustrated by Daniel Schwartz. New York, Viking, 1972; London, Bodley Head, 1973.
The 18th Emergency, illustrated by Robert Grossman. New York, Viking, 1973; London, Bodley Head, 1974.
The Winged Colt of Casa Mia, illustrated by Richard Cuffari. New York, Viking, 1973; London, Bodley Head, 1974.
After the Goat Man, illustrated by Ronald Himler. New York, Viking, 1974; London, Bodley Head, 1975.
The TV Kid, illustrated by Richard Cuffari. New York, Viking, and London, Bodley Head, 1976.
The Pinballs. New York, Harper, and London, Bodley Head, 1977.
The Cartoonist, illustrated by Richard Cuffari. New York, Viking, and London, Bodley Head, 1978.
Good-bye Chicken Little. New York, Harper, and London, Bodley Head, 1979.
The Night Swimmers, illustrated by Troy Howell. New York, Delacorte, and London, Bodley Head, 1980.
The Cybil War, illustrated by Gail Owens. New York, Viking, and London, Bodley Head, 1981.
The Animal, the Vegetable, and John D. Jones, illustrated by Ruth Sanderson. New York, Delacorte, and London, Bodley Head, 1982.
The Two-Thousand-Pound Goldfish. New York, Harper, and London, Bodley Head, 1982.
The Glory Girl. New York, Viking, and London, Bodley Head, 1983.
The Computer Nut, illustrated with computer graphics by Guy Byars. New York, Viking, and London, Bodley Head, 1984.
Cracker Jackson. New York, Viking, and London, Bodley Head, 1985.
The Blossoms Meet the Vulture Lady, illustrated by Jacqueline Rogers. New York, Delacorte, and London, Bodley Head, 1986.
The Not-Just-Anybody Family, illustrated by Jacqueline Rogers. New York, Delacorte, and London, Bodley Head, 1986.
A Blossom Promise, illustrated by Jacqueline Rogers. New York, Delacorte, 1987.
The Blossoms and the Green Phantom, illustrated by Jacqueline Rogers. New York, Delacorte, and London, Bodley Head, 1987.
The Burning Questions of Bingo Brown, illustrated by Cathy Bobak. New York, Viking, and London, Bodley Head, 1988.
Bingo Brown and the Language of Love, illustrated by Cathy Bobak. New York, Viking, 1989.
Bingo Brown, Gypsy Lover. New York, Viking, 1990.
The Seven Treasure Hunts. New York, Harper, 1991.
Wanted. . .Mud Blossom. New York, Delacorte, 1991.
Bingo Brown's Guide to Romance. New York, Viking, 1992.
Coast to Coast. New York, Delacorte, 1992.
The Dark Stairs : A Herculeah Jones Mystery. New York, Viking, 1994.

Tarot Says Beware: A Herculeah Jones Mystery. New York, Viking, 1995.

Dead Letter: A Herculeah Jones Mystery. New York, Viking, 1996.

The Joy Boys, illustrated by Frank Remkiewicz. New York, Yearling First Choice Chapter Book, 1996.

Tornado, illustrated by Doron Ben-Ami. New York, HarperCollins, 1996.

Disappearing Acts: A Herculeah Jones Mystery. New York, Viking, 1998.

PUBLICATIONS FOR CHILDREN

Fiction

Clementine, illustrated by Charles Wilton. Boston, Houghton, 1962.

The Dancing Camel, illustrated by Harold Berson. New York, Viking, 1965.

Rama, the Gypsy Cat, illustrated by Peggy Bacon. New York, Viking, 1966.

The Groober, illustrated by the author. New York, Harper, 1967.

Go and Hush the Baby, illustrated by Emily A. McCully. New York, Viking, 1971; London, Bodley Head, 1980.

The Lace Snail, illustrated by the author. New York, Viking, 1975.

The Golly Sisters Go West, illustrated by Sue Truesdale. New York, Harper, 1986.

Beans on the Roof, illustrated by Melodye Rosales. New York, Delacorte, and London, Bodley Head, 1988.

Hooray for the Golly Sisters, illustrated by Sue Truesdale. New York, Harper, 1990.

The Golly Sisters Ride Again, illustrated by Sue Truesdale. New York, HarperCollins, 1994.

My Brother, Ant, illustrated by Marc Simont. New York, Viking, 1996.

Ant Plays Bear, illustrated by Marc Simont. New York, Viking, 1997.

Other

The Moon and I (autobiography). Englewood Cliffs, New Jersey, Messner, 1991.

Editor, *Growing Up Stories,* illustrated by Robert Geary. New York, Kingfisher, 1995.

*

Media Adaptations: The following were adapted for ABC-TV as episodes of the *ABC Afterschool Special:* ''Pssst! Hammerman's After You,'' adapted from *The 18th Emergency,* 1973; ''Sara's Summer of the Swans,'' adapted from *The Summer of the Swans,* 1974; ''Trouble River,'' 1975; ''The Winged Colt,'' adapted from *The Winged Colt of Casa Mia,* 1976; ''The Pinballs,'' 1977; ''Daddy, I'm Their Mamma Now,'' adapted from *The Night Swimmers,* 1981.

Biography: Entry in *Dictionary of Literary Biography,* Volume 52: *American Writers for Children since 1960: Fiction,* Detroit, Gale, 1986.

Manuscript Collections: Clemson University, South Carolina.

Critical Studies: Entry in *Children's Literature Review,* Vol. 16, Detroit, Gale, 1989; entry in *Contemporary Literary Criticism,* Vol. 35, Detroit, Gale, 1985.

*   *   *

Betsy Byars has written many highly acclaimed books for young people. Her teenage characters are carefully drawn, their concerns in growing up clearly and sympathetically presented.

The Summer of the Swans is about one day in Sara's fourteenth summer. Sara lives in a coal mining area of West Virginia. Since her mother's death she and her siblings have been cared for by their aunt; her father works in Ohio and visits infrequently. This summer is a confusing one for Sara. Until now her life has flowed smoothly. Now she has to worry abut her enormous feet, her impossible body, her vivacious, beautiful older sister Wanda, and her burdensome mentally impaired younger brother Charlie. Sara's moods are as sudden as the appearance of the swans on the lake near their home. Sara takes Charlie to see the swans, and he delights in watching them glide silently about. That night Charlie disappears to look for the swans. Sara searches frantically for Charlie all the next day. Charlie, who cannot speak, is lost and helpless. During that long day Sara leaves her own miseries behind and concentrates on the needs of someone else. This strong, compassionate book, which won the Newbery award in 1971, addresses mental disability with honesty and courage.

The Night Swimmers is a story of three children whose mother is dead and whose father leaves them alone while he performs as a country-western singer. The father is set on becoming a star, and places his oldest child, Retta, in charge of feeding, clothing and entertaining her two younger brothers. It is Retta who finds the swimming pool belonging to a colonel who goes to bed early. She and her brothers sneak into his yard in the night, and with new bathing suits and inner tubes do the things that rich people do. Retta seems to have everything under control in their lives until the brothers struggle for their own independence, and one almost drowns while swimming alone in the pool. The crisis brings family members back together again to rethink their needs and relationships. This book, rich in family frustrations and affections, won the American Book Award for Juvenile Fiction in 1980.

The Cybil War is a lighthearted view of young love. Simon and Tony's friendship was sealed in second grade, when the class was asked to write essays on their fathers. Neither had a father. Simon falls in love with their red-haired classmate, Cybil, the first time he sees her cross her eyes. But Tony succeeds, with outrageous lies, in keeping them apart. Finally Simon finds out the truth, wins Cybil, and confronts Tony. The course of true love is simple, direct, and wonderful.

The Blossom Family stories recount the adventures of an atypical, spirited family. The father was a rodeo star; he is now dead. The mother and older daughter are on the rodeo circuit. In *Blossom Promise,* mother and daughter are at the Tucson Rodeo. Grandfather, Pap, remains on the farm with the two young sons. Junior is going for an overnight with his friend Mad Mary, who lives in a cave in the woods. Vern and his friend Michael have built a raft and are about to ride downstream on the Snake River. But when Pap has a sudden heart attack, all family members put their own pursuits on hold to address his needs. With love and determination, they see Pap and themselves through this emergency, becoming stronger individually and closer as a family.

Byar's Bingo Brown stories are rollicking good fun. Bingo is a young man learning about mixed-sex conversations, romance, and love. He is an intelligent young man who learns that young ladies require tact, understanding, and appropriate Christmas presents. In *Bingo Brown, Gypsy Lover,* Bingo must deal with Melissa, who finds him more romantic than a gypsy-lover, and his mother, whose major concern is his soon-to-be-born brother. The effect of a new sibling on a twelve-year-old is artfully and delightfully presented. First Bingo has to deal with his mother's own preoccupation with her body. Then he has to worry about her probable comparison of him, imperfect and clumsy, with arms that are too long, with a perfect younger child. He is certain that his mother will

do all the great, loving things with his brother that she has not done with him. The baby arrives, premature, and Bingo makes several trips to the hospital to look at Jamie in the nursery window. He worries over Jamie's health and he develops pride in Jamie. He wants to be a wonderful older brother, although he feels like a helpless young grandfather.

Byars presents well both the inner lives and outward behaviors of her characters. She shows them in a variety of settings, mostly rural and close to home. But she also shows their needs for adventure and exploration, as they move towards leaving home and taking on adult roles.

—Mary Lystad

C

CADNUM, Michael

Nationality: American. **Born:** Orange, California, 3 May 1949. **Family:** Married wife, Sherina. **Career:** Has worked as a teacher, a crisis counselor, and as a field assistant for archaeologists. Writer. **Awards:** Creative Writing Fellowship from the National Endowment for the Arts; Poetry Northwest's Helen Bullis Prize; Owl Creek Book Award. **Address:** c/o Katharine Kidde, Kidde, Hoyt & Picard, 335 East 51st St., New York, New York 10022.

PUBLICATIONS FOR YOUNG ADULTS

Fiction

Calling Home. New York, Viking, 1991.
Breaking the Fall. New York, Viking, 1992.
Taking It. New York, Viking, 1995.
Zero at the Bone. New York, Viking, 1996.
Edge. New York, Viking, 1997.
Heat. New York, Viking, 1998.

PUBLICATIONS FOR CHILDREN

Fiction

The Lost and Found House, illustrated by Steve Johnson and Lou Fancher. New York, Viking, 1997.

PUBLICATIONS FOR ADULTS

Novels

Nightlight. New York, St. Martin's Press, 1989.
Saint Peter's Wolf. New York, St. Martin's Press, 1991.
Sleepwalker. New York, Carroll & Graf, 1991.
Ghostwright. New York, Carroll & Graf, 1992.
The Horses of the Night. New York, Carroll & Graf, 1993.
Skyscape. New York, Carroll & Graf, 1994.
The Judas Glass. New York, Carroll & Graf, 1994.
In a Dark Wood. New York, Orchard Books, 1998.

Poetry

The Morning of the Massacre. Bieler Press, 1982.
Wrecking the Cactus. Salt Lick Press, 1985.
Invisible Mirror. Ommation Press, 1986.
Foreign Springs. Bakersfield, California, Amelia Press, 1987.
By Evening. Seattle, Washington, Owl Creek Press, 1992.
The Cities We Shall Never See. Canton, Connecticut, Singular Speech Press, 1993.

*

Michael Cadnum comments:

I sit down to write almost every morning, and I don't know what will happen. The brave, fresh voice of Bonnie Chamberlain, the platform diver in *Heat,* surprised my every day as I worked. Bonnie learned to climb to the top of a diving tower all over again as she recovered from her injury, and I was surprised at her courage. I was also surprised at her love for her father, a fraudulent attorney. I could not love the man as she does—I found myself disliking Mr. Chamberlain very much! But Bonnie had her own voice, and in being true to her point of view, perhaps I found myself feeling some compassion for everyone in the novel—even Bonnie's father.

Many of my novels are based on true stories. The shooting of a friend of mine in a car-jacking developed into the basic story of *Edge,* in which a young man's father is badly wounded. A true crime, with a young man killing his best friend by accident, branched out into the story for *Calling Home.*

I don't write "for" young adults, and I don't write "for" adults. My so-called young adult novels are in some ways more "adult" than any of my adult fiction. In a novel like *Zero at the Bone* I am experiencing with the reader how a family endures the terrible experience of having a child go missing. People on the margins of our lives—young people, children, human beings without power, without an established role in life—often see with clearer vision.

I have worked as a teacher, a crisis counselor, and as a field assistant for archaeologists. I have had many jobs which were very routine, but which gave me time to write. I live with my wife Sherina in Albany, California, and a green and yellow parrot name Luke often keeps me company when I write. When I look out my window I see San Francisco across the bay.

*   *   *

Although Michael Cadnum developed his literary reputation in the 1980s as a poet and an author of adult horror fiction, he has shifted his focus during the last decade almost exclusively to the genre of the teen suspense novel. His novels for young adults are set in the San Francisco Bay area and rely heavily upon careful twists in plot and in-depth psychological portraits of teenagers who attempt to reach maturity in an often violent and threatening world.

Cadnum's first YA novel, *Calling Home,* involves the aftermath of a violent murder of a teenage boy named Mead, whose life is ended by Peter, his best friend. Peter is drunk when he kills Mead, and in order to avoid detection and to protect his friend's family, Peter begins to impersonate Mead's voice in calls to his family. However, as his sense of guilt increases, Peter begins to hallucinate and experiences the sensation that Mead is literally taking possession of his body. Even after confessing, the boy is haunted by these hallucinations, and Cadnum does an excellent job of portraying the way that the suppression of guilt and terror can manipulate the psyche of an impressionable young mind. In

Breaking the Fall, Cadnum continues to focus on the psychological effects that violence and feelings of guilt have upon a young male protagonist, in this case, Stanley, a boy who is tempted into conducting a spree of house robberies by a dangerous acquaintance, Jared. It is only when Stanley is nearly killed by one of his intended victims that he is able to break through his dispassionate stance and confront his actions at face value.

In *Taking It,* Cadnum's third novel for young adults, a wealthy and seemingly self-possessed teenaged girl commands the attention of her divorced parents by engaging in chronic shoplifting. Not only does Anna Charles feel a sense of power by taking items, she comes to realize that she has begun to steal things without her own knowledge. This metaphor of suppression, so common to Cadnum's work, extends further into Anna's emotional life, as she hides from herself the fact that she is in love with her stepfather. Commenting on his protagonist, Cadnum has noted that ''I've always admired people who seemed perfectly self-assured, and often suspect they were hiding something even from themselves.'' Once Anna runs away from home and is unable to gain solace from her older brother, she wrecks her car, an action that enables her to recognize that she must confront her feelings and work toward gaining back control of her supposedly ''perfect'' life.

Zero at the Bone, published in 1996, marks a departure for Cadnum, as he shifts his focus to the effect that a random act of violence has upon a reasonably tight-knit and unified family. Narrated from the point of view of Cray Buchanan, a seventeen year-old who has always been close to his eighteen year-old sister Anita, the story builds in intensity as the family first suspects and then must admit that Anita has either been abducted or has decided to disappear. The only clues that the Buchanans can unearth are a few brief notes in Anita's diary that suggest that she had been having a secret affair and the eyewitness sighting of Anita at a subway session on the night of her disappearance. As Cray and his parents attempt to solve the mystery surrounding Anita's last days, they recognize that, in fact, it is often possible to live with someone for decades in an intimate family setting and still not know even the most basic elements of that person's life. More importantly, the Buchanans must eventually reconcile themselves to the idea that Anita may never return, and Cadnum does a fine job of tracing the steps that lead to this conclusion—from the family's disbelief to their anger to their regretful resignation.

An equally powerful treatment of a young person's reaction to random violence occurs in *Edge,* the story of seventeen year-old Zachary Madison's desire to avenge the crippling injuries that his father sustains after he is mugged in broad daylight in a supposedly ''safe'' San Francisco neighborhood. Cadnum's language conveys the depth of Zachary's misery as he contemplates his wounded parent: ''Straps held my father. His neck was captured by large white absorbent pads, his head held firm. His face was puffed into a Halloween joke by a white air tube.'' The motif of entrapment is carried over to Zachary's own situation once he learns that his father's assailant will most likely escape punishment. However, when Zachary attempts to shoot the guilty man and cannot bring himself to pull the trigger, he experiences a relief that, though mingled with shame, enables him to reaffirm his own values and beliefs.

Cadnum's novels are all written from the first person perspective and provide the reader with methodical descriptions of the steps that certain troubled young people follow as they decide to commit shocking crimes or to react to the violence from peers or adults. Often compared to Robert Cormier, Cadnum tackles the difficult questions surrounding teen violence, even when his conclusions are controversial and disturbing.

—Gwen Athene Tarbox

CALVERT, Patricia

Nationality: American. **Born:** Great Falls, Montana, 22 July 1931. **Education:** Winona State University, Minnesota, B.A. 1976, graduate study, since 1976. **Family:** Married George J. Calvert in 1951; two daughters. **Career:** Laboratory clerk, St. Mary's Hospital, 1948-49; clerk typist, General Motors Acceptance Corp., 1950-51; cardiac laboratory technician, Mayo Clinic, 1961-64; enzyme laboratory technician, 1964-70. Senior editorial assistant in publications, since 1970; instructor, Institute of Children's Literature, since 1987. **Awards:** Best book award from American Library Association, juvenile fiction award from Society of Midland Authors, and juvenile award from Friends of American Writers, all 1980, all for *The Snowbird*; award for outstanding achievement in the arts from Young Women's Christian Association (YWCA), 1981, for *The Snowbird*; Mark Twain Award nomination from Missouri Association of School Libraries, 1985, for *The Money Creek Mare*; Maude Hart Lovelace Award nomination, 1985, for *The Stone Pony*; Junior Library Guild selection and ALA Best Book for Young Adults, both 1986, both for *Yesterday's Daughter*; ALA Young Adult Best Book award, 1987; William Allan White Award, 1987, for *Hadder MacColl*; Best of 1990, Society of School Librarians International, 1991, for *When Morning Comes*; Junior Library Guild selection, 1993, for *Picking up the Pieces*. **Address:** Foxwood Farm, 6130 County Road, #7 S.E., Chatfield, Minnesota 55923, U.S.A.

PUBLICATIONS FOR YOUNG ADULTS

Fiction

The Snowbird. New York, Scribner, 1980.
The Money Creek Mare. New York, Scribner, 1981.
The Stone Pony. New York, Scribner, 1982.
The Hour of the Wolf. New York, Scribner, 1983.
Hadder MacColl. New York, Scribner, 1985.
Yesterday's Daughter. New York, Scribner, 1986.
Stranger, You and I. New York, Scribner, 1987.
When Morning Comes. New York, Macmillan, 1989.
The Person I Used to Be. New York, Macmillan, 1993.
Picking Up the Pieces. New York, Scribner, 1993.
Bigger. New York, Scribner, 1994.
Great Lives: The American West. New York, Atheneum, 1997.
Sooner. New York, Atheneum, 1998.

Other

Contributor, *Developing Reading Efficiency,* 4th edition, edited by Lyle L. Miller. Edina, Burgess, 1980.
A Hospital Just for Us. Rochester, Minnesota, Mayo Foundation for Medical Education and Research, 1996.

*

Biography: Essay in *Speaking for Ourselves, Too* compiled and edited by Donald R. Gallo, National Council of Teachers of English, 1993; essay in *Something about the Author Autobiography Series,* Volume 17, Detroit, Gale, 1994.

Patricia Calvert comments:

If I have entertained readers with my novels, that's what I intended to do. If I have informed their hearts, that's what I hoped might happen. One of the best letters I ever received was from a boy in a state far from mine who wrote: ''I never thought much about my own life until I read your book.'' The truth is, of course, that in the process of creating a story I have entertained and informed myself as well, a fact that continually astonishes and delights me. During the creation of fiction, I have been able to live so many other lives—to have been a variety of girls and boys, their parents, friends and enemies—even to have been a dog, a horse, a forest, a creek! At the moment, I am working on a book entitled *Writing to Ritchie,* about two young brothers, David and Ritchie, who are in foster care. I discovered that I shared their experiences as keenly as the experiences I share day to day with my co-workers, my husband, my children. I have occasionally referred to my career as an author as ''my other life,'' but when I am in a mood to be honest I admit the truth: It is my *real* life.

*   *   *

The main characters in Patricia Calvert's novels for young adults struggle with loss and change. Some, like JoBeth Cunningham in *The Stone Pony,* must deal with the death of a family member or friend. Others, Like *Hadder MacColl,* must embark on an entirely new way of life.

In *The Snowbird,* her first book, Calvert employs many of the themes and situations she explores in subsequent novels. Thirteen-year-old Willie (Willanna) Bannerman and her younger brother TJ are sent to live with their uncle Randall and his wife Belle in Dakota Territory in 1883 after their parents die in a fire. Willie tries to deal with her loss by nurturing her hatred for the men who had started the fire and makes up private stories to help her cope with her situation. She also tries to shield herself from additional pain by remaining emotionally distant.

However, in spite of herself, Willie comes to love the eccentric Belle, whose dreams will never materialize on the impoverished prairie. Willie also raises a silvery white filly, the Snowbird, that seems a dream personified. Both Belle and the Snowbird suffer horribly when Willie is forced to ride the young horse too far seeking help for Belle during childbirth. The loss of another baby pushes Belle beyond her endurance, and she abandons Randall and the children. Willie frees the Snowbird after she has nursed the mare to health. In rage and pain, she yells at TJ, ''Did it ever occur to you . . . that everybody I ever loved got up and left me?'' But Willie ultimately demonstrates her resilience.

Calvert's other historical novel, *Hadder MacColl,* deals with the loss of an entire way of life. Set in Scotland during Bonnie Prince Charlie's war to reclaim the throne, events move inexorably to the destruction of the Highlanders at the Battle of Culloden in 1746. Hadder, the fierce and independent daughter of Chieftain Big

Archibald, is appalled that her older brother Leofwin's Edinburgh education has convinced him that rebellion will bring disaster. Hadder despises his softness and insists that Highland traditions need never change.

Yet seeing hundreds of Highlanders, including Leofwin, dead on the battlefield makes Hadder question her assumptions Big Archibald's death. Chastened by despair, she severs her remaining tie to Scotland, and to survive she indentures herself and sails to Boston. Although parts of the Highlanders' way of life may seem strange to modern readers, Hadder's grief, particularly when she discovers Leofwin's body, cuts across time and place.

Like Hadder, JoBeth in *The Stone Pony* must work through the death of a sibling, in this case her talented older sister Ashleigh, who had suffered from cancer. Calvert effectively portrays the anger and guilt experienced by survivors. Images of Ashleigh's beauty and success haunt JoBeth, who feels she can never replace her sister and thinks she should have died instead. Learning to ride her sister's horse and developing a friendship with Luke, who exercises horses at the stable, draw JoBeth outside herself.

Jake Mathiessen in *The Hour of the Wolf* must deal not only with the death of his friend Danny Yumiat but also with memories of his own suicide attempt. After Danny drowns while running his sled dogs for the Iditarod race, Jake trains to enter the grueling competition himself. Danny's sister, Kamina, a staunch defender of native tradition, scoffs at Jake's chances and runs her own team. Facing hardships on the trail, Jake acknowledges that even someone as talented as Danny could be overtaken by fear and depression powerful enough to cause him to kill himself.

Sometimes loss can drive people to the kinds of behavior exhibited by Cat Kincaid in *When Morning Comes.* Her promiscuity stems from an endless search to experience the love she had never received from her father who died in Vietnam and her mother who had never recovered from her own grief.

Fifteen-year-old Ella Rae Carmody must adjust to a series of changes after her mother leaves her family in *The Money Creek Mare.* Leenie O'Brien in *Yesterday's Daughter* has to deal with the return of the mother who had left town sixteen years earlier after Leenie's birth. Raised by her grandparents, Leenie is unwilling to forgive her mother's long absence. *Stranger, You and I* presents the other side of the picture as Zee Crofton realizes she is too young to bring up a child alone and gives up her son for adoption.

In Calvert's worlds, adults are often weak and ineffective. Mothers, in particular, frequently abandon their children physically or psychologically. Jake's mother is more concerned about preserving an impeccable house than in helping her son cope with feelings of failure. Cat's mother, who has spent most of her life with cigarettes, alcohol, and men, tells Cat she no longer has a place for her daughter because she wants to remarry and move to California. Tired of dealing with poverty and family stress, Hugh McBride's mother rents a small apartment and leaves her family temporarily in *Stranger, You and I.*

Again and again, adult responsibilities fall on Calvert's young protagonists. Hugh plans a vacation for his parents in hopes of saving their marriage. Ella Rae schemes to help her father breed a successful race horse. Hadder maps her own future for herself and the woman who had raised her. Calvert portrays characters such as Leenie, JoBeth, and Hugh as more dependable, serious, and mature than the average adolescent. Just as Belle tells Willie that the girl has been ''older, my girl, than I'll ever be!'' so Cat's mother claims that she is not as strong as Cat. Hugh's mother describes him as the glue that holds the family together, and Ella Rae's mother entrusts the diner and younger siblings to her.

Often the adolescents maintain their self-control by rejecting emotional, especially romantic, involvement. Leenie denies her sexuality from fear that she will become pregnant as her mother had. JoBeth considers involvement with museum artifacts safer than emotional entanglements with people. In fact, JoBeth's declining interest in the stone pony whose inscription she had tried to decipher to impress her father corresponds to her increasing ease in riding Ashleigh's horse.

Animals play an important role in many of Calvert's plots. They can connect their owners with the past as Sionnach, the horse from Leofwin, ties Hadder to her brother. They can help a person care for another living creature as Cat discovers in her fondness for the old dog Peaches. Jake's survival depends on his care of his sled dogs, and he considers them closer friends than most humans he knows. Animals can represent dreams like the Snowbird and the unborn horse in *The Money Creek Mare.* Nature provides a refuge for Leenie when she enters the swamp to avoid her mother.

Many young adults in rural and small town settings exhibit remarkable innocence. Wholesome Hooter Lewis resists Cat's attempts at seduction which she had perfected in the city. Ella Rae's down-home speech and manners set her apart from the wealthy girls at the finishing school where she has been sent by adults who hope to adopt her. Hugh McBride offers to forfeit his plans in order to marry his best friend Zee even though he is not her baby's father.

Yet, Calvert makes clear that the future for both Hugh and Zee lies beyond small town Vandalia. In fact, the confines of that town had trapped Hugh's parents into early marriage. With its complex plot and well-realized characters, *Stranger, You and I* demonstrates Calvert's growth as a writer. Although certain themes and plot elements have remained constant in her novels, she has not exhausted the possible variations.

—Kathy Piehl

CAMERON, Eleanor (Frances)

Nationality: American. **Born:** Winnipeg, Manitoba, Canada, 23 March 1912. **Education:** University of California, Los Angeles, 1931-33; Art Center School, Los Angeles, one-year. **Family:** Married Ian Stuart Cameron in 1934; one son. **Career:** Library clerk, Los Angeles Public Library, 1930-36, and Los Angeles Schools Library, 1936-42; research librarian, Foote, Cone & Belding Advertising, Los Angeles, 1943-44; research assistant, Honing, Cooper & Harrington, Los Angeles, 1956-58; librarian, Dan B. Miner Co., advertising, Los Angeles, 1958-59; writer. Member of the editorial board, *Cricket* magazine, La Salle, Illinois, since 1973, and *Children's Literature in Education,* New York, since 1982; since 1977 member of the advisory board, Center for the Study of Children's Literature, Simmons College, Boston. Children's Literature judge, National Book awards, 1980. Gertrude Clarke Whittall Lecturer, Library of Congress, Washington, D.C., 1977. **Awards:** Hawaiian Children's Choice Nene award, 1960, for *The Wonderful Flight to the Mushroom Planet;* Mystery Writers of America Scroll award, 1964, for *A Spell Is Cast;*

California Literature Silver Medal award from Commonwealth Club of California, 1965, for *A Spell Is Cast,* and 1970, for *The Green and Burning Tree: On the Writing and Enjoyment of Children's Books;* Southern California Council on Literature for Children and Young People award, 1965, for distinguished contribution to the field of children's literature; *Boston Globe-Horn Book* award, 1971, for *A Room Made of Windows;* National Book award for children's literature, 1974, for *The Court of the Stone Children;* National Book award runner-up, 1976, for *To the Green Mountains;* FOCAL award, 1985, for *Julia and the Hand of God;* Kerlan award, 1985, for body of work; FOCAL award, 1990, for *A Room Made of Windows.* **Died:** 1996.

PUBLICATIONS FOR YOUNG ADULTS

Fiction

The Wonderful Flight to the Mushroom Planet, illustrated by Robert Henneberger. Boston, Little, Brown, 1954.
Stowaway to the Mushroom Planet, illustrated by Robert Henneberger. Boston, Little, Brown, 1956.
Mr. Bass's Planetoid, illustrated by Louis Darling. Boston, Little, Brown, 1958.
The Terrible Churnadryne, illustrated by Beth and Joe Krush. Boston, Little, Brown, 1959.
A Mystery for Mr. Bass, illustrated by Leonard Shortall. Boston, Little, Brown, 1960.
A Spell Is Cast, illustrated by Beth and Joe Krush. Boston, Little, Brown, 1964.
Time and Mr. Bass, illustrated by Fred Meise. Boston, Little, Brown, 1967.
A Room Made of Windows, illustrated by Trina Schart Hyman. Boston, Little, Brown, 1971; London, Gollancz, 1972.
The Court of the Stone Children. New York, Dutton, 1973.
To the Green Mountains. New York, Dutton, 1975.
Julia and the Hand of God, illustrated by Gail Owens. New York, Dutton, 1977.
Beyond Silence. New York, Dutton, 1980.
That Julia Redfern, illustrated by Gail Owens. New York, Dutton, 1982.
Julia's Magic, illustrated by Gail Owens. New York, Dutton, 1984.
The Private Worlds of Julia Redfern. New York, Dutton, 1988.

PUBLICATIONS FOR CHILDREN

Fiction

The Mysterious Christmas Shell, illustrated by Beth and Joe Krush. Boston, Little, Brown, 1961.
The Beast with the Magical Horn, illustrated by Beth and Joe Krush. Boston, Little, Brown, 1963.

PUBLICATIONS FOR ADULTS

Novel

The Unheard Music. Boston, Little, Brown, 1950.

Other

The Green and Burning Tree: On the Writing and Enjoyment of Children's Books. Boston, Little, Brown, 1969.
The Seed and the Vision: On the Writing and Appreciation of Children's Books. New York, Dutton, 1993.

*

Media Adaptations: *The Court of the Stone Children* has been adapted into a play.

Biography: Essay in *Something about the Author Autobiography Series,* Vol. 10, Detroit, Gale, 1990, 37-55; entry in *Dictionary of Literary Biography,* Vol. 52: *American Writers for Children since 1960: Fiction,* Detroit, Gale, 1986, 66-74.

Manuscript Collections: Kerlan Collection, University of Minnesota, Minneapolis.

Critical Studies: Entry in *Children's Literature Review,* Vol. 1, Detroit, Gale, 1976.

*   *   *

Eleanor Cameron wrote books for younger and older adolescents and for adults. Though she denied writing for any specific age level, her strong, realistic characters make her books particularly appropriate for bridging the gap between children's and adult literature. She has a good sense of how the world is perceived differently by young and old, how remarks of adults can be misunderstood by adolescents, and how behaviors of adolescents can be misinterpreted by adults. Her plots are well-paced and absorbing; she makes readers care about her characters and want to see how they make out.

Her series of books about Julia—*Julia's Magic, That Julia Redfern, Julia and the Hand of God, A Room Made of Windows,* and *The Private Worlds of Julia Redfern*—tell Julia's story from age six to age fifteen, showing changes in Julia herself and in her family constellation as she grows older. Julia is a forthright and determined young lady who reacts to life's challenges with strength and vigor. Throughout the series, she encounters a number of interesting characters and gradually develops her ambition to be a writer. The tone of the books is generally optimistic, although Cameron is often praised for her ability to mix in serious themes and real emotions. It should also be noted that Julia's age in the various books does not necessarily correspond to their publication dates; she is older in some of the earlier books.

In *A Room Made of Windows,* Julia is twelve and well along in her efforts to become a writer. She keeps a Book of Strangeness, which begins with a list of her most beautiful and most detested words. This is followed by another list of Dogs Alive and Dogs Dead and then a list of Cats Alive and Cats Dead, which give the names of all the dogs and cats she's ever known. A somewhat traumatic situation arises for Julia when her mother announces her intention to marry "Uncle Phil." On that same day Julia sees her story "The Mask"—about her deceased father being a writer and handing on his mask to her—in print. Julia must balance her desire to continue her father's legacy with the necessity of accepting her new stepfather.

In *The Private World of Julia Redfern,* Julia is fifteen years old, and her relationship with her stepfather continues to be rocky. But Julia becomes more successful with her writing, which allows her to express the loss she feels over the death of her father. Her first beau, John, encourages joyous and hopeful feelings. The impetuous younger Julia gradually becomes a more aware, a more tolerant, and a more secure human being. In some ways, Julia's development mirrors Cameron's own growth following her parents' divorce and her mother's remarriage.

Cameron's son inspired her to write a series of science-fiction fantasies with boy characters for younger adolescents, the Mushroom Planet books. Reviewers praised Cameron's skillful combination of fantasy with scientific fact, and predicted that the stories would appeal to young readers' need for a private place. The books describe the remarkable adventures of Chuck and David, the spaceships they build, and the friendships they develop with two scientists and the small green people who live on the planet Basidium. Chuck and David lead the sort of life most people only dream about, for they can reach Basidium in their spaceship in two hours. The planet is called Basidium partly because it is covered with mushrooms—some taller than five feet—and partly because the people who live there are spore, or Mushroom People.

In the first book of the series, *The Wonderful Flight to the Mushroom Planet,* the boys take their first trip, accompanied by the learned astronomer Mr. Tyco Bass. In the second book, *Stowaway to the Mushroom Planet,* they return to Basidium in an even better spaceship with Tyco's cousin, Mr. Theodosius Bass, also a gifted individual. This time they are joined by a stowaway who ridicules the idea of space travel yet wishes to obtain its secrets for his own glory. The trip is a huge success, for good triumphs over evil and the stowaway's plans are thwarted. Chuck and David, along with the Basses, remain the sole keepers of certain scientific verities.

Cameron wrote other distinguished novels of adolescent adventure, such as her National Book Award-winner *The Court of the Stone Children.* In this book and *The Terrible Churnadryne,* in which a young girl meets a ghost from Napoleon's era while visiting a French museum, Cameron moves toward pure fantasy. Her more realistic *A Spell Is Cast* involves Cory Winterslow taking a cross-country journey from her New York City home to California in order to spend Easter vacation with her uncle and grandmother, who live in a great old house on cliffs beside the Pacific Ocean. During her stay Cory finds out several troubling things about her family, but she also finds more love and friendship than she has ever known and learns to accept other people's needs and limitations.

Eleanor Cameron was a gifted storyteller who cared about her characters and described them skillfully, warts and all. Her best work is cognizant of the difficulties in growing up, but is also aware of the joys and challenges and absurdities life holds for everyone. She exposes the magic in the everyday world and captures the essence of her young readers' existence.

—Mary Lystad

CAPUTO, Philip

Nationality: American. **Born:** Chicago, Illinois, 10 June 1941.
Education: Purdue University, West Lafayette, Indiana; Loyola
University, Chicago, Illinois, B.A. 1964. **Military Service:** Served
in the United States Marine Corps, 1964-67. **Family:** Married Jill
Esther Ongemach in 1969; two sons. **Career:** Promotional writer
and member of staff of a house paper, 3-M Corp., Chicago, Illinois,
1968-69; local correspondent, *Chicago Tribune,* Chicago, 1969-
72; correspondent in Rome, Beirut, Saigon, and Moscow, 1972-
77; writer and lecturer. Notable assignments include coverage of
violence in Beirut, Yom Kippur War, Ethiopian Civil War, Turkish
invasion of Cyprus, fall of Saigon, 1975. **Awards:** Pulitzer Prize,
with William Hugh Jones, 1972, for coverage of primary election
fraud; George Polk award, 1973, for coverage of captivity by
Palestinian guerrillas; also received Illinois Associated Press award,
Illinois United Press award, and Green Gael award from American
Bar Association. **Address:** c/o Aaron Priest Literary Agency, 708
3rd Ave., New York, New York 10017-4103, U.S.A.

PUBLICATIONS

Fiction

A Rumor of War. New York, Holt, 1977; with a twentieth anniver-
sary postscript by the author, New York, Holt, 1996.
Horn of Africa. New York, Holt, 1980.
DelCorso's Gallery. New York, Holt, 1983.
Indian Country. New York, Bantam, 1987.
Means of Escape. New York, HarperCollins, 1991.
Equation for Evil: A Novel. New York, HarperCollins, 1996.
Exiles : Three Short Novels (includes "Standing In," "Paradise,"
and "In the Forest of the Laughing Elephant"). New York,
Knopf, 1997.

*   *   *

Philip Caputo's five book-length works are divided into two
categories, memoirs, and novels. The former, *A Rumor of War* and
A Means of Escape deal respectively with his career as a U.S.
Marines officer in Vietnam in the 1960s and his subsequent activity
as a journalist covering tumultuous military events in Lebanon,
Israel, Vietnam, Eritrea, and Afghanistan. The latter, *Horn of
Africa, DelCorso's Gallery,* and *Indian Country,* tend to derive
from his experiences as a reporter, although *Indian Country*
features a Vietnam Veteran's efforts to rebuild his life in the forests
of northern Michigan following a traumatic betrayal.

All of Caputo's works graphically explore the evil human
beings inflict on each other. Like two of his literary models, Joseph
Conrad and Ernest Hemingway, Caputo describes and analyzes the
hearts of darkness that turn ostensibly good people into casual
murderers and torturers. His world is filled with purposeful and
accidental mayhem as armed men shoot and eviscerate children,
women, and the elderly as well as their enemies. His depiction of
war erases any romance about what it does to participants, including himself.

Thus, Caputo's work is not for the fainthearted. Those offended
by verbal and visual obscenities, sexual exploitation, and graphic
descriptions of mutilated corpses should avoid his work, especially

his novels. Those mature enough for unflinching depiction of the
human condition will find him rewarding.

Ironically, his memoirs should prove the least objectionable to
the fastidious. *A Rumor of War* contains horrifying passages as
Caputo recounts his experiences as a Marine officer in Vietnam.
Caputo mercilessly analyzes his motives for joining the military.
His response to guerilla warfare and his participation in bureaucratic cover-ups makes for powerful, informative reading and redeems
the horrors he recounts. *Means of Escape,* written a decade later, is
less intense but equally valuable. Based on his career as a reporter
covering "bang bang" in Lebanon, Vietnam, Israel, Eritrea, and
Afghanistan, this memoir explores his motives for undertaking a
series of risky assignments that led to his being held as a spy and
later wounded by Palestinian guerillas, his reporting the North
Vietnamese capture of Saigon and his escape by helicopter, and his
trekking across the Afghan border with mujahadin as Soviet
gunships hover overhead. Increasingly bothersome to Caputo is the
realization that his marriage and fatherhood, plus his aging body,
make these assignments irresponsible if not foolhardy. Ultimately
Means of Escape is a vehicle for Caputo to determine why he
became the adult he is.

A Rumor of War and *Means of Escape* are valuable also in terms
of their less violent parts. Caputo in both writes lengthy segments
in which he recounts growing up in an Italian-American community in Chicago and its suburbs. His search for his Italian roots
eventually leads to an idyllic section of *Means of Escape* in which
he recounts a joyful visit to a Calabrian village where his distant
cousins still live. Thus extracts from each memoir can prove quite
informative on subjects besides war and allow readers to avoid the
more shocking segments.

Caputo's novels intensify the author's experiences as he creates
a series of memorable male characters who in restlessness, ruthlessness, and madness challenge the envelope of human possibility.
Horn of Africa, based loosely on his reporting of the Eritrean war of
independence against Ethiopia, follows three men purportedly on a
CIA-sponsored mission from Sudan into Eritrea. The point of view
character, Charles Gage, is a down-at-the-heels American
reporter looking for a job. He is joined on the mission by a sacked
British military officer Patrick Moody, and an American soldier of
fortune, Jeremy Norstrad. Their undercover mission develops into
a nightmare as Moody and Norstrad battle each other, and the three
face the dangers of the desert, tribal enmities, and the Ethiopian
military. In many ways comparable to Conrad's *Heart of Darkness,*
Horn of Africa explores the impact on westerners who are being
removed from their cultural moorings in a lawless land where force
is the only guarantee of survival.

DelCorso's Gallery is a thinly disguised autobiography in
which the main character, Nick DelCorso, a news photographer,
grapples with the conflicting claims of marriage, parenthood, and
photojournalism. DelCorso, like Caputo, has major assignments in
Vietnam and Lebanon that bring him face-to-face with death. His
acceptance of such assignments endangers his marriage. *DelCorso's
Gallery,* while full of the violence of war, offers insights into the
motives and ethics of journalists as they weigh the dangers of
getting stories, pictures, and professional fame in wartime.

Indian Country by contrast is the least autobiographical of
Caputo's novels. Set in the Upper Peninsula of Michigan, it follows
a Vietnam Veteran's efforts to build a normal life. Christian
Starkman, the son of a minister, initially did not want to join the
military but did so when his Ojibwa friend Bonny George St.

George was drafted. Starkman returns from Vietnam, but his friend does not because of a mistake Starkman made during a battle. Something of a recluse, Starkman works as an estimator for a timber company and eventually marries June, a divorcee, and sets up housekeeping with her and their children. However, Starkman is not at peace and his descent into illusion and paranoia creates a crisis in his career and marriage. Not until he comes to grips with his guilt does he find a way out of his predicament.

Like all of Caputo's writing, *Indian Country* strongly depicts the violence humans can commit. However, in this novel Caputo also develops in June his only strong female character, a woman whose tenacious will to help her husband and save their marriage is equally memorable. Caputo also provides insight into Native American customs as Starkman tries to gain peace of mind through contact with Bonnie George's elderly grandfather.

In conclusion, Caputo's memoirs and novels are aimed at mature readers who are willing to face the potential evil and madness in themselves and other humans. Those willing to understand the turmoil of the late twentieth century will gain humbling insight into what people can do. Caputo seeks to shed light on the evil he has observed in himself and humankind, and by facing it, lessen its power. In the process he spins some engrossing stories.

—Lawrence B. Fuller

CARD, Orson Scott

Pseudonyms: Brian Green. **Nationality:** American. **Born:** Richland, Washington, 24 August 1951. **Education:** Brigham Young University, B.A. (with distinction) 1975; University of Utah, M.A. 1981. **Family:** Married Kristine Allen in 1977; three sons and one daughter. **Career:** Worked as a volunteer Mormon missionary in Brazil, 1971-73; operated repertory theatre in Provo, Utah, 1974-75; Brigham Young University Press, Provo, editor, 1974-76; *Ensign,* Salt Lake City, Utah, assistant editor, 1976-78; free-lance writer and editor, since 1978. Senior editor, Compute! Books, Greensboro, North Carolina, 1983. Teacher at various universities and writers workshops. Local Democratic precinct election judge and Utah State Democratic Convention delegate. **Awards:** John W. Campbell Award for best new writer of 1977, World Science Fiction Convention, 1978; Hugo Award nominations, World Science Fiction Convention, 1978, 1979, 1980, for short stories, and 1986, for novelette, "Hatrack River"; Nebula Award nominations, Science Fiction Writers of America, 1979, 1980, for short stories; Utah State Institute of Fine Arts prize, 1980, for epic poem "Prentice Alvin and the No-Good Plow"; Hamilton/Brackett Award, 1981, for *Songmaster;* Nebula Award, 1985, Hugo Award, 1986, and Hamilton/Brackett Award, 1986, all for novel *Ender's Game;* Nebula Award, 1986, Hugo Award, 1987, and *Locus* Award, 1987, all for novel *Speaker for the Dead;* World Fantasy Award, 1987, for novelette, "Hatrack River"; Hugo Award, and Locus Award nomination, both 1988, both for novella "Eye for Eye"; Locus Award for best fantasy, Hugo Award nomination, and World Fantasy Award nomination, all 1988, all for novel *Seventh Son.* **Address:** Bova, 3951 Gulf Shore Boulevard North, PH 18, Naples, Florida 33940-3639, U.S.A.

PUBLICATIONS

Fiction

Hot Sleep. New York, Baronet, 1978; London, Futura, 1980.
A Planet Called Treason. New York, St. Martin's, 1979; London, Pan, 1981; revised edition, Dell, 1980; new revised edition published as *Treason,* St. Martin's, 1988.
Songmaster. New York, Dial, 1980; London, Futura, 1981.
Hart's Hope. New York, Berkley, 1982; London, Unwin, 1986.
The Worthing Chronicle. New York, Ace, 1983.
Wyrms. New York, Arbor House, 1987.
A Woman of Destiny (historical novel). New York, Berkley, 1983; published as *Saints,* New York, Tor, 1988.
The Abyss (screenplay novelization). New York, Pocket, and London, Century, 1989.
Worthing Saga. New York, Tor, 1990; London, Legend, 1991.
The Changed Man. New York, Tor, 1992.
Lost Boys. New York, HarperCollins, 1992.
Lovelock, with Kathryn H. Kidd. New York, Tor, 1994.
Children of the Mind. New York, Tor, 1996.
Pastwatch: The Redemption of Christopher Columbus. New York, Tor, 1996.
Treasure Box: A Novel. Thorndike, Maine, Thorndike Press, and New York, HarperCollins, 1996.
Stone Tables: A Novel (based on his play of the same name). Salt Lake City, Utah, Deseret Book Co., 1997.
Homebody: A Novel. New York, HarperCollins, 1998.

"Ender Wiggins" series:

Ender's Game. New York, Tor, 1985; London, Unwin, 1985.
Speaker for the Dead. New York, Tor, 1986; London, Century, 1987.
Xenocide. New York, Tor, 1991.

"Tales of Alvin Maker" series:

Seventh Son. New York, Tor, 1987; London, Century, 1988.
Red Prophet. New York, Tor, and London, Century, 1988.
Prentice Alvin. New York, Tor, and London, Century, 1989.
Alvin Journeyman. New York, Tor, 1995.

"Homecoming Saga" series:

The Memory of Earth. New York, Tor, 1993.
The Call of Earth. New York, Tor, 1993
The Ships of Earth. New York, Tor, 1994.
Earthborn. New York, Tor, 1995.
Earthfall. New York, Tor, 1995.

Short Stories

Capitol. New York, Ace, 1978.
Unaccompanied Sonata and Other Stories. New York, Dial, 1981.
Folk of the Fringe. West Bloomfield, Michigan, Phantasia Press, 1989; London, Century, 1990.

"Maps in a Mirror" series:

Maps in a Mirror. New York, Tor, 1990; London, Century, 1991.
Flux. New York, Tor, 1992.

Cruel Miracles. New York, Tor, 1992.
Monkey Sonatas. New York, Tor, 1993.

Plays

The Apostate (produced Provo, Utah, 1970).
In Flight (produced Provo, 1970).
Across Five Summers (produced Provo, 1971).
Of Gideon (produced Provo, 1971).
Stone Tables (produced Brigham Young University, Provo, 1973).
A Christmas Carol (adapted from the story by Charles Dickens; produced Provo, 1974).
Father, Mother, Mother, and Mom (produced Provo, 1974; published in *Sunstone,* 1978).
Liberty Jail (produced in Provo, 1975).
Rag Mission (as Brian Green); published in *Ensign,* July, 1977.

Other

Listen, Mom and Dad. Salt Lake City, Bookcraft, 1978.
Saintspeak: The Mormon Dictionary. Midvale, Utah, Signature, 1981.
Ainge. Midvale, Utah, Signature, 1982.
Compute's Guide to IBM PCjr Sound and Graphics. Greensboro, North Carolina, Compute, 1984.
Cardography. Eugene, Oregon, Hypatia Press, 1987.
Characters and Viewpoint. Cincinnati, Ohio, Writers Digest, 1988; London, Robinson, 1989.
How to Write Science Fiction and Fantasy. Cincinnati, Ohio, Writers Digest, 1990.
A Storyteller in Zion: Essays and Speeches. Salt Lake City, Bookcraft, 1993.

Editor, *Dragons of Darkness.* New York, Ace, 1981.
Editor, *Dragons of Light.* New York, Ace, 1983.
Editor, *Future on Fire.* New York, Ace, 1991.
Editor, with David Dollahite, *Turning Hearts: Short Stories on Family Life.* Salt Lake City, Utah, Bookcraft, 1994.

*

Biography: Entry in *Contemporary Literary Criticism,* Detroit, Gale, Vol. 44, 1987, Vol. 47, 1988, Vol. 50, 1988.

*   *   *

Orson Scott Card is a Mormon writer of fantasy and science fiction, most of which is suitable for and interesting to young adult readers. While Card's Mormon beliefs inform all of his works, his most popular fiction is not overtly religious or moralistic. His stories are usually highly engaging adventures, in which young people of extraordinary ability must deal with moral, political, intellectual, and social problems that test them and require personal growth that is often painful.

The most broadly appealing of his works are the novels in the "Tales of Alvin Maker" series: *Seventh Son, Red Prophet,* and *Prentice Alvin.* These books tell the story of Alvin Miller, the seventh son of a seventh son. He is born in 1800 in an alternative America, geographically recognizable as the frontier Midwest, but

historically different. The main difference is that some people are born with magical gifts, the abilities to mentally control the basic elements of earth, air, fire, and water. Alvin's special birth means he is a "maker," a possessor of the ability to master all forms of magic, not only controlling all the elements, but also able to learn the particular cultural forms of magic possessed by Native Americans and brought from Africa by the slaves. The three novels currently comprising the series tell Alvin's adventures growing up with his family, being caught up in the Indian wars that involved the historical figures of Tecumseh and his brother, the Prophet, and learning the trade of blacksmith while simultaneously learning how to use his magical powers in the service of making. Though cast as adventures, each of these novels focuses on Alvin's personal problems as a gifted young person, such as learning to get along with his family and his various teachers, to live in his society, to use his gifts for good ends, and discovering what he should ultimately do with his life. He learns that his mission in life is to defeat the "unmaker," an entropic force that wants all motion or making to cease. Card gives depth and reality to Alvin's struggles in part by presenting vivid, deep, and sympathetic portraits of a variety of characters, even those who are evil. These stories also explore major American themes such as race and slavery, gender roles, religious fanaticism, and humanity's relationship with nature. Of special interest in the series are the appearances of historical and mythical characters, such as William Blake, Napoleon, and Mike Fink. Card's narratives are fast-paced and gripping, but spiced with vivid descriptions and humorous episodes. Card has announced his intention of publishing two or three more books to complete this series.

While the *Alvin Maker* books and those in the science fiction series, *Homecoming,* are suitable for all young adult readers, educators should be aware that these books contain violent events and that Card's presentation of adult sexuality is frank, though morally serious. There is no gratuitous violence or sex in these books, but Card does deal realistically with both themes when it is appropriate to his stories. Among Card's novels that would be of interest to young adults, two are especially violent and, therefore, likely to offend less-sophisticated or sensitive readers: *Hart's Hope* and *Wyrms.*

Card's most successful science fiction series—winner of Hugo and Nebula awards—is aimed at older readers, but is appropriate to and widely admired by high school and college students. These are the three novels about Ender Wiggins: *Ender's Game, Speaker for the Dead,* and *Xenocide. Ender's Game* is the tale of a child genius who is trained to lead Earth's space fleet against a greatly feared and possibly overwhelming alien enemy. In the last phase of his training, when he thinks he is playing strategic games, he is actually leading the fleet by remote control, and he successfully wipes out the entire alien species. Because of the time distortions of light-speed space travel, Ender is still a young man thousands of years after the events of *Ender's Game,* when humans have realized that they were in error to think of the destroyed aliens as enemies. Ender himself is led to this realization because he has come into contact with a cocoon that contains the seeds of the rebirth of that race and he has become a speaker for the dead. In *Speaker for the Dead,* he is caught up in finding a new planet on which that species can start again, and this turns out to be a planet on which humanity has accidentally encountered another intelligent species. In *Xenocide,* a middle-aged Ender works with three non-human intelligent species, all of whom might be destroyed by a fearful and ignorant humanity. These books are also highly engaging adventures, characterized by social, political, spiritual, and intellectual puzzles and conflicts. One especially important central theme is the complex of problems posed by colonialism and imperialism in the modern world and how radically different cultures can relate to each other in mutually beneficial ways.

While Card is best known for his novels, his short stories are also excellent. *Maps in a Mirror: The Short Fiction of Orson Scott Card* collects most of his stories, and sections of this large collection have been published in separate paperbacks. The hardcover collection is a good resource since it contains introductions and afterwords in which Card talks about his life, career, and some of the ideas behind his stories. The best of these stories for young adults and classroom use are probably those in the sections ''Maps in a Mirror'' and ''Cruel Miracles,'' such as ''Unaccompanied Sonata,'' ''The Porcelain Salamander,'' ''Middle Woman,'' ''St. Amy's Tale,'' ''Kingsmeat,'' and ''Holy.'' Like the novels, these stories are sometimes quite violent but always have at least one challenging moral or intellectual dilemma at their center that can provoke serious thought and discussion.

—Terry Heller

CARTER, Alden R(ichardson)

Nationality: American. **Born:** Eau Claire, Wisconsin, 7 April 1947. **Education:** University of Kansas, B.A. 1969; Montana State University, teaching certificate, 1976. **Military Service:** Served in U.S. Navy, 1969-74; became lieutenant senior grade; nominated for Navy Achievement Medal. **Family:** Married Carol Ann Shadis in 1974; one son and one daughter. **Career:** Writer. Taught high school English and journalism for four years in Marshfield, Wisconsin. Speaker at workshops, including ALAN Workshop on Young Adult Literature of the National Council of Teachers of English, American Library Association, and International Reading Association. **Awards:** Best Book for Young Adults citation, American Library Association (ALA), 1984, for *Growing Season*; Best Book for Young Adults citations, ALA, New York Public Library, Los Angeles Public Library, and the Child Study Association, Best Book for Reluctant Readers citation, ALA Young Adult Services Committee, all 1985, all for *Wart, Son of Toad*; Best Book for Young Adults citations, ALA and Los Angeles Public Library, and Best Book for the Teenage citation, New York Public Library, all 1987, all for *Sheila's Dying*; Children's Book COuncil/National Science Teacher's Association Outstanding Science Trade Book for Children citation, 1988, for *Radio: From Marconi to the Space Age*; Best Book citation, ALA, and Best Book for the Teenage citation, New York Public Library, both 1989, and ALA ''Best of the Best'' citation, 1994, all for *Up Country*; Best Book for the Teenage citation and Best Children's Fiction Book of the Year citation, Society of Midland Authors, both 1990, both for *Robodad*; New York Public Library Best Book for the Teenage citations for *China Past—China Future, Dogwolf,* and *Between a Rock and a Hard Place*; *American Bookseller* Pick of the List, for *Dogwolf, Bull Catcher,* and *I'm Tougher than Asthma*; ALA Best Book for Young Adults, for *Between a Rock and a Hard Place*; Orbis Pictus Award nomination, for *I'm Tougher than Asthma*; *Oppenheim Toy Portfolio* Gold Seal Award, for *Big Brother Dustin*. **Address:** 1113 West Onstad Drive, Marshfield, Wisconsin 54449, U.S.A. **E-mail Address:** acarter@tznet.com. **Website:** http://www.tznet.com/busn/acarterwriter.

PUBLICATIONS FOR YOUNG ADULTS

Fiction

Growing Season. New York, Coward McCann, 1984.
Wart, Son of Toad. New York, Putnam, 1985.
Sheila's Dying. New York, Putnam, 1987.
Up Country. New York, Putnam, 1989.
Robodad. New York, Putnam, 1990; as *Dancing on Dark Water,* New York, Scholastic, 1993.
Dogwolf. New York, Scholastic, 1994.
Between a Rock and a Hard Place. New York, Scholastic, 1995.
Bull Catcher. New York, Scholastic, 1997.

Nonfiction

Supercomputers, with Wayne Jerome LeBlanc. New York, F. Watts, 1985.
Modern China, with photographs by Carol S. Carter and Alden R. Carter. New York, F. Watts, 1986.
Modern Electronics, with Wayne Jerome LeBlanc. New York, F. Watts, 1986.
Illinois. New York, F. Watts, 1987.
Radio: From Marconi to the Space Age. New York, F. Watts, 1987.
The Shoshoni. New York, F. Watts, 1989.
The Battle of Gettysburg. New York, F. Watts, 1990.
Last Stand at the Alamo. New York, F. Watts, 1990.
The Colonial Wars: Clashes in the Wilderness. New York, F. Watts, 1992.
The American Revolution: War for Independence. New York, F. Watts, 1992.
The War of 1812: Second Fight for Independence. New York, F. Watts, 1992.
The Civil War: American Tragedy. New York, F. Watts, 1992.
The Mexican War: Manifest Destiny. New York, F. Watts, 1992.
The Spanish-American War: Imperial Ambitions. New York, F. Watts, 1992.
Battle of the Ironclads: The Monitor and the Merrimack. New York, F. Watts, 1993.
China Past—China Future. New York, F. Watts, 1994.

The American Revolution Series

Colonies in Revolt. New York, F. Watts, 1988.
Darkest Hours. New York, F. Watts, 1988.
At the Forge of Liberty. New York, F. Watts, 1988.
Birth of the Republic. New York, F. Watts, 1988.

PUBLICATIONS FOR CHILDREN

I'm Tougher than Asthma, photographs by Dan Young. Morton Grove, Illinois, Albert Whitman, 1996.
Big Brother Dustin, photographs by Dan Young, with Carol Carter. Morton Grove, Illinois, Albert Whitman, 1997.

*

Biography: Entry in *Something about the Author,* Vol. 67, Detroit, Gale, 1992; essay in *Speaking for Ourselves, Too: More Autobiographical Sketches by Notable Authors for Young Adults* compiled and edited by Donald R. Gallo, National Council of Teachers of English, 1993; entry in *Something about the Author Autobiography Series,* Vol. 18, Detroit, Gale, 1994.

Critical Studies: Entry in *Children's Literature Review,* Vol. 22, Detroit, Gale, 1991.

Alden R. Carter comments:

I am always astonished by the courage of people, and young people in particular. I find the coming-of-age process endlessly intriguing, and if readers of my books come to share my fascination, then I have done my work well. I concentrate on characterization because the human soul matters more to me—and I think to serious readers whatever their age—than elaborate plots. Like people in real life, my characters do not survive their problems unscathed; all of us collect our store of disappointments, scars, and sad wisdom in the teenage years. Yet through their struggles, my characters grow and—like the vast majority of young people in real life—reach the threshold of adulthood triumphant in the realization of their own grit, resilience, and courage.

My nonfiction books also reflect my interest in the struggles of individuals and nations to overcome what often seem unscalable obstacles. History teaches the hard lesson that we fail more than we succeed. Yet we are a remarkably persistent and ingenious species, and ultimately we find the fingernail crack in the slippery surface, gain a toehold on the rock, and—inch by inch—work upward toward the summit and the open sky beyond.

*   *   *

The ability of young adults to adjust to difficult situations with the help of family and friends is a theme Alden R. Carter explores in each of his young adult novels. In *Growing Season,* seventeen-year-old Rick Simons reluctantly moves with his family from Milwaukee to a dairy farm in rural Wisconsin during his senior year. Rick only intends to stay for six months, to help get things going, and then return to Milwaukee to study architecture in college. But life on the farm is filled with daily chores, broken machinery, livestock problems, and family squabbles which demand his time and energy and Rick is unable to leave. Eventually, his resentment recedes and Rick comes to enjoy farm life. His family's determined acceptance of adversity and understanding of his feelings and mistakes, along with his friendship with Lorie, enable him to remain on the farm indefinitely. He may even find a way to use his architectural inclinations to improve their family farm and others like it. In this heart-warming novel, filled with familial love, supportive friendships, and the frustrations inherent in change and growth, Carter shows the advantages of life in the country, even for a city-bred teenager like Rick.

The question of the city vs. the country also figures in *Up Country.* Like Rick, sixteen-year-old Carl Staggers leaves Milwaukee to live in rural Wisconsin, but his situation is more severe than Rick's. Carl's stay up country is court-mandated when his mother is arrested for a hit-and-run accident and ordered into a recovery program for alcoholics. Carl does not want to leave his lucrative, but illegal electronics repair business and live with his

aunt, uncle, and cousin whom he has not seen for eight years. His relatives are kind to him, but Carl is annoyed by their countrified ways. His cousin Bob encourages him to date Signa, who becomes a loyal friend. When Carl's illegal activities are discovered, Signa and his country family stand by him throughout the legal proceedings. Even though his mother is now a recovering alcoholic and Carl can return to the city and live with her, he chooses to remain in the country where his friend Signa and a family he can count on will help him as he continues to learn how being the child of an alcoholic has affected his life.

Fourteen-year-old Shar's life has also been affected by an inadequate parent. Her father is a victim of brain damage caused by an aneurysm which has destroyed the part of his brain that controls higher emotions, like love. *RoboDad* is the story of how Shar learns to cope with a father who has no emotional connection to his family, a father who used to be her best buddy but now makes uncaring remarks about her physical appearance, a father who chooses to look for a lost ski rather than save her brother after a water-skiing accident, a father who makes people so uncomfortable that her best friend won't come to her home and her boyfriend breaks up with her, a father who has to be tranquilized so he doesn't hurt himself or anyone else. Shar and her family come to understand how each of them deals with their father's emotional detachment: Shar cries, Sid fights, Alex remains cheerful, and their mother works hard to pay the bills and keep things as calm as possible. Her mother's honesty helps Shar accept the fact that the father she loved so much is dead, but she can still go on caring for the man he has become even though he will never be able to love her back.

Steve Michaels in *Wart, Son of Toad* is also faced with a difficult situation involving his father. Steve and his father have lived alone since his mother and sister Roxy were killed in an automobile accident three years earlier. Steve attends the high school where his father is a very unpopular biology teacher. The students call his father the "Toad," and refer to Steve as "Wart." Unhappy students threaten his father and tease Steve. Mr. Michaels refuses to be intimidated, even when students vandalize his car. Steve, on the other hand, fights with one of the chiding jocks. Life is not easy for Steve and his father at home either; they argue constantly over Steve's grades and lack of desire to go to college. The shadow of Steve's mother and Roxy hovers over them as they both deal with their grief. Steve and his father eventually come to understand one another, and help each other put the past behind them and move on in new directions—Steve to pursue a course in auto mechanics and a relationship with his girlfriend Trish and Mr. Michaels to leave teaching and work as a guide for a wildlife foundation.

Dealing with death is also emphasized in *Sheila's Dying.* Jerry Kincaid has been dating Sheila Porter, but plans to break up with her. Before he tells her, however, she becomes ill, and he learns she is suffering from terminal cancer. Sheila's grandmother, her legal guardian, is alcoholic and unable to help Sheila, so Jerry supports Sheila through her medical ordeal. Bonnie Harper, Sheila's only other friend, wants to share in Sheila's care. Up to this point Jerry and Bonnie have had an adversarial relationship, but they manage to work together to meet Sheila's ever increasing needs. After a while they develop a friendship which sustains them through this trying time. Sheila knows she is dying and tells Jerry she hopes Bonnie will take her place as his steady girlfriend. By the end of the story, Jerry and Bonnie have fallen in love. Their mutual concern for Sheila has minimized any disagreements they may have had and made them appreciate the good in each other. They have not only helped Sheila through a difficult time, but themselves as well.

As Carter's characters struggle and adapt in various situations, they grow toward adulthood. The support of friends and family helps them in this process. Young adult readers find these characters real, their problems compelling, their feelings familiar, and their decisions satisfying. Such responses to his skillfully written stories consequently make Carter's young adult novels excellent fare for young adult readers.

—Elizabeth A. Poe

CASSEDY, Sylvia

Nationality: American. **Born:** Brooklyn, New York, 29 January 1930. **Education:** Brooklyn College, 1946-51, B.A. 1951; Johns Hopkins University, Baltimore, 1959-60. **Family:** Married 1) Leslie Verwiebe in 1949 (died 1950); 2) Edward Cassedy in 1952, three daughters and one son. **Career:** Teacher of creative writing to children, Queens College, City University of New York, Flushing, 1973-74, Great Neck Public Library, New York, 1975-79, and Manhasset Public Schools, New York, 1977-84. Instructor in teaching creative writing to children, Nassau County Board of Cooperative Education, New York, 1978-79. **Died:** 6 April 1989.

PUBLICATIONS FOR YOUNG ADULTS

Fiction

Behind the Attic Wall. New York, Crowell, 1983; London, Bodley Head, 1984.
M.E. and Morton. New York, Crowell, and London, Bodley Head, 1987.
Lucie Babbidge's House. New York, Crowell, 1989.

PUBLICATIONS FOR CHILDREN

Fiction

Little Chameleon, illustrated by Rainey Bennett. Cleveland, World, 1966.
Pierino and the Bell, illustrated by Evaline Ness. New York, Doubleday, 1966.
Marzipan Day on Bridget Lane, illustrated by Margot Tomes. New York, Doubleday, 1967.
The Best Cat Suit of All, pictures by Rosekranz Hoffman. New York, Dial, 1991.

Poetry

Roomrimes, illustrated by Michele Chessare. New York, Crowell, 1987.
Zoomrimes, illustrated by Michele Chessare. New York, Crowell, 1993.

Other

In Your Own Words: A Beginner's Guide to Writing. New York, Doubleday, 1979.

Editor, and Translator with Kunihiro Suetake, *Birds, Frogs, and Moonlight,* illustrated by Vo-Dinh. New York, Doubleday, 1967.
Editor, and Translator with Parvathi Thampi, *Moon-Uncle, Moon-Uncle: Rhymes from India,* illustrated by Susanne Suba. New York, Doubleday, 1973.
Translator with Kunihiro Suetake, *Red Dragonfly on my Shoulder: Haiku,* illustrated by Molly Bang. New York, HarperCollins, 1992.

*   *   *

Sylvia Cassedy wrote with a young eye. In her fiction the boundary between young people and adults—-a boundary often blurred or absent in literature for this age group—-is firmly present. On one side are the fantasies and helplessness of being young, on the other the rigidity and dreariness of being grown-up. Her preadolescent characters haven't yet developed the armour to shield themselves from the world's harsh realities nor have they lost their unique enjoyment of its physical details; they revel in odd, messy minutiae, such as smeary pink nail polish or soft corners of paper.

All of Cassedy's characters cope with reality through the transforming power of imagination. In her first book, *Behind the Attic Wall,* orphaned Maggie is stripped of love and security. Appropriately, she invents a game of domineering the imaginary "Backwoods Girls," who have even less than she. The talking dolls that Maggie discovers spring naturally out of this needy game; now instead of just pretending to, she can really give. The line between how much the dolls are Maggie's own creation and how much they are "real" is very fine, which makes their existence all the more haunting. The result is a remarkably powerful novel about caring and continuity.

In *M.E. and Morton,* Mary Ella—-or M. E., as she prefers to call herself—-also uses fantasy as a solace, in pretending that her bottles of paint are orphans. As well, she fantasizes that she is more popular and loved than she is. Her neighbour Polly pretends, too—-she imagines that the bugs on her ceiling are dancing and that she can shrink herself to fit into a toy train. Unlike the unhealthy fantasies of M. E., however, Polly's inventions enable her to transform her dull, poverty-stricken life into joy. M. E.'s slow older brother, Morton, is a perfect companion for Polly. He doesn't suffer from his sister's guilty confusion and can engage with Polly in simple play. It is easier to label this book realism than it is to call *Behind the Attic Wall* fantasy. The use of imagination, however, results in a similar "magic" in both: make-believe comes true through the healing power of love.

The author's final novel, *Lucie Babbidge's House,* digs deeper into the themes she has developed in her first two works, resulting in a more complex and cynical story. The utterly bleak orphanage where Lucie lives and goes to school is a symbol of both adult and child cruelty: Lucie's teacher verbally abuses her, and her classmates ape that bullying. Like Maggie, Lucie creates a fantasy around some dolls that she finds in a dollhouse in a hidden room where she escapes to whenever possible. She makes the dolls play all the roles she has known—-her over-literate teacher and beloved deceased parents, as well as herself as a child who was once happy. The dollhouse fantasy is gradually made obvious as the story proceeds, then a third level of reality is added as Lucie receives letters from Delia, a girl her own age in England. These three levels of reality—-Lucie's school life, her made-up dollhouse life, and Delia's life, which may or may not be fantasy—-begin to get mixed up, which threaten Lucie's sanity. The way she saves herself, by standing up to her teacher with words, provides a slender but strong thread of hope. This novel lacks the promise of love present at the end of Cassedy's first two novels, but its sadness is balanced by the black humour of the ridiculous restrictions in Lucie's daily life. The result is a brilliant comment on the gap between adults' and children's perceptions of reality.

Desperately lonely Maggie, posturing M. E., resilient Polly, stolid Morton, and pathetic but determined Lucie, all emerge as unforgettable personalities. While the leisurely pace of Cassedy's fiction may discourage readers looking for continuous action, each novel builds suspense in delicate layers to reach a surprise ending. The author's precise, measured language—-the language of the poet she was—-results in impeccable prose. Sylvia Cassedy was a compelling and original writer for young people.

—Kit Pearson

CAUDILL, Rebecca

Nationality: American. **Born:** Poor Fork (now Cumberland), Kentucky, 2 February 1899. **Education:** Sumner County High School, Portland, Tennessee, graduated 1916; Wesleyan College, Macon, Georgia, 1916-20, B.A. in English 1920; Vanderbilt University, Nashville, 1921-22, M.A. 1922. **Family:** Married James Sterling Ayars in 1931; one son (died 1956) and one daughter. **Career:** English and history teacher, Sumner County High School, Portland, Tennessee, 1920-21; English teacher, Collegio Benet, Rio de Janeiro, 1922-24; editor, *Torchbearer* magazine, Nashville, 1924-30; author of books for children and young people, since 1943. Originator of hospitality program for international students, University of Illinois; former alumni trustee, Wesleyan College; secretary of board of trustees, Urbana Free Library; Member of the Board of Trustees, Pine Mountain Settlement School, Kentucky, 1967-85. Teacher at writing workshops. Rebecca Caudill Public Library, Cumberland, Kentucky, named in 1965. **Awards:** Newbery award runner-up, 1949, for *Tree of Freedom;* "honor book" citations, *New York Herald-Tribune,* 1949, for *Tree of Freedom,* and 1954, for *House of the Fifers;* Wesleyan College Alumnae award for Distinguished Achievement, 1954; Nancy Bloch Memorial award for best juvenile book dealing with inter cultural relations, 1956, for *Susan Cornish;* Friends of American Writers award, 1965, for *The Far-Off Land;* author of Caldecott Honor Book, 1965, *A Pocketful of Cricket;* citation for most representative American book recommended for translation into other languages, Hans Christian Andersen award Committee, 1966, for *A Pocketful of Cricket;* Clara Ingram Judson award, Society of Midland Authors, 1966, for *A Certain Small Shepherd;* award for distinguished service in the field of children's reading (with husband, James Ayars), Chicago Children's Reading

Round Table, 1969; "Author of the Year" citation, Illinois Association of Teachers of English, 1972. **Died:** 2 October 1985.

PUBLICATIONS FOR YOUNG ADULTS

Fiction

Barrie and Daughter, illustrated by Berkeley Williams. New York, Viking, 1943.
Tree of Freedom, illustrated by Dorothy Bayley Morse. New York, Viking, 1949.
House of the Fifers, illustrated by Genia. New York, Longmans, 1954.
Susan Cornish, illustrated by E. Harper Johnson. New York, Viking, 1955.
The Far-Off Land, illustrated by Brinton Turkle. New York, Viking, 1964; London, Hart Davis, 1965.
Contrary Jenkins with husband, James Ayars, illustrated by Glen Rounds. New York, Holt, 1969.

Poetry

Come Along!, illustrated by Ellen Raskin. New York, Holt, 1969.
Wind, Sand, and Sky, illustrated by Donald Carrick. New York, Dutton, 1976.

Other

Florence Nightingale, illustrated by William Neebe. Evanston, Illinois, Row Peterson, 1953.

PUBLICATIONS FOR CHILDREN

Fiction

Happy Little Family, illustrated by Decie Merwin. Philadelphia, Winston, 1947.
Schoolhouse in the Woods, illustrated by Decie Merwin. Philadelphia, Winston, 1949.
Up and Down the River, illustrated by Decie Merwin. Philadelphia, Winston, 1951.
Saturday Cousins, illustrated by Nancy Woltemate. Philadelphia, Winston, 1953.
Schoolroom in the Parlor, illustrated by Decie Merwin. Philadelphia, Winston, 1959.
Time for Lissa, illustrated by Velma Ilsley. New York, Thomas Nelson, 1959.
Higgins and the Great Big Scare, illustrated by Beth Krush. New York, Holt, 1960.
The Best-Loved Doll, illustrated by Elliott Gilbert. New York, Holt, 1962.
A Pocketful of Cricket, illustrated by Evaline Ness. New York, Holt, 1964; London, Harrap, 1966.
A Certain Small Shepherd, illustrated by William Pène du Bois. New York, Holt, 1965; Edinburgh, Oliver and Boyd, 1966.
Did You Carry the Flag Today, Charley?, illustrated by Nancy Grossman. New York, Holt, 1966.
Somebody Go and Bang a Drum, illustrated by Jack Hearne. New York, Dutton, 1974.

PUBLICATIONS FOR ADULTS

Other

The High Cost of Writing. Cumberland, Kentucky, Southeast Community College, 1965.
My Appalachia: A Reminiscence, photographs by Edward Wallowtich. New York, Holt, 1966.

*

Manuscript Collection: University of Kentucky, Lexington; Kerlan Collection, University of Minnesota, Minneapolis; de Grummond Collection, University of Southern Mississippi, Hattiesburg; and May Massee Collection, Emporia State College, Kansas.

Media Adaptations: *A Pocketful of Cricket* (filmstrip and record), Miller-Brody, 1976.

Biography: Entry in *More Junior Authors,* edited by Muriel Fuller, New York, H.W. Wilson, 1963.

*   *   *

Rebecca Caudill has written books for elementary school, junior high school, and senior high school readers. Set in the Kentucky mountain country of her birth, these books bespeak former times in our country and of seldom-heralded rural areas. Caudill's characters are at one with their family, their animals, and their land.

The Tree of Freedom takes place in Kentucky in the spring of 1780, when homesteading is in full swing. Thirteen-year-old Stephanie Venable and her family make the long, hard journey from Carolina to Kentucky to take up their land grant claim of four hundred acres; they aim to build a house and start a farm. Stephanie brings with her an apple seed; her Grandmother Linney had carried an apple seed from France to Charleston, and planted it next to the house that her family built years before. Stephanie wanted to do the same at the family's new home in Kentucky, to plant a "tree of freedom," a link with her past and a symbol of her future. Kentucky in 1780 was full of promise, and full of hardship. Before winter the seven Venables would have to clear the land, build a cabin, and plant a crop. Talk of hostile Indians in the area, the call for Revolutionary Army volunteers to fight the British, and the threat of a Britisher's claim to the Venable's land, make the tasks more hazardous and difficult. But Stephanie goes ahead and plants her seed, and the Venables build a cabin and start their crops. Noel, the oldest child, goes off to join the Revolutionary Army. When he leaves, Stephanie shoulders more of the burden of family work. When Noel returns, he announces that he has been given the opportunity to read law in Williamsburg. He urges his family to allow Stephanie to study to be a teacher in Williamsburg. The book, which is well researched, ends with the hope of freedom and of opportunity for young people.

Barrie and Daughter is a fine story of understanding and affection between father and daughter. Fern's mother insists that a girl has one calling: to marry and run a household. She could also teach school, but that was the extent of a girl's options. This is not Fern's view of her future. The Barries live at Poor Fork, in the mountains of Kentucky, at the turn of the century. It is against the background of rigid mores of the mountain country that the novel is set. When Fern's father opens a store, Fern discovers that she enjoys the ordering and selling of goods. Fern and her father are similar in their imagination, their caring for others, and their courage. Their store is a new kind of store to the valley, one that is honest and one that puts the good of the neighbors first. Around the keeping of the store comes romance, and the strength to fight against hate and violence.

Caudill's "Happy Little Family" series includes *Happy Little Family, Schoolhouse in the Woods, Schoolhouse in Parlor, Saturday Cousins,* and *Up and Down the River.* In them Caudill writes to entertain and to provide readers with information on how life was led in an earlier time in a rural part of the country. Her books are not about community leaders, but about community members. They move at a slow, deliberate pace. Important in the activity is the change of seasons, for seasons direct to a large degree what one does in a life without central heat and air, without complex machines and public transportation. Relationships between family members in the books are positive and involve strong sets of reciprocal obligations. There are few social problems found in the books, and views of self, people, and the world are positive. Hostile forces appear, and the spectre of death is always there on the farm, but life itself is celebrated. If the pictures seem a little too perfect, they are still vibrant and plausible.

In *Up and Down the River,* summertime has finally arrived and the Fairchild family is ready for adventure. The family, consisting of two parents, three adolescents, and two younger children, has lots of work to do on the farm—there are animals to feed, eggs to gather, newborns to watch, stove wood to chop and carry. But Bonnie and Debbie have time to start a business venture, like their big sister who receives ten cents for every organ lesson she gives. Bonnie and Debbie decide to sell products ordered through their mother's magazines. They sell sensational new bluing at ten cents a package, and beautiful colored pictures at ten cents each. They are successful in selling their products up and down the river to their distant neighbors, who are not only pleased to buy thir wares, but who also give them presents—a newborn lamb, decorated dinner plates. The everyday activities of the two girls, while not climactic, are nonetheless good fun.

Caudill provides strong descriptions of a geographic region and its distinctive cultures that are not often seen in books for young adults. She reminds us of the diversity of our country, and also of its developmental history from a harsh, agricultural beginning.

—Mary Lystad

CAVANNA, Betty (Elizabeth Cavanna)

Pseudonyms: Betsy Allen; Elizabeth Headley. **Nationality:** American. **Born:** Camden, New Jersey, 24 June 1909. **Education:** Local schools, Haddenfield, New Jersey; Douglass College (now part of Rutgers University), New Brunswick, New Jersey, 1925-29, Litt.B. in journalism 1929 (Phi Beta Kappa). **Family:** Married 1) Edward Talman Headley in 1940 (died 1952), one son; 2) George Russell Harrison in 1957 (died 1979). **Career:** Reporter, Bayonne

Times, New Jersey, 1929-31; advertising manager and then art director, Westminster Press, Philadelphia, Pennsylvania, 1931-41; full-time writer, since 1941. **Awards:** Honor book, Spring Book Festival, 1946, for *Going on Sixteen,* and 1947, for *Secret Passage;* citation from New Jersey Institute of Technology and English Teachers Association of New Jersey, 1966, for *Mystery at Love's Creek;* runner-up, Edgar Allan Poe award, 1970, for *Spice Island Mystery,* and 1972, for *The Ghost of Ballyhooly;* citation from New Jersey Institute of Technology, 1976, for *Catchpenny Street.* **Address:** 45 Pasture Lane, Bryn Mawr, Pennsylvania 19010, U.S.A.

PUBLICATIONS FOR YOUNG ADULTS

Fiction

Puppy Stakes. Philadelphia, Westminster, 1943.
The Black Spaniel Mystery. Philadelphia, Westminster, 1945.
Going on Sixteen. Philadelphia, Westminster, 1946; revised, New York, Morrow, 1985.
Spurs for Suzanna, illustrated by Virginia Mann. Philadelphia, Westminster, 1947; London, Lutterworth, 1948.
A Girl Can Dream, illustrated by Harold Minton. Philadelphia, Westminster, 1948.
Paintbox Summer, illustrated by Peter Hunt. Philadelphia, Westminster, 1949.
Spring Comes Riding. Philadelphia, Westminster, 1950; London, Lutterworth, 1952.
Two's Company, illustrated by Edward J. Smith. Philadelphia, Westminster, 1951.
Lasso Your Heart. Philadelphia, Westminster, 1952.
Love, Laurie. Philadelphia, Westminster, 1953.
Six on Easy Street. Philadelphia, Westminster, 1954.
Passport to Romance. New York, Morrow, 1955.
The Boy Next Door. New York, Morrow, 1956.
Angel on Skis, illustrated by Isabel Dawson. New York, Morrow, 1957.
Stars in Her Eyes. New York, Morrow, 1958.
The Scarlet Sail. New York, Morrow, 1959; Leicester, Brockhampton, 1962.
Accent on April. New York, Morrow, 1960.
Fancy Free. New York, Morrow, 1961.
A Touch of Magic, illustrated by John Gretzer. Philadelphia, Westminster, 1961.
A Time for Tenderness. New York, Morrow, 1962.
Almost Like Sisters. New York, Morrow, 1963.
Jenny Kimura. New York, Morrow, 1964; Leicester, Brockhampton, 1966.
Mystery at Love's Creek. New York, Morrow, 1965.
A Breath of Fresh Air. New York, Morrow, 1966.
The Country Cousin. New York, Morrow, 1967.
Mystery in Marrakech. New York, Morrow, 1968.
Spice Island Mystery. New York, Morrow, 1969.
Mystery on Safari, illustrated by Joseph Cellini. New York, Morrow, 1970.
The Ghost of Ballyhooly. New York, Morrow, 1971.
Mystery in the Museum. New York, Morrow, 1972.
Petey, illustrated by Joe and Beth Krush. Philadelphia, Westminster, 1973.

Joyride. New York, Morrow, 1974.
Ruffles and Drums, illustrated by Richard Cuffari. New York, Morrow, 1975.
Mystery of the Emerald Buddha. New York, Morrow, 1976.
Runaway Voyage. New York, Morrow, 1978.
Stamp Twice for Murder. New York, Morrow, 1981.
The Surfer and the City Girl. Philadelphia, Westminster, 1981.
Storm in Her Heart. Philadelphia, Westminster, 1983.
Romance on Trial. Philadelphia, Westminster, 1984.
Wanted: A Girl for the Horses. New York, Morrow, 1984.
Banner Year. New York, Morrow, 1987.

Fiction as Elizabeth Headley

A Date for Diane, illustrated by Janet Smalley. Philadelphia, Macrae Smith, 1946.
Take a Call, Topsy!, illustrated by Janet Smalley. Philadelphia, Macrae Smith, 1947; revised as *Ballet Fever* (as Betty Cavanna), Philadelphia, Westminster, 1978.
She's My Girl! Philadelphia, Macrae Smith, 1949; as *You Can't Take Twenty Dogs on a Date* (as Betty Cavanna), Philadelphia, Westminster, 1977.
Catchpenny Street. Philadelphia, Macrae Smith, 1951; reprinted under name Betty Cavanna, Philadelphia, Westminster, 1975.
Diane's New Love. Philadelphia, Macrae Smith, 1955.
Tourjours Diane. Philadelphia, Macrae Smith, 1957.
The Diane Stories: All about America's Favorite Girl Next Door (contains *A Date for Diane, Diane's New Love,* and *Toujours Diane*). Philadelphia, Macrae Smith, 1964.

Fiction as Betsy Allen

The Clue in Blue. New York, Grosset, 1948.
Puzzle in Purple. New York, Grosset, 1948.
The Riddle in Red. New York, Grosset, 1948.
The Secret of Black Cat Gulch. New York, Grosset, 1948.
The Green Island Mystery. New York, Grosset, 1949.
The Ghost Wore White. New York, Grosset, 1950.
The Yellow Warning. New York, Grosset, 1951.
The Gray Menace. New York, Grosset, 1953.
The Brown Satchel Mystery. New York, Grosset, 1954.
Peril in Pink. New York, Grosset, 1955.
The Silver Secret. New York, Grosset, 1956.
The Mystery of the Ruby Queens. New York, Grosset, 1958.

Other

Compiler and Editor, *Pick of the Litter: Favorite Dog Stories.* Philadelphia, Westminster, 1952.
The First Book of Seashells, illustrated by Marguerite Scott. New York, Watts, 1955; London, Edmund Ward, 1965.
Arne of Norway, photographs by husband, George Russell Harrison. New York, Watts, and London, Chatto & Windus, 1960.
The First Book of Wildflowers, illustrated by Page Cary. New York, Watts, 1961.
Lucho of Peru, photographs by George Russell Harrison. New York, Watts, 1961; London, Chatto & Windus, 1962.
Paulo of Brazil, photographs by George Russell Harrison. New York, Watts, 1962; London, Chatto & Windus, 1963.

Pepe of Argentina, photographs by George Russell Harrison. New York, Watts, 1962; London, Chatto & Windus, 1963.

Lo Chau of Hong Kong, photographs by George Russell Harrison. New York, Watts, and London, Chatto & Windus, 1963.

Chico of Guatemala, photographs by George Russell Harrison. New York, Watts, and London, Chatto & Windus, 1963.

Carlos of Mexico, photographs by George Russell Harrison. New York, Watts, and London, Chatto & Windus, 1964.

Noko of Japan, photographs by George Russell Harrison. New York, Watts, 1964.

Doug of Australia, photographs by George Russell Harrison. New York, Watts, and London, Chatto & Windus, 1965.

Tavi of the South Seas, photographs by George Russell Harrison. New York, Watts, 1965; London, Chatto & Windus, 1967.

Ali of Egypt, photographs by George Russell Harrison. New York, Watts, and London, Chatto & Windus, 1966.

Demetrios of Greece, photographs by George Russell Harrison. New York, Watts, 1966, and London, Chatto & Windus.

The First Book of Wool, photographs by George Russell Harrison. New York, Watts, 1966; as *Wool,* London, Watts, 1972.

The First Book of Fiji, photographs by George Russell Harrison. New York, Watts, 1968; as *Fiji,* London, Watts, 1972.

Morocco, photographs by George Russell Harrison. New York, Watts, 1970; London, Watts, 1972.

*

Manuscript Collections: de Grummond Collection, University of Southern Mississippi, Hattiesburg.

Biography: Essay in *Something about the Author Autobiography Series,* Vol. 4, Detroit, Gale, 1987; entry in *More Junior Authors,* Bronx, New York, H.W. Wilson, 1963.

Critical Studies: Entry in *Contemporary Literary Criticism,* Vol. 12, Detroit, Gale, 1980.

*   *   *

Betty Cavanna, also known as Betsy Allen and Elizabeth Headley, is a prolific writer of books for children and young adults, having written more than seventy books. Though she began writing more than fifty years ago, many of her books are still among the favorites of today's young people—fond remembrances they share with their parents. An early love of reading was fostered when others read to her as a young child with infantile paralysis. Though she was captivated by fairy tales, she yearned for stories about ''real'' people. A journalism major in college, she honed her writing skills while aspiring to her ambition of working on a newspaper and writing children's books. She was able to achieve the first goal by being hired by the *Bayonne Times* within months of her graduation. She began writing short stories soon after that and within a few years, she had most ably achieved her second goal, becoming a popular author of books for children and young adults.

Recalling her childhood penchant for characters to whom she could relate, her books always seem to be about ''real'' people.

Cavanna uses much from her youthful memories in the detailed portrayals of both the characters and locales of her novels. Her book *Catchpenny Street* is set in Camden, New Jersey, the place of her birth and her earliest recollections. Another popular book, *Boy Next Door,* took its background from Haddonfield, a suburban town which was to serve as the Cavannas' home for the remainder of Betty's youth. Other books featured locales in New Jersey, Pennsylvania, Cape Cod, and Martha's Vineyard, where the author resided in later years. One of her historical novels, *Ruffles and Drums,* takes place in Concord, Massachusetts, where she lived in close proximity to the bridge and the battlefield which initiated the events in her book.

The circumstances of Cavanna's illness and its impact upon the experiences of her youth is generalized into the feeling of ''not belonging'' so common to many teenagers. As a young girl, she always wanted to conform and be a part of the crowd. As in the case of many of her characters, including Julie in *Going On Sixteen,* success in this task was not always achieved. A childhood acquaintance fostered an interest in horses and riding which later became the basis for the plots of *Banner Year, Wanted: A Girl for the Horses, Spring Comes Riding,* and *Spurs for Suzanna.* Many books highlight the author's love of the many dogs in her life, including *Going On Sixteen, Puppy Stakes, She's My Girl* (later revised as *You Can't Take Twenty Dogs on a Date*), *The Black Spaniel Mystery,* and *Pick of the Litter.* Keeping her characters close to her own knowledge and experience, Cavanna learned to fly in order to write *A Girl Can Dream.* She also tried skiing to write *Angel on Skis* and attempted sailing to add to the reality of *The Scarlet Sail.* Many of her books touch on other aspects and experiences of growing up such as loneliness, shyness, jealousy, mother-daughter rivalry and social maladjustment. Some books sensitively handle such tough topics as alcoholism, divorce, race, and prejudice.

Under the name of Betsy Allen, Cavanna wrote a series of mysteries, including *The Clue in Blue, The Riddle in Red, The Secret of Black Cat Gulch, The Green Island Mystery,* and *The Ghost Wore White.* Using the pseudonym Elizabeth Headley, the ''Diane'' stories were penned as well as several other titles. Cavanna employed her husband as photographer to author the ''Around the World Today'' series. These stories are about young people in several countries and include such titles as *Arne of Norway, Pepe of Argentina, Carlos of Mexico, Ali of Egypt,* and *Demetrios of Greece.* In later years, Cavanna's background research during her extensive travels empowered her to write novels of ''pure escape fiction in authentic settings'' such as *A Time for Tenderness* based in Brazil; *Jenny Kimura,* an acclaimed book about a Japanese-American girl; *Mystery at Love's Creek* in Australia; *Spice Island Mystery,* which takes place in Grenada; *Mystery on Safari,* based in East Africa; *The Ghost of Ballyhooly,* an Irish story; and *Mystery of the Emerald Buddha,* set in Bangkok, Thailand.

Cavanna's thirst for knowledge led her to write several nonfiction titles: *First Book of Seashells, First Book of Wildflowers, First Book of Wool, First Book of Fiji,* and *First Book of Morocco.* She has also contributed stories to several teenage magazines.

The author believes the longevity of her books is based on the universality and timelessness of the emotions she depicts in the lives of her characters. The popularity of her stories is evidenced by the sale of nearly a million copies of *Going on Sixteen* alone. Her books have been translated into twelve languages and have been incorporated into several school curriculums. She offers girls the chance to "slip away from the accelerated pace of school work, as I did once-upon-a-time, and read a book just for fun." Ms. Cavanna has amply succeeded in this endeavor. We all enjoy escaping into her adventures and look forward to passing this pleasure on to our daughters.

—Laurie Schwartz Guttenberg

CHAMBERS, Aidan

Pseudonyms: Malcolm Blacklin. **Nationality:** British. **Born:** Chester-le-Street, County Durham, 27 December 1934. **Education:** Queen Elizabeth I Grammar School, Darlington, County Durham, 1948-53; Borough Road College, London, 1955-57. **Military Service:** Served in the Royal Navy, 1953-55. **Family:** Married Nancy Harris Lockwood in 1968. **Career:** Teacher of English and drama in English schools, 1957-68. Since 1969 proprietor and publisher, Thimble Press, and publisher, *Signal: Approaches to Children's Books,* and *Young Drama: The Magazine about Child and Youth Drama,* South Woodchester, Gloucestershire; tutor, Further Professional Studies Department, University of Bristol, 1970-82. Columnist ("Young Reading"), *Times Educational Supplement,* London, 1970-72; columnist ("Letter from England"), *Horn Book,* Boston, 1972-84; writer and presenter, with Nancy Chambers, *Bookbox* programme, Radio Bristol, 1973-75; writer and presenter, *Children and Books* programme, BBC Radio, 1976; *Ghosts,* Thames-TV, 1980; and *Long, Short, and Tall Stories,* BBC-TV, 1981. General editor, Topliners, Club 75, and Rockets series, 1967-81, and 1977-1990, M Books series, Macmillan, London; since 1982 visiting lecturer for Westminster College, Oxford; cofounder and since 1989 editorial publisher of Turton & Chambers. **Awards:** Children's Literature Association award, 1978, for article "The Reader in the Book"; Eleanor Farjeon award, 1982; Silver Pencil award (Netherlands), 1985, 1986. **Address:** Lockwood, Station Rd., South Woodchester, Stroud, Gloucestershire GL5 5EQ, England.

PUBLICATIONS FOR YOUNG ADULTS

Fiction

Ghost Carnival: Stories of Ghosts in Their Haunts, illustrated by Peter Wingham. London, Heinemann, 1977.

Novels

Breaktime. London, Bodley Head, 1978; New York, Harper, 1979.
Seal Secret. London, Bodley Head, 1980; New York, Harper, 1981.
Dance on My Grave: A Life and Death in Four Parts. London, Bodley Head, 1982; New York, Harper, 1983, 1995.

The Present Takers. London, Bodley Head, 1983; New York, Harper, 1984.
Now I Know. London, Harper, 1987; as *NIK: Now I Know,* New York, Harper, 1988.
The Toll Bridge. London, Bodley Head, 1992; New York, Harper, 1994.

Plays

Johnny Salter (produced Stroud, Gloucestershire, 1965). London, Heinemann, 1966.
The Car (produced Stroud, Gloucestershire, 1966). London, Heinemann, 1967.
The Chicken Run (produced Stroud, Gloucestershire, 1967). London, Heinemann, 1968.
Ghosts (television play). 1980.
Long, Short and Tall Stories (television play). 1980-81.
The Dream Cage: A Comic Drama in Nine Dreams (produced Stroud, Gloucestershire, 1981). London, Heinemann, 1982.
Only Once (produced Cheltenham festival, 1997).

Other

Haunted Houses, illustrated by John Cameron Jarvies. London, Pan, 1971.
More Haunted Houses, illustrated by Chris Bradbury. London, Pan, 1973.
Great British Ghosts, illustrated by Barry Wilkinson. London, Pan, 1974.
Great Ghosts of the World, illustrated by Peter Edwards. London, Pan, 1974.
Book of Flyers and Flying, illustrated by Trevor Stubley. London, Kestrel, 1976.
Book of Cops and Robbers, illustrated by Allan Manham. London, Kestrel, 1977.

Editor, with Nancy Chambers, *Ghosts.* London, Macmillan, 1969.
Editor, *I Want to Get Out: Stories and Poems By Young Writers.* London, Macmillan, 1971.
Editor, with Nancy Chambers, *Hi-Ran-Ho: A Picture Book of Verse,* illustrated by Barbara Swiderska. London, Longman, 1971.
Editor, with Nancy Chambers, *World Minus Zero: An SF Anthology.* London, Macmillan, 1971.
Editor, with Nancy Chambers, *In Time to Come: An SF Anthology.* London, Macmillan, 1973.
Editor, *The Tenth [and Eleventh] Ghost Book.* London, Barrie and Jenkins, 2 vols., 1975-76; published together as *The Bumper Book of Ghost Stories,* London, Pan, 1976.
Editor, *Fighters in the Sky.* London, Macmillan, 1976.
Editor, *Funny Folk: A Body of Comic Tales,* illustrated by Trevor Stubley. London, Heinemann, 1976.
Editor, *Men at War.* London, Macmillan, 1977.
Editor, *Escapers.* London, Macmillan, 1978.
Editor, *War at Sea.* London, Macmillan, 1978.
Editor (as Malcolm Blacklin), *Ghosts 4.* London, Macmillan, 1978.
Editor, *Animal Fair,* illustrated by Anthony Colbert. London, Heinemann, 1979.
Editor, *Aidan Chambers' Book of Ghosts and Hauntings,* illustrated by Antony Maitland. London, Kestrel, 1980.

Editor, *Ghosts That Haunt You,* illustrated by Gareth Floyd. London, Kestrel, 1980.

Editor, *Loving You, Loving Me.* London, Kestrel, 1980.

Editor, *Ghost after Ghost,* illustrated by Bert Kitchen. London, Kestrel, 1982.

Editor, *Out of Time: Stories of the Future.* London, Bodley Head, 1984; New York, Harper, 1985.

Editor, *A Sporting Chance: Stories of Winning and Losing.* London, Bodley Head, 1985.

Editor, *Shades of Dark: Ghost Stories.* London, Hardy, 1984; New York, Harper, 1986.

Editor, *A Haunt of Ghosts.* New York, Harper, 1987.

Editor, *A Quiver of Ghosts.* London, Bodley Head, 1987.

Editor, *Love All.* London, Bodley Head, 1988.

Editor, *On the Edge.* London, Macmillan, 1990.

PUBLICATIONS FOR CHILDREN

Fiction

Cycle Smash. London, Heinemann, 1968.

Marle. London, Heinemann, 1968.

Don't Forget Charlie and the Vase, illustrated by Clyde Pearson. London, Macmillan, 1971.

Mac and Lugs, illustrated by Barbara Swiderska. London, Macmillan, 1971.

Ghosts 2 (short stories). London, Macmillan, 1972.

Snake River, illustrated by Peter Morgan. Stockholm, Almqvist och Wiksell, 1975; London, Macmillan, 1977.

Fox Tricks (short stories), illustrated by Robin and Jocelyn Wild. London, Heinemann, 1980.

PUBLICATIONS FOR ADULTS

Play

Everyman's Everybody (produced London, 1957).

Other

The Reluctant Reader. Oxford, Pergamon Press, 1969.

Introducing Books to Children. London, Heinemann, 1973; revised edition, Boston, Horn Book, 1983; London, Heinemann, 1984.

Axes for Frozen Seas (lecture). Huddersfield, Yorkshire, Woodfield and Stanley, 1981.

Editor, *Plays for Young People to Read and Perform.* Stroud, Gloucestershire, Thimble Press, 1982.

Editor, with Jill Bennett, *Poetry for Children: A Signal Bookguide.* Stroud, Gloucestershire, Thimble Press, 1984.

Editor, *Booktalk: Occasional Writing on Literature and Children.* London, Bodley Head, and New York, Harper, 1985.

The Reading Environment. Stroud, Gloucestershire, Thimble Press, 1990.

Tell Me: Children, Reading and Talk. Stroud, Gloucestershire, Thimble Press, 1993.

*

Biography: Essay in *Something about the Author Autobiography Series,* Volume 12, Detroit, Gale, 1991; essay in *Speaking for Ourselves, Too* compiled and edited by Donald R. Gallo, National Council of Teachers of English, 1993.

Critical Studies: Entry in *Contemporary Literary Criticism,* Volume 35, Detroit, Gale, 1985.

*   *   *

Aidan Chambers significantly combines the roles of critic and theorist with those of writer and anthologist for young adults. He has followed his early studies (*The Reluctant Reader* and *Introducing Books to Children*) with numerous papers and lectures, reflecting on the nature and values of adolescent fiction from the reader's, the writer's, and the teacher's standpoint. Although he may not be one of the top sellers, he is certainly one of the most challenging and influential authors for young people. His work implicitly denies any firm distinction between adult and juvenile fiction. He is prepared to write frankly about anything that his adolescent characters might experience, including Ditto's sexual encounter with Helen, Hal's homosexuality, or Nik's religious skepticism, and this openness has not been welcomed by all reviewers. Chambers has always emphasized the significance of stories as a way of discovering meaning, of changing lives. His awareness of Iser and other reader-response theorists has helped to shape what he knew instinctively from the act of composing: that readers must construct the meaning of stories for themselves, that authors do not always know what is to be found in the stories they have written. The technique of his novels suggests the influence of major experimental novelists, particularly B. S. Johnson, whose book *The Unfortunates* has been glowingly praised by Chambers, though *Albert Angelo* would also seem to have been a model.

After a number of books for younger readers, Chambers produced *Breaktime,* his first important novel for young adults. The story is itself about storytelling, about ways of telling. It centers on Ditto, a sixth-former who is challenged by the claims of Morgan, a contemporary and a rationalist, that fiction is simply a form of lying, a game rather than life. In one sense the book is Ditto's response: the story of his holiday break, camping, disturbing a political meeting, being involved in a burglary, losing his virginity. Like Morgan at the end, readers have to make their own sense of the narrative, to decide how much of it is true. The story is told in a mixture of external narrator and internal stream-of-consciousness styles, including a montage of headlines, typescript and handwriting, play text, cartoons, lists, and quotations. The effect is rather like Joyce or Vonnegut for adolescents. Chambers presents the literal and metaphorical climax with Helen in three-part counterpoint: the events, Ditto's thoughts, and—in a separate column—sections from a textbook describing the act of intercourse. Such framing devices and the way in which Ditto's story also incorporates the stories of others means that the reader feels simultaneously involved in and detached from the events described.

Published four years later, *Dance on My Grave* is also narrated in a cinematic montage of different documents, presenting Hal's account of his life as given to a social worker but involving the reader in evaluating the validity of what is being told. Hal capsizes a dinghy on the Thames and is rescued by the rather older Barry Gorman. The two are brought together as friends and lovers, but after Barry has casually slept with a Norwegian au pair girl, Hal is filled with anger and jealousy. After their quarrel, Barry goes off on his motorbike and is killed. Hal finally keeps the promise that they made each other, that the survivor would dance on the other's grave, and this bizarre episode was apparently drawn from an actual incident.

Now I Know, again told in a complex mixture of modes and parallel texts, is thematically even more demanding in its exploration of religious belief and other modes of knowing. A history teacher persuades Nik, a bright, inquisitive but uncommitted young man of seventeen, to undertake research for an amateur film about the Second Coming. He falls in love with a Christian feminist called Julie, but on the morning after her rejection of his sexual advances she is injured by a terrorist bomb and loses her sight. His ensuing attempts at induced mystical experiences end in organizing his own crucifixion in a scrap-yard. The text is assembled out of passages of third-person narration, extracts from Nik's notes, poems and doodles, tapes made by Julie from her hospital bed, and the report of an ambitious young policeman investigating the events. It is heavily intertextual, with quotations or echoes from the Bible, Joyce, Jung, Simone Weil, and others.

The repeated theme of these books is the painful passage from adolescence through greater understanding to maturity. Like Hal, Nik ends changed though not converted. The more recent novel *The Toll Bridge* similarly describes a young man's escape from the conformist pressures of parents, school, and girlfriend to become toll-keeper on a bridge far from home. There is a violent triangular relationship between three young people with names they give one another: Jan, Tess, and Adam. The form is again highly sophisticated and open to different ways of reading. It is impossible for bald outlines of plot to convey either the subtlety of the narration or the conviction with which adolescent dilemmas are presented. There is an element of truth in the criticisms advanced by some who find Chambers's themes unsuitable, the style self-conscious, the plots contrived, or the minor characters two-dimensional. Nevertheless, the originality and driving power of the novels are undeniable. Even the simpler stories for young people, like *Seal Secret* and *The Present Takers,* can be read at deeper and more metaphorical levels; beneath the exciting surface narrative run other stories about moral choice, motivation, and self-understanding. Everything that Chambers has written can be seen as demonstrating the power of language and of active reading where "the reader plays the text."

—Robert Protherough

"Man of letters" is a not a fashionable term, but if anyone deserves the distinction it is Aidan Chambers: playwright, novelist, publisher, and theorist. His work crosses national, linguistic, age and gender boundaries. He speaks to readers who believe that literature transforms, negotiates between "word stuff" and "world stuff" (to use Valentine Cunningham's terms).

Of the six novels Chambers projects for his "Dance Sequence"—each exploring a different kind of love and narrative shape—four are now complete. The most recent, *The Toll Bridge,* is a fugue, an intertwined dance of four characters, none of whom are as they seem. The book also contains what one reviewer/librarian describes as "the most erotic scene in children's literature." Although the scene is graphically on the page, the erotic

charge is in the voyeurism. The lovers, Adam and Tess, are unconscious of being watched through a window by the Tess's father. He, in turn, is silently watched by Jan (short for the two-faced Roman god Janus), the narrative focalizer. Both watchers are emblematic readers, trying to make sense of the scene they see being written before them.

As an author who cares about telling, hearing, and interpreting, Chambers has recently returned to his first love: drama. *Only Once,* a new play performed at the 1997 Cheltenham festival, is about the moral crises of eight adolescents in a group home. Chambers provides the words necessary for negotiating their world—a skill he also brings to his work as theorist and publisher.

In two recent theoretical books, *The Reading Environment* and *Tell Me: Children, Reading and Talk,* Chambers outlines his "tell me" strategy, a form of reader-response criticism that facilitates the development of literate readers. And through the publishing house of Turton and Chambers, anglophone audiences have access to the narrative brilliance of such international stars as Dutch author Ted van Lieshout and Swedish writer Peter Pohl.

—Lissa Paul

CHERRYH, C.J

Nationality: American. **Born:** Carolyn Janice Cherry in St. Louis, Missouri, 1 September 1942. **Education:** the University of Oklahoma, Norman, 1960-64, B.A. in Latin 1964 (Phi Beta Kappa); John Hopkins University, Baltimore (Woodrow Wilson Fellow, 1965-66), M.A. in classics 1965. **Career:** Taught Latin and ancient history in Oklahoma City public schools, 1965-76; freelance writer, since 1977. Artist-in-residence and teacher, Central State University, 1980-81. **Awards:** Woodrow Wilson fellow, 1965-66; John W. Campbell award, 1977, for Best New Writer in Science Fiction; Hugo award, World Science Fiction Convention, 1978, for short story "Cassandra," 1982, for novel *Downbelow Station,* and in 1988; Balrog award, for short story "A Thief in Korianth." **Address:** c/o Daw Books, 375 Hudson Street, 3rd Floor, New York, New York 10014-3658, U.S.A.

PUBLICATIONS

Science Fiction

The Book of Morgaine. New York, Doubleday, 1979; as *The Chronicles of Morgaine,* London, Methuen, 1985.
Gate of Ivrel. New York, DAW, 1976; London, Futura, 1977.
Well of Shiuan. New York, DAW, 1978; London, Magnum, 1981.
Fires of Azeroth. New York, DAW, 1979; London, Methuen, 1982.
Brothers of Earth. New York, DAW, 1976; London, Futura, 1977.
Hunter of Worlds. New York, DAW, 1976; London, Futura, 1977.
The Faded Sun: Kesrith. New York, DAW, 1978.
The Faded Sun: Shon'Jir. New York, DAW, 1979.
Hestia. New York, DAW, 1979; London, VGSF, 1988.
The Faded Sun: Kutath. New York, DAW, 1980.

Serpent's Reach. New York, DAW, 1980; London, Macdonald, 1981.

Downbelow Station. New York, DAW, 1981; London, Methuen, 1983.

Wave without a Shore. New York, DAW, 1981; London, VGSF, 1988.

Merchanter's Luck. New York, DAW, 1982; London, Methuen, 1984.

Port Eternity. New York, DAW, 1982; London, Gollancz, 1989.

The Pride of Chanur. New York, DAW, 1982; London, Methuen, 1983.

The Dreamstone. New York, DAW, 1983; London, VGSF, 1987.

40000 in Gehenna. Huntington Woods, Michigan, Phantasia Press, 1983; London, Methuen, 1986.

The Tree of Swords and Jewels. New York, DAW, 1983; London, VGSF, 1988.

Chanur's Venture. Huntington Woods, Michigan, Phantasia Press, 1984; London, Methuen, 1986.

Voyager in Night. New York, DAW, 1984; London, Methuen, 1985.

Angel with the Sword. New York, DAW, 1985; London, Methuen, 1987.

Cuckoo's Egg. Huntington Woods, Michigan, Phantasia Press, 1985; London, Methuen, 1987.

The Kif Strike Back (Chanur). Huntington Woods, Michigan, Phantasia Press, 1985; London, Methuen, 1987.

The Gates of Hell, with Janet Morris. New York, Baen, 1986.

Soul of the City, with Janet Morris and Lynn Abbey. New York, Ace, 1986.

Visible Light. West Bloomfield, Michigan, Phantasia Press, 1986; London, Methuen, 1988.

The Faded Sun Trilogy. London, Methuen, 1987.

Glass and Amber. Cambridge, Massachusetts, NESFA Press, 1987.

Kings in Hell, with Janet Morris. New York, Baen, 1987.

Legions of Hell. New York, Baen, 1987.

Chanur's Homecoming. New York, DAW, 1986; London, Methuen, 1988.

Cyteen. New York, Warner, 1988; London, New English Library, 1989.

The Betrayal. New York, Popular Library, 1989.

The Rebirth. New York, Popular Library, 1989.

The Vindication. New York, Popular Library, 1989.

Exile's Gate. New York, DAW, 1988; London, Methuen, 1989.

The Paladin. New York, Baen, 1988; London, Mandarin, 1990.

Smuggler's Gold. New York, DAW, 1988.

A Dirge for Sabis, with Leslie Fish. New York, Baen, 1989.

Ealdwood (includes *The Dreamstone* and *The Tree of Swords and Jewels*). London, Gollancz, 1989.

Reap the Whirlwind (Sword of Knowledge), with Mercedes Lackey. New York, Baen, 1989.

Rimrunners. New York, Warner, 1989; London, New English Library, 1990.

Rusalka. New York, Ballantine, 1989; London, Mandarin, 1990.

Wizard Spawn (Sword of Knowledge), with Nancy Asire. New York, Baen, 1989.

Chernevog. New York, Ballantine, 1990; London, Mandarin, 1991.

Heavy Time. New York, Warner, 1991; London, New English Library, 1991.

Yvgenie. New York, Ballantine, 1991.

Chanur's Legacy. New York, DAW, 1992.

The Goblin Mirror. New York, Ballantine, 1992.

Hellburner. New York, Warner, 1992.

Foreigner: A Novel of First Contact. New York, DAW, 1994.

Tripoint. New York, Warner Books, 1994.

Fortress in the Eye of Time. New York, HarperPrism, 1995.

Invader. New York, DAW, 1995.

Rider at the Gate. New York, Warner, 1995.

Cloud's Rider. New York, Warner, 1996.

Inheritor. New York, DAW, 1996.

Lois & Clark: A Superman Novel. Rocklin, California, Prima, 1996.

Fortress of Eagles. New York, HarperPrism, 1998.

Short Stories

Festival Moon. New York, DAW, 1987.

Troubled Waters. New York, DAW, 1988.

Other

Translator, *The Green Gods,* by Charles and Nathalie Henneberg. New York, DAW, 1980.

Translator, *Star Crusade,* by Pierre Barbet. New York, DAW, 1980.

Translator, *The Book of Shai,* by Daniel Walther. New York, DAW, 1984.

Contributor, *The Sword of Knowledge.* Riverdale, New York, Baen, 1995.

Editor, *Sunfall.* New York, DAW, 1981; London, Mandarin, 1990.

Editor, *Fever Season.* New York, DAW, 1987.

Editor, *Merovingen Nights.* New York, DAW, 1987.

Editor, *Divine Right.* New York, DAW, 1989.

Editor, *Flood Tide.* New York, DAW, 1990.

*   *   *

The talent that sets C.J. Cherryh apart from other authors is her ability to create, and make comprehensible, cultures and societies very different from our own—sometimes alien, sometimes human, always intriguing. It is a measure of her talent that she communicates these complex cultural structures within the context of fast-paced action/adventure stories. No ink is wasted on expository material; it often seems that the cultures were fully formed before her pen touched the paper.

Cherryh writes of universes, each with its own set of cultures and history. Most of her stories are set in the Alliance-Union universe, which includes the Chanur, Faded Sun, and Merovingen cultures. However, her body of work also includes multiple stories set in the Morgaine, the Ealdwood, and the Rusalka universes, plus a few single, unrelated stories.

Vivid characters populate Cherryh's universes, and it is the interactions of these characters that illuminate the cultures. This is not to say that the characters exist only to display the culture; generally, both the characters and the cultures exist to serve the story.

Young adults are most likely to be interested in Cherryh's portrayals of coming-of-age within the cultures she creates. While this is rarely the main theme—and is never the only theme— several of her stories focus on a young adult in the process of finding his or (more often) her place in the society Cherryh has created for the story.

Cyteen, set in the Alliance-Union universe, is one such book. It is the story of Ariane Emory, a powerful woman of the Union government, who dies unexpectedly. Her allies arrange to have her ''replicated''—not just genetically cloned, but mentally duplicated—by subjecting the clone Ari to the same experiences and events that shaped the original Ari. The axiom that children inherit the world their parents create finds its ultimate expression in Ari, who at sixteen must wield the power her predecessor amassed over a lifetime to fight inherited enemies and to complete inherited schemes.

In the "Faded Sun" trilogy, *Kesrith, Shon'Jir,* and *Kutath,* the coming of age of Melein and her brother Niun is precipitated by the near annihilation of their species. As the last two Mri in known space, Melein and Niun must find their place in a society which no longer exists anywhere but within themselves and perhaps on the legendary Mri home world—if it exists, if it can be found, and if Mri still live on it.

One of Cherryh's most fascinating stories of coming-of-age occurs in the "Rusalka" trilogy, *Rusalka, Chernevog,* and *Yvgenie.* The trilogy begins with Pyetr and the wizard Sasha fleeing the results of their adolescent mischief and growing into an adult view of life in the haunted forests of ancient Russia. The trilogy ends with Pyetr's daughter Illyana struggling against the rules her parents impose on her—rules which have their roots in her parents' own harsh coming-of-age experiences, rules which the reader fully understands. Young adult readers will, no doubt, be amazed to find themselves siding with the parents in this contention.

Merchanter's Luck, Angel with the Sword, and *The Paladin* are also primarily young adult stories. The family-crewed spaceships of the Alliance-Union universe are the setting for *Merchanter's Luck.* Young Sandy Kreja has to crew his small ship alone when pirates kill his family. Young Allison Reilly despairs of ever getting posted as crew on her family's huge multigenerational ship. A perfect match, if Sandy can overcome his distrust and Allison can overcome her big-ship arrogance. In *Angel with the Sword,* Altair Jones finds that caring for others is worthwhile, even in Merovingen, a harsh and unforgiving city designed to make fish bait out of unwary young orphans. In *The Paladin,* young Taizu is savagely catapulted out of childhood by the murder of her family and finds both the hazards and rewards of adulthood in her single-minded determination for revenge.

In all of these books, the characters' growth is the main story, and any other themes serve to support it. Usually, however, coming-of-age is too limited a theme for Cherryh's cultural creations. Young adults' stories are more often embedded within much larger stories. For example, in the "Chanur" series, young Hilfy Chanur is on her first voyage with her legendary Aunt Pyanfar to learn the family business, interstellar trade. In the adventures that follow, Hilfy learns what it takes to justify the swagger she affects as a daughter of the wealthy and powerful Chanur clan.

But the "Chanur" series is much more than Hilfy's story: it is Cherryh's tour de force of alien sociology. Pyanfar and her crew are Hani—a feline species very much like lions. (A male is only expected to fight for territory and stay out of the way while his sisters and daughters earn wealth and prestige for the clan.) In the course of the series, the Hani deal with eight different species, each with its own culture, and Chanur's fate rests on Pyanfar's understanding of those cultures.

Cherryh's talents for vivid characterization, insightful explorations of human nature and relationships, and absorbing storytelling are shared by many writers in many genres, but her ability to create and communicate comprehensible cultures stands, if not alone, then certainly in rare company. It is this ability that may ultimately

hold the greatest attraction for young adult readers. In comprehending that there is an underlying structure and coherence to even the most bizarre Cherryh culture, young adults may see that their own culture also has some kind of underlying structure; that their world is not just a jumble of unreasonable rules; that although the structure isn't as clear as Cherryh would make it, in some way, the world makes sense.

—Karen J. Gould

CHETWIN, Grace

Nationality: British. **Born:** Nottingham; immigrated to the United States in 1964. **Education:** University of Southampton, Highfield, B.A. (with honors) in philosophy. **Family:** Married Arthur G. Roberts; two daughters. **Career:** High school English and French teacher, Auckland, New Zealand, 1958-62; high school English teacher and department head, Devon, England, 1962-63; director, Group '72-'76 (drama group), Auckland, 1972-76; ran her own dance company in New Zealand for four years; produced operas at the amateur level; author of fantasy books since 1983. **Agent:** Jean V. Naggar, Jean V. Naggar Literary Agency, 216 East 75rd St., New York, New York 10021. **Address:** 37 Hitching Post Lane, Glen Cove, New York 11542, U.S.A.

PUBLICATIONS FOR YOUNG ADULTS

Fiction

On All Hallows' Eve. New York, Lothrop, 1984.
Out of the Dark World. New York, Lothrop, 1985.
Gom on Windy Mountain. New York, Lothrop, 1986.
The Riddle and the Rune. New York, Lothrop, 1987.
The Crystal Stair. New York, Bradbury, 1988.
The Starstone. New York, Bradbury, 1989.
Collidescope. New York, Bradbury, 1990.
Child of the Air. New York, Bradbury, 1991.
Friends in Time. New York, Bradbury, 1992.
The Chimes of Alyafaleyn. New York, Bradbury, 1993.
Jason's Seven Magnificent Night Rides. New York, Bradbury, 1994.

PUBLICATIONS FOR CHILDREN

Fiction

Mr. Meredith and the Truly Remarkable Stone, illustrated by Catherine Stock. New York, Bradbury, 1989.
Box and Cox, illustrated by David Small. New York, Bradbury Press, 1990.

PUBLICATIONS FOR ADULTS

Fiction

The Atheling. New York, Bluejay, 1987.

*   *   *

In the ten years since Grace Chetwin started writing for children and young adults, she has produced two picture books and ten books for older readers. Her young adult books all fall into the categories of either fantasy or science fiction. A competent writer with many enthusiasms, Chetwin has yet to hit a smooth stride in her writing style. She has a tendency to start writing a novel before she has completely assimilated her research and, as a result, the research calls undue attention to itself. Chetwin is at her best when she writes fantasies that are influenced by European folktales, such as the four books in her series about the wizard Gom.

The ''Gom'' books, which are all subtitled *From Tales of Gom in the Legends of Ulm,* are *Gom on Windy Mountain, The Riddle and the Rune, The Crystal Stair,* and *The Starstone. Gom on Windy Mountain* recounts Gom's boyhood as a woodcutter's youngest child. This first volume of the series owes much to nineteenth-century folktales and literary fairy tales, particularly to the German tales collected by the Grimms and the fairy tales of George MacDonald. As in a German fairy tale, the story contains a forest, a cottage, and a woodcutter, as well as a youngest son who must set out to seek his fortune. From MacDonald, Chetwin borrows labyrinthine caves and personified winds. Chetwin skillfully weaves these sources into an irresistible original fairy tale. The sequels maintain the atmosphere of ''long ago and far away'' as Gom seeks his destiny beyond the tiny village of his childhood. Unlike Chetwin's contemporary science fiction, these fantasies are based on a wide knowledge of traditional literature rather than on one or two areas of research grafted onto a story. The ''Gom'' tetralogy represents Chetwin's best work to date and has been well received by reviewers and critics.

Child of the Air is an ambitious fantasy novel set in a completely original secondary world with overtones of Dickens and Greek mythology. An orphaned brother and sister forced to live in a workhouse discover that they can fly, so they escape to seek others like themselves. Chetwin has created an intriguing geography for her world. The book suffers however, from an excess of invented words. Although there is a pronunciation guide at the end of the book and Chetwin attempts to define the words in context, there are simply too many neologisms for the reader to keep track of their meanings.

Two earlier books contain recurring characters. *On All Hallows' Eve* is a fantasy set in contemporary America. A preadolescent girl transplanted unwillingly from England stumbles into a menacing Otherworld on Halloween, and she must overcome a witch queen in order to rescue her sister and two local boys from the witch's evil power. The book is handicapped by an unlikable heroine who accepts her task grudgingly and ungraciously. In the sequel, *Out of the Dark World,* the heroine's temperament has improved a bit. Although she remains reluctant to take on heroic tasks, her reluctance is based on understandable fear and insecurity. *Out of the Dark World* adds science fiction to the fantasy of the earlier book. The heroine again must rescue someone from an evil power, but in this instance the victim is a male cousin who has been trapped inside a computer in the future. Chetwin's research into computers, New Age psychology, and Welsh mythology is a bit too obvious in the second book.

Another science fiction novel, *Collidescope,* contains touches of humor in the interaction between a pre-Colonial Native American and a twentieth-century teenager, brought together accidentally by an alien scout who works for an intergalactic environmental protection agency. The action is lively and fast-paced, especially in

the latter half of the book when the three main characters and one villain are chasing one another through time. In this book Chetwin's research into karate, robotics, and the history of Manhattan seems to be attached onto the story in large chunks instead of being a seamless part of the narrative. However, these awkward grafts do not diminish the story itself, and Chetwin proves adept at juggling three story lines at once.

There is a certain sameness about a number of Chetwin's books. Her heroines share a similar personality and learn the same lesson from their adventures. They are all whiney brats who have to overcome their self-absorption in order to rescue fellow beings from grave danger. Although real adolescents are sometimes unduly concerned with petty personal issues, characters who exhibit such a tendency quickly grow tiresome. Readers may weary of seeing an exciting fantasy adventure interrupted by a character's complaints about her mother. This is a further argument for the superiority of the ''Gom'' books. Gom, too, learns lessons in life, but he is a much more likeable character than Chetwin's female protagonists. He suffers from feelings of failure, overconfidence, shame, anger, guilt, and loneliness, but his concerns never seem petty.

—Donna R. White

CHILDRESS, Alice

Nationality: American. **Born:** Charleston, South Carolina, 12 October 1920. **Education:** schools in Harlem, New York; Radcliffe Institute for Independent Study (scholar), 1966-68, graduated 1968. **Family:** Married the musician Nathan Woodard in 1957; one daughter. **Career:** Playwright and novelist; actress and director, American Negro Theatre, New York, 1941-52; columnist (''Here's Mildred''), Baltimore *Afro-American,* 1956-58; artist-in-residence, University of Massachusetts, Amherst, 1984; also performed on radio and television. Lecturer at universities and schools; member of panel discussions and conferences on Black American theater at numerous institutions, including New School for Social Research, New York, 1965, and Fisk University, Nashville, Tennessee, 1966; visiting scholar at Radcliffe Institute for Independent Study (now Mary Ingraham Bunting Institute), Cambridge, Massachusetts, 1966-68. Member of governing board of France Delafield Hospital. **Awards:** Obie award for best original Off-Broadway play, *Village Voice,* 1956, for *Trouble in Mind;* John Golden Fund for Playwrights grant, 1957; Rockefeller grant, 1967; ''Outstanding Book of the Year'' citation, *New York Times Book Review,* 1973, Woodward School Book award, 1974, Jane Addams Children's Book Honor award, 1974, National Book award nomination, 1974, Lewis Carroll Shelf award, 1975, and ''Best Young Adult Book'' citation, American Library Association, 1975, all for *A Hero Ain't Nothin' but a Sandwich;* named honorary citizen of Atlanta, Georgia, 1975, for opening of *Wedding Band;* Sojourner Truth award, National Association of Negro Business and Professional Women's Clubs, 1975; Virgin Islands Film Festival award, 1977, for *A Hero Ain't Nothin' but a Sandwich;* Paul Robeson award, 1977, for *A Hero Ain't Nothin' but a Sandwich;* ''Alice Childress Week'' officially observed in Charleston and Columbia, South Carolina, 1977, to celebrate opening of *Sea Island Song;*

"Best Book" citation, *School Library Journal,* 1981, "Outstanding Books of the Year" citation, *New York Times,* 1982, "Notable Children's Trade Book in Social Studies" citation, National Council for the Social Studies and Children's Book Council, 1982, and Coretta Scott King Award honorable mention, 1982, all for *Rainbow Jordan.* Radcliffe Graduate Society medal, 1984; African Poets Theatre award, 1985; Audelco award, 1986; Harlem School of the Arts Humanitarian award, 1987. **Died:** 1994.

PUBLICATIONS FOR YOUNG ADULTS

Fiction

A Hero Ain't Nothin' but a Sandwich. New York, Coward McCann, 1973.
Rainbow Jordan. New York, Coward McCann, 1981.
Those Other People. New York, Putnam, 1989.

Plays

When the Rattlesnake Sounds, illustrated by Charles Lilly. New York, Coward McCann, 1975.
Let's Hear It for the Queen, illustrated by Loring Eutemey. New York, Coward McCann, 1976.

Screenplay: *A Hero Ain't Nothin' But a Sandwich,* 1977.

PUBLICATIONS FOR ADULTS

Novel

A Short Walk. New York, Coward McCann, 1979.

Plays

Florence (also director: produced New York, 1949). Published in *Masses and Mainstream* (New York), October 1950.
Just a Little Simple (adaptation of Langston Hughes's short story collection, *Simple Speaks His Mind*; produced in New York, 1950).
Gold through the Trees (produced New York, 1952).
Trouble in Mind (also director: produced New York, 1955). Published in *Black Theatre: A Twentieth-Century Collection of the Work of Its Best Playwrights,* edited by Lindsay Patterson, New York, Dodd Mead, 1971.
Wedding Band: A Love/Hate Story in Black and White (produced Ann Arbor, Michigan, 1966; televised, ABC-TV, 1973). New York, French, 1973.
String (adaptation of Maupassant's story "A Piece of String"; produced New York, 1969; televised, PBS-TV, 1979). With *Mojo,* New York, Dramatists Play Service, 1971.
Young Martin Luther King (produced on tour, 1969; originally entitled *The Freedom Drum*).
Wine in the Wilderness: A Comedy-Drama (televised 1969; produced New York, 1976). New York, Dramatists Play Service, 1970.
Mojo: A Black Love Story (produced New York, 1970). With *String,* New York, Dramatists Play Service, 1971.
Sea Island Song (produced Charleston, South Carolina, 1977).

Gullah (produced Amherst, Massachusetts, 1984).
Moms: A Praise Play for a Black Comedienne, music and lyrics by Childress and Nathan Woodard (produced New York, 1987).

Other

Like One of the Family: Conversations from a Domestic's Life. New York, Independence, 1956.
Many Closets. New York, Coward McCann, 1987.

Editor, *Black Scenes.* New York, Zenith, 1971.

*

Biography: Entry in *Dictionary of Literary Biography,* Vol. 7: *Twentieth-Century American Dramatists* by Rosemary Curb, Detroit, Gale, 1981; entry in *Dictionary of Literary Biography,* Vol. 38: *Afro-American Writers after 1955: Dramatists and Prose Writers* by Trudier Harris, Detroit, Gale, 1985; entry in *Fifth Book of Junior Authors and Illustrators* edited by Sally Holmes Holtze, Bronx, New York, Wilson, 1983.

Critical Studies: Entry in *Children's Literature Review,* Vol. 14, Detroit, Gale, 1988; entry in *Contemporary Literary Criticism,* Vol. 12, Detroit, Gale, 1980; Vol. 15, Detroit, Gale, 1980.

*   *   *

When the social agitation of the 1960s brought about the development of a new genre of hard-hitting problem novels aimed specifically at teenage readers, editor F.N. Monjo challenged dramatist Alice Childress to devote her writing skills to a book for young readers. The result was *A Hero Ain't Nothin' but a Sandwich,* which is such a powerful book that it helped shape the new genre as well as bring it respect.

The story circles around thirteen-year-old Benjie, a heroin addict, who may or may not make it out of the vicious cycle in which he finds himself. The twenty-three chapters consist of monologues from a dozen characters—Benjie, his mother, his stepfather, his teachers, his pusher, his grandmother, his friend. On the first page Benjie compares his life where "You best get over being seven or eight right soon" because "My block ain't no place to be a chile in peace," to that of a "rich chile like in some movin picture or like on TV—where everybody is livin it up and their room is perfect-lookin and their swimmin pool and their block and their house. . ." Benjie's comparison aptly illustrates the differences between the new realistic problem novel and the old romanticized fiction commonly offered to young readers. In the new books it was acceptable to have characters from lower-class families who lived in harsh and difficult settings rather than in idyllic and pleasant suburbia. These characters faced major problems and used colloquial and sometimes vulgar language. Many of the books had unhappy endings.

Some adults were shocked at this new realism, and *A Hero Ain't Nothin' but a Sandwich* was widely censored, eventually coming before the Supreme Court in a case against eight other books as well. But as movies, television, rock music, videos, magazines, and even the daily news made commonplace much that used to be considered obscene or at least inappropriate for young readers, critics began paying less attention to the controversial language in Childress's writing and more to its substance.

Childress uses the same dramatic technique of switching first-person viewpoints from chapter to chapter in *Rainbow Jordan* and *Those Other People*. The technique lets readers get into the minds of characters in ways that are more credible than if an omniscient narrator were describing the events. Since there's no narrator to tie together all the pieces, readers have to draw their own conclusions—a responsibility that censors fear teenage readers may not be prepared for.

Childress's greatest strength is in developing characters that make readers see such social issues as racism, sexism, drugs, and child abuse in personal terms. Few readers will forget the heroic Butler Craig, Benjie's unconventional stepfather, or fourteen-year-old Rainbow Jordan and fifty-seven-year-old Josephine who suffer together when Rainbow's childlike mother leaves for an out-of-town gig.

Childress has also written two one-act plays. *Let's Hear It for the Queen* is a humorous play for children that parodies the "Queen of Hearts" nursery rhyme. *When the Rattlesnake Sounds,* written for young adults, has a more serious intent. It takes viewers and performers beyond the stereotype of Harriet Tubman leading slaves through wilderness swamps to freedom. The setting is a hotel in Cape May, New Jersey, where Tubman is scrubbing, with two other young women, the hotel's linens and the guests' clothing to earn money for the support of the underground railway.

—Alleen Pace Nilsen

CHOYCE, Lesley

Nationality: Canadian. **Born:** Lesley Willis Choyce in Riverside, New Jersey, 21 March 1951. **Education:** Cinnaminson High School, Cinnaminson, New Jersey, 1965-69; East Carolina University, 1969-70; Rutgers University, 1970-72, B.A. 1972; Montclair State College, 1972-74, M.A. 1973; City University of New York, 1980-83, M.A. 1983. **Family:** Married Terry Paul, August 1974; two daughters. **Career:** Janitor, Cinnaminson Manor Nursing Home, 1968-72; instructor, Montclair State University, Bloomfield College, Queens College, 1972-83, and Mt. St. Vincent University, Nova Scotia Art College, St. Mary's University, 1978-80; professor, Dalhousie University, since 1983. **Awards:** Finalist, Canadian Science Fiction and Fantasy Award, 1981; Dartmouth Book Award, 1990 and 1995, short-listed, 1991, 1992, 1993; Ann Connor-Brimer Award for Children's Literature, 1994, shortlisted, 1992 and 1993; finalist, Manitoba's Young Reader's Choice Award, 1994; Authors Award, Foundation for the Advancement of Canadian Letters, 1995; First place, Canadian Surfing Championships, 1995. **Address:** 83 Leslie Road, E. Lawrencetown, Nova Scotia BZ2 1P8, Canada.

PUBLICATIONS FOR YOUNG ADULTS

Skateboard Shakedown. Halifax, Formac, 1989.
The Hungry Lizards. Toronto, Maxwell Macmillan, 1990.
Skatefreaks og Graesrodder. Copenhagen, Thorup, 1990.
Wave Watch. Halifax, Formac, 1990.

Wrong Time, Wrong Place. Halifax, Formac, 1991.
Some Kind of Hero. Toronto, Maxwell Macmillan, 1991.
Margin of Error: A Young Adult Short Story Collection. Ottawa, Borealis, 1992.
Clearcut Danger. Halifax, Formac, 1993.
Good Idea Gone Bad. Halifax, Formac, 1993.
Full Tilt. Toronto, Maxwell Macmillan, 1993.
Dark End of Dream Street. Halifax, Formac, 1994.
Big Burn. Saskatoon, Thistledown, 1995.
Falling Through the Cracks. Halifax, Formac, 1996.
The Trap Door to Heaven. Kingston, Quarry, 1996.

PUBLICATIONS FOR CHILDREN

Go for it, Carrie. Halifax, Formac, 1997.
Famous at Last. East Lawrencetown, Pottersfield, 1998.

PUBLICATIONS FOR ADULTS

Fiction

Eastern Shore. Halifax, Nimbus, 1981.
Billy Botzweiler's Last Dance. Toronto, Nightwood, 1984.
Downwind. St. Johns, Creative, 1984.
Conventional Emotions. St. Johns, Creative, 1985.
The Dream Auditor. Charlottetown, Ragweed Press, 1986.
Coming Up for Air. St. Johns, Creative, 1988.
The Second Season of Jonas MacPherson. Saslatoon, Thistledown Press, 1989.
Magnificent Obsessions: A Photonovel. Kingston, Quarry, 1991.
The Ecstacy Conspiracy. Montreal, NuAge, 1992.
The Republic of Nothing. Fredericton, Goose Lane, 1994.
The Trapdoor to Heaven. Kingston, Quarry, 1996.

Poetry

Reinventing the Wheel. Fredericton, Fiddlehead, 1980.
Fast Living. Fredericton, Fiddlehead, 1985.
The End of Ice. Fredericton, Goose Lane, 1985.
The Top of the Heart. Saskatoon, Thistledown, 1986.
The Man Who Borrowed the Bay of Fundy. Brandon, Brandon University, 1988.
The Coastline of Forgetting. East Lawrencetown, Pottersfield, 1995.
Beautiful Sadness. Victoria, Ekstasis, 1998.

Nonfiction

Edible Wild Plants of the Maritimes. West Chezzetoock, Wooden Anchor Press, 1977.
An Avalanche of Ocean. Fredericton, Goose Lane, 1987.
December Six/The Halifax Solution. East Lawrencetown, Pottersfield Press, 1988.
Transcendental Anarchy. Kingston, Quarry, 1993.
Nova Scotia: Shaped by the Sea. Toronto, Penguin, 1996.

Other

Editor, *Alternating Currents: Renewable Energy for Atlantic Canada.* Halifax, Wooden Anchor, 1977.
Editor with Phil Thompson, *ACCESS.* Porters Lake, Nova Scotia, Potterfield, 1979.

Editor, *The Pottersfield Portfolio, Volumes 1-7*. Porters Lake, Nova Scotia, Pottersfield, 1979-85.

Ediotr with John Bell, *Visions from the Edge*. Porters Lake, Nova Scotia, Pottersfield, 1981.

Editor, *The Cape Breton Collection*. Porters Lake, Nova Scotia, Pottersfield, 1984, 1989.

Editor, *Ark of Ice: Canadian Futurefiction*. Porters Lake, Nova Scotia, Pottersfielld, 1992.

Editor with Rita Joe, *The Mi'kmaq Anthology*. East Lawrencetown, Pottersfiled, 1997.

*

Lesley Choyce comments:

A career? I avoided one. To busy myself, I write novels and autobiographical books, host a TV show, teach part time at a university, run a publishing company, surf, freelance TV and radio work, perform and record alternative music and raise spinach.

Where do my ideas come from? Everything and anything. What makes me happy, what makes me scared. Bang, an idea arrives in the middle of the night.

How do I work? I don't work, never have. Mostly I just have fun and make stuff up.

Were I to offer advice, I'd say, "Do it. Forget about money and live. Make up your own life as it goes along. Don't let television or anybody do it for you."

*   *   *

A prolific author who writes in a wide variety of genres for audiences ranging from beginning readers to adults, Lesley Choyce has written a dozen titles for adolescents. In a non-didactic fashion, his fast-paced YA stories, which usually utilize a Nova Scotia setting, link the central characters' personal conflicts with larger social issues.

Skateboard Shakedown finds two 15-year-olds literally taking on city hall. Skateboard enthusiasts Gary Sutherland and his girlfriend, Sheila, enjoy the thrill of skateboarding down and around the sides of an abandoned swimming pool. Learning that the pool site is to be sold to developers rather than being maintained for public use, the pair visit the mayor and contact the media. The response of the adult "business" world is more than they expect, but eventually the teens, with parental support, prevail and expose the corruption infesting local politics.

Wave Watch sees Choyce at his writing best when describing the surfing experiences of 16-year-old Randy, a klutz at school but an expert on the surfing waves of the Eastern Shore. The book falters somewhat between Randy's water-based summer adventures, as characterization is inconsistent and Choyce introduces plot lines which remain undeveloped. For example, rural Randy's resentment of the monied Halifax, Nova Scotia, "townies'" invasion of his "private" surfing locale off the Lawrencetown headland evaporates too easily, and an ecological theme related to the beach's future development by the province's parks department remains unresolved. However, when Randy is skimming along on his surf board, the action moves swiftly.

The historical and contemporary treatment of Nova Scotia's black population by whites is a central theme in *Wrong Time, Wrong Place*. With a white father and a black mother, Corey Wheeler finds himself caught between two worlds, and his situation is exacerbated by his light skin colour which would allow him to reject his black heritage and "pass." Corey makes his racial choice when classroom hijinks result in a white student calling a black classmate a "nigger" and Corey identifies with his black friends. Escalating racial tensions lead to Corey's involvement in an incident with the same white student, Big John Barker. The high school's principal, "Heartless" Hartman, unreceptive to Corey's explanation, suspends Corey for a week. Upon Corey's return, Barker picks a fight but accidentally receives a concussion. Corey, assuming he will be blamed, hides from police. Ultimately, with family help, Corey's immediate problems are resolved positively although the school system must still take corrective race relations measures.

In *Clearcut Danger*, when a pulp and paper mill is proposed for East Harbour, a small town with a depressed economy, it initially seems like a good idea to high schooler Ryan Cooper, for it could mean jobs for himself and his father. However, Ryan's girlfriend, Alana, opposes the mill on environmental grounds and because it will be built on land sacred land to her people, the Micmacs. Reconsidering his initial position because of Alana's arguments and the contents of an official environmental study, Ryan joins Alana in campaigning against the mill, and the pair find themselves in the midst of a fight which threatens to divide their community.

A major societal concern—teen violence—is the focus of *Good Idea Gone Bad*. Mick, a Halifax, Nova Scotia, high school student, joins three skinhead-type friends in a senseless beating of a young man they believe to be gay. Dariana, the girl of Mick's dreams, characterizes Mick as a bigoted, racist, sexist pig. In a shallow attempt to get closer to Dariana, Mick becomes the drummer for Dariana's three person band, "Good Idea Gone Bad," in which Dariana is both keyboard player and song writer. Mick's band involvement becomes the catalyst for his gradual character change as he begins to "hear" and respond to the "social consciousness" lyrics of Dariana's songs.

In *Big Burn*, Choyce brings together *Wave Watch*'s surfing and *Clearcut Danger*'s environmental concerns, except the surfing is now windsurfing and the threat to the eco-system is toxic waste. Over a summer, Chris Knox, 16, comes to learn that, like *Skateboard Shakedown*'s Gary, you can successfully fight city hall. The issue driving Chris is the community's garbage dump, which has installed an incinerator to burn imported waste. Chris's father, an environmental engineer, had advised the government against the incinerator's construction, but his advice, which threatened the local economy, had only led to his job discontinuance. Chris's social conscience gets a boost with the arrival of Marina Ryerson, whose father has returned to his home community to die from cancer which Marina believes was caused by his 20 years of working in a chemical plant. Mr. Ryerson's death, coupled with the announcement of a second incinerator, leads the teens to greater action, including Chris's windsurfing attempt to block the first chemical-laden barge's arrival.

Although Choyce's YA novels always include a strong adolescent female character, in only two books is a teen girl the central figure, and, in both, they must learn to survive on the street. *Dark End of Dream Street* finds Halifax's Tara seemingly living a happy life, but, in one weekend, her life falls apart as her parents announce their separation, she breaks up with her boyfriend, and an elderly woman whom Tara had befriended through a weekend nursing home job dies. Tara's response is to join her troubled best friend,

Janet, on the streets, where Tara experiences another side of life, one which causes her to engage in self-evaluation. In *Falling Through the Cracks,* after years of verbal abuse, Melanie, 16, runs away from home. With her means of "earning" money apparently limited to panhandling, stealing, or hooking, Melanie considers participating in a break-and-entry when another runaway, Trent, needing someone to rent share, offers her a place to stay. Trent, who works at a donut shop, gets Melanie a waitressing job, and, until Trent is fired, the pair are just able to "survive" on their part-time incomes. As Melanie searches for help, she learns that adolescents who voluntarily leave home tend to fall through the cracks of the social services rules. To be eligible for welfare without having to quit school, Melanie must be pregnant, an option she considers. When a desperate Trent claims to have a full-time night job, Melanie accidently uncovers the truth—Trent is prostituting himself.

Margin of Error is a fine collection of 12 short stories. The male-centered stories explore issues of character and emotion that evolve out of relationships. Five of the stories present the many, often painful, faces of adolescent romance, while another four examine dimensions of adolescent male friendships. The remaining three stories show adolescents interacting with adults.

Choyce has also written three hi-lo titles for "Series 2000." *The Hungry Lizards* is the name of a band in which Jeremy, 16, plays lead guitar. Winning a "Battle of the Bands" contest means an eight month gig at a local bar, and Jeremy finds his life becoming complicated as he attempts to juggle his music career, school, family, and a new romance. *Some Kind of Hero* explores relationships through the familiar drama of the organ transplant. Rick and Alan play on the same soccer theme, and, while Rick had dated Tina, she is now going with Alan. A freak accident damages Alan's liver, and Rick shares Alan's blood type. On the way to donate blood, Rick is killed, and Tina convinces Rick's parents to donate his liver to save Alan's life. In *Full Tilt,* Newfoundlander Greg comes to the aid of a family of illegal Sri Lankan refugees who have barely survived being set adrift at sea by a ship that was supposed to bring them to Canada. While the hi-lo titles sometimes stretch plot credibility, their pell-mell action carries reluctant readers along.

—Dave Jenkinson

CHRISTIE, (Dame) Agatha (Mary Clarissa née Miller)

Pseudonyms: Agatha Christie Mallowan; Mary Westmacott. **Nationality:** British. **Born:** Torquay, Devon, 15 September 1890. Educated privately at home; studied singing and piano in Paris. **Family:** Married 1) Colonel Archibald Christie in 1914 (divorced, 1928, died, 1962), one daughter; 2) the archaeologist Max Edgar Lucien Mallowan in 1930 (died, 1978). Writer. During World War I, served as Voluntary Aid Detachment (V.A.D.) nurse in a Red Cross Hospital, Torquay, South Devon, England, and worked in the dispensary of University College Hospital, London, during World War II; also assisted her husband (Max Mallowan) on excavations in Iraq and Syria and on the Assyrian cities; worked in dispensary for University College Hospital, London, England. President, Detection Club. **Awards:** Fellow, Royal Society of Literature, 1950; Grand Master award, Mystery Writers of America, 1954; New York Drama Critics' Circle award, 1955, for *Witness for the Prosecution;* Commander of the British Empire, 1956; D.Litt., University of Exeter, 1961; Dame Commander, Order of the British Empire, 1971. **Died:** 12 January 1976.

PUBLICATIONS

Novels

The Mysterious Affair at Styles. London, Lane, 1920, New York, Dodd, 1927.

The Secret Adversary. London, Lane, 1920; New York, Dodd, 1922.

The Murder on the Links. London, Lane, and New York, Dodd, 1923.

The Man in the Brown Suit. London, Lane, and New York, Dodd, 1924.

The Secret of Chimneys. London, Lane, and New York, Dodd, 1925.

The Murder of Roger Ackroyd. London, Collins, and New York, Dodd, 1926.

The Big Four. London, Collins, and New York, Dodd, 1927.

The Mystery of the Blue Train. London, Collins, and New York, Dodd, 1928.

The Seven Dials Mystery. London, Collins, and New York, Dodd, 1929.

The Murder at the Vicarage. London, Collins, and New York, Dodd, 1930.

The Floating Admiral, with others. London, Hodder & Stoughton, 1931; New York, Doubleday, 1932.

The Sittaford Mystery. London, Collins, 1931; as *The Murder at Hazelmoor,* New York, Dodd, 1931.

Peril at End House. London, Collins, and New York, Dodd, 1932.

Lord Edgware Dies. London, Collins, 1933; as *Thirteen at Dinner,* New York, Dodd, 1933.

Murder in Three Acts. New York, Dodd, 1934; as *Three Act Tragedy,* London, Collins, 1935.

Murder on the Orient Express. London, Collins, 1934; as *Murder in the Calais Coach,* New York, Dodd, 1934.

Why Didn't They Ask Evans?. London, Collins, 1934; as *The Boomerang Clue,* New York, Dodd, 1935.

Death in the Clouds. London, Collins, 1935; as *Death in the Air,* New York, Dodd, 1935.

The A.B.C. Murders: A New Poirot Mystery. London, Collins, and New York, Dodd, 1936; as *The Alphabet Murders,* New York, Pocket Books, 1966.

Cards on the Table. London, Collins, 1936; New York, Dodd, 1937.

Murder in Mesopotamia. London, Collins, and New York, Dodd, 1936.

Death on the Nile. London, Collins, 1937; New York, Dodd, 1938.

Dumb Witness. London, Collins, 1937; as *Poirot Loses a Client,* New York, Dodd, 1937.

Appointment with Death: A Poirot Mystery. London, Collins, and New York, Dodd, 1938.

Hercule Poirot's Christmas. London, Collins, 1938; as *Murder for Christmas,* New York, Dodd, 1939; as *A Holiday for Murder,* New York, Avon, 1947.

Murder Is Easy. London, Collins, 1939; as *Easy to Kill,* New York, Dodd, 1939.

One, Two, Buckle My Shoe. London, Collins, 1940; as *The Patriotic Murders,* New York, Dodd, 1941; as *An Overdose of Death,* New York, Dell, 1953.

Sad Cypress. London, Collins, and New York, Dodd, 1940.

Ten Little Niggers. London, Collins, 1939; as *And Then There Were None,* New York, Dodd, 1940; as *Ten Little Indians,* New York, Pocket Books, 1965.

Evil Under the Sun. London, Collins, and New York, Dodd, 1941.

N or M?: A New Mystery. London, Collins, and New York, Dodd, 1941.

The Body in the Library. London, Collins, and New York, Dodd, 1942.

Five Little Pigs. London, Collins, 1942; as *Murder in Retrospect,* New York, Dodd, 1942.

The Moving Finger. New York, Dodd, 1942; London, Collins, 1943.

Death Comes as the End. New York, Dodd, 1944; London, Collins, 1945.

Towards Zero. London, Collins, and New York, Dodd, 1944.

Sparkling Cyanide. London, Collins, 1945; as *Remembered Death,* New York, Dodd, 1945.

The Hollow: A Hercule Poirot Mystery. London, Collins, and New York, Dodd, 1946; as *Murder After Hours,* New York, Dell, 1954.

Taken at the Flood. London, Collins, 1948; as *There Is a Tide. . . ,* New York, Dodd, 1948.

The Crooked House. London, Collins, and New York, Dodd, 1949.

A Murder Is Announced. London, Collins, and New York, Dodd, 1950.

They Came to Baghdad. London, Collins, and New York, Dodd, 1951.

Mrs. McGinty's Dead. London, Collins, and New York, Dodd, 1952; as *Blood Will Tell,* New York, Detective Book Club, 1952.

They Do It with Mirrors. London, Collins, 1952; as *Murder with Mirrors,* New York, Dodd, 1952.

After the Funeral. London, Collins, 1953; as *Funerals Are Fatal,* New York, Dodd, 1953; as *Murder at the Gallop,* London, Fontana, 1963.

A Pocket Full of Rye. London, Collins, 1953; New York, Dodd, 1954.

Destination Unknown. London, Collins, 1954; *So Many Steps to Death,* New York, Dodd, 1955.

Hickory, Dickory, Dock. London, Collins, 1955; as *Hickory, Dickory, Death,* New York, Dodd, 1955.

Dead Man's Folly. London, Collins, and New York, Dodd, 1956.

4:50 from Paddington. London, Collins, 1957; as *What Mrs. McGillicuddy Saw!,* New York, Dodd, 1957; as *Murder She Said,* New York, Pocket Books, 1961.

Ordeal by Innocence. London, Collins, 1958; New York, Dodd, 1959.

Cat Among the Pigeons. London, Collins, 1959; New York, Dodd, 1960.

The Pale Horse. London, Collins, 1961; New York, Dodd, 1962.

The Mirror Crack'd from Side to Side. London, Collins, 1962; as *The Mirror Crack'd,* New York, Dodd, 1963.

The Clocks. London, Collins, 1963; New York, Dodd, 1964.

A Caribbean Mystery. London, Collins, 1964; New York, Dodd, 1965.

At Bertram's Hotel. London, Collins, 1965; New York, Dodd, 1966.

Third Girl. London, Collins, 1966; New York, Dodd, 1967.

Endless Night. London, Collins, 1967; New York, Dodd, 1968.

By the Pricking of My Thumbs. London, Collins, and New York, Dodd, 1968.

Hallowe'en Party. London, Collins, and New York, Dodd, 1969.

Passenger to Frankfurt. London, Collins, and New York, Dodd, 1970.

Nemesis. London, Collins, and New York, Dodd, 1971.

Elephants Can Remember. London, Collins, and New York, Dodd, 1972.

Postern of Fate. London, Collins, and New York, Dodd, 1973.

Murder on Board. New York, Dodd, 1974.

Curtain: Hercule Poirot's Last Case. London, Collins, and New York, Dodd, 1975.

Sleeping Murder. London, Collins, and New York, Dodd, 1976.

The Scoop, and Behind the Screen, with others. London, Gollancz, and New York, Harper, 1983.

Short Stories

Poirot Investigates. London, Lane, 1924; New York, Dodd, 1925.

Partners in Crime. London, Collins, and New York, Dodd, 1929; as *The Sunningdale Mystery,* London, Collins, 1933.

The Under Dog, and Other Stories. London, Readers Library, 1929, New York, Dodd, 1951.

The Mysterious Mr. Quin. London, Collins, and New York, Dodd, 1930; as *The Passing of Mr. Quin.*

The Thirteen Problems. London, Collins, 1932; as *The Tuesday Club Murders,* New York, Dodd, 1933; selection, as *The Mystery of the Blue Geraniums, and Other Tuesday Club Murders,* New York, Bantam, 1940.

The Hound of Death, and Other Stories. London, Odhams Press, 1933.

The Listerdale Mystery, and Other Stories. London, Collins, 1934.

Parker Pyne Investigates. London, Collins, 1934; as *Mr. Parker Pyne, Detective,* New York, Dodd, 1934.

Murder in the News, and Other Stories. London, Collins, 1937; *Dead Man's Mirror, and Other Stories,* New York, Dodd, 1937.

The Regatta Mystery, and Other Stories. New York, Dodd, 1939.

The Mystery of the Baghdad Chest. Los Angeles, Bantam, 1943.

The Mystery of the Crime in Cabin 66. Los Angeles, Bantam, 1943; as *The Crime in Cabin 66,* London, Vallencey, 1944.

Poirot and the Regatta Mystery. Los Angeles, Bantam, 1943.

Poirot on Holiday. London, Todd, 1943.

Problem at Pollensa Bay [and] *Christmas Adventure.* London, Todd, 1943.

The Veiled Lady [and] *The Mystery of the Baghdad Chest.* London, Todd, 1944.

Poirot Knows the Murderer. London, Todd, 1946.

Poirot Lends a Hand. London, Todd, 1946.

Labours of Hercules: Short Stories. London, Collins, 1947; as *The Labours of Hercules: New Adventures in Crime by Hercule Poirot,* New York, Dodd, 1947.

Witness for the Prosecution, and Other Stories. New York, Dodd, 1948.

The Mousetrap and Other Stories. New York, Dell, 1949; as *Three Blind Mice, and Other Stories,* New York, Dodd, 1950.

The Adventure of the Christmas Pudding, and Selection of Entrees. London, Collins, 1960.

Double Sin, and Other Stories. New York, Dodd, 1961.

13 for Luck!: A Selection of Mystery Stories for Young Readers. New York, Dodd, 1961; London, Collins, 1966.

Star Over Bethlehem, and Other Stories (as Agatha Christie Mallowan). London, Collins, and New York, Dodd, 1965.

Surprise! Surprise!: A Collection of Mystery Stories with Unexpected Endings, edited by Raymond T. Bond. New York, Dodd, 1965.

13 Clues for Miss Marple. New York, Dodd, 1966.

Selected Stories. Moscow, Progress Publishers, 1969.
The Golden Ball, and Other Stories. New York, Dodd, 1971.
Poirot's Early Cases. London, Collins, 1974; as *Hercule Poirot's Early Cases,* New York, Dodd, 1974.
Miss Marple's Final Cases, and Two Other Stories. London, Collins, 1979.
The Agatha Christie Hour. London, Collins, 1982.
Hercule Poirot's Casebook: Fifty Stories. New York, Putnam, 1984.
Miss Marple, the Complete Short Stories. New York, Putnam, 1985.
English Country House Murders: Tales of Perfidious Albion, and others, edited by Thomas Godfrey. New York, Mysterious Press, 1989.

Plays

Black Coffee (produced London, 1930). London, Ashley, and Boston, Baker, 1934.
Ten Little Niggers, adaptation of her own novel (produced Wimbledon and London, 1943). London, French, 1944; as *Ten Little Indians* (produced New York, 1944), New York, French, 1946.
Appointment with Death, adaptation of her own novel (produced Glasgow and London, 1945). London, French, 1956; in *The Mousetrap and Other Plays,* 1978.
Murder on the Nile, adaptation of her novel *Death on the Nile* (as *Little Horizon,* produced Wimbledon, 1945; as *Murder on the Nile,* produced London and New York, 1946). London and New York, French, 1948.
The Hollow, adaptation of her own novel (produced Cambridge and London, 1951; Princeton, New Jersey, 1952; New York, 1978). London and New York, French, 1952.
The Mousetrap, adaptation of her story "Three Blind Mice" (broadcast 1952, produced Nottingham and London, 1952, New York, 1960). London and New York, French, 1954.
Witness for the Prosecution, adaptation of her own story (produced Nottingham and London, 1953; New York, 1954). London and New York, French, 1954.
Spider's Web (produced Nottingham and London, 1954; New York, 1974). London and New York, French, 1957.
Towards Zero, with Gerald Verner, adaptation of the novel by Christie (produced Nottingham and London, 1956). New York, Dramatists Play Service, 1957; London, French, 1958.
The Unexpected Guest (produced Bristol and London, 1958). London, French, 1958; in *The Mousetrap and Other Plays,* 1978.
Verdict (produced Wolverhampton and London, 1958). London, French, 1958; in *The Mousetrap and Other Plays,* 1978.
Go Back for Murder, adaptation of her novel *Five Little Pigs* (produced Edinburgh and London, 1960) London, French, 1960; in *The Mousetrap and Other Plays,* 1978.
Rule of Three: Afternoon at the Seaside, The Patient, The Rats (produced Aberdeen and London, 1962; *The Rats* produced New York, 1974; *The Patient* produced New York, 1978). London, French, 3 vols., 1963.
Fiddlers Three. (produced Southsea, 1971; London, 1972).
Akhnaton (as *Akhnaton and Nefertiti,* produced New York, 1979; as *Akhnaton,* produced London, 1980). London, Collins, and New York, Dodd, 1973.
The Mousetrap, and Other Plays (includes *Witness for the Prosecution, Ten Little Indians, Appointment with Death, The Hollow, Towards Zero, Verdict, Go Back for Murder*). New York, Dodd, 1978.

Radio Plays: *The Mousetrap,* 1952; *Personal Call,* 1960.

Novels as Mary Westmacott

Giant's Bread. London, Collins, and New York, Doubleday, 1930.
Unfinished Portrait. London, Collins, and New York, Doubleday, 1934.
Absent in the Spring. London, Collins, and New York, Farrar & Rinehart, 1944.
The Rose and the Yew Tree. London, Heinemann, and New York, Rinehart, 1948.
A Daughter's a Daughter. London, Heinemann, 1952; New York, Dell, 1963.
The Burden. London, Heinemann, 1956; New York, Dell, 1963.

Poetry

The Road of Dreams. London, Bles, 1925.
Poems. London, Collins, and New York, Dodd, 1973.

Other

Come, Tell Me How You Live (travel). London, Collins, and New York, Dodd, 1946; revised edition, 1975.
Editor, with others, *The Times of London Anthology of Detective Stories.* New York, John Day, 1973.
An Autobiography. London, Collins, and New York, Dodd, 1977.

*

Media Adaptations: *The Murder of Roger Ackroyd* (play by Michael Morton and first produced under the title *Alibi* on the West End at Prince of Wales Theatre), 1928; *Philomel Cottage* (play by Frank Vosper and first produced under the title *Love from a Stranger* on the West End at Wyndham's Theatre), in 1936; *Peril at End House* (play by Arnold Ridley and first produced on the West End at the Vaudeville Theatre), 1940; *Murder at the Vicarage* (play by Moie Charles and Barbara Toy and first produced in London at the Playhouse Theatre), 1949; *Towards Zero* (play by Gerald Verner and first produced on Broadway at the St. James Theatre), 1956; *Philomel Cottage* (filmed as *Love from a Stranger*), United Artists, 1937, and Eagle Lion, 1947; *And Then There Were None* (film), Twentieth Century-Fox, 1945; *Witness for the Prosecution* (film), United Artists, 1957; *Witness for the Prosecution* (television), Columbia Broadcasting System, 1982; *The Spider's Web* (film), United Artists, 1960; *Murder She Said* (film), Metro-Goldwyn-Mayer, 1962; *Murder at the Gallop* (film), Metro-Goldwyn-Mayer, 1963; *Mrs. McGinty's Dead* (filmed as *Murder Most Foul*), Metro-Goldwyn-Mayer, 1965; *Ten Little Indians* (film), Associated British & Pathe Film, 1965; *The Alphabet Murders* (film), Metro-Goldwyn-Mayer, 1967; *Endless Night* (film), British Lion Films, 1971; *Murder on the Orient Express* (film), EMI, 1974; *Death on the Nile* (film), Paramount, 1978; *The Mirror Crack'd* (film), EMI, 1980; *The Seven Dials Mystery* and *Why Didn't They Ask Evans?* (films), London Weekend Television, 1980; *Evil Under the Sun* (film), Universal, 1982; *Murder Ahoy,* (film, features the character Miss Jane Marple in a story not written by Christie), Metro-Goldwyn-Mayer, 1964.

Critical Study: *Studies in Agatha Christie's Writings* by Frank Behre, Gothenburg, Universitetet, 1967; *Agatha Christie: Mistress* *of Mystery* by Gordon C. Ramsey, New York, Dodd, 1967, revised edition, London, Collins, 1968; entry in *Contemporary Literary Criticism,* Detroit, Gale, Volume 1, 1973, Volume 6, 1976, Volume 8, 1978, Volume 12, 1980, Volume 39, 1986, Volume 48, 1988; *The Mysterious World of Agatha Christie* by Jeffrey Feinman, New York, Award Books, 1975; *An Agatha Christie Chronology* by Nancy Blue Wynne, New York, Ace Books, 1976; *The Mystery of Agatha Christie* by Derrick Murdoch, Toronto, Pagurian Press, 1976; *Agatha Christie: First Lady of Crime* edited by H.R.F. Keating, London, Weidenfeld & Nicolson, and New York, Holt, 1977; *The Mystery of Agatha Christie* by Gwyn Robyns, New York, Doubleday, 1978; *The Bedside, Bathtub, and Armchair Companion to Agatha Christie* edited by Dick Riley and Pam McAllister, New York, Ungar, 1979, London, Angus & Robertson, 1983, revised edition, Ungar, 1986; *A Talent to Deceive: An Appreciation of Agatha Christie* (includes bibliography by Louise Barnard) by Robert Barnard, London, Collins, and New York, Dodd, 1980; *The Agatha Christie Who's Who* by Randall Toye, New York, Holt, and London, Muller, 1980; *The Gentle Art of Murder: The Detective Fiction of Agatha Christie* by Earl F. Bargainnier, Bowling Green, Ohio, Bowling Green University Press, 1981; entry in *Dictionary of Literary Biography,* Detroit, Gale, Volume 13: *British Dramatists Since World War II,* Detroit, Gale, 1982, Volume 77: *British Mystery Writers, 1920-1939,* 1989; *Murder She Wrote: A Study of Agatha Christie's Detective Fiction* by Patricia D. Maida and Nicholas B. Spornick, Bowling Green, Ohio, Bowling Green University, 1982; *The Life and Crimes of Agatha Christie* by Charles Osborne, London, Collins, 1982, New York, Holt, 1983; *The Agatha Christie Companion: The Complete Guide to Agatha Christie's Life and Work* by Dennis Sanders and Len Lovalio, New York, Delacorte, 1984, London, W.H. Allen, 1985; *Agatha Christie: A Biography* by Janet Morgan, London, Cape, 1984, New York, Knopf, 1985; *The Life and Times of Miss Jane Marple: An Entertaining and Definitive Study of Agatha Christie's Famous Amateur Sleuth,* New York, Dodd, 1985, and *The Life and Times of Hercule Poirot,* New York, Putnam, and London, Pavilion, 1990, both by Anne Hart; *An A to Z of the Novels and Short Stories of Agatha Christie* by Ben Morselt, Phoenix, Arizona, Phoenix, 1986.

*   *   *

Judged by most conventional criteria, Agatha Christie is, at best, a mediocre writer. Her characterization is almost always two-dimensional, and in novel after novel she deploys the same troupe of pasteboard stereotypes (the peppery-but-gallant colonel, the poor little rich girl, the well-brought-up young man with half-baked radical notions, and so on). She seems convinced that all foreigners have funny and instantly recognizable national mannerisms (Italians are always excitable, and Germans are mostly stolid), and her sense of place is rudimentary. Her prose can be tersely economical but she lapses into cliche on the least provocation and tends, when trying to sound sophisticated, to stultify her sentences with French tags.

On the other hand, Christie's world sales have topped four hundred million (she is, after Shakespeare and the Bible, history's best-selling writer), so the relevance of conventional criteria to a discussion of her work seems questionable. There is little purpose

in berating oranges for not being bananas, and complaints that Christie is not George Eliot (or even, for that matter, Margery Allingham)seem so obviously true and so obviously beside the point as to be hardly worth making. It could, indeed, be plausibly argued that the very characteristics that deny her a place in the Great Tradition contribute largely to her phenomenal success in other areas and among young adult readers. For Christie's paramount concern is with the creation of plot, and anything which might tend to obscure the stark linear sequence of problematically related events (complex motivation, for example, or the pressure of social circumstance) is ruthlessly excised. The end towards which her narratives progress is not the private (and often provisional) closure of the conventional novel (the making and breaking of relationships), but the public revelation of factual truth (the identity of a murderer and the means by which the crime was committed). Moreover, although her fictional detectives undoubtedly share some common ground with the protagonists of other genres (the hero of the quest-romance, for example), they (and in Christie's case this mostly means the moustachioed Belgian Hercule Poirot or the prim, spinsterly Jane Marple) remain essentially unaffected, even by their most gruesome adventures. Christie's sleuths, that is, enter the narrative fully formed; their function is not to develop in response to events but only to analyse those events in order to distill apparent chaos into logical order. And as with the detectives so, mutatis mutandis with the other characters. The colonels, vicars, bright young things, and embittered old maids are of interest not for themselves but only in relation to the crimes for which each may turn out to be responsible. Even the hapless victims are seldom sufficiently distinctive to become objects of sympathy; indeed, the reader learns to look forward eagerly to their demise as a trigger for the progression of clues and deductions which it is the book's primary purpose to retail.

It is apparent that Christie's fiction (and indeed the classic English detective story in general) is founded upon a set of clearly established conventions. This, of course, is more or less true of all literary genres, but in Christie's novels the conventions operate primarily as rules in a game played between author (or narrator) and reader: the latter is provided by the former with all of the evidence necessary to solve a criminal mystery and is challenged to anticipate the detective's final revelation of the truth. And it is in the playing of this game that Christie is supremely successful. Unlike many of her contemporaries (Dorothy Sayers, for example), she never premises her solutions on the reader's possession of recondite knowledge but bases them on clearly visible and apparently commonplace clues (the state of the murdered girl's fingernails in *The Body in the Library,* for example). She is, in addition, extremely inventive in her manipulation (even, occasionally, transgression) of generic conventions. In *The Murder of Roger Ackroyd* the murderer is also the narrator; in *Murder on the Orient Express* all of the possible suspects turn out to be equally guilty; in *Hercule Poirot's Christmas* it is the investigating policeman who blurts out a confession in the penultimate chapter. No character can ever be safely exempted from suspicion and Christie, indeed, is adept at playing on and against the generically conditioned reflexes of even her most hardened readers. In *Death on the Nile,* for example, the solution to Linnet Doyle's murder is impossible to guess not only because the method of its commission is so diabolically original, but also because the killers are the two people whom our previous experience of Christie's writing would lead us to exclude as possibilities—the prime suspect and a clean-cut English gentleman.

At the height of her powers in the 1930s and 1940s (her later work shows some decline in ingenuity) Christie, then, is more sensibly regarded as a superb game-player than as a fourth-rate novelist. Her characters resemble chess pieces which she shifts about the board in dazzling variations on familiar strategies, and her objective—to frustrate the predictions of her reader while still providing a fully satisfying closure—is almost always realized. Hers, in the end, is a comfortingly orderly world, where all loose ends can be tied into neat bows and in which, once the murderer has been identified, no further or larger problems remain to be resolved.

—Robert Dingley

CHRISTOPHER, John

Pseudonym for Christopher Samuel Youd. **Other Pseudonyms:** Hilary Ford, William Godfrey, Peter Graaf, Peter Nichols, and Anthony Rye. **Nationality:** British. **Born:** Knowsley, Lancashire, 16 April 1922. **Education:** Peter Symonds' School, Winchester. **Military Service:** Served in the Royal Signals, 1941-46. **Family:** Married twice; four daughters and one son from first marriage. **Career:** Since 1958 full-time writer. **Awards:** Rockefeller-Atlantic award, 1946; Christopher award, 1971; *Guardian* award, 1971; Children's Literature prize (Germany), 1976; George G. Stone Center for Children's Books award, 1977. **Address:** c/o Society of Authors, 84 Drayton Gardens, London SW10 9SB, England.

PUBLICATIONS FOR YOUNG ADULTS

Fiction

The Tripods Trilogy. New York, Macmillan, 1980.
The White Mountains. London, Hamish Hamilton, and New York, Macmillan, 1967.
The City of Gold and Lead. London, Hamish Hamilton, and New York, Macmillan, 1967.
The Pool of Fire. London, Hamish Hamilton, and New York, Macmillan, 1968.
The Lotus Caves. London, Hamish Hamilton, and New York, Macmillan, 1969.
The Guardians. London, Hamish Hamilton, and New York, Macmillan, 1970.
The Sword of the Spirits Trilogy. New York, Macmillan, 1980; as *The Prince in Waiting Trilogy,* London, Penguin, 1983.
The Prince in Waiting. London, Hamish Hamilton, and New York, Macmillan, 1970.
Beyond the Burning Lands. London, Hamish Hamilton, and New York, Macmillan, 1971.
The Sword of the Spirits. London, Hamish Hamilton, and New York, Macmillan, 1972.
In the Beginning (reader for adults). London, Longman, 1972; revised edition (for children), as *Dom and Va,* London, Hamish Hamilton, and New York, Macmillan, 1973.

A Figure in Grey (as Hilary Ford). Kingswood, Surrey, World's Work, 1973.
Wild Jack. London, Hamish Hamilton, and New York, Macmillan, 1974; original version (reader for adults), London, Longman, 1974.
Empty World. London, Hamish Hamilton, 1977; New York, Dutton, 1978.
Fireball. London, Gollancz, and New York, Dutton, 1981.
New Found Land. London, Gollancz, and New York, Dutton, 1983.
Dragon Dance. London, Viking Kestrel, and New York, Dutton, 1986.
When the Tripods Came. New York, Dutton, 1988.
A Dusk of Demons. New York, Macmillan, 1994.

PUBLICATIONS FOR ADULTS

Novels

The Year of the Comet. London, Joseph, 1955; as *Planet in Peril,* New York, Avon, 1959.
The Death of Grass. London, Joseph, 1956; as *No Blade of Grass,* New York, Simon and Schuster, 1957.
Giant's Arrow (as Anthony Rye). London, Gollancz, 1956; as Samuel Youd, New York, Simon and Schuster, 1960.
Malleson at Melbourne (as William Godfrey). London, Museum Press, 1956.
The Friendly Game (as William Godfrey). London, Joseph, 1957.
The Caves of Night. London, Eyre and Spottiswoode, and New York, Simon and Schuster, 1958.
A Scent of White Poppies. London, Eyre and Spottiswoode, and New York, Simon and Schuster, 1959.
The Long Voyage. London, Eyre and Spottiswoode, 1960; as *The White Voyage,* New York, Simon and Schuster, 1961.
The World in Winter. London, Eyre and Spottiswoode, 1962; as *The Long Winter,* New York, Simon and Schuster, 1962.
Sweeney's Island. New York, Simon and Schuster, 1964; as *Cloud on Silver,* London, Hodder and Stoughton, 1964.
The Possessors. London, Hodder and Stoughton, and New York, Simon and Schuster, 1965.
A Wrinkle in the Skin. London, Hodder and Stoughton, 1965; as *The Ragged Edge,* New York, Simon and Schuster, 1966.
Patchwork of Death (as Peter Nichols). New York, Holt Rinehart, 1965; London, Hale, 1967.
The Little People. London, Hodder and Stoughton, and New York, Simon and Schuster, 1967.
Pendulum. London, Hodder and Stoughton, and New York, Simon and Schuster, 1968.

Novels as Samuel Youd

The Winter Swan. London, Dobson, 1949.
Babel Itself. London, Cassell, 1951.
Brave Conquerors. London, Cassell, 1952.
Crown and Anchor. London, Cassell, 1953.
A Palace of Strangers. London, Cassell, 1954.
Holly Ash. London, Cassell, 1955; as *The Opportunist,* New York, Harper, 1957.
The Choice. New York, Simon and Schuster, 1961; as *The Burning Bird,* London, Longman, 1964.
Messages of Love. New York, Simon and Schuster, 1961; London, Longman, 1962.
The Summers at Accorn. London, Longman, 1963.

Novels as Peter Graaf

Dust and the Curious Boy. London, Joseph, 1957; as *Give the Devil His Due,* New York, Mill, 1957.
Daughter Fair. London, Joseph, and New York, Washburn, 1958.
Sapphire Conference. London, Joseph, and New York, Washburn, 1959.
The Gull's Kiss. London, Davies, 1962.

Novels as Hilary Ford

Felix Walking. London, Eyre and Spottiswoode, and New York, Simon and Schuster, 1958.
Felix Running. London, Eyre and Spottiswoode, 1959.
Bella on the Roof. London, Longman, 1965.
Sarnia. London, Hamish Hamilton, and New York, Doubleday, 1974.
Castle Malindine. London, Hamish Hamilton, and New York, Harper, 1975.
A Bride for Bedivere. London, Hamish Hamilton, 1976; New York, Harper, 1977.

Short Stories

The Twenty-Second Century. London, Grayson, 1954; New York, Lancer, 1962.

*

Biography: Entry in *Something about the Author—Autobiography Series,* Vol. 6, Detroit, Gale, 1988; essay in *Speaking for Ourselves, Too* compiled and edited by Donald R. Gallo, National Council of Teachers of English, 1993.

John Christopher comments:

Before I started writing for young people, I had already published eleven adult books under the name of John Christopher. I was asked to try my hand at this different audience by an English publisher, who was quite happy with what I produced, the first draft of *The White Mountains.* The American publisher who saw it took a different view: she said the book started well but rapidly went off. She only professed herself as happy with the second rewrite, and I realized two things: that editors were stronger and more helpful in children's books, and that I had been assuming, quite wrongly, that this was an easier discipline. It is in fact a harder one, but extremely rewarding.

I only wrote one more adult novel before settling permanently into this new field. In those days, the late sixties, there was something else I found refreshing: children's books still treated story-telling as the quintessential basis for fiction. In the adult field, one had been either a serious writer or a story-teller. ("The novel tells a story," E. M. Forster said with weary cynicism, "—oh dear, I suppose it does.") In children's books, no story meant no publication.

The rot spread here eventually, along with such other factors as political correctness, but it was fun while it lasted. And maybe it will be again, for a new generation of writers. I hear tell that, even in his native France, Jacques Derrida is finally being recognized as a destructive fraud.

And it's not just story-telling, of course. There is the even more important question of a recognition of civilized values which, built up over centuries, even millennia, have painfully established and sustained decency and social sanity. Promulgation of these too

used to be a lynch-pin in writing for the young. I wish I could be optimistic that their present detractors would be as quickly seen through and dismissed as Derrida and his gang.

*   *   *

As the first important English writer of science fiction specifically for young adults, John Christopher is—like H.G. Wells before him—a skilled writer with a strong social conscience who uses the genre of science fiction to explore concerns about the direction of social and technological change, and the dangers presented by the fallibility of human nature. Looking to the past to help him envision the future, Christopher characteristically sees a regression, whereby in the England of the future most people live without machines, and technological power is controlled by a small elite. Christopher writes fluently and prolifically; not all of his novels meet the standards set by his best works, but his first two trilogies and *The Lotus Caves* and *The Guardians,* particularly, present memorable and troubling images of the future which stir the reader to question aspects of contemporary society and his or her role therein.

The subject of mind control, whether through indoctrination or by physical means, preoccupies Christopher throughout his work, and his central characters virtually always find themselves in rebellion against powerful figures who seek to impose or to maintain their control over human minds. In the "Tripods" trilogy, Christopher's first major work for young people, almost all human beings on Earth have come under the control of an alien race, the "Masters," who affix a metal cap to the skull of every adolescent boy and girl which enables their thoughts to be entirely subdued to the Masters's will throughout the rest of their lives. Capped humans live contentedly in quasi-medieval agrarian communities, avoiding the ruins of their cities and any sophisticated machinery, and willingly sending their most promising young people to spend short and painful lives as slaves in the Masters's domed cities. The young uncapped protagonists of *The White Mountains* are enlisted by a secret resistance movement, and in two subsequent novels they infiltrate the Masters's cities and destroy them. The great conclave held at the end of the trilogy, which hopes to establish a new world order, proves however that these leaders are in some ways their own worst enemies, as representatives of different races and factions begin quarrelling among themselves. Only in his young heroes' final determination to work together to heal these rifts among the nations does Christopher offer a slight hope that freed human beings can do anything other than squabble and seek to enslave each other anew.

Variations on this theme of mind control and rebellion are found in *The Lotus Caves,* set on a colonized Moon, and *The Guardians* and *Wild Jack,* both set in an England of the future. The tranquilizing and euphoric state induced in its human worshippers by the Plant, a vast, beautiful, and beneficent organism which has found a refuge in the Moon caves, is resisted by thirteen-year-old Marty because it will destroy his independent will and prevent him from returning to his family. He escapes from the Plant, however, with a certain sense of regret, and hopes to keeps its whereabouts secret from the other Moon colonists lest they interfere with it and destroy it. As this novel makes imaginative use of the Homeric story of the Lotus Eaters, so *Wild Jack* displaces the legend of Robin Hood into a futuristic England where the outlaw and his band have set up an active resistance to the complacent and privileged city-dwellers, who deploy Earth's seriously-depleted energy resources to benefit the ruling class, and condemn other humans to struggle for survival as best they can. A strong physical barrier also separates the classes in *The Guardians,* one of Christopher's bleakest and most powerful visions of the future. Rob runs away from the Conurbs, where industrial workers are crowded together in a passive society whose athletic spectacles and meaningless riots arising out of them provide the chief distractions from a numbing routine existence; in the County, however, Rob experiences the idyllic life of the privileged Edwardian country-house dweller, where all is serene, orderly, and beautiful. Accepted into this privileged class and world, Rob is utterly content, until his shattering discovery that social division is maintained by a ruling elite, the Guardians, who perform a sort of lobotomy on any members of the County set who question the status quo, thus ensuring their tranquillity and conformity. Rob is invited to become a Guardian, at the cost of betraying his friend; he chooses, instead, to join a band of rebels in their apparently hopeless task of unseating the Guardians and changing the social system.

The second of Christopher's trilogies, the "Winchester" trilogy which begins with *The Prince in Waiting,* also offers a bleak vision of the future of England and the part which scientific knowledge and technological power will play in it. At the outset, as in the beginning of the first trilogy, English society has returned to a medieval way of life: technology is feared and shunned, a priestly class shares power with a military elite, and city states such as Winchester wage sporadic warfare amongst themselves, led by knights on horseback. Luke, who finds himself unexpectedly in line to become his city's Prince, also learns that the scientific knowledge of the past is secretly preserved by the priests or Seers, who use it to keep the populace in awe of their apparent powers until they are able to find a strong ruler who will unite England once more and restore technology. Luke is to be this ruler, prepared to break the bonds of tradition and bring England enlightenment. Like the Arthurian story, which it partially recalls, Luke's venture turns to tragedy as love is betrayed, Luke cuts himself off from his friends, and eventually uses his technological power for brutal military purposes. Christopher seems to imply that history repeats itself in cycles, and this destructive use of technology will again eventually lead to disaster, and the rejection of all scientific knowledge.

Luke's inclination and training in the fields of masculine and military leadership lead to his failure, in his inability to understand and communicate with women. The need of men and women for each other, and for a greater understanding of each other, is directly addressed in two of Christopher's novels from the 1970s—*Dom and Va,* and *Empty World.* The setting of the first of these is not the future but the past, as a youth aggressively trained as a hunter and a girl from a gentle agrarian tribe come to recognize their need not only for each other as individuals but also for the contrasting qualities and strengths which each of them represents. The same recognition is experienced by the young couple in *Empty World,* who find themselves almost the sole survivors of a plague which has swept over the world. In this novel, however, it is not enough that they should find each other and begin the human race anew; the novel ends with them making a gesture of compassion to someone else, a desperate and hostile woman who had previously tried to kill

the boy. While their decision to let her rejoin them is a dangerous one, it offers hope that the new society which may arise will be one founded on compassion and forgiveness rather than jealousy and revenge.

Christopher's plots are skillfully constructed, and his spare direct story-telling keeps his novels consistently gripping. Characterization is not his strong point, although the central character in each of the first two trilogies does undergo significant development and change. Many of his young heroes, however, seem the same, and secondary characters are sketched in with a few attributes suiting their roles in the plot. Young women are generally confined to being decorative and sympathetic, although in his "Fireball" trilogy Christopher responds to the feminist awareness of the 1980s by creating at least two interesting females—one a Viking girl who retains her courage and aplomb when she is (rather improbably) transported to an Aztec kingdom and sets up court in a pyramid as chief bride of the gods, and the other an ancient Chinese mystic whose psychic powers enable her to appear as a seductive young woman. As these details might suggest, the geographical focus which gave intensity to many of Christopher's earlier novels is exchanged in this third trilogy for a fantastical exploration of how the twentieth century might look if history had developed differently: if, for example, the Romans had remained rulers of Britain, the Aztecs extended their empire far northwards, and the Industrial Revolution never occurred. The speculation is intriguing, but the trilogy does not carry the conviction of Christopher's earlier work.

In his latest work, *A Dusk of Demons,* Christopher continues his exploration of humankind's responses to technology. Perhaps reflecting a tendency in the 1990s to focus on religion in society, he has created a future world where superstition and the worship of Demons holds sway. In this world there are only villages, often pitted against each other, and machines are forbidden. The story opens with Ben living on an isolated island with a man he knows only as Master and the family that takes care of him. Ben is unsure of his parentage and when the Master dies, he is shocked to learn he is his son and that he is to inherit the island. Intrigue builds as several people try to control Ben and he takes to the open road, where danger surrounds him. It seems that Ben is the key to a return to knowledge for the world, and some want him dead while others want him to succeed. Christopher uses this book to set the stage for more to come, and as he tends to write trilogies, we should expect the story to gain momentum. *A Dusk of Demons* maintains a leisurely pace for the reader to get to know the mettle of the main character, who grows from a callow youth to one who is coming to know his own worth.

Christopher's novels, while they often explore the responses to technology possible in some future society, do not make detailed use of scientific knowledge or devices; they are concerned, rather, with human nature and society, and the ways in which one individual or group may attempt to impose and maintain its control over other people. Although they have no assurance of being able to establish a more just and truly free society themselves, Christopher's heroes inevitably choose to reject and actively rebel against the forces which seek to deprive their fellow humans of the right to choose and the spirit to rebel. This lack of any easy assurance or simple solution to the problems posed by human social organization has made Christopher's fiction seem pessimistic to some; on the other hand, their realistic, open-ended conclusions, which recognize human problems as ongoing and not to be resolved by one victory, give his novels a maturity of vision which makes them of continuing interest and relevance.

—M. Jean Greenlaw

CHUTE, Marchette (Gaylord)

Nationality: American. **Born:** Wayzata, Minnesota, 16 August 1909. **Education:** Central High School, Minneapolis, 1921-25; Minneapolis School of Art, 1925-26; University of Minnesota, Minneapolis, 1926-30, B.A. 1930 (Phi Beta Kappa). **Career:** Writer, mainly of biography and history. Member of executive board, National Book Committee, since 1954; judge for National Book awards, 1952, 1959. President, American PEN, 1955-57. **Awards:** American Library Association notable book award for *Geoffrey Chaucer of England;* Author Meets the Critics award for best nonfiction of 1950, American Library Association notable book award, and New York Shakespeare Club award, 1954, all for *Shakespeare of London;* Poetry Society of American Chap-Book award, Secondary Education Board award, American Library Association notable book award, and New York Shakespeare Club award, all in 1954, for *Ben Jonson of Westminster;* Outstanding Achievement award of University of Minnesota, 1957; co-winner of Women's National Book Association Constance Lindsay Skinner award, 1959. Litt.D.: Western College, Oxford, Ohio, 1952; Carleton College, Northfield, Minnesota, 1957; Dickinson College, Carlisle, Pennsylvania, 1964. Vice-President, 1961, and Secretary, 1962, National Institute of Arts and Letters; Member, American Academy; Benjamin Franklin Fellow, Royal Society of Arts. **Died:** 1994.

PUBLICATIONS FOR YOUNG ADULTS

Fiction

The Innocent Wayfaring, illustrated by the author. New York, Scribner, 1943; London, Phoenix House, 1956.
The Wonderful Winter, illustrated by Grace Golden. New York, Dutton, 1954; London, Phoenix House, 1956.

Poetry (illustrated by the author)

Rhymes about Ourselves. New York, Macmillan, 1932.
Rhymes about the Country. New York, Macmillan, 1941.
Rhymes about the City. New York, Macmillan, 1946.
Around and About. New York, Dutton, 1957.
Rhymes about Us, illustrated by the author. New York, Dutton, 1974.

Other

An Introduction to Shakespeare. New York, Dutton, 1951; as *Shakespeare and His Stage,* London, University of London Press, 1953.
Jesus of Israel, with Ernestine Perrie. New York, Dutton, 1961; London, Gollancz, 1962.
The Green Tree of Democracy. New York, Dutton, 1971.

PUBLICATIONS FOR ADULTS

Plays

Sweet Genevieve, with M.G. Chute (produced New York, 1945).
The Worlds of Shakespeare, with Ernestine Perrie (produced New York, 1963). New York, Dutton, 1963.

Other

The Search for God. New York, Dutton, 1941; London, Benn, 1946.
Geoffrey Chaucer of England. New York, Dutton, 1946; London, Hale, 1951.
The End of the Search. New York, North River Press, 1947.
Shakespeare of London. New York, Dutton, 1950; London, Secker & Warburg, 1951.
Ben Jonson of Westminster. New York, Dutton, 1953; London, Hale, 1954.
Stories from Shakespeare. Cleveland, World, 1956.
Two Gentle Men: The Lives of George Herbert and Robert Herrick. New York, Dutton, 1959; London, Secker & Warburg, 1960.
The First Liberty: A History of the Right to Vote in America 1619-1850. New York, Dutton, 1969; London, Dent, 1970.
P.E.N. American Center: A History of the First Fifty Years. New York, P.E.N. American Center, 1972.

*

Manuscript Collections: New York Public Library; Kerlan Collection, University of Minnesota, Minneapolis.

*   *   *

Chute is a scholarly writer who is well known for her meticulously researched adult biographies on such literary greats as Shakespeare, Chaucer, Herbert, and Ben Jonson. She has also drawn on this background of an earlier England for lively books for young people.

The Wonderful Winter is set for the most part in Elizabethan London. The major character, a young nobleman, runs away from home accompanied by his pet dog. After a few misadventures, he is taken on by Shakespeare's company of players. He helps behind the scenes and becomes a boy actor. In the process the reader becomes well acquainted with the business of theatre in this period. Descriptions of the Globe Theatre and of personalities of the time make the book excellent, easy-reading background for a study of the Shakespearian plays. As the young hero matures, he feels guilt at having run away from home. He admits his true identity and returns home.

The Innocent Wayfaring is set in the fourteenth-century countryside of Chaucer's England. To be precise, the story takes place during three days in June 1370 in Surrey. The scene opens on Midsummer Eve in the Manor of Rotheby where the Lord, Sir Hugh Richmond, and wife, Lady Emily, are engaged in an amusing discussion of redecorating. Lady Emily manages very neatly to have her husband select exactly the colors and styles upon which she has already decided. The conversation turns to their fifteen-year-old daughter, Anne, who for the past month has been residing in the convent headed by the Prioress, Dame Agatha, who is Sir Hugh's intimidating older sister. There Anne is to learn sewing, spinning, embroidery, and maidenly behavior. Both Anne and her father prefer hawking.

Anne, unhappy with the only career alternatives available to her—to be either a wife or a nun—runs away to London to become a traveling entertainer. To this end she takes the Prioress's pet monkey with her. Action follows rapidly as Anne finds her way to a country fair, loses her monkey, accuses a young man of stealing it, engages in a farcical and hilarious trial over the matter, and is rescued from the affair by the young man who literally carries her off. They travel on together and as they become acquainted discover that they are both running away. The young man, Nicholas Ware, seeks knowledge and wishes to be a poet rather than go into his father's business. Anne is attempting to escape a constrained existence as a wife. They increasingly feel that they have a great deal in common, and young adult readers will also feel they have a great deal in common with these lively and likeable teenagers.

They spend the night in an ale house, have an encounter with a highwayman, survive a violent summer storm, and arrive at the kitchen of the Castle Waring where they become acquainted, as does the reader, with the various residents of a medieval manor—the cook, reeve, miller, blacksmith, steward, plasterer, and peasants. The Lady of the Castle sees Anne as a prospective daughter-in-law and treats her well—-the description of the Lady's bedroom and her toilet articles gives an excellent picture of the personal life of a wealthy woman of the period. Anne escapes from the castle and rejoins Nick who persuades her both to agree to marry him and to return home. At the end of the book after being welcomed home, Anne announces that she is returning with Aunt Agatha to the convent to learn to be a good wife while Nick returns to London to enter his father's business.

Chute has also written of Biblical and early American times and for both children and adults. Besides being a historian and biographer, Chute is a published poet, playwright, and sometime illustrator of her own books.

—Reba Pinney

CISNEROS, Sandra

Nationality: American. **Born:** Chicago, Illinois, 20 December 1954. **Education:** Loyola University of Chicago, Illinois, B.A. 1976; University of Iowa, Iowa City, M.F.A. 1978. **Career:** Writer. Has taught at universities, including University of California, Berkeley, and University of Michigan. Worked previously as a high school teacher, counselor, college recruiter, and arts administrator. **Awards:** National Endowment for the Arts fellow, 1982 and 1987; Before Columbus Foundation award, 1985, for *The House on Mango Street;* Dobie-Paisano fellow, 1986; PEN/West Fiction award, and Lannan Foundation award, both 1991, for *Woman Hollering Creek and Other Stories.* **Address:** c/o Alfred A. Knopf Books, 201 East 50th Street, New York, New York 10022, U.S.A.

PUBLICATIONS

Poetry

Bad Boys. Mango Publications, 1980.
The Rodrigo Poems. Bloomington, Indiana, Third Women Press, 1985.
My Wicked, Wicked Ways. Bloomington, Indiana, Third Women Press, 1987.
Loose Woman: Poems. New York, Knopf, 1994.
Hairs = Pelitos, illustrated by Terry Ybanez (translated from English by Liliana Valenzuela). New York, Knopf, 1994.

Short Stories

The House on Mango Street. Arte Publico, 1983.
Woman Hollering Creek and Other Stories. Random House, 1991.

Other

Contributor, *Emergency Tacos: Seven Poets con Picante.* March/ Abrazo Press, 1989.

*

Biography: Essay in *Authors & Artists for Young Adults,* Volume 9, Detroit, Gale, 1992; *Dictionary of Literary Biography,* Vol. 122, *Chicano Writers,* Detroit, Gale, 1995; *Dictionary of Literary Biography,* Vol. 152, *American Novelists Since World War II,* Detroit, Gale, 1995.

*   *   *

Sandra Cisneros writes about life in the Latino communities of Mexican-American border towns, focusing particularly on the struggles of Latina women. In her short-story collections *The House on Mango Street* and *Woman Hollering Creek,* Cisneros creates female characters who seek identity and affirmation in the face of poverty and oppression. The subject matter is often harsh—many of the women in these stories suffer physical and emotional abuse within their male-dominated communities and beyond those borders, in the racist, classist mainstream society—but Cisneros' characters usually dream of and fight their way to independence and self-fulfillment. The language in all of the stories is vibrant and poetic, the narrators, speaking in a mixture of English and Spanish, evoke the tastes, smells, and colors of their environment.

The nameless girl narrating the stories in *The House on Mango Street* offers a clear-eyed, unsentimental account of life in and around her impoverished, Latino neighborhood. In the title story, the narrator's own desire for a "real house" reflects her need to be considered a "real" person in mainstream society, to be treated with dignity, and to live freely and creatively. Her observations and hopes shape the tone and theme of all the stories in the collection. To the narrator and her family ("Mama, Papa, Carlos, Kiki, my sister Nenny, and me"), having a "real house" means achieving a stereotypical white, upper-middle class standard of life. The narrator wants a house that is "white with trees around it, a great big yard and grass growing without a fence," but what she has on Mango Street is a house that is "small and red with tight steps in front and windows so small you'd think they were holding their breath." The poverty imposed on the narrator by race and class threatens to smother her, as it suffocates her friend Sally, a victim of child abuse and the central character in "What Sally Said."

The final story in *The House on Mango Street* suggests that the narrator finds a way out of this life through her imagination and writing. The collection ends on a very brief (two-paragraph) story of hope, entitled "A House of My Own." In this story, the narrator, focused and determined, visualizes her own place, her own identity as a female and a writer: "Not a flat. Not an apartment in back. Not a man's house. Not a daddy's. A house all my own. With my porch and my pillow, my pretty purple petunias. . . . Only a house quiet as snow, a space for myself to go, clean as paper before the poem."

The characters in *Woman Hollering Creek* also seek escape from the stigma of their race and class, at the same time, however, they celebrate the customs and language that bring them together as a unique community. The opening story, "My Lucy Friend Who Smells Like Corn," is a joyous description of the friendship between two young Latina girls. This story is a first-person, stream-of-consciousness appreciation of innocence and girlhood in a Texas border community. An example would be the narrator's proclamation: "I'm going to scratch your mosquito bites, Lucy, so they'll itch you, then put Mercurochrome smiley faces on them. We're going to trade shoes and wear them on our hands. . . . I'm going to peel a scab from my knee and eat it, sneeze on the cat, give you three M & M's I've been saving for you since yesterday, comb your hair with my fingers and braid it into teeny-tiny braids real pretty."

As the stories in the collection progress, however, the narrators grow more self-aware, more experienced, more exposed to the difficulties of coming-of-age as a female Latina in a white, male-dominated society. Bittersweet stories of childhood, such as "Eleven," "Barbie-Q," and "Mericans" give way to darker tales of adulthood, such as the title story, "Woman Hollering Creek." In this story a young bride, Cleofilas, dreams of romantic love and marriage as it is portrayed in the "telenovelas" she watches religiously. She imagines a life like that of the telenovela heroine, Lucia Mendez, who suffers "all kinds of hardships of the heart, separation and betrayal" for the sake of love, and is "always loving, no matter what, because *that* is the most important thing . . ." Instead Cleofilas finds herself in a physically abusive marriage, legally bound to "this husband whose whiskers she finds each morning in the sink, whose shoes she must air each evening on the porch. . .this man, this father, this rival, this keeper, this lord, this master, this husband till kingdom come." By the end of the story Cleofilas learns to distinguish romance from reality and, through the help of other women, finds the courage to start a new life for herself and her children.

Cisneros's stories are lively and bold, exposing young readers to the tales and voices of Latino culture, but also demonstrating the range of form and style possible in storytelling. Cisneros's experiments with language and content serve as models to young readers who may not see their experience reflected in "traditional" culture stories, and to young writers who wish to express their own experience in "alternative" narrative forms.

—Mary D. Esselman

CLAPP, Patricia

Nationality: American. **Born:** Boston, Massachusetts, 9 June 1912. **Education:** Kimberley School, Montclair, New Jersey; Columbia University School of Journalism, 1932. **Family:** Married Edward della Torre Cone in 1933; one son and two daughters. **Career:** Writer of adult and children's books and plays; member of the Board of Managers, Studio Players, Upper Montclair, New Jersey, since 1940. **Awards:** National Book Award runner-up, and Lewis Carroll Shelf Award, both 1969, both for *Constance: A Story of Early Plymouth;* American Library Association Best Young Adult Book citation, 1982, for *Witches' Children: A Story of Salem.* **Address:** 83 Beverley Rd., Upper Montclair, New Jersey 07043, U.S.A.

PUBLICATIONS FOR YOUNG ADULTS

Fiction

Constance: A Story of Early Plymouth. New York, Lothrop, 1968.
Jane-Emily. New York, Lothrop, 1969.
I'm Deborah Sampson: A Soldier in the War of the Revolution. New York, Lothrop, 1977.
Witches' Children: A Story of Salem. New York, Lothrop, 1982.
The Tamarack Tree. New York, Lothrop, 1986.

Plays

Peggy's on the Phone. Chicago, Dramatic Publishing, 1956.
Smart Enough to Be Dumb. Chicago, Dramatic Publishing, 1956.
The Incompleted Pass. Chicago, Dramatic Publishing, 1957.
Her Kissin' Cousin. Cedar Rapids, Iowa, Heuer Publishing, 1957.
The Girl out Front. Chicago, Dramatic Publishing, 1958.
The Ghost of a Chance. Cedar Rapids, Iowa, Heuer Publishing, 1958.
The Curley Tale. Cedar Rapids, Iowa, Art Craft, 1958.
Inquire Within. Evanston, Illinois, Row Peterson, 1959.
The Girl Whose Fortune Sought Her (published in *Children's Plays from Favorite Stories,* edited by S. E. Kamerman, Boston, Plays Inc., 1959).
Edie-across-the-Street. Boston, Baker, 1960.
The Honeysuckle Hedge. Franklin, Ohio, Eldridge, 1960.
Never Keep Him Waiting. Chicago, Dramatic Publishing, 1961.
Red Heels and Roses. New York, McKay, 1961.
If a Body Meet a Body. Cedar Rapids, Ohio, Heuer Publishing, 1963.
Now Hear This. Franklin, Ohio, Eldridge, 1963.
The Magic Bookshelf (published in *Fifty Plays for Junior Actors,* edited by S.E. Kamerman, Boston, Plays Inc., 1966).
The Other Side of the Wall (published in *Fifty Plays for Holidays,* edited by S.E. Kamerman, Boston, Plays Inc., 1969).
The Do-Nothing Frog (published in *100 Plays for Children,* edited by A.S. Burack. Boston, Plays Inc., 1970).
The Invisible Dragon. Chicago, Dramatic Publishing, 1971.
A Specially Wonderful Day. Chicago, Encyclopedia Britannica Educational Corp., 1972.
The Toys Take over Christmas. Chicago, Dramatic Publishing, 1977.
Mudcake Princess. Chicago, Dramatic Publishing, 1979.
The Truly Remarkable Puss in Boots. Chicago, Dramatic Publishing, 1979.

Also author of several other plays, including *A Feather in His Cap, The Wonderful Door, A Wish Is for Keeping, Susan and Aladdin's Lamp, The Signpost, The Friendship Bracelet, Christmas in Old New England, The Straight Line from Somewhere, Yankee Doodle Came to Cranetown,* and *When Ecstasy Cost a Nickel,* published in *Instructor Magazine, Plays Magazine, Grade Teacher Magazine,* and *Yankee Magazine,* 1958-81.

Nonfiction

Dr. Elizabeth: The Story of the First Woman Doctor. New York, Lothrop, 1974.

PUBLICATIONS FOR CHILDREN

Fiction

King of the Dollhouse, illustrated by Judith Gwyn Brown. New York, Lothrop, 1974.

Poetry

Popsical Song. Chicago, Encyclopedia Britannica Education Corp., 1972.

PUBLICATIONS FOR ADULTS

Plays

A Candle on the Table. Boston, Baker, 1972.
The Retirement. Franklin, Ohio, Eldridge, 1972.

Other

Contributor, *Through the Eyes of a Child,* edited by Donna E. Norton. Merrill, 1983.

*

Media Adaptations: *I'm Deborah Sampson: A Soldier in the War of the Revolution* has been optioned for filming by Walt Disney Studios.

Biography: Entry in *Fifth Book of Junior Authors and Illustrators,* New York, H.W. Wilson, 1983; essay in *Something about the Author Autobiography Series,* Vol. 4, Detroit, Gale, 1987; essay in *Speaking for Ourselves, Too,* compiled and edited by Donald R. Gallo, National Council of Teachers of English, 1993.

Manuscript Collections: Kerlan Collection, University of Minnesota, Minneapolis; De Grummond Collection, University of Southern Mississippi, Hattiesburg.

*   *   *

Much of Patricia Clapp's work in adolescent literature was preceded by years of writing plays for children. Active in theatre herself, in her play writing she developed an ear for dialogue, speech, and allowing a character to tell his own story. This was training which was essential when Clapp turned to writing novels,

for as she considered the stories of her characters, she heard them speaking. The result is a series of novels which avoided the obtrusive narrator and focused instead on the interior life of the character.

In combining this approach with meticulous historical research, Clapp used a form of historical fiction that had the advantage of being both immediate and dramatic—a throwback to writing for the theatre. It also provided Clapp with a unique point of reference in her historical stories; she could tell of the madness of the Salem witch trials from inside, expressing all the ambiguity, misunderstanding, and fear that her protagonist must have felt in the real event. She can allow the reader to experience almost simultaneously the bombardment of Vicksburg with Rosemary Leigh by having her character record the events as they happen. In short, such a technique moves a reader to the inside of the action.

The result is a novel that is not objective; it is not meant to be. It is instead a highly subjective recording of historical events, a recording which recounts some of the reactions and perceptions of other characters but which always keeps the filtering, subjective vision of the protagonist at the forefront. In Constance, the young girl may first view Plymouth Colony with disdain, but it is clear that others do not share her perceptions. Even the reader sees that some of her observations are colored and her perceptions incorrect—or deliberately misleading. At times, Clapp allows the reader to see things that the writer is not aware of, such as the malice and manipulation of Abigail Williams that Mary Warren seems to dismiss or ignore before the witch craze swept through Salem.

For three of her works—*Constance, The Tamarack Tree,* and *Dr. Elizabeth: The Story of the First Woman Doctor*—Clapp used a journal or diary as the means of recording her character's thoughts. *Constance* began as a question after Clapp found the name of the fourteen-year-old girl in a chart of her husband's genealogy: What must it have been like for a young adolescent to be ripped from her comfortable home in London and set on a bleak, wintry, desolate shore in a new world? The conventional understanding is that the first settlers arrived with spirited enthusiasm, but Clapp posits another perspective. By allowing Constance to speak to the reader from the privacy of her journal, Clapp allows her character to speak with an honesty and forthrightness which may not have had another vent in the context of Plymouth; she allows readers to see a very different vision of the Plymouth colony.

In *The Tamarack Tree,* Rosemary keeps a journal during the siege of Vicksburg; she begins it as a kind of therapy: it will take her mind off the constant bombardment and the horrendous exigencies of a siege. But here again Clapp, in letting Rosemary speak in the privacy of the diary, allows for a freedom of thought and expression which Rosemary might not have found in besieged Vicksburg: she is able to oppose slavery with a vehemence and force which would have isolated her in the city. The result is a more ambiguous, mixed vision of life in the South during the 1860s.

In two novels—*I'm Deborah Sampson: A Soldier in the War of the Revolution* and *Witches' Children*—Clapp abandons the journal device and has her characters speak in the first person. There is a different kind of immediacy here. In *Constance* and *The Tamarack Tree,* the journal stands between the reader and writer; the primary audience of Constance and Rosemary is the journal itself, with the suggestion that this is not only a record of events but a way of coming to understand them. In *I'm Deborah Sampson* and *Witches' Children,* the characters speak without that barrier, and at times it lends them an urgency which is vivid and convincing. The confusion and ambiguity which Marry Warren feels, for example, lends a complexity to the action of the ''possessed'' girls which conventional historical accounts may not include. Years after the trials, in a voice still filled with the pain, terror, and guilt for her role in the deaths of neighbors and even one she loved, Mary speaks as one still trying to make sense of what happened, still trying to understand how a game became an obsession. The complexities that she feels suggest the complexities of history, which is not a neat bundle of dates and events in Clapp's vision, but instead a messy jumble of people who feel and act out of those feelings. Mary does not assign blame, though it is tempting for the reader to blame the other girls, or the insensitive and terrorized townspeople, or the stern and unyielding judges. But Clapp does not allow Mary to do this, with the result that the book ends in an ambiguity that Mary too must have felt.

I'm Deborah Sampson has a similarly strong voice, and it too is told from the perspective of years. Here there is less ambiguity, however. The book's title suggests the strength and assertiveness of Deborah, a woman who could pry a musket ball out of her own wound. The concluding line of the novel—''I'm Deborah Sampson. I'm strong and I'm free.''—is stated by the sixty-year-old character and attests to the union of the first person narrator with the thematic issue of freedom.

That affirmation of Deborah Sampson is linked to another large consideration in Clapp's first-person narratives: the growth of the young woman to adulthood. In each of these novels, and most especially in *Constance,* Clapp combines the story of a young woman in a familiar historical setting with the story of a young woman coming to understand and celebrate her femininity. Constance moves from flirtatious crushes to deep and abiding love, overcoming even the strong strictures of her society to find that love. Rosemary Leigh comes to accept, though perhaps reluctantly, the need that others feel to accept and fulfill certain roles, a need which she too feels. The characters' speculation about their time and their world are mixed together with their musings of what it is like to be an adolescent in this remarkable setting, and it is that combination more than anything else which makes Clapp's characters vivid and real. (Clapp's protagonists are in fact real historical persons, with the exception of Rosemary Leigh, whom Clapp invented and put into Vicksburg so that she might be able to articulate an outside perspective on slavery.)

Dr Elizabeth: The Story of the First Woman Doctor is Clapp's biography of Elizabeth Blackwell, who was the first woman to graduate in the United States with a medical degree. Here, too, she is concerned with letting her character speak for herself, and so she turns to the journal form once again. The device again yields new perspectives; Clapp could have written a straightforward biography of a woman fighting for women's rights against a monolithic medical structure, but in using the journal form one sees not just the women's rights champion but the real woman, who had doubts and fears and frustrations.

Clapp's two fantasies—*Jane-Emily* and *King of the Dollhouse*—are less interesting works, lacking the strong historical context which gives so much power to the works of historical fiction. *Jane-Emily* focuses on the young Jane, who becomes possessed by the evil spirit of her dead Aunt Emily; *King of the Dollhouse* is an episodic novel of a miniature kind which watches over eleven babies in a young girl's dollhouse. Neither shows a protagonist in a

moment of growth; neither is completely convincing in its narrative voice.

Clapp's strength comes from the voices that dominate her books. They may be voices that are at times petulant, loving, argumentative, resolved, angry, or fearful. But in crafting those voices, Clapp produces vivid characters who work out of their historical context and who make that historical context clear and dramatic for the reader.

—Gary D. Schmidt

CLARK, Mary Higgins

Nationality: American. **Born:** New York City, 24 December 1929. **Education:** Villa Maria Academy; Ward Secretarial School; New York University; Fordham University, Bronx, New York, B.A. (summa cum laude) 1979. **Family:** Married 1) Warren F. Clark in 1949 (died 1964); three daughters and two sons; 2) Raymond Charles Ploetz in 1978 (marriage annulled). **Career:** Writer. Advertising assistant, Remington Rand, New York, 1946; stewardess, Pan American Airlines, 1949-50; radio scriptwriter and producer for Robert G. Jennings, 1965-70; vice-president, partner, creative director, and producer of radio programming, Aerial Communications, New York City, 1970-80; chairman of the board and creative director, David J. Clark Enterprises, New York City, since 1980. Chairman, International Crime Writers Congress, 1988; president, Mystery Writers of America. **Awards:** New Jersey Author award, 1969, for *Aspire to the Heavens,* 1977, for *Where Are the Children?,* and 1978, for *A Stranger Is Watching;* Grand Prix de Litterature Policiere (France), 1980; honorary doctorate, Villanova University, 1983. **Address:** c/o Eugene H. Winick, McIntosh and Otis, 475 Fifth Ave., New York, New York 10017, U.S.A.

PUBLICATIONS

Novels

Where Are the Children? New York, Simon & Schuster, and London, Talmy Franklin, 1975.

A Stranger Is Watching. New York, Simon & Schuster, and London, Collins, 1978.

The Cradle Will Fall. New York, Simon & Schuster, and London, Collins, 1980.

A Cry in the Night. New York, Simon & Schuster, 1982; London, Collins, 1983.

Stillwatch. New York, Simon & Schuster, and London, Collins, 1984.

Missing in Manhattan, with Thomas Chastain and others. New York, Morrow, 1986.

Weep No More, My Lady. New York, Simon & Schuster, and London, Collins, 1987.

Caribbean Blues, with others. South Yarmouth, Massachusetts, J. Curley, 1988.

While My Pretty One Sleeps. New York, Simon & Schuster, and London, Century, 1989.

Loves Music, Loves to Dance. New York, Simon & Schuster, 1991.

All around the Town. New York, Simon & Schuster, 1992.

I'll Be Seeing You. New York, Simon & Schuster, 1993.
Remember Me. New York, Simon & Schuster, 1994.
The Lottery Winner: Alvirah and Willy Stories. New York, Simon & Schuster, 1994.
Let Me Call You Sweetheart: A Novel. New York, Simon & Schuster, 1995.
Mary Higgins Clark: Three New York Times Bestselling Novels (includes "While my Pretty One Sleeps," "Loves Music, Loves to Dance," "All around the Town"). New York, Wings Books, 1996.
Moonlight Becomes You: A Novel. New York, Simon & Schuster, 1996.
Silent Night: A Novel. New York, Simon & Schuster, 1995.
Pretend You Don't See Her: A Novel. New York, Simon & Schuster, 1997.

Short Stories

The Anastasia Syndrome and Other Stories. New York, Simon & Schuster, 1989; London, Century, 1990.
My Gal Sunday (includes "A Crime of Passion," "They All Ran after the President's Wife," "Hail, Columbia," "Merry Christmas/Joyeux Noel"). New York, Simon & Schuster, 1996.

Other

Aspire to the Heavens: A Biography of George Washington (for children). New York, Meredith Press, 1969.

Contributor, *I, Witness.* New York, Times Books, 1978.

Editor, *Murder on the Aisle: The 1987 Mystery Writers of America Anthology.* New York, Simon & Schuster, 1987.
Editor and author of introduction, *The International Association of Crime Writers Presents Bad Behavior.* San Diego, Harcourt Brace, 1995.

*

Media Adaptations: *A Stranger Is Watching* (film), Metro-Goldwyn-Mayer, 1982; *The Cradle Will Fall* ("Movie of the Week"), CBS, 1984; *A Cry in the Night* (film), Rosten Productions, 1985; *Where Are the Children?* (film), Columbia, 1986; *Stillwatch* (broadcast), CBS, 1987; *Weep No More My Lady,* Ellipse; *A Cry in the Night* (which will star Clark's daughter Carol), Ellipse; two stories from *The Anastasia Syndrome,* Ellipse.

*   *   *

A masterful and popular storyteller, Mary Higgins Clark intricately laces suspense through tightly woven storylines to pull readers into her stories. Her novels deal with ordinary people who are suddenly catapulted into terrifying circumstances. One moment they are changing bedclothes, or standing near the street as a funeral procession passes; the next they seem to be living their worst nightmares.

The plots Clark creates are complex, providing many twists and turns, barricading the solution to the mystery from both reader and characters. Clues in the form of subtle details are placed along the way. The reader becomes involved in figuring out who the adversary is and cheering the characters on when they head for the same conclusions. When dramatic irony is employed, the reader agonizes that the characters are led away from the malefactor. The reader's involvement in the story is intense and the storyline extraordinarily entertaining.

In Clark's first and one of her best-known novels, *Where Are the Children?,* Nancy twice falls victim to the same crime committed by the same man: her two children are abducted and abused. Clark depicts the kind of man who would keep his wife so drugged up that she must be cared for as if she were a helpless little girl. She shows us what type of man would kidnap and kill his own children and then haunt their mother with the same crime seven years later. Many of Clark's themes deal with mental disorders. Her research is apparent in the facts she weaves into her novels. The reader learns about multiple-personality disorders and manipulative criminals.

Clark's victims often have a friend or relative dedicated to seeing their adversary punished. This character is usually a very strong woman who puts a great deal of pressure on herself to help her loved one. At several points in the plot the reader will seize a clue that this character has overlooked.

Darcy is the strong friend in *Loves Music, Loves to Dance.* When her dear friend Erin is killed, possibly by someone who placed a personal ad she had answered, Darcy is determined to find the killer. To ease her pain, Darcy has donated some of Erin's belongings to a sixteen-year-old, bedridden girl. As she places one of Erin's posters on the girl's bedroom wall, Darcy can't help feeling she's missing a clue. "Darcy stepped back to be sure the poster was hanging straight. It was. Then what was gnawing at her? *The personal ads.* But why now? Shrugging, she closed her toolbox." The reader knows what Darcy is overlooking and longs to point this out to her.

The extensive research Clark executes for her novels is evident. She succeeds in getting into the heads of the criminals in her novels. In *Loves Music, Loves to Dance* it is clear to the reader that Charley is the murderer and a sort of alter personality. "A long time had passed. Charley had become a blurred memory, a shadowy figure lurking somewhere in the recesses of his mind, until two years ago. . . ." The reader also knows that Charley is posing as a friend. "The look he'd been waiting for came into Erin's eyes. That tiny first flicker of awareness that something wasn't quite right. She recognized the subtle change in his tone and manner." But the reader does not know which of the men Erin and Darcy date harbors the alter personality named Charley. Though the reader doesn't know who killed Erin, many different suspects are presented and the reader is involved in trying to determine who is guilty before the FBI does.

In *All around the Town,* the reader knows who is guilty. The suspense builds as the strong character uncovers clues to identify the guilty party and the reader fervently hopes she will find out in time to save the victim. *All around the Town* is about a girl named Laurie who is abducted at the age of four and returned to her family after two years. Years later, she is arrested for killing one of her college professors, but has no memory of this crime. Her older sister Sarah, a prosecuting attorney, begins to build a case to defend her. Sarah is the strong character determined to avenge her loved one's injury. The amount of pressure she places on herself is intense. During the time Laurie is missing, Sarah makes pacts with God that if Laurie is returned she will forever take care of her. Now, years later she must hold up her end of the bargain and defend her sister's innocence. "That night when Sarah settled in bed, she had the nagging feeling that something she should have noticed had escaped her attention."

The reader worries both about Sarah and about Laurie's innocence, the key to which lies in her memory of those years she had been abducted. Again suspense is built because the reader knows what the key is, but cannot jump into the story to rescue Laurie and Sarah.

Clark keeps the reader guessing as to her novels' resolutions and a surprise twist always occurs at the end of each. The reader never feels cheated by Clark's economical but informative and entertaining prose. The intensity of the suspense and the intricate weavings of the plot keep the reader turning the pages.

—Lisa A. Wroble

CLARKE, Arthur C(harles)

Pseudonyms: E. G. O'Brien; Charles Willis. **Nationality:** British. **Born:** Minehead, Somerset, 16 December 1917. **Education:** Huish's Grammar School, Taunton, Somerset, 1927-36; King's College, London, 1946-48, B.Sc. (honours) in physics and mathematics 1948. **Military Service:** Flight Lieutenant in the Royal Air Force, 1941-46; served as Radar Instructor, and Technical Officer on the first Ground Controlled Approach radar; originated proposal for use of satellites for communications, 1945. **Family:** Married Marilyn Mayfield in 1954 (divorced 1964). **Career:** Assistant auditor, Exchequer and Audit Department, London, 1936-41; assistant editor, *Physics Abstracts,* London, 1949-50; from 1954, engaged in underwater exploration and photography of the Great Barrier Reef of Australia and the coast of Sri Lanka. Director, Rocket Publishing, London, Underwater Safaris, Colombo, and the Spaceward Corporation, New York. Has made numerous radio and television appearances (most recently as presenter of the television series *Arthur C. Clarke's Mysterious World,* 1980, and *World of Strange Powers,* 1985), and has lectured widely in Britain and the United States; commentator, for CBS-TV, on lunar flights of Apollo 11, 12 and 15; Vikram Sarabhai Professor, Physical Research Laboratory, Ahmedabad, India, 1980; acted role of Leonard Woolf in the film *Beddagama* ("The Village in the Jungle"), 1979. **Awards:** International Fantasy award, 1952, for *The Exploration of Space*; Hugo award, 1956, for "The Star"; Kalinga prize, 1961; Junior Book award, Boy's Club of America, 1961, for *The Challenge of the Sea*; Franklin Institute Ballantine Medal, 1963, for originating concept of communications satellites; Aviation-Space Writers Association Ball award, 1965, for best aerospace reporting of the year in any medium; American Association for the Advancement of Science-Westinghouse Science Writing award, 1969; Hugo award, Second International Film Festival special award, and Academy of Motion Picture Arts and Sciences award nomination, 1969, all for *2001: A Space Odyssey*; *Playboy* editorial award, 1971, 1982; Nebula award, 1972, for "A Meeting with Medusa"; Nebula award, 1973, Jupiter award, 1973, John W. Campbell

Memorial award, 1974, and Hugo award, 1974, all for *Rendezvous with Rama*; American Institute of Aeronautics and Astronautics award, 1974; Boston Museum of Science Washburn award, 1977, for "contributions to the public understanding of science"; GALAXY award, 1979; Nebula and Hugo awards, 1980, both for *The Fountains of Paradise*; National Academy of Television Arts and Sciences Emmy award, 1981, for contributions to satellite broadcasting; "Lensman" award, 1982; Marconi International Fellowship, 1982; Institute of Electrical and Electronics Engineers Centennial medal, 1984; American Astronautical Society E. M. Emme Astronautical Literature award, 1984; Science Fiction Writers of America Grand Master award, 1986; Vidya Jyothi medal, 1986; Charles A. Lindbergh award, 1987; named to Society of Satellite Professionals Hall of Fame, 1987; named to Aerospace Hall of Fame, 1988; Association of Space Explorers (Riyadh) Special Achievement award, 1989; C.B.E. (Commander, Order of the British Empire), 1989; Lord Perry Award for Distance Education, 1992; nominated for Nobel Peace Prize, 1994; NASA's Distinguished Public Service Award, 1995; BIS Space Achievement Medal and Trophy, 1995; International Academy of Astronautics' von Karman Award, 1996. D.Sc., Beaver College, Glenside, Pennsylvania, 1971; D.Litt., University of Bath, 1988; University of Liverpool, 1995. **Address:** "Leslie's House," 25 Barnes Place, Colombo 7, Sri Lanka; c/o Rocket Publishing Co. Ltd., Dene Court, Dene Road, Bishops Lydead, Taunton, Somerset TA4 3LT, England.

PUBLICATIONS

Novels

Prelude to Space. New York, Galaxy, 1951; London, Sidgwick and Jackson, 1953; as *Master of Space,* New York, Lancer, 1961; as *The Space Dreamers,* New York, Lancer, 1969.

The Sands of Mars. London, Sidgwick and Jackson, 1951; New York, Gnome Press, 1952.

Against the Fall of Night. New York, Gnome Press, 1953; revised edition, as *The City and the Stars,* London, Muller, and New York, Harcourt Brace, 1956.

Childhood's End. New York, Ballantine, 1953; London, Sidgwick and Jackson, 1954.

Earthlight. London, Muller, and New York, Ballantine, 1955.

The Deep Range. New York, Harcourt Brace, and London, Muller, 1957.

A Fall of Moondust. London, Gollancz, and New York, Harcourt Brace, 1961.

Glide Path. New York, Harcourt Brace, 1963; London, Sidgwick and Jackson, 1969.

2001: A Space Odyssey (novelization of screenplay). New York, New American Library, and London, Hutchinson, 1968.

Rendezvous with Rama. London, Gollancz, and New York, Harcourt Brace, 1973.

Imperial Earth: A Fantasy of Love and Discord. London, Gollancz, 1975; New York, Harcourt Brace, 1976.

The Fountains of Paradise. London, Gollancz, and New York, Harcourt Brace, 1979.

2010: Odyssey Two. New York, Ballantine, and London, Granada, 1982.

The Songs of Distant Earth. London, Grafton, and New York, Ballantine, 1986.

With Gentry Lee, *Cradle.* London, Gollancz, and New York, Warner, 1988.

2061: Odyssey Three. New York, Ballantine, and London, Grafton, 1988.

With Gentry Lee, *Rama II.* London, Gollancz, and New York, Bantam, 1989.

With Gregory Benford, *Beyond the Fall of Night.* New York, Putnam, 1990; with *Against the Fall of Night,* London, Gollancz, 1991.

The Ghost from the Grand Banks. New York, Bantam, and London, Gollancz, 1990.

With Gentry Lee, *The Garden of Rama.* London, Gollancz, and New York, Bantam, 1991.

With Gentry Lee, *Rama Revealed.* London, Gollancz, and New York, Bantam, 1993.

The Hammer of God. New York, Bantam, 1993.

With Mike McQuay, *Richter 10.* London, Vista, 1996.

3001: The Final Odyssey. New York, Ballantine, 1997.

Short Stories

Expedition to Earth. New York, Ballantine, 1953; London, Sidgwick and Jackson, 1954.

Reach for Tomorrow. New York, Ballantine, 1956; London, Gollancz, 1962.

Tales from the White Hart. New York, Ballantine, 1957; London, Sidgwick and Jackson, 1972.

The Other Side of the Sky. New York, Harcourt Brace, 1958; London, Gollancz, 1961.

Tales of Ten Worlds. New York, Harcourt Brace, 1962; London, Gollancz, 1963.

The Nine Billion Names of God: The Best Short Stories of Arthur C. Clarke. New York, Harcourt Brace, 1967.

Of Time and Stars: The Worlds of Arthur C. Clarke. London, Gollancz, 1972.

The Wind from the Sun: Stories of the Space Age. New York, Harcourt Brace, and London, Gollancz, 1972.

The Best of Arthur C. Clarke, 1937-1971, edited by Angus Wells. London, Sidgwick and Jackson, 1973.

The Sentinel: Masterworks of Science Fiction and Fantasy. New York, Berkley, 1983; London, Panther, 1985.

A Meeting with Medusa (published with *Green Mars,* by Kim Stanley Robinson). New York, Tor, 1988.

Dilemmas: The Secret (with *Flowers for Algernon,* by Daniel Keyes). New York, Houghton Mifflin, 1989.

Tales from Planet Earth. London, Century, 1989; New York, Bantam, 1990.

I Remember Babylon and Other Stories. Mattituck, New York, Amereon, n.d.

The Possessed and Other Stories. Mattituck, New York, Amereon, n.d.

Plays

With Stanley Kubrick, *2001: A Space Odyssey* (screenplay), 1968.

Arthur C. Clarke's Mysterious World (television series). Yorkshire Television, 1980; with Simon Welfare and John Fairley, A and W Publishers, 1980.

Arthur C. Clarke's World of Strange Powers (television series). ITV, 1984; with Simon Welfare and John Fairley, New York, Putnam, 1984.

Nonfiction

Interplanetary Flight: An Introduction to Astronautics. London, Temple Press, 1950; New York, Harper, 1951; revised edition, 1960.

The Exploration of Space. London, Temple Press, and New York, Harper, 1951, revised edition, 1959; revised edition, New York, Pocket Books, 1979.

The Exploration of the Moon, illustrated by R. A. Smith. London, Muller, 1954; New York, Harper, 1955.

The Young Traveller in Space (for children). London, Phoenix House, 1954; as *Going into Space,* New York, Harper, 1954; as *The Scottie Book of Space Travel,* London, Transworld, 1957; revised edition, with Robert Silverberg, as *Into Space: A Young Person's Guide to Space,* New York, Harper, 1971.

The Coast of Coral. London, Muller, and New York, Harper, 1956.

The Making of a Moon: The Story of the Earth Satellite Program. London, Muller, and New York, Harper, 1957; revised edition, New York, Harper, 1958.

The Reefs of Taprobane: Underwater Adventures Around Ceylon. London, Muller, and New York, Harper, 1957.

With Mike Wilson, *Boy Beneath the Sea* (for children). New York, Harper, 1958.

Voice across the Sea. London, Muller, 1958; New York, Harper, 1959; revised edition, London, Mitchell Beazley, and Harper, 1974.

The Challenge of the Spaceship: Previews of Tomorrow's World. New York, Harper, 1959; London, Muller, 1960.

The Challenge of the Sea. New York, Holt Rinehart, 1960; London, Muller, 1961.

With Mike Wilson, *The First Five Fathoms: A Guide to Underwater Adventure.* New York, Harper, 1960.

With Mike Wilson, *Indian Ocean Adventure.* New York, Harper, 1961; London, Barker, 1962.

Profiles of the Future: An Inquiry into the Limits of the Possible. London, Gollancz, 1962; New York, Harper, 1963; revised edition, New York, Harper, 1973; London, Gollancz, 1974, 1982; New York, Holt Rinehart, 1984.

With Mike Wilson, *Indian Ocean Treasure.* New York, Harper, 1964; London, Sidgwick and Jackson, 1972.

With the editors of *Life, Man and Space.* New York, Time, 1964.

The Treasure of the Great Reef. London, Barker, and New York, Harper, 1964; revised edition, New York, Ballantine, 1974.

Voices from the Sky: Previews of the Coming Space Age. New York, Harper, 1965; London, Gollancz, 1966.

The Promise of Space. New York, Harper, and London, Hodder and Stoughton, 1968.

With Neil Armstrong, Michael Collins, Edwin E. Aldrin, Jr., Gene Farmer, and Dora Jane Hamblin, *First on the Moon.* London, Joseph, and Boston, Little Brown, 1970.

With Chesley Bonestell, *Beyond Jupiter: The Worlds of Tomorrow.* Boston, Little Brown, 1972.

The Lost Worlds of 2001. New York, New American Library, and London, Sidgwick and Jackson, 1972.

Report on Planet Three and Other Speculations. London, Gollancz, and New York, Harper, 1972.

The View from Serendip (on Sri Lanka). New York, Random House, 1977; London, Gollancz, 1978.

Ascent to Orbit: A Scientific Autobiography: The Technical Writings of Arthur C. Clarke. New York and Chichester, Sussex, Wiley, 1984.

1984: Spring: A Choice of Futures. New York, Ballantine, and London, Granada, 1984.

With Peter Hyams, *The Odyssey File.* New York, Ballantine, and London, Granada, 1985.

Astounding Days: A Science Fictional Autobiography. London, Gollancz, 1989; New York, Bantam, 1990.

Other

Islands in the Sky (for children). London, Sidgwick and Jackson, and Philadelphia, Winston, 1952; revised edition, Penguin, 1972.

Across the Sea of Stars. New York, Harcourt Brace, 1959.

From the Oceans, From the Stars. New York, Harcourt Brace, 1962.

Dolphin Island: A Story of the People of the Sea (for children). New York, Holt Rinehart, and London, Gollancz, 1963.

An Arthur C. Clarke Omnibus. London, Sidgwick and Jackson, 1965.

Prelude to Mars. New York, Harcourt Brace, 1965.

Editor, *Time Probe: The Science in Science Fiction.* New York, Delacorte Press, 1966; London, Gollancz, 1967.

Editor, *The Coming of the Space Age: Famous Accounts of Man's Probing of the Universe.* London, Gollancz, and New York, Meredith, 1967.

The Lion of Comarre, and Against the Fall of Night. New York, Harcourt Brace, 1968; London, Gollancz, 1970.

A Second Arthur C. Clarke Omnibus. London, Sidgwick and Jackson, 1968.

Editor, *Three for Tomorrow.* Sphere, 1972.

Contributor, *Mars and the Mind of Man.* New York, Harper, 1973.

With others, *Technology and the Frontiers of Knowledge* (lectures). New York, Doubleday, 1973.

Four Great Science Fiction Novels. London, Gollancz, 1978.

Editor, with George Proctor, *The Science Fiction Hall of Fame 3: The Nebula Winners 1965-1969.* New York, Avon, 1982.

Selected Works. London, Heinemann, 1985.

Editor, *July 20, 2019: A Day in the Life of the 21st Century.* New York, Macmillan, 1986; London, Grafton, 1987.

Arthur C. Clarke's Chronicles of the Strange and Mysterious, edited by Simon Welfare and John Fairley. San Francisco, Collins, 1987.

Editor, *Project Solar Sail.* New York, Penguin, 1990.

How the World Was One: Towards the Tele-family of Man. New York, Bantam, and London, Gollancz, 1992.

The Hammer of God. New York, Bantam, 1993.

How the World Was One: The Turbulent History of Global Communications. London, Gollancz, 1993.

With Simon Welfare and John Fairley, *Arthur C. Clarke's A-Z of Mysteries: From Atlantis to Zombies.* London, HarperCollins, 1994.

Also author of introduction to *No Place Too Far;* of afterwords to Paul Preuss's *Venus Prime,* Volumes 1-6, Avon, 1988-91; of a movie treatment based on *Cradle;* contributor of over six hundred articles and short stories, occasionally under pseudonyms E. G. O'Brien and Charles Willis, to numerous magazines, including *Harper's, Playboy, New York Times Magazine, Vogue, Holiday,* and *Horizon.*

*

Media Adaptations: *A Fall of Moondust* (recording), Harcourt, 1976; *Arthur C. Clarke Reads from his 2001: A Space Odyssey* (recording), Caedmon, 1976; *The Nine Billion Names of God* (recording), Caedmon, 1978; *The Star* (recording), Caedmon, 1978; *Transit of Earth* (recording), Caedmon, 1978; *Childhood's End* (recording), 1979; *The Fountains of Paradise* (recording), Caedmon, 1979; *2010: Odyssey Two* (recording), Caedmon, 1983; *2010* (film, directed by Peter Hyams), MGM, 1984; *The Star* (television movie), CBS-TV, 1985; *The Snows of Olympus: A Garden on Mars* (computer simulation), HarperCollins, 1994; *The Arthur C. Clarke Audio Collection* (recording), Caedmon, 1995; *Childhood's End, The Songs of Distant Earth, The Fountains of Paradise,* and *Cradle* have all been optioned for films.

Biography: Essay in *Authors and Artists for Young Adults,* Volume 4, Detroit, Gale, 1990; *Arthur C. Clarke: The Authorized Biography* by Neil McAleer, Chicago, Contemporary Books, 1992.

Bibliography: *Arthur C. Clarke: A Primary and Secondary Bibliography* by David N. Samuelson, Boston, Hall, 1984.

Manuscript Collections: Mugar Memorial Library, Boston University.

Critical Studies: Entry in *Contemporary Literary Criticism,* Volume 1, Detroit, Gale, 1973, Volume 4, 1975, Volume 13, 1980, Volume 16, 1981, Volume 18, 1981, Volume 35, 1985; *Arthur C. Clarke* edited by Joseph D. Olander and Martin H. Greenberg, New York, Taplinger, and Edinburgh, Harris, 1977; *The Space Odysseys of Arthur C. Clarke* by George Edgar Slusser, San Bernardino, California, Borgo Press, 1978; *Arthur C. Clarke* (includes bibliography) by Eric S. Rabkin, West Linn, Oregon, Starmont House, 1979, revised edition, 1980; *Against the Night, The Stars: The Science Fiction of Arthur C. Clarke* by John Hollow, New York, Harcourt Brace, 1983, revised edition, Athens, Ohio University Press-Swallow Press, 1987; *Clarke's Odysseys* by Peter Stockill, London, Teesside Writers' Workshop, 1990; *Arthur C. Clarke: A Critical Companion* by Robin Anne Reid, Westport, Connecticut, Greenwood Press, 1997.

*   *   *

As the only novelist to win science fiction's coveted quartet— the Hugo, Nebula, Campbell, and Jupiter awards—for one work, *Rendezvous with Rama,* and as the co-creator of one of the more widely influential films of the twentieth century, *2001: A Space Odyssey,* Arthur C. Clarke is one of the most prophetic and significant writers in his chosen genre. Apart from his literary endeavors, however, Clarke may best be remembered as the inventor of the communication satellite, an idea he first expounded in a 1945 article entitled ''Extraterrestrial Relays.'' Although Clarke writes mostly fiction, he has written several nonfiction books, including the book that first brought him national attention, *The Exploration of Space.* It is Clarke's emphasis on science fiction, however, that allows his writing to transcend conventional age barriers. It is easy to note that he focuses within his vast body of work on two simple themes: spiritualism and technology. A study of these aspects and their relationship with each other reveals the traits and methods which make up Clarke's writing.

The aspect of "spiritualism" is an important one to Clarke as he feels that the search for man's place in the universe is humankind's fundamental quest. This quest takes many forms throughout Clarke's prose but the most prevalent is the Phoenix-like rebirth of childhood. This "spiritual" rebirth may appear as either a physical or a psychological entity but, regardless of the manifestation, Clarke commonly conceives it with the aid of technology.

Since his background is in science and mathematics, Clarke's infatuation with technology is considerable. The scientific details of his writing are lavishly illustrated, and at times Clarke may even seem preoccupied with the science of his fiction. But Clarke's description of technology is flawless; he pays particular attention to minute aspects and in doing so promotes realism. The "tech-speak" Clarke uses allows the fictional worlds he creates to function not as mere settings but almost as characters unto themselves. This literal-minded utilization of technology coupled with the "spiritual" quest is the crux on which Clarke's writing is based.

Clarke's greatest literary success, *Rendezvous with Rama,* also functions as an excellent example of his blend of spiritualism and technology. The novel chronicles the attempts of a research team sent to investigate a cylindrical object hurtling through the solar system. The UFO is given the name "Rama" and is eventually discovered to be an alien ship, although its crew has long since vanished. As the research team searches for clues to Rama's purpose and origin, they function as an allegory for the human need to question the meaning of life, bringing into play Clarke's spiritual quest. The depiction of Rama is beautifully achieved, making the mystery and elusiveness of the ship's purpose all the more alluring.

In both its effect and scope, Clarke's cinematic collaboration with Stanley Kubrick, *2001: A Space Odyssey,* often considered the greatest modern science fiction film, stands as his masterpiece. Although novels such as *Childhood's End* and *Rendezvous with Rama* have garnered more literary praise than *2001,* it remains the title most associated with Clarke. With its heavy reliance on technology and the inclusion of a healthy dose of Clarke's spiritual quest, *2001* is also emblematic of his writing overall. The plot and structure are similarly indicative of Clarke's other novels, thus providing a glimpse of Clarke's intent in the whole of his work.

Both the film and novel versions of *2001: A Space Odyssey* began when Kubrick contacted Clarke and proposed the idea of making the "proverbial good science fiction movie." Intrigued by the concept, Clarke began proposing possible plots; the pair eventually agreed on Clarke's 1951 short story "The Sentinel" as the basis for the film. The process of writing *2001* was a unique one, whereas the novelization was written in lieu of a script, thus binding the two works inextricably together. A short while after the film came out, the novelization was released; despite being written in tandem, the two works differ in certain respects, most notably in the film's negation of explanatory dialogue which is replaced by Kubrick's stunning visuals, whereas in the novel Clarke's "tech-speak" is ever-present. Throughout the writing process the original story changed dramatically, and although the film bears little resemblance to "The Sentinel," the gist of Clarke's "spiritual" message is still intact.

Episodic in construction, *2001* is the chronicle of man's first contact with sentient life, other than that found on earth. In the first section of the film, appropriately titled "The Dawn of Man," the concept of the monolith is introduced. Apes, arduously beginning the process of evolution, are hungrily grazing about a barren wasteland; they have not learned to hunt and are merely foragers, when they come across a giant black slab from which an ear-piercing sound is emanating. One of the apes is taught, presumably by the monolith, to use an elongated piece of bone as a tool, and later as a weapon. Thus the apes are forcefully nudged into evolution.

The film then progresses to the next stage in man's development in the year 2001, when another monolith is found, this time buried beneath the surface of the moon. When it is touched, it produces the same sound the apes had heard, except that the sound is now being directed towards Jupiter (another discrepancy between novel and film encroaches here, as the book substitutes Saturn for Jupiter). The next section of the film, "Jupiter Mission: 18 Months Later," chronicles two astronauts, Frank Poole and David Bowman, as they pilot their ship with the help of the super-computer HAL 9000 towards Jupiter, where the remaining members of the crew will be taken out of suspended animation and they will all be told the mission's objective. Subsequent malfunctions and accidents leave Bowman alone as the ship reaches Jupiter and he embarks on the final step in humankind's next developmental stage.

Through the monolith and Bowman's physical transformation, a tangible voice is given to Clarke's notion of the "spiritual" nature of humanity, and the quest for a metaphysical section of the universe to call humanity's own is the essence of Clarke's writing. The constant questioning of the bounds of the known is what makes Clarke's written journeys enthralling. In *2001,* although co-writing credit must be given to Kubrick, mainly for the visual impact of the film version and not the novelization, Clarke deftly conveys his fascination of "tech-speak" and his obsession with "spiritualism," making it a fine example of his literary genius.

Subsequent novels—*2010: Odyssey Two, 2061: Odyssey Three,* and *3001: The Final Odyssey*—extend Clarke's depiction of humanity's quest for answers to questions about the power behind the third monolith. The progressive accumulation of technological knowledge and experience across the millennium from 2001 to 3001 allows for the resurrection of Frank Poole in *3001.* Poole's connection with the first odyssey a thousand years earlier allows communication with Halman, an entity which encompasses the awarenesses of Bowman, the wisdom of Heywood Floyd (the protagonist of *2010* and *2061*), and the technology of HAL. This entity becomes the guardian of human interest in matters concerning the monolith. Through Frank Poole, humanity eventually reaps the benefit of Halman's thousand-year relationship with the monolith. Clarke's odysseys continue to merge the "tech-speak" with the "spiritual" as the writer explores the challenges facing humanity in its struggle for survival, a struggle which, as Clarke writes it, engages the intellect and the spirit to the fullest extent of each. Clarke tempers his largely optimistic stance that humans possess the qualities which will allow them to combine the elements of technological progress and spiritual growth with the implication that they must, lest they be found wanting when cosmic balances are finally weighed.

—Michael J. Tyrkus, updated by Linda Benson

CLEAVER, (Leroy) Eldridge

Nationality: American. **Born:** Wabbaseka, Arkansas, 31 August 1935. **Education:** junior college; also educated in Soledad Prison. **Family:** Married Kathleen Neal in 1967; one daughter and one son. **Career:** Prisoner at Soledad Prison, 1954-57, 1958-66; assistant editor and contributing writer, *Ramparts,* San Francisco, California, 1966-68; minister of information, Black Panther Party, Oakland, California, 1967-71; presidential candidate, Peace and Freedom Party, 1968; in exile in Cuba, Algeria, and France, 1968-75; owner of boutique in Hollywood, California, 1978-79; founder of Eldridge Cleaver Crusades, 1979; independent candidate for Congress in 8th Congressional District, California, 1984; contributor to *Commonweal, National Review,* and other periodicals. Lecturer at universities. **Awards:** Martin Luther King Memorial Prize, 1970, for *Soul on Ice.* **Died:** 3 May 1998 in Pomona, California.

PUBLICATIONS

Nonfiction

Soul on Ice, introduction by Maxwell Geismar. New York, McGraw, 1968.
Eldridge Cleaver: Post-Prison Writings and Speeches, edited by Robert Scheer. New York, Random House, 1969.
Eldridge Cleaver's Black Papers. New York, McGraw, 1969.
Author of introduction, *Do It!,* by Jerry Rubin. New York, Simon and Schuster, 1970.
Revolution in the Congo, with others. London, Revolutionary People's Communications Network, 1971.
Contributor, *The Black Panther Leaders Speak: Huey P. Newton, Bobby Seale, Eldridge Cleaver, and Company Speak Out through the Black Panther Party's Official Newspaper,* edited by G. Louis Heath. Metuchen, New Jersey, Scarecrow, 1976.
Soul on Fire. Waco, Texas, Word, 1978.

Also author, with others, of *War Within: Violence or Non-violence in Black Revolution,* 1971, of *Education and Revolution,* Center for Educational Reform, and of pamphlets for the Black Panther Party and People's Communication Network. Work appears in anthologies, including *Prize Stories, 1971: The O. Henry Awards.*

*

Critical Studies: Entry in *Contemporary Literary Criticism,* Vol. 30, Detroit, Gale, 1984.

*   *   *

Anger, outrage, the raw energy of the 1960s: these are the forces that burst from the pages of Eldridge Cleaver's *Soul on Ice,* a work widely popular among young adults during this time of social upheaval and civil-rights awareness. Published in 1968, this is not a series of somber disquisitions by a man in academic regalia. Quite the contrary. Here is a street-wise black, a man who has spent most of his adult life in California prisons, shouting into the faces of white Americans and telling them that a social revolution is at hand. No one doubts Cleaver's conviction, even if his literary credentials are unconventional.

Perhaps as much as anything, *Soul on Ice* has an odor—an odor of sweat, mean streets, sex, darkness, and blood. These are the qualities that triumph over Cleaver's uneven style. At times he is too learned, pedantic even, as if in compensation for his lack of formal education. In this mode he comments on the "man whose soul or emotional apparatus had lain dormant in a deadening limbo of desuetude. . . ." At the other extreme, he errs in using the sassy harangue, as when he calls the public opinion makers "a lot of coffee-drinking, cigarette-smoking, sly, suck-assing, status-seeking, cheating, nervous, dry-balled, tranquillizer-gulched, countdown-minded, out-of-style, slithering snakes." At its best, though, Cleaver's style is stark, indisputable. "I became a rapist," he matter-of-factly states in his first section. And later, " . . . I started to write. To save myself."

Loosely divided into four sections, *Soul on Ice* begins with "Letters from Prison," an account of Cleaver's life behind bars, his conversion to the Muslim religion, and his devotion to Malcolm X. Throughout this section, one experiences the routine, the boredom, the hopes, and the politics of prison life. The second section, "Blood of the Beast," argues that dissatisfaction among American Negroes is part of a worldwide revolutionary spirit. Cleaver insists that black Americans should not participate in the Vietnam War; only "fools . . . go to another country to fight for something they don't have for themselves." The third section houses a series of poignant letters between Cleaver and his attorney, Beverly Axelrod, who ultimately rallies enough public support to gain the writer parole. "White Woman, Black Man," the book's final section, may be its least convincing intellectually, but its most powerful emotionally. What Cleaver grapples with is the enigma of myth itself, in this case the myth of the Black Man as all body, White Man as all mind; Black Woman as fecund domestic, White Woman as dream maiden. Cleaver ends with an endorsement of love—whether generalized in the form of brotherhood or particularized in the form of miscegenation—as the only solution to class conflict, the same conclusion that has been argued for Malcolm X.

Eldridge Cleaver: Post-Prison Writings and Speeches, edited by Robert Scheer and published in 1969, is less satisfying than *Soul on Ice.* From a literary perspective the essays show little craftsmanship, much anger, and a penchant for obscene grandstanding, as in the writer's famous four-letter response to then-governor of California Ronald Reagan. The reader should realize, however, that following Cleaver's release from prison in 1966, he fell under the influence of Huey P. Newton and joined the Black Panther Party, an organization which operated free lunch programs for some inner-city children but which also advocated "total liberty for black people or total destruction for America." Cleaver became the Panthers' Minister of Information and frequently found himself embroiled in disputes with the police and FBI, even as he was giving lectures on college campuses. Then in 1968, he was wounded in a gunfight between the Panthers and the Oakland, California, police. A curious charge of assault and attempted murder was followed by an outpouring of support from around the world. During this same period, the Peace and Freedom Party nominated Eldridge Cleaver to be their candidate for President of the United

States. But Cleaver feared for his life. He had a solid defense against the Oakland indictments, but given the hostility and paranoia of the times, he doubted that he would survive another confinement. Someone would arrange to have him killed. He decided to jump bail and leave the country, a man on the run.

For the next seven years, Eldridge Cleaver visited such communist countries as Cuba, North Vietnam, China, and the Soviet Union, and lived more permanently in Algeria and France. Initially, he was regarded as a revolutionary hero, a spokesman for the disenfranchised blacks of the world. As the years passed, however, he became increasingly disillusioned with the communism he saw actually being practiced. Suicide was never far from his mind. Then he had a Christian mystical experience. *Soul on Fire,* published in 1978, is Cleaver's autobiography of his exile. The book concludes with his return to the United States, where a possible prison sentence is reduced to twelve hundred hours of community service.

From 1975 until his death in 1998 at age 62, Eldridge Cleaver was an active lecturer at universities and churches, telling the story of his life. His message was that secular zeal is not incompatible with religious zeal. *Soul on Fire* is neither as incendiary nor as immediate as *Soul on Ice,* and yet to those who would charge him with selling out his earlier principles, Cleaver wrote that "communism had nothing to offer me but another chapter in tyranny." His more careful followers remember that love is an essential focal point in *Soul on Ice.* Cleaver the Muslim and Cleaver the Christian meet at that point.

—Walker Rutledge

CLEAVER, Vera and Bill

Nationality: Americans. **Vera Cleaver (née Allen): Born:** Virgil, South Dakota, 6 January 1919. **Education:** schools in Kennebec, South Dakota, and Perry and Tallahassee, Florida. **Family:** Married Bill Cleaver in 1945. Free-lance accountant, 1945-54; accountant (civilian), United States Air Force, Tachikawa, Japan, 1954-56, and Chaumont, France, 1956-58. **Died:** 11 August 1992. **Bill Cleaver (William Joseph Cleaver): Born:** Hugo, Ohio, 24 March 1920. **Education:** schools in Vancouver, British Columbia, and Seattle, WA. **Military Service:** Served in the United States Army Air Corps, in Italy, 1942-45; United States Air Force, in Japan, 1954-56, and in France, 1956-58. Jeweler and watchmaker, 1950-54. **Died:** 20 August 1981. **Awards:** (Vera Cleaver) Children's Choice Award, 1986, for *Sweetly Sings the Donkey;.* (Vera and Bill Cleaver) Recipients: *Horn Book* Honor List, 1967, for *Ellen Grae; Horn Book* Honor List, 1969, American Library Association (ALA) notable book, 1970, Newbery Honor Book, and National Book award nomination, all for *Where the Lilies Bloom;* National Book award nomination, 1971, for *Grover; New York Times* outstanding book, ALA notable book, 1973, for *Me Too;* National Book award nomination, 1974, all for *The Whys and Wherefores of Littabelle Lee;* Golden Spur award, Western Writers of America, and Lewis Carroll Bookshelf award, and *New York Times* outstanding book citation, all 1975, all for *Dust of the Earth;* Western Writers of America Spur award, 1976. National Book award nomination, 1979, for *Queen of Hearts.*

PUBLICATIONS FOR YOUNG ADULTS

Fiction

Ellen Grae, illustrated by Ellen Raskin. Philadelphia, Lippincott, 1967; with *Lady Ellen Grae,* London, Hamish Hamilton, 1973.
Lady Ellen Grae, illustrated by E. Raskin, Philadelphia, Lippincott, 1968; with *Ellen Grae,* London, Hamish Hamilton, 1973.
Where the Lilies Bloom, illustrated by Jim Spanfeller. Philadelphia, Lippincott, 1969; London, Hamish Hamilton, 1970.
Grover, illustrated by Frederic Marvin. Philadelphia, Lippincott, 1970; London, Hamish Hamilton, 1971.
The Mimosa Tree. Philadelphia, Lippincott, 1970; London, Oxford University Press, 1977.
I Would Rather Be a Turnip. Philadelphia, Lippincott, 1971; London, Hamish Hamilton, 1972.
The Mock Revolt. Philadelphia, Lippincott, 1971; London, Hamish Hamilton, 1972.
Delpha Green and Company. Philadelphia, Lippincott, 1972; London, Collins, 1975.
Me Too. Philadelphia, Lippincott, 1973; London, Collins, 1975.
The Whys and Wherefores of Littabelle Lee. New York, Atheneum, 1973; Hamish Hamilton, 1974.
Dust of the Earth. Philadelphia, Lippincott, 1975; London, Oxford University Press, 1977.
Trial Valley. Philadelphia, Lippincott, and London, Oxford University Press, 1977.
Queen of Hearts. Philadelphia, Lippincott, 1978.
A Little Destiny. New York, Lothrop, 1979.
The Kissimmee Kid. New York, Lothrop, 1981.
Hazel Rye. New York, Lippincott, 1983.

Fiction by Vera Cleaver

Sugar Blue, illustrated by Eric Nones. New York, Lothrop, 1984.
Sweetly Sings the Donkey. New York, Lippincott, 1985.
Moon Lake Angel. New York, Lothrop, 1987.
Belle Pruitt. New York, Lippincott, 1988.

PUBLICATION FOR ADULTS by Vera Cleaver

Novel

The Nurse's Dilemma. New York, Bouregy, 1966.

*

Media Adaptations: *Where the Lilies Bloom* (film), United Artists, 1974.

Manuscript Collections: Kerlan Collection, University of Minnesota, Minneapolis; University of North Carolina, Chapel Hill.

Illustrator (Bill Cleaver): *Follow the Zookeeper* by Patricia Relf, 1984; *The Case of the Missing Mother* by James Howe, 1983.

Biography: Entry in *Dictionary of Literary Biography,* Detroit, Gale, Volume 52: *American Writers for Children since 1960: Fiction* by Jane Harper Yarbrough. Detroit, Gale, 1986, pp. 91-97.

Critical Study: Entry in *Children's Literature Review,* Volume 6. Detroit, Gale, 1984.

*   *   *

Together Vera and Bill Cleaver are known for their novels for young adults readers on contemporary themes that are full of humor, imagination, and a zest for life. After Bill Cleaver's death, Vera Cleaver continued to write books that have strong characters, rural and largely poverty-stricken settings, and real family groups.

The Cleavers' first book, *Ellen Grae,* was an immediate success. Eleven-year-old Ellen Grae is the sort of girl who takes off her starched petticoat after she gets to school and stuffs it in her desk because she doesn't like scratchy things. She lives with Mr. and Mrs. McGruder outside the village of Thicket because her mother and father are divorced. Ellen Grae has a special friend in Ira, a gentle person who lives with his pet goat Missouri in a tin shack by the river. Ira sells boiled and parched peanuts for a living and cannot seem to talk to anyone but Ellen Grae. When Ira tells Ellen Grae a violent secret of his childhood, she is faced with a real dilemma. Telling that secret will get Ira in terrible trouble. The young girl's sense of compassion and her sense of justice are beautifully described, and the outcome in a small compassionate community is a just one.

A courageous and strong fourteen-year-old girl struggles to preserve the dignity and independence of her family after the death of her parents, in *Where the Lilies Bloom.* Set in the Great Smoky Mountains of North Carolina—land described in an old hymn as "Where the Lilies Bloom So Fair"—it tells the story of human resourcefulness against the harshness of poverty and isolation. Mary Call, after burying her second parent in a tender, homemade service, must conceal his death from those who would send the four children to the county home. She also cares for a developmentally disabled older sister, goes to school, and supports the family. She does the latter by "wildcrafting," gathering medicinal plants and herbs on the slopes of the Great Smokies and selling them to pharmaceutical companies. The difficult and exhausting work provides a fair living and a unique education for a family. This gentle tale of adversity and love celebrates life.

The Mock Revolt is set in the town of Medina, Florida, and features thirteen-year old Ussy Mock, whose ambition in life is to get away from the deadly dullness of his town and family. He aims to earn enough money to buy a motorcycle so that he may travel to Pensacola, New Orleans, San Antonio, and San Francisco. When he gets to San Francisco, things do not work out the way he plans. Ussy meets up with a migrant labor family and the harsh realities of poverty. His own dreams of independence take second place to his sense of fairness and his need to help this family.

Belle Pruitt, written by Vera Cleaver, is about an eleven-year-old who is a gold-star student as long as she isn't asked to do anything creative. To create is not a part of her nature; she thinks that when she grows up she may become a reporter of facts. Belle's ordinary world turns upside down when her little brother dies of pneumonia and her spirited mother withdraws into a silent world. No one seems able to help her mother or pull the family back together. Belle realizes that she alone must take on the task, and she does so by transforming a weedlot into a beautiful garden. The wonderful new life which is emerging she hopes will help her mother recover.

In their books, the Cleavers juxtapose the world of the prosperous and the less-fortunate, yet both possess dignity. A number of their characters have deficits—they can't learn arithmetic, they are no good at English composition, they are unable to reason adequately—but these people are not pitiable because they find they do have some strengths and often others come forward to support them. It is not an idealized world, but one that by and large is compassionate and just.

—Mary Lystad

CLEMENTS, Bruce

Nationality: American. **Born:** New York City, 25 November 1931. **Education:** Columbia University, New York, A.B. 1954; Union Theological Seminary, New York, B.D. 1956; State University of New York, Albany, M.A. 1962. **Family:** Married Hanna Charlotte Margarete Kiep in 1954; one son and three daughters. Ordained Minister of the United Church of Christ: pastor in Schenectady, New York, 1957-64; instructor, Union College, Schenectady, New York, 1964-67. **Awards:** Nominated for the National Book Award, 1974, for *I Tell a Lie Every So Often.* **Address:** Department of English, Eastern Connecticut State College, Willimantic, Connecticut 06226, U.S.A.

Publications for Young Adults

Fiction

Two against the Tide. New York, Farrar Straus, 1967.
The Face of Abraham Candle. New York, Farrar Straus, 1969.
I Tell a Lie Every So Often. New York, Farrar Straus, 1974.
Prison Window, Jerusalem Blue. New York, Farrar Straus, 1977.
Anywhere Else But Here. New York, Farrar Straus, 1980.
Coming About. New York, Farrar Straus, 1984.
The Treasure of Plunderell Manor. New York, Farrar Straus, 1987.
Tom Loves Anna Loves Tom. New York, Farrar Straus, 1990.

Other

From Ice Set Free: The Story of Otto Kiep. New York, Farrar Straus, 1972.
Coming Home to a Place You've Never Been Before, with Hanna Clements. New York, Farrar Straus, 1975.

*

Biography: Essay in *Speaking for Ourselves, Too,* compiled and edited by Donald R. Gallo, Urbana, Illinois, National Council of Teachers of English, 1993.

Bruce Clements comments:

More than anything else, I am interested in the courage of ordinary young people, in the things they do to make their lives work and have meaning. The most important question I ask about any character, first and last, is: *What does he or she want?* If I can keep that clear to myself, and if I know the world in which that character has to act—its limitations, its possibilities—the story will come.

*   *   *

Bruce Clements's concern with moral order and his interest in teaching come through very clearly in his writings for young persons. Both his fiction and nonfiction strongly emphasize man's responsibility to his fellow man and society's need to support other societies. His writing style is crisp and clear; in a few words and phrases Clements conjures up vivid images of people, places, and times in conflict.

His novel *Two against the Tide* is a fantasy, set on an island near the coast of Maine. A community of middle-aged and elderly persons have stopped aging physically through a life-preserving drug discovered one hundred years before by a physician. Into this "utopia" come a brother and sister. The children must decide, after a summer on the island, whether or not to remain there and accept perpetual youth. The characters are sharply drawn; the plot is well paced, wise, and witty.

The Face of Abraham Candle is set in the Colorado of silver-mining days and focuses upon a young adolescent, suddenly orphaned and restless for adventure, who explores the caves of Mesa Verde in search of Indian relics. *Prison Window, Jerusalem Blue* focuses on a ninth-century English girl and her brother who are captured by Viking sailors and carried away to Denmark to become slaves. *Coming About,* set in the present, is a story of a young adolescent who is a loner and a mechanical genius, who thinks a lot about war and peace. To most of his peers he is "weird," but to one who becomes his friend, he is a complex individual trying to find, amidst good and evil, a meaningful place in his world.

The Treasure of Plunderell Manor is a fast-paced adventure tale, set in nineteenth-century England. A fourteen-year-old orphan girl begins a new job as maid to a seventeen-year-old orphan heiress, whose aunt and uncle keep her imprisoned in a tower room. The wicked aunt and uncle order the servant girl to spy on her mistress so as to discover the whereabouts of her family's hidden treasures. When instead, the servant and mistress become friends, the aunt and uncle plot to murder them both. Servant and mistress work together to prevent the aunt and uncle's evil schemes. It is the servant girl who finds the family treasures, secures her mistress's future, and in so doing secures her own as well. This book abounds with good and evil characterizations, chases and hair-raising escapes. Its ending is surprising and sensitive.

Tom Loves Anna Loves Tom is an honest and direct, modern-day love affair. It deals with aspects of adolescent affairs which are of great concern to teenagers: love and friendship, acquaintance rape, abortion. The book celebrates a love-at-first-sight relationship—tender and giving—between two sixteen-year-olds. All boy-girl relationships Tom and Anna know about, though, are not that successful. Acquaintance rape, as seen by both the victim and the victimizer, in its short and long-term effects, is poignantly presented. Abortion, as it affects a teenage mother and father, as well as adult relatives, is shown candidly and without rancor. There are other parts of this book that are moving and meaningful—adolescent relationships to pesky siblings, to parents, to elderly relatives. Of all Clements's books, this one may most closely touch young adult readers about to enter the twenty-first century.

Among the works of nonfiction, *From Ice Set Free* is a biography of Clements's father-in-law, a German raised in Scotland who was hanged by the Nazis in Berlin in 1944 as a resister to their regime. *Coming Home to a Place You've Never Been Before* is a documentary account of twenty-four hours in a halfway house for ex-junkies and ex-drug pushers.

Each of Clements's books shows considerable research; the historical and geographical backgrounds are detailed and complex. But more, the books show an understanding of persons living out their lives within the boundaries of special cultures, with their own needs and goals placed in juxtaposition to group demands and limitations. Clements is not easy reading, but he is worth the effort. His stories are powerful, with strong characters facing basic human choices.

—Mary Lystad

COATSWORTH, Elizabeth (Jane)

Nationality: American. **Born:** Buffalo, New York, 31 May 1893. **Education:** Park Street School, 1899-1907; Los Robles School, Pasadena, California, 1907-09; Buffalo Seminary, 1909-11; Vassar College, Poughkeepsie, New York, B.A. 1915 (Phi Beta Kappa); Columbia University, New York, M.A. 1916; Radcliffe College, Cambridge, Massachusetts. **Family:** Married Henry Beston in 1929 (died 1968); two daughters. **Career:** Author and poet. **Awards:** Newbery Medal, American Library Association, 1931, for *The Cat Who Went to Heaven;* Children's Spring Book Festival Honor award, 1940, for *The Littlest House,* and 1971, for *Under the Green Willow;* New England Poetry Club Golden Rose, 1967; Child Study Association of America Children's Books of the Year, 1968, for *Bob Bodden and the Good Ship Rover* and *The Lucky Ones: Five Journeys toward a Home,* 1971, for *The Snow Parlor and Other Bedtime Stories,* 1972, for *Good Night,* 1973, for *The Wanderers,* 1974, for *All-of-a-Sudden Susan,* and 1975, for *Marra's World;* Hans Christian Andersen award Highly Commended Author (U.S.), 1968; Kerlan award, University of Minnesota, 1975, for "recognition of singular attainments in the creation of children's literature." *Door to the North: A Saga of Fourteenth Century America, The Princess and the Lion,* and *The Sparrow Bush: Rhymes* were selected for the *Horn Book* honor list. Litt.D., University of Maine, Orono, 1955; L.H.D., New England College, Henniker, New Hampshire, 1958. **Died:** 31 August 1986.

PUBLICATIONS FOR YOUNG ADULTS

Fiction

Toutou in Bondage, illustrated by Thomas Handforth. New York, Macmillan, 1929.
The Boy with the Parrot: A Story of Guatemala, illustrated by Wilfred Bronson. New York, Macmillan, 1930.
Knock at the Door, illustrated by Francis D. Bedford. New York, Macmillan, 1931.
Cricket and the Emperor's Son, illustrated by Weda Yap. New York, Macmillan, 1932; revised edition, illustrated by Juliette Palmer, Surrey, World's Work, 1962.

Away Goes Sally, illustrated by Helen Sewell. New York, Macmillan, 1934; London, Woodfield, 1955; revised edition, illustrated by Caroline Sharpe, London, Blackie, 1970.

The Golden Horseshoe, illustrated by Robert Lawson. New York, Macmillan, 1935; revised edition, as *Tamar's Wager,* illustrated by R. Payne, London, Blackie, 1971.

Sword of the Wilderness, illustrated by Harve Stein. New York, Macmillan, 1936; London, Blackie, 1972.

Alice-All-by-Herself, illustrated by Marguerite de Angeli. New York, Macmillan, 1937; London, Harrap, 1938.

Dancing Tom, illustrated by Grace Paull. New York, Macmillan, 1938; London, Combridge, 1939.

Five Bushel Farm, illustrated by Helen Sewell. New York, Macmillan, 1939; London, Woodfield, 1958.

The Fair American, illustrated by Helen Sewell. New York, Macmillan, 1940; revised edition, illustrated by Caroline Sharpe, London, Blackie, 1970.

The Littlest House, illustrated by Marguerite Davis. New York, Macmillan, 1940; Kingswood, Surrey, World's Work, 1958.

A Toast to the King, illustrated by Forrest Orr. New York, Coward, 1940; London, Dent, 1941.

Tonio and the Stranger: A Mexican Adventure, illustrated by Wilfred Bronson. New York, Grosset, 1941.

You Shall Have a Carriage, illustrated by Henry Pitz. New York, Macmillan, 1941.

Forgotten Island, illustrated by Grace Paull. New York, Grosset, 1942.

Houseboat Summer, illustrated by Marguerite Davis. New York, Macmillan, 1942.

The White Horse, illustrated by Helen Sewell. New York, Macmillan, 1942; as *The White Horse of Morocco,* illustrated by Caroline Sharpe, London, Blackie, 1973.

Thief Island, illustrated by John Wonsetler. New York, Macmillan, 1943.

Twelve Months Makes a Year (stories), illustrated by Marguerite Davis. New York, Macmillan, 1943.

The Big Green Umbrella, illustrated by Helen Sewell. New York, Grosset, 1944.

Trudy and the Tree House, illustrated by Marguerite Davis. New York, Macmillan, 1944.

The Kitten Stand, illustrated by Kathleen Keeler. New York, Grosset, 1945.

The Wonderful Day, illustrated by Helen Sewell. New York, Macmillan, 1946; illustrated by Caroline Sharpe, London, Blackie, 1973.

Plum Daffy Adventure, illustrated by Marguerite Davis. New York, Macmillan, 1947; Kingswood, Surrey, World's Work, 1965.

Up Hill and Down: Stories, illustrated by James Davis. New York, Knopf, 1947.

The House of the Swan, illustrated by Kathleen Voute. New York, Macmillan, 1948; Kingswood, Surrey, World's Work, 1959.

The Little Haymakers, illustrated by Grace Paull. New York, Macmillan, 1949.

The Captain's Daughter, illustrated by Ralph Ray. New York, Macmillan, 1950; London, Collier Macmillan, 1963.

American Adventures 1620-1945, illustrated by Robert Frankenburg. New York, Macmillan, 1968.

First Adventure, illustrated by Ralph Ray. New York, Macmillan, 1950.

The Wishing Pear, illustrated by Ralph Ray. New York, Macmillan, 1951.

Boston Belles, illustrated by Manning Lee. New York, Macmillan, 1952.

Aunt Flora, illustrated by Manning Lee. New York, Macmillan, 1953.

Old Whirlwind: A Story of Davy Crockett, illustrated by Manning Lee. New York, Macmillan, 1953.

The Sod House, illustrated by Manning Lee. New York, Macmillan, 1954.

Cherry Ann and the Dragon Horse, illustrated by Manning Lee. New York, Macmillan, 1955.

Door to the North: A Saga of Fourteenth Century America, illustrated by Frederick T. Chapman. Philadelphia, Winston, 1950; Kingswood, Surrey, World's Work, 1960.

Dollar for Luck, illustrated by George Hauman and Doris Hauman. New York, Macmillan, 1951; as *The Sailing Hatrack,* illustrated by Gavin Rowe, London, Blackie, 1972.

The Last Fort: A Story of the French Voyageurs, illustrated by Edward Shenton. Philadelphia, Winston, 1952; London, Hamish Hamilton, 1953.

The Giant Golden Book of Cat Stories with Kate Barnes, illustrated by Feodor Rojankovsky. New York, Simon & Schuster, 1953; London, Publicity Products, 1955.

The Giant Golden Book of Dog Stories, illustrated by Feodor Rojankovsky. New York, Simon & Schuster, 1953; London, Publicity Products, 1954.

Horse Stories with Kate Barnes, illustrated by Feodor Rojankovsky. New York, Simon & Schuster, 1954.

Hide and Seek, illustrated by Genevieve Vaughan-Jackson. New York, Pantheon, 1956.

The Peddler's Cart, illustrated by Zhenya Gay. New York, Macmillan, 1956; as *The Pedlar's Cart,* illustrated by Margery Gill, London, Blackie, 1971.

The Giant Golden Books of Dogs, Cats, and Horses (contains *Horse Stories, The Giant Golden Book of Cat Stories,* and *The Giant Golden Book of Dog Stories*), with Kate Barnes. New York, Simon & Schuster, 1957.

The Cave, illustrated by Allen Houser. New York, Viking, 1958; as *Cave of Ghosts,* London, Hamish Hamilton, 1971.

The Dog from Nowhere, illustrated by Don Sibley. Evanston, Illinois, Row, Peterson, 1958.

Down Tumbledown Mountain, illustrated by Aldren Watson. Evanston, Illinois, Row, Peterson, 1958.

You Say You Saw a Camel!, illustrated by Brinton Turkle. Evanston, Illinois, Row, Peterson, 1958.

Desert Dan, illustrated by Harper Johnson. New York, Viking, 1960; London, Harrap, 1963.

Lonely Maria, illustrated by Evaline Ness. New York, Pantheon, 1960; London, Hamish Hamilton, 1967.

Ronnie and the Chief's Son, illustrated by Stefan Martin. New York, and London, Macmillan, 1962.

Jon the Unlucky, illustrated by Esta Nesbitt. New York, Holt, 1964; Chalfont St. Giles, Buckinghamshire, Sadler, 1968.

The Hand of Apollo, illustrated by Robin Jacques. New York, Viking, 1965; Kingswood, Surrey, World's Work, 1967.

The Fox Friend, illustrated by John Hamberger. New York, Macmillan, 1966.

The Place, illustrated by Marjorie Auerbach. New York, Holt, 1966.

The Ox-Team, illustrated by Peter Warner. London, Hamish Hamilton, 1967.

Troll Weather, illustrated by Ursula Arndt. New York, Macmillan, 1967; Kingswood, Surrey, World's Work, 1968.

Lighthouse Island, illustrated by Symeon Shimin. New York, Norton, 1968.

George and Red, illustrated by Paul Giovanopoulos. New York, Macmillan, 1969.

They Walk in the Night, illustrated by Stefan Martin. New York, Norton, 1969.

The Wanderers, illustrated by Trina Schart Hyman. New York, Four Winds, 1972.

Daisy, illustrated by Judith Gwyn Brown. New York, Macmillan, 1973.

All-of-a-Sudden Susan, illustrated by Richard Cuffair. New York, Macmillan, 1974.

Marra's World, illustrated by Krystyna Truska. New York, Greenwillow, 1975.

Other

Runaway Home, with Mabel O'Donnell, illustrated by Gustaf Tenggren. Evanston, Illinois, Row, Peterson, 1942.

Editor, *Tales of the Gauchos,* by William Henry Hudson, illustrated by Henry C. Pitz. New York, Knopf, 1946.

Editor, *Indian Encounters: An Anthology of Stories and Poems,* illustrated by Frederick T. Chapman. New York, Macmillan, 1960.

The Princess and the Lion, illustrated by Evaline Ness. New York, Pantheon, 1963; illustrated by Tessa Jordan, Philadelphia, Pennsylvania, Hamilton, 1971.

Daniel Webster's Horses, illustrated by Cary. Champaign, Illinois, Garrard, 1971.

PUBLICATIONS FOR CHILDREN

Fiction

The Cat and the Captain, illustrated by Gertrude Kaye. New York, Macmillan, 1927; revised edition, illustrated by Berniece Loewenstein, 1974.

The Cat Who Went to Heaven, illustrated by Lynd Ward. New York, Macmillan, 1930; London, Dent, 1949.

Pika and the Roses, illustrated by Kurt Wiese. New York, Pantheon, 1959.

The Noble Doll, illustrated by Leo Politi. New York, Viking, 1961.

Jock's Island, illustrated by Lilian Obligado. New York, Viking, 1963; London, Angus & Robertson, 1965.

The Secret, illustrated by Don Bolognese. New York, Macmillan, 1965; Kingswood, Surrey, World's Work, 1967.

Chimney Farm Bedtime Stories, with husband, Henry Beston, illustrated by Maurice Day. New York, Holt, 1966.

Bess and the Sphinx (includes verse), illustrated by Bernice Loewenstein. New York, Macmillan, 1967; London, Blackie, 1974.

Bob Bodden and the Good Ship "Rover," illustrated by Ted Schroeder. Champaign, Illinois, Garrard, 1968; London, Watts, 1972.

The Lucky Ones: Five Journeys toward a Home, illustrated by Janet Doyle. New York, Macmillan, 1968.

Indian Mound Farm, illustrated by Fermin Rocker. New York, Macmillan, and London, Collier, Macmillan, 1969.

Bob Bodden and the Seagoing Farm, illustrated by Frank Aloise. Champaign, Illinois, Garrard, 1970; London, Watts, 1972.

Grandmother Cat and the Hermit, illustrated by Irving Boker. New York, Macmillan, 1970; as *Grandmother Cat,* London, Bodley Head, 1971.

The Snow Parlor and Other Bedtime Stories, illustrated by Charles Robinson. New York, Grosset, 1971.

Under the Green Willow, illustrated by Janina Domanska. New York, Macmillan, 1971.

Good Night, illustrated by Jose Aruego. New York, Macmillan, 1972.

Pure Magic, illustrated by Ingrid Fetz. New York, Macmillan 1973; as *The Werefox,* New York, Collier, 1975; as *The Fox Boy,* London, Blackie, 1975.

Poetry

Night and the Cat, illustrated by Fougita. New York, Macmillan, 1950.

Mouse Chores, illustrated by Genevieve Vaughan-Jackson. New York, Pantheon, 1955.

The Peaceable Kingdom and Other Poems, illustrated by Fritz Eichenberg. New York, Pantheon, 1958.

The Children Come Running, illustrated by Roger Duvoisin and others. New York, Golden Press, 1960.

The Sparrow Bush: Rhymes, illustrated by Stefan Martin. New York, Norton, 1966.

Down Half the World, illustrated by Zena Bernstein. New York, Macmillan, 1968.

Other

UNICEF Christmas Book. Huntsville, Alabama, UNICEF, 1960.

Reading Round Table, Blue Book: Stories by Elizabeth Coatsworth, edited by George Manolakes. Brooklyn, New York, American Book, 1965.

Reading Round Table, Green Book. Brooklyn, New York, American Book, 1965.

PUBLICATIONS FOR ADULTS

Novels

Here I Stay, illustrated by Edwin Earle. New York, Coward, 1938; London, Harrap, 1939.

The Trunk. New York, Macmillan, 1941.

The Enchanted: An Incredible Tale, illustrated by Robert Winthrop. New York, Pantheon, 1951; London, Dent, 1952.

Silky: An Incredible Tale, illustrated by John Carroll. New York, Pantheon, and London, Gollancz, 1953.

Mountain Bride: An Incredible Tale. New York, Pantheon, 1954.

The White Room, illustrated by George W. Thompson. New York, Pantheon, 1958; London, Dent, 1959.

Poetry

Fox Footprints. New York, Knopf, 1923.

Atlas and Beyond: A Book of Poems, illustrated by Harry Cimino. New York, Harper, 1924.

Compass Rose. New York, Coward, 1929.

Country Poems. New York, Macmillan, 1942.

Summer Green, illustrated by Nora S. Unwin. New York, Macmillan, 1948.

The Creaking Stair, illustrated by William A. Dwiggins. New York, Coward, 1949.

Poems, illustrated by Vee Guthrie. New York, Macmillan, 1957.

Other

The Sun's Diary: A Book of Days for Any Year. New York, Macmillan, 1929.

Mary's Song. Nash, 1938.

Country Neighborhood, illustrated by Hildegard Woodward. New York, Macmillan, 1944.

Maine Ways, illustrated by Mildred Coughlin. New York, Macmillan, 1947.

South Shore Town. New York, Macmillan, 1948.

Maine Memories. Brattleboro, Vermont, Stephen Greene, 1968.

Editor, *Especially Maine: The Natural World of Henry Beston from Cape Cod to the St. Lawrence.* Brattleboro, Vermont, Stephen Greene, 1970.

Personal Geography: Almost an Autobiography. Brattleboro, Vermont, Stephen Greene, 1976; London, Prior, 1979.

*

Media Adaptations: *The Cat Who Went to Heaven* (record or cassette), Newbery Award Records, 1969; *The Cat Who Went to Heaven* (filmstrip with cassette), Miller/Brody, 1970; *Bob Bodden and the Good Ship "Rover"* (filmstrip with cassette), Taylor Associates, 1970. *Away Goes Sally, The Cat Who Went to Heaven, The Enchanted, Here I Stay, Lonely Maria, Personal Geography, Princess and the Lion, Pure Magic,* and *Ronnie and the Chief's Son* have been adapted as talking books; *The Cat Who Went to Heaven, Country Neighborhood, The Enchanted, Good Night, Houseboat Summer, Last Fort, Mountain Bride, Old Whirlwind, Poems, Ronnie and the Chief's Son, Silky, Toast to the King, White Room, Wishing Pear,* and *Trunk* have been adapted as Braille books.

Manuscript Collections: Kerlan Collection, University of Minnesota, Minneapolis; Bowdoin College Library, Brunswick, Maine.

*   *   *

Elizabeth Coatsworth's imagination was as boundless as her pen was prolific. The author of some ninety books for children, Coatsworth wrote on such diverse subjects as Viking-raided Ireland (*The Wanderers*), the ancient inhabitants of the fjords and mountains in Norway (*Troll Weather*), and a city boy's summer in *Lighthouse Island.* Her vision encompassed lonely children and their search for independence, magic dolls, refugees, forests where animals can turn into people, and, above all, nature.

Although she travelled widely, the bulk of her work concerns America in all its phases. History books aside, she wrote of the desert, the plains, the mountains, Indians, pioneers, immigrants. But it is from Maine that her finest books have come, and in Maine that she found for decades the resources to create one lapidary tale after another.

Although born in 1893, the author continued to understand the perceptions of the young throughout her long writing career. One of her most successful themes is that of the lonely and different child learning to cope in an adverse world. *Lonely Maria* and

Grandmother Cat and the Hermit both deal with this idea, as does *Marra's World* which combines the theme with Coatsworth's favorite setting—an island off the Maine Coast. With the subtle use of magic and fantasy, it conveys the mood of a legend. Marra is regarded as hopeless by her teacher and schoolmates and even by her father and grandmother: "Everything about her life bewildered her." But when it comes to nature, Marra excels. She knows everything about the island. Gradually, with the help of a friend, she accepts herself as different, and the enchantment begins. Marra's mother is Nerea, a seal who was human for a time and who returned to the sea. Here, and in *The Enchanted,* Coatsworth touches on the ancient mythic theme where one being is able to work extraordinary changes for love of another.

Coatsworth reached her apogee in her nature writing, notably "The Incredible Tales" tetralogy about New England originally written for adults. As critic Edmund Fuller observes: "As with all Miss Coatsworth's work, *Silky* is a poet's book, mystic, delicate, lovely. With these 'Incredible Tales' she has created a rich, fresh medium that is at once original and yet the revival of a tradition neglected or distorted in this material age." *The Enchanted,* the best of the four, begins: "There is in northern Maine a township or, as they say here, a 'plantation,' called the Enchanted. It lies in the heart of the forest country and is seldom entered except by lumbermen bound for some winter logging camp from which they return with curious stories." A young man, David Ross, decides to try farming and buys a place right next to the Enchanted. His neighbors are a warm, closely knit family named Perdry, and he falls in love with one of the daughters and marries her. For their honeymoon they camp in the forest: "The stream seemed to sing its continual braided song especially for them, and the big pine sheltered them as though it liked them. They sat for many hours between its curving roots, their backs to its wide trunk, looking out at the water flowing by, always new water, and new ripples of light, yet always essentially the same stream catching the sunlight in the same net of motion." The magic in this tale and in Coatsworth's others is not arbitrary. It is all planned, provided for. Her special gift was the weaving together of a local story and her own vivid characters. The events that conclude *The Enchanted,* the metamorphosis of the Perdrys, are at once anticipated and surprising.

It was Coatsworth's intention to instruct through her stories, but she was never pedantic. The works do not come together with quite the ease of a folktale that has been repeated from generation to generation, but are a combination of good New England common sense and modern legend. In *All-of-a-Sudden Susan,* building a feeling of danger, Coatsworth writes: "Everything was uneasy, except people, who are always the last to notice what's happening around them." A weakened dam bursts in a storm and Susan is carried away on the flood with her magic doll, Emelida, who talks to her. Susan sees uprooted houses, bloated animals, even a dead woman. "You can't keep people from dying," Emelida comforts her. "They do it all the time and we may be doing it, too, for all we know. But meantime, enjoy yourself."

The Sod House follows immigrants from their arrival in Boston to the settling of a community in Kansas. The New England Emigrant Aid Society helps the Traubels buy land on the Osage River. They are not welcome as Northerners at a time when North and South are angling for control of the territory. Political reasons are carefully explained. The Indians the Traubels meet are portrayed solemnly and informatively (Coatsworth was always interested in their way of life), and Ilse, the child in the story, is allowed to fulfill her possibilities, as are most of Coatsworth's fictive children.

The Lucky Ones, a collection of five stories about the homeless and the stateless from different parts of the world—Tibet, Algeria, Rwanda, Hungary, and Hong Kong—explains why they are refugees, and describes the adversity they meet in trying to adjust to another way of life. Each story is preceded by a poem, and while in some cases the political background is not given enough detail, the children in the stories, and the children who read them, are treated with the respect that marks all Coatsworth's work.

Using her considerable creativeness and knowledge, her love of the natural world, and her regard for children, Coatsworth was responsible for consistently fine literature for readers whose imaginations are as young and fresh as her own was.

—Angela Wigan

———

COBALT, Martin. *See* **MAYNE, William (James Carter).**

———

COFER, Judith Ortiz

Nationality: Puerto Rican **Born:** Hormigueros, Puerto Rico, 24 February 1952. **Education:** Augusta College, B.A. 1974; Florida Atlantic University, M.A. 1977; attended Oxford University, 1977. **Family:** Married Charles John Cofer, 13 November 1971; one daughter. **Career:** Bilingual teacher at public schools in Palm Beach County, Florida, 1974-75; adjunct instructor in English, Broward Community College, Fort Lauderdale, Florida, 1978-80; adjunct instructor, Palm Beach Junior College, 1978-80; instructor in Spanish, 1979, lecturer in English, 1980-84, University of Miami, Coral Gables, Florida; instructor in English, 1984-87, Georgia Center for Continuing Education; instructor in English, 1987-88, University of Georgia, Athens; instructor in English, Macon College, 1988-89; Special Programs coordinator, Mercer University College, Forsyth, Georgia, 1990; associate professor of Creative Writing, University of Georgia, Athens, since 1993. **Awards:** Scholar of English Speaking Union, Oxford University, 1977; Fellow of Fine Arts Council of Florida, 1980; Bread Loaf Writers' Conference Scholar, 1981; John Atherton Scholar in Poetry, 1982; Witter Bynner Foundation for Poetry grant, 1988; National Endowment for the Arts Fellowship in Poetry, 1989; Pulitzer Prize Nomination, 1990, for *Terms of Survival*; PEN Martha Albrand Special Citation for Non-Fiction, and Pushcart Prize, both 1991, both for *Silent Dancing: A Partial Remembrance of a Puerto Rican Childhood*; Pura Belpré Award and America's Award for Children's and Young Adult Literature honorable mention, both 1995, both for *An Island Like You: Stories of the Barrio.* **Agent:** Berenice Hoffman Literary Agency, 215 West 75th St., New York, New York 10023, U.S.A.

PUBLICATIONS FOR YOUNG ADULTS

Fiction

An Island Like You: Stories of the Barrio. New York, Orchard Books, 1995.

Non-Fiction

Silent Dancing: A Partial Remembrance of a Puerto Rican Childhood. Houston, Texas, Arte Publico Press, 1990.

PUBLICATIONS FOR ADULTS

Fiction

Terms of Survival. Houston, Texas, Arte Publico Press, 1985.
The Line of the Sun. Athens, Georgia, University of Georgia Press, 1989.

Poetry

Peregrina. West Chester, Pennsylvania, Riverstone Press, 1986.
With Robert Duran and Gustavo Perez Firmat, *Triple Crown: Chicano, Puerto Rican, and Cuban-American American Poetry.* Tempe, Arizona, Bilingual Press, 1987.
The Latin Deli: Prose and Poetry. Athens, Georgia, University of Georgia Press, 1993.

*   *   *

As the author of a number of poetry collections for adults and as a teacher of creative writing, Judith Ortiz Cofer brings a unique and masterful style to the composition of young adult texts. Most importantly, she is in tune with the subtle variations in accent and dialect that distinguish her protagonists, both those who are natives of the island of Puerto Rico and those who are first or second generation Puerto Ricans living in Patterson, New Jersey. Both locales provide the setting for her YA autobiographical work and her fiction, and her central themes include the examination of cultural differences between the island and the mainland, the description of intergenerational conflict, and the life lessons that young people learn, even amidst the chaos and poverty of the Patterson, New Jersey barrio.

Cofer's love of telling stories comes from her grandmother, and in her first book for young adults, *Silent Dancing: A Partial Remembrance of a Puerto Rican Childhood,* she recounts many of her ''Mama's'' tales as well as family stories that take place on the island of Puerto Rico and in Patterson. This autobiographical novel also concerns Cofer's reaction to living in two radically different cultures. During the time that her father, a member of the U.S. Navy, is based in the New York area, the family lives in Patterson, New Jersey. However, Cofer is not allowed to make friends with any of the children in her neighborhood because he does not want their manners or interests to rub off on his daughter. He hopes that his family will rise above the conditions in the barrio, so it is only on visits to her native Puerto Rico that Cofer is allowed any measure of freedom. Like the other prominent Puerto Rican YA writers of her generation, Nicholas Mohr and Esmeralda Santiago, Cofer expresses the sense that she is at home neither in her homeland nor in the United States. This sense of disconnectedness compels her to let out her feelings through the medium of poetry. Thus, in addition to including prose descriptions of her childhood, the volume also contains Cofer's juvenile poetry.

In her second work for young adults, the award-winning *An Island Like You: Stories of the Barrio,* Cofer creates twelve interconnected tales that feature the trials and triumphs of a number of teenagers who live in modern-day Patterson, a community that is ravaged by drugs, gang violence, and poverty. Some of her protagonists are gang "wanna-be's," shoplifters, and chronic underachievers; others are future poets and rising academic stars. However, Cofer manages to humanize each of her characters, no matter what his or her background or intentions. Thus Kenny Matoa, a punk who is first introduced to the reader as an antagonist for the scholarly Arturo, reappears later in the text as the victim of an unintentional drug overdose and a botched robbery. Anita, a young girl who helps to establish the self-esteem of her friend Sandra, is then shown to have self-esteem issues of her own, issues that threaten to make her the virtual slave of a corrupt and immoral Italian shop owner.

In each of these stories, an important life lesson is learned. For instance, in "Bad Influence," the only story set in Puerto Rico, loving and insightful grandparents manage to change the life of their granddaughter Rita, a girl who has been sent to the island because of "boy problems." Rather than preach to Rita about the dangers of becoming pregnant and getting married at a young age, the grandparents introduce her to another young girl, Angela, the anorexic and neglected daughter of Puerto Rican soap opera star. As the two girls interact, Rita learns that her grandparents have undertaken the task of saving Angela and her mother from the "mala influencia" in their home—the mother's abusive suitor. Not only does Rita come to respect her grandparents, she learns to recognize how lucky she is to have a wise and caring family.

In "An Hour with Abuelo," another wise grandparent figure, Abuelo Arturo, helps his young grandson and namesake to value his vocation as a poet by writing an autobiographical text entitled "Así es la vida" ("That's the way life is"). When the young Arturo is forced to visit his grandfather at "the old people's home," he is reluctant because he feels that he and his grandfather have nothing in common. However, when he listens to the sacrifices that his Abeulo made in order to ensure that the future generations of his family could succeed, Arturo is shocked. Not only did his grandfather have to give up an advanced education, he was forced to quit teaching in his village school once he was drafted into the U.S. Army during World War II. When he returns from the war, his "parents were sick, two of [his] brothers had been killed in the war, the [other siblings] had stayed in Nueva York. [He] was the only one left to help the old people. [He] became a farmer . . . and [he taught his children] how to read and write before they started school." "Así es la vida," his grandfather sighs, and perhaps for the first time, his grandson is able to put his own struggles into perspective. As his grandfather is wheeled off to give a poetry reading, Arturo feels less embarrassed regarding his own desires to become an author and a poet.

Another shared lesson between the generations occurs in "Beauty Lessons." Sandra, the protagonist, is an average-looking girl who is ridiculed by the popular girls in her high school because she has not yet "developed" and does not wear make-up. In an attempt to fit in, Sandra decides to ask her gorgeous aunt Modesto to give her beauty lessons. Standing in her aunt's doorway, Sandra watches Modesto transform into "an old woman": "I see her rub some white cream all over her face, and suddenly she starts to change. Her cheeks had been painted on . . . and it's like her expression is gone and she looks like a blank TV screen. . . [Then,] she squints, trying to see herself while she takes out a set of false teeth! Her face just sort of caves in when she does this." Rather than ask for beauty tips, Sandra slips away and musters up the courage to talk to a boy whom she likes. In addition to feeling sorry for her aunt, she realizes that her own youthful vigor is something to be grateful for because it is her own and does not come from a jar or a tube of make-up.

Perhaps the most poignant story of all is "White Balloons," the description of the final days of a successful Broadway actor who had grown up in the barrio, but is an outcast because he is an open homosexual. Ravaged by the AIDs virus, Rick Sanchez tries to give something back to his hometown by setting up a youth theater for Puerto Rican children. Unfortunately, the children's parents refuse to support his effort and take every opportunity to express their dislike, and even hatred, for the young man's lifestyle and disease. Cofer is particularly effective in pointing out the irony of this discriminatory behavior, and she uses the story to highlight the way that many of the teenagers in the barrio are able to put on a memorial for the actor after his death, thus unifying the community in the name of acceptance and tolerance.

An Island Like You provides an entertaining and moving perspective on life in the barrio and on the universal phenomenon of youthful alienation and eventual growth. The stories are brought to life with contemporary dialogue and realistic situations, making them an important addition to the genre of multiethnic adolescent narratives.

—Gwen A. Tarbox

COFFEY, Brian. *See* **KOONTZ, Dean R.**

COLE, Brock

Nationality: American. **Born:** Charlotte, Michigan, 29 May 1938. **Education:** Kenyon College, B.A.; University of Minnesota, Ph.D. **Family:** Married Susan. **Career:** Instructor in English composition, University of Minnesota; instructor in philosophy, University of Wisconsin, until 1975; writer and illustrator, from 1975. **Awards:**

Juvenile Award, Friends of American Writers, 1980, for *The King at the Door*; *New York Times* outstanding book, 1981, California Young Reader Medal, California Reading Association, 1985, and Young Reader's Choice Award, Pacific Northwest Library Association, all for *The Indian in the Cupboard*; Smarties "Grand Prix" for children's books, Book Trust, for *Gaffer Samson's Luck*; Parent's Choice Award, Parent's Choice Foundation, 1986, for *The Giant's Toe*; *New York Times* outstanding book, ALA Best Book for Young Adults, and ALA notable book, all 1987, and Carl Sandburg Award, Friends of Chicago Public Library, 1988, for *The Goats*; Booklist "Editors Choice" citation and Notable Children's Book of the Year citation by *Publishers Weekly,* both for *Celine*; *School Library Journal*'s Best Books of 1997 list, and National Book Award nominee, 1997, both for *the facts speak for themselves*.

PUBLICATIONS FOR YOUNG ADULTS

The Goats. New York, Farrar, Straus, Giroux, 1987.
Celine. New York, Farrar, Straus, Giroux, 1989.
the facts speak for themselves. Arden, North Carolina, Front Street, 1997.

PUBLICATIONS FOR CHILDREN (illustrated by the author)

The King at the Door. New York, Doubleday, 1979.
No More Baths. New York, Doubleday, 1980.
Nothing but a Pig. New York, Doubleday, 1981.
The Winter Wren. New York, Farrar, Straus, Giroux, 1984.
The Giant's Toe. New York, Farrar, Straus, Giroux, 1986.
Alpha and the Dirty Baby. New York, Farrar, Straus, Giroux, 1991.

*

Critical Studies: Essay by Patty Campbell, in *Wilson Library Bulletin,* January 1988; essays in *Horn Book,* January/February 1988, and September/October 1989; entry in *Children's Literature Review,* Vol. 18, Detroit, Gale, 1989.

Illustrator: *The Indian in the Cupboard* by Lynne Reid Banks, 1980; *Gaffer Samson's Luck* by Jill Paton Walsh, 1984.

*   *   *

Brock Cole began his career in children's and young adult literature as an illustrator. In an interview with Christine McDonnell for *Horn Book* Cole said he "tried to draw" like the illustrators he admired and studied—namely Maurice Sendek, Ernest Shepard, Margot Zemach and Edward Ardizzone. Several of these artists visually interpret well known traditional folktales. Cole took a similar interest in reworking folk narration in his first picture book, *The King at the Door*. Little Baggit, a chore-boy, shares his dinner with a ragged beggar who is the king in disguise, and for doing this he is richly rewarded. Cole's *The Giant's Toe* is a literary variant of

"Jack and the Beanstalk" only with a comical, magical twist since the dull-witted giant cuts off his toe by accident. The toe transforms into a trickster elf who plagues the giant by disposing of the giant's hen (that lays the golden eggs), and the magic harp. In similar manner the heroine from *Alpha and the Dirty Baby* must contend with a pesky, lazy family of imps. These lively animated, watercolor illustrations are suggestive of Margot Zemach's "oggily" creature in her humorous *Duffy and the Devil,* a variant of the German "Rumpelstiltskin." Cole's graceful and flowing watercolor illustrations for *The Winter Wren* are reminiscent of Edward Ardizzone's elegant style, while Cole's pen and ink sketches scattered throughout the *Indian in the Cupboard* resemble Sheperd's style in *The Wind in the Willows,* only Cole has more accuracy in depicting proportion between human and smaller characters. Cole broke free from these influences when he became a writer and found his own authentic voice.

Brock Cole's first venture into writing young adult fiction came with the publication of *The Goats*. In this survival/adventure narrative two thirteen year olds, Laura and Howie, find themselves abandoned by their parents for the summer at Camp Tall Pine. With implicit approval from the camp counselors, they are stripped naked and marooned on an island in a river by their peers as part of a cruel ritual to isolate the most socially backward girl and boy for the current term to see if any sexual interest can be aroused. But Laura and Howie instead develop a unique friendship as they strike back by successfully escaping from the island, the camp counselors, and other authorities who are trying to find them. Their vulnerable situation forces them to take food and clothing from an empty cottage and a public beach, as well as change from a car coin holder. They keep track of these items and vow eventually to make reparations. These infractions escalate when Howie becomes ill and Laura manipulates their way into a motel with no intent of paying for the room. Later, they commandeer a truck from a threatening male adult and proceed to run over his foot when he does not move out of the way. This is an action filled, fast-paced novel!

Cole alternately presents Laura and Howie as scapegoats and as successful bandits. Other kids sympathetic to their plight refer to them as Bonnie and Clyde. There is a strong indictment of adults through their seeming indifference and sometimes open hostility. Howie's dad, a college professor, is preoccupied with his research in Greece and can't be bothered with his kid. The motel manager assumes Laura and Howie want the room for sex. Fortunately, Laura's mom counterbalances this indifference and hostility when she responds to Laura's plight with understanding and love. Writing in the *Wilson Library Bulletin,* Patty Campbell called *The Goats* "a remarkable book to enjoy first and ponder later, and one that deserves to become a YA classic."

Celine is Coles second venture into young adult fiction written from a sixteen-year-old girl's narrative point of view. Celine's parents are preoccupied with separate lives after divorcing: her dad is a professor lecturing in Europe and her mom lives in South America. Celine lives in Chicago with her dad's second wife Catharine, who is only six years older than herself.

Celine's humorous and sometimes flippant spin on life makes her appealing to a young adult audience. When her dad admonishes her to "show a little maturity," she thinks, "If I was any more mature, I'd have Alzheimer's disease." In some ways she resembles Holden Caulfield from *Catcher in the Rye,* the subject of the paper she is slowly rewriting for her exasperated high school teacher. The narrative comes into focus as Celine befriends a five-year-old boy living next door who is struggling to cope with his parents' separation and divorce. Seeing in Jake Barker the hurt, betrayal, and anger that she experienced and still struggles with in her relationship with her parents, Celine becomes a surrogate parent and friend to Jake. Sprinkled throughout this narrative are Celine's encounters with males, including Jake's dad. Both Jake and Celine recognize the fallibility within Frank Barker. ''That's the great problem with maturity. One's escape routes become fewer and fewer.''

Celine's quirky, spontaneous insights keep readers interested. After a confrontation with a peer during school hours she flees to a storage closet:

> I sit down on a five-gallon drum of floor wax, fold my hands neatly on my lap, and consider staying in the janitor's closet for the rest of the day. But no. Mr. Mostella probably wouldn't welcome company. A silent, morose man, plagued by chewing gum, clogged toilets, starbursts of chocolate milk and catsup on the cafeteria walls, he has his own griefs.

Cole diligently captures the wonderful essence of this sixteen year old on the verge of adulthood.

Cole's most recent novel *the facts speak for themselves* is by far his darkest and most disturbing. As in *Celine* Cole once again selects a first person, female, narrative point of view, only this time thirteen-year-old Linda has been exploited and abused by several adult males, including her father. The opening chapter is absolutely riveting: Linda has just witnessed the murder of Jack Green, a real estate associate of her mothers, who has sexually assaulted Linda repeatedly over the past few months. Frank Perry, the man living with Linda's mother, guns down Green and then turns the gun on himself. Linda is taken into protective custody and recounts these events to the police in a very matter-of-fact manner. At the end of this chapter Linda persuades her social worker to allow her to write her own preliminary report since Linda feels that anyone else doing it would ''make me look like a fool.''

The remainder of the book is presented as Linda's written narrative of her life. Cole's presentation of Linda in this format is fairly plausible, suggesting how her abuse is intertwined with her mom's life as a sexual vagrant. Before his death, Linda's father encouraged his daughter's distorted and premature interest in sex, telling Linda very explicitly that her mom was at an airport motel with a lover. This discussion stimulates Linda's sexual interest in men, and at the age of ten she is raped by her mother's new boyfriend. Though Linda is sexually troubled and troublesome, she is also caring, especially toward her two younger brothers. There is a strong sense of order and decency within her as she narrates how she protects and cares for an old man her mother lived with and later deserted. Through her dispassionate narrative voice she simply moves forward through these terrible domestic situations to do what must be done. This novel is certain to attract controversy for its explicit presentation of sexual issues.

Of Cole's three young adult novels, *The Goats* should attract the widest audience; reluctant readers will especially be drawn to the consistent action and the depiction of Laura and Howie as victims.

—Richard Seiter

COLEMAN, Michael. *See* JONES, Allan Frewin.

COLLIER, Christopher and James Lincoln

Nationality: Americans. **Christopher Collier: Born:** New York, New York, 29 January 1930. **Education:** Clark University, Worcester, Massachusetts, B.A. 1951; Columbia University, New York, New York, M.A. 1955, Ph.D. 1964. **Military Service:** Served in United States Army, 1952-54. **Family:** Married 1) Virginia Wright in 1954, one son and one daughter; 2) Bonnie Bromberger in 1969, one son. **Career:** Teacher, Julian Curtiss School, Greenwich, Connecticut, 1955-58; teacher of social studies, New Canaan High School, Connecticut, 1959-61; instructor in history, Columbia University, Teachers College, New York City, 1958-59; instructor, University of Bridgeport, Connecticut, 1961-64, assistant professor, 1964-67, associate professor, 1967-71, professor of history, 1971-78, David S. Day Professor of History, 1978-84, chairman of department, 1978-81. Since 1984 professor of history, University of Connecticut, Storrs. Visiting professor, New York University, 1974; visiting lecturer, Yale University, 1977 and 1981; chairman, Columbia University Seminar on Early American History, 1978-79. Director, National Endowment for the Humanities Summer Institute for College Teachers, 1989. Consultant to numerous public and private organizations, including museums, historical societies, law firms, public utilities, and text, trade, and scholarly publishers. Since 1985 Connecticut State Historian; member of various historical commissions. **Address:** 344 West River Rd., Orange, Connecticut 06477, U.S.A. **James Lincoln Collier: Pseudonym:** Charles Williams. **Born:** New York, New York, 27 June 1928. **Education:** Hamilton College, Clinton, New York, A.B. 1950. **Military Service:** Served in the United States Army, 1950-51. **Family:** Married 1) Carol Burrows in 1952 (divorced), two sons; 2) Ida Karen Potash in 1983. **Career:** Writer; magazine editor, 1952-58. **Address:** 71 Barrow St., New York, New York 10014, U.S.A.

Awards: (Christopher Collier and James Lincoln Collier): Newbery Honor Book, a Jane Addams Honor Book, and a finalist for a National Book award, all 1975, for *My Brother Sam Is Dead;* Notable Children's Trade Book in the Field of Social Studies by the National Council for Social Studies and the Children's Book Council, 1981 and 1982 respectively, for *Jump Ship to Freedom* and *War Comes to Willy Freeman;* Phoenix award, 1994, for *My Brother Sam Is Dead.*

Awards: (Christopher Collier): Christopher award, 1987, for *Decision in Philadelphia: The Constitutional Convention of 1787.*

Awards: (James Lincoln Collier): Child's Study Association Book award, 1971, for *Rock Star;* London *Observer* Book of the Year award and American Book award nomination, both for *The Making of Jazz: A Comprehensive History*; Institute for Studies in American Music fellowship, 1985.

PUBLICATIONS FOR YOUNG ADULTS

Historical Novels (Christopher Collier and James Lincoln Collier)

My Brother Sam Is Dead. New York, Four Winds, 1974.
The Bloody Country. New York, Four Winds, 1976.
The Winter Hero. New York, Four Winds, 1978.
Jump Ship to Freedom. New York, Delacorte, 1981.
War Comes to Willy Freeman. New York, Delacorte, 1983.
Who Is Carrie?. New York, Delacorte, 1984.
The Clock, illustrated by Kelly Maddox. New York, Delacorte, 1992.
With Every Drop of Blood. New York, Delacorte Press, 1994.

Drama of American History Series; Nonfiction (Christopher Collier and James Lincoln Collier)

Clash of Cultures, Prehistory-1638. New York, Benchmark Books, 1998.
The Paradox of Jamestown, 1585-1700. New York, Benchmark Books, 1998.
Pilgrims and Puritans, 1620-1676. New York, Benchmark Books, 1998.
The French and Indian War, 1660-1763. Tarrytown, N.Y., Benchmark Books, 1998.
The American Revolution, 1763-1783. New York, Benchmark Books, 1998.
Creating the Constitution, 1787. New York, Benchmark Books, 1998.
Building a New Nation, 1789-1803. New York, Benchmark Books, 1998.
The Jeffersonian Republicans, 1800-1820. New York, Benchmark Books, 1998.
Andrew Jackson's America, 1821-1850. New York, Benchmark Books, 1998.
The Cotton South and the Mexican War, 1835-1850. New York, Benchmark Books, 1998.
The Civil War, 1860-1866. New York, Benchmark Books, 1998.

Fiction (James Lincoln Collier)

The Teddy Bear Habit; or, How I Became a Winner, illustrated by Lee Lorenz. New York, Norton, 1967.
Rock Star. New York, Four Winds Press, 1970.
Why Does Everybody Think I'm Nutty?. New York, Grosset and Dunlap, 1971.
It's Murder at St. Basket's. New York, Grosset and Dunlap, 1972.
Rich and Famous: The Further Adventures of George Stable. New York, Four Winds Press, 1975.
Give Dad My Best. New York, Four Winds Press, 1976.
Planet Out of the Past. New York, Macmillan, 1983.
When the Stars Begin to Fall. New York, Delacorte, 1986.
Outside Looking In. New York, Macmillan, 1987.
The Winchesters. New York, Macmillan, 1988.

My Crooked Family. New York, Simon & Schuster, 1991.
The Clock, illustrated by Kelly Maddox. New York, Delacorte, 1992.
The Jazz Kid. New York, Puffin, 1996.

Nonfiction (James Lincoln Collier)

Cheers. New York, Avon, 1960.
Battleground: The United States Army in World War II. New York, Norton, 1965.
A Visit to the Fire House, photographs by Yale Joel. New York, Norton, 1967.
Which Musical Instrument Shall I Play?, photographs by Yale Joel. New York, Norton, 1969.
Danny Goes to the Hospital, photographs by Yale Joel. New York, Norton, 1970.
Practical Music Theory: How Music Is Put Together from Bach to Rock. New York, Norton, 1970.
The Hard Life of the Teenager. New York, Four Winds Press, 1972.
Inside Jazz. New York, Four Winds Press, 1973.
Jug Bands and Hand Made Music. New York, Grosset and Dunlap, 1973.
The Making of Man: The Story of Our Ancient Ancestors. New York, Four Winds Press, 1974.
Making Music for Money. New York, Watts, 1976.
CB. New York, Watts, 1977.
The Great Jazz Artists, illustrated by Robert Andrew Parker. New York, Four Winds Press, 1977.
Louis Armstrong: An American Success Story. New York, Macmillan, 1985.
Duke Ellington. New York, Macmillan, 1991.
Jazz: An American Saga. New York, Oxford University Press, 1993.

PUBLICATIONS FOR ADULTS

Nonfiction (Christopher Collier)

Editor, *The Public Records of the State of Connecticut, 1802-03,* Volume 11, State Library of Connecticut, 1967.
Roger Sherman's Connecticut: Yankee Politics and the American Revolution. Middletown, Connecticut, Wesleyan University Press, 1971.
Connecticut in the Continental Congress. Chester, Connecticut, Pequot Press, 1973.
Roger Sherman: Puritan Politician. New Haven Colony Historical Society, 1976.
The Pride of Bridgeport: Men and Machines in the Nineteenth Century. Bridgeport Museum of Art, Science, and Industry, 1979.
The Literature of Connecticut History, with Bonnie B. Collier. Hartford, Connecticut Humanities Council, 1983.
Decision in Philadelphia: The Constitutional Convention of 1787, with James Lincoln Collier. New York, Random House, 1986.

Contributor to *Lyme Miscellany,* edited by George Willauer, Middletown, Connecticut, Wesleyan University Press, 1977; and *Long Island Sound: The People and the Environment,* Oceanic Society, 1978. Author of foreword to *Connecticut: A Bibliography of Its History,* edited by Roger Parks, Hanover, University Press of New England, 1986. Contributor to history and legal journals. Editor,

Monographs in British History and Culture, 1967-72, and *Connecticut History Newsletter,* 1967-73.

Novels (James Lincoln Collier)

Somebody up There Hates Me. New York, Macfadden 1962.
Fires of Youth (as Charles Williams). London, Penguin, 1968.

Nonfiction (James Lincoln Collier)

The Hypocritical American: An Essay on Sex Attitudes in America. Indianapolis, Bobbs-Merrill, 1964.
The Fine Art of Swindling, with others, edited by Walter Brown Gibson. New York, Grosset and Dunlap, 1966.
Sex Education U.S.A.: A Community Approach, with others. New York, Sex Information and Education Council of the United States, 1968.
The Making of Jazz: A Comprehensive History. Boston, Houghton Mifflin, and London, Hart Davis MacGibbon, 1978.
Louis Armstrong: An American Genius. New York, Oxford University Press, 1983, as *Louis Armstrong: A Biography,* London, Joseph, 1984.
Decision in Philadelphia: The Constitutional Convention of 1787, with Christopher Collier. New York, Random House, 1986.
Duke Ellington. New York, Oxford University Press, and London, Joseph, 1987.
The Reception of Jazz in America; A New View. Brooklyn, Institute for Studies in American Music, Conservatory of Music, Brooklyn College of the City University of New York, 1988.
Benny Goodman and the Swing Era. New York, Oxford University Press, 1989.
The Rise of Selfishness in the United States. New York, Oxford University Press, 1991.
Jazz; the American Theme Song. New York, Oxford University Press, 1993.

*

Media Adaptations: *My Brother Sam Is Dead* has been adapted as a record, a cassette, and a filmstrip with cassette.

Biography: Entry in *Fifth Book of Junior Authors and Illustrators,* edited by Sally Holmes Holtze, New York, H.W. Wilson, 1983; essays in *Speaking for Ourselves: Autobiographical Sketches by Notable Authors of Books for Young Adults,* Volume 1, compiled and edited by Donald R. Gallo, National Council of Teachers of English, 1990.

Critical Studies: Entry in *Children's Literature Review,* Volume 3, Detroit, Gale, 1978, p. 44; entry in *Contemporary Literary Criticism,* Volume 30, Detroit, Gale, 1984, p. 70.

Manuscript Collections: Kerlan Collection, University of Minnesota, Minneapolis.

Christopher Collier comments:
    The young adult books I write with my brother are intended to teach about important aspects of American history. They are as carefully researched as are the books I write for other historians. My brother, James, works just as hard to make our stories exciting and believable. It is our hope that young people will have a good time learning history so that they will remember it for the rest of their lives.

James Lincoln Collier comments:
    It seems to me that the best audience for fiction in the United States is young people. Unimpressed by prizes and reviews, they read what they like, and to a surprising extent they like the best. That this is so is crucially important for American literature, for if these, the young, do not come to appreciate the best writing, there will a generation hence be no audience for literature; and soon after the great tradition of Melville, Hawthorne, James, Faulkner, Hemingway, and so many others will be dead.

*   *   *

    Christopher Collier and James Lincoln Collier are a brother team of writers best known for two historical fiction trilogies about adolescents growing up in New England during the American Revolution and the early days of the Republic. Christopher (Kit), an American historian and professor, provides the historical theme and framework for the novels, while James (Jim), a musician, editor, and writer gives life to the characters and plot.
    The Colliers have a clear purpose for writing their historical fiction: to teach history to potential learners by flinging them "into a living past." They believe that writers of historical fiction for young readers must perform "an act of creation that vivifies on paper scenes no longer replicable in concrete fact" (*ALAN Review,* Winter 1987, p. 5).
    This combination of historian and writer has produced some of the most accurate, enjoyable-to-read, teachable historical fiction novels written for young adults. The first book of the Brother Sam trilogy, *My Brother Sam Is Dead,* won a Newbery honor for its hard recreation of fact and empathetic understanding of human relationships. Because many historians view the American War for Independence as much a civil war as a revolution, the Colliers selection of Redding, Connecticut, as the setting is appropriate not only because Christopher knows it well but also because the known number of Loyalists and Patriots there was about equal. Timmy, the twelve-year-old protagonist, reflects this division in his own thinking. He mentally switches sides numerous times in the novel, favoring at one time the Patriotism of his brother Sam who has run off to serve in the Continental army, and then the Loyalism to the Crown of his Tory father, and then switching back again. The novel makes it clear that the decision of which side to support was not an easy one. Timmy is caught up between the idealistic hero worship of Sam and his father Eliphalet's disapproval of a rebellion over no more than "a few pence in taxes." The novel shows a realistic relationship between a father and his sons. And, when Tim must become a man and take on the responsibility of caring for his mother and the family business, he finds his own private war to be no easier. The ironic conclusion of the novel may make some young readers wonder if any war is ever noble. Sam is arrested on a trumped-up charge of stealing cattle and shot by the Continental army he served so loyally and idealistically.
    The next two books in this trilogy, *The Bloody Country* and *The Winter Hero,* also deal with the question of war as a solution to human problems. *The Bloody Country* follows pioneers from

Connecticut to the Wyoming Valley of Pennsylvania in a dispute that the two states eventually go to war over. The valley was awarded to Pennsylvania by Congress in 1782. Ben Buck, the young protagonist of the novel, his parents, his sister Annie and her husband, and the family slave Joe Mountain, half Indian and half black, are a part of the group of Connecticut settlers whom the Pennsylvanians are trying to dispossess. The Bucks have worked hard to make a life for themselves, building a flour mill on the banks of the Susquehanna near Wilkes Barre. If they are driven back to Connecticut they will lose all they own and their sacrifice will count for nought. Ben begins to realize that his only future is as a servant with no chance for a family or land. This causes him to reflect on the plight of Joe, attempting to look at him for the first time as a person rather than chattel. The book's theme is the balance between property values and the value of human life. It is full of action which leads from an Indian raid that kills Ben's mother to the flooding of the Susquehanna and the destruction of the mill. However, through all the action and the eventual positive outcome for the family, the difficult questions still remain unanswered.

The Winter Hero, the third book in the trilogy, is set in Massachusetts in 1778 during another rarely studied historical event—Shays' Rebellion. The Revolution is over, but laws passed in faraway Boston are making western Massachusetts farmers, who have no representatives, poorer while the rich are getting richer. The story is told through the eyes of twelve-year-old Justin Conkey and is filled with lessons in basic political economics that can be understood by young readers. Likewise, the concept of the importance of representation rather than conflict is a major theme. Although not as rich in interesting relationships as the first two novels, Justin's desire to be a hero is typical of an adolescent boy. Throughout the novel, even after he is forced to become a serving boy for a wealthy creditor, Major Mattoon, Justin continues to attempt to understand why some people can rule over others and why the power structure makes a few people rich at the expense of everyone else. As in the two earlier novels, the questions are left to the readers to answer.

The Arabus family trilogy is the second by the Collier brothers. It relates the story of blacks during the Revolution; the focus of these three novels is on the relationship of the Constitution to black Americans. *Jump Ship to Freedom,* the middle book of the trilogy which was written first, attempts to show how the sectional division over the slavery question affected the writing of the Constitution. The book introduces readers to Daniel, the son of Jack Arabus, whose story is told in book one, *War Comes to Willy Freeman.* Daniel is the slave of a cruel Stratford, Connecticut, couple who confiscate government bonds belonging to Dan's mother and hide them in a family Bible. Throughout the narrative Dan fights against his self-concept as a stupid "nigger," beginning to realize as the book progresses that his worth is not measured by his sale price and that he is as honest and honorable as anyone. Dan bravely follows his neighbor William Samuel Johnson to Philadelphia and the Constitutional Convention in an attempt to get his help in gaining some cash from U.S. notes given Dan's father for fighting in the Revolution. He meets up with Fatherscreft who has been charged with carrying a message from the Congress in New York to the Philadelphia Congress. Just before Fatherscreft dies he entrusts Dan with the message. Dan has learned from Fatherscreft that if the Convention fails the U.S. will probably fall apart and Dan's bonds will be worthless and he will be unable to purchase his or his mother's freedom. Ironically, however, he also learns that the message he is carrying includes a plan to continue slavery in all the states and unsettled wilderness south of the Ohio River.

Dan's story is continued in book three of the trilogy *Who is Carrie?* Carrie, who doesn't know where she came from, lives the life of a slave in New York City. During the story she thinks she learns who her parents were and, if she is right, she should not be a slave. Although she is powerless, she is never without hope. The importance of this book and the other five is that each asks some of the difficult questions of U.S. history in a way that adolescents cannot only grasp them, but come to understand the human importance of them.

—Arthea J.S. Reed

COLMAN, Hila

Pseudonym: Teresa Crayder. **Nationality:** American. **Born:** New York City. **Education:** Radcliffe College, Cambridge, Massachusetts. **Family:** Married Louis Colman in 1945; two sons. **Career:** Publicity/promotion officer, Russian War Relief, New York, 1940-45; executive director, Labor Book Club, New York, 1945-47; free-lance writer, since 1949. Member of Democratic Town Committee, Bridgewater, Connecticut; former member of Bridgewater Board of Education, Connecticut; former chairperson of Zoning Board of Appeals, Bridgewater, Connecticut. **Awards:** Child Study Committee award, 1962, for *The Girl from Puerto Rico*; Garden State Children's Book award, New Jersey Library Association, 1979, for *Nobody Has to Be a Kid Forever.* **Address:** 76 Hemlock Rd., Box 95, Bridgewater, Connecticut 06752, U.S.A.

PUBLICATIONS FOR YOUNG ADULTS

Fiction

The Big Step. New York, Morrow, 1957.
A Crown for Gina. New York, Morrow, 1958.
Julie Builds Her Castle. New York, Morrow, 1959.
Best Wedding Dress. New York, Morrow, 1960.
The Girl from Puerto Rico. New York, Morrow, 1961.
Mrs. Darling's Daughter. New York, Morrow, 1962.
Watch That Watch. New York, Morrow, 1962; Kingswood, Surrey, World's Work, 1963.
Peter's Brownstone House, illustrated by Leonard Weisgard. New York, Morrow, 1963.
Phoebe's First Campaign. New York, Morrow, 1963.
Cathy and Lisette (as Teresa Crayder), illustrated by Evelyn Copelman. New York, Doubleday, 1964.
Classmates by Request. New York, Morrow, 1964.
Christmas Cruise. New York, Morrow, 1965.
The Boy Who Couldn't Make up His Mind. New York, Macmillan, 1965.
Bride at Eighteen. New York, Morrow, 1966.
Dangerous Summer. New York, Bantam, 1966.

Sudden Fame (as Teresa Crayder). New York, Macmillan, 1966.

Thoroughly Modern Millie (novelization of screenplay). Bantam, 1966.

Car-Crazy Girl. New York, Morrow, 1967.

Mixed-Marriage Daughter. New York, Morrow, 1968.

Something out of Nothing, illustrated by Sally Trinkle. New York, Weybright and Talley, 1968.

Andy's Landmark House, illustrated by Fermin Rocker. New York, Parents' Magazine Press, 1969.

Claudia, Where Are You?. New York, Morrow, 1969.

The Happenings at North End School. New York, Morrow, 1970.

Daughter of Discontent. New York, Morrow, 1971.

End of the Game, photographs by Milton Charles. Cleveland, World, 1971.

The Family and the Fugitive. New York, Morrow, 1972.

Benny the Misfit, illustrated by Elaine Raphael. New York, Crowell, 1973.

Chicano Girl. New York, Morrow, 1973.

Diary of a Frantic Kid Sister. New York, Crown, 1973.

Friends and Strangers on Location. New York, Morrow, 1974.

After the Wedding. New York, Morrow, 1975.

Ethan's Favorite Teacher, illustrated by John Wallner. New York, Crown, 1975.

That's the Way It Is, Amigo, illustrated by Glo Coalson, New York, Crowell, 1975.

The Amazing Miss Laura. New York, Morrow, 1976.

Nobody Has to Be a Kid Forever. New York, Crown, 1976.

The Case of the Stolen Bagels, illustrated by Pat Grant Porter. New York, Crown, 1977.

Sometimes I Don't Love My Mother. New York, Morrow, 1977.

Rachel's Legacy. New York, Morrow, 1978.

The Secret Life of Harold the Bird Watcher, illustrated by Charles Robinson. New York, Harper, 1978.

Tell Me No Lies. New York, Crown, 1978.

Ellie's Inheritance. New York, Morrow, 1979.

Accident. New York, Morrow, 1980.

What's the Matter with the Dobsons?. New York, Crown, 1980.

Confessions of a Storyteller. New York, Crown, 1981.

The Family Trap. New York, Morrow, 1982.

Girl Meets Boy. New York, Scholastic, 1982.

Don't Tell Me That You Love Me. New York, Archway, 1983.

My Friend, My Love. New York, Archway, 1983.

Not for Love. New York, Morrow, 1983.

Just the Two of Us. New York, Scholastic, 1984.

Nobody Told Me What I Need to Know. New York, Morrow, 1984.

Weekend Sisters. New York, Morrow, 1985.

A Fragile Love. New York, Pocket Books, 1985.

Triangle of Love. New York, Pocket Books, 1985.

Happily Ever After. New York, Scholastic, 1986.

Suddenly. New York, Morrow. 1987.

The Double Life of Angela Jones. New York, Morrow, 1988.

Rich and Famous Like My Mom. New York, Crown, 1988.

Forgotten Girl. New York, Crown, 1990.

Nonfiction

Beauty, Brains, and Glamour: A Career in Magazine Publishing, illustrated by Jacqueline Tomes. Cleveland, World, 1968.

A Career in Medical Research, illustrated by Edna Mason Kaula. Cleveland, World, 1968.

Making Movies: Student Films to Features, illustrated by George Guzzi. Cleveland, World, 1969.

City Planning: What It's All About—In the Planners' Own Words. Cleveland, World, 1971.

PUBLICATIONS FOR ADULTS

Nonfiction

The Country Weekend Cookbook, with Louis Colman. New York, Barrows, 1961.

Cleopatra (as Teresa Crayder). New York, Coward McCann, 1969.

Hanging On. New York, Atheneum, 1977.

*

Media Adaptations: *Tell Me No Lies* (Afterschool Specials, ''Unforgivable Secrets'' and ''Sometimes I Don't Love My Mother,'') ABC-TV, 1982.

Biography: Essay in *Authors and Artists for Young Adults,* Volume 1, by Hila Colman. Detroit, Gale, 1989; essay in *Speaking for Ourselves: Autobiographical Sketches by Notable Authors of Books for Young Adults,* Volume 1, compiled and edited by Donald R. Gallo, National Council of Teachers of English, 1990; essay in *Something about the Author Autobiography Series,* Volume 14, Detroit, Gale, 1992.

Hila Colman comments:

I love writing for adolescents because I find it an exciting age—something new is always happening. It is a dramatic time of life, a point when leaving childhood and becoming an adult are meeting head-on with all the accompanying conflicts of emotions, choices to be made, and new experiences to be enjoyed or feared. The number of stories to be written are endless, and as a writer I feel lucky to have so much rich material to choose from.

Now, as a grandmother, I thought I was finished writing for teenagers. But, like eating peanuts, I guess it is something that you find it difficult to stop. So, here I am, back at my typewriter (not a word processor) working on a new book. This time, however, I am writing without a contract, which I always had in the past, but going at my own pace. I do not want any more deadlines. But I am having fun with the book and I think it is a good one. It is called *My Father's Wife.* Fortunately, a writer does not have to retire, and I think that is a good thing. I find the current young generation diversified and full of surprises, and I am grateful to them for providing me with so much rich material to write about.

*   *   *

Hila Colman writes books about the interpersonal problems young adolescents have at home and with peers. She does this with clarity and directness, dealing with intergenerational and intragenerational concerns of grandparents, parents, and children.

Her grandmothers are usually strong people, some with conventional and some with unconventional views of social behavior. Her parents are shown with strengths, frailties, and self-doubts. Teenagers wrestle with the multiple social and personal crises of growing up.

Mixed-Marriage Daughter concerns the child of a Jewish mother and a Protestant father. Her Jewish grandmother desperately wants the child to believe in and to practice the orthodox Jewish faith. The child questions, rebels, and makes peace with her extended family. She manages in the end to be a friend of, but not bound to, her grandmother.

At some point many young people begin a secret diary. Sara begins *Diary of a Frantic Kid Sister* the week of her eleventh birthday and ends it as her twelfth birthday approaches. She vows that she will tell only the real truth here, because everyone she knows lies—her parents, her teachers, the principal of her school. The person who lies the most and thinks she gets away with it is Sara's sister Deirdre, four years her elder. Deirdre, Sara perceives, is more loved by their parents, more popular in school, and more accomplished in life. Sara's grief over Deirdre is all the more intense because of her own feelings of inadequacy and aimlessness. Her anger over her sister gives way in time to some understanding of her sister's complications in life. Only then are they able to coexist, almost peacefully. One particularly welcome aspect of the story is the serious professional interests of the three main characters—first mother and Deirdre, and then Sara. The former two are committed to music, the latter to literature. The needs of women for creativity and independence, as well as family connectedness, are clearly presented. And Sara herself, for all the daily hassles she must contend with, remains full of zest. This is a warm and very witty book.

Rachel's Legacy, set in the Jewish East Side of New York City in the early 1900s, is about the immigrant experience. The Ginsbergs arrive at Ellis Island from their Russian village with great hopes and expectations for the future. Their story, spanning three generations of family life, is full of strong and complex emotions, successes and failures, and support and betrayal as family members reach out in diverse ways to make their place in the new world.

Tell Me No Lies focuses upon a teenager who has never known her real father. She has been told by her mother that her father left for Saudi Arabia right after her birth. When her mother finally tells her the truth, she seeks to meet her father, who is now married with three more children and doesn't know she exists. The meeting is a painful one, and the teenager realizes that the settled stranger does not acknowledge her as his daughter. Once she gets to know her father, the daughter is more able to forgive her mother, accept her mother's affection for her, and accept her mother's new husband's desire to adopt her.

What's the Matter with the Dobsons? looks at a well-educated, well-to-do family that seemingly has everything. But look again— thirteen-year-old Amanda feels that her father favors her younger sister Lisa, and Lisa feels that her mother favors older sister Amanda. The parents quarrel over the children, and the quarrels become so intense that the parents separate. Amanda and Lisa want their parents back again; they want a whole family. But as mother explains, it isn't so simple when people get into situations they don't know how to get out of. The parents do reunite, but no great changes come about. Parents and children are the same people, with the same faults and virtues as before. Only now they know they have to make accommodations if their family life is to work;

they can't each have their own way. The book travels outside of the immediate family as well, presenting with compassion and restraint the problems of teenage dating and the issue of a widowed grandmother dating.

Colman's families and family members have real feelings and real problems. They do not all live happily ever after. But they are able to deal with adversity, alter courses in their lives, and provide comfort to those close to them. Colman's works reflect more accurately than most American books for adolescents the changing family structures and functions, and the meaning of these changes to family members. As such they are possible sources of comfort for some readers in personal and family crises, who will glean from these books identification, understanding, and support.

—Mary Lystad

CONFORD, Ellen

Nationality: American. **Born:** New York, New York, 20 March 1942. **Education:** Hofstra University, Hempstead, New York, 1959-62. **Family:** Married David H. Conford in 1960; one son. **Career:** Writer of books for children and young adults. **Awards:** One of the best books of the year from *School Library Journal,* 1971, for *Impossible, Possum*; one of the Children's Books of International Interest, 1974, for *Just the Thing for Geraldine*; one of the Library of Congress Children's Books of the Year, 1974, for *Me and the Terrible Two*; listed in Child Study Association of America Books of the Year, 1975, both *The Luck of Pokey Bloom* and *Dear Lovey Hart, I Am Desperate*; one of the Best Books for Young Adults by the American Library Association, 1976, for *The Alfred G. Graebner Memorial High School Handbook of Rules and Regulations*; Surrey School award, 1981, Pacific Northwest Young Reader's Choice Award, 1981, and California Young Reader's Medal, 1982, all for *Hail, Hail, Camp Timberwood*; One of *School Library Journal's* Best Books of the Year, 1983, and received a Parents' Choice award, 1983, for *Lenny Kandell, Smart Aleck* ; Parents' Choice award, 1985, for *Why Me?,* 1986, for *A Royal Pain;* South Carolina Young Adult Book award, 1986-87, and South Dakota Prairie Pasque award, 1989, both for *If This is Love, I'll Take Spaghetti.* **Agent:** McIntosh and Otis Inc., 310 Madison Ave., New York, New York 10017. **Address:** 26 Strathmore Rd., Great Neck, New York 11023, U.S.A.

PUBLICATIONS FOR YOUNG ADULTS

Fiction

Dreams of Victory, illustrated by Gail Rockwell. Boston, Little, Brown, 1973.

Felicia, the Critic, illustrated by Arvis Stewart. Boston, Little, Brown, 1973; London, Hamish Hamilton, 1975.

Me and the Terrible Two, illustrated by Charles Carroll. Boston, Little, Brown, 1974.

The Luck of Pokey Bloom, illustrated by Bernice Lowenstein. Boston, Little, Brown, 1975.

Dear Lovey Hart, I Am Desperate. Boston, Little, Brown, 1975.

The Alfred G. Graebner Memorial High School Handbook of Rules and Regulations. Boston, Little, Brown, 1976.

And This Is Laura. Boston, Little, Brown, 1977.

Hail, Hail, Camp Timberwood, illustrated by Gail Owens. Boston, Little, Brown, 1978.

Anything for a Friend. Boston, Little, Brown, 1979.

We Interrupt This Semester for an Important Bulletin. Boston, Little, Brown, 1979.

The Revenge of the Incredible Dr. Rancid and His Youthful Assistant, Jeffrey. Boston, Little, Brown, 1980.

Seven Days to a Brand New Me. Boston, Little, Brown, 1982.

To All My Fans, with Love, from Sylvie. Boston, Little, Brown, 1982.

If This Is Love, I'll Take Spaghetti. New York, Four Winds Press, 1983; London, Fontana, 1984.

Lenny Kandell, Smart Aleck, illustrated by Walter Gaffney-Kessell. Boston, Little, Brown, 1983.

You Never Can Tell. Boston, Little, Brown, 1984.

Strictly for Laughs. New York, Putnam, 1985.

Why Me?. Boston, Little, Brown, 1985.

A Royal Pain. New York, Scholastic, 1986.

The Things I Did for Love. New York, Bantam, 1987.

Genie with the Light Blue Hair. New York, Bantam, 1989.

Loving Someone Else. New York, Bantam, 1991.

Dear Mom, Get Me Out of Here! Boston, Little, Brown, 1992.

I Love You, I Hate You, Get Lost. New York, Scholastic, 1994.

PUBLICATIONS FOR CHILDREN

Fiction

Impossible, Possum, illustrated by Rosemary Wells. Boston, Little, Brown, 1971.

Why Can't I Be William?, illustrated by Philip Wende. Boston, Little, Brown, 1972.

Just the Thing for Geraldine, illustrated by John Larrecq. Boston, Little, Brown, 1974.

Eugene the Brave, illustrated by Larrecq. Boston, Little, Brown, 1978.

A Case for Jenny Archer, illustrated by Diane Palmisciano. Boston, Little, Brown, 1988.

A Job for Jenny Archer, illustrated by Diane Palmisciano. Boston, Little, Brown, 1988.

Jenny Archer, Author, illustrated by Diane Palmisciano. Boston, Little, Brown, 1989.

What's Cooking, Jenny Archer?, illustrated by Diane Palmisciano. Little Brown, 1989.

Jenny Archer to the Rescue. Boston, Little, Brown, 1990.

Can Do, Jenny Archer, illustrated by Diane Palmisciano. Boston, Springboard Books, 1991.

Nibble, Nibble, Jenny Archer, illustrated by Diane Palmisciano. Boston, Little, Brown, 1993.

Get the Picture, Jenny Archer? Boston, Little, Brown, 1994.

Norman Newman: My Sister the Witch. Troll/Little Rainbow, 1995.

Norman Newman and the Werewolf of Walnut Street. Troll/Little Rainbow, 1995.

The Frog Princess of Pelham. Boston, Little, Brown, 1997.

*

Media Adaptations: *And This Is Laura* and *The Alfred G. Graebner Memorial High School Handbook of Rules and Regulations* (television movie); "Getting Even: A Wimp's Revenge" (based on *The Revenge of the Incredible Dr. Rancid and His Youthful Assistant, Jeffrey*) (an "ABC Afterschool Special"), 1986. *Dear Lovey Hart, I Am Desperate* (an "ABC After School Special," also film), Walt Disney's Educational Media Co.; *Dreams of Victory* (sound recording disc); *If This Is Love, I'll Take Spaghetti, Lenny Kandell, Smart Aleck, The Luck of Pokey Bloom,* and *The Revenge of the Incredible Dr. Rancid and His Youthful Assistant, Jeffrey,* (sound recording cassettes.)

Biography: Essay in *Speaking for Ourselves: Autobiographical Sketches by Notable Authors of Books for Young Adults,* Volume 1, compiled and edited by Donald R. Gallo, National Council of Teachers of English, 1990.

Manuscript Collections: Kerlan Collection, University of Minnesota, Minneapolis.

Critical Studies: Entry in *Children's Literature Review,* Volume 10, Detroit, Gale, 1986.

*   *   *

Ellen Conford has explained that she writes books she hopes will lure readers away from television for a few hours, and her books are designed to do just that—compete with the streamlined world of videos and TV. Fast-paced and optimistic, Conford's stories offer engaging, sometimes quirky characters, uncomplicated plots, and simple solutions, complete with a generous dose of humor. Written in a style best described as comic realism, the majority of the books deal with the lighter problems of adolescence—especially romance—as seen through the eyes of teenagers.

Conford's works can be grouped into two categories, each with a slightly different approach. Her earlier works, embracing most of the publications from *Dear Lovey Hart, I Am Desperate* to *Hail, Hail, Camp Timberwood,* employ thirteen and fourteen-year-old girls as protagonists and treat the transition from childhood to adolescence, often incorporating romance as a plot complication. Several of these also include a change in the heroine's surroundings and use her gradual adjustment as a way of illustrating emotional growth. Conford returns to this strategy, but with a male protagonist, in a recent title, *Dear Mom, Get Me Out of Here.*

Love and the attendant complications become progressively more important in the works published after 1978, such as *The Things I Did for Love,* which humorously explores why people fall in love. The books from this period frequently feature girls aged fifteen to seventeen and are a logical continuation of Conford's previous stories. It is as if her earlier heroines have grown older and now confront a new set of problems; indeed, *We Interrupt This Semester for an Important Bulletin* actually continues the adventures of Carrie Wasserman, the protagonist from *Dear Lovey Hart.*

A number of the later publications also experiment with more improbable plots or settings, resulting in some of Conford's weakest works. Her recent fantasy novel, *Genie with the Light Blue Hair,* tries to blend romance and humor with a magic lamp, Aladdin-style; *A Royal Pain,* a strained variation of Mark Twain's *The Prince and the Pauper,* takes place in a fictitious European country.

Conford's protagonists narrate their own stories, with the cast of characters remaining much the same from book to book. The typical heroine is an average girl, mildly pretty, reasonably intelligent, and possessed of a wry sense of humor. Her biggest problem is unrequited love and/or a lack of self-confidence. Usually she has one or more close girlfriends. Practical and passive, they serve as a sounding board for her woes but rarely emerge as strong characters. In addition, the heroine often begins the story with a male as a platonic friend or convenient companion; he provides rides to school and casual conversation, then steps (or is shunted) aside once her love interest appears. As for the love interest, in many stories he is virtually faceless—attractive, but with little personality. Most protagonists come from happy, healthy families, complete with father, mother, and one or two siblings. Firmly ensconced in the middle class, they live in comfortable houses in suburbia, spending their time at school and shopping malls.

Conford deals with surfaces and the visible rather than complex psychological studies. Accordingly, her heroines usually have fairly straightforward goals: they want to be popular or they want a particular boy's affection. The actions taken to achieve this also affect exteriors—buying new clothes, trying new makeup, or learning to make small talk. Social success and physical attractiveness are important to them and are even sometimes equated. This is ironic since an underlying theme in many of the books is developing self-confidence by recognizing inner qualities. Occasionally Conford tries to invert the message: *Why Me?* and *You Never Can Tell* touch on the perils of loving someone for appearance rather than self. Unfortunately, neither story has the impact it should, perhaps because, like the protagonists themselves, Conford settles for surface rather than substance and neither develops the characters nor delves into the issues; indeed, in the latter, she undercuts her own point by ending with the protagonist still loving someone for his appearance.

Conford's plots have become progressively more streamlined, with fewer scenes devoted to developing characters or setting and greater emphasis on the heroine's internal monologues detailing her obsession with a particular boy. Accordingly, the early novels, most notably *The Alfred G. Graebner Memorial High School Handbook of Rules and Regulations* and *Dear Lovey Hart, I Am Desperate,* contain some of Conford's best writing. In the former, the story advances thorough a series of well-chosen vignettes; with the latter, strong secondary characters and subplots provide the necessary depth. Her approach occasionally backfires in later works where the subject matter could benefit from more complex plots, stronger characterizations, and/or less self-absorbed protagonists.

Conford's greatest asset is her humor, whether it be the wry commentary of her narrators, the one-liners in the dialogue, or the cleverly constructed incidents that leave the protagonist bewildered and the reader delighted. One of Conford's favorite and most effective techniques for treating a subject is to juxtapose the real and the imaginary. For example, *Seven Days to a Brand New Me* rests on the humorous contrast between the effervescent advice given in a self-help book, the exotic adventures described in a paperback romance, and the everyday life and frustrations of the narrator, a high school girl struggling to overcome shyness and gain the attention and affection of the boy at the next locker.

At her worst, Conford produces readable but forgettable fiction; at her best, warm and witty tales portraying the pitfalls of adolescence—well worth missing a few television shows to enjoy.

—Deidre Johnson

CONLY, Jane Leslie

Nationality: American. **Born:** Virginia. **Education:** Attended Smith College; attended Writing Seminars Program at Johns Hopkins University. **Family:** Married; one daughter. **Awards:** Newbery honor book, for *Crazy Lady!* **Address:** c/o HarperCollins Children's Books, 10 East 53rd St., New York, New York 10022, U.S.A.

PUBLICATIONS FOR YOUNG ADULTS

Fiction

Racso and the Rats of NIMH. New York, Harper, 1986.
RT, Margaret and the Rats of NIMH. New York, Harper, 1990.
Crazy Lady! New York, Harper, 1993.
Trout Summer. New York, Henry Holt and Co., 1995

*   *   *

Jane Leslie Conly's emerging career as a writer for young adults includes two animal/sci-fi titles, *Racso and the Rats of NIMH* and *RT, Margaret and the Rats of NIMH*. These titles are sequels to her father's (Robert C. O'Brien, pseudonym used by Robert Conly) highly acclaimed work *Mrs. Frisby and the Rats of NIMH*. All three books focus on a group of rats who have become a super intelligent life form through experimentation with their DNA at a laboratory named NIMH, the National Institute of Mental Health. Although these new life forms still look like rats physically, they are capable of reading and learning so successfully that they deliberately keep their knowledge from all humans, including the scientists at NIMH. As the rats become conscious of their continuing dependency on humans they courageously and secretly form their own civilization by growing their own food independent of man in a remote forest preserve named Thorn Valley. The direction in which their society evolves and their ultimate confrontation with man is the central focus of the Conly novels.

Jane Leslie Conly explores the struggles of the new NIMH civilization at Thorn Valley by introducing a new generation of young adult characters who are the offspring of the original group at NIMH. These characters, including Racso, Timothy, and Christopher, frequently find themselves in humorous predicaments. Spunky and outspoken Racso is a recognizable young adult with his cravings for candy bars, potato chips, and pop rock and his dislike for being told what to do, especially by adults. More importantly these young adults become aware of their social responsibility within the formation of their new utopian civilization "where work and pleasure are a part of everyone's life." Racso's contributions in saving the NIMH culture are notable because of the knowledge he brings about human use of computer technology.

Conly's second book *RT, Margaret and the Rats of NIMH* returns to the issue of human reaction to the rats as a new, intelligent life form. Their initial discovery by humans comes through two children when ten-year old Margaret and her younger, asthmatic brother RT (which stands for the name Artie or Arthur) become separated and lost from their parents while camping in Thorn Valley. Christopher, a young rat from NIMH, secretly takes food from the NIMH community and gives it to RT. When Margaret discovers Christopher and his capabilities as a new life form, she ineffectually holds him for ransom in exchange for guidance out of the wilderness. Ultimately the rats help the children return to their home and human civilization in exchange for helping with chores and tasks in the rat community. A sense of self-esteem and experience in cooperative learning between the human children and the NIMH rats suggests positive potential between the two intelligent civilizations. Conly appeals to a young adult audience through her ability to inject humor and lively action into the adventures and challenges of the younger NIMH generation in Thorn Valley.

Crazy Lady! is Conly's first venture into contemporary realism. Adult substance abuse and prejudice toward the developmentally disabled give this book a pensive tone. The central character, Vernon Dibbs, is an angry, overweight kid who lacks self esteem. His mom's recent death overwhelms him since she was his source of encouragement and comfort when he is held back a year in grade school. Eventually he receives help (tutoring) from a neighbor and in return he befriends an alcoholic mother, Maxine Flouter—the crazy lady—and her mentally challenged son, Ronald. With help from his family and buddies, Vernon organizes a neighborhood carnival to raise money for Ronald to attend a local Special Olympics event where he wears a wonderful pair of ''red and white checkered Converse running shoes.'' Vern gains a sense of compassion and self confidence through his relationship with Maxine and Ronald. The first person narrative from Vern's point of view gives authenticity, immediacy, and readability to the plot without being preachy. This book is worthy of its Newbery honor recognition.

Trout Summer, like the previous novel, deals with angry young adults. Shana Allen and her brother Cody reel from their dad's abrupt desertion and their mom's stubborn insistence that the family move to an urban location, away from the small town, country way of life they love. These events are partially offset when their mom allows them to spend the summer at a dilapidated shack along the banks of a remote river in western Pennsylvania. (Mom commutes to them on the weekends). Since both of them love the outdoors and fishing, they seem to thrive, despite a pesky old man, Henry Luck, who says he is a federal ranger in charge of protecting and restocking the river with trout. This frail old man becomes their mentor—teaching them about trout fishing, white water canoeing, and the original Algonquin people who once inhabited the area. These wilderness adventures make for pleasurable reading while Shana and Cody grow in emotional maturity as they respond to Mr. Luck's declining mental and physical health. The evolving, positive relationship between younger and older generations makes Conly's most recent novel a worthwhile reading experience.

—Richard D. Seiter

CONRAD, Pam

Nationality: American. **Born:** New York, New York, 18 June 1947. **Education:** Hofstra University, Hempstead, New York, 1977-79; New School for Social Research, New York, B.A. 1984. **Family:** Married Robert R. Conrad in 1967 (divorced, 1982); two daughters. **Career:** Writer, from 1979; teacher of writing courses at Queens College, New York. **Awards:** Society of Children's Book Writers grant, 1982; Western Writers of America Spur

award, American Library Association (ALA) notable book and best book for young adults citations, Society of Children's Book Writers Golden Kite award honor book citation, National Council for Social Studies and the Children's Book Council notable trade book in the field of social sciences citation, *Horn Book* honor list citation, National Cowboy Hall of Fame Western Heritage award, and Child Study Association of America's children's books of the year citation, all 1985; International Reading Association Children's Book award, *Boston Globe-Horn Book* award honor book, Women's National Book Association Judy Lopez Memorial award, and Society of Midland Authors' outstanding books about the Midwest or by midwestern authors citation, all 1986; and ALA *Booklist* ''Best of the '80s'' books for children citation, all for *Prairie Songs.* ALA recommended book for the reluctant young adult reader citation, 1987, and International Reading Association young adult choices citation, 1988, both for *Holding Me Here;* ALA best book for young adults citation, 1987, for *What I Did for Roman;* ALA *Booklist* children's editors' choices citation, 1988, for *Staying Nine;* ALA best books for young adults citation, ALA *Booklist* Children's Editors' Choices citation, Western Writers of America Spur award for best western juvenile, and National Council for the Social Studies and Children's Book Council notable children's trade book in social studies citation, all 1989, and International Reading Association teachers' choices citation, 1990, all for *My Daniel;* ALA notable children's book citation, and *New York Times* notable book citation, both 1989, *Horn Book* Fanfare honor list, and International Reading Association and Children's Book Council children's choice citation, both 1990, all for *The Tub People;* *Boston Globe-Horn* Book Fiction award honor book, 1990, Notable Trade Books for Language Arts, National Council of Teachers of English, 1990, and Edgar Allan Poe award, Mystery Writers of America, 1991, all for *Stonewords: A Ghost Story;* Orbis Pictus award honor book, National Council of Teachers of English, 1991, and Notable Children's Trade Books in Social Studies, National Council for Social Studies/Children's Book Council, 1991, for *Praire Visions;* *Publisher's Weekly* best books for children citation, ALA Best Books for children citation, Canada's Governor General's award, all 1996, all for *The Rooster's Gift.* **Agent:** Maria Carvainis, Maria Carvainis Agency, Inc., 235 West End Ave., New York, New York 10023, U.S.A. **Died:** 22 January 1996 in Rockville Center, New York.

PUBLICATIONS FOR YOUNG ADULTS

Fiction

Prairie Songs, illustrated by Darryl S. Zudeck. New York, Harper, 1985.
Holding Me Here. New York, Harper, 1986.
What I Did for Roman. New York, Harper, 1987; as *A Seal upon My Heart,* London, Oxford University Press, 1988.
Taking the Ferry Home. New York, Harper, 1988.
My Daniel. New York, Harper, 1989.
Stonewords: A Ghost Story. New York, Harper, 1990.
Pedro's Journal, illustrated by Peter Koeppen. Honesdale, Pennsylvania, Boyds Mills Press, 1991.
Prairie Visions: The Life and Times of Solomon Butcher, illustrated by Zudeck. New York, HarperCollins, 1991.
Our House: Stories of Levittown. New York, Scholastic, 1995.
Zoe Rising. New York, HarperCollins, 1996.

PUBLICATIONS FOR CHILDREN

Fiction

I Don't Live Here!, illustrated by Diane de Groat. New York, Dutton, 1983.

Pumpkin Moon. New York, Harcourt, 1984.

Seven Silly Circles, illustrated by Mike Wimmer. New York, Harper, 1987.

Staying Nine, illustrated by Mike Wimmer. New York, Harper, 1988.

The Tub People (picture book), illustrated by Richard Egielski. New York, Harper, 1988.

The Lost Sailor (picture book), illustrated by Richard Egielski. New York, HarperCollins, 1992.

The Tub Grandfather (picture book), illustrated by Richard Egielski. New York, HarperCollins, 1993.

Molly and the Strawberry Day (picture book), illustrated by Mary Szilagyi. New York, Harper, 1994.

Doll Face Has a Party! (picture book). New York, HarperCollins, 1994.

Animal Lingo (picture book). New York, HarperCollins, 1995.

Call Me Ahnighito (picture book). New York, HarperCollins, 1995.

The Rooster's Gift (picture book). New York, HarperCollins, 1996.

Animal Lullabies (picture book). New York, HarperCollins, 1997.

Is Anyone Here My Age? New York, Hyperion, 1997.

Kitchen Poem (picture book). New York, HarperCollins, 1998.

Doll Face Sequel (picture book). New York, HarperCollins, 1998.

Anna Roses Winkle John (picture book). New York, Scholastic, 1998.

Tub People Christmas (picture book). New York, HarperCollins, 1998.

The Mess (picture book). New York, Hyperion, 1998.

The Big Dog, the Big Rabbit, and the Old Man (picture book). New York, HarperCollins, 1998.

Blue Willow. New York, Philomel, forthcoming.

*

Biography: Entry in *Sixth Book of Junior Authors and Illustrators,* New York, H.W. Wilson, 1989; essay in *Speaking for Ourselves, Too* compiled and edited by Donald R. Gallo, National Council of Teachers of English, 1993.

Critical Studies: Entry in *Children's Literature Review,* Vol. 18, Detroit, Gale, 1989.

*   *   *

Pam Conrad's writing includes a wide variety of award-winning stories. She has created picture books, stories for young readers, and middle and young adult novels concerning a number of themes, settings, and situations.

Her first book, *I Don't Live Here!,* is for younger readers. While she was sending it to publishers she began developing her second book, *Prairie Songs.* Published in 1985, this historical novel has received numerous awards, including the 1986 International Reading Association Children's Book award.

A turn of the century novel, *Prairie Songs* takes place in Nebraska. The Downing family lives in a sod home, miles from any neighbors. To the narrator, Louisa, it is a beautiful place but lonely and desolate to the newcomer Emmeline Berryman. Through Louisa's eyes, we watch Emmeline change from a beautiful, hopeful lady expecting her first child to a miserable and pathetic figure. Tragically, she loses the baby and eventually succumbs to madness. This would be a profoundly sad story except the Downings are pioneer people of courage, strength, determination, loyalty, and resourcefulness. Their ability to endure provides a balance between the tragic experience of Emmeline and the heroic efforts of many prairie families.

In 1991, Conrad wrote *Prairie Visions: The Life and Times of Solomon Butcher.* We were introduced to Butcher in *Prairie Songs* when he photographed the Downing family. This nonfiction exploration of prairie life includes stories and photos collected by Butcher in the late 1800s. Taken together, *Prairie Visions* and *Prairie Songs* provide an important historical description of life in the sod houses. The excellent writing deserves to be read aloud and is especially appealing to younger adolescents.

Nebraska is also the setting for *My Daniel.* Julia Creath Summerwaite, eighty years old, has come east to see her grandchildren and take them to the Natural History Museum. The narration is alternated chapter by chapter between Julia and the author. Julia chronicles the adventures she shared with her brother during the prairie years, and Conrad describes the modern-day visit to the museum. This is an extraordinary story about sixteen-year-old Daniel who finds the remains of an enormous dinosaur in the creek bed of his farm. He tries to keep the knowledge from the fortune hunters but in the process loses his life when struck by lightening. Julia is eventually able to contact a reputable paleontologist who takes the bones to the museum and reconstructs them into an enormous brontosaurus. Her story, her memories, her love for Nebraska and her family make Julia a remarkable and memorable character.

For the younger adolescent reader, Conrad wrote *Stonewords: A Ghost Story.* Winner of the 1991 Edgar Award given by the Mystery Writers of America, the story is a complex, intricate plot of two girls who can travel back and forth through time. Zoe and Zoe Louise lived in the same house, separated by a staircase and one hundred years of time. Zoe lives with her grandparents because her mother is a shadowy person who periodically slips in and quickly out of her daughter's life. The reader will recognize the psychological undercurrents in what on the surface appears to be a time travel ghost story. Loneliness and the need for an imaginary playmate coupled with the need for a nurturing mother are critical pieces of Zoe's circumstances. These needs provide the motivation necessary for her to continue to seek out such a dangerous adventure. Suspenseful and strange, scary enough to hold interest, this mysterious ghost story proves how versatile Conrad can be as a writer.

Learning the truth about people is a theme that runs through three of Conrad's young adult novels. In *Holding Me Here,* Robin Lewis snoops to learn about a boarder in her home. Believing she can bring about a reconciliation between the woman and an estranged husband, Robin interferes and almost creates a disaster. Robin is so well defined that readers will ache for her when she realizes that good intentions aren't enough, and a little knowledge is a dangerous thing.

In *What I Did for Roman,* sixteen-year-old Darcie wants to discover the truth about her real father and discovers a very painful family secret. She also believes she has fallen in love with a man, Roman, who works in a zoo. Feeling desperate for affection and security she follows him around all summer and almost dies as he "tests death." In coming to terms with the loss of Roman, she realizes that she only knew one truth about him.

Ali Mintz learns the truth about the life of rich and beautiful Simone Silver in *Taking the Ferry Home.* Vacationing on a resort island, Ali meets the wealthy Simone and they attempt to become friends. This plot is based on the old themes and stereotypes about rich girls, and neither character has the qualities or depth found in Conrad's other works. The story includes adults who struggle with substance abuse, adding to the overall tone of heaviness and despair. Conrad once again effectively uses the narrative technique of alternating chapters between Simone and Ali. They take turns telling their story which provides each of them the opportunity to express their own point of view.

Taken together, Pam Conrad has produced a notable collection of works for young readers and young adults. Her words are imbued with meaning. She has demonstrated her understanding of the worries, concerns, and desires of young people and has provided realistic portraits of them. Her descriptions are fresh and wise, leaving the reader satisfied and perhaps inspired. Her phrases are memorable for their touching and simple truth. Her untimely death in 1996 has left a gap in the genre of Young Adult literature.

—Caroline S. McKinney

COONEY, Caroline B

Nationality: American. **Born:** 10 May 1947. **Education:** Attended Indiana University, 1965-66; Massachusetts General Hospital School of Nursing, 1966-67; University of Connecticut, 1968. **Awards:** Junior Literary Guild selection, for *Safe as the Grave, The Paper Caper,* and *Terrorist*; ALA Best Books for Young Adults citations, for *Whatever Happened to Janie?, Driver's Ed, Don't Blame the Music,* and *Voice on the Radio*; ALA Reluctant Reader citation, for *Driver's Education* and *Terrorist*; Anne Lindgergh Award, for *Out of Time*; Pacific States Award, Iowa Teen Award, Colorado Blue Spruce Award, IRA-CBC Children's Book Choice, for *The Face on the Milk Carton*; Iowa Teen Award, for *Whatever Happened to Janie?*. **Address:** c/o Bantam Doubleday Dell, 1540 Broadway, New York, New York 10036, U.S.A.

PUBLICATIONS FOR YOUNG ADULTS

Fiction

Safe as the Grave, illustrated by Gail Owens. Coward, 1979.
The Paper Caper, illustrated by Gail Owens. Coward, 1981.
An April Love Story. New York, Scholastic, 1981.
Nancy and Nick. New York, Scholastic, 1982.
He Loves Me Not. New York, Scholastic, 1982.
A Stage Set for Love. Archway, 1983.
Holly in Love. New York, Scholastic, 1983.
I'm Not Your Other Half. Putnam, 1984.
Sun, Sea, and Boys. Archway, 1984.
Nice Girls Don't. New York, Scholastic, 1984.
Rumors. New York, Scholastic, 1985.
Trying Out. New York, Scholastic, 1985.
Suntanned Days. Archway, 1985.

Racing to Love. Archway, 1985.
The Bad and the Beautiful. New York, Scholastic, 1985.
The Morning After. New York, Scholastic, 1985.
All The Way. New York, Scholastic, 1985.
Saturday Night. New York, Scholastic, 1986.
Don't Blame the Music. Putnam, 1986.
Saying Yes. New York, Scholastic, 1987.
Last Dance. New York, Scholastic, 1987.
The Rah Rah Girl. New York, Scholastic, 1987.
Among Friends. New York, Bantam, 1987.
Camp Boy-Meets-Girl. New York, Bantam, 1988.
New Year's Eve. New York, Scholastic, 1988.
Summer Nights. New York, Scholastic, 1988.
The Girl Who Invented Romance. New York, Bantam, 1988.
Camp Reunion. New York, Bantam, 1988.
Family Reunion. New York, Bantam, 1989.
The Fog. New York, Scholastic, 1989
The Face on the Milk Carton. New York, Bantam, 1990.
The Snow. New York, Scholastic, 1990.
The Fire. New York, Scholastic, 1990.
Camp Girl Meets Camp Boy. New York, Bantam, 1991.
The Cheerleader. New York, Scholastic, 1991.
Freeze Tag. New York, Scholastic, 1992.
Flight #116 Is Down. New York, Scholastic, 1992.
Operation-Homefront. New York, Bantam, 1992.
The Party's Over. New York, Scholastic, 1992.
The Return of the Vampire. New York, Scholastic, 1992.
Forbidden. New York, Scholastic, 1993.
Whatever Happened to Janie? New York, Bantam, 1993.
The Vampire's Promise. New York, Scholastic, 1993.
Driver's Ed. New York, Bantam, 1994.
Emergency Room. New York, Scholastic, 1994.
Twin's. New York, Scholastic, 1994.
Unforgettable. New York, Scholastic, 1994.
Both Sides of Time. New York, Bantam, 1995.
Flash Fire. New York, Scholastic, 1995.
Night School. New York, Scholastic, 1995.
Twenty Pageants Later. New York, Bantam, 1995.
Out of Time. New York, Delacorte, 1996.
The Voice on the Radio. New York, Delacorte, 1996.
Perfume. New York, Scholastic, 1997.
The Stranger. New York, Scholastic, 1997.
The Terrorist. New York, Scholastic, 1997.
Wanted. New York, Scholastic, 1997.
What Child Is This? A Christmas Story. New York, Delacorte, 1997.
Prisoners of Time. New York, Delacorte, 1998.

PUBLICATIONS FOR ADULTS

Fiction

Rear View Mirror. New York, Random House, 1980.
Sand Trap. New York, Avon, 1983.

*

Media Adaptations: "Rear View Mirror" (television movie), Warner Brothers, 1984; "The Face on the Milk Carton" (television movie), 1997.

*   *   *

Carolyn Cooney is a prolific writer best known for her young adult romantic novels. From childhood she remembers reading series books such as Cherry Ames and The Hardy Boys, which could explain her inspiration for writing the thriller trilogy that includes *The Fog, The Snow,* and *The Fire.* While writing this series she started on another series involving a character named Janie Johnson, a series which has expanded Cooney's popularity and recognition as a young adult writer.

Cooney's most popular series, *The Face on the Milk Carton* trilogy, integrates elements of romance, traumatic personal discovery, and mystery into the life of Janie Johnson. In *The Face on the Milk Carton* Janie inadvertently discovers her photograph as a missing three year old named Jennie Spring on the side of a milk carton. This photo initiates flashbacks to her life in the Spring family; in fact the polka dot dress Jennie Spring wears in the photo is tucked away in the Johnson attic. These memories combined with her mother's evasiveness at producing Janie's birth certificate in order for her to get a driving permit prompt Janie to speculate, "I'm somebody else, I'm adopted, they switched babies at the hospital." This archetypal pattern, found frequently in young adult fiction and fantasy, lures the reader into this narrative.

The mystery character introduced in *The Face on the Milk Carton* is Hannah, Janie's abductor and the Johnson's estranged daughter, who shows up at her parent's home and tells them the lie that Janie is their grandchild, and that a cult is pursuing them. Hannah disappears, leaving the family to protect themselves from the ambiguous menace by taking a new name and providing Janie with a new identity. Boy-next-door Reeve Shields gives Janie emotional support and soon becomes her romantic interest. His last name is quite appropriate for a character who functions in part as a protector, helping Janie make sense of her suddenly very insecure identity.

In the sequel, *Whatever Happened to Janie?*, Janie contacts her birth parents, the Springs, and volunteers to return to them. In fact this move is mandated according to law, since Janie is only fifteen: "She was a minor, and must obey her parents. And her parents were not Mr. and Mrs. Johnson. Her parents were Mr. and Mrs. Spring, who wanted her home. In their house, in their state." The disruption that this forced reunion causes is reflected in the anger of the older Spring siblings, who are intensely aware of the fear, pain, and anxiety their parents endured for thirteen years. Janie struggles to make the overwhelming adjustment to having two families: "And once more she could not sleep. A new nightmare surfaced. She did not have enough love to go around. Whatever love she gave these parents, she would have to take away from the others." The excitement in the novel picks up as abductor Hannah again comes into the picture. Her fingerprints show up in a two year old arrest record in New York City and the FBI continues to search for her. "It doesn't matter that you and the Johnsons and the Springs agreed to forget it. The law does not forget," Janie is told. The image of Hannah as a "doomed . . . ragdoll" sparks Jodie and Stephen to go on a perilous but futile trip to New York city to find her.

The Voice on the Radio, the last novel in this trilogy, chronicles Reeve's betrayal of Janie in his first term as a freshman at Hill College in Boston. He wants to make a big impression at the college radio station as a talk jockey so he narrates with considerable embellishment Janie's traumatic adventure. These twice a week late night narratives become so popular that they come to be known as "janies." Inevitably Janie discovers this treachery, much to Reeve's remorse. "'I've raped Janie,' thought Reeve. 'That's what talk shows are. The rape of the soul.'" Janie's ability to forgive Reeve and move on with her life give added dimension and development to her character.

With the publication of *Driver's Ed,* Cooney develops a situation that could happen to any young adult who, on the verge of becoming a driver, bends to peer pressure to prove they are cool. What makes this novel so painfully significant is that the young adult protagonists precipitate a tragedy for a young family in the community as well as themselves and their families. *Driver's Ed* begins casually with Remy Marland's romantic yearnings for Morgan Campbell, yearnings that are at their most intense when they are together during Driver's Education class. Remy is from a blue collar family while Morgan's parents are lawyers, with his dad aspiring to be nominated to run for governor. For the teens, stealing a traffic sign is the rebellious anti-diploma of finishing the class, but this quest for a sign soon leads to tragedy. Just two days after Remy, Morgan, and their driver "friend" Nicki remove several signs, the evening news covers Denise Thompson's death because of a missing stop sign.

As Morgan watches this breaking news on the television he is "screaming on the inside." A policeman being interviewed on this tragedy voices Cooney's major theme: "'They [kids] don't think. They forget that eventually it's the middle of the night . . . this Denise Thompson, she's a stranger to this road, she needs that stop sign.' The stop sign that stood on its side in Morgan's garage." Remy's moment of truth comes as she plays with her baby brother Henry, and thinks of Denise Thompson's son. "Denise Thompson's little boy isn't much older than this. She isn't crawling backward down the stairs with her baby son. She's dead. She'll never see her little boy grow up. Remy began sobbing, first soundlessly and then with huge bawling groans. Her little brother was stunned. He was the one who cried. Not his big sister! His world split open and he clung to his sister."

The rest of the novel is just as emotionally intense and draining as Remy and Morgan come to the decision of admitting to their rash behavior and taking responsibility for it. They come to realize how many families they have ruined but also the meaning of unconditional love. Legal terms such as "misdemeanor", "larceny", "reckless endangerment" and "felony sentence" take on a clarity of meaning in this particularly relevant young adult novel.

—Richard D. Seiter

COOPER, Susan (Mary)

Nationality: British. **Born:** Burnham, Buckinghamshire, England, 23 May 1935. **Education:** Somerville College, Oxford, M.A. 1956. **Family:** Married Nicholas J. Grant in 1963 (divorced, 1983), one son, one daughter, three stepchildren. **Career:** Writer. Reporter and feature writer, *Sunday Times,* London, England, 1956-63. **Awards:** *Horn Book* Honor List citation for *Over Sea, Under Stone; Horn Book* Honor List and American Library Association Notable Book citations, both 1970, both for *Dawn of Fear; Boston Globe-Horn Book* award, American Library Association Notable Book citation, Carnegie Medal runner-up, all 1973, and Newbery Award Honor Book, 1974, all for *The Dark Is Rising;* American

Library Notable Book citation, for *Greenwitch*; *Horn Book* Honor List and American Library Association Notable Book citation, Newbery Medal, Tir na N'og Award (Wales), and commendation for Carnegie Medal, all 1976, for *The Grey King*; Tir na N'og Award for *Silver on the Tree*; Christopher Award, Humanitas Prize, Writers Guild of America Award, and Emmy Award nomination from Academy of Television Arts and Sciences, all 1984, all for *The Dollmaker*; Emmy Award nomination, 1987, and Writers Guild of America Award, 1988, for teleplay *Foxfire*; *Horn Book* Honor List citation, 1987, for *The Selkie Girl*; B'nai B'rith Janusz Korczak Award, 1989, for *Seaward*. **Address:** c/o Margaret J. McElderry, Macmillan, 866 Third Ave., New York, New York 10022, U.S.A.

PUBLICATIONS FOR YOUNG ADULTS

Fiction

Dawn of Fear, illustrated by Margery Gill. New York, Harcourt, 1970; London, Chatto and Windus, 1972.
Jethro and the Jumbie, illustrated by Ashley Bryan. New York, Atheneum, 1979; London, Bodley Head, 1987.
Seaward. New York, Atheneum, and London, Bodley Head, 1983.
The Boggart. New York, McElderry/Macmillan, 1993.
Danny and the Kings. 1993.
The Boggart and the Monster. 1997.

"The Dark Is Rising" series:

Over Sea, Under Stone, illustrated by Margery Gill. London, Cape, 1965; New York, Harcourt, 1966.
The Dark Is Rising, illustrated by Alan E. Cober. London, Chatto and Windus, and New York, Atheneum, 1973.
Greenwitch. London, Chatto and Windus, and New York, Atheneum, 1974.
The Grey King, illustrated by Michael Heslop. London, Chatto and Windus, and New York, Atheneum, 1975.
Silver on the Tree. London, Chatto and Windus, and New York, Atheneum, 1977.

Other

Reteller, *The Silver Cow: A Welsh Tale,* illustrated by Warwick Hutton. New York, Atheneum, 1983.
Reteller, *The Selkie Girl,* illustrated by W. Hutton. New York, McElderry/Macmillan, 1986.

PUBLICATIONS FOR ADULTS

Fiction

Mandrake (science-fiction novel). London, Hodder, 1964.

Plays

Foxfire (with Hume Cronyn; first produced at Stratford, Ontario, 1980; Minneapolis and New York, 1982). New York and London, Samuel French, 1983.
Television Plays: author of *Dark Encounter,* 1976; author of teleplay version of Anne Tyler's novel *Dinner at the Homesick Restaurant.* (With Cronyn) *The Dollmaker* (adaptation of novel

of the same title by Harriette Arnow), produced by American Broadcasting Companies, Inc., 1984. *Foxfire* (teleplay), produced by Columbia Broadcasting System, Inc., 1987.

Other

Behind the Golden Curtain: A View of the U.S.A. London, Hodder, 1965, New York, Scribner, 1966.
J. B. Priestley: Portrait of an Author. London, Heinemann, 1970; New York, Harper, 1971.
Contributor, Michael Sissons and Philip French, editors, *The Age of Austerity: 1945-51.* London, Hodder, 1963.
Editor and author of preface, J. B. Priestley, *Essays of Five Decades.* Boston, Little, Brown, 1968.
Author of introduction, John and Nancy Langstaff, editors, *The Christmas Revels Songbook: In Celebration of the Winter Solstice.* Boston, David R. Godine, 1985.

PUBLICATIONS FOR CHILDREN

Fiction

Tam Lin, illustrated by Warwick Hutton. New York, McElderry / Macmillan, 1991.
Matthew's Dragon, illustrated by J.A. Smith. New York, McElderry / Macmillan, 1991.
Danny and the Kings, illustrated by J.A. Smith. New York, McElderry/Macmillan, 1993.

*

Media Adaptations: "The Dark Is Rising" (two-cassette recording), Miller-Brody, 1979; "The Silver Cow" (filmstrip), Weston Woods, 1985; "The Silver Cow" (recording), Weston Woods, 1986.

Biography: Entry in *Fourth Book of Junior Authors,* New York, H.W. Wilson, 1978; essay in *Something about the Author Autobiography Series* Vol. 6, Detroit, Gale, 1988; essay in *Speaking for Ourselves: Autobiographical Sketches by Notable Authors of Books for Young Adults,* Vol. 1, compiled and edited by Donald R. Gallo, National Council of Teachers of English, 1990.

Manuscript Collections: Osborne Collection, Toronto Public Library.

Critical Studies: Entry in *Children's Literature Review,* Vol. 4, Detroit, Gale, 1982.

*   *   *

Susan Cooper has come to be recognized as a major author of books for children and young adults. Her first work for children, *Over Sea, Under Stone,* came as a response to a contest designed to honor the memory of E. Nesbit. Set in Cornwall, this is a family adventure story concerning Simon, Barnabus, and Jane's search for a mysterious grail. The magic and myth, so much a part of the subsequent books of the ''Dark Is Rising'' series, is only hinted at here. The story draws upon the King Arthur legend and suggests connections to a world outside that of the contemporary environment.

Dawn of Fear calls upon the actual experiences of English childhood during World War II, but recasts them in the form of the fictional story of Derek and his friends Peter and Geoffrey. One of the strengths of this work lies in its ability to contrast the world of childhood play with the horrors of war without either losing the sense of innocent play or minimizing the atrocities of the world conflict.

Cooper's major contribution to young adult literature has been ''The Dark Is Rising'' series, which greatly expands the mythical theme suggested in *Over Sea, Under Stone* and reveals Cooper's extraordinary prowess as an author of fantasy. *The Dark Is Rising,* set in Buckinghamshire, is the second work in the sequence. Here the battle lines between good and evil are formally established as the forces of Light and Dark are drawn into conflict. The Light, aided by Will Stanton, youngest of the Old Ones, seeks to gather together the Six Signs of the Light that will enable Light to overcome Dark. Yet the drawing of lines between good and evil, Light and Dark, rather than completely clarifying the conflict, serves as a mechanism to cast doubt upon the nature of good and evil as concepts. The shadowy aspect of the conflict and the inability to ''read'' clearly the motivations of some of the characters are areas in which Cooper has been criticized. However, I feel that the ambiguity of protagonists and antagonists is a deliberate literary device. Rather than succumbing to artistic flaw, Cooper goes beyond the conventional expectations of her readers by inviting them to glimpse the complex, the unexplainable, and often the threatening aspects of mankind's nature. By offering the thesis that the human psyche may manifest itself in explicit actions or present itself in a mysterious and often frustrating manner, Cooper exceeds the traditional presentations of good versus evil often found in fantasy literature.

Greenwitch, the third book in the series, is quite different in mood from the earlier books. In this dreamlike novel set in Cornwall, magic often occurs during the hours of darkness and yet readers are not left with the feeling that experiences have been merely imagined. The Greenwitch, a figure created by village women, comes into possession of a great secret coveted by the powers of Light and Dark. Young Jane's innocence moves the creature to release the secret. Jane is an interesting figure because at first she appears to be a rather flat character who reacts according to convention. Yet as the story progresses, we learn that even those who are skilled and knowledgeable in fighting the powers of the Dark are powerless in this instance. Ironically it is Jane who is successful, not through dramatic means, but rather through communicating her compassion for the Greenwitch.

Will Stanton is the central figure in the suspense-filled *The Grey King,* fourth part of the sequence, set in Wales. Will is assisted in his quest for a golden harp by several people, including Bran, son of King Arthur, brought forward in time. Cooper continues her exploration of the many guises of evil and reiterates the theme that the Dark is a wily foe, capable of taking many forms.

Silver on the Tree rivals *The Dark Is Rising* in complexity. Set in Buckinghamshire, the book functions as the grand final conclusion of the series, combining intricate themes borrowed from previous books. The five children—Simon, Jane, Barnabus, Will, and Bran—are called together to assist in resolving the dramatic conflict between Light and Dark. In this book, Cooper is at her most powerful, drawing upon the full range of her creative genius. Characterizations are complex and there are surprises in store for both the reader and the characters.

Cooper's subsequent works are major departures from the preceding series. *Jethro and the Jumbie, The Silver Cow: A Welsh Tale, The Selkie Girl, Tam Lin,* and *Matthew's Dragon* are compact, imaginative works intended for a younger audience. In the first book set on a Caribbean island, Cooper introduces a black protagonist who must deal with the mischievous spirit called the Jumbie. *The Silver Cow, The Selkie Girl,* and *Tam Lin* form a picture book trilogy and return to the Celtic material used in Cooper's earlier works. In *The Silver Cow* a fairy cow given as a gift is misused by a young boy's father, with consequences to follow. *The Selkie Girl* is the tragic love story of the marriage of a mortal man and a Selkie girl. This is a story of transformation, a theme that intrigues Cooper and appears in many of her works. In *Tam Lin,* Cooper modifies the old story of Tam Lin, the enchanted knight, for a contemporary audience. Margaret is the adventurous king's daughter who finds sitting and waiting for someone to marry her, dull business and would rather seek adventure. She finds more than she bargained for (but not more than what she can cope with) when she meets Tam Lin in the off-limits Carterhays wood. On being informed of the manner in which she can save his enchanted soul from the fairies, Margaret holds fast (literally as well as figuratively), despite the dangerous transformations which he undergoes, ultimately winning the hand of the fair knight. *Matthew's Dragon* is a delightful picture book which stands alone in its subject matter. It is the story of a little boy who has a night adventure with a story book dragon. Matthew has an opportunity to meet all of the dragons who ever existed in story. The description of the celestial flying scene vaguely echoes some of the material to be found in Cooper's fantasy novels.

The novel *Seaward* is perhaps the most complex and least clearcut of all of Cooper's works for young people. Here she appears purposely to avoid explanations and instead chooses to offer the reader a world of possibilities, so many in fact that they create an extremely ambiguous text. This is a challenging novel, with subtleties which may perhaps be best appreciated by an adult audience. The protagonists, Cally and West, are adolescents caught up in the drama of having to cope with the deaths of their parents, events around which swirl mystery and innuendo. At the height of their personal tragedy they are transported to a Celtic world ruled by the old gods who would use the children should they be unable to resist the temptations placed before them. This is an allegorical tale about coming of age in a hostile world.

Vestiges of ancient Celtic ''Wild Magic'' haunt a Canadian family in the form of a Boggart in Cooper's recent work *The Boggart.* Having inherited the old Castle Keep in Scotland, the Volnik family also inherits an ancient prank-loving creature, the Boggart, who comes back to Canada with them via the conveyance of an old desk once housed in Castle Keep. Cooper exhibits a rare sense of humor in this story as protagonists Emily and Jessup cope with the often amusing but sometimes dark consequences of the Boggart's pranks. Cooper deftly interweaves folklore with new technology as the children must enter a computer game in order to rescue the Boggart and enable him to return to his homeland. She offers readers an amazingly clear-cut writing style free of the symbolic subtleties found in the *Dark Is Rising* sequence and, particularly, in *Seaward.*

Susan Cooper's work is fully illustrative of a richly creative imagination. Throughout her books major themes resurface, allowing the reader to experience and internalize the depth of her commitment to her social ideals as well as to her art. While she freely acknowledges her debt to the past, her fantasy writing for children and young people offers readers original perspectives in an area which continues to maintain a firm grasp upon the hearts of readers and authors alike.

—Karen Patricia Smith

CORMIER, Robert (Edmund)

Pseudonym: John Fitch IV. **Nationality:** American. **Born:** Leominster, Massachusetts, 17 January 1925. **Education:** St. Cecilia's Parochial School, Leominster; Leominster High School, graduated 1942; Fitchburg State College, Massachusetts, 1943-44. **Family:** Married Constance B. Senay in 1948; three daughters and one son. **Career:** Scriptwriter, WTAG Radio, Worcester, Massachusetts, 1946-48; reporter and columnist ("And So On"), Worcester *Telegram and Gazette,* 1948-55; reporter, columnist (as John Fitch IV), and associate editor, Fitchburg *Sentinel and Enterprise,* 1955-78; free-lance writer, 1978—. **Awards:** Best human interest story of the year award, Associated Press in New England, 1959 and 1973; Bread Loaf Writers Conference fellowship, 1968; best newspaper column award, K.R. Thomson Newspapers, Inc., 1974; outstanding book of the year awards, *New York Times,* 1974, for *The Chocolate War,* 1977, for *I Am the Cheese,* and 1979, for *After the First Death;* "Best Book for Young Adults" citations, American Library Association, 1974, for *The Chocolate War,* 1977, for *I Am the Cheese,* 1979, for *After the First Death,* and 1983, for *The Bumblebee Flies Anyway;* Maxi Award, *Media and Methods,* 1976; Woodward School Annual Book Award, 1978, for *I Am the Cheese;* Lewis Carroll Shelf Award, 1979, for *The Chocolate War;* "Notable Chidren's Trade Book in the Field of Social Studies" citation, National Council for Social Studies and Children's Book Council, 1980, for *Eight Plus One;* Assembly on Literature for Adolescents (ALAN) Award, National Council of Teachers of English, 1982; "Best of the Best Books, 1970-1983" citations, American Library Association, for *The Chocolate War, I Am the Cheese,* and *After the First Death;* "Best Books of 1983" citation, *School Library Journal,* for *The Bumblebee Flies Anyway;* Carnegie Medal nomination, 1983, for *The Bumblebee Flies Anyway;* Reader's Choice Award, 1983, for the *Eight Plus One* short story "President Cleveland, Where Are You?"; "Honor List" citation from *Horn Book,* 1986, for *Beyond the Chocolate War;* Young Adult Services Division "Best Book for Young Adults" citation, American Library Association, 1988, for *Fade;* World Fantasy Award nomination, 1989, for *Fade;* Margaret A. Edwards Award, American Library Association, 1991, for *The Chocolate War, I Am the Cheese,* and *After the First Death.* D.Litt.: Fitchburg State College, 1977. **Agent:** Curtis Brown, 10 Astor Place, New York, New York 10003. **Address:** 1177 Main Street, Leominster, Massachusetts 01453, U.S.A.

PUBLICATIONS FOR YOUNG ADULTS

Fiction

The Chocolate War. New York, Pantheon, 1974; London, Gollancz, 1975.
I Am the Cheese. New York, Pantheon, and London, Gollancz, 1977.
After the First Death. New York, Pantheon, and London, Gollancz, 1979.
The Bumblebee Flies Anyway. New York, Pantheon, and London, Gollancz, 1983.
Beyond the Chocolate War. New York, Knopf, and London, Gollancz, 1985.
Fade. New York, Delacorte Press, and London, Gollancz, 1988.
Other Bells for Us to Ring, illustrated by Deborah K. Ray. New York, Delacorte Press, 1990; as *Darcy,* London, Gollancz, 1990.
We All Fall Down. New York, Delacorte Press, and London, Gollancz, 1991.
Tunes for Bears to Dance To. New York, Delacorte Press, and London, Gollancz, 1992.
In the Middle of the Night. New York, Delacorte Press, 1995.
Tenderness: A Novel. New York, Delacorte Press, 1997.
Heroes: A Novel. New York, Delacorte Press, 1998.

Short Stories

Eight Plus One. New York, Pantheon, 1980.
Contributor, *Sixteen: Short Stories by Outstanding Writers for Young Adults.* New York, Delacorte Press, 1984.
Contributor, *Face to Face: A Collection of Stories by Celebrated Soviet and American Writers,* edited by Thomas Pettepiece and Anatoly Aleksin. New York, Philomel Books, 1990.

Other

I Have Words to Spend: Reflections of a Small Town Editor (autobiography). New York, Doubleday, 1991.

PUBLICATIONS FOR ADULTS

Novels

Now and at the Hour. New York, Coward McCann, 1960.
A Little Raw on Monday Mornings. New York, Sheed and Ward, 1963.
Take Me Where the Good Times Are. New York, Macmillan, 1965.

Nonfiction

Contributor, *Celebrating Children's Books: Essays in Honor of Zena Sutherland,* edited by Betsy Hearne and Marilyn Kay. New York, Lothrop, 1981.
Contributor, *Trust Your Children: Voices against Censorship in Children's Literature,* edited by Mark I. West. New York, Neal-Schuman, 1987.

*

Media Adaptations: *The Chocolate War, I Am the Cheese,* and *After the First Death* (recordings), Random House/Miller Brody, 1982; *I Am the Cheese* (film), Almi, 1983; *The Chocolate War* (film), Management Company Entertainment Group, 1989.

Biography: Entry in *Dictionary of Literary Biography* by Joe Stines, Volume 52, Detroit, Gale, 1986; entry in *Concise Dictionary of American Literary Biography: Broadening Views, 1968-1988* by Sylvia Patterson Iskander, Detroit, Gale, 1989; essay in *Authors and Artists for Young Adults* by Dieter Miller, Volume 3, Detroit, Gale, 1990; essay in *Speaking for Ourselves: Autobiographical Sketches by Notable Authors of Books for Young Adults,* Volume 1, compiled and edited by Donald R. Gallo, National Council of Teachers of English, 1990.

Manuscript Collections: Fitchburg State College, Massachusetts.

Critical Studies: *Presenting Robert Cormier* by Patricia J. Campbell, Boston, Twayne, 1985; ''An Interview with Robert Cormier'' by Anita Silvey, in *Horn Book,* March-April, May-June, 1985; entry in *Children's Literature Review,* Volume 12, Detroit, Gale, 1987; ''The Bland Face of Evil in the Novels of Robert Cormier'' by Nancy Vaglahn, in *The Lion and the Unicorn: A Critical Journal of Children's Literature,* June 1988, 12-18; ''Kind of a Funny Dichotomy: A Conversation with Robert Cormier'' by Roger Sutton, in *School Library Journal,* June 1991, 28-33.

Robert Cormier comments:

My books have been accepted by young readers for which I am grateful because young readers are a marvelous audience, open and responsive. I do not, however, write books for young people but about them. I write for the intelligent reader and this intelligent reader is often twelve or fourteen or sixteen years old. A work of fiction, if true to itself, written honestly, will set off shocks of recognition in the sensitive reader no matter what age that reader is. And I write for that reader.

*   *   *

The novels of Robert Cormier have added a new dimension to young adult literature. Dealing with evil, abuse of power, and corruption, they present a dark view of humanity, but one tempered by an underlying morality. All set in fictional Monument, Massachusetts, except for *We All Fall Down* and *Tunes for Bears to Dance To,* Cormier peoples his town with a variety of characters who breathe and experience life to the fullest. A first-rate stylist, Cormier commands and controls language through his fast-paced sentence structure, his vivid verbs, and his sparkling metaphors and similes. His award-winning books grab their readers' attention and compel them to think about the issues raised, long after the final pages have been turned.

After completing three adult novels (*Now and at the Hour, A Little Raw on Monday Mornings,* and *Take Me Where the Good Times Are*), Cormier began writing for the young adult audience with *The Chocolate War,* which recounts Jerry Renault's courageous stand—he refuses to participate in his school's annual fundraising chocolate sale—against a gang called the Vigils headed by manipulative Archie Costello, and against the corrupt headmaster of Trinity High School, Brother Leon. Jerry's crushing defeat at the novel's close made many adults question the role of the hero, note the absence of effective adult role models, and reject the novel as too pessimistic; yet teen readers accepted it, recognizing the pressures of peer conformity and the abuses of power, and begged for a sequel, which Cormier wrote eleven years later. The high school represents a microcosm of the world, a world teens face daily. The book makes an unforgettable impact; the reader questions whether Jerry will even survive.

In *I Am the Cheese,* the corruption and abuse of power become even more explicit and violent with the death of Anthony and Louise Delmonte (David and Louise Farmer) after Mr. Delmonte testifies against organized crime and the family is supposedly secure in the government's Witness Re-establishment Program. Their son, Adam, is trapped between two apparently equal evils: organized crime and corrupt government. No way out exists for Adam who continues to circle the grounds of the sanatorium when he is not drugged, looking for the father he believes to be still alive. He is the cheese left to stand alone at the end of the nursery song ''The Farmer in the Dell.'' Alternating points of view and narrative voices add to the complexity and mystery of this powerful novel's outcome, which defies the reader's expectations. Again Cormier leaves unanswered questions, such as what, if any role, did Amy Hertz, Adam's girlfriend, play in the discovery and consequent demise of the Farmers.

The narrative style of *After the First Death* alternates chapters and points of view from those centering on the Marchands—father and son—to those focusing on a hijacking of a busload of first graders. Cormier sensitively treats the dilemma of eighteen-year-old Kate Forrester, who chances to be driving the bus the day of the hijacking, and that of the youngest member of the terrorists, Miro Shantas. *After the First Death,* the title taken from Dylan Thomas's poem ''A Refusal to Mourn the Death, by Fire, of a Child in London,'' recounts a suspenseful story of betrayal and maturation, in which Cormier forces his readers to question father and son relationships, patriotism, and even the novel itself. Does the father narrate the son's chapters, or does General Marchand go insane only after his son's suicide? Is the General a patriot or a fool for sending his son as an intermediary with the terrorists? These unsettling questions contribute to making the novel unforgettable.

In contrast to the first three novels, *Eight Plus One,* a short-story collection, presents an entirely different side of Cormier. Written between 1965 and 1975 and set earlier—some during the Great Depression—these stories, although entertaining, are more family-oriented, occasionally sentimental, and very human. Introducing each story is a chapter discussing an aspect of writing which Cormier wished he had known when he was beginning to write seriously; for example, where ideas for stories originate and the value of figurative language. This book and *I Have Words to Spend: Reflections of a Small Town Editor,* also written prior to the novels, present the same side of Robert Cormier: a gentle man whose loving relations with his family often contribute to his narrative voice. *I Have Words to Spend,* not published until 1991, was not intended for a young adult audience and probably is not as enjoyable to them as are the novels. To adult readers, however, *I Have Words to Spend*—a collection of Cormier's human interest newspaper columns, carefully selected and most capably edited by his wife, Constance Senay Cormier—presents an entertaining, sometimes humorous, always revealing glimpse of small-town life and the philosophy and attitudes of a loving father and family-oriented man.

The gentle Cormier recedes in *The Bumblebee Flies Anyway,* another powerful novel. This one deals with teens in a hospital for the terminally ill where sixteen-year-old Barney Snow tries to make dreams come true, especially for Mazzio who is plugged into a machine and wants to be set free. Barney, who believes he loves Mazzio's twin sister, constructs a life-size model car nicknamed the Bumblebee after the heavy-bodied, short-winged bee who, according to the laws of aerodynamics, should not be able to fly but who flies anyway. The idea is to allow Mazzio to drive the car off the hospital roof, fly for one glorious moment, and thus leave this life in style. This extremely poignant novel, like *I Am the Cheese* and *After the First Death,* presents the reader with courageous characters but also with provocative problems, such as the reliability of the narrator who does not realize why he is hospitalized and who creates his own vocabulary to cover up unpleasantries in this sometimes brutal but always mesmerizing novel.

Cormier then turned his attention to a sequel. Although aware of the difficulties involved in writing sequels, he nevertheless acceded to multiple requests and produced *Beyond the Chocolate War,* a book not as shattering as *The Chocolate War* but still taut and suspenseful. Cormier does not just flesh out his characters from the earlier novel more; he creates new ones, such as Ray Bannister who has just moved to Monument, a talented magician whose act involves a guillotine. Set a few months after the close of its predecessor, *Beyond the Chocolate War* reveals Archie, who as a senior must choose his successor as leader of the Vigils. However, the book centers on Obie, who, revolted by Archie's evil, plans revenge against him with that guillotine and must confront evil himself. Again the abuses of power, evil, resentment, and hatred play a part but so does love as Cormier creates a tender first experience with love for Obie, reminiscent of Adam's love for Amy in *I Am the Cheese.* The novel does not seem as relentlessly honest as Cormier's others—almost as if the author is answering some of the criticism of the earlier book—but the violence and psychological suspense are as heavy, and the book is a compelling read.

In *Fade,* Cormier grips the reader once again, destroying myths. Into a completely realistic setting, Cormier injects an element of fantasy—the fade or the ability to become invisible that is passed down from uncle to nephew through the generations. In this his most autobiographical novel according to the author, Cormier portrays Paul Moreaux who inherits the fade but soon recognizes the painful responsibility that goes hand in hand with it, leaving Paul and the reader to question whether the fade is a gift or a curse. Never certain when an episode of the fade will overtake him, Paul becomes isolated from family and friends. He becomes a writer but must always be on the lookout for the next generation's fader. In the five-part structure, Cormier addresses issues of bigotry, evil, revenge, and murder, as well as the desire to be a writer and issues relevant to writers. *Fade* is a powerful book for both teen and adult readers—so powerful that readers may find themselves, along with the other characters, questioning whether faders can possibly exist.

Cormier's next novel, *We All Fall Down,* evokes the death and destruction of the plague which inspired the nursery rhyme, "Ring Around the Rosy," from which the novel's title is derived. Cormier depicts the far-reaching effects of evil in the lives of the innocent Jerome family, victims of a senseless house trashing. This novel, not one for the fainthearted, centers on Buddy Walker, a teenage

alcoholic facing his parents' impending divorce. Grief-stricken by his role in the trashing, Buddy seeks out one of his victims and begins a relationship with her that proves to be both touching and tragic. Multiple points of view are presented from Jane Jerome, whose sister Karen is hospitalized in a coma after accidentally confronting the trashers; to Buddy; to the Avenger, the primary character in the subplot, whose identity is not revealed until the novel's close when Cormier once again tricks his readers. The presentation of Buddy's and the Avenger's points of view, echoing that of terrorist Miro's in *After the First Death,* endows even the most evil characters with humanity and the readers of this electrifying novel with a broader perspective on life itself.

In *Tunes for Bears to Dance To* Cormier explores collective evil in the revelation of the horrors of the Holocaust on a Jewish survivor, Mr. Levine, and individual evil in the form of a bigoted, abusive grocer named Hairston. Eleven-year-old Henry Cassavant, whose family is still reeling from the death of Henry's brother Eddie, has left Monument and moved to Wickburg. Henry considers himself lucky to get a job at the grocery until the grocer forces Henry to commit a purely evil act of destruction. This book unites themes of previous novels, such as ineffectual parents, corruption of innocence, child abuse, death, and power. Although most of the characters are not well developed, the main themes of this novelette, which might almost be considered a parable, are forcefully delivered, particularly to a teenage audience.

Cormier in his only novel for younger children *Other Bells for Us to Ring* (entitled *Darcy* in England) presents a vivid account of life during World War II. He writes in the genteel manner that characterizes his short stories and newspaper columns but still depicts the achingly accurate feelings of the protagonist, eleven-year-old Darcy Webster. The title is drawn from Kenneth Patchen's moving poem "At the New Year," which serves as the novel's preface and deserves rereading at the novel's close. Set in Frenchtown, a part of Monument (in contrast to the two preceding novels which were set in Burnside and Wickburg (*We All Fall Down*) and Wickburg (*Tunes for Bears*), *Other Bells* is written from the perspective of Darcy, an outsider to Frenchtown. Darcy's new and adventuresome friend Kathleen Mary O'Hara, an Irish Catholic, introduces her to Catholicism and precipitates a painful spiritual crisis. Both girls must deal with alcoholic fathers, though the girls and their fathers differ considerably in their actions. In addition to questioning religion, Darcy must learn about wartime sacrifice, experience the absence of a father missing in action and a mother often depressed and withdrawn, and ultimately deal not only with death but also with miracles. After reading this poignant and revealing novel about adolescent insecurities, which in true Cormier fashion, raises issues and questions but leaves them unanswered, adult readers will recognize feelings they may have been out of touch with for years.

Cormier has written some powerful works—some suspenseful, thrilling novels and some quietly realistic, gentle stories and newspaper columns—all revealing his understanding of how evil and goodness work in the world. Although his outstanding reputation is based upon the former group of novels, the latter deserve praise too. His skill as a craftsman is undisputed. His impact on the field of young adult literature is immense and comparable only with the pleasure his readers derive from discovering another Cormier novel has been published.

—Sylvia Patterson Iskander

CRAYDER, Teresa. *See* COLMAN, Hila

CREECH, Sharon

Has also written as Sharon Rigg. **Nationality:** American. **Born:** Cleveland, Ohio, 29 July 1945. **Education:** Hiram College (Ohio), B.A. 1967; George Mason University, M.A. 1977. **Family:** Married 1) H. R. Leuthy, Jr. in 1967 (divorced 1977); one daughter, one son; 2) Lyle D. Rigg in 1982. **Career:** Federal Theater Project Archives, 1975-77; editorial assistant, *Congressional Quarterly,* 1977-79; literature and writing teacher, TASIS (The American School in Switzerland) English School, 1979-82, 1984-94; Switzerland School, 1982-84. **Awards:** Billee Murray Denny Poetry Award, Lincoln College, Lincoln, Illinois, 1988; Best Books, *School Library Journal* Best Books list, 1994, American Library Association (ALA) Notable Children's Books, 1995, Newbery Medal, 1995, Children's Book Award (England), 1995, UK Reading Association Award, 1995, W. H. Smith Award, 1996, Young Readers Award, Virginia State Reading Association, 1997, Heartland Award, 1997, Sequoia Award, 1997, and Austrian Literaturhaus Award, 1997, all for *Walk Two Moons*; Whitbread Award shortlist, 1997, for *Chasing Redbird.* **Address:** c/o HarperCollins, 10 East 53rd Street, New York, New York 10022, U.S.A.

PUBLICATIONS FOR YOUNG ADULTS

Fiction

Absolutely Normal Chaos. London, Macmillan, 1990; New York, HarperCollins, 1995.
Walk Two Moons. New York, HarperCollins, 1994.
Pleasing the Ghost, illustrated by Stacey Schuett. New York, HarperCollins, 1996; as *The Ghost of Uncle Arvie,* illustrated by Simon Cooper, London, England, Macmillan, 1996.
Chasing Redbird. New York, HarperCollins, 1997.
Bloomability. New York, HarperCollins, 1998.

Other

The Centre of the Universe: Waiting for the Girl (play). Produced, New York, 1992.
As Sharon Rigg, *The Recital* (novel). London, England, Pan-Macmillan, 1990.
As Sharon Rigg, *Nick Malley.* London, England, Pan-Macmillan, 1991.

*

Critical Studies: "Salamanca's Journey" by Hazel Rochman, in *New York Times Book Review,* 21 May 1995, 24; "Newbery Medal Acceptance" by Sharon Creech, in *Horn Book* (Boston), Vol. 71, No. 1, 1995, 418-425; "Sharon Creech" by Lyle D. Rigg, in *Horn Book,* Vol. 71, No. 1, 1995, 426-429.

Sharon Creech comments:

Readers occasionally comment on the frequency of journeys in my books. Journeys have always been important to me. When I was young, my family took a car trip each summer, and the one we took when I was thirteen—from Ohio to Idaho, nearly 3,000 miles in the car—was particularly dramatic. What a vast and varied country! I wanted to memorize everything I saw and heard. That journey was later recreated in *Walk Two Moons,* and I loved every minute of traveling with Salamanca across the States.

To me, every book, whether I'm writing it or reading it, is a journey. Each book is a chance to travel along with the characters, and to discover what matters to them, and how their journeys change them. I am intrigued by the way the physical journeys (from this place to that place) mirror interior journeys—how we are changed and shaped by where we go, who we meet, what we think along the way.

*   *   *

In her Newbery acceptance speech for *Walk Two Moons,* Sharon Creech spoke of her father who, after suffering a stroke, lived for six years without being able to speak or to understand words spoken to him. "A month after he died in 1986, I started my first novel, and when I finished it, I wrote another, and another, and another. The words rushed out. The connection between my father's death and my flood of writing might be that I had been confronted with the dark wall of mortality: we don't have endless time to follow our dreams; but it might also be that I felt obligated to use the words that my father could not." Though "the dark wall of mortality" figures largely in all of Creech's novels for young readers—all of her central characters deal with grief—it is the communication that cements relationships and the lively art of living that always triumph.

Even *Pleasing the Ghost,* whose nine-year old protagonist marks it as a book intended for an audience younger than the typical adolescent reader, depicts the process of a boy's grieving for the recent death of his father. As a way to say goodbye, Dennis wishes to see his father's ghost; instead, the ghost of the boy's dead Uncle Arvie literally breezes into the boy's life and asks him for three "pleases." Like Creech's father, Uncle Arvie suffered a stroke which left him unable to speak normally, so it is up to Dennis to decipher requests like "Dunder trampolink. Dunder boodled trampolink a gressapip." The serious process of dealing with grief takes a decidedly comic turn as Dennis works through the circumstances that will accomplish the three tasks that will please the ghost. It is out of love for his living wife, Dennis's aunt, that the ghost asks Dennis for the three "pleases." And it is out of love for Uncle Arvie that Dennis undertakes the "pleases" mission. By experiencing the love and accomplishing the "pleases," Dennis works through much of his grief. The message in this story of a nine-year-old boy whose father has died is, ultimately, the comforting one that though survivors may always miss those who have died, the loss can and indeed must be woven into the life yet to be lived.

Mary Lou Finney, the protagonist of Creech's first published novel for young readers, *Absolutely Normal Chaos,* also deals with grief, though in a less direct way than other of Creech's major characters. When Mr. Furtz, a neighbor even a thirteen-year-old can think of as too young to die, suddenly dies of a heart attack, Mary Lou faces mortality for the first time. Her shock and resulting reflections on life and death unfold as she writes the summer journal assigned by her English teacher. The journal convention lets readers have an especially intimate look at how this adolescent matures as she writes about her thoughts and feelings throughout a summer that brings her a series of unsettling experiences besides Mr. Furtz's death. Her parents and her four demanding siblings figure largely in her journal as part of what she herself terms the "absolutely normal chaos" of her life. But the chaos becomes less normal when, among other events, her best friend ignores her for, of all things, a boy. Then Mary Lou herself experiences her first love and develops some understanding of her friend's new focus. Her strange, quiet cousin Carl Ray comes to Easton, Ohio, to live with her family, a situation Mary Lou resents. Not until she visits his family on their no-electricity, no-phone, no-plumbing farm in West Virginia does she develop empathy for the difficulties involved in coping with entirely new people, surroundings, and circumstances. In the midst of all this "absolutely normal" chaotic emotional growth, Mary Lou has another summer assignment: she must read *The Odyssey*. This classic epic becomes the metaphor for the journey motif central to this young protagonist's development. As she writes her journal and reads *The Odyssey,* Mary Lou comes to the amazing conclusion that she, a typical adolescent female of the late twentieth-century, and Odysseus, the legendary hero of the ancient Greeks, share more common human concerns that she had imagined possible. She comes to realize that like Odysseus, her own life's journey will take her through loss and reward, connections and disconnections, with all kinds of challenges and incredible stops along the way.

The Newbery Award winning *Walk Two Moons* asks readers to sympathize with Salamanca Tree Hiddle's grief and confusion after her mother leaves the family so that she might better find her way through her own grief and confusion after a late-term miscarriage. The tragedy here is that the mother's journey ends with her death in a bus crash, which is a fact hidden from readers because Sal, the first-person narrator, cannot even think about it throughout most of the novel. She thinks about her mother coming home, about trees—how they sing and how they taste when she kisses them—about Ben and how it would taste to kiss him, and about any number of other things, but not about her mother never coming home. Thinking that a shift to new surroundings away from constant reminders of the mother will help Sal work through her determined denial, her father moves them from the family's farm near Bybanks, Kentucky, to Easton, Ohio. There Sal becomes friends with Mary Lou Finney and another thirteen-year-old, Phoebe Winterbottom, whose mother also leaves her family because she has problems to work through. Grim as all this sounds, the wry, humorous voices Creech creates for characters young and old and the engaging way Sal reports them invites the reader to enjoy Sal's narrative journey.

Walk Two Moons abandons the usual linear chronological plot found in novels for young readers and instead offers a complex narrative of multiple plots and frequent flashbacks. This narrative complexity mirrors the convolutions of Sal's feelings as she struggles against accepting the actuality of her mother's death. Readers move between vignettes of Sal's memories detailing the family's happy life together, Sal and her father's unhappiness after

the mother leaves, Sal's growing interest in Ben (Mary Lou's cousin, whose attention gives Sal "an odd sensation, as if a little creature was crawling up my spine"), tensions at school and about her father's friendship with a woman other than her mother, and Phoebe's story (which includes a stranger who leaves cryptic philosophical messages at the Winterbottom's front door and the revelation that Mrs. Winterbottom had as a teenager given up a baby for adoption). All of these storylines converge within Sal's account of the trip she makes across the country with her grandparents to visit her mother in Lewiston, Idaho. This journey from Ohio to Idaho serves as the frame within which Sal tells Phoebe's story to her grandparents; most important, telling the story becomes the stage upon which Sal plays out her own grief and confusion. The actual journey then parallels Sal's difficult metaphorical journey from denial to acceptance as along the way she tells, in bits and pieces, about the Winterbottom family's problems. As the words tumble out across the days in the car with her eccentric, exemplary grandparents, they give shape to Sal's reflections about how her own stormy feelings parallel Phoebe's anger and grief about her mother's absence. Sal begins to embrace the idea embodied in the American Indian proverb from which the novel's title is taken: "Don't judge a man until you've walked two moons in his moccasins." Discovering she can leave her anger behind frees her to enjoy her life's journey.

As do *Absolutely Normal Chaos* and *Walk Two Moons, Chasing Redbird* has a thirteen-year-old protagonist whose journey of self discovery takes her along an interesting path. In this case, the path Zinna Taylor discovers is the overgrown, two-hundred-year-old Bybanks-Chocton trail leading away from her family's Kentucky farm to the neighboring small town. As the third of seven children in a high-energy family, Zinna has loved the quiet company of her Uncle Nate and her red-haired Aunt Jessie, whom Nate calls his Redbird. When Jessie dies, Nate's overwhelming grief drives him to chase his Redbird, looking for Jessie's spirit in all the places they loved. Zinna's grief steels her determination to clear the whole twenty miles of the trail by herself. This project at first isolates her and then finally reconciles her to her family. It also keeps at bay the sixteen-year-old Jake Boone, whose attentions confuse and anger Zinna. The lonely, physical labor of clearing the trail gives Zinna a chance to literally and figuratively work through her guilt-ridden grief for her long-dead cousin Rose and newly-dead Aunt Jesse, whose deaths she mistakenly believes she caused. The days and weeks spent alone clearing the trail clear her mind; the burden of guilt dissipates and the girl develops a physical and mental strength that others, especially her mother, soon notice. Like Sal Hiddle, Zinna Taylor must work her way through suppressed memories and grief—but readers who've read more than one of Creech's books will notice other connections between the characters: the two Bybanks girls were best friends until Sal moved to Ohio. Zinna's excitement about the news that Sal and her father are returning to Bybanks makes clear that though the narratives are not connected by anything other than the girls' friendship and similar themes dealing with grief and self discovery, Sal's summer trip to Idaho coincides with Zinna's effort to clear the path between Bybanks and Chocton.

Sharon Creech is a writer whose talent draws her audience into situations which make dealing with some of the harsher vicissitudes of life seem not only possible but inviting. Though her characters must contend with a litany of coming-of-age motifs—budding sexuality and first loves, coming to terms with death and grief, illegitimacy, sibling rivalry, uncomfortable issues of self-recognition, and parents who for one reason or another are not part of their children's lives—Creech's understanding of loss and love and the importance of connections with other people draws readers into the characters' lives in the most sympathetic way. It is a testament to this writer's skill in approaching such serious issues with insight and humor that readers who enter these narratives emerge from the reading saying they *enjoyed* Creech's characters and stories.

—Linda Benson

CREW, Gary

Nationality: Australian. **Born:** Brisbane, Queensland, 23 September 1947. **Education:** Queensland Institute of Technology, Certificate of Engineering Drafting, 1970,; Queensland University, B.A. 1979, M.A. in literature 1985. **Family:** Married Christine Joy Willis in 1970; two daughters and one son. **Career:** Senior draftsman and drafting consultant, McDonald, Wapner, and Priddle, Brisbane, Queensland, Australia, 1963-73; English teacher, Everton Park State High School, Brisbane, 1974-78; Mitchelton State High School, Brisbane, 1978-81; Subject master in English, Aspley High School, Brisbane, 1982; Subject master in English and head of English department, Albany Creek High School, Brisbane, 1984-89; Creative writing lecturer and communication theory lecturer, Queensland University of Technology, contract literature and literacy consultant, primary and secondary schools throughout Australia, Children's book editor (Reed Books, Queensland University Press, Lothian Books), and series editor (*After Dark* children's series), all from 1989; **Awards:** Book of the Year award, Children's Book Council of Australia, Alan Marshall Prize for Children's Literature, and NSW Premier's Award, all 1991, all for *Strange Objects; Lucy's Bay* was short listed for the Children's Book Council of Australia's picture book of the year, 1993; Picture Book of the Year award, Children's Book Council of Australia, 1994, for *First Light*; National Children's Book Award and Children's Novel of the Year, Children's Book Council of Australia, 1994, for *Angel's Gate*; Picture Book of the Year, Children's Book Council of Australia, 1995, for *The Water Tower*. **Agent:** c/o Fran Kelly, 25 Panorama Crescent, Toowoomba 4350, Queensland, Australia. **Address:** P.O. Box 440, Maleny 4552, Queensland, Australia.

PUBLICATIONS FOR YOUNG ADULTS

Novels

The Inner Circle. Melbourne, Heinemann, 1985.
The House of Tomorrow. Melbourne, Heinemann, 1988.
Strange Objects. Melbourne, Heinemann, 1990; Simon and Schuster, 1993.
No Such Country: A Book of Antipodean Hours. Melbourne, Heinemann, 1991.
Angel's Gate. Melbourne, Heinemann, 1993.
With Michael O'Hara, *The Blue Feather.* Melbourne, Heinemann, 1997.

PUBLICATIONS FOR CHILDREN

Fiction

Tracks, illustrated by Gregory Rogers. Lothian, 1992.
Lucy's Bay, illustrated by Gregory Rogers. Jam Roll Press, 1992.
The Figures of Julian Ashcroft, illustrated by Hans DeHaas. Jam Roll Press, 1993.
First Light, illustrated by Peter Gouldthorpe. Lothian, 1993.
Gulliver in the South Seas, illustrated by John Burge. Lothian, 1994.
The Watertower, illustrated by Steven Wodman. Adelaide, ERA Publishers, 1994.
The Lost Diamonds of Killicrankie, illustrated by Peter Gouldthorpe. Lothian, 1995.
Caleb, illustrated by Steven Woolman. Adelaide, ERA Publishers, 1996.
The Figures of Julian Ashcroft, illustrated by Hans de Hass. Queensland University Press, 1996.
Bright Star, illustrated by Anne Spudvilas. Lothian (Australia) and Kane Miller (United States), 1997.
Tagged, illustrated by Steven Woolman. Adelaide, ERA Publishers, 1997.
The Viewer, illustrated by Shaun Tan. Lothian, 1997.

Other

Contributor, *At Least They're Reading! Proceedings of the First National Conference of the Children's Book Council of Australia.* Thorpe, 1992.
Contributor, *The Blue Dress,* edited by Libby Hathorne. Melbourne, Heinemann, 1992.
Contributor, *Hair Raising,* edited by Penny Matthews. Omnibus, 1992.
Contributor, *The Second Authors and Illustrators Scrapbook.* Omnibus, 1992.
Contributor, *The Lottery,* edited by Lucy Sussex. Omnibus, 1994.
Contributor, *Family,* edited by Agnes Nieuwenhuizen. Reed, 1994.
Contributor, *Crossing,* edited by Agnes Nieuwenhuizen and Tessa Duder. Reed, 1995.
Compiling editor, *Dark House.* Reed, 1995.
Contributor, *Nightmares in Paradise,* edited by R. Sheahan. Queensland University Press, 1995.
Contributor, *The Phone Book.* Random House, 1995.
Contributor, *Celebrate,* edited by M. Hillel and A. Hanzl. Viking, 1996.
Compiling editor, *Crew's 13.* ABC Books, 1997.
Contributor to periodicals, including *The Age, Australian Author, Imago, Magpies, Reading Time, Viewpoint,* and *World Literature Written in English.*

*

Media Adaptations: *Sleeping over at Lola's* (radio play), Australian Broadcasting Commission; *Strange Objects* (film), Zoic Films.

Biography: Essay in *The Second Authors and Illustrators Scrapbook* by Gary Crew, Omnibus, 1992.

Gary Crew comments:

From my earliest memories I recall that the happiest times for me were being curled up with a book or scraps of paper and coloured pencils—I suppose, when I look back that I was always escaping into, or creating, other worlds. I think that my ideas for the novels that I create today come from some of these earliest childhood times.

More than anything else I would like to be known as a writer of wonderful books, a writer who has enriched and opened up the imagination of young people so that now, in the present, they may see the world as a better place—and carry the phenomenal possibilities of youth into the future.

*   *   *

Even in his two picture books Gary Crew uses symbolism to make a universal statement relevant to young adults. *Tracks,* a seemingly simple illustrated poem, suggests, by tracing the slimy silver trail of a slug, that something mundane can create a great beauty. *Lucy's Bay* is a rites-of-passage picture story, in textured prose, about facing one's pains and fears, especially those that stem from the past, and moving forward. The image of regeneration here is a tuft of gossamer containing seeds from a reed pool.

Crew's first two novels are deliberate attempts to confront contemporary personal and societal problems through well-crafted literary models accessible to young people. Both *The Inner Circle* and *The House of Tomorrow* develop themes of personal and cultural identity, displacement and regeneration, through strong and thought-provoking plots which gain rich linguistic and literary texture by the conscious use of imagery and symbolism. His third book, *Strange Objects,* which was named Australian Book of the Year for older readers, is an archetypal post-modernist young adult novel using a variety of structures: a scrapbook diary, newspaper reports, extracts from library books, psychological studies, historical data and footnotes. *No Such Country: A Book of Antipodean Hours* is even more ambitious; a "big" contemporary novel of calculated literary intent. Here Crew elaborates past themes but in a very different context: Australia's search for identity by coming to terms with the Aboriginal presence. In a much more complex way it develops the theme of guilt and its consequences, embedded in *Lucy's Bay.*

The Inner Circle confronts Aboriginality in contemporary urban Australia and suggests that white Australians must not only co-exist with Aborigines but be prepared to take up the spiritual values that permeate Aboriginal culture. The novel focuses equally on two displaced urban teenagers, one white, one black, who come together when they each seek refuge in a disused powerhouse near a city park. Their stories are told through alternating and interlocking first-person narratives. Tony, the white boy, is calculatingly and cynically ambitious and has adopted a tough facade to hide the hurt he is suffering from his parents' fractured relationship and their separate buying of his favours. Joe, the Aborigine, is from a loving and supportive country family whom he keeps in ignorance of his impecunious finances and the racism that has driven him from his job. Despite a series of frustrations the boys' relationship is ultimately a healing one. The possibility of racial harmony is suggested by the recurring image of the wheel of the bicycle which Tony wants Joe to have, and by Joe's planting of an indigenous

palm to replace an exotic rosebush growing in a circular bed in the park. Black and white Australia can and must share the same soil.

The House of Tomorrow is the case-study, journal-like narrative of Mr. Mac, an aging English master, in which he includes the personal folio of a deeply disturbed pupil, Danny Coley. The boy's complex problems are ultimately revealed to stem from his being half Asian, born of his dead father's liaison, formed while fighting in Vietnam. The book's title comes from the words of the Prophet of Khalil Gibran, and its theme is expressed in that seer's quotation, "your children. . .are the sons and daughters of Life's longing for itself." The mysticism (Danny's ancestral voices and those of his senile Pentecostal grandfather); the death images, including two suicides; the Christian symbolism (baptism); and the implied regeneration through the child of Liz Murray—a colleague of Mr. Mac—are pointers to the richness of Crew's next two novels.

Both *The Inner Circle* and *The House of Tomorrow* are complex but not daunting, and already have a devoted young readership. *Strange Objects* and *No Such Country* are even more ambitious and challenging, in that both are multilayered, explore intricate philosophical concepts and weave their way through the natural and the supernatural. The "strange objects" of the former are present-day rediscoveries in Australia by a disturbed teenage boy, significantly called Steven Messenger, of a seventeenth-century "cannibal pot," a mummified hand wearing a ring which has strange psychological powers, and a leather journal. By appropriating and wearing the cursed ring Steven becomes identified with Pelgrom, a cabin boy from the *Batavia,* wrecked off Western Australia in 1629. Because Pelgrom and Steven have no real regard for Aboriginal life, art or spirituality, and scant interest in nature or the environment, both eventually vanish into the landscape.

Crime against Aborigines and the guilt engendered in a community by the cover-up of a tribal massacre trigger the action of Crew's *tour de force, No Such Country.* New Canaan is in bondage to an unscrupulous, manipulative Messianic figure, the Father. Only two white girls and the aptly named resurrected black, Sam Shadows, have the perception and courage to combat the pervasive evil of the Father. Together they bring about an Armageddon that cleanses and regenerates the Antipodean land, so that the earth breathes "warm and strong, as it had done since the beginning." Its biblical echoes, its recurring imagery—a foreboding fishing net to catch sinners, the Lamb's book of life, a white heron, an hour glass—its literary allusions, its intriguing mysticism and, above all, its lucid but evocative prose make *No Such Country* a highly significant contribution to young adult literature internationally.

—Maurice Saxby

CREW, Linda

Nationality: American. **Born:** Corvallis, Oregon, 8 April 1951. **Education:** Lewis and Clark College, Portland, Oregon, 1969-70; University of Oregon, Eugene, B.A. in journalism 1973. **Family:** Married Herb Crew in 1974; two sons, one daughter. **Career:** Writer. **Awards:** *Children of the River* was chosen as a Golden Kite Honor Book, 1989, a Michigan Library Association Young Adult Honor Book, and an American Library Association Best Book for Young Adults and "Best of the Best," and received the

International Reading Association Children's Book Award in the older readers category; *Nekomah Creek* was chosen as an ALA Notable Book for Children. **Agent:** Robin Rue, Anita Diamant Agency, 310 Madison Ave., New York, New York 10017, U.S.A.

PUBLICATIONS FOR YOUNG ADULTS

Fiction

Children of the River. New York, Delacorte, 1989.
Someday I'll Laugh about This. New York, Delacorte, 1990.
Fire on the Wind. New York, Delacorte, 1995.
Long Time Passing. New York, Delacorte, 1997.

PUBLICATIONS FOR CHILDREN

Fiction

Nekomah Creek, illustrated by Charles Robinson. New York, Delacorte, 1991.
Nekomah Creek Christmas, illustrated by Charles Robinson. New York, Delacorte, 1994.

PUBLICATIONS FOR ADULTS

Fiction

Ordinary Miracles. New York, Morrow, 1993.

*

Biography: Essay in *Speaking for Ourselves, Too* compiled and edited by Donald R. Gallo, National Council of Teachers of English, 1993.

Linda Crew comments:

I think of my writing process as the creating of a tapestry— the rough draft being the warp, the subsequent versions the weft, and finally, the finishing touches are the fancy French knots. My raw material is real life, which I weave with fictional threads into a story that I hope will express my feelings better than a strict recounting of the facts ever could. Because I've used so many incidents from my family's life in my books, we've all become confused over which details really happened and which were added in my embroidered version. That's why, when a reader asks me if one of my stories is true, the only honest answer is often that none of it really happened, but yes, it's all completely true!

*　　*　　*

Linda Crew entered the young adult literature scene with the publication in 1989 of her first book, *Children of the River.* With this novel, Crew gives young adults a glimpse into the experiences of Cambodian refugees and the struggles many faced when forced to flee their native land for the United States in search of a life free of tyranny. This is a thought-provoking, impressive novel that portrays believable characters and situations with whom readers can identify and sympathize.

The story of Sundara, the protagonist of *Children of the River,* begins in April 1975, with Sundara, age thirteen, fleeing her native Cambodia after the dreaded Khmer Rouge gain control of the country. Sundara heads for the United States with her aunt, uncle, and infant cousin, enduring a difficult ocean journey on a ship crowded with several hundred refugees. The story fast-forwards to September 1979. Sundara, now seventeen, is amazed at how different Americans are; after four years, she does not understand her American peers or their typically American teenage interests, hopes, and concerns. A class writing assignment illustrates the distance between the two cultures; Sundara's life centers on her struggles to deal with the circumstances of the life she left behind in Cambodia and with trying to find her place in a culture alien to her, while her classmates are concerned with video games, dress codes, and cafeteria food. Sundara fears her classmates will ridicule her because she is so different from them; but, in fact, they come to understand her, and even admire her courage. The story is subtle in showing that, despite cultural differences, young adult concerns about fitting in, love, and family relationships are experiences common to young people everywhere. It also shows how the struggle for power often results in the senseless destruction of a people, and how we, as Americans, have learned to take freedom for granted, allowing many of the values we once held dear to disappear.

Crew's second book, *Someday I'll Laugh about This,* is a lighter story about a coming-of-age summer vacation. Twelve-year-old Shelby wants this summer to be like the summers before; she wants nothing to change. But this summer everything will change. Her thirteen-year-old cousin, Kirsten, has a boyfriend she is moping about leaving for two weeks. Kirsten has also befriended the new girl whose father is ruining their ocean view with the condominiums he is building. And, much to Shelby's regret, the uncle she is fond of is bringing someone new to meet the family. Like everything and everyone around her, Shelby is changing—growing into a young woman. She learns to accept these changes and learns several lessons along the way about the importance of being yourself, and how standing up for what you believe in can make a difference.

In *Fire on the Wind,* published in 1995, Crew ventures into the genre of historical fiction. Set in Oregon during the summer of 1933, the bulk of the plot takes place in fifteen days, paralleling the great Tillamook Burn. Crew's meticulous research becomes the coming of age story of Estora (Storie) Faye Rendall, a thirteen-year-old logger's daughter struggling to find her own way. Storie's family lives in the logging camp far removed from most civilization, but Storie has enjoyed the beauty, peace, and solitude that the mountains provide. Still, she longs to attend the high school in the town down in the valley where she would have access to books and new ideas. Storie fluctuates between childhood and adolescence, torn between her love and respect for the forest and the life of logging, the only life she has known. She shuns dresses in favor of her baggy overalls, yet is intrigued with the new, young logger, Flynn Casey, who arrives in camp and of whom her father does not approve. Storie is forced to grow up quickly when a forest fire burns out of control and threatens to destroy their camp. While her father is off with the crews, Storie remains with her mother and brother as the fire moves closer and closer to the camp. Finally, the supervisor is forced to vacate the camp, but he insists that it is too late to inform the men who are off fighting the fire. Storie takes it upon herself to find her father and warn the crew, especially Flynn Casey, that unless they hurry, they will be left behind. Finally, she locates them and together with her father, but not Flynn, they rush to return. In Storie's last glimpse of the camp, she sees her beloved schoolhouse go up in flames.

Weeks later, the Rendall family is settled in town, and Storie is enrolled in eighth grade at the high school when Flynn Casey returns to town. The romance begins to blossom, this time with her father's permission. The plot jumps ahead to 1994. Storie, now widowed, tells the story of the forest fire to her two grandchildren who already are becoming advocates for forest preservation. The novel is fast-paced and the characters well-developed. We learn both about the characters and about logging life and its dangers through their dialogue which Crew generously sprinkles with logging terms.

Long Time Passing (1997) is set in the turbulent sixties. Fifteen-year-old Kathy Shay and her twin brother Kenny are high school sophomores in the small town of Chintimini, Oregon. In contrast to her brother's comfortable popularity, Kathy dreams of finding her own niche but is plagued by a series of what she perceives as failures. She is not selected for the junior varsity rally squad and meets with rejection when her art portfolio is returned from *Seventeen* magazine's contest. When she tries out for the lead in the school play, she loses to her best friend who only went to give her moral support. However, at tryouts, Kathy is reintroduced to James Holderread, another nonconformist, and their friendship develops into first love. She struggles to find herself and deal with issues of civil rights, Viet Nam, school, sexuality, and the role of women. She is devastated when James' father accepts another teaching position at a university in Massachusetts and James is forced to move. Kathy makes the difficult decision to not consummate their relationship and their letters become less frequent as time goes by.

Crew again uses the technique of fast-forwarding, and in the epilogue we next see Kathy and James, in their senior year of college, engaged to other people. James makes a last ditch drive up the coast in an effort to reconnect with Kathy, and within a month they decide to marry one another. The book ends with them still happily married twenty-four years later.

—Suzanne M. Valentic, updated by Susan B. Steffel

CRICHTON, (John) Michael

Pseudonyms: Jeffery Hudson; John Lange; Michael Douglas, a joint pseudonym. **Nationality:** American. **Born:** Chicago, Illinois, 23 October 1942. **Education:** Harvard University, Cambridge, Massachusetts, A.B. (summa cum laude) 1964 (Phi Beta Kappa); Harvard Medical School, M.D. 1969; Salk Institute, La Jolla, California, 1969-70. **Family:** Married 1) Joan Radam in 1965 (divorced 1971); 2) Kathleen St. Johns in 1978 (divorced 1980); 3) Suzanne Childs (divorced); 4) Anne-Marie Martin in 1987; one daughter. **Career:** Full-time writer of books and films; director of

films and teleplays. **Awards:** Mystery Writers of America Edgar Allan Poe award, 1968, for *A Case of Need,* and 1980, for *The Great Train Robbery;* Association of American Medical Writers award, 1970, for *Five Patients: The Hospital Explained.* **Agent:** International Creative Management, 40 West 57th Street, New York, New York 10019, U.S.A.

PUBLICATIONS

Fiction

The Andromeda Strain. New York, Knopf, and London, Cape, 1969.
The Terminal Man. New York, Knopf, and London, Cape, 1972.
Westworld. New York, Bantam, 1974.
The Great Train Robbery. New York, Knopf, and London, Cape, 1975.
Eaters of the Dead: The Manuscript of Ibn Fadlan, Relating His Experiences with the Northmen in A.D. 922. New York, Knopf, and London, Cape, 1976.
Congo. New York, Knopf, 1980; London, Allen Lane, 1981.
Sphere. New York, Knopf, and London, Macmillan, 1987.
Jurassic Park. New York, Knopf, 1990; London, Century, 1991.
Rising Sun. New York, Knopf, 1992.
Three Complete Novels, (contains *The Andromeda Strain, The Terminal Man,* and *The Great Train Robbery*). New York, Wing Books, 1993.
Disclosure. New York, Knopf, 1994.
A New Collection (includes selections from *Sphere, Congo,* and *Eaters of the Dead*). New York, Wings Books 1994.
The Lost World. New York, Knopf, 1995.
Two Complete Novels (includes *Disclosure* and *Rising Sun*). New York, Wings Books, 1996.
Airframe. New York, Knopf, 1996.
The Lost World, Jurassic Park: The Movie Storybook (based on the motion picture and the novel). New York, Grosset and Dunlap, 1997.

Screenplays

Westworld, MGM, 1973.
Coma, based on a novel by Robin Cook, United Artists, 1977.
The Great Train Robbery, United Artists, 1978.
Looker, Warner Bros., 1981.
Runaway, Tri-Star Pictures, 1984.
Jurassic Park, with John Koepp, Universal, 1993.
Rising Sun, with Philip Kaufman and Michael Backes, Twentieth Century Fox, 1993.
With Anne-Marie Martin, *Twister.* New York, Ballantine Books, 1996.

Fiction as John Lange

Odds On. New York, New American Library, 1966.
Scratch One. New York, New American Library, 1967.
Easy Go. New York, New American Library, 1968; London, Sphere, 1972; as *The Last Tomb,* as Michael Crichton, New York, Bantam, 1974.
The Venom Business. Cleveland, World, 1969.
Zero Cool. New York, New American Library, 1969; London, Sphere, 1972.
Drug of Choice. New York, New American Library, 1970; as *Overkill,* New York, Centesis, 1970.

Grave Descend. New York, New American Library, 1970.
Binary. New York, Knopf, and London, Heinemann, 1972.

Fiction as Jeffery Hudson

A Case of Need. Cleveland, World, and London, Heinemann, 1968.

Fiction as Michael Douglas

Dealing; or, the Berkeley-to-Boston Forty-Brick Lost-Bag Blues,
with Douglas Crichton. New York, Knopf, 1971.

Nonfiction

Five Patients: The Hospital Explained. New York, Knopf, 1970;
London, Cape, 1971.
Jasper Johns. New York, Abrams, and London, Thames and
Hudson, 1977; revised, New York, Abrams, 1994.
Electronic Life: How to Think about Computers. New York,
Knopf, and London, Heinemann, 1983.
Travels (autobiography). New York, Knopf, and London, Macmillan, 1988.

Theatrical Activities

Director: All films, *Westworld,* 1973; *Coma,* 1978; *The Great
Train Robbery,* 1978; *Looker,* 1981; *Runaway,* 1984; *Pursuit*
(television movie), 1972.

*

Media Adaptations: *The Andromeda Strain* (film), Universal in
1971; *Binary* (television movie entitled *Pursuit*), for ABC-TV,
1972; *A Case of Need* (film, *The Carey Treatment*), MGM, 1973;
The Terminal Man (film), MGM, 1974; *Jurassic Park* (film,
directed by Steven Spielberg), Universal, 1993; *Rising Sun* (film),
Twentieth Century Fox, 1993; *Congo* (film), Paramount, 1995;
Disclosure (film), 1995; *The Lost World, Jurassic Park: The
Complete Dinosaur Scrapbook,* by James Preller, with Molly
Jackel and Marilyn McCabe. New York, Scholastic, 1997.

Biography: Entry in *Dictionary of Literary Biography Yearbook:
1981,* Detroit, Gale, 1982.

Critical Studies: Entry in *Contemporary Literary Criticism,* Volume 2, Detroit, Gale, 1974; Volume 6, 1976; Volume 54, 1989; *The
Making of Jurassic Park* by Don Shay and Jody Duncan, New
York, Ballantine, 1993.

*   *   *

As the founder of a distinct literary genre (the techno-thriller)
and the author of several blockbuster novels, coupled with the
immense popularity of the 1993 film version of *Jurassic Park,*

Michael Crichton has ascended to an extremely high level of public
popularity. When Crichton began his writing career in the mid-
sixties he was producing mysteries under the names of John Lange
and Jeffery Hudson to pay his way through medical school. These
early novels (*Zero Cool, Overkill, Binary, A Case of Need,* etc.) are
all demonstrative of Crichton's writing style; he combines the
ability to write with cinematic fluidity and a critically technical
way of describing (courtesy of his medical school training) to
produce engaging and realistic novels. During this period, Crichton
debated whether to continue with medicine or pursue writing full-
time. Then, in 1969, he wrote what would become his greatest
literary achievement—*The Andromeda Strain,* the success of
which made his decision to quit medicine respectable.

Until this time Crichton's writing had been that of formulaic
thrillers, almost pulp fiction. In *The Andromeda Strain* Crichton
blended his scientific background and knowledge with his gift for
writing tight, suspenseful, and entertaining plots to produce his
trademark—the techno-thriller. Although the techno-thriller is
based primarily on science fiction, it is still, in terms of construction, the thriller and typically functions as such. Subsequent novels
such as *The Terminal Man, Sphere, Congo,* and *Eaters of the Dead*
follow the patterns and methods Crichton established in *The
Andromeda Strain* but fail to live up to the standards of this
predecessor. Even Crichton's return to classic thrillers with such
novels as *The Great Train Robbery* and *Rising Sun* display the
techno-thriller's reliance on science. Since Crichton's novels
exhibit similar characteristics, it is possible to explore the aspects
of one novel to examine his writing style.

The Andromeda Strain is the account of a group of scientists
desperately trying to keep an extraterrestrial micro-organism from
wreaking ecological Armageddon on an unsuspecting Earth. The
book is filled with scientific details, like glossaries, transcripts,
charts, graphs, printouts, etc., which make *The Andromeda Strain*
read more like science fact than science fiction. Furthermore, the
book is structured like a "Classified Government Document,"
making its premise more immediate. Consequently, Crichton's
fictional world is not one of far-off future-distant worlds, exotic
aliens, and fantastic machinery, it is rather a tale of man's survival
and his present state of affairs.

Crichton fills his novels with the dangers, horrors, and wonders
of what he feels is possible in the present day and the human ability
to cope with them. This blending of reality and fantasy make these
novels frightening not only in possibility but probability as well.
The journalistic stance Crichton commonly assumes is relatively
unbiased, although his sentiments ultimately underlie his works as
a whole. In this way Crichton transforms his novels into "wake-
up" calls in which he attempts to alert his readers to any scientific
discoveries or social processes he sees as potentially dangerous
(e.g. *The Andromeda Strain* proposes the notion of the abuse of
science in the guise of germ warfare). That blend of reality and
fiction is why Crichton's books are so popular (virtually all of his
novels have been best-sellers); they suspend disbelief, allow total
immersion in a fictional world, and, as a bonus, don't take too much
time to read.

The cinematic flow of Crichton's works is due to their lack of
text-bogging characterization, and this absence is the main criticism that has been levied against him. His characters have been
described as one-dimensional and mere plot puppets. But his use of
stereotypes stems from his desire to tell the story at hand and not
slow down for superfluous description. Crichton expects the reader

to bring into the novel a preconceived notion of any character they might encounter (in *The Andromeda Strain,* a scientist or politician), thus allowing the creation of a reader-identity for the character, rather than being force-fed an author's personal and rigid conception. By allowing reader identification with characters in this manner Crichton ensures the fluidity of the story since action is quicker than characterization.

Crichton's novels also display remarkable clarity and actuality in the portrayal of the cultures in which they are set. This trait is demonstrated prominently in the novels *The Great Train Robbery* and *Rising Sun.* These two novels are set respectively in Victorian England and the Japanese society of Los Angeles. Crichton's description of these cultures is not done through a sporadic introduction of ideas but rather by totally immersing the reader in these societies. Although Crichton refrains from distinct characterization of individuals, he does describe his subjects with some detail. He frequently interrupts the story with historically descriptive asides to clarify episodes (a device he also uses to explain scientific processes).

Although Crichton wrote prolifically after the publication of *The Andromeda Strain,* it was not until 1990 that he finally wrote a novel that rivals its intensity. *Jurassic Park* is the story of an amusement park run amuck. Crichton's park is not populated with rides, clowns, and a midway however, but rather with live dinosaurs. Like *The Andromeda Strain,* the novel tells of a group of scientists who desperately try to save themselves and society, but these characters are escaping from the jaws of hungry, biogenetically engineered dinosaurs, not a mutating germ. All of Crichton's conventions are intact, including a subtle warning against the misuse of science (biogenetics), making *Jurassic Park* his best work since *The Andromeda Strain.*

The traits of the techno-thriller combined with Crichton's scriptlike writing style make his novels easily transferrable to film. Many of his novels have in fact been made into motion pictures (*The Andromeda Strain, The Terminal Man, Jurassic Park,* etc.) and some even by Crichton himself (*Westworld, The Great Train Robbery*). These almost verbatim celluloid representations of his novels all display the stylistic fluidity of Crichton's writing. Although the films may come under the same attacks levied against his novels, they are nevertheless entertaining and serve as testaments to Crichton's desire to tell a good story, and if a message (or warning) happens to slip in, so be it.

—Michael J. Tyrkus

CROSS, Gillian (Clare)

Nationality: British. **Born:** Gillian Clare Arnold in London, England, 24 December 1945. **Education:** Somerville College, Oxford, B.A. (with first class honors) 1969, M.A. 1972; University of Sussex, Brighton, D. Phil. in English 1974. **Family:** Married Martin Cross in 1967; two daughters and two sons. **Career:** Various jobs including assistant to a village baker, teacher, office worker, and assistant to a member of Parliament; author of books for children and young adults. **Awards:** Carnegie highly commended book, 1982; Carnegie commended book, 1986; Guardian Award runner-up, 1983; Best Books for Young Adults list and Notable Children's Books list, 1985, 1987; Whitbread Award

runner-up, 1984; Edgar Award runner-up, 1986; Carnegie Medal, 1990, for *Wolf*; Smarties Book Prize, and Whitbread Children's Novel Award, both 1992, both for *The Great Elephant Chase.* **Address:** c/o Oxford Children's Books, Oxford University Press, Clarendon Street, Oxford OX2 6DP, England.

PUBLICATIONS FOR YOUNG ADULTS

Revolt at Ratcliffe's Rags, illustrated by Tony Morris. Oxford and New York, Oxford University Press, 1980; as *Strike at Ratcliffe's Rags,* London, Magnet, 1987.
A Whisper of Lace. Oxford and New York, Oxford University Press, 1981.
The Dark Behind the Curtain, illustrated by David Parkins. Oxford, Oxford University Press, 1982; New York, Oxford University Press, 1984.
Born of the Sun, illustrated by Mark Edwards. Oxford, Oxford University Press, 1983; New York, Holiday House, 1984.
On the Edge. Oxford, Oxford University Press, 1984; New York, Holiday House, 1985.
Chartbreak. Oxford, Oxford University Press, 1986; as *Chartbreaker,* New York, Holiday House, 1987.
Roscoe's Leap. Oxford, Oxford University Press, 1987; New York, Holiday House, 1987.
A Map of Nowhere. Oxford, Oxford University Press, 19866; New York, Holiday, House, 1989.
Wolf. Oxford, Oxford University Press, 1990; New York, Holiday House, 1991.
The Great Elephant Chase. Oxford, Oxford University Press, 1992; as *The Great American Elephant Chase,* New York, Holiday House, 1993.
New World. Oxford, Oxford University Press, 1994; New York, Holiday House, 1995.
Pictures in the Dark. Oxford, Oxford University Press, 1996; New York, Holiday House, 1996.

PUBLICATIONS FOR CHILDREN

The Runaway, illustrated by Reginald Gray. London, Methuen, 1979.
The Iron Way, illustrated by Tony Morris. Oxford and New York, 1979.
Save Our School, illustrated by Gareth Floyd. London, Methuen, 1981.
The Demon Headmaster, illustrated by Gary Rees. Oxford, Oxford University Press, 1982; New York, Oxford University Press, 1987.
The Mintyglo Kid, illustrated by Gareth Floyd. London, Methuen, 1983.
The Prime Minister's Brain, illustrated by Sally Burgess. Oxford, Oxford University Press, 1985; New York, Oxford University Press, 1987.
Swimathon!, illustrated by Gareth Floyd. London, Methuen, 1986.
Rescuing Gloria, illustrated by Gareth Floyd. London, Methuen, 1989.
Twin and Super-Twin, illustrated by Maureen Bradley. Oxford, Oxford University Press, 1990; New York, Holiday House, 1990.
Monster from Underground, illustrated by Peter Firmin. London, Heinemann, 1990.
Gobbo the Great, illustrated by Philippe Dupasquier. London, Methuen, 1991.
Rent-a-genius, illustrated by Glenys Ambrus. London, Hamish Hamilton, 1991.

Beware Olga!, illustrated by Arthur Robins. London, Walker, 1993,
The Furry Maccaloo, illustrated by Madeleine Baker, London, Heinemann, 1993.
The Tree House, illustrated by Paul Howard. London, Methuen, 1993.
What Will Emily Do?, illustrated by Paul Howard. London, Methuen, 1994.
Hunky Parker is Watching You, illustrated by Maureen Bradley. Oxford, Oxford University Press, 1994; as *The Revenge of the Demon Headmaster,* London, Puffin, 1995.
The Crazy School Shuffle, illustrated by Nick Sharratt. London, Methuen, 1995.
Posh Watson, illustrated by Mike Gordon. London, Walker, 1995.
The Roman Beanfeast, illustrated by Linzi Henry. London, Hamish Hamilton, 1996.
The Demon Headmaster Strikes Again. Oxford, Oxford University Press, 1996.
The Return of the Demon Headmaster. Oxford, Oxford University Press, 1997.

PUBLICATIONS FOR ADULTS

"How I Started Writing for Children," in *Books for Your Children* (Birmingham), Vol. 19, Summer 1984, 15-16.
"Twenty Things I Don't Believe about Children's Books," in *School Librarian* (London), Vol. 39, No. 2, 1991, 44-46.
"Carnegie Medal Acceptance Speech," in *Youth Library Review* (Birmingham), Vol. 12, Autumn 1991, 7-8.

*

Biography: "First, Catch Your Reader" by David Self, in *Times Educational Supplement Review: Children's Books* (London), No. 3999, 19 February 1993; essay in *Speaking for Ourselves, Too* compiled and edited by Donald R. Gallo, Urbana, Illinois, National Council of Teachers of English, 1993, 50-52.

Critical Studies: *Gillian Cross* by Keith Barker, Swindon, School Library Association, 1992; "The Novels of Gillian Cross" by Winifred Whitehead, in *The Use of English* (Edinburgh), Vol. 43 No. 1, 1992, 57-66.

Gillian Cross comments:

I think I became a writer for two reasons. First—I love reading. And I particularly love the sort of book that becomes a separate world while I'm reading it, so that I don't want it to end. Writing is like that too, but it goes on much longer. When I'm writing a book, I'm inside its special, separate world for nine months or a year.

The second reason for writing is that I love storytelling. When I was in my teens, travelling home from school on the train, I used to tell my friends a serial story, all about themselves. And when I got married and had children, there was more storytelling. Some writers are particularly concerned with character, or with social comment, but it's the actual story that I love.

The central things in my books are choices. My heroes and heroines tend to face tough situations where they have to make important and difficult decisions. The stories come out like that

because that's how life seems to me. What we do is important, not only to ourselves but to other people. The really exciting and dangerous moments are the ones when we have to choose what kind of people we want to be.

*   *   *

Gillian Cross offers varying blends of history, suspense, and social concern in her young adult novels designed to capture and hold readers' attention. Her fast-paced plots do not shy away from serious social issues or dark subjects such as violence, political intrigue, and death.

Her first novel, *The Iron Way,* appears to be a straightforward historical narrative, but the book contains themes that clearly relate to contemporary problems. Set in Victorian England, the novel deals with the coming of the railway to a rural society mistrustful of change and suspicious of the Irish railway workers. When 16-year-old Kate Penfold agrees to board laborer Conor O'Flynn, she does so out of a desperate need for funds to support herself and younger siblings. However, the Penfolds and Con find themselves caught between villagers and navvies as violent incidents escalate and eventually result in Con's death. Astute readers can easily recognize the application of the theme of the destructive power generated by fear of those who are different.

The mixture of history and suspense is more complex in *A Whisper of Lace,* which involves the nineteenth century smuggling of lace to England from the continent. Francis Merrowby and his sister are caught in an increasingly dangerous enterprise masterminded by a shadowy figure who turns out to be their long-absent older brother. Secret messages, nocturnal coach rides, and daring schemes to outwit the authorities supply plenty of intrigue. But Cross does not ignore the devastating economic consequences of such smuggling on the impoverished English lace workers.

Exploitation serves as a powerful theme in *The Dark Behind the Curtain,* in which ghosts of children from Victorian times seek revenge through contemporary children acting in a school production of "Sweeney Todd." Marshall, who portrays the evil Todd, bullies cast members and threatens his former friend Jackus, just as the stage character destroyed the lives of people in his day. Tension heightens as past and present, stage and school grow ever closer in a web of evil.

Exposing secrets of the past forms the basis of *Roscoe's Leap,* in which a family is literally divided and lives in separate wings of a huge mansion spanning a river. Only the arrival of an architecture student engaged in research about Samuel Roscoe, the ancestor who had constructed the house, starts a process of discovery for Stephen, who cannot understand memories of events from his early childhood. Mechanical toys, including a model of the French Terror, provide an explanation of how cruelty can affect several generations.

Questions about repression and the family fill *On the Edge,* one of Cross' most powerful novels. Tug, the son of a journalist who reports extensively on terrorist activities, is kidnapped by members of a group devoted to exposing the repressive power of families. Subject to brainwashing techniques at the country house where his captors have taken him, Tug grows increasingly uncertain about the identity of his "real" mother. Authorities are reluctant to interfere in what they perceive as a family unit. A parallel story of Jinny, a local girl convinced that Tug is held captive, points out the control exercised by many parents. Her own authoritative father dominates his children and provides little more freedom than Tug experiences in his prison. Even readers who overlook such comparisons will be enthralled by the mounting tension over what will happen to Tug.

Even more suspense permeates *Wolf,* which won the Carnegie medal. In this novel the terrorist is Cassy's own father, a member of the Irish Republican Army, who is willing to sacrifice anyone's life to advance his cause. Sent by her grandmother, with whom she usually stays, to Goldie, her beautiful but irresponsible mother, Cassy unknowingly carries with her the plastic explosive her father had brought to his mother's home. Goldie lives with a West African artist in an abandoned London house. As Lyall and his son do research on myths and facts about wolves for a school presentation they are preparing, the reader is increasingly aware that a human wolf is stalking Cassy. Cross intersperses fragments from the tale of Red Riding Hood to heighten the tension, and Cassy's fear affects the reader as well.

Cross incorporates other social issues besides political terrorism into her young adult novels. In *Pictures in the Dark,* she creates a chilling portrait of child abuse. Peter Luttrell's parents control his behavior so rigidly he is forced to withdraw psychologically. Charlie Wilcox, taking photos of the river for a Camera Club exhibit, spots an otter, though such animals haven't been seen along the banks in years. As he learns of Peter's familiarity with every inch of the river and his desperation to escape his father, Charlie concludes that boy and otter are intricately connected. *Revolt at Ratcliffe's Rags* documents what happens when three students bent on completing a school report investigate a local factory and get involved in labor unrest. The resulting strike tears apart the community and families and reveals that economic problems do not always have simple solutions.

In *Chartbreak* Cross uses the world of rock music to explore the search for identity of recording star Finch. Interspersing newspaper articles and magazine interviews with Finch's own account of her rise to fame, Cross contrasts public perceptions with personal reality. *Map of Nowhere* combines adolescents' fascination with adventure games with the necessity for making moral decisions in real life. Nick Miller, who wants to join the gang of which his older brother is a member, becomes their spy to help set up a robbery. However, his growing friendship with Joseph and Ruth Fisher makes him reluctant to betray the hard-working but poor family that refuses financial gain if it involves betraying moral principles.

New World explores the psychological dimensions and dangers of virtual reality games. Three teenagers serve as unwitting participants in a company's final tests of a game designed to exploit an individual's fears. Will Barrington doesn't realize that the two figures he is manipulating in a computer game are really virtual reality participants Miriam Enderby and Stuart Jones. Because Will's father has developed New World to provide maximum excitement to hook participants, he refuses to acknowledge its dangerous potential to players who learn how to bypass the cutoff mechanism activated by increased pulse rate. Dispassionate intercompany memos describing test results alternate with tense accounts of the teenagers' experiences.

Almost all Cross' books are set in England. However, *Born of the Sun* takes a family to South America in quest of an ancient city long sought by Paula Staszic's archeologist father. His growing irrationality on the journey reveals symptoms of his physical illness that receives an unexpected cure deep in the jungle. *The Great*

American Elephant Chase is set in the frontier days of the United States. Cissie Keenan and Tad Hawkins must take an elephant cross country to Nebraska after the animal's owner, Cissie's father, dies.

Cross continues to demonstrate her awareness of topics important to young adults, whether rock music or virtual reality games. Her apt blending of psychological elements with explorations of family dynamics enriches her work while holding readers' undivided attention. The variety and complexity of her young adult novels reveal her mastery of the form.

—Kathy Piehl

CROSSLEY-HOLLAND, Kevin (John William)

Nationality: British. **Born:** Mursley, Buckinghamshire, 7 February 1941. **Education:** Bryanston School; St. Edmund Hall, Oxford, M.A. (honours) in English language and literature 1962. **Family:** Two sons, two daughters. **Career:** Editor, Macmillan, publishers, London, 1962-71; talks producer, BBC, London, 1972; editorial director, Victor Gollancz Ltd., publishers, London, 1972-77; general editor, Mirror of Britain series, Andr Deutsch Ltd., publishers, London, 1975-80; editorial consultant, Boydell and Brewer, publishers, Woodbridge, Suffolk, 1983-90. Lecturer in English, Tufts in London programme, 1967-78; Gregory Fellow, University of Leeds, 1969-71; English Lecturer, University of Regensburg, 1978-80; Arts Council Fellow in English, Winchester School of Art, 1983, 1984; Visiting Fulbright Professor of English, St. Olaf College, Northfield, Minnesota, 1987-88; Endowed Chair in the Humanities and Fine Arts, University of St. Thomas, St. Paul, Minnesota, 1991-95. Chairman of the Literature Panel, Eastern Arts Association, 1986-89; Director, American Composers Forum, 1993-97. **Awards:** Arts Council award, 1968, for *The Green Children*; poetry award, 1972, for *The Rain-Giver*; Poetry Book Society Choice, 1976, for *The Dream-House*; Francis Williams award, 1977, for *The Wildman*; Carnegie Medal, 1986, for *Storm.* **Agent:** Rogers Coleridge and White, 20 Powis Mews, London W11 1JN, England. **Address:** Clare Cottage, Burnham Market, Norfolk PE31 8HE, England; 66 Ninth St. East, #2315, St. Paul, Minnesota 55101, U.S.A.

PUBLICATIONS FOR YOUNG ADULTS

Fiction

Havelok the Dane, illustrated by Brian Wildsmith. London, Macmillan, 1964; New York, Dutton, 1965.
King Horn, illustrated by Charles Keeping. London, Macmillan, 1965; New York, Dutton, 1966.
The Green Children, illustrated by Margaret Gordon. London, Macmillan, 1966; New York, Seabury Press, 1968; new edition, illustrated by Alan Marks, London, Oxford University Press, 1994.
Editor, *Winter's Tales for Children 3.* London, Macmillan, 1967.
The Callow Pit Coffer, illustrated by Margaret Gordon. London, Macmillan, 1968; New York, Seabury Press, 1969.

Wordhoard: Anglo-Saxon Stories, with Jill Paton Walsh. London, Macmillan, and New York, Farrar Straus, 1969.

Translator, *Storm and Other Old English Riddles,* illustrated by Miles Thistlethwaite. London, Macmillan, and New York, Farrar Straus, 1970.

The Pedlar of Swaffham, illustrated by Margaret Gordon. London, Macmillan, 1971; New York, Seabury Press, 1972.

The Sea-Stranger, illustrated by Joanna Troughton. London, Heinemann, 1973; New York, Seabury Press, 1974.

The Fire-Brother, illustrated by Joanna Troughton. London, Heinemann, and New York, Seabury Press, 1975.

Green Blades Rising: The Anglo-Saxons. London, Deutsch, 1975; New York, Seabury Press, 1976.

The Earth-Father, illustrated by Joanna Troughton. London, Heinemann, 1976.

The Wildman, illustrated by Charles Keeping. London, Deutsch, 1976.

Editor, *The Faber Book of Northern Legends [Northern Folktales],* illustrated by Alan Howard. London, Faber, 2 vols., 1977-80.

Translator, *Beowulf,* illustrated by Charles Keeping. London, Oxford University Press, 1982.

The Dead Moon and Other Tales from East Anglia and the Fen Country, illustrated by Shirley Felts. London, Deutsch, 1982.

Editor, *The Riddle Book,* illustrated by Bernard Handelsman. London, Macmillan, 1982.

Tales from the Mabinogion, with Gwyn Thomas, illustrated by Margaret Jones. London, Gollancz, 1984; Woodstock, New York, Overlook Press, 1985.

Axe-Age, Wolf-Age: A Selection from the Norse Myths, illustrated by Hannah Firmin. London, Deutsch, 1985.

The Fox and the Cat: Animal Tales from Grimm, with Susan Varley, illustrated by Varley. London, Andersen Press, 1985; New York, Lothrop, 1986.

Storm, illustrated by Alan Marks. London, Heinemann, 1985.

British Folk Tales: New Versions. London and New York, Orchard, 1987; selections as *Boo!, Dathera Dad, Piper and Pooka,* and *Small-Tooth Dog,* illustrated by Peter Melnyczuk, London, Orchard, 4 vols., 1988.

Northern Lights: Legends, Sagas and Folk-Tales, illustrated by Alan Howard. London, Faber, 1987.

The Quest for Olwen, with Gwyn Thomas, illustrated by Margaret Jones. Cambridge, Lutterworth Press, 1988.

Wulf. London, Faber, 1988.

Under the Sun and Over the Moon, illustrated by Ian Penney. London, Orchard, and New York, Putnam, 1989.

Sleeping Nanna, illustrated by Peter Melnyczuk. London, Orchard, 1989; New York, Ideal, 1990.

Sea Tongue, illustrated by Clare Challice. London, BBC/Longman, 1991.

Tales from Europe. London, BBC, 1991.

The Tale of Taliesin, with Gwyn Thomas, illustrated by Margaret Jones. London, Gollancz, 1992.

Long Tom and the Dead Hand, illustrated by Shirley Felts. London, Deutsch, 1992.

The Labours of Herakles, illustrated by Peter Utton. London, Orion, 1993.

The Green Children, illustrated by Alan Marks. London, Oxford University Press, 1994.

The Old Stories: Folk-Tales from East Anglis and the Fen Country. Cambridge, Colt, 1997.

Short! A Book of Very Short Stories. London, Oxford University Press, 1998.

The King Who Was and Will Be, illustrated by Peter Marone. London, Orion, 1998.

PUBLICATIONS FOR ADULTS

Poetry

On Approval. London, Outposts, 1961.

My Son. London, Turret, 1966.

Alderney: The Nunnery. London, Turret, 1968.

Confessional. Frensham, Surrey, Sceptre Press, 1969.

Norfolk Poems. London, Academy, 1970.

A Dream of a Meeting. Frensham, Surrey, Sceptre Press, 1970.

More Than I Am. London, Steam Press, 1971.

The Wake. Richmond, Surrey, Keepsake Press, 1972.

The Rain-Giver. London, Deutsch, 1972.

Petal and Stone. Knotting, Bedfordshire, Sceptre Press, 1975.

The Dream-House. London, Deutsch, 1976.

Between My Father and My Son. Minneapolis, Black Willow Press, 1982.

Time's Oriel. London, Hutchinson, 1983.

Waterslain and Other Poems. London, Hutchinson, 1986.

The Painting-Room and Other Poems. London, Century Hutchinson, 1988.

East Anglian Poems. Colchester, Jardine, 1988.

Oenone in January. Llandogo, Old Stile Press, 1988.

New and Selected Poems: 1965-1990. London, Hutchinson, 1991.

Eleanor's Advent. Llandogo, Old Stile Press, 1992.

The Language of Yes. London, Enitharmon, 1996.

Poems from East Anglia. London, Enitharmon, 1997.

Other

Translator, *The Battle of Maldon and Other Old English Poems,* edited by Bruce Mitchell. London, Macmillan, and New York, St. Martin's Press, 1965.

Editor, *Running to Paradise: An Introductory Selection of the Poems of W.B. Yeats.* London, Macmillan, 1967; New York, Macmillan, 1968.

Translator, *Beowulf.* London, Macmillan, and New York, Farrar Straus, 1968.

Editor, *Winter's Tales 14.* London, Macmillan, 1968.

Pieces of Land: Journeys to Eight Islands. London, Gollancz, 1972.

Editor, with Patricia Beer, *New Poetry 2.* London, Arts Council, 1976.

Translator, *The Exeter Riddle Book.* London, Folio Society, 1978; as *The Exeter Book of Riddles,* London, Penguin, 1979; revised edition, 1993.

The Norse Myths: A Retelling. London, Deutsch, and New York, Pantheon, 1980.

Translator, *The Anglo-Saxon World.* Woodbridge, Suffolk, Boydell Press, 1982; New York, Barnes and Noble, 1983.

Editor, *Folk-Tales of the British Isles.* London, Folio Society, 1985; New York, Pantheon, 1988.

Editor, *The Oxford Book of Travel Verse.* Oxford and New York, Oxford University Press, 1986.

Translator, *The Wanderer.* Colchester, Jardine, 1986.

Editor, *Medieval Lovers: A Book of Days.* London, Century Hutchinson, and New York, Weidenfeld and Nicolson, 1988.
Translator, *The Old English Elegies.* London. Folio Society, 1988.
The Stones Remain: Megalithic Sites of Britain, photographs by Andrew Rafferty. London, Rider, 1989.
Editor, *Medieval Gardens: A Book of Days.* New York, Rizzoli, 1990.
The Wildman (libretto). Woodbridge, Boydell and Brewer, 1995.
Translator, *Beowulf.* London, Oxford University Press, 1998.

*

Manuscript Collections: Brotherton Collection, University of Leeds; Lillian H. Smith and Osborne Collections, Toronto Public Library.

Biography: Entry in *Fourth Book of Junior Authors,* New York, H.W. Wilson, 1978; entry in *Dictionary of Literary Biography,* Volume 40, Detroit, Gale, 1985.

*   *   *

Kevin Crossley-Holland is a British author who writes across the spectrum of literature. He has written picture books, junior novels, poetry, and nonfiction; he has translated Norse and Old English myths, legends, folktales, and poetry; he has retold English folktales; he has collaborated on modern retellings of Welsh legends. With such a wide variety of interests, it is not surprising that his audience ranges widely too: from children and young adults to Anglo-Saxon scholars. If there is one theme that unites Crossley-Holland's work, it is his fascination with Britain's ancient past, particularly with the Anglo-Saxon period. Another consistent thread running throughout his work is his love of words. In all his writing, he attempts to render his stories into what he calls "lapidary English," referring to the smooth, polished facets of a gemstone. Since he is a poet, his poetic grasp of the sounds and nuances of words enables him to meet this goal more often than not.

Although Crossley-Holland's picture books are intended for younger readers, young adults will find much to interest them in books like *Beowulf* and *The Wildman.* Some critics feel that *Beowulf,* a masterly retelling of the Old English poem, is Crossley-Holland's best work. *The Wildman* is almost a prose poem, told in first person by a captured merman. Readers with an appreciation of art will enjoy Charles Keeping's evocative illustrations in both of these books. Similarly, the three Welsh legends retold in picture-book format by Crossley-Holland and Gwyn Thomas—*Tales from the Mabinogion, The Quest for Olwen,* and *The Tale of Taliesin*—have much to offer older readers. These tales were originally intended for adults, and the authors do not patronize their supposed audience of young readers by removing any of the adult motivations and actions. The illustrations by Margaret Jones provide a sophisticated and explicit accompaniment to the text.

Crossley-Holland's junior novels, such as *King Horn* and *Wulf,* are also historical. Although they generally deal with young adult protagonists, these books are written at a level more suited to younger readers: simple, direct sentences and little detail or description. More likely to appeal to teens is *Wordhoard: Anglo-Saxon Stories,* co-written by Jill Paton Walsh. A collection of original stories rather than a novel, this book successfully recreates an era so ancient as to be almost inaccessible. Using numerous Old English poems and histories as the basis of these stories, Crossley-Holland and Paton Walsh draw a sympathetic picture of Anglo-Saxon life, ending with the death of King Harold, the last Saxon king. Each story is independent, yet the consistent tone of the tales creates a unified volume.

Crossley-Holland's true genius lies in retelling ancient myths, legends, and tales. In *British Folk Tales* he retells fifty-five stories and ballads, mostly English (with one or two Scottish or Welsh tales). Some of the stories are familiar, such as "Jack and the Beanstalk" and "Goldilocks and the Three Bears"; others are more obscure: "The Last of the Picts" and "The Pedlar of Swaffham," for example. Although all the tales are well told, the collection is somewhat uneven because of the author's varied approaches to the material. This collection also includes "The Wildman," later reprinted as a picture book. Another book of British tales, *The Dead Moon and Other Tales from East Anglia and the Fen Country,* is a more unified collection. These are mostly scary or sad tales, beautifully told with a mere hint of the East Anglian dialect. Several of the stories in this volume have also been reprinted as picture books.

Britain's Viking heritage appears in several of Crossley-Holland's collections of tales. *Northern Lights: Legends, Sagas, and Folk-Tales* is his largest collection of Norse myths. Selections from *Northern Lights* were also printed as *Axe-Age, Wolf-Age.* Crossley-Holland does not have as strong a feel for these myths as he has for his native English folktales, but he successfully captures the tone of his medieval Icelandic sources.

Young adult readers who have an interest in ancient Britain may enjoy some of Crossley-Holland's adult works, such as his translations of Old English literature and his nonfiction books about Anglo-Saxon England. *Green Blades Rising,* for instance, introduces the Anglo-Saxon lifestyle in a direct manner that is easily accessible to older children, using many photographs and quotations from Old English literature.

All of Crossley-Holland's best work combines his storytelling skills with his mastery of the poetic elements of language. The most memorable tales in *The Dead Moon* and *British Folk Tales* benefit from this marriage of prose and poetry. *Beowulf,* originally a poem, retains the Anglo-Saxon poetic phrasing while fleshing out the characters and the story. Combining these skills creates and maintains an appropriate tone for each story, whether it is the rough and ready action of *Beowulf* or the sad, haunting lament of *The Wildman.*

—Donna R. White

CRUTCHER, Chris(topher C.)

Nationality: American. **Born:** Cascade, Idaho, 17 July 1946. **Education:** Eastern Washington State University, Cheney, B.A. 1968. **Career:** Teacher, Kennewick Dropout School, Kennewick, Washington, 1970-73; teacher, Lakeside School, Oakland, California, 1973-76, director of school, 1976-80; child protection team specialist, Community Mental Health, Spokane, Washington, 1980-82; child and family therapist, since 1982. **Awards:** Named to American Library Association's list of best books for young adults, 1983, for *Running Loose,* 1986, for *Stotan!,* and 1989, for *Chinese Handcuffs;* named to *School Library Journal*'s best books for young adults list, and to American Library Association's list of best books for young adults, both 1988, for *The Crazy Horse Electric Game;* Michigan Library Association Best Young Adult Book of 1992, for *Athletic Shorts;* ALAN award for Significant Contribution to Adolescent Literature. **Address:** East 3405 Marion Ct., Spokane, Washington 99223, U.S.A.

PUBLICATIONS FOR YOUNG ADULTS

Fiction

Running Loose. New York, Greenwillow, 1983.
Stotan!. New York, Greenwillow, 1986.
The Crazy Horse Electric Game. New York, Greenwillow, 1987.
Chinese Handcuffs. New York, Greenwillow, 1989.
Staying Fat for Sarah Byrnes. New York, Greenwillow, 1993.
Ironman: A Novel. New York, Greenwillow Books, 1995.

Other

Athletic Shorts: Six Short Stories. New York, Greenwillow, 1991.
The Deep End. New York, Morrow, 1992.

*

Media Adaptations: Screenplay for *Running Loose* and *The Crazy Horse Electric Game* is forthcoming. Options for the following: *The Deep End,* Interscope Pictures; *Staying Fat for Sarah Byrnes,* Columbia Pictures; "A Brief Moment in the Life of Angus Bethune" from *Athletic Shorts,* Disney Pictures.

Biography: Essay in *Speaking for Ourselves: Autobiographical Sketches by Notable Authors of Books for Young Adults,* Volume 1, compiled and edited by Donald R. Gallo, National Council of Teachers of English, 1990.

Chris Crutcher comments:

Though most of my books are considered young adult, that is never my consideration in writing them. My storytelling style does not change from a novel about so-called young adults to one about adults. I choose the story, tell it, and let the marketing people decide what it is. My mission is to write truths as I see them; reflect the world as it appears to me, rather than as others would have it. I would like to tell stories so "right on" that they punch a hole in the wall between young adult and adult literature.

*　　*　　*

Many authors have used sports as a metaphor for the ups and downs of life, but very few with the combined humor and poignancy of Chris Crutcher. In his four novels and the related book of short stories, Crutcher's characters engage in a wide variety of athletic activities while facing the typical and not so typical—yet sometimes very real—problems of adolescence. These are complex, sometimes irreverent, and deeply compelling works, in large part because the young male protagonists are portrayed so distinctly and with such realism. While the sporting events lend excitement and action, they are not really the central focus. Rather, these stories achieve their satisfaction and success from the characters' struggles to make sense of life and the depiction of friendship's power to aid in the struggle.

In Crutcher's first young adult novel, *Running Loose,* senior Louis Banks earns a starting position on the football team after a summer of hard training. But during the second game he takes a very public stand against the coach, who had ordered his team to injure the opponent's star player. Louis is disappointed that he won't be playing football, and only his girlfriend Becky seems to agree with his actions. When Becky is killed in an automobile accident, Louis finds coping with each day becomes a monumental challenge. With help from friends, adult and adolescent, Louis proves he's more than up to dealing with Becky's death.

The power of friendship is also strongly evident in *Stotan!* Walker, Lion, Nortie, and Jeff are four friends brought even closer by their shared experiences as swimmers, including Stotan week. (A stotan is a cross between a stoic and a spartan, and the swimming coach devises a week of training worthy of the name.) Walker, the narrator, has a drug addicted older brother who can make his life complicated, if not dangerous. Lion lives alone above a bar, a talented artist who lost his parents in a boating accident. Nortie attempts to break the pattern of an abusive father by working at a day care center, and Jeff develops leukemia. In the closing scenes at the state swim meet Walker, Lion, and Nortie defy a judge's ruling and swim three legs of the four-man relay without Jeff, leaving their lane eerily quiet while the other teams finish the race.

Willie Weaver's friends in *The Crazy Horse Electric Game* are an unlikely bunch: a principal at a high school in Oakland known as "Last Chance," students there called Telephone Man and Hawk, and a bus driver and part-time pimp named Lacey. Left with slurred speech and a physical handicap after a waterskiing accident, baseball hero Willie can't cope with the suffocating memories of his small hometown or the pity of his family and friends. He runs away, only to be beaten up by an Asian American gang when he arrives in Oakland. Willie does heal, both emotionally and physically, but returning home brings unpleasant revelations still to be faced.

Dillon Hemingway of *Chinese Handcuffs* has a shattering experience to understand: he witnessed his brother Preston's suicide. Preston's loss is especially difficult because of Dillon's attraction to his brother's girlfriend Stacey and further complicated when he discovers she is pregnant with his brother's baby. He also learns that Jennifer, a good friend and star basketball player, is being sexually abused by her stepfather, a talented lawyer. Dillon begins to find his own way as he helps Jennifer and Stacey, and his confidence returns as he trains for the triathlon.

Athletic Shorts is a book of six short stories, five of which focus on characters from the earlier works. These short works stand on their own but will be particularly appreciated with knowledge of the novels. Readers get Telephone Man's warped view of other racial groups, handed to him from his father, along with his perspective of events from a crucial day in *The Crazy Horse Electric Game.* In two other stories, readers gain insights into Willie Weaver's hometown friends Johnny and Petey, as Johnny wrestles his dad and Petey wrestles a girl. And in the final story, Louis Banks from *Running Loose* befriends his boss' nephew who is ill with acquired immuno-deficiency syndrome (AIDS). In so doing, Louis is forced to choose what he knows is right over his friendship with Carter.

These brief descriptions of Crutcher's works can only begin to capture their spirit. The humor, for example, ranges from outrageous (picture the results of eating a box of biscuit mix and drinking a bottle of strawberry shampoo) to wacky (Lion has a seatbelt on the toilet in his apartment) and from subtle (the English teacher's comments about the characters in a class novel apply directly to the characters of *The Crazy Horse Electric Game*) to groanable (Johnny composes intricate puns, among them the one based on *Bless the Beasts and Children* which results in "Bless the beets and the chilled wren"). But the humor is offset in Crutcher's stories by very serious and real issues: suicide, sexual abuse, racial prejudice, and alcoholism, among others.

Girls who read these books will respond to the humor and the serious issues. Teachers who read them will appreciate their "literacy"—as in Johnny's atrociously delightful puns and the letters that Dillon writes to his brother after reading the letters in Alice Walker's *The Color Purple*. Of course it's neither teachers or even girls who are the main target of these books. Most directly, Crutcher writes for boys, who all too often choose not to read because there aren't as many books that appeal to them—books with "real" characters in "real world" situations. In this goal, writing books that will hook young male readers, Crutcher is entirely successful. At the same time, he's created rich and complex works for all readers, adult and adolescent, male and female.

—Bonnie O. Ericson

CULPER, Felix. *See* **McCAUGHREAN, Geraldine.**

CURTIS, Christopher Paul

Nationality: American. **Born:** Flint, Michigan, 10 May 1954(?). **Education:** University of Michigan-Flint. **Family:** Married Kaysandra; one son and one daughter. **Career:** Writer. Worked previously as a factory worker, a campaign worker, a maintenance man, a warehouse clerk, and a purchasing clerk. **Awards:** Coretta Scott King Honor Book, Newbery Honor Book, American Library Association Best Book for Young Adults, and Golden Kite Award, all 1996, all for *The Watsons Go to Birmingham—1963*. **Address:** c/o Delacorte Press, 1540 Broadway, New York, New York 10036-4039, U.S.A.

PUBLICATIONS FOR YOUNG ADULTS

The Watsons Go to Birmingham-1963, New York, Delacorte Press, 1995.

*   *   *

Christopher Paul Curtis's award-winning first novel, *The Watsons Go to Birmingham—1963,* is a coming-of-age narrative set in the blue-collar town of Flint, Michigan, during the Civil Rights Movement. The subject matter is serious in nature and includes a description of the 1963 racially-motivated Birmingham church bombing that claimed the lives of four young African-American girls. By telling his tale through the eyes of Kenny Watson, a fourth grader, Curtis illustrates the way that momentous social events and political movements can impact the lives of even the youngest children. Moreover, like Mildred Taylor before him, Curtis provides a detailed and poignant description of the inner life of an African-American family, but he uses a humorous style that is unique and geared to appeal to young adults and well as to children.

The Watson family, or "the Weird Watsons," as they call themselves, live in one of Flint's segregated black neighborhoods. As a Flint native himself, Curtis underscores a number of the economic and social realities particular to the community. For instance, he chooses to emphasize the connection between urban, industrial Flint and the rural Southern roots of many of its inhabitants. Mrs. Watson is from Birmingham, Alabama, and a number of Kenny's school friends have recently moved up from the South as their parents try to better their lives and escape discrimination. Mr. Watson works for General Motors, the major Flint employer, and is an active member in the United Auto Workers. However, because the automobile industry is cyclical in nature, the Watsons and their neighbors have had hard times, often resorting to welfare (a fact that they attempt to conceal from their children), and they are forced to send their children to a somewhat dangerous school. Curtis's accurate description of the living conditions in Flint, as well as his use of actual business names and places, lend a realistic quality to the text.

This realism is carried over in Curtis's depiction of childhood experience as seen through the eyes of his narrator, Kenny Watson. Kenny uses language that is typical of a ten-year old, and many of his cultural references come from comic books and war movies. Moreover, the challenges that Kenny faces are ones that many readers can identity with. For instance, Kenny is teased by the other children because he has a "lazy eye" and because he is academically gifted—so gifted, in fact, that he is asked to give recitations in front of the other students and is held up as an example of racial pride. Although this acclaim pleases Kenny's parents, it makes him the least popular boy in school. The only thing that saves him from being beaten up on a regular basis is the fact that his older brother Byron is in a gang and is one of the most feared boys in school. As a result of the constant teasing, Kenny suffers from low self-esteem and is willing to play with boys who steal from him and hold him in contempt. Thus, when Rufus, a Southern transfer student, arrives at the elementary school, Kenny hopes that the new boy's poverty and thick accent will help to deflect attention away from himself. However, Rufus is unwilling to change his character in order to "fit in," and he helps Kenny to understand the importance of maintaining self-respect in the face of peer pressure.

Kenny's other life lessons come from observing the actions of his far less ambitious brother, thirteen-year old Byron "Daddy Cool" Watson. Even though Byron is intelligent and is especially compassionate in his treatment of the boys' five-year old sister Joetta, he tests the patience of his parents by flunking the fifth grade twice and hanging around with petty thieves. Byron's problems with authority come to form the primary focus of the story and cause the Watsons to travel down to Birmingham so that the matriarch of the family, Mrs. Watson's mother Grandma Sands, can "straighten him out." Based upon Mrs. Watson's stories about her upbringing, the Watson children imagine their grandmother to be a force of nature, akin to a tornado. Indeed, Kenny equates the meeting between Byron and Grandma Sands to that of Godzilla and King Kong. It is surprising, then, when the children reach her house in suburban Birmingham and find out that their grandma is a tiny, wrinkled, soft-spoken woman who gathers them up in an embrace and cries, "My fambly, my beautiful fambly." Rather than even try to defy Grandma Sands, Byron is awed by her presence and begins to reform his behavior. The maturation process is extended when Byron saves Kenny from drowning and witnesses the church bombing that claims the lives of four of his sisters' playmates. It is this act of racial violence that confirms for Byron what his parents have been telling him all along—that life will hold a number of challenges that he must prepare himself to face.

In addition to chronicling Byron's maturation, Curtis is also interested in depicting the way that younger children process complex and frightening events. Throughout the narrative, Kenny Watson is portrayed as a gullible boy who often falls for his father and brother's tall tales. In Birmingham, Byron creates a story about a monster called the *Wool Pooh,* Winnie the Pooh's evil twin, in order to discourage Kenny from swimming in a section of a river that actually contains a deadly whirlpool. However, Kenny has grown tired falling for Byron's tricks and decides to go swimming anyway. When he nearly drowns, Kenny imagines that he is visited underwater by two spirits: the first is his sister Joetta, dressed up as an angel, and the second is the dreaded *Wool Pooh,* who resembles a cartoon version of death—a faceless grey-black presence who tries to wrest Kenny's life away. By internalizing his near-death experience in the form of popular cultural icons, Kenny is able to accept the situation, and the reader is treated to a fine example of psychological realism.

Another phenomenon that Curtis considers is the way that some events in life are mystifying, even to adults. When the church in Birmingham is bombed, Joetta Watson is believed to be among the killed or injured; it was her Sunday school class that was meeting when the bomb went off. However, when Kenny reaches the scene, he is again confronted by the *Wool Pooh,* who appears to be taking possession of the dead. Kenny fights with him for the body of a girl he believes to be his sister, but when he sees a blood-covered shoe that resembles one of Joetta's, he is overcome with fear and flees the scene. A few minutes later, Joetta appears at the house and cannot understand why Kenny is so surprised to see her. Moreover, she claims that Kenny himself came to the church before the bombing and asked her to follow him home. What she cannot understand is why he has changed clothes—the Kenny she saw was dressed differently. Curtis makes no attempt to explain this conundrum, leaving the reader to decide whether Joetta was aided by divine intervention. While no one in the Watson family doubts that Kenny is telling the truth when he says that he did not go to the church prior to the bombing, Kenny is obsessed with finding out what really happened.

After the Watsons return to Flint safely, Kenny becomes withdrawn and depressed. He refuses to eat or to play with Rufus; instead, he hides out for days on end behind the living room sofa, because this is where the Watson's pets go when they become ill. Mr. Watson and Byron have perpetuated the myth that the sofa holds magic powers that heal the animals, and Kenny hopes that he

too can be healed. However, Byron is able to coax Kenny up to the bathroom, where the boy confesses his anger and fear over the bombing. Kenny is ashamed because he feels that he should have stood up to the *Wool Pooh,* and he is especially confused about why the other little girls were not visited by a spirit and thus saved from death. Although Byron cannot explain the puzzling phenomena, he helps Kenny to confront his feelings, an act that both rescues Kenny from depression and confirms Byron's maturity. Byron's message to Kenny is that while the Watsons cannot always control outside events, they do have each other to lean on.

The Watsons Go to Birmingham—1963 is an insightful and compelling first novel that has appeal for intermediate and young adult readers, alike. The text also includes a brief historical description of the events surrounding the church bombing, designed to contextualize the events of the novel and to encourage young readers to learn more about the Civil Rights Movement. Most importantly, Curtis treats his subject with respect, but also reaffirms the value of humor and love in the face of tragedy.

—Gwen A. Tarbox

CUSHMAN, Karen

Nationality: American. **Born:** Chicago, Illinois, 4 October 1941. **Education:** Stanford University, B.A. in English and Greek 1963; United States International University, San Diego, M.A. in Human Behavior 1977; John F. Kennedy University, Orinda, California, M.A. in Museum Studies 1986. **Family:** Married Philip Cushman, 6 September 1969; one daughter. **Career:** Adjunct professor in Museum Studies Department, JFK University, 1986-1996; writer, since 1990. **Awards:** Newbery Honor Book, Carl Sandburg Award for Children's Literature, Golden Kite Award, Bay Area Book Reviewers' Association Award for Children's Literature, Best Books list of *School Library Journal,* Ten Best Books list of Parent's Choice Foundation, and Cuffie Award from *Publishers Weekly,* all 1994, Young Adult Library Services Association Best Books for Young Readers and Recommended Books for Reluctant Readers, and Pick of the Lists award from the American Booksellers' Association, all 1995, and Honour List of the International Board on Books for Young People, 1996, all for *Catherine, Called Birdy;* Best Books, *School Library Journal,* 1995, and Newbery Medal, American Library Association, 1995, for *The Midwife's Apprentice;* Northern California Independent Booksellers Association California Author award, and John and Patricia Beatty award, California Library Association, both 1997, both for *Ballad of Lucy Whipple.* **Agent:** Marilyn Marlow, Curtis Brown, 10 Astor Place, New York, New York 10003, U.S.A. **Address:** 5480 College Avenue, Oakland, California 94618, U.S.A.

PUBLICATIONS FOR YOUNG ADULTS

Fiction

Catherine, Called Birdy. New York, Clarion, 1994.
The Midwife's Apprentice. New York, Clarion, 1995.
The Ballad of Lucy Whipple. New York, Clarion, 1996.

*

Critical Studies: ''Flying Starts: Seven Talents New to the Children's Book Scene Talk about their Debuts'' by Amy Umland Love, in *Publishers Weekly,* July 4, 1994; ''The Booklist Interview: Karen Cushman'' by Hazel Rochman, in *Booklist,* June 1-15, 1996; ''Newbery Medal Acceptance'' by Karen Cushman, in *Horn Book,* July/August 1996; ''Karen Cushman'' by Philip Cushman, in *Horn Book,* July/August 1996; ''A Talk with Karen Cushman'' by Sally Lodge, in *Publishers Weekly,* August 26, 1996; entry in *Something About the Author,* Volume 89, Detroit, Gale, 1997.

Karen Cushman comments:

I've always been a late bloomer but I always eventually bloom. Here I am making a new career late in life and having a wonderful time. I choose to write for young people because I can think of nothing more important to do and I hope to die with my hands on computer keys and hundreds of good ideas bouncing around in my head.

*   *   *

Karen Cushman has successfully blended her skill for storytelling with her career in museum studies to create historical fiction that in not only accurate but refreshingly entertaining. Her first novel, *Catherine, Called Birdy,* which she began at age fifty, took her three years to write and was named a Newbery honor book, in addition to receiving numerous other awards. She began to write it the day her daughter began filling out college applications. ''I wrote it,'' she said in her Newbery acceptance speech, ''because I needed to find out about things, about identity and responsibility, compassion and kindness and belonging, and being human in the world. How could I learn them if I didn't write about them?''

Catherine, Called Birdy is about a young woman living in an English manor in 1290 who struggles to control her life while her mother attempts to shape her into a lady and her ''father, the toad, conspires to sell me like a cheese to some lack-wit seeking a wife.'' Written in the form of a diary spanning one year, it recounts her adventures in avoiding marriage, fighting the docile fate of women in the thirteenth century, making mistakes and learning from them. The diary is a requirement made by her brother, a monk, to teach Catherine discipline and help her ''grow less childish and more learned.''

Subtle details add to the easy flow of the story as well as impart an authentic and humorous flavor to the medieval setting. ''I wanted to take a bath, thinking that the dirt on my skin made the rash worse, but the bathing tub had been turned upside down and is being used as an extra table in the kitchen and I cannot have it until spring.'' A spirited, head-strong young woman, Catherine devises plans and makes her own entertainment. Her frustrations in not having the skill or desire to be a proper lady sometimes lead to thoughtless action on her part: she throws her embroidery to the dogs, who fight and slobber over it; she throws her tangled spinning into the privy where it is discovered when the fields are fertilized; and she scares away suitors by blacking out her teeth, babbling of her father's hidden riches, and by setting fire to the privy. Her penance is more embroidery, stitching altar cloths for the church, and often confinement to her bedchamber, which she shares with a

variety of her caged birds, her nurse, and a multitude of visitors to the manor.

As the diary progresses, the reader sees growth in Catherine, but not lost hope for changing her future. Once ''Shaggy Beard,'' an older landowner, seeks her in marriage, Catherine devises plans for escaping this dreaded union, and succeeds only in getting extensions on the actual marriage date. In the end Catherine is mature enough to accept her fate, though to the less offensive son of Shaggy Beard. In her acceptance comes understanding and renewed hope.

After completing this novel, Cushman immediately began writing her next novel. She had thought of the title while working on *Birdy* and liked it. *The Midwife's Apprentice,* which earned the Newbery Medal, is about a homeless girl known as Brat, who finds a place to belong, finds a name, and finds that success is not about never failing, but about being willing to ''try and risk and fail and try again and not give up.'' The story takes place in a fourteenth century English village and opens with Brat sleeping on the dung heap for warmth. Jane Sharp, the village midwife, takes the girl in to help with chores in exchange for food.

Brat is timid, her only friend a stray cat. Slowly she emerges from her cocoon of protective distance. She makes friends and finds a place to belong. As her confidence grows she realizes she needs a real name and chooses ''Alyce,'' and then a name for her cat as well. Though she has learned only the art of gathering herbs and brewing tonics for the midwife, she is left to flounder through her first solo delivery and succeeds by using common sense. This boosts her confidence further, and the confidence of the villagers in her, but a failure drives her from her home in humiliation. She plays tricks on the villagers in revenge for the hurts she has suffered, then goes off to work at an inn. Alyce struggles with her identity and with finding the courage to persevere. She finally returns to Jane, refusing to let the woman decline in teaching her to become a midwife.

Like her previous novels, *The Ballad of Lucy Whipple* is about a young woman who has no control over her circumstances and takes her destiny into her own hands. Set during the California Gold Rush, *Ballad* again uses subtle details to draw an accurate picture of what life was like in the tent towns common during this period in history. California Morning Whipple is distraught at being dragged ''like a barrel of lard'' from her Massachusetts home to the noisy, dusty mining town of Lucky Diggings. In an effort to take control of her life she changes her name to Lucy, and sets up her own pie-baking business with the plan to earn enough money to return home. As obstacles prevent her she grows and learns and finally realizes ''home is where I am loved and safe and needed.'' Once she has figured this out she is able to achieve her heart's desire.

Cushman's characters are strong, spirited, willful, and independent young women. Though centuries distant, they have the same desires as contemporary young women. Cushman's inspiration to write these stories came from the emotional response to some historical fact, whether this was the differences between the social classes in the Middle Ages and the ownership of women by men, the emergence of learning in the dawn of the Renaissance, or the lack of attention given to the women and children brought unwillingly to California in the mid-nineteenth century. The result is powerful writing, strong in emotion, and balanced with the humor present in daily life. Through the hopes and dreams of her characters, the readers learn a great deal about identity, responsibility, compassion, kindness, belonging, and creating a place in the world through perseverance. Cushman imparts a wisdom she never knew she possessed until she began to write, and welcome wisdom it is.

—Lisa A. Wroble

CUSICK, Richie Tankersley

Nationality: American. **Born:** New Orleans, Louisiana, 1 April 1952. **Education:** University of Southwestern Louisiana, Lafayette, B.A. 1975. **Family:** Married Rick Cusick in 1980. **Career:** Ward clerk, Ochsner Foundation Hospital, New Orleans, Louisiana, summers, 1970-72; writer, Hallmark Cards, Inc., Kansas City, Montana, 1975-84; freelance writer, from 1984. **Awards:** Children's Choice award, IRA, 1989, for *The Lifeguard*; Book for the Teen Age, New York Public Library, 1990, for *Trick or Treat*; Edgar Award nomination, for *Help Wanted*. **Agent:** Mary Jack Wald Associates, Inc., Literary Representatives, 111 East 14th St., New York, New York 10003, U.S.A. **Address:** 7325 Quivira Road, #220, Shawnee, Kansas 66216, U.S.A.

PUBLICATIONS FOR YOUNG ADULTS

Horror Novels

Evil on the Bayou. New York, Dell, 1984.
The Lifeguard. New York, Scholastic, 1988.
Trick or Treat. New York, Scholastic, 1989.
April Fools. New York, Scholastic, 1990.
Teacher's Pet. New York, Scholastic, 1990.
Vampire. New York, Pocket Books, 1991.
Buffy the Vampire Slayer. New York, Pocket Books, 1992.
Fatal Secrets. New York, Pocket Books, 1992.
The Mall. New York, Pocket Books, 1992.
Silent Stalker. New York, Pocket Books, 1993.
Help Wanted. New York, Archway/Pocket Books, 1993.
The Drifter. New York, Archway/Pocket Books, 1994.
The Locker. New York, Archway/Pocket Books, 1994.
Someone at the Door. New York, Archway/Pocket Books, 1994.
Overdue. New York, Archway/Pocket Books, 1995.
Summer of Secrets. New York, Archway/Pocket Books, 1996.
Starstruck. New York, Archway/Pocket Books, 1996.
Buffy the Vampire Slayer: The Harvest. New York, Archway/
    Pocket Books, 1997.

PUBLICATIONS FOR ADULTS

Fiction

Scarecrow. New York, Pocket Books, 1990.
BloodRoots. New York, Pocket Books, 1992.

*

Richie Tankersley Cusick comments:

Writing—as well as reading—is the most wonderful kind of magic. There's nothing better than completely losing oneself in a book, being transported to a whole different world, meeting delightful and intriguing new characters, facing unexpected dangers, fears, and challenges, and—in the end—even being a bit disappointed when one finishes the last page and is forced to return to reality! It's very fulfilling to me when a reader says, "I felt like I was really *there*!" I *want* my readers to lose themselves in the story, to actually become one with the book for the duration of their reading.

In my books, things are seldom what they seem to be. My characters learn very early on that one can't judge things merely by appearances. My characters also stand up for what they believe in. They don't let themselves be easily swayed by what everyone else thinks is right or wrong.

The characters in my books usually find themselves encountering "bad surprises"—those tragic and frightening events which sometimes occur simply because we happen to be in the wrong place at the wrong time. And when this happens, these characters also discover resources within themselves which proves to them just how unique, special, and strong they really are. Another major theme in my books is friendship. There's nothing better than a good friend to help you through a crisis! As a matter of fact, that's usually when you find out who your real friends are!

I like to make my books both fun and frightening, both heartwarming and heartstopping! But in the process, I think it's very important for my readers to realize that they're not alone. That other young people have needs and concerns just like they do—similar fears, similar desires, similar insecurities, similar hopes and dreams. And that these fears can be overcome, that these dreams can come true.

As a writer, perhaps the best compliment I ever receive is when I hear from readers who tell me they've been inspired by a particular book of mine. That before they read my book, they didn't enjoy reading at all—but that now, they want to go on and read *more* books.

There's so *much* to read out there! So many wonderful and inspiring authors! When young people ask me for advice on how to write, I tell them "*Read!*" Read everything you can, read a variety of things, read to discover what inspires and enlightens you! My feeling is that one can learn so much about how to *write* books by reading them. Much more than by reading books on how to write!

I know I'm one of the very lucky ones, for I've been given the gift of making magic. Each time I write a new book, I have the opportunity to create something wondrous, unique, and entertaining.

But readers also have a special gift. A gift of discovering their *own* special magic each time they pick up a book, become one with it, and hold its meaning close to their hearts.

*   *   *

In all of her work, Cusick pays homage to the gothic style with dramatic plots, endangered heroines, weird mysteries, hints of the supernatural, and other gothic details not present in many contemporary thrillers. Most of Cusick's novels can be roughly classified as young adult thrillers, and even those horror novels written for adults, *Scarecrow* and *Blood Roots,* are read by young people, too.

Her first novel, *Evil on the Bayou* (number twenty-one in the Dell Twilight Series and later reissued separately), appeared in 1984 before the current popularity of young adult thrillers, most notably exemplified by the works of Cusick, Christopher Pike, and

R. L. Stine. Four years later, however, her second novel, *The Lifeguard,* appeared and enjoyed greater success in the marketplace than her first. Since then, she has published eighteen titles (her work has appeared on more than 70 bestseller lists) and earned a loyal following of young and adult readers.

Cusick's reliance on the English gothic tradition and the decadent, brooding feeling of the Southern gothic tradition distinguishes her work from other young adult thriller authors. For example, the setting (a decaying southern plantation house), first person narrative, and the presence of a wickedly dysfunctional family in her second novel for adults, *Blood Roots* (1993), is reminiscent of V.C. Andrews' work. Ironically, one of the weaker features of Cusick's writing is her use of the occult, which she has been unable, thus far, to incorporate successfully into her books. This may be due in part to her lack of accurate descriptions about particular occult practices. For example, the plentiful presence of snakes in *Evil on the Bayou* could be symbolic of voodoo rituals and African snake gods, but they appear only as sinister, nasty, and poisonous. In other titles, Cusick suggests the supernatural as a possible rationale for what is going on, but rarely presents it as the solution to the mystery. In *Trick or Treat,* real people, not ghosts, commit the murders in a spooky old house. In *Vampire* there are no supernatural vampires at all, just a disturbed, human murderer. The supernatural and the occult may be more interesting to Cusick as a backdrop for horrifying human behavior than as the main focus of her thrillers.

When Cusick does use the supernatural for its own sake, the results are not particularly effective. In her adult horror novel, *Scarecrow,* she relies on stereotype in her presentation of a bizarre hillbilly family in the Ozarks, complete with a psychic child. While menacing scarecrows abound, they pale in comparison to the far more frightening creatures in Robert Westall's *The Scarecrows. Buffy the Vampire Slayer* is also somewhat disappointing. Cusick novelizes a film from a story by Joss Wheldon, which may explain the the author's apparent lack of enthusiasm. Perhaps she is not as comfortable adapting other author's stories or writing a horror genre spoof. Her second contribution to the *Buffy* series, *The Harvest* (1997), however, suggests otherwise, as it has enjoyed enthusiastic responses from teen readers.

This criticism notwithstanding, Cusick is deservedly popular with teen readers. Her writing skills have sharpened over the years, resulting in fast-paced action stories. Her thrillers offer a mystery that includes many false leads, with the perpetrator of the crimes often turning out to be one of the more sympathetic—and least suspected—characters. Her novels are narrated by teenage female protagonists, making them appealing to young women who enjoy scary stories and strong heroines. Teen readers can also identify with her central characters, who often come from broken homes, and must deal with difficult relationships, some familial and some romantic. They often learn self-reliance in their struggles with the unknown evil and begin to understand the complexities of human behavior. In *Silent Stalker* (1993), for example, the heroine is unhappy because she is forced to spend the summer with an unloved and virtually unknown father, someone she will not be able to count on when she is thrust into danger. In *Vampire,* the heroine, Darcy, is sent to stay with an unknown uncle who runs a ''haunted house of horror.'' As people are killed, Darcy questions whether she can trust her uncle. Cusick's heroines must learn quickly how to make important judgments which may well determine if they will live or die. Cusick continues to address these themes and present assertive adolescent heroines in her more recent titles, including *The Drifter* (1994), *The Locker* (1994), and *Summer of Secrets* (1996).

Overall, Cusick has produced a number of exciting and popular young adult thrillers. Teen readers may be initially drawn to her stories more for their terrifying plots than for the adolescent developmental concepts she includes. Yet these concepts are important for creating three-dimensional, believable characters. It is not enough for an author to create a terrifying story. The writer of young adult books must also create individuals that readers care about and identify with as they devour the books. Richie Tankersley Cusick certainly succeeds in this aspect.

—Cosette Kies, updated by Rebecca R. Saulsbury

D

DAHL, Roald

Nationality: British. **Born:** Llandaff, Glamorgan, Wales, 13 September 1916. **Education:** Repton School, Yorkshire. **Military Service:** Served in the Royal Air Force, 1939-45: in Nairobi and Habbanyah, 1939-40; with a fighter squadron in the Western Desert, 1940 (wounded); in Greece and Syria, 1941; assistant air attaché, Washington, D.C., 1942-43; wing commander, 1943; with British Security Co-ordination, North America, 1943-45. **Family:** Married 1) the actress Patricia Neal in 1953 (divorced 1983), one son and four daughters (one deceased); 2) Felicity Ann Crosland in 1983. **Career:** Member of the Public Schools Exploring Society expedition to Newfoundland, 1934; member of the Eastern staff, Shell Company, London, 1933-37, and Shell Company of East Africa, Dar-es-Salaam, 1937-39. **Awards:** Mystery Writers of America Edgar Allan Poe award, 1954, 1959, and 1980; New England Round Table of Children's Librarians award, 1972, and Surrey School award, 1973, both for *Charlie and the Chocolate Factory;* Surrey School award, 1975, and Nene award, 1978, both for *Charlie and the Great Glass Elevator;* Surrey School award, 1978, and California Young Reader Medal, 1979, both for *Danny: The Champion of the World;* Federation of Children's Book Groups award, 1982, for *The BFG;* Massachusetts Children's award, 1982, for *James and the Giant Peach; New York Times* Outstanding Books award, 1983, Whitbread award, 1983, and West Australian award, 1986, all for *The Witches;* World Fantasy Convention Lifetime Achievement award, and Federation of Children's Book Groups award, both 1983, Maschler award runner-up, 1985, for *The Giraffe and the Pelly and Me; Boston Globe/Horn Book* nonfiction honor citation, 1985, for *Boy: Tales of Childhood;* International Board on Books for Young People awards for Norwegian and German translations of *The BFG,* both 1986; Smarties award, 1990, for *Esio Trot.* D.Litt.: University of Keele, Staffordshire, 1988. **Died:** 23 November 1990.

PUBLICATIONS

Fiction

The Gremlins, illustrated by Walt Disney Studio. New York, Random House, 1943; London, Collins, 1944.
James and the Giant Peach, illustrated by Nancy Ekholm Burkert. New York, Knopf, 1961; London, Allen and Unwin, 1967.
Charlie and the Chocolate Factory, illustrated by Joseph Schindelman. New York, Knopf, 1964; London, Allen and Unwin, 1967.
The Magic Finger, illustrated by William Pène du Bois. New York, Harper, 1966; London, Allen and Unwin, 1968.
Fantastic Mr. Fox, illustrated by Donald Chaffin. New York, Knopf, and London, Allen and Unwin, 1970.
Charlie and the Great Glass Elevator, illustrated by Joseph Schindelman. New York, Knopf, 1972; London, Allen and Unwin, 1973.
Danny: The Champion of the World, illustrated by Jill Bennett. London, Cape, and New York, Knopf, 1975.

The Wonderful Story of Henry Sugar and Six More. London, Cape, 1977; as *The Wonderful World of Henry Sugar,* New York, Knopf, 1977.
The Complete Adventures of Charlie and Mr. Willy Wonka, illustrated by Faith Jaques. London, Allen and Unwin, 1978.
The Enormous Crocodile, illustrated by Quentin Blake. London, Cape, and New York, Knopf, 1978.
The Twits, illustrated by Quentin Blake. London, Cape, 1980; New York, Knopf, 1981.
George's Marvellous Medicine, illustrated by Quentin Blake. London, Cape, 1981; New York, Knopf, 1982.
The BFG, illustrated by Quentin Blake. London, Cape, and New York, Farrar Straus, 1982.
The Witches, illustrated by Quentin Blake. London, Cape, and New York, Farrar Straus, 1983.
The Giraffe and the Pelly and Me, illustrated by Quentin Blake. London, Cape, and New York, Farrar Straus, 1985.
Matilda, illustrated by Quentin Blake. London, Cape, and New York, Viking Kestrel, 1988.
Roald Dahl: Charlie and the Chocolate Factory, Charlie and the Great Glass Elevator, The BFG. New York, Viking, 1989.
Esio Trot, illustrated by Quentin Blake. New York, Viking, 1990.
The Minpins. New York, Viking, 1991.
The Vicar of Nibbleswickle, illustrated by Quentin Blake. New York, Viking, 1992.

Recordings: *Bedtime Stories to Children's Books,* Center for Cassette Studies, 1973. *Charlie and the Chocolate Factory,* Caedmon, 1975; *James and the Giant Peach,* Caedmon, 1977; *Fantastic Mr. Fox,* Caedmon, 1978; *Roald Dahl Reads His "The Enormous Crocodile" and "The Magic Finger,"* Caedmon, 1980.

Poetry

Revolting Rhymes, illustrated by Quentin Blake. London, Cape, 1982; New York, Knopf, 1983.
Dirty Beasts, illustrated by Rosemary Fawcett. London, Cape, 1983; New York, Farrar Straus, 1984.
Rhyme Stew, illustrated by Quentin Blake. New York, Viking, 1990.

Other

Boy: Tales of Childhood. London, Cape, and New York, Farrar Straus, 1984.
Going Solo. London, Cape, and New York, Farrar Straus, 1986.
The Dahl Diary, 1992, illustrated by Quentin Blake. New York, Puffin, 1991.

PUBLICATIONS FOR ADULTS

Novels

Sometime Never: A Fable for Supermen. New York, Scribner, 1948; London, Collins, 1949.
My Uncle Oswald. London, Joseph, 1979; New York, Knopf, 1980.

Short Stories

Over to You: Ten Stories of Flyers and Flying. New York, Reynal, 1946; London, Hamish Hamilton, 1947.

Someone Like You. New York, Knopf, 1953; London, Secker and Warburg, 1954; revised edition, London, Joseph, 1961.

Kiss, Kiss. New York, Knopf, and London, Joseph, 1960.

Twenty-Nine Kisses. London, Joseph, 1969.

Selected Stories. New York, Random House, 1970.

Penguin Modern Stories 12, with others. London, Penguin, 1972.

Switch Bitch. New York, Knopf, and London, Joseph, 1974.

The Best of Roald Dahl. New York, Random House, 1978; London, Joseph, 1983.

Tales of the Unexpected. London, Joseph, and New York, Vintage, 1979.

More Tales of the Unexpected. London, Joseph, 1980; as *Further Tales of the Unexpected,* Bath, Chivers, 1981.

A Roald Dahl Selection: Nine Short Stories, edited by Roy Blatchford. London, Longman, 1980.

Two Fables. London, Viking, 1986; New York, Farrar Straus, 1987.

A Second Roald Dahl Selection: Eight Short Stories, edited by Hélène Fawcett. London, Longman, 1987.

Ah, Sweet Mystery of Life, illustrated by John Lawrence. London, Cape, 1988; New York, Knopf, 1989.

Plays

The Honeys (produced New York, 1955).

Screenplays: *You Only Live Twice,* with Harry Jack Bloom, 1967; *Chitty-Chitty-Bang-Bang,* with Ken Hughes, 1968; *The Night-Digger,* 1970; *The Lightning Bug,* 1971; *Willy Wonka and the Chocolate Factory,* 1971.

Television Play: *Lamb to the Slaughter* (*Alfred Hitchcock Presents* series), 1955.

Other

Editor, *Roald Dahl's Book of Ghost Stories.* London, Cape, and New York, Farrar Straus, 1983.

*

Media Adaptations: *36 Hours* (film, adaptation of "Beware of the Dog"), MGM, 1964; *Delicious Inventions* (film, excerpted from *Willie Wonka and the Chocolate Factory,* Paramount, 1971), Films, Inc., 1976; *Roald Dahl's Charlie and the Chocolate Factory: A Play* (play by Richard George), New York, Knopf, 1976; *Willie Wonka and the Chocolate Factory—Storytime* (filmstrip, excerpted from the 1971 Paramount film), Films, Inc., 1976; *Willie Wonka and the Chocolate Factory—Learning Kit* (filmstrip, excerpted from the 1971 Paramount film), Films, Inc., 1976; *The Great Switcheroo* (recording), Caedmon, 1977; *Tales of the Unexpected* (television movie), WNEW-TV, 1979; *Roald Dahl's James and the Giant Peach: A Play* (play by Richard George), Penguin, 1982; *The Witches* (film), Lorimar, 1990.

Critical Study: Entry in *Contemporary Literary Criticism,* Volume 1, Detroit, Gale, 1973; Volume 6, 1976; Volume 18, 1981; Entry in *Children's Literature Review,* Volume 1, Detroit, Gale, 1976; Volume 7, 1984; *Roald Dahl* by Chris Powling, London, Hamish Hamilton, 1983.

*   *   *

Clues to the origin of Roald Dahl's fictional world may be found in *Boy,* the first volume of his autobiography, where the author discusses his life at public schools in Wales and England. "I was appalled by the fact that masters and senior boys were allowed literally to wound other boys, and sometimes quite severely. I couldn't get over it. I never have got over it," he insists. Indeed, in story after story he administers sure and swift punishment to wantonly cruel adults, such as the horrible aunties in *James and the Giant Peach* or the evil headmistress in *Matilda.*

A second revealing description in *Boy* has young Roald being upbraided for not liking the rules. And why should he? What he sees is a sadistic, bandy-legged, sanctimonious headmaster whom the system rewards with England's highest Christian post: that of Archbishop of Canterbury. Early on, the six-foot, six-inch Dahl begins to see himself as an outsider, as one whose literary mission is to expose the mistakes of God and man and to present an order in which things operate as every young person knows they are supposed to operate.

To appreciate the Dahl outsider, one must recognize that he is someone who intuitively understands the controlling system. The difference is that he refuses to subscribe to it. At his best, he is the conman with a conscience, the individual who can skillfully defeat his adversaries at their own game. Willie Wonka in *Charlie and the Chocolate Factory* is this kind of person, becoming wonderfully wealthy by outwitting his unscrupulous competitors. A better example is the benign pickpocket in his story "The Hitchhiker," a man who can undo that most obvious of authority figures—a coarse, belligerent motorcycle cop.

The abiding principle in Dahl's work is one of schoolboy justice—poetic or otherwise. If, for example, the conman is neither an inspiring child nor worthy adult, Dahl takes great pleasure in having him generate his own comeuppance. This is the case with Uncle Oswald, a legendary seducer who gets seduced in "The Visitor." Similarly, in "Parson's Pleasure," an antique dealer who poses as an honest churchman and then dupes rural people out of their priceless furniture ends up collecting a pile of kindling instead of a rare Chippendale.

Too easily is Dahl's fiction segregated into adult and children's categories. In actual fact, both worlds are enormously similar, even though a certain sexual mischievousness is reserved for older readers. Elementary fair play is ever the issue at hand. So what if bizarre, improbable events are necessary in order to settle the score! Wild ducks train shotguns upon a family of hunters in *The Magic Finger.* And in "Lamb to the Slaughter," which became an *Alfred Hitchcock Presents* teleplay, a loving wife deftly decks her callous husband with a frozen leg of lamb. She and the unwitting officers then eat the evidence.

To insist that Dahl's world is too violent for young readers is to miss the point. All of his fiction is governed by an innocent, grand-scale reasoning: virtue is hyperbolically rewarded, while vice is rigorously punished. Of course Willie Wonka will freely give his fabulous chocolate factory to a kind, impoverished boy named

Charlie Bucket. Charlie deserves it. Unsophisticated logic demands no less. And of course the evil women in *The Witches* will be turned into mice. They deserve to be caught in traps and beheaded. After all, they have laid plans to kill every child in England.

Dahl's stories are distinguished by imaginative, free-wheeling plots, not by intense character development. Verbal ingenuity, however, is more evident in works for younger readers. Here, rhymes and alliterations are accompanied by outrageous puns and word coinages. Some of the cleverest neologisms appear in *The BFG*, where a gentle giant eats disgusting *snozzcumbers* while longing for something more *scrumdillyumptious*.

Another difference is that in the children's stories, magic is often needed to save the day. The heroine of *Matilda* discovers that she has psycho-kinetic powers, and the little girl in *The Magic Finger* can cast a spell by pointing with her index finger. In "The Swan," perhaps the most chilling piece that Dahl ever wrote, bullies tie young Peter Watson between two rails. Peter scrunches as low as he can and somehow survives being run over by a train. Still he is not set free. The bullies now kill a beautiful swan, cut off its wings, attach them to Peter, and make him climb a tall tree. They then start shooting at him with a .22-caliber rifle, taunting him to fly. And fly he does! He soars gracefully through the heavens to the safety of his own back garden.

"The Swan" is particularly interesting in that it corrects the notion that Dahl's natural adversaries are always children and adults. Here the enemies are Peter's schoolmates. Conversely, there are remarkably loving child-adult relationships depicted in *Danny: The Champion of the World, Matilda, The BFG,* and *Charlie and the Chocolate Factory.* One of the best involves a child hero and his cigar-smoking, Norwegian grandmother in *Witches.* When the lad is turned into a mouse, Dahl avoids the expected, sentimental trap of reversing the fate. The boy philosophically accepts his condition, telling his adoring grandmother, "It doesn't matter who you are or what you look like so long as somebody loves you." Such fundamental wisdom marks the timeless appeal of Roald Dahl's fiction for readers of all ages.

—Walker Rutledge

DALY, Maureen

Nationality: American. **Born:** Castlecaufield, County Tyrone, Ireland, 15 March 1921. **Education:** St. Mary Springs Academy, Fond du Lac, Wisconsin; Rosary College, River Forest, Illinois, B.A. 1942. **Family:** Married the writer William P. McGivern in 1946 (died 1983); one daughter (deceased) and one son. **Career:** Writer, 1938 to present. Police reporter and columnist, Chicago *Tribune,* 1941-44; reporter, Chicago City News Bureau, 1941-43; associate editor, *Ladies' Home Journal,* Philadelphia, 1944-49; editorial consultant, *Saturday Evening Post,* Philadelphia, 1960-69; since 1987 reporter and columnist, *Desert Sun,* Palm Desert, California. Screenwriter for Twentieth Century-Fox; lecturer on foreign lands and emerging nations. **Awards:** *Scholastic* magazine's short story contest, 1936, third prize for "Fifteen," 1937, first prize for "Sixteen"; O. Henry Memorial Award, 1938, for short story "Sixteen"; Dodd, Mead Intercollegiate Literary Fellowship Novel Award, 1942, and Lewis Carroll Shelf Award,

1969, both for *Seventeenth Summer;* Freedoms Foundation Award, 1952, for "humanity in reporting"; Gimbel Fashion Award, 1962, for contribution to U.S. fashion industry through *Saturday Evening Post* articles; one of *Redbook*'s ten great books for teens, 1987, for *Acts of Love.* **Address:** 73-305 Ironwood St., Palm Desert, California 92260, U.S.A.

PUBLICATIONS FOR YOUNG ADULTS

Fiction

Seventeenth Summer. New York, Dodd Mead, 1942; London, Hollis and Carter, 1947, illustrated edition, New York, Dodd Mead, 1948.

Sixteen and Other Stories, illustrated by Kendall Rossi. New York, Dodd Mead, 1961.

Acts of Love. New York, Scholastic, 1986; London, Gollancz, 1987.

First a Dream. New York, Scholastic, 1990.

Nonfiction

Smarter and Smoother: A Handbook on How to Be That Way, illustrated by Marguerite Bryan. New York, Dodd Mead, 1944.

What's Your P.Q. (Personality Quotient)?, illustrated by Ellie Simmons. New York, Dodd Mead, 1952; revised edition, 1966.

Twelve around the World, illustrated by Frank Kramer. New York, Dodd Mead, 1957.

Spanish Roundabout. New York, Dodd Mead, 1960.

Moroccan Roundabout. New York, Dodd Mead, 1961.

Other

Editor, *My Favorite Stories.* New York, Dodd Mead, 1948.

Editor, *My Favorite Mystery [Suspense] Stories.* New York, Dodd Mead, 2 vols., 1966-68.

PUBLICATIONS FOR CHILDREN

Fiction

Patrick Visits the Farm, illustrated by Ellie Simmons. New York, Dodd Mead, 1959.

Patrick Takes a Trip, illustrated by Ellie Simmons. New York, Dodd Mead, 1960.

Patrick Visits the Library, illustrated by Paul Lantz. New York, Dodd Mead, 1961.

Patrick Visits the Zoo, illustrated by Sam Savitt. New York, Dodd Mead, 1963.

The Ginger Horse, illustrated by Wesley Dennis. New York, Dodd Mead, 1964.

Spain: Wonderland of Contrasts. New York, Dodd Mead, 1965.

The Small War of Sergeant Donkey, illustrated by Wesley Dennis. New York, Dodd Mead, 1966.

Rosie, the Dancing Elephant, illustrated by Lorence Bjorklund. New York, Dodd Mead, 1967.

PUBLICATIONS FOR ADULTS

Nonfiction

The Perfect Hostess: Complete Etiquette and Entertainment for the Home. New York, Dodd Mead, 1950.

Mention My Name in Mombasa: The Unscheduled Adventures of an American Family Abroad (as Maureen Daly McGivern), with William P. McGivern, illustrated by Frank Kramer. New York, Dodd Mead, 1958.

A Matter of Honor, with William P. McGivern. New York, Arbor House, 1984.

Other

Editor, *Profile of Youth.* Philadelphia, Lippincott, 1951.

Also author of "High School Career Series," Curtis Publishing Co., 1942-49. Writer with husband of scripts for television series, including "Kojak," and of screenplay, *Brannigan.* Work represented in several textbooks and anthologies. Contributor of over two hundred articles to numerous periodicals, including *Vogue, Mademoiselle, Cosmopolitan, Woman's Day, Scholastic, Woman's Home Companion,* and *Redbook.*

*

Media Adaptations: *Seventeenth Summer* (film), Warner Bros., 1949; *The Ginger Horse* (film), Walt Disney Studios; Daly's short story, "You Can't Kiss Caroline," has also been dramatized.

Manuscript Collections: University of Oregon Library, Eugene.

Biography: Essay in *Something about the Author Autobiography Series,* Volume 1, Detroit, Gale, 1986; essay in *Speaking for Ourselves: Autobiographical Sketches by Notable Authors of Books for Young Adults,* Volume 1, compiled and edited by Donald R. Gallo, National Council of Teachers of English, 1990.

Critical Studies: Entry in *Contemporary Literary Criticism,* Volume 17, Detroit, Gale, 1981.

Maureen Daly comments:

My first novel, *Seventeenth Summer,* which was written when I was a teenager and published during my last year of college, has long been considered a "break through" book which established the Young Adult Literary category in the publishing business in the United States as that mammoth segment of publishing exists today.

I would like, at this late date, to explain that *Seventeenth Summer,* in my intention and at the time of publication, was considered a full adult novel and published and reviewed as such. It was given particular praise in *New York,* as well as hundreds of other publications, and was lauded by Sinclair Lewis in a lead review in the *New York Times Book Review.*

Recently, on a lecture/visit with Dr. Ray Crisp of the Lincoln Nebraska school system, I gleaned that *Seventeenth Summer* was considered a revolutionary up-start in the "young literature" field because it depicted drinking, smoking, heterosexual and homosexual activities as events in the lives of American teenagers,

unusual—I guess—in the prudish silences of my book's historic time slot.

(1997)Writing as a career can be challenging, interesting and often profitable enough to finance tickets to anywhere in the world. But it is also a tough self-assignment.

Good writers are never off the job. Since I began writing at fourteen, I have rarely been able to walk down a street, swim in a strange lake, wander through a supermarket, watch snow fall on a mountain without looking, seeing, feeling, recording and then thinking, "Now how am I going to say this? How am I going to put this scene, these people into words?"

Writers must always find the words, in their minds or on paper, for what they see and feel, a lifelong assignment.

*   *   *

Maureen Daly's major contribution to adolescent literature has been *Seventeenth Summer,* which helped to establish the romance novel among adolescent readers in the early 1940s. Although much of contemporary adolescent fiction has expanded to focus more heavily on the problem novel and its realism, many adolescent readers still prefer the romance.

Adolescent readers of romance novels identify readily with the protagonists, many of whom are the same age as the readers. The common themes in such novels, especially the possibility of leaving home and embarking on a new way of life as well as the seeking and securing of "true love," which always forms a major part of the plot, speak strongly to adolescents. Although some older readers may view such novels as exaggerated and larger than life, adolescence is a period of intense feelings and the emphasis upon emotion in the romance is an important ingredient for success with adolescent readers.

Unlike the old pattern of this genre—boy meets girl, boy loses girl, boy finally wins girl—the pattern in *Seventeenth Summer* focuses upon the role of the girl in the quest. This pattern is revealed through the actions of Angie, the main character, during Angie's seventeenth summer. Little actually happens in the novel: Angie falls in love, she dates a boy named Jack from her home town, and she eventually leaves him at the end of summer to go away to college. Significantly, however, the story is told from her point of view and she is the one to terminate the relationship.

The plot is not what holds the interest of readers. Instead, the sensitivity toward adolescent feelings which pervades the story leads readers to remember the book long after finishing it. The story is definitely female oriented and consequently has more appeal for female readers. Angie has no brothers, but her three sisters, two older, and one younger, serve as foils for Angie. One older sister, Margaret, has a steady boyfriend and is planning her wedding; Lorraine, the other older sister, has difficulty sustaining any relationships with men and sees herself as a failure. On the other side of Angie is Kitty, still young enough to wonder how butterflies fly and still wanting to play catch with her father. Angie's relationship with her mother is a warm and supportive one while her father is a more shadowy character for whom she has respect but no particular closeness. The family unit, however, provides a safe environment for Angie in which she can sort out her feelings.

The main focus of Angie's summer is her growing awareness of her feelings about boys and all the attendant misunderstandings and frustrations which accompany first love. Daly's treatment of every girl's daydream of having a boy ''fall'' for her might be compared to the fairy tale in which a wish for a new identity is granted. As Angie points out:

It's funny what a boy can do. One day you're nobody and the next day you're the girl that some fellow goes with and the other fellows look at you harder and wonder what you've got and wish that they had been the one to take you out first. And the girls say hello and want you to walk down to the drugstore to have Cokes with them because the boy who likes you might come along and he might have other boys with him. Going with a boy gives you a new identity—especially going with a fellow like Jack Daly.

Accompanying the love story, however, are elements which distinguish *Seventeenth Summer* from the usual romance. Although Daly's portrayal of society may seem tame by today's standards, she pushed the limits of what was socially acceptable in the 1940s. Jack smokes a pipe and drinks beer. During one of their dates, Jack takes Angie to a roadhouse where she asks him to explain why the male pianist has painted fingernails. He looks embarrassed, tries to respond, but offers no answer. Lorraine, Angie's older sister, depends upon traveling salesmen for dates and ends up being left behind each time the salesman moves on. The world created in the novel suggests that drinking, smoking and even dating do not necessarily lead to sin and damnation, a view quite avant garde for the time, and which was further enhanced by the fact that Daly was only seventeen herself when she wrote the major portion of the novel.

Daly also broke with the usual tradition of the omniscient author and chose to have Angie present her own story. Although the first person point of view today is an accepted form of narration, it was not used with great frequency in the writings of the 1940s. As a result of Daly's choice, however, readers experience a story that has a stronger and more believable sense of personal emotion and sensitivity than might otherwise have occurred. This sensitivity is heightened by Daly's prose, such as in Angie's description of her first kiss:

In the movies they always shut their eyes but I didn't. I didn't think of anything like that, though I do remember a quick thought passing through my mind again about how much he smelled like Ivory soap when his face was so close to mine. In the loveliness of the next moment I think I grew up. I remember that behind him was the thin, yellow arc of moon, turned over on its back, and I remember feeling my hands slowly relax on the rough lapels of his coat. Sitting on the cool grass in my sprigged dimity with the little blue and white bachelor's buttons pinned in my hair, Jack kissed me and his lips were as smooth and baby-soft as a new raspberry.

Some critics find Angie's innocence offensive and unbelievable. But the strength of the book and its staying power—over a million and a half copies have been sold since its publication—lie in readers remembering Angie as an individual, not as a representative of the 1940s. Readers many years after their first experience with *Seventeenth Summer* have written to Daly to tell her how well her portrayal of first love matched their own experiences. It is little surprise, therefore, that the book remains in print and is used so often by teachers of adolescent literature to represent the beginning of the American adolescent romance.

—Charles R. Duke

———

DANIEL, Colin. *See* WINDSOR, Patricia (Frances).

———

DANTICAT, Edwidge

Nationality: Haitian-American. **Born:** Port-au-Prince, Haiti, 19 January 1969; immigrated to the United States, 1981. **Education:** Attended Barnard College, New York, New York; Brown University, Providence, Rhode Island, M.F.A., 1993. **Career:** Writer/teacher, since 1994. **Awards:** National Book Award finalist, 1995, for *Krik? Krak!*; named one of *Granta*'s ''Best of American Novelists,'' 1996. **Address:** c/o Soho Press, 853 Broadway, No. 1903, New York, New York 10003, U.S.A.

PUBLICATIONS

Fiction

Breath, Eyes, Memory. New York, Soho Press, 1994.
Krik? Krak! New York, Soho Press, 1994.

*

Critical Studies: ''White Darkness/Black Dreams'' by Sal Scalora, in *Haiti: Feeding the Spirit,* New York, Aperture, 1992; ''My Father Once Chased Rainbows'' by Edwidge Danticat, in *Essence* (New York), November 1993, 48; ''Two Tales of Haiti'' by Joan Philpott, in *Ms.* (New York), March/April 1994, 77-78; ''Snapshots of Haiti'' by Jordana Hart, in *Ms.* (New York), March/April 1995, 75; ''Love and Haiti'' by Rebecca Carroll, in *Elle* (New York), April 1995, 80; ''Edwidge Danticat: Dreaming of Haiti'' by Deborah Gregory, in *Essence* (New York), April 1995, 56; ''A New Voice From Haiti'' by Edward Hower, in *World & I* (Washington, D.C.), July 1995; interview with Edwidge Danticat by Renee H. Shea, in *Callaloo* (Baltimore, Maryland), Spring 1996, 382-89.

*   *   *

Edwidge (pronounced ''Edweedge'' in the French style) Danticat was born in Haiti and lived there until she was twelve, and the people, the folklore, the landscape, even the vibrant colors and scents of her native land—along with a darkly running undercurrent of poverty, cruelty, and political turmoil—suffuse her fiction.

Danticat's first novel, *Breath, Eyes, Memory,* is dedicated "To the brave women of Haiti, grandmothers, mothers, aunts, sisters, cousins, daughters, and friends, on this shore and other shores. We have stumbled but we will not fall," and while the book's title evokes the novel's lyrical style, the dedication expresses the major themes of the novel and of her short stories as well: women and their myriad interrelationships, the exile of Haitian women, and Haitian women's courage and determination. As the novel opens, Sophie Caco, a young schoolgirl, is pressing a daffodil onto a Mother's Day card she has made for her Aunt Atie. Martine, Sophie's mother, left for the United States years before, and her unmarried aunt has raised Sophie. When Sophie gives her aunt the card, Atie hands it back: "Not this year," she says, sadly. "Why not this year?" "Sophie, it is not mine. It is your mother's. We must send it to your mother." Soon after, Martine sends for her, and a teary-eyed Sophie boards the plane for New York, leaving behind her beloved aunt, her grandmother Grandme Ife, and her happy childhood in Haiti. In New York, Sophie grows up fast. Her tormented mother awakens every night screaming from terrible nightmares, mostly, she says, of Sophie's rape-conception. Sophie faces discrimination from her American classmates, who accuse Haitians of having HBO—Haitian Body Odor—and carrying AIDS. But Sophie is strong and self-reliant. After she spends the night with the man she will marry and her mother "tests" her when she gets home, inserting two fingers into her vagina to see if Sophie is still pure, Sophie flees. She will survive.

In her prefatory note to *Krik? Krak!* Danticat explains her book's title with a quote from Sal Scalora's essay "White Darkness/Black Dreamings" in *Haiti: Feeding the Spirit*: "Krik? Krak! Somewhere by the seacoast I feel a breath of warm sea air and hear the laughter of children. An old granny smokes her pipe, surrounded by the village children. . . . We tell the stories so that the young ones will know what came before them. They ask Krik? we say Krak! Our stories are kept in our hearts." Although a few of the nine stories in this collection deal with distinctly adult concerns— "Night Women" is about a prostitute, for example—most speak to young adult readers as well. In "The Missing Peace," a motherless fourteen-year-old girl becomes her true self with the advice of an American journalist. In "Caroline's Wedding" a young women gets her naturalization papers at a Brooklyn courthouse and frames them, then goes on to help with her sister's wedding to a black American. When Josephine's mother is burned as a witch, in "Nineteen Thirty-Seven," the young Haitian woman implores: "May her flight be joyful."

Yes, there are massacres, rapes, horrible nightmares in Danticat's fiction, but above all these are the strength, hope, and joy of her poetic vision. At the end of *Breath, Eyes, Memory,* Sophie returns to Haiti for her mother's funeral, and her grandmother puts her hand on Sophie's shoulder and tells her:

Listen. Listen before it passes. Parol gin pie zel. The words can give wings to your feet. . . . There is a place where women are buried in clothes the color of flames, where we drop coffee on the ground for those who went ahead, where the daughter is never fully a woman until her mother has passed on before her. There is always a place where, if you listen closely in the night, you will hear your mother telling a story and at the end of the tale, she will ask you this question:

'Ou libere?' Are you free, my daughter?. . . . Now . . . you will know how to answer."

—Marcia Welsh

DANZIGER, Paula

Nationality: American. **Born:** Washington, D.C., 18 August 1944. **Education:** Montclair State College, New Jersey, B.A. 1967, M.A. **Career:** Substitute teacher, Edison, New Jersey, 1967; Title I teacher, Highland Park, New Jersey, 1967-68; junior-high school English teacher, Edison, New Jersey, 1968-70; English teacher, Lincoln Junior High School, West Orange, New Jersey, 1977-78; since 1978 full-time writer. Worked for the Educational Opportunity Program, Montclair State College, until 1977. **Awards:** New Jersey Institute of Technology award, and Young Reader Medal Nomination, California Reading Association, both 1976, Massachusetts Children's Book award, first runner-up, 1977, winner, 1979, and Nene award, Hawaii Association of School Librarians and the Hawaii Library Association, 1980, all for *The Cat Ate My Gymsuit;* Child Study Association of America's Children's Books of the Year citation, 1978, Massachusetts Children's Book award, Education Department of Salem State College, 1979, Nene award, 1980, California Young Reader Medal Nomination, 1981, and Arizona Young Reader award, 1983, all for *The Pistachio Prescription;* Children's Choice award, International Reading Association and the Children's Book Council, 1979, for *The Pistachio Prescription,* 1980, for *The Cat Ate My Gymsuit* and *Can You Sue Your Parents for Malpractice?,* 1981, for *There's a Bat in Bunk Five,* and 1983, for *The Divorce Express*; New Jersey Institute of Technology award, and New York Public Library's Books for the Teen Age citation, both 1980, and Land of Enchantment Book award, New Mexico Library Association, 1982, all for *Can You Sue Your Parents for Malpractice?;* Read-a-Thon Author of the Year award, Multiple Sclerosis Society, and Parents' Choice award for Literature, Parents' Choice Foundation, both 1982, Woodward Park School Annual Book award, 1983, and South Carolina Young Adult Book award, South Carolina Association of School Librarians, 1985, all for *The Divorce Express;* CRABbery award, Prince George's County Memorial Library System (Maryland), 1982, and Young Readers Medal, 1984, both for *There's a Bat in Bunk Five;* Parents' Choice award for Literature, Bologna International Children's Book Fair exhibitor, and Child Study Association of America's Children's Books of the Year citation, all 1985, all for *It's an Aardvark-Eat-Turtle World.* **Address:** c/o Delacorte Press, 1540 Broadway, New York, New York 10036-4039, U.S.A.

PUBLICATIONS FOR YOUNG ADULTS

Fiction

The Cat Ate My Gymsuit. New York, Delacorte, 1974.
The Pistachio Prescription. New York, Delacorte, 1978.
Can You Sue Your Parents for Malpractice?. New York, Delacorte, 1979.
There's a Bat in Bunk Five. New York, Delacorte, 1980.
The Divorce Express. New York, Delacorte, 1982.
It's an Aardvark-Eat-Turtle World. New York, Delacorte, 1985.

This Place Has No Atmosphere. New York, Delacorte, 1986.
Remember Me to Harold Square. New York, Delacorte, 1987.
Everyone Else's Parents Said Yes. New York, Delacorte, 1989.
Make Like a Tree and Leave. New York, Delacorte, 1990.
Earth to Matthew. New York, Delacorte, 1991.
Not for a Billion Gazillion Dollars. New York, Delacorte, 1992.
Amber Brown is Not a Crayon, illustrated by Tony Ross. New York, Putnam's, 1994.
Thames Doesn't Rhyme with James. New York, Putnam's, 1994.
You Can't Eat Your Chicken Pox, Amber Brown, illustrated by Tony Ross. New York, Putnam's, 1995.
Amber Brown Goes Fourth, illustrated by Tony Ross. New York, Putnam's Sons, 1995.
Amber Brown Wants Extra Credit, illustrated by Tony Ross. New York, Putnam's Sons, 1996.
Forever Amber Brown, illustrated by Tony Ross. New York, Putnam, 1996.
Amber Brown Sees Red, illustrated by Tony Ross. New York, Putnam, 1997.
With Ann M. Martin, *P.S. Longer Letter Later.* New York, Scholastic, 1998.
Amber Brown is Feeling Blue, illustrated by Tony Ross. New York, Putnam's, 1998.

*

Media Adaptations: *The Cat Ate My Gymsuit* (film, cassette), Cheshire, 1985; *The Cat Ate My Gymsuit* (cassette), *The Pistachio Prescription* (cassette), *There's a Bat in Bunk Five* (cassette), *Can You Sue Your Parents for Malpractice?* (cassette), and *The Divorce Express* (cassette), Listening Library, 1985-86.

Biography: Essay in *Authors and Artists for Young Adults,* Volume 4, Detroit, Gale, 1990; essay in *Speaking for Ourselves: Autobiographical Sketches by Notable Authors of Books for Young Adults,* Volume 1, compiled and edited by Donald R. Gallo, National Council of Teachers of English, 1990.

Critical Studies: Entry in *Children's Literature Review,* Volume 20, Detroit, Gale, 1990; entry in *Contemporary Literary Criticism,* Volume 21, Detroit, Gale, 1982.

*   *   *

Because Paula Danziger's books are fast-paced, easy reading, and filled with realistic situations that young adults recognize and with dialogue that they would love to deliver, critics of young adult literature often dismiss them as light entertainment. Even Danziger herself through such characters as Marcy Lewis, the protagonist of her first novel, *The Cat Ate My Gymsuit* (1974), is faintly apologetic of the fact that her novels may lack the depth of a heavyweight young adult offering. Marcy demurs, ''My life is not easy. I know I'm not poor. Nobody beats me. I have clothes to wear, my own room, a stereo, a TV, and a push button phone. Sometimes I feel guilty being so miserable, but middle class kids have problems too.'' Marcy sets the stage for the rest of Danziger's protagonists—the middle class kids of today, whose experiences include the modern restructuring of the family, the complications of changing

role models, fears of personal ineffectualness in a demanding world, and the universal challenges of adolescence.

The Cat Ate My Gymsuit is Paula Danziger's most representative work in terms of its comprehensive use of these important young adult themes. Furthermore, Danziger has revealed that her first novel was also her most angry and autobiographical since it was written in conjunction with events in her own life that forced her to deal with the leftover frustrations and fears of her youth. The author's personal success in facing up to those personal issues can be deduced from her method of resolving her characters' problems at the end of the novel. Marcy begins counseling with a psychiatrist while Ms. Finney, Marcy's teacher, decides to specialize in bibliotherapy.

Marcy's family life is classically and overbearingly patriarchal; her father is a bitter and unhappy man. Slowly we realize that the abuse Marcy receives from him, while not overtly physical, is the worst kind of verbal and emotional abuse. Mr. Lewis's favorite topics are Marcy's weight, her clumsiness, and eventually her support of her freethinking English teacher, Barbara Finney. Equally as subjugated by Mr. Lewis are Marcy's younger brother Stuart, who becomes practically invisible since Marcy is her father's favorite verbal target, and Marcy's mother. Mrs. Lewis's goal is to keep peace in the family, which she attempts to do by acting as the family's mediator; after each confrontation, she privately placates both her husband and Marcy. Mrs. Lewis maintains the family's delicate balance of artificial normality by prescribing tranquilizers for herself and huge bowls of ice cream for her children. The ice cream, of course, only exacerbates Marcy's weight problem and gives her father more ammunition for future confrontations. More ominously, Mrs. Lewis's dependence on prescription tranquilizers helps her convince herself that she has no other personal options than to endure the abusive situation in which she and her children suffer. The tranquilizers also serve as a form of emotional blackmail as Mrs. Lewis attempts to convince Marcy to follow her lead and accept the status quo.

Then, in the middle of the school year, Barbara Finney takes over Marcy's English class at school and begins a support group for her students which they name Smedley. From her involvement with Smedley, Marcy learns that her family is not functioning as it should. Her attempts to call this fact to the attention of her father meet with additional rebuffs and increased abuse. Marcy's mother, however, is more receptive—although hesitatingly so—to suggestions for improving family communication. Finally, Ms. Finney's refusal to pledge allegiance to the American flag and her consequent dismissal from the school system forces everyone to take a stand. Marcy's family is split between her father's ''follow the rules'' philosophy and Marcy's newfound courage to assert fledgling convictions. Mrs. Lewis, in the face of a family rift she cannot mediate, supports Marcy's efforts to reinstate Ms. Finney, and everyone's definitions of individual roles within the family are challenged. Mr. Lewis learns that his economic responsibility to his family, which he grudgingly fulfills, does not grant him the power to make them perform as he thinks they should. Marcy, and eventually her mother, challenge their dependence on that economic power—Marcy by refusing to be placated by binge-shopping with her mother after each argument with her father, and Mrs. Lewis by deciding to break from the homemaker mold and return to the workforce. Marcy and her friends learn through their banding together to save Ms. Finney's job that no one is too young to recognize injustice and wage effective battle against it. At the end of the novel and in keeping with its overall humorous tone, Marcy gets her first pimple, symbolic of her entrance into the world of adolescence. She welcomes this previously dreaded status now that she knows how to seek support and encouragement from her friends in Smedley.

Danziger's later novels rework one or all of her major themes. In *The Pistachio Prescription* (1978), for example, Cassie Stephens must face the disintegration of her parents' marriage while coping with her own insecurity as the self-proclaimed ugly duckling asthmatic of her family. Along the way, she and her friends unite to insure that the newly elected officers of the "freshperson" class will be people who are truly representative of their group and not the school snobs.

Lauren Allen asks *Can You Sue Your Parents for Malpractice?* (1979) when she takes a course entitled "Law for Children and Young People." Her teacher encourages his students to publish a newsletter about students' rights, teaching them that they can have some control over their own lives. Lauren's father, like Marcy's father from *The Cat Ate My Gymsuit*, feels his traditional patriarchal control over his family is threatened when his oldest daughter Melissa moves in with her boyfriend. As Lauren watches her sister struggle to create a relationship unlike their parents' tense marriage, Lauren herself challenges the socially acceptable by dating a boy younger than herself.

Marcy Lewis returns in *There's a Bat in Bunk Five* (1980). Her relationship with her father has progressed, although it's far from perfect. Spending the summer as a counselor-in-training at a creative arts camp directed by her former teacher Ms. Barbara Finney gives Marcy a chance to be on her own and practice some of the self-confidence she's learned since the ninth grade. Troubled campers and an attentive fellow counselor show her that she's got more to learn. Additionally, *There's a Bat in Bunk Five* is set near Woodstock, New York, a locale with which Danziger is personally familiar and which is used as the setting for her next two novels.

The Divorce Express (1982) and *It's an Aardvark-Eat-Turtle World* (1985) are about best friends who become "steps" when their parents decide to live together. Phoebe Brooks, the first-person narrator of *The Divorce Express*, must adjust to shuttling back and forth between her New York City mother and her Woodstock-based father. Her new friend Rosie Wilson shares Phoebe's divorce woes although Phoebe is still working through the many difficulties of her situation, and Rosie has adopted a more accepting and philosophical point of view. Rosie, a departure from Danziger's early protagonists, has more than mere adolescence to cope with: through her, Danziger deals not only with children of divorce but also with children of biracial marriage. When, in *It's an Aardvark-Eat-Turtle World*, Phoebe's father Jim and Rosie's mother Mindy decide to join their two households, Danziger switches the point of view to Rosie's first-person narration. Jim and Mindy are a warm and nurturing adult couple—Danziger's first—and the conflict in this novel is generated not by inflexible, tradition-minded grown-ups but by Phoebe's childish rejection of the new family structure. Phoebe's anger and rebelliousness are traits she shares with Danziger's early protagonists as she sorts through her confused feelings to achieve a final acceptance of the loving, cohesive family unit that Jim, Mindy, and Rosie offer her. Interestingly, Danziger has admitted that Phoebe's anger had been difficult to write about and that she had identified more with stable, self-knowledgeable Rosie during the writing of *It's an Aardvark-Eat-Turtle World*. Indeed, in identifying with Rosie, Danziger

shows a dramatic progression—both personally and creatively—from the early, angry, autobiographical *The Cat Ate My Gymsuit*.

As if to demonstrate that progression, anger and autobiography have been all but discarded in Danziger's latest novels, which focus on sixth-grader Matthew Martin. Matthew, whose adventures are related in evenhanded and reflective third person, is a distinct departure from Danziger's feminine protagonists, whose stories are narrated in energetic, if self-absorbed, first person. Matthew's most serious problems are loving-but-quirky parents who diverge philosophically on the topics of health food and junk food, an older sister who is charting an unsteady course through her own adolescence, and the disgruntled female members of his sixth-grade class who find him grossly immature.

As engaging a protagonist as Matthew is, however, Paula Danziger's earlier novels remain her best. Sometimes angry, but always honest and unfailingly humorous, characters like Marcy Lewis, Phoebe Brooks, and Rosie Wilson walk modern teenagers through situations similar to those in which they will sooner or later find themselves. In her most recent series of books, Danziger has introduced a new—and highly popular—character, Amber Brown. Although aimed at the elementary school reader, the series explores the problems, concerns, and triumphs of growing up on the eve of the twenty-first century through the eyes of the spunky, but very real, Amber Brown, who, like all of Paula Danziger's characters, lends young readers cheerful permission to be themselves and to look confidently into the future.

—Patricia L. Bradley

DAVIS, Jenny

Nationality: American. **Born:** Louisville, Kentucky, 29 June 1953. **Education:** Allegheny Community College, Pittsburgh, Pennsylvania, A.A. 1973; University of Kentucky, Lexington, B.A. 1976, M.A. 1983. **Family:** Married Dee Davis in 1975 (divorced 1981); two sons; married Charlie O'Neill in 1994. **Career:** Child advocate, Appalachian Regional Hospitals, Hazard, Kentucky, 1973-75; sex educator, Fayette County Health Department, Lexington, Kentucky, 1983-85; teacher, The Lexington School, Lexington, since 1985. **Address:** 723 Melrose, Lexington, Kentucky 40502, U.S.A.

PUBLICATIONS FOR YOUNG ADULTS

Novels

Goodbye and Keep Cold. New York, Orchard Books, 1987.
Sex Education. New York, Orchard Books, 1988.
Checking on the Moon. New York, Orchard Books, 1991.

*

Biography: Essay in *Speaking for Ourselves, Too* compiled and edited by Donald R. Gallo, National Council of Teachers of English, 1993.

*   *   *

Jenny Davis is not afraid to write about controversial subjects such as venereal disease, death, sex education, wife abuse, mental illness, and rape. Her books are not "simple problem" novels, but rather are complex creations where characters live realistic lives facing an assortment of difficulties which are not always solved but are dealt with satisfactorily.

Goodbye and Keep Cold is told by Edda Combs who has been out of college a year and is living in a beach house. Edda knows she will soon have to enter the adult world, but for now she sits and thinks about her life since the day her father was killed at a Kentucky strip mine. Edda's childhood world is full of complications: her mother (Frances) is romantically involved with the man (Henry John) who accidentally killed her husband; Edda learns that her father acquired herpes from her mother's best friend; her mother divorces her dead husband; a move to Lexington, Kentucky, and to schools where violence is the norm; her mother adopts Henry John's infant daughter; and her mother and Henry John marry.

The failings of adults are presented in a realistic fashion that young people will be able to accept, though Davis's characters do not face easy solutions to their problems. There is generally an older person, usually a relative, there to listen and to give advice when needed. Edda's family has Banker, a distant relative who has lived with them since Edda was two.

Sex Education, Davis's second novel, is told by sixteen-year-old Olivia Sinclair, who is in a psychiatric hospital. She writes about her past as a sort of therapy. (Davis herself spent her fifteenth year in a psychiatric hospital and, incidentally, once taught sex education classes.) Drawing from her own experiences Davis tells the story of two young people who get caught up in an outside class project of caring for someone else. They are assigned a pregnant woman who, as they later find out, has a husband who beats her. As the two young people try to help Maggie, her husband pushes David who falls down icy steps and breaks his neck. Livvy is so upset by David's death that she is institutionalized, where she retreats into sleep for seven months. Livvy's psychiatrist suggests that she write down everything that led to her admittance to the hospital and, as she is finishing, the teacher who had guided the class project comes to visit and asks Livvy's forgiveness for not realizing what might happen. Through this encounter Livvy is able to make peace with herself and accept that no one was really to blame for David's death. She realizes that she has not lost him completely, that a part of David will always be with her in her mind.

Again in *Checking on the Moon* the narrator is a young woman who is trying to make sense of a recent period in her life. Cab (who was born in one) and her brother Bill live with their grandmother in one of the ethnic areas of Pittsburgh while their mother travels through Europe with her new husband. Cab and Bill become involved with setting up a neighborhood crime-watch group after Bill's girlfriend Jessica is raped. Both Bill and Jessica's reactions are very true-to-life. Davis does not sugarcoat the situation by pretending the rape makes no difference to their relationship; it does, but both learn to deal with it.

Davis's subject matter and style of writing have strong appeal to teenage readers. All are told by young adults who are trying to understand themselves and their worlds. The problems they face are those common to many young adults, such as the search for identity, coping with parents, and dealing with friends. Accidents, illness, death, and disease are a part of the adult world young people

must also come to terms with. Davis's characters do so with varying degrees of success.

—Hazel K. Davis

DAVIS, Terry

Nationality: American.

PUBLICATIONS FOR YOUNG ADULTS

Fiction

Vision Quest. New York, Delacorte, 1979.
Mysterious Ways: A Novel. New York, Viking Press, 1984.
If Rock and Roll Were a Machine. New York, Delacorte, 1992.

Nonfiction

Presenting Chris Crutcher. New York, Twayne Publishers, and London, Prentice Hall International, 1997.

*   *   *

With his first novels, Terry Davis has carved a definite niche in the field of young adult literature. His works explore the lives of young men who confront seemingly insurmountable challenges and obstacles successfully. His protagonists are not perfect young men; they are adolescents who have seen their share of grief and failure. Yet, somehow, they manage to rise above what is lacking in their lives. They "gut it out" to utilize a phrase which would be in the vocabulary of both of Davis's young male protagonists, Louden and Bert. Each realizes victory in two arenas: the playing fields of his particular sport and in his quest for his own identity.

Vision Quest, Davis's first novel for young adult readers, relates the story of Louden Swain, a wrestler. Louden is attempting to drop two weight classes so that he can challenge the reportedly unbeatable Gordon Shute in their last year of high school competition. This feat requires tremendous physical discipline. Louden's mental discipline is also an integral part of the training. In his "vision quest," Louden must find his balance. Balance in life is a recurring theme in *Vision Quest*. Davis's characters must achieve the proper balance in their lives in order to find happiness and fulfillment. Louden cannot simply obsess about his sport. He has concerns in his personal life which require his attention as well: his relationship with his father, his teammates and friends, and his girlfriend Carla all have their place in Louden's life and in his quest to be the best he can be.

Bert Bowden, the protagonist of Davis's second novel, *If Rock and Roll Were a Machine,* is a fairly typical adolescent. He envisions himself as the star of the football team when, in reality he is too small for the sport. Sports are important in Bert's high school; it is the same high school attended by one Louden Swain some twenty years earlier. At one time Bert fancied himself a good student but the work of a rather sadistic teacher has all but destroyed Bert's self-image. The purchase of a motorcycle seems to signal Bert's separation from his childhood and the painful memories it holds for him. He discovers a freedom on the bike and an acceptance by other bikers which is important to his psyche. The motorcycle dealer becomes a friend and confidante; the other important influence in Bert's life is his English teacher who encourages Bert to continue working on his writing. Davis uses Bert's essays and other writing to provide insight into Bert's thoughts and feelings.

Both of Davis's novels focus on the important role which sports can play in an adolescent's life. Each person must find his (or her) own sport and work hard to become a skilled athlete. Not everyone wins every match, either. Davis ends *Vision Quest* with Louden and Shute taking the wrestling mat. It is not until *If Rock and Roll Were a Machine* that the reader learns what happened in that fateful match. In this novel, set twenty years after *Vision Quest,* Davis, in a move of wonderful irony, has Bert walk by the trophy case near the gym. There is a display case dedicated to the epitome of self-discipline, Louden Swain. Swain went on to become an Olympic wrestler. He later joined the Air Force and became an astronaut. He was killed in a shuttle explosion at the age of thirty-one. Bert does not always win his matches either. He has the opportunity to play against his nemesis, his former fifth-grade teacher Mr. Lawler. Bert is beating Lawler handily when Lawler simply refuses to continue the game. Bert's victory is a Pyrrhic one at best.

Davis is quick to puncture stereotypes as well. His characters are honest and lifelike, not simply cardboard cutouts or archetypes. There are few "dumb jocks" on the team. Both Louden and Bert are avid readers. Motorcyclists are not all tattooed, long-haired outlaws. Bert is certainly not the typical Harley rider; he is, however, confronted with the stereotypical response a motorcyclist receives when he goes off riding in unfamiliar territory. Finally, teachers are not always wonderful and supporting people. Certainly Bert has a caring teacher in Mr. Tanneran, but not all of Bert's teachers have been nurturing. The same is true for Louden Swain.

Perhaps the overriding theme of Davis's work deals with growth and change. Louden and Bert each are growing up and growing away from some of the things they held as precious when they were children. They are each a man-child, on the brink of adulthood. They waver between childhood and adulthood, reacting childishly in some circumstances then acting well beyond their years in others. Davis has captured that stage of growing up portrayed in other authors' works like Chris Crutcher and Judy Blume. His protagonists learn to face the truths, the tough truths. Davis has his "heroes" tell their truths to the reader. These truths are complex; they are frequently hurtful. Yet, by revealing these truths Davis's characters achieve that measure of growth which is not possible without pain: they are the truths which allow the characters to like themselves. Ultimately, then, Davis's message to readers is that one must be able to like oneself in order to be truly happy.

—Teri S. Lesesne

DEAVER, Julie Reece

Nationality: American. **Born:** Geneva, Illinois, 13 March 1953. **Career:** Writer for television series, 1973; teacher's aide in special education, Pacific Grove, California, 1978-88; illustrator for *Reader's Digest, New Yorker, Chicago Tribune,* and *McCall's*

Working Mother. **Awards:** Best Book for Young Adults citation; Books for the Teenage recommendation, New York Public Library; *Book List* Young Adult Editors' Choice citation; Books for Children recommendation, Library of Congress, 1988; Virginia State Reading Association Young Readers Award, 1991; ALA Quick Pick for Young Adults, 1995, for *Chicago Blues.* **Agent:** c/o HarperCollins, 10 East 53rd Street, New York, New York 10022. **Address:** 618 Sinex, Pacific Grove, California 93950, U.S.A. **E-mail Address:** Jdeaver886@aol.com.

PUBLICATIONS FOR YOUNG ADULTS

Fiction

Say Goodnight, Gracie. New York, Harper, 1988.
First Wedding, Once Removed. New York, Harper, 1990.
You Bet Your Life. New York, HarperCollins, 1993.
Chicago Blues. New York, HarperCollins, 1995.

*

Media Adaptations: Screenplay based on *Say Goodnight, Gracie.*

Julie Reece Deaver comments:

I love writing about young adults, but I never set out to write for that particular age group. As a teenager, I won a short story contest with *Seventeen Magazine,* and it was natural for me to write about characters my own age. But as I grew older, I found that my characters stayed teenagers, and that I really loved writing about that time of life when people are on the brink of adulthood.

In writing, I work without an outline, but just go where my characters want me to go. This means a lot of rewriting when the book is done, but I've found it hard to create and stick to any kind of structure or outline. The joy is in seeing what will happen to my characters.

I get a lot of fan mail asking me how to be a writer, and I like to tell my readers not to get too serious about their work, to find fun in it, and to take their inspiration not only from the classics but from all kinds of entertainment: picture books, comic strips, movies, television, songs. It all ends up adding spice to your writing.

When I was working in television, a screenwriter gave me some wonderful advice about writing. "Aim for the high," she told me, and I've found it to be true. If you write something that truly delights you, chances are your readers will be pleased, too.

* * *

Julie Reece Deaver's novels for young adults chronicle the pain and adjustments inherent in coping with change and loss. Set in Chicago and its suburbs, where Deaver grew up, the books focus on the relationships of middle-class teenagers with their friends and families.

Say Goodnight, Gracie represents an impressive writing debut. Morgan Hackett and Jimmy Woolf have been neighbors and best friends since babyhood. In fact, their mothers have maintained a close friendship since their own high school days. Now 17, Jimmy and Morgan share aspirations for stage careers and regularly travel to Chicago after school, he to dance class, she to an acting workshop. Jimmy's bid for a major stage part appears closer than Morgan's, especially when he lands an audition for a touring production of *Oklahoma.* When he blows his chance, he lashes out at Morgan, and their friendship suffers a major test. The greatest challenge is one Morgan must overcome without Jimmy. After dropping her off for class, Jimmy is killed by a drunken driver. Deaver's depiction of Morgan's denial, anger, and depression is telling and accurate. Parents and a school friend offer some help, but Morgan's healing begins only after she breaks down and acknowledges the pain to her aunt, a psychiatrist.

The novel's strength lies not only in the handling of loss and grief but in the creation of a genuine boy-girl friendship based on humor, shared interests, and deep affection. The dialogue between Morgan and Jimmy is casual, witty, and believable. Even though there are hints that romance might develop some day, the two have a strong relationship without that component. As Jimmy says, '''Lovers come and go, but friends go on and on.''' When he dies, readers join Morgan in missing him.

In contrast, *First Wedding, Once Removed* appears lightweight. As in her first novel, Deaver chooses first-person narration, this time revealing the events through the eyes of 14-year-old Alwilda (Pokie). She and her older brother Gib share intense interest in airplanes and spend hours watching planes and dreaming of flying lessons. The summer following Gib's high school graduation is bittersweet as Pokie realizes that his departure for college will signal an end to their daily camaraderie. When Gib assures her that he'll come home from college for holidays and summers, she protests that such visits won't be the same.

Her fears prove correct. Gib soon meets and falls in love with Nell, and his holidays are cut short to visit her. Pokie's second-place status is made apparent in Gib's declining interest in airplanes. When he takes the money he had saved for flying lessons to buy an engagement ring, Pokie's devastation is complete. During the same year Gib leaves for college, Pokie herself abandons her long-time friend Junior. When she begins high school, she suddenly considers the eighth grader immature.

Although there are no indications that the book is set in the past, certain aspects lend a nostalgic air. The idealized brother-sister relationship, however, fails to ring true. The refusal of Nell's parents to attend their daughter's wedding or even meet her future in-laws simply because they think she is too young to marry seems implausible. Equally unconvincing is the emphasis on the physical distance between Gib and his family, when the University of Missouri is only a day's drive away. However, the largest strain on readers' credulity is the immaturity of Pokie and Junior, who seem more like fifth and sixth graders than people in junior high and high school. For example, Junior insists on dressing up like a giant mouse for Halloween. Pokie's consistent disbelief about Gib's developing romance seems unlikely in a high-school student.

Deaver returns to surer footing in *You Bet Your Life.* While many seniors in Bess Milligan's high school class participate in work-study programs, her internship with comedy writers for the Les Komack show is unusual. Her commute to downtown Chicago gives her time to think about her mother's depression, which had led to her suicide six months earlier. Neither Bess nor her supportive father can make sense of how someone who enjoyed humor as much as her mother could sink into bouts of depression with which no one could help her cope. Understandably, Bess is reluctant to establish new relationships for fear they too will result in loss.

However, she eventually draws close to Georgia Fox, one of the comedy writers, who encourages and supports Bess. She also agrees to perform at a club with aspiring comic Elliott Heckart, although she insists that they avoid any romantic involvement. Bess' letters to her mother are searching and poignant, capturing the difficulty of dealing with the death of someone close.

In *Chicago Blues,* 17-year-old Lissa Hastings must handle abandonment, not death. Her mother, a former jazz singer and current alcoholic, decides she can no longer care for Lissa's 11-year-old sister Marnie, who is skipping school and getting into trouble. Lissa, the youngest student at a prestigious Chicago art school, has her own apartment but resents the added burden of caring for a sixth grader. Their father, a country singer, left years earlier and has provided little support of any kind, although he does contact them periodically.

Lissa provides some stability for Marnie, who in turn finds friends and makes progress in school. Their shaky finances are helped when Lissa's miniature rooms start to sell and she receives a bit of recognition for her work. The sisters' relationship deepens. Lissa communicates intermittently with her mother's friend Peggy, who chronicles the alcoholic woman's downward slide. Then Peggy changes to cautious optimism, as the girls' mother starts attending AA and struggles back to a healthy life and a steady job. Still, readers share Lissa's distrust, resentment, and sadness when the woman visits her daughters, and Marnie decides to return to her recovering mother.

Deaver is masterful at exploring the complex range of emotions engendered by loss and change in relationships among friends and family. Her inclusion of humor lightens the tone of her writing but does not diminish the insights she offers.

—Kathy Piehl

DE LINT, Charles

Has also written as Samuel M. Key. **Nationality:** Canadian. **Born:** Bussum, the Netherlands, December 22, 1951; family emigrated to Canada when author was four months old. **Family:** Married MaryAnn Harris, 1980. **Career:** Retail record store, Ottawa, Ontario, 1971-1983; musician, with Celtic bands Wickentree, 1970-1985, and Jump at the Sun, 1990-1997; small press editor/publisher, Triskell Press; regular reviewer for various fantasy magazines; full-time writer, since 1983. **Awards:** Small Press and Artisits Organization Award for fiction, 1982; First annual William L. Crawford Award for Best New Fantasy Author, International Association for the Fantastic in the Arts, 1984; Aurora (formerly known as the Casper) Canadian Science Fiction/Fantasy Award for Best Work in English, 1988, for *Jack the Giant Killer*; Readercon Small Press Award for Best Short Work, 1989, for ''The Drowned Man's Reel''; Reality 1 commendations Best Fantasy Author Award, TV Ontario's *Prisoners of Gravity,* 1991; HOMer Award for Best Fantasy Novel, CompuServe Science Fiction and Fantasy Forum, 1992, and New York Public Library's Best Books for the Teen Age, 1992, for *The Little Country*; Prix Ozone for Best Foreign Fantasy Short Story, 1997, for ''Timeskip''; YALSA Best Books for Young Adults, 1998, for *Trader.* **Address:** P. O. Box

9480, Ottawa, Ontario K1G 3V2, Canada. **Website:** http://
www.cyberus.ca/~cdl.

PUBLICATIONS FOR YOUNG ADULTS

Fiction

The Dreaming Place. New York, Atheneum, 1990.

Short Fiction

''Laughter in the Leaves,'' in *Dragons and Dreams,* edited by Jane
    Yolen, Martin H. Greenberg, and Charles G. Waugh. New
    York, Harper and Row, 1986.
''A Wish Named Arnold,'' in *Spaceships and Spells,* edited by
    Jane Yolen, Martin H. Greenberg, and Charles W. Waugh. New
    York, Harper and Row, 1987.
''One Chance,'' in *Werewolves,* edited by Jane Yolen and Martin
    H. Greenberg. New York, Harper and Row, 1988.
''Wooden Bones,'' in *Things That Go Bump in the Night,* edited by
    Jane Yolen and Martin H. Greenberg. New York, Harper and
    Row, 1989.
''There's No Such Thing,'' in *Vampires,* edited by Jane Yolen and
    Martin H. Greenberg. New York, HarperCollins, 1991.
''Fairy Dust,'' in *Wizard's Dozen,* edited by Michael Stearns. New
    York, Harcourt Brace, 1993; New York, Scholastic, 1997.
''Seven for a Secret,'' in *Immortal Unicorn,* edited by Peter S.
    Beagle and Janet Berliner. New York, HarperPrism, 1995.
''In the House of My Enemy,'' in *The Armless Maiden,* edited by
    Terri Windling. New York, Tor, 1996.

PUBLICATIONS FOR ADULTS

The Riddle of the Wren. New York, Ace, 1984.
Moonheart: A Romance. New York, Ace, 1984; London, Pan, 1990.
The Harp of the Grey Rose. Norfolk, Virginia, Donning/Starblaze, 1985.
Mulengro: A Romany Tale. New York, Ace, 1985; London,
    Macmillan, 1997.
Yarrow: An Autumn Tale. New York, Ace, 1986; London, Pan, 1992.
Jack the Giant Killer: A Novel of Urban Faerie. New York, Ace,
    1987; reprinted in *Jack of Kinrowan,* New York, Tor, 1995.
Greenmantle. New York, Ace, 1988; London, Pan, 1991.
Wolf Moon. New York, New American Library/Signet, 1988.
Svaha. New York, Ace, 1989.
Drink Down the Moon: A Novel of Urban Faerie. New York, Ace,
    1990; reprinted in *Jack of Kinrowan,* New York, Tor, 1995.
As Samuel M. Key, *Angel of Darkness.* New York, Jove, 1990.
The Little Country. New York, Morrow, 1991; London, Pan, 1993.
Spiritwalk (collected stories and novellas). New York, Tor, 1992;
    London, Macmillan, 1994.
As Samuel M. Key, *From a Whisper to a Scream.* New York,
    Berkley, 1992.
Dreams Underfoot: The Newford Collection (collected stories).
    New York, Tor, 1993.
Into the Green. New York, Tor, 1993.
The Wild Wood. New York, Bantam/Spectra, 1994.
Memory and Dream. New York, Tor, 1994.

As Samuel M. Key, *I'll Be Watching You.* New York, Jove, 1994.
The Ivory and the Horn: A Newford Collection (collected stories).
    New York, Tor, 1995.
Trader. New York, Tor, 1997.
Someplace to Be Flying. New York, Tor, 1998.

*

Critical Studies: Entry in the *St James Guide To Fantasy Writers,*
edited by David Pringle, Detroit, Gale, 1996; entry in the *Encyclopedia of Fantasy,* edited by John Clute and John Grant, New York,
St. Martin's Press, 1997.

Charles de Lint comments:

Because of my father's job with a surveying company, I grew
up in a lot of different places. We first moved from the Netherlands
to Britannia, Ontario (once on the outskirts but now pretty much
swallowed by Ottawa), lived in Western Canada for a short time,
then settled across the Ottawa River in Quebec in a rural area near
the town of Aylmer. For a three-year period we lived in Turkey and
Lebanon, but after that, my father travelled by himself and the
family stayed in Lucerne so that my older sister Kamé and I could
finally settle in and make some lasting friendships.

Having to amuse myself during those earlier years, I read
voraciously and widely. Mythic matter and folklore made up much
of that reading—retellings of the old stories (Mallory, White,
Briggs), anecdotal collections and historical investigations of the
stories' backgrounds—and then I stumbled upon the Tolkien
books which took me back to Dunsany, William Morris, James
Branch Cabell, E.R. Eddison, Mervyn Peake and the like. I was in
heaven when Lin Carter began the Unicorn imprint for Ballantine
and scoured the other publishers for similar good finds, delighting
when I discovered someone like Thomas Burnett Swann, who still
remains a favourite.

This was before there was such a thing as a fantasy genre, when
you'd be lucky to have one fantasy book published in a month, little
say the hundreds per year we have now. I also found myself reading
Robert E. Howard (the Cormac and Bran mac Morn books were my
favourites), Lovecraft, Clark Ashton Smith and finally started
reading science fiction after coming across Andre Norton's Huon
of the Horn. That book wasn't science fiction, but when I went to
read more by her, I discovered everything else was. So I tried a few
and that led me to Clifford Simak, Roger Zelazny and any number
of other fine science fiction writers.

These days my reading tastes remain eclectic, as you might
know if you've been following my monthly book review column in
The Magazine of Fantasy & Science Fiction. I'm as likely to read
Basil Johnston as Stephen King, Jeanette Winterson as Harlan
Ellison, Barbara Kingsolver as Patricia McKillip, Andrew Vachss
as Parke Godwin—in short, my criteria is that the book must be
good; what publisher's slot it fits into makes absolutely no difference to me.

But while I loved to read, I never considered making a living as
a writer. Instead I wanted to be a musician. The music I loved to
play was Celtic music, but at the time, there really wasn't much of a
career to be made from it. This was before Worldbeat, the Pogues,
Loreena McKennit and the like, so for fourteen years or so after
high school, I worked in various record stores during the day and
played gigs on the weekends.

I was writing all this time, but only for my own enjoyment. I kept up a voluminous correspondence, wrote great quantities of songs—which happily have returned to the ether from which they were drawn—and used to put together little hand-written pen & ink books of poetry that I sent to friends. My leanings towards the visual arts were absorbed with photography.

It wasn't until the mid-seventies, when I started getting together with John Charette, an artist friend of mine, on my days off from the record store, that I began to write with any seriousness, and even that only came about by chance. While John would draw, I'd write stories for him to illustrate. He passed some of my stories on to a writer he knew named Charles R. Saunders who, in turn, convinced me to send some out to one of the small press magazines that had sprung up in the wake of a growing interest in fantasy. I sold those first stories for the princely sum of $10.00 each and the proverbial light went on in my head. Here was something that I loved to do and people would actually pay me to do it.

Ah, the enthusiasm of youth. Six or seven years followed, during which I continued to work in record stores, played music on the weekends and wrote. I sent stories and novels out and back they came (except for those sold to the small press market). Finally, Andy Offutt picked up my novella ''The Fane of the Grey Rose'' for his Swords Against Darkness series and I later expanded that piece into my novel The Harp of the Grey Rose.

This is probably a good time to mention the importance of my wife MaryAnn to my career as a writer. I first moved to Ottawa to take care of a friend's apartment, but I stayed because of MaryAnn, who was born here. We've been married since 1980, but we've been together since 1975. I realized that we were meant to be together when she put up with my learning to play fiddle—she's never put me through anything remotely as irritating.

But a good relationship doesn't naturally translate into good fiction. What MaryAnn has always done, beyond editing and proofing my manuscripts before they're sent out, is make me stretch as an artist. She's the one who got me to start my first novel . . . and then finish it. She's the one who convinced me I should take my stories out of the faerie forest and see how well they might fare on a city street. And, in 1983, when I became one of the early victims of downsizing (the new owner of the record shop I was managing decided he wanted to run it himself), she's the one who convinced me to have a go at writing full-time.

Whether it was happy coincidence, or simply my own steam-engine time, I sold three novels that year and we haven't looked back since. I don't mean to imply that it's always been easy, for we've had some very lean years, but whatever else happens, we have the satisfaction of knowing that we follow our muses—MaryAnn with her art, I with my writing, both of us with our music.

These days I also dabble in art, but writing remains my first love and happily I've always been able to maintain my career in the manner that Leonard Cohen once put it when he spoke of art versus commerce: ''I didn't want to write for pay. I wanted to be paid for what I write.''

When it comes to writing ''young adult'' fiction, I don't approach it any differently than I do when writing adult fiction. I don't believe in ''writing down'' to kids. When I've been commissioned specifically to write a ''young adult'' piece, I simply keep cursing to a minimum and go for more subtle sex scenes. These are not really concessions for me, considering that I've won ''young adult'' library awards for novels that were actually written and marketed as adult fiction. I also get a lot of positive mail from

teenage readers about all of my work. I'm grateful that my work appeals to readers of all ages.

*   *   *

Poet, painter, Celtic musician, and inarguably Canada's most prolific fantasy author, Charles de Lint has been publishing verse, short stories, and novels for over twenty years. One of the pioneers in the development of ''urban'' or contemporary fantasy—fantasy which combines the motifs and themes of folklore and myth with contemporary settings and characters—de Lint writes fiction that is firmly grounded in a sense of place, often his native Ottawa and its environs. Although not known as a young adult author per se, de Lint has a wide following among those older teens who enjoy fantasy fiction, since he often uses young adults and their interests and concerns as characters and themes.

A voracious reader, as a child de Lint was attracted to the British folktales and legends, and he remembers Mallory, T. H. White, and British folklorist Katherine Briggs as his particular favorites. Later he turned to classic fantasy fiction through the works of J. R. R. Tolkien and to science fiction through the works of Andre Norton. This childhood reading has influenced de Lint's artistry in various ways. His very early writings were heavily imitative of the classic fantasy writers, both in style and content, and although he has long since developed his own unique literary vision, folklore and mythology continue to infuse his work.

De Lint's first published stories and two early novels (The Riddle of the Wren and The Harp of the Gray Rose) are of the high fantasy genre, set in secondary worlds. He still occasionally uses this type of setting—as in Wolf Moon and Into the Green, for example—but for the most part, his works are set in contemporary North American cities and are peopled with a mix of modern-day characters and figures drawn straight from Celtic and Native American folklore and mythology. De Lint credits his wife, MaryAnn, with the idea of using contemporary settings for his storylines, a suggestion that eventually led to Moonheart, published in 1984, a seminal work in the development of the genre of urban fantasy. His earlier urban fantasies—Moonheart, Spiritwalk, Yarrow, Greenmantle, Mulengro, and the Jack of Kinrowan novels—are set in various parts of his hometown of Ottawa. The Wild Wood is set in rural Quebec, where de Lint and his wife live in the summers. The Little Country, his only urban fantasy not set in North America, takes place in modern-day Cornwall, England. This use of a realistic setting for a work of fantasy allows de Lint to explore the idea of the magical in the mundane, to focus on how the mystical can interact with the physical world; this is the one theme that runs throughout the vast de Lint corpus.

More recently, de Lint has taken to setting his fiction in the imaginary city of Newford; The Ivory and the Horn and Dreams Underfoot are collections of short stories set in Newford, as are the events in Memory and Dream and de Lint's two most recent novels, Trader and Someplace to Be Flying. Newford is ''somewhere in North America''; according to de Lint, Canadians assume it in located in the United States, while Americans place it somewhere in Canada. Newford is intentionally ''Everycity,'' a typical mix of uptown neighborhoods and downtown slums, of homeless street people and middle-class WASPs—and supernatural beings. A sense of community and connectedness between these characters permeates the stories as the characters drift in and out of various storylines; the theme that runs throughout the Newford stories and novels is the interconnectedness of human relationships between people and with the environment.

Moonheart not only signalled de Lint's movement to contemporary settings for his fantasies; it also is prototypical of his use of mythology and folklore as narrative elements. In the beginning of *Moonheart,* de Lint's protagonist Sara Kendall finds a shaman's medicine pouch containing both Native American and Celtic talismans. This find, which precipitates the action of the novel, is the perfect metaphor for de Lint's works, which contain a unique mixture of North American and Celtic folkloric motifs and characters with which de Lint works his own peculiar brand of fantasy magic. This literary vision is colored by a belief in animism and the conviction that the Otherworld exists side by side with this world.

De Lint's early love of British folklore is brilliantly put to use in *Jack the Giant Killer,* the second entry in Terri Windling's ongoing Fairy Tale series of novels that recast fairy tales into new forms. This retelling of the British folktale has the story replayed out on the streets of contemporary Ottawa with a female Jack. Jacky Rowan takes on the title role in order to save the local Fairy Folk from the hounds of The Wild Hunt, a gang of motorcyclists commanded by two giants. Jacky of course wins, through a combination of a Trickster figure's luck, human bravery and determination, and a good bit of help from her friends, human and otherwise.

De Lint's only novel written expressly for young adults, *Dreaming Place,* draws primarily from Native American folklore concerning the manitou—spirits from the Otherworld—and totemism, along with images taken from the Tarot. Ash, one of the two main protagonists, is a rebellious teenager, and her closest friends are street people, one a fortune teller and the other a Native American shaman. *The Dreaming Place* belongs to the fairly recent subgenre of psychofantasy, fantasies that combine the problems of adolescence with the typical fantasy-novel elements of magic and the supernatural; here, Ash's anger at the world has helped open the door to a vampire manitou who attachs to Ash's cousin Nina, and Ash must conquer her inner anger in order to find a way to save Nina. This novel contains several of de Lint's signature elements: outsiders as protagonists, a contemporary setting, North American Indian mythology, and the overall theme of the importance of love, friendship, and compassion for one's fellow humans, as well as the idea of accepting responsibility for the consequences of one's actions.

Native American folklore also predominates in de Lint's latest novel, *Someplace to Be Flying,* a "corvid" (crow family) book based on the premise that the first race of beings were animal people, beings who could assume animal or human form. *Someplace* is a Trickster tale involving Raven and Coyote and a flock of punky "crow girls" who roam the streets of Newford looking for mischief. Colorful street people also predominate in this novel, as in many of de Lint's works.

De Lint's three Samuel Key novels all belong to the adult horror fantasy genre, as does *Mulengro,* a dark fantasy set in Newford and involving murder and Gypsy lore and for which de Lint won high praise for his accurate portrayal of this ethnic group. As in all his works, vivid characters, a contemporary setting, and the importance of being aware of the interactions between this world and the Otherworld mark these books as works of a gifted artist.

—Martha Hixon

DEUKER, Carl

Nationality: American. **Born:** San Francisco, California, 26 August 1950. **Education:** University of California at Berkeley, B.A. 1972; University of Washington, M.A. 1974; University of California at Los Angeles, teaching certificate, 1976. **Family:** Married Anne Mitchell, 1978; one daughter. **Career:** Teacher, Saint Luke School, Seattle, Washington, 1977-90; teacher, Northshore School District, Bothell, Washington, since 1991. Film and book critic, *Seattle Sun* (weekly newspaper), 1980-85. **Awards:** ALA Best Book for Reluctant Readers, 1988, for *On the Devil's Court,* and 1993, for *Heart of a Champion*; ALA Best Books for Young Adults citations, 1988, for *On the Devil's Court,* 1993, for *Heart of a Champion,* and 1997, for *Painting the Black*; South Carolina Young Adult Book Award, 1992, for *On the Devil's Court*; Golden Sower Young Adult Book of the Year (Nebraska), 1996, for *Heart of a Champion*; Pennsylvania Young Reader's Choice of the Year, 1997, for *Heart of a Champion*; Bulletin of the Center for Children's Books Blue Ribbon Book and New York Public Library Book for the Teenage, 1997, for *Painting the Black*. **Address:** 2827 Northwest 62nd St., Seattle, Washington 98107, U.S.A. **E-mail Address:** carl_deuker@norshore.wednet.edu.

PUBLICATIONS FOR YOUNG ADULTS

Fiction

On the Devil's Court. Boston, Little, Brown, 1988.
Heart of a Champion. Boston, Little, Brown, 1993.
Painting the Black. Boston, Houghton Mifflin, 1997.

Short Fiction

"If You Can't Be Lucky," in *Ultimate Sports: Short Stories by Outstanding Writers for Young Adults,* edited by Donald Gallo, New York, Delacorte, 1995.

*

Critical Studies: "On the Devil's Court" by Nancy Vasilakis, in *Horn Book,* March/April 1989, 92; "On the Devil's Court" by Gerry Larson, in *School Library Journal,* 11 November 1989, 60; "Heart of a Champion" by Diane Roback, in *Publisher's Weekly,* 31 May 1993, 56-57; "On the Devil's Court" by Ingeborg Urcia, in *Beacham's Guide to Young Adult Literature,* edited by Kirk Beetz, Vol. 7, Beacham, 1994; "Carl Deuker" by Elizabeth Bush, in *Bulletin for the Center for Children's Books* Homepage, September 1997 [Do you know if this site still exists?]; "Painting the Black," in *Book Report,* November 1997, 33.

Carl Deuker comments:

I try to write a good solid sports book that also encourages young adults to think about things that are more important than who made a basket or who hit a home run.

*   *   *

Carl Deuker's three novels for young adults, *On the Devil's Court* (1988), *Heart of a Champion* (1993), and *Painting the Black*

(1997), have established him as one of the most popular and critically-acclaimed contemporary writers of sports fiction for young adults. All three of his novels have been nominated for or have received state young reader awards and each has been cited by the American Library Association as a Best Book of the Year. In each of his works, Deuker employs teenage narrators who recount their experiences playing high school sports, as well as their struggles balancing teamwork with individuality, making ethical choices, and reconciling themselves with the flawed adults in their lives. Like the books of John Tunis, whom Deuker admires, and Chris Crutcher, Deuker's novels are more concerned with the psychology of young adults than with sports.

Deuker's first novel, *On the Devil's Court,* is also his most literary work. Overtly playing on the themes of Christopher Marlowe's *Dr. Faustus,* Deuker creates a high school senior, Joe Faust, who believes that he has sold his soul to the devil for a season of success on his basketball team. Joe's intense desire to succeed comes from two sources: his need to prove himself in a new school after his family moves from Boston to Seattle and his attempt to win the respect of his father, a world-famous geneticist. For Joe, becoming a star basketball player is one way to establish his individuality, especially when his father dictates the school he attends and even the books he reads. Joe's life is further complicated by the media frenzy surrounding his father's latest research, as well as his father's heart attack and his own ambivalence about his success on the basketball court. Joe ponders the price he may have paid for success, wondering whether or not it is the result of his own efforts or some supernatural force. Mixed with suspenseful descriptions of basketball games and discussions of Marlowe's play and Joe's values, the novel is carefully ambiguous about its supernatural elements. In the end, basketball becomes the catalyst for the new respect that Joe and his father gain for one another.

Heart of a Champion, Deuker's most powerful novel, explores the changing relationship between two boys, Seth Barham and Jimmy Winter, from age twelve, when Jimmy teaches Seth how to play ball, through their high school years as members of the same baseball team. As in *On the Devil's Court,* playing ball becomes a metaphor for the protagonists' struggles to establish their individuality and draw closer to absent fathers. In Seth's case, both he and his mother must cope with the death of Seth's father, while Jimmy's father, an alcoholic, abandons his family. As the story progresses, Seth's adulation for both Jimmy and for Mr. Winter is tempered by a growing recognition of their destructive behavior. Seth and Jimmy grow apart as the latter begins cutting classes and seeks solace in alcohol, which results in his temporary suspension from their team. Eventually, Jimmy, whose behavior has been largely countenanced because of his excellence on the ball field, is killed in an automobile accident, the result of drunk driving, and Seth and his team must rally to win the city championship. The novel ends somewhat didactically with Seth and his team playing to prove that "death doesn't happen, that everything goes on and on." For them, Jimmy has the "heart of a champion" and their win is really Seth's.

Deuker's fascination with the special treatment athletes receive continues in *Painting the Black.* According to Deuker, the book grew out of the fact that good athletes are sometimes led to believe that they are outside or above regular rules. Ryan Ward, the protagonist of *Painting the Black,* is caught up in the excitement of playing sports, but learns firsthand the dangers that come from idolizing those with athletic abilities. Like Seth Barham, Ryan

must decide what role he should take in ending the destructive behavior of his friend, Josh Daniels, the school's star quarterback and the pitcher of the Crown Hill High school baseball team. Ryan, like Deuker's other protagonists, is nearing the end of his public schooling and is confused about his future. He is also growing apart from his father, whose vision of his future is different than the one he sees for himself. When Josh moves in across the street from the Ward house in Seattle, he inspires Ryan to resurrect a childhood interest in baseball, one which ended when he broke an ankle. Daniels, it turns out, is an extraordinary player. According to Ryan, he is one of those unusual pitchers who can put "the ball right there on the borderline," which is called "painting the black."

As the year progresses, Ryan comes to idolize Josh, feeling lost when his friend tries out for the football team and living vicariously through Josh's wins. It is Josh who helps Ryan gain a spot as catcher on the baseball team and who becomes his partner as the team wins game after game. As Ryan gets to know Josh better, he discovers that his friend has flaws, though he tries to ignore them. Josh is obsessed with finding girls who "like to have some fun" and does not deal well with either anger or defeat. When Josh harasses flirtatious Celeste Honor, he draws the anger of class Valedictorian, Monica Roby. Ryan remains loyal to Josh, defending his actions to Monica, whom he subsequently rescues from two masked assailants. When Ryan recognizes one of them as Josh, he faces a moment of truth in which he discovers who he really is, the kind of event that he thought only happened in novels. Ultimately, Ryan identifies Josh to the police, but his friend is merely suspended for a couple of games and must do some community service. None of this prevents Josh from being called up to play for the Colorado Rockies. In the end, Ryan has matured and moves towards taking his charge of his own future.

Deuker's well-defined characters, carefully-crafted descriptions of baseball, football, and basketball games, and his own ambivalence about high school sports have gained him immense popularity with young adult readers. Deuker's ability to move beyond mechanical discussions of various sports and provide insight into the universal struggles of young adults have deservedly earned him the reputation as one of the most promising contemporary writers of sports fiction.

—Joel D. Chaston

DHONDY, Farrukh

Nationality: Indian. **Born:** Poona, Bombay, in 1944. **Education:** Wadia College, Poona, B.Sc.; Cambridge University, 1964-67, B.A. in English 1967; University of Leicester, M.A. in English. **Career:** English teacher, Henry Thornton Comprehensive School, Clapham, London; teacher, later head of English, Archbishop Temple School, Lambeth, London, 1974-80. Since 1985 commissioning editor for multicultural television programs, Channel Four Television, London. Writer of television scripts, plays, and fiction for adults and children. **Awards:** Children's Rights Workshop Other awards, 1977, for *East End at Your Feet,* and 1979, for *Come to Mecca, and Other Stories;* Collins/Fontana award for books for multi-ethnic Britain, for *Come to Mecca, and Other Stories;* Beckett prize, for television play, 1984; Dhondy's works were represented in "Children's Fiction in Britain, 1900-1990," an exhibition sponsored by the British Council's Literature Department, 1990.

PUBLICATIONS FOR YOUNG ADULTS

Fiction

East End at Your Feet. London, Macmillan, 1976.
Come to Mecca, and Other Stories. London, Collins, 1978.
The Siege of Babylon. London, Macmillan, 1978.
Poona Company. London, Gollancz, 1980.
Trip Trap. London, Gollancz, 1982.
Bombay Duck. London, Cape, 1990.
Black Swan. Boston, Houghton, 1992.
Janaky and the Giant and Other stories. London, Collins, 1993.

PUBLICATIONS FOR ADULTS

Plays

Mama Dragon (produced London, 1980).
Shapesters (produced London, 1981).
Kipling Sahib (produced London, 1982).
Trojans, adaptation of a play by Euripedes (produced London, 1982).
Romance, Romance; and The Bride. London, Faber, 1985.
Vigilantes (produced London, 1985). London, Hobo Press, 1988.
All the Fun of the Fair, with John McGrath and others (produced London, 1986).
Film, Film, Film (produced London, 1986).

Television Plays

Maids in the Mad Shadow, 1981.
No Problem series, with Mustapha Matura, 1983.
Good at Art, 1983.
Dear Manju, 1983.
The Bride, 1983.
Salt on a Snake's Tail, 1983.
Come to Mecca, 1983.
Romance, Romance, 1983.
The Empress of the Munshi, 1984.
Tandoori Nights series, 1985.
King of the Ghetto, 1986.
To Turn a Blind Eye, 1986.

Other

The Black Explosion in British Schools, with Barbara Beese and Leila Hassan. London, Race Today, 1982.
Editor, *Ranters, Ravers and Rhymers: Poems by Black and Asian Poets.* London, Collins, 1990.

*   *   *

Farrukh Dhondy's major works for young people appeared at a time when the United Kingdom market was crying out for quality, indigenous, multicultural writing, and he quickly became one of the leaders in this field.

Dhondy established himself with two short-story collections, *East End at Your Feet* and *Come to Mecca,* both characterized by snappy and realistic dialogue, as if the reader is overhearing a street conversation, and careful construction. The first book undoubtedly produced an impact as it was the subject of a notorious and largely racially motivated attack in a London school. Readers objected to the language used in the stories, although this was stoutly defended by local journalists and the series editor.

In *Come to Mecca* Dhondy shows a greater grasp of skill. There is a welcome variety in the style of each story: the defiance of the heroine of "Free Dinners" is as memorable as the character of Esther, who learns to grow up after taking part in a carnival, in "Go Play Butterfly"; the bitterness following racial attacks in "Salt on a Snake's Tail" is contrasted with the ironic title story, in which Dhondy ably demonstrates his dismay at "multiculturalism," a concept against which he often fulminates. In this story, Shahid, a naive Bengali teenager, becomes involved with a radical white girl, Betty, who has come to help in the strike at the clothing sweatshop where he works. When he asks her to "come to Mecca," meaning the local ballroom, Betty believes he wants to make a romantic pilgrimage to his roots, and Shahid's eyes are opened as he discovers that Betty sees him only as an issue and not as a person.

Dhondy followed these collections with a sharp and bitter novel, *The Siege of Babylon,* about a group of black adolescents who hold four hostages after a failed robbery. Although this is an angry and sometimes violent work, it loses none of the tight construction which is a hallmark of much of Dhondy's writing.

Poona Company is a much gentler book with serious undertones. Partly autobiographical, it offers fascinating vignettes of post-colonial India. Dhondy ably explores the curious mixture of class and caste and memorably portrays this eccentric, English-modelled public school. So clever is his use of words that the reader can almost feel and touch the atmosphere of the Poona bazaar. Memories that Dhondy evokes provide insight into this unfamiliar world for both black and white adolescent readers.

After an indifferent collection of stories, *Trip Trap,* in which he attempted to experiment with form, Dhondy turned his attention to other forms of media. Since then he has produced mainly scripts, although his adult novel, *Bombay Duck,* was nominated for a Whitbread Literary Award for a first novel. It is unlikely that he will write again for young adults, which is unfortunate, because voices like his need to be heard in the often insular world of children's publishing.

—Keith Barker

DICKINSON, Peter (Malcolm de Brissac)

Nationality: British. **Born:** Livingstone, Northern Rhodesia (now Zambia), 16 December 1927. **Education:** Eton College (King's scholar), 1941-46; King's College, Cambridge, B.A. 1951. **Military Service:** Served in the British Army, 1946-48. **Family:** Married 1) Mary Rose Barnard in 1953 (died 1988), two daughters and two sons; 2) Robin McKinley in 1992. **Career:** Assistant editor and reviewer, *Punch,* London, 1952-69. Chairman, Society of Authors Management Committee, 1978-80. **Awards:** Crime

Writers Association Gold Dagger award for best mystery of the year, 1968, for *The Glass-sided Ants' Nest,* and 1969, for *The Old English Peep Show*; American Library Association Notable Book Award, 1971, for *Emma Tupper's Diary*; Guardian Award, 1977, for *The Blue Hawk*; Boston Globe-Horn Book award for nonfiction, 1977; Whitbread Award and Carnegie Medal, both 1979, both for *Tulku*; *The Flight of Dragons* and *Tulku* were named to the American Library Association's ''Best Books for Young Adults 1979'' list; Carnegie Medal, 1982, for ''City of Gold''; Horn Book nonfiction award for *Chance, Luck, and Destiny*; Boston Globe-Horn Book award, 1989, for *Eva*; Whitbred Award, 1990, for *AK*. **Agent:** A.P. Watt Ltd., 20 John Street, London WC1N 2DL, England. **Address:** Bramdean Lodge, Bramdean, Alresford, Hants SO24 0JN, England.

PUBLICATIONS FOR YOUNG ADULTS

Fiction

The Weathermonger. London, Gollancz, 1968; Boston, Little Brown, 1969.

Heartsease, illustrated by Robert Hales. London, Gollancz, and Boston, Little Brown, 1969.

The Devil's Children, illustrated by Robert Hales. London, Gollancz, and Boston, Little Brown, 1970.

Emma Tupper's Diary. London, Gollancz, and Boston, Little Brown, 1971.

The Dancing Bear, illustrated by David Smee. London, Gollancz, 1972; Boston, Little Brown, 1973.

The Gift, illustrated by Gareth Floyd. London, Gollancz, 1973; Boston, Little Brown, 1974.

The Changes: A Trilogy (includes *The Weathermonger, Heartsease,* and *The Devil's Children*). London, Gollancz, 1975.

The Blue Hawk, illustrated by David Smee. London, Gollancz, and Boston, Little Brown, 1976.

Annerton Pit. London, Gollancz, and Boston, Little Brown, 1977.

Tulku. London, Gollancz, and New York, Dutton, 1979.

The Seventh Raven. London, Gollancz, and New York, Dutton, 1981.

Healer. London, Gollancz, 1983; New York, Delacorte Press, 1985.

Eva. London, Gollancz, 1988; New York, Delacorte Press, 1989.

Merlin Dreams, illustrated by Alan Lee. London, Gollancz, and New York, Delacorte Press, 1988.

AK. London, Gollancz, 1990; New York, Delacorte, 1992.

A Bone from a Dry Sea. London, Gollancz, 1992; New York, Delacorte Press, 1993.

Shadow of a Hero. London, Gollancz, 1994; New York, Delacorte Press, 1994.

Chuck and Danielle. London, Gollancz, 1994; New York, Delacorte Press, 1997.

The Lion Tamer's Daughter, and Other Stories. New York, Delacorte Press, 1997.

Other

Mandog (television series). BBC-TV, 1972.

Chance, Luck and Destiny, illustrated by David Smee and Victor Ambrus. London, Gollancz, 1975; Boston, Little Brown, 1976.

City of Gold and Other Stories from the Old Testament, illustrated by Michael Foreman. London, Gollancz, and New York, Pantheon, 1980.

Editor, *Presto! Humorous Bits and Pieces.* London, Hutchinson, 1975.

Editor, *Hundreds and Hundreds.* London, Penguin, 1984.

Contributor, *Guardian Angels,* edited by Stephanie Nettell. London, Viking, 1987.

PUBLICATIONS FOR CHILDREN

Fiction

Hepzibah, illustrated by Sue Porter. Twickenham, Middlesex, Eel Pie, 1978; Boston, Godine, 1980.

Giant Cold, illustrated by Alan E. Cober. London, Gollancz, and New York, Dutton, 1984.

A Box of Nothing, illustrated by Ian Newsham. London, Gollancz, 1985; New York, Delacorte Press, 1987.

Mole Hole, illustrated by Jean Claverie. London, Blackie, and New York, Bedrick, 1987.

Time and the Clock-mice, etcetera. Doubleday, London, 1993; Dell, New York, 1994.

PUBLICATIONS FOR ADULTS

Novels

Skin Deep. London, Hodder and Stoughton, 1968; as *The Glass-sided Ants' Nest,* New York, Harper, 1968.

A Pride of Heroes. London, Hodder and Stoughton, 1969; as *The Old English Peep Show,* New York, Harper, 1969.

The Seals. London, Hodder and Stoughton, 1970; as *The Sinful Stones,* New York, Harper, 1970,

Sleep and His Brother. London, Hodder and Stoughton, and New York, Harper, 1971.

The Iron Lion, illustrated by Marc Brown. Boston, Little Brown, 1972; London, Allen and Unwin, 1973.

The Lizard in the Cup. London, Hodder and Stoughton, and New York, Harper, 1972.

The Green Gene. London, Hodder and Stoughton, and New York, Pantheon, 1973.

The Poison Oracle. London, Hodder and Stoughton, and New York, Pantheon, 1974.

The Lively Dead. London, Hodder and Stoughton, and New York, Pantheon, 1975.

King and Joker. London, Hodder and Stoughton, and New York, Pantheon, 1976.

Walking Dead. London, Hodder and Stoughton, 1977; New York, Pantheon, 1978.

One Foot in the Grave. London, Hodder and Stoughton, 1979; New York, Pantheon, 1980.

A Summer in the Twenties. London, Hodder and Stoughton, and New York, Pantheon, 1981.

The Last House-Party. London, Bodley Head, and New York, Pantheon, 1982.

Hindsight. London, Bodley Head, and New York, Pantheon, 1983.

Death of a Unicorn. London, Bodley Head, and New York, Pantheon, 1984.

Tefuga: A Novel of Suspense. London, Bodley Head, and New York, Pantheon, 1986.

Perfect Gallows: A Novel of Suspense. London, Bodley Head, and New York, Pantheon, 1987.

Skeleton-in-Waiting. London, Bodley Head, 1989; New York, Pantheon, 1990.

Play Dead. London, Bodley Head, 1991; Mysterious Press, New York, 1992.

The Yellow Room Conspiracy. Little Brown, London, 1994; Mysterious Press, New York, 1994.

Other

The Flight of Dragons, illustrated by Wayne Anderson. New York, Harper, 1979.

Contributor, *The Great Detectives,* edited by Otto Penzler. Boston, Little Brown, 1978.

Contributor, *Verdict of Thirteen,* edited by Julian Symons. New York, Harper, 1979.

Contributor, *Imaginary Lands,* edited by Robin McKinley. Greenwillow, 1985.

"Fantasy: The Need for Realism," in *Children's Literature in Education* (New York), Vol. 17, No. 1, 39-51.

*

Media Adaptations: *A Box of Nothing* (cassette), G.K. Hall, 1988; *Changes* (television serial), BBC-TV, 1975; *The Flight of Dragons* (television movie), ABC-TV, 1982.

Biography: Entry in *Dictionary of Literary Biography,* Vol. 87, Detroit, Gale, 1989.

Critical Studies: Entry in *Contemporary Literary Criticism,* Detroit, Gale, Vol. 12, 1980, Vol. 35, 1985; "The Adolescent Novel of Ideas" by Peter Hollindale, in *Children's Literature in Education* (New York), Vol. 26, No. 1, 1995, 83-95.

Peter Dickinson comments:

I don't have much to say about my books, as I am a fairly instinctive writer, tending to go wherever the story leads me, without much by way of plan or theory. All successful books have their own voice, which establishes itself in the writer's head and keeps him on track. I like to tell stories, but any story involves more than itself. It involves its own society, and the ideas on which that is based, and a host of other complexities, all of which have to be dealt with and made to work as part of the story. I simply do the best I can to be honest about it all.

*   *   *

Peter Dickinson is a prolific author who has written almost equally for adults and for younger readers. The boundaries between the two groups of novels are hazy and young people may turn as readily to the contemporary adult tales (often variations on classical detection stories) as to the fantasies that are more remotely set. These adventures for young people can occur in the distant past or in a future post-industrial world of the "Changes." Because of the immediacy with which both are realised it is sometimes difficult to be sure (as in *The Blue Hawk*) whether the setting is in a vanished kingdom, like ancient Egypt, or in some future state.

Dickinson has a highly original, powerful imagination, which enables him to suggest the extraordinary with vivid conviction. We accept the possibility of a New Guinea tribe living in the attics of a London terrace or a chimpanzee being taught grammar in the palace of an oil sheik. He is equally capable of capturing sixth century Byzantium, China at the time of the Boxer rising, or contemporary Africa. He has a rare ability to get inside the thinking and to catch the speech styles of women as well as of men, of young and old. He is also an excellent writer of prose, with a wide vocabulary and a graphic style. Despite (or perhaps because of) his own sharp intelligence, his novels show repeated concern for the instinctual, for the hidden powers, against the coldly intellectual. Dickinson has said that young people have so much forced at them, both directly and through the media, that they need to sort out these bewildering perceptions and to fit them into some kind of structure. He believes that good fantasy novels can provide such "maps of coherence," and suggested when interviewed in *Children's Literature in Education* that "Fantasy is the poetry of ideas." Certainly such a judgement would be true of his own work.

The Seventh Raven, for example, is narrated convincingly in the voice of an articulate 17-year-old girl, involved in the excitement of an annual children's opera being presented in St. Andrews Church, Kensington. The first half of the book suggests that this will be a lively account of theatre, music, and family life built around the chaotic preparations for performing a work based on Elijah. At the dress rehearsal the novel shifts into another mode: violence intrudes into the civilised operatic world. A man is shot, terrorists burst in seeking the nephew of the future president of their country, Matteo, the unexpected arrival of the police forces them to take the children hostage, and the novel speeds towards climax in the threats of a show trial. It is not a simple thriller, with goodies and baddies, but a more complex exploration of the power of belief, for good or ill, of divided sympathies, and of human change.

Dickinson has always been interested in people with special powers (like Davy's telepathic ability to "see" the thoughts of others in *The Gift* or blind Jake's enhanced non-visual perceptiveness in *Annerton Pit*) and in cult religions (as in *The Seals*). These two concerns come together in *Healer.* The powers of healing are discovered in Pinkie Proudfoot, a girl of ten, but her story is seen through the eyes of Barry, a taciturn, unhappy boy of sixteen. Pinkie is exploited by her stepfather in the service of a dubious cult, the Foundation of Harmony, which charges the afflicted large sums for cures. Barry, whom Pinkie once cured of migraines, plans to rescue her. However, he is awkwardly uncertain of the nature of his relationship with her and very aware of another, violent side in his own nature, which he calls Bear, and is liable to break out of control. As so often in Dickinson, the story plunges towards a scene of confused violence. The novel poses questions about the nature of different, interlocking responsibilities for other people, and in a positive ending Pinkie succeeds in helping towards the integration of Barrie's personality.

Dickinson's experiences in Africa underlie a number of books. *Tefuga* is a multi-layered story in which a successful TV journalist, Nigel Jackland, is making a film in the 1980s about colonial life in northern Nigeria in the twenties, using his mother's journal as one of his sources. Cultural juxtapositions suggest that the rituals and fetishes of the British tribe are as strange as those of the Africans. Five years later, *AK* gives what one reviewer called a "flawlessly authentic" and "dreadfully real" picture of the imagined African country of Nagala at a time of continual revolution and tribal warfare. Paul, a young war orphan, becomes a kind of adoptive son to a soldier-politician, Michael Kagomi, who is by turns flung into and out of power. The greater part of the book describes the long journey of Paul and two young friends to free Michael from imprisonment in the capital, Dangoum.

Eva is a provocative and witty study of the self-destructive and life-affirming sides of human nature. In a future world where people have become effete and listless, Eva is the 13-year-old daughter of a scientist responsible for a group of chimpanzees that represents almost the last link with the animal world. Paralysed after a terrible car accident, Eva recovers after operations to discover that her parents have given permission for her "neurone memory" to be duplicated in the body of a chimpanzee. She develops a double identity between her human intelligence and her animal instincts and in an allusive conclusion leads the chimpanzees out of Egypt to begin the first cautious stages of creating a new culture.

Dickinson's interest in relating past and present has led to two novels which employ alternating narratives, one contemporary and one historical. In *A Bone from a Dry Sea* young Vinny joins her archaeologist father on an expedition to Africa, digging where once had been sea for evidence of early life. The other narrative makes an imaginative leap into the life of Li, a prehistoric creature who displays the embryonic forms of reasoning, imagination, and religious sense that will enable survival in a hypothetical version of evolution. Similarly, *Shadow of a Hero* tells two stories: one of the War of Independence waged by the fictional eastern European country of Varina against the Turks, the other a contemporary tale set in Winchester. Letta and her brothers are grandchildren of the one-time prime minister of Varina. They react in different ways to the uncertain nature of their nationalism, through politics, direct action, and cultural survival. Letta has studied Varinian poetry with her grandfather, and as his true heir has come to realise that the power of story embodied in people's memories is potentially more important than direct action.

Dickinson continues to push out the boundaries of young people's fiction both literally, in time and space, and metaphorically, in the concerns he explores and in the methods he employs. He transmutes such conventional genres as the thriller, fantasy, or science-fiction by making them channels for exploring questions of identity, morality, and ideology.

—Robert Protherough

DILLON, Eilis

Nationality: Irish. **Born:** Galway, 7 March 1920. **Education:** Ursuline Convent, Sligo. **Family:** Married 1) Cormac O Cuilleanain in 1940 (died 1970), one son and two daughters; 2) the writer Vivian Mercier in 1974. **Career:** Lecturer in Creative Writing, Trinity College, Dublin, 1971-72, and University College Dublin, 1988; lecturer at American universities and colleges on three tours, speaking on writing for children and Anglo-Irish literature, especially poetry. Fellow, Royal Society of Literature. **Awards:** *New York Herald Tribune* Children's Spring Book Festival Honorable Mention citations, 1960, for *The Singing Cave,* 1964, for *The Coriander,* and 1970, for *A Herd of Deer;* German Juvenile Book Prize Honor List citation, 1968, for *A Family of Foxes;* Notable Book citation, American Library Association, and Lewis Carroll Shelf Award, both 1970, for *A Herd of Deer;* Irish Book of the Year

award, 1991, for *The Island of Ghosts.* D.Litt.: National University of Ireland, 1992. **Died:** 1994.

PUBLICATIONS FOR CHILDREN AND YOUNG ADULTS

Fiction

An Choill Bheo (The Live Forest). Dublin, Government Publication Sale Office, 1948.

Midsummer Magic, illustrated by Stuart Tresilian. London, Macmillan, 1950.

Oscar agus an Cóiste Sé nEasóg (Oscar and the Six-Weasel Coach). Dublin, Government Publication Sale Office, 1952.

The Lost Island, illustrated by Richard Kennedy. London, Faber, 1952; New York, Funk and Wagnalls, 1954.

The San Sebastian, illustrated by Richard Kennedy. London, Faber, 1953; New York, Funk and Wagnalls, 1954.

Ceol na Coille (The Song of the Forest). Dublin, Government Publication Sale Office, 1955.

The House on the Shore, illustrated by Richard Kennedy. London, Faber, 1955; New York, Funk and Wagnalls, 1956.

The Wild Little House, illustrated by V.H. Drummond. London, Faber, 1955; New York, Criterion, 1957.

The Island of Horses, illustrated by Richard Kennedy. London, Faber, 1956; New York, Funk and Wagnalls, 1957.

Plover Hill, illustrated by Prudence Seward. London, Hamish Hamilton, 1957.

Aunt Bedelia's Cats, illustrated by Christopher Brooker. London, Hamish Hamilton, 1958.

The Singing Cave, illustrated by Richard Kennedy. London, Faber, 1959; New York, Funk and Wagnalls, 1960.

The Fort of Gold, illustrated by Richard Kennedy. London, Faber, and New York, Funk and Wagnalls, 1961.

King Big-Ears, illustrated by Kveta Vanecek. London, Faber, 1961; New York, Norton, 1963.

A Pony and a Trap, illustrated by Monica Brasier-Creagh. London, Hamish Hamilton, 1962.

The Cats' Opera, illustrated Kveta Vanecek. London, Faber, 1962; Indianapolis, Bobbs Merrill, 1963.

The Coriander, illustrated by Richard Kennedy. London, Faber, 1963; New York, Funk and Wagnalls, 1964.

A Family of Foxes, illustrated by Richard Kennedy. London, Faber, 1964; New York, Funk and Wagnalls, 1965.

The Sea Wall, illustrated by Richard Kennedy. London, Faber, and New York, Farrar Straus, 1965.

The Lion Cub, illustrated by Richard Kennedy. London, Hamish Hamilton, 1966; New York, Duell, 1967.

The Road to Dunmore, illustrated by Richard Kennedy. London, Faber, 1966.

The Cruise of the Santa Maria, illustrated by Richard Kennedy. London, Faber, and New York, Funk and Wagnalls, 1967.

The Key, illustrated by Richard Kennedy. London, Faber, 1967.

Two Stories: The Road to Dunmore and The Key, illustrated by Richard Kennedy. New York, Meredith Press, 1968.

The Seals, illustrated by Richard Kennedy. London, Faber, 1968; New York, Funk and Wagnalls, 1969.

Under the Orange Grove, illustrated by Richard Kennedy. London, Faber, 1968; New York, Meredith Press, 1969.

A Herd of Deer, illustrated by Richard Kennedy. London, Faber, 1969; New York, Funk and Wagnalls, 1970.

The Wise Man on the Mountain, illustrated by Gaynor Chapman. London, Hamish Hamilton, 1969; New York, Atheneum, 1970.

The Voyage of Mael Duin, illustrated by Alan Howard. London, Faber, 1969.

The King's Room, illustrated by Richard Kennedy. London, Hamish Hamilton, 1970.

The Five Hundred, illustrated by Gareth Floyd. London, Hamish Hamilton, 1972.

The Shadow of Vesuvius. New York, Nelson, 1977; London, Faber, 1978.

Down in the World, illustrated by Richard Kennedy. London, Hodder and Stoughton, 1983.

The Horse-Fancier. London, Macmillan, 1985.

The Seekers. New York, Scribner, 1986.

The Island of Ghosts. London, Macmillan, 1989.

Children of Bach. London, Macmillan, 1992.

Play

The Cats' Opera, adaptation of her own story (produced Dublin, 1981).

Other

Editor, *The Hamish Hamilton Book of Wise Animals,* illustrated by Bernard Brett. London, Hamish Hamilton, 1975.

Living in Imperial Rome, illustrated by Richard Kennedy. London, Faber, 1974; as *Rome under the Emperors,* Nashville, Nelson, 1975.

Editor, with others, *The Lucky Bag: Classic Irish Children's Stories,* illustrated by Martin Gale. Dublin, O'Brien Press, 1985.

PUBLICATIONS FOR ADULTS

Novels

Death at Crane's Court. London, Faber, 1953; New York, Walker, 1963.

Sent to His Account. London, Faber, 1954; New York, Walker, 1969.

Death in the Quadrangle. London, Faber, 1956; New York, Walker, 1968.

The Bitter Glass. London, Faber, 1958; New York, Appleton Century Crofts, 1959.

The Head of the Family. London, Faber, 1960.

Bold John Henebry. London, Faber, 1965.

Across the Bitter Sea. New York, Simon and Schuster, 1973; London, Hodder and Stoughton, 1974.

Blood Relations. London, Hodder and Stoughton, and New York, Simon and Schuster, 1978.

Wild Geese. New York, Simon and Schuster, 1980; London, Hodder and Stoughton, 1981.

Citizen Burke. London, Hodder and Stoughton, 1984.

The Interloper. London, Hodder and Stoughton, 1987.

Plays

A Page of History (produced Dublin, 1966).

Radio Play: *Manna,* 1960.

Other

Inside Ireland, photographs by Tom Kennedy. London, Hodder and Stoughton, 1982; New York, Beaufort, 1984.

Editor, *Modern Irish Literature: Sources and Founders.* Oxford, Clarendon Press, 1994.

*

Biography: Essay in *Contemporary Authors Autobiography Series* by Eilis Dillon. Volume 3, Detroit, Gale, 1986.

Critical Studies: Entry in *Contemporary Literary Criticism,* Volume 17, Detroit, Gale, 1981.

*   *   *

Eilis (pronounced El-eesh) Dillon, one of the most respected authors for young adults in Ireland, produced over forty novels and plays since the early 1950s. Her young adult works typically take the form of adventure tales set on or near the Aran Islands off the west coast of Ireland. Besides their settings, these novels have a number of other elements and themes in common, including: kidnappings, community loyalty, the treachery and beauty of the sea, superstition juxtaposed with religious belief, historical verisimilitude, resourceful young people who overcome great trials, and a writing style that is at once elegant and straightforward.

The salvaging of a drifting brig and the kidnapping of the protagonist, Pat Harmon, are featured events in *The San Sebastion.* In *The Lost Island,* belief in the supernatural (thought by many to be typically Irish) is an important element. *The House on the Island* finds the hero Jim O'Malley searching an Irish coastal village for his villainous uncle. *The Bitter Glass,* which takes its title from a poem by Irish poet William Butler Yeats, concerns the civil strife in 1922 Ireland. *The Singing Cave* relates the eccentric exploits of an egotistical recluse. In *The Fort of Gold* the boy heroes are forced to work for the villains Kelly and Crann. In a twist on the kidnapping theme, *The Coriander* tells of how two boys hold captive a doctor who is desperately needed by the islanders. In *The Cruise of the Santa Maria,* the young male protagonists are believed to be lost at sea on a boat classed as a "hooker." In *The Seekers,* Dillon relinquishes the Irish setting and sends her Pilgrim hero and heroine on a voyage from Yorkshire, England, to Plymouth colony in Massachusetts.

Dillon's *The Island of Ghosts* once again takes us to an Irish island village in the recent past and incorporates many of the same themes and conflicts highlighted in her earlier works. The story is narrated in part by Dara, one of the island boys, and in part by his sister Barbara. This shared narration carries out one of the obvious themes of the novel—that young women can be as capable, resourceful, and fearless as young men. In spite of the equal time granted the sexes, however, the story makes clear that there remains a tendency in these island communities to neglect the education and training of daughters in favor of sons.

Dara and his friend Brendan, who have been tutored in preparation for school on the mainland by Mr. Webb, an eccentric latecomer to the island, are subsequently kidnapped by that same

Mr. Webb. Tricked into sailing with him to the nearby "island of ghosts," which is said to be inhabited by the spirits of a long-deceased shipwrecked family, the boys are forced to become Mr. Webb's slaves. In the process, however, they learn what it means to become virtually self-sufficient, generating power and sustenance from what appears to be a sterile environment.

When, days after their secret departure, their sailing vessel is sighted empty and wrecked, the villagers are convinced that Mr. Webb and the boys have drowned. This belief, an example of a kind of islander fatalism about the fickleness of the sea, is exactly what Mr. Webb had sought to encourage. Left alone with his two protégés, he indulges in his reclusive tendencies while the boys maintain his minifarm. But not everyone believes the boys have drowned. Barbara and Cait, sisters to Dara and Brendan respectively, find that Mr. Lennon, the schoolmaster, shares their confidence that the boys—although perhaps victims of some strange plot—are alive and well and living on the island of ghosts. These three embark on a rescue mission and eventually the boys are found, and all, even Mr. Webb, live happily ever after.

Dillon manages to weave some rather complex issues into this spare plot. For example, her subtle indictment of unequal educational policies for boys and girls is quite effective. Her treatment of Mr. Webb and the varying responses of the two boys to his eccentricities reveal a man who is more disenchanted with the world than he is evil. The self-sufficiency Mr. Webb fosters turns out to be tremendously satisfying for Dara though Brendan resents every moment of his entrapment.

Besides such subtle revelations about the varieties of human response, *The Island of Ghosts* exposes young readers to certain Irish customs (for example "keening," a type of loud wailing lamentation for the dead), words, and attitudes that will expand their consciousness about a culture that has had deep and wide influences on our own. The cumulative effect of reading Dillon's works is a true feel for the Irish islanders and their mores. Dillon accomplishes this cultural transference in lucid accessible prose that never condescends or moralizes. If there is anything lacking in *The Island of Ghosts,* it is a convincing incorporation of the ghosts into the story. On balance, however, the effect of the novel is to reinforce confidence in the good instincts and competence of young people.

—Mary Lowe-Evans

DOHERTY, Berlie

Nationality: British. **Born:** Liverpool, Lancashire, 6 November, 1943. **Education:** Durham University, 1961-64, B.A. (honours) in English; Liverpool University, 1964-65, postgraduate certificate in social science; Sheffield University, 1977-78, postgraduate certificate in education. **Family:** Married Gerard Adrian Doherty in 1966 (divorced 1996); two daughters and one son. **Career:** Child care officer, Leicestershire County Council, 1966-67; home-maker, 1967-78; English teacher, schools in Sheffield, 1978-80; teacher with British Broadcasting Corp. (BBC) Radio, Sheffield, 1980-82; full-time writer, since 1983. Writer in residence at Calderdale Libraries, 1985, and Hall Cross Comprehensive School, Doncaster, England, 1986; member of Yorkshire Arts Literature

Panel, 1988-90; chair of Arvon Foundation at Lumb Bank, 1989-94. **Awards:** Library Association Carnegie Medal, 1986, Burnley/National Provincial Children's Book of the Year award, 1987, and *Boston Globe-Horn Book* Honor award, 1988, all for *Granny Was a Buffer Girl*; Television and Film award, New York, 1988, for *White Peak Farm*; Carnegie Medal, 1991, and Best Children's Play award, Writer's Guild of Great Britain, 1992, both for *Dear Nobody*; Nasen Award, 1995, for *The Golden Bird*; Carnegie commendation, 1995, for *Willa and Old Miss Annie*. **Agent:** David Higham Associates, 5-8 Lower John Street, Golden Square, London W1R 4HA, England.

PUBLICATIONS FOR YOUNG ADULTS

Fiction

How Green You Are!, illustrated by Elaine McGregor Turney. London, Methuen, 1982.
The Making of Fingers Finnigan, illustrated by John Haysom. London, Methuen, 1983.
White Peak Farm. London, Methuen, 1984.
Children of Winter, illustrated by Ian Newsham. London, Methuen, 1985.
Granny Was a Buffer Girl. London, Methuen, 1986; New York, Orchard, 1988.
Tough Luck. London, Hamish Hamilton, 1988.
Spellhorn. London, Hamish Hamilton, 1989.
Dear Nobody. London, Hamish Hamilton, 1992.
Street Child. London, Hamish Hamilton, 1993.
The Snake-Stone. London, Hamish Hamilton, 1995.
Daughter of the Sea, illustrated by Sian Bailey. New York, Hamish Hamilton, 1996, New York, Dorling Kindersley, 1998.
Running on Ice (short stories). London, Reed, 1997.

Plays

Howard's Field (first produced at Crucible Theatre, 1980).
Smells and Spells (first produced Sheffield Experimental Theatre, 1980.)
A Growing Girl's Story (first produced at Yorkshire Art Circus, Hartlepool, 1982).
A Case for Probation, in *Studio Scripts,* edited by David Self. Broadcast by BBC-Radio 4, 1983; London, Hutchingson, 1986.
The Amazing Journey of Jazz O'Neill (produced Hull, 1984).
Rock 'n' Roll Is Here to Stay (first produced at Graves Art Gallery, Sheffield, 1984).
Return to the Ebro (first produced in Manchester Library Theatre, 1985).
Tilly Mint and the Dodo, adaption of her own story (produced Doncaster, 1986).
How Green You Are!, adaption of her own story, in *Drama 1,* edited by John Foster. London, Macmillan, 1987.
Matthew, Come Home, in *Drama 2,* edited by John Foster. London, Macmillan, 1987.
Home, in *Stage Write,* edited by Gervase Phinn. London, Unwin Hyman, 1988.
Tribute to Tom, in *Drama 3,* edited by John Foster. London, Macmillan, 1988.
Dear Nobody (produced Crucible Theatre, 1993). Collins Educational, Plays Plus, 1995.

Memories (produced Calderdale, 1993).
The Sleeping Beauty (produced New Victoria Theatre, Stoke-on-Trent, 1993).

Radio Plays (for BBC Radio)

The White Bird of Peace, 1983; *The Sad Poet,* 1985; *The Mouse and His Child* (from the story by Russell Hoban), 1986; *Granny Was a Buffer Girl,* 1990; *There's a Valley in Spain,* 1990; *Dear Nobody,* 1993; *The Snow Queen* (from the story by Hans Christian Andersen), 1994; *Heidi* (from the novel by Johanna Spyr), 1996.

Television Plays

Fuzzball, BBC-TV 4, 1985; *White Peak Farm* (serial), BBC-TV 1, 1988; *Children of Winter,* BBC-TV 4, 1994.

PUBLICATIONS FOR CHILDREN

Fiction

Tilly Mint Tales, illustrated by Thelma Lambert. London, Methuen, 1984.
Paddiwak and Cosy (picture book), illustrated by Teresa O'Brien. London, Methuen, and New York, Dial Press, 1989.
Tilly Mint and the Dodo, illustrated by Janna Doherty. London, Methuen, 1989.
Snowy (picture book), illustrated by Keith Bowen. London, HarperCollins, 1992.
Old Father Christmas (picture book; from story by Juliana Horatia Ewing), illustrated by Maria Terea Meloni. London, HarperCollins, 1993.
Willa and Old Miss Annie, illustrated by Kim Lewis. London, Walker, 1994.
The Magical Bicycle (picture book), illustrated by Christian Birmingham. London, HarperCollins, 1995.
The Golden Bird, illustrated by John Lawrence. London, Heinemann, 1995.
Our Field (picture book; from story by Juliana Horatia Ewing), illustrated by Robin Bell Corfield. London, HarperCollins, 1996.
Tales of Magic and Wonder, illustrated by Juan Wijngaard. London, Walker, 1997.
Bella's Den, illustrated by Peter Melnyzcuk. London, Heinemann, 1997.

Radio Plays

The Drowned Village, 1978; broadcast by BBC-Radio 4, 1980; *Requiem,* 1982; broadcast by BBC-Radio 4, 1983; *Miss Elizabeth,* broadcast by BBC-Radio 4, 1984; 1986; *Sacrifice,* broadcast by BBC-Radio 4, 1985; 1986; *Children of Winter,* broadcast by BBC-Radio 4, 1988; 1989; *Dream of Unicorns,* 1988; broadcast by BBC-Radio 4, 1988.

Poetry

Walking on Air, illustrated by Janna Doherty. London, HarperCollins, 1993.
Big Bulgy Fat Black Slugs. London, Nelson, 1993.

PUBLICATION FOR ADULTS

Novel

Requiem. M. Joseph, 1991.
The Vinegar Jar. London, Hamish Hamilton, 1994; New York, St. Martin's Press, 1995.

*

Biography: Essay in *Something about the Author Autobiography Series,* Vol. 16, Detroit, Gale, 1993; essay in *Speaking for Ourselves, Too* compiled and edited by Donald R. Gallo, National Council of Teachers of English, 1993.

Critical Studies: Entry in *Children's Literature Review,* Vol. 21, Detroit, Gale, 1990.

Berlie Doherty comments:

Writing is such an important part of my life that I find it very difficult not to write. There is always something to write about! I don't feel quite comfortable with myself unless there are several things on the go at the same time.

There is a down-side to this compulsive writing, of course, and that is that you never really manage to take a holiday from it. When I go away I don't always remember to pack a camera (in fact I find it quite liberating to be on holiday without one) but I always pack my journal. If it gets left out I have to buy another or I'd never relax. Something, I don't know what, makes it necessary for me to record things—the meal, the sunset, the mood, the strangeness, the people, the wait in the airport. . . . I think there's an element of challenge there somehow—can I describe this scene just as it is, with all its sights and sounds and smells, can I describe how I feel about it right now, can I recreate this exotic, extraordinary/ordinary/friendly/aggressive stranger just as they are at this minute?

*   *   *

The intricacies of families—their joys, sorrows, secrets, dreams, expectations, rifts, and bonds—are at the heart of Berlie Doherty's three contemporary realistic novels (*Granny Was a Buffer Girl, White Peak Farm,* and *Dear Nobody*). Doherty's graceful, imagistic prose vividly evokes specific places, families, and individuals, but each description transcends time and place to make the particular universal. The drama in the novels, two of which were originally written for BBC radio, springs from character rather than plot; crystalline characterization resonates with lyrical emotion and keen observation. Interwoven through the novels, and hallmarking the lives of the characters, are the themes of independence and change.

The evening before her departure for a year of school in France, three generations of Jess's close-knit English family gather together in *Granny Was a Buffer Girl.* Jess, the story's narrator, feels like "a snake, shedding its skin." Both thrilled and scared, Jess looks forward to her approaching independence, but the accompanying, inevitable change causes her some anxiety. As her parents and grandparents share the family's "secrets, all its love stories, and all its ghost stories," Jess begins to understand the myriad complexions of love, and the strength of the bonds that connect and sustain family members. Even as she prepares to leave her family, she finds herself drawn closer to them. As her train departs, Jess, strengthened by the past and confident about her future, knows that "the snake had shed its skin." Deftly interwoven with the richly textured stories of her family, Jess's personal story of maturation is a celebration of the life-affirming power of familial ties.

White Peak Farm also explores the complexity of family relationships. Jeannie Tanner recounts how her family, headed by her sullen, hot-tempered father, is nearly shattered by dramatic change and lack of communication. Shattering their father's expectations, oldest daughter Kathleen elopes with the son of a neighboring enemy; Martin, the only son and heir to the farm, chooses art school over sheep farming; a tractor accident ultimately leaves Mr. Tanner crippled. Jeannie, too, faces painful decisions as she struggles with thoughts of her own future. Always independent, she decides to fulfill her long-time dream by going off to the university, but she knows that whatever she does with her life, she'll always make her way back to White Peak Farm. Ultimately it is the Tanners' attachment to the isolated Derbyshire farm—their life-blood for generations—that heals rifts and binds them together as much as their unspoken love for each other. While the novel's structure is episodic, Doherty's remarkable evocation of place and its influence on the Tanners solidly links the chapters.

In *Dear Nobody,* Helen and Chris are in their last year of high school and anticipating college when Helen discovers that she is pregnant. As the pair face impending parenthood, individual family complications are revealed: Chris works to reestablish a relationship with his mother, who deserted him years earlier; Helen discovers that her own mother was an illegitimate child. Helen refuses to have an abortion or give the baby up for adoption, choosing instead to break up with Chris, excluding him from her life even though she loves him. Initially angry and confused, Chris comes to share Helen's mature realization that "I'm not ready for forever. I'm not ready for him, and he's not ready for me." Alternating Chris's first-person perspective with the letters Helen writes to the unborn child she calls "Nobody," this emotionally charged novel, like Doherty's other works, probes the Byzantine nature of love and family relationships.

Berlie Doherty moved in a different direction with *Street Child. Children of Winter* linked the present and the distant past, but *Street Child* is a deliberate historical reconstruction of the life of Jim Jarvis, Dr. Barnado's first "client." As with the other teenage books Jim tells his own story. Eventually he finds security and an alternative family, so that his basically honest nature can re-assert itself.

Whatever the readership, the characters discover much about themselves and produce rounded solutions to their problems. *Willa and Old Miss Annie* tells of a lonely child in a new town; the old lady leads Willa through a concern for animals to a friend her own age. The book reveals a delightful sense of humour. *The Golden Bird* portrays Andrew, traumatised by the death of his father. A non-speaking role in the school play, given him by a sympathetic teacher, restores him to happiness by proving to him, as well as to his schoolfellows and his mother, that life has a lot to offer him.

In *The Snake-stone* James comes to terms with adoption. Adolescence brings problems of identity which James solves by tracing his natural mother, only to realise that his adoptive parents are his "real" parents. He knows his natural mother gave him ammonite, but she also gave him his skill as a diver; the reader learns her story simultaneously.

Berlie Doherty uses her diaries to obtain verisimilitude and bases her stories, with the exception of *Street Child,* firmly in the Derbyshire countryside near where she lives. Most have also been produced as plays and have been influenced by the comments and suggestions of local children and young people.

—Carolyn Shute, updated by Margaret Tye

DONOVAN, John

Nationality: American. **Born:** 1928. **Education:** University of Virginia, Charlottesville. **Career:** Writer. Executive director, Children's Book Council, New York, 1967-92; English teacher; examiner in U.S. Copyright Office; affiliated with St. Martin's Press. **Awards:** *Horn Book* honor list citation, Children's Book of the Year citation, Child Study Association of America, and *Book World*'s Children's Spring Book Festival honor book citation, 1969, all for *I'll Get There, It Better Be Worth the Trip; School Library Journal*'s Best Book citation, and *New York Times* Outstanding Book of the Year citation, both 1971, and National Book award, Children's Book category, 1972, all for *Wild in the World;* Children's Book of the Year citation, Child Study Association of America, 1976, for *Family;* Children's Reading Roundtable award, Children's Reading Roundtable of Chicago, 1983. **Died:** In 1992.

PUBLICATIONS FOR YOUNG ADULTS

Fiction

The Little Orange Book, illustrated by Mauro Caputo. New York, Morrow, 1961.
I'll Get There, It Better Be Worth the Trip. New York, Harper, 1969; London, Macdonald, 1970.
Wild in the World. New York, Harper, 1971.
Remove Protective Coating a Little at a Time. New York, Harper, 1973.
Good Old James, illustrated by James Stevenson. New York, Harper, 1974.
Family: A Novel. New York, Harper, 1976.
Bittersweet Temptation. New York, Zebra Books, 1979.
Translator, *Paul and Virginia.* Chester Springs, Dufour, 1983.

PUBLICATIONS FOR ADULTS

Other

The Businessman's International Travel Guide (nonfiction). New York, Stein and Day, 1971.
Editor, *U.S. & Soviet Policy in the Middle East.* New York, Facts on File, 1972.
Riverside Drive (play; produced New York, 1964).

*

Media Adaptations: *I'll Get There, It Better Be Worth the Trip* (film), 1973.

Critical Study: Entry in *Children's Literature Review,* Volume 3. Detroit, Gale, 1978, pp. 139-143; entry in *Contemporary Literary Criticism,* Volume 35. Detroit, Gale, 1985, pp. 51-56.

*   *   *

The late John Donovan was a poet of loneliness and alienation. Each of his five books, whether set on a remote mountain in New Hampshire or in the steel and glass canyons of Manhattan, features characters who are painfully isolated by circumstance or by their family's failures of communication.

In developing these themes, Donovan earned a reputation, as the British critic John Rowe Townsend put it, for being a "taboo buster." Donovan cheerfully employed expletives which had previously been deleted from books for young adults and dealt frankly with such subjects as sexual experimentation, parental alcoholism, death, and, in his first book, *I'll Get There, It Better Be Worth the Trip,* an (arguably) homosexual encounter between the thirteen-year-old protagonist Davy and his best friend, Douglas.

Since his parents' divorce, Davy has been living with his grandmother in a small Massachusetts town. When she dies, he is sent to live with his mother, a borderline alcoholic, in her Manhattan apartment. He is also reunited, during weekend visits, with his father, who has remarried. Davy's assessment of his parents' lack of enthusiasm for him is expressed in what he says of his much-loved dog, Fred: ". . .when you make a dog like Fred part of your family, he is a full-time member, not just someone who will be around when you want him to." Unfortunately Fred is killed by a hit-and-run driver soon after Davy and his new friend Douglas give physical expression to their friendship (they kiss each other and, spending the night together, do what is described as "it.") Davy is emotionally devastated and is consumed by guilt: "Nothing would have happened if I hadn't been messing around with (Douglas) Altschuler," he thinks bitterly. Eventually, in part through his father's support and in part through sharing his feelings with Douglas, Davy comes to terms with his guilt. "Life should be beautiful," Altschuler says, but most readers will realize that if that goal represents the "there" of the book's title, getting to it for these two emotionally vulnerable kids from fractured families will be a very difficult trip, indeed.

The family of John Gridley, the protagonist of Donovan's second novel, *Wild in the World,* is beyond fractured: its twelve members are dead. Indeed, the first six pages of the book are a laconic record of the deaths, by suicide, fire, fever, and accident, of John's parents and his six brothers and four sisters. John, the youngest, is left alone to manage the family farm on a remote mountain in New Hampshire. Emotionally he is a burnt-out case going through the motions of living but, in fact, simply waiting to die. This changes when a stray dog (or is it a wolf?) appears on the farm and John "adopts" it as a pet and calls it "Son." The name is symbolic of the emotions which Son awakens in John. These ripen as John nurses Son back to health after he is bitten by a rattlesnake. Reflecting on his newfound capacity for expressing emotion, John thinks, "Son taught me a lot. Human critters hold back." Ultimately it is John, not Son, who dies first. His untimely death, though it has tragic elements, is at least partially redeemed by his earlier discovery of his life-affirming love for Son. That the wolf/dog lives on gives tangible expression to the survival of that love. *Wild*

*in the World'*s powerful themes are expressed in an understated, almost laconic style which lends the story the timeless power of folklore or parable.

Donovan returns to the breezy, wry style and urban setting of *I'll Get There, It Better Be Worth the Trip* in his third novel, *Remove Protective Coating a Little At a Time.* Unlike Davy Ross, fourteen-year-old Harry Knight is not the product of a broken home, but his parents, Bud and Toots, are more like uncaring older siblings than father and mother. Though rich in material matters, Harry is obviously impoverished in terms of family love, support, and attention. He finds these, almost by accident, in the person of Amelia Myers, a seventy-two-year-old self-sufficient street person whom he meets in Central Park. Learning to care for Amelia and to feel responsible for her enables Harry to end his emotional isolation.

Donovan's fourth book, *Good Old James,* conveys a large message for all ages: in James, the retired protagonist, readers will discover that adolescents have no monopoly on loneliness—it is a regular and troubling visitor to the lives of the elderly, as well.

Donovan's consistent thematic concerns reach an apotheosis in his fifth and final book, *Family,* the story of the escape from a college lab of four apes who were to have been part of a scientific experiment. Three of the apes—Sasha, the narrator; Dilys, a mature female; and Lollipop, an infant, have been born in captivity. The fourth—the largest and most powerful, a male named Moses—is a "natural," born in the wild. From Moses the other three acquire not only the more sophisticated language of the wild apes but also a learned past consisting of stories, legend, and traditions. This establishes, for them, a context of connectedness and further nourishes the spirit of family which the apes increasingly experience, a spirit which few of Donovan's earlier human characters have known. Choosing to tell the apes' story in Sasha's first person voice gives Donovan the ironic distance he needs to comment on the failings of human society, especially its persistent equation of change with progress. Sasha is a brilliant creation—grave, compassionate and—despite his disingenuous denials—reflective. When winter arrives and Moses and Lollipop are killed by hunters, Sasha and Dilys have no choice but to return to the lab and their human captors, sustained by their memories and their hope, as Sasha states, "that Man is not lost." Donovan's sensitive handling of this theme in all of his books and his groundbreaking courage and candor in writing about important but formerly "taboo" subjects establishes his as a creative presence of enduring importance in the world of young adult literature.

—Michael Cart

DORRIS, Michael Anthony

Nationality: American. **Born:** Louisville, Kentucky, 30 January 1945. **Education:** Georgetown University, Washington, D.C., B.A. 1967; Yale University, New Haven, Connecticut, M.Phil. 1970. **Family:** Married Louise Erdrich, *q.v.,* in 1981; two sons and four daughters. **Career:** Assistant Professor, Johnston College, University of Redlands, California, 1970, and Franconia College,

New Hampshire, 1971-72; Instructor, 1972-76, Assistant Professor, 1976-79, Associate Professor, 1979, Professor of anthropology, 1979-88, Chair of Native American Studies Department, 1979-88, and Adjunct Professor, 1988-97, Dartmouth College, Hanover, New Hampshire. Director of urban bus program, summer, 1967, 1968, 1969; Native American Council chairman, 1973-76, 1979; visiting Assistant Professor, University of New Hampshire, 1973-74, and University of Auckland, 1980; consultant to National Endowment for the Humanities, 1976-97; consultant to television stations, including Los Angeles Educational Television stations, including Los Angeles Educational Television, 1976, and Toledo Public Broadcast Center, 1978. Editor, *Viewpoint,* 1967; member of editorial board, *American Indian Culture and Research Journal,* 1974-97; member of editorial advisory board, MELUS, 1977-79. **Awards:** Woodrow Wilson fellowship, 1967, 1980; National Institute of Mental Health research grant, 1971; Spaulding-Potter Program grant, 1973; Dartmouth College faculty fellowship, 1977; Guggenheim fellowship, 1978; Rockefeller fellowship, 1985; Indian Achievement award, 1985; National Endowment for the Arts fellowship, 1988; National Book Critics Circle award, for nonfiction, 1989; Scott O'Dell Award for Historical Fiction, 1993, for *Morning Girl.* **Died:** 11 April 1997.

PUBLICATIONS FOR YOUNG ADULTS

Fiction

Morning Girl. New York, Hyperion, 1992.
Guests. New York, Hyperion, 1994.
Sees Behind Trees. New York, Hyperion, 1996.
The Window. New York, Hyperion, 1997.

PUBLICATIONS FOR ADULTS

Fiction

A Yellow Raft in Blue Water. New York, Holt, 1987; London, Hamilton, 1988.
With Louise Erdrich, *Crown of Columbus.* New York, and London, Harper Collins, 1991.
Rooms in the House of Stone. Minneapolis, Minnesota, Milkweed, 1993.
Working Men: Stories. New York, Holt, 1993.
Cloud Chamber: A Novel. New York, Scribner, 1997.

Other

Native Americans: Five Hundred Years After. New York, Crowell, 1975.
Contributor, *Racism in the Textbook.* New York, Council on Interracial Books for Children, 1976.
Contributor, *Separatist Movements,* edited by Ray Hill. Elmsford, New York, Pergamon, 1979.
Guide to Research on North American Indians, with Arlene B. Hirschfelder and Mary Gloyne Byler. Chicago, American Library Association, 1983.
The Broken Cord, with foreword by Louise Erdrich. New York, Harper, 1987; London, Harper Collins, 1990.

Route Two. Northridge, California, Lord John Press, 1990.
Paper Trail: Essays. New York, HarperCollins, 1994.
Editor, with Emilie Buchwald, *The Most Wonderful Books: Writers on Discovering the Pleasures of Reading.* Minneapolis, Milkweed, 1997.

*

Critical Studies: *Conversations with Louise Erdrich and Michael Dorris,* edited by Allan Chavkin and Nancy Feyl Chavkin. Jackson, University Press of Mississippi, 1994.

*   *   *

An author of both fiction and nonfiction until his untimely death in 1997, Michael Dorris writes with intelligence, humor, and affection. He is an author who asks such questions as: What makes each person unique? What binds us together? What keeps us apart? What shapes our values, customs, traditions and defines our ethnicity?

Although the themes about which he writes are universal, Dorris, a member of the Modoc tribe, often uses Native Americans as the principal protagonists in his works of fiction. His three major nonfiction books deal in part or entirely with Native American subjects.

In 1975, Michael Dorris wrote: "There are many things that Indian people are not: They are not and never have been a unified, homogenous population; they are not represented by the stereotypes of Hollywood or most fiction; they are not people without history, languages, literatures, sciences, and arts; they are not vanished, and are not vanishing." This comes from the text, written by Dorris, which accompanies Joseph Farber's black and white photographs in the book, *Native Americans: Five Hundred Years After.*

Dorris has worked over the years to provide his readership with an expanded vision of what it means to be Native American, by moving beyond the stereotypes that mainstream Americans are served with typical Thanksgiving meals, or hear in some commonly used linguistic expressions like "Indian givers," or use as mascots for athletic teams like the "Redskins."

A source that enables readers to find high quality books on Native Americans without stereotypes is the 1983 American Library Association's *Guide to Research on North American Indians.* Dorris coauthored this book with Arlene Hirschfelder and Mary Gloyne Byler. The annotations included in this reference book provide a summary of the work, discuss the periods of time covered, and note inclusion of maps, artwork, photographs, appendix, and bibliography. The authors note if a work is based on field work or manuscript files, and indicate if sources are published or unpublished, primary or secondary.

In *The Broken Cord,* another nonfiction book, the author tells the story of his oldest son, Adam, from birth until he leaves home at the age of twenty. Adam is at the center of the book and is accompanied by a huge cast of characters. However, this is also Michael Dorris's story, the story of a proud, loving father, struggling to come to terms with his adopted son's multiple physical and mental problems caused by an alcoholic mother. On another level, *The Broken Cord* details the tragedy of Fetal Alcohol Syndrome (FAS), a set of preventable birth defects which are caused as a direct result of alcohol consumed during pregnancy and passed to developing babies. By making *The Broken Cord* Adam's story, Dorris gives FAS the face and name of a person for whom readers can come to care about. This focus raises the issue above the statistics and facts.

Throughout the book, Dorris mourns what could have been for his own child and others victimized by FAS, individuals who will be hindered or prevented from developing a joy for life and a curiosity for what goes on around them. Dorris does not explain as much as he paints a picture. In describing Adam's legacy, Dorris writes: "He came from a country that encouraged the farthest sight, but he forever stood in a well shaped by a bottle." Dorris made the transition from nonfiction to fiction in 1987 with *A Yellow Raft in Blue Water*, a story told in three voices. An adult novel, it also speaks to young adults. Rayona, fifteen years old, is the novel's first narrator. Tall like her largely absent dad and with skin that announces she's a blend of her African American father and her Native American mother, Rayona wonders where she will fit into the world. She lives with her mother, Christine. Mother and daughter have no money and have no prospects for getting any. They begin a journey home to the reservation and to Aunt Ida, Christine's mother.

Christine abandons Rayona on the reservation. Aunt Ida becomes all Rayona has. Ida, a large, forbidding woman, whose "real life is squeezed between the times of her programs on TV," refuses to speak English with Rayona but instead uses only her native Indian language. Rayona may know her family's native tongue, but everything else on the reservation is new and strange to her. She is forced to deal with a new school and no friends, her enigmatic Aunt Ida and other relatives whom she meets for the first time, comments and taunts on her mixed heritage, and the unwanted attention of a young priest. Fleeing from the priest, Rayona, completely on her own, finds help, gains confidence, earns money, and later respect. Rayona exhibits strength and persistence—qualities she has in common with her mother and grandmother, who each tell their own story before the novel ends.

Multiple viewpoints, intricate family dynamics, and complex characters keep *A Yellow Raft on Blue Water* absorbing, while allowing the readers to draw their own conclusions as to why the characters are the way they are and what their futures will be.

While continuing to utilize Native American society and culture, Michael Dorris changes settings and focus in his more recent novels, *Morning Girl* and *Crown of Columbus*. Both books focus on the effects Columbus's encounter with the indigenous people of the Americas. Set five hundred years apart, the two novels are directed toward different audiences.

Morning Girl is Dorris's first book directed at a younger audience, upper elementary through ninth graders. Set in 1492 in the Caribbean, it tells a story of the Tainos, the native people of a small Bahamian island. Michael Dorris won the O'Dell Award for Historical Fiction for *Morning Girl*. Taking turns doing the narration, Morning Girl, a twelve year old Taino, and Star Boy, her younger brother, tell of the beauty and hardships of their lives.

Morning Girl and Star Boy think of themselves as different as night is from day. But, together with their parents, they mourn the miscarriage of a new sibling, miss their deceased grandfather,

survive a powerful hurricane and public ridicule, and celebrate life with other community members. Morning Girl and Star Boy may see the world from different vantage points but they grow to appreciate and love each other in their nurturing environment.

Dorris captures the richness of his characters' culture in lyrical language. By depicting the Tainos' life clearly, Dorris helps the readers visualize the people that Columbus names incorrectly and considers only for servitude. Columbus expresses this thought in his diary, and Dorris quotes from the diary to end *Morning Girl*.

In *Crown of Columbus*, which Michael Dorris coauthored in 1991 with his wife, Louise Erdrich, the authors create a fictional couple who wrestle with Columbus's continued influence and the controversy the world faces on the quincentennial anniversary of his voyage. Written as an adult book, it has some appeal for young adults, although the only teen in the book is not fully developed. What *Crown of Columbus* has is adventure, intrigue, and mystery. The novel touches but does not dwell on the destructive elements of discovery and colonization.

Michael Dorris earlier combined his writing with teaching and developing the Native American studies program at Dartmouth College. His articles and reviews appeared in the *New York Times*, the *Washington Post*, the *Los Angles Times*, and various national magazines.

Dorris's books explored universal issues such as the quest for personal identity, coming of age, and the importance of personal accountability for behavior. Dorris created strong characters and wrote with a distinct sense of time and place, presenting multiple sides of complex issues. These factors combined with Michael Dorris's skillful use of language and imagery give readers fiction and nonfiction books that nourish and ask for additional consideration from their audience.

—Karen Ferris Morgan

———

DOUGLAS, Michael. *See* **CRICHTON, Michael.**

———

DOYLE, (Sir) Arthur Conan

Nationality: British. **Born:** Edingburgh, Scotland, 22 May 1859. **Education:** The Hodder School, Lancashire, 1868-70, Stonyhurst College, Lancashire, 1870-75, and the Jesuit School, Feldkirch, Austria (editor, *Feldkirchian Gazette*), 1875-76; studied medicine at the University of Edinburgh, 1876-81, M.B. 1881, M.D. 1885. **Career:** Served as senior physician at a field hospital in South Africa during the Boer War, 1899-1902; knighted, 1902. **Family:** Married 1) Louise Hawkins in 1885 (died 1906), one daughter and one son; 2) Jean Leckie in 1907, two sons and one daughter. Practised medicine in Southsea, Hampshire, 1882-90; full-time writer from 1891; stood for Parliament as Unionist candidate for Central Edinburgh, 1900, and tariff reform candidate for the Hawick Burghs, 1906. Member, Society for Physical Research, 1893-1930 (resigned). **Awards:** LL.D.: University of Edinburgh, 1905. Knight of Grace of the Order of St. John of Jerusalem. **Died:** 7 July 1930.

PUBLICATIONS

Novels

A Study in Scarlet. London, Ward Lock, 1888; Philadelphia, Lippincott, 1890.

The Mystery of Cloomber. London, Ward and Downey, 1888; New York, Fenno, 1895.

Micah Clarke. London, Longman, and New York, Harper, 1889.

The Firm of Girdlestone. London, Chatto and Windus, and New York, Lovell, 1890.

The Sign of the Four. London, Blackett, 1890; New York, Collier, 1891.

The White Company. London, Smith Elder, 3 vols., 1891; New York, Lovell, 1 vol., 1891.

The Doings of Raffle Haw. London, Cassell, and New York, Lovell, 1892.

The Great Shadow. New York, Harper, 1892.

The Great Shadow, and Beyond the City. Bristol, Arrowsmith, 1893; New York, Ogilvie, 1894.

The Refugees. New York, Longman, 3 vols., 1893; New York, Harper, 1 vol., 1893.

The Parasite. London, Constable, 1894; New York, Harper, 1895.

The Stark Munro Letters. London, Longman, and New York, Appleton, 1895.

Rodney Stone. London, Smith Elder, and New York, Appleton, 1896.

Uncle Bernac: A Memory of Empire. London, Smith Elder, and New York, Appleton, 1897.

The Tragedy of Korosko. London, Smith Elder, 1898; as *Desert Drama,* Philadelphia, Lippincott, 1898.

A Duet, with an Occasional Chorus. London, Grant Richards, and New York, Appleton, 1899; revised edition, London, Smith Elder, 1910.

The Hound of the Baskervilles. London, Newnes, and New York, McClure, 1902.

Sir Nigel. London, Smith Elder, and New York, McClure, 1906.

The Lost World. London, Hodder and Stoughton, and New York, Doran, 1912.

The Poison Belt. London, Hodder and Stoughton, and New York, Doran, 1913.

The Valley of Fear. New York, Doran, 1914; London, Smith Elder, 1915.

The Land of Mist. London, Hutchinson, and New York, Doran, 1926.

Short Stories

Mysteries and Adventures. London, Scott, 1889; as *The Gully of Bluesmandyke and Other Stories,* 1892.

The Captain of the Polestar and Other Tales. London, Longman, 1890; New York, Munro, 1894.

The Adventure of Sherlock Holmes. London, Newnes, and New York, Harper, 1892.

My Friend the Murderer and Other Mysteries and Adventures. New York, Lovell, 1893.

The Memoirs of Sherlock Holmes. London, Newnes, 1893; New York, Harper, 1894.

The Great Keinplatz Experiment and Other Stories. Chicago, Rand McNally, 1894.

Round the Red Lamp, Being Facts and Fancies of Medical Life. London, Methuen, and New York, Appleton, 1894.

The Exploits of Brigadier Gerard. London, Newnes, and New York, Appleton, 1896.

The Man from Archangel and Other Stories. New York, Street and Smith, 1898.

The Green Flag and Other Stories of War and Sport. London, Smith Elder, and New York, McClure, 1900.

Hilda Wade (completion of book by Grant Allen). London, Richards, and New York, Putnam, 1900.

Adventures of Gerard. London, Newnes, and New York, McClure, 1903.

The Return of Sherlock Holmes. London, Newnes, and New York, McClure, 1905.

Round the Fire Stories. London, Smith Elder, and New York, McClure, 1908.

The Last Galley: Impressions and Tales. London, Smith Elder, and New York, Doubleday, 1911.

His Last Bow: Some Reminiscences of Sherlock Holmes. London, Murray, and New York, Doran, 1917.

Danger! and Other Stories. London, Murray, 1918; New York, Doran, 1919.

Tales of Adventure and Medical Life. London, Murray, 1922; as *The Man from Archangel and Other Tales of Adventure,* New York, Doran, 1925.

Tales of Long Ago. London, Murray, 1922; as *The Last of the Legions and Other Tales of Long Ago,* New York, Doran, 1925.

Tales of the Ring and Camp. London, Murray, 1922; as *The Croxley Master and Other Tales of the Ring and Camp,* New York, Doran, 1925.

Tales of Terror and Mystery. London, Murray, 1922; as *The Black Doctor and Other Tales of Terror and Mystery* (selection), New York, Doran, 1925.

The Case-Book of Sherlock Holmes. London, Murray, and New York, Doran, 1927.

The Maracot Deep and Other Stories. London, Murray, and New York, Doubleday, 1929.

The Conan Doyle Historical Romances. London, Murray, 2 vols., 1931-32.

The Field Bazaar. Privately printed, 1934; Summit, New Jersey, Pamphlet House, 1947.

The Professor Challenger Stories. London, Murray, 1952.

Great Stories, edited by John Dickson Carr. London, Murray, and New York, London, House and Maxwell, 1959.

Strange Studies from Life, Containing Three Hitherto Uncollected Tales, edited by Peter Ruber. New York, Candlelight Press, 1963.

The Annotated Sherlock Holmes, edited by William S. Baring-Gould. New York, Schocken, 1976; as *The Sherlock Holmes Illustrated Omnibus,* London, Murray-Cape, 1978.

The Best Supernatural Tales of Arthur Conan Doyle, edited by E.F. Bleiler. New York, Dover, 1979.

Sherlock Holmes: The Published Apocrypha, with others, edited by Jack Tracy. Boston, Houghton Mifflin, 1980.

The Best Science Fiction of Arthur Conan Doyle, edited by Charles G. Waugh and Martin H. Greenberg. Carbondale, Southern Illinois University Press, 1981.

The Edinburgh Stories. Edinburgh, Polygon, 1981.

The Final Adventures of Sherlock Holmes, edited by Peter Haining. London, W.H. Allen, 1981.

Uncollected Stories, edited by John Michael Gibson and Roger Lancelyn Green. London, Secker and Warburg, and New York, Doubleday, 1982.

The Best Horror Stories of Arthur Conan Doyle, edited by Martin H. Greenberg and Charles G. Waugh. Chicago, Academy, 1988.

The Supernatural Tales of Sir Arthur Conan Doyle, edited by Peter Haining. Slough, Berkshire, Foulsham, 1988.

The Baker Street Dozen, edited by Pj Doyle and E.W. McDiarmid. New York, Congdon and Weed, 1989.

Memories and Adventures. Oxford, Oxford University Press, 1989.

The Red-Headed League. Mankato, Minnesota, Creative Education, 1989.

Sherlock Holmes: Two Complete Adventures. Philadelphia, Running Press, 1989.

Tales for a Winter's Night. South Yarmouth, Massachusetts, Curley, 1989.

When the World Screamed and Other Stories. San Francisco, Chronicle, 1990.

The Adventure of the Solitary Cyclist. Mankato, Creative Education, 1991.

The Adventures of the Speckled Band and Other Stories. Des Moines, Perfection Form, 1991.

The Horror of the Heights and Other Tales of Suspense. San Francisco, Chronicle, 1992.

Six Great Sherlock Holmes Stories. New York, Dover, 1992.

Plays

Jane Annie: or, The Good Conduct Prize, with J.M. Barrie, music by Ernest Ford (produced London, 1893). London, Chappell, and New York, Novello Ewer, 1893.

Foreign Policy, adaptation of his story ''A Question of Diplomacy'' (produced London, 1893).

Waterloo, adaptation of his story ''A Straggler of 15'' (as *A Story of Waterloo,* produced Bristol, 1894; London, 1895; as *Waterloo,* produced New York, 1899). London, French, 1907; in *One-Act Plays of To-Day,* 2nd series, edited by J.W. Marriott, Boston, Small Maynard, 1926.

Halves, adaptation of the story by James Payne (produced Aderdeen and London, 1899).

Sherlock Holmes, with William Gillette, adaptation of works by Doyle (produced Buffalo and New York, 1899; Liverpool and London, 1901).

A Duet (A Duologue) (produced London, 1902). London, French, 1903.

Brigadier General, adaptation of his stories (produced London and New York, 1906).

The Fires of Fate: A Modern Morality, adaptation of his novel *The Tragedy of Korosko* (produced Liverpool, London, and New York, 1909).

The House of Temperley, adaptation of his novel *Rodney Stone* (produced London, 1910).

The Pot of Caviare, adaptation of his story (produced London, 1910).

The Speckled Band: An Adventure of Sherlock Holmes (produced London and New York, 1910). London, French, 1912.

The Crown Diamond (produced Bristol and London, 1921). Privately printed, 1958.

It's Time Something Happened. New York, Appleton, 1925.

Poetry

Songs of Action. London, Smith Elder, and New York, Doubleday, 1898.

Songs of the Road. London, Smith Elder, and New York, Doubleday, 1911.

The Guards Came Through and Other Poems. London, Murray, 1919; New York, Doran, 1920.

The Poems of Arthur Conan Doyle: Collected Edition (includes play *The Journey*). London, Murray, 1922.

Other

Contributor, *The Fate of Fenella.* London, Hutchinson, 1892.

Contributor, *My First Book.* London, Chatto and Windus, and Philadelphia, Lippincott, 1894.

The Great Boer War. London, Smith Elder, and New York, McClure, 1900.

The War in South Africa: Its Cause and Conduct. London, Smith Elder, and New York, McClure, 1902.

Works. (Author's Edition). London, Smith Elder, 12 vols., and New York, Appleton, 13 vols., 1903.

The Fiscal Question. Hawick, Roxburgh, Henderdon, 1905.

An Incursion into Diplomacy. London, Smith Elder, 1906.

The Story of Mr. George Edalji. London, Daily Telegraph, 1907.

Through the Magic Door (essays). London, Smith Elder, 1907; New York, McClure, 1908.

The Crime of the Congo. London, Hutchinson, and New York, Doubleday, 1909.

Divorce Law Reform: An Essay. London, Divorce Law Reform Union, 1909.

Sir Arthur Conan Doyle: Why He Is Now in Favour of Home Rule. London, Liberal Publication Department, 1911.

The Case of Oscar Slater. London, Hodder and Stoughton, 1912; New York, Doran, 1913.

Contributor, *What the Worker Wants.* London, Hodder and Stoughton, 1912.

Divorce and the Church, with Lord Hugh Cecil. London, Divorce Law Reform Union, 1913.

Great Britain and the Next War. Boston, Small Maynard, 1914.

In Quest of Truth, Being Correspondence Between Sir Arthur Conan Doyle and Captain H. Stansbury. London, Watts, 1914.

To Arms! London, Hodder and Stoughton, 1914.

The German War. London, Hodder and Stoughton, 1914; New York, Doran, 1915.

Western Wanderings (travel in Canada). New York, Doran, 1915.

The Outlook on the War. London, Daily Chronicle, 1915.

An Appreciation of Sir John French. London, Daily Chronicle, 1916.

A Petition to the Prime Minister on Behalf of Sir Roger Casement. Privately printed, 1916.

A Visit to Three Fronts: Glimpses of British, Italian, and French Lines. London, Hodder and Stoughton, and New York, Doran, 1916.

The British Campaign in France and Flanders. London, Hodder and Stoughton, 6 vols., 1916-20; New York, Doran, 6 vols., 1916-20; revised edition, as *The British Campaigns in Europe 1914-18,* London, Bles, 1 vol., 1928.

The New Revelation; or, What Is Spiritualism? London, Hodder and Stoughton, and New York, Doran, 1918.

The Vital Message (on spiritualism). London, Hodder and Stoughton, and New York, Doran, 1919.

Our Reply to the Cleric. London, Spiritualists' National Union, 1920.

A Public Debate on the Truth of Spiritualism, with Joseph McCabe. London, Watts, 1920; as *Debate on Spiritualism,* Girard, Kansas, Haldeman Julius, 1922.

Spiritualism and Rationalism. London, Hodder and Stoughton, 1920.

Editor, *D. D. Home: His Life and Mission,* by Mrs. Douglas Home. London, Paul Trench Trubner, and New York, Dutton, 1921.

The Wanderings of a Spiritualist. London, Hodder and Stoughton, and New York, Doran, 1921.

Spiritualism: Some Straight Questions and Direct Answers. Manchester, Two Worlds, 1922.

The Case for Spirit Photography, with others. London, Hutchinson, 1922; New York, Doran, 1923.

The Coming of the Fairies. London, Hodder and Stoughton, and New York, Doran, 1922.

three of Them: A Reminiscence. London, Murray, 1923.

Our American Adventure. London, Hodder and Stoughton, and New York, Doran, 1923.

Memoirs and Adventures. London, Hodder and Stoughton, and Boston, Little Brown, 1924.

Translator, *The Mystery of Joan of Arc,* by Léon Denis. London, Murray, 1924; New York, Dutton, 1925.

Our Second American Adventure. London, Hodder and Stoughton, and Boston, Little Brown, 1924.

Editor, *The Spirtualist's Reader.* Manchester, Two Worlds Publishing Company, 1924.

The Early Christian Church and Modern Spiritualism. London, Psychic Bookshop, 1925.

Contributor, *My Religion.* London, Hutchinson, 1925; New York, Appleton, 1926.

Psychic Experiences. London and New York, Putnam, 1925.

The History of Spiritualism. London, Cassell, 2 vols., and New York, Doran, 2 vols., 1926.

Pheneas Speaks: Direct Spirit Communications. London, Psychic Press, and New York, Doran, 1927.

What Does Spiritualism Actually Teach and Stand For? London, Psychic Bookshop, 1928.

A Word of Warning. London, Psychic Press, 1928.

An Open Letter to Those of My Generation. London, Psychic Press, 1929.

Contributor, *If I Were a Preacher.* London, Cassell, and New York, Harper, 1929.

Our African Winter. London, Murray, 1929.

The Roman Catholic Church: A Rejoinder. London, Psychic Press, 1929.

The Edge of the Unknown. London, Murray, and New York, Putnam, 1930.

Works (Crowborough Edition). New York, Doubleday, 24 vols., 1930.

Conan Doyle's Stories for Boys. London, Cupples and Leon, 1938.

Sherlock Holmes: Selected Stories. Oxford, Oxford University Press, 1951.

Sherlock Holmes: A Definitive Text, edited by Edgar W, Smith. Heritage Press, 1957.

Famous Tales of Sherlock Holmes. Dodd, 1958.

The Glorious Hussar: The Best of the Exploits and Adventures of the Brigadier Gerard. New York, Walker, 1961.

The Boys' Sherlock Holmes: A Selection From the Works of A. Conan Doyle. New York, Harper, 1961.

Strange Studies from Life, edited by Peter Ruber. New York, Candlelight Press, 1963.

The Complete Adventures and Memoirs of Sherlock Holmes: A Facsimile of the Original Strand Magazine Stories, 1891-1893, illustrated by Sidney Paget. New York, C.N. Potter, 1975.

Arthur Conan Doyle on Sherlock Holmes. London, Favil, 1981.

Essays on Photography, edited by John Michael Gibson and Roger Lancelyn Green. London, Secker and Warburg, 1982.

Letters to the Press: The Unknown Conan Doyle, edited by John Michael Gibson and Roger Lancelyn Green. London, Secker and Warburg, and Iowa City, University of Iowa Press, 1986.

The Sherlock Holmes Letters, edited by Richard Lancelyn Green. London, Secker and Warburg, 1986.

*

Media Adaptations: *The Adventures of Sherlock Holmes* (film), Twentieth Century Fox, 1939; *The Hound of the Baskervilles* (film), Twentieth Century Fox, 1939; *A Study in Scarlet* (film); *His Last Bow* (film); *The Firm of Girdlestone* (film); *The Exploits of Brigadier Gerard* (film); Doyle's writings have also been adapted for plays, television broadcasts, and filmstrips, as well as numerous other film productions.

Biography: *Conan Doyle: His Life and Art* by Hesketh Pearson, London, Methuen, 1943, New York, Walker, 1961; *The Life of Sir Arthur Conan Doyle* by John Dickson Carr, London, Murray, and New York, Harper, 1949; *Conan Doyle: A Biography* by Pierre Nordon, London, Murray, 1966, New York, Holt Rinehart, 1967; *A Biography of the Creator of Sherlock Holmes* by Ivor Brown, London, Hamish Hamilton, 1972; *The Adventure of Conan Doyle: The Life of the Creator of Sherlock Holmes* by Charles Higham, London, Hamish Hamilton, and New York, Norton, 1976; *Conan Doyle: A Biographical Solution* by Ronald Pearsall, London, Weidenfeld and Nicolson, 1977; *Conan Doyle: Portrait of an Artist* by Julian Symons, London, G. Whizzard, 1979; *The Quest for Sherlock Holmes: A Biographical Study of the Early Life of Sir Arthur Conan Doyle* by Own Dudley Edwards, Edinburgh, Mainstream, 1982, Totowa, New Jersey, Barnes and Noble, 1983; *Arthur Conan Doyle* by Don Richard Cox, New York, Ungar, 1985; *The Unrevealed Life of Doctor Arthur Conan Doyle: A Study in Southsea* by Geoffrey Stavert, Horndean, Hampshire, Milestone, 1987; *Arthur Conan Doyle* by Jacqueline A. Jaffe, Boston, Twayne, 1987; *The Quest for Sir Arthur Conan Doyle: Thirteen Biographers in Search of a Life* edited by Jon L. Lellenberg, Carbondale, Southern Illinois University Press, 1987.

Bibliography: *A Bibliographical Catalogue of the Writings of Sir Arthur Conan Doyle* by Harold Locke, Tunbridge Wells, Kent, Webster, 1928; *The World Bibliography of Sherlock Holmes and Dr. Watson* by Ronald Burt De Waal, Boston, New York Graphic Society, 1975; *A Bibliography of A. Conan Doyle* by Richard

Lancelyn Green and John Michael Gibson, Oxford, Clarendor Press, 1983.

Manuscript Collection: Humanities Research Center, University of Texas, Austin.

Critical Study: *The Private Life of Sherlock Holmes* by Vincent Starrett, New York, Macmillan, 1933, London, Nicholson and Watson, 1934, revised edition, Chicago, University of Chicago Press, 1960, London, Allen and Unwin, 1961; *In the Footsteps of Sherlock Holmes* by Michael Harrison, London, Cassell, 1958, New York, Fell, 1960, revised edition, Newton Abbot, Devon, David and Charles, 1971, New York, Drake, 1972; *The Man Who Was Sherlock Holmes* by Michael and Mollie Hardwick, London, Murray, and New York, Doubleday, 1964; *A Sherlock Holmes Commentary* by D. Martin Dakin, Newton Abbot, Devon, David and Charles, 1972; *Sherlock Holmes in Portrait and Profile* by Walter Klinefelter, New York, Schocken, 1975; *The Sherlock Holmes File* by Michael Pointer, Newton Abbot, Devon, David and Charles, 1976; *Sir Arthur Conan Doyle's Sherlock Holmes: The Short Stories: A Critical Commentary* by Mary P. De Camara and Stephen Hayes, New York, Monarch, 1976; *The Encyclopedia Sherlockiana* by Jack Tracy, New York, Doubleday, 1977, London, New English Library, 1978; *Sherlock Holmes and His Creator* by Trevor H. Hall, London, Duckworth, 1978, New York, St. Martin's Press, 1983; *Sherlock Holmes: The Man and His World* by H.R.F. Keating, London, Thames and Hudson, and New York, Scribner, 1979; *Who's Who in Sherlock Holmes* by Scott R. Bullard and Michael Collins, New York, Taplinger, 1980; *The International Sherlock Holmes* by Ronald Burt De Waal, Hamden, Connecticut, Shoe String Press, and London, Mansell, 1980; *A Sherlock Holmes Compendium* edited by Peter Haining, London, W.H. Allen, 1980; *Sherlock Holmes in America* by Bill Blackbeard, New York, Abrams, 1981; *Sherlock Holmes: A Study in Sources* by Donald A. Redmond, Montreal, McGill-Queen's University Press, 1982; Entry in *Dictionary of Literary Biography,* Volume 18, Detroit, Gale, 1983; Volume 70, 1988; *A Study in Surmise: The Making of Sherlock Holmes* by Michael Harrison, Bloomington, Indiana, Gaslight, 1984; *The Complete Guide to Sherlock Holmes* by Michael Hardwick, London, Weidenfeld and Nicolson, 1986; *Sherlock Holmes: A Centenary Celebration* by Allen Eyles, London, Murray, 1986; *Elementary My Dear Watson: Sherlock Holmes Centenary: His Life and Times* by Graham Nown, New York, Ward Lock, 1986.

*   *   *

For the greater part of the twentieth century, the contributions of Sir Arthur Conan Doyle to young adult fiction have been at best underrated and at worst obscured by his Sherlock Holmes mysteries. It has been only in the recent past that the science fiction and adventure stories featuring Professor E. Challenger have resurfaced and become recognized for the quality works they are.

The exploits of Professor Challenger, chronicled in *The Lost World,* "The Poison Belt," "When the World Screamed," "The Disintegration Machine," and *The Land of Mist,* bear an important similarity to the Holmes stories. In both series, the escapades of a famous man are narrated from the viewpoint of a lesser man. Professor Challenger's chronicler is generally the young newspaper reporter Edward Malone, but the two are joined in some of their adventures by outdoorsman Lord John Roxton and Professor Summerlee. This larger cast of regular characters is not seen in the other works by Doyle.

The characters who make up the party itself are a great source of material for the author; their personalities and professions are diverse enough to create many an interesting interplay. Their interactions are not always of the civilized Holmes sort, as clashes of opinion and personality are commonplace. Challenger is a far cry from the Holmesian hero. As his title would denote, he is a teacher, a man of science, specializing in zoology. He is characterized as small and somewhat misshapen, but possessing enormous strength. His personality is volatile. He is given to argue with anyone on any subject, to become suddenly terribly violent, and to exhibit an enormous egotism. Given the sheer size and intensity of his personality, the other players can only react to and interact with him; Challenger is always the center of attention. Summerlee, for example, is also a scientist, a zoologist, and argues incessantly with Challenger on any and all scientific topics that arise. Roxton, on the other hand, is a hearty, even-tempered man who competently leads the group in dangerous situations. Lastly there is Malone, the seemingly naive man, who sees all with the wondering eyes of one who is carried along on the coattails of his fellows. It is Malone who reveals most of the joy of discovery and implications of human nature in the stories, and he is an excellent narrator with whom the reader may identify. The personalities of this intrepid group add a unique twist to the peculiar situations in which they find themselves.

Unlike the Holmes stories, Challenger adventures feature a much larger view of the world and deal with topics that are more far-reaching or have a greater bearing on the world at large. While Holmes and Watson rarely leave the microcosm of London, Challenger and his crew journey both the world and their own backyards, encountering many strange cultures and happenings as they go. The exotic locales, coupled with his lively and unusual characters, gives Doyle the freedom to incorporate more exciting adventure and science fiction plot elements. He creates fantasy worlds in these places where the reader is more prone to believe such strange events could occur. Challenger does use a keen sense of observation and superior reasoning skills, as does Holmes, but the added action appeals more to the younger reader.

In some ways, the exploits of Professor Challenger and his party are more complex in structure than their Holmesian counterparts. Along with their broader scope and greater physical action, the Challenger stories show far more wit and ironic humor than is normally seen in Doyle's work. Doyle uses this ironic humor to counter the main events in the story, accenting the gravity and horror of these events with just a touch of the farcical. As Charles Higham, in his biography of the author, *The Adventures of Conan Doyle,* points out, a particular scene of this type occurs in *The Lost World.* Upon returning from South America, Professor Challenger lectures at Queen's Hall on his discoveries, and presents a mysterious box:

Come then, pretty, pretty! [he said] in a coaxing voice.

An instant later, with a scratching, rattling sound, a most horrible and loathsome creature [a pterodactyl] appeared from below and perched itself upon the side of the case. Even the unexpected fall of the Duke of Durham into the orchestra, which occurred at that moment, could not distract the petrified attention of the vast audience.

The Duke's mishap, while comical in itself, serves to further stress the horror of the assembled crowd. More wry humor surfaces in "The Poison Belt," when Challenger expects all the inhabitants of the world to be exterminated by a huge cloud of gas from the heavens. He explains to his manservant, "I'm expecting the end of the world today, Austin," to which Austin replies, "Yes, sir, what time sir?"

Following the popular, if less successful release of "The Poison Belt," Challenger reappeared in the short story "When the World Screamed." In it, the professor believes that the earth is itself a living organism, wholly unaware of the pestilence of the human race upon itself. He drills a shaft through the earth's crust, eight miles down to a soft cortex. One writer suggested that the entire story hinged on a sexual symbolism in which the female earth is conquered by Challenger's penetrating, phallic drill. Challenger also appears in a short story entitled "The Disintegration Machine," in which he foils an evil scientist's plot to develop and sell to the highest bidder the ultimate weapon. Neither story appeared to be particularly popular, the latter having drifted almost entirely into obscurity.

Conan Doyle went on to explore the spirit world in *The Land of Mists*. Himself an avid spiritualist, he brought his beliefs to issue in this last Challenger novella. Spiritualism suffered then, as a science, from the same skepticism with which it is seen today. Edward Shanks, in reviewing the novella for *London Mercury* in 1926, attacked Conan Doyle's conviction of the truth of Spiritualism on the basis of his errors in getting the style and title of the Duke of Pomfret right! Wrote Shanks, "one cannot help feeling that a writer who can go so far astray with the usages of the tangible world might make serious mistakes with those of the intangible."

Along with the sin of being "an incurably inaccurate writer," Doyle was also accused of sinning by omitting a strong love interest in *The Lost World*. Indeed, the reviewer W. M. Payne in *The Dial* could find precious little else to criticize. However, the reviewer for *The Nation*, in 1912, applauded the work, stating: "To deal realistically with a theme of this kind requires no slight art. It would be easy enough to cram up a few books of geology and anthropology, and then imagine some way of getting a modern man back among the wild growths of the past; but to give the real thrill of living adventure to battles with flying elephants and ape-men is another matter. The creator of Sherlock Holmes has done this, and he has made the four adventurers in this lost world genuine men of distinct characters."

The Lost World became, for the most part, a critical and commercial success. Doyle so enjoyed his Challenger character that he dressed as the professor for publicity photos after the publication of the first story. Shortly before his death in 1930, Doyle described Challenger as "a character who has always amused me more than any other which I have created." Doyle's stories of Professor Challenger's exploits are rightly identified as science fiction and compare favorably to the works of Jules Verne. But equally his Challenger stories which have been out of print until recently, still appeal to adolescents today, with their unstuffy, irascible, fun-loving, childish hero.

—Nicholas Ranson

DOYLE, Brian

Nationality: Canadian. **Born:** Ottawa, Ontario, 12 August 1935. **Education:** York Street Public School, Ottawa; Glebe Collegiate Institute, Ottawa; Carleton University, Ottawa, B.A. in journalism 1957. **Family:** Married Jacqueline Doyle in 1960; one son and one daughter. **Career:** Journalist, Toronto *Telegram*; since 1969 high school English teacher at Glebe Collegiate, Ottawa, Ontario, and Ottawa Technical High School, Ottawa; also head of English department at Glebe Collegiate Institute; has worked variously as a waiter, taxi driver, bricklayer, and jazz singer; writer. **Awards:** Canadian Library Association Book of the Year awards, 1983, for *Up to Low,* and 1989, for *Easy Avenue;* Vicky Metcalf Body of Work award, Canadian Authors Association; Mr. Christie Book of the Year award; three times runner up, Governor General's award, Canadian Authors Association. **Address:** 539 Rowanwood, Ottawa, ON K2A 3C9, Canada.

PUBLICATIONS FOR YOUNG ADULTS

Fiction

Hey, Dad! Toronto, Groundwood Books, 1978.
You Can Pick Me up at Peggy's Cove. Toronto, Groundwood Books, 1979.
Up to Low. Toronto, Groundwood Books, 1982.
Angel Square. Toronto, Groundwood Books, 1984.
Easy Avenue. Toronto, Groundwood Books, 1988.
Covered Bridge. Toronto, Groundwood Books, 1990.
Spud Sweetgrass. 1992.
Uncle Ronald. Vancouver, British Columbia, and Buffalo, New York, Douglas & McIntyre, 1996

PUBLICATIONS FOR ADULTS

Other

Editor, *The Who's Who of Children's Literature.* London, Evelyn, 1968.
English and Englishness. London, and New York, Routledge, 1989.

*

Media Adaptations: *Angel Square* (film directed by Ann Wheeler).

Biography: Essay in *Something about the Author Autobiography Series,* Volume 16, Detroit, Gale, 1993.

Critical Studies: Entry in *Children's Literature Review,* Volume 22, Detroit, Gale, 1991.

*   *   *

Brian Doyle's work presents universal themes of adolescence in deceptively light and refreshingly humorous stories. Deeply grounded in both place and character, Doyle's blunt though careful articulation of detail and event results in fast-moving and enjoyable narratives. While in several of his novels there is a clear focus on child-father relationships, other themes such as self-determination, independence, grief, responsibility, and love are also raised.

Doyle's work can be divided into three groups. His first two novels, *Hey, Dad!* (1978) and *You Can Pick Me up at Peggy's Cove* (1979), are first person accounts told by a sister and younger brother respectively and set in contemporary times. *Hey Dad!* tells the story of a family car trip across Canada from Ottawa to the west coast of Vancouver Island. Megan, the adolescent narrator, describes in hilarious detail the characters they meet, the mishaps they encounter, and her own diminishing resentment towards her rambunctious father as she learns how to talk with him. In *You Can Pick Me up at Peggy's Cove*, Megan's younger brother Ryan is sent to stay with his aunt in Peggy's Cove, Nova Scotia, for the summer when their father temporarily "runs away" from the family. Colorful characters and a tentative exploration of Ryan's confusion at his father's abandonment carry this story through a somewhat tedious plot as Ryan falls in with a juvenile delinquent and tries to shock his father into coming back for him.

More successful and intriguing in their flirtation with fantastic characters and events, Doyle's next four novels all take place in Ottawa and the nearby Gatineau Hills at the end of, and shortly following, World War II. In *Up to Low* (1982), he introduces Tommy, the narrator, and a crowd of other characters including the fanatically neat Aunt Dottie, Mean Hughie, his wife Poor Bridget, daughter Baby Bridget, and old Willie the Hummer. A trip with his father out to the backwoods of Low to open up the family cabin involves Tommy in a strange series of events with strong symbolic undertones. Mean Hughie dies and Tommy finds himself in a rowboat with his first love, Baby Bridget, transporting Hughie's coffin up the Gatineau River. Tommy is also the main protagonist in *Angel Square* (1984), a story which precludes *Up to Low* chronologically. In a wonderful evocation of Lowertown, one of Ottawa's working class neighborhoods, Tommy describes Angel Square as "a dangerous square to cross four times a day" because of fights between the French Canadian "Pea Soups," the Jews, and the Catholic "Dogans." Not belonging to any of these groups, Tommy finds his identity in emulating "the Shadow," a radio mystery character. In this role, he sends notes to his love, Margot Lane, and investigates a neighborhood crime, only revealing his identity when he has established himself as a hero.

Doyle's light humor and intimate narrative style continue in a third series of two books, beginning with *Easy Avenue* (1988), the story of Hubbo O'Driscoll, a poor boy who moves away from Lowertown and starts hobnobbing with the rich. Colorfully named characters such as the wealthy golfer Mr. Donald D. DonaldmcDonald, Miss Collar-Cuff, the aristocratic old woman Hubbo reads to, and his first love, Fleurette Featherstone Fitchell, contribute to a thread of fantasy which weaves through this story and is further reinforced as an anonymous benefactor begins to send Hubbo monthly cheques. Hubbo's story continues in Doyle's next work, *Covered Bridge* (1990), but like *Up to Low*, this sequel moves into the rural setting of the lower Gatineau where the O'Driscoll family has relocated to a small farm. Hubbo takes a job as caretaker of the town's old covered bridge and in doing so embroils himself in a mystery involving a ghost, a lovelorn postman, a foolish priest, and a crazy goat. Lighter than his other stories, *Covered Bridge* presents a madcap ghost mystery for readers who like adventures.

In what is hopefully only the first of a third series of stories, Doyle's *Spud Sweetgrass* (1992) brings together all of his strongest elements: a quick-moving plot, a strong sense of place, slightly

fantastic characters, and an underlying foundation of deeper themes and moral conflicts. John or "Spud" Sweetgrass is still grieving for his trombone-playing father who died a few months before, and he is suspended from school for standing up to a bully teacher. Spud has a part-time job selling chips from a van in Chinatown and when he accidentally learns that oil from chip trucks all over the city is being dumped in the Ottawa River, he and his friends, Connie Pan and Dink the Thinker, organize themselves to solve this environmental crime. Multicultural elements are woven unobtrusively into the story as is Spud's growing awareness of the complexity of human nature.

Doyle's stories provide an atypically humorous and balanced view of adolescent adventures and coming of age experiences. His entertaining narratives capture the reader's attention while his intimate settings and strongly individualized characters beg sequels.

—Patricia Hill

DRAPER, Sharon Mills

Nationality: American. **Born:** Cleveland, Ohio, 1949. **Education:** Pepperdine University, Malibu, California, B.A. 1970; Miami University, Oxford, Ohio, M.A. 1973. **Family:** Married Larry Draper; two sons and two daughters. **Career:** English teacher and head of the English Department, Walnut Hills High School, Cincinnati, Ohio, since 1970; associate at Mayerson Academy for professional development of teachers; board of directors, National Board for Professional Teaching Standards, since 1997. **Awards:** First prize, *Ebony* magazine's Gertrude Williams Literary Contest, 1991, for short story, "One Small Torch"; Coretta Scott King Genesis Award for best new fiction, and Best Book for Young Adults citation, both 1995, both for *Tears of a Tiger*; Excellence in Teaching Award, National Council of Negro Women, 1997; Ohio Governor's Educational Leadership Award, 1997; Ohio Teacher of the Year, 1997; National Teacher of the Year, 1997. **Agent:** Janell Agyeman, Marie Brown Literary, Inc., 636 NE 72nd St., Miami, Florida 33138, U.S.A.

PUBLICATIONS FOR YOUNG ADULTS

Tears of a Tiger. New York, Atheneum, 1994.
Ziggy and the Black Dinosaurs, illustrated by James Ransome. East Orange, New Jersey, Just Us Books, 1994.
Ziggy and the Black Dinosaurs: Lost in the Tunnel of Time, illustrated by Michael Bryant. East Orange, New Jersey, Just Us Books, 1996.
Forged by Fire. New York, Atheneum, 1997.
Shadows of Caesar's Creek. East Orange, New Jersey, Just Us Books, 1997.

*

Critical Studies: "An 'A' for Creativity: Variety is on Teacher of the Year's Lesson Plan," in *USA Today,* 17 April 1997, D4; "America's Top Teacher Gives Tough Assignments—And Plenty of Support" by David Holmstrom, in *Christian Science Monitor*

(Boston), 5 May 1997, 12; ''Sharon Draper Named Teacher of the Year at White House Ceremony,'' in *Jet* (Chicago), 12 May 1997, 25; ''Two New Awards,'' in *American Libraries* (Chicago), June 1995, 487.

*   *   *

Didacticism permeates Sharon Mills Draper's fiction. Enlightening readers about African American heritage and its importance to modern life, Draper's works address the problems African Americans face in a predominantly white society, specifically stereotyping of black males. They also examine the dynamics of African American families and communities. Her themes and characters resemble those found in books by Walter Dean Myers and Bruce Brooks. Draper's fiction is energetic and intense, as characters become self aware and attain emotional growth. She often creates mystery plots as a means for characters to be introspective and explore their identities. She sets her books in Cincinnati where she lives and teaches, suggesting a familiarity with her characters and community that enhances their realism.

Draper introduces readers to four characters in *Tears of a Tiger.* Andrew Jackson, known as Andy, is the primary protagonist who begins to break down mentally when his best friend Robert Washington is killed in a car accident. Andy was the driver of the car and blames himself for Robert's death because he was drunk, celebrating a basketball victory. Tyrone Mills and B.J. Carson were also passengers, and they escaped from the burning car, watching helplessly as Robert, who was trapped, burned to death. Over a seven-month period, Andy begins to gradually self-destruct. He loses interest in basketball and school and succumbs to depression, but no one realizes the depths of Andy's despair. Draper reveals Andy's decline through the use of chapters consisting of police reports, news articles, letters, diary entries, poems, and phone conversations. Differing points of view are presented, including those of the boys' girlfriends, Hazelwood High School teachers, and Andy's counselor, Dr. Carrothers. These alternating narratives accurately capture the speech and idioms of high school students and African Americans.

Draper provides examples of subtle racism faced by the characters, including clerks who suggest that they leave stores and teachers who underestimate their intelligence and ambition. When Andy's friends approach the school counselor for help, she dismisses their concerns. Andy begins to strip off his clothes at a school talent show, an obvious cry for attention and metaphor for his loss of self, but he is rushed from the stage and ignored. His coach minimizes his loss and urges him to just concentrate on his game and have a positive attitude. Andy's younger brother Monty is the only one aware that Andy is desperately sad, providing the crying tiger metaphor that Draper appropriates for her title, but he is too immature to seek help. Andy's mother is preoccupied with her sorority and planning cotillions, and she refers to Robert's death as an ''unfortunate incident.'' Andy tells her that he needs help, but she is in denial and unable to comprehend his needs, remarking that he will be stronger and wiser for his pain. Andy's father can only harangue Andy about his poor grades, warning him that he must assimilate into the white professional world and telling him to ''Be a man. Be strong,'' instead of understanding why he is failing. Both of his parents attempt to maintain a facade to hide their family's reality which only worsens through neglect.

Gerald Nickelby, a minor character in *Tears of a Tiger,* is the protagonist of Draper's *Forged by Fire,* which is told primarily from his point of view. His mother, Monique, a drug addict, leaves three-year-old Gerald alone in their apartment and he accidentally sets a fire. When his mother is sent to prison for neglect, Gerald is raised by his Aunt Queen, who is the antithesis to Monique. Relying on a wheelchair because of her brittle bones, Aunt Queen nurtures Gerald and scrimps to provide him necessities and luxuries, including a bicycle. On his ninth birthday, Monique returns with a new husband, Jordan Sparks, and a daughter, Angel. Aunt Queen realizes that Angel has been traumatized but abruptly dies before she can protect the children. Gerald comes of age prematurely, assuming adult roles such as calling for paramedics in a vain attempt to save Aunt Queen.

Gerald's life experiences a sudden shift when he moves into his mother's home. He discovers that Jordan is molesting Angel. His mother is in denial about her husband, and Gerald seeks help from the father of his friend, Robert Washington. Gerald and Angel prevail in court, and while Jordan is in prison, Angel undergoes a rebirth through her study of ballet. Just when she earns the lead in a performance, Jordan returns. He promises that he will not hurt the children, but the family lives under the constant threat of domestic violence. Gerald determines to survive and save his sister and mother. He acquires strength through adversity and bears the burden of being responsible for everyone. He confronts and outsmarts Jordan to protect Angel and ultimately rescues her from death. Although the novel presents Gerald as a role model, much of it seems contrived and predictable. Jordan's last name, Sparks, perpetuates the fire imagery which symbolizes Gerald's and Angel's pain, strengthening, and salvation.

Draper's Black Dinosaurs series make her lessons most accessible and appealing to readers. Again, she uses four characters. *Ziggy and the Black Dinosaurs* introduces Rico, Ziggy, Rashawn, and Jerome, who form a club somewhat like the Black Heritage Club to which Rashawn's father belongs. Named for Rashawn's plastic dinosaur, the club has passwords representing black culture such as ''Tuskegee,'' and the boys build a clubhouse in Ziggy's backyard. While burying their treasures, they discover a box of human bones. At the same time, they are trying to solve the mystery of who cut down their basketball goals. Befriending Mr. Greene, the grandson of former slaves, they learn that corrupt developers destroyed an African American cemetery on the site to build houses. The book stresses ethnic pride and inter-generational friendships and promotes respect for heritage and sentiment over materialism and greed.

Two other Black Dinosaur mysteries extend beyond the home to the community. The boys are trapped underneath their school in *Lost in the Tunnel of Time* after Mr. Greene tells them about his grandfather who escaped slavery and provides a map that is the catalyst for their adventure. While waiting for rescuers, each boy has a dream representing some aspect of personal freedom; the imagery is symbolic, such as a golden eagle soaring above the earth. The boys recover artifacts from the underground railroad and begin to understand their personal history. In the *Shadows of Caesar's Creek,* the African Heritage Club sponsors a field trip for the four boys. They are joined by four girls and Noni, a counselor who instructs them about the woods and African American and Native American history. Declaring herself a descendant of Caesar, an escaped slave who became an Indian chief, she tries to teach the children about racial and gender stereotypes. Bored, the boys decide to explore the wilderness at night like young Indians did as manhood challenges. They use their ingenuity to solve problems and return home realizing that history books omit many details and are sometimes incorrect. Each Black Dinosaur book concludes with an instructive history article and also includes a bibliography and additional sources for information. Draper attempts to make history understandable and entertaining by creating a variety of characters with whom readers can identify.

Draper's focus on instruction sometimes overwhelms the stories. She also relies on exclamations, oversimplifications, and clichés to stress her points and characters' anger. The plots are predictable and conclusions are not always satisfactory. Many of her characters live in isolation and are misunderstood. Adults are mostly depicted as extremes, either abusive or nurturing. Yet most of her young adult characters, especially the Black Dinosaurs, are valuable role models who through example can empower readers.

—Elizabeth D. Schafer

DUANE, Diane

Nationality: American. **Born:** New York, New York, 18 May 1952. **Education:** Dowling College, New York, 1970-71; Pilgrim State Hospital of Nursing, 1971-74, R.N. 1974. **Family:** Married Robert Peter Smyth (who writes as Peter Morwood), 1987. **Career:** Psychiatric nurse, Payne Whitney Clinic, Cornell New York Hospital Medical Center, New York, 1974-76; assistant to writer, 1976-78; free-lance novelist and television writer, since 1978; staff writer, Filmation Studios, Reseda, California, 1983-84. **Awards:** *School Library Journal* Best Books, 1985, for *Deep Wizardry*; *Voice of Youth Advocates'* Best Science Fiction and Fantasy titles for Young Adults, 1986, for *Deep Wizardry* and *The Door into Shadow*; New York Public Library Books for the Teen Age citation, 1994, for *Dark Mirror*. **Agent:** Donald Maass Literary Agency, 157 West 57th Street, Suite 703, New York, New York 10019, U.S.A.

PUBLICATIONS FOR YOUNG ADULTS

Novels

So You Want to Be a Wizard? New York, Delacorte, 1983; London, Corgi, 1991.

The Wounded Sky. New York, Pocket Books, 1983; London, Titan, 1988.

My Enemy, My Ally. New York, Pocket Books, 1984; London, Titan, 1989.

Deep Wizardry. New York, Delacorte, 1985; London, Corgi, 1991.

With Peter Morwood, *The Romulan Way.* New York, Pocket Books, 1987; London, Titan, 1989.

Spock's World. New York, Pocket Books, 1988; London, Pan, 1992.

Doctor's Orders. New York, Pocket Books, and London, Titan, 1990.

High Wizardry. New York, Delacorte, 1990; London, Corgi, 1991.

Support Your Local Wizard (includes *So You Want to Be a Wizard?*, *Deep Wizardry*, and *High Wizardry*). New York, Guild American, 1990.

A Wizard Abroad. London, Corgi, 1993.

Dark Mirror. New York, Pocket Books, and London, Simon & Schuster, 1993.

Intellivore. New York, Pocket Books, 1997.

Plays

Author of television episodes for *Scooby-Doo, Captain Caveman, Space Ghost, Fonz and the Happy Days Gang, Laverne and Shirley in the Army, Biskitts, Glofriends, Transformers, My Little Pony, Dinosaucers, Batman,* and *Gargoyles,* 1979-94. Also author of screenplays for educational videos for children and story editor for various animated television series.

Other

Contributor, *Sixteen: Short Stories by Outstanding Young Adult Writers,* edited by Donald R. Gallo. New York, Delacorte, 1984.

Contributor, *Dragons and Dreams: A Collection of New Fantasy and Science Fiction Stories,* edited by Jane Yolen and others. New York, Harper, 1986.

PUBLICATIONS FOR ADULTS

The Door into Fire. New York, Dell, 1979; London, Magnum, 1981.

The Door into Shadow. New York, Bluejay, 1984.

With Peter Morwood, *Keeper of the City.* New York, Bantam, 1989.

With Peter Morwood, *Space Cops: Mindblast.* New York, Avon, 1991.

With Peter Morwood, *Space Cops: Kill Station.* New York, Avon, 1992.

With Peter Morwood, *Space Cops: High Moon.* New York, Avon, 1992.

The Door into Sunset. London, Corgi, 1992; New York, TOR, 1993.

With Peter Morwood, *SeaQuest DSV.* New York, Bantam, 1993; London, Millennium, 1994.

Spider-Man: The Venom Factor. New York, Putnam, 1994.

Spider-Man: The Lizard Sanction. New York, Putnam, 1996.

X-Com/UFO Defense: A Novel. Prima/Proteus, 1996.

Spider-Man: The Octopus Agenda. New York, Putnam, 1996.

The Outer Limits. 3 Vols. Prima, 1996-97.

The Book of Night with Moon. London, Hodder, and New York, Warner Aspect, 1997.

X-Men: Empire's End. New York, Putnam, 1997.

Plays

With Michael Reaves, "Where No One Has Gone Before" (television play; episode of *Star Trek: The Next Generation*). Paramount, 1987.

"Not in My Back Yard" (television play; episode of *Space Island One*). Bard Entertainments, 1998.

Other

Contributor, *Flashing Swords! 5,* edited by Lin Carter. New York, Dell, 1981.

Contributor, *Thieves' World 6: Wings of Omen.* New York, Ace, 1984.

Contributor, *Moonsinger's Friends,* edited by Susan Schwartz. New York, Bluejay, 1985.

Contributor, *Thieves' World 7: The Dead of Winter,* edited by Robert Asprin and Lynn Abbey. New York, Ace, 1985.

Star Trek: The Kobayashi Alternative (interactive text computer game). New York, Micromosaics and Simon & Schuster, 1985.

Contributor, *Thieves' World 10: Blood Ties,* edited by Robert Asprin and Lynn Abbey. New York, Ace, 1986.

Contributor, with Peter Morwood, *The Fleet: Break Through.* New York, Ace, 1989.

Contributor, with Peter Morwood, *The Fleet: Sworn Allies.* New York, Ace, 1990.

Contributor, with Peter Morwood, *The Fleet: Total War.* New York, Ace, 1990.

Contributor, *The Best of Star Trek: 20 Years.* New York, DC Comics, 1992.

Contributor, *Xanadu 2,* edited by Jane Yolen. Jane Yolen Books/Harcourt, 1994.

Contributor, *Don't Forget Your Spacesuit, Dear,* edited by Jody Lynn Nye. New York, Baen Books, 1996.

Privateer II: The Darkening (interactive movie/computer game). London, Electronic Arts UK, 1996.

*

Media Adaptations: *Spock's World* (audio cassette), Simon & Schuster, 1989; *Dark Mirror* (audio cassette), Simon & Schuster, 1993; *Spider-Man: The Lizard Sanction* (audio cassette), Simon & Schuster, 1996.

Critical Studies: ''Diane Duane'' by William M. Schuyler, Jr., in *Twentieth-Century Science-Fiction Writers,* 3rd. edition, edited by Noelle Watson and Paul E. Schellinger, Chicago and London, St. James Press, 1991; ''Diane Duane'' by Pauline Morgan, in *St. James Guide to Fantasy Writers,* edited by David Pringle, Detroit, St. James Press, 1996.

*   *   *

Diane Duane is not only highly talented but also unpredictable. She excels in three different genres and has also written TV scripts for *Star Trek: The Next Generation,* among others. The chronology of her writing shows an author switching genre and intended audience from one book to the next: between 1979 and 1985 she published two adult fantasies, two *Star Trek* novels, and the first two of her *Wizardry* children's fantasies. Then followed three more *Star Trek* novels (one in collaboration with her husband), another collaboration, third volumes in both the adult and children's fantasy series, and a fourth *Wizardry* book, *A Wizard Abroad.* She plans her work years ahead, particularly her fantasies. In 1979 *The Door into Fire* was published with a note that it was intended as the first of a quartet.

The *Wizardry* series is a *tour de force* of ''science fantasy.'' Although the wizards' power is magical, they go about their work scientifically by learning spells, by understanding the laws of nature, and also being knowledgeable about today's technological civilisation. Duane has also been compared to Madeleine L'Engle as her wizardry is infused with religion—a rather unorthodox Christianity. Religion is also bound up in her *Star Trek* and adult fantasy series. There are echoes of Tolkien and C. S. Lewis in her work: allusions deliberately positioned as homage to fantasists who, like Duane, concealed their Christianity beneath allegory or alternative mythology.

Wizardry, according to Duane, is not about selfish magic but about altruism: healing harms, helping the world run more smoothly, and occasionally saving the world from disaster. Wizardly science is acquired through ownership of the wizard's manual, a book which somehow gets into the hands of a person with magic potential, and which contains the awesome wizard's Oath. Once a wizard takes the Oath, s/he is faced with an ordeal. If passed, the manual is continually updated with fresh information and spells, plus a directory of other wizards with their status and power ranking. Wizards—both humans and intelligent animals—work under the authority of the Powers who created the universe (i.e. archangels, under Life [God]) and oppose the machinations of the Lone Power who invented Death at the dawn of time (i.e. Lucifer). This power confronts the thirteen-year-old heroine Nita and hero Kit in each volume.

In *So You Want to Be a Wizard,* Nita and Kit each come across a copy of the manual, say the Oath, become Novices, meet and become a team. Their initial dabbling in magic leads on to their ordeal, carried out in an alternative New York governed by the Lone Power. Their task is to recover a vital spellbook which he has stolen and hidden.

In *Deep Wizardry,* Kit and Nita, on a seaside holiday, encounter a whale who is also a wizard. Using wizardly speech—a special language—they discover that a group ritual is to be re-enacted in order to reduce environmental disasters affecting sea creatures, by generating a mass of good magic to hold down the Lone Power in its marine guise as the great Sea Serpent. If they fail, the eastern seaboard of the USA is likely to be flooded. Kit and Nita agree to shape-change into whales and join the ritual, and Nita volunteers to play the role of the sacrificed one, not realising that she will have to die as the food of the sinister Master-Shark. Luckily by another's substitution, Nita is freed of her fatal destiny.

High Wizardry is mainly the story of Nita's younger sister Dairine and her ordeal. Jealous of Nita's power, Dairine sneaks a look at her manual and rashly reads out the Oath. Next day, a new laptop computer arrives at home and Dairine discovers the wizard's manual stored in its memory, especially, as it will transpire, for her to use it. She begins a fantastic journey into space, at first thinking only of realising her fantasies of taking part in *Star Wars,* and then realising that there are actually real aliens, directed by the Lone Power, in chase of her. Little does she know that, as a computer expert, she has been chosen by the Powers to land on a silicon-based planet about to wake to sentience as a computer-style intelligence. The planet's mind then generates small silicon creatures which share its consciousness, and almost immediately the Lone Power arrives, having devised a way to tempt them to Fall. Homage to C. S. Lewis's *Perelandra (Voyage to Venus),* of course, but with a climax Lewis did not attempt, when the Lone Power is offered the chance to repent and return to Heaven. . .

A Wizard Abroad takes Nita and Kit to Ireland, in a tribute to Duane's new home. The plot recalls *Deep Wizardry* as wicked magic threatens the fabric of reality by bringing the past into the present, especially the violence of Irish legend. The Irish wizards decide to re-enact the Battle of Moytura, but first they must find the four treasures: the cup, sword, stone, and spear. The Lone Power returns in a grotesque guise as the Fomorian god Balor, and victory is barely won. This is a fresh treatment of the ''Celtic fantasy'' beloved of so many children's writers, and like the other *Wizardry* books it combines high poetic writing at the magical climaxes with down-to-earth American slang and cultural references. The latter will irritate fantasy purists, but one hopes it will help the average reader into the story.

Duane's more recent Wizardry novel, *The Book of Night with Moon,* published for adults, is magnificent. Taking up the concept of animals as wizards, it stars four intelligent cat-wizards living near New York's Grand Central Station, whose task is to supervise and repair "worldgates" invisible to ordinary humans which wizards use for instant transportation between certain places in our world and off the planet. The breakdown of the worldgates at Central Station leads to an expedition deep beneath the Station where lives a settlement of dinosaurs surviving from prehistoric times, about the make the choice between Good and Evil, and tempted by the "Lone Power" who wants to unleash their violence on the surface world, and on to other planets through the worldgates. Duane succeeds in convincing us of the seriousness of her vision of cat society, and the inner community of cat-wizards, including a sprinkling of cat-language and a final glossary.

Duane's adult works include several *Star Trek* novels. These are not "tie-in" versions of the TV scripts, which were turned into prose fiction by James Blish years ago, or the six films. They are new novels linking the TV and film adventures. Over fifty *Star Trek* novels have been published by several authors in a continuing series. The authors must be consistent with the media presentations, with authorised nonfiction material, and with other novels in the series. Diane Duane was a *Star Trek* fan for years before she turned professional author. She has studied astronomy, astrophysics, and medicine, and thus can well cope with the jargon of science and pseudo-science which a *Star Trek* author must scatter through his/her books, even mapping a galactic voyage using real astronomical data. With her instinctive feel for the relationships between the core personalities of *Star Trek*—Kirk, Spock, McCoy, Scotty, Uhuru, Sulu and Chekov—she has produced outstanding genre fiction which the *Star Trek* fan may conjure up in the "mind's eye" as authentic adventures. Because they are not straightforward space war scenarios, they will extend young readers who can cope with their length and intellectual demands.

In *The Wounded Sky,* Kirk's ship, the *Enterprise,* is chosen to test a new space drive, taking it far further than the warp drive used in *Star Trek* for faster-than-light travel. They discover that this new drive is damaging the fabric of the universe, leading to a breach, and contact with a new universe whose Supreme Being is just awakening to consciousness. It is a highly metaphysical novel with clear allusions to C.S. Lewis's Ransom trilogy and Narnia books. *My Enemy, My Ally* and *The Romulan Way* are linked stories about the Romulan Empire, traditional enemies of the Federation whose background history is detailed by Duane. They are descended from tribes of Vulcans who rejected the way of logic and emigrated into space two thousand years before the *Star Trek* era. Duane packs a strong message for peace between races into these two stories of treachery, espionage, and space combat.

Doctors's Orders is an enjoyable novel about McCoy's first time in command of the *Enterprise.* Kirk beams down onto a new planet in the hope of negotiating a treaty with its three alien species so that they join the Federation (as opposed to siding with, or being exploited by, the Klingons). Then he disappears, and McCoy has to captain the ship as it suddenly comes under Klingon attack. Finally *Spock's World* is set on the planet Vulcan, where there is a campaign to take Vulcan out of the Federation, and Kirk and Spock

are invited to speak at the public debate preceding the referendum. Chapters telling this story are interspersed with chapters about the history of Vulcan from the first awakening of hominid consciousness to the birth of Spock (who has a Vulcan father and Earthling mother). Again interplanetary politics is combined with philosophy: here, the history of how Vulcans coped with their inherently violent nature by developing an ethic of self-control.

More recently Duane has written two intellectually-challenging novels about the adventures of the *Next Generation* crew captained by Jean-Luc Picard. *Dark Mirror* builds on an original *Star Trek* episode "Mirror Mirror," where Kirk and Spock found that in an alternative universe they had counterparts also commanding the *Enterprise.* Years later it appears that the Empire plans to invade our universe and conquer our inhabited worlds. "Our" Picard, LaForge, and Deanna Troi go on a mission to sabotage the "other" *Enterprise,* involving them pretending to be their more evil counterparts; they find an ally in the "mirror" Worf who resents the Empire's subjugation of the Klingons.

Intellivore finds the *Enterprise* in a sparsely-populated area of the galaxy, supporting an archaeological survey ship suspicious about the disappearance of species, leaving whole planets uninhabited. It turns out that they must hunt down a mobile planet inhabited by a group mind which feeds on sentient minds in spaceships or on planets, and sucks them dry, leaving the people alive but mindless. Obviously this threat to the galaxy must be destroyed, but Starfleet crewmen risk losing their own minds as they approach the planet. Only Data has the necessary mental qualities to survive the experience.

In her *Door* adult fantasy series, Duane writes at full stretch without need to consider the restrictions of writing for juveniles or for *Star Trek* addicts who will pick on every minor deviation from the canon. The *Door* series is outstanding. Here is beauty, heroism, fear, magic, dragons, women warriors—and a wealth of fine writing. There is also an inherent eroticism, for these are genuine *adult* fantasies, though not as sexually explicit as those of Stephen Donaldson or Guy Kay. In this world ruled by the Goddess, lovemaking is good if done in love, friendship, or respect, and not unwillingly. Bisexuality is accepted, and the Goddess visits each individual once in his or her life in the form of a lover. Otherwise the ethic of the books is that of Good against Evil, with war as a necessity, sometimes a glorious endeavour, to bring about longed-for peace. I would suggest youngsters discover these books for themselves in the adult library or bookstore, rather than YA librarians shelving them alongside Duane's juveniles and *Star Trek* series.

—Jessica Yates

DUBOSARSKY, Ursula

Nationality: Australian. **Born:** Ursula Coleman, Sydney, New South Wales, 25 June 1961. **Education:** Studied literature and classical languages, University of Sydney; studied Hebrew while working on a kibbutz in Israel; Diploma in Education. **Family:** Married Avi Dubosarsky; one daughter and two sons. **Career:** Research Officer, Government Public Service, Canberra, Australia; researcher for *Readers Digest* books and magazines. **Awards:** Children's Book Award, New South Wales State Literary Awards,

1994; Children's Book Award, Victorian Premier's Literary Awards, 1994; Ethnic Affairs Commission Award, New South Wales Premier's Literary Awards, 1995; Honour Book, Children's Book Council of Australia Book of the Year, Older Readers, 1996. **Address:** c/o Penguin Books Australia, Ltd., 487 Maroondah Highway, Ringwood, Victoria 3134, Australia. **E-mail Address:** dubosar@ar.com.au.

PUBLICATIONS FOR YOUNG ADULTS

Fiction

High Hopes. Ringwood, Victoria, Penguin, and New York, Viking, 1990.
Zizzy Zing. North Ryde, New South Wales, Harper Collins, 1991; Ringwood, Victoria, and Harmondsworth, Penguin, 1998.
The Last Week in December. Ringwood, Victoria, and Harmondsworth, Penguin, 1993.
The White Guinea-Pig. Ringwood, Victoria, Viking, 1994; Harmondsworth and New York, Viking, 1995.
The First Book of Samuel. Ringwood, Victoria, and Harmondsworth, Penguin, 1995.
Bruno and the Crumhorn. Ringwood, Victoria, Viking, and Harmondsworth, Penguin, 1996.
Black Sails, White Sails. Ringwood, Victoria, Viking, 1997.
Honey and Bear, illustrated by Ron Brooks. Ringwood, Victoria, Viking, 1998.

PUBLICATIONS FOR CHILDREN

Fiction

Maisie and the Pinny Pig, illustrated by Roberta Landers. South Melbourne, Victoria, Macmillan, 1989.
The Strange Adventures of Isador Brown, illustrated by Paty Marshall-Stace. Ringwood, Victoria, Penguin, 1998.
Honey and Bear, illustrated by Ron Brooks. Ringwood, Victoria, Penguin, 1998.

*

Ursula Dubosarsky comments:

Whatever "age category" my books fall into, I think in the end I write more for a type of person than an age.

*   *   *

Ursula Dubosarsky's novels are family stories told from a child's perspective, often by a child who is puzzled or made anxious by the behaviour of the adults around him or her. Dubosarsky's two finest novels, *The White Guinea-Pig* and *The First Book of Samuel,* depict muddled or distracted adults involved in complex family relationships who rarely communicate effectively with their children. In *The White Guinea-Pig* both Geraldine's parents and the parents of her neighbour fail to discuss the circumstances of the death of a sibling, family financial troubles, or a father's imminent arrest, thereby causing immense stress and fear for their children who only know that something is wrong. Here the parent-child relationship is also linked to animal-human relationships through Geraldine's life-long pursuit of the perfect pet and the subsequent troubles caused by an escaping guinea-pig. Dubosarsky uses eating practices to illustrate these troubles, showing the poor and haphazard eating of Geraldine and her sister Violetta, who are left to fend for themselves while their parents deal with their difficulties, and the unvarying diet of pellets and slimy lettuce for the guinea-pigs caged in the back garden.

Similarly *The First Book of Samuel* focuses on misunderstanding others, even close relatives. Samuel's flamboyant opera singer father, Elkanah, says the family will move to Philadelphia as a ploy to flush out his wife's, Hannah's, supposed boyfriend, overlooking his own unfaithfulness. The idea of moving to another country upsets Samuel greatly but even more so his grandfather Elias, who loves Samuel above all other family, even his only daughter Hannah. Elias kidnaps Samuel on their shared birthday, the 21st of June, but they don't get far before finding out that Samuel has malaria, contracted many years before when a baby in Papua New Guinea. Elkanah's selfishness and dual family is contrasted to the suffering of people like Elias who lost everything in the Holocaust.

This conjunction of anxiety and families could be unappealing, but all Dubosarsky's novels are distinguished by humorous situations, a gallery of eccentrics, exotic details, irony, and witty references. Her baroque touches are made evident in *The Last Week in December* by the character's names—Bernardo, Nestor, Demelza, Lettice, and Bella—and unexpected references, "You mean like the Council of Trent, where they make up prayers". The novel is an insightful and humorous depiction of childhood guilt. Young Bella is haunted by the theft of her English grandfather's, Ernest's, tobacco pouch, a spur of the moment thing, but she is able to forget about her crime for three years until a return visit by the grandparents is announced. Bella's secret is the focus of an amusing look at how different families work. After an eventful summer when grandmother Dorothy reveals that she has known of Bella's crime all along, Bella decides that "families were really very strange" but that finding she can be mistaken about people "made the world seem somehow bigger, more exciting, unexpected. . . ."

Dubosarsky's heroes and heroines are innocent characters, children who seem to expect the adult world to be haphazard and so are unsurprised when their expectations are fulfilled. Their fallible viewpoint adds to the ironic tone of the novels and is reminiscent of Robin Klein's guileless characters. Even an assertive heroine like Julia in *High Hopes* finds adults are tricky to handle. Julia arranges an English tutor for her Argentinian father whose English is poor but what can she do when her father, George, falls in love with the teacher! Unlike Julia, Bruno from *Bruno and the Crumhorn* is a rather weak-willed child, unwilling to assert himself in any way and so when his mother insists he learn the crumhorn with his odd Great Aunt Ilma he can't refuse. But then he loses the unusual medieval instrument on a bus and the girl who finds it, Sybil, not only learns the crumhorn but becomes Bruno's special friend. Phyllis in *Zizzy Zing* goes to what seems remarkable lengths to convince herself of the normality of other's bizarre behaviour. The first book written by Dubosarsky but the third to be published, *Zizzy Zing* is unique in having a fantasy element but is nevertheless indicative of her style, for an apparently ordinary recount of a contemporary child's summertime experience is layered with unconventional detail. While Phyllis is staying with the nuns who had cared for her orphaned mother as a child, a letter addressed to the mother arrives. The letter is very old and the envelope empty, but Phyllis and Sister Monica decide to go to the address printed on the back. At some point in the train journey Phyllis experiences a time shift and arrives at the town, Katoomba, in 1938. A strange lady cares for Phyllis and provides clues to the family background of Phyllis's mother.

The title of *Black Sails, White Sails* refers to the legend of Theseus who, after defeating the Minotaur, neglects to hoist white sails on his return, causing his grieving father Aegeas to cast himself into the sea. A teenage girl living a confined life with her reclusive mother meets a girl, Olivia, she had known at school many years before and they begin a new relationship based, the heroine thinks, on this tenuous past link. The girl (not named) believes that life consists of patterns and meanings, but she discovers that all the supposed relationships, links, and patterns she had taken for granted are entirely false—just as in the legend where, despite the black sails, Theseus lived. On reflection this rejection of meaning and purpose prompts a great release: "I sensed some peculiar humour in the universe, something windy and airborne like a seagull. . . ." Perhaps the author is making a comment here about how her previous books were read, or on the novel form generally, but regardless of intention this is an entertaining tale, every character and incident both ordinary and peculiar!

—Kerry White

DUDER, Tessa

Nationality: New Zealander. **Born:** Tessa Staveley, Auckland, 13 November 1940. **Education:** Diocesan High School for Girls, Auckland, 1946-57; University of Auckland. **Family:** Married John Nelson Duder in 1964; four daughters. **Career:** Journalist, Auckland *Star,* 1959-64; feature writer, *Daily Express,* London, 1964-66; book reviewer and columnist for literary magazines *Quote Unquote* (Auckland) and *Viewpoint* (Melbourne). Since 1986 editor and trustee, Spirit of Adventure Trust, Auckland. National vice-president, 1992-96, president, since 1996, New Zealand Society of Authors; panelist, Arts Council of New Zealand Children's Writing Programme, 1987-1993. Script consultant for 1993 feature film *Alex,* Isambard Productions, New Zealand, and Total Film, Australia; founder and actor of *Metaphor,* a drama quartet of four writers/actors formed in 1993. Since 1993 professional actor and writer. **Awards:** Cardiff Empire Games silver medal, for swimming, 1958; Choysa bursary, 1985; New Zealand Library Association Esther Glen award, 1988. 1990, 1992; New Zealand Children's Book of the Year award, 1988, 1990, 1993; New Zealand Literary Fund travel grant, 1989; Arts Council of New Zealand travel grant, 1989, and special writing bursary, 1990; New Zealand Commemorative medal, 1990; writer-in-residence, University of Waikato, 1991; Australia-New Zealand Literary Exchange Fellow, 1993; Order of the British Empire for services to literature. **Agent:** Ray Richards, Richards Literary Agency, 3/43 Aberdeen Road, Castor Bay, Auckland. **Address:** 6/169 Jervois Rd., Herne Bay, Auckland, New Zealand.

PUBLICATIONS FOR YOUNG ADULTS

Fiction

Night Race to Kawau. Auckland, Oxford University Press, 1982; London, Penguin, 1985.
Jellybean. Auckland and Oxford, Oxford University Press, 1985; New York, Viking Kestrel, 1986.
Alex. Auckland, Oxford University Press, 1987; Oxford, Oxford University Press, 1988; Boston, Houghton Mifflin, 1989.
In Lane Three, Alex Archer. Auckland, Oxford University Press, 1987; Boston, Houghton, 1989.
Alex in Winter. Auckland, Oxford University Press, 1989; New York, Penguin, 1991.
Alessandra: Alex in Rome. Auckland, Oxford University Press, 1991; as *Alex in Rome,* Boston, Houghton Mifflin, 1992.
Songs for Alex. Auckland, Oxford University Press, 1992.
Mercury Beach. Auckland, Penguin, 1997.

Other

The Book of Auckland. Auckland, Oxford University Press, 1985.
Play It Again, Sam (reader), illustrated by Kelvin Hawley. Auckland, Shortland, 1987.
Dragons (reader), illustrated by Kelvin Hawley. Auckland, Shortland, 1987.
Simply Messing About in Boats (reader). Auckland, Shortland, 1988.
Journey to Olympia: The Story of the Ancient Olympics. Scholastic, 1992.
The Making of Alex: The Movie. Auckland, Ashton Scholastic, 1993.
Editor and contributor, *Nearly Seventeen* (short stories and one-act plays). Auckland, Penguin, 1993.
Editor and contributor, *Falling in Love* (short stories). Auckland, Penguin, 1995.
Editor, with Agnes Nieuwenhuizen, and contributor, *Crossing* (short stories). Melbourne, Reeds, 1995.
Editor, with Peter McFarlane, and contributor, *Personal Best* (short stories). Melbourne, Reeds, 1997.

Also contributor of short stories "Not Just a Pretty Face" in *Zig-Zag,* edited by William Taylor, Auckland, Penguin, 1993, "A Sea Change," in *Ultimate Sports,* edited by Donald R. Gallo, New York, Delacorte, 1995, and "A Stroke of Luck," in *The First Time, Volume 1,* edited by Charles Montpetit, Melbourne, Hodder Headline, 1996.

PUBLICATIONS FOR ADULTS

Other

Kawau. Auckland, Bush Press, 1980; revised edition, as *Discover Kawau,* 1984.
Spirit of Adventure: The Story of New Zealand's Sail Training Ship. Auckland, Century Hutchinson, 1985.
Waitemata: Harbour of Sail. Auckland, Century Hutchinson, 1989.
Contributor, *The Written World,* edited by Agnes Nieuwenhuizen. Melbourne, D.M. Thorpe, 1994.

Plays

With Martin Baynton, *The Warrior Virgin,* music by Laughton Pattrick. New Zealand, Heinneman, 1996.

Author, with Martin Baynton, of plays *Foreign Rites,* 1992, *Five Go to the Dogs,* 1993, and *Ghost Writers,* 1994, all performed by drama quartet *Metaphor* in New Zealand and Australia.

*

Theatrical Activities: Actress: *Foreign Rites,* 1992, *Five Go to the Dogs,* 1993, and *Ghost Writers,* 1994, all performed with drama quartet *Metaphor* in New Zealand and Australia; *Shortland Street* (soap opera), 1997.

Media Adaptations: *Alex* (film based on her novel of the same title), Isambard Productions, New Zealand, and Total Film, Australia, 1993.

Tessa Duder comments:

I began creative writing 18 years ago and at the time of writing am still best-known as the creator of Alex. Ten years after its publication, *Alex* is still far and away the best-selling children's novel ever produced in New Zealand and all four books are still in print, widely read by adults as well as children.

But since I said goodbye to Alex in 1992, other areas have opened up: acting study and part-time career as a professional actor (including, in 1997, in New Zealand's longest running medical soap on television), writing plays, children's television scripts, a regular column on children's literature, a heavy programme as a speaker in schools, conferences, and elsewhere, and of course answering those letters from readers, which are both a joy and sometimes a burden for children's writers. I've edited—and contributed stories to—four anthologies for young adults which have done well in both Australia and New Zealand. My Australian connection has strengthened with visits to writers' festivals in Melbourne and Adelaide, and from 1996 I've been spending much time on literary politics as president of the NZ Society of Authors (PEN Inc.). It was a relief when, in April of 1997, I finally published *Mercury Beach,* my first junior novel for five years, and even more of a relief to find it well received. It was, deliberately, about as far away from Alex as I could get. A sequel is on the way, and a young adult novel and an adult play. I'd love to do some more acting, stage and TV. Long-term ambitions now are to write a novel which will be as firmly attached to my name as Alex is now; and to be a good grandmother to my first grandchild Clare Sedef, born to my third daughter and Turkish son-in-law in December of 1996. As often happens, I'm finding a renewed interest in picture book!

*　　*　　*

Tessa Duder's wide experiences have contributed to the growth of her ability to write with convincing power, and to her constant concern with the struggle and triumph of strong female characters. In *Night Race to Kawau,* when Sam's father is knocked unconscious while trying to haul down the spinnaker, Sam, her mother, and young sister Jane have to sail their yacht through the stormy night of the race from Auckland to Kawau Island in the Hauraki Gulf. Then Sam and Jane have to hike over the bush-clad hills of Kawau Island for help. Fluent readers find this an exciting story of achievement with already tense family relationships frayed through stress, danger, and exhaustion. For yachting enthusiasts there is the added pleasure of authentic nautical details.

''Musicians are never ordinary, least of all conductors.'' Beautifully controlled and moving, *Jellybean* captures agony and ecstasy in a fine study of a musical child set apart from society by her ''impossible yearning,'' and reveals with compassion the emotional conflicts of a busy solo mother and daughter. Geraldine, alias Jellybean, aged 10, often goes reluctantly with her cellist mother when she plays in the orchestra and, as well, in pubs for extra money. Yet by going to her mother's rehearsals and concerts, Jellybean develops a longing to be a conductor of the ''real music'' she hears there. At the attainable level of a school performance, Jellybean's achievement is credible and triumphant. The arrival of Gerald, the mysterious cellist, adds mystery to the storyline. Could he be Jellybean's father? She doesn't want to know. Images spring clear in the immediacy of the narrative's present tense. Humour enhances several occasions, notably Jellybean's unofficial orchestra-pit-eye view of a ballet dress rehearsal. The frightful ''competition mum'' is the only stereotype in a story where women can achieve even as conductors, and a man can be sensitive and caring. The whole story is illuminated by the music and ballet of Tchaikovsky's *The Nutcracker.*

Duder's first two novels use a simple chronological timeline. The development of a double timeline gives *Alex* an appropriately complex structure for, again, a study of female achievement, with risk-taking, unashamed ambition, and punishing hard work. Alex, aged 15 and very mature, is a competitive swimmer, aiming for the 1960 Olympic Games in Rome. The prologue in italics introduces her at the crisis of being called to the blocks for the final selection race: ''In a few minutes I will dive into that artificially turquoise water waiting at my feet. A minute later I'll be either ecstatic or a failure.'' That minute lasts the length of the novel. Between each phase of the race printed in italics, Alex's life is recounted in chronological flashbacks printed in ordinary type. Both timelines maintain tension as they move forward through humorous and dramatic happenings, disaster and despair, to the climatic moment of success. To add to the complexity, Alex bears in her mind throughout the race the voice of Andy, the young man with whom she has fallen in love and who meets his death with the unexpectedness of real life.

Because of its strong structure, *Alex* can fully embrace the teenage world of family, school, friends, and society. Alex is multi-talented—on the school stage, in class, on the hockey field as well as in the swimming pool. Her poignant love affair with the also talented Andy is handled with tenderness and passion. Attitudes and issues are confronted—dangerous driving, alcohol, parental and peer pressure, group dynamics, comradeship in competition, society's expectations of girls, and concepts of femaleness and femininity. Adults are portrayed mainly as generous and supportive. A few have their own suffering to deal with; a few are insensitive and scheming. Setting a precedent by winning both the

Esther Glen award and the Government Printer's award of 1988, and with rights to TV already sold, this skilful and most moving novel seems certain to reach the readership it deserves. A sequel is already in progress to cover the Olympic Games themselves.

Duder's writing also includes impressive short stories and, in non-fiction, *The Book of Auckland* and *Spirit of Adventure,* all a valuable contribution to our indigenous literature in which we express "our identity as a nation, something very precious."

—Diane Hebley

DUNCAN, Lois

Pseudonyms: Lois Kerry. **Nationality:** American. **Born:** Philadelphia, Pennsylvania, 28 April 1934. **Education:** Duke University, Durham, North Carolina, 1952-53; University of New Mexico, Albuquerque, B.A. (cum laude; Phi Beta Kappa) in English 1977. **Family:** Married Donald Wayne Arquette in 1965; one daughter (deceased) and one son; three children from first marriage. **Career:** Writer; lecturer in journalism, University of New Mexico, 1971-82; contributing editor for *Woman's Day,* 1986-90; magazine photographer; lecturer at writers' conferences. **Awards:** Three-time winner during high school years of *Seventeen* magazine's annual short story contest; Seventeenth Summer Literary award, Dodd, Mead & Co., 1957, for *Debutante Hill*; Best Novel award, National Press Women, 1966, for *Point of Violence*; Edgar Allan Poe award Runner-up, Mystery Writers of America, 1967, for *Ransom,* 1969, for *They Never Came Home,* 1985, for *The Third Eye,* 1986, for *Locked in Time,* and 1989, for *The Twisted Window*; Zia award, New Mexico Press Women, 1969, for *Major Andre: Brave Enemy*; grand prize winner, Writer's Digest Creative Writing Contest, 1970, for short story; Theta Sigma Phi Headliner award, 1971; American Library Association (ALA) Best Books for Young Adults citations, 1976, for *Summer of Fear,* 1978, for *Killing Mr. Griffin,* 1981, for *Stranger with My Face,* 1982, for *Chapters: My Growth as a Writer,* 1990, for *Don't Look Behind You,* and 1992, for *Who Killed My Daughter?*; *New York Times* Best Books for Children citations, 1981, for *Stranger with My Face,* and 1988, for *Killing Mr. Griffin*; Ethical Culture School Book award, Library of Congress' Best Books citation, and *English Teacher's Journal* and University of Iowa's Best Books of the Year for Young Adults citation, all 1981, and Best Novel award, National League of American Pen Women, 1982, all for *Stranger with My Face*; Notable Children's Trade Book in the Field of Social Studies, National Council for Social Studies and the Children's Book Council, 1982, for *Chapters: My Growth as a Writer*; Child Study Association of America's Children's Books of the Year citation, 1986, for *Locked in Time* and *The Third Eye*; Children's Book award, National League of American Pen Women, 1987, for *Horses of Dreamland*; Young Reader award, Essex-Hudson Regional Library Cooperative, 1989, for a body of work; Margaret A. Edwards award, for a distinguished body of work for Young Adults, from the Young Adult Services Committee of the *School Library Journal,* 1992. **Agent:** Wendy Schmalz, Harold Ober Associates, 425 Madison Ave., New York, New York 10017, U.S.A.

PUBLICATIONS FOR YOUNG ADULTS

Novels

Debutante Hill. New York, Dodd Mead, 1958.
Love Song for Joyce (as Lois Kerry). New York, Funk and Wagnalls, 1958.
A Promise for Joyce (as Lois Kerry). New York, Funk and Wagnalls, 1959.
The Middle Sister. New York, Dodd Mead, 1960.
Game of Danger. New York, Dodd Mead, 1962.
Season of the Two-Heart. New York, Dodd Mead, 1964.
Ransom. New York, Doubleday, 1966; as *Five Were Missing,* New York, New American Library, 1972.
They Never Came Home. New York, Doubleday, 1969.
A Gift of Magic, illustrated by Arvis Stewart. Boston, Little Brown, 1971.
I Know What You Did Last Summer. Boston, Little Brown, 1973; London, Hamish Hamilton, 1982.
Down a Dark Hall. Boston, Little Brown, 1974.
Summer of Fear. Boston, Little Brown, 1976; London, Hamish Hamilton, 1981.
Killing Mr. Griffin. Boston, Little Brown, 1978; London, Hamish Hamilton, 1980.
Daughters of Eve. Boston, Little Brown, 1979.
Stranger with My Face. Boston, Little Brown, 1981; London, Hamish Hamilton, 1983.
The Third Eye. Boston, Little Brown, 1984; as *The Eyes of Karen Connors,* London, Hamish Hamilton, 1985.
Locked in Time. Boston, Little Brown, 1985; London, Hamish Hamilton, 1986.
The Twisted Window. New York, Delacorte Press, and London, Hamish Hamilton, 1987.
Don't Look behind You. New York, Delacorte Press, and London, Hamish Hamilton, 1989.
Gallows Hill. New York, Delacorte Press, and London, Hamish Hamilton, 1997.

Nonfiction

Major Andre: Brave Enemy, illustrated by Tran Mawicke. New York, Putnam, 1969.
Peggy (on Margaret Arnold). Boston, Little Brown, 1970.

Other

Psychic Detectives in Action (cassette), RDA Enterprises, 1993.
Editor, *Night Terrors: Stories of Shadow and Substance.* New York, Simon and Schuster, 1996.
Editor, *Trapped!* New York, Simon and Schuster, 1998.

PUBLICATIONS FOR CHILDREN

Fiction

The Littlest One in the Family, illustrated by Suzanne K. Larsen. New York, Dodd Mead, 1960.
Silly Mother, illustrated by Suzanne K. Larsen. New York, Dial Press, 1962.
Giving Away Suzanne, illustrated by Leonard Weisgard. New York, Dodd Mead, 1963.

Hotel for Dogs, illustrated by Leonard Shortall. Boston, Houghton Mifflin, 1971.

Wonder Kid Meets the Evil Lunch Snatcher, illustrated by Margaret Sanfilippo. Boston, Little Brown, 1988.

The Magic of Spider Woman, illustrated by Shonto Begay. New York, Scholastic, 1996.

Poetry

From Spring to Spring: Poems and Photographs, photographs by the author. Philadelphia, Westminster Press, 1982.

The Terrible Tales of Happy Days School, illustrated by Friso Henstra. Boston, Little Brown, 1983.

Horses of Dreamland, illustrated by Donna Diamond. Boston, Little Brown, 1985; London, Hamish Hamilton, 1986.

The Birthday Moon, illustrated by Susan Davis. New York, Viking, 1989.

Songs from Dreamland, music by Robin Arquette, illustrated by Kay Chorao. New York, Knopf, 1989.

Nonfiction

The Circus Comes Home, photographs by Joseph Janney Steinmetz. New York, Delacorte, 1992.

PUBLICATIONS FOR ADULTS

Fiction

Point of Violence. New York, Doubleday, 1966; London, Hale, 1968.

When the Bough Breaks. New York, Doubleday, 1973.

Nonfiction

How to Write and Sell Your Personal Experiences. Cincinnati, Writer's Digest, 1979.

Chapters: My Growth as a Writer. Boston, Little Brown, 1982.

Who Killed My Daughter? The True Story of a Mother's Search for her Daughter's Murderer. New York, Delacorte Press, 1992.

With Dr. William Roll, *Psychic Connections: A Journey into the Mysterious World of Psi.* New York, Dell, 1995.

Recordings

A Visit with Lois Duncan (videotape). Albuquerque, NM, RDA Enterprises, 1985.

Dream Songs from Yesterday (cassette). Albuquerque, NM, RDA Enterprises, 1987.

Our Beautiful Day (cassette). Albuquerque, NM, RDA Enterprises, 1988.

The Story of Christmas (cassette). Albuquerque, NM, RDA Enterprises, 1989.

Psychics in Action (series of cassettes). Albuquerque, NM, RDA Enterprises, from 1992.

Other

Contributor of over five hundred articles and stories to periodicals, including *Good Housekeeping, Redbook, McCall's, Woman's Day, The Writer, Reader's Digest, Ladies' Home Journal, Saturday Evening Post,* and *Writer's Digest.*

*

Media Adaptations: *Summer of Fear* (television movie, *Strangers in Our House*), NBC-TV, 1978; *Down a Dark Hall* (cassettes), Listening Library, 1985; *Killing Mr. Griffin, Summer of Fear,* and *Stranger with My Face* (cassettes), Listening Library, 1986; *Selling Personal Experiences to Magazines* and *Songs from Dreamland* (cassettes), RDA Enterprises, 1987; *Killing Mr. Griffin* (television movie), NBC-TV, 1997; *I Know What You Did Last Summer* (film), Mandalay, 1997; *Gallows Hill* (television movie), NBC-TV, 1998.

Biography: Essay in *Something about the Author Autobiography Series,* Volume 2, Detroit, Gale, 1986; essay in *Authors and Artists for Young Adults,* Volume 4, Detroit, Gale, 1986; entry in *Something About the Author,* Volume 36, Detroit, Gale, 1986; essay in *Speaking for Ourselves: Autobiographical Sketches by Notable Authors of Books for Young Adults,* Volume 1, compiled and edited by Donald R. Gallo, National Council of Teachers of English, 1990; ''A Conversation with Lois Duncan'' by Roger Sutton, in *School Library Journal,* June 1992; *Presenting Lois Duncan* by Cosette Kies, New York, Twayne Publishing, and Toronto, Maxwell Macmillan Canada, 1993.

Critical Studies: Entry in *Contemporary Literary Criticism,* Volume 26, Detroit, Gale, 1983.

*   *   *

Lois Duncan began her writing career very early in life, shortly after she learned to print at age five or so. At age ten she submitted her first typed manuscript to *Ladies' Home Journal.* The editor did not publish it, but his kindly rejection letter encouraged her to keep trying. Some sage advice from a new neighbor, who turned out to be MacKinlay Kantor, led her to stop writing what he called romantic ''trash'' and write about what she knew. She did, and as a result sold her first short story to a teen magazine at age thirteen. A decade later Duncan's first novel, *Debutante Hill,* a piece of ''sweet and sticky ... pap,'' won a literary competition that awarded her one thousand dollars and a book contract from Dodd Mead.

The world of adolescent fiction by the mid-1960s was not a world of books like *Debutante Hill,* however. Fiction of this period was characterized by an often gritty realism; plots were no longer concerned solely with sports, dating, and horses. Their subject matter involved things happening in the real world—drugs, peer pressure, social and psychological problems, sex, divorce, etc. This new freedom to write more realistically for young readers appealed to Duncan, and her first novel written ''under the new set of ground rules'' was *Ransom,* a taut adventure story about a group of teenagers kidnapped by their school-bus driver. How different *Ransom* was from Duncan's earlier teen novels is indicated by the fact that Dodd Mead refused to publish it because it "wasn't Duncan's style;" Doubleday then took it on, and it become a runner-up for the Edgar Allan Poe award. A second realistic teen novel, *They Never Came Home,* was also an Edgar runner-up, and Duncan was firmly set in the writing style that was to prove so successful for her over the next several decades.

The style Duncan uses is a simple one. She places an individual or a group of normal, believable young people in what appears to be a prosaic setting such as a suburban neighborhood or an American high school; on the surface everything is as it should be until Duncan introduces an element of surprise that gives the story an entirely new twist. In her novel *Down a Dark Hall,* for example, a young woman goes off to what appears to be a normal boarding school. It proves, however, to be run by a headmistress who is herself a medium, and the school is haunted by malevolent ghosts of artists and writers who invade the minds and bodies of the innocent students. *Summer of Fear* is about an average family in Albuquerque, New Mexico, who "inherit" a seventeen-year-old girl, Julia, from relatives who have died in a car crash. Rachael, the narrator, first suspects Julia of being strangely sinister, but when she finds out that Julia cannot be photographed, Rachael begins to realize that Julia is not merely different but is a witch, and an evil one at that. *Stranger with My Face* introduces astral projection when an evil young woman tries to take over the mind and body of her identical twin sister. *The Third Eye* tells the story of Karen, who must summon the courage to use her gift of extrasensory perception to stop the evil machinations of an older couple who kidnap babies to sell them on the baby market. One of Duncan's most exciting and sophisticated novels, *Locked in Time,* finds Nore spending the summer with her new step-relations and her father on her step-mother's Louisiana plantation. Strange events and unlikely occurrences lead her to believe her new relatives are "locked in time"—ageless—but her discovery of their secret leads to terrible danger for Nore. In each of these books, an element of the occult is an integral part of a fast-moving plot, but it is always believable because Duncan never carries her depiction of the supernatural into the sometimes goofy realms that some other authors do. Character and plot are always predominant; the books are first and foremost good mysteries made even more interesting for young readers by some aspect of the unusual.

Not all Duncan's novels depend on use of the supernatural, however. Some of her best works for young adults use the depths of human nature as an unexpected fillip that raises them above the level of the average teen novel. In *I Know What You Did Last Summer,* four teenage friends, riding in a car which is going too fast on a dark road, hit and kill a young boy on a bike. Barry, the driver, persuades the others that nothing will be gained by confessing what they have done, especially since they'd been coming from a party where they had smoked a little pot and drunk some beer. They all manage to put the incident out of their minds until a year later, when each receives a letter saying simply, "I know what you did last summer." A succession of letters follow, each more threatening than the last, until the young people realize that their very lives are in danger from a psychopath bent on revenge. This book was released as a mass-market movie in 1997 in the wake of the revival of teen horror flicks heralded by the hit movie *Scream.*

In *Killing Mr. Griffin,* a group of high-school students set out to scare a hated English teacher into being a little more reasonable by taking him to a remote spot in a woods, tying him to a tree, and leaving him overnight. It soon becomes apparent that Mark, the charismatic leader of the group, would like to go even further than frightening Mr. Griffin, but the rest refuse to go along with him. The next morning when they go to release the teacher they find him dead; without his life-sustaining medication he has succumbed to a heart attack. This time Mark does prevail by convincing the others that nothing is to be gained by telling the truth about what has happened. It is only when Mark begins to pressure the group to kill again that they recognize him for the evil person he is, but by then it's almost too late.

One of Duncan's most chilling examples of the power of an evil person is in her portrayal of Irene Stark in *Daughters of Eve,* who uses the members of a high-school girls' service club as instruments of revenge on all men. Her pathological hatred results in tragic consequences for the naive young women she is ostensibly guiding as their advisor and mentor. In *The Twisted Window,* Tracy Lloyd, abandoned by her father after her mother's death, is drawn into helping a strange young man, Brad Johnson, rescue his baby sister, who was kidnapped by their stepfather and now living in the same town as Tracy. The plot backfires for Tracy, though, when she begins to realize that Brad is seriously disturbed and she finds herself and the child in terrible danger.

In each of these novels, it is a mark of Duncan's ability as a writer that the evils she describes are perfectly plausible and believable. As in her use of the occult, her use of warped human nature as a tool to move the plot along briskly never seems contrived or used solely for shock effect; it is integral to the story. In this respect, Duncan is strongly reminiscent of Robert Cormier in her no-holds-barred portraits of the consequences of human evil and perversity.

Duncan's work is shocking to many adult critics who refuse to believe that so much evil exists, but a tragic incident in Duncan's own life belies their unbelief. In April 1989, Duncan's twenty-one-year-old daughter was shot to death by an as-yet unidentified killer. For several years Duncan's grief over the murder left her unable to write another novel for young readers. During this period, however, she was at work on a new book, *Who Killed My Daughter? The True Story of a Mother's Search for Her Daughter's Murderer,* in which Duncan writes of the many suspicious aspects of the killing and the ineptitude of the crime's investigators. It is Duncan's hope that this book will help to bring to light the strange and terrible true story of why her child was murdered.

"The greatest tragedy of my life has also proven to be the most bizarre experience in my life," Duncan said in a 1992 interview with Roger Sutton for *School Library Journal.* Her investigations into this tragedy revealed incredible parallels between the murder and the events depicted in Duncan's 1989 novel, *Don't Look Behind You,* released one month before Kaitlyn's death. "These connections began to pile up to such a degree that I wondered if I was going crazy," Duncan told Sutton. She contacted Dr. William Roll, director of the Psychical Research Foundation, for reassurance and understanding of these coincidences. Duncan later collaborated with Roll on a nonfiction book, *Psychic Connections,* that investigates psychic phenomena. Though fans may have wondered if Duncan would ever again write the fast-moving murder suspense novels she is so popular for, these two nonfiction books were something Duncan apparently needed to write in order to work through her grief for her daughter.

After editing a volume of short suspense stories titled *Night Terrors,* and writing a children's book for Scholastic, Duncan's long awaited suspense novel *Gallows Hill* was published. In the novel, Sarah has moved from California to a small Missouri town. She agrees to tell fortunes at a school Halloween carnival and is so successful the other kids convince her to continue telling fortunes. When her visions become unsettling, however, she is labeled a witch. Because she and her only friend, Charlie, experience recurring nightmares about the Salem witch trials, Sarah becomes convinced her visions are somehow connected to those long ago events. *Gallows Hill* has been criticized for not living up to Duncan's usual quality: at points the plot and circumstances stretch beyond credibility and the ending is wrapped up too quickly and neatly. Sarah's character, however, is well-drawn. Her perception and emotions in dealing with the cruelty of the other students endear her to the reader. *Gallows Hill* is a welcome addition to the fast-moving plots, fine characterization, and excruciating suspense that characterize most of Duncan's fiction. Lois Duncan remains one of the most popular writers for this age group on the contemporary scene.

—Audrey Eaglen, updated by Lisa A. Wroble

DUNLOP, Eileen (Rhona)

Nationality: British. **Born:** Alloa, Clackmannan, Scotland, 13 October 1938. **Education:** Alloa Academy, 1943-56; Moray House College of Education, Edinburgh, 1956-59, diploma (honours) in primary education 1959. **Family:** Married Antony Kamm in 1979. **Career:** Teacher and writer. Assistant teacher, Eastfield Primary School, Penicuik, Midlothian, 1959-62, and Abercromby Primary School, Tullibody, Clackmannan, 1962-64; assistant headmistress, Sunnyside School, Alloa, 1964-79; headmistress of Preparatory School of Dollar Academy, Clackmannan, 1980-90. **Awards:** Edgar Allan Poe award nomination, 1983, for *The Maze Stone*; Scottish Arts Council Book awards, 1983, for *The Maze Stone,* and 1986, for *Clementina*; American Library Association Notable Book citation, and Carnegie Medal commendation, both 1987, for *The House on the Hill*; McVitie's Scottish Writer of the Year commendation, for *Finn's Island,* 1991. **Address:** 46 Tarmangie Drive, Dollar, Clackmannan, FK14 7BP, Scotland.

PUBLICATIONS FOR YOUNG ADULTS

Fiction

Robinsheugh, illustrated by Peter Farmer. London, Oxford University Press, 1975; as *Elizabeth Elizabeth,* New York, Holt Rinehart, 1976.
A Flute in Mayferry Street, illustrated by Phillida Gili. London, Oxford University Press, 1976; as *The House on Mayferry Street,* New York, Holt Rinehart, 1977.
Fox Farm. London, Oxford University Press, 1978; New York, Holt Rinehart, 1979.
The Maze Stone, illustrated by Martin White. Oxford, Oxford University Press, 1982; New York, Coward, McCann & Geohegan, 1983.

Clementina. Oxford, Oxford University Press, 1985; New York, Holiday House, 1987.
The House on the Hill. Oxford, Oxford University Press, and New York, Holiday House, 1987.
The Valley of Deer. Oxford, Oxford University Press, and New York, Holiday House, 1989.
Finn's Island. London, Blackie & Son, 1991; New York, Holiday House, 1992.
Tales of St. Columba. Chester Springs, Pennsylvania, Dufour Editions, 1992.
Green Willow. New York, Holiday House, 1993.
Finn's Roman Fort. London, Blackie & Son, 1994; as *Finn's Search,* New York, Holiday House, 1994.
Websters' Leap. New York, Holiday House, 1995.
Tales of St. Patrick. New York, Holiday House, 1996.
The Ghost by the Sea. New York, Holiday House, 1997.

Other (with Antony Kamm)

Edinburgh, illustrated by Helen Herbert. Cambridge University Press, 1982.
The Story of Glasgow, illustrated by Maureen and Gordon Gray. Glasgow, Drew Publishing, 1983.
Editor, with Antony Kamm, *A Book of Old Edinburgh.* Edinburgh, Macdonald Publishers, 1984.
Kings and Queens of Scotland, illustrated by Maureen and Gordon Gray. Glasgow, Drew Publishing, 1984.
Scottish Heroes and Heroines of Long Ago, illustrated by Maureen and Gordon Gray. Glasgow, Drew Publishing, 1984.
Editor, with Antony Kamm, *The Scottish Collection of Verse to 1800.* Glasgow, Drew Publishing, 1985.
Scottish Homes through the Ages, illustrated by John Harrold. Glasgow, Drew Publishing, 1985.
Editor, *Scottish Traditional Rhymes for Children.* Glasgow, Drew Publishing, 1985.
Stones of Destiny. Dublin, Poolbeg Press, 1994.
Waters of Life. Dublin, Poolbeg Press, 1996.

*

Biography: Essay in *Something about the Author Autobiography Series,* Vol. 12, Detroit, Gale, 1991.

Eileen Dunlop comments:

From time to time, I am asked whether I have ever had the kind of experience which I describe in my books. This surprises me, since I believe in a reasoned universe, and subscribe to Coleridge's dictum, *The imagination is the servant of reason.* I believe that our experience of the past must be cerebral, or imaginative, or both. I do not believe that ghosts have any objective validity; if they exist at all, they must be products of minds and imaginations pushed by abnormal stress to their limits, and it is this symbolic function which they have in my work.

There are two reasons why I choose to write in the way I do. The first relates to my chosen audience of younger readers, and the other to myself, as an adult working out adult perceptions through the medium of stories in which adults and children are characters of equal importance.

The first reason is simple. Children love a ghost story. Whether or not they admit to believing in ghosts, they enjoy being frightened within a secure environment. They also love the idea of being able to go back into the past. Any of my books can be read on the level of a weird tale; I have suspended my disbelief in writing it, and the measure of my success is the extent to which young readers can do the same.

The second reason is more complex. Although I write in the first instance for children, for my own satisfaction I try to enrich my work by employing a wide range of symbolism and allusion. In *The House on the Hill,* many of the motifs echo the *Four Quartets* of T.S. Eliot, a writer whose ideas of time and its significance have greatly influenced my own. In *Robinsheugh,* the range of literary and historic allusion is wider. I am interested also in adult, as well as child psychology, in the relation of children to adults, and of childhood to adult experience. I am fascinated by the past, and how the influence of the past makes us what we are, as individuals, as families, as a nation. I do not believe that we can go back into the past, in any real sense, but I believe that the past can be very intensely experienced through memory, mind, and imagination. This is what I try to convey in my books—my ghosts are symbolic of the power of imagination to evoke the most vivid images, and excursions into the past are to be understood as feats of imagination taken—for conventional and artistic reasons—far beyond the limits of normal possibility. The suggestion in my fiction that a child's "occult" experience may arise from some tumult in the mind of an adult character, as in the relationship between Kate and Elizabeth in *Robinsheugh,* or between Jane and Philip in *The House on the Hill,* underlines the close affinity there may be between different generations of one family. It also emphasises the fact that, while an openness of response may be one of the blessings of youth, an informed mind and the power of recall are among the compensations of maturity.

I am a Scottish writer. While I am aware of the dangers of narrowness and insularity, I find that I can write with greatest conviction when I choose Scottish themes and settings; my sense of the "spirit of place" is very strong. A strongly-imagined, realistic background seems to me indispensable, if I am to achieve in my readers the 'willing suspension of disbelief' which fantasy writing requires. The intertwining of fantasy with humdrum reality, and the evocation of real places, is a common facet of Scottish folklore and literature; from Burns's *Tam O' Shanter* to Fred Urqruart's *Proud Lady in a Cage,* the chilling effect of the magical and macabre arises from its juxtaposition with the utterly commonplace. I should like to feel that my writing finds a place in this tradition.

*   *   *.

Three threads run through Eileen Dunlop's books for young adults: her love of her native Scotland (the setting of all her books), her interest in the links between past and present, and her use of the supernatural. These elements, combined with traditional romantic themes, make her books particularly appealing to young adults. Dunlop's skills as a storyteller have developed gradually through-out her career, though in her later novels she shows a greater ability

to draw her reader into the story and is less inclined to overwhelm them with too much detail and explanation as in her earlier works.

Dunlop's first published book, *Robinsheugh,* is a time-travel story and a very dense and demanding read; only the fact that events are seen from the viewpoint of twelve-year-old Elizabeth Martin marks it as a book for young people. Elizabeth is spending the summer with her older, scholarly cousin Kate, who is carrying out research on the Melville family of Robinsheugh in the Scottish border country. An old mirror provides a link to the past and to a woman named Elizabeth who lived at Robinsheugh in the 1770s. The past becomes so real that present-day Elizabeth's relationship with Kate disintegrates into animosity.

Published the following year, *A Flute in Mayferry Street* is set in Edinburgh, where Colin Ramsay lives with his widowed mother and invalid sister, Marion. His ambition to play in the school orchestra seems futile because he does own a flute. The unravelling of a family mystery provides a solution; first a letter, then a photograph, and later a trunk containing a flute are found and Marion and Colin gradually piece together the story of their great-uncle Charles Ramsay and Alan Farquhar, who had been friends in the early part of the twentieth century.

After a gap of some years, during which Dunlop published *Fox Farm* for younger children, she produced *The Maze Stone,* in which the prose is more finely honed. The opening is dramatic, "On the twenty-fourth of June, in the year 1914, a young man went into a house, and never came out again." The date is significant; in the changes brought about by World War I, this mysterious happening is forgotten. Seventy years later, the area is vastly different around the Bieldlaw, and the hill which dominates the landscape is threatened through exploitation by a mining company. Central to the story are Fanny and Hester, stepsisters through the marriage of Fanny's father and Hester's mother. Alongside the re-enactment of the legend of the mortal who is enticed into fairyland is a very modern concern about the environment.

In *Clementina,* another modern institution, a time-share proper-ty, provides the setting for the story and a link with the past; changes in relationships are also important. Bridget Graham has persuaded her mother to spend a legacy on four weeks in a chalet in the newly developed Benalmond Forest Park. Bridget's best friend, Daisy, and the slightly older Clementina, an orphan from a child-ren's home befriended by Mrs. Graham, are invited to join them for their holiday there. Clementina is, however, far from the stereotypical poor orphan; her strong personality, musical gifts, and her mysteri-ous links with the Drummonds, whose family home is at the centre of the Park, make it a disturbing holiday for them all. The invasion of the present by the past is seen from the viewpoint of ordinary Daisy whose best-friend relationship with Bridget is ruined forever by the events of the summer.

Like *Clementina, The Valley of the Deer* is a powerful story about a girl growing up. It includes another dramatic opening: "For Anne Farrar, it all began on the night when her bedroom wall fell down." As a result of the collapsed bedroom wall, Anne finds an old family Bible and is fascinated by the entry for Alice Jardyne, born in 1701 and "blottit out of the Boke of Lyffe" in 1726. Anne wonders what Alice has done to deserve such a terrible epitaph. Sharing her parents' interest in the past, Anne begins to research Alice's story and thereby meets Polly Jardine, a young woman in a wheelchair and a contemporary representative of the Jardyne family.

Dunlop's books for young adults, set firmly in time and space, show young people maturing through experience; she always provides a clear viewpoint from which the reader can observe, but does not dictate the conclusions they should draw. She examines relationships, not only between siblings or friends or children and their parents, but between people of different ages. The reader feels that Dunlop's characters have a life outside of her books; Dunlop's books also have a satisfying pattern, whether it takes the form of past events repeated in the present or of some physical token, such as the pattern on the maze stone which manifests itself in various ways.

Since 1989 Dunlop, perhaps partly because of the declining British market for young adult novels of this quality, has published only stories for younger children and nonfiction. These stories have many of the qualities of her work for older children while her nonfiction is about Scotland, its past and its traditions.

—Sheila Ray

———

DWYER, Deanna. *See* **KOONTZ, Dean R.**

———

DWYER, K.R. *See* **KOONTZ, Dean R.**

———

E

EDDINGS, David

Nationality: American. **Born:** Spokane, Washington, 7 July 1931.
Education: Everett Junior College, 1950-52; Reed College, B.A.
1954; University of Washington, Seattle, M.A. 1961. **Military
Service:** United States Army, 1954-56. **Family:** Married Judith
Leigh Schall, 27 October 1962. **Career:** Writer; has worked as a
buyer for Boeing Co., Seattle, as a grocery clerk, and as a college
English teacher. **Agent:** Eleanor Wood, Blasingame, McCauley,
and Wood, 111 Eighth Avenue, Suite 1501, New York, New York
10011, U.S.A.

PUBLICATIONS FOR YOUNG ADULTS

Fiction

Pawn of Prophecy. New York, DelRey, 1982.
Queen of Sorcery. New York, DelRey, 1982.
Magician's Gambit. New York, DelRey, 1984.
Castle of Wizardry. New York, DelRey, 1984.
Enchanter's Endgame. New York, DelRey, 1984.
Guardians of the West. New York, DelRey, 1987.
King of the Murgos. New York, DelRey, 1988.
Demon Lord of Karanda. New York, DelRey, 1988.
Sorceress of Darshiva. New York, DelRey, 1989.
The Diamond Throne. New York, DelRey, 1989.
The Ruby Knight. New York, DelRey, 1990.
The Seeress of Kell. New York, DelRey, 1991.
The Sapphire Rose. New York, DelRey, 1991.
Domes of Fire. New York, DelRey, 1993.
The Shining Ones. New York, DelRey, 1993.
The Hidden City. New York, DelRey, 1994.
With Leigh Eddings, *Belgarath the Sorcerer.* New York,
    Ballantine, 1995.
With Leigh Eddings, *Polgara the Sorceress.* New York,
    Ballantine, 1997.
The Rivan Codex. New York, Ballantine, 1998.

PUBLICATIONS FOR ADULTS

Fiction

High Hunt. New York, Putnam, 1973.
The Losers. New York, Fawcett Columbine, 1992.
Two Complete Novels (includes *The Losers* and *High Hunt*). New
    York, Wing Books, 1994.

*

Critical Studies: "David Eddings," in *Twentieth-Century Science-Fiction Writers,* Detroit, St. James Press, 1991; review of
Belgarath the Sorcerer by Sally Estes, in *Booklist,* July 1995; entry
in *Contemporary Authors New Revision Series,* Volume 45, Detroit, Gale, 1996; entry in *Authors and Artists for Young People,*
Detroit Gale, 1997.

*   *   *

David Eddings is a prolific and widely read author of fantasy
whose "Belgariad," "Malloreon," and "Elenium" series are
especially popular with young adult readers. Though his second
novel, *Pawn of Prophecy,* was published nine years after his first, it
launched his success as a fantasy novelist. The long-running saga
spans four separate series and concludes with two tomes covering
the prehistory of the saga: *Belgarath the Sorcerer* and *Polgara the
Sorceress.*

Eddings has created a world that never was, complete with
improbable geology, preposterous theology in which mortals are
given the task of killing gods with the help of immortals, and a
sprinkling of magic. "Many of my explanations of how magic is
supposed to work are absurdities—*but* my characters all accept
these explanations as if there was no possibility of quibbling about
them, and if the characters believe, then the readers seem also to
believe. Maybe that's the *real* magic," Eddings stated in *Contemporary Authors.*

As often occurs when the popularity of a series dictates its
continuance, Eddings has been criticized for repetition in the plot
line and characters that lack originality. For those readers, however, who avidly follow the saga, the mix of war, politics, persuasive
dialogue, and intriguing action amounts to well-plotted stories and
winning characters with each novel an "installment" to the total
story line encompassing each "separate" series.

In the "Belgariad" series the adventures of Garion, a young
orphan, are chronicled. Garion gradually recognizes his magical
abilities and realizes his fate to fight the evil god Torak and become
King of Riva. He enlists the help of sorcerers and warriors, and
takes possession of the Orb of Aldur to fulfill the ancient prophecies. Garion's adult life is covered in the "Malloreon" series in
which he battles the sorceress Zandramas and a talisman of dark
magic called the Sardion.

The characters are well drawn and minor plot threads add a
realism that shows Eddings's skill in observation and handling of
the day-to-day concerns that make his created world believable.
Garion's life is filled with events that move the plot forward but
that also mirror the realistic concerns of the average person:
balancing work, responsibility, and recreation; following the current events of other countries; pressures to conceive an heir for the
throne; solving disputes brought before him; and wondering at the
rise in the number of people joining an ancient religion referred to
as the Bear-cult.

In the first book of the "Malloreon," *Guardians of the West,*
Garion continues to learn about his powers while learning also to be
ruler, especially of his fiery-spirited wife Ce' Nedra. He is
counseled by his aunt, the sorceress Polgara, and his grandfather,
the crotchety sorcerer Belgarath, both thousands of years old.
Using his powers he is able to decipher part of the prophecies to
learn that his destiny within them did not close when he defeated

Torak. Zandramas and the Sardion threaten the balance between good and evil and Garion is called upon a quest to prevent his kidnapped son from becoming the keeper of the dark just as he himself is the keeper of the light. His entourage includes warriors, princes, and noblemen of various countries whose political bickering, distrust, and varying customs adds a realism within their created realm. These details do not distract from the story, nor bog it down, but make it more believable.

The "Elenium" series shifts focus to Spearhawk, a Pandion knight, who is on a quest for the jewel Bhelliom which will free his queen from imprisonment. His saga continues for three novels which follow his search for the sapphire-rose jewel and his battle with the evil god Azash. Spearhawk, of course, triumphs and marries the Queen Ehlana and returns her home.

The fourth series, the "Tamuli" series, is again three-part and continues the story of Spearhawk. This time he is called upon by the Tamul empire to aid them in their fight against fabled ghost warriors that have returned to wreak havoc and revenge with a magic that threatens to enter Queen Ehlana's domain. To save their own country they agree to travel across the continent to offer aid but find only treachery. In order to defeat these ancient warriors the Bhelliom jewel must be retrieved from where it has been hidden beneath the ocean. In retrieving the jewel Spearhawk encounters a second set of evil beings, The Shining Ones, who appear human and friendly, but he senses their loyalty lies with the sapphire-rose and not the defeat of the Tamuli. The characters are well-rounded, intelligent, and likable. The plot is action-packed, intricately blending the simple and complex, the mortal with formidable magic, and internal strife with external politics. In the conclusion, *The Hidden City,* Spearhawk must again rescue his queen who has been kidnapped by the demented god Cyrgon. Cyrgon has called forth Klael, the ancient embodiment of evil, and Spearhawk must again use the Bhelliom to save his queen and the world as he knows it.

The history of this world and its struggle to balance good and evil in battles between gods and between god and mortal are explained in the prequels. *Belgarath the Sorcerer* and *Polgara the Sorceress* are two hefty volumes which tell the life stories of the immortals who are paramount in fulfilling the prophecy to balance good and evil. Though they could be enjoyed alone, these novels are best read at the end of the other series because of references to the present in telling their histories. These volumes are fitting conclusions to the saga, especially since Leigh Eddings, now recognized as a long-time collaborator, is listed as co-author. "The Eddingses temper larger-than-life violence and intrigue with a healthy dose of wit," said Sally Estes in a *Booklist* review of *Belgarath.* With characters so real and such a well-thought-out history as the Eddingses have created, few lovers of fantasy will leave this world behind without having made many friends, developed fortitude, and felt fulfilled by vicarious experiences.

—Lisa A. Wroble

EDGERTON, Clyde (Carlyle)

Nationality: American. **Born:** Durham, North Carolina, 20 May 1944. **Education:** University of North Carolina at Chapel Hill, B.A. 1966, M.A.T. 1972, Ph.D. 1977. **Military Service:** Served in U.S. Air Force, 1966-71; piloted reconnaissance and forward air control missions in Southeast Asia during Vietnam War; received Distinguished Flying Cross. **Family:** Married Susan Ketchin in 1975; one daughter. **Career:** English teacher, Southern High School, Durham, North Carolina, 1972-73; co-director, English Teaching Institute, Chapel Hill, North Carolina, 1976; associate professor, Campbell University, Buies Creek, North Carolina, 1977-81, assistant professor of education and psychology, 1981-85; associate professor of English and education, St. Andrews Presbyterian College, Laurinburg, North Carolina, 1985-89; writer. Visiting lecturer in English at North Carolina Central University, 1977; writer in residence at Agnes Scott College, 1990; creative writing instructor, Duke University, Durham, North Carolina, 1992; co-chair, Eudora Welty Chair of Southern Studies, Millsaps College, Jackson, Mississippi; lecturer at conferences and workshops. Guest on television and radio programs, including *Today* and National Public Radio's *Sunday Weekend Edition, Morning Edition,* and *Good Evening with Noah Adams.* Musician; member of Tarwater Band. **Awards:** *Publisher's Weekly* named *The Floatplane Notebooks* one of the best books of 1988; Guggenheim fellow, 1989; Lyndhurst fellow, 1991; Fellowship of Southern Writers, 1997; North Carolina Award for fiction, 1997. **Address:** c/o Dusty's Air Taxi, 714 Ninth Street, G-7, Durham, NC 27705, U.S.A.

PUBLICATIONS FOR YOUNG ADULTS

Fiction

Raney. Chapel Hill, North Carolina, Algonquin Books, 1985.
Walking across Egypt. Chapel Hill, North Carolina, Algonquin Books, 1987.
Understanding the Floatplane. Chapel Hill, North Carolina, Mud Puppy Press, 1987.
The Floatplane Notebooks. Chapel Hill, North Carolina, Algonquin Books, 1988.
Cold Black Peas. Chapel Hill, North Carolina, Mud Puppy Press, 1990.
Killer Diller. Chapel Hill, North Carolina, Algonquin Books, 1991.
In Memory of Junior. Chapel Hill, North Carolina, Algonquin Books, 1992.
Redeye. Chapel Hill, North Carolina, Algonquin Books, 1995.
Where Trouble Sleeps. Chapel Hill, North Carolina, Algonquin Books, 1995.

Recordings: *Walking across Egypt: Songs and Readings from the Books "Raney" and "Walking across Egypt,"* music performed by Edgerton and other members of the Tarwater Band, Flying Fish Records, 1987; *Clyde Edgerton Reads "The Floatplane Notebooks,"* Random House Audiobooks, 1989; *The "Killer Diller" Tapes,* Durham, North Carolina, Dusty's Air Taxi, 1991; *The Devil's Dream,* by Lee Smith and the Tarwater Band, Durham, North Carolina, Dusty's Air Taxi, 1993; Edgerton has recorded all his novels for The Freeman Group, Durham, North Carolina.

Other

Contributor, *Weymouth: An Anthology of Poetry,* edited by Sam Ragan. Laurinburg, North Carolina, St. Andrews Press, 1987.

Contributor, *Family Portraits: Remembrances by Twenty Distinguished Writers,* edited by Carolyn Anthony. New York, Doubleday, 1989.

Contributor, *New Stories from the South: The Year's Best, 1990,* edited by Shannon Ravenel. Chapel Hill, North Carolina, Algonquin Books, 1990.

Also contributor, *Best American Short Stories,* 1997, and *On Faith and Fiction,* edited by W. Dale Brown.

*

Media Adaptations: *Walking across Egypt* (play, adapted by John Justice, produced 1989); *Raney* (play, adapted by John Justice, produced North Carolina 1990; film, Castleway Productions, Atlanta, Georgia); *The Floatplane Notebooks* (play, adapted by Jason Moore and Paul Fitzgerald, produced Chicago 1992).

Critical Studies: Entry in *Contemporary Literary Criticism,* Volume 39, Detroit, Gale, 1986.

Clyde Edgerton comments:

I recently received letters from two eleventh-grade classes in South Carolina. They had just read *The Floatplane Notebooks* and their letters were a response to my story. I was gratified that they found the story interesting and had raised important issues and questions related to the story. I am happy that young adults are able to bring their own lives and experiences to my writing and thus find pleasure and perhaps insights into their own relationships. So far, all my books have had young adults as main characters. I feel about these characters the same way I feel about young readers in general—their youth provides energy, enthusiasm, and fresh insights—and what writer doesn't need readers with these qualities?

*   *   *

Clyde Edgerton is a funny and a profound novelist. In the span of eight years he has published five rollicking stories of small town Southern life. His beat is the Piedmont area of North Carolina. His books are adult novels; individual imperfections and social problems are presented clearly and with humor, and there is no attempt to pass judgment on them. Young adults in their twenties are featured prominently, as are older adults in their seventies, and often the relationships between the two are central to the plot. Edgerton's characters have more faults than most, but they also have considerable virtues, and they are so likable that you want to invite them over for a cup of coffee, a piece of homemade apple pie, and a nice long chat.

Raney is the story of the first two years, two months, and two days in a modern marriage. Set in Listre, North Carolina, it begins just before the wedding, at the K and W Cafeteria, where Raney discovers that her mother-in-law-to-be is a vegetarian. She thought somehow that people were born vegetarians, and she is surprised that Mrs. Shepherd just changed over after some programs on simple living put on by the Episcopalians. Raney herself is Baptist. There are other things Raney learns about, and some adjustments she makes, to life with another family, another approach to class, religion and race, another way of doing the dishes

and defining pornography. The need for adjustments continue until the end of the book, when Raney and Charles's first child is born. But throughout, love, and the joys and perplexities of living, are described in detail, with wit and wisdom.

In *Walking Across Egypt* we meet Mattie Rigsbee, a strong-willed senior citizen who at seventy-eight is slowing down, just a bit. Mattie still cooks three meals a day and her house in Listre always smells good from homemade biscuits, fried chicken, pound cake, and apple pie. When a stray dog comes into her yard, she knows she has as much business keeping him as she has Walking across Egypt, which is the title of her favorite hymn. But she warms him up some beef stew and he does not wish to leave. When Wesley Benfield enters her life, or rather when she enters Wesley's life with pieces of cake and pie, he is even less likely a companion than the stray dog. Wesley is a sixteen-year-old delinquent in the Young Men's Rehabilitation Center, there for stealing a car. But in the end Mattie keeps the dog and Wesley, and you can bet with her good spirit and her good cooking, they both will be better off. And maybe Mattie will be better off too. This book is about reaching out, about caring, and about the best southern cooking there is. Edgerton, also a folk musician, has thoughtfully supplied Mattie with the words and music to "Walking across Egypt." It is gratifying to have a new hymn to sing.

The Floatplane Notebooks chronicles the lives of five generations of the Copelands of Listre. There are a fair number of relatives to account for, so the author provides a genealogical chart in the beginning of the book. The time frame is 1956 to 1971, and the book is written from the perspectives of a number of younger family members, a single event being interpreted differently by different individuals. Building a floatplane is the hobby, obsession of the present head of the family, Albert. He writes frequently about its progress in his notebooks. If the plane should crash, he can look through the notebooks to determine why. The notebooks also contain the secrets of family yearning and love. The Copelands enjoy a family isolation until the Vietnam War, and the bonds of love and caring continue after that war, through tragedy and triumph.

In *Killer Diller,* Mattie Rigsbee, somewhat frailer, and Wesley Benfield, somewhat rehabilitated, return. And Edgerton gives us two more songs—"Sour Sweetheart Blues" and "When I Sleep in Class." Listre is a beehive of activity in this book because the Baptist college, Ballard University, has two new programs: Nutrition House, for overweight Christians, and Project Promise, for special education students of the county. Project Promise uses the residents of the rehabilitation halfway house adjacent to the Ballard campus to teach special ed students job-related skills of masonry and plumbing. Wesley is now a halfway house resident and project participant. He teaches bricklaying, while also writing songs for his Baptist band, preaching, and lusting for a certain girl in Nutrition House. Meanwhile Mattie becomes ill and after a hospital stay, ends up in the Shady Grove Nursing Home. Mattie hates the home because she can't cook there. It is Wesley, of course, who finds a way for her to escape to her home.

In Memory of Junior is about four generations of the Bales and McCord families. It has a genealogical chart in opening pages, and it too is written from the perspective of several family members and of other persons, a single event being interpreted differently by different individuals. Grove McCord was Albert Copeland's daddy's sister's boy. Grove was flying his own little plane before Albert started on his floatplane. The improbable plot of this novel focuses on three elderly people, contemplating their final resting places: Laura and Glen Bales and Grove McCord. The families end up with too many graves and too few tombstones. The importance of the grave site to family continuity has come up before in *The Floatplane Notebooks*. In this latter book the importance is explained simply by Uncle Grove, "You're history longer than you are fact." This book too is about day-to-day family life, described with kindhearted humor.

Edgerton, like a number of Southern writers, credits his family with providing him with great family stories, told over and over, for as long as he could remember. His novels about family are full of likable, outrageous, and very human characters. They show love and tenderness, strong feelings of connection, despite death and divorce and desertion. The books are hilarious, touching, wonderful.

—Mary Lystad

EHRLICH, Amy

Nationality: American. **Born:** New York City, 24 July 1942. **Education:** Bennington College, Bennington, Vermont, 1960-62, 1963-65. **Family:** Married Henry Ingraham in 1985; one son. **Career:** Has worked as a teacher in a day care center, fabric colorist, and hospital receptionist; roving editor, *Family Circle* magazine, New York, 1976-77; senior editor, Delacorte Press, New York, 1977-78; senior editor, 1978-82, executive editor, 1982-84, Dial Books for Young Readers, New York; vice president, editor-in-chief, Candlewick Press, Cambridge, Massachusetts, since 1991. **Awards:** Best Book of the Year list, *School Library Journal*, 1972, *New York Times*, 1972, ALA Children's Books of Exceptional Interest citation, all for *Zeek Silver Moon*; Reviewer's Choice, *Booklist*, 1979, IRA-CBC Children's Choice, Child Study Association Children's Book of the Year, and *American Bookseller* Pick of the Lists citations, all for *Thumbelina*; IRA-CBC Children's Choice citation, for *The Everyday Train*; *American Bookseller* Pick of the Lists, Kansas State Reading Circle, Best Book of the Year list, *School Library Journal*, 1981, and Reviewer's Choice, *Booklist*, 1981, all for *Leo, Zack, and Emmie*; *Redbook* Children's Book of the Year citation, 1987, for *The Wild Swans*; *American Bookseller* Pick of the Lists and *Booklist* Reviewer's Choice citations, both for *The Snow Queen*; Child Study Association Children's Book of the Year, and Kansas State Reading Circle citations, all for *Cinderella*; *Booklist* Young Adult Reviewer's Choice and Best of the Decade citations, and Dorothy Canfield Fisher award, 1990, all for *Where It Stops, Nobody Knows*. **Agent:** F. Joseph Spieler, 154 West 57th Street, New York, New York 10019. **Address:** Box 73, RFD 3, St. Johnsbury, Vermont 05819, U.S.A.

PUBLICATIONS FOR YOUNG ADULTS

Fiction

Where It Stops, Nobody Knows. New York, Dial, 1988.
The Dark Card. New York, Viking, 1991.

Other

Editor, *When I Was Your Age: Original Stories about Growing Up.* Cambridge, Massachusetts, Candlewick Press, 1996.

PUBLICATIONS FOR CHILDREN

Zeek Silver Moon, illustrated by Robert Andrew Parker. New York, Dial, 1972.
Adapter, *Wounded Knee: An Indian History of the American West* (originally published as *Bury My Heart at Wounded Knee),* by Dee Brown. New York, Holt, 1974.
The Everyday Train, illustrated by Martha Alexander. New York, Dial, 1977.
Reteller, *Thumbelina,* by Hans Christian Andersen, illustrated by Susan Jeffers. New York, Dial, 1979.
Leo, Zack, and Emmie, illustrated by Steven Kellogg. New York, Dial, 1981.
Reteller, *The Wild Swans,* by Hans Christian Andersen, illustrated by Susan Jeffers. New York, Dial, 1981.
Annie and the Kidnappers, illustrated by Leonard Shortall. New York, Random House, 1982.
Annie Finds a Home, illustrated by Leonard Shortall. New York, Random House, 1982.
Adapter, *Annie: The Storybook Based on the Movie.* New York, Random House, 1982.
Reteller, *The Snow Queen,* by Hans Christen Andersen, illustrated by Susan Jeffers. New York, Dial, 1982.
Adapter, *Bunnies All Day Long,* illustrated by Marie H. Henry. New York, Dial, 1985.
Adapter, *Bunnies and Their Grandma,* illustrated by Marie H. Henry. New York, Dial, 1985.
Adapter, *Cinderella,* by Charles Perrault, illustrated by Susan Jeffers. New York, Dial, 1985.
Adapter, *The Ewoks and the Lost Children.* New York, Random House, 1985.
Editor and adapter, *The Random House Book of Fairy Tales,* illustrated by Diane Goode. New York, Random House, 1985.
Adapter, *Bunnies On Their Own,* illustrated by Marie H. Henry. New York, Dial, 1986.
Adapter, *Bunnies at Christmastime,* illustrated by Marie H. Henry. New York, Dial, 1986.
Buck-Buck the Chicken, illustrated by R.W. Alley. New York, Random House, 1987.
Leo, Zack, and Emmie Together Again, illustrated by Steven Kellogg. New York, Dial, 1987.
Emma's New Pony, photographs by Richard Brown. New York, Random House, 1988.
Adapter, *Pome and Peel: A Venetian Tale,* illustrated by Laszlo Gal. New York, Dial, 1989.
Adapter, *Rapunzel,* by the Brothers Grimm, illustrated by Kris Waldherr. New York, Dial, 1989.
The Story of Hanukkah, illustrated by Ori Sherman. New York, Dial, 1989.
Lucy's Winter Tale, illustrated by Troy Howell. New York, Dial, 1991.
Parents in the Pigpen: Pigs in the Tub, illustrated by Steven Kellogg. New York, Dial, 1993.

Maggie and Silky Joe, illustrated by Robert Blake. New York, Viking, 1994.

Hurry Up, Mickey, illustrated by Miki Yamamoto. Cambridge, Massachusetts, Shaw's Candlewick Press, 1996.

*

Amy Ehrlich comments:

Writing my two young adult novels meant a great deal to me. In them I wanted to tell truly gripping stories and to portray the pain and the searing discoveries of adolescence. This is a pivotal time in a human life and adults often flinch at remembering it. But I loved the intensity of recollection that came over me as I worked. The characters are made up and the stories of course are fiction, but I tried to tell the truth.

*   *   *

Amy Ehrlich's expansive involvement in children's and young adult literature includes both writing and editing. She earns acclaim for writing original picture books and early readers such as *The Everyday Train* and *Leo, Zack, and Emmie Together Again.* Her interest in language and story infuses retellings of classic fairy tales such as Hans Christian Andersen's *Thumbelina* and the Grimm Brothers' *Hansel and Gretel.* In her two young adult novels, *Where It Stops, Nobody Knows,* and *The Dark Card,* Ehrlich turns to an older audience in an extended storytelling form in which she challenges these readers with intricate plots, psychologically complex characters, and enigmatic, provocative conclusions.

Both novels operate superficially as mysteries. Nina Lewis, the adolescent protagonist in *Where It Stops, Nobody Knows,* begins to question the reasons for her frequent relocations. Why must Joyce, her mother, always uproot them? Why is she so protective? Compelled by Nina, and equipped with the authorial tone of doubt and secrecy, readers face even more puzzles. What relationship do Joyce and Nina have? What motivates Joyce? Why does she fear stability and commitment? Will her undeniable love for Nina suffocate the girl?

In *The Dark Card,* seventeen-year-old Laura flirts with danger and Atlantic City's extravagance and exploitation. She leads a double life: in daylight, she's a blossoming adolescent innocently living in the family summer home; at night, she costumes herself in experience and enters the lurid surrealism of casinos. Ehrlich begs readers to question here, too. Will Laura pass the limits of safety? How far can the mature gambler Ari be trusted? What happened to Laura's mother's bracelet?

Despite the complex plots, use of past tense, and dialogue written above the level of comprehension of the characters, Ehrlich masterfully involves the intelligent reader as observer and participant in the characters' lives. One cares about Nina and Joyce; about Laura, her boyfriend, her sister, and their father.

Both novels break the traditional expectations of fiction for young people. While Ehrlich invites readers to solve the enigmas, in fact, complete understanding may prove elusive and illusory. Disturbance, even profound disturbance, lies at the heart of these novels. Nina experiences frequent disruption with each new move; Joyce acts oddly at times. Instead of mourning her mother, Laura dresses in her clothes and acts dramatically unlike herself. Ehrlich crosses additional boundaries by writing of socially inappropriate and deviant behavior. The end of *Where It Stops, Nobody Knows* finds Joyce imprisoned for kidnapping. And in *The Dark Card,* Laura strips for Ari in a hotel room—a scene which shocks some readers with its explicitness—revealing this adolescent's profound psychological infirmity. Again, this ambitiousness to push the parameters of young-adult fiction testifies to Ehrlich's faith in her audience's intelligence and their ability to confront complexity.

These disturbances take on additional strength because Ehrlich contrasts them to the recognizable. Joyce may be troubled, but she loves Nina fully. And Nina exists completely within a realistic young-adult sphere. She wants to succeed in school; she wants to have friends; she experiences first love and boyfriends. Even the disquieting wrinkles of their mother-daughter relationship gain power because Ehrlich sets them against the normalcy of that relationship: Joyce makes the rules and Nina rebels; they understand each other and still struggle with each other. Similarly, Laura's double life pits the expected against the unexpected. Laura discovers the typical difficulties of her relationship with her mother when she begins to act outrageously outside that relationship. She can see the perverseness of her involvement with Ari because it deviates from her satisfying experiences with Billy.

In the characters of Nina and Laura, Ehrlich presents portraits of adolescents on the edge of womanhood. Unlike characters in much other fiction (e.g., Beverly Cleary's female protagonists), these young women strive for individuality against profoundly confused and confusing circumstances. Ehrlich uses a common experience of a girl's young adulthood—separation from mother—and explores it in hyperbolic ways. Joyce's love threatens to consume Nina. Nina dares to break out in little ways only because she finds safety in Joyce's protection. With detailed images of masks, makeup, and costuming, Laura almost totally fuses with her mother in order to separate from her. Female readers will recognize themselves similarly engaged. Ehrlich offers them confirmation and release.

Crossing yet another boundary, Ehrlich does not orchestrate that release for the reader. Secrecy dominates the novels to their very end. The characters hold secrets; the drive to discover their extent and the truth behind the secrets undeniably compels readers to keep turning the pages, but these novels conclude with only possible, not definite, resolution. The reader must bring her own experiences to articulate her individual conclusion—wherein lies Ehrlich's true impact as a writer.

—Cathryn M. Mercier

———

ELLEN, Jaye. *See* **NIXON, Joan Lowery.**

———

ELLIS, Sarah

Nationality: Canadian. **Born:** Vancouver, British Columbia, Canada, 19 May 1952. **Education:** University of British Columbia,

B.A. 1973, M.L.S. 1975; Simmons College, Boston, M.A. 1980. **Career:** Librarian, Toronto Public Library, c. 1975; children's librarian, Vancouver Public Library, Vancouver, British Columbia, 1976-81; children's librarian, North Vancouver District Library, North Vancouver, British Columbia, from 1981. **Awards:** Sheila A. Egoff Award, 1987, for *The Baby Project,* and 1997, for *Back of Beyond*; Governor-General's Award for Children's Literature, 1991, for *Pick-Up Sticks*; Mr. Christie Book Award and Violet Downy L.O.D.E. Award, both 1994, both for *Out of the Blue*; Canadian Authors' Association Vicky Metcalf Award, for body of work. **Address:** 4432 Walden Street, Vancouver, British Columbia, V5V 3S3, Canada.

PUBLICATIONS FOR YOUNG ADULTS

Fiction

The Baby Project. Toronto, Ontario, Groundwood Books, 1986; as *A Family Project,* New York, Macmillan, 1988.
Next-Door Neighbours. Toronto, Groundwood Books, 1989; as *Next-Door Neighbors,* New York, Macmillan, 1990.
Putting Up with Mitchell, illustrated by Barbara Wood. Brighouse Press, 1989.
Pick-Up Sticks. Toronto, Groundwood Books, 1991; New York, Macmillan, 1992.
Out of the Blue. Toronto, Groundwood Books, 1994; New York, McElderry Books, 1995.
Back of Beyond. Toronto, Groundwood Books, 1996; New York, McElderry Books, 1997.

*   *   *

Sarah Ellis writes about ordinary people and their commonplace situations with a careful skill which illuminates and clarifies many of the basic themes and concerns of adolescence and family life. With a distinctive fidelity to a child-centered perspective, Ellis tells the stories of female protagonists who struggle with the daily issues of maturing as well as learning to face challenges of moving neighborhoods, dealing with new schools and friendships, and coping with death.

In *A Family Project,* winner of the Canadian Governor General's Award, eleven-year-old Jessica and her best friend, Margaret, change the subject of their animal project from platypuses to babies when Jessica's mother unexpectedly announces she is pregnant. Minute details of characterization and convincing dialogue sketch the members of Jessica's family, their renter downstairs, and Margaret and Jessica themselves. With humor and laughter communicated through subtle anecdotes, Ellis chronicles the family's adjustment to the pregnancy and eventual birth of Baby Lucie. When the tragedy of crib death suddenly takes Lucie away from them, Jessica has to fight to make sense of the "complicated hurt inside her."

Different themes are handled with the same sensitivity and humour in *Next-Door Neighbors,* a story of moving to a new neighborhood and trying to feel at home. Twelve-year-old Peggy struggles with shyness and has trouble fitting into her new school. She becomes further alienated from her classmates when she is caught lying to impress them. Peggy slowly develops an unlikely friendship with her two neighbors: George, whose family has

immigrated from Eastern Europe, and Sing, the live-in gardener for the elderly lady next door. As she gets to know George and Sing, Peggy begins to recognize their unique talents and appreciate some of the cultural differences between them. She also learns to assert herself, and standing up to an adult for the first time, challenges the blatant racism of Sing's employer. Ellis weaves all of these issues into an entertaining and probing story of a young adolescent.

In her third novel, *Pick-Up Sticks,* Ellis moves away from traditional (though not typical) families, to the story of Polly, a thirteen-year-old who lives alone with her mother. Rather than focusing exclusively on this now commonplace family grouping, Ellis raises other issues connected to coming of age, financial security, and peer pressure. While her mother hunts for affordable housing, Polly lives with her wealthy uncle and aunt, an experience which calls into question all her previous longings for money and stability. Again, Ellis's characters are vividly and realistically drawn: Polly's scatterbrained, spontaneous mother; Stephanie, her overindulged cousin who turns to petty theft and vandalism for fun; Eric, the mentally handicapped neighbor; and Vanessa, Polly's best friend. A detectable maturing of perception and attitudes in the context of these relationships rounds out Polly's character and sustains the strong narrative drive.

Ellis's stories are all firmly rooted in place and supported by a wealth of realistic detail. Her themes though basic, elucidate concerns shared by her readers, while her self-possessed and hopeful protagonists lead the way into adolescence.

—Patricia Hill

ELLISON, Ralph (Waldo)

Nationality: American. **Born:** Oklahoma City, Oklahoma, 1 March 1914. **Education:** Attended high school in Oklahoma City; Tuskegee Institute, Alabama, 1933-36. **Military Service:** Served in the United States Merchant Marine, 1943-45. **Family:** Married Fanny McConnell in 1946. **Career:** Writer, from 1937; worked as a researcher and writer on Federal Writers' Project in New York City, 1938-42; edited *Negro Quarterly,* 1942; lecture tour in Germany, 1954; lecturer at Salzburg Seminar, Austria, fall, 1954; U.S. Information Agency, tour of Italian cities, 1956; instructor in Russian and American literature, Bard College, Annandale-on-Hudson, New York, 1958-61; Albert Schweitzer Professor in Humanities, 1970-79, emeritus, 1979-94, New York University, New York City. Chairman, Literary Grants Committee, American Academy, 1964-67; Alexander White Visiting Professor, University of Chicago, 1961; visiting professor of writing, Rutgers University, New Brunswick, New Jersey, 1962-64; visiting fellow in American studies, Yale University, New Haven, Connecticut, 1966; lecturer in American Negro culture, folklore, and creative writing at other colleges and universities throughout the United States, including Columbia University, Fisk University, Princeton University, Antioch University, and Bennington College. Gertrude Whittall Lecturer, Library of Congress, Washington, D.C., 1964; Ewing Lecturer, University of California, Los Angeles, 1964; member, Carnegie Commission on Educational Television, 1966-67; honorary consultant in American letters, Library of Congress, Washington, D.C., 1966-72; Trustee, John F. Kennedy Center for the Performing Arts, Washington, D.C., Educational Broadcasting Corp., New School for Social Research, Bennington College, New York, Vermont, and Colonial Williamsburg Foundation; member, National Council on the Arts, 1965-67. **Awards:** Rosenwald grant, 1945; National Book award and National Newspaper Publishers' Russwurm award, both 1953, both for *Invisible Man;* Certificate of award, *Chicago Defender,* 1953; Rockefeller Foundation award, 1954; Prix de Rome fellowships, American Academy of Arts and Letters, 1955 and 1956; *Invisible Man* selected as the most distinguished postwar American novel and Ellison as the sixth most influential novelist by *New York Herald Tribune Book Week* poll of two hundred authors, editors, and critics, 1965; recipient of award honoring well-known Oklahomans in the arts from governor of Oklahoma, 1966; Medal of Freedom, 1969; Chevalier de l'Ordre des Arts et Lettres (France), 1970; Ralph Ellison Public Library, Oklahoma City, named in his honor, 1975; Member, American Academy, 1975; National Medal of Arts, 1985, for *Invisible Man* and for his teaching at numerous universities; Coordinating Council of Literary Magazines-General Electric Foundation award, 1988. Ph.D. in Humane Letters: Tuskegee Institute, 1963; Litt.D.: Rutgers University, 1966; University of Michigan, Ann Arbor, 1967; Williams College, Williamstown, Massachusetts, 1970; Long Island University, New York, 1971; College of William and Mary, Williamsburg, Virginia, 1972; Harvard University, Cambridge, Massachusetts, 1974; Wake Forest College, Winston-Salem, North Carolina, 1974; L.H.D.: Grinnell College, Iowa, 1967; Adelphi University, Garden City, New York, 1971; University of Maryland, College Park, 1974; Bard College, Annandale-on-Hudson, New York, 1978; Wesleyan University, Middletown, Connecticut, 1980; Brown University, Providence, Rhode Island, 1980. **Died:** 16 April 1994.

PUBLICATIONS

Novels

Invisible Man. New York, Random House, 1952; London, Gollancz, 1953.

Other

Contributor, *The Living Novel: A Symposium,* edited by Granville Hicks. London, Macmillan, 1957.

Shadow and Act (essays). New York, Random House, 1964; London, Secker & Warburg, 1967.

With Karl Shapiro, *The Writer's Experience.* Washington, D.C., Library of Congress, 1964.

Contributor, *Education of the Deprived and Segregated.* New York, Bank Street College of Education, 1965.

Contributor, *Who Speaks for the Negro?,* by Robert Penn Warren. New York, Random House, 1965.

With Whitney M. Young and Herbert Gans, *The City in Crisis.* New York, Randolph Educational Fund, 1968.

Contributor, *To Heal and to Build: The Programs of Lyndon B. Johnson,* edited by James MacGregor Burns. New York, McGraw, 1968.

Contributor, *American Law: The Third Century, The Law Bicentennial Volume,* edited by Bernard Schwartz. Littleton, Colorado, F.B. Rothman for New York University School of Law, 1976.

Going to the Territory (essays). New York, Random House, 1986.

The Collected Essays of Ralph Ellison, edited with an introduction by John F. Callahan; preface by Saul Bellow. New York, Modern Library, 1995.

Flying Home and Other Stories, edited with an introduction by John F. Callahan. New York, Random House, 1996.

*

Media Adaptations: "Ralph Ellison: An Interview with the Author of Invisible Man" (sound recording), Center for Cassette Studies, 1974; "Is the Novel Dead?: Ellison, Styron and Baldwin on Contemporary Fiction," with William Styron and James Baldwin (sound recording), Center for Cassette Studies, 1974.

Biography: Entry in *Concise Dictionary of American Literary Biography: The New Consciousness, 1941-1948,* Detroit, Gale, 1987; *Contemporary Fiction in America and England, 1950-1970,* 1976; entry in *Dictionary of Literary Biography,* Volume 2: *American Novelists since World War II,* Detroit, Gale, 1978.

Bibliography: "A Bibliography of Ralph Ellison's Published Writings" by Bernard Benoit and Michel Fabre, in *Studies in Black Literature* (Fredericksburg, Virginia), Autumn 1971.

Critical Studies: *The Negro Novel in America,* revised edition, by Robert A. Bone, New Haven, Connecticut, Yale University Press, 1958; *Five Black Writers: Essays* by Donald B. Gibson, New York, University Press, 1970; *Twentieth-Century Interpretations of Invisible Man* edited by John M. Reilly, Englewood Cliffs, New Jersey, Prentice Hall, 1970; *The Merrill Studies in Invisible Man* edited by Ronald Gottesman, Columbus, Ohio, Merrill, 1971; entry in *Contemporary Literary Criticism,* Detroit, Gale, Volume 1, 1973, Volume 3, 1975, Volume 11, 1979; *Ralph Ellison: A Collection of Critical Essays* edited by John Hersey, Englewood Cliffs, New Jersey, Prentice Hall, 1973; *Folklore and Myth in Ralph Ellison's Early Works* by Dorothea Fischer-Hornung, Stuttgart, Hochschul, 1979; *The Craft of Ralph Ellison,* Cambridge, Massachusetts, Harvard University Press, 1980; *New Essays on Invisible Man* edited by Robert G. O'Meally, London, Cambridge University Press, 1988; *Ralph Ellison: The Genesis of an Artist* by Rudolf F. Dietze, Nuremberg, Carl, 1982; introduction by the author to thirtieth anniversary edition of *Invisible Man,* New York, Random House, 1982; *Speaking for You: The Vision of Ralph Ellison* edited by Kimberly W. Benston, Washington, D.C., Howard University Press, 1987; *Invisible Criticism: Ralph Ellison and the American Canon* by Alan Nadel, Iowa City, University of Iowa Press, 1988; *Creative Revolt: A Study of Wright, Ellison, and Dostoevsky* by Michael F. Lynch, New York, Lang, 1990; *Conversations with Ralph Ellison* edited by Maryemma Graham and Amritjit Singh, Jackson, University Press of Mississippi, 1995.

*   *   *

Although Ralph Waldo Ellison did not write *Invisible Man* directly for young adults, it is assigned in schools and colleges across the United States and is one of the most widely read novels of the African American experience. It has attained the status of a literary classic, almost as well known as *Huckleberry Finn* and *Moby Dick,* though more often read than the latter. Ellison was virtually unknown as a writer when it was published, having only contributed to a number of magazines. He began working on the novel in 1945 and continued over the next seven years, a period of enormous change in the recognition of the role of African Americans in society. The armed forces and major sports were desegregated in this period, and the momentous, unanimous Supreme Court ruling of *Brown v. Board of Education* was soon to follow. *Invisible Man* became part of the growing civil rights movement of the postwar period and has informed all subsequent struggles for equal rights. It instantly made him one of the most celebrated authors in the world. He won the National Book Award with it, as well as several other awards, and though he published little other than essays and a few short stories since, he remained among the most famous writers of the late twentieth century.

Ellison grew up in Oklahoma City, which was, he thought, a fairly tolerant community, and though his time at the Tuskegee Institute and in New York after 1936 must have made him see the social situation differently, he insists he wrote *Invisible Man* thinking not of its brilliant sociological insights into injustice, but strictly of the art of writing. This concern with aesthetics derived at least partly from the strong influence of T. S. Eliot's *The Waste Land,* which Ellison was highly impressed with as a student at Tuskegee. He was also deeply interested in the works of Russian authors, about whom he lectured and wrote, with the most obvious influence being Feodor Dostoyevsky's *Notes from the Underground* and its parallel "The Man Who Lived Underground" by Richard Wright, who exerted a great influence on Ellison during his New York stay. Ellison's invisible man also owes quite a bit to Joseph K. of Franz Kafka's *The Trial.*

The philosophical influences of transcendentalism and postwar French existentialism have also been argued, primarily because *Invisible Man* can be read as a novel of self-discovery as much, if not more than, a novel of racial identity. The narrator comes to recognize that if an individual accepts the role other members of society (black and white) impose upon him, he is doomed as a man, his invisibility made permanent. Interpreted in this way the novel is a universal statement about the human condition which is set in the black experience, but not limited to it. While this makes *Invisible Man* a novel for all people, it has caused criticism by commentators who feel Ellison played into the establishment's hands by putting the burden of equality upon the individual, without appreciating the onerous burden of societal pressure. It is for this reason, these critics argue, that the novel has been so blatantly praised and widely taught.

Despite Ellison's aesthetic intentions and the rich variety of literary allusions and references that *Invisible Man* contains, it is usually read for its illumination of the situation of the black man in America. In the paint company in which the narrator works, there is an old black man, deep in the bowels of the factory, who controls the machinery. Further, there is the imagery of the black additive which is mixed into white paint so that it will dry properly. Black people, Ellison is obviously saying, have made enormous contributions to white society which are absorbed and ignored, just like the additive. The races have a symbiotic relationship which white society refuses to acknowledge, imposing invisibility upon African Americans.

However, unlike many novels which are read for their social commentary, it is not a novel which could be described as realistic.

The characters are fascinating, but represent an array of types rather than individuals. From Ras, a proselytizer for the back-to-Africa movement, to Bledsoe, the establishment black leader, the characters of the novel have a highly symbolic quality, and the words "dreamlike" and "surreal" are often used to describe it. As in Kafka, however, the distortions are all firmly within a particular milieu, which relates it more to the naturalistic novel of Emile Zola and Frank Norris. Ellison's scenes and settings are exaggerated, but still plainly recognizable as particular places in the black American's landscape, whether the southern Negro college or Harlem. Unlike Norris or Zola at their worst, however, Ellison never allows himself to become preachy, nor does he reduce his characters and events to simple allegory, though in most instances the characters seem to lack free will in the same way that Zola's and Norris's do. Determined by circumstances of birth and environment, they seem unable to escape. In a non-naturalistic revolt against determinism, however, the narrator himself, the invisible man, transcends his circumstances by stepping outside of normal human society in an act of will comparable to the absurd acts of the heroes of Jean-Paul Sartre and Albert Camus, and he becomes quite literally enlightened in his underground hiding place amongst his 1,369 lights operated on stolen power. Overt symbolism such as that of the light bulbs or the earlier image of the paint factory may be an important reason why *Invisible Man* appears on so many school reading lists, but it is also one reason it is so accessible to a large reading public, despite the sophisticated interlayering of literary techniques and allusions. Such a potent combination assures it a long life as a literary classic.

—J. Madison Davis

EMERSON, Zack. *See* **WHITE, Ellen Emerson.**

ENGDAHL, Sylvia (Louise)

Nationality: American. **Born:** Los Angeles, California, 24 November 1933. **Education:** Pomona College, Claremont, California, 1950; Reed College, Portland, Oregon, 1951; University of Oregon, Eugene, 1951-52, 1956-57; University of California, Santa Barbara, B.A. in education 1955; graduate work in anthropology, Portland State University, Oregon, 1978-80. **Career:** Elementary school teacher, Portland, 1955-56; programmer, then computer systems specialist, SAGE Air Defense System, Lexington, Massachusetts, Madison, Wisconsin, Tacoma, Washington, and Santa Monica, California, 1957-67; full-time writer, 1968-78; Member of online faculty, Connected Education Inc., New York,

1985-1997. **Awards:** Notable Book citation from American Library Association, Honor List citation from *Horn Book,* and Newbery Honor Book award, 1971, all for *Enchantress from the Stars;* Christopher Award, 1973, for *This Star Shall Abide;* Phoenix Award, 1990, for *Enchantress from the Stars.* **E-mail Address:** sengdahl@teleport.com. **Website:** http://www.teleport.com/~sengdahl.

PUBLICATIONS FOR YOUNG ADULTS

Fiction

Enchantress from the Stars, illustrated by Rodney Shackell. New York, Atheneum, 1970; London, Gollancz, 1974.
Journey between Worlds, illustrated by James and Ruth McCrea. New York, Atheneum, 1970.
The Far Side of Evil, illustrated by Richard Cuffari. New York, Atheneum, 1971; London, Gollancz, 1975.
This Star Shall Abide, illustrated by Richard Cuffari. New York, Atheneum, 1972; as *Heritage of the Star,* London, Gollancz, 1973.
Beyond the Tomorrow Mountains, illustrated by Richard Cuffari. New York, Atheneum, 1973.
The Doors of the Universe. New York, Atheneum, 1981.

Other

The Planet-Girded Suns: Man's View of Other Solar Systems, illustrated by Richard Cuffari. New York, Atheneum, 1974.
Editor, with Rick Roberson, *Universe Ahead: Stories of the Future,* illustrated by Richard Cuffari. New York, Atheneum, 1975.
Editor, *Anywhere, Anywhen: Stories of Tomorrow.* New York, Atheneum, 1976
The Subnuclear Zoo: New Discoveries in High Energy Physics, with Rick Roberson. New York, Atheneum, 1977.
Tool for Tomorrow: New Knowledge about Genes, with Rick Roberson. New York, Atheneum, 1979.
Our World Is Earth (for children), illustrated by Don Sibley. New York, Atheneum, 1979.

*

Biography: Essay "An Observer of Planet Earth," in *Something about the Author Autobiography Series,* Volume 5, Detroit, Gale, 1988; essay "The Mythic Role of Space Fiction," in *The Phoenix Award of the children's Literature Association 1990-1994,* Lanham, Maryland, and London, Scarecrow Press, 1996.

Critical Studies: Entry in *Children's Literature Review,* Volume 2, Detroit, Gale, 1976; "Knowledge, Truth, and Faith in Sylvia Louise Engdahl's Star Trilogy" by Alethea Helbig, in *The Phoenix Award of the Children's Literature Association 1990-1994,* edited by Alethea Helbig and Agnes Perkins, Lanham, Maryland, and London, Scarecrow Press, 1996; "The Peril and Power of Love in Sylvia Louise Engdahl's *Enchantress from the Stars*" by Kathy Piehl, in *The Phoenix Award of the Children's Literature Association 1990-1994,* edited by Alethea Helbig and Agnes Perkins, Lanham, Maryland, and London, Scarecrow Press, 1996.

Sylvia Engdahl comments:

In many libraries my books fail to reach the audience for which they are most appropriate. Because of the success of *Enchantress from the Stars* they are usually shelved with children's books, although the other novels are enjoyed most by readers fourteen or older. Also, they are frequently shelved with science fiction, whereas they appeal more to a general audience than to science fiction fans. Both teenagers and adults who don't like other science fiction often like mine, while science fiction enthusiasts tend to dismiss mine as not being "far out" enough for their taste; this was one of my main reasons for choosing to publish in the young people's field rather than the science fiction genre.

*   *   *

One of Sylvia Louise Engdahl's primary strengths as a writer of science fiction for adolescents lies in her employment of this form to comment on personal and political questions both contemporary and timeless. While she is hardly unusual among science-fiction authors—from H.G. Wells onward—in using the future to illuminate the present, the restraints she places upon her didactic impulses and the sympathy she brings to her complex portraits of people and cultures, make her an interesting social observer.

Engdahl's novels vary in the challenge they offer readers. *Journey between Worlds,* for instance, straightforwardly describes its heroine's passage to adulthood as she moves from Earth to Mars, from fear of the unknown to acceptance of experience, and from her domineering Oregon fiancé to new love on Mars. Melinda's phobia about not being able to breathe when off her native planet is turned inside out as the narrative makes plain that real suffocation consists of denying growth—refusing to leave home. That Melinda's quest is predominantly framed in the terms of the teen romance, however, directs the story toward a different audience than that addressed by Engdahl's more characteristic works.

In *Enchantress from the Stars* (a 1971 Newbery Honor Book), Engdahl foregrounds concerns that extend throughout her works: the importance of empathy, intelligence, and moral courage; the individual's role in effecting change; and the need to approach problems on a symbolic as well as a literal level and to combine the mundane with the spiritual. *Enchantress* tells the story of a young anthropology student, Elana, who finds herself involved in the effort to save a feudal world from colonization by a technology-absorbed interstellar empire. While Elana is the primary narrator, we also share the viewpoints of representatives from the other cultures: Georyn, the woodcutter's son, and Jarel, the doctor.

This shifting narration underscores one of the novel's chief values, respect for others. Elana may belong to the most advanced culture—that which unites technological and mental powers—but her command of telepathy does not make her personally superior to Georyn or Jarel. The human element is always more important than material trappings; indeed, she and Georyn fall in love, although their separate responsibilities make continuing the romance impossible. While the three young people may "read" the situation differently (Georyn's narrative is cast in fairy-tale language, Jarel's in technological terms), we are constantly reminded that each viewpoint has its own truth.

The Anthropological Service to which Elana belongs is dedicated to preserving that truth, to studying cultures without changing them. Nonintervention, the service has learned, must take priority over the desire to help; like adolescents, cultures cannot grow if others do their thinking for them. To an idealist like Elana, this principle often appears harsh, as in *The Far Side of Evil* when she is sent to observe a planet apparently on the brink of nuclear annihilation. The emphasis is not on the Torisian Cold War but on Elana's progress toward self-knowledge, her friend Kari's progress toward courage, and her colleague Randil's progress toward responsibility. As in *Enchantress from the Stars,* the individual's spiritual quest mirrors that of the world: the totalitarians of Toris share Kari's lack of faith and Randil's unconscious arrogance, so that as each character evolves toward maturity, we are given hope that society may follow.

In addition to her novels, Engdahl has edited or coedited collections of science-fiction stories and written or collaborated on a number of nonfiction works on scientific subjects such as physics or genetics. The latter interest plays an important role in the tale unfolded in Engdahl's trilogy: *This Star Shall Abide, Beyond the Tomorrow Mountains,* and *The Doors of the Universe.* These novels take place on a metal-poor planet colonized generations previously by a group of scientists whose home sun had subsequently gone nova, presenting the colonists with the problem of surviving in a world whose biology is unfriendly and which cannot support the technology developed on the mother planet.

As is gradually revealed, the solution devised by the chief scientist among the initial group of settlers has required the establishment of a peculiar caste system that purports to be a theocracy but is in fact a meritocracy in which those demonstrating intelligence and independence of mind are chosen for the ''priesthood''—actually, a secret cadre of scientists. What we learn about this world keeps pace with the discoveries made by the trilogy's protagonist, Noren. His rebellious questioning of his Stone Age society puts him at odds with his fellow villagers in the first volume, with a group of subhuman mutants in the second (descendants of people who have drunk untreated water), and in the third with those whose ''heresies,'' like his own, have permitted their elevation to the rank of scientist. Similarly, he moves from self-discovery to romantic love to leadership of his world, a sequence of widening understanding that parallels the individual's attainment of maturity.

The trilogy is an extended meditation on the need for total commitment to an ideal, for willingness to challenge assumptions, and for change. Again the individual is paramount; Noren's intelligent iconoclasm finds a solution to his people's problem, while his own quest to learn to fit into his world parallels the colony's effort to become part of an alien environment. Likewise, these three novels consistently acknowledge the terrifying complexity of life—the awareness that what is necessary may not always be fair and that growth often involves hurt.

Engdahl's emphasis on being different, on the painfulness of responsibility, and on coming to terms with oneself and one's world accounts for much of her success as a writer for adolescents: the concerns she addresses on a symbolic level are indeed important. In their refusal to condescend to their readers, her novels practice the same respect for others that they preach. The consistently high quality of her prose and the unity of her moral vision make Engdahl's works exciting and deserving of addition to the canon of young-adult science fiction.

—Claudia Nelson

EYERLY, Jeannette Hyde

Pseudonyms: Jeannette Griffith, a joint pseudonym with Valeria Winkler Griffith; has also written as Linda Lee, Miriam Carlock, and Sandy McTavish. **Nationality:** American. **Born:** Topeka, Kansas, 7 June 1908. **Education:** Drake University, 1926-29; University of Iowa, A.B. 1930. **Family:** Married Frank Rinehart Eyerly in 1932; two daughters. **Career:** Writer. Publicity director, Des Moines Public Library, 1930-32; creative writing teacher, Des Moines Adult Education Program, 1955-57. Des Moines Child Guidance Center, member of board of directors, 1949-54, president, 1953-54; St. Joseph Academy Guild, member of board of directors, 1954-57, president, 1957; member of acquisition committee, Des Moines Art Center, 1960-63; Polk Mental Health Center, member of board of directors, 1968-78, president, 1977-78, 1982—; Iowa Commission for the Blind, member of board, 1977-80, chairman, 1978-79. **Awards:** Susan Glaspell Award, 1965, for *Gretchen's Hill;* Christopher Award, 1970, for *Escape from Nowhere; Radigan Cares* selected as one of the Child Study Association's Books of the Year, 1970. **Agent:** Curtis Brown Ltd., 10 Astor Place, New York, New York 10003, U.S.A.

PUBLICATIONS FOR YOUNG ADULTS

Fiction

Dearest Kate, with Valeria Winkler Griffith, under joint pseudonym Jeannette Griffith. Philadelphia, Pennsylvania, Lippincott, 1961.
More Than a Summer Love. Philadelphia, Lippincott, 1962.
Drop-Out. Philadelphia, Lippincott, 1963.
The World of Ellen March. Philadelphia, Lippincott, 1964.
A Girl Like Me. Philadelphia, Lippincott, 1966.
The Girl Inside. Philadelphia, Lippincott, 1968.
Escape from Nowhere. Philadelphia, Lippincott, 1969.
Radigan Cares. Philadelphia, Lippincott, 1970.
The Phaedra Complex. Philadelphia, Lippincott, 1971.
Bonnie Jo, Go Home. Philadelphia, Lippincott, 1972.
Goodbye to Budapest: A Novel of Suspense. Philadelphia, Lippincott, 1974.
The Leonardo Touch. Philadelphia, Lippincott, 1976.
He's My Baby, Now. Philadelphia, Lippincott, 1977.
See Dave Run. Philadelphia, Lippincott, 1978.
If I Loved You Wednesday. Philadelphia, Lippincott, 1980.
Seth and Me and Rebel Make Three. Philadelphia, Lippincott, 1983.
Angel Baker, Thief. Philadelphia, Lippincott, 1984.
Someone to Love Me. Philadelphia, Lippincott, 1987.

PUBLICATIONS FOR CHILDREN

Fiction

Gretchen's Hill, illustrated by Burmah Burris. Philadelphia, Lippincott, 1965.
The Seeing Summer, illustrated by Emily McCully. Philadelphia, Lippincott, 1981.

PUBLICATIONS FOR ADULTS

Nonfiction

Writing Young Adult Novels, with Hadley Irwin. Cincinnati, Ohio, Writer's Digest, 1988.

*

Biography: Entry in *Fifth Book of Junior Authors and Illustrators,* New York, H.W. Wilson, 1983; essay in *Something about the Author Autobiography Series,* Volume 10, Detroit, Gale, 1990; essay in *Speaking for Ourselves, Too* compiled and edited by Donald R. Gallo, National Council of Teachers of English, 1993.

Jeannette Eyerly comments:

How could I be so lucky? In my long life, I've had the best of both possible worlds. Not only have I been a wife, a mother, a grandmother (and now a great-grandmother!) but I have been a writer of many kinds of things. Under three different "pen names" I have been "Linda Lee" (she wrote flippantly), "Miriam Carlock" (a serious writer), and, when a male point of view needed, I became "Sandy McTavish." When necessary I've even been "anonymous." Very convenient.

Soon after this phase, I found my true niche was writing for children and young adults.

Nearly all of my novels have come from things that have interested me: The welfare of the young in today's troubled society, kids dropping out of school, kids dealing with drugs, the break-up of their families, unmarried motherhood (and fatherhood—see *He's My Baby Now*), and deep depression. A teen-ager who lived two doors away and mowed our lawn committed suicide. So did my fictional Dave in *See Dave Run.* And so the story goes.

It was Anthony Trollope who said no one should ever say that he/she *had* to tell a story. They should say, "I have a story to tell." And everyone does.

*   *   *

Jeannette Hyde Eyerly, who also wrote under the name of Jeannette Griffith, possesses extensive writing experience, beginning with magazine articles and a syndicated column then moving on to include short stories and novels in her repertoire. Her books have been adapted as educational resources both in the written format and in a television movie. Her insightful handling of the contemporary problems of youth has garnered her several prestigious literary awards.

Eyerly primarily relies on her life's encounters and experiences to generate ideas for her books and stories. An early book written for children, *Gretchen's Hill,* relates incidents from her childhood. As a mother of two daughters, she heard their complaints about the "gumdrop" teenage novels with patently happy endings and complete resolution of all conflicts. Her wisdom and experience led her to believe teenagers might prefer books which were somewhat closer to the truth. Her earliest book, *More Than a Summer Love,* dealt with the problems of teenagers in love. Several later books also addressed this theme. In *More Than a Summer Love,* this story of romance subtly enlightens teenagers on the "dangers" of becoming too seriously involved when they are too

young to understand the future ramifications of their actions. Marriage is difficult enough without adding the concomitant obstacles faced by young people such as education and employment.

Beginning with *A Girl Like Me,* then *Bonnie Jo, Go Home, He's My Baby, Now,* and finally *Someone to Love Me,* Eyerly expands upon the "problems of teenage love" theme by dealing with the issue of teenage pregnancy. In *A Girl Like Me* she writes to teens in their own words as they communicate their fears to each other. She utilizes dialogue and vocabulary common to youth when they discuss issues in confidence. Though this book was written almost thirty years ago, teenage boys still try to persuade their girlfriends to "go all the way," and "you would if you loved me" is still a popular phrase. Teenage girls (and in some cases, younger now) can certainly relate to these sentiments. Though issues of birth control today may be clouded by the more pressing issue of sexually transmitted diseases, unwanted pregnancy is still a concern. Of course in some ways the stigma placed on the unmarried pregnant woman may be less today than it was years ago, the primary considerations remain the same as those which troubled Eyerly's characters. What does the girl do? What about school, her social life, her friends, her future? What about the boy? What about his plans? What about the baby? Are marriage and abortion options to consider? In *Bonnie Jo, Go Home,* Bonnie Jo decides to go to New York and seek an illegal (at that time) abortion. Without lecturing to readers, the book leaves teenagers with the frightening reality that there are consequences to their actions. Abortion, though legal in most areas now, is still not without a serious emotional, if not financial, price. This book allows the reader to go inside the characters' minds to experience their pain, their suffering, and their questioning of themselves and their actions.

In *Someone to Love Me,* Patrice decides to keep her baby. This choice is also fraught with repercussions. When a young, unmarried girl becomes pregnant—whether through ignorance, foolishness, or both—her life must change in one way or another. If she decides to bear and keep her baby, she sacrifices her youth for motherhood. Eyerly researched her writing of this book in alternative high schools and groups for unwed teenage mothers. It was there she gained the understanding of the plights of these women she so skillfully conveys to her readers. Life is irrevocably changed when "children have children." She explicitly details her character's daily trials perhaps with the thought that she may one day save a reader from the same fate.

Finally, *He's My Baby, Now* deals with the problem of teenage pregnancy by taking an unconventional tact. This book is told from the young unmarried father's perspective. In this story, the young man does not wish to have his child placed up for adoption and refuses to sign the legal papers. The teens are forced to realize that the product of their union is a living, breathing human being that requires love and care that will last a lifetime. Once again Eyerly shows the readers the consequences their lack of responsibility can have on their futures. Teenagers broaden their thinking when they realize the wide-ranging effects of an unexpected pregnancy on both the boy and the girl involved. The book was somewhat unique in its time in that it dealt with the feelings boys usually tried to hide. In writing the book from the boy's point of view, her message gained the wider audience to make it more educational, but in a palatable way. So great was the response to this book that it was eventually the basis for a special television program.

Eyerly has also addressed other problems faced by youth. *Drop-Out,* another critically acclaimed book, led to many classroom discussions on the virtues of staying in school. Most teenagers can relate to the feelings of frustration and of wanting to "get out." Those without the experiences of the outside world may not know what's waiting for them unless they can see it through the eyes of the character. Another book which relates to escaping the everyday problems is *Seth and Me and Rebel Make Three.* This book is of a lighter fare than *See Dave Run,* which realistically portrays a teenage loner with real characters we might find in "Anytown, U.S.A." This story of a runaway boy who eventually takes his own life was written long before teenage suicide became the problem it is today. The author also looks at a teenager's attempted suicide due to her mental health in *The Girl Inside.*

Another award-winning book was *Escape from Nowhere,* which was frequently used in classrooms to discuss the issue of drug abuse. Eyerly's extensive research is evidenced by her exacting details and descriptions. The author also saw the problems of teenagers coming from broken homes. In *The World of Ellen March,* a teenager suffers through the divorce of her parents but eventually realizes life does go on and she will survive. Though divorce is more common today than it once was, children are no more ready to see it in their own homes.

We see many other sides to Eyerly. One book, *The Seeing Summer,* vividly describes the experience of blindness by capturing the friendship between a blind child and a sighted friend. This book was later adapted into a short classroom play used for instructing both sighted and blind students as well as teachers of the blind. Other books have students involved in politics as in *Radigan Cares.* Add intrigue and you have *Goodbye to Budapest: A Novel of Suspense* and *The Leonardo Touch.* It is no wonder that Eyerly eventually wrote (with Hadley Irwin) *Writing Young Adult Novels,* which was most favorably reviewed.

—Laurie Schwartz Guttenberg

F

FARLEY, Walter (Lorimer)

Nationality: American. **Born:** Syracuse, New York, 26 June 1915. **Education:** Erasmus High School, Brooklyn, New York; Mercersburg Academy, Pennsylvania, 1931-35; Columbia University, New York, 1941. **Military Service:** Served in the Fourth Armored Division, and as staff member of *Yank* magazine, United States Army, 1942-46. **Family:** Married Rosemary Lutz in 1945; two daughters (one deceased) and two sons. **Career:** Writer. Advertising copywriter, Batten Barton Durstine and Osborn, New York, 1941; Arabian horse breeder, Earlville, Pennsylvania, 1946-65. Consultant and promoter for films, ''The Black Stallion'' and ''The Black Stallion Returns.'' **Awards:** Pacific Northwest Library Association's Young Reader's Choice award, 1944, for *The Black Stallion,* and 1948, for *The Black Stallion Returns;* Boys Club Junior Book award, 1948, for *The Black Stallion Returns;* literary landmark established in Farley's honor by Venice Area Public Library, Venice, Florida. **Died:** 16 October 1989.

PUBLICATIONS FOR YOUNG ADULTS

Fiction

The Black Stallion, illustrated by Keith Ward. New York, Random House, 1941; London, Lunn, 1947; abridged edition, as *The Black Stallion Picture Book,* Random House, 1979.

Larry and the Undersea Raider, illustrated by P.K. Jackson. New York, Random House, 1942; London, Muller, 1944.

The Black Stallion Returns, illustrated by Harold Eldridge. New York, Random House, 1945; London, Lunn, 1947.

Son of the Black Stallion, illustrated by Milton Menasco. New York, Random House, 1947; 2nd edition with drawings by Hofbauer, London, Collins, 1950.

The Island Stallion, illustrated by Keith Ward. New York, Random House, 1948; London, Hodder & Stoughton, 1973.

The Black Stallion and Satan, illustrated by Milton Menasco. New York, Random House, 1949; revised edition, London, Hodder & Stoughton, 1974.

The Blood Bay Colt, illustrated by Milton Menasco. New York, Random House, 1950; as *The Black Stallion's Blood Bay Colt,* New York, Random House, 1978.

The Island Stallion's Fury, illustrated by Harold Eldridge. New York, Random House, 1951; London, Knight, 1975.

The Black Stallion's Filly, illustrated by Milton Menasco. New York, Random House, 1952; London, Knight, 1979.

The Black Stallion Revolts, illustrated by Harold Eldridge. New York, Random House, 1953; London, Knight, 1978.

The Black Stallion's Sulky Colt, illustrated by Harold Eldridge. New York, Random House, 1954.

The Island Stallion Races, illustrated by Harold Eldridge. New York, Random House, 1955.

The Black Stallion's Courage, illustrated by Allen F. Brewer, Jr. New York, Random House, 1956; London, Knight, 1978.

The Black Stallion Mystery, illustrated by Mal Singer. New York, Random House, 1957; London, Hodder & Stoughton, 1973.

The Horse-Tamer, illustrated by James Schucker. New York, Random House, 1958.

The Black Stallion and Flame, illustrated by Harold Eldridge. New York, Random House, 1960; revised edition, London, Hodder & Stoughton, 1974.

The Black Stallion Challenged!, illustrated by Angie Draper. New York, Random House, 1964; as *The Black Stallion's Challenge,* London, Hodder & Stoughton, 1983.

The Great Dane, Thor, illustrated by Joseph Cellini. New York, Random House, 1966.

The Black Stallion's Ghost, illustrated by Angie Draper. New York, Random House, 1969.

The Black Stallion and the Girl, illustrated by Angie Draper. New York, Random House, 1971.

Walter Farley's Black Stallion Books (includes *The Black Stallion, The Black Stallion Returns, The Black Stallion and Satan,* and *The Black Stallion Mystery*). New York, Random House, 4 vols., 1979.

The Black Stallion Legend. New York, Random House, 1983.

Other

Man O'War, illustrated by Angie Draper. New York, Random House, 1962.

How to Stay Out of Trouble with Your Horse, photographs by Tim Farley. New York, Doubleday, 1981.

PUBLICATIONS FOR CHILDREN

Fiction

Big Black Horse, with Josette Frank (adaptation of *The Black Stallion*), illustrated by P.K. Jackson. New York, Random House, 1953.

Little Black, a Pony, illustrated by James Schucker. New York, Random House, 1961; London, Collins, 1963.

Little Black Goes to the Circus, illustrated by James Schucker. New York, Random House, 1963; London, Collins, 1965.

The Horse That Swam Away, illustrated by Leo Summers. New York, Random House, 1965.

The Little Black Pony Races, illustrated by James Schucker. New York, Random House, 1968.

The Black Stallion Picture Book, illustrated with photographs from the motion picture. New York, Random House, 1979.

The Black Stallion Returns: A Storybook Based on the Movie, edited by Stephanie Spinner. New York, Random House, 1982.

The Black Stallion: An Easy-to-Read Adaptation, illustrated by Sandy Rabinowitz. New York, Random House, 1986.

The Black Stallion Beginner Book. New York, Random House, 1987.

*

Media Adaptations: *The Black Stallion* (movie), United Artists, 1979; *The Black Stallion* (filmstrip with cassette), Media Basics, 1982; *The Black Stallion Returns* (movie), United Artists, 1983.

Biography: Entry in *Dictionary of Literary Biography,* Volume 22: *American Writers for Children, 1900-1960,* Detroit, Gale, 1983.

Manuscript Collections: Butler Library, Columbia University, New York; Venice Area Public Library, Venice, Florida.

Critical Study: Entry in *Contemporary Literary Criticism,* Volume 17, Detroit, Gale, 1981.

*   *   *

Animal stories for young adult readers frequently focus on the bonds of love and loyalty which develop between a character and an animal. Walter Farley's series of books describe the unbridled love between a boy, Alec Ramsey, and his horse, a wild Arabian stallion who appears in the first book of the series, *The Black Stallion.* Other books in the series feature a different racehorse, either a descendant or a rival of the Black.

The plots of Farley's books are fast-paced as the human protagonist, Alec Ramsey, recognizes the outstanding speed of each of his horses and then prepares it for racing. Conflict arises when some aspect of the horse's temperament threatens to undermine its success in the race. Resolution of the conflict is achieved through Alec's insights and loving, patient treatment of the horse. The climax of the story is usually the thrilling narration of the race itself. Victory is achieved despite obstacles, usually in a come-from-behind finish; the win can be attributed not only to the talent but also to the heart and courage of horse and rider.

Only in *Man O'War,* Farley's biography of the legendary race horse, does the pace of the story drag. It is a thoroughly researched piece; however, the facts weight the story and the author's attempts to introduce tension and conflict for each race seem contrived.

The development of character and setting take a back seat to plot in Farley's books. These are not coming-of-age stories; in fact, Alec's only growth is as a jockey. Introspection is infrequent and limited to concern about the horse's ability to race. The reader does not come to know Alec except as a horseman. As a student, he waits for the clock to signal dismissal so that he can be with his horse. When schoolmates come to see his horse and are frightened by its wild behavior, they leave and do not return. Alec doesn't miss them. His closest friend is Henry Daily, an older man who shares Alec's love and knowledge of horses and helps train them for racing. Daily is impressed by Alec's extraordinary ability to communicate with horses.

Alec's parents are also undeveloped characters. They do not share their son's passion for horses or feel comfortable about it for that matter. In *The Black Stallion* they are such background figures that they don't realize that their son is racing his horse in clandestine midnight training sessions at Belmont Park. Alec's father isn't informed that his son will compete in a nationally acclaimed challenge stakes until a week before the race and his mother is never told. Both parents do end up at the track to share in his triumph, however.

In *The Son of the Black Stallion,* Alec's father assumes a more prominent role, resisting, then finally supporting, his son's ambition to race the Black's fiery colt. Still, it is the trainer, Henry, who has the most influence on Alec.

In *The Black Stallion and Flame* an older Alec Ramsey is still racing partners with Henry Daily and his parents don't appear in the story. A disaster at sea occurs in this story as it did in *The Black Stallion.* This time Alec and his horse reach safety separately and Farley indulges in some anthropomorphism as he describes the Black's pleasure at running free on a desert island, competing with another stallion for control of a herd of wild horses. Farley notes that the Black looked at the broodmares "lovingly" and that he preferred the dark brown mares.

Setting assumes some significance in *The Black Stallion Returns* because Alec visits the desert fortress of the Black's Arabian owner, who reclaims his horse and takes it home. Although Alec must relinquish his beloved Black, he is promised the first foal of the bloodline. In only a few other stories in this series does setting change from a horse barn and racetrack.

Travel by ship and airplane reveal the age of these tales. In addition, Farley's portrayal of females and ethnic groups is indicative of the era in which his books were written. His use of dialect is offensive by today's standards and so is his depiction of women as simple-minded homemakers (in *The Black Stallion*) or vacuous socialites (in *Man O'War*).

Despite these shortcomings young readers will vicariously thrill to Alec's ability to tame a wild stallion by virtue of the kindness and love which he transmits through a secret language of touches, whispers and whistles. Readers will identify with an average boy, who is the only person able to command the love and tame the savagery of that wildest of creatures—the wild stallion.

Farley's affection for horses is evident in his descriptions of sleek, muscular creatures that carry themselves with power, grace and dignity. All of the horses are lovingly portrayed: stallions; trotters; broodmares; colts; and even Napoleon, the cart horse who acts as the steadying influence for the high-strung stallions. Farley is the master of the horse story, and those who love horses or seek fast-paced adventure will treasure these books.

—Anne Drolett Creany

FARMER, Nancy

Nationality: American. **Born:** Nancy Coe in Phoenix, Arizona, 9 July 1941. **Education:** Phoenix College, Phoenix, Arizona, A.A. 1961; Reed College, Portland, Oregon, B.A. 1963; attended Merritt College, Oakland, California, and University of California at Berkeley, Berkeley, California, 1969-71. **Family:** Married Harold Farmer in 1976; one son. **Career:** Worked in the Peace Corps in India, 1963-65; lab technician, University of California at Berkeley, Berkeley, California, 1969-72; chemist and entomologist, Loxton, Hunting and Associates, Songo, Mozambique, 1972-74; lab technician and entomologist, University of Zimbabwe, Rukomeche, Zimbabwe, 1975-78; freelance scientist and writer in Harare, Zimbabwe, 1978-88; lab technician, Stanford University Medical School, Palo Alto, California, 1991-92; freelance writer, since 1992; member, Society of Children's Book Writers and Illustrators. **Awards:** Writers of the Future Gold Award, Bridge Publications, 1988; National Endowment for the Arts grant, 1992; Newbery Honor Book award, 1995, for *The Ear, the Eye and the Arm*; National Book Award nominee, 1996, Newbery Honor Book Award, 1997, and Commonwealth Club Silver Medal, 1997, Notable Children's Book, 1997, and Top Ten Best Book for Young

Adults, American Library Association, 1997, for *A Girl Named Disaster*.

PUBLICATIONS FOR YOUNG ADULTS

Fiction

The Ear, the Eye and the Arm. Zimbabwe, College Press, 1989;
  New York, Orchard Books, 1994.
A Girl Named Disaster. New York, Orchard Books, 1996.

Contributor to *Writers of the Future Anthology, #4* (Los Angeles, California, Bridge Publications, 1988) and *Best Horror and Fantasy of 1992* (New York, St. Martin's Press, 1993).

PUBLICATIONS FOR CHILDREN

Fiction

Lorelei. Zimbabwe, College Press, 1988.
Tsitsi's Skirt. Zimbabwe, College Press, 1988.
Tapiwa's Uncle. Zimbabwe, College Press, 1992.
Do You Know Me, illustrated by Shelley Jackson. New York, Orchard Books, 1993.
The Warm Place. New York, Orchard Books, 1994.
Runnery Granary, illustrated by Jos. A. Smith. New York, Greenwillow Books, 1996.

*

Media Adaptations: ''Tapiwa's Uncle'' (play adapted by Aaron Shepard), in *Stories on Stage,* H. W. Wilson, Co., 1993; *The Ear, the Eye and the Arm* (sound recording), Recorded Books, 1995; *A Girl Named Disaster* (sound recording), Recorded Books, 1996; ''Resthaven'' (play adapted by Aaron Shepard), in *Aaron Shegard's Reader's Theatre,* http://www.aaronshep.com/rt, March 1998.

Critical Studies: *Something About the Author,* Detroit, Gale, Vol. 79, 1995, 70-71; review of *The Ear, the Eye and the Arm,* in *Black Enterprise* (New York), February 1996, 243; review of *Runnery Granary* by Lolly Robinson, in *Horn Book* (Boston), September/October 1996, 575; review of *The Ear, the Eye and the Arm* by Freeman Levinrad, in *Cricket* (LaSalle, Illinois), March 1997, 37.

Nancy Farmer comments:

I have little to say about my career or motivation. Writing is as natural as breathing to me, and I don't think about where it comes from. Instead, I'd like to tell you something about my childhood. This has got to be more interesting than any philosophical ideas I could come up with.

I grew up in a small town on the Arizona/Mexico border, where my father managed a hotel. The guests included rodeo riders and the circus crowd. I remember cages of lions and wolves in the parking lot. Once, when I was nine, the circus vet invited me to attend the autopsy of a young elephant that had fallen over dead. He discovered that the animal had two hearts. As an adult I realize that it was a strange way to entertain a child, but as a child I found the experience fascinating.

Life at the hotel was a wonderful preparation for writing. I worked at the desk from age nine, renting rooms and listening to the stories the patrons told each other in the lobby. One man, who only had one eye, told me he lost it in a fight with a grizzly bear. He had a postcard of the stuffed grizzly in front of a trading post. One of the desk clerks painted a mural on the hotel wall of an Aztec princess being sacrificed to the sun god. It was a great painting, but the princess looked a lot like my sister. My mother made him paint clothes on the princess, and my father fired him.

There were never any children in the hotel. Because it was in a tough area, none of my school friends was allowed to visit me. I spent most of my time with cowboys, railroad men, truck drivers and fruit packers. At the end of the street was a giant fruit-packing factory. Assembly lines clanked all day, and the packers put only medium-sized fruit into the crates. Anything too large or small was ground up and fed into the Colorado River. One of my jobs was to rescue baskets of rejects for us to eat. Sometimes we ate cantaloupes for breakfast, lunch and dinner. At other times we had figs three times a day. My mother created a recipe for pickled figs after we complained about the monotony. This is one of the most horrible dishes ever invented.

The only writer in the hotel was a man who wrote a western every month and was paid $300, a decent salary in those days. He lived on egg sandwiches and whiskey. One of my jobs was to make sure he got enough sandwiches to dilute the whiskey. His heroes all had ice-blue eyes, and just before they got into a fight they would tell the villains, ''Look into my ice-blue eyes''. This was a signal to start breaking up the furniture. One day I couldn't rouse the writer. He was collapsed on the floor. I was alone in the hotel, only nine or ten years old, and I thought he was dying. I didn't know anything about alcoholism. I called an ambulance. The ambulance drivers got there just as the writer was waking up. He was a very large man. He crawled to his feet and said, ''Look into my ice-blue eyes''. Then he proceeded to break up the furniture and threw the drivers downstairs. The hospital was very angry at me.

Another time, the police hid out behind the desk to catch a bank robber, who was staying in one of the rooms. He wasn't in the room at the moment, though. I was supposed to hand him the key when he came in, just as though nothing had happened. All around my feet were policemen flattened on the floor. Then they charged upstairs after the robber. My mother found teddy bears in the room later. The robber had broken out of jail and was going home to see his kids. She felt so bad about this, she sent the teddy bears and some money on to the children.

My bedroom window overlooked a highway. Outside was a pink neon sign that flashed *Beer . . . Beer . . . Beer.* I used that sign in *The Ear, the Eye and the Arm.* Up and down the street were bars and liquor stores. At midnight the bars closed, and all the drunks piled out to drive to California across the river, where the bars stayed open until one a.m. I could hear the cars driving over the sidewalks, the sound of bottles being smashed and the happy screams of the party-goers. I fell asleep until one a.m. when the drunks came back. Then I slept another hour until the eighteen-wheeler trucks showed up from California. The drivers preferred to travel in the middle of the night to avoid the heat.

On a diagonal from my window was a large, abandoned building. This had been owned by an Italian who was the mortal enemy of the man who owned our hotel. When the Italian died, he put it in his will that his building couldn't be used for anything. It couldn't be painted or fixed up. It was to sit there and rot, as an insult to the man who owned our hotel.

On the top floor of this building lived a colony of bats. At sundown, they came forth in a large cloud. They spent the night snapping up insects that were attracted to the beer sign. This didn't bother me until the day my sister took me to see *Dracula. I* came home in a daze. I asked my brother, who was older and college-educated, whether there were such things as vampire.

"Sure," he said, hauling down a biology book. He showed me a photograph of an evil-looking creature lapping up blood from a bowl.

"Vampires live a long way off, don't they?" I asked.

"Oh, no. They live in Mexico, which is," my brother waved his arm, "about five miles in that direction."

From that night on I couldn't sleep. It was so hot, I couldn't breath under the sheet I had pulled over my head. I could still hear the sound of leathery wings as the bats flitted around the beer sign. I didn't want to admit I was scared, because I didn't want my brother and sister to laugh at me.

Finally, Amelia, who was the hotel maid, noticed I was looking sick. She was a Cocopah Indian, which meant that she was six feet tall and weighed 300 pounds—average for Cocopah women. I figured Amelia wouldn't laugh at me, so I told her the problem.

"That's bad," she agreed. "What you need is garlic in the window. Vampires don't like garlic." She brought me a silver cross that had been blessed by the priest and told me to wear it around my neck. "Vampires won't bite anyone who wears a silver cross. It makes their teeth fall out."

For the first time in weeks I got a good night's sleep. Then Amelia went too far. She figured I needed something more to get over my fear of bats, so she brought me a dead bat to play with. I stretched out its wings, swung it around and inspected its little, sharp teeth.

But there are only so many things you can do with a dead bat. After a while I became bored. Then I thought of my sister. Mary was much older than I, and very beautiful. More importantly, she was afraid of bugs and snakes. She would even scream if you dropped a kitten on her. Mary had a cedarwood jewelry box of which she was very proud. It was full of necklaces, rings, bracelets and belts made of Navajo silver. I laid the bat, wings outstretched, on top of the jewelry. I closed the lid and waited.

And then I forgot about it. Mary didn't wear any jewelry for two weeks. It was summer, and the temperature outside was over 100 degrees. One morning I heard a scream from the bedroom. Without thinking twice, I raced for the ladder that led up to the hotel roof. I knew Mary was afraid of heights. I hid on the roof for hours. I drank the water that dripped from the mossy sides of the coolers. I was waiting for everyone to become so worried that they would forgive me.

Finally, around sundown, Amelia came up the ladder. I was astounded. I didn't know Amelia could use the ladder. I didn't know it could bear her weight. "You better come down and apologize," she said. "Mary has stopped threatening to kill you."

So I went down and apologized. I had to boil and wash all the jewelry, but nothing could get the smell out of the cedar box. After a month, Mary gave it to me for my coin collection. She was a very forgiving girl.

*   *   *

Nancy Farmer spent seventeen years working in remote areas of Mozambique and Zimbabwe, and the culture, customs, and folklore of these African countries form the basis of her award-winning books for young adults.

The Ear, the Eye and the Arm is set in a futuristic Zimbabwe in the year 2194. Tendai (13), his sister Rita (11), and their little brother Kuda (4), the children of General Amadeus Matsika, Zimbabwe's Chief of Security, live in a grand mansion surrounded by searchlights and alarms. An automatic Doberman helps scare away intruders, a house robot serves breakfast and keeps everyone on schedule, a holophone serves as high-tech telephone, and a (human) Mellower helps make the family members feel calm and good about themselves by singing their praises. As the story opens, Tendai is just awakening from a dream: "Someone was standing by his bed, a person completely unlike anyone Tendai had ever met. In the predawn light his features were unclear. He was simply a presence of darker blue than the sky behind him. But there was about him a scent of woody smoke and new leaves and the honey of far-off, unseen flowers. The presence pointed at Tendai and said, 'You!'" The image leaves him with a strange sense that something important is about to happen. And indeed it does. In order to earn the explorer's badge he needs to become an Eagle Scout, Tendai decides to sneak out for the day and explore the city of Harare (his security-conscious father would never allow it). Rita and Kuda beg to go along on Tendai's adventure. They take a bus to the capital, where they are kidnapped by Fist and Knife at an open-air market, taken to the She Elephant, the human "queen" of a toxic waste dump inhabited by the nasty "vlei" people, and sold to the notorious Masks gang; they escape to Resthaven, a walled community dedicated to following the ancient traditions of the Shona people; and finally, with the help of the three mutant detectives their mother has hired (the Ear, Eye, and Arm of the title), make it back home—just in time to celebrate Tendai's fourteenth birthday. "You'll love this exciting, fun, awesome, and truly delightful book," wrote Freeman Levinrad (age nine) in the March 1997 "Cricket Readers Recommend" column in *Cricket* magazine.

Like *The Ear, the Eye and the Arm, A Girl Named Disaster* is an adventure-filled coming-of-age story. Not quite twelve, Nhamo (whose named indeed means "disaster" in the Shona language) flees from her traditional village in Mozambique when she is about to be married to a cruel man with three wives. Following her grandmother's advice, she takes off in the middle of the night in a dead fisherman's battered canoe down the Musengezi River. For many days, she follows the river, catches fish to eat, camps in secluded places, and communes with the spirits of her dead mother, the canoe's dead owner ("Crocodile Guts"), and an imaginary witch ("Long Teats"), and repeats to herself the stories and folklore of her people. Suddenly, she is swept by raging currents into Lake Cabora Basso and cannot see land in any direction. She eventually comes across a small island inhabited only by small wildlife—mostly dassies (rock rabbits that she traps and eats) and baboons. She settles down for a while, builds herself little sleeping and food-storage areas (away from the greedy baboons), and soon, in her loneliness, finds herself talking to the baboons, too. When she is attacked by a leopard, she knows it is time to move on. Sick, hungry, exhausted, she rebuilds her leaking boat and goes back into the lake in search of human civilization. When she reaches it, in the form of a scientific research station on the border of Zimbabwe, she finds it as hard to readjust to human society as it was to survive in the wild.

Both of these novels include glossaries and notes on the history, peoples, and traditions of Zimbabwe and Mozambique. Both present an unsentimental yet utterly fascinating view of the traditional tribal life, while casting a wary eye at modern lifestyles. And both demonstrate the lifesaving power of story. In these powerful stories, Nancy Farmer has shown herself to be a storyteller *par excellence*.

—Marcia Welsh

FARMER, Penelope (Jane)

Nationality: British. **Born:** Westerham, Kent, 14 June 1939. **Education:** St. Anne's College, Oxford, Degree in History (with second-class honors) 1960; Bedford College, London, Diploma in Social Studies 1962; doctoral study at Keele University, since 1988. **Family:** Married 1) Michael John Mockridge in 1962 (divorced, 1977), one daughter and one son; 2) Simon Shorvon in 1984. **Career:** Writer. Teacher for London County Council Education Department, 1961-63, sociological researcher, 1985-90. **Awards:** American Library Association notable book, 1962, and Carnegie Medal commendation, 1963, both for *The Summer Birds*. **Agent:** Deborah Owen, 78 Narrow St., London E14. **Address:** 30 Ravenscourt Rd., London W6 0UG, England.

PUBLICATIONS FOR YOUNG ADULTS

Novels

The China People, illustrated by Pearl Falconer. Stroudsburg, Pennsylvania, Hutchinson, 1960.
The Summer Birds, illustrated by James J. Spanfeller. New York, Harcourt, 1962.
The Magic Stone, illustrated by John Kaufmann. New York, Harcourt, 1964.
The Saturday Shillings, illustrated by Prudence Seward. London, Hamish Hamilton, 1965; as *Saturday by Seven,* New York, Penguin, 1978.
The Seagull, illustrated by Ian Ribbons. London, Hamish Hamilton, 1965; New York, Harcourt, 1966.
Emma in Winter, illustrated by James J. Spanfeller. New York, Harcourt, 1966.
Charlotte Sometimes, illustrated by Chris Connor. New York, Harcourt, 1969.
Dragonfly Summer, illustrated by Tessa Jordan. London, Hamish Hamilton, 1971; New York, Scholastic Book Services, 1974.
A Castle of Bone. New York, Atheneum, 1972.
William and Mary. New York, Atheneum, 1974.
Year King. New York, Atheneum, 1977.
Thicker Than Water. New York, Walker, 1989.
Stone Croc. New York, Walker, 1991.
Penelope: A Novel. New York, Margaret K. McElderry Books, 1996.

Other

Editor, *Beginnings: Creation Myths of the World,* illustrated by Antonio Frasconi. London, Chatto & Windus, 1978; New York, Atheneum, 1979.
Translator, *Soumchi,* by Amos Oz, illustrated by William Papas. New York, Harper, 1980; with illustrations by Quint Buchholz, San Diego, Harcourt Brace, 1995.
Editor, *Two, or, The Book of Twins and Doubles, an Autobiographical Anthology.* London, Virago Press, 1996.

PUBLICATIONS FOR CHILDREN

Fiction

The Serpent's Teeth: The Story of Cadmus (picture book), illustrated by Chris Connor. London, Collins, 1971, New York, Harcourt, 1972.
Daedalus and Icarus (picture book), illustrated by Chris Connor. New York, Harcourt, 1971.
The Story of Persephone (picture book), illustrated by Graham McCallum. London, Collins, 1972; New York, Morrow, 1973.
August the Fourth, illustrated by Jael Jordon. London, Heinemann, 1975; East Orleans, Massachussetts, Parnassus, 1976.
Heracles (picture book), illustrated by Graham McCallum. London, Collins, 1975.
The Coal Train, illustrated by William Bird. London, Heinemann, 1977.
The Runaway Train, illustrated by William Bird. London, Heinemann, 1979.

PUBLICATIONS FOR ADULTS

Novels

Standing in the Shadow. London, Gollancz, 1984.
Eve: Her Story. London, Gollancz, 1985; San Francisco, Mercury House, 1988.
Away from Home: A Novel in Ten Episodes. London, Gollancz, 1987.
Glasshouses. London, Gollancz, 1988; North Pomfret, Vermont, Trafalgar Square, 1989.
Snakes & Ladders. London, Little, Brown, 1993.

*

Biography: Entry in *Fourth Book of Junior Authors and Illustrators,* New York, H.W. Wilson, 1978, pp. 124-126.

Critical Studies: Entry in *Children's Literature Review,* Volume 8, Detroit, Gale, 1985; entry in *The Marble in the Water* by David Rees, Boston, Horn Book, 1980, 1-13.

Penelope Farmer comments:

Adolescence is a very interesting age to me: there's so much raw power in kids of that age, before their instincts—sexual energies in particular—are understood and focussed. Some of the power, maybe, is dissipated now in the much greater sophistication of late twentieth-century teenagers. All the same I am interested in exploring the tensions, the aggressions, the passions, and the search for identity arising from the physical changes at puberty. And precisely because these emotions are so powerful, I have till now found it easier to do so using mythological or supernatural themes. I feel strongly that fiction which attempts to corral all such feelings into stories of teenage romance—will she get the boy or won't she?—or which make the most controversial aspect a matter of how explicit you can make the details of the sexual act in a young adult novel diminish the characters it depicts and those for whom it is written. A lot of science fiction, on the other hand, gets it right—in that it confronts the young with real worlds, real issues of life and death, real levels of responsibility. Maybe that's where I will head next, therefore. Who knows!

*   *   *

Penelope Farmer's reputation as a children's writer has long rested securely on two books, *Charlotte Sometimes* and *A Castle of Bone,* published in 1969 and 1972 respectively. Farmer began to write while still at university, and *Charlotte Sometimes* was her seventh book. For all the grace and skill of her earlier books, *Charlotte Sometimes* was, however, breaking new ground, both for the author and in its genre. It is after all a "school story" opening with the first day at boarding school; and it must be the profoundest and most subversive such ever written, for the mechanism of the time slip is not really the little bed with wheels, but the disorientation, the displacement, the suppression of the self imposed by authoritarian contexts such as school. Changing places with Clare, who slept in the same bed forty years earlier, Charlotte loses a clear sense of who she is. Farmer's profound personal involvement in her work has often been remarked upon; the impression arises because the centre of awareness in the narration is interior to the central character, and the illumination offered by the fantasy is cast on the psyche, not primarily on the time or place or society portrayed by the story, in spite of the skill with which England in 1918 is evoked. Charlotte is simultaneously afraid of failing to achieve a return to her own time—failure to be herself—and afraid of being found out to be herself and not Clare, a most touching and realistic portrayal of the uncertainties of adolescence.

A Castle of Bone is still Farmer's masterpiece. Hugh's battered second-hand cupboard—it is never called a wardrobe—plays tricks, converting things put in it to earlier phases of themselves. It is in his room that he dreams, or perhaps hallucinates, moving across a mysterious landscape dominated by a castle, which both attracts and repels him. Hugh, his sister Jean, his friend Penn, and Penn's sister Anna together play with the cupboard and struggle to understand it, experimenting till disaster strikes; Hugh travels the hallucinatory landscapes alone, not recognising what he sees there. The Celtic tree alphabet controls the dreams and gradually unfolds a choice between life and death, or immortality, which the children must make. Most unusual for a work of fantasy, *A Castle of Bone* is both witty and funny. From a bolting pig nearly smashing banisters, to desperate attempts to stop a mother seeing her baby in case she recognises him, it is full of joyful relish for the funny side of the story.

It was nearly ten years before Farmer attempted such an ambitious work again, and then with *Year King* she tackled the edgy margins of psychology and fantasy to explore the nature of identity. Lan and Lew are identical twins, though not alike in character. The struggle between them, accompanied by terrifying telepathic episodes, is played out against the sensuous landscape of West Somerset and the ancient mythological patterning of the theme of the Year King. Farmer is herself a twin, and this book has passages of power and depth. But the freighting of her story with mythological material of huge import and the developing sexuality of her adolescent hero make this an unwieldy book, which Farmer has not entirely ordered and controlled, and it lacks the clarity and grace of which Farmer is capable.

The direction in which Farmer's talent was unfolding propelled her, after *Year King,* onto the adult list, to which she has made distinguished contributions. But she did not cease to write the shorter books for younger readers which she had been writing from the first alongside her books for older children. In this difficult field her command of simplicity and her power to suggest hidden meaning stand her in good stead, and her craftsmanship is immaculate.

In 1989 Farmer published *Thicker than Water,* a full-scale children's novel coming at a time when her public must have expected her to have moved permanently to the adult list. Once again twins are at the centre of the tale, which is a ghost story of sinister power. Becky doesn't know that her mother was a twin until her aunt dies and her mother takes in her sister's son—waiflike, sensitive Will. The pleasant country house in Derbyshire, with a worked out mine in the nearby field, is haunted for Will, though not for anyone else, by the voice of a child, crying and saying "Help me" and then, horribly, "Bury me." This complicates Will's already difficult choice between his family, till now unknown to him, and a foster home in London. In the end his attempts to save the ghost child, lost down the mine many years ago, nearly costs his own life. Against this dramatic story, the tug of resentment and love between the cousins is quietly explored and resolved. The use of alternating narration—Becky and Will taking turns in the first person—is effective, though Farmer's power to mimic a London voice is shaky here and there; but this is a genuinely frightening ghost story and a powerful one.

It is to be hoped that Farmer will not desert children's books, but continue to work in this genre, as well as in other literary forms. Her unique combination of reality and fantasy makes for challenging and rewarding reading.

—Jill Paton Walsh

FAST, Howard (Melvin)

Pseudonyms: E.V. Cunningham; Walter Ericson. **Nationality:** American. **Born:** New York City, 11 November 1914. **Education:** George Washington High School, New York, graduated 1931; National Academy of Design, New York. **Military Service:** Served with the Office of War Information, 1942-43, and the Army Film Project, 1944. **Family:** Married Bette Cohen in 1937; one daughter and one son. **Career:** War correspondent in the Far East for *Esquire* and *Coronet* magazines, 1945; taught at Indiana University, Bloomington, Summer 1947; imprisoned for contempt of Congress, 1947; owner, Blue Heron Press, New York, 1952-57; weekly columnist, New York *Observer,* since 1989. **Member:** Founder, World Peace Movement, and member, World Peace Council, 1950-55; American-Labour Party candidate for Congress for the 23rd District of New York, 1952; member, Fellowship for Reconciliation. **Awards:** Bread Loaf Writers Conference award, 1933; Schomburg Race Relations award, 1944; Newspaper Guild award, 1947; Jewish Book Council of America award, 1948; Stalin (now Soviet) International Peace prize, 1954; Screenwriters award, 1960; National Association of Independent Schools, award, 1962; American Library Association Notable Book citation, 1972, for *The Hessian;* Emmy award, for television play, 1976. **Address:** c/o Sterling Lord Agency, 65 Bleecker St., New York, New York 10012, U.S.A.

PUBLICATIONS

Novels

Two Valleys. New York, Dial Press, 1933; London, Dickson, 1934.
Strange Yesterday. New York, Dodd Mead, 1934.
Place in the City. New York, Harcourt Brace, 1937.
Conceived in Liberty: A Novel of Valley Forge. New York, Simon and Schuster, and London, Joseph, 1939.
The Last Frontier. New York, Duell, 1941; London, Lane, 1948.
The Tall Hunter. New York, Harper, 1942.
The Unvanquished. New York, Duell, 1942; London, Lane, 1947.
Citizen Tom Paine. New York, Duell, 1943; London, Lane, 1946.
Freedom Road. New York, Duell, 1944; London, Lane, 1946.
The American: A Middle Western Legend. New York, Duell, 1946; London, Lane, 1949.
The Children. New York, Duell, 1947.
Clarkton. New York, Duell, 1947.
My Glorious Brothers. Boston, Little Brown, 1948; London, Lane, 1950.
The Proud and the Free. Boston, Little Brown, 1950; London, Lane, 1952.
Spartacus. Privately printed, 1951; London, Lane, 1952.
Silas Timberman. New York, Blue Heron Press, 1954; London, Lane, 1955.
The Story of Lolu Gregg. New York, Blue Heron Press, 1956; London, Lane, 1957.
Moses, Prince of Egypt. New York, Crown, 1958; London, Methuen, 1959.
The Winston Affair. New York, Crown, 1959; London, Methuen, 1960.
The Golden River, in *The Howard Fast Reader.* New York, Crown, 1960.
Power. New York, Doubleday, 1962; London, Methuen, 1963.
Agrippa's Daughter. New York, Doubleday, 1964; London, Methuen, 1965.
Torquemada. New York, Doubleday, 1966; London, Methuen, 1967.
The Hunter and the Trap. New York, Dial Press, 1967.
The Crossing. New York, Morrow, 1971; London, Eyre Methuen, 1972.
The Hessian. New York, Morrow, 1972; London, Hodder and Stoughton, 1973.
The Immigrants. Boston, Houghton Mifflin, 1977; London, Hodder and Stoughton, 1978.
The Second Generation. Boston, Houghton Mifflin, and London, Hodder and Stoughton, 1978.
The Establishment. Boston, Houghton Mifflin, 1979; London, Hodder and Stoughton, 1980.
The Legacy. Boston, Houghton Mifflin, and London, Hodder and Stoughton, 1981.
Max. Boston, Houghton Mifflin, 1982; London, Hodder and Stoughton, 1983.
The Outsider. Boston, Houghton Mifflin, 1984; London, Hodder and Stoughton, 1985.
The Immigrant's Daughter. Boston, Houghton Mifflin, 1985; London, Hodder and Stoughton, 1986.
The Call of Fife and Drum: Three Novels of the Revolution. Secaucus, New Jersey, Citadel Press, 1987.
The Dinner Party. Boston, Houghton Mifflin, and London, Hodder and Stoughton, 1987.
The Pledge. Boston, Houghton Mifflin, 1988; London, Hodder and Stoughton, 1989.
The Confession of Joe Cullen. Boston, Houghton Mifflin, 1989; London, Hodder and Stoughton, 1990.
Sylvia: A Novel. Secaucus, New Jersey, Carol Publishing, 1992.
The Trial of Abigail Goodman. New York, Crown, 1993.
Seven Days in June: A Novel of the American Revolution. Secaucus, New Jersey, Carol Publishing, 1994.
The Bridge Builder's Story: A Novel. Armonk, New York, M.E. Sharpe, 1995.
An Independent Woman. New York, Harcourt Brace & Co., 1997.

Short Stories

Patrick Henry and the Frigate's Keel and Other Stories of a Young Nation. New York, Duell, 1945.
Departure and Other Stories. Boston, Little Brown, 1949.
The Last Supper and Other Stories. New York, Blue Heron Press, 1955; London, Lanc, 1956.
The Edge of Tomorrow. New York, Bantam, 1961; London, Corgi, 1962.
The General Zapped an Angel. New York, Morrow, 1970.
A Touch of Infinity: Thirteen Stories of Fantasy and Science Fiction. New York, Morrow, 1973; London, Hodder and Stoughton, 1975.
Time and the Riddle: Thirty-One Zen Stories. Pasadena, California, Ward Ritchie Press, 1975.

Poetry

Never to Forget the Battle of the Warsaw Ghetto, with William Gropper. New York, Jewish Peoples Fraternal Order, 1946.
Korean Lullaby. New York, American Peace Crusade, n.d.

Plays

The Hammer (produced New York, 1950).
Thirty Pieces of Silver (produced Melbourne, 1951). New York, Blue Heron Press, and London, Lane, 1954.
George Washington and the Water Witch. London, Lane, 1956.
The Crossing (produced Dallas, 1962).
David and Paula (produced New York, 1982).
Citizen Tom Paine: A Play in Two Acts, adaptation of his own novel (produced Williamstown, Massachusetts, 1985). Boston, Houghton Mifflin, 1986.
The Novelist (produced Williamstown, Massachusetts, 1987).
The Second Coming (produced Greenwich, Connecticut, 1991).

Screenplays: *The Hill,* Doubleday, 1964; *Spartacus* (with Dalton Trumbo), 1965; *The Hessian,* 1971.

Television Plays: *What's a Nice Girl Like You. . . ?,* 1971; *The Ambassador* (*Benjamin Franklin* series), 1974; *21 Hours at Munich,* with Edward Hume, 1976.

Nonfiction

Haym Salomon, Son of Liberty. New York, Messner, 1941.
Lord Baden-Powell of the Boy Scouts. New York, Messner, 1941.
Goethals and the Panama Canal. New York, Messner, 1942.
The Picture-Book History of the Jews, with Bette Fast. New York, Hebrew Publishing Company, 1942.
The Incredible Tito. New York, Magazine House, 1944.
Intellectuals in the Fight for Peace. New York, Masses and the Mainstream, 1949.
Literature and Reality. New York, International Publishers, 1950.
Tito and His People. Winnipeg, Contemporary Publishers, 1950.
Peekskill, U.S.A.: A Personal Experience. New York, Civil Rights Congress, and London, International Publishing Company, 1951.
Spain and Peace. New York, Joint Anti-Fascist Refugee Committee, 1952.
The Passion of Sacco and Vanzetti: A New England Legend. New York, Blue Heron Press, 1953; London, Lane, 1954.
The Naked God: The Writer and the Communist Party. New York, Praeger, 1957; London, Bodley Head, 1958.
The Howard Fast Reader. New York, Crown, 1960.
The Jews: Story of a People. New York, Dial Press, 1968; London, Cassell, 1970.
The Art of Zen Meditation. Culver City, California, Peace Press, 1977.
Being Red: A Memoir. Boston, Houghton Mifflin, 1990.
The Novelist: A Romantic Portrait of Jane Austen. New York, French, 1992.
War and Peace: Observations on Our Times. Armonk, New York, Sharpe, 1993.

Other

The Romance of a People (for children). New York, Hebrew Publishing, 1941.
Editor, *The Selected Works of Tom Paine.* New York, Modern Library, 1946; London, Lane, 1948.
Editor, *The Best Short Stories of Theodore Dreiser.* Cleveland, World, 1947.
Tony and the Wonderful Door (for children). New York, Blue Heron, 1952; as *The Magic Door,* Culver City, California, Peace Press, 1979.
April Morning (for children). New York, Crown, and London, Methuen, 1961.
Contributor, *The Human Almanac: People Through Time,* by Richard Burrill. Sierra Pacific Press, 1983.

Novels as E.V. Cunningham

Sylvia. New York, Doubleday, 1960; London, Deutsch, 1962.
Phyllis. New York, Doubleday, and London, Deutsch, 1962.
Alice. New York, Doubleday, 1963; London, Deutsch, 1965.
Lydia. New York, Doubleday, 1964; London, Deutsch, 1965.
Shirley. New York, Doubleday, and London, Deutsch, 1964.
Penelope. New York, Doubleday, 1965; London, Deutsch, 1966.
Helen. New York, Doubleday, 1966; London, Deutsch, 1967.
Margie. New York, Morrow, 1966; London, Deutsch, 1968.
Sally. New York, Morrow, and London, Deutsch, 1967.
Samantha. New York, Morrow, 1967; London, Deutsch, 1968; as *The Case of the Angry Actress,* New York, Dell, 1984.
Cynthia. New York, Morrow, 1968; London, Deutsch, 1969.

The Assassin Who Gave Up His Gun. New York, Morrow, 1969; London, Deutsch, 1970.
Millie. New York, Morrow, 1973; London, Deutsch, 1975.
The Case of the One-Penny Orange. New York, Holt Rinehart, 1977; London, Deutsch, 1978.
The Case of the Russian Diplomat. New York, Holt Rinehart, 1978; London, Deutsch, 1979.
The Case of the Poisoned Eclairs. New York, Holt Rinehart, 1979; London, Deutsch, 1980.
The Case of the Sliding Pool. New York, Delacorte Press, 1981; London, Gollancz, 1982.
The Case of the Kidnapped Angel. New York, Delacorte Press, 1982; London, Gollancz, 1983.
The Case of the Murdered Mackenzie. New York, Delacorte Press, 1984; London, Gollancz, 1985.
The Wabash Factor. New York, Delacorte Press, 1986; London, Gollancz, 1987.

Novels as Walter Ericson

Fallen Angel. Boston, Little Brown, 1951; as *The Darkness Within,* New York, Ace, 1953; as *Mirage* (as Howard Fast), New York, Fawcett, 1965.

*

Media Adaptations: *Man in the Middle* (film, based on *The Winston Affair),* 1964; *Mirage* (film), 1965; *Penelope* (film), 1966; *Jigsaw* (film, based on *Fallen Angel),* 1968; *The Immigrants* (television miniseries), 1979. *Freedom Road* (film), 1980.

Manuscript Collections: University of Pennsylvania, Philadelphia; University of Wisconsin, Madison.

Biography: Entry in *Dictionary of Literary Biography,* Volume 9, Detroit, Gale, 1981; essay in *Contemporary Authors Autobiography Series,* Volume 18, Detroit, Gale, 1993.

Critical Studies: *History and Conscience: The Case of Howard Fast* by Hershel D. Meyer, Princeton, New Jersey, Anvil Atlas, 1958; *Counterpoint* by Roy Newquist, New York, Rand McNally, 1964; entry in *Contemporary Literary Criticism,* Volume 23, Detroit, Gale, 1983.

*   *   *

Howard Fast, who has written under the names E.V. Cunningham and Walter Ericson, is as multifaceted as he is multitalented. His writings are so diverse that the use of pseudonyms would be appropriate if they were indeed used to differentiate between the categories and periods of his works. This is, however, not the case. Fast used pseudonyms so that his work might be published during a time in which he was blacklisted by J. Edgar Hoover's FBI and the House Committee on Un-american Activities because of the alleged contents of his biographical novel *Citizen Tom Paine.*

Fast was active politically and even ran for Congress on the American Labor Party ticket. These activities, coupled with his interest in history, led him to serve as a war and foreign correspondent as well as to write factually based books. His early repertoire contains both historical works as well as novels that have their basis in historical fact. Some of these titles include (but are by no means limited to): *Conceived in Liberty: A Novel of Valley Forge; The Romance of a People; Lord Baden-Powell of the Boy Scouts; Haym Salomon, Son of Liberty; The Picture-Book History of the Jews; Goethals and the Panama Canal; Freedom Road;* and *Patrick Henry and the Frigate's Keel.*

At the time of his blacklisting, Fast had just finished writing the book that was eventually made into the award-winning film *Spartacus.* This novel, which also has its basis in history, is about the slave revolt against the Romans approximately seventy-five years before Christ. Spartacus was a slave whose thirst for freedom compelled him to lead the uprising. As in all of Fast's work, his vividly detailed descriptions of the characters and the events oblige the reader to form mental images as the stories unfold. Another book in this genre is *Moses, Prince of Egypt.*

A later historically based novel popular with young adults is *April Morning.* This story is set in Lexington, Massachusetts, during the American Revolution. A self-absorbed young boy is suddenly thrust into the responsibilities of manhood while the nation is fighting for its independence. The boy's maturation and desire to win the respect of his elders is dramatically represented by Fast's distinctive characterizations.

Under the name of E.V. Cunningham, the pseudonym he used in the United States during his blacklisting, Fast wrote many books in the suspense-murder-mystery genre. The first in this group, *Sylvia,* about a beautiful and mysterious woman, sparked an entire series of "mystery lady" books, including *Phyllis, Alice, Shirley, Lydia, Penelope,* etc., which in turn inspired a series of crime stories, including *The Case of the Kidnapped Angel* and *The Case of the Russian Diplomat.* The film *Mirage* was based upon a mystery written by Fast under the pseudonym of Walter Ericson.

The book *The Pledge* was based upon the author's own professional experiences and his tribulations during the McCarthy Era. Fast has also written nonfiction books on both the Jewish people and the Buddhist religion.

Young adults may be most familiar with Fast's intense character studies in the recent book *Max,* and in the series of novels beginning with *The Immigrants,* which was also made into a movie. This saga of the Lavette family, which courses through several decades, begins in *The Immigrants,* then continues with *Second Generation, The Establishment, The Legacy,* and *The Immigrant's Daughter.* These stories all vibrantly depict the emotionally charged scenes in which the characters find themselves. The appropriate political climate is also included to set the story in its proper framework. At first glance, these ponderous novels seem insurmountable to the average reader. Once begun, however, the "pages seem to fly," and readers are absorbed into Fast's telling of the tale. Even when the novel is finished, readers may be anxious to begin reading the next book in the series. It should be noted that although the books are written in time sequence, they "stand alone" and each may be read independently, though this is not preferable.

Fast has stated that he is "always delighted when any book of mine is read widely by young people." He feels the books they read "will endure." It is obvious that Fast's extensive literary talents most certainly will.

—Laurie Schwartz Guttenberg

FEELINGS, Tom

Nationality: American. **Born:** Brooklyn, New York, 19 May 1933. **Education:** Received a scholarship to Cartoonist and Illustrators' School, New York City, 1951-53; School of Visual Arts, New York, 1957-60. **Military Service:** Graphics Division, U. S. Air Force, 1953-57. **Family:** Married 1) Muriel Grey in 1968 (divorced, 1974); two children; 2) Diane Johnson. **Career:** Freelance illustrator, from 1959; illustrator for *African Review,* Ghana Publishing Company, Ghana, 1964-66; illustration instructor for Ministry of Education and head of children's book project, Government of Guyana, 1971-74; freelance illustrator for Ghana television and newspapers; Associate Professor of Art, University of South Carolina, Columbia, 1989-95. Contributor of articles to *Black World, Horn Book, Cricket, Freedom Ways, Harper's/Liberator, Look,* and *Pageant;* contributor of illustrations to various classroom texts. **Awards:** Certificate of Merit, Society of Illustrators, 1961, 1962, and 1968; Nancy Bloch Memorial award, Downtown Community School, 1968, Newbery Honor Book award, American Library Association, 1969, and Lewis Carroll Shelf award, 1970, all for *To Be a Slave;* Caldecott Honor Book award, American Library Association, 1972, and Art Books for Children citations, Brooklyn Museum and Brooklyn Public Library, 1973, 1974, 1975, all for *Moja Means One;* Caldecott Honor Book award, American Library Association, 1972, Boston Globe-Horn Book award, 1974, Art Books for Children citation, 1976, and American Book award nomination, 1981, all for *Jambo Means Hello;* Outstanding Achievement Award, The School of Visual Arts, 1974; Woodward School annual book award, 1973; Brooklyn Museum citation, 1973; American Library Association notable book citation, and Horn Book honor list, for *Black Pilgrimage;* Children's Book Showcase award, Children's Book Council, 1977, for *From Slave to Abolitionist;* Coretta Scott King award and American Library Association Notable Book award, American Library Association, 1979, for *Something on My Mind;* Visual Arts Grant, National Endowment for the Arts, 1982; Award of Excellence, Multicultural Publishers Exchange, 1991, for *Tommy Traveler in the World of Black History;* Coretta Scott King award, 1994, for *Soul Looks Back in Wonder;* Coretta Scott King Honor award and American Library Association Notable Book award, 1982, for *Daydreamers;* Coretta Scott King award, 1996, for *The Middle Passage;* Honorary Doctor of Arts Degree: The School of Visual Arts, New York, 1996; Honorary D.H.L.: John Jay College of Criminal Justice, New York, 1997. **Agent:** Marie Brown, 625 Broadway, New York, New York 10012, U.S.A. **Address:** 180 Wateree Ave., Columbia, South Carolina 29205, U.S.A.

PUBLICATIONS FOR YOUNG ADULTS (illustrated by the author)

Black Pilgrimage. New York, Lothrop, 1972.
Tommy Traveler in the World of Black History. New York, Writers & Readers, 1991.
Editor, *Soul Looks Back in Wonder.* New York, Dial, 1993.
The Middle Passage. New York, Dial, 1995; (note: this was adapted from an earlier comic strip, "Tommy Traveler in the World of Negro History," New York, New York Age [bygone], 1958).

*

Critical Studies: "The Artist at Work: Technique and the Artist's Vision" by Tom Feelings, in *Horn Book,* Vol. 61, No. 6, 1985, 685-95; "Tom Feelings and *The Middle Passage*" by Rudine Sims Bishop, in *Horn Book,* Vol. 72, No. 4, 1996, 436-42; review of *The Middle Passage* by Kathleen Leonardson, in *Marblehead Advocate,* 4 April 1996; review of *The Middle Passage* by Karin Schill, in *Augusta Chronicle* (Augusta, Georgia), 8 August 1996.

Illustrator: *Samory Toure* by Roland Snellings, 1963; *Bola and the Oba's Drummers* by Letta Schatz, 1967; *When the Stones Were Soft: East African Folktales* complied by Eleanor Heady, 1968; *The Congo: River of Mystery* by Robin McKown, 1968; *Song of the Empty Bottles* by Osmond Molarsky, 1968; *To Be a Slave* by Julius Lester, 1968; *The Tuesday Elephant* by Nancy Garfield, 1968; *Black Folktales* compiled by Julius Lester, 1969; *Panther's Moon* by Ruskin Bond, 1969; *A Quiet Place* by Rose Blue, 1969; *Tales of Temba: Traditional African Stories* by Kathleen Arnot, 1969; *African Crafts* by Jane Kerina, 1970; *Zamani Goes to Market* by Muriel Feelings, 1970; *Moja Means One: Swahili Counting Book* by Muriel Feelings, 1971; *Jambo Means Hello: Swahili Alphabet Book* by Muriel Feelings, 1974; *From Slave to Abolitionist: The Life of William Wells Brown* by Lucille Schulberg Warner, 1976; *Something on My Mind* by Nikki Grimes, 1978; *Black Child* by Joyce Carol Thomas, 1981; *Daydreamers* by Eloise Greenfield, 1981; *Now Sheba Sings the Song* by Maya Angelou, 1987; *Talking with Artists* edited by Pat Cummings, 1992.

Tom Feelings comments:

When I am asked what kind of work I do, my answer is that I am a storyteller in picture form, who tries to reflect and interpret the lives and experiences of the people who gave me life. When I am asked who I am, I say I am an African who was born in America. Both answers connect me specifically with my past and present . . . therefore I bring to my art a quality which is rooted in the culture of Africa . . . and expanded by the experience of being Black in America. I use the vehicle of "fine art" and "illustration" as a viable expression of form, yet striving always to do this from an African perspective, an African world view, and above all to tell the African story; this is my content. The struggle to create artwork, as well as to live creatively under any conditions and survive (like my ancestors), embodies my particular heritage in America.

Throughout the centuries Africa's powerful celebratory rites have always acted as a spiritually strong balancing force to counter the painful experience of slavery. Clearly evident in Black music, Black dance, and the world of athletics, wherever there is a level playing field, we innovate, we improvise within that restrictive form, then transcend it, raising the level of excellence. In the words of writer Paule Marshall, "we are a people who transformed humiliating experiences into creative ones."

As a storyteller in picture form, as an African who was born in America, how could I do anything else but try and live up to that legacy and become a vehicle for this profound, dramatic histroy to pass through.

*   *   *

As eloquent as the words that Tom Feelings uses to describe the source of his art are the actual illustrations that strive to tell the story of his people. By appealing to the reader's visual perceptions in the stories he tells through art, Tom Feelings creates an awareness of the complexity of the experience of African Americans both past and present. Drawing from his own experiences both in the United States and Africa, his personal life is deeply embedded in his literary creations, as he struggles to seek a balance of both joy and sorrow in his personal perceptions of his own heritage. His need to create pictures that reflect the complexity of the African experience combine with movement and rhythm found in music as he uses an improvisational approach to his drawing. "In black culture, joy and pain don't just sit side by side, they interact, and build on each other," Feelings told Rudine Sims Bishop in *Horn Book.* Bishop added: "This interaction of the opposing forces of joy and pain is, in Feelings' view, a characteristic of black life and culture in America, and it is basic to all of his work with African-American themes."

As a young artist, Feelings began drawing the faces of people in his community in New York. In *Black Pilgrimage* he describes the dark, somber intense moods that became evident in the portraits he drew. He blamed these moods on negative self-images, frustration, and a vivid awareness of the direct and indirect struggle between the races. However, drawings of children reflected the beauty of joy, as they were not aware of these struggles. In *Black Pilgrimage* he says that children as subjects had less time to be exposed to the pain of being Black in a white country and that they reflect the best in us before it is changed or corrupted. He decided to go to Ghana to find more of this spirit in his people as a whole. His art gradually reflected the joy he found in the people there through brighter colors and lilting lines. When he returned to the United States he was challenged to find within his art a balance of both the sorrow and exuberance of his people. This he felt he first achieved in the illustrations for the young adult book *To Be A Slave.*

Feelings expresses concern for young people in his sensitively phrased comments within the pages of *Soul Looks Back in Wonder.* "My soul looks back in wonder at how African creativity has sustained us and how it still flows—seeking, searching for new ways to connect the ancient with the new, the young with the old, the unborn with the ancestors." In this richly illustrated volume, thirteen poems by outstanding African-American poets were specifically created for Feelings art. Both poetry and accompanying illustrations celebrate the strength, beauty, creativity and endurance of African-American heritage. "Too many teenagers are growing up in an environment where indifference and hostility are bullets aimed straight at the core of their spirits," Feelings says in his closing comments. He strives to create literature which reflects in pictures and words the heritage of African-American youth.

While discovering the joy among people in Ghana, a friend inquired as to what happened to the millions of people who were taken to the United States, West Indies, and South America as slaves. As he pondered the answer, so began a work which would take twenty years to complete. While illustrating many books for other African-American authors, Feelings prepared the illustrations that were to tell the story of *The Middle Passage.* This book consists of sixty-four narrative paintings of the tragic journey of enslaved Africans across the Atlantic. In reviewing this book, Kathleen Leonardson wrote in the *Marblehead Advocate,* "The book itself is a graphic panorama, with images, full of emotion and suffering. . . . The artwork has a surreal quality, a beauty of form, which belies the horror depicted. . . . White men are depicted as ghost-like beings, not fully human, perhaps not fully incarnate.

Blacks are drawn with depth, both emotionally and physically.... It is only through such a vehicle that the impact of slavery can be experienced at a visceral level.'' Feelings helps readers to sense the horror, depravity, greed, and cruelty of this era of history. The authenticity of *The Middle Passage* is grounded in his extensive research, and his use of books and black music from all continents where slaves were taken. Even the artistic medium and techniques used by Feelings reflect his culture. Having only tissue and black and white tempera paint available in Ghana, he determined to do more with less. The spontaneity of the paintings reveals the triumph as felt in the music he collected. Within the pictures, the reader senses the triumph of spirit and beauty in spite of the evil of the circumstances.

When asked why he felt he needed to go back to the horrors of the past, Feelings replied in an *Augusta Chronicle* interview, ''I do it because unless we deal with the past, we won't understand what's happening now. Some things in our community happen over and over again because we never did deal with the past.'' He feels to address the past will help address problems of crime and poverty facing the his people today.

Tom Feelings tells stories in his books that are for all ages and all races. He portrays especially the beauty and strength of a people whose experience is heavy with sorrow and pain. Young readers of African-American heritage can find affirmation of their race, while readers of other ethnicities can nurture their understanding of African-American history from an authentic perspective. The visual experience extends the literary experience beyond what printed text can offer.

—Janelle B. Mathis

FERRIS, Jean

Nationality: American. **Born:** Fort Leavenworth, Kansas, 24 January 1939. **Education:** Stanford University, Palo Alto, California, B.A. 1961, M.A. 1962. **Family:** Married Alfred G. Ferris; two children. **Career:** Clinical audiologist, Veterans Administration Hospital, San Francisco, California, 1962-1963, San Diego Speech and Hearing Association, San Diego, California, 1963-1965, and in a doctor's office, San Diego, 1975-1976; free-lance writer, since 1977; secretary and office assistant, San Diego, 1979-1984. **Awards:** Society of Children's Book Writers grant, 1984, 1987; American Library Association (ALA) Best Books for Young Adults, *School Library Journal*'s Best Books of the Year, *Booklist* Editor's Choices for Young Adults, and Southern California Council on Literature for Children and Young People award for distinguished fiction, all 1987, all for *Invincible Summer*; ALA Recommended Book for Reluctant Young Readers, International Reading Association Young Adults Choice, Iowa Young Readers Award, and Virginia Young Readers Award nomination, 1988, all for *Looking for Home*; ALA Best Book for Young Adults, and California Young Readers Medal nomination, 1992, both for *Across the Grain*; Utah Children's Book Award nomination, and South Carolina Young Adult Book Award nomination, 1995, for *Relative Strangers*; Junior Library Guild selection, 1995, and New York Public Library's Books for the Teenage selection, 1997, for *Signs of Life*; ALA Best Books nomination, Junior Library Guild selection, Texas Library Association selection for high school

reading, 1998, for *All that Glitters*. **Address:** 2278 San Juan Road, San Diego, California 92103, U.S.A.

PUBLICATIONS FOR YOUNG ADULTS

Fiction

Amen, Moses Gardenia. New York, Farrar, Straus, Giroux, 1983.
The Stainless Steel Rule. New York, Farrar, Straus, Giroux, 1986.
Invincible Summer. New York, Farrar, Straus, Giroux, 1987.
Looking for Home. New York, Farrar, Straus, Giroux, 1989.
Across the Grain. New York, Farrar, Straus, Giroux, 1990.
Relative Strangers. New York, Farrar, Straus, Giroux, 1993.
Signs of Life. New York, Farrar, Straus, Giroux, 1995.
All That Glitters. New York, Farrar, Straus, Giroux, 1996.
Into the Wind. New York, Avon Books, 1996.
Song of the Sea. New York, Avon Books, 1996.
Weather the Storm. New York, Avon Books, 1996.
Bad. New York, Farrar, Straus, Giroux, 1998.
Love Among the Walnuts. New York, Harper Collins, 1998.

*

Critical Sources: Entry in *Contemporary Authors New Revision Series,* Vol. 38, Detroit, Gale, 1993, 129-130; entry in *Something About the Author,* Vol. 56, Detroit, Gale, 1989, 47-48; review of *Amen, Moses Gardenia,* in *Bulletin of the Center for Children's Books* (Chicago), January 1984, 85-86; review of *Invincible Summer* by Zena Sutherland, in *Bulletin of the Center for Children's Books* (Chicago), July-August 1987, 206; review of *Looking for Home* by Zena Sutherland, in *Bulletin of the Center for Children's Books* (Chicago), July-August 1989, 274; review of *Across the Grain* by Robert Strang, in *Bulletin of the Center for Children's Books* (Chicago), February 1991, 140; review of *Relative Strangers* by Deborah Stevenson, in *Bulletin of the Center for Children's Books* (Chicago), November 1993, 79.

Jean Ferris comments:

Culture changes. Fads change. Clothing styles and hairdos and language change. But emotions do not. The way I felt about family, boys, school and my future when I was 13, 14, 15, 16 and 17 is the same as today's teens feel about the same concerns. True, they have things on their minds that I did not—should I have sex? When? With whom? How do I respond when someone offers me drugs? Why is my family splitting up? But I wondered what to do about alcohol, cigarettes, kissing on the first date, and my parent's arguments—still in the same ballpark. And many of today's kids have less support than I did, from family, church and community. They need help, and the answers to some hard questions, just as I did—and still do. Often, I found, and continue to find, my help and my answers, and some comfort, too, in books. I try to write the kinds of books I wanted to read, to meet the needs that I had, and that I believe today's young people still have. And I want my books to be entertaining, as well. Today's young people have many compelling demands for their attention—jobs, video games, the Internet. Books can seem very slow, and dull and difficult to someone who is used to speed, and flash and change. But books stay with you, in your mind, the way a video game or sitcom do not. What you put inside your head makes you into who you become. So it is important to read rich, thought-provoking, spirited books in order to become a rich, thought-provoking, spirited person. They don't have to be my books, just as long as they're somebody's.

*   *   *

Jean Ferris's novels present a range of female characters, from autonomous to dependent teenage girls. Some of these books benefit from her strong characterizations and examination of family dynamics and the role of love, while others seem formulaic and trite. Many of her characters are creative, resolving their problems with intelligence and humor. They rely on themselves. Romance, however, often becomes a priority for Ferris's female characters, or is their only source of a sense of well being.

Farrell, the depressed and insecure protagonist of Ferris's first book, *Amen, Moses Gardenia,* is isolated from her peers by her alcoholic, social-climbing mother who insists that the family keep moving to newer and bigger houses. Raised in poverty, Farrell's mother is obsessed with possessions and is oblivious to her daughter's solitude. Despite Farrell's efforts, she is unable to make any friends at school, feeling intimidated by the popular cheerleaders whom she labels "the Blondes." Farrell copes by dreaming of being surrounded by friends playing what she calls grayball, a game in which she is always the center of attention. In reality, she suffers "dark spells" of intense and prolonged depressed moods. Earl Mae, the family's maid, serves as Farrell's primary nurturer and confidante; she has her own tragic background, having lost her husband and children in a fire. Her companion, Moses Gardenia, a salesman who considers himself a "persuader" because he convinces people what he thinks is best for them, also befriends Farrell and attempts to alleviate her pain through humorous stories.

When she acts out in school, Farrell encounters another mentor, Niele Sparks, the school counselor who tries to help Farrell secure friendships. She takes Farrell to a nature group outing, where Farrell finally meets Ted Kittredge, whom she has admired from afar. They begin a romantic relationship which alleviates Farrell's melancholy. Her happiness peaks during a weekend ski trip with Ted which she terms "perfect." Returning home, Farrell is again alone and in conflict with her illogical mother when Earl Mae leaves town for a cooking contest. Misinterpreting a phone call from Ted and believing that he favors his former girlfriend, one of the despised "blondes," over her, Farrell attempts suicide on her birthday but is saved by Niele and redeemed by her family and Ted who soothes her with the comment that he prefers an intelligent girl to a pretty one. Assured of Ted's commitment to her, Farrell finds life bearable. Although Ferris's efforts to depict teenage depression are admirable, the suggestion that romance can cure emotional illness is unsatisfactory, causing the reader to ponder Farrell's fate if Ted ever leaves her.

Ferris's second book, *The Stainless Steel Rule,* presents a stronger protagonist, high school swimmer Kitty, who reexamines her friendships with Fran and Mary and her relationship with her father. Kitty wants a responsible father, but she is more of a parent to her immature and often absent father than he is to her. At school, Kitty admires a handsome new student, Nick, but he chooses Mary as his girlfriend. When Nick realizes that Mary is diabetic, he encourages her to abandon her insulin and try mind control to regulate her body. Although she is concerned about Mary's well-being and aware that Nick is mean and manipulative, Kitty is

unsure of herself and hesitates to act because of Fran's "stainless steel rule," which suggests that they should never interfere in someone else's life because that person will not forgive them. Finally, motivated by a dream, Kitty tells Mary's foster parents who discover Mary in a coma. Although aware that their relationship has been altered, the girls manage to reconcile and reestablish their trust in each other and themselves.

Health is also an issue in *Invincible Summer,* in which Robin, an Iowa high school student anxious to leave her small town, is diagnosed with leukemia. In the hospital she meets Rick who suffers from a similar condition. Together they cope with the despair of their illnesses and hope for the future. Their friendship evolves into a sexual relationship, and their intimacy offers them courage and life despite their bleak prognoses. Ferris effectively reveals their story in sections, divided into seasons of the year, and the weather and holidays serve as metaphors for their recovery: Robin is weakest in fall and winter then revives in spring and summer.

Daphne Blake finds love where she least expects it in *Looking for Home.* Coping with an abusive father, she works to earn money to attend college. Desiring affection absent in her home, she agrees to have sex with her boyfriend Scott on prom night and becomes pregnant. Daphne decides not to tell Scott about the baby and escapes to a bigger city, named Lincoln, where she is alone except for her unborn child. She locates housing in the YWCA and finds a job in a restaurant where she befriends a retired doctor and a college student. After a fainting spell reveals her pregnancy, Daphne confides in Mattie, an artist who prepares collages of garbage that all have one spot of red to symbolize her focus. Through her friendships, Daphne learns that one mistake does not ruin her life and that family consists of the people that you love. Her choices win her independence from fear and isolation and offer her hope of an education and a focus for the future.

Perhaps Ferris's strongest female protagonist is Berkeley in *Relative Strangers.* An intelligent high school senior, Berkeley, named for the school her mother had wanted to attend, is mature and independent. She and her mother Lily have a loving bond and respect each other's individuality. Berkeley's father, known as Ace, is a successful insurance salesman who divorced Lily when Berkeley was young and has little contact with his daughter. Berkeley idealizes her father until he invites her on a trip to Europe, and she gets to know him. On the trip she meets his materialistic new wife and embittered stepdaughter, Shelby, who is coping with the suicide of her father. Ace remains self-centered and aloof from Berkeley and is inconsiderate of her feelings. He does not respect Berkeley's relationship with her boyfriend Spike, who is also touring Europe. Spike maturely realizes that he and Berkeley have plenty of time in America to be a couple and suggests that she give her father a chance to be a parent despite his imperfections. Berkeley becomes aware of her charming and manipulative father's deceit and lies, learning about his true identity rather than her idealized image. She recognizes and accepts that she is both "lioness and rabbit," sometimes courageous and sometimes a coward, and reinforces her self respect and faith in herself.

Hannah in *Signs of Life* resembles Berkeley in terms of character. Intelligent, creative, and adventurous, Hannah is unable to grieve for her identical twin sister Molly who was killed by a drunk driver. Hannah accompanies her parents to France where they hope to heal while touring such sites as the Lascaux cave paintings. Feeling paralyzed by her grief, Hannah believes that Molly was her mother's favorite child, creating a conflict with her parents. She meets Stefan, a gypsy circus performer, who helps her accept her loss and risk loving again. Stefan, like Spike, is nurturing of Hannah without expecting her to sacrifice her personal needs for his happiness. During her visit, Hannah dreams of living during prehistoric times, and her visions give her strength to mourn for Molly, accept a second loss with the departure of Stefan, and reconcile with her mother.

Will in *Across the Grain* and Brian in *All That Glitters* are both strong male characters. Will takes care of his erratic older sister Paige, moving to the desert to help her manage a diner. Parentless, he needs Paige to be an emotional support, but she is too busy dating men and avoiding work. Will meets Sam Webb, a middle-aged man who acts as a father figure and guides Will's emotional maturation by teaching him to carve wood and build a house. Mike, the daughter of a visiting anthropologist, also affects Will's life through her anger, intensity, and encouragement. Tia in *All That Glitters* resembles Mike in personality. She is brooding and mysterious to Brian, who is spending several weeks in the Florida Keys with his father while his mother remarries. Tia's and Brian's friendship focuses on the absence of fathers and role of substitute father figures in their lives. Brian helps Tia readjust her attitudes toward men and her self perception as an African American in a predominantly white society. Tia, Brian, and his father help locate and protect a sunken ship filled with treasure from scavengers. Father and son are aloof toward each other until a hurricane forces them to work together to avoid drowning. Although both stories are suspenseful, at times the plot twists are predictable and the characters seem stereotypical.

Ferris's American Dreams trilogy, *Into the Wind, Song of the Sea,* and *Weather the Storm,* deviates from her strong, conflict resolution novels. These books, instead, are sentimental historical romances, featuring teenaged Rosie and her adventures with privateer Captain Robert Lyons, his crew, and his nemesis Captain Lawrence in the 1814 Caribbean. Rosie is first featured as a girl who can make her own decisions then is ultimately transformed into a passive wife to Lyons, relying on him instead of herself. Her submission to masculine authority seems to fit a fictional formula, creating a disappointing heroine when compared with Ferris's other proactive protagonists. Although Ferris creates complex characters and intriguing situations in most of her books, her weaker novels detract from her best work.

—Elizabeth D. Schafer

FISK, Nicholas

Pseudonym for David Higginbottom. **Nationality:** British. **Born:** London, 14 October 1923. **Education:** Ardingly College, Sussex. **Military Service:** Served in the Royal Air Force during World War II. **Family:** Married Dorothy Antoinette Richold in 1949; twin daughters and two sons. **Career:** Writer and illustrator; has worked as an actor, journalist, musician, editor, publisher, and speaker to children and adults; former advertising creative director, head of creative groups, and consultant. **Agent:** Laura Cecil, 17 Alwyne Villas, Canonbury, London N1 2HG. **Address:** 59 Elstree Road, Bushey Heath, Hertfordshire WD2 3QX, England.

PUBLICATIONS FOR YOUNG ADULTS

Science Fiction

Space Hostages. London, Hamish Hamilton, 1967; New York, Macmillan, 1969.

Trillions. London, Hamish Hamilton, 1971; New York, Pantheon, 1973.

Grinny. London, Heinemann, 1973; Nashville, Nelson, 1974.

High Way Home. London, Hamish Hamilton, 1973.

Little Green Spacemen. London, Hamish Hamilton, 1974.

Time Trap. London, Gollancz, 1976.

Wheelie in the Stars. London, Gollancz, 1976.

Antigrav. London, Kestrel, 1978.

Escape from Splatterbang. London, Pelham, 1978; New York, Macmillan, 1979; as *Flamers,* London, Knight, 1979.

Monster Maker. London, Pelham, 1979; New York, Macmillan, 1980.

A Rag, A Bone, and a Hank of Hair. London, Kestrel, 1980; New York, Crown, 1982.

The Starstormer Saga (Starstormers, Sunburst, Catfang, Evil Eye, Volcano). London, Knight, 5 vols., 1980-83.

Robot Revolt. London, Pelham, 1981.

On the Flip Side. London, Kestrel, 1983.

You Remember Me! London, Kestrel, 1984; Boston, Hall, 1987.

Bonkers Clocks, illustrated by Colin West. London, Viking Kestrel, 1985.

Dark Sun, Bright Sun, illustrated by Brigid Marlin. London, Blackie, 1986.

Mindbenders. London, Viking Kestrel, 1987.

Backlash. London, Walker, 1988.

The Talking Car, illustrated by Ann John. London, Macmillan, 1988.

The Telly Is Watching You. London, Macdonald, 1989.

The Worm Charmers. London, Walker, 1989.

The Back-yard War. London, Macmillan, 1990.

The Model Village. London, Walker, 1990.

A Hole in the Head. London, Walker, 1991.

Pig Ignorant. London, Walker, 1991.

Extraterrestrial Tales. London, Puffin, 1991.

Editor, *The Puffin Book of Science Fiction.* London, Viking, 1993.

Fiction

The Bouncers. London, Hamish Hamilton, 1964.

The Fast Green Car. London, Hamish Hamilton, 1965.

There's Something on the Roof! London, Hamish Hamilton, 1966.

Emma Borrows a Cup of Sugar. London, Heinemann, 1973.

Der Ballon. Germany, Junior Press, 1974.

The Witches of Wimmering. London, Pelham, 1976.

Leadfoot. London, Pelham, 1980.

Snatched. London, Hodder & Stoughton, 1983.

Broops! Down the Chimney. London, Walker, 1992.

Fantastico, illustrated by Mick Reid. Harlow Longman 1994.

Not a Dicky Bird. London Red Fox, 1996.

Short Stories

Sweets from a Stranger and Other Science Fiction Stories. London, Kestrel, 1982.

Living Fire. London, Corgi, 1987.

Other

Look at Cars, illustrated by the author. London, Hamish Hamilton, 1959; revised edition, London, Panther, 1969.

Look at Newspapers, illustrated by Eric Thomas. London, Hamish Hamilton, 1962.

The Young Man's Guide to Advertising. London, Hamish Hamilton, 1963.

Making Music, illustrated by Donald Green. London, Joseph, 1966; Boston, Crescendo, 1969.

Lindbergh the Lone Flier, illustrated by Raymond Briggs. London, Hamish Hamilton, and New York, Coward McCann, 1968.

Richthofen the Red Baron, illustrated by Raymond Briggs. London, Hamish Hamilton, and New York, Coward McCann, 1968.

*

Illustrator: *A Fishy Tale* by Beryl Cooke, 1957; *Look at Aircraft* by Sir Philip Joubert de la Ferte, 1960; *The Bear Who Was Too Big* by Lettice Cooper, 1963; *Tea with Mr. Timothy* by Geoffrey Morgan, 1966; *Menuhin's House of Music* by Eric Fenby, 1969; *Skiffy* by William Mayne, 1972.

*   *   *

Nicholas Fisk's prodigious output of books for over thirty years, for children and young adults, has been characterised by a fierce narrative drive, a lucid and resonant style, an exceptionally free-ranging imagination which coheres round a number of urgent and consistent themes, a down-to-earth practicality which tempers the fantasy, and—above all—a respect for the enterprise and as yet untrammelled originality of the minds of the young. His major genre is science fiction: his stories range far in time and space—though *Grinny, Antigrav, Monster Maker, You Remember Me,* and *The Worm Charmers* are among his strongest novels and are set in recognisably contemporary surroundings. There is sometimes a return to a time of great personal significance for him—the 1940s. Not only is this period superbly evoked in his teenage memoir *Pig Ignorant,* but it is also reproduced movingly in what is probably his science fiction masterpiece, *A Rag, a Bone, and a Hank of Hair.*

The perennial science fiction device of outside threat based on an advanced technology becomes in Fisk's work a means of dramatising two of his most important themes: a technical expertise together with a trust in the clear thinking of children who are not yet forced into deadening adult moulds. Thus, in *Trillions,* Scott knows that the invading objects can be used creatively: the general's obsession with more and more force to get rid of them is a depressingly familiar adult reaction. In *Wheelie in the Stars,* a twentieth-century motorcycle alone saves an advanced but failed technology. In *Antigrav,* the young adults discover a red stone with the ability to defy gravity. They set up ingenious and crystal-clear experiments to both prove and illustrate the principle, and then fall foul of warring adults representing the futilities of the Cold War at its height. *Grinny* and *You Remember Me,* though separated by eleven years, form a sequence. Timothy and Beth, brother and sister, twice repel attempts by aliens to take over Earth. In each

story, adults are manipulated with frightening ease but children see the truth and can counter it by commonsense, ingenuity, and bravery. There is no hint here of Eileen Colwell's devastating comment on Enid Blyton: "What chance has a gang of desperate criminals against three children and a dog?" The events, though fantastic, are entirely credible within the contract laid down between author and reader (in Fisk's own words: "One thumping lie only"). Their implications are thought through with disciplined exactitude.

Grinny has remained an unfailingly popular book. The family is visited unexpectedly by the self-proclaimed Great Aunt Emma (Grinny). Only Tim and Beth are not taken in. Discovering Grinny's true, nonhuman nature, elucidating "her" purpose and then finding a way of destroying her, forms a narrative of great power which remains compulsively readable. *You Remember Me* is just as compelling but is also a more reflective work. "Grinny" is replaced by Lisa Treadgold, the beautiful, idealistic leader of a growing mass movement, "The Rollers." Significantly, Timothy and Beth are now older. Timothy is nearer to adulthood: his mind is clouded, less proof against the wiles of the alien forces. Beth now bears the weight of the truth. There is another element in this more serious sequel. The Rollers, founded on "Rule of Law" and "Decency, Discipline, Dedication," have all the hallmarks of totalitarianism. There is undoubtedly a hint of political allegory in this compelling narrative. Beth's thwarting of Lisa is based on the same resourcefulness as the destruction of Grinny.

A similar seriousness underlies the magnificent *A Rag, a Bone, and a Hank of Hair.* In Fisk's dying future world, where youth is scarce and revered, genetic coding is used to prolong the species by producing the "Reborns," humans reconstituted from the ingredients listed in the book's title. Brin, a boy of startling intelligence, is set to live with three Reborns from the 1940s, as a sort of working trial. London Blitz conditions are reproduced: Brin finds himself identifying with his new companions. Their dirty, dangerous, emotional world contrasts with the anodyne luxury of his own. When they burst out of their bonds and create a new character by sheer force of imagination they must—with Brin—be destroyed. But they live on: their voices haunt their creators and the story becomes a defiant statement about human qualities and potentialities.

The pervasive themes of trust in the undistorted clarity of the young mind and the dangerous soullessness of alien technology (which seems equated with any human technology which is not based on craftsmanship) are shown in the collection of short stories *Sweets from a Stranger.* As a short-story writer, Fisk shows point and economy. The title story ironically rehearses the extraterrestrial menace of Grinny: "Mind Milk" (a truly virtuoso piece of plotting) shows this menace deliberately closing in on the minds of the young: "Space Invaders" and "Oddiputs" show the machines with minds and lives of their own.

A different version of the artefact with a life of its own is seen in *Monster Maker,* where Matt works with Chancey Balogh, builder of film monsters, and meets the reverberatingly sinister Ultragorgon. Among other virtues, this story celebrates careful craftsmanship and respect for a job well done—qualities which typify Fisk's own authorial achievement. Matt's ingenuity rivals that of his hero, Chancey Balogh—an ingenuity matched by the four Worm Charmers in the novel of that name, an urgent contemporary thriller about the discovery and foiling of a drug trafficker.

Nicholas Fisk is one of the few authors for young adults who approaches the unforced popularity of Blyton, Blume, or Dahl, who uses popular and accessible genres but who also possesses serious concern and a consistent world view to a profound degree.

—Dennis Hamley

FITCH, Clarke. *See* SINCLAIR, Upton (Beall).

FLEISCHMAN, Paul

Nationality: American. **Born:** Monterey, California, 5 September 1952. **Education:** University of California, Berkeley, 1970-72; University of New Mexico, Albuquerque, 1975-77, B.A. in university studies 1977. **Family:** Married Becky Mojica in 1978; two sons. **Career:** Has worked as janitor, bagel baker, bookstore clerk, and proofreader; author. **Awards:** Silver Medal, Commonwealth Club of California, Golden Kite honor book, Society of Children's Book Writers, and *New York Times* outstanding book citation, all 1980, all for *The Half-a-Moon Inn;* Newbery honor book, American Library Association (ALA), 1983, for *Graven Images: Three Stories;* Golden Kite honor book, Society of Children's Book Writers, and Parents' Choice award, Parents' Choice Foundation, both 1983, both for *Path of the Pale Horse; Boston Globe-Horn Book* award honor book, best books for young adults nomination, ALA, both 1988, and Newbery Medal, ALA, 1989, all for *Joyful Noise: Poems for Two Voices; Boston Globe-Horn Book* award honor book, 1990, and ALA notable book, 1991, both for *Saturnalia;* ALA notable book and Golden Kite Honor Book, both 1991, both for *The Borning Room;* Scott O'Dell award, Silver Medal, Commonwealth Club of California, both 1994, both for *Bull Run.* **Address:** 855 Marino Pines, Pacific Grove, CA 93950, U.S.A.

PUBLICATIONS FOR YOUNG ADULTS

Fiction

The Half-a-Moon Inn, illustrated by Kathy Jacobi. New York, Harper, 1980.
Graven Images: Three Stories, illustrated by Andrew Glass. New York, Harper, 1982.
Path of the Pale Horse. New York, Harper, 1983.
Coming-and-Going Men: Four Tales of Itinerants, illustrated by Randy Gaul. New York, Harper, 1985.
Rear-View Mirrors. New York, Harper, 1986.
Saturnalia. New York, Harper, 1990.
The Borning Room. New York, HarperCollins, 1991.
Bull Run, woodcuts by David Frampton. New York, HarperCollins, 1993.
Dateline: Troy. Cambridge, Massachusetts, Candlewick Press, 1996.
Seedfolk. New York, HarperCollins, 1997.

Poetry

I Am Phoenix: Poems for Two Voices, illustrated by Ken Nutt. New York, Harper, 1985.
Joyful Noise: Poems for Two Voices, illustrated by Eric Beddows. New York, Harper, 1988.

Other

Townsend's Warbler. New York, HarperCollins, 1992.
Copier Creations. New York, HarperCollins, 1993.

PUBLICATIONS FOR CHILDREN

Fiction

The Birthday Tree, illustrated by Marcia Sewall. New York, Harper, 1979.
The Animal Hedge (picture book), illustrated by Lydia Dabcovich. New York, Dutton, 1983.
Finzel the Farsighted, illustrated by Marcia Sewall. New York, Dutton, 1983.
Phoebe Danger, Detective, in the Case of the Two-Minute Cough, illustrated by Margot Apple. Boston, Houghton Mifflin, 1983.
Rondo in C, illustrated by Janet Wentworth. New York, Harper, 1988.
Shadow Play (picture book), illustrated by Eric Beddows. New York, Harper, 1990.
Time Train, illustrated by Claire Ewart. New York, HarperCollins, 1991.
A Fate Totally Worse than Death. Cambridge, Massachusetts, Candlewick Press, 1995.

*

Biography: Entry in *Fifth Book of Junior Authors and Illustrators,* New York, H.W. Wilson, 1983; essay in *Speaking for Ourselves, Too* compiled and edited by Donald R. Gallo, National Council of Teachers of English, 1993.

Critical Studies: Entry in *Children's Literature Review,* Volume 20, Detroit, Gale, 1990.

*　　*　　*

Paul Fleischman's writing style is powerful, distinctive. His concise, yet lyrical use of language glides young readers through intriguing plots, appealing characters, and unique content. In his poetry and prose the author skillfully employs rhyme, alliteration, and metaphor to evoke aural and visual imagery. Fleischman reports that he tries to create an atmosphere in his writings, spending more time tinkering with the harmony of the sounds than the sense of a story. The writer gives credit to his father, author Sid Fleischman, for his recognition of the importance of a story's sound "shape" and for his love of research to uncover the past. His fascination with "out-of-the-way corners of American history" is apparent in his many stories that feature period settings and carefully compiled historical facts.

Nowhere is Fleischman's mastery of language more evident than in his poetry. *I Am Phoenix* and *Joyful Noise* are companion poetry publications written to be read aloud, separately and simultaneously, by two people. Composed in free verse, these imaginative musical duets demonstrate the author's ingenious wordsmanship. *I Am Phoenix* includes fifteen verses on bird song and flight. His Newbery Medal-winning *Joyful Noise* presents first-person profiles of fourteen different insects. When read aloud as intended, the spoken poems in *Joyful Noise* create the cadence of insect voices, producing a rhythm reminiscent of the humming, buzzing, droning noises made by crickets, honey bees, and cicadas.

The author's historical novels not only illustrate how skillfully he crafts the sound "shape" of a story, but also the "sense," or plot, of it. *Path of the Pale Horse, Saturnalia, The Borning Room,* and *Bull Run* are four of Fleischman's young adult novels that portray interesting aspects of Early American life. In addition to his figurative prose, each offers engaging characters, important themes, and provocative plots.

Path of the Pale Horse takes place in Philadelphia during the 1793 yellow fever epidemic. Fourteen-year-old Lep is the protagonist, and Dr. Peale is his medical mentor. In this story of Lep's search for his sister Clara, Fleischman subtly integrates the plot with historical facts and makes the characters, especially Lep, come to life.

Saturnalia is a satiric novel full of humor, atmosphere, and suspense. It is set in Puritan Boston in 1681 and focuses on the white man's treatment of Indians and servants. The hero is a poor Indian boy apprenticed to the town printer. The antagonist is a fanatical tithingman whose job is to root out evil and blasphemy. The title comes from the pagan Roman ritual of Saturnalia, a day in December when slaves and masters exchange roles.

The Borning Room is a convincing first-person narrative that deftly weaves historical events—the Underground Railroad, the Civil War, the suffragettes, and the rise of technology—into the everyday life of one Ohio family. Georgina Lott, birthed in her family's borning room, summarizes these important events to a portrait painter who has been hired to sketch her picture before she dies, in the same room. The borning room, a symbol in this story, was common in the 1800s. It was usually located off the kitchen and reserved for births, illnesses, and deaths.

In *Bull Run,* fictional characters give first-person accounts of the first major battle of the Civil War. Through the sixteen individual voices of men and women, blacks and whites, Northerners and Southerners, Fleischman paints a vivid portrait of the bloodiest U.S. war. The writer's character development is at its best here. These people seem real, believable; they elicit sympathy and understanding from the reader.

Fleischman's short story collections present the same lyrical prose, Early American settings, and mysterious atmospheres as his novels. They are yet another vehicle for displaying his artistry in the use of language, as well as his ability to create deceptively simple tales that challenge the reader to discover hidden meaning.

Graven Images is an apt title for Fleischman's collection of three stories that focus on a wooden sailor boy, a copper weathervane, and a marble statue. In each of the tales, the graven image influences the characters' actions and faith. "The Binnacle Boy" is a chilling murder mystery involving a deaf serving girl, her fussy mistress, and a sailing ship's dead crew. In the humorous "Saint Crispin's Follower," the shoemaker's apprentice finds his own true love through happenstance. "The Man of Influence" is a suspenseful story of an arrogant stone carver and his ghost patron.

Reviewers praised Fleischman's powerful and mysterious narratives, claiming that they held a timeless quality.

The stories in *Coming and Going Men* describe four travellers passing through New Canaan, Vermont, in 1800. The travellers each leave an impression but are also affected by the town. Cyrus Snype (silhouette cutter), Mr. Hamby (ballad seller), Simeon and Patrick Fyfe (exhibitors), and Jonathan Wardwell (peddler) are all well-drawn and authentic. They transport young readers to previous times and give them new insights into the human condition.

Paul Fleischman is a master of his craft. His lyrical language and remarkable imagery enable him to create convincing characters and time periods. An added appeal of his work is that his protagonists often share young readers' powerful emotional needs, and therefore help them make discoveries about themselves. The success of his long list of young adult works shows that his attention to the sound and the sense of his writing—whether poetry, historical fiction, or short stories—is appreciated by his audience.

—Catherine Price

FLEMING, Ian (Lancaster)

Nationality: British. **Born:** London, 28 May 1908. **Education:** Durnford School, Isle of Purbeck, Eton College; Royal Military Academy, Sandhurst; studied languages at the University of Munich and the University of Geneva. **Military Service:** Served in the Royal Naval Volunteer Reserve, as personal assistant to the Director of Naval Intelligence, 1939-45: Lieutenant. **Family:** Married Anne Geraldine Charteris in 1952; one son. **Career:** Writer. Moscow correspondent, Reuters Ltd., London, 1929-33; associated with Cull & Co. (merchant bankers), London, 1933-35; stockbroker, Rowe & Pitman, London, 1935-39; Moscow correspondent, the *Times,* London, 1939; foreign manager, Kemsley (later Thomson) Newspapers, 1945-59; publisher, *Book Collector,* London, 1949-64. Order of the Dannebrog, 1945. **Awards:** Young Readers' Choice award, 1967, for *Chitty Chitty Bang Bang.* **Died:** 12 August 1964.

PUBLICATIONS

Fiction

Casino Royale. London, Cape, and New York, Macmillan, 1954; as *You Asked for It,* New York, Popular Library, 1955.

Live and Let Die. London, Cape, 1954; New York, Macmillan, 1955.

Moonraker. London, Cape, and New York, Macmillan, 1955; as *Too Hot to Handle,* New York, Permabooks, 1957.

Diamonds are Forever. London, Cape, and New York, Macmillan, 1956.

The Diamond Smugglers. London, Cape, 1957; New York, Macmillan, 1958.

From Russia, With Love. London, Cape, and New York, Macmillan, 1957.

Doctor No. London, Cape, and New York, Macmillan, 1958.

Goldfinger. London, Cape, and New York, Macmillan, 1959.

Thunderball. London, Cape, and New York, Viking, 1961.

The Spy Who Loved Me. London, Cape, and New York, Viking, 1962.

On Her Majesty's Secret Service. London, Cape, and New York, New American Library 1963.

You Only Live Twice. London, Cape, and New York, New American Library, 1964.

The Man with the Golden Gun. London, Cape, and New York, New American Library, 1965.

Octopussy, and The Living Daylights. London, Cape, and New York, New American Library, 1966.

Short Stories

For Your Eyes Only: Five Secret Exploits of James Bond. London, Cape, and New York, Viking, 1960.

Other

Thrilling Cities (thirteen essays). London, Cape, 1963; New York, New American Library, 1964.

Ian Fleming Introduces Jamaica, edited by Morris Cargill. London, Deutsch, 1965; New York, Hawthorn, 1966.

Screenplay: *Thunderball,* with Kevin McClory and Jack Whittington, 1965.

PUBLICATION FOR CHILDREN

Fiction

Chitty Chitty Bang Bang, illustrated by John Burningham. New York, Random, 1964.

*

Media Adaptations: Many of Fleming's James Bond books have been filmed, usually with Sean Connery, Roger Moore, or Timothy Dalton playing the lead; in addition, *Chitty Chitty Bang Bang* was adapted into a musical and into a film starring Dick Van Dyke.

Bibliography: *Ian Fleming: A Catalogue of a Collection: Preliminary to a Bibliography* by Iain Campbell, privately printed, 1978.

Critical Studies: *007 James Bond: A Report* by O.F. Snelling, London, Spearman, 1964, New York, New American Library, 1965; *The James Bond Dossier,* by Kingsley Amis, London, Cape, and New York, New American Library, 1965; *The Life of Ian Fleming,* London, Cape, and New York, McGraw Hill, 1966, *007 James Bond,* London, Sidgwick and Jackson, and New York, Morrow, 1973, and *James Bond: The Authorised Biography of 007,* London, Granada, 1985, New York, Grove Press, 1986, all by John Pearson; *The Bond Affair* by Oreste Del Buono and Umberto Eco, London, Macdonald, 1966; *Ian Fleming: The Spy Who Came in with the Gold* by Henry Zieger, New York, Duell, 1966; *You Only Live Once: Memories of Ian Fleming* by Ivar Bryce, London, Weidenfeld and Nicolson, 1975, Frederick, Maryland, University Publications of America, 1985; *The James Bond Films* by Steven

Jay Rubin, London, Arlington, 1982; *Murder in the Millions: Erle Stanley Gardner, Mickey Spillane, Ian Fleming* by J. Kenneth Van Dover, New York, Ungar, 1984; *The James Bond Bedside Companion* by Raymond Benson, New York, Dodd Mead, 1984; *Secret Agents in Fiction: Ian Fleming, John Le Carré, and Len Deighton* by L.O. Saverberg, London, Macmillan, 1984; *James Bond: A Celebration* by Peter Haining, London, W.H. Allen, 1987; *Ian Fleming's James Bond* by John E. Gardner, New York, Avenel, 1987.

Best known for his James Bond thrillers, Ian Fleming's writing reflects both his time spent in the British Intelligence Service and his experience as a journalist. Plot-driven and with an emphasis on setting, the Bond adventure stories all follow a similar pattern: Bond encounters an easily defined enemy, and with the help of incredible gadgets, his unstoppable car, and his license to kill, he triumphs, conquering beautiful women along the way. Judging literature of past decades by modern standards poses innumerable problems, and seems somewhat unfair; but an intelligent young adult reader will move beyond Fleming's sometimes xenophobic and sexist undertones and enjoy the Bond novels for what they are—thrilling, outrageous, exciting spy stories. Unfortunately, many young people only know of the abundance of James Bond movies, and miss the insights into 007's character and the descriptions of setting and weaponry that the books offer.

The huge popularity of these novels defined the character of Bond as the quintessential spy. His enigmatic side, his physical endurance, and his abilities as a lover became standards by which to judge all superspies. To today's reader, or rereader, he seems almost a cliche. The dangerous and highly dramatic confrontations with foreign enemies seem dated in this post-Cold War age of corporate espionage and savings-and-loan debacles. Fleming's portrayal of women also poses some problems. Some are ruthless, sophisticated spies themselves, but all fall victim to Bond's endless charm and sex appeal—a chauvinistic ideal.

Fleming's success is not limited to his Bond novels. Younger readers continue to enjoy Fleming's timeless adventure story of the Pott family and their magical green car in *Chitty Chitty Bang Bang.* The delightfully improbable chain of events that begins with the purchase of the dilapidated buggy, which ultimately proves to have the capacity to speed, fly, swim, think, and, most importantly, feel, greatly appeal to young people. When Jeremy and Jemima are kidnapped, the young twins save themselves through quick thinking and resourcefulness. Young people feel empowered when children, of any age, triumph over adults.

While older readers may be reluctant to pick up a book about a magical car, even the most sophisticated reader will find this story captivating. This is Fleming's spoof on spy novels—perhaps on Bond himself—and shows his love of weaponry and the unexpected. Just when the Potts think their doom is sealed, Chitty Chitty Bang Bang proves to have another knob to pull or twist that saves the family. Commander Pott (retired) possesses extensive knowledge of explosive devices, and gangsters come complete with nicknames (Joe the Monster) and a big, black shiny car. The story moves quickly, and Fleming's chatty narrative voice, with its conspiratorial tone, involves the reader directly with the events. The open ending lets the reader's imagination take the Potts and their car wherever he or she desires. The movie adaptation of this book, like those of the Bond stories, is more familiar to most than the book, but, while amusing, it does not deliver the same rich detail the book provides.

Both the Bond books and *Chitty Chitty Bang Bang* quickly enthrall the reader with their action-oriented plots and amazing gadgets, and give the satisfaction of a good read.

—Karen E. Walsh

FOLEY, June

Nationality: American. **Born:** Trenton, New Jersey, 6 June 1944. **Education:** Montclair State College, Upper Montclair, New Jersey, B.A. in anthropology, 1974, teacher's certificate in social studies 1976; New York University, M.A. in English and American Literature, 1990, Ph.D. 1995. **Family:** Married in 1970 (divorced 1976); one son. **Career:** Member of editorial staff, 1978-94, *World Almanac,* New York; adjunct assistant professor of literature and writing, New York University, Fordham University, and New School for Social Research, all New York City, from 1995. **Agent:** Marilyn Marlow, Curtis Brown Ltd., 10 Astor Pl., New York, New York 10003 U.S.A.

PUBLICATIONS FOR YOUNG ADULTS

Novels

It's No Crush, I'm in Love! New York, Delacorte, 1982.
Love by Any Other Name. New York, Delacorte, 1983.
Falling in Love Is No Snap. New York, Delacorte, 1986.
Susanna Siegelbaum Gives up Guys. New York, Scholastic, 1991.

Other

Editor, with Mark Hoffman and Tom McGuire, *The World Almanac: The Complete 1868 Original and Selections from 25, 50, and 100 Years Ago.* New York, Pharos, 1992.

*

Media Adaptations: *It's No Crush, I'm in Love* (ABC Afterschool Special), ABC-TV, 1983.

June Foley comments:

I returned to school myself while writing *Susanna Siegelbaum* and earned the Ph.D. in English and American Literature in 1995. A specialist in the 19th-century British novel, I am hoping to write a young adult novel about the first visit to New York City by the great English novelist Charles Dickens in 1842. The main character, Molly Dunn, will be an adolescent based on my own ancestors, who came to the United States from Ireland. I want to write about the way reading and writing can change lives.

*   *   *

June Foley writes about adolescence because she considers it to be one's most awkward yet exciting time of life. She enjoys writing about young love, and her *Falling in Love Is No Snap* about perky, likable Alexandra Susskind is a good example.

Foley's first novel, *It's No Crush, I'm in Love!,* is another example of her exemplary writing for young adults. She has written a humorous but touching story of Annie Cassidy, a fourteen-year-old who falls in love with her English teacher, David Angelucci. Annie's favorite book is *Pride and Prejudice,* and she imagines herself as the book's heroine, Elizabeth Bennet, and Mr. Angelucci as Elizabeth's love, Mr. Darcy. Annie has a communication problem with her mother whose life is filled with raising four girls by herself, Mr. Cassidy having died in a car accident some time ago. So Annie confides her feelings to her best friend, Susanna Siegelbaum, a fun-loving, outgoing girl who is just the opposite of Annie, but basically the same since both girls are oddballs. Susanna listens to Annie, doesn't really encourage her but supports her because Annie is finally overcoming her shyness and letting her feelings out. However, Annie's life changes when she becomes a writer for the school newspaper and meets Robby Pols, a fellow student and the editor-in-chief of the newspaper. Annie's rejection by Mr. Angelucci is painful, but Annie recovers, faces reality, learns that there are many kinds of love, and even finds a new warm and loving relationship with her mother, who is finally emerging from her cocoon. Foley's well-written story shows her understanding of young adults as they reach toward maturity, accompanied by the painful and frustrating emotions of adolescence.

Susanna Siegelbaum Gives Up Guys takes up where *It's No Crush, I'm In Love!* ends. This amusing story is about Susanna Siegelbaum and her promise to give up boys because she suddenly finds she has never really been part of any boy-girl couple. She has never known any boy well, and doesn't really stick with anyone long enough, anyway. So she decides to give up boys altogether, makes a bet with Annie Cassidy, her best friend, that she can do without boys, not even kiss or flirt with one for three months. However, Susanna also finds herself without a friend, because Annie has become engrossed in her boyfriend, Robby Pols, and doesn't spend time with Susanna anymore. When Susanna's parents become concerned because Susanna hasn't been going out, Susanna makes a deal with class clown Ben Green to pretend to be her new boyfriend. In return Susanna will tutor him in English and support him in the sports he participates in. The two learn to share thoughts and feelings and to boost each other's spirits when things get gloomy. However, when each criticizes the other for always wanting to be the center of attention and showing off, each decides to change and to grow up. Much to Susanna's astonishment, she discovers she really cares for Ben and he for her. Foley has written an appealing story about an enduring friendship between two girls who don't let boyfriends or personality differences come between them. Filled with sparkling dialogue, unpredictable characters, and topped by a surprise ending, the book keeps the reader laughing throughout.

Billie Quinn, just starting high school, has found she has matured physically, but not quite mentally and emotionally in *Love By Any Other Name.* Bubba Umlauf, a blond, handsome, number-one sports star of Central High, has two things on his self-centered mind—sports and making out with Billie Quinn. Billie loves the attention she receives from being Bubba's girl. She spends all her extra time with Bubba, neglecting her family and other responsibilities, barely getting by in school, and seems oblivious to anything but Bubba and her popularity. When Billie is paired with Cameron Ingersoll in her drama class, she is certain she is going to have a problem. Cameron is a tall, skinny boy Billie didn't even know existed, but Billie learns more from Cameron than how to act a part in a school play. She learns to grow up, to think for herself, to accept responsibilities, to become a supportive family member, and to realize there is more to life than being popular and dating a conceited high school jock. Foley has written a winner, portraying family problems along with peer pressures, sexual urges and how to handle them, and many other concerns that adolescents face. She has also written about a young girl who learns to care about the feelings of others and to stop thinking of herself all the time.

Although Foley hasn't written many books, each that she has written makes for good reading, with happy endings of young people conquering difficulties faced during the turbulent adolescent years, problems that young adults can easily identify with because they encounter them each and every day themselves.

—Carol Doxey

FORBES, Esther

Nationality: American. **Born:** Westborough, Massachusetts, 28 June 1891. **Education:** Bradford Junior College, graduated 1912; University of Wisconsin, Madison, 1916-18. **Family:** Married Albert Learned Hoskins in 1926 (divorced 1933). **Career:** Author of historical novels. Staff member, editor, Houghton Mifflin Co. (publishers), Boston, Massachusetts, 1920-26, 1942-46. **Awards:** Pulitzer Prize (history), 1943, for *Paul Revere and the World He Lived In;* American Library Association Newbery Medal, 1944, for *Johnny Tremain: A Novel for Young and Old;* Metro-Goldwyn-Mayer Novel award, 1948. **Died:** 12 August 1967.

PUBLICATIONS FOR YOUNG ADULTS

Fiction

Johnny Tremain: A Novel for Young and Old, illustrated by Lynd Ward. Boston, Houghton, 1943; London, Chatto & Windus, 1944.

Other

America's Paul Revere, illustrated by Lynd Ward. Boston, Houghton Mifflin, 1946.

PUBLICATIONS FOR ADULTS

Novels

O Genteel Lady! Boston, Houghton Mifflin, 1926; London, Heinemann, 1927.
Miss Marvel. Boston, Houghton Mifflin, 1935.
Paradise. New York, Harcourt Brace, and London, Chatto & Windus, 1937.
The General's Lady. New York, Harcourt, 1938; London, Chatto & Windus, 1939.
Paul Revere and the World He Lived In. Boston, Houghton Mifflin, 1942.
The Boston Book, with Arthur Griffin. Boston, Houghton Mifflin, 1947.

The Running of the Tide. Boston, Houghton Mifflin, 1948; London, Chatto & Windus, 1949.
Rainbow on the Road. Boston, Houghton Mifflin, 1954; London, Chatto & Windus, 1955.

Other

A *Mirror for Witches in Which is Reflected the Life, Machinations, and Death of Famous Doll Bilby, Who, With a More than Feminine Perversity, Preferred a Demon to a Mortal Lover,* woodcuts by Robert Gibbings. Boston, Houghton Mifflin, 1928.
Anne Douglas Sedgwick: An Interview. Boston, Houghton Mifflin, 1947.

*

Media Adaptations: *Johnny Tremain* (film), Walt Disney Productions, 1957; *Johnny Tremain* (cassette), Caedmon, 1974, and the Center for Literary Review, 1978; *Rainbow on the Road* adapted for Broadway as *Come Summer,* 1969; *A Mirror for Witches* adapted for Broadway as *Bilby's Doll,* 1976; *A Mirror for Witches* (ballet), Sadler Wells Company, London.

Biography: Essay in *Dictionary of Literary Biography,* Volume 22: *American Writers for Children: 1900-1960,* Detroit, Gale, 1983; essay in *Something about the Author Autobiography Series,* Volume 2, Detroit, Gale, 1986; essay in *Contemporary Authors Autobiography Series,* Volume 25, revised, Detroit, Gale, 1989.

Manuscript Collections: American Antiquarian Society, Worcester, Massachusetts; Clark University Library, Worcester, Massachusetts.

Critical Studies: Entry in *More Junior Authors,* edited by Muriel Fuller, New York, Wilson, 1963; *Esther Forbes* by Margaret Erskine, Worcester, Massachusetts, Worcester Bicentennial Committee, 1976; entry in *Contemporary Literary Criticism,* Volume 12, Detroit, Gale, 1980.

*   *   *

The reputation of Esther Forbes as a writer for children has been established by one book—*Johnny Tremain.* It is her only work of fiction for young adults. Young people who are interested in historical fiction, however, would enjoy her other works, particularly *Rainbow on the Road.*

Forbes had several unique advantages in writing *Johnny Tremain* which helped to make the book one of the most solid choices to win the Newbery Medal in the history of the award; they have also helped to make the book still worthwhile—even enabling it to survive the "trauma" of being required reading in many a school system.

The first advantage was her detailed knowledge of Paul Revere's world—its physical conditions, its contemporary events, its political figures and their influences. Information of all kinds, gathered in her exhaustive research for her earlier *Paul Revere and the World He Lived In* was so firm in her mind that complete scenes for *Johnny Tremain,* accurately detailed and furnished, could arise spontaneously. The creative process did not have to be interrupted and reaffirmed by research. The richness and liveliness added to the story by this ability are as rewarding as the plot and characters.

The second advantage derived also from her historical research: the curiosity and insight with which she considered people and the reasons for their behavior. She was always titillated by the quirk of thought or misunderstanding which could precipitate a historical incident. As she studied the Boston of the 1760s and 1770s, the role played by apprentices of all trades intrigued her—and she promised herself the indulgence of writing a piece of fiction about them in time.

When World War II brought the issue of freedom and fighting for it once more into daily consciousness, she found the crux for her story. She could reveal the universal and timeless problems of making difficult choices, believing in a cause, being responsible for one's actions, overcoming a handicap (Johnny's burned hand), and facing grief and loss (the death of Rab) by telling the story of Johnny Tremain, apprentice to a silversmith in Boston during the American Revolution. In her Newbery Medal acceptance speech, Forbes said, "I was anxious to show young readers something of the excitement of human nature, never static, always changing, often unpredictable, and endlessly fascinating." She might well have been defining the elements needed to produce a classic—which is what she did.

The text for *America's Paul Revere* is a distillation of the man and the most important facts of his life and times, prepared for younger readers as a counterpart for Lynd Ward's illustrations.

—Lee Kingman

FORD, Hilary. *See* **CHRISTOPHER, John.**

FORMAN, James D(ouglas)

Nationality: American. **Born:** Mineola, Long Island, New York, 12 November 1932. **Education:** A.B. Princeton University, 1954; LL.B. Columbia University, 1957. **Family:** Married Marcia Fore, 1956; one daughter. **Career:** Attorney, from 1957; Writer. **Awards:** Children's Spring Book Festival Award, 1965 and 1969; Lewis Carroll Shelf Award, 1972; American Library Association Best Book Award, 1979. **Agent:** Theron Raines, Raines & Raines, 71 Fourth Ave., New York, New York 10016, U.S.A. **Address:** 2 Glen Road, Sands Point, Port Washington, New York 11501, U.S.A.

PUBLICATIONS FOR YOUNG ADULTS

Fiction

The Skies of Crete. New York, Farrar, Straus, 1963.
Ring the Judas Bell. New York, Farrar, Straus, 1968.
The Shield of Achilles. New York, Farrar, Straus, 1966.
Horses of Anger. New York, Farrar, Straus, 1967.
The Traitors. New York, Farrar, Straus, 1968.
The Cow Neck Rebels. Farrar, Straus, 1969.
My Enemy, My Brother. New York, Meredith, 1969.
Ceremony of Innocence. New York, Hawthorn, 1970.
So Ends This Day. New York, Farrar, Straus, 1970.
Song of Jubilee. New York, Farrar, Straus, 1971.
People of the Dream. New York, Farrar, Straus, 1972.
The Life and Death of Yellow Bird. New York, Farrar, Straus, 1973.
Follow the River. New York, Farrar, Straus, 1975.
The White Crow. 1976.
The Survivor. New York, Farrar, Straus, 1976.
A Fine, Soft Day. New York, Farrar, Straus, 1978.
Freedom's Blood. New York, F. Watts, 1979.
A Ballad For Hogskin Hill. New York, Farrar, Straus, 1979.
That Mad Game: War and the Chances for Peace. New York, Scribner, 1980.
The Pumpkin Shell. New York, Farrar, Straus, 1981.
Call Back Yesterday. New York, Scribner, 1983.
Doomsday Plus Twelve. New York, Scribner, 1984.
Cry Havoc. New York, Scribner, 1988.
The Big Ban. New York, Scribner, 1989.
Prince Charlie's Year. New York, Scribner, 1991.
Becca's Story. New York, Scribner, 1992.
The Blunderbuss. New York, Scribner, 1994

Nonfiction

With Marcia Forman, *Islands of the Eastern Mediterranean* (booklet). New York, Doubleday, 1959.
Law and Disorder. New York, Thomas Nelson, 1971.
Capitalism: Economic Individualism to Today's Welfare State. New York, F. Watts, 1972.
Communism: From Marx's Manifesto to Twentieth Century Reality. New York, F. Watts, 1972.
Socialism: Its Theoretical Roots and Present-Day Development. New York, F. Watts, 1972.
Code Name Valkyrie: Count Claus von Stauffenberg and the Plot to Kill Hitler. New York, S.G. Phillips, 1973.
Fascism: The Meaning and Experience of Reactionary Revolution. New York, F. Watts, 1974.
Anarchism: Political Innocence or Social Violence? F. Watts, 1975.
The White Crow. New York, Farrar, Straus, 1976.
Inflation. New York, F. Watts, 1977.
Nazism. New York, F. Watts, 1978.

*

Critical Studies: "Life Models: Of Heroes and Hopes" by Kenneth L. Donelson and Alleen Pace Nilsen in *Literature for Today's Young Adults*, First Edition, New York, Scott, Foresman, and Company, 1980, 283-316; entry in *Something about the Author* edited by Donna Olendorf and Diane Telgen, Detroit, Gale Research, Vol. 70, 1993, 61-65; entry in *Contemporary Literary Criticism* edited by Sharon R. Gunton, Detroit, Gale Research, Vol.

21, 1982, 115-123; "James D. Forman, On Becoming a Storyteller" in *Literature for Today's Young Adults*, Third Edition, by Kenneth L. Donelson and Alleen Pace Nilsen, HarperCollins, 1989, 237.

*　*　*

An only child without nearby neighbors, James D. Forman grew up entertaining himself. He has described his main source of childhood entertainment as the fantasies of his own imagination. His home was filled with books and he read everyday. As he grew up Forman considered writing a scholarly and respected vocation. He felt fortunate to have had teachers who encouraged his writing by focusing more on content than mechanical aspects of language. While attending Princeton, his focus was psychology and later law. His career as an attorney was mainly in the area of real estate management within a family firm. Forman has shared that he never thought he had the "properly combative temperament" to be a lawyer.

Feeling quite discontent with the realities of law, he pursued his interest in photography. One photographic assignment for the American Geographic Society involved four months in Greece preparing pictures and text. This experience ultimately led to his writing for adolescents and setting numerous novels in Greece.

The Skies of Crete, a juvenile novel focusing on the Greek Civil war, began Forman's writing career. Many of his later books also deal with the moral and ethical problems of war. *The Skies of Crete* vividly portrays the futility of war while showing the universality of the characters and plot. *Ring the Judas Bell* and *The Shield of Achilles* continued his focus on war in Greece. Both were praised for complexity of plot, authenticity and richness of setting, and the depth to which courage, loyalty, friendship, good, and evil are treated in a young adult book. In each novel Forman presents his adolescent protagonists with tests within the context of their war-torn country. Forman does not sacrifice the historical integrity of events during the Greek civil war, but uses the events to further his own stories.

In *My Enemy, My Brother,* Forman combines war with other social issues. Daniel Barantz, a Jewish survivor of the Holocaust, begins a new life in Israel only to be caught up in another war as Jewish settlers and Arabs struggle over territory disputes. His best friend is Arab and both youth prepare for war in opposite camps. Critics have noticed Forman's purposeful lack of resolution at the end of this book as symbolic of the unresolved Arab-Israel conflict. Even without a strong conclusion, it powerful prose and imagery and the message it extends on the evils of war have been praised. Questions that young people continue to ponder dealing with the purpose of war are seen from both young male protagonists in this novel.

War has also been explored from an American perspective in *The Cow Neck Rebels* and *Song of Jubilee.* The former takes place during the Revolutionary War as Bruce Cameron, a sixteen-year old, comes of age following his decision to enter the struggle for independence. *Song of Jubilee* examines the debilitating influence of slavery on all people during the Civil War. Although some felt the characterization of Jim, a slave in Virginia whose first-person account frames the plot, does not provide accurate insights into his

motivations to remain with his master during the war, the book is still acknowledged for its portrayal of the demoralizing effects of war on all involved.

World War II is the setting for *Ceremony of Innocence*, a novel based on a true story of a brother and sister who are caught in the dilemma of whether or not to stand up for their convictions when they disagree with the government. In *Ceremony of Innocence,* Forman masterfully depicts the lives of two siblings, Sophie and Hans Scholl, in 1942 Germany when the two decide to produce and disseminate leaflets attacking Nazism. This is Forman's "best book," according to Ken Donelson and Alleen Pace Nilsen in the first edition of *Literature for Today's Young Adults,* who have called Forman the best war novelist for young adults. Donelson and Nilsen praise Forman's books for their ability to catch "the misery and stink of war coupled with the pathos of real people caught up in events they cannot comprehend or manage." But more importantly, according to Donelson and Nilsen, Forman's writing creates strong, noble, believable heroes, "acting as heroes might, unsure, frightened, bewildered, and horrified."

While Forman is highly acknowledged for his realistic portrayal of war and the people involved in its misery, he also has written both science fiction and nonfiction books for young adults. *Cry Havoc* and *Doomsday Plus Twelve* both extend the author's creativity. *Cry Havoc* describes a heroine's plot to destroy a pack of genetically engineered dogs who are raiding a small town. *Doomsday Plus Twelve* takes place in the year 2000 and provides insight into the world of a post nuclear holocaust. Forman's nonfiction has been praised for being easily understood introductions of topics as Nazism, communism, and anarchism. His focus stresses the relationship between government and people as well as the history and development of these forms of government.

"Forman's most successful works," as stated in *Contemporary Literary Criticism,* "examine the reactions of people caught up in the death and destruction of war, focusing especially on young adults who are forced into maturity by events beyond their control. Although his young heroes and heroines feel horror, disgust, and fear, they act with unfaltering strength and honor." In his exploration of racism, ecology, and war, he provides not only realistic descriptions of historical contexts but also exposes the human element at the heart of these issues. Forman shared in the third edition of *Literature for Today's Young Adults* that, "I like to preach a bit . . . a rather pacifistic theme hoping that my fervor on behalf of humanity and the preservation of this fragile globe which we share with so many other creatures will rub off on the next generation."

—Janelle B. Mathis

FOX, Paula

Nationality: American. **Born:** New York City, 22 April 1923; daughter of the writer Paul Hervey Fox. **Education:** Columbia University, New York, 1955-58. **Family:** Married 1) Richard Sigerson in 1948 (divorced 1954), two sons: 2) Martin Greenberg in 1962. **Career:** Writer; has worked in numerous occupations, including model, saleswoman, public relations worker, machinist, staff member for the British publisher Victor Gollancz, and reader for a film studio. News service correspondent, Paris and Warsaw, for the British wire service Telepress, late 1940s; English-as-a-second-language instructor at the Ethical Culture School, New York City; teacher for emotionally disturbed children, Dobbs Ferry, New York; from 1963 teacher of writing workshops and professor of literature, University of Pennsylvania, Philadelphia. **Awards:** Finalist in National Book award children's book category, 1971, for *Blowfish Live in the Sea;* National Institute of Arts and Letters award, 1972; Guggenheim fellowship, 1972; National Endowment for the Arts grant, 1974; Newbery Medal, American Library Association, 1974, for *The Slave Dancer;* Hans Christian Andersen International Medal, 1978; National Book award nomination, 1979, for *The Little Swineherd and Other Tales;* one of *New York Times*'s Outstanding Books, 1980, and American Book award, for paperback fiction, 1983, for *A Place Apart*; Child Study Children's Book award from the Bank Street College of Education and one of *New York Times*'s Notable Books, both 1984, Christopher award and Newbery Honor Book, both 1985, and International Board on Books for Young People Honor List for Writing, 1986, all for *One-Eyed Cat;* Brandeis Fiction Citation, 1984; Rockefeller Foundation grant, 1984; one of the *New York Times*'s Notable Books, 1986, and one of the Child Study Association of America's Children's Books of the Year, 1987, for *The Moonlight Man;* Silver Medallion, University of Southern Mississippi, 1987; *Boston Globe/Horn Book* award for fiction and Newbery Honor Book, 1989, for *The Village by the Sea*. **Address:** 306 Clinton Street Brooklyn, New York 11201, U.S.A.

PUBLICATIONS FOR YOUNG ADULTS

Fiction

A *Likely Place,* illustrated by Edward Ardizzone. New York, Macmillan, 1967; London, Macmillan, 1968.

Portrait of Ivan, illustrated by Saul Lambert. Englewood Cliffs, New Jersey, Bradbury Press, 1969; London, Macmillan, 1970.

Blowfish Live in the Sea. Englewood, New Jersey, Bradbury Press, 1970.

The Slave Dancer, illustrated by Eros Keith. Englewood, New Jersey, Bradbury Press, 1973; London, Macmillan, 1974.

A Place Apart. New York, Farrar Straus, 1980; London, Dent, 1981.

The Moonlight Man. New York, Bradbury Press, and London, Dent, 1986.

Lily and the Lost Boy. New York, Orchard Books, 1987; as *The Lost Boy,* London, Dent, 1988.

Western Wind. New York, Orchard Books, 1993.

The Eagle Kite. New York, Orchard Books, 1995.

Radiance Descending. New York, DK Ink, 1997.

PUBLICATIONS FOR CHILDREN

Fiction

Maurice's Room, illustrated by Ingrid Fetz. New York, Macmillan, 1966.

How Many Miles to Babylon?, illustrated by Paul Giovanopoulos. New York, David White, and London, Macmillan, 1967.

The Stone-Faced Boy, illustrated by Donald A. Mackay. Englewood Cliffs, New Jersey, Bradbury Press, 1968; London, Macmillan, 1969.

Dear Prosper, illustrated by Steve McLachlin. New York, David White, 1968.

The King's Falcon, illustrated by Eros Keith. Eaglewood Cliffs, New Jersey, Bradbury Press, 1969; London, Macmillan, 1970.

Hungry Fred, illustrated by Rosemary Wells. Englewood, New Jersey, Bradbury Press, 1969.

Good Ethan, illustrated by Arnold Lobel. Englewood, New Jersey, Bradbury Press, 1973.

The Little Swineherd and Other Tales (short stories), illustrated by Leonard Lubin. New York, Dutton, 1978; London, Dent, 1979; with illustrations by Robert Byrd, New York, Dutton Children's Books, 1996.

One-Eyed Cat. New York, Bradbury Press, 1984; London, Dent, 1985.

The Village by the Sea. New York, Orchard Books, 1988.

In a Place of Danger. New York, Orchard Books, 1989.

Monkey Island. New York, Orchard Books, 1991.

Reteller, *Amzat and His Brothers: Three Italian Tales* (short stories), as remembered by Florence Vecchi, illustrated by Emily McCully. New York, Orchard Books, 1993.

PUBLICATIONS FOR ADULTS

Novels

Poor George. New York, Harcourt Brace, and London, Bodley Head, 1967.

Desperate Characters. New York, Harcourt Brace, and London, Macmillan, 1970; reprinted with an afterword by Irving Howe, Boston, Nonpareil, 1980.

The Western Coast. New York, Harcourt Brace, 1972; London, Macmillan, 1973.

The Widow's Children. New York, Dutton, 1976.

A Servant's Tale. Berkeley, California, North Point Press, 1984; London, Virago Press, 1986.

The God of Nightmares. Berkeley, California, North Point Press, 1990.

*

Media Adaptations: *Desperate Characters* (motion picture), Paramount, 1970; *One-Eyed Cat* (cassette and film with cassette), Random House.

Biography: Entry in *Dictionary of Literary Biography,* Volume 52: *American Writers for Children since 1960: Fiction,* Detroit, Gale, 1986; essay in *Speaking for Ourselves: Autobiographical Sketches by Notable Authors of Books for Young Adults,* Volume 1, compiled and edited by Donald R. Gallo, National Council of Teachers of English, 1990.

Critical Studies: Entry in *Children's Literature Review,* Volume 1, 1976, Volume 44, 1997, Detroit, Gale; entry in *Contemporary Literary Criticism,* Volume 2, 1974, Volume 8, 1978, Detroit, Gale.

Paula Fox comments:

Why am I a writer? I can only answer that by saying that I tell stories; I am a storyteller and have been one for more than thirty years. When I finish one story, I watch the drift in my head and very soon am thinking of another story. All of one's experience shapes one's stories. Imagination is unifying, not separating. If I were to say that I wrote a book, for example *The Village by the Sea,* because a sand village I had built as a child had been knocked down, I would falsify terribly what is a complicated, intuitive process of imagination into which I am only afforded an occasional glimpse. I love writing—though it can be wearisome. I especially love writing for young people, although as I write, I do not think of ages, only of people.

*   *   *

Paula Fox is an author with tremendous versatility. Her works include picture and chapter books for the youngest readers, such as *Maurice's Room;* books for intermediate readers, like *How Many Miles to Babylon?, The Stone-Faced Boy,* and *Village by the Sea;* folktale retellings, including *Amzat and his Brothers: Three Italian Folktales;* and novels for adults, such as *Desperate Characters* and *A Servant's Tale.* Her realistic fiction for young adults complements this range with literary excellence. She received the Newbery Medal for *The Slave Dancer,* a Newbery Honor Award for *One-Eyed Cat,* and the prestigious Hans Christian Andersen Medal for her entire body of work for children and young adults.

Recurring aesthetic and ideological concerns pattern Fox's novels for young adults. In essays, lectures, and interviews, Fox reveals a prevailing respect for her audience. She addresses young readers frankly and helps them to understand the lives of other people. Isolation is a common theme of her work: characters often start out insecure and develop self-knowledge through their relationships with others. Her use of language—to establish mood, to evoke and extend images—speaks to her stylistic coherence and uniqueness. Using specific, telling details, she creates vivid settings with precision. However, the skillful vitality of her character portrayals also reveals an author plumbing the depths of human individuality. Her style, setting, plot, and character have a seamless unity.

The Slave Dancer stands as Fox's most externally directed novel. Beginning in the New Orleans of 1840, it traces with historical accuracy the slave trade. Thirteen-year-old Jessie Bollier is kidnapped and indentured to serve as fife player on the slave ship *Moonlight.* His first-person, retrospective narrative speaks intensely of the horrors and dehumanization he witnesses and in which he participates. His sensual descriptions of the city and the ship actualize the experience for readers. More than anything, his interactions with the ship's crew and his ability to see the ship's ''cargo'' as individual human beings structure Jessie's story. He moves beyond disdain for the intense personalities he meets to realize his own capacity for evil and eventually to demand accountability of himself.

Isolation plagues thirteen-year-old Victoria in *A Place Apart.* After her father's death, her comfort and security are gone. When she and her mother move to a small town, she experiences even deeper separation. Unlike Jessie, Victoria lives in a relatively understandable moral world. School and friends begin to fill her emptiness and Hugh, a new friend, helps her develop undiscovered attributes in herself. Her confidence grows and her isolation dissipates. However, Victoria learns that her strength always must stem from an inner force of stability. While Hugh, her friends, and her mother can appreciate who she is, only Victoria can create, sustain, or change that essence. She learns to maintain a tension between her need to be close to others and her need to have a private place.

In *One-Eyed Cat,* guilt consumes eleven-year-old Ned Wallis and forces him to stand alone after he shoots a forbidden air rifle. Thinking he maimed a one-eyed stray cat, Ned must find his way back to himself through forgiveness. He charts that course by slow, steady contact with others: his morally daunting minister father, his patient, ailing mother, and a supportive listener, elderly Mr. Scully. When he finally confesses and receives an equal confession from his mother in return, the family's recognition of each other's imperfections leads to reconciliation.

The essential bond between child and adult permeates all Fox's young adult novels in various combinations: child and mother, child and father, child and adult mentor. In *The Moonlight Man,* fifteen-year-old Catherine Ames yearns to establish a connection to her alcoholic father. Harry proves as unapproachable as Reverend Wallis, though his remoteness stems from physical distance and unreliability rather than high moral expectations. Like other Fox characters who must cope with human failings, Catherine must accommodate the facts of her father and discover a love strong enough to allow his weaknesses.

A quiet, emotionally withdrawn child also appears in *Lily and the Lost Boy.* Placed in contemporary times on the Greek island of Thasos, Lily feels abandoned when her older brother Paul turns to a mysterious boy for companionship. The island setting highlights Lily's sense of desertion, though it also provides a warm, inclusive community in which Lily gains perspective on her relationship with Paul. Like all Fox characters, her thoughtfulness and introspection enable her to perpetuate a friendship with Paul when his new comrade disappoints him.

Disappointment, abandonment, intergenerational bonds, and forgiveness unite in *Monkey Island.* Forsaken by his pregnant mother, Clay begins to live on the streets of New York City, a place in some ways as isolated as a Greek island. The eleven-year-old child discovers community with two homeless men he meets in the park. More important than the survival skills Calvin and Buddy teach him, Clay rediscovers his capacity to love and be loved. Fortified by them, Clay returns to his mother knowing he has discovered ''a place beyond forgiveness,'' a nurturing place in its recognition of family as the fundamental link between imperfect human beings.

In every novel, Fox attributes significant capabilities to her readers. She pays tribute to their emotional, intellectual, and psychological abilities with layered, probing narratives, identifiable characters who achieve genuine illumination, and lucid, striking prose. Although critics occasionally label her work ''depressing,'' most praise her integrity in writing honestly about relationships and emotional development. Her craft seems effortless; her vision essential and eloquent.

—Cathryn M. Mercier

FRANK, Anne

Nationality: German. **Born:** Frankfort-am-Main, 12 June 1929. **Died:** In Bergen-Belsen concentration camp, March 1945.

PUBLICATIONS

Anne Frank: The Diary of a Young Girl, translated by B.M. Mooyaart-Doubleday, introduction by Eleanor Roosevelt. Garden City, New York, Doubleday, 1952.

Anne Frank's Tales from the Secret Annex, translated by Ralph Mannheim and Michel Mok. New York, Doubleday, 1959.

The Works of Anne Frank, introduction by Ann Birstein and Alfred Kazin. New York, Doubleday, 1959; Westport, Connecticut, Greenwood Press, 1977.

The Diary of Anne Frank: The Critical Edition, edited by David Baranouw and Gerrold de Stroom, translated by Arnold J. Pomerans and B.M. Mooyaart-Doubleday, prepared by the Netherlands State Institute for War Documentation. New York, Doubleday, 1989.

The Diary of a Young Girl: The Definitive Edition, edited by Otto H. Frank and Mirjam Pressler, translated by Susan Massotty. New York, Doubleday, 1995.

*

Media Adaptations: *Diary of Anne Frank* (play, adapted by Frances Goodrich and Albert Hackett, produced New York, 1995), New York, Random House, 1955; *Diary of Anne Frank* (film), Twentieth Century-Fox, 1959; *The Diary of Anne Frank* (recording), Spoken Arts, 1974; *The Diary of Anne Frank* (recording), Caedmon, 1977; *The Diary of Anne Frank* (television movie), 1980; *Anne Frank Remembered* (film), 1996.

Critical Studies: *Anne Frank: A Portrait In Courage* by Ernst Schnabel, translated by Richard and Clara Winston, New York, Harcourt, 1958; *The Obsession* by Meyer Levin, New York, Simon and Schuster, 1977; *Anne Frank in the World* by Stephen Cohen, Amsterdam, Anne Frank Foundation, 1985; *Anne Frank Remembered: The Story of the Woman Who Helped Hide the Frank Family* by Miep Gies with Alison Leslie Gold, New York, Simon and Schuster, 1987; *Anne Frank, Beyond the Diary: A Photographic Remembrance* by Rund vander Rol and Rian Verhoeven, translated by Tony Langham and Plym Peters, introduced by Anna Quindlen, New York, Viking, 1993; *Dear Anne Frank* by Anne Frank Educational Trust, London, Puffin Books, 1995; *An Obsession with Anne Frank: Meyer Levin and the Diary* by Lawrence Graver, Berkeley, University of California Press, 1995; *Anne Frank* by Sandor Katz, New York, Chelsea House, 1996; *Anne Frank* by Rachel Epstein, New York, Franklin Watts, 1997; *Readings on the Diary of a Young Girl,* San Diego, Greenhaven Press, 1998.

*   *   *

Anne Frank is most likely the only author represented in this volume who has published only one book. Her diary detailing her and her family's daily struggles coping with life as fugitives from Nazism over a two year period has become a legend for readers all over the world, young and old.

Anne's father, Otto Frank, was a German-Jewish businessman who, when Hitler came to power, moved his family to Holland in 1933 and set up a very successful business selling pectin, drugs, and herbs. When Hitler's soldiers and stormtroopers invaded Holland, Anne's father moved his family to a ''secret annex'' (an attic) above his business offices. With the courageous help of Miep Gies (Otto Frank's office manager) and her family and other workers in his office, eight people went into hiding simply because they were Jewish: the Frank Family (Anne, her older sister Margot, and her mother and father); the Van Pels family (called the ''van Daans'' by Anne), consisting of Peter—a teenage boy two and a half years older than Anne—and his mother and father; and an unmarried dentist named Fritz Pfeffer (whom Anne named ''Alfred Dussel'').

All around Anne, Jews were being rounded up daily by the Nazis and carted off to concentration camps throughout Nazi-occupied Europe or murdered in remote areas of Holland. Anne began her diary (''The Diary of a Young Girl'') on her thirteenth birthday, just about a month before her family went into hiding. She called her diary Kitty, and it became the ''confidante'' to whom Anne could bare her soul, telling secrets about herself and her family, her thoughts and feelings. The diary, in effect, became her own ''secret annex''.

In the diary, Anne vents her most personal feelings about the people with whom she shares her cramped living quarters for two years. Almost daily, she complains about her mother, whom she resents because Anne believes Mrs. Frank treats her like a friend instead of a daughter and doesn't understand her needs and appreciate her worth. In contrast, Anne idealizes her caring and sensitive father, often pitting her adulation for him against her alienation from her mother. She also repeatedly compares and contrasts herself with her suave and more passive older sister Margot, at times criticizing her and at other times empathizing with her. Anne clearly dislikes and disrespects Mrs. Van Daan, whose son Peter Anne gradually becomes attracted to. She also lashes out in her diary at Alfred Dussel, the prudish, middle-aged dentist who finds refuge with the Frank and Van Daan families.

Anne frequently comments on the crazy world she and her family are hiding from: ''I could spend hours telling you about the suffering the war has brought, but I'd only make myself more miserable. . . . Jews and Christians alike are waiting. The whole world is waiting, and many are waiting for death.''

Despite her temperamental outbursts and her self-absorption, Anne displays an unusual proclivity for being self-critical and for apologizing to people she has hurt. Near the end of her family's ordeal—only three weeks before being captured by the Nazis—Anne writes in her diary: ''I watch myself as if I were a stranger. I've cured myself by holding my behavior up to the light and looking at what I was doing wrong''. Another aspect of Anne's complex personality is her deep and wide-ranging intellectual curiosity; she loves to read classic works, study foreign languages, and contemplate the meaning of life, even under the most difficult of situations.

The tensions of her life create mood upswings and downswings that result in poignant descriptions of despair and hope—all in the same breath—and of sensitivity to the dangers facing her father's employees who have helped hide them and care for their needs: "I've asked myself again and again whether it wouldn't have been better if we hadn't gone into hiding, if we were dead now and didn't have to go through this misery especially so that the others could be spared the burden. But we all shrink from this thought. We still love life, we haven't yet forgotten the voice of nature, and we keep hoping for . . . everything."

Anne Frank wrote these words in her diary on May 26, 1944 as she looked out at "the world transformed into a wilderness," as she heard the "approaching thunder that one day will destroy us," and as she witnessed the "suffering of millions." It was just nine weeks before the S.S. and their Dutch collaborators stormed the annex, arrested its eight occupants, and carted them off to concentration camps. Only Anne's father, Otto Frank, survived. Anne and her sister were sent to the Bergen-Belsen death camp, near Hannover, Germany; during a typhus outbreak, Anne and Margot—along with thousands of other prisoners—perished a month before British troops liberated the camp on April 12, 1945.

After the war, Otto Frank located his former secretary Miep Gies, who had found Anne's diary pages strewn over the annex floor and saved them. She never read the diary but gave what she had saved to Anne's father who, after careful deliberation, decided to publish a condensed version of the diary, omitting Anne's frequent references to sexuality and her more intemperate criticism of others living in the annex. Otto Frank died in 1980 and left the diary manuscripts to the Netherlands State Institute for War Documentation, who substantiated the authenticity of the documents. With the approval of the Anne Frank Foundation, which owned the copyright to the diary, later editions of the diary restored most of what had been deleted by Anne's father.

Of all the primary documents that have emerged from the horrendous events of the Holocaust, *The Diary of a Young Girl* has become the most read first-person account of this nightmare of history. It personalizes the tragedy of the genocide because it shows how the life of such a promising young woman was cut short simply because she was a Jew. Many, however, question how Anne's precocious and moving diary has been used since it was published, especially as adapted in the Goodrich and Hackett play based on her diary. They believe the play takes Anne's diary out of the Holocaust context, turning it into an often melodramatic statement of universalism emphasizing her love of life, her hope for the future, and her antagonism to prejudice generally. What is lost, they believe, is the awful reality of the anti-semitic genocide, the extermination camps, the death marches and mass shootings—the stuff of Elie Wiesel's agonizing novels.

Nonetheless, Anne Frank's diary—especially in its "definitive edition"—lives on and speaks to millions throughout the world about a time not so long ago, an experience few today could even imagine, and a young, promising life snuffed out. The book has endured because of the spirit of Anne Frank—a spirit that believes in the goodness of humanity and the fundamental importance of right in the world even while witnessing the mass murder of millions of her Jewish brothers and sisters (and other minorities) and a world that often acted indifferent to the carnage: "It's a wonder that I haven't abandoned my ideals. They seem so absurd and impractical. Yet I cling to them because I still believe in spite of everything that people are truly good at heart."

—Jack Forman

FREEDMAN, Russell (Bruce)

Nationality: American. **Born:** San Francisco, California, 11 October 1929. **Education:** San Jose State College (now University), California, 1947-49; University of California, Berkeley, B.A. 1951. **Military Service:** Served in the U.S. Army, Counter Intelligence Corps, 1951-53; served in infantry in Korea. **Career:** Reporter and editor, Associated Press, San Francisco, California, 1953-56; publicity writer for television, J. Walter Thompson Co. (advertising agency), New York City, 1956-60; associate staff member, *Columbia Encyclopedia,* Columbia University Press, New York City, 1961-63; free-lance writer, particularly for juveniles, since 1961; editor, Crowell-Collier Educational Corp., New York City, 1964-65; writing workshop instructor, New School for Social Research, New York City, 1969-86. **Awards:** Western Heritage award, National Cowboy Hall of Fame, 1984, for *Children of the Wild West*; Spur award Honor Book, Western Writers of America, 1985, and Jefferson Cup Honor Book, 1986, both for *Cowboys of the Wild West*; Jefferson Cup Honor Book, 1988, for *Indian Chiefs*; Golden Kite award Honor Book, Society of Children's Book Writers, 1987, American Library Association Newbery Medal and Jefferson Cup award, both 1988, International Board on Books for Young People (IBBY) Honor List choice, 1990, all for *Lincoln: A Photobiography*; Golden Kite award Honor Book, 1988, for *Buffalo Hunt*; Orbis Pictus award, 1990, for *Franklin Delano Roosevelt*; *Boston Globe/Horn Book* award (nonfiction), 1991, Newbery Honor award, 1992, Golden Kite award for nonfiction, 1992, Jefferson Cup award, 1992, all for *The Wright Brothers: How They Invented the Airplane*; Golden Kite Honor for nonfiction, 1992, and Western Heritage award, 1993, for *An Indian Winter*; *Washington Post*/Children's Book Guild award for nonfiction, 1992; Knickerbocker award for Juvenile Literature, New York Library Association, 1993; Empire State award for Excellence in Literature for Young People, New York Library Association, 1993; Golden Kite award for nonfiction, 1993, Newbery Honor award, 1994, and *Boston Globe/Horn Book* award for nonfiction, 1994, all for *Eleanor Roosevelt: A Life of Discovery*; Golden Kite award for nonfiction, 1994, and Jane Addams Children's Book award, Jane Addams Peace Association, and *School Library Journal* Best Books citation, both 1995, all for *Kids at Work: Lewis Hine and the Crusade against Child Labor*; Spur Award, Western Writers of America, 1996, for *Life and Death of Crazy Horse*; Regina Medal for juvenile literature, Catholic Library Association, 1996; Laura Ingalls Wilder Award for body of work, 1998. **Address:** 280 Riverside Dr., New York, New York 10025, U.S.A.

PUBLICATIONS FOR YOUNG ADULTS

Nonfiction

Teenagers Who Made History, portraits by Arthur Shilstone. New York, Holiday House, 1961.

Two Thousand Years of Space Travel. New York, Holiday House, 1963.

Jules Verne: Portrait of a Prophet. New York, Holiday House, 1965.

Thomas Alva Edison. New York, Study-Master, 1966.

Scouting with Baden-Powell. New York, Holiday House, 1967.

How Animals Learn, with James E. Morriss. New York, Holiday House, 1969.

Animal Instincts, with James E. Morriss, illustrated by John Morris. New York, Holiday House, 1970.

Animal Architects. New York, Holiday House, 1971.

The Brains of Animals and Man, with James E. Morriss. New York, Holiday House, 1972.

The First Days of Life, illustrated by Joseph Cellini. New York, Holiday House, 1974.

Growing Up Wild: How Young Animals Survive, illustrated by Leslie Morrill. New York, Holiday House, 1975.

Animal Fathers, illustrated by Joseph Cellini. New York, Holiday House, 1976.

Animal Games, illustrated by St. Tamara. New York, Holiday House, 1976.

Hanging On: How Animals Carry Their Young. New York, Holiday House, 1977.

How Birds Fly, illustrated by Lorence F. Bjorklund. New York, Holiday House, 1977.

Getting Born, illustrated with photographs and drawings by Corbett Jones. New York, Holiday House, 1978.

How Animals Defend Their Young. New York, Dutton, 1978.

Immigrant Kids. New York, Dutton, 1980.

They Lived with the Dinosaurs. New York, Holiday House, 1980.

Tooth and Claw: A Look at Animal Weapons. New York, Holiday House, 1980.

Animal Superstars: Biggest, Strongest, Fastest, Smartest. Englewood Cliffs, New Jersey, Prentice Hall, 1981.

Farm Babies. New York, Holiday House, 1981.

When Winter Comes, illustrated by Pamela Johnson. New York, Dutton, 1981.

Can Bears Predict Earthquakes? Unsolved Mysteries of Animal Behavior. Englewood Cliffs, New Jersey, Prentice Hall, 1982.

Killer Fish. New York, Holiday House, 1982.

Killer Snakes. New York, Holiday House, 1982.

Children of the Wild West. New York, Clarion Books, 1983.

Dinosaurs and Their Young, illustrated by Leslie Morrill. New York, Holiday House, 1983.

Rattlesnakes, illustrated by the author. New York, Holiday House, 1984.

Cowboys of the Wild West. New York, Clarion Books, 1985.

Holiday House: The First Fifty Years (adult). New York, Holiday House, 1985.

Sharks, illustrated by the author. New York, Holiday House, 1985.

Indian Chiefs. New York, Holiday House, 1987.

Lincoln: A Photobiography. New York, Clarion Books, 1987.

Buffalo Hunt. New York, Holiday House, 1988.

Franklin Delano Roosevelt. New York, Clarion Books, 1990.

The Wright Brothers: How They Invented the Airplane, photographs by Orville and Wilbur Wright. New York, Holiday House, 1991.

An Indian Winter, paintings and drawings by Karl Bodmer. New York, Holiday House, 1992.

Eleanor Roosevelt: A Life of Discovery. New York, Clarion, 1993.

Kids at Work: Lewis Hine and the Crusade against Child Labor. New York, Clarion, 1994.

The Life and Death of Crazy Horse. New York, Holiday House, 1996.

Out of Darkness: The Story of Louis Braille. New York, Clarion, 1997.

Martha Graham, A Dancer's Life: A Photo-Biography of the American Dancer, Teacher, Choreographer. New York, Clarion, 1997.

Other

Wendell Berry: A Bibliography. Occasional Paper 12, Lexington, University of Kentucky, 1998.

*

Media Adaptations: *Newbery/Caldecott Medal Acceptance Speeches* (sound recording), Westport, Connecticut, Weston Woods, 1988; *Lincoln: A Photobiography* (filmstrip and video), McGraw-Hill Media, 1989; *Out of the Darkness: The Story of Louis Braille* (sound recording), Prince Frederick, Maryland, Recorded Books, 1998; *Newbery/Caldecott Medal, Laura Ingalls Wilder Award Acceptance Speeches* (sound recording), Westport, Connecticut, Weston Woods, 1998.

Biography: Essay in *Authors and Artists for Young Adults,* Vol. 4, Detroit, Gale, 1990; entry in *Sixth Book of Junior Authors and Illustrators,* New York, H.W. Wilson, 1989.

Critical Studies: Entry in *Children's Literature Review,* Vol. 20, Detroit, Gale, 1990, 71-89.

Russell Freedman comments:

It seems that I was predestined to be a writer. My parents met in a bookshop and held their first conversation over a stack of bestsellers. She was a sales clerk, and he was the West Coast representative of a large publishing house. They married soon afterward, and I grew up in a house filled with books and with the lively conversations and disputes of visiting authors.

When I went to work as a cub reporter for the Associated Press, I learned to meet deadlines and respect facts. Later, as a television publicity writer, I learned that if you fail to capture and hold the reader's interest, you're just blowing in the wind.

Today I enjoy studying and writing about subjects that for some reason excite my curiosity, enthusiasm, or concern. Starting a new book is like trying to solve a puzzle. You have to decide what to include, and what to leave out, how to begin, what to emphasize and where, how to balance facts and interpretation, how to breathe life into the subject and convey your own enthusiasm to the reader. The process of viewing the material, of seeing what belongs where, is a mystery I never resolve once and for all.

Like every writer, a nonfiction writer is essentially a storyteller. Whatever my subject, I always feel that I have a story to tell that is worth telling, and so I want to tell it as clearly and simply and effectively as I can, in a way that will stretch the reader's imagination and make that reader care.

*   *   *

When Russell Freedman was a boy, he and his family visited the Lincoln Memorial in Washington, D.C. There, his father counseled him to walk around the impressive statue, to observe Lincoln from different angles. The youthful Russell recalls that Lincoln looked somber and strong from one vantage point, more animated and soft from another. His father's advice, to examine a subject from a multiplicity of viewpoints, still serves as a benchmark for all of Russell Freedman's writings. His consistently inventive and multivalent interpretation of diverse subject matter elevates nonfiction for young adults to a new level of excellence.

His earliest book, *Teenagers Who Made History,* was motivated—as Freedman claims so much of his work has been—by chance. For this title, Freedman was inspired by an article he read in the *New York Times* about the Braille typewriter and its adolescent inventor. With his inquisitive journalistic mind, he wondered about other youth who had made striking contributions while still in their teens. A second title in the beginning of his career traced space travel over a two thousand year period. This definitive exploration was to intrigue and satisfy Freedman for a short time; he learned he was far less interested in such full treatment, that his attention lay in much more narrowly defining his focus. Still, the space travel book clearly led the way to his first biography detailing a single individual, that of Jules Verne. In both that biography and the one of Baden Powell, the founder of the boy scouts, Freedman was to reveal his consummate talents as a researcher and selector of material.

For the next fifteen years, Freedman confined his writings almost exclusively to the exploration of animal behavior. In these books for younger readers, he honed those skills that serve to distinguish his most memorable later work.

Another chance event marked a critical advance in his work. Attending a turn-of-the-century photography exhibit, Freedman was deeply moved by several photographs of immigrants whose faces spoke vividly and poignantly from the past. His *Immigrant Kids,* a perfect "picture book," integrates photographs and text with lucidity and grace. The success of that volume in which the photographs serve as powerful text, not as embellishment, convinced Freedman that evocative photography was underutilized as a potent means of communicating stories to young people, particularly young people engaged by the visual medium of television. With the same integrity and thoroughness that distinguishes his best writing, Freedman sought out those authentic pictures which would best reveal his subject. His commitment to choice photography as integral to the telling of story certainly applies to his companion books, *Children of the Wild West* and *Cowboys of the Wild West,* in which period photographs expose with striking authority the settlement of Western America. In both books, what emerges is Freedman's resolution to combat stereotype, to correct some egregious myths about our history and its people. Indeed, asked to comment on what characterizes his work, Freedman names his unrelenting desire for justice—justice for the Native American Indian, for immigrants, for cowboys, for all those too simply perceived as heroes and villains in history. In these particular books, and in *Indian Chiefs,* images seamlessly integrated with words help us to understand the violation which one group of people suffered at the hands of another. A haunting pair of photographs of Indian boys and girls, first in their native clothes on arrival at boarding school and then a year later, looking dazed and emotionless in their Americanized garb; a grim pile of buffalo hides, estimated at some forty thousand, purchased by the white man at the expense of the Indian who venerated the buffalo; and the prideful dignity revealed in the portrait photographs of Indian chiefs: these images impact the reader, commanding both attention and compassion for those against whom profound wrongs were committed.

Setting the historical record straight is representative of the best of Freedman's work. Not surprisingly, his first biography committed to amending the record of a legendary hero undertakes the man most venerated among Americans, the man about whom more has been written, perhaps, than any other American. In *Lincoln: A Photobiography,* Freedman hoped to uncover the man behind the myth. This Newbery award winning volume documents Freedman's meticulous research skills, his artful selective process as he sifts among inexhaustible material, and his brilliance in providing stunning images to deepen and broaden his portrayal. Few who read this remarkable portrait will forget the juxtaposition of five photographs which show the ravages of the presidency on the embattled and struggling Lincoln during his four years in office.

Freedman turned once again to an American president in *Franklin Delano Roosevelt,* a volume that further demonstrates the author's mastery in revealing not only the man in his complexity, but also the times which he shaped and which shaped him. Freedman's deft handling of the intensity and pain of the Civil War years of Lincoln is matched by his skillful treatment of the Roosevelt years, the times of the Depression through the Second World War. Without sentiment or bathos, Freedman looks honestly and directly at the man and his times. The portrait that emerges commands our respect for its passion and its intelligence: one never feels overloaded with facts, but gets a keen sense of balance and form in the composition and arrangement of information instead.

The Wright Brothers: How They Invented the Airplane once again shows Freedman as a creative artist, shaping his material for dramatic effect without ever compromising accuracy. From its effective opening sentence, "No one had ever seen what Amos Root [a curious beekeeper who travelled 200 miles to eyewitness the first airplane in controlled flight] saw on that September afternoon in 1904," to its poignant closing, detailing that a century later Neil Armstrong "stepped onto the lunar surface . . . carrying with him a piece of the original cotton wing covering from the Wright flyer," Freedman crafts a theater of genuine excitement. Original photographs by Wilbur and Orville Wright increase the tension. Nine internal pages of wordless photographs showing a glider in free flight remind one of the mounting exhilaration of Max cavorting with the wild things in the wordless pages of Maurice Sendak's classic.

Expert use of visuals finds Freedman turning occasionally away from photography when another art form would serve better. For *Buffalo Hunt* Freedman employs paintings of those artist adventurers who traveled West in the 1800s when Indians depended on the buffalo to fulfill all their material and spiritual needs. His *Indian Winter* records the adventures of German prince Alexander Phillip Maximilian among the Mandan Indians and utilizes the painting and drawings of Karl Bodmer, the Swiss painter who accompanied the prince on his travels. Freedman's text itself relies judiciously on the actual journal writings of the prince. His ability to use the words

297

of others (often quotations serve to introduce his chapters) meshed with his own, foster his creation of all these tapestries of history which earn him a unique place in young adult literature.

—Susan P. Bloom

———————

FRENCH, Paul. *See* ASIMOV, Isaac.

———————

FRENCH, Simon

Nationality: Australian. **Born:** Sydney, New South Wales, 26 November 1957. **Education:** Mitchell College, Bathurst, New South Wales, 1976-79, diploma in teaching 1979. **Career:** Has worked as library clerical assistant and fruitpicker; infants' teacher, Willow Tree, 1980, and St. Clair, 1981-84, both New South Wales; youth worker, 1984-87. Since 1988 teacher in New South Wales. **Awards:** Special mention from the Australian Children's Book of the Year awards, 1976, for *Hey, Phantom Singlet;* commendations in Australian Children's Book of the Year competition, 1982, for *Cannily, Cannily;* Australian Children's Book of the Year award, 1987, for *All We Know;* honour book, Australian Childrens' Book Awards, Book of the Year, Australian Family Therapy Association, Book of the Year nomination, Bank Street School, New York, all 1992, all for *Change the Locks.* **Address:** 1735 East Kurrajong Rd., East Kurrajong, New South Wales 2758, Australia.

PUBLICATIONS FOR YOUNG ADULTS

Fiction

Hey, Phantom Singlet, illustrated by Alex Nicholas. Sydney and London, Angus & Robertson, 1975.
Cannily, Cannily. Sydney and London, Angus & Robertson, 1981.
All We Know. Sydney and London, Angus & Robertson, 1986.
Change the Locks. New York, Scholastic, 1993.

*   *   *

Hey, Phantom Singlet, Simon French's first novel, written while he was still at school and published when he was seventeen, contains many of the typical characteristics of the young adult novel, such as down-to-earth classroom dialogue. Math, a youth who suffers from growing pains and sees himself as an outsider, feels the need to establish a forceful presence by adopting bizarre gear—in this instance an orange singlet (vest) and a fur cap. Math is suffering because his father is in jail and his mother, married at seventeen, "sometimes felt that life had become too much for her."

In this, and each of his succeeding books, French is recording one step on a journey toward maturity. Because his novels are

skillfully crafted and his prose finely honed, he is a writer both for those who are in the process of breaking free and stepping across the boundaries of childhood, and for adults, young or old, who have experienced the pain and the excitement of growing up.

French writes from his experience, as a schoolboy in Sydney in the 1960s, a teacher, a welfare worker with disturbed children, and as an astute and sympathetic observer of the human condition. In particular he is concerned with those who are "different"—the loners, the rejected, the emotionally deprived. All of these French dignifies as individuals to be valued and accepted for their own personal worth.

There is a growing maturity to his writing, both in subject matter and style. *Hey, Phantom Singlet* uses some now dated colloquialisms. Since then, while not eschewing idiom, French is careful to avoid that particular trap. So while he explores the contemporary scene and can be topical (as in raising the issue of competitive sport in *Cannily, Cannily)* he writes for all times and places. His young protagonists, their peers, their parents, and teachers are to be found the world over, not only in Australia.

Teachers have a high profile in his first three books. In *Hey, Phantom Singlet* and *Cannily, Cannily* they can be crass, authoritarian, and insensitive like Mad Dog Preston in the former, or bullies like Fuller, the sadistic football coach in *Cannily, Cannily.* But it is a sympathetic English teacher, Mr. Boon, who helps Math through his confusion and directs him forward to some degree of maturity. Mr. Boon is a forerunner to Mr. Clifton in *All We Know,* one of the most likeable teachers in contemporary fiction, who in his genuine concern for his students could well be a self-portrait of the author. In the same book, Arkie's mother and her stepfather, Michael, are both committed teachers and wise parents.

Parents, however, in French's books have shortcomings even when they are caring and understanding. Math's harassed mother is a shadow of Steven's mother in *Change the Locks.* Kath and Buckley, Trevor's parents in *Cannily, Cannily,* are concerned and loving but are itinerants whose casual life-style puts Trevor in jeopardy at a new school: his hair is all wrong, his patchwork shoulder bag brings ridicule. So he lies about his prowess as a footballer in a bid for acceptance. In *All We Know,* Arkie's friend Kylie is sad because her father only comes to take her out on weekends and her mother is constantly loading her with responsibility. Little Ian, in the same book, hangs around Arkie's house and often stays over because his mother is a drunk and his father is not around. Steven, in *Change the Locks,* takes responsibility for his irresponsible and disorganized mother who confesses that as a single teenage parent she was only "a kid with kids." But French does not cast stones. Like Arkie with her camera, he photographs life, but is selective enough to show its many facets. Math's life is influenced positively not only by Mr. Boon but by Steve Kerr, an artist who lives across the street. Trevor and his father, toward the end of *Cannily, Cannily* crack a wave together and an "inexplicable optimism" runs through the boy. Arkie, near the end of *All We Know* composes a letter to the dad whom she still misses and who is still very much a part of her inner life. Then at the close of the book she catches a glimpse of Ian, looking "forlorn and distant," part of a group of children in a state institution. For French, time is a continuum and life is made up of pluses and minuses. This is most apparent in *Change the Locks* which embodies his recurring theme of "breaking free" and moving on. Steven, at his most troubled, has a school friend whose family provide him sanctuary.

French's novels are socially relevant without being tracts. His plots, in the first three books, particularly, are contemplative but not static. Although written in the third person the reader is told in the first two what Math and Trevor are thinking. In *All We Know*, Arkie's introspective mental monologue is printed in italics. We are privy to her obsession with detail, her examination of the minutiae of life. *Change the Locks* is in the first person but there are sentences and snippets in italics which bring the past into the present—a kind of subconscious thought-stream. Steven's preoccupation is with unrecalled past events which constantly haunt him. His mother's fecklessness is a burden, a situation similar to French's short story "Peace and Quiet." In *Change the Locks* there is a mystery and a solution, therefore more action and suspense than in the earlier works. It is a more robust book, more obviously concerned with social issues and personal problems, but it is never polemic or didactic. Again, it is a sympathetic unravelling of the threads of the characters' lives. Steven finally discovers the full story of his mother's teenage pregnancy and their life together in squalid city squats, and this in turn becomes a catharsis for both mother and son. There has been a "connection," and life can move forward as it always does in a Simon French novel.

The tolerance that French extends to his characters is not an easy acknowledgement that life is often difficult. Rather it is an optimistic statement of belief in the complexities of relationships and a sympathetic understanding of the ongoing struggle that is life.

—Maurice Saxby

FRITZ, Jean

Pseudonyms: Ann Scott. **Nationality:** American. **Born:** Hankow, China, 16 November 1915; lived in China until 1928. **Education:** Wheaton College, Norton, Massachusetts, 1933-37, A.B. 1937; Columbia University Teachers College, New York, 1938-39. **Family:** Married Michael G. Fritz in 1941; one son and one daughter. **Career:** Author of historical biographies and novels for young people. Associate editor, Wheaton *News*, 1933-37; research assistant, Silver Burdett, publishers, New York, 1937-41; researcher, Boy Scouts of America, New York, 1941; reviewer, San Francisco *Chronicle,* and Tacoma *Ledger-News-Tribune,* Washington, and free-lance writer, Macmillan and Prang publishers, 1940s-early 1950s; children's librarian, Dobbs Ferry Library, New York, 1955-57; founder and teacher, Jean Fritz Writers' Workshops, Katonah, New York, 1962-70; teacher, Board of Cooperative Educational Service, Westchester County, New York, 1971-73; faculty member, Appalachian State University, Boone, North Carolina, summers 1981-83. Book reviewer, *San Francisco Chronicle,* 1941-43, and *New York Times,* since 1970, and *Washington Post*; lecturer. **Awards:** Named *New York Times* outstanding book of the year, 1973, for *And Then What Happened, Paul Revere?,* 1974, for *Why Don't You Get a Horse, Sam Adams?,* 1975, for *Where Was Patrick Henry on the 29th of May?,* 1976, for *What's the Big Idea, Ben Franklin?,* 1981, for *Traitor: The Case of Benedict Arnold,* and 1982, for *Homesick: My Own Story*; named *Boston Globe-Horn Book* honor book, 1974, for *And Then What Happened, Paul Revere?,* 1976, for *Will You Sign Here, John Hancock?,* and 1980, for *Stonewall*; named outstanding Pennsylvania author, Pennsylvania School Library Association, 1978; Honor award for Nonfiction, Children's Book Guild, 1979, for the "body of her creative writing"; American Book award nomination, 1980, for *Where Do You Think You're Going, Christopher Columbus?,* and 1981, for *Traitor: The Case of Benedict Arnold*; Child Study award and Christopher award, both 1982, Newbery Honor Book award, American Book award, and named *Boston Globe-Horn Book* honor book, all 1983, all for *Homesick: My Own Story*; *Boston Globe-Horn Book* Nonfiction award, 1984, and Knickerbocker award for Juvenile Literature, 1992, both for *The Double Life of Pocahontas*; Regina award, 1985; Laura Ingalls Wilder award, 1986; Orbis Pictus award, National Council of English Teachers, 1989, and Boston Globe/Horn Book award, 1990, both for *The Great Little Madison*; LL.D.: Washington and Jefferson College, 1982; Wheaton College, 1987; **Address:** 50 Bellewood Ave., Dobbs Ferry, New York 10522, U.S.A.

PUBLICATIONS FOR YOUNG ADULTS

Nonfiction

Stonewall, illustrated by Stephen Gammell. New York, Putnam, 1979.
Traitor: The Case of Benedict Arnold. New York, Putnam, 1981.
The Double Life of Pocahontas, illustrated by Ed Young. New York, Putnam, 1983.
Make Way for Sam Houston!, illustrated by Elise Primavera. New York, Putnam, 1986.
Homesick: My Own Story, illustrated by Margot Tomes. New York, Putnam, 1982.

PUBLICATIONS FOR CHILDREN

Fiction

Bunny Hopwell's First Spring, illustrated by Rachel Dixon. New York, Wonder Books, 1954.
Fish Head, illustrated by Marc Simont. New York, Coward McCann, 1954; London, Faber, 1956.
Help Mr. Willy Nilly, illustrated by Jean Tamburine. New York, Treasure Books, 1954.
Hurrah for Jonathan!, illustrated by Violet La Mont. Racine, Wisconsin, Whitman, 1955.
121 Pudding Street, illustrated by Sofia. New York, Coward McCann, 1955.
The Late Spring, illustrated by Erik Blegvad. New York, Coward McCann, 1957.
The Cabin Faced West, illustrated by Feodor Rojankovsky. New York, Coward, 1958.
Champion Dog, Prince Tom, with Tom Clute, illustrated by Ernest Hart. New York, Coward McCann, 1958.
How to Read a Rabbit, illustrated by Leonard Shortall. New York, Coward McCann, 1959.
Brady, illustrated by Lynd Ward. New York, Coward McCann, 1960; London, Gollancz, 1966.
December Is for Christmas (as Ann Scott), illustrated by Alcy Kendrick. New York, Wonder Books, 1961.
Tap, Tap, Lion—1, 2, 3, illustrated by Leonard Shortall, New York, Coward McCann, 1962.

I, Adam, illustrated by Peter Burchard. New York, Coward McCann, 1963; London, Gollancz, 1965.

Magic to Burn, illustrated by Beth and Joe Krush. New York, Coward McCann, 1964.

Early Thunder, illustrated by Lynd Ward. New York, Coward McCann, 1967; London, Gollancz, 1969.

George Washington's Breakfast, illustrated by Paul Galdone. New York, Coward McCann, 1969 and 1984; Boston, Houghton-Mifflin, 1989..

The Secret Diary of Jeb and Abigail: Growing Up in America, 1776-1783, illustrated by Kenneth Bald and Neil Boyle. Pleasantville, New York, Reader's Digest Association, 1976.

Other

Growing Up, illustrated by Elizabeth Webbe. Chicago, Rand McNally, 1956.

The Animals of Doctor Schweitzer, illustrated by Douglas Howland. New York, Coward McCann, 1958; Edinburgh, Oliver and Boyd, 1962.

San Francisco, illustrated by Emil Weiss. Chicago, Rand McNally, 1962.

Surprise Party (reader), illustrated by George Wiggins. New York, Initial Teaching Alphabet Publications, 1965.

The Train (reader), illustrated by Jean Simpson. New York, Grosset and Dunlap, 1965.

And Then What Happened, Paul Revere?, illustrated by Margot Tomes. New York, Coward McCann, 1973; New York, Paperstar, 1996.

Why Don't You Get a Horse, Sam Adams?, illustrated by Trina Schart Hyman. New York, Coward McCann, 1974.

Where Was Patrick Henry on the 29th of May?, illustrated by Margot Tomes. New York, Coward McCann, 1975.

Who's That Stepping on Plymouth Rock?, illustrated by J. B. Handelsman. New York, Coward McCann, 1975.

What's the Big Idea, Ben Franklin?, illustrated by Margot Tomes. New York, Coward McCann, 1976.

Will You Sign Here, John Hancock?, illustrated by Trina Schart Hyman. New York, Coward McCann, 1976.

Can't You Make Them Behave, King George?, illustrated by Tomie dePaola. New York, Coward McCann, 1977.

Brendan the Navigator: A History Mystery about the Discovery of America, illustrated by Enrico Arno. New York, Coward McCann, 1979.

Where Do You Think You're Going, Christopher Columbus?, illustrated by Margot Tomes. New York, Putnam, 1980.

Back to Early Cape Cod. Philadelphia, Eastern Acorn Press, 1981.

The Man Who Loved Books, illustrated by Trina Schart Hyman. New York, Putnam, 1981.

The Good Giants and the Bad Pukwudgies (folktale), illustrated by Tomie dePaola. New York, Putnam, 1982.

China Homecoming, photographs by Mike Fritz. New York, Putnam, 1985.

Shh! We're Writing the Constitution. illustrated by Tomie dePaola. New York, Putnam, 1987.

China's Long March: 6000 Miles of Danger, illustrated by Yang Zhr Cheng. New York, Putnam, 1988.

The Great Little Madison. New York, Putnam, 1989.

Bully for You, Teddy Roosevelt!. New York, Putnam, 1991.

George Washington's Mother, illustrated by DyAnne DiSalvo-Ryan. New York, Grosset & Dunlap, 1992.

The Great Adventures of Christopher Columbus; A Pop-up Book, illustrated by Tomie dePaola. New York, Putnam, 1992.

(contributor) *The World in 1492.* New York, Holt, 1992.

Around the World in a Hundred Years: Henry the Navigator—Magellan. New York, G.P. Putnam's Sons, 1993.

Harriet Beecher Stowe and the Beecher Preachers. New York, Putnam, 1994.

You Want Women to Vote, Lizzie Stanton?, illustrated by DyAnne DiSalvo. New York, Putnam, 1995.

PUBLICATIONS FOR ADULTS

Other

Cast for a Revolution: Some American Friends and Enemies, 1728-1814. Boston, Houghton Mifflin, 1972.

Contributor, *Worlds of Childhood: The Art and Craft of Writing for Children,* edited by William Zinsser. Boston, Houghton Mifflin, 1990.

*

Manuscript Collections: Kerlan Collection, University of Minnesota, Minneapolis; Children's Literature Collection at the University of Oregon Library, Eugene; University of Southern Mississippi.

Biography: Entry in *Dictionary of Literary Biography,* Vol. 52: *American Writers for Children since 1960: Fiction,* Detroit, Gale, 1986; essay in *Something About the Author Autobiography Series,* Vol. 2, Detroit, Gale, 1986.

Critical Studies: Entry in *Children's Literature Review,* Detroit, Gale, Vol. 2, 1976, Vol. 14, 1988.

*   *   *

Jean Fritz is a literary craftsman who writes exceptional biographies for young adults. Noted for her meticulous research, she brings the facts to life with an abundance of humor and conversational style. She gives a concise historical interpretation of the times while imparting a sensitive glimpse into the character. Her research in American history satisfies her own curiosity about her roots, for Fritz, the daughter of missionaries, was reared in China until she was thirteen. As she herself explains, "Most of my childhood was spent . . . as far away as I could get [from America]—in China. Indeed, I think it is because I was so far away that I developed a homesickness that made me want to embrace not just a given part of America at a given time but the whole of it. No one is more patriotic than the one separated from his country; no one is as eager to find roots as the person who has been uprooted."

Fritz's historically correct biographies show her as a master writer and a creative researcher going beyond the facts to explain the real person. Following her award-winning American Revolutionary War biography series for children, she wrote *Traitor: The Case of Benedict Arnold* (1981) for young adults. Fritz skillfully intertwines the historical events of the American Revolution with Arnold's character and personality. Her eloquent style and compelling recreation of Arnold's twisted character widen one's understanding of his treasonable behavior. This anti-hero is portrayed as an unloved individual who is vain, jealous, and greedy. His seditious betrayal, acted out of self-pity rather than any noble principle, eventually causes his rejection by the very people he sought to serve. Fritz's extensive Revolutionary War research evidences itself in the authenticity of this biography.

The Double Life of Pocahontas (1983) imaginatively explores an earlier period of American history. Fritz develops a concise historical interpretation of a sensitive heroine. Pocahontas, the favorite daughter of an Algonquian Indian chief, befriends the English colonists in Jamestown. When she subsequently saves Captain John Smith from death at the hands of her father, she is considered Smith's sponsor into her tribe. Relations between the colonists and the Indians later deteriorate to the point where the colonists resort to kidnapping Pocahontas. Feeling rejected by her people, she marries colonist John Rolfe and moves to England. Fritz's poignant story recreates the troubled life of a young woman trapped between her Indian heritage and a strange English lifestyle. The extensive research by Fritz into a shadowy part of American history accurately depicts the double life of a remarkable Indian princess.

Stonewall (1979) is the life of the Civil War hero Thomas (Stonewall) Jackson. Fritz scrutinizes Stonewall's complex personality from his impoverished childhood to his idolized leadership role in the Confederate army. This eccentric military genius is a curious mixture of toughness and humanity. Such a well-documented biography allows the reader to see Jackson's early years, particularly his inflexibility during his discouraging tenure as a teacher, with compassion. In the end Jackson's love for God and country, together with his toughness and determination, make him the hero he was always afraid to be. Fritz thoughtfully and skillfully reveals the intricate no nonsense life of Jackson in her no nonsense style.

Another eccentric hero is the subject of *Make Way for Sam Houston* (1986). Sam Houston is realistically depicted with his hot temper and drunkenness contrasted against his charming, flamboyant, and patriotic lifestyle. Fritz gives a very human study of a shrewd leader and politician who became a United States congressman, governor of Tennessee, commander-in-chief of the Texas army, and eventually governor of Texas. Fritz's dependable research gives Houston credit for his devotion to the cause of Indian rights and the founding and preservation of Texas. Ingeniously she acquaints the readers with a remarkable Texas hero they will respect.

In addition to the engrossing biographies that capture the spirit of their subjects, Fritz has contributed to *The World in 1492* and written a collective biography *Around the World in a Hundred Years* which examines the voyages of early explorers including Prince Henry the Navigator, Bartholemew Diaz, Christopher Columbus, Juan Ponce de Leon, and Ferdinand Magellan. Fritz portrays the events of these and other explorers in chronological order with a lively tone, humor, and description that flows like an adventure story. She includes an overview of the misleading view of the world in the fourteenth and fifteenth centuries, and the knowledge contributed by these explorers that was gained through "cruelty, arrogance, and greed" in their dealings with the natives they encountered.

Fritz's books have consistently garnered numerous awards, prizes, and honors for more than forty years for their substantial and lasting contribution to literature. In addition to her biographies for young adults, Fritz has written critically acclaimed fiction and nonfiction for younger children. She has devoted her literary career to "surprising children into learning," a task she has done very well indeed for children and young adults. Most important, however, is her success in encouraging young readers to share in her passion for historical fact.

—Linda Garrett, updated by Lisa A. Wroble

FURLONG, Monica (Mavis)

Nationality: English. **Born:** Harrow, Middlesex, England, 17 January 1930. Author; reporter for several London newspapers, 1956-68; producer, BBC, 1974-78; moderator of the Movement for the Ordination of Women, 1982 **Agent:** c/o Anthony Sheil Associates, 2/3 Morwell Street, London W.C.1, England.

PUBLICATIONS FOR YOUNG ADULTS

Fiction

The Cat's Eye. London, Weidenfield and Nicolson, 1976.
Cousins. London, Weidenfield and Nicolson, 1983.
Wise Child. London, Gollancz, and New York, Knopf, 1987.
Juniper. New York, Random House, 1991.
A Year and a Day. London, Gollancz, 1990.
Robin's Country. New York, Knopf, 1995
Bird of Paradise. London, Mowbray, 1995.
Flight of the Kingfisher. London, HarperCollins, 1996.

Poetry

God's a Good Man and Other Poems. London, Mowbray, 1974.

Nonfiction

Contributor, *Ourselves Your Servants: The Church's Ministry.* London, Advisory Council for the Church's Ministry, 1967.
Contemplating Now. London, Hodder and Stoughton, and Philadelphia, Pennsylvania, Westminster Press, 1971.
Travelling In. London, Hodder and Stoughton, 1971.
The End of Our Exploring. London, Hodder and Stoughton, 1973.
Puritan's Progress. A Study of John Bunyan. London, Hodder and Stoughton, and New York, Coward, 1975.
Burrswood, Focus of Healing. London, Hodder and Stoughton, 1978.
Editor, *The Trial of John Bunyan and the Persecution of the Puritans.* London, Folio Society, 1978.
Merton: A Biography. New York, Harper, 1980.
Christian Uncertainties. Cambridge, Massachusetts, Cowley, 1982.
Editor, *Feminine in the Church.* London, Society for Promoting Christian Knowledge, 1984.
Zen Effects: The Life of Alan Watts. Boston, Houghton Mifflin, 1986.
Therese of Lisieux. London, Virago, and New York, Pantheon, 1987.
Dangerous Delight: Women and Power in the Church. London, Society for Promoting Christian Knowledge, 1991.

301

Editor, *Visions and Longings: Medieval Women Mystics*. Boston, Shambhala; New York, Random House, 1996.
Author of introduction, *The Pilgrim's Progress* by John Bunyan. Rockport, Massachusetts, Element, 1996.
Compiler and author of introduction, *The Wisdom of Julian of Norwich*. Grand Rapids, Michigan, W.B. Eerdmans, 1996.

*   *   *

Well-known as a broadcaster and writer for adults, Monica Furlong has produced one of the most complete historical/fantasy novels for young adults. *Wise Child* is set on the Isle of Mull in the seventh century, although its setting and period often appear to be timeless. Told through the voice of the wise child, the story describes the adoption and training of this young girl by Juniper, a white witch and pagan. The child's father is away on a long voyage when her mother uses her and scars her mentally before running away and deserting her. In the first of several of the book's set pieces, the child is auctioned off. Juniper, recognizing the wise child (whose name refers to her being "old beyond her years") as a healer in the making, casts the highest bid and takes her to her white house. There, life is often hard and the two work physically on the land. The child is torn between this torturing life and the glamorous world of her mother, who comes to reclaim her. However, after a trial for witchcraft following a severe winter for which Juniper is blamed by the villagers, the wise child discovers where her true loyalties lie.

Wise Child is a remarkable book in many ways, subtly drawn and told with a quiet urgency. While set firmly in the past, it manages to draw upon emotions with which many young adults can identify. The dismay felt by the wise child at her many problems is touchingly real, while the conflict produced due to her loyalty both to Juniper and her feckless mother is bound to provoke empathy.

Another of Furlong's books for young adults, *A Year and a Day*, continues the events in *Wise Child* and tells of the early life of Juniper. Known as Ninnoc to her family, she is the daughter of King Mark and niece of Mark's evil sister who is training her supposed son Gamal to take over the kingdom. Ninnoc is persuaded to live for a year and a day with her mysterious, shabby undemonstrative godmother, Euny, who oversees her initiation as a doran—a wise woman. Ninnoc rebels against her firm treatment at the hands of her godmother and the poverty-stricken life she is forced to lead and is seduced into the glamorous life of her aunt. However, Ninnoc's aunt's motives become all too obvious, resulting in a power struggle between the forces of good and evil.

A Year and a Day, while lacking the outstanding qualities of *Wise Child*, is a skillful piece of work. Hopefully Furlong will continue to write about these strong women and continue the sequence of novels set in this period.

—Keith Barker

G

GAINES, Ernest J(ames)

Nationality: American. **Born:** Oscar, Louisiana (some sources cite River Lake Plantation, near New Roads, Pointe Coupee Parish, Louisiana), 15 January 1933. **Education:** Vallejo Junior College, California; San Francisco State College (now University), California, B.A. 1957; graduate study at Stanford University, California, 1958-59. **Military Service:** Served in U.S. Army, 1953-55. **Career:** Writer. Writer in residence, 1971, Denison University Granville, Ohio; writer in residence, 1981, Stanford University; visiting professor, 1983, writer in residence, 1986, Whittier College, California; professor of English and writer in residence, since 1983, University of Southwestern Louisiana. **Awards:** Wallace Stegner Fellow, 1957, Stanford University; Joseph Henry Jackson Award, 1959, for ''Comeback'' (short story), from San Francisco Foundation; award from National Endowment for the Arts, 1967; Rockefeller grant, 1970; Guggenheim fellowship, 1971; award from Black Academy of Arts and Letters, 1972; fiction gold medal, 1972, for *The Autobiography of Miss Jane Pittman,* and 1984, for *A Gathering of Old Men,* from Commonwealth Club of California; award from Louisiana Library Association, 1972; award for excellence of achievement in literature from San Francisco Arts Commission, 1983; literary award from American Academy and Institute of Arts and Letters, 1987. D.H.L.: Denison University, 1980, Brown University, 1985, Bard College, 1985, Whittier College, 1986, and Louisiana State University, 1987. **Address:** 15155 Garcal Dr., San Jose, California 95127-2612, U.S.A.

PUBLICATIONS FOR ADULTS and Young Adults

Fiction

Catherine Carmier. New York, Atheneum, 1964.
Of Love and Dust. New York, Dial, 1967; New York, Vintage Books, 1994.
Bloodline (short stories). New York, Dial, 1968.
The Autobiography of Miss Jane Pittman. New York, Dial, 1971.
In My Father's House. New York, Knopf, 1978.
A Gathering of Old Men. New York, Knopf, 1983.
A Lesson before Dying. New York, Knopf, 1993.

PUBLICATIONS FOR CHILDREN

Fiction

A Long Day in November (story originally published in author's collection *Bloodline*; illustrated by Don Bolognese). New York, Dial, 1971.

*

Media Adaptations: *The Autobiography of Miss Jane Pittman* (film), Columbia Broadcasting System (CBS-TV), 1974; *The Sky Is Gray* (film for public television), 1980; *A Gathering of Old Men* (film), CBS-TV, 1987.

Biography: *Dictionary of Literary Biography,* Detroit, Gale, Volume 2: *American Novelists since World War II,* 1978, Volume 33: *Afro-American Fiction Writers after 1955,* 1984; *Dictionary of Literary Biography Yearbook: 1980,* Detroit, Gale, 1981; *Concise Dictionary of American Literary Biography: Broadening Views, 1968-1988,* Detroit, Gale, 1989; *Porch Talk with Ernest Gaines: Conversations on the Writer's Craft,* edited by Marcia Gaudet and Carl Wooton, Baton Rouge, Louisiana State University Press, 1990.

Bibliography: *Contemporary Literary Criticism,* Detroit, Gale, Volume 3, 1975, Volume 11, 1979, Volume 18, 1981, Volume 86, 1996.

Manuscript Collections: Dupree Library, University of Southwestern Louisiana, Lafayette.

Critical Studies: *Interviews with Black Writers,* edited by John O'Brien, Liveright, 1973; *The Way of the New World: The Black Novel in America* by Addison Gayle, Jr., Doubleday, 1975; *The Black American Short Story in the Twentieth Century: A Collection of Critical Essays,* edited by Peter Bruck, B.R. Gruner (Amsterdam), 1977; *In the Singer's Temple: Prose Fictions of Barthelme, Gaines, Brautigan, Piercy, Kesey, and Kosinski* by Jack Hicks, University of North Carolina Press, 1981; *Conversations with Ernest Gaines,* edited by John Lowe, Jackson, University Press of Mississippi, 1995.

*   *   *

Just as Isaac Bashevis Singer wrote about a European Jewish culture that had been destroyed before he began writing, so too has Ernest Gaines written about a culture that almost has been destroyed by economic and social changes in Louisiana. While *The Autobiography of Miss Jane Pittman* moves from the antebellum South to the beginning of the civil rights movement of the 1950s and 1960s, Gaines's other five novels and short stories (*A Long Day in November* is short enough to appear in the short story collection *Bloodline*) are mostly set between 1930 to 1970 on plantations with black and Cajun sharecroppers or in towns near such plantations. While whites are on top in this world, whites, Cajuns, and blacks are torn apart living under racist ''rules.'' Many of the whites and Cajuns on which Gaines focuses benefit from these rules, but love, usually of a black man or woman, makes these rules problematic even to them. For the black people in Gaines's works, a constant struggle exists between the demands of survival and the desire for dignity and self-respect.

Catherine Carmier explores the biases in the black community itself once white blood has been introduced into black families. Jackson, who is black, returns to his aunt who lives on a plantation. While trained to be a teacher or political leader, Jackson resists those roles that no longer seem appropriate to his identity, only to fall in love with Catherine Carmier, a Creole, whose father thinks his family a cut above blacks in the former slave quarters. As in so many of Gaines's novels, the dilemmas of the characters crystallize into a scene: in this case, it is a fight between Catherine's father and Jackson over Catherine's love and identity as a black person.

Set earlier than *Catherine Carmier, Of Love and Dust* occurs in 1948. The code of behavior for blacks is solidly in place, but interracial love upsets the fragile order. Bonbon, a Cajun overseer, uses the code in trying to break the spirit of Marcus, a young black man bonded to the plantation following his killing of another black man. Marcus to get even with Bonbon, tries to take Bonbon's black mistress away from him, but failing at that seduces Bonbon's white wife. The exploitation of both Bonbon and Marcus gives way to love, as Bonbon grows to love his black mistress and Marcus grows to love Bonbon's wife. While Bonbon kills Marcus, he does so more from the pressure of his Cajun background than from a desire for revenge. Though the black narrator, Jim, rejects Bonbon, Bonbon is a changed man who must leave the South—with his mistress and not his wife. Marcus grows from fool to hero in the eyes of the black people on the plantation, as they sense his quest for respect.

The Autobiography of Miss Jane Pittman, like Ellison's *Invisible Man,* is a fictive portrait of black people in America from the Civil War to the time of Martin Luther King, Jr. Gaines's ploy of having the work supposedly composed of tapes by a historian recording the words of Miss Jane Pittman, who is 108 or 109, as she and her friends look back at their lives allows this imaginative history to be created. Unlike Ellison's novel, in which the protagonist-narrator travels to college and then to New York, Miss Jane never leaves Louisiana. History is not simply given through Jane's life but through those who are important to her such as Ned whose maturity covers the turn of the century and Jimmy, who is a follower of King. The interracial love of earlier novels is present in a white and Creole liaison that ends in suicide as the "code" claims another victim.

In My Father's House, a novel set in 1970, also ends with a suicide, when the illegitimate son of a minister active in the civil rights movement takes his life. Before the minister, Phillip Martin, had become a responsible man following his conversion fifteen years earlier, he had left a woman he loved and his three children by her. Forced by a white power broker sheriff to trade a civil rights goal of equal pay for equal work for his incarcerated illegitimate son, Phillip chooses his son's freedom, but he loses everything he has worked for except his second legitimate family. The attempt by Phillip to achieve a unified character for the whole of his fragmented life is brave, however, and mirrors the growing pains of thousands of black Americans.

A Gathering of Old Men, like *The Autobiography of Miss Jane Pittman,* was made into a film. Just as the earlier novel had a great historical sweep because of Jane's age, so too is there a historical sweep to the later novel for a similar reason—the age of the nearly twenty old men who are in their seventies and eighties. They gather to provide protection to a revered friend by each claiming to have murdered the same Cajun. Mathu, their friend, is in turn shielding another man, only to find that unnecessary when Big Charlie admits to the murder and claims their respect. The character of the law and society are changing in this novel, as blacks, whites, and Cajuns cheer black and white running-backs for Louisiana State University's football team. As old black men, used to being

humiliated, rise to claim their manhood, the code begins to be buried.

As in *Of Love and Dust* and *A Gathering of Old Men, A Lesson before Dying,* Gaines's latest novel, shows a black man achieving dignity and pride. Jefferson, a young black man reluctantly involved in the killing of a white man, is going to the electric chair. Tormenting him are the words of his defense attorney who calls Jefferson a hog. Grant Wiggins, a plantation school teacher who is college educated, is compelled by his own and Jefferson's relatives to educate Jefferson to self-respect before he dies. As the novel closes black and white witness Jefferson's transformation.

Gaines's novels and stories are dramatically powerful. Values always collide in powerful scenes featuring excellent dialogue. Gaines, distrustful of the symbol and the romance, writes gripping realistic narratives. Seldom in Gaines is there omniscience; his mostly first-person narrators establish authenticity through our reading of their tone of voice. While Gaines is not enamored of film or television, one can readily understand why his novels and stories attract producers, directors, and actors.

—Craig W. Barrow

GARD, Janice. *See* LATHAM, Jean Lee.

GARDAM, Jane

Nationality: British. **Born:** Jane Pearson in Coatham, Yorkshire, 11 July 1928. **Education:** Saltburn High School for Girls; Bedford College, London, 1946-49, B.A. (honours) 1949, graduate study, 1949-52. **Family:** Married David Gardam in 1952; two sons and one daughter. **Career:** Red Cross librarian, 1951; sub-editor, *Weldons Ladies Journal,* London, 1952-53; assistant literary editor, *Time and Tide,* London, 1952-54. **Awards:** *A Long Way from Verona* received special mention from the Guardian award for children's fiction, and was selected an honor book by *Book World's* Spring Book Festival award, both 1972, and won the Phoenix award, 1991; *Boston Globe-Horn Book* honor book for text, 1974, for *The Summer after the Funeral;* David Higham Prize for fiction and Winifred Holtby Memorial prize for fiction, both 1977, both for *Black Faces, White Faces;* runner-up citation, Booker Prize, 1978, for *God on the Rocks;* Whitbread Literary award, 1981, for *The Hollow Land;* Carnegie Medal "highly recommended" award, for *The Hollow Land* and "commended" award, for *Bridget and William,* both 1983; Katherine Mansfield award, 1984, for *The Pangs of Love;* Whitbread Novel of the Year award, for *The Queen of the Tambourine,* 1991. Fellow, Royal Society of Literature, 1976. **Agent:** Bruce Hunter, David Higham Associates, 5-8 Lower John Street, London, W1R 4HA. **Address:** Haven House, Sandwich, Kent, England.

PUBLICATIONS FOR YOUNG ADULTS

Fiction

A Few Fair Days, illustrated by Peggy Fortnum. London, Hamish
Hamilton, 1971; New York, Macmillan, 1972.
A Long Way from Verona. London, Hamish Hamilton, and New
York, Macmillan, 1971.
The Summer after the Funeral. London, Hamish Hamilton, and
New York, Macmillan, 1973.
Bilgewater. London, Hamish Hamilton, 1976; New York,
Greenwillow, 1977.
The Hollow Land, illustrated by Janet Rawlins. London, MacRae,
1981; New York, Greenwillow, 1982.
Through the Dolls' House Door. London, MacRae, and New York,
Greenwillow, 1987.
Going into a Dark House. London, Sinclair-Stevenson, 1994.
Faith Fox: A Nativity. London, Sinclair-Stevenson, 1996.

PUBLICATIONS FOR CHILDREN

Fiction

Bridget and William, illustrated by Janet Rawlins. London, MacRae,
1981; as *Bridget and William: Black Woolly Pony, White Chalk
Horse.* London, Walker, 1993.
Horse, illustrated by Janet Rawlins. London, MacRae 1982.
Kit, illustrated by William Geldart. London, MacRae, 1983.
Kit in Boots, illustrated by William Geldart. London, MacRae, 1986.
Swan, illustrated by John Dillow. London, MacRae, 1987.

PUBLICATIONS FOR ADULTS

Novels

Black Faces, White Faces. London, Hamish Hamilton, 1975; as
The Pineapple Bay Hotel, New York, Morrow, 1976.
God on the Rocks. London, Hamish Hamilton, 1978; New York,
Morrow, 1979.
Crusoe's Daughter. London, Hamish Hamilton, 1985; New York,
Atheneum, 1986.

Short Stories

The Sidmouth Letters. London, Hamish Hamilton, and New York,
Morrow, 1980.
The Pangs of Love and Other Stories. London, Hamish Hamil-
ton, 1983.
Showing the Flag. London, Hamish Hamilton, 1989.
The Queen of the Tambourine. London, Sinclair-Stevenson, 1991.

Other

The Iron Coast: Notes from a Cold Country, photographs by Peter
Burton and Harland Walshaw. London, Sinclair-Stevenson, 1994.

*

Media Adaptations: Film, *God on the Rocks,* ITV, 1992.

Biography: Entry in *Dictionary of Literary Biography,* Volume
14, Detroit, Gale, 1983; essay in *Something about the Author
Autobiography Series,* Volume 9, Detroit, Gale, 1990.

Critical Studies: Entry in *Children's Literature Review,* Volume
12, Detroit, Gale, 1987; entry in *Contemporary Literary Criticism,*
Volume 43, Detroit, Gale, 1987.

*   *   *

Jane Gardam's work as a whole is distinguished by a clearly
delineated, often satiric representation of historical and cultural
moments of English life and British educational, religious, and
class institutions. Many of her characters are drawn from the milieu
of Anglican church and school communities. The favoured chronology for her stories is the period during and immediately
surrounding the Second World War. Gardam's concentration on a
particular class, political, and professional group and its values
accounts for the somewhat nostalgic feeling about much of her
work. She offers us a perspective on changes in English culture,
moments in time now lost. A sense of history, and of history within
the lives of particular persons and groups, structures the progression of the narrative in works such as *The Hollow Land, Through
the Dolls' House Door,* and *Crusoe's Daughter.*

A sense of place and period is also an important feature of
Gardam's fiction. The landscape and customs of the north of
England of her childhood form a backdrop to many stories. In
addition, as the publisher's dustjackets of her books remind us,
Gardam is a much-travelled writer. The depiction of the "English[wo]man abroad" is a facet of her adult fiction—influenced,
no doubt, by the writings of Somerset Maugham, whose work she
has admired.

One of the conventions of this tradition is the depiction of the
eccentric or "larger than life" individual, and this is a trademark of
Gardam's fiction. The dramatic representation of this category of
character (usually female) often borders on the grotesque or the
black comic.

Many of these eccentrics are genteel paupers of the superannuated
middle classes, living as seedy, anachronistic reminders of a
bygone age of privilege. Gardam reserves her harshest satire for the
status-conscious backbiting and parsimony of the upper-middle
classes, the last vestiges of a society upon the margins of which her
young heroines and their families live.

Jane Gardam is not only a very English writer, she is also a very
self-consciously literary one. Her works make constant allusion to
classical myth and literature, English literature, and to art: Shakespeare, Brontë, Hardy, Joyce, Gauguin, Botticelli—all these make
themselves felt as influences in her texts. Often her protagonists
identify with these intertextual literary models to structure their
quest for self-definition. Athene Price, in *The Summer after the
Funeral,* feels herself to be a tragic alter ego of Emily Brontë, while
Folly Flint imaginatively defines herself as "Crusoe's Daughter."
Allusive games, or games invoking the literary system, also
abound. Proper names frequently have mythological or symbolic
significance. The title story of *The Sidmouth Letters,* in which a
collection of Jane Austen's letters to a lover are discovered, utilizes
the mode of the fictional (literary) historical to satirize academic
pretensions and obsessions.

Gardam is a writer for whom genre is flexible. Some of her works, such as *The Hollow Land; Black Faces, White Faces;* and *A Few Fair Days,* can be seen either as short stories or as episodic novels. Gardam favours the use of vignettes to capture moments in place and time, to covey the flavour of experience, placing them in an episodic narrative structure rather than relying on the primacy of complex traditional plotting. Her strength lies in the sense of balance between the comic impetus and the incisive scrutiny she brings to bear on matters of social hierarchy and the anxieties of the socio-sexual maturation process.

Gardam's status as a writer for young adults rests on three major texts, *A Long Way from Verona, The Summer after the Funeral,* and *Bilgewater,* to which can be linked her adult novel, *Crusoe's Daughter,* which shares the focus on the representation of adolescence and developing sexuality. She favours the first-person narrative in her dramatizations of the anxieties of the young female protagonist: a misfit saddled with a chaotic and eccentric family, anxiously aware of her existence on the margins of acceptable affluence and social respectability. The narratives enact the heroine's painful progress towards autonomy and identity against the odds of repressive religious or educational structures, and awkward social and economic horizons, which are often related to the equivocal status of her father.

The writer's novels have been described as "plotless," but they are not without a narrative trajectory, one which can be seen in the deliberate interruption or transgression of the romantic quest pattern. The protagonist's increasing disaffection with her father/family, leading to a literal or symbolic flight/separation, is linked to the increasing pressures of her own sexuality. Her search for autonomy is linked in her imagination to a romantic icon, a young male figure, often explicitly associated with a literary precursor in the romance mode. The novels exploit both romantic and antiromantic tendencies. However, the romance pattern is never successfully completed. The young male idol is discovered to have feet of clay: thus the heroine's existential quest is rerouted from its traditional trajectory towards a less ideal, though nevertheless autonomous conclusion.

The title of *A Long Way from Verona* announces the distance this text will place between itself and the conventions of Shakespearean love tragedy, while other references also signal the importance of *Romeo and Juliet* as a major intertext against which the failure of the ideal of romance in wartime in the north of England is to be read. At the same time, the dangers of impending sexual maturity for the young heroine, Jessica Vye, are suggested by Mrs. Looney Hopkins's description of her as "a little Juliet"—"younger than she are married mothers made." The world of Cleveland/Durham and the Tees District is, however, a long way from Juliet's Verona. It is a world where ideals are proved unreliable, where adolescent longing for the perfect beloved is revealed as wish-fulfillment fantasy, and where the dark side of sexuality, frightening but attractive, is revealed by the furtive admiration of the Italian POW Jessica meets in the Valley Gardens.

The novel is set in the district and period of Gardam's own adolescence, thinly disguised. The Vye family are forced to cope with the radical father's abrupt vocational change from a well-to-do schoolmaster's position to the lower hierarchy of the Anglican pastoral economy. Jessica's mother had functioned well enough as a comfortable professional's mate, with domestic help, but is completely ineffectual when confronted by the considerable domestic and parish duties of a poor curate's wife.

Though denigrated by her English mistress, Miss Dobbs, Jessica has literary ambitions and has been told by Arnold Hanger, a writer visiting her school, that she is "a writer beyond all possible doubt." The heroine is aware of the appeal of great art, and of herself as an artist. While her later discovery of Hanger's status as a third-rate practitioner deflates her pride and her romantic idea of attachment to art, her subsequent success in the poetry competition, judged by the highly reputable Walter de la Mare, affirms the validity of the claims of her story to be read as a portrait of the artist as a young woman.

Socially Jessica is seen as a misfit and a rebel at her school. She is an inappropriate Juliet with a fetish for Rupert Brooke, whose works are given to her by the (possibly lesbian) Miss Philemon, who is something of a mentor and a muse. Another of Gardam's eccentric marginalized spinster ladies, Miss Philemon not only gives Jessica a copy of *Romeo and Juliet,* she also shocks and titillates her with the implications of innocent sexual enjoyment and aesthetic pleasure suggested by the copy of Gauguin's painting of two naked Tahitians which hangs in her home.

The "Romeo" figure appears in the person of Christian Fanshawe, son of her father's old college friend. Jessica's first sight of the male Adonis strikes her like an epiphany: a revelation of the romantic ideal embodied, which has previously been represented in her imagination by the figure of Rupert Brooke. In Gardam's fiction, the presence of such perfect male beauty usually signals the circumvention of romantic aspirations. Like that of Jack Rose in *Bilgewater* and the "Heathcliff of the Summerhouse" in *The Summer after the Funeral,* Christian's promise of fulfillment is illusory. The reform-minded Christian is interested in Jessica only because of her father's reputation as a Fabian commentator. His idea of a date is a visit to the slums, while the clammy misadventure of the hand-holding episode, signals the antiromantic embarrassments of adolescent sexual forays. When Christian deserts Jessica during the bomb attack, leaving her to fend for herself and to make her own way home, the unreliability of the male hero figure and of patriarchal protection as a valid option is brought home remorselessly to the young female. Romantic idealization is forced to give way to self-sufficiency and painful autonomy.

For the beautiful Athene Price, the main protagonist of *The Summer after the Funeral,* the search for autonomy is impelled by sexual maturation and the necessity for escape from the post mortem influence of her father, an Anglican patriarch who "positively ate her up," attempting to possess her both intellectually and emotionally. Her quest for identity during the summer following his death takes the form of a journey in which she must negotiate a path between two stultifying possibilities. She must avoid the fate of the bitter and frustrated spinsters—Posie Dixon, Sybil Bowles, and Primrose Clark—while at the same time escaping seduction by older men who resemble her father in their desire to possess her: Basil, the fiftyish painter, and Henry Bell, the classicist schoolmaster.

Athene also represents her identity in terms of literary models. She identifies with Emily Brontë, resonating to the possibilities of tragic romantic passion and recoiling from the spectre of sterility represented by the life at the Haworth Parsonage under the structures of religious and patriarchal control, escape from which seems to be promised only by sexual initiation. Metaphors of natural fecundity are utilized to signal Athene's ripening into sexual anticipation: flowers (red hot pokers), the luxuriance of summer growth, fruit (the blood-red berries in Basil's pantry, which represent Athene's recoil from the grotesque suggestion of her own defloration). Her fear of the possibility of having been possessed by Basil while sleeping and her attraction to Henry Bell are staging posts in a quest whose perceived goal is the grand romantic potential signified by ''the Heathcliff of the Summer-house,'' the dark ''gypsy'' lover of her imagination, who turns out to be, in actuality, the more prosaic Lucian, a Jewish school friend of her brother, Sebastian.

Bilgewater demonstrates its author's affection for the writing of James Joyce: its title announces to be as a *jeu d'esprit,* a parcel of nonsense. The playful human tendency towards corruption of language leads to the humiliating renaming of its heroine. Marigold Green, an unlikely flower, becomes ''Bilgewater'' (a corruption of ''Bill's daughter''), a label which signals her frumpish lack of allure to the boys at the school at which her father teaches, and at which she is the only adolescent female interloper.

The first epigraph to the book—''Youth is a blunder''—points to the wryly, self-deprecating narrative stance, as the eighteen-year-old Marigold, now safely established in the intellectual haven of Cambridge with a reliable, if unexotic, partner, looks back to the mistakes and wrong-turnings of her earlier youth.

Bilgewater follows the ''mythic'' narrative model of *Ulysses,* structuring the quest upon the search of the child for its ''true'' parent. In Gardam's novel, the quest is not for the father, as it is in Joyce's work and in the classical Greek model of the Telemachus myth, but for the child's true mother. Marigold's father is a rather absent-minded scholar who has little regard for his daughter's existence, her needs as a female, and for her emerging sexuality. She seeks a sense of belonging and feminine identity through pursuit of the mystery surrounding the nature of her dead mother, Daisy. The name, Daisy Green, is the source of her daughter's romantic illusion about her mother's pastoral innocence and perfection. Flowers traditionally represent youth, purity, and beauty: a beauty without stain which is rendered sentimentally more desirable because of its inevitable transience. The sordid worldliness of the Rose family cast a sensual slur over the notion of the pure and perfect mother, and Bilgewater finds her true female parent in the practical school matron, Paula Rigg—with her reliable if rather unsentimental care for Bilgewater and her father—just as she will find her future partner in the reliable but unremarkable Boakes. Her developing sexuality leads her to veer between a schoolgirl idolization of Jack Rose, the most beautiful and popular boy in the school, and the ambiguously attractive Terrapin, a trickster figure who is more nearly her intellectual soul mate, but who offers a dangerous sexual intensity and an intermittent commitment. The whimsical, somewhat contrived ending of the narrative allows the heroine to find a ''middle way'' between these extremes. Her eventual husband is somewhat of a surprising choice, but less of a grotesque misalliance than those made by the other potential mates.

Crusoe's Daughter is another example of Gardam's literary self-reflexiveness. It deals with the nature of feminine isolation and with the nature of fictional narrative. Its feminist agenda is seen in its focus on the motif of the woman/everywoman, alone on an existential island which is at once austere and in touch with the landscape of abandonment. Polly Flint is stranded and imprisoned at six years of age, when she comes to live with her two maiden aunts in the yellow house, on the edge of a salt marsh somewhere on the Northumbrian coast. The story follows the changes in culture, landscape, industrial growth, times and manners, until Polly's death in 1985. Though she sees herself as ''Crusoe's daughter,'' resolved to get on with the business of living in an unpromising environment for human fulfillment, she nevertheless dreams of rescue. The relationship with the dashing (Jewish) young man who engages her imagination as potential hero and rescuer never comes to fruition. He is finally returned to her an old and broken man, a victim of Hitler's concentration camps. Once more Gardam circumvents the romantic quest pattern, while dramatizing the pains and potential of adult female autonomy.

In addition to her works for young adults, Gardam has written fiction for younger readers and for adults.

—Leonie Margaret Rutherford

GARDEN, Nancy

Nationality: American. **Born:** Boston, Massachusetts, 15 May 1938. **Education:** Columbia University, New York, B.F.A. 1961, M.A. 1962. **Career:** Contributing editor, *Junior Scholastic,* New York, 1969-70; *American Observer,* Washington, D.C., 1970-72; associate editor, Houghton Mifflin Co., New York, 1972, assistant editor, 1973, editor, 1974-76; teacher and free-lance writer, 1976—. Has also worked in the theatre as an actress and lighting designer, taught at various levels, and done free-lance editorial work for various publishers. Lecturer at schools and libraries to children on writing. **Awards:** *Annie on My Mind* was selected to the 1982 *Booklist* Reviewer's Choice, the 1982 ALA Best Books, and the 1970-83 ALA Best of the Best lists; *Fours Crossing* was selected to the 1983-84 William Allen White award Master List. **Address:** c/o McIntosh & Otis, Inc., 310 Madison Ave., New York, New York 10017, U.S.A.

PUBLICATIONS FOR YOUNG ADULTS

Fiction

Berlin: City Split in Two. New York, Putnam, 1971.
What Happened in Marston, illustrated by Richard Cuffari. New York, Four Winds, 1971.
The Loners. New York, Viking, 1972.
Vampires. Philadelphia, Pennsylvania, Lippincott, 1973.
Werewolves. Philadelphia, Pennsylvania, Lippincott, 1973.
Witches. Philadelphia, Pennsylvania, Lippincott, 1975.
Devils and Demons. Philadelphia, Pennsylvania, Lippincott, 1976.
Fun with Forecasting Weather. Boston, Massachusetts, Houghton Mifflin, 1977.
Fours Crossing. New York, Farrar Straus, 1981.
The Kids' Code and Cipher Book. Hamden, Connecticut, Linnet, 1981.
Maria's Mountain. Boston, Massachusetts, Houghton Mifflin, 1981.
Annie on My Mind. New York, Farrar Straus, 1982.
Adaptor, *Favorite Tales from Grimm,* illustrated by Mercer Mayer. New York, Four Winds, 1982.
Watersmeet. New York, Farrar Straus, 1983.
Prisoner of Vampires, illustrated by Michele Chessare. New York, Farrar Straus, 1984.
Peace, O River. New York, Farrar Straus, 1986.
The Door Between. New York, Farrar Straus, 1987.
Mystery of the Night Raiders. New York, Farrar Straus, 1987.
Mystery of the Midnight Menace. Farrar Straus, 1988.
Mystery of the Secret Marks. New York, Farrar Straus, 1989.

Lark in the Morning. New York, Farrar Straus, 1991.
My Sister, the Vampire. New York, Knopf, 1992.
Mystery of the Kidnapped Kidnapper. New York, Pocket Books, 1994.
Dove and Sword: A Novel of Joan of Arc. New York, Farrar, Straus, and Giroux, 1995.
My Brother, the Werewolf. New York, Bullseye Books, 1995.
Good Moon Rising. New York, Farrar Straus Giroux, 1996.

*

Biography: Essay in *Speaking for Ourselves, Too* compiled and edited by Donald R. Gallo, National Council of Teachers of English, 1993.

*   *   *

Much of the body of Nancy Garden's work demonstrates a tendency towards the intriguing and the fantastic. Her books for younger readers well illustrates this as they delve, within the genre of both fiction and nonfiction, into the supernatural and unexplained. Her nonfiction ties itself closely with her fiction as occult characters are featured in both. Garden's fantasy literature for young adults also explores the mystical realm. Her realistic fiction for older readers bravely departs from this trend to confront current issues with tact and sensitivity.

The "Fours Crossing" books create fantasy rooted in the city of Fours Crossing, a town steeped in history and mysticism. The series follows the adventures of Melissa and her friend Jed as they work against the evil will of a powerful hermit to maintain the balance of nature. A taste of one of Garden's works for younger readers, *The Kids' Code and Cipher Book,* pervades the series as mystical signs and symbols require decoding in order to overcome the evil. These well-constructed ciphers challenge the reader to participate in the adventure, creating an interactive reading experience. Though primarily plot-driven, intriguing fantasy elements make these books satisfying.

The internal struggles of Kate in *Peace, O River* make her one of Garden's most engaging young adult characters. Kate returns to her childhood home after a four-year absence to discover a feud raging between the two towns bordering the river. The feud manifests itself in Kate's high school as explosive gang violence. Kate struggles to unite the two towns in the face of a proposed local nuclear waste disposal site and in so doing learns about the nature of conflict and the price of peace. The cross-river relationships prove intriguing as does the character development of the protagonist. Occasionally approaching maudlin, the overall sentiment of the tale manages to convince and prove poignant.

Annie on My Mind depicts with clarity and sensitivity the first homosexual relationship of two young women. Garden takes no aspect of the relationship for granted—the reader participates in the wonder, the bliss, and the fear of the two characters coming to terms with their sexuality. This careful plotting combined with strong characterization allows for the development of a realistic dynamic between the couple, rendering the romance highly convincing. The romance turns bittersweet, though, when the couple must face the fear and hatred of a disapproving community.

Garden's depiction of a homophobic society tends toward caricature as the antagonists are all extreme. A spectrum of opposition may have added balance to the conflict that reads as too black and white. The book remains highly valuable in its successful portrayal of teen romance.

Lark in the Morning presents a fresh presence in young adult fiction in its inclusion of a homosexual character whose struggle with sexuality is not central to the narrative. Seventeen-year-old Gillian reflects on the realization of her sexuality that took place the summer before, but focuses her attention on the two runaways she discovers hiding near her family's summer home. In an effort to respect the young siblings' fear of returning to their abusive parents, Gillian decides to help them on her own; it is a task that proves more than she bargained for. Garden deals with sexuality with tact, as Gillian's homosexuality is never treated as a random aspect of her character. Instead, her identity as a lesbian becomes relevant in a way that balances well with the plot's central issues.

Garden's success in the creation of dynamic and engaging works in the genres of both fantasy and realistic fiction demonstrates a breadth of ability. The topics explored in her writing show her making an important contribution to young adult libraries.

—Susan Rich

GARFIELD, Leon

Nationality: British. **Born:** Brighton, Sussex, 14 July 1921. **Education:** Brighton Grammar School in England. **Military Service:** Served in the Royal Army Medical Corps, 1940-46: private; served in Belgium and Germany. **Family:** Married Vivien Dolores Alcock in 1948; one daughter. Biochemical technician, Whittington Hospital, London, 1946-66; part-time biochemical technician in a hospital in London, 1966; since 1966 novelist. **Awards:** Gold Medal, Boys' Clubs of America, 1966, for *Jack Holborn;* first *Guardian* award for children's fiction, 1967, for *Devil-in-the-Fog;* Arts Council of Great Britain award for the best book for older children, and American Library Association (ALA) Notable Book citation, both 1967, *Boston Globe-Horn Book* honor book citation, 1968, and Phoenix award, 1987, all for *Smith;* Carnegie Medal runner-up, 1967, for *Smith,* 1968, for *Black Jack,* and 1970, for *The Drummer Boy;* *New York Times* Best Illustrated Book citation, 1968, for *Mister Corbett's Ghost;* Carnegie Medal for the most outstanding book of the year, and Kate Greenaway Medal commendation, both 1970, both for *The God beneath the Sea;* Kate Greenaway Medal commendation, and ALA Notable Book citation, both 1972, both for *The Ghost Downstairs;* Child Study Association of America's Children's Books of the Year citation, 1976, for *The House of Hanover: England in the Eighteenth Century;* Whitbread Literary award, 1980, for *John Diamond;* *Boston Globe-Horn Book* Fiction Honor citation, 1981, for *Footsteps;* Federation of Children's Book Groups award, 1981, for *Fair's Fair;* Hans Christian Andersen award nomination, 1981; Prix de la Fondation de France, 1984; Golden Cat award (Sweden), 1985; runner-up for Maschlev awards, 1985, for *Shakespeare Stories* and *The Wedding Ghost;* Children's Literature Association Phoenix award, 1987. Fellow, Royal Society of Literature, 1985. **Died.**

PUBLICATIONS FOR YOUNG ADULTS

Fiction

Jack Holborn, illustrated by Antony Maitland. London, Constable, 1964; New York, Pantheon, 1965.

Devil-in-the-Fog, illustrated by Antony Maitland. London, Constable, and New York, Pantheon, 1966.

Smith, illustrated by Antony Maitland. London, Constable, and New York, Pantheon, 1967.

Black Jack, illustrated by Antony Maitland. London, Longman, 1968; New York, Pantheon, 1969.

Mr. Corbett's Ghost, illustrated by Alan E. Cober. New York, Pantheon, 1968.

The Boy and the Monkey, illustrated by Trevor Ridley. London, Heinemann, 1969; New York, Watts, 1970.

The Drummer Boy, illustrated by Antony Maitland. New York, Pantheon, 1969; London, Longman, 1970.

Mister Corbett's Ghost, and Other Stories, illustrated by Antony Maitland. London, Longman, 1969.

The Restless Ghost: Three Stories by Leon Garfield, illustrated by Saul Lambert. New York, Pantheon, 1969.

The Strange Affair of Adelaide Harris, illustrated by Fritz Wegner. London, Longman, and New York, Pantheon, 1971.

The Captain's Watch, illustrated by Trevor Ridley. London, Heinemann, 1972.

The Ghost Downstairs, illustrated by Antony Maitland. London, Longman, and New York, Pantheon, 1972.

Lucifer Wilkins, illustrated by Trevor Ridley. London, Heinemann, 1973.

The Sound of Coaches (with Edward Blishen), illustrated by John Lawrence. London, Kestrel, and New York, Viking Press, 1974.

The Prisoners of September. London, Kestrel, and New York, Viking Press, 1975.

The Pleasure Garden, illustrated by Fritz Wegner. London, Kestrel, and New York, Viking Press, 1976.

An Adelaide Ghost. London, Ward Lock, 1977.

The Confidence Man. London, Kestrel, 1978; New York, Viking Press, 1979.

Bostock and Harris; or, The Night of the Comet, illustrated by Martin Cottam. London, Kestrel, 1979; as *The Night of the Comet: A Comedy of Courtship Featuring Bostock and Harris,* New York, Delacorte Press, 1979.

John Diamond, illustrated by Antony Maitland. London, Kestrel, 1980; as *Footsteps,* New York, Delacorte Press, 1980.

Fair's Fair, illustrated by Margaret Chamberlain. London, Macdonald, 1981; American edition illustrated by S. D. Schindler, New York, Doubleday, 1983.

King Nimrod's Tower, illustrated by Michael Bragg. London, Constable, and New York, Lothrop, 1982.

The Writing on the Wall, illustrated by Michael Bragg. London, Methuen, 1982, New York, Lothrop, 1983.

Guilt and Gingerbread, illustrated by Fritz Wegner. London, Viking Kestrel, 1984.

The King in the Garden, illustrated by Michael Bragg. London, Methuen, 1984; New York, Lothrop, 1985.

The Wedding Ghost, illustrated by Charles Keeping. Oxford, Oxford University Press, 1985; New York, Oxford University Press, 1987.

The December Rose (novelization of his own television series). London, Viking Kestrel, 1986; New York, Viking Kestrel, 1987.

Blewcoat Boy. London, Gollancz, 1988; as *Young Nick and Jubilee,* illustrated by Ted Lewin, Delacorte Press, 1989.

The Empty Sleeve. London, Viking Kestrel, and New York, Delacorte Press, 1988.

Revolution! London, Collins, 1989.

The Saracen Maid, illustrated John Talbot. London and New York, Simon & Schuster, 1991.

Sabre-tooth Sandwich. New York, Simon & Schuster, 1994.

"Apprentices" series:

The Cloak, illustrated by Faith Jaques. London, Heinemann, 1976.

The Lamplighter's Funeral, illustrated by Antony Maitland. London, Heinemann, 1976.

Mirror, Mirror, illustrated by Antony Maitland. London, Heinemann, 1976.

Moss and Blister, illustrated by Faith Jaques. London, Heinemann, 1976.

The Dumb Cake, illustrated by Faith Jaques. London, Heinemann, 1977.

The Fool, illustrated by Faith Jaques. London, Heinemann, 1977.

Labour in Vain, illustrated by Faith Jaques. London, Heinemann, 1977.

Rosy Starling, illustrated by Faith Jaques. London, Heinemann, 1977.

Tom Titmarsh's Devil, illustrated by Faith Jaques. London, Heinemann, 1977.

The Valentine, illustrated by Faith Jaques. London, Heinemann, 1977.

The Enemy, illustrated by Faith Jaques. London, Heinemann, 1978.

The Filthy Beast, illustrated by Faith Jaques. London, Heinemann, 1978.

The Apprentices. New York, Viking Press, 1978; London, Heinemann, 1982.

Editor

Editor, *Baker's Dozen: A Collection of Stories.* London, Ward Lock, 1973; as *Strange Fish and Other Stories,* New York, Lothrop, 1974.

Editor, *A Swag of Stories: Australian Stories,* illustrated by Caroline Harrison. London, Ward Lock, 1977.

Editor, *Hamlet,* illustrated by Natalia Orlova, Peter Kotov, and Natasha Demidova. New York, Knopf, 1993.

Editor, *Macbeth,* illustrated by Nikolai Serebriakov. New York, Knopf, 1993.

Editor, *A Midsummer Night's Dream,* illustrated by Elena Prorokova. New York, Knopf, 1993.

Editor, *Romeo and Juliet,* illustrated by Igor Makarov. New York, Knopf, 1993.

Editor, *The Tempest,* illustrated by Elena Livanova. New York, Knopf, 1993.

Editor, *Twelfth Night,* illustrated by Ksenia Prytkova. New York, Knopf, 1993

Other

The God beneath the Sea, with Edward Blishen, illustrated by Charles Keeping. London, Longman, 1970; American edition illustrated by Zevi Blum, New York, Pantheon, 1971.

Child O'War: The True Story of a Sailor Boy in Nelson's Navy, with David Proctor, illustrated by Antony Maitland. London, Collins, and New York, Holt Rinehart, 1972.

The Golden Shadow, with Edward Blishen, illustrated by Charles Keeping. New York, Pantheon, 1973.

Editor, *The Book Lovers: A Sequence of Love-Scenes.* London, Ward Lock, 1976; New York, Avon, 1978.

The House of Hanover: England in the Eighteenth Century. London, Deutsch, and New York, Seabury Press, 1976.

Shakespeare Stories, illustrated by Michael Foreman. London, Gollancz, and New York, Schocken, 1985.

Tales from Shakespeare, illustrated by Michael Foreman. New York, Schocken, 1985.

Tales from Shakespeare II, illustrated by Michael Foreman. New York, Schocken, 1994.

Six more Shakespeare Stories. London, Oxford/Heinemann New Windmills, 1994.

PUBLICATIONS FOR ADULTS

Novels

The Mystery of Edwin Drood (completion of the novel by Charles Dickens). London, Deutsch, 1980; New York, Pantheon, 1981.

The House of Cards. London, Bodley Head, 1982; New York, St. Martin's Press, 1983.

Other

Editor, *Sketches from Bleak House,* with Mervyn Peake and Edward Blishen. London, Methuen, 1983.

*

Media Adaptations: *John Diamond* (film), BBC-TV, 1981; *Jack Holborn* (a Taurus Film), 1982; *The Ghost Downstairs* and *The Restless Ghost* (dramatized for TV), 1982 and 1983, respectively; *The December Rose* (six-part series), BBC-TV, 1986-87; *Mr. Corbett's Ghost* (film), 1987. Several of Garfield's other books have been dramatized for film and television. *Devil-in-the Fog, Smith* and *The Strange Affair of Adelaide Harris* (TV serials-British TV), and *Black Jack* (film), produced by Tony Garnett and directed by Ken Loach.

Biography: Essay in *Speaking for Ourselves, Too* compiled and edited by Donald R. Gallo, National Council of Teachers of English, 1993.

Critical Studies: Entry in *Children's Literature Review,* Volume 21. Detroit, Gale, 1990; entry in *Contemporary Literary Criticism,* Volume 12. Detroit, Gale, 1980.

*   *   *

Leon Garfield's novels vividly evoke another place and time, the England of the eighteenth century. Historical backgrounds and lifestyles are convincingly shown, but historical research never intrudes on the exciting plots of these fast-paced adventure stories, told in a strong narrative style.

The central characters are usually male adolescents who are at first naive children, taking others at face value and accepting whatever adults tell them. But as the heroes gain experience of the adult world and its changing values, they are forced to develop their own identities, deciding what to believe and whom to trust. In *Footsteps,* young William Jones sets out to right a wrong done by his dead father, so the father's troubled ghost will no longer walk at night. But people such as the law clerk Jenkins who seem eager to help turn out to be untrustworthy, while people he initially discounts, such as the unfriendly porter Seed, become his true friends. Deceptiveness of appearances and ambiguity between good and evil are refrains running through Garfield's works, encouraging the young adult reader to evaluate people as individuals, not as members of groups.

Travel is important in most of the novels, journeys which symbolize their young heroes' quests for identity and truth. *Jack Holborn* is a shipboard adventure. Stowaway Jack must decide whom, of several ambiguous men, including the paradoxical captain who turns out to be twins identical in appearance but differing in character, to believe. In *The Sound of Coaches* young Sam Chichester confronts problems of growing up, establishing an adult relationship with his adoptive father, and coming to terms with his disappointment on meeting the biological father he had romanticized. The passage of time and Sam's developing independence are symbolized by the constantly turning wheels of the London Chichester coach Sam drives in his disabled adoptive father's stead.

Garfield's novels show humans surviving however they must, sometimes forced by circumstances into undesired actions but capable of great generosity and even heroism. *The Sound of Coaches* illustrates the interdependence of human beings and their ability to bring happiness to each other, while *Black Jack* shows the power of love to transform an individual. In the latter, the title character is a criminal who evades the hangman's noose, captures young Tolly Dorking, and forces the boy to help him escape. Tolly grows fond of his captor and patiently urges him toward a better life.

Echoes of classic authors can be seen in Garfield's writing, not surprising since he learned to write fiction by studying such giants as Henry Fielding, Jonathan Swift, and Daniel Defoe, but he never merely copies any other writer. *Jack Holborn* has obvious parallels with Robert Louis Stevenson's *Treasure Island,* and several Garfield works recall those of Charles Dickens. *Smith,* like *Oliver Twist,* chronicles the adventures of a young pickpocket, while the French-Revolution story *The Prisoners of September* suggests *A Tale of Two Cities.* Like Dickens, Garfield writes of the plight of London's poor and satirizes institutions such as doctors and law courts. Also like Dickens, he often treats events melodramatically and invents eccentric characters. In *Black Jack* the people Tolly meets include a twelve-year-old blackmailer, a troop of traveling hucksters of "magical" elixir, and a "professional widow" who makes a living claiming and selling the corpses of hanged criminals.

Garfield writes in a highly readable, lively, and literate style. His plots are complex, his descriptions extravagant and filled with colorful imagery. Readers not only see and hear scenes but touch and smell them, whether it's the stench and filth of underworld London in *Smith* or the quiet damp of a mist-hung thicket in *Devil-in-the-Fog.* Settings vary from the chaotic, noisy, unspeakably awful, insane asylum where young Belle lives in *Black Jack,* to the London-rooftop "castle" the urchin Shot-in-the-Head builds of old clothing and stolen trinkets in *Footsteps.* Garfield is a master of the well-chosen detail and the apt figure of speech. Barnacle, the spunky chimney sweep of *The December Rose,* is described thus: "A boy, white as a chicken bone, stood outside St. Marylebone Public Baths, trying to hold up his trousers, which hung on him, loose as cobwebs." People of all walks of life are differentiated by their speech, as when the stableman in *Footsteps* tells William to "go dahn that way. . .then 'long Bishopsgit. . .and 'long past Bedlam 'orspittle.''

Garfield's novels fall somewhere between literature for children and that for adults, being understandable to young people but with a mature point of view. He does not simplify or sweeten the world for adolescents; situations are often macabre, and his young heroes sometimes journey through dark and threatening passages before emerging into the light of self-knowledge and understanding of the adult world. But he writes with warmth, emphasis on moral choice, and tolerance for human frailty. Reading his works can prepare young readers for the complexity of feelings and masterful use of language found in writers such as Jane Austen, Fyodor Dostoevsky, and William Shakespeare.

—Elbert R. Hill

GARNER, Alan

Nationality: British. **Born:** Congleton, Cheshire, England, 17 October 1934. **Education:** Magdalen College, Oxford. **Military Service:** Served two years in the Royal Artillery; became second lieutenant. **Family:** Married Ann Cook, 1956 (marriage dissolved); one son, two daughters; married Griselda Greaves, 1972; one son, one daughter. **Career:** Writer. **Awards:** Carnegie Medal commendation, 1965, for *Elidor;* Carnegie Medal, 1967, and *Guardian* Award for children's fiction, 1968, both for *The Owl Service;* Lewis Carroll Shelf Award, 1970, for *The Weirdstone of Brisingamen;* selected as a highly commended author by the Hans Christian Andersen Awards committee of the International Board on Books for Young People, 1978; first prize, Chicago International Film Festival, 1981, for *Images;* Mother Goose Award, 1987, for *A Bag of Moonshine.* **Address:** ''Toad Hall,'' Blackden-cum Goostrey, Cheshire CW4 8BY, England.

PUBLICATIONS FOR YOUNG ADULTS

Fiction

The Weirdstone of Brisingamen: A Tale of Alderley. London, Collins, 1960; as *The Weirdstone: A Tale of Alderley,* New York, F. Watts, 1961; revised edition, London, Penguin, 1963; New York, Walck, 1969.
The Moon of Gomrath (sequel to *The Weirdstone of Brisingamen*). London, Collins, 1963; New York, Walck, 1967.
Elidor, illustrated by Charles Keeping. London, Collins, 1965; New York, Walck, 1967.
The Old Man of Mow, illustrated with photographs by Roger Hill. London, Collins, 1966; New York, Doubleday, 1970.
The Owl Service. London, Collins, 1967; New York, Walck, 1968.
Red Shift. London, Collins, and New York, Macmillan, 1973.
The Breadhorse, illustrated by Albin Trowski. London, Collins, 1975.
Alan Garner's Fairy Tales of Gold (The Golden Brothers, The Girl of the Golden Gate, The Three Golden Heads of the Well, The

Princess and the Golden Mane), illustrated by Michael Foreman. London, Collins, four volumes, 1979; one-volume edition, Collins, and New York, Philomel, 1980.
Once upon a Time, Though It Wasn't in Your Time and It Wasn't in My Time, and It Wasn't in Anybody Else's Time. London, Dorling Kindersley, 1993.
Strandloper. London, Harvill, 1996.
Little Red Hen, illustrated by Norman Messenger. New York, DK Publishing, 1997.
The Well of the Wind, illustrated by Herve Blondon. New York, DK Publishing, 1998.

''The Stone Book'' Quartet (illustrated with etchings by Michael Foreman)

The Stone Book. London, Collins, 1976; New York, Collins & World, 1978.
Tom Fobble's Day. London, Collins, 1977; New York, Collins & World, 1979.
Granny Reardun. London, Collins, 1977; New York, Collins & World, 1978.
The Aimer Gate. London, Collins, 1978; New York, Collins & World, 1979.
The Stone Book Quartet (The Stone Book, Granny Reardun, The Aimer Gate, Tom Fobble's Day). London, Collins, 1983; New York, Dell, 1988.

Plays

Holly from the Bongs: A Nativity Play, music by William Mayne; photographs by Roger Hill (produced in Goostrey, Cheshire, 1965). London, Collins, 1966; revised version, music by Gordon Crosse (produced in London, 1974), published in *Labrys 7* (Frome, Somerset), 1981.
The Belly Bag, music by Richard Morris (produced in London, 1971).
Potter Thompson, music by Gordon Crosse (produced in London, 1975). London, Oxford University Press, 1975.
To Kill a King (televised, 1980). Published in *Labrys 7,* 1981.
The Green Mist (dance drama). Published in *Labrys 7,* 1981.

Additional Plays: *Lurga Lom,* 1980; *Sally Water,* 1982.

Screenplays: *Places and Things,* 1978; *Images,* 1981.

Radio Plays: *Have You Met Our Tame Author?,* 1962; *Elidor,* 1962; *The Weirdstone of Brisingamen,* 1963; *Thor and the Giants,* 1965, revised, 1979; *Idun and the Apples of Life,* 1965, revised as *Loki and the Storm Giant,* 1979; *Baldur the Bright,* 1965, revised, 1979; *The Stone Book, Granny Reardun, Tom Fobble's Day,* and *The Aimer Gate,* 1980.

Television Plays: *The Owl Service,* 1969; (with John Mackenzie) *Red Shift,* 1978; *Lamaload,* 1979; *To Kill a King, (Leap in the Dark* series), 1980; *The Keeper,* 1982.

Other

Editor, *The Hamish Hamilton Book of Goblins: An Anthology of Folklore,* illustrated by Krystyna Turska. London, Hamish Hamilton, 1969; as *A Cavalcade of Goblins,* New York, Walck, 1969; as *A Book of Goblins,* London, Penguin, 1972.

Compiler, *The Guizer: A Book of Fools.* London, Hamish Hamilton, 1975; New York, Greenwillow, 1976.

The Lad of the Gad (folktales). London, Collins, 1980; New York, Philomel, 1981.

Alan Garner's Book of British Fairy Tales (retellings), illustrated by Derek Collard. London, Collins, and New York, Delacorte, 1984.

Jack and the Beanstalk, illustrated by Julek Heller (for children; retelling). London, Collins, 1985, New York, Delacorte, 1992.

A Bag of Moonshine (folktales), illustrated by Patrick James Lynch. London, Collins, and New York, Delacorte, 1986.

*

Manuscript Collections: Brigham Young University, Provo, Utah.

Biography: Essay in *Speaking for Ourselves: Autobiographical Sketches by Notable Authors of Books for Young Adults,* Volume 1, compiled and edited by Donald R. Gallo, National Council of Teachers of English, 1990.

Critical Studies: *A Fine Anger: A Critical Introduction to the Work of Alan Garner* by Neil Philip, London, Collins, and New York, Philomel, 1981; ''Alan Garner Issue'' of *Labrys 7,* 1981; *Children's Literature Review,* Volume 20, Detroit, Gale, 1990.

*   *   *

Intensely individual, often demanding, repeatedly innovative, Alan Garner is an outstanding writer for young adults. Books that seem simple and even naive on the surface, like the ''Stone Book'' quartet, can challenge adult readers by the resonance with which they explore universal themes within a brilliantly realised sense of time, place, and identity. Three novels (*Elidor, The Owl Service, Red Shift*), progressively more complex to read and morally demanding, transmute elements of myth and folklore into metaphors for significant experiences and relationships. They are particularly aimed at young adults and vividly realise the difficulties and pain of adolescence. Garner has said that, while writing primarily for himself, he finds readers from the ages of ten to eighteen ''the most important of all, and. . .the best audience. Few adults read with a comparable involvement.''

After his first two children's books, fantasies somewhat in the Tolkien mode, Garner pushed C.S. Lewis's rather timid conjunction of the everyday and fabulous (which he found ''insufferable'') to dramatically new limits in *Elidor.* Whereas for Lewis the contemporary world simply provided a prologue to the real, moralising story in Narnia, Garner achieves the infinitely trickier task of realising fantasy in a Manchester of slum clearance, home

life, and television. Because the magic in the novel is only seen through children's eyes, *Elidor* can be read as their fantasy game. However, the everyday objects with which the children return—stone, railing, cracked cup—which they see as ritual treasures like lance and grail, also seem to have an unsettling power that interferes with the television, washing-machine, and father's electric razor.

In *The Owl Service,* three adolescents holidaying in a Welsh valley become possessed by the spirits of characters in a local myth and reenact elements of the tragedy. Garner has said that the Mabinogion story of Lleu Llaw Gyffes and the wife who was made for him out of flowers, who betrayed him and was herself turned into an owl, was animated for him by the discovery of a dinner service with a flower pattern that could be reassembled into the face of an owl. However, this myth is kept in the background, and the narrative concentrates on the bewildering emotions that take over Alison, her stepbrother Roger, and Gwyn, the cook's son: sexual tensions, class and national resentments, and the painful awareness of adult frailty. The novel is marked from the very beginning by a high proportion of dialogue, so that the characters reveal themselves and their attitudes by speech styles. There is a recurrent concern with what it means to ''speak properly.'' The reader has to fill in the gaps in the talk and must also reconstruct what has gone before. Garner has said that his characters can be identified with their mythic equivalents in two distinct ways, and critics have varied in their evaluation of the ending. Most readers have admired the way in which Roger resists the dark feelings within him, forgives, and admits his responsibility, thus transforming the owls back into flowers. However, some feel that they have been tempted by the author to identify with Gwyn, that the conclusion is manipulated, and that in view of his character Roger's behaviour is implausible. Such disagreements may testify to the openness and intensity of the novel.

Perhaps a deliberately more problematic text, *Red Shift* requires more than a single reading. Some adolescent readers become frustrated by hunting for clues in the text and feel that they are missing the hidden key that will unlock it for them. The novel abandons many of the conventional devices of young adult fiction (chapter divisions, descriptions of characters, explanation of events) in favour of a multi-layered cinematic technique emphasising dialogue, abrupt cutting between scenes, and allusive references to other works. The narrative, although placed in a single locality in and around Mow Cop, switches between three different periods: the Roman occupation of Britain, the Civil War, and the present day. In each of these periods a similar narrative develops: a love triangle in which the sensitive man in a couple is threatened both by his own self-doubt and the intrusion of a stronger figure who eventually helps save the other two. The character sets are virtually interchangeable. The ultimate impression is one of timelessness: everything that has happened exists simultaneously in some eternal present.

Although his reputation as an author for adolescents rests at present chiefly on only three books, Garner is acknowledged as a seminal figure, whose works are quite unlike those of any other writer. His idiosyncratic power, his ability as a storyteller, his outstanding sense of place, and his meticulous craftsmanship assure him a leading place in any current account of literature for young adults.

—Robert Protherough

GARNETT, Eve

Nationality: British. **Born:** Worcestershire. **Education:** The Convent, Bideford, Devon; West Bank School, Devon; Alice Ottely School, Worcester; Chelsea Polytechnic School of Art, London; Royal Academy Schools, London (studentship; Creswick Prize and Silver Medal). **Career:** Artist: murals for Children's House, Bow, London; exhibitions at the Tate Gallery, 1939, Le Fevre Gallery, and New English Art Club, all London. **Awards:** Library Association Carnegie Medal, 1938, for *The Family from One End Street and Some of Their Adventures;* Creswick Prize and Silver Medal. **Died:** 1991.

PUBLICATIONS FOR YOUNG ADULTS (illustrated by the author)

Fiction

"Is It Well with the Child?", illustrated by the author. London, Muller, 1938.
The Family from One End Street and Some of Their Adventures. London, Muller, 1937; New York, Vanguard Press, 1939.
In and Out and Roundabout: Stories of a Little Town. London, Muller, 1948.
Further Adventures of the Family from One End Street. London, Heinemann, and New York, Vanguard Press, 1956.
Holiday at the Dew Drop Inn: A One End Street Story. London, Heinemann, 1962; New York, Vanguard Press, 1963.
Lost and Found: Four Stories. London, Muller, 1974.

Other

Editor, *A Book of Seasons: An Anthology.* London, Oxford University Press, 1952; Boston, Bentley, 1953.
Contributor, *Chosen for Children.* British Library Association, 1952.
Contributor, *A Golden Land.* Constable, 1958.
Contributor, *Naughty Children.* Gollancz, 1962.
To Greenland's Icy Mountains: The Story of Hans Egede, Explorer, Coloniser, Missionary. London, Heinemann, and New York, Roy, 1968.
First Affections: Some Autobiographical Chapters of Early Childhood. London, Muller, 1982.

*

Illustrator: *The London Child* by Evelyn Sharp, 1927; *The Bad Barons of Crashbania* by Norman Hunter, 1932; *A Child's Garden of Verses* by Robert Louis Stevenson, 1948; *A Golden Land* edited by James Reeves, 1958.

*   *   *

Eve Garnett is both an author and artist, and her writing and illustrations are equally important in her books, stories, and poems. Each book that Garnett has written for young adults is enhanced by her peaceful, beautiful pencil illustrations. Garnett's writing and art can be described as nostalgic glimpses into simple times of the past when life was less complicated.

Garnett's writing typically focuses on common human experiences that occur within the context of the family. Her books, *The*

Family from One End Street, Further Adventures of the Family from One End Street, and *Holiday at the Dew Drop Inn,* tell of the triumphs and trials of the Ruggles family; a large, poor family in England. In these books, each chapter is a complete episode that can be read like a short story.

Though her characters are often faced with what could be called trivial problems today, Garnett's ability to develop characters that the reader can easily identify with permits these problems to be presented as familiar, real-life situations. By focusing on the emotions and thoughts of the characters facing the problems, Garnett is able to create a connection between reader and character. Humor often plays an important role in how the characters deal with these problems. When the Ruggles children get the measles in *The Family from One End Street,* and Olav must give Fisker to the trader in "The Rusty-Eyed Seal," a happy ending occurs. Suitable, clever solutions to problems and happy endings characterize Garnett's fiction.

In *Is It Well with the Child?* she deals with the uncharacteristically serious issues of cruelty, poverty, and indifference toward children. Most of Garnett's verses and illustrations in this book are cheerful on the surface; upon closer look, however, they depict the pain and helplessness that some children are forced to experience in their lives.

In her fiction, Garnett develops her characters by describing their actions, words, thoughts, and by supplementing these with illustrations. In *Holiday at the Dew Drop Inn,* Lily Rose comes alive for the reader as Garnett eloquently tells of the thoughts, concerns, and fears of this adolescent as she realizes that she has just helped two prisoners escape. In *The Family from One End Street,* Garnett thoroughly develops the character of Kate so that the reader can empathize with Kate's concern over not having the appropriate clothes for entering the prestigious secondary school to which she has won a scholarship.

Garnett's main characters tend to be strong, resilient women and girls like Mrs. Ruggles, Lily Rose, and Kate. In addition, the most developed of her characters are young adults and children, such as Lily Rose and Kate in the three books dealing with the Ruggles family. Because Garnett tends to focus on and develop female characters more than male characters, her fiction may be more appealing to female readers. She also fully develops the characters in her nonfiction book *To Greenland's Icy Mountains* and goes beyond the traditional confines of nonfiction, including the feelings and thoughts that Hans Egede may have experienced during the events described therein.

Aware that many readers may not be familiar with the places and time periods she writes of, Garnett provides the necessary background information within the context of her stories. Garnett's settings, usually in England, often play important roles in her stories. The beach becomes a major character as it steals Kate's hat and disrupts a family gathering at the park in *The Family from One End Street.* The short story "Silver Treasure," about good fortune and hidden treasure, is appropriately set in Ireland. In "The Kind Visitor," the blueberry patch plays an important role in the loss and eventual return of My-Thomas. The two short stories mentioned above were originally intended for younger readers; however, they have many elements that may appeal to young adult readers.

A great respect for nature is evident in her poetry, fiction, and nonfiction. In the anthology *A Book of Seasons,* Garnett celebrates the quiet beauty of nature as it changes from season to season. Her books and short stories involve many situations and problems that occur in connection with nature. *Holiday at the Dew Drop Inn* describes the experiences of Kate, a town girl, as she learns about nature while spending the summer in the country. In her nonfiction book *To Greenland's Icy Mountains,* nature is an important character that challenges Hans Egede throughout his life.

The use of old-fashioned words and colloquial expressions helps to set the mood and illustrates pictures of the characters and settings for the reader, though some of the language may be confusing to the young adult reader. In addition, some of the language used by Garnett now carries negative connotations that may interfere with the reader's understanding and appreciation of certain passages. For example, the phrase ''ten little nigger boys'' in *Further Adventures of the Family from One End Street,* refers to ten black piglets. In addition, many of her characters speak in dialects that may be unfamiliar to some readers.

Garnett's books, stories, poetry, and illustrations are all endearing and enduring. Garnett's works have delighted and entertained several generations of young readers. Because of her focus on the commonality of human emotions and experiences within the family, Garnett's works continue to appeal to today's young adult readers.

—Laurie Elish-Piper

GARRISEN, Paul. *See* **PAULSEN, Gary.**

GARRISON, Frederick. *See* **SINCLAIR, Upton (Beall).**

GEORGE, Jean Craighead

Nationality: American. **Born:** Washington, D.C., 2 July 1919. **Education:** Pennsylvania State University, State College, B.A. 1941; Louisiana State University, Baton Rouge, 1941-42, and University of Michigan, Ann Arbor. **Family:** Married John Lothar George in 1944 (divorced 1963); one daughter and two sons. **Career:** Reporter, International News Service, 1942-44, and Washington *Post,* 1943-44, both in Washington, D.C., and United Features (Newspaper Enterprise Association), 1945-46; artist, *Pageant Magazine,* New York, 1945; continuing education teacher in Chappaqua, New York, 1960-68; staff writer, 1969-74, and roving editor, 1974-82, *Reader's Digest,* Pleasantville, New York; author and illustrator of books and articles on natural history. **Awards:** Aurianne award, American Library Association, 1956, for *Dipper of Copper Creek;* Newbery Medal honor book award

and ALA notable book citation, both American Library Association, 1960, International Hans Christian Andersen award honor list, 1962, Lewis Carroll Shelf citation, 1965, and George G. Stone Center for Children's Books award, 1969, all for *My Side of the Mountain;* Woman of the Year, Pennsylvania State University, 1968; Claremont College award, 1969; Eva L. Gordon Award, American Nature Study Society, 1970; *Book World* First Prize, 1971, for *All upon a Stone;* Newbery Medal, National Book award finalist citation, German Youth Literature Prize from West German section of International Board on Books for Young People, and Silver Skate from Netherlands Children's Book Board, all 1973, and listing by Children's Literature Association as one of ten best American children's books in two hundred years, 1976, all for *Julie of the Wolves;* School Library Media Specialties of South Eastern New York award, 1981; Irvin Kerlan award, University of Minnesota, 1982; University of Southern Mississippi award, 1986; Grumman award, 1986; Washington Irving award, Westchester Library Association, 1991; Knickerbocker for Juvenile Literature, School Library Media Section, New York Public Library Association. **Agent:** Curtis Brown Ltd., 10 Astor Place, New York, New York 10003. **Address:** 20 William St., Chappaqua, New York 10514, U.S.A.

PUBLICATIONS FOR YOUNG ADULTS

Novels (illustrated by the author)

Vulpes, the Red Fox (as Jean George), with John L. George. New York, Dutton, 1948.
Vison, the Mink (as Jean George), with John L. George. New York, Dutton, 1949.
Masked Prowler: The Story of a Raccoon (as Jean George), with John L. George. New York, Dutton, 1950.
Meph, the Pet Skunk (as Jean George), with John L. George. New York, Dutton, 1952.
Bubo, the Great Horned Owl (as Jean George), with John L. George. New York, Dutton, 1954.
Dipper of Copper Creek (as Jean George), with John L. George. New York, Dutton, 1956.
The Hole in the Tree (as Jean George). New York, Dutton, 1957.
Snow Tracks (as Jean George). New York, Dutton, 1958.
My Side of the Mountain (as Jean George). New York, Dutton, 1959; London, Bodley Head, 1962.
The Summer of the Falcon. New York, Crowell, 1962; London, Dent, 1964.
Gull Number 737. New York, Crowell, 1964.
Hold Zero! New York, Crowell, 1966.
Water Sky. New York, Harper, 1987.
On the Far Side of the Mountain. New York, Dutton, 1990.

Fiction

Tree House (play, music by Saul Aarons). Chappaqua, New York, 1962.
Coyote in Manhattan, illustrated by John Kaufmann. New York, Crowell, 1968.
All upon a Stone, illustrated by Don Bolognese. New York, Crowell, 1971.
Who Really Killed Cock Robin? An Ecological Mystery. New York, Dutton, 1971.

Julie of the Wolves, illustrated by John Schoenherr. New York, Harper, 1972.

All upon a Sidewalk, illustrated by Don Bolognese. New York, Dutton, 1974.

Hook a Fish, Catch a Mountain. New York, Dutton, 1975.

Going to the Sun. New York, Harper, 1976.

The Wentletrap Trap, illustrated by Symeon Shimin. New York, Dutton, 1978.

The Wounded Wolf, illustrated by John Schoenherr. New York, Harper, 1978.

River Rats, Inc. New York, Dutton, 1979.

The Cry of the Crow. New York, Harper, 1980.

The Grizzly Bear with the Golden Ears, illustrated by Tom Catania. New York, Harper, 1982.

The Talking Earth. New York, Harper, 1983.

Shark beneath the Reef. New York, Harper, 1989.

Missing Gator of Gumbo Limbo: An Ecological Mystery. New York, HarperCollins, 1992.

Famous Animals (stories), pictures by Christine Merrill. New York, HarperCollins, 1994.

The Case of the Missing Cutthroat Trout: An Ecological Mystery. New York, HarperCollins, 1994.

Julie. New York, HarperCollins, 1994.

There's an Owl in the Shower. New York, HarperCollins, 1995.

Julie's Wolf Pack. New York, HarperCollins, 1997.

Look to the North: A Wolf Pup Diary, illustrated by Lucia Washburn. New York, HarperCollins, 1997.

Arctic Son, illustrated by Wendell Minor. New York, Hyperion, 1997.

Rhino Mom. Forthcoming, 1998.

Giraffe Trouble. Forthcoming, 1998.

"Thirteen Moons" nonfiction series:

The Moon of the Salamanders, illustrated by John Kaufmann. New York, Crowell, 1967, new edition illustrated by Marlene Werner, New York, HarperCollins, 1992.

The Moon of the Bears, illustrated by Mac Shepard. New York, Crowell, 1967, new edition illustrated by Ron Parker, New York, HarperCollins, 1993.

The Moon of the Owls, illustrated by Jean Zallinger. New York, Crowell, 1967, new edition illustrated by Wendell Minor, New York, HarperCollins, 1993.

The Moon of the Mountain Lions, illustrated by Winifred Lubell. New York, Crowell, 1968, new edition illustrated by Ron Parker, New York, HarperCollins, 1991.

The Moon of the Chickarees, illustrated by John Schoenherr. New York, Crowell, 1968, new edition illustrated by Don Rodell, New York, HarperCollins, 1992.

The Moon of the Fox Pups, illustrated by Kiyoaki Komoda. New York, Crowell, 1968, new edition illustrated by Norman Adams, New York, HarperCollins, 1992.

The Moon of the Wild Pigs, illustrated by Peter Parnall. New York, Crowell, 1968, new edition illustrated by Paul Mirocha, New York, HarperCollins, 1992.

The Moon of the Monarch Butterflies, illustrated by Murray Tinkelman. New York, Crowell, 1968, new edition illustrated by Kam Mak, New York, HarperCollins, 1993.

The Moon of the Alligators, illustrated by Adrina Zanazanian. New York, Crowell, 1969, new edition illustrated by Michael Rothman, New York, HarperCollins, 1991.

The Moon of the Gray Wolves, illustrated by Lorence Bjorklund. New York, Crowell, 1969, new edition illustrated by Sal Catalano, New York, HarperCollins, 1991.

The Moon of the Deer, illustrated by Jean Zallinger. New York, Crowell, 1969, new edition illustrated by Sal Catalano, New York, HarperCollins, 1992.

The Moon of the Moles, illustrated by Robert Levering. New York, Crowell, 1969, new edition illustrated by Michael Rothman, New York, HarperCollins, 1992.

The Moon of the Winter Bird, illustrated by Kazue Mizumura. New York, Crowell, 1969, new edition illustrated by Vincent Nasta, New York, HarperCollins, 1992.

"One Day" nonfiction series:

One Day in the Desert, illustrated by Fred Brenner. New York, Crowell, 1983.

One Day in the Alpine Tundra, illustrated by Walter Gaffney-Kessell. New York, Crowell, 1984.

One Day in the Prairie, illustrated by Bob Marstall. New York, Crowell, 1986.

One Day in the Woods, illustrated by Gary Allen. New York, Crowell, 1988.

One Day in the Tropical Rain Forest, illustrated by Gary Allen. New York, HarperCollins, 1990.

Dear Rebecca, Winter is Here, pictures by Loretta Krupinski. New York, HarperCollins, 1993.

The Fire Bug Connection: An Ecological Mystery. New York, HarperCollins, 1993.

Nonfiction

Spring Comes to the Ocean, illustrated by John Wilson. New York, Crowell, 1966.

Beastly Inventions: A Surprising Investigation into How Smart Animals Really Are, illustrated by the author. New York, McKay, 1970; as *Animals Can Do Anything,* London, Souvenir Press, 1972.

The Wild, Wild Cookbook: A Guide for Young Wild-Food Foragers, illustrated by Walter Kessell. New York, Crowell, 1982.

The First Thanksgiving, illustrated by Thomas Locker. New York, Philomel Books, 1993.

The Everglades, paintings by Wendell Minor. New York, HarperCollins, 1994.

Acorn Pancakes, Dandelion Salad and 38 Other Wild Recipes, illustrated by Paul Mirocha. New York, Harper Collins, 1995.

To Climb a Waterfall, illustrated by Thomas Locker. New York, Philomel, 1995.

Everglades, illustrated by Wendell Minor. New York, HarperCollins, 1995.

The Tarantula in My Purse and 172 Other Wild Pets. New York, HarperCollins, 1996.

PUBLICATIONS FOR ADULTS

Other

Everglades Wildguide, illustrated by Betty Fraser. Washington D.C., National Park Service, 1972.

New York in Maps 1972-73, with Toy Lasker. New York, New York Magazine, 1974.

New York in Flashmaps 1974-75, with Toy Lasker. Chappaqua, New York, Flashmaps, 1976.

The American Walk Book: An Illustrated Guide to the Country's Major Historic and Natural Walking Trails from New England to the Pacific Coast. New York, Dutton, 1978.

Journey Inward (autobiography). New York, Dutton, 1982.

Exploring the Out-of-Doors. Chicago, American Library Association, 1983.

How to Talk to Your Animals, illustrated by the author. San Diego, Harcourt Brace, 1985; London, Hodder and Stoughton, 1986.

How to Talk to Your Dog (originally published in *How to Talk to Your Animals*), illustrated by the author. New York, Warner, 1986.

How to Talk to Your Cat (originally published in *How to Talk to Your Animals*), illustrated by the author. New York, Warner, 1986.

Editor, *The Big Book for the Planet,* with Ann Durell and Katherine Paterson. New York, Dutton Children's Books, 1993.

Contributor to books, including *Marvels and Mysteries of Our Animal World,* Reader's Digest Association, 1964. Contributor of articles on natural history and children's literature to periodicals, including *Audubon, Horn Book, International Wildlife,* and *National Wildlife.* Consultant for science books.

*

Media Adaptations: *My Side of the Mountain* (film), starring Teddy Eccles and Theodore Bikel, Paramount, 1969; *Julie of the Wolves* (recording), read by Irene Worth, Caedmon, 1977; *One Day in the Woods* (musical video), music by Fritz Kramer and Chris Kubie, Kunhardt Productions, 1989; *My Side of the Mountain* (film), 1995; *One Day in the Woods,* (musical for children), music by Chris Kubie, 1997.

Biography: Entry in *Dictionary of Literary Biography,* Volume 52: *American Writers for Children since 1960: Fiction.* Detroit, Gale, 1986, pp. 168-74; essay in *Speaking for Ourselves: Autobiographical Sketches by Notable Authors of Books for Young Adults,* Volume 1, compiled and edited by Donald R. Gallo, National Council of Teachers of English, 1990.

Manuscript Collections: Kerlan Collection, University of Minnesota, Minneapolis.

Critical Studies: Entry in *Children's Literature Review,* Volume 1, Detroit, Gale, 1976, pp. 89-94; entry in *Contemporary Literary Criticism,* Volume 35, Detroit, Gale, 1985, pp. 175-80; *Children's Books and their Creators,* edited by Anita Silvey, Boston, Houghton Mifflin, 1995; "Look to the North: A Wolf Pup Diary" by Patricia Manning, in *School Library Journal,* Vol. 43, No. 4, 1997, 123-124; "Julie's Wolf Pack" by Caroline Wood, in *School Library Journal,* Vol. 43, No. 9, 1997, 216-217; "Arctic Son" by Mollie Bynum, in *School Library Journal,* Vol. 43, No. 11, 1997, 81-82; "Julie's Wolf Pack" by Terri Schmitz in *Horn Book,* Vol. 74, No. 1, 1998, 71.

Illustrator: *Hawks, Owls, and Wildlife* by John J. Craighead and Frank C. Craighead, Jr., 1969.

Jean Craighead George comments:

One day I built a pond and a waterfall in my backyard. The next day as I stood there admiring it a story began. A frog appeared on its shore. A dragonfly flew over it. I was delighted and so I watched for new life every day. In a short time the pond was occupied by diving beetles, mosquito larva, and salamanders. I had not put them there. They had heard the call of water through their miraculous senses and had come to my pond to give it meaning. I began to write.

These are the everyday things that get me writing. Each morning is rich with new material. I go for a walk, climb a mountain, or sit with my grandchildren and the books come from the world around me through my head to my fingers. The only thing that I do that nonwriters do not is feel the fire of the material and write it down with love. And it is love.

*　　*　　*

Jean Craighead George's fiction comes from a lifelong love of the outdoors and of writing. Both of her parents were naturalist-entomologists, and growing up she was surrounded by animals and spent much time exploring nature. Through her young adult novels about the natural environment, she teaches and informs, and shows young people that they can learn from nature and live comfortably in the natural environment. She writes only what she has seen or experienced, resulting in vivid descriptions, such as when fifteen-year-olds Joe and Crowbar run the Grand Canyon's Lava Fall rapids on their backs after abandoning their raft in *River Rats, Inc.* Perhaps best known for *My Side of the Mountain* and *Julie of the Wolves,* George is at her best putting adolescents in nature where they rely on their own ingenuity and learn to listen to and respect nature in order to survive.

Ingenious survival techniques are abundant in George's books. Sam Gribley, thirteen-year-old narrator of *My Side of the Mountain,* whittles a fish hook out of a green twig, makes a tent and bed out of hemlock boughs, makes snowshoes out of ash saplings and deer hide, and burns out the inside of a living tree to make a home. In his sequel, *On the Far Side of the Mountain,* he makes a waterwheel-driven sawmill, and his sister, Alice, builds a plumping mill to grind acorns into flour, an idea from a book she has read. This, like much information passed on by George characters, is remembered from books those characters have read, sending a clear message of the importance of reading to readers. Another survival skill, garnered from books as well as from characters's own ingenuity, is the ability to trap or collect natural foods on which to live. Sam shows that an astute and resourceful nature observer can eat a balanced diet straight from nature. He explains how to make salt, recognize hawthorn berries, smoke fish, and how to cook cattails, which he explains directly to the reader. "If you ever eat cattails, be sure to cook them well, otherwise the fibers are tough and they take more chewing to get the starchy food from them than they are worth". In *River Rats, Inc.,* Walter, the wild boy, survives on live lizards and other natural foods, as well as human garbage that he finds.

George illustrates the connection between nature and people when her characters learn to understand and heed nature's messages. By close observation of a wolf pack, thirteen-year-old Miyax, in *Julie of the Wolves,* learns to communicate with the wolves and is accepted by the pack. They supply her with food, give her comfort and companionship, and protect her from a bear and a lone wolf. Listening to nature is carried even further in *Who Really Killed Cock Robin?*, an ecological mystery solved by fourteen-year-old Tony Isidoro and friends as they carefully observe wildlife behavior and plant colonization to determine the origins and spread of various environmental pollutants. George explains the path of toxic chemicals up the food chain and its effects on both animals and humans. In *The Talking Earth*, thirteen-year-old Billie Wind, a Seminole Indian girl, is sent into the Everglades alone because she doesn't believe that nature talks to people. Through her experiences she learns to listen to the natural world and realizes that "all living things are a family, and one can not live without the other." The Eskimos of *Water Sky* survive on the ice during whaling season by watching the clouds and the wind, and are better able to predict whale behavior than are scientists who have modern equipment.

Another message which George presents is that of the wildness of nature and preservation of that wildness. Thirteen-year-old Mandy Tressel learns a hard lesson about wildlife in *The Cry of the Crow* when she raises an orphaned crow chick but refuses to let it return to the wild, and must kill it to protect her brother. In *Coyote in Manhattan*, characters are split between those who would kill the coyote in Central Park and those who would let it live wild. The wild side prevails when the coyote is set free outside the city.

George shows her respect for nature when she describes the ecology of wildlife in accurate and interesting detail. She immerses readers in the lemming cycle of the far north, nuthatch behavior in the Catskills, the food chain in the Everglades, and stream ecology in the Rocky Mountains, drawing rich descriptions of the natural balance of nature. However, she also points out where humans upset that balance. In *Hook a Fish, Catch a Mountain*, she details how timber clear-cutting destroys cutthroat trout fisheries, heating stream water, and silting natural pools.

Although some experiences are implausible, such as parents allowing thirteen-year-old Sam Gribley to live alone in the mountains for a year, Jean Craighead George writes reverently about the natural environment, conveying to readers its beauty and complexity. She places readers in the environment of her characters, teaching about the interaction of people and nature in engrossing tales, without being didactic. Tony Isidoro sums up the interrelationship between humans and nature in *Who Really Killed Cock Robin?* when he says "A team of people killed Cock Robin and a team of people solved the crime. And that's how it's going to be from now until the day we live in balance with all beasts and plants, and air and water." The necessity of teamwork between humans and nature to protect the environment is consistent in all of Jean Craighead George's young adult novels.

Readers have confidence in the authenticity of George's writing, knowing that it is thoroughly researched and borne of experience. Fortunately, her experiences are both vast and diverse. George states in *Children's Books and Their Creators* that her stories come from three sources: her childhood; research in books and in the field; and wild creatures she has raised or studied in the wilds. She also recognizes a new source: her children and grandchildren. George expresses the conviction that children should be initiated into the process of learning about and loving nature. Her writing is instrumental in developing children's understanding of and affection for nature.

Everglades is one of the books that emanated from her childhood. In *Booklinks*, George explains that she wrote this elegant picture book as a tribute to her father who studied that unique ecosystem. George recalls paddling the Florida waterways with her parents, both entomologists, as they collected plant and animal specimens for their research. George explains the ending she used in *Everglades* by quoting her father's philosophy, "Teach the kids about nature and they will take care of the Earth." Another book that springs from George's childhood is *Acorn Pancakes, Dandelion Salad and 38 Other Wild Recipes*, in which she gives young readers advice on foraging and the pleasure derived from finding wild foods. She tells her audience, "the greatest unsought gift is that you become aware of the interdependency of plant, bird, beast, and human."

George is an impeccable researcher whose study of wolves has lead to several books on the subject. Her knowledge of wolves, their behavior, and their social hierarchy is shared with older readers in *Julie's Wolf Pack*, George's third book dealing with an Inupiat Eskimo girl, Julie, and the wolf pack that befriended her. However, it is the wolf pack that is the main character in this story and George portrays the wolves convincingly. Since the perspective of the wolves is maintained throughout the story, Julie is merely a peripheral character. For the most part, George describes only the wolves' behaviors, only rarely straying into anthropomorphism. However, in this book, she ascribes human emotions to the wolves, noting that Kapu, alpha male in the pack, ". . .loves pups. Pups aroused the most tender emotions in him and all wolves." George's descriptions of the Arctic tundra and its wild inhabitants are vivid. She passes no judgment on the behavior of humans who come into contact with the wolves, allowing readers to make up their own minds.

The picture book, *Look to the North: A Wolf Pup Diary* enables children to see how a wolf pack welcomes and cares for new pups. She connects milestones in the pups' development with natural events which take place in the young reader's world. In the author's note, George comments that she loves the wolf pups because in these children of the wild she sees all children and to her, "they are wonderful." George invites young readers to love them, too.

The Tarantula in My purse and 172 Other Wild Pets provides readers with clear insights into the extent of George's involvement with wild animals. They have been a part of her day-to-day life since childhood and she made them a part of her children's lives as well. Among the myriad of wild animals with whom she has shared her home, we learn about the owl that liked to get in the shower but, once there, became too waterlogged to move. From this relationship came the book, *There's an Owl in the Shower*, a fictional account of an out-of-work logger's family that takes in a baby owl only to discover, as the owl matures, that it is one of the spotted owls that has caused the logger to lose his job. In this book, George effectively conveys the complex environmental and social issues that surround this topic, but her character development is not as strong as one would expect.

Arctic Son is based upon the life of her grandson and his parents, living in Alaska. Her text is affectionate but not sentimental and, instead, provides an informative and insightful view of warm, loving families and of Inupiat Eskimo culture. Through the child's experiences, readers are introduced to the seasons of the Arctic and recognize that, in the Arctic, things are different. However, George concludes with a universal similarity, joy at dawn, greeting the rising sun.

Jean Craighead George is keenly aware of her readership, of their demand for lively, informative stories, and of her responsibility to them. She creates for her readers a world she knows well—the natural world, filled with wild creatures, dependent on each other and influenced by the hand of humanity. Her ability to bring the natural world to life within the framework of a well-crafted story is noteworthy. Her touch is nearly always deft. When it is not, the reader is surprised. There is such a surprise at the end of *To Climb a Waterfall,* a picture book that chronicles a young girl's efforts to reach the top of a waterfall. George describes the wild beauty that awaits at every step of her journey and when the child attains her goal, George commends her achievement and notes, "The waterfall is now part of you. Take it with you wherever you go, and you'll never be bored again." The last phrase of the book is uncharacteristic of George's writing. Rather than concerning herself with keeping children occupied, George strives to transmit her own love of nature to children so that they will internalize the wonders of the natural world, becoming transformed and strengthened for the challenges of life.

—Susanne L. Johnston, updated by Anne Drolett Creany

GERAS, Adèle (Daphne)

Nationality: British. **Born:** Jerusalem, Israel, 15 March 1944. **Education:** St. Hilda's College, Oxford, 1963-66, B.A. (honors) in modern languages 1966. **Family:** Married Norman Geras in 1967; two daughters. **Career:** French teacher, Fairfield High School, Droylsden, Lancashire, 1968-71; writer, since 1976. **Awards:** Taylor award, 1991, for *My Grandmother's Stories*; National Jewish Book Award, 1994, for *Golden Windows.* **Agent:** Laura Cecil, 17 Alwyne Villas, London N1 2HG. **Address:** 10 Danesmoor Road, Manchester M20 3JS, England.

PUBLICATIONS FOR YOUNG ADULTS

Fiction

The Girls in the Velvet Frame. London, Hamish Hamilton, 1978; New York, Atheneum, 1979.
The Green behind the Glass. London, Hamish Hamilton, 1982; as Snapshots of Paradise: Love Stories, New York, Atheneum, 1984.
Other Echoes. New York, Atheneum, 1982.
Voyage. London, Hamish Hamilton, and New York, Atheneum, 1983.
Letters of Fire and Other Unsettling Stories. London, Hamish Hamilton, 1984.
Happy Endings. London, Hamish Hamilton, 1986; San Diego, Harcourt, 1991.
Daydreams on Video. London, Hodder & Stoughton, 1989.
The Tower Room. London, Hamish Hamilton, 1990; San Diego, Harcourt, 1992.
Pictures of the Night. San Diego, Harcourt, 1992; London, Hamish Hamilton, 1992.
Watching the Roses. San Diego, Harcourt, 1992; London, Hamish Hamilton, 1991.
A Lane to the Land of the Dead. London, Hamish Hamilton, 1994.

Other

Yesterday (autobiographical memoir). London, Walker Books, 1992.

PUBLICATIONS FOR CHILDREN

Fiction

Tea at Mrs. Manderby's, illustrated by Doreen Caldwell. London, Hamish Hamilton, 1976.
Apricots at Midnight and Other Stories from a Patchwork Quilt, illustrated by Doreen Caldwell. London, Hamish Hamilton, 1977; New York, Atheneum, 1982.
Beyond the Cross Stitch Mountains, illustrated by Mary Wilson. London, Hamish Hamilton, 1977.
The Painted Garden, illustrated by Doreen Caldwell. London, Hamish Hamilton, 1979.
The Rug That Grew, illustrated by Priscilla Lamont. London, Hamish Hamilton, 1981.
A Thousand Yards of Sea, illustrated by Joanna Troughton. London, Hodder & Stoughton, 1981.
The Christmas Cat, illustrated by Doreen Caldwell. London, Hamish Hamilton, 1983.
Little Elephant's Moon, illustrated by Linda Birch. London, Hamish Hamilton, 1986.
Ritchie's Rabbit, illustrated by Vanessa Julian-Ottie. London, Hamish Hamilton, 1986; New York, Random House, 1987.
Finding Annabel, illustrated by Alan Marks. London, Hamish Hamilton, 1987.
Fishpie for Flamingoes, illustrated by Linda Birch. London, Hamish Hamilton, 1987.
The Fantora Family Files, illustrated by Tony Ross. London, Hamish Hamilton, 1988; New York, William Morrow, 1998.
The Strange Bird, illustrated by Linda Birch. London, Hamish Hamilton, 1988.
The Coronation Picnic, illustrated by Frances Wilson. London, Hamish Hamilton, 1989.
Bunk Bed Night, illustrated by Bernice McMullan. London, Dent, 1990.
My Grandmother's Stories: A Collection of Jewish Folk Tales, illustrated by Jael Jordan. New York, Knopf, 1990; London, Heinemann, 1990.
Nina's Magic, illustrated by Mary Norman. London, Hamish Hamilton, 1990.
Pink Medicine, illustrated by Bernice McMullan. London, Dent, 1990.
A Magic Birthday, illustrated by Adriano Gon. London, Simon & Schuster, 1992.
The Fantora Family Photographs, illustrated by Tony Ross. London, Hamish Hamilton, 1993; New York, Avon, 1999.
Golden Windows and Other Stories of Jerusalem. New York, HarperCollins, 1993; London, Heinemann, 1993.
Toey, illustrated by Duncan Smith. London, Heinemann, 1994.
The Return of Archibald Gribbet, illustrated by Sumiko Davies. Harlow, Longman, 1994.
Gilly the Kid, illustrated by Sue Heap. Brighton, Macdonald, 1995
Candle in the Dark, illustrated by Elsie Lennox. London, A&C Black, 1995
Little Swan, illustrated by Karen Popham. New York, Random House, 1995, London, Random House 1997.
Beauty and the Beast, illustrated by Louise Brierley. London, Hamish Hamilton, 1996
Kingfisher Book of Jewish Stories, illustrated by Jane Cope. London, Kingfisher, 1995.

The Magical Storyhouse, illustrated by Joanna Walsh. Brighton, Madonald, 1996.

Chalk and Cheese, illustrated by Adriano Gon. London, Transworld, 1996.

Cinderella, illustrated by Gwen Tourret. Brighton, Macdonald, 1996.

From Lullaby to Lullaby, illustrated by Kathryn Brown. New York, Simon and Schuster, 1997

Orchard Book of Favourite Opera Stories, various illustrators. London, Orchard, 1997.

Picasso Perkins, illustrated by Tony Ross. London, Transworld, 1997.

Louisa's Secret, illustrated by Karen Popham. London, Random House, 1997.

Louisa in the Wings, illustrated by Karen Popham. London, Random House, 1997

Louisa and Phoebe, illustrated by Karen Popham. London, Random House, 1997.

Blossom's Revenge, illustrated by Tony Ross. London, Transworld, 1997.

Silent Snow, Secret Snow. London, Hamish Hamilton, 1998.

Callie's Kitten, illustrated by Tony Ross. London, Transworld, 1998

Geejay the Hero, illustrated by Tony Ross. London, Transworld, 1998.

The Gingerbread House. Edinburgh, Barrington Stoke, 1998.

Lolly. London, Orchard, 1998.

PUBLICATIONS FOR ADULTS

Poetry

With Pauline Stainer, *Up on the Roof.* Huddersfield, Smith Doorstep, 1987.

Voices from the Dolls' House. Rockingham Press, 1994.

*

Theatrical Activities: Acted in *Four Degrees Over* by David Wood and John Gould, London, 1966.

Adèle Geras comments:

Although my work is published on the children's lists (or the list for young adults), I would hope that it could be enjoyed by everyone. I don't believe in writing for children as being an easy option—indeed I'd even say that the younger the child is and the shorter a text is, the more difficult it is to get it exactly right! All that white space around a word means it has to be the right word. Also it is worth remembering that short texts for young children are read aloud maybe thousands of times, and therefore need to have the power and resonance of the best poetry. Try reading a paragraph of an adult novel (the same paragraph!) over and over again, and see how it stands up.

I like writing for young adults because they have all the best qualities of both adults and small children. That is, they are grown-up enough to understand most things, and still young enough to believe in STORIES, in the magic of a wonderful tale, in justice, in other worlds, in ghosts, in the possibility of a better life for everyone . . . in everything that's around. . . .

*   *   *

Although she writes successfully for all ages, Adèle Geras is outstanding as a writer for young adults. One of her finest achievements is the "Egerton Hall" trilogy about girls growing up in the 1960s. She makes good use of her own experiences; born in Jerusalem, she travelled the world as a child, and then had an English, upper-middle-class girlhood, progressing from Roedean, a leading girls' boarding school, to Oxford. Her travels, Jewish heritage, and school and university days are all reflected in her work although they seldom feature in the same book. Her well-crafted short stories, in particular, show her interest in traditional tales. Other important influences are the sea and the past, both of which pervade much of her writing.

An early short story, "A Thousand Yards of Sea," told in the style of a traditional tale, which linked the origins of taffeta material to the sea, appeared in *Cricket,* the American children's magazine, in 1976, and was later extended and published as a picture book. Her first young adult novel, *The Girls in the Velvet Frame,* is set in Jerusalem in 1913 and features five sisters who plan to have their photograph taken as a present for their widowed mother. No word has come from their brother, Isaac, who has emigrated to the United States, and they decide that a copy of the photograph sent to the brother of their own rabbi, who is in New York, may help to find him.

There is much evocative detail in the descriptions of their home, the way in which clothes are passed down, the dressing up for special occasions, and above all the food. The sisters emerge from the pages of the book as very different personalities. Rifka the eldest, capable and responsible, starts work and begins to fall in love with David. Claudia is a feminist in the making, and through her eyes, the reader observes the preferential treatment given to males in this society. Although only eight, the imaginative and adventurous Naomi intends to go to America herself when she is sixteen; meanwhile, she weaves stories for the two youngest girls Dvora and Shoshie, who take great delight in feeding and playing with the rabbits belonging to the boy next door. The domestic details and the characters are given shape by the framework of the story; it begins and ends with a photograph. First, a neighbor shows them the photograph of her daughter, and then she in turn is shown their photograph and hears of the letter which has come from Isaac. The large cast of characters, youthful and adult, enables Geras to paint a very clear picture of the pre-First World War Jewish community in Jerusalem.

Voyage, in which the hardships facing Jewish immigrants to the United States in the early years of the twentieth century are described, lacks the strong focus of the earlier book. Events are seen mainly through the eyes of three unrelated girls: Mina, Golda, and Rachel. They are at different stages of growing up, but in order to give a realistic and wide-ranging picture of the people who might have sailed on a boat such as the S.S. Danzig, looking for a new and better life away from the persecution and hostility of central Europe, Geras has introduced other important characters, and the viewpoint is continually shifting. Golda's baby provides a unifying link between the many passengers, Jewish and non-Jewish, but the book is also held together by the images of the sea, described in all its manifestations at the end of each chapter. The book ends with the boat's arrival in a New York harbour and a final comment on the sea. "Blue enough," said Mina. "Not exactly what I expected, but blue enough."

The "Egerton Hall" trilogy, set in 1962, consists of *The Tower Room, Watching the Roses,* and *Pictures of the Night,* which tell the stories of three friends, Megan, Alice, and Bella, who meet at Egerton Hall School. Their lives parallel those of three fairy tale heroines—Rapunzel, the Sleeping Beauty, and Snow White. The events in the books overlap as each girl tells her own tale, looking backwards to the events and influences which have shaped her life and attitudes. The fairy tale parallels become more apparent as the trilogy proceeds, gradually moving through the momentous year when the girls fall in love and face their emerging sexuality, creating a powerful tour de force, outstanding in young adult literature.

Geras's short stories have appeared in a variety of anthologies and magazines. Her skills in this field can be sampled in three collections, *The Green behind the Glass, Daydreams on Video,* and *A Lane to the Land of the Dead.* The theme of the first is love, but the manner of the telling varies considerably. "Bounce the Moon," for example, has powerful sea images which provide a counterpoint to the story of Miranda and her mother; "The Whole Truth," set in North Borneo is a supernatural tale; and "Alice" foreshadows the fairy tale influences of the "Egerton Hall" trilogy. The title story in *Daydreams on Video* is set against the background of a pop music concert; "Vamp till ready or Zuleika Who?" in the same collection uses the author's experience of student drama activities at Oxford. "Plain Miss," a romantic story about an older woman, also has links to the "Egerton Hall" books. The stories in *A Lane to the Land of the Dead* are all about the supernatural: here the author's strong sense of place is used both as setting and inspiration. Manchester provides a rich and colourful background for stories that range from the funny "The Phantom of the Library" to the lingering horror of the title story, "A Lane to the Land of the Dead."

Storytelling of this quality retains the reader's attention. It is not surprising that when Walker Books decided to initiate their series of "Teenage Memoirs" and invite young adult authors to write about their own teenage experiences, Adèle Geras was one of the first authors to do so. In *Yesterday* (1992), she describes her three years at Oxford and incidentally reveals some of the sources and influences which she later used in her novels and short stories.

—Sheila Ray, updated by Felicity Trotman

GIBSON, William (Ford)

Nationality: American. **Born:** Conway, South Carolina, 17 March 1948. **Education:** University of British Columbia, B.A. 1977. **Family:** Married Deborah Jean Thompson in 1972; one daughter and one son. **Career:** Writer. **Awards:** Nebula award nomination, c. 1983, for short story "Burning Chrome"; Hugo award, Philadelphia Science Fiction Society Philip K. Dick Memorial award for best U.S. original paperback, Nebula award, and Porgie award for best paperback original novel in science fiction from *West Coast Review of Books,* all 1985, and Australian National Science Fiction Convention Ditmar award, all for *Neuromancer*; Nebula award nomination and Hugo award nomination, both for *Count Zero.* **Agent:** Martha Millard Literary Agency, 204 Park Avenue, Madison, New Jersey 07940, U.S.A.

PUBLICATIONS FOR YOUNG ADULTS

Novels

Neuromancer. New York, Ace, 1984.
Count Zero. New York, Arbor House, 1986.
Mona Lisa Overdrive. New York, Bantam, 1988.
With Bruce Sterling, *The Difference Engine.* London, Gollancz, 1990; New York, Bantam, 1991.
Virtual Light. New York, Bantam/Spectra, 1993.

Other

Contributor, *Shadows 4.* New York, Doubleday, 1981.
Contributor, *Universe 11.* New York, Doubleday, 1981.
Contributor, *Nebula Award Stories 17.* New York, Holt Rinehart, 1983.
Contributor, with John Shirley, Bruce Sterling, and Michael Swanwick, *Burning Chrome.* New York, Arbor House, 1986.
Contributor, *Mirrorshades: The Cyberpunk Anthology.* New York, Arbor House, 1986.
Dream Jumbo (text to accompany performance art by Robert Longo), produced Los Angeles, 1989.

*

Media Adaptations: *Johnny Mnemonic* (film), 1995.

Critical Studies: Entry in *Contemporary Literary Criticism,* Detroit, Gale, Volume 39, 1986; Volume 63, 1991.

*   *   *

The youthful, speeding, slangy world invented by William Gibson in *Neuromancer, Count Zero,* and *Mona Lisa Overdrive* has an irresistible appeal for the young-adult audience. In a Bladerunner-style future, these toughs survive in a world barely recognizable to adults, but predicated on the kinds of changes that television and computer technology have made familiar to teenagers. At the same time, elements of current culture are incorporated into these novels in such a way that they lurk beneath the surface, haunting the characters in much the same way that events like Vietnam and Watergate haunt the edges of many young adults' consciousness.

Gibson's plots reflect a vision in which the future world moves in real space at speeds mirroring computer speeds; in which the depersonalization of the computer world is completed by the longing of artificial intelligences to become persons; in which incidents, persons, and places become so dependent on one another for meaning that meaning becomes a gestalt. Travel is almost constant in these novels; the characters are as restless as computer cursors. Large portions of all three novels could be interpreted as chase scenes—complex, involving, metaphoric chases, but chases nonetheless. The characters whisk themselves from one impersonal environment to another, as Case does in *Neuromancer*; those who linger long enough to leave their mark on a space are in danger, as Bobby discovers in *Count Zero.* Their lack of personal place may account for their need to provide themselves with constant points of reference. The reader shares this search for place through a constant stream of allusions to his (the reader's) world.

Some provide simple coloring, such as the use of Rastafarian culture; others are critical moorings in the dizzy plot free-fall, such as references to the work of Joseph Cornell and the use of voodoo theology in *Count Zero*. In these plots, events may happen sequentially, but the reader and the characters experience them as one simultaneous rush. Only afterward are we and the characters able to sort out which events occurred concurrently and which were the result of cause and effect.

The characters who inhabit this literature are shaped by the same forces that shape today's youth. These speeding travelers are young and street-smart. Bobby Newmark, the cyberdeck cowboy of *Count Zero*, is typical. Bobby struggles to be tough and hip, to use the appropriate slang that will signal his belonging on the inner track. Like most of Gibson's human characters, he is engaged in an active pursuit of goals that he will understand only too late. Molly, the "hired gun" of *Neuromancer* and *Mona Lisa Overdrive*, is a slightly older and wiser version of this character; having protected herself as best she can with skills and weapons, she seeks further safety in studied ignorance. Desiring nothing, she hopes to become invulnerable. Typically, these tough punks are revealed to have both a moral sense and human feelings—if the reader can recognize them under the devil-may-care surface. Older characters, like Armitage in *Neuromancer* or the Finn in *Count Zero* are incomprehensible fanatics, some dangerous, some benign. Others, like Turner or Marly in *Count Zero* are destroyed by their essential humanity, never having learned to protect themselves. The artificial intelligences struggle to inherit this future earth from humanity, meek or otherwise.

This struggle is also a struggle to redefine the meaning of activity and passivity. Computers, having gained independence of thought, now seek to throw off their responsive role and take a directing part in humanity's future. This struggle and tension not only shapes the plots and characters, but also informs Gibson's prose style. Human characters express themselves in computer slang (even Bobby's nickname, Count Zero, is borrowed from "antique" computer jargon), and their conversations and thoughts are littered with words like "black ice" and "flat-lines," and imported Japanese terms. Contemplation is an activity for the artificial intelligences. Short, abrupt sentences convey the constant defensive responses of the human characters and move the plots along in a blinding rush of speed that gives the reader little more time for comprehension than the bewildered protagonists. Yet, young adults will recognize and embrace this slangy, confusing style, for it mirrors the reality of their own lives.

Gibson is not an author for the reluctant reader or for those who need their plots and prose straight up, but for the adventurous reader willing to be challenged by a not always pleasant view of humanity's future, a soul mate is waiting.

—Cathy Chauvette

GIOVANNI, Nikki (Yolande Cornelia Giovanni)

Nationality: American. **Born:** Nashville, Tennessee, 7 June 1943. **Education:** Fisk University, Nashville, Tennessee, 1960-61, 1964-67, B.A. (honors) in history, 1967; University of Pennsylvania Social Work School, Philadelphia; Columbia University School of the Arts, New York. **Family:** One son. **Career:** Poet, writer, lecturer. Assistant Professor of Black Studies, Queens College of the City University of New York, Flushing, 1968; Associate Professor of English, Rutgers University, Livingston College, New Brunswick, New Jersey, 1968-72; visiting Professor of English at Ohio State University, 1984; Professor of Creative Writing at Mount St. Joseph on the Ohio, 1985; Professor, Virginia Polytechnic Institute and State University, 1987—; Director, Warm Hearth Writer's Workshop, 1988—. Editorial Consultant, *Encore* magazine and *Encore American and Worldwide News,* Albuquerque, New Mexico; founder of publishing firm, Niktom Ltd., 1970; co-chair of Literary Arts Festival for State of Tennessee Homecoming, 1986; author of columns "One Woman's Voice," for Anderson-Moberg Syndicate of the *New York Times,* and "The Root of the Matter," in *Encore American and Worldwide News.* **Awards:** Ford Foundation grant, 1967; National Endowment for the Arts grant, 1968; Harlem Cultural Council grant, 1969; named one of ten most admired black women by the *Amsterdam News,* 1969; *Mademoiselle* award for outstanding achievement, 1971; Omega Psi Phi Fraternity award for outstanding contribution to arts and letters, 1971; Meritorious Plaque for Service, Cook County Jail, 1971; Prince Matchabelli Sun Shower award, 1971; life membership and scroll, National Council of Negro Women, 1972; National Association of Radio and Television Announcers award for best spoken word album, for *Truth Is on Its Way,* 1972; Woman of the Year Youth Leadership award, *Ladies' Home Journal,* 1972; National Book award nomination for *Gemini,* 1973; American Library Association commendation for *My House,* 1973; Cincinnati Chapter YWCA Woman of the Year, 1983; elected to Ohio Women's Hall of Fame, 1985; named Outstanding Woman of Tennessee, 1985; Post-Corbett Award, 1986; Ohioana Book Award, 1988; Woman of the Year, NAACP (Lynchburg chapter), 1989; Jeanine Rae Award for the Advancement of Women's Culture, 1995; Langston Hughes Award, 1996; awarded keys to numerous cities, including Lincoln Heights, Ohio, Dallas, Texas, and Gary, Indiana, all 1972, New York City, 1975, Buffalo, New York, and Cincinnati, Ohio, both 1979, Savannah, Georgia, and Clarksdale, Mississippi, both 1981, Miami, Florida, 1982, New Orleans, Louisiana, Monroe, Louisiana, Fort Lauderdale, Florida, and Los Angeles, California, all 1984; Honorary Doctorates: Wilberforce University, 1972, University of Maryland, Princess Anne Campus, 1974, Ripon University, 1974, Smith College, 1975, and Mount St. Joseph on the Ohio, 1983, Fisk University, 1988, Indiana University, 1991, Otterbein College, 1992, Widener University, 1993, Albright College, 1995, Cabrini College, 1995, and Allegheny College, 1997. **Address:** Department of English, Virginia Polytechnic Institute and State University, P.O. Box 0112, Blacksburg, Virginia 24063-0112, U.S.A.

PUBLICATIONS FOR YOUNG ADULTS

Poetry

Black Feeling, Black Talk. Detroit, Broadside Press, 1968.
Black Judgement. Detroit, Broadside Press, 1968.
Black Feeling, Black Talk/Black Judgement. New York, Morrow, 1970.
Poem of Angela Yvonne Davis. New York, Afro Arts, 1970.

Re:Creation. Detroit, Broadside Press, 1970.
My House, with foreword by Ida Lewis. New York, Morrow, 1972.
The Women and the Men. New York, Morrow, 1975.
Cotton Candy on a Rainy Day, with introduction by Paula Giddings. New York, Morrow, 1978.
Those Who Ride the Night Winds. New York, Morrow, 1983.
Sacred Cows . . . and Other Edibles. New York, Morrow, 1988.
The Selected Poems of Nikki Giovanni. New York, Morrow, 1996.
Love Poems. New York, Morrow, 1997.

Other

Editor, *Grandmothers: Poems, Reminiscences, and Short Stories about the Keepers of Our Traditions.* New York, Holt, 1994.
Racism 101. New York, Holt, 1994.
Editor, *Shimmy, Shimmy, Shimmy Like My Sister Kate: Looking at the Harlem Renaissance through Poems.* New York, Henry Holt, 1996.

Recordings: *Truth Is on Its Way,* Right-On Records, 1971; *Like A Ripple on a Pond,* Niktom, 1973; *The Way I Feel,* Atlantic Records, 1974; *Legacies: The Poetry of Nikki Giovanni,* Folkways Records, 1976; *The Reason I Like Chocolate,* Folkways Records, 1976; *Cotton Candy on a Rainy Day,* Folkways Records, 1978.

PUBLICATIONS FOR CHILDREN

Poetry

Spin a Soft Black Song: Poems for Children, illustrated by Charles Bible. New York, Hill & Wang, 1971; reprinted with illustrations by George Martin, Westport, Connecticut, Lawrence Hill, 1985; revised edition, New York, Farrar, Straus, 1987.
Ego-Tripping and Other Poems for Young People, illustrated by George Ford. Westport, Connecticut, Lawrence Hill, 1973.
Vacation Time: Poems for Children, illustrated by Marisabina Russo. New York, Morrow, 1980.
Knoxville, Tennessee, illustrated by Larry Johnson. New York, Scholastic, 1994.
The Genie in the Jar, illustrated by Chris Raschka. New York, Holt, 1996.
The Sun is So Quiet, illustrated by Ashley Bryan. New York, Holt, 1996.

PUBLICATIONS FOR ADULTS

Nonfiction

Gemini: An Extended Autobiographical Statement on My First Twenty-five Years of Being a Black Poet. Indianapolis, Bobbs-Merrill, 1971.
A Dialogue: James Baldwin and Nikki Giovanni, with James Baldwin. Philadelphia, Lippincott, 1973; London, Joseph, 1975.
A Poetic Equation: Conversations Between Nikki Giovanni and Margaret Walker, with Margaret Walker. Washington, D.C., Howard University Press, 1974.

Other

Editor, *Night Comes Softly: An Anthology of Black Female Voices.* Newark, New Jersey, Medic Press, 1970.
Editor, *Appalachian Elders: A Warm Hearth Sampler.* Blacksburg, Virginia, Pocahontas Press, 1991.
Author of foreword, *The Abandoned Baobob: The Autobiography of a Woman,* Chicago, Chicago Review Press, 1991.

*

Media Adaptations: *Spirit to Spirit: The Poetry of Nikki Giovanni* (television film, featuring the poet reading from her published works), Public Broadcasting Corporation, 1986.

Manuscript Collections: Mugar Memorial Library, Boston University, Massachusetts.

Biography: Entry in *Authors in the News,* Volume 1, Detroit, Gale, 1976; *Dictionary of Literary Biography,* Detroit, Gale, Volume 5: *American Poets since World War II,* 1980, Volume 41: *Afro-American Poets since 1955,* 1985.

Critical Studies: *Dynamite Voices I: Black Poets of the 1960s* by Don L. Lee, Broadside Press, 1971; *Modern Black Poets: A Collection of Critical Essays* edited by Donald B. Gibson, Prentice-Hall, 1973; *Understanding the New Black Poetry: Black Speech and Black Music as Poetic References* by Stephen Henderson, Morrow, 1973; entry in *Contemporary Literary Criticism,* Detroit, Gale, Volume 2, 1974, Volume 4, 1975, Volume 19, 1981, Volume 64, 1991; *Beautiful, Also, Are the Souls of My Black Sisters: A History of the Black Woman in America* by Jeanne Noble, Prentice-Hall, 1978; *Black Women Writers at Work* by Claudia Tate, Crossroad Publishing, 1983; entry in *Children's Literature Review,* Volume 6, Detroit, Gale, 1984; *Black Women Writers, 1950-1980: A Critical Evaluation* edited by Mari Evans, Doubleday, 1984; *Black Literature Criticism,* Detroit, Gale, 1992; *Nikki Giovanni* by Virginia Fowler, Boston, Twayne, 1992; *Conversations with Nikki Giovanni* by Virginia Fowler, Jackson, University Press of Mississippi, 1992.

*   *   *

Nikki Giovanni is a poet for persons young and old, a poet for persons of all races. And she is a songstress for children. Her songs are of the spirit. They concentrate on blackness, womanhood, and also on living. They beat the drums of Martin Luther King, Jr., drums of triumph and of pain, drums of peace. They celebrate the mother who doesn't care if she owns the whole world; her universe is her little son. They tell what it's like to eat fresh corn and okra and greens in the South in the summertime.

All of Giovanni's works may be enjoyed by the young adult. Those found in the children's section of the library are among her more joyous and lyrical. Young adults will respond to her references of growing up, to her dreams of running faster than any gazelle, outswimming any fish, and beating a falcon up to the top of the mountain.

Spin a Soft Black Song includes a variety of poems—poems about love and friendship, hopes and dreams. In "Poem for

Rodney,'' Rodney is always being asked what he is going to be when he grows up; he just thinks he'd like to grow up. In ''Poem for Debbie,'' we meet a young girl who is tall and bold, with sneakers to make her run faster. In ''If'' a young man thinks about being Matthew Henson and exploring the North Pole or the man in Harriet Tubman's life who gives her support on her journeys south. The illustrations of children in this book are all of black children, and some of the words are descriptive of the children's blackness. But most of the emotions, happy and sad, apply to all young people.

Ego-Tripping and Other Poems for Young incorporate black history, past and current, more than the former book. ''Poem for Black Boys'' asks where are the heroes for black boys and suggests that they play run-away-slave or Mau Mau rather than cowboys and Indians. ''Revolutionary Dreams'' speaks of militant dreams of blacks taking over America, stopping the riots and negotiating the peace. ''Revolutionary Music'' digs Sly and the Family Stone and James Brown. Other poems are not about race. ''Alone'' is about loneliness and about communicating with others—universal concerns. Again, the illustrations are of black people, with the addition of one white cop.

Giovanni gained widespread popularity with two early works, *Black Feeling, Black Talk* and *Black Judgement,* because of their strident and often angry verse. She made her poems accessible to young people through public readings at colleges and through best-selling recordings accompanied by gospel music. In much of these works, Giovanni focuses on the individual's search for love and acceptance, reflecting what she considers a major struggle in the black community. ''Nikki-Rosa,'' from *Black Judgement,* is often cited as her signature poem. It recounts her happy childhood, asserting that happiness depends on love rather than material possessions, that black love is black wealth.

The personal perspective of ''Nikki-Rosa'' is continued in her next work, *Re-Creation,* and in the essay collection, *Gemini: An Extended Autobiographical Statement on My First Twenty-five Years of Being a Black Poet.* These works, influenced by the birth of her son in 1969 and by her increasing affection for rhythm and blues, are less angry than her previous volumes. In them Giovanni views the black revolution more from a personal than a collective perspective and speaks to the need for change in order to address the possibilities of life. These works will have particular meaning to black youth, but they will also have meaning to all youth who are impatient for social change and who intend to devote energies to achieve it.

Those Who Ride the Night Winds is a collection of poems about people who have tried to affect change, who went against the status quo, who were willing to test their wings. Included are poems about Lorraine Hansberry, John Lennon, Billie Jean King, Charles White, Robert Kennedy, Rosa Parks. Lorraine Hansberry made it possible for all of us to look a little deeper. Robert Kennedy reminds us that trees should never be felled in the summer, before the promise is fulfilled.

Giovanni's poems are found in a number of popular anthologies, such as *Sing a Song of Popcorn: Every Child's Book of Poems* (selected by Beatrice Schenk de Regniers, et al., Scholastic Inc., New York, 1988) and *The Poetry of Black America: Anthology of the 20th Century* (edited by Arnold Adoff, Harper and Row, New York, 1973). These poems deserve to be read; they will be enjoyed in whichever book cover they are found.

—Mary Lystad

GIPSON, Fred(erick Benjamin)

Nationality: American. **Born:** Mason, Texas, 7 February 1908. **Education:** Mason High School, graduated 1926; University of Texas, Austin, 1933-37. **Family:** Married Tommie Eloise Wynn in 1940 (divorced 1964); two sons. **Career:** Farm and ranch hand, and clerk, 1926-33; reporter and columnist, Corpus Christi *Caller-Times,* San Angelo *Standard-Times,* and Paris *News,* all in Texas, 1938-40; associate editor, *True West* magazine, Austin, 1953-59; editorial director, *Frontier Times,* Bandera, Texas, 1958-59. President, Texas Institute of Letters, 1960. **Awards:** McMurray Bookshop award, Dallas, Texas, 1949, for *Hound-Dog Man,* and 1950, for *Recollection Creek;* Cokesbury Book Store award, Dallas, Texas, for children's book by Texas writer on Texas subject, 1956, for *The Trail-Driving Rooster;* Newbery Medal runner-up, 1957, Maggie award for Western book, 1958, and William Allen White Children's Book award, 1959, all for *Old Yeller;* First Sequoyah award, Oklahoma, 1959; Northwest Pacific award, 1959; lifetime fellowship to Texas Institute of Letters, 1970. **Died:** 14 August 1973.

PUBLICATIONS FOR YOUNG ADULTS

Fiction

Hound-Dog Man. New York, Harper, 1949.
The Home Place. New York, Harper, 1950; London, Joseph, 1951; abridged edition, as *Return of the Texan,* Edinburgh, Oliver and Boyd, 1962.
Recollection Creek. New York, Harper, 1955; revised edition, for children, 1959.
Old Yeller, illustrated by Carl Burger. New York, Harper, 1956; London, Hodder and Stoughton, 1957.
Savage Sam, illustrated by Carl Burger. New York, Harper, and London, Hodder and Stoughton, 1962.

Screenplays: *Old Yeller,* with William Tunberg, 1957; *Hound-Dog Man,* with Winston Miller, 1959; *Savage Sam,* with William Tunberg, 1962.

Television Play: *Brush Roper.*

Other

Fabulous Empire: Colonel Zack Miller's Story. Boston, Houghton Mifflin, 1946; as *Circles Round the Wagon,* London, Joseph, 1949.
Big Bend, with J. Oscar Langford. Austin, University of Texas Press, 1952.
Cowhand: The Story of a Working Cowboy. New York, Harper, 1953; London, Corgi, 1957.
The Cow Killers: With the Aftosa Commission in Mexico. Austin, University of Texas Press, 1956.
An Acceptance Speech. New York, Harper, 1960.
Fred Gipson before Old Yeller, edited by C. Richard King. Austin, Texas, Eakin Press, 1980.

PUBLICATIONS FOR CHILDREN

Fiction

The Trail-Driving Rooster. New York, Harper, 1955.
Little Arliss, illustrated by Ronald Himler. New York, Harper, 1978.
Curly and the Wild Boar, illustrated by Ronald Himler. New York, Harper, 1979.

*

Critical Study: *Fred Gipson* by Sam H. Henderson, Austin, Texas, Steck Vaughn, 1967; *Fred Gipson, Texas Storyteller* by Mike Cox, Austin, Texas, Shoal Creek, 1980.

* * *

In an author's note to his biography *Cowhand,* Fred Gipson wrote, "I am, by profession and by nature, a collector and writer of tales, and for me, a good tale, well told, is enough." This is an outlook that throughout his writing makes itself as unmistakable and clear as any of the rosy, storm-signalling sunsets or ringing hound-dog calls he describes in his books about boyhood adventures in the wilds of late nineteenth and early twentieth century Texas. For Gipson, the achievement of literary significance was not the thing. It was the good tale he was after. Using plain-talking, shoot-howdy language that gets simply to the beauty, humor, longing, or pain of a matter, Gipson wrote about what he knew: hard work, hard play, the way old folks tell stories, and boys, dogs, and other creatures in their natural habitats. Through the telling of the specifics of these things—the chase and kill of a coon hunt, a faithful dog in a fight, losing oneself in a starry sky, bucking against a mother's wishes, bringing home meat for the family—Gipson gets at basic desires that have meaning for young readers, things like independence, adventure, companionship, connection with nature, receiving recognition for one's accomplishments.

Also elemental in Gipson's work is the boyhood passage from innocence to experience, described by the philosophical music maker Fiddling Tom in *Hound-Dog Man:* "There's a time when a boy can lay his belly on the ground and feel the heartbeats of the earth coming up to him through the grass roots. That's his time to prowl. That's his time to smell the par-fume of the wild flowers, to hear the wind singing wild in his ears, to hurt with the want of knowing what's on the yonder side of the next ridge."

Old Yeller, Gipson's best known and well loved book, a Newbery Honor book which has won a majority of awards for which young people do the voting, best exemplifies Gipson's boy into man theme. Because Old Yeller the dog meets an untimely death, the sentimentality that can come with adulthood crystallizes that climactic event in the mind so that many remember *Old Yeller* as a tearjerker of a dog story. But if it were only that, young people would not find the meaning and relevance in it that they do. The reasons they cite for liking this bare bones coming-of-age story have to do with interest in the hard details of daily survival on the 1860s Texas frontier, like carrying water in a cowhide pail, marking dangerous wild hogs, or sewing up a wound with horse hair, and the exciting adventures and newly tried independence of the main character, Travis. *Old Yeller* is not essentially about a dog

that dies. It is about the young man he leaves behind. While Papa, along with most of the men in Salt Licks, is away driving a pooled herd of area cattle to Kansas markets, fourteen-year-old Travis gets a task enviable and romantic to most young readers: he is made man in charge until his father returns. Travis's companion through this trial is Old Yeller. The meat-stealing stray bravely proves his worth through fierce, life-threatening encounters and becomes a part of the family. As Travis's narrative unfolds, the early tone of little boy bravado and self-satisfied pride matures. Being man of the place entails more than the hard physical work of providing for and protecting the family. Travis learns about patience, discipline, restraint, and the unconditional caring required by family relationships.

Family and neighbor relationships are further tested in the sequel, *Savage Sam,* in which Travis, his feisty, comic-relief-providing younger brother Little Arliss, and a neighbor girl are captured by Apaches and carried away on a harrowing journey across the Texas plains. Other Gipson books with young adult themes are *Hound-Dog Man,* another coming-of-age/boy-dog companionship story about young Cotton who learns a number of life lessons when he and his friend Spud embark on a once-in-a-lifetime hunting trip with the good-hearted scoundrel Blackie Scantling; *Recollection Creek,* a humorous collection of episodes from an uproarious year in the life of the extended Creech family, as told by young Hopper Creech; and *Cowhand: The Story of a Working Cowboy,* a biography based on the life of west Texas cowboy Ed "Fat" Alford. *Little Arliss, Curly and the Wild Boar,* and *The Trail-Driving Rooster* are shorter, one-adventure tales for younger readers.

A Texan Mark Twain to some degree, Gipson, in writing so honestly and distinctly about an earlier time and a specific region, inevitably presents their inherent biases. His books are about a man's world, and unfortunately, his women characters, while clearly just as hard working, intelligent, and strong willed as his men, remain in the background, are often referred to as so-and-so's woman rather than by name, and are notable chiefly for their cooking abilities, for being pretty enough to frame for the mantel, or for their usefulness as a point of comparison for things weak, impractical, or confining. Ethnic slurs are also a part of his characters' vernacular. The collision of white and Native American cultures brought about by white man's westward expansion is an important underlying theme in *Savage Sam,* and the "Injun killing" in the book is a highly uncomfortable matter. This is offset only slightly by Travis's late realization that all creatures' lives are important and ". . .each of us would fight to keep them just as long as we could—and try to help those we loved to do the same." Through his well-told tales—tall ones and small ones—Gipson reminds us of society's slow, painful coming-of-age. Through the kinds of people we know—friends, enemies, family, and neighbors—he shows us, for better and for worse, what we have been. It is enough.

—Tracy J. Sukraw

GLENN, Mel

Nationality: American. **Born:** Zurich, Switzerland, 10 May 1943. **Education:** New York University, A.B. 1964; Yeshiva University,

M.S. 1967. **Family:** Married Elyse Friedman in 1970; two sons. **Career:** Peace Corps volunteer, Sierra Leone, West Africa, 1964-66; teacher, Junior High School 240, Brooklyn, New York, 1967-70; English teacher, Abraham Lincoln High School, Brooklyn, from 1970; author, from 1980. **Awards:** Best Books for Young Adults citation, American Library Association, and Golden Kite Honor Book, Society of Children's Book Writers, for *Class Dismissed!: High School Poems,* 1982; Christopher Award, for *Class Dismissed II,* 1982; Best Books for Young Adults citation, American Library Association, for *My Friend's Got This Problem, Mr. Candler,* 1992; Top Ten Best Books for Young Adults citation, American Library Association, and Edgar Allan Poe award nomination, Mystery Writers of America, for *Who Killed Mr. Chippendale?: A Mystery in Poems,* 1997; Best Books for Young Adults citation, American Library Association, for *The Taking of Room 114* and *Jump Ball,* 1998. **Address:** 4288 Bedford Ave., Brooklyn, New York 11229, U.S.A.

PUBLICATIONS FOR YOUNG ADULTS

Fiction

One Order to Go. New York, Clarion, 1984.

Poetry

Class Dismissed!: High School Poems, photographs by Michael J. Bernstein. New York, Clarion, 1982.
Class Dismissed II: More High School Poems, photographs by Michael J. Bernstein. New York, Clarion, 1986.
Back to Class, photographs by Michael J. Bernstein. New York, Clarion, 1988.
My Friend's Got This Problem, Mr. Candler, photographs by Michael J. Bernstein. New York, Clarion, 1991.
Who Killed Mr. Chippendale?: A Mystery in Poems. New York, Lodestar, 1996.
The Taking of Room 114: A Hostage Drama in Poems. New York, Lodestar, 1997.
Jump Ball: A Basketball Season in Poems. New York, Lodestar, 1997.

PUBLICATIONS FOR CHILDREN

Fiction

Play-by-Play. Clarion, 1986.
Squeeze Play: A Baseball Story. Clarion, 1989.

*

Critical Studies: "Back to Class Again" by Mel Glenn, in *ALAN Review,* March 1990, no. 3, 2-4; *Kirkus Reviews,* 15 August 1997; "Books for Adolescents: Interview" by Teri S. Lesesne, in *Journal of Adolescent and Adult Literacy,* March 1997, no. 6, 502-506; *Something About the Author,* Vol. 93, Detroit, Gale, 1997.

Mel Glenn comments:

I write to remember. I write to open up the lines of communication, to explain my past to myself and others. On a certain level we are all emotionally fourteen. Good writing can put us in touch with who we were and who we are.

I write because I want to remember how it felt not making the basketball team, worrying about my future, agonizing over final exams. If, because of what I have written some reader says "Oh, I've felt *exactly* like that" then I've succeeded in showing that we have all been touched by the same emotional brush.

Of late, I've been incorporating my poems into stories and have met with some success. I am still writing for teenagers; I am still teaching teenagers and have been in the classroom so long that one of my students asked whether I taught Fred Flintstone. My last book, *Jump Ball,* is a fictionalized version of our 1995 state championship team. One member of that team, Stephon Marbury, now plays in the NBA for the Minnesota Timberwolves. My next book will be about an Asian girl who works in the school library and has a secret life. It is tentatively titled, *Laura Li, Will You Marry Me?*

For those teens wishing to write, there is no substitute for just doing it. Keep a pencil handy and your minds open.

*   *   *

Mel Glenn's poetry collections highlight the trials and tribulations, the angst and anxiety, and the joys and wonders of adolescence. His poems echo the voices of young adults who are struggling in two separate worlds: the world of adults and the world of children. They do not possess full membership in either; hence, the frustration which is adolescence. Glenn's poems seem to capture the essence of the adolescent: the emotions which sometimes seem to run out of control, the changing relationships with parents and other adults as the adolescent struggles for independence, the myriad of decisions which need to be made.

Glenn refers to *Class Dismissed!* as his literary firstborn. Subtitled *High School Poems,* this first collection was to establish the format for the books to follow. The poems, each titled with the name of a fictitious student, are accompanied by Michael J. Bernstein's photographs of actual students. Reminiscent of Edgar Lee Masters's *Spoon River Anthology,* by which Glenn claims he may have been inspired, the poems are short, one page. While the language is spare, the poems reveal much. Each takes on the persona of an individual student. "Benjamin Haywood," for example, exhibits an outward cool which belies the uncertainties he hides within. "Hildy Ross" lies to her teacher about the bruise on her cheek; she cannot confide in him about her father's abuse. These poems are vignettes, allowing readers a glimpse into the very center of an individual before snapping shut.

Class Dismissed II: More High School Poems deals with topics such as getting the keys to the car, picking out the correct college, and finding a job. The voices of each of the students resonate with candor. It is as if Glenn were eavesdropping inside the heads of adolescents; here are their thoughts and feelings without any of the artifice. Simile and metaphor are present. In "Robert Ashford," parents pore over college catalogs as if they were picking out a summer camp while Robert wonders if he will ever have some say on the subject of college. "Vinnie Robustelli" describes his new sports car in terms so seductive the reader is led to believe that he is describing his steady girlfriend. "Amanda Butler" laments that her mother's notes on the refrigerator are their only means of conversations; they leave her cold. "Paul Hewitt" asks his English teacher if he has any books that deal with real life because he never plans on going hunting for white whales or living in the Dust Bowl. This sly use of humor is also a hallmark of Glenn's work.

Perhaps Glenn's ironic sense of the absurd is best evidenced in *Back to Class*. What sets this book aside is the inclusion of poems about teachers who reveal a great deal about their personal and professional lives. Mr. Winograd who teaches first period English wonders why people are able to identify him as an English teacher so easily when he is *outside* of the school. Does he have a verb for a vein, a noun for a nose, a fragment for a forehead he wonders? Wouldn't it be "a novel experience" if someone mistook him for a baseball player instead? Mr. Pressman who teaches fine arts marvels at his best creation to date, his six-year-old son, who is just now trying his own hand at drawing. Accounting teacher Ted Sage wonders about his net worth after all the years he has spent working in a system which is educationally bankrupt. The inclusion of the teachers and their points of view strengthens the collection as they provide an opportunity for adolescents to draw parallels between themselves and adults.

My Friend's Got This Problem, Mr. Candler is the fourth collection of high school poems. Mr. Candler, a fictitious high school counselor, takes readers through a typical week in his office. Readers watch as students and parents share their joy and anguish with Mr. Candler. One of the overriding themes of this collection is that there are two sides to every story. Glenn reinforces this theme in several ways. First, he provides poems about one situation from two or more perspectives. Maureen and Hugh McDermott each took Mr. Pettis's history exam. Maureen shares her exhilaration at her 92 percent on the test; she respects Pettis even though he made her work so hard. On the other hand, her brother Hugh (his score was 29 percent) hates history and dislikes Pettis as well. Here is one of the hard truths about school and teaching. Perhaps even more moving are the accounts given by parents and their children when they call or visit Mr. Candler. Matthew Egan sees Mr. Candler because he is having difficulty dealing with the pressure his father applies for him to get better grades. Mr. Egan sees things a bit differently. He grew up in a household where he was beaten for not doing better in school. From his point of view, he only wants what is best for his son, just the way his father wanted what was best. Another parent who refuses to give his name tells Candler that his daughter is lying when she talks about his abuse. He is just using discipline; Candler had better not interfere if he's smart.

Who Killed Mr. Chippendale?, with its strong storyline unifying the poems spoken by individual voices, marked a move toward plot in Glenn's writing. Centering on the murder of Tower High School English teacher Robert Chippendale, who is shot in the head while running around the school track early one morning, the individual voices telling the story include those of Chippendale, of guidance counselor Angela Falcone with whom he once had a relationship, the policeman investigating the case, the principal, and the students. Several of the voices belong to possible suspects. As in Glenn's other books, the poems reveal not only varying points of view about the murder, but also insights into the individual characters and their hidden lives. However, in comparison with the earlier books, with their powerful black and white photos of each speaker, the voices here are less compelling, less intimate, less fully developed and less involving.

The Taking of Room 114 is more successful in both plot and characterization. On the last day of school, Mr. Wiedermeyer, a long-time history teacher at Tower High, goes berserk and holds his senior history class hostage. A preliminary section introduces the reader to the characters and setting as students reveal their thoughts while waiting to pick up their yearbooks. The developing hostage situation is relayed through the voices of school officials, teachers, other students, bystanders, police investigators, news reporters, and strange notes from Mr. Wiedermeyer himself. The bulk of the book consists of groups of five poems spoken by each of the twenty students in the class, capturing their thoughts during each one of their four high school years, and on June 16th, the day of the crisis. These poems, which include some successful experiments with shaped verse, rap rhythms, and varying type faces, provide insight into the complex lives and interrelationships of each one of these students. The students seem real, as if you went to school with them. A final section reveals what may have triggered Mr. Wiedermeyer's breakdown.

In *Jump Ball: A Basketball Season in Poems,* the voices of players, teachers, parents, fans, and bystanders tell what happens when the bus of the Tower High basketball team goes out of control on an icy road. According to *Kirkus Reviews,* "Indifferent adults and the imminent crushing of so many hoop dreams give the story a bitter, discouraging cast."

Glenn's poems reach out to adolescents, even those who are not ordinarily readers of poetry. One of his greatest contributions to the field of young adult literature is that he has made poetry accessible to more readers, especially male readers. The honesty of the poems and the emotions Glenn conveys make for crisp reading. The simple language allows readers to clearly identify the themes of the works. Glenn does not avoid unpleasant topics; he addresses them head-on. The refreshing candor and range of personae are part of the reason for his continued popularity with adolescents and those who work with adolescents. Glenn's fictional students and teachers should help readers as they deal with their own personal dilemmas of adolescence. In his more recent works the combination of strong story lines with the poems provides an interesting mixing of genres, as his subtitles suggest.

—Teri S. Lesesne, updated by Linnea Hendrickson

GODFREY, William. *See* **CHRISTOPHER, John.**

GOLDING, William (Gerald)

Nationality: British. **Born:** St. Columb, Cornwall, 19 September 1911. **Education:** Marlborough Grammar School; Brasenose College, Oxford, B.A. 1935, M.A. 1960. **Military Service:** Served in the Royal Navy, 1940-45; became rocket ship commander. **Family:** Married Ann Brookfield in 1939; one son and one daughter. **Career:** Writer. Was a settlement house worker after graduating from Oxford University; writer, actor, and producer in small theatre companies, 1934-40, 1945-54; taught English and philosophy, 1939-40, schoolmaster, 1945-61, both at Bishop Wordsworth's

School, Salisbury, Wiltshire; Visiting Professor and writer in residence, Hollins College, Virginia, 1961-62. **Awards:** Commander, Order of the British Empire, 1965; James Tait Black Memorial Prize, 1980, for *Darkness Visible;* Booker McConnell Prize, 1981, for *Rites of Passage;* Nobel Prize for Literature, 1983, for body of work; D.Litt., University of Sussex, Brighton, 1970; University of Kent, Canterbury, 1974; University of Warwick, Coventry, 1981; Oxford University, 1983, the Sorbonne, Paris, 1983; LL.D.: University of Bristol, 1984. Honorary Fellow, Brasenose College, 1966. Fellow, 1955, and Companion of Literature, 1984, Royal Society of Literature. C.B.E. (Commander, Order of the British Empire), 1966. Knighted, 1988. **Died:** 19 June 1993.

PUBLICATIONS

Fiction

Lord of the Flies. London, Faber, 1954; New York, Coward McCann, 1955.
The Inheritors. London, Faber, 1955; New York, Harcourt, 1962.
Pincher Martin. London, Faber, 1955; as *The Two Deaths of Christopher Martin,* New York, Harcourt, 1957.
Free Fall. London, Faber, 1959; New York, Harcourt, 1960.
The Spire. London, Faber, and New York, Harcourt, 1964.
The Pyramid. London, Faber, and New York, Harcourt, 1967.
Darkness Visible. London, Faber, and New York, Farrar, Straus, 1979.
Rites of Passage. London, Faber, and New York, Farrar, Straus, 1980.
The Paper Men. London, Faber, and New York, Farrar, Straus, 1984.
Close Quarters. London, Faber, and New York, Farrar, Straus, 1987.
Fire Down Below. London, Faber, and New York, Farrar, Straus, 1989.

Short Stories

The Scorpion God. London, Faber, 1971; New York, Harcourt, 1972.

Plays

The Brass Butterfly, adaptation of his story "Envoy Extraordinary" (produced London, 1958; New York, 1970). London, Faber, 1958; Chicago, Dramatic Publishing Company, n.d.

Radio Plays: *Miss Pulkinhorn,* 1960; *Break My Heart,* 1962.

Poetry

Poems. London, Macmillan, 1934; New York, Macmillan, 1935.

Other

Contributor, *Sometimes, Never.* New York, Ballantine, 1956.
The Hot Gates, and Other Occasional Pieces. London, Faber, and New York, Harcourt, 1965.
Talk: Conversations with William Golding, with Jack I. Biles. New York, Harcourt, 1970.
A Moving Target (essays). London, Faber, and New York, Farrar, Straus, 1982.
Nobel Lecture. Leamington Spa, Warwickshire, Sixth Chamber, 1984.
An Egyptian Journal. London, Faber, 1985.

*

Media Adaptations: *Pincher Martin* (radio play), British Broadcasting Corp., 1958; *Lord of the Flies* (film), Continental, 1963, and Castle Rock Entertainment, 1990.

Biography: Entry in *Dictionary of Literary Biography,* Volume 15: *British Novelists, 1930-1959,* Detroit, Gale, 1983; entry in *Dictionary of Literary Biography Yearbook: 1983,* Detroit, Gale, 1984.

Bibliography: *William Golding: A Bibliography* by R.A. Gekoski and David Hughes, London, Deutsch, 1990.

Critical Studies: *A Review of English Literature* by Peter Green, London, Longman, 1960; *The Modern Novel* by Walter Allen, New York, Dutton, 1964; *William Golding* by Samuel Hynes, New York, Columbia University Press, 1964; *The Art of William Golding* by Bernard S. Oldsey and Stanley Weintraub, New York, Harcourt, 1965; *William Golding: A Critical Study* by James R. Baker, New York, St. Martin's, 1965, and *Critical Essays on William Golding* edited by James R. Baker, Boston, Hall, 1988; *The Modern Confessional Novel* by Peter M. Axthelm, New Haven, Connecticut, Yale University Press, 1967; *William Golding* by Bernard F. Dick, New York, Twayne, 1967; *William Golding: A Critical Study* by Mark Kinkead-Weekes and Ian Gregor, London, Faber, 1967, New York, Harcourt, 1968, revised edition, Faber, 1984; *The Tragic Past* by David Anderson, Louisville, Kentucky, John Knox Press, 1969; *William Golding* by Leighton Hodson, Edinburgh, Oliver and Boyd, 1969, New York, Putnam, 1971; *The Novels of William Golding* by Howard S. Babb, Columbus, Ohio State University Press, 1970; *Harvest of a Quiet Eve: The Novel of Compassion* by James Gindin, Bloomington, Indiana University Press, 1971; entry in *Contemporary Literary Criticism,* Detroit, Gale, Volume 1, 1973, Volume 2, 1974, Volume 3, 1975, Volume 8, 1978, Volume 10, 1979, Volume 18, 1981, Volume 27, 1984; *William Golding: The Dark Fields of Discovery* by Virginia Tiger, London, Calder & Boyars, and Atlantic Highlands, New Jersey, Humanities Press, 1974; *Number and Nightmare: Forms of Fantasy in Contemporary Fiction* by Jean E. Kennard, Hamden, Connecticut, Archon Books, 1975; *William Golding* by Stephen Medcalf, London, Longman, 1975; *William Golding: Some Critical Considerations* edited by Jack I. Biles and Robert O. Evans, Lexington, University Press of Kentucky, 1979; *Of Earth and Darkness: The Novels of William Golding* by Arnold Johnston, Columbia, University of Missouri Press, 1980; *A View from the Spire: William Golding's Later Novels* by Don Crompton, Oxford, Blackwell, 1985; *William Golding Novels: A Casebook 1954-1967* edited by Norman Page, London, Macmillan, 1985; *William Golding: The Man and His Books: A Tribute on His 75th Birthday* edited by John Carey, London, Faber, 1986, New York, Farrar, Straus, 1987; *William Golding: A Structural Reading of His Fiction* by Philip Redpath, London, Vision Press, 1986; *William Golding: A Study* by V.V. Subbarao, London, Oriental University Press, 1987; *The Novels of William Golding* by Stephen Body, Brighton, Sussex, Harvester Press, and New York, St. Martin's Press, 1988; *William Golding* by James Gindin, London, Macmillan, and New York, St. Martin's Press, 1988; *William Golding Revisited: A Collection of Original Essays* edited by B.L. Chakoo, New Delhi, Arnold, 1989;

The Modern Allegories of William Golding by L.L. Dickson, Tampa, University of South Florida Press, 1990.

*   *   *

Because William Golding's *Lord of the Flies* and *The Inheritors* frequently appear in American high school English curricula, along with Knowles's *A Separate Peace* or Salinger's *Catcher in the Rye,* Golding is sometimes considered a young adult novelist or a science fiction writer. Neither of these genres really fits the majority of Golding's novels, however, which have more in common with the ethical romances of Hawthorne or Melville than Judy Blume's books. Even Goldings two early works suggest a greater complexity since in each the mythic archetypal qualities represent symbolic patterns outside their texts—typical of Golding—rather than within, as is frequently the case with adolescent novels. Also, unlike most young adult novels or science fiction, Golding's characters and narrative situations concretely portray spiritual and moral assumptions in conflict: Golding is a Christian novelist with an awareness of the spiritual and ethical dimension of cultural forces.

Lord of the Flies was Golding's first published novel after four previous attempts. Set in the near future during wartime, the adolescent boys on Golding's island revert to atavistic tribal and later savage impulses in the manner of Jack London. The values that the boys have been raised by, the rationality of preparing for rescue, providing for shelter, and caring for the very young are nothing compared to their desire to hunt, to rule autocratically, or to kill a scapegoat. Ralph's Apollonian rationality is only preserved from the Dionysian hunters by the ironic *deus ex machina* of a warship and a uniformed officer.

The Inheritors shows a similar clash in pre-history, in which a Neanderthal extended family is supplanted by a Cro-Magnon tribe. Golding, faithful to what was known about the Neanderthals when he composed the novel, portrays them initially as caring, compassionate, communal—Edenlike inhabitants of our genetic past. They are discovered by, and in turn learn from the Cro-Magnons who stalk them and are eventually led by example into selfishness and sin. Lok, the early Neanderthal point-of-view character, wills his own death in an effort to join the others of his group, as a new point-of-view character, Tuami, of the "new people" takes over, describing the bleak voyage as Eden is lost once again. *The Inheritors* demands more reader participation than *Lord of the Flies* does. Lok is an unreliable narrative agent, and so too is Tuami. The shift between point-of-view characters is a gap the reader must fill. As Golding's career progressed, he demanded more and more of readers to determine the meaning behind his novels.

In *Pincher Martin,* a novel of memories and dreams, Christopher Hadley Martin, winds up living a fantasy of survival after his ship is torpedoed. The novel, much like Ambrose Bierce's "Occurrence at Owl Creek Bridge," shows Christopher imagining his survival on a rock island in the middle of the ocean. Not until the novel's end is the reader certain that Christopher's story is a fantasy of survival by a man unable to accept his death. Christopher's disjointed memories and fantasies portray him as an adult version of Jack from *Lord of the Flies,* a man who must destroy those whose lives represent an altruism or goodness foreign to his nature. Christopher's hell is living in his own value system. He is the total

opposite of Lok in *The Inheritors,* who accepts death and chooses it as a natural consequence of life.

Like *Pincher Martin, Free Fall* is a "memory" novel and has its artist-narrator, Sammy Mountjoy, examine episodes from his past to determine when he lost his freedom. The answer is not provided by his background in either the slums or a concentration camp, but his college seduction of a young girl, Beatrice, as he barters her sanity for his pleasure. Unlike Golding's previous novels, *Free Fall* utilizes sets of polarized characters demonstrating values throughout its episodes, although they are inadequately represented therein.

Set in the Middle Ages, *The Spire* is the story of Jocelyn, dean of a cathedral, whose goal is to erect a 400-foot spire on the cathedral before his death. The problem with this goal is that neither the foundation nor the ground on which the cathedral rests will support such a spire. Jocelyn, in pursuing his quest, the result of what he considers a divine vision, entails sacrifice and risk, and though the spire is erected for the greater glory of God, its construction causes sacrifice of others, treachery, and murder; it represents Jocelyn's vicarious sexuality and will as well as divine glory. With each step, the costs and sacrifices of building the spire mount, accentuating Jocelyn's blind willfulness in carrying out his priestly duties. The consequences of Jocelyn's choices are presented with the artistic economy of a Greek tragedy in this powerful novel.

The three episodes covering about thirty years in *The Pyramid* are tied together by Oliver, the narrator, and the stratified provincial town, appropriately named Stilbourne, in which his family lives. In its three sections *Pyramid* emphasizes social divisions in a story about sexual initiation and class and in two stories shows the inadequate call of art through characters in theatre and music. In *Pyramid* the narrative center does not hold, however. A similar problem occurs in a much more ambitious novel, *Darkness Visible,* also divided into three sections. The first part deals with Matty Windrove, a child burned in the Blitz of World War II, whose parents are unknown; the second deals with Sophy Stanhope and her sister, raised by a father and a series of his mistresses; the third deals with the interaction of these characters, where Sophy as terrorist kills Matty. Matty and Sophy have a combined identity, one representing feeling and the other intellect. Neither is a successful human being because of this; each represents social forces of the 1960s and 1970s that Golding detests. Because of the symbolic and allegorical density of the novel, and because Matty at best attracts pity and Sophy disgust, even horror, *Darkness Visible* is a difficult novel to enter.

Golding's best novel since *The Spire, Rites of Passage* is composed of two narratives: the upper-class Edmund Talbot's journal addressed to his patron-godfather, and an extended letter by the Reverend James Colley to his sister. Both deal with life onboard the *Britannia,* bound for the Antipodes near the end of the Napoleonic era. The ship is a microcosm of shifting British society, which the snobbish Talbot explores from the top and Colley from the middle, looking up. The motive for the action is the discovery of the reasons for Colley's death, shame caused by others, and Colley's own nature.

The familiar dichotomies of Golding—Apollonian reasonableness and Dionysian feeling—are in part represented by the narrators and in the spiritual testing and measurement of person and class, in a time of real and metaphoric translation.

The Paper Men hopes to be a serious novel about writers and their critics, and art and its relation to life; however, none of the penetration or the humor of these authors results. The writer, Sir Wilfred Barclay, is somewhat limited, and the American would-be biographer, Rick L. Tucker, is caricature beyond belief. Better representation of both by Golding would have made for a dynamic novel, although the book has two memorable moments: Barclay's shooting of Tucker and Tucker's shooting of Barclay.

Surprising for a writer who loves the novel because no other medium exists in which readers may "live for so long and so intimately with a character" is that Golding should produce so few sympathetic characters. Perhaps the essential conflict in Golding is between scientific pessimism and what spiritual optimism science chooses to ignore.

—Craig W. Barrow

GORDIMER, Nadine

Nationality: South African. **Born:** Springs, Transvaal, 20 November 1923. **Education:** Attended convent school, and the University of the Witwatersrand, Johannesburg. **Family:** Married 1) Gerald Gavronsky in 1949 (divorced, 1952), one daughter; 2) Reinhold H. Cassirer in 1954, one son. **Career:** Writer. Ford Foundation visiting professor, under auspices of Institute of Contemporary Arts, Washington, D.C., 1961; lecturer, Hopwood awards, University of Michigan, Ann Arbor, 1970; writer in residence, American Academy in Rome, 1984; has also lectured and taught writing at Harvard (1969), Princeton (1969), Northwestern (1969), Columbia (1971), and Tulane universities; presenter, *Frontiers* television series, 1990. **Awards:** W.H. Smith & Son Literary award, 1961, for short story collection *Friday's Footprint, and Other Stories;* Thomas Pringle award, 1969, James Tait Black Memorial Prize, 1972, for *A Guest of Honour;* Booker Prize for Fiction, National Book League, 1974, for *The Conservationist;* Grand Aigle d'Or (France), 1975; CNA award, 1975; Honorary Member, American Academy of Art and Sciences, 1980; Neil Gunn fellowship, Scottish Arts Council, 1981; Common Wealth award for Distinguished Service in Literature, 1981; Modern Language Association of America award, 1981; Premio Malaparte (Italy), 1985; Nelly Sachs Prize (Germany), 1985; Honorary Fellow, Modern Language Association (U.S.A.), 1985; Bennett award (U.S.A.), *Hudson Review,* 1986; Commandeur de l'Ordre des Arts et des Lettres (France), 1986; Royal Society of Literature Benson medal, 1990. D.Litt., University of Leuven, 1980, Smith College, City College of the City University of New York, and Mount Holyoke College, all 1985, and honorary degrees from Harvard University and Yale University, both 1987, and New School for Social Research, 1988; University of York, 1987; Cambridge University, 1992; Nobel Prize for literature, 1991. **Agent:** Russell & Volkening, Inc., 50 West 29th St., New York, New York 10001, U.S.A.

PUBLICATIONS

Novels

The Lying Days. London, Gollancz, and New York, Simon & Schuster, 1953.
A World of Strangers. London, Gollancz, and New York, Simon & Schuster, 1958.

Occasion for Loving. London, Gollancz, and New York, Viking, 1963.
The Late Bourgeois World. London, Gollancz, and New York, Viking, 1966.
A Guest of Honour. New York, Viking, 1970; London, Cape, 1971.
The Conservationist. London, Cape, 1974; New York, Viking, 1975.
Burger's Daughter. London, Cape, and New York, Viking, 1979.
July's People. New York, Viking, 1981.
A Sport of Nature. London, Cape, and New York, Knopf, 1987.
My Son's Story. London, Bloomsbury, and New York, Farrar, Straus, 1990.
None to Accompany Me. New York, Farrar, Straus, and Giroux, 1994.
Harald, Claudia, and Their Son Duncan. London, Bloomsbury, 1996.
The House Gun. New York, Farrar, Straus and Giroux, 1998.

Short Stories

Face to Face. Johannesburg, Silver Leaf Books, 1949.
The Soft Voice of the Serpent, and Other Stories. New York, Simon & Schuster, 1952; London, Gollancz, 1953.
Six Feet of the Country. London, Gollancz, and New York, Simon & Schuster, 1956.
Friday's Footprint, and Other Stories. London, Gollancz, and New York, Viking, 1960.
Not for Publication, and Other Stories. London, Gollancz, and New York, Viking, 1965.
Penguin Modern Stories 4, with others. London, Penguin, 1970.
Livingstone's Companions. New York, Viking, 1971; London, Cape, 1972.
Selected Stories. London, Cape, 1975; New York, Viking, 1976; as *No Place Like: Selected Stories,* London, Penguin, 1978.
Some Monday for Sure. London, Heinemann Educational, 1976.
A Soldier's Embrace. London, Cape, and New York, Viking, 1980.
Town and Country Lovers. Los Angeles, Sylvester & Orphanos, 1980.
Something Out There. London, Cape, and New York, Viking, 1984.
Crimes of Conscience. London, Heinemann, 1991.
Jump and Other Stories. New York, Farrar, Straus, 1991.
Why Haven't You Written?; Selected Stories, 1950-1972. New York, Penguin, 1992.

Other

Editor, with Lionel Abrahams, *South African Writing Today.* London, Penguin, 1967.
African Literature: The Lectures Given on This Theme at the University of Cape Town's Public Summer School, February, 1972. Cape Town, Board of Extra Mural Studies, University of Cape Town, 1972.
The Black Interpreters: Notes on African Writing. Johannesburg, Spro-Cas/Ravan, 1973.
On the Mines, photographs by David Goldblatt. Cape Town, Struik, 1973.
What Happened to Burger's Daughter; or, How South African Censorship Works, with others. Johannesburg, Taurus, 1980.
Lifetimes Under Apartheid, photographs by David Goldblatt. London, Cape, and New York, Knopf, 1986.
Reflections of South Africa, edited by Kirsten Egebjerg and Gillian Stead Eilersen. Herning, Denmark, Systime, 1986.
The Essential Gesture: Writing, Politics and Places, edited and introduced by Stephen Clingman. New York, Knopf, 1988.

Conversations with Nadine Gordimer, edited by Nancy Topping Bazin and Marilyn Dallman Seymour. Jackson, University Press of Mississippi, 1990.

Three in a Bed: Fiction, Morals, & Politics. Bennington, Vermont, Bennington College, 1991.

Writing and Being. Cambridge, Harvard University Press, 1995.

Television Plays and Documentaries: *A Terrible Chemistry,* (*Writers and Places* series), 1981 (UK); *Choosing for Justice: Allan Boesak,* with Hugo Cassirer, 1985 (USA and UK); *Country Lovers, A Chip of Glass Ruby, Praise,* and *Oral History* (all in *The Gordimer Stories* series), 1985 (USA); *Frontiers* series, 1990 (UK).

Contributor to *The Heinemann Book of Contemporary African Short Stories,* London, Heinemann Educational, 1992; *Best Short Stories of 1991, 1992, 1993,* and numerous other anthologies.

*

Theatrical Activities: Director, with Hugo Cassirer, *Choosing for Justice: Allan Boesak* (TV), 1985.

Bibliography: *Nadine Gordimer, Novelist and Short Story Writer: A Bibliography of Her Works* by Racilia Jilian Nel, Johannesburg, University of the Witwatersrand, 1964.

Critical Studies: *Nadine Gordimer* by Robert F. Haugh, New York, Twayne, 1974; *Nadine Gordimer* by Michael Wade, London, Evans, 1978; *Nadine Gordimer* by Christopher Heywood, Windsor, Berkshire, Profile, 1983; *The Novels of Nadine Gordimer: Private Lives/Public Landscapes* by John Cooke, Baton Rouge, Louisiana State University Press, 1985; *The Novels of Nadine Gordimer: History from the Inside* by Stephen Clingman, London, Allen & Unwin, 1986; *Nadine Gordimer* by Judie Newman, London, Macmillan, 1988; entry in *Contemporary Literary Criticism,* Detroit, Gale, Volume 3, 1975, Volume 5, 1976, Volume 7, 1977, Volume 10, 1979, Volume 18, 1981, Volume 33, 1985, Volume 51, 1989; *Critical Essays on Nadine Gordimer* edited by Rowland Smith, Boston, Hall, 1990.

*   *   *

There is nothing easy about Nadine Gordimer's fiction. Her characters, themes, narrative strategies, and—for one who is not South African—even her vocabulary are complicated. The difficulty of her texts arises naturally from the shaky, troubled historical ground she visits again and again in her stories: "Apartheid. . .the dirtiest social swindle the world has ever known," as she states in *Burger's Daughter.*

Burger's Daughter, the Gordimer novel most concerned with the young-adult problem of establishing a consistent set of values, was published in 1979, just three years after the infamous Soweto Uprising, a benchmark in modern South African history. When some fifteen thousand black schoolchildren assembled in Soweto on June 16, 1976, to protest the enforced use of Afrikaans (the language of their oppressors) in their schools, they were met with brutal suppression. In the year-long hostilities that followed, hundreds of blacks were killed. Significantly, the original protest was directed not only at the ruling white class, but also at black parents who, it seemed to the children, had to some extent colluded in their own subordination by passively accepting their degraded roles. It was the height of the Black Consciousness movement when even the authenticity of white, liberal commitment to black equality—like Gordimer's—was being questioned. Apartheid, the policy undergirding white supremacy, was being turned on its head as militant blacks insisted on a new kind of separatism, one in which blacks were dominant.

The Black Consciousness movement and its culminating event, the Soweto Revolt, profoundly affected Gordimer. She found the generational aspects of the conflict—children turning on their parents—particularly upsetting. Also, the betrayal by the blacks of white liberals like herself who had spent their lives working for equity between the races disturbed her. Yet she could certainly grasp the arguments of the Black Consciousness activists and even see the need for their firm self-assertion. She was thus forced to examine her own conscience regarding the role whites should expect to play in liberating black South Africans and even in liberating themselves from the collective guilt of their race. *Burger's Daughter* is the site of that self-examination, for it centers on the conflicts, personal and historical, that arise from this period in the life of Gordimer and South Africa.

Focusing on the generational conflict between young Rosa Burger and her father, Lionel, the novel examines apartheid and its ideological opposite, Black Consciousness, through Rosa's developing personality. Daughter of a doctor whose dedication to the South African Communist Party lands him, time and again, in prison where he eventually dies while serving a life sentence, Rosa becomes, in effect, an extension of her father. As a child and adolescent, she is able to reach people and places that her father cannot in order to deliver Party messages. She furthermore is absorbed into the communal life chosen for her by both parents. Consequently, she becomes subject to the loss of privacy and individual attention that such communality entails.

For a time, Rosa "defects" from her father's influence. Ironically though, she flees to France and the Bohemian digs of her father's ex-wife, Katya. Thus she has escaped only to be united with another extension of her father—this time from his past. In France she experiences a community of a different sort, one committed to the trivialities of everyday life rather than the apocalyptic vision of Marxism. But she also encounters a lover, Bernard, the one person who (although married to another) declares, "You are the dearest thing in the world to me." Before Rosa and Bernard are able to carry out their plans for Rosa's permanent defection to Paris, Rosa encounters Baasie—a black, who, as a boy, was treated as a son by the Burgers and who was Rosa's closest childhood friend until she lost track of him after her father's death—and her past catches up with her, turns her around, and sends her back to South Africa where she lives out her own version of her father's social commitment.

From the opening of the novel outside the prison where Rosa's mother is incarcerated the reader assumes the posture of a surveillant, although at first it is not clear what we are watching for. The story progresses erratically, sometimes through the words of a government watchdog, other times by way of Rosa's private notes to a long-lost roommate/analyst, sometimes possibly via her father's biographer, eventually through her direct address to her dead father. Picking our way among these discordant voices, we come to realize that what we are seeking is an integrated Rosa, just as she is.

We watch and listen to see if she will devote herself to her parents' dream of a future, integrated, socialized South Africa at the expense of her own private need for an intimate, exclusive relationship. Before the conclusion of the novel Rosa ends up in prison, but in the meantime she answers both the public and private demands of her nature.

Besides the various narrators or recorders Gordimer employs, her mode of providing background information is eccentric. She releases details into the plot piecemeal, almost surreptitiously, so that Rosa—and through Rosa, her father—comes to us in fragments. For example, we learn that Rosa's brother has died; only later do we realize that he has drowned; later still that he drowned in the family's private swimming pool.

This novel requires close, serious attention, but the rewards for the diligent reader are great. Not only does it absorb one in the most private aspects of Rosa Burger's life, it involves the reader in a twenty-five-year period of South African history. That history in many ways mirrors the history of Black civil rights in the United States, a period when our social consciences were stripped bare.

—Mary Lowe-Evans

GRAAF, Peter. *See* **CHRISTOPHER, John.**

GRAHAM, Lorenz (Bell)

Nationality: American. **Born:** New Orleans, Louisiana, 27 January 1902. **Education:** the University of Washington, Seattle, 1921; University of California, Los Angeles, 1923-24; Virginia Union University, Richmond, 1934-36, B.A. 1936; Columbia University, New York; New York University. **Family:** Married Ruth Morris in 1929; two daughters and two sons. **Career:** Teacher, Monrovia College, Liberia, 1924-29, and Richmond Adult Schools, Virginia, 1930-33; educational adviser, Civilian Conservation Corps, Virginia and Pennsylvania, 1936-42; housing manager, Newport News Housing Authority, Virginia, 1942-46; real estate salesman and building contractor, Long Island, New York, 1946-49; social worker, Queens Federation of Churches, New York, 1948-56; probation officer, Los Angeles County, California, 1957-67; lecturer, California State University, Pomona, 1970-78. **Awards:** Thomas Alva Edison Foundation special citation for *The Ten Commandments;* Charles W. Follett award, 1958, and Child Study Association of America award, 1959, both for *South Town;* Association for Study of Negro Life and History award, 1959; Los Angeles City Council award, 1966; Vassie D. Wright award, 1967; Southern California Council on Literature for Children and Young People award for significant contribution to the field of literature for young people, 1968; first prize from *Book World,* 1969, for *Whose Town?;* California Association of Teachers of English citation, 1973; Martin Luther King award from Southern California region of Christian Church, 1975; *Boston Globe-Horn Book*

award, and Children's Book Showcase award, both 1976, both for *South Town.* D.H.L.: Virginia University, 1983. **Died:** 11 September 1989.

PUBLICATIONS FOR YOUNG ADULTS

Fiction

South Town. Chicago, Follett, 1958.
North Town. New York, Crowell, 1965.
Whose Town? New York, Crowell, 1969.
Carolina Cracker. Boston, Houghton Mifflin, 1972.
Detention Center. Boston, Houghton Mifflin, 1972.
Stolen Car. Boston, Houghton Mifflin, 1972.
Runaway. Boston, Houghton Mifflin, 1972.
Return to South Town. New York, Crowell, 1976.

PUBLICATIONS FOR CHILDREN

Fiction

Tales of Momolu, illustrated by Letterio Calapai. New York, Reynal, 1946.
I, Momolu, illustrated by John Biggers. New York, Crowell, 1966.
Song of the Boat, illustrated by Leo and Diane Dillon. New York, Crowell, 1975.

Other

How God Fix Jonah, illustrated by Letterio Calapai. New York, Reynal, 1946.
The Story of Jesus, illustrated by William Walsh. New York, Gilberton, 1955.
The Ten Commandments, illustrated by Norman Nodel. New York, Gilberton, 1956.
John Brown's Raid: A Picture History. New York, Scholastic, 1972.
Directions 3-4, with John Durham and Elsa Graser. Boston, Houghton Mifflin, 2 vols., 1972.
John Brown: A Cry for Freedom. New York, Crowell, 1980.

*

Manuscript Collection: Kerlan Collection, University of Minnesota, Minneapolis; North Carolina Central University Library, Durham.

Biography: Entry in *Dictionary of Literary Biography,* Volume 76, Detroit, Gale, 1988; essay in *Something about the Author Autobiography Series,* Volume 5, Detroit, Gale, 1988.

Critical Study: Entry in *Children's Literature Review,* Volume 10, Detroit, Gale, 1985.

*   *   *

In his series of four novels that begins with *South Town,* Lorenz Graham has a message to give, more than a story to tell. It's a message that encourages understanding and reconciliation between whites and blacks, rich and poor, powerful and weak. But the message needs a story—a vehicle to carry it and connect it, through the imagination, to the reader's life and actions. The danger of course is that the message drives the story rather than vice versa. Graham does not altogether escape that danger.

The story starts in *South Town* where we meet the Williams family, a model black family with their own piece of land and a lot of pride. David, sixteen, has ambitions to become a doctor plus a strong sense of mission to help those who can't help themselves and to right the wrongs of the South Town society. But David learns about the white power structure, personified by the Boyds, and how it intends to keep uppity blacks permanently subservient. David's father is forced to render equal work for unequal pay. When he protests, he is thrown in jail and nearly beaten to death. To make sure the Williams family gets the message, the whites, with the law's help, organize a night riders gang and terrorize those in the family home by threats and gunfire. Graham avoids a simple white versus black conflict, however. Several of the white community folk reject racism and stand with the Williams family against their own people, willing to risk both reputation and life. Yet, David's faith in white acceptance and racial equality is severely shaken. The family decides that the North may offer more opportunity for good employment, a better education, and a kinder acceptance within the human community. Reluctantly, feeling sad but hopeful, the Williams family leaves South Town and its nightmares behind.

We meet them again in *North Town*. The father has found a factory job, and David is enrolled at an integrated but mostly white North Town Central High where, like the character in Ralph Ellison's *Invisible Man,* he learns some painful lessons about his own invisibility. David's cynicism about race relations, justice, and his own prospects deepens. When he finds himself implicated in a stolen car incident, his future seems doomed. And when his father can no longer work because of a serious illness, David has to assume the role of breadwinner. Yet the bad times don't prevail. David is exonerated from guilt in the crime of his friends. He is able to stay in school even when he takes over his father's factory job. And he learns enough about football to have his own shining moment of game-winning heroics. Gradually David gains a sense of belonging to the human family, both black and white. Add to that Pa Williams's eventual recovery and the family's move out of the run-down ghetto that stigmatized them as inferior, and the wisdom of the migration north seems confirmed.

Though the plot, as in *South Town,* is not well integrated, the action line is stronger here and a range of characters again represents Graham's balanced emphasis, avoiding the danger of stereotyping and reducing the human relationships to simply a racial one. But he still too often presents his characters more as case studies than as dynamic individuals.

In *Whose Town?* that flaw is perpetuated. David, now eighteen and a senior, remains as principal character but now functions mostly as a passive victim and detached observer. It's the decade of the sixties with much racial unrest and violent eruptions into race riots. North Town is not exempt. David gets involved in an ugly racial incident, his friend is killed, and David spends a couple of nights in jail. What hurts especially is his discovery that most whites presume his guilt. His South Town bitterness resurfaces. He tries to find his way by listening to the voices of the radical black militants as well as to the more moderate voices of his father and his pastor. He vacillates. But the author's thematic intent manipulates both plot and character development. David graduates from high school, his conviction that "we're all Americans" shaken but not destroyed, and his professional aspirations still intact. Girlfriend Jeannette Lenoir answers the book title's question: "It's everybody's town."

Unfortunately, Lorenz Graham's literary inspiration and craft forsake him nearly altogether in *Return to South Town.* Apparently the author was eager to document the impact of the civil rights movement on the South during the sixties and seventies. Hence the plot becomes incidental and the characters function mostly as mouthpieces for the observations of the author.

David has completed his doctor's training and, true to his boyhood dreams, returns to South Town to establish himself as family physician. He is warmly welcomed by old friends but coldly rejected by Harold Boyd, the nemesis of his youth and now director of the Boyd Memorial Hospital. He finds that much has changed, except the human heart. But David distinguishes himself as hero at a serious accident scene and later at a fiery plane crash. And when, despite Harold Boyd's objections, the state ultimately grants him a license to practice medicine, David's noble dream comes true and his mission can begin, a mission in which Joyce Palmer, professor of sociology at the community college, is eager to join him. And as David's girlfriend did earlier, now it is Joyce, his future wife, who sums up the author's theme of the whole "Town" series: "I claim to be a human with problems living among a lot of other human beings who also have problems."

It is true that Lorenz Graham can hardly be acclaimed as a literary stylist or gifted writer. It is also true that in the nineties this series appears badly dated. Yet these books retain their value for they constitute an honest documentary of pre-to post-civil rights times, from the point of view of a struggling family whose humanity consistently strikes the reader more tellingly than the blackness of their skin.

—Henry J. Baron

GRANT, Cynthia D.

Nationality: American. **Born:** Brockton, Massachusetts, 23 November 1950. **Family:** Married 1) Daniel Heatley, one son; 2) Erik Neel, one son. **Career:** Writer, from 1974. **Address:** Box 95, Cloverdale, California 95425, U.S.A.

PUBLICATIONS FOR YOUNG ADULTS

Fiction

Joshua Fortune. New York, Atheneum, 1980.
Summer Home. New York, Atheneum, 1981.
Big Time. New York, Atheneum, 1982.
Hard Love. New York, Atheneum, 1983.
Kumquat May, I'll Always Love You. New York, Atheneum, 1986.
Phoenix Rising, or, How to Survive Your Life. New York, Atheneum, 1989.
Keep Laughing. New York, Atheneum, 1991.
Shadow Man. New York, Atheneum, 1992.

Uncle Vampire. New York, Atheneum, 1993.
Mary Wolf. New York, Atheneum, 1995.
The White Horse. New York, Atheneum, 1998.

Cynthia D. Grant comments:

One reason I write for teenagers is because those years remain so vivid in my mind. Junior high and high school were difficult times. The kids were so mean to each other! If you stuck out in any way, by being especially smart, or handicapped, or saddled with a hideous home permanent, you were picked on until you bled to death of a thousand tiny cuts. Kids who were picked on took it out on smaller kids. Hurt people hurt people, and themselves. Is this a system?

In my writing I try to reach out to readers and let them know that they are not alone; that, unique as each of us is, we all feel lonely and scared and confused sometimes. And to say, in the words of an anonymous author: Be kind; everyone you meet is fighting a hard battle.

*   *   *

In her realistic fiction for young adults, Cynthia D. Grant demonstrates genuine insight to the young adult world. In *Joshua Fortune* she creates a title character on the verge of adolescence. In addition to the emotional, psychological, and physical changes shared by adolescents, Joshua also finds himself burdened by his name, resentful of his parents' sixties' attitudes, angry at his father's consistent absence, and struggling to accept the reality of his mother's impending marriage. Joshua's world lacks the stability he craves when his family moves to a new town. Grant allows Joshua his anger and frustration as understandable reactions to a befuddling, uncontrollable world; however, these negative emotions never overwhelm him. He vents, but he does not wallow. He lashes out, but he also releases compassion and understanding.

When his home life alienates him, he turns to his peers. Joshua finds himself surprisingly attracted to new friends in school. By observing other families, he realizes the solidity and love within his own family. His friends Alexa and Richard provide Joshua with the perspectives which often elude young adults. Alexa's quirkiness, her verbal banter, and her extravagant sense of humor pull Joshua out of himself. With her, he learns to laugh again. While Richard's own desperation seems familiar to Joshua, the two boys command a unique ability to understand each other implicitly.

Friendship is just what sixteen-year-old Dory lacks in *Big Time*. Like Joshua Fortune, Dory has a challenging younger sister. But unlike Joshua's appropriately named sister Sarah Sunshine, Dory's sister Missy offers no emotional relief. Her parents dwell on Missy, leaving Dory feeling excluded. The family's resources and aspirations center on nine-year-old Missy's potential to make it big in Hollywood. Behind the scenes, Dory knows her sister is difficult and excessively self-absorbed.

Although Dory cannot escape her family as they venture from Deadwood, Oklahoma, to Hollywood with a fast-talking, promise-making talent scout, she does learn about the idiosyncrasies of backstage life and personalities. She participates in this new arena with a healthy skepticism and a heavy dose of humor. As the lights fade in Missy's dream of stardom, Dory discovers her own resilience and individuality—she even gets asked to do a TV sitcom.

Dory's final words, that life may be strange but "it's always good for a few laughs," take on multifaceted intensity in Grant's two novels *Phoenix Rising, or, How to Survive Your Life* and *Keep Laughing*. In each of these novels, laughter operates as the freeing catalyst to emotional health. In them, Grant also exposes the imprisonment of laughter. After her sister has died from cancer, Jessie locks herself away from all she cares about and all who care about her. Her delightful, easy sense of humor no longer offers levity and perspective—it frightens her and burdens her. How can she laugh when Helen is dead? Will she ever deserve to be happy and lighthearted again?

And for the unfortunately named Shepherd Youngman, humiliation, rejection, and exclusion make up life's jokes. On the verge of his sixteenth birthday, Shep leaves the safety of home and his mother to travel with his comedian father, Joey. Armed with a comedy club and television deals, a swank apartment and financial comfort, Joey promises to give Shep the home and father he's put on hold for so long. Shep soon realizes the fragility of Joey's life and the hollowness of these promises. He hears himself used as material in Joey's act; he finds himself needing a father but being treated like a buddy, not a son. Like Joshua Fortune, Shep Youngman establishes a peaceful, if uneven, relationship with his father due to the loving, stable family created by his mother.

Grant's *Phoenix Rising* stands as an artistically ambitious undertaking in which she departs from a chronologically straight-forward narrative to reveal the intricacies of Jessie and Helen's relationship with an equally complex way of storytelling. She alternates Jessie's ongoing grieving process in the past tense with parcels of Helen's journal. The past tense assures readers that Jessie will get well. This structure fortifies the novel by including Helen's living voice. Grant shapes Helen as a character through the journal, articulating her hopes, dreams, ambitions, disappointments, and frustrations. As readers come to know Helen, they mourn her loss with Jessie and her brother Lucas.

Shadow Man does not prove as gratifying in its structure. It, too, opens with the death of a character whose absence dominates the novel. As the many people who loved him learn of and react to eighteen-year-old Gabriel McCloud's death, he becomes the ultimate shadow man. However, unlike Helen, he never takes on any substance at all. Other people's responses to him never quite intersect; the reader learns the variety of Gabe's personality, but cannot unite them into a full character. As a result, one reads of others mourning him, but never personally participates in the grieving process.

In all her novels, Grant conveys an understanding of young adulthood as a time of challenge and growth. She displays and creates believable young adult characters. Her frequent use of dialogue as a crafting tool evokes a range of adolescent voices. In every novel, she places her young adult characters firmly within the spheres of family and friends. She presents the family as an essential, life-giving community. And, even when threatened by a negligent parent or untimely death, Grant's families always support the young adult. The truth of her families comes from their fragility which she dares to share with readers. Grant's characters, like most adolescents, may wish for the nuclear family, but they flourish in alternate forms; however shaken or wobbly, these families do not shatter—they remain the arena of sustenance and love. Absence—of a father, sister, a friend, or brother—demands attention in these novels. The characters recognize their loss and struggle to overcome it. The absence cannot be filled; the loss cannot be replaced. Yet, each character learns that, with the perspective afforded by laughter and the foundation established by family, they can be made whole again.

—Cathryn M. Mercier

GRAY, Elizabeth Janet. *See* **VINING, Elizabeth Gray.**

GREEN, Hannah. *See* **GREENBERG, Joanne (née Goldenberg).**

GREENBERG, Joanne

Pseudonyms: Hannah Green. **Nationality:** American. **Born:** Born Joanne Goldenberg in Brooklyn, New York, 24 September 1932. **Education:** American University, Washington D.C., B.A. **Family:** Married Albert Greenberg in 1955; two sons. **Career:** Writer; medical officer, Lookout Mountain Fire Department; certified emergency medical technician. Adjunct professor of anthropology, Colorado School of Mines, 1983—. **Awards:** National Jewish Welfare Board Harry and Ethel Daroff Memorial Fiction award, 1963, and William and Janice Epstein Fiction award, 1964, both for *The King's Persons;* New York Association of the Deaf Marcus L. Kenner award, 1971; Christopher Book award, 1971, for *In This Sign;* Frieda Fromm-Reichman Memorial award, 1967; Rocky Mountain Women's Institute award, 1983; Denver Public Library Bookplate award, 1990; Colorado Author of the Year, 1991. D.L., Western Maryland College, 1977; D.H.L., Gallaudet College, 1979; J.H.L., University of Colorado, 1987. **Agent:** Lois Wallace, Wallace Literary Agency, 1977 E. 70th Street, New York, New York 10021. **Address:** 29221 Rainbow Hill Road, Golden, Colorado 80401, U.S.A.

PUBLICATIONS FOR YOUNG ADULTS

Fiction

The King's Persons. New York, Holt, 1963.
The Monday Voices. New York, Holt, 1965.
In This Sign. New York, Holt, 1968.
Founder's Praise. New York, Holt, 1976.
A Season of Delight. New York, Holt, 1981.
The Far Side of Victory. New York, Holt, 1983.
Simple Gifts. New York, Holt, 1986.
Age of Consent. New York, Holt, 1987.

Of Such Small Differences. New York, Holt, 1988.
No Reck'ning Made. New York, Holt, 1993.

Short Stories

Summering. New York, Holt, 1966.
Rites of Passage. New York, Holt, 1971.
High Crimes and Misdemeanors. New York, Holt, 1979.
With the Snow Queen and Other Stories. New York, Arcade, 1991.

Nonfiction as Hannah Green

I Never Promised You a Rose Garden. New York, Holt, 1964.

*

Media Adaptations: *I Never Promised You a Rose Garden* (film), New World Pictures, 1977.

Critical Study: Entry in *Contemporary Literary Criticism,* Detroit, Gale, Volume 7, 1977; Volume 30, 1984.

*   *   *

Joanne Greenberg, also known as Hannah Green, is a writer of versatility and verve. She is a writer with whom one can enjoy a rainy day at a vacation resort. Her style lends itself to the mature reader while simultaneously presenting themes suitable for all ages. Greenberg addresses the persistent doubts that plague all of us by relating stories of others in need. Though the scenarios in which her characters find themselves may be unfamiliar to the average reader, the emotions they feel while enmeshed in the plotlines are universal in appeal and scope. Her works include magazine publications, short stories, novels, and a movie adaptation of her book *I Never Promised You a Rose Garden.*

Greenberg wrote *I Never Promised You a Rose Garden* under the pseudonym of Hannah Green. In this book, she details the struggle of a sixteen-year-old girl fighting for her sanity. The descriptive and, at times, poetic use of language brings the reader inside the character's world of fantasy. The depiction of the brilliant psychiatrist grappling with the reality of her own life while immersed in the treatment of her patient is explicitly detailed and well written. One can sense the underlying common thread of the need for acceptance so familiar to all adolescents. We sense the character's desire for the unconditional love that all human beings need. We can see ourselves confronting the confusion of youth along with the feelings of isolation and rejection. Greenberg's personal encounter with mental problems was a basis for the character's ordeal with psychosis and schizophrenia. Her empathy for her character is clearly evident in the portrayal of the teen's pilgrimage through failure and success.

Another popular book deals once again with the theme of isolation—in the world of the deaf. The book *In This Sign* was heralded and awarded by those both within and outside of the deaf community. The themes of loneliness and of being different are dramatically brought to life by the experiences of Greenberg's characters. She is able to take the reader on a journey inside her characters' minds. She does not just bring their thoughts into the open, but she allows us to feel their emotions. She transforms the occurrences within the realm of her deaf character into common circumstances with which we can all identify. Readers can gain an affinity for the handicapped through edification and education which is expertly interwoven into the storyline.

In another book, *Of Such Small Differences,* Greenberg expands the reader's minds to encompass the daily trials and tribulations of a character who in this story is not only deaf, but also blind. Once again we see the universality of isolation. In this case it is related, as in the previous book, to a physical disability. The leading character's experiences and ensuing love affair are portrayed as one might relate a story told by one friend to another. The primary difficulties handled by the protagonist are those of anyone involved in a growing relationship. It is a love story. The physical disabilities are secondary in the development of the characters' union. We see the individuals expressing almost a degree of freedom in their solitude. Once again, the handicapping condition has been used to relate to the universality of the emotion. Everyone, especially adolescents, can relate to feeling as though they are different; when in fact, that is what makes us all the same. As indicated by Greenberg, we are "of such small differences."

In *Simple Gifts* we also see people somewhat out of sync with the world around them. Love, for these "misfits," comes after much turmoil. Greenberg describes feelings we have all had through the eyes of her characters. We see the meanness as well as the kindness in the secrets of those in our lives. When we receive love, it usually comes as a surprise, when it is least expected.

One of Greenberg's sadder stories is described in *The Far Side of Victory.* This book examines such themes as crime and punishment of the human soul. Our guilt or innocence is primarily determined by our own abilities to cope with life's adversities. In our search for truth and meaning, we must experience love and loss.

Another book which also includes references to actual historical events is *Founder's Praise.* This book details the climb of a family through hard times in the history of the United States. Their belief in the goodness of people through religion and morality guides them into their future.

Greenberg has also written several collections of short stories. In one book, *Summering,* her tales again reflect the themes of love and misunderstanding, loneliness and friendship. We are subsequently captivated by her imaginative characterizations and narratives which uniquely embody her freshness and innovation. In another book of short stories, *With the Snow Queen and Other Stories,* she writes of people we know. We can relate to people with basic human needs, even in peculiar situations. In one story, she employs the unconventional tact of having a character break through the "third wall" to "speak" directly to the reader. Her range of unusual topics runs the gamut from time travel to the solemnity of the life of a monk. Another collection, *High Crimes and Misdemeanors,* utilizes much humor and fantasy. At the same time, Greenberg is still able to embroil the readers in the particulars of her characters which most closely link us all to the hopes, fears, and dreams of life. Additionally, this book also contains several stories which come from Greenberg's religious background.

Greenberg's popularity lies in both her creativity and her originality. Her ability to incorporate common themes into uncommon situations makes her a most readable author.

—Laurie Schwartz Guttenberg

GREENE, Bette

Nationality: American. **Born:** Memphis, Tennessee, 28 June 1934. **Education:** University of Alabama, 1952; Memphis State University, 1953-54; Alliance Française (Paris), 1954; Columbia University, 1955; Harvard University, 1972. **Family:** Married Donald Sumner Greene in 1959; one daughter and one son. **Career:** Reporter, Memphis *Hebrew Watchman,* 1950, Memphis *Commercial Appeal,* 1950-52, and United Press International, Memphis bureau, 1953-54; public information officer, American Red Cross, Memphis, 1958-59, and Boston State Psychiatric Hospital, 1959-61. **Awards:** *New York Times*' outstanding book award, Golden Kite award, Society of Children's Book Writers, and American Library Association (ALA) notable book citation, all 1973, and National Book award nomination for best children's book, 1974, all for *Summer of My German Soldier;* Children's Choice Book award, *New York Times*' outstanding book award, and ALA notable book citation, all 1974, and Newbery Honor Book award, 1975, all for *Philip Hall Likes Me. I Reckon Maybe; Parents' Choice* award, 1983, for *Them That Glitter and Them That Don't.* **Address:** 338 Clinton Road, Brookline, Massachusetts 02146, U.S.A.

PUBLICATIONS FOR YOUNG ADULTS

Fiction

Summer of My German Soldier. New York, Dial Press, 1973; London, Hamish Hamilton, 1974.
Philip Hall Likes Me. I Reckon Maybe, illustrated by Charles Lilly. New York, Dial Press, 1974; London, Hamish Hamilton, 1976.
Morning Is a Long Time Coming. New York, Dial Press, and London, Hamish Hamilton, 1978.
Get on out of Here, Philip Hall. New York, Dial Press, 1981; London, Hamish Hamilton, 1982.
Them That Glitter and Them That Don't. New York, Knopf, 1983.
I've Already Forgotten Your Name, Philip Hall! New York, Knopf, 1983.
The Drowning of Stephan Jones. New York, Bantam, 1991.

*

Media Adaptations: *Summer of My German Soldier* (television movie, starring Kristy McNichol, Bruce Davison, and Esther Rolle), National Broadcasting Company (NBC-TV), 1978; *Summer of My German Soldier* (audiocassette); *Philip Hall Likes Me. I Reckon Maybe* (audiocassette).

Biography: Essay in *Speaking for Ourselves: Autobiographical Sketches by Notable Authors of Books for Young Adults,* Volume 1, compiled and edited by Donald R. Gallo, National Council of Teachers of English, 1990; essay in *Authors and Artists for Young Adults,* Volume 7, Detroit, Gale, 1991; essay in *Something about the Author Autobiography Series,* Volume 16, Detroit, Gale, 1993.

Manuscript Collections: Kerlan Collection, University of Minnesota, Minneapolis.

Critical Studies: Entry in *Children's Literature Review,* Volume 2, Detroit, Gale, 1976; entry in *Contemporary Literary Criticism,* Volume 30, Detroit, Gale, 1984.

*   *   *

Celebrated for her emotionally powerful books and her strong characters, Bette Greene has left an indelible mark on twentieth-century young adult literature. A very intense woman who feels strongly that children "are the most important part of our world," Greene devotes much of her writing to themes that deal with hypocrisy, prejudice, and the many forms of abuse—physical, emotional, and religious—that exist in society, and how they affect people, especially children and young adults. Hers voice comes from her heart and dares to question what many don't want to think about.

People react so strongly to Greene's writing because she herself is intensely involved with her books. Her writing is steeped in human emotion and experience. "The best ideas," says Greene, "come from your response to living—to what makes you wake up in the morning wanting to break out into song and what makes you want to break out into tears." Anything else is "formula writing" which, according to Greene, is less difficult to write. "If you follow a template," explains Greene, "clearly writing and life are a lot easier for you. The really difficult thing about writing is the motivation of the characters, how people respond, what's going on inside—and that stuff is never formula." To Greene, writing is all about "trying to understand things which might not be really understandable—trying to understand this journey that we all take called life."

Greene's characters are born out of her life's experiences and are enhanced by what she sees in daily life. Seeing a parent yank a child's arm in a store can leave a lasting impression on her. "I hate violence towards children," she says. "I can write about those themes all day long because that is an issue that is very disturbing to me." When she wrote *Summer of My German Soldier,* probably Greene's best-known novel, she wrote it to try to understand abuse and life as she had partly experienced it. The childhood experiences of Greene's twelve-year-old character, Patty Bergen, are similar to those in Greene's own life. Like Patty, Greene grew up as a Jewish girl in a small town in Arkansas during World War II amidst the hatred and violence directed toward anyone who wasn't a white, Christian American. Patty offers a lot of insight into what it feels like to be mistreated, especially after she befriends a black woman and an escaped German prisoner and finds them kinder to her than her own parents. The sequel, *Morning Is a Long Time Coming,* continues with Patty's personal journey to find love and acceptance within herself and from others after graduation from high school.

Two of Greene's most popular books for younger readers may also be the funniest. *Philip Hall Likes Me. I Reckon Maybe* and *Get on out of Here, Philip Hall* are episodic novels about Beth Lambert, who likes a boy all of the time while he only likes her some of the time. Every year letters pour in to the author from young girls from around the globe who explain that the boys they know act an awful lot like Philip Hall.

Greene wrote *The Drowning of Stephan Jones* to try to understand what, to her, is "totally incomprehensible"—why people hate just because a person's sexuality is different from theirs. In this novel, Greene focuses on the treatment of homosexuals—the "designated victims" of our society. "Too much hate is coming from the pulpit," she says, "and people cannot separate the supposed sin from the sinner." These concerns are certainly evident in *The Drowning of Stephan Jones,* where a gay couple, Stephan Jones and Frank Montgomery, are the victims of hatred and harassment by people who believe that their violent actions are right and religious.

"People can easily identify and disapprove of political tyranny, but religious tyranny is much more difficult to pinpoint and discuss objectively." She recalls her own personal experience of what she considers religious abuse when she became a "born-again Christian" as a child. Greene said she spent six years trying to convert her Jewish parents to Christianity and cried because she actually believed that her parents' souls were going to hell. The irony is that the minister probably felt that he served Bette well, but Greene feels that, in her case, religion was carried too far—that "we each have a right to our own God."

Greene strongly feels that people need more moral courage—the courage to stand up to any form of violence, hatred, and abuse and say, "This [injustice] is wrong!" When people do not speak out, they are indirectly condoning the abuse by allowing it to continue. People often wait to see who will say something first because "people often find physical courage easier to come by than moral courage." In other words, people are more apt to physically risk their lives to save someone than publicly say something contrary to the "moral majority's" views on controversial religious issues.

Greene likens literature to "a mirror on the souls of readers" which has the potential of increasing people's "awareness, social skills, and compassion." Regarding her own writing, Greene says the biggest compliment people can give her after reading one of her books is that they feel and understand more about life than they did before the reading. Given the response to her writing, Greene often achieves that goal. While her novels generally deal with adolescent protagonists, Greene's audience is not limited to teenagers. She notes that in response to *The Drowning of Stephan Jones,* she received a letter which opened, "Thank you for opening the eyes of a sixty-two-year-old farm woman." Perhaps this wide range of readers exists because the issues that Greene deals with aren't limited by age, race, religion, or gender.

Greene can't imagine being anything but a writer. She loves what she does and would like to be remembered as having helped children. It is evident that Bette Greene has already exceeded that aspiration through her writing.

—Joan F. Kaywell and Heidi M. Quintana

GREENWALD, Sheila

Nationality: American. **Born:** New York City, 26 May 1934. **Education:** Sarah Lawrence College, Bronxville, New York, B.A. 1956. **Family:** Married George Green in 1960; two sons. **Career:** Writer and illustrator. **Address:** 175 Riverside Drive, New York, New York 10024, U.S.A.

PUBLICATIONS FOR YOUNG ADULTS

Fiction (illustrated by the author)

A Metropolitan Love Story. New York, Doubleday, 1962.
Willie Bryant and the Flying Otis. New York, Grosset, 1971.
The Hot Day. Indianapolis, Indiana, Bobbs Merrill, 1972.
Miss Amanda Snap. Indianapolis, Indiana, Bobbs Merrill, 1972.
Mat Pit and the Tunnel Tenants. Philadelphia, Pennsylvania, Lippincott, 1972.
The Secret Museum. Philadelphia, Pennsylvania, Lippincott, 1974.
The Secret in Miranda's Closet. Boston, Houghton Mifflin, 1977.
The Mariah Delany Lending Library Disaster. Boston, Houghton Mifflin, 1977.
The Atrocious Two. Boston, Houghton Mifflin, 1978.
All the Way to Wits' End. Boston, Little, Brown, 1979.
It All Began with Jane Eyre, or, the Secret Life of Franny Dillman. Boston, Little, Brown, 1980.
Give Us a Great Big Smile, Rosy Cole. New York, Atlantic Monthly Press, 1981.
Blissful Joy and the SATs: A Multiple-Choice Romance. New York, Atlantic Monthly Press, 1982.
Will the Real Gertrude Hollings Please Stand Up? New York, Atlantic Monthly Press, 1983.
Valentine Rosy. New York, Atlantic Monthly Press, 1984.
Rosy Cole's Great American Guilt Club. New York, Atlantic Monthly Press, 1985.
Alvin Webster's Sure Fire Plan for Success and How It Failed. Boston, Little, Brown, 1987.
Write On Rosy!: A Young Author in Crisis. Boston, Little, Brown, 1988.
Rosy's Romance. Boston, Little, Brown, 1989.
The Mariah Delany Author of the Month Club. Boston, Little, Brown, 1990.
Here's Hermione, A Rosy Cole Production. Boston, Little, Brown, 1991.
Rosy Cole Discovers America! Boston, Joy Street, 1992.
My Fabulous New Life. New York, Browndeer Press, 1993.
Rosy Cole! She Walks in Beauty. Boston, Little, Brown, 1994.
Rosy Cole: She Grows and Graduates. New York, Orchard Books, 1997.

*

Illustrator: *Pocketful of Poems* by Marie L. Allen, 1957; *The Pink Motel* by Carol Ryrie Brink, 1959; *The Little Leftover Witch* by Florence Laughlin, 1960; *Brave Betsy* by Miriam Dreifus, 1961; *Come A-Witching* by Grace V. Curl, 1964; *Amy and the Sorrel Summer* by Laura H. Fisher, 1964; *The Remarkable Ramsey* by Barbara Rinkoff, 1965; *The Boy Who Couldn't Make Up His Mind* by Hila Colman, 1965; *Who'll Mind Henry?* by Anne Mallet, 1965; *The Seventh Cousin* by Florence Laughlin, 1966; *The Pretender Princess* by Mary J. Roth, 1967; *When I Was Jersey* by James Playsted Wood, 1967; *Jump the Rope Jingles* by Emma V. Worstell, 1967; *The Mystery Cup* by Jean Bothwell, 1968; *The New Boy on the Sidewalk* by M. Jean Craig, 1968; *Veronica the Show Off* by Nancy K. Robinson, 1982; *Henny Youngman's Book of Jokes* by Henny Youngman, 1992.

Sheila Greenwald comments:

I can't remember a time when I wasn't drawing. Writing came later and was harder. In college I loved classes in creative writing, but was aware of the fact that at the time I didn't have much to write about. I began to illustrate books after college. Most of them were for children. By the time my own two sons started school, I had plenty of things I wanted to write about. My books are generated by issues involving values about which I either feel strongly or am unresolved. Sometimes the books help me to explore an issue, sometimes they are to expound on one. Humor helps both me and my characters achieve a necessary perspective.

*   *   *

Sheila Greenwald's sheer joy in her craft is evident in her many books for young people. Although she enjoys inventing characters and situations rather than recording actual events and emotions, Greenwald is not unsympathetic toward her characters. They must cope with difficult issues—such as divorce, anorexia, and mental illness—but Greenwald also injects a healthy dose of humor into her books, endowing her characters with the rare ability to laugh at themselves and their seemingly hopeless situations. The effortless quality of Greenwald's prose allows her characters to assume the guise of old friends. Greenwald also claims to be highly opinionated, and she admits that inventing stories allows her to showcase her beliefs.

One subject she obviously has strong feelings about is the annual rite of passage for high schoolers, the Scholastic Aptitude Test, which figures prominently in *Blissful Joy and the SATs: A Multiple-Choice Romance,* one of her most popular books. Greenwald's native New York is central to the story, though the setting is unobtrusive; Greenwald's familiarity with the city allows it to function as a backdrop against which the story develops. Blissful Joy Bowman prides herself on her good sense and responsibility. As the daughter of amicably divorced actors, Bliss has always played the parental role with her rather childlike parents. While they dart from one job to another, Bliss attends the proper school and achieves good grades to ensure herself a safe and secure future. Bliss is determined to have "a normal life." Bliss succeeds in keeping her life completely in order until the day she is befriended by Blackball, a stray dog, on the subway. This seemingly insignificant event sets into motion a chain of events over which she has no control. With the help of Blackball and the quirky group of people he introduces, Bliss learns that in the real world people do not always fit into her neatly assigned pigeonholes.

Greenwald creates an impressive array of characters in *Blissful Joy.* Many of the characters have amusing, even outrageously flamboyant names like Delphi Pilpel, the homely veterinarian. Yet though these people are unique, they are also very human. Despite their familiar contemporary problems, Greenwald's characters are not stereotypes. Sibyl's anorexia and Louisa's mother's mental illness and desertion are not depicted in a heavy-handed, moralistic manner, but with honesty and in keeping with their characters. The issues raised are well-integrated within the context of the story. In the same fashion, Bliss's first experience with that which she and her fellow amateur psychologist and best friend, Jenny, call MPRWOS (Meaningful Peer Relationship With the Opposite Sex), is both touching and funny. Her relationships with Howard and Colin expose Bliss to the hurt and disappointment, as well as to the fulfillment, of a relationship. Greenwald provides a sensitive and witty account of the problems, real and imagined, of first love.

Another important theme in the book involves Bliss's feelings about her parents' divorce. Like many children of divorce, Bliss remains hopeful that her parents will reconcile. Although she is resigned to the reality of their relationship—thanks to numerous self-help books—Bliss still feels uneasy with her parents' romantic relationships with others. In the process of accepting her parents' weaknesses while appreciating their uniqueness, Bliss confronts her own prejudice and shallowness. When she adopts Blackball, Bliss begins to admit that she has ordinary emotions that she does not need to submerge. Bliss acknowledges that, while she should not allow her life to be run by her emotions, the capacity to feel is not a weakness. By giving of herself to relationships and to Blackball, whom she needs as much, if not more, than he needs her, Bliss becomes human. Allowing her parents the freedom to be themselves eventually leads to their increased responsibility for her and for themselves.

The concepts of reality and illusion also play a significant role in *Blissful Joy*. The Bowman adults treat their lives as theatrical roles; those roles parallel and intersect with the lives of those around them. For example, Colin, infatuated with Bliss, rehearses tender lines with her mother, and Bliss mistakenly thinks the two are involved. Mr. Bowman romances sensible Delphi under false pretenses (for the sake of Blackball), not realizing he is falling in love with her. Greenwald's expert use of irony and satire is one of the qualities that lifts this novel above other, more mundane "problem novels."

Greenwald has also created a compelling young character in Rosy Cole, who in 1994's *Rosy Cole! She Walks in Beauty* discovers that beauty may not be so alluring once it is achieved. Rosy wants to become a work of art just like the ones she views at the Metropolitan Museum, and taking the suggestions of Donald—with whom she becomes infatuated—she makes some changes to her appearance that result in a sudden upsurge in her popularity. But Rosy is stranded by her own instant success, and decides it isn't worth it. Later she *Rosy Cole: She Grows and Graduates* (1997), a tale in which Greenwald continues some of the themes explored in books such as *Blissful Joy and the SATs*. She wrote this book, she says, "out of a heartfelt desire to clue young people in on the fact that there is more involved in their acceptance or rejection at [private] schools than innate ability. . . . What is lost in the race to gain admission to boast-worthy prestige schools is the importance of finding the right school for each student and the likelihood that there are many fine options."

Sheila Greenwald writes seamlessly. With a virtually invisible hand, she makes her points. It is through her characters' interaction that Greenwald conveys such messages as the importance of not stereotyping people, of accepting one's own and others' limitations, and above all, of maintaining a sense of humor.

—Maryclare O'Donnell Himmel, updated by Judson Knight

GUY, Rosa (Cuthbert)

Nationality: American. **Born:** Trinidad, West Indies, 1 September 1925; moved to the United States, 1932. **Education:** New York University. **Family:** Married Warner Guy (deceased); one son.

Career: Worked with the American Negro Theatre, New York, mid-1940s; since 1950 writer; founding president, Harlem Writer's Guild. Lecturer. **Awards:** American Library Association "Best Book for Young Adults" citations, 1973, for *The Friends,* 1976, for *Ruby,* 1978, for *Edith Jackson,* 1979, for *The Disappearance,* and 1981, for *Mirror of Her Own;* "Children's Book of the Year" citations from Child Study Association, 1973, for *The Friends,* and 1986, for *Paris, Pee Wee, and Big Dog;* "Outstanding Book of the Year" citation from the *New York Times,* 1973, for *The Friends,* and 1979, for *The Disappearance; The Friends* was selected one of *School Library Journal*'s "Best of the Best" Books, 1979; *The Disappearance* and *Edith Jackson* were selected among the New York Public Library's Books for the Teen Age, 1980, 1981, and 1982; Coretta Scott King award, 1982, for *Mother Crocodile;* Parents' Choice award for Literature from the Parents' Choice Foundation, 1983, for *New Guys around the Block;* Other award, 1987, for *My Love, My Love; or, The Peasant Girl.* **Address:** c/o Ellen Levine Literary Agency Inc., 15 E. 26th St., Suite 1801, New York, New York 10001, U.S.A.

PUBLICATIONS FOR YOUNG ADULTS

Fiction

Bird at My Window. Philadelphia, Lippincott, and London, Souvenir Press, 1966.
The Friends. New York, Holt, Rinehart, 1973; London, Gollancz, 1974.
Ruby. New York, Viking Press, 1976; London, Gollancz, 1981.
Edith Jackson. New York, Viking Press, 1978; London, Gollancz, 1979.
The Disappearance. New York, Delacorte Press, 1979; London, Gollancz, 1980.
Mirror of Her Own. New York, Delacorte Press, 1981.
New Guys around the Block. New York, Delacorte Press, and London, Gollancz, 1983.
Paris, Pee Wee, and Big Dog, illustrated by Caroline Binch. New York, Delacorte Press, and London, Gollancz, 1984.
And I Heard a Bird Sing. New York, Delacorte Press, and London, Gollancz, 1987.
The Ups and Downs of Carl Davis III. New York, Delacorte Press, 1989.
Billy the Great, illustrated by Caroline Binch. New York, Doubleday, 1992.
The Music of Summer. New York, Delacorte Press, 1992.
The Sun, the Sea, a Touch of the Wind. New York, Dutton, 1995.

Other

Translator, *Mother Crocodile: An Uncle Amadou Tale from Senegal,* illustrated by John Steptoe. New York, Delacorte Press, 1981.

PUBLICATIONS FOR ADULTS

Novels

A Measure of Time. New York, Holt, Rinehart, 1983; London, Virago Press, 1984.
My Love, My Love; or, The Peasant Girl. New York, Holt, Rinehart, 1985; London, Virago Press, 1987.

Play

Venetian Blinds (produced at Topical Theatre, New York, 1954).

Other

Editor, *Children of Longing.* New York, Holt, Rinehart, 1971.

Contributor to *Ten Times Black,* edited by Julian Mayfield, New York, Bantam, 1972; and to *Sixteen: Short Stories by Outstanding Writers for Young Adults,* edited by Donald R. Gallo, New York, Delacorte, 1984.

*

Media Adaptations: *The Friends* (documentary), Thames Television, 1984.

Biography: Entry in *Dictionary of Literary Biography* Volume 33: *Afro-American Fiction Writers after 1955.* Detroit, Gale, 1984; essay in *Speaking for Ourselves: Autobiographical Sketches by Notable Authors of Books for Young Adults,* Volume 1, compiled and edited by Donald R. Gallo, National Council of Teachers of English, 1990.

Critical Studies: Entry in *Children's Literature Review,* Volume 13, Detroit, Gale, 1987; entry in *Contemporary Literary Criticism,* Volume 26, Detroit, Gale, 1983.

*   *   *

In a voice full of probing and anguished sensitivity, Rosa Guy examines the intersection of race and class in twentieth-century urban America. The lives of the forgotten ones haunt her world, taking and shaping for themselves identities which society would deny and destroy. The civilizing influence at the heart of her books is a call to compassion, a sustained imperative to care for one another, well and deeply and across all boundaries.

In her singular attention to the realities of inner-city adolescence, Rosa Guy claims a courageous place among contemporaries. Her stories demonstrate where and when the nation's vision fails its children, and the best of them illuminate the dark underside of the middle-class dream, laying bare the horrible irony of living with so little alongside those who seem to have so much. Poverty is the fault line shattering the lives of Guy's characters, turning friend against friend, neighbor against neighbor, brother against brother. While she tells the stories of those who survive, she never forgets and cannot condemn those who do not. A deep and empathic understanding of the forces which shape young lives informs Rosa Guy's work, shining like signal fire from the depths of her writer's soul.

Love is her fundamental concern. Her books beg the question of how love survives in the face of fear, poverty, betrayal, and hatred. *Edith Jackson* finds an answer in its heroine, an orphaned schoolgirl whose deep and responsible concern for siblings forms the story's moral compass. In a world where caring cannot logically endure, Edith roots like a sapling in cement, sprouting tough green shoots of growth.

Bird at My Window is another of Rosa Guy's sinewy, spiritual hymns to the lives of the ghetto born. Crushing poverty and prejudice strip Wade Williams of everything but his will to live, leaving him with little to live for in the end. The novel traces his descent into madness, borne of agonizing rejection by whites unwilling to tolerate the presence of a gifted black boy in their school. He is the brilliant fruit, ripened past season, falling heavy and far from the tree of life. He symbolizes all who live and die facelessly, their talents untapped, in the reaches of the inner city. If they are to survive, Rosa Guy's characters reach inside to that place where trust and love lie inviolate. Imamu Jones, the teenage hero of *The Disappearance, New Guys around the Block,* and *And I Heard a Bird Sing,* finds in himself the compassion to nurse an alcoholic mother, the courage to reveal the stunning blood-guilt of a murdering friend, and the strength to face down his own emerging adolescent fears. Because Imamu cares, he is horrified by the eruptions of violence which mark the passing of days in his neighborhood. Caring will disturb his dreams, cast long shadows on his waking hours, but sear pain and understanding permanently into his soul. Imamu will move out of the ghetto, but his destiny is bound to the lives of those who cannot.

Guy's stories invariably raise the disturbing question of race consciousness in America. Readers unfamiliar with her kind of relentless portrayal of inner-city devastation will find these books a harrowing surprise. A nightmarish sense of unreality pervades, in particular, the setting of *New Guys around the Block,* where homeless addicts live and raise children in burned out and deserted rubble-strewn buildings. In *Edith Jackson* a young orphaned woman is charged with the care of her siblings. Rosa Guy claims these young ones and celebrates survival in spite of all odds, claiming each success as her own, fixing our sights on the drama played out daily in the streets of the forgotten neighborhoods.

Into the same cloth as somber strains of death, loss, and betrayal, Guy deftly weaves the lighter elements of a comic touch, the poignant and aching excitement of a first love's stirring. The schoolboy hero of *The Ups and Downs of Carl Davis III* takes readers along for a magic carpet ride, inviting us to forget the tough streets he's left behind, while the adventurous *Paris, Pee Wee, and Big Dog* entertains mightily back in the big city. The laughter which Phyllisia and Edith share in *The Friends* echoes up and down the streets of New York City, pealing like bells, healing the loneliness of their separate lives. *Ruby*'s young lovers share the same secret; in one another's company they are safe, they are real, they know joy at last.

Guy's ear attends with delight to the snap and sensuousness of young adult dialogue, idiom, and inflection, whether the visceral jive of the street, the low, mourning cadence of disappointment, or the half-trembling voice of a teenager coming square up against life and authority. This is the sound of life happening all around, never stopping, always rushing on, and rushing in. Her heroes and heroines are compassionate, although they have seen much that is inhumane. They are doers and thinkers, feelers and believers. They are dreamers and lovers, sons and daughters, sisters and brothers. They are all of us.

—Laurie Ann Eno

H

HADLEY, Lee. *See* IRWIN, Hadley.

HALAM, Ann

Pseudonym for Gwyneth A(nn) Jones. **Nationality:** British. **Born:** Manchester, Lancashire, 14 February 1952. **Education:** The University of Sussex, Brighton, B.A. (honors) 1973. **Family:** Married Peter Gwilliam in 1976; one son. **Career:** Executive officer, Manpower Services Commission, Hove, Sussex, 1975-77; author of books for young people and adults since 1977; editor of the Star (South-coast Telematics Aspirational Reader) at: http://www.star.org.uk/star. **Awards:** First prize from *Manchester Evening News* children's story competition, 1967, for "The Christmas Church Mice"; runner-up for *Guardian* Children's Fiction award, 1981, for *Dear Hill*; *Guardian* Children's Fiction award short list, 1986, for *King Death's Garden*; Horn Book Notable children's book nomination, for *The Daymaker*; co-winner of James Tiptree Award, 1991, for *White Queen*; W. H. Smith's Mind Boggling Books short list, 1994, for *The Haunting of Jessica Raven*; Arthur C. Clarke Award nomination, 1995, for *North Wind*; Dracula Society's Children of the Night award, 1995, for *The Fear Man*; World Fantasy Award, 1996, for *Seven Tales and a Fable*. **Agent:** Anthony Goff, David Higham Associates Ltd., 5-8 Lower John Street, Golden Square, London W1R 4HA. **Address:** 139 Ditchling Rise, Brighton, East Sussex BN1 4QQ, United Kingdom.

PUBLICATIONS FOR YOUNG ADULTS

Fiction

The Alder Tree. London, Allen & Unwin, 1982.
King Death's Garden. London, Orchard, 1986.
The Daymaker. London, Orchard, 1987.
Transformations. London, Orchard, 1988.
The Skybreaker. London, Orchard, 1990.
The Haunting of Jessica Raven. London, Orion 1994.
Fear Man. London, Orion, 1995.
The Powerhouse. London, Orion, 1997.
Crying in the Dark. London, Orion, 1998.

Fiction as Gwyneth A. Jones

Water in the Air. London, Macmillan, and New York, Macmillan, 1977.
The Influence of Ironwood. London, Macmillan, 1978.
The Exchange. London, Macmillan, 1979.

The Hidden Ones. London, Women's Press, 1988.
Seven Tales and a Fable (fairy tales), edited by Steven Pasechnik. Cambridge, Massachusetts, Edgewood Press, 1995.

PUBLICATIONS FOR CHILDREN

Fiction

Dear Hill. London, Macmillan, 1980.
Ally Ally, Aster. London, Allen & Unwin, 1981.

PUBLICATIONS FOR ADULTS

Novels as Gwyneth A. Jones

Divine Endurance. London, Allen & Unwin, 1984; New York, Arbor House, 1987. Reissued London, Headline, 1993, New York, Tor
Escape Plans. London, Allen & Unwin, 1986.
Kairos. London, Unwin Hyman, 1988.
White Queen. London, Gollancz, 1991, New York, Tor, 1993.
Flowerdust. London, Headline, 1993, New York, Tor,
North Wind. London, Gollancz, 1994, New York, Tor,
Phoenix Cafe. London, Gollancz, 1997, New York, Tor, 1998.

Other

Deconstructing the Starships (essays), Liverpool, Liverpool University Press, 1998.

Author of short stories, reviews, and critical essays in *Foundation: Journal of the Science Fiction Foundation, Interzone,* and *The New York Review of Science Fiction.*

*

Ann Halam comments:

I was born in Blackley, Manchester. But I never felt I lived in the city, though it was only a short bus ride away. I used to be a member of a gang called The Clover Club, consisting of me, my two sisters, my brother and three friends of ours. There was farmland quite close to where we lived and some big wild parks: we usually played at being explorers, and naturalists. I loved being outdoors, but I was often ill when I was a child. I had bronchitis every winter, which meant I would spend long days in bed, alone, reading. It was good preparation for a writer's life because you do spend a lot of time on your own.

I've always liked ghost stories. When I was ten, I bought a book called *Great Tales of Terror and the Supernatural* from a jumble sale, and that's where I found some of the stories that still inspire the Ann Halam books. I remember that my mother was horrified: but she likes my ghost stories now, so it wasn't such a bad idea.

I never thought I'd make writing my career. After university I did a teacher training course, but I wasn't very good at that, so I started working at a job centre. A friend of mine showed some stories I had written to a London publisher, and she suggested I should try to write a school story. That's how I came to write my first published book, *Water in the Air*. You could say I've never looked back, though it was a few more years before I could give up my day job and make a living out of writing.

I still love exploring, and being outdoors. I travel whenever I can. As well as writing Ann Halam books, I write science fiction for grown ups under my own name. People often ask me which books I like best, and I always say "Both!"

*   *   *

Having published several critically acclaimed fantasies for children, Gwyneth Jones wrote *Ally Ally, Aster*. Rejected by her first publisher, it was accepted by Allen and Unwin, who also encouraged her ambition to write adult science fiction for their own list. Gwyneth Jones therefore decided to write all her children's books as "Ann Halam," a family name, and use her real name for her adult fiction. Later, she revealed her identity, resolving the mystery of where the talented children's author Gwyneth Jones had gone!

King Death's Garden is neither fantasy nor science fiction, but a ghost story with a chilling climax. Lonely Maurice discovers traces of an eccentric Professor's research: he had found out how to raise the dead. Maurice, absorbed in the strange dreams which come to him whenever he goes to a special part of the cemetery, "King Death's Garden," is increasingly aware of being spied on—haunted—and one evening he lingers too late in the cemetery and is nearly trapped for ever.

Ann Halam's next work for young people was a major science fantasy, the "Inland" trilogy. It is set in a future about three centuries ahead of ours. Twentieth-century civilisation has collapsed, following the exhaustion of all modern ways of producing energy, particularly electricity. Instead, women have rediscovered magic, which keeps the desolation of the destroyed world at bay, but magic only works as long as people do not turn back to science. In *The Daymaker*, Zanne is found to have strong magical powers. She is sent to magic school to learn to use them for society's good, eventually to become a Covener, the head of a community who supervises the use of magic in that locality.

Attracted by machines left over from the age of technology, Zanne is tempted to make them work again, by magic instead of electricity. This results in the gradual drying-up of magic in her area. The villagers smash the machines, but Zanne runs away to the "badlands" to find a rumoured Daymaker (i.e. electric power station) to set it going by magic. Just in time she learns that this would neutralise everyone else's magic powers, and her whole country of "Inland" would lose its fertility.

Four years later, in *Transformations*, Zanne is sent to the mountainous region of Minith to find and destroy another Daymaker. The puritanical sect of miners inhabiting the mountains refuses to help her: they would rather suffer blighted lives than reveal the truth to a stranger. The blight affects teenagers most. Zanne and her friend, the lonely girl Sirato, watch how the teenagers are temporarily transformed into monsters by an evil power lurking in the old mines. Zanne exercises magic to pull Sirato back when she shapechanges into a rat. She explains to Sirato that: "The people of the past . . . found a power that belongs neither to them nor to us. . . . They took that force and made it work for them, made it heat water

and turn wheels. But when they'd taken what they wanted, what was left over was poison to them . . . they hid it away, buried it under a mountain. . . .'' The reader must put a name to the evil (nuclear waste) which in Inland causes magical transformations and lingering death. The fanatical miners refuse Zanne's offered help, and try to kill her, but all ends well.

In *The Skybreaker* Zanne has a companion, Holne of Minith, once one of the transformed teenagers, now training as a Covener. They travel by sea to Magia, rumoured to have a "skybreaker." Zanne finds a European city culture where magic is harnessed centrally by the constant repetition of formulae (recalling the medieval church) to maintain the network of waterways and hold back the sea. This production line has generated extra magic which the Great Mage, Lady Monkshood, has siphoned off, not to awake a "skybreaker" from the olden days but to manufacture a new one: a rocket to fly through space by magic. Zanne realises that the launch and flight of the rocket would destroy the world's magic networks. Its very existence has already caused Holne to revert to his beast-shape.

The "Daymaker" trilogy is an outstanding achievement in the genre. Ann Halam's style rises to the challenge of describing the supernatural effects Zanne encounters, and each book can stand several re-readings. She describes a world where the equality of the sexes, and sometimes the superiority of women, is natural (as are strong differences in skin colour); and a world where the results of the twentieth-century demand for electricity, disregarding consequent pollution, are dramatically brought home.

Ann Halam's most recent books have contemporary settings, and are about teenagers who, at odds with society for various reasons, have terrifying experiences with the supernatural world. Thirteen-year-old Jessica, in *The Haunting of Jessica Raven*, cannot help her beloved older brother, who is dying. On holiday she meets Jean-Luc, a young Frenchman who is always with a gang of terrifying children. In her state of highly charged emotional stress, Jessica is receptive to Jean-Luc's searing memories of past events, and her desire to help him brings benefits to everyone.

Other titles are for older readers. Andrei's family, in *The Fear Man*, is permanently on the move to escape from the father Andrei has never known. They live in squalid conditions, with neurotic Mum taking dead-end jobs. Andrei has to face his inheritance as a night person, and retrieve the cloak of darkness his father stole years ago, in a genuinely scary, surprising, but ultimately very satisfying story.

Murder and demonic possession face Robs, Jef, and Maddy in *The Powerhouse*, as musically gifted Robs becomes increasingly concerned with Maddy's obsession with Sophie Raeburn, who died horribly, possibly murdered, twenty-five years ago. The three rehearse their techno-art numbers in the old powerhouse where Sophie lived: all have frightening experiences with her ghost, but it is Robs who has to face Maddy and wrestle with the evil that has taken her over. There are parallels between Robs' band and Sophie's, and there are parallels between Elinor and the two-hundred-year-old ghost of Nellie in *Crying in the Dark*. Elinor, scarred in the fire that killed her father, is the bullied and abused cousin of the Madisons, a family whose extreme nastiness is conveyed with understated brilliance. Living in the old Dower House, Elinor constantly hears a child crying. She is drawn into the two-hundred-year-old world of Nellie, the poor relation of the local Wicked Lady, Deborah Revelle. Treated worse than a kitchen skivvy, Nellie dies in prison after being charged with the murder of eight-year-old Richard Revelle. It is Elinor's concerned and loyal African friend, Oya, who by chance triggers a happy ending for Elinor, and the solution of the old mystery.

Ann Halam's characters are well-drawn and conveyed with perception. Her convincing stories start from a well-laid basis of normality, and then take one step that plunges the reader into a frightening, unfamiliar, supernatural world. Each of her books is a little gem.

—Jessica Yates, updated by Felicity Trotman

HALL, Barbara

Nationality: American. **Born:** Danville, Virginia, 17 July 1960. **Education:** James Madison University, Harrisonburg, Virginia, B.A. 1982. **Family:** Married Nick Harding in 1985; one daughter. **Career:** Screenwriter for television, Los Angeles, California, since 1982; writer/developer, Castle Rock Entertainment; children's writer. **Awards:** *Booklist* editors list citation, *School Library Journal*'s Ten Best of Books of 1990 citation, American Library Association Notable Book and Best Books of 1990 citations, all 1990, for *Dixie Storms;* ALA Best Books for Reluctant Readers citation, 1992, for *Fool's Hill;* Humanities award, 1992, for "Comfort and Joy," episode of *I'll Fly Away.* **Agent:** Cynthia Manson, 444 East 86th St., New York, New York 10028. **Address:** 10720 Le Conte Ave., Los Angeles, California 90024, U.S.A.

PUBLICATIONS FOR YOUNG ADULTS

Fiction

Skeeball and the Secret of the Universe. New York, Richard Jackson/Orchard Books, 1987.
Dixie Storms. Orlando, Florida, Harcourt, 1990.
Fool's Hill. New York, Bantam, 1992.
A Better Place. New York, Simon & Schuster, 1994.
Close to Home. New York, Simon & Schuster, 1997.

Screenplays (television episodes)

Story editor, *Newhart.* CBS, 1982-83.
Executive story editor, *A Year in the Life.* NBC, 1986-87.
Producer, *Moonlighting.* ABC, 1989.
Producer, *Anything but Love.* ABC, 1990.
Co-executive producer, *I'll Fly Away.* NBC, 1992.
Creative consultant, *Northern Exposure.* CBS, from 1993.

Barbara Hall comments:

I've heard that a writer keeps writing about any part of his or her life which is unresolved. That certainly has something to do with why I write about adolescence. Every time I explore that age, I have the opportunity to go back and fix something that never got fixed, confront someone I never confronted, or reaffirm a desire or conviction that I possessed back then, and might be in danger of losing.

* * *

In Barbara Hall's first novel, *Skeeball and the Secret of the Universe,* Matty Collier, a rebel without a cause in his own right who idolizes James Dean and spends the summer before his final year of high school searching for "the Thing," thinks and talks a lot about teenage angst: "I was all the time praying to something that had no name, that had no real definition in my mind at all. More than anything else, I prayed to this feeling I had that there was some kind of great pattern, the one that kept things from falling apart, that rescued kids like me from working in a hot-dog joint." Who hasn't felt this way? In *Skeeball* and in two other novels, *Dixie Storms* and *Fool's Hill,* Hall presents common coming-of-age questions about self-identity, personal purpose, and interpersonal relationships through the stories of memorable, likeable characters like Matty. The constraints and standard peculiarities of small town or rural life influence these young people's quests; in fact, setting is a key component of their world views. Hall's novels are driven by character, action, and emotion in a scene-to-scene construction that makes the overall experience of them not unlike the experience of television drama.

As in teledramas, where stories are told largely through the things characters do and say rather than through significant exploration of the inner life a character might have but for which there is little or no visual evidence, Hall's novels present character and action as two sides of the same coin. Her characters are not without "mind life"; certainly each presents his or her own reasoned outlook and musings. But for the most part, Hall depends on plot action to motivate and reveal. The characters—genuine, strongly voiced, and often funny—begin with a premise of what they believe their lives should be like, which is then tested by reality. Matty, an only child who discovers he is the "accident" that caused his parents to marry as teenagers, bounces like one of his beloved skeeballs around his small, beach resort hometown with idealistic disdain for the inevitable responsibilities of adulthood. He believes that jobs, marriage, and families cause people to give up and glaze over before they have discovered and experienced that which gives their lives unique purpose.

In *Dixie Storms,* Dutch Peyton is an empathetic mix of woman and child. Without a mother, Dutch lives on a Virginia farm with her hard-working father, a difficult adult brother whose wife has left him with their young son, and a nervous aunt. Dutch is responsible and practical to a fault, taking on the weight of household duties and looking after her wise-cracking, trouble-making nephew. But she is uncertain about matters of growing up and yearns for someone to show her the way. Finally, in *Fool's Hill,* Hall presents eager-to-please Libby, who from her vantage point in a small rural Virginia town, sees the world as being made up of the people who fall down (plain, awkward people like herself) and the people who laugh at them (perfect people like her older sister Gloria). With Gloria away in Chicago, which to Libby is as much an exotic idea as it is a place, she spends the summer trying to become a "laugher" and gets mixed up with the wrong crowd in the process.

What these characters have in common, and what makes them interesting and easy to identify with, is a quality of loneliness. They stand somewhat outside the circle of their peers and, to some extent, seem removed even from their own situations. As a result, they possess both a real longing to be a part of a meaningful whole and a special ability to comment on the adolescent condition. In each novel, Hall heightens plot tension by bringing in an outsider— a beautiful summer tourist, a worldly cousin, a pair of rough and tumble sisters willing to take a "faller" along for the ride. The technique provides contrast for her characters' positions and increases their sense of isolation. Hall links this character isolation with small town settings, which are knowingly created and full of local sound and color. Sense of place is most convincing in *Dixie Storms,* where she fleshes out the relationship between modern farming families and their land. Using the theme of "The Country Mouse and the City Mouse," she brings in Dutch's city cousin Norma, who seems for a time to be everything Dutch wishes to become. Hall drops the fable's moralism, however, and gives it an original twist: even after Norma's superior facade crumbles, revealing undesirable superficial qualities, Dutch finds that it is still possible to like her.

Hall's novels appeal to emotions more often than to intellect. In each, she uses a teledrama-like method of setting up a scene where the balance of forces has been upset. There are no accidents or coincidences and few surprises. Secondary characters serve mainly to advance the main character's story to the climactic point where his or her false goal is revealed and new understanding is reached: Matty realizes that doing something important to him and doing it well is the "Thing"; Dutch learns to accept that people—herself included—can't always live up to her "hard hopes" of them; Libby finds, too, that there are no perfect people and that being herself takes courage but is right for the long run. Forces are brought back into balance. Hall's is an efficient method of storytelling and, on an emotional level, it satisfies.

—Tracy J. Sukraw

HALL, Lynn

Nationality: American. **Born:** Lombard, Illinois, 9 November 1937. **Education:** Attended schools in Iowa. **Family:** Married Dean W. Green in 1960 (divorced 1961). **Career:** Secretary, Fort Worth, Texas, 1955-57; secretary and veterinarian's assistant, Des Moines, Iowa, 1957-66; copywriter, Ambro Advertising Agency, Des Moines 1966-68; full-time writer, since 1969. **Awards:** Book of the year selections from Child Study Association of America include *Ride a Wild Dream,* 1969, *Too Near the Sun,* 1970, *Gently Touch the Milkweed,* 1970, *To Catch a Tartar,* 1973, *Barry the Bravest St. Bernard,* 1973, *New Day for Dragon,* 1975, *Just One Friend,* 1985, and *Mrs. Portree's Pony,* 1987; Charles W. Follett award, 1971, for *A Horse Called Dragon;* Best Young Adult Books selections by American Library Association, 1972, for *Sticks and Stones,* 1980, for *The Leaving,* and 1984, for *Uphill All the Way;* Netherlands' Silver Quill award, 1976, for *Sticks and Stones;* Edgar Allan Poe award runner up from the Mystery Writers of America, 1980, for *The Whispered Horse; The Leaving* was selected as one of the best young adult books by American Library Association, 1980, received the *Boston Globe-Horn Book* award for fiction, 1981, and was selected as one of New York Public Library's books for teenagers, 1981 and 1982; Tennessee Children's Choice award from Tennessee Library Association, 1981, for *Shadows; The Horse Trader* was selected as one of New York Public Library's books for teenagers 1982; *Uphill All the Way* was selected as one of the best young adult books by American Library Association, 1984; *Tazo and Me* was selected an Outstanding

Science Trade Book for Children by the National Science Teachers Association and the Children's Book Council, 1985; Golden Kite award Honor Book for Fiction from the Society of Children's Book Writers, 1986, for *The Solitary;* Children's Literature award from the Society of Midland Authors, 1987, for *Mrs. Portree's Pony;* Johnson Brigham award from the Iowa State Historical Society, 1989, for *The Secret Life of Dagmar Schultz.* **Address:** Touchwood, Route 2, Elkader, Iowa 52043, U.S.A.

PUBLICATIONS FOR YOUNG ADULTS

Fiction

The Shy Ones, illustrated by Greta Elgaard. Chicago, Follett, 1967.
Gently Touch the Milkweed, illustrated by Rod Ruth. Chicago, Follett, 1970.
Too Near the Sun, illustrated by Stefan Martin. Chicago, Follett, 1970.
A Horse Called Dragon, illustrated by Joseph Cellini. Chicago, Follett, 1971; as *Wild Mustang,* New York, Scholastic, 1976.
Dog Stories, illustrated by Joseph Cellini. Chicago, Follett, 1972.
The Siege of Silent Henry. Chicago, Follett, 1972.
Sticks and Stones, illustrated by Milton Glaser. Chicago, Follett, 1972.
Riff Remember. Chicago, Follett, 1973.
Troublemaker, illustrated by Joseph Cellini. Chicago, Follett, 1974.
New Day for Dragon, illustrated by Joseph Cellini. Chicago, Follett, 1975.
Flowers of Anger, illustrated by Joseph Cellini. Chicago, Follett, 1976.
Dragon Defiant, illustrated by Joseph Cellini. Chicago, Follett, 1977.
Shadows, illustrated by Joseph Cellini. Chicago, Follett, 1977.
Dog of the Bondi Castle, illustrated by Michael Mariano. Chicago, Follett, 1979.
The Whispered Horse. Chicago, Follett, 1979.
The Leaving, illustrated by Lloyd Bloom. New York, Scribner, 1980.
Danza!, illustrated by Sandra Rabinowitz. New York, Scribner, 1981.
Dragon's Delight. Chicago, Follett, 1981.
The Ghost of the Great River Inn, illustrated by Allen Davis. Chicago, Follett, 1981.
The Horse Trader, illustrated by Ted Lewin. New York, Scribner, 1981.
Half the Battle. New York, Scribner, 1982.
Tin Can Tucker, illustrated by Ruth Sanderson. New York, Scribner, 1982.
Denison's Daughter. New York, Scribner, 1983.
The Boy in the Off-White Hat. New York, Scribner, 1984.
Uphill All the Way. New York, Scribner, 1984.
The Giver. New York, Scribner, 1985; London, Macmillan, 1987.
Just One Friend. New York, Scribner, 1985.
The Something-Special Horse, illustrated by Sandy Rabinowitz. New York, Scribner, 1985.
Danger Dog. New York, Scribner, 1986.
If Winter Comes. New York, Scribner, 1986; London, Viking Kestrel, 1987.
Mrs. Portree's Pony. New York, Scribner, 1986.
The Solitary. New York, Scribner, 1986; London, Viking, 1988.
Flyaway. New York, Scribner, 1987.
In Trouble Again Zelda Hammersmith?, illustrated by Ray Cruz. San Diego, Harcourt Brace, 1987.
Letting Go. New York, Scribner, 1987.
Ride a Dark Horse. New York, Morrow, 1987.
Dagmar Schultz and the Powers of Darkness. New York, Scribner, 1988.
A Killing Freeze. New York, Morrow, 1988.

Murder at the Spaniel Show. New York, Scribner, 1988.
The Secret Life of Dagmar Schultz. New York, Scribner, 1988.
Zelda Strikes Again! San Diego, Harcourt Brace, 1988.
Dagmar Schultz and the Angel Edna. New York, Scribner, 1989.
Here Comes Zelda Claus and Other Holiday Disasters. San Diego, Harcourt Brace, 1989.
Where Have All the Tigers Gone? New York, Scribner, 1989.
Fair Maiden. New York, Scribner, 1990.
Halsey's Pride. New York, Scribner, 1990.
Murder in a Pig's Eye. San Diego, Harcourt Brace, 1990.
The Tormentors. San Diego, Harcourt Brace, 1990.
Dagmar Schultz and the Green-Eyed Monster. New York, Scribner, 1991.
Flying Changes. San Diego, Harcourt Brace, 1991.
The Soul of the Silver Dog. San Diego, Harcourt Brace, 1992.
Windsong. New York, Scribner, 1992.

PUBLICATIONS FOR CHILDREN

Fiction

The Secret of Stonehouse, illustrated by Joseph Cellini. Chicago, Follett, 1968.
Ride a Wild Dream, illustrated by George Roth. Chicago, Follett, 1969.
The Famous Battle of Bravery Creek. Champaign, Illinois, Garrard, 1972.
Barry the Bravest St. Bernard, illustrated by Richard Amundsen. Champaign, Illinois, Garrard, 1973.
Flash Dog of Old Egypt, illustrated by Taylor Oughton. Champaign, Illinois, Garrard, 1973.
To Catch a Tartar, illustrated by Joseph Cellini. Chicago, Follett, 1973.
Bob Watchdog of the River, illustrated by Taylor Oughton. Champaign, Illinois, Garrard, 1974.
The Stray, illustrated by Joseph Cellini. Chicago, Follett, 1974.
Captain: Canada's Flying Pony, illustrated by Tran Mawicke. Champaign, Illinois, Garrard, 1976.
Owney the Traveling Dog, illustrated by Barbara Erikson. Champaign, Illinois, Garrard, 1977.
The Mystery of Pony Hollow, illustrated by Ruth Sanderson. Champaign, Illinois, Garrard, 1978.
The Mystery of the Lost and Found Hound, illustrated by Alan Daniel. Champaign, Illinois, Garrard, 1979.
The Mystery of the Schoolhouse Dog, illustrated by William Hutchinson. Champaign, Illinois, Garrard, 1979.
The Mystery of the Plum Park Pony, illustrated by Alan Daniel. Champaign, Illinois, Garrard, 1980.
The Mystery of the Stubborn Old Man, illustrated by Herman Vestal. Champaign, Illinois, Garrard, 1980.
The Disappearing Grandad, illustrated by William Jefferson. Chicago, Follett, 1981.
The Haunting of the Green Bird, illustrated by David Cunningham. Chicago, Follett, 1981.
The Mysterious Moortown Bridge, illustrated by Ruth Sanderson. Chicago, Follett, 1981.
The Mystery of the Caramel Cat, illustrated by Ruth Sanderson. Champaign, Illinois, Garrard, 1981.
Megan's Mare. New York, Scribner, 1983.
The Mystery of Pony Hollow Panda, illustrated by William Hutchinson. Champaign, Illinois, Garrard, 1983.

Barry, the Bravest Saint Bernard, illustrated by Antonio Castro. New York, Random House, 1992.
Shadows, illustrated by Dave Henderson. New York, Bullseye Books, 1992.
The Mystery of the Phantom Pony, illustrated by Marie DeJohn. New York, Random House, 1993.

Nonfiction

Kids and Dog Shows. Chicago, Follett, 1975.
Careers for Dog Lovers. Chicago, Follett, 1978.
Tazo and Me, photographs by Jan Hall. New York, Scribner, 1985.
Dog Showing for Beginners. New York, Howell Book House, 1994.

*

Biography: Essay in *Something about the Author Autobiography Series,* Volume 4, Detroit, Gale, 1987; essay in *Speaking for Ourselves: Autobiographical Sketches by Notable Authors of Books for Young Adults,* Volume 1, compiled and edited by Donald R. Gallo, National Council of Teachers of English, 1990.

Manuscript Collections: Kerlan Collection, University of Minnesota, Minneapolis.

*   *   *

A prolific author of books for young adults, Lynn Hall specializes in gentle and well-detailed stories about young people coming of age and their family relationships.

Hall shows her experience as a professional dog handler in the quietly written *The Shy Ones,* the story of Robin, a young girl so painfully shy she is without friends at school, a situation that worries her parents. Taming a lost, hurt, golden retriever leads Robin outside of her shyness: first she gets a job with the veterinarian who mends the dog, and then she unexpectedly finds a boyfriend while she is standing in front of the local drugstore teaching the dog not to fear people. When the dog turns out to be purebred and to have an owner, Robin conquers her fear, defies the dog's abusive owner, and shows the dog. Robin is a realistic character, and the reader is drawn to empathize with her struggle to accept both herself and her shyness while longing to be like the other teens around her. Her emergence from her shell is profoundly moving.

Flyaway is the story of seventeen-year-old Ariel, her younger sister, Robin, and their dysfunctional family. The father is a disguised dictator, perfect in the public eye but ruthless in his control of the family. Ariel's mother is so dominated that she betrays Ariel in her first bid for freedom. Ariel and Robin both hate their father but choose different ways to escape his control. Ariel works secretly, debating marriage and looking for a job. Robin, pushed to the breaking point, runs away with the father of her best friend and turns to prostitution. While well-written, *Flyaway* is not an easy book. The things that go unsaid by Hall are the more difficult for the unspoken understandings. Ariel is a determined character, but without the sharp edge of desperation that drives her sister to an even uglier life than the one with her family. When Ariel finally escapes her father's domination by selling the skis that previously had been her escape, relief is mixed with anxiety for the remaining child, alone and unsupported in the empty home.

In *Fair Maiden,* Hall uses a Renaissance fair as the setting for a teenager's first love, weaving the fantasy of the fair into Jenny's feelings for the man she hardly knows in real life but who, as John the Lutanist, is everything she dreamed. John has a history of falling in love with young girls, but Jenny is the first with whom he is intimate, and instead of Jenny ending the relationship, John does, afraid of the reality of what they have done.

Hall again uses a dog theme in *Halsey's Pride,* in which thirteen-year-old March moves in with her father, a breeder of purebred collies, after her mother's new husband rejects her. March falls in love with her father's prized stud dog, Halsey's Pride, who returns March's love with the uncritical adoration March wants from her father. When Pride's puppies prove to have a genetic flaw, proving Pride is not as good as her father believes, March learns the hard lesson of acceptance that her father has failed to find.

A pony is the animal catalyst in *Mrs. Portree's Pony.* Addie Harvey finds herself an unwanted foster child until she comes upon a pony who belonged to the long-gone daughter of a local recluse. Addie and Mrs. Portree strike up a friendship, and the two find love and support in each other when Addie is eventually asked to leave her foster home.

Hall changes gears in *Murder in a Pig's Eye,* a mystery set in farm country in Wisconsin. Bodie Tureen and his sister, Gracie, stumble on a mystery in their small town and set out to solve it. Along the way, Bodie manages nearly to get arrested and cut in half by a chain saw, and gets covered in pig manure. While amusing, this book lacks the character involvement of Hall's more serious works. The delicate details of character so readily available in *Flyaway* or *The Shy Ones* is lacking, and Hall strives so hard for humor that the characters never seem to experience actual growth.

Most of Hall's books are quick reads, perfect for a reluctant reader. The characters' problems are easily empathized with and involving. Hall's works describing unusual careers, hobbies, or settings are meticulously researched and rich in detail, teaching while at the same time telling a story.

—Melanie Belviso

HALVORSON, Marilyn

Nationality: Canadian. **Born:** Olds, Alberta, 17 January 1948. **Education:** Sundre High School, Sundre, Alberta, 1961-64; University of Calgary, B.Ed. 1981. **Career:** Teacher, County of Mountain View, Alberta, 1968-1990; rancher, since 1977. **Awards:** Clarke Irwin/Alberta Culture Writing for Youth Competition, 1983; R. Ross Annett Award for Children's Literature, 1987. **Address:** Box 9, Site 14, RR2, Sundre, Alberta T0M 1X0, Canada.

PUBLICATIONS FOR YOUNG ADULTS

Cowboys Don't Cry. Toronto, Clarke Irwin, and New York, Delacorte, 1984.
Let It Go. Toronto, Irwin, and New York, Delacorte, 1985.
Nobody Said It Would Be Easy. Toronto, Irwin, 1987; as *Hold On, Geronimo,* New York, Delacorte, 1987.
Dare. Toronto, Stoddart, 1988.

Bull Rider, illustrated by Greg Ruhl. Don Mills, Ontario, Collier Macmillan Canada, 1989.
Brothers and Strangers. Toronto, Stoddart, 1991.
Stranger on the Run. Toronto, Stoddart, 1992.
Blue Moon. Don Mills, Ontario, Maxwell Macmillan Canada, 1994.
Cowboys Don't Quit. Toronto, Stoddart, 1994.
Stranger on the Line. Toronto, Stoddart, 1997.

PUBLICATIONS FOR CHILDREN

But Cows Can't Fly and Other Stories. Toronto, General, 1993.

PUBLICATIONS FOR ADULTS

To Everything a Season: A Year in Alberta Ranch Country. Toronto, Stoddart, 1991.

*

Media Adaptations: *Cowboys Don't Cry, Cowboys Don't Quit, Dare, Stranger on the Run, Let It Go,* and *Nobody Said It Would Be Easy* have all been recorded on cassette; *Cowboy's Don't Cry* has been adapted as a made-for-TV movie.

Marilyn Halvorson comments:

With nearly 20 years experience teaching young adults and a lifetime spent riding and ranching it's only natural that kids and horses play a big role in most of my books. Although I no longer teach I'm still running my cow-calf operation in the semi-wild wooded country of the foothills north west of Calgary and enjoying all my furred and feathered neighbors, both wild and tame.

*   *   *

Since the appearance of *Cowboys Don't Cry* in the early 1980s, rancher/writer Marilyn Halvorson has produced a string of successful novels which utilize Alberta, Canada, ranch-based storylines that normally revolve about troubled but sensitive adolescent males. Like S. E. Hinton's protagonists, Halvorson's characters find a ready audience amongst adolescents of both genders.

In *Cowboys Don't Cry,* which has also become a made-for-TV movie, Shane Morgan, 14, has still not forgiven his father, Josh, for the alcohol-related accident which killed his mother four years previously. At that time Josh was a two-time North American Bull Riding Champion, but following his wife's death he increasingly turned to drinking for solace and his career plummeted until he was forced to become a rodeo clown to make a living. Paralleling Josh's occupational decline is his deteriorating relationship with Shane. Though an inheritance of an Alberta ranch gives the pair a fresh start, Josh's drinking continues to separate him from his son who tries to heed his mother's advice from his childhood days: "Cowboys don't cry."

A decade later, Halvorson revisited Shane in *Cowboys Don't Quit.* Shane, now 15, is concerned because Josh is late in returning from Bozeman, Montana. Shane imagines various explanatory scenarios, including one involving his greatest fear: Josh's resuming drinking. To assuage his anxiety, Shane heads south accompanied by his stowaway neighbour, Casey Sutherland. The early portion of the duo's in-search-of-Josh odyssey provides engaging, occasionally lighthearted reading, but the book's tone darkens as Shane approaches Bozeman and circumstantial evidence apparently confirms Shane's alcohol-based suspicions. When Casey chastises a demoralized Shane, her words remind him of his deceased mother's advice, "Cowboy's don't quit, Shane." A re-energized Shane continues on, eventually rescuing his father from a gang of poachers who are illegally selling animal parts to Asia. Though aspects of the plot rely on chance, readers will still be satisfied with the book's ending, which reaffirms the father-son bond.

Another set of paired novels are *Let It Go* and *Nobody Said It Would Be Easy* (published in the United States as *Hold On, Geronimo*). Best friends Red Cantrell and Lance "Geronimo" Ducharme, both 15, each have a secret. Due to a drug overdose, Red's brother is in a vegetative state in a Calgary hospital, a situation which has caused so much stress in the Cantrell family that Red and his father are almost estranged. Lance, meanwhile, believes that his mother, a country singing star, abandoned him and his father 10 years before to pursue her career. When she returns and wants to spend time with him, he refuses, but Red tests the strength of their friendship by arranging a mother-son meeting. *Nobody Said It Would Be Easy* introduces a third major character, Kat, Lance's cousin who joins the pair of boys on a flight taking them to a horse drive. When the plane crashes and the pilot is killed, the adolescent trio must work together to survive.

To date, *Dare* is the only full length Halvorson novel in which the main character has not returned in a sequel. When his grandmother suddenly dies, 15-year-old Darren "Dare" Jamieson fears that he and his brother Ty, 12, both now technically orphans, will be placed in separate foster homes. However, Laura McConnell, rancher and substitute teacher, had already befriended Ty and she volunteers to take care of the two boys. Like Laura's rebellious horse, Smoke, Dare fights against being "broken" but ultimately he and Smoke are no match for Laura's version of tough love.

Brothers and Strangers is the first of a series of novels which follow the story of Steve Garrett. The opening volume, however, features Steve's younger brother, Beau, 16, who, because he is dependable and academically capable, is an atypical Halvorson protagonist. Beau's family life is a disaster; his parents had separated following their ranch's financial collapse, and now Beau runs the home, his older brother Steve having run away. The stability Beau has been able to recreate is disrupted by both Steve's sudden reappearance and his learning that Steve's life is at risk because Steve, now 19, had betrayed a Vancouver drug dealer, Carlos Romero. In *Stranger on the Run*, Steve, now the central character, encounters Jesse Firebird and begins to work on a ranch owned by the Johannesons. Steve gains maturity as he works with animals and begins to identify with Jesse's attempts to save the land from exploitation by a gas company.

While the first two instalments of Steve Garrett's story were lively, *Stranger on the Line* suffers somewhat from a lengthy timeline. Though the plot continues action introduced by the previous title's "Epilogue," the book's year-long time span causes some of the happenings to be treated superficially. Steve, 20 and still on the run from his vengeful pursuer, illegally enters the United States where he hooks up with Reece Kelly, an ex-jockey who owns a Montana ranch stocked with racetrack rejects. Recognizing Reece's financial difficulties, Steve suggests entering a chuckwagon in the Calgary Stampede, and the pair spend three seasons assembling a team from Reece's misfit horses. At the Stampede, Steve's wagon reaches the "final four," and he encounters his lost love, Lynne Tremayne, and, unfortunately, Romero. At story's end, for Lynne's safety, the pair separate, and Steve is again in flight from Romero.

Halvorson has also authored two hi-lo "Series 2000" titles. *Bull Rider* features Layne McQueen, 16, whose father had been killed six years before while on the verge of achieving a championship season in rodeo bull riding. Now Layne wants to take up the sport, but his mother is adamantly opposed. In *Blue Moon,* 17-year-old Bobbie-Jo Brooks, in search of a horse for barrel racing, purchases a run-down blue roan mare at an auction. After Bobbie-Jo successfully nurses Blue Moon back to health and achieves some barrel racing success, she learns that her horse may have originally been stolen.

—Dave Jenkinson

HAMILTON, Virginia (Esther)

Nationality: American. **Born:** Yellow Springs, Ohio, 12 March 1936. **Education:** Antioch College, Yellow Springs, 1952-55, B.A. 1955; Ohio State University, Columbus, 1957-58; New School for Social Research, New York, 1958-60. **Family:** Married Arnold Adoff in 1960; one daughter and one son. **Career:** Whittall lecturer, Library of Congress, Washington, D.C., 1975; visiting professor, Queens College, Flushing, New York, 1986-87. **Awards:** American Library Association's (ALA) list of notable children's books of 1967, Nancy Block Memorial award of the Downtown Community School awards Committee, New York, both for *Zeely*; Edgar Allan Poe award for best juvenile mystery, 1969, for *The House of Dies Drear*; Ohioana Literary award, 1969; John Newbery Honor Book award, 1971, for *The Planet of Junior Brown*; Lewis Carroll Shelf award, *Boston Globe-Horn Book* award, 1974, John Newbery Medal and National Book award, both 1975, and Gustav-Heinemann-Friedinspreis fur kinder und Lugendbucher (Dusseldorf, Germany), 1991, all for *M.C. Higgins, the Great*; John Newbery Honor Book award, Coretta Scott King award, *Boston Globe-Horn Book* award, and American Book award nomination, all 1983, all for *Sweet Whispers, Brother Rush*; *Horn Book* Fanfare award in fiction, 1985, for *A Little Love*; Coretta Scott King award, *New York Times* Best Illustrated Children's Book award, Children's Book Bulletin Other award, and *Horn Book* Honor List selection, all 1986, all for *The People Could Fly: American Black Folktales*; *Boston Globe-Horn Book* award, 1988, and Coretta Scott King award, 1989, both for *Anthony Burns: The Defeat and Triumph of a Fugitive Slave*; John Newbery Honor Book award, 1988, for *In the Beginning: Creation Stories from around the World*; Jane Addams Children's Book award, 1990, for *Anthony Burns*; Catholic Library Association Regina Medal, 1990; Coretta Scott King award, 1992, for *The Bells of Christmas*; Hans Christian

Andersen award U.S. nominee, 1992, for body of work; Honorary D.H.L., Bank St. College, 1990. **Agent:** Arnold Adoff Agency, Box 293, Yellow Springs, Ohio 45387, U.S.A.

PUBLICATIONS FOR YOUNG ADULTS

Fiction

Zeely, illustrated by Symeon Shimin. New York, Macmillan, 1967.

The House of Dies Drear, illustrated by Eros Keith. New York, Macmillan, 1968.

The Planet of Junior Brown. New York, Macmillan, 1971; London, Gollancz, 1987.

M.C. Higgins, the Great. New York, Macmillan, 1974; London, Hamish Hamilton, 1975; published with teacher's guide by Lou Stanek, Dell, 1976.

Arilla Sun Down. New York, Greenwillow, 1976; London, Hamish Hamilton, 1977.

Justice and Her Brothers. New York, Greenwillow, 1978; London, Hamish Hamilton, 1979.

Dustland. New York, Greenwillow, and London, MacRae, 1980.

The Gathering. New York, Greenwillow, and London, MacRae, 1981.

Sweet Whispers, Brother Rush. New York, Philomel, 1982; London, Walker, 1987.

The Magical Adventures of Pretty Pearl. New York, Harper, 1983.

Willie Bea and the Time the Martians' Landed. New York, Greenwillow, 1983.

A Little Love. New York, Philomel, 1984; London, Gollancz, 1985.

The Mystery of Drear House: The Conclusion of the Dies Drear Chronicle. New York, Greenwillow, 1987.

A White Romance. New York, Philomel, 1987; London, Gollancz, 1988.

Cousins. New York, Philomel, 1990.

Plain City. New York, Scholastic, 1993.

Other

W.E.B. DuBois: A Biography. New York, Crowell, 1972.

Paul Robeson: The Life and Times of a Free Black Man. New York, Harper, 1974.

Editor, *The Writings of W.E.B. Du Bois.* New York, Crowell, 1975.

The People Could Fly: American Black Folktales, illustrated by Leo and Diane Dillon. New York, Knopf, 1985; London, Walker, 1986; published with cassette, 1987.

Anthony Burns: The Defeat and Triumph of a Fugitive Slave. New York, Knopf, 1988.

In the Beginning: Creation Stories from around the World, illustrated by Barry Moser. San Diego, Harcourt Brace, 1988.

The Dark Way: Stories from the Spirit World, illustrated by Lambert Davis. San Diego, Harcourt Brace, 1990.

Many Thousand Gone: African Americans from Slavery to Freedom, illustrated by Leo and Diane Dillon. New York, Knopf, 1992.

Her Stories: African American Folktales, Fairy Tales, and True Tales, illustrated by Leo and Diane Dillon. New York, Blue Sky Press, 1995.

When Birds Could Talk and Bats Could Sing. illustrated by Barry Moser. New York, Blue Sky Press, 1996.

A Ring of Tricksters: Animal Tales from America, the West Indies, and Africa. Forthcoming.

PUBLICATIONS FOR CHILDREN

The Time-Ago Tales of Jahdu, illustrated by Nonny Hogrogian. New York, Macmillan, 1969.

Time-Ago Lost: More Tales of Jahdu, illustrated by Ray Prather. New York, Macmillan, 1973.

Jahdu, illustrated by Jerry Pinkney. New York, Greenwillow, 1980.

Junius over Far. New York, Harper, 1985.

Bells of Christmas, illustrated by Lambert Davis. San Diego, Harcourt Brace, 1989.

The All Jahdu Storybook, illustrated by Barry Moser. San Diego, Harcourt Brace, 1991.

Drylongso, illustrated by Jerry Pinkney. San Diego, Harcourt Brace, 1992.

*

Media Adaptations: *The House of Dies Drear* (television series, "Wonderworks"), Public Broadcasting Service, 1984.

Biography: Entry in *Dictionary of Literary Biography,* Vol. 52: *American Writers for Children since 1960: Fiction,* Detroit, Gale, 1986, 174-184; entry in *Dictionary of Literary Biography,* Vol. 33: *Afro-American Fiction Writers after 1955,* Detroit, Gale, 1984, 107-110; essay in *Speaking for Ourselves: Autobiographical Sketches by Notable Authors of Books for Young Adults,* Vol. 1, compiled and edited by Donald R. Gallo, National Council of Teachers of English, 1990.

Critical Studies: Entry in *Children's Literature Review,* Detroit, Gale, Vol. 1, 1976, and Vol. 11, 1986; entry in *Contemporary Literary Criticism,* Vol. 26, Detroit, Gale, 1983.

*   *   *

Virginia Hamilton is a gifted writer, known for her versatility and command of the art of storytelling. Her works encompass every genre of prose and all of them reflect her experiences as an African American.

The characters in her realistic fiction books are vividly drawn. *The Planet of Junior Brown* revolves around three memorably unique outcasts. Mr. Pool is the teacher turned custodian who attempts to teach the boys in his underground hideaway in the school basement. Junior Brown is a huge, dreamy, musically talented boy who is psychologically fragile. Buddy Clark serves as his foil: he is rooted in the day-to-day business of survival—his own. The development of the boys is bittersweet; as Junior Brown becomes increasingly psychotic, Buddy Clark ceases to think only of his own well-being and takes responsibility for his friend and the other homeless boys in his neighborhood, as well.

In *M.C. Higgins, the Great,* the protagonist is another striking character who continuously seeks a way to convince his parents to leave their ancestral home, Sarah's Mountain, because he fears that the spoil heap, a residue of strip-mining, will one day smother them all. One avenue of escape is the possibility that his mother's beautiful voice will be discovered. The characters in both stories are survivors, concerned with the safety of those they love.

Other characters deal with personal issues. Geeder (in *Zeely*) is a dreamy, imaginative girl who concludes that the statuesque daughter of her uncle's tenant farmer, Zeely, must be a Watusi queen. Zeely herself helps Geeder grow in awareness of her own identity and appreciation for her African American heritage.

In *Cousins,* Cammy must cope with grief and guilt when her outwardly perfect cousin drowns accidentally. Hamilton convincingly portrays all sides of a child who is, by turns, devoted to her invalid grandmother and teenage brother, jealous of her bulimic cousin's perfection, and insecure about her own inadequacies. Although the complexity of some of Hamilton's books is difficult for young readers, this book is among the most accessible. Buhlaire Sims in *Plain City* is a thirteen-year-old mixed-race child who has been going through life without a past. She tries to find her father, but her mother will not help her, so she dreams about her reunion with her father. When she does find him she realizes all her dreams are wrong: her father is homeless and mentally ill, and he will not stay indoors; the first night after she found him Buhlaire never slept because she was worrying about how cold he might be. Buhlaire soon comes to the realization that she was like her father in many ways. Once she finds her father, everything seems changed, though not necessarily for the worst. Though her actual father is difficult to understand, Buhlaire Sims will be okay because she is a survivor. Another fictional character with strong appeal for young readers is Thomas Small. Small overcomes his fear of bizarre events to uncover the mystery of Drear House, a former station on the Underground Railroad in *The House of Dies Drear*.

Hamilton's characters ring true for many reasons. The characters are prototypes for children who wrestle with similar issues of searching for identity and place in the family. They also come to life through Hamilton's skillful use of dialogue and, when appropriate, dialect. For example, in *Cousins,* Cammy's language usage, typical of her age-mates, is continually corrected by Gram who mutters about what schools must be teaching these days.

The historical characters in Hamilton's biographies and historical fiction do not come to life as vividly as her fictional characters. A meticulous researcher, Hamilton relates the lives and accomplishments of W.E.B. DuBois and Paul Robeson without bringing them to life as she does with her fictional protagonists. An exception is the book *Many Thousand Gone,* which provides true accounts of slaves who fled to freedom. Perhaps the recording of a single heroic act provides more cohesion than attempting to describe famous people with multiple accomplishments. *Her Stories: African American Folktales, Fairy Tales, and True Tales* focusses on the magical lore and wondrous imaginings of African American women. Hamilton provides notes at the end of each tale that allow the reader to see the African American heritage from slave times to the present. *When Birds Could Talk and Bats Could Sing* is a collection of stories featuring sparrows, jays, buzzards, and bats, based on African American tales. This collection of tales focusses on the shared qualities of birds and humans; the folktales have been passed down from the era around the Civil War when the African Americans told tales like the Brer Rabbit stories.

Just as her characters are convincingly developed, Hamilton's settings are varied but realistic. Although most of Hamilton's books are set near her Yellow Springs, Ohio, home each imparts its own unique, vividly described flavor to the reader. *The House of Dies Drear* is a fine example; the tranquil college town stands in contrast to the impressive, yet forbidding Drear House. Hamilton brings to life the drafty old house riddled with secret passages and the tensions of countless slaves who hovered in its chambers poised between capture and freedom. The reader's awe parallels the Small family's as the underground chamber is revealed, filled with antique treasures.

The sights and sounds of the nursing home where Cammy visits Gram are as poignantly real as the classroom where a shrine of sorts is created for her drowned cousin. Likewise, the home of M.C. Higgins conveys images of isolated mountain hollows. In addition to visualizing M.C. swaying atop the flagpole in front of his home, Hamilton also provides readers with the metaphor of a boy who attempts to rise above the environmental disaster he fears.

Hamilton's talents as a writer are not restricted to fiction and nonfiction. As a folklorist, Hamilton weds her scholarly research with her gift for telling tales. *In the Beginning* demonstrates both the uniqueness and the universality of various cultures' explanations of how this world came to be. *The People Could Fly* is a noteworthy chronicle of the tales African slaves brought to this land and the stories that evolved during their enslavement. Many of the stories focused on the people's overwhelming desire for freedom—none more poignantly than the title story. Some of the stories incorporate Gullah dialect. The author's notes about the dialect and origin of the stories are a welcome addition.

Hamilton's Jadhu stories are literary folktales—born of the folk tradition but a product of the author's rich imagination. Originally, these stories were told in the framework of a caregiver who told stories to a little boy. Recently, Hamilton has streamlined the stories to make them more accessible to a contemporary audience.

Both the fantasy *Sweet Whispers, Brother Rush* and the historical *Anthony Burns: The Defeat and Triumph of a Fugitive Slave* employ a similar story-within-a-story device. In the former story, a young girl slips through a time warp to learn about her past; in the latter, an imprisoned victim of the Fugitive Slave Act evades his captors by retreating to childhood memories. Both of these books (along with *The Planet of Junior Brown*) reveal Hamilton's penchant for the surreal, which may limit their appeal to less mature or culturally aware readers.

Many themes, motifs, and symbols recur in Hamilton's work. The themes of self-understanding and the importance of family are evident in many of her books. However, family does not always fit the traditional ''father knows best'' mold. Mothers are frequently distant and fathers often absent (as in *The Planet of Junior Brown*; *Sweet Whispers, Brother Rush*; and *Cousins*). On the other hand, *Drylongso* and *The House of Dies Drear* depict a ''traditional'' family. As a motif, music resonates in Hamilton's books, revealing her own musical background. Many main characters are musical— Junior Brown is a pianist, as is Mac Darrow in *The House of Dies Drear*; Drylongso plays a harmonica; M.C.'s mother sings and Cammy plays the piano, and her cousin plays it better in *Cousins*. Another motif is that of the traveler. From *Zeely,* in which Geeder tells about the night traveler, to *Drylongso,* in which a mysterious boy brings an end to the drought, travel (whether physical or psychic like Junior Brown and Tree's in *Sweet Whispers, Brother Rush*) plays a prominent role. The ultimate traveler is the slave who travels to freedom. Her folktales support this motif of the traveler. Her continuous writings provide the readers with many historical and inspirational tales. Readers can thank Virginia Hamilton for freeing their minds by passing along her stories.

—Anne Creany, updated by Rosanne Donahue

HARNETT, Cynthia (Mary)

Nationality: British. **Born:** London, 22 June 1893. **Education:** private schools: Chelsea School of Art, London; studied with the artist G. Vernon Stokes. Author and illustrator of children's books, 1930-49, and of historical novels for young people, since 1949. **Military Service:** Served in the British Censorship during both world wars. **Awards:** Library Association Carnegie Medal, 1951, for *The Wool-Pack;* Spring Book Festival, 1954, for *The Drawbridge Gate;* Carnegie (commended) 1959, for *The Load of the Unicorn;* Spring Book Festival, 1973, for *The Writing on the Hearth.* **Died:** 25 October 1981.

PUBLICATIONS FOR YOUNG ADULTS

Fiction

Junk, the Puppy, with G. Vernon Stokes, illustrated by the authors. London, Blackie, 1937.

The Pennymakers, with G. Vernon Stokes, illustrated by the authors. London, Eyre & Spottiswoode, 1937.

Velvet Mask, illustrated by G. Vernon Stokes. London, Medici Society, 1937.

Banjo, the Puppy, with G. Vernon Stokes, illustrated by the authors. London, Blackie, 1938.

To Be a Farmer's Boy, with G. Vernon Stokes, illustrated by the authors. London, Blackie, 1940.

Mountaineers, with G. Vernon Stokes, illustrated by the authors. London, Collins, 1941.

Mudlarks, with G. Vernon Stokes, illustrated by the authors. London, Collins, 1941.

Ducks and Drakes, with G. Vernon Stokes, illustrated by the authors. London, Collins, 1942.

Bob-Tail Pup, with G. Vernon Stokes, illustrated by the authors. London, Collins, 1944.

Sand Hoppers, with G. Vernon Stokes, illustrated by the authors. London, Collins, 1946.

Two and a Bit, with G. Vernon Stokes, illustrated by the authors. London, Collins, 1948.

Follow My Leader, with G. Vernon Stokes, illustrated by the authors. London, Collins, 1949.

The Great House, illustrated by the author. London, Methuen, 1949; Cleveland, World, 1968.

Pets Limited, with G. Vernon Stokes, illustrated by the authors. London, Collins, 1950.

The Wool-Pack, illustrated by the author. London, Methuen, 1951; as *Nicholas and the Woolpack,* New York, Putnam, 1953; as *The Merchant's Mark,* Minneapolis, Lerner, 1984.

Ring Out, Bow Bells!, illustrated by the author. London, Methuen, 1953; as *The Drawbridge Gate,* New York, Putnam, 1954; as *The Sign of the Green Falcon,* Minneapolis, Lerner, 1984.

The Green Popinjay, illustrated by the author. Oxford, Blackwell, 1955.

Stars of Fortune, illustrated by the author. London, Methuen, and New York, Putnam, 1956.

The Load of Unicorn, illustrated by the author. London, Methuen, 1959; as *Caxton's Challenge,* Cleveland, World, 1960; as *The Cargo of Madalena,* Minneapolis, Lerner, 1984.

A Fifteenth Century Wool Merchant, illustrated by the author. London, Oxford University Press, 1962, and New York, Clarendon Press, 1962.

The Writing on the Hearth, illustrated by Gareth Floyd. London, Methuen, 1971; New York, Viking Press, 1973.

Other

Editor, *In Praise of Dogs: An Anthology in Prose and Verse,* illustrated by G. Vernon Stokes. London, Country Life, 1936.

David's New World: The Making of a Sportsman, with G. Vernon Stokes, illustrated by the authors. London, Country Life, 1937.

Getting to Know Dogs, illustrated by G. Vernon Stokes. London, Collins, 1947.

Monasteries and Monks, illustrated by Edward Osmond. London, Batsford, 1963; Cincinnati, Ohio, Soccer Associates, 1965.

* * *

Cynthia Harnett's historical novels combine meticulous research and believable characters. For each of these stories, from her first attempts in *The Great House* to her final work, *The Writing on the Hearth,* Harnett spent long periods of time getting all the details right. The result is always an accurate portrayal of the English past, populated by real and likeable characters to whom interesting things happen.

Before publishing the series of historical novels for which she is best known, Harnett had collaborated with her cousin G. Vernon Stokes on text and illustrations for a number of books for somewhat younger children. Her background as an illustrator greatly influenced the historical novels, where her method of bringing the past to life is primarily visual. Unlike many earlier practitioners of the historical genre for young readers, Harnett, along with Rosemary Sutcliff, Geoffrey Trease, and Henry Treece, strove for accuracy. She was especially interested in presenting ordinary people of other times, not merely the aristocracy and royalty. Harnett, even more than the other pioneers in good juvenile historical fiction, strove to make her readers *see* what her characters would have seen. Thus the objects and practices of the wool trade, or of early printing, or of castle life, are so accurate and so easy to visualize that history teachers often use Harnett's books as background reading for the medieval period.

The Great House, Harnett's first venture into the juvenile historical field, concerns architecture at the end of the seventeenth century—a period when much rebuilding was under way and new architectural styles came into vogue. Her beautifully detailed line drawings are carried out with the same meticulous accuracy as the text. Though the plot is somewhat thin, the characters, Barbara and Geoffrey and their architect father, are plausible. Countryside and London city life contrast nicely. Though well received, *The Great House* has never been as successful as Harnett's fifteenth-century novels, which spanned a period of more than twenty years.

Nicholas and the Wool-Pack, the first historical novel to win the Carnegie Medal, focuses on the only son of a wool trading family in the Cotswolds. The plot concerns Nicholas's efforts to find out what the Lombards and his father's employee, Simon Leach, are plotting; in the end, somewhat predictably, Nicholas and his friends succeed in solving the puzzle and clearing his father of a serious charge of wrongdoing. Along the way, Nicholas grows from irresponsible boy to steady young man and acquires a fiancée who is also an equal and a friend. The charm of the book, though, lies not so much in its tidy and satisfying plot as in its loving evocation of the Cotswolds and the wool trade in the fifteenth century. Harnett makes this information simply fascinating, from details of manufacture to economic exchanges to subtle class distinctions and how they influenced trade.

Caxton's Challenge (British title *The Load of Unicorn*) carries out the same general scheme of a young man unravelling a plot against a businessman and his enterprise, but this time it is Caxton and printing rather than the Fetterlocks and wool shipping. Again the characters belong to the various strata of the middle class, and again the details of the printing trade are revealed in compelling detail: the machinery, the terminology, the texts, and even, surprisingly, the paper. For paper, something which modern readers regard as cheap and always available, is at the center of the plot in this exciting story. *Stars of Fortune* and *Ring Out, Bow Bells!* depart from the basic Harnett plot line as they are based on the lives of real people (George Washington's ancestors in the reign of Queen Mary and Dick Whittington about 1415, respectively).

In her last book, which required ten years of research, Harnett returned to the mid fifteenth century and to the themes and general plot line of her two most successful historical novels. *The Writing on the Hearth* presents Stephen, a schoolboy on the estate of William de la Pole, Earl of Suffolk. The setting shifts from the Chiltern Hills to the bustle of London, with some particularly exciting scenes set along the river. Unlike earlier books, this one shows a good deal about intrigues and rivalries among the aristocracy, with de la Pole's wife, Alice (granddaughter of the poet Chaucer) involved in the central secret. Glimpses of fifteenth century schoolroom education of several kinds, and the lure of Oxford, also offer more variety than is usual with Harnett. As Harnett was nearly eighty when *The Writing on the Hearth* appeared, she did not illustrate the book herself; the drawings are by Gareth Floyd and, though adequate, they are by no means the equal of Harnett's own sensitive and charming illustrations in her previous works. Even the cover painting by Trina Schart Hyman for the American edition does not equal the perfect match of text and picture that the author herself had achieved.

Harnett announced that *The Writing on the Hearth* would be her last book, and it was. Several of the historical novels were reissued in 1984, and *Nicholas and the Wool-Pack* has been reprinted many times in paperback.

—Caroline C. Hunt

HARTNETT, Sonya

Nationality: Australian. **Born:** 23 March 1968. **Education:** Royal Melbourne Institute of Technology, Melbourne, Victoria, Australia, B.A. in Media Studies 1988. **Family:** Unmarried. **Career:** Bookseller. **Awards:** IBBY Ena Noël Award, 1996, for *Wilful Blue*; Shaeffer Pen Prize, Victorian Premier's Literary Awards, Miles Franklin Inaugural Kathleen Mitchell Award, and Children's Book Council Book of the Year, all 1996, all for *Sleeping Dogs*. **Address:** 15A Cain Avenue, Northcote, Victoria 3070, Australia.

PUBLICATIONS FOR YOUNG ADULTS

Trouble All the Way. Melbourne, Rigby, 1984.
Sparkle and Nightflower. Melbourne, Rigby, 1986.
The Glass House. Sydney, Pan McMillan, 1990.
Wilful Blue. Ringwood, Penguin Viking, 1994.
Sleeping Dogs. Ringwood, Penguin Viking, and New York, Viking, 1995.
The Devil Latch. Ringwood, Penguin Viking, 1996.
Black Foxes. Ringwood, Penguin Viking, 1996.
Princes. Ringwood, Penguin Viking, 1997; New York, Viking, 1998.
All My Dangerous Friends. Ringwood, Penguin Viking, 1998.

*

Sonya Hartnett comments:

I like writing for young adults because they are readers who are not yet jaded, who can still be shocked and surprised and find newness in what they read. I like their open-mindedness: adults are always telling me that my books are overly bleak and severe, but no young adult has ever said this to me. It's a forgiving audience that has a sense of humour and is prepared to suspend its disbelief. I often write about people who feel awkward with the world, and I think teenagers sometimes feel that way, so they're better able to recognise the characters I write about, and to understand what drives them.

*   *   *

Sonya Hartnett's three early novels *Trouble All the Way* (1984), *Sparkle and Nightflower* (1986), and The *Glass House* (1990)—are now out of print and she has no special wish to see them reprinted. They deal with young people and the problems of growing up; the first one was published when the author was fifteen. Even so they are impressive as the work of a young writer and show the promise of her future writing career.

Hartnett's 1994 novel *Wilful Blue* deals with the issue of suicide and its effect on others. Set in an artists' colony that was once a monastery and by the gently bullying Harriet Finch, the novel centers around the efforts of seven artists as they prepare an exhibition and deal with the suicide of one of their fellow artists, Guy Alexander Defoe. The novel dramatizes the complex nature of the people we meet, how people present different sides of themselves to others, and how we never know their inner selves and secrets. Jesse McGee feels especially guilty as he was closest to Defoe as they painted a huge picture of four famous Australian painters of the Heidelberg School in the Chapel at Sanquedeet. Jesse has failed to read Defoe's signals of self destruction and wonders why he feels this way about a man he hardly knew. The allusions suggested through Defoe's name imply the isolation of the individual who needs to find some fruitful purpose for staying alive. Though he is talented, Defoe doubts that this is enough and the painting he is engaged upon seems to enforce this; it is concerned with figures of a famous past, but what really seems to be lacking in his life is spiritual belief signified by the ruined monastery and 'forgotten' chapel where Defoe and McGee work. Once art and talent may have supplied a raison d'etre, but they do so no longer.

Though the other artists share some blame for the painter's death, they have offered no help and put the event behind them, unwilling to share McGee's obsession. Hartnett subtly lets us see their contribution without being heavy handed about it. Guy reads T. S. Eliot's 'The Waste Land' and his wilful use of blue in his painting is the image for how he sees his world. Though some have complained that Hartnett's stories offer no hope, she is an honest writer who refuses to present life to young adults as a series of happy endings. She acknowledges there are people with ''a blackness of mind'' who want to die and ''who retire from living long before . . . the blood [stops] flowing,'' but the dialogue in the novels reveals alternative views of the issue. Defoe's beliefs seem summed up by the verse on the tattered altar cloth found in the chapel's confessional:

> Nothing on earth I call my own—
> A stranger to the world unknown
> I all their goods despise—
> I trample on their whole delight
> And seek a country out of sight—
> A country in the skies.

Guy sees the message as ''so sure of itself, it is so zealous!'' while Jesse calls it narrow minded and fanatical. To Harriet it means nothing more than words of a hymn she sang as a child, the sentiments of which she has never thought much about.

Hartnett's strength lies in presenting a view of life opposed to the one with which we are most comfortable. *Sleeping Dogs* (1995) presents a family at the extreme end of what is regarded as normal family life. The institution here is dark and ruinous, perverted and destructive, anything but wholesome. The Willow family and their dogs live in a broken down grey house filled with fear and ruled by the father, Griffin Willow, an alcoholic loser and misfit. Willow is not without education—he once studied law—but he seems never to have succeeded at anything because of his overbearing personality. The family members have no control over their lives, no freedom and no independence. All fear leaving the security of the family. The mother has opted out mentally and physically and lives in what is practically a catatonic state. Edward, the oldest son, runs the farm and has some spirit and at times is able to control the bashings 19-year-old Jordan receives from his father. Jordan carries on an incestuous relationship with his 23-year-old sister Michelle. He comes to her bed in a room ''dark and chill, dewy with its own shade.'' Oliver, another son, can't make friends and is seen by his school fellows as weird, and Jennifer, known as Speck, whose existence is almost overlooked, enjoys playing cruel jokes on children. Into this twisted situation arrives an artist, Bow Fox, a Brer Fox type who in befriending Oliver discovers Jordan's and Michelle's guilty secret. His refusal to let sleeping dogs lie leads to tragedy.

Sleeping Dogs is a complex poetic novel, rich with allusion and imagery. It raises issues of crime and punishment and notions of what is right and wrong and who makes decisions about the construction of ethics. Bow Fox is appalled at the ''Willow way of doing things,'' as are most of the book's readers, but Oliver refuses to simply admit that their way of life is wrong. He points out that his father reads books, went to school, and watches television. The Willows love their father, though they realize he is a hard man to love. Fox is unable to come to terms with the depth of his concern for the family, and the views and attitudes he puts forward are glib

and out of touch with what really happens in the family. *Sleeping Dogs* reveals how difficult it is to escape a present existence for something better and how most people are content to remain in a known situation even if it is uncomfortable. The book also discloses how the human spirit may be robbed of its right to independence and freedom, a theme that recurs in Hartnett's later novels.

The Devil Latch and *Black Foxes* continue Hartnett's preoccupation with parent-child-relations and the sense of loss felt when these are lacking. Kitten Latch goes through the world, independent as a cat, aloof and disdainful of the everyday. Abandoned by his parents, he is brought up by his bullying grandfather Paul Latch, once a man of iron but now bedridden. In revenge for his insensitive treatment, Kitten torments his paralysed grandfather at the instigation of the voices in his head that he refers to as the twins. The motif of the wasp and its prey supports the idea of how people feed on each other. Kitten's increasing irrational behavior finally erupts in tragedy. The epigraph at the beginning of the book points out how easy it is to break a man's spirit and suggests that whoever is guilty of this is doing the devil's work for him.

Black Foxes, set in the early 19th century, reflects Hartnett's interest in the Romantic Age. Lord Tyrone Sully epitomizes the Byronic hero, embodying individualism, revolt, emotion, humor and imagination. In outlook, dress, and appearance Tyrone defies conventions and fate. Though he is resentful over the death of his parents, who ''died young, still strong and able minded'', his friendship with Oscar Herringbone keeps him stable. Oscar can ''almost feel the blood tumbling through Tyrone's veins'' but he realizes at one point that after all these years they don't know one another at all. Oscar's family has ''never known death'' and he sees Tyrone's life ''signposted by death.'' Even so he realizes that Tyrone is much more alive ''in a vital way'' than he feels himself to be. Tyrone is described as ''rampant, like a vengeful spirit.'' The fox metaphor which runs through Hartnett's earlier books is taken up here once again and extended to reveal the many facets of this potent symbol.

Princes is set in a decaying, rat-infested Gothic mansion inhabited by identical twins. Hartnett is expert at describing enclosures, whether they be decaying monasteries, run-down farms, or the decline of suburbia. The twins, Indigo and Ravel, are in their twenties and rich; their parents have ''gone on a journey'' and it's obvious they are not expected back. The twins are obsessed with one another and play endless mind games, mostly vicious. Trouble begins when Ravel decides to get a job. This upsets the dominant twin Indigo and soon the reader begins to suspect it is not only the rats that are being poisoned.

Though this situation is familiar the way the story is structured makes it compelling. Hartnett interrupts the story's suspense—where are the parents? will Indigo's scheme succeed?—with factual information about the role of the doppelgänger, Richard III and the princes in the tower, and the horror of a pig eating living flesh. This information lends richness to the characters' behavior and helps to suggest that truth can be stranger than fiction. People, like pigs, can devour one another. The twin's house with the tower as its highest point suggests that while they think they are controlling their lives, they are in actual fact prisoners. For Hartnett's princes, their run-down mansion, though palatial, is a kind of prison.

Hartnett's books are not soothing to read but once begun they are difficult to put down. They show the injuries society can inflict and the way the injured can become a threat to society. The novels expose the exploiters and the exploited, "them and us"; every cloud may have its own silver lining but Hartnett is only too readily aware that every silver lining has its cloud.

—Michael Stone

HASKINS, James S.

Also writes as Jim Haskins. **Nationality:** American. **Born:** Montgomery, Alabama, 19 September 1941. **Education:** Georgetown University, Washington, D.C., B.A. 1960; Alabama State University, Montgomery, B.S. 1962; University of New Mexico, Alburquerque, M.A. 1963; New School for Social Research, New York, 1965-67; Queens College of the City University of New York, 1967-68. **Career:** Stock trader, Smith Barney & Co., New York City, 1963-65; teacher, New York City Board of Education, New York City, 1966-68; visiting lecturer, New School for Social Research, New York City, 1970-72; associate professor, Staten Island Community College of the City University of New York, Staten Island, NY, 1970-77; professor of English, University of Florida, Gainsville, since 1977. Reporter, New York *Daily News,* 1963-64. Visiting lecturer, Elisabeth Irwin High School, 1971-73; visiting professor, Indiana University/Purdue University, Indianapolis, 1973-76; visiting professor, College of New Rochelle, 1977. Director, Union Mutual Life, Health and Accident Insurance, 1970-73. Member of board of advisors, Psi Systems, 1971-72; member of board of directors, Speedwell Services for Children, 1974-76. Member of Manhattan Community Board No. 9, 1972-73, academic council for the State University of New York, 1972-74, New York Urban League Manhattan Advisory Board, 1973-75, and National Education Advisory Committee and vice-director of Southeast Region of Statue of Liberty, Ellis Island Foundation, 1986. Consultant, Education Development Center, since 1975, Department of Health, Education and Welfare, 1977-79, National Research Council, 1979-80, and Grolier, Inc., 1979-82. Member of National Education Advisory Committee, Commission on the Bicentennial of the Constitution. **Awards:** Notable children's book in the field of social studies citations from *Social Education,* 1971, for *Revolutionaries: Agents of Change,* from *Social Studies,* 1972, for *Resistance: Profiles in Nonviolence* and *Profiles in Black Power,* and 1973, for *A Piece of the Power: Four Black Mayors,* from National Council for the Social Studies-Children's Book Council Book Review Committee, 1975, for *Fighting Shirley Chisholm,* and 1976, for *The Creoles of Color of New Orleans* and *The Picture Life of Malcolm X,* from Children's Book Council, 1978, for *The Life and Death of Martin Luther King, Jr.;* World Book Year Book literature for children citation, 1973, for *From Lew Alcindor to Kareem Abdul Jabbar;* Books of the Year citations, Child Study Association of America, 1974, for *Adam Clayton Powell* and *Street Gangs;* Books for Brotherhood bibliography citation, National Council of Christians and Jews book review committee, 1975, for *Adam Clayton Powell: Portrait of a Marching Black;* Spur award finalist, Western Writers of America, 1975, for *The Creoles of Color of New Orleans;* Eighth Annual Coretta Scott King award, and Books Chosen by Children citation, Children's Book Council, both 1977, both for *The Story of Stevie Wonder;* Woodson Outstanding Merit award, National Council for

the Social Studies, 1980, for *James Van Der Zee: The Picture-Takin' Man;* American Society of Composers, Authors and Publishers-Deems Taylor award, 1980, for *Scott Joplin: The Man Who Made Ragtime;* Ambassador of Honor book, English-Speaking Union Books-Across-the-Sea, 1983, for *Bricktop;* Coretta Scott King honorable mention, 1984, for *Lena Horne;* American Library Association (ALA) Best Book for Young Adults citation, 1987, for *Black Music in America;* Alabama Library Association best juvenile work citation, 1987, for "Count Your Way" series; "Bicentennial Reading, Viewing, Listening for Young Americans" citations, ALA and National Endowment for the Humanities, for *Street Gangs: Yesterday and Today, Ralph Bunche: A Most Reluctant Hero,* and *A Piece of the Power: Four Black Mayors;* certificates of appreciation, Joseph P. Kennedy Foundation, for work with the Special Olympics program; Coretta Scott King Book award, 1990, for *A Black Dance in America: A History through Its People.* **Address:** 325 West End Ave., Apt. 7D, New York, New York 10023, U.S.A.

PUBLICATIONS FOR YOUNG ADULTS

Fiction

Resistance: Profiles in Nonviolence. New York, Doubleday, 1970.
Religions. Philadelphia, Lippincott, 1971.
Revolutionaries: Agents of Change. Philadelphia, Lippincott, 1971.
The War and the Protest: Vietnam. New York, Doubleday, 1971.
Jobs in Business and Office. New York, Lothrop, 1974.
Street Gangs: Yesterday and Today. Mamaroneck, New York, Hastings House, 1974.
Witchcraft, Mysticism and Magic in the Black World. New York, Doubleday, 1974.
The Consumer Movement. New York, F. Watts, 1975.
The Creoles of Color of New Orleans. New York, Crowell, 1975.
Who Are the Handicapped? New York, Doubleday, 1978.
The Quiet Revolution: The Struggle for the Rights of Disabled Americans, with J.M. Stifle. New York, Crowell, 1979.
The New Americans: Vietnamese Boat People. Hillside, New Jersey, Enslow, 1980.
Black Theatre in America. New York, Crowell, 1982.
The New Americans: Cuban Boat People. Hillside, New Jersey, Enslow, 1982.
The Guardian Angels. Hillside, New Jersey, Enslow, 1983.
Double Dutch, with David A. Walker. Hillside, New Jersey, Enslow, 1986.
Black Music in America: A History through Its People. New York, Crowell, 1987.
A Sixties Reader, with Kathleen Benson. New York, Viking, 1988.
The Autobiography of Rosa Parks, with Rosa Parks. New York, Dial, 1990.
Black Theater in America. New York, HarperCollins, 1991.
Religions of the World. New York, Hippocrene Books, 1991.
The Scottsboro Boys. New York, H. Holt and Co., 1994.
The Headless Haunt and Other African-American Ghost Stories. New York, HarperCollins, 1994.
Black Eagles. New York, Scholastic Inc., 1995.
The Day Fort Sumter Was Fired on. New York, Scholastic, 1995.
The Freedom Rides. New York, Hyperion Books for Children, 1995.
From Afar to Zulu. New York, Walker, 1995.

The Harlem Renaissance. Brookfield, Connecticut, Millbrook Press, 1996.

Power to the People. New York, Simon & Schuster Books for Young Readers, 1997.

Separate, But not Equal. New York, Scholastic, 1997.

African Beginnings. New York, Lothrop, 1998.

African American Military Heroes. New York, John Wiley, 1998.

Moaning Bones. New York, Lothrop/Morrow, 1998.

African American Entrepreneurs. New York, J. Wiley & Sons, 1998.

Black, Blue, and Gray. New York, Simon & Schuster Books for Young Readers, 1998.

Biographies

From Lew Alcindor to Kareem Abdul Jabbar. New York, Lothrop, 1972.

A Piece of the Power: Four Black Mayors. New York, Dial, 1972.

Profiles in Black Power. New York, Doubleday, 1972.

Deep Like the Rivers: A Biography of Langston Hughes, 1902-1967. New York, Holt, 1973.

Adam Clayton Powell: Portrait of a Marching Black. New York, Dial, 1974.

Babe Ruth and Hank Aaron: The Home Run Kings. New York, Lothrop, 1974.

Fighting Shirley Chisholm. New York, Dial, 1975.

Dr. J: A Biography of Julius Irving. New York, Doubleday, 1975.

The Picture Life of Malcolm X. New York, F. Watts, 1975.

Always Movin' On: The Life of Langston Hughes. New York, F. Watts, 1976.

Pele: A Biography. New York, Doubleday, 1976.

The Story of Stevie Wonder. New York, Doubleday, 1976.

Barbara Jordan. New York, Dial, 1977.

The Life and Death of Martin Luther King, Jr. New York, Lothrop, 1977.

Bob McAdoo: Superstar. New York, Lothrop, 1978.

George McGinnis: Basketball Superstar. Mamaroneck, New York, Hastings, 1978.

Andrew Young: Man with a Mission. New York, Lothrop, 1979.

I'm Gonna Make You Love Me: The Story of Diana Ross. New York, Dial, 1980.

''Magic'': A Biography of Earvin Johnson. Hillside, New Jersey, Enslow, 1981; as *Sports Great Magic Johnson,* 1992.

Katherine Dunham. New York, Coward-McCann, 1982.

Donna Summer. New York, Atlantic Monthly Press, 1983.

About Michael Jackson. Hillside, New Jersey, Enslow, 1985.

Diana Ross: Star Supreme. New York, Viking, 1985.

Corazon Aquino: Leader of the Philippines. Hillside, New Jersey, Enslow, 1988.

Leaders of the Middle East. Hillside, New Jersey, Enslow, 1988.

The Magic Johnson Story. Hillside, New Jersey, Enslow, 1988, as *Sports Great Magic Johnson,* Hillside, New Jersey, Enslow, 1989.

Shirley Temple Black: Actress to Ambassador, illustrations by Donna Ruff. New York, Puffin Books, 1988.

I Am Somebody! A Biography of Jesse Jackson. Hillside, New Jersey, Enslow, 1992.

Colin Powell. New York, Scholastic Inc., 1992.

The March on Washington. New York, HarperCollins, 1993.

Louis Farrakhan and the Nation of Islam. New York, Walker and Co., 1996.

Bayard Rustin. New York, Hyperion Books for Children, 1997.

I am Rosa Parks. New York, Dial Books for Young Readers, 1997.

Spike Lee. New York, Walker and Co., 1997.

Other as Jim Haskins

Jokes from Black Folks. New York, Doubleday, 1973.

Ralph Bunche: A Most Reluctant Hero. New York, Hawthorne, 1974.

Your Rights, Past and Present: A Guide for Young People. New York, Hawthorne, 1975.

The Long Struggle: The Story of American Labor. Louisville, Westminster, 1976.

Teen-Age Alcoholism. New York, Hawthorne, 1976.

Gambling—Who Really Wins? New York, F. Watts, 1978.

Real Estate Careers. New York, F. Watts, 1978.

James Van Der Zee: The Picture Takin' Man, illustrations by James Van Der Zee. New York, Dodd, Mead, 1979.

The Child Abuse Help Book, with Pat Connolly. Reading, Massachusetts, Addison Wesley, 1981.

Editor, *The Filipino Nation.* Three volumes, Danbury, Connecticut, Grolier International, 1982.

Sugar Ray Leonard. New York, Lothrop, 1982.

Werewolves. New York, Lothrop, 1982.

Donna Summer: An Unauthorized Biography, with J.M. Stifle. Boston, Little, Brown, 1983.

Space Challenge: The Story of Guion Bluford, an Authorized Biography, with Kathleen Benson. Minneapolis, Carolrhoda Books, 1984.

Break Dancing. Minneapolis, Lerner, 1985.

The Statue of Liberty: America's Proud Lady. Minneapolis, Lerner, 1986.

Count Your Way through . . .[Africa, Arab World, Brazil, Canada, China, France, Germany, Greece, India, Ireland, Israel, Italy, Japan, Korea, Mexico, Russia]. Minneapolis, Carolrhoda Books, 16 vols., 1987-96.

Bill Cosby: America's Most Famous Father. New York, Walker, 1988.

Christopher Columbus: Admiral of the Ocean Sea. New York, Scholastic, 1991.

Scatman: An Authorized Biography of Scatman Crothers, with Helen Crothers. New York, Morrow, 1991.

Against All Opposition: Black Explorers in America. New York, Walker, 1992.

Amazing Grace: The Story behind the Song. Brookfield, Connecticut, Millbrook, 1992.

The Day Martin Luther King, Jr. Was Shot: A Photo History of the Civil Rights Movement. New York, Scholastic, 1992.

I Have A Dream: The Life & Words of Martin Luther King, Jr. Brookfield, Connecticut, Millbrook Press, 1992.

One More River to Cross: Twelve Black Americans. New York, Scholastic, 1992.

Get on Board: The Story of the Underground Railroad. New York, Scholastic, 1993.

PUBLICATIONS FOR ADULTS

Nonfiction as Jim Haskins

Diary of a Harlem Schoolteacher. Grove, 1969, 2nd edition, Briarcliff Manor, New York, Stein & Day, 1979.

Editor, *Black Manifesto for Education.* New York, Morrow, 1973.

The Psychology of Black Language, with Hugh F. Butts. New York, Barnes & Noble, 1973.

Snow Sculpture and Ice Carving. London, Macmillan, 1974.

The Cotton Club. Random House, 1977, 2nd edition, New York, New American Library, 1984.

The Great American Crazies, with Kathleen Benson and Ellen Inkelis. Ashland, Massachusetts, Condor, 1977.

The Stevie Wonder Scrapbook, with Kathleen Benson. New York, Grosset & Dunlap, 1978.

Voodoo and Hoodoo: Their Tradition and Craft as Revealed by Actual Practitioners. London, Briarcliff Manor, New York, Stein & Day, 1978.

Richard Pryor, a Man and His Madness: A Biography. Beaufort Books, New York, 1984.

Queen of the Blues: A Biography of Dinah Washington. New York, Morrow, 1987.

Outward Dreams: Black Inventors and Their Inventions. New York, Walker, 1991.

Other

Pinckney Benton Stewart Pitchback: A Biography. London, Macmillan, 1973.

A New Kind of Joy: The Story of the Special Olympics. New York, Doubleday, 1976.

Contributor, *Understanding Human Behavior in Health and Illness* by Emily Mumford. Baltimore, Williams & Wilkins, 1977.

Scott Joplin: The Man Who Made Ragtime, with Kathleen Benson. New York, Doubleday, 1978.

Contributor, *New York Kid's Catalog.* New York, Doubleday, 1979.

Contributor, *Notable American Women Supplement.* Cambridge, Massachusetts, Radcliffe College, 1979.

Lena: A Personal and Professional Biography of Lena Horne, with Kathleen Benson. New York, Stein & Day, 1984.

Nat King Cole, with Kathleen Benson. New York, Stein & Day, 1984.

Contributor, *Clearings in the Thicket: An Alabama Humanities Reader* by Jerry Brown. Kennebunkport, Maine, Mercer University Press, 1985.

Mabel Mercer: A Life. New York, Atheneum, 1988.

Mr. Bojangles: The Biography of Bill Robinson. New York, Morrow, 1988.

Winnie Mandela: Life of Struggle. New York, Putnam, 1988.

Hamp: An Autobiography (with discography), with Lionel Hampton. New York, Warner, 1989.

India Under Indira and Rajiv Gandhi. Hillside, New Jersey, Enslow, 1989.

Black Dance in America: A History through its People. New York, Crowell, 1990.

Lena: A Biography of Lena Horne, with Kathleen Benson. Lanham, Maryland, Scarborough House, 1990.

Editor, *Judaism.* New York, Hippocrene Books, 1991.

Editor, *The Catholic Church.* New York, Hippocrene Books, 1992.

The Methodists. New York, Hippocrene Books, 1992.

Thurgood Marshall: A Life for Justice. New York, Holt, 1992.

Hippocrene U.S.A. Guide to Historic Black South. New York, Hippocrene Books, 1993.

*

Media Adaptations: *Diary of a Harlem Schoolteacher* recorded by Recordings for the Blind; *The Cotton Club* inspired the 1984 film of the same name.

Biography: Entry in *Sixth Book of Junior Authors,* edited by Sally Holmes Holtze, New York, Wilson, 1989, pp. 115-17; essay in *Something about the Author Autobiography Series,* Volume 4, Detroit, Gale, 1987, pp. 197-209.

Critical Studies: Entry in *Children's Literature Review,* Volume 3, Detroit, Gale, 1978, pp. 63-69.

*   *   *

James Haskins has written a prodigious number of nonfiction books, more than eighty to date. Haskins writes for adults, young adults, and children; his books are wide-ranging in their subject matter. One book, *The Cotton Club,* was made into a major movie. The majority of Haskins's books are for young adults, and through them he has tackled such topics as child abuse, street gangs, the war in Vietnam, the disabled, and Cuban boat people. Yet, for the most part, he has used his young adult books to explore the black experience in America. It is these books on the African American experience that represent Haskins's most important contribution to young adult nonfiction. They sensitively treat a multitude of diverse topics having to do with African American life and culture.

A great many of Haskins's books are biographies. He has written about athletes, entertainers, and high achievers in other fields. From Scott Joplin to Stevie Wonder, from Kareem Abdul Jabbar to Magic Johnson, from Ralph Bunche to Barbara Jordan, Haskins has not been content to record the "glitz and glitter," but has sought out the real person. In *The Life and Death of Martin Luther King, Jr.,* for example, Haskins writes about the man behind the image. He seeks to reveal King's feelings, his confusions, and his failings. In the process, Martin Luther King, Jr., is revealed, an extraordinary leader who is appealing and enormously strong emotionally, but a man with faults. In Haskins's hands, King becomes a real person, not a plaster saint.

The same can be said of *Scott Joplin: The Man Who Made Ragtime.* Written with Kathleen Benson, this book brings life and vitality to a man who died over seventy years ago. Haskins identifies Joplin as a major creator of a black musical form, but does more than merely chronicle the events of Joplin's life. Placing Joplin within a historical context, Haskins describes a man driven to make music, plagued by poverty and racism, but also a man who fought to make the larger white society accept ragtime.

Katherine Dunham introduced traditional West African and Afro-Caribbean dance to western audiences. In *Katherine Dunham,* Haskins tells how she did this. The problems she encountered were enormous, but Haskins manages to dig beneath the surface and never allows events to overwhelm his portrait of Dunham the person. He portrays her as a woman of deep convictions and strong emotions, who had to fight her middle-class family's disapproval to become a dancer and who had to endure life in a segregated America as well. Despite beauty and intelligence, Lena Horne had no easy time of it either. Written also with Kathleen Benson, *Lena: A Personal and Professional Biography of Lena Horne* tells the story of Horne's difficult childhood and her emergence from anger and repression into a black woman fully aware of her power and her own worth.

James Van Der Zee: The Picture Takin' Man is the life of the photographer who worked during the 1920s and 1930s taking pictures of the residents of Harlem. Little known and unappreciated until his enormous cache of pictures was made into an exhibition at the New York Metropolitan Museum of Art, he told his life story to Haskins. What emerges from the book through the use of those interview materials and a number of Van Der Zee's actual pictures is a wonderful portrait of a man who simply worked from day to day, trying to make a living at work he loved. Married twice and always on the edge of poverty, he made his living by taking pictures and did well for awhile. The Great Depression, changing lifestyles, and age finally caught up with him. He and his wife were evicted from their Harlem apartment when they were in their eighties because they were unable to pay the rent. What emerges from this book is a richly detailed view of one man's life, a view that also reflects black life in America in the last years of the nineteenth and the first half of the twentieth century. In addition to biography, Haskins has written books dealing with a number of different aspects of black life. All are characterized by an insider's detail and the use of little known or disregarded facts that take the reader behind the scenes. Haskins's most recent books, *The March on Washington* and *Get on Board: The Story of the Underground Railroad,* are two examples. Both books speak to the African American's quest for freedom, one in the antebellum South and the other in America in the 1960s.

Get on Board profiles the many personalities who worked on the Underground Railroad as conductors and stationmasters and the slaves who traveled the train's route. Haskins gives these people names and feelings. He recounts the well-known exploits of Harriet Tubman but includes the stories of others as well. Haskins emphasizes the efforts that slaves, ex-slaves, and free black men and women exerted on their own behalf, feeling that their contributions to their own freedom have too frequently been overlooked.

The March on Washington is filled with details, details that explain not only why the march was organized, but how. Bayard Rustin, the consummate civil rights organizer, emerges as the hero of this piece. In two short months, he was able to pull together all the thousands of pieces of organizational detail that enabled the march to succeed, from the provision of portable toilets to the provision of refreshments for 250,000 people. One also gets a glimpse of the many conflicts and tensions that existed among the leaders of the march, one such conflict nearly derailing the march minutes before it was to begin.

Black Music in America: A History through Its People is a collection of sketches of the many black Americans who have created and performed music, from opera to soul, from spirituals to blues and gospel. There are chapters on the music the slaves created and on the evolution of the blues. But perhaps the most fascinating chapters discuss the contributions to black music of more contemporary musicians. James Brown, Aretha Franklin, Michael Jackson, Wynton Marsalis, and Tina Turner are all here. *Black Theater in America* and *Black Dance in America: A History through Its People* similarly treat the contributions of African Americans to theater and dance by concentrating on personalities.

Departing from the arts, *The Creoles of Color of New Orleans* describes the rich history and culture of a New Orleans people of mixed African, French, and Spanish descent. On the other hand, the place of the supernatural in black America is traced in *Witchcraft,*

Mysticism and Magic in the Black World. Haskins argues that African slaves brought their religious beliefs with them to this country and that these beliefs have survived in various ways. As a result, superstitions and mysticism are more accepted by blacks than by those in the larger society.

It is obvious that James Haskins is both a prolific and eclectic writer. Through his many books, he has been able to investigate and report on African American subject areas long ignored or undervalued by other writers. He has been able to a profile the lives of prominent African Americans in ways that highlight their uniqueness as human beings but still point to the additional burdens they incur by being black in America. He has been able to bring back from obscurity black people who have made enduring contributions to the arts, to sports, and to politics, showing them to be real people. He has written books on well-known and little-known events in black history and has been adept at taking an always unique insider's perspective. This is Haskins's great strength, to take little-known or seemingly unimportant facts about an event or a person and weave them into a fascinating whole, a whole that never fails to inform, educate, and entertain.

—Carol Jones Collins

HAUTZIG, Esther (née Rudomin)

Nationality: American. **Born:** Vilna, Poland (now Vilnius, Lithuania), 18 October 1930. Came to the United States in 1947, naturalized U.S. citizen in 1951. **Education:** Hunter College (now Hunter College of the City University of New York), 1948-50. **Family:** Married Walter Hautzig in 1950; one daughter and one son. **Career:** Secretary, G.P. Putnam's Sons, New York City, 1951-52; publicity assistant, Children's Book Council, New York City, 1953; director of children's book promotion, 1954-59, consultant, 1961-68, Thomas Y. Crowell Co., New York City; free-lance children's book consultant, New York City, since 1959. Three-time speaker at the Summer Institutes of the Children's Literature Center, Simmons College, Boston, Massachusetts; lecturer and speaker on writing, reading and bookmaking at many schools, libraries, and professional association meetings, including the Westchester County Library Association, Annual Children's Book Meeting for the Association of New York City Children's Book Librarians, University of Minnesota book banquet, 1982, University of Arkansas/Little Rock Children's Book Author Festival, 1988, Central Missouri University in Warrensburg 23rd Annual Book Festival, 1991, and at many others. Support group member for the Division of Young Adult Services, and general volunteer, New York Public Library, New York City; volunteer, New York City School Volunteer Program: Authors-Read-Aloud Program. **Awards:** American Library Association (ALA) notable children's book citation, 1968, *Boston Globe-Horn Book* honor book, 1968, *New York Times* outstanding children's book citation, 1968, National Book Award for Children's Literature finalist, 1969, *Horn Book* Fanfare honor list, 1969, Shirley Kravitz Children's Book award from the Association of Jewish Libraries, 1969, Jane Adams award, 1969, "Best Jewish Novel" by the Synagogue School and Center Division of Jewish Libraries, 1970, Lewis Carroll Shelf award, 1971, German Youth Literature Prize honorable list (Deutsche Jugenliteraturpreis), 1987, Children's Book

Prize of the Foundation of France (Le Prix du Livre Pour La Jeunesse), 1987, and Grand Prize of the "Thirteen" [jurors] of the Christian Media (Le Grand Prix des Treize, Chrétiens-Medias), 1987, all for *The Endless Steppe*; ALA Notable Children's Book, for *A Gift for Mama*; Parents' Choice Remarkable Book in the literature category, for *The Seven Good Years and Other Stories*; notable book citation, Children's Trade Books in Social Studies from the National Council of Social Studies/Children's Book council, 1992, Jewish Book awards for Children's Literature from the Jewish Book Council, 1993, and honor book, Sydney Taylor Book Awards of the Association of Jewish Libraries, 1993, all for *Riches*. **Address:** 505 West End Ave., New York, NY 10024, U.S.A.

PUBLICATIONS FOR YOUNG ADULTS

The Endless Steppe: Growing up in Siberia (autobiography). New York, HarperCollins, 1968.

Other

Translator and adaptor, *The Case against the Wind and Other Stories* by I.L. Peretz, illustrated by Leon Shtainmets. New York, Macmillan, 1975.
Translator and adaptor, *The Seven Good Years and Other Stories* by I.L. Peretz, illustrated by Deborah Kogan Ray. Philadelphia, Pennsylvania, Jewish Publication Society, 1984.
Remember Who You Are: Stories about Being Jewish (biographical sketches). New York, Crown, 1990.

PUBLICATIONS FOR CHILDREN

Fiction

A Gift for Mama, illustrated by Donna Diamond. New York, Viking, 1981.
Riches, illustrated by Donna Diamond. New York, HarperCollins, 1992.

"Four Languages" series (all contain text in English, Spanish, French, and Russian):

At Home: A Visit in Four Languages, illustrated by Aliki. New York, Macmillan, 1968.
In the Park: An Excursion in Four Languages, illustrated by Ezra Jack Keats. New York, Macmillan, 1968.
In School: Learning in Four Languages, illustrated by Nonny Hogrogian. New York, Macmillan, 1969.

Nonfiction

Let's Cook without Cooking: 55 Recipes without a Stove (as Esther Rudomin), illustrated by Lisl Weil. New York, Crowell, 1955.
Let's Make Presents: 100 Easy-to-Make Gifts under $1.00, illustrated by Ava Morgan. New York, Crowell, 1962.
Redecorating Your Room for Practically Nothing, illustrated by Sidonie Coryn. New York, Crowell, 1967.
Cool Cooking: 16 Recipes without a Stove, illustrated by Jan Pyk. New York, Lothrop, 1973.
Let's Make More Presents: Easy and Inexpensive Gifts for Every Occasion, illustrated by Ray Skibinski. New York, Macmillan, 1973.

Life with Working Parents: Practical Hints for Everyday Situations, illustrated by Roy Doty. New York, Macmillan, 1976.
Christmas Goodies, illustrated by Ronald Fritz. New York, Happy House Books/Random House, 1981.
Holiday Treats, illustrated by Yaroslava. New York, Macmillan, 1983.
Make It Special, illustrated by Martha Weston. New York, Macmillan, 1986.
On the Air: Behind the Scenes at a TV Newscast, illustrated with photographs by David Hautzig. New York, Macmillan, 1991.

*

Biography: Entry in *Third Book of Junior Authors,* Wilson, 1972; essay in *Something about the Author Autobiography Series,* Vol. 15, Gale, 1993.

Critical Studies: Entry in *Children's Literature Review,* Vol. 22, Gale, 1991.

Esther Hautzig comments:

What I always wanted and loved to do was write. I did not expect to be an AUTHOR! Whether I write craft books, or cookbooks, or picture books or translations, they are all part of ME and I could not have written any of them without having lived in and written about Siberia, and Vilna, and translated from Yiddish. Everyone's story is unique. I urge young people to keep a journal and write down their story, whatever it may be. Wondrous things can happen each day, to be savored and shared with others.

*   *   *

Esther Hautzig is best known for her autobiographical account *The Endless Steppe: Growing Up in Siberia,* which is not only about her life in exile for the five years from age ten to fifteen, but is a magnificent survival story in both the physical and spiritual sense.

The story begins in Vilna, Poland, in 1941 when Hautzig and her parents and grandparents are transported by the invading Russians to Rubtsovsk, Siberia. The family run a prosperous jewelry store and are considered dangerous capitalists by the Russians. They are transported to Siberia in railway cattle cars, a journey which requires weeks. Hautzig's powers of detailed description are evident in the description of this harrowing journey and in the descriptions of the extremes of heat and cold, the hard work, the crowded living conditions, and the constant threat of starvation. There is also the grief for a grandfather reported dead in another labor camp and for the father ordered to work behind the Russian front lines in the war against the Germans.

In counterbalance against these constant deprivations are the optimism, the endurance, the persistence, and the sheer resilience of the female members of the Hautzig family—Esther, her mother, and her grandmother. This untiring effort to overcome obstacles is illustrated in Esther's learning Russian, developing a love for the Russian classics, and becoming editor of the school paper. Early in their stay in Siberia, when the members of the family are working in a gypsum mine, the grandmother persistently manicures her nails at night—attempting to maintain something of the standard of her former life.

One of the most amusing incidents in the book occurs after Hautzig discovers her ability as a trader at the Sunday market. When an old peasant closely examines a book of Russian verse she is attempting to sell, she points out the virtues of the poems while he feels the thickness and quality of the paper. Upon her exclaiming that the paper makes no difference, he responds that different people see different things in books—this one, he contends, is not suitable as the pages are not right for rolling cigarettes. Hautzig is appalled at this and delighted that he did not buy the book.

Hautzig has given us not only a detailed, accurate, and poignant account of the Second World War with all its dangers and deprivations, but also the story of a young girl finding a best friend, going to a dance, having a boyfriend, in short, of a girl growing from childhood to maturity surrounded by love in the midst of hardship.

Although Hautzig finds at the end of the war that many of their family members and friends have been killed, miraculously she and her mother and grandmother are reunited with her father in Vilna, and she realizes Siberia will always hold a special place in her heart.

Hautzig has authored a number of craft books for young people growing out of her experience in Siberia making do with little or nothing. Out of her conviction of the importance of early language lessons, she pioneered a series of picture books in four languages. She has also translated from the Yiddish and has written a book for adults, *Remember Who You Are: Stories about Being Jewish,* which was recommended for young adults in *School Library Journal, The Book Report,* and *Books for the Teen Age, 1991,* by the New York Library. A collection of short sketches about various people she has known, it includes tales about some who perished and some who survived, some inspiring accounts and some funny. It acts as a fitting sequel and supplement to *The Endless Steppe.*

—Reba Pinney

HEAD, Ann

Pseudonym for Anne Christensen Morse. **Nationality:** American. **Born:** Beaufort, South Carolina, 30 October 1915. **Education:** Antioch College, student for three years. **Family:** Married Stanley F. Morse, Jr. (second marriage); one daughter from each marriage. **Career:** Writer, since 1943.

PUBLICATIONS FOR YOUNG ADULTS

Fiction

Fair With Rain. New York, McGraw, 1957.
Always in August. New York, Doubleday, 1961.
Everybody Adored Cara. New York, Doubleday, 1963.
Mr. and Mrs. Bo Jo Jones. New York, Putnam, 1967.

Nonfiction

Good Dog! Educating the Family Pet. North Pomfret, Vermont, Trafalgar, 1988.

*   *   *

Ann Head's novels are engaging overall. She is skilled at supplying wonderful detail and interesting characters. The bulk of her work could be classified as enjoyable, light reading material, providing romance, suspense, mystery, and humor. *Always in August, Fair With Rain,* and *Everybody Adored Cara* are similar in style and contain engaging descriptions and scenery, while their characters explore different facets of human relationships, whether it be a cheating husband or the prospect of a son becoming engaged. Although adults will no doubt enjoy taking any of these books to the beach, young adults will most likely be uninterested in these novels. While young adults are fully capable of reading and understanding the matter of these novels, they will not be totally engaged in the stories. The narrators are all older, either mothers or married women, mostly interested in what revolves around their lives: their children, husbands, friends and themselves.

Head's only true young adult novel, *Mr. and Mrs. Bo Jo Jones,* should capture the attention of its intended audience. The story involves two teenagers whose relationship progresses to the point of parenthood. What follows is a tale of the tumultuous decision to have the baby, the upset parents of the teenagers, a breakup of the couple, and their eventual reuniting as the mother becomes Mrs. Bo Jo Jones and the family goes to college together. The story is gripping and the worn copies in libraries attest to its popularity.

The teenagers' choice, while a difficult one, ends well: they are back in love, still have their child, and are pursuing their education. Head has tied the novel up a little too neatly, giving a very idealistic portrayal of what very few teenage pregnancies result in. The title alone, a feminist's nightmare, gives way to fantasy and simplistic notions of teenage pregnancy. Although *Mr. and Mrs. Bo Jo Jones* seems dated, the story is enough to interest young adults.

—Kate Lentz

HEADLEY, Elizabeth. *See* **CAVANNA, Betty.**

HEINLEIN, Robert A(nson)

Nationality: American. **Born:** Butler, Missouri, 7 July 1907. **Education:** Central High School, Kansas City, graduated 1924; University of Missouri, Columbia, 1924-25; United States Naval Academy, Annapolis, Maryland, B.S. 1929; University of California, Los Angeles, 1934-35. **Military Service:** Served in the United States Navy, 1929 until retirement because of physical disability,

1934. **Family:** Married 1) Leslyn McDonald (divorced 1947); 2) Virginia Doris Gerstenfeld in 1948. Owner, Shively and Sophie Lodes silver mines, Silver Plume, Colorado, 1934-35; worked in mining and real estate, 1936-39; Civilian Engineer, Philadelphia Navy Yard, 1942-45. Candidate for California State Assembly, 1938; Forrestal Lecturer, United States Naval Academy, 1973. Guest commentator during Apollo lunar landing, Columbia Broadcasting System, 1969. **Awards:** Guest of Honor, World Science Fiction Convention, 1941, 1961, 1976; Hugo award, 1956, for *Double Star*, 1960, for *Starship Troopers*, 1962, for *Stranger in a Strange Land*, 1967, for *The Moon Is a Harsh Mistress*; Boys' Clubs of America Best Liked Book Award, 1959; Sequoyah Children's Book Award of Oklahoma, Oklahoma Library Association, 1961, for *Have Space Suit—Will Travel*; named best all-time author, *Locus* magazine readers' poll, 1973 and 1975; Grand Master Nebula award, 1974; Humanitarian of the Year award, National Rare Blood Club, 1974; American Association of Blood Banks Award, 1977; Council of Community Blood Centers Award, 1977; Inkpot award, 1977; L.H.D.: Eastern Michigan University, Ypsilanti, 1977; *Locus* award, 1985; Distinguished Public Service Medal, National Aeronautics and Space Administration (NASA), 1988 (posthumously awarded); the Rhysling Award of the Science Fiction Poetry Association is named after the character in Heinlein's story, "The Green Hills of Earth"; Tomorrow Starts Here award, Delta Vee Society; numerous other awards for his work with blood drives. **Died:** 8 May 1988.

PUBLICATIONS FOR YOUNG ADULTS

Fiction

Rocket Ship Galileo, illustrated by Thomas Voter. New York, Scribner, 1947; London, New English Library, 1971.

Space Cadet, illustrated by Clifford Geary. New York, Scribner, 1948; London, Gollancz, 1966.

Red Planet, illustrated by Clifford Geary. New York, Scribner, 1949; London, Gollancz, 1962; expanded edition, New York, Del Rey, 1989.

Farmer in the Sky, illustrated by Clifford Geary. New York, Scribner, 1950; London, Gollancz, 1962.

Between Planets, illustrated by Clifford Geary. New York, Scribner, 1951; London, Gollancz, 1968.

The Rolling Stones, illustrated by Clifford Geary. New York, Scribner, 1952; as *Space Family Stone,* London, Gollancz, 1969.

Starman Jones, illustrated by Clifford Geary. New York, Scribner, 1953; London, Sidgwick and Jackson, 1954.

The Star Beast, illustrated by Clifford Geary. New York, Scribner, 1954; London, New English Library, 1971.

Tunnel in the Sky. New York, Scribner, 1955; London, Gollancz, 1965.

Time for the Stars. New York, Scribner, 1956; London, Gollancz, 1963.

Citizen of the Galaxy. New York, Scribner, 1957; London, Gollancz, 1963.

Have Space Suit—Will Travel. New York, Scribner, 1958; London, Gollancz, 1970.

Starship Troopers. New York, Putnam, 1959; London, New English Library, 1961.

Podkayne of Mars: Her Life and Times. New York, Putnam, 1963; London, New English Library, 1969.

PUBLICATIONS FOR ADULTS

Novels

Beyond This Horizon. Reading, Pennsylvania, Fantasy Press, 1948; London, Panther, 1967.

Sixth Column. New York, Gnome Press, 1949; as *The Day After Tomorrow,* New York, New American Library, 1951; London, Mayflower, 1962.

Waldo, and Magic Inc. New York, Doubleday, 1950; as *Waldo, Genius in Orbit,* New York, Avon, 1958.

The Puppet Masters. New York, Doubleday, 1951; London, Museum Press, 1953.

Double Star. New York, Doubleday, 1956; London, Joseph, 1958.

The Door into Summer. New York, Doubleday, 1957; London, Panther, 1960.

Methuselah's Children. New York, Gnome Press, 1958; London, Gollancz, 1963.

The Robert Heinlein Omnibus. London, Sidgwick and Jackson, 1958.

Stranger in a Strange Land. New York, Putnam, 1961; London, New English Library, 1965; revised and uncut edition with preface by wife, Virginia Heinlein, New York, Putnam, 1990.

Glory Road. New York, Putnam, 1963; London, New English Library, 1965.

Farnham's Freehold. New York, Putnam, 1964; London, Dobson, 1965.

Three by Heinlein (includes *The Puppet Masters, Waldo,* and *Magic, Inc.*), New York, Doubleday, 1965; as *A Heinlein Triad,* London, Gollancz, 1966.

A Robert Heinlein Omnibus. London, Sidgwick and Jackson, 1966.

The Moon Is a Harsh Mistress. New York, Putnam, 1966; London, Dobson, 1967.

I Will Fear No Evil. New York, Putnam, 1971; London, New English Library, 1972.

Time Enough for Love: The Lives of Lazarus Long. New York, Putnam, 1973; London, New English Library, 1974.

The Number of the Beast. New York, Fawcett, and London, New English Library, 1980.

Friday. New York, Holt Rinehart, and London, New English Library, 1982.

Job: A Comedy of Justice. New York, Ballantine, and London, New English Library, 1984.

The Cat Who Walks through Walls: A Comedy of Manners. New York, Putnam, 1985; London, New English Library, 1986.

To Sail Beyond the Sunset: The Life and Loves of Maureen Johnson, Being the Memoirs of a Somewhat Irregular Lady. New York, Putnam, and London, Joseph, 1987.

Short Stories

The Man Who Sold the Moon. Chicago, Shasta, 1950; London, Sidgwick and Jackson, 1953.

The Green Hills of Earth. Chicago, Shasta, 1951; London, Sidgwick and Jackson, 1954.

Universe. New York, Dell, 1951; as *Orphans of the Sky,* London, Gollancz, 1963; New York, Putnam, 1964.

Assignment in Eternity. Reading, Pennsylvania, Fantasy Press, 1953; London, Museum Press, 1955; abridged edition, as *Lost Legacy,* London, Digit, 1960.

Revolt in 2100. Chicago, Shasta, 1953; London, Digit, 1959.

The Menace from Earth. New York, Gnome Press, 1959; London, Dobson, 1966.

The Unpleasant Profession of Jonathan Hoag. New York, Gnome
Press, 1959; London, Dobson, 1964; as *6 x H: Six Stories,* New
York, Pyramid, 1962.

The Worlds of Robert A. Heinlein. New York, Ace, 1966; London,
New English Library, 1970.

The Past through Tomorrow: Future History Stories. New York,
Putnam, 1967; abridged edition, London, New English Library,
2 vols., 1977.

The Best of Robert Heinlein, 1939-1959, edited by Angus Wells.
London, Sidgwick and Jackson, 2 vols., 1973.

Destination Moon. Boston, Gregg Press, 1979.

Expanded Universe: The New Worlds of Robert A. Heinlein. New
York, Grosset and Dunlap, 1980.

Screenplays: *Destination Moon,* with Rip Van Ronkel and James
O'Hanlon (based on *Rocket Ship Galileo;* produced by George Pal/
Eagle Lion, 1950), edited by David G. Hartwell, Gregg Press,
1979; *Project Moonbase,* with Jack Seaman, Galaxy Pictures/
Lippert Productions, 1953.

Television Plays: scripts for *Tom Corbett, Space Cadet* series,
1950s.

Other

The Discovery of the Future (address). Los Angeles, Novacious, 1941.

Of Worlds Beyond: The Science of Science Fiction, with others,
edited by Lloyd Arthur Eshbach. Reading, Pennsylvania, Fantasy Press, 1947; London, Dobson, 1965.

Editor, *Tomorrow, the Stars: A Science Fiction Anthology.* New
York, Doubleday, 1952.

Famous Science Fiction Stories, with others. New York, Random
House, 1957.

The Science Fiction Novel: Imagination and Social Criticism, with
others, edited by Basil Davenport. Chicago, Advent, 1959.

The Notebooks of Lazarus Long. New York, Putnam, 1978.

Author of preface, *High Frontier: A Strategy for National Survival,*
by Daniel O. Graham. Chicago, Pinnacle Books, 1983.

Grumbles from the Grave (correspondences), edited by V. Heinlein.
New York, Ballantine, 1989.

Robert A. Heinlein Requiem (collection of fiction and nonfiction),
edited by Yoji Kondo. New York, Tor Books, 1992.

Tramp Royale (travel). New York, Putnam, 1992.

*

Media Adaptations: The television series *Tom Corbett: Space
Cadet,* which aired from 1951-1956, was based on Heinlein's
novel *Space Cadet;* television, radio, and film rights to many of
Heinlein's works have been sold; a military simulation board game
has been created based on *Starship Troopers.*

Biography: Entry in *Dictionary of Literary Biography* by Joseph
Patrouch, Volume 8, Detroit, Gale, 1981.

Bibliography: *Robert A. Heinlein: A Bibliography* by Mark Owings,
Baltimore, Croatan House, 1973.

Manuscript Collection: University of California Library, Santa Cruz.

Critical Study: *Seekers of Tomorrow* by Sam Moskowitz, Cleveland, World, 1966; *Heinlein in Dimension: A Critical Analysis*
(includes bibliography) by Alexei Panshin, Chicago, Advent, 1968;
entry in *Contemporary Literary Criticism,* Detroit, Gale, Volume
1, 1973, Volume 3, 1975, Volume 8, 1978, Volume 14, 1980,
Volume 26, 1983, Volume 55, 1989; *Robert A. Heinlein, Stranger
in His Own Land,* San Bernardino, California, Borgo Press, 1976,
and *The Classic Years of Robert A. Heinlein,* Borgo Press, 1977,
both by George Edgar Slusser; *Robert A. Heinlein* edited by Martin
H. Greenberg and Joseph D. Olander, New York, Taplinger, and
Edinburgh, Harris, 1978; *Robert A. Heinlein: America as Science
Fiction* by H. Bruce Franklin, New York, Oxford University Press,
1980, Oxford, Oxford University Press, 1981; *Robert A. Heinlein*
by Peter Nicholls, New York, Scribner, 1982; *Yesterday or Tomorrow? The Work of Robert A. Heinlein* by R. Reginald, San
Bernardino, California, Borgo Press, 1984.

*   *   *

Known as the dean of science fiction, Robert A. Heinlein was a
prolific writer of believable characters engaged in meaningful
struggles even when placed in the most unbelievable situations.
From Nazis plotting World War III on the moon to Venerian
Dragons speaking Cockney English and debating issues of individual liberty, all are cast in what has long been recognized as a
cogent vision of a future history that is rich in exploring the
potential for individual achievement.

Although now seriously dated, Heinlein's 1947 *Rocket Ship
Galileo* was among the first modern science fiction novels for
young adults to be critically acclaimed, and its success led Heinlein
to write a novel a year for the next thirteen years. The success of
each lay primarily in Heinlein's combination of a straightforward
narrative leading its protagonists to growth and maturity with
detailed descriptions of very plausible future societies. In *Space
Cadet,* Matt Dodson, initiated into the rules and regulations of the
Space Patrol, struggles with learning how difficult it is to adjust to
leaving home for the first time as well as coping with an entirely
new set of demands and expectations as he helps police the Solar
Federation of Earth, Mars, Venus, Luna, and Ganymede. Similarly,
Rod Walker, in *Tunnel in the Sky,* is unexpectedly stranded on a
primitive planet when a high school test in basic survival goes
awry. Not only must Walker make sure that he and his classmates
survive the dangers of their new world but also must find the
maturity to place the group's needs above his own. Tom Bartlett,
hero of *Time for the Stars,* helps explore the galaxy while maintaining a telepathic communications link first with his twin brother and
then with successive generations of his family since he ages at a
much slower rate than those on Earth. A convincing evocation of
life on board a space ship, yet the novel's central conflict is Tom's
internal battle with the psychological complexes that allowed his
twin to dominate him throughout his life.

Not written as a series, twelve of the thirteen early novels do,
nevertheless, present a consistent story about the conquest of space
without the didacticism or cynicism that so often weakens Heinlein's

later works. In these future worlds hunger, war, political corruption, or oppression can all be overcome by eager, capable individuals who see science, technology, reason, and service to others as central to creating better worlds. Jim Marlowe of *Red Planet* runs away from his boarding school to warn fellow Martian colonists of the treachery planned by the Mars Company, a corporation modeled on the British East India Company. Jim's trip across the Martian deserts and the actions he takes to protect the colonists and native Martians test his maturing courage, tolerance, and altruism. *Between Planets,* a more complex novel with a plot and theme that Heinlein explores thoroughly in *The Moon Is a Harsh Mistress,* has as its hero Don Harvey, an unwitting courier for a secret group of Venusian freedom fighters who discovers that the fight for political freedom is a fight for individual liberty.

The last of the novels written specifically for young adults and winner of a Hugo Award, *Starship Troopers,* is profoundly different from all the others. Having an adult protagonist, it traces the making of a starship soldier. Set in a time of a vicious space war, it is a dark, disturbing novel which glorifies war and the fighting man with vivid, convincing detail. Nonetheless, its idealization of military leaders as concerned, paternalistic men coupled with its original yet plausible military equipment makes the novel highly popular.

While not written for young adults, *Double Star, Stranger in a Strange Land,* and *The Moon Is a Harsh Mistress,* all winners of Hugo Awards, are of particular appeal to older adolescents. Political and social revolution or intrigue are the central focus of each, and each contains a hero who must mature. In *Double Star,* Lorenzo Smythe, a down and out actor, substitutes for one of the Solar System's most powerful political figures when he is kidnapped. Carrying out the charade successfully, Lorenzo discovers the reality of power politics: No single person is ever in control, so he, a charlatan, along with a team of astute political advisors, is perfectly capable of exercising power effectively. In *Stranger in a Strange Land,* a work that has become something of a cult classic, Michael Valentine Smith, a human male raised from birth by a race of brilliantly advanced Martians, is returned in his twenties to what is, to him, an alien Earth. Because he is believed to hold legal rights to most of the wealth of Mars, the government tries unjustly to imprison him in a hospital. He escapes and ultimately forms a quasi-religious organization dedicated to teaching the Martian disciplines that have made Michael superior to most other human beings. Since these disciplines diverge radically from existing sexual and social mores, Michael is eventually killed by a rioting mob, leaving his disciples to continue his work. Younger readers are not likely to find this novel entertaining, however, since it not only is didactic but also is lacking in action and its pacing is slow. In contrast, *The Moon Is a Harsh Mistress* tells the engrossing tale of war between the Lunar Colony and Earth. A logical product of circumstance, the Lunar culture Heinlein develops is an intriguing mix of the familiar and the alien that nonetheless never fails to emphasize human values. Manuel Garcia O'Kelly, known as Mannie, a lunar-born computer expert, discovers that the moon's main computer has become a sentient being. Mannie and the computer, Mike, become friends as the two are drawn into a rebellion to free the moon from Earth's tyranny. One of Heinlein's most endearing characters, Mike learns friendship, love, and self-sacrifice as he helps his human friends achieve freedom.

A work quite unlike Heinlein's others is *Glory Road,* yet it remains one of his most well read by both adults and adolescents. A

heroic fantasy, it sets Oscar Gordon, a former military advisor in Vietnam, on the road to adventure with a beautiful woman, Star, and a gnomish old man, Rufo, whom he meets in response to a help-wanted advertisement. Needed to help rescue the mysterious "Egg of the Phoenix," he joins the two armed only with a sword, and the three undergo a series of unlikely and extraordinary adventures that culminate in Oscar's discovery that Star is actually the Empress of Twenty Universes, Rufo her son, and the egg a sophisticated recording device necessary to her governing. What makes this novel transcend the ordinary is that Heinlein addresses what happens to a hero once the adventure has ended and the universe has been saved and, although fantastic in plot, once again Heinlein focuses on what he does best: individuals, their growth, and their relationships.

With characters who learn from both their mistakes and their successes, who build, use, and enjoy their technologies, who reach beyond today to redefine tomorrow, Robert A. Heinlein insists that religious hypocrisy, corporate avarice, and political chicanery exist only so long as good people tolerate them and that individuals dedicated to improving themselves and their worlds can make a difference in everything that they do. Thus, Heinlein's fictive world is a positive one, one where everything is possible.

—Marlene San Miguel Groner

HELLER, Joseph

Nationality: American. **Born:** Brooklyn, New York, 1 May 1923. **Education:** Abraham Lincoln High School, New York, graduated 1941; University of Southern California, Los Angeles, 1945-46; New York University, B.A. 1948 (Phi Beta Kappa); Columbia University, New York, M.A. 1949; Oxford University (Fulbright scholar), 1949-50. **Military Service:** Served in the United States Army Air Force in World War II; Lieutenant. **Family:** Married twice; 1) Shirley Held in 1945 (divorced); one daughter and one son. **Career:** Instructor in English, Pennsylvania State University, University Park, 1950-52; advertising writer, *Time* magazine, New York City, 1952-56, and *Look* magazine, New York, 1956-58; promotion manager, *McCall's* magazine, New York, 1958-61; former teacher of fiction and dramatic writing at Yale University and University of Pennsylvania; City College of the City University of New York, New York City, Distinguished Professor of English, until 1975; full-time writer, since 1975. Has worked in the theater, movies, and television. **Awards:** Fulbright scholar, 1949-50; National Institute of Arts and Letters grant in literature, 1963; American Academy grant, 1963; Prix Interallie (France) and Prix Médicis Etranger (France), both 1985, both for *God Knows.* **Address:** 390 West End Ave., New York, New York 10024, U.S.A.

PUBLICATIONS

Novels

Contributor, *Nelson Algren's Own Book of Lonesome Monsters,* New York, Lancer, 1960; London, Panther, 1964.
Catch-22. New York, Simon & Schuster, 1961, critical edition, edited by Robert M. Scotto, Dell, 1973.

Something Happened. New York, Knopf, and London, Cape, 1974.
Good as Gold. New York, Simon & Schuster, and London, Cape, 1979.
God Knows. New York, Knopf, and London, Cape, 1984.
Picture This. New York, Putnam, and London, Macmillan, 1988.
Closing Time: A Novel. New York, Simon & Schuster, 1994.

Plays

We Bombed in New Haven (produced New Haven, Connecticut, 1967; New York, 1969; London, 1971). New York, Knopf, 1968; London, Cape, 1969.
Catch-22: A Dramatization, adaptation of his own novel. New York, Delacorte Press, and London, French, 1973.
Clevinger's Trial, adaptation of chapter 8 of his novel *Catch-22* (produced London, 1974). New York, French, 1973; London, French, 1974.

Screenplays: *Sex and the Single Girl,* with David R. Schwartz, 1964; *Casino Royale* (uncredited), 1967; *Dirty Dingus Magee,* with Tom and Frank Waldman, 1970.

Other

No Laughing Matter (autobiography), with Speed Vogal. New York, Putnam, and London, Cape, 1986.
Dear God: Children's Letters. New York, Doubleday, 1987.
Conversations with Joseph Heller, edited by Adam J. Sorkin. Jackson, University Press of Mississippi, 1993.
Now and Then, from Coney Island to Here (autobiography). by Joseph Heller. New York, Knopf, 1998.

*

Media Adaptations: *Catch-22* (motion picture, directed by Mike Nichols, adapted by Buck Henry, and starring Alan Arkin as Yossarian), Paramount, 1970.

Biography: Entry in *Dictionary of Literary Biography,* Detroit, Gale, Volume 2: *American Novelists since World War II,* 1978, *Yearbook: 1980,* 1981, Volume 28: *Twentieth-Century American Jewish Fiction Writers,* 1984.

Bibliography: *Three Contemporary Novelists: An Annotated Bibliography* by Robert M. Scotto, New York, Garland, 1977; *Joseph Heller: A Reference Guide* by Brenda M. Keegan, Boston, Hall, 1978.

Critical Studies: "Joseph Heller's *Catch-22*" by Burr Dodd, in *Approaches to the Novel* edited by John Colmer, Edinburgh, Oliver and Boyd, 1967; "The Sanity of *Catch-22*" by Robert Protherough, in *Human World* (Swansea), May 1971; *A Catch-22 Casebook* edited by Frederick T. Kiley and Walter McDonald, New York, Crowell, 1973; entry in *Contemporary Literary Criticism,* Detroit, Gale, Volume 1, 1973, Volume 3, 1975, Volume 5, 1976, Volume 8, 1978, Volume 11, 1979, Volume 36, 1986; *Critical Essays on*

Catch-22, Encino, California, Dickinson Seminar Series, 1974, and *Critical Essays on Joseph Heller,* Boston, Hall, 1984, both edited by James Nagel; "Something Happened: A New Direction" by George J. Searles, in *Critique* (Atlanta), vol. 18, no. 3, 1977; *From Here to Absurdity: The Moral Battlefields of Joseph Heller* by Stephen W. Potts, San Bernardino, California, Borgo Press, 1982; *Joseph Heller* by Robert Merrill, Boston, Twayne, 1987; *Joseph Heller: An Interview* by David Middleton, Dallas, Northouse & Northouse, 1988; *The Fiction of Joseph Heller: Against the Grain* by David Seed, London, Macmillan, 1989; *Understanding Joseph Heller* by Sanford Pinsker, Columbia, University of South Carolina Press, 1991.

*   *   *

Despite its World War II setting, Joseph Heller's *Catch-22* may well be the quintessential 1960s novel. Noisy, brash, anti-establishment, and profoundly moving, it captures the bureaucratic quagmire from which Captain John Yossarian seeks to escape. A bombardier, Yossarian is told that when he completes a certain number of missions, he can return home. The problem is that this number keeps increasing. Yossarian then adopts a more elemental mission, that of survival. He believes that if he can convince his superiors he is insane, he can be grounded. But there's a catch: Catch-22.

As Doc Daneeka patiently explains, government policy does indeed stipulate that an insane pilot must be relieved of duty: all the pilot has to do is officially declare his insanity. The "catch" is that if the pilot is rational enough to insist upon his insanity, he obviously must not be insane at all. Military doublespeak, with rules that seemingly address a problem and then tautologically shift around to deny their solution, implies more than linguistic chaos, according to Heller; it portends the death of civilization. Such language provides a screen from personal responsibility for the horror and meaninglessness of war, while paradoxically perpetuating that same barbarism.

Yossarian's choices are limited: like young Snowden, he can keep flying missions until he is killed; like Milo Minderbinder, he can gleefully learn to manipulate the system and gain enormous profit at the expense of his colleagues' lives; or like Orr, he may make a separate peace. His decision is a moral one, for he learns that mere survival is not enough. He cannot change the world, but he can make a statement of personal worth, since Snowden's death taught him that "The spirit gone, man is garbage."

Something Happened, published thirteen years after Heller's first novel, presents a comfortably hollow businessman who is Yossarian's antithesis. Bob Slocum, the book's protagonist and first-person narrator, has opted for being "garbage." He is somewhat likable, occasionally colorful, but nevertheless garbage, having lost his spirit long ago. That was the "something" that happened, and with this loss came the loss of his core identity (even his handwriting was stolen from someone else). In this novel, Heller continues to evaluate the question of life versus survival. Slocum does survive, but as a simpleton, the spiritual counterpart to his mentally retarded second son.

With *Good As Gold,* Heller initially seems to be scrutinizing the world of Washington in the same way he examined the military and the business community in his first two novels. It too is a bleak institution amazingly absurd and devoid of affirmation, a place where one is informed that he can do "Anything you want, as long as it's everything we tell you to say and do. . . ." The single difference between this and the earlier novels is that Heller begins an exploration of his Jewish heritage. Bruce Gold, an English professor who has written a favorable review of the President's book, is rewarded with an invitation to join the White House staff. Although he cares nothing about politics, he would like to be the Secretary of State, specifically the first Jewish Secretary of State— not counting Henry Kissinger, whom he accuses of having sold out his Jewish roots in favor of praying with Richard Nixon and waging war upon oppressed people. Apart from government office, Gold is preoccupied with writing a book entitled *The Jewish Experience in America.* What is soon realized is that *Good As Gold* is Heller's book on the Jewish experience in America. More precisely, Heller's purpose is to satirize those individuals, Jews and Gentiles alike, who renounce their cultural and religious heritage in order to be assimilated into the power elite.

Heller enlarges his absurdist perspective in *God Knows,* espousing the theory that it's not just man's social institutions that defy purpose and meaning, the flaw is cosmic. The narrator of this unusual work is the Biblical King David, lying on his deathbed and anachronistically reviewing his life. His historical omniscience is amusingly evident in his criticism of Michelangelo's famous uncircumcised statue: "It may be a good piece of work, taken all in all, but it just isn't me." Linguistic anachronisms also abound in the frequent shifts from a King James diction to contemporary slang. Heller's point is that his David is not merely the Hebrew king; he is both an Everyman and a primordial hero. His dilemma is the universal one of loneliness and isolation, made particularly acute after a lifetime of stunning achievements.

Like *God Knows, Picture This* also contains meticulously researched history. One such topic is Rembrandt's "Aristotle Contemplating the Bust of Homer," while another is the world of Dutch mercantilism in the seventeenth century. And yet a third is Greek culture from the Age of Pericles through the fourth century B.C. Heller's actual concern, however, is ontological, the nature of reality itself. Thus, a painting of a model who is posing as a man who may never have contemplated a bust of Homer, achieves its own philosophical legitimacy completely separate from its historical coordinates. So too does the reader who contemplates a book about a painting about contemplating. With the question of the nature of reality, Heller masterfully continues the intellectual probing that he successfully began with *Catch-22.*

—Walker Rutledge

HENTOFF, Nat(han Irving)

Nationality: American. **Born:** Boston, Massachusetts, 10 June 1925. **Education:** Northeastern University, Boston, B.A. (summa cum laude) 1945; Harvard University, Cambridge, Massachusetts, 1946; the Sorbonne, Paris (Fulbright fellow), 1950. **Family:** Married 1) Miriam Sargent in 1950 (divorced 1950); 2) Trudi Bernstein in 1954 (divorced 1959), two daughters; 3) Margot Goodman in 1959, two sons. **Career:** Writer, producer, and announcer, WMEX Radio, Boston, 1944-53; associate editor, *Downbeat* magazine,

New York, 1953-57; co-founding editor, *Jazz Review,* 1959-60. Since 1958 staff writer and columnist, *Village Voice,* New York; since 1960 staff writer, the *New Yorker;* since 1984 columnist, Washington *Post.* Faculty member, New School for Social Research, New York, and New York University. Reviewer for several magazines, including *New York Herald Tribune Book Week, Peace News,* and *Reporter.* Lecturer at schools and colleges. **Awards:** Children's Spring Book Festival award, *New York Herald Tribune,* and Nancy Bloch award, both 1965, both for *Jazz Country;* Woodward Park School award, 1966, for *Jazz Country;* Golden Archer award, 1980, for *This School Is Driving Me Crazy;* Hugh M. Hefner First Amendment award, Deadline Club, 1981, for *The First Freedom: The Tumultuous History of Free Speech in America;* Cranberry Award List, Acton Public Library, 1983, for *The Day They Came to Arrest the Book.* **Address:** 37 West 12th Street, New York, New York 10011, U.S.A.

PUBLICATIONS FOR YOUNG ADULTS

Fiction

Jazz Country. New York, Harper, 1965.
Journey into Jazz, illustrated by David Stone Martin. New York, Coward McCann, 1968.
I'm Really Dragged but Nothing Gets Me Down. New York, Simon and Schuster, 1968.
In the Country of Ourselves. New York, Simon and Schuster, 1971.
This School Is Driving Me Crazy. New York, Delacorte, 1976; London, Angus and Robertson, 1977.
Does This School Have Capital Punishment? New York, Delacorte, 1981; London, Angus and Robertson, 1982.
The Day They Came to Arrest the Book. New York, Delacorte, 1982; London, Angus and Robertson, 1985.

Nonfiction

American Heroes: In and Out of School. New York, Delacorte, 1987.

PUBLICATIONS FOR ADULTS

Novels

Call the Keeper. New York, Viking Press, 1966; London, Secker and Warburg, 1967.
Onwards! New York, Simon and Schuster, 1968.
Blues for Charlie Darwin. New York, Morrow, 1982; London, Constable, 1983.
The Man from Internal Affairs. New York, Mysterious Press, 1985.
Speaking Freely: A Memoir. New York, Knopf, 1997.

Other

Editor, with Nat Shapiro, *Hear Me Talking to Ya: The Story of Jazz by the Men Who Made It.* New York, Rinehart, and London, Davies, 1955.
Editor, with Nat Shapiro, *The Jazz Makers: Essays on the Greats of Jazz.* New York, Rinehart, 1957; London, Davies, 1958.

Editor, with Albert McCarthy, *Jazz: New Perspectives on the History of Jazz by Twelve of the World's Foremost Jazz Critics and Scholars.* New York, Rinehart, 1959; London, Cassell, 1960.

Jazz Street, photography by Dennis Stouk. London, Deutsch, 1960.

The Jazz Life. New York, Dial, 1961; London, Davies, 1962.

Peace Agitator: The Story of A.J. Muste. New York, Macmillan, 1963.

The New Equality. New York, Viking, 1964.

Our Children Are Dying. New York, Viking, 1966.

Editor, *The Essays of A. J. Muste.* Indianapolis, Bobbs Merrill, 1967.

A Doctor among the Addicts. Chicago, Rand McNally, 1968.

A Political Life: The Education of John V. Lindsay. New York, Knopf, 1969.

State Secrets: Police Surveillance in America, with Paul Cowan and Nick Egleson. New York, Holt, Rinehart, 1974.

Jazz Is. New York, Random House, 1976; London, W.H. Allen, 1978.

Does Anybody Give a Damn? On Education. New York, Knopf, 1977.

The First Freedom: The Tumultuous History of Free Speech in America. New York, Delacorte, 1980.

The 1984 Calendar: An American History, with Tim Keefe and Howard Levine. Lansing, Michigan, Point Blank Press, 1983.

Boston Boy (memoir). New York, Knopf, 1986.

John Cardinal O'Connor: At the Storm Center of a Changing American Catholic Church. New York, Scribner, 1988.

Free Speech for Me—But Not for Thee: How the American Left and Right Relentlessly Censor Each Other. New York, HarperCollins, 1992.

*

Biography: Entry in *Third Book of Junior Authors,* New York, H.W. Wilson, 1972, p. 124; essay in *Contemporary Authors Autobiography Series,* Volume 6, Detroit, Gale, 1988, pp. 165-74; essay in *Speaking for Ourselves: Autobiographical Sketches by Notable Authors of Books for Young Adults,* Volume 1, compiled and edited by Donald R. Gallo, National Council of Teachers of English, 1990.

Manuscript Collections: Boston University, Massachusetts.

Critical Studies: Entry in *Children's Literature Review,* Volume 1, Detroit, Gale, 1976, pp. 107-109.

Nat Hentoff comments:

I am no longer writing novels for young readers. I very much want to continue because of the satisfaction of hearing from the readers—sometimes decades after a book has been published. But I cannot get a publisher for the novel I very much want to do even though all my YA novels have made back their advances and are still selling in various parts of the world. Moreover, until I stopped, I had spoken at the state library associations in half the states and some of its members have indicated that they had been waiting for my next YA novel.

The novel that has been turned down by some 15 publishers—including some that have published previous books of mine—is

about the growing separatism in high schools and colleges. Blacks stay by themselves, whites are in another place, and Asian-Americans in yet another state of isolation. A novel is a particularly apt place to explore—with humor and narrative power—why this is happening. But my idea would seem to be too controversial in a time when the goals are harmony and mutual understanding—rather than the reality of what's actually happening. So I am no longer a writer of books for young adults.

* * *

The 1960s and 1970s were a time of cultural revolution in the United States. The seemingly idyllic "happy days" of the fifties ended suddenly with the deaths of John, Martin, and Bobby and with bloody civil rights marches, drugs, generation gaps, student demonstrations, and Vietnam. These years were also a time of the Beatles and Woodstock, lunar exploration, and the genesis of the information age. They began with the youngest American president in office and vanished as a vapor one thousand days later. This was a time when baby boomers—the largest group of youthful Americans of any generation—came of age. This was a time in which a writer such as Mark Twain would have reveled, a time for analytical literary skill, wit, humor, and even a touch of sarcasm. It was a time for Nathaniel Irving Hentoff.

Like Mark Twain, Nat Hentoff views life from both the perspective of one who has lived it and one who writes about it. His young adult fiction is the shadow image of his interests—jazz, education, journalism, and civil rights. The majority of book reviewers praise Hentoff's first novel for a young adult audience, *Jazz Country,* as his best. In one of his latest, *The Day They Came to Arrest the Book,* his unique style unites with that of the remarkable Mr. Twain. Both writers were zealots for freedom of the press and censorship issues. Under the setting of a school book review committee meeting, Hentoff skillfully recreates many of the adverse attitudes faced by *The Adventures of Huckleberry Finn* when that American classic was published over one hundred years ago.

Hentoff was raised and educated in the Boston area and moved to New York City as a young man. It is, therefore, not surprising that his characters are based in New York, or similar metropolitan environs, and frequently attend college in Massachusetts. We meet the majority of Hentoff's protagonists via third person narrative. However, Tom, the son of a corporate lawyer from New York, is discussed in the first person in *Jazz Country.* The author's youthful personal experiences with jazz greats such as Duke Ellington come across with the clarion tones of a trumpet solo. The language and dialect are "cool!" In fact, all of Hentoff's use of narrative in his novels evidences a knowledge of the thoughts and speech of contemporary teenagers.

Hentoff has been criticized for being a topically oriented writer. But if this is a weakness, it is also a strength. In a sense, he has chronicled a turbulent era in America for young adults. The sixties and seventies were a time for crusaders. Many of the teenagers in Hentoff's works are politically and socially conscious. Written at a time when the draft did not mean basketball players and money or beer and party times, *I'm Really Dragged but Nothing Gets Me Down* examines the threat of enforced military service that teenage males faced at the height of the Vietnam War, a concern which many adults—and even many of their peers—did not understand. Jeremy, a high school senior, is thrust into an exploration of conscience and differing views between his father and himself on the army and on life itself. *In the Country of Ourselves* continues the preceding theme of the alienation of youth and the questioning of authority. Revolutionaries and pacifists are skillfully portrayed. Conflict is conducted through dialogue rather than via violence.

While the sixties and seventies were times of turbulence, the winds of change for many teenagers had begun earlier as depicted by two young men, James Dean in the movie *Rebel without a Cause* and Elvis Presley. The appeal and persuasion of these two artists are frequently seen in the themes, plots, and even the characters of young adult novels. The protagonist in *Jazz Country* is a young white man who wants to learn jazz from black musicians just as Elvis drew his inspiration from black rhythm and blues artists. *I'm Really Dragged but Nothing Gets Me Down* and *In the Country of Ourselves* both deal with causes and with youth who are considered rebels in their time.

Even though concerned with serious topics, Hentoff also incorporates humor in his writings. Both *This School Is Driving Me Crazy* and its sequel *Does This School Have Capital Punishment?* examine themes of considerable importance to teenagers and to Mr. Hentoff—truth, friendship, education, relationships between fathers and sons, and jazz (although not necessarily in that order). We follow the antics and frustrations of Sam and his friends through puberty into adolescence. Hentoff started his literary career as a jazz critic, so it is not surprising that jazz is a major component of the school curriculum at Burr Academy.

Nat Hentoff has the ability to present social and political problems through fictional dialogue. His passion for the rights to free speech and expression are also documented in two works of young adult nonfiction, *The First Freedom: The Tumultuous History of Free Speech in America* and *American Heroes: In and Out of School*. The need that young Americans have to learn to think for themselves is the underlying philosophy of Hentoff's writing.

—Albert Spencer

HERALD, Kathleen. *See* **PEYTON, K.M.**

HERBERT, Frank (Patrick)

Nationality: American. **Born:** Tacoma, Washington, 8 October 1920. **Education:** the University of Washington, Seattle, 1946-47. **Family:** Married 1) Flora Parkinson in 1941 (divorced 1945), one daughter; 2) Beverly Ann Stuart in 1946, two sons; 3) Theresa. **Career:** Reporter and editor for west coast newspapers; lecturer in general and interdisciplinary studies, University of Washington, 1970-72; social and ecological studies consultant, Lincoln Foundation and the countries of Vietnam and Pakistan, 1971. Director-photographer of television show, "The Tillers," 1973. **Awards:** International Fantasy award, 1956, for *The Dragon in the Sea*; Nebula award, 1965, for *Dune*; Hugo award, 1966, for *Dune*; Prix Apollo, 1978; Doctor of Humanities, Seattle University, Washington, 1980. **Died:** 12 February 1986.

PUBLICATIONS

Fiction

The Dragon in the Sea. Doubleday, 1956; London, Gollancz, 1960; as *21st Century Sub,* New York, Avon, 1956; as *Under Pressure,* New York, Ballantine, 1974.
Dune. Philadelphia, Chilton, 1965; London, Gollancz, 1966.
Destination: Void. New York, Berkley, 1966; London, Penguin, 1967.
The Eyes of Heisenberg. New York, 1966; London, Sphere, 1968.
The Green Brain. New York, Ace, 1966; London, New English Library, 1973.
The Heaven Makers. New York, Avon, 1968; London, New English Library, 1970.
The Santaroga Barrier. New York, Berkley, 1968; London, Rapp and Whiting, 1970.
Dune Messiah. New York, Putnam, 1969; London, Gollancz, 1971.
Whipping Star. New York, Putnam, 1970; London, New English Library, 1972; revised edition, New York, Berkley, 1977.
The God Makers. New York, Putnam, and London, New English Library, 1972.
Soul Catcher. New York, Putnam, 1972; London, New English Library, 1973.
Hellstrom's Hive. New York, Doubleday, 1973; London, New English Library, 1974; as *Project 40,* New York, Bantam, 1973.
Children of Dune. New York, Berkley, and London, Gollancz, 1976.
The Dosadi Experiment. New York, Putnam, 1977; London, Gollancz, 1978.
The Illustrated Dune. New York, Berkley, 1978; as *The Great Dune Trilogy* (includes *Dune, Dune Messiah,* and *Children of Dune*). London, Gollancz, 1979.
The Jesus Incident, with Bill Ransom. New York, Berkley, and London, Gollancz, 1979.
Direct Descent. New York, Ace, 1980; London, New English Library, 1982.
God Emperor of Dune. New York, Putnam, and London, Gollancz, 1981.
The White Plague. New York, Putnam, 1982; London, Gollancz, 1983.
The Lazarus Effect, with Bill Ransom. New York, Putnam, and London, Gollancz, 1983.
Heretics of Dune. New York, Putnam, and London, Gollancz, 1984.
Chapterhouse: Dune. New York, Putnam, and London, Gollancz, 1985.
Man of Two Worlds, with Brian Herbert. New York, Putnam, and London, Gollancz, 1986.
The Second Great Dune Trilogy (includes *God Emperor of Dune, Heretics of Dune,* and *Chapterhouse: Dune*). London, Gollancz, 1987.
Worlds beyond Dune: The Best of Frank Herbert (includes *The Jesus Incident, Whipping Star, Destination: Void, The God Makers,* and *The Dosadi Experiment*). New York, Berkley, 1987.

The Ascension Factor, with Bill Ransom. New York, Putnam, and London, Gollancz, 1988.
Songs of Muad'Dib: The Poetry of Frank Herbert, edited by Brian Herbert. New York, Ace, 1992.

Short Stories

Five Fates, with others. New York, Doubleday, 1970.
The Worlds of Frank Herbert. London, New English Library, 1970; New York, Ace, 1971.
The Book of Frank Herbert. New York, DAW, 1973; London, Panther, 1977.
The Best of Frank Herbert, edited by Angus Wells. London, Sidgwick and Jackson, 1975.
The Priests of Psi and Other Stories. London, Gollancz, 1980.
Eye, edited Byron Preiss. New York, Berkley, 1985; London, Gollancz, 1986.

Other

Editor, *New World or No World.* New York, Ace, 1970.
Threshold: The Blue Angels Experience. New York, Ballantine, 1973.
Editor, with others, *Tomorrow, and Tomorrow, and Tomorrow....* New York, Holt, Rinehart, 1974.
Without Me You're Nothing: The Essential Guide to Home Computers, with Max Barnard. New York, Simon and Schuster, and London, Gollancz, 1981; as *The Home Computer Handbook,* London, New English Library, 1985.
Editor, *Nebula Winners 15.* New York, Harper, 1981; London, W.H. Allen, 1982.

*

Media Adaptations: "Sandworms of Dune" (recording), Caedmon, 1978; "The Truths of Dune" (recording), Caedmon, 1979; "The Battles of Dune" (recording), Caedmon, 1979; *The Art of Dune* (book), New York, Berkley, 1984; *Dune* (film, screenplay by David Lynch), Universal, 1984; *The Dune Storybook* (book) by Joan Vinge, New York, Putnam, 1984; *Dune: The Making of Dune* (book), by Ed Naha, New York, Berkley, 1984; "The World of Dune" (teaching kit), Life-time Learning Systems, Inc., 1984.

Manuscript Collection: California State University Library, Fullerton.

Critical Study: *Herbert's Dune and Other Works* by Louis David Allen, Nebraska, Cliff's Notes, 1975; entry in *Contemporary Literary Criticism,* Detroit, Gale, Volume 12, 1980, Volume 23, 1983, Volume 35, 1985, Volume 44, 1987; essay in *Dictionary of Literary Biography,* Volume 8, Detroit, Gale, 1981; *Frank Herbert* by Timothy O'Reilly, New York, Ungar, 1981; *The Dune Encyclopedia* edited by Willis E. McNelly, New York, Putnam, and London, Corgi, 1984; *The Maker of Dune: Insights of a Master of Science Fiction* edited by Timothy O'Reilly, New York, Berkley, 1987; *The Notebooks of Frank Herbert's Dune* edited by Brian Herbert, New York, Perigree Books, 1988.

*   *   *

Frank Herbert was a prolific writer, mainly of science fiction, producing more than twenty novels and dozens of short stories in his fifty-year career. Nearly all of his novels and story collections are accessible to and appropriate for young adults even though they were written for an older audience and, therefore, occasionally contain depictions of violence and sexual behavior that may not be appropriate for younger readers. Most readers agree that the six novels in the Hugo and Nebula award-winning "Dune" series comprise Herbert's main achievement, while opinions vary about which of Herbert's other works are most worth reading.

Though the "Dune" series is appropriate for young adults, the opening novel, *Dune,* is fairly daunting. Herbert plunges the reader into an alien future centered around a complex interplanetary civilization. The social and political organization of this civilization is based on feudal models and seems strange at first because of the technologies and the socio-political consequences Herbert has imagined. The characters are driven by familiar human motives: love, power, and the need for self-knowledge. Duke Leto Atreides finds himself caught up in a subtle and highly complex power struggle that brings his family and forces to the planet Arrakis, or Dune, which is the source of "the spice," a kind of drug that releases the human mind into a hyper-perceptive state and lengthens the lifespan of its user. This drug is crucial to this civilization because it allows space travel between two points without moving while simultaneously allowing an accident-free course projection. The economic structure of this society is based on the "spice." Likewise, the spiritual organization of this civilization depends on this drug allowing women trained in its use, called Bene Gesserit, to share the literal memories of their foremothers. The vividness, completeness, and complexity of Herbert's universe are its most attractive features, but the fact that he opens the novel by dropping the reader into events already taking place makes the series difficult to begin. Readers must persist despite confusion for perhaps a quarter of the novel before gaining enough knowledge of Herbert's world to feel at home. A teacher might introduce students to this novel by viewing the David Lynch film adaptation.

Herbert encourages his readers to endure their confusion at the beginning of *Dune* by involving them quickly and deeply in the inner lives of the main characters, especially fifteen-year-old Paul, the Duke's son, and his mother, Jessica. All of the novels in the series focus on the relations between individuals in conflict over political power, so they are both political and personal. Herbert wants the reader to care for those characters who are trying to make and preserve affectionate relationships and who are trying to use political power for humane goals. He also reveals the inner lives of characters who live for personal power and those who have been forced or seduced into being the tools of power-seekers. The result is a combination of intense personal drama and political, economic, and military intrigue. This combination raises many questions and themes about the nature and limits of political power and about the qualities of a proper society.

Dune tells how the Atreides family is almost destroyed on the planet Arrakis. The Duke is killed, while Paul and his mother are lost and presumed dead in the desert that covers most of the planet. However, Paul and Jessica succeed in becoming leaders of the Fremen, the powerful but reticent native population of the planet. Eventually, they are able to work with the ecology, wildlife, and people of Arrakis to defeat and replace the interplanetary emperor who has plotted their destruction all along.

The next three novels in the series span thousands of years, telling in the same compelling fashion the story of how humanity manages to spread itself among planets in such a way as to ensure the ultimate survival of the species, yet in each, stories of the personal struggle for love and the realization of humanity's best impulses are balanced with political and military adventure. In *Dune Messiah,* a central problem is Paul's wish to disengage from the restrictions of his being emperor in order to have an ordinary family life with his beloved Chani. This is complicated by a conspiracy to dethrone and kill him, by his loss of sight, and by his unique ability to infer and envision future events. In *Children of Dune,* Paul's son, Leto II, becomes the main character. He shares his father's power of prescience, but he sees a way to ensure increasing unpredictability in the behavior of human masses by fragmenting the species into widely separated groups inhabiting planets unknown to each other. This plan he calls ''the golden path.'' *God Emperor of Dune* takes place 3500 years after *Children of Dune.* To achieve humanity's golden path, Leto has physically bonded with a sand-trout, and has become a sandworm, the animal responsible for producing the spice. This bonding has made him virtually invulnerable. He rules a boringly stable empire in which he secretly foments the rebellion that leads to the golden path. *Heretics of Dune* and *Chapter House: Dune* take up future human history thousands of years after the success of the golden path. These last two novels, in a series that would have included another had Herbert lived, develop a new and different story set in the universe of the first four.

None of Herbert's other works is so well-known as the ''Dune'' series. *The Dragon in the Sea, The Eyes of Heisenberg, The God Makers, The Green Brain, Hellstrom's Hive,* and *Whipping Star* are among the most popular, all having been translated into several European languages. Like the *Dune* series, these novels emphasize complex adventure plots with attention to cosmic questions about human nature and society.

—Terry Heller

HERMES, Patricia

Nationality: American. **Born:** Brooklyn, New York, 21 February 1936. **Education:** St. John's University, Jamaica, New York, B.A. 1957. **Family:** Married Matthew E. Hermes in 1957 (divorced 1984), four sons and one daughter. **Career:** Teacher of English and social studies, Rollingcrest Junior High School, Takoma Park, Maryland, 1957-58; teacher of home-bound children, Delcastle Technical High School, Delcastle, Delaware, 1972-73; writer, 1977—; writer in residence, Norfolk Public School System, Norfolk, Virginia, 1981—; teacher of English and writing, Scared Heart University, Fairfield, Connecticut, 1986-87. **Awards:** California Young Reader Medal, for *You Shouldn't Have to Say Goodbye;* Best Book for young adults, America Library Association, 1985, for *A Solitary Secret;* several Children's Choice awards. **Agent:** Dorothy Markinko, McIntosh and Otis, Inc., 310 Madison Avenue, New York, New York 10017, U.S.A. **Address:** 1414 Melville Avenue, Fairfield, Connecticut 06430, U.S.A.

PUBLICATIONS FOR YOUNG ADULTS

Fiction

What If They Knew. San Diego, California, Harcourt, 1980.
Nobody's Fault. San Diego, California, Harcourt, 1981.
You Shouldn't Have to Say Goodbye. San Diego, California, Harcourt, 1982.
Who Will Take Care of Me? San Diego, California, Harcourt, 1983.
Friends Are Like That. San Diego, Harcourt, 1984.
A Solitary Secret. San Diego, Harcourt, 1985.
Kevin Corbett Eats Flies, illustrated by Carol Newsom. San Diego, Harcourt, 1986.
A Place for Jeremy. San Diego, Harcourt, 1987.
A Time to Listen: Preventing Youth Suicide. San Diego, Harcourt, 1987.
Heads, I Win, illustrated by Carol Newsom. San Diego, Harcourt, 1988.
Be Still My Heart. New York, Putnam, 1989.
I Hate Being Gifted. New York, Putnam, 1990.
Mama, Let's Dance. Boston, Little Brown, 1991.
My Girl. New York, Simon and Schuster, 1991.
Take Care of My Girl. Boston, Little Brown, 1992.
Someone to Count On. Boston, Little Brown, 1993.
I'll Pulverize You, William. New York, Minstrel Books, 1994.
Nothing but Trouble, Trouble, Trouble. New York, Scholastic, 1994.
Everything Stinks. New York, Minstrel Book, 1995.
On Winter's Wind. Boston, Little Brown, 1995.
Christmas Magic, illustrated by John Steven Gurney. New York, Scholastic, 1996.
Fly Away Home (novel based on the autobiography of Bill Lishman). New York, Newmarket Press, 1996.
When Snow Lay Soft on the Mountain, illustrated by Leslie Baker. Boston, Little Brown, 1996.
Boys Are Even Worse than I Thought. New York, Minstrel, 1997.
Zeuss and Roxanne. New York, Minstrel, 1997.
Calling Me Home. New York, Avon Book, 1998.
Cheat the Moon. Boston, Little Brown, 1998.

*

Media Adaptations: *Fly Away Home* (screenplay) by Robert Rodat and Vince McKewin.

Biography: Essay in *Speaking for Ourselves, Too* compiled and edited by Donald R. Gallo, National Council of Teachers of English, 1993.

Patricia Hermes comments:

I *love* to write! It's *very* hard work, but it's such fun, too. Writing for young people gives me the opportunity to connect, to make the connection between my life and the life of the reader. It also gives me the opportunity to *live* other lives. I can be any character I want. Sometimes I can be silly and frivolous. Other times I'm serious. I can write about things that scare me—but in the book, I can be brave. I can do things in a book that I wouldn't dare do in real life—and I can make everything work out. But best of all, I can sometimes—in a very small way—make a difference in the life of a young reader, as authors made a difference in my life when I was a young adult—as they continue to do today.

* * *

The body of Patricia Hermes's work consists of realistic young adult fiction. Mainly contemporary, her novels focus on common adolescent concerns, including moving to a new town or making new friends, and more specific situations, such as incest or parental abandonment. Problem novels such as these tend to condescend to readers, focusing on a specific issue at the expense of plot and character development, and offering solutions where sometimes none can be reached. Hermes attempts to avoid these foibles by implementing a first-person narrative voice in the majority of her books. Allowing a character to tell his or her own story adds dimension and complexity to the character. A young reader recognizes the motivations of the characters because of their simultaneous experience of incidents. Tracy's shabby treatment of her lifelong friend Kelly in *Friends Are Like That* and her desire to be part of the popular crowd mirrors the experience of many young adults—her voice rings true.

Hermes's use of the first-person narrative unfortunately results in a lack of development of the other characters. Angela, the popular girl Tracy encounters, never goes beyond stereotype. The peripheral characters in most of Hermes's novels suffer from the same shallowness. The concentration on one individual interior voice also leads to weaker plots and settings.

The concentration on one young adult allows Hermes, in many of her works, to explore the idea of hidden shame. Most young people do not want to be different; conformity becomes almost an obsession. A step toward maturity comes with the realization that everyone has secrets, problems they will not tell even their "best friend." Hermes's writing becomes didactic in her desire to emphasize this point. *A Solitary Secret,* written in journal form, tells the story of a young, nameless incest victim. The novel is set during World War I, perhaps to remove the immediacy for a contemporary reader, and uses imagery to soften the horrifying abuse. A new girl, Sheila, moves to town, and the girls begin a game of sharing secrets. It quickly becomes obvious Sheila also has something to hide—a fatal illness. By creating such dramatic instances of secrecy, Hermes's writing becomes heavy-handed. This overkill also occurs in *You Shouldn't Have to Say Goodbye.* While dealing with her mother's cancer, Sarah also discovers that her best friend's mother suffers from agoraphobia. When tackling illness within a family—epilepsy, mental retardation, cancer, etc.—Hermes explores all the emotions of her character. The anger and selfish worry of a youngster sounds authentic. Death and illness force young people to grow up quickly. Sarah becomes frightened and angry when her mother teaches her how to do laundry because she knows what the lesson signifies.

Hermes also recognizes the pain of abandonment, either by death or by a parent leaving. In both *Take Care of My Girl* and *Mama, Let's Dance,* children are abandoned by a parent. When Brady attempts to find her father, she learns that he lives only about an hour from the house where she and her grandfather live. Acknowledging that her father does not want her, while painful, allows Brady to rework her definition of a family, and recognize her special relationship with her grandfather. When Mary Belle's mother abandons her three children, they attempt to survive on their own so that they will not be placed in separate foster homes. Both young girls gain a sense of worth and self-reliance from a painful lesson—that adults can, and do, fail.

Many of Hermes's protagonists also achieve self-reliance when their faith in God falters. Mary Belle wishes she could find peace in prayer like her brother Ariel, but she needs more tangible assurances. This doubt in the existence of a God who lets siblings and parents die will echo in the minds of some young readers, and Hermes does a commendable job of balancing lack of conviction with respect for religion.

Although many adults in these novels fail the children around them, some operate as saviors. The incest victim gives her journal to a kind neighbor who steers her toward help; Mary Belle's neighbors take her and her brother in once their secret is discovered. For younger readers, this assurance that adults can help provides security. Many problems like the ones Hermes's deals with in her novels cannot be solved by adolescents alone. The helping adult figure only becomes problematic when it offers a neat, clean resolution. The tidy endings seem preachy, and overly sentimental. Readers know that all situations do not resolve themselves easily, and may feel cheated by happy endings. Clean endings contrast with cluttered beginnings. Hermes sometimes tries to tackle too much, and she tends to concentrate on issues rather than characters. For example, in *Take Care of My Girl,* every page seems to contain some message about environmental responsibility.

What Hermes's novels may lack in literary value, they compensate for in their strong narrative voices and accurate portrayals of the pain of adolescence. Her dedication to young people also manifests itself in her nonfiction work, *A Time to Listen: Preventing Youth Suicide.* Indeed, many of her books of fiction occasionally read like self-help manuals, but will nonetheless reach young readers with their honesty and empathy.

—Karen Walsh

HERRIOT, James

Pseudonym for James Alfred Wight. **Nationality:** English. **Born:** Sunderland, County Tyne and Werr, England, 3 October 1916. **Education:** Glasgow Veterinary College, M.R.C.V.S. 1938. **Military Service:** Served in Royal Air Force, 1943-45. **Family:** Married Joan Catherine Danbury in 1941; one daughter and one son. **Career:** General practitioner in veterinary medicine, Yorkshire, England, 1938—; writer, 1966—. **Awards:** *All Things Bright and Beautiful* was chosen one of ALA's Best Young Adult Books, 1974, and *All Creatures Great and Small,* 1975; Officer of the British Empire, 1979; D.Litt., Watt University, Scotland, 1979; honorary D. Vsc., Liverpool University, 1984. **Died** 23 February 1995.

PUBLICATIONS FOR ADULTS and Young Adults

Nonfiction

If Only They Could Talk. London, M. Joseph, 1970.
It Shouldn't Happen to a Vet. London, M. Joseph, 1972.
All Creatures Great and Small (includes *If Only They Could Talk* and *It Shouldn't Happen to a Vet*). New York, St. Martin's, 1972.

Let Sleeping Vets Lie. London, M. Joseph, 1973.
Vet in Harness. London, M. Joseph, 1974.
All Things Bright and Beautiful (includes *Let Sleeping Vets Lie* and *Vet in Harness*). New York, St. Martin's, 1974.
Vets Might Fly. London, M. Joseph, 1976.
Vet in a Spin. London, M. Joseph, 1977.
All Things Wise and Wonderful (includes *Vets Might Fly* and *Vet in a Spin*). New York, St. Martin's, 1977.
James Herriot's Yorkshire. New York, St. Martin's, 1979.
Animals Tame and Wild, with others. New York, Sterling, 1979; as *Animal Stories: Tame and Wild,* New York, Sterling, 1985.
The Lord God Made Them All. New York, St. Martin's, 1981.
The Best of James Herriot. New York, St. Martin's, 1983.
James Herriot's Dog Stories. New York, St. Martin's, 1986.
Every Living Thing. New York, St. Martin's, 1992.

PUBLICATIONS FOR CHILDREN

Fiction

Moses the Kitten, illustrated by Peter Barrett. New York, St. Martin's, 1984.
Only One Woof, illustrated by Peter Barrett. New York, St. Martin's, 1985.
The Christmas Day Kitten, illustrated by Ruth Brown. New York, St. Martin's, 1986.
Bonny's Big Day, illustrated by Ruth Brown. New York, St. Martin's, 1987.
Blossom Comes Home, illustrated by Ruth Brown. New York, St. Martin's, 1988.
The Market Square Dog, illustrated by Ruth Brown. New York, St. Martin's, 1989.
Oscar: Cat-About-Town, illustrated by Ruth Brown. New York, St. Martin's, 1990.
Smudge: The Little Lost Lamb, illustrated by Ruth Brown. New York, St. Martin's, 1991.
James Herriot's Treasury for Children, illustrated by Peter Barrett and Ruth Brown. New York, St. Martin's, 1992.

*

Media Adaptations: *All Creatures Great and Small* (film), EMI Productions, 1975; (television movie), NBC-TV, 1975; (television series), BBC, 1978; PBS-TV, 1979; (cassette), Listen for Pleasure, 1980; *All Things Bright and Beautiful* (film), BBC-TV, 1979; (cassette), Listen for Pleasure, 1980; *The Lord God Made Them All* (cassette), Listen for Pleasure, 1982; *All Things Wise and Wonderful* (cassette), Cassette Book; *Stories from the Herriot Collection* (cassette), Listen for Pleasure.

Biography: Essay in *Authors and Artists for Young Adults,* Volume 1, Detroit, Gale, 1989.

Critical Study: Entry in *Contemporary Literary Criticism,* Volume 12, Detroit, Gale, 1980.

*   *   *

Alf Wight may have been born in 1916 to be a veterinarian, but readers throughout the world can be grateful that in 1966 James Herriot the writer was born. The works of this gifted author have such a broad appeal that even the classification of children's works and adult publications is arbitrary. Each of his works appeals to the most fundamental values in the reader so that only the length, not the thematic sophistication, of such novels as *All Creatures Great and Small* would deter younger readers. And in all James Herriot's writing, the earthy portraits of both human and animal characters, combined with a delightful humor, attract an older reader.

Herriot's primary works are the five novels which detail his life as a veterinarian in the rural Yorkshire town of Darrowby where he and his partners Tristan and Sigfried Farnon treat the animals of the village folk and rugged farmers of the region. *All Creatures Great and Small* begins the reader's odyssey through the career of young James Herriot, and *Every Living Thing* brings this journey to a close. Herriot's stories are not just about animals and the difficulties faced by a veterinarian in the rugged north country of England. In each novel, the reader meets extremely well-drawn characters: the peculiar senior partner in the veterinarian practice Sigfried, his reckless younger brother Tristan, the gentle Helen (later Herriot's wife), a range of elderly ladies with their beloved cats, and gruff farmers doubting the ability of a young veterinarian to heal their prized bulls, horses, and sheep. Combining this array of characters, Herriot builds a rich texture in his novels which makes them more than fine animal books; instead he creates a tapestry of human behavior as reflected by the relationships people have with the animals they rely on for both companionship and livelihood.

The simple didactic quality in Herriot's work emerges from the vignettes dealing with the life of a country veterinarian, many of which rely on an effective, understated humor. Memorable among these are the episodes involving the pampered Tricki Woo and his indulgent owner Mrs. Pumphrey, the scene when Herriot and Tristan mishandle an effort to milk a bull for the purposes of artificial insemination (with painful result), the episode when Herriot accidentally injects one of his helpers while attending to a large cow, and the many efforts made by Herriot to save an animal from the folk medicine diagnoses of various pretenders to medical skill. These episodes also give the reader a familiar look into the lifestyle of the Yorkshire farmer who scrapes out a living in a rugged country and the life of a small English village with its tiny shops and open air markets; they introduce the inspiring character of Granville Bennet whose skill in animal surgery is matched only by his Epicurean excesses and the knacker Jeff Mallock who picks up the remains of Herriot's unsuccessful efforts.

Herriot's descriptive skill is excellent. The reader is transported through his words to the snow-covered hillsides in the Yorkshire dales and the bustling streets and rowdy pubs on market day in the county's villages. And all this material—on the practice of veterinary medicine and the country lifestyle of Yorkshire—fuses well with the first person narratives of Herriot's life as he began a profession, courted and married Helen, served in the British Royal Air Force during World War II, raised his children, and, always, remained close to the animals he loves.

Herriot will not receive the critical accolades that his popularity would argue he deserves. But the very lack of a "literary" style is the most attractive feature of his work. He is a simple storyteller, somewhat in the vein of some of literary history's finest writers, such as Twain, Scott, and Poe. And if the literary scholars have not taken particular notice, readers throughout the world have, which for Herriot was no doubt the purpose for providing a glimpse into his life in the first place.

—Gerald W. Morton

HESSE, Karen

Nationality: American. **Born:** Baltimore, Maryland, 29 August 1952. **Education:** University of Maryland, College Park, Maryland, B.A. 1975. **Family:** Married Randy Hesse in 1971; two daughters. **Career:** Writer, from 1969; leave benefit coordinator, University of Maryland, 1975-76; worked variously as a teacher, librarian, advertising secretary, typesetter, and proofreader. Affiliated with Mental Health Care and Hospice, from 1988; chair of the Newfane, Vermont, elementary school board; board member of the Moore Free Library, Newfane, Vermont, 1989-91; member of the Society of Children's Book Writers and Illustrators (leader of South Vermont chapter, 1985-92). **Awards:** *Hungry Mind Review* Children's Book of Distinction citation, 1992, for *Wish on a Unicorn*; Christopher Medal, *Horn Book* Fanfare citation, *School Library Journal* Best Book citation, New York Public Library Book for Sharing citation, American Library Association Best Book for Young Adults, International Reading Association Book of the Year citation, all 1992, all for *Letters from Rifka*; *School Library Journal* Best Book of the Year citation, 1992, for *Sable*; American Library Association Best Books for Young Adults citation, 1994, for *Phoenix Rising*; *Publisher's Weekly* Best Book citation, and *School Library Journal* Best Book citation, both 1996, both for *The Music of Dolphins*; *Booklist* Editors' Choice citation, *Book Links* Best Book of the Year citation, and New York Public Library 100 Titles for Reading and Sharing selection, all 1997, and American Library Association Newbery Medal, 1998, all for *Out of the Dust*; poetry awards from Writer's Digest and Poetry Society of Vermont.

PUBLICATIONS FOR YOUNG ADULTS

Fiction

Wish on a Unicorn. New York, Holt, 1991.
Letters from Rifka. New York, Holt, 1992.
Phoenix Rising. New York, Holt, 1994.
A Time of Angels. New York, Hyperion Books for Children, 1995.
The Music of Dolphins. New York, Scholastic, 1996.
Out of the Dust. New York, Scholastic, 1997.

PUBLICATIONS FOR CHILDREN

Fiction

Poppy's Chair, illustrated by Kay Life. New York, Macmillan, 1993.
Lester's Dog, illustrated by Nancy Carpenter. New York, Crown, 1993.

Lavender, illustrated by Andrew Glass. New York, Holt, 1993.
Sable, illustrated by Marcia Sewall. New York, Holt, 1994.
Just Juice, illustrated by Robert Andrew Parker. New York, Scholastic, 1998.

*

Critical Studies: *Something About the Author,* Vol. 74, Detroit, Gale, 1993, 120-21; review of *Phoenix Rising* by Nancy Vasilakis, in *Horn Book* (Boston, Massachusetts), September 1994, 599; review of *Phoenix Rising* by Donna Pool Miller, in *The Book Report* (Worthington, Ohio), November/December 1994, 43-44; review of *A Time of Angels* by Brooke Selby Dillon, in *The Book Report,* May/June 1996, 36-37; review of *The Music of Dolphins* by Carol Burbridge, in *The Book Report,* November/December 1996, 40-41; "Letters in Biographies and Novels" by Elizabeth Paterra, in *Book Links* (Chicago, Illinois), May 1997, 37-39; review of *Out of the Dust* by Brooke Selby Dillon, in *The Book Report,* November 1997, 35; "Girls' Stressful Tales Draw Newbery and Caldecott Awards" by Eden Ross Lipson, in *New York Times,* 13 January 1998, E8; "Welcome to the Newbery Medal Home Page!," American Library Association, http://www.ala.org/alsc/newbery.html (3 July 1998); "Karen Hesse: The 1998 Newbery Award Winner and Author of *Out of the Dust*" by Michelle Picard, Riverdale School District (Portland, Oregon) web site, http://www.riverdale.k12.or.us/~cmaxwell/hesse.htm (3 July 1998); "Author Characteristics Essay" by Candice C., Virginia Department of Education web site, http://pen1.pen.k12.va.us/Anthology/Div. . .udentPublishing/authorEssays/hesse.html (3 July 1998).

Karen Hesse comments:

I have a cat's curiosity about the world. When something, some issue, some era, some person or group of people catches my attention, I am riveted to that point. Every sense, every muscle, every thought adheres to that very specific object of focus. Perhaps readers feel drawn to my work in the same way we are drawn to a cat with heightened senses. We are fascinated by the movement of its muscles under the fur, by the fire in its eye, by the fluid movement, the liquid posture as it follows up on a rustling, on an inaudible, imperceptible sound. Interestingly, just as the cat walks away after its curiosity has been satisfied, so do I turn from a subject after I've exhausted my curiosity. But with that turning away I am also turning toward the next subject.

*   *   *

As a girl growing up, Karen Hesse was "thin and pasty" (her own description), read a lot, and felt that she didn't really fit in. The young heroines in her award-winning novels for young adults are outsiders, too, who overcome their lack of acceptance and the difficulties to which they are subjected with a rare and admirable courage and level-headedness to which any teenager might aspire.

Maggie, the sixth-grade heroine of *Wish on a Unicorn,* lives in a tiny, run-down trailer with her widowed mother, her retarded younger sister Hannie (who is nearly eight), and her brother Mooch (who is six). When Hannie discovers an abandoned—and very dirty—stuffed animal on her and Mags' walk home from school one day, she talks Maggie into bringing it home: "Unicorn got magic, Mags." "No, Hannie. That's just in stories . . . fairy tales . . . make-believe. You got a stuffed unicorn there. It's not real. . . . And it doesn't have one bit of magic in it." When the girls get home, Mooch sees the unicorn, makes his wish right away—for something to eat—and gets his wish immediately when Mags tosses her uneaten lunch bag to him. Maggie knows for sure that wishes never come true. She gives Mooch her uneaten sandwiches every day after school. But what if they could? If wishes could come true, Maggie would just like "to be like everyone else, living in a house big enough so we wouldn't be tiptoeing around Mama sleeping on the living-room couch in the middle of the day [Mama works nights]." She would just like "to look and act and be like the other kids at school and not be embarrassed about who I am." In fact, she wants too many things: "Where would I ever begin?" Hannie persuades Maggie to go ahead and make one wish. She looks down at her pants, cuffed almost to her knees to hide that they are too short, twists the unicorn's horn in her hand, and makes her wish: "I wish I had some decent clothes to wear so Patty Jo and Alice would like me." Well, that very afternoon Aunt Laine had sent a whole box of clothes in the mail, and Mama's been trying them on and dividing them up—a great big pile for herself and a smaller pile of clothes that were too small and that might fit Maggie, a pile that includes a pretty pink sweater with penguins on it! Maggie wears the pink sweater—"too pretty for painting"—to school the very next day and is instantly befriended by Patty Jo and Alice, who invite her home with them after school. Hannie may be retarded, but she has wisely saved her own wish until she can think of something really special, and when she has to walk home from school all by herself that day and face the local bully as well as the big, scary highway, she wishes that Maggie would come and rescue her—and the unicorn's final wish amazingly comes true.

While Wish on a Unicorn was written from Maggie's first-person perspective, Hesse's next novel, Letters from Rifka, was written in an even more immediate epistolary style—a genre always popular with young adults. The year is 1919. When the Russian soldiers begin to torment the Jews in the Ukraine, twelve-year-old Rifka and her family decide they must leave their homeland for America, where Rifka's three oldest brothers already live. But Jews are not allowed to travel within the Ukraine, so they must hide in boxcars to get to the Polish border. The family makes it safely through the perilous trip to Poland, only to contract typhoid fever. They all recover, but after an act of kindness to a Polish peasant woman, Rifka contracts a highly contagious case of ringworm and is not allowed to board the ship with her parents. With the help of the Hebrew Immigrant Aid Society, they find a family in Belgium willing to take Rifka in until her ringworm is healed, and Rifka's parents and two brothers board the ship for America. Finally, after over nine months, Rifka's ringworm is all cleared up—although the treatments have caused her to lose her hair—and she is ready to join her family in America. The ocean voyage is long and hazardous, and Rifka almost doesn't make it past Ellis Island when the immigration officials notice her bald head, but in the end Rifka is allowed to enter the United States. Rifka's adventures are told through the letters she has written to her older cousin Tovah in the margins of the volume of Pushkin Tovah has given her. Once she is settled in the United States, Rifka wraps up her precious book and sends it back to her cousin: ". . .so you will know of my journey. I hope you can read all the tiny words squeezed onto the worn pages. I hope they bring you the comfort they have brought to me. I send you my love, Tovah. At last I send you my love from America. Shalom, my dear cousin, Rifka." Dedicated to the "memory of Zeyde and Bubbe, my beloved grandparents," Letters From Rifka is based on the true-life story of Hesse's great-aunt Lucy.

Hesse dedicated her next book, Phoenix Rising, "For the children of Three Mile Island. For the children of Chernobyl. For all of us, children of a nuclear age." This is the first-person narrative of thirteen-year-old Nyle, who discovers another kind of courage when she befriends the dying Ezra, a fifteen-year-old victim of radiation exposure whom her grandmother has taken in.

With A Time of Angels, Hesse returns to the earlier part of the twentieth century, to the 1918 influenza epidemic which swept through the country and killed over twenty-two million people. After her Tanta Rosa dies of the epidemic and her two younger sisters Eve and Libby are stricken by it, fourteen-year-old Hannah Gold is sent from her family's tenement in Boston to stay with Tanta Rosa's cousin outside of Albany. Already feverish from the flu herself, Hannah barely makes it to the train station, where she is led by a mysterious girl with violet eyes onto the train to Brattleboro, Vermont, instead of Albany. When she arrives in Brattleboro, she is really sick and taken to the overflowing hospital there. She recovers, and is taken in by an old German farmer. Scorned by his neighbors for being German in the wake of the First World War, "Uncle" Klaus takes loving care of the frail young Jewish girl. But Hannah's violet-eyed angel returns and leads her back to Boston and her sisters. In her review of the book for The Book Report, Brooke Selby Dillon called A Time of Angels "children's literature at its finest. . . . modern readers will find themselves spellbound."

In her comments on Out of the Dust as it was awarded the 1998 Newbery Medal, Newbery Committee chair Ellen Fader said of the novel, the story of fifteen-year-old Billie Jo's coming to terms with her mother's accidental death, the Oklahoma dust storms, and the Great Depression: "Hesse's painstaking first-person narration of Billie Jo's withering and, finally, taking root is spare and gritty. She creates a stark and piercing rhythm in a free verse form that naturally and immediately communicates this story of Billie Jo's fierce spirit and growing self-understanding." A truly wonderful achievement for what Candice C., Grade 6, aptly described in her Spring 1998 essay on Hesse for the Virginia Department of Education web site as "a wonderful young adult author."

—Marcia Welsh

HILL, Douglas (Arthur)

Pseudonyms: Martin Hillman. **Nationality:** Canadian. **Born:** Brandon, Manitoba, Canada, 6 April 1935. **Education:** Schools in Prince Albert, Saskatchewan; University of Saskatchewan, Saskatoon, 1952-57, B.A. (honours) in English 1957; University of Toronto, 1957-59. **Family:** Married Gail Robinson in 1958 (divorced 1978); one son. **Career:** Series editor, Aldus Books, London, 1962-64. Since 1964 freelance writer. Literary editor, Tribune, London, 1971-84. Science fiction advisor, Rupert Hart-Davis, 1966-68, Mayflower Books, 1969-71, J.M. Dent and Sons, 1972-74, and Pan Books, 1974-80, all London. British Guest of Honour at Albacon, a science fiction convention, Scotland, 1994; Chair of the Children's Writers and Illustrators Group, Society of Authors, 1995-97. **Awards:** Canada Council grant, 1966, 1969, 1970. **Agent:** Sheila Watson, Watson Little Ltd., Capo di Monte, Windmill Hill, London NW3 6RJ, England. **Address:** 3 Hillfield Ave., London N8 7DU, England.

PUBLICATIONS FOR YOUNG ADULTS

Fiction

Galactic Warlord. London, Gollancz, 1979; New York, Atheneum, 1980.

Deathwing over Veynaa. London, Gollancz, 1980; New York, Atheneum, 1981.

Day of the Starwind. London, Gollancz, 1980; New York, Atheneum, 1981.

Planet of the Warlord. London, Gollancz, 1981; New York, Atheneum, 1982.

Young Legionary: The Earlier Adventures of Keill Randor. London, Gollancz, 1982; New York, Atheneum, 1983.

The Huntsman. London, Heinemann, and New York, Atheneum, 1982.

Have Your Own Extraterrestrial Adventure. London, Sparrow, 1983.

Warriors of the Wasteland. London, Heinemann, and New York, Atheneum, 1983; as *Creatures of the Claw,* London, Macmillan, 1998.

Alien Citadel. London, Heinemann, and New York, Atheneum, 1984.

Exiles of ColSec. London, Gollancz, and New York, Atheneum, 1984.

The Caves of Klydor. London, Gollancz, 1984; New York, Atheneum, 1985.

ColSec Rebellion. London, Gollancz, and New York, Atheneum, 1985.

Blade of the Poisoner. London, Gollancz, and New York, McElderry, 1987.

Master of Fiends. London, Gollancz, 1987; New York, McElderry, 1988.

Penelope's Pendant, illustrated by Steve Johnson. London, Macmillan, and New York, Doubleday, 1990.

Penelope's Protest, illustrated by Annabel Spenceley. London, Pan Macmillan, 1994.

Penelope's Peril, illustrated by Annabel Spenceley. London, Pan Macmillan, 1994.

World of the Stiks. London, Bantam, 1994.

Cade: Galaxy's Edge. London, Bantam, 1996.

Cade: The Moons of Lannamur. London, Bantam, 1996.

The Dragon Charmer, illustrated by Peter Melnyczuk. London, Hodder, 1997.

Cade: The Phantom Planet. London, Bantam, forthcoming.

Other

Coyote the Trickster: Legends of the North American Indians, with Gail Robinson, illustrated by Graham McCallum. London, Chatto and Windus, 1975; New York, Crane Russak, 1976.

The Exploits of Hercules, illustrated by Tom Barling. London, Pan, 1978.

Editor, *Alien Worlds.* London, Heinemann, 1981.

Editor, *Planetfall.* Oxford, Oxford University Press, 1986.

The Young Green Consumer Guide, with John Elkington, Joel Merkower, and Julia Hailes. London, Gollancz, 1990; as *Going Green: A Kid's Handbook to Saving the Planet,* New York, Viking, 1990.

Witch and Wizard. London, Dorling Kindersley, 1997; as *Watches and Magic-makers,* New York, Knopf, 1997.

PUBLICATIONS FOR CHILDREN

Fiction

The Moon Monsters, illustrated by Jeremy Ford. London, Heinemann, 1984.

How Jennifer (and Speckle) Saved the Earth, illustrated by André Amstutz. London, Heinemann, 1986.

Goblin Party, illustrated by Paul Demayer. London, Gollancz, 1988.

The Tale of Trellie the Troog, illustrated by Cathy Simpson. London, BBC Radio and Longman, 1991.

Unicorn Dream, illustrated by D. S. Aldridge. London, Heinemann, 1992.

The Voyage of Mudjack, illustrated by Anthony Lewis. London, Methuen, 1993.

Fireball and the Hero, illustrated by Anthony Lewis. London, Methuen, 1995.

The Magical Tree-castle. London, Heinemann, 1995.

Malcolm and the Cloud-stealer. London, Scholastic, 1995.

Space Girls Don't Cry, illustrated by Michael Reid. London, Reed, 1998.

PUBLICATIONS FOR ADULTS

Fiction

The Fraxilly Fracas. London, Gollancz, 1989.

The Colloghi Conspiracy. London, Gollancz, 1990.

The Lightless Dome. London, Pan, 1993.

The Leafless Forest. London, Pan, 1994.

Other

Contributor, *Poetmeat Anthology of British Poetry.* Blackburn, Lancashire, Screeches Publications, 1965.

The Supernatural, with Pat Williams. London, Aldus, 1965; New York, Hawthorn, 1966.

Editor, *The Peasants' Revolt: A Collection of Contemporary Documents.* London, Jackdaw, 1966.

Editor, *The Way of the Werewolf.* London, Panther, 1966.

Editor, *Window on the Future.* London, Hart Davis, 1966.

Editor, *The Devil His Due.* London, Hart Davis, 1967; New York, Avon, 1969.

The Opening of the Canadian West. London, Heinemann, and New York, Day, 1967.

Contributor, *Young British Poets.* Geneva, Poésie Vivante, 1967.

Magic and Superstition. London, Hamlyn, 1968.

John Keats. London, Morgan Grampian, 1968.

Contributor, *Poems from Poetry and Jazz in Concert.* London, Souvenir Press, 1969.

Regency London. London, Macdonald, 1969.

Fortune Telling. London, Hamlyn, 1970.

A Hundred Years of Georgian London. London, Macdonald, 1970; New York, Hastings House, 1971.
Return from the Dead. London, Macdonald, 1970; as *The History of Ghosts, Vampires, and Werewolves,* New York, Harrow, 1973.
Bridging a Continent (as Martin Hillman). London, Aldus, 1971; revised edition, London, Reader's Digest Association, 1978, 1979.
Editor, *Warlocks and Warriors.* London, Mayflower, 1971.
The Scots to Canada. London, Gentry, 1972.
The Comet. London, Wildwood, 1973.
Witchcraft, Magic, and the Supernatural, with others. London, Octopus, 1974.
The English to New England. London, Gentry, and New York, Potter, 1975.
Editor, *Tribune 40.* London, Quartet, 1977.
Fortune Telling: A Guide to Reading the Future. London, Hamlyn, 1978.
Editor, *The Shape of Sex to Come.* London, Pan, 1978.
The Illustrated "Faerie Queene" (retelling). New York and London, Newsweek, 1980.
The Fraxilly Fracas. London, Gollancz, 1989.
The Colloghi Conspiracy. London, Gollancz, 1990.
The Lightless Dome. London, Pan, 1993.
The Leafless Forest. London, Pan, forthcoming.

*

Biography: Essay in *Speaking for Ourselves, Too* compiled and edited by Donald R. Gallo, National Council of Teachers of English, 1993.

Douglas Hill comments:

Since no youthful reading habit comes into existence in a single, fully formed leap from (say) Ninja Turtles to the novels of Dickens, I think of myself as constructing some lower rungs on the ladder that is needed for that sort of ascent. At the same time, because I specialize in science fiction and fantasy, I like to think that I'm doing my bit towards maintaining the health of the imagination—which may be the only thing that distinguishes the human mind from another item of information technology.

*   *   *

Douglas Hill, a Canadian, came to London as a young man to further his writing career and was for years a journalist and author of popular nonfiction. A lifelong science-fiction fan, he was deploring the lack of SF for young readers in the hearing of a publisher, who took him at his word and challenged him to write some himself. Then began a period of intense midlife creativity, in which Hill produced thirteen science fiction/fantasy novels for ten- to fourteen-year-olds in nine years, plus some short fantasies for beginning readers. Now he is writing longer adult novels and, judging by the first two, they are accessible to teenage readers as well.

All Hill's YA novels are composed in the series format: first a quartet, with a prequel written afterwards, then two trilogies, and finally a two-parter. The "Last Legionary" quartet presents a tough fighting hero, a kind of space mercenary, but with a heart and conscience. Looking for a rationale for his hero's fighting superiority and relative invulnerability, Hill invented the planet Moros, where youngsters were trained in survival and combat skills in order to cope with their planet's hostile environment and native "monsters." Then adults from Moros would hire themselves out to other planets to help win wars, in conflicts chosen on a strictly ethical basis. When all living things on Moros are destroyed by radiation, Keill Randor, the only survivor, is recruited by a secret group of scientists to discover the cause, whom they have called the "Warlord," an evil genius bent on sowing dissent and eventually ruling the galaxy.

Because Keill is also dying of radiation, the scientists replace his bones "molecule by molecule" with "an organic alloy." This completely fantastic concept does however render plausible Keill's survival in his many hand-to-hand combats without even a broken bone. Eventually, by intelligence, strength, and guts, Keill slogs his way to the heart of the Warlord's empire, aided by a female telepathic alien who pilots his spaceship and warns him of danger. Hill's punchy, exaggerated style is best shown by quotation:

> The ship lurched sideways, metal screeching against stone like a death cry, and toppled with a slow finality into the yawning mouth of the pit that had opened beneath it."
> (From *Day of the Starwind*)

OS-9 sprawled on the moss like a stringless puppet, his broken jaw askew and his head twisted in a manner that showed how cleanly his neck had been snapped. (From *Starwind*)

Hill had successfully identified a gap in the market. Juvenile SF was overliterary, full of "message" books about nuclear war and the destruction of civilisation. It needed an injection of traditional "space opera" to encourage the average reader, written in a professional "pulp" style. The time was right: the *Star Wars* craze had made reading SF fashionable among the young.

One could criticise the "Last Legionary" series for its overdetailed combat scenarios and lack of positive human female characters. Hill's following books remedied these faults. The "Huntsman" trilogy has a post-nuclear-war scenario. Earth has in fact suffered two disasters: centuries after the horror of nuclear war and radioactivity, Earth has been invaded by alien Slavers for its mining potential. Earthpeople are worked to death and regarded as barely sentient vermin. Set in Hill's native North America, the trilogy shows how two genetically altered humans bred in the Slavers' laboratories, the heroic Finn Ferral and the shaggy hair-covered beast-man Baer, team up to fight the Slavers. They journey to the Wastelands, the deserts of Central North America, where they join tribes of native Americans resisting the Slavers, and Finn meets his kidnapped foster-sister, now a woman-warrior. Success in the struggle against the Slavers restores humankind's pride, and eventually Planet Earth regains its freedom.

Hill's third trilogy returns to space opera with a theme from Heinlein: teenagers dispatched through space to colonise new planets. Sent as a punishment by ColSec—Colonization Section— five teenagers, three from street gangs and two minor offenders against the law, bond together on the planet Klydor, fight or make truce with aliens, defeat the ColSec inspectors, and lead a rebellion of the colonised planets to win self-govern'nent and the right to sell their products at market value. The teenagers include Cord, the hero, exceptionally strong, from the Scottish highlands; Samella, a girl who is a computer expert; and Heleth, a street-fighting girl.

Hill's fourth series switched to fantasy, using the Dungeons-and-Dragons formula of several questers, each possessing special powers, which Hill calls Talents. Four gifted people (two male, two female) are recruited by a good wizard to combat the forces of evil, presented here as hideous demons. Three have aided him before. The fourth is twelve-year-old Jarral, the young hero, who possesses the special Talent of being able to call up the forces of nature, for example earthquakes and thunderstorms. In this two-parter, Hill imports into young people's literature the conventions of sword-and-sorcery, that popular genre of adult fantasy born in the United States SF magazines decades before *The Lord of the Rings* was published, and offers a vigorous alternative to the literary fantasies of Lewis, Garner, and Cooper. And one of Hill's drawbacks, the way that his evil characters usually *look* ugly too, is irrelevant when the evil characters are demons or long-lived sorcerers who have worked evil for centuries.

Making the jump to adult SF, Hill wrote two comic space operas about Del Curb, an Intergalactic Courier, a fellow who thinks he's attractive to women. Accustomed to making sexist observations, he can't fool an intelligent woman, though he encounters a few females who make advances to *him,* some welcome, some not. Curb narrates himself, with throwaway lines like: "He seems crazy as a Phyquollian thorn-leaper" and "I felt as if I'd been kicked in the stomach by a Naspiddoric stone-tail." In this future, the galaxy is populated throughout, either by settlers from Earth or sentient aliens, and faster-than-light travel is essential. Earth itself was ruined by nuclear war centuries before, Curb tells us noncommittedly, and is now ruled by giant mutant cockroaches. Aided by his superintelligent ship's computer-pilot, Curb's aim to make a profit from his shady deals is usually frustrated by pirates and criminal gangs, but in both books he wins out. Lacking explicit sex, these might go into YA SF collections, though not as good as Harry Harrison's humorous SF, their more accomplished model.

Hill returned to juvenile space adventure with *World of the Stiks,* about trade and colonisation. A team of traders from Earth, legally trading with the forest-dwelling "Stiks" for their fine-woven cloth, finds itself competing with illegal traders who are dealing in "easy-dust," an addictive drug which is bound to ruin the innocent Stiks. Our teenage hero Jonmac survives the shoot-out between the adults, is captured by the criminals while the Earth ship takes off, escapes and lives in the forest with the Stiks, learning their language and culture, until the Earth traders return. This rite-of-passage novel combines Heinleinian toughness with the eco-logical concerns of Hughes or Hoover.

Hill's new trilogy is space opera featuring an interstellar rogue, Cade, in search of a "Phantom Planet" rumoured to be rich in the mineral necessary for spacflight technology. We meet Cade's great-uncle and mentor, "the galaxy's greatest hacker—the Datamaster," and Raishe, a bounty-hunter with an implant which gives her enhanced fighting powers. There is a cast of aliens, human gangsters, and an Artificial Intelligence. The milieu recalls Han Solo's early life-style, and the thrills and spills are punchily recounted.

Hill has also written shorter fantasies to bridge the gap between picture-books and full-length children's novels; some of these could appeal to reluctant YA readers. The "Penelope" trilogy, set in our world, is about a girl with a magic pendant which obeys her wishes, but in a distorted fashion, which generally gets her into

trouble. Two stories set in fantasy worlds could also interest the older reader; *The Dragon Charmer* is about a girl who conquers her fear of dragons to protect a dragon's egg and its newly-hatched baby dragon. *Malcolm and the Cloud-stealer* is about a boy with the power to communicate with animals, birds and insects. Al-though his powers were scorned by the Lord High Wizard when he applied to wizard School, Malcolm defeats a magical enemy "where larger powers have failed." All these shorter books have a strongly identified child hero/ine, and positive messages about courage and good versus evil.

Douglas Hill writes more from the head (and the thesaurus) than the heart, but when both combined, as in the "Huntsman" and "Blade of the Poisoner" series, he deserves much praise for creating ethical fantasy which appeals to reluctant readers. The eagerness with which youngsters return a Douglas Hill book to demand the sequel justifies his midcareer change.

—Jessica Yates

HILL, John. *See* **KOONTZ, Dean R.**

HILLERMAN, Tony

Nationality: American. **Born:** Sacred Heart, Oklahoma, 27 May 1925; raised among Pottawatomie and Seminole Indians. **Education:** Educated at Indian boarding school for eight years; Oklahoma State University, Stillwater; University of Oklahoma, Norman, B.A. in journalism 1948; University of New Mexico, Albuquerque, M.A. in English 1965. **Military Service:** Served in the United States Army Infantry, 1943-45; Silver Star, Bronze Star, Purple Heart. **Family:** Married Marie E. Unzner in 1948; three daughters and three sons. **Career:** Reporter, *News Herald,* Borger, Texas, 1948; news editor, *Morning Press,* 1949, and city editor, *Constitution,* 1950, Lawton, Oklahoma; political reporter, United Press International, Oklahoma City, 1950-52; bureau manager, United Press, Santa Fe, New Mexico, 1952-54; political reporter, later executive editor, *New Mexican,* Santa Fe, 1954-62. Assistant to the President, 1963-66, 1976-81, Associate Professor, 1965-66, Professor of Journalism and chair of Department, 1966-85, Professor Emeritus, from 1985, University of New Mexico; writer and lecturer. **Awards:** Shaffer award from the New Mexico Press Association, 1952, for reporting; Burrows award from the New Mexico Press Association, 1960, for editorial writing; American Library Association's Best Books for Young Adults selection, 1970, for *The Blessing Way* and 1988, for *A Thief of Time;* Edgar Allan Poe award from the Mystery Writers of America, 1974, for *Dance Hall of the Dead;* Navajo Special Friend award, 1986, for "authentically depicting the strength and dignity of the Navajo culture in his books"; Western Writers of America Honor for Children's Literature, 1986, for *The Boy Who Made Dragonfly;* Grand Prix de Litterature Policiere (France), and Golden Spur award from the Western Writers of America for Best Novel of the Year, both 1987, both for *Skinwalkers*; Special Friend of Dineh award, Navajo Tribal Council, 1987; Ambassador award, Center for the Indian, 1992. D.Litt.: University of New Mexico, 1990, and Arizona State University, 1991. **Address:** 2729 Texas NE, Albuquerque, New Mexico 87110, U.S.A.

PUBLICATIONS FOR ADULTS and Young Adults

Mystery Novels

The Blessing Way. New York, Harper, and London, Macmillan, 1970.
The Fly on the Wall. New York, Harper, 1971.
Dance Hall of the Dead. New York, Harper, 1973.
Listening Woman. New York, Harper, 1978; London, Macmillan, 1979.
People of Darkness. New York, Harper, 1980; London, Gollancz, 1982.
The Dark Wind. New York, Harper, 1982; London, Gollancz, 1983.
The Ghostway. New York, Harper, and London, Gollancz, 1985.
Skinwalkers. New York, Harper, 1987; London, Joseph, 1988.
A Thief of Time. New York, Harper, 1988; London, Joseph, 1989.
Talking God. New York, Harper, 1989; London, Joseph, 1990.
Coyote Waits. New York, Harper, 1990; London, Joseph, 1991.
Sacred Clowns. New York, HarperCollins, 1993.
Finding Moon. New York, HarperCollins, 1995.
The Fallen Man. New York, HarperCollins, 1996.

Collections

The Joe Leaphorn Mysteries. New York, Harper, 1989.
The Jim Chee Mysteries. New York, Harper, 1992.
Leaphorn and Chee: Three Classic Mysteries. New York, HarperCollins, 1992.

Other

The Great Taos Bank Robbery: And Other Indian Country Affairs. Albuquerque, University of New Mexico Press, 1973.
New Mexico, photographs by David Muench. Portland, Oregon, Belding, 1974.
Rio Grande, photographs by Robert Reynolds. Portland, Oregon, Belding, 1975.
Editor, *The Spell of New Mexico.* Albuquerque, University of New Mexico Press, 1976.
Indian Country: America's Sacred Land, photographs by Béla Kalman. Flagstaff, Arizona, Northland Press, 1987.
Hillerman Country: A Journey through the Southwest with Tony Hillerman, photographs by Barney Hillerman. New York, HarperCollins, 1991.
Talking Mysteries: A Conversation with Tony Hillerman, illustrated by Ernest Franklin. Albuquerque, University of New Mexico Press, 1991.
Editor, *The Best of the West: An Anthology of Classic Writing from the American West.* New York, HarperCollins, 1991.
New Mexico, Rio Grande, and Other Essays, photography by David Muench and Robert Reynolds. Portland, Oregon, Graphic Arts Center Press, 1992.
Mudhead Kiva: A Novel. New York, Harper, 1993.
Sacred Clowns. New York, HarperCollins, 1993.

Editor, *The Mysterious West.* New York, HarperCollins, 1994.
Editor, with Rosemary Herbert, *The Oxford Book of American Detective Stories.* New York, Oxford University Press, 1996.

PUBLICATIONS FOR CHILDREN

Fiction

The Boy Who Made Dragonfly: A Zuni Myth, illustrated by Laszlo Kubinyi. New York, Harper, 1972; new edition, illustrated by Janet Grado, University of New Mexico Press, 1986.

*

Media Adaptations: *Dance Hall of the Dead* (cassette), Simon & Schuster, 1985; *A Thief of Time* (cassette), Caedmon, 1988; *Fly on the Wall* (cassette), Caedmon, 1989; *Talking God* (cassette), Caedmon, 1990.

Manuscript Collections: Zimmerman Library, University of New Mexico.

Critical Studies: *Tony Hillerman: Blessing Way to Talking God,* by Louis A. Heib, n.p., Press of the Gigantic Hound, 1990; *Tony Hillerman,* Avenel, New Jersey, Outlet Book Company, 1992; *The Tony Hillerman Companion: A Comprehensive Guide to His Life and Work* edited by Martin Henry Greenberg, New York, HarperCollins, 1994; *Tony Hillerman: A Public Life* by John Sobol, Toronto, ECW Press, 1994; *Tony Hillerman: A Critical Companion* by John M. Reilly, Westport, Greenwood Press, 1996.

*   *   *

Tony Hillerman writes mystery novels heavily salted with the myths and culture of the Navajo culture. *Newsweek* comments: "Hillerman consistently evokes nature and place. . . . He creates morality plays that are as subtly colored as their landscape." By exploring the places where the Navajo world abuts the white world, the author creates fascinating tales.

Hillerman concentrates on two major characters, both members of the Tribal Police: Joe Leaphorn, introduced in *The Blessing Way,* fiftyish, married to a traditional Navajo woman but insisting on rational explanations for the more primitive beliefs of his people; and Jim Chee, in his twenties, introduced in *The People of Darkness,* studying to be a yataalii, a shaman. In Hillerman's work it is the older man, rather than the younger, who is more skeptical, more inclined to question the cultural dictates of his people. Both men are steeped in their culture, but Leaphorn is less inclined to seek traditional measures to combat his ills. A Navajo ceremony, a Blessing Way, is needed after a person has been contaminated by the presence of a dead body. Chee undergoes this ritual several times in the course of the novels, Leaphorn only once. The shaman who holds the Way for Leaphorn is Jim Chee. Navajo beliefs about death and dying are very prevalent in Hillerman's novels, naturally enough, since most popular mysteries involve murder, and Hillerman's are no exception. The Navajo do not believe in an afterlife, merely in the presence of a ghost after death whose appearance contaminates a dwelling. Should a person die within a hogan, the home is abandoned, with a hole cut in the north wall to allow the ghost to escape.

The author addresses ecological and archeological concerns as well as cultural ones. Particularly in *A Thief of Time* and *Talking God,* Hillerman explores the dark underside of anthropologists' excavations in the southwest. Archeology for profit—disregarding the traditions of the descendants of the culture being explored—is the focus of *Talking God.* A member of the Smithsonian Institution is the focus of the inquiry. An Indian seeking to restore some of the bones in the museum's collections to their heirs, Henry Highhawk becomes a victim of the very forces he sought to enlist in his cause. Hillerman explores the morality of displaying Indian burials, by having his character, Highhawk, disinter the grandparents of a blue-blooded WASP who is Museum spokesperson. Highhawk sends her her grandparents' remains by UPS. His arrest for grave robbing (handled by Jim Chee) points up the difference between excavating ancient graves and opening modern ones. The title *A Thief of Time* refers to persons who steal artifacts from an archaeological site to sell for their own profit.

Hillerman's characters are given the opportunity to grow with each new adventure. Leaphorn's wife has died, and Chee has gone from an Anglo-Saxon, blue-eyed, blonde girlfriend to an uneasy relationship with a young Navajo woman who is a lawyer. The two men have gone from working separately to appearing together. Although they work for different offices of the Tribal Police, they make an effective team. By the finish of *Coyote Waits,* Joe Leaphorn is contemplating a trip to China with an Associate Professor of American Studies from Arizona State, Louisa Bourebonette, and Jim Chee ponders his relationship with the lawyer, Janet Pete. Leaphorn is also contemplating retirement; in fact his involvement in the case stems not from his role as a policeman, but from the fact that the accused criminal is a relative of Leaphorn's late wife.

The world of the modern Navajo provides the setting for the novels and plays almost as important a role as do the two protagonists. The vast arid land, populated by shepherds and horsemen, presents an entirely different aspect to the "detective" novel. Hillerman was an innovator in this respect, making the ethnic hero and setting popular with modern readers. In *Talking God,* for example, a great deal of the action fluctuates between cosmopolitan Washington, D.C. and the emptiness of the desert reservation. The crime was plotted in the city, but the wasteland of Arizona provides the perfect spot for the murderer to dispose of his target.

Leaphorn and Chee, as Tribal Police, are constantly running into conflicts of interest with the FBI and the Anglo police forces. Questions of jurisdiction often occupy the two men. Frequently, Leaphorn or Chee must figure out how to investigate a case that is not legitimately theirs without stepping on any other law enforcement officer's toes. The conflicts thus created add dimension to the characters and enhance the plot.

Tony Hillerman is a master of his craft. His work is well-constructed and well-plotted. The *Boston Globe* book review calls him "one of the finest and most original craftsmen at work in the genre today." He is that—and more.

—Louise J. Winters

HILLMAN, Martin. *See* **HILL, Douglas (Arthur).**

HINTON, S(usan) E(loise)

Nationality: American. **Born:** Tulsa, Oklahoma, in 1950. **Education:** University of Tulsa, B.S. in education 1970. **Family:** Married David E. Inhofe in 1970; one son. **Career:** Writer of young adult novels since age sixteen. Consultant on film adaptations of her novels; minor acting roles in some film adaptations of her novels. **Awards:** *New York Herald Tribune* best teenage books list, 1967; *Chicago Tribune Book World* Spring Book Festival Honor Book, 1967; American Library Association Best Young Adult Books, 1975, *Media and Methods* Maxi Award, 1975, American Library Association Newcott Caldeberry award, 1976, Massachusetts Children's Book Award, 1979, all for *The Outsiders*; ALA Best Books for Young Adults list, 1971, *Chicago Tribune Book World* Spring Book Festival Honor Book, 1971, and Massachusetts Children's Book Award, 1978, all for *That Was Then, This Is Now*; ALA Best Books for Young Adults list, 1975, *School Library Journal* Best Books of the Year list, 1975, and Land of Enchantment award, New Mexico Library Association, 1982, all for *Rumble Fish*; ALA Best Books for Young Adults List, 1979, *School Library Journal* Best Books of the Year list, 1979, New York Public Library Books for the Teen-Age, 1980, American Book Award nomination for children's paperback, 1981, Sue Hefly Honor Book, Louisiana Association of School Libraries, 1982, California Young Reader Medal nomination, California Reading Association, 1982, and Sue Hefly Award, 1983, all for *Tex*; Golden Archer Award, 1983; recipient of first ALA Young Adult Services Division/*School Library Journal* Author Award, 1988, for body of work. **Address:** c/o Delacorte Press, 1540 Broadway, New York, New York 10036-4039, U.S.A.

PUBLICATIONS FOR YOUNG ADULTS

Fiction

The Outsiders. New York, Viking Press, 1967; London, Gollancz, 1970.
That Was Then, This Is Now. New York, Viking Press, and London, Gollancz, 1971.
Rumble Fish. New York, Delacorte Press, 1975; London, Gollancz, 1976.
Tex. New York, Delacorte Press, 1979; London, Gollancz, 1980.
Taming the Star Runner. New York, Delacorte Press, 1988.

Screenplay: *Rumble Fish,* with Francis Ford Coppola, 1983.

PUBLICATIONS FOR CHILDREN

The Puppy Sister, illustrated by Jacqueline Rogers. New York, Delacorte Press, 1995.
Big David, Little David, illustrated by Alan Daniel. New York, Doubleday Books for Young Readers, 1995.

*

Media Adaptations: *Rumble Fish* (recording), Viking, 1977; *The Outsiders* (filmstrip with cassette), Current Affairs and Mark Twain Media, 1978; *The Outsiders* (cassette), Random House, 1978; *That Was Then, This Is Now* (filmstrip with cassette), Current Affairs and Mark Twain Media, 1978; *Tex* (film), Walt Disney Productions, 1982; *The Outsiders* (film), Warner Brothers, 1983; *Rumble Fish* (film), Universal, 1983; *That Was Then, This Is Now* (film), Paramount, 1985; *The Outsiders* (television series), Fox, 1990.

Biography: Essay in *Authors and Artists for Young Adults,* Volume 2, Detroit, Gale, 1989; essay in *Speaking for Ourselves: Autobiographical Sketches by Notable Authors of Books for Young Adults,* Volume 1, compiled and edited by Donald R. Gallo, National Council of Teachers of English, 1990.

Critical Studies: Entry in *Children's Literature Review,* Volume 3, Detroit, Gale, 1978, Volume 23, 1991; entry in *Contemporary Literary Criticism,* Volume 30, Detroit, Gale, 1984; *Presenting S. E. Hinton* by Jay Daly, Boston, Twayne, 1987; teacher's guides are available for *The Outsiders, That Was Then, This Is Now, Rumble Fish,* and *Tex,* all written by Lou Willett Staneck and published by Dell.

*   *   *

One of the most popular twentieth-century writers for young adults, S.E. Hinton has produced a number of novels about sensitive "greasers," "hoods," and abandoned teenagers which have become best-sellers, spawning four film adaptations and a television series. All of Hinton's novels are similar, both in their choice of characters and in their themes. Her characters are frequently larger than life, almost mythic, and are social outcasts, such as Dallas Winston of *The Outsiders* and Motorcycle Boy of *Rumble Fish.*

Hinton's books are usually narrated by macho, poor, and "cool" teenage boys who are also vulnerable and occasionally cry. They are often orphans, as in *The Outsiders,* or have been abandoned by their parents, as in *Tex.* Despite the fact that Hinton's protagonists often skip school and get into trouble with their teachers, they frequently enjoy reading and three of them, Ponyboy Curtis, Tex McCormick, and Travis Harris, are presented as potential poets or writers. Indeed, Hinton's characters make frequent allusions to their favorite books which include works as diverse as *Great Expectations, Gone with the Wind, Smokey the Cowhorse,* and the poems of Robert Frost. While Hinton's books often border on the melodramatic, they tackle issues important to many young adults, including prejudice and the struggle to maintain innocence and hope in an often corrupt world.

The Outsiders, written when Hinton was only sixteen, is narrated by Ponyboy Curtis who is supposedly writing his story as a term paper for his English class. He and his two older brothers have been orphaned and are part of a gang of what Ponyboy describes as "greasers." Throughout the book, Ponyboy and his friends are in conflict with the town's wealthy teenagers, known as "Socs." When Ponyboy's best friend, the innocent and abused Johnny Cade, kills a Soc in self-defense, he and Ponyboy flee the town and embark on an odyssey in which they learn that even Socs are human beings (after all, they see the same sunsets). Ponyboy also learns the importance of "staying gold" or maintaining some innocence, an idea expressed in his favorite poem.

The Outsiders has often been identified as one of the "groundbreaking" young adult books which helped usher in an era of realistic, and sometimes pessimistic, books about teenagers and their problems. While it has been criticized as cliched and somewhat melodramatic, *The Outsiders* provides a believable and likeable narrator who wrestles with the very real problems of prejudice and acceptance faced by many young adults. Despite the deaths of Johnny Cade and the more dangerous Dallas Winston at the end of the novel, *The Outsiders* suggests that if anyone does stay gold, it will be dreamers like Ponyboy.

Hinton's next two novels, *That Was Then, This Is Now* and *Rumble Fish* are less optimistic. While Ponyboy Curtis and some of his friends reappear in *That Was Then, This Is Now,* it is not a direct sequel to *The Outsiders.* The novel is related by a boy named Byron who ultimately decides to turn in his foster brother and best friend, Mark, for dealing drugs when their young friend, M&M, has a bad LSD trip. There are no pat solutions in this novel; going to prison only hardens Mark further. At the end of the novel, Byron longs for the past when he did not have to make such difficult choices. Rusty James, the narrator of *Rumble Fish,* also loses his innocence and becomes as emotionless and hardened as his older brother, Motorcycle Boy, who, like Dallas Winston, meets a violent death. Like Hinton's first two novels, *Rumble Fish* takes place in a relatively short period of time, one which changes the main character forever.

Both of Hinton's later novels, *Tex* and *Taming the Star Runner,* feature protagonists with uncertain futures who must deal with family problems and first romances. Tex McCormick lives with his older brother, Mace, and keeps hoping that their father will return. His brother clearly wants to go on to college but has become Tex's surrogate father. Tex, who despite appearances is somewhat naive, is shocked when his brother sells their horses in order to survive. Eventually, Tex is able to help his brother let go and seek his dream. Along the way, Tex moves from innocence to experience, learning his true parentage and gaining a more realistic perspective of "Pop." As part of Tex's initiation into adulthood, he and Mace are abducted by an escaped convict (the now murderous Mark of *That Was Then, This Is Now,* who may be Tex's real brother) and Tex is shot by a drug dealer.

In *Taming the Star Runner,* Hinton provides a fictionalized version of her own success as a young adult writer. Sixteen-year-old Travis McCormick, like Hinton, has a novel accepted for publication, despite the fact that he is failing English. One part of the novel deals with Travis' growth as a writer and his interactions with his editor, Ms. Carmichael. *Taming the Star Runner,* however, is also a novel of maturation and loss. Travis has been forced to go live with his uncle because of an altercation with his abusive stepfather. As a newcomer to his high school, he is an outsider until he becomes involved with helping Casey Kencaide as she tries to tame her horse, Star Runner. Although the horse ultimately dies and Travis loses his intense feelings for Casey, the novel ends with Travis finally looking forward to life, having resolved some of his feelings about his family and personal situation.

While Hinton's earlier books contain references that might seem to date them, they are still popular, partly because the topics they explore continue to be important to young adults. All of Hinton's novels suggest how young adults are frequently shaped by their environment and are concerned with their struggles, only sometimes successful, to leave the past behind and face the future. Hinton has the great ability to create authentic characters who sound like real young adults and their journeys towards adulthood will likely remain popular with future readers, whether "Socs" or "greasers."

—Joel D. Chaston

HO, Minfong

Nationality: Burmese. **Born:** Rangoon, 7 January 1951. **Education:** Tunghai University, Taichung, Taiwan, 1968-69; Cornell University, Ithaca, New York, B.A. in history and economics (honors) 1973, and M.F.A. in creative writing, 1980. **Family:** Married John Value Dennis, Jr. in 1976; two sons and one daughter. **Career:** manual worker, Starlight Plywood Factory, Singapore, 1973; journalist, *Straits Times,* Singapore, 1973-75; lecturer in English, 1975-76, Chiengmai University, Chiengmai, Thailand; trade union representative, 1973-75; teaching assistant in English literature, 1978-80, Cornell University; nutritionist and relief worker, Catholic Relief Services, Thai-Cambodian border, 1980; writer-in-residence, Singapore University, 1983; presenter of writing workshops in Switzerland, Indonesia, Thailand, Malaysia, and New York, 1990-96; **Member:** Authors Guild, PEN America. **Awards:** First prize from Council on Interracial Books for Children for *Sing to the Dawn,* 1973; first prize, Annual Short Story Contest of Singapore, Ministry of Culture, 1982, and first prize Annual Short Story Contest, *AsiaWeek Magazine,* Hong Kong, 1983, both for *Tanjong Rhu*; second place, prose section, Commonwealth Book Awards, Commonwealth Book Council, 1987; first prize, National Book Development Council of Singapore, 1988; Parents Choice Award, 1990, and American Library Association Best Books for Young Adults list, 1991, for *Rice without Rain*; National Council of Social Studies/Children's Book Council Notable Children's Books in the Field of Social Studies, and Best Books selection, *Parents Magazine,* 1991, and Notable Children's Trade Books in the Language Arts, 1992, all for *The Clay Marble*; Southeastern Asian Writer Award, conferred by the Crown Prince of Thailand, 1996; American Library Association Notable Book and Caldecott Honor Award for *Hush! A Thai Lullaby,* 1997; American Library Association Notable Book for *Maples in the Mist,* 1997. **Agent:** Renee Cho, McIntosh and Otis, Incorporated, 310 Madison Avenue, New York, New York, 10017, U.S.A. **Address:** 893 Cayuga Heights Road, Ithaca, New York 14850, U.S.A.

PUBLICATIONS FOR YOUNG ADULTS

Fiction

Sing to the Dawn. New York, Lothrop, Lee and Shepard, 1975.
Rice without Rain. London, Andre Deutsch, 1986, and New York, Lothrop, Lee and Shepard, 1990.
The Clay Marble. New York, Farrar, 1991.

Other

With Stephen Clark, *Sing to the Dawn* (libretto; produced Singapore Repertory Theatre, Singapore Arts Festival, 1996), music by Dick Lee. Singapore, Times Books International, 1996.

PUBLICATIONS FOR CHILDREN

Translator and compiler, *Maples in the Mist: Children's Poems from the Tang Dynasty,* illustrated by Jean and Mou-Sien Tseng. New York, Lothrop, Lee and Shepard, 1995.
Reteller, with Saphan Ros, *Two Brothers,* illustrated by Jean and Mou-Sien Tseng. New York, Lothrop, Lee and Shepard, 1995.
Hush!: A Thai Lullaby (poetry), illustrated by Holly Meade. New York, Lothrop, Lee and Shepard, 1996.
Reteller, with Saphan Ros, *Brother Rabbit: A Cambodian Tale,* illustrated by Jennifer Hewitson. New York, Lothrop, Lee and Shepard, 1997.

PUBLICATIONS FOR ADULTS

Tanjong Rhu and Other Stories. Singapore, Federal Publications, 1986.

*

Biography: *Something about the Author,* Vol. 94. Detroit, Gale, 1997.

*   *   *

In Minfong Ho's novel, *The Clay Marble* (1991), twelve-year-old Dara's most earnest wish is to return home to Cambodia, to repair their house, establish a family, and plant rice seed. During the relentless hardships that she endures, and despite all the horror that she sees, she keeps this hope alive. Finally, at the novel's conclusion, it is this hope which in fact maintains the integrity of the family, forcing Dara's brother to choose home over becoming a soldier.

This focus on home is dominant in the work of Minfong Ho. Having grown up in Singapore and Burma, she was later concerned that the books written especially for the young reader depicted Asia and Thailand as something out of *The King and I:* an unrealistic and anachronistic vision. When she came to Cornell University for her college education, she decided to write about the Asia that she knew, and she creates a world of great beauty and gentleness, with loving family relationships and ancient customs. But she also creates a world of poverty, drought, dreadful injustice, starvation, and death. Her protagonists are set between these two visions, but in that situation they discover their pride, integrity, and determination to love the land and overcome injustice.

Sing to the Dawn (1975), Ho's first and in some ways gentlest novel, tells of Dawan, a young girl who wins a scholarship to study in the city. Her teacher recognizes that she is a perceptive and sensitive student; she understands the injustice of the rent paid to the landlords: half of the rice harvest, leaving the farmers with little to eat. She also understands the responsibility of the scholarship; if Dawan is to study in the city, she must return and make life better for her village. But before Dawan can accept the scholarship, she must first overcome all of the prejudices built up by centuries of tradition; she is a girl, and consequently, it is presumed, she does not need an education.

Here is where Dawan's strength and determination develop, or, to use the major metaphor of the novel, where the lotus bud begins to open up and bloom. Blocked by what she sees as an almost irrational resistance by her father as well as the intransigence of the religious community, she forces her brother to recognize the injustice of making her refuse the scholarship. This is extraordinarily difficult for Kwai, for if she refuses the scholarship, he will receive it instead. Reluctantly, and with some bitterness, he becomes her advocate, and the novel closes with Dawan on the bus, heading toward the city.

This is in a microcosm what all of Ho's work is about: a young girl overcoming established practices and finding her own way. At the same time, that protagonist is tied closely to a love for the land and for the culture. Dawan does not go off merely for herself; she goes for her village, as well as for her family. The result is a set of novels where Dawan, and later Dara and Jinda, come to understand something about themselves—how they are growing and developing—at the same time that they come to understand something about the needs of their culture. This dual growth makes each of the novels compelling; Ho has created real characters in real situations which may be unfamiliar to most Western readers.

In *The Clay Marble* and *Rice without Rain* (1990), Ho places her characters in situations more troublesome than those of *Sing to the Dawn*. Here the stakes are more than a scholarship; they are survival itself, both on the individual level and on the level of the culture. In *The Clay Marble,* the war between four or five factions in Cambodia has driven Dara and what remains of her family to the border refugee camps between Thailand and Cambodia. Despite the relative safety of the camp, there is still the danger of shelling and when that begins, Dara is separated from her family. To recover her family, she must display a courage and determination that she had not known she had.

In *Rice without Rain,* Jinda meets five university students who come to her village to learn what it is like to be a farmer in northern Thailand. When her father is arrested for leading the resistance against the highland rents, he is arrested and Jinda becomes part of the student movement that is urging reforms in the government. Her purpose is to free her father, but the other students' goals are more cloudy: they see him principally as a political symbol. But soon the struggle becomes more tangible as the peaceful rally is disrupted by government forces, and a massacre ensues—the massacre that occurred at Thammasart University in October, 1976. Jinda, fleeing, returns home and must then deal with the death of her father, as well as her disillusionment with the students.

The vividness of these novels comes from their portrayal of individual characters, not just economic and political realities. In *Rice without Rain,* Jinda is a young woman aware of her growing sexuality and her attraction to Ned, one of the university students. Her love for him is balanced against her perception that his cause is

the foremost element in his life. She must deal with the realities of the drought, the injustice of the land rental, and the corruption of the government, but for her these are realities that affect everything about her life, from the land she works to the food she eats. Ned and the other students have, for much of the novel, an academic and social distance from that reality.

Dara and Dawan are much alike. Dawan, for perhaps the first time in her life, is confronted with the prejudice against women in society, and it is only through her own determination that she is able to win out against that prejudice. Dara is confronted by a mindless militarism that threatens to suck in her brother. Through the strength that she finds in her friendship with Jantu, she is able to combat that militarism with an assertion of the importance of family. This interaction of the individual with the large forces of her society and culture provides much of the conflict within the novels.

If there is one consistent center in the three novels, it is the family. *The Clay Marble* is, in fact, about the nature of the family. Dara has fled Cambodia with her brother and mother; she meets a friend with a sister and a grandfather. They recognize that they now have fragments of families, as do most of the refugees. The great task of the novel is to return home and forge new families, which in fact happens in the afterword of the novel. Like the rice harvest, the family is the thing most prized in each of the novels.

Again and again, the female protagonists of Ho's novels work out of the contexts of their families. Here is the repository of tradition. Here is the authority. Here is the group for which one works and which in turn gives one identity. To move outside of the family—like Dao who abandons the family to live in the city in *Rice without Rain*—is to risk ostracism and loss of identity, as well as culture. To stay within the family is to stay within the culture, and to find a kind of love and acceptance that gives strength even as it allows the individual to grow.

Ho's novels can be as brutal as they can be sensitive. There is the image of the opening lotus blossom, but also the image of the corpse dangling from a limb. There is the image of a baby bathing in a river, but also an image of that same baby with a swollen stomach, dead. There's new love, and there is hideous murder. Ho does not hold back in presenting a land of stark contrasts. What enables the reader to leave the novels with a sense of hope is the strength of the central characters to endure the brutality and hardships, to overcome them, and to return stronger to the family to plant the rice fields, to marry, and to love.

Since the publication of *The Clay Marble* in 1991, Ho has retold folktales and written and translated poetry for an audience of younger children. *The Two Brothers* (1995), a familiar Cambodian folktale, reflects "the rich texture of Cambodian life" and "the age-old conflict between predestination and free will," as Ho points out in her author's note. This conflict can also be seen in the lives of contemporary Cambodians where "stoic fatalism" combines with activism. Inspired by a desire to pass on to her own children the poems from her Chinese heritage, in *Maples in the Mist* (1996) Ho has collected and translated poems from the Tang Dynasty (618-907 A.D.), a time known as the Golden Age of China. These short, simple poems, beautifully illustrated, appear in Chinese characters as well as in English, and are followed by notes on each of the poets. *Hush!: A Thai Lullaby* (1996) won a Caldecott Honor Award for Holly Meade's striking illustrations of collage and cut paper that tell one story, while the text tells another. While the pictures show the baby playing, the mother tells all the animals,

"Hush!" and "My baby's sleeping." *Brother Rabbit* (1997), another Cambodian folktale retold in collaboration with Saphan Ros, features a trickster rabbit similar to the cunning creature found in the folklore of other cultures. The bold and dramatic lines of illustrations suggest both wood-cut and batik, and reflect the folkloric nature as well as the motion and energy of the story.

—Gary D. Schmidt, updated by Linnea Hendrickson

HOBBS, Will

Nationality: American. **Education:** Stanford University, B.A. 1969, M.A. 1971. **Family:** Married Jean Loftus in 1972. **Career:** Reading and English teacher, Durango, Colorado, public schools, 1973-89; writer since 1990. **Awards:** Notable Book, Children's Book Council, 1989, Best Book for Young Adults, American Library Association, 1989, and Teachers' Choice Award, International Reading Association, 1990, all for *Bearstone;* Best Book for Young Adults and Best Book for Reluctant Young Adult Readers, American Library Association, 1992, for *Downriver.* **Address:** c/o Atheneum, 1230 Avenue of the Americas, New York, New York 10020, U.S.A.

Publications for Young Adults

Fiction

Changes in Latitudes. New York, Atheneum, 1988.
Bearstone. New York, Atheneum, 1989.
Downriver. New York, Atheneum, 1991.
The Big Wander. New York, Atheneum, 1992.
Beardance. New York, Atheneum, 1993.
Kokopelli's Flute. New York, Atheneum, 1995.
Far North. New York, Morrow Junior Books, 1996.
Beardream, illustrated by Jill Kastner. New York, Atheneum, 1997.
River Thunder. New York, Delacorte Press, 1997.
Ghost Canoe. New York, Morrow Junior Books, 1997.
Howling Hill, illustrated by Jill Kastner. New York, Morrow Junior Books, 1998.

*

Biography: Essay in *Speaking for Ourselves, Too* compiled and edited by Donald R. Gallo, National Council of Teachers of English, 1993.

*   *   *

Will Hobbs uses his personal outdoor experiences in Colorado, Mexico, and the canyon lands of the Southwest as the basis for the settings in his novels. For example, The Window and the Rio Grande Pyramid rock formations in *Bearstone* and *Bear Dance* are real places in the San Juan Mountains, and Hobbs has taken Colorado River raft trips in the Grand Canyon, as did the young people in *Downriver.*

Hobbs has also been influenced by his reading of natural history books and of early books written about the various areas. *Vagabond for Beauty* by Everett Bruce, written in the early 1930s, is one such book. In addition to providing unique settings for the action in his novels, Hobbs uses the environment as the background to voice his concern for nature. In his novels he interweaves human relationships and relationships with the natural world.

As a reading and English teacher of adolescents, Hobbs learned that young readers, as well as reluctant readers, were fascinated with adventure stories. His close association with adolescents assists him in providing accurate depictions of them in his novels. For instance, the character of Cloyd in *Bearstone* and *Bear Dance* developed from a composite of students he taught in his junior high reading class. As in many young adult novels, the adults are conveniently absent from the action, with only a few exceptions. Walter, the old rancher in *Bearstone* and *Bear Dance,* is based on a rancher friend of Hobbs's with whom he spent summers helping to bring in the hay crop. His characters are believable in their dialogue and their motivations.

Hobbs's first novel, *Changes in Latitudes,* involves the disintegration of the family structure and the parallel theme of the extinction of the sea turtle, viciously hunted for its oils. Told through the eyes of Travis, a "cool" sixteen-year-old teenager, the reader identifies with the pain of the father staying behind when the mother, Travis, and two other children (Jennifer, fourteen, and Teddy, nine) head for a holiday in Mexico. The mother, who is involved in an affair, allows the children to fend for themselves. Teddy's fascination with the sea turtles leads him to a friendship with a marine biologist and to adventure and tragedy. Guilt, a powerful emotion in the story, is experienced by several of the characters and provides a basis for significant discussion by readers of the novel.

Bearstone introduces a young Native American boy, Cloyd Atcitty, to a crusty old rancher/miner named Walter Landis. Walter is cautious about dealing with Cloyd, and neither of them is very communicative. When Cloyd is exploring the mountains near Walter's ranch, he finds Indian burial artifacts, including a turquoise stone in the shape of a bear. Cloyd thinks this will bring him luck, but he makes the mistake of telling one of Walter's visitors about seeing a grizzly bear in the mountains and that man goes out to kill the bear. When Walter is injured in a mine accident, Cloyd gets the visitor to pick Walter up in the helicopter which has come for the bear carcass. Cloyd has the opportunity to tell the game warden that the bear had been killed deliberately, but he decides not to out of his friendship for Walter. A rite of passage story, Cloyd learns to trust and love someone, in spite of his stubbornness. As a symbol of this love, he gives Walter the bear stone in the hospital.

In *Bear Dance,* a sequel to *Bearstone,* Cloyd wants to look in the mountains for the mother bear and her three cubs while Walter goes back to his neglected mine. Cloyd meets Ursa, a part-Indian woman, who is a professor at the University of Montana. She wants to find evidence of a grizzly, since that will permit the Wildlife division to reintroduce bears into Colorado. Cloyd saves the two surviving bear cubs and learns about the bear dance and bear dreams, both of which are important for his survival.

Downriver is told through the eyes of Jessie, a fifteen-year-old who is rebelling against her father, a professor at the university in Boulder. Her mother has died, and Jessie is experimenting with the wrong crowd. Her father sends her on an outdoor experimental program where she is one of eight alienated young people. Rebellious, the kids decide to take their counselor Al's car and equipment and go down the Grand Canyon on their own. With no map but carrying the supplies Al had arranged for them, they board the boats and head down the treacherous river. They learn how to trust each other to succeed. In this survival story, the young people begin to understand peer pressure and other people's values. Young readers will be encouraged to look at their own motives and those of families and friends. The descriptions of the area and the excitement of running the rapids are evidence that the author has had those experiences himself.

The Big Wander is set in the desert canyon lands of Utah and Arizona where Clay Lancaster, fourteen, and his older brother Mike have gone in their creaky 148 Studebaker to search for their Uncle Clay. The time of the novel is 1962 and accurate references to songs, politics, and the Peace Corps could encourage dialogue with parents of young readers. The boys' mother is spending the summer with the Peace Corps in Guatemala, and the father has been killed in the Korean War. Departing for his summer job in Seattle, Mike is convinced Clay will be looked after by a family who run a trading post. But Clay is undaunted in his search for his uncle and, with a burro named Pal and his dog Curly for company, he gets involved with Indians who are trying to save wild mustangs as well as with a Mormon family who are ranchers. Their daughter Sarah provides a love interest for Clay. This exciting book is a journey of discovery, in which readers will learn along with Clay about wild creatures, wild places, and a diversity of life.

Will Hobbs has established himself as a careful researcher for books that have unique settings and determined young characters. His use of strong images, careful selection of words, and well-developed plots and characters have made his books popular with young adults, who have nominated his books in a number of states for reader awards. Teachers and librarians are cognizant of their appeal and have included his books on "Teachers' Choices" and "Best Young Adult" lists. Although a fairly new author for young adults, Will Hobbs is a popular speaker at meetings for teachers and librarians, as well as inspiring to student authors. Because his books deal with universal values and his characters are memorable, his reputation will deservedly grow in the years to come.

—Ruth K. J. Cline

———

HOLDEN, Elizabeth Rhoda. *See* **LAWRENCE, Louise.**

———

HOLEMAN, Linda

Nationality: Canadian. **Born:** Linda Gay Freeman in Winnipeg, Manitoba, 24 December 1949. **Education:** River East Collegiate,

Winnipeg, Manitoba, 1968; University of Winnipeg, 1969-72, B.A. 1972; University of Manitoba, Winnipeg, 1972-73, Cert. in Ed. 1973; University of Manitoba, 1978-83, M.Ed. 1983. **Family:** Married to Jon Holeman in 1971; two daughters and one son. **Career:** Classroom and resource teacher, Frontier School Division, South Indian Lake, Manitoba, 1974-76; classroom and resource teacher, Ryerson School, Fort Garry School Division, Winnipeg, 1977-84; creative writing instructor, Continuing Education Division, University of Winnipeg, since 1996. **Awards:** *Canadian Living Magazine* Short Story Prize, 1991; First Runner-up, Thistledown Press Young Adult Short Story Competition, 1992; *Winnipeg Free Press*/Canadian Author Association Nonfiction Competition Winner, 1993; Thistledown Press Young Adult Short Story Competition Winner, 1995. **Address:** 728 South Drive, Winnipeg, Manitoba R3T 0C3, Canada.

PUBLICATIONS FOR YOUNG ADULTS

Saying Good-bye (short stories). Toronto, Lester, 1995.
Promise Song (novel). Toronto, Tundra Books, 1997.
Mercy's Birds (novel). Toronto, Tundra Books, 1998.

PUBLICATIONS FOR CHILDREN

Frankie on the Run. Toronto, Boardwalk Books, 1995

PUBLICATIONS FOR ADULTS

Flying to Yellow (short stories). Toronto, Turnstone Press, 1986.
Devil's Darning-needle (short stories). Erin, Ontario, The Porcupine Quill, 1999.

Linda Holeman comments:

I don't know who started the lie, the one that tells young people that "these are the best years of your life." They aren't. When I talk to audiences of young adults, I'm quick to dispel that myth. The ages twelve through eighteen are some of the most difficult years of life, in terms of trying to get a grip on emotions and ego and beliefs and hopes and all the rest that goes into the complicated and delicate concoction that makes up the self. It is a time of confusion, a time of trying to make sense of who you are and who everyone else is and how you fit into the whole mess that is called life. And this sense of discomfort, of questioning, of uncertainty, is timeless for young people. Regardless of year of birth, the "coming of age" ritual has always been a universal one.

I believe that I never really and truly grew up. And maybe this is why I find the young adult voice one that echoes and reverberates in my head, louder than all the other voices I hear when I am writing. Oh, I put on a good act; I'm a wife and mother of three children—two of them teenagers right now. I love to watch them; they are often a source of inspiration for me. But INSIDE, in this deep place, is a feeling that my life, like theirs, is still a bit of a muddle. And so for me, the young adult voice isn't unnatural. I'm not searching for it when I write. It's here, now, and my constant hope is that it is honestly portrayed in my writing for young adults.

These is a sense of aloneness in being a young adult—that feeling of being on the outside, even if you are in the midst of a group of people you consider your friends. It is a fragile time, a time when your world can come undone by a word, a look. This sense of aloneness is a common one for the writer, as well. We tend to be loners, by choice. Writers are most often the people that hang back, that listen, and watch. To be the centre of attention means that people are watching YOU; there is no chance to learn by watching others. So there is a parallel that can be drawn between the young adult and the writer—this sense of self-imposed wariness, of standing a little apart.

I remember my own growing-up years clearly—not only the events and situations, but the feelings they produced in me. I don't know if this ability to recall is just because of the way I am, or whether I have nurtured this. Certainly, since I began writing for the teen audience, I have been able to call back incidents that had previously been deeply buried. I'm not talking about trauma here. I'm talking about the small, everyday things that happen to us and affect the way we think about ourselves and the world. The minuscule but important stories of our lives.

There is a certain single-mindedness in being a young adult. The word is solipsism—meaning that things are viewed from a sole inward viewpoint. It is the opposite of being objective, when you can stand back and clearly view a situation from all angles and perspectives. To the young adult, everything is personal and immediate and huge. The young person does not have the many layers of adult experiences to gauge and cushion his or her own against. Everything is done for the first time, and first times, whether it's starting junior high, or driving a car, or kissing, are always exhilarating and frightening.

So when I write for young adults, I leave my grown-up world and fly back through the decades. I hear, and see, and smell and touch and taste with my teenage soul. This is my way, my experience, and it is the only way that works for me. Young words roll from my less-than-young fingertips. And I am eternally grateful for this gift.

*   *   *

In addition to her anthologized short stories, Linda Holeman has written two volumes of short stories, one for adults and the other for YA's, plus an historical YA novel. Dealing with the recurring themes of change and loss and the accompanying emotional pain, *Saying Goodbye* is a collection of ten short stories, nine of which have adolescent female central characters. Each story focuses on a critical time in the life of a young person. For example, in "Something Fishy," Rachel Olchowecki makes a bid for attention at school by claiming to be related to an MTV star. When the lie takes on a life of its own, Rachel rides the crest of her new found popularity only to have to deal ultimately with the lie's aftermath when she is found out. In the title story, "Saying Goodbye," Liza, the 15-year-old daughter from an interracial marriage, goes to a remote Lake Winnipeg island to fulfill her Ojibwa father's last wish and scatter his ashes there. On the island where she had shared summers with her father, Liza realizes she must now dwell alone in her mother's world. Sometimes, however, the story's central character is not the individual who experiences the loss. In "Sweet Bird of Youth," for instance, Blake senses that

his younger cousin is at risk of sexual abuse and "rescues" him while, in "Shasta," Hayley is passively present as a classmate is date-raped. Though the stories lack happy endings, they do offer realistic glimpses into aspects of adolescent life.

While *Saying Goodbye* was contemporary in its content, *Promise Song* is developed around an actual happening in Canadian history. Between 1868 and 1925, more than 80,000 children were sent to Canada, principally from British orphanages or "Homes." During this period, Canada required much manual labour, especially in its rural areas, and consequently many of these Home children ended up working on small, isolated farms in Eastern Canada. In *Promise Song,* the Westley sisters, Rosetta and Flora, had been orphaned four years previously when their surviving parent died, and the girls were then placed in the Manchester Refuge. Now, in May, 1900, they find themselves "home children" being shipped to Canada. Rosetta, 14, who has become her six-year-old sister's surrogate mother, comforts Flora by singing the "Promise Song," in which she pledges, "I promise you . . . we'll stay together. . . ." However, shortly after their arrival in Belleville, Ontario, the sisters are separated; Flora is adopted by a childless couple while Rosetta is sent to a backwoods Ontario farm. There, Rosetta learns she will not be adopted but rather is to be bound by a contract of indenture to the bullying, taciturn Albert Thomas and his frail, subdued, and submissive wife, Gudrun. After an unsuccessful attempt to run away in search of Flora, Rosetta decides to work at the house and farm chores until November, when she is to receive her six month wage of $2.00. However, Albert's manipulation of Rosetta's "expenses" leaves her in debt to him, and so another half year's demanding physical dawn-to-dusk toil is required.

While Rosetta's concern about her promise to Flora remains before readers, the plot really revolves about the happenings at the Thomas farm as Rosetta gradually uncovers the sources of the couple's seemingly loveless relationship. Gudrun, an Icelandic immigrant, was "given" to Thomas in marriage when her older sister, Albert's intended, ran off with another man. Only 15 when she married, Gudrun, now 20, has already experienced several miscarriages plus the deaths of two infants within weeks of their birth. During the time Rosetta is at the Thomas farm, Gudrun again becomes pregnant, and Rosetta, now quite fond of Gudrun, agrees to remain with her until the baby's birth. The infant's premature arrival adds suspense as does Gudrun's failing health after the birth. While Rosetta has found a form of sisterhood with Gudrun, she ultimately fulfills her promise to Flora, and the book concludes, possibly unsatisfactorily for those who want "tidy" endings, with the two sisters again meeting. Subplots include an emerging romance between Rosetta and a neighbour lad, plus Rosetta's having to deal with the unwanted, "nasty" attentions of Eli, the hired hand.

—Dave Jenkinson

HOLM, (Else) Anne (Lise)

Nationality: Danish. **Born:** Aal, Jutland, 10 September 1922. **Family:** Married second husband, Johan Christian Holm in 1949;

one child. **Career:** Writer. **Awards:** Gyldendal Prize for best Scandinavian children's book, 1963, American Library Association notable book citation, 1965, and Gold Medal, Boys' Club of America Junior Book award, all for *David*. **Address:** Strandvejen 661, Klampenborg, Denmark.

PUBLICATIONS FOR YOUNG ADULTS

Translated Fiction

David. Copenhagen, Gyldendal, 1963; as *North to Freedom*, translation from the Danish by L. W. Kingsland. New York, Harcourt, 1965; as *I Am David*. London, Methuen, 1965.
Peter. Copenhagen, Gyldendal, 1965; New York, Harcourt, 1968.
The Hostage, translation from the Danish by Patricia Crampton. London, Methuen, 1980.
The Sky Grew Red, translation from the Danish by Patricia Crampton. London, Methuen, 1991.

Untranslated Fiction

Dina fra Apotekergaarden. St. John's, Jespersen & Pio, 1956.
Familien i Apotekergaarden. St. John's, Jespersen & Pio, 1958.
Komtessen fra Baekkeholm. St. John's, Jespersen & Pio, 1959.
Adam og de voksne. Copenhagen, Gyldendal, 1967.

*

Media Adaptations: A British Broadcasting Corporation (BBC) television series was based on *David,* and the book has also been optioned for film.

Biography: Essay in *Something about the Author Autobiography Series,* Volume 7, Detroit, Gale, 1989, pp. 123-37.

*   *   *

Danish writer Anne Holm is best known for her young adult novel *David,* which has been translated into over twenty languages. In the United States it is known as *North to Freedom,* and in the United Kingdom as *I Am David*. This highly introspective story, called both a "journey of discovery" and an "allegory of freedom" by reviewer Alberta Eiseman, begins in a political internment camp in the Balkans where twelve-year-old David has lived since infancy. For some unknown reason one day, the camp commander arranges for him to escape and instructs him to travel south to Salonica, hide on a ship bound for Italy, and then go north to Denmark, where he will be safe. David, well aware of the evil of the camp, suspects that this escape will be an excuse to kill him. However, he decides that he prefers death to continued captivity and thus escapes.

He makes many discoveries on his harrowing flight, one being that he is strong and able to survive on little food. Then there is the matter of learning to deal with people. For a boy who has gone from childhood to a wary adulthood very quickly in a prison camp this is extremely difficult. Though David concludes that he can never be a normal boy, he maintains his integrity and gradually overcomes his fear of people, making good use of the languages he has learned in the camp—what *they* spoke, and French, German, Italian, and English. Finally, David comes to understand *them*—their treachery, brutality, and methods of operation. (Throughout the book the word Communist is never used and this adds to the pervading horror of this ever-present force which is referred to as *they* or *them*.)

Though she has been criticized for occasional factual inaccuracies in her novels, as in depicting "a carefree, peaceful Europe which did not exist during the years described," as Eiseman points out in *David,* Holm's novels are praised for their affirmations of life that will stimulate and challenge young adult readers.

—Reba Pinney

HOLMAN, Felice

Nationality: American. **Born:** New York City, 24 October 1919. **Education:** Syracuse University, New York, B.A. 1941. **Family:** Married Herbert Valen in 1941; one daughter. **Career:** Advertising copywriter, New York, 1944-50. **Awards:** Austrian Book Prize, Lewis Carroll Shelf Award, Best Book for Young Adults award, and American Library Association Notable Book award, all 1978, for *Slake's Limbo;* American Library Association Notable Book award, 1979, for *The Murderer;* Best Book for Young Adults award, 1985, for *The Wild Children;* Child Study Committee Book Award, 1990, for *Secret City, U.S.A.* **Address:** c/o Atheneum, 1230 Avenue of the Americas, New York, New York 10022, U.S.A.

PUBLICATIONS FOR YOUNG ADULTS

Fiction

Slake's Limbo. New York, Scribner, 1974; London, Macmillan, 1980.
The Murderer. New York, Scribner, 1978.
The Wild Children. New York, Scribner, 1983.
Secret City, U.S.A. New York, Aladdin, 1990.
Real. New York, Atheneum, 1997.

Poetry

At the Top of My Voice and Other Poems, illustrated by Edward Gorey. New York, Norton, 1970.
I Hear You Smiling and Other Poems, illustrated by Laszlo Kubinyi. New York, Scribner, 1973.
The Song in My Head and Other Poems, illustrated by James Spanfeller. New York, Scribner, 1985.

Other

The Drac: French Tales of Dragons and Demons, with Nanine
Valen, illustrated by Stephen Walker. New York, Scribner, 1975.

PUBLICATIONS FOR CHILDREN

Fiction

Elizabeth, the Bird Watcher, illustrated by Erik Blegvad. New
York, Macmillan, 1963.

Elizabeth the Treasure Hunter, illustrated by Erik Blegvad. New
York, Macmillan, 1964.

Silently, the Cat, and Miss Theodosia, illustrated by Harvey
Dinnerstein. New York, Macmillan, and London, Collier Macmillan, 1965.

The Witch on the Corner, illustrated by Arnold Lobel. New York,
Norton, 1966; London, Lutterworth Press, 1967.

Victoria's Castle, illustrated by Lillian Hoban. New York, Norton, 1966.

Elizabeth and the Marsh Mystery, illustrated by Erik Blegvad. New
York, Macmillan, 1966; London, Collier Macmillan, 1974.

Professor Diggins' Dragons, illustrated by Ib Ohlsson. New York,
Macmillan, and London, Collier Macmillan, 1966.

The Cricket Winter, illustrated by Ralph Pinto. New York, Norton, 1967.

The Blackmail Machine, illustrated by Victoria de Larrea. New
York, Macmillan, 1967; London, Collier Macmillan, 1968.

A Year to Grow, illustrated by Emily McCully. New York, Norton, 1968.

The Holiday Rat, and the Utmost Mouse, illustrated by Wallace
Tripp. New York, Norton, 1969.

Solomon's Search, illustrated by Mischa Richter. New York,
Grosset and Dunlap, 1970.

The Future of Hooper Toote, illustrated by Gahan Wilson. New
York, Scribner, 1972.

The Escape of the Giant Hogstalk, illustrated by Ben Shecter. New
York, Scribner, 1974; as *The Escape of the Giant Hogweed,*
London, Abelard Schuman, 1978.

Terrible Jane, illustrated by Irene Trivas. New York, Scribner, 1987.

*

Biography: Essay in *Speaking for Ourselves, Too* compiled and
edited by Donald R. Gallo, National Council of Teachers of
English, 1993; essay in *Something about the Author Autobiography Series,* Volume 17, Detroit, Gale, 1994.

Manuscript Collections: Kerlan Collection, University of Minnesota, Minneapolis.

Felice Holman comments:

In recent years I have been writing what have been called
"survival stories" about children with unusual obstacles or difficult situations to cope with. The best known of these is *Slake's*
Limbo, about a boy who lives for 121 days in a subway tunnel.
Another is *The Wild Children* about the wandering gangs of
children in Russia. More recent is *Secret City, U.S.A.,* which tells
about homeless kids who try to start a new city. In each of these
books, I get drawn in while I am writing. I become very involved in
the life of the characters I am writing about and I suffer a lot of wear
and tear. In the end, though, I feel terrific: I get a great deal of
satisfaction from the feeling that I may have done a little something. Writing for young adults (a whole new generation) keeps me
hopeful that the things I worry about—things that make my
characters have such a tough time—will be improved. It is those
young adult readers who will be the ones who fix things.

*   *   *

Though she has written stories and poems for young children
(*At the Top of My Voice*) and co-authored a collection of mythic
tales about dragons and supernatural beings (*The Drac*), Felice
Holman is best known for her works of young adult literature. Here
she has focused on characters that are, in some ways, completely
foreign to most of her readers—a refugee in a subway station, a
Russian child hiding from the government, a Jewish boy growing
up in a Polish mining town. Yet all of these characters are familiar:
each yearns for family and the peace to grow up and enjoy life, and
each character struggles to find these in very different ways.

Holman explores these needs in the context of their deprivation.
These characters are frequently brought into situations which
would have been difficult to imagine at the beginning of their
respective novels. Each finds a darkness in the human soul that is
terrible and frightening, yet at the same time finds, both within
himself and in others, elements of unexpected grace. This grace,
suggests Holman, is nurturing to the giver as well as its receiver.
The result is a compellingly hopeful vision. Having seen and been
plunged down into the worst, the characters emerge to new hope,
new life. At times this can be quite explicit, as when Slake emerges
from his limbo in the subway and heads upward, both literally and
metaphorically.

The Wild Children is arguably Holman's best-known work.
Painstakingly researched, the novel focuses on the children abandoned during the early days of the Soviet Union, following one
boy's sojourn among the wild children. Alex comes down from his
hidden bedroom one morning to find that his entire family has been
taken away. There is no place to turn—he fears the authorities, and
others fear being connected to Alex. He turns to a beloved teacher
who helps Alex get to his uncle in Moscow. But when he arrives
there, he finds that his uncle has also disappeared. He is alone in
Moscow, with no money, and no place to go.

In establishing this situation, Holman has deprived Alex not
only of those things he must have to be happy—notably, a
family—but also of those things he must have simply to survive.
His situation is one of almost utter loss and loneliness. But this is
where Holman allows grace to enter; he is taken up by one of the
gangs of wild children who steal to survive. They lie and thieve, but
they will not hurt, nor will they run drugs, as so many of the other
gangs do. They do what must be done to survive. It is here that Alex
finds what he has least expected and what he refuses at first to
believe: a nurturing family. They feed him, shelter him, care for
him when he is sick, and protect him from the situation in which he

finds himself. Eventually they will help him to a new life outside of Russia, as he in turn helps most of them to join him.

The suggestion is very strong here that the family is crucial to the well-being of the adolescent, even if that family is not necessarily a biological one. No individual can truly live alone, and Alex knows that if he abandons the gang, he could not live long on the streets of Moscow.

This same theme is prominent in *Slake's Limbo,* where Slake, frustrated and wearied by the evils that encroach upon his life, escapes to a small room between two pillars down a subway tunnel. He is at first content with this life: structuring his days around the search for newspapers that he resells, taking the subway to all the many New York stations, finding treasures in trash cans to decorate his room, and making a true friend—a rat.

But he also finds that life cannot be lived alone—that is, if he hopes for a life with any meaning and joy. Soon he has regular customers for his newspapers, and is surprised to learn that they seem to care about him (one brings him a warm jacket). The waiters where he buys a daily sandwich begin to increase his order, though not its cost, seeing his need. And eventually, when he falls ill, he is brought to the hospital and a social worker by a subway engineer who finds him. He is in fact surrounded by a caring community. And though he will reject the formal help of the social worker, he will, at the novel's conclusion, emerge from the subway into the bright air, having learned an important truth—one that Alex would affirm as well.

Though the great power of Holman's narratives comes from the struggle of the protagonist to survive against very long odds, some comes from the vivid imagery she depicts: the abandoned cellar where Alex first meets the wild children, the overturned rocking chair that announces his family has been taken away, the rat peering into Slake's small room. Each image is arresting because of its moment in the plot, but also because of its thematic significance: the cellar is Alex's introduction to a new family, the rat a suggestion of mutual need.

Perhaps one of Holman's starkest images appears in *The Murderer,* where Hershey Marks is tied to a clothespole by some Polish kids, one of them Lorsh, whom Hershey had admired and tried to emulate. He is, as the narrator suggests, "mortified, disappointed, and scared." The disappointment is crucial here. Hershey is the only one of the Jewish children to attempt to make a connection with the Polish boys. He has wanted to be like Lorsh, to be accepted by him. But here Lorsh shows a kind of evil that is frightening in its carelessness and cruelty.

But here too grace interposes. Throughout the novel there has been a conflict between the miners, who are mostly Polish, and the merchants, who are predominantly Jewish. Set during the Depression, it is a time when most of the miners cannot pay their bills; they seem trapped forever by the need to use credit. At the end of the novel, Lorsh, who has just started to work in the mines, comes to Hershey's store and must ask for credit. Hershey's response is to give it immediately, but once Lorsh leaves, Hershey realizes that Lorsh is becoming trapped in the same cycle in which the others are trapped. Hershey wishes he could have given him the merchandise as a gift but it is too late. Hershey's response to his mock crucifixion on the clothespole is not rejection, but the yearning to respond with grace.

Hershey does not share the loss of a family with Alex and Slake, but like those two characters he yearns for a world in which he has a

real place, where he is not constantly trying to survive. The dangers in his world come from a clash of cultures, and although those dangers are not as life-threatening as those which Alex faces, they are still dramatic parts of Hershey's life.

The needs that each of Holman's characters face are universal; she makes them vivid by placing her characters in a microcosm of the real world. All of her plots use confined settings: a room in a subway tunnel, a cellar, a small town surrounded by mountains. Within that microcosm, under the sharpened focus of fiction, Holman's characters play out elemental human needs. Their escape from those settings suggests not that those needs have been fulfilled, but instead their new awareness that those needs cannot be filled in isolation.

—Gary D. Schmidt

HOOVER, H(elen) M(ary)

Nationality: American. **Born:** Stark County, Ohio, 5 April 1935. **Education:** Louisville High School; Mount Union College, Alliance, Ohio; Los Angeles County School of Nursing. **Career:** Writer. **Awards:** Children's Book of the Year, the Child Study Association of America, and one of the American Library Association's "Best Books for Young Adults," both 1974, for *The Lion's Cub;* one of the American Library Association's "Best Books for Young Adults," 1981, and received the Ohioana award, 1982, for *Another Heaven, Another Earth;* Central Missouri State College award for outstanding contribution to children's literature, 1984; Parents Choice Honor award, 1987, for *Orvis;* one of the American Library Association's "Best Books for Young Adults," named to Enoch Pratt Library's "Youth to Youth Books List," and received Parents Choice Honor award, all 1988, and also named to the Library of Congress best books for children list and a notable children's trade book by *Social Education,* both 1989, for *The Dawn Palace: The Story of Medea;* "Best of the Best 100 Books of the past 25 Years," American Library Association, 1994, for *Another Heaven, Another Earth;* Parent's Choice Gold Medal award, 1995, for *The Wind of Mars.* **Address:** 9405 Ulysses Ct., Burke, Virginia 22015, U.S.A.

PUBLICATIONS FOR YOUNG ADULTS

Science Fiction

Children of Morrow. New York, Four Winds Press, 1973; London, Methuen, 1975.
The Lion's Cub. New York, Four Winds Press, 1974.
Treasures of Morrow. New York, Four Winds Press, 1976.
The Rains of Eridan. New York, Viking, 1977; London, Methuen, 1978.
The Delikon. New York, Viking, 1977; London, Methuen, 1978.
The Lost Star. New York, Viking, 1979; London, Methuen, 1980.
The Return to Earth. New York, Viking, 1980; London, Methuen, 1981.
This Time of Darkness. New York, Viking, 1980; London, Methuen, 1982.
Another Heaven, Another Earth. New York, Viking, 1981; London, Methuen, 1983.
The Bell Tree. New York, Viking, 1982.

The Shepherd Moon: A Novel of the Future. New York, Viking, and London, Methuen, 1984.
Orvis. New York, Viking Kestrel, and London, Methuen, 1987.
The Dawn Palace: The Story of Medea. New York, Dutton, 1988.
Away Is a Strange Place to Be. New York, Dutton, 1990.
Only Child. New York, Dutton, 1992.
The Winds of Mars. New York, Dutton, 1995.

Other

The Whole Truth . . . Retelling Ancient Tales, Washington D.C., National Gallery of Art, 1996.
Contributor, edited by Aileen Pace Nilsen and Kenneth L. Donelson, *Literature for Today's Young Adults.* Glenview, Illinois, Scott, Foresman, 1985.
Anatomy of Wonder: A Critical Guide to Science Fiction. New York, Bowker, 1987.
Contributor, *Innocence and Experience: Essays and Conversations on Children's Literature.* New York, Lothrop, 1987.
Contributor, *But That's Another Story: Famous Authors Introduce Popular Genres,* edited by Sandy Asher. New York, Wallace & Company, 1996.
Contributor, *The Big Book for Our Planet,* New York, Dutton, forthcoming.

*

Biography: Essay in *Something about the Author Autobiography Series,* Volume 8, Detroit, Gale, 1989; essay in *Speaking for Ourselves: Autobiographical Sketches by Notable Authors of Books for Young Adults,* Volume 1, compiled and edited by Donald R. Gallo, National Council of Teachers of English, 1990.

Manuscript Collections: Kerlan Collection, University of Minnesota, Minneapolis.

H. M. Hoover comments:

"Could an old woman live in a shoe?" I asked, pointing to the picture in *Mother Goose.*

"A man in Pennsylvania built a shoe house," Dad said. "He lives in it. It has a spiral staircase. Even a bathroom."

I considered that, then turned the page. "Could a cow really jump over the moon?"

"Anything can happen in a story," Dad said.

He was right.

From *Mother Goose* I went on to read fairy stories, *The Arabian Nights, Tarzan,* and *Oz,* all the myths I could find. They were wonderful, timeless stories of distant worlds, supernatural people and beast and odd forms of transportation. By the time I began reading science fiction, space ships weren't that big a jump from flying carpets or winged horses. Godzilla was just a bigger dragon.

I write science fiction because fantasy and science fiction are the most fun to write. They're stories set out of time—just like the stories I loved most as a child.

*   *   *

One attribute of good science fiction is that it presents a good adventure tale while stimulating consideration of more serious

matters relating to science, technology, and social science. H. M. Hoover's works are a reflection of this attribute. In *The Shepherd Moon,* privileged thirteen-year-old Merry discovers a being from one of Earth's artificial satellite moons, who is plotting to conquer the Earth until the plan is thwarted by Merry and her grandfather. The novel's underlying message is an exploration of the uses of power and privilege and the consequences of overcrowding on Earth, a dual thrust found in all of Hoover's science fiction.

Hoover's early books all feature a strong, young female protagonist. These characters are isolated in some way from their parents, and in most of the books are preoccupied with themselves until they establish a growing relationship with an elder mentor. In *The Delikon,* Varina, a Delikon and a three hundred and seven-year-old child, reveres Sidra, the t'kyna on a conquered Earth ruled by the Delikon. In *The Rains of Eridan,* Karen is orphaned in a mutiny and is befriended by Theo, a biologist. Together they unravel the many mysteries of the planet Eridan. Though there is a supportive adult, the youth is always the main focus and each character is fully realized. The youths of these novels all have qualities that make them special in some way, but each also behaves in the way a young adult would, with the attendant fears, hurts, and joys.

A frequent criticism of science fiction is that it consists of plot and no characterization. Hoover, however, presents the reader with a strong plot and her characters are as alive as the action. An exploration of emotions and interactions is an important element in each of her books, and there is always the development of some kind of caring relationship between characters. One could even say that Hoover writes love stories, when love is defined in terms of caring about another being. Lian, a teenage astrophysicist who is on the planet Balthor with her parents to study a supernova, is rescued from a crash by the leader of an archeological expedition. She finds satisfaction and possibly a new career when her trust and caring for supposedly native creatures called lumpies leads to the discovery that these beings are sentient travellers from another planet and that the site of the excavation is actually a starship. These travellers in *The Lost Star* evolve for the reader, through Lian's perspective, from endearing pets to intelligent beings.

Hoover's books are replete with imagery and her skill in crafting phrases and sentences that create vivid mental representations is marvelous. Her interest in nature is evident in the detailed descriptions of the landscapes of the worlds she has created, including Earth in future centuries. The reader never strains to enter these worlds because the land, with its flora and fauna, is so expressively presented. In *The Lost Star,* the exotic creatures on Balthor are seen through the eyes of humans on that planet. The description is so much a part of the action that it is not tedious.

Recently, Hoover has included male protagonists in her works. In *Away Is a Strange Place to Be,* Abby and Bryan have been kidnapped and transported to a developing world to aid in the construction of a space habitat. The conditions they live in are horrible and the resourceful Abby and spoiled Bryan finally work together to escape, and return to Earth. Not content with her own escape, Abby works to free the other children who are imprisoned in the habitat. As always, Hoover explores the ramifications of technology and its effects on human beings. Hoover takes the concept of an *Only Child* one step further when she introduces us to Cody, the only child living on a spaceship. In his first visit to the planet, Cody is kidnapped by aliens and discovers that they are sentient beings and that the code of colonization that decrees that a planet with intelligent life cannot be colonized has been breached. Hoover's handling of this moral question is deft.

The concept of myth is a feature in much of Hoover's science fiction. Because she is writing of a future time, Hoover enables the reader to see that much of the knowledge and many of the behaviors of the present will become myths centuries from now. The alert reader will make the connection to the myths shared today and realize that these myths were grounded in fact but have evolved into stories over time. This interest in myth has led Hoover into a new direction: a novel about Medea and the calamities that befell her.

Extensive research and an awareness of the cultural mores of the Greek world in the time of Medea led Hoover to present, in *The Dawn Palace,* an account that is atypically sympathetic to Medea. Using her talent for rich detail, Hoover allows the reader to be present in a world of long ago and to participate in the pain and frustration that Medea felt throughout her life. Young adults will relate to this finely crafted novel and will gain an appreciation for events in another time.

Whether travelling to the past or the future, Hoover carries her readers along by creating a vivid world that is immediately accessible, producing satisfying plots, and creating characters that readers care about.

—M. Jean Greenlaw

HOUSTON, Gloria

Nationality: American. **Born:** 24 November 19(??) in Marion, North Carolina. **Education:** Appalachian State University, Boone North Carolina, B.S. in Music Education 1963; University of South Florida, Tampa, M. Ed. 1983, Ph.D. in Curriculum and Instruction 1989. **Family:** (divorced); two daughters. **Career:** Flight attendant, Delta Airlines, Atlanta; teacher, Winston-Salem, North Carolina, 1963-64, Irving Independent Schools, Texas, 1967-72, Riverview, Florida, 1972-73, Brandon, Florida, 1974-79 and 1983, and Plant City, Florida, 1981-1982; instructor, visiting assistant professor, and author-in-residence, University of South Florida, Tampa, 1983-1994, and Western Carolina University, Cullowhee, North Carolina, from 1994. International Board of Governors, Computer Pals Around the World (CPAW). **Awards:** Notable Children's Book nomination, American Library Association, 1983, for *My Brother Joey Died*; ''Most Likely to Become a Classic'' citation, *Publisher's Weekly,* Best Book of the Decade, *Booklist,* New York Public Library's 101 Books-Not-To-Be Missed, and Teachers' Choice citation, International Reading Association (IRA), all 1988, all for *The Year of the Perfect Christmas Tree*; Notable Trade Books in the Field of Social Studies list, Teachers' Choice citation, IRA, and Texas Bluebonnet Award list, all 1990, all for *Littlejim*; Notable Children's Book citation, American Library Association, 1992, Teachers' Choice citation, IRA, Children's Choice citation, IRA, Notable Trade Books in the Language Arts, The Family Channel Seal of Quality, 1997, all for *My Great Aunt Arizona*; Distinguished Alumni Award, Appalachian State University, 1990; National Literacy Award, Partnerships in Education, 1990; Cuffie Award, *Publisher's Weekly,* 1995, for *Mountain Valor*; North Carolina Junior book Award list, 1995, South Carolina Children's Book Award list, 1996, and Kansas

State Reading Circle-Recommended list, 1995, for *Littlejim's Gift: an Appalachian Christmas Story*; Distinguished Educator, IRA, 1997; Juvenile Literature Award, North Carolina American Association of University Women, 1997, Best Book for Social Studies, Children's Book Council and the National Council of Social Studies Educators, 1998, and Society of School Librarians International Best Book Award, 1998, all for *Littlejim's Dreams.* **Member:** Author's Guild, Society of Children's Book Writers and Illustrators, National Council of Teachers of English, Children's Literature Council, International Reading Association, Phi Kappa Phi. **Agent:** Cheryl Thompson, 3022 Planters Walk Court, Charlotte, North Carolina 28210, U.S.A. **Address:** 214 Killian Hall, Western Carolina University, Cullowhee, North Carolina 28723, U.S.A. **E-mail Address:** ghinc@ioa.com. **Website:** http://152.30.12.86/houston/homehouston.html.

PUBLICATIONS FOR YOUNG ADULTS

Fiction

My Brother Joey Died, photographs by Harvey Kelman. New York, Messner, 1982.
Littlejim, illustrated by Thomas B. Allen. New York, Philomel, 1990.
Mountain Valor, illustrated by Thomas B. Allen. New York, Philomel, 1994.
Littlejim's Dreams, illustrated by Thomas B. Allen. San Diego, Harcourt Brace, 1997.

PUBLICATIONS FOR CHILDREN

Fiction

The Year of the Perfect Christmas Tree, illustrated by Barbara Cooney. New York, Dial, 1988.
But No Candy, illustrated by Lloyd Bloom. New York, Philomel, 1992.
My Great Aunt Arizona, illustrated by Susan Condie Lamb. New York, HarperCollins, 1992.
Littlejim's Gift, illustrated by Thomas B. Allen. New York, Philomel, 1994.

*

Media Adaptations: *The Perfect Christmas Tree* (film; Houston acted as associate producer), Sanmar Productions, 1996.

Critical Studies: ''Gloria Houston and the Burden of the 'Old Culture''' by Roberta Herrin, in *Appalachian Journal* (Boone, North Carolina), Vol. 24, No. 1, 1996, 31-42; ''Portraits: Gloria Houston'' by Mary Berry, in *The Emergency Librarian,* May-June, 1997.

*   *   *

Gloria Houston's picture books and novels for young readers bring to life the rural communities of North Carolina where she and her parents grew up. Many of her works about Appalachia incorporate details of family history.

Houston's first book, *My Brother Joey Died,* uses a contemporary setting. A preadolescent girl recounts her brother's sudden illness and death. She expresses guilt over her last angry words to him, her anger at the trite phrases of comfort offered by adults, and her bewilderment over the speed of events. Understanding grandparents help her cope initially, but when they return home, she gets into trouble at school and home. She eventually finds help from a counselor and support group. Although the book sometimes has a "textbook" feeling, the narrator's honesty saves the text from didacticism. The black-and-white photographs create an outdated appearance.

Houston was much more fortunate in the illustrator for her first work about Appalachia, *The Year of the Perfect Christmas Tree.* Barbara Cooney traveled to North Carolina to help her visualize the setting near Spruce Pine. The story tells how in the spring of 1918 Ruthie and her father find the perfect balsam high on Grandfather Mountain so their family can take its turn supplying the church's Christmas tree. Then Ruthie's father is called to fight in World War I. The Armistice offers hope he can return in time to cut the tree, but in the end, Ruthie and Mama must make the long trek to fetch the balsam. Using her wedding dress, Mama also contrives to fashion an angel costume for Ruthie for the pageant and an angel doll who looks just like her. The immensely popular book went immediately to a second printing.

Ruthie's separation from her father is paralleled in a later picture book, *But No Candy,* set during World War II. Sunny Brook General Store, around which much of the story revolves, is based on the store of the same name owned by Houston's parents. Six-year-old Lee enjoys her daily trip to the candy counter to select a special treat, usually a Hershey bar. She notices the worried faces of neighbors who gather around the radio to hear news of war. One day Uncle Ted leaves to fight. The candy supply dwindles and disappears. Daddy tells Lee that sugar goes to the soldiers as part of the "war effort." Ration cards, newsreels, headlines bring the war into Lee's life, but nothing is as constant a reminder as the lack of candy. When her uncle returns—with Hershey bars—Lee realizes that the years have changed her. She values the person more than the candy. Houston deftly portrays the home front experience in a child's terms.

Houston uses a longer format for two novels based on her father's life. In *Littlejim,* the twelve-year-old title character already demonstrates his love of learning and facility with words. His promise as a scholar delights his mother but displeases his father. Bigjim, the finest logger around, constantly belittles his son, calling him a "no-account boy" because he thinks his son should emulate him. He discourages Littlejim from entering a regional essay contest about "What it Means to be an American." Supported by his mother, Littlejim writes about people from many countries who had come to his region for various reasons. Even his dour father has to concede that publication of the winning essay in the *Kansas City Star* and a $10 check demonstrate talent that makes Littlejim "'right much of a man.'"

Details of daily life—such as preparing foods for winter—enrich the book. Houston does not avoid danger and violence. Littlejim witnesses the death of a gaffer cut in two by the saw at the lumber mill. Littlejim's memories of that awful sight recur forcefully during hog butchering, where he earns his father's scorn by vomiting. In fact, Bigjim ridicules Littlejim so often that his sister Nell asks why his father doesn't love Littlejim as he does her and baby May. Mama's reassurances and the community's support bolster Littlejim, but Bigjim's negativity is wearisome and distasteful.

The encroachment of the outside world is a prominent theme in *Littlejim's Dreams.* In 1920, Littlejim is 14 and hopes to continue his education. Bigjim still disparages book learning and ridicules dreaming. Times are hard because Bigjim refuses to cooperate with the large timber companies who want to clearcut the land. Bigjim's need for funds becomes urgent when Mama requires hospitalization. To pay for her care, Bigjim sells mineral rights to his land, but he is tricked by an unscrupulous neighbor. The virgin timer is logged to "'prepare the lands for prospecting and mining.'" The combination of a letter from Littlejim published in the *Inquirer* and the work of the lawyer-uncle of a young man who had boarded with Littlejim's family brings a halt to logging and a large cash settlement. But nothing can replace the trees. Mama's return from the hospital and Bigjim's words of pride in his son bring some happiness at the story's conclusion.

The picture book *Littlejim's Gift* relates to the novels. Originally part of *Littlejim,* the story recounts how the boy uses money he had saved for a set of tools to buy a doll for Nell. After he wins a school competition, he recites at the Christmas observance at the Missionary Baptist Church. Bigjim disapproves of celebrating Christmas and is angry with Littlejim but joins his family. Because this story was published after *Littlejim,* there are puzzling references to some of its details in the novel that are clarified only by reading the picture book.

My Great-Aunt Arizona, however, clearly stands alone. Aunt Zony appears in *Littlejim's Dreams,* and her nephew admires her learning and spirit. But even those who know nothing of Littlejim will appreciate Arizona's joy in learning and her exuberance in sharing her knowledge with others. From childhood she loves to learn and eventually realizes her dream of teaching. She returns to Henson Creek, marries, has a family, but keeps teaching. For 57 years, she shares her life with her students and encourages them to pursue their own dreams. Like most women in Houston's books, Arizona is energetic, hard-working, and competent.

The theme of strong women is most obvious in *Mountain Valor,* a novel for upper-elementary and junior high readers. Set in the same area of North Carolina but during the Civil War, the novel portrays a region and people split by the conflict. Valor McAimee's father and brother Tom are away fighting for the Confederacy. Her brother Jeff and uncle Joe are fighting for the Union. Eleven-year-old Valor admires the exploits of Melinda Blaylock, who dressed like a man to accompany her husband to the army, and Rebecca Linkerfelt, who offers healing cures to her neighbors, even though some consider her a "witch woman." Valor, her mother, cousin Jed, and free black servants Savannah and Ben struggle to keep the farm going. Marauders from both armies raid and destroy farms in the area. But the notorious band of Colonel Kirk most disrupts life for Valor. The first raid sends her mother into early labor, and the loss of the baby leads to her depression. Months later, the band returns. This time they kill Ben and steal all the livestock. Desperate to avoid starvation, Valor disguises herself as a boy and manages to recover the animals by drugging the soldiers with Aunt Becky's herbs. Houston notes that the book is based on a true incident from the life of Matilda Houston. As in her other works, Houston pays exceptional attention to the language of her characters. Her notes explain some of the variant forms of English spoken in Appalachia at the time her novels are set.

—Kathy Piehl

HOUSTON, James A(rchibald)

Nationality: Canadian. **Born:** Toronto, Ontario, 12 June 1921. **Education:** John Wanless Primary School and Northern Vocational High School, both Toronto; Ontario College of Art, 1938-40; L'Academie de la Grand Chaumière, Paris, 1947-48; studied with printmaker Unichi-Hiratsuka, Tokyo, 1958-59; studied engraving with William Hayter, Atelier 17, 1961. **Military Service:** Served in the Toronto Scottish Regiment, 1940-45; became warrant officer. **Family:** Married 1) Alma G. Bardon in 1950 (divorced 1966), two sons; 2) Alice Daggett Watson in 1967. **Career:** Author and illustrator. Arctic adviser, Canadian Guild of Crafts, 1949-52; first civil administrator, Government of Canada, West Baffin, Eastern Arctic, Northwest Territories, 1952-62. Associate director of design, 1962-72, and since 1972 master designer, Steuben Glass, New York. Visiting lecturer at Wye Institute and Rhode Island School of Design. Chairman of board of directors of Canadian Arctic Producers, 1976-77, and American Indian Art Center; member of board of directors of Canadian Eskimo Arts Council; president of Indian and Eskimo Art of the Americas; vice-president of West Baffin Eskimo Cooperative and Eskimo Art, Inc. Member of primitive art committee of Metropolitan Museum of Art. Artist: individual shows—Canadian Guild of Crafts, 1953, 1955, 1957; Robertson Galleries, Ottawa, 1953; Calgary Galleries, 1966; Canadiana Galleries, Edmonton, 1977; Yaneff Gallery, Toronto, 1983, 1986; Steuben Glass, 1987, 1991, 1997; Century Association, New York, 1991; Takashimaya, Tokyo, 1991; represented in collections of Glenbow-Alberta Museum of Art, Montreal Museum of Fine Arts, National Gallery of Art, Ottawa. **Awards:** Canadian Library Association Book of the Year Medal, 1966, for *Tikta'liktak: An Eskimo Legend,* 1968, for *The White Archer: An Eskimo Legend,* 1980, for *River Runners: A Tale of Hardship and Bravery,* and runner-up, 1982, for *Long Claws: An Arctic Adventure;* American Indian and Eskimo Cultural Foundation award, 1966; American Library Association Notable Books awards, 1967, for *The White Archer,* 1968, for *Akavak,* and 1971, for *The White Dawn;* decorated officer of Order of Canada, 1972; Amelia Frances Howard-Gibbon award runner-up, 1973, for *Ghost Paddle;* Vicky Metcalf award, 1977; Queen Elizabeth Silver Anniversary Medal, 1977; Inuit Kuavati award of merit, 1979; Vicky Metcalf Short Story award, 1980, for "Long Claws" in *The Winter Fun Book;* Honorary Fellow, Ontario College of Art, and Fellow, Royal Society of Arts, London, 1981; Canadian nominee, Hans Christian Andersen award, 1987, 1991; Canada Council's Children's Literature Prize, 1986, for *The Falcon Bow;* Citation of Merit award, Royal Canadian Academy of Art, 1987; Max and Gretta Ebel award, Canadian Society of Children's Authors, Illustrators, and Performers, 1989; Canadian Authors Association Literary Award for fiction, 1990, for *Running West;* Governor General's Literary Award nominee and Ontario Library Association Silver Birch Award, 1992, for *Drifting Snow.* D.Litt., Carleton University, Ottawa, 1972; D.H.L., Rhode Island College, Providence, 1975; D.F.A., Rhode Island School of Design, Providence, 1979; D.D.L., Dalhousie University, Halifax, Nova Scotia, 1987; named as one of the 125 most significant Canadians, 1992; Massey Medal, Royal Canadian Geographical Society, 1997. **Address:** 24 Main St., Stonington, Connecticut 06378, U.S.A.; Queen Charlotte Islands, Tlell, Box 43, British Columbia V0T 1Y0, Canada.

PUBLICATIONS FOR YOUNG ADULTS

Fiction (illustrated by the author)

Tikta'liktak: An Eskimo Legend. Toronto, Longman, and New York, Harcourt, 1965.
Eagle Mask: A West Coast Indian Tale. Toronto, Longman, and New York, Harcourt, 1966.
The White Archer: An Eskimo Legend. Toronto, Longman, and New York, Harcourt, 1967.
Akavak: An Eskimo Journey. Toronto, Longman, and New York, Harcourt, 1968.
Wolf Run: A Caribou Eskimo Tale. Toronto, Longman, and New York, Harcourt, 1971.
Ghost Paddle: A Northwest Coast Indian Tale. Toronto, Longman, and New York, Harcourt, 1972.
Editor, *Songs of the Dream People: Chants and Images from the Indians and Eskimos of North America.* Toronto, Longman, and New York, Atheneum, 1972.
Kiviok's Magic Journey: An Eskimo Legend. Toronto, Longman, and New York, Atheneum, 1973.
Frozen Fire: A Tale of Courage. Toronto, McClelland & Stewart, and New York, Atheneum, 1977; London, Penguin, 1979.
River Runners: A Tale of Hardship and Bravery. Toronto, McClelland & Stewart, and New York, Atheneum, 1979; London, Penguin, 1981.
Long Claws: An Arctic Adventure. Toronto, McClelland & Stewart, and New York, Atheneum, 1981.
Black Diamonds: A Search for Arctic Treasure. Toronto, McClelland & Stewart, and New York, Atheneum, 1982.
Ice Swords: An Undersea Adventure. Toronto, McClelland & Stewart, and New York, Atheneum, 1985.
The Falcon Bow: An Arctic Legend. Toronto, McClelland & Stewart, and New York, McElderry, 1986.
Whiteout. Toronto, Greey de Pencier, 1988.
Drifting Snow. Toronto, McClelland & Stewart, and New York, McElderry, 1992.

PUBLICATIONS FOR ADULTS

Novels (illustrated by the author)

The White Dawn: An Eskimo Saga. Toronto, Longman, New York, Harcourt, and London, Heinemann, 1971.
Ghost Fox. Toronto, McClelland & Stewart, New York, Harcourt, and London, Collins, 1977.
Spirit Wrestler. Toronto, McClelland & Stewart, New York, Harcourt, and London, Collins, 1980.
Eagle Song. Toronto, McClelland & Stewart, and New York, Harcourt, 1983.
Running West. Toronto, McClelland & Stewart, and New York, Crown, 1989.
Confessions of an Igloo Dweller. Toronto, McClelland & Stewart, 1995; Boston, Houghton Mifflin, 1996.
The Ice Master. Toronto, McClelland & Stewart, 1997.

Other

Canadian Eskimo Art. Ottawa, Queen's Printer, 1955.
Eskimo Graphic Art. Ottawa, Queen's Printer, 1960.
Eskimo Prints. Barre, Massachusetts, Barre Publishers, 1967.

America Was Beautiful, edited by Alice Watson. Barre, Massachusetts, Barre Publishers, 1970.

Ojibwa Summer, photographs by B. A. King. Barre, Massachusetts, Barre Publishers, 1972.

Screenplays: *The White Dawn,* 1973; *The Mask and the Drum,* 1975; *Kalvak,* 1976; *So Sings the Wolf,* 1976; *Art of the Arctic Whaleman,* 1978; *Legends of the Salmon People,* 1978; *Ghost Fox,* 1979; *Whiteout,* 1987.

*

Media Adaptations: *Ghost Fox* (eight cassettes), Crane Memorial Library, 1978.

Manuscript Collections: National Library of Canada, Ottawa.

Critical Studies: "James Houston: The Neglected Hero" by John Ayre, in *Saturday Night,* May 1974, 25-30; *The Republic of Childhood* by Sheila Egoff, Toronto, Oxford, 1975; *Six Journeys: A Canadian Pattern* by Charles Taylor, Toronto, House of Anansi, 1977, 73-104; entry in *Children's Literature Review,* Vol. 3, Detroit, Gale, 1978; "The Man" by Mary D. Kierstead, in *New Yorker,* 29 August 1988, 33-47; entry in *Something About the Author: Autobiography Series,* Vol. 17, Detroit, Gale, 1994.

Illustrator: *Shoot to Live,* 1944; *Nuki* by Alma Houston, 1955; *Ayorama* by Raymond de Coccola and Paul King, 1956; *Tuktut/Caribou,* 1957; *The Unicorn Was There* by Elizabeth Pool, 1966; *The Private Journal of Captain G.F. Lyon of H.M.S. Hecla, During the Recent Voyage of Discovery under Captain Parry, 1821-1823* by George Francis Lyon, 1970; *The American Heritage Book of Fish Cookery* by Alice Watson Houston, 1980; *First Came the Indians* by Mary Jo Wheeler-Smith, 1982; *The Incredible Eskimo* by R. de Coccola and P. King, 1986; *Place Names of the Eastern Shore of Maryland* by J. Kenneth Keatley, 1987; *Confessions of an Igloo Dweller,* 1996; *The Ice Master,* 1997.

James Houston comments:

It is gratifying to me to write adventure stories for young adults. These stories are almost always based on true events. Beginning when I was young, I have had the good fortune to live for long periods of my life with Indian and Inuit/Eskimo people in the north. I choose to write about some of these first people in North America because of the unfamiliar way in which they have lived their lives and the many special skills they have developed.

To hold the attention of one's readers, I believe an author should try to tell a story that possesses truth and interesting characters, and is perhaps enhanced by an unusual environment. It should possess as well a driving sense of purpose and excitement.

*   *   *

James Houston has written several books for the junior high school audience; his adult novels are also of interest to young adults. His stories are set in Canada and the Arctic, showing a depth of understanding for the people there and their legends and customs. His characters include Inuit-Eskimos and also Indians of the Cree, Dene, Naskapi, Abnaki, and other tribes that once populated the northern part of the continent.

According to *Children's Literature Review* (Gale, 1978), Houston is a Canadian artist who lived for twelve years with the Eskimos of the Canadian Arctic. This "influenced both his fiction and the world of visual art. Houston uses his artistic talent to include sharp pen-and-ink drawings at the end of each chapter of the books for young teens. It was Houston who 'discovered' and promoted the sculpture of the Eskimos and introduced printmaking to them." Although Houston now spends much time in Canada, he lives in the United States, also.

Most of his books of interest to young adults are fiction. However, one book which he edited, *Songs of the Dream People,* is a collection of chants and poems for readers of all ages. The short selections in this book reflect the legends, feelings, cultures, and philosophies of the Native Americans of the far north. They represent the oral traditions of these people and are grouped by regions into four sections: Eskimo, Eastern, Central, and Northwest Coast Indians. Striking pen-and-ink drawings by Houston show weapons and other artifacts.

Many people feel that Houston's writings about Eskimo life and customs are what distinguishes him from other writers for young people, but some of his best books deal not with the Eskimo, but with Indians. *River Runners* is set among the Naskapi, a tribe living along the rivers of subarctic Quebec and northern Labrador. Several Indian tribes are brought into *Running West* and *Ghost Fox.*

It is interesting to note that although the settings are rugged and in places that are associated with men, several of Houston's protagonists are female, among them, Elizabeth of *Drifting Snow,* Sara, who was captured by hostile Indians in *Ghost Fox,* and Thana, also captured by hostile Indians in *Running West.* Thana proved to be a knowledgeable guide to the fur traders. *Running West, River Runners, Frozen Fire,* and *Drifting Snow* are based on true incidents.

Many of Houston's protagonists are in pairs: a native youth and a young friend new to the region. Survival is a theme that runs through much of his fiction, especially surviving the harsh environment of the Arctic winters in isolated locations where a person must depend on him or herself for everything: finding food, finding directions to travel, struggling against wild beasts and hostile people, and enduring chilling storms, all in places where there are few settlers and fewer signposts.

Running West is a powerful adult novel of survival in unexplored territory during the years 1715-17. It's a love story of Thana, a Dene Indian, and William Stewart, a Scotsman who becomes indentured as a servant at the English fur trading fort in the Hudson Bay Territory. He is ordered to let Thana lead him and a company of traders to the tribe from which she was stolen by a band of very cruel Indians. In Dene country, Thana says, they will find furs of marten, fisher, otter, and ermine as well as the yellow pebbles (gold) which were used to make the handle of her special scraper, a tool for handling furs. This is all she has from her mother, an Indian who was murdered at the time Thana was stolen away.

The trip to Dene country is a perilous nine-moon trek filled with danger from enemy tribes, starvation, exhaustion, and fierce winter weather. Early on, most of her accompanying traders turn back. When the journey ends, Thana is pregnant with William's child. She and William become husband and wife when she weaves a wedding veil of beads and string and William asks her to remove it.

When William's navigational instruments are deliberately destroyed by an angry "carrier" or porter, William becomes frantic. However, Thana says that "Wolf Star" will guide them. Thana uses all her native skills to lead them and help them find food along the way. Starvation is a daily threat.

Thana's eagerness to learn the English or "Ballahouly" language adds humor to the narrative. Also amusing are her naive observations of the English customs. "All the Ballahouly ate in curious ways that always interested me. They used iron knives and scoops instead of fingers. The fat soup stirrer never once sat down with us. At home, our Dene women prepared all food. I would ask Williyumm why had they not brought any Ballahooly women with them? How did they get their babies?"

Alternating chapters narrated first by William and then by Thana carry the story from the perspective of each without slowing down the action. Thana's chapters show insight into the traditions and customs of the Indian people. Each "voice" describes the environment, some of which is rich with plants, fish, birds, and animal life. Much of it is desolate. *Running West* is recommended as historical fiction in *Best Books for Senior High Readers*.

Both *Running West* and *Ghost Fox* tell of the Indians' cruelty to a girl whose family and tribespeople are destroyed by other hostile tribes. Both are well written with insight into the culture of the people, plenty of action, and memorable characters. In *Ghost Fox*, Sara, the young Indian woman, eventually marries into the tribe who kidnapped her and finds a place there so that when she's given a chance to return to her people she does not want to do so.

Another adult novel recommended for teens is *Spirit Wrestler*. In this story, a friendless Eskimo boy is befriended by a female shaman. The boy named Shoona is introduced first as a dying man carried into the camp of the Northern Service Officer, the administrator of that vast barren arctic area of Canada known as Baffin Island, where Houston himself spent twelve years as an officer.

Houston's novel *Drifting Snow* is for children up through the junior-high age, but it is not as convincing in its depiction of people struggling to survive as some of his earlier books. It's the story of a young teenage girl's search for her biological parents among the Eskimos. The strength of this book is in the description of Eskimo life on a remote island where people cling to old customs and experience life-threatening travel on icy waters as their ancestors once did.

Three of Houston's junior novels, *Frozen Fire, River Runners: A Tale of Hardship and Bravery,* and *Ice Swords* are recommended by John T. Gillespie in his *Best Books for Junior High Readers*. *Frozen Fire* is the story of an Eskimo boy and his white friend who set out to find the Eskimo boy's father, a prospector who has disappeared. A sequel to this novel is *Black Diamonds*.

River Runners is an exciting contemporary novel about fifteen-year-old Andrew, a Scot, and his new friend Paskak, a Naskapi Indian youth. They meet at the far northern fur trading post of Fort Chimo. Paskak teaches Andrew, an apprentice fur trader, the Arctic survival skills of his native tribe. After a brief training period at the fort, the two boys set out on snowshoes, accompanied by Indian packmen and dog-drawn toboggans loaded with supplies, for a new fur trade outpost at Ghost Lake far into the interior of Quebec. Andrew struggles with every ounce of energy he can muster to keep up with the natives as they follow the frozen Kiksoak River south until they finally reach Ghost Lake. The packmen and their dogs return to Ft. Chimo and civilization. They leave the boys and

scattered Naskapi Indian families searching against great odds for food and furs during the long hard winter in the frozen north.

Ice Swords is a third book in the series which starts with *Frozen Fire*. In this book the same boys, Matthew and his Inuit friend Kayak, are invited to spend the summer in the Arctic studying the migration of whales. They live and work with Dr. Lunan and his daughter Jill, who teaches the boys to deep-sea dive. This is an interesting story which soon turns into a scary adventure.

—Virginia L. Gleason

HOWKER, Janni

Nationality: British. **Born:** Nicosia, Cyprus, 6 July 1957. **Education:** Kendal High School, Westmorland; Lancaster University, Lancashire, B.A. (honours) in independent studies, 1980, M.A. in creative writing, 1984. **Family:** Married Mick North in 1988 (second marriage). **Career:** Writer; creator of writing workshops. Editor of the poetry magazine, *Brew,* for the Brewery Arts Centre in Kendal, England, 1978-79; worked variously as assistant in hostel for the mentally ill, research assistant in sociology department at Lancaster University, examiner at Open University, census officer, park attendant, landlady, housemother for mentally handicapped children, tutor, and assistant on an archeological site. **Awards:** International Reading Association children's book award and *Burnley Express* award, both 1985, for *Badger on the Barge,* which also was named Best Book of the Year by the American Library Association, 1984, shortlisted for the Carnegie Medal Award, 1984, commended by the Whitbread Literary Awards, 1985, and listed by *School Library Journal* as a "Best Book of 1985"; Tom-Gallon Trust Award, 1985, for short story "The Egg-Man"; Whitbread Literary Award, children's fiction category, *Young Observer* (now *Observer*) teenage fiction prize, and *Observer*-Rank Organisation prize, all 1985, and Silver Pencil award, 1987, all for *The Nature of the Beast,* which also was named an ALA Notable Book, 1985, highly commended by the Carnegie Medal Awards, 1985, and placed on *Horn Book*'s honor list, 1986; *Boston Globe-Horn Book* fiction honor award and Somerset Maugham award, both 1987, for *Isaac Campion,* which also was highly commended by the Carnegie Medal Awards, 1986, and named Best Book of the Year by the ALA, a *New York Times* Notable Book, and a Best Book for Young Adults by *School Library Journal,* all 1987. **Address:** c/o Julia MacRae Books, 20 Vauxhall Bridge Road, London SW1V 2SA, England.

PUBLICATIONS FOR YOUNG ADULTS

Fiction

Badger on the Barge and Other Stories. London, MacRae, and New York, Greenwillow, 1984.
The Nature of the Beast. London, MacRae, and New York, Greenwillow, 1985.
Isaac Campion. London, MacRae, and New York, Greenwillow, 1986.
The Topiary Garden, pictures by Anthony Browne. New York, Orchard Books, 1995.
Walk with a Wolf, illustrated by Sarah Fox-Davies. Cambridge, Massachusetts, Candlewick Press, 1998.

Plays

Badger on the Barge (television play; from her own story). 1987.
The Nature of the Beast (screenplay). 1988.

*

Media Adaptations: *Badger on the Barge* (television movie),
ITV, 1987; *The Nature of the Beast* (film), 4/British Screen, 1988.

Biography: Essay in *Something about the Author Autobiography
Series* by Janni Howker, Volume 13, Detroit, Gale, 1992.

Critical Studies: Entry in *Children's Literature Review,* Volume
14, Detroit, Gale, 1988.

*   *   *

Janni Howker was the most remarkable British writer of fiction
for young people to emerge in the mid-1980s, a time when new
talent was scarce. Her first book, *Badger on the Barge and Other
Stories,* was highly acclaimed and won several awards; her second
and third, *The Nature of the Beast* and *Isaac Campion,* swiftly
consolidated her reputation. Though praise for these books was
high, it was not excessive; they are of true quality.

Badger on the Barge is in no way apprentice work; the writer,
though young and decidedly regional, was already very accomplished. The book consists of a group of five longish short stories,
all of which are about relationships between young and old people.
Helen in the title story befriends a crusty old woman who lives on a
barge and is fighting for her independence; Liz in "The Topiary
Garden" meets old Sally Beck who could only make a life for
herself by pretending to be a boy. Jane in "The Egg-Man"
glimpses the depth and vulnerability of love through a crazy old
man's grief for a long-dead wife. Yet none of the stories are
concerned only with the young-old relationship; each has also a
subtheme, interwoven with the main one and resolved with it. They
are ingeniously organized and limpidly written, and at the same
time subtle and perceptive. The most poignant and atmospheric is
"Jakey," in which an old boatman is about to die and his young
friend Steven, dreaming, sees a dark shape following Jakey's boat:
"a great grey shape, like a shark, swimming behind, slowly,
secretly." It is Jakey's death.

In *The Nature of the Beast* Howker adapted her gift for the apt
and sounding phrase to a first-person narration by a rough
working-class boy. The setting is northern, on the edge of an
industrial town; the Haverstock Beast—if it exists—prowls
around, savaging farmers' stock and spreading fear among the
people. Is the beast real or symbolic? The mill on which the town
depended has closed; unemployment is also a beast that is ravaging
the community. In the end it seems that a beast of anger and
frustration is inside the boy himself: "I'm going to take over where
the Beast left off," he says. Though there is warmth in the story,
there is a chilling conclusion.

Isaac Campion has a similar setting to that of *The Nature of the
Beast,* but it is set back in time to the limits of living memory, for
Isaac is supposedly telling his story to the author, just before his
death in 1984 at the age of ninety-six. The year is 1901. Isaac's
older brother has been killed as the result of a foolish dare from the
son of his father's hated enemy; Isaac must leave school to work
without pay for Father, a horse dealer and a harsh, violent man. On
impulse Isaac frustrates Father's plan to take a hideous revenge.
Immediately afterwards the steamboat carrying a cargo of Irish
mares for Father is thought to have sunk in a storm. Father comes
home drunk, defeated, apparently ruined, yet hard and bitter still.
Later the steamer is seen to be safe, riding at anchor; but Isaac has
had enough, and will be off to America by the end of summer.

This is a brief, emotionally intense novel, full of the passionate
power of hatred and the close but often suffocating or infuriating
relationships between members of a family. There is compassion
too for the horses that "dragged the whole weight of work behind
them. . .until they were done for, and sent to the knacker's, or
buried in a ditch." It gives a gritty, wholly convincing picture of a
bleak world of hard-driven people. "I know I can endure it,"
thinks Isaac. "I was put on the earth to endure it. But there must be
more to living a life than this." The book is not in the end
pessimistic, however. In Isaac himself—poor, ordinary lad though
he is—the human spirit shines. There's nothing shining about
Father, but even in him there is something heroic: a fierce determination to fight, survive, and win in grim surroundings.

Howker's first three books suggest that hers is a major talent,
but the second and third could be said to belong to general as much
as to young people's fiction, and it remains to be seen whether she
will stay within the bounds of the young adult's list.

—John Rowe Townsend

HOY, Linda

Nationality: British. **Born:** Sheffield, 27 March 1946. **Education:**
Sheffield Polytechnic, Certificate of Education, 1973, B.Ed. (with
honors), 1974. **Family:** Divorced; three children. **Career:** Worked
as a shop assistant, barmaid, and civil servant; English teacher,
Gosforth Comprehensive School, near Sheffield, England, 1974-
83; lecturer, Sheffield City Polytechnic, 1986-1990. **Agent:** Gina
Pollinger, 222 Old Brompton Rd., London SW5 OB2, England.

PUBLICATIONS FOR YOUNG ADULTS

Novels

Your Friend Rebecca. London, Bodley Head, 1981.
The Damned. London, Bodley Head, 1983.
Kiss File JC 100. London, Walker, 1988.
Nightmare Park. London, Collins, Armada, 1989.
Ring of Death. London, Collins, Armada, 1990.
Haddock 'n' Chips. London, Walker, 1993.
The Pit. Aylesbury, Ginn, 1995.
Nightmare Express. London, Collins, 1996.
Dear Poltergeist, illustrations by Tony Kenyon. London, Walk-
er 1996.

Other

The Alternative Assembly Book (for teachers). Essex, Longman, 1985.
Emmeline Pankhurst. London, Hamish Hamilton, 1985.

Emily (television play), TV South, 1985.
Editor, *Poems for Peace.* Leichhardt, Australia, Pluto Press, 1986.
Emmeline Pankhurst. London, Evans, 1993.

*   *   *

Linda Hoy is a Quaker committed to showing her young adult readers how to survive and keep the faith. Each of her books contains spiritual tools for readers to take with them as they try to construct their own lives. She explores the problems, rewards, and overall necessity of believing in something.

Her sole work of nonfiction, *Emmeline Pankhurst,* seems a natural biography for Hoy to write. Pankhurst, the founder of the militant women's suffrage movement, endured many hardships, including prison, for her belief. Hoy shows that although it wasn't an easy road for Pankhurst, it was a necessary one. It is because of the unfaltering faith of Pankhurst and others like her that women were granted the right to vote. Hoy avoids fictionalizing by allowing Pankhurst's life to shine on its own, thus giving the reader a straightforward and naturally inspiring story.

Hoy's heavy hand proves problematic in her works of fiction. Her strengths and weaknesses are perhaps best exemplified in *Your Friend, Rebecca.* Rebecca is an instantly likable character with a wonderfully adolescent sense of humor. She calls her principal— Miss Hoggit—the Hog, burns cod fries, and ridicules teen fashion magazines. Because the story is told in the first person, we are privy to all private jokes and thoughts. Instead of letting Rebecca's engaging character flourish on its own, however, Hoy acts as a puppeteer, conveniently pulling the strings she finds appropriate to her ends.

Hoy loads the novel with overt references to *King Lear.* Each chapter begins with a quote from the play. When Rebecca's drama teacher, Mrs. Gloucester, tells Rebecca, who has not read the play, to play Cordelia and ad lib lines, she can't act, but says what she feels: "I have the feelings you'd expect a daughter to have for a father." When Rebecca is mad at Darren, whom she both has a crush on and must do the scene with, she plays Regan and tells him to get lost. Rebecca conveniently acts out all her frustrations through drama, letting all her pent-up emotions loose at just the right time in the play.

Drama class allows Rebecca to explore and release her true feelings. She becomes a new, improved person who goes to Quaker Meetings and starts liking her dad. Somewhere in the midst of her transformation, however, the real Rebecca becomes lost and Linda Hoy takes over. Hoy's descriptions, characters, and sharp sense of humor become overshadowed by the messages she unveils. Even in her novels that don't end happily, Hoy's voice, rather than that of her characters, is loudest. For example, in *Kiss File JC 110,* Julian's character is one the reader can easily relate to; however, from the start and throughout the story, Hoy's obvious symbolism and religious agenda prevail.

Hoy is at her best in the genre of nonfiction and, if she can find more characters from history that inspire her, perhaps that is where she will find her niche. Interestingly, her only book left in print in the United States is *Emmeline Pankhurst.* Although Hoy's message is important, it will most likely be lost on readers too old or too young to appreciate it. While older YA readers will most likely feel patronized by Hoy's loaded references, younger teen readers of

Hoy's fiction may be able to enjoy her appealing characters, lively dialogue, and apt descriptions without feeling her authorial control.

—Kate Lentz

———

HUDSON, Jeffery. *See* **CRICHTON, Michael.**

———

HUGHES, Dean

Nationality: American. **Born:** Ogden, Utah, 24 August 1943. **Education:** Weber State College, Ogden, Utah, B.A. 1967; University of Washington, Seattle, M.A. 1968, Ph.D. 1972; postdoctoral study at Stanford University, Stanford, California, summer, 1975, and Yale University, New Haven, Connecticut, summer, 1978. **Family:** Married Kathleen Hurst in 1966; one daughter and two sons. **Career:** Associate professor of English, Central Missouri State University, Warrensburg, 1972-80; part-time visiting professor, 1980-82, and guest professor, 1997-98, Brigham Young University, Provo, Utah; writer, part-time editor, and consultant, 1980-89. Guest author, speaker, and workshop leader at writing conferences. **Awards:** National Endowment for the Humanities summer seminar stipend, 1975 and 1978; Outstanding Faculty Achievement award from Central Missouri State University, 1980; nominated for state awards in Tennessee, Missouri, Kansas, South Carolina, West Virginia, Kentucky, and Wyoming; Utah Children's Book award nominations for *Nutty for President, Switching Tracks, Nutty and the Case of the Ski-Slope Spy,* and *Family Pose; Honestly, Myron* was selected one of the "Best Books for Kids" by Children's Book Committee; *Family Pose* received an Editors' Choice award from *Booklist.* **Address:** 1466 West 1100 North, Provo, Utah 84604, U.S.A.

PUBLICATIONS FOR YOUNG ADULTS

Fiction

Nutty for President, illustrated by Blanche Sims. New York, Atheneum, 1981.
Hooper Haller. Salt Lake City, Utah, Deseret, 1981.
Honestly, Myron, illustrated by Martha Weston. New York, Atheneum, 1982.
Switching Tracks. New York, Atheneum, 1982.
Jenny Haller. Salt Lake City, Utah, Deseret, 1983.
Millie Willenheimer and the Chestnut Corporation. New York, Atheneum, 1983.
Nutty and the Case of the Mastermind Thief. New York, Atheneum, 1985.
Nutty and the Case of the Ski-Slope Spy. New York, Atheneum, 1985.
Brothers. Salt Lake City, Utah, Deseret, 1986.
Nutty Can't Miss. New York, Atheneum, 1987.
Theo Zephyr. New York, Atheneum, 1987.

Nutty Knows All. New York, Atheneum, 1988.
Family Pose. New York, Atheneum, 1989; as *Family Picture,* New York, Scholastic, 1990.
Jelly's Circus. New York, Aladdin, 1989.
Nutty the Movie Star. New York, Atheneum, 1989.
End of the Race. New York, Atheneum, 1993.
Nutty's Ghost. New York, Atheneum, 1993.
Re-Elect Nutty! New York, Atheneum, forthcoming.
One-Man Team. New York, Random House, 1994.
The Trophy. New York, Knopf, 1994.
Backup Soccer Star. New York, Random House, 1995.

Angel Park All-Stars Series

Volume 1, *Making the Team,* illustrated by Dennis Lyall. New York, Knopf, 1990.
Volume 2, *Big Base Hit,* illustrated by Dennis Lyall. New York, Knopf, 1990.
Volume 3, *Winning Streak,* illustrated by Dennis Lyall. New York, Knopf, 1990.
Volume 4, *What a Catch!,* illustrated by Dennis Lyall. New York, Knopf, 1990.
Volume 5, *Rookie Star,* illustrated by Dennis Lyall. New York, Knopf, 1990.
Volume 6, *Pressure Play,* illustrated by Dennis Lyall. New York, Knopf, 1990.
Volume 7, *Line Drive,* illustrated by Dennis Lyall. New York, Knopf, 1990.
Volume 8, *Championship Game,* illustrated by Dennis Lyall. New York, Knopf, 1990.
Volume 9, *Superstar Team,* Dennis Lyall. New York, Knopf, 1991.
Volume 10, *Stroke of Luck,* illustrated by Dennis Lyall. New York, Knopf, 1991.
Volume 11, *Safe at First,* illustrated by Dennis Lyall. New York, Knopf, 1991.
Volume 12, *Up to Bat,* illustrated by Dennis Lyall. New York, Knopf, 1991.
Volume 13, *Play-Off,* illustrated by Dennis Lyall. New York, Knopf, 1991.
Volume 14, *All Together Now,* illustrated by Dennis Lyall. New York, Knopf, 1991.

Angel Park Soccer Stars Series

Volume 1, *Kickoff Time,* illustrated by Dennis Lyall. New York, Knopf, 1991.
Volume 2, *Defense!,* illustrated by Dennis Lyall. New York, Knopf, 1991.
Volume 3, *Victory Goal,* illustrated by Dennis Lyall. New York, Knopf, 1992.
Volume 4, *Psyched!,* illustrated by Dennis Lyall. New York, Knopf, 1992.
Volume 5, *Backup Goalie,* illustrated by Dennis Lyall. New York, Knopf, 1992.
Volume 6, *Total Soccer,* illustrated by Dennis Lyall. New York, Knopf, 1992.
Volume 7, *Shake Up,* illustrated by Dennis Lyall. New York, Knopf, 1993.
Volume 8, *Quick Moves,* illustrated by Dennis Lyall. New York, Knopf, 1993.

Angel Park Hoop Stars Series

Volume 1, *Nothing but Net,* illustrated by Dennis Lyall. New York, Knopf, 1992.
Volume 2, *Point Guard,* illustrated by Dennis Lyall. New York, Knopf, 1992.
Volume 3, *Go to the Hoop!,* illustrated by Dennis Lyall. New York, Knopf, 1993.
Volume 4, *On the Line,* illustrated by Dennis Lyall. New York, Knopf, 1993.

Angel Park Karate Stars Series

Volume 1, *Find the Power.* New York, Random House, 1994.

Angel Park Football Stars Series

Volume 1, *Quarterback Hero.* New York, Random House, 1994.

Lucky Series

Lucky Breaks Loose. Salt Lake City, Utah, Deseret, 1990.
Lucky's Crash Landing. Salt Lake City, Utah, Deseret, 1990.
Lucky's Gold Mine. Salt Lake City, Utah, Deseret, 1990.
Lucky Fights Back. Salt Lake City, Utah, Deseret, 1991.
Lucky's Mud Festival. Salt Lake City, Utah, Deseret, 1991.
Lucky the Detective. Salt Lake City, Utah, Deseret, 1992.
Lucky's Tricks. Salt Lake City, Utah, Deseret, 1992.
Lucky's Cool Club. Salt Lake City, Deseret, 1993.
Lucky in Love. Salt Lake City, Deseret, 1993.
Lucky Comes Home. Salt Lake City, Deseret, 1994.

Mormon Historical Fiction Series

Under the Same Stars. Salt Lake City, Utah, Deseret, 1979.
As Wide as the River. Salt Lake City, Utah, Deseret, 1980.
Facing the Enemy. Salt Lake City, Utah, Deseret, 1982.
Cornbread and Prayer. Salt Lake City, Utah, Deseret, 1988.

Other

Contributor, *Monsters, Ghoulies, and Creepy Creatures,* edited by Lee Bennett Hopkins. Morton Grove, Illinois, Whitman, 1977.
Contributor, *Merrily Comes Our Harvest In,* edited by Lee Bennett Hopkins. Orlando, Florida, Harcourt Brace, 1978.
Romance and Psychological Realism in William Godwin's Novels. Salem, New Hampshire, Arno, 1981.
The Mormon Church: A Basic History. Salt Lake City, Utah, Deseret, 1986.
Baseball Tips (nonfiction), with Tom Hughes, illustrated by Dennis Lyall. New York, Random House, 1993.
Great Stories from Mormon History (nonfiction), with Tom Hughes, Salt Lake City, Utah, Deseret, 1995.
We'll Bring the World His Truth (nonfiction), with Tom Hughes, Salt Lake City, Utah, Deseret, 1995.

PUBLICATIONS FOR ADULTS

Fiction

Lullaby and Goodnight (as D.T. Hughes). New York, Pocket Books, 1992.

Children of the Promise Series

Volume 1, *Rumors of War*. Salt Lake City, Utah, Deseret, 1997.
Volume 2, *Since You Went Away*. Salt Lake City, Utah, Deseret, 1997.

Dean Hughes comments:

I've always had a wide variety of interests. As a kid, I was as rough-and-tumble as the next boy, without the slightest fear of dirt. But my mom taught me to embroider, and I loved that too. Of course, I also love to read. In high school I played football, was on the debate team, and I wrote for the school literary magazine. And now, I write middle-grade humor; a sports series; historical fiction; mysteries; and serious, literary books for young adults. I have also published nonsense verse and an adult true-crime book.

I might be better off, commercially, to find a niche and stay with it. But I get so many ideas for stories for different ages and audiences, and I hate to limit myself to one kind of book. I happen to believe that an author can do excellent, important work in a book of humor, in a sports novel, or in a series book. I will admit, however, that my greatest love is to write serious fiction as I have done in books like *Family Pose* and *End of the Race*.

*   *   *

Dean Hughes has written a wide variety of books for children and young adults. In most of his books, Hughes focuses on the day-to-day struggles of growing up. Occasionally, however, he addresses some of the larger issues that young people face, treating them with sensitivity and understanding. While he primarily concentrates on books for upper elementary and middle school students, his stories frequently span several grade levels by introducing characters of different ages.

The ability to create honest and believable characters—characters with whom young readers can empathize and relate—is Hughes' main strength as a writer. The interest generated by particular characters has led to several series for Hughes, including his ''Lucky Ladd,'' books, his ''Nutty'' books, ''The Angel Park All Stars'' books, ''The Angel Park Soccer'' books, and his sports series. Although these books primarily feature grade-school children, interest in them often continues into the middle school, and they usually exemplify his themes of love, unity, and growing up.

Brothers (1986) brings together nine-year-old Dokey and his nineteen-year-old brother, Rob. While the book would not appeal to many high school students, it is certainly beyond the ability of most nine-year-olds. The adventure of hunting and the excitement of surviving in the snow makes it an interesting book for many students.

In the book, Rob is confronted with his own personal set of self-doubts, even though the story is told in third person from Dokey's point of view. Both boys struggle with their own conflicts as they attempt to reach out to one another through the differences created by time and age. Rob is struggling with his lifetime plan of spending two years doing missionary work and must also wrestle with the emotional conflicts brought about by his shaky relationship with his girlfriend. Dokey is simply trying to outgrow his nickname and redefine his position in his family. In this way, both brothers are struggling with growing up and this draws in readers of all ages who are faced with some of the same problems.

Many of his books, including *Brothers,* include references to Hughes' Mormon background without becoming overly didactic or preachy. His Mormon history trilogy, *Under the Same Stars* (1979), *As Wide as the River* (1980), and *Facing the Enemy* (1982) deals with the Mormon expulsion from Missouri and the ordeal of establishing a new colony as a part of the American westward expansion. It is a historical tale, an adventure story, a character study, and a religious history. The focus is not on the religion but on the characters. As in many of his books, he is able to involve readers of several ages by not stressing the age of the protagonist.

In the first book, the Williams' family has been called to be a part of the new settlement, and young Joseph has been told by the Prophet Joseph Smith that God has a special job for him. Joseph Williams is not an extraordinary boy—he gets into trouble, is willing to fight, and frequently resents his strict religious training. Although Joseph is only nine, his struggles and resentments can be appreciated by an audience which is much older and, in fact, should be older. Facing bigotry and hatred of those who do not want the Mormons to settle in Missouri, Joseph grows up much faster than his years might suggest.

In the last two parts of the trilogy, Joseph continues to grow, discovering that he must continue to struggle, sometimes with his own people. After facing the fact that the world can be wrong, he finally must face the knowledge that his own people may be wrong—a major obstacle in growing up for most young adults.

Two of Hughes' finest novels for the young adult audience never mention his interest in Mormon religion but are consistent in their repetition of his themes of love, family, and unity. One of his first young adult novels is *Switching Tracks* (1982). It is the story of a young boy who lives with guilt after his father's suicide, and an old man who is facing cancer and death. Although the resolution seems almost too simple in this realistic novel of facing mortality, Hughes' strength in developing believable and honest characters is at its pinnacle in this book. Mark's development as a troubled teenager fighting to protect his sanity, blocking all attempts by his mother to help him, and dealing with his horror of daring his father to kill himself is contrasted effectively with the characterization of Willard, a tired, old, railroad worker who knows he is dying. Neither man nor boy can cure the problems, but they find comfort in helping each other.

Family Pose (1989) is also about lonely people crossing barriers of age to find comfort. David is only eleven, but he is an orphan and a runaway. Paul is a forty-year-old alcoholic who works at a small hotel. As the story develops, so do the characters. Inside the hotel there are several workers; most of them are loners, most of them are very sad. In their effort to help David, they are brought together, and Paul and David both find a family to fill their lives.

Hooper Haller (1981) and *Jenny Haller* (1983), books in which the title characters are descendants of Joseph Williams from the Mormon trilogy, are directed at older readers. Both characters discover that the struggles to grow up do not end with high school graduation. Hooper goes directly to the major leagues after high school, while Jenny decides between law school and marriage.

Throughout his books Hughes concentrates on messages of unity, truth, and love, but the primary tie which pulls all of his works together is the note of hope on which they usually end. While it detracts from the realism in some cases, it also makes them very satisfying.

—Judith Gero John

HUGHES, (James Mercer) Langston

Nationality: American. **Born:** Joplin, Montana, 1 February 1902. **Education:** Columbia University, New York, 1921-22; Lincoln University, Jefferson City, Montana, A.B. 1929. Poet, novelist, short story writer, playwright, song lyricist, radio writer, translator, author of juvenile books, and lecturer. In early years worked as assistant cook, launderer, busboy, and at other odd jobs; worked as seaman on voyages to Africa and Europe. Madrid correspondent for *Baltimore Afro-American,* 1937; visiting professor in creative writing, Atlanta University, Georgia, 1947; poet in residence, Laboratory School, University of Chicago, Illinois, 1949. **Awards:** *Opportunity* magazine literary contest, first prize in poetry, 1925; Amy Spingarn Contest, *Crisis* magazine, poetry and essay prizes, 1925; Witter Bynner undergraduate poetry prize contests, first prize, 1926; *Palms* magazine Intercollegiate Poetry award, 1927; Harmon Gold Medal for Literature, 1931, for *Not without Laughter;* Rosenwald Fellowships, 1931, 1941; Guggenheim fellowship for creative work, 1935; Litt.D., Lincoln University, 1943, Howard University, 1960, Western Reserve University, 1964; National Institute and American Academy of Arts and Letters grant, 1947; Anisfeld-Wolfe award for best book on racial relations, 1954; Spingarn Medal, National Association for the Advancement of Colored People, 1960. **Died:** 22 May 1967.

PUBLICATIONS FOR ADULTS and Young Adults

Poetry

The Weary Blues. New York, Knopf, 1926.
Fine Clothes to the Jew. New York, Knopf, 1927.
Dear Lovely Death. Amenia, New York, Troutbeck Press, 1931.
The Negro Mother and Other Dramatic Recitations. New York, Golden Stair Press, 1931.
Scottsboro Limited: Four Poems and a Play. New York, Golden Stair Press, 1932.
A New Song. New York, International Workers Order, 1938.
Shakespeare in Harlem, with Robert Glenn. New York, Knopf, 1942.
Freedom's Plow. New York, Musette Publishers, 1943.
Jim Crow's Last Stand. Negro Publication Society of America, 1943.
Lament for Dark Peoples and Other Poems. Azusa, California, Holland, 1944.
Fields of Wonder. New York, Knopf, 1947.
One-Way Ticket. New York, Knopf, 1949.
Montage of a Dream Deferred. New York, Holt, 1951.
Ask Your Mama: 12 Moods for Jazz. New York, Knopf, 1961.
The Panther and the Lash: Poems of Our Times. New York, Vintage, 1967.

Novels

Not without Laughter. New York, Knopf, 1930.
Tambourines to Glory. New York, John Day, 1958.

Short Stories

The Ways of White Folks. New York, Knopf, 1934.
Simple Speaks His Mind. New York, Simon & Schuster, 1950.
Laughing to Keep from Crying. New York, Holt, 1952.

Simple Takes a Wife. New York, Simon & Schuster, 1953.
Simple Stakes a Claim. New York, Rinehart, 1957.
Something in Common and Other Stories. New York, Hill & Wang, 1963.
Simple's Uncle Sam. New York, Hill & Wang, 1965.

Autobiography

The Big Sea. New York, Knopf, 1940.
I Wonder as I Wander. New York, Rinehart, 1956.

Nonfiction

A Negro Looks at Soviet Central Asia. Co-operative Publishing Society of Foreign Workers in the U.S.S.R., 1934.
The Sweet Flypaper of Life, with Roy De Carava. New York, Simon & Schuster, 1955.
A Pictorial History of the Negro in America, with Milton Meltzer. New York, Crown, 1956; 4th edition published as *A Pictorial History of Blackamericans,* 1973.
Fight for Freedom: The Story of the NAACP. New York, Norton, 1962.
Black Magic: A Pictorial History of the Negro in American Entertainment, with Milton Meltzer. Englewood Cliffs, New Jersey, Prentice-Hall, 1967.
Black Misery. Middlebury, Vermont, Paul S. Eriksson, 1969.

Editor

Four Lincoln University Poets. Jefferson City, Montana, Lincoln University, 1930.
The Poetry of the Negro, 1746-1949, with Arna Bontemps. New York, Doubleday, 1949; revised edition, as *The Poetry of the Negro, 1746-1970,* 1970.
Lincoln University Poets, with Waring Cuney and Bruce M. Wright. Fine Editions, 1954.
The Book of Negro Folklore, with Arna Bontemps. New York, Dodd, 1958.
An African Treasury: Articles, Essays, Stories, Poems by Black Africans. New York, Crown, 1960.
Poems from Black Africa. Bloomington, Indiana University Press, 1963.
New Negro Poets: U.S. Bloomington, Indiana University Press, 1964.
The Book of Negro Humor. New York, Dodd, 1966.
The Best Short Stories by Negro Writers: An Anthology from 1899 to the Present. Boston, Little, Brown, 1967.

Omnibus Volumes

Selected Poems. New York, Knopf, 1959.
The Best of Simple. New York, Hill & Wang, 1961.
Five Plays by Langston Hughes, edited by Webster Smalley. Bloomington, Indiana University Press, 1963.
The Langston Hughes Reader. New York, Braziller, 1968.
Don't You Turn Back (poems), edited by Lee Bennett Hopkins. New York, Knopf, 1969.
Good Morning Revolution: The Uncollected Social Protest Writing of Langston Hughes, edited by Faith Berry. Brooklyn, New York, Lawrence Hill, 1973.

Other

Translator, with Mercer Cook, *Masters of Dew,* by Jacques Roumain. New York, Reynal & Hitchcock, 1947.

Translator, with Frederic Carruthers, *Cuba Libre,* by Nicolas Guillen. Los Angeles, Anderson & Ritchie, 1948.

Translator, *Selected Poems of Gabriela Mistral.* Bloomington, Indiana University Press, 1957.

Arna Bontemps-Langston Hughes Letters: 1925-1967, with Arna Bontemps, edited by Charles H. Nichols, New York, Dodd, 1980.

Also author of numerous plays (most have been produced), including *Little Ham,* 1935, *Mulatto,* 1935, *Emperor of Haiti,* 1936, *Troubled Island,* 1936, *When the Jack Hollers,* 1936, *Front Porch,* 1937, *Joy to My Soul,* 1937, *Soul Gone Home,* 1937, *Little Eva's End,* 1938, *Limitations of Life,* 1938, *The Em-Fuehrer Jones,* 1938, *Don't You Want to Be Free,* 1938, *The Organizer,* 1939, *The Sun Do Move,* 1942, *For This We Fight,* 1943, *The Barrier,* 1950, *The Glory Round His Head,* 1953, *Simply Heavenly,* 1957, *Esther,* 1957, *The Ballad of the Brown King,* 1960, *Black Nativity,* 1961, *Gospel Glow,* 1962, *Jericho-Jim Crow,* 1963, *Tambourines to Glory,* 1963, *The Prodigal Son,* 1965, *Soul Yesterday and Today, Angelo Herndon Jones, Mother and Child, Trouble with the Angels,* and *Outshines the Sun.*

Also author of screenplay, *Way Down South,* 1942. Author of libretto for operas, *The Barrier,* 1950, and *Troubled Island.* Lyricist for *Just Around the Corner,* and for *Kurt Weill's Street Scene,* 1948. Columnist for *Chicago Defender* and *New York Post.* Poetry, short stories, criticism, and plays have been included in numerous anthologies.

PUBLICATIONS FOR CHILDREN

Popo and Fifina: Children of Haiti, with Arna Bontemps. London, Macmillan, 1932.

The First Book of Negroes. New York, F. Watts, 1952.

Famous American Negroes. New York, Dodd, 1954.

The First Book of Rhythms. New York, F. Watts, 1954.

Famous Negro Music Makers. New York, Dodd, 1955.

The First Book of Jazz. New York, F. Watts, 1955.

The First Book of the West Indies. New York, F. Watts, 1956; as *The First Book of the Caribbean,* London, E. Ward, 1965.

Famous Negro Heroes of America. New York, Dodd, 1958.

The First Book of Africa. New York, F. Watts, 1960.

*

Biography: Entries in *Dictionary of Literary Biography,* Detroit, Gale, Volume 4: *American Writers in Paris, 1920-1939,* 1980; Volume 7: *Twentieth-Century American Dramatists,* 1981; Volume 48: *American Poets, 1880-1945, Second Series,* 1986; Volume 51: *Afro-American Writers from the Harlem Renaissance to 1940,* 1987;

Manuscript Collections: James Weldon Johnson Memorial Collection, Beinecke Library, Yale University, New Haven, Connecticut; Schomburg Collection of the New York Public Library;

Lincoln University Library, Pennsylvania; Fisk University Library, Nashville, Tennessee.

Critical Studies: Entry in *Children's Literature Review,* Volume 17, Detroit, Gale, 1989; entry in *Contemporary Literary Criticism,* Detroit, Gale, Volume 1, 1973, Volume 5, 1976, Volume 10, 1979, Volume 15, 1980, Volume 35, 1985, Volume 44, 1987.

*   *   *

During the Harlem Renaissance when the work of African-American writers was initially acknowledged as a significant feature of American literature, Langston Hughes achieved a position of prominence that eventually led to his recognition as "the Laureate of Black America." A wider historical perspective indicates that Hughes was an important contributor to an American poetic renaissance in which a singularly American voice—initially introduced by Walt Whitman—emerged as a distinct variant to the lingering strain of the British tradition still dominant in the United States. Hughes's poetry encompasses some of the experimentalism of such contemporaries as e. e. cummings and Marianne Moore, as well as the more immediately accessible lyricism of Carl Sandburg and the authenticity of community speech found in Robert Frost. He was driven by a desire to "explain and illuminate the Negro condition in America," and he was a pioneer in combining the rhythms of street speech, the blues, and the language of the black community with the formal patterns and structural conventions of the traditional English poetry he had mastered.

Hughes is not generally regarded as a poet whose work is specifically addressed to young adult readers and listeners, but in his attempt to address the concerns of African Americans while exploring the universal questions of human existence, he has excluded no part of an audience with a degree of literacy and a grasp of the fundamentals of language. Almost all of his poetry is accessible and engaging because Hughes was influenced by such popular American poets as Sandburg, Vachel Lindsay, and Edgar Lee Masters who were interested in reaching a wide audience rather than a literary elite, but certain aspects of Hughes's poetry have a particular appeal for younger readers. The spirit of optimism and his faith in human beings pervades most of his work, but it is tempered by realistic assessment of the effects of racial hatred. There is a sense of a justifiable grievance in Hughes's writing, but it almost never shades into bitterness, so that the positive elements don't seem shallow or spurious. Instead, they reflect a determination to transcend the destructive and soul-crushing tendencies of poems written in rage and frustration.

With a title that echoes Sandburg, "I, too, sing America" is a call for inclusion, an anticipation of multicultural diversity that Hughes saw as one of the strengths of an American society that had tried to deny its rich ethnic mix. In spite of the history of racial terror and violence that Hughes knew from his own experience as well as from his reading, he saw himself in the spirit of Whitman as a poet who would not turn away from an idealistic vision of the promise of America. Hughes's self-description as "the darker brother" suggests the guilt haunting the American conscience but it is balanced by his belief in a true family that isn't riven by superficial differences but joined by the decency latent in most people. His appeal to this quality depends on his conviction that "They'll see / How beautiful I am / And be ashamed." His conclusion to the poem, "I, too, am America" is a testament of faith in his countrymen and women to recognize and appreciate the contributions of African-American citizens.

The poem "The Negro Speaks of Rivers" is a corollary in which Hughes suggests the richness of the historical legacy that African-Americans have brought to American society. Blending the history and heritage of black people who "bathed in the Euphrates when dawns were young," who "looked upon the Nile and raised the pyramids above it," with their lives in America where they "heard the singing of the Mississippi when Abe Lincoln / went down to New Orleans," Hughes opens a passage of centuries previously ignored by school texts. The concluding line, "My soul has grown deep like the rivers," is an attempt to project the elusive but powerful spirit of black culture that has enriched American lives into an image that can touch all Americans.

"Harlem" operates around the crucial question of "What happens to a dream deferred?" and offers the unsettling suggestion that it can "dry up / like a raisin in the sun," or that it can "explode" into violence. This prophetic poem, written in 1951, is not only a perceptive assessment of the psychological impact of racist policies, but a statement of the fragility of a young person's dreams. Characteristically, Hughes sees the counter-possibilities that can preserve the dream until it is realized, offering in "Dream Boogie" the awakening of the dream into the "good morning" of a "boogie-woogie rumble." Here, the irrepressible spirit of African-American vitality is projected in jazz rhythms—the sounds of survival—leading the poet to say, encouragingly: Sure, / I'm happy! / Take it away!/ He, pop! / Re-bop! / Mop! / Y-e-a-h!"

The energy, exuberance and playful sense of language illustrated here is one of the features that Hughes purposefully incorporated into his poetry as a literary equivalent of the verbal dexterity and intricate rhythmic structures of black music and colloquial speech. The poem "Children's Rhymes" skillfully weaves street chants and pointed commentary about how opportunity is often dependent on racial status: By what sends / the white kids / I ain't sent: / I know I can't / be President.

Hughes adjusts a familiar patriotic phrase by a sarcastic insertion—"Liberty And Justice— / Huh—For All."—before concluding the poem with the jump-rope chant: "Oop-pop-a-da! / Skee! Daddle-de-do! / Be-bop! / Salt' peanuts! / De-dop!"

A more meditative mood occurs in some of Hughes's reflective poems which focus on a young person near the beginning of life's journey. In "Mother to Son," the trials of the speaker ("Life for me ain't been no crystal stair") are acknowledged as basic, but the thrust of the poem is toward guidance and encouragement. The mother's example of perseverance ("I'se been a-climbin' on. . .And sometimes goin' in the dark / Where there ain't been no light") leads to an exhortation ("So boy, don't you turn back") stressing the necessity for endurance, exemplified by the older black woman who is still "climbin' on." The uncertainty and expectancy of a youth approaching adulthood is conveyed by Hughes's "Theme for English B," where he expresses the perennial doubt of an inquisitive young person who observes, "It's not easy to know what is true for you or me"—a universal exclamation—and proceeds with a series of meditative queries about life, skillfully joining youthful questions ("Me-who?") with the additional burden of racial consciousness. Even the poems like "Uncle Tom" or "Ballad of the Landlord" which are more caustic in their criticism of American society are cast in the mode of an observer commenting in sorrow rather than direct exhortations to action, and

the lament "Song for a Dark Girl" places the horrifying image of a lynching in lyric form, which ameliorates the effect to some degree.

The same spirit of generosity and hope that informs Hughes's poetry is also present in his short fiction and in his two-volume autobiography. The occasionally anthologized story "On the Road" in which a black man is denied shelter at Christmastime and meets Christ on the highway combines Hughes's rueful humor and tempered judgement of the faults in American society, while the autobiography is generally a positive record of accomplishment and perseverance. In addition, Hughes invented a kind of voice-of-the-common-man he called Jesse B. Semple ("Just Be Simple") in 1943 who became very popular as a source of down-home wit and good sense in newspaper sketches Hughes eventually collected in four volumes. As in his poetry, these prose pieces are inspired by the same fundamental belief in the possibilities of American democracy that has made Hughes such an important and enduring figure in American literary history.

—Leon Lewis

HUGHES, Monica (Ince)

Nationality: Canadian. **Born:** Liverpool, England, 3 November 1925; daughter of the mathematician E.L. Ince; became Canadian citizen, 1957. **Education:** the Convent of the Holy Child Jesus, Harrogate, Yorkshire, graduated 1942; Edinburgh University, 1942-43. **Military Service:** Served in the Women's Royal Naval Service, 1943-46. **Family:** Married Glen Hughes in 1957; two daughters and two sons. Dress designer, London, 1948-49, and Bulawayo, Rhodesia (now Zimbabwe), 1950; bank clerk Umtali, Rhodesia, 1951; laboratory technician, National Research Council, Ottawa, 1952-57. Since 1975 full-time writer; writer in residence at several universities, including University of Alberta, 1984-85. **Awards:** Vicky Metcalf award from Canadian Authors Association, 1981, for body of work, 1983, for short story "The Iron-Barred Door" in *Anthology 2*; Alberta Culture Juvenile Novel award, Bay's Beaver award, both 1981, for *Hunter in the Dark*; Canada Council prize for children's literature, 1982, a best book for young adults by the American Library Association and Young Adult Canadian Book award, both 1983; Canada Council prize for children's literature, 1981, for *The Guardian of Isis*; *The Keeper of the Isis Light* was named a best book for young adults by the American Library Association, 1981, and named to International Board on Books for Young People's honor list, 1982; Guardian award runner-up, 1983, for *Ring-Rise, Ring-Set*; Alberta R. Ross Annett award from Writers Guild of Alberta, 1983, 1984, 1986, 1992; Hans Christian Andersen award nomination, 1984. **Agent:** Pamela Paul Agency Inc., 253 High Park Avenue, Toronto, Ontario MGP 255. **Address:** 13816 110A Ave., Edmonton, Alberta T5M 2M9, Canada.

PUBLICATIONS FOR YOUNG ADULTS

Fiction

Gold-Fever Trail: A Klondike Adventure, illustrated by Patricia Peacock. Edmonton, Alberta, LeBel, 1974.
Crisis on Conshelf Ten. Toronto, Methuen, and London, Mammoth, 1992; New York, Atheneum, 1977.

Earthdark. London, Mammoth, 1991; Toronto, Methuen, 1981.

The Ghost Dance Caper. London, Mammoth, 1978; Toronto, Methuen, 1986.

The Tomorrow City. London, Mammoth, 1992; Toronto, Methuen, 1982.

Beyond the Dark River. London, Mammoth, 1979; New York, Atheneum, 1981.

The Beckoning Lights, illustrated by Richard A. Conroy. Edmonton, Alberta, LeBel, 1982, and New York, Watts, 1982.

Hunter in the Dark. Toronto, Irwin, 1982; New York, Atheneum, 1982.

Ring-Rise, Ring-Set. London, MacRae, and New York, Watts, 1992; Toronto, Methuen, 1983.

The Treasure of the Long Sault, illustrated by Richard A. Conroy. Edmonton, Alberta, LeBel, 1982.

My Name Is Paula Popowich!, illustrated by Leoung O'Young. Toronto, Lorimer, 1983.

Space Trap. Vancouver, Groundwood/Douglas & McIntyre, and London, MacRae, 1983; New York, Watts, 1984.

Devil on My Back. London, MacRae, 1984; New York, Atheneum, 1985; Don Mills, Collier MacMillan, 1985.

Sandwriter. London, MacRae, 1984; Markham, Ontario, Franklin Watts, 1986; and New York, Holt, 1988.

Blaine's Way. Toronto, Irwin, 1986; London, Severn House, 1988.

The Dream Catcher. London, MacRae, 1986; New York, Atheneum, 1987.

Log Jam. Toronto, Irwin, 1987; as *Spirit River,* London, Methuen, 1988.

The Promise. Toronto, Stoddart, and London, Methuen, 1989; New York, Simon & Schuster, 1992.

The Refuge. Toronto, Doubleday, 1989; Don Mills, Stoddart, 1992.

Invitation to the Game. Toronto, HarperCollins, 1990; New York, Simon & Schuster, 1990; London, Methuen, 1991.

The Crystal Drop. London, Methuen, 1992; New York, Simon & Schuster, 1993; Toronto, HarperCollins, 1992.

A Handful of Seeds. Toronto, Lester, 1993.

The Golden Aquarians. Toronto, HarperCollins, and New York, Simon & Schuster, 1994.

Castle Tourmandyne. Toronto, HarperCollins, and New York, Simon & Schuster, 1995.

Where Have You Been, Billy Boy? Toronto, HarperCollins, 1995.

The Seven Magpies. Toronto, HarperCollins, 1996.

The Faces of Fear. Toronto, HarperCollins, 1997.

With Carlos Freire, *Jan's Big Bang.* Halifax, Formac, 1997.

The Story Box. Toronto, HarperCollins, forthcoming.

"Isis" Trilogy

The Keeper of the Isis Light. London, Mammoth, 1980; New York, Atheneum, 1981.

The Guardian of Isis. London, Mammoth, 1981; New York, Atheneum, 1982.

The Isis Pedlar. London, Mammoth, 1982; New York, Atheneum, 1983.

Contributor

Magook. Toronto, McClelland & Stewart, 1977.

Out of Time. London, Bodley Head, 1984; New York, Harper, 1985.

Dragons and Dreams. New York, Harper, 1985.

The Windows of Dreams. London, Methuen, 1986.

Take Your Knee Off My Heart. London, Methuen, 1990.

Mother's Day. London, Methuen, 1992.

The Unseen: Scary Stories, selected by Janet Lunn. Toronto, Lester, 1994.

Short stories are included in *Owl's Fun Book for Spring, Summer and Fall,* Grey de Pencier, 1982; *Canadian Children's Annual,* Grolier, 1988; *Canadian Children's Treasury,* Key Porter, 1988.

PUBLICATIONS FOR CHILDREN

Fiction

Little Fingerling: A Japanese Folk Tale, illustrated by Brenda Clark. Toronto, Kids Can Press, 1989.

Dipper in Danger, illustrated by Robert McPhillips. Oxford, Heinemann, 1996.

Dipper Gets Stuck, illustrated by Robert McPhillips. Oxford, Heinemann, 1996.

Dipper and the Old Wreck, illustrated by Robert McPhillips. Oxford, Heinemann, 1996.

The Dirty Car, illustrated by Julie Park. Aylesbury, Ginn, 1996.

Lost at the School Fair, illustrated by Julie Park. Aylesbury, Ginn, 1996.

Woof woof!, illustrated by Julie Park. Aylesbury, Ginn, 1996.

Nonfiction

With Betty Root, *All Abroad: Map and Characters.* Aylesbury, Ginn, 1994.

With Betty Root, *Guinea Pigs.* Aylesbury, Ginn, 1994.

With Betty Root, *Hedgehogs.* Aylesbury, Ginn, 1994.

With Betty Root, *Odd One Out,* photographs by Steve Gorton. Aylesbury, Ginn, 1995.

With Betty Root, *What's in Here?,* photographs by Steve Gorton. Aylesbury, Ginn, 1995.

With Betty Root, *Living in the Garden,* illustrated by Karen Hiscock. Aylesbury, Ginn, 1995.

With Betty Root, *Animal Homes,* illustrated by Alan Male. Aylesbury, Ginn, 1995.

With Betty Root, *Look Where I Live,* illustrated by David Price. Aylesbury, Ginn, 1995.

With Betty Root, *Animals that Hide,* illustrated by Gail Rose. Aylesbury, Ginn, 1995.

With Betty Root, *People Who Help Us,* illustrated by Lesley Smith. Aylesbury, Ginn, 1995.

Publications for Adults

"Towards Empowerment: Reflections on Children's Literature," in *Images of the Child,* edited by Harry Eiss. Bowling Green, Ohio, Popular, 1994.

*

Biography: Essay in *Something about the Author Autobiography Series,* Volume 11, Detroit, Gale, 1991; entry in *Sixth Book of Junior Authors and Illustrators,* New York, Wilson, 1989; essay in *Speaking for Ourselves, Too* compiled and edited by Donald R. Gallo, National Council of Teachers of English, 1993; entry in

Writing Stories, Making Pictures, Canadian Children's Book Centre, Toronto, CCBC, 1994 .

Manuscript Collections: University of Calgary, Alberta.

Critical Studies: Entry in *Children's Literature Review,* Volume 9, Detroit, Gale, 1985, pp. 61-79.

Monica Hughes comments:

I write in response to my excitement at the wonder of our world, and sometimes in response to my dismay at what we are doing to it. About two-thirds of my novels are in the science fiction genre, and, like the myths of old, may be a metaphor for contrary ideas that resonate with young people: independence and loneliness, adventure and responsibility, technology and the environment.

I don't search for ideas; they find me—in ordinary events, in people I meet, in articles in magazines or items in the newspaper. What they have in common is that they catch my interest and I find myself asking: What would happen if. . . ?

—What if a carousel could send one into the future?

—What if a doll-house were haunted by its evil designer?

—How might a virtual-reality game affect a disabled girl?

These questions find a place in my "Ideas" file and may eventually become another book.

*   *   *

From her first young adult novel, *Gold-Fever Trail: A Klondike Adventure,* set during Canada's Gold Rush, Monica Hughes demonstrates the extensive research and careful attention to background detail that characterize her work; in fact, because of its authenticity, *Gold-Fever Trail* has been used as a supplemental history text in Alberta (Canada) schools. Hughes's recurring theme of self-reliance is central, as Harry and Sarah set out alone to find their father in the goldfields. Resourceful like all Hughes's protagonists, these motherless siblings find success far beyond their expectations.

In *The Ghost Dance Caper,* praised for its realistic description of the crime scene but criticized for its stereotypical Indian dialogue, Hughes depicts the search for individual identity, one of her favorite themes. Caught between the contempt of the "pureblood" Indians and the indifference of those who completely reject Indian ways, Tom, a young half-Blackfoot Indian, sets out to find his "spirit"—a task requiring access to a mystic "ghost bundle," available only through a museum burglary.

Identity is likewise the issue in *My Name Is Paula Popowich!,* as Paula Herman finds her paternal grandmother and discovers her half-Ukrainian heritage. Nearly twelve years old, Paula feels like a misfit in her mother's German-Canadian community; she even bleaches her hair to be blonde like everyone else. Gradually winning concessions from a mother embittered by the trials of single parenthood, Paula embraces her new identity.

Hughes sets several novels in the near future, describing technology that seems a plausible extension of what exists today. *Crisis on Conshelf Ten* and *Earthdark* relate adventures of young Kepler Masterman. Born on the Moon, he cannot adapt to the Earth's gravity; so his Earth visit is spent in an undersea colony which, like his lunar colony, is being exploited by the technocrats who initiated and support it. Hughes's concerns about the desirable limits of

technology and the exploitation of underdeveloped countries can be seen as Kepler discovers that humans have been transformed into "gillmen," better adapted to working underwater. In *Earthdark* Kepler returns to the Moon colony with news of governmental reform. Inspired by the alienation, fear, and loneliness she felt upon first seeing the Canadian prairie landscape, Hughes creates a forbidding lunar landscape as backdrop for the power struggle in this colony. *The Crystal Drop,* set in 2011, explores the vulnerability of the environment as global warming transforms the Canadian prairies while *The Golden Aquarians* depicts the conflict Walt Elliott faces as his father destroys planets' environments in order to make them habitable for human beings.

Another power struggle figures in *Beyond the Dark River,* Hughes's account of Canadian life after a nuclear holocaust. Again drawing inspiration from the bleak Canadian prairies, Hughes describes a world, populated primarily by urban mutants, in which only isolated, self-sufficient groups like the German Hutterites and the Cree Indians are relatively unaffected. The Hutterites live simple, communal farm lives, but theirs is a closed society, characterized by bigotry. More admirable to Hughes is the natural wisdom seen in the lifestyle of the Cree, who follow ancient tribal customs. Like many of Hughes's youthful protagonists, fifteen-year-old Benjamin is dispatched on a mission, dangerous but vital to his community: the Hutterites, who have rejected all knowledge except the Bible, now need information from urban libraries. With the help of a young Cree who is training to become a medicine woman, Benjamin gains not only the scientific data, but also an appreciation of another culture and the independence to oppose his community's bigotry.

In an equally bleak picture of the near future, *Ring-Rise, Ring-Set,* technology again is both a necessity and an evil. Hughes's fears about environmental pollution have been fulfilled: Earth is surrounded by dust rings which block the sun's rays, threatening a new ice age. The conflict between developed and primitive societies recurs as the City People possess the technology to dissolve the rings, but the procedure would endanger the Ekoes, who live close to nature. Ultimately the Ekoes choose their values over physical survival, while the City People debate whether preserving their civilization is worth the cost.

Although Hughes's weakest novels *(The Beckoning Lights* and *Space Trap)* involve interplanetary travel and alien beings, she skillfully portrays the results of space colonization in the "Isis" trilogy. *The Keeper of the Isis Light,* the first of these and generally considered Hughes's masterpiece, is the story of sixteen-year-old Olwen Pendennis, who has grown up on the planet of Isis, attended only by Guardian, an anthropomorphic robot programmed by her dying parents to provide for her every need. Olwen experiences no loneliness until she is rejected by Mark London, a young settler newly arrived from Earth. Since the Isis environment has proven fatal to Olwen's parents, Guardian attempts—perhaps unwisely—to ensure her welfare by physical modifications that enable her to adapt to the planet's atmosphere: wider nostrils, larger lungs, and reptilian skin. Hughes suggests that Mark's rejection is based on ethnic prejudice; the colonists, and especially he, urge Olwen to have these modifications reversed. However, Olwen is secure in her own individuality; so she chooses isolation over conformity and retreats to the upland area of the planet, leaving the more hospitable valley for the settlers, who increasingly spurn her help.

The Guardian of Isis, the second "Isis" novel, is set approximately four generations later, when the colony has regressed to a primitive agricultural society bound by myths and taboos. Jody N'Kumo, an intelligent and inquisitive young misfit, challenges these taboos by reinventing simple mechanical devices and investigating supposedly supernatural occurrences. Alarmed by danger that, in typical Hughes fashion, only he sees, Jody challenges the taboos once too often, and the President (Mark London) exiles him to the Ugly One's realm. Though the colonists consider this a virtual death sentence, Jody finds that the Ugly One (Olwen) has been trying to warn of an impending flood. Again Hughes shows a self-absorbed adolescent required to become altruistic; and, as is usually the case, Jody is the only one able to act at the crucial moment. Neither Olwen nor Guardian can dive to the lakebottom and remove the obstruction; so Jody must use all his courage, endurance, and concentration to save his people.

In *The Isis Pedlar,* the final "Isis" novel and also the weakest and most controversial, David N'Kumo, the nephew of Jody, falls in love with the daughter of Michael Flynn, an unscrupulous itinerant pedlar. Using drugs and conjuring tricks, the outsider Flynn exploits the primitive Isis colonists, and to save him from their rebellion, Jody is forced finally to become the colony's leader. Perhaps because Flynn is a rather unlikable rogue, the emphasis upon his Irish nationality has brought charges of ethnic stereotyping.

Where Have You Been, Billy Boy? begins in 1908 when orphaned Billy is taken in by elderly Johannes, carousel-operator at a carnival. Billy is thrilled about his new home, but wonders about the old man's nightly disappearances. Johannes' illness lets him learn the carousel's secret, that it's a time-machine. But when it transports him to 1993, Billy has difficulty trying to return because the decrepit carousel has been locked away in a barn.

In *The Seven Magpies,* set during World War II, fourteen-year-old Maureen Frazer is sent from eastern England to the supposedly safer west. There she confronts the Seven Magpies, a secret society of girls who participate in clandestine rituals, and a connection to the past helps solve a puzzle in the present. The novel is a many-leveled mystery blending ancient Celtic magic, standing stones and an ancient counting rhyme with the harshness of wartime and the possibility of spies.

Monica Hughes's novels are characterized by depth of characterization and plausibility of plot. Her protagonists are often literal or spiritual outsiders who must weigh the values of their societies. As her young adults struggle to become mature and responsible, they face universal young adult problems, but they also confront contemporary social and moral dilemmas for which Hughes offers some optimistic possibilities but no easy solutions.

—Charmaine Allmon Mosby, updated by Elbert R. Hill

HUGHES, Ted (Edward James Hughes)

Nationality: British. **Born:** Mytholmroyd, Yorkshire, 17 August 1930. **Education:** Mexborough Grammar School, Yorkshire; Pembroke College, Cambridge, 1951-54, B.A. in archaeology and anthropology 1954, M.A. 1959. **Military Service:** Served in the Royal Air Force, 1948-50. **Family:** Married 1) the poet Sylvia Plath in 1956 (died 1963); one daughter and one son; 2) Carol Orchard in 1970. **Career:** Worked as a rose gardener, night watchman in a steelworks, zoo attendant, teacher, and reader for the Rank Organisation, in the 1950s; taught at the University of Massachusetts, Amherst, 1957-58. Founding editor, with Daniel Weissbort, *Modern Poetry in Translation* magazine, London, 1964-71. **Awards:** First Prize, Young Men's and Young Women's Hebrew Association Poetry Center contest, 1957, and first prize, Guinness Poetry Awards, 1958, both for *The Hawk in the Rain*; Guggenheim fellow, 1959-60; Somerset Maugham award, 1960, Hawthornden Prize, 1961, and Abraham Wonsell Foundation awards, 1964-69, all for *Lupercal*; City of Florence International Poetry prize, 1969, for *Wodwo*; Premio Internazionale Taormina Prize, 1972; Etna-Taormina prize, 1973; Queen's Medal for Poetry, 1974; *Season Songs* was a Children's Book Showcase Title, 1976; O.B.E. (Officer, Order of the British Empire), 1977; *Signal* Poetry award, 1979, for *Moon-Bells and Other Poems,* 1981, for *Under the North Star,* and 1983, for *The Rattle Bag: An Anthology of Poetry*; Royal Society of Literature Heinemann award, 1980, for *Moortown*; Poet Laureate, 1984; *The Iron Man: A Story in Five Nights* (new edition) was exhibited at the Bologna International Children's Book Fair, and received the Kurt Maschler Emil award from the National Book League, both 1985; *Guardian* award, 1985, for *What Is the Truth? A Farmyard Fable for the Young*; Honorary Fellow, Pembroke College, Cambridge, 1986. Honorary doctorates: Exeter College, 1982, Open University, 1983, Bradford College, 1984, and Pembroke College, 1986. **Agent:** c/o Faber and Faber Ltd., 3 Queen's Square, London WC1N 3AU, England. Lives in North Tawton, Devon, England.

PUBLICATIONS FOR YOUNG ADULTS

Fiction

How the Whale Became and Other Stories, illustrated by George Adamson. London, Faber, 1963; illustrated by Rick Schreiter, New York, Atheneum, 1964.

The Iron Man: A Story in Five Nights, illustrated by George Adamson. London, Faber, 1968; as *The Iron Giant: A Story in Five Nights,* illustrated by Robert Nadler, New York, Harper, 1968.

Ffangs the Vampire Bat and the Kiss of Truth, illustrated by Chris Riddell. London, Faber, 1986.

Tales of the Early World, illustrated by Andrew Davidson. London, Faber, 1988.

The Iron Woman: A Sequel to The Iron Man, illustrated by Andrew Davidson. London and New York, Faber and Faber, 1994.

Poetry

Meet My Folks!, illustrated by George Adamson. London, Faber, 1961; Indianapolis, Bobbs-Merrill, 1973; revised edition, Faber, 1987.

The Earth-Owl and Other Moon-People, illustrated by R.A. Brandt. London, Faber, 1963; New York, Atheneum, 1964; as *Moon-Whales and Other Moon Poems,* illustrated by Leonard Baskin, New York, Viking Press, 1976; revised edition, as *Moon-Whales,* London, Faber, 1988.

Nessie, the Mannerless Monster, illustrated by Gerald Rose. London, Faber, 1964; as *Nessie the Monster,* illustrated by Jan Pyk, Indianapolis, Bobbs-Merrill, 1974.

Five Autumn Songs for Children's Voices, illustrated by Phillida Gili. Crediton, Devon, Gilbertson, 1969.

Autumn Song, illustrated by Nina Carroll. Kettering, Northamptonshire, Steane, 1971.

Spring, Summer, Autumn, Winter. London, Rainbow Press, 1974; revised edition, as *Season Songs,* illustrated by Leonard Baskin, New York, Viking Press, 1975; London, Faber, 1976; revised edition, Faber, 1987.

Earth-Moon, illustrated by the author. London, Rainbow Press, 1976.

Moon-Bells and Other Poems. London, Chatto and Windus, 1978.

Under the North Star, illustrated by Leonard Baskin. London, Faber, and New York, Viking Press, 1981.

What Is the Truth? A Farmyard Fable for the Young, illustrated by R.J. Lloyd. London, Faber, and New York, Harper, 1984.

The Cat and the Cuckoo. Winchester, Wykeham Press, 1988.

Plays

The Coming of the Kings (broadcast 1964; produced London, 1972). Included in *The Coming of the Kings and Other Plays, 1970.*

The Tiger's Bones (broadcast 1965). Included in *The Coming of the Kings and Other Plays, 1970.*

Beauty and the Beast (broadcast 1965; produced London, 1971). Included in *The Coming of the Kings and Other Plays, 1970.*

The Price of a Bride (broadcast 1966). Excerpt published in *Here, Now and Beyond,* edited by Nancy Coniston Martin, London, Oxford University Press, 1968.

The Demon of Adachigahara, music by Gordon Crosse (cantata; produced Shrewsbury, 1968). London, Oxford University Press, 1969.

Sean, The Fool, The Devil and the Cats (broadcast 1968; produced London, 1971). Included in *The Coming of the Kings and Other Plays, 1970.*

The Coming of the Kings and Other Plays (includes *Beauty and the Beast, Sean, the Fool, The Devil and the Cats, The Coming of the Kings,* and *The Tiger's Bones*). London, Faber, 1970; augmented edition as, *The Tiger's Bones and Other Plays for Children* (includes *Orpheus*), illustrated by Alan E. Cober, New York, Viking Press, 1974.

The Iron Man (televised 1972). London, Faber, 1973.

Orpheus (broadcast 1971). Chicago, Dramatic Publishing Company, 1973. Included in *The Tiger's Bones and Other Plays for Children,* 1974.

The Pig Organ; or, Pork with Perfect Pitch, music by Richard Blackford (produced London, 1980).

Radio Plays: *The Coming of the Kings,* 1964; *The Tiger's Bones,* 1965; *Beauty and the Beast,* 1965; *The Price of a Bride,* 1966; *The Head of Gold,* 1967; *Sean, The Fool, The Devil and the Cats,* 1968; *Orpheus,* 1971.

Other

Poetry in the Making: An Anthology of Poems and Programmes from "Listening and Writing". London, Faber, 1967; abridged edition, as *Poetry Is,* New York, Doubleday, 1970.

Editor, with Seamus Heaney, *The Rattle Bag: An Anthology of Poetry.* London, Faber, 1982.

PUBLICATIONS FOR ADULTS

Poetry

The Hawk in the Rain. London, Faber, and New York, Harper, 1957.

Pike. Northampton, Massachusetts, Gehenna Press, 1959.

Lupercal. London, Faber, and New York, Harper, 1960.

With Thom Gunn, *Selected Poems.* London, Faber, 1962.

The Burning of the Brothel. London, Turret, 1966.

The Recklings. London, Turret, 1967.

Scapegoats and Rabies: A Poem in Five Parts. London, Poet and Printer, 1967.

Animal Poems. Crediton, Devon, Gilbertson, 1967.

Gravestones (6 broadsides), linocuts by Gavin Robbins. Exeter, Devon, Exeter College of Art, 1967; as *Poems,* 1 volume, 1968.

Poems: Ted Hughes, Fainlight, and Sillitoe. London, Rainbow Press, 1967.

I Said Goodbye to Earth. London, Turret, 1969.

A Crow Hymn. Frensham, Surrey, Sceptre Press, 1970.

The Martyrdom of Bishop Farrar. Crediton, Devon, Gilbertson, 1970.

A Few Crows. Exeter, Devon, Rougemont Press, 1970.

Four Crow Poems. Privately printed, 1970.

Crow: From the Life and Songs of the Crow. London, Faber, 1970; New York, Harper, 1971; revised edition, London, Faber, 1972.

Fighting for Jerusalem. Ashington, Northumberland, Mid-NAG, 1970.

Amulet. Privately printed, 1970.

Corgi Modern Poets in Focus I, with others, edited by Dannie Abse. London, Corgi, 1971.

Crow Wakes: Poems. Woodford Gree, Essex, Poet and Printer, 1971.

Poems, with Ruth Fainlight and Alan Sillitoe. London, Rainbow Press, 1971.

In the Little Girl's Angel Gaze. London, Steam Press, 1972.

Selected Poems, 1957-1967, illustrated by Leonard Baskin. London, Faber, 1972; New York, Harper, 1973.

Prometheus on His Crag: 21 Poems, illustrated by Leonard Baskin. London, Rainbow Press, 1973.

The Interrogator: A Titled Vulturess. London, Scolar Press, 1975.

Cave Birds. London, Scolar Press, 1975; revised edition, as *Cave Birds: An Alchemical Cave Drama,* illustrated by Leonard Baskin, London, Faber, 1978; New York, Viking Press, 1979.

The New World, music by Gordon Crosse. London, Oxford University Press, 1975.

Eclipse. Knotting, Bedfordshire, Sceptre Press, 1976.

Gaudete. London, Faber, and New York, Harper, 1977.

Chiasmadon. Baltimore, Seluzicki, 1977.

Sunstruck. Knotting, Bedfordshire, Sceptre Press, 1977.

Calder Valley Poems. London, Rainbow Press, 1978.

A Solstice. Knotting, Bedfordshire, Sceptre Press, 1978.

Orts. London, Rainbow Press, 1978.

Moortown Elegies. London, Rainbow Press, 1978.

Adam and the Sacred Nine. London, Rainbow Press, 1979.

All Around the Year, photographs by Michael Morpurgo. Murray, 1979.

Remains of Elmet: A Pennine Sequence, photographs by Fay Godwin. London, Rainbow Press, 1979; revised edition, London, Faber, and New York, Harper, 1979; revised edition published as *Elmet: Poems,* London and Boston, Faber and Faber, 1994.

Night-Arrival of Sea-Trout, The Iron Wolf, Puma, Brooktrout, Pan, Woodpecker, Wolverine, Eagle, Mosquito, Tapir's Saga, Wolf-Watching, Mice Are Funny Little Creatures, Weasels at Work, Fly Inspects (broadsides). North Tawton, Devon, Morrigu Press, 1979-83.

Four Tales Told by an Idiot. Knotting, Bedfordshire, Sceptre Press, 1979.

In the Black Chapel (poster). London, Victoria and Albert Museum, 1979.

Moortown. London, Faber, 1979; New York, Harper, 1980.

Sky-Furnace, painting by Roger Vick. North Tawton, Devon, Caricia Fine Arts, 1981.

A Primer of Birds: Poems, illustrated by Leonard Baskin. Lurley, Devon, Gehenna Press, 1981.

Selected Poems: 1957-1981. London, Faber, 1982; as *New Selected Poems,* New York, Harper, 1982.

River, photographs by Peter Keen. London, Faber, 1983; New York, Harper, 1984.

Flowers and Insects: Some Birds and a Pair of Spiders, illustrated by Leonard Baskin. London, Faber, and New York, Knopf, 1986.

Wolfwatching. London and Boston, Faber and Faber, 1989.

Cappriccio: Poems by Ted Hughes, engravings by Leonard Baskin. Searsmont, Maine, Gehenna Press, 1990.

New Selected Poems, 1957-1994. London, Faber and Faber, 1995.

Plays

The House of Aries (broadcast 1960). Published in *Audience,* (Cambridge, Massachusetts), Spring 1961.

The Calm (produced Boston, 1961).

The Wound (broadcast 1962). Included in *Wodwo,* 1967; revised version (produced London, 1972).

Epithalamium (produced London, 1963).

The House of Donkeys (broadcast 1965). Published in *Living Language,* Autumn 1974.

Seneca's Oedipus (produced London, 1968; Los Angeles, 1973; New York, 1977). London, Faber, 1969; New York, Doubleday, 1972.

Orghast (produced Persepolis, 1971). Excerpt published in *Performance* (New York), December 1971.

Eat Crow. London, Rainbow Press, 1971.

The Story of Vasco, music by Gordon Crosse, adaptation of a play by Georges Schehadé (produced London, 1974). London, Oxford University Press, 1974.

Radio Plays: *The House of Aries,* 1960; *A Houseful of Women,* 1961; *The Wound,* 1962; *Difficulties of a Bridegroom,* 1963; *Dogs,* 1964; *The House of Donkeys,* 1965.

Short Stories

The Threshold. London, Steam Press, 1979.

Difficulties of a Bridegroom. London, Faber and Faber, and New York, Picador, 1995.

Other

Editor, with Patricia Beer and Vernon Scannell, *New Poems 1962.* London, Hutchinson, 1962.

Editor, *Here Today.* London, Hutchinson, 1963.

Editor, with Thom Gunn, *Five American Poets.* London, Faber, 1963.

Editor, *Selected Poems,* by Keith Douglas. London, Faber, 1964; New York, Chilmark Press, 1965.

Editor, with Olwyn Hughes, *Ariel,* by Sylvia Plath. London, Faber, 1965; New York, Harper, 1966.

Wodwo (miscellany). London, Faber, and New York, Harper, 1967.

Editor, *A Choice of Emily Dickinson's Verse.* London, Faber, 1968.

Translator, with Assia Gutmann, *Selected Poems,* by Yehuda Amichai. London, Cape Goliard Press, 1968; expanded edition, as *Poems,* New York, Harper, 1969; London, Penguin, 1971.

Editor, *Crossing the Water,* by Sylvia Plath. London, Faber, 1971; as *Crossing the Water: Transitional Poems,* New York, Harper, 1971.

Editor, *Winter Trees,* by Sylvia Plath. London, Faber, 1971; New York, Harper, 1972.

Editor, *With Fairest Flowers While Summer Lasts: Poems from Shakespeare.* New York, Doubleday, 1971; as *A Choice of Shakespeare's Verse,* London, Faber, 1971; introduction published as *Shakespeare's Poem,* London, Lexham Press, 1971.

Contributor, *Cricket's Choice.* Chicago, Open Court, 1974.

Editor, and translator with János Csokits, *Selected Poems,* by János Pilinszky. Manchester, Carcanet, 1976.

Editor, and Translator with Yehuda Amichai, *Amen,* by Yehuda Amichai. New York, Harper, 1977; London, Oxford University Press, 1978.

Translator, *Another Republic,* edited by Charles Simic and Mark Strand. New York, Ecco Press, 1977.

Editor, and author of introduction, *Johnny Panic and the Bible of Dreams, and Other Prose Writings,* by Sylvia Plath. London, Faber, 1977; augmented edition, London, Faber, and New York, Harper, 1979.

Henry Williamson: A Tribute. London, Rainbow Press, 1979.

Translator, with Yehuda Amichai, *Time,* by Yehuda Amichai. New York, Harper, and London, Oxford University Press, 1979.

Editor, *New Poetry 6.* London, Hutchinson, 1980.

Editor, *The Collected Poems of Sylvia Plath.* London, Faber, and New York, Harper, 1981.

Editor, with Seamus Heaney, *1980 Anthology: Arvon Foundation Poetry Competition.* Todmorden, Lancashire, Kilnhurst, 1982.

Consulting editor, *The Journals of Sylvia Plath,* edited by Frances McCullough. New York, Dial Press, 1982.

Editor, *Sylvia Plath's Selected Poems.* London, Faber, 1985.

Translator, *The Early Books of Yehuda Amichai.* New York, Sheep Meadow Press, 1988.

Translator, with János Csokits, *The Desert of Love,* by János Pilinszky. London, Anvil Press Poetry, 1989.

Editor, *The Essential Shakespeare.* New York, Ecco Press, 1991.

Ruin-charm for the Duchy and other Laureate Poems. London, Faber, 1992.

Shakespeare and the Goddess of Complete Being. London, Faber and Faber, 1992; New York, Farrar Straus Giroux, 1992.

A Dancer to God: Tributes to T. S. Eliot. New York, Farrar Straus Giroux, 1993.

Winter Pollen: Occasional Prose, edited by William Scammell. London, Faber and Faber, 1994; New York, Picador, 1995.

Editor, *A Choice of Coleridge's Verse.* London, Faber and Faber, 1996.

Translator, *Tales from Ovid.* New York, Farrar Straus Giroux, 1997.

*

Media Adaptations: *Poets Reading 5,* Jupiter, 1962; *The Poet Speaks 5,* Argo, 1965; *Crow,* Claddagh, 1973; *The Poetry and Voice of Ted Hughes,* Caedmon, 1977; *Selections from Crow and Wodwo,* Caedmon, 1979.

Biography: Entry in *Dictionary of Literary Biography,* Volume 40, Detroit, Gale, 1985.

Bibliography: *Ted Hughes: A Bibliography 1946-1980* by Keith Sagar and Stephen Tabor, London, Mansell, 1983.

Critical Studies: *Ted Hughes,* London, Longman, 1972, and *The Art of Ted Hughes,* London, Cambridge University Press, 1975, revised edition, 1978, both by Keith Sagar, and *The Achievement of Ted Hughes* edited by Keith Sagar, Manchester, Manchester University Press, and Athens, University of Georgia Press, 1983; "Dark Rainbow: Reflections on Ted Hughes" by John Adams, in *Signal,* May 1971, 65; entries in *Contemporary Literary Criticism,* Detroit, Gale, Vol. 2, 1974, Vol. 4, 1975, Vol. 9, 1978, Vol. 14, 1980, Vol. 37, 1986; *Thom Gunn and Ted Hughes* by Alan Bold, Edinburgh, Oliver and Boyd, 1976; entry in *Children's Literature Review,* Vol. 3, Detroit, Gale, 1978; *Sylvia Plath and Ted Hughes* by Margaret Dickie Uroff, Urbana, University of Illinois Press, 1979; *Ted Hughes: The Unaccommodated Universe, with Selected Critical Writings by Ted Hughes and Two Interviews* by Ekbert Faas, Santa Barbara, California, Black Sparrow Press, 1980; *Ted Hughes: A Critical Study* by Terry Gifford and Neil Roberts, London, Faber, 1981; *Myth in the Poetry of Ted Hughes: A Guide to the Poems* by Stuart Hirschberg, Portmarnock, County Dublin, Wolfhound Press, and Totowa, New Jersey, Barnes and Noble, 1981; *Ted Hughes* by Thomas West, London, Methuen, 1985; *Ted Hughes* by Dennis Walder, Milton Keynes, Buckinghamshire, Open University Press, 1987; *Ted Hughes as Shepherd of Being* by Craig Robinson, London, Macmillan, 1989.

*   *   *

Ted Hughes has written poetry, prose, and plays for young adults. The central themes in his works are life, death, and the power and mystery of the cosmos. Hughes's works have a sense of urgency as he tries to communicate his vision of the world to his young readers. Though full of humor, Hughes' writing typically reflects this deeper purpose, and he uses a variety of poetic and prose forms to match the diversity and richness he finds in nature. For example, his play *The Tiger's Bones* is a satire that warns about the dangers of the modern scientific mentality, and his book *Iron Giant: A Story in Five Nights* is a myth that deals with the issues of sacrifice and redemption. His collection of poems, *Season Songs,* encourages the reader to have an openness to nature and its processes.

Hughes believes, as he states in *Poetry in the Making,* that there is no ideal form of poetry or writing, and this is reflected in his varied pieces and styles of writing. His poetry ranges from free verse ("New Year Song") to highly structured forms and rhyme schemes ("The Loon" and "The Black Bear"). Hughes has used a wide variety of styles and formats for his writing, varying these at least as often as the themes about which he is writing.

Hughes's central focus is on nature, complete with the violence, destruction, purity, dignity, and harmony that make up the natural world. Hughes' books of poetry, *Under the North Star, The Cat and the Cuckoo, Moon-Whales and Other Moon Poems,* and *Season Songs,* all focus on various aspects of nature. In addition, his fable *What Is the Truth?* and his book *Tales of the Early World* also deal with the creation and existence of various creatures in nature. Within these natural settings, Hughes deals unblinkingly with death, violence, and destruction. He portrays these happenings in a realistic manner, and as a necessary and inevitable part of the cycle of life.

The cycles of nature form the theme of his popular and well-received collection of poetry *Season Songs.* The element of death is present as a part of the cycles of nature in all of these poems. This collection begins with "A March Calf" as it first experiences its mother and surroundings. But sentimentality has no place in this world. Hughes introduces the inevitability of death for the calf near the end of the poem by writing:

> Hungry people are getting hungrier,
> Butchers developing expertise and markets.

There is no sentiment again in the poem "There Came a Day," where Hughes pins autumn with these lines:

> There came a day that caught the summer
> Wrung its neck
> Plucked it
> And ate it.

Season Songs ends with "The Warm and the Cold," a poem full of opposites that focuses on the impending death and destruction that winter brings. The poem begins with the following description:

> Freezing dusk is closing
> Like the slow trap of steel
> On trees and roads and hills and all
> That can no longer feel.

The ineluctable intertwining of nature, mankind, fate and man's abuse of the earth are sharply present. Animals are both metaphor and meaning when Hughes writes about them. In *Poetry in the Making,* Hughes devotes an entire chapter to the processes he goes through when writing his animal poems. He explains that his first animal poem, "Thought Fox," is based on real observations of and experiences with a fox that he recalled from his memory. He then thoroughly describes how he uses his five senses to capture the various aspects and dimensions of the animals so the reader can see, hear, smell, and actually experience the animal to the degree language permits.

Hughes is a highly imaginative writer, as one would expect from such an accomplished poet. Yet as he describes the grotesque, amazing creatures, plants, and events on the moon in his collection *Moon-Whales,* an element of comedy is often present in the poems. The majority of the poems in this collection focus on a specific animal or plant as it would be on the moon. "The Burrow Wolf" is a hideous, frightening creature at the beginning of the poem when Hughes tells the reader: ''And the wolf's eyes start clean out of his head on eleven-inch stalks.'' The comic element in these poems often takes on an ironic tone. ''The Burrow Wolf'' ends with these unexpected lines:

And he might lunatically mistake this wolf for his wife.
So the man in the moon ended his life.

In fact, there are so many horrible creatures and events on the moon that Hughes has written an entire poem entitled ''Moon Horrors.''

Hughes' passionate involvement in nature extends to include the celestial bodies, especially the Moon. Clearly, *Moon-Whales* is replete with cosmic references. In addition, cosmic imagery informs almost all of the poems in *Under the North Star*. In fact, Keith Cushman, in *The Achievement of Ted Hughes,* called this collection of poems Hughes' own ''poetic constellation.'' The first poem in *Under the North Star* is ''The Loon,'' and it begins with these lines: ''The Loon, the Loon / Hatched from the moon''— thus setting the tone and meaning from the beginning. ''The Wolverine'' describes the wolverine as he ''Bobs up in the Northern Lights.'' Cosmic images are overt also throughout Hughes' prose works *Tales of the Early World* and *What Is the Truth?*

In *Meet My Folks!* (1987 edition), Hughes writes about his ''other'' granny, the one who doesn't appear in his 1961 menagerie of relatives. She's an octopus—and she's come for tea. From a child's perspective, what could be more granny-like than the huge slithery wetness of this tentacled, many-armed creature? With typical dead-accurate aim, Hughes targets the perfect image. But he is too gifted a poet to leave it as a shallow joke.

Granny, because she is an octopus, can't talk. When she does attempt ''a WORD,'' she is so overwhelmed that she only manages two tears—which plop into the saucer of her teacup. The final close-up focuses on the trace of her presence: ''For the sea-tears in her saucer / And a man's tears are the same.'' Hughes affirms the humanity of his comic sea monster of a granny, wakens a sympathetic response to her, and reminds us of our fishy pasts in evolutionary seas. In this poem, as in everything Hughes writes, readers are compelled to participate: to see, hear, feel and remember.

Now in his late sixties, Hughes has authored ''a canon of work on a Victorian scale,'' as Sean O'Brien says (*London Sunday Times Books* 5 March 1995). *Ted Hughes: New and Selected Poems 1957-1994* (1995), contains poems from collections published for children—unlike the two earlier volumes (1972 and 1982) from which they were excluded. For the first time, the substantial and growing body of Hughes's work for children is read as part of the whole.

Ted Hughes has written a wide variety of finely illustrated, fiercely wrought, passionate poetry, prose, and plays for young adults. Hughes values the youth of the world too much to hide from them the bewildering and fantastic; his poet's eye and mind is everywhere probing the beauty and strangeness of nature in all its forms. His work cumulatively reveals his faith and respect in the abilities of children everywhere to make a sense of life. Hughes is quoted as saying, ''Every new child is nature's chance to correct culture's error,'' and his books for young adults are implicit texts to help in this recovery.

—Nicholas Ranson, updated by Lissa Paul

HUNT, Irene

Nationality: American. **Born:** Newton, Illinois, 18 May 1907. **Education:** the University of Illinois, Urbana, B.A. 1939; University of Minnesota, Minneapolis, M.A. 1946; University of Colorado, Boulder. **Career:** French and English teacher, Oak Park public schools, Illinois, 1930-45; instructor in psychology, University of South Dakota, Vermillion, 1946-50; teacher, 1950-65, and director of language arts, 1965-69, Cicero public schools, Illinois. **Awards:** Charles W. Follett award, 1964, Newbery Honor Book, 1965, Dorothy Canfield Fisher award, 1965, Clara Ingram Judson Memorial award, 1965, Lewis Carroll Shelf award, 1966, and ALA Notable Book citation, all for *Across Five Aprils;* Newbery Medal, 1967, and International Board on Books for Young People Honor List, 1970, both for *Up a Road Slowly;* Friends of Literature award, and Charles W. Follett award, both 1971, both for *No Promises in the Wind;* Omar's Book award, for *The Lottery Rose;* Parents' Choice award, 1985, for *The Everlasting Hills.*

PUBLICATIONS FOR YOUNG ADULTS

Fiction

Across Five Aprils. Chicago, Follett, 1964; London, Bodley Head, 1965.
Up a Road Slowly. Chicago, Follett, 1966; London, Macdonald, 1967.
Trail of Apple Blossoms, illustrated by Don Bolognese. Chicago, Follett, 1968; London, Blackie, 1970.
No Promises in the Wind. Chicago, Follett, 1970.
The Lottery Rose. New York, Scribner, 1976.
William. New York, Scribner, 1977.
Claws of a Young Century. New York, Scribner, 1980.
The Everlasting Hills. New York, Scribner, 1985.

*

Media Adaptations: *No Promises in the Wind* has been optioned for production as a film.

Manuscript Collection: Kerlan Collection, University of Minnesota, Minneapolis.

Biography: Entry in *Dictionary of Literary Biography* by Philip A. Sadler, Volume 52, Detroit, Gale, 1986.

Critical Study: Entry in *Children's Literature Review,* Volume 1, Detroit, Gale, 1976.

*   *   *

Irene Hunt's novels are notable works for young people for their wide-ranging diversity. She demonstrates her virtuosity as a storyteller by never duplicating her use of characters, setting, and plot within the genre of historical fiction. In addition, all of Hunt's novels consistently demonstrate other important elements such as poetic yet simple language and a delicate appreciation of the natural world. Most outstanding of all, Hunt never fails to reveal to her reader the complexities and rewards of human relationships, especially within the context of the family.

In fact, family issues dominate Hunt's novels. Her characters struggle to construct stable family situations for themselves, sometimes in the absence of anything faintly resembling a nurturing family environment. Perhaps the death of Hunt's father and the consequent disruption of her childhood was a personal source for her novelistic explorations of family dynamics. In any case, she frequently juxtaposes the disrupted traditional family with its hopeful reconstruction. Of major importance to Hunt seems to be the overwhelming need young people have for stable role models; indeed, these individuals often assume the roles of surrogate parents to her main characters.

Hunt's first novel, the widely acclaimed *Across Five Aprils,* is a perfect illustration of her concern for the support which the family and the surrogate family can offer an adolescent. In it, she masterfully depicts the dissolution and reconstruction of the country during the Civil War and establishes the Creighton family as a microcosm of that internal conflict. Hunt's research of historical details is impeccable, and her use of her grandfather's memories of his childhood during the war gives the reader a sense of great intimacy with the lives of the characters. More importantly, Hunt's use of the Civil War and the corresponding tensions between North and South becomes a paradigm for the processes by which personal needs are met or left unfulfilled within the American family.

The Creightons are touched by the war even on their backwoods southern Illinois farm. Jethro Creighton, the youngest of his large family, sees the men he loves and admires leave one by one for wartime service. Their letters home gradually awaken in Jethro an awareness of the cruel and divisive nature of war. Once the pampered baby of the family, Jethro advances to adult status amid the disintegration of the family unit in which he had once felt security. Jethro's successful transition is made possible by the many father surrogates with whom he identifies: his sensitive brother Bill, his teacher Shadrach, astute and compassionate Ross Milton, the much-maligned Dave Burdow, and even President Abraham Lincoln, whose stern leadership tempered with mercy leaves an indelible mark on young Jethro.

Up a Road Slowly was Hunt's second novel and the one for which she received the Newbery Award. In it, Julie Trelling recounts her ten years with her aunt Cordelia, after the death of her mother and her father's inability to raise her on his own. Willful and adventurous, Julie clashes frequently with her aunt, a strict and duty-bound woman who nonetheless exerts a loving and powerful influence over Julie. Julie's development is placed in meaningful counterpoint with the personality of her uncle Haskell, who has been rendered perpetually childlike as well as alcoholic by his permissive mother. As Julie overtakes and surpasses her uncle in maturity and self-acceptance, she finally realizes that she owes much to Aunt Cordelia, who has risen to her needs and provided the surrogate guidance that Julie's own parents could not.

In *Trail of Apple Blossoms* Hunt tells the story of folk-hero John Chapman (Johnny Appleseed), who befriended both native Americans and westward-looking settlers during the early 1800s. Chapman's efforts to plant apple trees throughout the Ohio Valley are familiar even to young children. To the well-known legends Hunt adds a fictional encounter with the Bryant family, whom Chapman befriends when he saves their small daughter's life. The lives of the Bryants and Johnny Appleseed cross several more times as if to remind Chapman of his purpose: to encourage

families to further settlements of the new country, for in the family lies the country's strength.

The Depression era, a time when economic hardships placed unusual tensions on the American family, is the setting for *No Promises in the Wind.* For Josh Grondowski, the stresses of adolescence and the hopelessness of his family's poverty combine to make his relationship with his demanding father unendurable. Josh decides to run away, trusting his own strengths and abilities to make a new life for himself. He does not leave alone, however; with Josh is his younger brother Joey. As Josh fights not only for his survival but Joey's as well, he learns to understand his father's anger at his failures as a parent and as a person. Josh's growth to this level of empathy with his father is facilitated by the two people to whom he unconsciously looks as surrogate parents during his journey: Emily, who teaches Josh to look beyond superficialities to the nobility which lies within, and Lonnie, whose personal losses show Josh the value of his relationship, however troubled, with his father.

Hunt's last few novels continue to demonstrate her versatility. All, with one exception, abandon the genre of historical fiction while still maintaining her novelistic focus on family and surrogate family. In *The Lottery Rose,* Georgie Burgess's family life is a nightmare of abuse and neglect. Georgie's love for beauty survives his mistreatment and creates the avenue by which he is drawn back into a world of love and trust. The premise of *William* involves three orphaned black children who are cared for after their parents' deaths by a white, unwed, teenaged mother. Race, however, becomes a nonissue as Hunt again explores the loss of the traditional family structure and its replacement. *In Claws of a New Century* Hunt returns to historical fiction but with a feminist theme. Finally, *The Everlasting Hills* deals with the struggle of a neurologically impaired child to achieve selfhood. Family issues still remain at the forefront as twelve-year-old Jeremy Tydings learns that he is a product both of the family he has been given and of the family he has chosen.

Both modern parents and their children alike have the tendency to see the current shifts and changes in family dynamics as the unique products of their generation's cultural problems. Hunt's novels indicate otherwise; while the individual problems may be different, their influences on the family remain the same. Hunt's adolescent protagonists, regardless of the era in which they live, continually demonstrate the value of changed family relationships in contrast to the ones that have always been considered traditional. What remains important is not the normality or typicality of the family in which growth from adolescence to adulthood is achieved, but how the existing family structure supports and guides that transition.

—Patricia L. Bradley

HUNTER, Kristin (Elaine)

Has also written as Kristin Hunter Lattany. **Nationality:** American. **Born:** Kristin Eggleston in Philadelphia, Pennsylvania, 12 September 1931. **Education:** Charles Sumner School, Camden, and Magnolia Public School, both New Jersey; Haddon Heights High School, New Jersey, graduated 1947; University of Pennsylvania, 1947-51, B.S. in education 1951. **Family:** Married 1) Joseph

Hunter in 1952 (divorced 1962); 2) John I. Lattany in 1968.
Career: Columnist and feature writer, *Pittsburgh Courier,* 1946-52; teacher, Camden, New Jersey, 1951; copywriter, Lavenson Bureau of Advertising, Philadelphia, 1952-59, and Werman & Schorr, Inc., Philadelphia, 1962-63; research assistant, School of Social Work, University of Pennsylvania, 1961-62; information officer, City of Philadelphia, 1963-64, 1965-66; director of health services, Temple University, Philadelphia, 1971-72; director, Walt Whitman Poetry Center, Camden, 1978-79. Lecturer in Creative Writing, University of Pennsylvania, Philadelphia, 1972-79, Adjunct Associate Professor of English, 1981-83, Senior Lecturer in English, University of Pennsylvania, 1983-1995. Writer-in-residence, Emory University, Atlanta, 1979. **Awards:** Fund for the Republic Prize, 1955, for television documentary, *Minority of One;* John Hay Whitney fellowship, 1959-60; Philadelphia Athenaeum award, 1964; Bread Loaf Writers Conference De Voto fellowship, 1965; National Council on Interracial Books for Children award, 1968, Mass Media Brotherhood award from National Conference of Christians and Jews, 1969, and Lewis Carroll Shelf award, 1971, all for *The Soul Brothers and Sister Lou;* Sigma Delta Chi reporting award, 1968; Spring Book Festival award, 1973, Christopher award, and National Book award finalist, both 1974, all for *Guests in the Promised Land;* Drexel Children's Literature Citation, 1981; New Jersey State Council on the Arts prose fellowship, 1981-82, 1985-86; Pennsylvania State Council on the Arts literature fellowship, 1983-84; Lifetime Achievement award, Moonstone, Philadelphia, 1996. **Address:** 721 Warwick Road, Magnolia, New Jersey 08049, U.S.A.

PUBLICATIONS FOR YOUNG ADULTS

Fiction

The Soul Brothers and Sister Lou. New York, Scribner, 1968; London, Macdonald, 1971.
Boss Cat, illustrated by Harold Franklin. New York, Scribner, 1971.
The Pool Table War. Boston, Houghton Mifflin, 1972.
Uncle Daniel and the Raccoon. Boston, Houghton Mifflin, 1972.
Guests in the Promised Land: Stories. New York, Scribner, 1973.
Lou in the Limelight. New York, Scribner, 1981.
Kinfolks (as Kristin Hunter Lattany). New York, Ballantine, 1996.

PUBLICATIONS FOR ADULTS

Fiction

God Bless the Child. New York, Scribner, 1964; London, Muller, 1965.
The Landlord. New York, Scribner, 1966.
The Survivors. New York, Scribner, 1975.
The Lakestown Rebellion. New York, Scribner, 1978.

Other

Minority of One (documentary/television play, Columbia Broadcasting System, 1956).
The Double Edge (play, produced Philadelphia, 1965).
Contributor, *The Best Short Stories by Negro Writers* with Langston Hughes, editor. Boston, Little, Brown, 1967.

*

Media Adaptations: *The Landlord* (motion picture), United Artists, 1970.

Biography: Essay in *Something about the Author Autobiography Series,* Volume 10, Detroit, Gale, 1990; entry in *Dictionary of Literary Biography,* Volume 33: *Afro-American Fiction Writers after 1955,* Detroit, Gale, 1984.

Critical Studies: Entry in *Children's Literature Review,* Volume 3, Detroit, Gale, 1978; entry in *Contemporary Literary Criticism,* Volume 35, Detroit, Gale, 1985.

Kristin Hunter comments:
I have fun. I hope my readers do.

*   *   *

Kristin Hunter, a pioneer in the field of young adult literature, began writing books about African-American teenagers in the mid-1960s. Her works deal with the black community as a self-contained entity and to a lesser extent with the impingement on that world by the larger, white-dominated society. The subtle caste distinctions of skin tone and hair color among people of color are mentioned frankly. Her characters are ordinary teenagers who learn to adjust their lives in response to a variety of circumstances.

The Soul Brothers and Sister Lou, published in 1968, is about Louretta Hawkins, a light-skinned African-American girl. She begins playing the piano with some friends who have formed a singing group. Blind Eddie Bell, a blues musician, teaches her how to compose music. When one member of the singing group is accidentally killed, another friend writes a poem about his death. Louella puts it to music; a music teacher contacts a recording company, and a single is cut. Thanks to a local disc jockey, "Lament for Jethro" becomes a big hit and life changes for the "Soul Brothers and Sister Lou." The black power movement is discussed sympathetically but is not offered as a solution to the problems of the ghetto. Although Jethro's accidental death is caused by a policeman, the antagonism towards authority figures already existed. Even though Louretta's family now has enough money to move out of the ghetto, discrimination prevents their relocation. In the end, the more things change, the more they remain the same.

The sequel, *Lou in the Limelight,* appeared in 1981. The title refers to the attempts by Marty Ross, the singing group's agent, to split the group apart. Lou and her friends resent this, but this becomes the least of their problems. Their first performances in New York lead to appearances in Las Vegas. The dangers of New York pale in comparison to the Mafia-sponsored threats in Nevada. Drugs and prostitution are only two of the problems facing them. After nearly being entrapped, the children testify for the government and help convict some of the criminals. Next, the Soul Brothers and Sister Lou go on a Southern tour to repay some of their debts. The drug problems catch up with Lou, though. After nearly dying from an unintentional overdose, she finds some unknown relatives. A newfound cousin adopts her and plans to send her to college. In this sequel, unfortunately, the action never stops. Little consideration is paid to the likelihood of all these terrible things happening to one group of musicians. The fairy-tale ending is probably the most unrealistic thing. It is an interesting story but lacking in credibility.

Guests in the Promised Land is a collection of short stories. The title story is about a young black boy who is treated to a day at an all-white country club. He oversteps the invisible bounds and gets kicked out. The problem was caused because he did not realize he was just a "guest in the Promised Land." Another story, "Two's Enough of a Crowd," deals with two young people who are misfits. When they find each other, they realize that they are not the only nonconformists. "Debut" is the story of a debutante who is trying to break into the society of light-skinned blacks. She finds out that in her own way she is more important than any of the flighty girls around her. A teenager's older brother comes home from prison in "Hero's Return," and dispels the myths about criminal life. The younger brother learns that education and honesty are more important than any short-lived benefits from crime. "The Scribe" is a thirteen-year-old boy who comes up with his own solution to the problem of illiteracy in his city. Six other stories cover such topics as integration and gang relations. The ideas in the stories are interesting: some themes are rendered very well. Unfortunately, many of the plots are trite and almost all the stories are dated.

Hunter's young adult fiction was undoubtedly fresh and original when it first appeared. With the exception of *The Soul Brothers and Sister Lou,* it has not stood the test of time. Even this novel is not really a classic, but it still is an entertaining book. Her real contribution has been to show that fiction for teenagers can be written about all types of people. Although most of her work deals with poor blacks, a good number of middle-class African Americans are also depicted. The ghetto society of the 1960s is accurately described, complete with slang and jive talk. Although certainly not intended that way, her fiction becomes historical. So, finally, these works become of interest to young people of today because they portray the way their parents lived.

—Sharon Clontz Bernstein

HUNTER, Mollie

Nationality: Scottish. **Born:** Maureen McVeigh, in Longniddry, East Lothian, 30 June 1922. **Education:** Preston Lodge School, East Lothian. **Family:** Married Thomas "Michael" McIlwraith in 1940; two sons. **Military Service:** Volunteered services in a serviceman's canteen during World War II. **Career:** Writer since 1953. May Hill Arbuthnot Lecturer in the United States in 1975, and in 1976 toured New Zealand and Australia lecturing under the joint auspices of the British Council, the International Reading Association, and the education authorities for New Zealand and Australia; writer-in-residence, Dalhousie University, Halifax, Nova Scotia, 1980, 1981; organized and taught in writers' workshops for both adults and children; 29th Anne Carroll Moore Spring Lecturer, 1986; teacher of creative writing, Aberlour Summer School for Gifted Children, 1987, 1988. **Awards:** Child Study Association of America's Children's Books of the Year citations, 1968, for *The Ferlie,* 1970, for *The Walking Stones,* 1971, for *The Thirteenth Member,* both 1972, for *A Sound of Chariots* and *The*

Haunted Mountain, 1974, for *The Stronghold,* 1975, for *A Stranger Came Ashore,* 1976, for *Talent Is Not Enough,* 1977, for *A Furl of Fairy Wind,* and 1987, for *Cat, Herself; Book World's* Children's Spring Book Festival honor book citation, 1970, for *The Lothian Run; New York Times* Outstanding Book of the Year citations, for *The Haunted Mountain* and *A Sound of Chariots,* both 1972, and *A Stranger Came Ashore,* 1975; Children's Book award from the Child Study Association of America, 1973, for *A Sound of Chariots;* Scottish Arts Council award, 1973, for *The Haunted Mountain;* Carnegie Medal for Children's Book of Outstanding Merit, British Library Association, 1974, and Silver Pencil award (Holland), 1975, both for *The Stronghold; A Stranger Came Ashore* was selected one of *School Library Journal's* Best Children's Books, 1975, and was a *Boston Globe-Horn Book* award Honor Book, 1976; *The Wicked One* was selected one of *School Library Journal's* Best Books for Spring and was selected a Scottish Arts Council award Book, both 1977; *You Never Knew Her as I Did!* was selected one of the New York Public Library's Books for the Teen Age, and a Notable Children's Trade Book in the Field of Social Studies by the National Council of Social Studies and the Children's Book Council, both 1982; *Cat, Herself* was chosen one of the American Library Association's Best Books for Young Adults, and one of *School Library Journal's* Best Books for Young Adults, both 1986; Phoenix award, Children's Literature Association, 1992, for *A Sound of Chariots.* **Address:** Rose Cottage, 7 Mary Ann Court, Inverness IV3 5BZ, Scotland.

PUBLICATIONS FOR YOUNG ADULTS

Historical Adventures

Hi Johnny, illustrated by Drake Brookshaw. London, Evans, 1963; new edition illustrated by M. Christopherson, Byway Books, 1986.

The Spanish Letters, illustrated by Elizabeth Grant. London, Evans, 1964; New York, Funk and Wagnalls, 1967.

A Pistol in Greenyards, illustrated by Elizabeth Grant. London, Evans, 1965; New York, Funk and Wagnalls, 1968.

The Ghosts of Glencoe. London, Evans, 1966; New York, Funk and Wagnalls, 1969.

The Lothian Run. New York, Funk and Wagnalls, 1970. London, Hamish Hamilton, 1971.

The Thirteenth Member: A Story of Suspense. New York, Harper, and London, Hamish Hamilton, 1971.

The Stronghold. New York, Harper, and London, Hamish Hamilton, 1974.

You Never Knew Her as I Did! London, Hamish Hamilton, and New York, Harper, 1981, as *Escape from Loch Leven,* Edinburgh, Canongate, 1987.

A Furl of Fairy Wind, illustrated by M. Christopherson. Byway Books, 1986.

Fantasy

Patrick Kentigern Keenan, illustrated by Charles Keeping. London, Blackie, 1963; as *The Smartest Man in Ireland,* New York, Funk and Wagnalls, 1965.

The Kelpie's Pearls, illustrated by Charles Keeping. London, Blackie, 1964; illustrated by Joseph Cellini, New York, Funk and Wagnalls, 1966.

Thomas and the Warlock, illustrated by Charles Keeping. London, Blackie; illustrated by Joseph Cellini, New York, Funk and Wagnalls, 1967.

The Ferlie, illustrated by Michal Morse. London, Blackie, 1968; illustrated by Joseph Cellini, New York, Funk and Wagnalls, 1968; as *The Enchanted Whistle,* London, Methuen, 1985.

The Bodach, illustrated by Gareth Floyd. London, Blackie, 1970, as *The Walking Stones: A Story of Suspense,* illustrated by Trina Schart Hyman, New York, Harper, 1970.

The Haunted Mountain: A Story of Suspense, illustrated by Trevor Ridley. London, Hamish Hamilton; illustrated by Lazslo Kubinyi, New York, Harper, 1972.

A Stranger Came Ashore: A Story of Suspense. London, Hamish Hamilton, and New York, Harper, 1975; produced as a play, Royal Lyceum Theatre, Edinburgh, 1998.

The Wicked One: A Story of Suspense. London, Hamish Hamilton, and New York, Harper, 1977.

The Mermaid Summer. London, Hamish Hamilton, and New York, Harper, 1988.

Fiction

A Sound of Chariots. New York, Harper, 1972; London, Hamish Hamilton, 1973.

The Third Eye. London, Hamish Hamilton, and New York, Harper, 1979.

The Dragonfly Years. London, Hamish Hamilton, 1983; as *Hold on to Love,* New York, Harper, 1984.

I'll Go My Own Way. London, Hamish Hamilton, 1985; as *Cat, Herself,* New York, Harper, 1986.

Publications for Children

Fiction

A Furl of Fairy Wind: Four Stories, illustrated by Stephen Gammell. New York, Harper, 1977.

The Knight of the Golden Plain, illustrated by Marc Simont. London, Hamish Hamilton, and New York, Harper, 1983.

The Three-Day Enchantment, illustrated by Marc Simont. New York, Harper, 1985.

The Brownie, illustrated by M. Christopherson. Byway Books, 1986.

The Enchanted Boy, illustrated by M. Christopherson. Byway Books, 1986.

Day of the Unicorn, illustrated by Donna Diamond. New York, Harper, 1994.

Gilly Martin the Fox, illustrated by Dennis McDermott. New York, Hyperion Books, 1994.

The King's Swift Rider. New York, Hyperion Books, 1998.

Publications for Adults

Essays

Talent Is Not Enough: Mollie Hunter on Writing for Children. New York, Harper, 1976.

The Pied Piper Syndrome (essays). New York, Harper, 1992.

Plays

A Love-Song for My Lady (produced Inverness, 1961). London, Evans, 1961.

Stay for an Answer (produced Inverness, 1962). London, French, 1962.

*

Media Adaptations: *The Kelpie's Pearls* (BBC-Radio program series); *The Lothian Run* (BBC-Radio program series); "The Enchanted Whistle" (BBC-Radio program series); *The Ferlie* (radio, U.S., also on BBC-Radio); *A Stranger Came Ashore* has been read in serial form on Swedish radio, and also produced as a musical on a Swedish stage; *A Furl of Fairy Wind* (cassette, U.K.); *The Walking Stones* and *The Wicked One* were featured in Yorkshire TV's "Book Tower" program.

Manuscript Collections: National Library of Scotland.

Biography: "Profile: Mollie Hunter," by Patricia Dooley, in *Children's Literature Association Newsletter* (Villanova, Pennsylvania), Vol. 3, Fall 1978, 3-6; "Mollie Hunter: An Interview," in *Top of the News* (Chicago), Winter 1985, 141-46; entry in *Something About the Author—Autobiographical Series,* edited by Joyce Nakamura, Vol. 7, Detroit, Gale, 1988, 139-153; entry in *Speaking for Ourselves, Too,* edited by Donald R. Gallo, Urbana, National Council of Teachers of English, 1993, 100-102; "Mollie Hunter" by Joel D. Chaston, in *Dictionary of Literary Biography,* Vol. 161, *British Children' Writers Since 1960,* Detroit, Gale, 1996, 210-161.

Critical Studies: "World Enough and Time: The Work of Mollie Hunter" by Peter Hollindale, in *Children's Literature in Education* (New York), Autumn 1977, 109-119; "Unself-Conscious Voices: Larger Contests for Adolescents" by Geraldine DeLuca, in *Lion and the Unicorn* (Brooklyn), Fall 1978, 92-96; "Mollie Hunter" by Stanley Cook, in *School Librarian* (London), June 1978, 108-111; "Profile: The Person Behind the Book—Mollie Hunter" by Janet Hickman, in *Language Arts* (Urbana), March 1979, 302-306; "The Spirit of Old Scotland: Tone in the Fiction of Mollie Hunter" by R. S. Ryan, in *Orana* (Australia), May 1984, 93-101, and August 1984, 138-45; "The Truth of Autobiographical Fiction for Children" by Roni Natov, in *Children's Literature in Education* (New York), Summer 1986, 112-25; "Springs of Hope: Recovery of the Primordial Myth in 'Mythic Novels' for Young Readers" by M. Sarah Smedman, in *Children's Literature* (New Haven), No. 16, 1988, 91-107; "Mollie Hunter: Underrated Downunder?" by Jenny Mutton, in *Orana* (Australia), Vol. 24, No. 3, August 1988, 157-65; "The Work of Keeping Writing Play: A View Through Children's Literature" by George Shannon, in *Children's Literature in Education* (New York), Vol. 21, No. 1, March 1990, 37-43; "*Cat* Herself" by Joel D. Chaston, in *Beacham's Guide to Young Adult Literature,* edited by Kirk Beetz, Washington, D. C., Beacham, 1994, 2910-2917; "The Morphing of Mollie Hunter or Folklore as the Root of Fantasy" by Betty Greenway, in *ALAN Review* (Athens, Georgia), Vol. 23, No. 3, Spring 1996, 20-21.

Mollie Hunter comments:

Being a Scot means, among other things, being heir to a distinctive literary tradition—much of which is concerned with the historical novel and with tales of the supernatural. In that same literary tradition, also, there has never been the clear-cut distinction between books for children and books for adults generally accepted in other cultures—a fact that suits very well with my own belief that a good book for children should simply be a good book per se.

I have always therefore used whatever gift I have by indulging my natural empathy with young people at the same time as I unleash the inborn impulse to tell a story—sometimes that of an adventure set at some particular period of my own country's history, sometimes that of some weird experience of the supernatural, and latterly in novels of the kind that could be expected to have particular appeal for teenage girl readers, since the changing face of publication has made this possible. Also, although Scotland is little known beyond its own geographical bounds, I have always tried in all such books to make its culture open and accessible to all young readers—thereby, I should say, giving myself as much pleasure as I hope will ultimately also be theirs.

*   *   *

Mollie Hunter, one of the most popular and influential contemporary Scottish writers of fiction for young adults, has written many award-winning books which have been almost universally praised for their suspenseful plots, evocation of Scottish settings, and effective use of folk customs, folktales, and historical references. Most of Hunter's books for young adults fall into three categories—literary folktales, historical novels, and realistic biographical fiction—and she has been praised for work in each of these genres.

Hunter's fantasies draw heavily on Scottish and Irish folklore and often involve characters who learn to control the supernatural and come to appreciate their own special gifts and talents. Often, they also involve conflicts between old beliefs and modern technology or the struggle between good and evil. Invariably, they validate the importance of storytelling and folk traditions.

In four of Hunter's fantasies, *The Smartest Man in Ireland, The Haunted Mountain, Thomas and the Warlock,* and *The Wicked One,* fathers and husbands come to value their wives' common sense or patience, eventually realizing that their families are more important than fairy gold. Several of Hunter's other fantasies feature characters with special gifts or talents who find themselves involved with supernatural creatures. In *The Kelpie's Pearls,* a seventy-two-year-old woman, Morag MacLeod, befriends a water sprite and learns that special gifts and talents are often misunderstood and unappreciated. Like many of Hunter's characters, the protagonist of *The Bodach* has "second sight" which he is supposed to use to enable thirteen ancient stones to walk about again as they have every hundred years.

Both *A Stranger Came Ashore* and *The Mermaid Summer* are about children who confront malevolent creatures from the sea. *A Stranger Came Ashore,* Hunter's best fantasy, is a deceptively simple work about a boy who suspects that a newcomer to his home in the Shetland Islands is a "selkie," a great seal who has taken the form of a human. The novel, which is filled with descriptions of traditional Shetland customs, is carefully ambiguous about the reality of the supernatural events it describes. In *The Mermaid Summer,* two children's love for their grandfather helps them defeat a proud mermaid. In recent years, Hunter has also produced the texts for several short picture books, either retelling Scottish folktales or legends as in *Gilly Martin, the Fox,* or creating literary fairytales of her own, as in *A Furl of Fairy Wind, The Knight of the Golden Plain, The Three Day Enchantment,* and *Day of the Unicorn.*

Hunter's historical novels are noted for their extensive research and appealing teenage protagonists. Critic Peter Hollindale has suggested that in Hunter's earliest historical novels, such as *Hi Johnny, The Spanish Letters,* and *The Lothian Run,* plot is sometimes more important than historical setting. *The Spanish Letters,* which involves a sixteenth-century plot against the Scottish king, is also one of several novels in which historical events are presented from the point of view of a teenage boy. Hunter also features characters who are at odds with society or who are torn by divided loyalties. Both *A Pistol in Greenyards* and *The Ghosts of Glencoe* recount fictionalized versions of massacres involving Scottish Highlanders, and are also told by teenage boys. In *The Thirteenth Member,* sixteen-year-old stablehand Adam Lawrie encounters a coven of witches which is being used to help depose King James VI, and explores the difficulty of knowing who to trust.

Two of Hunter's best historical novels are *The Stronghold* and *You Never Knew Her as I Did! The Stronghold,* winner of the Carnegie Medal, describes the attempts by the early inhabitants of the British Isles to protect themselves against Roman invaders. A lame boy, Coll, saves his people by creating a series of "strongholds." In *You Never Knew Her as I Did!,* young Will Douglas struggles with his desires to help the imprisoned Mary Queen of Scots and his loyalty to his family who are her jailers. In the course of the novel, Will learns the necessity of play-acting in order to survive.

In 1972, Hunter's *A Sound of Chariots* was published, one of her best and most moving books in which she provides an account of her childhood and her father's death. Her alter ego, Bridie McShane, eventually learns to openly grieve for her father and uses her feelings to write poetry, her one goal in life. In 1992, *A Sound of Chariots* was awarded the Children Literature Association's Phoenix Award for a book published twenty years earlier which has stood the test of time. In the sequel, *Hold on to Love,* Bridie continues her development as a writer and eventually marries a young man who encourages her and helps her deal with her continued sorrow over her father's death.

Besides these autobiographical works, Hunter has also written two other realistic books whose female protagonists face many of the same struggles as Bridie McShane and who also have the gift of second sight. In *The Third Eye,* a compelling look at Ballinford, West Lothian, during the early 1930s, Jinty Morrison learns to use her own "third eye" to better understand the world around her. The novel also explores the fine line between social classes. *Cat, Herself* focuses on Cat McPhie, a young "traveller" or "tinker," whose attitudes towards herself and her family change through the course of the novel. The novel also explores the persecution of those who are perceived as being different and the value of folk traditions.

Few writers for young adults have produced a body of work which encompasses so many genres and which appeals to such a wide audience. Mollie Hunter is as gifted a storyteller as the characters in her books. She invariably entertains her readers while helping them to gain what she calls the "third eye," the ability to clearly see the world. She also effectively introduces young adults to her own culture, educating them about Scotland both past and present.

—Joel D. Chaston

HURSTON, Zora Neale

Nationality: American. **Born:** Eatonville, Florida, 7 January 1891(?). **Education:** Howard University, Washington, D.C., 1923-24; Barnard College, New York, B.A. 1928; graduate study at Columbia University, New York. **Family:** Married 1) Herbert Sheen in 1927 (divorced 1931); 2) Albert Price III in 1939 (divorced). **Career:** Writer and folklorist. Collected folklore in the South, 1927-31; instructor in drama, Bethune-Cookman College, Daytona, Florida, 1933-34; collected folklore in Jamaica, Haiti, and Bermuda, 1937-38; collected folklore in Florida for the Works Progress Administration, 1938-39; staff writer, Paramount Studios, Hollywood, California, 1941; collected folklore in Honduras, 1946-48; worked as a maid in Florida, 1950; free-lance writer, 1950-56; librarian, Patrick Air Force Base, Florida, 1956-57; writer for *Fort Pierce Chronicle* and part-time teacher at Lincoln Park Academy, both in Fort Pierce, Florida, 1958-59; librarian at the Library of Congress, Washington, D.C.; professor of drama at North Carolina College for Negroes, Durham; assistant to writer Fannie Hurst. **Awards:** Guggenheim fellowship, 1936 and 1938; Annisfield award, 1943, for *Dust Tracks on a Road;* D.Litt. **Died:** 28 January 1960.

PUBLICATIONS

Fiction

Jonah's Gourd Vine. Philadelphia, Pennsylvania, Lippincott, 1934.
Mules and Men. Philadelphia, Pennsylvania, Lippincott, 1935.
Their Eyes Were Watching God. Philadelphia, Pennsylvania, Lippincott, 1937.
Moses, Man of the Mountain. Philadelphia, Pennsylvania, Lippincott, 1939.
Seraph on the Suwanee. New York, Scribner, 1948.
I Love Myself When I Am Laughing . . . And Then Again When I Am Looking Mean And Impressive, edited by Alice Walker. New York, Feminist Press, 1979.
The Sanctified Church. Berkeley, California, Turtle Island Foundation, 1983.
Spunk: The Selected Stories of Zora Neale Hurston. Berkeley, California, Turtle Island Foundation, 1985.
The Gilded Six-Bits. Minneapolis. Minnesota, Redpath Press, 1986.
The Complete Stories. New York, Harper, 1992.

Plays

Fast and Furious, with Clinton Fletcher and Time Moore; published in *Best Plays of 1931-32,* edited by Burns Mantle and Garrison Sherwood, 1931.
Mule Bone: A Comedy of Negro Life in Three Acts, with Langston Hughes. New York, Harper, 1931.
Stephen Kelen-d'Oxylion Presents Polk County: A Comedy of Negro Life on a Sawmill Camp with Authentic Negro Music, with Dorothy Waring, (produced New York, 1944).

Nonfiction

Tell My Horse. Philadelphia, Pennsylvania, Lippincott, 1938; as *Voodoo Gods: An Inquiry into Native Myths and Magic in Jamaica and Haiti,* Dent, 1939.
Dust Tracks on a Road. Philadelphia, Pennsylvania, Lippincott, 1942.

Contributor to various anthologies, including, *Black Writers in America, Story in America, American Negro Short Stories, The Best Short Stories by Negro Writers, From the Roots,* and *Anthology of American Negro Literature.*

*

Biography: Entries in *Dictionary of Literary Biography,* Detroit, Gale, Volume 51, 1987; Volume 86, 1989; *Zora Neale Hurston: A Literary Biography* by Robert E. Hemenway, Champaign, University of Illinois Press, 1977.

Critical Study: Entries in *Contemporary Literary Criticism,* Detroit, Gale, Volume 7, 1977; Volume 30, 1984; Volume 61, 1990.

*   *   *

Zora Neale Hurston was a novelist, anthropologist, and the most important collector of black folklore from the rural South. Hurston compiled this folklore into two books. She also wrote four novels, over fifty short stories and essays, and a prize-winning autobiography, and was twice the recipient of a Guggenheim award.

Although Hurston's work is primarily considered adult literature, some of her books are not only appropriate for a young adult audience, but necessary to provide an important voice, rich in a heritage too long disregarded. She is one of the major writers of the twentieth century to whom we should be grateful for capturing a uniquely imaginative and creative style of telling stories "before everybody forgets all of 'em."

Hurston was born on 7 January, though there are vast discrepancies as to the exact year. According to a biography written by Robert E. Hemenway in 1977, research could not confirm Hurston's birth year: Hurston's brother claimed she was born in 1891, her gravestone reads 1901, and her second marriage certificate lists 1910.

Regardless of the year, the location of her birth and early childhood is a major factor in her subsequent work. Eatonville, Florida, was said to be the first all-black incorporated town. She grew up in a community of black people who, through self-governing, had tremendous confidence and a sense of wholeness that comes from a healthy environment—one free from persecution and violence. This was an unusual experience for the blacks of the early South.

The heart of the town was the general store owned by Joe Clarke. It was on the porch of this store where the tales were told and songs were sung. It was there that Hurston heard the "big old lies" that she later incorporated into her work. From the tales of Brer Rabbit and "lying" sessions at the general store, to the confidence and strength instilled in Hurston by her parents and community; these experiences were woven into the fabric that gave us the celebration and joy, the lyrical prose of Zora Neale Hurston.

Mules and Men, Hurston's first book of folklore, was published in 1935. The product of extensive research in Florida and Louisiana, this was a popular and very important work of reference. She returned to her hometown of Eatonville to begin gathering information, choosing this as her starting point "because [she] knew that the town was full of material and that [she] could get it without hurt, harm or danger." She was happy to find the "same love of talk and song."

Now considered a classic of black literature, *Their Eyes Were Watching God* was met with great criticism when published in 1937, including that of her contemporary, the influential Richard Wright. Wright said the novel "carries no theme, no message, no thought." Other black writers of the Harlem Renaissance were writing serious novels of protest and social realism. While these writers were trying to distance themselves from their rural origins, Hurston was recreating the Southern blacks of her youth, dialect and all.

Their Eyes Were Watching God tells the story of Janie Crawford, a young woman who discovers that the black woman need not be "de mule uh de world" as was her grandmother's experience. Overcoming two oppressive marriages—the first arranged by her grandmother who has hoped for a better life for Janie; the second to a man with a vision and a promise, ultimately unkept, to always treat her like a lady—Janie marries a third man, Tea Cake, who treats her as an equal. It is through this loving relationship that she realizes all that life has to offer. Janie experiences a self-awakening and love of self she has not known before. While *Their Eyes Were Watching God* celebrates black culture and its oral tradition, it more importantly explores the pain of a young woman's search for her own identity in a racially oppressed culture, within a male-dominated world.

Her life forgotten, her books decades out of print, the work of Hurston was resurrected mostly thanks to the efforts of Alice Walker and Robert Hemenway. In an essay entitled "Looking for Zora," published in *Ms.* (1975), Alice Walker describes her August 1973 search through a neglected cemetery for Hurston's unmarked grave. Upon what she thought was the approximate location, Walker placed a gravestone with an epitaph that reads:

Zora Neale Hurston
"A Genius of the South"
1901-1960
Novelist, Folklorist, Anthropologist

For her independent achievement of a college education against all odds, her courageous efforts in the pursuit for the preservation of black folklore, and for the accomplishment of having published more than any other black woman of her time—the life of Zora Neale Hurston proves to be as much an inspirational study as her art.

—Suzanne M. Valentic

HURWITZ, Johanna

Nationality: American. **Born:** Johanna Frank, New York City, 9 October 1937. **Education:** Queens College, Flushing, New York, 1955-58, B.A. in English 1958; Columbia University, New York, 1958-59, M.L.S. 1959. **Family:** Married Uri Levi Hurwitz in 1962; one daughter and one son. **Career:** Children's librarian, New York Public Library, 1959-64; lecturer in children's literature, Queens College, 1965-68; librarian, Calhoun School, 1968-75, and New Hyde Park school district, 1975-77, both New York; children's librarian, Great Neck Public Library, New York, 1978—. Visiting storyteller, New York Public Library, 1964-67; teacher of writer's workshops in children's literature, Hofstra University, Hempstead, New York, 1981, 1986. **Awards:** *Parents' Choice* award, Parents' Choice Foundation, 1982, for *The Rabbi's Girls,* and 1984, for *The Hot and Cold Summer;* Texas Bluebonnet award and Wyoming Indian Paintbrush award, both 1987, both for *The Hot and Cold Summer;* Swedish Institute grant, 1988; Kentucky Bluegrass award, West Virginia Children's Book award, and Mississippi Children's Book award, all 1989, all for *Class Clown;* Florida Sunshine State award, 1990, and New Jersey Garden State award, 1991, both for *Teacher's Pet.* **Address:** 10 Spruce Place, Great Neck, New York 11021, U.S.A.

PUBLICATIONS FOR YOUNG ADULTS

Fiction

Busybody Nora, illustrated by Susan Jeschke. New York, Morrow, 1976.

Nora and Mrs. Mind-Your-Own-Business, illustrated by Susan Jeschke. New York, Morrow, 1977.

The Law of Gravity, illustrated by Ingrid Fetz. New York, Morrow, 1978.

Much Ado about Aldo, illustrated by John Wallner. New York, Morrow, 1978.

Aldo Applesauce, illustrated by John Wallner. New York, Morrow, 1979.

New Neighbors for Nora, illustrated by Susan Jeschke. New York, Morrow, 1979.

Once I Was a Plum Tree, illustrated by Ingrid Fetz. New York, Morrow, 1980.

Superduper Teddy, illustrated by Susan Jeschke. New York, Morrow, 1980.

Aldo Ice Cream, illustrated by John Wallner. New York, Morrow, 1981.

Baseball Fever, illustrated by Ray Cruz. New York, Morrow, 1981.

The Rabbi's Girls, illustrated by Pamela Johnson. New York, Morrow, 1982.

Tough-Luck Karen, illustrated by Diane deGroat. New York, Morrow, 1982.

Rip-Roaring Russell, illustrated by Lillian Hoban. New York, Morrow, 1983.

DeDe Takes Charge!, illustrated by Diane deGroat. New York, Morrow, 1984.

The Hot and Cold Summer, illustrated by Gail Owens. New York, Morrow, 1984.

The Adventures of Ali Baba Bernstein, illustrated by Gain Owens. New York, Morrow, 1985.

Russell Rides Again, illustrated by Lillian Hoban. New York, Morrow, 1985.

Hurricane Elaine, illustrated by Diane deGroat. New York, Morrow, 1986.

Yellow Blue Jay, illustrated by Donald Carrick. New York, Morrow, 1986.

Class Clown, illustrated by Sheila Hamanaka. New York, Morrow, 1987.

Russell Sprouts, illustrated by Lillian Hoban. New York, Morrow, 1987.

The Cold and Hot Winter, illustrated by Carolyn Ewing. New York, Morrow, 1988.

Teacher's Pet, illustrated by Sheila Hamanaka. New York, Morrow, 1988.

Hurray for Ali Baba Bernstein, illustrated by Gail Owens. New York, Morrow, 1989.

Russell and Elisa, illustrated by Lillian Hoban. New York, Morrow, 1989.

Class President, illustrated by Sheila Hamanaka. New York, Morrow, 1990.

Aldo Peanut Butter, illustrated by Diane deGroat. New York, Morrow, 1990.

"E" Is for Elisa, illustrated by Lillian Hoban. New York, Morrow, 1991.

School's Out, illustrated by Sheila Hamanaka. New York, Morrow, 1991.

Ali Baba Bernstein: Lost and Found, illustrated by Karen Milone. New York, Morrow, 1992.

Roz and Ozzie, illustrated by Eileen McKeating, 1992.

New Shoes for Sylvia, illustrated by Jerry Pinkney. New York, Morrow, 1993.

The Up and Down Spring, illustrated by Gail Owens. New York, Morrow, 1993.

Make Room for Elisa, illustrated by Lillian Hoban. New York, Morrow Junior Books, 1993.

School Spirit, illustrated by Karen Dugan. New York, Morrow Junior Books, 1994.

A Llama in the Family, illustrated by Mark Graham. New York, Morrow Junior Books, 1994.

Ozzie on His Own, illustrated by Eileen McKeating. New York, Morrow Junior Books, 1995.

Elisa in the Middle, illustrated by Lillian Hoban. New York, Morrow Junior Books, 1995.

Even Stephen, illustrations by Michael Dooling. New York, Morrow Junior Books, 1996.

The Down & Up Fall, illustrated by Gail Owens. New York, Morrow Junior Books, 1996.

Spring Break, illustrated by Karen Dugan. New York, Morrow Junior Books, 1997.

Ever-clever Elisa, illustrated by Lillian Hoban. New York, Morrow Junior Books, 1997.

Starting School, illustrated by Karen Dugan. New York, Morrow Junior Books, 1998.

Faraway Summer, illustrated by Mary Azarian. New York, Morrow Junior Books, 1998.

Other

Anne Frank: Life in Hiding, illustrated by Vera Rosenberry. Philadelphia, Jewish Publication Society, 1988.

Astrid Lindgren: Storyteller to the World, illustrated by Michael Dooling. New York, Viking, 1989.

Leonard Bernstein: A Passion for Music, illustrated by Sonia O. Lisker. Philadelphia, Jewish Publication Society, 1993.

Helen Keller, Courage in the Dark, illustrated by Neverne Covington. New York, Random House, 1997.

Editor, *A Word to the Wise, and Other Proverbs,* illustrated by Robert Rayevsky. New York, Morrow Junior Books, 1994.

*

Manuscript Collections: Kerlan Collection, University of Minnesota, Minneapolis.

*   *   *

Johanna Hurwitz has a special gift for understanding young adults intimately. She manages to tell her stories through the perspective of characters, whatever their ages, sharing their thoughts, emotions, and concerns. Prominent themes include growing up and friendship. In her novels for early adolescents these themes continue, yet the elements of responsibility and learning to like oneself are added. The tone is not at all philosophical, but friendly, like good friends confiding to each other, admitting mistakes, offering each other advice and consolation. Perhaps this is the reason she is so well-liked as an author and seems to hit the bull's-eye every time in dealing with the concerns of eleven- through fifteen-year-olds.

In *The Cold and Hot Winter* Derek is anxiously awaiting the arrival of his next-door neighbor's niece, Olivia, who had visited the previous summer and had added some spice to Derek and his best friend's lives. Now, driving to the airport with his neighbors to pick up Olivia, he worries she has changed and won't like him, or that he won't like her. While he worries, the adults discuss the weather and express their desire for no more snow. "How silly grown-ups were, Derek thought. It was a cold day but that didn't bother him. Winter was supposed to be cold. And if they were lucky they would get a couple of good snow storms before the season ended."

Tough-Luck Karen describes the misfortunes of thirteen-year-old Karen Sossi. It seems everything goes wrong for her. She forgets her gym-locker key, accidently takes the beef intended for the family dinner in place of her school lunch, and struggles through her first baby-sitting job. Adolescence is difficult enough, but for Karen, her problems seem to be complicated further. Though she tells her mother she'll outgrow this phase of her life, Karen actually wonders if her luck will ever change. She thinks it has when she meets a new girl at school and invites her over. Unfortunately, Annette turns out to be allergic to the Sossi family cats. "Karen stood about awkwardly. She didn't know if she should apologize or pretend that everything was normal. What was the etiquette for causing someone to have an allergic reaction? she wondered."

In *Hurricane Elaine* the speech and actions of both fifteen-year-old Elaine and her mother are realistic. Elaine is Karen Sossi's older sister. Their father refers to Elaine as a hurricane because she rushes into action without thinking about the consequences. Elaine is a very typical teenager. Her complaints about household rules and intolerance for her younger siblings is a characteristic with which many readers will relate: "Even if she doesn't want to make a call and she's not expecting one, my mother won't let me stay on the phone longer than five minutes." Then when Elaine gets a phone call from a boy in her class who wants to ask for a date, her mother clocks the call and shouts up the stairs, "Time's up."

Mrs. Sossi handles her adolescent charges with humorous firmness. When Elaine has a miserable day at school, she storms into the house, ignoring her mother's greeting, and takes her frustration out on the family cat. When Mrs. Sossi requests her help in the kitchen, Elaine shouts "I'm busy" just as the phone rings. Mrs. Sossi explains to the caller that Elaine is very busy and can't be disturbed. When Elaine complains about this, Mrs. Sossi's response is very typical of that of parents of teenagers: "Why did you come home, if you won't greet anyone and won't answer me when I speak to you?"

Though struggling to grow up, learning to like oneself, and learning to be responsible are difficult for both her characters and real-life adolescents, Hurwitz adds humor that makes the ups and downs of that period of life bearable. Readers may feel their own lives are quite boring, but when compared to Elaine, Karen, or Derek's life, many similarities surface. Readers also gain confidence that they too can face difficulties and are not alone in their struggles to gain self-confidence and to be taken seriously by the adults in their lives.

—Lisa A. Wroble

HUXLEY, Aldous (Leonard)

Nationality: British. **Born:** Godalming, Surrey, 26 July 1894. **Education:** Hillside School, Godalming 1903-08; Eton College, 1908-13; Balliol College, Oxford, 1913-15, B.A. (honours) in English 1915. **Family:** Married 1) Maria Nys in 1919 (died, 1955); 2) Laura Archera in 1956; one son. **Career:** Worked in the War Office, 1917; taught at Eton College, 1918; member of the editorial staff of the *Athenaeum,* London, 1919-20; Drama Critic, *Westminster Gazette,* 1920-21; full-time writer from 1921; travelled and lived in France, Italy, and the United States, 1923-37; settled in California, 1937, and worked as a free-lance screenwriter. **Awards:** Award of Merit and Gold Medal, American Academy of Arts and Letters, 1959; D.Litt., University of California, 1959. Companion

of Literature, Royal Society of Literature, 1962. **Died:** 22 November 1963.

PUBLICATIONS

Novels

Crome Yellow. London, Chatto and Windus, 1921; New York, Doran, 1922.

Antic Hay. London, Chatto and Windus, and New York, Doran, 1923.

Those Barren Leaves. London, Chatto and Windus, and New York, Doran, 1925.

Point Counter Point. London, Chatto and Windus, and New York, Doubleday, 1928.

Brave New World. London, Chatto and Windus, and New York, Doubleday, 1932.

Eyeless in Gaza. London, Chatto and Windus, and New York, Harper, 1936.

After Many a Summer. London, Chatto and Windus, 1939; as *After Many a Summer Dies the Swan,* New York, Harper, 1939.

Time Must Have a Stop. New York, Harper, 1944; London, Chatto and Windus, 1945.

Ape and Essence. New York, Harper, 1948; London, Chatto and Windus, 1949.

The Genius and the Goddess. London, Chatto and Windus, and New York, Harper, 1955.

Antic Hay and The Gioconda Smile. London, Chatto and Windus, and New York, Harper, 1957.

Brave New World and Brave New World Revisited. London, Chatto and Windus, and New York, Harper. 1960.

Island. London, Chatto and Windus, and New York, Harper, 1962.

Short Stories

Limbo: Six Stories and a Play. London, Chatto and Windus, and New York, Doran, 1920.

Mortal Coils: Five Stories (includes play *Permutations among the Nightingales*). London, Chatto and Windus, and New York, Doran, 1922.

Little Mexican and Other Stories. London, Chatto and Windus, 1924; as *Young Archimedes and Other Stories,* New York, Doran, 1924.

Two or Three Graces and Other Stories. London, Chatto and Windus, and New York, Doran, 1926.

Brief Candles. London, Chatto and Windus, and New York, Doubleday, 1930; as *After the Fireworks,* New York, Avon, n.d.

The Gioconda Smile. London, Chatto and Windus, 1938.

Twice Seven: Fourteen Selected Stories. London, Reprint Society, 1944.

Collected Short Stories. London, Chatto and Windus, and New York, Harper, 1957.

The Crows of Pearblossom, illustrated by Barbara Cooney. London, Chatto and Windus, and New York, Random House, 1967.

Plays

Liluli, adaptation of a play by Romain Rolland, in *Nation* (London), 20 September-29 November 1919.

Albert, Prince Consort: A Biography Play for Which Mr. John Drinkwater's Historical Dramas Serve as a Model, in *Vanity Fair* (New York), March 1922.

The Ambassador of Capripedia, in *Vanity Fair* (New York), May 1922.

The Publisher, in *Vanity Fair* (New York), April 1923.

The Discovery, adaptation of the play by Frances Sheridan (produced London, 1924). London, Chatto and Windus, 1924; New York, Doran, 1925.

The World of Light: A Comedy in Three Acts (produced London, 1931). London, Chatto and Windus, and New York, Doubleday, 1931.

The Gioconda Smile, adaptation of his own story (produced London, 1948; New York, 1950). London, Chatto and Windus, 1948; as *Mortal Coils,* New York, Harper, 1948.

The Genius and the Goddess, with Ruth Wendell, adaptation of the novel by Huxley (produced New York, 1957).

Screenplays: *Pride and Prejudice,* with Jane Murfin, 1940; *Madame Curie,* 1943; *Jane Eyre,* with John Houseman and Robert Stevenson, 1944; *A Woman's Vengeance,* 1948.

Poetry

The Burning Wheel. Oxford, Blackwell, 1916.

Jonah. Oxford, Holywell Press, 1917.

The Defeat of Youth and Other Poems. Oxford, Blackwell, 1918.

Leda and Other Poems. London, Chatto and Windus, and New York, Doran, 1920.

Selected Poems. Oxford, Blackwell, and New York, Appleton, 1925.

Arabia Infelix and Other Poems. New York, Fountain Press, and London, Chatto and Windus, 1929.

Apennine. Gaylordsville, Connecticut, Slide Mountain Press, 1930.

The Cicadas and Other Poems. London, Chatto Doubleday, 1931.

Verses and a Comedy. London, Chatto and Windus, 1946.

The Collected Poetry of Aldous Huxley, edited by Donald Watt. London, Chatto and Windus, and New York, Harper, 1971.

Nonfiction

On the Margin: Notes and Essays. London, Chatto and Windus, and New York, Doran, 1923.

Along the Road: Notes and Essays of a Tourist. London, Chatto and Windus, and New York, Doran, 1925.

Jesting Pilate: The Diary of a Journey. London, Chatto and Windus, 1926; as *Jesting Pilate: An Intellectual Holiday,* New York, Doran, 1926.

Essays New and Old. London, Chatto and Windus, 1926; New York, Doran, 1927.

Proper Studies: The Proper Study of Mankind Is Man. London, Chatto and Windus, 1927; New York, Doubleday, 1928.

Do What You Will: Essays. London, Chatto and Windus, and New York, Doubleday, 1929.

Holy Face and Other Essays. London, The Fleuron, 1929.

Vulgarity in Literature: Digressions From a Theme. London, Chatto and Windus, 1930.

Music at Night and Other Essays. London, Chatto and Windus, and New York, Doubleday, 1931.

T.H. Huxley as a Man of Letters (lecture). London, Macmillan, 1932.

Beyond the Mexique Bay: A Traveller's Journal. London, Chatto and Windus, and New York, Harper, 1934.

1936 . . . Peace? London, Friends Peace Committee, 1936.

The Olive Tree and Other Essays. London, Chatto and Windus, 1936; New York, Harper, 1937.

What Are You Going to Do About It? The Case for Constructive Peace. London, Chatto and Windus, 1936; New York, Harper, 1937.

An Encyclopedia of Pacifism. New York, Harper, 1937.

Ends and Means: An Inquiry into the Nature of Ideals and into the Methods Employed for Their Realization. London, Chatto and Windus, and New York, Harper, 1937.

The Most Agreeable Vice. Los Angeles, Ward Ritchie Press, 1938.

Words and Their Meanings. Los Angeles, Ward Ritchie Press, 1940.

Grey Eminence: A Study in Religion and Politics. London, Chatto and Windus, and New York, Harper, 1941.

The Art of Seeing. New York, Harper, 1942; London, Chatto and Windus, 1943.

The Perennial Philosophy. New York, Harper, 1945; London, Chatto and Windus, 1946.

Science, Liberty, and Peace. New York, Harper, 1946; London, Chatto and Windus, 1947.

Food and People, with John Russell. London, Bureau of Current Affairs, 1949.

Prisons, with the Carceri Etchings by G.B. Piranesi. London, Trianon Press, and Los Angeles, Zeitlin and Ver Brugge, 1949.

Themes and Variations. London, Chatto and Windus, and New York, Harper, 1950.

Joyce, the Artificer: Two Studies of Joyce's Methods, with Stuart Gilbert. London, Chiswick Press, 1952.

The Devils of Loudun. Chatto and Windus, and New York, Harper, 1952.

A Day in Windsor, with J.A. Kings. London, Britannicus Liber, 1953.

The Doors of Perception. London, Chatto and Windus, and New York, Harper, 1954.

The French of Paris, photographs by Sanford H. Roth. New York, Harper, 1954.

Adonis and the Alphabet, and Other Essays. London, Chatto and Windus, 1956; as *Tomorrow and Tomorrow and Tomorrow and Other Essays,* New York, Harper, 1956.

Heaven and Hell. London, Chatto and Windus, and New York, Harper, 1956.

A Writer's Prospect—III: Censorship and Spoken Literature. London, 1956.

Brave New World Revisited. New York, Harper, 1958; London, Chatto and Windus, 1959.

"Chemical Persuasion," in *Fantasy and Science Fiction* (New York), April 1959.

Collected Essays. London, Chatto and Windus, and New York, Harper, 1959.

On Art and Artists: Literature, Painting, Architecture, Music, edited by Morris Philipson. London, Chatto and Windus, and New York, Harper, 1960.

Selected Essays, edited by Harold Raymond. London, Chatto and Windus, 1961.

Literature and Science. London, Chatto and Windus, and New York, Harper, 1963.

The Politics of Ecology: The Question of Survival. Santa Barbara, California, Center for the Study of Democratic Institutions, 1963.

New Fashioned Christmas. N.p., Hart Press, 1968.

America and the Future. Austin, Texas, Jenkins, 1970.

Moksha: Writings on Psychedelics and the Visionary Experience 1931-1963, edited by Michael Horowitz and Cynthia Palmer. New York, Stonehill, 1977; London, Chatto and Windus, 1980.
The Basic Philosophy of Aldous Huxley. American Institute of Psychology, 1984.

Other

Rotunda: A Selection From the Works of Aldous Huxley. London, Chatto and Windus, 1932.
Retrospect: An Omnibus of His Fiction and Non-Fiction Over Three Decades. New York, Doubleday, 1933.
Stories, Essays, and Poems. London, Dent, 1937.
The World of Aldous Huxley: An Omnibus of His Fiction and Non-Fiction over Three Decades, edited by Charles J. Rolo. New York, Harper, 1947.
Great Short Works of Aldous Huxley, edited by Bernard Bergonzi. New York, Harper, 1969.
The Letters of Aldous Huxley, edited by Grover Smith. London, Chatto and Windus, 1969; New York, Harper, 1970.
Collected Works. London, Chatto and Windus, 1970.
Science, Liberty and Peace. London, Chatto and Windus, 1970.
The Human Situation: Lectures at Santa Barbara 1959, edited by Piero Ferrucci. New York, Harper, 1977; London, Chatto and Windus, 1978.
The Wisdom of the Ages. Found Class Reprints, 2 volumes, 1989.
Huxley and God: Essays on Mysticism, Religion, and Spirituality, edited by Jacqueline Bridgeman. San Francisco, Harper, 1991.
Contributor, *This I Believe.* New York, Simon and Schuster, 1952.
Editor, with W.R. Childe and T.W. Earp, *Oxford Poetry 1916.* Oxford, Blackwell, 1916.
Editor, *The Letters of D.H. Lawrence.* London, Heinemann, and New York, Viking Press, 1932.
Editor, *Text and Pretexts: An Anthology with Commentaries.* London, Chatto and Windus, 1932; New York, Harper, 1933.
Editor, *An Encyclopedia of Pacifism.* London, Chatto and Windus, and New York, Harper, 1937.
Translator, *A Virgin Heart,* by Rémy de Gourmont. New York, Brown, 1921; London, Allen and Unwin, 1926.

*

Media Adaptations: *Point Counter Point* (play), London, 1930; *Prelude to Fame* (film; based on ''Young Archimedes''), Universal, 1950; *Brave New World* (television movie), NBC-TV, 1978; *Brave New World* (cassette; filmstrip with cassette), Current Affairs and Mark Twain Media, 1978.

Biography: *Aldous Huxley* by Jocelyn Brook, Longmans, Green, 1954; *The Huxleys* by Ronald W. Clark, New York, McGraw, 1968; *The Timeless Moment: A Personal View of Aldous Huxley* by Laura Huxley, New York, Farrar Straus, 1968, London, Chatto and Windus, 1969; *Aldous Huxley* by Harold H. Watts, New York, Twayne, 1969; *Aldous Huxley* by Keith M. May, London, Elek, 1972, New York, Harper, 1973; *Aldous Huxley: A Biography* by Sybille Bedford, London, Chatto and Windus-Collins, 2 volumes, 1973-74, New York, Knopf, 1 volume, 1974; *Huxley: A Biographical Introduction* by Peter Thody, New York, Scribner, 1973; entries in *Dictionary of Literary Biography,* Detroit, Gale, Volume

36, 1985; Volume 100, 1990; entry in *Concise Dictionary of British Literary Biography,* Volume 6, Detroit, Gale, 1991.

Bibliography: *Aldous Huxley: A Bibliography 1916-1959* by Claire John Eschelbach and Joyce Lee Shober, Berkeley, University of California Press, 1961; supplement by Thomas D. Clareson and Carolyn S. Andrews, in *Extrapolation 6* (Wooster, Ohio), 1964; *Aldous Huxley: An Annotated Bibliography of Criticism* by Eben E. Bass, New York, Garland, 1981.

Critical Study: *Aldous Huxley: A Literary Study* by John Atkins, London, Calder, and New York, Roy, 1956, revised edition, London, Calder, and Boyars, 1967, New York, Orion Press, 1968; *Aldous Huxley: A Memorial Volume* by Julian Huxley, New York, Harper, 1965; *Aldous Huxley: A Study of the Major Novels* by Peter Bowering, London, Athlone Press, 1968, New York, Oxford University Press, 1969; *Aldous Huxley: Satire and Structure* by Jerome Meckier, London, Chatto and Windus, and New York, Barnes and Noble, 1969; *Aldous Huxley: A Critical Study* by Laurence Brander, Lewisburg, Pennsylvania, Bucknell University Press, 1970; *Aldous Huxley and the Way to Reality* by Charles M. Holmes, Bloomington, Indiana University Press, 1970; *Aldous Huxley's Quest for Values* by Milton Birnbaum, Knoxville, University of Tennessee Press, 1971; *Aldous Huxley: A Satirist and Novelist* by Peter Firchow, St. Paul, University of Minnesota Press, 1972; *Dawn and the Darkest Hour: A Study of Aldous Huxley* by George Woodcock, London, Faber, and New York, Viking Press, 1972; entries in *Contemporary Literary Criticism,* Detroit, Gale, Volume 1, 1973; Volume 3, 1975; Volume 4, 1975; Volume 5, 1976; Volume 8, 1978; Volume 11, 1979; Volume 18, 1981; Volume 35, 1985; *Aldous Huxley: A Collection of Critical Essays* edited by Robert E. Kuehn, Englewood Cliffs, New Jersey, Prentice Hall, 1974; *Aldous Huxley: The Critical Heritage* edited by Donald Watt, London, Routledge, 1975; *Demon and Saint in the Novels of Aldous Huxley* by Lilly Zahmer, Bern, Schweizer Anglistische Arbeiten, 1975; *Aspects of Structure and Quest in Aldous Huxley's Major Novels* by Bharathi Krishnan, Uppsala, Sweden, University of Uppsala, 1977; *Aldous Huxley, Novelist* by Christopher S. Ferns, London, Athlone Press, 1980; *The Dark Historic Page: Social Satire and Historicism in the Novels of Aldous Huxley 1921-1939* by Robert S. Baker, Madison, University of Wisconsin Press, 1982.

*   *   *

As the grandson of eminent Victorian scientist Thomas Henry Huxley (a celebrated agnostic and popularizer of Darwinism), Aldous Huxley could have been expected to continue the family tradition as a rationalist and a skeptical advocate of empirical science. But Huxley was also descended from the famous Victorian schoolmaster Dr. Thomas Arnold, who was an ordained minister, an uncompromising moralist, and an exponent of the virtues of an education in the Greek and Roman classics, and it was this family tradition which Huxley ultimately embraced in his own idiosyncratic way. When failing eyesight in his adolescence became an obstacle to the study of science, Huxley, a lonely youth, turned to the study of literature. During his university years, unable to serve in the British army during World War I, he undertook a period of almost solitary study of English literature at Balliol College, Oxford. After an apprentice period as an undistinguished neo-romantic poet, he became an ironic novelist who will long be remembered as both a brilliant satirist of social behavior in the 1920s, and as a dedicated seeker of religious faith who rejected conventional religion, but chose the difficult path of private spiritual search and contemplative mysticism.

Huxley's early satirical fiction does not offer much of interest to young adult readers, although *Crome Yellow* presents a young poet's emotional confusion effectively, and *Antic Hay* treats London's social trends of the early twenties as the basis for grotesque comedy. A more probing effort to explore the disenchantment and amoral behavior of British intellectuals in the Jazz Age is *Point Counter Point;* but this fictional anatomy of modern disillusionment might have benefitted from a lighter tone and more of Huxley's humor. Instead, the influence of Fyodor Dostoyevsky and Huxley's contemporary, D. H. Lawrence, provide this novel with weighty themes.

As a prophetic critic of the twentieth-century obsession with science, technological development, and commercial and industrial advancement, Lawrence had become Huxley's mentor. An evangelist of sexual mysticism and a throwback to primitivist religious feeling, Lawrence was not only a great novelist, but a controversial social critic who continued to influence Huxley's thinking well after his death in 1930. Huxley resurrects Lawrence's passionate spirit in his next novel, his celebrated entry into the realm of speculative fiction. In *Brave New World,* Huxley produced a major dystopian novel which establishes a memorable opposition between behaviorist social programming, and a Lawrencian individualism, embodied in John, "the Savage," who serves as the novel's heroic and self-immolating protagonist.

Reared on a Pueblo reservation in northern New Mexico, and nurtured both by Native American mysticism and by his intense reading of the collected works of Shakespeare, John readily assaults the mindless pretenses of a supposed utopia, the programmed society described ironically by the title (a quotation taken from a romantic context in Shakespeare's *The Tempest*). This "brave new world," set six hundred years in the future from Huxley's time, is caustically attacked by "the Savage" in the ferocious tone exhibited by Lawrence in many of his expository essays, especially *Studies in Classic American Literature,* which Lawrence composed while living near Taos, New Mexico, not far from the Savage's own native grounds.

Armed with the humanist emotions in Shakespeare's verse, John levels scorching and withering criticism of a smug, self-satisfied world which has eliminated the nuclear and established social family order through the application of Henry Ford's mass production techniques to the nurturing of test-tube babies, who are given subliminal social training and educated to accept their predetermined social roles through the methods of Watsonian behaviorism. As adults, the citizens of this false utopia are indoctrinated to the belief that they are happy, while their psychological frustrations are relieved by easily obtained sexual experience and mind-soothing drugs. But in the climactic debate of the novel, John, "the Savage," rejects the rhetoric justifying this behaviorist social tyranny. In response to the arguments of Mustapha Mond, the administrator of this future society, who echoes Dostoyevsky's Grand Inquisitor in claiming that human beings need to be protected from their own unhappiness, John asserts the classic humanist argument that human dignity requires "the right to be unhappy."

In *Brave New World,* Huxley produced an enduring novel in the science fiction genre, and one of the most brilliant satires in English literature. Although other intellectuals before Huxley—H. G. Wells, E. M. Forster, Yugeny Zamiatin, Karel Capek—had experimented with science fiction romances as a method of social criticism, Huxley's novel remains a seminal work and a remarkable achievement which influenced many later writers from George Orwell to Robert Silverberg.

After *Brave New World,* Huxley's fiction and nonfiction both became increasingly concerned with his interest in religious mysticism. Like Lawrence, Huxley left England to become a citizen of the world, settling ultimately in Southern California. The influence of Lawrence, however, was gradually replaced by that of Gerald Heard, a more conventional religious mystic. Although *Eyeless in Gaza* and *Time Must Have a Stop* are both concerned with religious quests, *After Many a Summer Dies the Swan,* which satirizes the popular culture of Southern California and a foolish attempt to gain physical immortality through technological innovation, displays some of Huxley's vintage comic irony.

Much of Huxley's later energy was devoted primarily to nonfiction, both in essays presenting social criticism, and in works like *The Perennial Philosophy,* which collects and comments on the texts that Huxley considered the vital essence of the world's mystical writings. *The Devils of Loudon,* a study of religious repression and sexual perversity, was adapted by John Whiting into a play and later transformed into an impressive film, *The Devils.*

In his final important novel, *Island,* Huxley presented a fictional counterpoint to *Brave New World* in a utopian novel which offered mystical experience stimulated by such drugs as mescaline and LSD as one of the goals of human experience. Unlike the drug called "soma" of *Brave New World,* which provides merely a temporary and pleasurable relief from social tension, the drug induced experience of *Island* reaches deeper levels of contemplation and vision. As a result, the novel had some influence on the cult of "mind expanding" drugs in the sixties; but this aspect of its teaching has not been appealing in the climate of the current reaction against drug usage.

Since *Island,* like many utopian novels, tends to substitute exposition for drama, it has never achieved the popularity of Huxley's other major venture into speculative fiction. But the novel remains important as a revelation of Huxley's intellectual development.

Although Huxley wanted to be remembered as a social novelist and essayist, he was aware that his extraordinary emotional detachment limited his ability to create sympathetic characters. In addition to his limitations as a fiction writer, many critics who admired his satire deplored his rejection of rationalism and his long devotion to the cause of mysticism. Yet Huxley's later work testifies to the seriousness of his religious quest. However, Huxley will probably owe his enduring reputation not to the writing describing his spiritual search but to his efforts as a satirist, and ultimately, perhaps, to the brilliant, imaginative satire in *Brave New World.*

—Edgar L. Chapman

IRWIN, Hadley

Joint pseudonym for Lee Hadley and Ann Irwin. **Lee Hadley: Nationality:** American. **Born:** Earlham, Iowa, 10 October 1934. **Education:** Drake University, Des Moines, Iowa, B.A. 1956; University of Wisconsin-Madison, M.A. 1961. **Career:** Writer. Copywriter, Younkers of Des Moines (department store), 1955-58; high school English teacher, De Soto, Iowa, 1959-60; instructor in English, Ocean County Community College, Toms River, New Jersey, 1965-68; assistant, then associate, then full professor of English, Iowa State University, Ames, 1969-95. **Died:** 1995. **Ann Irwin: Nationality:** American. **Born:** Peterson, Iowa, 8 October 1915. **Education:** Morningside College, Sioux City, Iowa, B.A. 1937; University of Iowa, Iowa City, M.A. 1967. **Family:** Married Keith C. Irwin, 1943; three daughters and one son. **Career:** Writer. High school English teacher, Iowa, 1937-67; instructor in English, Buena Vista College, Storm Lake, Iowa, 1967-68; instructor in English, Midwestern College, Denison, Iowa, 1968-1970; associate professor of English, Iowa State University, Ames, 1970-85. **Awards:** Honor Book award, Jane Addams Peace Association, 1981, for *We Are Mesquakie, We Are One*; Society of Midland Authors award, 1982, for *Moon and Me*; Notable Children's Trade Book in the Field of Social Studies award from joint committee of the National Council on Social Studies and Children's Book Council and Best Young Adult Book award from American Library Association, both 1982, for *What about Grandma?* and both 1985, for *Abby, My Love*; Children's Choice Book award, joint committee of Children's Book Council and International Reading Association, 1986, for *Abby, My Love*. **Address:** Department of English, Iowa State University, Ames, Iowa 50011, U.S.A.

PUBLICATIONS FOR YOUNG ADULTS

Fiction

The Lilith Summer. New York, Feminist Press, 1979.
We Are Mesquakie, We Are One. New York, Feminist Press, 1980.
Bring to a Boil and Separate. New York, Atheneum, 1980.
Moon and Me. New York, Atheneum, 1981.
What about Grandma? New York, Atheneum, 1982.
I Be Somebody. New York, Macmillan, 1984.
Abby, My Love. New York, Macmillan, 1985.
Kim/Kimi. New York, Macmillan, 1987.
So Long at the Fair. New York, Macmillan, 1988.
Can't Hear You Listening. New York, Macmillan, 1990.
The Original Freddie Ackerman. New York, Macmillan, 1992.
Jim Dandy. New York, Macmillan, 1994.
Sarah with an H. New York, Macmillan, 1996.

Nonfiction

Writing Young Adult Novels. Cincinnati, Ohio, Writer's Digest Books, 1988.

Other (Ann Irwin)

Hawkeye Adventure, with Bernice Reida. Graphic Publishing, 1966.
Hawkeye Lore, with Bernice Reida. Graphic Publishing, 1968.
One Bite at a Time. New York, F. Watts, 1973.
Moon of the Red Strawberry, with Bernice Reida. Aurora, 1977.
Until We Reach the Valley, with Bernice Reida. New York, Avon, 1979.

*

Media Adaptation: *The Lilith Summer* was released with a teaching guide by Aims, 1984.

Biography: Essay in *Speaking for Ourselves: Autobiographical Sketches by Notable Authors of Books for Young Adults,* Vol. 1, compiled and edited by Donald R. Gallo, National Council of Teachers of English, 1990; essay in *Something about the Author Autobiography Series,* Vol. 14, Detroit, Gale, 1992.

*   *   *

Hadley Irwin is the pen name for Lee Hadley and Ann Irwin. Together, as a "single identity," Hadley Irwin has authored a number of books for young adults. Like other works in this age class, her fiction addresses issues of concern to teenagers, including suicide, incest, and alcohol abuse. Particularly successful are *What about Grandma?, Abby, My Love,* and *Kim/Kimi.* These novels, as well as *So Long at the Fair* and *Can't Hear You Listening,* are not action-packed works that are sped through; rather, they're books a reader strolls with while contemplating a central problem and caring for various characters.

In *What about Grandma?,* sixteen-year-old Rhys and her mother find themselves looking after Grandma Wyn, who refuses to stay in a nursing home. The three women, initially "a pyramid of age locked into one house," gradually come to terms with the hurts and misunderstandings of the past, and find joy in their relationships.

In *Abby, My Love,* Irwin's focus is the sensitive issue of sexual abuse. The story is narrated by Chip, who reflects on his longtime friendship with Abby. For years, Chip had desired a closer relationship, but Abby would withdraw so that she simply couldn't be reached. When Abby finally turns to Chip in desperation, telling him that her father sexually abused her, Chip relies on his mother and her boyfriend for help. But as is often sadly true in such situations, Abby's mother is unable or unwilling to take any action to protect her daughter, so it is Chip's love and strength which ultimately prod Abby to seek the professional assistance she needs.

situations, Abby's mother is unable or unwilling to take any action to protect her daughter, so it is Chip's love and strength which ultimately prod Abby to seek the professional assistance she needs.

Kim/Kimi addresses the notion of identity, but with an important twist. Kim Andrews/Kimi Yoguchi is half Japanese. In response to her crisis of mixed racial identity, she travels to Sacramento to locate her Japanese family, armed only with an old photograph and her deceased father's name, Yoguchi. There Kimi learns about the parts of her heritage not covered in textbooks, including the forced internment of Japanese citizens in camps like Manzanar and Tule Lake during World War II. She is ultimately successful in her quest to locate her father's family, but the relationship established is very uncertain, although hopeful.

The conclusions of *So Long at the Fair* and *Can't Hear You Listening* are also fragile endings. Joel's slow and painful acceptance of his best friend Ashley's suicide is the subject of *So Long at the Fair*. After spending a week at the state fairgrounds, Joel is ready to begin his personal healing process. In *Can't Hear You Listening,* Tracy deals with her parents' separation, her mother's successful writing career, and the abuse of alcohol and drugs by her friend Stanley. While the family relationships have stabilized by the end of the novel, Stanley still has difficult times to face.

In addition to dramatizing teen concerns, several other recurring ideas emerge from Irwin's works. The first of these is the portrayal of the elderly as human beings with hopes, fears, loves, and problems. This is especially evident in *What about Grandma?* which features Grandma Wyn, her fun-loving and energetic neighbor Virene, the Reverend Baddeley, and others. Similarly, Mrs. Mueller in *Kim/Kimi,* while less fully developed as a character than Grandma Wyn, leads an interesting life and helps Kim in her search. Tracy's grandmother in *Can't Hear You Listening* abandons her role as a farm wife following her husband's death and transforms into a bridge-playing Arizona condo dweller, just to see if she still has the gumption to make such a change. In all these novels, the elderly are not only present, but portrayed realistically and humanly, an accomplishment of note in young adult fiction.

A second commonality in Irwin's novels is setting. Grandma Wyn's beloved Iowa lake could well be considered an additional character in *What about Grandma?* The lake brings back memories for all three women and serves as the backdrop for important conversations between the generations. Kim's quest to locate her Japanese family becomes more understandable given her upbringing in a small Iowa town. Abby's abuse within a middle-class family living in an Iowa town is all the more chilling for its occurrence in such a "safe" environment. And Joel's retreat from his comfortable and upscale home to the state fair is a believable escape. The choice of Iowa towns for the settings is a natural one, since both Irwin and Hadley are longtime residents. While the settings may appear somewhat idyllic to urban readers, their depiction is never negative or stereotypically provincial.

A third motif is the value of a strong parent-adolescent relationship. In *What about Grandma?* the relationship that slowly develops among the three women is what makes the work satisfying. This same type of generational trio appears in *Can't Hear You Listening* and again, these characters struggle to understand and respect one another. Similarly Chip's close relationship with his mother not only gives him the strength to help Abby, it also provides the support both Chip and his mother themselves require to cope with Abby's abuse.

A final thread running through Irwin's works is the self-worth that a number of characters find when they assume nurturing or teaching roles. Kimi's friend Ernie volunteers at a center for recent Asian immigrants, Joel coaches the Little League Baseball Bombers, and Ashley tutors at an alternative school. In fact, it is a newspaper article's focus on her, instead of her students, that precipitates Ashley's suicide.

Hadley Irwin's works sensitively and successfully portray adolescent concerns. There is occasional heavy-handedness ("Life is growth. To grow, you have to learn who you *were,* who you *are,* and what you *will become.''*), and several descriptions, while humorous, appear to be parodies of the romance novels Kim reads ("I had to admit he was kind of cute in a beefy way and had the biggest biceps of anyone on the team. His pectorals weren't bad, either"). But these faults are minor when considered in the greater context of the novels' characters and issues.

In the end, the great strength of Hadley Irwin's fiction can perhaps be reduced to a single concept: respect. In all her works, respect for others is a central theme, whether the respect is for the elderly, a parent, an adolescent, or persons different, younger, or less fortunate. This is indeed a valuable message for young adult readers.

—Bonnie O. Ericson

JACKSON, Sam. *See* **TRUMBO, Dalton.**

JACQUES, Brian

Nationality: British. **Born:** Liverpool, 15 June 1939. **Education:** Attended Roman Catholic school in Liverpool. **Family:** Two sons. **Career:** Seaman, 1954-57; railway fireman, 1957-60; longshoreman, 1960-65; long-distance truck driver, 1965-75; docks representative, 1975-80; free-lance radio broadcaster, 1980—. Radio broadcasts for BBC-Radio Merseyside include the music programs "Jakestown" and "Saturday With Brian Jacques" and documentaries "We All Went Down the Docks," "Gangland Anthology," "The Eternal Christmas," "Centenary of Liverpool," "An Eyeful of Easter," "A Lifetime Habit," and "The Hollywood Musicals," a six-part series; broadcaster for BBC-Radio 1 and BBC-Radio 2; member of BBC Northwest Television Advisory Council. Presents humorous lectures at schools and universities. Patron of Royal Wavertree School for the Blind. **Awards:** National Light Entertainment award for Radio from Sony Company, 1982, for BBC-Radio Merseyside's "Jakestown"; Rediffusion award for Best Light Entertainment Program on Local Radio, 1982, and Commendation, 1983; Parents' Choice Honor Book for Literature, 1987, and Children's Book of the Year award from Lancashire County Library, 1988, both for *Redwall;* W.A. Young Readers Book award, 1991, for *Mossflower.* **Address:** c/o from Lancashire County Library, 1988, both for *Redwall;* W.A. Young Readers Book award, 1991, for *Mossflower.* **Address:** c/o Putnam Publishing Corp., 200 Madison Ave., New York, New York 10016, U.S.A.

PUBLICATIONS FOR YOUNG ADULTS

Novels

Redwall, illustrated by Gary Chalk. New York, Philomel, 1987.
Mossflower, illustrated by Gary Chalk. New York, Philomel, 1988.
Mariel of Redwall, illustrated by Gary Chalk. New York, Philomel, 1991.
Mattimeo. New York, Avon, 1991.
Seven Strange & Ghostly Tales. New York, Philomel, 1991.
The Redwall Trilogy. N.p., Red Fox, 1991.
Salamandastron. New York, Philomel, 1992.
Martin the Warrior. London, Hutchinson, 1993; New York, Ace, 1995.
The Bellmaker, illustrated by Allan Curless. London, Hutchinson, 1994.
Outcast of Redwall, illustrated by Allan Curless. London, Hutchinson, 1995.
The Pearls of Lutra: A Tale of Redwall, illustrated by Allan Curless. London, Hutchinson, 1996.
The Great Redwall Feast, illustrated by Christopher Denise. London, Random House, 1996.

*　　*　　*

Brian Jacques has made the world of woodland and meadow his own. His books are populated with the creatures of the forest, and not a human among them. The heroes are the little folk, the "gentlebeasts" to use his own term: mice, voles, moles, squirrels, and badgers. Against these gentle creatures the author pits the predators: rats, foxes, and wildcats. The animals are generally true to their natures, but a bit anthropomorphized.

The tales center themselves on a community consisting primarily of mice who live in the Abbey of Redwall. Although the mice seem organized on standard monastic lines, religion plays no part in the narratives. The Redwall community practices charity and love for all creatures, even those about whom it might be best to be a bit less charitable. In *Salamandastron,* for example, two renegade sea-rats (a loathsome variety of pirate) come to the Abbey for shelter. They steal the magical sword of Martin the Warrior and slink off into the night, leaving one of the brother mice dead. The theft is not their only legacy: one of them was carrying the germs of Dryditch Fever. Soon most of the Abbey residents are ill and dying.

Jacques has a standard approach to each of his works. Two problems are set: one for an individual or group of individuals, and a second for the entire Abbey. In *Salamandastron* a young badger and a young hare from the Mountain of Dragons have crept off with a smooth-talking weasel. They are met by Samkin Squirrel and Arula Mole from Redwall, who are trying to track the thieves who stole the sword. In the meantime Thugg, the otter, and Baby Dumble, the dormouse, have set out for the mountains of the north to find the Flowers of Icetor, the only cure for the fever. The

narrative flows smoothly between the adventures of the various groups, eventually bringing all of them together.

Jacques gives his creatures individual "racial" characteristics by a unique use of language. Moles, for example, speak a dialect much like cockney English: "Ee be a gurt noisy trowt that un, eh?" The eagles and falcons of the northern mountains speak Scots: "We were searchin' for that young rip, mah son Rocangus, but six braw sojers like us wid be shamed if we couldnae give some crows a good tanning!" Less intelligent creatures, like the sparrows in *Redwall,* speak a variety of pidgin English: "Me hunt worms. Bring dandelions for Matthias. Mouse like eat flowers."

The tales are peppered with poetry and rhymes, often in the form of puzzles that the protagonists must solve to resolve their problem, like this piece from *Redwall:*

> Who says that I am dead
> Knows nought at all.
> I—am that is
> Two mice within Redwall.
> The Warrior sleeps
> 'Twixt Hall and Cavern Hole
> I—am that is
> Take on my mighty role.
> Look for the sword
> In moonlight streaming forth,
> At night, when day's first hour
> Reflects the North.
> From o'er the threshold
> Seek, and you will see;
> I—am that is
> My sword will wield for me.

The mouse Matthias and his abbot must decipher the rhyme to find the lost sword and reclaim the Abbey from the Sparrows that have infested its upper regions. Among the minor characters in *Mattimeo* is a poetical owl, Sir Harry the Muse, whose comments are always in rhymes:

> Dread words do not alarm me
> When food is on its way
> No parchment threat can harm me
> Lead on, lead on I say.

Jacques makes his tales palatable to the younger reader by sprinkling them with accounts of fabulous feasts. Any excuse to celebrate in Mossflower County means a lavish meal prepared by the cooks of Redwall: "Our Abbot . . . has declared that his first anniversary shall be marked by a huge feast . . . I never told him . . . of the wonderful feast when the main gate was raised. . . . The feast of The Autumn of the Warriors' Return began just after dawn." The hares and moles are particularly interested in eating until they are ready to burst. Good October ale, salads, jams, and jellies are the stuff upon which the Redwallers feed.

Jacques pictures a quiet simple time when virtue is always triumphant over evil. There is always a price, but it is paid with few recriminations.

—Louise J. Winters

JAMES, Mary. *See* KERR, M.E.

JANECZKO, Paul B(ryan)

Pseudonyms: P. Wolny. **Nationality:** American. **Born:** Passaic, New Jersey, 27 July 1945. **Education:** St. Francis College, Biddeford, Maine, A.B. 1967; John Carroll University, Cleveland, Ohio, M.A. 1970. **Family:** Married Nadine Edris; one daughter. **Career:** Poet and anthologist. High school English teacher in Parma, Ohio, 1968-72, and Topsfield, Massachusetts, 1972-77; guest editor of *Leaflet,* Spring 1977; Gray-New Gloucester High School, Gray, Maine, teacher of language arts, 1977-90, visiting writer, 1990—. **Awards:** *Postcard Poems* was selected one of New York Public Library's Books for the Teen Age, 1980 and 1981, and *Don't Forget to Fly: A Cycle of Modern Poems,* 1982; *Don't Forget to Fly,* 1981, *Poetspeak,* 1983, *Strings: A Gathering of Family Poems,* 1984, *Pocket Poems: Selected for a Journey,* 1985, and *Going over to Your Place,* 1987, were selected by the American Library Association as Best Young Adult Books of the Year; *Don't Forget to Fly* was selected one of *School Library Journal*'s Best Books, 1981, and *Poetspeak: In Their Work, about Their Work,* 1983; English-Speaking Union Books-across-the-Sea Ambassador of Honor Book award, 1984, for *Poetspeak; Pocket Poems* was chosen one of Child Study Association of America's Children's Books of the Year, 1985. **Address:** RR 1, Box 260, Marshall Pond Rd., Hebron, Maine 04238, U.S.A.

PUBLICATIONS FOR YOUNG ADULTS

Poetry

Brickyard Summer, illustrated by Ken Rush. New York, Orchard, 1989.
Stardust Hotel, illustrated by Dorothy Leech. New York, Orchard, 1993.
That Sweet Diamond: Baseball Poems, illustrated by Carole Katchen. New York, Atheneum, 1998.

Editor and Compiler

The Crystal Image. New York, Dell. 1977.
Postcard Poems. Scarsdale, New York, Bradbury, 1979.
It's Elementary. New York, Bantam, 1981.
Don't Forget to Fly: A Cycle of Modern Poems. Scarsdale, New York, Bradbury, 1981.
Poetspeak: In Their Work, about Their Work. Scarsdale, New York, Bradbury, 1983.
Strings: A Gathering of Family Poems. Scarsdale, New York, Bradbury, 1984.
Pocket Poems: Selected for a Journey. Scarsdale, New York, Bradbury, 1985.
This Delicious Day: 65 Poems. New York, Franklin Watts, 1987.

Going over to Your Place: Poems for Each Other. Scarsdale, New York, Bradbury, 1987.
The Music of What Happens: Poems That Tell Stories. New York, Franklin Watts, 1988.
The Place My Words Are Looking For: What Poets Say about and through Their Work. Scarsdale, New York, Bradbury, 1990.
Preposterous: Poems of Youth. New York, Orchard, 1991.
Looking for Your Name. New York, Orchard, 1993.
Poetry from A to Z: A Guide for Young Writers, illustrated by Cathy Bobak. New York, Bradbury Press, 1994.
Wherever Home Begins: 100 Contemporary Poems. New York, Orchard Books, 1995.
With Naomi Shihab Nye, *I Feel a Little Jumpy Around You: A Book of Her Poems & His Poems Collected in Pairs.* New York, Simon and Schuster, 1996.
Home on the Range: Cowboy Poetry, pictures by Bernie Fuchs. New York, Dial Books, 1997.

Fiction

Bridges to Cross, illustrated by Robert J. Blake. New York, Macmillan, 1986.

Nonfiction

Loads of Codes and Secret Ciphers. New York, Simon and Schuster, 1981.

Other

Contributor, *Censorship: A Guide for Teachers, Librarians, and Others Concerned with Intellectual Freedom,* edited by Lou Willett Stanek. New York, Dell, 1976.
Contributor, *Children's Literature Review,* edited by Gerard J. Senick. Volume 3, Detroit, Gale, 1978.
Contributor, *Young Adult Literature in the Seventies,* edited by Jana Varlejs. Metuchen, New Jersey, Scarecrow, 1978.

Author of ''Back Pages,'' a review column in *Leaflet,* 1973-76. Author of numerous articles, stories, poems (under pseudonym P. Wolny), and reviews to newspapers, professional and popular magazines, including *Armchair Detective, New Hampshire Profiles, Modern Haiku, Dragonfly, Friend, Child Life,* and *Highlights for Children.*

*

Biography: Essay in *Authors and Artist for Young Adults,* volume 9, Detroit, Gale, 1992.

Paul B. Janeczko comments:

I started writing when I was in the fifth or sixth grade. But, unlike many writers, I didn't begin with poems or short stories or ''novels.'' No, I started by writing postcards to get free stuff. Stuff I didn't really need—e.g., a sample of tarnish remover, a moving kit, a stain removal chart—but had to have.

When I started teaching high school English nearly twenty-five years ago, I figured I could write a novel like the young adult novels

I was teaching. I was wrong, so I started writing for teacher magazines and spent a lot of years developing my writing skills in that area.

Strictly speaking, my poems are not autobiographical. Oh, I borrow from people I've known and from experiences I've had, but then my imagination kicks in and I create new people who have new experiences. I spend a great deal of time developing the characters in my books because I know if I can create interesting characters, they will, more than likely, do interesting things. And that's what readers are looking for.

*   *   *

It is difficult to imagine where, in the late 1970s, 1980s, and the beginning of the 1990s, young adults might have found exciting collections of contemporary poetry were it not for Paul Janeczko and his many anthologies. Others have compiled a variety of thematic collections but Janeczko's ability to ferret out the unusual, the relevant, is an amazing gift to students (as well as to teachers, librarians, families, and friends) who wish to be introduced to the latest in poetry.

Janeczko's instinct, both for the individual poem and the shape of a collection, is that of a fine anthologist; poems with strong images stand by themselves, yet relate and dovetail into each other, one enriching the next, occurring in a progression which crescendos toward an end and still seems to circle back to the beginning. Thus, in *Preposterous,* the opening poem, Gary Hyland's "Zip on Good Advice," which begins with the line "What do parents know anyhow?" is a lead into "Dodo" by Henry Carlile, just as the last of the 108 selections, William Stafford's "Runaway Teen"—which ends with "It's hard being a person. We all know that" recalls and echoes the first line of the Hyland.

Within the anthologies, many among the American Library Association's Best Books of the Year, Janeczko chooses the work of hundreds of contemporary poets. There is certainly William Stafford, X.J. Kennedy, Richard Eberhart, Donald Hall, and Randall Jarrell but there is also a wealth of lesser known poets Janeczko often uses—David Allan Evans, Jonathan Holden, Sheryl L. Helms, Mark Vinz, Ronald Wallace, Keith Wilson, and Paul Zimmer to name only a few. Each anthology bears its own special mark of distinction. *Pocket Poems: Selected for a Journey* is in a "pocket-size format for travelers and others on the move." *Strings: A Gathering of Family Poems* centers around the experiences of family life; *Going over to Your House: Poems for Each Other* is heralded by Peter Meinke's "The Heart's Location" wherein the narrator seeks "a poem full of ordinary words/about simple things/in the inconsolable rhythms of the heart." Janeczko's *Looking for Your Name* is an arresting collection of poems about life in America today, ranging in subject from acquired immunodeficiency syndrome (AIDS) to pacifism, violence, the nuclear freeze, unemployment, sports, love, peace, family, and offshore drilling.

Janeczko's first book of his own poetry, *Brickyard Summer,* is rich with the people and places of a New England milltown; high school chums "hanging out in front of Manny's," the nuns who warn of the Seven Deadly Sins and the realisms of a dying cat, petty thievery, a first kiss. Friendship, comradery, and encounters with unusual adults also mark his second collection, *Stardust Hotel* (1993):

The H fell nearly 14 years ago:
the day I was born
Nick swung on it in joy
until it snapped off in his hands.
He never replaced it,
saying he liked to be reminded
of how he felt that day.

Janeczko remembers the small, telling details. There are "aunts smelling of rose water," Patrick who "spit into the pocket of his glove," Brady who chewed "Juicy Fruit" and Eduardo who "gave samba lessons/to ladies in a rented room/over Owen's Auto Parts." He writes of the elixir for Wayne's "damaged aura," the dare to meet at a cemetery and "press dry lips to the polished marble," and "girls in spike heels,/leopard pants snug/as a stamp on a first-class parcel," Charlie Hooper whose voice "was quiet but wild like pigeons taking flight" and Rusty, who:

. . . mostly
works at the A&P
fielding questions
about chicken thighs,
Cornish hens,
and leg of lamb.

Certainly Janeczko is the poet of youth—casual, callow, alternately blustering and frightened—probing for life's discoveries; encountering its petty larcenies and pragmatism, its joys and pains, its important and abiding friendships, and often, moments of epiphany and serendipity. His nonfiction work *Loads of Codes and Secret Ciphers* seems almost as a footnote to the delicious puzzles and secrecy of youth, as does in a certain sense, *Bridges to Cross* a work of fiction in which the theme of hidden, untold secrets echoes with the quiet pain of salad days. Reading his poetry one not only realizes Janeczko's extreme sensitivity to the young but equally important encounters, head-on, a wry, delicious sense of humor which is all too rare in many poets who are apt to take themselves too seriously. For Janeczko life is not simple, but neither is it, as George Bernard Shaw took pains to tell us, wasted on the young. Janeczko's work makes this abundantly clear.

—Myra Cohn Livingston

JINKS, Catherine

Nationality: Australian. **Born:** Brisbane, Queensland, 1963. **Education:** Studied medieval history, University of Sydney. **Family:** Married; one child. **Career:** Journalist; full-time writer. **Awards:** Children's Book Council of Australia Book of the Year, Older Readers, 1996; Sheaffer Pen Prize for Young Adult Fiction, Victorian Premier's Literary Awards, 1997; Best Young Adult Novel, Aurealis Award for Excellence in Australian Speculative Fiction, 1997. **Address:** c/o Penguin Books Australia, Ltd., 487 Maroondah Highway, Ringwood, Victoria 3134, Australia.

PUBLICATIONS FOR YOUNG ADULTS

Fiction

This Way Out. Norwood, South Australia, Omnibus, 1991.
Pagan's Crusade. Melbourne, Oxford University Press, 1992; Oxford, Oxford University Press, 1993.
The Future Trap. Norwood, South Australia, Omnibus, 1993.
Pagan in Exile. Norwood, South Australia, Omnibus, 1994.
Pagan's Vows. Norwood, South Australia, Omnibus, 1995.
Witch Bank. Ringwood, Victoria, Penguin, 1995.
Pagan's Scribe. Norwood, South Australia, Omnibus, 1996.
Eye to Eye. Ringwood, Victoria, Penguin, 1997.
Piggy in the Middle. Ringwood, Victoria, Penguin, 1998.

PUBLICATIONS FOR CHILDREN (illustrated by author)

Fiction

The Secret of Hermitage Isle. Sydney, ABC Books, 1997.
The Horrible Holiday. Ringwood, Victoria, Penguin, 1998.

PUBLICATIONS FOR ADULTS

Fiction

An Evening with the Messiah. Ringwood, Victoria, and New York, Penguin Books, 1996.
Little White Secrets. Ringwood, Victoria, Penguin Books, 1996.

*   *   *

Catherine Jinks has written in a number of genres but it is her distinctive historical novels, the four Pagan books, that have attracted notice and awards. Drawing on her knowledge of medieval history, Jinks recreates twelfth century life as experienced by sixteen-year-old Pagan Kidrouk, a "street kid" in Jerusalem in 1187 at the time of the Crusades. Pagan becomes squire to Templar knight Lord Roland Roucy de Bram, described by Pagan as looking, "...like something off a stained-glass window", a contrast to Pagan with, "Skin the colour of braised almonds. Built like a horsewhip. Black hair. Black eyes." Pagan's crusade, of course, is survival and he is blessed with all that is necessary to get by in a hard and dangerous world, including sharp wits and a monastery education. This is not so with Roland who, although of noble birth, is illiterate, and whose trustfulness and moral code cause endless frustration to the worldly Pagan. In the first of the series, *Pagan's Crusade,* Pagan provides an amusingly cheeky commentary on the pilgrims to Jerusalem who require the Templar's protection. He uses these same wits to survive Saladin's siege and achieve freedom for Roland, whom he comes to love.

In *Pagan in Exile,* Pagan and Lord Roland return to the latter's family home in France. But what a home, and what a jealous, dirty, and grasping family the de Bram's prove to be! Roland has to confront family tensions and re-examine his own actions and involvement with violence, particularly in light of his love for a local woman, Esclaramonde, who is a member of an heretical religious sect. In *Pagan's Vows* it is still 1188 but Pagan and Lord Roland have left the latter's brawling family and the tragedy of

Esclaramonde's death to seek solace and refuge as novices in an abbey. Roland is a broken reed but Pagan flourishes as a student (although he wouldn't admit this) and also flushes out a blackmailing racket which results in the death of a friend, Raymond. *Pagan's Scribe* moves to 1209 when Pagan is in his late thirties and Archdeacon of Carcassone, but little else has changed. Roland remains in the Abbey of St. Martin, most clerics are still greedy, lazy, and stupid, and the Pope, responding to worries about the rising popularity of the religious heretics, the Cathars in Languedoc, orders a crusade. Despite all Pagan's rhetorical skills the papal forces descend bloodily on Carcassone. After a long siege the town is taken and Roland is killed.

Each of the Pagan books revolves around an ethical question in the context of Christian philosophy. In *Pagan's Vows* Pagan's lessons in rhetoric, in particular his readings from Boethius, provide a commentary on the secret life of the monastery, where truth takes on many appearances and it is ironic that Pagan, the supposed sinner, is the catalyst for bringing evil into the light. Despite the somber subjects and tragic events such a wealth of information about religious battles and historical figures sits lightly on the reader because of Pagan's first person delivery. His relentless wisecracking about the characters, sights, and smells of life around him, a joyful response in the face of so much ugliness, sin, and stupidity, carries the narrative along at an almost bewildering pace. Some scenes, such as when Pagan washes paupers' feet as a penance for swearing in *Pagan's Vows,* are not for the faint of heart.

Lively, spirited heroes and heroines are a feature of Jink's other novels. In *This Way Out* Bron hates living in the outer western Sydney suburb of Deberfield and thinks modelling will be the way to escape. Despite setbacks and cruel awakenings she keeps trying. *Witch Bank* is an unusual fantasy set in a large city bank. Heather is a nondescript mouse-like girl who somehow gets a job in the bank and is taken under the wing of Pam, a modern witch. There are several witches in the bank and they recognise in Heather a girl with special powers of invisibility. But how is it that mysterious Jasper can see her so clearly?

In contrast to the historical setting of the Pagan titles, three of Jinks' novels have futuristic settings. In *The Future Trap* an ordinary Australian girl, Paula, is kidnapped and taken to a space station 5000 years in the future to provide blood for medical purposes. Even in this strange world of genetically engineered humanity there are people who care passionately about human rights. A communicator, Sellian, and a soldier, Julz, risk their own lives to ensure Paula is returned unharmed to her own time. Before she leaves Gnosis-10, however, she discovers that this ugly and poisoned place is Earth. The ethics of genetic engineering also informs *Piggy in the Middle,* which is set in the near future, when young Dallas, a feral pig shooter, discovers that a pig owned by a research company contains human genes—her genes! Jansi, the hero of *Eye to Eye,* is close kin to Pagan, both in style of dialogue and in the situation of a wise protector who comes to rely on a young streetwise boy. In this futuristic otherworld arguments about the limits of technology substitute for the religious debates of the Pagan series. Jansi, an unwanted tag-end of a desert tribe, finds a star ship which he presumes to be a temple to Shaklat, the tribe's god. Controlling the damaged ship is PIM, a computer whose characteristics blur the boundary between machine and human. Boy and computer take turns telling the story and though they are alien to each other they find a way to communicate. Jinks skillfully builds towards the suspenseful showdown between these unlikely colleagues and the galaxy bosses who want them destroyed.

—Kerry White

JOHNSON, Annabel and Edgar

Pseudonyms: Have also written as A.E. Johnson.

ANNABEL. Nationality: American. **Born:** Annabel Jones, in Kansas City, Missouri, 18 June 1921. **Education:** William and Mary College, Williamsburg, Virginia, 1939-40; Art Students' League, New York. **Family:** Married Edgar Johnson in 1949. **Career:** Worked in publishing houses, as a librarian, legal secretary, and in other secretarial posts prior to 1957; writer, 1957—.

EDGAR (RAYMOND). Nationality: American. **Born:** Washoe, Montana, 24 October 1912. **Education:** Billings Polytechnic Institute, Montana; Kansas City Art Institute, Missouri; Alfred University, New York. **Family:** Married Annabel Jones in 1949. **Career:** Ceramic artist and head of the Ceramics Department, Kansas City Art Institute, 1948-49; model-maker, jeweler, and woodcarver with work exhibited in one-man show in New York City and included in Museum of Modern Art exhibition of American handcrafts; freelance writer in collaboration with wife, Annabel Jones Johnson. Sometime restorer of antique musical instruments for Smithsonian Institution, Washington, D.C. **Died:** 2 December 1990.

Awards (joint): Spring Book Festival award, 1959, for *The Black Symbol,* and 1960, for *Torrie;* Friends of American Writers award, 1962, for *The Secret Gift;* Golden Spur award, Western Writers of America, 1966, for *The Burning Glass;* William Allen White Children's Book award, 1967, for *The Grizzly.* **Address:** 2925 South Teller, Denver, Colorado 80227, U.S.A.

PUBLICATIONS FOR YOUNG ADULTS

Fiction

As a Speckled Bird (by Annabel Johnson alone). New York, Crowell, 1956; London, Hodder and Stoughton, 1958.
The Big Rock Candy. New York, Crowell, 1957.
The Black Symbol, illustrated by Brian Saunders. New York, Harper, 1959; Leicester, Brockhampton, 1960.
The Bearcat. New York, Harper, and London, Hamish Hamilton, 1960.
Torrie, illustrated by Pearl Falconer. New York, Harper, 1960; Leicester, Brockhampton, 1961.
Pickpocket Run. New York, Harper, 1961.
The Rescued Heart. New York, Harper, 1961.
The Secret Gift (as A.E. Johnson). New York, Doubleday, and London, Hodder and Stoughton, 1961.
Wilderness Bride. New York, Harper, 1962.

A Golden Touch. New York, Harper, 1963.
The Grizzly, illustrated by Gilbert Riswold. New York, Harper, 1964; Bath, Chivers, 1973.
A Peculiar Magic, illustrated by Lynd Ward. Boston, Houghton, 1965.
The Burning Glass. New York, Harper, 1966.
Count Me Gone. New York, Simon and Schuster, 1968.
A Blues I Can Whistle (as A.E. Johnson). New York, Four Winds, 1969.
The Last Knife. New York, Simon and Schuster, 1971.
Finders, Keepers. New York, Four Winds, 1981.
An Alien Music. New York, Four Winds, 1982.
The Danger Quotient. New York, Harper, 1984.
Prisoner of Psi. New York, Atheneum, 1985.
A Memory of Dragons. New York, Atheneum, 1986.
Gamebuster, illustrated by Stephen Marchesi. Bergenfield, New Jersey, Dutton, 1990.
I Am Leaper, illustrated by Stella Ormai. Portland, Oregon, Galley, 1990.
Niner. N.p., Browndeer Press, 1994.

*

Manuscript Collections: Kerlan Collection, University of Minnesota.

Biography: Entry in *Third Book of Junior Authors,* New York, H.W. Wilson, 1972.

*   *   *

Annabel and Edgar Johnson's historically located stories are distinguished by a highly economical use of detail which, without any evident laboring to do so, brings home to us just what life must have been like on the American frontier in the nineteenth century. Even more impressive is the unobtrusive but wholesomely insistent moral concern which is discreetly embodied in the narrative texture itself: as the story unfolds we find ourselves sharing the young protagonist's discovery of the realities of human nature in other people and in himself or herself. In *Torrie* the fourteen-year-old heroine is unwillingly uprooted from her comfortable home in St. Louis to undertake a 2000-mile trek by ox-drawn wagon to California. As the hardships of the journey unroll, only slowly does she learn to value the qualities of leadership now revealed in her insignificant-looking schoolmaster father, the staunchness and selflessness of her mother, the love of her parents for each other and for herself and her brother. It is not till the climax of the journey, when she accidentally learns that the true purpose of her parents in undertaking their migration has been concern for her own health, that the full extent of her misconception of herself and her parents is made clear to her. The rigors of the dangerous and eventful journey have brought a new stature as well as a new self-knowledge to each member of the family; and we leave them established in a cabin in California, with the prospect of a new pioneering farming life ahead of them, and a securely founded love burgeoning between Torrie and Jess, the family's young hired teamster.

Torrie has a strong emotional appeal for girls of any age above twelve, whereas *The Black Symbol* is rather more of a boys' book, though not exclusively so. The central character is Barney, who runs away from his uncle to search for his gold-miner father, and joins a travelling medicine show run by the smooth-talking Dr. Cathcart. Dr. Cathcart and his assistant Hoke Wilson clearly owe something to "The King" and "The Duke" in *Huckleberry Finn*, and the core of the book is Barney's gradual discovery of the coldhearted sadistic ruthlessness of these two villains. The detailed trickery of the carnival is neatly worked into the plot, which involves two other members of the troupe, the frightened negro boy Billy, and the blind "Strong Man" Steve.

In their later fiction the Johnsons moved increasingly towards the present day, and in their later novels together, into the future. In *Finders, Keepers* two independent-minded teenagers struggle desperately to survive in the aftermath of a catastrophic explosion at a nuclear power plant near Denver; there is a graphic and disturbing depiction of panic and savagery among the city dwellers who swarm westward into mountainous country to escape the radioactive fallout. In *An Alien Music* the ecological disaster is a manmade build-up of carbon dioxide in the atmosphere which heats the earth's surface to a point where it becomes uninhabitable. Jesse, a fifteen-year-old orphan girl with Indian blood, bluffs her way onto the NASA Sky-Lab which her brother has helped design to carry a select group of people to the planet Mars to form a human colony there. The excitements of the ensuing space voyage are exceptionally convincing, both in their technological aspects and in the treatment of human tensions within the crew. In particular Jesse's shifting and ambivalent relationship with the commander, Ben Hammond, brings into focus important questions concerning the nature of leadership, democracy, and self-discipline. *The Danger Quotient* starts in the year 2127 in an underground colony built as refuge from the nuclear holocaust, whence the young narrator journeys by means of a "time refractor" to Denver in 1981, 1945, and 1918 seeking insight into factors that could decide his own fate as well as that of his fellow-survivors. His contacts at these different dates with members of the same American family are interwoven with great ingenuity into a pattern adding an absorbing human dimension to the temporal jigsaw puzzle. Each of these three novels is told in the first person, in the authentic-sounding idiom of an American teenager yet with a linguistic flair which is able to encompass subtle moral and social issues.

Prisoner of Psi achieves similar effects through a slightly more complex narrative structure in which segments of third-person narrative are intercut with excerpts from the diary kept by Tris, the psychically gifted son of a noted television psychic who has been kidnapped, in 2000 A.D., by a ruthless terrorist organization. The gripping story of his eventual rescue makes skillful use of E.S.P. paraphernalia and at the same time explores subtly and sensitively (not for the first time in the Johnsons' fiction) the topic of misunderstanding and conflict between parent and child. *A Memory of Dragons* is set in an unspecified future of world conflict and shortages, with an impending secession from the United States by its western states actively on the cards. Sought as an ally by both sides on account of his flair for inventing high-tech gadgetry, Paul Killian's involvement is complicated by an inchoate burden of personal guilt which he is able to exorcise only after a series of time-travel excursions into an ancestor's experiences of the earlier American Civil War. As with its immediate predecessors, the intricate and absorbing narrative is conveyed through a series of brief, enticingly readable cameos which are brilliantly orchestrated into a complex yet coherent whole.

—Frank Whitehead

JOHNSON, Marguerita Annie. *See* ANGELOU, Maya.

JOHNSTON, Julie

Nationality: Canadian. **Born:** Julia Ann Dulmage, in Smith Falls, Ontario, 21 January 1941. **Education:** Smith Falls District Collegiate Institute, Ontario, 1955-60; University of Toronto, 1960-63, Diploma in Physio and Occupational Therapy 1963; Trent University, 1976-84, B.A. (Honors) 1984. **Family:** Married Basil William Johnston in 1963; four daughters. **Career:** Occupational therapist, Ontario Hospital School for Retarded Children, Smith Falls, Ontario, 1963-65; occupational therapist, Rehab Centre, Kingston, Ontario, 1965-67; writer. **Awards:** Canadian Playwriting Competition, 1979; Sears Festival Best Play Award, 1983; Sears Festival Best Play Award, 1985; Governor General's Literary Award for Children's Literature, 1992, 1994; National I.O.D.E. Award, 1993; Ruth Schwartz Children's Book Award, 1995; CLA Young Adult Canadian Book Award, 1995; Honorary D.Litt.: Trent University, 1996. **Address:** 463 Hunter St. W., Peterborough, Ontario K9H 2M7, Canada.

PUBLICATIONS FOR YOUNG ADULTS

Hero of Lesser Causes. Toronto, Lester, 1992; Boston, Little Brown, 1993.
Adam and Eve and Pinch-Me. Toronto, Lester, 1994.

*

Julie Johnston comments:

I write Young Adult novels, perhaps because I have strong memories of my own adolescence. It's an easy step for me to back up into the lives of my characters. A child hesitating on the border of adulthood is like a newly emerging character in a story. Many possibilities open up. At this age, kids waffle back and forth between infancy and maturity which lends an air of suspense. Will the fledgling fly? Teenagers have definite problems, intricate problems that affect their future lives, each one filled with story possibilities.

My first attempts at public writing began in high school with a couple of plays I wrote for my class to produce in front of the whole school. These went over very well, as I recall. We tried to turn one into a movie using my father's eight millimeter home movie camera and two flood-lights. It was not a box office success. This was followed by a short novel in serial form about the adventures of teenagers at a summer cottage. A chapter of the story appeared each week in our town's newspaper. As the weeks wore on I began to go through agony. Oh, I loved writing the story; that wasn't the cause of the agony. My problem was that I didn't know how to end it. (I didn't want to end it!) My advice to young writers: before you begin, plan, even roughly, how it will end. And then, painful as it may be, learn to say good-bye to your work.

*   *   *

Although Julie Johnston has only written two novels, both have received Canada's highest critical recognition, the Governor General's Literary Award for Children's Literature. While *Hero of Lesser Causes,* Johnston's engaging account of the emotional confusions surrounding growing up, will principally appeal to a middle school audience, it will also attract some adult readers who remember when the word "polio" evoked an emotional response similar to what "AIDS" presently generates. Set in Channing, Ontario, a small lower Ottawa Valley town, in the mid-1940s, the story focuses on the changing relationship between siblings, Keely and Patrick Connor, aged 12 and 13 1/2.

Of prime importance to Keely are her fantasy life and her beloved brother Patrick, from whom she claims to derive her identity. Keely's rich imaginative world includes the heroic warrior image of "Keely the Connor" crisscrossing the Ottawa Valley on a silver-white stallion "fixing things, making everything all better." When Patrick contracts the body-withering disease polio, the once carefree Keely determines to save her almost totally paralysed and emotionally demoralized brother from losing hope in his future and committing suicide; however, Keely, who is trying to discard her childhood behaviours and be recognized as a responsible adult, keeps "getting sidetracked and caught up in causes of lesser magnitude," such as uniting Patrick's private nurse, Peggy Doyle, with her fiance, who was missing in action in World War II.

The actions of the well developed principal characters lead readers to recognize that, irrespective of Patrick's physical state, the siblings' "best pals" relationship would have had to change simply because of maturation's effects. Johnston populates the novel with a strong supporting cast, including Charlotte Hodge, the community newcomer who provides some comic relief in what could have easily become a depressing read. Small, unobtrusive details, such as radio show names, remind readers of the novel's historic time setting. Despite Patrick's claim that "in real life you don't get happy endings," this fine first book concludes optimistically.

Johnston definitely avoided the sophomore jinx with *Adam and Eve and Pinch-Me,* another fine character study which won three national prizes. At the story's February opening, Sara Moone, a ward of the Children's Aid and someone who is angry at the world, eagerly awaits her sixteenth birthday, some six months away, for it marks the date she can legally leave school and live independently. Sara's experiences in countless foster homes have taught her not to get close to people for they keep on disappearing. Instead, she has decided that "the way to get along in the world is to be invisible." Continuing to confide her innermost thoughts only to her computer's memory, Sara moves to the small community of Ambrose, Ontario, where she encounters another, hopefully final, set of foster parents, the childless Huddleston's, loquacious "Ma" and laconic "Hud," plus their other two foster children, Josh, 4, and Nick, age indeterminate. Living with the quartet, Sara unwillingly, but increasingly, finds herself behaving like a participant in the family and not just a captive spectator. Compounding Sara's disquietude is her knowledge that her birth mother is trying to make contact with her. When a stranger searching for a daughter comes to Ambrose, Sara is convinced "The Woman" is her mother. As a

child must discover the correct answer, "Pinch-me-not," to the painful children's riddle, Sara must learn a better response than invisibility to life's real puzzles. Johnston's ability to reproduce the varying styles of people's speech contributes much to the book's character development, and her scenes involving the habitués of the Elite Cafe, the small town's local gather-and-gossip coffee shop, are superb.

—Dave Jenkinson

JONES, Allan Frewin

Pseudonyms: Steven Saunders, Fiona Kelly, and Michael Coleman. **Nationality:** British. **Born:** London, 30 April 1954. **Education:** Lowden Road Primary School, London; The Strand Grammar School, London; mature student at Middlesex Polytechnic, 1981-83, received Diploma of Higher Education. **Family:** Married Claudia Duwendag in 1991. **Career:** Various clerical jobs, including Civil Service, Local Government, and a Trade Union. Active in local Group of Amnesty International. **Awards:** Shortlisted for Children's Section of Whitbread Prize, 1991. **Agent:** Laurence Pollinger Ltd., 18 Maddox Street, Mayfair, London, W1R OEU, England.

PUBLICATIONS FOR YOUNG ADULTS

Fiction

The Mole and Beverley Miller. London, Hodder and Stoughton, 1987.
The Cost of Going Free. London, Hodder and Stoughton, 1988.
Rabbit Back and Doubled. London, Hodder and Stoughton, 1989.
Bad Penny. London, Bodley Head, 1990.
Millions of Lisa. London, Hodder and Stoughton, 1990.
The Half-Good Samaritan. London, Hodder and Stoughton, 1991.
Tommy and the Sloth. London, Simon and Schuster, 1992.
Wishing Bird & Co. London, Simon and Schuster, 1993.
Burning Issues. London, Bodley Head, 1994.

"Little Sister" series

The Great Sister War. London, Red Fox, 1995.
My Sister, My Slave. London, Red Fox, 1995.
Stacy the Matchmaker. London, Red Fox, 1995.
Copycat. London, Red Fox, 1995.
Sneaking Out. London, Red Fox, 1995.
Sister Switch. London, Red Fox, 1995.
Full House. London, Red Fox, 1996.
Bad Boy. London, Red Fox, 1996.
The New Stacy. London, Red Fox, 1996.
Summer Camp. London, Red Fox, 1996.
Start Search. London, Red Fox, 1996.
Parent Trouble. London, Red Fox, 1996.

"The Hunter & Moon" Mysteries

The Weird Eyes File. London, Hodder and Stoughton, 1997.
The Alien Fire File. London, Hodder and Stoughton, 1997.
The Skull Stone File. London, Hodder and Stoughton, 1997.

The Time Traveller File. London, Hodder and Stoughton, forthcoming.
The Thunderbolt File. London, Hodder and Stoughton, forthcoming.
The Star Ship File. London, Hodder and Stoughton, forthcoming.

Fiction as Steven Saunders

Dark Secrets, Red Ink. London, Macdonald, 1988.
Kisschase. London, Macdonald, 1989.
Blind Ally. London, Macdonald, 1989.

Fiction as Fiona Kelly

"The Mystery Club" series

Secret Clues. London, Hodder and Stoughton, 1993.
Dangerous Tricks. London, Hodder and Stoughton, 1993.
Hide & Seek. London, Hodder and Stoughton, 1994.
Secret Treasure. London, Hodder and Stoughton, 1994.
Crossed Line. London, Hodder and Stoughton, 1994.
Poison! London, Hodder and Stoughton, 1994.
Out of Control. London, Hodder and Stoughton, 1994.
The Secret Room. London, Hodder and Stoughton, 1994.

"The Mystery Kids" series

Spy-catchers. London, Hodder and Stoughton, 1995.
The Empty House. London, Hodder and Stoughton, 1995.
Blackmail! London, Hodder and Stoughton, 1996.
Hostage! London, Hodder and Stoughton, 1996.

Fiction as Michael Coleman

Virus Attack. London, Macmillan, 1997.
Access Denied. London, Macmillan, 1997.

Other

With Lesley Pollinger, *Teach Yourself Writing Children's Books.* London, Hodder and Stoughton, 1997.

Publications for Children

Anna's Birthday Adventure. London, Wayland, 1997.

*

Allan Frewin Jones comments:

I started writing books for a very simple reason: so that I could read them. I write about teenagers because I am fascinated by how young people cope for the first time with all the turmoil that life flings at them. It is a time of immense upheaval, conflict, pressure and passion—the perfect recipe for disasters and triumphs in the raw; unencumbered by hindsight or perspective. The only desire I

have is that my writing should attempt to reflect my perception of reality. If I feel that I have managed that, I am marginally contented—until the next bunch of characters come along to keep me awake at night with their problems.

*   *   *

At a time when the teenage novel had revolved for years around sexual initiation and what happened afterwards: falling in love, out of love, pregnancy, abortion, keeping the baby . . . Allan Frewin Jones began to publish a fresh, comparatively innocent kind of teenage novel about first love, especially the "crush" period when one or both parties nurses unrequited love for the other. He charts the revelation which comes as a boy realises he is in love, his embarrassment about asking the girl out, his rapture when he learns that she loves him too. His characters may make love, but don't usually go all the way: in any case Frewin Jones is not an explicit writer, and in only one book does his heroine get pregnant (without full intercourse!). Within what is a shaped narrative he produces the effect of absolutely natural behaviour and dialogue. Teachers and parents looking for something to shock them will find it more in his characters' language, i.e. the swearwords and frank sex talk, than in their relatively modest sexual behaviour.

Frewin Jones is also an accurate observer of the class-based nuances of British society: the relatively secure, but hardly "posh" lower middle classes; society's young outcasts living in cardboard boxes in the subway; the working classes housed in high-rise flats plagued by criminals. He is also good on political trends and youngsters' disillusionment with their parents.

Frewin Jones's first book, *The Mole and Beverley Miller,* charts the impact on a shy boy of his and Beverley's mutual love, and of her bicycle accident and subsequent coma in hospital. The book is structured in two time streams, telling the story from their first meeting, and from her accident, in alternating units of one or two chapters each, a device which heightens our awareness of the Mole's suffering. Beverley's feminist grandmother is also a pleasantly original character.

In his second book, *The Cost of Going Free,* Sally, the daughter of a divorced mother, is attracted to a fairground worker. Her mother fears that her outright disapproval might bring about the outcome she least desires—pregnancy or elopement, perhaps. Horrible family rows ensue. Sally nearly loses her virginity at a party, but discovers that he doesn't care for her, and she and her mother are reconciled.

Frewin Jones found that he was writing more books than his publisher could handle, and so submitted three in quick succession elsewhere, taking the name of Steven Saunders for what turned out to be a rather racy trio of novels, with more candid sexuality and swearwords. *Dark Secrets, Red Ink* starts off as a comedy: Jax, daughter of a trade union official, has become an extreme left-wing activist, working for the newspaper *Red Ink,* but she has to choose between her politics and giving support to her newly pregnant sister while she decides what to do about the baby.

Blind Ally and *Kisschase* both describe a relationship between a boy from a conventional background and a girl who has gone "off the rails," recalling novels by Zindel such as *I Never Loved Your Mind.* Alasdair (Ally), sharing a holiday with his parents, meets a strange girl on the beach. They fall in love, but she has a weakness for drink and a criminal record. Ally wants to live with her and reform her, but the police catch up with her, and they are forever separated.

In *Kisschase,* Paul, an office worker, chats up Naomi, a student, in a snack bar at lunchtime. Their growing friendship is complicated by the girl's violent ex-boyfriend, who beats Paul up and vandalises Naomi's flat. Then her college project on London's homeless gets her into deep trouble with drug dealers and pimps. There could be a little more warning about forms of V.D. including AIDS. Paul's sexually experienced friend doesn't care about catching V.D. at all, though his viewpoint about girls is shown to be crude and far inferior to Paul's belief that sexual intercourse should be kept for a long-term relationship. Naomi then admits to Paul that although she has currently vowed celibacy, being weary of instant sex with every new boyfriend, she has had a number of sexual partners. However, committed relationships are shown to be superior to promiscuous ones, without preaching to the teenage reader.

Returning to his first publisher, Frewin Jones also returned to the innocent mode of his first two books. *Rabbit Back and Doubled* is one of his best. A boy and girl of sixteen and seventeen are starting an art course at school. The girl, Rachel Ronchetti, is known as Spag Bol for her Italian ancestry, but assumes it is because of her overweight appearance. She determines to be more positive about her appearance, goes for her young man, and gets him in the end. Unusually this story is told from both teenagers' viewpoints.

In *Millions of Lisa* we have the boy's side again. While Danny's girlfriend is away with her parents, his parents take in a lodger, Lisa, an attractive girl six years his senior. Soon Danny is completely overwhelmed by his feelings for both girls simultaneously; fortunately Lisa is mature enough to sort him out, though not before his girlfriend returns unexpectedly and finds him kissing Lisa!

Frewin Jones's last two teenage novels to date are both written from the girl's viewpoint, and take us into the sleazy world of council high-rise flats, filth and petty crime, recalling for me the clash between Rosa Guy's Harlem and the more respectable suburban culture to which characters like Edith Jackson and Imamu aspire. Frewin Jones is extremely accurate about poverty—material and spiritual—in today's Britain. Here indeed is an enviable body of work: eleven teenage novels, each with a distinct plot and three-dimensional characters (including the adults), published over only five years!

—Jessica Yates

JONES, Diana Wynne

Nationality: British. **Born:** London, England, 16 August 1934. **Education:** Friends' School, Saffron Walden, Essex, 1946-53; St. Anne's College, Oxford, 1953-56, B.A. 1956. **Family:** Married John A. Burrow in 1956; three sons. **Career:** Writer, since 1965. **Awards:** Carnegie commendation, 1975, for *Dogsbody; Guardian* commendation, 1977, for *Power of Three;* Carnegie commendation, 1977, and *Guardian* award, 1978, for *Charmed Life;* Boston *Globe-Horn Book* Honor Book award, 1984, for *Archer's Goon; Horn Book* Honor List, 1984, for *Fire and Hemlock; Horn Book* Fanfare List, 1987, for *Howl's Moving Castle;* Mythopaeic Society

of California Award, 1996, for *The Crown of Dalemark.* **Agent:** Laura Cecil, 17 Alwyne Villas, London N1 2HG. **Address:** 9, The Polygon, Clifton, Bristol BS8 4PW, England.

PUBLICATIONS FOR YOUNG ADULTS

Fiction

The Ogre Downstairs. London, Macmillan, 1974; New York, Dutton, 1975.
Dogsbody. London, Macmillan, 1975; New York, Greenwillow, 1977.
Eight Days of Luke. London, Macmillan, 1975; New York, Greenwillow, 1988.
Power of Three. London, Macmillan, 1976; New York, Greenwillow, 1977.
The Homeward Bounders. London, Macmillan, and New York, Greenwillow, 1981.
Archer's Goon. London, Methuen, and New York, Greenwillow, 1984.
Fire and Hemlock. New York, Greenwillow, 1984; London, Methuen, 1985.
Warlock at the Wheel and Other Stories. London, Macmillan, and New York, Greenwillow, 1984.
Howl's Moving Castle. London, Methuen, and New York, Greenwillow, 1986.
A Tale of Time City. New York, Greenwillow, and London, Methuen, 1987.
Black Maria. London, Methuen, 1991; as *Aunt Maria,* New York, Greenwillow, 1991.
Castle in the Air. New York, Greenwillow, 1991.
A Sudden Wild Magic. New York, Morrow, 1992.
The Crown of Dalemark. New York, Greenwillow, 1993.
Hexwood. London, Methuen, and New York, Greenwillow, 1993.
Fantasy Stories. Kingfisher, 1994.

"Chrestomanci" cycle

Charmed Life. London, Macmillan, and New York, Greenwillow, 1977.
The Magicians of Caprona. London, Macmillan, and New York, Greenwillow, 1980.
Witch Week. London, Macmillan, and New York, Greenwillow, 1982.
The Lives of Christopher Chant. London, Methuen, and New York, Greenwillow, 1988.

"Dalemark" cycle

Cart and Cwidder. London, Macmillan, 1975; New York, Atheneum, 1977.
Drowned Ammet. London, Macmillan, 1977; New York, Atheneum, 1978.
The Spellcoats. London, Macmillan, and New York, Atheneum, 1979.
The Crown of Dalemark. London, Mammoth, 1993.

Plays

The Batterpool Business (produced London at Arts Theatre, October, 1967).
The King's Things (produced London at Arts Theatre, February, 1969).
The Terrible Fisk Machine (produced London at Arts Theatre, January, 1970).

Other

The Skiver's Guide, illustrated by Chris Winn. London, Knight Books, 1984.
Editor, *Hidden Turnings: A Collection of Stories through Time and Space.* London, Methuen, 1989; New York, Greenwillow, 1990.
Editor, *The Tough Guide to Fantasyland.* London, Gollancz, 1996.

Contributor

The Cat-Flap and the Apple Pie. London, W. H. Allen, 1979.
Hecate's Cauldron. New York, DAW Books, 1981.
Hundreds and Hundreds. New York, Puffin, 1984.
Dragons and Dreams. New York, Harper, 1986.
Guardian Angels. New York, Viking Kestrel, 1987.

PUBLICATIONS FOR CHILDREN

Fiction

Wilkins' Tooth, illustrated by Julia Rodber. London, Macmillan, 1973; as *Witch's Business,* New York, Dutton, 1974.
Who Got Rid of Angus Flint?, illustrated by John Sewell. London, Evans, 1978.
The Four Grannies, illustrated by Thelma Lambert. London, Hamish Hamilton, 1980.
The Time of the Ghost. London, Macmillan, 1981.
Chair Person, illustrated by Glenys Ambrus. London, Hamish Hamilton, 1989.
Wild Robert, illustrated by Emma C. Clark. Boston, Hall, 1992.
Yes, Dear, illustrated by Graham Philpot. New York, Greenwillow, 1992.
Stopping for a Spell, illustrated by Joseph A. Smith. New York, Greenwillow, 1993.
Everard's Ride. Boston, NESFA, 1995.

PUBLICATIONS FOR ADULTS

Changeover (novel). London, Macmillan, 1970.
Stopping for a Spell (novel). New York, Greenwillow, 1993.
Minor Arcana (short stories). London, Gollancz, 1996.
Deep Secret (novel). London, Gollancz, 1997.

*

Biography: Entry in *Fifth Book of Junior Authors,* New York, H.W. Wilson, 1983; essay in *Something about the Author Autobiography Series,* Volume 7, Detroit, Gale, 1989; essay in *Speaking for Ourselves, Too* compiled and edited by Donald R. Gallo, National Council of Teachers of English, 1993.

Critical Studies: Entry in *Contemporary Literary Criticism,* Volume 26, Detroit, Gale, 1983.

*   *   *

Diana Wynne Jones did not set out to become a "YA author." The literary form she chose was the longer children's fantasy, as perfected by E. Nesbit in which children, often undergoing some family stress (e.g. separation from their parents, poverty, illness), encounter magic, which causes them further problems. The resolution of the magical problems also deals with the real-life crisis in *The Ogre Downstairs:* remarriage forces five step-siblings to share the same household, and their continual feuding is complicated by the gift of a magic chemistry set to each sibling group.

In *Eight Days of Luke,* David, the orphaned boy-hero, accidentally summons up the Norse god Loki and finds the other gods in hot pursuit, while Loki pleads for David's protection. A reader ignorant of Norse mythology will learn more by reading the book, which is also notable for its incomplete happy ending more suited to a YA novel than a children's book: David's wicked cousins revealed as criminals make their getaway, and he becomes the responsibility of his (good) cousin's wife, who will presumably divorce, maybe remarry.

Dogsbody also looks forward to a future after the book's conclusion. The child-heroine is not the leading character: the immortal Sirius, the Dog Star, is sent to Earth to search for a cosmic weapon and enchanted into a puppy's body. He is taken into a family of Earth children, becoming the special pet of Kathleen, treated as a "dogsbody" or Cinderella-type by her foster family. When Sirius discovers his own starry Companion betrayed him and caused his punishment on Earth, he realises he would now only choose Kathleen as his new Companion—and how can that be? After her earthly death?

With *Cart and Cwidder, Power of Three,* and *Charmed Life,* Diana Wynne Jones introduced a theme into her fantasies which has now become her trademark. The hero/ine of her books is likely to grow up among magical folk, often in an alternative world where history ran differently, or a secondary fantasy world, but this hero/ine feels inadequate because s/he does not appear to have magic powers. Using his/her own resources to cope with the problems magic is causing, at the climax a crisis reveals that our hero/ine does truly possess magic powers, sometimes superior to the others, and certainly unique. This plot twist also occurs in *The Magicians of Caprona, Archer's Goon, The Spellcoats,* and *Howl's Moving Castle,* and in a modified way *Aunt Maria* (British title, *Black Maria*) where the heroine rejects the power offered because it is tainted.

Charmed Life, which introduces the good enchanter Chrestomanci, has several sequels, as Wynne Jones became fond of her alternative fantasy world where magic is real, licensed and run by the government to make sure it is used for good. Various crooked sorcerers try to operate independently and even overthrow Chrestomanci. *The Magicians of Caprona* is set in an alternative Italy, using a Romeo-and-Juliet plot with a happy ending. *The Lives of Christopher Chant* is about Chrestomanci's childhood.

Nearly all Wynne Jones's books may be classified as domestic fantasy, as magic disrupts ordinary life, sometimes combined with high fantasy, as gods and goddesses become involved. Only a few belong to other supernatural genres: *Witch Week* and *The Time of the Ghost* are ghost-horror stories, with a twist: the witches in the former are children, desperately hiding their powers from a hostile State; the ghost in the latter is benign, but under the curse of a pagan goddess. Wynne Jones's two science fiction novels are based on the concept of alternative worlds (*The Homeward Bounders*) and the Time Patrol which prevents the bad guys changing history (*A Tale of Time City*).

Although most of her leading characters are too young for romance, Wynne Jones may nevertheless be claimed as a young adult author for her development of the "rite-of-passage" theme in a fantasy context. The youngster, aged between ten and thirteen, undergoes a crisis which results in the recognition of his/her powers, enhanced stature within the family, and feet set firmly on a career of using magic for good. It is also clear from the length of her books, their complex plots, and range of literary allusions to myths and other cultures that many youngsters will not be ready for them until they are teenagers. One must stress here how readable, funny, enjoyable, and "unputdownable" they are: they extend their readers, and the taste for her books is known to be addictive, for her adult fans as well as teenagers.

This is not all she offers young adult readers. In 1985 she began a series of romantic fantasies about a girl's (or boy's) first love, which is eventually requited. These are *Fire and Hemlock, Howl's Moving Castle,* and *Castle in the Air. Fire and Hemlock* is set in our world, now, and precisely charts the experience of the teenage "crush" on an older student or teacher. In real life, of course, the "crush" is best left unspoken and is generally unrequited, and even in this fantasy the girl cannot become an independent person until she turns her back on her dream lover. Maybe, after the book's ending, they reunite. . . The story describes a network of witchcraft centred on the court of the Faerie Queen, as in the "Tam Lin" ballad. Every nine years she takes a new lover, and the old lover is sacrificed to extend her consort's life, or her own life every eighty-one years. The Fairy Court schemes to prevent our heroine Polly saving Tom's life, and then to recruit her as the next female sacrifice: all is gradually revealed in this extraordinarily long, addictive read.

Howl's Moving Castle, of a more manageable length, is one of Wynne Jones's most perfect works. Attractive Sophie is cursed by the Witch of the Waste into the shape of an old woman, and bluffs her way into Wizard Howl's castle in search of a counter-spell. The wizard turns out to be youthful and immature; his fire demon promises to remove the spell if Sophie does him a good turn, but can't explain how she is to perform it. In the sequel, *Castle in the Air,* Wynne Jones creates a superb pastiche of the world of the Arabian Nights, and also provides a glimpse of Sophie's married life.

So far Wynne Jones has hardly written for adults, though she would say that most of her children's fantasies also function on an adult level; however, in publishing terms, she has written a few commissioned short stories and one adult fantasy. This, *A Sudden Wild Magic,* defies generic rules. It is for adults; the leading characters are all ages from late teenage upwards, and their partnerings are relevant to the plot; but sexual behaviour is not explicitly described, so it may be stocked in a young adult library. It has an extravagant plot and a typical surprise climax. The plot concerns dealings between our world and an alternate world which is plundering our scientific ideas, and is a fascinating mix of science fiction and sorcery which Wynne Jones's readers will eagerly devour.

Finally to Diana Wynne Jones's contribution to the "secondary world" aspect of high fantasy, the Dalemark Quartet. Dalemark resembles Scandinavia in its North, South Wales, and the Cotswolds in the South and, although it may be situated in our world, it has remained isolated. Magic is occasionally wielded by the Undying, by their favoured humans, or by renegade mages. As the epic opens, Dalemark has been divided for centuries into free North and authoritarian South, each split into several earldoms. The Southern earls are tyrants and their citizens dream of being liberated by the North. In the first book, *Cart and Cwidder,* a boy minstrel, Moril, is involved in smuggling a Northern earl's son from South to North; in the second, *Drowned Ammet,* a young spy, Mitt, narrowly escapes becoming an assassin, and flees North by sea. Both encounter or wield magic during their adventures. In the third, *The Spellcoats,* we go back to the founding of Dalemark when the chief God, the One, struggles to unite feuding tribes against the evil mage Kankredin, who wishes to enslave them and rule Dalemark forever. In the fourth book, *The Crown of Dalemark,* Moril and Mitt team up to look for the Crown and discover the person who will become the new king. In their quest they meet several Undying from *The Spellcoats.* Some useful points are made about political manipulation and the drive for power versus the impulse towards altruism: the good characters know that an uprising to liberate the South will result in many innocent deaths, but to do nothing leaves the Southerners prey to tyranny, while the Northern earls are corrupted by the need to employ spies and assassins. A vision of Dalemark 200 years after, in modern times, reveals a peaceful country which reveres the memory of the king who united it. Only recently completed, the Dalemark Quartet must stand as one of our author's greatest achievements.

—Jessica Yates

JONES, Gwyneth A(nn). *See* **HALAM, Ann.**

JORDAN, June

Has also written as June Meyer. **Nationality:** American. **Born:** New York City, 9 July 1936. **Education:** Midwood High School, Brooklyn, New York; Northfield School for Girls, Massachusetts, 1950-53; Barnard College, New York, 1953-55, 1956-57; University of Chicago, 1955-56. **Family:** Married Michael Meyer in 1955 (divorced 1966), one son. **Career:** Assistant to the producer of the film *The Cool World,* 1964; research associate, Mobilization for Youth Inc., New York, 1965-66; director, Voice of the Children, 1967-70; member of the English Department, City College, New York, 1967-70, 1972-75, and 1977-78, Connecticut College, New London, 1968, Sarah Lawrence College, Bronxville, New York, 1971-75, and Yale University, New Haven, Connecticut, 1974-75; Associate Professor, 1978-82, Professor of English, 1982-89, and director of the Poetry Center and the Creative Writing Program, 1986-89, State University of New York, Stony Brook. Chancellor's Lecturer, 1986, and since 1989 Professor of Afro-American studies and women's studies, University of California, Berkeley. Poet-in-residence, Teachers and Writers Collaborative, New York, 1966-68, MacAlester College, St. Paul, Minnesota, 1980, Loft Mentor Series, Minneapolis, 1983, and Walt Whitman Birthplace, Huntington, New York, 1988; Reid Lecturer, Barnard College, 1976; playwright-in-residence, New Dramatists,

New York, 1987-88; Visiting Professor, Department of Afro-American Studies, University of Wisconsin, Madison, summer 1988. Political columnist, *The Progressive* magazine, since 1989, and *City Limits,* London, since 1990. **Awards:** Rockefeller grant, 1969; American Academy in Rome Environmental Design prize, 1970; American Library Association Best Young Adult Book, 1970, for *Soulscript,* and 1971, for *His Own Where;* Nancy Bloch Memorial award, 1971, for *The Voice of the Children;* National Book award finalist, and selected one of *New York Times'* Outstanding Young Adult Novels, both 1971, both for *His Own Where; New Life: New Room* was selected a Notable Children's Trade Book in the Field of Social Studies by the National Council for Social Studies and the Children's Book Council, and one of Child Study Association of America's Children's Books of the Year, both 1975; New York Council of the Humanities award, 1977; Creative Artists Public Service grant, 1978; Yaddo fellowship, 1979, 1980; *His Own Where* was selected one of New York Public Library's Books for the Teen Age, 1980; National Endowment for the Arts fellowship, 1982; National Association of Black Journalists award, 1984; New York Foundation for the Arts fellowship, 1985; Massachusetts Council on the Arts award, 1985, for essay "On the Difficult Miracle of Black Poetry, or Something Like a Sonnet for Phillis Wheatley"; MacDowell Colony fellowship, 1987; Nora Astorga Leadership award, 1989. **Address:** Department of Afro-American Studies, 690 Barrows Hall, Berkeley, California 94720, U.S.A.

PUBLICATIONS FOR YOUNG ADULTS

Fiction

His Own Where. New York, Crowell, 1971.
New Life: New Room, illustrated by Ray Cruz. New York, Crowell, 1975.
Kimako's Story, illustrated by Kay Burford. Boston, Houghton Mifflin, 1981.

Verse

Who Look at Me? New York, Crowell, 1969.

Other

Dry Victories. New York, Holt Rinehart, 1972.
Fannie Lou Hamer (biography), illustrated by Albert Williams. New York, Crowell, 1972.
Editor, with Terri Bush, *The Voice of the Children.* New York, Holt Rinehart, 1970.
Editor, *Soulscript: Afro-American Poetry.* New York, Doubleday, 1970.

PUBLICATIONS FOR ADULTS

Plays

In the Spirit of Sojourner Truth, (produced New York, 1979).
For the Arrow That Flies by Day, (produced New York, 1981).
Freedom Now Suite, music by Adrienne B. Torf (produced New York, 1984).
The Break, music by Adrienne B. Torf (produced New York, 1984).

The Music of Poetry and the Poetry of Music, music by Adrienne B. Torf (produced Washington, D.C., and New York, 1984).
Bang Bang Über Alles, music by Adrienne B. Torf, lyrics by Jordan (produced by Atlanta, 1986).
I Was Looking at the Ceiling and Then I Saw the Sky (libretto), music by John Adams, 1995.

Poetry

Some Changes. New York, Dutton, 1971.
Poem: On Moral Leadership as a Political Dilemma (Watergate, 1973). Detroit, Broadside Press, 1973.
New Days: Poems of Exile and Return. New York, Emerson Hall, 1973.
Okay Now. New York, Simon and Schuster, 1977.
Things That I Do in the Dark: Selected Poetry. New York, Random House, 1977; revised edition, Boston, Beacon Press, 1981.
Passion: New Poems, 1977-1980. Boston, Beacon Press, 1980.
Living Room. New York, Thunder's Mouth Press, 1985.
High Tide—Marea Alta. Willimantic, Connecticut, Curbstone Press, 1987.
Lyrical Campaigns: Selected Poems. London, Virago Press, 1989.
Naming Our Destiny: New and Selected Poems. New York, Thunder's Mouth Press, 1989.
Kissing God Good-Bye. New York, Doubleday, 1997.
Recordings: *Things That I Do in the Dark and Other Poems,* Spoken Arts, 1978; *For Somebody to Start Singing,* with Bernice Reagon, Black Box-Watershed, 1979.

Other

Civil Wars (essays). Boston, Beacon Press, 1981.
Bobo Goetz a Gun. Willimantic, Connecticut, Curbstone Press, 1985.
On Call: Political Essays 1981-1985. Boston, South End Press, 1985.
Moving Towards Home: Political Essays. London, Virago Press, 1989.
Technical Difficulties: African American Notes on the State of the Union. New York, Pantheon Books, 1992.

*

Biography: Entry in *Dictionary of Literary Biography,* Detroit, Gale, Volume 38, 1985; Essay in *Authors and Artists for Young Adults,* Detroit, Gale, Volume 2, 1989.

Manuscript Collections: Radcliffe Schlesinger Archives, Harvard University, Cambridge, Massachusetts.

Critical Studies: Entry in *Children's Literature Review,* Volume 10, Detroit, Gale, 1986.

Also author of *The Issue.* Author of column "The Black Poet Speaks of Poetry," *American Poetry Review,* 1974-77; contributing editor for *Chrysalis, First World,* and *Hoo Doo.* Contributor of stories and poems (prior to 1969 under name June Meyer) to national periodicals, including *Esquire, Nation, Evergreen, Partisan Review, Negro Digest, Harper's Bazaar, Library Journal, Encore, Freedomways, New Republic, Ms., American Dialog, New Black Poetry, Black World, Black Creation, Essence,* and to newspapers including *Village Voice, New York Times,* and *New York Times Magazine.*

* * *

June Jordan is a versatile writer known primarily as a poet who is also recognized as a political commentator. Her book *Civil Wars* was the first collection of political essays "to be published by a black woman in the United States." She has combined her artistic vision as a poet and her social commitment as an educator and activist in several books for young readers which concentrate on some of the circumstances facing African American children growing up on the streets of America's older cities. These works have been written with an attentive ear for the rhythms and vocabulary of black colloquial speech and join the social and cultural details of African American life with situations and problems common to young people anywhere. While these books are directed toward an audience approximately the age of their oldest characters, a sense of pervasive pressures accelerating the process of maturation makes them appropriate for young adult readers. *Kimako's Story* is narrated by a girl "seven going on eight" whose introduction to the exhilarating strangeness of street life in New York City carries her beyond the familiar concerns of someone her age, while *New Life: New Room* shows three children ages six through ten who must rearrange their already cramped living space to accommodate a new baby. Their ingenious, cooperative responses to the limits they face and the decisions they are forced to make indicate a maturity exceeding their relative youth.

Similarly, while her short novel *His Own Where* follows its sixteen-year-old protagonist Buddy Rivers for several months at a pivotal point in his life, Jordan's goals and strategies tend to restrict its potential audience to those young adults who are inquisitive, intellectually adventurous, and emotionally mature enough to appreciate an unconventional and distinctly original approach. Jordan has set the entire narrative focus within the mind of her protagonist and the novel advances as a series of image-impressions and thoughts akin to a Joycean stream-of-conscious projection of personality. In addition, she has chosen to use the narration as a demonstration of the linguistic vitality and literary possibilities of so-called "Black English," deftly fusing more conventional syntactic patterns with a carefully nuanced, creative and poetic "voice" that is effective in conveying Buddy's reactions and ideas. Although Buddy is often reflective and philosophical, the narration is almost entirely set in an ongoing present that infuses it with an energy and immediacy that enables Jordan to give Buddy a singularly individual style as well as a representative responsiveness to the emergence of Black Pride in the 1960s.

As the novel begins, Buddy's father is in critical condition in a hospital following a serious automobile accident. During his vigil at his father's bedside, Buddy meets Angela Figueroa, the daughter of a nurse on the hospital staff, and their relationship is dramatically intensified at an early stage when her father beats her in an alcoholic explosion of misguided disciplinary desperation. After Buddy takes her to the emergency room following her father's attack, they both realize that they are essentially removed from the protection and support of their families and that the various social services set up to provide some assistance are basically irrelevant. Instinctively, they move toward each other in an attempt to form a new family unit. They are teenagers on the threshold of adulthood forced to make choices without adequate preparation but aware that they are on a track toward a life of acquiescence, suppressed anger, and constant frustration interrupted by aimless outbursts of indulgence leading to incarceration, addiction, or death. Jordan has employed the traditional coming-of-age theme in a setting which demands an unusually rapid reaction to the changes brought on by physical maturity. One of the most appealing aspects of the two central characters is their understanding of the responsibilities of an adult's freedom to choose. Nonetheless, their choices are difficult and their time spent together is marked by uncertainty.

Jordan has made both Buddy and Angela sympathetic and engaging, writing with a straightforward candor that avoids condescension. As they struggle to find a place for themselves—the *Where* of the title—Jordan emphasizes their resilience, decency, and consideration for each other. The goal of their journey is a kind of private sanctuary (ironically located in a cemetery), a safe space both within and around them, and Jordan's social critique has made it clear that the various institutions supposed to provide guidance and assistance have failed due to the inherent hostility, indifference, and racism embedded in the authoritarian structures that reflect contemporary society. In their tentative steps toward selfhood and a measure of independence, Buddy and Angela are supported by their dreams of a community of fellowship, their vision of beauty amidst grime and decay, and their developing feelings for each other. Jordan does not underplay the force of their physical attraction, and their desire to conceive a child is acknowledged as an effort to fashion a new beginning but not endorsed as a wise choice. In her use of vivid poetic imagery, however, Jordan suggests that their mutual sensuality transcends the merely physical, expanding their sexual impulses into an emblem of a sustaining life force. Because she never avoids the most unsettling aspects of their life, her brief, intense glimpse at Buddy and Angela resonates with a kind of truth that an accomplished young adult can recognize and appreciate.

—Leon Lewis

JUDY, Stephen. *See* **TCHUDI, Stephen N.**

JUSTER, Norton

Nationality: American. **Born:** Brooklyn, New York, 2 June 1929. **Education:** University of Pennsylvania, Philadelphia, B. Arch. 1952; University of Liverpool (Fulbright scholar), 1952-53. **Military Service:** Served in the United States Naval Reserve Civil Engineer Corps, 1954-57. **Family:** Married Jeanne Ray in 1964. **Career:** Architect, Juster and Gugliotta, New York, 1960-68; adjunct professor in environmental design, Pratt Institute, New York, 1960-70; architect, Juster-Pope-Frazier Associates, Shelburne Falls, Massachusetts, 1969—; Emeritus Professor of Design, Hampshire College, Amherst, Massachusetts, 1992—. **Awards:** Ford Foundation grant, 1960-61; National Academy of Arts and Sciences award for outstanding achievement, 1968-69; Guggenheim fellowship, 1970-71; George G. Stone Center for Children's

Books Seventh Recognition of Merit, 1971. **Address:** 259 Lincoln Avenue, Amherst, Massachusetts 01002, U.S.A.

PUBLICATIONS FOR YOUNG ADULTS

Fiction

The Phantom Tollbooth, illustrated by Jules Feiffer. New York, Epstein and Carroll, 1961; London, Collins, 1962.
The Dot and the Line: A Romance in Lower Mathematics. New York, Random House, 1963; London, Nelson, 1964.
Alberic the Wise and Other Journeys, illustrated by Domenico Gnoli. New York, Pantheon, 1965; London, Nelson, 1966; reprinted as *Alberic the Wise,* illustrated by Leonard Baskinow, Saxonville, Massachusetts, Picture Book Studios, 1992.

Verse

Otter Nonsense, illustrated by Eric Carle. New York, Philomel, 1982; London, Faber, 1983.
As: A Surfeit of Similes, illustrated by David Small. New York, Morrow, 1989.

Other

Stark Naked: A Paranomastic Odyssey, illustrated by Arnold Roth. New York, Random House, 1969.
So Sweet to Labor: Rural Women in America 1865-1895. New York, Viking Press, 1979; as *A Woman's Place: Yesterday's Women in Rural America,* Golden, Colorado, Fulcrum Publishing, 1996.

*

Media Adaptations: *The Dot and the Line* (film), MGM, 1965; *The Phantom Tollbooth* (film), MGM, 1970.

*   *   *

Norton Juster's *The Phantom Tollbooth* has proven to be timeless. Its survival on the shelves for over thirty years attests to its success. This fantasy novel presents a rare combination of a convincing, well-rounded secondary world with a rollicking use of wordplay that proves both entertaining and provocative. The Lands Beyond presents a unique world where nonsense is grounded in logic. The tale explores the fantasy quest of the young, disenchanted Milo who overcomes his discontent through his adventure in the fantasy realm. As is common to many young protagonists of this mode of fantasy, including Alice of *Alice in Wonderland,* and Dorothy of *The Wizard of Oz,* Milo is bored to distraction. Through a quest in the fantasy reality, Milo gains the survival tactics to find inspiration in his real world.

Milo proves himself ripe for adventure as he suffers from a consuming disinterest in all things. The crown of his apathy is his belief that the pursuit of knowledge presents the greatest waste of time. His summons into the fantasy realm occurs one typically dull day when a mysterious package containing a scaled-down genuine turnpike tollbooth appears in Milo's bedroom. As there seems to be nothing better to do, Milo assembles the package. He passes through the tollbooth in his small electric car and finds himself racing along a beautiful highway in the Lands Beyond.

Within the fantasy reality, Milo's experiences allow him to achieve insight and ability that will prove relevant in his real world. Milo meets his first challenge in the Doldrums where he must overcome the temptation of the Lethargarians—a species of apathetic creatures whose lifestyle is reminiscent of Milo's own. He manages to escape by utilizing his intellectual might. In so doing, Milo effectively leaves his old lifestyle behind and begins his journey towards learning the power of knowledge.

Milo is joined by a guide, a ticking watchdog named Tock. Together they journey to the city of Dictionopolis and learn that something is amiss in this kingdom founded on knowledge. Since the banishment of the princesses, Rhyme and Reason, wisdom has been robbed of its logic, and nonsense is sweeping the land. Milo takes on the task of rescuing the princesses. His quest takes him across the Lands Beyond towards the Mountains of Ignorance.

His journey allows him to collect the tools of knowledge that will allow him to battle the demons who rule in the realm of Ignorance. He receives from King Azaz, ruler of Dictionopolis, a box containing all the words the king knows. In the Forest of Sight, Milo learns that perception depends on point of view, and receives a telescope that will allow him to see things as they are. In the valley of sound, Milo receives from the Soundkeeper a collection of beautiful sounds. From the Mathemagician, ruler of Digitopolis, Milo receives a magic staff—a gleaming pencil with which to calculate. Thus equipped, Milo ventures into the Mountains of Ignorance in search of the Castle in the Air where the princesses are imprisoned.

In this realm where wisdom does not rule, Milo encounters and overcomes various demons who are the manifestations of ignorance. He overcomes the Everpresent Wordsnatcher, the Terrible Trivium, the Demon of Insincerity, the Gelatinous Giant, and the Senses Taker, all by employing the gifts of knowledge he had received throughout his journey. Upon finding the Princesses, Milo confides in them his new discovery—"there's so much to learn." He brings Rhyme and Reason back to the kingdom and returns to the city of Wisdom a hero.

Milo has also succeeded in returning rhyme and reason to his own existence, as is evident upon his return home. Now, even in absence of a quest that requires the use of his wit and intelligence, Milo's mind is open to the pursuit of knowledge. Milo realizes that there in his own room exists "all the puzzle and excitement of everything he didn't know." He brings into his reality the boon of his fantasy adventure—the appreciation of the pursuit of knowledge that will alleviate his life of his once profound boredom. Milo demonstrates his recovery from his affliction of apathy, when despite his desire to return to the Lands Beyond, he admits, "I really don't know when I'll have the time. There's just so much to do right here."

In conveying this theme with clarity, Juster employs in his narrative a brilliant use of language that renders concepts literal through wordplay. For example, Milo travels in a vehicle that runs only when all is quiet, for "it goes without saying." At a banquet in Dictionopolis, he regrets his dry pre-meal speech, for everyone there must eat their words. In Digitopolis, Milo only gets hungrier as he feasts on subtraction stew. Despite this nonsense that renders the obscure literal and the literal obscure, the theme of wisdom versus ignorance gives clear sense and logic to this fantasy realm where art and science become two distinct cities, and the senses translate into places on the map. In all cases, knowledge serves as power and ignorance proves debilitating. The entertaining and provoking presence of nonsense and wordplay harken back to Carroll's *Alice in Wonderland,* while the precision with which Juster creates a logical fantasy reality has more in common with the secondary world creators, Le Guin and Tolkien.

The narrative about a young protagonist presents the plot with clarity, rendering the novel accessible to younger readers. Yet, with age and repeated readings, the book reveals depth in its layers of meaning, creating a tale that promises to engage all ages. The same holds true for Juster's shorter works, directed more specifically to younger children, yet still satisfying for more advanced readers.

—Susan Rich

K

KAMM, Josephine

Nationality: British. **Born:** London, 30 December 1905. **Education:** Queen's College School, London, 1915-17; Parents' National Educational School, Burgess Hill, Sussex, 1917-23; Triangle Secretarial College, London, 1923. **Family:** Married George Emile Kamm in 1929 (died); one son. **Career:** Shorthand typist, British Commonwealth Union, London, 1924-26; assistant secretary, Empire Industries Association, London, 1926-29; shorthand typist, then senior information officer, Ministry of Information, London, 1939-46; senior information officer, Central Office of Information, London, 1946; writer. Member of National Council, 1957-69, and Executive Committee, 1963-69, National Book League; member of Executive Committee, London Centre of PEN International, 1965-69; member of Committee of Management, Fawcett Library, London, 1967-75; Society of Authors. **Awards:** Jewish Book Council of America Isaac Siegel Memorial award, 1962, for *Return to Freedom*. **Died:** 31 August 1989.

PUBLICATIONS FOR YOUNG ADULTS

Fiction

He Went with Captain Cook, illustrated by G.S. Ronalds. London, Harrap, 1952.
Janet Carr, Journalist. London, Lane, 1953; revised edition, Leicester, Brockhampton Press, 1972?
Student Almoner. London, Lane, 1955.
Out of Step, illustrated by Jillian Willett. Leicester, Brockhampton Press, 1962.
Return to Freedom, illustrated by William Stobbs. London and New York, Abelard Schuman, 1962.
Young Mother. Leicester, Brockhampton Press, and New York, Duell, 1965.
No Strangers Here. London, Constable, 1968.
First Job. Leicester, Brockhampton Press, 1969.
Where Do We Go from Here? Leicester, Brockhampton Press, 1972.
The Starting Point. Leicester, Brockhampton Press, 1975.
Runaways. London, Hodder & Stoughton, 1978.

Other

Abraham: A Biography, with Philip Cohen. London, Union of Liberal and Progressive Synagogues, 1948.
They Served the People (biographies). London, Lane, 1954.
Men Who Served Africa, illustrated by G.S. Ronalds. London, Harrap, 1957.
Leaders of the People. London and New York, Abelard Schuman, 1959.
The Story of Sir Moses Montefiore. London, Vallentine Mitchell, 1960.
The Story of Mrs. Pankhurst, illustrated by Faith Jaques. London, Methuen, 1961; as *The Story of Emmeline Pankhurst,* New York, Meredith Press, 1968.
Malaria Ross, illustrated by Anne Linton. London, Methuen, 1963; New York, Criterion, 1964.

Malaya and Singapore, illustrated by W.B. White and A.W. Gatnell. London, Longman, 1963.
A New Look at the Old Testament, illustrated by Gwyneth Cole. London, Gollancz, 1965; as *Kings, Prophets, and History,* New York, McGraw-Hill, 1966.
The Story of Fanny Burney, illustrated by Val Biro. London, Methuen, 1966; New York, Meredith Press, 1967.
The Hebrew People: A History of the Jews from Biblical Times to the Present Day. London, Gollancz, 1967; as *The Hebrew People: A History of the Jews,* New York, McGraw-Hill, 1968.
Joseph Paxton and the Crystal Palace, illustrated by Faith Jaques. London, Methuen, 1967.
Explorers into Africa. London, Gollancz, and New York, Crowell Collier, 1970.
The Slave Trade. London, Evans, 1980.
Editor, *A Tale of Two Cities,* by Charles Dickens, illustrated by Barry Wilkinson. London, Collins, 1973.

PUBLICATIONS FOR ADULTS

Novels

All Quiet at Home. London, Longman, 1936.
Disorderly Caravan. London, Harrap, 1938.
Nettles to My Head. London, Duckworth, 1939.
Peace, Perfect Peace. London, Duckworth, 1947.
Come, Draw This Curtain. London, Duckworth, 1948.

Other

Progress Toward Self-Government in the British Colonies. London, Fosh & Cross, 1945.
African Challenge: The Story of the British in Tropical Africa. London, Nelson, 1946.
Daughter of the Desert: The Story of Gertrude Bell. London, Lane, 1956; as *Gertrude Bell, Daughter of the Desert,* New York, Vanguard Press, 1956.
How Different from Us: A Biography of Miss Buss and Miss Beale. London, Bodley Head, 1958.
Hope Deferred: Girls' Education in English History. London, Methuen, 1965.
Rapiers and Battleaxes: The Women's Movement and Its Aftermath. London, Allen & Unwin, 1966.
Indicative Past: A Hundred Years of the Girls' Public Day School Trust. London, Allen & Unwin, 1971.
John Stuart Mill in Love. London, Gordon & Cremonesi, 1977.

*   *   *

When Josephine Kamm died in 1989, one of her obituarists, while acknowledging that in the 1960s she "pushed back the frontiers of teenage fiction" in Britain with her novels *Out of Step, Young Mother,* and *No Strangers Here,* also remarked that these books appear "squeaky clean and innocent" compared with present-day writing for young adults. This is true, if it means that

Kamm examined teenage life within a context of social values which are less widely agreed upon today, but the comment also pinpoints the principal problem in evaluating Kamm's novels within this genre. It is the fate of any book which strives to deal with contemporary problems through a meticulous re-creation of life that, thirty years on, will have become literally a "period piece." It is therefore impossible to understand the impact of Kamm's work in the 1960s if one reads it as if it were written in and for the 1990s; *Out of Step* and *Young Mother,* along with the other books published between 1962 and 1978, are now best viewed historically, as a response to the challenge of writing for young adults at the time when the genre was in its infancy in America, and in Britain was virtually nonexistent.

Before embarking on the series of young adult novels for which she is probably best remembered Kamm had already written for adolescents as well as for adults. In the 1950s she published biographies intended for a young readership, reflecting her interest in Jewish affairs (*Leaders of the People; The Story of Sir Moses Montefiore*) and the British Commonwealth (*They Served the People; Men Who Served Africa*). The most ambitious of these is *Daughter of the Desert,* an account of the life of the British scholar and traveller Gertrude Bell. Although perhaps too respectful toward its subject for modern taste, the beginnings of the insight and scholarship which would mark Kamm's later biographies for adults are present. This prolific writer continued to publish books on these themes throughout the 1960s and 1970s. Her patient research is most evident in her one historical novel, *Return to Freedom,* an award-winning book, set in seventeenth-century London, which tells the story of Oliver Cromwell's attempts to revoke a 400-year-old edict prohibiting Jews from settling in England. Although the narrative is initially slowed down by more historical detail than present-day teenagers find palatable, the story is unusual and told with both skill and sympathy. The character of Cromwell, not superficially attractive, is particularly well-drawn.

In the 1950s, Kamm also wrote two "career novels," *Janet Carr, Journalist* and *Student Almoner,* titles in a series intended to give teenage girls insight into a variety of careers. Although the series is interesting historically, as one of the first attempts in Britain to cater to a specifically young adult readership, the characterisation of Janet Carr and Barbara Henderson, the trainee hospital social worker, inevitably suffers because Kamm's remit was to convey career information. These are not among her most successful novels, but they were important in Kamm's development as a writer for young adults. They gave her the idea for other books in which, unconstrained by formulaic conventions, she could choose and develop her own themes.

It is difficult now to realise just how revolutionary Kamm's teenage novels seemed in Britain in the early 1960s; the wonder is not that, in accordance with the convention of the day, they were inexplicit, but that they were so frank. During the 1950s the book establishment had been edging towards the perception that teenagers, as a recently defined "group," might merit a literature of their own; Kamm's stories of young adults coping with single parenthood, mixed-race relationships, adoption, and early marriage established her as a pioneer in this genre. There are, perhaps, "stock situations," but the narratives are strong and there are no stock characters—although the need to explore problems in depth sometimes means that characters are less fully rounded than an adult reader might wish. Thus her most successful books are those with the fewest characters.

Young Mother, the most famous of Kamm's books and still in print in 1992, tells the story of schoolgirl Pat Henley's pregnancy with a brave honesty, remarkable when one reflects that Kamm was in her late fifties when she wrote it. The embarrassment and tedium of Pat's experience, and her doomed efforts to keep her child, are well described; although changes in social attitudes have inevitably dated her stories, Kamm's nonjudgmental view of the young, her humanity and determination to eschew facile resolutions, give them lasting appeal.

Only those young in the 1960s can fully appreciate Kamm's evocation of that restless decade—the loving observation of London life, the self-importance and self-doubt of a young generation sensing emancipation, the determination of their parents to criticise what they could understand perfectly well. This atmosphere is caught most poignantly in *Out of Step,* the love story of Betty Fielding and her West Indian boyfriend, Bob Francis, which unfolds against a working-class background, at a time of low aspirations, full but undemanding employment, and cruel prejudice. British racism is indignantly exposed, and this excellent novel is read with an awareness that, although Kamm's work may be taking its place in history, many of the questions she raised then are yet to be answered.

—Eileen Dunlop

KATZ, Welwyn

Nationality: Canadian. **Born:** Welwyn Wilton, London, Ontario, 7 June 1948. **Education:** University of Western Ontario, London, 1966-69, B.S.C. (honours) in mathematics 1969; Althouse College of Education, London, 1969-70, diploma in education 1970. **Family:** Married Albert N. Katz in 1973; one daughter. **Career:** Mathematics teacher, London secondary schools, 1970-77. **Awards:** International Children's Fiction Contest prize, 1987; Canada Council grant, 1981, 1983, 1985, 1988; Canadian Library Association Book of the Year for Children runnerup, 1989. **Address:** 103 Windsor Avenue, London, Ontario N6C 1Z8, Canada.

PUBLICATIONS FOR YOUNG ADULTS

Fiction

The Prophecy of Tau Ridoo, illustrated by Michelle Desbarats. Edmonton, Alberta, Tree Frog Press, 1982.
Witchery Hill. Vancouver, Douglas and McIntyre, and New York, Atheneum, 1984; London, Angus and Robertson, 1988.
Sun God, Moon Witch. Vancouver, Douglas and McIntyre, 1986.
False Face. Vancouver, Douglas and McIntyre, 1987; New York, McElderry, 1988.
The Third Magic. Vancouver, Douglas and McIntyre, 1988; New York, McElderry, 1989.
Whalesinger. Douglas and McIntyre, 1990; New York, Macmillan, 1991.
Come Like Shadows. New York, Viking, 1993.
Time Ghost. New York, Margaret K. McElderry Books, 1995.
Out of the Dark. Vancouver, Douglas and McIntyre, 1995; New York, Margaret K. McElderry Books, 1996.

*

Welwyn Katz comments:

I am particularly interested in the ancient legends that have been passed down for hundreds, even thousands of years. For these stories of past times to be kept alive from generation to generation, there must be something "true" about them, something of modern validity. What I try to do in my novels is enmesh the truths of legend with ordinary reality. I write books that, for the most part, are set on modern-day Earth, but I make ancient superstitions and legends parallel the ordinary realism of the plot. My characters resolve modern problems by brushing against the ancient.

*   *   *

The novels of Welwyn Katz all deal with some aspect of the supernatural or mythic. The characters are either physically transported to another realm where much of the action takes place, as in *The Prophecy of Tau Ridoo* and *The Third Magic,* or, as in *Witchery Hill, Sun God, Moon Witch,* and *False Face,* they are confronted by supernatural forces in ordinary and familiar surroundings. The plots generally revolve around the ancient conflict of good against evil—an evil that is either externalized and focused in a specific character or internalized within the main character, as he or she unknowingly falls under evil influences.

The Prophecy of Tau Ridoo is a fairly standard fantasy adventure in which the five Aubrey children are transported to the mysterious and dangerous world of Tau Ridoo. Separated and pursued by agents of the evil Red General, the children manage to survive with the help of the sorceress Cooky and her magic, and struggle to defeat the evil force that has kept Tau Ridoo in darkness for almost 700 years. The action is brisk and enlivened by touches of humor.

A dark and sinister tale, *Witchery Hill* brings 14-year-old Mike and his divorced journalist father to Guernsey for a prolonged stay with his father's friends, the St. George family. Outwardly all is happy and serene, but as Mike slowly befriends the rather sullen daughter Lisa, he becomes aware of hostile undercurrents. Thirteen-year-old Lisa, a diabetic and deeply devoted to her father, reveals her suspicions that her beautiful stepmother is a practicing witch, engaged in a deadly struggle for control of the local coven. As the action unfolds, Mike's unsatisfactory relationship with his father and his struggle to understand the psychic power of evil bring matters to a head in a climactic scene in which he is left alone to prevent a terrible sacrifice and destroy the ancient power that holds the coven together.

This theme continues in *Sun God, Moon Witch.* Dreading the thought of spending the summer with her cousin Patrick in a sleepy English village, Thorny McCabe quickly discovers that, far from being quiet and dull, the village is the center of a dramatic controversy over the ancient stone circle of Awen-Ur. All too soon she finds herself caught in a terrible struggle between a mysterious lady in white and the fiery local squire as the powers of light battle the forces of dark for control of the world.

Departing somewhat from this theme, *False Face* is set in present-day Canada and has as its protagonists two unhappy adolescents brought together in an uneasy alliance through their discovery of a rare pair of Iroquois false face masks belonging to an outcast medicine man. Troubled by the acrimonious divorce of her parents, 13-year-old Laney finds comfort in the small face mask she has found. Fourteen-year-old Tom, half-Indian and determined to preserve his ethnic identity, is deeply resentful of Laney's casually ignorant attitude to the masks, which represent an important aspect of Indian culture. As the emotional conflicts with the adults in their lives grow, so does their understanding of the true and terrifying power of the masks.

The Third Magic returns to more familiar themes, drawing its inspiration from Arthurian legends. On a visit to England, 15-year-old Morgan Lefevre is mistaken for one of her ancestors and is summoned to the alien world of Nwm where she finds herself caught between the opposing forces of two magics.

Reminiscent in tone and theme to early Robert Westall, particularly *The Wind Eye* and *The Watch House,* Katz's books are compelling reading. She is a strong storyteller (though there are occasional touches of melodrama in her earlier books), and her characters are well drawn. She seems to be in tune with the adolescent psyche and is able to convey the painful confusions of that time of life in a succinct and sympathetic manner. She is harder on the adult characters who, if they are not the actual embodiment of evil, are somewhat remote and slow to understand or respond to the situations around them, almost as if life had deadened their feelings and perceptions.

In keeping with her chosen themes, Katz's next three books, *Whalesinger, Come Like Shadows,* and *Time Ghost,* further explore the relationships between the known world and the supernatural as well as the interrelationship of all living things. As in her earlier books, her central characters are teenagers, usually troubled by a difficult problem that makes them more vulnerable to the often evil forces of nature.

Essentially a love story, *Whalesinger* is set against the magnificent backdrop of the Point Reyes National Seashore in California. A scientific expedition studying aspects of ecology brings together a varied group of people including two older teenagers, an emotionally isolated boy determined to avenge his older brother's death on a similar expedition, and a withdrawn girl who discovers she shares an empathetic bond with a gray whale and her calf. The complicated relationships that evolve between the human and animal protagonists and the natural setting in which they find themselves give a rich texture to this novel that, despite a somewhat somber cast, has a generally positive resolution. This is a particularly good story with strong characterization, an absorbing plot, and wonderful descriptions of the isolated coastline whose character is subject to sudden and sometimes violent changes. The description of an earthquake that occurs at a climactic point in the story attests to the author's particular strength in evoking the awesome power of nature.

Come Like Shadows, Katz's 1993 novel set in Canada and Scotland, has a somewhat more complicated and, often, unruly plot. Sixteen-year-old Kinny, determined to be an actress, is thrilled to be hired as assistant to the brilliant director of a new production of Macbeth set in mid-18th-century Canada. Things go wrong almost immediately: the director behaves strangely, the actors are hostile, and Kinny soon realizes that her only use to the company is to find and keep track of the props. One of her finds, a junk shop mirror, turns out to be the catalyst that makes a bad situation worse by releasing the malevolent spirit of the witches that destroyed the real Macbeth in the 11th century. The story moves to its inexorable climax when the company goes to perform in Scotland and the witches, now in modern guise, are finally ready to renew their coven with Kinny, who, although aware of their sinister plan, seems to be powerless to resist.

Time Ghost, her latest book for somewhat younger readers, is set 50 years into the future in a Canada much changed by the ravages of pollution. Here again are the familiar themes of respect for nature and acceptance of the interrelationship of all living things.

Two sets of siblings in their early teens, Sara and her older brother Karl, and Dani and her brother Josh, who have always lived in the protected confines of the city, accompany Sara's and Karl's grandmother to the still unspoiled North Pole. Everyone is eager for the adventure but a rebellious Sara, overwhelmed by a fear of the vast open spaces, finds it impossible to appreciate her grandmother's cheerful admonitions to appreciate her surroundings. A confrontation with her grandmother on her birthday sends Sara and her friend Dani back in time to the late 20th century before pollution irrevocably changed the character of the countryside.

As in *Whalesinger,* Katz is very much attuned to the natural setting she is describing. She conveys the visual as well as the sensual beauty of the vast frozen spaces—the sun shining on the snow, the feel of the clean air—very effectively. The supernatural aspects of travelling back in time are handled in a believable way and Sara's and Dani's wonder at finding themselves in a place where nature is not to be feared is both touching and sobering. Although the underlying theme of environmental protection is quite strong it does not overwhelm this lively and entertaining story.

Although she has had some lapses, Katz's strongest books, *False Face, Whalesinger,* and to some extent, *Time Ghost,* all display her particular talent for inventive plots, strong writing style, and interesting characters. Her love of nature and fascination with the supernatural animates these, as well as all her novels, and her sensitive portrayals of adolescents are particularly compelling. She is always a pleasure to read.

—Divna Todorovich

KEITH, Harold (Verne)

Nationality: American. **Born:** Lambert, Oklahoma Territory, 8 April 1903. **Education:** Lambert High School, graduated 1921; Northwestern State College, Alva, Oklahoma (Scroll scholarship, 1922), 1921-24; University of Oklahoma, Norman, B.A. in history 1929, M.A. 1938, special courses in professional writing, 1953-56. **Family:** Married Virginia Livingston in 1931; one son and one daughter. **Career:** Elementary school teacher, Amorita Consolidated School System, Oklahoma, seventh-grade, 1922-23; sports correspondent, *Daily Oklahoman, Tulsa World, Kansas City Star,* and *Omaha World-Herald,* 1922-29; assistant to grain buyer, Red Star Milling Co., Hutchinson, Kansas, 1929-30; sports publicity director, University of Oklahoma, Norman, 1930-69. President, College Sports Information Directors, 1964-65. Set U.S. Masters national records for the two- and three-mile runs, 1973, and 10,000 meter run, 1974. **Awards:** Helms Foundation Sports Publicist of the Year, 1950; American Library Association Newbery Medal for *Rifles for Watie,* 1958; Arch Ward Memorial Trophy for outstanding achievement in sports publicity, 1961; Charlie May Simon award for *The Runt of Rogers School;* Western Writers of

America Spur award and Western Heritage award for *Susy's Scoundrel,* 1975; Western Heritage award for *The Obstinate Land,* 1979. **Address:** 2318 Ravenwood Lane, Hall Park, Route 4, Norman, Oklahoma 72071, U.S.A.

PUBLICATIONS FOR YOUNG ADULTS

Fiction

Shotgun Shaw: A Baseball Story, illustrated by Mabel Jones Woodbury. New York, Crowell, 1949.
A Pair of Captains, illustrated by Mabel Jones Woodbury. New York, Crowell, 1951.
Rifles for Watie. New York, Crowell, 1957.
Komantcia. New York, Crowell, 1965.
Brief Garland. New York, Crowell, 1971.
The Runt of Rogers School. Philadelphia, Lippincott, 1971.
The Bluejay Boarders, illustrated by Harold Berson. New York, Crowell, 1972.
Go Red, Go!, illustrated by Ned Glattauer. Nashville, Nelson, 1972.
Susy's Scoundrel, illustrated by John Schoenherr. New York, Crowell, 1974.
The Obstinate Land. New York, Crowell, 1977.
The Sound of Strings. Norman, Oklahoma, Levite of Apache Publishing, 1992.

Nonfiction

Boys' Life of Will Rogers, illustrated by Karl S. Woerner. New York, Crowell, 1937; revised as *Will Rogers: A Boy's Life,* illustrated by Karl S. Woerner. Norman, Oklahoma, Levite of Apache, 1991.
Sports and Games. New York, Crowell, 1941; revised edition, 1960.

PUBLICATIONS FOR ADULTS

Nonfiction

Oklahoma Kickoff. Privately printed, 1948.
Forty-Seven Straight: The Wilkinson Era at Oklahoma. Norman, University of Oklahoma Press, 1984.

*

Biography: Entry in *Children and Books,* 3rd edition, edited by May Hill Arbuthnot, Glenview, Illinois, Scott, Foresman & Co., 1964; *Books and the Teen-Age Reader* by G. Robert Carlson, New York, Harper, 1967; *Children's Literature in the Elementary School* edited by Charlotte S. Hack, New York, Holt, 1961; *Newbery and Caldecott Medal Books: 1956-1965* edited by Lee Kingman, Boston, Massachusetts, Horn Book, 1965.

Manuscript Collections: Northwestern State College Library, Alva, Oklahoma; University of Oklahoma Library, Norman.

*   *   *

Harold Keith's father was a grain buyer, so the family moved many times and Harold attended nine different schools. Perhaps this satisfied any wanderlust the young boy ever had, because for well over half a century he has been deeply rooted in the soil and history of Oklahoma, living in Norman for sixty-seven years and earning his state's Lifetime Achievement Book Award and membership in the Oklahoma Writer's Hall of Fame. Beginning writers are often advised to write what they know, and Keith thoroughly embraced this old principle, writing almost entirely for boys, about sports, and setting his stories in the heartland of America.

Sports have been his lifelong interest, both as observer and participant. He was sports editor of his high-school magazine and spent thirty-nine years as varsity publicist for the University of Oklahoma. His athletic career is incredible. He won the Penn Relays steeplechase as an undergraduate—despite having never run one before—the Oklahoma Athletic Union's cross-country race at age forty-two, and he set a U.S. Masters Association record for the three-mile run for men seventy and over. For much of his career, he wrote almost entirely about sports in article and book form. One of his earliest books, *Sports and Games,* surveyed various recreational activities and sold well, becoming a Junior Literary Guild selection.

As a teacher for the Amorita school district he had close experience with the interests and dreams of children, and other than his publicity and a behind-the-scenes book about University of Oklahoma football, most of his writing has been for adolescent boys. *The Runt of Rogers School,* for instance, concerned boys of short stature attempting to compete in athletics. Of normal height himself, Keith talked with numerous short athletes to gain insight into the particular problems they might face. This concern with the reality of the characters and settings is one of the most important reasons Keith's writings stand out. His genuine interest in other people has allowed him to get close to his subjects and to use their experiences as the background of his fiction. This method of writing began with the work on his master's thesis, ''Clem Rogers and His Influence on History,'' during which he made a large number of visits to eastern Oklahoma to interview people who had known the Rogers family. He then adapted his thesis into his first book, *Boy's Life of Will Rogers.*

His greatest fame was to come from his historical writings. Despite publishing regularly, he was dissatisfied with the level of his writing. He spent summers in the Professional Writing Program at the university, a course of study he still praises at every opportunity, saying he learned more in one class session than he had learned in years of trial and error. He had always considered plotting to be the easiest part of writing, whereas characters and the creation of scenes bedeviled him. As his characterization has always been one of his strong suits, one can assume the remark mainly illustrates his care in that area. The program emphasized the scene and sequel method, and combined with his research skills, historical interests, and insight into motivation, Keith soon reached the upper echelon of young adult authors.

In 1958, *Rifles for Watie* was awarded the thirty-seventh Newbery medal and its success illustrates how Keith's continuing attempts to improve his writing paid off. Young Jeff Bussey serves four years in the western Civil War, and becomes involved in finding out how General Stand Watie, who has been harrying Federal troops with Cherokee raiders, has gotten his rifles. This combination *Red Badge of Courage* and spy novel germinated through Keith's usual careful research. Not many veterans still lived from that war but Keith hunted up twenty-two of them, most nearly one hundred years old, and all Confederates. He immersed himself in the Western history materials of the university library, and while travelling with the football team visited historical societies and carefully read the diaries and letters of Union veterans. The result was highly praised for its vivid authenticity. One reviewer recommended it as supplemental historical reading for young adults, and the book is still used for that purpose. In 1992, for example, Keith was asked to speak to high schools students in several states about the book. What reviewers also highly praised, however, was his ability to convey all of this authenticity by means of a series of scenes which hurtled forward, never pausing in its action.

His *Komantcia,* a New York Times Best Book of 1965, was set among the Comanches. In his characteristic method he mined the collections at the university library and visited the tribe, who once ranged from Wyoming to Texas but had been forcibly resettled in Oklahoma. He even interviewed one of the wives of the Comanches' most famous chiefs, Quanah Parker. He gathered so much material that the publisher forced Keith to shorten the novel, and it was 1992 before *The Sound of Strings* was released as a sequel.

In the 1970s, Keith continued to win awards. *Susy's Scoundrel* won the Spur and Western Heritage Award. *The Obstinate Land* won a Western Heritage Award and was praised for being a convincing portrayal of a family striving to make a living in the harsh surroundings of the Cherokee Strip, an area in northern Oklahoma. Though his output was limited by his work as a publicist, Keith's careful attention to details and craftsmanship would probably have never allowed him to be a rapid writer. He approached writing doggedly, likening it to a long-distance run in which the competitor must keep moving even when exhausted. The high quality of his work and his amiable personality nonetheless has made him one of the most beloved writers in his home state and elsewhere.

—J. Madison Davis

KELL, Joseph. *See* BURGESS, Anthony.

KELLEHER, Victor (Michael Kitchener)

Nationality: British. Born: London, 19 July 1939. Education: University of Natal, Pietermaritzburg, South Africa, B.A. in English 1961; University of St. Andrews, Fife, Diploma in Education,

1963; University of the Witwatersrand, Johannesburg, B.A. (honors) 1969; University of South Africa, Pretoria, M.A. 1970, D.Litt. et Phil., 1973. **Family:** Married Alison Lyle in 1962; one son and one daughter. **Career:** Junior Lecturer in English, University of the Witwatersrand, 1969; Lecturer, 1970-71, Senior Lecturer in English, 1972-73, University of South Africa; Lecturer in English, Massey University, Palmerston North, New Zealand, 1973-76; Lecturer, 1976-79, Senior Lecturer, 1980-83, Associate Professor of English, from 1984, University of New England, Armidale, New South Wales; writer. **Awards:** Patricia Hackett Prize from *Westerly* magazine, 1978, for story "The Traveller"; senior writer's fellowship from the Literature Board of the Australia Council, 1982; West Australian Young Readers' Book award from the West Australian Library Association, 1982, for *Forbidden Paths of Thual;* West Australian Young Readers' Special award from the West Australian Library Association, 1983, for *The Hunting of Shadroth;* Australian Children's Book of the Year award from the Children's Book Council of Australia, 1983, for *Master of the Grove;* Australian Science Fiction Achievement award from the National Science Fiction Association, 1984, for *The Beast of Heaven;* Honour award from the Children's Book Council of Australia, 1987, for *Taronga;* Australian Children's Book Honor award, 1991, for *Brother Night.* **Address:** 149 Wigram Rd., Glebe, NSW 2037, Australia.

PUBLICATIONS FOR YOUNG ADULTS

Fiction

Forbidden Paths of Thual, illustrated by Antony Maitland. London, Viking Kestrel, and New York, Penguin Books, 1979.
The Hunting of Shadroth. London, Viking Kestrel, and New York, Penguin Books, 1981.
Master of the Grove. London, Viking Kestrel, and New York, Penguin Books, 1982.
The Green Piper. Melbourne, Viking Kestrel, and New York, Penguin Books, 1984; London, Viking Kestrel, 1985.
Papio: A Novel of Adventure. London, Viking Kestrel, and New York, Penguin Books, 1984.
Rescue! New York, Dial, 1985.
The Makers. New York, Penguin Books, 1986; Melbourne, Viking Kestrel, 1987.
Taronga. Melbourne, Viking Kestrel, and New York, Penguin Books, 1986; London, Hamish Hamilton, 1987.
Baily's Bones. Melbourne, Viking Kestrel, and New York, Dial, 1988.
Em's Story. St. Lucia, University of Queensland Press, 1988.
The Red King. New York, Dial, 1990.
Brother Night. New York, J. MacRae, 1991.
Voices from the River. St. Lucia, University of Queensland Press, 1991.
Del-Del, illustrated by Peter Clarke. New York, Walker, 1992.
Micky Darlin'. St. Lucia, University of Queensland Press, 1992.
To the Dark Tower. New York, J. MacRae, 1992.
Parkland. Victoria and New York, Viking, 1994.
Where the Whales Sing, illustrations by Vivienne Goodman. Victoria, Viking, 1994; as *Riding the Whales,* New York, Dial Books for Young Readers, 1995.

PUBLICATIONS FOR ADULTS

Novels

Voices from the River. London, Heinemann, 1979.
The Beast of Heaven. St. Lucia, University of Queensland Press, 1984.
Wintering. St. Lucia, University of Queensland Press, 1990.

Short Stories

Africa and After. Brisbane, University of Queensland Press, 1983; as *The Traveller: Stories of Two Continents,* St. Lucia, University of Queensland Press, 1987.

*   *   *

Victor Kelleher is one of Australia's most outstanding writers of fantasy. Of his books for young people nine are fantasy novels, and seven of these have imaginary settings and involve quests. The adventure story *Papio,* a modern quest story, is the only novel without some supernatural element, whereas the effects of belief in the supernatural is a theme of the horror thriller *Del-Del.* Kelleher's writing for adults is more diverse in style and genre, but the intellectual and emotional challenges of his books are certainly not diminished for his younger readers.

The central precept of Victor Kelleher's writing is that things are not always what they seem. In all his novels the heroes struggle with hindrances to clear perception. His first three fantasy/quest adventures, *Forbidden Paths of Thual, The Hunting of Shadroth,* and *Master of the Grove,* involve young men setting out on dangerous although apparently straightforward missions. All find that the beliefs of their communities are based on false premises and each have to confront complex enemies, make difficult moral choices, and acknowledge the part chance plays in human lives. In the award-winning *Master of the Grove,* truth and falsehood are the heart of the novel. Derin, the hero, sets out on a quest accompanied by an old woman (Marna) and a raven to find his missing father. He doesn't know it, but Derin's mission is to unseat the evil Krob and restore peace to a war-torn land. But is witch Marna a friend or an enemy? He finds, right when he needs to know, that deception is his only protection from evil.

Concepts of truth, deception, and evil are related to control and power in the early novels and also in *The Makers, The Red King,* and *Brother Night.* All three are quest novels. *The Makers* is a disturbing book about a carefully controlled society which takes young children and trains them as warriors, telling them they have been made specifically for this purpose. There is a lighter touch in *The Red King* where Petie (a magician), Timkin (an acrobat), Crystal (a monkey), and Bruno (a bear) seem an unlikely group to defeat the tyrant Red King who controls the forest kingdom. There is much trickery and confusion about good and evil as in *Master of the Grove.* Confusion also taunts the hero of Kelleher's most outstanding fantasy quest adventure to date, the richly symbolic *Brother Night.* The hero, Ramon, finds out that his mother is Pilar, the woman known by the village as the Moon Witch, and that he had a twin brother killed at birth because of his monstrous appearance. Ramon believes his father is the Sun Lord, Semlock, but why is Semlock trying to kill him? Ramon's giant and ugly brother, Lal, is not dead and together they set out for the Twin cities on tellingly different quests—Ramon to kill his father and compassionate, loving Lal to bury Pilar's bones.

Two novels, *Papio* and *Taronga,* look at animal-human relationships and *The Green Piper* is a horrific account of a strange plantlike creature with a hatred for flesh. Like the Pied Piper this creature attracts living things to it and destroys them. In *Papio* David and Jem save two baboons, Papio and Upi, from death at a laboratory but then need to stay with them once they're free, learning that freedom has a price. The setting of *Taronga* is postapocalypse Sydney where all social systems have broken down, and desperate gangs roam the city and countryside. An orphaned boy, Ben, has a special ability to communicate with animals and influence their actions which he uses to good effect when stalked through Taronga Park Zoo by a tiger. Previously Ben had used his powers to lure animals to their death, providing food for survivors. There is a strong antiviolence stance, with an emphasis on how violence always escalates. The novel ends on an exciting and positive note with the zoo animals freed and Ben and an Aboriginal girl, Ellie, heading for the mountains to start a new life although neither know what this life might be like. As Ben says, "It's not only the animals that'll have to adapt. We'll have to as well. Anything can happen now. Anything."

The nature of truth is also a major theme in this author's contemporary adventures *Baily's Bones, Papio,* and the thriller *Del-Del.* In fast-moving, often violent narratives the faces of deception, be they superstition, nostalgia, or sentimentality, are revealed as dangerous shams and traps for soft thinkers. The intricacies of love and, of necessity, hate are an important part of *Brother Night* and this theme, too, is further explored in *Baily's Bones* and especially in *Del-Del.* The historical background to *Baily's Bones* is the massacre of a whole tribe of Aborigines in the mid-nineteenth century. A white man, escaped convict Frank Baily, sees it happen and swears revenge against the murderer, Walter Arnold. The hatred draws in others and in modern times Alex and Dee are involved when their "simple" brother Kenny, reminiscent of Lal, seems to be possessed by the spirit of Frank Baily. Supernatural possession is also the key to Kelleher's widely admired and controversial novel *Del-Del.* Sam, a year after the death of his much loved sister, starts to act in a very peculiar manner and gradually his family come to believe he is possessed by a demon. Sam's mother resists this idea, but his grandmother urges them to use priests to rid Sam of the demon. The family starts to come apart, and Sam's behaviour gets worse but fortunately Beth, the eldest child, finds a solution. In this book about the power of grief Kelleher cleverly uses the form of the horror genre to point out the deceptiveness of superstition.

The dust-jacket notes for Kelleher's book, *To the Dark Tower,* describe this novel as "challenging" and a reviewer more forthrightly said she found the book "a bit of a haul" whilst admiring the technical achievement. The hero, Tom, lives his waking life in the grimness of an industrial city, but in his dreams he is The Carrier bearing the mysterious Sleeper's spirit in the form of a beautiful child. Tom realises, just before his task is accomplished, that the Sleeper represents a grim past, worse by far than the difficult present. The dangers of yearning for a past golden age is a fine theme, but the road to the gripping conclusion is tediously repetitive. This is a very sophisticated fantasy quest book but the characterisation of Tom and his heroic companions is a disappointment compared to the riches of *Del-Del.*

—Kerry White

KELLY, Fiona. *See* **JONES, Allan Frewin.**

KENDALL, Carol

Nationality: American. **Born:** Carol Seeger in Bucyrus, Ohio, 13 September 1917. **Education:** Ohio University, Athens, A.B. (Phi Beta Kappa) 1939. **Family:** Married Paul Murray Kendall in 1939 (died 1973); two daughters. **Awards:** Ohioana Award and Newbery Medal Honor Book Award, American Library Association Honor Book, all for *The Gammage Cup,* 1960; Parents' Choice Award, 1982, and Mythopoeic Society Aslan Award, 1983, both for *The Firelings.* **Address:** 928 Holiday Drive, Lawrence, Kansas 66049, U.S.A.

PUBLICATIONS FOR YOUNG ADULTS

Fiction

The Other Side of the Tunnel, illustrated by Lilian Buchanan. London, Lane, 1956; New York, Abelard, 1957.
The Gammage Cup, illustrated by Erik Blegvad. New York, Harcourt, 1959; as *The Minnipins,* London, Dent, 1960.
The Big Splash, illustrated by Lilian Obligado. New York, Viking, 1960.
The Whisper of Glocken, illustrated by Imero Gobatto. New York, Harcourt, 1965; London, Bodley Head, 1967.
The Firelings. London, Bodley Head, 1981; New York, Atheneum, 1982.

Other

With Yao-wen Li, *Sweet and Sour: Tales from China,* illustrated by Shirley Felts. London, Bodley Head, 1978; New York, Houghton, 1979.
Reteller, *Haunting Tales from Japan.* Lawrence, Spencer Museum of Art, University of Kansas, 1985.

PUBLICATIONS FOR CHILDREN

The Wedding of the Rat Family (Chinese folktale; picture book), illustrated by James Watts. New York, Macmillan, 1988.

PUBLICATIONS FOR ADULTS

Novels

The Black Seven. New York, Harper, 1946; London, Lane, 1950.
The Baby-Snatcher. London, Lane, 1952.

*

Biography: Essay in *Something about the Author Autobiography Series,* Volume 7, Detroit, Gale, 1989.

Manuscript Collections: Ohio University Library, Athens.

Carol Kendall comments:

People ask me ''What made you decide to be a writer?'' and laugh knowingly when I answer ''Six older brothers.''

Those six brothers were as fine a set of boys and young men as one could want, but they did talk a lot. By the time I made my belated appearance into the family, they were so well gifted in the flow of conversation that there were few pauses for the addition of one small female voice. So I grew up listening. Family recollections would indicate that I was just one sentence short of being completely mute—my single comment of record (at age four) was ''Thank goodness that noisy thing is gone.'' The noisy thing was my brother Arden, whose goings and comings were as turbulent as a high wind gusting through the house.

But then came school! I loved school. The teachers also talked a lot, but they did it to me instead of to each other, and their words were about reading and writing—worth all the missed conversations in the world. My voice could be heard at last! Before the year was out, I started to write a ''diary-book'' with my new power. The opening line was ''I saw my first robin today.'' It was also the last line, for clearly I had run out of words I knew how to write. The rest of my thoughts would have to wait a spell.

I am still not adept at entering conversations when there are more than three competing talkers, but I don't mind much because I know I can put my own offerings into the computer and fish them out when the time is ripe.

*   *   *

Carol Kendall is one of the twentieth century's most underrated fantasy writers, possibly because she is not as prolific as many of her contemporaries. Although she has written two run-of-the-mill adventure stories and retold several Chinese folk tales, she is primarily known as the author of three fantasy novels: *The Gammage Cup* (first published in 1959); its sequel, *The Whisper of Glocken* (1965); and *The Firelings* (1981). These sparse publication dates help to explain her relative obscurity. In 1960 *The Gammage Cup* received recognition as a Newbery Honor book, but during the following decade Lloyd Alexander remolded American fantasy into a new genre with his Prydain books. As a result, gentler fantasies like *The Gammage Cup* and its sequel fell out of favor. However, Kendall's obscurity is not deserved. Her books weave important social themes and moral concepts into well-paced fantasy adventures with a thread of subtle humor running throughout.

The Gammage Cup introduces a society of small hobbit-like beings called Minnipins, who live along a river in the Land Between the Mountains. According to their oral history, the Minnipins emigrated there in ancient times, led by the legendary hero Gammage, to escape their enemies. Few Minnipins in the enlightened town of Slipper-on-the-Water believe the legends; they prefer to believe the stories about Fooley the Balloonist, who flew beyond the mountains and returned with several mysterious relics. Fooley's descendants have become the town leaders—the conservative, narrow-minded Council of Periods. When the twelve Minnipin villages hold a contest for the finest village, the Periods decide they must do something about the five nonconformists in Slipper-on-the-Water. The rest of the novel deals with the adventures of these five characters after they are banished from the village.

The novel abounds in subtle social satire. The Minnipins' misunderstanding of the Fooley artifacts sheds humorous light on the nature of art and on social stratification, and their disdain for history and creativity provides a parody of contemporary American society. The efforts of Walter the Earl to convince the Minnipins to embrace their own glorious history rather than the false Fooley history and the efforts of the other four nonconformists to establish lives of creative individualism highlight the natural enmity between society and the individual. Kendall does not favor one over the other, however. The underlying theme of all her books is balance, so she attempts to balance the needs of an inherently conservative society with the needs of artistic individuals. Although the Council of Periods is held up to ridicule, all the Minnipins rise to heroism when their traditional enemies reappear, and the somewhat chastened Periods remain in charge of the village at the end of the book despite their lack of vision.

The sequel, *The Whisper of Glocken,* begins with the flooding of the village of Water Gap. Five Minnipins from Water Gap are reluctantly thrust into the role of heroes, sent beyond the mountains to determine the cause of the flood. Whereas *The Gammage Cup* dealt with issues of conformity and individualism, the theme of *The Whisper of Glocken* is the nature of heroism. Glocken, the young bell ringer from Water Gap, has so thoroughly idealized the Five Heroes of Slipper-on-the-Water that he is sorely disappointed when he finally meets them. Glocken has dreamed of becoming a hero himself, but he finds that the reality is not as glorious as his dreams. His four Water Gap companions also learn valuable lessons about themselves—lessons about mutual need and support. When Glocken finally becomes a hero, he does not even recognize the moment because he is intent on doing what must be done.

A third and more recent fantasy explores Kendall's most daring theme to date: the nature of religious faith. *The Firelings* are a cooperative society of small beings very like the Minnipins, but living on the side of a volcano called ''Belcher,'' which is their god. On occasions the Firelings have pacified Belcher with a ''Morsel,'' or human sacrifice. Now Belcher is acting up again, and the villagers are discussing ways to pacify him. The adults cling to the old ways, but the young people are free of these superstitions. Five young firelings help a sixth escape his sacrificial fate, and they all desperately search for the legendary Way of the Goat that will lead their people to safety. Kendall does not make religion a black and white issue by pitting enlightened youngsters against superstitious elders; rather she seeks to create a balance between trust in tradition and a legitimate questioning of authority. Although she seems to cast MudLar, the hereditary religious leader and mystic, as a mountebank who preys on the fears of his ignorant society, later events prove the hermit to be an intelligent man devoted to freeing his people from their own need of him. Many of the misunderstood religious beliefs of the firelings are the means by which they eventually escape the enslavement of the volcano. Mysticism also plays a role in the events of the novel. For example, there are tendrils of ESP between several of the younger firelings. This novel is darker and more ambitious than Kendall's earlier works. There are undercurrents of shame, guilt, madness, and drug addiction, although they barely disturb the surface of the fantasy adventure.

—Donna R. White

KERR, M.E

Pseudonym for Marijane (Agnes) Meaker. **Other Pseudonyms:** Ann Aldrich, Mary James, M. J. Meaker, Vin Packer. **Nationality:** American. **Born:** Auburn, New York, 27 May 1927. **Education:** Vermont Junior College, the New School for Social Research, and the University of Missouri, Columbia, B.A. 1949. **Career:** Freelance writer, from 1949; held several jobs, including assistant file clerk, E. P. Dutton and Fawcett, 1949-51, and volunteer writing teacher at Commercial Manhattan Central High, 1968. Founding member of the Ashawagh Writers' Workshop. **Awards:** American Library Association (ALA) notable book, one of *School Library Journal's* best books of the year, both 1972, and winner of the *Media and Methods* Maxi awards, 1974, all for *Dinky Hocker Shoots Smack!*; *Book World's* Children's Spring Book Festival honor book, one of Child Study Association's Children's books of the year, and one of *New York Times'* outstanding books of the year, all 1973, all for *If I Love You, Am I Trapped Forever?*; one of *School Library Journal's* best books of the year, 1974, for *The Son of Someone Famous*; ALA notable book, one of ALA's best books for young adults, and one of *New York Times* outstanding books of the year, all 1975, all for *Is That You, Miss Blue?*; one of *School Library Journal's* best books of the year, 1977, for *I'll Love You When You're More Like Me*; Christopher award, 1979, and The Christophers, *School Library Journal's* book of the year award, one of *New York Times'* outstanding books of the year, both 1978, and one of New York Public Library's best books for the teen age, 1980 and 1981, all for *Gentlehands*; Golden Kite award, Society of Children's Book Writers, one of *School Library Journal's* best books of the year, both 1981, and one of New York Public Library's books for the teen age, 1982, all for *Little Little*; one of *School Library Journal's* best books of the year, 1982, for *What I Really Think of You*; one of ALA best books for young adults, 1983, for *Me, Me, Me, Me, Me: Not a Novel*; one of ALA best books for young adults, 1985, for *I Stay Near You*; one of ALA recommended books for the reluctant young adult reader, 1986, and California Young Reader Medal, 1991, both for *Night Kites*; Margaret A. Edwards award, 1993, for body of work; Best Book Honor Award, Michigan Library Assoication, 1994; Recommended Books for Reluctant Young Adult Readers citation, American Library Association, 1995; Fanfare Honor List, *Horn Book,* 1995. **Agent:** Eugene Winick, McIntosh & Otis, Inc., 310 Madison Ave., New York, New York 10017, U.S.A. **Address:** 12 Deep Six Dr., East Hampton, New York 11937, U.S.A.

PUBLICATIONS FOR YOUNG ADULTS

Fiction as M. E. Kerr

Dinky Hocker Shoots Smack!. New York, HarperCollins, 1972.
If I Love You, Am I Trapped Forever?. New York, HarperCollins, 1973.
The Son of Someone Famous. New York, HarperCollins, 1974.
Love is a Missing Person. New York, HarperCollins, 1975.
Is That You, Miss Blue? New York, HarperCollins, 1975.
I'll Love You When You're More Like Me. New York, HarperCollins, 1977.
Gentlehands. New York, HarperCollins, 1978.
Little Little. New York, HarperCollins, 1981.
What I Really Think of You. New York, HarperCollins, 1982.
Him She Loves? New York, HarperCollins, 1984.
I Stay Near You. New York, HarperCollins, 1985.
Night Kites. New York, HarperCollins, 1986.
Fell. New York, HarperCollins, 1987.
Fell Down. New York, HarperCollins, 1989.
Fell Back. New York, HarperCollins, 1989.
Linger. New York, HarperCollins, 1993.
Deliver Us from Evie. New York, HarperCollins, 1994.
Hello, I Lied. New York, HarperCollins, 1997.

Other

Me Me Me Me Me, Not a Novel (autobiography, as M. E. Kerr). New York, Harper, 1983.
Foreword (as M. E. Kerr), *Hearing Us Out, Voices from the Gay and Lesbian Community,* by Roger Sutton. New York, Little, Brown and Company, 1994.
"We Might as Well All Be Strangers" (short story), in *Am I Blue?: Coming Out from the Silence,* edited by Marion Dane Bauer. New York, HarperCollins, 1994.

PUBLICATIONS FOR CHILDREN

Fiction as Mary James

Shoebag. New York, Scholastic, 1990.

The Shut-Eyes. New York, Scholastic, 1993.

Frankenlouse. New York, Scholastic, 1994.

Shoebag's Return. New York, Scholastic, 1996.

PUBLICATIONS FOR ADULTS

Fiction as Vin Packer

Dark Intruder. New York, Gold Medal Books, 1952.
Spring Fire. New York, Gold Medal Books, 1952.
Look Back to Love. New York, Gold Medal Books, 1953.
Come Destroy Me. New York, Gold Medal Books, 1954.
Whisper His Sins. New York, Gold Medal Books, 1954.
The Thrill Kids. New York, Gold Medal Books, 1955.
The Young and Violent. New York, Gold Medal Books, 1956.
Dark Don't Catch Me. New York, Gold Medal Books, 1956.

Three-Day Terror. New York, Gold Medal Books, 1957.
The Evil Friendship. New York, Gold Medal Books, 1958.
5:45 to Suburbia. New York, Gold Medal Books, 1958.
The Twisted Ones. New York, Gold Medal Books, 1959.
The Girl on the Best Seller List. New York, Gold Medal Books, 1961.
The Damnation of Adam Blessing. New York, Gold Medal Books, 1961.
Something in the Shadows. New York, Gold Medal Books, 1961.
Intimate Victims. New York, Gold Medal Books, 1962.
Alone at Night. New York, Gold Medal Books, 1963.
The Hare in March. New York, New American Library, 1967.
Don't Rely on Gemini. New York, Delacorte Press, 1969.

Fiction for Adults

Game of Survival (as M. J. Meaker). New York, New American Library, 1968.
Shockproof Sydney Skate. New York, Little, Brown, 1972.

Nonfiction for Adults as Ann Aldrich

We Walk Alone. New York, Gold Medal Books, 1955.
We Too Must Love. New York, Gold Medal Books, 1958.
Carol in a Thousand Cities. New York, Gold Medal Books, 1960.
We Two Won't Last. New York, Gold Medal Books, 1963.
Take a Lesbian to Lunch. New York, MacFadden-Bartell, 1972.

Nonfiction for Adults as M. J. Meaker

Sudden Endings. New York, Doubleday, 1964; paperback edition under name Vin Packer, New York, Fawcett, 1964.

*

Media Adaptations: *Dinky Hocker Shoots Smack!* (film and was a television afternoon special), Learning Corporation of America, 1978; *If I Love You Am I Trapped Forever?* (audio cassette), Random House, 1979.

Biography: Essay in *Something about the Author Autobiography Series,* Volume 1, Detroit, Gale, 1986; essay in *Speaking for Ourselves: Autobiographical Sketches by Notable Authors of Books for Young Adults,* Volume 1, compiled and edited by Donald R. Gallo, National Council of Teachers of English, 1990.

Critical Sources: Entry in *Contemporary Literary Criticism,* Detroit, Gale, Volume 12, 1980, Volume 35, 1985; *Presenting M. E. Kerr* by Alleen Pace Nilsen, Twayne Publishers, 1986.

M.E. Kerr comments:

Although I had a long career writing suspense and regular novels for adults, my work aimed at young adults has given me the most pleasure and challenge. The teenage years fascinate me, for they are the beginning of the man and of the woman, and here we glimpse them unmasked and forming.

The too-tall nerd in the ill-fitting suit, hunched over in an attempt to hide himself, lopes into a future where he is the CEO of a major corporation. . .the brilliant beauty queen becomes a suburban wife/mother and a champion tennis player at the local country club. . .the big hero sports star is selling cars now. . .the one in the

class that no one really remembers that well is a Nobel prize-winning scientist. . .the black sheep/cutup is a rock star, or a TV talk host or a children's writer—all of that sort of thing intrigues me.

Whole decades can be forgotten by people, but I know very few who forget what happened during those four vital years of high school.

*   *   *

Romance, humor, mystery, and a fascination with the underdog are the hallmarks of M. E Kerr's popular and highly respected writing for young adults. An expert manipulator of the conventions of the contemporary teen novel—troubled or vulnerable young protagonist, problematic parents, and an ironic stance towards reality—Kerr chronicles the self-absorption of adolescence with equal parts of sympathy and good-natured satire. Her sympathy with teen tunnel vision proceeds from the belief expressed in her 1993 autobiography, *Me Me Me Me Me: Not a Novel,* that "What's going on in the world is secondary to what's going on in high school, for in those vulnerable teen years high school *is* the world." At the same time, Kerr confesses that "whenever you find a little smart-mouth, tomboy kid in any of my books, you have found me from long ago. . . ." (75). Humor helps the smart-mouth character cope with her situation while it suggests to the young reader that high school is not forever; it will be "the world" for just a few years. In Kerr's hands, being a teenager is significant, but more importantly, it is survivable.

Kerr's focus on high school or prep school as the world should not, however, be taken to mean that her characters never leave the halls of their respective schools. Kerr takes her characters to their favorite teen hang-outs, locales which reverberate with multiple associations in the context of the other novels. Eight of the books are set or partly set in Seaville, New York, a plush resort town modeled after East Hampton, Long Island where Kerr now lives. Three other novels take place either in Kerr's old hometown of Auburn, rechristened "Cayuta," or in La Belle, another one-factory town in upstate New York. If the setting is Seaville, Sweet Mouth is the place to go for a coke, The Surf Club is the place to dance, snobs belong to The Hadefield Club (a.k.a. The Hatefilled Club), and The Witherspoon Funeral Home is the last stop before burial for half the citizenry. A major character in one Seaville novel may reappear as a bit player in another. The three upstate New York novels are less identically referential but the institutions mentioned in their respective pages—a prison, an orphanage, and a high-priced recovery haven for alcoholics—evoke the same claustrophobia.

Despite Kerr's frequent returns to familiar locales, only the mystery/thriller novels featuring John Fell *(Fell, Fell Back,* and *Fell Down)* could be termed series novels. Fell's adventures start in Seaville, with most of the action then taking place at Fell's prep school in Cottersville, Pennsylvania. The other Seaville books and the novels set in upstate New York do lend themselves to being read differently, however, than they might be read if they did not overlap in some of their particulars. One clue to the reading they invite is suggested by the profession of a main character in *I'll Love You When You're More Like Me,* the second Seaville novel. Young Sabra St. Amour stars in a daytime soap opera named "*Hometown,*" and has a large and loyal following of teenage fans, as does M.E.

Kerr. Each of her hometown locales provides a familiar and therefore inviting setting for her readers and allows her, life Fedora Foxe, the producer of *Hometown,* to introduce new plotlines and characters to retain fans' interest.

But just as the plotlines of soap operas are not so much new as they are "topical and updated," so too are Kerr's plots timely, and in some cases, eccentric refurbishings of standard soap opera fare. Romance shares top billing with domestic/familial ruptures, and there are plenty of dark family secrets and life-threatening or even fatal illnesses and accidents. The books featuring John Fell combine the romance plot with stock elements from the mystery and thriller genre: espionage, secret societies, conspiracy, and murder, with the answers to mysteries in earlier books revealed in their ever-more sensational sequels.

Kerr's characters are often familiar types as well, sometimes regrettably familiar in their perpetuation of negative images of young women. More important are the numerous well-realized characters who populate her books, many of whom make their appearances outside of Kerr's standard hometown locales and plots. Dinky Hocker, of *Dinky Hocker Shoots Smack,* lives in Brooklyn Heights with her sensitive cousin Natalia, lawyer father and do-gooder mother, Helen Hocker. Grossly overweight, Dinky drugs herself with food, not heroin; the book takes its title from the graffiti Dinky paints as a public act of revenge to embarrass her mother the night of a community awards banquet honoring Mrs. Hocker's volunteer work with recovering drug addicts. At home, Mrs. Hocker has mistaken manipulation for loving concern. Supposedly for Dinky's own good, Helen has cut her off from her politically conservative fellow weight watcher P. John, the one friend who supports Dinky's dieting but whom Mrs. Hocker views as being little better than a fat fascist. Although P. John plays second lead to Tucker Woolf, whose romance with Dinky's cousin Natalia occupies much of the book, P. John is a real scene stealer when he reappears near the end of the novel as a slimmed-down liberal who had shed prejudices along with pounds.

Even more arresting are the characters who come to life in *Is That You, Miss Blue?* Flanders Brown, uprooted by the break-up of her parents' marriage, has been sent to an Episcopalian boarding school in Virginia. On her own for the first time, she discovers who she is as she makes friends with several of the school's nonconformists and observes the self-serving exclusivity of many of her fellow students. The paradox of their exclusivity is their conformity to peer pressure and the standards set by class leaders such as sophisticated France Shipp. France helps engineer the dismissal of Miss Blue, an inspired science teacher whose equally inspired religious experiences strike the headmistress of this ostensibly religious school as incipient insanity. Flanders's attitude towards Miss Blue mirrors her own growing maturity as she moves from mocking Miss Blue to respect and empathy for her former teacher.

Kerr also takes up the subject of religious belief vs. religious hypocrisy in two later novels. *Little Little,* set in upstate New York, is narrated alternately by Little Little La Belle and Sydney Cinnamon, two young people whose friendship might become a romance once Little Little's fiance runs off with another woman. Knox Lionel, Little Little's sometime fiance, is better known as Little Lion, a popular evangelical preacher whose religion is pure show biz. All four characters (including the "other" woman) are dwarves, a fact which only heightens the novel's carnival atmosphere because here Kerr is too much the smart-mouth kid. The jokes and frenetic

pace of the novel inadvertently work to deny Sydney and Little Little their humanity. Kerr is much more successful in persuading readers to see past labels and stereotypes in *What I Really Think of You.* This novel's two narrators, Opal Ringer and Jesse Pegler, learn to come to terms with their own spirituality and the social, economic, and religious complexities of being preacher's kids.

Preacher's kids are not the only Kerr adolescents whose fathers (or, as in the case of *Gentlehands,* grandfather) provoke identity crises. In *The Son of Someone Famous,* Adam Blessing finds himself more cursed than blessed by having a politically powerful father who is celebrated for his shuttle diplomacy. *Him She Loves* features a professional comedian who revives his career by ridiculing his daughter's boyfriend on national television, while *If I Love You, Am I Trapped Forever* portrays an absentee and alcoholic father who is still too much of a child himself to be a parent to his son. *Love Is A Missing Person* depicts a dad who favors one child over the other, with negative consequences for all involved. None of these dads is much of a role model, but that is just as well since the one father figure who invites emulation is the most problematic of all; he's the infamous "Gentlehands" of Auschwitz.

Given these troubled family histories, it is no wonder that the course of love does not run smoothly for the protagonists of most of the novels. Breaking up, rather than living happily ever after is the order of the day. For example, the three-generation saga *I Stay Near You* devotes the greater part of each of its interlocked narratives to detailing the unhappy consequences of the passionate emotions precipitated by a romantic misalliance in the summer of 1943. By the time the story reaches the present, love has become a ghost from summers past. *Night Kites,* another densely textured story, follows the romantic fortunes of its young male protagonist, but Erick Rudd's loving and losing Nicki Marr is less important than the fact that he loves and will soon lose his older brother. Pete has AIDS and has come home to spend his last months with his family. Kerr's presentation of Pete's story is multilayered, empathetic, and embedded within his family's reactions. Kerr provides no easy answers or consolations because there aren't any answers beyond a few all-important grace notes of understanding and love. And finally, no such grace notes characterize John Fell's experience. He discovers that his lover romanced him as part of a scheme to benefit the man she really loves.

Kerr's habitually ironic stance towards the possibilities of romance is modulated by the positive relationships the Peel brothers eventually enjoy with their respective girlfriends in Kerr's most recent novel, *Linger.* Those relationships are, however the result of putting aside their earlier fascination with Lynn Dunlinger, the beautiful daughter of a wealthy and influential restaurant owner. Bobby, the older brother, writes to Lynn from Saudia Arabia where he has been sent to fight in Operation Desert Storm. Back home, Bobby's younger brother Gary experiences his own crush on Lynn but realizes that she is completely absorbed by her love affair with their high school English teacher, a vocal opponent of Desert Storm. Although Lynn's romance ends in disillusionment, the Peel brothers' loss of illusions is accompanied by an energized political consciousness and a shedding of chauvinist responses to the young women who care deeply about them. Bobby's is the true baptism by fire—his tank was hit, injuring him and his friend Gus, and killing their buddy, Sugar—but Gary's love for his brother causes Gary to question his own habitually apolitical mind set. *Linger,* like so many of Kerr's books for young adults, entertains while at the same time prompting its readers to question their own habitual frames of thought.

—Janice M. Alberghene

KERRY, Lois. *See* DUNCAN, Lois.

KESEY, Ken (Elton)

Nationality: American. **Born:** La Junta, Colorado, 17 September 1935. **Education:** Attended high school in Springfield, Oregon; University of Oregon, Eugene, B.A. 1957; Stanford University, California (Woodrow Wilson fellow), 1958-59, graduate study, 1958-61, 1963. **Family:** Married Faye Haxby in 1956; four children (one deceased). **Career:** Multi-media artist and farmer. Night attendant in psychiatric Veterans Administration Hospital, Menlo Park, California, 1961; president, Intrepid Trips, Inc. (motion picture company), 1964; publisher, *Spit in the Ocean* magazine, Pleasant Hill, Oregon, 1974—. Served prison term for marijuana possession, 1967. **Awards:** Woodrow Wilson fellowship; Saxton Fund fellowship, 1959; Distinguished Service award, State of Oregon, 1978. **Address:** 85829 Ridgeway Rd., Pleasant Hill, Oregon 97401, U.S.A.

PUBLICATIONS FOR ADULTS AND YOUNG ADULTS

Novels

One Flew over the Cuckoo's Nest. New York, Viking, 1962; London, Methuen, 1963.
Sometimes a Great Notion. New York, Viking, 1964; London, Methuen, 1966.
Demon Box. New York, Viking, and London, Methuen, 1986.
With others, *Caverns.* New York, Viking, 1990.
The Further Inquiry. New York, Viking, 1990.
Sailor Song. New York, Viking, 1992.
With Ken Babbs, *Last Go Round.* New York, Viking, 1994.

Other

Kesey. Eugene, Oregon, Northwest Review, 1977.
Contributor, *The Last Whole Earth Catalog: Access to Tools.* Portola Institute, 1971.
Editor and contributor, *The Last Supplement to the Whole Earth Catalog,* with Paul Krassner. Portola Institute, 1971.
Compiler and contributor, *Kesey's Garage Sale* (miscellany; includes screenplay *Over the Border*). New York, Viking, 1973.

PUBLICATIONS FOR CHILDREN

Fiction

Little Tricker the Squirrel Meets Big Double the Bear, illustrated by Barry Moser. New York, Puffin, 1990.
The Sea Lion. New York, Viking, 1991.

*

Media Adaptations: *One Flew over the Cuckoo's Nest* was adapted for the stage by Dale Wasserman and produced on Broadway at the Cort Theatre on 13 November 1963, revived in 1971, and adapted for film by United Artists in 1975; *Sometimes a Great Notion* (film), Universal, 1972.

Manuscript Collections: University of Oregon, Eugene.

Biography: Entry in *Concise Dictionary of American Literary Biography, 1968-1988,* Detroit, Gale, 1989; entry in *Dictionary of Literary Biography,* Detroit, Gale, Volume 2: *American Novelists since World War II,* 1978; Volume 16: *The Beats: Literary Bohemians in Postwar America,* 1983.

Critical Studies: *The Electric Kool-Aid Test* by Tom Wolfe, New York, Farrar Straus, 1968, London, Weidenfeld & Nicolson, 1969; entries in *Contemporary Literary Criticism,* Detroit, Gale, Volume 1, 1973; Volume 3, 1975; Volume 6, 1976; Volume 11, 1979; Volume 46, 1987; *Ken Kesey* by Bruce Carnes, Boise, Idaho, Boise State College, 1974; "Ken Kesey Issue" of *Northwest Review* (Eugene, Oregon), vol. 16, nos. 1-2, 1977; *Ken Kesey* by Barry H. Leeds, New York, Ungar, 1981; *The Art of Grit: Ken Kesey's Fiction,* Columbia, University of Missouri Press, 1982, and *One Flew over the Cuckoo's Nest: Rising to Heroism,* Boston, Twayne, 1989, both by M. Gilbert Porter; *Ken Kesey* by Stephen L. Tanner, Boston, Twayne, 1983; *On the Bus: The Legendary Trip of Ken Kesey and the Merry Pranksters* by Ken Babbs, photographs by Rob Bivert, New York, Thunder's Mouth Press, 1989, London, Plexus, 1991.

*   *   *

Ken Kesey's appeal to young adults resides perhaps as much in the "text" of his personal life as that of his novels. As a precociously brilliant sixties' novelist, Kesey published his famous *One Flew over the Cuckoo's Nest* (1962) and the less well known *Sometimes a Great Notion* (1966). As a guru of the hallucinogenic drug culture of that time, he lived a wildly uninhibited and free-spirited life, not unlike the chief characters, McMurphy and Hank Stamper, in his novels. Although not about the drug culture, both works grew out of the sense of eroding individualism that permeated that era.

Told from the viewpoint of a huge Amerindian schizophrenic called Big Chief, *Cuckoo's Nest* depicts the plight of inmates in a mental ward presided over by a physically imposing matriarch named Big Nurse Ratched. Despite the "wretchedness" of their existence under the influence of what Big Chief calls "the Combine," most of these inmates ironically choose to remain in the degradation of harshly imposed routines rather than face the insecurities of the world outside the institution.

Kesey brilliantly fuses the thought and language of an authentically paranoid schizophrenic with a comic-book style narration in which the atmosphere seems "like a cartoon world, where the characters are flat and outlined in black, jerking through some kind of goofy story." Yet, for all its smart-aleck humor, the story is anything but wholly funny. Recognizing this tonal oppositeness, the young-adult reader is faced with an early example of the same dissonance found in films, where modern comic-book characters and settings often express serious social messages.

Big Chief perceives the hospital as a totally unnatural environment in which the essential spiritual bond between Indian and nature is blocked by a series of nightmarish, technological evil spirits. Into this inimical world steps McMurphy, dancing to the beat of a free-spirit drummer, an obvious perennial favorite character to many young adults who share that identity. Because of his obdurate dedication to free-willed, individual consent, McMurphy contends diametrically against the depersonalizing authority of Nurse Ratched, confounding her with his clever belligerence. He is her antithesis, the quintessential rebel against the unaccountable use of power. In effect, McMurphy becomes for Big Chief "a giant come out of the sky to save us from the Combine that was net-working the land with copper wire and crystal." This mythic allusion hyperbolically extends McMurphy's hero status into the neverending allegory where a youthful hero contends against an unloving and unjust monarch within a natural or social wasteland.

As in many such mythic allegories, however, the hero must be scapegoated in order to show the reader the brutality of oppressive authority and allow the reader to hold in reverence the indomitability of the hero's human spirit. Kesey has a treat for the young reader here in that he fashions this scapegoating both as externally imposed on and internally accepted by McMurphy. Externally imposed is McMurphy's lobotomy by order of Nurse Ratched as penance for his dissidence. Internally, though, McMurphy had already realized that his hero status was fated by its being an overburdened projection of all the inmates' expectations. In brief, McMurphy had earlier given up taking heroic responsibility for those who would not be responsible for themselves. Thus neutralized by both parent-like authority and personal consent, McMurphy must be freed and his heroic boon carried on by Big Chief, whom he has freed to return to his homeland. The Indian smothers the former hero's helpless body in an act of humane dispatch. Though at first a difficult concept for some youth, this segment of the novel provides some serious contemplation about individual action and consequences.

A parallel theme links *Cuckoo's Nest* with Kesey's second novel, *Sometimes a Great Notion,* a story of rugged naturalism in a northwest logging town and of the conflict between two aspects of human nature. In this novel, Hank Stamper portrays a man of action and nature, the individualistic free spirit contending against intellectual authority. His nemesis is Draeger, a union official attempting to force local loggers into conformity. In a clear analogy, the young reader is revisiting McMurphy and Nurse Ratched in a different venue.

By contrast with Big Chief's isolation from nature, however, Hank's brother Lee has freely accepted a retreat into his intellect brought about by his attending an eastern university. Another interesting variation is found in Viv, Hank's wife, controlled and protected by Stamper, the later love object of Lee, who tries to reach out to what he wants her to be. Viv is the "viv-acious," life-loving, female counterpart of McMurphy, who cannot allow herself to become someone else's projected expectation of her. In these particular distinctions, *Great Notion* enlarges Kesey's message to contemporary young adults who are attempting to raise their intelligent identity and to find gender-free ways of empathy and relationship.

Kesey's works tell stories from varied viewpoints of traditionally overlooked characters, befitting the postmodern critical idea that all stories have multiple vantage points and are only the composite of all of them. For this and the unsentimentalized romanticism of his plots, Kesey remains good reading for young adults.

—Ron Evans

KEY, Samuel M. *See* **DE LINT, Charles.**

KINCAID, Jamaica

Nationality: American. **Born:** Elaine Potter Richardson in St. John's, Antigua, West Indies, 25 May 1949; immigrated to United States, naturalized U.S. citizen. **Education:** Princess Margaret girls' school, Antigua; New School for Social Research, New York; Franconia College, New Hampshire. **Family:** Married Allen Evan Shawn; one daughter and one son. **Career:** Contributor, and currently staff writer, the *New Yorker,* 1974—. **Awards:** American Academy Morton Dauwen Zabel award, 1984, for *At the Bottom of the River.* **Address:** *The New Yorker,* 25 West 43rd Street, New York, New York 10036, U.S.A.

PUBLICATIONS

Novels

Annie John. New York, Farrar, Straus, and London, Pan, 1985.
Lucy. New York, Farrar, Straus, 1990; London, Cape, 1991.
The Autobiography of My Mother. New York, Farrar, Straus, and Giroux, 1996.
My Brother. New York, Farrar, Straus, and Giroux, 1997.

Short Stories

At the Bottom of the River. New York, Farrar, Straus, 1983; London, Pan, 1984.
Annie, Gwen, Lily, Pam, and Tulip, illustrated by Eric Fischl. New York, Library Fellows of the Whitney Museum of American Art, 1986.

Other

A Small Place. New York, Farrar, Straus, and London, Virago Press, 1988.

*

Critical Studies: Entry in *Contemporary Literary Criticism,* Volume 43, Detroit, Gale, 1987.

*　　*　　*

Best known for her works of fiction, Jamaica Kincaid is a writer with a clear, illuminating vision of humanity, who scrutinizes the complex layers that exist in the mother and daughter relationship. Because Kincaid vividly remembers both the beauty and pain of childhood and adolescence, her female protagonists speak with a sense of powerful authenticity.

Utilizing prose that on occasion is reminiscent of poetry or the rhythm and repetition of folkloric chants, Kincaid's work has received wide critical acclaim. She writes as every woman's daughter who both loves and harshly judges every mother. At other times she writes as an outsider, observing American life. Even though she has lived in the United States more than half her life, Kincaid, who was born on the West Indian island of Antigua, views contemporary society with cool detachment. Of Americans, like the upper-middle class employers of her character Lucy, in the novel of the same name, Kincaid observes they make "no connections between their comforts and the decline of the world that lay before them."

Kincaid deals with such universal themes as coming-of-age and the necessity of separation from parents and establishing identity. The protagonists in *At the Bottom of the River, Annie John,* and *Lucy* experience the pain and pleasure of growing up as they strive to become women who are not shadows of their mothers but separate and distinct individuals.

In her nonfiction book, *A Small Place,* Kincaid continues these themes as she writes of her birthplace, the island country of Antigua, which has come of age and has had to establish independence after years of colonial British rule. Kincaid writes with anger about slavery, colonization, racism, and corruption. "Nothing can erase my rage—not an apology, not a large sum of money, not the death of the criminal—for this wrong can never be made right." *A Small Place* enables readers to look at Antigua and the greater issues Kincaid raises.

Kincaid's three most important novels, *At the Bottom of the River, Annie John,* and *Lucy,* if read together, act as companion pieces for one another. *Annie John* is the narrative of a young girl growing up and separating from her mother. The details of Annie's story seem to fill in some information not given by the young female narrator in the stories that comprise *At the Bottom of the River. Lucy* continues to explore the mother-daughter theme with a different protagonist, slightly older than the one in the other two books.

At the Bottom of the River consists of ten short stories. Some of the stories, like "Girl" and "The Letter from Home," are written in chant-like form, with folkloric repetition of certain refrains. "Girl," the first story in the collection, appears as one startlingly long, extended sentence, three pages in length, and consists of the orders a mother gives her daughter for how to live life. Suggestions for proper behavior in a wide variety of circumstances make up the story. Of primary importance to the mother is that everything be done her way, society's way, and done "not like the slut you are so bent on becoming."

In *Annie John,* Kincaid takes a long hard look at the end of childhood and the beginning of adolescence. At ten, Annie thought "only people I did not know died." Living near a cemetery for a summer, Annie learns that death comes even to children. After her mother prepares a young child for burial and her father makes the coffin, Annie begins to look at both parents, especially her mother, differently. The mother-daughter relationship begins to unravel, Annie's body changes as she begins puberty, and her life away from her parents becomes increasingly more important. Annie begins a secret life which includes lying, stealing, and the beginnings of sexual experimentation.

At the beginning of Kincaid's novel, *Lucy,* the young female protagonist has just arrived in the United States from her Caribbean home. All appears new to the nineteen-year-old woman, from changing seasons and cold weather, to buildings with elevators. She says: "The undergarments that I wore were all new . . . and as I sat in the car, twisting this way and that . . . I was reminded of how uncomfortable new can make you feel."

In the United States to work as an au pair for an attractive, upper-middle class couple with four children, Lucy finds her homesickness to be surprising. She thought she could leave home completely behind like "an old garment" which she had outgrown. Readers sense the ambivalence and the strength Lucy possesses as she faces life. At the end of the novel, Lucy's future remains as uncertain as that of Annie John but both protagonists have stretched, expanded their vision, and gone beyond their mothers.

Lengthy sentences, unusual sentence structure, singular imagery, and vivid descriptions of sights, sounds, and smells characterize Kincaid's writing. Her young narrators comment with blunt honesty on what they see around them, without the societal constraints of their elders. For some readers, Kincaid's frankness about her protagonists' relationships with friends of the same sex as in *Annie John,* or with male lovers in *Lucy,* might be surprising. For others, these scenes will add to the complexity and authenticity of the novels.

Kincaid uses powerful symbolism, poetic language, and imagery. From a simple description of peals of laughter that "would fly up into the air wrapped around each other like a toffee twist" in *Lucy,* to the complicated transformation of mother and daughter into large reptiles in "My Mother," from *At the Bottom of the River,* Kincaid takes great care in her use of language. Her books can be read, enjoyed, and interpreted on many levels. With a strong, distinctive voice and style, Kincaid appeals across generations and national boundaries.

Can a mother ever concede that her daughter will grow up to become the person she needs to be and not the person the mother wants her to be? Do the bonds between mothers and daughters endure despite years of separation, denial, and even death? These questions may not have a single answer. Neither do Kincaid's novels, but they raise important questions.

—Karen Ferris Morgan

KING, Stephen (Edwin)

Also writes as Steve King. **Pseudonyms:** Richard Bachman; John Swithen. **Nationality:** American. **Born:** Portland, Maine, 21 September 1947. **Education:** University of Maine at Orono, B.Sc., 1970. **Family:** Married Tabitha Jane Spruce; one daughter and two sons. **Career:** Full-time writer. Worked as a janitor, a laborer in an industrial laundry, and in a knitting mill. English teacher, Hampden Academy, Hampden, Maine, 1971-73; writer in residence, University of Maine, Orono, 1978-79. Owner, Philtrum Press, a publishing house, and WZON-AM, a rock 'n' roll radio station, both in Bangor, Maine. Has made cameo appearances in films *Knightriders*, as Steven King, 1980, *Creepshow*, 1982, *Maximum Overdrive*, 1986, and *Pet Sematary*, 1989; has also appeared in American Express credit card television commercial. Served as judge for 1977 World Fantasy Awards, 1978. Participated in radio honor panel with George A. Romero, Peter Straub, and Ira Levin, moderated by Dick Cavett on WNET in New York, October 30-31, 1980. **Awards:** *Carrie* named to *School Library Journal*'s Book List, 1975; World Fantasy award nominations, 1976, for *'Salem's Lot*, 1979, for *The Stand* and *Night Shift*, 1980, for *The Dead Zone*, 1981, for "The Mist," and 1983, for "The Breathing Method: A Winter's Tale" in *Different Seasons*; Hugo award nomination, and Nebula award nomination, both 1978, both for *The Shining*; Balrog awards, second place in best novel category for *The Stand*, and second place in best collection category for *Night Shift*, both 1979; *The Long Walk* was named to the American Library Association's list of best books for young adults, 1979; World Fantasy award, 1980, for contributions to the field, and 1982, for story "Do the Dead Sing?"; Career Alumni award, University of Maine at Orono, 1981; *Firestarter* was named to the American Library Association's list of best books for young adults, 1981; Nebula award nomination, 1981, for story "The Way Station"; special British Fantasy Society award for outstanding contribution to the genre, 1982, for *Cujo*; Hugo award, World Science Fiction Convention, 1982, for *Stephen King's Danse Macabre*; named *Us* Magazine Best Fiction Writer of the Year, 1982; Locus award for best collection, Locus Publications, 1986, for *Stephen King's Skeleton Crew*. **Agent:** Arthur Greene, 101 Park Avenue, New York, New York 10178, U.S.A. **Address:** P.O. Box 1186, Bangor, Maine 04001, U.S.A.

PUBLICATIONS

Novels

Carrie: A Novel of a Girl with a Frightening Power. New York, Doubleday, and London, New English Library, 1974; as *Carrie*, New York, New American Library/Times Mirror, 1975.

'Salem's Lot. New York, Doubleday, 1975; London, New English Library, 1976.

The Shining. New York, Doubleday, and London, New English Library, 1977.

The Stand. New York, Doubleday, 1978; London, New English Library, 1979; revised edition with illustrations by Berni Wrightson, New York, Doubleday, and London, Hodder and Stoughton, 1990.

The Dead Zone. New York, Viking, and London, Macdonald and Jane's, 1979; as *The Dead Zone: Movie Tie-In*, New York, New American Library, 1980.

Firestarter. New York, Viking, and London, Futura, 1980.

Cujo. New York, Viking, 1981; London, Macdonald, 1982.

The Dark Tower: The Gunslinger, illustrated by Michael Whelan. Hampton Falls, New Hampshire, Grant, 1982; as *The Gunslinger,* New York, New American Library, 1988; London, Sphere, 1989.

Christine. New York, Viking, and London, Hodder and Stoughton, 1983; with illustrated by Stephen Gervais in a limited edition, West Kingston, Rhode Island, Grant, 1983.

Cycle of the Werewolf, illustrations by Berni Wrightson. New York, New American Library, 1983; London, New English Library, 1986.

Pet Sematary. New York, Doubleday, and London, Hodder and Stoughton, 1983.

The Talisman, with Peter Straub. New York, Viking Press/Putnam, and London, Viking, 1984.

The Eyes of the Dragon (for young adults), limited edition illustrated by Kenneth R. Linkhauser. Bangor, Maine, Philtrum Press, 1984; new edition illustrated by David Palladini, New York, Viking, 1987; London, Macdonald, 1988.

It. New York, Viking, and London, Hodder and Stoughton, 1986; first edition as *Es.* Munich, West Germany, Heyne, 1986.

Misery. New York, Viking, and London, Hodder and Stoughton, 1987.

The Tommyknockers. New York, Putnam, 1987; London, Hodder and Stoughton, 1988.

The Dark Half. New York, Viking, 1989; London, Hodder and Stoughton, 1990.

The Drawing of Three, illustrated by Phil Hale. New York, New American Library, and London, Sphere, 1989.

Needful Things. Boston, G.K. Hall, 1991; London, Hodder and Stoughton, 1992.

The Waste Lands, illustrated by Ned Dameron. Hampton Falls, New Hampshire, Grant, 1991.

Dolores Claiborne. Boston, G.K. Hall, 1992.

Gerald's Game. New York, Viking, 1992; London, Hodder and Stoughton, 1993.

Insomnia. New York, Viking, 1994.

Rose Madder. New York, Viking, 1995.

Desperation. New York, Viking, 1996.

Novels as Richard Bachman

Rage. New York, New American Library/Signet, 1977.

The Long Walk. New York, New American Library/Signet, 1979.

Roadwork: A Novel of the First Energy Crisis. New York, New American Library/Signet, 1981.

The Running Man. New York, New American Library/Signet, 1982; London, New English Library, 1988.

Thinner. New York, New American Library, 1984; London, New English Library, 1987.

The Regulators. New York, Dutton, 1996.

Short Stories

The Star Invaders (as Steve King). Durham, Maine, Triad, Inc., and Gaslight Books, 1964.

Night Shift. New York, Doubleday, and London, New English Library, 1978; as *Night Shift: Excursions into Horror,* New York, New American Library/Signet, 1979.

Different Seasons. New York, Viking, and London, Futura, 1982.

The Breathing Method. Bath, Chivers Press, 1984.

Rita Hayworth and Shawshank Redemption: A Story from "Different Seasons." Thorndike, Maine, Thorndike Press, 1983.

Stephen King's Skeleton Crew, illustrated by J.K. Potter. New York, Viking, and London, Macdonald, 1985.

My Pretty Pony, illustrated by Barbara Kruger. New York, Knopf, 1989.

Four Past Midnight. Boston, G.K. Hall, and London, Hodder and Stoughton, 1990.

Nightmares and Dreamscapes (collection of short stories). New York, Viking, 1993.

Screenplays

Stephen King's Creep Show: A George A. Romero Film (adaptation of short stories "Father's Day," "Weeds," "The Crate," and "They're Creeping Up on You," released by Warner Brothers as *Creepshow,* 1982), illustrated by Berni Wrightson and Michele Wrightson. New York, New American Library, 1982.

Cat's Eye (adaptation of short stories "Quitters, Inc.," "The Ledge," and "The General," MGM/UA, 1984).

Silver Bullet (adaptation of *Cycle of the Werewolf,* released by Paramount Pictures/Dino de Laurentiis's North Carolina Film Corp., 1985).

Director, *Maximum Overdrive* (adaptation of short stories "The Mangler," "Trucks," and "The Lawnmower Man," released by Dino de Laurentiis' North Carolina Film Corp., 1986). New York, New American Library, 1986.

Pet Sematary (adaptation of novel, Laurel Production, 1989).

Also author of teleplay *Sorry, Right Number* for *Tales from the Dark Side* series, and of screenplay *The Stand,* based on his novel of same title. Author of unproduced versions of screenplays, including *Children of the Corn, Cujo, The Dead Zone, The Shotgunners, The Shining, Something Wicked This Way Comes,* and *Daylight Dead,* (based on short stories "Strawberry Spring," "I Know What You Need," and "Battleground").

Other

Contributor, *Frankenstein, Dracula, Dr. Jekyll and Mr. Hyde,* by Mary Shelley, Bram Stoker, and Robert Louis Stevenson. New York, New American Library/Signet, 1978.

Contributor, *Shadows,* edited by Charles L. Grant. New York, Doubleday, Volume 1, 1978; Volume 4, 1981.

Contributor, *The Year's Finest Fantasy,* edited by Terry Carr. New York, Putnam, 1978.

Another Quarter Mile: Poetry. Pittsburgh, Pennsylvania, Dorrance, 1979.

Contributor, *Nightmares,* edited by Charles L. Grant. Playboy, 1979.

Contributor, *More Tales of Unknown Horror,* edited by Peter Haining. London, New English Library, 1979.

Contributor, *Murderess Ink: The Better Half of the Mystery,* edited by Dilys Winn. East Brunswick, New Jersey, Bell, 1979.

Contributor, *New Tales of the Cthulhu Mythos,* edited by Ramsey Campbell. Sauk City, Wisconsin, Arkham House, 1980.

Contributor, *The Shapes of Midnight,* by Joseph Payne Brennan. New York, Berkley, 1980.

Contributor, *The 17th Fontana Book of Great Ghost Stories,* edited by R. Chetwynd-Hayes. Centerport, New York, Fontana, 1981.

Contributor, *The Arbor House Treasury of Horror and the Supernatural,* compiled by Bill Pronzini, Barry N. Malzberg, and Martin H. Greenberg. New York, Arbor House, 1981.

Contributor, *A Fantasy Reader: The Seventh World Fantasy Convention Program Book,* edited by Jeff Frane and Jack Rems. Seventh World Fantasy Convention, 1981.

Stephen King (includes *The Shining, 'Salem's Lot, Night Shift,* and *Carrie*). North Pomfret, Vermont, W.S. Heinemann/Octopus Books, 1981.

Stephen King's Danse Macabre. Everest House, 1981; London, Futura, 1982.

Contributor, *Tales from the Nightside,* by Charles L. Grant. Sauk City, Wisconsin, Arkham House, 1981.

Contributor, *When Michael Calls,* by John Farris. New York, Pocket Books, 1981.

Contributor, *New Terrors,* edited by Ramsey Campbell. New York, Pocket Books, 1982.

Contributor, *Terrors,* edited by Charles L. Grant. Playboy, 1982.

Contributor, *Death,* edited by Stuart David Schiff. Playboy, 1982.

Contributor, *The Do-It-Yourself Bestseller,* edited by Tom Silberkleit and Jerry Biederman. New York, Doubleday, Dolphin, 1982.

Contributor, *Fear Itself: The Horror Fiction of Stephen King,* edited by Tim Underwood and Chuck Miller. Lancaster, Pennsylvania, Underwood-Miller, 1982; London, Pan, 1991.

Contributor, *Mr. Monster's Movie Gold,* by Forrest J. Ackerman. Norfolk, Virginia, Donning, 1982.

The Plant. Bangor, Maine, Philtrum Press, Part I, 1982; Part II, 1983; Part III, 1985.

Contributor, *Stalking the Nightmare,* by Harlan Ellison. West Bloomfield, Michigan, Phantasia Press, 1982.

Contributor, *World Fantasy Convention '82,* edited by Kennedy Poyser. Eighth World Fantasy Convention, 1982.

Black Magic and Music: A Novelist's Perspective on Bangor. Bangor Historical Society, 1983.

Contributor, *Frankenstein, or The Modern Prometheus,* by Mary Wollstonecraft Shelley, illustrated by Berni Wrightson. New York, Dodd, 1983.

Contributor, *Grand Illusions,* by Tom Savini. Pittsburgh, Pennsylvania, Imagine, Inc., 1983; as *Bizarro,* Crown, 1983.

Contributor, *Satyricon II Program Book,* edited by Rusty Burke. Satyricon II/DeepSouthCon XXI, 1983.

Contributor, *Shadowings: The Reader's Guide to Horror Fiction, 1981-82,* edited by Douglas E. Winter. Mercer Island, Washington, Starmont House, 1983.

Contributor, *Tales by Moonlight,* edited by Jessica Amanda Salmonson. Chicago, Robert L. Garcia, 1983.

Contributor, *World Fantasy Convention 1983,* edited by Robert Weinberg. Weird Tales Ltd., 1983.

Contributor, *The Blackboard Jungle,* by Evan Hunter. New York, Arbor House, 1984.

Contributor, *The Writer's Handbook,* edited by Sylvia K. Burack. Boston, Writer, Inc., 1984.

Contributor, *The Year's Best Horror Stories, Series XII,* edited by Karl Edward Wagner. New York, DAW, 1984.

The Bachman Books: Four Early Novels (includes *Rage, The Long Walk, Roadwork,* and *The Running Man,* with introduction "Why I Was Richard Bachman"). New York, New American Library, 1985; London, Hodder and Stoughton, 1986.

Stephen King's Year of Fear 1986 Calendar. New York, New American Library, 1985.

Contributor, *Kingdom of Fear: The World of Stephen King,* edited by Tim Underwood and Chuck Miller. Lancaster, Pennsylvania, Underwood-Miller, 1986.

Contributor, *Now and On Earth,* by Jim Thompson. Belen, New Mexico, Dennis Macmillan, 1986.

Contributor, *The Dark Descent,* edited by David G. Hartwell. New York, Doherty Associates, 1987.

Contributor, *Masques II: All New Stories of Horror and the Supernatural,* edited by J.N. Williamson. Maclay and Associates, 1987.

Contributor, *The New Adventures of Sherlock Holmes: Original Stories by Eminent Mystery Writers,* edited by Martin Harry Greenberg and Carol-Lynn Roessel Waugh. New York, Carroll and Graf, 1987.

Contributor, *Stephen King Goes to Hollywood.* New York, New American Library, 1987.

Contributor, *Genuine Man,* by Don Robertson. Bangor, Maine, Philtrum Press, 1988.

Nightmares in the Sky: Gargoyles and Grotesques, photographs by f.Stop FitzGerald. London, Viking, 1988.

Contributor, *Prime Evil: New Stories by the Masters of Modern Horror,* edited by Douglas E. Winter. New York, New American Library, 1988; London, Bantam, 1989.

Contributor, *Dark Visions.* London, Gollancz, 1989.

Contributor, *Feast of Fear: Conversations with Stephen King,* edited by Tim Underwood and Chuck Miller. New York, Carroll and Graf, 1992.

Contributor, *Midnight Graffiti.* London, Svern Ho, 1993.

Also contributor of stories to numerous other anthologies, including "Squad D" to Harlan Ellison's *The Last Dangerous Visions.* Author of weekly column "King's Garbage Truck" for *Maine Campus* (February 20, 1969 through May 21, 1970), and of monthly book review column for *Adelina,* (June through November, 1980). Contributor of short fiction and poetry to numerous periodicals.

*

Media Adaptations: *Carrie* (film, directed by Brian De Palma), United Artists, 1976; (musical, adapted by Lawrence D. Cohen and Michael Gore), produced England, 1988; *'Salem's Lot* (television miniseries), Warner Brothers, 1979; *The Shining* (film, directed by Stanley Kubrick), Warner Brothers/Hawks Films, 1980; *Christine* (film), Columbia Pictures, 1983; *Cujo* (film), Warner Communications/Taft Entertainment, 1983; *The Dead Zone* (film, directed by David Cronenberg), Paramount Pictures, 1983; *Children of the Corn* (film), New World Pictures, 1984; *Firestarter* (film), Universal Pictures, 1984; *Rita Hayworth and Shawshank Redemption: Different Seasons I, The Body: Different Seasons II, Apt Pupil: Different Seasons III,* and *The Breathing Method: Different Seasons IV* (cassettes), Recorded Book, 1984; *The Word Processor* (television adaptation of *The Word Processor of the Gods* for *Tales from the Darkside* television show), Laurel Productions, 1984; *Night Shift* (cassette), Recorded Books, 1985; *Skeleton Crew* (cassette, including *The Ballad of the Flexible Bullet, Gramma,* and *The Mist),* Recorded Books, 1985; *Two Mini-Features from Stephen King's Nightshift Collection* (videotape, includes *The Woman in the Room* and *The Boogeyman),* Granite Entertainment Group, 1985; *Gramma* (television episode of *The Twilight Zone),* CBS-TV, 1986; *The Mist* (radio dramatization), Boston; (cassette), Simon and Schuster Audioworks, 1986; (computer game), Mindscape, Inc.; *The Monkey, Mrs. Todd's Shortcut, The Reaper's Image,* and *Gramma* (cassettes), Warner Audio, 1986; *Stand by Me* (film, adaptation of novella *The Body),* Columbia Pictures, 1986; *Strawberry Spring, The Boogeyman, Graveyard Shift, The Man Who Loved Flowers, One for the Road, The Last Rung on the Ladder, I Know What You Need, Jerusalem's Lot,* and *I Am the Doorway* (cassettes), Walden, 1986; *Thinner* (cassette), Listen for Pleasure, 1986; *Creepshow 2* (film, including *The Raft, Old Chief Woodn'head* and *The Hitchhiker),* New World Pictures, 1987; *Graveyard Shift* (film), 1987; *The Running Man* (film), Taft Entertainment/Barish Productions, 1987; *The Gunslinger* and *The Drawing of Three* (cassettes), New York, New American Library, 1988; *Misery* (film), Castle Rock, 1990; *It* (television miniseries), ABC-TV, 1990; *The Lawnmower Man* (film), 1992; *Sometimes They Come Back* (television movie), 1992; *The Dark Half* (film, directed by George A. Romero), 1993; *The Tommyknockers* (television miniseries), 1993; *Sorry, Right Number* (television episode of *Tales from the Darkside); The Cat from Hell* (film, episode in four-segment film entitled *Tales from the Darkside—The Movie),* Laurel Productions, 1990; *Needful Things* (film), Castle Rock, 1993.

Several additional short stories have also been adapted for the screen. King's screenplay *The Stand* is in production as a television miniseries; *Battleground* has been optioned by Martin Poll Productions for NBC-TV; *The Long Walk* has been optioned for a film production; a film based upon a treatment by King of *Training Exercise* is scheduled for production by Dino De Laurentiis's North Carolina Film Corporation; *Apt Pupil: Summer of Corruption* is being developed for production by Richard Kobritz; *The Talisman* has been optioned for a television miniseries.

Biography: Entry in *Dictionary of Literary Biography Yearbook: 1980,* Detroit, Gale, 1981; essay in *Authors and Artists for Young Adults,* Volume 1, Detroit, Gale, 1989.

Bibliography: *The Annotated Guide to Stephen King: A Primary and Secondary Bibliography of the Works of America's Premier Horror Writer* by Michael R. Collings, Mercer Island, Washington, Starmont House, 1986.

Critical Studies: Entry in *Contemporary Literary Criticism,* Volume 12, Detroit, Gale, 1980; Volume 26, 1983; Volume 37, 1985; *Stephen King: The Art of Darkness* by Douglas E. Winter, New York, New American Library, 1984; *Discovering Stephen King* edited by Darrell Schweitzer, Mercer Island, Washington, Starmont House, 1985; *The Many Facets of Stephen King* by Michael R. Collings, Mercer Island, Washington, Starmont House, 1985; *The Shorter Works of Stephen King* by Michael R. Collings and David Engebretson, Mercer Island, Washington, Starmont House, 1985; *Stephen King as Richard Bachman* by Michael R. Collings, Mercer Island, Washington, Starmont House, 1985; *The Films of Stephen King* by Michael R. Collings, Mercer Island, Washington, Starmont House, 1986; *Stephen King: At the Movies* by Jessie Horsting, New York, Signet/Starlog, 1986; *The Stephen King Phenomenon* by Michael R. Collings, Mercer Island, Washington, Starmont House, 1987; *Bare Bones: Conversations on Terror with Stephen King* edited by Tim Underwood and Chuck Miller, New York, McGraw-Hill, 1988; *The Stephen King Companion* edited by George Beahm, Kansas City, Missouri, Andrews and McMeel, 1989; *The Shape under the Sheet: The Complete Stephen King Encyclopedia* by Stephen J. Spignesi, Popular Culture, Ink., 1991; *Stephen King: The Second Decade* by Tony Magistrale, New York, Twayne Publishers, 1992.

*   *   *

Called "a one-man entertainment industry" by critic Curt Suplee, Stephen King's tales of horror, science fiction, and fantasy have been public favorites since he published his first novel, *Carrie,* in 1974. In the six years that followed, he published *'Salem's Lot* (based on his short story "Jerusalem's Lot"), *The Shining, The Stand, The Dead Zone,* and *Firestarter;* had film versions of *Carrie* and *The Dead Zone* released; and had a television version of *'Salem's Lot* produced. By 1980, he had become the first writer to have three works listed simultaneously on the *New York Times'* best-seller list—*Firestarter, The Dead Zone,* and *The Shining.* To paraphrase his own words, Stephen King had become a "brand-name" author.

Young adults figure prominently in King's writing and make up a good portion of his readership. His novel *Carrie* centers around the peculiar life of sixteen-year-old Carrie White. Encompassing the problems of adolescence and peer pressure, the story opens in a high school gym class where, while showering, Carrie begins menstruating. She not only suffers the shock of this incident, having never been told about menstruation, but is humiliated by the other girls in her class, as they taunt her mercilessly. In addition to the constant harassment of her peers at school, Carrie must cope at home with the fanaticisms of her religious mother, in addition to controlling her own telekinetic powers. The story turns into a real bloodbath at a prom, but in spite of the horrors in plot that develop, *Carrie* has been compared to classic fairy tales like the Brothers Grimm's "Little Snow White" and "the Goose-Girl."

Though King writes primarily for adults, many of his works are accessible to a mature young adult audience; and his strong depictions of children, in novels like *Firestarter,* and *The Shining,* are strikingly realistic. The fact that his books are frequently banned from school libraries for their adult content doesn't faze the author at all since King feels teenagers will not be harmed by them, and they are more likely to go out of their way to seek out those titles to read anyway. In an interview for *High Times,* King explains: "We start kids off on things like 'Hansel and Gretel,' which features child abandonment, kidnapping, attempted murder, forcible detention, cannibalism, and finally murder by cremation. And the kids love it." Exposing children to tales of horror does not affect them adversely, he feels, for it's easier for children to suspend their beliefs when reading, whereas adults can clearly distinguish between what is real and what is not.

Some people think that King is not really a horror writer because horror fiction needs to be about the supernatural. *'Salem's Lot, Cycle of the Werewolf, Pet Sematary, It,* and other King novels contain these elements, but many of King's works are based on psychic phenomena, not supernatural monsters. In *Carrie,* Carrie uses telekinesis and pyrokinesis to gain revenge on her high school tormentors. Johnny Smith uses precognition in *Dead Zone* when he realizes that a presidential candidate is actually a potential dictator.

Coincidences in *Apt Pupil* allow Todd Bowden to grow in evil from a bright thirteen-year-old fascinated by Nazi atrocities in the death camps to a seventeen-year-old murderer.

Carrie, Apt Pupil, and other novels by King could be classified as psychological thrillers, but to do so would ignore the fact that horror fiction's main purpose is to evoke uneasiness and fear in readers, and that King's novels repeatedly do so. King presents well-defined characters who are in surroundings like those his readers know. "The more frightened people become about the real world," said King in an interview, "the easier they are to scare." These familiar worlds in the novels are disrupted by dangers ranging from the slobbering werewolf in *Cycle of the Werewolf* to the monster which can take many forms in *It* to the homicidal car in *Christine* to a bizarre set of coincidences in *Apt Pupil.* By intruding into everyday life, rather than appearing in exotic settings and distant places, these dangers increase in shock value.

King evokes an even more complex set of reactions to these stories by his matter-of-fact telling and his tongue-in-cheek tone. In a passage in *Christine* he balances the horror by humorously describing a garage office as "Early American Carburetor." This casualness and humor disarms the reader, and makes the premise of a homicidal car in a familiar world more believable and unsettling than if the premise were presented by a more distant narrator using a less amiable tone. By repeatedly presenting the extraordinary and shocking in such a casual manner, Stephen King has established himself as the late twentieth century's master of colloquial horror.

Although it cannot be said that Stephen King's works are universally critically acclaimed, his works' overwhelming success with readers and moviegoers prove his enduring popularity and literary contribution.

—Harold Nelson

KLASS, David

Nationality: American. **Born:** Vermont, 8 March 1960. **Education:** Yale University, B.A. 1982; University of Southern California School of Cinema and Television, M.A. 1989. **Career:** Novelist and screenwriter; director of short films and live theater. **Awards:** Fiction for Young Adults Award, Southern California Council, and named to "1OO Best of the Best" list, American Library Association (ALA), both 1990, both for *Wrestling with Honor*; *School Library Journal* Best Book of Year, Children's Book Council Notable Trade Book, National Council for Social Studies, ALA Best Book for Young Adult Readers, *Voice of Youth Advocates* Outstanding Trade Book, and Runner-up, Bank Street Annual Children's Book Award, all 1994, and Texas Lone Star Book Award shortlist, 1995-1996, all for *California Blue*; ALA Best Book for Young Adult Readers, 1995, for *Danger Zone*. **Agent:** c/o Scholastic Inc., 555 Broadway, New York, New York 10012, U.S.A.

PUBLICATIONS FOR YOUNG ADULTS

The Atami Dragons. New York, Scribner, 1984.
Breakaway Run. New York, E. P. Dutton, 1986.
A Different Season. New York, E. P. Dutton, 1988.

Wrestling with Honor. New York, E. P. Dutton, 1989.
Samurai, Inc. New York, Fawcett, 1992.
California Blue. New York, Scholastic, 1994.
Danger Zone. New York, Scholastic, 1995.
Screen Test. New York, Scholastic, 1997.

*

Critical Studies: Review of *The Atami Dragons,* in *Booklist,* 1 December 1984; *Bulletin of the Center for Children's Books,* December 1984, and December 1987; review of *Breakaway Run,* in *Booklist,* August 1987; review of *A Different Season,* in *Kirkus Reviews,* 1 November 1987; review of *A Different Season,* in *Publisher's Weekly,* 27 November 1987; review of *A Different Season,* in *Booklist,* 1 January 1988; review of *Wrestling with Honor,* in *Publisher's Weekly,* 30 September 30 1988; review of *California Blue,* in *Publisher's Weekly,* 14 February 1994; review of *California Blue,* in *Kirkus Reviews,* 15 February 1994.

*   *   *

David Klass's young adult novels treat a variety of sports: soccer, baseball, wrestling, basketball, and long distance running. While presenting crisp, fast-moving sports stories, Klass also presents real young people who deal with a variety of social problems. He is adept at developing active plots and also presenting complex social problems with perception and with an even-handed treatment of different opinions and points of view concerning these problems. Characterization is never sacrificed to the treatment of social issues. The underlying theme of all his books is the developing maturity of the protagonist and his efforts to be true to himself.

In *Breakaway Run,* Klass's first novel, Tony Ross goes to Atami, Japan, for five months study. He suffers the usual frustrations of high school exchange students in adjusting to his host family, the language difficulty, and Japanese culture. Tony's personal qualities and his athletic ability, especially in soccer, soon earn him acceptance from his host family and from his schoolmates. During his stay in Japan Tony also manages to cope with the news that his parents are getting a divorce.

The Atami Dragons tells the story of Jerry Sanders, who accompanies his father and sister to Japan during the summer following the death of his mother. He is missing the summer baseball season at home and is happy to avail himself of the opportunity to play in Japan. He makes new friends, learns about baseball in another culture, and begins to adjust to his mother's death.

A Different Season presents the conflict experienced by Jim "Streak" Roark, a talented high school baseball pitcher. He is attracted to an outstanding girl athlete, Jennifer Davis. Their relationship suffers when she tries to join the baseball team. Jim maintains that girls have no business playing baseball. The private debate between the two becomes a public issue. Jennifer is allowed to join the team but the integrated team is not successful in its final big game. Klass presents arguments for and against the gender integration of sports teams, but leaves the reader to form their own conclusion without resolving this central conflict.

Wrestling with Honor treats the issue of drug testing high school athletes. The protagonist, Ron Woods, is an honor student, captain of the wrestling team, and an Eagle Scout. When his drug test returns a false positive, he refuses to take another test because he believes the tests are a violation of his right to privacy. His moral stand is not understood: he is banned from the wrestling team, and his relations with his family, his teammates and his girl friend deteriorate. Before the rather contrived ending Ron discovers why his test was positive, explores his feelings about his father (who was killed in Vietnam), and confronts his most challenging wrestling competitor.

California Blue is set in a lumber mill town in Northern California where John Rodgers has always lived with his family. John is a long distance runner who enjoys doing his practice runs through the old growth redwood forest which is part of the mill company land. He is a keen observer of nature and hopes to further his scientific interests by attending an East Coast university. As the story opens the three major conflicts of the novel emerge. John's father announces that he has been diagnosed with lukemia and has, his doctor says, a thirty percent chance of survival. Next John discovers a new species of butterfly which he wants to protect on the lumber mill land. He knows that the steps he takes to identify the butterfly and protect it through environmentalist forces will be bitterly resented by the whole town and his parents. He does not realize the violence with which his discovery will cause him to be treated. To add to his problems John feels that he has fallen in love with his favorite teacher, Miss Merrill, the high school biology teacher. He indicates his feelings to her. Miss Merrill handles his feelings with respect and indicates that she is fond of him.

The debate between loggers and environmentalists over the preservation of rare or endangered creatures is handled with empathy for both sides although the reader will be aware that Klass is an environmentalist. A *Publisher's Weekly* reviewer described this as "a beautifully rendered novel" which transforms an environmental issue into a compelling story of a boy in transition from adolescence to adulthood. There are some brief but lovely descriptive accounts of the virgin growth forest and the animals that live there as John has observed them at different times of day and at different seasons. The story ends with John introducing his father to his butterflies in their home in the forest on the mill land. The butterfly has been named Rodgers' California Blue. This is usually considered the best of Klass's young adult novels and has been the winner of numerous awards.

Danger Zone is a highly suspenseful basketball story with an international setting. It also treats racism and terrorism as first hand experiences for the protagonist, Jimmy Doyle. Jimmy is the best shooting guard ever to come out of his small town high school in Granham, Minnesota. He is selected for the "Dream Team" to represent the United States in an International Tournament for players seventeen and under in Rome. Jimmy is concerned about his ability to play at this level, but looks forward to playing with the best players in the country, making new friends, and visiting new places. When he arrives in Los Angeles for a week of training before going to Italy he is faced with the problem of convincing both himself and his predominantly African American teammates that he deserves a place on the team. He is also puzzled by the antagonism of the team's superstar, Augustus LeMay. Jimmy becomes aware of racial issues and life styles which he has not encountered before and comes to understand something of Augustus's antagonism.

Once in Italy competition with other teams grows intense and tensions mount. Basketball fans will be delighted with the vivid descriptions of the floor play. Death threats are made against the team, they are moved to a more secure location, and at their final tournament game the terrorist appears and Jimmy is wounded. The story ends with Jimmy back home, at peace with himself, reunited with his girlfriend, Janey, and about to have an operation on his wounded knee.

Screen Test is the first of Klass's novels to feature a female protagonist. Elizabeth Wheaton is a beautiful, green-eyed, chestnut-haired sixteen year old in a small town in northern New Jersey. She has a happy home life with her parents who are both teachers, dreams of becoming a veterinarian, and is enjoying getting to know her first boyfriend, Eric. Liz appears in a short film which is being produced and directed by a young neighbor as part of his master's program. The film is seen by a Hollywood producer who offers Liz a role in a Hollywood movie they are producing during the summer. She is reluctant to accept. The producer points out that she will be paid $30,000 for five weeks work in the movie *Beach Getaway,* and adds that college is expensive and one summer of acting could save her parents using their savings for her college expenses. Liz does not share this conversation with her parents, but it is a deciding factor in her acceptance of the offer.

Her co-star, Tommy Fletcher, is handsome, helpful, and attentive. The movie goes well, and Liz is urged by Tommy and by his superagent, Samantha Wong, to stay in Hollywood and pursue an acting career. The experience of glittering premieres, star treatment on the set, beautiful clothes, and Tommy's romantic attentions all make Liz believe there are many things she would enjoy in a Hollywood career. Soon, however, she discovers that Tommy has lied to her: he said he was nineteen, and that his parents were killed in an auto accident. In fact, she meets his mother and learns that he is twenty-four. With the realization that Tommy programs his life as if it were a movie script, with no regard for reality, she makes the decision to return to New Jersey and take up her regular life. The story is fast moving and provides some interesting characters. Throughout the book Liz seems surprisingly mature and level-headed for a sixteen year old swept up in such an exciting summer adventure.

—Reba Pinney

KLASS, Sheila Solomon

Nationality: American. **Born:** Sheila Solomon in Brooklyn, New York, 6 November 1927. **Education:** Brooklyn College, Brooklyn, New York, B.A. 1949; University of Iowa, M.A. 1951, M.F.A. 1953. **Family:** Married Morton Klass; three children. **Career:** Worked as an aide in a psychopathic hospital in Iowa City, Iowa, 1949-51; English teacher in junior high school in New York City, 1951-57; Manhattan Community College of the City University of New York, New York City, assistant professor, 1968-73, associate professor, 1973-82, professor of English, since 1982. Guest at Yaddo colony, 1974; contributor of short stories and humorous articles to *Hadassah, Bergen Record, New York Times,* and other publications. **Awards:** Leonia Drama Guild Bicentennial Prize, for one-act play, 1976. **Agent:** Ruth Cohen P.O. Box 7626, Menlo Park, California 94025, U.S.A. **Address:** Department of English, Manhattan Community College of the City University of New York, 199 Chambers Street, New York, New York 10007, U.S.A.

PUBLICATIONS FOR YOUNG ADULTS

Fiction

Nobody Knows Me in Miami (middle-grade readers). New York, Scribner's, 1981.
To See My Mother Dance. New York, Scribner's, 1981.
Alive and Starting Over. New York, Scribner's, 1983.
The Bennington Stitch. New York, Scribner's, 1985.
Page Four. New York, Scribner's, 1986.
Credit-Card Carole. New York, Scribner's, 1987.
Kool Ada (middle-grade) New York, Scholastic, 1991.
Rhino. New York, Scholastic, 1993.
Next Stop: Nowhere! New York, Scholastic, 1995.
A Shooting Star: A Novel About Annie Oakley (mid-grade). New York, Holiday House, 1996.
The Un-Civil War (middle-grade). New York, Holiday House, 1997.

PUBLICATIONS FOR ADULTS

Come Back on Monday. New York, Abelard Schuman, 1960.
Everyone in This House Makes Babies. Garden City, New York, Doubleday, 1964.
Badahur Means Hero. New York, Gambit, 1969.
"Otherwise It Only Makes One Hundred Ninety-Nine" (one-act play; produced Leonia, New Jersey, 1976).
A Perpetual Surprise. Cambridge, Massachusetts, Apple-Wood, 1981.
In a Cold Open Field. New York, Black Heron Press, 1997.

*

Critical Studies: Something About the Author, Vol. 45, Detroit, Gale, 1986.

Sheila Solomon Klass comments:

I've always written. As a child, it was my only sport. I was overweight, nearsighted, and uncoordinated. Making up stories was what I did best and loved best. So I simply made my life's work what interested me and gave me the most pleasure—creating worlds of my own in my head! Which is really what a writer of fiction does. To this day, the hours spent writing are my best time.

In the schools I attended (P.S. 16, Eastern District High School, Brooklyn College), I wrote for the newspapers and magazines: feature stories, humor columns, and news. My graduate degrees are in writing.

Since I came from a poor family and knew very early that I had to earn my own living, I became a teacher, and that is what I am, still, today: teacher and writer; it is a happy combination for me. I started out in the 1950s teaching English in a Harlem junior high school, and from the 1960s to the present, I have been teaching at Manhattan Community College.

Young people challenge, stimulate, entertain and often puzzle me. I hope I do as much for them. I certainly try.

I actually began my career as a novelist writing only adult fiction. During a very difficult time in my life, I decided to try a new genre. I wrote *Nobody Knows Me in Miami* about ten-year-old Miriam whose rich relatives want to adopt her and take her away from her Depression-poor home and family; she gets to choose which kind of life she wants. Scribner's bought it enthusiastically, and since I'd enjoyed writing the juvenile novel so much, I just kept on going.

I've written about children and young adults, often in difficult situations, whose resourcefulness and strength and humor see them through: *To See My Mother Dance* is about Jess, who at thirteen seeks her run-away mother, and then *Alive and Starting Over* picks up Jess's story several years later.

In *The Bennington Stitch,* I dealt with parents' unrealistic academic expectations; Amy's mother wants her to go to Bennington, an artsy college, while Amy isn't sure she wants college at all. *Page Four* followed; the book is Dave's extended essay on page four of a college application; in it he explains how and why he messed up in high school and asks the college for admission. In *Credit-Card Carole,* an affluent suburban teenager learns a leaner style of life so her father can pursue his dream.

Kool Ada, my first book for Scholastic, follows orphaned eleven-year-old Ada from Appalachia to Chicago and the rigors and triumphs of her new life. In *Rhino,* Annie, an adolescent who hates her nose, is determined to have plastic surgery. *Next Stop: Nowhere!* is the story of fourteen-year-old Beth, who is sent by her wealthy New York mother to live with her divorced, eccentric father in Vermont.

I became interested in writing historical novels; *A Shooting Star: A Novel About Annie Oakley,* my first Holiday House book, was a pleasure to research and write. Annie, who grew up to be the best sharpshooter in the world, was the daughter of peaceful farmers, poor Quakers. At ten she lived in the poorhouse; at eleven she was house servant to cruel masters who starved and beat her till she ran away. At fifteen she won the Thanksgiving Day Shooting Match in Cincinnati beating the best shot there—and she was on her way.

Two notable publishing events happened to me in 1997. My adult novel about parents who lose a son in the Korean War, *In a Cold Open Field,* was published by Black Heron Press—this after thirty-five years of rejections! And my juvenile novel, The *Uncivil War,* appeared. It is a novel about twelve-year-old Asa who has to contend with many things: she loves to eat and hates being overweight; her mother is pregnant and the premature baby is in danger; a cute boy in school is driving her crazy with his teasing.

I have finished the manuscript of a humorous novel about one remarkable summer in the life of Louisa May Alcott when the Alcott family tried communal living in an idealistic vegetarian "paradise" (no beverages but cold water; no animal products) with some very odd other folks.

As a member of the School Volunteer Program, I visit the New York public schools regularly to read my work to students and to talk to them and teach them about writing. These visits are a great delight.

My enthusiasm about writing is infectious; I have three grown children, all of whom are professional writers. My daughter, Perri Klass, a pediatrician, is a novelist and writer of non-fiction; *Baby Doctor* is her latest publication. My son, David Klass is a screenwriter ("Kiss the Girls") and author of many Young Adult novels, and my youngest child, Judy Klass is a playwright, poet, and author of *The Cry of the Onlies,* a Star Trek novel. This pleases me; I can't think of a higher calling.

*   *   *

Who am I? Where am I going? These are questions that perpetually preoccupy teenagers, and these are the questions that provide the thematic focus of the young adult novels of Sheila Solomon Klass.

Amy Hamilton, the protagonist of *The Bennington Stitch,* has known all her life that her mother is determined that she go to Bennington College: "Seconds after I was born, my intellectual mother, who had been given only a spinal anaesthetic and therefore claims that her mind was perfectly clear, made a solemn twofold vow: 'This child will be called Amelia Bloomer Hamilton, and she will study the arts at Bennington College. Nothing will prevent this!'" The trouble is, Amy is not an intellectual, she has trouble taking tests and doubts very much that she'll do well enough on her S.A.T.s to get into Bennington, and she doesn't want to go to Bennington anyhow. But what does she want to do? She doesn't really know—until she embarks on her senior project, helping a peppery but frail old lady with her patchwork quilts. Amy learns a lot about quilting—and herself. She designs a quilt for her mom with a special beaded stitch she and "Aunt Edna" name after her mother's favorite college, and she decides to return to Aunt Edna and their quilting after graduation. And Mom, deprived of her lifetime dream for her daughter, finally gets to pursue it for herself, as she enrolls in a new non-resident M.F.A. program at Bennington.

"Imagine a normal father who is forty-two years old, a bookworm, sensible, a successful dentist, short and slim with a young Walter Matthau kind of face, a dentist with a light-as-a-feather touch, his patients say. Imagine that this Dr. Tooth blows his circuits. Without any warning one afternoon he announces that he is about to 'Fly after the bluebird of happiness! Have a rendezvous with destiny! Chase rainbows!'" When Carole (*Credit-Card Carole*) Warner's father decides to leave his dental practice and pursue his dream of an acting career, Carole is forced to take a good look at herself and where she is going. No more all-day trips to the mall with her other credit-card carrying pals, buying a few new tapes, a new top at the Gap, lunch at a mall restaurant. No more housecleaning help at home. Now it's house-cleaning for Carole on Saturdays—at home, and, for a bit of spending money, at her friend Jim's house. As she adjusts to this initially painful new lifestyle and watches her father go from one fruitless audition to another—but at last getting his big role—Carole learns that family, friends, and following your own dreams are far more important than new tops or tapes.

Who is Ada? What is she? The school bullies call her a "ree-tart," she's in Ms. Walker's "Dumbo class," she doesn't speak, and she keeps getting into fights. Who is this silent, skinny, poor Appalachian girl? And what is she doing on the mean, ugly streets of Chicago? "Things were so different back home. I was born in a holler tucked in right beside Flat Top Mountain . . . [with] woods and birds and fishes and millions of wildflowers." Ada's mother died a minute after Ada was born. Her brother, playmate, and "best and closest friend" Will Junior died, of "Newmonia," when he was nine, opening up a "big empty space in the world." When her father dies in his bed of black lung disease, Ada tries to scream, but no sound emerges: "I couldn't. I just couldn't. That was when I just stopped listening to words. The sound of folks talking bounced around in the air outside my understanding. . . . I stopped listening. I took shelter in the cave of my mind where it was warm and safe. I just sat and sucked my thumb and bit my cuticles until they bled. I stopped talking and I lived back inside my head where I was a little bit protected.'' That was when Ada was sent to Chicago to live with her only relative, her Great-Aunt Lottie.

The reader knows—from Ada's eloquent narration—that Ada cannot be retarded. And so does her devoted but no-nonsense teacher, who is determined to get Ada to start talking, to start thinking and stop fighting, and to take her real place in the world. Ms. Walker talks to Ada. She listens to Ada's silence, and then to her first, painful words. When Ada finds a way to trick a bully out of fighting by pretending she has a knife, Ms. Walker tells her that ''pretending that way was brave and brilliant'' and, ''At that word brilliant, a warm breeze brushed my face, touched my cheeks light as a feather, and I took it as a sign . . . [that] said to me: The cold wind is gone for now, Ada. You are safe. The big hole punched in the world when Will Junior died is mostly shrunk up.'' Ada trembles all over with happiness. Ms. Walker goes on to tell her, ''Girl, you're going to be all right. You're going to be just fine. I know it. You know how I know it?. . . Because a lot of your trouble came from not thinking, from being too quick, too ready to fight. From being Hot Ada. . . . But a girl who finds her way out of trouble is something else. She's using her mind. . . . Now . . . and you must always remember I said this—whenever I think of you, in my mind you will always be Kool Ada.''' Kool Ada—that's Ada!

Annie Trevor, protagonist of *Rhino,* has a problem, and while it may seem small compared with Ada's problems, it's big to her. In fact it's too big—her too-big nose. Her family likes her just as she is (of course, her father and grandfather have the same nose, but they're big men and it looks all right on them). So does her boyfriend Bob. But every time she looks in the mirror, Annie sees ''an okay face and in the middle of it a clunky nose. I can't deal with myself as a girl with that kind of nose.'' So, despite everyone's advice, Annie decides to save up from her job at the health food store for a nose job (rhinoplasty). It will cost much more than she'll be able to save, though, even by working extra hours. Finally, on her fifteenth birthday, her grandfather gives her an early inheritance: ''To my . . . granddaughter, Annie Trevor, whose fifteenth birthday we are celebrating today, I give three thousand dollars from my savings account to be added to her own money to meet the cost of a plastic surgery operation.'' Annie sobs, ''You were so against it—'' ''In principle, I'm still against it,'' Grandpa replies. ''It's a good and honorable nose. . . . What happened, Annie, is I had time here to realize that I don't understand a lot of what is going on today. It's all too fast. But I do understand something that grabs you and you can't shake free of it and it drives you crazy and whittles you down and won't let go. With me it was the smoking, and with you it's this nose business. So I decided if this operation will make you happy and make your life better, then you should have it. You'd get the money anyway when I died. This way I'll be around to see my happy grandchildren. I get my reward here and now.''

''I was a teenage girl myself!'' Sheila Solomon Klass reminds us in her note ''About the Author'' at the end of *Rhino.* She was also a junior high school teacher in New York City for six years, and is the mother of three grown children. She clearly knows teenagers—what they think about, what they worry about, how they feel—and she clearly knows what they like to read about, and how to write especially for them.

—Marcia Welsh

KLAUSE, Annette Curtis

Nationality: American. **Born:** Bristol, England, 20 June 1953; came to the United States, June, 1968. **Education:** University of Maryland, B.A., 1976, M.L.S., 1978. **Family:** Married Mark Jeffrey Klause, 11 August, 1979. **Career:** Various positions for library contracting companies, Montgomery County, Maryland, Department of Public Libraries, 1981—; Silver Spring Community Libraries, Department of Public Libraries, Silver Spring, Maryland, children's librarian I, 1981; Montgomery County Department of Public Libraries, substitute librarian, 1981-82; Kensington Park Community Library, Kensington Park, Maryland, part-time children's librarian I, 1982-84; Bethesda Regional Library, Bethesda, Maryland, full-time children's librarian I, 1984-89; Olney Community Library, Olney, Maryland, head of children's services, 1989-91; Kensington Park Community Library, head of children's services, 1991-92; Aspen Hill Community Library, Rockville, Maryland, head of children's services, from 1992. Writer. **Awards:** American Library Association (ALA) Best Book for Young Adults and Best Book for Reluctant Readers, 1990, *School Library Journal* Best Book, 1990, Booklist Best Book and Editor's Choice, 1990, Best Book of the Year Honor Book, Michigan Library Association Young Adult Division, 1990, Maryland Library Association Black-eyed Susan award for grades six through nine, 1992-93, California Young Reader Medal, young adult category, 1993, Sequoyah Young Adult Book Award, Oklahoma Library Association, 1993, and South Carolina Library Association Young Adult Award, all for *The Silver Kiss; Alien Secrets* was named an ALA Notable Book for Children, a *Booklist* Editor's Choice, one of the *School Library Journal Best Books,* and one of New York Public Library's 100 Best Children's Books, all 1993. **Address:** c/o Bantam Doubleday Dell, Books for Young Readers, 1540 Broadway, New York, New York 10036, U.S.A.

PUBLICATIONS FOR YOUNG ADULTS

Fiction

The Silver Kiss. New York, Delacorte, 1990.
Alien Secrets. New York, Delacorte, 1993.
Blood and Chocolate. New York, Delacorte Press, 1997.

Also author of short stories, including ''Librarians from Space,'' published in *The U*n*a*b*a*s*h*e*d Librarian,* number 51, 1984; and ''The Hoppins,'' published in *Short Circuits,* edited by Donald Gallo, Delacorte, 1992. Author of poetry published in *Takoma Park Writers 1981,* Downcounty Press, 1981; *Cat's Magazine; Aurora; Visions;* and others. Contributor of articles to professional journals; contributor of book reviews to *School Library Journal,* 1982-94.

*

Critical Studies: ''Growing Up To Be A Writer'' by Annette Curtis Klause, in *Voice of Youth Advocates,* Vol. 14, No. 1 (April 1991), 19-20, 22; *Speaking For Ourselves, Too: More Autobiographical Sketches By Notable Authors of Books For Young Adults* edited by Donald Gallo, Urbana, Illinois, National Council of Teachers of English, 1993; essay in *Speaking for Ourselves, Too* compiled and edited by Donald R. Gallo, National Council of Teachers of English, 1993; entry in *Something about the Author,* Volume 79, Gale, 1995.

*   *   *

Rarely does a first novel generate such positive critical response as did Annette Curtis Klause's *The Silver Kiss,* a deceptively simple, yet seductive story that has been called the quintessential young adult novel. This hauntingly beautiful story combines modern realism and traditional vampire lore in a multifaceted tale. Zoë is attempting to deal with her mother's pending death from cancer, with her feelings of desertion by her father who is having his own problems coping, and with the fact that her best friend is moving away. She is fascinated and comforted by the mysterious, silver-haired Simon and is drawn into believing what she does not want to believe, that this handsome young man is a vampire on a mission to avenge his own mother's death by killing his vampire brother, Christopher. Alternating chapters present Zoë's and Simon's perspectives on events and draw readers into their thoughts and feelings. Simon is a convincing character, a vampire with human emotions, yearning for affection in spite of his underlying anger and violence. There is a great deal of tension created by this clash of two worlds as well as restraint in dealing with both the tempting sexuality and violence. All of these layers of complexity are so skillfully crafted in language with such compelling simplicity that the book was named a Best Book for Reluctant Readers as well as a Best Book for Young Adults by the American Library Association.

Klause's second book, *Alien Secrets,* is a vivid science fiction adventure for younger adolescent readers that capitalizes on her ability to create multidimensional characters. Puck is a young heroine who makes mistakes but continues to meet her commitments and accomplish her goals. Hush, a Shoowa, is an alien portrayed with humor, honor, dignity, and caring. Hush is tentative in reaching out, but, with Puck's help, learns the value of trust. This is a fast-moving mystery, a complex "whodunit" set in outer space that is not easy to solve. There are subtle clues, disguises, mistaken identities, and a search for a stolen object—in this case, the Soo, a religious symbol from Hush's homeland. There are also ghosts, the spirits of Hush's comrades killed by the evil Grakk who are trapped on the refitted spaceship on which they originally met their fate. Within the form of this mystery, Klause explores hyperspace and gives readers a sensitivity to the mathematical and scientific concepts involved. Especially appealing is her description of hyperspace from both an artistic and mathematical context. Klause seems to play with the imagery of the Soo and the hyperspace visualizations, implying an emotional and scientific relationship. It is no surprise that the ghosts who inhabit the spaceship, Cat's Cradle, are essential to plot movement. They are given peace by following the Soo, regained by Hush and Puck, to their home. Klause provides a crystalline image in the passages describing this: "Far above, ragged shreds tore off, sparkled for a moment, then turned to mist and disappeared, until the whole bolt of ghost cloth was unfurled and gone, back into the life force of its own world."

In both of these novels, Klause creates very appealing aliens who reach out to sensitive human characters in ways that benefit both. Her young protagonists are strong females who cope with realistic adolescent problems but still have the interest and the

energy to help those outsiders rejected by others. Klause writes a good yarn, but she does much more than that; she has the ability to attract, fascinate, and thrill readers with exciting plots and memorable characters. The beauty of her language creates vivid images of those times and places where the real world touches the non-real, but very believable, world of magic and the imagination.

—Kay E. Vandergrift

KLEIN, Norma

Nationality: American. **Born:** New York City, 13 May 1938. **Education:** the Dalton School, New York, 1941-51; Elizabeth Irwin High School, 1952-56; Cornell University, Ithaca, New York, 1956-57; Barnard College, New York, 1957-60, B.A. (cum laude) in Russian 1960 (Phi Beta Kappa); Columbia University, New York, 1960-63, M.A. in Slavic languages 1963. **Family:** Married Erwin Fleissner in 1963; two daughters. **Career:** Author of novels, short stories, poetry, and children's fiction. Instructor of fiction at Yale and Wesleyan universities. **Awards:** One of Child Study Association of America's Children's Books of the Year, 1973, *Girls Can Be Anything; Media & Methods* Maxi award for Paperbacks, 1975, and selected one of New York Public Library's Books for the Teen Age, 1980, both for *Sunshine;* one of *School Library Journal*'s Best Books of the Year, 1978, for *Love Is One of the Choices;* O. Henry award, 1983, for short story "The Wrong Man." **Died:** 25 April 1989.

PUBLICATIONS FOR YOUNG ADULTS

Novel

Mom, the Wolf Man and Me. New York, Pantheon, 1972; London, Heinemann, 1986.
It's Not What You Expect. New York, Pantheon, 1973; London, Pan, 1986.
Coming to Life. New York, Simon & Schuster, 1974.
Confessions of an Only Child, illustrated by Richard Cuffari. New York, Pantheon, 1974.
Taking Sides. New York, Pantheon, 1974.
What It's All About. New York, Dial Press, 1975.
Girls Turn Wives. New York, Simon & Schuster, 1976.
Hiding. New York, Four Winds Press, 1976.
It's Okay If You Don't Love Me. New York, Dial, 1977.
Love Is One of the Choices. New York, Dial, 1978; London, Futura, 1981.
Tomboy. New York, Four Winds Press, 1978.
French Postcards (novelization of screenplay). New York, Fawcett, 1979; London, Coronet, 1980.
Breaking Up. New York, Pantheon, 1980; London, Pan, 1986.
A Honey of a Chimp. New York, Pantheon, 1980.
Robbie and the Leap Year Blues. New York, Dial, 1981.
Beginner's Love. New York, Dial, 1982; London, Pan, 1986.
The Queen of the What Ifs. New York, Fawcett, 1982.
Bizou. New York, Viking, 1983.
Angel Face. New York, Viking, 1984; London, Pan, 1987.
Snapshots. New York, Dial, 1984.
The Cheerleader. New York, Knopf, 1985.

Family Secrets. New York, Dial, 1985.
Give and Take. New York, Viking, 1985.
Going Backwards. New York, Scholastic, 1986; London, Pan, 1987.
My Life as a Body. New York, Knopf, 1987.
Older Men. New York, Dial, 1987; London, Women's Press, 1988.
No More Saturday Nights. New York, Knopf, 1988.
Now That I Know. New York, Bantam, 1988.
That's My Baby. New York, Viking, 1988.
Learning How to Fall. New York, Bantam. 1989.
Just Friends. New York, Knopf, 1990.

PUBLICATIONS FOR ADULTS

Novel

Give Me One Good Reason. New York, Putnam, 1973.
Sunshine (novelization of a TV play). New York, Holt Rinehart, 1975; London, Everest, 1976.
The Sunshine Years. New York, Dell, 1975; London, MacDonald, 1984.
Sunshine Christmas. Mount Kisco, New York, Futura, 1977.
Domestic Arrangements. New York, Evans, 1981; London, Futura, 1982.
Wives and Other Women. New York, St. Martin's, 1982; London, MacDonald, 1983.
The Swap. New York, St. Martin's, 1983.
Lovers. New York, Viking, 1984; London, Piatkus, 1986.
American Dreams. New York, Dutton, 1987.
The World as It Is. New York, Dutton, 1989.

Short Stories

Love and Other Euphemisms. New York, Putnam, 1972.
Sextet in A Minor: A Novella and Thirteen Short Stories. New York, St. Martin's, 1983.

PUBLICATIONS FOR CHILDREN

Fiction

Girls Can Be Anything, illustrated by Roy Doty. New York, Dutton, 1973.
Dinosaur's Housewarming Party, illustrated by James Marshall. New York, Crown, 1974.
If I Had It My Way, illustrated by Ray Cruz. New York, Pantheon, 1974.
Naomi in the Middle, illustrated by Leigh Grant. New York, Dial, 1974.
A Train for Jane (verse), illustrated by Miriam Schottland. Old Westbury, New York, Feminist Press, 1974.
Blue Trees, Red Sky, illustrated by Pat Grant Porter. New York, Pantheon, 1975.
Visiting Pamela, illustrated by Kay Chorao. New York, Dial, 1979.

Other

Baryshnikov's Nutcracker, photographs by Ken Regan, Christopher Little, and Martha Swope. New York, Putnam, 1983.
First Down & a Billion. New York, St. Martin's Press, 1987.

*

Media Adaptations: *Mom, the Wolf Man and Me* (cassette), Caedmon, 1977; *Mom, the Wolf Man and Me* (film), Time-Life Productions, 1979; *Confessions of an Only Child* (cassette), Caedmon, 1977.

Biography: Essay in *Authors and Artists for Young People,* Volume 2, Detroit, Gale, 1989, pp. 139-50; essay in *Speaking for Ourselves: Autobiographical Sketches by Notable Authors of Books for Young Adults,* Volume 1, compiled and edited by Donald R. Gallo, National Council of Teachers of English, 1990.

Critical Studies: *Children's Literature Review,* Volume 2, Detroit, Gale, 1976; entry in *Contemporary Literary Criticism,* Volume 30, Detroit, Gale, 1984.

*   *   *

When Norma Klein died from a heart infection at the age of fifty-one in 1989, she left the world of young adult literature a poorer place. Klein was a prolific American author who wrote for children, young adults, and adults. While all her books met with success, it was as a writer of children's and young adult fiction that Klein enjoyed the greatest recognition, becoming a superstar second only to Judy Blume when it came to having a large coterie of loyal young readers. Klein, like Blume, wrote with uncompromising frankness about issues that are of concern to contemporary youth: sex and sexism, single or gay parents, disintegrating families, pornography, feminism—all have been grist for Klein's mill. As a result, she shares another honor with Blume; Klein's books for young readers are second only to Blume's when it comes to censorship attempts in the United States, a fact of which Klein was quite proud.

In the 1970s, Klein wrote a number of children's books. These included *Girls Can Be Anything,* an expression of her strong feminist sentiments and a precursor of the firm feminist position that became clear in her later writings for older children and young adults. One of the books she wrote during this period was a taboo-breaking novel for its time for early adolescent readers, *Mom, the Wolf Man, and Me.* In it, Brett is the eleven-year-old daughter of an unmarried mother; their relationship is warm and mutually respectful. Her mother, to the consternation of many critics, relishes her life, and Brett suffers not at all from her highly unorthodox family situation. But into this tranquil situation comes a problem in the form of an unusual red-haired man with a wonderful Irish wolfhound called Norma. It becomes obvious early on that Brett's mother, Deborah, is not only interested in "The Wolf Man," as Brett has named him, but is considering marrying him. How Brett handles her jealousy and fears of the new relationship makes a warm, funny, and loving family story that many consider Klein's finest work, its controversial aspects notwithstanding.

Over the course of her career, Klein wrote over two dozen novels for teenage readers, almost all of which are still in print and read avidly by this age group. Klein said that her aim in writing young adult books was to present central characters who are "strong and interesting" in the face of the problems of growing up in American society; in this she succeeded admirably for the most part, as her legion of loyal young adult readers attests. *It's Not What You Expect* is a good example of how she managed to accomplish that aim. Fourteen-year-old twins Oliver and Carla decide to capitalize on Oliver's gourmet-cooking skills by opening a restaurant in a house the two are caring for over the summer and serve one dinner each evening at a reasonable price. They involve family and friends, and the restaurant is a success from the beginning, to the delight of everyone involved. Family problems arise, however: Dad, in a mid-life crisis, decides to leave and go to New York City to write a novel, picking up a new girlfriend in the process. Mom must cope with Dad's absence but also with the amorous advances of a neighbor, while older brother Tom's girlfriend is found to be pregnant. The twins offer Tom the restaurant's proceeds to pay for Sara Lee's abortion, but he angrily refuses. Carla, a strong young woman, is at first angry and hurt by all this, but eventually begins to realize that life just isn't always "what you expect," and grows as a result of her new understanding. The family is eventually reunited, but at some cost—and some acquired maturity—to all.

It's Okay If You Don't Love Me, another ground-breaking young adult book, is the story of Jody, an urbane, liberated Jewish young woman from a liberal, divorced New York family, who meets Lyle, a straightlaced midwestern Roman Catholic who has come to New York to live with his sister and her family. They fall in love despite their differences, and Jody attempts the difficult task of seducing Lyle. However, when Jody betrays Lyle with her former boyfriend Whitney, Lyle is alienated and deeply hurt. The clash of values arising from their differing backgrounds is not strong enough to keep Jody and Lyle apart forever, however, and eventually they are reconciled. What made *It's Okay* controversial to critics was its explicit and frank details about the young people's sexual activity; the book's publisher, in fact, went so far as to issue it as an adult book despite the fact that it was clearly written for teenagers, a not unusual occurrence with Klein's more explicit tales. In spite of this, the book remains one of Klein's most popular books among the young adult audience.

In the 1980s Klein began shifting from female protagonists' viewpoints in many of her young adult novels to young males' viewpoints. In *Snapshots,* for example, Sean and Marc, fine amateur photographers, take nude photographs of Marc's beautiful younger sister, not out of salaciousness but simply because Tiffany is an exquisite child who is a natural model. The boys get into trouble when the person developing the photos reports them to the district attorney, who accuses them of producing child pornography. In *Give and Take,* Spence, an eighteen-year-old naif, has to fend off the attentions of women who seek to seduce him. In *Beginner's Love,* the protagonist is Joel, a virgin who has his first affair, and *Angel Face* features Jason, who is not doing too well in either his school life or his love life, and whose family is falling apart. Klein has said that she writes from the boy's viewpoint because she wishes "there were more good novels about teenage boys, particularly about what boys feel about girls, their families, schools, the future."

Reviewers have occasionally faulted Klein for writing young adult books on "trendy" subjects; it can just as easily be argued that she wrote topical books, discussing in a way accessible to teenage readers, some of the issues of concern to kids today. Some of these topics she wrote of so well are Alzheimer's disease and its effects on a teenager and his family who take his grandmother into their home when she can no longer live alone *(Going Backwards);* a boy whose life is forever changed by a paralyzing accident but who still manages to reach out and help liberate a shy, insecure young woman who is his tutor *(My Life as a Body);* the effects of a mother's serious mental disease on a young woman and her father

(Older Men); a thirteen-year-old's struggle to deal with not only her divorced parents but also her father's new life as a gay man *(Now That I Know);* an unmarried seventeen-year-old boy's successful fight to win custody of his infant son and parenthood's effects on his formerly carefree college life *(No More Saturday Nights);* and another seventeen-year-old boy, whose father is a recovering alcoholic and divorced from the boy's lesbian mother *(Learning How to Fall).* She wrote frankly, honestly, and usually with a leavening of humor to get the reader through the serious themes.

In all her books for young adults, Klein struck a note with her readers that few other authors for this age group do consistently. She wrote about the things that concern young people, both boys and girls: sexuality, sex roles and sexual behavior, love, peer relations, and family ties. Her portrayals of teenage angst always rang true, and like her friend Judy Blume, she respected and cared for her readers, who respond in kind to her books.

—Audrey Eaglen

KLEIN, Robin

Nationality: Australian. **Born:** Kempsey, New South Wales, 28 February 1936. **Education:** Kempsey Primary School, 1941-47, and Newcastle Girls High School, 1948-51, both New South Wales. **Family:** Married Karl Klein in 1956 (divorced 1978); two sons and two daughters. **Career:** Writer. Worked as a "tea lady" at a warehouse, and as a bookshop assistant, nurse, copper enamelist, and program aide at a school for disadvantaged children. **Awards:** Special Mention, Critici in Erba, Bologna Children's Book Fair, 1979, for *The Giraffe in Pepperell Street*; Australian Junior Book of the Year award, Children's Book Council of Australia, 1983, for *Thing*; Australian Children's Book Council Awards shortlist, 1984, for *Junk Castle* and *People Might Hear You,* 1985, for *Hating Alison Ashley* and *Penny Pollard's Letters,* 1986, for *Halfway Across the Galaxy and Turn Left* and *The Enemies,* 1987, for *Boss of the Pool,* 1988, for *Birk the Berserker,* and 1994, for *Seeing Things*; Book of the Year award Highly Commended Citation from the Children's Book Council of Australia, 1984, for *Penny Pollard's Diary*; senior fellowship grant from the Arts Council of Australia Literature Board, 1985; Australian Human Rights award for Literature, 1989, and Australian Book of the Year award for older readers from the Children's Book Council of Australia, 1990, for *Came Back to Show You I Could Fly*; Honour Book, Children's Book Council Awards, 1992, for *Borish and Borsch*; New South Wales State Literary Award, 1992, for *All in the Blue Unclouded Weather*; Dromkeen Medal, 1992. **Agent:** Curtis Brown, P.O. Box 19, Paddington, Sydney, NSW 2021. **Address:** Belgrave, VIC 3160, Australia.

PUBLICATIONS FOR YOUNG ADULTS

Fiction

Junk Castle, illustrated by Rolf Heimann. Melbourne, New York, and Oxford, Oxford University Press, 1983.
Penny Pollard's Diary, illustrated by Ann James. Melbourne and Oxford, Oxford University Press, 1983.

People Might Hear You. Melbourne and London, Penguin, 1983; Middlesex, England and New York, Viking Kestrel, 1987.

Penny Pollard's Letters, illustrated by Ann James. Melbourne and Oxford, Oxford University Press, 1984.

The Tomb Comb, illustrated by Heather Potter. Melbourne, Oxford University Press, 1984.

The Enemies, illustrated by Noela Young. North Ryde, New South Wales, Angus & Robertson, 1985; as *Enemies,* New York, Dutton, 1989.

Halfway Across the Galaxy and Turn Left. Melbourne and London, Viking Kestrel, 1985; New York, Viking, 1986.

Separate Places, illustrated by Anna Lacis. Kenthurst, New South Wales, Kangaroo Press, 1985.

Boss of the Pool, illustrated by H. Panagopoulos. Adelaide, Omnibus Books, 1986.

Games. . . , illustrated by Melissa Webb. Melbourne, Viking Kestrel, 1986.

Penny Pollard in Print, illustrated by Ann James. Melbourne, Oxford University Press, 1986.

Get Lost, illustrated by June Joubert. Melbourne, Macmillan, 1987.

The Last Pirate, illustrated by Rick Armor. Melbourne, Rigby, 1987.

With Max Dunn, *The Lonely Hearts Club.* Melbourne, Oxford University Press, 1987; New York, Oxford University Press, 1988.

Parker-Hamilton, illustrated by Gaston Vanzet. Melbourne, Rigby, 1987.

Laurie Loved Me Best. Melbourne and London, Viking Kestrel, 1988.

Penny Pollard's Passport, illustrated by Ann James. Melbourne, Oxford University Press, 1988.

Against the Odds, illustrated by Bill Wood. Melbourne and London, Viking Kestrel, 1989.

Boris and Borsch. Sydney, Allen & Unwin, 1990.

Came Back to Show You I Could Fly. Ringwood, Victoria, Australia, Viking Kestrel 1989; New York, Viking, 1990.

All in the Blue Unclouded Weather. New York, Viking, 1991.

Dresses of Red and Gold. Melbourne, Viking Kestrel, 1993.

Seeing Things. Ringwood, Victoria, Australia, Viking, 1992; New York, Viking, 1994.

Turn Right for Syrgon. New York, Puffin, 1994.

The Sky in Silver Lace. Ringwood, Victoria, Australia and New York, Viking, 1995.

The Listmaker. Ringwood, Victoria, Australia and New York, Viking, 1997.

PUBLICATIONS FOR CHILDREN

Fiction

Honoured Guest, illustrated by Margaret Power. Melbourne, Macmillan, 1979.

Sprung!, illustrated by Margaret Power. Willoughby, New South Wales, Rigby, 1982.

Thing, illustrated by Alison Lester. Melbourne and Oxford, Oxford University Press, 1982.

Oodoolay, illustrated by Vivienne Goodman. Flinders Park, South Australia, Era Publications, 1983.

Brock and the Dragon, illustrated by Rodney McRae. Rydalmere, New South Wales, Hodder & Stoughton, 1984.

Hating Alison Ashley. Melbourne and London, Penguin, 1984; New York, Penguin, 1985.

Ratbags and Rascals, illustrated by Alison Lester. Melbourne, Dent, 1984.

Thalia the Failure, illustrated by Rhyll Plant. Gosford, New South Wales, Ashton Scholastic, 1984.

Thingnapped!, illustrated by Alison Lester. Melbourne and Oxford, Oxford University Press, 1984.

The Princess Who Hated It, illustrated by Marie Smith. Adelaide, Omnibus Books, 1986.

Birk the Berserker, illustrated by Alison Lester. Adelaide, Omnibus Books, 1987.

I Shot an Arrow, illustrated by Geoff Hocking. Melbourne, Viking Kestrel, 1987.

Amy's Bed, illustrated by Coral Tulloch. Adelaide, Omnibus Books, 1992.

Thingitis, illustrated by Alison Lester. Hodder Headline Australia, 1996.

Thing's Concert, illustrated by Alison Lester. Hodder Headline Australia, 1996.

Thing's Birthday, illustrated by Alison Lester. Hodder Headline Australia, 1996.

Thing Finds a Job, illustrated by Alison Lester. Hodder Headline Australia, 1996.

Poetry

The Giraffe in Pepperell Street, illustrated by Gill Tomblin. Rydalmere, New South Wales, Hodder & Stoughton, 1978.

Snakes and Ladders: Poems about the Ups and Downs of Life, illustrated by Ann James. Melbourne, Dent, 1985.

Other

Annabel's Ghost (stories). Melbourne, Oxford University Press, 1985.

Christmas, illustrated by Kristen Hilliard. Sydney, Methuen, 1987.

Don't Tell Lucy, illustrated by Kristen Hilliard. Sydney, Methuen, 1987.

Robin Klein's Crookbook, illustrated by Kristen Hilliard. Sydney, Methuen, 1987.

Dear Robin. . .: Letters to Robin Klein. Sydney, Allen and Unwin, 1988.

Tearaways: Stories to Make You Think Twice. New York, Viking, 1991.

*

Media Adaptations: *Battlers* (includes *Good for Something, Serve Him Rights,* and *You're On Your Own*), Edward Arnold Audiobooks, 1985.

Critical Studies: *How Writers Write* by Pamela Lloyd, Methuen, 1987; *The Inside Story: Creating Children's Books,* edited by Belle Alderman, Children's Book Council of Australia, 1987; entry in *Children's Literature Review,* Volume 21, Detroit, Gale, 1991.

*   *   *

Robin Klein is one of Australia's most prolific and versatile writers for young adults. Her work includes picture books, short stories, and fiction for both younger and older readers. Although the predominately female protagonists of Klein's young adult fiction range in age from around eleven to eighteen, the implied readership of her work seems to be a younger teenaged group. The author keeps sexual tension at a distance and the novels generally employ a child focalization, eschewing the dangerous complexities of developing adolescent sexuality. The anxieties of Klein's characters centre on peer-group exclusivity and family embarrassments: anxieties about being acceptable to the right "in-crowd" rather than to romantic soul mates.

Klein writes with humour and irony. Her characters frequently display a rueful or ironic mode of self-presentation. Their language is wry, witty, and knowing rather than sentimental—though lyric and nostalgic moments are to be found in the author's writing, particularly in her more recent autobiographically-based novels, such as *All in the Blue Unclouded Weather* and *Dresses of Red and Gold*. Klein generally employs a collusive, even conspiratorial narrative stance. It is not her usual mode to challenge her audience's sense of reality, or its social and cultural assumptions. She writes at her reader's level, forging a comfortable alliance between "us" and "them." Her stories are full of characters one loves to hate: more fortunate classmates, glamorous older sisters (like Dovis, in *Halfway Across the Galaxy and Turn Left*), loutish boy-bullies, smart-alecky teachers, etc., who conspire to humiliate the luckless and envious heroine.

Child characters in Klein's novels frequently suffer from an acute sense of responsibility toward the less-than-capable adults in their lives, and are often represented as little old men and women for whom the burden of holding things together in their dysfunctional families seems to weigh with a guilty imperative. For example, Patricia Miggs, the heroine of *Games...*, bears the burden of caring for her widowed, invalid, and morbidly possessive mother, and is consumed with guilt as she makes her escape to spend a weekend away with two treacherous girlfriends.

The comic version of this ultra-responsible character type is found in X, the young female "Family Organizer" in Klein's science fiction spoof, *Halfway Across the Galaxy and Turn Left*. Family roles are reversed in this alien ménage: X literally does have the burden of the family on her incompetent shoulders. In this story of a family of remarkable aliens, with an ordinary (if officious) daughter, Klein portrays a parodic inversion of the drama of the adolescent outcast who sees him/herself as an alien in a society into which other (more glamorous or fortunate) souls seem to fit easily.

Science fiction is not Klein's usual mode; her stories and novels more commonly inhabit the territory of social realism wherein she depicts an urban society, with its contemporary social problems: broken homes and single parents, working-class deprivation, middle-class emotional deprivation, drug-referral centers, peer-group "territories" which outsiders must avoid, homeless teenagers, and those who have homes which are not "homes."

More recently, however, Klein has turned to the past and her own life for inspiration. *All in the Blue Unclouded Weather* and *Dresses of Red and Gold* are set in "Wilgawa," a fictional town in rural Australia in the late 1940s. These novels are composed of vignettes from the lives of a family of working-class girls, with their youthful ambitions toward great and glamorous lives. The stories enact the girls' negotiation of hierarchies of class and adolescent social prestige, depicting their fascination for the attractions of wealth and elegance represented to them in magazines, and their embarrassment for their families and the makeshift gracelessness of their homes.

Klein's fictional world is one in which appearances deceive. Her characters are often afflicted with selective blindness, misinterpreting the evidence in front of them. The plots turn on the protagonist's reversal of previous, mistaken opinions or expectations. The reader in *Hating Alison Ashley,* for example, is alerted quite early in the narrative to the possibility that Alison (Erica Yurken's rival and enemy) is really her secret ally. Long before Erica's eyes are opened, the reader is made privy to the knowledge that Alison has her own social discomforts and a deep need for intelligent female friendship. Similarly, while eleven-year-old Seymour, in *Came Back to Show You I Could Fly,* sees eighteen-year-old Angie as an elegant and exotic "flower" suffering from a mysterious "flu," the reader identifies her as a disorganized junkie, fired by imaginative but futile illusions and scarred by the rejection on the part of her well-to-do family.

Often Klein employs the device of the juxtaposition of narrative "voices," providing conflicting or revisionist focalizations. In *Laurie Loved Me Best,* the two friends, Andre and Julia, relate, by turns, their perceptions of events. The juxtaposed narrations reveal the flaws in each girl's representation of the other's home life; illusory utopias are revealed to be nothing of the sort.

In Klein's world, enemies turn out to be friends; longed-for social triumphs prove to be deliberately-planned humiliations; rich little girls with "nice" families turn out to be "poor little rich girls," while poor and unfashionable homes turn out to have hidden "riches" of love and communality. Thus Klein's stories reveal a deep sense of class division. Her heroines are exposed as would-be social climbers, who are desperate to escape into an imagined world of wealth and glamour. They are conscious of their relative poverty and social deprivation and are anxious to be included into the cliques of rich and popular girls who seem to perpetually scorn and exclude them. These protagonists commonly find their redemption in a true friend—usually another unfashionable type—and in realizing that wealth is often merely a social facade. Moreover, wealth is usually equated with emotional poverty. Alison Ashley is a beautifully dressed, beautifully behaved interloper in the deprived world of Barringa East Primary School: she is also a lonely latchkey child whose high-powered executive mother has no time to give her the love she craves. Similarly, Angie's mother, in *Came Back to Show You I Could Fly,* has erased all evidence of her wayward daughter's presence from her former room in the spotless and elegant middle-class home, much as the family has apparently cut the disappointing teenage drug addict out of their elegant and well-regulated lives.

This plot tendency may display a predilection on Klein's part towards wish-fulfillment fantasy; the clichés, however, are not always acted out (Angie's parents do not, in the end, abandon her, while Seymour's domestic circumstances demonstrate that less-privileged homes may be as impoverished in love as rich ones). Fortunately, Klein's more mature writing demonstrates that she is flexible enough to show that these social and moral oppositions are never absolute.

She shows, too, the reality of life. In *Seeing Things,* Miranda's parents have died and she lives with a grandmother who struggles to make ends meet. Miranda seeks solace in her imagination and soon learns she has some clairvoyant ability, which brings her both the positive attention she craves, as well as negative attention. She is able to earn money, however, and this will help her grandmother. Miranda is at times contrary and seems to constantly complain, to the distraction of the reader. Yet, people do complain, and there is something very real in how Klein has handled this character.

People do also sometimes surprise us by acting out of character, as happens in *Dresses of Red and Gold.* Dad can't hold a job and doesn't exactly dote on his girls, but when Cathy boasts about the plans being made for her nonexistent birthday party, Dad improvises a treasure hunt for all the kids who show up uninvited. And Vivienne, too, has grown tremendously when she finally buys her long-coveted red-and-gold dress only to give it away to the sister of her most despised classmate.

Klein's girls are strong. They dream and have hope they can change their futures. In *The Sky in Silver Lace,* which continues the story of the Melling sisters begun in *All in the Blue Unclouded Weather,* the family has moved from the small town of Wilgawa to the large city. Their father is off to make his fortune and their mother struggles to raise the girls alone and find a permanent home while receiving both charity and spiteful remarks from a city relative. Each chapter focuses on the aspirations of one of the girls and her struggles to make a place in the world. Each girl learns and grows through her struggles and handles her own problems with inner strength and determination. In the end, even Vivienne, the youngest, realizes their father will not be returning and so they must become self-reliant. Klein's characters possess strengths as well as flaws that are realistic. Her characters have spunk and soon realize, as do the readers, that life is often a matter of what we make of it. Growth and hope are underlying threads in Klein's works that serve as inspiration for her readers.

—Leonie Margaret Rutherford, updated by Lisa A. Wroble

KNIGHT, Kathryn Lasky. *See* **LASKY, Kathryn.**

KNOWLES, John

Nationality: American. **Born:** Fairmont, West Virginia, 16 September 1926. **Education:** Phillips Exeter Academy, Exeter, New Hampshire, graduated 1945; Yale University, New Haven, Connecticut, B.A. 1949. **Career:** Reporter, Hartford *Courant,* Connecticut, 1950-52; freelance writer, 1952-56; associate editor, *Holiday* magazine, Philadelphia, 1956-60. Writer-in-residence, University of North Carolina, Chapel Hill, 1963-64, and Princeton University, New Jersey, 1968-69. **Awards:** Rosenthal Foundation award, William Faulkner Foundation award, both 1961, for *A Separate Peace;* National Association of Independent Schools award, 1961. **Address:** c/o Curtis Brown Ltd., 10 Astor Place, New York, New York 10003-6935, U.S.A.

PUBLICATIONS FOR YOUNG ADULTS

Novels

A Separate Peace. London, Secker and Warburg, 1959; New York, Macmillan, 1960.
Morning in Antibes. New York, Macmillan, and London, Secker and Warburg, 1962.
Indian Summer. New York, Random House, and London, Secker and Warburg, 1966.
The Paragon. New York, Random House, 1971.
Spreading Fires. New York, Random House, 1974.
A Vein of Riches. Boston, Little Brown, 1978.
Peace Breaks Out. New York, Holt Rinehart, 1981.
A Stolen Past. New York, Holt Rinehart, 1983; London, Constable, 1984.
The Private Life of Axie Reed. New York, Dutton, 1986.

Short Stories

Phineas: Six Stories. New York, Random House, 1968.

Other

Double Vision: American Thoughts Abroad. New York, Macmillan, and London, Secker and Warburg, 1964.

*

Media Adaptations: *A Separate Peace* (film), Paramount, 1972.

Biography: Entry in *Dictionary of Literary Biography,* Volume 6, Detroit, Gale, 1980.

Manuscript Collections: Beinecke Library, Yale University, New Haven, Connecticut.

Critical Studies: Entry in *Contemporary Literary Criticism,* Volume 1, Detroit, Gale, 1973; Volume 4, 1975; Volume 10, 1979.

*   *   *

John Knowles is best known for his first opus: *A Separate Peace.* The awards granted this work suggest one reason for its enormous popularity and persistence, especially in the academic milieu: it is a very useful text with which to teach students how a good book should be written.

Knowles's other novels have generally been judged by critics to display a pleasing style, a clear plot line, and a fine sense of place (perhaps a partial result of his work for *Holiday Magazine*)—but, *A Separate Peace* adds, in great measure, to these qualities three other elements of fiction that carry it beyond the other titles: a focused, useful point of view; a superb realization of character; and, a substantial, wholesome, and satisfying theme.

These attributes blend well in this minor classic. The first-person narrator, Gene Forrester (perhaps representing Knowles himself, at an earlier age), provides the point of view (the reader can know and feel only what the narrator observes and experiences), and this works to the novel's benefit, since the most important thrust in the text is Gene's feeling about, reaction to, and final understanding of the hero of the book: the delightful, admirable, charming Phineas (''Finny'').

Making such a truly amiable figure believable is one of the great triumphs of *A Separate Peace*. Knowles accomplishes this by combining the characteristics of a superb athlete, an indifferent student, a wildly daring young man, and a profoundly extroverted character all in one. The setting is the Devon School (based on Phillips Exeter Academy, attended by Knowles) in the summer of 1942. Since the Second World War has begun for the United States, the world conflict becomes a sort of analogue for the conflicts in the novel.

The salient feature of Finny's character—and a thematic force in the book—is his refusal to accept conflict: ''. . .there might be a flow of simple, unregulated friendliness between them, and such flows were one of Finny's reasons for living.'' This naturally charismatic boy (all but a few of the lads at the school are just a year or two too young to enlist in the military) is a credible counterpoise to the more introverted and intellectual Gene, who becomes his best friend and, indirectly, causes his death.

Since the events are told in retrospect, as Gene recalls them on a return visit to the school fifteen years later, the story gains substance from the more thoughtful recounting and interpreting of the plot and the people by an older person. Perhaps the most important interpretation is Gene's realization that Phineas was one of a kind: as he comments at the close of the book, regarding the difference between his friend and other people, ''All of them, all except Phineas, constructed at infinite cost to themselves these Maginot Lines against this enemy they thought they saw across the frontier, this enemy who never attacked that way—if he ever attacked at all; if he was indeed the enemy.''

Finny has shown his wonderful acceptance of people and his rejection of evil in his unwillingness to blame Gene for his disastrous fall from the tree, or for his friend's action when he does face the reality. In their last conversation, where Gene manages to convince Finny of his guilt, Finny interprets the motives in his typically generous way: ''Something just seized you. It wasn't anything you really felt against me, it wasn't some kind of hate you've felt all along. It wasn't anything personal.'' To make such a saintly character believable is possibly one of the great accomplishments in modern literature. Nowhere can one find, also, such a lively and engaging picture of adolescence. How many readers would like to find a friend, as Gene does, of whom he or she could say, ''Only Phineas was never afraid, only Phineas never hated anyone.''

Knowles's other works are less known, though his third novel, *Indian Summer*, was a selection of the Literary Guild. The prime complaint among critics is that the characters in these later works are not developed as fully and vigorously as those in *A Separate Peace*. In *The Paragon*, the central character, Lou Colfax, emerges with considerable clarity; however, the other personages (such as Gordon Durand and the other moneyed people in the plot) seem stereotyped.

In *Peace Breaks Out*, Knowles wisely returns to the Devon School, this time with a World War II veteran who is an instructor at the academy. Since the instructor is an alumnus of Devon, much is familiar; the students now attending are not so, however. Hallam is a less appealing protagonist than either Phineas or Gene Forrester, and once more the scattered point of view distracts the reader's attention. The plot somewhat echoes that of *A Separate Peace*, but the ambiance is far more grim and even sinister, as Hallam comes to grips with the fact that the war is not really over; treachery, hatred, and cruelty still exist, even in this idyllic setting. At the close, he thinks of the monstrous boy Wexford that he has encountered here. ''He is an incipient monster,. . .and I can't stop him. For the last dozen years we've seen in the world how monsters can come to the top and just what horrors they can achieve. And these monsters were once adolescents.'' He sees that monsters are forming even at Devon and that ''people will have to try to cope with them, confront them, risk everything in defeating them, defeating them once again, for a time.''

Clearly, this grimmer tone reveals adolescence—and, indeed, human nature—in a much darker fashion than *A Separate Peace*. However, the pervasiveness of war is keenly represented. While the personalities of the unappealing Wexford and Hochschwender are not fully outlined, their evil and misguided energy come to light, as in this observation by Hallam: ''Nothing could be more vicious than a fight between boys, lacking any trace of the caginess or caution of men.'' While the events and the people in *Peace Breaks Out* fail to attain the force to be found in *A Separate Peace*, this tightly woven story seems to come closest to that high achievement. In any judgment of Knowles's work, one fact is certain: one would have to look far to find an author who can so ably set forth the feelings, thoughts, and actions of young men, especially in crisis situations.

—Fred McEwen

KNUDSON, R.R

Pseudonym for Rozanne Knudson. **Nationality:** American. **Born:** Washington, D.C., 1 June 1932. **Education:** Brigham Young University, Provo, Utah, B.A. 1954; University of Georgia, Athens, M.A. 1958; Stanford University, Stanford, California, Ph.D. 1967. **Career:** English teacher in various public high schools in Florida, 1957-60; assistant professor of English, Purdue University, West Lafayette, Indiana, 1965-67; coeditor, *Quartet,* 1966-68; supervisor of English, Hicksville Schools, Long Island, New York, 1967-70; instructor in English, University of Lethbridge, Lethbridge, Alberta, summer 1969; assistant professor, York College of the City University of New York, Jamaica, New York, 1970-71; full-time writer, 1972—; writer-in-residence, Kean College, 1986. **Awards:** Nominee for Maud Lovelace Book award, for *Zanboomer*; nominee for Dorothy Canfield Fisher Book award, for *Zanbanger*; Fellow at MacDowell Colony, Virginia Center for the Creative Arts, Ragdale, Dorland Mountain Colony, Cummington Community of the Arts, Villa Montalvo, and Gell House. **Address:** 73 The Boulevard, Sea Cliff, New York 11579, U.S.A.

PUBLICATIONS FOR YOUNG ADULTS

Fiction

Sports Poetry, with P.K. Ebert. New York, Dell, 1971.
Zanballer. New York, Delacorte, 1972.
Jesus Song. New York, Delacorte, 1973.
You Are the Rain. New York, Delacorte, 1974.
Fox Running. New York, Harper, 1975.

Zanbanger. New York, Harper, 1977.
Zanboomer. New York, Harper, 1978.
Rinehart Lifts. New York, Farrar Straus, 1980.
Just Another Love Story. New York, Farrar Straus, 1982.
Speed. New York, Dutton, 1983.
Zan Hagan's Marathon. New York, Farrar Straus, 1984.
Frankenstein's 10K. New York, Viking, 1986.
Rinehart Shouts. New York, Farrar Straus, 1987.

Nonfiction

Selected Objectives for the English Language Arts, with Arnold
    Leslie Lazarus. Boston, Houghton Mifflin, 1967.
Books for You, with J.A. Wilson and others. New York, Washing-
    ton Square Press, 1971.
Starbodies, with Franco Columbo. New York, Elesvier-Dutton, 1978.
Weight Training for Young Athletes, with Franco Columbo. Chica-
    go, Illinois, Contemporary Books, 1979.
Muscles! New York, Avon, 1983.
Punch! New York, Avon, 1983.
Babe Didrikson: Athlete of the Century, illustrated by Ted Lewin.
    New York, Viking, 1985.
A Waterpower Workout, with Lynda Huey. New York, New
    American Library, 1986.
Martina Navratilova: Tennis Power, illustrated by George Angelini.
    New York, Viking, 1987.
Julie Brown: Racing against the World. New York, Viking, 1988.
Coaching Evelyn, with Pat Connolly. New York, Harper, 1990.
The Wonderful Pen of May Swenson. New York, Macmillan, 1993.
May Swenson: A Poet's Life in Photos. Logan, Utah, Utah State
    University Press, 1997.
Editor with May Swenson, *American Sports Poems.* New York,
    Orchard Books/F. Watts, 1988.

Other

Contributor, *The Scribner's Anthology for Young People.* New
    York, Scribner, 1976.

*

Manuscript Collections: Kerlan Collection, University of Minnesota.

R.R. Knudson comments:

I've written in silent rooms on Long Island and in Delaware,
Virginia, Georgia, Florida, Arizona, California, and in New Hampshire. I've written only about my obsessions, and almost all of my
characters are myself. Read my novels if you want to know more.

*　　*　　*

Most of R.R. Knudson's books deal with sports in one form or
another, but they are so enjoyably written that even a nonparticipant
can read them and be engrossed in the wants and needs of
Knudson's characters. Her writing is clean and straightforward,
lacking in lavish detail but filled with action and goals.

Her best known books are perhaps her series about the good-at-
all-sports Suzanne Hagan, called ''Zan'' by her peers. Zan lives for

sports of all kinds and is supported by her parents and best friend,
the bookish Arthur Rinehart.

The first book in the series is *Zanballer* and is devoted to girls
playing the man's sport of football. When the Robert E. Lee High
School's gym is being refurbished, the girl's gym class is relegated
to the home economics wing to learn to dance. Zan refuses to dance
and begs to use the lacrosse field. Through Zan's begging and
Rinehart's scheming, enough girls are coaxed from dancing to
make a football team, and the coach takes notice. Once the girl's
team, Catch-11, ties in a game with his junior varsity squad, even
the reluctant principal bows to pressure from the press, and Catch-
11, led by Zan, wins a special exhibition game played against the
Richmond Redskins Junior Varsity.

Zanballer touches on some issues of concern to teenagers,
especially girls, and reflects the growing willingness of schools to
integrate girls into the previously all-male teams. Zan's fight
against the principal, who tries through the entire series to force her
into his idea of what a girl should be, is encouraging. That she wins
in the end is even more so, since her victory is only achieved by
being as good as the boys.

In *Zanbanger,* Zan and her friend E.J. are preparing for the
girl's basketball season with delight. The gym floor is repaired, and
the girl's team is ready to go—until Mrs. Butor, *Zanballer's* dance
teacher, is named as the coach. Mrs. Butor coaches polite, restrained play, and Zan is cut from the team for being ''too
aggressive.'' When Zan practices with the boys' team, she excels,
and that gives her the idea to try out for boys' basketball. The
principal forbids it, the community is outraged, and Zan goes to
court to win the right to be allowed to play. Rinehart, acting as her
lawyer, defends not only Zan's right to play with the boys, but the
right of any girl who wants to, anywhere. Even though Zan's court
battle is won, her troubles are only beginning since the boys' team
is hostile toward both Zan and E.J. and refuses to help the two girls
on the court. By the book's end, Zan and E.J. have won over the
team, and the Generals have won the championship, once again
beating the Redskins.

In *Zanboomer,* Zan, E.J., and Aileen, the prom queen turned
player, reunite on the boys' baseball team. In a game with the
Redskins, Zan is injured by Joe Donn Joiner, her enemy throughout
the books. Shoulder separated, Zan can no longer play baseball,
and in an attempt to keep her from eating her heart out over the loss
of her team, Rinehart introduces her to long-distance running. Zan
practices diligently, and by the end of the school year, she has once
again defeated the Redskins, and Joe Donn Joiner's attempt to
cheat Zan out of the race ends in failure.

Zan Hagan's Marathon puts Zan on the Olympic Team as a
long-distance runner again, where instead of winning her race, she
ties it, finally learning that winning is not all there is.

The first three books are written from Zan's point of view, with
Rinehart getting a chapter for his opinions and view of what is
happening to Zan. Each character is distinctly written, and Rinehart's
scientific approach to sports is humorous and amusing. Knudson
portrays the feelings of winning, losing, and almost being good
enough with the intensity of a young person, and is careful not to
bring adult responses to adolescent characters.

Another very noteworthy book is *Fox Running,* the story of Fox
Running, a Mescalero Apache girl who runs away from her
reservation after the death of her grandfather. Found by Kathy
''Sudden'' Hart, a former Olympic sprinter who has lost her nerve
to race, and Sudden's coach, Fox's potential as a runner is

discovered. Brought back to the University of Arizona, Fox proves to be useless to the coach since she is gun-shy and cannot bear the sound of the starter's pistol. Sudden will not give up on Fox, just as Fox refuses to allow Sudden to let her fears manipulate her future as a sprinter. Both learn from each other's pasts, and the book culminates triumphantly at the Olympics, where both Fox and Sudden win their races—Fox setting a new women's world record for the mile.

Fox Running is a gently told story of two hurt people, and how each finds the courage to go on. Fear of the past is the primary theme, with a secondary theme of perseverance. Both Sudden and Fox are well-drawn and distinct characters, people in their own right, and easy to care about. Knudson's secondary characters are also as clearly drawn, and memorable. All of R.R. Knudson's books are good, well-written sports stories, about believable, real people.

—Melanie Belviso

KOERTGE, Ron(ald)

Nationality: American. **Born:** Olney, Illinois, 22 April 1940. **Education:** University of Illinois, Urbana, B.A. 1962; University of Arizona, Tucson, M.A. 1965. **Family:** Married 1) Cheryl Vasconcellos; 2) Bianaca Richards. **Career:** Professor of English, Pasadena City College, California, from 1965. **Awards:** American Library Association Best Book citation and ALA book for reluctant readers, for *Where the Kissing Never Stops*; ALA Best Book citation, *Booklist*'s Books of the Decade, and Young Adult Library Association's 100 Best of the Best, for *Arizona Kid*; ALA Best Book citation, for *The Boy in the Moon*; Maine Student Book Award choice, for *Mariposa Blues*; National Endowment for the Arts Fellowship, 1990; California Arts Council grant, 1993; ALA Best Book citation, ALA Notable Book citation, New York Public Library choice for books for the Teen Age, all for *The Harmony Arms*; ALA Best Book citation, New York Library 100 Best Children's Books list, Bulletin for the Center for Children's Books Blue Ribbon Book, Bank Street Child Study Children's Book Committee Choice for Book of the Year, Judy Lopez Memorial Award Honor Book, YALSA Best Books for Young Adults list, all 1994, all for *Tiger, Tiger Burning Bright*; *School Journal*'s Best Books citation, 1996, for *Confess-O-Rama*. **Address:** Department of English, Pasadena City College, 1560 Colorado Boulevard, Pasadena, California 91106, U.S.A.

PUBLICATIONS FOR YOUNG ADULTS

Fiction

Where the Kissing Never Stops. New York, Atlantic Monthly, 1987.
The Arizona Kid. Boston, Joy Street, 1988.
The Boy in the Moon. Boston, Joy Street, 1990.
Mariposa Blues. Boston, Joy Street, 1991.
The Harmony Arms. Boston, Joy Street, 1992.
Tiger, Tiger, Burning Bright. New York, Orchard Books, 1994.
Confess-O-Rama. New York, Orchard Books, 1996.
The Heart of the City. New York, Orchard Books, 1998.

Poetry

Meat: Cherry's Market Diary. Mag Press, 1973.
The Father Poems. Fremont, Michigan, Sumac Press, 1974.
The Hired Nose. Mag Press, 1974.
My Summer Vacation. Venice Poetry Company, 1975.
Men under Fire. Fallon, Nevada, Duck Down Press, 1976.
Twelve Photographs of Yellowstone. San Francisco, California, Red Hill Press, 1976.
How to Live on Five Dollars a Day. Venice Poetry Company, 1976.
Cheap Thrills. Stockton, California, Wormwood Review Press, 1976.
Sex Object. Los Angeles, Little Caesar Press, 1979.
The Jockey Poems. Cape Elizabeth, Maine, Maelstrom Press, 1980.
Diary Cows. Los Angeles, Little Caeser Press, 1982.
Life on the Edge of the Continent: Selected Poems. Fayetteville, Arkansas, University of Arkansas Press, 1982.
High School Dirty Poems. Los Angeles, California, Red Wind, 1991.
Making Love to Roget's Wife. Fayetteville, Arkansas, University of Arkansas Press, 1997.

PUBLICATIONS FOR ADULTS

Fiction

The Boogeyman. New York, Norton, 1980.

*

Biography: Entry in *Dictionary of Literary Biography,* Vol. 105, Detroit, Gale, 1991; essay in *Speaking for Ourselves, Too,* compiled and edited by Donald R. Gallo, Urbana, Illinois, National Council of Teachers of English, 1993.

Ron Koertge comments:

I never intended to be a young adult writer, so it's a surprise to me and a lot more fun than if I'd become the sort of writer I'd planned. In a sense it was the failure to write a second novel after *The Boogeyman* that made it possible for me to succeed as a YA novelist. I like writing for kids, and as long as ideas for books keep showing up, I'll keep writing.

*   *   *

With eight thoughtful and inspiring coming-of-age young adult novels under his belt, Ron Koertge has established himself as a talented and popular author of contemporary realistic fiction that aptly chronicles the adolescent experience. Koertge's style is direct and natural; a remarkable ear for, and an emphasis on, dialogue serves to immediately engage the reader in the story. Enormously likeable, Koertge's fully-realized characters are convincingly honest, loyal to family and friends, and display a strong sense of integrity despite their teenage angst. One of Koertge's greatest gifts to his readers is his irresistibly witty sense of humor. While he frequently uses humor to reveal character, Koertge never downplays the seriousness of universal adolescent concerns. His books are both affecting and funny—a rare feat in a field deluged with issue-oriented books often overwhelmed by sentimentality or triteness.

"God, I thought about sex a lot," says sixteen-year-old Walker in Koertge's first novel, *Where the Kissing Never Stops.* Walker's preoccupation with sex introduces a concern important to many of Koertge's characters. In a frank and funny exploration of sexuality, Walker struggles to nurture a romantic, fulfilling relationship with his girlfriend Rachel and to keep his mother's embarrassing occupation as a roadhouse stripper a secret from her. The consummation of Walker and Rachel's relationship is caring and respectful; Walker moves toward a mature acceptance of his mother's job when he realizes how happy it makes her. Dialogue about masturbation and body image is candid, but Koertge depicts Walker as both vulnerable and tender, much more than just a horny teenager out for some action.

Sexuality also plays an important role in *The Arizona Kid*. The story's narrator—sixteen-year-old Billy, self-conscious about being too short, too pale, and too virginal—arrives in Tucson to spend the summer with his gay Uncle Wes. Billy faces a summer of change and discovery as he experiences firsthand the colorful world of horse racing, falls head-over-heels in love, loses his virginity, and learns about his uncle's gay lifestyle. Billy's relationship with his feisty, understanding girlfriend Cara Mae boosts his shaky self-confidence; warm, witty, and generous Uncle Wes fosters Billy's growing sense of independence. Billy, at first uncertain how to behave in his uncle's company, quickly overcomes his discomfort as he and Wes develop a natural rapport and share frank, often funny discussions about romance, AIDS, and birth control. Koertge presents a range of sexuality with sensitivity and openness, but leavens serious themes with plentiful doses of humor. At summer's end a newly confident and assured Billy tells Uncle Wes that "I'm as tall as I am. It's okay."

High school seniors Nick, Freida, and Kevin have been best friends forever, but suddenly things change dramatically in *The Boy in the Moon*. First Kevin turns into a bleached-blond musclehead with whom the acne-riddled, insecure, self-effacing Nick has trouble relating. Then Nick finds himself romantically attracted to Freida. Nick and Freida's mutual attraction culminates in their first awkward but loving sexual experience. As Freida's caring and commitment help Nick overcome his insecurity and instill in him a sense of self-worth, Nick and Freida's support of Kevin help him deal with an abusive, alcoholic father. At summer's finish the trio part company, their friendship solidified and strengthened by their shared, transforming experiences.

Mariposa Blues, set against the backdrop of a southern California racetrack, also chronicles a summer of change and confusion. After years of being considered a "chip off the old block," thirteen-year-old Grahame struggles to establish an identity separate from that of his father and finds himself engaged in constant confrontations with him. By summer's end, father and son move toward reconciliation and a fuller understanding of each other. Grahame's confusion and alienation from his father is portrayed in a vivid and credible manner, especially in the stormy confrontational scenes.

The Harmony Arms focuses on some of Koertge's quirkiest characters. Fourteen-year-old Gabriel McKay's father Sumner, an eccentric who uses a ubiquitous handpuppet named Timmy the Otter as his mouthpiece and pretends his suitcase is a dog named Rover, causes Gabriel endless embarrassment. Then father and son move temporarily to Los Angeles, where Gabriel discovers his neighbors—a ninety-year-old vegetarian nudist; a mostly offtarget psychic; an actress/animals-rights activist; and her daughter Tess, a fourteen-year-old aspiring filmmaker who carries a camcorder everywhere to film her life as it takes place—are just as offbeat as his father. As Gabriel and Tess develop a romantic friendship, they commiserate together over the mortifying and often unfathomable actions of their parents. Anything-goes L.A. helps to give Gabriel a new perspective on himself and his father; when Tess remarks about her mother that "you gotta throw away a lot of weird stuff, but what's left is pretty good," Gabriel comprehends that her comment holds true for Sumner as well. Infused with humor and snappy dialogue, Koertge's funniest novel offers the reader an oddball, unconventional, but enormously appealing coming-of-age story.

Koertge explores similar themes in *Tiger, Tiger, Burning Bright* (1994) and *Confess-O-Rama* (1996) that appear in his earlier work, but he delves into new territory in his most recent title, *The Heart of the City* (1998), a novel that moves away from the male adolescent coming-of-age story to explore the lives of two ten-year-old African-American girls living in inner-city Los Angeles. Joy Fontaine and her parents move from the upscale suburban Woodland Hills to Ibarra Street, a move that Joy and her mother furiously protest. Although quite unhappy, Joy learns to adjust to her new environment with the help of Neesha, her next-door neighbor, who teaches her the importance of street smarts, "rappin'," and striking an attitude. When the neighborhood is threatened by gang members who want to take over an abandoned house for their drug deals, Joy and Neesha organize their community and triumph, at least temporarily. In his chronicle of the girl's experiences, Koertge promotes racial harmony, community solidarity, and exposes economic, racial, and cultural prejudices. Unfortunately, his praiseworthy efforts are overshadowed by almost unbearable political correctness and lessons too great even for 10-year-olds to understand. Indeed, Koertge is uncharacteristically preachy and heavy-handed in his social messages. Most disappointing is the absence of his trademark humor, which often balances the seriousness of the issues he addresses in his work.

Needless to say, these criticisms do not mar Koertge's well-earned and deserving reputation as a fine young adult writer. His spirited, funny stories, uniquely attuned to contemporary adolescent concerns, offer their readers easy companionship while providing them with provocative explorations of sexuality and self-identity. As readers navigate the perilous realms of their own adolescence, they will surely want Koertge's books along to help ease their way.

—Carolyn Shute, updated by Rebecca R. Saulsbury

KONIGSBURG, E(laine) L(obl)

Nationality: American. **Born:** New York City, 10 February 1930. **Education:** Farrell High School, Pennsylvania; Carnegie Institute of Technology (now Carnegie-Mellon University), Pittsburgh, B.S. 1952; University of Pittsburgh, 1952-54. **Family:** Married David Konigsburg in 1952; two sons and one daughter. **Career:** Writer. Bookkeeper, Shenango Valley Provision Company, Sharon, Pennsylvania, 1947-48; science teacher, Bartram School, Jacksonville, Florida, 1954-55, 1960-62. Worked as manager of a dormitory laundry, playground instructor, waitress and library page while in college; research assistant in tissue culture lab and organic chemistry while in graduate school at the University of Pittsburgh. **Awards:** Honor book in *Book Week* Children's Spring

Book Festival, 1967, and Newbery Honor Book, 1968, for *Jennifer, Hecate, Macbeth, William McKinley, and Me, Elizabeth*; Newbery Medal, 1968, and William Allen White award, 1970, both for *From the Mixed-Up Files of Mrs. Basil E. Frankweiler*; Carnegie-Mellon Merit award, 1971; American Library Association notable children's book and National Book award nomination, both 1974, both for *A Proud Taste for Scarlet and Miniver*; American Library Association best book for young adults, for *The Second Mrs. Giaconda*, and *Father's Arcane Daughter*; American Library Association notable children's book and American Book award nomination, 1980, both for *Throwing Shadows; Jennifer, Hecate, Macbeth, William McKinley, and Me, Elizabeth, About the B'nai Bagels, A Proud Taste for Scarlet and Miniver*, and *Journey to an 800 Number* were all chosen Children's Books of the Year by the Child Study Association of America. **Address:** c/o Atheneum, 1230 Avenue of the Americas, New York, New York 10020, U.S.A.

PUBLICATIONS FOR YOUNG ADULTS (illustrated by the author)

Fiction

From the Mixed-Up Files of Mrs. Basil E. Frankweiler. New York, Atheneum, 1967; London, Macmillan, 1969.

Jennifer, Hecate, Macbeth, William McKinley, and Me, Elizabeth. New York, Atheneum, 1967; as *Jennifer, Hecate, MacBeth, and Me*, London, Macmillan, 1968.

About the B'nai Bagels. New York, Atheneum, 1969.

(George). New York, Atheneum, 1970; as *Benjamin Dickenson Carr and His (George)*, London, Penguin, 1974.

Altogether, One at a Time (stories), illustrated by Gail E. Haley, Mercer Meyer, Gary Parker, and Laurel Schindelman. New York, Atheneum, 1971; 2nd edition, London, Macmillan, 1989.

A Proud Taste for Scarlet and Miniver. New York, Atheneum, 1973; London, Macmillan, 1974.

The Dragon in the Ghetto Caper. New York, Atheneum, 1974; London, Macmillan, 1979.

Father's Arcane Daughter. New York, Atheneum, 1976; London, Macmillan, 1977.

Throwing Shadows (stories). New York, Atheneum, 1979.

Journey to an 800 Number. New York, Atheneum, 1982; as *Journey by First Class Camel*, London, Hamish Hamilton, 1983.

Up from Jericho Tel. New York, Atheneum, 1986.

Samuel Todd's Book of Great Colors. New York, Macmillan, 1990.

Samuel Todd's Book of Great Inventions. New York, Atheneum, 1991.

Amy Elizabeth Explores Bloomingdale's. New York, Atheneum, 1992.

T-Backs, T-Shirts, COAT and Suit. New York, Atheneum, 1993.

The View from Saturday. New York, Atheneum, 1996.

Other

Contributor, *Expectations 1980* (braille anthology). E. Falmouth, Massachusetts, Braille Institute, 1980.

The Mask beneath the Face; Reading about and with, Writing about and for Children. Washington, D.C., Library of Congress, 1990.

Talktalk: A Children's Book Author Speaks to Grown-ups. New York, Atheneum, 1995.

*

Media Adaptations: *From the Mixed-Up Files of Mrs. Basil E. Frankweiler* (record; cassette), Miller-Brody/Random House, 1969; *From the Mixed-Up Files of Mrs. Basil E. Frankweiler* (motion picture) starring Ingrid Bergman, Cinema 5, 1973, released under new title *The Hideaways*, Bing Crosby Productions, 1974; *Jennifer and Me* (television movie; based on *Jennifer, Hecate, Macbeth, William McKinley, and Me, Elizabeth*), NBC-TV, 1973; *The Second Mrs. Giaconda* (play), first produced in Jacksonville, Florida, 1976. *Jennifer, Hecate, Macbeth, William McKinley, and Me, Elizabeth* (cassette), Listening Library, 1986; *Caroline?* (based on *Father's Arcane Daughter*), Hallmark Hall of Fame Presentation, 1990.

Manuscript Collections: University of Pittsburgh, Pennsylvania.

Biography: Entry in *Third Book of Junior Authors*, New York, H.W. Wilson, 1972; essay in *Authors and Illustrators of Children's Books: Writings on Their Lives and Works*, New York, Bowker, 1972; entry in *Dictionary of Literary Biography*, Volume 52, Detroit, Gale, 1986; *E. L. Konigsburg* by Dorrel Thomas Hanks, Jr., New York, Twayne, 1992; essay in *Speaking for Ourselves, Too* compiled and edited by Donald R. Gallo, National Council of Teachers of English, 1993.

Critical Studies: Entry in *Children's Literature Review*, Volume 1, Detroit, Gale, 1976; *Your Arcane Novelist: E. L. Konigsberg* by David Rees, Horn Book, 1978.

*   *   *

E. L. Konigsburg writes warm, funny books about young people who are searching for independence and adventure. Her style is crisp and clear, peppered with humorous details.

Her first book, *Jennifer, Hecate, Macbeth, William McKinley and Me, Elizabeth*, finds Elizabeth in a new apartment in suburban New York City. She always walks the back road to school alone and she feels very lonely. Enter Jennifer, a witch who also happens to go to William McKinley Elementary School and is also in the fifth grade. Jennifer allows Elizabeth to become her apprentice; Elizabeth has to learn, among other things, how to eat raw eggs and uncooked oatmeal, cast short spells, and get along with Jennifer. Over the school year the girls meet each Saturday at the library and go from there to the park, where they read books on witchcraft and hold special ceremonies. Hecate, the queen of the witches in *Macbeth*, is one of the witches that Jennifer looks to for instruction in the finer accomplishments of witchcraft. In the end, Jennifer and Elizabeth's best joint effort in witchcraft does not work, but by then the girls find that they don't have to be witches anymore, they can just be friends.

From the Mixed-Up Files of Mrs. Basil E. Frankweiler won the Newbery award in 1968 and later a William Allen White award. It was made into a major motion picture by Westfall Productions. This story is about Claudia Kincaid, who runs away from home to teach her parents a lesson in Claudia appreciation. She invites her young brother, Jamie, to go with her, to be a companion and to help finance the trip. They leave Greenwich, Connecticut, for the Metropolitan Museum of Art, to live comfortably and interestingly. Claudia's choice of the Met as a getaway proves to be a good one. Thousands of school children visit the museum every day, so

Claudia and Jamie walk unnoticed. The Met has a snack bar for sustenance and ample rest rooms. And there are rooms of fine French and English furniture from which to choose comfortable bedding. Claudia chooses a wonderful French bed dating from the sixteenth century. Once the fun of settling in is over though, Claudia is disappointed that she doesn't feel differently. Then she finds a statue at the museum so beautiful that she has to discover its maker. The former owner of the statue is Mrs. Basil E. Frankweiler, and with Mrs. Frankweiler's help, she learns about the statue and finds a way to go back home gracefully.

About the B'nai Bagels stars Mark Setzer, who is twelve years old and worries about his performance at his Bar Mitzvah. He also worries about his performance on the Little League baseball team, the B'nai B'rith (everyone calls it the B'nai Bagels). Mark has a special reason for concern with his baseball playing, because the manager of the team is his mother Bessie (everyone calls her Mother Bagel) and the coach of the team is his brother Spencer (everyone calls him Brother Bagel). In the end, the B'nai Bagels have a good season. Mark plays a good center field, and he and the manager and the coach gain a closer appreciation of one another.

Journey to an 800 Number is a beguiling story of love and friendship. Seventh grader Maximillian Stubbs is sent to stay with his father while his mother is on a first-class honeymoon cruise with a rich elderly man from Philadelphia. Max's father is a camel-keeper; his camel's name is Ahmed. Max does not like the fact that his father is a camel-keeper, he does not like Ahmed, and he does not appreciate sharing a less-than-first-class way of life in a trailer park in the American southwest. During the month Max spends with his father, Ahmed gives rides in a shopping center, takes part in a travel agents' convention and a state fair, and performs in a Las Vegas night club act. Max makes friends with people who run a taco stand at the fair, summer ranch hands, and a young girl named Sabrina whose mother pretends a lot. Sabrina explains that in real life, "my mother is an eight hundred number." Her mother is one of a hundred people who sit in a room taking orders from about eighty mail catalogues. She is always a polite voice, never a face. By the end of this month, Max has learned some things about first-class, the art of pretending, kindness, and loyalty. This is a deeply moving book about survival and about connectedness.

Up from Jericho Tel is about two sixth-grade latchkey children who live with single parents in the Empire Estates Mobile Homes Park on Long Island. These children are different from the clones of Singer Grove Middle School who live in houses, have two parents, and whose mothers make cakes for PTA bake sales. Jeanmarie Troxell and Malcolm Soo are independent and ambitious—she to be a famous actress and he to be a famous scientist. And they are adventurous, adventurous enough to meet a quite dead actress named Tallulah, who allows them mysteries to solve and the ability, for short periods, to be invisible. Being invisible starts something inside them, and Jeanmarie and Malcolm learn things about their inner selves. The two do solve the mysteries and importantly, they gain confidence to become the famous people they wish to be.

Konigsburg's books are fresh and spirited, filled with delightful humor. Her plots are original and suspenseful, her characters are colorful and strong. The reader should look carefully at her sparse illustrations (Konigsburg is also an artist), for they often reveal additional dimensions to the fine stories.

—Mary Lystad

KOONTZ, Dean R.

Pseudonyms: David Axton; Brian Coffey; Deanna Dwyer; K. R. Dwyer; John Hill; Leigh Nichols; Anthony North; Owen West. **Nationality:** American. **Born:** Everett, Pennsylvania, 9 July 1945. **Education:** Shippensburg State College, B.A. in English, 1966. **Family:** Married Gerda Ann Cerra in 1966. **Career:** Worked as teacher and counselor in Appalachian Poverty Program, Saxton, Pennsylvania, 1966-67; English teacher, Mechanicsburg school district, Pennsylvania, 1967-69. Full-time writer, from 1969. **Awards:** Creative writing award, *Atlantic Monthly,* 1966, for "The Kittens"; Hugo award nomination, 1971, for *Beastchild.* D.Litt.: Shippensburg State College, 1989. **Agent:** Robert Gottlieb, William Morris Agency, 1325 Avenue of the Americas, New York, New York, 10019, U.S.A. **Address:** P.O. Box 9529, Newport Beach, California 92658-9529, U.S.A.

PUBLICATIONS

Novels

Star Quest. New York, Ace, 1968.
The Fall of the Dream Machine. New York, Ace, 1969.
Fear That Man. New York, Ace, 1969.
Anti-Man. New York, Paperback Library, 1970.
Beastchild. New York, Lancer, 1970.
Dark of the Woods. New York, Ace, 1970.
The Dark Symphony. New York, Lancer, 1970.
Hell's Gate. New York, Lancer, 1970.
The Crimson Witch. New York, Curtis, 1971.
A Darkness in My Soul. New York, DAW, 1972; London, Dobson, 1979.
The Flesh in the Furnace. New York, Bantam, 1972.
Starblood. New York, Lancer, 1972.
Time Thieves. New York, Ace, 1972; London, Dobson, 1977.
Warlock. New York, Lancer, 1972.
A Werewolf among Us. New York, Ballantine, 1973.
Hanging On. New York, Evans, 1973; London, Barrie and Jenkins, 1974.
The Haunted Earth. New York, Lancer, 1973.
Demon Seed. New York, Bantam, 1973; London, Corgi, 1977.
After the Last Race. New York, Atheneum, 1974.
Nightmare Journey. New York, Berkley, 1975.
Night Chills. New York, Atheneum, 1976; London, W.H. Allen, 1977.
The Vision. New York, Putnam, 1977; London, Corgi, 1980.
Whispers. New York, Putnam, 1980; London, W.H. Allen, 1981.
Phantoms. New York, Putnam, and London, W.H. Allen, 1983.
Darkness Comes. London, W.H. Allen, 1984; as *Darkfall,* New York, Berkley, 1984.
Twilight Eyes. Plymouth, Michigan, Land of Enchantment, 1985.
Strangers. New York, Putnam, and London, W.H. Allen, 1986.
Watchers. New York, Putnam, and London, Headline, 1987.
Oddkins: A Fable for All Ages, illustrated by Phil Parks. New York, Warner, and London, Headline, 1988.
Lightning. New York, Putnam, and London, Headline, 1988.
Midnight. New York, Putnam, and London, Headline, 1989.
The Bad Place. New York, Putnam, and London, Headline, 1990.
Cold Fire. New York, Putnam, and London, Headline, 1991.

Dean R. Koontz: Three Complete Novels, The Servants of Twilight, Darkfall, Phantoms. Avenel, New Jersey, Outlet Book Company, 1991.
Dean R. Koontz: A New Collection. New York, Wings Books, 1992.
Hideaway. New York, Putnam, 1992.
Dragon Tears. New York, Putnam, 1993.
Mr. Murder. New York, Putnam, 1993.
Dark Rivers of the Heart. New York, Knopf, 1994.
Winter Moon. New York, Ballantine, 1994.
Intensity. New York, Knopf, 1996.
Sole Survivor. New York, Knopf, 1997.
Ticktock. New York, Ballantine, 1997.
Fear Nothing. New York, Bantam, 1998.

Novels as David Axton

Prison of Ice. Philadelphia, Lippincott, and London, W.H. Allen, 1976.

Novels as Brian Coffey

Blood Risk. Indianapolis, Bobbs Merrill, 1973; London, Barker, 1974.
Surrounded. Indianapolis, Bobbs Merrill, 1974; London, Barker, 1975.
The Wall of Masks. Indianapolis, Bobbs Merrill, 1975.
The Face of Fear. Indianapolis, Bobbs Merrill, 1977; as K. R. Dwyer, London, Davies, 1978.
The Voice of the Night. New York, Doubleday, 1980; London, Hale, 1981.

Novels as Deanna Dwyer

The Demon Child. New York, Lancer, 1971.
Legacy of Terror. New York, Lancer, 1971.
Children of the Storm. New York, Lancer, 1972.
The Dark of Summer. New York, Lancer, 1972.
Dance with the Devil. New York, Lancer, 1973.

Novels as K.R. Dwyer

Chase. New York, Random House, 1972; London, Barker, 1974.
Shattered. New York, Random House, 1973; London, Barker, 1974.
Dragonfly. New York, Random House, 1975; London, Davies, 1977.

Novels as Anthony North

Strike Deep. New York, Dial Press, 1974.

Novels as Aaron Wolfe

Invasion. Don Mills, Ontario, Laser Books, 1975.

Novels as John Hill

The Long Sleep. New York, Popular Library, 1975.

Novels as Leigh Nichols

The Key to Midnight. New York, Pocket Books, 1979; London, Magnum, 1980.
The Eyes of Darkness. New York, Pocket Books, 1981; London, Fontana, 1982.

The House of Thunder. New York, Pocket Books, 1982; London, Fontana, 1983.
Twilight. New York, Pocket Books, and London, Fontana, 1984; as Dean R. Koontz as *The Servants of Twilight,* New York, Berkley, 1988.
Shadowfires. New York, Avon, and London, Collins, 1987.

Novels as Owen West

The Funhouse (novelization of screenplay). New York, Jove, 1980; London, Sphere, 1981.
The Mask. New York, Jove, 1981; London, Coronet, 1983.

Novels as Richard Paige

The Door to December. New York, New American Library, 1985; as Leigh Nichols, London, Fontana, 1987.

Short Stories

Soft Come the Dragons. New York, Ace, 1970.

Other

The Pig Society, with Gerda Koontz. Los Angeles, Aware Press, 1970.
The Underground Lifestyles Handbook, with Gerda Koontz. Los Angeles, Aware Press, 1970.
Contributor, *Again, Dangerous Vision,* edited by Harlan Ellison. New York, Doubleday, 1972.
Contributor, *Infinity 3,* edited by Robert Haskins. New York, Lancer, 1972.
Contributor, *Infinity 4,* edited by Robert Haskins. New York, Lancer, 1972.
Contributor, *Androids, Time Machines, and Blue Giraffes,* edited by Roger Elwood and Vic Ghidalia. Follett, 1973.
Contributor, *Flame Tree Planet,* edited by Roger Elwood. St. Louis, Missouri, Concordia, 1973.
Contributor, *Future City,* edited by Roger Elwood. New York, Simon and Schuster, 1973.
Contributor, *Infinity 5,* edited by Robert Haskins. New York, Lancer, 1973.
Writing Popular Fiction. Cincinnati, Writer's Digest, 1973.
Contributor, *Children of Infinity,* edited by Roger Elwood. New York, Putnam, 1974.
Contributor, *Final Stage,* edited by Edward L. Ferman and Barry N. Malzberg. Charterhouse, 1974.
How to Write Best-selling Fiction. Cincinnati, Writer's Digest, and London, Poplar Press, 1981.
Contributor, *Night Visions Four.* Arlington Heights, Illinois, Dark Harvest, 1987.
Contributor, *Night Visions Six.* Arlington Heights, Illinois, Dark Harvest, 1988.
Contributor, *Stalkers: All New Tales of Terror and Suspense* (stories), edited by Ed Gorman and Martin H. Greenberg, illustrated by Paul Sonju. Arlington Heights, Illinois, Dark Harvest, 1989.
Cold Terror: The Writings of Dean R. Koontz, edited by Bill Munster. Lancaster, Pennsylvania, Underwood Miller, 1990.
Santa's Twin. New York, HarperCollins, 1996.

*

Media Adaptations: *Demon Seed* (film), MGM/UA, 1977; *Shattered* (film), Warner Bros., 1977; *Watchers* (film), Universal, 1988; *Intensity* (miniseries), Fox Network, 1997; *Phantoms* (film), Miramax/Dimension, 1998; *Mr. Murder* (miniseries), ABC television, 1998.

Biography: Essay in *Authors and Artists for Young Adults,* Volume 9, Detroit, Gale, 1992.

*   *   *

Many thriller or horror novelists achieve their success through strong plotting and description. Dean R. Koontz takes this genre a step further by pulling readers into his stories emotionally. His characters seem real, with fears and desires readers can relate to. He builds suspense not only through plot but through the use of foreshadowing. These hints about the possible outcome of the story plunge readers forward, as if they are detectives who must find out if their instincts prove true. Koontz also appeals to readers' senses with skillfully drawn metaphors and similes. But to prevent his work from becoming too overbearing, Koontz often includes elements of romance, humor, and spirituality in his books. As a result, Koontz engages readers with various interests, which has propelled many of his novels of dark suspense to the top of bestseller lists.

Koontz often elevates the theme of good versus evil, elements of which we all possess, through the use of unique metaphors. In *Visions,* for example, the sound of leathery wings fluttering against the air represents an evil lingering on the threshold of the occult. It recurs throughout the book, remaining mysterious, yet with each occurrence gaining strength and revealing more clues as to its origin. Like the clairvoyant whose visions it invades, the reader can almost recognize the object making the sound, yet fears identifying it.

In *The Voice of the Night,* evil is represented by a sound in the dark only shy, fearful Colin seems to hear. It murmurs and whispers, mixing with the natural night sounds. In the novel, fourteen-year-old Colin is befriended by Roy, his total opposite. Roy is strong, confident, and fearless, but Colin senses there is something else very different about Roy. Colin struggles with the gray areas between good and evil.

Koontz uses another metaphor, evil in the form of a dark secret, in *The Mask* and *The House of Thunder.* In each story, a secret from the past haunts the main character, threatening to push her over the edge of sanity. In *The House of Thunder,* Susan constantly relives the nightmare of witnessing her boyfriend's murder thirteen years before. Since she has never come to terms with the event, it remains her secret fear. This dark secret ripples through her mind, merging reality and delusion. It seems that the living dead have returned to take their vengeance on her, their accuser.

Koontz's use of simile and strong descriptive passages provide a further sensation that bonds readers to his stories and characters. His fascinating similes for fear invoke foreboding and often grip more than one of the senses. Koontz's novels are filled with the horrors our anxieties ignite: murder, death, phobias, the occult, insanity, the evils that lurk in the shadows of our rooms and our minds. Yet a positive sense of hope also graces his pages. Though readers are distressed by the uncertainty, in the recesses of their minds they know good will prevail in the end. Perhaps this is what draws young adult readers to Koontz's novels. The uncertainty, the struggle to gain control of one's life is the very element young adult readers are struggling with in their own lives. They can identify with the characters, the action, and the themes. Like Colin in *The Voice of the Night,* young adults are coming to grips with the gray areas in life.

Though most of his books are read by adults or young adults, Koontz did write one book targeted to younger readers on the edge of adolescence. *The Oddkins,* labeled "a fable for all ages," adds the element of fantasy to the good versus evil theme. It speaks to the child within us all; the child who is reluctant to deal with the complexities of gray areas in life, and the child who wishes the world could again be simple black and white.

The Oddkins is about magical toys created for special children who need a friend to survive a crisis in their young lives. Though soft and stuffed, the Oddkins are alive and can speak to and comfort their child until that time when he no longer needs a secret friend. Then the Oddkins become merely stuffed toys and the child's memories of his secret friend fade into the innocence of childhood fantasy. When their creator dies, evil toys, created decades earlier to hurt children, emerge from the subcellar of his toy factory to spread harm and fear once more. The evil toys must be stopped, and a new toymaker must be found so the Oddkins can continue spreading hope.

Whether writing using a simple plot and clean-cut, black-and-white themes, or sketching a complex plot using numerous shades of gray, Koontz's strength emerges in his ability to involve readers in his stories emotionally. His sensory descriptions trap readers, further involving them in the outcome of the story. Koontz creates a unique juxtaposition in which readers are so caught up in the story that they must see it through to resolution, yet their fears and intuition warn them against turning the pages.

—Lisa A. Wroble

KOTZWINKLE, William

Nationality: American. **Born:** Scranton, Pennsylvania, 22 November 1938. **Education:** Attended Rider College and Pennsylvania State University, 1955-1957. **Family:** Married Elizabeth Gundy. **Career:** Worked as a short-order cook, department store Santa Claus, promotional copywriter for Prentice-Hall, and tabloid journalist, 1957-1969; freelance writer of novels, short fiction, poetry, novelizations of films, and screenplays, since 1969. **Awards:** National Magazine Awards for fiction, 1972, 1975; O'Henry Prize, 1975; World Fantasy Award for best novel, 1977, for *Doctor Rat;* North Dakota Children's Choice Award, 1983, and Buckeye Award, 1984, both for *E. T. The Extra-Terrestrial: A Novel.* **Agent:** Henry Denow, Harold Ober Associates, 425 Madison Avenue, New York, New York 10017, U.S.A.

PUBLICATIONS FOR YOUNG ADULTS

Fiction

The Leopard's Tooth. New York, Seabury, 1976.
Jack in the Box. New York, Putnam, 1980.
E. T. The Extra-Terrestrial: A Novel. New York, Putnam, 1982.
Trouble in Bugland: A Collection of Inspector Mantis Mysteries. New York, Godine, 1983.
E. T. The Book of the Green Planet: A New Novel. New York, Putnam, 1985.
Hearts of Wood and Other Timeless Tales. Boston, Godine, 1986.

PUBLICATIONS FOR CHILDREN

Fiction

The Fireman. New York, Pantheon, 1969.
The Day the Gang Got Rich. New York, Viking, 1970.
Elephant Boy. New York, Farrar, Straus & Giroux, 1970.
The Ship that Came Down the Gutter. New York, Pantheon, 1970.
The Return of Crazy Horse. New York, Farrar, Straus & Giroux, 1971.
The Oldest Man and Other Timeless Stories. New York, Pantheon, 1971.
The Supreme, Superb, Exalted and Delightful, One and Only Magic Building. New York, Viking, 1973.
Up the Alley with Jack and Joe. New York, Macmillan, 1974.
The Ants Who Took Away Time. Garden City, New York, Doubleday, 1978.
Dream of Dark Harbor. Garden City, New York, Doubleday, 1979.
The Nap Master. New York, Harcourt Brace Jovanovich, 1979.
The World Is Big and I'm So Small. New York, Crown, 1986.
The Empty Notebook. Boston, Godine, 1990.
The Million Dollar Bear. New York, Knopf, 1994.
Tales from the Empty Notebook. New York, Marlowe, 1996.

PUBLICATIONS FOR ADULTS

Fiction

Elephant Bangs Train. New York, Pantheon, 1971.
Hermes 3000. New York, Pantheon, 1972.
The Fan Man. New York, Harmony, 1974.
Nightbook. New York, Avon/Hearst, 1974.
Swimmer in the Secret Sea. New York, Avon/Hearst, 1975.
Doctor Rat. New York, Knopf, 1976.
Fata Morgana. New York, Knopf, 1977.
Christmas at Fontaine's. New York, Putnam, 1982.
Superman III. New York, Warner, 1983.
Queen of Swords. New York, Putnam, 1983.
Jewel of the Moon. New York, Putnam, 1985.
The Exile. New York, Dutton, 1987.
The Midnight Examiner. New York, Houghton Mifflin, 1989.
The Hot Jazz Trio. New York, Houghton Mifflin, 1989.
The Game of Thirty. New York, Houghton Mifflin, 1994.
The Bear Went Over the Mountain. New York, Doubleday, 1996.

Poetry

Herr Nightingale and the Satin Woman. New York, Knopf, 1978.
Great World Circus. New York, Putnam, 1983.
Seduction in Berlin. New York, Putnam, 1985.

*

Media Adaptations: *Jack in the Box* filmed as *The Book of Love,* 1990.

Critical Studies: ''An Interview with William Kotzwinkle'' by R. E. Nowicki, in *San Francisco Review of Books,* spring 1985, 7-8; ''William Kotzwinkle'' interview with Walter Gelles, in *Publisher's Weekly,* 7 November 1989, 46-47; unpublished interview with Leon Lewis, March 1996.

William Kotzwinkle comments:
Only in recent time have we had a classification called ''children's books,'' and it isn't a particularly good thing to have. *Treasure Island, Alice in Wonderland,* and *Tom Sawyer* didn't come in that way, and people of all ages were free to read them and find a new piece of their soul. . . . Once they became a separate category, it unleashed a river of trash. So much of this writing is condescending, permeated with an austere sense of looking down at the child, or of deliberately writing *for* the child.

* * *

Although by most measures of success William Kotzwinkle has had a very productive career as a writer, he remains a somewhat obscure, even mysterious figure, his books so widely varying in style and subject that instead of one significant audience, he has a number of different groups of enthusiastic readers each essentially unaware of his other interests. Since the publication of *The Fireman* in 1969, Kotzwinkle has written more than twenty books marketed primarily for children. Beginning with his first collection of short stories, *Elephant Bangs Train* (1971), he has also written more than twenty books for adults, books ranging from the classic evocation of the ethos of the Sixties, *The Fan Man* (1974) to his riveting vision of evil in Nazi Germany, *The Exile* (1987) to his very contemporary version of a hard-boiled detective story in *The Game of Thirty* (1994). He is probably best known, however, for his novelization of the film *E. T.,* which Stephen Spielberg (who liked *The Fan Man)* asked Kotzwinkle to write, and which sold more than 3,000,000 copies.

One of the reasons that Kotzwinkle has remained so elusive as an author is that his conception of *E. T.,* which he wrote from E. T.'s point of view, rather than Elliott's as in the film, does not fit easily into any specific category. Some reviewers assumed that it was targeted for children, but Kotzwinkle, who has commented that the separate division of books into children/adult areas ''isn't a particularly good thing to have,'' said that he adopted Melissa Mathison's screenplay to communicate to adults as much as children, and told Walter Gelles that he saw E. T. as ''a powerful archetype that is dawning for humanity, the little helper from the stars. . . . The alien is a missing link for us, a missing piece of our awareness.''

The confusion of classification with regard to many of Kotzwinkle's works has not been an impediment to his readers, although it has made it more difficult to establish his identity as a marketable author. When it was published in 1976, *The Leopard's Tooth* was described as Kotzwinkle's "first novel for young readers," though little distanced it from his adult novels. Though none of his books specified the young adult reader as a primary audience, several of them might be most accurately located in this area and discussed in terms of issues commonly raised by such a classification.

In accordance with the range of his interests and his facility with different styles and voices, Kotzwinkles's books in the young adult area cover the full spectrum of this field. *The Leopard's Tooth* seems to be designed for the mid-teen reader; the thematically linked stories in *Trouble in Bugland* tend to be for younger teens; his short story collections cover the entire reading range; his novel *Jack in the Box* moves from the late-teen years toward conspicuously adult issues; and both of the E. T. books defy limiting categorization.

For many boys reaching adolescence in the 1950s (when Kotzwinkle was just entering his teen years), the approved reading included books by authors like John R. Tunis and Ralph Henry Barbour, books which offered a guide for behavior based on the traditional values and virtues of a Victorian English education. The views presented in such books were sensible and idealized, if somewhat simplistic and unrealistic, especially in comparison with current YA literature. Kotzwinkle's *The Leopard's Tooth* is an attempt to preserve the positive attributes of this kind of writing, joining the enduring essence of Victorian virtue with a post-Imperial perspective, enjoying a degree of nostalgia for a vanished world without a blind obeisance to its destructive demands. It is designed as a classic coming-of-age narrative, including models for proper behavior, challenges that must be met to enter the world of early adulthood, and a setting in an exotic foreign land which is linked to the even wider, stranger landscape of the imagination.

Set in 1911, far enough back in time to remove it from the immediate and the mundane, it sends a young man from a relatively privileged background on an expedition to Africa, fulfilling a dream of exploration he has developed from the adventures and artifacts his mother(!), an archeologist, has brought home from her travels. Led by the intrepid Sir Henry Turnbull, a pleasing caricature of an explorer straight out of H. Rider Haggard— "Charles could see Sir Henry's huge pith helmet. . . . He was a gray-bearded giant of a man, with a voice like a foghorn and the handshake of a bear"—the party must solve the mystery of the leopard's tooth, an amulet with powers that can be used for good or evil.

The jungle setting is sufficiently exotic to evoke a realm of wonder, and Charles realizes instinctively that he is at home in the wild. During the course of the story Kotzwinkle deftly introduces considerable factual information about history and origins, as Sir Henry tells Charles his mission is to "show them their past and make it live," offering the kind of excitement that one may experience in the great exhibition halls of the Museum of Natural History, or in a book that recreates a prehistoric setting.

The crux of the adventure involves human/animal interconnections, as Sir Henry is *apparently* transformed into a leopard as the result of a misunderstanding concerning the powers of magic and the intrusion of the explorers into another kind of civilization. Confronting the fundamental issue of cultural despoilage, Sir Henry explains that a shaman "may feel he is doing his duty is

protecting the sacred relics of his people." Kotzwinkle balances the need to know with the need to respect other ways of being, and as is the custom in the cosmos of most young people's literature, all of the elements of the story are pulled into a neat, elegant mosaic at the conclusion. Sir Henry establishes an equality of cultures when he acknowledges that he and the shaman are "fellow seekers" and Charles realizes that his destiny is to become a *seeker* as well. For Kotzwinkle, *The Leopard's Tooth* is the book that an earlier time could have produced if it hadn't had its vision obscured by some residual cultural baggage.

In a collection of linked short stories directed toward the early teen reader, Kotzwinkle returns to an idealized world of Victorian virtue in *Trouble in Bugland,* a mid-nineteenth century, evidently "British" land of mystery, intrigue, and menace where melodramatic evil is everpresent but where an intrepid hero can defeat the forces of darkness through strength of character and the application of a keen intelligence. The five stories in "A Collection of Inspector Mantis Mysteries" are conceived as an ingenious transmutation of Arthur Conan Doyle's Sherlock Holmes tales into a land of insects, with Holmes recreated as the hyper-perceptive Mantis and his stolid, dependable assistant Dr. Watson as Dr. Hopper. Kotzwinkle's conceit is to take the actual characteristics of the insects on which the characters are based and use them as the basis for the physical and psychological traits of each "person" in the series. The linkage is etymologically accurate and totally consistent with the behavior of the characters in situations that brilliantly build on the behavior of each species. In "The Case of the Frightened Scholar," Professor Channing Booklouse literally eats books (just as a scholar devours the intellectual contents of a book), but finds the new knowledge dangerous since is contains a coded message sought by enemies of the realm. In "The Case of the Caterpillar's Head," Rodney Damselfly, a kind of sporting blade whose expertise at tennis is a result of his extraordinary vision (like the fly with 30,000 retinal units), is plagued by debt due to his inability to live beyond a moment's impulse. Utilizing one of the characteristic techniques of his books for young adults, Kotzwinkle takes the lure of arcane phenomena (the world of insects), applies it to a fundamental element in human psychology (the capacity for rational deduction), and integrates these components in a gripping narrative that combines the excitement of a mystery/adventure tale with some satisfying insights about human need and desire.

Initially, Mantis and Hopper resemble the anthropomorphic equivalents of animated cartoons, cute creatures with human attributes. As the tales progress, the characters, especially Mantis, assume an allegorical ambiguity closer to the complexity of human nature than the single-trait dominance required by children's books. The struggle to overcome evil and seek justice has an essential appeal to any reader not consumed by cynicism, while the satisfaction inherent in seeing a riddle revealed is an important element of a story for young adults discovering the increasingly ambiguous nature of almost everything. When Mantis observes, "The imagination is a powerful force," he is expressing one of Kotzwinkle's central themes, and the Inspector's fascination with the intricate details of the social structure in Bugland—a parallel for the Dickensian milieu that Kotzwinkle draws on—is designed to draw the reader into a landscape of the imagination. When Mantis says, "The adventure is its own reward," he is referring not only to the pursuit of villains but also to the reader's involvement in a foreign place and time. Although Mantis's powers of deduction and observation are striking, it is his "human" side—his foibles and semi-vices—that give his character the dimension of authenticity. He is far from perfect, but still formidable, a heroic presence in a fictive world that offers some consolation for a young adult whose own life might be somewhat less interesting and more frustrating than the "Bugland" of the author's imagination.

Kotzwinkle is particularly fond of the short story form since its compression suits his proclivity for the fantastic or surrealistic. He is able to maintain the mood of an alternative aspect of reality very effectively within the bounds of shorter pieces, and has commented, "There are safe, ordinary mental images, and there are unsafe, extraordinary ones. The last kind interest me." His short fiction frequently moves into realms that he characterizes with John Keats's reference to "faery lands forlorn," and although the majority of his work in this area is closer to traditional children's literature, several short stories might be accurately located in the YA range. The title story from the collection *Hearts of Wood and Other Timeless Tales* is a whimsical but heartfelt exploration of the powers of love, characteristically beginning as a child's fairy tale about a carousel whose wooden animals yearn to roam the earth, and then turning toward a narrative of the love of a grotesque troll for a beautiful lady dragon on the carousel. The uncertainty that the troll feels about his love for the seemingly unattainable, gorgeous creature of another species matches a familiar motif in YA literature, and Kotzwinkle has invested it with a kind of bizarre humor built on word play, incongruity, and zaniness that can suit the self-protective sensibility of young people sensitive about their doubts and feelings. Similarly, "The Dream of Chuang" also takes a fairy-tale premise as its subject—the interchange of identity between a butterfly and a collector—but proceeds into a more sophisticated philosophical reflection on the nature of identity itself and is presented with a tone that suggests a kind of zen-like involvement with the world, making it more appealing to a YA reader than the subject might indicate.

A number Kotzwinkle's stories have a particular interest for YA readers as their protagonist is a boy in his mid-teens dealing with the weirdness of an apparently absurd world. "The Bird Watcher," for example, sets up a comic contrast between the supposedly wholesome intentions of a boy scout outing and the protagonist's confused and curious response to nascent sexual awareness; "Stroke of Good Luck; a true nurse romance" is a racy account of a boy's sexual fantasies apparently becoming real. These stories mix poignancy with absurdity to convey the turmoil and uncertainty of mid-teen years, while in "Star Cruisers, Welcome" invading aliens threatening to literally devour Earth are repulsed when their space ship is stripped like an abandoned car by an inner-city gang who leave a signature graffiti on the ship as a defiant statement of turf pride.

Kotzwinkle's best known and most successful venture into the realm of the imagination is his novelization of Spielberg's film *E. T.,* which Kotzwinkle extended in a sort of sequel that followed E. T. to his home on the Green Planet. As is evident from *E. T.*'s widespread, continuing popularity, its appeal is universal (as Kotzwinkle intended), offering some things for readers of any age. The "space geek" (as Kotzwinkle affectionately called him) is a classic outsider, misunderstood, distrusted and exploited by adults. His odd appearance, problems with communication, desire to find home ground, instinctive but confused impulses of love, and susceptibility to a cosmic sorrow akin to a teen's feelings of loneliness are elements that correspond to many YA reader's

concerns. In *The Book of the Green Planet,* E. T.'s occupation as a cosmic botanist concerned with the environmental health of the entire universe operates as a strong argument for current ecological concerns and in both books, Kotzwinkle's off-beat humor, gentle satire, very inventive use of names, and characteristically agile merging of "fantasy" and "reality" are aspects that can work especially well with a YA audience. The presentation of the family in *E. T.* and its recollection in *The Book of the Green Planet* might also connect with readers growing up in similar situations. Characters include Gertie (age 5), an endearing combination of precocity, self-enclosing logic, and untainted innocence; Elliott, a "blossoming neurotic" whose destiny was "mediocrity, miserliness and melancholy," who resembles many young boy's image of themselves; and Michael, essentially likeable but quickly becoming a soured cynic. Their mother Mary has been bruised by divorce and is struggling to raise the family as a single parent. E. T.'s love for Mary has about it the plaintive, doomed yearning of an impossible romance. The entire family (including E. T.) is alienated from the authorities (government scientists, school principals, law officers) who are in charge. The arrival of E. T.'s ship—"It was E. T. multiplied a millionfold, the greatest heart-light the world has ever seen"—is an inspiring testament to the miraculous, a magical apparition validating a young person's belief in the possibility of something existing beyond the mundane and of a future more promising than the disappointments of the past.

From his recreation of a vanishing boyhood dream in *The Leopard's Tooth* through the evocation of exotic realms where mystery and adventure quicken the pulse and captivate the imagination, Kotzwinkle has presented a decidedly positive picture for the YA reader. The darker side of existence has been kept on the fringes, controllable and comprehensible, but in *Jack in the Box,* a novel that Chris Lynch has said is about "the great lurch from childhood to adulthood," Kotzwinkle has shifted his perspective to explore some of the less wholesome features of late teen life. Set in the coal mining/manufacturing region of Pennsylvania's Lackawana Valley, *Jack in the Box* is a kind of working-class version of the classic of the genre, Salinger's *The Catcher in the Rye.* The protagonist, Jack Twiller, "has been living inside a box and now he's popped out." The "box" is the innocence of childhood, and the outer world is a confusing flux of angry adults, polluted sidewalks, obtuse acquaintances, unattainable girls, and complicated situations which seem to have no satisfactory solutions. What keeps the book from becoming as bleak as Twiller's prospects ("The button factory?" he asks a guidance counselor in disbelief) is the full exercise of Kotzwinkle's "lunatic humor," an exercise in incongruity and absurdity that keeps everything, including Twiller, off balance most of the time. The essential theme of the novel is Twiller's growing awareness of himself and a corresponding awareness of others, the first step in the maturing process from instinctive love to appreciative love.

The novel is an audacious attempt to join the ends of the spectrum of YA literature, the fading wonder of the child's world with the bleakness of a looming adult life stretching onward through decades of boredom. Characteristic of Kotzwinkle's work, *Jack in the Box* is an unsettling amalgam that carries the exuberant spirit of youth beyond childhood's end and similarly infects the relatively innocent joys of childhood with premonitions of adult life and its discontents. While it might tend to disconcert those looking for a compartmentalized version of teen life, Kotzwinkle's narration of Twiller's maturation, full of screw-ups and failed schemes, is an illuminating account of how small gains in self-awareness and a deepening understanding of the world can lead to a construction of the self that can withstand the inevitable further screw-ups and failures of existence.

—Leon Lewis

KRISHER, Trudy

Nationality: American. **Born:** Trudy Butner in Macon, Georgia, United States, 22 December 1946. **Education:** College of William and Mary, Williamsburg, Virginia, B.A. 1968; Trenton State College, New Jersey, M.Ed. 1972. **Family:** Two daughters and one son. **Career:** Assistant professor and campus writing center coordinator, University of Dayton, Ohio, from 1985. Member of the board of directors, Miami Valley Literacy Council, and member, Miami Valley Unitarian Fellowship. **Awards:** Miami Valley Cultural Alliance Arts Award, 1994; *Publisher's Weekly* Cuffie Award for Most Promising New Author, 1994; Parents Choice Honor Book selection, American Library Association Best Book for Young Adults selection, both 1994, International Reading Association Best Young Adult Novel award, Virginia Library Association Jefferson Cup Honor Book, both 1995, all for *Spite Fences.* **Agent:** Jane Jordan Browne, Multimedia Product Development, 410 South Michigan Ave., Suite 724, Chicago, Illinois 60605-1465, U.S.A.

PUBLICATIONS FOR YOUNG ADULTS

Fiction

Spite Fences. New York, Delacorte, 1994.
Kinship. New York, Delacorte, 1997.

PUBLICATIONS FOR CHILDREN

Fiction

Kathy's Hats: A Story of Hope, illustrated by Nadine Bernard Westcott. Morton Grove, Illinois, Albert Whitman, 1992.

PUBLICATIONS FOR ADULTS

Nonfiction

Writing for a Reader. Paramus, New Jersey, Prentice-Hall, 1995.

*

Critical Studies: Review of *Spite Fences* by Lee Diane Gordon, in *The Book Report* (Worthington, Ohio), March/April 1995, 38; review of *Spite Fences* by Lois Stover, in *English Journal* (Urbana, Illinois), January 1996, 88; entry in *Something About the Author,* Vol. 86, Detroit, Gale, 1996, 132-34; "Local Writer Earns Literary Kudos," in *University of Dayton News,* http://www.udayton.edu/news/nr/012898/html (4 May 1998).

*   *   *

Born in Macon, Georgia, and raised in South Florida, Trudy Krisher has given her young adult novels—both set in rural Georgia—an authentic Southern accent and realistic Southern settings and situations.

With her very first book—*Kathy's Hats,* a children's picture book—Krisher began dealing with personally difficult, often painful subjects in a frank and honest yet positive and hopeful way. Inspired by her own daughter's battle with cancer at age nine, *Kathy's Hats* is the poignant story of how a little girl's love of hats helps her cope with the hair loss she experiences as a result of her chemotherapy treatments.

Spite Fences, Krisher's powerful, award-winning first book for young adults, deals with racial tensions in the South in the 1960s, as well as with poverty, family strife, and a mother's cruelty and physical abuse of her daughter. Magnolia Pugh—"Maggie"—is a thirteen-year-old white girl who lives in Kinship, Georgia. Her daddy has just lost his job as a salesman for Johnson & Johnson. In her anger and frustration, Maggie's mother fights constantly with her husband, beats Maggie mercilessly, even swatting her in the face with an armful of thorny rose bush stems, and focuses all of her attention on getting her younger daughter, Gardenia, prepared to win the Hayes County Little Miss Pageant. Maggie's outlets are escaping to her room, climbing up into the pecan tree in a corner of the yard, going on a "sneak" with her best friend Pert Wilson—and looking at things through the lens of the old camera given to her by Zeke, a young black peddler. To make ends meet, Maggie's mother takes in laundry, and Maggie gets a cleaning job through Zeke for George Andrew Hardy, Ph.D., Assistant Professor of Mathematics. When she discovers that George Hardy is black, Maggie knows that her parents would forbid her to continue working for him, but she likes working for him, she likes him, and her family needs the money. So, she keeps the secret.

In the meantime, the Pughs' neighbor, Virgil Boggs, tears apart Gardenia's favorite doll, Angel, and threatens to do the same to Maggie and Gardenia. In self-defense, the Pughs put up a big, solid fence around their whole yard, but even a tall fence cannot protect their girls all of the time—they must go to school, to the store, to work. And the fence becomes a slate for terrible hate words when Virgil's sister discovers pictures Maggie took when she and Pert were secretly watching a party at the blacks' park. In town, the blacks stage a peaceful "eat-in" at the drugstore, where they're allowed to shop but not to sit. With George Hardy's help, Maggie learns that it takes "a lifetime to build both a relationship and a community," that the world is "a curious place, full of change and wonder," and that it doesn't really matter what side you're on: "Somehow, we're all kin."

In her next novel for young adults, *Kinship,* Krisher focuses on Maggie's spunky, fun-loving friend Pert Wilson. Fifteen-year-old Pert (short for "Perty," the name her daddy wrote on her birth certificate) has different problems. She has a loving mother, Rae Jean, and a good home, but her father took off soon after she was born and she yearns for him, and her home is a run-down trailer in a run-down trailer park that is facing demolition by the Kinship zoning officials. Pert thinks it is the most wonderful day imaginable when her daddy pulls into their trailer lot, and so do her neighbors at the Happy Trails trailer park when Pert's smooth-talking daddy promises to help them fix up their trailers and lots to reverse the zoning officials' eviction ruling. But when Daddy stands Pert up at her school's Father-Daughter dance and takes off with the money the neighbors had given him for repairs and improvements as well as with his wife's hard-earned "rainy day" cache, Pert learns a hard lesson about the difference between family and kin. In the stuttered but so eloquent words of neighbor Alice Potter: "...families is different from k-k-kin. . . . Kin drops by now and again. They sends letter or sometimes money. They comes around holidays. . . . Family's folks what builds a f-f-foundation under you—folks what s-s-stays.''

In 1994, Trudy Krisher won the *Publisher's Weekly* Cuffie Award for Most Promising New Author. Her first three books show not only great promise, but great accomplishment, and her readers will look forward to her next gripping and heart-felt literary achievement.

—Marcia Welsh

KROPP, Paul

Nationality: Canadian. **Born:** Buffalo, New York, 22 February, 1948. **Education:** Hutchinson-Central Technical School, Buffalo, New York, 1966; Columbia College, Columbia University, New York, 1966-70, B.A. 1970; University of Western Ontario, London, Ontario, 1970-72, M.A. 1972; University of Western Ontario, London, Ontario, 1971-72, Cert. Ed. 1972. **Family:** Married 1) Marsha Atwood in 1968 (divorced); three sons; 2) Gale Bildfell in 1989. **Career:** Teacher, Burlington, Ontario, 1972-74; teacher, Hamilton, Ontario, 1974-94. **Address:** 391 Wellesley Street East, Toronto, Ontario M4X 1H5, Canada.

PUBLICATIONS FOR YOUNG ADULTS

Fiction

Wilted. New York, Coward, McCann & Geoghelan, 1980; revised as *You've Seen Enough,* Toronto, Maxwell Macmillan, 1992.
Getting Even. New York, Simon & Schuster, 1986.
Moonkid and Liberty. Boston, Little Brown, 1989.
The Rock. Toronto, Stoddart, 1989.
Ellen, Elena, Luna. Maxwell Macmillan, 1992.
Moonkid and Prometheus. Stoddart, 1997.

Series Canada

Burn Out. Toronto, Collier Macmillan, 1979.
Dope Deal. Collier Macmillan, 1979.
Hot Cars. Collier Macmillan, 1979.
Runaway. Collier Macmillan, 1979.
Fair Play. Collier MacMillan, 1980.
Dead On. Collier MacMillan, 1980.
Dirt Bike. Collier MacMillan, 1980.
No Way. Collier Macmillan, 1980.
Baby, Baby. Collier Macmillan, 1982
Gang War. Collier Macmillan, 1982.
Snow Ghost. Collier Macmillan, 1982.
Wild One. Collier Macmillan, 1982.
Amy's Wish. Collier Macmillan, 1984.
Micro Man. Collier Macmillan, 1984.
Take Off. Collier Macmillan, 1986.
Get Lost. Maxwell Macmillan, 1987.

Head Lock. Maxwell Macmillan, 1988.
Tough Stuff. Maxwell Macmillan, 1988.
Split Up. Maxwell Macmillan, 1989.

Series 2000

Death Ride. Collier Macmillan, 1986.
Jo's Search. Collier Macmillan, 1986.
Not Only Me. Maxwell Macmillan, 1987.
Under Cover. Maxwell Macmillan, 1987.
Baby Blues. Maxwell Macmillan, 1989.
We Both Have Scars. Maxwell Macmillan, 1990.
The Victim Was Me. Maxwell Macmillan, 1991.
Riot on the Street. Maxwell Macmillan, 1993.
Blizzard. Maxwell Macmillan, 1995.

PUBLICATIONS FOR CHILDREN

Justin, Jay-Jay and the Juvenile Dinkent. Toronto, Scholastic-Tab, 1986; reprinted as *Fast Times With Fred,* Scholastic, 1990.
Cottage Crazy. Toronto, Scholastic, 1988.
Ski Stooges. Toronto, Scholastic, 1992.

PUBLICATIONS FOR ADULTS

Nonfiction

The Reading Solution: Make Your Child a Reader. Toronto, Random House, 1993; as *Raising a Reader,* New York, Doubleday, 1996.
With Lynda Hodson, *The School Solution: Getting Canada's Schools to Work for Your Children.* Toronto, Random House, 1995.
I'll Be the Parent, You Be the Kid. Toronto, Random House, 1998.

*

Paul Kropp comments:

I've been writing for kids ever since I began teaching at a boy's vocational high school—back in the days when we still had such things. The "boys" weren't much interested in updated by *Scuffy the Tugboat,* so I wrote *Burn Out, Hot Cars* and *Dope Deal* for them. After that I began working on longer and more difficult young-adult novels like *Wilted, Moonkid and Liberty* and others— books that have been translated and published around the world. All the stories begin with something from real life—a character, an incident, a moment in time—and then get developed with imagination and continual rewriting. The process takes three to five years, but produces a book that ultimately has a life of its own.

*		*		*

Paul Kropp can legitimately be called the "father" of the Canadian hi-lo genre. While teaching in a Hamilton, Ontario, vocational high school in the mid-1970s, Kropp discovered that many of his students were reading at an elementary grade level; however, when he sought reading material which was appropriate to their demonstrated reading ability but which also contained content relevant to their age and interests, he could not find anything. Kropp pitched the concept of a series of high interest-low vocabulary books to a number of Canadian publishers, with Collier Macmillan being the first to respond positively.

Beginning in 1982 the "Series Canada" ("Encounter Series" in the United States) books, released in sets of four, were printed in large print on oversized pages. Three books from each quartet were directed at a male audience, for Kropp recognized that there were more weak male than female readers amongst high-schoolers. To attract reluctant readers, the books' "packaging" included wrap-around covers consisting of full-colour photographs of objects connected to the storylines. In the books' usual 10 chapters, readers would normally encounter an illustration every second page. Titles were short and "punchy" while subject matter was meant to be relevant to the world of adolescents. For example, works dealt with such issues as premarital pregnancy (*Baby, Baby*), racism (*Fair Play*), teen shoplifting (*No Way*), and running away from home (*Take Off* and *Runaway*). Because of their low reading level and a format which resembled the typical elementary paperback, "Series Canada" titles were often erroneously purchased by teachers and librarians in elementary schools who were then sometimes "offended" by the titles' older subject matter.

In 1986, Kropp introduced an "advanced" hi-lo series, "Series 2000," which had a higher reading level than "Series Canada." Additionally, "Series 2000" books utilized smaller print, longer titles and fewer illustrations than did "Series Canada," and they were also published in a more "adult," mass-market paperback size. Content was grittier with, for instance, *Not Only Me* exploring incest, *The Victim Was Me*, date rape, and *Jo's Search*, the quest for a birth mother.

Although both series were commercially successful, they were not always critical successes in the eyes of some reviewers who elected to apply the same standards to these hi-lo titles that they would employ in evaluating mainstream YA fiction. Not surprisingly, these brief works would often fall short in terms of depth of characterization or sophistication of plot. However, when judged as examples of the hi-lo genre, "Series Canada" and "Series 2000" fare extremely well.

Originally the sole author of both series, Kropp recruited additional authors as demand for titles increased, and consequently reluctant readers were introduced to other mainstream YA writers, such as William Bell, Lesley Choyce and Marilyn Halvorson. Unfortunately, because of a corporate merger, "Series Canada" and "Series 2000" were discontinued. While no new titles have been published since 1995, earlier titles are still commercially available.

While authoring more than two dozen hi-lo books, Kropp also wrote another half dozen titles for the wider teen audience. Alienated adolescents, especially those who do not fit into the school's social scene, frequently appear in Kropp's novels. *You've Seen Enough* is an updated version of Kropp's first YA novel, *Wilted*, in which Danny Morrison, 14, is concerned that his classmates will consider him a "wilt," a loser, because he has to wear glasses. Danny's problems go beyond physical appearance for, at home, his parent's deteriorating marriage finally comes apart. At school, when Danny's interest in Samantha Morgan is reciprocated, he is threatened by 200-pound Ron Masten who claims Samantha as his territory. While glasses have improved Danny's vision, the recent happenings in his life also cause him to see more clearly and less egocentrically, but, for the moment, as Samantha says, "You've seen enough." A comparative reading of the novel's two versions

reveals that Kropp, as well as making Danny more self-confident, has tightened the original story, thereby making it a crisper read, while modifying content detail to reflect new teen symbols.

An admirer of Paul Zindel, Kropp admits to being influenced by Zindel's device of having a male and female adolescent alternate narrating chapters, something Kropp utilized in *Getting Even* and *Moonkid and Liberty*. In the former, Jane Flemming, a bright, attractive newcomer to Wagnalls High School, categorizes fellow grade 11 student Keith Hartman as just another "Piggie," one with whom she wants to get even because of a crude remark made about her body. Keith, actually shy, lives in the shadow of his older brother who had been a "god" at Wagnalls. Jane also brings some emotional family baggage with her, but gradually the two believably move from antagonism to friendship to romance.

Ian "Moonkid" McNaughton, 13, and older sister, Liberty, react to a new school and peers in contrasting ways in *Moonkid and Liberty*. Ian antagonizes his classmates by flaunting his superior intelligence and using it to insult those he dislikes. Liberty, however, desperately tries to blend in by conforming to the in-crowd's norms of dress and behaviour. When the pair's hippy father is arrested, the siblings again react differently, but the event causes them to re-examine their values and each other. As well, Moonkid, while seeking vengeance on his tormentors, realizes the frightening power of his intelligence. Almost a decade later, Kropp returned to Ian, now 15, in *Moonkid and Prometheus,* a longer than normal YA novel. Still a social isolate, Moonkid must choose: "volunteer" to tutor an elementary school student, or be sent to a "tough" secondary school. Electing the former, Ian is matched with a pupil who needs help with reading and writing—Prometheus "Pro" John Gibbs, a six-foot-tall black seventh grade student from the projects. Over one term, this odd couple frequently swap their tutor/pupil roles while becoming close friends. As Moonkid addresses Pro's learning needs, Pro reciprocates by helping an uncoordinated Ian with his basketball skills as well as his social deficiencies. Kropp does not repeat the alternating narrator technique but supplements Moonkid's first person narration with Pro's journal entries which provide both Pro's keen insights into events and proof of his growth in writing and vocabulary skills.

Ellen/Eléna/Luna offers an interesting twist on the alternating narrator device by providing three central characters in one. Ellen Bertrand, a grade 11 reporter for a student newspaper, is tired of being a wannabe and decides, "I've got to become more interesting" by doing something unusual. Ellen's best friend, the paper's editor-in-chief, suggests a story idea calling for Ellen to place an ad in the "Personal Classifieds," date some of the responses, and then write about her experiences. The remainder of the book follows Ellen as she follows through on two dates: Tooner, a 20-year-old punk cartoonist, and Garrett Watson, an amateur film maker attending an exclusive private school. Reluctant to use her own identity, Ellen adopts a different persona for each date. With Tooner, she becomes Luna Hilton, invents an "artsy" history, and overhauls her appearance. Ellen dates Garrett in the guise of the sophisticated, worldly Eléna Hilton and transforms her taxi-driving-father and supermarket-cashier-mother into a famous poet and watercolour painter who run an art colony in Mexico. Though Luna's date with Tooner is essentially disastrous, Eléna and Garrett become strongly attracted to each other. Having created a fiction, Eléna does not know how to admit her lies without losing Garrett. Everything seemingly unravels at a major social event when Ellen/Eléna/Luna encounter her father, Garrett, and Tooner.

The Rock departs from the rest of Kropp's work in terms of its style and content. Via a "Prologue," Kropp informs readers that one of the book's characters, the Rock, is dead and then takes the plot back in time and works forward to a concluding point just after Rock's death. Readers meet four long-time childhood friends, Brian, aka the Beak, Simon, Tony La Roche, aka The Rock, and Rock's younger sister, Nikki. Rock, a year older than the other two guys, is the quartet's natural leader. Although at one point, Beak, the book's narrator, asserts, "We'll always be friends," as the three males, and later Nikki, move into high school, their friendship gradually begins to alter as changing academic and personal interests pull them in different directions. Rock's accidental death becomes the visible proof that their close friendship is over and that they will just have to accept warm memories of what once was.

—Dave Jenkinson

KRUMGOLD, Joseph (Quincy)

Nationality: American. **Born:** Jersey City, New Jersey, 9 April 1908. **Education:** New York University, B.A. 1928. **Family:** Married Helen Litwin in 1947; one son. **Career:** Novelist and author of children's books. Publicity writer, Metro-Goldwyn-Mayer, New York City, 1928; screenwriter and producer for film companies, including Paramount, RKO, Columbia, and Republic, in New York, Hollywood, California, and Paris, France, 1929-40; producer and director, Film Associates, New York City, and Office of War Information, 1940-46; president in charge of production, Palestine Films, New York City and Jerusalem, Israel, 1946-52; Joseph Krumgold Productions (producer of motion pictures and television films), Hope, New Jersey, proprietor, 1952-60; writer, director, and producer for Columbia Broadcasting System, Inc., National Broadcasting Company, Inc., National Educational Television, and Westinghouse Television, New York, Rome, and Istanbul, 1960-70. Press agent. Member, Freling Huysen Township (New Jersey) school board. **Awards:** American Library Association Newbery Medal, 1954, for . . .And Now Miguel, and 1960, for Onion John; Boys' Club of American Junior Book award, 1954, and Freedoms Foundation award, 1973, both for . . .And Now Miguel; Robert Flaherty award honorable mention, 1954, for movie . . .And Now Miguel; Lewis Carroll Shelf award, 1960, for Onion John; The Most Terrible Turk was chosen as one of Child Study Association's Children's Books of the Year, 1969; first prizes for films and documentaries at Venice, Edinburgh, and Prague film festivals. **Died:** 10 July 1980.

PUBLICATIONS FOR YOUNG ADULTS

Fiction

Sweeney's Adventure, illustrated by Tibor Gergely. New York, Random House, 1942.
. . .And Now Miguel, illustrated by Jean Charlot. New York, Crowell, 1953.
Onion John, illustrated by Symeon Shimin. New York, Crowell, 1959.
Henry 3, illustrated by Alvin Smith. New York, Atheneum, 1967.

Other

The Most Terrible Turk: A Story of Turkey, illustrated by Michael Hampshire. New York, Crowell, 1969.

PUBLICATIONS FOR ADULTS

Novel

Thanks to Murder. New York, Vanguard Press, and London, Gollancz, 1935.

Screenplays: The Blackmailer, with Lee Loeb and Harold Buchman, 1936; Adventure in Manhattan, with others, 1936; Lady from Nowhere, with Fred Niblo, Jr., Arthur Strawn, and Ben G. Kohn, 1936; Lone Wolf Returns, with Bruce Manning and Lionel Houser, 1936; Jim Hanvey—Detective, with Olive Cooper and Octavus Roy Cohn, 1937; Join the Marines, with Olive Cooper and Karl Brown, 1937; Speed to Burn, with others, 1938; Lady Behave, with Olive Cooper, 1938; Main Street Lawyer, 1939; The Phantom Submarine, 1940; The Crooked Road, with Garnett Weston, E.E. Paramore, and Richard Blake, 1940; Seven Miles from Alcatraz, 1942; Hidden Hunger (documentary), with Henwar Rodakiewicz, 1942; Magic Town with Robert Riskin, 1947; Dream No More, 1950; . . .And Now Miguel, 1953; One Tenth of a Nation (documentary), with Henwar Rodakiewicz, 1940; Mr. Trull Finds Out (documentary), 1941; The Autobiography of a Jeep (documentary), 1943.

Other

Where Do We Grow From Here: An Essay on Children's Literature. New York, Atheneum, 1968.
Editor, The Oxford Furnace, 1741-1925. Belvidere, New Jersey, Warren County Historical Society, 1976.

*

Media Adaptations: Audio cassette versions of Krumgold's work include . . .And Now Miguel (filmstrip with record or cassette), Miller-Brody, 1978; and Onion John (filmstrip with record or cassette, or record or cassette only), Miller-Brody, 1978.

Biography: Entry in More Junior Authors, edited by Muriel Fuller, New York, H.W. Wilson, 1963.

Critical Study: Entry in Contemporary Literary Criticism, Volume 12, Detroit, Gale, 1981.

* * *

In his two best books for young people, . . .And Now Miguel and Onion John, Joseph Krumgold succeeds in directing the genre of realistic fiction for a young audience to the same purpose of exposition and exploration that identifies the best novels for adults.
. . .And Now Miguel explores the developing awareness of a Mexican boy who lives on a sheep farm and, through Miguel's consciousness, gives us the texture and design of such a life. Krumgold was also a professional filmmaker and the subject of this

widely acclaimed book evolved during a filmmaking trip when Krumgold had the opportunity to live among families like Miguel's. Working as a filmmaker yielded not only subject matter, but also particular techniques. While Krumgold's writing is not really "cinematic," he had an intensely visual sense for the telling detail which may well have evolved from his experience with the camera.

In some ways *Onion John* is a more unusual book, dealing, again through the consciousness of a young boy, with the way in which Onion John, an eccentric East European, part-hobo, part-wizard, interrelates with the highly conventional expectations of small-town Middle America. Onion John has lived happily for years in his tiny self-built house using candles as his only form of lighting and storing his vegetables in numerous bathtubs in his living room. The townspeople decide to build Onion John a "proper" house. No one realises that such a house embodies a mass of expectations about how everyday life is to be conducted and eventually Onion John, unable to accommodate himself to these narrow expectations, sadly takes to the road again. A story of this kind is unusual in a book for young people, and Krumgold sustains a moving narrative without dropping into sentimentality.

More alert readers are likely to find Krumgold's preoccupations excessively macho. He was, for example, almost exclusively concerned with father-son relationships and, rather laughably, in *Henry 3* manages to discover that flabby businessmen are really heroes under the skin when faced with a hurricane, while he turns their wives into caricatures of weakness and greed, hysterical over the loss of their furs. In this respect he can be viewed as the inheritor of such early writers of the boys' adventure tale as R.M. Ballantyne and G.A. Henty who, like Krumgold, celebrate a bonding of boys and men and an exclusion of females.

Krumgold's contribution rests less on such preoccupations than on his development of sophisticated narrative techniques. Few writers for children use the first person narrative with comparable conviction or have a comparable sense of how that form of narrative may be employed as a lens for exploring the world surrounding the "I."

—Gillian Thomas

L

LACKEY, Mercedes R.

Nationality: American. **Born:** Chicago, Illinois, 24 June 1950. **Education:** Purdue University, West Lafayette, Indiana, B.S. 1972. **Family:** Married 1) Anthony Lackey in 1972 (divorced 1990); 2) Larry Dixon in 1990. **Career:** Artist's model in and near South Bend, Indiana, 1975-81; Associates Data Processing, South Bend, computer programmer, 1979-82; surveyor, layout designer, and analyst, CAIRS (survey and data processing firm), South Bend, 1981-82; computer programmer, American Airlines, Tulsa, Oklahoma, since 1982. **Address:** P.O. Box 8309, Tulsa, Oklahoma 74101-8309, U.S.A.

PUBLICATIONS FOR YOUNG ADULTS

Novels

Arrows of the Queen. New York, DAW Books, 1987.
Arrow's Flight. New York, DAW Books, 1987.
Arrow's Fall. New York, DAW Books, 1988.
Oathbound. New York, DAW Books, 1988.
Burning Water. New York, Tor Books, 1989.
Oathbreakers. New York, DAW Books, 1989.
Magic's Pawn. New York, DAW Books, 1989.
Reap the Whirlwind. Riverdale, New York, Baen, 1989.
A Knight of Ghosts & Shadows, with Ellen Guon. Riverdale, New York, Baen, 1990.
Magic's Promise. New York, DAW Books, 1990.
Magic's Price. New York, DAW Books, 1990.
By the Sword. New York, DAW Books, 1991.
The Elvenbane: An Epic High Fantasy of the Halfblood Chronicles, with Andre Norton. New York, T. Doherty, 1991.
Jinx High. New York, Tor, 1991.
Winds of Fate. New York, DAW Books, 1991.
Bardic Voices: The Lark & the Wren. Riverdale, New York, Baen, 1992.
Born to Run, with Larry Dixon. Riverdale, New York, Baen, 1992.
Children of the Night. New York, Tor Books, 1992.
Freedom Flight, with Ellen Guon. Riverdale, New York, Baen, 1992.
Summoned to Tourney, with Ellen Guon. Riverdale, New York, Baen, 1992.
Winds of Change. New York, DAW Books, 1992.
Winds of Fury. New York, DAW Books, 1992.
Fortress of Frost & Fire: The Bard's Tale II, with Ru Emerson. Riverdale, New York, Baen, 1993.
If I Pay Thee Not in Gold, with Piers Anthony. Riverdale, New York, Baen, 1993.
Rediscovery: A Novel of Darkover, with Marion Zimmer Bradley. New York, DAW Books, 1993.
The Ship Who Searched, with Anne McCaffrey. Riverdale, New York, Baen, 1993.
When the Bough Breaks, with Holly Lisle. Riverdale, New York, Baen, 1993.
The Robin & the Kestrel. Riverdale, Baen, 1993.
Sacred Ground. New York, TOR, 1994.

With Larry Dixon, *The Black Gryphon.* New York, DAW Books, 1994.
Storm Warning. New York, DAW Books, 1994.
With Marion Zimmer Bradley and Andre Norton, *Tiger Burning Bright.* New York, Morrow, 1995.
The Eagle & the Nightingales. Riverdale, Baen, 1995.
With Andre Norton, *Elvenblood: An Epic High Fantasy.* New York, TOR, 1995.
The Fire Rose. Riverdale, Baen Books, 1995.
With Larry Dixon, *The White Gryphon.* New York, DAW Books, 1995.
Storm Rising. New York, DAW Books, 1995.
Firebird. New York, Tor, 1996.
With Larry Dixon, *The Silver Gryphon.* New York, DAW Books, 1996.
Storm Breaking. New York, DAW Books, 1996.
Four and Twenty Blackbirds. Riverdale, Baen Books, 1997.
The Free Bards (contains *The Lark & the Wren, The Robin & the Kestrel,* and *The Eagle & the Nightingales*). Riverdale, Baen, 1997.

*   *   *

Mercedes Lackey is one of the most prolific writers in the current science-fiction and fantasy field. Her popular fantasy novels set in the land of Valdemar and its surrounding countries are filled with magic, mystery, love, and laughter. She currently has twelve books set in this world of wonders.

Lackey has taken an historical perspective as the approach to her novels. This causes the reader to be in the unique position to know before reading a trilogy exactly how the story is going to end. An example is her second published series "The Last Herald Mage." The first few pages of *Arrows of the Queen* reveals the protagonist's fate quite clearly. Yet "The Last Herald Mage" series contains many of the writer's best character creations and is among the strongest of her work.

The author has populated her lands with a large variety of fascinating races both human and nonhuman. The magic-using, bird-loving Tayledras, for example, are contrasted with their cousins the plains-dwelling horse-breeders, the Shin'a'in. Both groups are strongly reminiscent of American Indians. Their histories are fascinatingly intertwined, each tribe having been assigned a specific task by the Goddess who is taskmistress to their people.

Lackey's strength is in her characters rather than her plots. The historical perspective allows her to reuse her characters; thus Talia, the protagonist of *Arrows of the Queen, Arrow's Flight,* and *Arrow's Fall* reappears in *By the Sword* as well as in the "Mage Winds" trilogy. In the latter works, however, Talia plays only a very minor role. Princess Elspeth, the heroine of the "Mage Winds" trilogy, is placed in the unique position of being an antagonist in *Arrows of the Queen,* while assuming the major role in the latter works.

The author's crowning triumph in characterization is the protagonist of "The Last Herald Mage," Vanyel Ashkevron. The young hero is foundering under the expectations of his father and mother. Longing to be a Bard, he possesses only a trace of the "gift" of Bardic musical talent. He does not measure up to his father's image of the ideal son. Lord Ashkevron fears that the boy is at best effeminate, if not deliberately homosexual. Vanyel must grapple with his own uncertainty about his sexual orientation in addition to his other problems. When he is sent to the capital city of Haven to study, his life changes. Under the tutelage of his Aunt Savil, one of the most important and influential of the Herald Mages, the boy expands. He meets the love of his life and is trapped in an intolerable situation by the boy he loves. The result is the death of his lover, and the barriers in Vanyel's mind are torn open, making him the most powerful of all the Herald Mages. His reaction to his new powers and his attempts to learn to control them make the novels fascinating to read, even though a reader of the previous work knows that Vanyel is doomed.

The vast panorama of races and countries make Mercedes Lackey's novels well worth reading. Even her nonhuman characters become lifelike and realistic, while retaining enough mystery to be exotic. The gryphons of *Winds of Fate, Winds of Change,* and *Winds of Fury* are a prime example. Treyvan, the male, gives an entertaining account of how he met Darkwind, the Tayledras protagonist, when Darkwind was a child of eight. The boy was playing "monster" in the ruins outside his village when the Gryphon arrived. After watching curiously for a while, the bird-beast crept up behind the child and uttered a soft "Boo." The boy fled, screaming, leaving an apologetic gryphon to deal with the elders of his tribe.

Mercedes Lackey promises to keep readers enthralled with her tales of Valdemar for many years to come. She keeps her creative skills sharpened with a variety of other work, all characterized by the same attention to personality that is her hallmark. She continues to create creatures and people that delight, regardless of the setting in which she places them.

—Louise J. Winters

LANG, T.T. *See* **TAYLOR, Theodore.**

LANGE, John. *See* **CRICHTON, Michael.**

LANGTON, Jane

Nationality: American. **Born:** Jane Gillson in Boston, Massachusetts, 30 December 1922. **Education:** Wellesley College, Massachusetts, 1940-42; University of Michigan, Ann Arbor, 1942-45,

B.S. (Phi Beta Kappa), 1944, M.A. 1945; Radcliffe College, Cambridge Massachusetts, 1945-46, 1947-48, M.A. 1948; Boston Museum School of Art, 1958-59. **Family:** Married William Langton in 1943; three sons. **Career:** Writer. Prepared art work and visual material for educational program in the natural sciences entitled *Discovery,* WGBH, Channel 2, Boston, 1955-56; taught children's literature, Graduate Center for the Study of Children's Literature, Simmons College, 1979-80, and suspense novel writing at the Radcliffe Seminars, 1981. **Awards:** Mystery Writers of America Edgar award nomination, 1962, for *The Diamond in the Window;* American Library Association Newbery Honor Book award, 1980, for *The Fledgling;* Nero Wolfe award, 1984, and Mystery Writers of America Edgar award nomination, 1985, both for *Emily Dickinson Is Dead.* **Address:** 9 Baker Farm Rd., Lincoln, Massachusetts 01773, U.S.A.

PUBLICATIONS FOR YOUNG ADULTS

Fiction

The Majesty of Grace, illustrated by the author. New York, Harper, 1961; as *Her Majesty, Grace Jones,* 1974.

The Diamond in the Window, illustrated by Erik Blegvad. New York, Harper, 1962; London, Hamish Hamilton, 1969.

The Swing in the Summerhouse, illustrated by Erik Blegvad. New York, Harper, 1967; London, Hamish Hamilton, 1970.

The Astonishing Stereoscope, illustrated by Erik Blegvad. New York, Harper, 1971.

The Boyhood of Grace Jones, illustrated by Emily McCully. New York, Harper, 1972.

Paper Chains. New York, Harper, 1977.

The Fledgling. New York, Harper, 1980.

The Fragile Flag. New York, Harper, 1984.

The Hedgehog Boy, illustrated by Ilse Plume. New York, Harper, 1985.

Salt: From a Russian Folktale, illustrated by Ilse Plume. New York, Hyperion, 1992.

The Queen's Necklace: A Swedish Folktale, illustrated by Ilse Plume. New York, Hyperion, 1994.

PUBLICATIONS FOR ADULTS

Novels

The Transcendental Murder. New York, Harper, 1964.

Dark Nantucket Noon, illustrated by the author. New York, Harper, 1975.

The Memorial Hall Murder, illustrated by the author. New York, Harper, 1978.

Natural Enemy, illustrated by the author. New Haven, Connecticut, Ticknor & Fields, 1982.

Emily Dickinson Is Dead, illustrated by the author. New York, St. Martin's Press, 1984.

Good and Dead. New York, St. Martin's Press, 1986; London, Penguin, 1987.

Murder at the Gardner: A Novel of Suspense, illustrated by the author. New York, St. Martin's Press, 1988.

The Dante Game, illustrated by the author. New York, Viking, 1991.

God in Concord, illustrated by the author. New York, Viking, 1992.
Divine Inspiration, New York, Viking, 1993.
The Shortest Day: Murder at the Revels, New York, Viking, 1995.
Dead as a Dodo, New York, Viking, 1996.
The Face on the Wall, New York, Viking, 1998.

OTHER

Contributor of prose, *Acts of Light* (includes poems by Emily Dickinson and painting and drawings by Nancy Ekholm Burkert). New York Graphic Society, 1980.

*

Biography: Essay in *Something about the Author Autobiography Series,* Vol. 5, Detroit, Gale, 1988.

Manuscript Collections: Kerlan Collection, University of Minnesota, Minneapolis; Boston University.

*   *   *

While Jane Langton is known as a writer of mysteries for adults which appeal to older teenagers, most of her works for young adults are aimed at readers aged ten to fourteen. Whether chronicling Grace Jones's bumpy journey into adolescence or the mystical adventures of the Hall family, Langton's works glow with a sense of history, place, and the value of the individual spirit.

The sense of history and place is strongest in Langton's fantasies set in Concord, Massachusetts, where eighteenth-century colonists fired the opening shots of the American Revolution and nineteenth-century transcendentalists rethought the goals of human endeavor. Concord's transcendentalist history permeates *The Diamond in the Window, The Astonishing Stereoscope, The Swing in the Summerhouse,* and *The Fledgling; The Fragile Flag* carries its message out to the rest of the world. Together, these five stories chronicle the continuing saga of the Hall family—Eddy and Eleanor, their uncle Freddy, and their stepcousin Georgie—in physical and metaphorical adventures that teach the children about themselves and the world. Particularly in the first work, Langton uses Concord and its past to great advantage. In their magical dreams Eddie and Eleanor become toys Louisa May Alcott and her sisters loved and mice who share Henry David Thoreau's cabin beside Walden pond; their quest to free relatives who vanished years before ends as Concord celebrates the anniversary of the revolution's opening shots.

These works are, in effect, transcendentalist novels. The Hall family, unique and somewhat shabby, eschews monetary treasures for the greater riches of warm hearts and wide-ranging minds. The words of Thoreau and of Ralph Waldo Emerson echo through the novels in Freddy's conversations, a great—if unhinged—transcendentalist scholar. In their dreams Eddy and Eleanor listen to Emerson's aeolian harp, hearing through it the sounds of the universe, and escape from inside a chambered nautilus only by

"building more stately mansions" of intellect and soul; they learn the wonder of even the least significant creature by finding the representation of the universe in an atom in the cell of a kitten and evolve from fish to human to see truth-seeking humans as the pinnacle of natural progress. Georgie's friendship with a Canada goose emblematizes her stewardship of the earth, which she acts out by leading a children's crusade against nuclear holocaust.

A major theme of Langton's works is the ultimate value of the individual human spirit. Grace Jones is one such spirit in *The Boyhood of Grace Jones,* set in the late 1930s. Suffused with the works of Arthur Ransome and reluctant to give up her individuality to become a painted doll giggling over boys and movie stars, Grace charts a choppy course through early adolescence, wearing her father's World War I middy over her clothes and imagining herself as adventure-seeking sailor "True Blue Tom." Grace's silent champion, as she swaggers through the halls of junior high school as if on the deck of a rolling ship, is handsome music teacher Mr. Chester, who values her "vital spark." Though she gives up the middy and the mental image of Tom by the end of the book, the spark remains. Grace knows herself and has become infatuated with the power of words, with the "clashing together of the hot and the cold" inside her at the images in "Kubla Khan" and "The Rime of the Ancient Mariner" and with her own power to create those feelings with words.

Emphasis on the value of the individual is central to the fantasies Langton creates. Many of Eddy and Eleanor's adventures teach them the value of their own individuality, and the Hall family adults guide them in working out their own identities. Faced with Georgie's intensity, her parents quell their misgivings and help her start her antinuclear march to Washington, D.C.

Langton constantly contrasts the impractical, individualistic, large-hearted Halls with their community. The Concord of the books—in the persons of Mr. Preek and Miss Prawn, the local banker and his secretary is the one Thoreau fled: complacent, conforming, smug about its history, and barren of imagination. Preek and Prawn plot to eliminate the Halls' exotic Victorian house, planted among Concord's square white houses like a "tropical plant in a field of New England daisies," and Prawn is as proud of being descended from the man who jailed Thoreau for not paying his poll tax as she is of signing papers to commit the most individual man in Concord: Uncle Freddy.

Freddy is the ideal transcendentalist, Thoreau's "once-and-a-half-witted" man who is thought half-witted by his neighbors. Maddened in the first novel by the disappearance of his brother, sister, and best friend, Freddy acts out transcendentalist metaphors, becoming the poor but spiritual man in the hollow tree who Thoreau would visit, blowing bubbles emblematic of Emerson's concentric circles that imprison the individual until a new idea breaks him free. Knocked back into reason by a bust of Louisa May Alcott—a delightful image, given Alcott's hardheaded stance against nonsense and fairy tales—Freddy remains the man who marches to his own drummer. Loving and lovable, rejoicer in nature and the spirit, he cares not what society thinks of him. Freddy lacks the dignity which Emerson may have felt essential, but his life is tinged by a rainbow as Thoreau wished his to be. Freddy literally slides down a rainbow and is left with a piece of it, symbolic of, in Thoreau's words, the "true harvest of [his] daily life."

Theme-rich as Langton's novels are, they also are rich in humor and in fascinating characters. The engaged reader glides happily through lucent prose in her layered novels. The setting of Langton's novels is precisely delineated from the beauties of Thoreau's Walden to the grimy landscape through which the Children's Crusade marches. Describing the bumpy course of young adolescence, Langton never forgets that each adolescence is unique. Eddy, Eleanor, Grace, and Georgie are three-dimensional individuals surrounded by secondary characters who come alive, from boisterous and irrepressible Oliver Winslow to practical and officious Frieda Caldwell. The result is that the reader comes away not just with messages, but with memories of lively, characters with all their humor and warts—individual spirits all.

—Pat Pflieger, updated by Rebecca R. Saulsbury

LASKY, Kathryn

Pseudonym: Also writes as Kathryn Lasky Knight. **Nationality:** American. **Born:** Indianapolis, Indiana, 24 June 1944. **Education:** University of Michigan, Ann Arbor, B.A. 1966; Wheelock College, Boston, Massachusetts, M.A. 1977. **Family:** Married Christopher Knight in 1971; one daughter and one son. **Career:** Writer. **Awards:** *Boston Globe-Horn Book* award, 1981, for *The Weaver's Gift*; ALA notable book citations, 1981, for *The Night Journey* and *The Weaver's Gift*, 1984, for *Sugaring Time*, and 1985, for *Puppeteer*; National Jewish Book award, Jewish Welfare Board Book Council, and Sydney Taylor Book award, Association of Jewish Libraries, both 1982, both for *The Night Journey*; ALA best books for young adults citations, 1983, for *Beyond the Divide*, 1984, for *Prank*, and 1986, for *Pageant*; *New York Times* notable book citation, 1983, for *Beyond the Divide*; Newbery Honor Book, ALA, 1984, for *Sugaring Time*; *Washington Post*/Children's Book Guild Nonfiction award, 1986, for body of work; ''Youth-to-Youth Books: A List for Imagination and Survival'' citation, Pratt Library's Young Adult Advisory Board, 1988, for *The Bone Wars*; Western Writers of America Best Western Juvenile Nonfiction Award, 1993, for *Searching for Laura Ingalls*; Parent's Choice Honor Book, 1993, for *Monarchs*; Parent's Choice award, 1994, for *The Librarian Who Measured the Earth*; Children's Bookseller's Choice, NCSS/CBC Notable Book in Social Studies, IRA/CBC Children's Choices selection, 1996, for *She's Wearing a Dead Bird on Her Head*; Jefferson Cup, 1997, for *A Journey to the New World*; National Jewish Book award, 1997, for *Marven of the Great North Woods*. **Address:** 7 Scott Street, Cambridge, Massachusetts 02138, U.S.A.

PUBLICATIONS FOR YOUNG ADULTS

Fiction

The Night Journey, illustrated by Trina Schart Hyman. New York, Warne, 1981.
Beyond the Divide. New York, Macmillan, 1983.
Prank. New York, Macmillan, 1984.
Home Free. New York, Four Winds Press, 1985.
Pageant. New York, Four Winds Press, 1986.

The Bone Wars. New York, Morrow, 1988.
Double Trouble Squared. San Diego, California, Harcourt, 1991.
Shadows in the Water. San Diego, California, Harcourt, 1992.
Voice in the Wind. San Diego, California, Harcourt, 1993.
Beyond the Burning Time. New York, Scholastic, 1994.
Memories of a Bookbat. San Diego, California, Harcourt, 1994.
A Journey to the New World: The Diary of Remember Patience Whipple. New York, Scholastic, 1996.
True North: A Novel of the Underground Railroad. New York, Scholastic, 1996.
Dreams of the Golden Country: The Diary of Zipporah Felman. New York, Scholastic, 1998.

PUBLICATIONS FOR CHILDREN

Fiction

Agatha's Alphabet, with Lucy Floyd, illustrated by Dora Leder. Chicago, Rand McNally, 1975.
I Have Four Names for My Grandfather, illustrated with photographs by Christopher Knight. Boston, Little Brown, 1976.
Tugboats Never Sleep, photographs by Christopher Knight. Boston, Little Brown, 1977.
My Island Grandma, illustrated by Emily McCully. New York, Warne, 1979.
Jem's Island, illustrated by Ronald Himler. New York, Scribner, 1982.
Sea Swan, illustrated by Catherine Stock. New York, Macmillan, 1988.
Fourth of July Bear, illustrated by Helen Cogancherry. New York, Morrow, 1991.
I Have an Aunt on Marlborough Street, illustrated by Susan Guevara. New York, Macmillan, 1992.
The Tantrum, illustrated by Bobette McCarthy. New York, Macmillan, 1993.
Cloud Eyes, illustrated by Barry Moser. San Diego, California, Harcourt, 1994.
The Solo, illustrated by Bobette McCarthy. New York, Macmillan, 1994.
Pond Year, illustrated by Michael Bostock. Cambridge, Massachusetts, Candlewick Press, 1995.
The Gates of the Wind, illustrated by Janet Stevens. San Diego, California, 1995.
She's Wearing a Dead Bird on Her Head, illustrated by David Catrow. New York, Hyperion, 1995.
Lunch Bunnies, illustrated by Marilyn Hafner. Boston, Joy Street, 1996.
Grace the Pirate, illustrated by Karen Lee Schmidt. New York, Hyperion, 1997.
Marven of the Great North Woods, illustrated by Kevin Hawkes. San Diego, California, Harcourt, 1997.
Hercules: The Man, the Myth, the Hero, illustrated by Mark Hess. New York, Hyperion, 1997.
Alice Rose and Sam. New York, Hyperion, 1998.

Nonfiction

Tall Ships, photographs by Christopher Knight. New York, Scribner, 1978.
Dollmaker: The Eyelight and the Shadow, photographs by Christopher Knight. New York, Scribner, 1981.

The Weaver's Gift, photographs by Christopher Knight. New York, Warne, 1981.

Sugaring Time, photographs by Christopher Knight. New York, Macmillan, 1983.

A Baby for Max, photographs by Christopher Knight. New York, Scribner, 1984.

Puppeteer, photographs by Christopher Knight. New York, Macmillan, 1985.

Traces of Life: The Origins of Humankind, illustrated by Whitney Powell. New York, Morrow, 1989.

Dinosaur Dig, photographs by Christopher Knight. New York, Morrow, 1990.

Surtsey: The Newest Place on Earth, photographs by Christopher Knight. New York, Hyperion, 1992.

Think Like an Eagle: At Work with a Wildlife Photographer, photographs by Christopher Knight and Jack Swedberg. Boston, Little Brown, 1992.

Monarchs, photographs by Christopher Knight. San Diego, California, Harcourt, 1993.

With Meribah Knight, *Searching for Laura Ingalls: A Reader's Journey,* photographs by Christopher Knight. New York, Macmillan, 1993.

Days of the Dead, photographs by Christopher Knight. New York, Hyperion, 1994.

The Librarian Who Measured the Earth, illustrated by Kevin Hawkes. Boston, Little, Brown, 1994.

The Most Beautiful Roof in the World: Exploring the Rainforest Canopy, photographs by Christopher Knight. San Diego, California, Harcourt, 1997.

Shadows in the Dawn: The Lemurs of Madagascar, photographs by Christopher Knight. San Diego, California, Harcourt, 1998.

A Brilliant Streak: The Making of Mark Twain, illustrated by Barry Moser. San Diego, California, Harcourt, 1998.

PUBLICATIONS FOR ADULTS

Fiction as Kathryn Lasky Knight

Atlantic Circle, photographs by Christopher Knight. New York, Norton, 1985.

Trace Elements. New York, Norton, 1986.

The Widow of Oz. New York, Norton, 1989.

Mortal Words. New York, Simon and Schuster, 1990.

Mumbo Jumbo. New York, Simon and Schuster, 1991.

Dark Swan. New York, St. Martin's Press, 1994.

*

Media Adaptations: *Sugaring Time* (filmstrip and cassette), Random House, 1986, (videocassette), 1988.

Biography: Essay in *Speaking for Ourselves: Autobiographical Sketches by Notable Authors of Books for Young Adults,* compiled and edited by Donald R. Gallo, Vol. 1, National Council of Teachers of English, 1990; essay in *Writers for Young Adults,* edited by Ted Hipple, Vol. 2, New York, Scribners, 1997.

Critical Studies: Entry in *Children's Literature Review,* Vol. 11, Detroit, Gale, 1986.

Kathryn Lasky comments:

To me, the whole point of being an artist is being able to get up every morning and reinvent the world.

*   *   *

Kathryn Lasky is a versatile writer of books including fiction and nonfiction, picture books and novels for young adults. Her desire is that the readers will appreciate the world in which they live and come away with a sense of wonderment and joy. She also writes books under her married name of Kathryn Lasky Knight. As a very young girl, she was a voracious reader and "spinner of tales" who constantly wrote stories in secret and shared them with no one. She recalled, "I think I always felt that [writing] was my profession, announced or unannounced, paid or unpaid." Her mother noticed her creative expressions in talking and writing and encouraged her to be a writer.

Lasky's clear style, well-developed characterizations, and poetic imagery combine to produce books of facts that involve the reader and appeal to a wide audience. One of the themes in Kathryn Lasky's books has to do with Jewish culture. Writing directly from her own experiences, she explores the world with an artist's eye and imagination. *The Night Journey* (1981) is a true family story about her grandmother's escape from czarist Russia when Jews were being murdered or forced to serve in the army. Well written and exciting, switching from the present to past events adroitly, with memorable characters, the book won the National Jewish Book Award. Kathryn Lasky continues the Jewish autobiographical theme in *Pageant* (1986). Set at an exclusive girls' school in Indianapolis, it features Sarah Benjamin, who has hilarious adolescent problems while growing up, losing her sister to college, her best friend to a boy, and making decisions about what she really believes. For this work, Mrs. Lasky researched violins, plastic surgery, and ballet.

The Jewish theme is continued in *Prank* (1984). This book is set in Boston and opens with the desecration of a synagogue by the brother of the main character, Birdie. While trying to help her brother, Birdie researches the Nazi treatment of the Jews during World War II, and becomes increasingly aware of problems of anti-Semitism at home as well as of severe family problems. Though criticized for a weak plot, this book was distinguished for vital characterization and development of a topic not often addressed in young adult literature.

Another book that has been controversial is *Memoirs of a Bookbat.* Harper's early memories are of her parents fighting and her father filled with anger and drink. When Harper was seven her parents "got religion" and became part of the fundamentalist movement. They eventually became missionaries, traveling in a trailer from small town to town, organizing against anything they thought was evil. Their fights to censor books conflicts with teenaged Harper's love of books and starts her on the path to a duplicitous life. The final straw comes when her parents make Harper and her little sister Weezie march against an abortion clinic. Harper plots with a friend and runs away to live with her grandmother. Lasky is a bit heavy-handed, but she captures the closed and single-minded nature of faces we often see on the news.

The theme of dinosaurs is explored with great enthusiasm by Kathryn Lasky. This interest started when she was in charge of the tape recorder on an archaeology dig with her photographer husband in Nevada. "I was so fascinated by what these guys were digging up that I forgot I was doing the sound. After that, I became an armchair archaeologist and read everything about it I could." *The Bone Wars* (1988) was a result of Lasky finding the story of Cope and Marsh, the real life archaeologists upon which the story is based. Set during the Sioux Indian Wars and the Battle of the Little Bighorn, this novel follows the adventures of a young man talented in discovering and uncovering the bones of dinosaurs. Based on true events leading to the establishment of dinosaur bones being placed in museums, this book is fascinating and fast-paced, informing the reader not only about fossils, geography, and geology, but also about the traditions and sacred heritage of some of our Native Americans.

Continuing with her research, Ms. Lasky found drawings by Whitney Powell, who is one of the first artists to illustrate early cave women. After taking a course in anthropology and studying in the bone labs at Harvard University for a year, Lasky wrote *Traces of Life: The Origins of Humankind* (1989) with illustrations by Whitney Powell. This book explains the history of research on hominids, evolution, and the scientists who had a part in that research.

The dinosaur theme harmonizes with another of her interests in the westward movement. *Beyond the Divide* (1983) tells the story of a young Amish girl, Meribah, who finds herself alone and starving in the wilderness of the Sierras. Assisted by Indians, she survives to become a strong woman and return to a valley found while on the wagon train. The novel is so realistic it would be easy to believe that *Beyond the Divide* is directly from a diary of a young girl going West.

Extending the concept of the diary as a format, Kathryn Lasky has recently become involved with Scholastic's "Dear America" series, books written by a variety of authors that reflect the viewpoint of characters placed within authentic historical context. Lasky's first entry in this series, *A Journey to the New World: The Diary of Remember Patience Whipple,* is told from the point of view of a young woman who sailed on the Mayflower in 1620. As Lasky has sailed the Atlantic twice herself in a thirty-foot boat, she is able to empathize with the experiences of storms, fear, and sickness that she relates so well. Covering the period of the voyage and the first year in the new world, "Mem" lets us see each of the voyagers in their courage, pettiness, steadfastness, and guile. These are real people, not cardboard characters. The language and behaviors are true to the period and history comes alive in a fascinating manner.

This ability to use authentic language and behavior is what makes Lasky such an outstanding writer of historical fiction. It is obvious that there is a strong foundation of research underlying her work, but it never gets in the way of good storytelling. Two recent historical novels exemplify Lasky's control of this medium. *Beyond the Burning Time* is a powerful story set in the time of the Salem witch trials. Lasky presents action, but the heart of the story is in the exploration of the reactions of the characters as they try to cope with the hysteria of the time and seek the meaning of justice. *True North* is told through dual points of view; Afrika is a young slave running for freedom in the underground railroad and Lucy is an inhabitant of Boston who is buffeted by the anti- and pro-slavery debates of the time. It is obvious that Kathryn Lasky

presents strong female protagonists. Her young women are of their time, but are questioning, thinking characters.

Kathryn Lasky has made and continues to make an impact on young adult literature. Her well-researched books provide a thorough, accurate picture of whatever theme is being presented. Her use of lyrical language captures the moods as well as facts leaving the reader with "a sense of joy—indeed celebration" of the world in which they live.

—M. Jean Greenlaw, updated by Laura M. Zaidman

LATHAM, Jean Lee

Pseudonyms: Janice Gard; Julian Lee. **Nationality:** American. **Born:** Buckhannon, West Virginia, 19 April 1902. **Education:** West Virginia Wesleyan College, Buckhannon, A.B. 1925; Ithaca Conservatory (now College), New York, B.O.E. 1928; Cornell University, Ithaca, New York, M.A. 1930; West Virginia Institute of Technology, Montgomery, 1942. **Career:** Served as a trainer of inspectors, United States War Department Signal Corps, 1943-45: Silver Wreath, 1944. Teacher and professional speaker. Head of English department, Upshur County High School, West Virginia, 1926-28; substitute teacher of speech, West Virginia Wesleyan College, summer, 1927; teacher of English, history, and play production, Ithaca College, New York, 1928-29; editor-in-chief, Dramatic Publishing Co., Chicago, Illinois, 1930-36; freelance writer, 1936-41 and since 1945; trainer, U.S. War Department, Signal Corps Inspection Agency, 1943-45; director of workshops in juvenile writing, Indiana University Writers' Conference, Bloomington, 1959-60, and Writers' Conference in the Rocky Mountains, 1963. **Awards:** American Library Association John Newbery Medal for most distinguished contribution to children's literature, 1956, for *Carry On, Mr. Bowditch;* D.Litt.: West Virginia Wesleyan College, 1956; Boys' Clubs of America Junior Book award, 1957, for *Trail Blazer of the Seas;* Dade County Women of the Year awards, Theta Sigma Phi, 1961, *Miami News,* 1962. **Died** 13 June 1995.

PUBLICATIONS FOR YOUNG ADULTS

Fiction

Carry On, Mr. Bowditch, illustrated by John Cosgrave. Boston, Houghton Mifflin, 1955.
This Dear-Bought Land, illustrated by Jacob Landau. New York, Harper, 1957.
The Frightened Hero: A Story of the Siege of Latham House, illustrated by Barbara Latham. Philadelphia, Chilton, 1965.

Nonfiction

555 Pointers for Beginning Actors and Directors. Chicago, Dramatic Publishing, 1935.
The Story of Eli Whitney, illustrated by Fritz Kredel. New York, Aladdin, 1953.
Medals for Morse: Artist and Inventor, illustrated by Douglas Gorsline. New York, Aladdin, 1954.

Trail Blazer of the Seas, illustrated by Victor Mays. Boston, Houghton Mifflin, 1956.

On Stage, Mr. Jefferson!, illustrated by Edward Shenton. New York, Harper, 1958.

Young Man in a Hurry: The Story of Cyrus W. Field, illustrated by Victor Mays. New York, Harper, 1958.

Drake, the Man They Called a Pirate, illustrated by Frederick Chapman. New York, Harper, and London, Hamish Hamilton, 1960.

Samuel F.B. Morse: Artist-Inventor, illustrated by Jo Polseno. Champaign, Illinois, Garrard, 1961.

Translator, *Wa O' Ka,* by Pablo Ramirez, illustrated by Ramirez. Indianapolis, Bobbs Merrill, 1961.

Man of the Monitor: The Story of John Ericsson, illustrated by Leonard Everett Fisher. New York, Harper, 1962.

Eli Whitney: Great Inventor, illustrated by Louis F. Cary. Champaign, Illinois, Garrard, 1963.

The Chagres: Power of the Panama Canal. Champaign, Illinois, Garrard, 1964.

George W. Goethals: Panama Canal Engineer, illustrated by Hamilton Green. Champaign, Illinois, Garrard, 1965.

Retreat to Glory: The Story of Sam Houston. New York, Harper, 1965.

Sam Houston: Hero of Texas. Champaign, Illinois, Garrard, and London, Harper, 1965.

The Columbia: Powerhouse of North America. Champaign, Illinois, Garrard, 1967.

David Glasgow Farragut: Our First Admiral, illustrated by Paul Frame. Champaign, Illinois, Garrard, 1967.

Anchor's Aweigh: The Story of David Glasgow Farragut, illustrated by Eros Keith. New York, Harper, 1968.

Far Voyager: The Story of James Cook. New York, Harper, 1970.

Rachel Carson: Who Loved the Sea, illustrated by Victor Mays. Champaign, Illinois, Garrard, 1973.

Elizabeth Blackwell: Pioneer Woman Doctor, illustrated by Ethel Gold. Champaign, Illinois, Garrard, 1975.

Plays

The Alien Note. Chicago, Dramatic Publishing, 1930.

The Christmas Party, adaptation of the story by Zona Gale. Chicago, Dramatic Publishing, 1930.

Crinoline and Candlelight. Chicago, Dramatic Publishing, 1931.

The Giant and the Biscuits. Chicago, Dramatic Publishing, 1934.

The Prince and the Patters. Chicago, Dramatic Publishing, 1934.

Tommy Tomorrow. Chicago, Dramatic Publishing, 1935.

All on Account of Kelly. Chicago, Dramatic Publishing, 1937.

And Then What Happened? Chicago, Dramatic Publishing, 1937.

Mickey the Mighty. Chicago, Dramatic Publishing, 1937.

The Ghost of Rhodes Manor. New York, Dramatists Play Service, 1939.

Nine Radio Plays (includes *With Eyes Turned West, Mac and the Black Cat, Stew for Six, For Mister Jim, Debt of Honor, Cupid on the Cuff, Voices, The Way of Shawn,* and *Discipline by Dad*). Chicago, Dramatic Publishing, 1940.

Plays as Julian Lee

Another Washington. Chicago, Dramatic Publishing, 1931.

The Christmas Carol, adaptation of the story by Charles Dickens. Chicago, Dramatic Publishing, 1931.

A Fiancé for Fanny. Chicago, Dramatic Publishing, 1931.

I Will! I Won't! Chicago, Dramatic Publishing, 1931.

Keeping Kitty's Dates. Chicago, Dramatic Publishing, 1931.

Washington for All. Chicago, Dramatic Publishing, 1931.

Christmas for All. Chicago, Dramatic Publishing, 1932.

Thanksgiving for All, with Genevieve and Elwyn Swarthout, adaptation of *The Pompion Pie,* by Jane Tallman. Chicago, Dramatic Publishing, 1932.

The Children's Book, with Harriette Wilburr and Nellie Meader Linn. Chicago, Dramatic Publishing, 1933.

Just for Justin. Chicago, Dramatic Publishing, 1933.

Lincoln Yesterday and Today. Chicago, Dramatic Publishing, 1933.

Tiny Jim. Chicago, Dramatic Publishing, 1933.

He Landed from London. Chicago, Dramatic Publishing, 1935.

Christmas Programs for the Lower Grades, with Ann Clark. Chicago, Dramatic Publishing, 1937.

Thanksgiving Programs for the Lower Grades, with Ann Clark. Chicago, Dramatic Publishing, 1937.

Big Brother Barges In. Chicago, Dramatic Publishing, 1940.

The Ghost of Lone Cabin. Chicago, Dramatic Publishing, 1940.

PUBLICATIONS FOR CHILDREN

Fiction

The Cuckoo That Couldn't Count, with Bee Lewi, illustrated by Jacqueline Chwast. New York, Macmillan, 1961.

The Dog That Lost His Family, with Bee Lewi, illustrated by Karla Kuskin. New York, Macmillan, 1961.

When Homer Honked, with Bee Lewi, illustrated by Cyndy Szekeres. New York, Macmillan, 1961.

The Man Who Never Snoozed, with Bee Lewi, illustrated by Sheila Greenwald. New York, Macmillan, 1961.

What Tabbit the Rabbit Found, illustrated by Bill Dugan. Champaign, Illinois, Garrard, 1974.

Story Adaptations

Aladdin, illustrated by Pablo Ramirez. Indianapolis, Bobbs Merrill, 1961.

Ali Baba, illustrated by Pablo Ramirez. Indianapolis, Bobbs Merrill, 1961.

Hop O' My Thumb, illustrated by Arnalot. Indianapolis, Bobbs Merrill, 1961.

Jack the Giant Killer, illustrated by Pablo Ramirez. Indianapolis, Bobbs Merrill, 1961.

The Magic Fishbone, illustrated by Pablo Ramirez. Indianapolis, Bobbs Merrill, 1961.

Nutcracker, illustrated by Jose Correas. Indianapolis, Bobbs Merrill, 1961.

Puss in Boots, illustrated by Pablo Ramirez. Indianapolis, Bobbs Merrill, 1961.

The Brave Little Tailor, Hansel and Gretel, and Jack and the Beanstalk, illustrated by Pablo Ramirez and José Correas. Indianapolis. Bobbs Merrill, 1962.

The Ugly Duckling, Goldilocks and the Three Bears, and The Little Red Hen, illustrated by José Correas and Pablo Ramirez. Indianapolis, Bobbs Merrill, 1962.

Poetry

Who Lives Here?, illustrated by Benton Mahan. Champaign, Illinois, Garrard, 1974.

Plays

Thanks, Awfully! Chicago, Dramatic Publishing, 1929.
Christopher's Orphans. Chicago, Dramatic Publishing, 1931.
Lady to See You. Chicago, Dramatic Publishing, 1931.
A Sign unto You. Chicago, Dramatic Publishing, 1931.
The Blue Teapot. Chicago, Dramatic Publishing, 1932.
Broadway Bound. Chicago, Dramatic Publishing, 1933.
Master of Solitaire (produced in New York, 1936). Chicago, Dramatic Publishing, 1935.
The Bed of Petunias. Chicago, Dramatic Publishing, 1937.
Have a Heart! Chicago, Dramatic Publishing, 1937.
Here She Comes! Chicago, Dramatic Publishing, 1937.
Just the Girl for Jimmy. Chicago, Dramatic Publishing, 1937.
Smile for the Lady! Chicago, Dramatic Publishing, 1937.
Talk Is Cheap. Chicago, Dramatic Publishing, 1937.
Well Met by Moonlight. Chicago, Dramatic Publishing, 1937.
What Are You Going to Wear? Chicago, Dramatic Publishing, 1937.
They'll Never Look There! New York, Dramatists Play Service, 1939.
The Arms of the Law. Chicago, Dramatic Publishing, 1940.
Old Doc. Chicago, Dramatic Publishing, 1940.
Gray Bread. Evanston, Illinois, Row Peterson, 1941.
Minus a Million. New York, Dramatists Play Service, 1941.
People Don't Change. Chicago, Dramatic Publishing, 1941.
Señor Freedom. Evanston, Illinois, Row Peterson, 1941.
The House without a Key, adaptation of the novel by Earl Derr Biggers. Chicago. Dramatic Publishing, 1942.
The Nightmare. New York, Samuel French, 1943.

Radio Plays: for *First Nighter, Grand Central Station* and *Skippy Hollywood Theatre* programs, 1930-41.

Plays as Janice Gard

Lookin' Lovely. Chicago, Dramatic Publishing, 1930.
Listen to Leon. Chicago, Dramatic Publishing, 1931.
Depend on Me. Chicago, Dramatic Publishing, 1932.

*

Media Adaptations: *Old Doc* (television and presented on "Kraft Theatre" series), 1951.

Manuscript Collection: Kerlan Collection, University of Minnesota, Minneapolis.

Critical Study: Entry in *Contemporary Literary Criticism,* Volume 12, Detroit, Gale, 1980.

*   *   *

Jean Lee Latham is one of the most prolific biographers in children's and young adult literature, writing a series of substantial biographies for young adult readers whose length is astonishing, given the number of works she has published and the research that went into each. She was the first biographer to earn a Newbery Award, winning it in 1956 for *Carry on, Mr. Bowditch.* Her work spanned decades, but each biography is marked by one consistent factor: Latham's sense of story.

Latham's work is no longer as popular as it once was, both in public libraries and in critical circles. Following the work of writers like Jean Fritz and Milton Meltzer, biography for young readers began to become more rigorous in its application of scholarship. For Fritz, research is to mark every sentence; for Latham, research is only a foundation upon which one might build a large and wonderfully complex story.

The result is that Latham's work carries with it many techniques abhorred by biographers: fictionalized dialogue, fictionalized scenes and characters, interior thought which suggests motivations but which is not recorded in any historical document. In addition, Latham's characters each seem to have an annoyingly tidy life; each carries the seeds of his future in his childhood, and to anyone who might look hard enough, that future is evident. The result of these techniques is that Latham wrote what today would be called fictionalized biography, in which the central facts of the work are accurate, but much of the material built around those facts is conjecture or even pure fiction.

Latham's work focuses principally—though not exclusively—upon American male characters; her British characters, such as Sir Francis Drake, James Cook, and John Smith (of Jamestown fame) are explorers who never seem comfortable in England once their careers have begun. Latham treats these characters with remarkable consistency. Each, for example, begins as a young boy who shows little promise except to a single person—the Yankee peddler who senses Eli Whitney's technical skills, the teacher who perceives Matthew Maury's stubborn persistence, the tutor who recognizes the brilliant mind of Nathaniel Bowditch—but are unfortunately surrounded by other characters who do not see these qualities, and who in fact block the fulfillment of those qualities, with all good intentions.

However, each of the characters is also endowed with an extraordinary ability to persevere through and overcome the elements set in his path. And Latham gives each a phrase or symbol which is often repeated throughout the biography to stress that perseverance. "Carry on, Mr. Bowditch" is a line spoken by Bowditch's captain. Latham uses this phrase to suggest Bowditch's ability to overcome all difficulties—or, to put it in his own nautical terms, to not become becalmed. For James Cook, Latham suggests that he was determined to "keep on keeping on." At the end of *Medals for Morse,* when Samuel Morse is finally being cheered for inventing the telegraph, an admirer tells him that this is his hour of triumph. His reply is typical of a Latham character: "It's the only one that counts—the one when you finish what you set out to do."

This is biography cum fairy tale. A despised younger brother or son, faced with ridicule and abuse, finds the willing services of the larger-than-life character who perceives the son's true worth. After a time of difficulty and trial, the character's value is suddenly made dramatically manifest, and those who before had despised him cannot help but recognize his very special abilities. This is the pattern that Latham uses over and over again. James Cook, for example, the son of a common laborer, must prove his special abilities by serving aboard ships for twenty years before the navy grants him the commission which it gives to virtually any gentleman, whether or not it has been earned. But in the end, each one of these characters triumphs and overcomes poverty or accidents of birth or the ignorance and shortsightedness of those around him. The message in all of this is that by hard work and application, even a day laborer can become a captain. One needs only to exploit one's gifts and at the same time, suppress negative qualities. As in the fairy tale, goodness will win out.

This implicit didacticism in Latham's work is based on the proposition that a biography can in fact present models for behavior. In her work, Latham presents distinctly American role models in characters who are adventurous, eager, anxious to get ahead, technically competent, curious, and confident in their abilities as well as their natural goodness. The titles of Latham's biographies suggest these characteristics. Cyrus Field is the ''Young Man in a Hurry.'' James Cook is the ''Far Voyager.'' Matthew Maury is the ''Trail Blazer of the Seas,'' etc.

The sense of a character functioning as role model appears vividly in Latham's biography of John Smith, *This Dear-Bought Land.* This story of the founding of Jamestown and the difficult years in which the settlers faced death by illness, starvation, Indian raids, and suicidal madness is quite different in technique from Latham's other works. She presents Smith only in his mature years, though he too follows the pattern of being despised until his true worth is demonstrated. But what is significantly different in this biography is the use of the character David Warren, a young boy, nobly born, who is despised by those around him for his weakness and dependence upon his noble birth, rather than his own qualities. When his father is killed, David goes to Jamestown in his place, and at first fears, and then admires John Smith for his stubborn insistence that the colony must survive, and for his willingness to make all contribute to the welfare of the colony, even the gentlemen who have come and wish to have others work for them. John Smith thusly becomes a strong model for David; Latham seems to conjecture a similar relationship between her characters and her readers.

Latham's characters were explorers like James Cook, inventors like Eli Whitney, men of political acumen like Sam Houston, and those who combined those characteristics, like Thomas Jefferson. Certainly she set out to present them as archetypal Americans. But she also set out to tell an entertaining and vivid story, one that would capture the attention of her young readers. If Latham's work is not so well regarded today because of the fictionalization that she uses, her sense of story in biography still merits some recognition. Though some of her characters led lives that lent themselves to drama, many did not. And yet Latham crafted those lives into stories by using the pattern of pain and frustration leading to fulfillment and accomplishment. The very qualities she wished to promote were the qualities that generated good stories. Her characters may not be the accurate representations of Jean Fritz or Milton

Meltzer, but they are nonetheless real characters who struggle, who have doubts, who yearn for something, and who eventually achieve their goals.

—Gary D. Schmidt

———

LATTANY, Kristin Hunter. *See* HUNTER, Kristin.

———

LAWRENCE, Louise

Pseudonym for Elizabeth Rhoda Holden. **Nationality:** British. **Born:** Leatherhead, Surrey, 5 June 1943. **Education:** Poplar Road Primary School, Leatherhead, 1948-54; Lydney Grammar School, Gloucestershire, 1955-60. **Family:** Married twice; two daughters and one son. **Career:** Assistant librarian, Gloucestershire Country Library, 1961-63, and at Forest of Dean branches, 1969-71; writer, since 1971. **Agent:** A.M. Heath, 79 St. Martin's Lane, London, WC2N 4AA. **Address:** 22 Church Road, Cinderford, Gloucestershire GL14 2EA, England.

PUBLICATIONS FOR YOUNG ADULTS

Fiction

Andra. London, Collins, 1971.
The Power of Stars. London, Collins, and New York, Harper, 1972.
The Wyndcliffe. London, Collins, 1974; New York, Harper, 1975.
Sing and Scatter Daisies. New York, Harper, 1977.
Star Lord. New York, Harper, 1978; London, Bodley Head, 1987.
Cat Call. New York, Harper, 1980.
The Earth Witch. New York, Harper, 1981; London, Collins, 1982.
Calling B for Butterfly. New York, Harper, 1982; London, Bodley Head, 1988.
The Dram Road. New York, Harper, 1983.
Children of the Dust. London, Bodley Head, and New York, Harper, 1985.
Moonwind. London, Bodley Head, and New York, Harper, 1986.
The Warriors of Taan. London, Bodley Head, 1986; New York, Harper, 1988.
Extinction Is Forever and Other Stories. New York, HarperCollins, 1990.
Ben-Harran's Castle. London, Bodley Head, 1992; as *The Keeper of the Universe,* New York, Clarion Books, 1992.
The Dispossessed. London, Bodley Head, 1994; as *The Patchwork People,* New York, Clarion Books, 1994.
Journey Through Llandor. London, HarperCollins, 1995.
The Road to Irriyan. London, HarperCollins, 1996.

The Shadow of Mordican. London, HarperCollins, 1996.
The Dreamweaver. London, HarperCollins, 1996; New York, Clarion Books, 1997.

*

Biography: Essay in *Speaking for Ourselves, Too* compiled and edited by Donald R. Gallo, National Council of Teachers of English, 1993.

*   *   *

The late 1960s and early 1970s saw a tremendous increase in young adult fantasy writing. Tolkien's impact had been digested, authors were setting trilogies and longer sequences in fantasy worlds like Earthsea and Prydain, but more significant was Alan Garner's example: the Celtic or folklore fantasy set in the modern era. Of the many authors who made a science fiction/fantasy debut then, few have remained faithful either to the genre or the age group. Louise Lawrence, however, has persisted in her art, moving away from Garnerian fantasy towards pure science fiction, to the point where she should be recognised as Britain's senior woman practitioner of young adult science fiction. It has been a long and dogged journey, each accomplished novel giving no hint of the struggle to write it and to have it published.

In her first decade of writing, Louise Lawrence wrote in three genres: science fiction, fantasy, and horror (more specifically the "ghost story"). She began with *Andra,* set in the future when all humans live in underground cities because Earth's climate and orbit around the sun have been seriously damaged by war. The war continues: the Uralians intend to sabotage Sub-City One's plan to emigrate in spaceships to settle on an Earth-type planet. Andra, a girl whose brain transplant gives her memories of Earth before the disaster, becomes a rebel and inspires the young people. But—in a twist typical of Lawrence—there is no happy ending.

Next came *The Power of Stars,* blending science fiction and Garnerian fantasy. Bacteria from space infects a rabbit; the rabbit bites a girl; she becomes possessed by "the power of stars." Two teenage boys investigate the girl's strange behaviour. The clash between rich boy and poor local boy, the clipped dialogue, the sudden shifts of scene, and the Welsh border setting all recall Garner's *The Owl Service.*

Her third book was *The Wyndcliffe,* a ghost story about a girl haunted by the spirit of a dead Romantic poet, John Hollis. The sequel, *Sing and Scatter Daisies,* carried the story into the next generation, but British readers could not know this since the book was only published in the United States. Lawrence's British publisher turned down nearly everything she wrote while her American publisher continued to publish her writing. British audiences consequently missed her return to science fiction with *Star Lord,* and her powerful fantasy *Cat Call. The Earth Witch,* set in Wales, another Celtic fantasy in the Garnerian mode, was her last book for the British publisher Collins. It is about a teenager trapped in a love affair with the pagan Earth Witch. Collins then turned down her science fiction novel *Calling B for Butterfly* and her ghost

story *The Dram Road,* in which a violent teenager is redeemed by an old man's love, the forces of nature, and a friendly village community, with the ghosts of the man's wife and son hovering in the background.

Lawrence continued her career in Britain with *Children of the Dust,* signalling a commitment to science fiction and a stronger emphasis on political and environmental issues. In the early 1980s the protest against nuclear weapons and the Cold War became an enormously popular movement in Western Europe. Inspired by the involvement of her own children in peace marches, Lawrence wrote about a nuclear attack on Britain, showing the effect it had on one family living near Bristol: those who went underground into the bunkers prepared for a nuclear war, and those who remained to try to survive the nuclear winter. Eventually in a fantastic conclusion, humankind evolves physically and mentally (with psychokinetic powers) to cope with nuclear radiation.

Lawrence's new British publisher, Bodley Head, encouraged more science fiction combining the rite-of-passage of a teenager with a political theme. Returning to her favourite Welsh background, she wrote *Moonwind,* about a boy from Wales awarded a holiday on the Moon. There he encounters an alien spirit-woman stranded for 10,000 years by a fault in her starship. He helps to repair the smashed piece of equipment, and she offers a hint of escape from Earth's pollution by voyaging back to her beautiful home planet. But to do this, he would have to leave his physical body—die—and trust her assurance that his spirit would live on.

Next came *The Warriors of Taan.* Set on a planet colonized by Earthlings, it is still science fiction, but as the natives have a feudal culture, with women living separate from men and worshipping a Goddess, it is also something of a heroic, feminist fantasy. The sisterhood of Taan plots to take over the male culture and even tame the Earthlings. Bodley Head also republished several of Lawrence's science fiction novels, including *Star Lord,* about an alien starship crashing into a Welsh mountain, with hints that the mountain's power caused the crash (Celtic fantasy again), and *Calling B for Butterfly,* about six children surviving a starship disaster who are rescued by an alien force—but their fate is not to return to Earth, but to voyage on into space.

The characteristics of a mature Lawrence novel are now apparent: a setting in Wales or the Welsh borders, near Gloucestershire where she has lived for most of her life; a prophetic element, warning against pollution, nuclear war, and the overuse of technology, and hence a feminist outlook; the ethical dilemma of the central young adult character, posed directly to the reader; a downbeat ending, perhaps a temporary victory, or redemption through death. Finally a special way with words: poetic prose and the occasional "purple passage" describing the landscape, the forces of nature, the joy of music, or the incredible beauty of a nebula in deep space.

Having published a few short stories in a couple of anthologies, Lawrence's next project was a book of stories, entitled *Extinction Is Forever.* By the end of the book her talents and obsessions have been fully showcased. The title story is a chiller: nuclear war has nearly wiped out all life on earth; humans have mutated to become sea creatures; a time traveller discovers this, but the mutants destroy his time machine to stop him from returning to the past with this vital warning. Another story, "The Death Flower," suggests that only by destroying most of Earth's population—everyone with an aggressive streak—can the planet be saved.

Human aggression is also the theme of her novel, *Ben-Harran's Castle*. The book depicts a universe where each planet is controlled by a mild, hypnotic system to control aggression, to keep them crime-free and ensure that wars never happen, apart from the planets in the galaxy where the Galactic Controller, Ben-Harran, has decreed that free will is God's will. But the High Council wants the population to stop destroying one another, and after another of Ben-Harran's planets has exploded in nuclear conflagration, the Council recalls him and puts him on trial. The book suggests that if planetary controls are imposed on Earth, humans would lose their artistic creativity and potential for spiritual development, for under these controls people are unaware of their souls and lose their awareness of God. The conflict is seen through the eyes of two teenagers, one from Earth, the other from a "controlled" planet, kidnapped by Ben-Harran to debate the issue with him and the Council. With this powerful metaphysical work Lawrence reaches the current height of her powers.

Lawrence returns to Wales for the setting of her futuristic novel *The Dispossessed,* published as *The Patchwork People* in the United States. The outlook is grim when the novel opens, the gap between rich and poor overwhelming because of pollution, technology, and the overuse of irreplaceable resources. The water level is rising along with mortality rates because of the greenhouse effect. There is a world-wide depression, and riots erupt as frustration mounts. When Hugh rescues Helena during a riot, the stage for subsequent meetings is set. She arranges for her father, a colliery manager, to get Hugh and his friends jobs, but that only creates more problems. Hugh realizes that he must find a way of life that will last, but he doubts that Helena will be able to give up her luxurious lifestyle to share it with him. The ending is upbeat, however, as Helena shows that she is more than capable of adapting as a potential solution is offered to those willing to work for it in a return to the land.

Lawrence next worked on the Llandor trilogy, beginning with *Journey through Llandor.* In it Roderick, Craig, and Carrie are transported from England to a fantasy world where they are helped by an elf girl and others as Grim Thane threatens them. The story continues in *Road to Irriyan* as the three awaken from a long sleep to learn that the evil Grim Thane continues to pursue them. He wants to wrest from them their knowledge of modern weapons. The third book of the trilogy, *The Shadow of Mordican,* finds Craig and Carrie under the spell of Irriyan until Craig begins to realize that all is not as it seems. This fantasy trilogy, published only in England, is a sharp departure from the stark reality of *The Dispossessed.*

The Dreamweaver contains many of the characteristics mentioned earlier: warnings against war and violence, pollution and the overuse of technology, and the "ethical dilemma of the young adult character." There are differences, however. The primary setting is no longer Wales but Arbroth, similar to Earth before it was destroyed by technology, pollution, and wars. Approaching Arbroth is a spaceship with over 3000 Earth inhabitants and their technology ready to start the destructive process all over again. When the Earthling Troy expresses his anguish over the destruction he foresees the ship's occupants committing against a lovely planet and its agrarian people, he connects to Eth on Arbroth. Although the people on Arbroth have returned to the land and forsaken most technology, some like Eth have telepathic and other mindpowers. By the time the spaceship arrives—a span of seven years—a solution is found that leaves the reader hopeful and with the knowledge that technology is not all bad. These last two books offer a positive outlook for the human condition as Louise Lawrence continues to warn readers of the dangers of human destruction in compelling and talented novels.

—Jessica Yates, updated by Marilyn F. Apseloff

LEE, (Nelle) Harper

Nationality: American. **Born:** Monroeville, Alabama, 28 April 1926. **Education:** Huntington College, Indiana, 1944-45; University of Alabama, Tuscaloosa, 1945-49; Oxford University, Wellington Square. **Career:** Airline reservation clerk with Eastern Air Lines and British Overseas Airways, New York, during the 1950s; left to devote full time to writing. Member, National Council on Arts, 1966-72. **Awards:** Pulitzer Prize, 1961, Alabama Library Association award, 1961, Brotherhood award of National Conference of Christians and Jews, 1961, *Bestsellers'* paperback of the year award, 1962, all for *To Kill a Mockingbird.*

PUBLICATIONS

Novel

To Kill a Mockingbird. Philadelphia, Lippincott, 1960; London, Heinemann, 1960.

*

Media Adaptations: *To Kill a Mockingbird* (movie), Horton Foote, 1962. The book was adapted into a play by Christopher Sergel and produced in England in 1987.

Biography: Entry in *Dictionary of Literary Biography,* Volume 6: *American Novelists since World War II, Second Series,* Detroit, Gale, 1980.

Critical Studies: Entry in *Contemporary Literary Criticism,* Volume 12, Detroit, Gale, 1980.

*   *   *

Harper Lee's only novel, *To Kill a Mockingbird,* won the 1961 Pulitzer Prize for Fiction and established her place in young adult literature. Universal themes of justice, compassion, racism, and family love enrich this drama set in Maycomb, Alabama (inspired by Lee's Monroeville, Alabama, home) in the 1930s. Transcending place and time, this modern American classic celebrates the courage of people who face adversity with dignity.

Narrator Jean Louise (Scout) Finch recollects three years of events leading to her brother Jem's accident: one arm was broken so badly that it healed shorter than the other. Scout obviously has emotional scars from this event twenty-five years ago. She begins the story when she was six, the summer their friend Dill encouraged them to make the reclusive Boo Radley emerge from his house. Neighborhood legend said this six-foot-six-inch terror dined on raw squirrels and stray cats, had rotten teeth, and drooled most of the time. After the novel's climactic scene on a frightening Halloween night, the children know more about the mysterious Boo who does indeed come out, yet their questions about the greater mystery of racism remain unanswered. The events following that summer of innocent play initiate the children into the darker experiences of social prejudice, cruelty, and fears. Scout and Jem witness the tragic consequences of persecuting people who are different, for Boo was very nice once they met him.

Not only are recluses such as Boo unfortunately branded as menacing threats to society, but blacks also suffer from social injustice. Some of the novel's most dramatic scenes occur in the courtroom as their father, Atticus Finch, a highly respected lawyer and citizen, defies townspeople's prejudice and heroically defends a black man falsely accused of raping a white woman. Before the trial, Atticus explains to Scout and Jem his belief in personal integrity: how people conduct themselves in trying times shows their true character. Atticus defends his unpopular decision to defend a black man accused of a heinous crime by telling his daughter that the only thing that does not abide by majority rule is a person's conscience.

In a Southern town dominated by whites, the ultimate crime is said to have been committed when Tom Robinson, a poor black laborer, is accused of raping Mayella Ewell, a poor white woman. Atticus proves that Tom is clearly innocent, and Bob Ewell, Mayella's father, is obviously guilty of beating her for making sexual advances toward Tom. However, as Atticus states, social injustice will prevail in a system ruled by white men convinced from childhood that "*all* Negroes lie, that *all* Negroes are basically immoral beings, that *all* Negro men are not to be trusted around our women. . . ." His impassioned plea to let the court treat all races equally falls on the all-male, all-white jury's unsympathetic ears. Because "a court is only as sound as its jury, and a jury is only as sound as the men who make it up," Tom is murdered—the scapegoat of society's prejudice and violence.

By the same token, racism also destroys the lives of whites. Mayella, victimized by her father, helps crucify an innocent man to save herself. Although Bob Ewell may be a victim of the poverty, ignorance, and bigotry that create racism, he proves to be a truly malevolent character who warrants no sympathy for his fate. In addition to the destructive impact on the Ewells, Scout and Jem also suffer from Maycomb's racism by enduring the insults of both children and adults. After Jem confesses to vandalizing Mrs. Dubose's camellias (retaliating for her saying that Atticus was "no better than the niggers and trash he works for!"), Atticus explains that the sick old woman should not be held responsible for what she says; she is one more pitiable victim of society's bigotry. Jem is punished by having to read aloud two hours to the woman everyday

after school and on Saturdays for a month; as a result, he gains greater insight into the woman he once despised. The lessons learned undoubtedly will strengthen his character as an adult.

All these experiences over the three-year period validate the truth of Atticus's remark that "it's a sin to kill a mockingbird." The analogy between the senseless slaughter of innocent songbirds and Tom's tragic death becomes clear to Scout. She suddenly understands that not protecting Boo Radley from being implicated in Bob Ewell's death would "be sort of like shootin' a mockingbird." Although Atticus fails to save Tom, he teaches his children about racial justice and human dignity. Harper Lee's *To Kill a Mockingbird* has remained popular with young adults because it dramatizes so well the best and worst in human nature.

—Laura M. Zaidman

LEE, Julian. *See* **LATHAM, Jean Lee.**

LEE, Mildred

Nationality: American. **Born:** Blocton, Alabama, 19 February 1908. **Education:** Cairo High School, Georgia; Bessie Tift College, Forsyth, Georgia, 1925-26; Troy Normal College, Alabama, 1927; Columbia University, New York, 1936; New York University; University of New Hampshire, Durham, 1944. **Family:** Married 1) Edward Cannon Schimpff in 1929 (divorced), one daughter and one son; 2) James Henry Scudder in 1947, one daughter. **Awards:** Child Study Association Children's Book Award, 1964, for *The Rock and the Willow;* Austrian National Award and Alabama Association Award, 1971, for *The Skating Rink.* **Address:** 1361 52 Avenue North, St. Petersburg, Florida 33703, U.S.A.

PUBLICATIONS FOR YOUNG ADULTS

Fiction

The Rock and the Willow. New York, Lothrop, 1963; London, Oxford University Press, 1975.
Honor Sands. New York, Lothrop, 1966.
The Skating Rink. New York, Seabury Press, 1969; London, Abelard Schumann, 1972.
Fog. New York, Seabury Press, 1972.
Sycamore Year. New York, Lothrop, 1974.
The People Therein. New York, Clarion, 1980.

PUBLICATIONS FOR ADULTS

Fiction

The Invisible Sun. Philadelphia, Westminster Press, 1946.

*

Biography: Entry in *Third Book of Junior Authors,* New York, H.W. Wilson, 1972; essay in *Something about the Author Autobiography Series,* Volume 12, Detroit, Gale, 1991.

Manuscript Collections: University of Wyoming Library, Laramie; Kerlan Collection, University of Minnesota, Minneapolis.

Mildred Lee comments:

The Rock and the Willow was in a sense the beginning, though the desire and need to write goes back almost to the beginning of my life. There was nothing strange or even particularly serious about it to me. No more than the games and fantasies of my friends. I shared this characteristic of "making things up" with my younger siblings and, as I grew older, with those of my friends who were interested. Not many were; it was a very personal and private longing.

I was very greedy for life. Much as I wanted to write, it never occurred to me that I might sacrifice practically everything to achieve success. I wanted the same things other people had: marriage, a home, children. These I had and would not have missed the experience however much more time for writing I might have had had I made that choice. Still, when I neglected what I still call my Proper Work I carried a considerable burden of guilt. After I had had several short stories and a novel, *The Invisible Sun,* published I went through a staggeringly long barren time but I never gave up the idea of writing, not once.

It must have been some time in the 1950s when I began the novel I called "The Big Road" but later changed to *The Rock and the Willow.* I took an interminable time with it. The story was told from the viewpoint of the eldest daughter of a poor Alabama farm family. I had no thought in writing it of age or classification. The Singleton family were people. I lived close to them and they became very real to me. Somehow I managed eventually to finish it and send it forth to begin its many journeys—always round trips. I did not even know the term "Young Adult." I knew there were children's books and probably thought of them as juveniles—though no one could have derived more pleasure from the young people's books of my adolescence than I had.

I had copied a list of book publishers from a publication in the library and when *The Rock and the Willow* came back from one I sent it to another. Several times it had almost made it; I'd get a note instead of a rejection slip which softened the blow and some of the notes were downright encouraging. E.P. Dutton kept the manuscript for weeks and made the complaint that it was difficult to categorize it without, however, suggesting it be turned over to the young people's department (maybe they didn't have one then, I don't know).

I sent it to fifteen publishing houses and hope was ebbing if not nearly gone. I remember thinking, "It isn't going to be published." In my heart I knew it was a good book and told myself this, but it wasn't going to be published. Of course I'd had other books that had not been published but they had not hurt like this one that I knew was good. One blue Monday morning the phone rang and it was Beatrice Creighton, editor in chief of Lothrop, Lee and Shepard in New York, and she was saying "Miss Lee, we would *love* to publish your beautiful book . . ." I waited for the inevitable "but." It did not come. Instead she proffered an invitation to me to come to New York to discuss some possible slight changes in the book. I had not known that Lothrop was a publisher of books for young people only!

Through the haze of my delirious joy there was a recurring tinge of. . .what? Disappointment? Discontent? Dissatisfaction? I had intended my book for a general public's reading—not tucked into a pigeonhole. Well, it wasn't; I could not have asked for a more gracious, surprising, splendid reception than it got. Also it opened the door that must have been waiting for me. My only regret is that I have not a greater achievement—a longer list of books. Anything I have written that has been of help in the often difficult job of growing up cannot have been wasted.

*   *   *

Spanning two decades of her life, from her fifties to her seventies, Mildred Lee wrote six novels for young adults. In many ways, it seems remarkable that a woman at that age could have written so accurately and perceptively about the feelings and behavior of teenagers—both male and female, underprivileged and privileged, present-day and in the past.

All of Lee's main characters are adolescents who are introspective and sensitive, aware of their feelings of self-doubt and loneliness. In the course of the stories, all of them experience confusing and contradictory emotional, intellectual, and sexual awakenings. They survive death, loss, or abuse. All of them grow and are strengthened through these experiences, but their triumphs are never forced or flashy. Lee's style is quiet; her stories unfold naturally. Her closures are never final, pointing toward further pain, hope, and growth.

Two of Lee's main characters have physical disabilities—Tuck Faraday in *The Skating Rink* stutters and Ailanthus Farr in *The People Therein* limps—and Lee uses these handicaps to emphasize the sense of being different and the resulting alienation these characters feel. In some ways, their physical imperfections are metaphors for the limitations of all individuals, for even the more typical adolescents of her novels, such as *Fog, Sycamore Year,* and *Honor Sands,* seem very aware of circumstances, such as poverty, which they perceive as making them different or keeping them from realizing their potential.

All of Lee's novels are set in the southeastern United States, either in rural areas or small towns. Two, however, *The Rock and the Willow* and *The People Therein,* take place in the mountains of southern Appalachia and are strongly evocative of the beauty of the place and the values of the inhabitants. Earline "Enie" Singleton, the main character in *The Rock and the Willow,* grew up in Tired Creek, Alabama, in the 1930s, while *The People Therein,* which begins in 1910, is the story of Ailanthus "Lanthy" Farr who lived near Dewfall Gap, North Carolina. Although the novels are separated by two decades and several state borders, the sense of place and lifestyles of the families are similar. In both stories, Lee has presented young women who are strong and independent, hardworking and poor, women who love their families and homes but rebel against the rigid customs and beliefs of their parents and forge their own ways.

Through the encouragement and interest of a teacher, Enie discovers her passion for learning and writing, but her decision to go to college and become a teacher herself seems doomed due to lack of money, her mother's death, and her father's resistance.

Although Enie remained skeptical whenever her mother would say, ''God moves in mysterious ways His wonders to perform,'' in the end she comes to acknowledge the fact that things sometimes do work out in totally unanticipated ways.

Lee's novels definitely have an old-fashioned flavor about them, although the themes of alienation and developmental growth toward wholeness transcend time and place. Even those that are set in contemporary times depict a quieter and slower paced life, far removed from modern-day MTV (Music Television) and Nintendo. While her books predate these particular phenomena, she did write most of them during the sixties and seventies, certainly turbulent times for many young adults. That her books do not mirror contemporary historical events is certainly an intentional choice on her part. She seems content to focus on the smaller, more personal, and more universal issues of family relations and self-identity. Her novels have never appealed to all adolescents, but they have been and will continue to be satisfying and comforting reading experiences for more contemplative young adults.

—Linda J. Wilson

LEE, Tanith

Nationality: British. **Born:** London, 19 September 1947. **Education:** Attended Prendergaste Grammar School; Catford Grammar School, London, and an art college. **Career:** Librarian, writer. **Awards:** August Derleth award, 1980; World Fantasy Convention award, 1983. **Agent:** c/o Macmillan London Ltd., 4 Little Essex Street, London WC2R 3LF, England.

PUBLICATIONS FOR YOUNG ADULTS

Fiction

The Dragon Hoard, illustrated by Graham Oakley. London, Macmillan, and New York, Farrar Straus, 1971.
Princess Hynchatti and Some Other Surprises, illustrated by Helen Craig. London, Macmillan, 1972; New York, Farrar Straus, 1973.
Companions on the Road. London, Macmillan, 1975.
The Winter Players. London, Macmillan, 1976.
Companions on the Road [and] *The Winter Players.* New York, St. Martin's Press, 1977.
East of Midnight. London, Macmillan, 1977; New York, St. Martin's Press, 1978.
The Castle of Dark. London, Macmillan, 1978.
Shon the Taken. London, Macmillan, 1979.
Prince on a White Horse. London, Macmillan, 1982.
Black Unicorn, illustrated by Heather Cooper. New York, Atheneum, 1991.
Dark Dance. New York, Dell, 1992.
Gold Unicorn. Sutton, Severn House, 1994.

PUBLICATIONS FOR CHILDREN

Fiction

Animal Castle, illustrated by Helen Craig. London, Macmillan, and New York, Farrar Straus, 1972.

PUBLICATIONS FOR ADULTS

Novels

The Birthgrave. New York, DAW, 1975; London, Futura, 1977.
Don't Bite the Sun. New York, DAW, 1976.
The Storm Land. New York, DAW, 1976; London, Futura, 1977.
Drinking Sapphire Wine. New York, DAW, 1977.
Volkhavaar. New York, DAW, 1977; London, Hamlyn, 1981.
Night's Master. New York, DAW, 1978; London, Hamlyn, 1981.
The Prince of Demons. DAW, 1978.
Quest for the White Witch. New York, DAW, 1978; London, Futura, 1979.
Vazkor, Son of Vazkor. New York, DAW, 1978; as *Shadowfire,* London, Futura, 1979.
Death's Master. New York, DAW, 1979; London, Hamlyn, 1982.
Drinking Sapphire Wine (includes *Don't Bite the Sun*). London, Hamlyn, 1979.
Electric Forest. New York, DAW, 1979.
Day by Night. New York, DAW, 1980.
Kill the Dead. New York, DAW, 1980.
Sabella; or, The Blood Stone. New York, DAW, 1980.
Delusion's Master. New York, DAW, 1981.
The Silver Metal Lover. New York, DAW, 1982; London, Unwin, 1986.
Anackire. New York, DAW, 1983; London, Futura, 1985.
Sung in Shadow. New York, DAW, 1983.
Days of Grass. New York, DAW, 1985.
Dark Castle, White Horse. New York, DAW, 1986.
Delirium's Mistress. New York, DAW, 1986.
Night's Sorceries. New York, DAW, 1987.
The White Serpent. New York, DAW, 1988.
Forests of the Night. London, Unwin Hyman, 1989.
A Heroine of the World. New York, DAW, 1989.
Lycanthia. London, Legend, 1990.
The Blood of Roses. Century, 1990.
Heart-beast. London, Headline, 1992.
Nightshades. London, Headline, 1993.
Elephantasm. London, Headline, 1993.
Personal Darkness. Little, Brown, 1993.
Darkness, I. London, Warner Books, 1994.
Eva Fairdeath. London, Headline, 1994.
Vivia. London, Little, Brown, 1995.
Reigning Cats and Dogs. London, Headline, 1995.

Short Stories

The Betrothed. Sidcup, Kent, Slughorn Press, 1968.
Cyrion. New York, DAW, 1982.
Red as Blood; or Tales from the Sisters Grimmer. New York, DAW, 1983.
The Beautiful Biting Machine. New Castle, Virginia, Cheap Street, 1984.
Tamastara; or, The Indian Nights. New York, DAW, 1984.
The Gorgon and Other Beastly Tales. New York, DAW, 1985.
Dreams of Dark and Light: The Great Short Fiction of Tanith Lee. Sauk City, Wisconsin, Arkham House, 1986.
The Book of the Beast. London, Unwin, 1988.
The Book of the Damned. London, Unwin, 1988.
Women as Demons: The Male Perception of Women through Space and Time. London, Women's Press, 1989.

The Book of the Dead. Woodstock, New York, Overlook Press, 1991.
The Book of the Mad. Woodstock, New York, Overlook Press, 1993.

Other

Unsilent Night (miscellany). Cambridge, Massachusetts, NESFA Press, 1981.

Radio Plays: *Bitter Gate,* 1977; *Red Wine,* 1977; *Death Is King,* 1979; *The Silver Sky,* 1980.

Television Plays: *Sarcophagus,* 1980, and *Sand,* 1981 (both *Blake's Seven* series).

*

Bibliography: by Mike Ashley, in *Fantasy Macabre 4* (London), 1983.

*   *   *

Tanith Lee is a prolific writer of adult and juvenile fantasy books. Since the early 1970s, she has generated more than twenty volumes filled with tales of witches, fairies, demons, and hidden realms. Lee creates highly descriptive prose and well-formed, engaging characters who usually happen upon some sort of magical adventure. She has often received praise for the originality of her work and her highly descriptive writing style.

The success of her first book for the young adult market, *The Dragon Hoard* was a harbinger of praise to come for following volumes. It tells the story of Prince Jasleth and his sister Princess Goodness who are bewitched by an evil fairy. Once they are freed from her spell, Jasleth sets off on a quest for the Dragon Hoard with Prince Fearless and his companions. In good fairy-tale fashion, all are married off in the end and live happily ever after. *Princess Hynchatti* followed this first success with ample acclaim of its own. This series of twelve short fantasies is geared toward the younger end of the young adult reading scale—appealing to those in the nine to twelve year old range. The tales are built around typical plots involving princes, princesses, witches, and fairies yet each contains a twist or two that adds freshness and originality to potentially hackneyed subject matter. The humor in these tales boarders on silliness, but this is an attractive feature to many young readers.

Companions on the Road did not fair as well as Lee's earlier works. Although the writing and characterization were viewed as adequate, general critical consensus held that both seemed forced. *Companions* also revealed Lee's dark side. Her next young adult work, *East of Midnight,* a tale of exchanged identity and its consequences, continued this darker mood. Once again, the work received mixed reviews although this book was regarded as more carefully crafted. Because it contained violent and terrifying episodes, reviewers classified it as a horror story rather than a fantasy.

The shift in Lee's writing style was indicative of her move to adult fantasy. From 1978 to 1991, her efforts were completely devoted to an adult audience. In 1991, however, she published another work for young adults, *Black Unicorn.* Her hiatus from the market produced a positive result. This adventurous tale relates the story of Taniquil (the daughter of a sorceress) and a beautiful black unicorn she brings to life. Though the work still reflects elements of Lee's darker side, the overall tone of the work is positive.

In this book, as in others, Lee addresses themes such as the search for identity, coping with inept or uncaring authority figures, abandonment, loneliness, and many other issues that face adolescent readers. Her characters are often young adults who, in the end, emerge victorious from struggles with these issues. In each of her novels, Lee constructs worlds in which these characters can call on magical powers to assist them in their struggles. One fresh aspect of Lee's work, however, is that her characters show vulnerability. They express feelings of self consciousness, inadequacy, fear, and being overwhelmed by circumstances. For example, when Taniquil is lost in the desert, Lee portrays her as a scared, vulnerable, and overwhelmed young girl who just hours earlier had informed her mother that she was ready to set out on her own. Fortunately, Lee is in control of the universe she has created and Taniquil is saved by the unicorn. In this as in every other conflict in Lee's work, the character emerges victorious yet transformed. This growth of the characters through conflict is an insightful and refreshing aspect of Lee's work. It places her stories in the realm of classic fairy tales which were intended to teach young readers about the difficulties they would find in life.

Lee's inability to maintain a consistent vision of her audience is the major drawback to her work. In her *Don't Bite the Sun,* her dialogue is too sophisticated for adolescents yet too self-conscious for adults. The same is true on occasion in *Black Unicorn.* The inconsistencies caused by this flaw can result in confusion that requires the reader to reread the confusing passage several times until they understand the meaning. This weakness, however, is overshadowed by the generally dynamic nature of her prose.

—Linda Ross

LEESON, Robert (Arthur)

Nationality: British. **Born:** Barnton, Cheshire, England, 31 March 1928. **Education:** Sir John Deane's Grammar School (scholar), 1939-44; University of London, External B.A. (honors) 1972. **Military Service:** Served in British Army in the Middle East, 1946-48. **Family:** Married Gunvor Hagen in 1954; one son, one daughter. **Career:** Journalist on local newspapers and magazines in England and Europe, 1944-56; reporter, 1956-58, parliamentary correspondent, 1958-61, feature writer, 1961-69, literary editor, 1961-80, children's editor, 1969-84, *Morning Star,* London, England; free-lance writer and editor, since 1969. Chairman, Writer's Guild of Great Britain, 1985-86. **Awards:** Eleanor Farjeon award, 1985. **Address:** 18 McKenzie Rd., Broxbourne, Hertfordshire, England.

PUBLICATIONS FOR YOUNG ADULTS

Fiction

The Last Genie. London, Collins, 1973.
The Third Class Genie. London, Collins, 1975.
Silver's Revenge. London, Collins, 1978; New York, Philomel, 1979.
It's My Life. London, Collins, 1980.
Candy for King. London, Collins, 1983.

Genie on the Loose. London, Collins, 1984.

Time Rope series (*Time Rope, Three against the World, At War with Tomorrow, The Metro Gangs Attack*). London, Longman, 4 vols., 1986.

Slambash Wangs of a Compo Gormer. London, Collins, 1987.

Jan Alone. London, Collins, 1989.

Coming Home. London, Collins, 1990.

Zarnia Experiment series (*Landing, Fire, Deadline, Danger Trail, Hide and Seek, Blast Off*). London, Reed Children's Book, 6 vols., 1993.

Red, White & Blue. London, Harper Collins, 1995.

Doomwater. London, Reed Children's Books, 1997.

Historical Fiction

Bess, illustrated by Christine Nolan. London, Collins, 1975.

The White Horse. London, Collins, 1977.

Nonfiction

The Cimaroons. London, Collins, 1978.

PUBLICATIONS FOR CHILDREN

Fiction

The Demon Bike Rider, illustrated by Jim Russell. London, Collins, 1976.

Challenge in the Dark, illustrated by Jim Russell. London, Collins, 1978.

Harold and Bella, Jammy and Me. London, Collins, 1980.

The Reversible Giant, illustrated by Chris Smedley. London, A. & C. Black, 1986.

Wheel of Danger, illustrated by Anthony Kerins. London, Collins, 1986.

Never Kiss Frogs!, illustrated by David Simonds. London, Hamish Hamilton, 1988.

Hey Robin!, illustrated by Helen Leetham. London, A. & C. Black, 1989.

How Alice Saved Captain Miracle, illustrated by Gary Rees. London, Heinemann, 1989.

Burper, illustrated by Caroline Crossland. London, Heinemann, 1989.

Right Royal Kidnap, illustrated by Chris Smedley. London, A. & C. Black, 1990.

One Frog Too Many, illustrated by David Simonds. London, Hamish Hamilton, 1991.

Pancake Pickle, illustrated by Caroline Crossland. London, Hamish Hamilton, 1991.

Swapper, illustrated by Anthony Lewis. London, Heinemann, 1991.

April Fool at Hob Lane School, illustrated by Caroline Crossland. London, Hamish Hamilton, 1992.

No Sleep for Hob Lane, illustrated by Caroline Crossland. London, Hamish Hamilton, 1992.

Ghosts at Hob Lane, illustrated by Caroline Crossland. London, Hamish Hamilton, 1993.

Karlo's Tale, illustrated by Hilda Offen. London, Collins, 1993.

Smart Girls, illustrated by Axel Scheffler. London, Walker Books, 1993.

The Story of Robin Hood. London, Kingfisher Books, 1994.

The Dog Who Changed the World, illustrated by Alison Forsythe. London, Hamish Hamilton, 1994.

Geraldine Gets Lucky, illustrated by Susie Poole. London, Hamish Hamilton, 1995.

The Amazing Adventures of Idle Jack, illustrated by Axel Schefler. London, Walker, 1995.

Smart Girls Forever, illustrated by Axel Schefler. London, Walker Books, 1996.

Also wrote several books based on the British Broadcasting Corp. (BBC) television series *Grange Hill* published by Fontana Books, 1980-82, including: *Grange Hill Rules, O.K.?, Grange Hill Goes Wild, Grange Hill for Sale, Grange Hill Home and Away; Forty Days of Tucker J* (based on the BBC television series *Tucker's Luck* by Redmond), Fontana Books, 1983.

Historical Fiction

Beyond the Dragon Prow, illustrated by Ian Ribbons. London, Collins, 1973.

'Maroon Boy, illustrated by Michael Jackson. London, Collins, 1974.

All the Gold in the World, illustrated by Anna Leplar. London, A. and C. Black, 1995.

Nonfiction

Mum and Dad's Big Business, illustrated by Ken Sprague. Manchester, Cooperative Union, 1982.

The People's Dream, illustrated by Ken Sprague. Manchester, Cooperative Union, 1982.

PUBLICATIONS FOR ADULTS as R.A. Leeson

Other

United We Stand: An Illustrated Account of Trade Union Emblems. Bath, Adams & Dart, 1971.

Strike: A Live History, 1887-1971. London, Allen & Unwin, 1973.

Children's Books and Class Society: Past and Present, edited by Children's Rights Workshop. London, Writers and Readers Publishing Cooperative, 1977.

Travelling Brothers: The Six Centuries Road from Craft Fellowship to Trade Unionism. London, Allen & Unwin, 1978.

Reading and Righting: The Past, Present, and Future of Fiction for the Young. London, Collins, 1985.

*

Media Adaptations: *The Third-Class Genie* (play), London, BBC Schools Radio, 1986, and Leicester, England, 1987; *Slambash Wangs of a Compo Gormer,* London, BBC Schools Radio, 1989; *It's My Life,* Manchester, BBC Radio Five, 1992.

Robert Leeson comments:

Writing for Young Adults is writing for people crossing a frontier zone, badly mapped and studded with minefields. We made this frontier zone, we made these young people. We taught them to explore, to question, to find out, yet often we are alarmed at their loss of innocence.

The writer stands in a fortunate position in relation to many young people, who often cannot communicate with the adults closest to them, of being the friendly older person they may feel free to listen to. That means a great opportunity for the writer and a great responsibility.

*   *   *

Robert Leeson writes from a consistent and firmly held set of views on society and childhood, views which he sets out clearly in *Reading and Righting*. Briefly, these are that books are a vital means of liberating and empowering humans—especially children and young adults—within a society which has been structured to deny a voice to a considerable proportion of its members. The paradox that the book, symbol of this restrictive culture, should be the desired agent of change accounts for the variety, energy, and sheer popularity of Leeson's work. His understanding and qualified acceptance of an existing literary tradition has led to a stream of historical, school, science fiction, humorous, and realistic novels which give central roles to characters previously denied recognition—whether because of gender, ethnic origin or social position—and at the same time redefine and revitalise conventional forms.

Thus his early historical trilogy (*'Maroon Boy, Bess,* and *The White Horse*) presents a segment of history—concerning the Cimaroons—not encountered in any official view of the subject. *Silver's Revenge* provides a daring, subversive, wryly humorous sequel to Stevenson's *Treasure Island* and epitomises Leeson's affectionately critical attitude to the literary tradition (now reinforced by *Karlo's Tale*, his sequel to Browning's *The Pied Piper*). *Candy for King,* partly reflecting Leeson's own army experience, stands as a contemporary *Candide*. The "Time Rope" quartet (*Time Rope, Three against the World, At War with Tomorrow,* and *The Metro Gangs Attack*) using a science fiction convention, involves three young people from undervalued, disenfranchised backgrounds, and sustaining but unacknowledged roots at war within a future dystopia of disturbing logic and likelihood. The "Grange Hill" series of novels, based on a popular television series about an English comprehensive school, but always original works in themselves, moved the school story genre decisively into new territory. The final book in the series, *Forty Days of Tucker J,* took a character who, over his television school career and in Leeson's books, had achieved nationally recognised inimitability and was subjected searchingly to a contemporary world outside school. Leeson's acute ear for the language and lore of young adults shows itself to great advantage here, continuing the sensitivity to voice and register established in earlier books such as *The Demon Bike Rider, The Third Class Genie,* and continued in *Genie on the Loose.*

Leeson himself regards *Candy for King,* the "It's My Life" trilogy—*It's My Life, Jan Alone,* and *Coming Home*—the "Time Rope" quartet, and *Slambash Wangs of a Compo Gormer* as his major works for young adults.

Leeson's *Candy for King* portrays with all the relentless consistency of Voltaire a hero of complete innocence and absolute trust. Kitchener Candeford, anxious always to put into literal practice the great principles of "love, liberty, loyalty and leadership," goes through school, work, and into the army as an oblivious, gentle giant unwittingly leaving a trail of disaster behind him. An often anarchically funny novel, its wandering sequence unified by its extraordinary hero makes it a picaresque masterpiece. Candy

himself remains unsullied but the story's undoubted message is that the world is not ready for his brand of nobility.

In *It's My Life,* Jan Whitfield is sixteen, attending a comprehensive school in the north of England, attracted to Peter Carey at the same school, and living an apparently normal life with parents and brother. But her mother, without warning or seeming reason, walks out on the family. The story concerns Jan's attempts to come to terms with this. This quiet, perceptively written, entirely convincing novel quickly gained a large following both in schools and with independent readers. The appearance in 1989 of a sequel, *Jan Alone,* surprising after so long an interval, was in retrospect inevitable. The trilogy, completed in 1990 with *Coming Home,* stands as one of the great achievements in recent years in the realistic novel. Jan develops through the books to responsibility, adulthood, and understanding. The process is not easy: it involves self-knowledge of a high order. At the end of *It's My Life* the mother's disappearance was a given: its significance was that it "had everything to do with what was to happen to Jan." At the end of *Coming Home,* with the superbly realised episode of the mother's return ("Why should I have to do the unforgivable to get away from the unbearable?") the situations of the two women are set in contrast and a whole, satisfying structure for the trilogy appears. There is an assertion of human continuity and also need for change: in Jan there is an acute dramatisation of the possibilities for young women in contemporary society. Leeson would not call this trilogy "feminist." However, there are several reasons for regarding it in this way. Jan's involvement in a male-dominated world is active: she makes her own luck against great odds.

A literal translation of *Slambash Wangs of a Compo Gormer* from the original Klaptonian would be "fighting fantasies of a complete idiot." This novel is an imaginative *tour-de-force,* funny, ingenious, with several contemporary targets neatly hit. Arnold's life in Denfield, with uncomprehending parents and inimical schoolfellows who regard him as a "wally" because he does not seem to inhabit their world, is relieved only by his private fantasy: the planet Klaptonia, where the Replic Dornal triumphs in one elemental, heroic adventure after another. Little does he know that his fantasy actually exists. There is trouble in Klaptonia, and Arnold and Replic Dornal are about to change places. Arnold's adventures on Klaptonia and Dornal's attempts to cope with life at Denfield Comprehensive School form an absorbing, resonant, highly comic narrative. There is a gallery of caricatured characters who have an uncomfortable ring of truth. Leeson provides a complete Klaptonian language which is a linguistic—as well as a comic—achievement in its own right. The whole novel stands as a remarkable feat of invention. Once again, established genres—science fiction, fantasy, and the school story—are reworked, affectionately mocked, and given new life.

His output since 1993 has consisted more of books for younger readers than for young adults. Geraldine the frog, of *Geraldine Gets Lucky,* has been especially popular. In writing for young adults, Leeson has turned to suspense with *Doomwater,* an exciting tale of female art students in a dangerous situation.

Leeson's entire achievement—varied in tone, content, and genre; consistent in honesty, seriousness, and concern for giving voice to the usually unheard—stands as unique in contemporary literature for young adults. It is unfortunate that so many of his books are unavailable outside the United Kingdom.

—Dennis Hamley, updated by Caroline C. Hunt

LE GUIN, Ursula K(roeber)

Nationality: American. **Born:** Berkeley, California, 21 October 1929. **Education:** Radcliffe College, Cambridge, Massachusetts, A.B. in French 1951 (Phi Beta Kappa); Columbia University, New York (Faculty fellow; Fulbright fellow, 1953), M.A. in romance languages 1952. **Family:** Married Charles A. Le Guin in 1953; two daughters and one son. **Career:** Instructor in French, Mercer University, Macon, Georgia, 1954, and University of Idaho, Moscow, 1956; department secretary, Emory University, Atlanta, 1955; taught writing workshops at Pacific University, Forest Grove, Oregon, 1971, University of Washington, Seattle, 1971-73, Portland State University, Oregon, 1974, 1977, 1979, in Melbourne, Australia, 1975, at the University of Reading, England, 1976, Indiana Writers Conference, Bloomington, 1978 and 1983, University of California, San Diego, 1979, Kenyon College, Tulane University, Bennington Writing Program, Beloit College, and Flight of the Mind. Creative consultant for Public Broadcasting Service, for television production of *The Lathe of Heaven,* 1979. **Awards:** Fulbright fellowship, 1953; *Boston Globe-Horn Book* award, 1968, Lewis Carroll Shelf award, 1979, *Horn Book* honor list citation, and American Library Association Notable Book citation, all for *A Wizard of Earthsea;* Nebula Award nomination, novelette category, 1969, for "Nine Lives"; Nebula Award, Science Fiction Writers Association, and Hugo Award, International Science Fiction Association, both 1970, for *The Left Hand of Darkness;* Newbery Silver Medal Award, and National Book Award for Children's Literature finalist, both 1972, and American Library Association Notable Book citation, all for *The Tombs of Atuan;* Child Study Association of America's Children's Books of the Year citation, 1972, and National Book Award for Children's Books, 1973, both for *The Farthest Shore;* Hugo Award for best novella, 1973, for *The Word for World Is Forest;* Hugo Award nomination, Nebula Award nomination, and *Locus* Award, all 1973, all for *The Lathe of Heaven;* Hugo Award for best short story, 1974, for "The Ones Who Walk Away from Omelas"; American Library Association's Best Young Adult Books citation, 1974, for *The Dispossessed: An Ambiguous Utopia;* Nebula Award, and Jupiter Award, both 1975, for short story "The Day before the Revolution"; Nebula Award nomination and Jupiter Award, both 1976, for short story "The Diary of the Rose"; National Book Award finalist, American Library Association's Best Young Adult Books citation, Child Study Association of America's Children's Books of the Year citation, and *Horn Book* honor list citation, all 1976, and Prix Lectures-Jeunesse, 1987, all for *Very Far Away from Anywhere Else;* Gandalf Award nomination, 1978; Gandalf Award (Grand Master of Fantasy), 1979; Balrog Award nomination for best poet, 1979; University of Oregon Distinguished Service award, 1981; *Locus* Award, 1984, for *The Compass Rose;* American Book Award nomination, 1985, and Janet Heidinger Kafka Prize for Fiction, University of Rochester English Department and Writer's Workshop, 1986, both for *Always Coming Home.* Guest of Honor, World Science Fiction Convention, 1975; International Fantasy Award and Hugo Award, for *Buffalo Gals,* 1988; Nebula Award, for *Tehanu,* 1990; Pushcart Prize, for "Bill Weisler," 1991; Harold D. Vursell Award, American Academy & Institute of Arts & Letters, 1991; OILA Award for *Searoad,* 1992. D.Litt.: Bucknell University, Lewisburg, Pennsylvania, 1978; Lawrence University, Appleton, Wisconsin, 1979; D.H.L.: Lewis and Clark College, Portland, 1983; Occidental College, Los Angeles, 1985; Emory University, Kenyon College, Portland State University. **Agent:** Virginia Kidd, P.O. Box 278, Milford, Pennsylvania 18337, U.S.A.

PUBLICATIONS FOR YOUNG ADULTS

Novels

A Wizard of Earthsea, illustrated by Ruth Robbins. Berkeley, California, Parnassus Press, 1968; London, Gollancz, 1971.
The Tombs of Atuan, illustrated by Gall Garraty. New York, Atheneum, 1971; London, Gollancz, 1972.
The Farthest Shore, illustrated by Gail Garraty. New York, Atheneum, 1972; London, Gollancz, 1973.
Very Far Away from Anywhere Else. New York, Atheneum, 1976; as *A Very Long Way from Anywhere Else,* London, Gollancz, 1976.
Earthsea (includes *A Wizard of Earthsea, The Tombs of Atuan,* and *The Farthest Shore*). London, Gollancz, 1977; as *The Earthsea Trilogy,* London, Penguin, 1979.
The Beginning Place. New York, Harper, 1980; as *Threshold,* London, Gollancz, 1980.
Tehanu: The Last Book of Earthsea. New York, Atheneum, 1990.

PUBLICATIONS FOR CHILDREN

Fiction

Leese Webster, illustrated by James Brunsman. New York, Atheneum, 1979; London, Gollancz, 1981.
The Adventures of Cobbler's Rune, illustrated by Alicia Austin. New Castle, Virginia, Cheap Street, 1982.
Adventures in Kroy. New Castle, Virginia, Cheap Street, 1982.
Solomon Leviathan's Nine Hundred Thirty-first Trip around the World, illustrated by Alicia Austin. New Castle, Virginia, Cheap Street, 1983.
A Visit from Dr. Katz, illustrated by Ann Barrow. New York, Atheneum, 1988; as *Dr. Katz,* London, Collins, 1988.
Catwings, illustrated by S.D. Schindler. New York, Orchard, 1988.
Catwings Return, illustrated by S.D. Schindler. New York, Orchard, 1989.
Fire and Stone, illustrated by Laura Marshell. New York, Atheneum, 1989.
A Ride on the Red Mare's Back, illustrated by Julie Downing. New York, Orchard, 1992.
Fish Soup, illustrated by Patrick Wynne. New York, Atheneum, 1992.
Wonderful Alexander and the Catwings, illustrations by S.D. Schindler. New York, Orchard Books, 1994.

PUBLICATIONS FOR ADULTS

Novels

Rocannon's World, with *The Kar-Chee Reign,* by Avram Davidson. New York, Ace, 1966; London, Tandem, 1972.
Planet of Exile, with *Mankind Under the Lease,* by Thomas M. Disch. New York, Ace, 1966; London, Tandem, 1972.
City of Illusions. New York, Ace, 1967; London, Gollancz, 1971.
The Left Hand of Darkness. New York, Ace, and London, Macdonald, 1969; with a new afterword and appendixes by the author, New York, Walker, 1994.

The Lathe of Heaven. New York, Scribner, 1971; London, Gollancz, 1972.

The Dispossessed: An Ambiguous Utopia. New York, Harper, and London, Gollancz, 1974.

The Word for World Is Forest. New York, Putnam, 1976; London, Gollancz, 1977.

Three Hainish Novels (includes *Rocannon's World, Planet of Exile,* and *City of Illusions*). New York, Doubleday, 1978.

Malafrena. New York, Putnam, 1979; London, Gollancz, 1980.

The Eye of the Heron and Other Stories. New York, Harper, and London, Gollancz, 1983.

Always Coming Home (includes cassette of *Music and Poetry of the Kesh*), illustrated by Margaret Chodos, diagrams by George Hersh. New York, Harper, 1985; London, Gollancz, 1986; without cassette, New York, Bantam, 1987.

Five Complete Novels. New York, Avenel, 1985.

The New Atlantis, with *The Return from Rainbow Bridge,* by Kim Stanley Robinson. New York, Tor, 1989.

Searoad: The Chronicles of Klatsand. New York, Harper Collins, 1991.

Four Ways to Forgiveness. New York, HarperPrism, 1995.

Worlds of Exile and Illusion (contains *Rocannon's World, Planet of Exile,* and *City of Illusions*).New York, Orb, 1996.

Short Stories

The Wind's Twelve Quarters. New York, Harper, 1975; London, Gollancz, 1976.

The Water Is Wide. Portland, Oregon, Pendragon Press, 1976.

Orsinian Tales. New York, Harper, 1976; London, Gollancz, 1977.

The Compass Rose. New York, Harper, 1982; London, Gollancz, 1983.

The Visionary. The Life Story of Flicker of the Serpentine, with *Wonders Hidden,* by Scott Russell Sanders. Santa Barbara, California, Capra Press, 1984.

Buffalo Gals and Other Animal Presences (includes verse). Santa Barbara, California, Capra Press, 1987; as *Buffalo Gals,* London, Gollancz, 1990.

The Ones Who Walk Away from Omelas. Mankato, Minnesota, Creative Education, 1992.

A Fisherman of the Inland Sea: Science Fiction Stories. New York, HarperPrism, 1994.

Unlocking the Air and Other Stories. New York, HarperCollins, 1996.

Poetry

Wild Angels. Santa Barbara, California, Capra Press, 1974.

Tillai and Tylissos, with Theodora K. Quinn. N.p., Red Bull Press, 1979.

Torrey Pines Reserve. Northridge, California, Lord John Press, 1980.

Gwilan's Harp. Northridge, California, Lord John Press, 1981.

Hard Words and Other Poems. New York, Harper, 1981.

In the Red Zone, with Hank Pander. Northridge, California, Lord John Press, 1983.

Wild Oats and Fireweed. New York, Harper, 1988.

No Boats. Ygor & Buntho, 1992.

Blue Moon Over Thurman Street, photographs by Roger Dorband. Portland, Oregon, NewSage Press, 1993.

Going Out with Peacocks and Other Poems. New York, HarperPerennial, 1994.

Plays

No Use to Talk to Me, in *The Altered I: An Encounter with Science Fiction,* edited by Lee Harding. Melbourne, Nostrilia Press, 1976; New York, Berkley, 1980.

King Dog: A Screenplay, with *Dostoevsky: A Screenplay,* by Raymond Carver and Tess Gallagher. Santa Barbara, California, Capra Press, 1985.

Other

From Elfland to Poughkeepsie (lecture). Portland, Oregon, Pendragon Press, 1973.

Dreams Must Explain Themselves, illustrated by Tim Kirk. New York, Algol Press, 1975.

Editor, *Nebula Award Stories 11.* London, Gollancz, 1976; New York, Harper, 1977.

The Language of the Night: Essays on Fantasy and Science Fiction, edited by Susan Wood. New York, Putnam, 1979; revised edition, London, Women's Press, 1989, New York, HarperCollins, 1992.

Editor, with Virginia Kidd, *Interfaces: An Anthology of Speculative Fiction.* New York, Ace, 1980.

Editor, with Virginia Kidd, *Edges: Thirteen New Tales from the Borderlands of the Imagination.* New York, Pocket Books, 1980.

Contributor, *Burning with a Vision: Poetry of Science and the Fantastic,* by Thomas M. Disch. Philadelphia, Pennsylvania, Owlswick Press, 1984.

Uses of Music in Uttermost Parts, music by Elinor Armer (performed in part in San Francisco, California, 1986).

Dancing at the Edge of the World: Thoughts on Words, Women, Places. New York, Grove Press, and London, Gollancz, 1989.

Way of the Water's Going: Images of the Northern California Coastal Range, photographs by Ernest Waugh and Alan Nicholson. New York, Harper, 1989.

Contributor, *A Home-Concealed Woman: The Diaries of Magnolia Wynn Le Guin,* edited by Charles A. Le Guin. Athens, Georgia, University of Georgia Press, 1990.

Editor, with Brian Attebery, *The Norton Book of Science Fiction: North American Science Fiction, 1960-1990.* New York : W.W. Norton, 1993.

Earthsea Revisioned (lecture). Cambridge, Massachusetts, Children's Literature New England, and Cambridge, England, Green Bay Publications, 1993.

Translator, *The Twins, the Dream: Two Voices; Las gemelas, el sueno, dos voces,* by Diana Bellessi. Houston, Arte Publico Press, 1996.

Reteller, with J. P. Seaton, *Tao Te Ching: A Book about the Way and the Power of the Way,* by Lao-tzu. Boston, Shambhala, 1997.

Steering the Craft: Exercises and Discussions on Story Writing for the Lone Navigator or the Mutinous Crew. Portland, Oregon, Eighth Mountain Press, 1998.

Recordings: *The Lathe of Heaven,* Alternate World, 1976; *The Ones Who Walk Away from Omelas and Other Stories,* Alternate World, 1976; *Gwilan's Harp and Intercom,* Caedmon, 1977; *The Earthsea Trilogy,* Colophone, 1981; *Music and Poetry of the Kesh,* with Todd Barton, Valley Productions, 1985; *Rigel Nine: An Audio Opera,* with David Bedford, Charisma, 1985; *The Left Hand of Darkness,* Warner, 1985; *The Word for World Is Forest,* Book of the Road, 1986.

*

Media Adaptations: *The Word for World Is Forest* (recording), Book of the Road, 1968; *The Lathe of Heaven* (television broadcast), PBS-TV, 1979; *The Tombs of Atuan* (filmstrip with record or cassette), Newbery Award Records, 1980; *The Earthsea Trilogy* (recording), Colophone, 1981; *The Ones Who Walk Away from Omelas* (stage drama), performed at the Portland Civic Theatre, 1981.

Biography: Entry in *Dictionary of Literary Biography* by Brian Attebery, Volume 8, Detroit, Gale, Volume 8, 1981; *Ursula K. Le Guin* by Charlotte Spivack, Boston, Twayne, 1984; entry in *Dictionary of Literary Biography* by Andrew Gordon, Volume 52, Detroit, Gale, 1986; entry in *Concise Dictionary of American Literary Biography 1968-1988,* Detroit, Gale, 1989; essay in *Authors and Artists for Young Adults,* Volume 9, Detroit, Gale, 1992; essay in *Speaking for Ourselves, Too* compiled and edited by Donald R. Gallo, National Council of Teachers of English, 1993.

Bibliography: *Ursula K. Le Guin: A Primary and Secondary Bibliography* by Elizabeth Cummins Cogell, Boston, Hall, 1983.

Manuscript Collections: University of Oregon Library, Eugene.

Critical Studies: *The Farthest Shores of Ursula K. Le Guin* by George Edgar Slusser, San Bernardino, California, Borgo Press, 1976; ''Ursula Le Guin Issue'' of *Science-Fiction Studies* (Terre Haute, Indiana), March 1976; Entry in *Children's Literature Review* Volume 3, Detroit Gale, 1978; Volume 28, 1992; Entry in *Contemporary Literary Criticism* Volume 8, Detroit, Gale, 1978; Volume 13, 1980; Volume 22, 1982; Volume 45, 1987; Volume 71, 1992; *Ursula Le Guin* by Joseph D. Olander and Martin H. Greenberg, New York, Taplinger, and Edinburgh, Harris, 1979; *Ursula K. Le Guin: Voyage to Inner Lands and to Outer Space* edited by Joseph W. De Bolt, Port Washington, New York, Kennikat Press, 1979; *Ursula K. Le Guin* by Barbara J. Bucknall, New York, Ungar, 1981; *Approaches to the Fiction of Ursula K. Le Guin* by James Bittner, Ann Arbor, Michigan, UMI Research Press, and Epping, Essex, Bowker, 1984; *Understanding Ursula K. Le Guin* by Elizabeth Cummins Cogell, Columbia, University of South Carolina Press, 1990.

*   *   *

Ursula Le Guin's immense reputation as a fantasy writer for children is founded essentially on the Earthsea trilogy—*A Wizard of Earthsea, The Tombs of Atuan,* and *The Farthest Shore.* Few writers have received more critical attention, and though this is partly due to her work as an adult science-fiction writer of great repute, it is mainly a well-justified tribute to the qualities of the Earthsea books.

The hero of all three books is Ged—a young magician in the first book, at the height of his powers in the second, and as the aging Archmage in the third. Misusing his powers in the first book *A Wizard of Earthsea,* he releases into the world a nameless shadow—an evil which he must then chase and battle with to the ends of the earth. When he finally finds and confronts it, it bears his own

name. In the second volume, *The Tombs of Atuan,* searching for the missing half of a talismanic ring, he is captured and entombed in an underground labyrinth by the young priestess Tenar who is dedicated to death. His own fate and the fate of all the world depend on his being able to persuade her to choose life and reject the power of death. In the third volume, *The Farthest Shore,* he and his young companion, a future Great King, are pitched against an enemy whose evil-doing is sapping the power of all the magicians in the world, the power of hope and joy and ritual and craftsmanship among the people. To secure his own immortality the corrupt magician has made a hole in the barrier between life and death, and light and joy are flowing out through it.

No paraphrase of plot or setting can do justice to the profound originality of these books, which have been repeatedly imitated. In the first place, although there are wizards and dragons and other clear similarities to the medieval literary landscape used by Tolkien among many others, the setting, an elaborate huge archipelago of varied islands, is wholly invented and fully circumstantial. It is full of magic—magic used for high and commonplace purposes alike—but the magic is never arbitrary, and instead of convincing the reader that Earthsea is unlike the real world, it breathes a contagious sense that the real world, too, is full of wonders. More profound yet is the nature of the adventures that befall the characters. Imaginary the perils may be, as the magical defence for dealing with them are, but the adventures are real; they are the moral dangers and triumphs of the inner world seen with a fierce clarity. Far from being escapist, Le Guin's story turns the reader round to face him or herself. The language and imagery are extremely beautiful: ''My name, and yours, and the true name of the sun, or a spring of water, or an unborn child are all syllables of the great word that is very slowly spoken by the shining of the stars. . . ,'' but the moral vision of the work is challengingly bleak and austere. ''You thought as a boy that a mage is one who can do anything. And the truth is that as a man's real power grows and his knowledge widens, ever the way he can follow grows narrower; until at last he chooses nothing, but does only and wholly what he *must* do. . .''

After an interval of seventeen years, in 1990, Le Guin published *Tehanu,* the fourth and last book of Earthsea. There was a book about young Ged, and a book about old Ged; now there is a book about young Tenar, and a book about Tenar as an old woman. We learn that Tenar left the Mage Ogion, and deliberately chose to live an obscure life as a farmer's wife. Now a widow, she is fostering a child who has been horribly scarred by acts of cruelty. Ged, no longer archmage, burnt out by the great crisis in The Farthest Shore, comes home to her, and in the world outside the High Magic, struggling with the humdrum difficulties of life and the danger to the child, the two of them at last consummate their love. *Tehanu* is a book of great depth and subtlety, deliberately confronting and altering the bedrock values of the old high fantasy on which the first three Earthsea books were based. It rejects the male-gendered tales of heroism, and in their place builds on women's experiences as the benchmarks of virtue, courage, love. The damaged child is at the centre of the book, and the triumph over evil is hers. Of course, the change of vision is the result of feminism, which has changed the weather in many minds since the early Earthsea books were written, and the author is very aware of that. But in two other ways *Tehanu* is unlike the earlier titles. Though it shares their dreamlike quality and many of their beauties, it is deeply self-conscious. Wrestling with the implied values in heroic narrative, it bring values above the subliminal, into view as a major part of the subject of the story. The thought process shaping the book is no longer innocent and implicit but urgently right-minded. The other great difference is that *Tehanu* can almost be defined as not being a book for young adults. The struggle between good and evil, as represented here, is not simple, though the powers of good and evil are more than ever frightening when evil is not a vast cosmic mysterious thing but something as familiar and realistic as the abuse of a child; but the child at the centre of the story is seen always through the eyes of the aging Tenar—in short the Earthsea sequence seems now to contain three young people's books and one adult novel. Le Guin has provided a powerful and in the strong sense self-critical commentary on the completed Earthsea sequence, and *Tehanu* in particular, in ''Earthsea Revisioned.''

The last thing one would have expected of the author of Earthsea was a realistic adolescent novel, such as *Very Far Away from Anywhere Else.* The two young protagonists, Natalie and Owen, are each highly individual—he wholly unable to be the car-loving, normal, tear-away son his parents yearn for, but instead desperate to study at a serious college; she a serious musician. Though he resists the pressure to conform to stereotype in other ways, Owen succumbs to it in his relationship with Natalie and nearly ruins everything with an unwelcome attempt to transform their friendship into a sexual one. Le Guin's admirers have objected to the didactic tone of this book, which is undoubtedly present as it is in so many other adolescent novels. But the rage which is palpable in the book—alongside a lot of human tenderness—is not really against the corrupting pressure on the young to advance too quickly into their sexual adulthood, rather it is against all the pressures by which individuals in their glorious oddity and variety are crushed into a few standard shapes by a society that hates nonconformity. With *The Beginning Place,* Le Guin twisted together the Earthsea strand and the realist strand in her imagination. A kind of place-slip happens when Hugh crosses a stream on the edge of the dismal modern city where he lives; he enters a wilderness of forest and stream and mountain. It is inhabited by another modern teenager, Irene, and by an ancient people living simple lives. Then there is a dragon that turns everything foul and that must be found and killed. Hugh plays Sigurd's part, and the two are released from the suffocating control of their parents to live in the real world and rent an apartment together. There are multiple resonances in this book—Oedipus and Sigurd among many others—and the position of the fantasy geography as a land of the inner world and of the mind is clearer than in Earthsea, though less compellingly beautiful.

In various miniature works for much younger readers, Le Guin shows a salty sense of humour that is barely apparent in the grander stories. It is less than ever possible to predict what she might do next, or put a limit on her possibilities. Hers is certainly one of the most powerful talents ever exercised in writing for the young.

—Jill Paton Walsh

L'ENGLE, Madeleine

Nationality: American. **Born:** New York City, 29 November 1918. **Education:** Smith College, A.B. (with honors) 1941; New School for Social Research, 1941-42; Columbia University, New York, 1960-61. **Family:** Married Hugh Franklin in 1946 (died 1986); two daughters and one son. **Career:** Worked in the theatre, New York, 1941-47; teacher with Committee for Refugee Education, during World War II; teacher, St. Hilda's and St. Hugh's School, Morningside Heights, New York, 1960-66; librarian, Cathedral of St. John the Divine, New York City, 1966—; member of the faculty, University of Indiana, Bloomington, summers, 1965-66, 1971; writer-in-residence, Ohio State University, Columbus, 1970, and University of Rochester, New York, 1972; since 1970 president, Crosswicks Ltd, New York; since 1976 lecturer, Wheaton College, Illinois; president, Authors Guild of America. **Awards:** American Library Association Newbery Medal, Hans Christian Andersen Award runner-up, 1964, Sequoyah Children's Book Award from the Oklahoma State Department of Education, and Lewis Carroll Shelf Award, both 1965, all for *A Wrinkle in Time; Book World*'s Spring Book Festival Honor Book, and one of *School Library Journal*'s Best Books of the Year, both 1968, both for *The Young Unicorns;* Austrian State Literary Prize, 1969, for *The Moon by Night;* University of Southern Mississippi Silver Medallion, 1978, for ''an outstanding contribution to the field of children's literature''; American Book Award for paperback fiction, 1980, for *A Swiftly Tilting Planet;* Smith Medal, 1980; Newbery Honor Book, 1981, for *A Ring of Endless Light;* Books for the Teen Ager selection, New York Public Library, 1981, for *A Ring of Endless Light,* and 1982, for *Camilla;* Sophie Award, 1984; Regina Medal from the Catholic Library Association, 1984; National Council of Teachers of English ALAN award, 1986. **Agent:** Robert Lescher, 67 Irving Place, New York, New York 10009. **Address:** Crosswicks, Goshen, Connecticut 06756, U.S.A.

PUBLICATIONS FOR YOUNG ADULTS

Fiction

The Small Rain: A Novel (for adults). New York, Vanguard, 1945; abridged edition (for young adults) as *Prelude,* New York, Vanguard, 1968; London, Gollancz, 1972.
And Both Were Young. New York, Lothrop, 1949.
Camilla Dickinson. New York, Simon & Schuster, 1951, as *Camilla,* New York, Crowell, 1965.
Meet the Austins, illustrated by Gillian Willett. New York, Vanguard, 1960.
A Wrinkle in Time. New York, Farrar, Straus, 1962.
The Moon by Night. New York, Farrar, Straus, 1963.
The Arm of the Starfish. New York, Farrar, Straus, 1965.
The Young Unicorns. New York, Farrar, Straus, 1968.
Intergalactic P.S.3. New York, Children's Book Council, 1970.
A Wind in the Door. New York, Farrar, Straus, 1973.
Dragons in the Waters (sequel to *The Arm of the Starfish*). New York, Farrar, Straus, 1976.
A Swiftly Tilting Planet. New York, Farrar, Straus, 1978.
A Ring of Endless Light. New York, Farrar, Straus, 1980.
A House Like a Lotus. New York, Farrar, Straus, 1984.
Many Waters. New York, Farrar, Straus, 1986.
An Acceptable Time. New York, Farrar, Straus, 1988.
Troubling a Star. New York, Farrar, Straus, Giroux, 1994.
A Live Coal in the Sea. New York, Farrar, Straus, and Giroux, 1996.

PUBLICATIONS FOR CHILDREN

Picture Books

The Twenty-four Days before Christmas: An Austin Family Story, illustrated by Inga. New York, Farrar, Straus, 1964.

Dance in the Desert, illustrated by Symeon Shimin. New York, Farrar, Straus, and London, Longman, 1969.

Everyday Prayers, illustrated by Lucille Butel. New York, Morehouse, 1974.

Prayers for Sunday, illustrated by Lizzie Napoli. New York, Morehouse, 1974.

Ladder of Angels: Scenes from the Bible Illustrated by the Children of the World. New York, Seabury, 1979.

The Anti-Muffins, illustrated by Gloria Ortiz. New York, Pilgrim Press, 1980.

The Sphinx at Dawn: Two Stories, illustrated by Vivian Berger. New York, Harper, 1982.

The Glorious Impossible, illustrated by Giotto. New York, Simon & Schuster, 1990.

Plays

18 Washington Square, South: A Comedy in One Act (first produced in Northhampton, Massachusetts, 1940). Boston, Baker, 1944.

How Now Brown Cow, with Robert Hartung (first produced in New York). 1949.

The Journey with Jonah, illustrated by Leonard Everett Fisher (produced in New York, 1970). New York, Farrar, Straus, 1967.

Poetry

Lines Scribbled on an Envelope and Other Poems. New York, Farrar, Straus, 1969.

Other

Anytime Prayers, photography by Maria Rooney. Wheaton, Illinois, Harold Shaw Publishers, 1994.

Miracle on 10th Street, and Other Christmas Writings. Wheaton, Illinois, Harold Shaw Publishers, 1998.

Also author of *Once Upon a Christmas,* 1994.

PUBLICATIONS FOR ADULTS

Fiction

Ilsa. New York, Vanguard, 1946.

A Winter's Love. Philadelphia, Lippincott, 1957.

The Love Letters. New York, Farrar, Straus, 1966.

The Other Side of the Sun. New York, Farrar, Straus, 1971.

A Severed Wasp (sequel to *The Small Rain*). Farrar, Straus, 1982.

Certain Women. New York, Farrar, Straus, 1992.

Poetry

The Weather of the Heart. Wheaton, Illinois, Shaw, 1978.

Walking on Water: Reflections on Faith and Art. Wheaton, Illinois, Shaw, 1980.

A Cry like a Bell. Wheaton, Illinois, Shaw, 1987.

Nonfiction

A Circle of Quiet. New York, Farrar, Straus, 1972.

The Summer of the Great-Grandmother. New York, Farrar, Straus, 1974.

Editor with William B. Green, *Spirit and Light: Essays in Historical Theology.* New York, Seabury, 1976.

The Irrational Season. New York, Seabury, 1977.

And It Was Good: Reflections on Beginnings. Wheaton, Illinois, Shaw, 1983.

Dare to Be Creative. Washington, D.C., Library of Congress, 1984.

Trailing Clouds of Glory: Spiritual Values in Children's Books, with Avery Brooke. Philadelphia, Westminster, 1985.

A Stone for a Pillow: Journeys with Jacob. Wheaton, Illinois, Shaw, 1986.

Two Part Invention. New York, Farrar, Straus, 1988.

Sold Into Egypt: Joseph's Journey into Human Being. Wheaton, Illinois, Shaw, 1989.

A Rock That is Higher: Story as Truth. Wheaton, Illinois, Shaw, 1992.

Walking on Water: Reflections on Faith and Art. New York, North Point Press, 1995.

With Carole F. Chase, *Glimpses of Grace: Daily Thoughts and Reflections.* San Francisco, HarperSanFrancisco, 1996.

With Luci Shaw, *Wintersong: Christmas Readings.* Wheaton, Illinois, Harold Shaw, 1996.

Penguins and Golden Calves: Icons and Idols. Wheaton, Illinois, Harold Shaw Publishers, 1996.

Mothers & Daughters, photography by Maria Rooney. Wheaton, Illinois, Harold Shaw Publishers, 1997.

With Luci Shaw, *Friends for the Journey: Two Extraordinary Women Celebrate Friendships Made and Sustained through the Seasons of Life.* Ann Arbor, Michigan, Vine Books/Servant Publications, 1997.

Bright Evening Star: Mystery of the Incarnation. Wheaton, Illinois, H. Shaw, 1997.

My Own Small Place: Developing the Writing Life. Wheaton, Illinois, H. Shaw Publishers, 1998.

A Winter's Love. Wheaton, Illinois, Harold Shaw Publishers, 1998.

*

Media Adaptations: *A Wrinkle in Time* was recorded by Newbery Award Records, 1972, and adapted as a filmstrip with cassette by Miller-Brody, 1974; *A Wind in the Door* was recorded and adapted as a filmstrip with cassette by Miller-Brody; *Camilla* was recorded as a cassette by Listening Library; *A Ring of Endless Light* was recorded and adapted as a filmstrip with cassette by Random House. *And Both Were Young, The Arm of the Starfish, Meet the Austins, The Moon by Night, A Wrinkle in Time,* and *The Young Unicorns* have been adapted into Braille; *The Arm of the Starfish, Camilla, Dragons in the Waters, A Wind in the Door,* and *A Wrinkle in Time* have been adapted into talking books; *The Summer of the Great-Grandmother* is also available on cassette.

Manuscript Collections: Wheaton College; Kerlan Collection, University of Minnesota, Minneapolis; de Grummond Collection, University of Southern Mississippi.

Biography: Entry in *More Junior Authors,* New York, H.W. Wilson, 1963; essay in *Authors and Artists for Young Adults,*

Volume 1, Detroit, Gale, 1989; essay in *Speaking for Ourselves: Autobiographical Sketches by Notable Authors of Books for Young Adults,* Volume 1, compiled and edited by Donald R. Gallo, National Council of Teachers of English, 1990; essay in *Something about the Author Autobiography Series,* Volume 15, Detroit, Gale, 1993.

Critical Studies: *Children's Literature Review,* Detroit, Gale, Volume 1, 1976, Volume 14, 1988. *Contemporary Literary Criticism,* Volume 12, Detroit, Gale, 1980; *The Swiftly Tilting Worlds of Madeleine L'Engle: Essays in Her Honor,* edited by Luci Shaw, Wheaton, Illinois, Harold Shaw Publishers, 1998.

Madeleine L'Engle comments:

It was the first time that I'd been forced to think consciously about creativity in connection with little children, rather than the older ones for whom I often write. I was trying to think out loud about the concentration essential for all artists, and in the very little child I found the perfect example. The concentration of a small child at play is analogous to the concentration of the artist of any discipline. In real play, which is real concentration, the child is not only outside time, he is outside *himself.* He has thrown himself completely into whatever it is that he is doing. A child playing a game, building a sand castle, painting a picture, is completely *in* what he is doing. His *self*-consciousness gone; his consciousness is wholly focused outside himself.

I had just witnessed this in Crosswicks, observing an eighteen-month-old lying on her stomach on the grass watching a colony of ants, watching with total, spontaneous concentration. And I had played ring-around-a-rosy with her; we skipped around in a circle, grandparents, parents, assorted teenagers, wholly outside ourselves, holding hands, falling in abandon onto the lawn, joining in the child's shrieks of delighted laughter.

And with her we were outside self and outside time.

When we are *self*-conscious, we cannot be wholly aware; we must throw ourselves out first. This throwing ourselves away is the act of creativity. So, when we wholly concentrate, like a child in play, or an artist at work, then we share in the act of creating. We not only escape time, we also escape our self-conscious selves. (From *A Circle of Quiet,* 1972.)

*   *   *

The award-winning author of more than forty published books including plays, poems, essays, autobiographies, and novels, Madeleine L'Engle is one of America's most popular writers of books for young adults. L'Engle's literate stories are ageless, weaving family life, values, science, history, and theology into complex, often suspenseful plots with life-affirming messages.

L'Engle's popularity mushroomed after winning the Newbery Medal in 1963 for *A Wrinkle in Time,* the first in her time-fantasy trilogy (including *A Wind in the Door* and *A Swiftly Tilting Planet).* L'Engle said winning the Newbery was especially rewarding because the book had been rejected by almost every publisher in New York because of its difficulty level and uncertainty about the audience.

L'Engle's books do offer young adults a reading challenge. She writes for intelligent readers, using carefully chosen vocabulary and literary allusions throughout her stories. She blends references to mythology and carefully researched details of history, science, architecture, and philosophy into her tales. The reader must accept references to the principles of physics, cellular biology, and extra-sensory communication in the time-fantasy series. L'Engle tackles such concepts as human communication with dolphins, the future impacting the past, and regeneration in other novels.

Young adults rise to L'Engle's literary challenges because she creates recurring families and characters that readers befriend and care about, and fast-paced plots that engage readers in following several intertwining threads to satisfying conclusions. In *A Wrinkle in Time,* Meg Murray, the oldest child of the family featured in the time-fantasy series, must "tesser," travel through a wrinkle in time, to save her father and ultimately the world from the evil force IT. In the third book in the series, Meg's younger brother Charles Wallace travels back in time guided by a unicorn to inhabit the bodies of two brothers of ancient Welsh mythology in order to change the course of history. In *Many Waters,* Meg's other brothers, twins Sandy and Dennys, sketchily developed in the time-fantasy series, land in a world inhabited by seraphim, cherubim, fallen angels, and Japheth, Noah's father, where they must save themselves from the biblical Flood. In *The Arm of the Starfish,* Meg is a famous scientist married to Calvin O'Keefe of the time-fantasy series and is the mother of Polly O'Keefe, a secondary character in *Starfish* and a primary character in *An Acceptable Time,* in which she and Zachary, a young man she encountered in Greece in *A House like a Lotus,* find a door into another circle of time where a Druid priest saves Polly from becoming a human sacrifice after Zachary has betrayed her. The Austin family and their friends appear in *Meet the Austins, The Moon by Night,* and *The Young Unicorns.* Dr. Austin and his family play an important part in helping Dave of *The Young Unicorns* survive the violence and hatred of his former gang and begin a new life. Part of the great joy of reading L'Engle's books is the opportunities readers have to renew friendships and learn more about L'Engle's believable characters.

L'Engle writes about what is important to young adults. In an interview, L'Engle stressed the importance of teachers, librarians, and authors helping youngsters ask and search for answers to the big questions Why am I on the earth? Does my life matter? Does anybody care? Is there meaning to my existence? Am I really a human being? These questions are central to L'Engle's stories. The protagonists are intelligent, thoughtful, moral, and spiritual young people. Vicky Austin, in *A Ring of Endless Light,* deals bravely with the death of her beloved grandfather and family friend. Vicky's sensitivity and understanding of poetry allow her to communicate with the dolphins being studied by the scientists on her grandfather's island. Her abilities to communicate with these beautiful creatures provide her the energy to understand and accept the naturalness of death. In *The Young Unicorns,* Dave befriends Emily, a young, blind girl, and it is her enhanced sense of hearing that saves their lives when trapped in the tunnels of the Cathedral Church of St. John the Divine. In *The Arm of the Starfish,* Adam risks his life to save his friend and the world, and in *A House like a Lotus,* Polly O'Keefe travels to Greece and Cyprus where she struggles to make sense of the confusing events of her life, learning about love, pain, and anger in the process.

The greatest pleasures in L'Engle's novels come from her commitment to sometimes frightening, always thought-provoking, optimistic situations and themes. L'Engle's stories emphasize mankind's oneness with everything in the universe, the idea that everything affects everything else. This idea of connectedness among peoples, even across universes and time, provides readers with a sense of belonging to something much larger than self. Christian allusions are prevalent in L'Engle's novels; however, even those readers who don't recognize these allusions sense the spirituality of L'Engle's stories and are uplifted by the predominant message of her works: the power of love can cross all boundaries of time and space to transform and save mankind.

—Hollis Lowery-Moore

LESTER, Julius (Bernard)

Nationality: American. **Born:** St. Louis, Missouri, 27 January 1939. **Education:** Fisk University, Nashville, Tennessee, 1956-60, B.A. 1960. **Family:** Married 1) Joan Steinau in 1962 (divorced 1970), one daughter and one son; 2) Alida Carolyn Fechner in 1979, one son and one stepdaughter. **Career:** Musician and singer, recorded with Vanguard Records; associate editor, *Sing Out,* New York, 1964-69; contributing editor, *Broadside of New York,* 1964-70; director, Newport Folk Festival, Rhode Island, 1966-68; lecturer, New School for Social Research, New York, 1968-70; producer and host, WBAI radio, New York, 1968-75; host, *Free Time,* WNET-TV, New York, 1971-73; Professor of Afro-American Studies, 1971-88, Professor of Near Eastern and Judaic Studies, since 1982, acting director and associate director of Institute for Advanced Studies in Humanities, 1982-84, University of Massachusetts, Amherst. Writer-in-residence, Vanderbilt University, 1985. **Awards:** Newbery Honor Book citation, 1969, and Lewis Carroll Shelf Award, 1970, both for *To Be a Slave;* Lewis Carroll Shelf Award, 1972, and National Book Award finalist, 1973, both for *The Long Journey Home: Stories from Black History;* Lewis Carroll Shelf Award, 1973, for *The Knee-High Man and Other Tales;* honorable mention, Coretta Scott King Award, 1983, for *This Strange New Feeling,* and 1988, for *Tales of Uncle Remus: The Adventures of Brer Rabbit;* Distinguished Teacher's Award, 1983-84; Faculty Fellowship Award for Distinguished Research and Scholarship, 1985; National Professor of the Year Silver Medal Award, Council for Advancement and Support of Education, 1985; Massachusetts State Professor of the Year and Gold Medal Award for National Professor of the Year, both from Council for Advancement and Support of Education, both 1986; Distinguished Faculty Lecturer, 1986-87. **Office:** University of Massachusetts—Amherst, Amherst, Massachusetts 01002, U.S.A.

PUBLICATIONS FOR YOUNG ADULTS

Fiction

The Long Journey Home: Stories from Black History. New York, Dial Press, 1972; London, Longman, 1973.
Two Love Stories. New York, Dial Press, 1972; London, Kestrel, 1974.
This Strange New Feeling (short stories). New York, Dial Press, 1982; as *A Taste of Freedom: Three Stories from Black History,* London, Longman, 1983.

And All Our Wounds Forgiven. New York, Arcade, 1994.
Shining, illustrated by Terea Shaffer. San Diego, Silver Whistle, 1997.
What a Truly Cool World, illustrated by Joe Cepeda. New York, Scholastic, 1998.

Other

Editor, with Mary Varela, *Our Folk Tales: High John, The Conqueror, and Other Afro-American Tales,* illustrated by Jennifer Lawson. Privately printed, 1967.
Editor, *To Be a Slave,* illustrated by Tom Feelings. New York, Dial Press, 1968; London, Longman, 1970.
Black Folktales, illustrated by Tom Feelings. New York, Baron, 1969; with new introduction by author, New York, Grove Press, 1992.
The Knee-High Man and Other Tales, illustrated by Ralph Pinto. New York, Dial Press, 1972; London, Kestrel, 1974.
The Tales of Uncle Remus: The Adventures of Brer Rabbit, illustrated by Jerry Pinkney. New York, Dial Press, and London, Bodley Head, 1987.
More Tales of Uncle Remus: The Further Adventures of Brer Rabbit, illustrated by Jerry Pinkney. New York, Dial Press, 1988.
Further Tales of Uncle Remus: The Misadventures of Brer Rabbit, Brer Fox, Brer Wolf, the Doodang, and Other Creatures, illustrated by Jerry Pinkney. New York, Dial Press, 1990.
How Many Spots Does a Leopard Have? and Other Tales, illustrated by David Shannon. New York, Scholastic, 1990.
The Last Tales of Uncle Remus, illustrated by Jerry Pinkney. New York, Dial, 1994.
John Henry, illustrated by Jerry Pinkney. New York, Dial Books, 1994.
The Man Who Knew Too Much: A Moral Tale from the Baila of Zambia, illustrated by Leonard Jenkins. New York, Clarion Books, 1994.
Othello: A Novel (retelling of the play by William Shakespeare). New York, Scholastic, 1995.
Sam and the Tigers: A New Telling of Little Black Sambo, pictures by Jerry Pinkney. New York, Dial Books for Young Readers, 1996.
From Slave Ship to Freedom Road, paintings by Rod Brown. New York, Dial Books, 1998.
Black Cowboy, Wild Horses: A True Story, illustrated by Jerry Pinkney. New York, Dial Books, 1998.
When God Made the World: Stories Based on Jewish Legends. San Diego, Harcourt Brace, 1999.

PUBLICATIONS FOR ADULTS

Novels

Do Lord Remember Me. New York, Holt Rinehart, 1985; London, Dent, 1987.

Poetry

The Mud of Vietnam: Photographs and Poems. New York, Folklore Press, 1967.
Who I Am, with David Gahr. New York, Dial Press, 1974.

Other

The 12-String Guitar as Played by Leadbelly: An Instructional Manual, with Pete Seeger. New York, Oak, 1965.
The Angry Children of Malcolm X. Nashville, Tennessee, Southern Student Organizing Committee, 1966.
Editor, with Mary Varela, *To Praise Our Bridges: An Autobiography,* by Fanny Lou Hamer. Jackson, Mississippi, KIPCO, 1967.
Look Out Whitey! Black Power's Gon' Get Your Mama! New York, Dial Press, 1968; London, Allison and Busby, 1970.
Editor, *Ain't No Ambulances for No Nigguhs Tonight,* by Stanley Couch. New York, Baron, 1969.
Search for the New Land: History as Subjective Experience. New York, Dial Press, 1969; London, Allison and Busby, 1971.
Revolutionary Notes. New York, Baron, 1969.
Editor, *The Seventh Son: The Thoughts and Writings of W.E.B. Du Bois.* New York, Random House, 2 vols., 1971.
Compiler, with Rae Pace Alexander, *Young and Black in America.* New York, Random House, 1971.
All Is Well: An Autobiography. New York, Morrow, 1976.
Lovesong: Becoming a Jew. New York, Holt Rinehart, 1988.
Falling Pieces of the Broken Sky. New York, Arcade, 1990.

*

Critical Studies: Entry in *Children's Literature Review,* Volume 2, Detroit, Gale, 1976.

*   *   *

Julius Lester established his reputation by writing biographies of African Americans and by retelling collections of black folktales. The biographies include *The 12-String Guitar as Played by Leadbelly, To Be a Slave, Who I Am,* and *The Seventh Son: The Thought and Writings of W.E.B. Du Bois.* The folktales include *Black Folktales, The Knee-High Man and Other Tales* and *The Tales of Uncle Remus: The Adventures of Brer Rabbit.* Many of these books are collaborations. Lester worked with the singer Pete Seeger on *The 12-String Guitar as Played by Leadbelly,* with the artist Tom Feelings on several books, and with the photographer David Gahr on *Who I Am.*

Lester achieved his first critical success with *To Be a Slave,* published in 1968. The book was an ALA Notable Book and a Newbery Honor Book, and it received the Nancy Bloch Award. The book received this recognition during the decade in which the Civil Rights Movement was significant. Also, during this decade, historians including Jacqueline Bernard and Milton Meltzer had begun to consult original sources and, on the basis of these sources, to challenge accepted historical truths. In *To Be a Slave* Lester challenged the assumption prevalent at the time that African-American history is relatively unimportant in American history. He quotes an ex-slave as an epigraph for the book: ''In all the books that you have studied you never have studied Negro history, have you?. . .'' The book's success helped Lester establish himself as a major ''social advocacy'' historian.

Lester frames slaves' and ex-slaves' recorded statements with his own comments in the book. In one of his first comments, Lester writes:

To be a slave. To know, despite the suffering and deprivation, that you were human, more human than he who said you were not human.

To know joy, laughter, sorrow, and tears and yet be considered only the equal of a table. To be a slave was to be a human being under conditions in which that humanity was denied. They were not slaves. They were people. Their condition was slavery.

This passage is simultaneously passionate and thought-provoking. Lester begins the first paragraph with a sentence fragment to make his prose sound conversational, he repeats ''human'' three times in the second sentence to emphasize that the slaves were human beings and not inanimate objects like tables, and he lists the common human emotions the slaves felt to illustrate their membership in the human family. The passage is rich in feeling.

But Lester makes the passage intellectually rich as well by introducing two significant ethical ideas. First, he suggests that the institution of slavery debases slave and slave owner alike, and that by trying to limit their slaves' humanity the slave owners limited their own humanity. Second, he highlights the absurdity of considering slaves to be equal to inanimate objects like tables when slaves felt joy, laughter, sorrow, and tears. In his book Lester shows his thinking to be consistent with the Judeo-Christian tradition of finding meaning in suffering. The central idea uniting the slave reminiscences is that slavery is horrible and is wrong. Lester gives dignity and significance to these brief reminiscences by reinforcing and interpreting this idea in his comments. Ella Wilson's suffering would have been even more horrible if it would have gone unnoticed, if others could not have learned from it:

My master used to throw me in a buck and whip me. He would put my hands together and tie them. Then he would strip me naked. Then he would squat me down. Then he would run a stick through behind my knees and in front of my elbows. My knee was up against my chest. My hands was tied together just in front of my shins. The stick between my arms and my knees held me in a squat. That what they call a buck. You couldn't stand up and you couldn't get your feet out. You couldn't do nothing but just squat there and take what he put on. You couldn't move no way at all. Just try to. You just fall over on one side and have to stay there till you were turned over by him. He would whip me on one side till that was sore and full of blood and then he would whip me on the other side till that was all tore up.

The first chapter, titled ''To Be a Slave,'' contains this and other brief reminiscences. The other seven chapters are equally loosely organized under general headings including ''The Auction Block'' and ''The Plantation.'' *To Be a Slave* is similar to Lester's other books in this looseness of overall organization, power of particular passages, and reliance on Lester's voice to unify it.

Black Folktales, a collection he published in 1969, again contains stories loosely grouped under general headings. Lester writes in the Foreword:

It is in stories like these that a child learns who his parents are and who he will become. . . . The stories in this book come from the black people of Africa and Afro-America. . . . These stories are told here not as they were told a hundred years ago, but as I tell them now. And I tell them now only because they have meaning now.

Lester has repeatedly proven through his biographies of famous and anonymous African Americans and his retellings of black folktales that African Americans' lives and stories have meaning long after the original living or telling.

—Harold Nelson

LEVENKRON, Steven

Nationality: American. **Born:** New York City, 25 March 1941. **Education:** Queens College of the City University of New York, B.A. 1963; Brooklyn of the City University of New York, M.S. 1969. **Family:** Married Abby Rosen in 1963; two daughters. **Career:** Social studies teacher at secondary schools in New York, 1963-68; guidance counselor at secondary schools in New York, 1968-74; in part-time private practice of psychotherapy, 1972-74; visiting psychotherapist, Montefiore Hospital and Medical Center, Bronx, New York, 1975—; clinical consultant, Center for the Study of Anorexia, New York, 1981—. **Awards:** Annual award from the National Association of Anorexia Nervosa and Associated Disorders, 1981, for bringing anorexia nervosa to public attention; *The Best Little Girl in the World* was named best book for young adults by the American Library Association, 1978-79. **Address:** 16 East 79th Street, New York, New York 10021, U.S.A.

PUBLICATIONS FOR YOUNG ADULTS

Fiction

The Best Little Girl in the World. Chicago, Contemporary Books, 1978.
The Luckiest Girl in the World. New York, Scribner, 1997.

Nonfiction

Treating and Overcoming Anorexia Nervosa. New York, Scribner, 1982.
Obsessive-Compulsive Disorders: Treating and Understanding Crippling Habits. New York, Warner, 1991.

*   *   *

Given the fact that Levenkron is a psychologist and not a professional writer of literature for young adults, his one excursion into the world of the novel is quite impressive. *The Best Little Girl in the World* is the excruciatingly painful story of a teenage anoretic who nearly dies as a result of her illness. The book joins the Dietrich family—a typical white, middle-class family—just as fifteen-year-old Francesca's disease is beginning to climax. She clearly feels alienated from her family because her older brother and sister have seemingly gotten the lion's share of attention from their parents. Francesca was always "the good child" compared to her more confrontational sister Susanna and conceited but adored brother Gregg. Francesca's life has begun to revolve around the

opinion of her ballet instructor—the sole adult in Francesca's life who seems to notice her. At the suggestion of the teacher, Francesca begins dieting with the hope that she will qualify for a position at a prestigious ballet camp. This suggestion, however, plays into Francesca's low self-esteem, and the girl becomes obsessed with the weight loss as a means of solving all of the unpleasant realities of her life.

The troubled youth even takes on a new identity, "Kessa," to cope with the pain of her circumstances. Levenkron describes with keen insight the thoughts and feelings of the slowly deteriorating Francesca as well as the experience of her concerned parents and physicians. As Francesca's disease progresses, her thinking becomes obscured partly because of malnutrition. Once her mother realizes her daughter is terribly ill, the rate of Francesca's deterioration increases. Eventually the girl is hospitalized. Her only hope comes from the relationship she has established with a psychologist who has just begun working with anorexic patients. As they realize the seriousness of Francesca's condition, the family is forced to deal with the dynamics within the unit that contributed to her illness. As it turns out, Francesca's behavior is motivated largely by a desire for attention. Since being the "good girl" obviously did not work, she turned to a negative, self-destructive behavior instead. In the end, a combination of a near-death experience, peer pressure, counseling, and family support make rehabilitation a feasible option for Francesca. When the novel closes, her prognosis is good.

The characters in this novel are somewhat flat and stereotypical. However, since the work is actually a modern morality play that presents a common dilemma and its successful resolution, the flatness of the characters enhances the work. Levenkron's glimpses into the depth of the secondary characters creates a bas relief against which the more fully formed Francesca is showcased. Throughout the book, Levenkron speaks primarily from Francesca's point of view. He provides his audience with a poignant image of a teenage girl in excruciating emotional, and eventually physical, pain. In so doing, he provides a vehicle of communication for those readers who experience this pain or know someone who does.

The Best Little Girl in the World is an excellent tool for counselors or lay people dealing with anorexia. Levenkron's clear depictions of each stage of the disease serve to warn would-be anoretics of the terrible consequences of their choices, while demonstrating that there are people who understand the fear and pain that lies at the root of their condition. It also dispels some of the fear of the unknown for those travelling this long, dark road. Perhaps most significantly, Levenkron provides a lively, easily accessible, and cogent argument against the societal values that contribute to this disease.

For those interested in a more technical discussion of anorexia and other obsessive/compulsive behaviors, Levenkron has written several nonfiction works on the subject. His accessible style is evident in these works as well.

—Linda Ross

LEVITIN, Sonia

Pseudonym: Also writes as Sonia Wolff. **Nationality:** American. **Born:** Sonia Wolff in Berlin, Germany, 18 August 1934; brought to the United States, 1938. **Education:** the University of California, Berkeley, 1952-54; University of Pennsylvania, Philadelphia, 1954-56, B.S. in education 1956; San Francisco State University, 1957-60. **Family:** Married Lloyd Levitin in 1953; one son and one daughter. **Career:** Elementary school teacher, Mill Valley, California, 1956-57; adult education teacher, Daly City, California, 1962-64, and Acalanes Adult Center, Lafayette, California, 1965-72; creative writing teacher, Palos Verdes Peninsula, California, 1973-76. Since 1978 teacher, Writers' Program, University of California at Los Angeles Extension. Since 1989 instructor in American Jewish literature, University of Judaism. Founder, STEP adult education corporation. Performed volunteer work, including publicity, for various charities and educational institutions. **Awards:** *Journey to America* received the Charles and Bertie G. Schwartz award for juvenile fiction from the Jewish Book Council of America, 1971, and American Library Association Notable Book honors; *Roanoke: A Novel of the Lost Colony* was nominated for the Dorothy Canfield Fisher award, Georgia Children's Book award, and Mark Twain award; *Who Owns the Moon?* received American Library Association Notable Book honors; *The Mark of Conte* received the Southern California Council on Literature for Children and Young People award for fiction, 1976, and was nominated for California Young Reader Medal award in the junior high category, 1982; Golden Spur award from Western Writers of America, 1978, and Lewis Carroll Shelf award, both for *The No-Return Trail;* Southern California Council on Literature for Children and Young People award for a distinguished contribution to the field of children's literature, 1981; National Jewish Book award in children's literature, PEN Los Angeles award for young adult fiction, Association of Jewish Libraries Sydney Taylor award, Austrian Youth Prize, Catholic Children's Book Prize (Germany), Dorothy Canfield Fisher award nomination, Parent's Choice Honor Book citation, and American Library Association Best Book for Young Adults award, all 1988, all for *The Return*; Edgar Allen Poe award from Mystery Writers of America, Dorothy Canfield Fisher award nomination, and Nevada State award nomination, all 1989, all for *Incident at Loring Groves*; ALA-YASD Best Book for Young Adults award and Sidney Taylor award honor book, Jewish Library Association, both 1989, both for *Silver Days*; YALSA Recommended Book for Reluctant Young Adult Readers, for *The Golem and the Dragon Girl*; Riverside County Author's award, 1993, for *Annie's Promise*; National Conference on Christians and Jews Recommended list, *Booklist* Editor's Choice, Voice of Youth Advocates Outstanding Books, all 1994, YALSA Best Books for Young Adults list, 1995, all for *Escape from Egypt*; Southern California Council on Literature for Children, 1994; Young People Distinguished Body of Work award; Parents' Choice honor book, 1996, for *Evil Encounter*; Best of the Year selection, *School Library Journal*, 1996, for *Nine for California*. **Agent:** Toni Mendez, Inc., 141 East 56th St., New York, New York 10022, U.S.A.

PUBLICATIONS FOR YOUNG ADULTS

Fiction

Journey to America, illustrated by Charles Robinson. New York, Atheneum, 1970; London, Macmillan, 1987.
Rita the Weekend Rat, illustrated by Leonard Shortall. New York, Atheneum, 1971.

Roanoke: A Novel of the Lost Colony, illustrated by John Gretzer. New York, Atheneum, 1973.
Who Owns the Moon?, illustrated by John Larrecq. Berkeley, California, Parnassus, 1973.
Jason and the Money Tree, illustrated by Pat Grant Porter. New York, Harcourt Brace, 1974.
A Single Speckled Egg, illustrated by John Larrecq. Berkeley, California, Parnassus, 1975.
The Mark of Conte, illustrated by Bill Negron. New York, Atheneum, 1976.
Beyond Another Door. New York, Atheneum, 1977.
The No-Return Trail. New York, Harcourt Brace, 1978.
A Sound to Remember, illustrated by Gabriel Lisowski. New York, Harcourt Brace, 1979.
Nobody Stole the Pie, illustrated by Fernando Krahn. New York, Harcourt Brace, 1980.
The Fisherman and the Bird, illustrated by Francis Livingston. Boston, Houghton Mifflin, 1982.
All the Cats in the World, illustrated by Charles Robinson. New York, Harcourt Brace, 1982.
The Year of Sweet Senior Insanity. New York, Atheneum, 1982.
Smile Like a Plastic Daisy. New York, Atheneum, 1984.
A Season for Unicorns. New York, Atheneum, 1986.
The Return. New York, Atheneum, 1987.
Incident at Loring Groves. New York, Dial Press, 1988.
Silver Days. New York, Atheneum, 1989.
The Man Who Kept His Heart in a Bucket. New York, Dial Press, 1991.
Annie's Promise. New York, Macmillan, 1993.
The Golem and the Dragon Girl. New York, Dial Press, 1993.
Adam's War. New York, Dial Press, 1994.
A Piece of Home. New York, Dial Press, 1996.
Evil Encounter. New York, Simon and Schuster, 1996.
Nine for California. New York, Orchard, 1996.
Yesterday's Child. New York, Simon and Schuster, 1997.
The Singing Mountain. New York, Simon and Schuster, 1998.
Boom Town. New York, Orchard, 1998.
The Cure. San Diego, Harcourt Brace, forthcoming.

PUBLICATIONS FOR ADULTS

Novels

Reigning Cats and Dogs, illustrated by Joan Berg Victor. New York, Atheneum, 1978.
What They Did to Miss Lily (as Sonia Wolff). New York, Harper, 1981; London, New English Library, 1982.

*

Biography: Essay in *Something about the Author Autobiography Series,* Volume 2, Detroit, Gale, 1986; essay in *Speaking for Ourselves, Too* compiled and edited by Donald R. Gallo, National Council of Teachers of English, 1993.

Critical Studies: Entry in *Contemporary Literary Criticism,* Volume 17, Detroit, Gale, 1981.

Sonia Levitin comments:

Through my writing I try to create bridges—between childhood and adulthood, between peoples of different beliefs and cultures. My desire is to invite the reader to cross that bridge and to discover not only the Other, but himself. Learning, knowing, and loving go together. It is so with all things. So I try to make it easy for the reader to know and learn while I entertain him, hoping that he will also find new passions.

* * *

Versatility is a hallmark of Sonia Levitin's work. Her ability to write historical as well as realistic fiction captures a wide range of readers. She is an author who unfolds a story carefully and with attention to the details that bring life and caring to characters.

Her trilogy, based on Levitin's own life, takes the reader through the war years and offers rich insight into the survival of one family in the midst of horrendous upheaval and personal tragedy. *Journey to America,* is the story of the Platt family's escape from Nazi Germany in 1938, told from the perspective of Lisa Platt. The courage of each member of the family and their willingness to leave everything held dear to seek freedom and safety capture the reader's attention. Levitin uses Lisa's fears and language that binds the reader to the story as the family arrive in Switzerland on their way to America. *Silver Days* lacks the strength of the earlier work, but it is still a fine portrayal of what it was like to come to America and struggle through the early days of learning English and conforming to different ways. Again, the story is told from Lisa's point of view and explores the concept of adaptability, not only of Lisa but also of the family itself. *Annie's Promise* brings the story of the Platt family full circle. Annie is the youngest and this is clearly her story. Her summer at "Quaker Pines," a Quaker-sponsored camp, is her chance to test herself and determine who she will be as a young woman. Although she fails in her antagonistic relationship with the angry street kid, Nancy Rae, she learns a great deal from that hateful encounter. Perhaps the most powerful scene in the book is Annie's angry confrontation with her parents over their treatment of Tally, her young black friend from camp. Annie screams: "You are just like the Nazis. This is why there are wars!. . .Because people hate for no reason—how could you?"

In *Beyond Another Door* Daria comes to grips with the frightening power of extrasensory perception. A nondescript object, a glass dish won at a fair, acts as the catalyst to call her grandma's spirit back to help her cope with this ability. Throughout the story her mother is frightened and tries to push her away from anything that encourages this talent. She won't speak of the problem or of the grandmother's reputation as a gifted psychic. Most of Daria's friends turn away from her in fear of weird happenings, but new ones like Rob and Man believe in her. Levitin makes the distinction, so important to the story, of knowing something and causing it, which is a burden that gifted people such as Daria carry. She makes a tremendous impact on the reader in having Daria say towards the end of the story: "I can't just accept things without asking questions. It wouldn't be logical. Some people go too far, believing everything without even thinking." But it is also Daria's decision to commit herself to her painting and at the same time to seek help from Rob's father who is a psychologist studying psychic phenomena that brings the unfolding of this story to a fullness.

Levitin continues her interest in the preternatural with *The Golem and the Dragon Girl* which, while it forces the reader to consider cultural roots and heritage in a ghost-filled ancestral home, still offers insights into the unstable world of adolescence. Jonathan and Laurel each want to avoid moving from their homes and each becomes involved in a sharing of Jewish and Chinese cultures. Music is one key in this novel that helps the reader focus on both the protagonists' personal problems as well as the larger issues.

Levitin moves into historical fiction in *The No-Return Trail,* the story, based on fact, of Nancy Kelsey, a seventeen-year-old wife and mother and the first American woman to make the journey to California in the Bidwell-Bartleson expedition of 1841. Nancy grows and changes a great deal as she moves with the wagon train across the land and struggles with her womanhood and her relationship to her husband. In *Roanoke: A Novel of the Lost Colony,* sixteen-year-old William Wythers joins emigrants bound for Virginia. Levitin uses what little factual material is known about the colony at Roanoke as the backdrop for William's growth into manhood.

A Season of Unicorns and *Incident at Loring Groves* offer insight into adolescent concerns. Inky the protagonist of the first gathers the strength to face her fears by changing herself, and Cassiday and Ken risk peer pressure and their popularity to accept responsibility and report the murder of a classmate in the second story.

In *The Return* Desta, a young Ethiopian Jewish girl, struggles to make the long journey to join "Operation Moses," the secret Exodus of Ethiopian Jews from the Sudan to Israel between 1984 and 1985. As in many of her books, prejudice, oppression, and racial hatreds are explored. In this instance it is against the "Falasha," the derogatory term other Ethiopians called the Ethiopian Jews. Having endured so much pain and suffering, it is Desta who releases Dan from engagement bonds and leads in enunciating their common need to study before they consider marriage. Told in the first person, this powerful and haunting story of thirst, starvation, and death is grim in parts but lyrical in its portrayal of the power of the human spirit—a power that permeates all of Levitin's work and gives her stories their clarity and richness.

—Jane Anne Hannigan

LEVOY, Myron

Nationality: American. **Born:** New York City, 30 January 1930. **Education:** City College, New York, B.S. in chemical engineering 1952; Purdue University, West Lafayette, Indiana, M.S. in chemical engineering 1953. **Family:** Married Beatrice Fleischer in 1952; one daughter and one son. **Career:** Has worked as a chemical engineer; now a full-time writer. **Awards:** *Book World*'s Children's Spring Book Festival honor book, and one of Child Study Association of America's Children's Books of the Year, both 1972, and a Children's Book Showcase selection, 1973, all for *The Witch of Fourth Street, and Other Stories;* New Jersey Institute of Technology Authors award, 1973, for *Penny Tunes and Princesses; Boston Globe-Horn Book* award honor book for fiction, American Book award finalist, Woodward Park School Annual Book award, Jane Addams Children's Book award honor book,

New Jersey Institute of Technology Authors award, all 1978, Dutch Silver Pencil award, Austrian State Prize for Children's Literature, both 1981, Buxtehuder Bulle award, Buxtehuder, West Germany, German State Prize for Children's Literature, both 1982, ALA Best of the Best List, 1992, Young Adult Library Services Association Best of the Best List, 1994, all for *Alan and Naomi;* ALA Best Books for Young Adults, 1981, Woodward Park School Annual Book award and New York Public Library's Books for the Teen Age, both 1982, all for *A Shadow Like a Leopard;* ALA Best Book for Young Adults and International Reading Association Young Adult Choice, both 1986, for *Pictures of Adam.* **Agent:** Susan Cohen, Writers House Inc., 21 West 26th Street, New York, New York 10010.

PUBLICATIONS FOR YOUNG ADULTS

Fiction

Alan and Naomi. New York, Harper, 1977; London, Bodley Head, 1979.
A Shadow like a Leopard. New York, Harper, 1981.
Three Friends. New York, Harper, 1984.
Pictures of Adam. New York, Harper, 1986; London, Bodley Head, 1987.
Kelly 'n' Me. New York, Harper, 1992.

PUBLICATIONS FOR CHILDREN

Fiction

The Witch of Fourth Street and Other Stories, illustrated by Gabriel Lisowski. New York, Harper, 1972.
Penny Tunes and Princesses, illustrated by Ezra Jack Keats. New York, Harper, 1972.
The Hanukkah of Great-Uncle Otto, illustrated by Donna Ruff. Philadelphia, Pennsylvania, Jewish Publication Society, 1984.
The Magic Hat of Mortimer Wintergreen. New York, Harper, 1988; London, Macmillan, 1989.

PUBLICATIONS FOR ADULTS

Novels

A Necktie on Greenwich Village. New York, Vanguard Press, 1968.

Plays

The Penthouse Perspective (produced Northport, New York, 1967).
Eli and Emily (produced New York, 1969).
The Sun Is a Red Dwarf (produced New York, 1969).
Sweet Tom (produced New York, 1969).
Footsteps (produced New York, 1970). New York, Breakthrough Press, 1971.
Smudge (produced New York, 1971).

*

Media Adaptations: *The Witch of Fourth Street and Other Stories* (recording), Listening Library; *Alan and Naomi* (film), Leucadia Film Corporation and the Maltese Companies, Inc., 1992.

Biography: Essay in *Speaking for Ourselves: Autobiographical Sketches by Notable Authors of Books for Young Adults,* Volume 1, compiled and edited by Donald R. Gallo, National Council of Teachers of English, 1990.

Myron Levoy comments:

In my novels for young adults, I have a special interest in exploring the loner and outsider. From the ghetto boy who writes his own brand of poetry yet yearns for the security and camaraderie of the gang (*A Shadow Like a Leopard*) to the wealthy girl who rejects her family's elitist values for her own compassionate view of life (*Kelly 'n' Me*), my teenagers must face a central decision of their lives: to conform or to be truly their own selves. I should add that I call them *my* teenagers because they are, in a sense, my children, or, indeed, me. Their stories are open-ended; as in most lives, their struggles are never fully resolved. It's my hope that from this, my readers can gain new insight into their own struggles and the courage to be truer to their own inner selves.

*   *   *

The consistent question that Myron Levoy poses in his novels for adolescent readers is this: What is it like to be on the outside of things? Again and again he creates characters who find themselves separated from what they perceive to be the normal experience of a North American adolescent. This difference may be generated by events from the past, by ethnicity, by social status, or by sexuality, but for the character the reason makes little difference; the enormity of the separation is what is paramount. It is that sense of difference which causes many of the plot situations in Levoy's novels. And it is a coming to grips with that sense of difference which leads to the novels' moving resolutions.

It would not have been easy to guess this direction in Levoy's work from his first fiction for young readers, *The Witch of Fourth Street and Other Stories* (1972). This set of stories focuses on a group of children living on the Lower East side of New York City, all of them coming from recently immigrated families. There are Italians, Jews, Greeks, Russians, and Irish, all united by their bonds of family love, their desire to make a new and better life, and their memories of the old country. Here are stories of fathers scrimping to buy their son an electric Lionel train and the joy that that train brings to the neighborhood children, street vendors and their aging horses, young girls coming to accept their parents' roles, matchstick bridges, children who find evil reminiscent of that left behind in the old country. And there is a story of a gentle falling into death, a moving back into memory until one is again in one's mothers arms. There is nothing like this in any of Levoy's later work.

And yet perhaps there is. Here is a group of children who are themselves apart. Their parents yearn to bring them into the mainstream American experience as they perceive it, yet they also yearn to remember the old country, to remember the past which gives the family its history, its meaning, and even its story. The children are caught in the tension, partly in one world partly in another, but not fully in either.

In some ways these stories about young protagonists set apart are not dissimilar to the story of Ramon Santiago in *A Shadow Like a Leopard* (1981). In this novel, Ramon is getting sucked into a vision of being "macho" as his father and peers define it, so that he seems to be on the verge of losing his own chance to forge an identity. The one thing which is distinctly his—his writing—is something he hides from his father and friends. He robs an old woman, wanders the streets of New York City, and abandons school—such as it is—in search of something. His father in Attica, his mother in a hospital, Ramon seems to need the gang which beckons to him as a way of finding a place.

But Ramon finds, reluctantly, that he is different, not only from the mainstream culture that inhabits Fifth Avenue, but also from those around him. His writing is important to him, and he finds it to be cathartic. He has a vision which seems to generate metaphor easily: "a shadow like a leopard." Even his daydreams suggest his difference: he dreams of a nice white house and a sister and parents who all sit down with him at an evening meal, far away from the streets of New York City. Not until he meets Arnold Glasser does he come to recognize his own artistic tendencies and to value them, not see them as impediments to being macho. By the end of the novel he is able to affirm that he is who he is; his situation has not changed, but his acceptance of his differences has strengthened him to go beyond his situation: "Ramon Santiago! That's me!".

It is this affirmation—"That's me!"—that rings through all of Levoy's work; characters must work through their differences, understand the causes of their differences, and come to accept them. Thus, in *Three Friends* (1984) Karen and Joshua are able to affirm Lori, an artistic and sensitive girl confused about her sexuality, not by changing themselves and their relationship but by accepting Lori for who she is. In *Kelly 'n' Me* (1992) Anthony helps Kelly to both understand and accept who she is, going beyond the surfaces generated by money, social status, and dark secrets held closely. And in *Pictures of Adam* (1986) Lisa can take Adam down to a lake, both of them naked, and declare that they are who they are and everything else is irrelevant. The statement may not be completely true, but it is an affirmation of what comes first when one considers one's identity.

Levoy does not resolve his endings with complete ease. In *A Shadow like a Leopard,* Ramon still must deal with his father who tries to define his macho nature, Adam still dreams of killing his abusive father each night, and Kelly leaves Port Authority on a bus, searching for an identity that she may or may not find. But in no novel is the conclusion left so poignantly unresolved as in *Alan and Naomi* (1977), Levoy's most acclaimed book. Here Alan is persuaded by his parents to befriend a young war refugee, Naomi, who has seen her father beaten to death by the Gestapo. The sight has left her withdrawn and uncommunicative; she spends her days shredding tiny pieces of paper—representing the memory of the papers she and her father were shredding before the Nazis found them.

At first resentful of this duty and embarrassed by it, Alan visits Naomi only grudgingly. But as they begin to communicate through the use of puppets, Alan comes to truly see her as a friend and perhaps even more than that. Eventually he is able to speak directly with her, rather than through puppets, and he takes her to visit an airfield where they fly his toy plane. She returns to school. But when Alan and Naomi are attacked by a bully and Alan's face is bloodied, Naomi runs back home and hides in the coal, murmuring that the dead should be buried. She is more withdrawn than ever before, and must eventually be hospitalized. Not even Alan can reach her, and though Alan's father expresses some hope for her recovery, the novel ends with Alan's conviction that she will not recover. Some events in the past, Levoy suggests, cannot be resolved.

If Levoy's novels celebrate any one thing, they celebrate friendship. It is friendship, an intimate closeness with another, that Levoy uses to bring his characters to their resolutions. When Ramon first encounters Glasser, whom he has come to rob, he finds a man more alone, more outside than he is, an artist who sees his entire career as a failure and who is ready to die not because he is brave, but because he is tired and worn out. It takes Ramon to affirm Glasser, as it takes Glasser to affirm Ramon; each finds the validity of his artistic expression through the other. In *Pictures of Adam,* Lisa is beset with a family that seems to be breaking apart and a mother who seems to be becoming an alcoholic; though ostensibly she sets out to help Adam overcome his own horrific background—a father who beat him with a chain—as well as the fantasies he uses to shield himself from that horror, she too is affirmed by Adam's innocent love; she too does not need to be what others define her to be. Joshua and Karen help Lori cope with her sense of being outside of normal experience, but they too help each other to accept who they are. Their willingness to see themselves as "weirdos" sets up their later willingness to help each one be what he or she wants to be. Kelly learns to accept her past and to search for herself because of the unquestioning love of Anthony, who is himself struggling with an alcoholic mother whom he must learn to love.

If the friendships in Levoy's novels do not always lead to successful resolutions, as in *Alan and Naomi,* they nevertheless do point towards healing and growth. Adam and Lori will grow with Lisa's and Joshua's help; Kelly will be able to depend upon and remember Anthony's love; and Ramon will find new possibilities that he had never imagined under the guidance of Glasser. If the novels of Myron Levoy are filled with pain—and they are—then it is the pain of healing, the stretching of wounds to allow for growth.

—Gary D. Schmidt

LEWIS, C(live) S(taples)

Pseudonyms: Also wrote as Clive Hamilton; N.W. Clerk. **Nationality:** British. **Born:** Belfast, Northern Ireland, 29 November 1898. **Education:** Wynyard House, Watford, Hertfordshire, 1908-10; Campbell College, Belfast, 1910; Cherbourg School, Malvern, Worcestershire, 1911-13, and Malvern College, 1913-14; privately, in Great Bookham, Surrey, 1914-17; University College, Oxford (scholar; Chancellor's English Essay prize, 1921), 1917, 1919-23, B.A. (honours) 1922. **Military Service:** Served in the Somerset Light Infantry, 1917-19: First Lieutenant. **Family:** Married Joy Davidman Gresham in 1956 (died 1960); two stepsons. **Career:** Philosophy tutor, 1924, and lecturer in English, 1924, University College, Oxford; fellow and tutor in English, Magdalen College, Oxford, 1925-54; professor of medieval and renaissance English, Cambridge University, 1954-63. Lecturer, University College of North Wales, Bangor, 1941; Riddell Lecturer, University of Durham, 1943; Clark lecturer, Cambridge University, 1944. **Awards:** Gollancz prize, 1937; Library Association Carnegie Medal, 1957. D.D.: University of St. Andrews, Fife, 1946; Docteur-es-Lettres, Laval University, Quebec, 1952; D. Litt.: University of Manchester, 1959; Hon. Dr.: University of Dijon, 1962; University of Lyon, 1963. Honorary Fellow, Magdalen College, Oxford, 1955; University College, Oxford, 1958; Magdalene

College, Cambridge, 1963. Fellow, Royal Society of Literature, 1948; Fellow, British Academy, 1955. **Died:** 22 November 1963.

PUBLICATIONS FOR YOUNG ADULTS (illustrated by Pauline Baynes)

Fiction

"Chronicles of Narnia" series:

The Lion, The Witch, and the Wardrobe. London, Bles, and New York, Macmillan, 1950.
Prince Caspian: The Return to Narnia. London, Bles, and New York, Macmillan, 1951.
The Voyage of the "Dawn Treader." London, Bles, and New York, Macmillan, 1952.
The Silver Chair. London, Bles, and New York, Macmillan, 1953.
The Horse and His Boy. London, Bles, and New York, Macmillan, 1954.
The Magician's Nephew. London, Lane, and New York, Macmillan, 1955.
The Last Battle. London, Lane, and New York, Macmillan, 1956.

Other

Letters to Children, edited by Lyle W. Dorsett and Marjorie Lamp Mead. New York, Macmillan, and London, Collins, 1985.

PUBLICATIONS FOR ADULTS

Novels

Out of the Silent Planet. London, Lane, 1938; New York, Macmillan, 1943.
Perelandra. London, Lane, 1943; New York, Macmillan, 1944; as *Voyage to Venus,* London, Pan, 1953.
That Hideous Strength: A Modern Fairy-Tale for Grown-Ups. London, Lane, 1945; New York, Macmillan, 1946; abridged edition, as *The Tortured Planet,* New York, Avon, 1958.
Till We Have Faces: A Myth Retold. London, Bles, 1956; New York, Harcourt Brace, 1957.
Of Other Worlds: Essays and Stories, edited by Walter Hooper. London, Bles, 1966; New York, Harcourt Brace, 1967.
The Dark Tower and Other Stories, edited by Walter Hooper. London, Collins, and New York, Harcourt Brace, 1977.

Verse

Spirits in Bondage: A Cycle of Lyrics (as Clive Hamilton). London, Heinemann, 1919.
Dymer (as Clive Hamilton). London, Dent, and New York, Dutton, 1926.
Poems, edited by Walter Hooper. London, Bles, 1964; New York, Harcourt Brace, 1965.
Narrative Poems, edited by Walter Hooper. London, Bles, 1969; New York, Harcourt Brace, 1972.

Other

The Pilgrim's Regress: An Allegorical Apology for Christianity, Reason, and Romanticism. London, Dent, 1933; New York, Sheed and Ward, 1935; revised edition, London, Bles, 1943; Sheed and Ward, 1944.
The Allegory of Love: A Study in Medieval Tradition. Oxford, Clarendon Press, and New York, Oxford University Press, 1936.
Rehabilitations and Other Essays. London and New York, Oxford University Press, 1939.
The Personal Heresy: A Controversy, with E.M.W. Tillyard. London and New York, Oxford University Press, 1939.
The Problem of Pain. London, Bles, 1940; New York, Macmillan, 1944.
The Weight of Glory. London, S.P.C.K., 1942.
The Screwtape Letters. London, Bles, 1942; New York, Macmillan, 1943; revised edition, as *The Screwtape Letters and Screwtape Proposes a Toast,* London, Bles, 1961; New York, Macmillan, 1962.
Broadcast Talks: Right and Wrong: A Clue to the Meaning of the Universe, and What Christians Believe. London, Bles, 1942; as *The Case for Christianity,* New York, Macmillan, 1943.
A Preface to "Paradise Lost" (lectures). London and New York, Oxford University Press, 1942; revised edition, 1960.
Christian Behaviour: A Further Series of Broadcast Talks. London, Bles, and New York, Macmillan, 1943.
The Abolition of Man; or, Reflections on Education with Special Reference to the Teaching of English in the Upper Forms of Schools. London, Oxford University Press, 1943; New York, Macmillan, 1947.
Beyond Personality: The Christian Idea of God. London, Bles, 1944; New York, Macmillan, 1945.
The Great Divorce. A Dream. London, Bles, and New York, Macmillan, 1946.
Miracles: A Preliminary Study. London, Bles, and New York, Macmillan, 1947.
Vivisection. London, Anti-Vivisection Society, and Boston, New England Anti-Vivisection Society, 1947.
Transposition and Other Addresses. London, Bles, 1949; as *The Weight of Glory and Other Addresses,* New York, Macmillan, 1949.
The Literary Impact of the Authorized Version (lecture). London, Athlone Press, 1950; Philadelphia, Fortress Press, 1963.
Mere Christianity. London, Bles, and New York, Macmillan, 1952.
Hero and Leander (lecture). London, Oxford University Press, 1952.
English Literature in the Sixteenth Century, Excluding Drama. Oxford, Clarendon Press, 1954.
De Descriptione Temporum (lecture). London, Cambridge University Press, 1955.
Surprised by Joy: The Shape of My Early Life. London, Bles, 1955; New York, Harcourt Brace, 1956.
Reflections on the Psalms. London, Bles, and New York, Harcourt Brace, 1958.
Shall We Lose God in Outer Space? London, S.P.C.K., 1959.
The Four Loves. London, Bles, and New York, Harcourt Brace, 1960.
The World's Last Night and Other Essays. New York, Harcourt Brace, 1960.
Studies in Words. London, Cambridge University Press, 1960; revised edition, 1967.
An Experiment in Criticism. London, Cambridge University Press, 1961.

A Grief Observed (as N.W. Clerk; autobiography). London, Faber, 1961; Greenwich, Connecticut, Seabury Press, 1963.

They Asked for a Paper: Papers and Addresses. London, Bles, 1962.

Beyond the Bright Blur (letters). New York, Harcourt Brace, 1963.

Letters to Malcolm, Chiefly on Prayer. London, Bles, and New York, Harcourt Brace, 1964.

The Discarded Image: An Introduction to Medieval and Renaissance Literature. London, Cambridge University Press, 1964.

Screwtape Proposes a Toast and Other Pieces. London, Fontana, 1965.

Letters, edited by W.H. Lewis. London, Bles, and New York, Harcourt Brace, 1966.

Studies in Medieval and Renaissance Literature, edited by Walter Hooper. London, Cambridge University Press, 1966.

Spenser's Images of Life, edited by Alastair Fowler. London, Cambridge University Press, 1967.

Christian Reflections, edited by Walter Hooper. London, Bles, and Grand Rapids, Michigan, Eerdmans, 1967.

Letters to an American Lady, edited by Clyde S. Kilby. Grand Rapids, Michigan, Eerdmans, 1967; London, Hodder and Stoughton, 1969.

Mark vs. Tristram: Correspondence Between C.S. Lewis and Owen Barfield, edited by Walter Hooper. Cambridge, Massachusetts, Lowell House Printers, 1967.

A Mind Awake: An Anthology of C.S. Lewis, edited by Clyde S. Kilby. London, Bles, 1968; New York, Harcourt Brace, 1969.

Selected Literary Essays, edited by Walter Hooper. London, Cambridge University Press, 1969.

God in the Dock: Essays on Theology and Ethics, edited by Walter Hooper. Grand Rapids, Michigan, Eerdmans, 1970; as *Undeceptions: Essays on Theology and Ethics,* London, Bles, 1971.

The Humanitarian Theory of Punishment. Abingdon, Berkshire, Marcham Books Press, 1972.

Fern-Seed and Elephants and Other Essays on Christianity, edited by Walter Hooper. London, Fontana, 1975.

The Joyful Christian: 127 Readings, edited by William Griffin. New York, Macmillan, 1977.

They Stand Together: The Letters of C.S. Lewis to Arthur Greeves 1914-1963, edited by Walter Hooper. London, Collins, and New York, Macmillan, 1979.

C.S. Lewis at the Breakfast Table and Other Reminiscences, edited by James T. Como. New York, Macmillan, 1979; London, Collins, 1980.

The Visionary Christian: 131 Readings, edited by Chad Walsh. New York, Macmillan, 1981.

On Stories and Other Essays on Literature, edited by Walter Hooper. New York, Harcourt Brace, 1982.

Of This and Other Worlds, edited by Walter Hooper. London, Collins, 1982.

The Cretaceous Perambulator, with Owen Barfield, edited by Walter Hooper. Oxford, C.S. Lewis Society, 1983.

The Business of Heaven: Daily Readings from C.S. Lewis, edited by Walter Hooper. London, Fount, and New York, Harcourt Brace, 1984.

Boxen: The Imaginary World of the Young C.S. Lewis, edited by Walter Hooper. London, Collins, and San Diego, Harcourt Brace, 1985.

Present Concerns, edited by Walter Hooper. London, Fount, and San Diego, Harcourt Brace, 1986.

Timeless at Heart: Essays on Theology, edited by Walter Hooper. London, Fount, 1987.

The Essential C.S. Lewis, edited by Lyle W. Dorsett. New York, Macmillan, 1988.

Letters: C.S. Lewis and D.G. Calabria, edited and translated by Martin Moynihan. London, Collins, 1989.

Editor, *George MacDonald: An Anthology.* London, Bles, 1946; New York, Macmillan, 1947.

Editor, *Arthurian Torso, Containing the Posthumous Fragment of "The Figure of Arthur,"* by Charles Williams. London, and New York, Oxford University Press, 1948.

*

Bibliography: "A Bibliography of the Writings of C.S. Lewis" by Walter Hooper, in *Light on C.S. Lewis* edited by Jocelyn Gibb, London, Bles, 1965; *C.S. Lewis: An Annotated Checklist of Writings about Him and His Works* by Joe R. Christopher and Joan K. Ostling, Kent, Ohio, Kent State University Press, 1974.

Manuscript Collections: Bodleian Library, Oxford; Wheaton College, Illinois.

Critical Studies (selection): *C.S. Lewis* by Roger Lancelyn Green, London, Bodley Head, and New York, Walck, 1963, revised edition, in *Three Bodley Head Monographs,* Bodley Head, 1969, *C.S. Lewis: A Biography* by Green and Walter Hooper, London, Collins, and New York, Harcourt Brace, 1974, revised edition, 1988, and *Past Watchful Dragons: The Narnian Chronicles of C.S. Lewis,* New York, Macmillan, 1979, and *Through Joy and Beyond: A Pictorial Biography of C.S. Lewis,* New York, Macmillan, 1982, both by Hooper; *Light on C.S. Lewis* edited by Jocelyn Gibb, London, Bles, 1965; *The Lion of Judah in Never-Never Land: The Theology of C.S. Lewis Expressed in His Fantasies for Children,* Grand Rapids, Michigan, Eerdmans, 1973, and *The C.S. Lewis Hoax,* Portland, Oregon, Multinomah, both by Kathryn Ann Lindskoog; *The Secret Country of C.S. Lewis* by Anne Arnott, London, Hodder and Stoughton, 1974, Grand Rapids, Michigan, Eerdmans, 1975; *The Longing for Form: Essays on the Fiction of C.S. Lewis* edited by Peter J. Schakel, Kent, Ohio, Kent State University Press, 1977, and *Reading with the Heart: The Way into Narnia* by Schakel, Grand Rapids, Michigan, Eerdmans, 1979; *The Inklings: C.S. Lewis, J.R.R. Tolkien, Charles Williams and Their Friends* by Humphrey Carpenter, London, Allen and Unwin, 1978, Boston, Houghton Mifflin, 1979; *The Literary Legacy of C.S. Lewis* by Chad Walsh, New York, Harcourt Brace, and London, Sheldon Press, 1979; *A Guide Through Narnia* by Martha C. Sammons, Wheaton, Illinois, Shaw, and London, Hodder and Stoughton, 1979; *Narnia Explored* by Paul A. Karkainen, Old Tappan, New Jersey, Revell, 1979; *Companion to Narnia* by Paul F. Ford, New York, Harper, 1980; *C.S. Lewis, Spinner of Tales: A Guide to His Fiction* by Evan K. Gibson, Grand Rapids, Michigan, Christian University Press, 1980; *C.S. Lewis* by Margaret Patterson Hannay, New York, Ungar, 1981; *C.S. Lewis: The Art of Enchantment* by Donald E. Glover, Athens, Ohio University Press, 1981; *C.S. Lewis* by Brian Murphy, Mercer Island, Washington, Starmont

House, 1983; *The Politics of Fantasy: C.S. Lewis and J.R.R. Tolkien* by Lee D. Rossi, New York and Epping, Essex, Bowker, 1984; *Clive Staples Lewis: The Drama of a Life* by William Griffin, New York, Harper, 1986; *C.S. Lewis: His Literary Achievement* by C.N. Manlove, London, Macmillan, 1987; *C.S. Lewis* by Joe R. Christopher, Boston, Twayne, 1987; *C.S. Lewis, Man of Letters: A Reading of His Fiction* by Thomas Howard, Worthing, Sussex, Churchman, 1987; *Jack: C.S. Lewis and His Times* by George Sayer, London, Macmillan, 1988; *C.S. Lewis and His World* by David Barratt, Grand Rapids, Michigan, Eerdmans, 1988.

*   *   *

In 1950, twenty-five years after accepting a post as an Oxford don, C.S. Lewis embarked on a project that was unusual for a man of his position: he published the first in a series of novels for children. The first book in the "Chronicles of Narnia," *The Lion, the Witch, and the Wardrobe,* introduces the Pevencie children, four English youngsters who have been sent to the countryside to stay with a wise old professor during the World War II bombing of London. During a game of hide-and-seek one stormy day, the youngest child, Lucy, hides in a wardrobe only to discover that it is really a doorway into the land of Narnia.

Thus begin the adventures of Peter, Susan, Edmund, and Lucy in a world inhabited by talking animals, mythical creatures, and a few humanlike beings. The children soon discover that something sinister has taken place in this newfound world: the evil White Witch has cast a spell on Narnia, condemning it to eternal winter. The only one who can break the power of the spell is Aslan, the great lion-king; and, since signs of spring have just begun to appear, the inhabitants of the land are sure "Aslan is on the move." The four Pevencie children and later a younger cousin and his friend become intricately involved in the future of Narnia as Lewis masterfully weaves an entire world from its creation to its close throughout the rest of the series *(Prince Caspian, The Voyage of the "Dawn Treader," The Silver Chair, The Horse and His Boy, The Magician's Nephew,* and *The Last Battle).*

Lewis crafted the books specifically for children, including, as he later said, "no love interest and no close psychology." The books encourage a child's imagination by presenting ideas that appeal to young people. Children are the main characters with adults rarely appearing. Narnia is a completely separate world from our own—one that can only be entered by children (we find out in *The Magician's Nephew* that the professor himself entered Narnia as a boy). Time in Narnia is totally unrelated to time in our world. One year in Narnia, for example, may be only a few minutes in England and vice versa. Above all of the events of Narnia presides the great king Aslan, the creator, savior, protector, and eventual finisher of Narnia.

Through his writings, Lewis fixes himself in opposition to a point of view that he considered "modern" and distressing, and in doing so, he forces his reader to come to terms with his view of truth. In her *The Lion of Judah in Never-Never Land: The Theology of C.S. Lewis Expressed in His Fantasies for Children,* Kathryn Ann Lindskoog states: "In Lewis's opinion, the modern conception of progress, as popularly imagined, is simply a delusion supported by no evidence. . . . He calls the idea of the world slowly ripening to perfection a myth not a generalization from experience. He feels this myth distracts from our real duties and our real

interests. [This] attitude is illustrated by the depressing picture of [the dying world of Charn] given in *The Magician's Nephew.*"

Harkening back to a premodern era, Lewis's works, particularly his fiction, address such themes as betrayal and forgiveness, good and evil, the nature of life and death, courage, loyalty, tradition, and the existence of absolute truth and a fixed moral order. He consciously rejects such contemporary themes as the endless quest for fulfillment, relative truth, innovation as a positive force, individuality, and self-actualization. Thomas Howard maintains in his *C.S. Lewis: Man of Letters* that Lewis "wanted to lead his readers to a window, looking out from the dark and stuffy room of modernity, and to burst open the shutters and point us all to an enormous vista stretching away from the room in which we are shut." To Lewis, the noble ideas he espoused represented freedom rather than the imprisonment suggested by some of his critics.

Those who read Lewis's writings—especially the "Chronicles of Narnia"—generally embrace his ideas or reject them outright. Helen Gardner summarized critical response to Lewis: "He aroused warm affection, loyalty, and devotion. . . . [but] he also aroused strong antipathy, disapproval, and distaste among his colleagues and pupils, and among some readers. It was impossible to be indifferent to him." Most of Lewis's detractors objected to his fantasy writings on ideological not literary grounds. Some took issue with Lewis's ideas on conventional virtues and his use of violence in the "Chronicles of Narnia," viewing them as detrimental to children. Among those was Peter Hollindale who wrote in *Use of English,* "The structure of power in Narnia, with Aslan as its head, is enforced by battle, violence, retributive justice, pain and death. Anything which challenges the power is either evil or stupid, and frequently both."

Others who took issue with Lewis's writings, such as his friend and fellow Inkling J.R.R. Tolkien, objected to what they interpreted as an overuse of allegory. In response to this, Lewis insisted that Narnia was not an allegory of human experience. It was, he maintained, a story of what might happen if there were a place like Narnia and God wanted to relate to that world. Lewis argued that by looking at Narnia's experience, we might be able to examine our own situation apart from religious trappings that Lewis felt often interfere with an honest human relationship with God.

His supporters have seen his work as brilliant in both its literary and theological aspects. Chad Walsh observed in his *The Literary Legacy of C.S. Lewis* that "Lewis brought to traditional mythology as much as he took from it. . . . This absolute clarity of visual imagination is one of the main appeals of his more fantastic books. Anyone reading, say, *The Lion, the Witch, and the Wardrobe* is given so distinct a picture of Aslan's death that he could reproduce the scene on canvas with photographic detail." Walsh continues "Lewis is not the first writer to attempt serious fantasy, but he is one of the most powerful, haunting and successful. He makes this genre a means of dramatizing the human condition and posing the everlasting questions. He converts fantasy into a presentation of philosophic and theological insights."

Lewis, however, did not look to critics for success, his concern was a larger audience. It was with this audience that Lewis achieved his greatest influence as witnessed by the *Times Literary Supplement* critic who said "[for] the past thirty years of his life, no other Christian writer in [England] had such an influence on the general reading public. . . . Each new book from his pen was awaited with an eagerness which showed that thousands of intelligent men and women had acquired a taste for his distinctive idiom and had come to rely on him as a source of moral and intellectual insight.''

—Linda Ross

LEWIS, Elizabeth Foreman

Nationality: American. **Born:** Baltimore, Maryland, 24 May 1892. **Education:** Tome School, 1906-09; Maryland Institute of Fine Arts, 1909-10; Bryant and Stratton Secretarial School, Baltimore, Maryland 1916-17; Bible Seminary of New York, 1917. **Family:** Married John Abraham Lewis in 1921 (died 1934); one son. **Career:** Author of books for children. Associate mission treasurer, Women's Foreign Missionary Society, Shanghai, China, 1917-18; district supervisor of schools, Chunking, China, and teacher for schools in Nanking, China, 1918-21. **Awards:** American Library Association Newbery Medal, 1933, for *Young Fu of the Upper Yangtze.* **Died:** 7 August 1958.

PUBLICATIONS FOR YOUNG ADULTS

Fiction

Young Fu of the Upper Yangtze, illustrated by Kurt Wiese. Philadelphia, Winston, 1932; London, Harrap, 1934.
Ho-Ming, Girl of New China, illustrated by Kurt Wiese. Philadelphia, Winston, 1934; London, Harrap, 1935.
China Quest, illustrated by Kurt Wiese. Philadelphia, Winston, 1937; London, Harrap, 1938.
When the Typhoon Blows, illustrated by Kurt Wiese. Philadelphia, Winston, 1942; London, Harrap, 1944.
To Beat a Tiger, One Needs a Brother's Help, illustrated by John Huehnergarth. Philadelphia, Winston, 1956; London, Harrap, 1957.

PUBLICATIONS FOR ADULTS

Other

Portraits from a Chinese Scroll, illustrated by Virginia Hollinger Stout. Philadelphia, Winston, 1938; London, Harrap, 1939.
Test Tubes and Dragon Scales, with George C. Basil. Philadelphia, Winston, 1940.

*

Media Adaptations: *Young Fu of the Upper Yangtze* (recording and filmstrip).

Biography: Entry in *Junior Book of Authors,* second edition, Stanley J. Kunitz and Howard Haycraft, editors, New York, H.W. Wilson, 1951.

*   *   *

Elizabeth Foreman Lewis grew up amid a closely knit family whose love of church and of books influenced her choice of careers. As a young woman she studied religious education and

literature and was active in church and settlement activities. In 1917 she was sent to China by the Methodist Women's Board. After her return to the United States, Lewis used her experiences in China as a background for her writings, both juvenile and adult. She saw opportunities in the first cultural revolution while portraying problems people have at times of social change. Her heroes and heroines have hope and determination; they make good use of opportunities for social and geographic mobility.

Lewis's most important novel for children is *Young Fu of the Upper Yangtze,* which won the Newbery Medal for 1933. This is the story of a thirteen-year-old Chinese country boy who is brought by his widowed mother to the bustling city of Chungking and apprenticed to a skilled coppersmith. As he delivers his master's wares Fu explores the large metropolis and finds everywhere the conflicts born of superstition and prejudice, of Civil War, of old and new ideas. Fu is not an idealized hero: he is brave and honest, but he also wastes his master's time and his own. The book contains many Confucian proverbs which are employed by adult characters to point out to Fu the folly of his ways: ''Laziness never filled a rice bowl.'' ''There is no merit worthy of boasting.''

Others of Lewis's children's books are for older children. They too focus on individual response to social change. *Ho-Ming, Girl of New China* is the story of a young girl who must free herself from primitive beliefs before she can begin a new education in public-health nursing. As a girl not encouraged to think for herself, she must meet family resistance while retaining family loyalties. *To Beat a Tiger, One Needs a Brother's Help* is about young boys from different social backgrounds living in Shanghai. They witness disease, starvation, and violent death and become close friends as they pull together for survival during the Japanese invasion of China.

Lewis stated that by the time illness forced her to return to America, China and her people had become a major concern in her life. In time she had to write about them, she had to convince a few readers of the inherent greatness of the Chinese, who overcame mass torture and killing, poverty and disease, determined to structure a better world. Lewis's books were well received in America and in Europe. Indeed, through her sympathetic character portrayal, her swift plots, and her compelling prose, she has affected many young readers for several decades.

—Mary Lystad

LILLINGTON, Kenneth (James)

Nationality: British. **Born:** Catford, London, 7 September 1916. **Education:** St. Dunstan's College, London, 1927-35; Wandsworth Training College, London, 1948-49. **Military Service:** Served in the Royal Army Pay Corps, 1941-43; Royal Corps of Signals, 1943-46; became sergeant. **Family:** Married Dulcie E. Lock in 1942; two daughters and two sons. **Career:** Advertising copywriter, Temple Press, London, 1938-39; teacher, Walton-on-Thames School for Boys, Surrey, 1949-56; lecturer in French and English, Brooklands Technical College, Weybridge, Surrey, 1956-81; lecturer on modern literature, Workers' Educational Association, from 1950, on poetry for Poetry Society of London, 1950-57. **Agent:** c/o Faber and Faber, 3 Queen Square, London WC1N 3AU, England.

PUBLICATIONS FOR YOUNG ADULTS

Fiction

Soapy and the Pharaoh's Curse, illustrated by Julia Faithful. London, Heinemann, 1957.
Conjurer's Alibi. London, Nelson, 1960.
The Secret Arrow, illustrated by Robert Hodgson. London, Nelson, 1960.
A Man Called Hughes, illustrated by D.L. Mays. London, Nelson, 1962.
Young Man of Morning. London, Faber, 1979.
What Beckoning Ghost? London, Faber, 1983.
Isabel's Double. London, Faber, 1984.
Selkie. London, Faber, 1985.
Full Moon. London, Faber, 1986.
An Ash-Blonde Witch. London, Faber, 1987.
Jonah's Mirror. London, Faber, 1988.
Josephine. London, Faber, 1989.
Give up the Ghost. London, Faber, 1991.
The Mad Detective. London, Faber, 1992.
A Trick of the Dark. London, Faber, 1993.

Plays

Blue Murder, in *The Windmill Book of One-Act Plays,* edited by E.R. Wood. London, Heinemann, 1960.
My Proud Beauty, in *The Second Windmill Book of One-Act Plays,* edited by E.R. Wood. London, Heinemann, 1963.
The First Book of Classroom Plays (includes *The Case of the Golden Cockerel, Words Fail Me, The Cat Princess, Professor Tugnutt's Time Machine, The Perfect Customer, In Darkest Britain, The Christmas Spirit, The Stove, Skeleton Plays*) London, Hale, 1967.
The Fourth Windmill Book of One-Act Plays (includes *Make Your Play, Bring Out Your Dead, I'll Ring for More Toast, Is Horror Your Neighbour?, A Villa on Venus, You Never Heard Such Unearthly Laughter, The Cinderella Story*). London, Heinemann, 1967.
The Second Book of Classroom Plays (includes *The Blackfeet and the Cree, The Knocking on the Wall, The Picts Drop In, Professor Tugnutt's Truth Gas, For Crying Out Loud, The Boy Next Door, Robin Hood and the Jester, End of Part One*). London, Hale, 1968.
Cantaloup Crescent, in *The Fifth Windmill book of One-Act Plays,* edited by E.R. Wood. London, Heinemann, 1970.
Olaf and the Ogre, in *The Sixth Windmill Book of One-Act Plays,* edited by E.R. Wood. London, Heinemann, 1972.
The Seventh Windmill Book of One-Act Plays (includes *Mockery Hollow, The Avenging Phoenix, I Am a Dustbin, Postman's Knock, A Latin Lesson, The Devil's Grandson, The Adventures of Chastity Pewke, Come What May*). London, Heinemann, 1972.
There's an End of May, in *The Eighth Windmill Book of One-Act Plays,* edited by E.R. Wood. London, Heinemann, 1975.

Other (retellings)

A Christmas Carol. London, Faber Music, 1988.
The Mikado, music by Arthur Sullivan. London, Faber Music, 1988.

PUBLICATIONS FOR CHILDREN

Fiction

The Hallowe'en Cat, illustrated by Gareth Floyd. London, Faber, 1987.
Gabrielle, illustrated by Gareth Floyd. London, Faber, 1988.
The Real Live Dinosaur and other Stories, illustrated by Gareth Floyd. London, Faber, 1990.

PUBLICATIONS FOR ADULTS

Other

Editor, *Nine Lives: An Anthology of Poetry and Prose Concerning Cats.* London, Deutsch, 1977.
Editor, *For Better for Worse.* London, Angus & Robertson, 1979.
Read and Understand: Famous Stories, with Paul Snowden and Hiroshi Tsuchiya. Tokyo, Kirihara Shoten, 1988.

*

Kenneth Lillington comments:

I became a children's writer by accident. In 1951 the school library possessed a miserable collection of books (*The Gorilla Hunters,* a late Victorian novel by Ballantyne, was one of its liveliest) and my class of twelve-year-olds sat through their Friday afternoon free-reading period bored and fidgety. Comics were not allowed. So I began writing a story for them myself. They lapped it up. This doesn't necessarily mean that it was any good; I was on good terms with my pupils and they'd praise anything that moved quickly and was reasonably exciting. We got through three or four chapters, then my class moved on and I forgot about this story for several years. But my wife, some time in 1955, read what I'd written and persuaded me to finish it. I sent it to Heinemann and it was published in 1957 as *Soapy and the Pharaoh's Curse.* I cannot read it now without a shiver. Life has changed a lot since the 'fifties and its terribly out of date. But it started me off. Nearly all my books since then have been for children.

Or rather, with three exceptions, for "Young Adults"—the hardest market of all, because young adults prefer books that are for adults. I've wondered from time to time who *did* read them, apart from librarians and teachers, but by the grace of God plenty of young readers have read them and still do. I've never tried to write down (which I consider a crime) nor have I written with any particular kind of reader in mind. I write with a sort of idealised reader in mind. It pays off. I've had any number of appreciative letters from readers, especially from America, and the PLR returns are gratifying.

One of the liabilities of writing for children is that people patronise you—"Are you going to write for adults when you grow up?" sort of thing—and the writers, in their defence, are liable to make extravagant claims for their craft. It requires special skills; children are never fooled . . . and so on. I won't go as far as this; children can be attracted to rubbish as much as any adult—but it is true that you cannot *indulge* yourself as a writer for adults can. You must have a story to tell and you must stick to it. It imposes that same discipline as does making a vase or a piece of furniture. I find this stimulating. I write to amuse myself, yes, but I watch out not to bore myself.

*   *   *

Kenneth Lillington's teenage novels contain a good helping of the supernatural and usually have a strong romantic element. Lillington's female characters are always intelligent and resourceful, not to mention forceful; his male characters are weaker, less decisive, and require support and leadership from the women they meet. Whether or not these are created with tongue-in-cheek humour, they make his books immensely attractive to teenage girls, who will find these inspiring role models. His books are always refreshing, bubbly, and intellectually quite demanding, but appeal to those who enjoy the lively exploration of ideas as much as the development of character and plot.

Whether the supernatural element is in the form of magic, ghosts, science fiction, or simply legend, the books are firmly rooted in reality. In *Selkie,* this encompasses the problems related to unemployment, growing up, changing relationships, class consciousness, and superstition. Catherine, the heroine, resents having to leave her boyfriend and move to Cornwall. She gets involved with Joe, a young labourer, and together they try to solve the mystery of the legend of the Selkie, or seal girl, that is at the centre of the book. Lillington captures the strong emotions of an adolescent girl trying to deal with her feelings about two boys from very different backgrounds. The book also presents a realistic portrait of the effects of unemployment on families that is relevant today as it was in 1935 when the book is set.

An Ash-Blonde Witch and *Jonah's Mirror* contain rather more of the supernatural than the natural. *An Ash-Blonde Witch* is set in the twenty-second century, when there are pockets of the world that have not changed, called Conservation Areas. When Sophie and her father are sent to study one of these areas—Urstwhile—the effect is like stepping back in time. The scientific skills of psychological healing and levitation that are commonplace in Sophie's world are taken to be magic by the people of Urstwhile and she is deemed a witch. On the other hand, emotions like love and jealousy are no longer felt outside of Urstwhile and Sophie's punishment for interfering in a Conservation Area is to suffer these emotions. The balance between science fiction and fairy-tale is nicely held and the ending, in which the witch Dorcas is transported out of the old-fashioned Urstwhile because her skills are thought to be valuable to the more advance society provides a humorous twist.

In *Jonah's Mirror* the two main characters, Jonah Sprockett, a millionaire and chairman of Sprockett Electricals, and his partner and fiancée Miss Wingbone, "arguably the cleverest woman in the world," are caught up in an elaborate fantasy. As a result of an experiment with a magic mirror, Jonah finds himself locked in the strange world of Sudonia which is inhabited by fairy-tale princesses, mythical beasts, and strange marauding knights, where he falls in love with the beautiful Princess Miranda. Jonah thinks he has spirited himself into a parallel universe, but Miss Wingbone's theory is that it is all a dream and therefore a figment of his imagination. This ingenious explanation is rather complex to follow at times, particularly when Miss Wingbone herself enters Sudonia, but it provides endless opportunities for some wonderful tongue-in-cheek humour.

What Beckoning Ghost?, Full Moon, Isabel's Double and *Give up the Ghost* all deal with ghosts or apparitions. *What Beckoning Ghost?* is a romance with a touch of the supernatural in which Emma finishes her O-levels and breaks up with her boyfriend. She is sent to stay with her godmother, where she meets a ghost and finds another boyfriend. In *Full Moon* Lillington creates an intricate web of relationships between twins, sisters, parent and child, boyfriend and girlfriend, old and young, living and dead, through which she explores the kind of tensions that exist in such very close relationships.

Isabel's Double is about the apparition of Isabel that has haunted her since childhood, which starts to haunt Mike who becomes her boyfriend. After some help from a psychiatrist, the "doppelganger" is finally conquered in a chilling climax involving psychic powers, spirits, and a painting of Isabel. *Give up the Ghost* begins, "Every night before going to bed, Mrs. Mason would drink a cup of Instant Postum and play a game of Scrabble with her husband, who had been dead for five years." Through her paranormal powers Mrs. Mason is introduced to the ghost of Fred Hopper and drawn into a wrangle with his sisters about his will, when he leaves all his money to a fellow gardener, Miss Grayling. The books dealing with ghosts and apparitions are perhaps more disturbing than Lillington's others, because it is not as easy to dismiss such psychic phenomena as pure fantasy.

The prevalence of romantic themes and strong female characters in Lillington's books makes them generally more appealing to teenage girls than to boys, but *Josephine* appeals to both groups. Set in the 1930s, it is the story of a young girl who is sent to a boys' boarding school where her uncle is the headmaster, when her own school is closed, where she affects the lives of all the boys she comes into contact with. The various under-plots—for example, the legend of the wolf-boy who has been seen around the school—fill the book with mystery and make this an immensely enjoyable read.

The Mad Detective is an engaging mixture of the Agatha Christie thriller and a comical farce. When two couples turn up in a hotel a murder is about to occur, according to clairvoyant Norman Norval. But what he can't determine is the victim. The intricate plot is peppered with highly original and amusing characters, and Lillington's dry wit and love of wordplay are given full rein here.

His characters are often working out their feelings for a boyfriend or girlfriend, which makes them particularly appealing to young adults at a time in their lives when they too may be experiencing similar anxieties.

In *A Trick of the Dark* Lillington returns to the supernatural and creates a book that is both amusing and disturbing, depending on how much the reader believes in the existence of "little people". The plot hinges on one R. J. Bodkin, a professor of medieval literature, who has written a 1,100-page fantasy novel called the *Gnomes of Yggsdragarth,* which has become the centre of a cult. It doesn't take much to work out the irony of that reference! The main female character, 18-year-old Kate, sees an elf reflected in her bedroom window. She has seen the same elf in a picture in a magazine ten years before. This sets up a chain of events that draws her and various members of her family into a dangerous relationship with forces that they do not understand. The professor has been taken over by these elves and paralyzed, cared for by an obsessive woman, who was once his secretary. She and the gardener strive to keep the elves at bay. Once again, Lillington questions our perceptions of reality and fantasy. Some of the scenes in which the malevolent forces attempt to win control are particularly menacing, making this a more sinister book overall than many of Lillington's others.

—Fiona Lafferty

LINGARD, Joan (Amelia)

Nationality: British. **Born:** Edinburgh, Scotland, 1932. **Education:** Bloomfield Collegiate School, Belfast; Moray House Training College, General Certificate of Education. **Family:** Three children. **Career:** Schoolteacher, Midlothian, 1953-61; novelist and television scriptwriter. Member, Scottish Arts Council, since 1979. **Awards:** Scottish Arts Council bursary, 1969; Buxtehude Bulle prize (West Germany), 1987; Scottish Arts Council Award, 1994, for *After Colette*. **Agent:** David Higham Associates, 5-8 Lower John Street, London W1R 4HA, England. **Address:** 72 Great King Street, Edinburgh EH3 6QU, Scotland.

PUBLICATIONS FOR YOUNG ADULTS

Fiction

The Twelfth Day of July. London, Hamish Hamilton, 1970; Nashville, Nelson, 1972.
Across the Barricades. London, Hamish Hamilton, 1972; Nashville, Nelson, 1973.
Into Exile. London, Hamish Hamilton, and Nashville, Nelson, 1973.
Frying as Usual, illustrated by Priscilla Clive. London, Hamish Hamilton, 1973.
The Clearance. London, Hamish Hamilton, and Nashville, Nelson, 1974.
A Proper Place. London, Hamish Hamilton, and Nashville, Nelson, 1975.
The Resettling. London, Hamish Hamilton, and Nashville, Nelson, 1975.
Hostages to Fortune. London, Hamish Hamilton, 1976; Nashville, Nelson, 1977.
The Pilgrimage. London, Hamish Hamilton, 1976; Nashville, Nelson, 1977.
The Reunion. London, Hamish Hamilton, 1977; Nashville, Nelson, 1978.
Snake among the Sunflowers. London, Hamish Hamilton, and Nashville, Nelson, 1977.
The Gooseberry. London, Hamish Hamilton, 1978; as *Odd Girl Out,* New York, Elsevier Nelson, 1979.
The File on Fraulein Berg. London, MacRae, and New York, Elsevier Nelson, 1980.
Strangers in the House. London, Hamish Hamilton, 1981; New York, Dutton, 1983.
The Winter Visitor. London, Hamish Hamilton, 1983.
The Freedom Machine. London, Hamish Hamilton, 1986.
The Guilty Party. London, Hamish Hamilton, 1987.
Rags and Riches. London, Hamish Hamilton, 1988.
Tug of War. New York, Dutton, 1990.
Between Two Worlds. New York, Dutton, 1991.
Hands Off Our School! London, Hamish Hamilton, 1992.
Night Fires. London, Hamish Hamilton, 1993.
Lizzie's Leaving. London, Hamish Hamilton, 1995.

Other

Maggie (television series). 1981, 1982.

PUBLICATIONS FOR ADULTS

Novels

Liam's Daughter. London, Hodder and Stoughton, 1963.
The Prevailing Wind. London, Hodder and Stoughton, 1964.
The Tide Comes In. London, Hodder and Stoughton, 1966.
The Headmaster. London, Hodder and Stoughton, 1967.
A Sort of Freedom. London, Hodder and Stoughton, 1969.
The Lord on Our Side. London, Hodder and Stoughton, 1970.
The Second Flowering of Emily Mountjoy. Edinburgh, Harris, 1979; New York, St. Martin's Press, 1980.
Greenyards. London, Hamish Hamilton, and New York, Putnam, 1981.
Sisters by Rite. London, Hamish Hamilton, and New York, St. Martin's Press, 1984.
Reasonable Doubts. London, Hamish Hamilton, 1986.
The Women's House. London, Hamish Hamilton, 1989.
After Colette. London, Sinclair, Stevenson, 1993.
Dreams of Love and Modest Glory. London, Sinclair, Stevenson, 1995.

Other

The Sandyford Place Mystery and *A Kiss, A Fond Embrace* (television plays; adapted from the novel *Square Mile of Murder* by Jack House). 1980.
Her Mother's House (television play). 1982.

*

Biography: Essay in *Something about the Author Autobiography Series* by Joan Lingard, Volume 5, Detroit, Gale, 1988.

Joan Lingard comments:

I began to write when I was eleven years old. I was an avid reader from early childhood and could never find enough to read. One day when I was complaining to my mother about having nothing to do and nothing to read, she turned to me and said, "Why don't you write a book of your own?" I thought, "Why not? Why shouldn't I?" So I got some lined, foolscap paper, filled my fountain pen with green ink, thinking that would be an artistic color for a writer to use, and I began to write my very first novel. I was never in two minds that it would have to be a novel, for that was what I enjoyed reading most. Short stories ended too quickly for me; I liked the depth and breadth of the novel.

My first novel concerned a girl finding secret passages and secret caves and tracking down and capturing smugglers: a highly improbable story. (I was very much under the influence of the English children's writer Enid Blyton at that stage.) These are not the kind of books I write now. I want my stories to be not only probable but credible so that readers, even if they have not experienced similar situations, can say, "Yes, I believe that could happen. I can understand this happening. I can *feel* it." Good writing should set up echoes of recognition. Young people throughout the world have many common experiences. The children of Northern Ireland might be different in some ways from their contemporaries elsewhere, but it is the universality of much of the human experience that enables the reader to identify with the characters in a novel and find those echoes. . . .

The crossroads of change interest me very much as a writer. Adolescence in itself is a major crossroad in life, a time of great upheaval and change, which can be both exciting and stressful. The emerging teenager no longer accepts everything their elders practice or preach; they are looking for ideas of their own, different standards. They are looking for a different identity from that of the child protected by the family home. It is a time of displacement. When people are displaced from their pattern of living, they have to readjust, to take stock of old values and assess new ones. What will they do? Which way will they go?

I have written a great deal about displaced people in my fiction for young adults. In my quintet about Ulster, beginning with *The Twelfth Day of July* and *Across the Barricades,* Protestant Sadie and Catholic Kevin have to leave their Belfast homes because of the Troubles and go into exile. As do Astra and her twin Hugo in *Tug of War,* followed by its sequel *Between Two Worlds.* The Soviets are advancing into their country, Latvia, and so they must leave everything and flee. That is the ultimate form of displacement: to be a refugee and give up your home and all your possessions and go into the wilderness, like leaves blown before the wind, not knowing where you will end up.

There are other forms of displacement: less dramatic and more personal. In my novel *Lizzie's Leaving,* fifteen-year-old Lizzie leaves home to go and live with the father she has never seen, and who has never seen her. In this way she opens herself up to new experiences and new emotions. In *Strangers in the House,* Calum's mother, who is divorced, marries a man called Tom, who is a widower and has a daughter, Stella, the same age as Calum. The two young ones suddenly find they have to share their parents with other people and come to terms with acquiring a step-sibling. Experiences such as these are unfortunately common in our society today. But young people can gather strength from reading about others in similar situations and knowing that they are not alone in what they are experiencing.

Life is limited: this is something that struck me very early on in my childhood. We inhabit one body, one mind, see the world through one pair of eyes, but by writing and by reading, we can live in different worlds, get inside the skins and minds of different people, and in so doing push out the boundaries of our own. It is vital for all of us, whether young or not so young, to keep pushing out the boundaries. And that is why books are so important.

*   *   *

Joan Lingard had written six adult novels before, on the suggestion of a friend, she embarked on *The Twelfth Day of July* in the 1960s. Although its main characters are children, this famous book—with the then incipient Catholic-Protestant ''Troubles'' of Ulster as its background—was the beginning of a distinguished career as a writer for young adults. Since the book's publication in 1972, Lingard has published continuously for this age group, some ''one-off'' titles, others in series—notably the ''Kevin and Sadie'' novels that began with *Twelfth Day*; the ''Maggie'' books with their sprightly Glasgow heroine; and, most recently, books about the Latvian Petersons who settle in Canada after World War II.

Lingard has a natural empathy with adolescent readers, understanding their hopes, aspirations, and emotional uncertainties, yet paying her readers the compliment of engaging them on an intellectual level as adults. There is no condescension in her uncompromising, humorous, and dramatic narratives; she creates a world which young readers instantly recognize as their own, and they compliment her in return: she is one of the few quality writers whose books teenagers, notoriously unbookish, eagerly buy for themselves.

Joan Lingard's themes relate directly to the experience of her readers. They view working-class life, family tensions, the destructive effect of social prejudice on community relations, and the necessity of young adults beginning to make decisions and take control of their own lives. These were themes which Josephine Kamm pioneered in Britain in the 1960s; Lingard, a very different kind of writer, has carried them on and developed them for a more troubled and complex age.

All of these themes make their first appearance in the series of novels featuring Kevin and Sadie, the young couple from opposite factions in Ulster, a province torn apart by religious bigotry with roots in the distant past. Their extended story—from their childhood in the now universally familiar back streets of Belfast, through their struggle to find fulfillment in a Belfast riven by virtual civil war to their flight to London—is told with an appealing mixture of toughness, nonjudgemental realism, and tender understanding. Probably the best and most powerful of these novels is *Across the Barricades* (awarded the German Buxtehuder Bulle Prize for Children's Literature in 1987). The development of Kevin and Sadie's love against a bitter background of family disapproval and civil disintegration is a moving variation on a classic theme of young love under a comfortless star.

Lingard has stated that she began to write her ''Maggie'' quartet as a respite from thinking about Ulster and its problems. Certainly this series, which has been televised, is much lighter in tone, although its concerns are perhaps closer to the experience of most young readers. Told with humor and panache in the first person, the series follows the doings of Maggie, a working-class girl who wants to go to university and fulfil her potential. The career of Maggie, whose vigor and enterprise enable her to establish her father in a plumbing business and house her grandmother after a fire, is contrasted with the life of her middle-class boyfriend, James. The complexities of Glaswegian social life are personified by James's mother and Maggie's granny, two archetypal, vastly entertaining characters. Nowhere does Lingard display her talent for seeing the world through young eyes more amusingly than in these books. (Incidentally, Maggie really existed, and Lingard bought the real Maggie's former school as a summer home.)

Lingard's passionate belief in tolerance and social justice runs through all her writing, and strikes a chord in the hearts and minds of young people. In *The Guilty Party,* which recalls a famous protest of women against nuclear missiles at Greenham Common in the 1980s, Jodie, a teenage Belfast girl living in an English village, campaigns against the siting there of a nuclear power plant.

This gripping story, like the ''Kevin and Sadie'' and ''Maggie'' books, is vividly contemporary, but Lingard is also adept at making the somewhat more distant past—particularly the period around World War II—relevant to modern young people. This is significant, since the moral issues that seem clear-cut in one era appear confusing to another. In *The File on Fraulein Berg,* set in wartime Belfast, three schoolgirls take their teacher's name at face value and behave badly, failing to consider that Fraulein Berg, a Jewish refugee, might herself be a victim of Nazi persecution. The distinction between ''Nazi'' and ''German,'' still often blurred after fifty years, is at the heart of this thought-provoking and ultimately somber book.

More recently Lingard, who is married to a Latvian-Canadian, has embarked on a sequence of novels set in Europe and Canada during and after World War II. *Tug of War* begins the story of the Peterson family, who have to flee their home in Latvia as the Russians advance, suffering the horrors of separation and becoming "displaced persons" in Europe after 1944. The disintegrating continent is poignantly evoked through images of rural life and family love, contrasted with the mechanized, destructive forces of bombers and submarines. In 1948, at the opening of *Between Two Worlds,* the reunited family arrives in Toronto, where their struggle to survive continues in a scarcely less hostile environment. The tables are turned as the children have to support their parents, and the story tells of hardships surmounted and family affection firmly sealed. The battle of the Petersons to preserve their identity as Latvians while becoming good Canadians makes this story relevant to other, more recent attempts of minority groups to assimilate with larger societies.

Lingard's objectivity on the Irish situation, remarkable in a writer who spent her formative years in Belfast, is explained in a 1986 essay published in *A Portrait of the Artist as a Young Girl.* There she attributes her lack of sectarian prejudice to her upbringing by a mother who was a Christian Scientist, adding that since she left Belfast at the age of eighteen, she was not drawn emotionally into the turmoil which has darkened Ulster life since then. Thus she has been able, uniquely, to combine the knowledge of an insider with the observation of an outsider; one feels that this informed detachment, tied to a warm concern for human beings, has stood her in good stead when transferring her attention to other conflicts and moral dilemmas. "My themes are universal," Lingard has said, "enabling readers to identify with my characters, regardless of where a book is set. I often show teenagers with verve who are caught at the crossroads of social or historical change."

—Eileen Dunlop, updated by Judson Knight

LIPSYTE, Robert (Michael)

Nationality: American. **Born:** New York City, 16 January 1938. **Education:** Columbia University, New York, 1953-59, B.A. in English 1957, M.S. in journalism 1959. **Military Service:** Served in the United States Army, 1961. **Family:** Married Katherine L. Sulkes; one son and one daughter by a previous marriage. **Career:** *New York Times,* copyboy, 1957-59, sports reporter, 1959-67, sports columnist, 1967-71 and 1991—; *New York Post,* columnist, 1977; sports essayist for program *Sunday Morning,* Columbia Broadcasting Service, Inc. (CBS-TV), New York City, 1982-86; correspondent, National Broadcasting Company, Inc. (NBC-TV), New York City, 1986-88; host of program *The Eleventh Hour,* Public Broadcasting Service (PBS-TV), New York City, 1989-90; writer. Has also worked as a journalism teacher and radio commentator. **Awards:** Dutton Best Sports Stories award, E.P. Dutton, 1964, for "The Long Road to Broken Dreams," 1965, for "The Incredible Cassius," 1967, for "Where the Stars of Tomorrow Shine Tonight," 1971, for "Dempsey in the Window," and 1976, for "Pride of the Tiger"; Mike Berger award, Columbia University Graduate School of Journalism, 1966; Wel-Met Children's Book

award, Child Study Children's Book Committee at Bank Street College of Education, 1967, for *The Contender; One Fat Summer* was named an outstanding children's book of the year by the *New York Times* and was selected as one of the American Library Association's best young adult books, both 1977; New Jersey Author citation, New Jersey Institute of Technology, 1978; Emmy award for on-camera achievement, Academy of Television Arts and Sciences, 1990, as host of the television program *The Eleventh Hour.* **Agent:** Theron Raines, Raines and Raines, 71 Park Avenue, Suite 4A, New York, New York 10016. **Address:** 126 E. 1657, New York, New York 10003, U.S.A.

PUBLICATIONS FOR YOUNG ADULTS

Fiction

The Contender. New York, Harper, 1967; London, Pan, 1969.
One Fat Summer. New York, Harper, 1977.
Summer Rules. New York, Harper, 1981.
Jock and Jill. New York, Harper, 1982.
The Summerboy. New York, Harper, 1982.
The Brave. New York, Harper, 1991.
The Chemo Kid. New York Harper, 1992.
The Chief. New York, Harper, 1993.

Other

Assignment: Sports. New York, Harper, 1970; revised edition, 1984.
Free to Be Muhammad Ali. New York, Harper, 1978.
Arnold Schwarzenegger: American Hercules. New York, Harper, 1993.
Jim Thorpe: 20th Century Jock. New York, Harper, 1993.
Michael Jordan: A Life above the Rim. New York, HarperCollins, 1994.
Joe Louis: A Champ for All America. New York, HarperCollins, 1994.

PUBLICATIONS FOR ADULTS

Novels

Something Going, with Steve Cady. New York, Dutton, 1973.
Liberty Two. New York, Simon and Schuster, 1974.

Other

Nigger, with Dick Gregory. New York, Dutton, 1964; London, Allen and Unwin, 1965.
The Masculine Mystique, illustrated by Tim Lewis. New York, New American Library, 1966.
Sportsworld: An American Dreamland. Chicago, Quadrangle, 1975.
Advisory editor, *Sports and Society,* edited by Gene Brown. New York, Arno Press, 1980.
Malady: A Traveler's Guide to the Country of Illness. New York, Alfred Knopf, 1998.
With Peter Levine, *Idols of the Game: A Sporting History of the American Century.* Atlanta, Turner Publishing, 1995.

Screenplays: *That's the Way of the World* (*Shining Star*), 1975; *The Act,* 1982.

Scriptwriter for *Saturday Night with Howard Cosell;* contributor to periodicals, including *TV Guide, Harper's Magazine, Nation, New York Times, New York Times Book Review,* and *Esquire.*

*

Biography: Essay in *Speaking for Ourselves: Autobiographical Sketches by Notable Authors of Books for Young Adults,* Volume 1, compiled and edited by Donald R. Gallo, National Council of Teachers of English, 1990; essay in *Authors and Artists for Young Adults,* Volume 7, Detroit, Gale, 1991.

Manuscript Collections: De Grummond Collection, University of Southern Mississippi; Kerlan Collection, University of Minnesota.

Critical Studies: Entry in *Contemporary Literary Criticism,* Volume 21, Detroit, Gale, 1982; entry in *Children's Literature Review,* Volume 23, Detroit, Gale, 1991.

Robert Lipsyte comments:

Boys don't read as much as we'd like them to, because (1) current books tend not to deal with the real problems and fears of boys, and (2) there is a tendency to treat boys as a group—which is where males are at their absolute worst—instead of as individuals who have to be led into reading secretly and one at a time.

Boys need reassurance that their fears of violence and humiliation and competition are shared fears. Books can reassure them, but to be able to read a book—properly—you have to be able to sink into a scene, to absorb characters, to care, to empathize. You have to be willing to make yourself vulnerable to a book as surely as you need to make yourself vulnerable to a person. This is not easy for a male in this society to do, particularly an adolescent male who is unsure of his own identity, his sexuality, his future.

*   *   *

Robert Lipsyte, a widely read sports journalist, has made his mark on young adult literature with three breezily funny novels (*One Fat Summer, Summer Rules,* and *The Summerboy*) about teenager Bobby Marks, whose summers spent getting in and out of trouble while growing up in the fifties reflect some of the author's own experiences. Through the course of these first-person narratives, Bobby changes and grows—from a spoiled, 200-pound fourteen-year-old whom kids call The Crisco Kid "because he's fat in the can," through a summer as a sixteen-year-old camp counselor and would-be lover. Finally, in *The Summerboy,* Bobby shows his true character when he sacrifices his cherished summer job folding laundry to help his fellow employees get even with an unscrupulous and womanizing boss.

One of the ways that Lipsyte overcame his own early teen fat summers of overeating and over-reading was to dive into sports; his high school years were saturated with swimming, softball, track, and judo. When he graduated from college, he welded his compulsive interest in sports with his love for writing. He has utilized his journalistic skills to write two very successful nonfiction sports books for young adults—*Free to Be Muhammad Ali,* a biography of the famous boxer and *Assignment: Sports,* a collection of colorfully written articles on athletes and sports.

Even Lipsyte's romantic fantasy novel for younger readers, *Jock and Jill,* deals with sports. The story contains unlikely plot twists and turns, but Lipsyte's heroes—a suburban high school pitching star named Jack Ryder and Jillian, the unpredictably likeable and stubborn girl whose camera he smashes into while chasing a foul pop-up—are so believably portrayed that they convince even the more skeptical readers to accept the story's plot implausibilities. Jillian involves Jack the Jock in a scheme to help poor and hungry New York City kids, and soon the Mayor and a Puerto Rican street gang get pulled into the story. Jack's reputation is threatened, and his baseball career is put in jeopardy. Although Jack falls down, he doesn't break his crown.

The Chemo Kid combines some of the romantic elements of *Jock and Jill* with a Bobby Marks-type teenager—a self-described "wimp" named Fred Bauer—who manages to acquire superhero powers. Bobby gains these powers of character through sheer will, while Fred acquires momentary physical super-strength as the unintended result of an experimental chemotherapy he has been taking to fight a virulent cancer. With the support of his environmental-activist girlfriend Mara (who resembles Jill in some respects), his two selfishly scheming buddies, and his newly made bizarre friends from the "cancer ward" of the hospital where Fred is being treated, Fred's wimpy life is transformed by his medically induced superpowers and he enters a sort of "twilight zone." He takes on his two classmate nemeses (a drug dealer and a brain-dead, bully football captain), a multitude of foolish adult authority figures (the mayor, Fred's doctor, the football coach, the police, etc.), and a corporation that is polluting the city's water supply. The story's end parallels that of *Jock and Jill:* the hero again emerges a victor.

Lipsyte's best and most-read novel is probably his first published story, *The Contender.* It is about a young Harlem high school dropout named Alfred Brooks who fights against the pull of drugs and gangs, the guilt of abandoning his best friend caught by police in a robbery of a store where Alfred works, and against the pervasive despair he feels as a prisoner in a place with no future. One day, he wanders into Donatelli's gym and accepts the challenge that Donatelli throws at him: "Everyone wants to be a champion. That's not enough. You have to start by wanting to be a contender. . . . It's the climbing that makes the man. Getting to the top is an extra reward." These words guide and strengthen Alfred in his darkest moments. He stands his ground not only against seasoned boxers but also against heavy peer pressure to rob the grocery store where he works. When Alfred faces the truth about himself—he's a good boxer but not a champion—he displays the grit of a contender: he stays three rounds in the ring with a champion fighter and win's Donatelli's respect and a new-found self-respect.

Lipsyte wrote *The Contender* in 1967, the same year that saw the publication of S.E. Hinton's groundbreaking realistic young adult novel *The Outsiders* and a year before the publication of *The Pigman,* Paul Zindel's trendsetting novel for teenagers. *The Contender* is also a trailblazer because it transformed the junior sports novel from an action-packed, predictable story of sports heroics into a realistic, coming-of-age story with sports serving as a metaphor for the real action in the novel: coping with life. Although today Lipsyte's first novel seems too dependent on plot coincidences and too filled with stereotyped secondary characters, *The Contender* set the stage for more sophisticated sports metaphor novels for teen readers, such as Bruce Brooks' *The Moves Make the Man* and Robert Lehrman's *Juggling.*

More recently, Lipsyte has written two sequels to *The Contender.* In *The Brave,* Alfred Brooks—now a police officer—interrogates Sonny Bear, a rebellious and confused runaway Moscondaga Nation Native American who has been arrested on a drug charge. Like Brooks twenty years before, Sonny is a promising young boxer who is faced with the conflict that Brooks also faced: the immediate but risky rewards of street life versus the discipline and training required to be a champion boxer. Brooks becomes Sonny's manager and helps guide him through this conflict. *The Chief,* published in 1993, continues Sonny's story. Brooks has become a paraplegic via a police shooting incident, although he is still Sonny's manager. The story is narrated by Marty Witherspoon, a young black college student and aspiring writer who is Sonny's close friend and publicist. Marty is responsible for getting Sonny back on track after the boxer loses his focus when he is cheated of a boxing victory. But when Sonny becomes involved in a plan to help heal deep wounds within the Moscondaga Nation as a result of their flirtation with gambling, Marty's counseling powers are sorely tested. As *The Chief* ends, there is no resolution to Sonny's boxing ambitions and his new interest in Moscondaga politics; readers also don't know what will become of Marty's writing ambitions and his romantic interest in Robin Bell, a gutsy young film producer.

''It's the climbing that makes the man. . . .'' Lipsyte is clearly not finished with Sonny and Marty because they still have more climbing to do.

—Jack Forman

LITTLE, (Flora) Jean

Nationality: Canadian. **Born:** T'ai-nan, Formosa, now Taiwan, 2 January 1932. **Education:** University of Toronto, B.A. 1955; attended Institute of Special Education, Salt Lake City; received teaching certificate from University of Utah. **Career:** Teacher of children with motor handicaps, Canada; specialist teacher at Beechwood School for Crippled Children, Guelph, Ontario; children's writer. Visiting instructor at Institute of Special Education and Florida University, Tallahassee; summer camp director and leader of church youth groups. **Awards:** Canadian Children's Book Award, joint award of American and Canadian branches of Little, Brown, 1961, for *Mine for Keeps;* Vicky Metcalf Award, Canadian Authors Association, 1974, for body of work inspirational to Canadian boys and girls; Governor General's Literary Award for Children's Literature, Canada Council, 1977, for *Listen for the Singing;* Children's Book Award, Canada Council, 1979; Children's Book of the Year Award, Canadian Library Association, and Ruth Schwartz Award, both 1985, for *Mama's Going to Buy You a Mockingbird; Boston Globe-Horn Book* Honor Award, 1988, for *Little by Little: A Writer's Education;* Order of Canada, 1993; IODE award, 1995; numerous Junior Literary Guild awards. **Address:** RR #2 R.P.O., Elora, Ontario, Canada N0B 1S0.

PUBLICATIONS FOR YOUNG ADULTS

Fiction

Spring Begins in March, illustrated by Lewis Parker, Boston, Little, Brown, 1966.
One to Grow On, illustrated by Jerry Lazare. Boston, Little, Brown, 1969.
Look through My Window, illustrated by Joan Sandin. New York, Harper, 1970.
Kate. New York, Harper, 1971.
Listen for the Singing. New York, Dutton, 1977.
Mama's Going to Buy You a Mockingbird. Markham, Ontario, Penguin, 1984; New York, Viking Kestrel, 1985.

Nonfiction

Little by Little: A Writer's Education. Markham, Ontario, and New York, Viking, 1987.
Stars Come out Within. New York, Penguin, 1990.

PUBLICATIONS FOR CHILDREN

Fiction

Mine for Keeps, illustrated by Lewis Parker. Boston, Little, Brown, 1962.
Home from Far, illustrated by Jerry Lazare. Boston, Little, Brown, 1965.
Take Wing, illustrated by Lazare. Boston, Little, Brown, 1968.
From Anna, illustrated by Sandin. New York, Harper, 1972.
Stand in the Wind, illustrated by Emily Arnold McCully. New York, Harper, 1975.
Lost and Found, illustrated by Leoung O'Young. Markham, Ontario, Penguin and New York, Viking, 1985.
Different Dragons, illustrated by Laura Fernandez. Markham, Ontario, Penguin, and New York and London, Viking Kestrel, 1986.
Once upon a Golden Apple. illustrated by Phoebe Gilman. New York, Viking, 1991.
Jess Was the Brave One, illustrated by Janet Wilson. New York, Viking, 1992.
Revenge of the Small Small, illustrated by Janet Wilson. New York, Viking, 1993.
With Claire McKay, *Bats about Baseball,* illustrated by Kim LeFevre. New York, Viking, 1995.
His Banner Over Me. Toronto and New York, Viking Kestrel, 1995.
Jenny and the Hanukkah Queen, illustrated by Suzanne Mogensen. Toronto, Viking, 1995.
Gruntle Piggle Takes Off, illustrated by Johnny Wales. Toronto, Viking, 1996; New York, Viking Kestrel, 1996.
The Belonging Place. Toronto and New York, Viking Kestrel, 1997.
Emma's Magic Winter. New York, HarperCollins, 1998.

Poetry

It's a Wonderful World. Privately printed, 1947.
When the Pie Was Opened. Boston, Little, Brown, 1968.
Hey World, Here I Am!, illustrated by Barbara DiLella. Toronto, Kids Can Press, 1986; illustrated by Sue Truesdell, New York, Harper, 1989.

*

Media Adaptations: *Hey World, Here I Am* and *Little by Little: A Writer's Education* are available on audiocassette; *Mama's Going to Buy You a Mockingbird* was adapted as a television movie; *Home from Far* was adapted as a television movie.

Biography: Entry in *Fourth Book of Junior Authors and Illustrators,* New York, H.W. Wilson, 1978; essay in *Something about the Author Autobiography Series,* Volume 17, Detroit, Gale, 1994; *The Mind's Eye* (movie), Scholastic.

Manuscript Collections: Kerlan Collection, University of Minnesota, Minneapolis.

Critical Studies: *Children's Literature Review,* Volume 4, Detroit, Gale, 1982.

*   *   *

Jean Little's writing appeals to a wide audience, however, many of her novels are more appropriate for those within the younger age range of the young adult reader category. In 1961, she won the Canadian Children's Book Award for *Mine for Keeps,* a book for younger readers. However, her two books of memoirs, *Little by Little* and *Stars Come out Within* are appropriate for those at the older range of the young adult reader category.

In her memoirs, Little tells about growing up within a close and warm family, about becoming a writer, and about living with her own severe visual impairment. Little was born with very limited vision in both eyes and has had to adapt to this. As an adult, she became a teacher of children with handicaps before she became a published author. Her students encouraged her to write children's books in which a main character had a physically challenging condition. They wanted to read books about children similar to themselves. While reading these memoirs, the reader realizes not only the physical difficulties of having very limited sight, but also the emotional strain it places on a child and adolescent when this condition interferes with forming relationships with peers. Little's recollections of her own youth also help the reader gain insight into the feelings of those who are physically challenged.

Stars Come out Within, the second of her memoirs, continues with stories of her adult life by describing her experiences as a writer, her response to losing more of her vision, and finally, her reaction to becoming totally blind. She also recounts the joy of regaining independence through her Seeing Eye dog, Zephyr, and her talking computer, SAM.

Because Little has always been an avid reader, she creates main characters who enjoy reading. Throughout her own books, there are references to titles or other authors of children's books.

In Little's novels, the main character is usually a girl who differs from her peers, learns to accept this difference, and goes on to establish close relationships with others. The books are rich both in characterization and in examples about the importance of family and peer relationships. The contents, instead of dwelling on the limitations which may be imposed by being handicapped, focus on the inner struggles of the main characters as they adapt to the environment and form close relationships. The main characters struggle to solve personal problems, and through this, gain insight and strength.

In *Look through My Window,* Emily Blair, a lonely, only child, learns to live with other children when four young cousins come to stay with her family. At the same time, the family moves to a new house in a new town and she must adapt to this changing outside world as well. She finally realizes her dream of having a best friend, Kate. Both Emily and Kate are poets.

Kate, Emily Blair's best friend, has a book of her own, *Kate.* In it, Kate learns about the rift between her father and his family. There is also a rift between Kate and her best friend, Emily. Kate comes to appreciate her parents who had seemed "unusual" to her, to accept her Jewish background, and to recognize the importance of her friendship with Emily. *Spring Begins in March* is the story of Meg who is not doing well in school and who had to adjust to the fact that the promised room of her own will not happen because her grandmother must move in with the family. At first, Meg resents her grandmother. Having found and read her grandmother's diary, Meg learns there are common experiences between her grandmother's girlhood and her own. In the end, Meg comes to understand not only the difficulty the grandmother had of finding a place in their family but also what her grandmother offered to the family, especially to her.

One to Grow On is the story of twelve-year-old Jamie Chisholm who tells so many lies or exaggerations that her family does not always believe her. Tillie, Jamie's godmother, takes her on a vacation away from the rest of the family. During the time she spends with Tillie, Jamie gains insight into her own and a friends' behavior and through this learns her own strengths.

From Anna and *Listen for the Singing* are about Anna Solden, a visually-impaired immigrant from Germany to Canada. In *From Anna,* she struggles to become familiar with the ways of her new country. In the sequel, *Listen for the Singing,* set at the beginning of World War II, she leaves the security of a special class to attend a regular high school. Here, in addition to learning to make friends and to adjusting to the classroom, she experiences prejudice because of her family's German name. When her brother, Rudi, is blinded while in the navy, Anna helps him to accept this condition. Making friends, confronting the teacher who is prejudiced, and helping Rudi—all cause Anna to gain maturity and insight into herself.

Mama's Going to Buy You a Mockingbird is the story of a family coping with a father's illness and death as seen through the eyes of the twelve-year-old son Jeremy. As he comes to accept his father's death, Jeremy makes friends with Tess, a girl who is considered to be different from the other students in his class. They offer friendship and support to each other.

To avoid the pain of loss when he remembers his father, Jeremy tries to forget and never to talk about his father. However, the book ends with a Christmas scene in which Jeremy realizes the tenderness of the relationship between his parents and that his father's legacies to him are the happy memories.

Because the main characters struggle to overcome problems within themselves or have physically challenging handicaps, there may be a tendency to recommend certain titles for bibliotherapy. However, there is some criticism of Little's work for that use because the character's problems are solved quickly or limitations are too easily accepted. Little writes in the *Stars Come out Within* that in *Listen for the Singing,* Anna's brother adapts to his blindness very easily with Anna's help, in contrast to her own struggle to accept complete blindness.

—Etta Miller

LOHANS, Alison

Nationality: Canadian. **Born:** Reedley, California, 13 July 1949. **Education:** Reedley High School, Reedley, California, 1963-67; Whittier College, Whittier, California, 1967-69; California State University, Los Angeles, California, 1969-71, B.A. 1971; University of Victoria, British Columbia, 1975-76, Postgrad. Dip. in Elem. Ed. 1976; University of Regina, Saskatchewan, 1984-88, since 1996. **Family:** Married Michael A. Pirot, 1969 (deceased, 1985); one son (adopted); married Stewart Raby; one son. **Career:** Clerk-typist, 1971-73, and pharmacist's assistant, 1974-76, McGill and Orme Pharmacy, Victoria, British Columbia; teacher and house parent, Argenta Friends School, Argenta, British Columbia, 1973-74; instrumental music teacher, Regina Public Board of Education, Saskatchewan, 1976-79; day care worker, Regina, Saskatchewan, and Reedley, California, 1982-84; research assistant, Saskatchewan Instructional Development and Research Unit, Faculty of Education, University of Regina, 1986-88; correspondence instructor in writing for children, Division of Fine Arts and Humanities, University of Regina Extension Department, 1990-95, and Saskatchewan Writers Guild, from 1995. **Awards:** Saskatchewan Writers Guild Literary Award, 1989 and 1991; South Saskatchewan Reading Council/Saskatchewan Writers Guild Young Readers' Choice Award, 1994 and 1996; Volunteer Leadership Award, Saskatchewan Writers Guild, 1996. **Address:** 76 Dolphin Bay, Regina, Saskatchewan S4S 4Z8, Canada.

PUBLICATIONS FOR YOUNG ADULTS

Who Cares About Karen? Richmond Hill, Scholastic, 1983.
Can You Promise Me Spring? Richmond Hill, Scholastic, 1991.
Foghorn Passage. Don Mills, Stoddart, 1992.
Laws of Emotion. Saskatoon, Thistledown, 1993.
Don't Think Twice. Saskatoon, Thistledown, 1997.

PUBLICATIONS FOR CHILDREN

Mystery of the Lunchbox Criminal. Richmond Hill, Scholastic, 1990.
Germy Johnson's Secret Plan. Richmond Hill, Scholastic, 1992.
The Secret Plan. Richmond Hill, Scholastic, 1995.
Nathaniel's Violin, illustrated by Marlene Watson. Victoria, Orca, 1996.
Getting Rid of Mr. Ribitus. Edmonton, Hodgepog Books, 1998.

*

Alison Lohans comments:

I made my first commitment to writing for young adults when I was in junior high school, and sadly disappointed by the library books featuring teenage girl protagonists. At the time, the majority of books for young women were romance novels.

A steady diet of teen romance simply wasn't enough for me; it did little to nurture me, as I was in the porcess of awakening to the realities of societal and racial inequities, and world issues such as the Cold War and the Cuban missile crisis, the aftermath of Hiroshima and Nagasaki, and then the earliest beginnings of the Vietnam War. Accustomed as I was to looking to books to expand my understanding of important issues, I looked, but found few significant life questions in the teen fiction of the time. I felt both cheated and disillusioned; as a young woman, I wanted to read about other young women who were doing meaningful things with their lives, and perhaps helping to make the world a better place.

In frustration, I quit reading almost entirely—why waste my time on mindless romance that went nowhere?—and at the same time vowed, when I grew up, to write books that would "make kids think". In short, I decided my calling was to write the sort of books that were missing from the library shelves.

The teen years are among the most intense stages of a person's life. Many important questions are asked and strong emotions felt as every young person tries to determine how she or he fits into not only the immediate social worlds of peers and family, but also the socio-cultural milieu we live in. It is a time of searching for self, a time of challenge and defiance, of pain, of leaping hope and idealism, and at times, of despair. It is also a time of empowerment, as a young person in the process of *becoming* makes his or her first real strides toward being a functioning individual within society.

Real life contains important questions, often clothed in bumps and bruises, and always rough edges. It is these things I seek to address, through the lens of a teen protagonist, hoping always to repect that bright flame of the spirit of youth.

*   *   *

With the exception of Alison Lohans' first novel, *Who Cares About Karen?,* the impact of serious illness and/or death on families appears to be a recurring theme in Lohans' writing for young adults. *Who Cares About Karen?* finds five high school students returning home by car one rainy spring night after a school band tour. Driving along a winding British Columbia mountain road, the group unexpectedly encounters a rock slide which forces their car off the cliff road into a steep ravine. Readers follow the characters over nearly a 24 hour period as they deal with both their physical predicament and changing interpersonal relationships. The first three chapters are narrated by shy Karen McConnachie, 14, a self-professed "complete dud," who sees herself as a burden to the group. The remaining ten chapters are alternately told by Karen and Stan Lewis, also 14. Stan must cope with the reputation of his older brother Ward, another of the car's occupants, who, according to community gossip, spent time in a mental hospital. Stan's chapters inform readers of the true nature of Ward's violent character, and, as the day passes, a growing affection emerges between Stan and Karen as they begin to see the people behind the outward appearances.

The question in the title of Lohans' second book, *Can You Promise Me Spring?* would be a legitimate one for Jamie Carmichael, 12, to ask in October when it is discovered that he has Hodgkin's disease, a form of cancer, and must undergo chemotherapy treatments. Told from the perspective of Jamie's sister, Lori, 16, the story follows the impact Jamie's possibly fatal illness has on the members of this Regina, Saskatchewan, family up until the point that Jamie's cancer is diagnosed as being in remission. In one of the subplots, Lori breaks up with her self-centred boyfriend who cannot relate to her emotional situation, and she then finds a new relationship with another teen whose grandfather is dying of cancer. Lohans writes with authority about cancer for it was part of her family life for 14 years prior to her husband's death.

Cancer's effects on families reappears in *Foghorn Passage*. Following a five year battle with cancer, William Franklin's death has brought about numerous changes in the lives of his survivors: daughters "Sammy," 16, and Deena, 13, plus widow Carolyn. In the 10 months since William's death, the surviving family trio have sold the family home and moved first into a cramped apartment and then into a run-down house in a seedy part of town. Financial realities force Carolyn to hold down two jobs, thereby reducing her time to be a supportive mother. The more significant effects of William's death, however, are emotional, and, for central character Sammy, her unresolved grief finds varied expressions including nightmares. Another tragedy touches Sammy when a fellow youth orchestra member, Matt Bruckner, is involved in a car accident which leaves Matt's sister dead and Matt paraplegic. At a time when Sammy is still coping with her own confused emotions, she finds herself becoming involved in helping Matt find a reason to live. Although the plot perhaps attempts to do too much, Lohans ties up her major storylines in satisfactory yet realistic ways.

Laws of Emotion is a fine collection of 10 short stories whose contents, as the title paradoxically suggests, deal with the spectrum of unpredictable and ungovernable emotions encountered by maturing adolescents. Eight of the stories feature female central characters. Including personal triumphs and tragedies, the stories' subject matter ranges in scope from life's first to last events. For example, in "Beginnings," unwed Tara, 16, unexpectedly finds herself giving birth at the family's lake cottage during a prairie thunderstorm while Joan, in "Of Time and Teeth," experiences her initial personal encounter with death while working as a part-time nurse's aide in a seniors home. Attraction between the sexes serves as the source of many emotions, and virtually all of the stories explore romance's various forms from the "crush" in "It Wasn't My Fault" to the hate/love relationship found in "Truce." The collection's only slightly jarring note is "Red Tide," a science fiction piece which seems out of place amidst all the realism. In an "Afterword," Lohans describes the sources of her stories' ideas.

Don't Think Twice is Lohans' most sophisticated and challenging work, both in structure and content. At 283 pages, it is longer than the typical YA novel, and, unlike most books for adolescents, its narrator is an adult, a mother looking for her runaway daughter. In her late forties, Saskatchewanite Jan Crowther is most upset that the youngest of her four children, Lisa, 16, has, angrily run off, likely to Vancouver, British Columbia. As Jan waits for news about Lisa, who, Jan fears, might be involved in prostitution, she begins to write to her, telling of her own "rebellious" year, 1967, when she was 17 and still living at home with her parents in Sierra Vista, a conservative California farming community. Into Jan's ordered life came new neighbours, the Crowther family—parents Ben and Dorothy and their sons, Tim, 17 and Rob, 16—all committed activists against the war in Vietnam. A "good" student in every sense of that word, Jan finds her values challenged by the romance she discovers first with Tim and then Rob and by the Crowthers' willingness, despite the enormous pro-war sentiment around them, to act publicly on their beliefs. Again death enters Lohans' writing as Tim is accidentally killed while hitchhiking to Canada to avoid

the war. The effects of Tim's death still resonate years later in Jan's marriage with Rob. While Jan does make contact with Lisa by the story's conclusion, readers realize that the book's ending is really another beginning in the relationship of these women from two different generations. Like many of Robert Cormier's books, *Don't Think Twice* has the potential to cross over into the adult market.

—Dave Jenkinson

LONDON, Jack (John Griffith London)

Nationality: American. **Born:** San Francisco, California, 12 January 1876. **Education:** a grammar school in Oakland, California; Oakland High School, 1895-96; University of California, Berkeley, 1897-98. **Family:** Married 1) Bessie Mae Maddern in 1900 (separated 1903; divorced 1905), two daughters; 2) Clara Charmain Kittredge in 1905; one daughter (died 1910). Novelist, short story writer, and political essayist. **Career:** Worked at a succession of odd jobs, including salmon canner, oyster pirate, patrol agent of San Francisco shore police, seal fisher, jute millworker, coal shoveler, and laundry worker, 1889-90; oyster "pirate" then member of the California Fisheries Patrol, 1891-92; sailor on the *Sophie Sutherland*, sailing to Japan and Siberia, 1893; joined Coxey's Army (a band of jobless men who marched to Washington, D.C.), and tramped throughout the United States and Canada, 1893-96; arrested for vagrancy in Niagara Falls, New York and sentenced to one month in Erie County Penitentiary in New York; gold miner in the Yukon Territory, 1897-98; worked as a journalist and reported the Russo-Japanese War for the San Francisco *Examiner,* 1904; ran for mayor of Oakland, California, on the Socialist ticket, 1905; lecturer throughout the United States, 1905-06; attempted to sail round the world on a 45-foot yacht, 1907-09; reported the Mexican Revolution for *Collier's,* 1914. **Died:** 22 November 1916.

PUBLICATIONS

Novels

The Cruise of the Dazzler. New York, Century, 1902; London, Hodder & Stoughton, 1906.
A Daughter of the Snows, illustrated by Frederick C. Yohn. Philadelphia, Lippincott, 1902; London, Isbister, 1904.
The Call of the Wild, illustrated by Philip Goodwin and Charles Livingston Bull. New York, Macmillan, and London, Heinemann, 1903.
The Kempton-Wace Letters (published anonymously), with Anna Strunsky. New York, Macmillan, and London, Isbister, 1903.
The Sea Wolf, illustrated by W.J. Aylward. New York, Macmillan, 1904, and London, Heinemann, 1904.
The Game, illustrated by Henry Hutt and T.C. Lawrence. New York, Macmillan, and London, Heinemann, 1905.
Before Adam. New York, Macmillan, 1906; London, Laurie, 1908.
White Fang. New York, Macmillan, 1906; London, Methuen, 1907.
The Iron Heel. New York, Macmillan, 1907; London, Everett, 1908.

Martin Eden. New York, Macmillan, 1909; London, Heinemann, 1910.

Burning Daylight. New York, Macmillan, 1910; London, Heinemann,, 1911.

Adventure. London, Nelson, and New York, Macmillan, 1911.

The Abysmal Brute. New York, Century, 1913; London, Newnes, 1914.

John Barleycorn, illustrated by H.T. Dunn. New York, Century, 1913; as *John Barleycorn; or, Alcoholic Memoirs,* London, Mills & Boon, 1914.

The Valley of the Moon. New York, Macmillan, and London, Mills & Boon, 1913.

Mutiny of the Elsinore. New York, Macmillan, 1914; London, Mills & Boon, 1915.

The Jacket. London, Mills & Boon, 1915; as *The Star Rover,* New York, Macmillan, 1915,

The Scarlet Plague, illustrated by Gordon Grant. New York, Macmillan, and London, Mills & Boon, 1915.

The Little Lady of the Big House. New York, Macmillan, and London, Mills & Boon, 1916.

Jerry of the Islands. New York, Macmillan, and London, Mills & Boon, 1917.

Michael, Brother of Jerry. New York, Macmillan, 1917; London, Mills & Boon, 1918.

Hearts of Three. London, Mills & Boon, 1918; New York, Macmillan, 1920.

The Assassination Bureau, Ltd., completed by Robert L. Fish. New York, McGraw, 1963; London, Deutsch, 1964.

Short Stories

The Son of the Wolf: Tales of the Far North. Boston, Houghton, 1900; London, Isbister, 1902; as *An Odyssey of the North,* London, Mills & Boon, 1915.

The God of His Fathers, and Other Stories. New York, McClure, 1901; as *The God of His Fathers: Tales of the Klondyke,* London, Isbister, 1902.

Children of the Frost, illustrated by Raphael M. Reay. New York, Macmillan, 1902.

The Faith of Men, and Other Stories. New York, Macmillan, and London, Heinemann, 1904.

Tales of the Fish Patrol, illustrated by George Varian. New York, Macmillan, 1905; London, Heinemann, 1906.

The Apostate (also as *The Apostate: A Parable of Child Labor*). Chicago, Kerr, 1906.

Moon-Face, and Other Stories. New York, Macmillan, and London, Heinemann, 1906.

Love of Life, and Other Stories. New York, Macmillan, 1906; London, Everett, 1908.

Lost Face. New York, Macmillan, 1910; London, Mills & Boon, 1915.

South Sea Tales. New York, Macmillan, 1911; London, Mills & Boon, 1912.

The Strength of the Strong (story). Chicago, Kerr, 1911.

When God Laughs, and Other Stories. New York, Macmillan, 1911; London, Mills & Boon, 1912.

The Dream of Debs. Chicago, Kerr, 1912(?).

The House of Pride and Other Tales of Hawaii. New York, Macmillan, 1912; London, Mills & Boon, 1914.

Smoke Bellew, illustrated by P.J. Monahan. New York, Century, 1912; as *Smoke and Shorty,* London, Mills & Boon, 1920.

A Son of the Sun, illustrated by A.O. Fischer and C.W. Ashley. New York, Doubleday, 1912; London, Mills & Boon, 1913; as *The Adventures of Captain Grief,* Cleveland, World, 1954.

The Night-Born. . . . New York, Century, 1913; London, Mills & Boon, 1916.

The Strength of the Strong (collection). New York, Macmillan, 1914; London, Mills & Boon, 1917.

The Turtles of Tasman. New York, Macmillan, 1916; London, Mills & Boon, 1917.

The Human Drift. New York, Macmillan, 1917; London, Mills & Boon, 1919.

The Red One. New York, Macmillan, 1918; London, Mills & Boon, 1919.

On the Makaloa Mat. New York, Macmillan, 1919; as *Island Tales,* London, Mills & Boon, 1920.

Dutch Courage, and Other Stories. New York, Macmillan, 1922; London, Mills & Boon, 1923.

Jack London's Tales of Adventure, edited by Irving Shepard. New York, Hanover House, 1956.

Short Stories, edited by Maxwell Geismar. New York, Hill & Wang, 1960.

Great Short Works of Jack London, edited by Earle Labor. New York, Harper, 1965.

Stories of Hawaii, edited by A. Grove Day. New York, Appleton-Century, 1965.

Goliah: A Utopian Essay. Berkeley, California, Thorp Springs Press, 1973.

Curious Fragments: Jack London's Tales of Fantasy Fiction, edited by Dale L. Walker. Port Washington, New York, Kennikat Press, 1975.

The Science Fiction of Jack London: An Anthology, edited by Richard Gid Powers. Boston, Gregg Press, 1975.

Jack London's Yukon Women. New York, Belmont, 1982.

Young Wolf: The Early Adventure Stories of Jack London, edited and introduced by Howard Lachtman. Santa Barbara, California, Capra, 1984.

In a Far Country: Jack London's Western Tales, edited by Dale L. Walker. New York, Jameson, 1986.

Plays

The Great Interrogation, with Lee Bascom (produced San Francisco, 1905).

Scorn of Women: In Three Acts. New York, Macmillan, 1906; London, Macmillan, 1907.

Theft: A Play in Four Acts. New York, and London, Macmillan, 1910.

The Acorn-Planter: A California Forest Play. . . . New York, Macmillan, and London, Mills & Boon, 1916.

Daughters of the Rich, edited by James E. Sisson. Oakland, California, Holmes, 1971.

Gold: A Play, with Herbert Heron, edited by James E. Sisson. Oakland, California, Holmes, 1972.

Other

The People of the Abyss. New York, Macmillan, and London, Isbister, 1903.

The Scab. Chicago, Kerr, 1904.

The Tramp. New York, Wilshire's Magazine, 1904.

Jack London: A Sketch of His Life and Work. London, Macmillan, 1905.

War of the Classes. New York, Macmillan, and London, Heinemann, 1905.

What Life Means to Me. Princeton, New Jersey, Intercollegiate Socialist Society, 1906.

The Road. New York, Macmillan, 1907; London, Mills & Boon, 1914.

Jack London: Who He Is and What He Has Done. New York, Macmillan, 1908(?).

Revolution. Chicago, Kerr, 1909.

Revolution, and Other Essays. New York, Macmillan, 1910; London, Mills & Boon, 1920.

The Cruise of the Snark. New York, Macmillan, and London, Mills & Boon, 1911.

London's Essays of Revolt, edited by Leonard D. Abbott. New York, Vanguard Press, 1926.

Jack London, American Rebel: A Collection of His Social Writings, Together With an Extensive Study of the Man and His Times, edited by Philip S. Foner. New York, Citadel Press, 1947.

The Fitzroy Editions of the Works of Jack London, edited by I.O. Evans. London, Arco, New York, Archer House, and Horizon Press, 18 vols., 1962-68.

The Bodley Head Jack London, edited by Arthur Calder-Marshall. London, Bodley Head, Volume 4 vols., 1963-66; as *The Pan Jack London,* London, Pan, 2 vols., 1966-68.

Letters from Jack London: Containing an Unpublished Correspondence Between London and Sinclair Lewis, edited by King Hendricks and Irving Shepard. New York, Odyssey Press, 1965; London, MacGibbon and Kee, 1966.

Reportage, the San Francisco Quake: Two Accounts, with Will Irwin. Perfection Form Co., 1968.

Jack London Reports: War Correspondence, Sports Articles, and Miscellaneous Writings, edited by King Hendricks and Irving Shepard. New York, Doubleday, 1970.

Jack London's Articles and Short Stories in The (Oakland) High School Aegis, edited by James E. Sisson, illustrated by Holly Janes. Cedar Springs, Michigan, London Collector, 1971.

Daddy Boy: A Series of Dedications to His First Wife by Jack London. Stockton, California, Holt-Atherton Pacifica Center for Western Studies, 1976.

Jack London on the Road: The Tramp Diary, and Other Hobo Writings, edited by Richard W. Etulain. Logan, Utah University Press, 1979.

No Mentor But Myself: A Collection of Articles, Essays, Reviews, and Letters on Writings and Writers, edited by Dale L. Walker. Port Washington, New York, Kennikat Press, 1979.

Revolution: Stories and Essays, edited by Robert Barltrop. London, Journeyman Press, 1979.

Sporting Blood: Selections From Jack London's Greatest Sports Writing, edited by Howard Lachtman. Novato, California, Presidio Press, 1981.

The Unabridged Jack London, edited by Lawrence Teacher and Richard E. Nicholls. Philadelphia, Running Press, 1981.

Novels and Stories and *Novels and Social Writings* (Library of America), edited by Donald Pizer. New York, Literary Classics of the United States, and London, Cambridge University Press, 2 vols., 1982-84.

Jack London's California: The Golden Poppy and Other Writings, edited by Sal Noto. New York, Beaufort, 1986.

Greater Nowheres: A Journey through the Australian Bush, with Dave Finkelstein. New York, Harper & Row, 1988.

*

Media Adaptations: *The Abysmal Brute* (film), Universal, 1923, later version released as *Conflict,* Universal, 1936; *Adventure* (film), Paramount, 1925; *The Call of the Wild* (film), United Artists, 1935; *White Fang* (film), Twentieth Century-Fox, 1936; *The Sea-Wolf* (film), Warner Brothers, 1941; *The Adventures of Martin Eden* (film based on *Martin Eden*), Columbia, 1942; *A Piece of Steak* and *To Kill a Man* (films), both Balboa Amusement Co., both 1913; *John Barleycorn* (film), Bosworth, Inc., 1914; *The Mutiny of the Elsinore* (film released under the title *The Mutiny),* Shurtleff, Inc., 1920; *The Star Rover* (film), Shurtleff, Inc., 1920; Burning Daylight, Rowland Distributors, 1928; *Smoke Bellew* (film), First Division, 1929; *Alaska* (film based on *Flush of Gold*), Monogram, 1944; *The Fighter* (film based on *The Mexican*), United Artists/Gottlieb, 1952; and *The Assassination Bureau Ltd.* (film), Paramount, 1969; *Jack London: The Sea Wolf* (recordings), read by Anthony Quayle, Caedmon, 1981; *To Build a Fire* (recordings), read by Robert Donly, Miller-Brody; *Jack London Cassette Library* (recordings), read by Jack Dahlby, Listening Library; *The Call of the Wild* (recordings), read by Arnold Moss, Miller-Brody; *The Iron Heel* (play), adapted by W.G. Henry, produced by the Karl Marx players in Oakland, California, 1911.

Biography: Entry in *Dictionary of Literary Biography,* Detroit, Gale, Volume 8: *Twentieth-Century American Science Fiction Writers,* 1981, Volume 12: *American Realists and Naturalists,* 1982, Volume 78, *American Short-Story Writers, 1880-1910,* 1989.

Bibliography: *Jack London: A Bibliography* by Hensley C. Woodbridge, John London, and George H. Tweney, Georgetown, California, Talisman Press, 1966; supplement by Woodbridge, Milwood, New York, Kraus, 1973; in *Bibliography of American Literature 5* by Jacob Blanck, New Haven, Connecticut, Yale University Press, 1969; *The Fiction of Jack London: A Chronological Bibliography* by Dale L. Walker and James E. Sisson, El Paso, University of Texas, 1972; *Jack London: A Reference Guide* by Joan R. Sherman, Boston, Hall, 1977.

Manuscript Collections: Huntington Library, San Marino, California; Merrill Library at Utah State University, Logan.

Critical Studies: *Jack London: A Biography,* by Richard O'Connor, Boston, Little, Brown, 1964, London, Gollancz, 1965; *The Alien Worlds of Jack London* by Dale L. Walker, Grand Rapids, Michigan, Wolf House, 1973; *Jack London* by Earle Labor, Boston, Twayne, 1974; *Jack London: The Man, the Writer, the Rebel,* by Robert Baltrop, London, Pluto, 1976; *Jack: A Biography of Jack London* by Andrew Sinclair, New York, Harper, 1977, London, Weidenfeld & Nicolson, 1978; *Jack London and the Klondike: The Genesis of an American Writer* by Franklin Walker, San Marino,

California, Huntington Library Publications, 1978; *Jack London: Essays in Criticism* edited by Ray Wilson Ownbey, Layton, Utah, Peregrine Smith, 1978; *Jack London: An American Myth* by John Perry, Chicago, Nelson Hall, 1981; *Solitary Comrade: Jack London and His Work* by Joan D. Hedrick, Chapel Hill, University of North Carolina Press, 1982; *The Novels of Jack London: A Reappraisal* by Charles N. Watson, Jr., Madison, University of Wisconsin Press, 1983; *Jack London* by Gordon Beauchamp, Mercer Island, Washington, Starmount House, 1984; *Jack London—An American Rebel?* by Carolyn Johnston, Westport, Connecticut, Greenwood Press, 1984; *The Tools of My Trade: The Annotated Books in Jack London's Library* by David Mike Hamilton, Seattle, University of Washington Press, 1986; *Jack London* by James Lundquist, New York, Ungar, 1987.

*   *   *

The works of Jack London, author of some twenty novels and novellas and over one hundred short stories, are marked by an enormous amount of preparation; he once asserted that he suffered a "lack of origination" and had to gather facts from sources such as newspaper accounts and his own voracious reading, much of it in his fifteen-thousand-volume personal library. A diligent, careful, and committed writer, London also relied on his own experiences for material, ranging from his travels in the United States, the Yukon, and the Pacific to his stint in jail for vagrancy to a boat trip halfway around the world. His works focus on a cluster of themes—what he liked to call his "philosophy of life"—which stress the survival of the fittest, especially in inhospitable environments, and the virtues of courage, strength, determination, and a healthy respect for the truth.

London stands in the lofty tradition of such giants as Robert Louis Stevenson, as an able storyteller; Joseph Conrad, with whom he shared a love and respect for the sea; and Rudyard Kipling, whose sense of conflict echoes throughout London's pages. Three types of conflict can often be identified in the works of London—Man versus Nature, Man versus Man, and Man versus Himself. These are clearly depicted in the representative novels *Call of the Wild, The Sea Wolf, Martin Eden, Adventure, Jerry of the Islands, Smoke Bellew,* and the classic short story "To Build a Fire."

"To Build a Fire" demonstrates the conflict of Man against Nature, in which Nature story, like *Call of the Wild* and *White Fang,* reveals London's sense of the awesome appearance of Nature, sometimes harsh but always impressive. A passage from *White Fang* illustrates the power of London's descriptive images of the northern regions of the United States that he knew so well: "Dark spruce forest frowned on either side of the frozen waterway. The trees had been stripped by the wind of their white covering of frost, and they seemed to lean to each other, black and ominous, in the fading light." It is a tribute to London's skill as a writer that as readers identify with and hope for the survival of the man in "To Build a Fire," they develop an increased appreciation and respect for the tremendous power of Nature.

While Nature is often a grim force in London's works, it plays no favorites, and those who measure up to its demands prevail, as does Buck, the canine hero of *Call of the Wild* Buck seems almost like a human being, as readers have access to his thoughts and dreams. He overcomes terrible hardships and engages in fierce battles with both men and other animals, displaying a high level of courage and cunning, as when he attacks a bull moose in the forest: "Three hundred-weight more than a half a ton he weighed; he had lived a long, strong life, full of fight and struggle, and at the end he faced death at the teeth of a creature whose head did not reach beyond his great knuckled knees."

London's ability to humanize animals, to penetrate their minds and hearts, makes their struggles and triumphs more poignant and more accessible to the reader. This is best represented in *The Sea Wolf.* In this novel, the central character, Wolf Larsen is a powerful (in one scene, he crushes a raw potato with one hand), ruthless, and brutal sea captain. He readily permits the beating of a cabin boy, beats a sailor nearly to death, almost cripples two seal hunters for quarreling, and has the cook tossed overboard, where he loses part of his leg to a shark. Though Larsen is typically harsh and sometimes appears insane, London adds dimension to his character by making him an avid reader who can speak standard English when he chooses—for example, in the presence of "gentleman" Humphrey Van Weyden, who has the misfortune of finding himself on Larsen's aptly named ship, the *Ghost.*

In London's works, the internal conflict of Man against Himself is well developed in both men and animals, usually dogs. As Wolf Larsen in *The Sea Wolf* is made up of two selves at odds with one another, the noble dogs in *White Fang* and *Call of the Wild* also revolt against their roots. White Fang shifts from a life in the wild to one of domesticity, while Buck flees a tame existence in favor of the wilderness.

London's fiction is not without heroism and occasional self-sacrifice, as when his master saves the life of the dog Jerry in *Jerry of the Islands,* or when John Thornton saves Buck's life in *Call of the Wild,* or when White Fang saves his master's family from an intruder, at the near loss of his own life. If these narratives have a flaw, it is in the linearity of the plots; one adventure follows hard upon another, as seen in the progression of incidents in *Adventure,* and *Smoke Bellew.* However, the energy and movement of the story lines, the development of interesting and rounded characters, and the eloquence of a highly expressive style usually outweigh this deficiency.

Much of the appeal and popularity of London's fiction can be attributed to the universal themes made available to readers of all ages. The raging battles that exist between human and natural forces in these works erode the layers of civilization to reveal glimpses of the most primeval impulses inherent in men and their environments. London once complained that when he began writing, he had "no one to give me tips, no one's experience to profit by." He was compelled to labor hard for his subject matter, his story lines, and his forceful style, the results of which are well worth the effort that went into them.

—Fred McEwen

LOWRY, Lois

Nationality: American. **Born:** Lois Hammersberg in Honolulu, Hawaii, 20 March 1937. **Education:** Brown University, Providence, Rhode Island, 1954-56; University of Southern Maine, Portland, B.A. in English 1972. **Family:** Married Donald Grey

Lowry in 1956 (divorced 1977); two daughters and two sons (one deceased). **Career:** Free-lance writer and photographer, since 1972. **Awards:** Children's Literature award, International Reading Association, 1978, for *A Summer to Die*; American Library Association Notable Book citation, 1980, for *Autumn Street*; American Book Award nomination, 1983, for *Anastasia Again!*; *Boston Globe-Horn Book* award, Golden Kite award, and Child Study award, Children's Book Committee of Bank Street College, all 1987, all for *Rabble Starkey*; Christopher award, 1988; Newbery Medal, National Jewish Book award, and Sidney Taylor award, National Jewish Libraries, all 1990, all for *Number the Stars*; Newbery Medal, 1994, for *The Giver*. **Agent:** Wendy Schmalz, Harold Ober Associates, 425 Madison Avenue, New York, New York 10017, U.S.A. **Address:** 205 Brattle Street, Cambridge, Massachusetts 02138, U.S.A.

PUBLICATIONS FOR YOUNG ADULTS

Fiction

A Summer to Die, illustrated by Jenni Oliver. Boston, Houghton Mifflin, 1977; London, Kestrel, 1979.
Find a Stranger, Say Goodbye. Boston, Houghton Mifflin, 1978; London, Kestrel, 1980.
Anastasia Krupnik. Boston, Houghton Mifflin, 1979; London, Fontana, 1986.
Autumn Street. Boston, Houghton Mifflin, 1980; as *The Woods at the End of Autumn Street,* London, Dent, 1987.
Anastasia Again!, illustrated by Diane deGroat. Boston, Houghton Mifflin, 1981; London, Fontana, 1986.
Anastasia at Your Service, illustrated by Diane deGroat. Boston, Houghton Mifflin, 1982; London, Fontana, 1987.
The One Hundredth Thing about Caroline. Boston, Houghton Mifflin, 1983.
Taking Care of Terrific. Boston, Houghton Mifflin, 1983.
Anastasia, Ask Your Analyst. Boston, Houghton Mifflin, 1984.
Us and Uncle Fraud. Boston, Houghton Mifflin, 1984.
Anastasia on Her Own. Boston, Houghton Mifflin, 1985.
Switcharound. Boston, Houghton Mifflin, 1985.
Anastasia Has the Answers. Boston, Houghton Mifflin, 1986.
Anastasia's Chosen Career. Boston, Houghton Mifflin, 1987.
Rabble Starkey. Boston, Houghton Mifflin, 1987; as *The Road Ahead,* London, Dent, 1988.
Number the Stars. Boston, Houghton Mifflin, 1989.
Your Move, J.P.! Boston, Houghton Mifflin, 1990.
Anastasia at This Address. Boston, Houghton Mifflin, 1991.
The Giver. Boston, Houghton Mifflin, 1993.
Anastasia, Absolutely. Boston, Houghton Mifflin, 1995.

PUBLICATIONS FOR CHILDREN

All about Sam, illustrated by Diane deGroat. Boston, Houghton Mifflin, 1988.
Attaboy, Sam! illustrated by Diane deGroat. Boston, Houghton Mifflin, 1992.

See You Around, Sam! Boston, Houghton Mifflin, 1996.
Stay! Keeper's Tale, illustrated by True Kelley. Boston, Houghton Mifflin, 1997.

PUBLICATIONS FOR ADULTS

Other

Black American Literature (textbook). Portland, Maine, Weston Walsh, 1973.
Literature of the American Revolution (textbook). Portland, Maine, Weston Walsh, 1974.
Values and the Family (booklet). Portland, Maine, Weston Walsh, 1977.

Photographer, *Here in Kennebunkport,* text by Frederick H. Lewis. Brattleboro, Vermont, Durrell, 1978.

*

Manuscript Collections: Kerlan Collection, University of Minnesota, Minneapolis.

Biography: *A Visit with Lois Lowry* (videotape), Boston, Houghton Mifflin, 1985; ''*PW* Interviews: Lois Lowry,'' in *Publishers Weekly,* 21 February 1986, 152-53; essay in *Something about the Author Autobiography Series,* Volume 3, Detroit, Gale, 1986; ''Lois Lowry'' by Shirley Haley-James, in *Horn Book,* July/August 1990, 422-24; ''Lois Lowry'' by Walter Lorraine, in *Horn Book,* July/August 1994, 423-26.

Critical Studies: Entry in *Children's Literature Review,* Volume 6, Detroit, Gale, 1984; ''Lois Lowry'' by Laura M. Zaidman, in *Dictionary of Literary Biography,* Volume 52, *American Writers for Children Since 1960: Fiction,* Detroit, Gale, 1987; essay in *Authors and Artists for Young Adults,* Volume 5, Detroit, Gale, 1990; ''Newbery Medal Acceptance'' by Lois Lowry, in *Horn Book,* July/August 1990, 412-21; essay in *Speaking for Ourselves, Too,* edited by Donald R. Gallo, National Council of Teachers of English, 1993; ''Newbery Medal Acceptance'' by Lois Lowry, in *Horn Book Magazine,* July/August 1994, 414-22; *Lois Lowry* by Joel D. Chaston, New York, Twayne, 1997.

Lois Lowry comments:
For my own two grandchildren—and for all those of their generation—I try, through writing, to convey my passionate awareness that we live intertwined on this planet and that our future depends upon our caring more, and doing more, for one another.

*   *   *

Lois Lowry uses her fascination with life's beginnings, transitions, and endings to create outstanding fiction for young adults. This two-time Newbery Medalist portrays realistically the difficulties of living in a sometimes frightening, confusing world.

Half of Lowry's twenty-four novels published from 1977 to 1997 focus on Anastasia Krupnik and her family—parents Myron (Harvard English professor) and Katherine (free-lance artist) and brother Sam (featured in three books for younger children). The Anastasia series offers superb characterization, realistic dialogue, clever humor, and relevant themes reminiscent of Beverly Cleary's popular Ramona series. In the nearly twenty years separating the initial *Anastasia Krupnik* and *Anastasia, Absolutely,* she matures from ten to thirteen and faces typical adolescent worries. With sensitivity and wit the writer presents issues relevant to children: assignments and peer relationships in school, sibling rivalry, crushes on teachers, death of grandparents and birth of siblings, religious identity, moving and making new friends, boredom, independence, money, peer pressure, and career decisions. In *Anastasia, Absolutely,* for example, Lowry juxtaposes ethical decisions with a humorous situation. While walking her dog, thirteen-year-old Anastasia thinks she has mailed a package for her mother, a Caldecott Honor Book artist, but she accidentally tosses the dog waste bag into the mailbox instead of the important book sketches. Anastasia applies the lessons learned in her eighth-grade ethics class to deal with her anguish over inadvertently tampering with the U.S. mail. As with the other Anastasia books, ending each chapter is a page of Anastasia's writing that weaves the narrative thread throughout; here she writes her assignment on situations presenting ethical dilemmas. The many decisions Anastasia faces all emphasize strong family values that nurture children's self-esteem and enable them to grow into responsible adults.

In her Tate series, Lowry has created equally endearing characters who enjoy close family ties. Caroline, eleven, her thirteen-year-old brother, J.P., and mother, Joanna Tate, affirm the single-parent family's ability to solve problems with humor and love. The title *The One Hundredth Thing about Caroline* is taken from Mrs. Tate's frequent praise of her children, such as finding 100 wonderful things to love about Caroline. The siblings explore the mysteries of their world, creating zany situations. In the sequel, *Switcharound,* Caroline and J.P., spending the summer with their father, stepmother, and their children, resolve their differences to survive their visit. In *Your Move, J.P.!,* first love creates havoc in J.P.'s life, but his sense of humor and creativity serve him well in getting out of embarrassing situations.

In contrast to this light-hearted tone, *A Summer to Die* (inspired by her sister's death from cancer) depicts how the Chalmers family deals with a child's dying of leukemia. The father teaches college English and writes books, the mother is warm and understanding, and the younger daughter Meg is precocious (reminding one of Anastasia's family). Because Meg, thirteen, resents her popular older sister Molly, she feels tremendous guilt when Molly dies. Supported by her parents and friends, Meg understands eventually "the jagged edges of sadness are softened by memories."

Two other works provide poignant visions of lost childhood. In *Autumn Street* Elizabeth Lorimer and her mother live with grandparents while her father serves in World War II. Elizabeth recalls aching memories of fear and the trauma of her grandfather's stroke, two playmates' deaths, news of the Holocaust, and her father's injuries. In *Us and Uncle Fraud* a child's near-death experience ends the age of innocence for Louise Cunningham, eleven. Almost losing her older brother, Louise appreciates her family, even Uncle Claude, whose dream-weaving fantasy world destroys her naive faith in all-powerful, ever-truthful adults. At the novel's end, Louise listens to "the regular sounds of family life and of the love that bound us together, despite our flaws."

Other Lowry novels focus on teenagers seeking their identity. In *Find a Stranger, Say Goodbye* Natalie Armstrong, seventeen, searches for her biological parents after she graduates from high school. Having learned the truth about her past, she discards her emotional baggage and packs for college with a freed spirit, ready to soar. *Taking Care of Terrific* portrays another confused teenager looking for her identity. Enid Crowley (who prefers Cynthia over Enid) babysits Joshua (who prefers Tom Terrific) and tries to give him the adventure his absent working mother cannot. With their adult friends, they explore the magical night world of Boston's Public Garden in the swan boats and get arrested. *Rabble Starkey* shows other harsh realities disrupting family unity. After love-struck Sweet Hosanna had left home at thirteen to marry, she returned without a husband—but with baby Parable (Rabble). The single mother supports Rabble, now twelve, by working as a housekeeper and eventually decides to get a college education. Lowry's parable of family love praises the strength of the human spirit to seek a better tomorrow.

Winner of the 1990 Newbery Medal, *Number the Stars,* set in 1943 Copenhagen, pays tribute to the courage of Danish Christians who risked their lives to save Denmark's seven thousand Jews from the Holocaust which destroyed six million Jews and millions of others across Europe. Lowry depicts how bravely Annemarie Johansen, ten, helps her Jewish friend Ellen Rosen and her family escape to safety in Sweden. In her Newbery acceptance speech, Lowry explains that her editor wanted to delete repeated references to Nazis' black boots, but she succeeded in keeping these terrifying images, because "those high shiny boots had trampled on several million childhoods and I was sorry I hadn't had several million more pages on which to mention that."

Her second Newbery Medal—for the fantasy *The Giver*—firmly establishes her reputation for creativity, diversity, and excellence as she explores new territory. Her fictional society appears perfect, without violence, overpopulation, poverty, unemployment, pain, sexual feelings, or even bad manners; yet without emotions, feelings, colors, or sense of history, this utopia turns out to be a dystopia from which twelve-year-old Jonas, Receiver of Memory for a totalitarian community, must escape. His courage to survive allows him to find "places where families created and kept memories, where they celebrated love." Lowry's Newbery acceptance speech describes how life reflects "the magic of the circular journey" because "we go out and come back, and that what we come back to is changed, and so are we. . . . Things come together and become complete."

Lowry has mastered the storyteller's art of recreating life's funny and bewildering experiences. She believes that the power of language shapes our future by retelling our stories about pivotal moments connecting people. Skillfully balancing tragedy with humor, Lowry offers the laughter, compassion, and wisdom young adults need to survive the difficult transition from childhood to adulthood.

—Laura M. Zaidman

LUCAS, Victoria. *See* PLATH, Sylvia.

LYLE, Katie Letcher

Nationality: American. **Born:** Peking, China, 12 May 1938. **Education:** Hollins College, Virginia, B.A. 1959; Johns Hopkins University, Baltimore, Maryland, M.A. 1960; graduate study at Vanderbilt University, Nashville, Tennessee, 1961-62. **Family:** Married Royster Lyle, Jr. in 1963; one daughter and one son. **Career:** Teacher in Baltimore, Maryland, 1960-61, 1962-63; member of English faculty, 1963-87, chairman of English department, 1968-80, chairman of liberal arts division, 1971-73, Southern Seminary Junior College, Buena Vista, Virginia. Guest instructor, Washington and Lee University, 1987; writer in residence, 1989, guest instructor, 1989-93, Hollins College. Elderhostel instructor, Southern Seminary, Mary Baldwin College, and other places, 1984—. Has been a professional folk singer in Baltimore and Nashville. **Awards:** Bread Loaf fellowship, 1973, 1974; Newbery Award finalist, 1973, 1974; Irene Leach Memorial Essay Contest winner, 1984, runner-up, 1985, and honorable mention, 1993; Sherwood Anderson Short Story Contest runner-up, 1987; third prize, Hackney Literary Awards, 1989; third prize, Virginia Highlands Festival Contest, 1992; . **Address:** 110 West McDowell, Lexington, Virginia 24450, U.S.A.

PUBLICATIONS FOR YOUNG ADULTS

Fiction

I Will Go Barefoot All Summer for You. Philadelphia, Pennsylvania, Lippincott, 1973.
Fair Day, and Another Step Begun. Philadelphia, Pennsylvania, Lippincott, 1974.
The Golden Shores of Heaven. Philadelphia, Pennsylvania, Lippincott, 1976.
Scott's Marathon. New York, Coward, 1980.
Dark but Full of Diamonds. New York, Coward, 1981.
Finders Weepers. New York, Coward, 1982.

PUBLICATIONS FOR ADULTS

Nonfiction

Lyrics of Three Women, with Maude Rubin and May Miller. Baltimore, Linden Press, 1964.
On Teaching Creative Writing. National Defense Education Act, 1968.
Scalded to Death by the Steam: Authentic Stories of Railroad Disasters and the Ballads That Were Written about Them. Chapel Hill, North Carolina, Algonquin, 1983.
The Man Who Wanted Seven Wives. Chapel Hill, North Carolina, Algonquin, 1986.

The Wild Berry Book. Minocqua, Wisconsin, Northword, 1994.
The Foraging Gourmet. Lyons and Burford, 1997.
When the Fighting Is All Over (memoir). Longstreet, 1997.

Editor, with Roger Jeans, *Goodbye to Old Peking, 1936-1939.* Miami, Ohio University Press, 1998.

Other

Contributor, *Beyond the Square,* edited by Robert K. Rosenburg. Hollywood, California, Linden Press, 1972.

Also author of ''Footsteps,'' a television series. Author of ''A Foreign Flavor,'' a weekly column on food and humor, for *Roanoke Times,* 1970-74. Contributor to *A Guide to Chessie Trail,* 1988, and to *Virginia Wild Rivers Study,* edited by Paul Dulaney; of poems and short stories to *Shenandoah,* the *Virginia Quarterly Review,* and other literary magazines, and of articles and reviews to newspapers and magazines, including *Newsweek.*

*

Biography: Essay in *Speaking for Ourselves: Autobiographical Sketches by Notable Authors of Books for Young Adults,* Volume 1, compiled and edited by Donald R. Gallo, National Council of Teachers of English, 1990.

*   *   *

Katie Letcher Lyle is a writer whose prose has an exceptionally fine, often poetic quality and who is able to imagine believable and fascinating characters. Lyle likes to create young adult characters who are highly individual, have an unusual love of language, and are rooted in their Southern communities, which become more specific and well-realized with each book she writes (witness, for example, the movement from the generic Nashville setting in *The Golden Shores of Heaven* to the unspecified Southern state in *Dark but Full of Diamonds* to the highly particular southwestern Virginia setting of *Finders Weepers).* Lyle treats her characters' experiences of romance and sexuality with a mixture of sympathy, romanticism, and hardheaded insight.

One of the strengths of Lyle's writing is the self-possession of her young adult characters. Whether it is Scott Dabney in *Dark but Full of Diamonds* seeking to come to terms with his romantic feelings for his drama teacher who is also his father's fiancée, or Lee Eldridge in *Finders Weepers,* calmly arguing with a kidnapper who is trying to force her to show him where the hidden treasure she has found is located, Lyle's main characters are young people who certainly have struggles, doubts, and difficulties, but seem to possess, at some level, a remarkably strong and healthy sense of self. That strong sense of self is not unrelated to their sense of humor. It also may have something to do with their Southern sense of being rooted in a community, which includes but is not limited to an extended family. Lyle is at her best when she is demonstrating, as she often does, that her rural and Southern characters, anchored as they are in their small-town societies, are by no means necessarily provincial. Her principal characters are, in general, exceptionally smart, highly verbal, imaginative, and sane, even when they are doing crazy things. Her young adults face their share (or more) of teenage upheavals, but there is a hopefulness running like an indestructible ribbon through the fabric of Lyle's fiction.

Lyle's characters do much more than survive the angst of growing up. They invent ways to cope with disappointment and adversity, often through humorous fantasies or wild escapades. Jessie in *I Will Go Barefoot All Summer for You* makes a secret love vow to go barefoot for the boy she is in love with and, when she fails to keep her vow, decides to run away and live with him. Ellen Burd in *Fair Day, and Another Step Begun* virtually wills John Waters, the young man she loves, into loving her and acknowledging their unborn child, even though he has no inclination to do either. Ellen is stubborn and persistent, but she is also curiously sensible and free from self-pity. Her vision of what John will be to her and their child is strong enough to make his love become a reality—a romantic idea, surely, but also powerfully attractive and perhaps not without wisdom. Mary Curlew in *The Golden Shores of Heaven* similarly has the single-minded determination to make her dream of becoming a country music singer in Nashville come true. Though Scott in *Dark but Full of Diamonds* fails in his desperate effort to win the love of the woman who loves his father, his love of theater, of assuming and creating dramatic roles, is the positive force in his life which enables him to begin healing himself. It is safe to say that though Lyle's main characters may suffer many doubts and anxieties, they do not doubt their self-worth. Not as superficial or alienated as Judy Blume's characters, they are on the whole wittier and wiser (or at least smarter). Although they may not be as profound or spiritually symbolic as some of Katherine Paterson's young people, they are as highly individuated as characters and at least equally complicated and genuine in their social relationships.

Lyle also brings to the young adult novel an intriguing mixture of romanticism and tough-mindedness. The romanticism is reflected in the sometimes extravagant (if not clichéd) premises of her novels: the quest for fame and fortune as a singer, for example, or a young man's hopeless love for an attractive older woman; or hidden treasure, surrounded by legend and folklore. The sources of Lyle's inspiration, on one level at least, often seem to lie close to myth, folklore, and sometimes even popular culture (with the exception of television which seems notably absent from or insignificant in the lives of her characters). The mythic or folkloric plot premises in Lyle's novels are given original and intriguing twists: Jessie in effect runs away from a home that doesn't exist in *I Will Go Barefoot All Summer for You;* Scott's oedipal attraction in *Dark but Full of Diamonds* does *not* result in the classical denouement; and Lee's real treasure in *Finders Weepers* is her relationship with the people of southwestern Virginia, particularly her grandmother, a possession threatened by her preoccupation with the hidden treasure. The tough-mindedness lies partly in the pervasive knowledge in Lyle's fiction that happiness does not result from easy gratifications but rather from lasting, genuine relationships and from satisfying pursuits of difficult-to-attain goals. And the psychological good sense of her fiction, of particular value to young people, is the persistent awareness that her characters reveal of the importance of being true to themselves. Her characters often realistically combine paradoxical qualities, as in Lee Eldridge's combination of sense and sensibility.

The strengths of Lyle's fiction, then, include strong, clear, often poetic prose writing, well-realized characters who are not represented in isolation but placed in believable social contexts, a vivid and affectionate sense of humor, and, a romantic imagination balanced by common sense about human nature. Lyle's novels for young adults received mixed reviews from critics when they first appeared, partly because she has not been content to stick to formulas or repeat her successes, and has experimented with forms and themes (for example, mixing comic misadventures with serious flashbacks and dreams or blending romantic ballad and realistic contemporary novel), but she is an engaging, talented writer whose novels deserve a broader audience.

—J.D. Stahl

LYNCH, Chris

Nationality: American. **Born:** Boston, Massachusetts, 2 July 1962. **Education:** Suffolk University, Boston, Massachusetts, 1979-1983, B.A. in journalism 1983; Emerson University, Boston, Massachusetts, M.A. in professional writing and publishing 1991. **Family:** Married Tina Coviello; two children. **Career:** Worked as a house painter and moving van driver, then as a proof-reader of financial reports, 1985-1989; teacher of writing, Emerson University, Boston, Massachusetts, 1995; teacher of writing, Vermont College, Burlington, Vermont, from 1997. **Awards:** American Library Association award, Best Books for Young Adults and Quick Picks for Reluctant Young Adult Readers citations, 1993, for *Shadow Boxer*, 1994, for *Iceman* and *Gypsy Davey*, and 1996, for *Slot Machine*; Best Books of the Year list, *School Library Journal*, 1993, for *Shadow Boxer*; Blue Ribbon Award, *Bulletin of the Center for Children's Books*, 1994, for *Iceman* and *Gypsy Davey*; Editor's Choice award, *Booklist*, 1994, for *Gypsy Davey*; finalist, Dorothy Canfield Fisher Award, finalist, Book of the Year Award from *Hungry Mind Review*, Young Adult Choices Citation, International Reading Association, all 1997, all for *Slot Machine*. **Agent:** c/o HarperCollins Children's Press, 10 East 53rd St., New York, New York 10022, U.S.A.

PUBLICATIONS FOR YOUNG ADULTS

Fiction

Shadow Boxer. New York, HarperCollins, 1993.
Iceman. New York, HarperCollins, 1994.
Gypsy Davey. New York, HarperCollins, 1994.
Slot Machine. New York, HarperCollins, 1995.
Political Timber. New York, HarperCollins, 1996.

"Blue-eyed Son" Series

Mick. New York, HarperCollins, 1996.
Blood Relations. New York, HarperCollins, 1996.
Dog Eat Dog. New York, HarperCollins, 1996.

Short Stories

"The Hobbyist," in *Ultimate Sports,* edited by Donald Gallo. New York, Delacorte, 1995.
"Story," in *Night Terrors,* edited by Lois Duncan. New York, Simon and Schuster, 1996.

*

Critical Studies: "Slot Machine" by Stephanie Zvirin, in *Booklist,* 1 September 1995, 74; "On a Constituency" by Chris Lynch, in *Literature for Today's Young Adults,* edited by Kenneth L. Donelson and Alleen Pace Nilsen, New York, Addison Wesley Longman, 1997, 100; "Chris Lynch" by J. Sydney Jones, in *Authors & Artists for Young Adults,* Vol. 19, Detroit, Gale, 1996, 175-182; entry in *Something About the Author,* Vol. 95, Detroit, Gale, 1997.

Chris Lynch comments:

I don't know for sure. A writer is not supposed to say this, but I should. There are some days when I doubt what I'm doing. I doubt the value, doubt the effect, doubt the sense and the meaning of writing fiction for a living. Fortunately, these demons come, blast away at the psyche, then go on their way to assault the next unfortunate writer.

By the next morning I see it again, the real stuff, and I know why I do it. And I do it.

But this much I do know, and I know it every day. It is *not* worth less to create work for a 15-year-old than for a 40-year-old.

*   *   *

With the same fervor that energizes his fiction, Chris Lynch described his essential credo as a writer for young adults: "*15-year-olds are not children!*" he declared in a statement about his work prepared for *Literature for Today's Young Adults,* and they have "a set of concerns and interests as serious and complex as any other population." This seriousness of purpose and intensity of expression has marked Lynch's work from his first novel, *Shadow Boxer,* an unflinchingly realistic exploration of the seductive appeal of controlled violence justified by a sporting setting or required by the macho code of the streets. Lynch has talked about the "hovering menace" he sees in urban life, and the two brothers who are the narrative focus of *Shadow Boxer* must deal with constant challenges on the street, as well as the lure of the ring where their father suffered the injuries that led to his early death. Prior to the publication of *Shadow Boxer,* Lynch had not been successful with the conventional forms of standard adult fiction that he was trying to write, and when a class assignment at Emerson University called for an account of a childhood incident, Lynch said in an interview with J. Sydney Jones that he "had a vague idea of writing about some things my brother and I had done in our youth, but as soon as I sat down with it, I was off to the races. The stuff just poured out." The key, Lynch felt, was "matching yourself and your material," and while the book was only "about twenty percent autobiographical," it introduced several of the themes which have remained crucial to his work.

The working-class neighborhood in Boston, the struggling single parent trying to combine a job with the demands of raising two decent but unruly children, the appeal of an aggressive attitude as a means of settling everything, the longing for an absent father, and the inner turmoil of a mid-teen young man trying to make sense of his life are all elements which recur in Lynch's books. *Shadow Boxer* also utilizes Lynch's fascination with and deep knowledge of an athletic discipline as a centering device, and its riveting scenes of action in the ring or on the street have the clarity

and graphic power which Lynch brings to all of his recreations of a sporting event. The episodic arrangement of the narrative troubled some reviewers, but as Lynch commented to Jones, "I don't see transitions in my life. I see moments." Lynch cited Joan Didion's *Play It As It Lays* and Sherwood Anderson's *Winesburg, Ohio* as "incredibly liberating" examples that "made me understand how scenes assemble." His willingness to deviate from more conventional modes of organization was typical of Lynch's refusal to accede to the expectations of a genre, and is an important aspect both of his employment of original methods of structure and of his willingness to push the boundaries of what Young Adult writing can cover or include.

Lynch's second book, *Iceman,* also had its origins in his own early life, but not as much in terms of the situation as in what he calls "the whole inability to express yourself. Where does that go," he asked in the Jones interview, "the frustration? It's got to go someplace. Writing it, I tapped into something very adolescent American male where anger is cool." In the case of the fourteen-year-old protagonist, it has gone into a viciousness in the rink and a doom-driven death fixation that parallels the coldness he feels in his family. The harshness of the psychological setting is both unnerving and compelling as Lynch does not retreat from the consequences of the protagonist's efforts to escape from the grip of a numbing home and the perverse thrill of terrorizing people on the ice. The intimation of hope at the conclusion is only partially convincing, but the central character is always authentic. Characterization is one of the strongest components of Lynch's writing in *Iceman,* as it was in *Shadow Boxer,* and it functions as the starting point for all of his fiction.

In discussing his work with Jones, Lynch emphasized this point. "One of the great things we can do as novelists is to take a good close-up view of characters. . . . I don't really plot my books. I write characters; that where it all starts." *Gypsy Davey,* his third book, begins, continues, and ends literally within the chaotic mind of a boy in his early teens forced to become the responsible person in a collapsing family with no adult guidance. To the world, he is nearly mute, riding his bike endlessly and apparently aimlessly. From the perspective on his inner consciousness which Lynch presents in alternate chapters set in a different type, his intelligence, compassion, and confusion are heart-rending evidence of a different but not inferior perspective, a boy whose swirl of thoughts is an indication of some degree of clinical brain-damage as well as what Lynch calls his "charming sweetness." While Davey's attempts to care for the neglected child of his older sister are the central focus of the narrative, the long section which describes the sister's marriage is a riveting mix of lacerating satire and poignant sociological analysis. Here, and in his depiction of Davey's father, the wayward rogue known as "Sneaky Pete," Lynch is stretching the limits of the Young Adult genre, writing passages that would not be out of place in the most adult of novels. As he has said, "If you talk down to your audience . . . They will reject you." Lynch is confident enough in the capability of his audience to introduce material that might be unfamiliar in literature, but which is not likely to be beyond the experience of the reader's own lives.

Lynch's first three novels dealt with families that were damaged to some degree, and in each case, the bleakness of the protagonist's background resulted in a relatively grim depiction of existence, although the conclusion of each book points toward a somewhat brighter future. While *Slot Machine* also involves a difficult situation, its mood is comic and exuberant. Elvin Bishop, a relatively unathletic young man about to enter high school, spends three weeks at a camp designed to find a ''slot'' or niche for each student, ideally on a team but ultimately in a category that provides a convenient, conformist label. Lynch said that he experienced a similar program (although for only two days), and told Jones that ''what makes this book funny is Elvin's filtering of events. The dark underbelly is still there . . . [but] he's making jokes about what's happening to him.'' Revealingly, Lynch also mentions that ''Elvin's voice more closely represents the way I talk than the other narrators.'' In other words, he is very witty, in love with language, self-reflective without resorting to self-pity, proud of what he can accomplish, tolerant and friendly; in sum, a tremendous pleasure to be with.

In contrast to the gripping narration of the first three books, *Slot Machine* is both more relaxed and more difficult to resist or to put at a distance. It is hard to avoid some degree of identification with Elvin, to not root for him, to not feel a glow of satisfaction at his efforts, accomplishments, and ultimate location of the place where he belongs. After enduring semi-humiliation at various athletic venues and other activities engineered by the control-freak coaches who run the camp, Elvin finds a home in the realm of the arts with the other ''misfits'' who are actually the most appealing people in the book. It is clear that Elvin is close to Lynch's heart as well as his mind/voice, although it stretches the imagination to some degree to actually expect a young teen to be able to use the language as impressively as Elvin does. During the course of the narrative, however, such doubts are less likely to occur as the propelling power of the events sweeps the reader along.

Slot Machine launched another narrative direction for Lynch, and after its completion he said, ''I'm going to do more with Elvin as a narrator.'' However, he also commented that ''I plan to get back to Davey sometime.'' The next two projects Lynch worked on demonstrated his plans to proceed on both paths. His ''Blue-Eyed Son'' trilogy— which is actually a single book divided into three separate publications to satisfy the commercial realities of the Young Adult market—is a withering indictment and insider's expose of ethnic insularity and the blinding hatred of bigotry endemic to an old cultural community losing its power and influence. *Political Timber,* which was also published in 1996, is set in the affluent, culturally-refined precincts of the same ethnic group, the Boston Irish. Its protagonist is a ''fortunate son'' of a prosperous, well-educated, and humane family who has been asked to stand as a surrogate candidate for mayor by his old politician grandfather, ineligible for election due to his present status as an inhabitant of a local prison. Both Mick, from the trilogy, and Gordon Foley, from *Political Timber,* are moving toward their senior year in high school, Foley looking forward to the privileges of that position, Mick marking time in school while he tries to come to terms with the demands for tribal loyalty of his ''friends'' and family—a group of thugs substituting violence for common sense and a household of contentious weaklings retreating into tiny personal prisons as refuges against a changing world that threatens their meager self-esteem. Lynch, who grew up in the

Jamaica Plains district of Boston when it was in transition from an Irish enclave to a mostly Hispanic neighborhood, has conceived the two books as a kind of Boston ''High'' and ''Low'' and has followed the dark vision of his earliest books and the sprightly comic stance of *Slot Machine* to create a contrasting tableau that follows two seemingly dissimilar young men through ''the great lurch from childhood to adulthood.''

The almost unrelenting violence of the ''Blue-Eyed Son'' trilogy, and its hyperrealistic depiction of the miseries, hard times, and no-exit outlook of Mick's family, may have encouraged Lynch to reach for a degree of balance in *Political Timber,* a book which Lynch said grew out of a picture in a newspaper of a boy who ran for mayor of a small town. ''He was a goof. It was all a lark for him. I loved that spirit and I went with it.'' Foley's problems are nothing like Mick's, but Lynch takes him seriously even while placing him in a one comic predicament after another. Interestingly, Lynch sees the book as written for high teens, ''a woefully under-served constituency. I wanted to portray an eighteen-year-old, someone who is on the cusp between the adult and kid world,'' he told Jones. The outcome of *Political Timber* is very up-beat, and for all of his uncertainty, Foley has a fine future to look forward to, while the troublingly unsettled situation Mick remains in at the close of *Dog Eat Dog* offers no guarantees that he will ever even reach the adult world.

One of the reasons for Lynch's success as a writer for Young Adults is his often reiterated commitment to what he calls his ''constituency.'' He is not coy about admitting that he has a specific personal philosophy to express. ''Soft-pedal your message and they will reject you,'' he asserts. Assessing his ''body of work,'' Lynch summarized the central concern of his books by saying to Jones, ''They deal with the whole idea of identity and individuality.'' In the ''Blue-Eyed Son'' trilogy, he addressed himself to the way in which individual identity can be crushed by a ''very overt racism,'' joining a perennial theme of Young Adult literature with a strong moral statement. ''I wanted to put the spotlight on us,'' Lynch said of the Irish community he grew up in, and this willingness to look directly at the often harsh facts of existence for young people who are finding it difficult to ''be who you are'' gives his writing an honesty and verisimilitude that, as Stephanie Zvirin put it in a review for *Booklist,* ''speaks with wisdom and heart to the victim and outsider in us all.'' In an account of his career for HarperCollins, Lynch remarked: ''In much of my work I describe people who are struggling with who they are, with people's perceptions of them. . . . So it is up to the individual to escape the label. To grow out of it. To be more than the label says. I sort of tell my readers that all the time.'' As a writer speaking directly to readers who are often under tremendous pressure to accept some powerful person's or institution's version of themselves, Lynch has, in book after book, helped to make it ''okay to be who you are.''

—Leon Lewis

M

MacAVOY, R(oberta) A(nn)

Nationality: American. **Born:** Cleveland, Ohio, 13 December 1949. **Education:** Case Western Reserve University, Cleveland, 1967-71, B.Sc. 1971. **Family:** Married Ronald Allen Cain in 1978. **Career:** Financial aid officer's assistant, Columbia College, New York, 1975-78; computer programmer, SRI International, Menlo Park, California, 1979-83; since 1982, full-time writer. **Awards:** John W. Campbell Best New Writer award, 1984. **Agent:** Richard Curtis Associates, 171 East 74th Street, New York, New York 10021. **Address:** Underhill at Nelson Farm, 1669 Nelson Road, House 6, Scotts Valley, California 95066, U.S.A.

PUBLICATIONS FOR YOUNG ADULTS

Novels

Tea with the Black Dragon. New York and London, Bantam, 1983.
A Trio for Lute. New York, Doubleday, 1984.
Damiano. New York, Bantam, 1984; London, 1985.
Damiano's Lute. New York, Bantam, 1984; London, 1985.
Raphael. New York, Bantam, 1984; London, 1985.
The Book of Kells. New York, Bantam, 1985.
Twisting the Rope: Casadh and t'Sugain. New York, Bantam, 1986.
The Great Horse. New York, Bantam, 1987.
The Third Eagle: Lessons Along a Minor String. New York, Doubleday, 1989.
Lens of the World. New York, Morrow, 1990, London, Headline, 1991.
King of the Dead. New York, Morrow, and London, Headline, 1991.
The Belly of the Wolf. New York, William Morrow, 1994.

*   *   *

In the work of R. A. MacAvoy, young adult readers will find familiar forms in the service of some of the themes they find most intriguing. MacAvoy explores the eternal questions of meaning, personal identity, and the "right" way of life through characters who embody and personalize these questions. These are books for the thoughtful reader, one who is willing to study character and enjoy the author's crafted prose.

The language employed in these novels is not difficult, but it is conscious. An appreciation for digression and simile will add to the reader's enjoyment. Sentences like, "I awoke before dawn for the whole week before Baron Howdl's next winnowing," from *Lens of the World,* will be much more effective for the reader who understands not only the meaning but the nuances of "winnowing." Similarly, "Less promptly, the bumblebees followed" *(Lens of the World),* will reveal itself only to the reader who has supplied both imagination and attention. The literalist will see only departing soldiers, while those who have missed previous references to the black-and-yellow uniforms will find themselves truly at sea. This poetic prose adds a dimension too often missing from works intended for the young adult audience.

MacAvoy frequently makes use of standard forms. *Tea with the Black Dragon* and *Twisting the Rope* are mysteries. It is a daring mystery reader, however, who will be willing to tolerate protagonists who are mystics and philosophers, one of whom also claims a previous life as a dragon. The "Damiano" trilogy follows the familiar fantasy format of coming-of-age quest, but again, the introspective character of the hero turns the form on its head. In *Lens of the World* and its sequel, *King of the Dead,* MacAvoy again uses a familiar form, the epistolary novel, to reveal her characters in ways that plot cannot.

Indeed, it is the similarities in her protagonists which are MacAvoy's most salient characteristic. They are inward-turning, self-questioning, thoughtful people. Not afraid of contemplation, they are most likely to respond to difficulties with thought rather than action. Life (and plot complications) may force them to act, but they will question those actions later. They are unable to see only one side of a question and, one and all, are seekers—of truth, peace, harmony, or inner balance. External warfare is often a metaphor for internal character struggles. The search for internal balance is played out in political complications, kidnappings, journeys into hostile territory. Mastery over one's self, whether as a musician, warrior, or lens grinder, yields mastery in the external world.

Zhurrie, in *Lens of the World,* is in many ways an ultimate creation in this embodiment of thematic development of character. His search for identity and belonging shape the plot. He is forced into action against his will when he hesitates to operate in a world he so imperfectly understands. Yet his self comprehension informs all of his acts and his reports of them. Although Zhurrie's life is full of battles, travels, and invention, this is never his focus. He is always examining these experiences for reasons, causes, and meaning. It is when Zhurrie is uniquely qualified to interpret this reality that the full force of the thematic meaning is revealed to the reader. Because *Lens of the World* deals so successfully with many important themes of young adult literature, including coming-of-age, self-identity, relationships, and responsibility to the community, it deserves special mention. In it, young adult readers will find models and metaphors for many of their experiences.

—Cathy Chauvette

MAGORIAN, Michelle

Nationality: British. **Born:** Portsmouth, England, 6 November 1947. **Education:** Rose Bruford College of Speech and Drama, diploma, 1969; London University, certificate in film studies, 1984; Ecole Internationale de Mime, 1969-70. **Family:** Married in 1987; one son. **Career:** Writer and actress. Appeared in several television programs and the film *McVicar;* has performed mime shows and was a member of a repertory theatre group. **Awards:** Carnegie Medal commendation, 1981, for *Good Night, Mr. Tom;* International Reading Association Children's Book award, American Library Association Best Book for Young Adults, and British

Guardian award for Children's Literature, all 1982, all for *Good Night, Mr. Tom*; West Australian Young Readers' Book award, Library Association of Australia, 1983, for *Good Night, Mr. Tom*, and 1987, for *Back Home*; American Library Association Best Book for Young Adults, for *Back Home*, 1984. **Agent:** Patricia White, Rogers, Coleridge & White, 20 Powis Mews, London W11 1JN, England. **Address:** 803 Harrow Rd., Wembley, Middlesex HA0 2LP, England.

PUBLICATIONS FOR YOUNG ADULTS

Fiction

Good Night, Mr. Tom. London, Kestrel, and New York, Harper, 1981.
Back Home. New York, Harper, 1984; London, Kestrel, 1985.
Waiting for My Shorts to Dry (poetry), illustrated by Jean Baylis. London, Kestrel, 1989.
Who's Going to Take Care of Me?, illustrated by James Graham Hale. New York, HarperCollins, 1990.
A Little Love Song. New York, Methuen, 1991.
Orange Paw Marks (poetry), illustrated by Jean Baylis. London, Kestrel, 1991.
Not a Swan. New York, HarperCollins, 1992.
Jump! New York, Walker Books, 1992.
In Deep Water and Other Stories. London, Viking, 1992.
Cuckoo in the Nest. London, Methuen Children's, 1994.

*

Media Adaptations: *Back Home* (television film).

*   *   *

Although all of Michelle Magorian's young adult novels take place during World War II, their subjects would have been unmentionable in juvenile fiction of the 1940s: child abuse, illegitimacy, sexuality, gender roles, and class differences. Yet these are not harsh books, thanks to Magorian's engaging protagonists, her sensitive yet powerful writing style, and her emotional honesty. The war and its aftermath provide a setting of crisis and change in which believable characters and their struggles engage the reader's interest compellingly.

Magorian rose to fame with *Good Night, Mr. Tom*, the story of an abused London boy billeted on a gruff, elderly widower. It would seem unlikely that the well worn plot of a lonely child meeting an emotion-starved older person, to the lasting benefit of both, could excite readers and critics alike in the 1980s—but it did, moving many to tears. Showing the dark side of human nature, and of the war, *Good Night, Mr. Tom* succeeds by the power of its message: hope. Willie Beech, whose mother has sewn him into his clothes and packed a belt for his hosts to beat him with, is assigned to Tom Oakley simply because Tom lives near the church. That the transformation of Willie into a normal boy and Tom into a loving parent surrogate avoids sentimentality is almost miraculous. The narrative gradually reveals the extent of Willie's victimization at the hands of his mother, a religious fanatic; his bruises and his fear of everything and everyone are the outward signs of profound deprivation, for Willie has never eaten nourishing food, been

allowed to play, or learned to read. As the nature of Willie's problems becomes clear, Tom experiences flashbacks to the terrible loss of his young wife and infant son.

Magorian places her central fable in a meticulously detailed rural setting with other fully rounded characters: Carrie, who wins a scholarship but faces hostility from her working class family; Mrs. Hartridge, whose husband is missing in action; Zach (Will's best friend), a Jewish evacuee from a theatrical family. Finally, Magorian does not simply end the story with the transformation of Will and Tom; Will's return to London, his rescue by Tom, his prolonged recuperation, and the loss of Zach take up the second part of the book. The healing powers of the countryside are balanced by those of art, as Will learns to express himself in theatre and drawing.

Magorian's second young adult book, *Back Home*, also portrays complex characters from several generations. In addition to Rusty, who is returning from a wartime stay with American relatives, there are two compelling elderly women: the eccentric Beatie, who functions as a fairy godmother, and her malevolent counterpart, Rusty's grandmother. The transformation of Rusty from repressed child to happy young adolescent has already happened before the story begins; her attempts to fit into the conditions of postwar England are balanced by the freer ideals she has learned abroad.

Unlike *Good Night, Mr. Tom*'s focus on childhood and old age, *Back Home* also includes a searching examination of the generation between. Rusty's mother Peggy, sheltered and repressed, finds new strengths and abilities under wartime conditions. As Virginia has become Rusty overseas, so Margaret has turned into Peggy, skilled driver and mechanic, in Devon. Peggy's inarticulate love for Rusty, her unhappiness with her tyrannical mother-in-law and coldly conventional husband, and her eventual decision to make a new life are shown with understanding and skill.

Gender roles, barely mentioned in the earlier book, permeate *Back Home*. Rusty, with her androgynous name and skill in woodcutting and carpentry, has difficulty with British customs. Peggy, herself a mechanic, at first supports traditional gender roles for her children and only gradually comes to reject them after both Rusty and her younger brother Charlie run afoul of societal expectations. The scene in which Charlie is shorn of his thick hair, then caned by his father as Rusty tries to protect him, brings these questions into sharp focus.

Back Home examines issues of class and nationality in many ways, one of them education—as exemplified by the differences between Rusty's American school and the unspeakable Benwood House, a monument to institutional meanness unequalled since Jane Eyre's Lowood. In typical Magorian fashion, one of the most telling features of Benwood is its treatment of art and music as extras, and even at that, subjects to be learn by rote. By contrast, Rusty and Charlie's later school in Devon is run on progressive lines and vaguely resembles a West Country Summerhill. Particularly significant is the difference between the ostracism accorded to a scholarship student at Benwood and the unquestioned acceptance of Rusty's friend Beth at the Devon school, which she attends free because her parents work there. Also developed in detail is the question of sexual repression. The difference between Rusty's casual acceptance of male friends and the attitudes of most of the English characters is striking. Bertie's pleasure at seeing the children dance naked in the rain contrasts sharply with the grandmother's view that pregnancy must not be mentioned in front of children, especially at teatime. Rusty's classmates can be expelled for talking to any man, and one of them believes Rusty will have a baby because she spent the night talking to a boy.

After a hiatus of seven years, Magorian returned to World War II with *Not a Swan.* More lyrical than *Good Night, Mr. Tom,* more optimistic than *Back Home,* the story focuses for the first time on an adolescent main character, Rose, youngest of three sisters evacuated to Devon. The double plot balances Rose's maturation in wartime against her gradual discovery of the fate of Mad Hilda, whose cottage she and her sisters are living in. At sixteen, Rose has almost complete autonomy. For the first time, Magorian has a chance to develop her ideas about sexuality and repression with direct reference to the main character; for, after reading Hilda's journal and discovering the tragedy of her life after illegitimate pregnancy, Rose herself goes through sexual initiation and the growth of love in a very different fashion. Bridging the two stories is the saga of Dot, a young woman from a nearby home for pregnant evacuees, whose fiance has been killed. The graphically described birth of Dot's baby and the subsequent acceptance of Dot by her fiance's parents are high points. In all three of these plot strands, questions of love versus sex, true legitimacy versus respectability, and birth versus literal or metaphorical death are examined.

Women's roles, class distinctions, and the role of art come in for discussion once again in *Not a Swan.* The enforced seclusion of Mad Hilda by her wealthy family contrasts with the freedom enjoyed by Rose and her sisters and, indeed, by their absent mother, who is away entertaining the troops. The working-class characters, particularly Dot and her fiance's parents, have a conspicuously practical and unconventional response to crisis. Also as in *Good Night, Mr. Tom,* art has power to heal. Will draws; Rose, like Hilda before her, writes. The central position accorded to writing throughout the book makes the coincidence of Alec's identity seem not merely coincidental but inevitable.

—Caroline C. Hunt

MAHY, Margaret

Nationality: New Zealander. **Born:** Whakatane, New Zealand, 21 March 1936. **Education:** University of Auckland, B.A. 1957, Diploma of Librarianship 1958. **Family:** two daughters. **Career:** Writer. Petone Public Library, New Zealand, assistant librarian, 1958-59; School Library Service, Christchurch, New Zealand, librarian in charge, 1967-76; Canterbury Public Library, Christchurch, children's librarian, 1976-80. Writer in Residence, Canterbury University, 1984, and Western Australian College of Advanced Education, 1985. **Awards:** Esther Glenn award, New Zealand Library Association, 1970, for *A Lion in the Meadow,* 1973, for *The First Margaret Mahy Story Book,* 1983, for *The Haunting;* New Zealand Literary Fund grant, 1975; *School Library Journal* Best Book citation, 1982, for *The Haunting;* Carnegie Medals, British Library Association, 1983, for *The Haunting,* 1985, for *The Changeover: A Supernatural Romance,* and 1987, for *Memory;* Notable Children's Book citation, 1984, Association for Library Service to Children, Children's Book of the Year citation, and Best Books for Young Adults award, American Library Association, all 1986, for *The Changeover;* Honor List citation, *Horn Book,* 1985, for *The Changeover,* and 1987, for *The Catalogue of the Universe; Observer* prize, 1987; Books of 1987 citation, ALA Young Adult Services

Division, for *The Tricksters,* and 1989, for *Memory;* Society of School Libraries International Book award, and *Boston Globe/ Horn Book* award, both 1988, for *Memory.* May Hill Arbuthnot Lecturer, ALSC, 1989. **Agent:** Vanessa Hamilton, The Summer House, Woodend, West Stoke Chichester, West Sussex PO18 9BP, England. **Address:** 23 Merlincote Crescent, Governor's Bay, Lyttelton Harbor, Canterbury, South Island, New Zealand

PUBLICATIONS FOR YOUNG ADULTS

Novels

The Haunting, illustrated by Bruce Hogarth. London, Dent, 1982; New York, Atheneum, 1983.

The Changeover: A Supernatural Romance. London, Dent, and New York, Atheneum, 1984.

The Catalogue of the Universe. London, Dent, 1985; New York, Atheneum, 1986.

Aliens in the Family. London, Methuen, and New York, Scholastic, 1986.

The Tricksters. London, Dent, 1986; New York, McElderry, 1987.

Memory. London, Dent, and New York, McElderry, 1987.

The Pirate Uncle, illustrated by Barbara Steadman. Woodstock, New York, Overlook Press, 1994.

The Other Side of Silence. New York, Viking, 1995.

Other

My Mysterious World (autobiography), photographs by David Alexander. Katonah, New York, R.C. Owen Publishers, 1995.

PUBLICATIONS FOR CHILDREN

Fiction

The Dragon of an Ordinary Family, illustrated by Helen Oxenbury. New York, Watts, and London, Heinemann, 1969.

A Lion in the Meadow, illustrated by Jenny Williams. New York, Watts, and London, Dent, 1969; augmented edition, as *A Lion in the Meadow and Five Other Favorites,* London, Dent, 1976.

Mrs. Discombobulous, illustrated by Jan Brychta. New York, Watts, and London, Dent, 1969.

Pillycock's Shop, illustrated by Carol Barker. New York, Watts, and London, Dobson, 1969.

The Procession, illustrated by Charles Mozley. New York, Watts, and London, Dent, 1969.

The Little Witch, illustrated by Charles Mozley. New York, Watts, and London, Dent, 1970.

Sailor Jack and the 20 Orphans, illustrated by Robert Bartelt. New York, Watts, and London, Dent, 1970.

The Boy with Two Shadows, illustrated by Jenny Williams. New York, Watts, and London, Dent, 1971.

The Princess and the Clown, illustrated by Carol Barker. New York, Watts, and London, Dobson, 1971.

The Man Whose Mother Was a Pirate, illustrated by Brian Froud. London, Dent, 1972; New York, Atheneum, 1973; revised edition illustrated by Margaret Chamberlain, New York, Viking, 1986.

The Railway Engine and the Hairy Brigands, illustrated by Brian Froud. London, Dent, 1973.

Clancy's Cabin, illustrated by Trevor Stubley. London, Dent, 1974.

The Rare Spotted Birthday Party, illustrated by Belinda Lyon. London, Watts, 1974.

Rooms to Rent, illustrated by Jenny Williams. New York, Watts, 1974; as *Rooms to Let,* London, Dent, 1975.

Stepmother, illustrated by Terry Burton. London, Watts, 1974.

The Witch in the Cherry Tree, illustrated by Jenny Williams. London, Dent, and New York, Parents' Magazine Press, 1974.

The Boy Who Was Followed Home, illustrated by Steven Kellogg. New York, Watts, 1975; London, Dent, 1977.

The Bus Under the Leaves, illustrated by Margery Gill. London, Dent, 1975.

The Great Millionaire Kidnap, illustrated by Jan Brychta. London, Dent, 1975.

Ultra-Violet Catastrophe! or, The Unexpected Walk with Great-Uncle Mangus Pringle, illustrated by Brian Froud. London, Dent, and New York, Parents' Magazine Press, 1975.

David's Witch Doctor, illustrated by Jim Russell. London, Watts, 1976.

Leaf Magic, illustrated by Jenny Williams. London, Dent, 1976; New York, Parents' Magazine Press, 1977.

The Wind Between the Stars, illustrated by Brian Froud. London, Dent, 1976.

Look under V, illustrated by Deidre Gardiner. Wellington, Department of Education School Publications Branch, 1977.

The Nonstop Nonsense Book, illustrated by Quentin Blake. London, Dent, 1977; New York, McElderry, 1989.

The Pirate Uncle, illustrated by Mary Dinsdale. London, Dent, 1977.

The Great Piratical Rumbustification, and The Librarian and the Robbers, illustrated by Quentin Blake. London, Dent, 1978; Boston, Godine, 1986.

Raging Robots and Unruly Uncles, illustrated by Peter Stevenson. London, Dent, 1981.

Cooking Pot, with Joy Cowley and June Melser, illustrated by Deidre Gardiner. Auckland, Shortland, 1982; Leeds, Arnold Wheaton, 1985.

The Crocodile's Christmas Sandals, illustrated by Deidre Gardiner. Wellington, Department of Education School Publications Branch, 1982; as *The Crocodile's Christmas Thongs,* Melbourne, Nelson, 1985.

Fast and Funny, with Joy Cowley and June Melser, illustrated by Lynette Vondruska. Auckland, Shortland, 1982; Leeds, Arnold Wheaton, 1985.

Roly-Poly, with Joy Cowley and June Melser, illustrated by Deidre Gardiner. Auckland, Shortland, 1982; Leeds, Arnold Wheaton, 1985.

Sing to the Moon, with Joy Cowley and June Melser, illustrated by Isabel Lowe. Auckland, Shortland, 1982; Leeds, Arnold Wheaton, 1985.

Tiddalik, with Joy Cowley and June Melser, illustrated by Philip Webb. Auckland, Shortland, 1982; Leeds, Arnold Wheaton, 1985.

The Bubbling Crocodile, illustrated by Deidre Gardiner. Wellington, Department of Education School Publications Branch, 1983.

A Crocodile in the Library, illustrated by Deidre Gardiner. Wellington, Department of Education School Publications Branch, 1983.

Mrs. Bubble's Baby. Wellington, Department of Education School Publications Branch, 1983.

The Pirates' Mixed-Up Voyage: Dark Doings in the Thousand Islands, illustrated by Margaret Chamberlain. London, Dent, 1983.

Shopping with a Crocodile. Wellington, Department of Education School Publications Branch, 1983.

The Birthday Burglar, and A Very Wicked Headmistress, illustrated by Margaret Chamberlain. London, Dent, 1984; Boston, Godine, 1988.

The Dragon's Birthday, illustrated by Philip Webb. Auckland, Shortland, 1984.

Fantail, Fantail, illustrated by Bruce Phillips. Wellington, Department of Education School Publications Branch, 1984.

Going to the Beach, illustrated by Dick Frizzell. Wellington, Department of Education School Publications Branch, 1984.

The Great Grumbler and the Wonder Tree, illustrated by Diane Perham. Wellington, Department of Education School Publications Branch, 1984.

The Spider in the Shower, illustrated by Rodney McRae. Auckland, Shortland, 1984.

Ups and Downs and Other Stories, illustrated by Philip Webb. Auckland, Shortland, 1984.

Wibble Wobble and Other Stories. Auckland, Shortland. 1984.

The Adventures of a Kite, illustrated by David Cowe. Auckland, Shortland, 1985; Leeds, Arnold Wheaton, 1986.

The Cake, illustrated by David Cowe. Auckland, Shortland, 1985; Leeds, Arnold Wheaton, 1986.

The Catten, illustrated by Jo Davies. Auckland, Shortland, 1985; Leeds, Arnold Wheaton, 1986.

Clever Hamburger, illustrated by Rodney McRae. Auckland, Shortland, 1985; Leeds, Arnold Wheaton, 1986.

A Crocodile in the Garden, illustrated by Deidre Gardiner. Wellington, Department of Education of Education School Publications Branch, 1985.

The Earthquake, illustrated by Dianne Perham. Auckland, Shortland, 1985; Leeds, Arnold Wheaton, 1986.

Horrakopotchin. Wellington, Department of Education School Publications Branch, 1985.

Jam: A True Story, illustrated by Helen Craig. London, Dent, 1985; Boston, Atlantic Monthly Press, 1986.

Out in the Big Wild World, illustrated by Rodney McRae. Auckland, Shortland, 1985.

Rain, illustrated by Elizabeth Fuller. Auckland, Shortland, 1985.

Sophie's Singing Mother, illustrated by Jo Davies. Auckland, Shortland, 1985; Leeds, Arnold Wheaton, 1986.

Arguments, illustrated by Kelvin Hawley. Auckland, Shortland, 1986.

Baby's Breakfast, illustrated by Madeline Beasley. Auckland, Heinemann, 1986.

Beautiful Pig. Auckland, Shortland, 1986; Leeds, Arnold Wheaton, 1987.

An Elephant in the House, illustrated by Elizabeth Fuller. Auckland, Shortland, 1986.

Feeling Funny, illustrated by Rodney McRae. Auckland, Heinemann, 1986.

The Fight on the Hill, illustrated by Jan van der Voo. Auckland, Shortland, 1986; Leeds, Arnold Wheaton, 1987.

The Funny Funny Clown Face, illustrated by Miranda Whitford. Auckland, Heinemann, 1986.

The Garden Party, illustrated by Rodney McRae. Auckland, Heinemann, 1986.

Grow Up Sally Sue. Auckland, Heinemann, 1986.

Jacko, The Junk Shop Man, illustrated by Jo Davies. Auckland, Shortland, 1986.

The King's Treasure. Auckland, Heinemann, 1986.

The Long Grass of Tumbledown Road. Auckland, Shortland, 1986; Leeds, Arnold Wheaton, 1987.

The Man Who Enjoyed Grumbling, illustrated by Wendy Hodder. Auckland, Heinemann, 1986.

Mr. Rooster's Dilemma, illustrated by Elizabeth Fuller. Auckland, Shortland, 1986; as *How Mr. Rooster Didn't Get Married,* Leeds, Arnold Wheaton, 1986.

Mr. Rumfitt, illustrated by Nick Price. Auckland, Heinemann, 1986.

The Mouse Wedding, illustrated by Elizabeth Fuller. Auckland, Shortland, 1986.

Muppy's Ball, illustrated by Jan van der Voo. Auckland, Heinemann, 1986.

My Wonderful Aunt, illustrated by Dierdre Gardiner. Auckland, Heinemann, 4 vols., 1986; revised edition, Chicago, Children's Press, 1988.

The New House Villain, illustrated by Elizabeth Fuller. Auckland, Heinemann, 1986.

A Pet to the Vet, illustrated by Philip Webb. Auckland, Heinemann, 1986.

The Pop Group, illustrated by Madeline Beasley. Auckland, Heinemann, 1986.

The Robber Pig and the Ginger Beer [Green Eggs], illustrated by Rodney McRae. Auckland, Shortland, 2 vols., 1986; Leeds, Arnold Wheaton, 2 vols., 1987.

Shuttle 4. Auckland, Heinemann, 1986.

Squeak in the Gate, illustrated by Jo Davies. Auckland, Shortland, 1986.

The Terrible Topsy-Turvy, Tissy-Tossy Tangle, illustrated by Vicki Smillie-McItoull. Auckland, Heinemann, 1986.

The Three Wishes, with others, illustrated by Rodney McRae and others. Auckland, Shortland, 1986.

Tinny Tiny Tinker, illustrated by David Cowe. Auckland, Shortland, 1986.

The Tree Doctor, illustrated by Wendy Hodder. Auckland, Heinemann, 1986.

Trouble on the Bus, illustrated by Wendy Hodder. Auckland, Heinemann, 1986.

The Trouble with Heathrow, illustrated by Rodney McRae. Auckland, Heinemann, 1986.

A Very Happy Birthday, illustrated by Elizabeth Fuller. Auckland, Shortland, and Leeds, Arnold Wheaton, 1986.

Tai Taylor and His Education, illustrated by Nick Price. Auckland, Heinemann, 1986-87.

Tai Taylor and the Sweet Annie, illustrated by Nick Price. Auckland, Heinemann, 1986-87.

Tai Taylor Goes to School, illustrated by Nick Price. Auckland, Heinemann, 1986-87.

Tai Taylor Is Born, illustrated by Nick Price. Auckland, Heinemann, 1986-87.

Elliott and the Cats Eating Out. Auckland, Heinemann, 1987.

The Girl Who Washed in Moonlight, illustrated by Robyn Belton. Auckland, Heinemann, 1987.

Guinea Pig Grass, illustrated by Kelvin Hawley. Auckland, Shortland, 1987.

The Haunting of Miss Cardamon, illustrated by Korky Paul. Auckland, Heinemann, 1987.

Iris La Bonga and the Helpful Taxi Driver, illustrated by Vicki Smillie-McItoull. Auckland, Heinemann, 1987.

The Mad Puppet, illustrated by Jon Davis. Auckland, Heinemann, 1987.

The Man Who Walked on His Hands, illustrated by Martin Bailey. Auckland, Shortland, 1987.

No Dinner for Sally, illustrated by John Tarlton. Auckland, Shortland, 1987.

As Luck Would Have It, illustrated by Deidre Gardiner. Auckland, Shortland, 1988.

A Not-So-Quiet Evening, illustrated by Glenda Jones. Auckland, Shortland, 1988.

Sarah, The Bear and the Kangaroo, illustrated by Elizabeth Fuller. Auckland, Shortland, 1988.

When the King Rides By. Glasgow, Thornes, 1988.

The Blood and Thunder Adventure on Hurricane Peak, illustrated by Wendy Smith. London, Dent, 1989.

The Great White Man-Eating Shark: A Cautionary Tale, illustrated by Jonathan Allen. New York, Dial, 1990.

Making Friends, illustrated by Wendy Smith. New York, McElderry, 1990.

Seven Chinese Brothers, illustrated by Jean and Mou-sien Tseng. New York, Scholastic, 1990.

Dangerous Spaces. New York, Viking, 1991.

Keeping House. New York, Macmillan, 1991.

Pumpkin Man and the Crafty Creeper. New York, Greenwillow, 1991.

The Queen's Goat, illustrated by Emma Chichester Clark. New York, Dial Press, 1991.

The Horrendous Hullabaloo, illustrated by Patricia MacCarthy. New York, Viking, 1992.

Underrunners. New York, Viking, 1992.

The Good Fortunes Gang, illustrated by Marion Young. New York, Delacorte, 1993.

A Busy Day for a Good Grandmother, illustrated by Margaret Chamberlain. London, Hamish Hamilton, and New York, Margaret K. McElderry Books, 1993.

The Rattlebang Picnic, illustrated by Steven Kellogg. New York, Dial Books for Young Readers, 1994.

The Christmas Tree Tangle, illustrated by Anthony Kerins. New York, Margaret K. McElderry Books, and Toronto, Maxwell Macmillan Canada, 1994.

The Greatest Show Off Earth, illustrated by Wendy Smith. New York, Viking, 1994.

Tick Tock Tales: Stories to Read around the Clock, illustrated by Wendy Smith. New York, Margaret K. McElderry Books, 1994.

Tingleberries, Tuckertubs and Telephones: A Tale of Love and Ice-cream, illustrated by Robert Staermosc. New York, Viking, 1995.

The Five Sisters, illustrated by Patricia MacCarthy. New York, Viking, 1996.

Boom, Baby, Boom, Boom, illustrated by Patricia MacCarthy. New York, Viking, 1997.

Screenplays: Adaptor, *The Haunting of Barrey Palmer* (based on *The Haunting*). New Zealand, 1987.

Television Scripts: *A Land Called Happy Wooly Valley, Once upon a Story,* and *The Margaret Mahy Story Book Theatre.*

Poetry

Seventeen Kings and Forty Two Elephants, illustrated by Charles Mozley. London, Dent, 1972; revised edition edited by Phyllis J. Fogelman with illustrations by Patricia MacCarthy, New York, Dial Press, 1987.

The Tin Can Band and Other Poems, illustrated by Honey de Lacey. London, Dent, 1989.

Collections

The First Margaret Mahy Story Book: Stories and Poems, illustrated by Shirley Hughes. London, Dent, 1972.

The Second Margaret Mahy Story Book: Stories and Poems, illustrated by Shirley Hughes. London, Dent, 1973.

The Third Margaret Mahy Story Book: Stories and Poems, illustrated by Shirley Hughes. London, Dent, 1975.

The Great Chewing-Gum Rescue and Other Stories, illustrated by Jan Ormerod. London, Dent, 1982.

Leaf Magic and Five Other Favourites, illustrated by Margaret Chamberlain. London, Dent, 1984.

The Downhill Crocodile Whizz and Other Stories, illustrated by Ian Newsham. London, Dent, 1986.

Mahy Magic: A Collection of the Most Magical Stories from the Margaret Mahy Story Books, illustrated by Shirley Hughes. London, Dent, 3 vols., 1986.

The Horrible Story and Others, illustrated by Shirley Hughes. London, Dent, 1987.

The Door in the Air and Other Stories, illustrated by Diana Catchpole. London, Dent, 1988; New York, Delacorte, 1991.

Chocolate Porridge and Other Stories, illustrated by Shirley Hughes. London, Puffin, 1989.

Bubble Trouble and Other Poems and Stories, illustrated by Margaret Mahy. New York, Macmillan, 1992.

The Girl With the Green Ear: Stories About Magic in Nature, illustrated by Shirley Hughes. New York, Knopf, 1992.

A Tall Story and Other Tales, illustrated by Jan Nesbitt. New York, Macmillan, 1992.

Nonfiction

New Zealand: Yesterday and Today. London, Watts, 1975.

*

Media Adaptations: *The Haunting* (cassette), G.K. Hall, 1986; *The Chewing Gum Rescue and Other Stories* (cassette), G.K. Hall, 1988; *The Pirate's Mixed-Up Voyage* (cassette), G.K. Hall; *Nonstop Nonsense.* (cassette), G.K. Hall.

Biography: Essay in *Authors and Artists for Young Adults,* Volume 8, Detroit, Gale, 1992.

Manuscript Collections: J.M. Dent and Sons Ltd., London.

Critical Studies: Entry in *Children's Literature Review,* Volume 7, Detroit, Gale, 1984.

*   *   *

The opening sentence of Margaret Mahy's *Aliens in the Family* gives as good a summary of the author's theory of fiction as is to be found in all the pages of criticism that have so far been written about this prolific and engaging writer of literature for children and young adults: "Even the most ordinary days can be full of secrets and mysteries...." Indeed, if one can take her fiction as an accurate measure, Mahy sees fantastic possibilities in almost all of life. The work of this librarian-turned-writer is often referred to as "Mahy Magic," an alliterative reference to the many fantastical elements that appear in much of her work for young adults. The appellation also does double duty in describing the artistic nature of her writing, for, indeed, there is a magical, a lyrical, a poetical quality to her work, which ranges from children's picture books to problem novels with threads of the supernatural expertly woven into the fabric of the story. The author's energy, zest, and imagination are evident from just a cursory glance at the catalogue of her published works: more than one hundred books with titles ranging from the fanciful (*An Elephant in the House, The Great Piratical Rumbustification*) to the alliterative (*Raging Robots and Unruly Uncles, Tinny Tiny Tinker*) to the provocative (*The Changeover: A Supernatural Romance, Catalogue of the Universe*).

Mahy's style in her young adult books is essentially to take a realistic theme within a family setting and to supercharge it with fantastical or supernatural elements; this she does expertly in *Aliens in the Family.* The story concerns a seemingly normal New Zealand family that is invaded by aliens, both literally and figuratively. As the story unfolds, we meet David Raven and his newly acquired family: Philippa, his wife; Dora and Lewis, his stepchildren. Then enters the figurative alien: Jake, his tomboyish daughter from a previous marriage whose rough exterior is decidedly at odds with Dora's fluffy, beauty-shop persona. The appearance of Bond, the real alien, interjects a supernatural dimension to the plot and gives the fractious Raven children something to focus on besides their own internecine conflicts. Bond, who is an information gatherer from another world, has traveled through space and back through time to absorb information about late twentieth-century culture in New Zealand. He is being pursued by dark and mysterious forces who want to gain access to Bond's database for their own nefarious purposes. In the process of helping Bond, the family, in fact, helps itself. There is something about this process that allows grace to flood into the family, so that the alien becomes not just a supernatural trick but a metaphor graphically portraying the movement of goodness in ordinary lives. In this sense, Mahy is not unlike the adult author Flannery O'Connor who distorted reality in another away—toward the grotesque—in an effort to get her readers to see more clearly the relationships between her characters and the forces (social, historical, religious) which propel them along to their destinies.

The alien in this case is typical of most of Mahy's supernatural characters in that rather than being threatening or frightening, he is appealing and engaging. In fact, most of her supernatural characters are ordinary persons who have supernatural characteristics added to their personalities. This was very much the case in *The Haunting,* Mahy's first young adult novel which earned her her first Carnegie medal. This story seems a simple fantasy at the outset, the tale of a young boy who has inherited a family tendency toward wizardry from a shadowy uncle no one has heard from for years but who was known to have the same magical powers the young boy seems to possess. However, in a masterful twist toward the end of the book, we discover that it is the boy's older sister who actually has the magical powers; she has used the powers to create for the boy the impression that he has magical abilities, thus drawing attention away from her own mysterious self. But the twisting is not over yet. We further discover that it is the grandmother, a fractious but seemingly harmless old lady, who is the most malevolent power holder in the family. Because it invests its female characters with so much power, the story has been applauded by many critics as being a feminist breakthrough in young adult fiction.

Like other literary stylists before her, Mahy makes frequent and effective use of the ironical device of juxtaposing opposites as a means of revealing the deeper truth inherent in both extremes, thereby casting a bright and incisive light on the beauty and ambiguity of the whole. This device is particularly evident in *Memory,* the story of a young man haunted by the death of his sister. His memory of the accidental death, which occurred when the two of them plus his sister's best friend were playing near a precipice, is in fragments as a result of the emotional trauma. For several years the event has haunted him to the point of alcoholism and, as the story opens, he is beginning a desperate search to piece the tragic event back together in an effort to purge his guilt. He finds unexpected help in the person of an elderly woman whose memory is being ravaged by Alzheimer's disease.

In *The Changeover: A Supernatural Romance,* which also won a Carnegie medal, Mahy tells the story of a fourteen-year-old girl with psychic powers. She has a romance with a boy some four years older than she, but the real story here is the heroine's decision to become a witch in order to protect her younger brother from school bullies. In *The Catalogue of the Universe* Mahy eschews the overtly fantastical to tell a story that is pretty fantastic on its nonsupernatural merits. Angela, the daughter of an unwed mother, is a ravishing eighteen-year-old whose best friend, Tycho, is very odd looking and self-conscious. Angela's mother neither wants nor needs a man in her life, but Angela is determined to learn more about her father. Tycho helps her and in the process Angela comes to realize that her feelings for him have gone beyond friendship.

As was previously noted, Mahy writes some books that are clearly aimed at children and others that are clearly aimed at young adults. Between these two extremes is a broad literary estuary where Mahy writes wildly fantastical, whimsical tales which can be appreciated by children, young adults, and adults. Representative of this category is *The Birthday Burglar and a Very Wicked Headmistress,* a slight novel in which Mahy creates an alliterative tour-de-force. Rendered with wit, whimsy, and extraordinary literary finesse, the story concerns a boy named Bassington who lives on Barleycorn Island where he is cared for by a butler named Baker. Bassington has everything he could possibly want except a birthday as his neglectful parents (a bank robber and a black sheep) failed to give him one. So Bassington—travelling by hot air balloon—begins stealing birthdays in a nearby town. The children whose birthdays are stolen are upset, but Bassington might have gotten away with the deed had he not stolen the birthday of ninety-nine-year-old Mrs. Herringbone. She had been anxiously awaiting her "Happy Hundredth Birthday" message from the Queen, but with no birthday to celebrate there will be no message. So Mrs. Herringbone rouses the children to action and plans are laid to thwart the birthday burglar. By the time the final chapter ("Bliss for Baker, Bright Beginnings for Bassington—Happy Birthday Everyone") is reached, the burglar is reformed, and everyone is having a rollicking good time, including the reader.

Mahy is obviously fascinated by the supernatural and the fantastic; however, she refrains from writing books that are fantasies in a vacuum. In her books for young adults, Mahy uses fantasy as a light to illuminate aspects of our so-called ordinary lives. The ordinary lives Mahy writes about are those with which children in the late twentieth century can readily identify: they are the lives of children who live in homes ranging from happy and whole to homes headed by divorced parents or parents who are single by choice. In her books for children at the lower end of the young adult age range, Mahy uses fantasy as a tool to explore the wildest possibilities of the human imagination. Mahy writes with power and intelligence; she invests her characters with dignity, wit, and enormous appeal, and, in the process, she gives her readers an often wild and exhilarating ride through her unpredictable universe.

—Bill Buchanan

MAJOR, Kevin (Gerald)

Nationality: Canadian. **Born:** Stephenville, Newfoundland, 12 September 1949. **Education:** Memorial University of Newfoundland, St. John's, B.Sc. 1973. **Family:** Married Anne Crawford in 1982; two sons. **Career:** Teacher, Roberts Arm, Newfoundland, 1971-72, and Carbonear, Newfoundland, 1973; teacher of special education and biology, Eastport Central High School, Newfoundland, 1974-76; writer, since 1976. Substitute teacher, since 1976-88. **Awards:** Children's Literature Prize from Canada Council, and Ruth Schwartz Children's Book award from Ruth Schwartz Charitable Foundation and Ontario Arts Council, both 1978, Canadian Association of Children's Librarians Book-of-the-Year Award, 1979, Hans Christian Andersen Honor List, International Board on Books for Young People, and *School Library Journal* Best Books of the Year list, both 1980, all for *Hold Fast;* Canadian Young Adult Book award from the Young Adult Caucus of the Saskatchewan Library Association, and *School Library Journal* Best Books of the Year list, both 1981, for *Far from Shore;* Young Adult Canadian Book award runner-up, 1990, for *Blood Red Ochre;* Book-of-the-Year award, Canadian Association of Children's Librarians, and Ann Conner Brimer award, both 1992, both for *Eating Between the Lines;* Vicky Metcalf award for outstanding body of work for children in Canada, 1992. **Agent:** Westwood Creative Artists, 94 Harbord St., Toronto, Ontario M5S 1G6, Canada. **Address:** 27 Poplar Avenue, St. John's, Newfoundland A1B 1C7, Canada; web site: www.newcomm.net/kmajor; e-mail: kmajor@thezone.net.

PUBLICATIONS FOR YOUNG ADULTS

Fiction

Hold Fast. Toronto, Clarke, Irwin, 1978; New York, Delacorte, 1980.
Far from Shore. Toronto, Clarke, Irwin, 1980; New York, Delacorte, 1981.
Thirty-six Exposures. New York, Delacorte, 1984.
Dear Bruce Springsteen. Toronto, Doubleday, 1987; New York, Delacorte, 1987; London, Viking Kestrel, 1989.
Blood Red Ochre. Toronto, Doubleday, and New York, Delacorte, 1989.
Eating between the Lines. Toronto, Doubleday, 1991.
Diana: My Autobiography. Toronto, Doubleday, 1993.

Other

Editor and contributor of illustrations, *Doryloads: Newfoundland Writings and Art.* Portugal Cove, Newfoundland, Breakwater Books, 1974.

PUBLICATION FOR ADULTS

Terra Nova National Park: Human History Study, with James A. Tuck. Ottawa, Parks Canada, 1983.
No Man's Land (novel). Toronto, Doubleday, 1995.
Gaffer (novel). Toronto, Doubleday, 1997.

PUBLICATIONS FOR CHILDREN

The House of Wooden Santas. Red Deer, Red Deer College Press, 1997.

*

Biography: *Speaking for Myself: Canadian Writers in Interview* edited by Andrew Garrod, Breakwater Books, 1986; entry in *Dictionary of Literary Biography,* Volume 60: *Canadian Writers since 1960, Second Series,* Detroit, Gale, 1987; essay in *Speaking for Ourselves: Autobiographical Sketches by Notable Authors of Books for Young Adults,* Volume 1, compiled and edited by Donald R. Gallo, National Council of Teachers of English, 1990.

Critical Studies: Entry in *Contemporary Literary Criticism,* Volume 26, Detroit, Gale, 1983; entry in *Children's Literature Review,* Volume 11, Detroit, Gale, 1986, pp. 123-133; entry in *Contemporary Authors New Revision Series,* Vol. 38, Detroit, Gale, 1993; *Meet the Authors and Illustrators* by Deborah Kovacs, Vol. 2, Scholastic, 1993; *Meet Canadian Authors and Illustrators* edited by Allison Gertridge, Scholastic Canada, 1994; *Writing Stories, Making Pictures* edited by Stacey Noyes and Nancy Pearson, Canadian Children's Book Centre, 1994; *Children's Voices in Atlantic Literature and Culture* edited by Hilary Thompson, Canadian Children's Press, 1996.

Kevin Major comments:

I see my audience as both young people and adults. Each new book I like to be fresh in style and content—a challenge for me to write and offering something of the unexpected to the reader. I find it's the reinventing of myself as author that keeps me in front of the blank screen.

*   *   *

Kevin Major's first novel, *Hold Fast,* met immediate critical acclaim in Canada and received a number of national awards. Such a beginning could have lured the novice author into repeating a successful formula. Instead, Major has deliberately challenged himself by departing markedly from *Hold Fast*'s style in each of his six subsequent novels. By doing this successfully, Major has established himself as one of Canada's premier writers for adolescents.

Hold Fast begins and ends with death. When fourteen-year-old Michael's parents are accidentally killed, Michael and his younger brother Brent are separated. Brent remains with Aunt Flo and Grandfather while Michael moves to the city to live with his aunt and uncle and their two teenage children, Curtis and Marie. Curtis and Michael, who initially share few common interests, gradually discover mutual concerns, including a growing dislike for Curtis's dictatorial father. Michael's environment becomes increasingly unbearable, reaching crisis proportions following a school incident in which Michael accidentally injures another student. Uncle Ted orders an expelled Michael to apologize to the victim. Unwilling to accept further injustices in this overly controlled house, Michael runs away to his old home and, surprisingly, is joined by Curtis. Death, which separated the brothers, reunites them: Grandfather's death allows Michael to remain with Aunt Flo and Brent. Curtis returns to his father with no guarantee that the message inherent in his running away has been heard.

Far from Shore follows Chris, fifteen, over an eleven-month period as his life and family disintegrate. Chris's father, unable to find work in Newfoundland, seeks employment in Alberta. Without his father's influence, Chris's behaviour deteriorates. He fails grade ten, and his increased drinking causes him to lose his old friends whom he replaces with an older, tougher crowd. Following one drunken spree, Chris is charged with vandalizing the local school. Given an opportunity to redeem himself as a summer camp counsellor, Chris displays poor judgment and almost kills a young camper. Sobered by the incident, Chris, at the book's conclusion, resumes his schooling while his father returns to seek work or to take the family to Alberta. The book's impact is enhanced by Major's multinarrator technique which involves five characters.

Each of the thirty-six chapters in *Thirty-six Exposures* serves as a snapshot revealing a side of seventeen-year-old Lorne, who is concluding grade twelve in Marten, Newfoundland. When Lorne's friend Trevor is unjustly suspended from Mr. Ryan's history class, the normally shy Lorne leads a classroom strike and a school walkout until Trevor is reinstated. Beginnings include Lorne's not using his valedictory address as a vehicle of revenge against Mr. Ryan, and a romance with Elaine wherein sex and love become confused. Endings involve not only school and changed relationships with parents, but Trevor's accidental death. Not wanting to find himself saying at age sixty-five, "If only. . . ," Lorne questions conforming to the pattern of further education, marriage, and local employment.

Dear Bruce Springsteen is the salutation of fifty-one letters that fourteen-year-old Terry Blanchard directs to the rock superstar over a seven-month period. While the letters treat many of Terry's egocentric problems—poor grades, girl anxieties, physique—the theme of a boy trying to "find" his father runs through the unanswered correspondence. Abandoned by his father some six months before, Terry lives in an apartment with his working mother and younger sister. Despite Terry's father's leaving to play in a country music band, Terry defends him against his mother's criticisms. Home tensions increase when Terry buys a guitar and his mother fears his father's "dreamer" pattern is being repeated. The longest letter, a nine-pager, describes Terry's physical journey to seek out his father and their discovery of each other.

Blood Red Ochre utilizes a pair of fifteen-year-old narrators who alternate chapters in relating two stories, one contemporary, the other historic, which merge at the book's conclusion via time fantasy elements. David, from present day Marten, Newfoundland, is coping with his discovery that the man he calls father is not his birth father; Dauoodaset, a nineteenth-century Beothuk, is struggling with fellow tribe members to survive a harsh winter in an area yet unsettled by whites whose diseases and guns have decimated Newfoundland's indigenous people. Each youth embarks on a journey, one to discover a father; the other to find food to provide a future for his starving people. Each meets disappointment. Uniting the two stories is Nancy/Shanawdithit. To David, Nancy is the school's new, mysterious dark complexioned girl, someone he finds romantically interesting; to Dauoodaset, Shanawdithit is his future wife and mother to his children. In the book's penultimate chapter, Shanawdithit/Nancy becomes the narrator as David is swept into the past to be present when Dauoodaset is killed on Red Ochre Island by a white settler. Though David's story will hold readers' interest, the tragic tale of Dauoodaset's heroic struggle and Shanawdithit's inability to change the past will grab readers' emotions.

Eating between the Lines, Major's first venture into humour, won him his second Canadian Library Association Book of the Year award. Jackson, sixteen, faces a double-barrelled dose of romance problems. While his parents' marriage has lost its romance, Jackson cannot find any with Sara, the girl of his dreams and fantasies. Informed by his mother that she intends to leave her husband who is mired in a methodical, dull job, Jackson attempts to prevent his parents' separation while simultaneously trying to separate Sara from boyfriend Adam. Jackson unknowingly acquires the magical vehicle for achieving both ends when, as the "028th" customer of "Masterpizza," a restaurant run by an ex-librarian, he receives the grand opening prize, a pizza-shaped gold medal. Later, Jackson accidentally discovers that holding the medal in one hand while making contact with more gold completes a circuit that carries him into the setting and action of whatever he is reading. Jackson's visits into *The Odyssey, The Adventures of Huckleberry Finn, Romeo and Juliet,* plus his mother's journal, ultimately resolve everyone's problems in fun-filled ways.

Diana: My Autobiography, another humorous read, features Major's first female central character, his fictional about-to-enter-junior-high daughter who is obsessed with the Royal Family. Reading Andrew Morton's *Diana: Her True Story* gives Major's Diana the idea of writing her own autobiography. The preteen's overwritten version of her own "true" story is hilarious in its egocentrism. When an English boy, Willard Smith, and his family spend the summer in St. John's, Newfoundland, Diana's overactive imagination leads her to conclude that Will is really disguised royalty and that she, naturally, is to be his future bride. Each chapter consists of two parts: the first, in italics, is the autobiographical entry while the rest of the chapter, in ordinary type, chronicles Diana's everyday life as seen through her royal-coloured glasses.

—David Jenkinson

MARK, Jan(et Marjorie)

Nationality: British. **Born:** Janet Marjorie Brisland in Welwyn, Hertfordshire, 22 June 1943. **Education:** Ashford Grammar School, Kent, 1954-61; Canterbury College of Art, 1961-65, National Diploma in Design 1965. **Family:** Married Neil Mark in 1969 (divorced 1989); one daughter and one son. **Career:** Teacher, Southfields School, Gravesend, Kent, 1965-71. Writer-in-residence, Oxford Polytechnic, 1982-84. **Awards:** Penguin/*Guardian* award, 1975, and Library Association Carnegie Medal, 1976, both for *Thunder and Lightnings; The Ennead* was named a Notable

Children's Trade Book in the field of social studies by the National Council for Social Studies and the Children's Book Council, 1978; runner-up for Library Association Carnegie Medal, 1981, for *Nothing to Be Afraid Of;* co-winner of Young *Observer*/Rank Teenage Fiction Prize, 1982, for *Aquarius;* Library Association Carnegie Medal, 1983, for *Handles;* Angel Literary award for fiction, 1983, for *Feet,* and 1987, for *Zeno Was Here;* British nominee for International Hans Christian Andersen Medal, 1984; runner-up for *Guardian* award for Children's Fiction, 1986, for *Trouble Halfway.* **Agent:** David Higham Associates Ltd, 5/8 Lower John Street, Golden Square, London W1R 4HA, England. **Address:** 98 Howard Street, Oxford OX4 3BG, England.

PUBLICATIONS FOR YOUNG ADULTS

Fiction

Thunder and Lightnings, illustrated by Jim Russell. London, Kestrel, 1976; New York, Crowell, 1979.
Under the Autumn Garden, illustrated by Colin Twinn. London, Kestrel, 1977; New York, Crowell, 1979.
The Ennead. London, Kestrel, and New York, Crowell, 1978; translated into Spanish as *La eneada,* Mexico City, Espasa-Calpe : Consejo Nacional para la Cultura y las Artes,1990.
Divide and Rule. London, Kestrel, 1979; New York, Crowell, 1980.
Aquarius. London, Kestrel, 1982; New York, Atheneum, 1984.
Handles. London, Kestrel, 1983; New York, Atheneum, 1985.
Trouble Half-Way, illustrated by David Parkins. London, Viking Kestrel, 1985; New York, Atheneum, 1986.
At the Sign of the Dog and Rocket. London, Longman, 1985.
Dream House. London, Viking Kestrel, 1987.
Man in Motion, illustrated by Jeff Cummins. London, Viking Kestrel, 1989; translated into French as *Allo, c'est moi,* Paris, Gallimard jeunesse, 1992.
The Hillingdon Fox. Turton and Chambers, 1991.
Great Frog and Mighty Moose. London, Walker, 1992.
A Fine Summer Knight, illustrated by Bob Harvey. London, Viking, 1995.
My Frog and I. London, Reed, 1997.
The Sighting. London, Viking, 1997.

Short Stories

Nothing to Be Afraid Of, illustrated by David Parkins. London, Kestrel, 1980; New York, Harper, 1981.
Hairs in the Palm of the Hand, illustrated by Jan Ormerod. London, Kestrel, 1981; as *Bold as Brass,* London, Hutchinson, 1984.
Feet and Other Stories, illustrated by Bert Kitchen. London, Kestrel, 1983.
Frankie's Hat, illustrated by Quentin Blake. London, Viking Kestrel, 1986.
Enough Is Too Much Already and Other Stories. London, Bodley Head, 1988.
A Can of Worms. London, Bodley Head, 1990.
Finders, Losers. New York, Orchard, 1990; London, Lion, 1991.
In Black and White. London, Viking, 1991.
Do You Read Me? Eight Stories. London, Heinemann/New Windmills, 1994.
They Do Things Differently There. London, Bodley Head, 1994.

Plays

Izzy (televised 1983). London, Longman, 1985.
Interference (televised 1986). London, Longman, 1987.
Captain Courage and the Rose Street Gang, with Stephen Cockett. London, Collins, 1987.
Time and the Hour; and, *Nothing to Be Afraid Of: Two Plays by Jan Mark.* London, Longman, 1990.

Other

Editor, *School Stories.* New York, Kingfisher, 1989.
Editor, *The Puffin Book of Song and Dance.* London, Viking, 1992.
Editor, *The Oxford Book of Children's Stories.* London and New York, Oxford, 1993.

Reteller, *God's Story: How God Made Humankind,* illustrated by David Parkins. London, Walker, 1997; Cambridge, Massachusetts, Candlewick, 1998.

PUBLICATIONS FOR CHILDREN

The Short Voyage of the Albert Ross, illustrated by Gavin Rowe. London, Granada, 1980.
The Long Distance Poet, illustrated by Steve Smallman. Cambridge, Dinosaur, 1982.
The Dead Letter Box, illustrated by Mary Rayner. London, Hamish Hamilton, 1982.
Fur, illustrated by Charlotte Voake. London, Walker, and New York, Harper, 1986.
Out of the Oven, illustrated by Antony Maitland. London, Viking Kestrel, 1986.
Fun, illustrated by Michael Foreman. London, Gollancz, 1987.
The Twig Thing, illustrated by Sally Holmes. London, Viking, 1988.
Strat and Chatto, illustrated by David Hughes. London, Walker, 1989.
The Snow Maze, illustrated by Jan Ormerod. London, Walker, 1992.
All the Kings and Queens, illustrated by Lis Toft. London, Heinemann, 1993.
Fun with Mrs. Thumb, illustrated by Nicola Bayley. Cambridge, Massachusetts, Candlewick, 1993; translated into Spanish as *Cric, crac, catacrac,* Barcelona, Lumen, 1993.
Carrot Tops and Cotton Tails, illustrated by Tony Ross. London, PictureLions, and New York, Atheneum, 1993.
This Bowl of Earth, illustrated by Gay Shephard. London, Waler, 1993.
Harriet's Turn, illustrated by Jane Cope. Harlow, Longman, 1994.
Haddock, illustrated by Fiona Moodie. Hemel Hempstead, Simon & Schuster, 1994.
Taking the Cat's Way Home, illustrated by Paul Howard. London, Walker, 1994.
A Worms-Eye View, illustrated by Jan Smith. London, Picadilly, 1994.
Under the Red Elephant, illustrated by Jeffrey Reid. London, HarperCollins, 1995.
The Tale of Tobias, illustrated by Rachel Merriman. London, Walker, 1996.
The Coconut Quins, illustrated by Anna C. Leplar. London, Viking, 1997.

PUBLICATIONS FOR ADULTS

Novels

Two Stories, illustrated by Clive King. Oxford, Inky Parrot Press, 1984.
Zeno Was Here. London, Cape, and New York, Farrar Straus, 1987.

*

Media Adaptations: *The Dead Letter Box* (cassette), Puffin/Cover to Cover, 1987; *Frankie's Hat, Hairs on the Palm of the Hand,* and *Nothing to Be Afraid Of* (cassettes), Chivers Press, 1987, 1988, and 1989; *Izzy* (television movie), 1983; *Interference* (television movie), 1986; *Handles* (television movie), 1989; *If You Meet a Fairy* (television play), 1997.

Interviews: "Read," Mark, Learn, in *Times Education Supplement,* 3 June 1983, 37; "Authorgraph No. 25: Jan Mark," in *Books for Keeps,* March 1984, 12-13.

Critical Studies: "Whatever Happened to Jan Mark?" by Peter Hunt, in *Signal,* January 1980, 11-19; "Jan Mark," by Winifred Whitehead, in *The Use of English,* spring 1982, 32-39; "Letters from England: A Mark of Distinction," by Peter Hunt, in *Horn Book,* September-October 1984, 665-670; Entry in *Children's Literature Review,* Volume 11, Detroit, Gale, 1986.

*   *   *

Jan Mark's novels and short stories for young adults are notable for unconventional themes and a variety of styles. A prolific author whose work ranges from picture books to adult novels, Mark's writings for young adults contain some of her best work.

The most controversial novels Mark has written comprise an informal trilogy. *The Ennead, Divide and Rule,* and *Aquarius* all consider issues of friendship and betrayal and offer a bleak perspective on how people manipulate each other.

Set in the future, *The Ennead* depicts a society where the primary motivation for action is self-preservation. The desolate planet Erato has solved its unemployment problem by banishing the unproductive. But the arrival of a sculptor unwilling to sacrifice her artistic integrity challenges the prevailing social controls and causes the adolescent protagonist Isaac to reconsider his values.

Divide and Rule explores the repressive aspects of institutional religion. Eighteen-year-old Hanno, a self-proclaimed unbeliever, is nevertheless selected to spend a year as the temple's ritual shepherd. Increasingly horrified by his discoveries about how religious leaders manipulate the gullible population, Hanno finds he cannot outwit those who consistently turn his words and actions against him.

In her third book for young adults, *Aquarius,* Mark deliberately set out to subvert the reader's identification with the main character, Viner. After establishing sympathy for him when he is forced to flee his rain-soaked country for a kingdom paralyzed by drought, Mark reveals Viner as a character with no moral scruples. Viner uses his powers to find water to secure a position of power and supplants the rain-king Morning Light. Unable to express his growing love for the king, he then tricks the king into returning to his water-soaked homeland.

The themes of these books seem to blur the boundaries between writing for young adults and adults. *At the Sign of the Dog and Rocket,* however is clearly written for young adults. It describes a series of misadventures when Lilian Goodwin has to manage the family pub with the help of a student teacher, Tom Collins, whom she had bedeviled when he taught her class. Their wariness and animosity develop into friendship as Tom demonstrates his ability with both customers and Lilian's disobedient younger siblings.

In other novels Mark has experimented with narrative style. *Man in Motion,* for example, records numerous telephone conversations that document the adjustments Lloyd must make following his move from a village to a large city school with a racially diverse population. Lloyd's diminishing conversations with his former friends reveal a divergence of interests and show how people can grow apart. Lloyd's insights into other cultures expand his awareness of different ways of life.

In *The Hillingdon Fox,* Mark includes journal entries of two brothers. In 1990, Hugh Marshall begins a diary on his seventeenth birthday, when Saddam Hussein invades Kuwait. Hugh's observations alternate with excerpts from the journal his older brother Gerald kept in 1982 during the Falklands' war, when Gerald had been eighteen. The commentary on the political situation intertwines with discussions of school and family, and the complex plot lines converge in Gerald's desperate attempts to enlist Hugh in recovering a time capsule that had been buried when Gerald was in school.

While Gerald and Hugh offer two perceptions of the same people at different time periods, *Finders, Losers* includes accounts by six young people whose lives intersect in various ways on a single day. All the characters are connected in some way to Shapton College, where much of the action occurs. However, each person can provide only one interpretation of events, and the reader must figure out how the lives of the people intersect.

In addition to her novels, Mark has written numerous short stories which reveal her facility with humor, her ability to create suspense, and her insights into human relationships. The collection *Enough Is Too Much Already* includes a series of stories told by three friends, Maurice, Nazzer, and Nina. Their re-creation of incidents at school and home contain both humorous anecdotes and wry commentary on their own lives, particularly their ability to draw on the inexhaustible supply of useless information they are amassing in preparation for re-sits of exams. The first and last stories provide a frame of sorts since both deal with Maurice's failure to meet Nazzer and Nina at a disco as he had promised.

Most of Mark's collections are less interconnected, although the nine stories of *In Black and White* relate thematically since all deal with the supernatural. "Grow Your Own" describes a compost heap that slowly assumes a life of its own while "Birthday Girl" considers the mysterious yearly appearance of a young girl lying underwater in a bathtub. Mark's tales of ghosts and suspense appear in other collections of her own such as "Resurgam" in *A Can of Worms* as well as in anthologies of stories by many authors. For example, *Shades of Dark,* compiled by Aidan Chambers, contains Mark's "The Gnomon," a tale of revenge based on a betrayal of love.

Some of Mark's best short stories take place in school settings. The masterful "Time and the Hour" in *Hairs in the Palm of the Hand* reveals the useless waste of time that occurs during the school day and includes the surprising revelation for students that at least some teachers share their feelings. "The Choice Is Yours" in *Nothing to Be Afraid Of* describes how a student can be part of a senseless power struggle between adults. Play rehearsals provide the setting for "I Was Adored Once Too" in *Feet and Other Stories.* The poignant juxtaposition of lines from the play with contemporary experience reveals the pain of adolescents uncertain about establishing relationships.

Mark's characters gain insights about others in a variety of places besides school. Indeed, many of her stories involve young adults' acquisition of new perspectives about members of their own families. *You're Late, Dad,* an anthology edited by Tony Bradman, contains "Dan, Dan, the Scenery Man." Attending play practice at a community theater, June sees her reserved father as an indispensable part of the theater company. In fact, all the adults appear so far removed from their everyday occupations that June questions what their "real selves" are. "'Acting isn't just pretending, is it?'" she asks her father.

"Frankie's Hat" chronicles Frankie's seventeenth birthday, which is spent in the company of her younger sister Sonia. Freed from home responsibilities, Frankie quickly assumes the carefree behavior of her pre-marriage days only to revert to a more staid personality in the presence of her husband and baby son. The title story in *A Can of Worms* reveals to Dora her respectable grandmother's kleptomania while "Too Old to Rock and Roll" in the same collection explores how Greg's success in overcoming his widowed father's grief produces unexpected results.

Recently, Mark has concentrated more on books for middle-grade and younger readers. Two collections, *The Oxford Book of Children's Stories* and *God's Story,* are for all ages—including young adults. The latter, a retelling of stories from the Midrash, presents a series of provocative questions and conclusions, starting with creation and ending with the restoration of Jerusalem. Except for *A Fine Summer Knight,* which is not available in the United States, Mark's original fiction of the last few years consists of picture books: *Fun with Mrs. Thumb* and *Silly Tails* have been especially popular on both sides of the Atlantic.

Mark punctuates her stories with plot twists and pungent comments on wide-ranging matters from school bullies to slow-witted tourists to snobs preoccupied with social distinctions. Her high levels of invention and productivity assure her a place of continuing importance in contemporary fiction for young adults.

—Kathy Piehl, updated by Caroline C. Hunt

MARSDEN, John

Nationality: Australian. **Born:** Melbourne, Victoria, Australia, 27 September 1950. **Education:** Mitchell College, Bathurst, Australia, Diploma in Teaching, 1978; University of New England, Armidale, Australia, B.A. 1981. **Career:** English teacher, Geelong Grammar School, Geelong, Victoria, Australia, 1982-90; writer, since 1991. **Awards:** Children's Book of the Year award (Australia), 1988, Premier's award (Victoria), 1988, Young Adult Book award (New South Wales), 1988, Christopher award, 1989, and ALA Notable Book, 1989, all for *So Much to Tell You. . .*; Grand Jury Prize (Vienna), for *Letters from the Inside*; National Children's Book Award (Australia), for *A Killing Frost*; Young

Australians' Book Award and National Multicultural Children's Book Award, for *Tomorrow, When the War Began*; Australian Booksellers Association Book of the Year Award, 1998, for *Burning for Revenge*. **Address:** Level 18, 31 Market St., Sydney 2000, Australia.

PUBLICATIONS FOR YOUNG ADULTS

Fiction

So Much to Tell You. . . . Montville, Walter McVitty, 1988; Boston, Little, Brown, 1989.
The Journey. Sydney, Pan, 1988.
The Great Gatenby. Sydney, Pan, 1989.
Staying Alive in Year 5. Sydney, Piper, 1989.
Out of Time. Pan Australia, 1990.
Letters from the Inside. Chippendale, Pan Macmillan, 1991; Boston, Houghton Mifflin, 1994.
Take My Word for It. Chippendale, Pan Macmillan, 1992.
Looking for Trouble. Chippendale, Pan Macmillan, 1993.
Tomorrow When the War Began. Chippendale, Pan Macmillan, 1993; Boston, Houghton Mifflin, 1995.
The Dead of the Night. Chippendale, Macmillan, 1994; Boston, Houghton Mifflin, 1997.
Cool School: You Make it Happen. Sydney, Pan Macmillan, 1995.
Checkers, Sydney, Macmillan, 1996; Boston, Houghton Mifflin, 1998.
Creep Street. Sydney, Macmillan, 1997.
Darkness, Be My Friend. Sydney, Macmillan, 1996.
The Third Day, the Frost. Sydney, Pan Macmillan, 1996; as *A Killing Frost,* Boston, Houghton Mifflin, 1998.
Burning for Revenge. Sydney, Macmillan, 1997.
Dear Miffy. Sydney, Macmillan, 1997.
The Night is For Hunting. Sydney, Macmillan, 1998.
Norton's Hut. Port Melbourne, Lothian, 1998.
The Rabbits. Port Melbourne, Lothian, 1998.

Other

Everything I Know about Writing. Port Melbourne, Reed Books/ Mandarin, 1993.
So Much to Tell You. . .: the Play. Port Melbourne, McVitty/ Lothian, 1994.
A Prayer for the 21st Century. Port Melbourne, Lothian Books, 1997.
Secret Men's Business. Sydney, Macmillan, 1998.
The 'Tomorrow Series' 1999 Diary. Sydney, Macmillan, 1998.

Editor, *Tomorrow: 20 Visions for the Future.* Sydney, Pan, 1994.
Editor, *For Weddings and a Funeral: Special Poems for Special Occasions.* Sydney, Macmillan, 1996.
Editor, *This I Believe: Over 100 Eminent Australians Explore Life's Big Question.* Milsons Point, Random House, 1996.

*

Media Adaptations: *Letters from the Inside* (audio tape), Sydney, Macmillan, 1997; *Looking For Trouble* (audio tape), Sydney, Macmillan, 1998; *Staying Alive in Year 5* (audio tape), Sydney, Macmillan, 1998.

John Marsden comments:

My books vary a good deal. Most are contemporary, realistic novels dealing with average Australians—though they're often in extraordinary situations. I try to deal with universal experiences, universal feelings. I try to write with a light touch, so that the books are very readable, but there's usually something serious there for the reader to reflect on, too.

A teenager wrote to me recently saying: "When I read your books I feel that you're reading my mind." I certainly aim for authenticity, so I am pleased to get responses like that.

I started writing for teenagers by accident. I was teaching an English class in the mid-eighties and realized with much disappointment that they weren't very interested in reading. When I looked at the books available for them I could understand why. The books didn't seem very interesting compared to computers, videos, and television.

I wrote *So Much to Tell You. . .* for that class, thinking it might have more appeal than some of the titles they had been stuck with. The book had a big impact in Australia and that encouraged me to keep writing for this age group.

Since that time I have sold over a million copies in Australia, a country with a population of only 18 million. The most popular have been the series beginning with *Tomorrow, When the War Began.* I think their popularity comes from the fact that they show teenagers acting bravely, and they encourage readers to see themselves in a heroic light. In their real lives most teenagers nowadays seem to get little opportunity to display courage, responsibility, or initiative, so it is perhaps not surprising that they respond so strongly to a book which attributes these qualities to them.

Some of my books, especially *Letters from the Inside* and *Dear Miffy,* have been very controversial with adults. It's partly because of the swear words in them, partly because of the sex and violence in *Dear Miffy,* but mostly because the books explore dark areas and do not necessarily offer hope for their protagonists. I believe that it is important to shed light on those dark areas, for only by doing so will we relieve the darkness. Adults who build walls around teenagers, trying to protect them from reality, or adults who lie to them, pretending that everything is sweet and lovely, are not doing young people any favours. I'm interested in understanding. I have no brief for ignorance.

*   *   *

John Marsden's years of living and teaching in Australia's private schools have given him the capacity to breathe new life into the venerable form of the boarding school story, extending it to encompass much harsher institutions, and an unparalleled ability to render the language of young adult Australians of both sexes. He is acutely aware of their fears, needs, and aspirations, and understands their ambiguous status as people legally little more than children but physically and mentally little less than adults. Until recently Australian authors for young adults have depicted the relatively secure lives of children of the ordinary people highly valued in an aggressively egalitarian society. Marsden's characters, however, are often the daughters and sons of the wealthy; many of them are children of failed or faltering marriages; and some are members of families in which emotional and physical violence have caused enormous damage. Almost all are candid in discussing their sexuality and that of their peers. Marsden frequently requires his readers to piece together a story from hints and implications; he is drawn to the journal and the letter as ways of controlling the release of information while maintaining interest and suspense.

So Much to Tell You. . . ., Marsden's first novel, is ostensibly the private journal of a fourteen-year-old girl who is an elective mute. Eventually the reader can piece together her story: her face has been scarred by acid intended for her mother, thrown by her father after an acrimonious divorce, and she has come to Warrington School as an alternative to entering a psychiatric institution. The device of the journal allows Marsden to reveal information with the tight control of a thriller-writer, and at the same time to describe the intense, shifting alliances of a girls' dormitory group from the viewpoint of a detached observer. Marina's withdrawal slowly alters to a limited trust, and her growing awareness of the loneliness and the difficulties of her peers enables her to understand that she has much in common with others—even with her father.

Underlying *The Journey* is Marsden's interest in rites of passage from adolescence to adulthood. The novel is set in a vaguely European, pre-industrial society which encourages adolescents of both sexes to leave home on a journey of self-discovery and return with seven stories that will, if accepted in their community, admit them to full adult status. Through experiences of sensual, sexual, and psychological awakening the aptly named Argus learns to see truths of value for all young adults: that the outlines of a fulfilling life for all human beings, even the apparently abnormal, are broadly similar, and that human beings and human problems are usually more complex than they at first appear. Despite the importance of its themes, the generality, occasional didacticism, and obvious symbolism of *The Journey* reduce its emotional impact.

The Great Gatenby returns to the world of the boarding school in the wise-cracking, self-opinionated, first-person narrative of Erle Gatenby, whose parents have made some sacrifices to send him to a private school where, they hope, he will find some sense of direction. He does, but not until he has gone through several scrapes with authority in a funny but fairly predictable narrative. Erle learns some self-discipline: he responds to good coaching, and makes something of his swimming prowess; he learns to see his teachers as people; he meets Melanie, and finds that falling in love with her brings him experiences he did not bargain for.

Technically more demanding, *Out of Time* presents brief descriptions of people who seem to have fallen out of existence: missing persons, orphans whose histories are unknown, children whose early deaths have left their siblings without memory of them. Across these meditative flashes Marsden lays a narrative that uses the well-worn device of a time-machine to enable a young adult narrator, psychologically devastated by blame for his sister's death, to return to the past to help others and, eventually, himself. James cannot change events, but he can bring together separated people and can assure himself of the accuracy of his own memory of his sister's last night alive.

In *Letters from the Inside* Marsden gives new life to the old form of the epistolary novel, exploiting his ear for the language of young Australians and the intimacy of personal letters in a story that questions the comfortable belief that Australian society is relatively free from violence. An advertisement for a pen-pal brings together what appear to be two young women from middle-class households until inconsistencies in one girl's letters provoke questions leading to an admission: Tracey is writing from a penal institution. More than that—she is a leader in its brutal world. Not all of the violence is "inside," however; Mandy's brother is obsessed with firearms and increasingly prone to attack his sister physically. Tracey's tough exterior begins to soften as she finds in Mandy an unsentimental but sympathetic friend whose optimism gives her a reason to rehabilitate herself. But Tracey's long acquaintance with violence also leads her to fear the outcome of Mandy's brother's worsening behaviour. The novel comes to a despairing and controversial end that is all the more chilling because it is implied rather than stated.

With *Tomorrow, When the War Began,* Marsden started something quite different. Teenagers in an Australian country town go on a Christmas-summer camping holiday—a latterday Enid Blyton adventure. But their adult-free idyll soon turns to nightmare when they discover that Australia has been invaded and occupied by a powerful Asian army. Suddenly, terrifyingly, they have become some of the few Australians not yet rounded up by the invaders. So begins a slow, brutal guerrilla campaign, fought by the gaggle of isolated teenagers raiding from their remote wilderness hideout. The story is told by one of the girls. Throughout the adventures there are continual references back to school days, the soap opera world of teenagers and parents and authorities, while boyfriend-girlfriend relationships simmer in the war zone. The business of actually killing other people (usually Asian, usually young and male) is recounted unflinchingly. The teenagers suffer psychologically, perhaps suitably so in this age of counselling and post traumatic shock syndrome, AIDS and safe sex. Marsden always handles controversial material with a teacher-like sense of responsibility. He wants to tell it like it is, but not sensationalise, or condone violence for its own sake.

Though this book has been wildly popular it suffers compared to the best examples of speculative war fiction. The attempt to sketch a larger international context, in which the inept exiled Australian government wrings its hands in anguish and New Zealand mounts a counter-invasion, is handled rather clumsily. Worse, Marsden treats the invading Asian troops as ciphers, not human beings, failing to show one redeeming feature in any of the invaders.

Marsden has written some of the strongest teenage novels in Australia, or elsewhere, and needs to be reckoned with. In 1998 the Australian Booksellers Association recognized Marsden's achievement with its prestigious Book of the Year Award for *Burning for Revenge,* the first time a young adult title won the award in open competition with adult titles.

—John Murray, updated by John Gough

MARTINEZ, Victor

Nationality: American. **Born:** Fresno, California. **Education:** California State University, Fresno. **Career:** Writer. Previously worked as a field laborer, welder, truck driver, fire fighter, office clerk, and teacher. **Awards:** National Book Award for Young People's Literature, 1996; Belpre Author Honor Award, 1998. **Address:** c/o HarperCollins Children's Books, 10 East 53rd St., New York, New York 10022, U.S.A.

PUBLICATIONS FOR YOUNG ADULTS

Parrot in the Oven: mi vida (fiction). New York, HarperCollins, 1996.

PUBLICATIONS FOR ADULTS

Caring for a House (poetry). San Jose, California, Chusma House Publications, 1992.

*　　*　　*

Writing in a highly fluid and poetic style, Victor Martinez has made a significant contribution to the genre of adolescent fiction with his first novel, the award-winning *Parrot in the Oven: mi vida*. In many respects, Martinez shares an artistic and political sensibility with Gary Soto, the author of a number of memorable multi-ethnic coming-of-age narratives in which a young Mexican-American male protagonist loses his innocence, but develops in its place a determination to stave off bitterness and cynicism. Both authors use descriptive and evocative imagery to create a compassionate and realistic portrayal of the Central California region and its people.

Set in Fresno, California during the early 1970s, *Parrot in the Oven* chronicles the maturation of Manuel Hernandez, a fourteen year-old boy who desires more than anything the opportunity to become a vato firme, a respected man. Ostensibly, Manny embarks upon his quest with few role models and with little chance of success. One of four children, he lives in the projects with his drunken, insecure father and his weary mother. While the older Hernandez family members have seemingly resigned themselves to lives of quiet desperation, Manny remains determined to achieve a measure of status and success. This naivete prompts Mr. Hernandez to label Manny a "perico" or "a parrot that complains how hot it is in the shade, while all along he's sitting inside an oven." However, during his ninth grade-year, Manny undergoes a number of life-changing events that, ultimately, provide him with the answer to his quest and enable him to shed the label of "perico."

Perhaps Manny's greatest challenge comes from living with parents and siblings who are addicted to escapism. His father, feeling guilty for being fired from his job, spends his days and nights drinking cheap beer at Rico's, a local pool parlor. When Mrs. Hernandez is not engaged in compulsive cleaning, she sits for hours in front of the television set, creating fantasies in which she is rescued by white actors such as Cary Grant. Nardo, Manny's older brother, is lazy and self-indulgent, and Magda, his older sister, spends all of her earnings on rock 'n roll records that she listens to whenever she is at home. When Manny is given $20.00 for school supplies by a sympathetic teacher, his father takes it and spends it all on alcohol; when Manny is invited to the birthday party of his white employer's daughter, he is harrassed and driven out by her drunken white friends. Everywhere Manny turns, he is forced to confront despair, opposition, and discrimination.

However, like his maternal grandfather before him, Manny is a realist who possesses "useful blood," meaning that he cannot help but to work "like a man trying to fill all of his tomorrows with one solid day's work." He picks chili peppers, helps his mother around the house, and earns excellent grades at school. Most importantly, he abhors violence, a trait that spares him from acting out in abusive ways—even when he is the victim of parental and peer abuse.

Manny's character is tested when his desire to gain sexual experience and the status of a vato firme leads him to join a gang run by Eddie, a young man who promises Manny will have access to Rita and Patty, the girls in the gang. Gang membership is often described as a refuge for adolescents who are searching for a sense of family life and a sense of belonging. Although Manny makes it through the initiation, he is sickened by the way Eddie treats his sister Magda and the way that he is able to rob a woman without any remorse or concern. For Manny, joining the gang would simply expose him to the very violence and cynicism that he is trying to avoid at home.

Even though Manny is often treated with contempt, he learns not to view himself or his prospects through others' eyes. It is compassion, not physical strength or selfish aggression, that transforms a boy into a man, a fact that Martinez underscores in the final pages of the novel by equating Manny's return home after deciding to quit the gang to the return of warmth and peace to his household: "Shadows lifted from the floor like a flock of birds rising into the horizon, and light guttered through the room, slapping away dark for good." The metaphor is extended when Manny takes his (rightful) place in his father's chair and gazes sympathetically, and with wonder, upon his home. Manny has lost his innocence, but he has managed to avoid the cynicism and ethical compromise that can often accompany such a change.

Throughout his novel, Martinez is careful to show Manny's situation in a realistic light. While the novel concludes on an optimistic note, the dehabilitating effects of poverty and discrimination are always there in the background, threatening to undermine Manny's life. However, Martinez shows through his portrayal of Manny, that young people are not necessarily prisoners of their environment and are often able to build upon feelings of hope, compassion, and determination.

—Gwen A. Tarbox

MASON, Bobbie Ann

Nationality: American. **Born:** Mayfield, Kentucky, 1 May 1940. **Education:** University of Kentucky, Lexington, 1958-62, B.A. 1962; State University of New York, Binghamton, M.A. 1966; University of Connecticut, Storrs, Ph.D. 1972. **Family:** Married Roger B. Rawlings in 1969. **Career:** Writer, Mayfield *Messenger,* Kentucky, 1960; contributor to magazines *Movie Stars, Movie Life,* and *T.V. Star Parade,* Ideal Publishers, New York, 1962-63; Assistant Professor of English, Mansfield State College, Pennsylvania, 1972-79. **Awards:** National Book Critics Circle award nomination and American Book award nomination, both 1982, PEN-Faulkner award for fiction nomination and Ernest Hemingway Foundation award, both 1983, all for *Shiloh and Other Stories;* National Endowment for the Arts fellowship, 1983; Pennsylvania Arts Council grant, 1983, 1989; Guggenheim fellowship, 1984; American Academy and Institute for Arts and Letters award, 1984; National Book Critics Circle Award nomination and Southern Book Award, both 1994, both for *Feather Crowns.* **Agent:** Amanda Urban, International Creative Management, 40 West 57th Street, New York, New York 10019.

PUBLICATIONS

Novels

In Country. New York, Harper, 1985; London, Chatto and
    Windus, 1986.
Spence + Lila. New York, Harper, 1988; London, Chatto and
    Windus, 1989.
Feather Crowns. New York, Harper, and London, Chatto and
    Windus, 1993.

Short Stories

Landscapes, with Martha Bennett. Monterey, Kentucky, Larkspur
    Press, 1984.
Shiloh and Other Stories. New York, Harper, 1982; London,
    Chatto and Windus, 1985.
Love Life: Stories. New York, Harper, and London, Chatto and
    Windus, 1989.
Midnight Magic: Selected Stories. Princeton, New Jersey, Ecco
    Press, 1998.

Other

*The Girl Sleuth: A Feminist Guide to the Bobbsey Twins, Nancy
    Drew, and Their Sisters.* New York, Feminist Press, 1975.
Nabokov's Garden: A Guide to Ada. Ann Arbor, Michigan,
    Ardis, 1976.

Also contributor of short stories to awards anthologies, including
Best American Short Stories, 1981 and 1983, *The Pushcart Prize,*
1983 and 1997, and *The O. Henry Awards,* 1986 and 1988

*

Media Adaptations: *In Country* (film; directed by Norman
Jewison), 1989.

Biography: Entry in *Dictionary of Literary Biography Yearbook:
1987,* Detroit, Gale, 1988.

Manuscript Collections: University of Kentucky, Lexington.

Critical Studies: Entry in *Contemporary Literary Criticism,* Detroit, Gale, Volume 28, 1984, Volume 43, 1987.

*   *   *

Combining detailed description of everyday western Kentucky
life with her characters' uneasy consideration of larger philosophical issues, Bobbie Ann Mason portrays people's search for individual identity in times of social and personal transition. Some, as
in her story "Nancy Culpepper," turn to their ancestral past for
clues, while others, like nine-year-old Peggy Jo of "Detroit
Skyline, 1949" *(Shiloh and Other Stories)* lack the vocabulary to
define their concerns for themselves, much less express their
conflicts to others.

Mason's stories also emphasize the fragility of modern marriages. Mary Lou and Mack ("The Rookers") find communicating
difficult after their youngest daughter leaves for college. Cleo
("Old Things") worries about her daughter's impending divorce.
After "The Retreat," Georgeann ends her marriage as unemotionally
as she decapitates a sick chicken. Norma Jean ("Shiloh") leaves
Leroy when she realizes that the basis for their marriage is merely
social conformity. Even Nancy ("Lying Doggo") briefly questions the security of her fifteen-year marriage.

Some of Mason's characters face an uncertain future without
the support of tradition. There is no customary Christmas celebration to temper Carolyn's resentment of her constantly bickering
family ("Drawing Names"), and her suspicions of her boyfriend's
unreliability increase her sense of isolation. For others, however,
traditions provide security. When Joe McClain ("Graveyard Day")
fulfills his obligation to clean his family's burial plot, he wins the
trust of Waldeen Murdock and her daughter, Holly. Tradition has
likewise strengthened the Culpeppers' marriage *(Spence + Lila)*;
not even Lila's life-threatening illnesses can separate them permanently from each other or from their land. Likewise tradition has
helped them cope with the divorce of one daughter and the
somewhat unorthodox marriage of the other, just as they have
adjusted to fast-food restaurants, discount stores, shopping malls,
Top-40 radio stations, and the factory where their son now works.

Mason further treats the issues of individual identity and social
change in her short-story collection *Love Life.* This volume too
contains a coming-of-age story, "State Champions," the first-
person narrator's nostalgic account of her schooldays, especially
during the Cuba Cubs' remarkable season; however, generally the
stories in this volume are darker in tone, and most involve some
actual or impending loss. Joann ("Hunktown") must choose
between her husband's ambition to be a musician in Nashville and
her own desire to keep her job and live on her father's farm.
Jeannette ("Big Bertha Stories") must commit her husband to a
mental hospital because their son is terrorized by his father's
stories, which confuse a strip-mining machine with the war
machines in Vietnam. Mental instability also threatens Lynette
Johnson ("Coyotes"), who wonders if someday she may repeat
her mother's suicide attempt. In the title story, Opal has preserved
her equilibrium by avoiding most emotional attachments, but she is
distressed to see that same emotional pattern repeated in the life of
the one person for whom she feels affection.

Not all losses have been openly acknowledged, though. In
"Private Lies" Mickey becomes obsessed with finding the daughter given up for adoption eighteen years ago. After a clandestine
affair, Barbara ("The Secret of the Pyramids") must deal secretly
with her grief and guilt when her lover dies in a traffic accident.
Ruth ("Bumblebees") refuses to grieve openly for her husband
and daughter, killed in a car wreck. The alternating voices of
mother and daughter ("Marita") also deny any loss as they react to
Marita's pregnancy and subsequent abortion.

In Country, Mason's first novel, addresses the concerns of
young adult readers, exploring questions of personal identity and
family relationships. After high school graduation, seventeen-
year-old Samantha ("Sam") Hughes attempts to make sense of
her past so she can determine her future. Her mother, Irene—
recently remarried and living in Lexington—wants Sam to enroll
at the University of Kentucky in the fall, but Sam is contemptuous
of her stepfather and resentful of what she considers her mother's
abandonment. Thus, she insists she will live in Hopewell, commute

to nearby Murray State University, and continue to assume responsibility for her mother's brother, Emmett, a psychologically disabled Vietnam veteran. Through Emmett, Sam meets other Vietnam veterans, and in each she searches for hints of her father's identity. She also examines her father's pictures and letters, but until she reads his long-ignored personal journal, Sam sees no link between her idealistic soldier father and the cynical veterans she knows.

Disillusioned by knowledge of her father, Sam further breaks with the past, initially deciding to deny her paternity by severing all ties with the Hughes family. Sam finds she cannot escape the past, however, until she can accept the flaws in both her biological father, Dwayne, and her surrogate father, Emmett. Understanding requires symbolic reenactment, and finally a healing pilgrimage to the Vietnam Memorial in Washington, D.C.

—Charmaine Allmon Mosby

MATAS, Carol

Nationality: Canadian. **Born:** Winnipeg, Manitoba, 14 November 1949. **Education:** Grant Park High School, Winnipeg, 1963-66; University of Winnipeg Collegiate, 1966-67; York University, Toronto, Ontario, 1967; University of Western Ontario, London, 1968-70, B.A. 1970; Actor's Lab, London, England, 1972. **Family:** Married Per Brask, 1977; one daughter and one son. **Career:** Actress, since 1972. **Awards:** Geoffrey Bilson Award for Historical Fiction for Young People, 1988; Sydney Taylor Book Award, 1989, 1993; Silver Birch Award, 1994; Manitoba Young Reader's Choice Award, 1996; Jewish Book Award, 1996. **Address:** c/o Writers Union of Canada, 24 Ryerson Ave., Toronto, Ontario M5T 2P3, Canada.

PUBLICATIONS FOR YOUNG ADULTS

Lisa. Toronto, Lester & Orpen Dennys, 1987; as *Lisa's War,* New York, Scribner's, 1987.
Jesper. Toronto, Lester & Orpen Dennys, 1989; as *Code Name Kris,* New York, Scribner's, 1990.
The Race. Toronto, HarperCollins, 1991.
Daniel's Story. Toronto and New York, Scholastic, 1993.
Sworn Enemies. Toronto, HarperCollins, 1993.
The Burning Time. Toronto, HarperCollins, and New York, Delacorte, 1994.
The Primrose Path. Winnipeg, Bain & Cox, 1995.
After the War. Richmond Hill, Ontario, Scholastic, and New York, Simon & Schuster, 1996.
The Garden. Toronto, Scholastic, 1997.
The Freak. Toronto, Key Porter, 1997.
Telling. Toronto, Key Porter, 1998.

PUBLICATIONS FOR CHILDREN

The DNA Dimension, illustrations by Greg Ruhl. Toronto, Gage, 1982.
The Fusion Factor. Saskatoon, Fifth House, 1986; as *It's Up to Us,* Toronto, General, 1991.
Zanu. Saskatoon, Fifth House, 1986.

Me, Myself and I. Saskatoon, Fifth House, 1987.
Adventure in Legoland, illustrated by Mark Teague. Richmond Hill, Ontario, Scholastic Canada, 1991.
Safari Adventure in Legoland, illustrated by Elroy Freem. Richmond Hill, Ontario, Scholastic Canada, 1993.
The Lost Locket, illustrations by Susan Gardos. Richmond Hill, Ontario, Scholastic Canada, 1994.
With Perry Nodelman, *Of Two Minds.* Winnipeg, Bain & Cox, 1994.
Greater than Angels. Richmond Hill, Ontario, Scholastic Canada, 1998.

*

Media Adaptations: *Sworn Enemies, Lisa's War, Daniel's Story,* and *The DNA Dimension* have all been recorded on cassette.

*   *   *

Beginning by writing science fiction for younger children, Carol Matas has gone on to author books in a variety of genres and for a wide range of ages, but she is best known for her award-winning historical fiction which has focused on persecuted peoples.

The Second World War and its aftermath have been central to five of Matas's novels. *Lisa* and *Jesper,* a pair of connected novels, revolve about the German occupation of Denmark during World War II. *Lisa* reveals how most Danish Jews were rescued from deportation to German death camps. The narrator, Lisa, a 12-year-old Jewish girl living in Copenhagen, initially finds the German invasion to be a minor inconvenience, but as she becomes more personally aware of the war, especially its violence, she takes up the resistance cause before reluctantly escaping with her family to the safety of Sweden. *Jesper* indirectly continues Lisa's story, for the title character is someone Lisa fell in love with while part of the Danish resistance. Jesper, 17, who has been captured by the Germans and is awaiting execution, discovers that one of his interrogators is Frederik, once an admired mentor and now a committed Nazi. Jesper's attempts to reconcile these two images of his ''friend'' are central to the story, which is largely told via flashbacks.

Matas gives another face to the war via *Daniel's Story,* an emotionally powerful novel that spans the period from 1933 to 1945. Daniel, a 14-year-old Jewish boy living in Frankfurt, Germany, is deported with his parents and younger sister to a series of internment camps including the infamous Auschwitz and Buchenwald. Daniel tells his story via a series of pictures in his mind, pictures which include the deaths of many of his relatives.

Likely numerous adolescents are unaware of war's aftermath and may even assume that with the carnage over, everyone lived ''happily ever after.'' Via a pair of novels, Matas reveals that, for many, the conclusion of the horrors of World War II marked the beginnings of new trials. In *After the War,* when Ruth Mendenberg, a Buchenwald survivor at age 15, returns to her home in Poland, she finds that none of her 80 relatives have apparently survived the Holocaust. Emotionally dead, Ruth allows herself to be recruited by an underground organization involved in the dangerous task of smuggling refugee Jewish children across Europe to Eretz Israel (Palestine). Ruth's story is continued in *The Garden,* which finds her on a kibbutz in Palestine but still not at peace. A United Nation's vote to partition Palestine into two states, one for the

Arabs and the other for Jews, was about to occur, and the area appeared ready to be plunged into war. Ruth becomes a member of the haganah, a group only prepared to fight in defensive causes, while her brother becomes part of the Irgun, radical terrorists. While telling a good story, Matas presents a balanced picture of the political events surrounding Israel's creation.

Sworn Enemies puts a personal face on an historical event little known to North Americans. In an 1827 attempt to assimilate and Christianize Polish Jews who had become "Russian" through conquest, Czar Nicholas I decreed that 18-year-old Jewish males could be drafted into the Russian army for a period of 25 years while 12-year-old Jewish boys could be recruited into youth battalions in preparation for adult military service. Local authorities in some Jewish communities resorted to khappers/captors to kidnap males when quotas could not be reached by legitimate means. The book's sworn enemies are two 16-year-olds Jews from Odessa: Aaron Churchinsky, a well-to-do jeweller's son and yeshiva student about to be married to Miriam, and Zev Lobonsky, an apprentice butcher and seasonal khapper. Zev, jealous of Aaron's intelligence and community reputation, plus his relationship with Miriam, kidnaps Aaron and gives him over to the Russian army where Aaron is subjected to numerous brutal psychological and physical abuses aimed at causing him to convert to Christianity. Prior to the kidnapping, Aaron had borne Zev no animosity, but now Aaron wanted Zev dead. Ironically, Zev himself becomes an involuntary conscript, and the paths of the two boys cross in the story.

While the Salem witch trials may be familiar to most Western teens, France's 16th century witch burnings dealt with in *The Burning Time* may not. The Roman Catholic Church's attempts to eliminate witches became a convenient vehicle for unscrupulous people to accuse their neighbours of witchcraft. When Madame Rives, the mother of Rose, 15, and a healer and midwife, is widowed, she becomes especially vulnerable. With the arrival of a witch-hunting judge, Madame Rives finds herself charged with witchcraft and condemned to death by burning. Though the witch hunts had obvious religious connections, Matas shows how they were also intimately entangled in male attempts to maintain women in subjugated states.

Adult politics is not the usual stuff of YA literature, but *The Race* uses a five-day national Liberal Leadership Convention in Calgary, Alberta, as the setting for an adolescent romance. Reminiscent of Romeo and Juliet's family problems, the plot's romance linking Winnipeg's Ali Green, 14, and Montreal's Paul James, 15, finds Ali's mother and Paul's father as principal leadership rivals. The budding romance encounters its biggest challenge when the couple overhears Paul's father accepting a bribe for future government contracts. Questions of family loyalty and right and wrong come to the fore as the two must decide what to do with the information while also considering the effects any decision may have both on the political race and their own personal relationship. Matas's lively style, which captures the colour and political drama of a leadership race, should so engage her audience that they will become almost as interested in discovering the new national leader's identity as they are in knowing the outcome of the teen romance.

Matas has also written about complex contemporary issues. *The Primrose Path*'s title is found in *Hamlet,* wherein Ophelia expresses her concern about pastors who preach to others "the steep and thorny way to Heaven" while treading "the primrose path" of pleasure themselves. Following her grandmother's death, Debbie Mazur, 14, moves with her family across country where Debbie's grieving mother finds solace in Rabbi Werner, the handsome and charismatic leader of a neighborhood synagogue. Mrs. Mazur decides that Debbie would benefit from attending the Hebrew school attached to this ultra-Orthodox synagogue, but Debbie, who had worshipped at a Reform temple, feels alienated by the unfamiliar rituals. Her attitudes change, though, when she is befriended by four grade nine girls who appear to enjoy a special relationship with Rabbi Werner, their Hebrew teacher and the school's principal. As Debbie discovers personally, however, Rabbi Werner, while "innocently" tickling the girls, "accidentally" touches their breasts. Initially embarrassed, Debbie explains away the touching, but, when the tickling extends to her "privates," she recognizes the Rabbi's behaviours to be clearly inappropriate. Matas effectively captures Debbie's confused emotional state as she vacillates about what to do. Adults wanting "justice" may be disappointed by the book's ending, for the wrongdoer is not clearly punished. Nonetheless, Matas realistically reveals what can occur when questions of morality become entwined in adult "politics" and reputation.

Telling refers to the ritual three sisters in a single parent family have of sharing the intimate happenings in their lives. Sandwiched between Sue, 17, and Corey, 13, is Alex, the narrator. Over the summer, each young woman has been called upon to make a number of moral choices, and each now wishes she had the opportunity to revisit those decisions. At the heart of the girls' problems is ultimately the question of the place of women in today's society. Like the porridge in the cabin of the Three Bears, each sister was of a different "temperature" in terms of her commitment to "feminism," but each discovered that she was willing to sacrifice principles in order to be seen as "nice." Though some adults may find Matas' message too blatant, teen readers of both genders will enjoy exploring the issues *Telling*'s characters raise.

The Freak borders on fantasy for the central character, Jade, 15, has psychic powers following a bout of meningitis. Knowing what people are thinking and then acting on this information makes Jade appear to be a freak both in her own eyes and in the eyes of her school mates. However, Jade accepts her special "gift" after she uses it to track down the source of anti-Semitic hate literature and saves the local synagogue from being bombed. While an acceptable read, *The Freak* reinforces that Matas is at her best when writing historical fiction.

—Dave Jenkinson

MATHABANE, Mark

Nationality: Naturalized U.S. citizen (originally South African.) **Born:** Johannes Mark Mathabane in Alexandra, South Africa, 1960. **Education:** Attended Limestone College, 1978, St. Louis University, 1979, and Quincy College, 1981; Dowling College, B.A. 1983; Columbia University, 1984. **Family:** Married Gail Ernsberger in 1987. **Career:** Freelance lecturer and writer, since 1985. **Awards:** Christopher award, 1986, for *Kaffir Boy;* nominated Speaker of the Year by the National Association of Campus Activities, 1993; White House Fellow, U.S. Department of Education, 1996-97. **Agent:** Fifi Oscard Agency, 24 West 40th Street,

New York, New York 10018, U.S.A. **Address:** 341 Barrington Park Ln., Kernersville, North Carolina 27284, U.S.A.

PUBLICATIONS FOR YOUNG ADULTS

Nonfiction

Kaffir Boy: The True Story of a Black Youth's Coming of Age in Apartheid South Africa. New York, Macmillan, 1986; as *Kaffir Boy: Growing out of Apartheid.* London, Bodley Head, 1987.
Kaffir Boy in America: An Encounter with Apartheid. New York, Scribner, 1989.
Love in Black and White: The Triumph of Love over Prejudice and Taboo, with Gail Mathabane. New York, HarperCollins, 1992.
African Women: Three Generations. New York, HarperCollins, 1994.

*

Media Adaptations: *Kaffir Boy* (cassette), Dove Books on Tape, 1988.

Biography: Entry in *Contemporary Black Biography,* Detroit, Gale Research, 1994.

Critical Studies: Sketch in *Black Writers,* Detroit, Gale Research, 1994; entry in *The Schomberg Center Guide to Black Literature,* Detroit, Gale Research, 1996.

Mark Mathabane comments:

During my senior year at Dowling College on Long Island, I grew convinced that Americans did not understand what the term "apartheid" meant in human terms. Other black South African students I met in the United States seemed afraid to speak out against apartheid for fear of endangering their families still trapped in South Africa. In my case, however, my urge to expose the horrors of apartheid outweighed my fear of reprisals by South Africa's terrorist regime. I felt compelled to sit down at my typewriter and try to explain to the world, and to myself, all the terrors, struggles, and deprivation I had survived. My friends called me mad for thinking I could write a book. My professors discouraged me from continuing. But once I started writing, the book possessed me wholly. I opened myself to remembering all the painful experiences I had forced myself to forget.

I wrote best in the mornings, when my mind was still fresh with dream fragments and alive with childhood memories. After graduating, I rented a small room in someone's house near campus and spent hours in the computer lab writing and revising. I had about 600 pages completed when a friend asked me if I would speak about growing up in South Africa at Bellport Unitarian Church one Sunday. As fate would have it, two published authors were in the audience who were eager to introduce me to their editors and agents. In a matter of weeks, to my amazement, several publishers were bidding on the manuscript.

I still base my writing on my convictions, on what James Baldwin called "the fire in the belly." I believe that all powerful, moving writing must be totally honest and based on getting at the gist of life's eternal truths. Currently my writing springs from my strong belief that all of us—regardless of race, gender, creed, or ethnic origin—share a common humanity. I hope my writing and speaking will inspire people to heal the racial divide, respect and celebrate individual differences, communicate better and with more open minds, and work toward building a nation in which diversity is an asset and everyone feels included and valued.

*   *   *

South African writer Mark Mathabane's life is the subject of his writing. Though still in his thirties, he has already written three volumes of autobiography: *Kaffir Boy, Kaffir Boy in America,* and *Love in Black and White* (co-authored with his wife, Gail Mathabane). Together the books document his unlikely and inspiring journey from hungry, hopeless, suicidal child to articulate, confident, successful adult. Each volume portrays a particular era in his life and is distinguished by unique experiences and feelings.

Significant people and themes promote unity throughout the series. Foremost are Mathabane's family and American tennis stars Arthur Ashe and Stan Smith. Ashe provides inspiration by example, as tennis player and as human rights activist, while Smith and his wife provide financial and emotional support and a "home away from home" in the United States. These relationships reinforce two central themes: the importance of the family unit, and the need to respect individuals regardless of race.

Although written for an adult audience, Mathabane's books nonetheless offer valuable historical and cultural information, as well as inspiration, to young adults. Determined and courageous, Mathabane has repeatedly refused to be intimidated when the odds are against him. From the anonymous squalor of his black South African childhood to his very public life as a best-selling author in America, Mathabane documents reality as he lives it.

In *Kaffir Boy in America,* Mathabane describes his "momentous discovery" of Richard Wright's *Black Boy,* which led him to become a writer: "I mentally replaced 'white South' with 'white South Africa' and 'nigger' with 'Kaffir' [Arabic for 'infidel'; a derogatory term for blacks] and was intrigued by how Richard Wright's feelings mirrored my own." Overwhelmed by the experience, Mathabane went on to read Malcolm X, Claude Brown, Maya Angelou, and every other black writer he could find.

Parallels with *Black Boy* are apparent in the title of *Kaffir Boy* and in many of its themes: the violence of life in the ghetto, fear and anger at whites, conflict between father and son, love of books, education as an escape, and the determination to succeed. The first and most emotionally powerful of Mathabane's books, *Kaffir Boy* portrays unflinchingly the brutality of his childhood in the black shantytown of Alexandra, just ten miles north of Johannesburg. A harrowing early scene finds five-year-old Johannes (he later changed his name to Mark), awakened in darkness from his "bed of cardboard, under the kitchen table." Soon, he is wetting his ragged shorts in terror as his mother, who lacks the "right" papers, flees a police raid, leaving him in charge of two younger siblings.

Johannes's nightmare continues as the police reappear the following night, arresting and humiliating his father and other adults, who stand half-naked while their children watch in shame and fear. Later scenes depict more raids, murders, robberies, trips to the dump for food, childhood prostitution, and other events so painful that at age ten Johannes contemplates suicide. But his mother never gives up hope, and she inspires him as well. His grandmother, too, encourages Mathabane and brings him books from her white employers. A white nun helps Mark obtain the right papers, and despite his father's objections, much red tape, and enormous financial sacrifice, Mathabane's mother sends him to school. He excels in his classes, and wins a tennis scholarship to an American college. *Kaffir Boy* ends as he heads for the airport to "follow destiny" to America—the Promised Land.

Kaffir Boy in America documents Mathabane's gradual adjustment to life in a less idealized America. Equally direct but less powerful than *Kaffir Boy,* this volume is more exploratory than explosive. In it, Mathabane struggles to find himself and his place in the world. Caught between fears for his family in South Africa and the desire to succeed in America, Mathabane moves from college to college, attending four before deciding to stop fleeing and "confront [his] fate." He becomes a student leader, a speaker about South Africa, a graduate student, and ultimately a writer. Along the way, he considers both black and white racism and other social problems, offering fresh insights into an America he has come to know well. He also marries Gail Ernsberger, a white American writer, and brings his siblings to the United States to be educated when the success of *Kaffir Boy* makes this financially possible.

Love in Black and White continues the story of Mark and Gail Mathabane with warmth and candor. In alternating chapters, the authors describe the development of their relationship, sometimes recounting the same events from two perspectives. They address honestly their personal doubts and fears and the continuing societal reaction to them as an interracial couple. Mostly personal narrative, the book also includes some analysis of race relations and interracial marriage in the United States and South Africa. It ends on a note of hope for their biracial children and for the world.

Though the moral power of Mathabane's message has not been blunted, his delivery of it in *African Women: Three Generations* is much weaker than in previous works. Perhaps drawing on the success of the *Wild Swans: Three Daughters of China* by Jung Change (Simon and Schuster, 1991), Mathabane sets out to tell the story of three women in his own family: his sister Florah, mother Geli, and grandmother Ellen or "Granny." Written in the first person, ostensibly in the voices of the three women speaking successively, the book suffers from the fact that the voice throughout always sounds like Mathabane himself—educated, urbane, Western—instead of the authentic tone of a woman who has known little beyond the misery of Alexandra. Gail Mathabane's photographs add dimension to the book, but the text is nonetheless stifled by the inauthentic tone.

And yet throughout his work, Mathabane offers young adults the opportunity to see victims of injustice overcome pain and regain their human dignity. He also invites readers to join the struggle for justice to which he has dedicated his life. In the concluding lines of *Love in Black and White,* the Mathabanes suggest that "Racism is essentially a problem of the heart. . . . If in our hearts we truly accept one another as fellow human beings, many of our intractable problems would have solutions, and there would be no limit to the good we could do in making our world a better place for all." Using his own life as example, Mark Mathabane offers evidence and insight into major problems besetting today's world, but he also demonstrates an unwavering belief in the resilience of the human spirit. This is a message young adults cannot hear too often.

—Lois Rauch Gibson, updated by Judson Knight

MATHIS, Sharon Bell

Nationality: American. **Born:** Atlantic City, New Jersey, 26 February 1937. **Education:** Morgan State College (now Morgan State University), Baltimore, B.A. in sociology (magna cum laude) 1958; D. C. Teachers College; Catholic University of America, Washington, D.C., M.Sc. in library science 1975. **Family:** Married Leroy Franklin Mathis in 1957 (divorced, 1979); three daughters. **Career:** Interviewer, Children's Hospital of District of Columbia, 1958-59; teacher, Holy Redeemer Elementary School, Washington, D.C., 1959-65; special education teacher, Bertie Backus Junior High School, 1965-66, Charles Hart Junior High School, 1966-72, and Stuart Junior High School, 1972-75, all in Washington, D.C.; librarian, Benning Elementary School, Washington, D.C., librarian, 1975-76; library media specialist, Friendship Education Center (now called the Patricia Roberts Harris Educational Center), Washington, D.C., library media specialist, since 1976; author of children's books. Writer in charge of children's literature division, Washington, D.C., Black Writers Workshop, 1970-73; member of board of advisers, Lawyers Committee of District of Columbia Commission on the Arts, 1972-73; writer-in-residence, Howard University, Washington, D.C., 1972-74; member of Black Women's Community Development Foundation, 1973-74. **Awards:** Award for a children's book manuscript, Council on Interracial Books for Children, 1969, and chosen one of Child Study Association of America's Children's Books of the Year, 1971, both for *Sidewalk Story;* Bread Loaf Writers Conference Fellow, 1970; *Teacup Full of Roses* was chosen one of Child Study Association of America's Children's Books of the Year, one of *New York Times*' Best Books of the Year, and one of the American Library Association's (ALA) Best Young Adult Books, all 1972, and Coretta Scott King award, runner up, 1973; Coretta Scott King award, 1974, for *Ray Charles; Listen for the Fig Tree* was selected one of ALA's Best Young Adult Books, 1974; *Boston Globe-Horn Book* Honor Book for Text, one of Child Study Association of America's Children's Books of the Year, Notable Children's Trade Book in the Field of Social Studies, National Council of Social Studies and the Children's Book Council, and one of the *New York Times*' Outstanding Books, all 1975, and Newbery Honor Book, 1976, all for *The Hundred Penny Box;* Arts and Humanities award, Club Twenty, 1975; District of Columbia Association of School Librarians award, 1976; Arts and Humanities award, Archdiocese of Washington, D.C., 1978; MacDowell fellowship, 1978; Wallace Johnson Memorial award, 1984, for "Outstanding Contributions to the Literary Arts"; Arts and Letters award, Boys and Girls Clubs of Greater Washington, 1984; Arts and Letters award, Delta Sigma Theta Sorority, 1985; Outstanding Writer award, Writing-to-Read Program, D.C. Public Schools, 1986. **Agent:** Marilyn Marlow, Curtis Brown Ltd., 10 Astor Place, New York, New York 10003. **Address:** P.O. Box 44714, Fort Washington, Maryland 20744, U.S.A.

PUBLICATIONS FOR YOUNG ADULTS

Fiction

Brooklyn Story, illustrated by Charles Bible. New York, Hill & Wang, 1970.
Teacup Full of Roses. New York, Viking, 1972.

Listen for the Fig Tree. New York, Viking, 1974.
Running Girl: The Diary of Ebonee Rose. San Diego, Harcourt Brace, 1997.

Other

Ray Charles, illustrated by George Ford. New York, Crowell, 1973.
Cartwheels. New York, Scholastic, 1977.
Red Dog, Blue Fly: Football Poems. New York, Viking, 1991.

PUBLICATIONS FOR CHILDREN

Fiction

Sidewalk Story, illustrated by Leo Carty. New York, Viking, 1971.
The Hundred Penny Box, illustrated by Leo and Diane Dillon. New York, Viking, 1975.

Work included in anthology *Night Comes Softly: Anthology of Black Female Voices,* edited by Nikki Giovanni.

*

Media Adaptations: *Teacup Full of Roses* (record; cassette), Live Oak Media, 1977; *The Hundred Penny Box* (cassette; record; filmstrip), Random House.

Biography: Entry in *Dictionary of Literary Biography,* Volume 33: *Afro-American Fiction Writers after 1955,* Detroit, Gale, 1984; essay in *Something about the Author Autobiography Series,* Volume 3, Detroit, Gale, 1987; essay in *Speaking for Ourselves: Autobiographical Sketches by Notable Authors of Books for Young Adults,* Volume 1, compiled and edited by Donald R. Gallo, National Council of Teachers of English, 1990.

Critical Studies: Entry in *Children's Literature Review,* Volume 3, Detroit, Gale, 1978.

*   *   *

Sharon Bell Mathis is a novelist, poet, and biographer. In her work she celebrates black children, teenagers, and black families. Her style is clear and crisp, and her message is one of strength, of triumph over adversity, of joy in living.

Although many of her books are for younger children, including her biography *Ray Charles* and her poetry, *Brooklyn Story* was to be "a high-interest, low-vocabulary novel for teenagers with reading deficiencies," written in the aftermath of the assassination of Martin Luther King, Jr., and dealing with responses to love and death. Published in 1970 after the success of her children's book *Sidewalk Story,* it led the way to other books for young adults.

Teacup Full of Roses, an ALA Notable Book, was praised by critics as a tribute not only to black youth, but to all youth of any race, and that the truths it related about a black world could be just as true for any other ethnic-American group. Seventeen-year-old Joe is the mainstay of a brilliant younger brother, an older brother on drugs, a disabled father, and a blindly devoted mother. How he deals with this responsibility is eloquently told, underscoring the

values of hard work, education, and the hope for a better life, even as the story line leads to the inevitably tragic end.

In her second ALA Notable Book, *Listen for the Fig Tree,* Mathis portrays a blind teenager, Muffin, who must also contend with an alcoholic mother and the memory of her father's murder the Christmas before. Her determination to attend the Kwanza celebration, symbolizing black pride, is realized through the combination of her own prodigious efforts and the help of good neighbors, including one who is a homosexual.

Three girls in *Cartwheels* vie for the fifty-dollar prize in a gymnastic competition. The ensuing events reveal the aspirations and frustrations of each but conclude satisfactorily for all three, although only one wins the award. Mathis is a black author who cares about black young people and the black community. She treats both with great dignity and good humor. She is a joyous writer, and her characters are spirited and competent.

—Mary Lystad

MAYNE, William (James Carter)

Pseudonyms: Martin Cobalt; Dynely James; Charles Molin. **Nationality:** British. **Born:** Kingston upon Hull, Yorkshire, 16 March 1928. **Education:** Cathedral Choir School, Canterbury, 1937-42. **Career:** Writer of children's books; lecturer, Deakin University, Geelong, Victoria, 1976, 1977; Fellow in Creative Writing, Rolle College, Exmouth, Devon, 1979-80. **Awards:** Carnegie Medal from British Library Association for best children's book of year, 1957, for *A Grass Rope; Boston Globe-Horn Book* Honor award, 1989, for *Gideon Ahoy;* Phoenix award honor, 1991, for *A Game of Dark.* **Agent:** David Higham Associates Ltd., 5-8 Lower John St., Golden Square, London W1R 4HA, England.

PUBLICATIONS FOR YOUNG ADULTS

Novels

Follow the Footprints, illustrated by Shirley Hughes. London, Oxford University Press, 1953.
The World Upside Down, illustrated by Shirley Hughes. London, Oxford University Press, 1954.
A Swarm in May, illustrated by C. Walter Hodges. London, Oxford University Press, 1955; Indianapolis, Bobbs-Merrill, 1957.
Choristers' Cake, illustrated by C. Walter Hodges. London, Oxford University Press, 1956; Indianapolis, Bobbs-Merrill, 1958.
The Member of the Marsh, illustrated by Lynton Lamb. London, Oxford University Press, 1956.
The Blue Boat, illustrated by Geraldine Spence. London, Oxford University Press, 1957; New York, Dutton, 1960.
A Grass Rope, illustrated by Lynton Lamb. London, Oxford University Press, 1957; New York, Dutton, 1962.
The Long Night, illustrated by D.J. Watkins-Pitchford. London, Blackwell, 1957.
Underground Alley, illustrated by Marcia Lane Foster. London, Oxford University Press, 1958; New York, Dutton, 1961.
The Gobbling Billy (as Dynely James), with R.D. Caesar. London, Gollancz, and New York, Dutton, 1959; by William Mayne and Dick Caesar, Leicester, Brockhampton Press, 1969.

The Thumbstick, illustrated by Tessa Theobald. London, Oxford University Press, 1959.

Cathedral Wednesday, illustrated by C. Walter Hodges. London, Oxford University Press, 1960.

The Fishing Party, illustrated by Christopher Brooker. London, Hamish Hamilton, 1960.

The Rolling Season, illustrated by Christopher Brooker. London, Oxford University Press, 1960.

Thirteen O'Clock, illustrated by D.J. Watkins-Pitchford. Oxford, Blackwell, 1960.

The Changeling, illustrated by Victor Adams. London, Oxford University Press, 1961; New York, Dutton, 1963.

The Glass Ball, illustrated by Janet Duchesne. London, Hamish Hamilton, 1961; New York, Dutton, 1962.

Summer Visitors, illustrated by William Stobbs. London, Oxford University Press, 1961.

The Last Bus, illustrated by Margery Gill. London, Hamish Hamilton, 1962.

The Twelve Dancers, illustrated by Lynton Lamb. London, Hamish Hamilton, 1962.

The Man from the North Pole, illustrated by Prudence Seward. London, Hamish Hamilton, 1963.

On the Stepping Stones, illustrated by Prudence Seward. London, Hamish Hamilton, 1963.

A Parcel of Trees, illustrated by Margery Gill. London, Penguin, 1963.

Plot Night, illustrated by Janet Duchesne. London, Hamish Hamilton, 1963; New York, Dutton, 1968.

Words and Music, illustrated by Lynton Lamb. London, Hamish Hamilton, 1963.

A Day without Wind, illustrated by Margery Gill. London, Hamish Hamilton, and New York, Dutton, 1964.

Sand, illustrated by Margery Gill. London, Hamish Hamilton, 1964; New York, Dutton, 1965.

Water Boatman, illustrated by Anne Linton. London, Hamish Hamilton, 1964.

Whistling Rufus, illustrated by Raymond Briggs. London, Hamish Hamilton, 1964; New York, Dutton, 1965.

The Big Wheel and the Little Wheel, illustrated by Janet Duchesne. London, Hamish Hamilton, 1965.

Pig in the Middle, illustrated by Mary Russon. London, Hamish Hamilton, 1965; New York, Dutton, 1966.

Dormouse Tales (The Lost Thimble, The Steam Roller, The Picnic, The Football, The Tea Party) (as Charles Molin), illustrated by Leslie Wood. London, Hamish Hamilton, 5 vols., 1966.

Earthfasts. London, Hamish Hamilton, 1966; New York, Dutton, 1967.

The Old Zion, illustrated by Margery Gill. London, Hamish Hamilton, 1966; New York, Dutton, 1967.

Rooftops, illustrated by Mary Russon. London, Hamish Hamilton, 1966.

The Battlefield, illustrated by Mary Russon. London, Hamish Hamilton, and New York, Dutton, 1967.

The Big Egg, illustrated by Margery Gill. London, Hamish Hamilton, 1967.

The House on Fairmont, illustrated by Fritz Wegner. London, Hamish Hamilton, and New York, Dutton, 1968.

Over the Hills and Far Away. London, Hamish Hamilton, 1968; as *The Hill Road,* New York, Dutton, 1969.

The Toffee Join, illustrated by Shirley Hughes. London, Hamish Hamilton, 1968.

The Yellow Aeroplane, illustrated by Trevor Stubley. London, Hamish Hamilton, 1968; Nashville, Nelson, 1974.

Ravensgill. London, Hamish Hamilton, and New York, Dutton, 1970.

A Game of Dark. London, Hamish Hamilton, and New York, Dutton, 1971.

Royal Harry. London, Hamish Hamilton, 1971; New York, Dutton, 1972.

The Incline. London, Hamish Hamilton, and New York, Dutton, 1972.

Skiffy, illustrated by Nicholas Fisk. London, Hamish Hamilton, 1972.

The Swallows (as Martin Cobalt). London, Heinemann, 1972; as *Pool of Swallows,* Nashville, Nelson, 1974.

The Jersey Shore. London, Hamish Hamilton, and New York, Dutton, 1973.

A Year and a Day, illustrated by Krystyna Turska. London, Hamish Hamilton, and New York, Dutton, 1976.

It. London, Hamish Hamilton, 1977; New York, Greenwillow, 1978.

Max's Dream, illustrated by Laszlo Acs. London, Hamish Hamilton, and New York, Greenwillow Books, 1977.

Party Pants, illustrated by Joanna Stubbs. London, Knight, 1977.

While the Bells Ring, illustrated by Janet Rawlins. London, Hamish Hamilton, 1979.

The Mouse and the Egg, illustrated by Krystyna Turska. London, MacRae, 1980; New York, Greenwillow Books, 1981.

Salt River Times, illustrated by Elizabeth Honey. Melbourne, Nelson, and London, Hamish Hamilton, 1980; New York, Greenwillow Books, 1980.

The Patchwork Cat, illustrated by Nicola Bayley. London, Cape, and New York, Knopf, 1981.

All the King's Men. London, Cape, 1982; New York, Delacorte, 1988.

Skiffy and the Twin Planets. London, Hamish Hamilton, 1982.

Winter Quarters. London, Cape, 1982.

The Mouldy, illustrated by Nicola Bayley. London, Cape, and New York, Random House, 1983.

A Small Pudding for Wee Gowrie, illustrated by Martin Cottam. London, Macmillan, 1983.

Underground Creatures. London, Hamish Hamilton, 1983.

Drift. London, Cape, 1985; New York, Delacorte, 1986.

Animal Library (Come, Come to My Corner, Corbie, Tibber, Barnabas Walks, Lamb Shenkin, A House in Town, Leapfrog, Mousewing), illustrated by Kenneth Lilly, Peter Visscher, Martin Baynton, Jonathan Heale, Barbara Firth, and Sarah Fox-Davies. London, Walker, 8 vols., 1986-87; first 3 vols. published Englewood Cliffs, New Jersey, Prentice-Hall, 1987.

The Blemyahs, illustrated by Juan Wijngaard. London, Walker, 1987.

Gideon Ahoy! London, Viking Kestrel, 1987; New York, Delacorte, 1989.

Kelpie. London, Cape, 1987.

Tiger's Railway, illustrated by Juan Wijngaard. London, Walker, 1987.

The Farm that Ran Out of Names. London, Cape, 1989.

Antar and the Eagles. New York, Doubleday, 1990.

The Second-hand Horse and Other Stories. London, Heinemann, 1990.

Rings on Her Fingers. London, Hamish Hamilton, 1991.

With Nicola Bayley, *The Patchwork Cat.* London, Cape, 1992.

And Never Again, illustrated by Kate Aldous. London, Hamish Hamilton, 1992.

The Egg Timer. London, Heinemann, 1993.

Low Tide. New York, Delacorte, 1993.

Cuddy. London, Cape, 1994.

Bells on Her Toes, illustrated by Maureen Bradley. London, Hamish Hamilton, 1994.
Earthefasts. London, Hodder Children's Books, 1995.
Cradlefasts. London, Hodder Children's Books, 1995.

Other

Editor, with Eleanor Farjeon, *The Hamish Hamilton Book of Kings,* illustrated by Victor Ambrus. London, Hamish Hamilton, 1964; as *A Cavalcade of Kings,* New York, Walck, 1965.
Editor, with Eleanor Farjeon, *The Hamish Hamilton Book of Queens,* illustrated by Victor Ambrus. London, Hamish Hamilton, 1964; as *A Cavalcade Queens,* New York, Walck, 1965.
Editor (as Charles Molin), *Ghosts, Spooks, Spectres.* London, Hamish Hamilton, 1967; New York, David White, 1968.
Editor, *The Hamish Hamilton Book of Heroes,* illustrated by Krystyna Turska. London, Hamish Hamilton, 1967; as *William Mayne's Book of Heroes,* New York, Dutton, 1968.
Editor, *The Hamish Hamilton Book of Giants,* illustrated by Raymond Briggs. London, Hamish Hamilton, 1968; as *William Mayne's Book of Giants,* New York, Dutton, 1969.
Editor, *Ghosts.* London, Hamish Hamilton, and New York, Nelson, 1971.
Composer, music for *Holly from the Bongs,* by Alan Garner, 1965.
Editor, *Supernatural.* Kingfisher, 1995.

PUBLICATIONS FOR CHILDREN

Fiction

No More School, illustrated by Peter Warner. London, Hamish Hamilton, 1965.
Robin's Real Engine, illustrated by Mary Dinsdale. London, Hamish Hamilton, 1972.
Hob Stories (*Red Book, Green Book, Yellow Book, Blue Book*), illustrated by Patrick Benson. London, Walker, and New York, Philomel, 4 vols., 1984.
Hob and the Goblins, illustrated by Norman Messenger. London, Dorling Kindersley, 1994.
Lady Muck, illustrated by Jonathan Heale. London, Heinemann, 1997.

*

Biography: Essay in *Something about the Author Autobiography Series,* Volume 11, Detroit, Gale, 1991.

Critical Studies: Entry in *Contemporary Literary Criticism,* Volume 12, Detroit, Gale, 1979.

*   *   *

William Mayne has been extraordinarily prolific and has won many literary prizes; at the same time, he is an example of the kind of writer who is much admired by reviewers and librarians but ignored or even disliked by young adults. His work is difficult to

tie-down, because he has written, using several pen names, for a range of age-groups in very different styles and genres. Early in his career Mayne was most at home with stories set in the Yorkshire Dales where he lives, effectively meshing realism and fantasy, but he has recently widened his settings to include America, New Zealand, and an anonymous Balkan country. He repeatedly writes of young people undertaking demanding tasks, and has written, particularly in the seventies and beyond, a number of unusual and challenging novels for young adults. The best of these are demanding and oblique, and can be read in more than one way.

Two of Mayne's earliest novels are powerful naturalistic stories set in a remote, rugged countryside marked with the decaying remains of nineteenth century industrialisation. One of Mayne's chief strengths has always been his ability to realise places, seasons, and weather vividly and to charge them with feeling. Both stories deal with passionate emotions: thwarted love, anger and jealousy, and tensions between the generations and between the sexes. In both, young people find that uncovering the truth is harder and more hazardous than it seems. In *Ravensgill* the young members of two village families try to probe the origins of a feud still bitterly kept alive by their grandparents. *The Incline* is set in a community whose livelihood is the slate quarry and where tensions arise when workers are laid off after an accident with the machinery.

Perhaps the greatest critical disagreement concerning Mayne has been prompted by *A Game of Dark,* a Freudian allegory about David Jackson, an introverted young man, overconscious of his own thoughts and feelings, grappling with the inability to love his dying father, who is emotionally and physically crippled. David's guilt and sexual fears are increased by his uneasy relationship with his mother, who is also his teacher at school. The fantasy world into which David retreats is a chivalric community threatened by a marauding worm. In this domain, the trendy vicar and father-substitute "becomes one" with the chivalric lord and features of the worm are associated with David's father. There is also an emotional complexity about the inglorious killing of the worm, symbolically linked as it is to David's father's death. In a strange way, David is left "consolate," but his sudden discovery that he is now able to love his father seems contrived rather than growing out of what has gone before.

A critically popular novel, *The Jersey Shore* essentially consists of two long journeys (each "lasted all night and all day") that frame the long central reminiscences of a grandfather talking to a small boy as they sit beside the sea in New Jersey. The novel can be read as a subtle exploration of memory and history, of family and race, in which Arthur is "growing his own history." Readers, like Arthur, have to piece together the real story from the dense cross-references and the insistent parallels between past and present. In the conclusion, a grown-up Arthur's return to the Norfolk from which his grandfather came repeats the pattern of love and freeing from slavery about which he has been learning.

There are weaknesses in parts of Mayne's extensive work. Some reviewers complain of the lack of narrative drive and coherence. Story lines can be contorted with contrived endings, and at times Mayne deliberately but implausibly withholds significant information, like the revelation that Grandma Florence in *The Jersey Shore* was black. At its best, Mayne's style is direct, using short sentences powerfully and conveying experiences or his characters' perceptions in clear images. At other times his writing can be mannered, whimsical, or oversophisticated, and the dialogue can seem not just quirky but unconvincing, like the pidgin put into the mouths of the Indian characters in *Drift* or the attempt at Welsh styles in *The Farm that Ran Out of Names*. Mayne expects his readers to construct knowledge and understanding from elliptical hints and vivid images. One repeated theme in his work is the need to find language with which to realise an undefined awareness, to cope with experience. In *A Game of Dark* Donald begins with "no throat to speak of and nothing to say." Rafe Considine in *Drift* discovers that he has "forgotten how to speak," and events force him to learn a new attitude to language. Most challengingly of all, *Gideon Ahoy!* centres on a deaf, brain-damaged teenager who cannot speak except in unintelligible sounds, but whose development is sensitively charted. In his best work, Mayne triumphantly solves the major technical problems he sets himself and thoroughly deserves his reputation.

—Robert Protherough

MAZER, Harry

Nationality: American. **Born:** New York City, 31 May 1925. **Education:** Union College, Schenectady, New York, B.A. 1948; Syracuse University, New York, M.A. 1960. **Military Service:** Served in the U.S. Army Air Forces, 1943-45; became sergeant; received Purple Heart and Air Medal with four bronze oak leaf clusters. **Family:** Married Norma Fox in 1950; three daughters and one son. **Career:** New York Central, railroad brake man and switchtender, 1950-55; New York Construction, Syracuse, New York, sheet metal worker, 1957-59; Central Square School, Central Square, New York, teacher of English, 1959-60; Aerofin Corp., Syracuse, New York, welder, 1960-63; full-time writer, since 1963. **Awards:** American Library Association (ALA) Best of the Best Books list, 1970-73, for *Snowbound;* Kirkus Choice list, 1974, for *The Dollar Man;* (with Norma Fox Mazer) ALA Best Books for Young Adults list, 1977, and International Reading Association-Children's Book Council Children's Choice, 1978, both for *The Solid Gold Kid;* ALA Best Books for Young Adults list, and Dorothy Canfield Fisher Children's Book Award nomination, both 1979, both for *The War on Villa Street; New York Times* Best Books of the Year list, 1979, New York Public Library Books for the Teen Age list, 1980, ALA Best Books for Young Adults list, 1981, and ALA Best of the Best Books list, 1970-83, all for *The Last Mission; Booklist* Contemporary Classics list, 1984, and German "Preis der Lesseratten," both for *Snowbound;* Arizona Young Readers award nomination, 1985, for *The Island Keeper;* ALA Best Books for Young Adults list, 1986, for *I Love You, Stupid!;* New York Library Books for the Teen Age list, 1986, and International Reading Association-Children's Book Council Young Adult Choice list, 1987, both for *Hey Kid! Does She Love Me?;* ALA Best Books for Young Adults list, 1987, Iowa Teen award Master list, 1988, and West Australian Young Reader's Book award, 1989, all for *When the Phone Rang;* ALA Best Books for Young Adults list, ALA Books for Young Adult Reluctant Readers list, 1988, and New York Public Library Books for the Teen Age list, 1988, all for *The Girl of His Dreams;* (with Norma Fox Mazer) New York Public Library Books for the Teen Age list, 1989, for *Heartbeat;* ALA Books for Young Adult Reluctant Readers list, 1989, for *City Light.* **Agent:** George Nicholson, Sterling Lord Literistic, 65 Bleecker Street, New York, New York 10012, U.S.A

PUBLICATIONS FOR YOUNG ADULTS

Novels

Guy Lenny. New York, Delacorte, 1971.
Snow Bound. New York, Delacorte, 1973.
The Dollar Man. New York, Delacorte, 1974.
The Solid Gold Kid, with Norma Fox Mazer. New York, Delacorte, 1977.
The War on Villa Street. New York, Delacorte, 1978.
The Last Mission. New York, Delacorte, 1979.
The Island Keeper: A Tale of Courage and Survival. New York, Delacorte, 1981.
I Love You, Stupid! New York, Crowell Junior Books, 1981.
Hey Kid! Does She Love Me? New York, Crowell Junior Books, 1985.
When the Phone Rang. New York, Scholastic, Inc., 1985.
Cave under the City. New York, Crowell Junior Books, 1986.
The Girl of His Dreams. New York, Crowell Junior Books, 1987.
City Light. New York, Scholastic, Inc., 1988.
Heartbeat, with Norma Fox Mazer. New York, Bantam, 1989.
Someone's Mother Is Missing. New York, Delacorte, 1990.
Bright Days, Stupid Nights, with Norma Fox Mazer. New York, Bantam, 1992.
Who Is Eddie Leonard? New York, Delacorte, 1993.
The Dog in the Freezer. New York, Simon & Schuster, 1997.

Other

Editor, *Twelve Shots.* New York, Delacorte, 1997.

*

Media Adaptations: *Snowbound* ("After School Special"), National Broadcasting Company, 1978; *Snowbound* (audiocassette), Listening Library, 1985; *The Last Mission* (audiocassette), Listening Library, 1985.

Biography: Essay in *Authors and Artists for Young Adults,* Volume 5, Detroit, Gale, 1990; essay in *Speaking for Ourselves: Autobiographical Sketches by Notable Authors of Books for Young Adults,* Volume 1, compiled and edited by Donald R. Gallo, National Council of Teachers of English, 1990; essay in *Something about the Author Autobiography Series,* Volume 11, Detroit, Gale, 1991.

Critical Studies: Entry in *Children's Literature Review,* Volume 16, Detroit, Gale, 1989; *Presenting Harry Mazer* by Arthea J.S. Reed, New York, Twayne, 1996.

*   *   *

Harry Mazer writes fast-paced novels about young people coping with ordinary daily hassles and extraordinary life-threatening problems. Despite their predicaments, Mazer's protagonists usually emerge morally victorious.

Snow Bound is a story of survival in a treacherous snowstorm, not unusual in upstate New York. Tony Laporte, age fifteen, leads an easy life because his parents want him to have all the things they didn't have. When his parents refuse to let him keep the stray dog he brings home with him, Tony decides to teach them a lesson by running off in his mother's old car. In the middle of a tremendous snowstorm, he picks up Cindy Reichart, who is hitchhiking home because she needs freedom after a weekend of being cooped up at her grandmother's house. Tony tries to impress Cindy by showing off his driving skills, only to end up wrecking the car in a desolate area far from the main highway. The two spend the first days bickering with each other and waiting to be rescued. When help doesn't come, they realize they must cooperate in order to survive. Snowbound, they are faced with starvation, frost bite, wild dogs, and broken limbs. In the process of finding a way out of the wilderness, they become caring and supportive of one another, developing a friendship likely to endure after their eleven-day ordeal.

The Dollar Man is about Marcus Rosenbloom, an overweight thirteen-year-old who dreams he is Marcus the Magnificent, the Great Invisible Man. In his invisible dream, Marcus is transformed from a fat, clumsy boy to a lean, athletic young man like his father, the father he has never seen except in dreams. Marcus lives with his feisty, unmarried, working mother on the east side of New York. When his mother refuses to tell him anything about his father, Marcus rejects her and hangs out with older boys who experiment with drugs and alcohol. He is expelled from school, charged with smoking marijuana on school grounds. It is his friends rather than he who were doing the smoking, but they neither own up to their offense nor stand up for him. Despondent, Marcus determines to find his father and live a new, better life with him. He finds his father, who is worth many dollars, and the confrontation between the two allows him to learn much about his father and about himself.

The War on Villa Street is about a boy growing up in New York City, with a passive mother and an alcoholic father. Willis Pierce and his family are always moving because of his father's alcoholic behavior, and Willis is always an outsider. On the street, in school, in the grocery store, he has to guard against a snub or negative remark. Willis sticks to himself, minds his own business—for him it's the only way. Gradually, however, Willis's closed-off world falls apart. His father beats him up one Friday night in a fit of anger; the gang on Villa Street are out to get him. Willis challenges one of the gang members in a running race on Field Day, but his father, drunk and disorderly, comes to Field Day and Willis loses. Ashamed, Willis takes his father home where his father beats him. Willis turns on his father, punching him again and again, fighting for his life, then runs terrified from his apartment. Eventually he does return, finds a way to be free of his father, and to reach out to persons his own age for companionship and comfort.

Cave under the City is set during the 1930s in the heart of the Depression, and yet it seems a story of today when homelessness in many big cities is a major social problem. Tolley Holtz and his younger, dyslexic brother live with their parents in New York City. More and more people are out of work, and when their father can't find work anymore, he leaves for Baltimore to find a job. The mother becomes ill, collapses, and is taken by ambulance from work to a hospital. The hospital calls the apartment building to say that their mother wants the boys to go to their grandmother's, but Tolley and Bubber go, only to find their grandmother gravely ill.

They return to their house, buy food on credit, try to survive. They also write their father to come home. When they decide to visit their mother at the hospital, the social service department steps in and tries to place the boys in a children's center, but Tolley resists, and the children run away. They live in an abandoned cellar with no lights, no windows, and call it a cave. They suffer hunger and starvation, wanting and smelling food, drinking lots of water. They steal food and milk, though they dislike doing so. Finally their father comes home and they go back to their apartment, back to school, and Tolley starts making money to repay the grocer.

Harry Mazer has also written books with his wife, Norma Fox Mazer. *The Solid Gold Kid,* one of their collaborations, is a striking thriller involving the kidnapping of a millionaire's son. The book is swift-moving, vibrant, believable.

Mazer's forte is the emotional turmoil, the humor and pain of adolescent years. His characters are resilient and strong. His endings emphasize compassion, understanding, resourcefulness, and honesty.

—Mary Lystad

MAZER, Norma Fox

Nationality: American. **Born:** New York City, 15 May 1931. **Education:** Antioch College, Yellow Springs, Ohio, 1949-50; Syracuse University, New York, 1957-59. **Family:** Married Harry Mazer in 1950; three daughters and one son. **Career:** Writer, since 1964. Worked as a secretary at a radio station, punch press operator, waitress, and cashier. **Awards:** National Book award nomination, 1973, for *A Figure of Speech;* Lewis Carroll Shelf award, University of Wisconsin, 1975, for *Saturday the Twelfth of October;* Christopher award, *New York Times* Outstanding Books of the Year list, *School Library Journal* Best Books of the Year list, American Library Association (ALA) Best Books for Young Adults list, ALA Notable Book, Lewis Carroll Shelf award, all 1976, all for *Dear Bill, Remember Me? and Other Stories;* (with Harry Mazer) ALA Best Books for Young Adults list, 1977, and Children's Book Council-International Reading Association Children's Choice, 1978, both for *The Solid Gold Kid;* ALA Best Books for Young Adults list, 1979, *School Library Journal* Best Books of the Year list, 1979, ALA Best of the Best Books 1970-83 list, and ALA 100 Best of the Best, 1968-93, all for *Up in Seth's Room;* Austrian Children's Books list of honor, and German Children's Literature prize, both 1982, both for *Mrs. Fish, Ape, and Me, the Dump Queen;* Edgar award, Mystery Writers of America, 1982, and California Young Readers Medal, 1985, both for *Taking Terri Mueller;* ALA Best Books for Young Adults list, 1983, for *Someone to Love;* ALA Best Books for Young Adults list, *New York Times* Outstanding Books of the Year list, and New York Public Library Books for the Teenage list, all 1984, all for *Downtown;* Iowa Teen award, 1985-86, for *When We First Met;* Children's Book Council-International Reading Association Children's Choice, 1986, for *A, My Name Is Ami;* Newbery Honor Book, *School Library Journal* Best Books of the Year list, ALA Notable Book, ALA Best Books for Young Adults list, Canadian Children's

Books Council Choice, *Horn Book* Fanfare Book, and Association of Booksellers for Children Choice, all 1988, all for *After the Rain*; ALA Best Books for Young Adults list, 1989, Iowa Teen award, 1990, New York Public Library Books for the Teenage list, and ALA 100 Best of the Best 1968-93, all for *Silver*; (with Harry Mazer) Children's Book Council-International Reading Association Children's Choice, New York Public Library Books for the Teen Age list, and Literature Prize ZDF (Germany), all 1989, all for *Heartbeat*; New York Public Library Books for the Teenage list, 1989 and 1990, for *Waltzing on Water*, 1993 for *Out of Control*, and 1994, for *Missing Pieces*; American Bookseller's Pick of the Lists, New York Public Library Books for the Teenage list, and IRA Teacher's Choice Award, all 1990, all for *Babyface*; American Booksellers Pick of the Lists, 1992, for *Bright Days, Stupid Nights*, 1993, for *Out of Control*, and 1994, for *Missing Pieces*; ALA Best Books for Young Adults, 1993, for *Out of Control*. **Agent:** Elaine Markson, 44 Greenwich Avenue, New York, New York 10011. **Address:** 7626 Brown Gulf Road, Jamesville, New York 13078, U.S.A.

PUBLICATIONS FOR YOUNG ADULTS

Fiction

I, Trissy. New York, Delacorte, 1971.
A Figure of Speech. New York, Delacorte, 1973.
Saturday, the Twelfth of October. New York, Delacorte, 1975.
Dear Bill, Remember Me? and Other Stories. New York, Delacorte, 1976.
The Solid Gold Kid, with Harry Mazer. New York, Delacorte, 1977.
Up in Seth's Room. New York, Delacorte, 1979.
Mrs. Fish, Ape, and Me, the Dump Queen. New York, Dutton, 1980.
Taking Terri Mueller. New York, Avon, 1981, London, Methuen, 1988.
Summer Girls, Love Boys, and Other Short Stories. New York, Delacorte, 1982.
When We First Met. New York, Four Winds. 1982.
Someone to Love. New York, Delacorte, 1983.
Downtown. New York, Morrow, 1984.
Supergirl (novelization of screenplay). New York, Warner Books, and London, Severn House, 1984.
A, My Name Is Ami. New York, Scholastic, Inc., 1986; as *A for Ami,* London, Penguin, 1988.
Three Sisters. New York, Scholastic, Inc., 1986.
After the Rain. New York, Morrow, 1987; London, Macmillan, 1988.
B, My Name Is Bunny. New York, Scholastic, Inc., 1987; as *A Name Like Bunny.* London, Penguin, 1988.
Silver. New York, Morrow, 1988.
Heartbeat, with Harry Mazer. New York, Bantam, 1989.
Babyface. New York, Morrow, 1990.
C, My Name Is Cal. New York, Scholastic, Inc., 1990.
D, My Name Is Danita. New York, Scholastic, Inc., 1991.
E, My Name Is Emily. New York, Scholastic, Inc., 1991.
Bright Days, Stupid Nights, with Harry Mazer. New York, Bantam Doubleday Dell, 1992.
Out of Control. New York, Morrow, 1993.
Missing Pieces. New York, Morrow, 1994.
When She Was Good. New York, Scholastic, 1997.
Crazy Fish. New York, Morrow, 1998.

Other

Editor, with Margery Lewis, *Waltzing on Water: Poetry by Women.* New York, Dell, 1989.
Editor, with Jacqueline Woodson. *Just a Writer's Thing: A Collection of Prose and Poetry from the National Book Foundation's 1995 Summer Writing Camp.* New York, National Book Foundation, 1996.

Contributor to *Sixteen: Short Stories by Outstanding Writers for Young Adults,* edited by Donald R. Gallo, New York, Delacorte, 1984; *Short Takes: A Short Story Collection for Young Readers,* edited by Elizabeth Segal, New York, Lothrop, 1986; and *Visions: Nineteen Short Stories by Outstanding Writers for Young Adults,* edited by Don Gallo, New York, Delacorte, 1987; *Ultimate Sports,* edited by Don Gallo, New York, Delacorte, 1995; *Night Terrors,* edited by Lois Duncan, New York, Simon & Schuster, 1996.

*

Media Adaptations: *When We First Met* (film), Home Box Office, 1984; *Taking Terri Mueller* (audiocassette), Listening Library, 1986; *Dear Bill Remember Me? and Other Stories* (audiocassette), Listening Library, 1987; *After the Rain* (audiocassette), Listening Library, 1988.

Biography: Essay in *Something about the Author Autobiography Series,* Vol. 1, Detroit, Gale, 1986; essay in *Authors and Artists for Young Adults,* Vol. 5, Detroit, Gale, 1990; entry in *Fifth Book of Junior Authors and Illustrators,* New York, H.W. Wilson, 1983.

Critical Studies: Entry in *Contemporary Literary Criticism,* Vol. 26, Detroit, Gale, 1983; *Children's Literature Review,* winter 1991-92.

Norma Fox Mazer comments:

At the age of thirteen I was seized by love: the love of writing. From that time on, I never wanted anything but to be a writer of fiction, of stories that would enthrall readers as stories enthralled me. All my dreams of the future became wrapped around this thought: "Someday, when I'm a real writer...." Twenty-six books and many years later, I still love writing as much as I did when I was thirteen. Every day, I feel blessed to have this life, to be able to sit at my desk and dream and write stories that other people are going to read.

*   *   *

Norma Fox Mazer has written a number of highly acclaimed books for young adults. Her main characters are young people on the verge of adulthood, struggling with self-image and interest in the opposite sex. Some lead ordinary lives; some have to face enormous social problems, such as drunken driving, teenage sex, discrimination against the poor and handicapped, and care of the elderly. Mazer's characters are not all admirable, but they are believable and provide insight into why people behave the way they do. Because of her strong characterizations, Mazer is one of the most widely read writers for young adults today.

Up in Seth's Room is about an adolescent boy and girl who fall in love, with the boy demanding an active sexual relationship and the girl refusing because she wants to wait until she is older. Seth persists. "If at first you don't succeed . . . that's the male creed," he tells her. The girl, Finn, holds firm. And they find they can remain friends, good friends.

Mrs. Fish, Ape, and Me, the Dump Queen is about people who are on the fringe of society. Mrs. Fish is a middle-aged spinster and cleaning woman; Ape is an older bachelor who runs the town dump; and Me, the dump queen, is an orphan adolescent, ridiculed by her peers and desperate for affection. Eventually these three come together as a family unit; they are not your stereotypical family, but they are a functioning one, providing love and comfort to one another.

Taking Terri Mueller won the Edgar Allan Poe award for Best Juvenile Mystery in 1981. It is about a father who kidnaps his daughter in the aftermath of divorce. The father is afraid that he would never see his daughter again and that a stepfather would take his place in her affections. The father is forced to move a lot with his child—to big cities like New York and Chicago, to small towns such as Hap Falls and Amberville—to avoid being discovered. Father and daughter have a warm and caring relationship, but as the child becomes a teenager, she wonders about the mother she has been told died in a car accident when the daughter was four. What was her mother like? The father refuses to discuss her, and there are no pictures. Finally the child realizes that something in his story is wrong. She asks questions and she demands answers. As thirteen-year-old Terri struggles to find out about the mother she doesn't remember, and to figure out the father she has always loved, she solves the mystery. But then she finds herself torn between father and mother. The child's bewilderment and anger are real, but her choices for the remainder of her life, though difficult, are now hers to make.

In *When We First Met,* Jenny Pennoyer falls in love with the son of the drunken driver who killed her older sister. Emotions of hatred, guilt, forgiveness, and caring are expressed. Relationships are complex, often explosive, and they ring true.

After the Rain is a stunning portrait of two human beings, a grandfather and a granddaughter, who begin to take walks together every afternoon when the grandfather's health is not such that he can safely go out alone anymore. For fifteen-year-old Rachel these after-school visits begin as a duty, but in time they become a source of comfort, growth, and strength.

Norma Fox Mazer has written several books with her husband, Harry Mazer. *Heartbeat* is about teenage friendship, romance, and death, bringing together the joys and sorrows, fun, and frustrations of growing up. This novel, too, is fast-paced, moving, and believable.

Mazer's descriptive ability is excellent. The reader is able to see vividly what her characters look like, what their physical environment consists of, and most importantly, how they feel about themselves and others. In addition to addressing their responses to social problems and adversity, Mazer tackles ordinary concerns of teenagers. What's life all about? Supposing I don't get married, then what do I do? Will I be able to earn my keep? What do I do besides work? Will I even grow up before the world blows up? And if so, do I want to? Do I want to be old? Why did that boy or girl walk past me in the hall without speaking today? What should I wear to school tomorrow? Mazer tackles these issues with concern, understanding, and humor.

—Mary Lystad

McCAFFREY, Anne (Inez)

Nationality: Irish. **Born:** Cambridge, Massachusetts, 1 April 1926. **Education:** Stuart Hall, Staunton, Virginia; Montclair High School, New Jersey; Radcliffe College, Cambridge, Massachusetts, B.A. (cum laude) in Slavonic languages and literature 1947; studied meteorology at City of Dublin University; also studied voice for nine years. **Family:** Married H. Wright Johnson in 1950 (divorced 1970); two sons and one daughter. **Career:** Copywriter and layout designer, Liberty Music Shops, New York, 1948-50; copywriter, Helena Rubinstein, New York, 1950-52. Currently runs a thoroughbred horse stud farm in Ireland; since 1978, director, Dragonhold Ltd., and since 1979, director, Fin Film Productions; has performed in and directed several operas and musical comedies in Wilmington and Greenville, Delaware; Secretary-Treasurer, Science Fiction Writers of America, 1968-70. **Awards:** Hugo award for best novella, World Science Fiction Society, 1968, for "Weyr Search"; Nebula award for best novella, Science Fiction Writers of America, 1969, for "Dragonrider"; E.E. Smith award for fantasy, 1975; American Library Association notable book citations, 1976, for *Dragonsong,* and 1977, for *Dragonsinger; Horn Book* Fanfare Citation, 1977, for *Dragonsong;* Hugo award, Ditmar award, Gandalf award, and Eurocon/Streso award, all 1979, all for *The White Dragon;* Balrog citation, 1980, for *Dragondrums;* Golden Pen award, 1981; Science Fiction Book Club award, 1986, for *Killashandra,* 1989, for *Dragonsdawn,* and 1990, for *The Renegades of Pern* and *The Rowan.* **Agent:** Virginia Kidd, P.O. Box 278, Milford, Pennsylvania 18337, U.S.A. **Address:** Dragonhold-Underhill, Newcastle, Co. Wicklow, Republic of Ireland.

PUBLICATIONS FOR ADULTS AND YOUNG ADULTS

Novels

Restoree. New York, Ballantine, 1967; London, Rapp and Whiting, 1968.

Dragonflight. New York, Ballantine, 1968; London, Rapp and Whiting, 1969.

Decision at Doona. New York, Ballantine, 1969; London, Rapp and Whiting, 1970.

The Ship Who Sang. New York, Walker, 1969; London, Rapp and Whiting, 1971.

The Mark of Merlin. New York, Dell, 1971; London, Millington, 1979.

The Ring of Fear. New York, Dell, 1971; London, Millington, 1979.

Dragonquest: Being the Further Adventures of the Dragonriders of Pern. New York, Ballantine, 1971; London, Rapp and Whiting-Deutsch, 1973.

To Ride Pegasus. New York, Ballantine, 1973; London, Dent, 1974.

The Kilternan Legacy. New York, Dell, 1975; London, Millington, 1976.

Dragonsong. New York, Atheneum, and London, Sidgwick and Jackson, 1976.

Dragonsinger. New York, Atheneum, and London, Sidgwick and Jackson, 1977.

Dinosaur Planet. London, Futura, 1977; New York, Ballantine, 1978.

The Dragonriders of Pern. New York, Doubleday, 1978.

The White Dragon. New York, Ballantine, 1978; London, Sidgwick and Jackson, 1979.

Dragondrums. New York, Atheneum, and London, Sidgwick and Jackson, 1979.

The Harper Hall of Pern. New York, Doubleday, 1979.

Crystal Singer. New York, Ballantine, and London, Severn House, 1982.

The Coelura. Columbia, Pennsylvania, Underwood Miller, 1983; with *Nerilka's Story,* London, Bantam, 1987.

Moreta: Dragonlady of Pern. New York, Ballantine, and London, Severn House, 1983.

Dinosaur Planet Survivors. New York, Ballantine, and London, Futura, 1984.

Stitch in Snow. Columbia, Pennsylvania, Underwood Miller, 1984.

The Girl Who Heard Dragons. New Castle, Virginia, Cheap Street, 1985.

The Ireta Adventure (includes *Dinosaur Planet* and *Dinosaur Planet Survivors*). New York, Doubleday, 1985.

Killashandra. New York, Ballantine, 1985; London, Bantam, 1986.

Nerilka's Story. New York, Ballantine, 1986; with *The Coelura,* London, Bantam, 1987.

Habit Is an Old Horse. Seattle, Dryad Press, 1986.

The Year of the Lucy. New York, Tor, 1986; London, Corgi, 1987.

The Lady. New York, Ballantine, 1987; as *The Carradyne Touch,* London, Macdonald, 1988.

Dragonsdawn. New York, Del Rey, 1988; London, Bantam, 1989.

The Renegades of Pern. New York, Ballantine, 1989; London, Bantam, 1990.

With Jody Lynn Nye, *The Death of Sleep.* New York, Baen, 1990.

Pegasus in Flight. New York, Ballantine, and London, Bantam, 1990.

The Rowan. New York, Ace, and London, Bantam, 1990.

With Elizabeth Moon, *Sassinak.* New York, Baen, 1990.

Three Gothic Novels (includes *The Mark of Merlin, The Ring of Fear,* and *The Kilternan Legacy*). Columbia, Pennsylvania, Underwood Miller, 1990; as *Three Women,* New York, Tor, 1990.

All the Weyrs of Pern. New York, Ballantine, 1991.

Damia. New York, Putnam, 1991.

With Elizabeth Moon, *Generation Warriors.* New York, Baen, 1991.

Wing of Pegasus (includes *To Ride Pegasus* and *Pegasus in Flight*). Garden City, Guild America Books, 1991.

With Jody Lynn Nye, *Crisis on Doona.* New York, Ace, 1992.

Crystal Line. New York, Ballantine, 1992.

With Margaret Ball, *The Partnered Ship.* New York, Ace, 1992.

With Elizabeth Ann Scarborough, *Powers That Be.* New York, Ballantine, 1992.

The Ship Who Searched. New York, Simon and Schuster, 1992.

Damia's Children. New York, Putnam, 1993, and Ace Books, 1994.

The City Who Fought. New York, Baen Books, 1993.

The Chronicles of Pern: First Fall. New York, Del Rey, 1993.

Lyon's Pride. New York, Ace Books, 1994.

Treaty at Doona. New York, Ace Books, 1994.

The Dolphins of Pern. New York, Ballantine, 1994.

With Elizabeth Ann Scarborough, *Power Lines.* New York, Ballantine, 1994.

With Jody Lynn Nye, *The Ship Who Won.* New York, Baen, 1994.

Freedom's Landing. New York, Putnam, 1995.

An Exchange of Gifts. Newark, Wildside Press, 1995.

With Elizabeth Ann Scarborough, *Power Play.* New York, Ballantine, 1995.

Black Horses for the King. New York, Harcourt, 1996.

No One Noticed the Cat. New York, ROC, 1996.

Freedom's Choice. New York, Putnam, 1997.

Dragon's Eye. New York, Ballantine, 1997.

With Margaret Ball, *Acorna: The Unicorn Girl.* New York, HarperPrism, 1997.

With Margaret Ball, *Acorna's People,* New York, HarperPrism, 1997.

With Richard Woods, *A Diversity of Dragons.* 1997.

Masterharper of Pern. New York, Ballantine, 1998.

Freedom's Challenge. New York, Putnam, 1998.

Short Stories

A Time When, Being a Tale of Young Lord Jaxom, His White Dragon, Ruth, and Various Fire-Lizards. Cambridge, Massachusetts, NESFA Press, 1975.

Get off the Unicorn. New York, Ballantine, 1977; London, Corgi, 1979.

The Worlds of Anne McCaffrey. London, Deutsch, 1981.

Other

Editor, *Alchemy and Academe: A Collection of Original Stories Concerning Themselves with Transmutations, Mental and Elemental, Alchemical and Academic.* New York, Doubleday, 1970.

Editor, *Cooking out of This World.* New York, Ballantine, 1973.

The People of Pern, with Robin Wood. Norfolk, Virginia, Donning, 1988.

The Dragonlover's Guide to Pern, with Jody Lynn Nye. New York, Ballantine, 1989.

Editor, with Elizabeth Ann Scarborough, *Space Opera.* New York, DAW Books, 1996.

Contributor to anthologies, including *Infinity One,* 1970, *Future Love,* 1977, and *Once Upon a Time,* 1991, *Masters of Fantasy,* 1992, and to magazines, including *Analog, Galaxy,* and *Magazine of Fantasy and Science Fiction.*

*

Media Adaptations: *Dragonsong* and *Dragonsinger* have been adapted as children's stage plays by Irene Elliott and produced in Baltimore, Maryland; the "Pern" books have also inspired a cassette of music, *Dragonsongs,* a board game, and two computer games. *The White Dragon, Moreta, Dragonlady of Pern, Nerilka's Story,* and *The Rowan* are all available on cassette. *Freedom's Landing* and *Lyon's Pride* as audio books by Brilliance Corp., 1994 and 1995.

Manuscript Collections: Syracuse University, New York; Kerlan Collection, University of Minnesota, Minneapolis.

Biography: Entry in *Dictionary of Literary Biography,* Vol. 8, Detroit, Gale, 1981; essay in *Speaking for Ourselves: Autobiographical Sketches by Notable Authors of Books for Young Adults,* Vol. 1, compiled and edited by Donald R. Gallo, National Council of Teachers of English, 1990; essay in *Authors and Artists for Young Adults,* Vol. 6, Detroit, Gale, 1991; essay in *Something about the Author Autobiography Series,* Vol. 11, Detroit, Gale, 1991.

Bibliography: *Leigh Brackett, Marion Zimmer Bradley, Anne McCaffrey: A Primary and Secondary Bibliography* by Rosemarie Arbur, Boston, Hall, 1982; *Anne McCaffrey: A Reader's Guide* by Mary T. Brizzi, Mercer Island, Washington, Starmont, 1986; *Anne Inez McCaffrey: Forty Years of Publishing, An International Bibliography* by Mathew D. Hargreaves, Seattle, Washington, 1992; *Anne Inez McCaffrey: Two More Years of Publishing* by Mathew D. Hargreaves, Seattle, 1994.

Critical Studies: Entry in *Contemporary Literary Criticism,* Vol. 17, Detroit, Gale, 1981; ''Backed by Popular Demand,'' in *Library Journal,* 15 February 1994; ''The Booklist Interview: Anne McCaffrey,'' in *Booklist,* 15 March 1994; *Anne McCaffrey: A Critical Companion* by Robin Roberts, Westport, Connecticut, Greenwood Press, 1996.

*   *   *

Anne McCaffrey is a prolific writer in the field of young adult fiction. Her well-loved works include science fiction and fantasy, as well as adult romances.

Her most widely known books are what McCaffrey herself classifies as ''soft sf,'' the ''Dragonriders of Pern'' series which includes fifteen titles; they have fantasy elements but hardcore science is in the background in the stories set on the planet Pern. Once a colony of Earth, the people of P.E.R.N. (Parallel Earth Resources Negligible) have lost the little technology they chose to possess in their efforts to fight Thread, a deadly spore that consumes all organic matter. The only thing standing between the people and the menace Thread are the dragonriders, men and women bound for life to the genetically engineered, telepathic, fire-breathing dragons. Pern has become a feudal society, in which the drangonriders serve as lords, with songs and harpers used to keep their history alive in the 50-year spans when no thread falls.

The first two books in the ''Dragonrider'' series, *Dragonflight* and *Dragonquest,* deal with the efforts and politics of Pern's protectors and people. In *Dragonflight,* Lessa, the heir to Ruatha Hold, watches as her parents are killed, and pursues their killer. Having succeeded, she searches for something to fill the void her victory has left, and becomes the female leader of Benden Weyr, the preeminent dragon home. *Dragonquest* shows the conflict between old ways and new, as the dragonriders, who Lessa has brought two hundred years forward into their future, try to force an evolved society back into the old mold. The third book in the trilogy, *The White Dragon,* showcases a minor character from the previous works, and follows the maturing and coming-of-age of Jaxom and his unusual white dragon, Ruth.

The dragon books tend to lean heavily on the theme of heroism, since the dragonriders are indeed Pern's heroes. McCaffrey tends to emphasize that the reason her characters cannot reach a goal is not a flaw in their personalities, but in their circumstances. With the dragons, McCaffrey speaks to teenagers who have ever longed for a friend who will instantly know their hurts and unhappiness, and always be there. McCaffrey depicts her dragons as large, gentle children, totally devoted to their riders, and the dragons bring both

humor and life to the stories, as well as the necessary touch of the fantastic.

The next three books focus on Harper Hall, and follow a pattern similar to those focusing on the Dragonriders. The first two books follow a theme, and the third explores a supporting character's life. *Dragonsong* and *Dragonsinger* tell the story of Menolly, a girl who wants to be a Harper more than anything in the world. Menolly achieves her goal, becoming Pern's first female Harper against all odds. *Dragondrums* tells the story of Menolly's best friend, Piemur, an apprentice who can't seem to find his place. Both Menolly and Piemur are engaging, generously drawn characters who evoke a genuine desire to read more about them.

The remaining nine books in the series address the history preceding the first six. *Moreta: Dragonlady of Pern, Nerilka's Story, Dragonsdawn,* and *Renegades of Pern* seem rushed in both tone and style compared to the first books. Though written intermittently with other series, fans impatient for the next installment in the saga (which is a curious blend of science fiction, fantasy, and romance) will overlook the flaws. Characters who were rich in nuance become the cardboard versions of themselves, lacking the originality of detail that made them so well-loved in the first books. *Moreta* and *Nerilka's Story* tell the story of a flu epidemic striking Pern. With the dragonriders ill, there is no one to repel the attacking Thread, and Pern's Healers race to discover the long-lost medical techniques that will combat the plague. *Moreta* has an unhappy ending, the heroine dying as she completes her task of vaccine delivery. *Nerilka's Story* was designed to be an ancillary tale, answering the questions left unresolved in *Moreta. Moreta's* characters, while well-written, lack sympathy, and *Nerilka's* are primarily stiff and dull.

The later books *All the Weyrs of Pern, The Chronicles of Pern: First Fall, The Dolphins of Pern,* and *Dragon's Eye* are more devoted to the science that brought the low-tech colony to the agrarian culture known to the dragonriders. *The Chronicles of Pern: First Fall* tells of how P.E.R.N. was colonized, the technology available and how it was abandoned when the first thread began to fall. *The Dolphins of Pern* recounts the abandonment of the first colony on Pern and the establishment of the first weyr. *All the Weyrs of Pern* tells of the discovery and reclamation of their ancestors' lost technology and how the dragonriders work to defeat Thread for a final time. The characters and the storytelling are strongest in those books about the dragonriders such as Lessa, F'lar, and those who began the series in *Dragonflight.*

Also popular with teen readers are *The Rowan* and *Damia* books about a technological space-going society that relies on telekinetics and telepathies to support technology. These psychics are the defense of their solar system, as well as the freight-handling workhorses. *The Rowan* and *Damia* deal with a mother and daughter's search for love among equals, when they have none.

Occupying the same universe are McCaffrey's hugely popular ''Ship Who Sang'' series, including books co-written with Mercedes Lackey and Margaret Ball. The ''Ship'' books follow the lives of shell persons, crippled men and women who choose to give up their useless bodies and run ships and installations with their minds, and their ''brawns,'' the mobile people chosen to aid them. The ''Ship'' protagonists are all female, and their brawns are all male. In one title, however, *The City Who Fought,* the roles are reversed with the ''shell'' being a male. Eventually, like most of McCaffrey's works, there is a happy ending, in which brawn and shell person find love in spite of the physical barriers.

McCaffrey's writing on the whole is entertaining and crisp, with attention paid to the details of anything new to the reader. Her characters are appealing for their perseverance and use of natural gifts. In several of her books, difficult topics such as death and rape are glossed over, concealed by delicate wording, so only careful and aware reading indicates the underlying action. Though many of her earlier works contained technical flaws, McCaffrey has increasingly relied on the help of experts. Her novels delve into her interests in psychology, psychic ability, and the ethics of whether future technologies will enhance life or create new conflicts. She continues to weave compelling stories, ranging from softer science-based fantasy to near-future and advanced technological galaxies, in which there is something to be enjoyed by all ages.

—Melanie Belviso, updated by Lisa A. Wroble

McCAUGHREAN, Geraldine

Pseudonym: Has also written as Felix Culper. **Nationality:** British. **Born:** Geraldine Jones, in Enfield, Middlesex, 6 June 1951. **Education:** Enfield County Grammar School for Girls, 1963-69; Southgate Technical College, Middlesex, 1969-70; Christ Church College of Education, Canterbury, Kent, 1973-77, B.Ed. (honours) 1977. **Family:** Married John McCaughrean in 1988; one daughter, Ailsa. **Career:** Secretary, Thames Television, London, 1970-73; secretary, 1977, and sub-editor, 1978-79 and 1983-88, Marshall Cavendish, publishers, London; editorial assistant, Rothmans, Ware, Hertfordshire, 1980-82; editor, Banbury Focus, Oxfordshire, 1982. **Awards:** All-London Literary Competition, 1979, for short story "The Pike"; Whitbread Children's Book Award, 1987, and Katholischen Kinderbuchpreis (Germany), 1991, for *A Little Lower than the Angels*; Library Association Carnegie Medal and *Guardian* award, both 1989, both for *A Pack of Lies*; *Parenting* Reading Magic Award, 1993, for *Greek Myths*; Beefeater Children's Novel Award, 1994, for *Gold Dust*; Smarties Book Prize Bronze Award, 1996, for *Plundering Paradise*. **Agent:** Jacqueline Korn, David Higham Associates, 5-8 Lower John Street, Golden Square, London W1R 4HA. **Address:** The Bridge House, Great Shefford, Berkshire, RG17 7DA, England.

PUBLICATIONS FOR YOUNG ADULTS

Fiction

A Little Lower than the Angels. Oxford, Oxford University Press, 1987.
A Pack of Lies. Oxford, Oxford University Press, 1988; New York, Oxford University Press, 1989.
Gold Dust. Oxford, Oxford University Press, 1993.
Plundering Paradise. Oxford, Oxford University Press, 1996.
Forever X. Oxford, Oxford University Press, 1997.
The Pirate's Son. New York, Scholastic Press, 1998.
Hatching the Stones. Forthcoming.

Other (retellings)

1001 Arabian Nights, illustrated by Stephen Lavis. Oxford, Oxford University Press, 1982.
The Canterbury Tales, illustrated by Victor Ambrus. Oxford, Oxford University Press, 1984; Chicago, Rand McNally, 1985.
El Cid. Oxford, Oxford University Press, 1989.
The Orchard Book of Greek Myths, illustrated by Emma Chichester Clark. London and New York, Orchard, 1992.
The Odyssey, illustrated by Victor G. Ambrus. Oxford, New York, Oxford University Press, 1993.
The Orchard Book of Stories from the Ballet, illustrated by Angela Barrett. London, Orchard, 1994; as *Random House Book of Stories from the Ballet,* New York, Random House, 1995.
Stories from Shakespeare, illustrated by Antony Maitland. London, Orion Children's Books, 1994.
On the Day the World Began, illustrated by Norman Bancroft-Hunt. Harlow, Essex, Longman, 1995.
The Quest of Isis, illustrated by David Sim. Harlow, Essex, Longman, 1995.
Myths and Legends of the World: The Golden Hoard, illustrated by Bee Willey. London, Orion Children's Books, 1995; New York, McElderry, 1996.
Myths and Legends of the World: The Silver Treasure, illustrated by Bee Willey. London, Orion Children's Books, 1996; New York, McElderry, 1997.
Moby Dick, Or, The White Whale, illustrated by Victor G. Ambrus. Oxford and New York, Oxford University Press, 1996.
King Arthur and the Round Table, illustrated by Alan Marks. Hove, Macdonald Young Books, 1996.
Myths and Legends of the World: The Bronze Cauldron, illustrated by Bee Willey. London, Orion Children's Books, 1997.
God's People: Stories from the Old Testament, illustrated by Anna Leplar. London, Orion Children's Books, and New York, M.K. McElderry Books, 1997.
The Orchard Book of Greek Gods and Goddesses, illustrated by Emma Chichester Clark. London, Orchard Children's Books, 1997.
The Doubleday Book of Princess Stories, illustrated by Lizzie Sanders. London, Doubleday, 1997.
Beauty and the Beast, illustrated by Gary Blythe, San Diego, Harcourt Brace, 1999.
Myths and Legends of the World: The Crystal Pool. Forthcoming.
God's Kingdom. Forthcoming.

Also contributor to numerous anthologies and collections.

PUBLICATIONS FOR CHILDREN

Adaptor, *Who's That Knocking on My Door?,* by Michel Tilde. Oxford, Oxford University Press, 1986.
The Story of Noah and the Ark, illustrated by Helen Ward. Dorking, Surrey, Templar, 1987.
The Story of Christmas. Dorking, Surrey, Templar, 1988.
My First Space Pop-up Book, illustrated by Mike Peterkin. London, Guild Publishing, and New York, Little Simon, 1989.
My First Earth Pop-up Book, illustrated by Mike Peterkin. London, Guild Publishing, 1989; New York, Little Simon, 1990.
Saint George and the Dragon, illustrated by Nicki Palin. New York, Doubleday, 1989.

Adaptor, *The Snow Country Prince,* by Daisuka Ikeda, illustrated by Brian Wildsmith. Oxford, Oxford University Press, 1990; New York, Knopf, 1991.

Adaptor, *The Princess and the Moon,* by Daisuka Ikeda, illustrated by Brian Wildsmith. Oxford, Oxford University Press, and New York, Knopf, 1991.

Adaptor, *The Cherry Tree,* by Daisuka Ikeda, illustrated by Brian Wildsmith. Oxford, Oxford University Press, 1991; New York, Knopf, 1992.

Adaptor, *Over the Deep Blue Sea,* by Daisuka Ikeda, illustrated by Brian Wildsmith. Oxford, Oxford University Press, 1992.

Blue Moon Mountain, illustrated by Nicki Palin. Dorking, Surrey, Templar, 1994.

Blue Moo, illustrated by Colin Smithson. Harlow, Essex, Longman, 1994.

Baabra Lamb, illustrated by Colin Smithson. Harlow, Essex, Longman, 1994.

Good Dog, illustrated by Colin Smithson. Harlow, Essex, Longman, 1994.

Gregorie Peck, illustrated by Colin Smithson. Harlow, Essex, Longman, 1994.

Little Angel, illustrated by Ian Beck. London, Orchard Books, 1995.

Cowboy Jess. London, Orion Children's Books, 1995.

Cowboy Jess Saddles Up. London, Orion Children's Books, 1996.

Unicorns! Unicorns!, illustrated by Sophie Windham. London, Orchard Children's Books, and New York, Holiday House, 1997.

Noah and Nelly. London, Orion Children's Books, 1997.

Casting the Gods Adrift, illustrated by Paul Fisher-Johnson. London, A & C Black, 1998.

Never Let Go, illustrated by Jason Cockcroft. London, Hodder, 1998.

Too Big. London, Transworld, 1998.

Beauty and the Best, illustrated by Gary Blythe. London, Transworld, forthcoming.

Other, as Felix Culper

Seaside Adventure, illustrated by Chrissie Wells. London, Hamlyn, 1986.

Tell the Time, with Chrissie Wells, illustrated by Wells. London, Hamlyn, 1986.

Orville and Cuddles (eight titles). London, Dragon Books, 1986.

In the Town, Having Fun, On the Move, illustrated by Shelagh McGee. London, Hamlyn, 1986.

The Infinite Beyond, illustrated by Mike Peterkin, paper engineering by Paul Wilgress. New York, Warner Books, 1989.

The Mighty Deep, illustrated by Mike Peterkin, paper engineering by Paul Wilgress. New York, Warner Books, 1989.

PUBLICATIONS FOR ADULTS

Novels

The Maypole. London, Secker & Warburg, 1989.
Fires' Astonishment. London, Secker & Warburg, 1990.
Vainglory. London, Cape, 1991.
Lovesong. London, Richard Cohen Books, 1996.
The Ideal Wife. London, Richard Cohen Books, 1997.

Textbooks (as Geraldine Jones)

Adventure in New York. London, Oxford University Press, 1979.
Raise the Titanic. Oxford, Oxford University Press, 1980.
Sabre Tooth. Oxford, Oxford University Press, 1980.

Radio Plays

Last Call. BBC Radio 4 and BBC World Service, 1991.
A Little Lower than the Angels (adapted for radio by Barbara Minchin). BBC Radio 4, 1992.

*

Media Adaptations: Audio Tapes—*Greek Myths* (read by Andrew Sachs), Chivers Audio Books, 1993; *Stories from Shakespeare* (read by Anton Rodgers and Imelda Staunton), Abbey, 1995; *The Golden Hoard* (read by Nigel Lambert), Chivers Audio Books, 1996; *The Silver Treasure* (read by Nigel Lambert), Chivers Audio Books, 1997; *The Bronze Cauldron,* forthcoming.

*   *   *

Geraldine McCaughrean is a writer difficult to categorize in terms of "age suitability." The universality of her novels for the young, *A Little Lower than the Angels* and *A Pack of Lies,* brings to mind C. S. Lewis's dictum that a children's story enjoyed only by children is a bad children's story. Yet her adult work, especially the novel *Vainglory,* is accessible to teenagers with an interest in history and a zest for challenging prose. Reading McCaughrean reinforces the belief that a good book is written for anyone capable of reading it, regardless of the intended primary audience.

McCaughrean entered the field of books for young people as a reteller of tales; her versions of *1001 Arabian Nights* and Chaucer's *The Canterbury Tales* first marked her as an exciting new talent, a writer capable of inspired storytelling. Although she has continued to work in this field, her novels give readers the uncomfortable sense that McCaughrean's gift is to some degree wasted on the re-creation of other writers' material. She has a rare power to evoke wonderfully imagined worlds of her own.

A Little Lower than the Angels, McCaughrean's first novel, was published to immediate acclaim, winning the Whitbread Children's Novel Award in 1987. Set in medieval England, it tells the story of golden-haired Gabriel, a stonemason's apprentice who runs away from his evil master and takes refuge with a troupe of travelling players. The pageant cart on which they perform biblical plays is a dominating presence in the story. On one level, the book can be read as an exciting adventure tale, recounting what happens to Gabriel after he is wheedled into acting the part of an angel by the superficially beneficent playmaster, Garvey, in a wicked confidence trick. Shunning the friendship of Lucie, who plays Lucifer and seems devilish to innocent Gabriel, the boy comes very close to believing that he has miraculous, angelic powers. His rude awakening begins when his former master, the villainous mason, arrives and allies himself with Garvey, and his disillusionment is completed when he is confronted by dying plague victims, desperate for the miracle he cannot perform. This brilliantly imagined, terrifying episode is the climax of the story; thereafter Gabriel, facing the truth about Garvey, casts his lot with Lucie and his daughter Izzie. The story moves toward a warm, satisfying conclusion—and one of the most moving final sentences in literature.

A short summary cannot do justice to the texture and variety of this novel. As well as being a story full of action and dramatic incident, it is an exploration of good and evil, reality and illusion, truth and falsehood in relationships. The prose is ravishing, the dialogue pithy and believable. Images burn themselves into the reader's mind—the young Gabriel plunging on a rope through the dusty air of the church, prefiguring other falls; the pageant cart with its burden of truth and illusion, heaven and hell, lurching over the rainswept moor; the peacock's feathers brightening the angel's wings. Like all the best historical novels, *A Little Lower than the Angels* convinces by the sheer power of its writing; Geraldine McCaughrean sustains a richly imagined, consistent world.

The same may be said of *Vainglory*, a long novel published for adults, but well within the grasp of a historically minded teenager. Set in France during the fifteenth and sixteenth centuries and featuring both historical and fictional characters, it recounts the fortunes of the family de Gloriole, whose passion for their chateau, Gloriole-sur-Sablois in the Loire Valley, poisons their love for one another. Just as the pageant cart played a powerful symbolic role in *A Little Lower Than the Angels,* the chateau, ungrateful recipient of so much ostentatious devotion, haunts *Vainglory* and defines the book's moral thrust. The background appears in loving, colorful detail, recalling the stylized art of Jean duc de Berry's *Très Riches Heures,* but the characters refuse to be confined in the landscape. Cruel, obsessed, and larger than life, they roam a world where terror and peril are incarnated in birds with curved beaks and creatures with sharp teeth. But the pervading motif of the book is fire, from the ominous pyre that consumes Jeanne d'Arc to a final conflagration brought about by the determination of the last de Gloriole to escape the thrall of the lovely, murderous chateau. *Vainglory* suspends our belief that the past is a foreign country; in McCaughrean's treatment, it is thoroughly credible and underpinned by a deep moral sensibility.

It is proof of Geraldine McCaughrean's versatility that *A Pack of Lies,* winner of the *Guardian* Children's Fiction Award and the Carnegie Medal in 1988, is as different from the aforementioned books as can be imagined. Both a novel and a collection of short stories, *A Pack of Lies* concerns a mysterious young man, MCC Berkshire, who meets Ailsa Povey in a public library and arranges to work unpaid in her mother's unsuccessful antiques shop. There he displays his (and Geraldine McCaughrean's) brilliance as a storyteller, weaving tales around items of stock in which customers have shown—in the main, tepid—interest. So good are the stories that the enthralled customers invariably buy, to the embarrassment of Ailsa and Mrs. Povey, who regard MCC's stories as ''a pack of lies.'' This gleeful, good-humored tour de force may be read simply for fun. Anyone can enjoy a spoof detective story, a ''moral tale,'' or the hilarious Gothic horror story that features Baron Greefenbludd, the hunchbacked Fowlstrangler, and the Reverend Lovegood Divine. But this is really a sophisticated book. The author moves confidently from one country, one period, and one genre to another, and one must be widely read to fully experience the pleasure of its constant literary echoing. The problem posed by the conclusion is a tricky one: MCC Berkshire's ''pack of lies''

turns out to have been a pack of truth, and his disappearance from the shop forces the Poveys and the reader to consider the complex relationship between the teller of a story and the characters he creates.

Admirers of Geraldine McCaughrean's work will return to books they have already read, and find new riches in them. They will also be hungry for new stories. Taking another brave leap away from familiar ground, McCaughrean in 1993 published *Gold Dust,* a novel about two children caught up in a rush for gold in modern Brazil. McCaughrean has also continued her work as a reteller of old tales, from the Odyssey to Melville's *Moby Dick.* In 1996, for instance, she published *The Golden Hoard,* which recounts stories as familiar as Midas and as obscure as the Kikuyu legend of how men and women came to agree. *Publisher's Weekly* placed high blessing not only on this volume, but on the author's whole career: ''McCaughrean could probably weave a mesmerizing tale from the copy on the back of a cereal box.''

—Eileen Dunlop, updated by Judson Knight

McCULLERS, (Lula) Carson (Smith)

Nationality: American. **Born:** Columbus, Georgia, 19 February 1917. **Education:** Columbia High School, graduated 1933; attended classes at Columbia University, New York, and New York University, 1935-36. **Family:** Married 1) James Reeves McCullers, Jr., in 1937 (divorced, 1940); 2) remarried McCullers in 1945 (died, 1953). Writer. **Awards:** Fiction fellowship, Houghton Mifflin, 1939; Bread Loaf Writers Conference fellowship, 1940; Guggenheim fellow, 1942, 1946; National Institute of Arts and Letters grant in literature, 1943; *Mademoiselle* award, 1948; New York Drama Critics Circle award, two Donaldson awards, and the Theatre Club, Inc. gold medal, all 1950, all for the stage adaptation of *The Member of the Wedding;* prize of the younger generation from German newspaper *Die Welt,* 1965, for *The Heart Is a Lonely Hunter;* University of Mississippi grant, 1966; Henry Bellamann award, 1967. Member, American Academy, 1952. **Died:** 29 September 1967.

PUBLICATIONS

Novels

The Heart Is a Lonely Hunter. Boston, Houghton, 1940; London, Cresset Press, 1943.
Reflections in a Golden Eye. Boston, Houghton, 1941; London, Cresset Press, 1942.
The Member of the Wedding. Boston, Houghton, and London, Cresset Press, 1946.
The Ballad of the Sad Cafe: The Novels and Stories of Carson McCullers. Boston, Houghton, 1951; as *The Ballad of the Sad Cafe and Other Stories,* New York, Bantam, 1967; as *The Shorter Novels and Stories of Carson McCullers,* London, Barrie & Jenkins, 1972.
Clock without Hands. Boston, Houghton, and London, Cresset Press, 1961.

Short Stories

The Ballad of the Sad Cafe: The Novels and Stories of Carson McCullers. Boston, Houghton, 1951; London, Cresset Press, 1952; as *Collected Short Stories,* Houghton, 1961; as *The Shorter Novels and Stories of Carson McCullers,* London, Barrie & Jenkins, 1972.
Seven. New York, Bantam, 1954.

Plays

The Member of the Wedding, adaptation of her own novel (produced Philadelphia, 1949; New York, 1950; London, 1957). New York, New Directions, 1951.
The Square Root of Wonderful (produced Princeton, New Jersey, and New York, 1957; London, 1970). Boston, Houghton, 1958; London, Cresset Press, 1958.

Television Plays: The Invisible Wall, from her story, ''The Sojourner,'' 1953; *The Sojourner,* from her own story, 1964.

Poetry

The Twisted Trinity, music by David Diamond. Philadelphia, Elkan Vogel, 1946.
Sweet as a Pickle and Clean as a Pig (for children). Boston, Houghton, 1964; London, Cape, 1965.

Other

The Mortgaged Heart: The Previously Uncollected Writings of Carson McCullers, edited by Margarita G. Smith. Boston, Houghton, 1971; London, Barrie & Jenkins, 1972.

*

Media Adaptations: *The Member of the Wedding* (film), Columbia, 1952; *Reflections in a Golden Eye* (film), Seven Arts, 1967; *The Heart Is a Lonely Hunter* (film), Warners-Seven Arts, 1968.

Biography: Entry in *Dictionary of Literary Biography,* Detroit, Gale, Volume 2: *American Novelists Since World War II,* 1978, Volume 7: *Twentieth-Century American Dramatists,* 1981.

Bibliography: *Katherine Anne Porter and Carson McCullers: A Reference Guide* by Robert F. Kiernan, Boston, Hall, 1976; *Carson McCullers: A Descriptive Listing and Annotated Bibliography of Criticism* by Adrian M. Shapiro, Jackson R. Bryer, and Kathleen Field, New York, Garland, 1980.

Manuscript Collection: Humanities Research Center, University of Texas, Austin.

Critical Studies: *Carson McCullers: Her Life and Work* by Oliver Evans, London, Owen, 1965, as *The Ballad of Carson McCullers,* New York, Coward McCann, 1966; *Carson McCullers* by Lawrence Graver, Minneapolis, University of Minnesota Press, 1969;

Carson McCullers by Dale Edmonds, Austin, Texas, Steck Vaughn, 1969; *The Lonely Hunter: A Biography of Carson McCullers* by Virginia Spencer Carr, New York, Doubleday, 1975, London, Owen, 1977; *Carson McCullers* by Richard M. Cook, New York, Ungar, 1975; *Carson McCullers* by Margaret B. McDowell, Boston, Twayne, 1980; entry in *Contemporary Literary Criticism,* Detroit, Gale, Volume 1, 1973, Volume 4, 1975, Volume 10, 1979, Volume 12, 1980.

*   *   *

Although Carson McCullers did not consider herself a writer for young adults her fictions provide such notable adolescent heroines that they have become favorites of young readers and a staple of high school and college literature courses. Moreover, the writer, who published her first novel at twenty-three, infused her work with the emotional energy of her own troubled adolescence. In fact, gangling adolescent girls are just some of the misfit characters with whom McCullers peoples her works, making her pictures of kids and teens universally appealing to younger and older readers.

The gawky adolescent in her first novel, *The Heart Is a Lonely Hunter,* is Mick Kelley, whose nickname reveals her ambivalent sexual identity. The Kelley family operates a boarding house in the white working-class section of an unnamed Southern mill city, and the boarders form a group of lonely misfits who often puzzle and frighten the maturing young girl. Mick has matured beyond her twelve years because she is pressed into caring for her younger siblings by her busy, distracted mother. She finds some companionship with her weary, worked-out father, but in her awakening adolescence she adopts a surrogate father in the person of Mr. Singer, a deaf-mute boarder who repairs watches at a local jewelry store.

McCuller's original title for the novel was *The Mute,* since the ironically silent Singer becomes the central symbolic character around whom the other characters orbit. In addition to Mick, they include Biff Brannon, the owner of a nearby café and a childless widower who sees Mick as a surrogate daughter. The town's two intellectuals—Jake Blount, a white radical, and Dr. Copland, a black physician—also regard Singer with sympathy. Both of them believe the mute to be a Jew, which is not the case; in fact, Singer understands little of their intellectual ramblings, nor is he much more concerned with Biff or Mick. Actually he is devoted to another mute who has been institutionalized in a nearby mental hospital. When the friend dies suddenly, Singer commits suicide, leaving the others to puzzle out some meaning for their existence.

Although Mick is only one of the major characters in *The Heart Is a Lonely Hunter,* she remains the most fully developed and least symbolic, but also the most hopeful. With her interests in music and narrative as well as her desire to travel and create, Mick represents something of the author's own adolescence. Similar girls appear in many of McCullers's short fictions including many unpublished stories written before her successful first novel. Her first published story, ''Wunderkind,'' concerns a young musician who is hailed as such by her overbearing mentor, another surrogate father who later abandons her to the confusions of adolescence. Later stories would see the reappearance of this adolescent character as well, often enough as a teenaged boy, though these stories seem less successful as serious literature.

However, the best example of the adolescent remains Frankie Addams, the protagonist of McCullers's novel *The Member of the Wedding*. Several characters in this novel are near analogues of those depicted in *The Heart Is a Lonely Hunter*. The most obvious pairing involves the female adolescents Frankie Addams and Mick Kelley, girls similar in age, appearance, and, to some extent, motivation. Frankie's father recalls Mick's in that both men are ineffective and estranged from their daughters; Frankie's mother is dead, while Mick's, busy caring for her small children and the boarders, was virtually nonexistent. Thus Frankie, like Mick, lacks a primary female role model. Both girls are alienated from other children by differences in age and interests, while they maintain a fitfully meaningful relationship with younger children, especially Mick with Bubber and Frankie with John Henry West. The relationship between Frankie and the family's cook, Berenice Sadie Brown, develops that of Mick and Portia in the earlier novel.

While McCullers used Mick Kelley as this type of symbolic adolescent in her first novel, in *The Member of the Wedding* she concentrates entirely on the adolescent and presents the story more completely and from the girl's point of view. Yet adolescence remains a metaphor and larger issues are present.

As the novel opens, Frankie feels that her recent and rapid growth spurt has made her a real freak, like the tall man in the carnival's Freak House. Frankie's physical maturation has made her unsure of her sexuality, so she is also fascinated by the Half-Man/Half-Woman in the Freak House. Her nickname again proves ambiguous in terms of gender, symbolizing as well her precarious state between childhood and adolescence. Her hair is cropped short, and her summer outfit consists of Boy Scout shorts and a BVD undershirt. In this transitional state, Frankie feels lost; she is not a "member" of anything in her own view.

Of course, she is still a member of her extended family, though she is an only child with a dead mother and a distant father. During the summer, she is part of a surrogate family consisting of Berenice, the family's black cook, and John Henry, her younger cousin. This mundane "family" is not romantic enough for her, however, and she wants to escape the Addams's kitchen to a more glamorous world of wartime adventure and romance. She believes her older brother who is stationed in Alaska has achieved this goal.

When her brother announces his marriage on an upcoming army leave, Frankie becomes fascinated with the idea that she will somehow be a "member of the wedding." Although she is included in the wedding party, the newly wedded couple have no intention of inviting her on their honeymoon. Frankie "throws a fit" of childish anger and later contemplates suicide. The novel's final section serves as a sort of coda, set some three months after the wedding. Frankie is leaving her situation at last; she and her father are moving to a new suburb, leaving behind Berenice, who is too old to move with them, and John Henry, who has died from meningitis in the interim. Her change is symbolized by her name— she prefers to be called Frances now—as well as by her new friendship with her suburban neighbor, Mary Littlejohn.

Critics have disagreed on how ironically McCullers intends her ending, but all agree that it rings true in both realistic and symbolic terms. The writer's fictions accurately depict the desires and disappointments of adolescence, and at the same time she portrays the young adult as an American "everyman" in the tradition of Huck Finn, bewildered by a world of dangerous choices and adult responsibilities. Adolescent characters populate McCullers's fiction from her first story to her final novel and although she did not create these characters for the pleasure of younger readers alone, these intriguing portraits have placed her fictions among the favorites of teenagers and their teachers alike.

—Joseph R. Millichap

McCULLOCH, John Tyler. *See* **BURROUGHS, Edgar Rice**

McGRAW, Eloise Jarvis

Nationality: American. **Born:** Houston, Texas, 9 December 1915. **Education:** Classen High School, Oklahoma City, graduate 1932; Principia College, Elsah, Illinois, B.A. in art 1937; Oklahoma University, Norman, 1938; Colorado University, Boulder, 1939; Museum Art School, Portland, Oregon (now Pacific Northwest College of Art), Portland, Oregon, 1970-78. **Family:** Married William Corbin McGraw in 1940; one son and one daughter. **Career:** Instructor in portrait and figure painting, Oklahoma City University, Oklahoma City, 1943-44; writer since 1949; voluntarily corrected and graded English compositions for local district high school, 1961-62; teacher of adult education fiction writing classes, Lewis & Clark College, Portland, 1965-66, and Portland State University, summers, 1970-78; teacher at University of Oregon Haystack conference, manuscript clinic, summers, 1965-67. Has directed juvenile workshops in Portland, Oregon, Seattle, Washington, La Jolla, California, and elsewhere; speaks frequently on writing at schools and literary gatherings; featured in writers' "Teleconferences" broadcast on educational channels. **Awards:** *New York Herald-Tribune* Children's Book Festival honor book, 1951, for *Crown Fire*; Newbery Honor Book, 1952, for *Moccasin Trail*, 1962, for *The Golden Goblet*; Lewis Carroll Shelf award, 1963; William Allen White award nominations, 1973, for *Master Cornhill* and 1983, for *The Money Room*; Mystery Writers of America Edgar Allan Poe award for best juvenile mystery of the year, 1978, for *A Really Weird Summer*; Mark Twain award, Sequoyah award, and Bluebonnet award nominations, all 1983, for *The Money Room*; Western Writers Golden Spur award nomination, 1983-84, for *Hideaway*; L. Frank Baum Memorial award, with daughter Lauren Lynn McGraw, International Wizard of Oz Club, 1983, for contributions to the Oz saga; Evelyn Sibley Lampman award, Oregon Library Association, 1984, for "significant contribution to children's literature"; Iowa Children's Choice award and Tennessee Volunteer State Book award nominations, and West Virginia Children's Book award, all 1990-91, for *The Seventeenth Swap*; Oregon Literary Arts Award, 1992, for *Striped Ships*; Edgar Allen Poe Award finalist and ALA Recommended Books for the Reluctant Young Adult Reader, both 1994, for *Tangled Webb*; Charles Erskine Scott Wood Award for Lifetime Achievement, Oregon Literary Arts, 1996; *Boston Globe-Horn Book* Honor Book, Society of Children's Book Writers and Illustrators Golden Kite Award, Parents' Choice Silver Honor, Best

Book List, *School Library Journal,* and named to New York Public Library 100 Best Books List and *Parenting Magazine*'s Reading Magic Awards list, all 1996, and Oregon Literary Arts Book award and Newbery Honor Book, both 1997, all for *The Moorchild.* **Agent:** Curtis Brown Ltd., 10 Astor Pl., New York, New York 10003. **Address:** 1970 Indian Trail, Lake Oswego, Oregon 97034, U.S.A.

PUBLICATIONS FOR YOUNG ADULTS

Fiction

Sawdust in His Shoes. New York, Coward McCann, 1950.
Crown Fire. New York, Coward McCann, 1951.
Moccasin Trail. New York, Coward McCann, 1952.
Mara, Daughter of the Nile. New York, Coward McCann, 1953; London, Penguin, 1986.
The Golden Goblet. New York, Coward McCann, 1961; London, Methuen, 1964.
Merry Go Round in Oz, with Lauren Lynn McGraw, illustrated by Dick Martin. Chicago, Reilly & Lee, 1963.
Greensleeves. New York, Harcourt Brace, 1968.
Master Cornhill. New York, Atheneum, 1973; London, Penguin, 1987.
A Really Weird Summer. New York, Atheneum, 1977.
Joel and the Great Merlini, illustrated by Jim Arnosky. New York, Pantheon, 1979.
The Forbidden Fountain of Oz, with Lauren Lynn McGraw, illustrated by Dick Martin. N.p., International Wizard of Oz Club, 1980.
The Money Room. New York, Atheneum, 1981.
Hideaway. New York, Atheneum, 1983.
The Seventeenth Swap. New York, Atheneum, 1986; London, Viking Kestrel, 1988.
The Trouble with Jacob, illustrated by Jon Riley. New York, McElderry, and London, Viking Kestrel, 1988.
The Striped Ships. New York, Macmillan, 1991.
Tangled Webb. New York, McElderry, and Toronto, Maxwell Macmillan Canada, 1993.
The Moorchild. New York, McElderry, 1996.

Play

Steady, Stephanie. Chicago, Dramatic Publishing, 1961.

PUBLICATIONS FOR ADULTS

Novel

Pharaoh. New York, Coward McCann, 1958.

Other

Techniques of Fiction Writing. Boston, The Writer, 1959.

*

Media Adaptations: *Moccasin Trail* (sound recording and film-strip), Newbery Award Records, 1973; *The Golden Goblet* (sound recording and filmstrip), Newbery Award Records, 1975.

Biography: Essay in *Something about the Author Autobiography Series,* Vol. 6, Detroit, Gale.

Manuscript Collections: University of Oregon Library, Eugene; Kerlan Collection, University of Minnesota.

*   *   *

With a forty-year writing career and some twenty juvenile titles to her credit, Eloise Jarvis McGraw is a widely respected author of young-adult fiction. As a rule, her novels are carefully and realistically plotted; invariably, a reader is made to care about her sharply drawn and appealing protagonists. At her best, McGraw demands much of the youthful readers she rigorously avoids talking down to, engaging in frequent wordplay, supporting her plots with understated foreshadowing and symbolism.

With the possible exception of McGraw's "Oz tales," her novels are concerned with adolescent loners—characters whose rebelliousness, prejudice, or scant assets block meaningful social interaction and who must learn to fit into their environments, to trust and appreciate other people. While the majority of her novels have male protagonists, five of her best works tell the stories of strong and highly individualized adolescent women: *Mara, Daughter of the Nile, Greensleeves, The Striped Ships, Tangled Webb,* and *The Moorchild.*

McGraw's first novel, *Sawdust in His Shoes,* is a kind of *Toby Tyler* in reverse, and tells the story of Joe Lang, a young bareback rider who temporarily leaves the circus and learns trust and lasting confidence from a family on a small farm. Contemporary adolescent readers would likely complain about the novel's occasionally cloying scenes and about its idealized portraits of family life. Nevertheless, the novel remains a moving and rather enchanting portrait of rural America in the early 1900s, as does a subsequent novel, *Crown Fire,* the tale of a quick-tempered young lumberjack/boxer who must learn self-control.

The most satisfying works from the first decade of McGraw's career are her historical novels. Three of these are set in ancient Egypt, providing a convincing glimpse of ancient Egyptian religion and culture: *Mara, Daughter of the Nile*; *Pharaoh,* sometimes considered an "adult" version of the history forming the basis of *Mara*; and *The Golden Goblet.* The best of these, *Mara,* combines a love story with political intrigue to underscore a young woman's gradual apprehension of her moral responsibility to herself and others. *Moccasin Trail,* set on the eighteenth-century American frontier, shows the struggles of a white youth raised by Indians to reintegrate himself in white society. It includes some of McGraw's finest scenes of daring adventure; its depiction of Indian society, while not always entirely accurate, is surprisingly objective. Nevertheless, the conclusion of the novel (wherein the protagonist throws off his Indian background) is abrupt and unconvincing.

Greensleeves marks a turning point in McGraw's career. Written in first person, set in contemporary America, and covering parts of two years in the life of its protagonist, the novel is the richest, the most immediate, the most "adult" of all McGraw's fiction. Employing as backdrop a mild mystery story where nothing is what it seems, *Greensleeves* is concerned with appearances vs. realities, especially those in the mind of its protagonist, Shannon Lightly. The reader immediately recognizes Shannon as a strong, intelligent, witty, and very cosmopolitan eighteen-year-old; Shannon herself, however, is convinced she is gawky and socially inept. Ironically, it is only after she assumes the persona of a gum-popping, heavily mascaraed bimbo named Georgette that Shannon learns to live outside herself, gaining confidence in her ability to make and keep friends, to live a meaningful life. Eventually, she must face the question of her true identity, one apart from "Georgette" or the old Shannon. The delightful plot and characterizations make the novel immensely readable; its central issues—the ramifications of divorce, the changing nature of the modern family, the often agonizing process of self-discovery, the distinctions between sexual attraction and love—provide it with timeless viability.

With the exception of one of her most recent novels, *The Striped Ships,* and her "Oz" stories, McGraw's fiction following *Greensleeves* has been set in contemporary society and has dealt with contemporary issues, particularly the influences of parental separation or divorce on adolescent children. These later novels, beginning with *Master Cornhill,* are about half the length of McGraw's earlier works; their language is simpler; their protagonists are generally twelve or thirteen rather than sixteen or older. While long-time readers of McGraw may miss the relative complexity and stylistic richness of her earlier novels, it is important to recognize that her readership has shifted from older to younger adolescents, the majority of them pre-teens.

The best of these later "contemporary novels" is *A Really Weird Summer* which, despite its innocuous title, is a serious symbolic representation of the psychological impact of parental divorce, together with subsequent familial role shifting, on an oldest child. The novel's protagonist, unable to cope with the new dynamics of his family or the resulting responsibilities that seem to be falling upon him, creates his own "safe" reality in an imaginary world of increasingly vivid and "real" hallucinations. On the point of abandoning himself to his created world, he finally recognizes its danger and pulls back from it, acquiring a maturity that will see him through his real-life challenges.

Also engagingly original is the most recent of McGraw's "contemporary novels," *Tangled Webb,* which describes the twelve-year-old protagonist's grief at the death of her mother and her conflicted emotions when her father decides to remarry. The protagonist correctly intuits that her new stepmother is hiding something, and she is determined to uncover the secret. But as the process of revelation is set in motion, the protagonist finds herself aligned with her stepmother, fervently hoping that the secret—whatever it is—will not disrupt their family. While this short novel might be faulted for failing to develop the difficult social issues it introduces, like alcoholism and poverty, or for failing to explore more convincingly the complex family dynamics at its center, it is nevertheless a moving and efficiently narrated story that speaks to children who have themselves experienced family transformation.

Other later novels include *Hideaway,* a novel with two adolescent protagonists who help one another understand personal responsibility in the face of nonexistent or unsuitable parental role models; *The Seventeenth Swap,* an entertaining but thematically superficial tale of a boy who "swaps" his way to a gift for a handicapped friend; and *The Money Room* and *The Trouble with Jacob,* lighthearted mysteries concerned with sibling rivalry and the working out of personal identity in single-parent households.

In *The Striped Ships,* McGraw returns to historical fiction, recounting the adventures of an eleven-year-old Norman British girl who is separated from her family and who eventually determines to center herself through art—through helping to create the Bayeux tapestry. Though the novel is intended for a younger audience than McGraw's early novels, it approximates their length; it also resembles them in its deft characterizations and its carefully developed plot. McGraw's latest novel, *The Moorchild,* is an absorbing fantasy about a changeling who, despite being shunned and mistreated by the people of the village in which she has grown up, determines to find the human child for whom she was exchanged and to restore the child to its parents. Both *The Striped Ships* and *The Moorchild* convincingly echo the themes of McGraw's earliest novels: the difficulty of acquiring independence while demonstrating morally responsible socialization, and the necessity of reaching outside oneself in order to achieve true self-discovery.

—Keith Lawrence

McINTYRE, Vonda N(eel)

Nationality: American. **Born:** Louisville, Kentucky, 28 August 1948. **Education:** University of Washington, Seattle, B.S. in biology 1970, graduate study in genetics, 1970-71. **Career:** Writer, from 1969. Conference organizer, and riding and writing instructor. **Awards:** Nebula award, 1973, for "Of Mist, and Grass, and Sand"; Hugo award and Nebula award, both 1978, both for *Dreamsnake.* **Address:** P.O. Box 31041, Seattle, Washington 98103-1041, U.S.A.

PUBLICATIONS

Novels

The Exile Waiting. New York, Doubleday, 1975; London, Gollancz, 1976.
Dreamsnake. Boston, Houghton Mifflin, and London, Gollancz, 1978.
The Entropy Effect. New York, Pocket Books, and London, Macdonald, 1981.
Star Trek II: The Wrath of Khan (novelization of screenplay). New York, Pocket Books, and London, Futura, 1982.
Superluminal. Boston, Houghton Mifflin, 1983; London, Gollancz, 1984.
Star Trek III: The Search for Spock (novelization of screenplay). New York, Pocket Books, and London, Panther, 1984.
The Bride (novelization of screenplay). New York, Dell, 1985.
Barbary. Boston, Houghton Mifflin, 1986.
Enterprise: The First Adventure. New York, Pocket Books, 1986.
Star Trek IV: The Voyage Home (novelization of screenplay). New York, Pocket Books, 1986; London, Grafton, 1987.
Starfarers, illustrated by Byron Taylor. Norwalk, Connecticut, Easton Press, 1989.
Screwtop, with *The Girl Who Was Plugged In,* by James Tiptree, Jr. New York, Tor Books, 1989.
Transition. Norwalk, Connecticut, Easton Press, 1991.
Metaphase. New York, Bantam, 1992.
Nautilus. New York, Bantam, 1994.
The Crystal Star. New York, Bantam Books, 1994.
The Moon and the Sun. New York, Pocket Books, 1997.

Short Stories

Fireflood and Other Stories. Boston, Houghton Mifflin, 1979; London, Gollancz, 1980.

Contributor, *Lythande,* by Marion Zimmer Bradley (includes novelette "Looking for Satan"). London, Sphere, 1988.

Other

Editor, with Susan Janice Anderson, *Aurora: Beyond Equality.* New York, Fawcett, 1976.

Contributor, *The Crystal Ship: Three Original Novellas of Science Fiction,* edited by Robert Silverberg. Nashville, Tennessee, Nelson, 1976.

Contributor, *Interfaces,* edited by Ursula K. Le Guin and Virginia Kidd. New York, Ace, 1980.

Contributor to science fiction magazines, including *Analog: Science Fiction/Science Fact.* Currently working on novel entitled *Changeling.*

*

Critical Studies: Entry in *Contemporary Literary Criticism,* Volume 18, Detroit, Gale, 1981.

Vonda N. McIntyre comments:

I don't label myself a young adult writer—only a writer. I've written one children's book, *Barbary,* and a novel, *Dreamsnake,* that earned some notice in young adult publications. But *Dreamsnake,* like *Superluminal* and the "Starfarers" quartet *(Starfarers, Transition, Metaphase,* and *Nautilus),* were written as novels for grown-ups. I don't myself believe that young readers would be hurt by reading anything I've ever written, including the scenes dealing directly with sexuality. But others would disagree, so you ought to be aware that you might take some heat, in our increasingly puritanical social climate, for mentioning books in which violence hurts, in which when people die, their deaths affect all the people around them for more than the forty-two minutes of the average TV episode, and in which people who love each other engage in sexual activity and enjoy it. (And in which people sometimes have sex just for fun and aren't punished for it afterwards.)

*   *   *

Nebula and Hugo award winner Vonda N. McIntyre, an astute storyteller who creates possible future worlds that often draw on her scientific background in genetics, is noted for her realistic characters who have believable flaws and strengths. Her short stories and novels most often center on the importance of being responsible for one's own choices and the realization of individual potential through commitment to oneself and others.

When McIntyre began publishing in the early 1970s, she was one of several new female science fiction writers with a strong feminist stance. McIntyre, however, avoids plots centered directly on the inequalities facing women in a society dominated by men. Her more subtle approach demands characters prove themselves in situations where being female is not the main issue—finding a way to live up to their fullest potential is. They may face challenging, repressive circumstances, but those circumstances grow from personal and social situations like those currently confronted in contemporary society. Instead of centering on gender issues, the focus is instead on the strength of mind and spirit necessary to move beyond inhibiting circumstances.

In her early work, McIntyre created young female protagonists who demonstrate the intelligence, ingenuity, and tenacity necessary to meet difficult goals. Characters like Mischa, the mutant telepath who must free herself from a dystopian city on a postholocaust world in McIntyre's first novel, *The Exile Waiting,* and Kylis, a spaceport "rat" serving time doing hard labor in a penal colony on another future world in *Screwtop,* survive on their intelligence and courage. Both learn the importance of commitment to other people—Mischa risks her life to save her tutor and Kylis passes up a chance for freedom because it requires she betray the men with whom she has partnered.

Snake is the healer serving her proving year in the Nebula-winning novelette "Of Mist, and Grass, and Sand" and *Dreamsnake,* the Nebula and Hugo award-winning novel developed from it. Snake becomes McIntyre's prototype female whose dedication to her personal goals in no way diminishes her concern for others. As a healer, Snake uses her knowledge of genetics and molecular biology to manipulate the biochemistry of the genetically altered snakes Mist and Sand so they create venoms which heal. Grass, a rare off-world dreamsnake, produces venom that allows the terminally ill to die peacefully. After a lapse in judgment which results in Grass's death, the grief-stricken Snake must face the realization that without the dreamsnake she cannot function as a healer. She recognizes her responsibility for her failure, but, in *Dreamsnake,* turns her regret and anger to strength as she faces the mental and physical challenges of a quest for a new dreamsnake.

In the course of Snake's journey, McIntyre introduces elements she develops in most all her subsequent writing: the importance of community and personal responsibility, conflicts about the use of technology, "partnerships" in which three or more adults form a relationship analogous to traditional marriages but free of the sex role stereotyping, the naturalness of the need for sexual expression, the importance of contraception (achieved in McIntyre's future worlds through biofeedback techniques taught to both males and females as children), and the necessity of moving beyond loss and grief in one's life.

Starfarers and its sequels, *Transition, Metaphase,* and *Nautilus,* extend these themes and explore the problems and consequences inherent in mixing science and technology with human needs and goals. Technophobia, the politics of research, the perversion of peaceful technology to destructive purposes, and conflicts between nationalistic factions combine and contrast with the joy of pure research, exploration, and discovery as the spaceship *Starfarer* transitions along cosmic strings between star systems on a search for intelligent alien life forms. Contact occurs in *Transition* and *Metaphase,* but "civilization" is closed to groups who practice war. Victoria MacKenzie, a brilliant mathematician, develops an equation that allows the Earth ship to travel the strings faster than civilization ships can. Civilization, it turns out, is old and existing on the technology of its creators. Victoria's algorithm offers significant progress and may be the "gift" required from new cultures. Humans, with their ingenuity, may be welcome after all.

Barbary, the only one of McIntyre's books written expressly for young readers, uses an alien contact event as a cover for a very human action. Barbary, a streetwise orphan being placed with a new family, uses the adults' distraction to sneak her pet cat Mickey aboard the ship taking her to her new home on the space research station *Einstein.* The clever ways she and her new sister deal with the problems of secretly caring for Mickey mark them as very young exemplars of McIntyre's strong females and fit them nicely into the tradition of the child in young adult literature who rebels against and subverts adult authority.

In 1982, McIntyre began writing novelizations of the Star Trek films. *Star Trek II: The Wrath of Khan, Star Trek III: The Search for Spock,* and *Star Trek IV: The Voyage Home* parallel the film plots, and *Enterprise: The First Adventure* provides backstory for the whole series by telling how Jim Kirk becomes captain and the crew becomes cohesive when their routine shakedown cruise encounters a new life form near Romulan space. Though the optimistic Star Trek view that science and technology clearly serve humankind's best interests and the fast-paced adventure remain intact, the deft, detailed characterization clearly stamps these books as McIntyre's work. She makes Spock's continuous struggle to control his human responses and Jim Kirk's insecurities sympathetic and realistic. In *Enterprise,* she introduces an element of jealousy in the ranks when one among the crew is promoted out of sequence to become the captain's yeoman. This quirk departs a bit from the usual Star Trek dictate that the crew never conflicts, but it certainly demonstrates a keen knowledge about how people actually relate to each other.

McIntyre shares with the Star Trek philosophy a basic optimism about the ultimate advantages of technology. Her worlds, however, are undercut by a dark element that suggests a cautionary approach. *Dreamsnake* and *The Exile Waiting* take place on a world recovering from the ruin of a nuclear war. In *Screwtop,* vastly superior people called "tetraparentals" are created by combining the genetic traits of four parents. They must spend their lives working on projects decided for them before they were born and are allowed no individuality. The novella "Aztecs" introduces a starship pilot who must have her heart replaced with pluseless electronic pumps so she can survive the faster-than-light-speed velocities required by interstellar travel. The technology allows the pilot to achieve her goals, but, because of some basic biomechanical incompatibility, it isolates her from normal humans. Ruin, enslavement, and alienation, then, can result as readily as the beneficent progress Star Trek promises.

—Linda G. Benson

McKILLIP, Patricia A(nne)

Nationality: American. **Born:** Salem, Oregon, 29 February 1948. **Education:** San Jose State University, B.A. 1971, M.A. in English 1973. **Career:** Writer. **Awards:** World Fantasy award for best novel, 1975, for *The Forgotten Beasts of Eld;* Hugo award nomination, 1979, for *Harpist in the Wind.*

PUBLICATIONS FOR YOUNG ADULTS

Fiction

The House on Parchment Street, illustrated by Charles Robinson. New York, Atheneum, 1973.
The Throme of the Erril of Sherill, illustrated by Julie Noonan. New York, Atheneum, 1973.
The Forgotten Beasts of Eld. New York, Atheneum, 1974; London, Futura, 1987.
The Night Gift, illustrated by Kathy McKillip. New York, Atheneum, 1976.
Harpist in the Wind. New York, Atheneum, and London, Sidgwick and Jackson, 1979.
Heir of Sea and Fire. New York, Atheneum, 1977; London, Sidgwick and Jackson, 1979.
The Riddle-Master of Hed. New York, Atheneum, 1976; London, Sidgwick and Jackson, 1979.
Riddle of Stars (includes *The Riddle-Master of Hed, Heir of Sea and Fire,* and *Harpist in the Wind*). New York, Doubleday, 1979; as *The Chronicles of Morgon, Prince of Hed,* London, Sidgwick and Jackson, 1981.
The Quest of the Riddlemaster. New York, Ballantine, 1980.
Moon-Flash. New York, Atheneum, 1984.
The Moon and the Face. New York, Atheneum, 1985.
The Changeling Sea. New York, Atheneum, 1988.
The Sorceress and the Cygnet. New York, Ace, 1991.
The Cygnet and the Firebird. New York, Ace, 1993.
Something Rich and Strange. New York, Bantam Books, 1994.
The Book of Atrix Wolfe. New York, Ace Books, 1995.
Winter Rose. New York, Ace Books, 1996.
Song for a Basilisk. New York, Ace Books, 1998.

PUBLICATIONS FOR ADULTS

Novels

Stepping from the Shadows. New York, Atheneum, 1982.
Fool's Run. New York, Warner, and London, Macdonald, 1987.

*   *   *

One of the best contemporary fantasy writers for young adults is Patricia McKillip. Her distinctive writing voice sets her books apart from more traditional fantasies. A mood of dreamy mysticism pervades most of her works, and her heroes and heroines are loners isolated from others by their own immense supernatural powers and/or by their search for some ultimate truth. Greed, the abuse of power, and the struggle between love and hate are all recurring themes for McKillip.

Two of McKillip's early works do not display the unique style that is the strength of her later novels. Her first book, *The House on Parchment Street,* is a standard ghost story inspired by McKillip's childhood in England. This book and *The Night Gift* (McKillip's only realistic novel, in which a group of young people try to make a hideaway for a teenager who has attempted suicide) are her only young adult works set in the real world.

McKillip found her voice in her second book, *The Throme of the Erril of Sherill,* a novelette in which a Cnite searches for a legendary song of unsurpassed beauty in order to win the hand of his beloved princess. This book set the tone for her future fantasies and introduced her favorite scenario: the king's greed creates the need for the quest and the power of love brings it to an end.

Following *The Throme of the Erril of Sherill* was *The Forgotten Beasts of Eld,* another fantasy of greed, power, hate, and love. The isolated sorceress of Eld Mountain finds her intellectual life interrupted by the arrival of a baby and a young lord. Her powers eventually become the focus of a war for control of the kingdom— a war reflected in her personal struggle between her strong mental powers and her awakening emotions. In a sense the book is a parable about the need for balance between pure reason and deep emotions.

A similar struggle is the basis for McKillip's well-known fantasy trilogy: *The Riddle-Master of Hed, Heir of Sea and Fire,* and *Harpist in the Wind.* Using the riddle concept she introduced in *The Forgotten Beasts of Eld,* McKillip creates a society in which asking and answering riddles represents the highest intellectual achievement. The trilogy follows the destiny of Morgon of Hed, a riddle master faced with the greatest riddle of all: his identity. Filled with prophecy, battles, sorcery, noble warriors, and ladies, the trilogy is an epic tale of one man's struggle between his need for the truth and his fear of it as he is pulled between his love and hatred for the mysterious harpist who directs his destiny.

McKillip turns her talents to science fiction in *Moon-Flash* and *The Moon and the Face,* in which she builds a living cultural museum on a planet that may or may not be Earth. The tribes who live on the planet are unaware of one another and of the advanced civilization that watches over them. In *Moon-Flash* a curious young girl from one of the tribes decides to follow a river to the world's end, where she and a friend discover the truth about their society. *The Moon and the Face* continues the story after the protagonists have uncovered the true nature of the annual moon-flash their people worship. Even in science fiction, McKillip maintains her mysticism: the primitive tribe has dreams about the more advanced civilization, even though they cannot interpret the dreams, and the young heroine can sense the stories behind alien artifacts by a mere touch.

Like *Moon-Flash,* McKillip's return to fantasy, *The Changeling Sea,* concerns one adolescent girl, Peri, a misfit in her society, who becomes involved in events beyond her understanding. To punish the sea for drowning her father, Peri hexes the sea, not realizing she actually has the power to do so. As the spells unravel, mythical sea creatures rise to the world of men and Peri becomes the unwitting catalyst in breaking the enchantments over two young princes. As in *Moon-Flash,* there is a touch of romance.

Because of their sexual content, McKillip's more recent books are more suited to an older audience. *Fool's Run* is a science fiction novel about a rock band that performs on a penal space station and gets involved in an escape. McKillip is at her most mystic in this novel, leaving the reader confused about what has actually happened in the story. The many characters are driven by hate, love, and a need for truth, but this is also a book about the power of music and of vision. *The Sorceress and the Cygnet* is similarly overladen with intuitive mysticism. In this fantasy, a young man from a gypsy-like tribe is coerced into freeing a group of mythical beings from their eternal prisons and helping them find a source of power protected by his distant relative. Again, the mystic element is so heavy that the reader is unsure of what transpires during the story's climax.

At her best McKillip is a powerful writer adept at juggling universal themes and subjects. No one is better at exploring the imperative of truth and its high personal cost.

—Donna R. White

McKINLEY, (Jennifer Carolyn) Robin

Nationality: American. **Born:** Warren, Ohio, 16 November 1952. **Education:** Dickinson College, Carlisle, Pennsylvania, 1970-72; Bowdoin College, Brunswick, Maine, B.A. (summa cum laude) in English 1975. **Family:** Married Peter Dickinson in 1992. **Career:** Editor and transcriber, Ward & Paul, Washington, D.C., 1972-73; research assistant, Research Associates, Brunswick, 1976-77; bookstore clerk, Maine, 1978; teacher and counselor in private secondary school, Natick, Massachusetts, 1978-79; editorial assistant, Little, Brown, Inc., Boston, Massachusetts, 1979-81; barn manager on horse farm, Holliston, Massachusetts, 1981-82; clerk, Books of Wonder, New York, 1983; freelance reader and editor, 1983-85. **Awards:** one of the New York Public Library's Books for the Teen Age, 1980, 1981, and 1982, American Library Association Notable Book, and Horn Book Honor List, for *Beauty: A Retelling of the Story of Beauty and the Beast*; one of the American Library Association's Best Young Adult Books, 1982, and Newbery Honor Book, 1983, for *The Blue Sword*; Newbery Medal, 1985, and named a Notable Book by the Association for Library Service to Children of the American Library Association, for *The Hero and the Crown*; Best Anthology designation from World Fantasy awards, 1986, for *Imaginary Lands*; Horn Book Honor List, 1988, for *The Outlaws of Sherwood*; D.Let., Bowdoin College, 1986. **Agent:** Merrilee Heifetz, Writers House, Inc., 21 West 26th St., New York, New York 10010, U.S.A. **Address:** 33 Queensdale Rd., London W11 4SB, England.

PUBLICATIONS FOR YOUNG ADULTS

Fiction

The Door in the Hedge. New York, Greenwillow, 1981.
The Blue Sword. New York, Greenwillow, 1982; London, MacRae, 1983.
The Hero and the Crown. New York, Greenwillow, and London, MacRae, 1985.
The Outlaws of Sherwood. New York, Greenwillow, 1988.
Deerskin. New York, Putnam, 1993.
A Knot in the Grain and Other Stories. New York, Greenwillow, 1994.
Rose Daughter. New York, Greenwillow, 1997.
The Stone Fey, illustrated by John Clapp. San Diego, Harcourt, 1998.
Kirith. New York, Greenwillow, forthcoming.

Other

Beauty: A Retelling of the Story of Beauty and the Beast. New York, Harper, 1978; London, MacRae, 1983.
Contributor, Terri Windling and Mark Arnold, editors, *Elsewhere II.* New York, Ace Books, 1982.
Contributor, Terri Windling and Mark Arnold, editors, *Elsewhere III.* New York, Ace Books, 1984.
Editor, *Faery.* New York, Ace Books, 1985.
Editor, *Imaginary Lands.* New York, Greenwillow, 1985; London, MacRae, 1987.
Adapter, *Tales from the Jungle Book.* New York, Random House, 1985.
Adapter, *Black Beauty,* illustrated by Susan Jeffers. New York, Random House, 1986; London, Hamish Hamilton, 1987.
Adapter, *The Light Princess,* illustrated by Katie Thamer Treherne. San Diego, Harcourt, 1988.
The Little Mermaid. San Diego, Harcourt, 1989.

PUBLICATIONS FOR CHILDREN

Picture Books

My Father Is in the Navy. New York, Greenwillow, 1992.
Rowan. New York, Greenwillow, 1992.

*

Media Adaptations: *The Blue Sword* (cassette), Random House, 1984; *The Hero and the Crown* (cassette), Random House, 1986.

Critical Studies: Entry in *Children's Literature Review,* Volume 10, Detroit, Gale, 1986.

Biography: Entry in *Dictionary of Literary Biography,* Volume 52: *American Writers for Children since 1960: Fiction,* Detroit, Gale, 1986; essay in *Speaking for Ourselves: Autobiographical Sketches by Notable Authors of Books for Young Adults,* Volume 1, compiled and edited by Donald R. Gallo, National Council of Teachers of English, 1990.

*   *   *

Robin McKinley, whose young-adult works include fairy tales, legends, and fantasies, creates female characters who are intelligent, loyal, and courageous—eager to cross the physical and psychological barriers that lie between them and the fulfillment of their destinies. In her acceptance speech for the Newbery Medal, which she received in 1985 for *The Hero and the Crown,* McKinley commented that she "can't remember a time when the stories I told myself weren't about shy, bumbling girls who turned out to be heroes." Such characters escape and defy the limiting spheres to which they seem confined, sometimes through extraordinary feats of prowess and endurance. As they become aware of their hidden strengths and potential, McKinley's inspirational young heroines mature, beginning to view the world around them with a "new clarity of perception."

In *Beauty,* a retelling of the "Beauty and the Beast" tale—McKinley keeps many of the traditional elements while bringing a freshness and intensity to the story, told from the viewpoint of Beauty, the youngest of three sisters, who is ever conscious of the inappropriateness of her chosen nickname. Beauty, who describes herself as "thin, awkward, and undersized," is nevertheless a courageous and determined heroine. During her enforced sojourn in the castle of the Beast, her image shifts from a tomboy to a beautiful, mature young woman able to wear the silver dress of a princess and to see, as she develops trust and sympathy for the Beast, with a "new depth or roundness." Beauty's love of books, her care and affection for her horse Greatheart, and the progression of her sisters' own romances are woven into the treatment of theme.

The seductive power of evil is broken by perceptive characters in McKinley's retellings of the fairy tales "The Frog Prince" and "The Twelve Dancing Princesses": in the first story, a princess fears rather than is dazzled by a necklace that "gleamed and seemed to shiver with life," and in the second, a soldier sees past the "grace and scintillation of gems and precious things beyond counting" to the deadness that lies across the underground "black lake," where the twelve princesses dance all night. As in *Beauty,* the protagonists in these stories possess the qualities of courage, clear-eyed intelligence, and a capacity for goodness and love, as McKinley retains the spirit of beauty and fairy tale in her imaginative retellings.

Adventure and romance abound in the fantasies *The Blue Sword* and *The Hero and The Crown* both of which are set in the imaginary kingdom of Damar and relate the story of a "damalur-sol," or "lady hero." In *The Blue Sword,* Harry Crewe is kidnapped from the outermost post of the Homelanders by Corlath, king of the hillfolk of Damar. Harry holds fast to her courage and gradually becomes aware of her inherited gift of "kelar"—the "gift of seeing." She is trained to ride and wield a sword in battle, earning a place as one of Corlath's elite riders. Possessing qualities similar to McKinley's other heroines, Harry is a vivacious, forthright, and determined leader in combat and diplomacy and a worthy inheritor of Gonturan, the legendary sword of the flame-haired Lady Aerin. Aerin, is the daughter of the king of Damar and "the witchwoman," who wins her title as "swordbearer" in her father's court by fighting the dragons that plague the kingdom. Almost destroyed by the great dragon Maur, Aerin travels to the valley of Luthe, an immortal "mage," who helps her physically and spiritually overcome the "dragon" of despair and acknowledge her inner strength and power. In a striking passage, Aerin meets Agsded—her uncle and the evil counterpart of herself—in an inner sanctuary and wrests from him the "hero's crown," which holds the strength of Damar. Triumphant in battle against the northerners who threaten Damar, Aerin returns to her home to claim her rightful position as queen.

Landscapes become integral elements in McKinley's work: in *The Blue Sword* and *The Hero and the Crown,* the harsh sand and gritty winds of the desert, and the Stone City and the Damarian Hills of the imaginary kingdom of Damar figure prominently. The haunting quality of landscape and its strong impetus to keep those who love it within its boundaries is felt by Maddie, a young woman who raises sheep in the "Hills" in "The Stone Fey," a short story found *Imaginary Lands,* a book of fantasy stories edited by McKinley. Like her landscapes, McKinley's narratives are richly descriptive. Whether she is describing the colorful, luxurious interior of a king's tent, a deathly combat against the scorching fire of a great dragon, or the warm breath and soft nose of a favorite horse, her attention to detail brings a vitality and vividness to her text.

In *The Outlaws of Sherwood,* McKinley's Robin Hood is an anxious, cautious, and somewhat enigmatic character, whose necessary escape after killing a fellow forester is seen by Lady Marian and the philosophizing much as an opportunity to establish a rebel Saxon band deep within Sherwood Forest. Lady Marian dons Robin Hood's mantle of decisive leadership, while other members of his band exude high spirit and a sense of adventure. Lady Cecily, disguised as a boy outlaw, is another of McKinley's courageous heroines, and her love for Little John adds a tender note. The tale contains both traditional and original elements, and life in Sherwood Forest for the "green young outlaws" is vividly presented in a version that McKinley hopes is "historically unembarrassing."

Written in a rich stylistic prose, McKinley's works range from retellings of fairy tales and legends to original renderings of fantasies and romances. A common thread tying her stories together is the memorable characters she creates whose external journeys and adventures are paralleled by their psychological growth and insistence on integrity at all costs. These stories invite young-adult readers not only to respond to inspirational role models who dare to "do things" but to venture, like McKinley's characters, beyond the borders of their own lands and across the boundaries of their own imaginations.

—Hilary S. Crew

McMILLAN, Terry

Nationality: American. **Born:** 1951. **Education:** University of California, Berkeley, B.A.; attended MFA Film Program at Columbia University, New York. **Career:** Columnist, *New York Times;* book reviewer *New York Times Book Review, The Atlanta Constitution,* and the *Philadelphia Inquirer.* Visiting professor of creative writing, University of Wyoming, Laramie; associate professor of English, University of Arizona, Tucson; teacher of writer's workshop, Stanford University, Stanford, California. **Awards:** New York Foundations for the Arts award for fiction, 1986; Before Columbus Foundation National Book award, 1987, for *Mama;* Women in Communication Matrix Award for Career Achievement in Books, 1993. Fellow, Yaddo Artist Colony, 1982, 1983, and 1985, MacDowell Colony, 1983; Doubleday literary fellowship, Columbia University, 1985; National Endowment for the Arts Fellowship and Rockland Center for the Arts Fellowship, both 1988; Tucson/Pima Arts Council Literary Arts Fellowship, 1990.

PUBLICATIONS

Fiction

Mama. Boston, Houghton Mifflin, and London, Cape, 1987.
Disappearing Acts. New York, Viking, 1989; London, Cape, 1990.
Editor, *Breaking Ice: An Anthology of Contemporary African-American Fiction.* New York, Viking, and London, Cape, 1990.

Waiting to Exhale. New York, Viking, 1992.
How Stella Got Her Groove Back. New York, Viking, 1996.

Nonfiction

Contributor, *Five for Five: The Films of Spike Lee.* New York, Stewart, Tabori and Chang, 1991.

*

Critical Studies: Entry in *Contemporary Literary Criticism,* Volume 50, Detroit, Gale, 1988; Volume 61, 1990.

*   *   *

Terry McMillan is best known for her novel, *Waiting to Exhale,* about four black professional women, their friendships, and their search for fulfilling relationships with men. Although this novel was a best-seller, its subject matter seems a bit adult for young adult readers (and its language a bit graphic). Still, given the dearth of contemporary novels, films, plays, etc., by and about professional black women, perhaps young adult readers, especially young women, would welcome a story of black upper-middle-class experience. In *Waiting to Exhale* they may find, at last, a novel about black women who are not stereotypes. These women pursue careers and relationships because they are educated, independent, and full of humor, self-awareness, and the desire to live fully.

The appeal of McMillan's work lies in her ability to create fresh, original black characters who lead intensely diverse lives. Although McMillan writes about the black community in general, she focuses particularly on the stories and struggles of young black women. McMillan's female characters are survivors—tough, hip, self-directed; with each novel, her female protagonists seem a bit stronger and a bit more focused.

McMillan's first novel, *Mama,* tells the story of the mother-daughter bond between Mildred, a hard talker, drinker, and fighter, and Freda, her oldest daughter, a thoughtful and conscientious young woman. The novel opens in 1964 in industrial Point Haven, Michigan, a fictional town that closely resembles Port Huron, Michigan, where McMillan grew up. Twenty-seven-year-old Mildred is in the midst of another brutal fight with her alcoholic husband, Crook, and thirteen-year-old Freda tries to shelter the younger children from their parents' violence. Throughout the first few chapters of the novel, Freda plays mother to Bootsey, Money, Angel, and Doll, as Mildred tries to find a steady job and a steady man. As the years go by, Mildred goes through jobs and men, struggling to help her children as they confront their own problems, such as drug addiction, unexpected pregnancy, and sexual assault. In particular, Mildred tries to maintain a close relationship with Freda, even after Freda moves to California for school and then to New York for work.

Mildred's fierce love for her children motivates her every move; she explains, "These is *my* kids. . .and this ain't half the shit they gon' see in this world, so they might as well find out from me now what's going on out there before some ignorant ass in the streets gives it to 'em wrong and then they'll really end up catching hell.'' Despite her mother's efforts and her own ambitions, Freda finds herself ''catching hell'' in the form of cocaine abuse, alcoholism, and bad relationships with men. But in the end, when Mildred is forty-eight, and Freda is thirty-four, both mother and daughter have sobered up and redirected their lives. They learn to heal each other: ''Freda pressed her head into Mildred's bare shoulder. . . . Mildred's breasts felt full against her own, and Freda couldn't tell whose were whose. They held each other up. . . . It seemed as if they hugged each other for the past and for the future.''

Another McMillan novel of interest to young adult readers (though again, the themes are definitely adult) is *Disappearing Acts,* the story of a love affair between Zora Banks, a teacher and singer, and Franklin Swift, a construction worker. At the beginning of the novel, both characters are wary of the opposite sex. Franklin, a divorced father of two, is cynical about his ability to sustain a relationship with a woman; he explains: ''[Women] complicate shit. . . . All they do is throw me off track. It takes me too damn long to swing back.'' Zora, however, wants to be in a relationship but finds that her involvement with men keeps her from developing her talents as a teacher and singer. Like Franklin, Zora feels that romantic relationships complicate her life and ambitions, so she decides to avoid such entanglements, stating: ''Instead of wasting my time wishing and hoping, sleeping with self-pity and falling in love over and over again with ghosts, I'm going to stop concentrating so hard on what's missing in my life and be grateful for what I've got. For instance, this organ inside my chest. God gave me a gift, and I'd be a fool not to use it.''

Despite both characters' resistance, a passionate relationship develops between them. Each character alternates the role of narrator as the story of their relationship evolves through courtship, disagreements, moving in together, abortion, pregnancy and childbirth, and sex. But in dealing so explicitly with sexual issues, McMillan realistically addresses the challenges of contemporary relationships.

In fact, the novel is about love and commitment, and the characters' struggles to achieve both. Near the novel's end, Zora tells Franklin, ''. . .understand this: I love you just as much now as I did three years ago. We've had some rough times, and maybe time might help us both; I don't know. But you see that little boy over there? He's ours. We made him. And if you ever get your divorce and you feel like you're ready, come get us.'' Franklin's choice, to live with Zora and his son as a family, reflects the theme running throughout all of McMillan's work, from *Mama* to *How Stella Got Her Groove Back*: emotional fulfillment and stability can be achieved through committed love relationships.

In *How Stella Got Her Groove Back,* McMillan continues her exploration of the effects of love. Stella, a financially independent single mother, discovers happiness unexpectedly on her Jamaican vacation. Falling in love with a man almost half her age, Stella questions social mores and her own need for emotional support as her relationship with this man deepens. Eventually she realizes that though this man may not appear to be a logical mate because of his age, he has enhanced her life by cherishing her unique approach to life, helping her to recapture her love of design and art, and supporting her as she embarks on a new career. And as McMillan has underscored in her other works, accepting what makes you happy in life is the key to true happiness.

—Mary D. Esselman, updated by Sara Pendergast

MEAKER, M.J. *See* KERR, M.E.

MEANS, Florence Crannell

Nationality: American. **Born:** Baldwinsville, New York, 15 May 1891. **Education:** Henry Read School of Art, Denver, 1910-11; Kansas City Theological Seminary, 1912; Macpherson College, Kansas, summers 1922-29; University of Denver, 1923-24. **Family:** Married Carleton Bell Means in 1912 (died 1973); one daughter. **Career:** Lecturer, Writer's Conference in the Rocky Mountains, Boulder, Colorado, 1947-48, and University of Denver Writers' Workshop, 1947-54. **Awards:** Child Study Association annual award for character-building book, 1945, and Newbery Honor Book, 1946, for *The Moved-Outers;* Nancy Bloch Annual award for a book dealing with intercultural relations, 1957, for *Knock at the Door, Emmy;* Central Baptist Seminary churchmanship citation, 1962. **Died:** 19 November 1980.

PUBLICATIONS FOR YOUNG ADULTS

Fiction

Rafael and Consuelo: Stories and Studies about Mexicans in the United States for Primary Children, with Harriet Fullen. New York, Friendship Press, 1929.
A Candle in the Mist, illustrated by Marguerite de Angeli. Boston, Houghton Mifflin, 1931.
Ranch and Ring, illustrated by Henry Peck. Boston, Houghton Mifflin, 1932.
Dusky Day, illustrated by Manning Lee. Boston, Houghton Mifflin, 1933.
A Bowlful of Stars, illustrated by Henry Pitz. Boston, Houghton Mifflin, 1934.
Rainbow Bridge, illustrated by Eleanor Lattimore. New York, Friendship Press, 1934.
Penny for Luck, illustrated by Paul Quinn. Boston, Houghton, 1935.
Tangled Waters, illustrated by Herbert Morton Stoops. Boston, Houghton Mifflin, 1935.
The Singing Wood, illustrated by Manning Lee. Boston, Houghton Mifflin, 1937.
Shuttered Windows, illustrated by Armstrong Sperry. Boston, Houghton Mifflin, 1938.
Adella Mary in Old New Mexico, illustrated by Herbert Morton. Boston, Houghton Mifflin, 1939.
Across the Fruited Plain, illustrated by Janet Smalley. New York, Friendship Press, 1940.
At the End of Nowhere, illustrated by David Hendrickson. Boston, Houghton Mifflin, 1940.
Children of the Promise, illustrated by Janet Smalley. New York, Friendship Press, 1941.
Whispering Girl, illustrated by Oscar Howard. Boston, Houghton Mifflin, 1941.

Shadow over Wide Rain, illustrated by Lorence Bjorklund. Boston, Houghton Mifflin, 1942.

Teresita of the Valley, illustrated by Nicholas Panesis. Boston, Houghton Mifflin, 1943.

Peter of the Mesa, illustrated by Janet Smalley. New York, Friendship Press, 1944.

Wither the Tribes Go Up. New York, Northern Baptist Convention, 1944.

The Moved-Outers, illustrated by Helen Blair. New York, Walker, 1945.

Great Day in the Morning, illustrated by Helen Blair. Boston, Houghton Mifflin, 1946.

Assorted Sisters, illustrated by Helen Blair. Boston, Houghton Mifflin, 1947.

The House under the Hill, illustrated by Helen Blair. Boston, Houghton Mifflin, 1949.

The Silver Fleece, with Carl Means, illustrated by Edwin Schmidt. Philadelphia, Winston, 1950.

Hetty of the Grande Deluxe, illustrated by Helen Blair. Boston, Houghton Mifflin, 1951.

Alicia, illustrated by William Barss. Boston, Houghton Mifflin, 1953.

The Rains Will Come, illustrated by Fred Kabotie. Boston, Houghton Mifflin, 1954.

Knock at the Door, Emmy, illustrated by Paul Lantz. Boston, Houghton Mifflin, 1956.

Reach for a Star. Boston, Houghton Mifflin, 1957.

Borrowed Brother, illustrated by Dorothy Bayley Morse. Boston, Houghton Mifflin, 1958.

Emmy and the Blue Door, illustrated by Frank Nichoas. Boston, Houghton Mifflin, 1959.

But I Am Sara. Boston, Houghton Mifflin, 1961.

That Girl Andy. Boston, Houghton Mifflin, 1962.

Tolliver. Boston, Houghton Mifflin, 1963.

It Takes All Kinds. Boston, Houghton Mifflin, 1964.

Us Maltbys. Boston, Houghton Mifflin, 1966.

Our Cup Is Broken. Boston, Houghton Mifflin, 1969.

Smith Valley. Boston, Houghton Mifflin, 1973.

PUBLICATIONS FOR CHILDREN

Stories

All 'Round Me Shinin'. New York, Baptist Board of Education, c. 1940.

Frankie and Willie Go a Far Piece. New York, Baptist Board of Education, c. 1940.

Some California Poppies and How They Grew. New York, Baptist Board of Education, c. 1940.

Plays

The Black Tents: A Junior Play of Life among the Bedouins of Syria. New York, Friendship Press, 1926.

Tara Finds the Door to Happiness. New York, Friendship Press, 1926.

Pepita's Adventures in Friendship: A Play for Juniors about Mexicans in the United States. New York, Friendship Press, 1929.

Other

Children of the Great Spirit: A Course on the American Indian, with Frances Somers Riggs. New York, Friendship Press, 1932.

Carvers' George: A Biography of George Washington Carver, illustrated by Harve Stein. Boston, Houghton Mifflin, 1952.

PUBLICATIONS FOR ADULTS

Nonfiction

Sagebrush Surgeon (biography of Clarence G. Salsbury). New York, Friendship Press, 1955.

Sunlight on the Hopi Mesas: The Story of Abigail E. Johnson. Philadelphia, Judson Press, 1960.

Biography of Frederick Douglass. Imperial International, 1969.

*

Biography: Entry in *The Junior Book of Authors,* second edition, New York, H.W. Wilson, 1951.

Manuscript Collection: University of Colorado Library, Boulder.

*   *   *

As more children's book departments were established in American publishing companies during the 1930s, a new need also grew: books for "young adults." One of the first writers to fill this need was Florence Crannell Means. Moreover, she went far beyond the "career" type of story which soon became popular to tackle difficult real-life situations with characters presented in depth. She was one of the first to write sympathetically about minority groups, articulating their struggle for dignity, security, and education—or just plain survival.

Her first stories, such as *A Candle in the Mist,* were in the pioneer genre. But though her plots may have been built out of typical frontier activities, her characters are not stereotyped. They have individuality and strength.

It was probably natural to follow pioneer stories with Indian stories; but Means did not write typical Indian stories. A Baptist minister's daughter, she grew up in a household where people of many nationalities and races were welcomed wholeheartedly; thus she developed sympathy and insight into the problems of minorities, with a special interest in Indians of the southwest. Among others, she portrayed Navajos (*Tangled Waters*) and Hopis (*Whispering Girl*). She took time to observe people in their home territory before writing about them. She always put her characters first, bringing out their habits and problems as an integral part of their personalities and their stories.

This concern for human values accounts for the survivability of her stories. Although *Shuttered Windows* and *Great Day in the Morning* are now "period pieces" (blacks are called negroes, and their worlds are basically separate from whites), the books are still valid as to story and character, and valuable as social history. The same can be said of *The Moved-Outers* which deals with nisei (American-born children of Japanese parents) in internment camps on the West Coast during World War II. Reading this now, one wonders if the young people could really have been so mild and cooperative with officials; but they were patriotic, as well as heartbroken; it is still a moving story—and it stands as an obvious yardstick for the change to the cynical outspokenness of today's young people.

In later books, Means presented with great honesty the discouragement and bitterness of a twenty-year-old Hopi Indian girl (*Our Cup Is Broken*) and the unflattering selfishness in desperate times of some members of a young girl's family in Colorado in the early 1900s (*Smith Valley*). In other words, her multilayered stories of all kinds of people are not goody-goody, missionary-inspirational; they are honest, realistic, and, always, interesting and well-written.

—Lee Kingman

MEIGS, Cornelia Lynde

Pseudonym: Adair Aldon. **Nationality:** American. **Born:** Rock Island, Illinois, 6 December 1884. **Education:** Bryn Mawr College, Pennsylvania, A.B. 1908. English teacher, St. Katherine's School, Davenport, Iowa, 1912-13; Instructor, Professor of English, and Professor Emeritus, Bryn Mawr College, 1932-50; civilian employee, U.S. War Department, Washington, D.C., 1942-45; writing instructor, New School for Social Research, New York City, 1951. **Awards:** Drama League prize, 1915, for *The Steadfast Princess;* American Library Association named *The Windy Hill* a Newbery honor book in 1922, *Clearing Weather* in 1929, and *Swift Rivers* in 1933; Newbery Medal, 1934, for *Invincible Louisa,* which was also named to the Lewis Carroll Shelf, 1963; Spring Book Festival middle honor, 1943, for *Mounted Messenger;* Little, Brown & Company prize for *The Trade Wind;* L.H.D., Plano University, Texas, 1967; Jane Addams award, 1971, for *Jane Addams: Pioneer for Social Justice.* **Died:** 8 October 1973.

PUBLICATIONS FOR YOUNG ADULTS

Fiction

The Kingdom of the Winding Road, illustrated by Frances White. New York, Macmillan, 1915.
Master Simon's Garden. New York, Macmillan, 1916.
The Windy Hill. New York, Macmillan, 1921.
The New Moon, illustrated by Marguerite de Angeli. New York, Macmillan, 1924.
Rain on the Roof, illustrated by Edith Ballinger Price. New York, Macmillan, 1925.
As the Crow Flies. New York, Macmillan, 1927.
The Trade Wind, illustrated by Henry Pitz. Boston, Little Brown, 1927; London, Hodder and Stoughton, 1928.
Clearing Weather, illustrated by Frank Dobias. Boston, Little Brown, 1928.
The Wonderful Locomotive, illustrated by Berta and Elmer Hader. New York, Macmillan, 1928.
The Crooked Apple Tree, illustrated by Helen Mason Grose. Boston, Little Brown, 1929.
The Willow Whistle, illustrated by E. Boyd Smith. New York, Macmillan, 1931.

Swift Rivers, illustrated by Forrest Orr. Boston, Little Brown, 1932.
Wind in the Chimney, illustrated by Louise Mansfield. New York, Macmillan, 1934.
The Covered Bridge, illustrated by Marguerite de Angeli. New York, Macmillan, 1936.
Young Americans: How History Looked to Them While It Was in the Making. Boston, Ginn, 1936.
The Scarlet Oak, illustrated by Elizabeth Orton Jones. New York, Macmillan, 1938; Birmingham, Combridge, 1939.
Call of the Mountain, illustrated by James Daugherty. Boston, Little Brown, 1940.
Mother Makes Christmas, illustrated by Lois Lenski. New York, Grosset and Dunlap, 1940.
Vanished Island, illustrated by Dorothy Bayley. New York, Macmillan, 1941.
Mounted Messenger, illustrated by John Wonsetler. New York, Macmillan, 1943.
The Two Arrows. New York, Macmillan, 1949.
The Dutch Colt, illustrated by George and Doris Hauman. New York, Macmillan, 1952.
Fair Wind to Virginia, illustrated by John Wonsetler. New York, Macmillan, 1955.
Wild Geese Flying, illustrated by Charles Geer. New York, Macmillan, 1957.
Mystery at the Red House, illustrated by Robert Maclean. New York, Macmillan, 1961.

Fiction as Adair Aldon

The Island of Appledore, illustrated by W. B. King. New York, Macmillan, 1917.
The Pirate of Jasper Peak. New York, Macmillan, 1918.
The Pool of Stars. New York, Macmillan, 1919.
At the Sign of the Two Heroes, illustrated by S. Gordon Smyth. New York, Century, 1920.
The Hill of Adventure, illustrated by J. Clinton Shepherd. New York, Century, 1922.

Plays

The Steadfast Princess. New York, Macmillan, 1916.
Helga and the White Peacock. New York, Macmillan, 1922.

Other

Invincible Louisa: The Story of the Author of "Little Women." Boston, Little Brown, 1933; as *The Story of Louisa Alcott,* London, Harrap, 1935.
Editor, *Glimpses of Louisa: A Centennial Sampling of the Best Short Stories,* by Louisa May Alcott. Boston, Little Brown, 1968.
Jane Addams: Pioneer for Social Justice: A Biography. Boston, Little Brown, 1970.

PUBLICATIONS FOR ADULTS

Novel

Railroad West. Boston, Little Brown, 1937.

Other

The Violent Men: A Study of Human Relations in the First American Congress. New York, Macmillan, 1949.

Editor and part author, *A Critical History of Children's Literature.* New York, Macmillan, 1953, revised edition, 1969; London, Collier Macmillan, 1969.

What Makes a College?: A History of Bryn Mawr. New York, Macmillan, 1956.

Saint John's Church, Havre de Grace, Maryland, 1809-1959. Havre de Grace, Democratic Ledger, 1959.

The Great Design: Men and Events in the United Nations from 1945 to 1963. Boston, Little Brown, 1963.

Louisa May Alcott and the American Family Story. London, Bodley Head, 1970; New York, Walck, 1971.

*   *   *

Although Cornelia Meigs, who also wrote under the pseudonym of Adair Aldon, is best remembered for her Newbery Medal biography of Louisa May Alcott, *Invincible Louisa,* and for her comprehensive, astute *A Critical History of Children's Literature* (revised in 1969), she also made a significant contribution in several genres to children's literature with historical fiction, mysteries, and drama. Her particular interest in the development of the United States was reflected in many books; her experiences of storytelling within the family circle were a source of her sense of narrative flow; her empathy for children was echoed repeatedly in stories in which they are faced with obstacles and rise to conquer their problems.

Meigs's first book for young adults, *The Kingdom of the Winding Road,* was published in 1915 but is now out of print, as are many of her other titles. Her second book, *Master Simon's Garden,* received wider critical acclaim; it is a strikingly effective message about intolerance: in a rigidly Puritan Massachusetts town, Master Simon is reviled for wasting time and space on a beautiful garden—an expression of his love and tolerance—but his legacy is appreciated by future generations. Her interest in the past is also evident in *The Willow Whistle,* a tale of pioneer life in the midwest; in *Wind in the Chimney,* two English children are instrumental in helping their widowed mother keep her new home in America just after the American Revolution; and *The Covered Bridge,* set in Vermont in 1788, has a strong sense of local history and the New England countryside.

Meigs's play *The Steadfast Princess* won the Drama League Prize in 1915, and her dramatic flair is repeatedly clear in such mystery stories as *Mystery at the Red House,* which has a plot that is exciting despite the book's slow pace. In this book, as well as in *The Dutch Colt* and *Wild Geese Flying,* young protagonists rise to the occasion and solve problems in an exciting but believable manner.

While Meigs seldom created memorable characters or drew her characters in depth, her plots are absorbing, her historical backgrounds authoritative but unobtrusive, and her themes—especially in historical fiction—strong. She wrote with perspective and polish. If all her writing is not great, many of her books have elements of greatness. Reviewing another author's book, she wrote, "No book can be said to have even the elements of greatness unless it can stand the task of recollection," and many of Meigs's stories can indeed stand that task.

—Zena Sutherland

MELLING, O. R.

Pseudonym for Geraldine Valerie Whelan. **Nationality:** Irish/Canadian. **Born:** Dublin, Ireland, 2 December, 1956. **Education:** Malvern Collegiate, Toronto, Ontario; University of Toronto, 1973-76, B.A. 1976; University of Toronto, 1982-83, B.A. (Honors) 1983; University of Toronto, 1983-84, M.A. 1984. **Family:** Divorced; one daughter. **Military Service:** Canadian Naval Reserve, 1973-78; Sub-lieutenant. **Career:** Literary critic, *The Irish Times* and *Books Ireland,* since 1992. **Awards:** CLA Young Adult Canadian Book Award, 1984; Ruth Schwartz Children's Book Award, 1993. **Agent:** c/o Westwood Creative Artists, 94 Harboard St., Toronto, Ontario M5S 1G6. **Address:** c/o Penguin Books Canada Ltd., Suite 300, 10 Alcorn Ave., Toronto, Ontario M4V 3B2, Canada.

PUBLICATIONS FOR YOUNG ADULTS

The Druid's Tune. Harmondsworth, Middlesex, and Markham, Ontario, Kestrel, 1983.

The Singing Stone. Markham, Ontario, Viking Kestrel, 1986.

The Hunter's Moon. Toronto, HarperCollins, 1993.

My Blue Country. New York, Penguin, and Toronto, Viking, 1996.

PUBLICATIONS FOR ADULTS

Falling Out of Time. Markham, Ontarion, Viking, 1989; New York, Penguin, 1990.

*

Media Adaptations: *The Singing Stone* (sound recording), Toronto, CNIB, 1989, and Vancouver, British Columbia, Library Services Branch, 1992.

*   *   *

Geraldine Valerie Whelan, who writes as O. R. Melling, is best known for her first three books, all fantasies set in Ireland with a Canadian adolescent main character. *The Druid's Tune,* a time slip fantasy which won the 1984 Young Adult Canadian Book Award, finds Torontonians Jimmy Redding, 15, and his sister Rosemary, 17, visiting present-day Ireland but travelling back in time to the Iron Age, Celtic society where they become involved in the invasion of Ulster by Queen Maeve of Connaught. The pair's conduit to the earlier time is the farmhand Peter Murphy, who, the siblings come to learn, is a Druid, a priest or magician with special powers. When Jimmy becomes the charioteer of the adolescent warrior hero Cuculaan—also known as the Hound of Ulster—and Rosemary falls in love with the Queen's son, brother and sister find themselves on opposing sides. The book contains much bloody action as Cuculaan guards Ulster's northern border by conducting guerilla warfare against Maeve's invading armies. Despite the gore, the book can be read as a strong antiwar statement.

The Singing Stone initially takes Kay Warrick, 18 and an orphan, to Ireland on a personal quest to discover who she is. Transported some 3000 years into the Bronze Age, Kay finds herself companion to a young girl, Aherne, and the pair embark on a quest quite different from what Kay had originally envisioned. The two young women are to recover the ancient treasures of the people known as the Tuatha De Danaan: the Spear, the Cauldron, the Sword, and—the finest of the treasures—the Stone of Destiny. In the past, the treasures had worked in harmony, but with the passage of time and abuse by the Danaan, the Spear of Truth and the Cauldron of Charity and Generosity had been subordinated to the Sword of War so that the people were cut off from their rightful destiny. Though *The Singing Stone* is about the conquest of the Danaan people, it is virtually bloodless for Melling speaks to the idea of surrender as an acceptable alternative to war.

Torontonian Gwen Woods, 16, comes to Dublin to visit her cousin, Findabhair, also 16, in *The Hunter's Moon.* Ever since the pair were young girls they have shared a love of fantasy and have wanted to visit another world. They decide to explore the sites in Ireland that are connected to the Celtic myths of fairy hills. On their first night on the road the pair sleep in the Mound of Hostages at Tara, and Gwen has a dream in which she is warned to leave this sacred place. When Gwen awakens, she finds Findabhair gone and eventually learns that she has been stolen by the fairies to become Queen to Finvarra, High King to the fairies. Throughout the rest of the novel, Gwen, with the assistance of various "helpers," attempts to rescue Findabhair while avoiding being trapped, herself, in the faerie world. Gwen's quest takes on new urgency when she discovers that every seventh year, during the time of the Hunter's Moon, the Great Worm, which had been driven from Fairyland, demands a human sacrifice, and that sacrifice is about to be Findabhair. The book's surprising conclusion is believably noble.

After her three YA fantasies set in Ireland, Melling switched genres and settings in *My Blue Country* and addressed a more contemporary subject, the experiences of Jessica (Jesse) Catherine McKinnock, 17, a member of CUSO (Canadian University Students Overseas). Jesse's diary entries chronicle her group's training period in Canada and their eventual CUSO field experience in Malaysia. The Canada portion follows Jesse and her fellow CUSO volunteers as they are educated in Malaysian culture and language, focussing on Jesse's learning how to function as part of a project team of eight, a group readers come to know as individuals. Jesse's culture shock begins in Canada as she encounters the cultural, linguistic, and socioeconomic diversity exhibited by the CUSO contingent, and it continues as she leaves Canada and confronts Malaysia's differences. While readers will enjoy the novelty of Jesse's Malaysian happenings, they will be captivated by the doomed Romeo and Juliet-type romance between Christian Jesse and Ahmed, President of the National Federation of Islamic Youth.

—Dave Jenkinson

MELTZER, Milton

Nationality: American. **Born:** Worcester, Massachusetts, 8 May 1915. **Education:** Columbia University, New York, 1932-36. **Military Service:** Served in the U.S. Army Air Force, 1942-46; became sergeant. **Family:** Married Hilda Balinky in 1941; two daughters. **Career:** Staff writer, Federal Theatre Project of the Works Projects Administration, New York City, 1936-39; researcher and writer, Columbia Broadcasting System Inc. (CBS-Radio), New York City, 1946; Public Relations Staff of Henry A. Wallace for President, 1947-49; account executive, Medical and Pharmaceutical Information Bureau, New York City, 1950-55; assistant director of public relations, Pfizer Inc., New York City, 1955-60; editor, Science and Medicine Publishing Co. Inc., New York City, 1960-68; full-time writer of books, since 1968; historian; biographer. Consulting editor, Thomas Y. Crowell Co., 1962-74, Doubleday & Co. Inc., 1963-73, and Scholastic Book Services, 1968-72; adjunct professor, University of Massachusetts, Amherst, 1977-80; lecturer at universities in the United States and England and at professional meetings and seminars; writer of films and filmstrips. **Awards:** Thomas Alva Edison Mass Media award for special excellence in portraying America's past, 1966, for *In Their Own Words: A History of the American Negro,* Volume 2, *1865-1916;* Children's Literature award of the National Book award, finalist, 1969, for *Langston Hughes: A Biography,* 1975, for *Remember the Days: A Short History of the Jewish American* and *World of Our Fathers: The Jews of Eastern Europe,* and 1977, for *Never to Forget: The Jews of the Holocaust;* Christopher award, 1969, for *Brother, Can You Spare a Dime? The Great Depression, 1929-1933,* and 1980, for *All Times, All Peoples: A World History of Slavery, Slavery: From the Rise of Western Civilization to the Renaissance* was selected one of *School Library Journal's* Best Books, 1971; Charles Tebeau award from the Florida Historical Society, 1973, for *Hunted Like a Wolf: The Story of the Seminole War;* Jane Addams Peace Association Children's Book award Honor Book, 1975, for *The Eye of Conscience: Photographers and Social Change; Boston Globe-Horn Book* Nonfiction Honor Book, 1976, for *Never to Forget: The Jews of the Holocaust,* and 1983, for *The Jewish Americans: A History in Their Own Words, 1650-1950;* Association of Jewish Libraries Book award, 1976, Jane Addams Peace Association Children's Book award, 1977, Charles and Bertie G. Schwartz award for Jewish Juvenile Literature from the National Jewish Book awards, 1978, Hans Christian Andersen Honor List, 1979, and selected by the American Library Association as a "Best of the Best Books 1970-1983," all for *Never to Forget: The Jews of the Holocaust; Dorothea Lange: A Photographer's Life* was selected one of the *New York Times'* Best Adult Books of the Year, 1978; Washington Children's Book Guild Honorable Mention, 1978 and 1979, and Nonfiction award, 1981, all for his total body of work; American Book award finalist, 1981, for *All Times, All Peoples: A World History of Slavery;* Carter G. Woodson Book award from the National Council for Social Studies, 1981, for *The Chinese Americans;* Jefferson Cup award from the Virginia State Library Association, 1983, for *The Jewish Americans: A History in Their Own Words, 1650-1950;* Children's Book award special citation from the Child Study Children's Book Committee, one of *School Library Journal's* Best Books for Young Adults, both 1985, and Olive Branch award from the Writers' and Publishers' Alliance for Nuclear Disarmament, Jane Addams Peace Association Children's

Book award, and New York University Center for War, Peace, and the News Media, all 1986, all for *Ain't Gonna Study War No More: The Story of America's Peace-Seekers;* John Brubaker Memorial award from the Catholic Library Association, 1986; Golden Kite award for nonfiction, Society of Children's Book Writers, 1987, for *Poverty in America;* Jane Addams Peace Association Children's Book award Honor Book, 1989, for *Rescue: The Story of How Gentiles Saved Jews in the Holocaust.* Many of Meltzer's books have been selected as Library of Congress' Best Children's Books of the Year, Notable Children's Trade Book in Social Studies from the National Council for Social Studies, and *New York Times* Outstanding Children's Books of the Year. **Agent:** Harold Ober Associates, 425 Madison Ave., New York, New York 10017, U.S.A. **Address:** 263 West End Ave., New York, New York 10023, U.S.A.

PUBLICATIONS FOR YOUNG ADULTS

Nonfiction

In Their Own Words: A History of the American Negro. New York, Crowell, Volume 1, *1619-1865,* 1964; Volume 2, *1865-1916,* 1965; Volume 3, *1916-1966,* 1967; abridged edition, as *The Black Americans: A History in Their Own Words, 1619-1983,* New York, Crowell, 1984, New York, Trophy, 1987.

A Light in the Dark: The Life of Samuel Gridley Howe. New York, Crowell, 1964; Cleveland, Ohio, Modern Curriculum Press, 1991.

Tongue of the Flame: The Life of Lydia Maria Child. New York, Crowell, 1965.

Bread—and Roses: The Struggle of American Labor, 1865-1915. New York, Knopf, 1967, New York, Facts on File, 1991.

Thaddeus Stevens and the Fight for Negro Rights. New York, Crowell, 1967.

Langston Hughes: A Biography. New York, Crowell, 1968.

Brother, Can You Spare a Dime? The Great Depression, 1929-1933. New York, Knopf, 1969, New York, Facts on File, 1991.

Margaret Sanger: Pioneer of Birth Control, with Lawrence Lader. New York, Crowell, 1969.

Freedom Comes to Mississippi: The Story of Reconstruction. Chicago, Illinois, Follett, 1970.

Slavery: From the Rise of Western Civilization to the Renaissance. New York, Cowles, 1971; Volume 2, *Slavery: From the Renaissance to Today,* New York, Cowles, 1972; one-volume edition, as *Slavery: A World History,* New York, Da Capo, 1993.

To Change the World: A Picture History of Reconstruction. New York, Scholastic Book Services, 1971.

Hunted Like a Wolf: The Story of the Seminole War. New York, Farrar, Straus, 1972.

Underground Man (novel). Scarsdale, New York, Bradbury Press, 1972, New York, Harcourt, 1990.

The Right to Remain Silent. New York, Harcourt, 1972.

Bound for the Rio Grande: The Mexican Struggle, 1845-1850. New York, Knopf, 1974.

The Eye of Conscience: Photographers and Social Change, with Bernard Cole. Chicago, Illinois, Follett, 1974.

Remember the Days: A Short History of the Jewish American, illustrated by Harvey Dinnerstein. Garden City, Doubleday, 1974.

Taking Root: Jewish Immigrants in America. New York, Farrar, Straus, 1974.

World of Our Fathers: The Jews of Eastern Europe. New York, Farrar, Straus, 1974.

Never to Forget: The Jews of the Holocaust. New York, Harper, 1976, New York, Trophy, 1991.

Violins and Shovels: The WPA Arts Projects. New York, Delacorte, 1976.

The Human Rights Book. New York, Farrar, Straus, 1979.

All Times, All Peoples: A World History of Slavery, illustrated by Leonard Everett Fisher. New York, Harper, 1980.

The Chinese Americans. New York, Crowell, 1980.

The Hispanic Americans, photographs by Morrie Camhi and Catherine Noren. New York, Crowell, 1982.

The Jewish Americans: A History in Their Own Words, 1650-1950. New York, Crowell, 1982.

The Truth about the Ku Klux Klan. New York, F. Watts, 1982.

The Terrorists. New York, Harper, 1983.

A Book about Names: In which Custom, Tradition, Law, Myth, History, Folklore, Foolery, Legend, Fashion, Nonsense, Symbol, Taboo Help Explain How We Got Our Names and What They Mean, illustrated by Mischa Richter. New York, Crowell, 1984.

Ain't Gonna Study War No More: The Story of America's Peace-Seekers. New York, Harper, 1985.

Betty Friedan: A Voice for Women's Rights, illustrated by Stephen Marchesi. New York, Viking, 1985.

Dorothea Lange: Life through the Camera, illustrated by Donna Diamond and photographs by Dorothea Lange. New York, Viking, 1985.

The Jews in America: A Picture Album. Philadelphia, Pennsylvania, Jewish Publication Society, 1985.

Mark Twain: A Writer's Life. New York, F. Watts, 1985.

George Washington and the Birth of Our Nation. New York, F. Watts, 1986.

Poverty in America. New York, Morrow, 1986.

Winnie Mandela: The Soul of South Africa, illustrated by Stephen Marchesi. New York, Viking, 1986.

The American Revolutionaries: A History in Their Own Words, 1750-1800. New York, Crowell, 1987.

The Landscape of Memory. New York, Viking, 1987.

Mary McLeod Bethune: Voice of Black Hope, illustrated by Stephen Marchesi. New York, Viking, 1987.

Benjamin Franklin: The New American. New York, F. Watts, 1988.

Rescue: The Story of How Gentiles Saved Jews in the Holocaust. New York, Harper, 1988, New York, Trophy, 1991.

Starting from Home: A Writer's Beginnings. New York, Viking, 1988, New York, Puffin, 1991.

American Politics: How It Really Works, illustrated by David Small. New York, Morrow, 1989.

Voices from the Civil War: A Documentary History of the Great American Conflict. New York, Crowell, 1989.

The American Promise: Voices of a Changing Nation, 1945-Present. New York, Bantam, 1990.

The Bill of Rights: How We Got It and What It Means. New York, Harper, 1990.

Columbus and the World Around Him. New York, F. Watts, 1990.

Crime in America. New York, Morrow, 1990.

Thomas Jefferson: The Revolutionary Aristocrat. New York, F. Watts, 1991.

The Amazing Potato. New York, HarperCollins, 1992.

Lincoln: In His Own Words, illustrated by Stephen Alcorn. New York, Harcourt, 1993.

Andrew Jackson and His America. New York, F. Watts, 1993.

Gold. New York, HarperCollins, 1993.

Theodore Roosevelt and His America. New York, F. Watts, 1994.

Frederick Douglass: In His Own Words, illustrated by Stephen Alcorn. New York, Harcourt, 1995.

Hold Your Horses. New York, HarperCollins, 1995.

Tom Paine: Voice of Revolution. New York, F. Watts, 1996.

Publications for Adults

Nonfiction

A Pictorial History of the Negro in America, with Langston Hughes. New York, Crown, 1956; 5th revised edition, with C. Eric Lincoln, as *A Pictorial History of Black Americans,* 1983; revised as *African American History: Four Centuries of Black Life,* New York, Scholastic Textbooks, 1990.

Mark Twain Himself. New York, Crowell, 1960.

Editor, *Milestones to American Liberty: The Foundations of the Republic.* New York, Crowell, 1961, revised edition, 1965.

Editor, with Walter Harding, *A Thoreau Profile.* New York, Crowell, 1962.

Editor, *Thoreau: People, Principles and Politics.* New York, Hill & Wang, 1963.

Time of Trial, Time of Hope: The Negro in America, 1919-1941 with August Meier, illustrated by Moneta Barnett. Garden City, New York, Doubleday, 1966, Cleveland, Ohio, Modern Curriculum Press, 1991.

Black Magic: A Pictorial History of the Negro in American Entertainment, with Langston Hughes. Englewood Cliffs, New Jersey, Prentice-Hall, 1967; as *Black Magic: A Pictorial History of the African-American in the Performing Arts,* with Langston Hughes, C. Eric Lincoln, and Jon Michael Spencer. New York, Da Capo Press, 1990; sixth updated and revised edition, 1995.

Dorothea Lange: A Photographer's Life. New York, Farrar, Straus, 1978, reprinted, 1985.

Editor, with Patricia G. Holland and Francine Krasno, *The Collected Correspondence of Lydia Maria Child, 1817-1880: Guide and Index to the Microfiche Edition.* Kraus Microform, 1980.

Editor, with Patricia G. Holland, *Lydia Maria Child: Selected Letters, 1817-1880.* Amherst, University of Massachusetts Press, 1982.

Cheap Raw Material: How Our Youngest Workers Are Exploited and Abused. New York, Viking, 1994.

Nonfiction for the Classroom: Milton Meltzer on Writing, History, and Social Responsibility. Teachers College Press, 1994.

Who Cares? Millions Do: A Book about Altruism. New York, Walker, 1994.

A History of Jewish Life from Eastern Europe to America. Aronson, 1996.

Weapons & Warfare: From the Stone Age to the Space Age. New York, HarperCollins, 1996.

Editor of ''Women of America'' series, New York, Crowell, 1962-74, ''Zenith Books'' series, Garden City, Doubleday, 1963-73, and ''Firebird Books'' series, New York, Scholastic Book Services, 1968-72. Also author of documentary films, including *History of the American Negro* (series of three half-hour films), Niagara Films, 1965; *Five,* Silvermine Films, 1971; *The Bread and Roses*

Strike: Lawrence, 1912 (filmstrip), District 1199 Cultural Center, 1980; *The Camera of My Family,* Anti-Defamation League, 1981; *American Family: The Merlins,* Anti-Defamation League, 1982. Member of U.S. editorial board of *Children's Literature in Education,* from 1973, and of *Lion and the Unicorn,* from 1980.

*

Biography: Essay in *Something about the Author Autobiography Series,* Volume 1, Detroit, Gale, 1986, pp. 203-221; entry in *Dictionary of Literary Biography,* Volume 61: *American Writers for Children since 1960: Poets, Illustrators, and Nonfiction Authors,* edited by Glenn E. Estes, Gale, 1987, pp. 214-223.

Critical Studies: Entry in *Children's Literature Review,* Volume 13, Detroit, Gale, 1987; entry in *Contemporary Literary Criticism,* Volume 26, Detroit, Gale, 1983.

Milton Meltzer comments:

What I hope my books do is to raise questions in the minds of young readers about the world they live in. Why do things come out this way? Do they have to be this way? Could they be changed? How do people go about changing their lives? Change is always taking place, whether we wish it or not. But shouldn't we, as thinking, feeling beings, grow conscious of it and try to shape change to more human ends? If my books raise the reader's consciousness of what freedom and equality and justice mean, then it will be one small step toward helping us all lead richer and more fulfilling lives.

* * *

Milton Meltzer is a man with a mission, the quintessential crusader. A perusal of the titles of his books, spanning close to forty years, gives evidence of the zealous dedication with which Meltzer documents the human struggle for justice and freedom, not only here and now in America, but everywhere throughout mankind's history. His strong belief that the function of literature is to disturb, not to ease or placate, explains what he writes: his books intentionally unsettle the reader and advocate change and action. Armed with the intelligence of a lifetime of reading and research, Meltzer lends his passionate voice to awaken young people especially, to the truths of history, truths not reflected in textbooks which gloss over or dismiss the difficult and the ugly. His social conscience demands that truth must embrace the vision of the underdog.

His first book, *A Pictorial History of the Negro in America,* a collaborative effort with Langston Hughes, traces the role of the African American in the history of this country. Meltzer expresses great pride in this book, not because it was his first, but because he thinks it has probably had the greatest influence of anything he has written. Leafing through the index at the back of the book reveals the names and topics of many subsequent volumes he has written, Meltzer himself acknowledged that ''the material is rich enough to be mined for many other useful books.''

A companion book, *Black Magic: A Pictorial History of the Negro in American Entertainment,* also written with Langston Hughes, catalogues names and events in the arts; yet its cumulative effect is a powerful and poetic evocation of the creativity in all phases of entertainment as African Americans struggle and rise triumphant against overwhelming odds. With the publication of these two volumes, Meltzer has become known as a graphic historian. Subsequent work relies heavily on visual material to deepen and enrich text. A much more recent book, *African American History: Four Centuries of Black Life,* a revision of *A Pictorial History of the Negro in America,* is directed to a largely young adult and more contemporary audience.

While the majority of Meltzer's earliest titles are aimed at an adult audience, his discovery of a young adult public thrills him: "They care more, respond more quickly, are more open to new ideas." He finds himself clearly excited about introducing young people to names like Lydia Maria Child, Margaret Sanger, Dorothea Lange, Thaddeus Stevens, and Samuel Gridley Howe, all of whom stand as subjects of his biographies, all of whom fought against injustice, oppression, and suppression. "My subjects choose action," Meltzer asserts. As biographer, Meltzer tackles such prominent Americans as George Washington and Thomas Jefferson. Here his emphasis is to present a balanced portrait whose selectivity reveals the fullness of the man, not just the mythology surrounding him. Turning from portraiture, Meltzer invests events with similar integrity; he wishes to present lesser known happenings about which the textbooks tell little, or tell it incorrectly—such titles include *Bound for the Rio Grande: The Mexican Struggle, 1845-1850, Hunted Like a Wolf: The Story of the Seminole War, Violins and Shovels: The WPA Arts Projects.*

Meltzer returns to the time of his own adolescence to record for a young adult audience what it was like growing up in the Depression. He was himself involved in the WPA Arts Project, as a writer in the press department, but the larger canvas of poverty and want, of a nation at risk, truly compels Meltzer. His thoughtful portrait *Brother, Can You Spare a Dime? The Great Depression, 1929-1933* draws liberally on eye-witness narratives of the Depression to recreate what happened. Here, as elsewhere, Meltzer reveals his consummate skill as a selector of convincing and illuminating material. Those whose voices he calls upon include such well known figures as John Steinbeck and Edmund Wilson, but the sounding of ordinary men and women presents parallel poignancy and power.

The technique of embedding his story with the kind of primary source material typically given to an older audience—diaries, letters, memoirs, speeches, news accounts—becomes Meltzer's signature. Over the years, he produced a number of books subtitled *A History in Their Own Words.* The first-person accounts of men, women, and children whose lives make up the underside of history elevates his books to a new plane of quality and authenticity, what he describes as a "giant step up and out of the textbook swamp." Over his illustrious career, Meltzer effectively uses this format to examine the lives of Jewish and Black Americans, of Hispanic and Chinese Americans. When a single issue rather than a people demand his focus, Meltzer's impeccable research unearths that information which will best convey his conviction. *The Right to Remain Silent, The Human Rights Book, Poverty in America,* and *Ain't Gonna Study War No More: The Story of America's Peace-Seekers* all make their case for the need for greater understanding and responsible, moral action.

In *Starting from Home: A Writer's Beginnings,* Meltzer turns to autobiography to reach back into his own early history to better understand himself and his roots. A child of immigrant parents caught in the Depression, Meltzer speaks of those people, those

forces which empowered him. In school, an occasional teacher moved him outside of facts and memorization, and excited him with the world of ideas. Born with curiosity, an inveterate questioner, Meltzer needed only a spark to self-ignite. As an American, such a flame was inspired with his high school discovery of the antislavery poets. As a Jew, such a spark was inspired by a newspaper article citing the Nazi slogan "Jew perish!" Many of Meltzer's books deepen our understanding of both Black and Jewish history, two subjects which he returns to again and again.

With perhaps his most praised book, *Never to Forget: The Jews of the Holocaust,* winner of innumerable awards, Meltzer articulates passionately his conviction in the power and importance of nonfiction. Saddened and outraged both by high school textbooks whose treatment of Nazism is "brief, bland, superficial, and misleading" and whose treatment of the Holocaust is dismissive, Meltzer set out to write a book for Jew and non-Jew alike, whose presentation corrects such egregious errors. Searing first-person documents, many from children, complement Meltzer's unrelenting examination of the forces of hatred and destruction. Meltzer's artistry in communicating the unthinkable without resorting to other than the facts—and presenting those facts with such intelligence and sensitivity—respects the reader. This book cries out as a moral call to remembrance—and beyond, it is a moral call to action, lest history repeat itself.

Meltzer's partisan voice, heard on behalf of the disenfranchised and the neglected, speaks lucidly and fervently on behalf of nonfiction—he decries its status as the stepchild of literature for young people. His work serves as a model for the best of literature: his books consistently empower facts with enviable style and imagination.

—Susan P. Bloom

MERRIAM, Eve

Nationality: American. **Born:** Philadelphia, Pennsylvania, 19 July 1916. **Education:** Cornell University, Ithaca, New York; University of Pennsylvania, Philadelphia, A.B. 1937; University of Wisconsin, Madison; Columbia University, New York. **Family:** Married Waldo Salt; two sons. **Career:** Author, poet, playwright. Copywriter, 1939-42; radio writer, mainly of documentaries and scripts in verse for Columbia Broadcasting System and other networks, and conductor of weekly program on modern poetry for station WQXR, New York City, 1942-46; daily verse columnist, *PM,* New York City, 1945; feature editor, *Deb* magazine, New York, 1946; fashion copy editor, *Glamour* magazine, 1947-48; free-lance magazine and book writer, since 1949; taught courses in creative writing at City College of the City University of New York, 1965-69. Member of the field project staff, Bank Street College of Education, New York, 1958-60. Public lecturer, 1956-92. **Awards:** Yale Younger Poets Prize, 1945, for *Family Circle; Collier's* Star Fiction award for "Make Something Happen," 1949; William Newman Poetry award, 1957; grant to write poetic drama, Columbia Broadcasting System, 1959; *New York Times'* Best Illustrated award, 1970, for *Finding a Poem;* National Council of Teachers of English awards, 1970 and 1981, for excellence in poetry for children; Obie award, *Village Voice,* 1977, for play *The Club;* Parents' Choice award, 1985, for *Blackberry Ink; New York*

Times' Best Illustrated award, 1987, for *Halloween ABC.* **Died:** 11 April 1992.

PUBLICATIONS FOR YOUNG ADULTS

Poetry

Family Circle. New Haven, Connecticut, Yale University Press, 1946.

The Inner City Mother Goose, photographs by Lawrence Ratzkin. New York, Simon & Schuster, 1969.

Finding a Poem, illustrated by Seymour Chwast. New York, Atheneum, 1970.

The Nixon Poems. New York, Atheneum, 1970.

I Am a Man: Ode to Martin Luther King, Jr., illustrated by Suzanne Verrier. New York, Doubleday, 1971.

Out Loud, illustrated by Harriet Sherman. New York, Atheneum, 1973.

Rainbow Writing. New York, Atheneum, 1976.

A Word or Two with You: New Rhymes for Young Readers, illustrated by John Nez. New York, Atheneum, 1981.

If Only I Could Tell You: Poems for Young Lovers and Dreamers, illustrated by Donna Diamond. New York, Knopf, 1983.

Fresh Paint, illustrated by David Frampton. New York, Macmillan, 1986.

Fiction

The Wise Woman and Her Secret, illustrated by Linda Graves. New York, Simon & Schuster, 1991.

Other

The Real Book about Franklin D. Roosevelt, illustrated by Bette J. Davis. New York, Garden City, 1952; London, Dobson, 1961.

Editor, with Nancy Larrick, *Male and Female under Eighteen: Frank Comments from Young People about Their Sex Roles Today.* New York, Discus Books, 1973.

Ab to Zogg: A Lexicon for Science-Fiction and Fantasy Readers, illustrated by Al Lorenz. New York, Atheneum, 1977.

PUBLICATIONS FOR CHILDREN

Poetry

There Is No Rhyme for Silver, illustrated by Joseph Schindelman. New York, Atheneum, 1962.

Funny Town, illustrated by Evaline Ness. New York, Crowell Collier, 1963.

It Doesn't Always Have to Rhyme, illustrated by Malcolm Spooner. New York, Atheneum, 1964.

Don't Think about a White Bear, illustrated by Murray Tinkelman. New York, Putnam, 1965.

Catch a Little Rhyme, illustrated by Imero Gobbato. New York, Atheneum, 1966.

Independent Voices, illustrated by Arvis Stewart. New York, Atheneum, 1968.

The Birthday Cow, illustrated by Guy Michel. New York, Knopf, 1978.

Jamboree: Rhymes for All Times, illustrated by Walter Gaffney-Kessel. New York, Dell, 1984.

Blackberry Ink, illustrated by Hans Wilhelm. New York, Morrow, 1985.

A Book of Wishes for You. Norwalk, Connecticut, Gibson, 1985.

A Sky Full of Poems. New York, Dell, 1986.

Halloween ABC, illustrated by Lane Smith. New York, Macmillan, 1987.

You Be Good and I'll Be Night: Jump-on-the-Bed Poems, illustrated by Karen Schmidt. New York, Morrow, 1988.

Chortles: New and Selected Wordplay Poems, illustrated by Sheila Hamanaka. New York, Morrow, 1989.

A Poem for a Pickle, illustrated by Sheila Hamanaka. New York, Morrow, 1989.

Fiction

What Can You Do with a Pocket?, illustrated by Harriet Simon. New York, Knopf, 1964.

Do You Want to See Something?, illustrated by Abner Graboff. New York, Scholastic, 1965.

Small Fry, illustrated by Garry Mackenzie. New York, Knopf, 1965.

Miss Tibbett's Typewriter, illustrated by Rick Schreiter. New York, Knopf, 1966.

Andy All Year Round, illustrated by Margo Hoff. New York, Funk & Wagnalls, 1967.

Epaminondas, illustrated by Trina S. Hyman. New York, Follett, 1968, as *That Noodle-Head Epaminondas,* illustrated by Trina S. Hyman, New York, Scholastic, 1972.

Project One-Two-Three, illustrated by Harriet Sherman. New York, McGraw, 1971.

Boys and Girls, Girls and Boys, illustrated by Harriet Sherman. New York, Holt, 1972.

Unhurry Harry, illustrated by Gail Owens. New York, Four Winds, 1978.

Good Night to Annie, illustrated by John Wallner. New York, Four Winds, 1979.

The Christmas Box (picture book), illustrated by David Small. New York, Morrow, 1985.

The Birthday Door (picture book), illustrated by Peter J. Thornton. New York, Morrow, 1986.

Where Is Everybody? (picture book), illustrated by Diane de Groat. New York, Simon & Schuster, 1989.

Fighting Words (picture book), illustrated by David Small. New York, Morrow, 1991.

Other

The Real Book about Amazing Birds, illustrated by Paul Wenck. New York, Garden City, 1954; London, Dobson, 1960.

The Voice of Liberty: The Story of Emma Lazarus. New York, Farrar Straus, 1959.

A Gaggle of Geese, illustrated by Paul Galdone. New York, Knopf, 1960.

Mommies at Work, illustrated by Beni Montresor. New York, Knopf, 1961.

What's in the Middle of a Riddle?, illustrated by Murray Tinkelman. New York, Collier, 1963.

The Story of Benjamin Franklin, illustrated by Brinton Turkle. New York, Four Winds, 1965.

Translator, *Animal Tales,* by Hana Doskocilova, illustrated by Mirko Hanak. New York, Doubleday, 1971.

Translator, *Christmas,* by Dick Bruna, illustrated by Dick Bruna. New York, Doubleday, 1971.

Bam! Zam! Boom!: High Rise Going Up, illustrated by William Lightfoot. New York, Walker, 1972.

Daddies at Work, illustrated by Eugenie Fernadez. New York, Simon & Schuster, 1989.

PUBLICATIONS FOR ADULTS

Poetry

Tomorrow Morning. New York, Twayne, 1953.

The Double Bed: From the Feminine Side. New York, Cameron, 1958.

The Trouble with Love. New York, Macmillan, 1960.

Basics: An I-Can-Read-Book for Grownups. New York, Macmillan, 1962.

A Husband's Notes about Her: Fictions. New York, Macmillan, 1976.

Plays

Inner City, music by Helen Miller, adaptation of *The Inner City Mother Goose* by Eve Merriam (produced New York, 1971).

Out of Our Father's House, with Paula Wagner and Jack Hofsiss, music by Ruth Crawford Seeger and others, adaptation of the book *Growing Up Female in America* edited by Eve Merriam (produced New York, 1975). New York, French, 1975.

We the Women (television play), 1975.

The Club (produced New York, 1976; London, 1978). New York, French, 1976.

At Her Age. New York, French, 1979.

Dialogue for Lovers: Sonnets of Shakespeare Arranged for Dramatic Presentation (produced New York, 1980). New York, French, 1981.

And I Ain't Finished Yet (produced New York, 1981).

Plagues for Our Time, music by Tom O'Horgan (produced New York, 1983).

Woman Alive: Conversation Against Death (libretto), music by Patsy Rogers (also director; produced New York, 1983).

Street Dreams, music by Helen Miller (produced New York, 1984).

Other

Emma Lazarus: Woman with a Torch. New York, Citadel, 1956.

Figleaf: The Business of Being in Fashion. Philadelphia, Lippincott, 1960.

After Nora Slammed the Door: American Women in the 1960's: The Unfinished Revolution. Cleveland, World, 1964.

Equality, Identity, and Complementarity: Changing Perspectives of Man and Woman, with others, edited by Robert H. Amundson. Denver, Research Center on Women, 1968.

Man and Woman: The Human Condition. Denver, Research Center on Women, 1968.

Editor, *Growing Up Female in America: Ten Lives.* New York, Doubleday, 1971.

*

Media Adaptations: ''Catch a Little Rhyme'' (recording), 1976; ''Out Loud'' (recording), 1988.

Biography: Entry in *Dictionary of Literary Biography,* Volume 61: *American Writers for Children Since 1960: Poets, Illustrators, and Nonfiction Authors,* Detroit, Gale, 1987, pp. 224-233.

Manuscript Collections: Kerlan Collection, University of Minnesota, Minneapolis; de Grummond Collection, University of Southern Mississippi, Hattiesburg; Schlesinger Library, Radcliffe College, Cambridge, Massachusetts.

Critical Study: Entry in *Children's Literature Review,* Volume 14, Detroit, Gale, 1988, pp. 187-204.

*   *   *

Eve Merriam's versatility was astounding. A keen observer of contemporary life, she brought to her poetry, plays, and prose a fresh outlook on all phases of the modern world, its delights as well as absurdities. Agile and penetrating, she continually beguiled her poetry readers with a variety of rhythms, rhymes, word play, and inventive forms which had their roots in traditional prosody, yet breathed with a twentieth-century sophistication refreshing to read, delightful to hear. She was an outstanding performer whose training in the theatre enhanced all of her poetry readings.

Merriam's poetic themes ranged from the joy of words and word-play through a gamut of observations on contemporary life. Her concerns for humanity, the planet, ecology, the moot value of some phases of technology, science, and love often found a voice in the part played by poetry itself with its seemingly limitless possibilities for self-expression. What underlay all of her writing was the art of asking her readers to extend their horizons, develop their sensibilities, cultivate curiosity, and become aware of their potential both as individuals and members of a community. Artfully, she warned against mediocrity. ''A cliché,'' she explained, ''is what we all say when we're too lazy to find another way.'' A unique talent enabled her to avoid didacticism by playing a dual role as both poet and reader. Writing of *it* and *they,* she commented that ''*They* just make it all up, / and *we* go along.'' By thus becoming part of the *we* she never pointed an accusing finger at her readers.

For those who enter into Merriam's work, there will be the love of words and sounds for their own sake as well as challenges to the intellect. In her poem ''Having Words,'' she listed the things that the word *umbrage* is not, and advised her readers that ''You'll have to find out for yourself what it is.'' She played with numbers, the alphabet, punctuation, the points of the compass, and a myriad of other objects and ideas, always asking the reader to join in the fun. As a playwright, she wrote for stage and television; as a nonfiction writer, she was engaged in work on such topics as fashion, American women in the 1960s, racial and gender equality, and biography. In a playful mood, she wrote *Ab to Zogg, A Lexicon for Science-Fiction and Fantasy Readers,* 1977, introducing readers to creatures like XIVLCMXXXVILXVM (''Reincarnated Roman gladiator whose quarked tunic conceals deadly microwaves and whose name none dare pronounce aloud'') and Hovvers (''Half souls who inhabit a zone midway between the mushroom caps and the sequoia tops. . . .''). Such inventiveness was at the heart of one of her most beloved poems, ''Mean Song,'' which begins ''Snickles and podes, / Ribble and grodes: / That's what I wish you. . . .''

She could be delightfully caustic, attacking television and its ridiculous commercials—the supermarket with its "banana detergent," "deodorant pie," plastic plants that "keep us germ-proof dirt-free," "artificial lawns with real crab grasses," and the "cult" of bargain sales. "You can take away my mother, / you can take away my sister, / but don't take away / my little transistor." Here, again, her pose is that of one with the reader. Often she used personification. All of the things of the day make us hurry and deprive us of time to speak. Yet, "slowly, says the darkness, / you can talk to me."

Eve Merriam wrote for all ages. Her *Inner City Mother Goose,* 1969, portrays the problems of city life: dirty streets, drugs, poverty programs, and political corruption, aspects of life certainly not for the nursery rhyme age for which she also wrote stories and verse. In a charming book for "young lovers and dreamers" *If Only I Could Tell You,* 1983, she, herself, becomes the lyric lover and dreamer: "At night / in the dark / thinking of you / the sky / becomes / so bright / I have to / put on / sunglasses." She wrote about people whose "independent voices" have wrought meaningful changes in the world. Many poems and some articles span all age categories; "Inside a Poem" and "What Can a Poem Do?" were first published as broadsides for the young, and later as adult articles in *The Writer* magazine.

Her poems on poetry are memorable. In "How to Eat a Poem" she advised the reader to "bite in." The poem is "ready and ripe now, whenever you are." In "Reply to the Question: *How Can You Become a Poet?*" she suggested that young writers observe the varying phases of a leaf in spring, summer and autumn, and then "in winter / when there is no leaf left / invent one."

A prodigious talent and recipient of the Yale Series of Younger Poets Award in 1945, the National Council of Teachers of English Excellence in Poetry Award in 1981, and an Obie Award in 1977, Eve Merriam will be remembered by those who have heard and watched as she read her work, conducted workshops for the young, or walked with her in Central Park or on the New York streets observing life at every level.

—Myra Cohn Livingston

MEYER, Carolyn (Mae)

Nationality: American. **Born:** Lewistown, Pennsylvania, 8 June 1935. **Education:** Bucknell University, Lewisburg, Pennsylvania, B.A. (cum laude) 1957. **Family:** Married 1) Joseph Smrcka in 1960 (divorced 1973); 2) Ernest A. "Tony" Mares in 1987; three sons, one daughter. **Career:** Secretary, late 1950s; free-lance writer of articles, book reviews, and books, 1963—; Columnist *McCall's* magazine, 1967-72; Institute of Children's Literature, instructor, 1973-79; Alpha Lambda Delta Lecturer, Bucknell University, 1974; Guest lecturer in children's literature, 1976-78; Children and young adult book reviewer, *Los Angeles Times,* 1989-90. Gives talks and workshops in elementary, junior and senior high schools, and colleges. Presenter at history, library, literary, and reading conferences. Workshop leader for writing groups. **Awards:** Notable Book citations from American Library Association, 1971, for *The Bread Book,* 1976, for *Amish People,* and 1979, for *C.C. Poindexter;* Best Book for Young Adults citations from American Library Association, 1979, for *C.C. Poindexter,* 1980, for *The*

Center: *From a Troubled Past to a New Life,* 1985, for *The Mystery of the Ancient Maya,* 1986, for *Voices of South Africa* and *Denny's Tapes,* 1992, for *Where the Broken Heart Still Beats,* 1993, for *White Lilacs; New York Times* Best Book Citation, 1977, for *Eskimos: Growing Up in a Changing Culture;* Voice of Youth Advocates YASD Best Books Citation, 1988, for *Denny's Tapes* and *Voices of South Africa;* Author of the Year award from Pennsylvania School Librarians Association, 1990. **Agent:** Amy Berkower, Writers House Inc., 21 W. 26th St., New York, New York 10010, U.S.A. **Address:** 202 Edith Boulevard, N.E., Albuquerque, New Mexico 87102-3526, U.S.A.

PUBLICATIONS FOR YOUNG ADULTS

Fiction

C.C. Poindexter. New York, Antheneum, 1979.
Eulalia's Island. New York, Antheneum, 1982.
The Summer I Learned about Life. New York, Antheneum, 1983.
The Luck of Texas McCoy. New York, Antheneum, 1984.
Elliott & Win. New York, Antheneum, 1986.
Denny's Tapes. New York, McElderry, 1987.
Wild Rover. New York, McElderry, 1989.
Because of Lissa. Hotline Series #1. New York, Bantam, 1990.
Killing the Kudu. New York, McElderry, 1990.
Japan—How Do Hands Make Peace? Earth Inspectors No. 10, illustrated by Barbara Carter. New York, McGraw, 1990.
The Problem with Sidney. Hotline Series #2. New York, Bantam, 1990.
Gillian's Choice. Hotline Series #3. New York, Bantam, 1991.
The Two Faces of Adam. Hotline Series #4. New York, Bantam, 1991.
Where the Broken Heart Still Beats: The Story of Cynthia Ann Parker. New York, Harcourt, 1992.
White Lilacs. New York, Harcourt, 1993.
Rio Grande Stories. New York, Harcourt, 1994.
Drummers of Jericho. New York, Harcourt, 1995.
Gideon's People. New York, Harcourt, 1996.
Jubilee Journey. New York, Harcourt, 1997.
Mary, Bloody Mary. New York, Harcourt, forthcoming.

Nonfiction

Miss Patch's Learn-to-Sew Book, illustrated by Mary Suzuki. New York, Harcourt, 1969.
Stitch by Stitch: Needlework for Beginners, illustrated by the author. New York, Harcourt, 1970.
The Bread Book: All about Bread and How to Make It, illustrated by Trina Schart Hyman. New York, Harcourt, 1971.
Yarn: The Things It Makes and How to Make Them, illustrated by Jennifer Perrott. New York, Harcourt, 1972.
Saw, Hammer, and Paint: Woodworking and Finishing for Beginners, illustrated by Toni Martignoni. New York, Morrow, 1973.
Christmas Crafts: Things to Make the 24 Days Before Christmas, illustrated by Anita Lobel. New York, Harper, 1974.
Milk, Butter, and Cheese: The Story of Dairy Products, illustrated by Giulio Maestro. New York, Morrow, 1974.
The Needlework Book of Bible Stories, illustrated by Janet McCaffery. New York, Harcourt, 1975.

People Who Make Things: How American Craftsmen Live and Work. New York, Antheneum, 1975.

Rock Tumbling: From Stones to Gems to Jewelry, photographs by Jerome Wexler. New York, Morrow, 1975.

Amish People: Plain Living in a Complex World, photographs by Michael Ramsey, Gerald Dodds, and the author. New York, Antheneum, 1976.

Coconut: The Tree of Life, illustrated by Lynne Cherry. New York, Morrow, 1976.

Lots and Lots of Candy, illustrated by Laura Jean Allen. New York, Harcourt, 1976.

Eskimos: Growing Up in a Changing Culture, photographs by John McDougal. New York, Antheneum, 1977.

Being Beautiful: The Story of Cosmetics from Ancient Art to Modern Science, illustrated by Marika. New York, Morrow, 1977.

Mask Magic, illustrated by Melanie Gaines Arwin. New York, Harcourt, 1978.

The Center: From a Troubled Past to a New Life. New York, Antheneum, 1980.

Rock Band: Big Men in a Great Big Town. New York, Antheneum, 1980.

The Mystery of the Ancient Maya, with Charles Gallenkamp. New York, Antheneum, 1985; revised edition, Simon and Schuster, 1995.

Voices of South Africa: Growing Up in a Troubled Land. New York, Harcourt, 1986.

Voices of Northern Ireland: Growing Up in a Troubled Land. New York, Harcourt, 1987.

A Voice from Japan: An Outsider Looks In. New York, Harcourt, 1988.

In a Different Light: Growing Up in a Yup'ik Eskimo Village in Alaska, photographs by John McDonald, New York, Simon and Schuster, 1996.

*

Biography: Essay in *Something about the Author Autobiography Series* Volume 9, Detroit, Gale, 1990; essay in *Something About the Author* Volume 70, Detroit, Gale, 1993; essay in *Speaking for Ourselves, Too* compiled and edited by Donald R. Gallo, National Council of Teachers of English, 1993; essay in *Authors & Artists for Young Adults* Volume 16, edited by E.A. Des Chenes, Detroit, Gale, 1995.

Carolyn Meyer comments:

The two things I enjoy most are researching a subject, or maybe a cluster of subjects, and telling a story. The research part got me started in writing, nonfiction in the beginning. Then I discovered that the stories I most liked to tell were stories that required a lot of preliminary digging—sometimes in libraries, sometimes in conversations with all kinds of people. In the twenty-five years I've been writing for children and young adults, there has been a steady march toward more complex subjects, each book demanding more and more of me as researcher and storyteller. If readers share in even a part of what I have discovered in the process, I'm happy.

*　　*　　*

The young adult works of Carolyn Meyer come from her curiosity and her sense of place. She has been successful in writing both fiction and informational books, with selections in both forms being designated by the American Library Association as "Best Books for Young Adults." In her fiction, Meyer frequently imbues her characters with the social and personal problems they must face to attain maturity and self-acceptance. Characterization is a strong facet of her writing, and most are unconventional, creating the focus for the novel. The topics are timely, yet universal, and are stimulating to the teenage reader. Meyer does not duck controversial issues but rather presents them to the reader in a straightforward manner with realistic dialogue. Because she is thorough in her research there is a verisimilitude that resonates for the reader.

Meyer explains that the gawky protagonist of *C.C. Poindexter* is based on her own teenage feelings as a misfit, and her other early novels were inspired by experiences she and her children had. An unconventional relationship and the consequences of stereotyping in society are the basis for the story of *Elliott and Win.* Win is a teenager, newly arrived in Santa Fe, whose only friend is Paul, a bully who dresses in battle gear. Win hasn't seen his father in seven years, so his mother enrolls him in a Big Brothers program, where he meets Elliott. Elliott is not what Win expected; he likes gourmet food and opera, and takes Win to kayak races and teaches him photography. Of course Paul is sure Elliott is gay and torments Win with these insinuations. Win struggles with his anger with Paul, his own uncertainties, and his adjustments to the new world that is being opened to him. An additional plot line is the relationship of Win and Heather, a girl beset with the problems of puberty and a bad reputation. The only incident that rings untrue is the revelation that Paul's father is gay, which seems a bit too coincidental.

Two other realistic fiction novels that present interesting premises are *Denny's Tapes* and *Killing the Kudu.* One month in the life of Dennis James Brown is recorded on tape as he flees his home in search of who he is to become. This device allows for the use of flashback as well as the dramatic presentation of the present. Denny reveals that he has been brought up white by his mother, but he has a black father he hasn't seen in years. Denny's mother has tried to protect him from cruelty, but his stepfather throws him out of the house with a racial epithet when he discovers Denny and his daughter embracing. Denny sets out to find three people: his black grandmother, his white grandmother, and his father. Through his search, he discovers much about his family, about black culture, and gains a direction for his life.

In *Killing the Kudu,* two cousins are emotionally separated by tragedy. When the boys were young, Scott accidently shot Alex, leaving him a paraplegic in a wheelchair. Now Alex is eighteen and comes to stay with his grandmother for part of the summer, where the boys are reunited. Meyer realistically portrays the tension of their relationship, including their rivalry for the affection of Claire, an Irish au pair with nurses' training, who has come to work for the summer. There are questions of the effects of paraplegia, including sexual capacity, as well as touching scenes of friendship. In time, Alex grows from a sheltered mama's boy to a young man determined to have a life of his own.

Meyer's historical fiction shines. Her sense of place is strong and she is able to give it free rein in novels that require greater development of setting. Couple this with her adept characterizations and the resulting stories thoroughly engage the reader. *Where the Broken Heart Still Beats: The Story of Cynthia Ann Parker* is a moving example of Meyer's gift of asking "what if." Many of the facts of Parker's life have been lost, but her legend lives on. Meyer has created a fictional cousin, whose diary conveys the reactions of the "civilized world" to Parker, who, in 1860, is returned to her family after twenty-five years of living with the Comanches. This alternates with chapters told from Naduah's (Parker's Comanche name) point of view. A tragic and poignant narrative of a clash of cultures, Meyer has combined excellent storytelling with information about the time and the Comanches to create a gripping book. The essence of the novel is revealed in the following quote: "But this woman who Grandfather insists is his brother's daughter does not look like one who has been rescued. She looks like one who is imprisoned."

In *White Lilacs,* Rose Lee is twelve the summer she learns her life will be changed forever; that the "white lilacs" her grandfather lovingly tends in his garden in Freedomtown will have to be transplanted along with all the lives of the blacks who live there. Freedomtown is a thriving black community within a small Texas town, but as the town has grown, the land has become more desirable and the whites want it for a city park. Because Rose Lee works for one of the prominent white families, these events are told through her viewpoint. In the end, the only thing left of Freedomtown are the sketches made by Rose Lee. There are memorable characters, including Rose Lee's brother Henry, who refuses to accept inferior status, and visiting Aunt Susanna, inspired by the Langston Hughes poem, "When Sue Wears Red" that Meyer first included in *Denny's Tapes.* There can be no happy ending because the story adheres to its nonfiction roots, but there is fortitude and integrity in its telling. *Jubilee Journey,* the sequel to *White Lilacs,* features Emily Rose, Rose Lee's thirteen-year-old great granddaughter who lives in Connecticut. Invited to Texas to celebrate Juneteenth with Rose Lee, Emily Rose, whose father is French Canadian, discovers her African American heritage and encounters discrimination, including when her brother Steven is arrested for dating a white girl. Meyer presents many viewpoints and characters to illuminate the diversity of Emily Rose's life and provides resolution for readers of both books.

Meyer capably explains cultures and groups that she encounters as well as showing how individuals mature and learn to approve of themselves and others and seek direction in their lives. One of her strongest books, *Rio Grande Stories,* depicts the Heritage Project class at Rio Grande Middle School in Albuquerque, New Mexico. Each student is expected to contribute a chapter for a book featuring the multicultural heritage of New Mexico. Through their projects, including recipes, histories, and crafts, the students understand and accept themselves and by sharing their information gain an appreciation for each other and their diverse community.

Such acceptance is absent in *Drummers of Jericho* in which Pazit Trujillo moves from Denver to a small Texas town to live with her father because she constantly argues with her mother. Pazit, who has just returned from a year at an Israeli kibbutz, embraces Judaism, her mother's religion, while her father, a Latino professor, and his second wife and their children are aloof toward religion. Joining the high school marching band, Pazit plays on the sideline while the band assembles in a cross formation. Her father complains to the American Civil Liberties Union, and Pazit becomes the target of hostile anti-Semitism. Billy Harper, a drummer and member of a conservative family, publicly supports Pazit, and they are both ostracized as they defend the right to religious freedom. Meyer stresses the conflicts teenagers find in their families and communities as they seek individual expression. This theme is also crucial to the plot of *Gideon's People* in which Amish teenager Gideon Stoltzfus yearns to escape the restrictive traditions of his culture and family in 1911 Lancaster County, Pennsylvania.

He meets Isaac Litvak, an Orthodox Jew, who also wants personal freedom. Although Meyer's portrayal of these religious communities sometimes seems stereotypical, her characters exhibit similarities as well as differences in their attempt to mature as individuals.

Reality is a major aspect of Meyer's fiction. Her Hotline series reveals issues such as drug abuse and suicide faced by a high school counseling hotline. Meyer's non-fiction also provides facts about a wide variety of topics from sewing, woodworking, rock bands, and other cultures. Her collections of observations about South Africa, Northern Ireland, and Japan give voice to people who have been previously ignored because of their race, gender, or age. *Eskimos: Growing Up in a Changing Culture* and its sequel *In a Different Light: Growing Up in a Yup'ik Eskimo Village in Alaska* examine how traditions are threatened as technology and Western culture are introduced to an isolated region. Meyer revises and reissues her books when significant new knowledge is available such as archaeologists understanding of Mayan hieroglyphics.

Meyer's work for young adults always eschews the easy plotline and delves into the uncomfortable realities of our world. Her books are often among the first published for young adults on controversial topics. She is increasingly deft in her ability to tell her stories, and one awaits her new works with a sense of anticipation.

—M. Jean Greenlaw, updated by Elizabeth D. Schafer

MIKLOWITZ, Gloria D.

Nationality: American. **Born:** New York City, 18 May 1927. **Education:** Hunter College (now Hunter College of the City University of New York), 1944-45; University of Michigan, Ann Arbor, B.A. 1948; New York University, 1948. **Family:** Married Julius Miklowitz in 1948; two sons. **Career:** Writer, since 1952. Scriptwriter, 1952-57; wrote documentary films for the U.S. Naval Ordinance Test Station, Pasadena, California; Pasadena City College, Pasadena, instructor, 1971-80; instructor for Writer's Digest School. **Awards:** One of Child Study Association of America's Children's Books of the Year, 1969, for *The Zoo Was My World,* and 1975, for *Harry Truman;* Outstanding Science Book for Children from the National Council for Social Studies and the Children's Book Council, 1977, for *Earthquake!,* and 1978, for *Save That Raccoon!;* one of New York Public Library's Books for the Teen Age, 1980, for *Did You Hear What Happened to Andrea?,* 1981, for *The Love Bombers,* and 1982, for *The Young Tycoons;* Western Australia Young Reader Book award, 1984, for *Did You Hear What Happened to Andrea?;* Iowa Books for Young Adults Poll, 1984, for *Close to the Edge,* 1986, for *The War between the Classes,* 1989, for *After the Bomb,* and 1989, for *Good-Bye Tomorrow;* Humanitas Prize (awarded to scriptwriter) for humanitarian values, 1985, for "CBS Schoolbreak Special: The Day the Senior Class Got Married;" Emmy (awarded to film producers) for Best Children's Special, 1986, for "CBS Schoolbreak Special: The War Between the Classes"; Recommended Books for Reluctant Young Adult Readers for *Good-Bye Tomorrow* and *Secrets Not Meant to Be Kept,* both 1987; IRA Young Adult Choices, 1989, for *Secrets Not Meant to Be Kept.* **Agent:** Marilyn Marlow, Curtis Brown Ltd., 10 Astor Place, New York, New York 10003, U.S.A. **Address:** 5255 Vista Miguel Dr., La Canada, California 91011, U.S.A.

PUBLICATIONS FOR YOUNG ADULTS

Fiction

Turning Off. New York, Putnam, 1973.
A Time to Hurt, A Time to Heal. New York, Tempo Books, 1974.
Paramedic Emergency. New York, Scholastic Book Services, 1977.
Runaway. New York, Tempo Books, 1977.
Unwed Mother. New York, Tempo Books, 1977.
Did You Hear What Happened to Andrea? New York, Delacorte, 1979.
The Love Bombers. New York, Delacorte, 1980.
Before Love. New York, Tempo Books, 1982.
Carrie Loves Superman. New York, Tempo Books, 1983.
Close to the Edge. New York, Delacorte, 1983.
The Day the Senior Class Got Married. New York, Delacorte, 1983.
After the Bomb. New York, Scholastic, 1985.
The War between the Classes. New York, Delacorte, 1985.
Love Story, Take Three. New York, Delacorte, 1986.
After the Bomb: Week One. New York, Scholastic, 1987.
Good-Bye Tomorrow. New York, Delacorte, 1987.
Secrets Not Meant to Be Kept. New York, Delacorte, 1987.
The Emerson High Vigilantes. New York, Delacorte, 1988.
Anything to Win. New York, Delacorte, 1989.
Suddenly Super Rich. New York, Bantam, 1989.
Standing Tall, Looking Good. New York, Delacorte, 1991.
Desperate Pursuit. New York, Bantam, 1992.
The Killing Boy. New York, Bantam, 1993.
Past Forgiving. New York, Simon & Schuster, 1994.
Camouflage. New York, Harcourt Brace, 1998.
The Last Fortress. Michigan, Eerdmans, 1998.

Nonfiction

The Zoo Was My World, with Wesley A. Young. New York, Dutton, 1969.
Harry Truman, illustrated by Janet Scabrini. New York, Putnam, 1975.
Earthquake!, illustrated by Jaber William. New York, Messner, 1977.
Dr. Martin Luther King, Jr. New York, Tempo Books, 1977.
Nadia Comaneci. New York, Tempo Books, 1977.
Steve Cauthen. New York, Tempo Books, 1978.
Tracy Austin. New York, Tempo Books, 1978.
Natalie Dunn, Roller Skating Champion. New York, Harcourt Brace Jovanovich, 1979.
Roller Skating. New York, Tempo Books, 1979.
Movie Stunts and the People Who Do Them. New York, Harcourt Brace Jovanovich, 1980.
The Young Tycoons. New York, Harcourt Brace Jovanovich, 1981.

PUBLICATIONS FOR CHILDREN

Fiction

Barefoot Boy, illustrated by Jim Collins. Chicago, Follett, 1964.
The Zoo That Moved, illustrated by Don Madden. Chicago, Follett, 1968.
The Parade Starts at Noon, illustrated by Don Madden. New York, Putnam, 1969.

The Marshmallow Caper, illustrated by Cheryl Pelavin. New York, Putnam, 1971.
Sad Song, Happy Song, illustrated by Earl Thollander. New York, Putnam, 1973.
Ghastly Ghostly Riddles, with Peter Desberg, illustrated by Dave Ross. New York, Scholastic Book Services, 1977.
Save That Raccoon!, pictures by St. Tamara. New York, Harcourt, 1978.
Win, Lose, or Wear A Tie; Sports Riddles, with Peter Desberg, pictures by Dave Ross. New York, Random House, 1980.
Good Sport Jokes, with Peter Desberg, illustrated by Laurie Burruss. New York, Readers Digest Services, 1977.
Riddles for a Scary Night, with Peter Desberg, illustrated by Laurie Burruss. New York, Readers Digest Services, 1977.

*

Media Adaptations: ''Andrea's Story: A Hitchhiking Tragedy'' (television movie; based on *Did You Hear What Happened to Andrea?*), ''Afterschool Special,'' ABC-TV, September, 1983; ''The Day the Senior Class Got Married'' (television movie), ''Schoolbreak Special,'' CBS-TV, 1985; ''The War Between the Classes'' (television movie), ''Schoolbreak Special,'' CBS-TV, 1986.

Biography: Essay in *Speaking for Ourselves: Autobiographical Sketches by Notable Authors of Books for Young Adults,* Volume 1, compiled and edited by Donald R. Gallo, National Council of Teachers of English, 1990; essay in *Authors and Artists for Young Adults,* Volume 6, Detroit, Gale, 1991; essay *Something about the Author Autobiography Series,* Volume 17, Detroit, Gale, 1994.

Manuscript Collections: de Grummond Collection, University of Southern Mississippi.

Gloria D. Miklowitz comments:

I feel a special kinship with young adults, maybe because my own teen years are still vivid. Today's young people, however, face much more difficult problems and issues than any previous generation. That's what I like to write about—kids trying to come to terms with life today, trying to find healthy options to what seem insurmountable problems.

*   *   *

Gloria Miklowitz's fiction for young adults deals with contemporary social issues and problems confronting adolescents. Her fiction explores topics such as rape, child abuse, AIDS, religious cults, nuclear bombs, and suicide. Miklowitz carefully researches each topic from different perspectives. Her message is clear, but not overly didactic and she attempts to show teenagers that they have alternative choices in life. Her books tend to evolve from problems and probe issues rather than spotlight individual characters.

In *Did You Hear What Happened to Andrea?* Miklowitz deals with rape from the perspectives of a number of people. For research, she answered phones for a rape hotline center, and interviewed rape victims, families of victims, police, and doctors.

Consequently, she depicts the reactions of Andrea, the rape victim; her boyfriend; her brother and sister; her removed parents; acquaintances and friends at school; the investigating policeman; and the rapist. Because the rape happened early in the book, after Andrea and her boyfriend recklessly hitchhiked, the remainder of the book deals with how characters emotionally handle the aftermath.

Secrets Not Meant to Be Kept investigates a headline topic: child abuse in a day-care center. Adri, a teenager who has blotted out memory of her first six years of life and has trouble expressing affection, slowly remembers her experience as her three-year-old sister shows signs of abuse that she recognizes. Adri and her friend Ryan gather evidence about the abuse that shocks her parents and others in the community.

The topic of AIDS or ARC (AIDS-related complex) is treated in *Good-bye Tomorrow*. The story is told through three people: Alex Weiss, a teenage swimmer who had a blood transfusion the year before; Shannon, his girlfriend; and Christy, his younger sister. They relate their discovery or knowledge of Alex's ARC and the resulting reactions to and uncertainty of dealing with it. John, Alex's closest friend, provides a different perspective through the other three. Miklowitz's research on the topic and her open honesty are apparent in this novel.

In *The Love Bombers,* Miklowitz uses her reading, interviews, and time spent with the Moonies to create an inside view of a religious cult. The book centers around Jenna's quest to find her brother Jeremy, who has dropped out of college to join the cult. Jeremy's low self-esteem and his desire to win the approval he never felt he had at home make him a target of the cult. Jenna and her friend Rick experience how cult members bombard recruits with "love," constant supervision, exercise, and involvement so that they have no time to think for themselves. Although Jeremy remains with the cult, Jenna wonders if he will ever be able to leave and become independent.

The threat of nuclear war is the subject of *After the Bomb* and its sequel, *After the Bomb: Week One*. Miklowitz creates realistic descriptions of the desolate homes, land, and people after the Russians mistakenly release a bomb on Los Angeles. The novel forms the background for Philip Singer, a runner who is overshadowed by a handsome brother, to take leadership and overcome his sense of inadequacy as he rescues his mother, helps at the hospital, and aids in supplying water to the hospital. In the sequel Philip and Matt look for their father, who was working at the California Institute of Technology when the nuclear attack began.

The War between the Classes reveals prejudice and offers a classroom experiment as a means of enlightening people—one step in overcoming this social ill. The teacher uses the "Color Game," a social studies experience. Students are divided into four socio-economic groups, labeled by color codes, and follow strict behavior rules of intergroup actions. During the experiment, Amy (Emiko) Sumoto and Adam Tarcher, who are in love, and their classmates gain insight by tolerating and inflicting humiliations and abuses on each other. In this novel, Miklowitz confronts readers with questions of social class, ethnic prejudice, and sexism.

Miklowitz's carefully researched books for young adults illustrate the diversity of her curiosity and wide interests. They focus on the contemporary headline issues and problems young adults may face and provide ways to deal with these.

—Edna Earl Edwards

MILES, Betty

Nationality: American. **Born:** Chicago, Illinois, 16 May 1928. **Education:** Antioch College, B.A. 1950. **Family:** Married Matthew B. Miles in 1949; two daughters, one son. **Career:** Assistant kindergarten teacher at New Lincoln School, 1950-51; Bank Street College of Education, New York, instructor in children's language and literature, 1971-75; currently free-lance author. Frequent speaker to various parent, teacher, library, and classroom groups. Consultant to Beginner Books of Random House, National Coordinating Council on Drug Education, and "Sesame Street," Children's Television Workshop. **Awards:** Distinguished Achievement award, Educational Press Association, 1973; Child Association Book of the Year award and Outstanding Science Books for Children award, both 1974, both for *Save the Earth! An Ecology Handbook for Kids;* Child Association Book of the Year award, 1974; for *The Real Me;* Mark Twain award, 1984, and Georgia Children's Book award, 1986, both for *The Secret Life of the Underwear Champ.* **Address:** 94 Sparkill Ave., Tappan, New York 10983, U.S.A.

PUBLICATIONS FOR YOUNG ADULTS

Fiction

The Real Me. New York, Knopf, 1974.
All It Takes Is Practice. New York, Knopf, 1976.
Just the Beginning. New York, Knopf, 1976.
Looking On. New York, Knopf, 1978.
The Trouble with Thirteen. New York, Knopf, 1979.
Maudie and Me and the Dirty Book. New York, Knopf, 1980.
The Secret Life of the Underwear Champ, illustrated by Dan Jones. New York, Knopf, 1981.
I Would If I Could. New York, Knopf, 1982.
Sink or Swim. New York, Knopf, 1986.

Nonfiction

Save the Earth: An Ecology Handbook for Kids, illustrated by Claire A. Nivola and with photographs. New York, Knopf, 1974.
Save the Earth: An Action Handbook for Kids, illustrated by Nelle Davis. New York, Knopf, 1991.

PUBLICATIONS FOR CHILDREN

Picture books

A House for Everyone, illustrated by Jo Lowrey. New York, Knopf, 1958.
What Is the World? illustrated by Remy Charlip. New York, Knopf, 1958.
The Cooking Book, illustrated by Jo Lowrey. New York, Knopf, 1959.
Having a Friend, illustrated by Eric Blegvad. New York, Knopf, 1959.
A Day of Summer, illustrated by Remy Charlip. New York, Knopf, 1960.
A Day of Winter, illustrated by Remy Charlip. New York, Knopf, 1961.
Mr. Turtle's Mystery, illustrated by Margaret Tomes. New York, Knopf, 1961; London, Hamish Hamilton, 1961.

The Feast on Sullivan Street, illustrated by Kurt Werth. New York, Knopf, 1963.

Associate Editor, *The Bank Street Readers.* New York, Macmillan, 1965-69.

A Day of Autumn, illustrated by Marjorie Auerbach. New York, Knopf, 1967.

Joe Finds a Way, with Joan Blos; illustrated by Lee Ames. New York, Singer, 1967.

A Day of Spring, illustrated by Marjorie Auerbach. New York, Knopf, 1970.

Just Think, with Joan Blos; illustrated by Pat Grant Porter. New York, Knopf, 1971.

Around and Around—Love, illustrated with photographs. New York, Knopf, 1975.

Hey I'm Reading! illustrated by Sylvie Wickstrom. New York, Knopf, 1994.

The Sky Is Falling! illustrated by Cynthia Fisher. New York, Aladdin, 1998.

The Tortoise and the Hare, illustrated by Paul Meisel. New York, Aladdin, 1998.

*

Biography: Entry in *Fifth Book of Junior Authors and Illustrators,* New York, H.W. Wilson, 1983; essay in *Something about the Author Autobiography Series,* Volume 9, Detroit, Gale, 1990; essay in *Speaking for Ourselves, Too* compiled and edited by Donald R. Gallo, National Council of Teachers of English, 1993.

Betty Miles comments:

Reading is one way all of us—young adults and older ones, too—discover how other ordinary people learn to make choices, take stands and try to do what they think is right. I always hope that my books, along with all the others, will help to support and encourage young people as they are growing. I'm grateful for the dedicated parents, librarians, and teachers who—despite hard times and low budgets—work to bring books and young readers together.

*   *   *

It is apparent that Betty Miles writes about contemporary issues, making her a popular twentieth-century writer for young adults. She wrote *Save the Earth!* because she wanted people to care as she does about environmental problems. She also cares about young people and the problems they are faced with every day.

The Real Me is really about Betty Miles and the way she feels and thinks, but it is written about an adolescent girl, Barbara Fisher, fighting to end sex discrimination in PE classes in her school. Barbara wants to take tennis, but only boys are allowed to take that class, so Barbara pushes the school to allow girls to choose classes other than slimnastics, field hockey, modern dance, or acrobatics. Barbara also wants to be a paper carrier, but once again she faces sex discrimination because paper delivery is for boys only. Barbara's mother, a writer for the local newspaper, is fighting for women's rights, too, and the two females are all of a sudden treated like nuts. However, neither back down in what they believe. They find, to their delight and satisfaction, that they can and do help

make changes in their community and make life more bearable for the female population in general. This is a comfortable story of a loving family that sticks together, works and plays together, and celebrates together the accomplishments of each member of the family. Young people will learn about justice and equality after reading this book and will see the importance of the women's liberation movement for everyone.

A real eye-opener, *Maudie and Me and the Dirty Book* portrays Kate Harris and Maudie Schmidt who volunteer for a special project in English class. The project involves working with first graders, helping them learn to read. Kate is not happy being paired with Maudie, because Maudie is not one of Kate's crowd and one who most kids tend to avoid. But the two girls go to the library where Kate, with the help of the librarian, innocently picks out a book about a dog that has puppies. She reads the book to the first graders, and an innocent discussion on sexual anatomy follows the reading. Later, Kate is shocked to find herself in the middle of a protest at a town meeting where some of the narrow-minded citizens object to the book Kate read, saying it was smut. Kate bravely stands up in front of the crowded auditorium and voices her beliefs on the rights of kids to learn and to state that the book is not smut but is educational. Kate is warmly supported by her family and teacher, and a lasting friendship with Maudie develops. Both entertaining and enlightening, the story is humorous, educational, and well-written, subtly teaching a lesson in democracy.

A group of kids from New York City are chosen to spend two weeks with families in New Hampshire and are known as the Fresh Air kids in *Sink or Swim.* B.J. Johnson seems to be the only black kid in the New Hampshire town and finds himself with a white family, Jackie and Norm Roberts and their two children. B.J. is happy when everyone welcomes him and makes him feel right at home, but he has never been to the country and finds it a trifle frightening. Betty Miles has written an enjoyable story about new experiences, accepting and being accepted, and the joy with which B.J. greets each new day in the country. The reader can smell the chickens, the flowers and fresh air, and feel the fear as B.J. learns the hard way to swim to the raft at the swimming pond. The book is appealing with its undercurrent of inter-racial love and good feeling despite differences.

Cathy Myers is thirteen years old, her mother just became a cleaning lady, and Cathy is going to be suspended from school for leaving the school grounds to go to a local coffee shop in *Just the Beginning.* Besides that, George Waldman picks on Cathy constantly, even though she tries to avoid him. Cathy faces her suspension, learns to deal with her mother being a cleaning lady, and then has to face the trauma of George Waldman dying a violent death. Ms. Miles has written about growing up and facing responsibilities and of a teenager learning that life isn't always what we want it to be. Through Cathy's eyes we see the importance of family love and sharing, the pressure of trying to be like others, and the knowledge that one has to face growing up, regardless of obstacles. Although the pace is slow, the theme is clear.

The Trouble with Thirteen is full of changes. It is a story about two best friends, Annie Morrison and Rachel Weiss. Annie is very self-conscious about her changing body, her moods, and her feelings. She's not quite sure she's ready to grow up, but finds she really doesn't have any choice. Rachel's parents are getting a divorce and the family is moving to New York City, and Annie is devastated that Rachel is leaving her. Then the Morrison's dog dies in Annie's arms, and things seem too much for her to deal with all at once. Ms. Miles has written a perceptive story of a young girl coping reluctantly with changes in her life but accepting them because she has to. The story touches one's heart with the sadness of losing a beloved pet that dies and a beloved friend that moves away, but the story shows that young people can deal with these things and life does go on.

Rosalie Hudnecker in *Looking On* is a fourteen-year-old, tall, overweight junior high girl seeking love and happiness as does every young person. When a young married couple moves into a small trailer next door, Rosie sees a possible place to go to find a sense of belonging and sharing that she so desperately craves. She discovers she doesn't fit in with the Judsons because she has a life of her own to live. She goes on a diet, gets her hair cut, and becomes more involved with friends her own age. This is a quiet, slow-moving story of a girl growing up, determined to change herself for the better.

Whether the background issue is ecology or women's liberation, racial discrimination or censorship, Ms. Miles writes stories that appeal to youthful readers because ultimately her books are about changing and growing and helping young people to learn about themselves.

—Carol Doxey

MILLER, Frances A.

Nationality: American. **Born:** New York City, 15 October 1937. **Education:** Wellesley College, Wellesley, Massachusetts, B.A. 1959; California State University, Hayward, Teaching Credential, 1976; graduate study at San Jose State University, California. **Family:** Married John David Miller; two daughters and two sons. **Career:** Reading tutor and volunteer worker at public schools in Oakland and San Ramon, California, 1966-75; reading and English teacher at middle school in Hayward, California, 1976-77; member of executive board, Adult Literacy Program, Sydney, Australia, 1979-83; writer and public speaker, since 1983. Coordinator of "Aussie Books for Kids" exhibit, 1984-88. **Awards:** ALA Best Book for Young Adults, California Young Reader Medal, both 1985, both for *The Truth Trap*.

PUBLICATIONS FOR YOUNG ADULTS

Fiction

The Truth Trap. New York, Dutton, 1980.
Aren't You the One Who. . . ? New York, Atheneum, 1983.
Losers and Winners. New York, Fawcett, 1986.
Cutting Loose. New York, Fawcett, 1991.

*   *   *

Frances A. Miller has written four novels which follow the same character through two-and-a-half years of living. *The Truth Trap* is the first in the series that follows Matt McKendrick on a quest beginning when he is fifteen-years-old. Until that time he had lived with a strong and loving family in a small town where they kept a cattle ranch. Suddenly everything changes for him

when his parents are killed in an accident. Fearing that the authorities will take his younger sister away, Matt runs to Los Angeles believing he can take care of her if he finds work. Deaf since birth, his sister has a close relationship with Matt. While he is searching for a job she is murdered; Matt is accused of the crime, arrested, and although not found guilty, has his own recriminations to deal with. The policemen arresting Matt represent the two forces in society with which he will need to contend from then on: those who believe him, and those who don't. The officer who trusts Matt is the only real support he has, and Matt is eventually adopted by him.

Miller does a masterful job of climbing into her character and letting the reader hear his thoughts. Matt's inner voice is realistic, strong, and relentless as it responds to the complexities of grief, anger, and resentment, and most of all to the outrageous injustices inflicted on him. As *The Truth Trap* is essentially a story of survival, Matt is necessarily a self-absorbed character. In the next novel in the series, *Aren't You the One Who. . . ?*, Matt begins to move forward in an attempt to establish relationships with the larger community, but the outside world is often hostile and people remember what he was accused of. Thus, the title is an appropriate question for Matt's conflict, since people are inclined to remember only the accusations, not the outcome of the case. Thus, Matt is believed to be guilty until he is able to prove that he is innocent and worthy of trust.

In this book, Matt becomes friends with the Schuylers, a family of four children who have lost their mother and are facing enormous adjustments and responsibilities of their own. In becoming friends with the Schuylers, Matt begins to take risks, to give to others, and to establish trust again. As he develops a greater acceptance for himself, he gains the courage to face the future and the challenges of going to high school. Unfortunately, school offers a new series of problems, including an insensitive running coach. Through dealing with this problem in his own way, Matt builds the confidence that he can continue to face the consequences of his decisions.

Losers and Winners takes the reader into Matt's senior year in high school and his competition for "Runner of the Year." The story further develops his relationship with the Schuylers as they continue to fill the empty spaces in his life. The fourth novel of the series, *Cutting Loose,* takes Matt home to Idaho where he and his friends work on a guest ranch. As it turns out, the guest ranch was once his family home, and Matt must now face the task of literally learning to let go of the past.

The plot in each of these novels is strong and appealing to young adult readers. Underlying the extraordinary events of the novels are numerous themes and messages. Although never didactic, Miller has strong convictions about her characters, young people and the relationships between them. She strives to create in Matt a character who in spite of atrocious odds is a winner, and who is able to grow, change, and learn. She provides a protagonist the reader cares about, because Matt is a problem solver who develops tenacity, possesses a strong sense of justice and fairness, and remains loyal and caring.

These stories can be read independently of each other, but following the growth of Matt is rewarding if the four are read in order. The thematic thread that connects them all is the fact that society often judges everything at face value rather than taking the time to learn and understand. Miller demonstrates her belief that all ages and stages of development are of value, and adults and young people need to share mutual respect. Making mistakes and taking risks are valued as agents of growth. The characters the reader does not care for are those who are unwilling to change, and who refuse to look beyond their preconceptions and stereotypical judgments.

As a parent of four children, a teacher of middle school students and an avid reader, Miller has accrued a storehouse of knowledge about young people. She gives voice to their strong emotions, and allows her characters a full range of feelings, reactions, and reflections. Her dialogues ring true, and readers believe the words of her characters. Miller is exceptionally gifted in capturing the intensity of youth and the conflicts of the teenage years. She describes so well how quickly emotions can give way to other feelings; the ever changing emotional landscape of youth is what she knows best. Miller's words are clear, strong and succinct and she spends them generously on Matt's feelings; she provides enough knowledge about him to make the reader care about her character. Thus, Miller awards the reader with a sense of hope, and confirms the need to believe that anyone can overcome even the most difficult of circumstances.

—Caroline S. McKinney

MILLER, Jim Wayne

Nationality: American. **Born:** Leicester, North Carolina, 21 October 1936. **Education:** Berea College, A.B. 1958; Vanderbilt University, Ph.D. 1965. **Family:** Married Mary Ellen Yates in 1958; two sons and one daughter. **Career:** German and English teacher, Fort Knox Dependent Schools, Fort Knox, Kentucky, 1958-60; assistant professor, 1963-66, associate professor, 1966-70, professor, since 1970, Western Kentucky University, Bowling Green. Affiliated with Poet-in-the-Schools Program, Virginia public schools, beginning 1977; poet-in-residence, Centre College of Kentucky, 1984. Staff member, Hindman Settlement School Writers Workshop, since 1978; fellow of the corporation of Yaddo, 1983-84. Invited reader, fiftieth anniversary meeting of South Atlantic Modern Language Association, 1978. Visiting professor, Appalachian Studies Workshop, Berea College, 1973-80, and James R. Stokely Institute for Liberal Arts Education, University of Tennessee, 1984-85. Chairman, Kentucky Humanities Council, Inc., 1973-74; board member, Appalachian Community Service Network. Consultant to poetry workshops in Kentucky, Virginia, North Carolina, Tennessee, Indiana, and West Virginia; consultant to Appalachian studies programs at colleges and universities throughout the Appalachian South; member of advisory board of "An Appalachian Experience," Children's Museum, Oak Ridge, Tennessee. **Awards:** Alice Lloyd Memorial Prize for Appalachian Poetry from Alice Lloyd College, 1967, for poems in *Copperhead Cane;* Sigma Tau Delta Topaz award for Distinguished Service to the University, Western Kentucky University, 1969, Western Kentucky University faculty award for research and creativity, 1976; Thomas Wolfe Literary award, for *The Mountains Have Come Closer,* 1980; received honorary doctorate of letters, Berea College, 1981; Western Kentucky University faculty award for public service, 1982; Distinguished Alumnus award, Berea College Alumni Association, 1983; Appalachian Writers Association Book of the

Year award, 1989, for *Newfound;* Zoe Kincaid Brockman Memorial award for Poetry, North Carolina Poetry Society, 1989; Appalachian Writers Association award for Outstanding Contributions to Appalachian Literature, 1990; Educational Service to Appalachia award, Carson-Newman College, Jefferson City, Tennessee, 1990; Laurel Leaves award, Appalachian Consortium of Colleges and Universities, 1991; literary awards for poetry, short stories, and translations from Kentucky Writers Guild, *Green River Review, Appalachian Harvest,* and *Kentucky Poetry Review.* **Died:** 18 August 1996.

PUBLICATIONS

Poetry

Copperhead Cane. Nashville, Tennessee, Robert Moore Allen, 1964.
The More Things Change, the More They Stay the Same (ballads). Frankfort, Kentucky, Whippoorwill Press, 1971.
Dialogue with a Dead Man. Athens, Georgia, University of Georgia Press, 1974, reprinted Saginaw, Michigan, Green River Press, 1978.
The Mountains Have Come Closer. Boone, North Carolina, Appalachian Consortium, 1980, reprinted 1991.
Vein of Words. Big Timber, Montana, Seven Buffaloes Press, 1984.
Nostalgia for 70. Big Timber, Montana, Seven Buffaloes Press, 1986.
His First Best Country. Frankfort, Kentucky, Gnomon, 1987.
Brier, His Book. Frankfort, Kentucky, Gnomon, 1988.
Round and Round with Kahlil Gibran. Blacksburg, Virginia, Rowan Mountain, 1990.

Novel

Newfound. New York, Orchard, 1989, reprinted, 1991.

Other

Translator, *The Figure of Fulfillment,* by Emil Lerperger. University Center, Michigan, Green River, 1975.
Contributor, *Voices from the Mountains,* edited by Guy and Candie Carawan. New York, Knopf, 1975.
Contributor, *Voices from the Hills,* edited by Robert J. Higgs and Ambrose Manning. New York, F. Ungar, 1977.
Contributor, *A Geography of Poets,* edited by Edward Field. New York, Bantam, 1979.
Editor, *I Have a Place.* Pippa Passes, Kentucky, Appalachian Learning Laboratory, 1980.
Reading, Writing, Region: A Checklist and Purchase Guide for School and Community Libraries. Boone, North Carolina, Appalachian Consortium, 1984.
Contributor, *Strings: A Gathering of Family Poems,* edited by Paul B. Janeczko. Scarsdale, New York, 1984.
Contributor, *United States in Literature.* Glenview, Illinois, Scott, Foresman, 1984.
Contributor, *Geography and Literature: A Meeting of the Disciplines,* edited by Paul Simpson-Housley and William E. Mallory. Syracuse, New York, Syracuse University Press, 1986.
Contributor, *Going over to Your Place,* edited by Paul B. Janeczko. New York, Bradbury, 1987.
Editor, *A Jesse Stuart Reader.* Ashland, Kentucky, Jesse Stuart Foundation, 1988.

Editor, *A Ride with Huey the Engineer.* Ashland, Kentucky, Jesse Stuart Foundation, 1988.

Contributor, *The Music of What Happens: Poems That Tell Stories,* edited by Paul B. Janeczko. New York, Orchard Books, 1988.

Editor, *The Beatinest Boy.* Ashland, Kentucky, Jesse Stuart Foundation, 1989.

Contributor, *An Ear to the Ground: An Anthology of Contemporary American Poetry,* edited by Marie Harris and Kathleen Aguero. Athens, Georgia, University of Georgia Press, 1989.

The Examined Life: Family, Community, and Work in American Literature. Boone, North Carolina, Appalachian Consortium, 1989.

Editor, *The Rightful Owner.* Ashland, Kentucky, Jesse Stuart Foundation, 1989.

Contributor, *Our Words, Our Ways: Reading and Writing in North Carolina,* edited by Sally Buckner. Durham, North Carolina, Carolina Academic Press, 1991.

Contributor, *Preposterous: Poems of Youth,* edited by Paul B. Janeczko. New York, Orchard Books, 1991.

Contributor, *Perspectives* (grade 8 language arts anthology), edited by Ed Hannan and others. Toronto, Holt, 1991.

Contributor, *Men of Our Time: Male Poetry in Contemporary America,* edited by Fred Moramarco and Al Zolynas. Athens, Georgia, University of Georgia Press, 1992.

Editor, *Southern Mountain Speech.* Kentucky, Berea College Press, 1992.

Editor, *A Penny's Worth of Character,* by Jesse Stuart, illustrated by Rocky Zornes. Ashland, Kentucky, Jesse Stuart Foundation, 1993.

*

Jim Wayne Miller comments:

For me, writing has never been a matter of having something to say and then saying it. Rather, writing is an attempt to clarify concerns I have, questions I put to myself. Thinking of writing in this way, I've made experiments and probes, said a lot of things, and then decided which of those things I meant! Instead of knowing in advance what I want to say, I always have to discover my meaning in and through the process of writing.

But no matter how much or how little I write in the future, I know the quality I want the work to possess. Growing up in western North Carolina, I was often amused, along with other natives, at tourists who fished the trout streams. The pools, so perfectly clear, had a deceptive depth. Fishermen unacquainted with them, wearing hip waders, were forever stepping off into pools they judged to be knee-deep—and going in up to their waists or even their armpits, sometimes being floated right off their feet. I want to make my writing like those pools, so simple and clear its depth is deceptive. I want the writing to be transparent, so readers forget they are reading and are aware only that they are having an experience. They are suddenly plunged deeper than they expected and come up shivering.

*   *   *

Jim Wayne Miller, a professor of German at Western Kentucky University until his death in 1996, published essays, poetry, fiction, and drama, translated the poetry of an Austrian poet, and edited and introduced some of the works of Jesse Stuart. He is best known as an exceptionally gifted poet and as a wonderfully entertaining reader of his own poetry. His touching works about growing up in a rural area and about changing family relationships also appeal to young adult readers.

Central to his accomplishments is his emphasis on place. The specific place most often called up in his poetry is the southern Appalachian Mountains, particularly western North Carolina, where he was born. He dedicated his book *Dialogue with a Dead Man* to "the people of Appalachia wherever they are." Miller's poetic persona who embodies that culture is "the Brier." Much like a Kentucky hillbilly, the Brier has roots in rural, farming America. From the 1930s to 1960s, he may have gone north to places like Detroit, Chicago, and Cincinnati to make a living, but he never forgot his home nor the wisdom he gained from his ancestors. Nevertheless, the lore and ballads are in danger of being lost if someone does not commit them to paper. Even the places may no longer exist—as Miller expresses in his poem "Small Farms Disappearing in Tennessee" from *Brier, His Book.*

Fortunately, the Brier records in easily accessible language the essence of Appalachian culture. The first stanza of "Squirrel Stand," from *Dialogue with a Dead Man,* provides a good example:

> Now burley's curing in the high-tiered barn
> and yellow leaves ride out on slow black water.
> Cold wind moving in the rows of corn
> rattles the blades like an old man pulling fodder.
> Down from the mountain pastures overnight,
> cattle stand by the yellow salt block bawling.
> Now it's September in the world; fine rain is falling.

From the perspective of his otherness, the Brier describes, sometimes satirically, what's wrong with modern man. In "Brier Sermon," from *The Mountains Have Come Closer,* the Brier berates his audience for forgetting about the past, about their innocent, childlike selves, and for losing touch with nature. A clever reversal occurs in the self-mocking poem "The Brier Losing Touch with His Traditions," from the same collection. An "authentic mountain craftsman," the Brier goes north to be closer to his market. But his northern customers are dismayed to find that he uses electric power tools to make those authentic chairs, so he has to move back to Kentucky "to have some time for himself" and to keep his customers believing in his authenticity.

In addition to his emphasis on place, Miller believes that metaphor is the literal soul of poetry. In "From the Brier Glossary of Literary Terms," in *Brier, His Book,* he defines a poem as Thoreau might have: "A cold spring. Sweet water nobody knows is / there but you. You stand, looking down, and / see yourself outlined against the sky." And in "The Brier Plans a Mountain Vision Center," from the same collection, the Brier tells what poems do: unlike rose-colored glasses, they make "gentle contact with the mind's eye, / like a soft lens, lining up then with now, now with then, news with news that stays news, like front and / rear gun sights."

Miller "aims" various poems at death, for instance "Aunt Gladys's Home Movie No. 31, Albert's Funeral," from *Dialogue with a Dead Man.* This poem describes a family gathered after their uncle Albert's funeral to view a home movie eulogizing Albert and his love of flowers:

Our chairs drawn to one end of the living
room, we sit like faithful at a Sunday evening
service, viewing a miracle. Before our eyes
Albert stirs in the ticking coil of dark
film and comes riding a beam of light,
a smear of colors, finger painting—flowers.

Part of the attraction of the poem is its esoteric pattern: it is a sestina, an amazingly complex French lyric form.

A large number of Miller's poems focus on the concerns of middle-class Americans—the joys of raising children, the sound of a vacuum cleaner on Saturday morning, dreams, living and dying. The persona of a poem called "Skydivers," in *The Mountains Have Come Closer,* uses two apt metaphors to sum up the changing relationship between a parent and his family. Life, the poem suggests, is like riding a chair-lift in an amusement park. Everyone enjoys the ride and the thrills it provides, although each member of the family is ultimately separated from the others. As time passes, the metaphor changes. Now the family is skydiving, and the thrills are even greater, but so, finally, is the separation:

It is pleasant and so still but we are falling
farther and farther apart through private corridors
of air. The earth grows under us, and begins
to be patches of ground the size of our shadows.

The pleasure of skydiving, of living, is always modified by the persona's knowledge of the coming "shadows," or final separation places—their graves.

Provocative images, delightful, clarifying metaphors, gentle satire, insights into family living, and celebrations of his Appalachian past all mark Jim Wayne Miller as an accomplished writer. His poetry is well worth reading and comprehending.

—John Reiss

MITCHELL, Margaret (Munnerlyn)

Pseudonyms: Also wrote as Peggy Mitchell; Margaret Mitchell Upshaw, Elizabeth Bennett. **Nationality:** American. **Born:** Atlanta, Georgia, 8 November 1900. **Education:** Washington Seminary, Atlanta, 1914-18; Smith College, Northampton, Massachusetts, 1918-19. **Family:** Married 1) Berrien Kinnard Upshaw in 1922 (annulled 1924); 2) John Robert Marsh in 1925. **Career:** Feature writer and reporter, Atlanta *Journal and Constitution* and *Sunday Journal Magazine,* 1922-26. Free-lance columnist, 1926; novelist, 1926-36; homemaker, 1936-49. Volunteer selling war bonds during World War II; volunteer for the American Red Cross in the 1940s. **Awards:** Pulitzer Prize from Columbia University Graduate School of Journalism, 1937, for *Gone with the Wind;* Bohmenberger Memorial award, 1938; M.A.: Smith College, 1939; named honorary citizen of Vimoutiers, France, 1949, for helping the city obtain American aid after World War II. **Died:** 16 August 1949.

Fiction

Gone with the Wind. New York and London, Macmillan, 1936.

Other

Margaret Mitchell's "Gone with the Wind" Letters, edited by Richard Harwell. New York, Macmillan, and London, Collier Macmillan, 1976.
Margaret Mitchell, A Dynamo Going to Waste: Letters to Allen Edee, 1919-1921, edited by Jane Bonner Peacock. Atlanta, Peachtree Publications, 1985.

*

Media Adaptation: *Gone with the Wind* (film, starring Clark Gable, Vivien Leigh, Leslie Howard, and Olivia De Havilland), Metro-Goldwyn-Mayer, 1939.

Biography: Entry in *Dictionary of Literary Biography,* Volume 9: *American Novelists, 1910-1945,* Detroit, Gale, 1981.

Manuscript Collections: University of Georgia, Athens; Atlanta Public Library.

Critical Studies: *Margaret Mitchell of Atlanta* by Finis Farr, New York, Morrow, 1965; *The Road to Tara: The Life of Margaret Mitchell* by Anne Edwards, New Haven, Connecticut, Ticknor and Fields, and London, Hodder & Stoughton, 1983; *Gone with the Wind as Book and Film* edited by Richard Harwell, Columbia, University of South Carolina Press, 1983.

*   *   *

Although Margaret Mitchell did not consider herself a writer for young adults, her single masterpiece, *Gone with the Wind,* and its blockbuster film version have been perennial favorites of American teenagers, to the point that both are often included in high school and college curriculums. The increased interest of recent years following the fiftieth anniversaries of both the novel (1986) and the film (1989), as well as the publication of an authorized sequel (1992) will surely extend the popularity of *Gone with the Wind* into the next century. This popular phenomenon proves most interesting as Mitchell's masterwork seems a nineteenth-century book in subject, theme, and style—a twentieth-century reincarnation of the Victorian "triple-decker" romance. Thus the book's remarkable popularity is a combination of tradition and change much like the narrative it relates.

In critical terms, it is possible to read *Gone with the Wind* as a female development novel. At the novel's opening in 1861, Scarlett O'Hara is a sixteen-year-old coquette; when it concludes in 1873 she is a twenty-eight-year-old woman. In the twelve year span of the novel, she experiences Secession, Civil War, and Reconstruction, as well as romance, love, marriage, and motherhood. Scarlett lives through the adolescent trauma of American culture, which is matched by a traumatic personal history as much or more tumultuous. Energized by her own life, Mitchell created one of the most arresting tales of troubled adolescence in American literature and in so doing created a novel which will continue to captivate teenagers and fascinate their teachers well into the next century.

For younger readers, Scarlett O'Hara's development from teenaged girl to mature woman proves as fascinating now as it did when the book was first published in 1936 or when the movie first appeared in 1939. The particular, indeed peculiar energy of the story proceeds from Mitchell's own girlhood, adolescence, and young adult life. During these years she heard the family legends of the Civil War era into which she projected her own development toward womanhood. The novel combines Mitchell's family and personal romances with historical facts to create powerful and popular fiction.

The popular image of Mitchell was as a Southern matron who turned to writing as her contemporaries might cultivate bridge, golf, or gardening. Although descended from old Georgia families and raised in comfortable circumstances, the future author was no simple Southern belle. Her mother's feminist leanings clashed with her father's conservatism, and a young Mitchell became a somewhat willful, rebellious tomboy, given to flights of imaginative fancy and a series of serious, debilitating accidents and illnesses. After the death of her first beloved on the Western Front and of her mother in the influenza epidemic, Mitchell became "a flapper," both living the wild times of the Jazz age and writing about them in nonfiction. Her first marriage was a disaster, climaxed by spousal rape and scandalous divorce, while her second marriage mirrored her dependent, and sometimes stressful relationships with her father and brother. The writer's social, psychological, and sexual ambiguities found expression in her greatest creation, Scarlett O'Hara, while other people in her life provided models for other characters in *Gone with the Wind*.

The critical history of *Gone with the Wind* is contradictory, as might be expected from the writer's conflicted biography. The reaction of reviewers and of general readers was quite positive in 1936, for no one would deny that the novel was a great "read." Even the initial response of the literary community seemed laudatory. Comparisons were made with the great novelists and novels of the nineteenth century—such as Thackeray and *Vanity Fair,* Tolstoy and *Anna Karenina,* and Flaubert and *Madame Bovary.* In terms of memorable characters, sweeping action, colorful settings, and grand themes the novel was a success. At the same time, qualifying statements about style, sentiment, racism, and melodrama raised legitimate questions about the book's literary status.

Unfortunately, the novel's existence as a cultural artifact subsumed its identity as a literary text and the immense power and popularity of the film version only complicated the situation. Book and film were conflated into a phenomenon of American and later international popular culture. Thus criticism was arrested at the levels of basic appreciation, often in the opposite poles of love and/or hate, and evaluation, again often in bipolar terms of praise and/or scorn. On the popular level the novel was lauded and in the literary world it was defamed.

This critical neglect continued well into the 1960s when reconsiderations of American culture and society elicited new readings of classic texts. Mitchell and her novel were seen as important symbols of American cultural forces. A serious biography in 1965 sparked reconsideration simply by the assumption of Mitchell's importance as a writer. Other reevaluations followed which asserted the literary quality of the work, notably in feminist terms. The critical neglect of the novel thus was explained in terms

of the largely male critical establishment, and Mitchell became the subject of articles and dissertations in the 1970s. Finally, in the 1980s, the half-century anniversaries of both novel and film provided new perspectives for critical focus in a number of important critical works, including a definitive biography.

—Joseph R. Millichap

MOERI, Louise

Nationality: American. **Born:** Klamath Falls, Oregon, 30 November 1924. **Education:** Stockton Junior College, A.A. 1944; University of California, Berkeley, B.A. 1946. **Family:** Married Edwin Albert Moeri in 1946; one daughter and two sons. **Career:** Library assistant, Manteca Branch Library, Manteca, California, 1961-78; writer. **Address:** 18262 South Austin Road, Manteca, California 95336, U.S.A.

PUBLICATIONS FOR YOUNG ADULTS

Fiction

The Girl Who Lived on the Ferris Wheel. New York, Dutton, 1979.
Save Queen of Sheba. New York, Dutton, 1981.
First the Egg. New York, Dutton, 1982.
Downwind. New York, Dutton, 1984.
Journey to the Treasure. New York, Scholastic, 1986.
Forty-third War. Boston, Houghton Mifflin, 1989.

PUBLICATIONS FOR CHILDREN

Fiction

Star Mother's Youngest Child, illustrated by Trina Schart Hyman. Boston, Houghton Mifflin, 1975.
A Horse for XYZ, illustrated by Gail Owens. New York, Dutton, 1977.
How the Rabbit Stole the Moon, illustrated by Marc Brown. Boston, Houghton Mifflin, 1977.
The Unicorn and the Plow, illustrated by Diane Goode. New York, Dutton, 1982.

*

Biography: Essay in *Something about the Author Autobiography Series,* Detroit, Gale, Vol. 10, 1990, and Vol. 93, 1998; essay in *Speaking for Ourselves, Too* compiled and edited by Donald R. Gallo, National Council of Teachers of English, 1993.

Louise Moeri comments:

I consider writing to be one of the hardest jobs in the world, and if I weren't compelled to do it, I'd take up some other line of work. But the fact is, I was born to be a writer, as I feel most creative people are born to paint, compose, or whatever medium reaches out to them. Whatever your talents are, they are included in the package that you come into the world with, and it is up to you to look into that package and discover what it is you are meant to be. My particular obsession with words and sentences began very early in my life, and shows no sign of abatement as I grow older. Picking up a pencil or sitting down at my typewriter marks the beginning of just one more chapter in my struggle to put some piece of human life into printed words to make a difference in someone's understanding of the world around him. Creative people are like lenses—they reveal details and patterns in life that might otherwise be missed.

But as difficult, unrewarding, and unnoticed as it often is, there is nothing I can do that is as exiting as watching a story emerge from my pencil onto a piece of paper. Since I am not one of those masterful writers who knows exactly what is going to happen in the story from the first word, I am fascinated as each incident, each chapter appears. It is a wonder-filled experience as I live it along with the characters who tug at my sleeve and say—"Hey! Let me tell you what happened. . ." and no matter how hard it is, I'm going to go right on doing it.

(1997)As the years have gone by, my vision has grown darker. Mesmerized by headlines and high-tech developments, my fear is that the people who have it in their power to make society function well are abandoning the task. So many "leaders" fail to lead in any meaningful way toward self-control and responsibility, fairness and accountability. Instead, what counts for success is often only flagrant public consumption for the sole purpose of attracting and holding the limelight. It has been said that people get the government (and society) they deserve. The same can be said of families. Families disintegrate when parents are unwilling to accept the burdens and responsibilities of parenting. As Walt Kelly once said through his character, Pogo, "We have met the enemy and he is us."

I have always written and will continue to write stories that I hope will enable people—both adults and children—to see themselves in a clear, truthful light and to build better lives for themselves. As the Author of Proverbs, 29:18 put it: "Where there is no vision, the people perish. . . ."

My goal is to help people see more clearly. Nothing else is worth doing.

*   *   *

When asked to recommend an author for a middle grade or junior high reader with a penchant for fast-paced adventure plots and books with page-turning appeal, Louise Moeri comes to mind. Moeri creates believable characters that foster empathy in readers. In contrast to many young adult novels with protagonists free of family responsibilities, Moeri's characters are children with adult challenges. Although Moeri's stories center on a variety of subject matter and themes, most of which are relevant and sometimes controversial, the novels are essentially about human nature and refrain from sensationalism.

The Girl Who Lived on the Ferris Wheel is described by the publisher as a psychological thriller. How will Clotilde (Til for short) continue to bear her mother's beatings? Won't her loving but unseeing father recognize Til's misery and danger? What will happen to Til's deeply disturbed mother? The suspense intensifies

and the reader is breathless waiting to discover if Til escapes her mother's butcher knife. Divorce, child abuse, and mental illness are the topics of this novel, but the real story is eleven-year-old Til's struggle to survive in a world where the adults seem unable to help.

In *First the Egg* Sarah Webster and David Hanna become the unwilling parents of an egg. In order to complete their marriage and family class project, Sarah and David must protect and nurture the egg for an entire week; they can never leave it alone, and they must complete a baby book chronicling the egg baby's development. Sarah's responsibilities open her eyes to the disturbing patterns within her own family that she has previously ignored and helps her reach out to David, who is headed for trouble. Natural language and everyday situations help the reader identify with Sarah. Moeri's realistic descriptions of Sarah's frustration with the silliness of the project when it is first assigned to actually "missing" the egg when the project is over enhances the credibility of the story. It is easy for readers to put themselves in Sarah's place.

Twelve-year-old King David and his six-year-old sister Queen of Sheba are the only survivors of a Sioux Indian attack on their Oregon Trail wagon train. David takes charge of his whiny, sulky sister and follows the trail of some wagons that may have gotten away, hoping to find his parents. Starving and exhausted David faces the temptations of abandoning the petulant Sheba. *True Queen of Sheba* is suspenseful and engaging. The reader respects David's responsibility and yearns for a happy ending even when the youngsters' plight seems hopeless.

In *Downwind* it is twelve-year-old Ephraim Dearborn who must act as an adult and take responsibility for his three younger siblings. Ephraim's family lives downwind of the local nuclear power plant and meltdown is imminent according to the local news. In panic, the Dearborns attempt to escape, only to find chaos and traffic jams blocking the road to safety. Ephraim's mother breaks down and is unable to take care of the two children hurt in the scramble. *Downwind* is another page turner with an admirable young protagonist who rises to meet the challenges of an adult situation. Ephraim's world does not collapse, but he is changed forever.

Uno, Lolo, and Macio have managed to escape the soldiers—both the Revolutionaries and the Loyalists—who periodically round up all the boys in their Central American village and force them to become soldiers. War has always been a part of their lives, and the fathers and older men were taken long ago. No one in the villages goes untouched. Uno's sister is raped by the soldiers, and there is little food or money for the village families. During a surprise raid Uno, Lolo, and Macio are "recruited" at gunpoint to join the revolutionaries. Uno has never understood the reasons for fighting, but during eight days of training, patrol, and battles he sees villagers massacred by the government's Loyalist troops and becomes committed to the rebel cause. In *The Forty-third War*, Moeri once again uses realistic dialogue and emotion to create a novel which allows young adults to read with caring and belief the story of boys who must become men in order to survive.

In all of Moeri's thin but powerful books, the protagonists not only survive but develop an understanding of the transience of life and the complexities of human nature. Cynical readers may scoff at the happy endings achieved in Moeri's chronicles of adverse conditions and unthinkable hardships, but the careful construction of credible characters and the tense plots ensure that most readers are cheering for these stalwart youngsters and will be dissatisfied with anything less than favorable resolutions. For the young adolescent the message is clear: life is often a struggle, but you, too, can overcome the hardships.

—Hollis Lowery-Moore

MOHR, Nicholasa

Nationality: American. **Born:** New York City, 1 November 1938. **Education:** Art Students' League, 1957-58; Taller de Grafica, Mexico City, 1956; New School for Social Research, New York, New York, 1959; Brooklyn Museum of Art School, 1965-67; Pratt Center for Contemporary Printmaking, 1967-70. **Family:** Married Irwin Mohr in 1958 (deceased), two sons. **Career:** Fine arts painter in New York, California, Mexico, and Puerto Rico, 1957-58; printmaker in New York, Mexico, and Puerto Rico, 1965—; teacher in art schools in New York, 1968-69. Art instructor, Art Center of Northern New Jersey, 1971-73; writer in residence, MacDowell Colony, Peterborough, New Hampshire, 1972, 1974, and 1976; artist in residence, New York City public schools, 1973-74; lecturer in Puerto Rican studies, State University of New York at Stony Brook, 1977; distinguished visiting professor at Queens College of the City University of New York, 1988-91; also visiting lecturer in creative writing for various educator, librarian, student, and community groups. Head creative writer and co-producer of videotape series *Aqui y Ahora.* Member of New Jersey State Council on the Arts; member of board of trustees, and consultant, of Young Filmmakers Foundation; consultant on bilingual media training for Young Filmmakers/Video Arts. **Awards:** Outstanding book award in juvenile fiction, *New York Times,* 1973, Jane Addams Children's Book award, Jane Addams Peace Association, 1974, citation of merit for book jacket design, Society of Illustrators, 1974, and *School Library Journal*'s "Best of the Best 1966-78" citation, all for *Nilda;* outstanding book award in teenage fiction, *New York Times,* 1975, best book award, *School Library Journal,* 1975, and National Book award finalist for "most distinguished book in children's literature," 1976, all for *El Bronx Remembered;* best book award, *School Library Journal,* best book award in young adult literature, American Library Association, and Notable Trade Book award, joint committee of National Council for the Social Studies and Children's Book Council, all 1977, all for *In Nueva York;* Notable Trade Book award, joint committee of National Council for the Social Studies and Children's Book Council, 1980, and American Book award, Before Columbus Foundation, 1981, both for *Felita;* commendation from the Legislature of the State of New York, 1985, for *Rituals of Survival: A Woman's Portfolio;* Hispanic Heritage Award for Literature, 1997; honorary doctorate of letters, State University of New York at Albany, 1989. **Address:** 727 President St., Brooklyn, NY 11215, U.S.A.

PUBLICATIONS FOR YOUNG ADULTS

Novels

Nilda, illustrated by the author. New York, Harper, 1973; updated edition, Houston, Texas, Arte Publico, 1986.
Felita, illustrated by the author. New York, Dial Press, 1979.

Going Home. New York, Dial Press, 1986.
El Bronx Remembered: A Novella and Stories, illustrated by the author. New York, Harper, 1975; updated edition, Houston, Texas, Arte Publico, 1986.
All for the Better: A Story of el Barrio, illustrated by Rudy Gutierrez. Austin, Texas, Raintree, 1992.
Isabel's New Mom. New York, Macmillan, 1993.
The Magic Shell, illustrated by Rudy Gutierrez. New York, Scholastic, 1994.

Short Stories

In Nueva York. New York, Dial Press, 1977; updated edition, Houston, Texas, Arte Publico, 1988.

Radio Play: *Inside the Monster,* New York, Film Video Arts, 1981.

Television Play: *Aqui Y Ahora,* New York, Film Video Arts, 1975.

PUBLICATIONS FOR CHILDREN

Picture Books

Old Letivia and the Mountain of Sorrows, illustrated by Rudy Gutierrez. New York, Viking, 1994.
The Song of El Coqui and Other Tales of Puerto Rico, illustrated by Antonio Martorell. New York, Viking, 1995.

PUBLICATIONS FOR ADULTS

Fiction

Rituals of Survival: A Women's Portfolio. Houston, Texas, Arte Publico, 1985.
A Matter of Pride and Other Stories. Houston, Arte Publico, 1997.

Nonfiction

Growing Up Inside the Sanctuary of My Imagination. New York, J. Messner, 1994.

Also author, with Ray Blanco, of *The Artist* (screenplay). Contributor of stories to textbooks and anthologies, including *The Ethnic American Woman: Problems, Protests, Lifestyles.* Contributor of short stories to *Children's Digest, Scholastic Magazine,* and *Nuestro.* Member of board of contributing editors, *Nuestro.*

*

Biography: Essay in *Something about the Author Autobiography Series,* Vol. 8, Detroit, Gale, 1989; essay in *Speaking for Ourselves: Autobiographical Sketches by Notable Authors of Books for Young Adults,* Vol. 1, compiled and edited by Donald R. Gallo, National Council of Teachers of English, 1990.

Critical Studies: Entry in *Contemporary Literary Criticism,* Vol. 12, Detroit, Gale, 1980; entry in *Children's Literature Review,* Vol. 22, Detroit, Gale, 1991.

Illustrator: *Hispanic Temas* edited by Hilda Hidalgo and Joan McEniry, 1985.

Nicholasa Mohr comments:

Because of who I am, I feel blessed by the work I do, for it permits me to use my talents and continue to "make magic." I can recreate those deepest of personal memories as well as validate and celebrate my heritage and my future.

*   *   *

Nicholasa Mohr, the first Puerto Rican woman born on the U.S. mainland to write about her ethnic roots in New York City's Lower East Side and the South Bronx, is an artist as well as an author of young adult novels. She attended art schools and worked as a freelance painter and graphic artist for years before she began writing novels and short stories for young adults. Therefore, it is not surprising that Mohr drew the colorful, eye-catching cover art for her first two books—*Nilda* and *El Bronx Remembered*—and the expressive character drawings in each book. Her writing, in fact, simulates her art—rich in descriptive and evocative detail, vivid in its realistic word-pictures depicting slices of life from her poverty-stricken El Barrio childhood.

Mohr's first novel, *Nilda,* describes four years in the life of a ten-year-old second-generation Puerto Rican girl living in New York City during World War II. From this story, one gets a clear sense of the hurt and humiliation suffered by migrating Puerto Ricans. Because of the Jones Act of 1917, Puerto Ricans born in Puerto Rico are automatically American citizens. As a result, their language and culture have been heavily influenced by American culture and the English language. Subsequently, when Nilda's parents move to the U.S. mainland during the 1920s, they are more open to social assimilation than immigrants from other countries because of this Americanization. But they and their children are greeted by racism, gang violence, drugs, job discrimination, and pervasive poverty and are made to feel unwelcome. Nilda is one of six children whose brave and strong mother holds together a large, extended family consisting of a physically sick father, a mentally ill aunt, a brother in prison, and his pregnant girlfriend. Nilda also has to contend with a school that questions her absence to mourn her father's death according to Puerto Rican custom, a policeman who brutalizes her neighbors and who denigrates her ethnic background, and a church that exploits the trust its Puerto Rican parishioners put in it. Permeating the novel are the twin themes of inner strength and ethnic survival; Nilda's mother's last words to her daughter are "You have something all yours. . .keep it." In the face of social adversity and family tragedy, Nilda draws on her self-esteem and sensitivity. She copes with her father's death by meditating on the beauty of spring, the season of new life. And when her mother dies, she consoles herself by recollecting special private moments in her mother's life.

This optimism during times of travail is further developed in Mohr's second book, *El Bronx Remembered*—a collection of short

stories and a novella continuing Nilda's life. Set in the 1950s, the stories concern problems similar to those appearing in her first novel: broken families, out-of-wedlock pregnancies, unfulfilled gay relationships, gang violence, and school insensitivity to the needs of Puerto Rican students. These stories focus on the second generation of Puerto Ricans in New York City whose connection to their homeland is increasingly remote. More and more they form friendships with members of other ethnic groups, sharing their problems, hopes, and dreams. Mohr's characters in this melange of stories seem to draw strength from one another. Her main message is: Life goes on.

In her third book, *In Nueva York,* the characters are older and the time is later—the 1970s. But the social problems of New York's Puerto Rican communities persist and in some cases have worsened. Like its predecessor, this book is a collection of interconnected stories and survival is its main theme. Forty years before, Old Mary—a domestic servant in Puerto Rico—had given birth to William, a son fathered by her master. Now near the end of her unhappy and unfulfilled life, she has located William. The stories deal with Mary's shock and initial disappointment upon learning that her son is a dwarf and a variety of personal and family problems. Throughout these stories, a stray street cat appears, disappears and reappears, serving as the book's controlling metaphor of survival.

Felita and its sequel *Going Home* are novels written for older children about a nine-year-old girl whose family moves out of their predominantly Puerto Rican neighborhood in New York City to a middle-class, ethnically mixed area. But Felita and her family are singled out and harassed by prejudiced neighbors from the day of their move—and eventually they return to their old neighborhood.

Although Mohr's striking and memorable visual imagery and realistic writing lay bare the underside of life in New York's Puerto Rican communities from the 1940s to the 1980s, she introduces her readers to sympathetic, sensitive characters (many of whom are adults) who love deeply, help others, and are proud of their ethnic identity even when it comes under attack. Mohr would view the proverbial cup that is half-empty and half-full as being half-full . . . and getting fuller all the time.

—Jack Forman

MOLONEY, James

Nationality: Australian. **Born:** Manly, New South Wales, 20 September 1954. **Education:** Villanova College, Brisbane, Queensland, 1964-72; Griffith University, Queensland, Diploma in Teaching 1975; Queensland University of Technology, Graduate Diploma Teacher Librarianship, 1979; Queensland University of Technology, Graduate Diploma in Computer Education 1988. **Family:** Married Kate Hickey in 1983; three children. **Career:** Primary teacher, 1976-78; teacher and librarian, Marist College, Ashgrove, since 1983. **Awards:** Family Award, Relationships Australia, 1992, and Children's Book Council of Australia Notable Book Award, 1993, both for *Crossfire*; Family Award, Relationships Australia, Honour Book, Children's Book Council's of Australia, and International Youth Library's selection of notable new books, all 1994, all for *Dougy*; Australian Multicultural Children's Literature Award, Honour Book, Children's Book Council of Australia, and Human Rights Award commendation in Children's Literature, all 1995, all for *Gracey*; Book of the Year Award, Children's Book Council, 1996, for *Swashbuckler*; Book of the Year Award for Older Readers, Children's Book Council of Australia's, Family Award, Relationships Australia, Peace Prize, Psychologists for the Prevention of War, 3M Talking Book Award shortlist, and Victorian Premier's Award shortlist, all 1997, all for *A Bridge to Wiseman's Cove*; Aurealis Speculative Fiction Award shortlist, Children's Book Council of Australia Notable Book, and Ned Kelly Award shortlist, 1997, all for *The Pipe*. **Address:** 142 Buena Vista Ave, Coorparoo, Queensland 4151, Australia. **Agent:** Margaret Connolly, P.O. Box 945, Wahroonga, NSW 2076, Australia.

PUBLICATIONS FOR YOUNG ADULTS

Fiction

Crossfire. Brisbane, University of Queensland Press, 1992.
Dougy. Brisbane, University of Queensland Press, 1993.
Gracey. Brisbane, University of Queensland Press, 1994.
The House on the River Terrace. Brisbane, University of Queensland Press, 1995.
Swashbuckler. Brisbane, University of Queensland Press, 1995.
The Pipe, illustrated by Shaun Tan. Melbourne, Lothian, 1996.
A Bridge to Wiseman's Cove. Brisbane, University of Queensland Press, 1996.
The Snake Man. Melbourne, Lothian, 1998.
Buzzard Breath and Brains. Brisbane, University of Queensland Press, 1998.
Angela. Brisbane, University of Queensland Press, forthcoming.

Short Stories

"The Cat and the Crow," in *Dark House,* edited by Gary Crew. Melbourne, Reed, 1995.
"Examination Results," in *Celebrate,* edited by Margot Hillel. Melbourne, Penguin, 1996.

*

Critical Studies: "Know the Author: James Moloney" by Kevin Steinberger, in *Magpies* (Hamilton, Queensland, Australia), May 1994, 5-7; "The World in Children's Literature: Life as It Is or Life as It Should Be" by Maureen Nimon and John Foster, in *Magpies,* November 1994, 7-9; "What Is a Multicultural Book?" by Ruth Starke, in *Viewpoint* (University of Melbourne), autumn 1995, 22-24; "Reading Matters" by Kate Veitch, in *Viewpoint,* winter 1995, 24-25.

*   *   *

James Moloney's first novel, *Crossfire* (1992), shows how a teenage boy's admiration for his father decreases when he comes to realise the man's true character. Luke Aldridge worships his father and his love and knowledge of guns and believes his mother criticises her husband's behaviour unnecessarily. Luke's father, Wayne "Armalite" Aldridge, is a boy who has never grown up and in spite of being a good shot treats his guns like toys. Luke regards his father as a "good bloke" while his mother and her sister see him as undependable, always stuck in the pub, and never giving a thought to anyone but himself. Incidents that reveal his father's character—such as the sweat shirt his father is always going to buy him but never does, arriving late to pick him up, and trying to beat the breathalyser—help Luke lean toward his mother's view but it is the father's behaviour on the shooting trip that makes him see his dad as he really is.

In this episode Moloney makes the reader aware of the dangers of handling guns carelessly and the senseless killing that shooting from trucks involves. Luke sees his father ignore basic rules which could have resulted in death for either of them and he sees animals unnecessarily humiliated. The arrival of a Vietnam veteran who tells what it is like to be stalked is the outstanding milestone in Luke's growing up. The boy realises that guns are for killing and the trip is nothing but a pathetic game, cruel killing for the sake of killing. A gun confrontation at the end of the novel nearly ends in tragedy but provides Luke and his mother with the opportunity to force Wayne to see some truth about his life.

Dougy (1993) is the first of three books in which Moloney considers relations between blacks and whites in a small country town. Dougy is a 13-year-old Aboriginal boy who doesn't think much of himself; he is not good at school and sees little direction in his life. The second book *Gracey* (1994) is about his 14-year-old sister, the fastest runner in town. Each book is self contained but to read both gives a deeper insight into Moloney's themes concerning family, racism, and reconciliation. The children's mother wants her children to be part of the present and future, not the past. Her life is not easy: her husband drinks and another son, 16-year-old Raymond, seems bent on a path of self destruction. The Aboriginal legend Dad tells to the group of Aborigines at the riverbank is listened to attentively but Mum rejects it as a silly story, Gracey tries to weigh up its value, and Dougy is not sure. In both books the characters are torn between two worlds.

Both books show the unfairness, discrimination, jealousy, and prejudice that exist in this small rural town. Both novels have dramatic scenes of action, including Raymond's death in jail in *Gracey* and the siege and escape from the flood in *Dougy*. Moloney points out that rather than fight each other, white and black should be united in fighting the flood disaster which ultimately destroys the town.

In *Gracey,* the central character's running ability has won her a sporting scholarship to a Brisbane school. Now a state athletics champion, she returns home on the death of her mother to realise she has been living a white life and has almost ignored her Aboriginality. Her efforts to come to terms with her racial identity are made more difficult by the discovery of human bones on a building site. Are these the bones of a massacre or do they mean something else? Characters in the novel explain and exploit the situation to suit their own ends and Moloney makes a plea to see the whole picture rather than lay blame on an individual. The book has elements of mystery and history and the author begs the reader to learn from the past.

Gracey is interesting for its narrative structure, which reveals attitudes from different perspectives. The story is told through three narrators: Dougy, Gracey, and a young policeman, Trent Foster, who leaves messages on his father's answering machine. Despite his attempt at the beginning of his service in the town to understand the Aboriginal point of view, in the end Foster finds himself confused, overwhelmed, and so out of his depth that he leaves the police service.

The House on River Terrace (1995) tells the story of 16-year-old Ben whose father, a politician, is the shadow minister for justice, a man proud of his position in Brisbane society. For political purposes Rob Fielding plans to exploit his family's now deserted but once grand house by making a television documentary about the family's past. This brings him into conflict with his son, who realises from documents found in the house that the family's wealth was based on exploitation of the Aborigines. The diaries also give insights into the family's past and management of the conscription debate during World War I. Ben sees his father's campaign against the homeless as a vote winning exercise when he evicts squatters, especially an Aboriginal girl, Jess, that Ben had befriended. This girl is related to the Aborigines that Ben's forbears exploited and ultimately this association lends itself to tragedy. In the end Ben's confrontation with his father has a positive outcome and the framing device of family tree and diaries make this a well constructed and effective family saga.

A Bridge To Wiseman's Cove (1996) is Moloney's most engaging book to date. The story centres upon the Matt Family, 15-year-old Carl, his younger brother Harley, and older sister Sarah, children "sired by different fathers long gone." Their mother frequently takes off for "holidays," leaving them alone for some weeks, but when the book opens she has been away longer than usual and it seems she may have left for good. Sarah strikes out to make a life of her own, leaving her two brothers at Wattle Beach with Aunt Beryl, who uses her nephews' Social Security cheques to support her habit with the poker machines, her layabout boyfriend, and her bowling activities. The boys are left to their own devices and the younger one is soon in trouble.

The feeling of abandonment pervades the book. "Who will love you if your own mother doesn't?" is a question Carl asks and the unspoken answer sums up his view of himself. The mystery of the mother's disappearance is solved at the end as is the question of why the Matts are seen as "trash" and outcasts in the small community of Wattle Beach. Ultimately Carl finds refuge at Wiseman's Cove, a short barge ride from Wattle Creek, with a family who help him find employment, friendship, and self esteem. All of Moloney's books are fast paced and make for engrossing and challenging reading.

—Michael Stone

MOMADAY, N(avarre) Scott

Nationality: American. **Born:** Lawton, Oklahoma, 27 February 1934. **Education:** Augusta Military Academy, University of New Mexico, Albuquerque, A.B. 1958; Stanford University, California (creative writing fellow, 1959), A.M. 1960, Ph.D. 1963. **Family:** Married 1) Gaye Mangold in 1959 (divorced), three daughters; 2) Regina Heitzer in 1978, one daughter. **Career:** Assistant Professor, University of California, Santa Barbara, 1963-65; Associate

Professor of English, 1968-69, Associate Professor of English and Comparative Literature, 1969-73, University of California, Berkeley; Professor of English, Stanford University, 1973-82; Professor of English, University of Arizona, Tucson, since 1982. Professor, University of California Institute for the Humanities, 1970; Whittall Lecturer, Library of Congress, Washington, D.C., 1971; Visiting Professor, New Mexico State University, Las Cruces, 1972-73, State University of Moscow, Spring 1974, Columbia University, New York, 1979, and Princeton University, New Jersey, 1979; writer-in-residence, Southeastern University, Washington, D.C., 1985, and Aspen Writers' Conference, Colorado, 1986. Artist: has exhibited drawings and paintings. Consultant, National Endowment for the Humanities and National Endowment for the Arts, since 1970. Member of the Board of Trustees, Museum of the American Indian, Heye Foundation, New York City, since 1978. **Awards:** Academy of American Poets prize, 1962, for poem "The Bear"; Guggenheim fellowship, 1966-67; Pulitzer Prize for fiction, 1969, for *House Made of Dawn;* National Institute of Arts and Letters grant, 1970; American Academy award, 1970; shared Western Heritage award with David Muench, 1974, for nonfiction book *Colorado, Summer/Fall/Winter/Spring;* Premio Letterario Internazionale Mondelo, Italy, 1979. Western Literature Association award, 1983. D.H.L.: Central Michigan University, Mt. Pleasant, 1970; University of Massachusetts, Amherst, 1975; Yale University, New Haven, Connecticut, 1980; Hobart and Williams Smith Colleges, Geneva, New York, 1980; College of Santa Fe, New Mexico, 1982; D.Litt.: Lawrence University, Appleton, Wisconsin, 1971; University of Wisconsin, Milwaukee, 1976; College of Ganado, 1979; D.F.A.: Morningside College, Sioux City, Iowa, 1980. **Address:** 5675 Camino Esplendora #2211, Tucson, Arizona 85718-4583, U.S.A.

PUBLICATIONS

Novels

House Made of Dawn. New York, Harper, 1968.
The Ancient Child. New York, Doubleday, 1989.

Poetry

Before an Old Painting of the Crucifixion, Carmel Mission, June 1960. San Francisco, Valenti Angelo, 1975.
Angle of Geese and Other Poems. Boston, David Godine, 1974.
The Gourd Dancer, illustrated by the author. New York, Harper, 1976.

Other

Editor, *The Complete Poems of Frederick Goddard Tuckerman.* New York, Oxford University Press, 1965.
The Journey of Tai-me (Kiowa Indian tales), etchings by Bruce S. McCurdy. Privately printed, 1967; revised edition, as *The Way to Rainy Mountain,* illustrated by father, Alfred Momaday, Albuquerque, University of New Mexico Press, 1969.
Colorado, Summer/Fall/Winter/Spring, illustrated with photographs by David Muench. Chicago, Rand McNally, 1973.
Editor, *American Indian Authors.* Boston, Houghton Mifflin, 1976.

The Names: A Memoir. New York, Harper, 1976.

Editor, *A Coyote in the Garden,* by Ann Painter. Lewiston, Idaho, Confluence, 1988.

In The Presence of the Sun: Stories and Poems, 1961-1991, illustrated by the author. New York, St. Martin's, 1992.

The Native Americans: Indian Country. Atlanta, Georgia, Turner Publishing, 1993.

Circle of Wonder: A Native American Christmas Story. Santa Fe, Clear Light Publishers, 1994.

The Man Made of Words, Essays, Stories, Passages. New York, St. Martin's Press, 1997.

The Man Who Killed the Deer (screenplay; adaptation of a novel by Frank Waters) N.d.

*

Manuscript Collections: Bancroft Library, University of California, Berkeley.

Critical Studies: Entry in *Contemporary Literary Criticism,* Detroit, Gale, Volume 2, 1974, Volume 19, 1981; *Four American Indian Literary Masters* by Alan R. Velie, Norman, University of Oklahoma Press, 1982; *N. Scott Momaday: The Cultural and Literary Background* by Matthias Schubnell, Norman, University of Oklahoma Press, 1986; *Approaches to Teaching Momaday's The Way to Rainy Mountain* edited by Kenneth M. Roemer, New York, Modern Language Association of America, 1988; *Ancestral Voice: Conversations with N. Scott Momaday* by Charles L. Woodard, Lincoln, University of Nebraska Press, 1989; *Conversations with N. Scott Momaday* edited by Matthias Schubnell, Jackson, University Press of Mississippi, 1997.

*   *   *

In *The Way to Rainy Mountain,* arguably his most important work, Scott Momaday establishes the patterns of theme and technique which have characterized his novels, poems, and memoirs. An expansion of the Kiowa folktales retold from *The Journey of Tai-me* is Momaday's attempt to develop a myth which incorporates individual lives as part of an overall ancestral past.

Each of the three sections (''The Setting Out,'' ''The Going On,'' and ''The Closing In'') progresses from the most inclusive and remote to the most personal and recent: Momaday begins with Kiowa legends, followed by tribal history, then personal memoir. Using different typefaces to indicate the transitions, Momaday retells Kiowa origin myths, retraces the history of the tribe's three-century migration from Yellowstone to the Great Plains, and finally links these stories with personal memories and stories passed down by his paternal ancestors. Each layer of the narrative explains and so adds significance to those which precede it, as the psychic journey of Momaday the teller reenacts the wanderings of the Kiowa. Literally traveling to his grandmother's grave, he realizes that her lifespan encompassed the decline in tribal identity.

The Names: A Memoir continues the exploration of personal identity in the larger context of the family and the tribe. Again Momaday combines Kiowa tradition with genealogical exploration

and almost idyllic memories, as he describes his boyhood among the Kiowas, who give names to every object in, and every characteristic of, their environment. Momaday's name, Tsoaitalee, is the Kiowa name for a spot important in tribal legends—a massive rock known in Anglo-American culture as the Devils Tower. Since the name was supposedly prophetic of an individual's character and fate, Momaday had been given a great honor and a profound responsibility.

This memoir emphasizes the importance of names, through those names tracing Momaday's Anglo-American heritage as well as the Kiowa. His mother's family included not only a Cherokee great-grandmother, but also a grandfather, Theodore Scott, who was a sheriff in Kentucky. In identifying with his Indian ancestors, however, Momaday is following the lead of his mother, who chose an Indian name, Indian dress, and an Indian school. Initially among the Kiowa, Momaday's paternal grandfather had only one name, Mammeday, but with the adoption of Christian names, the name John was added. Alfred, Scott's father, modified the family name to Momaday. The development of the family surname seems symbolic of the family's ability to remain Native Americans but to incorporate the best elements of the Anglo culture.

Momaday also treats the issue of cultural identity in his best known work, *House Made of Dawn,* winner of the 1969 Pulitzer prize for fiction. In this novel, praised for its mythic themes but criticized for its difficult narrative structure, a Native American veteran (interestingly, named Abel) cannot re-adapt to reservation life upon his return from World War II. After killing a man and serving a prison sentence, he is paroled to a halfway house in Los Angeles.

Unlike his roommate Ben, a narrative voice who appears to be a Momaday spokesman, Abel remains outside the Anglo-American culture; his attitude causes trouble on the job and with the police. Although the local groups he discovers do not practice the Native American ceremonies in their pure form, the sermons of medicine man/priest John Tosamah lead ultimately to Abel's return to the reservation and his dying grandfather. The novel's resolution is the ritual race at dawn, in which Abel's true opponents are evil and death. Thus, coinciding with his grandfather's death is Abel's symbolic rebirth into his culture.

Like his character Abel, Momaday finds strength and beauty in traditional Native American life, which he sees as an antidote to the prevailing modern mood of individual isolation. A part of their belief in the principle of harmony in the universe, the Kiowa's oral tradition links them to the land and establishes it as a spiritual entity, similar to themselves and worthy of reverence. The retelling of history and legends also taps into the tribal memory, providing a sense of personal and group identity.

Momaday's poems, which have received less attention than his prose, likewise recast traditional Kiowa legends in terms of family history. In *The Gourd Dancer* and *Angle of Geese and Other Poems,* Momaday draws upon ''blood memories,'' becoming in effect the successor to ancient medicine men as he interprets for his contemporary audience the Native American consciousness.

In attempting to express his essentially intuitive perceptions about the Kiowa, however, Momaday is hampered by the limitations imposed in using the language of an alien culture. Nevertheless, Momaday, who does not speak Kiowa himself, understands how the language not only reflects but also influences the way a people think, and he believes that in relating these tales, he is offering hope and spiritual healing to modern American society.

This process of translating his ancient myths to benefit modern society is the subject of Momaday's second novel, *The Ancient Child,* which is primarily autobiographical. Using the myth associated with his own Kiowa name, Momaday portrays a Native American artist's efforts to maintain his culture and interpret it for the Anglo world. While the artist generally is an outsider in his society, the Native American can draw upon his advantage of an alternate world view found in tribal legends. Thus, like Momaday himself, the artist can use the traditional vehicles of dreams and visions to forge an identity which is at once personal and universal.

—Charmaine Allmon Mosby

MORI, Kyoko

Nationality: Japanese. **Born:** Kobe, 1957; immigrated to United States, 1977. **Education:** Rockford, Illinois, B.A. 1979; University of Wisconsin-Milwaukee, M.A. 1981, Ph.D. 1984. **Career:** Associate Professor of English and Creative Writing, Saint Norbert College, De Pere, Wisconsin, since 1985. **Awards:** Editor's Award, *Missouri Review,* 1992, for poem "Fallout"; *New York Times* Notable Book, Council of Wisconsin Writers Best Novel, Elizabeth Burr award, Wisconsin Library Association, Best Books For Young Adults Award, American Library Association (ALA) Young Adult Services Association, all 1994, all for *Shizuko's Daughter*; Best Books For Young Adults Award, ALA Young Adult Services Association, Council of Wisconsin Writers Best Novel, *Hungry Mind Review* Notable Book for Young Adults, Passaic Community Poetry Center Best Book for Young Adults, 1996, for *One Bird.* **Agent:** Ann Rittenberg, Literary Agency, Inc., 14 Montgomery Place, Brooklyn, New York 11215, U.S.A.

PUBLICATIONS FOR YOUNG ADULTS

Fiction

Shizuko's Daughter. New York, Holt, 1993.
One Bird. New York, Holt, 1995.

PUBLICATIONS FOR ADULTS

Poetry

Fallout. Chicago, Tia Churcha Press, 1994.

Other

"Address," in *USSBY Newsletter,* spring 1994, 6-7.
The Dream of Water: A Memoir (autobiography). New York, Holt, 1995.
"Brave Outsiders: Multicultural Writers on Adolescence," in *CBC Features,* Vol. 48, No. 1, spring-summer 1995, 84-85.
"Landscapes" (speech), in *Journal of Youth Services in Libraries* (Chicago), Vol. 9, No. 2, 1996, 135-139.
Polite Lies: On Being a Woman Caught Between Cultures (essays). New York, Holt, 1998.

Contributor of short stories to *Maryland Review, South-East Review, Crosscurrents, Prairie Schooner, Kenyon Review, New Series,* and *Apalachee Quarterly.*

*

Biography: Entry in *Something About the Author,* Vol. 82, Detroit, Gale, 1995, 164-167.

Kyoko Mori comments:
I have written two coming-of-age novels because growing up, as a theme, is inherently full of dramatic possibilities. In all of my writing—fiction, poetry, non-fiction—I strive for vividness of imagery and language, heartfelt truths anchored in disciplined and well-crafted writing.

*   *   *

Describing her philosophy of life and writing in an address for USBBY, Kyoko Mori explained how her work has been informed by her experience of feeling like an outsider to her own Japanese culture and traditions. Brought up in a Westernized family and social setting, Mori left Japan at the age of twenty to live in the United States. In a *Dream of Waters: A Memoir,* Mori describes her first visit to Japan after thirteen years. She did not think of it as returning home; it was, rather, a "foreign country" where she could speak the language. In narrating her experiences and feelings as she meets her family and friends and immerses herself in remembering and re-constructing her past, Mori writes from both *without* and *within* Japanese life and culture. As she explained in her USSBY address, it is the "balance between belonging and not belonging" that she wishes to convey in her work.

Strands from her own life are woven into the story of Yuki, the main protagonist in her first novel, *Shizuko's Daughter.* The suicide of Yuki's mother, Shizuko; the marriage of Yuki's father, Hideki, to Hanae, who had been his mistress for several years; and the cold relationship between Yuki and her step-mother and father follow a pattern of events and relationships narrated by Mori in her autobiography so that one text serves to illumine the other. A variant form of this pattern structures a story in Mori's second novel, *One Bird,* in which fifteen-year-old Megumi Shimizu's mother, unable to live with her husband any longer, packs up and returns to her old home to live with her elderly father. Megumi, desolate at being parted from her mother, is left to live with an uncompromising grandmother and a father who spends much of his time with his mistress in Hiroshima and gives his daughter little time and support.

In her essay "Brave Outsiders," Kyoko Mori makes the comparison between adolescent protagonists portrayed as outsiders and multicultural writers who also share the experience of seeing from the outside. Yuki in *Shizuko's Daughter* and Megumi in *One Bird* are, in some respects, mirror-images. They are described as academically bright, creative, and independent girls who feel alienated from their fathers and their father's families—the patrilinear line—while feeling the immeasurable loss of their mothers. Yuki, especially, is represented as being an outsider in her own home once her stepmother, Hanae, comes to live with the family. In one chapter, "Grievances," Hanae vents her bitterness about her barrenness and her resentment of a stepdaughter who does not even pretend to like her and who shuts herself up in her room, locking everything away from her. Through the symbolic act of breaking Yuki's mother's pottery—the "heirloom that should be passed on to mother and daughter"—and her ordering of Yuki's father to burn his former wife's clothes and the mementoes she had saved of Yuki's childhood, Hanae attempts to eradicate Yuki and her mother from her life with Yuki's father. Finally, Yuki leaves her father's home to attend art school in Nagasaki, echoing Mori's own departure from family and Japan in *The Dream of Water.*

What is not broken in *Shizuko's Daughter* and *One Bird,* however, are the strong, loving bonds between daughters and mothers that lie at the heart of each story. Throughout *Shizuko's Daughter,* Yuki constantly recreates the memories of her mother and the times they shared together so that Shizuko becomes a vivid presence in the text: "Yuki could still see her mother running up the stairway in her white dress, the roses a blur of pink and green." To keep her mother's memory fresh, Yuki makes colored drawings in a sketchbook of the embroidered clothes Shizuko had made for her together with sketches of her mother's pottery that had been thrown out by her stepmother. A daughter's recording of the treasured objects associated with her mother is parallel with Shizuko's loving sketches of Yuki in Shizuko's own sketchbook, the one legacy which Yuki's father saves and passes on to his daughter. The love of a mother for her daughter is also heard through the voice of Shizuko at the commencement of the novel. In a note, she tells her daughter that she loves her and that her decision to commit suicide is done for her daughter's sake as well as her own: "People will tell you that I've done this because I did not love you. Don't listen to them." The story of Shizuko and her daughter is told from different perspectives in a plural narrative including the narrated thoughts and feelings of Hideki as he remembers his earlier marriage and thinks about his relationship with his daughter.

Loving connections between a teenage daughter and her mother are also described in *One Bird.* Against the orders of her father, Megumi keeps in touch with her mother who leaves because of her unhappy marriage. If she does not leave, she tells her daughter, she will not be able to go on living; this way she can see her daughter when Megumi is old enough to leave her father's house. As in *Shizuko's Daughter,* we hear the angry voice of a daughter who feels that her mother has let her down by leaving: "Will my mother and I ever get over our years of separation? When I am forty years old, will I still be angry at her for leaving me?" In both novels, a mother is forgiven and the daughter mother relationship is envisioned as a continuing emotional bond. Megumi, in *One Bird,* finds the courage to defy her father's injunctions and visits her mother with the help of Dr. Mizutani who offers Megumi a part-time job in her bird clinic. The closeness between daughter and mother is articulated through their physical likeness. As Megumi hold her mother at their reunion, she notices how their "hands and wrists are the same." She is "her mother's daughter," Megumi narrates, "no-one is going to keep us apart for seven years."

Matrilinear bonds are privileged in Mori's feminist daughter-mother narrative in the face of a Japanese culture that has given deference and privilege to fathers and sons. Mori shows in both novels the oppression experienced by the mothers of Yuki and Megumi in a patriarchal culture—each bound by her dependence on a husband who felt free to neglect his wife for a mistress. In these novels as in Mori's autobiography, the leaving of a mother means that daughters must live with their father's family—an economic necessity but an arrangement that is also expected as a matter of form. In contrast to the cold relationships between Yuki and Megumi and their fathers' families, there are warm memories and portraits of maternal grandparents. Takeo, grandfather to Yuki, who taught her the constellations in the sky in *Shizuko's Daughter,* is also present by name in *One Bird* and *The Dream of Water.* Mori shows how the lives of Yuki and Megumi are enriched with an appreciation of art and the beauty of nature, a legacy from their mothers. Woven in and out of Mori's young adult novels and autobiography are the vibrant colors of flowers and the beautiful "luminous" stitches of a mother's embroidery. In *Shizuko's Daughter,* Shizuko hopes that her loss will lead to her daughter's freedom—a hope that is reiterated in Mori's autobiography. While the texts of Mori's young adult novels speak, with evocative imagery and metaphors, to the pain of this loss, they also testify to the sustaining love between mothers and daughters that enables daughters to move on—changed by their experiences—but not daunted in spirit.

—Hilary S. Crew

MORPURGO, Michael

Nationality: British. **Born:** St. Albans, Herts, 5 October 1943. **Education:** The Kings School, Canterbury, Kent, 1957-62; King's College, London, 1964-67. **Military Service:** Royal Military Academy, Sandhurst. **Family:** Married Clare Lane; two sons and one daughter. **Career:** Has worked as an army officer, farmer, and primary school teacher for 10 years; founder and director of Farms for City Children (educational charity); writer. **Awards:** Silver Pencil award (Holland); Circle d'Or prize (France); Whitbread Prize (UK), 1995; Smarties award (UK), 1996; Children's Book award (UK), 1996; *Booklist* Book of the Year. **Agent:** Jacqueline Korn, David Higham Associates Ltd., 5-8 Lower John Street, Golden Square, London W1R 4HA, England. **Address:** Langlands, Iddesleigh, Winkleigh, Devon EX19 8SN, England.

PUBLICATIONS FOR YOUNG ADULTS

Fiction

It Never Rained, illustrated by Isabella Hutchins. London, Macmillan, 1974.

Thatcher Jones, illustrated by Trevor Ridley. London, Macmillan, 1975.

Friend or Foe, illustrated by Trevor Stubley. London, Macmillan Education, 1977.

"Do All You Dare," with photographs by Bob Cathmoir. London, Ward Lock Educational, 1978.

The Ghost-Fish. London, Ward Lock Educational, 1979.

That's How. London, Ward Lock Educational, 1979.

Love at First Sight. London, Ward Lock Educational, 1979.

The Day I Took the Bull by the Horn. London, Ward Lock Educational, 1979.

The Nine Lives of Montezuma. London, Heinemann, 1980.

The Marble Crusher, illustrated by Trevor Stubley. London, Macmillan, 1980.

Miss Wirtle's Revenge, illustrated by Graham Clarke. London, Kaye & Ward, 1981.

War Horse. London, Kaye & Ward, 1982; New York, Greenwillow, 1983.

The White Horse of Zennor. London, Kaye & Ward, 1982.

Twist of Gold. London, Kaye & Ward, 1983; New York, Viking, 1993.

Little Foxes, illustrated by Gareth Floyd. London, Kaye & Ward, 1984.

Why the Whales Came. London, Heinemann, 1985; New York, Scholastic, 1990.

Tom's Sausage Lion, illustrated by Robina Green. London, A. & C. Black, 1986.

King of the Cloud Forests. London, Heinemann, 1987; New York, Viking, 1988.

Jo-Jo the Melon Donkey, illustrated Chris Molan. London, Malin Books/Deutsch, 1987.

Conker, illustrated by Linda Birch. London, Heinemann Bananas, 1987.

Mossop's Last Chance, illustrated by Shoo Rayner. London, A. & C. Black, 1988.

My Friend Walter. London, Heinemann, 1988.

Mr. Nobody's Eyes. London, Heinemann, 1989; New York, Viking, 1990.

Waiting for Anya. London, Heinemann, 1990; New York, Viking, 1993.

And Pigs Might Fly!, illustrated by Shoo Rayner. London, A. & C. Black, 1990.

Albertine, Goose Queen, illustrated by Shoo Rayner. London, A. & C. Black, 1990.

Martians at Mudpuddle Farm, illustrated by Shoo Rayner. London, A. & C. Black, 1991.

The Sandman and the Turtles. London, Heinemann, 1991; New York, Philomel, 1994.

Colly's Barn, illustrated by Claire Colvin. London, Heinemann, 1991.

Jigger's Day Off, illustrated by Shoo Rayner. London, A. & C. Black, 1992.

The King in the Forest, illustrated by Tony Kerins. London, Simon & Schuster Young Books, 1993.

The War of Jenkins' Ear. London, Heinemann, 1993; New York, Philomel, 1995.

Snakes and Ladders, illustrated by L. Smith. London, Heinemann, 1994.

The Wreck of the Zanzibar, illustrated by Christian Birmingham. London, Heinemann, 1994; New York, Viking, 1995.

The Dancing Bear, illustrated by Christian Birmingham. London, Collins, 1994; Boston, Houghton Mifflin, 1996.

Arthur, High King of Britain (retelling), illustrated by Michael Foreman. London, Pavilion, 1994; San Diego, Harcourt Brace, 1995.

Mum's the Word, illustrated by Shoo Rayner. London, A. & C. Black, 1995.

Blodin the Beast, illustrated by Christina Balit. London, Frances Lincoln, 1995; Golden, Colorado, Fulcrum, 1995.

Long Way Home. London, Heinemann, 1996 .

The Ghost of Grania O'Malley. London, Heinemann, and New York, Viking, 1996.

Robin of Sherwood (retelling), illustrated by Michael Foreman. London, Pavilion Books, 1996; San Diego, Harcourt Brace, 1996.

The Butterfly Lion, illustrated by Christian Birmingham. London, Collins, 1996; New York, Viking, 1997.

Sam's Duck, illustrated by Keith Bowen. London, Collins, 1996.

Red Eyes At Night, illustrated by Tony Ross. London, Hodder, 1997.

Escape from Shangri-La. London, Heinemann, 1998; New York, Philomel, 1998.

Joan of Arc of Domremy (retelling), illustrated by Michael Foreman. London, Pavilion, 1998; San Diego, Harcourt Brace, 1999.

Other

Editor, with Clifford Simmons, *Living Poets.* London, Murray, 1974.

Editor, *All Around the Year,* with photographs by Robin Ravilious and poems by Ted Hughes. London, Murray, 1979.

Editor, with Graham Barrett, *The Story-Teller,* 2 Vols. London, Ward Lock, 1979, 1981.

Editor, *Ghostly Haunts,* illustrated by Nilesh Mistry. London, Pavilion, 1994.

Editor, *Muck and Magic.* London, Heinemann, 1996.

Editor, *Beyond the Rainbow Warrior,* illustrated by Michael Foreman. London, Pavilion Books, 1996.

Farm Boy, illustrated by Michael Foreman. London, Pavilion Books, 1997.

*

Media Adaptations: *Friend or Foe* (film), 1984; *Why the Whales Came* (film), 1990; *Sam's Duck* (TV), 1992; *My Friend Walter* (TV), 1993.

*   *   *

Michael Morpurgo is a prolific and increasingly successful writer; in addition to the prizes he has won, his books have been on numerous award shortlists and have been translated into a dozen languages. Far from the wacky zaniness of so much current children's writing, his novels offer a wholesome and satisfying read. They are set in a wide variety of authentic backgrounds, from Cornwall to California; his characters are always convincing, and his stories are engrossing.

A crucial influence on Morpurgo's writing has been his experience as a farmer, and the contact with children which his Farms for City Children scheme has provided (parties of schoolchildren come to the Devon farm for a week at a time to learn about farming first hand—from milking through mucking out stables). His aim is to open up the horizons of children who may never have seen the countryside, and to put them in touch with nature. He believes there is a strong emotional link between children and animals, which bring out a strong sense of fairness in them.

A relationship between a child and an animal forms the subject of several of his novels. In *Little Foxes* a boy who is unhappy with his latest foster mother runs away with an orphaned fox cub. In *Mr. Nobody's Eyes,* a boy, again unhappy at home because of his stepfather, takes charge of a chimpanzee who has been separated from her owner. The situations are unusual, but they gain credibility because the emotions involved ring true. Perhaps the greatest suspension of disbelief is required for *King of the Cloud Forests,* in which a young Englishman lost in the Himalayas is adopted by a band of yetis—gentle, lumbering creatures who treat him as their leader. But again the situation is strangely believable, and the reader shares Ashley's sense of loss when he has to return to civilization.

His novels also raise issues and dilemmas for the characters to resolve, and there is both balance and subtlety in the resolution. In *Friend or Foe* (1977), which was his first longer story, David and his friend Tucky are evacuated to a Devon farm during the Second World War, and one day discover two German pilots hiding on the moor. David's life is saved by one of them and he wonders, should he report the Germans' presence, as his patriotic instincts would dictate, or is it his moral duty to give help to two decent men?

The terrible illogicality of war is explored in other books, in particular *War Horse,* which depicts the First World War through the eyes of a thoroughbred horse parted from his beloved young master. The novel has been called the *Black Beauty* of the Great War, and Joey's adventures are indeed varied, showing the full horror of conditions on the front line as well as acts of kindness from men on both sides.

Waiting for Anya is set during the Second World War in a small village in the French Pyrenees which is occupied by the Germans. The kindly Corporal, who loves eagle watching, befriends 12-year-old Jo, but Jo is actively engaged in helping Jewish children escape over the border to Spain. This novel contains possibly the most heartstopping moments in Morpurgo's work. His climaxes are if anything understated and never overwritten, but the drama speaks for itself.

A struggle for survival is the subject of *Twist of Gold* in which two Irish children are able to escape from the potato famine of the 1840s and make their way to America. The rough passage in steerage, the streets of Boston teeming with immigrants, and especially the great trek west to California are all vividly conveyed, and tension is maintained throughout with many reversals of fortune.

Several of Morpurgo's novels are set in and off the coast of Cornwall, an area he knows very well, but as always he does extra research into the background, often speaking to old people with long memories of events early in the century. Local superstitions inspired by a basis of fact play a part in *Why the Whales Came,* one of his most atmospheric books, which was made into a film. *The Wreck of the Zanzibar* is written as the diary of Laura—who lived on the island of Bryher at a time of great hardship—which is read by her great nephew in the present day. Sparely written and evocative, this novel won several awards.

Morpurgo brings immediacy to his historical novels either by means of a foreword linking the narrative with the present or a postscript which brings events up to the present day. In *Arthur, High King of Britain,* for instance, a boy in the present day nearly drowns off the coast of Cornwall, and he finds himself in a sea cave where Arthur has been in residence for 1,400 years, waiting for the time to return. Deprived of an audience for so long, Arthur regales the boy with a vivid firsthand narrative of the Round Table tales.

My Friend Walter is a ghost story with a difference, for it is no less than the ghost of the Elizabethan adventurer Sir Walter Raleigh who appears to Bess at the Tower of London. Sir Walter is a ghost of flesh and blood who speaks his mind and expects to get his way, and his actions provide the scope for much humour in the telling. If *The Ghost of Grania O'Malley* features the rumbustious ghost of a legendary Irish queen as well as a time slip to the past, it also involves environmental issues in the present day, and, in an unusual twist, features a heroine who is disabled but takes full part in the action.

In some ways the most complex of Morpurgo's novels is *The War of Jenkins' Ear,* set in an exclusive English "public" school. It is an enclosed and claustrophobic world, and the class warfare against the village boys is in serious danger of escalating. But the major theme concerns the relationship between Toby and Simon, a boy who claims to be Christ and to have special powers. What is Toby to believe? Simon is expelled when the headmaster hears of the matter, but the novel ends on an enigmatic note. There is food here for much thought and discussion.

If the children who are the central characters of his novels are always plucky and resourceful, many of Morpurgo's adult characters are three-dimensional: particularly memorable are the mysterious Birdman in *Why the Whales Came,* Signor Blondini in *Mr. Nobody's Eyes,* the former slave Little Luke in *Twist of Gold,* and Popsicle in *Escape from Shangri-La.* Heartwarming and sensitive, Morpurgo's imaginative empathy, whether writing about animals or people, makes for pure gold. His novels certainly open up horizons for young readers.

—Jennifer Taylor

MORRISON, Toni

Nationality: American. **Born:** Chloe Anthony Wofford, in Lorain, Ohio, 18 February 1931. **Education:** Howard University, Washington, D.C., B.A. 1953; Cornell University, Ithaca, New York, M.A. 1955. **Family:** Married Harold Morrison in 1958 (divorced 1964); two sons. **Career:** Instructor in English, Texas Southern University, Houston, 1955-57, and Howard University, 1957-64; senior editor, Random House, New York, 1965-84; Associate Professor of English, State University of New York, Purchase, 1971-72; State University of New York at Albany, Visiting lecturer, Yale University, New Haven, Connecticut, 1976-77, Rutgers University, New Brunswick, New Jersey, 1983-84, and Bard College, Annandale-on-Hudson, New York, 1986-88. Schweitzer Professor of the Humanities, State University of New York, Albany, 1984-89; Regents' Lecturer, University of California, Berkeley, 1987; Santagata Lecturer, Bowdoin College, Brunswick, Maine, 1987. Since 1989, Robert F. Goheen Professor of the Humanities, Princeton University, New Jersey. **Awards:** National Book award nomination and Ohioana Book award, both 1975, both for *Sula;* National Book Critics Circle award and

American Academy and Institute of Arts and Letters award, both 1977, both for *Song of Solomon;* New York State Governor's Art award, 1986; National Book award nomination and National Book Critics Circle award nomination, both 1987, and Pulitzer Prize for fiction and Robert F. Kennedy award, both 1988, all for *Beloved;* Elizabeth Cady Stanton award from the National Organization of Women; Book of the Month Club award, 1986; Before Columbus Foundation award, 1988; Melcher award, 1988; Honorary degree: College of Saint Rose, Albany, 1987; Nobel Prize for literature, 1993. **Agent:** Lynn Nesbit, International Creative Management, 40 West 57th St., New York, New York 10019, U.S.A.

PUBLICATIONS

Novels

The Bluest Eye. New York, Holt, 1969; London, Chatto & Windus, 1980.
Sula. New York, Knopf, 1973; London, Allen Lane, 1974.
Song of Solomon. New York, Knopf, 1977; London, Chatto & Windus, 1978.
Tar Baby. New York, Knopf, and London, Chatto & Windus, 1981.
Beloved. New York, Knopf, and London, Chatto & Windus, 1987.
Jazz. New York, Knopf, 1992.
Paradise. New York, Knopf, 1998.

Play

Dreaming Emmett (produced Albany, New York, 1986).

Other

Editor, *To Die for the People: The Writings of Huey P. Newton.* New York, Random House, 1972.
Editor, *The Black Book.* New York, Random House, 1974.
Editor, *Race-ing Justice, En-gendering Power: Essays on Anita Hill, Clarence Thomas, and the Construction of Social Reality.* New York, Pantheon, 1992.
Playing in the Dark: Whiteness and the Literary Imagination. Cambridge, Massachusetts, 1992.
Contributor, *Arguing Immigration: The Debate over the Changing Face of America,* edited by Nicolaus Mills. New York, Simon and Schuster, 1994.
The Dancing Mind: Speech upon Acceptance of the National Book Foundation Medal for Distinguished Contribution to American Letters on the Sixth of November, Nineteen Hundred and Ninety-six. New York, Knopf, 1996.
Editor and author or preface, *Deep Sightings and Rescue Missions: Fiction, Essays, and Conversations* by Toni Cade Bambara. New York, Pantheon Books, 1996.
Editor with Claudia Brodsky Lacour and author of introduction, *Birth of a Nation'hood, Gaze, Script, and Spectacle in the O.J. Simpson Case.* New York, Pantheon Books, 1997.

*

Bibliography: *Toni Morrison: A Bibliography* by Mod Mekkawi, Howard University Library, 1986; *Toni Morrison: An Annotated Bibliography* by David L. Middleton, New York, Garland, 1987.

Critical Studies: Entry in *Contemporary Literary Criticism,* Detroit, Gale, Volume 4, 1975, Volume 10, 1979, Volume 22, 1982, Volume 55, 1989; entry in *Dictionary of Literary Biography,* Detroit, Gale, Volume 6: *American Novelists since World War II,* 1980, Volume 33: *Afro-American Fiction Writers after 1955,* 1984; entry in *Dictionary of Literary Biography Yearbook: 1981,* Detroit, Gale, 1982; *New Dimensions of Spirituality: A Biracial and Bicultural Reading of the Novels of Toni Morrison* by Karla F.C. Holloway, Westport, Connecticut, Greenwood Press, 1987; *The Crime of Innocence in the Fiction of Toni Morrison* by Terry Otten, Columbia, University of Missouri Press, 1989; *Toni Morrison* by Wilfred D. Samuels, Boston, Twayne, 1990; *Conversations with Toni Morrison,* edited by Danille Taylor-Guthrie, Jackson, University Press of Mississippi, 1994.

*   *   *

Of the many adolescent readers captivated by the award-winning and very adult novels of Toni Morrison, the vast majority are high school females. And while Morrison is especially popular among young African Americans, her stories, characters, and themes are not bound by race or ethnicity. Young or old, Morrison's female readers are inclined to say similar things about the appeal of her works: they know real people *exactly* like the characters in her novels; her writings embrace contemporary life—the triumphs and failures, the hectic anxiety, the social strictures and pressures, the excitement, fears, and remorse; her writings present racial issues in ways that clarify and purge, in ways that lead to healing; she is not afraid to describe women and men as sexual beings; she knows precisely what it means to be a woman; and she helps illuminate the relative truth of the values which male society—and women themselves—have assigned to womanhood.

Adolescent readers point to yet another of Morrison's qualities they find important; she remembers what it means to be young. It is true that most of Morrison's protagonists are well beyond high school and in their twenties or thirties. Nevertheless, their concerns are those often associated with late adolescence: establishment of self-identity; formation of long-term social, familial, and professional goals; validation of a personal moral code; and creation of meaningful and enduring male-female and same-gender relationships.

The nightmare influences of democracy on the establishment of self-identity, where democracy can demand conformity to the frequently discriminatory ideals of the majority, is an important theme of Morrison's first novel, *The Bluest Eye.* This unforgettable parable of a young black woman who grows up believing that blonde hair and blue eyes would make her beautiful and bring social acceptance and familial harmony, is also concerned with the idea that "love is never any better than the lover." At the structural heart of the novel is an incestuous rape, at least partially the result of false ideals; for the novel's protagonist, the consequences of this love gone utterly wrong are self-rejection, despair, and finally madness.

Sula, very much a product of the early 1970s, was highly controversial when it first appeared—not only because of its authority-and-tradition-flouting protagonist and its unusual portraits of feminine bonding, but for its depictions of black males. There isn't a strong or admirable male character in the novel; instead, there are men with names like BoyBoy and Chicken Little. Leaving aside overly emotional responses to the novel, readers have come to see *Sula* as an exploration of traditional and contemporary values, an exploration ending in an implicit merging of the two worlds where some values on each side are preserved, and others discarded.

Morrison's third novel, *Song of Solomon,* has a male protagonist Macon (Milkman) Dead III; in part, perhaps, it is a response to critics of *Sula.* In simplest terms the novel recounts Milkman's search for his legacy (rumored to be a hidden cache of gold) in an effort to come into his own and escape the insignificance of his family. Eventually he comes to understand precisely who he is—not, ironically, through discovering his father's gold, but through learning his cultural history by uncovering his roots. In the end the novel is perhaps Morrison's most poetic, most complete exploration of the search for self; it suggests that the successful passage to adulthood ends in a merging of the intellectual, physical, spiritual, sexual, and cultural/historical selves.

In some respects, *Tar Baby* revisits the themes of *The Bluest Eye.* The story of a light-skinned African American woman who denies her blackness, *Tar Baby* is a moving analysis of the costs of self-denial, of seeing life in terms of duty and obligations rather than loyalty and love, of turning one's back on the sources of personal redemption. The deepest tragedy of the novel is that, in running from herself, the protagonist also maims or destroys the lives of those who know and care about her.

Beloved is Morrison's most ambitious, most highly imagined novel. Intentionally mimicking traditional slave narratives, *Beloved* is the nineteenth-century history of Sethe, an escaped slave who, while still in slavery, slashed the throat of her infant daughter in a "mercy killing." The ghost of her daughter haunts Sethe, eventually becoming flesh and confronting her as a twenty-year-old woman/child. The novel has a marvelous cast of characters and involved subplots; among its many themes are economic slavery, cultural and racial alienation, and the potentially oppressive, monstrous nature of traditional society.

Uncharacteristically lyrical in plot and structure, sharing more of the spirit of *Song of Solomon* than any other Morrison novel, *Jazz* tells of a middle-aged couple who are obsessed with the husband's dead lover: the husband, who kills his lover so she won't desert him, is overwhelmed by guilt and sorrow that nothing can dispel, not even his wife; the wife, cut off from her husband spiritually, attacks the dead lover in her coffin with a knife and then, in effect, makes her home and heart shrines to the dead woman's memory. The bulk of the novel tells how the couple eventually transcend the immediate past by returning to their historical pasts, learning where their lives began, how they evolved, and by whom they have been shaped. It is a story of profound emotions, simply and compassionately—even sweetly—told.

Morrison is also the author of *Playing in the Dark,* a critical history of African American writers, one which assesses black artistic accomplishment in a society whose tastes, methods, and impulses are all-too-obviously white.

—Keith Lawrence

MORSE, Anne Christensen. *See* **HEAD, Ann.**

MOWAT, Farley (McGill)

Nationality: Canadian. **Born:** Belleville, Ontario, 12 May 1921. **Education:** public schools in Trenton, Belleville, Windsor, Richmond Hill, and Toronto, Ontario, and Saskatoon, Saskatchewan; University of Toronto, B.A. 1949. **Military Service:** Served in the Canadian Army Infantry and Intelligence Corps, 1940-46: Captain. **Family:** Married 1) Frances Thornhill in 1947, two sons; 2) Claire Angel Wheeler in 1965. **Career:** Freelance writer. **Awards:** President's Medal for best Canadian short story of 1952 from the University of Western Ontario, for "Eskimo Spring"; Anisfield-Wolfe award for contribution to interracial relations, 1954, for *People of the Deer*; Governor General's Medal for juvenile literature, 1957, for *Lost in the Barrens*; Book of the Year for Children award from the Canadian Association of Children's Librarians, and International Board on Books for Young People Honour List, Canada, both 1958, both for *Lost in the Barrens*; Canadian Women's Clubs award, 1958, for *The Dog Who Wouldn't Be*; Boys' Club Junior Book award from the Boys' Club of America, 1963, for *Owls in the Family*; National Association of Independent Schools award, 1963, for juvenile books; Hans Christian Andersen Honour List, 1965, for juvenile books; Canadian Centennial Medal, 1967; Leacock Medal from the Stephen Leacock Foundation, 1970, and L'Etoile de la Mer Honours List, 1972, for *The Boat Who Wouldn't Float*; Metcalf award from the Canadian Authors' Association, 1971, for his body of work; Curran award, 1977, for "contributions to understanding wolves"; Queen Elizabeth II Jubilee Medal, 1978; Knight of Mark Twain, 1980; New York Public Library's Books for the Teen Age, 1980, for *The Great Betrayal,* and 1981, for *And No Birds Sang;* Officer, Order of Canada, 1981. D. Litt.: Laurentian University, Sudbury, Ontario, 1970; University of Victoria, British Columbia, 1982; Lakehead University, Thunder Bay, Ontario, 1986; LL.D.: University of Toronto, 1973; University of Lethbridge, Alberta, 1973; University of Prince Edward Island, Charlottetown, 1979. Officer, Order of Canada, 1981. **Agent:** Herta Ryder, c/o Toby Eady Associates, 7 Gledhow Gardens, London SW5 0BL, England. **Address:** c/o McClelland and Stewart Ltd., 481 University Avenue, Suite 900, Toronto, Ontario M5G 2E9, Canada.

PUBLICATIONS FOR YOUNG ADULTS

Short Stories

The Snow Walker. Toronto, McClelland and Stewart, 1975; Boston, Little Brown, 1976; London, Heinemann, 1978.

Other

People of the Deer (on the Ihalmiut Eskimos). Boston, Little Brown, and London, Joseph, 1952; revised edition, Toronto, McClelland and Stewart, 1975.

The Regiment (on the Hastings and Prince Edward Regiment). Toronto, McClelland and Stewart, 1955.

The Dog Who Wouldn't Be. Boston, Little Brown, 1957; London, Joseph, 1958.

Editor, *Coppermine Journey: An Account of Great Adventure,* by Samuel Hearne. Toronto, McClelland and Stewart, and Boston, Little Brown, 1958.

The Grey Seas Under. Boston, Little Brown, 1958; London, Joseph, 1959.

The Desperate People (on the Ihalmiut Eskimos). Boston, Little Brown, 1959; London, Joseph, 1960; revised edition, Toronto, McClelland and Stewart, 1976.

Editor, *The Top of the World: Ordeal by Ice.* Toronto, McClelland and Stewart, 1960; Boston, Little Brown, and London, Joseph, 1961.

The Serpent's Coil (on salvaging ships). Toronto, McClelland and Stewart, 1961; Boston, Little Brown, and London, Joseph, 1962.

Never Cry Wolf. Toronto, McClelland and Stewart, and Boston, Little Brown, 1963; London, Secker and Warburg, 1964.

Westviking: The Ancient Norse in Greenland and North America. Boston, Little Brown, 1965; London, Secker and Warburg, 1966.

Canada North. Boston, Little Brown, 1967; revised edition, as *Canada North Now: The Great Betrayal,* Toronto, McClelland and Stewart, 1976; as *The Great Betrayal,* Little Brown, 1976.

Editor, *The Top of the World: The Polar Passion—The Quest for the North Pole, with Selections from Arctic Journals.* Toronto, McClelland and Stewart, 1967; Boston, Little Brown, 1968.

This Rock within the Sea: A Heritage Lost (on Newfoundland), photographs by John de Visser. Boston, Little Brown, 1968.

The Boat Who Wouldn't Float. Toronto, McClelland and Stewart, 1969; Boston, Little Brown, and London, Heinemann, 1970.

Sibir: My Discovery of Siberia. Toronto, McClelland and Stewart, 1970; as *The Siberians,* Boston, Little Brown, 1971; London, Heinemann, 1972.

A Whale for the Killing. Toronto, McClelland and Stewart, and Boston, Little Brown, 1972; London, Heinemann, 1973.

Editor, *The Top of the World: Tundra—Selections from the Great Accounts of Arctic Land Voyages.* Toronto, McClelland and Stewart, 1973.

Wake of the Great Sealers. Boston, Little Brown, 1973.

And No Birds Sang (war memoirs). Toronto, McClelland and Stewart, 1979; Boston, Little Brown, and London, Cassell, 1980.

The World of Farley Mowat: A Selection, edited by Peter Davison. Boston, Little Brown, 1980.

Sea of Slaughter. Toronto, McClelland and Stewart, and Boston, Atlantic Monthly Press, 1984; London, Bantam, 1986.

My Discovery of America. Toronto, McClelland and Stewart, and Boston, Atlantic Monthly Press, 1985.

Virunga: The Passion of Dian Fossey. Toronto, McClelland and Stewart, 1987; as *Woman in the Mists: The Story of Dian Fossey and the Mountain Gorillas of Africa,* New York, Warner, 1987; London, Macdonald, 1988.

The New Founde Land. Toronto, McClelland and Stewart, 1989.

Rescue the Earth. Toronto, McClelland and Stewart, 1990.

My Father's Son: Memories of War and Peace. Boston, Houghton Mifflin, 1992.

Born Naked. Toronto, Key Porter Books, 1993.

Aftermath: Travels in a Post-war World. Boulder, Colorado, Roberts Rinehart, 1996.

The Farley Mowat Reader, edited by Wendy Thomas. Toronto, Key Porter Books, 1997.

Television Scripts: *Sea Fare* (*Telescope* series), 1964; *Diary of a Boy on Vacation,* 1964; and others.

PUBLICATIONS FOR CHILDREN

Fiction

Lost in the Barrens, illustrated by Charles Geer. Boston, Little Brown, 1956; London, Macmillan, 1957.

The Black Joke, illustrated by D. Johnson. Toronto, McClelland and Stewart, 1962; Boston, Little Brown, 1963; London, Macmillan, 1964.

The Curse of the Viking Grave, illustrated by Charles Geer. Boston, Little Brown, 1966; London, Pan, 1979.

Other

Owls in the Family, illustrated by Robert Frankenberg. Boston, Little Brown, 1961; London, Macmillan, 1963.

Contributor to *Cricket's Choice,* Open Court, 1974, and to magazines, including *Saturday Evening Post, Argosy, Maclean's,* and *Cricket.*

*

Media Adaptations: *A Whale for the Killing* (film), ABC-TV, 1980; (cassette), Books on Tape; *Never Cry Wolf* (film), Disney, 1983; (cassette), Books on Tape, 1986; (cassette, voice by Mowat), Bantam, 1988; *Grey Seas Under* (cassette), Books on Tape, 1986; *The Snow Walker* (cassette), Books on Tape, 1986; *Lost in the Barrens* (cassette), Books on Tape; *People of the Deer* (cassette), Books on Tape; *My Father's Son: Memories of War and Peace* (cassette), Vancouver, B.C., Library Services Branch, 1993.

Manuscript Collections: McMaster University, Hamilton, Ontario.

Biography: Entry in *Dictionary of Literary Biography,* Volume 68, Detroit, Gale, 1988; Essay in *Authors and Artists for Young Adults,* Volume 1, Detroit, Gale, 1989.

Critical Studies: *Farley Mowat* by Alex Lucas, Toronto, McClelland and Stewart, 1976; Entry in *Children's Literature Review,* Volume 20, Detroit, Gale, 1990.

*   *   *

Sometimes referred to as "the Canadian Jack London," Farley Mowat nevertheless defies categorization or easy description. It is true that he shares with London a fascination for the Arctic. But while London saw only Arctic harshness and frigidity, turning the white land into a vast naturalistic metaphor, Mowat perceives delicately balanced ecosystems teeming with life, inspiration, and beauty. And unlike London, who is known primarily as a writer of fiction, Mowat's most respected works are nonfiction, the product of rich, varied and adventurous living. Mowat is also important for his political positions, especially his stance on the environment. He has become perhaps the most articulate spokesperson for Canada's Green Movement; his is one of the world's strongest voices demanding protection for wilderness lands and endangered wildlife.

Of the more than thirty books he has written or edited, Mowat has addressed only four to juvenile audiences. *Lost in the Barrens* is the story of two teenage males, a white and a Cree Indian, whose curiosity about legends of a "stone house" (which turns out to be a Viking tomb) causes them to become separated from their hunting party. Consequently, they are forced to spend much of one winter in the barrens of Canada's Keewatin District, preserved through their ingenuity and their cool-headed preparations for the winter snows. *Owls in the Family*, generally categorized as nonfiction and most often read by pre-teens, is an illustrated and greatly embellished version of the Wol and Weeps stories in *The Dog Who Wouldn't Be*. Mowat's other two juvenile novels, *The Black Joke* and *The Curse of the Viking Grave*, are out of print. *The Black Joke* is the story of three adolescent males who steal back a sloop that whisky smugglers have, in effect, "stolen" from the father of one of the boys. But the plot is contrived, the characterizations and dialogue are weak, and the book never attracted a large audience. The sequel promised in the final lines of *Lost in the Barrens* was the ill-fated *The Curse of the Viking Grave*, a novel so poorly put together that Mowat himself is said to have condemned it.

Of Mowat's self-proclaimed juvenile novels only *Lost in the Barrens* is widely known to the many adolescents who have appropriated Mowat's popular "adult" books as their own, especially *The Dog Who Wouldn't Be* and *Never Cry Wolf*. A mildly fictionalized memoir of Mowat's childhood on the Canadian prairies near Saskatoon, *The Dog Who Wouldn't Be* recounts a boy's adventures with his dog, Mutt, and two owls, Wol and Weep. In the end, however, the book is as much about the boy's relationship with his family, especially his father, as it is about the boy and his pets. The book has the timeless appeal of James Herriot's works—and is much funnier. Some of the humor is derived from situations that make adult readers squeamish, but it is exactly right for adolescent males. What it says about father-son relationships affords it a human richness that few passages in Herriot achieve. But the Mowat work most popular among adolescents, males in particular, is *Never Cry Wolf*. Initially conceived by its author as a satire of bureaucracy, of governmental bungling and its impact on the environment, the book became instead, according to Mowat's preface, "a plea for understanding, and preservation, of an extraordinarily highly evolved and attractive animal." The account of the government-hired biologist whose fear of Arctic wolves is replaced by admiration, whose assignment to study the wolves gives way to a self-imposed mission to preserve them, is one of the finest contemporary statements on the human capacity to bond with other animals and thrive in the natural world, no matter how threatening either appears.

Other Mowat works enjoyed by adolescents twelve and older include *The Boat Who Wouldn't Float*, a Twain-inspired travelogue of Mowat's capricious voyage to sundry ports in the Maritime Provinces and eventually to Montreal, a voyage hazarded in a rebellious if not unseaworthy vessel named the *Happy Adventure*; *Siberia*, an appreciation of the environs, wildlife, and indigenous peoples of the regions often considered Russian wastelands; *A Whale for the Killing*, which recounts Mowat's efforts to save a fin whale trapped in a saltwater pond near Burgeo, Newfoundland, and which has been called the best animal story in Canadian literature; and *My Discovery of America*, a humorous account of a Canadian innocent dropping by America.

Mature adolescents also enjoy *People of the Deer*, Mowat's successful (and highly controversial) first book, and *The Desperate People*, its sequel, which together form an intensely detailed and moving portrait of the Barren Land Eskimos and suggest that the Canadian government and other white influences have resulted in the near-decimation of a once-proud tribe; *The Serpent's Coil*, which records Mowat's experiences on a small salvage boat operating out of the Halifax harbor; *The Snow Walker*, a collection of stories, memoirs and essays about Canada's Eskimos; *And No Birds Sang*, a narrative of Mowat's combat experiences in Italy and Sicily during World War II; *Sea of Slaughter*, an indictment of Canadian/U.S. fishing practices and environmental policies wreaking havoc on the sea life and coastline of Eastern Canada and New England; and *Woman in the Mists*, a biography of Dian Fossey. Mowat devotees may also read his ambitious history/appreciation of the Arctic known as "The Top of the World Trilogy," *Ordeal by Ice*, *The Polar Passion*, and *Tundra*. High school English teachers sometimes rely on *The World of Farley Mowat*, a selection of his works, to introduce Mowat to their students.

—Keith Lawrence

MOWRY, Jess

Nationality: American. **Born:** Oakland, California, 27 March 1960. **Education:** Attended elementary school in Oakland. **Career:** Writer; worked with children at a private community center; also held a number of jobs, including garbage hauling and yard cleaning. **Address:** c/o Simon and Schuster Books for Young Readers, 1230 Avenue of the Americas, New York, New York 10020, U.S.A.

PUBLICATIONS FOR YOUNG ADULTS

Fiction

Rats in the Trees: Stories. Santa Barbara, California, J. Daniel and Co., 1990.
Children of the Night. New York, All America Distributors, 1991.
Way Past Cool: A Novel. New York, Farrar Straus Giroux, 1992.
Six Out Seven. New York, HarperCollins, 1993.
Babylon Boyz. New York, Simon & Schuster, 1997.

PUBLICATIONS FOR CHILDREN

Fiction

Ghost Train. New York, Henry Holt, 1996.

*

Biography: Interview with Paul Tullis, www.buzznet.com/people/tullis/index.html, January 1995.

* * *

In each of his novels, Jess Mowry challenges young readers to view inner city life in ways designed to counteract the stereotypical catalog of angry young men, smoking guns, and back alley crack houses. To be certain, these elements make their appearance in Mowry's texts, but the focus is on the strategies that average teenagers use in order to maintain their dignity and their senses of humor in a society that is out of their control. Mowry's best heroes, Corbitt in *Six Out Seven* or Pook in *Babylon Boyz,* may have been robbed of their innocence, but not of their compassion. Friends stick together, and parents do their best to help their children. However, as Mowry conveys the daily compromises and negotiations that constitute life in the modern urban wasteland, he steers away from romanticizing his protagonists' decisions or lifestyles. Unlike many of his contemporaries, Mowry wants his readers to identify with his protagonists for who they are inside, not for where they live. There is nothing to envy in Mowry's West Oakland or Babylon.

One of the distinguishing features of Mowry's novels is his use of contemporary dialect and slang. For the most part, his characters' accents and turn of phrase ring true. Mowry himself grew up in Oakland, and he emphasizes the importance of using language carefully. In an interview with Paul Tullis, Mowry comments, "there's nothing stupider to a kid than an adult trying to talk their language. If you know what the words mean and they know it, that's fine, but if you try to get down and talk what they're talking this particular week, it's ridiculous. I don't talk to kids no different than when I'm talking to you or to anybody else, and I guess some kids can handle that, some kids can't. But if you're going to be on the same level as kids, you can't go retreating to the great mountain of adulthood every time they say something you don't like or they put you down or something."

As part of his commitment to realism, Mowry includes a number of graphically violent drive-by shootings and gang fights. *Way Past Cool* begins as a group of school children are sprayed with bullets from a passing van, and *Six Out Seven* ends with a somewhat awkwardly choreographed shoot-out in a crack house. For the most part, however, the violence remains in the background, almost as another character. While the themes of each novel vary, all of them chronicle the struggles of basically good kids who are threatened by poverty, drug discrimination, and sudden death.

In *Way Past Cool,* Mowry focuses on the destruction that erupts after Deek, a sixteen year-old drug dealer, attempts to shakedown the Friends and the Crew, rival gangs in a small West Oakland neighborhood. Although he is successful in the short term, he is ultimately killed. A stronger parallel storyline follows the experiences of Ty, Deek's unwilling bodyguard. Ty is able to redeem himself by saving his brother Danny from becoming a drug dealer and by starting a new life with Markita, a young single mother who works at Burger King in order to support her baby. As in all of his novels, Mowry pays careful attention to the way that economics impact behavior. Deek's greediness is punished, and Markita's determination in the face of poverty is rewarded. While the gun battles are a bit drawn out and the plot is somewhat formulaic, the novel contains moving depictions of individuals who are caught up in an intricate web of violence and anguish surrounding the guilty and the innocent, alike.

Six Out Seven, Mowry's follow-up to the highly successful *Way Past Cool,* is a less structurally satisfying novel. Set in Mowry's native Mississippi and in West Oakland, the novel depicts the experiences of Corbitt Wainwright, a teenager who must flee the South when he engages in a deadly confrontation with Bates, a racist pedophile whose false accusations have led to Corbitt's father's imprisonment. Once in Oakland, he links up with Lactameon ("Tam"), a streetwise, intelligent, and compassionate boy who faces the daily struggle of surviving the mean streets. While Mowry is effective at pointing out the challenges facing both urban and rural African-American youth, *Six Out Seven* lumbers to its bloody conclusion, lacking the pace of *Way Past Cool* or the intricate characterizations of *Babylon Boyz.*

In *Ghost Train,* Mowry turns his attention to a slightly younger audience. His protagonist Remi is a thirteen year-old Haitian refugee who is terrorized on his first night in Oakland by what appears to be an out of control freight train heading for his bedroom window. With the help of his neighbor Niya, Remi discovers a way to trace the origins of the "ghost train," and in the process solves a murder mystery that is connected to the train's appearance. What is most notable about this text is the way that Mowry is able to interest young readers in the relevance of history. By going back into the past, Remi and Niya are able to uncover the roots of much of the racism that they face in the present.

In *Babylon Boyz,* Mowry's fourth full-length novel, three best friends, Pook, Dante, and Wyatt, face a moral dilemma when they uncover a large package of cocaine. Dante, who was born with a heart ailment that resulted from his mother's crack addiction, is in desperate need of an operation, and the boys must decide if they will join the ranks of the crack dealers in order to earn the necessary money. Although the cocaine is taken back by the white pushers who lost it, the boys' debate highlights the sort of choices that confront the very poor.

As part of his desire to remain true to his subject matter, Mowry has entered the ongoing debate over the suitability of including depictions of graphic sex, violence, and strong language in his novels. However, despite the protest of some reviewers and librarians, Mowry's texts are a perennial favorite with adolescent readers, many of whom appreciate his candor and honesty.

—Gwen A. Tarbox

MOYES, Patricia

Nationality: British. **Born:** Bray, County Wicklow, Ireland, 19 January 1923. **Education:** Overstone School, Northampton, 1934-39, Cambridge School Certificate, 1939. **Military Service:** Served in the radar section of the British Women's Auxiliary Air Force, 1940-45; Flight Officer. **Family:** Married 1) John Moyes in 1951 (divorced 1959); 2) John S. Haszard in 1962. **Career:** Company secretary, Peter Ustinov Productions Ltd., London, 1945-53; assistant editor, *Vogue,* London, 1953-58; writer, since 1956. **Awards:** Mystery Writers of America Edgar Allan Poe award, 1970, for *Many Deadly Returns.* **Agent:** Curtis Brown Ltd., 162-168 Regent Street, London WIR 5TB, England. **Address:** P.O. Box 1, Virgin Gorda, British Virgin Islands, West Indies.

PUBLICATIONS FOR YOUNG ADULTS

Novels (series: Henry and Emmy Tibbett in all books)

Dead Men Don't Ski. London, Collins, 1959; New York, Holt, 1960.
The Sunken Sailor. London, Collins, 1961; as *Down among the Dead Men,* New York, Holt, 1961.
Death on the Agenda. London, Collins, and New York, Holt, 1962.
Murder à la Mode. London, Collins, and New York, Holt, 1963.
Falling Star. London, Collins, and New York, Holt, 1964.
Johnny under Ground. London, Collins, 1965; New York, Holt, 1966.
Murder by 3's (omnibus volume). New York, Holt, 1965.
Murder Fantastical. London, Collins, and New York, Holt, 1967.
Death and the Dutch Uncle. London, Collins, and New York, Holt, 1968.
Who Saw Her Die? London, Collins, 1970; as *Many Deadly Returns,* New York, Holt, 1970.
Season of Snows and Sins. London, Collins, and New York, Holt, 1971.
The Curious Affair of the Third Dog. London, Collins, and New York, Holt, 1973.
Black Widower. London, Collins, and New York, Holt, 1975.
To Kill a Coconut. London, Collins, 1977; as *The Coconut Killings,* New York, Holt, 1977.
Who Is Simon Warwick? London, Collins, 1978; New York, Holt, 1979.
Angel Death. London, Collins, 1980; New York, Holt, 1981.
A Six-Letter Word for Death. London, Collins, and New York, Holt, 1983.
Night Ferry to Death. London, Collins, and New York, Holt, 1985.
Black Girl, White Girl. New York, Holt, 1989; London, Collins, 1990.
Twice in a Blue Moon. New York, Holt, 1993.

Plays

Time Remembered, adaptation of a play by Jean Anouilh, (broadcast, 1954; produced London, 1954; New York, 1957). London, Methuen, 1955.
School for Scoundrel (screenplay), with Peter Ustinov and Hal E. Chester, 1960.

Other

Helter-Skelter. New York, Holt, 1968; London Macdonald, 1969.
After All, They're Only Cats. New York, Curtis, 1973.
Contributor, *Techniques of Novel Writing.* Boston, The Writer, 1973.
How to Talk to Your Cat. London, Barker, and New York, Holt, 1978.

*   *   *

A leading contemporary practitioner of the classic British mystery, Patricia Moyes is known for carefully plotted puzzles which her sleuths solve through a combination of clues, intuition, persistence, logical thinking, physical courage, and calculated risk. To draw the reader into the detection game, Moyes provides an abundance of clues, several red herrings, and sometimes—as in *Who Is Simon Warwick?*—a final plot twist. Another device characteristic of Moyes is the epilogue which, like the denouement in plays, provides a final restoration of order in her fictional world.

Perhaps because of her experience in writing for movies and the stage, Moyes relies heavily upon dialogue. She has a good ear for everyday speech; her characters seem believable because they use diction and syntax appropriate to their age and social position. Even her favorite point of view, first person, becomes an extended dramatic monologue in her novels.

Also adding to the verisimilitude of Moyes' novels is her accurate depiction of the places and activities which provide a backdrop for the mystery. Because these situations reflect her own interests and experiences, Moyes can not only describe them in the manner of an expert, but also construct a mystery which seems to evolve logically from that background. For instance, her movie work is reflected in *Falling Star,* her days at *Vogue* in *Murder à la Mode,* her travels with her husband in *Night Ferry to Death,* her enthusiasm for crossword puzzles in *A Six-Letter Word for Death,* her love of skiing in *Dead Men Don't Ski,* and her passion for sailing in *Down among the Dead Men* and *Helter-Skelter.*

Moyes' best-known mysteries feature Chief Inspector Henry Tibbett and his wife Emmy. The obvious respect and affection between these two characters add a note of domesticity to these mysteries, and frequently the Tibbetts stumble upon a mystery during the course of their usual activities (*Night Ferry to Death*) or while vacationing with family (*The Curious Affair of the Third Dog*) or friends (*Down among the Dead Men*). Generally these friends are, like the Tibbetts, genteel and sophisticated; even criminal masterminds usually are superficially charming, though emotionally unbalanced to some degree. Lower-class characters are at best humorous eccentrics and many are at least technically guilty of violating the law.

Criminals typically underestimate the soft-spoken Henry, who usually downplays his reputation at Scotland Yard. He is particularly adept at recognizing hidden crimes, and his logical mind allows him to quickly deduce the identity of the perpetrators. Since he rarely takes another character completely into his confidence, neither the criminals nor his allies realize the extent of his knowledge until he can prove his case. Relying upon his instincts about individuals and their misdeeds, Henry shrewdly lays traps so that the culprits will reveal their own guilt. Often these stratagems are a calculated gamble which involve physical risk to Henry and sometimes to others.

While Henry usually solves the mystery and provides the final explanation, Emmy is his most valuable ally. She too is clever, courageous, and resourceful; and often her tact and sympathy are essential in gaining a significant bit of information. Emmy relies more on intuition, while Henry is more logical; thus, she provides the balance to make this a true partnership.

With their well-developed humor and relative lack of graphic violence, most of Moyes' mysteries are appropriate for readers of any age, but *Helter-Skelter* was written specifically for a young adult audience. Without sacrificing the intricate plotting and keen suspense of Moyes' other mysteries, it addresses a number of familiar teenage concerns, such as maturation, sibling rivalry, and conflict with parents and other authority figures.

Helter-Skelter takes on elements of the contemporary cloak-and-dagger novel when Felicity Bell, ''Cat,'' realizes that a local murder is linked to a spy operation and enlists the help of several of her friends to solve the crime. Moyes provides abundant clues for any reader even slightly aware of the deep-seated conflict between the Irish and the English. Thus the reader can guess the murderer's identity long before Cat does, and suspense builds as the reader roots for Cat to solve the puzzle before it is too late. In her customary epilogue Moyes ties up some loose ends and prepares for a sequel—revealing that, after testifying at the murder trial, all the principle characters of the book are all well and good and ready for more adventures.

—Charmaine Allmon Mosby

MURPHY, Shirley Rousseau

Nationality: American. **Born:** Oakland, California, 20 May 1928. **Education:** the California School of Fine Arts (now San Francisco Art Institute), California, 1947-51, A.A. in fine art and commercial art 1951. **Family:** Married Patrick J. Murphy in 1951. **Career:** Packaging designer, Sam Kweller, Los Angeles, 1953-55; teacher of mosaics, San Bernardino Valley College, California, 1953-61; documents assistant, Canal Zone Library Museum, Panama, 1964-67. Painter and sculptor. Individual shows: Jack Carr Gallery, South Pasadena, California, 1957; San Bernardino Valley College, and Whittier Art Association, California, both 1958; Ojai Valley Art Center, California, and Ash Grove Gallery, Los Angeles, both 1959; Cherry Gallery, San Bernardino, and Light House Gallery, Hermosa Beach, California, both 1960; Richmond Museum, California, 1963. Since 1963 freelance writer. **Awards:** Received eight awards for sculpture and four for painting at San Francisco Museum and other exhibitions, 1959-62; Dixie Council of Authors and Journalists' award, 1977, for *The Ring of Fire* and *Silver Woven in My Hair,* 1979, for *The Flight of the Fox,* 1981, for *Mrs. Tortino's Return to the Sun,* 1986, for *Nightpool,* and 1988, for *The Ivory Lyre.* **Address:** 1977 Upper Grandview Rd., Jasper, Georgia 30143, U.S.A.

PUBLICATIONS FOR YOUNG ADULTS

Fiction

Carlos Charles, with Patrick J. Murphy. New York, Viking, 1971.
Poor Jenny, Bright as a Penny. New York, Viking, 1974.
The Grass Tower, illustrated by Charles Robinson. New York, Atheneum, 1976.
The Ring of Fire. New York, Atheneum, 1977.
Silver Woven in My Hair, illustrated by Alan Tiegreen. New York, Atheneum, 1977; London, Macdonald and Jane's, 1978.
The Wolf Bell. New York, Atheneum, 1979.
The Castle of Hape. New York, Atheneum, 1980.
Caves of Fire and Ice. New York, Atheneum, 1980.

The Joining of the Stone. New York, Atheneum, 1981.
Nightpool. New York, Harper, 1985.
The Ivory Lyre. New York, Harper, 1987.
The Dragonbards. New York, Harper, 1988.
Medallion of the Black Hound, with Welsh Suggs. New York, Harper, 1989.

Other

Contributor, *Anywhere, Anywhen,* edited by Sylvia Engdahl. New York, Atheneum, 1976.

PUBLICATIONS FOR CHILDREN

Fiction

The Sand Ponies, illustrated by Erika Weihs. New York, Viking, 1967.
White Ghost Summer, illustrated by Barbara McGee. New York, Viking, 1967.
Elmo Doolan and the Search for the Golden Mouse, illustrated by Fritz Kredel. New York, Viking, 1970.
The Flight of the Fox, illustrated by Don Sibley. New York, Atheneum, 1978.
Soonie and the Dragon, illustrated by Susan Vaeth. New York, Atheneum, 1979.
The Song of the Christmas Mouse, illustrated by Donna Diamond. New York, Harper, 1990.

Picture Books

The Pig Who Could Conjure the Wind, illustrated by Mark Lefkowitz. New York, Atheneum, 1978.
Mrs. Tortino's Return to the Sun, with Patrick J. Murphy, illustrated by Susan Russo. New York, Lothrop, 1980.
Tattie's River Journey, illustrated by Tomie de Paola. New York, Dial Press, and London, Methuen, 1983.
Valentine for a Dragon, illustrated by Kay Chorao. New York, Atheneum, 1984.
Wind Child, illustrated by Leo and Diane Dillon. New York, Harper, 1998.

Other

Contributor, *The Unicorn Treasury,* edited by Bruce Coville. New York, Doubleday, 1988.
Herds of Thunder, Manes of Gold, edited by Bruce Coville. New York, Doubleday, 1989.

PUBLICATIONS FOR ADULTS

The Catswold Portal, New York, Roc, 1992.
Cat on the Edge. New York, HarperCollins, 1996.
Cat under Fire. New York, HarperCollins, 1996.
Cat Raise the Dead. New York, HarperCollins, 1997.
Cat in the Dark. New York, HarperCollins, 1998.

*

Media Adaptations: *Tattie's River Journey* (videotape), Listening Library, 1984.

Biography: Essay in *Speaking for Ourselves, Too* compiled and edited by Donald R. Gallo, Urbana, Illinois, National Council of Teachers of English, 1993; essay in *Something About the Author Autobiography Series* by Shirley Rousseau Murphy, Volume 18, Detroit, Gale, 1994.

Manuscript Collections: de Grummond Collection, University of Southern Mississippi, Hattiesburg.

Shirley Rousseau Murphy comments:

Why write fantasy? My own reason for this indulgence is to bring the numinous "other" world, that we sense somewhere beyond, together with the real, hard, factual world of everyday. Neither half of mankind is complete without the other. Tolkien's fantasy worlds that "open your hoard and let all the locked things fly away like cage birds," reflects only half of what we are; and even Tolkien's wonderful fantasies could not exist without the everyday, the mundane—chopping the firewood, kneading the bread, the discomfort of sleeping on the cold earth, our unending labor to keep our families secure. Man is half dreamer and half level-minded workman: nurturer of children, builder of bridges. This mix is what I find exciting. And I seek in my hero that deep core of integrity and sturdiness that is the stuff of all real heroes, and is the salvation of humanity. Fantasy feeds our yearning and tickles our questions. Fantasy whispers to us what we are and where we might be headed—and that we can only get there if we have, within us, the strength of heroes.

*   *   *

Shirley Murphy's young adult fiction runs the gamut: realistic family stories, problem novels, animal stories, modernized folk/ fairy tales, and original high fantasy. Strong, independent female heroines, varied plots and styles, and often complicated narratives distinguish her fiction. Her realistic novels use simple prose, but her fantasy novels of time travel, talking animals, telepathy among people and also between people and animals, flying horses, and fierce dragons matched to mystical bards can be quite mannered.

The only child of an artistic mother and a horsetrainer father, she learned to express her fantasies through art and literature and to exercise practical self-discipline. At age thirty-five, after a successful career as an artist she began to master writing distinctive books for children. Always testing her limits, at times she lets her plots become overly episodic and complicated and lets her shifting points of view get confusing. In some of her fantasy novels, the sustained telepathic dialogues of peoples and animals diminishes their individuality of characters. But her best books repay rereading and rethinking. All are filled with graphic details—often violent in the fantasy novels—and their plots conclude neatly.

White Ghost Summer (1967) and *The Sand Ponies* (1967), her first two books, are realistic family stories set on the coast of her California childhood. In *White Ghost Summer,* the mother, her four adolescent girls, and her preadolescent boy move from a city apartment to a commodious Victorian house near the Pacific Ocean, a city park, and a zoo. There eleven-year-old Melani, "Mel," from whose point of view the story is told, glimpses a ghostly white horse early one morning in the fog and later discovers that this and two other horses hidden in a secret valley belong to a young man. She and her family help establish his legal claim. Her riding lessons at Mr. Blake's riding school nearby lead to prizes. But all is not perfect. The delinquent behavior of her brother, nine-year-old Spence, and some neighbor boys causes some difficulties. But at the end all is well, and the family is even reconciled with strict, disapproving Aunt Vivian.

Sand Ponies starts simply with the running away of two orphans—thirteen-year-old Karen and her twelve-year-old brother Tom—from their drunken guardians Aunt Hester and Uncle Tom and their dingy city apartment. But their journey by bus and on foot back to the California coast gets complicated by a mysterious tramp, actually a disguised policeman, who follows them, and by the children's accidentally learning that a group of men from the Black Turtle Inn are stealing and selling wild ponies. The children aid in the arrest. They are also taken in by the Tillman family who are remodeling a barn for a house. This leads to the romances of four adults. The point of view shifts widely including not only most of these characters, but also Karen and Tom's former horses who coincidentally find their way to Mr. Tillman's ranch, and even a watchful crow who sees part of the action of the story. Despite a nice simple style and tone, the plot is too episodic, coincidental, complex, and confusing.

The problem novels *Carlos Charles,* (1971) written with husband Patrick J. Murphy, and *Poor Jenny, Bright as a Penny* (1974) draw upon his experience as a career probation officer. The first is a sparse story of the arrest and rehabilitation of the twelve-year-old Carlos, a shoeshine boy of Jamaican-American birth, who lives on the streets of the Panama Canal Zone after his grandmother dies and his mother abandons him. Sergeant Romeros befriends Carlos and sees the boy placed on probation with a gruff boatbuilder, who gives him a home and a chance to learn a skill. As the story advances, Carlos meets Mexican-American geologist and pilot Vincente Baroja, who takes him flying and encourages him to go to school and seek a better life. Carlos helps bring a band of gunrunners to justice and rescues Vincente when his plane crashes in the jungle. A believable, honest book filled with action and moral choices, it gets realistic flavor from the many Spanish words— both translated and left in context—and from a spare style like Joseph Krumgold's *. . .and Now Miguel.*

Poor Jenny, Bright as a Penny is just as graphic about an American welfare family, which drifts from one dingy furnished apartment to another. It is told from the point of view of fifteen-year-old Jenny Middle, who wants to be a writer but has been forced to act as surrogate mother for her younger siblings since the death of her father three years ago when her irresponsible mother sold their home, wasted the money, and took Lud Merton as lover and drinking companion. Jenny struggles heroically to keep the family together despite their mother's neglect, frequent shifts from one school to another, and a life in cramped apartments and juvenile halls. This life leads Crystal, Jenny's older sister, into promiscuity, drug addiction, delinquency, and finally death. The mother cheats on welfare and later is imprisoned for fraudulent use of a credit card. As in *Carlos,* an interested police officer and his wife, a writer, rescue Jenny and her nine-year-old brother Bingo, giving them a home and later becoming their foster parents.

The Grass Tower (1976) marks a transition in Murphy's realistic novels. Its strong-minded Californian heroine is fifteen-year-old Bethany, a horse lover gifted with telepathic powers. As the complicated plot unravels, Bethany is first frightened and then fascinated as her strong telepathic powers, stimulated by the false storefront of the Church of Zagdeska. It leads her to discover who her real parents were, to communicate telepathically, and then be reunited with Ninea Ruiz.

As in *Poor Jenny,* two of Murphy's animal books concern research and writing. In the charming and educational *Elmo Doolan and the Search for the Golden Mouse* (1970), the entire Doolan mouse family researches the history of mice, using the resources of the public library where they live; they leave their manuscript on microfilm for the librarian to find, who types a copy and gets it published. The book includes the reference notes compiled by the Doolans. *The Flight of the Fox* (1978) details how after Rory a kangaroo rat becomes friends with twelve-year-old Charlie Gribble and Crispin his lemming, they learn from aircraft manuals how to repair a model airplane found in a town dump, so that Rory and Crispin can fly it and defeat the dastardly starlings who try to ruin the plane and soil the whole town.

The Song of the Christmas Mouse (1990) is partly realistic animal story and partly a sensitive family story. Rick, a single adolescent small town boy, discovers during Christmas vacation a strange silver-colored mouse living in the woodpile. From reading and his veterinarian father, he learns that its grey and white stripes are the result of crossbreeding of an escaped pet white mouse and a common wild one. When his pesky city cousin seven-year-old Hattie and her divorced mother arrive from the city, the two square off about the mouse as well as Rick's new Canadian Blazer sled, which Hattie steals and wrecks. When the mouse is discovered climbing the Christmas tree and singing "a long, trilling cry," the stage is set for reconciliation.

Murphy reworks traditional dragons tales in the three parts of *Soonie and the Dragon* (1979), which has the sixteen-year-old independent heroine Soonie, going out into the world, using her skills at dancing, singing, and storytelling to rescue three princesses, to find a mate for herself, and to claim from the king the reward for saving his three daughters. Likewise blond, blue-eyed, sixteen-year-old Thursey is too independent to wait for a fairy godmother in Murphy's reworking of the Cinderella story in *Silver Woven in My Hair* (1977). Significantly we first see her searching for her old white horse. Abused by her stepmother Augusta and stepsisters Delilah "fat as a young stoat" and Druscilla "thin as a saw blade," Thursey has been educated by the village monk Anwin. For her own instruction she has compiled books of the variants of the Cinderella story as well as writing her own stories. She first meets the prince, disguised as Gillie, a goatherd, whose stories inspire her to attend the ball, using the invitation gotten by Anwin. This reworking pushes literary parallels and erudition to extremes, but Thursey remains an admirable, independent, innkeeper's daughter.

The majority of Murphy's young adult novels are works of high fantasy, consisting of a quintet, a trilogy, and a single co-authored novel. *The Ring of Fire* (1977) begins the quintet about the conflict of the repressive state religion and culture of the land of Ere and invaders from Kubal with the telepathic, red-haired seers and Children of Ynell and the mysterious Luff Eresi and their winged horses. A map, an elaborate history, and a genealogy help to tie the

five books together, along with a continuing quest to reunite the shards of a jade runestone. *The Ring of Fire* establishes the conflict and shows how the telepathic and visionary Children of Ynell are led by the girls Meahta and Zephy, the goatherd Thorn, and the magician Anchorstar in an escape from the corrupt village of Burdeeth and its Kubalese invaders to safety in Carriol.

The Wolf Bell (1979) set prior to *The Ring of Fire* traces the birth and boyhood of Ramad, a red-haired seer of Ynell, the legendary hero of the five books, and the love child of aristocratic, sensual, wilful thirteen-year-old Tayba who bares the child to spite her father and prevent an arranged marriage. Mother and child are taken in and educated by Gredillon, the witchlike bell woman, until they have to escape to Burgdeeth, where Tayba becomes the lover of Vinniver, its cruel ruler-seer, who institutes the land's false religion and oppressive culture. Ramad uses as weapons against enemies both his telepathic powers and Gredillon's wolf bell with a fragment of the runestone which calls both real and spirit wolves. He meets the slave Skeelie and her brother Jerthon, who is casting the bronze statue of the Luff Eresi beneath which the Children of Ynell are constructing the escape tunnel to be used in *The Ring of Fire*. Ramad gets the runestone but then lightning splits it into nine pieces.

In *The Castle of Hape* (1980), twelve years after Ramad's defeat of Vinniver, Seers of Carriol led by Ramad, Jerthon, and twenty-year-old Skeelie attack the evil forces led by the Pellian Seer BroogArl, whose chief weapon—the monster Hape—has the heads of a serpent, an eel, and a horned man (or cat). Ramad solicits aid from the Luff Eresi, who agree to institute a way to save future victims only if Ramad will be a willing sacrifice in Burgdeeth. One subplot deals with Ramad's search for Telien, a girl he has seen in a vision in *The Ring of Fire* as they travel through time. Another subplot concerns the romance triangle of Ram, Telien, and Skeelie. With the Hape, BroogArl, and the other Pellian Seers dead, Ramad is free to seek Telien through time with the aid of three starfire stones given by Anchorstar.

In *Caves of Fire and Ice* (1980), nine years in the future, Skeelie and a friendly wolf companion Tore, with whom she communicates telepathically, go on various quests. One is a journey to Gredillion's derelict bell house and a cell where an older Telien is captive having had a baby by a surviving Seer of the Castle of Hape. Evil characters continue to search for shards of the runestone as Ramad and Skeelie collect more fragments. Telien reappears possessed by a lustful wraith. When it is exorcised, she dies and Ram sets out for Carriol with Skeelie. *The Joining of the Stone* (1981), set twelve years after the death of Ramad, completes the quintet. Lobon, the grown son of Ramad and Skeelie, has taken on his dead father's quest to collect the remaining jade shards. Skeelie has married the Cutter of Stones, who shaped some of the shards. Zephy and Thorn, now the leaders of Carriol, organize a dive to get a shard from the sea to use against an evil trio: Kish, a woman; RilkenDal, an exile; and the dragon Dracvadrig. After an apocalyptic scene, Lobon kills Kish and restores the runestone except for a shard lost in *The Ring of Fire*. Lobon and Meahta fly off to the future. Skeelie and the Cutter of the Stones travel to the past. Time rolls back; continents reappear; and the inscription of the stone is restored. The novels of this series have much action. Inventive details about foods, herbs, and animals make this alternate world different but recognizable. Yet the shifts in time call for many recapitulations and explanations and the extended telepathic communications reduce the narrative largely to a mind trip.

The high fantasy trilogy about the land of Tirror with its singing dragons, visionary bards, and their defeat of the forces of evil—told in Attic style with touches of Old Norse and medieval romance—attempts less and succeeds better as a narrative. In *Nightpool* (1985), the sixteen-year-old hero and rightful heir to the kingdom of Auric, Tebriel, "Teb," is completing his education among the talking otters who saved him from being the usurper Sivich's bait for the sea monster Hydrus. Teb's charming life among the otters, especially their leader Thakkur, and his rescue by the talking foxes have both realistic and fantastic detail. The last flying dragon Dawncloud has five young, setting the stage for each bard to be united with a dragon. Teb gets Seastrider. Dawncloud searches other worlds for her bard, Meriden. In *The Ivory Lyre* (1987), Teb, disguised as a prince and with the young dragons changed to horses, visits the Kingdom of Dacia. Dacia is a land in collusion with the evil humans and un-men, agents of the evil forces that have come to the land through the Castle of Doors to kill all singing dragons and talking animals, especially in grotesque gladiatorial games. In Dacia, Teb meets Keri, daughter of the former horsemaster, makes contact with the resistance forces, and learns news of Camery, his sister left behind in Auric. Camery and Keri's father Colewolf get their singing dragons. Teb and Keri retrieve the ivory lyre of the dragon Bayzum from a sea cave below the castle of Dacia and defeat the evil forces as the people remember their heroic past and cast away their drugged mithnon liquor and the drug cadacus. Teb and Camery leave on their dragons through the Castle of Doors to search for Meriden.

After a lot of recapitulation, *The Dragonbards* (1988) completes the trilogy. Teb and four dragonbards find five more singing dragons in Yoorthed. He is caught trying to rescue two more bard children from the evil Quazelzeg's castle and must be rescued by Marshy and Keri. Though he feeds Sivich to the sharks, Teb's mind is enslaved by the dark forces and lets them through. After much self-struggle, Teb assumes his rightful role as dragonbard and King of Auric in the final battle where the Graven Light defeats Quazelzeg. At the end, men and talking animals and dragons are living in harmony as in the past.

Medallion of the Black Hound (1989), a fantasy adventure book co-authored with Welch Suggs the twelve-year-old son of a close friend, alternates between and compares the American present and a parallel but primitive Celtic one. David Shepherd, the twelve-year-old son of a history teacher and athletic coach, also the descendant of the eldest of three sons of the Celtic king Finn Mac Cumhal for whom three magical medallions were made, finds himself thrust back in time and space just after his father has given him the hound medallion before leaving to check on the raising of a twelfth Viking ship with its treasure cargo. David meets the girl Jendyfi in the Cymru forest, is introduced to evil ogres, droowgs, the zombie-like Degras, and the good beasts like the wyverlyn Haun. He has been called to use his medallion to help King Kastinoe, owner of another of the medallions, to defeat the evil Balcher, who has the third. After finding Siarl Kastinoe's missing son, killing the Chimotaur (a blend of Minotaur and Chimera), and calling up the avenging spirit hounds to defeat the enemy, David is suddenly transported back to the soccer field two weeks later.

This story's synthesis of action—a modern American family and an ancient Celtic society—is typical of Murphy's experimentation with language, integration of research materials, inventiveness of incidents, and vivid, morally distasteful monsters. Murphy's *Flight of the Fox* was a Literary Guild selection, and her novels have received five awards from the Council of Authors and Journalists.

—Hugh T. Keenan

MYERS, Walter Dean

Nationality: American. **Born:** Martinsburg, West Virginia, 12 August 1937. **Education:** Empire State College, New York, B.A. 1984. **Military Service:** United State Army, 1952-1954. **Family:** Married Constance Brendel, 1973 (second marriage); one daughter and one son from first marriage. **Career:** Employment Supervisor, New York State Department of Labor, Brooklyn, 1966-1969; Senior Editor, Bobbs-Merrill Publishers, New York, 1970-1977; part-time teacher of creative writing and black history, New York, 1974-1975; freelance writer, since 1977. **Awards:** Council on Interracial Books for Children Award, 1968, for *Where Does the Day Go?*; Child Study Association of America's Children's Books of the Year, 1972, for *The Dancers,* and 1987, for *Adventure in Granada*; American Library Association (ALA) Notable Children's Books List, 1975, for *Fast Sam, Cool Clyde and Stuff,* 1978, for *It Ain't All for Nothin',* 1979, for *The Young Landlords,* 1981, for *Legend of Tarik,* 1982, for *Hoops,* 1988, for *Me, Mop, and the Moondance Kid* and *Scorpions,* and 1993, for *Somewhere in the Darkness*; ALA Best Books For Young Adults List, 1978, for *It Ain't All for Nothin',* 1979, for *The Young Landlords,* 1981 for *The Legend of Tarik,* 1982, for *Hoops,* 1988, for *Fallen Angels* and *Scorpion,* 1992, for *Now Is Your Time,* 1993, for *Somewhere in the Darkness,* and 1998, for *Harlem*; Coretta Scott King Award, 1980, for *The Young Landlords,* 1985, for *Motown and Didi,* 1989, for *Fallen Angels,* 1992, for *Now Is Your Time,* 1993, for *Somewhere in the Darkness,* 1994, for *Malcolm X,* 1997, for *Slam!,* and 1998, for *Harlem*; National Endowment of the Arts grant, 1982, 1989; Notable Children's Trade Book in the Field of Social Studies from the National Council for Social Studies and the Children's Book Council, 1982, for *The Legend of Tarik*; Edgar Allan Poe Award runner-up, 1982, for *Hoops*; Parents' Choice Foundation Award, 1982, for *Won't Know Til I Get There,* 1984, for *The Outside Shot,* and 1988, for *Fallen Angels*; New Jersey Institute Technology Authors Award, 1983, for *Tales of a Dead King*; MacDowell Fellowship, 1988; Newbery Honor Book, 1989, for *Scorpions,* and 1993, for *Somewhere in the Darkness*; Boston Globe/Horn Book Award, 1992, for *Somewhere in the Darkness*; ALAN Award, 1994; Margaret A. Edwards Award, 1994, for *Hoops, Motown and Didi, Fallen Angels,* and *Scorpion*; Caldecott Honor Book, 1998, for *Harlem.* **Address:** 2543 Kennedy Blvd., Jersey City, New Jersey 07304, U.S.A.

PUBLICATIONS FOR YOUNG ADULTS

Fiction

Fast Sam, Cool Clyde, and Stuff. New York, Viking Press, 1975.
Brainstorm, photographs by Chuck Freedman. New York and London, Watts, 1977.
Mojo and the Russians. New York, Viking Press, 1977.

Victory for Jamie, illustrated by Norm Walker. New York, Scholastic, 1977.

It Ain't All for Nothin'. New York, Viking Press, 1978.

The Young Landlords. New York, Viking Press, 1979.

The Black Pearl and the Ghost: or, One Mystery After Another, illustrated by Robert Quackenbush. New York, Viking Press, 1980.

The Golden Serpent, illustrated by Alice and Martin Provensen. New York, Viking Press, 1980; London, MacRae, 1981.

Hoops. New York, Delacorte Press, 1981.

The Legend of Tarik. New York, Viking Press, 1981.

Won't Know Till I Get There. New York, Viking Press, 1982.

The Nicholas Factor. New York, Viking Press, 1983.

Tales of a Dead King. New York, Morrow, 1983.

Motown and Didi: A Love Story. New York, Viking Kestrel, 1984.

Mr. Monkey and the Gotcha Bird, illustrated by Leslie Morrill. New York, Delacorte Press. 1984.

The Outside Shot. New York, Delacorte Press, 1984.

Adventure in Granada. New York, Viking Kestrel, 1985.

The Hidden Shrine. New York, Viking Kestrel, 1985.

Duel in the Desert. New York, Viking Kestrel, 1986.

Ambush in the Amazon. New York Penguin, 1986.

Crystal. New York, Viking Kestrel, 1987.

Shadow of the Red Moon. New York, HarperCollins, 1987; New York, Scholastic, 1995.

Sweet Illusions. New York, Teachers and Writers Collaborative, 1987.

Fallen Angels. New York, Scholastic, 1988.

Me, Mop, and the Moondance Kid, illustrated by Rodney Pate. New York, Delacorte Press, 1988.

Scorpions. New York, HarperCollins, 1988.

The Mouse Rap. New York, HarperCollins, 1990.

Somewhere in the Darkness. New York, Scholastic, 1992.

Mop, Moondance, and the Nagasaki Knights. New York, Delacorte Press, 1992.

The Righteous Revenge of Artemis Bonner. New York, HarperCollins, 1992.

Glory Field. New York, Scholastic, 1994.

Slam! New York, Scholastic, 1996.

Nonfiction

The World of Work: A Guide to Choosing a Career. Indianapolis, Bobbs Merrill, 1975.

Social Welfare: A First Book. New York, Watts, 1976.

Now Is Your Time!: The African-American Struggle For Freedom. New York, HarperCollins, 1992.

A Place Called Heartbreak: A Story of Vietnam, illustrated by Frederic Porter. Austin, Texas, Raintree, 1992.

Young Martin's Promise, Austin, Texas, Raintree, 1992.

Malcolm X: By Any Means Necessary. New York, Scholastic, 1993.

Remember Us Well: An Album of Pictures and Verse. New York, HarperCollins, 1993.

Brown Angels: An Album of Pictures and Verse. New York, HarperCollins, 1993.

Glorious Angels: An Album of Pictures and Verse. New York, HarperCollins, 1995.

One More River To Cross: An African-American Photograph Album. New York, Harcourt, Brace, 1996.

Toussaint L'Ouverture: The Fight For Haiti's Freedom. New York, Simon & Schuster, 1996.

Harlem, illustrated by Christopher Myers. New York, Scholastic, 1997.

Amistad: A Long Road To Freedom. New York, Dutton, 1998.

Other

Contributor to *What We Must See: Young Black Storytellers,* Dodd, 1971, and *We Be Word Sorcerers: Twenty-five Stories by Black Americans.* Also contributor of articles and fiction to periodicals, including *Black Creation, Black World, Scholastic, McCall's, Espionage, Alfred Hitchcock Mystery Magazine, Essence, Ebony Jr.,* and *Boy's Life.*

PUBLICATIONS FOR CHILDREN

Where Does the Day Go?, illustrated by Leo McCarty. New York, Parents' Magazine Press, 1969.

The Dancers, illustrated by Anne Rockwell. New York, Parents' Magazine Press, 1972.

The Dragon Takes a Wife, illustrated by Ann Grifalconi. Indianapolis, Bobbs Merrill, 1972; New York, Scholastic, 1995.

Fly, Jimmy, Fly!, illustrated by Moneta Barnett. New York, Putnam, 1974.

Story of the Three Kingdoms, illustrated by Ashley Bryan. New York, HarperCollins, 1995.

How Mr. Monkey Saw the Whole World, illustrated by Synthia Saint James. New York, Bantam, Doubleday, Dell for Young Readers, 1997.

*

Media Adaptations: *The Young Landlords* (film), Topol Productions.

Biography: Entry in *Dictionary of Literary Biography,* Vol. 33, Detroit, Gale, 1984; essay in *Something About the Author Autobiography Series,* Vol. 2, Detroit, Gale, 1986; essay in *Speaking for Ourselves: Autobiographical Sketches by Notable Authors of Books for Young Adults,* Vol. 1, compiled and edited by Donald R. Gallo, National Council of Teachers of English, 1990; ''Margaret A. Edwards Award Acceptance Speech'' by Walter Dean Myers, in *Journal of Youth Services in Libraries,* Vol. 8, No. 2, Winter 1995, 129-133.

Critical Studies: Entry in *Children's Literature Review,* Vol. 4, 1982, Vol. 16, 1989, Detroit, Gale; *Presenting Walter Dean Myers* by R. Bishop, Boston, Twayne, 1990; ''Making Intellect Cool'' by Nancy R. Needham, in *NEA Today,* December 1991, 9; ''Walter Dean Myers: This Award-Winning Author for Young People Tells It Like It Is'' by Amanda Smith, in *Publisher's Weekly,* 20 July 1992, 217-218; ''Threads In Our Cultural Fabric: A Conversation with Walter Dean Myers'' by Roger Sutton, in *School Library Journal,* June 1994, 24-29.

*   *   *

''Harlem was a promise/Of a better life, of a place where a man didn't/Have to know his place/Simply because he was/Black.''

Harlem, Walter Dean Myers's recent book for young readers, is a picture book for all ages that expresses through its colorful poetry and art (painted by his son Christopher) the central role Harlem plays in the author's popular novels for teenagers. Harlem, in fact, permeates Myers's fiction. In *Fallen Angels,* for example, Myers writes about the Vietnam War and a black seventeen-year old recruit named Richie Perry who enlists because he can't afford college and because he wants to get out of the crime-ridden Harlem neighborhood where he grew up. Although the agony and tragedy of the war take place in the hinterlands of Vietnam, Richie's thoughts are often of his family and friends who are still trying to cope with life in Harlem. One of the few in his unit to survive his tour of duty, Richie can't wait to return to the place from where he once fled.

The setting for *The Righteous Revenge of Artemis Bonner* takes place mostly in the Wild West during the 1880s, but the story ends with a sentiment for New York City that is similar to Richie's. Artemis is a fifteen-year-old New Yorker who treks from the East Coast to the western frontier in order to even the score with the killer of his uncle. There's also an exciting subplot about unearthing a family treasure hidden someplace in the West. Artemis and a half-Cherokee friend named Frolic eventually do return to New York City. "New York City," Artemis tells Frolic,"has more sights than all of Tombstone and San Francisco put together, plus it is a safe place to live."

Perhaps contrasting New York City favorably with the Vietnam War and the Wild West is faint praise, but Myers remembers from his own Harlem childhood many positive experiences (such as reading from the newspaper to his mother while she did housework and getting his first typewriter from his father). However, he doesn't tone down the dangerous and dead end reality of Harlem—the deadly, violent gangs (such as he depicts in *Scorpions*); the families torn apart by crime and poverty (as in *Somewhere in the Darkness*); the drugs; school dropouts; and pervasive hopelessness. In *Motown and Didi,* one of the author's most adult-oriented novels, Myers creates two products of the Harlem tragedy: Didi, a girl stymied in her attempt to enter college because of a brother who eventually drugs himself to death and a mother who has a nervous breakdown; and Motown, a likeable boxer who is homeless. What these two young people do to survive demonstrates how Myers uses the harsh realities of Harlem to provide a proving ground in which his characters can mature. Didi and Motown employ their street smarts to overcome their environment while developing a capacity to love and at the same time creating an ethical code that emphasizes a commitment to help others.

In *Hoops,* seven-year old Lonnie Jackson plays basketball to earn his ticket out of Harlem. His troubled but wise coach tells him, "You got to learn to use your talent and you got to cover yourself." When he and his coach are offered large sums of money to shave points off a game, Lonnie—who is used to depending solely on his athletic skills to resolve problems—is forced to draw on his sense of right and wrong. The next year, to help pay off his college tuition debts, Lonnie helps an autistic child relate to the outside world (in a sequel entitled *The Outside Shot*), but he again has to fight off repeated bribes to fix basketball games.

Myers transforms the Harlem world of abandoned apartments into a business opportunity for the five bright, enterprising teenage heroes of *The Young Landlords* as well as a chance to improve their neighborhood, and he provides four of them with the challenge of exonerating the fifth member of the group who has been accused of stealing. This scenario of Harlem neighborhood buddies extricating themselves from a crisis brought on by youthful irresponsibility and exuberance is repeated in three of his other novels—*Mojo and the Russians, Fast Sam, Cool Clyde and Stuff,* and *Won't Know Till I Get There.* And in *The Mouse Rap,* Myers focuses on a Harlem fourteen-year-old half-pint boy who meets his father for the first time in eight years, gets wowed by a new girl from California, and involves his small circle of friends in a dangerous search for lost treasure. There is a certain sameness to these lighthearted, humorous, and relatively innocent adventures, but they provide readers with evidence that kids are kids, even in Harlem.

The author's repertoire of stories also includes two science fiction and fantasy novels whose spiritual roots can be traced to Myers's Harlem experiences. *The Legend of Tarik* is ostensibly about a young knight in medieval North Africa who was orphaned early in life because of a genocidal attack on his people by a warrior-tyrant named El Muerte (The Death). In this mixture of Don Quixote and The Lone Ranger, Tarik seems like a medieval Motown who—inspired by love for a woman and by vengeance for crimes against his loved ones—fights an uphill battle against Evil. Tarik does realize, though almost too late, the dehumanizing effect that even killing for "good" reasons can have. And, in a somewhat implausible and wooden novel called *The Nicholas Factor,* Myers tackles the issue of elitist, secret societies that depend on willing, unthinking followers—a characteristic common to both racist groups like the Ku Klux Klan and urban youth gangs.

In 1992 and 1993, Myers wrote two nonfiction books for young adults on African-Americans. One is an episodic and personalized history of black Americans entitled *Now Is Your Time: The African-American Struggle for Freedom,* which focuses on particular events (such as John Brown's Raid and the Dred Scott Supreme Court decision) and on slices of life of both the famous and the lesser-known that show the richness and variety of the black American experience and culture. The other is a respectful and accurate examination of Malcolm X entitled *Malcolm X: By Any Means Necessary.* In his fiction for teenagers, Myers has always placed a premium on character development in his protagonists; likewise, in this biography he emphasizes the important changes of belief Malcolm made near the end of his short life, changes that were responsible for his long-lasting influence on the lives of black and white Americans.

Exploring the African-American heritage and describing the powerful emotions connected to one's family are important elements of Myers's writings. He has also endeavored to paint evocative verbal images of people and events. In 1993, he published *Brown Angels*—a striking photo album of pictures depicting black Americans at the turn of the century accompanied by expressive prose poetry celebrating children. Two years later, he put together a similarly configured photo album called *Glorious Angels* that pictures children from ethnic groups around the world.

In his prolific and entertaining fiction and instructive, expressive nonfiction, Myers has opened up a part of America that once was closed to young readers. He has at once illuminated the hopelessness of black urban life and pointed out ways it can be overcome. Just as importantly, he has helped narrow the gap between black and white youths.

—Jack Forman

N

NAIDOO, Beverley

Nationality: British and South African. **Born:** Johannesburg, South Africa, 21 May 1943. **Education:** University of Witwatersrand, South Africa, B.A., 1963; University of York, B.A. (with honors) 1967; University of York, postgraduate certificate of education (PGCE) 1968; University of Southampton, Ph.D. 1991. **Family:** Married Nandhagopaul Naidoo in 1969; two children. **Career:** Kupugani Non-Profit Nutrition Corporation. Field worker, Johannesburg, South Africa; Primary and secondary teacher, London, 1969-85; writer, since 1985; researcher, 1988-91; Advisory Teacher for Cultural Diversity and English, Dorset, U.K., 1992-1997; Development Officer for Arts, Bournemouth Education Directorate, U.K., 1997-98; part-time tutor for creative writing, Goldsmith college, University of London, from 1997; freelance writer-educationalist, from 1997. **Awards:** Other award, *Children's Book Bulletin*, 1985; Children's Book award, Child Study Book Committee at Bank Street College of Education, 1986; one of Child Study Association for American's Children's Books of the Year, 1987, and Parents' Choice Honor Book for Paperback literature from the Parents' Choice Foundation, 1988, for *Journey to Jo'burg: A South African Story*; Notable Children's Trade Book in the Field of Social Studies, 1990, and Best Books for Young Adults list, American Library Association, 1991, all for *Chain of Fire*; shortlisted for Smarties Prize for Children's Books, 1996, The Guardian Children's Fiction Award, 1996, Josette Frank Award, Children's Book Committee at Bank Street College of Education, 1997, International Reading Association Teachers' Choice, 1998, Notable Children's Trade Books in the field of Social Studies, 1998, all for *No Turning Back*. **Address:** 13 Huntly Rd., Bournemouth, Dorset BH3 7HF, England. **E-mail Address:** bn3@soton.ac.uk.

PUBLICATIONS FOR YOUNG ADULTS

Fiction

Journey to Jo'burg: A South African Story, illustrated by Eric Velasquez. Harlow, Longman, 1985, New York, Lippincott, 1986.
Chain of Fire. London, Collins, 1989; New York, Lippincott, 1990.
No Turning Back. London, Viking, 1995; New York, HarperCollins, 1997.

Other

Editor, *Free as I Know.* London, Bell & Hyman, 1987.
Co-editor, *Global Tales: Stories from Many Cultures.* Harlow, Longman, 1997.

PUBLICATIONS FOR CHILDREN

Fiction

Letang's New Friend [Trouble for Letang and Julie; Letang and Julie Save the Day], illustrated by Petra Röhr-Rouendaal. Harlow, Longman, 1994.
Where Is Zami?, illustrated by Petra Röhr-Rouendaal. Basinstoke, Macmillan, 1998.

PUBLICATIONS FOR ADULTS

Other

Censoring Reality: An Examination of Books on South Africa. London, ILEA Centre for Anti-Racist Education and British Defence/Aid Fund for Southern Africa, 1985.
Through Whose Eyes? Exploring Racism: Reader, Text, and Context. Stoke on Trent, Trentham Books, 1992.

*

Biography: Essay in *Speaking for Ourselves, Too* compiled and edited by Donald R. Gallo, National Council of Teachers of English, 1993.

Beverley Naidoo comments:

Writing for me is a journey. It is a way of exploring the country of my childhood from the perspective of the child I was not. I was brought up with the usual ideas most white South Africans had at the time, completely taking for granted the services of our cook-cum-nanny, who was like a second mother to me, while her own children were prevented by apartheid laws from living with her. I still feel intensely angry about my ''miseducation''—and how racism distorted my vision and segregated my experience from that of the majority of other young South Africans who were black. I was just very fortunate that after leaving school I met people who challenged my inability to see what was all around me.

South Africa is now in the process of great historical change but, as in the U.S., the rifts and scars of racism run deep. Writing allows me to use my imagination to challenge the segregation of experience caused through discrimination. While I am beginning to diversify, sometimes moving my focus away from South Africa, I want my writing always to be primarily a way of extending the limits of my own understanding. Hence the journey. Obviously I hope it is one my readers will find worth following.

*   *   *

In her juvenile novel *Journey to Jo'burg* (1986), Beverley Naidoo introduces the characters of Naledi, Tiro, and Dineo, as well as their grandmother, Nono, and their Mama. In this short story, Naledi and Tiro walk and ride to Johannesburg in order to find their mother and bring her back to their village to help nurse Dineo back to health. It is an important journey for Naledi, but not just in the sense that she expected: she also learns of the darkness of apartheid and comes to a new resolve to fight its influences.

By the time *Journey to Jo'burg* was published, Naidoo had already written *Censoring Reality* (about nonfiction books that discussed South Africa for young readers). Having grown up in South Africa, with a cook and nanny whose children lived hundreds of miles away, she had come to see the injustices of her situation as a white child versus that of black children. She began to write fiction quite consciously as a means of educating the world's children about apartheid.

In 1989, this purpose continued in *Chain of Fire,* a novel for adolescent readers and "dedicated to all those who have struggled to resist." It is a novel filled with pain, sorrow, anger, and frustration. But it is not mere propaganda; the story is never manipulated and distorted to gain a sympathetic response. It continues the story of Naledi, a strong, capable, and complex young woman, who comes to new awareness about justice and her own role in securing justice. It is a painful role she takes on.

The novel opens with the announcement that the South African government plans to evict all of the residents of Bophelong, including Naledi, Tiro, Dineo, and their grandmother, Nono, and to send them to what is termed a homeland but what is truly a barren desert. Abandoned by their chief, the residents are at a loss; there seems to be no way to fight the injustice. Encouraged by a growing relationship with Taola Dikobe, Naledi becomes a part of a student group that tries to fight back, organizing a large student march against the evictions. Pit against the students are the headmaster of their school, their village chief, informers and spies, black policemen pressured by the government, and all the forces of the government itself, replete with tanks and weapons.

The march is broken up but not before the children are filled with a firm resolve to stand against the government and its policy of apartheid. But despite their resistance, inexorably the government closes in. Arrests are made in the night, pensions are cut off, water is cut off, the school is closed down, the church is destroyed, Taola is beaten up, and finally his father, an outspoken opponent of the government, is assassinated. The government trucks come, and the families are removed to a deserted rocky place, there to live in tin huts.

Though *Journey to Jo'burg* concludes with the hopeful presence of Mama, Naledi's mother is not able to appear at the end of *Chain of Fire* to fix things. Taola and Naledi are separated, Naledi's friends are in prison, hospitals, or hiding, the community has indeed been removed, and Nono grows weaker with each day as though she has no more strength to deal with the government's atrocities. But in the same manner that Naledi came to understand the evil of apartheid in *Journey to Jo'burg,* she comes to understand in *Chain of Fire* the power of resistance; a powerful chain of resistance has been built between the hearts of those who would fight against the government, no matter what the government does. She realizes that she is not alone in the fight, that she is not an impotent victim.

The title of the novel is suggestive. The image of the chain recalls the sense of community that is so important in the novel.

Bophelong is clearly a village where each family is closely linked to the others; it has been this way for generations. The community is weakened when links fall away: when Chief Sekete abandons them, when Rra Thopi informs against them. But the chain is not destroyed. Again and again Naledi discovers that the community must indeed stay together and must resist together. This fact remains true even when community is dispersed.

The image of fire is especially suggestive. This is in many ways a spiritual battle as much as it is a physical one; the government has all of the advantages in terms of brute force. But the battle is also one of a group of people refusing to have its spirit destroyed, refusing to be cowed and manipulated and abused. It is a battle for the soul of South Africa. And at the same, the fire suggests the depths of passion and commitment which those who resist must feel. Saul Dikobe is killed because he refuses to live as the government insists that he should live. "No! They are not going to make me run like a frightened dog. . . . Will they destroy me, my family, my people while I must sit quietly by and watch? Oh no!" This is the fire that fills the resistors.

If this novel was only about this struggle, seen from a distanced narrator, it would be a powerful indictment of the South African government. There is no happy ending to save the day, no resolution but the resolve to keep on fighting. But what makes this novel even more powerful is that it is consistently told from the point of view of Naledi. Naidoo does present other perspectives: the raging bitterness of Tiro, the despairing acceptance of Nono, the sheer terror of Dineo, the quiet courage and steel of Mama Dikobe. But the perspective that emerges most powerfully is that of Naledi.

It is significant that Naidoo does not make Naledi into a larger-than-life figure; she is in many ways quite ordinary, with ordinary concerns and interests—at first. When the government's announcement comes into her life, she must come to a difficult decision: should she work against the government despite her Nono's prohibitions? If such activities threaten her school career, should she still continue? She chooses to resist and to work for justice, despite the cost to herself and to her family. At first she simply deceives her grandmother, but when Nono finds out, she reprimands Naledi, who is more hurt by this than by the whips of government soldiers. But little by little she is drawn into the resistance, at first out of a sense of emergency when she must find Tiro, then because of her growing relationship with Tiro, and then because of the rightness of the cause. Elected a student leader, she is given responsibilities because of her commitment and willingness to do something about that commitment. Even her grandmother comes to accept Naledi's role, dangerous as it might be.

Thus, the ending of the novel is full of hope, despite the success of the government's plans and the destruction of Bophelong. "Naledi's heart burned. It was a fierce fire within her, as fierce as the sun bearing down on her now, forever welding new links in a chain. . . . Each day the chain was lengthening, strengthening. She was not alone. They were not alone." The novel concludes with Naledi moving towards a group to share this knowledge with them—a sign that her role has not diminished, that she will continue to resist and to help others resist. She is someone who has grown into this role, and her growth is an important part of the power of *Chain of Fire.*

—Gary D. Schmidt

NAMIOKA, Lensey

Nationality: Chinese. **Born:** Beijing, 14 June 1929. **Education:** Radcliffe College, Cambridge, Massachusetts, 1947-49; University of California, Berkeley, B.A., 1951, M.A., 1952. **Family:** Married Isaac Namioka in 1957; two daughters, Aki and Michi. **Career:** Instructor in mathematics, Wells College, Aurora, New York, 1957-58; instructor in mathematics, Cornell University, Ithaca, New York, 1958-61; broadcasting monitor, Japan Broadcasting Corp., 1969. Translator for American Mathematical Society, 1958-66. **Awards:** Washington State Governor's Award, 1976, for *White Serpent Castle,* and 1996, for *April and the Dragon Lady;* runner-up, Edgar Allan Poe Award, 1982, for *Village of the Vampire Cat;* Certificate of Merit, *Parenting* magazine, 1994, for *The Coming of the Bear;* Parents' Choice recognition, 1995, for *Yang the Third and Her Impossible Family.* **Agent:** Ruth Cohen Inc. Literary Agency, Box 7626, Menlo Park, California 94025. **Address:** 2047 23rd Ave. E., Seattle, Washington 98112, U.S.A.

PUBLICATIONS FOR YOUNG ADULTS

Fiction

The Samurai and the Long-Nosed Devils. New York, McKay, 1976.
White Serpent Castle. New York, McKay, 1976.
Valley of Broken Cherry Trees. New York, Delacorte, 1980.
Village of the Vampire Cat. New York, Delacorte, 1981.
Who's Hu? New York, Vanguard, 1981.
Phantom of Tiger Mountain. New York, Vanguard, 1986.
Island of Ogres. New York, Harper, 1989.
The Coming of the Bear. New York, HarperCollins, 1992.
Yang the Youngest and his Terrible Ear, illustrated by Kees de Kieffe. Boston, Joy Street Books, 1992.
April and the Dragon Lady. San Diego, Browndeer, 1994.
Yang the Third and Her Impossible Family, illustrated by Kees de Kieffe. Boston, Little, Brown, 1995.
Den of the White Fox. San Diego, Browndeer, 1997.
Yang the Second and Her Secret Admirers, illustrated by Kees de Kieffe. Boston, Little, Brown, 1998.

PUBLICATIONS FOR CHILDREN

The Loyal Cat, illustrated by Aki Sogabe. San Diego, Browndeer, 1995.
The Laziest Boy in the World. New York, Holiday House, 1998.

PUBLICATIONS FOR ADULTS

Translator, *How to Order and Eat in Chinese,* by Buwei Y. Chao. New York, Vintage, 1974.
Japan: A Traveler's Companion. New York, Vanguard, 1979.
China: A Traveler's Companion. New York, Vanguard, 1985.

Contributor of plays to *Center Stage,* edited by Donald Gallo.

*

Lensey Namioka comments:

As a child, my greatest pleasure was reading. My aim is to write books that will give the same pleasure to young people today.

While my books contain messages—the need for understanding and tolerance—I also try to make them as entertaining as possible. If my readers agree with my message, then they deserve to have some fun. If they disagree, I'm certainly not going to convert them by being preachy and boring.

* * *

Lensey Namioka claims not to have had a young adult audience in mind when she wrote her first novel, *The Samurai and the Long-Nosed Devils,* in 1976. Perhaps her claim suggests why adolescent readers are inclined to criticize her style, plots, and characterizations—and why her primary audience is in the eleven through fifteen age range rather than among the older teens her publishers also target. Her male protagonists are not entirely believable, especially in terms of their sexuality: though in their late teens or early twenties, they are content to do no more than carry on mild flirtations with the women they admire from a safe distance. Dialogue in her historical novels is invariably forced, unconvincing, and idiomatically anachronistic. The plots of her least satisfying novels seem little more than thrown together admixtures of characters and situations; structural unity is further eroded by narrative digressions and the occasional failure to resolve a secondary or tertiary plot line. Finally, Namioka's historical novels often incorporate contrived "culture lessons," rather stiff doses of aesthetic medicine that, all too obviously, have been spooned into the text for the reader's good.

Ironically, Namioka's claim not to have written specifically to a young adult audience may also explain the loyalty of young readers who enjoy her novels. Except for *The Coming of the Bear,* Namioka's historical fiction addresses its adolescent audience with respect, challenging their vocabulary skills and considering (however superficially) such issues as political corruption, racial prejudice, social and familial violence, and rape. And, at her best, Namioka tells engrossing tales of bravado and adventure in exotic settings. These qualities, in the view of her loyal readers, more than offset her stylistic or structural deficiencies.

Of Namioka's nine published novels to date, seven are historical novels read by teens ages fifteen and younger, especially males. Other than *Phantom of Tiger Mountain,* a "Robin Hood" tale of well-born outlaws who subvert untoward political forces in eleventh-century China, the historical novels are set in late sixteenth-century feudal Japan (about 1575-1600) and recount the continuing adventures of Konishi Zenta and Ishihara Matsuzo, two young and homeless *ronin.* The best of the Zenta/Matsuzo novels are *Valley of Broken Cherry Trees,* which establishes a believable bond between Zenta and a fourteen-year-old aristocrat who is utterly devoid of self-confidence and parental approval but who learns courage, pride, and self-acceptance from his association with the *ronin;* and *Island of Ogres,* which relegates Zenta and Matsuzo to its secondary plot lines, focusing on the coming-of-age (including the partially believable romantic awakening) of a young swordsman who has nearly drowned his potential in alcohol.

Zenta/Matsuzo novels dealing with racial issues are *The Samurai and the Long-Nosed Devils,* concerned with relations between Portuguese missionaries and the Japanese of sixteenth-century Kyoto, and *The Coming of the Bear,* which recounts tensions between the Ainu of Hokkaido and the Japanese encroaching on their territory. Unfortunately, the first of these is guilty of reverse racism in its portrayal of what must be defined as the condescending acceptance of the Portuguese by "open-minded" Japanese; as previously suggested, the second is the least satisfying of all Namioka's novels, its subject matter trivialized by a hastily concocted plot, lifeless dialogue, and one-dimensional characterizations. *White Serpent Castle,* which anticipates a central tension of *Valley of Broken Cherry Trees* (the imminent disempowering of a warlord's rightful heir), is perhaps the most carefully plotted of Namioka's historical novels; *Village of the Vampire Cat,* the tale of a disguised warrior terrorizing a village through his brutal murders of young women, is the most "exciting"—and the most disturbingly sexist in its depictions of cruelty and violence.

Namioka's novels for preteens, *Who's Hu?,* and her humorous series chronicling a family of Chinese musicians who have recently immigrated from China, *Yang the Youngest and his Terrible Ear, Yang the Second and Her Secret Admirers,* and *Yang the Third and Her Impossible Family,* are Namioka's best works in terms of stylistic consistency: the dialogue rings truer; the characters are more believable and individualistic; the plots seem less contrived. Despite expectations aroused by its title, *Yang the Youngest* is the story of a tone-deaf boy whose musician father forces him to study the violin. *Yang the Third* tells the story of Yingmei, who learns to come to terms with the difficulties and embarrassments that cultural differences bring to her life, while *Yang the Second* depicts Yinglan Yang's resistance to adapt to American culture. *Who's Hu?* focuses on Emma, a Chinese teenager, who struggles with the competing gender expectations of her Chinese heritage and the United States, and learns to forge an identity based on what she herself values.

Namioka's most recent young adult novel, *April and the Dragon Lady,* similarly documents the difficulties of April Chen who struggles to negotiate an identity between her Chinese cultural heritage and contemporary American expectations. At issue are her plans to go to college versus her loyalty and responsibilities to her grandmother (the "dragon lady"), as well as her wish to date a white boyfriend versus her respect for her family's values.

Namioka has published plays for adolescents and her travel books for adults, *Japan: A Traveler's Companion* and *China: A Traveler's Companion,* are used and appreciated by English-speaking adolescents participating in study abroad programs in Asia.

—Keith Lawrence, updated by Rebecca R. Saulsbury

NAPOLI, Donna Jo

Nationality: American. **Born:** Miami, Florida, 28 February 1948. **Education:** Harvard University, B.A. 1970, Ph.D. 1973. **Family:** Married Barry Ray Furrow, 1968; five children. **Career:** Lecturer in philosophy and Italian, Smith College, Northampton, Massachusetts, 1973-74; lecturer in mathematics and Italian, University of North Carolina, Chapel Hill, 1974-75; assistant professor of linguistics, Georgetown University, Washington, D.C., 1975-80; professor of linguistics, University of Michigan, Ann Arbor, 1980-87; professor of linguistics, Swarthmore College, Swarthmore,

Pennsylvania, since 1987. **Awards:** One Hundred Titles for Reading and Sharing selection, New York Public Library, 1992, Children's Book of the Year, Bank Street Child Study Children's Book Committee, 1993, and New Jersey Reading Association's Jerry Award, 1996, all for *The Prince of the Pond*; Publisher's Weekly Best Book of the Year, 1993, Blue Ribbon Book designation, *Bulletin of the Center for Children's Books,* 1993, and Best Books for Young Adults selection, Young Adult Library Services Association (YALSA), 1994, all for *The Magic Circle*; Children's Book of the Year, Bank Street Child Study Children's Book Committee, 1995, for *When the Water Closes Over My Head,* and 1996, for *Jimmy, the Pickpocket of the Palace*; Pick of the List, American Booksellers Association, 1996, for *Zel*; Hall of Fame Sports Book for Kids, Library of Philadelphia, 1996, for *Soccer Shock*; Best Books for Young Adults selection, 1997, for *Song of the Magdalene,* and 1998, for *Stones in Water.*

PUBLICATIONS FOR YOUNG ADULTS

The Hero of Barletta, illustrated by Dana Gustafson. Minneapolis, Carolrhoda Books, 1988.
Soccer Shock, illustrated by Meredith Johnson. New York, Dutton, 1991.
The Prince of the Pond; Otherwise Known as De Fawg Pin, illustrated by Judy Schachner. New York, Dutton, 1992.
The Magic Circle. New York, Dutton, 1993.
When the Water Closes Over My Head, illustrated by Nancy Poydar. New York, Dutton, 1994.
Jimmy, the Pickpocket of the Palace, illustrated by Judy Schachner. New York, Dutton, 1995.
The Bravest Thing. New York, Dutton, 1995.
Zel. New York, Dutton, 1996.
Song of the Magdalene. New York, Scholastic, 1996.
Trouble on the Tracks. New York, Scholastic, 1996.
On Guard. New York, Dutton, 1997.
Stones in Water. New York, Dutton, 1997.
Albert, illustrated by Jim Lamarche. New York, Harcourt, forthcoming.
Changing Tunes. New York, Dutton, forthcoming.
Sirena. New York, Scholastic, forthcoming.

Other

Also author of several scholarly papers on linguistics and the editor of several collections of poetry.

*

Biography: Entry in *Something about the Author Autobiography Series* Vol. 23, Detroit, Gale, 1997, 161-178; entry in *Something about the Author* Vol. 92, Detroit, Gale, 1997, 161-166.

*   *   *

Donna Jo Napoli leads two seemingly disparate lives: one as a linguistics scholar and chair of the linguistics department of Swarthmore College, Pennsylvania, and the other as an increasingly popular and successful author of children's and young adult novels. Yet she herself says that these are not two separate lives, but rather two aspects of a single love, the love of writing and of putting thoughts on paper.

Napoli's fiction can be broadly divided into two types: contemporary realistic novels and fairy-tale retellings. In both, her strong points as a writer are her genuine, believable characters and the situations they find themselves involved in. *Soccer Shock,* her first published novel, and its sequel, *Shark Shock,* both concern ten-year-old Adam, who, due to an unexpected strong electric shock, discovers that he can hear his freckles talking and can communicate with them when underwater. In *Soccer Shock* he attempts to use this special secret to become a star soccer player, and in *Shark Shock,* to alleviate his fear of sharks during the family vacation at the beach. Some adult reviewers have found the idea of talking freckles a bit too much of a stretch, but the two novels are otherwise so grounded in the realistic, everyday situations of family life and childhood that as a whole, the plots are entirely believable. In general, Napoli's ability to get inside the mind of her child characters and to narrate the story from that point of view, complete with the fears, concerns, and frustrations of modern childhood, has gained her a large and faithful reading audience.

Napoli's second realistic novel, *When the Water Closes Over My Head,* and its sequel, *On Guard,* lightly explore the frustrations of sibling rivalry and a child's lack of self-confidence as nine-year-old Mikey learns first to overcome his fear of drowning in the swimming pool and later to develop his individuality and self-confidence through the sport of fencing. *Trouble on the Tracks,* an adventure novel, takes place on a twenty-two-hour train ride across the Australian outback as thirteen-year-old Zack and his younger sister learn to work together to solve a mystery, rescue a priceless endangered cockatoo, and prevent a planned train wreck. She turns to the heavier problems of loss and mortality in *The Bravest Thing* as Lila learns to accept the death of her pet baby rabbits and the diagnosis of cancer in her favorite aunt and of scoliosis in herself.

Napoli switches gears in *Stones in Water,* which deals with her most somber subject yet: the incarceration of Italian children in Nazi concentration camps. The honest, understated tone of the narrative as events unfold for Roberto and others caught up in the horrors of this war makes Napoli's message of the strength which hope and friendship and compassion can impart all the more impressive.

In *Song of the Magdalene,* Napoli continues to address the hard facts of life, this time using historical fiction to explore the issues of rape, loss, and prejudice against women and the handicapped as she presents a possible early life history for the famous biblical figure of Mary Magdalene. Although the plot of the novel itself is fictionalized—the story ends even before the Biblical accounts of Mary Magdalene begin—the background of the story is accurately depicted; Napoli spent nearly a year doing research for this book.

Napoli's first published work was a picturebook retelling of a well-known Italian folktale, *The Hero of Barletta,* in which a resourceful giant saves his village from an encroaching army. Her subsequent ventures into folklore retellings took a very different approach. *The Prince of the Pond; Otherwise Known as de Fawg Pin,* a inventive twist to the classic German fairy tale "The Frog Prince," is told from the point of view of the female frog who teaches the enchanted prince how to cope in his new environment. Jade, the female froggy rescuer, and "Pin," whose unfamiliar long tongue gives him a definite lisp, create a happy life together and set about raising their fifty new froglets, until Fate and the classic storyline step in and a princess accidently kisses Pin, breaking the enchantment. As a whole, the story is light-hearted and humorous as Pin learns to cope with his unfamiliar state, but the ending is bittersweet: Jade mourns the loss of her mate without ever understanding who or what he really is. This imaginative novel is only somewhat marred by the rather obviously placed facts of natural history concerning frog life and behavior that the author worked into the narrative. Napoli eventually produced a sequel, *Jimmy, the Pickpocket of the Palace,* in which Pin's oldest froglet, Jimmy, tries to save his pond from the same old troublesome witch, is turned into a human boy, and meets his father.

Napoli's next fairy-tale retelling and her first young adult novel take a distinctly darker twist. *The Magic Circle* is a powerfully written retelling of the story of Hansel and Gretel's witch and how she came to be such a horrific creature. Told from the witch's point of view, the novel originated from Napoli's daughter Eva's question as to why there were so many evil women in traditional fairy tales. In *The Magic Circle,* "The Ugly One" is a hunchback and a gifted healer who learns how to exorcise demons and eventually is condemned to burn as a witch. In order to save her beloved daughter from the same fate, The Ugly One agrees to become the demons' servant and a true witch. In the emotionally intense ending, she finds final salvation in the fiery oven of the traditional tale. The novel is set in Reformation Germany of the late 1600s, and Napoli's meticulous research into the German medieval mind, culture, and folklore, plus her spare, poetic narrative voice combine to make *The Magic Circle* her most intense and haunting tale to date. Her next retelling, *Zel,* is another psychological interpretation of the motivation of a seemingly evil character and also of mother-daughter relationships as she retells, through multiple narrators, the Rapunzel story. This novel also carries the message of forgiveness and the nature of true love.

Napoli says that she does not write in order to preach her particular world view but rather to depict the world as honestly as possible while also imparting a sense of hope and the possibility of a decent and happy future. This belief in the ability of ordinary people to overcome and to survive permeates each of her novels.

—Martha P. Hixon

NAYLOR, Phyllis Reynolds

Pseudonym: Also writes as Phyllis Naylor. **Nationality:** American. **Born:** Anderson, Indiana, 4 January 1933. **Education:** Joliet Junior College, Illinois, 1951-53; American University, Washington, D.C., 1959-63, B.A. in psychology 1963. **Family:** Married Rex V. Naylor in 1960 (second marriage); two sons. **Career:** Clinical secretary, Billings Hospital, Chicago, 1953-56; elementary school teacher in Hazelcrest, Illinois, 1956; assistant executive secretary, Montgomery County Education Association, Rockville, Maryland, 1958-59; editorial assistant, National Education Association, *NEA Journal,* Washington, D.C., 1959-60. Full-time writer, since 1960. Active in civil rights and peace organizations. **Awards:** Children's Books of the Year from Child Study Association of America, 1971, for *Wrestle the Mountain,* 1979, for *How Lazy Can You Get?,* and 1986, for *The Agony of Alice; Wrestle the Mountain* was a Junior Literary Guild selection, 1971; *To Walk the Sky Path* was a Weekly Reader Book Club selection, 1973;

Walking through the Dark was a Junior Literary Guild selection, 1976; *Crazy Love: An Autobiographical Account of Marriage and Madness* was a Literary Guild selection, 1977; Golden Kite award for Nonfiction from Society of Children's Book Writers, 1978, and Children's Choice from International Reading Association and Children's Book Council, 1979, both for *How I Came to Be a Writer; How Lazy Can You Get?* was a Weekly Reader Book Club selection, 1979; Children's Choice, 1980, for *How Lazy Can You Get?,* and 1986, for *The Agony of Alice;* Best Book for Young Adults from Young Adult Services Division of American Library Association, and Notable Children's Book in the Field of Social Studies from National Council for Social Studies and Children's Book Council, both 1982, and South Carolina Young Adult Book award, 1985-86, all for *A String of Chances;* Child Study award from Bank Street of College of Education, 1983, for *The Solomon System;* Edgar Allan Poe award from Mystery Writers of America, 1985, for *Night Cry; The Agony of Alice* was an American Library Association (ALA) Notable book, 1985; Notable Children's Book in the Field of Social Studies, 1985, for *The Dark of the Tunnel,* 1985; *The Keeper* was a Junior Literary Guild selection, 1986; Best Book for Young Adults from Young Adult Services Division of the American Library Association, 1986, for *The Keeper,* and 1987, for *The Year of the Gopher;* Joan G. Sugarman award, 1987, for *Beetles, Lightly Toasted;* Creative Writing Fellowship Grant from National Endowment for the Arts, 1987; Society of School Librarians International Book award, 1988, for *Maudie in the Middle;* Best Young Adult Book of the Year from Michigan Library Association, 1988, for *The Year of the Gopher;* Christopher award, 1989, for *Keeping a Christmas Secret; Send No Blessings* was an ALA Notable Book for Young Adults, 1990; Hedda Seisler Mason award, 1991, for *Alice in Rapture, Sort of;* Newbery Medal, 1992, ALA Notable Book, and 27 different state awards, all for *Shiloh; All But Alice* was an ALA Notable book, and a Recommended Book for Reluctant Readers, 1993; Kerlan Award, University of Minnesota, 1995; Appalachian Medallion, University of Charleston, West Virginia, 1997. **Agent:** John Hawkins & Associates, Inc., 71 West 23rd St., Suite 1600, New York, New York 10010, U.S.A. **Address:** 9910 Holmhurst Rd., Bethesda, Maryland 20817, U.S.A.

PUBLICATIONS FOR YOUNG ADULTS

Fiction

To Shake a Shadow, illustrated by Gloria Kamen. Nashville, Abingdon, 1967.

When Rivers Meet, illustrated by Allan Eitzen. New York, Friendship, 1968.

Making It Happen, illustrated by Joe De Velasco. Chicago, Follett, 1970.

No Easy Circle, illustrated by Lou Aronson. Chicago, Follett, 1972.

Walking through the Dark, illustrated by James and Ruth McCrea. New York, Atheneum, 1976.

Shadows on the Wall, illustrated by Ruth Sanderson. New York, Atheneum, 1980.

Faces in the Water, illustrated by Ruth Sanderson. New York, Atheneum, 1981.

Footprints at the Window, illustrated by Ruth Sanderson. New York, Atheneum, 1981.

A String of Chances, illustrated by Ruth Sanderson. New York, Atheneum, 1982.

The Solomon System, illustrated by Ronald Himler. New York, Atheneum, 1983.

Night Cry, illustrated by Ruth Sanderson. New York, Atheneum, 1984.

The Dark of the Tunnel, illustrated by Ronald Himler. New York, Atheneum, 1985.

The Keeper, illustrated by Ronald Himler. New York, Atheneum, 1986.

The Year of the Gopher, illustrated by John Steven Gurney. New York, Atheneum, 1987.

Send No Blessings. New York, Atheneum, 1990.

Alice in Between. New York, Atheneum, 1994.

The Fear Place. New York, Atheneum, 1994.

Alice the Brave. New York, Atheneum, 1995.

Alice in Lace. New York, Atheneum, 1996.

Outrageously Alice. New York, Atheneum, 1997.

Achingly Alice. New York, Atheneum, 1997.

Sang Spell. New York, Atheneum, 1998.

Alice on the Outside. New York, Atheneum, 1999.

Jade Green: A Ghost Story. New York, Atheneum, 1999.

Nonfiction

How to Find Your Wonderful Someone, How to Keep Him/Her If You Do, How to Survive If You Don't. Philadelphia, Fortress, 1972.

An Amish Family, illustrated by George Armstrong. Chicago, O'Hara, 1974.

Short Stories

Grasshoppers in the Soup: Short Stories for Teen-agers, illustrated by Elsa Bailey. Philadelphia, Fortress, 1965.

Knee Deep in Ice Cream and Other Stories, illustrated by Johanna Sperl. Philadelphia, Fortress, 1967.

The Dark Side of the Moon, illustrated by Joseph Papin. Philadelphia, Fortress, 1969.

The Private I and Other Stories, illustrated by Elsa Bailey. Philadelphia, Fortress, 1969.

Ships in the Night, illustrated by Otto Reinhardt. Philadelphia, Fortress, 1970.

Change in the Wind. Minneapolis, Augsburg Press, 1980.

Never Born a Hero. Minneapolis, Augsburg Press, 1982.

A Triangle Has Four Sides. Minneapolis, Augsburg Press, 1984.

PUBLICATIONS FOR CHILDREN

Fiction

The Galloping Goat and Other Stories, illustrated by Robert Jefferson. Nashville, Abingdon Press, 1965.

Jennifer Jean, The Cross-Eyed Queen (as Phyllis Naylor), illustrated by Harold K. Lamson. Minneapolis, Lerner, 1967.

The New Schoolmaster, illustrated by Mamoru Funai. Morristown, New Jersey, Silver Burdett, 1967.

A New Year's Surprise, illustrated by Jack Endewelt. Morristown, New Jersey, Silver Burdett, 1967.

What the Gulls Were Singing, illustrated by Jack Smith. Chicago, Follett, 1967.

Meet Murdock, illustrated by Gioia Fiammenghi. Chicago, Follett, 1969.

To Make a Wee Moon, illustrated by Beth and Jo Krush. Chicago, Follett, 1969.

Wrestle the Mountain, illustrated by Paul Giovanopoulos. Chicago, Follett, 1971.

To Walk the Sky Path, illustrated by Jack Endewelt. Chicago, Follett, 1973.

Witch's Sister, illustrated by Gail Owens. New York, Atheneum, 1975.

Witch Water, illustrated by Gail Owens. New York, Atheneum, 1977; London, W.H. Allen, 1979.

The Witch Herself, illustrated by Gail Owens. New York, Atheneum, 1978; London, W.H. Allen, 1979.

How Lazy Can You Get?, illustrated by Alan Daniel. New York, Atheneum, 1979; London, Hamish Hamilton, 1980.

Eddie, Incorporated, illustrated by Blanche Sims. New York, Atheneum, 1980.

All Because I'm Older, illustrated by Leslie Morrill. New York, Atheneum, 1981.

The Boy with the Helium Head, illustrated by Kay Chorao. New York, Atheneum, 1982.

The Mad Gasser of Bessledorf Street, illustrated by Andrew Rhodes. New York, Atheneum, 1983.

Old Sadie and the Christmas Bear, illustrated by Patricia Montgomery Newton. New York, Atheneum, 1984.

The Agony of Alice, illustrated by Blanche Sims. New York, Atheneum, 1985.

The Bodies in the Bessledorf Hotel, illustrated by Gail Owens. New York, Atheneum, 1986.

The Baby, the Bed, and the Rose, illustrated by Mary Szilagyi. New York, Clarion, 1987.

Beetles, Lightly Toasted, illustrated by Melodye Rosales. New York, Atheneum, 1987.

Maudie in the Middle, with Lura Schield Reynolds, illustrated by Judith Gwyn Brown. New York, Atheneum, 1988.

One of the Third Grade Thonkers, illustrated by Walter Gaffney-Kessell. New York, Atheneum, 1988.

Alice in Rapture, Sort Of, illustrated by Blanche Sims. New York, Atheneum, 1989.

Keeping a Christmas Secret, illustrated by Lena Shiffman. New York, Atheneum, 1989.

Bernie and the Bessledorf Ghost. New York, Atheneum, 1990.

Witch's Eye. New York, Delacorte, 1990.

Reluctantly Alice. New York, Atheneum, 1991.

Shiloh. New York, Atheneum, 1991.

King of the Playground, illustrated by Nola Langner Malone. New York, Atheneum, 1991.

Witch Weed. New York, Delacorte, 1991.

Josie's Troubles. New York, Atheneum, 1992.

The Witch Returns. New York, Delacorte, 1992.

All But Alice. New York, Atheneum, 1992.

The Grand Escape. New York, Atheneum, 1993.

The Face in the Bessledorf Funeral Parlor. New York, Atheneum, 1993.

The Boys Start the War. New York, Delacorte, 1993.

The Girls Get Even. New York, Delacorte, 1993.

Boys Against Girls. New York, Delacorte, 1994.

Being Danny's Dog. New York, Atheneum, 1995.

Ice. New York, Atheneum, 1995.

Shiloh Season. New York, Atheneum, 1996.

The Bomb in the Bessledorf Bus Depot. New York, Atheneum, 1996.

The Healing of Texas Jake, illustrated by Alan Daniel. New York, Atheneum, 1997.

I Can't Take You Anywhere, illustrated by Jef Kaminsky. New York, Atheneum, 1997.

Saving Shiloh. New York, Atheneum, 1997.

Danny's Desert Rats. New York, Atheneum, 1998.

The Treasure of Bessledorf Hill. New York, Atheneum, 1998.

The Girls' Revenge. New York, Atheneum, 1998.

Other

Getting Along in Your Family, illustrated by Rick Cooley. Nashville, Abingdon Press, 1976.

How I Came to Be a Writer, illustrated by Lou Carbone. New York, Atheneum, 1978.

Getting Along with Your Friends, illustrated by Rick Cooley. Nashville, Abingdon Press, 1980.

Getting Along with Your Teachers, illustrated by Rick Cooley. Nashville, Abingdon Press, 1981.

Ducks Disappearing, pictures by Tony Maddox. New York, Atheneum, 1997.

Strawberries. New York, Atheneum, 1999.

PUBLICATIONS FOR ADULTS

Novels as Phyllis Naylor

Revelations. New York, St. Martin's, 1979.

Unexpected Pleasures. New York, Putnam, 1986.

Other, as Phyllis Naylor

Crazy Love: An Autobiographical Account of Marriage and Madness. New York, Morrow, 1977.

In Small Doses (essays). New York, Atheneum, 1979.

The Craft of Writing the Novel (as Phyllis Reynolds Naylor). Boston, The Writer, 1989.

*

Media Adaptations: *The Keeper* (''Afterschool Special,'' ''My Dad Can't Be Crazy, Can He?''), American Broadcasting Companies (ABC-TV), 1989; *Witch's Sister* (television special), Blue Marble Program.

Biography: Essay in *Something About the Author Autobiography Series,* Volume 10, Detroit, Gale, 1990; *A Talk With Phyllis Reynolds Naylor* (audiotape), Scarborough, New York, Tim Podell Productions, 1991.

Manuscript Collections: Kerlan Collection, University of Minnesota, Minneapolis; de Grummond Collection, University of Southern Mississippi, Hattiesburg.

Critical Studies: *Contemporary Authors, Vols. 21-22,* Detroit, Gale Research, 1969; *Something About the Author,* Detroit, Gale Research, Vol. 6, 1977, Vol. 66, 1991; *Children's Literature Review,* Vol. 17, Detroit, Gale, 1989; *Something About the Author, Autobiography Series,* Vol. 10, Detroit, Gale Research, 1990; *Authors and Artists for Young Adults,* Vol. 4, Detroit, Gale Research, 1990; *Meet the Authors and Illustrators,* Vol. 2. Scholastic, 1993; *Presenting Phyllis Naylor* by Lois Thomas Stover, New York, Twayne, 1997.

Phyllis Reynolds Naylor comments:

I know that I carry many different people inside me, and I call on them from time to time when needed. There are moments I still feel like a scared child, yet I can draw on this panic when I need to in my writing. I also know what it is like to be the strong one when necessary, the supportive one, and sometimes I have to talk to myself like a reassuring mother. If I never experienced fear or jealousy, could I write about them convincingly? Maybe not. And so, when I go through a difficult time, I tell myself, "Remember this; perhaps you can use it in a book."

All of us, authors and readers alike, have both joy and pain in our lives. I have never been one to think, "Why *me*?" but rather, "Why *not* me?" since I've seen many tragedies happen to friends. The difference between author and reader, I guess, is that after going through a hard time, the writer is less likely to give himself a good shake and get on with his life; he grabs hold of the thought, the worry, the experience, the feeling and doesn't let go, painful though it may be. He insists on dissecting, examining, and recreating it on paper in a way that will provide release. And the more he can touch upon universals, the more his experience will speak to others.

When I wrote *Crazy Love,* a friend said to me, "I really don't know how you could put all that personal stuff down on paper; you told us things not even your family doctor should know!"

Perhaps so. In novels, of course, no one else need know just how much of ourselves we are exposing. Often not even writers realize the degree to which their writing is autobiographical. But we are able to do this—we take this risk—because we accept the fact that everything we have ever felt or seen or heard or experienced, no matter how marvelous or disgusting or cowardly or brave, someone else has experienced too. And we can therefore trust the generosity of our readers when we put our thoughts and feelings down on paper.

*　　*　　*

A versatile and prolific author of young-adult novels, Phyllis Reynolds Naylor's work is distinguished by her skill at diversity. From comedy to tragedy, from books for younger readers to older young adults, from rural settings to urban landscapes, from fantasy to realism, she reveals a fine sense of the unexpected difficulties and rewards of life through her authentically drawn characters. Some of her novels have strong autobiographical elements, but others—no less convincing—are not based on her own experiences.

One of her best novels is *A String of Chances,* in which sixteen-year-old Evie experiences a summer away from home, living with a cousin and the cousin's husband, who are expecting a baby. Evie has her first serious romance, gains insights into her family's patterns of behavior, and struggles with her long-standing dislike of a boy who is living at her parents' home for the summer. Evie's father is a country preacher, and she confronts her own religious doubts and questions, especially when the beloved baby Joshua suddenly dies. What might easily have become trite and stereotypical is not at all so: Evie's father is loving and genuine and has a sense of humor; the baby's death and the consequent grief of all involved are presented with truthfulness and depth; and Evie emerges stronger and wiser but without easy resolutions to her religious questions or to her difficulties in romance. The milieu of the small town is aptly brought to life, and even the minor characters are intriguing and vital.

In *The Year of the Gopher,* seventeen-year-old George Richards's well-to-do suburban Minneapolis family suffers from performance expectations that have ruled family behavior for three generations. George revolts against these expectations by refusing to go to an Ivy League college (as his lawyer father did) and chooses to find blue-collar work instead, at least for a year. Naylor draws the world of George's teenage peers with observant, accurate detail: George's first sexual relationship, his relationships with his siblings, and his maturing realizations about life all are presented without clichés or sensationalism.

Focusing directly on sibling relationships, *The Solomon System* is a story about loyal brothers Ted and Nory Solomon. Their closeness is threatened, however, by the tension between their parents, who are headed for divorce, and by the two brothers' growing apart in other ways. Naylor creates plausible and interesting characters in a Jewish family, sympathetically and sensitively portrayed.

Some of Naylor's novels can be described as problem novels, with a difficult social or psychological issue forming the central theme. *The Keeper* deals with the recognition and consequences of mental illness. This novel tells the terrifying story of Nick, whose father behaves more and more strangely, until Nick is forced to recognize that his father is mentally ill. *The Keeper* has its roots in Naylor's own experience: her first husband was seriously mentally ill. *Crazy Love* is her compelling account of her traumatic first marriage. Another novel dealing with problems is the Gothic *Night Cry,* in which Naylor explores the predicament of Ellen, who lives on a Mississippi farm and is often alone when her father, a traveling salesman, is away. Through her loneliness and involvement with a superstitious neighbor, she allows her fears to take on larger dimensions than they should.

Naylor treats her characters with an admirable mixture of sympathy and critical insight, gives them depth, individuality, and complexity, and has the power to make the reader care for them. Naylor earned the prestigious Newbery Medal for her moving novel *Shiloh,* the story of a West Virginia boy and his friendship with an abused dog. Naylor's portrayal of the boy's struggle to hide his involvement with the dog without being any more dishonest than necessary; his economically poor, but loyal family; and the West Virginia setting all contribute to this outstanding novel. Naylor created an especially popular character in Alice, whose humorous and touching misadventures began in *The Agony of Alice* and *Alice in Rapture, Sort of* and continue in several further novels. Her mother dead, Alice lives with her father and brother, and yearns for a female role model—for whom she has in mind the glamorous Miss Cole, not her own dumpy teacher, Mrs. Plotkin.

Alice in Lace continues the Alice saga, moving the heroine into ever more sensitive ground as she matures. But as always, Naylor handles the subject matter—emerging sexuality—with good humor. Alice and her boyfriend Patrick pretend that they are engaged, but it's all for the sake of education, specifically to fulfill a class assignment. The experience gets Alice thinking about growing up, marriage . . . and sex. She and her friends speculate as to what their wedding nights will be like, and they dress up in sexy clothes (at least, they think they're sexy) to serve Alice's brother breakfast in bed.

Willing to present complex religious, ethical, and psychological issues in her fiction, Naylor does so without a hidden—or, for that matter, obvious—agenda, but with simple honesty and sensitivity.

—J.D. Stahl, updated by Judson Knight

NEEDLE, Jan

Nationality: British. **Born:** Holybourne, 8 February 1943. **Education:** Victoria University of Manchester, drama degree (with honors), 1971. **Career:** Reporter, *Portsmouth Evening News,* Portsmouth, England, 1960-64; reporter and sub-editor for *Daily Herald and Sun,* 1964-68; freelance writer, since 1971. **Agent:** David Higham Associates, 5-8 Lower John Street, Golden Square London WIR 4HA, England.

PUBLICATIONS FOR YOUNG ADULTS

Fiction

Albeson and the Germans. Tubingen, Deutsch, 1977.
My Mate Shofiq. Tubingen, Deutsch, 1978.
A Sense of Shame and Other Stories. Tubingen, Deutsch, 1980.
Losers Weepers, illustrated by Jane Bottomley. New York, Methuen, 1981.
Another Fine Mess. Armada, 1982.
Piggy in the Middle. Tubingen, Deutsch, 1982.
Going Out. Tubingen, Deutsch, 1983.
A Pitiful Place and Other Stories. Tubingen, Deutsch, 1984.
Tucker's Luck. Tubingen, Deutsch, 1984.
Behind the Bike Sheds. New York, Methuen, 1985.
A Game of Soldiers. Tubingen, Deutsch, 1985.
Great Days at Grange Hill. Tubingen, Deutsch, 1985.
Tucker in Control. New York, Methuen, 1985.
Skeleton at School. New York, Heinemann, 1987.
Uncle in the Attic. New York, Heinemann, 1987.
Wagstaffe the Wind-Up Boy. Tubingen, Deutsch, 1987.
In the Doghouse. New York, Heinemann, 1988.
The Sleeping Party. New York, Heinemann, 1988.
The Thief. London, Hamish Hamilton, 1989
Mad Scramble. New York, Heinemann, 1990.
As Seen on TV. New York, Heinemann, 1990.
Bogeymen. Tubingen, Deutsch, 1992.
The War of the Worms. London, Hamish Hamilton, 1992.
Wagstaffe and the Life of Crime. Lions, 1992.
The Bully. London, Hamish Hamilton, 1993.

PUBLICATIONS FOR CHILDREN

Rottenteeth (picture book), illustrated by Roy Bentley. Tubingen, Deutsch, 1979.
The Bee Rustlers, illustrated by Paul Wright. New York, Collins, 1980.
The Size Spies, illustrated by Roy Bentley. Tubingen, Deutsch, 1980.

PUBLICATIONS FOR ADULTS

Novels

A Fine Boy for Killing. Tubingen, Deutsch, 1979.
Wild Wood, illustrated by William Rushton. Tubingen, Deutsch, 1981.

Other

Brecht (criticism), with Peter Thompson. Illinois, University of Chicago Press, 1981.
Rebels of Gas Street, with others. New York, Collins, 1986.

*   *   *

Jan Needle's diverse work for young adults represents the compromise which gifted modern writers must often make if they wish to win and entertain a large readership but also to make serious moral and political statements about issues which confront young citizens in our time. Needle is a conspicuously political writer, personally committed to what might be termed the "humanitarian left," and a number of his novels and stories are deeply concerned with questions of racial, class, and sexual identity, and with the moral dimension of nationality, patriotism, and war. In several of his books the immediate setting is contemporary Britain or places with which Britain is politically enmeshed (*A Game of Soldiers,* for example, is set in the Falkland Islands during the 1982 war with Argentina) but his themes are universal, and the common denominator of these stories is the writer's indignation at the folly and cruelty of people and societies who refuse to recognise their shared humanity.

Not all of Needle's work is as solemn as these themes make it sound. He is also a brilliant humorist and has produced a number of books which are sheer comic entertainment. Some of them, such as *The Size Spies,* are for pre-teenage children, but that book's appealing mode of zany and iconoclastic science fiction mixed with satire has also been adapted in some of Needle's recent work—*Wagstaffe the Wind-Up Boy* and *Wagstaffe and the Life of Crime*—in a form which also attracts older readers. These stories concern the adventures of a boy who, having been squashed flat by a truck on the motorway, is reconstructed as a machine. This is comedy of extravagant ruthlessness and hilarious bad taste which owes something to Roald Dahl and to comic book traditions but has a distinctive mockery of convention and satiric relish for absurdity which teenage readers enjoy.

More serious are Needle's novels on contemporary social issues. At their most accessible these are stories which originated in television scripts and were subsequently novelised. Books such as

Great Days at Grange Hill are recast from Needle's scripts for a long-running television series about a state comprehensive school, for which many other writers have also written. Because an urban secondary school necessarily reflects many tensions which arise from class, race, and anti-social behaviour, the scripts and books gave Needle a chance to combine undemanding entertainment with social realism. *A Game of Soldiers,* which began life as a television serial, is a far more serious book, and reflects Needle's determination to exploit the available media which reach a mass young adult audience, and to use the screen as a way into the novel. Brief, vivid and moving, this tense, unsparing story describes the experience of three young Falklands children who find a severely wounded Argentinean boy-soldier and have to face the resulting crisis in their lives. The book's theme is, in Wilfred Owen's phrase, "war, and the pity of war."

Perhaps the most controversial of Needle's "documentary" novels is *Piggy in the Middle.* The protagonists in the book are all adults, mostly members of the police, and the book's theme is race prejudice in the police force. *Piggy in the Middle* is therefore a regional depiction of an almost universal problem which affects young adults deeply. By choosing as his key figure a young, inexperienced but intelligent and tolerant policewoman, Needle is able to demonstrate how sexual prejudices intertwine with racial ones, and to illustrate the problem when looking at frontline law enforcement of distinguishing between on the one hand understandable grievance and provocation and on the other naked and vindictive prejudice. Sandra, the young policewoman, is finally unable to reconcile her police role with her painfully acquired political insights, and has to resign. The book is utterly uncompromising in its implicit anti-racist stance, but it is educative rather than propagandist because Needle scrupulously shows us the faults and duplicities on both sides, the confusion of good and bad within the single individual—in short, the sheer complexity of urban social tensions. Needle can be an accusatory, unaccommodating writer, carefully sealing off the moral escape-routes which his readers might seek, but he articulates conflicting viewpoints and lets us see why anti-social forces, however mistaken, feel and act as they do. The anti-racist novel *My Mate Shofiq* and the stories in the collection *A Sense of Shame* (notably the fierce indictment of defective courtroom justice, "The Common Good") are other powerful explorations of prejudice in its many guises.

The peak of Needle's literary achievement to date, however, consists of two novels with less evident topicality and mass appeal but with much to offer to more advanced young adult readers. *Wild Wood* is a magnificent satiric reversal of Kenneth Grahame's *The Wind in the Willows,* presenting the misdoings of Toad and the unearned pleasure-filled lives of the River Bankers from the viewpoint of the impoverished proletarian weasels, stoats, and ferrets who inhabit the Wild Wood. Needle's version of the insurrection and takeover of Toad Hall (renamed "Brotherhood Hall" by its captors) is modelled like Orwell's *Animal Farm* on the Russian revolution, and it makes some shrewd political thrusts. But these are gently understated, and the book is a rich and spirited comedy, affectionately disrespectful to its great forerunner. Finest of all Needle's books is the superb historical novel *A Fine Boy For Killing,* set in the time of the Napoleonic War and depicting the brutality of press gangs and the intense suffering of life at sea under vicious captains, material hardships and a barbarous disciplinary regime. The book outshines such celebrated equivalent novels for adults as C. S. Forester's "Hornblower" series in its mingling of compulsive excitement with bleak realism and moral intelligence. *A Fine Boy For Killing* is a minor classic, and we must hope that Needle's populist fiction, however successful, will not impede him from giving his imagination such major expression in the future.

—Peter Hollindale

NELSON, Theresa

Nationality: American. **Born:** Beaumont, Texas, 15 August 1948. **Education:** University of St. Thomas, Houston, Texas, B.A. in English (magna cum laude) 1972. **Family:** Married Kevin Cooney; three children. **Career:** Actress and teacher of dramatic arts, Theatre Under the Stars, Houston, 1971-80; Glee Club director, St. Mary's School, Katonah, New York, 1983-90; freelance writer and speaker, from 1983. **Awards:** Best Book of the Year citation, *School Library Journal,* 1986; Notable Children's Trade Book in the Field of Social Studies citation, National Council for the Social Sciences/Children's Book Council, 1987; Washington Irving Children's Choice Award, 1988; Notable Children's Book citation and Best Book for Young Adults citation, both from American Library Association, 1990; Best Book of the Year citation, *School Library Journal,* 1990; Editor's Choice citation, *Booklist,* 1990; Fanfare citation, *Horn Book,* 1990; Pick of the Lists citation, *American Bookseller,* 1990; Books for Children citation, Library of Congress/Children's Literature Center, 1990; Teacher's Choice citation, International Reading Association, 1990; Books for the Teen Age citation, New York Public Library, 1990; Notable Children's Trade Books in the Field of Social Studies citation, National Council for the Social Sciences/Children's Book Council, 1990; Notable Children's Book citation and Best Books for Young Adults citation, American Library Association, 1992; Best Book of the Year citation, *School Library Journal,* 1992; Fanfare citation, *Horn Book,* 1992; Books for the Teen Age citation, New York Public Library, 1992; Children's Literature Center: Books for Children citation, Library of Congress, 1992.

PUBLICATIONS FOR YOUNG ADULTS

Fiction

The Twenty-Five Cent Miracle. New York, Bradbury Press, 1986.
Devil Storm. New York, Orchard Books, 1987.
And One for All. New York, Orchard Books, 1989.
The Beggars' Ride. New York, Orchard Books, 1992.
"Andrew, Honestly," in *Don't Give Up the Ghost: The Delacorte Book of Original Ghost Stories,* edited by David Gale. New York, Delacorte Press, 1993.
Earthshine. New York, Orchard Books, 1994.
The Empress of Elsewhere. New York, DK Publishers, 1998.

*

Media Adaptations: "Andrew, Honestly" (sound recording), American Printing House for the Blind, 1993.

Critical Studies: *And One for All by Theresa Nelson* by Judith R. Cooper, Literature/Social Studies Program series, Littleton, Massachusetts, Sundance, 1992; entry in *Something About the Author,* Vol. 79, Detroit, Gale Research, 154-158; entry in *Contemporary Authors,* Vol. 148, Detroit, Gale Research, 321-324.

*   *   *

If the settings of Theresa Nelson's novels are varied and, at times, terrifying, so are the emotions that drive the actions of the complex and diverse family of characters that populate her fiction. A native of coastal Texas, Nelson is married to an engineer-turned-actor whose career has led the family first to New York and most recently to California. Each of these locations provides settings for Nelson's novels, the plots of which are as different as the locales.

The body of Nelson's work provides fiction that has a refreshing combination of literary and social value. Focusing intentionally on themes or problems that are directly relevant to the lives of young adults, Nelson examines with care and compassion issues such as poverty, AIDS, homelessness, and myriad other issues, all detailed through the actions and insights of a cast of finely drawn characters.

Appropriately set in a small Texas town which she acknowledges having modeled on her own hometown of Beaumont, Texas, Nelson's first novel, *The Twenty-Five Cent Miracle,* focuses on Hank, an alcoholic widower, and his eleven-year-old daughter, Elvira, who is desperately seeking both to help her father and to establish a loving, father-daughter relationship with him. His failure to adequately provide for Elvira has left the door open for his rich and domineering sister, Darla, to take Elvira to live with her. For Elvira the ideal solution is a marriage between her father and Miss Ivy, the beautiful and kind town librarian who has taken an interest in the young girl. When, predictably, Miss Ivy kindly but firmly rejects Elvira's idea, the young girl's dream world collapses and she is left to face the inevitable—life with Aunt Darla. Elvira responds by running away from home and becoming ill as a result of exposure. Elvira's actions make Hank realize the young girl's attachment to him and how much he would miss her if she were removed from his life. When she is finally returned to him, Hank sits by her sickbed and nurses the daughter he almost lost. As she recuperates, Hank embraces Elvira and she realizes that in his own way her father does love her, suggesting that the story, as it progresses beyond the last page into the reader's imagination, will result in Elvira's hoped for solution—a loving relationship with a reformed father. The ending is a bit too neat and the peripheral characters a bit too stereotypical, but the core of the book and the relationship between father and daughter is both strong and insightful. The book is particularly useful for exploring a seldom explored subculture, i.e., the world of poverty associated with house trailers and mobile homes.

In another novel set on the Texas coast, *Devil Storm,* Nelson uses the devastating hurricane of 1900 as the setting for an historical adventure that combines the mystique of Galveston Island's pirate past with the Carroll family's struggle to survive the storm that killed 6,000 Texans. The human drama being played out against the backdrop of the storm involves a mysterious former slave named Tom who befriends and is befriended by the Carroll children, 13-year-old Walter and his younger sister, Alice. The children are intrigued by his tales of pirating and slavery, but their

father, having accepted local gossip that Tom is both unstable and dangerous, mistrusts the 82-year-old man. As the tension over their relationship with Tom builds, the strength of the storm also builds, and one dramatic situation becomes metaphor for the other. When the storm finally hits, Mr. Carroll is trapped on the other side of Galveston Bay from the family, and, in an ironic twist, it is Tom, the man whom he had distrusted, who steps in to save the family. As in her earlier novel, Nelson's sense of place and local dialect is strong and true. She places believable characters in a dangerous and dramatic situation which both entertains with its pulsing storm drama and enlightens with the window it opens onto slavery and subsequent relations between the races.

In *And One for All* Nelson turns to another historical setting to examine the homefront conflict generated by the Vietnam War through the eyes of Geraldine Brennan, a seventh-grader whose brother, Wing, volunteered for the Marines on his 18th birthday. While Wing goes to boot camp and then to Vietnam, his best friend, Sam Daily, becomes a radical anti-war protester, an action which alienates him from the Brennan family. When Wing is killed in action Geraldine blames Sam for his death and takes a bus from her upstate New York home to Washington D.C. where she confronts Sam, who is involved in yet another peace march. She finally realizes that both Sam and Wing—each in their own ways—were seeking the same thing, the end of the war. Through skillful characterization and carefully controlled development of the conflict, Nelson weaves yet another tale which gives her readers insight into an important historic era and a major issue that continues to confront the world—what is the price of peace?

Nelson's next novel, *The Beggars' Ride,* examines the contemporary problem of runaway teenagers and the street life style which many of them adopt. The setting here is Atlantic City, New Jersey, to which 12-year-old Clare has fled to escape the neglect of her alcoholic mother and the sexual abuse of her mother's boyfriend. In a bleak look at the life such children are forced into, Nelson details the development of relationships among these young street people, showing how they resort to petty thievery, shoplifting, and pickpocketing to eke out an existence. As the drama unfolds the reader gets to know a varied cast of characters within the young girl's adopted street "family." Though the book ends on a hopeful note, it is the despair and danger in the daily lives of these children that will remain with the reader long after the book is finished.

In her most recent book, *Earthshine,* Nelson turns to the west coast and to a tragedy that is continuing to be played out, the AIDS crisis. A magical book that is perhaps her best writing to date, *Earthshine* is at once both heartbreaking and uplifting. The story is told through the eyes of 12-year-old Margery Grace ("Slim") McGranahan whose father, "Mack," is dying of AIDS. The book takes the reader inside what might be described as the culture of AIDS, that is, the network of personal, helping, and professional relationships that Mack, Slim, and Mack's partner, Larry, develop in their attempts to cope with the inevitable. Though Mack dies in the end, it is not his death that stays with the reader but the strong and growing sense of family within the group and their determination to save Mack, even though they know on a logical level that their efforts will not forestall the inevitable. However, in their struggles—which include a last minute trip into the desert to visit a modern day medicine man—the people trying to help Mack grow beyond their limited selves to become stronger and more aware of their need for each other. The overarching agony of Mack's progressing disease is beautifully and skillfully balanced by his determined clowning—an effort to shift the family's focus off his disease—and by the birth of Angelina's (another AIDS victim) healthy baby. The author almost never makes a false step in this wonderfully realized telling of a modern tragedy. The central characters are finely drawn and, as a group, are well balanced, but even the peripheral characters are strong and believable; there is hardly a stereotype to be found in the book.

In her one departure to date from full-length fiction, Nelson shows up to good critical advantage in the company of a stellar group of other young adult writers. Her entry ("Honestly, Andrew") in *Don't Give Up the Ghost,* a volume of original ghost stories which also included entries by Gary Soto, Walter Dean Myers, and Joan Lowry Nixon, was described by the *School Library Journal* reviewer as the "most absorbing" story in the collection. The story tells of a young boy who time travels to the future to meet himself as an older man. Her forthcoming (1998) novel, *The Empress of Elsewhere,* focuses on the efforts of a brother and sister to help their elderly neighbor care for a pet monkey who keeps escaping. In the process of helping the neighbor with her monkey problem, they befriend and help her granddaughter whose has emotional problems stemming from the family's troubled past.

In her career to date Nelson has drawn on her knowledge of local settings to create a body of fictional literature that both entertains and systematically focuses the readers attention on painful social problems. From sexual abuse, to race relations, to the AIDS epidemic, Nelson uses the skill of the literary artist to take her young readers into a meaningful encounters with characters who struggle with problems which, unfortunately, many of the readers themselves also struggle. As good reading, as bibliotherapeutic tools, as aids to learning more about social problems and history, Nelson's books deliver and should be on the shelves of all serious young adult collections.

—William E. Buchanan

NEUFELD, John (Arthur)

Pseudonym: Joan Lea. **Nationality:** American. **Born:** Chicago, Illinois, 14 December 1938. **Education:** Yale University, New Haven, Connecticut, B.A. 1960. **Military Service:** Served in the United States Army; discharged honorably. **Career:** Editor, teacher television scriptwriter, and author. Advertising copy writer, Harcourt, Brace, and World, New York City; publicist, Franklin Watts, Inc., McGraw-Hill, Holt, and Western Publishing. **Awards:** Notable Book award, American Library Association, for both *Edgar Allan* and *Lisa, Bright and Dark.* Fellowship, Macdowell Colony, Peterborough, New Hampshire. **Address:** 210 Indian Mountain Road, Lakeville, Connecticut 06039-2006, U.S.A.

PUBLICATIONS FOR YOUNG ADULTS

Fiction

Edgar Allan. New York, S. G. Phillips, 1968.
Lisa, Bright and Dark. New York, S. G. Phillips, 1969.

Touching. New York, S. G. Phillips, 1970.
Sleep Two, Three, Four! New York, Harper, 1971.
Freddy's Book. New York, Random House, 1973.
Sunday Father. New York, New American Library, 1975.
The Fun of It. New York, Putnam, 1977.
A Small Civil War. New York, Fawcett, 1982.
Sharelle. New York, New American Library, 1983.
Almost a Hero. New York, Atheneum, and Toronto, Maxwell Macmillan Canada, 1995.
Gaps in Stone Walls. New York, Atheneum, 1996.

Other

Lisa, Bright and Dark (teleplay; *Hallmark Hall of Fame* presentation). NBC-TV, 1973.

PUBLICATIONS FOR ADULTS

Fiction

For All the Wrong Reasons. New York, Norton, 1973.
Trading Up, (as Joan Lea). New York, Atheneum, 1975.
Family Fortunes. New York, Atheneum, 1988.

Also author of television scripts *Death Sentence,* and *You Lie So Deep My Love,* both ABC-TV.

*

Media Adaptations: *Edgar Allan, Freddy's Book, For All the Wrong Reasons, The Fun of It, A Small Civil War,* and *Sharelle* have all been optioned for television.

Biography: Essay in *Something about the Author Autobiography Series,* Volume 3, Detroit, Gale, 1986, pp. 175-87.

Manuscript Collections: Kerlan Collection, University of Minnesota.

John Neufeld comments:

As a child, I began to learn about life as an adult by reading fiction. I can't believe I was, or am, alone. The topics I select to address are those I feel strongly that young people should begin to consider as they mature . . . i.e., often my books center around problems or ideas or conflicts a young person has yet to meet. My hope is that, later, when they do meet these struggles, my work will have been of some help in making constructive, suitable decisions for themselves and for those around them. I'm also crazy about my characters and their stories. One has to be in order to face the page day after day.

* * *

John Neufeld tackles sensitive issues—such as mental illness, physical handicaps, and racial prejudice—with tremendous insight that accurately and honestly addresses each issue's impact on society. He credits young adults with a perceptiveness and depth of character that contrasts sharply with the ineptitude of the adult world.

Attitudes toward mental illness are explored in *Lisa, Bright and Dark,* one of Neufeld's best-known works. When Lisa Shilling tells her parents she thinks she may be going crazy, they see it as a ploy for more attention. Her friends, however, become alarmed as Lisa's condition deteriorates and her behavior shows signs of being drastic cries for help from the adults in her life. Even after walking through a plate-glass window, however, her parents won't believe anything is seriously wrong. While they continue to try to get the adults to listen, her friends set up a "therapy session," in which Lisa receives some relief by talking about what is happening to her. Though the ending is too magically resolved, with one adult stepping in at the request of his daughter, who is trying to help Lisa, the book sufficiently deals with mental illness without belaboring the technical details.

Neufeld addresses racial prejudice in *Edgar Allan,* which is based on the true story of a white family that adopts a black boy in the late 1960s. The story is told honestly, in a straightforward style, from the perspective of twelve-year-old Michael Fickett. The son of a minister in a small, but privileged white suburb in California, Michael chronicles the events surrounding the adoption of three-year-old Edgar Allan which causes disunion within the family, antagonism from the community, and an ultimatum from the church board of directors.

Michael is analytical, slightly introverted, and open-minded and balances the account of Edgar Allan's stay with the Ficketts by adding insights into the reactions of the family members. The two younger children seem not to notice the color of Edgar Allan's skin; Michael is at first shocked but his older sister is absolutely furious and refuses to acknowledge the child's presence. This story is not simply about the taking in and the "giving back" of one black child, though. It is also about failure, decisions, and how all of these resulting issues affect and develop Michael's life.

Touching tells the story of a courageous sixteen-year-old girl with cerebral palsy and her refusal to be denied dignity or love. Twink's family realize the intelligence of their daughter and diligently search for a school that will meet her needs. Twink expresses a desire to write about her life, and in a desperate attempt to remain in control of the few faculties left to her, she agrees to undergo an experimental technique to control her arm spasms. Though her parents try to discourage her, she insists on going through with the experiment, for her sake as well as for the sake of others. Unfortunately the result leaves her blind, but her determination to write is not hindered despite the loss.

Neufeld succeeds in showing each teen's perspective in part by telling the story from mixed viewpoints. The narrative is told simply, yet it can be highly emotive. Twink's courage is admirable, but more importantly readers come to understand the needs and desires of the physically handicapped, and also learn to reevaluate attitudes about people they know little about.

John Neufeld creates teenage characters who are perceptive and make decisions to take action. They are willing to learn about and understand situations unfamiliar to them. Neufeld's reputation for portraying teens as more capable of facing complex problems than adults is an appealing affirmation for young adult readers.

—Lisa A. Wroble

NEVILLE, Emily Cheney

Nationality: American. **Born:** Manchester, Connecticut, 28 December 1919. **Education:** Oxford School, 1931-36; Bryn Mawr College, Pennsylvania, A.B. 1940; Albany Law School, New York, J.D. 1976; admitted to the New York bar, 1977. **Family:** Married Glenn T. Neville in 1948 (died 1965); three daughters and two sons. **Career:** Office worker 1940-41, and feature writer, 1941-44, New York *Daily Mirror.* Currently in private law practice. **Awards:** American Library Association Newbery Medal, 1964, for *It's Like This, Cat;* Women's International League for Peace and Freedom Jane Addams award, 1966, for *Berries Goodman.* **Address:** Keene Valley, NY 12943, U.S.A.

PUBLICATIONS FOR YOUNG ADULTS

Fiction

It's Like This, Cat, illustrated by Emil Weiss. New York, Harper, 1963; London, Angus and Robertson, 1969.
Berries Goodman. New York, Harper, 1965; London, Angus and Robertson, 1970.
The Seventeenth-Street Gang, illustrated by Emily McCully. New York, Harper, 1966.
Traveler from a Small Kingdom, illustrated by George Mocniak. New York, Harper, 1968.
Fogarty, New York, Harper, 1969.
Garden of Broken Glass. New York, Delacorte Press, 1975.
The Bridge, illustrated by Ronald Himler. New York, Harper, 1988.
The China Year. New York, Harper, 1991.

*

Media Adaptations: *It's Like This, Cat* (recording), American School Publishers and (videotape), Newbery Productions.

Biography: Essay in *Something about the Author Autobiography Series* by Emily Cheney Neville, Volume 2, Detroit, Gale, 1986.

Manuscript Collections: Kerlan Collection, University of Minnesota, Minneapolis.

Critical Studies: Entry in *Contemporary Literary Criticism,* Volume 12, Detroit, Gale, 1980.

*　　*　　*

Emily Cheney Neville writes primarily for young adults, though she has published one picture book. She is best known for her first book, *It's Like This, Cat,* a sensitive, funny story about Dave Mitchell, an ordinary teenage boy in an ordinary middle-class family in New York City.

Dave can't seem to do anything right as far as his father is concerned. He and his father argue a lot, and the arguments result in his mother having asthma attacks and Dave walking out of the house. His father says a dog can be educational for a boy, so Dave walks out and comes home with a cat. In the course of a summer,

Dave and the cat have ordinary and not-so-ordinary adventures. They meet new people, and Dave, at age fourteen, finds the first girl that he feels comfortable with. Dave learns, through observing the relationship between his father and an older teenage male friend, that his father is not a bad guy after all. Seeing his family through the eyes of others, gives Dave understanding and compassion. A simple, straightforward story, *It's Like This, Cat* is memorable for its brilliant teenage dialogue, humor, and realism. New York City, with its dirt and its danger, its stray cats and stray people, is eloquently described.

Berries Goodman is about a nine-year-old boy who has a laid-back family and lives in an ethnically diverse big-city neighborhood. Berries accepts people as they are. After his family moves to the suburbs, with its "restricted communities," he is introduced to anti-Semitism. It puzzles and disturbs him since he values his best friend, a Jewish boy named Sidney Fine. The characters in this book are well delineated and the plot unfolds naturally. The first-person dialogue is as fresh and spirited as that of *It's Like This, Cat*. And the underlying subject of prejudice and its effects on children's lives is presented honestly and clearly.

Another fast-paced New York City story, *The Seventeenth-Street Gang* has believable characters too; the children talk as children and the adults talk as adults. The girls and boys of mixed ages are led by a strong-willed girl, Minnow. Minnow can be alternately charming and hostile; she is always resilient. The shifting power struggles within the gang are artfully described. The children's strategies for maintaining privacy and independence from adults are also well presented.

Neville's early childhood included a world of relatives, games and adventures with cousins, holidays celebrated with an extended family, and memories of a variety of family pets. *Travelers from a Small Kingdom* is an autobiographical account describing Neville's close-knit family living in a small town in the 1920s. This world may seem to some modern readers who are accustomed to a world of technology, speed, overcrowding, and violence, as uneventful and dull. But Neville makes her childhood and its setting real and satisfying.

Fogarty, like *It's Like This, Cat,* is strong in candor, pithy characterizations, and surprising situations. Dan Fogarty, twenty-three, a college graduate and law school drop-out, is first met loafing around in front of Malone's garage in Wilbur Flats. He describes himself as "the town flop"; his old school teacher, the preacher, and almost everyone around would like him to "be something." Next, Dan is seen in the East Village of New York City, sleeping with a young lady and facing an unsuccessful play production. *Fogarty* speaks of the emotional hold of a small town on even the most rebellious citizens, and describes a sensitive young man as he gets over an unhappy romance and deals with his artistic talents.

The China Year is the story of Henri, an eighth-grade New York City child who lives in a loft apartment with her painter mother and college professor father, and who summers in the Poconos. One day Henri is studying for finals, wondering about summer. The next day her father announces an exchange appointment for him to teach English literature in Beijing. Henri's China year is a year of school lessons by mail, no friends, no phone, no pizza, and throngs of people who do not speak her language. Henri explores Beijing on her bike, and at a busy corner meets Minyuan. Minyuan speaks English; he went to school in Philadelphia for a year while his mother taught Chinese at a college there. Minyuan

offers to show Henri Tienanmen Square, "very important Chinese place." Later she wants to go to the Peking Hotel to use the bathroom and eat ice cream. He explains that ordinary Chinese people are not allowed in this elegant place. Through Minyuan and his family, Henri and her family get a close look at Chinese culture and its constrictions. Importantly, they make real Chinese friends. Because of Henri's mother's illness, the family leaves Beijing before the year is up, and before the Tienanmen Square massacre. Back in New York, Henri sees the TV footage of fighting and fears for Minyuan's safety. She sends him a letter, not mentioning the massacre but cautiously only writes of their friendship. She receives a letter back from him which is also only about their friendship. By describing cultural differences through day-to-day experiences of teenagers, Neville is able to give them intimacy and meaning. For those who do not have the unique opportunity of observing life in the Third World, this book may be a particularly enriching experience.

—Mary Lystad

NICHOLS, Leigh. *See* **KOONTZ, Dean R.**

NICHOLS, Peter. *See* **CHRISTOPHER, John.**

NIX, Garth

Nationality: Australian. **Born:** Melbourne, Victoria, 1963. **Education:** Major in script and freelance writing, Canberra College of Advanced Education (now University of Canberra). **Career:** Bookshop sales assistant; publisher's sales representative; book editor; and public relations consultant in information technology; full-time writer, from 1998. **Awards:** Best Fantasy Novel, Aurealis Award for Excellence in Australian Speculative Fiction, 1996; Best Young Adult Novel, Aurealis Award for Excellence in Australian Speculative Fiction, 1996; American Library Association Notable Book. **Address:** c/o Allen & Unwin, 9 Atchison St., St. Leonards, NSW 2065, Australia.

PUBLICATIONS FOR YOUNG ADULTS

Fiction

The Ragwitch. Chippendale, New South Wales, Pan, 1990; New York, Doherty, 1994.
Sabriel. Pymble, New South Wales, Harper Collins, 1995; New York, HarperCollins, 1996.

The Calusari (novelization of an episode of the television show *The X Files*). Pymble, New South Wales, and London, HarperCollins, 1997.

Shade's Children. St. Leonards, New South Wales, Allen & Unwin, and New York, HarperCollins, 1997.

Lirael: Daughter of the Clayr. St. Leonards, New South Wales, Allen & Unwin, and New York, HarperCollins, 1999.

PUBLICATIONS FOR ADULTS

Very Clever Baby's First Reader: A Simple Reader for Your Child Featuring Freddy the Fish and Easy Words. Sydney, Nix Books, 1988.

Very Clever Baby's Ben Hur: Starring Freddy the Fish as Charlton Heston. Sydney, Nix Books, 1989.

Very Clever Baby's Guide to the Greenhouse Effect. Sydney, Nix Books, 1992.

PUBLICATIONS FOR CHILDREN

Bill the Inventor, illustrated by Nan Bosworth. Mascot, New South Wales, Koala Book Company, 1998.

*　　*　　*

Garth Nix is one of Australia's most original writers of fantasy for young readers. Both *Sabriel* and *Shade's Children* have attracted considerable positive critical notice because of the breadth and detail of Nix's imaginary worlds. The worlds he creates and the situations of his characters are frightening, but Nix objects to his writing being labelled as horror fiction, pointing out that his heroes are not helpless but always triumph over evil. In *The Ragwitch,* his first novel, Julia and her brother Paul find an ugly rag doll in a nest on top of an ancient Aboriginal midden. Unwittingly Julia releases and is possessed by the evil North-Queen, who transports her to another world. Paul follows and, helped by a varied group of people, magicians, and creatures, destroys the witch and restores his sister. Incidents and characters remind the reader of a host of famous fantasy works but equally striking is the inventiveness evident in the creation of even minor details such as the "death leaf" Julia's companions absorb into their bodies.

The setting for *Sabriel* is two adjoining lands: Ancelstierre, much like our world but reminiscent of the 1920s, and the Old Kingdom, a place of magic where the living and the dead are in close contact. Sabriel is a young necromancer able to enter Death at will. She has to save her father, Abhorsen (the name of the executioner in *Measure For Measure*), a particularly skilled magician, from Death and help restore the Old Kingdom which is being destroyed by an evil creature who inhabits both Death and Life. Although structured around the familiar motif of a quest, of note is the imaginative construction of death as a cold, fast-flowing river and the remarkable detail of this strange world. Most memorable perhaps is Sabriel's bandolier with its seven bells that, when rung in combination, can send an unsettled spirit through the river gates to final rest, an idea prompted by the tools of excommunication—"bell, book and candle"—and a Dorothy Sayers' novel, *The Nine*

Tailors, that features church bells with Latin names. *Daughter of the Clayr* continues the story of the Old Kingdom about twenty years on from Sabriel's adventures. Again someone, this time a scientist, is brought into the Old Kingdom as an aid to strange magical forces. This novel features the lovely twins, Ryelle and Sanar, who help Sabriel towards the end of her quest by bringing a Paperwing, a magical aircraft, at a time of great need.

The Calusari is a novelization of an episode from the television series *The X Files,* the first title in the new Young Adult X-Files novel series. With half a dozen murders in a few short pages and a setting in the present, it is nevertheless not as unsettling as *Shade's Children.* The setting for *Shade's Children* is the near-future in a decaying city (partly inspired by Sydney and San Francisco) where fifteen years previously all people over the age of fourteen have suddenly disappeared. In the place of adults after The Change are a small group of Overlords who breed specialized creatures, fueled with the brains of fourteen-year-old humans, for war games which they watch on screens from their headquarters. The four heroes, Ella, Drum, Ninde, and Gold-Eye, are some of the few escapees from the children's dormitories who are found and cared for by Shade, once a research scientist at a university now, remarkably, a computer program, whose altruism seems increasingly suspect.

The novel has a more elaborate structure than *Sabriel.* With databases, interview dialogue, computer records, and Shade's own internal "conversations," each of the major characters is given a voice and important past events are related to action in the present. This futuristic *Oliver Twist* is disturbing but it is ultimately a moral tale with the heroes' successes dependent on trust, cooperation, and actions for the common good. Of course their supernormal abilities (called Change Talents as they are somehow connected with the Overlords manipulation of reality) are useful! As in *The Ragwitch* and *Sabriel,* there is a lot of action with escapes, fight scenes, and chases. Counterpointing the grim world is the relationship of the four, which includes some romance, and, of course, the writer's wit. Only a re-reading will highlight the black humor of the first-page description of Ella's liberation from the dorms, achieved with a razor blade labelled, "Not for use by children." Recalling the author's penchant for jokes, note that despite their titles, Nix's "Clever Baby" books—tiny readers featuring fish with remarkable vocabularies including easy words like "perfidious" and "lust"—are humorous works for adults.

—Kerry White

NIXON, Joan Lowery

Pseudonym: Jaye Ellen. **Nationality:** American. **Born:** Los Angeles, California, 3 February 1927. **Education:** the University of Southern California, Los Angeles, 1944-47, B.A. in journalism 1947; California State College, 1948-49, elementary teaching certificate. **Family:** Married Hershell H. Nixon in 1949; three daughters and one son. **Career:** Writer. Elementary school teacher, Los Angeles, 1947-50; creative writing instructor, Midland College, Texas, 1971-73, and University of Houston, 1974-78; taught creative writing in numerous public schools in Texas. Member of the Board of Directors, Society of Children's Book Writers, Los

Angeles, 1976-79. **Awards:** Steck-Vaughn award, Texas Institute of Letters, 1975, for *The Alligator under the Bed*; Edgar Allan Poe award for best juvenile novel, Mystery Writers of America, 1980, for *The Kidnapping of Christina Lattimore*, 1981, for *The Seance,* and 1987, for *The Other Side of Dark,* and 1994, for *The Name of the Game Was Murder*; Edgar Allan Poe award nominee, Mystery Writers of America, 1975, for *The Mysterious Red Tape Gang,* 1985, for *The Ghosts of Now,* and 1993, for *The Weekend Was Murder!,* 1995, for *Shadowmaker,* and 1996, for *Spirit Seeker*; Outstanding Science Trade Book for children, National Science Teachers Association and Children's Book Council Joint Committee, 1979, for *Volcanoes: Nature's Fireworks,* 1980, for *Glaciers: Nature's Frozen Rivers,* and 1981, for *Earthquakes: Nature in Motion*; Crabbery award, Oxon Hill branch of Prince George's County (MD) Library, 1984, for *Magnolia's Mixed-Up Magic*; Young Hoosier award, 1988, for *A Deadly Game of Magic*; Golden Spur, Western Writers of America, 1988, for *A Family Apart,* and 1989, for *In the Face of Danger*; Young Hoosier award, 1989, for *The Dark and Deadly Pool*; Colorado Blue Spruce Young Adult award, 1988, Virginia Young Adult Silver Cup, 1989, Oklahoma Sequoyah Young Adult Book award, 1989, Iowa Teen award, 1989, California Young Readers Medal, 1990, and Utah Young Adult award, 1991, all for *The Other Side of Dark*; California Young Readers Medal, 1990, for *The Stalker*; Virginia Young Reader's award, 1992, for *A Family Apart*; Nevada's Young Readers award, 1992, and Nebraska's Golden Sower award, 1993, both for *Whispers From the Dead*; Arizona Young Readers award, 1997, and Black-eyed Susan award, 1997, for *The Name of the Games Was Murder.* **Agent:** Amy Berkower, Writers House Inc., 21 West 26th St., New York, New York 10010, U.S.A. **Address:** 10215 Cedar Creek Dr., Houston, Texas 77042, U.S.A.

PUBLICATIONS FOR YOUNG ADULTS

Fiction

The Kidnapping of Christina Lattimore. New York, Harcourt, 1979.
The Seance. New York, Harcourt, 1980; London, Granada, 1983.
The Spectre. New York, Delacorte, 1982; London, Granada, 1983.
The Trouble with Charlie (as Jaye Ellen). New York, Bantam, 1982.
Days of Fear, photographs by Joan Menschenfreund. New York, Dutton, 1983.
A Deadly Game of Magic. New York, Harcourt, 1983; London, Corgi, 1988.
The Ghosts of Now. Delacorte, 1984; London, Corgi, 1987.
The Stalker, illustrations by Wendy Popp. Delacorte, 1985.
The Other Side of Dark. New York, Delacorte, 1986; London, Hodder and Stoughton, 1988.
The Dark and Deadly Pool. New York, Delacorte, 1987.
A Family Apart. New York, Bantam, 1987.
Caught in the Act. New York, Bantam, 1988.
In the Face of Danger. New York, Bantam, 1988.
Secret, Silent Screams. New York, Delacorte, 1988.
The Island of Dangerous Dreams. New York, Dell, 1989.
A Place to Belong. New York, Bantam, 1989.
Star Baby. New York, Bantam, 1989.
Whispers from the Dead. New York, Delacorte, 1989.
Encore. New York, Bantam, 1990.
Overnight Sensation. New York, Bantam, 1990.

Candidate for Murder. New York, Delacorte, 1991.
High Trail to Danger. New York, Bantam, 1991.
A Deadly Promise. New York, Bantam, 1992.
Land of Hope. New York, Bantam, 1992.
The Weekend Was Murder! New York, Delacorte, 1992.
Land of Promise. New York, Bantam, 1993.
The Name of the Game was Murder. New York, Delacorte, 1993.
Land of Dreams. New York, Delacorte, 1994.
Shadowmaker. New York, Delacorte, 1994.
A Dangerous Promise. New York, Delacorte, 1994.
Keeping Secrets. New York, Delacorte, 1995.
Spirit Seekers. New York, Delacorte, 1995.
Don't Scream. New York, Delacorte, 1996.
Murdered, My Sweet. New York, Delacorte, 1997.
A Circle of Love. New York, Delacorte, 1997.

Other

Oil and Gas: From Fossils to Fuels, with Hershell H. Nixon, illustrated by Jean Day Zallinger. New York, Harcourt, 1977.
Volcanoes: Nature's Fireworks, with Hershell H. Nixon. New York, Dodd, 1978.
Glaciers: Nature's Frozen Rivers, with Hershell H. Nixon. New York, Dodd, 1980.
Earthquakes: Nature in Motion, with Hershell H. Nixon. New York, Dodd, 1981.
Land under the Sea, with Hershell H. Nixon. New York, Dodd, 1985.

PUBLICATIONS FOR CHILDREN

Fiction

The Mystery of Hurricane Castle, illustrated by Velma Ilsley. New York, Criterion, 1964.
The Mystery of the Grinning Idol, illustrated by Alvin Smith. New York, Criterion, 1965.
The Mystery of the Hidden Cockatoo, illustrated by Richard Lewis. New York, Criterion, 1966.
The Mystery of the Haunted Woods, illustrated by Theresa Brudi. New York, Criterion, 1967.
The Mystery of the Secret Stowaway, illustrated by Joan Drescher. New York, Criterion, 1968.
Delbert, the Plainclothes Detective, illustrated by Philip Smith. New York, Criterion, 1971.
The Mysterious Red Tape Gang, illustrated by Joan Sandin. New York, Putnam, 1974, in paperback as *The Adventures of the Red Tape Gang,* illustrated by Steven H. Stroud, Scholastic, 1983.
The Secret Box Mystery, illustrated by Leigh Grant. New York, Putnam, 1974.
The Mysterious Prowler, illustrated by Berthe Amoss. New York, Harcourt, 1976.
The Boy Who Could Find Anything, illustrated by Syd Hoff. New York, Harcourt, 1978.
Danger in Dinosaur Valley, illustrated by Marc Simont. New York, Putnam, 1978.
Muffie Mouse and the Busy Birthday, illustrated by Geoffrey Hayes. New York, Seabury, 1978, as *Muffy and the Birthday Party,* New York, Scholastic, 1979.
Bigfoot Makes a Movie, illustrated by Syd Hoff. New York, Putnam. 1979.

Casey and the Great Idea, illustrated by Amy Rowen. New York, Dutton, 1980.

Gloria Chipmunk, Star!, illustrated by Diane Dawson. Boston, Houghton, 1980.

If You Say So, Claude, illustrated by Lorinda Bryan Cauley. New York, Warne, 1980.

The New Year's [Halloween, Valentine, Happy Birthday, April Fool, Thanksgiving, Easter, Christmas Eve] Mystery, illustrated by Jim Cummins. Chicago, Whitman, 8 vols., 1979-81.

Kidnapped on Astarr, illustrated by Paul Frame. Champaign, Illinois, Garrard, 1981.

Mysterious Queen of Magic, illustrated by Paul Frame. Champaign, Illinois, Garrard, 1981.

Mystery Dolls from Planet Urd, illustrated by Paul Frame. Champaign, Illinois, Garrard, 1981.

The Spotlight Gang and the Backstage Ghost. Tarrytown, New York, Harlequin, 1981.

The Gift, illustrated by Andrew Glass. New York, Macmillan, 1983.

Magnolia's Mixed-Up Magic, illustrated by Linda Bucholtz-Ross. New York, Putnam, 1983.

The House on Hackman's Hill. New York, Scholastic Inc., 1985.

Maggie, Too, illustrations by Darrel Millsap. San Diego, Harcourt, 1985.

And Maggie Makes Three. San Diego, Harcourt, 1986.

Beats Me, Claude, illustrated by Tracey Campbell Pearson. New York, and London, Viking, 1986.

Fat Chance, Claude, illustrated by Tracey Campbell Pearson. New York, Viking Kestrel, 1987.

Haunted Island. New York, Scholastic Inc., 1987.

Maggie Forevermore. San Diego, Harcourt, 1987.

You Bet Your Britches, Claude, illustrated by Tracey Campbell Pearson. New York, Viking, 1989.

The Haunted House on Honeycutt Street. New York, Dell, 1991.

Honeycutt Street Celebrities. New York, Dell, 1991.

Mystery Box. New York, Dell, 1991.

Watch Out for Dinosaurs. New York, Dell, 1991.

That's the Spirit, Claude. New York, Viking, 1992.

The Statue Walks at Night. New York, Disney Press, 1995.

The Legend of the Lost Mine. New York, Disney Press, 1995.

Backstage with a Ghost. New York, Disney Press, 1995.

Check in to Danger. New York, Disney Press, 1995.

The House Has Eyes. New York, Disney Press, 1996.

No Time for Danger. New York, Disney Press, 1996.

Beware of the Pirate Ghost. New York, Disney Press, 1996.

Catch a Crooked Clown. New York, Disney Press, 1996.

Fear Stalks Grizzly Hill. New York, Disney Press, 1996.

Sabotage on the Set. New York, Disney Press, 1996.

Search for the Shadowman. New York, Delacorte, 1996.

Internet Escapade. New York, Disney Press, 1997.

Bait for a Burglar. New York, Disney Press, 1997.

Picture Books

The Alligator under the Bed, illustrated by Jan Hughes. New York, Putnam, 1974.

The Butterfly Tree, illustrated by James McIlrath. Huntington, Indiana, Our Sunday Visitor, 1979.

Will You Give Me a Dream?, illustrated by Bruce Degen. New York, Four Winds Press, 1994.

When I Am Eight, illustrated by Dick Gackenbach. New York, Dial, 1994.

Other

Five Loaves and Two Fishes: Feeding of Five Thousand for Beginning Readers; John 6:1-15 for Children, illustrated by Aline Cunningham. St. Louis, Concordia, 1976.

Who Is My Neighbor?: The Good Samaritan for Beginning Readers; Luke 10:29-37 for Children, illustrated by Aline Cunningham. St. Louis, Concordia, 1976.

The Son Who Came Home Again: The Prodigal Son for Beginning Readers; Luke 15:11-32 for Children, illustrated by Aline Cunningham. St. Louis, Concordia, 1977.

When God Listens, illustrated by James McIlrath. Huntington, Indiana, Our Sunday Visitor, 1978.

When God Speaks, illustrated by James McIlrath. Huntington, Indiana, Our Sunday Visitor, 1978.

Before You Were Born, illustrated by James McIlrath. Huntington, Indiana, Our Sunday Visitor, 1980.

If You Were a Writer, illustrated by Bruce Degen. New York, Four Winds Press, 1988.

PUBLICATIONS FOR ADULTS

Other

People and Me (textbook), with others. New York, Benefic, 1975.

This I Can Be (textbook), with others. New York, Benefic, 1975.

Writing Mysteries for Young People. Boston, The Writer, 1977.

The Grandmother's Book. Nashville, Abingdon Press, 1979.

*

Biography: Essay in *Something about the Author Autobiography Series,* Volume 9, Detroit, Gale, 1990; essay in *Speaking for Ourselves: Autobiographical Sketches by Notable Authors of Books for Young Adults,* Volume 1, compiled and edited by Donald R. Gallo, National Council of Teachers of English, 1990.

Joan Lowery Nixon comments:

From the time I was very young I wanted to be a writer. In fact, I *knew* I would be a writer. I wrote nearly every day—diary entries, stories, poems—and I used to read, read, read. I began writing short nonfiction articles for magazines while I was still in high school, and at the University of Southern California I majored in journalism. It was later, while I was a busy mother of four young children that I wrote my first book for children and loved the experience. My memories of childhood and teenaged years are vivid, and I write for young people of today through my emotions. While today's problems are different from problems of my generation, the emotions involving fear, uncertainty, joy, sorrow, excitement, the desire to love and be loved remain the same. I was always the optimist, strengthened by hope, and I try to pass along this same hope to my readers.

*   *   *

Joan Lowery Nixon is a prolific writer of books for children at elementary, junior high, and high school levels. She is best known for her fast-paced, ingenious mystery stories and is a three-time winner of the Mystery Writers of America Edgar Allan Poe Award.

Her mysteries for older children are psychological thrillers, involving complicated characterizations and plots that demand the reader's participation in solving the crime. In *The Kidnapping of Christina Lattimore,* Christina and a young reporter set out to prove Christina's innocence when her kidnappers claim that she was an accomplice to their crime. In *The Seance,* what begins as a game, with Lauren and five other girls gathered in a candlelight circle, develops into murder of the participants.

The Spectre is about nine-year-old Julie, an abused child, and the friend she makes in the hospital, seventeen-year-old Dina, a victim of Hodgkins disease. Julie and Dina share feelings of fear and despair, but eventually their support of each other allows them to feel hopeful towards the future.

A Deadly Game of Magic tells about Lisa and her friends caught in a violent storm. The storm leaves them stranded by an old deserted house, strewn with odd tricks and gadgets, the paraphernalia for a practiced magician. Lisa has always dreamed of being a magician; now her life depends on it.

Nixon also writes funny, rollicking books about people, their predicaments, and their relationships. *Beats Me, Claude* is about a happy couple who live quietly in a cabin in the rolling hills of Texas. Shirley attempts to make an apple pie for Claude and ends up using the pie both to capture escaped criminals and to cajole Claude into adopting two deserving orphans.

In quite a different vein, Nixon has written a series of historical novels, *The Orphan Train Quartet.* During the period from 1854 to 1929, the Children's Aid Society sent more than 100,000 children on orphan trains from the slums of New York City to new homes in the West. This out-placing was judged successful and other child welfare groups, such as the New York Foundling Hospital, followed its example. *The Orphan Train Quartet* was inspired by true stories of these children. It follows the six Kelly children, whose poverty-stricken widowed mother sends them West from New York in 1856 because she feels she cannot adequately care for them. The children go to various homes around St. Joseph, Missouri. The books are: *A Family Apart, Caught in the Act, In the Face of Danger,* and *A Place to Belong.*

In *A Place to Belong,* Danny and Peg Kelly feel lucky to be adopted by Alfrid and Olga Swenson. But when Olga dies unexpectedly they fear for their future. Danny comes up with a solution: Alfrid should marry their own mother. This does not come to pass, but another satisfactory solution is found. The book takes place just before the outbreak of the Civil War and critical aspects of a family's history are juxtaposed with those of American history. *The Orphan Train Quartet* offers readers a glimpse of other times in America where young people faced different kinds of family and community crises, as well as similar needs for self-esteem, love, and adventure.

More recently Nixon has written a trilogy, *Hollywood Daughters,* telling the stories of three generations of mothers and daughters who dream and struggle within the glamorous world of Hollywood. *Star Baby, Overnight Sensation,* and *Encore* describe fifty years of Hollywood history, as played out within one family. Gladys Baynes is a beautiful and ambitious woman who does not succeed in a career as a serious actress; she hopes though to achieve success vicariously through her daughter, Abby Grant. Abby subsequently becomes a superstar TV comic. Now comes Abby's daughter, Cassie Martin, who is interested in becoming a serious still photographer. Cassie falls in love with Marc and agrees to play the leading role in his first film. She is sensational. The plots of

these three books are fast-paced, filled with grueling hours of studio work and glittering Beverly Hills play. The reader is pulled from Gladys to Abby to Cassie, and finally to Cassie's children.

Nixon's skillful writing and boundless imagination make young readers want to read on, to find out what surprises wait on the next page and discover if their solutions to her never-ending puzzles are the correct ones. She is also a writer of warmth, understanding young people's serious concerns about self and life, as well as their need for excitement and fun.

—Mary Lystad

NOLAN, Han

Nationality: American. **Born:** Birmingham, Alabama. **Education:** University of North Carolina at Greensboro, B.S. in dance education; Ohio State University, M.A. in dance. **Family:** Married Brian Nolan; two daughters. **Career:** Writer. **Awards:** National Book Award finalist, 1996, for *Send Me Down a Miracle*; *Send Me Down a Miracle* and *Dancing on the Edge* were named to New York Public Library's Books for the Teen Age list; National Book Award for Young People's Literature, 1997, and *Parents'* Choice Storybook Award, for *Dancing on the Edge.* **Address:** c/o Rosemarie Rauch, 525 B St., Ste. 1900, San Diego, California 92101, U.S.A.

PUBLICATIONS FOR YOUNG ADULTS

Fiction

If I Should Die Before I Wake. New York, Harcourt Brace, 1994.
Send Me Down A Miracle. New York, Harcourt Brace, 1996.
Dancing on the Edge. New York, Harcourt Brace, 1997.

*   *   *

Combining historical fiction with fantasy, Han Nolan's powerful first novel *If I Should Die Before I Wake* leaves a lasting impression. The reader is immediately engaged with the main character, Hilary Burke, an angry sixteen-year-old who joins a neo-Nazi gang in an effort to belong. The gang goes on a rampage one night, desecrating the Jewish cemetery and kidnapping a young Jewish boy and locking him in a school locker. Late that same night, a serious motorcycle accident leaves Hilary in a coma. Ironically, she finds herself in a Jewish hospital being cared for by those she professes to hate.

Still in a coma and unable to communicate, Hilary nevertheless retains her hatred of Jews and just about everything else. She senses herself spinning backward in time to find herself a young, thirteen-year-old Polish girl named Chana who is terrorized by the Nazi regime at the onset of World War II and later tries to flee the country. Nolan deftly moves back and forth between the stories of Hilary and Chana, and we learn the details of each of their hard lives. In alternating chapters, each girl tells her own tragic story, and each becomes increasingly aware of the other.

As she becomes more familiar with Chana and her struggle to survive, Hilary begins to change. The memories of Chana that she's been experiencing can't help but affect her, and she begins to reevaluate her own life. The two girls merge into a seemingly single struggle to survive. Hilary awakes from the coma after three days, her life forever changed by what she's experienced through Chana. In a surprise ending, Hilary solves the remaining puzzle of Chana's identity, and the reader is left to ponder that significance. Nolan juxtaposes these seemingly different but strikingly similar lives in a powerful dual narrative that blends history, fantasy, and adolescent desire to simultaneously separate from and connect to the past.

Nolan's second book, *Send Down a Miracle,* was a National Book Award finalist. In this compelling story, Charity Pittman is fourteen years old in Casper, Alabama, where her father is the local preacher. Her mother leaves town to attend a birdcage collectors' convention, but Charity senses there is more to her departure. Charity is further intrigued when Adrienne Dabney arrives in town from New York. An artist and colorful free-spirit, Adrienne has returned to her hometown for a sensory deprivation experiment designed to inspire her creativity.

After Adrienne emerges from her month-long experiment and announces that she has seen Jesus Christ sitting in her wooden chair, the plot catapults forward with the town dividing itself between those eager to believe and those who are convinced it is the work of the devil. People line up to visit the chair and to pray for their own miracles while Charity's father rails against the vision, the gullibility of the townspeople, and Adrienne, whom he proclaims as the antichrist.

Meanwhile, Charity's mother has decided not to return from her convention, and Charity and her younger sister are left to sort it all out. Although Charity is proud to be her father's daughter and convinced he is a good man, she begins to question the wisdom of his way of life. She longs to break away and live her own life and silently understands why her mother has fled.

As Charity watches the antics of the townspeople with more poise than most adults, she gradually learns that for her, the truth lies somewhere in the middle and that religion and life are not always easily defined. She concludes that it is no longer enough to please only her father and that it is people's attempts to find happiness in other things and other people that is giving them difficulty. Charity discovers that the answer is not to run away but to stay and fight to be her own person.

Nolan again examines the struggles of coming of age in her third novel *Dancing on the Edge,* winner of the National Book Award. Miracle McCloy lives with her grandmother Gigi in a world of mystics, Ouiji boards, and seances. At sixteen, Miracle recounts her story from the age of ten to the present. Over and over she hears the story of how she was rescued from her mother's dead body after a tragic accident. She is, indeed, a miracle. Her father, Dane, is a brooding novelist, given to his own compulsions and eccentricities. When he is discovered missing, the family insists that he melted in the midst of a ring of candies. Miracle devotes her life to reconnecting with her father and somehow bringing him back.

Convinced that she is somehow to blame for both her mother's and father's disappearance, Miracle is haunted by what she is not being told. She begins to construct an alternative world that will somehow make up for her own dysfunctional family. With the help of her grandfather, Miracle secretly takes dance lessons. In her passion for dance, Miracle escapes the confusion and pain of daily life. She is driven to be so good that her father would come back to see her perform. Ironically, while dancing Miracle is compelled to injure herself in order to remind herself that she is real. The bruises become the proof. She does not believe in love because you can't touch it, but while dancing, she escapes to a special place where she talks to her father and feels safe.

In part two of the novel, Miracle is severely burned when her clothes catch on fire as she dances in a circle of candles. She wakes up in the hospital, and with the help of a psychiatrist, she begins to find her way back to reality. She discovers the truth about her mother and father and the reason for her grandmother's silence about it. Miracle moves in with her Aunt Casey, and together they learn how to deal with the power of love. By facing the truth, Miracle reclaims her own life. She believes in miracles and now believes in herself, recognizing, after all, that love is the realest thing she has ever known.

—Susan B. Steffel

NORTH, Andrew. *See* **NORTON, Andre.**

NORTH, Anthony. *See* **KOONTZ, Dean R.**

NORTH, Sterling

Nationality: American. **Born:** near Edgerton, Wisconsin, 4 November 1906. **Education:** the University of Chicago, A.B. 1929. **Family:** Married Gladys Buchanan in 1927; one son and one daughter. **Career:** Reporter, 1929-31, and literary editor, 1932-43, Chicago *Daily News;* literary editor, New York *Post,* 1943-49, and New York *World Telegram and Sun,* 1949-56; founding editor, North Star Books, Houghton Mifflin, publishers, Boston, 1957-64. **Awards:** Witter Bynner Poetry award; *Poetry* magazine's Young Poet's Prize; *New York Herald Tribune*'s Spring Book Festival honor book, 1956, for *Abe Lincoln: Log Cabin to White House;* Dutton Animal Book award, New Jersey Institute of Technology Authors award, both 1963, Newbery Honor Book, 1964, Lewis Carroll Shelf award, 1964, Dorothy Canfield Fisher Children's Book award, 1965, Aurianne award, 1965, William Allen White Children's Book award, 1966, Pacific Northwest Library Association Young Readers' Choice award, 1966, Sequoyah Children's Book award, 1966, ALA Notable Book citation, and *Horn Book* honor citation, all for *Rascal: A Memoir of a Better Era;* New Jersey Institute of Technology Authors award, 1965, for *Little Rascal;* New Jersey Institute of Technology Children's Book Writer of the Year award, 1966; Dutton Animal Book award, 1969, for *The Wolfling.* **Died:** 21 December 1974.

PUBLICATIONS FOR YOUNG ADULTS

Fiction

So Dear to My Heart. New York, Doubleday, 1947; London, Odhams Press, 1949.

Rascal: A Memoir of a Better Era, illustrated by John Schoenherr. New York, Dutton, 1963; as *Rascal: The True Story of a Pet Raccoon,* London, Hodder and Stoughton, 1963; abridged edition, as *Little Rascal,* New York, Dutton, 1965; Leicester, Brockhampton Press, 1966.

PUBLICATIONS FOR CHILDREN

The Five Little Bears, illustrated by Clarence Biers and Hazel Frazee. Chicago, Rand McNally, 1935; London, Shaw, 1940.

The Zipper ABC Book, illustrated by Keith Ward. Chicago, Rand McNally, 1937.

Greased Lightning, illustrated by Kurt Wiese. Philadelphia, Winston, 1940.

Midnight and Jeremiah, illustrated by Kurt Wiese. Philadelphia, Winston, 1943.

The Birthday of Little Jesus, illustrated by Valenti Angelo. New York, Grosset and Dunlap, 1952; Manchester, World Distributors, 1953.

Son of the Lamp-Maker: The Story of a Boy Who Knew Jesus, illustrated by Manning Lee. Chicago, Rand McNally, 1956.

The Wolfling, illustrated by John Schoenherr. New York, Dutton, 1969; London, Heinemann, 1970.

Other

Abe Lincoln: Log Cabin to White House, illustrated by Lee Ames. New York, Random House, 1956.

George Washington, Frontier Colonel, illustrated by Lee Ames. New York, Random House, 1957.

Young Thomas Edison, illustrated by William Barss. Boston, Houghton Mifflin, 1958.

Thoreau of Walden Pond, illustrated by Harve Stein. Boston, Houghton Mifflin, 1959.

Captured by the Mohawks and Other Adventures of Radisson, illustrated by Victor Mays. Boston, Houghton Mifflin, 1960.

Mark Twain and the River, illustrated by Victor Mays. Boston, Houghton Mifflin, 1961.

The First Steamboat on the Mississippi, illustrated by Victor Mays. Boston, Houghton Mifflin, 1962.

PUBLICATIONS FOR ADULTS

Novels

Midsummer Madness. New York, Grosset and Dunlap, 1933.

Tiger. Chicago, Reilly and Lee, 1933.

Plowing on Sunday. New York, Macmillan, 1934.

Night Outlasts the Whippoorwill. New York, Macmillan, 1936; London, Cobden Sanderson, 1937.

Seven Against the Years. New York, Macmillan, 1939.

Reunion on the Wabash. New York, Doubleday, 1952.

Poetry

Poems. Chicago, University of Chicago Press, 1925.

Other

The Pedro Gorino: The Adventures of a Negro Sea-Captain in Africa, with Harry Dean. Boston, Houghton Mifflin, 1929; as *Umbala,* London, Harrap, 1929.

The Writings of Mazo De La Roche. Boston, Little Brown, n.d.

Editor, with Carl Kroch, *So Red the Nose; or, Breath in the Afternoon: Literary Cocktails* (recipes). New York, Farrar and Rinehart, 1935.

Being a Literary Map of These United States Depicting a Renaissance No Less Astonishing Than That of Periclean Athens or Elizabethan London, with Gladys North, map by Frederic J. Donseif. New York, Putnam, 1942.

Editor, with C.B. Boutell, *Speak of the Devil: An Anthology of the Appearances of the Devil in the Literature of the Western World.* New York, Doubleday, 1945.

Hurry Spring! New York, Dutton, 1966.

Raccoons Are the Brightest People. New York, Dutton, 1966; as *The Raccoons of My Life,* London, Hodder and Stoughton, 1967.

*

Media Adaptations: *So Dear to My Heart* (film), RKO, 1948; *Rascal: A Memoir of a Better Era* (film), Disney Studios, 1969; (record/cassette), Miller-Brody, 1979.

Manuscript Collection: Boston University Library.

*   *   *

Although Sterling North wrote a considerable body of literature, mostly for young readers, he is primarily known for two of his works, *So Dear to My Heart* (1947) and *Rascal: A Memoir of a Better Era* (1963), with the raccoon Rascal being the most memorable of this gifted writer's creations. So clearly is North in his element when writing stories which bring the essential truths we learn from nature into a context which young readers understand, that even his well-written biographies about notable Americans have been largely ignored. In these, as well as his better known works, however, Sterling North displays such a command of literary technique and a clarity of theme that his writing appeals to a diverse audience, from young readers to adults.

Rascal: A Memoir of a Better Era is somewhat presented as an autobiography, although the techniques of fiction-writing are well in command. The time is the World War I era, the setting rural Wisconsin, and the conflict that of a maturing boy who has lost his mother and is being raised by a gentle but somewhat preoccupied father. Told from the child's perspective, the story allows the reader to see the difficulties and joys of such a life, the loneliness of a child left much on his own and the freedom of this lifestyle which allows him to bring into his home a raccoon kit who, like the child, is prepared to test life's possibilities, to experience its joys, and to deal with its sorrows. For North, however, the parallels go further; in one poignant passage the child narrator refers to his decision to put away his traps, and to forgo the income derived from the suffering of animals. As he says, if nations could bring the killing in

Europe to an end, he could sign—and keep—a pact with the animals who, like his pet raccoon, sought only to live out their lives in natural, secure surroundings. The parallel is profound and only heightens the reader's awareness that the maturing child will keep his oath; nations will not.

Such depth of theme strikes the older reader immediately and emerges from the rich texture of this novel. For the younger reader, the adventures of the child and his pet raccoon are perhaps more fulfilling. In these adventures, however, lie the simpler truths of life. From the moment the narrator takes on the time-consuming responsibility of raising the raccoon kit, the reader sees a bond develop which reveals that the child's maturing process is intact. The raccoon's explorations of the world are those of the engrossed narrator who shares in the adventures of his pet, marveling at the animal's refined instincts and delighting at its lessons, such as learning to overcome a raccoon's instinct to wash its food, rather than losing a second sugar cube to this natural behavior.

The impending crisis of the novel arrives when Rascal passes his companion in the maturing process, and the call of nature—of a mate—overcomes the ties of a yearlong friendship. Even in that crisis, however, a fundamental truth about life emerges, and the narrator takes a further step, releasing his pet despite the overwhelming sense of loss that doing so gives him.

North tries in his biographies of Abraham Lincoln, Thomas Edison, and other notables to point up the same basic moral truths which give *Rascal* and *So Dear to My Heart* their thematic quality. The young reader will find in these works a celebration of curiosity, determination, and gentleness as well as sound history. These basic qualities—a respect for fact and accuracy and a deep appreciation for the struggles of youth—make Sterling North's works especially worthwhile reading for any generation of young people and proper reminders of essential values for adults.

—Gerald W. Morton

NORTON, Andre

Pseudonym for Alice Mary Norton. **Other Pseudonyms:** Andrew North; Allen Weston. **Nationality:** American. **Born:** Cleveland, Ohio, 17 February 1912. **Education:** Western Reserve University, Cleveland, 1930-32. **Career:** Children's librarian, Cleveland Public Library, 1932-50; special librarian, Library of Congress, Washington, D.C., during World War II; editor, Gnome Press, New York, 1950-58. **Awards:** Award from Dutch government, 1946, for *The Sword Is Drawn*; Ohioana Library Juvenile award honor book, 1950, for *Sword In Sheath*; Boys Club of America Medal, 1951, for *Bullard of the Space Patrol,* and Certificate of Merit, 1965, for *Night of Masks*; Hugo award nominations, 1962, for *Star Hunter,* 1964, for *Witch World,* and 1968, for *Wizard's World*; Headliner award, Theta Sigma Phi, 1963; Invisible Little Man award for sustained excellence in science fiction, 1963; Phoenix award, 1975; Gandalf Master of Fantasy award, 1977, for lifetime achievement in fantasy; Andre Norton award, Women Writers of Science Fiction, 1978; Balrog Fantasy award, 1979; Ohioana award, 1980, for body of work; Ohio Women's Hall of Fame, 1981; Fritz Leiber award for work in the field of fantasy, 1983; Lensman award, 1983 and 1987; Nebula Grand Master award for lifetime achievement, 1984; Jules Verne award for work in the field of

Science Fiction, 1984; Daedalus award, 1986; Guest of honor, World Science Fiction Earescon, 1989. **Agent:** Russell Galen, Scovil-Chichak-Qalen Agency.

PUBLICATIONS FOR YOUNG ADULTS

Fiction

The Prince Commands, illustrated by Kate Seredy. New York, Appleton Century, 1934.

Ralestone Luck, illustrated by James Reid. New York, Appleton Century, 1938.

Follow the Drum. New York, Penn, 1942.

The Sword Is Drawn, illustrated by Duncan Coburn. Boston, Houghton Mifflin, 1944; London, Oxford University Press, 1946.

Scarface, illustrated by Lorence Bjorklund. New York, Harcourt Brace, 1948; London, Methuen, 1950.

Sword in Sheath, illustrated by Lorence Bjorklund. New York, Harcourt Brace, 1949; as *Island of the Lost,* London, Staples Press, 1953.

Star Man's Son, 2250 A.D., illustrated by Nicolas Mordvinoff. New York, Harcourt Brace, 1952; London, Staples Press, 1953; as *Daybreak, 2250 A.D.,* New York, Ace, 1954.

Star Rangers. New York, Harcourt Brace, 1953; London, Gollancz, 1968; as *The Last Planet,* New York, Ace, 1955.

At Swords' Point. New York, Harcourt Brace, 1954.

The Stars Are Ours! Cleveland, World, 1954.

Yankee Privateer, illustrated by Leonard Vosburgh. Cleveland, World, 1955.

Star Guard. New York, Harcourt Brace, 1955; London, Gollancz, 1969.

The Crossroads of Time. New York, Ace, 1956; London, Gollancz, 1967.

Stand to Horse. New York, Harcourt Brace, 1956.

Sea Siege. New York, Harcourt Brace, 1957.

Star Born. Cleveland, World, 1957; London, Gollancz, 1973.

Star Gate. New York, Harcourt Brace, 1958; London, Gollancz, 1970.

The Time Traders. Cleveland, World, 1958.

The Beast Master. New York, Harcourt Brace, 1959; London, Gollancz, 1966.

Galactic Derelict. Cleveland, World, 1959.

Storm over Warlock. Cleveland, World, 1960.

The Sioux Spaceman. New York, Ace, 1960; London, Hale, 1976.

Shadow Hawk. New York, Harcourt Brace, 1960; London, Gollancz, 1971.

Ride Proud, Rebel! Cleveland, World, 1961.

Catseye. New York, Harcourt Brace, 1961; London, Gollancz, 1962.

The Defiant Agents. Cleveland, World, 1962.

Lord of Thunder. New York, Harcourt Brace, 1962; London, Gollancz, 1966.

Rebel Spurs. Cleveland, World, 1962.

Key Out of Time. Cleveland, World, 1963.

Judgment on Janus. New York, Harcourt Brace, 1963; London, Gollancz, 1964.

Ordeal in Otherwhere. Cleveland, World, 1964.

Night of Masks. New York, Harcourt Brace, 1964; London, Gollancz, 1965.

The X Factor. New York, Harcourt Brace, 1965; London, Gollancz, 1967.

Quest Crosstime. New York, Viking Press, 1965; as *Crosstime Agent,* London, Gollancz, 1975.

Steel Magic, illustrated by Robin Jacques. Cleveland, World, 1965; London, Hamish Hamilton, 1967; as *Gray Magic,* New York, Scholastic, 1967.

Moon of Three Rings. New York, Viking Press, 1966; London, Longman, 1969.

Victory on Janus. New York, Harcourt Brace, 1966; London, Gollancz, 1967.

Octagon Magic, illustrated by Mac Conner. Cleveland, World, 1967; London, Hamish Hamilton, 1968.

Operation Time Search. New York, Harcourt Brace, 1967.

Dark Piper. New York, Harcourt Brace, 1968; London, Gollancz, 1969.

Fur Magic, illustrated by John Kaufmann. Cleveland, World, 1968; London, Hamish Hamilton, 1969.

The Zero Stone. New York, Viking Press, 1968; London, Gollancz, 1974.

Postmarked the Stars. New York, Harcourt Brace, 1969; London, Gollancz, 1971.

Uncharted Stars. New York, Viking Press, 1969; London, Gollancz, 1974.

Dread Companion. New York, Harcourt Brace, 1970; London, Gollancz, 1972.

Ice Crown. New York, Viking Press, 1970; London, Longman, 1971.

Android at Arms. New York, Harcourt Brace, 1971; London, Gollancz, 1972.

Exiles of the Stars. New York, Viking Press, 1971; London, Longman, 1972.

The Crystal Gryphon. New York, Atheneum, 1972; London, Gollancz, 1973.

Dragon Magic, illustrated by Robin Jacques. New York, Crowell, 1972.

Breed to Come. New York, Viking Press, 1972; London, Longman, 1973.

Forerunner Foray. New York, Viking Press, 1973; London, Longman, 1974.

Here Abide Monsters. New York, Atheneum, 1973.

The Jargoon Pard. New York, Atheneum, 1974; London, Gollancz, 1975.

Lavender-Green Magic, illustrated by Judith Gwyn Brown. New York, Crowell, 1974.

Iron Cage. New York, Viking Press, 1974; London, Kestrel, 1975.

Outside, illustrated by Bernard Colonna. New York, Walker, 1975; London, Blackie, 1976.

The Day of the Ness, with Michael Gilbert, illustrated by Gilbert. New York, Walker, 1975.

Knave of Dreams. New York, Viking Press, 1975; London, Kestrel, 1976.

No Night Without Stars. New York, Atheneum, 1975; London, Gollancz, 1976.

Red Hart Magic, illustrated by Donna Diamond. New York, Crowell, 1976; London, Hamish Hamilton, 1977.

Wraiths of Time. New York, Atheneum, 1976; London, Gollancz, 1977.

Star Ka'at, with Dorothy Madlee, illustrated by Bernard Colonna. New York, Walker, 1976; London, Blackie, 1977.

The Opal-Eyed Fan. New York, Dutton, 1977.

Trey of Swords (short stories). New York, Grosset and Dunlap, 1977; London, Star, 1979.

Star Ka'at World, with Dorothy Madlee, illustrated by Jean Jenkins. New York, Walker, 1978.

Quag Keep. New York, Atheneum, 1978.

Seven Spells to Sunday, with Phyllis Miller. New York, Atheneum, 1979.

Star Ka'ats and the Plant People, with Dorothy Madlee, illustrated by Jean Jenkins. New York, Walker, 1979.

Voorloper, illustrated by Alicia Austin. New York, Ace, 1980.

Star Ka'ats and the Winged Warriors, with Dorothy Madlee, illustrated by Jean Jenkins. New York, Walker, 1981.

Gryphon in Glory. New York, Atheneum, 1981.

Ten Mile Treasure. New York, Pocket Books, 1981.

House of Shadows, with Phyllis Miller. New York, Atheneum, 1984.

Ride the Green Dragon, with Phyllis Miller. New York, Atheneum, 1985.

Elvenblood: An Epic High Fantasy, with Mercedes Lackey. New York, TOR, 1995.

The Monster's Legacy, illustrated by Jody A. Lee. New York, Atheneum, 1996.

The Warding of Witch World. New York, Warner Books, 1996.

Derelict for Trade: A Great New Solar Queen Adventure, with Sherwood Smith. New York, TOR, 1997.

A Mind for Trade: A Great New Solar Queen Adventure, with Sherwood Smith. New York, Tor, 1997.

Fiction as Andrew North

Sargasso of Space. New York, Gnome Press, 1955; as Andre Norton, London, Gollancz, 1970.

Plague Ship. New York, Gnome Press, 1956; as Andre Norton, London, Gollancz, 1971.

Voodoo Planet. New York, Ace, 1959.

Other

Rogue Reynard, illustrated by Laura Bannon. Boston, Houghton Mifflin, 1947.

Huon of the Horn, illustrated by Joe Krush. New York, Harcourt Brace, 1951.

Bertie and May, with Bertha Stenn Norton, illustrated by Fermin Rocker. New York, World, 1969; London, Hamish Hamilton, 1971.

Editor, with Ernestine Donaldy, *Gates to Tomorrow: An Introduction to Science Fiction.* New York, Atheneum, 1973.

Editor, *Small Shadows Creep: Ghost Children.* New York, Dutton, 1974; London Chatto and Windus, 1976.

PUBLICATIONS FOR ADULTS

Novels

Murder for Sale (as Allen Weston, with Grace Hogarth). London, Hammond, 1954; as *Sneeze on Sunday,* by Andre Norton and Grace Allen Hogarth, New York, Tor, 1992.

Secret of the Lost Race. New York, Ace, 1959; as *Wolfshead,* London, Hale, 1977.

Star Hunter. New York, Ace, 1961.

Eye of the Monster. New York, Ace, 1962.

Witch World. New York, Ace, 1963; London, Tandem, 1970.

Web of the Witch World. New York, Ace, 1964; London, Tandem, 1970.

Three Against the Witch World. New York, Ace, 1965; London, Tandem, 1970.

Year of the Unicorn. New York, Ace, 1965; London, Tandem, 1970.

Warlock of the Witch World. New York, Ace, 1967; London, Tandem, 1970.

Sorceress of the Witch World. New York, Ace, 1968; London, Tandem, 1970.

Merlin's Mirror. New York, DAW, 1975; London, Sidgwick and Jackson, 1976.

The White Jade Fox. New York, Dutton, 1975; London, W.H. Allen, 1976.

Velvet Shadows. New York, Fawcett, 1977.

Yurth Burden. New York, DAW, 1978.

Zarsthor's Bane. New York, Ace, 1978; London, Dobson, 1981.

Snow Shadow. New York, Fawcett, 1979.

Iron Butterflies. New York, Fawcett, 1980.

Horn Crown. New York, DAW, 1981.

Forerunner. New York, Tor, 1981.

Moon Called. New York, Simon and Schuster, 1982.

Caroline, with Enid Cushing. New York, Pinnacle, 1982.

Ware Hawk. New York, Atheneum, 1983.

Wheel of Stars. New York, Simon and Schuster, 1983.

Stand and Deliver. New York, Dell, 1984.

Gryphon's Eyrie, with A.C. Crispin. New York, Tor, 1984.

Were-Wrath. New Castle, Virginia, Cheap Street, 1984.

Forerunner: The Second Venture. New York, Tor, 1985.

Flight in Yiktor. New York, Tor, 1986; London, Methuen, 1988.

The Gate of the Cat. New York, Ace, 1987.

Imperial Lady: A Fantasy of Han China, with Susan Shwartz. New York, Tor, 1989.

Black Trillium, with Marion Zimmer Bradley and Julian May. New York, Doubleday, 1990; London, Grafton, 1991.

Dare to Go A-Hunting. New York, Tor, 1990.

The Jekyll Legacy, with Robert Bloch. New York, Tor, 1990.

The Elvenbane. New York, Tor, 1991.

Storms of Victory, with Pauline Griffin. New York, Tor, 1991.

Flight of Vengeance, with P.M. Griffin and Mary H. Schaub. New York, Tor, 1992.

Mark of the Cat. New York, Ace, 1992.

Songsmith, with A.C. Crispin. New York, Tor, 1992.

Golden Trillium. New York, Bantam, 1993.

Redline the Stars, with P.M. Griffin. New York, Tor, 1993.

Short Stories

High Sorcery. New York, Ace, 1970.

Garan the Eternal. Alhambra, California, Fantasy, 1972.

Spell of the Witch World. New York, DAW, 1972; London, Prior, 1977.

The Many Worlds of Andre Norton, edited by Roger Elwood. Radnor, Pennsylvania, Chilton, 1974; as *The Book of Andre Norton,* New York, DAW, 1975.

Perilous Dreams. New York, DAW, 1976.

Lore of the Witch World. New York, DAW, 1980.

Serpent's Tooth. Winter Park, Florida, Andre Norton Ltd., 1987.

Moon Mirror. New York, Tor, 1988.

Wizards' Worlds, edited by Ingrid Zierhut. New York, Tor, 1989.

Other

Editor, *Bullard of the Space Patrol,* by Malcolm Jameson. Cleveland, World, 1951.

Editor, *Space Service.* Cleveland, World, 1953.

Editor, *Space Pioneers.* Cleveland, World, 1954.

Contributor, *Best Science Fiction Stories and Novels, 1955,* edited by T.E. Dikty. Hollywood, Florida, Frederick Fell, 1955.

Editor, *Space Police.* Cleveland, World, 1956.

Contributor, *Swordsmen in the Sky,* edited by Donald A. Wollheim. New York, Ace, 1964.

Contributor, *The Time Curve,* edited by Roger Elwood and Sam Moskowitz. Portland, Maine, Tower, 1968.

Contributor, *Alien Earth and Other Stories,* edited by Roger Elwood and Sam Moskowitz. Macfadden-Bartell, 1969.

Contributor, *Many Worlds of Science-Fiction,* edited by Ben Bova. New York, Dutton, 1971.

Contributor, *Zoo 2000: Twelve Stories of Science-Fiction and Fantasy Beasts,* edited by Jane Yolen. Seabury, 1973.

Contributor, *In Saving Worlds: A Collection of Original Science-Fiction Stories,* edited by Roger Elwood and Virginia Kidd. New York, Doubleday, 1973.

Contributor, *Science-Fiction Adventures from Way Out,* edited by Roger Elwood. Racine, Wisconsin, Western Publishing, 1973.

Contributor, *Flashing Swords! #2,* edited by Lin Carter. New York, Doubleday, 1973.

Contributor, *The Long Night of Waiting by Andre Norton and Other Stories,* edited by Roger Elwood. Santa Fe, New Mexico, Aurora, 1974.

Contributor, *The Gifts of Asti and Other Stories,* edited by Roger Elwood. Crystal Lake, Illinois, Follett, 1975.

Editor, *Baleful Beasts and Eerie Creatures.* Chicago, Rand McNally, 1976.

Contributor, *The DAW Science-Fiction Reader,* edited by Donald A. Wollheim. New York, DAW, 1976.

Contributor, *Flashing Swords! #3: Warriors and Wizards,* edited by Lin Carter. New York, Dell, 1976.

Contributor, *Sisters of Sorcery: Two Centuries of Witchcraft Stories by the Gentle Sex,* edited by Seon Manley and Gogo Lewis. New York, Lothrop, 1976.

Contributor, *Swords Against Darkness II,* edited by Andrew J. Offrett. New York, Zebra, 1977.

Contributor, *Phantasmagoria: Tales of Fantasy and the Supernatural,* edited by Jane Mobley. Homer, Arkansas, Anchor Books, 1977.

Editor, with Robert Adams, *Magic in Ithkar.* New York, Tor, 2 vols., 1985.

Editor, *Tales of Witch World.* New York, Tor, 2 vols., 1987-88.

Editor, *Four from the Witch World.* New York, Tor, 1989.

Editor, with Martin H. Greenberg, *Catfantastic.* New York, DAW, 1989.

Editor, with Ingrid Zierhut, *Grand Master's Choices.* Cambridge, Massachusetts, NESFA, 1989.

Editor, with Martin H. Greenberg, *Catfantastic II.* New York, DAW, 1991.

Contributor of stories to *Fantasy Book* and *Fantastic Universe* (as Andrew North), *Magazine of Fantasy and Science-Fiction, Phantom Magazine, Golden Magazine for Boys and Girls, Worlds of If, Spaceway Science-Fiction,* and *The World of Fantasy.*

*

Media Adaptations: *The Beastmaster* (film), MGM/UA, 1982; *Witch World* (recording); Norton has also authorized numerous *Witch World* items, such as maps, acrylic sculptures, and stationery.

Biography: Entry in *Dictionary of Literary Biography,* Volume 8, Detroit, Gale, 1981; Volume 52, 1986.

Bibliography: *Andre Norton: A Primary and Secondary Bibliography* by Roger C. Schlobin, Boston, Hall, 1980.

Manuscript Collections: Andre Norton Ltd., Winter Park, Florida; George Arents Research Library, Syracuse University, New York.

Critical Studies: Entry in *Contemporary Literary Criticism,* Volume 12, Detroit, Gale, 1980.

*   *   *

One of America's more prolific young adult writers, Andre Norton also ranks as one of the earliest, having started her career in 1934—long before publishers singled out young adults as a specialized market in the 1960s. During her most productive years (1954-85) she averaged three books a year, and most of her books remain in print. Although she has written a number of historical adventures and gothics for adolescents *(Scarface, Ride Proud, Rebel!, The White Jade Fox, The Opal-Eyed Fan,* to name a few), Norton is best known for her science fiction, or as some critics prefer to call it, "science fantasy." In these books she has created a complex universe in which elements of science fiction interact with the kind of supernatural events usually found in fantasy.

Norton's first science fiction book for young adults, *Star Man's Son, 2250 A.D.,* introduces many of the themes that pervade her created universe. On a planet decimated by nuclear war, the descendants of the survivors attempt to make a new life for themselves and avoid the mistakes of the Old Ones. Fors, a young mutant cast out by his tribe, is caught in the middle of a brewing conflict between two other tribes, while the Beast Things from the destroyed cities prey on all the humans. His telepathic cat and a young black warrior from another tribe are his only friends as he seeks his destiny in a ravaged world.

Like Fors, most of Norton's heroes (and her few heroines) are outcasts in their society. Sometimes they are isolated by physical deformities, sometimes by unusual mental powers. Often they are part or wholly of alien blood. Usually orphaned, these heroes strike out on their own across a hostile, alien landscape, pursuing a personal quest even as they are pursued by enemies. Their journey brings them self-knowledge and self-acceptance and generally ends with group acceptance into their true society, which is not always their original one. Sometimes the society in which the hero finds a place for himself is itself isolated in space or time. In *Operation Time Search,* for instance, the hero remains trapped in the past, and the heroine of *Ice Crown* is quite content to be stranded forever on a planet whose medieval culture cuts it off from interstellar contact.

Some of the recurring elements in these novels are survivalism, underground labyrinths, time travel, parallel universes, supernatural powers, mutants, telepathic animals, and ethnic heroes. The animals are usually feline, but Norton has also used telepathic wolverines and dolphins as well as created a number of alien animal species with telepathic powers. Other supernatural powers appear in her protagonists and in alien communities, such as the Wyverns of *Storm Over Warlock.*

The universe Norton has created is a macrocosm of Earth (or "Terra," as she calls the home planet). It contains postwar ghettoes like the Dipple, which appears in several books as the original community from which the hero sets out, and which is a stronghold of the Thieves' Guild, the organized criminals of the future. Keeping an eye on the Guild and its operations is the Patrol, an intergalactic police corps that often appears in the nick of time to rescue the hero. The Free Traders are the licensed merchants who carry goods from planet to planet, and Survey is an elite corps of scientific explorers who map the universe. One recurring theme is the existence of the Forerunners, a mysterious race of star travellers who lived eons before the Terrans and who have left incomprehensible and often powerful artifacts behind on a number of planets. A search for Forerunner treasure provides the plot for a number of Norton's books.

Many of the novels are linked in some way, although few of the links are strong enough to create a series. For example, two of the characters from *Moon of Three Rings* and *Flight in Yiktor* also appear in *Dare to Go A-Hunting,* but each story is independent and the books can be read in any order. A minor character in *Forerunner Foray* is the son of the hero of *Storm Over Warlock.* An early series about Time Agents includes *The Time Traders, Galactic Derelict, The Defiant Agents,* and *Key Out of Time;* although they contain overlapping characters, these books too can be read out of sequence. The "Witch World" series, written for adults, is also of interest to adolescent readers. This series includes *Witch World, Web of the Witch World, Three Against the Witch World, Year of the Unicorn, Warlock of the Witch World,* and *Sorceress of the Witch World.* Although the "Witch World" series is fantasy rather than science fiction and does not seem to be set in the same universe as Norton's science fiction books, many familiar themes and elements appear in the series.

Most of Norton's more recent titles have been co-authored by writers such as Dorothy Madlee, Phyllis Miller, Mercedes Lackey, Susan Shwartz, and P. M. Griffin. These books continue Norton's science fantasy tradition.

—Donna R. White

NÖSTLINGER, Christine

Nationality: Austrian. **Born:** Vienna, Austria, 13 October 1936. **Education:** Attended art school in Vienna, Austria. **Family:** Married in 1959; two daughters. **Career:** Journalist for a Vienna daily newspaper; writer. **Awards:** Friedrich-Boedecker Prize, 1972, for contribution to children's literature; Buxtehuder Bulle award, 1973, for *Fly Away Home*; German Youth Literature Prize, 1973, for *The Cucumber King*; Oesterreichischer Staatspreis fuer Kinder-und Jugendliteratur, 1975, for *Achtung! Vranek sieht ganz harmlos aus,* 1979, for *Guardian Ghost,* and 1987, for *A Dog's Life; The Cucumber King* was selected for the International Board on Books for Young People (IBBY) honor list in the translator's category, 1978; Mildred L. Batchelder award, 1979, for *Konrad*; Kinder-und Jugendbuchpreis der Stadt Wien, 1980, for *Dschi Dsche-i Dschunior; Luke and Angela* was selected as an American

Library Association Notable Book, 1981; Hans Christian Andersen Medal from the IBBY, 1984, for body of work; Children's Book award, City of Vienna, 1987, for *Der geheime Grossvater*; Fourteenth Children's Book Prize of Zurich, 1991, for *Der Zwerg in Kopf.*

PUBLICATIONS FOR YOUNG ADULTS

Novels (with translations from the German by Anthea Bell)

Marrying Off Mother. London, Andersen Press, 1978, Orlando, Florida, Harcourt, 1982; as *Ein Mann fuer Mama,* Hamburg, Germany, F. Oetinger, 1972.

Fly Away Home. New York, F. Watts, 1975; as *Maikaefer, flieg! Mein Vater, das Kriegsende, Cohn und ich,* Weinheim, Germany, Beltz & Gelberg, 1973.

Girl Missing. New York, F. Watts, 1976; as *Ilse Janda, 14,* Hamburg, Germany, F. Oetinger, 1974.

Four Days in the Life of Lisa. New York, Abelard-Schuman, 1977; as *Studentplan,* Weinheim, Germany, Beltz & Gelberg, 1975.

Die unteren sieben Achtel des Eisbergs. Weinheim, Germany, Beltz & Gelberg, 1978.

Luke and Angela. London, Andersen Press, 1979; Orlando, Florida, Harcourt, 1981; as *Luki-live,* Hamburg, Germany, F. Oetinger, 1978.

Pfui Spinne! Weinheim, Germany, Beltz & Gelberg, 1980.

Zwei Wochen im Mai: Mein Vater, der Rudi, der Hansi und ich. Weinheim, Germany, Beltz & Gelberg, 1981.

But Jasper Came Instead. London, Andersen Press, 1983; as *Das Austauschkind,* Germany, 1982.

PUBLICATIONS FOR CHILDREN

Fiction (with translations from the German by Anthea Bell)

Fiery Frederica, illustrated by David McKee. New York, Abelard-Schuman, 1975; as *Die feuerrote Friedrike,* Vienna, Austria, Jugend & Volk, 1970.

The Disappearing Cellar: A Tale Told by Pia Maria Tiralla, a Viennese Nanny, illustrated by Heidi Rempen. New York, Abelard-Schuman, 1975; as *Die Kinder aus dem Kinderkeller: Aufgeschrieben von Pia Maria Tiralla,* Weinheim, Germany, Beltz & Gelberg, 1971.

Mr. Bat's Great Invention, illustrated by F. J. Tripp. London, Andersen Press (London), 1978; as *Mr. Bats Meisterstueck; oder, Die total verjuengte Oma.* Hamburg, Germany, F. Oetinger, 1971.

The Cucumber King: A Story With a Beginning, a Middle, and an End, in Which Wolfgang Hogelmann Tells the Whole Truth, illustrated by Werner Maurer. New York, Abelard-Schuman, 1975; as *Wir pfeifen auf den Gurkenkoenig,* Weinheim, Germany, Beltz & Gelberg, 1972.

Der kleine Herr greift ein, illustrated by Rolf Rettich. Hamburg, Germany, F. Oetinger, 1973.

Sim Sala Bim, illustrated by Wolfgang Zoehrer. Vienna, Austria, Jugend & Volk, 1973.

Achtung! Vranek sieht ganz harmlos aus (title means "Careful! Vranek Seems to Be Totally Harmless"). Vienna, Austria, Jugend & Volk, 1974.

Gugerells Hund, with Hans Arnold. Bethesda, Maryland, Betz, 1974.

Iba de guanz oaman Kinda (poem), woodcut illustrated by Thomas Bewick. Vienna, Austria, Jugend & Volk, 1974.

Das Leben der Tomanis, illustrated by Helme Heine. Cologne, Germany, G. Middelhauve, 1974-76.

Conrad: The Factory Made Boy, illustrated by Frantz Wittkamp. London, Andersen Press, 1976; as *Konrad,* illustrated by Carol Nicklaus, New York, F. Watts, 1977; as *Konrad; oder, Das Kind aus der Konservenbuechse,* Hamburg, Germany, F. Oetinger, 1975.

Der kleine Jo (title means "Little Jo"), illustrated by Bettina Anrich-Woelfel. Lucerne, Switzerland, H. Schroedel, 1976.

Das will Jenny haben, illustrated by Anrich-Woelfel. H. Lucerne, Switzerland, Schroedel, 1977.

Lollipop, illustrated by Angelika Kaufmann. London, Andersen Press, 1982; as *Lollipop,* Weinheim, Germany, Beltz & Gelberg, 1977.

Pit und Anja entdecken das Jahr: Der Fruehling kommt (title means "Pit and Anja Discover the Year: Spring Comes"), illustrated by Bernadette Parmentier. Lucerne, Switzerland, H. Schroedel, 1978.

Pit und Anja entdecken das Jahr: Im Sommer (title means "Pit and Anja Discover the Year: In the Summer"), illustrated by Bernadette Parmentier. Lucerne, Switzerland, H. Schroedel, 1978.

Guardian Ghost. London, Andersen Press, 1986; as *Rosa Reidl, Schutzgespenst,* Vienna, Austria, Jugend & Volk, 1979.

Dschi Dsche-i Dschunior. Vienna, Austria, Jugend & Volk, 1980.

Einer, illustrated by Janosch. Weinheim, Germany, Beltz & Gelberg, 1980.

Brainbox Sorts It Out. London, Andersen Press, 1985; as *Brainbox Cracks the Case,* New York, Bergh, 1986; as *Der Denker greift ein,* Vienna, Austria, Jugend & Volk, 1981.

Gretchen Sackmeier. Hamburg, Germany, F. Oetinger, 1981.

Rosalinde hat Gedanken im Kopf (title means "Rosalinde Has Thoughts in Her Head"). Hamburg, Germany, F. Oetinger, 1981.

Anatol und die Wurschtelfrau. Vienna, Austria, Jugend & Volk, 1983.

Gretchen hat Haenschen-Kummer: Eine Familiengeschichte. Hamburg, Germany, F. Oetinger, 1983.

Jokel, Jula, und Jericho, two volumes, illustrated by Edith Schindler. Weinheim, Germany, Beltz & Gelberg, 1983.

Der geheime Grossvater (title means "The Secret Grandfather"), illustrated by Christine Nöstlinger, Jr. Vienna, Austria, Jugend & Volk, 1986.

A Dog's Life, illustrated by Jutta Bauer. London, Andersen Press, 1990; as *Der Hund kommt!,* Weinheim, Germany, Beltz & Gelberg, 1987.

Echt Susi. Wien, Dachs-Verlag, 1988.

Die nie geschriebenen Briefe der Emma K. Wien, Dachs-Verlag, 1988.

Der gefrorene Prinz, Marchenroman. Weinheim, Beltz & Gelberg, 1990.

Hauhaltsschnecken leben langer. Munchen, DTV, 1991.

Wie ein Ei dem anderen. Weinheim, Beltz & Gelberg, 1991.

Liebe Tochter, werter Sohn. Wien, Jugend und Volk, 1992.

Am Montag ist alles ganz anders. Wien, Jugend und Volk, 1992.

Mit zwei linken Kochloffeln: Ein kleiner Kochlehrgang fur Kuchenmuffel. Wien, Jugend und Volk, 1993.

*

Critical Studies: Entry in *Children's Literature Review,* Vol. 11, Detroit, Gale, 1987, 179-189.

*   *   *

Christine Nöstlinger is probably Austria's most renowned writer of books for young people. Winner of the international Hans Christian Andersen award, her books have been translated into a variety of languages and have proven to be popular wherever they are read. This is not surprising as the themes she writes about are universal and her strong, often anti-authoritarian characters are likely to appeal to young people all over the world.

Her young adult books with a contemporary setting stand comparison with those of Judy Blume and Paula Danziger. In *Marrying Off Mother,* Sue and Julia face a situation with which many young people have to contend: their parents' separation. The girls are sent to live in their grandmother's house, an all-female establishment. Their grandmother is a tyrant, while one of their aunts is neurotically houseproud and the other scatterbrained. Sue and Julia decide that if they cannot get their parents together again (and they do try strenuously to do so), they will have to find a suitable spare male to marry their mother. The events which occur when they try to put this plan into operation often end in farce of the broadest type. The theme of this book is similar to many ''prob-lem'' novels produced for young adults. However, it is told in such a light way that any moralising is conveyed far more subtly than is usual with this kind of book. Young adult readers in a similar situation to the heroines could both sympathise with and laugh gently at Sue and Julia's reactions.

In *Luke and Angela,* the hero returns from a summer school in England with some highly original ideas—such as wearing pyjamas to school. However, Luke's behaviour tests his relationship with Angela, who has previously been his closest friend; and the book, through its use of comedy, raises many issues about friendship. Another interesting feature about this book, and others written by Nöstlinger, is its strong anti-authoritarian streak, particularly in Luke's clashes with his Latin teacher. In English-speaking countries, young adult novels, particularly in recent years, have sidestepped this subject, perhaps to avoid the wrath of parents.

Nöstlinger is most firmly on the side of her adolescent hero as he struggles to take an individual stance.

Another book likely to be of interest to young people deals with exchange visits. In *But Jasper Came Instead* the Mittermeier family is expecting an English boy, Tom, to come on a visit to Vienna. However, Jasper, Tom's younger brother, appears instead and this truculent English boy, who appears to have an aversion to washing, is something of a shock to the staid and conventional Mittermeier parents. It is their daughter Billie who discovers the insecurity which lies at the heart of Jasper's behaviour problems as well as finding strength within herself to stand up to her parents. As with the previous books discussed, the story is told with such a light touch that any didacticism on the author's part is easily subsumed in the narrative.

Fly Away Home is partly autobiographical, tells of the World War II years in Vienna, and was published at a time when writers in other parts of the world (such as Nina Bawden in Great Britain and Esther Hautzig in America) were recounting their war lives through the use of fiction. One thing in common with all these authors is the emotion of the characters. It is the minutiae which count in Christel's life as the Nazis retreat from Vienna and the Russians advance near the end of the war. Christel's father has deserted from the army and has to go into hiding. This situation is made all the more precarious when a group of Russian soldiers commandeers the country villa in which the family is living. Christel makes friends with Cohn, the gentle cook whose behaviour is totally different from the other brutish soldiers. The style of *Fly Away Home* varies from Nöstlinger's normal narrative structure and its short, staccato sentences mirror the urgency of the family's situation almost as in a newsreel.

Young adult readers will gain much from the work of Christine Nöstlinger. The emotions her characters demonstrate are universal and sympathetic to any adolescent, whatever their background. The style of writing is sufficiently central European, and her unique handling of anti-authoritarian situations will undoubtedly be attractive to young adults struggling with these feelings themselves.

—Keith Barker

O

O'BRIEN, E. G. *See* CLARKE, Arthur C(harles).

O'BRIEN, Robert C.

Pseudonym for Robert Leslie Conly. **Nationality:** American.
Born: Brooklyn, New York, 11 January 1918. **Education:** schools
in Amityville, Long Island, New York; Williams College,
Williamstown, Massachusetts, 1935-37; Juilliard School of Music, New York, Columbia University, New York; University of
Rochester, New York, B.A. in English 1940. **Family:** Married
Sally McCaslin in 1943; one son and three daughters. **Career:**
Author and editor. Worked in an advertising agency, 1940; researcher and writer, *Newsweek* magazine, New York, 1941-44;
rewrite man, *Times-Herald*, 1944-46, and *Pathfinder* magazine,
1946-51, both Washington, D.C.; staff member, rising to senior
assistant editor, *National Geographic* magazine, Washington, D.C.,
1951 73. **Awards:** "Children's Books of the Year" citation, Child
Study Association of America, 1971, Lewis Carroll Shelf award,
1972, Newbery Medal, American Library Association (ALA),
1972, runner-up for National Book award, 1972, "Honor Book"
citation, *Boston Globe*-Horn Book, 1972, Mark Twain award,
1973, Young Readers' Choice award, Pacific Northwest Library
Association, 1974, and William Allan White Children's Book
award, 1974, all for *Mrs. Frisby and the Rats of NIMH;* "Best
Young Adult Books" citation, ALA, 1972, for *A Report from
Group 17;* "Children's Books of the Year" citation, Child Study
Association of America, 1975, "Best Young Adults Books"
citation, ALA, 1975, Jane Addams Children's Book award, 1976,
best juvenile novel, Mystery Writers of the America, 1977, "Books
for the Teen Age" citations, New York Public Library, 1980, 1981,
and 1982, and "Honor Book" citation, *Boston Globe-Horn Book,*
all for *Z for Zachariah*. **Died:** 5 March 1973.

PUBLICATIONS FOR YOUNG ADULTS

Fiction

The Silver Crown, illustrated by Dale Payson. New York, Atheneum,
1968; London, Gollancz, 1973.
Mrs. Frisby and the Rats of NIMH, illustrated by Zena Bernstein.
New York, Atheneum, 1971; London, Gollancz, 1972.
Z for Zachariah. New York, Atheneum, 1975; London, Gollancz, 1975.

PUBLICATIONS FOR ADULTS

Novel

A Report from Group 17. New York, Atheneum, 1972; London,
Gollancz, 1973.

*

Manuscript Collection: Kerlan Collection, University of Minnesota, Minneapolis.

Media Adaptations: *Mrs. Frisby and the Rats of NIMH* (record
and cassette), Newbery Award Records, 1972; *Mrs. Frisby and the
Rats of NIMH* (filmstrip with cassette), Miller-Brody, 1973; *The
Secret of NIMH* (motion picture; based on *Mrs. Frisby and the Rats
of NIMH*), Metro-Goldwyn-Mayer/United Artists, 1982; *Mrs.
Frisby and the Rats of NIMH, A Report from Group 17,* and *Z for
Zachariah* are all available as "talking books."

*   *   *

Robert Leslie Conly, using the pseudonym Robert C. O'Brien,
began his writing career for young adults in his late forties, after
spending most of his professional life as a journalist and editor.
Although he wrote only four young adult novels before his death at
age fifty-six, his reputation remains as a significant writer of
science fiction and fantasy, especially for his multiple award
winning *Mrs. Frisby and the Rats of NIMH*. All of his novels have
an adventure/survival core with three of them directly exploring
the nature of evil in man and man's obsession for violence,
destruction, control, and power. However, O'Brien's most creative
and provocative work emerges with the NIMH title as he speculates
on the possibility of new life forms created by man on Earth, and
the irony that these new life forms would have more humane
sensibilities than their human counterpart.

O'Brien's initial novel *The Silver Crown* blends adventure and
survival in a present day American setting with historical allusions
linked to malevolent power, strangely derived from the fifth
century and St. Jerome. A group or sect, who align themselves to
the influence of St. Jerome, perpetrates destructive acts on contemporary society—first with arson and muggings, then with race riots
with the eventual goal to gain control over everybody's minds. The
silver crown, the talisman in the possession of a young girl named
Ellen, can either be used for good or evil according to the mind of
its possessor. The crown becomes the object the sect pursues along
with Ellen, and this becomes the primary action in this lively, albeit
predictable plot.

With the publication of his second work *Mrs. Frisby and the
Rats of NIMH,* O'Brien established himself as a skillful and
significant writer blending elements of traditional animal fantasy

with science fiction. A group of super intelligent rats are developed by rearranging their DNA at the NIMH (National Institute of Mental Health) laboratory. Although the rats are not changed physically, they keep their growing intellectual capacities such as learning to read and to reason from Dr. Schultz and his colleagues. When the rats learn to unlock their cages by reading the instructions for unlatching the doors, their escape from the lab is imminent. Once escaping they must confront more complex issues such as their new identity: "We don't know where to go, because we don't know who we are." As they accept their identity as a new life-form they know they cannot return to being rats living off garbage. At the same time they don't want to depend on humans so they devise "the Plan" which is "to live without stealing" and to grow their own food in their new civilization in a remote forest preserve away from human detection. Human response may be one of fear and loathing which is implied when the scientists from NIMH try to exterminate the rats before they are completely prepared to initiate "the Plan." Compassion, courage, and ingenuity form the moral personality of the rats from NIMH as they help other animals such as the mother mouse Mrs. Frisby in saving the life of one of her children. This novel is saturated with delightful surprises and wonders and probably inspired former Disney animator Don Bluth to create the feature length animated film "The Secret of NIMH" in the early eighties.

In his third novel, *A Report from Group 17,* O'Brien recycles and blends narrative elements from his earlier novels into a cold war atmosphere of political intrigue between the United States and Russia. The evil conspiracy to take over the world in *The Silver Crown* is transposed to the Russians in *A Report from Group 17* as they attempt to contaminate the water supply of Washington, D.C. with mutagens that will eventually render a population indifferent to being taken over by a foreign power. This variation of germ warfare which gradually introduces its effects through the genes of succeeding generations is used by O'Brien in a similar way as that used by the scientist in the NIMH novel. In fact, the name of the former Nazi scientist now working for Russia who coordinates this plan is Schultz, the same name of the scientist at NIMH, although, the character is much more malevolent in *A Report from Group 17*. The plot remains fairly taut since O'Brien once again uses a young female adolescent in peril, this time named Allie Adams, who is captured by the evil scientist Schultz and kept partially sedated with Pentothal and curare. Overall the novel belongs to the cold war spy thriller genre.

O'Brien's last novel *Z for Zachariah,* set in the eastern United States, discloses a world where super powers have exchanged nuclear attacks and only two characters have survived the aftermath. Sixteen-year-old Ann Burden is confronted by the menacing adult John Loomis who, as he wanders about in the life suit he has claimed by killing others, discovers her protected valley that was spared the desolation of the rest of the continent. Through Ann Burden's journals, O'Brien creates macabre and terrifying experiences as Loomis asserts himself initially through sexual innuendos, and ultimately through outright attempts for domination. What shines through this narrative is Ann's resiliency, decency, and humanity in this solid, well-paced, science fiction thriller. Although O'Brien's young adult novel legacy is brief, they are worthy of attention since they confront relevant issues that will be with us well into the twenty-first century.

—Richard D. Seiter

O'DELL, Scott

Nationality: American. **Born:** Los Angeles, California, 23 May 1898. **Education:** Occidental College, Los Angeles, 1919; University of Wisconsin, Madison, 1920; Stanford University, California, 1920-21; University of Rome, 1925. **Military Service:** Served in the United States Air Force during World War II. **Career:** Writer, 1934-89. Formerly worked as a technical director for Paramount and as a cameraman for Metro-Goldwyn-Mayer, 1920s; book editor of a Los Angeles newspaper, 1940's. Established Scott O'Dell award for historical fiction, 1981. Also grew citrus fruit and taught a mail-order course in photoplay writing. **Awards:** Rupert Hughes award, 1960, John Newbery Medal, American Library Association (ALA), Lewis Carroll Shelf award, and Southern California Council on Literature for Children and Young People Notable Book award, all 1961, Hans Christian Andersen award of Merit, International Board on Books for Young People, 1962, William Allen White award, and German Juvenile International award, both 1963, Nene award, Hawaii Library Association, 1964, OMAR award, 1985, and ALA Notable Book Citation, all for *Island of the Blue Dolphins;* Newbery Honor Book, 1967, German Juvenile International award, 1968, and *Horn Book* honor citation, all for *The King's Fifth;* Newbery Honor Book, 1968, ALA Notable Book citation, and *Horn Book* honor citation, all for *The Black Pearl;* Newbery Honor Book, 1971, ALA Notable Book citation, and *Horn Book* honor citation, all for *Sing Down the Moon;* Hans Christian Andersen Medal for lifetime achievement, 1972. "Children's Books of the Year" citations, Child Study Association of America, 1970, for *Sing Down the Moon,* 1972, for *The Treasure of Topo-el-Bampo,* 1974, for *Child of Fire,* 1975, for *The Hawk That Dare Not Hunt by Day,* 1976, for *Zia* and *The 290,* and 1987, for *Streams to the River, River to the Sea: A Novel of Sacagawea;* Freedoms Foundation award, 1973, for *Sing Down the Moon; New York Times* Outstanding Book citation, 1974, and ALA Notable Book citation, both for *Child of Fire;* University of Southern Mississippi Medallion, 1976; ALA Notable Book citation, for *Zia;* Regina Medal, Catholic Library Association, 1978, for body of work; *Focal* award, Los Angeles Public Library, 1981, for "excellence in creative work that enriches a child's understanding of California"; Parents Choice award for Literature, Parents Choice Foundation, 1984, for *Alexandra,* and 1986, for *Streams to the River, River to the Sea;* Scott O'Dell award for Historical Fiction, 1986, for *Streams to the River, River to the Sea;* School Library Media Specialist of Southeastern New York award for contribution to children's literature, 1989; Northern Westchester Center for the Arts award, 1989. **Died:** 15 October 1989.

PUBLICATIONS FOR YOUNG ADULTS

Fiction

Island of the Blue Dolphins. Boston, Houghton, 1960; London, Constable, 1961.
The King's Fifth, illustrated by Samuel Bryant. Boston, Houghton, 1966; London, Constable, 1967.
The Black Pearl, illustrated by Milton Johnson. Boston, Houghton, 1967; London, Longman, 1968.
The Dark Canoe, illustrated by Milton Johnson. Boston, Houghton, 1968; London, Longman, 1969.

Journey to Jericho, illustrated by Leonard Weisgard. Boston, Houghton, 1969.

Sing Down the Moon. Boston, Houghton, 1970; London, Hamish Hamilton, 1972.

The Treasure of Topo-el-Bampo, illustrated by Lynd Ward. Boston, Houghton, 1972.

Child of Fire. Boston, Houghton, 1974.

The Hawk That Dare Not Hunt by Day. Boston, Houghton, 1975.

The 290. Boston, Houghton, 1976; London, Oxford University Press, 1977.

Zia, illustrated by Ted Lewin. Boston, Houghton, 1976; London, Oxford University Press, 1977.

Carlota. Boston, Houghton, 1977; as *The Daughter of Don Saturnino,* London, Oxford University Press, 1979.

Kathleen, Please Come Home. Boston, Houghton, 1978.

The Captive. Boston, Houghton, 1979.

Sarah Bishop. Boston, Houghton, 1980.

The Feathered Serpent. Boston, Houghton, 1981.

The Spanish Smile. Boston, Houghton, 1982.

The Amethyst Ring. Boston, Houghton, 1983.

The Castle in the Sea. Boston, Houghton, 1983.

Alexandra. Boston, Houghton, 1984.

The Road to Damietta. Boston, Houghton, 1985.

Streams to the River, River to the Sea: A Novel of Sacagawea. Boston, Houghton, 1986.

The Serpent Never Sleeps: A Novel of Jamestown and Pocahontas, illustrated by Ted Lewin. Boston, Houghton, 1987.

Black Star, Bright Dawn. Boston, Houghton, 1988.

My Name Is Not Angelica. Boston, Houghton, 1989.

Thunder Rolling in the Mountains, with Elizabeth Hall. Boston, Houghton, 1992.

Other

The Cruise of the Arctic Star, illustrated by Samuel Bryant. Boston, Houghton, 1973.

PUBLICATIONS FOR ADULTS

Novels

Woman of Spain: A Story of Old California. Boston, Houghton, 1934.

Hill of the Hawk. Indianapolis, Bobbs-Merrill, 1947; London, Corgi, 1955.

The Sea Is Red. New York, Holt, 1958.

Other

Representative Photoplays Analyzed: Modern Authorship. Hollywood, Palmer Institute of Authorship, 1924.

Man Alone, with William Doyle. Indianapolis, Bobbs-Merrill, 1953; as *Lifer,* London, Longman, 1954.

Country of the Sun, Southern California: An Informal History and Guide. New York, Crowell, 1957.

The Psychology of Children's Art, with Rhoda Kellogg. San Diego, California, Communications Research Machines, 1967.

*

Media Adaptations: *Island of the Blue Dolphins* (film), Universal, 1964; *The Black Pearl* (film), Diamond Films, 1976; *Island of the Blue Dolphins* (filmstrip/cassette set), Pied Piper Productions, 1965; *Island of the Blue Dolphins* (filmstrip), Teaching Films, 1965; *The Black Pearl, Sing Down the Moon, The King's Fifth, Child of Fire,* and *Zia* (record/cassette/filmstrip sets), Miller-Brody, 1974-77; *Child of Fire* (filmstrip/cassette sets), Random House, 1979; *Zia,* (filmstrip/cassette sets), Random House, 1982; *Island of the Blue Dolphins, The Black Pearl, The Dark Canoe,* and *The King's Fifth* (all available in Braille); *Island of the Blue Dolphins, The King's Fifth, Child of Fire, The Cruise of the Arctic Star, Sing Down the Moon,* and *Zia* (all available as talking books).

Biography: Entry in *Dictionary of Literary Biography,* Volume 52: *American Writers for Children since 1960: Fiction,* Detroit, Gale, 1986; essay in *Authors and Artists for Young Adults,* Volume 3, Detroit, Gale, 1990; essay in *Speaking for Ourselves: Autobiographical Sketches by Notable Authors of Books for Young Adults,* Volume 1, compiled and edited by Donald R. Gallo, National Council of Teachers of English, 1990.

Manuscript Collection: University of Oregon Library, Eugene.

Critical Studies: Entry in *Children's Literature Review,* Detroit, Gale, Volume 1, 1976, Volume 16, 1989; entry in *Contemporary Literary Criticism,* Volume 30, Detroit, Gale, 1984.

*   *   *

Scott O'Dell is a magnificent storyteller. For thirty years, he has woven wondrous tales of human struggle for independence and connectedness. His adolescent heroines and heroes are courageous and strong, and they enrich the world around them. His settings are usually historical, with rich and carefully researched details. O'Dell was raised in California, and most of his novels are set on the West Coast or in the southwestern United States.

His first and most acclaimed book, *Island of the Blue Dolphins,* is set on a remote island in the Pacific, off the coast of California, which was first settled by Indians about 2000 B.C. When the Indians left and sailed to the east in 1835, one twelve-year-old girl was left behind. This is Karana's story; she lives for eighteen years in isolation on the Island of the Blue Dolphins. Year after year she watches the seasons pass and waits for a ship to take her away too. She keeps herself alive by building shelters, making weapons, scavenging for food, and fighting her enemies—wild dogs. This is a story not only of unusual survival, but also of natural beauty and personal discovery. When she is found, Karana is wearing a necklace of black stones, an otter cape, and a cormorant skirt. The girl whose story O'Dell tells actually lived upon the island during this period and is known historically as the Lost Woman of San Nicolas. She is buried on a hill near the Santa Barbara Mission, where she was befriended when brought to California. *Island of the Blue Dolphins* won many awards, among which was the John Newbery Medal.

O'Dell's Seven Serpents Trilogy looks at the Spanish colonization of the Southwest and the conflicts between explorers and native peoples. Consisting of *The Captive, The Feathered Serpent,* and *The Amethyst Ring,* the trilogy focuses on the story of a young

New World missionary in conflict with his compatriots' cruel treatment of Mayan Indians.

Another of O'Dell's highly acclaimed historical novels is *The King's Fifth,* a dramatic account of the steel-helmeted conquistadors of Spain, who strike out into unknown territories—what is now the state of Arizona—to find gold. Their greed causes them to sacrifice blood, honor, life itself, for a lake of gold. The story is passionate, setting white men against red men, Spaniard against Spaniard. No characters are all good or all bad, they are deeply complex, committed, and human.

The sequel to *Island of the Blue Dolphins, Zia* is an excellent novel in its own right, its narrator, fourteen-year-old Zia, lives in a California Mission and wants to rescue her Aunt Karana, left behind on the Island nearly twenty years ago. Though longing to see and help her aunt, Zia fears that Karana might not wish to live at the Mission, might miss the freedom of her own place far away from the white people who tell Indians what to do. Zia and Karana are united and Zia's fears are realized. Karana cannot sleep in a dormitorio. She runs away to the beach, becomes ill, and dies there. Zia feels she dies because she misses her island home.

Alexandra is about a modern girl living in a Florida village. Like O'Dell's historical heroines, Alexandra is strong, courageous, and determined. Under the guidance of her grandfather Stefanos, who in his day was a renowned fisherman, she learns the dangerous craft of the sponge diver. In addition to learning the ways of watermen, she learns about those who use the waters for drug trafficking. She has to decide whether to remain silent or to implicate her close friends.

My Name Is Not Angelica is a stunning novel, set on the Island of St. John in the Atlantic Ocean, at the time of the African slave revolt of 1733-34. Sixteen-year-old Raisha is kidnapped and sold by a West African king to Danish planters on St. John. Raisha becomes a house servant, and the planter's wife calls her "Angelica" because she has the smile of an angel from Heaven. But even as a sheltered house servant, Raisha is caught up in the terrible suffering of other slaves. Many of these slaves at the time of the revolt lose all hope and leap over a cliff to death in the sea. Raisha's husband holds out his strong hand to her so they may leap together. This surprising ending is a compelling portrayal of the human spirit as well as an effective indictment of slavery.

O'Dell is a master of historical fiction. His sense of time and place, and his understanding of human beings and human societies, are truly remarkable. His works will surely be enjoyed by many generations to come.

—Mary Lystad

OKIMOTO, Jean Davies

Nationality: American. **Born:** 14 December 1942. **Education:** Attended DePauw University, 1960-63, and University of Washington, Seattle, 1971-72; Antioch College, M.A. 1977. **Family:** Married 1) Peter C. Kirkman, 1961 (divorced, 1971), two daughters; Joseph T. Okimoto, 1973, two sons. **Career:** High school teacher of remedial reading in Seattle, Washington, 1972-73; University of Washington, Seattle, editorial consultant in child psychiatry, 1973-74; Mount Baker Youth Service Bureau, Seattle, assistant to director, 1974-75; private practice of psychotherapy in

Seattle, from 1975. Seattle Public Schools, volunteer tutor, 1969; Franklin Area School Council, chairman, 1970; Mount Baker Youth Service Bureau, chairman, 1973. Creator and chairperson of Mayor's Reading Awards. **Awards:** Washington State Governor's Writers' Award, 1982, for *It's Just Too Much*; American Library Association Best Book for Young Adults and International Reading Association Choice Book, both 1987, both for *Jason's Women*; Maxwell Medallion for Best Children's Book of the Year, 1993; Parents' Choice Award, two Smithsonian Notable Books. **Address:** 2700 East Madison, Seattle, Washington 98112, U.S.A.

PUBLICATIONS FOR YOUNG ADULTS

Fiction

My Mother Is Not Married to My Father. New York, Putnam, 1979.
It's Just Too Much. New York, Putnam, 1980.
Norman Schnurman, Average Person. New York, Putnam, 1982.
Who Did It, Jenny Lake? New York, Putnam, 1983.
Jason's Women. New York, Atlantic Monthly Press, 1986.
Boomerang Kids. New York, Little Brown, 1987.
Blumpoe the Grumpoe Meets Arnold the Cat. New York, Little Brown, 1990.
Molly by Any Other Name. New York, Scholastic, 1990.
Take a Chance, Gramps! New York, Little Brown, 1990.
A Place for Grace. Seattle, Sasquatch Books, 1990.
No Dear, Not Here. Seattle, Sasquatch Books, 1995.
Talent Night. New York, Scholastic, 1995.
The Eclipse of Moonbeam Dawson. New York, Tor, 1997.

Contributor of short stories to books, including *Visions,* edited by Don Gallo, Delacorte, 1988; and *Connections,* edited by Gallo, Delacorte, 1989; contributor of play to *Hum it Again, Jeremy* (one-act play), published in *Center Stage,* edited by Gallo, Harper, 1990.

*

Biography: Essay in *Speaking for Ourselves, Too* compiled and edited by Donald R. Gallo, National Council of Teachers of English, 1993.

*   *   *

Writing as a psychotherapist as well as a twice-married mother of a blended family, Jean Davies Okimoto brings both theoretical and practical knowledge to the body of literature she has created for young adults. Most of her novels are so-called problem novels and deal with many of the real situations which teens today encounter in their domestic and school environments, including the trauma of divorce, conflict with step siblings, fear of failure, and loss of friends.

Okimoto brings a light, easy style to her books. This, coupled with the fact that most of her books are around one hundred pages in length, makes them very approachable reading material for virtually all intermediate and middle school children. Okimoto's basic approach in her problem fiction is to set up an emotional, adjustment, or some other sort of problem or set of problems in the first chapter and then to take the characters through to the resolution of those difficulties. Occasionally, Okimoto has a tendency to allow her fiction to become subservient to her psychotherapeutic interests; consequently, at times one gets the feeling that the story has been created as a means of showcasing a problem, and then the story begins to sound like a case study. Fortunately, the author keeps a fairly tight rein on these tendencies, and the majority of her fiction avoids the case-study pitfalls.

In her first novel, *My Mother Is Not Married to My Father,* Okimoto begins setting the problem up in the first sentence of the first chapter: "I knew something was wrong." In the ninety-odd pages which follow the opening, Okimoto gets the parents divorced, has the protagonist (eleven-year-old Cynthia) resolve her fears that the divorce was all her fault, pairs the father off with a new girlfriend, and ends with the mother (a self-employed potter) announcing her engagement to a seemingly ideal mate, an earth-sensitive medical doctor.

In *It's Just Too Much,* a sequel to *My Mother Is Not Married to My Father,* Okimoto has Cynthia resolving her adjustment problems to blended-family living, particularly her resentment of what she perceives to be the favored treatment received by her two step-siblings, who visit on weekends. To this domestic mix is added Cynthia's embarrassment over being a no-bra adolescent in a school full of girls who are wearing bras.

In one of her more ambitious undertakings, *Take A Chance, Gramps!,* Okimoto attempts—with varying degrees of success—to link the adjustment problems of adolescence with the adjustment problems of aging. Janie, the protagonist, has always relied on her best friend Alicia in all social situations, and when she learns that Alicia is moving to another town on the eve of her first day in junior high school, she feels helpless and dejected. These feelings are veritable mirror images of the feelings her grandfather has been having since the death of his wife. "Gramps" now lives with Janie and her family but has become a virtual recluse, and everything he says is garbled beyond recognition as a result of his not wearing his false teeth. The book explores the relationship between these two characters and shows how they are able to help each other overcome their fears and begin enjoying life. At her mother's encouragement, Janie talks Gramps into taking an outing downtown where they happen upon a senior citizens' dance; it is, they learn, a weekly affair. Gramps is taken by the vision of all these older people having fun but is embarrassed because he does not have his teeth in. So he and Janie plan a return trip, complete with teeth. One thing leads to another, and the two finally meet and develop romantic interests in an elderly woman and her grandson who comes regularly to the dances. In the meantime, Gramps has told Janie that if she wants to develop friends on her own at school without Alicia, she has to extend herself. So she devises a plan whereby she forces herself to say "Hi" to every third person she meets in the hall. Sure enough, it works. Before the first term is over Janie has become popular enough to be elected to the student council.

In her more recent problem novels (*Jason's Women* and *Molly by Any Other Name*), Okimoto addresses the adjustment difficulties faced by Asian Americans and weaves in a variety of other problems not related to Asian culture, such as adoption and death.

The concerns which Okimoto identifies in her novels are real enough; however, her determination to sew everything up neatly and produce a happy ending results in her plots becoming fairly predictable, even if they are well-rendered and enjoyable. The result is a diminution of the tension that is needed to drive a strong piece of fiction. To her credit, Okimoto does present viable solutions to many problems teens are likely to encounter during the arduous process of growing up. Many adolescents experiencing adjustment problems will find welcome solace in the pages of Okimoto's fiction.

Perhaps Okimoto's finest piece of writing is not a problem-novel per se, but a humorous slice-of-life novel (*Norman Schnurman, Average Person*) which details the exploits of a sixth-grade boy who is trying to find his own identity within the towering shadow of his father, the former star running back of the University of Washington's football team. The book's protagonist, Norman Schnurman, is more interested in scavenging in junk stores than in playing football. On one of his junk store outings, he finds a bare-chested Hawaiian hula-doll lamp with light bulbs for breasts. He and his best friend, P.W., devise an after-school peep show featuring the doll, a poster of a girl in a wet tee shirt, and various other artifacts. The humor which ensues from this situation is good-natured and infectious; it is representative of the consistently high quality of writing to be found in the rest of the book. The character development in this novel is perhaps the strongest in her writing to date, with the relationship between Norman and P.W. being particularly well realized.

In 1983 Okimoto stepped out of her problem-novel persona entirely to write a young-adult mystery/romance, *Who Did It, Jenny Lake?* The plot of the mystery is well crafted, and there are enough red herrings to keep even a die-hard Agatha Christie fan jumping to wrong conclusions in an effort to figure out whodunit. However, for the romance part of the book, the author seems to have resorted to the Sweet Valley High school of fiction writing wherein every girl is as cute as a button and every guy is a bronze god. It is rather as if Barbie and Ken have gone sleuthing.

Okimoto's problem novels should be high on anyone's list who is counseling middle schoolers through adjustment problems related to relationships in the home or school setting. The books are generally well written, and, because of their sympathetic and insightful treatment of adolescent problems, they are excellent bibliotherapeutic tools. The books which are not aimed quite so obviously at psychotherapeutic problem solving are more interesting as pieces of literature and will have broader appeal among young adult readers.

—Bill Buchanan

ONEAL, Zibby

Nationality: American. **Born:** Elizabeth Bisgard in Omaha, Nebraska, 17 March 1934. **Education:** Stanford University, 1952-55; University of Michigan, B.A. 1970. **Family:** Married Robert Moore Oneal in 1955; one daughter and one son. Lecturer in English, University of Michigan, Ann Arbor, 1976-85. Member of board of trustees, Greenhills School, Ann Arbor, 1975-79. **Awards:** Friends of American Writers award, 1972, for *War Work;* "Notable Book" citations and "Best Books for Young Adults" citations, American Library Association, 1980, for *The Language of Goldfish,* 1982, for *A Formal Feeling,* and 1985, for *In Summer Light;* "Best Books of the Year" citation, *New York Times,* 1982, and Christopher award, 1983, both for *A Formal Feeling; Horn Book* Honor Book, and *Boston Globe/Horn Book* award, both 1986, both for *In Summer Light.* **Address:** 501 Onondaga St., Ann Arbor, Michigan 48104, U.S.A.

PUBLICATIONS FOR YOUNG ADULTS

Fiction

War Work, illustrated by George Porter. New York, Viking, 1971.
The Language of Goldfish. New York, Viking, 1980; London, Gollancz, 1987.
A Formal Feeling. New York, Viking, 1982; London, Gollancz, 1983.
In Summer Light. New York, Viking, 1985.

Other

Grandma Moses: Painter of Rural America, illustrated by Donna Ruff. New York, Viking, 1986.

PUBLICATIONS FOR CHILDREN

Fiction

The Improbable Adventures of Marvelous O'Hara Soapstone, illustrated by Paul Galdone. New York, Viking, 1972.
Turtle and Snail, illustrated by Margot Tomes. Philadelphia, Lippincott, 1979.
Maude and Walter, illustrated by Maxie Chambliss. New York, Lippincott, 1985.
A Long Way to Go, illustrated by Michael Dooling. New York, Viking, 1990.

*

Biography: Entry in *Sixth Book of Junior Authors and Illustrators,* edited by Sally Holmes Holtze, New York, H.W. Wilson, 1989; essay in *Speaking for Ourselves: Autobiographical Sketches by Notable Authors of Books for Young Adults,* Volume 1, compiled and edited by Donald R. Gallo, National Council of Teachers of English, 1990.

Manuscript Collections: Kerlan Collection, University of Minnesota, Minneapolis.

Critical Studies: Entry in *Children's Literature Review,* Volume 13, Detroit, Gale, 1987; entry in *Contemporary Literary Criticism,* Volume 30, Detroit, Gale, 1984.

*   *   *

Zibby Oneal is most noted for her three young adult novels, *The Language of Goldfish, A Formal Feeling,* and *In Summer Light.*

Though each book is a distinct entity, they share common threads. There is a female protagonist in each book whose struggle to find out who she is and what her place in the world will be is the focus of the book. Art also plays a major role in two of the books, and images of color, line, and shape abound in all three of these novels. Though there is the expected misconnection between the protagonist and the adults in her life, each has a supportive sibling who ameliorates the sense of isolation. Oneal also makes use of flashback, which allows the reader to gain a context for the protagonists' ordeals. Each book is one of intense conflict, though there is a coolness of style that permeates them; the reader watches as if at a play, and ultimately applauds the resolution.

For Carrie, in *The Language of Goldfish,* growing up is very hard and she fights the changes that are happening to her body and to her emotions; she can't seem to fit in anywhere. Carrie and her sister had enjoyed a secret language that they used with a goldfish in the pond in their yard, which becomes a symbol of the aspects of childhood that Carrie wants to remain the same. She wants nothing to change, while her sister Moira is eagerly accepting maturity and considers their secret language to be a thing of the past. This powerful internal struggle causes Carrie anxiety attacks and she attempts suicide. *The Language of Goldfish* reflects the trauma of growing up that many young adults face. The feeling of being on the outside, of having no one to talk to who understands the sense of isolation and fear, is paramount in the book. The use of rich metaphor in descriptive passages and short sentences in dialogue heightens the sensation of personal isolation within a vibrant world. The only device that doesn't work is the image of the island in the middle of the pond. It plays a central role as the metaphor for Carrie's anguish, yet the image keeps slipping and is never fully recognized.

Emily Dickinson wrote "After great pain, a formal feeling comes," which functions as the metaphor for Oneal's second novel. Anne is home from boarding school and is still trying to come to terms with the sudden death of her mother the year before, and the unexpected remarriage of her father. She runs compulsively in an attempt to forget, and as the book progresses it becomes obvious that she has repressed a great many incidents of her relationship with her mother as well as the attendant emotions. Oneal maintains a formal feeling in images such as Anne perceiving everyone as being on the other side of a glass pane, and in the repetition of the feeling that to lose control is the worst thing possible. Oneal makes excellent use of detail and creates suspense by using small incidents to build to the climax. This is a powerful novel that probes human emotions with insight and an elegant style.

A modern rendition of the fairy tale of Sleeping Beauty, *In Summer Light* is the story of Kate, a young woman forced by a bout of mono to spend her summer at her parents' island home, where a conflict with her artist father and her lack of understanding of her mother fosters a feeling of oppression. Kate finally wins release when a visiting graduate student, there to catalog her father's work, encourages her to resume her painting. Oneal once again uses the elements of conflict with a parent, a sense of separateness, the need to be liked, and the need to please. She has also made use of the image of an island, and color flows throughout the story. There is a warmth to this book that is reflected in the hot summer setting as well as in the relationships of the characters.

Oneal has carved a niche for herself in young adult literature. Though her books are about the travails of adolescents, they are written with elegance and style and transcend the popular offerings that come with monotonous regularity from so many authors within this genre.

—M. Jean Greenlaw

O'NEILL, Judith (Beatrice)

Nationality: Australian. **Born:** Judith Lyall in Melbourne, Victoria, 30 June 1930. **Education:** Mildura High School, Victoria, 1942-47; University of Melbourne (Derham prize, 1950; Rotary Foundation fellowship, 1952), 1948-52, B.A. (honors) in English 1951, M.A. in English 1952; University of London (Story-Miller prize, 1953), 1952-53, postgraduate certificate in education 1953. **Family:** Married John Cochrane O'Neill in 1954; three daughters. **Career:** Tutor in English, University of Melbourne, 1954-56 and 1960-62; tutor, Open University, Cambridge, England, 1971-72; English teacher, St. Mary's School, Cambridge, 1973-82; freelance writer, since 1982. **Awards:** Third prize, Rigby Anniversary Literary Contest (Australia), 1982, for *Jess and the River Kids;* shortlisted for Australian Children's Book Council award, 1989, for *Deepwater;* shortlisted for Carnegie award and *Guardian* Children's Fiction award, 1993, for *So Far from Skye.* **Agent:** A.P. Watt Ltd., 20 John Street, London WC1N 2DL, England. **Address:** 9 Lonsdale Terrace, Edinburgh EH3 9HN, Scotland.

PUBLICATIONS FOR YOUNG ADULTS

Fiction

Jess and the River Kids. London, Hamish Hamilton, 1984.
Stringybark Summer, illustrated by Valerie Littlewood. London, Hamish Hamilton, 1985.
Deepwater. London, Hamish Hamilton, 1987.
The Message. London, Hamish Hamilton, 1989.
So Far from Skye, London, Hamish Hamilton, 1992.
Hearing Voices. London, Hamish Hamilton, 1996.
Spindle River. Cambridge, Cambridge University Press, 1998.

Other

Martin Luther. London, Cambridge University Press, 1975; Minneapolis, Lerner, 1979.
Transported to Van Diemen's Land: The Story of Two Convicts. London, and New York, Cambridge University Press, 1977.

Critical Studies

Editor, *Critics on Keats.* London, Allen & Unwin, 1967; Coral Gables, Florida, University of Miami Press, 1968.
Editor, *Critics on Charlotte and Emily Brontë.* London, Allen & Unwin, and Carol Gables, Florida, University of Miami Press, 1968.

Editor, *Critics on Pope.* London, Allen & Unwin, and Carol Gables, Florida, University of Miami Press, 1968.
Editor, *Critics on Jane Austen.* London, Allen & Unwin, and Carol Gables, Florida, University of Miami Press, 1969.
Editor, *Critics on Blake.* London, Allen & Unwin, and Carol Gables, Florida, University of Miami Press, 1970.
Editor, *Critics on Marlowe.* London, Allen & Unwin, and Carol Gables, Florida, University of Miami Press, 1970.

*

Judith O'Neill comments:

I am an Australian, but for thirty years I have lived in Britain. My stories are often set in Australia and in the past, drawing on my own childhood and on the childhoods of my parents, grandparents, and great-grandparents. *Spindle River* is a new departure. It is set in Scotland in 1819, at robert Owen's famous cotton mills at New Lanark. I enjoy writing for young adults because I so clearly remember my own years as a teenager with their mixture of hope, excitement and anguish. I am working on the filmscript of *So Far from Skye.*

*   *   *

Judith O'Neill's family history is particularly relevant to her writing. Her great-great grandparents were among the crofters who emigrated from the Isle of Skye in Scotland to Victoria, Australia, in the "famine clearances" of 1852. O'Neill was born and brought up in Australia and she uses her own experiences and those of her ancestors for much of the background of her novels, which are vivid portrayals of life in Australia.

The novels are all set in the past, and although the setting is always important, historical details are so deftly woven into the whole, they can seem incidental to the story from time to time. O'Neill writes with strong feeling about her subjects making her books quite compelling. She brings the past alive and makes the reader feel as if he or she is learning something about life in another country, and another time. The stories all deal with family relationships, friendships, and the domestic details that are part of everyday life, which makes them particularly accessible to young adults. They chronicle the type of adventures and dramas that adolescents identify with and enjoy vicariously, and they end happily in the safety and warmth of loving families.

Two of O'Neill's earlier novels, *Stringybark Summer* and *Jess and the River Kids,* are aimed at younger adolescents. They are both straightforward adventure stories peopled with close-knit, happy, hard-working families, who live tough lives in the outback. *Stringybark Summer,* set in turn-of-the-century Australia, is the story of Sophie, the only daughter of a farming couple, who is sent to stay with her aunt's family miles away on a sawmill, while her mother is having another baby. She goes reluctantly but ends up enjoying herself as she joins a large, rather chaotic family and their work. The children, Sophie's cousins, run free, watching the logging, helping with the horses, and generally being part of the community. Various episodes, such as getting a sick baby to the doctor in the middle of a stormy night, or saving a horse that has been bitten by a snake, will have readers captivated throughout this realistic portrayal of life in Australia. Progress is at the forefront of the novel, too, when the steam train is brought in to replace the horses, with disastrous consequences. Sophie learns a lot about herself and understands why her father has been so sullen and depressed; her older brother was killed at the age of six months when he was kicked by a horse accidentally. Sophie returns home to see her new baby brother and finds her father a changed man, enthusiastically looking forward to the future.

Jess and the River Kids, is set during the World War II, although this impinges little on the events of the story. The real story centres around Jess and the two boys she meets by the river. The boys' father, a gold prospector, and mother are away at the time, and they live in a houseboat, next to a deaf old lady, Lizzie. The three spend a fairly ordinary summer playing games, camping out, and listening to Lizzie's tales of her past, until their boat is broken into and a golden nugget brooch is stolen. In the process Lizzie's houseboat is set alight and cast off into the river and the children must rescue her from the burning boat.

The Message, features Don, whose father is off fighting in New Guinea, and who feels ignored and unappreciated at home. He runs away and finds himself in a strange town with no money, where he is befriended by Sal and Gray, who take him back to their community, Arcady. Don gradually realises there is something strange about the group. They keep talking about the good Waves that they believe control events, bringing people to them and making things happen, and they believe that the radio news bulletin contains a special message just for them. But the whole thing is beginning to go sour; several of the group's leading members have left, or leave shortly after Don arrives, and the community that was founded on truth and trust is being destroyed by suspicion and deceit. They have been remarkably adept in illegally printing petrol coupons, thinking they were helping the war effort. Don manages to escape as the police find out about the forgery and is reunited with his family, having learnt a few lessons about himself and life in the process. This is an extremely thought-provoking book, which raises some interesting questions about the problems of such alternative religious cults founded on the strong beliefs of one charismatic leader.

In *Deepwater,* O'Neill uses World War I as an integral part of the story. The families who live in the small farming community of Deepwater in the Australian bush are all touched by the outbreak of war. One by one the eldest sons go off to fight, while at home the farmers are facing the worst drought in years, which is threatening to ruin many of them. When Charlotte's elder brother enlists she has to give up the idea of going away to high school and do her brother's share of the farmwork. Then a woman teacher comes to the school and takes a very jingoistic stance on the war. An anti-German feeling develops against the Henschke family causing bitterness, distress, and chaos in what was a close community. Even with this sort of subject O'Neill manages to make "good" prevail in the form of Charlotte and her family who are determined that the community must survive. Ideas of what nationalism and patriotism actually mean are played out and the final ghastly tragedy of Gallipoli touches everyone.

In *So Far from Skye,* O'Neill tells her own family history and incorporates a little-known story. It is the account of the crofting families who were forcibly rounded up and sent to Australia after the famines in the Highlands of Scotland in 1852. Bewildered, half-starved, badly clothed and dirty, many speaking only the Gaelic,

they were transported on ships to begin new lives working for Australian farmers. Hundreds died on the long voyage, but for those who survived it was a complete change of lifestyle, from the harsh weather and subsistence on the tiny island of Skye to the blistering heat, strange animals, the struggle with a new language, and the vast distances of the Australian outback. This is a very moving account of the long, painful journey from one culture to another. Plenty of adventure on the voyage makes for exciting reading.

Not surprisingly she has written a sequel to this family history in *Hearing Voices.* This moves rapidly into the present and hinges on a grand family reunion of all the descendants of the MacDonald family who were sent to Australia all those years ago. One family has moved back to Scotland and the eldest son, Malcolm, is sent to the reunion. It is an interesting device that O'Neill uses to do two things. Firstly, she pieces together the story of what happened to the MacDonalds when they started their new lives in Australia by way of memories and evidence found in letters. Then there is a secondary plot and intrigue when Malcolm is kidnapped and we discover why his family returned to Scotland and why his father could not come back to Australia. Instrumental in solving the mysteries is the family gift of second sight that has been handed down from Morag to Eileen. The issues at the heart of the story are, once again, relationships, divided loyalties and the strength of family ties.

In all her novels, O'Neill captures the feelings, fears and hopes of the people. Their overwhelming spirit and bravery shine through and their strong faith in God and an intense commitment to family and friends enable them to weather the fiercest storms and come through together, ready to make the best of what life has to offer them.

—Fiona Lafferty

ORGEL, Doris (née Adelberg)

Pseudonym: Also writes as Doris Adelberg. **Nationality:** American. **Born:** Vienna, Austria, 15 August 1929; emigrated to the United States, 1940. **Education:** Radcliffe College, Cambridge, Massachusetts. 1946-48; Barnard College, New York, B.A. (cum laude) 1950 (Phi Beta Kappa). **Family:** Married Shelley Orgel in 1949; two sons and one daughter. **Career:** Author and translator of children's books. Worked for magazine and book publishers, 1950-55; taught writing workshops, Bridgeport University and Fairfield University, both Connecticut; frequent contributor, *Cricket Magazine;* children's book reviewer, *New York Times.* **Awards:** Lewis Carroll Shelf award, 1960, for translation of *Dwarf-Long-Nose; Sarah's Room* was named one of *New York Times* best 100 books, 1963; *Book World* Children's Spring Festival First Prize in picture book division, 1972, for *Little John;* American Library Association Notable Book award, for *A Certain Magic; New York Times* Best Illustrated Book award, for *Merry, Merry Fibruary;* Child Study Association award, Golden Kite Honor Book award, American Library Association Notable Book award, all 1978, and Association of Jewish Libraries award, 1979, all for *The Devil in Vienna.* **Agent:** Writers House Inc., 21 West 26th Street, New York, New York 10010, U.S.A.

PUBLICATIONS FOR YOUNG ADULTS

Fiction

The Mulberry Music, illustrated by Dale Payson. New York, Harper, 1971.

A Certain Magic. New York, Dial Press, 1976.

The Devil in Vienna. New York, Dial Press, 1978; London, Simon and Schuster, 1989.

Risking Love. New York, Dial Press, 1985.

PUBLICATIONS FOR CHILDREN

Fiction

Sarah's Room, illustrated by Maurice Sendak. New York, Harper, 1963; London, Bodley Head, 1972.

Cindy's Snowdrops, illustrated by Ati Forberg. New York, Knopf, 1966; London, Hamish Hamilton, 1967.

Cindy's Sad and Happy Tree, illustrated by Ati Forberg. New York, Knopf, 1967.

In a Forgotten Place, illustrated by James McMullan. New York, Knopf, 1967.

Whose Turtle?, illustrated by Martha Alexander. Cleveland, World, 1968.

On the Sand Dune, illustrated by Leonard Weisgard. New York, Harper, 1968.

Merry, Rose, and Christmas-Tree June, illustrated by Edward Gorey. New York, Knopf, 1969.

Next Door to Xanadu, illustrated by Dale Payson. New York, Harper, 1969; as *Next-Door Neighbors,* 1979.

Phoebe and the Prince, illustrated by Erik Blegvad. New York, Putnam, 1969.

The Uproar, illustrated by Anita Lobel. New York, McGraw Hill, 1970.

Bartholomew, We Love You!, illustrated by Pat Grant Porter. New York, Knopf, 1973.

My War with Mrs. Galloway, illustrated by Carol Newsom. New York, Viking Kestrel, 1985.

Whiskers Once and Always, illustrated by Carol Newsom. New York, Viking Kestrel, 1986.

Midnight Soup and a Witch's Hat, illustrated by Carol Newsom. New York, Viking Kestrel, 1987.

Crack in the Heart. New York, Fawcett, 1989.

Starring Becky Suslow, illustrated by Carol Newsom. New York, Viking Kestrel, 1989.

Nobodies and Somebodies. New York, Viking Press, 1991.

The Mouse Who Wanted to Marry, illustrated by Holly Hannon. New York, Bantam, 1993.

Don't Call Me Slob-o, illustrated by Bob Dorsey. New York, Hyperion Books for Children, 1996.

Friends to the Rescue, illustrated by Bob Dorsey. New York, Hyperion Books for Children, 1996.

The Princess and the God. New York, Orchard Books, 1996.

Poetry

Grandma's Holidays (as Doris Adelberg), illustrated by Paul Kennedy. New York, Dial Press, 1963.

Lizzie's Twins (as Doris Adelberg), illustrated by N.M. Bodecker. New York, Dial Press, 1964.

The Good-byes of Magnus Marmalade, illustrated by Erik Blegvad. New York, Putnam, 1966.

Merry, Merry Fibruary, illustrated by Arnold Lobel. New York, Parents' Magazine Press, 1977.

Other (retellings)

Translator, *Dwarf-Long-Nose,* by Wilhelm Hauff, illustrated by Maurice Sendak. New York, Random House, 1960; London, Bodley Head, 1979.

The Tale of Gockel, Hinkel, and Gackeliah, illustrated by Maurice Sendak. New York, Random House, 1961.

Schoolmaster Whackwell's Wonderful Sons: A Fairy Tale, illustrated by Maurice Sendak. New York, Random House, 1962.

The Heart of Stone: A Fairy Tale, illustrated by David Levine. New York, Macmillan, and London, Collier Macmillan, 1964.

The Story of Lohengrin, The Knight of the Swan, illustrated by Herbert Danska. New York, Putnam, 1966.

A Monkey's Uncle, illustrated by Mitchell Miller. New York, Farrar Straus, 1969.

Translator, *The Enchanted Drum,* by Walter Grieder, illustrated by Walter Grieder. New York, Parents' Magazine Press, 1969.

Translator, *The Grandma in the Apple Tree,* by Mira Lobe, illustrated by Judith Gwyn Brown. New York, McGraw Hill, 1970.

Baron Munchausen: Fifteen Truly Tall Tales, illustrated by Willi Baum. Reading, Massachusetts, Addison Wesley, 1971.

The Child from Far Away, illustrated by Michael Eagle. Reading, Massachusetts, Addison Wesley, 1971.

Little John, illustrated by Anita Lobel. New York, Farrar Straus, 1972.

Godfather Cat and Mousie, illustrated by Ann Schweninger New York, Macmillan, 1986.

Next Time I Will: An Old English Tale, illustrated by Betsy Day. New York, Bantam, 1993.

The Flower of Sheba, with Ellen Schecter, illustrated by Laura Kelly. New York, Bantam, 1994.

Translator, *Nero Corleone: A Cat's Story,* by Elke Heidenreich, illustrated by Quint Buchholz. New York, Viking, 1997.

*

Manuscript Collections: Kerlan Collection, University of Minnesota, Minneapolis.

Doris Orgel comments:

As the field of children's books becomes increasingly mass-market-driven, gimmicky and reductive, I feel grateful that it remains possible to write out of inwardness and singularity, and still hope to stir responses in individual children.

*   *   *

Doris Orgel's writing for young adults encompasses two very different historical and social settings: Austria in the 1930s, and the United States in the 1980s, but her work is more united thematically than one might imagine at first glance, namely by her characters' coming to terms with loss, fear, and painful love. Through her fiction, Orgel has made a major contribution to understanding the destructive effects of anti-Semitism and fascism in Europe in this century. Her realistic works set in America also add to her list of valuable contemporary novels for young adults.

Born Doris Adelberg in Vienna, Austria, in 1929, she emigrated to the United States in 1940, barely escaping the Nazi threat. In her novel *A Certain Magic,* Orgel addresses the legacy of mid-twentieth-century events in Europe. Through the symbols of a magical emerald and a special doll, the device of a wartime journal kept by the refugee girl Gertrude Ehrenteil, and the affectionate, inquisitive friendship of eleven-year-old Jenny for her Aunt Trudl (the Gertrude of the journal), Orgel recreates, in an interesting synthesis, a contemporary American young person's realization of what Hitler's threat was like to an Austrian child in 1938. The distance between Jenny's comparatively innocent life and Trudl's dislocated, threatened existence is bridged with honesty and imagination.

In the award-winning *The Devil in Vienna* Orgel transforms her own experience into powerful fiction most directly and completely. In this novel, told partially through letters between Inge Dornenwald, who is Jewish, and Lieselotte Vessely, who is Catholic, the period of the Austrian *Anschluss* is vividly recreated, not only in its political but also in its cultural and mundane personal details. The friendship of Inge and Lieselotte undergoes severe testing, but it endures. It is a dramatic and moving story, complex, realistic, and suspenseful. The novel effectively shows the links between personal and political values under the pressures of a totalitarian movement. *The Devil in Vienna* is a major achievement and a book of considerable significance for young people seeking to understand what happened in Europe under Hitler's rule. It has been published in many languages in Europe and has been made into a television movie titled *A Friendship in Vienna.*

Orgel has also written young adult novels set in the contemporary American milieu. In her acclaimed novel *Risking Love,* Dinah Moskowitz, Barnard student, tells the story of her self-discovery and evolution through therapy. Her humor and defensiveness, her experience of sexuality and romance, her fear—rooted in her parents' divorce—that love is not lasting, and the exploratory digressions of psychotherapy are absorbingly created.

Less highly praised by critics, *Crack in the Heart* is the story of seventeen-year-old Zanna, who moves to New York City with her mother after Zanna's father dies. Isolated at the privileged girls' school where her mother works, Zanna meets a college student named Jeff who is creative, musical, and charismatic, but also involved in drugs. Though Zanna experiments with drugs, she does not get hooked. The deeper theme of her life is coming to terms with the loss of her father.

Orgel is a skillful writer who has bridged her European origins and American experience with insight and imagination, creating a legacy of historical awareness, humor, and shared humanity through her fiction.

—J.D. Stahl

ORLEV, Uri

Nationality: Polish. **Born:** Warsaw, 24 February 1931. **Military Service:** Served in the Israeli Army, 1949-51. **Awards:** Awards

from Israeli Broadcast Authorities, 1966, for "The Great Game," 1970, for "Dancing Lesson," and 1975, for "The Beast of Darkness," and Television Prize, 1979, for youth program "Who Will Ring First?"; Youth Alia prize, 1966, for *The Last Summer Vacation;* Prime Minister Prize (Israel), 1972 and 1989, for body of work; Ze-ev Prize from Israel Ministry of Education and Culture, 1977, and International Board on Books for Young People (IBBY) Honor List (Israel), 1979, both for *The Beast of Darkness;* Haifa University Prize for Young Readers, 1981; IBBY Honor List (Israel), 1982, *Horn Book* honor list citation, 1984, and Sydney Taylor Book award from the Association of Jewish Libraries, Mildred L. Batchelder award for Translation, Edgar Allan Poe award runner-up from the Mystery Writers of America, and Jane Addams Children's Book award, all 1985, Silver Pencil Prize for best book translated to Dutch, 1986, and Honor award from the Ministry of Youth, Family, Women and Health of the Federal Republic of Germany and West Berlin, 1987, and first recipient of Janusz Korczak Literary Prize (Poland), 1990, all for *The Island on Bird Street;* IBBY Honor List (Israel) for translation of *Kaitush Hamehachef* (*Kaitush the Wizard*) by J. Korczak, 1988; high commendation by the jury of the Collective Promotion of the Dutch Book (CPNB), 1989; Preis der Leseratten, Germany, Honor List of the Auswahlliste Deutscher Jugendliteraturpreis, Honor List of the Catholic Youth Book Prize, Story Book Honor Title by *Parent's Choice* (U.S.A.), Children's Books Notable Children's Trade Book in Field of Social Studies, Bulletin Blue Ribbons, all 1991, all for *The Man From the Other Side*; Mildred L. Batchelder award for foreign language book translated into English, 1991, for *The Man from the Other Side,* translated by Hillel Halkin; Jewish Book Council National Jewish Book Award in the children's literature category, 1992, and Batchelder Award for the best translation into English, 1996, both for *The Lady with the Hat*; *New York Times Book Review* Notable Book of 1993, and Israeli Ministry of Science and Art, and Ministry of Education, Culture, and Sport Annual Book Parade Prize, 1995, both for *Lydia, Queen of Palestine;* Hans Christian Andersen Award, 1996; Holon Municipality Prize, 1997, for *The Song of the Whales*; Yad Vashem Bruno Brandt Award, 1997 and Ministry of Education Zeew Prize, 1997, both for *The Sandgame.* **Address:** Yemin Moshe, 4 Ha-berakhah, Jerusalem, Israel.

PUBLICATIONS FOR YOUNG ADULTS

Novels, translated into English

The Lead Soldiers. Tel Aviv, Sifriat-Poalim, 1956; translated from the original Hebrew by Hillel Halkin, Battle Ground, Washington, P. Owen, 1979.

The Island on Bird Street, translated from the original Hebrew by Hillel Halkin. Boston, Massachusetts, Houghton, 1984.

The Man from the Other Side, translated from original Hebrew by Hillel Halkin. Boston, Massachusetts, Houghton, 1991.

Lydia, Queen of Palestine, translated from original Hebrew by Hillel Halkin. Boston, Massachusetts, Houghton, 1993.

The Lady with the Hat, translated from the original Hebrew by Hillel Halkin. Boston, Massachusetts, Houghton, 1995.

The Sandgame, translated from the original Hebrew by Hillel Halkin. Israel, Ghetto Fighters' House, 1997.

Fiction

The Beast of Darkness. Tel Aviv, Am Oved, 1976.
The Big-Little Girl. Jerusalem, Keter, 1977.
The Driving-Mad Girls. Jerusalem, Keter, 1977.
Noon Thoughts. Tel Aviv, Sifriat-Poalim, 1978.
It's Hard to Be a Lion. Tel Aviv, Am Oved, 1979.
The Lion Shirt. Givatayim, Massada, 1979.
Siamina. Tel Aviv, Am Oved, 1979.
The Black Cloud. Tel Aviv, Massada/Modan, 1979.
How Mr. Cork Made the Brain Work. Tel Aviv, Massada/Modan, 1979.
The Good Luck Passy. Tel Aviv, Am Oved, 1980.
Granny Knits. Givatayim, Massada, 1980.
Mr. Mayer, Let Us Sing. Givatayim, Massada, 1980.
The Island on Bird Street. Jerusalem, Keter, 1981.
Wings Turn. Givatayim, Massada, 1981.
Big Brother. Jerusalem, Keter, 1983.
The Dragon's Crown. Jerusalem, Keter, 1985.
Journey to Age Four. Tel Aviv, Am Oved, 1985.
Shampoo on Tuesdays. Jerusalem, Keter, 1986.
The Wrong Side of the Bed. Jerusalem, Keter, 1986.
The Man from the Other Side. Jerusalem, Keter, 1988.
The Lady with the Hat. Jerusalem, Keter, 1990.
Lydia, Queen of Palestine. Jerusalem, Keter, 1991.
A Mouthful of Meatball. Jerusalem, Keter, 1995.
The Sandgame. Jerusalem, Keter, 1996.
Last of Kin. Jerusalem, Keter, 1996.
The Wandering Family. Jerusalem, Keter, 1997.
The Song of the Whales. Jerusalem, Keter, 1997.

PUBLICATIONS FOR ADULTS

Fiction

The Lead Soldiers. Sifriat Poalim, 1956; Jerusalem, Keter, 1989.
Till Tomorrow. Tel Aviv, Am Oved, 1958.
The Last Summer Vacation. Daga, 1966.

Translator from Polish to Hebrew

In the Desert and Jungle, by Henryk Sienkiewicz. Paris, Y. Marcus, 1970.
King Matthew I, by Janusz Korczak. Jerusalem, Keter, 1979.
King Matthew on a Deserted Island, by Janusz Korczak. Jerusalem, Keter, 1979.
The Stories of Bruno Schulz. Tel Aviv, Schocken, 1979.
Kaitush the Wizard. Tel Aviv, Am Oved, 1993.
Eden, by Stanislaw Lem. Givatayim, Massada, 1980.
The Invincible, by Stanislaw Lem. Tel Aviv, Schocken, 1981.
Pirx the Pilot, by Stanislaw Lem. Tel Aviv, Schocken, 1981.
The Little Jack's Bankruptcy, by Janusz Korczak. Hakibutz Hameuchad, 1985.
The Devil of the Junior Year, by Kornel Makuszinski. Tel Aviv, Zmora-Bitan, 1990.

*

Biography: *Something About the Author, Autobiography Series,* Detroit, Gale Research, 1995.

Critical Study: *Children's Literature Review,* Detroit, Gale Research, 1993.

Uri Orlev comments:

From an early age, I read a lot. Whenever I went to the library, there were two things I wanted to know: did it have illustrations, and was it scary? If the answers were yes, I borrowed the book. The more I read, the more jealous I became. Why did such exciting things happen to the heroes of the books, while all that ever happened to me was being forced to eat, to take my afternoon nap, and to go to school every day? School was what I hated most.

And then the war broke out. My father went off in an officer's uniform, and I felt very proud. After a month of German shelling, my family found itself fleeing a building that had gone up in flames. We ran down the street, my mother holding my brother and me by the hands. Fire shot out the windows around us, timbers cracked from the heat, walls came crashing down, a screaming woman jumped from the top story. And it was then I realized that it was happening to me too: I had become the hero of an adventure story myself.

Of course, there were many painful and frightening things in my childhood, but others were amazing and exciting, the kinds of things one can experience only in wartime, like a lost cannon my friends and I accidentally exploded by sticking a shell up its barrel, or a dead horse that opened its mouth and laughed at us. But beyond it all, there were the memories of my mother surrounding us with her love in the most trying situations, and treating us with great patience—and sometimes with a spanking too.

A journalist once asked me if I view myself as a writer of teenage Holocaust novels. I was stunned. I have written twenty-five books for different age groups, of which only four deal directly with the Holocaust—and these four were not written for the purpose of instructing young people in the subject. The Holocaust was simply part of my childhood. . . .

I have received many letters from children who have read my books through the eyes of their own experience. I would like to mention in particular one I received in November 1992. It was written by Ramon Stewart, a 12-year-old black boy from Columbus, Ohio in the United States, after reading my book *The Island of Bird Street,* and it said: "The same kind of stuff that was happening in Poland has happened here. There are drive-by shootings and people are killed in front of their families. . . ."

[Another boy asked me] "Does writing about what happened to you in the past help you to get over it?" My answer was that I don't know. What I do know is that, for me, there is no grown-up way to talk, tell, or think about the things that happened. I can remember them only as if I were still a boy.

*   *   *

To read the novels of Uri Orlev is in some ways to read the story of Orlev's life. Like many of his characters he was born in Warsaw, Poland, and he spent his childhood in part behind the Ghetto walls, and then in hiding beyond them. His father was captured by the Russians, his mother murdered by the Nazis. He was loved and protected by his aunt, with whom he was sent to Bergen-Belsen, where he and his brother were among the few that survived. After the war he and his brother emigrated to what was then Palestine, where he lived on a kibbutz in Galilee.

Parts of this story—particularly the years in the Warsaw Ghetto—are in all of Orlev's work. Fathers are consistently absent; mothers are brave and loving but often separated by circumstances from their children; children themselves must struggle to survive. This struggle is particularly prominent in Orlev's work; he consistently depicts the struggle of the human soul towards love, family, joy, and childhood, and away from the horror represented by the faceless Nazis who bring death and terror.

Though Orlev is prolific and is much published in Israel, only a handful of his works have been published in North America, all of them translated by Hillel Halkin. The first of these was *The Lead Soldiers,* the most clearly autobiographical of all of his novels. "The hero of this story, which is more than half true," Orlev writes in the prologue, "is a small boy who hadn't seen very much of anything in life, which may be why he wasn't afraid to see more." The union between author, narrator, and character is very strong here. This novel in fact deals with the period in Orlev's life when he moved from the suburbs of Warsaw to the Ghetto, and from there to the concentration camp at Bergen-Belsen.

The point of view of the novel is significant, for unlike many stories dealing with the Holocaust, this one is told from a child's perspective. It is written in an impressionistic style, where scenes shift quickly from one moment to another, each representing a moment which would imprint itself upon a small child's memory: hiding in a bin to escape those searching for him; finding a box of photographs—all that is left of a family—and flinging them out the window; being hit and arrested by a man in a grey suit, and being held against a wall with his brother, knowing that they are about to be shot.

The child protagonist, Yurik, tries to make sense of what is happening to his family, but ultimately he cannot; instead, he turns to his imagination to bring order to the things he sees happening around him. Yurik and his brother bring their lead soldiers to play at war every place they go, endowing them with heroic names along the way. All the while they seem to be watched by Orlev the narrator, who even enters into the story at times to interact with the children. Only when they are safely out of Poland and in a kibbutz in Palestine is the narrator able to leave the children, able to leave himself: "My story is finished and a new story, it would seem, is about to begin."

The Island on Bird Street is more straightforward in its narrative approaches, but it too deals with the experience of Jews in Poland; here the experience is much more focused, for the setting remains the Warsaw Ghetto. Where the father had been gone in *The Lead Soldiers,* here the mother has been taken away in the beginning of the novel. Alex is in hiding with his father, one of those left behind after deportations from the Ghetto in order to work in the factories. They are discovered and marched off, together with others. But Alex's father and Boruch, another worker in the factory, help Alex to escape. Boruch is killed protecting Alex, and when he hears shots, his father assumes that Alex too is dead.

The rest of the novel is a vivid description of Alex's life of hiding in the Ghetto. He refuses to leave the ruined house to which he has escaped, believing his father will come back; as the months go by, however, and his father does not return, Alex begins to lose this dream. Nevertheless, Orlev is once again concerned with the story of survival. Against all hope, Alex is able to find food, protect himself against a soldier, rig a clever hiding-place, and even occasionally escape from the Ghetto and meet a girl over on the Polish side of the wall. He refuses all chances of escaping the

Ghetto entirely, for he is waiting for his father. In the end Alex's struggle to survive is successful, and his father does indeed return.

The power of this novel does not lie merely in its dramatic adventures and escapes, nor in its ability to depict life in the Ghetto—though both of these are important elements of the novel. Instead, the impact comes from Alex's unwavering hope, his sense that he will do whatever it takes to survive and wait for his father. All those he meets seem marked by desperation, as though they hide out with no real hope. But Alex maintains his hope, and that hope consequently gives him purpose.

The Man from the Other Side also depicts life in the Warsaw Ghetto, though here the story is not Orlev's, but that of his friend Marek, whom Orlev names as the protagonist. Marek's stepfather smuggles food to the Jews in the Ghetto by carrying it through the sewer system, and eventually Marek begins to help him. He seems to feel little sympathy for those on the other side of the wall, but this changes when his mother tells him that his father, who was killed under torture—another absent father—was Jewish. Marek suddenly feels a kinship with those in the Ghetto, and this leads him to help hide Pan Jozek until the uprising in the Ghetto. Then he helps him return to the Ghetto to participate in the revolt, and Marek, who is trapped there with him, sees firsthand what has been happening all this time on the other side of the wall.

Each of these three novels uses a child protagonist to mediate the experience of the war. Each of the children are aware of what is happening to a limited extent; not until real separation comes upon them do they realize the enormity of the war. They deal with the horrors of the war through the imagination (like Yurik), or through finding someone to care for (like Alex and Marek), or through focusing on their family's life. But for each, the war forces itself upon them completely, utterly, and terrifyingly.

Like *The Island on Bird Street* and *The Man from the Other Side, Lydia, Queen of Palestine* uses a first-person narrator to show how a young child deals with the events of the war, this time in Romania. More than any other narrator, Lydia is unaware of what the war means. She does not seem to understand why she and her mother are growing poorer, why she is no longer allowed to attend the public school, or why the Iron Guard is dangerous. She too is faced with the prospect of surviving the war—this she does when her mother puts her on a train to Turkey and then to Palestine—but she must also survive the breakup of her family, as her father divorces her mother and heads off to Palestine on his own. This betrayal overshadows all else that has gone on before.

Much of the story is about Lydia's escape to Palestine and her life on a kibbutz, learning to adjust to an entirely new way of thinking. The caring community that surrounds her is in stark contrast to that of Bucharest. It takes some time before Lydia is able to accept this new community. Her defense against her losses lies in her imagination—she dreams of marrying the prince of Romania and becoming the queen of Palestine—and in her strong character, which is manipulative, assertive, and dominant. These are not qualities particularly useful on a kibbutz, but they are ones useful in surviving.

In *The Lady with the Hat,* 17-year-old Yulek survives the concentration camps and returns to his village in Poland, only to discover that a mysterious Englishwoman in a hat has been searching for him. This may be his aunt Malka, he reasons, but he is headed to Rome, not England, and from Rome to Palestine. At that time, the British, who still held control over the site of the future State of Israel, were preventing Jews from travelling to Palestine, so the trip had to be made in secret, much like the slaves' journey on the ''Underground Railroad'' in antebellum America. Three things haunt Yulek on his secret journey: memories of his deceased family members, longing for his future life in Palestine, and the desire to be joined with his aunt Malka, who reappears later in the story.

In each of these novels the war is always in the foreground. There are scenes of betrayal and loss of hope—the man who throws himself and his two children off a burning roof, the family that sits down at a beautiful meal to take poison and end their plight, the dying grandmother waiting to hear news of her granddaughter's escape, the two boys taken from a train leading to freedom and brought back to who knows what. But overpowering these are the stories of Yurik and Alex and Marek and Lydia, who find the means to live and to remember and—perhaps like Orlev himself— to tell a story so their ordeals might not be forgotten.

—Gary D. Schmidt, updated by Judson Knight

ORWELL, George

Pseudonym for Eric (Arthur) Blair. **Nationality:** British. **Born:** of English parents in Motihari, Bengal (now Bihar), India, 25 June 1903; brought to England, 1904. **Education:** Attended convent school, Henley-on-Thames, Oxfordshire; St. Cyprian's, Eastbourne, Sussex, 1911-16; Wellington School, 1917; Eton College, (King's Scholar), 1917-21. **Military Service:** Served in the United Marxist Workers' Party militia in Catalonia, 1937; served on Aragon front during Spanish Civil War; became lieutenant. Wounded in action; served in the Home Guard, Local Defence Volunteers, 1940-43; served in England during World War II; became sergeant. **Family:** Married 1) Eileen O'Shaughnessy in 1936 (died 1945), one adopted son; 2) Sonia Brownell in 1949. **Career:** Writer. Police officer for Indian Imperial Police in Burma at Police Training School, Rangoon, 1922-23, assistant superintendent of police at Myaungmya, 1923, Twante, 1924, Syriam, 1925, Insein, 1925-26, Moulmein, 1926, and Katha, 1927 (resigned 1927); dishwasher in Paris, France, 1929; teacher, The Hawthorns (private school), Hayes, Middlesex, England, 1932-33; teacher, Frays College (private school), Uxbridge, England, 1933; clerk, Booklovers' Corner (used book store), London, England, 1934-36; shopkeeper in Wallingford, Herfordshire, England, beginning in 1936; began as assistant, became producer of educational radio programs, British Broadcasting Corp. (BBC), London, 1941-43; literary editor, 1943-45, author of ''As I Please'' column, 1943-47, *Tribune,* London; correspondent in France, Germany, and England, 1945, *Observer,* London. **Died:** 21 January 1950.

PUBLICATIONS

Novels

Burmese Days. New York, Harper, 1934; London, Gollancz, 1935.
A Clergyman's Daughter. London, Gollancz, 1935, New York, Harper, 1936.
Keep the Aspidistra Flying. London, Gollancz, 1936; New York, Harcourt, 1956.

Coming Up for Air. London, Gollancz, 1939; New York, Harcourt, 1950.
Animal Farm: A Fairy Story. London, Secker & Warburg, 1945, New York, Harcourt, 1946.
1984. London, Secker & Warburg, and New York, Harcourt, 1949; edited by Bernard Crick, Oxford, Oxford University Press, 1984.

Other

Down and Out in Paris and London. London, Gollancz, and New York, Harper, 1933.
The Road to Wigan Pier. London, Gollancz, 1937; New York, Harcourt, 1958.
Homage to Catalonia. London, Secker & Warburg, 1938; New York, Harcourt, 1952.
Inside the Whale, and Other Essays. London, Gollancz, 1940.
The Lion and the Unicorn: Socialism and the English Genius. London, Secker & Warburg, 1941; New York, AMS Press, 1976.
Editor, *Talking to India: A Selection of English Language Broadcasts to India.* London, Allen & Unwin, 1943.
Critical Essays. London, Secker & Warburg, 1946; as *Dickens, Dali, and Others: Studies in Popular Culture,* New York, Reynal, 1946.
James Burnham and the Managerial Revolution. London, Socialist Book Centre, 1946.
The English People. London, Collins, 1947; New York, Haskell House, 1974.
Editor, *British Pamphleteers 1: From the Sixteenth Century to the French Revolution.* London, Wingate, 1948.
Shooting an Elephant, and Other Essays. London, Secker & Warburg, and New York, Harcourt, 1950.
Such, Such Were the Joys. New York, Harcourt, 1953; as *England Your England, and Other Essays,* London, Secker & Warburg, 1953.
A Collection of Essays. New York, Doubleday, 1954.
The Orwell Reader, edited by Richard H. Rovere. New York, Harcourt, 1956.
Selected Essays. London, Penguin, 1957; as *Inside the Whale and Other Essays,* 1975.
Selected Writings, edited by George Bott. London, Heinemann, 1958.
Collected Essays. London, Secker & Warburg, 1961.
Decline of English Murder and Other Essays. London, Penguin, 1965.
The Collected Essays, Journalism, and Letters of George Orwell, 4 vols., edited by wife, Sonia Orwell, and Ian Angus. London, Secker & Warburg, and New York, Harcourt, 1968.
The Complete Works. New York, Harcourt, 17 vols., 1984.
The War Broadcasts and *The War Commentaries,* edited by W.J. West. London, British Broadcasting Corp. Publications-Duckworth, 2 vols., 1985; as *George Orwell: The Lost Writings,* New York, Avon, 1988.

Radio Plays: *The Voyage of the Beagle,* from work by Darwin, 1946; *Animal Farm,* from his own novel, 1947.

*

Media Adaptations: *Animal Farm* (animated film), 1955; *Animal Farm* (play by Nelson Slade Bond), Samuel French, 1964; *1984* (films), 1956 and 1984; *1984* (play), Dramatic Publishing, 1963.

Biography: Entry in *Dictionary of Literary Biography,* Volume 15: *British Novelists, 1930-1959,* Detroit, Gale, 1983.

Manuscript Collection: University College, London.

Critical Studies (selection): *George Orwell* by Tom Hopkinson, London, Longman, 1953, revised edition, 1962; *George Orwell: A Literary Study* by John Atkins, London, Calder & Boyars, 1954, New York, Ungar, 1955, revised edition, London, Calder & Boyars, 1971; *A Study of George Orwell, The Man and His Works* by Christopher Hollis, London, Hollis & Carter, and Chicago, Regnery, 1956; *The Crystal Spirit: A Study of George Orwell* by George Woodcock, Boston, Little Brown, 1966, London, Cape, 1967; *The Making of George Orwell: A Study in Literary History* by Keith Alldritt, London, Arnold, and New York, St. Martin's Press, 1969; *Orwell's Fiction* by Robert A. Lee, Notre Dame, Indiana, University of Notre Dame Press, 1969; *The World of George Orwell* edited by Miriam Gross, London, Weidenfeld and Nicolson, 1971, New York, Simon & Schuster, 1972; *Orwell* by Raymond Williams, London, Fontana, and New York, Viking Press, 1971, and *George Orwell: A Collection of Critical Essays* edited by Williams, Englewood Cliffs, New Jersey, Prentice Hall, 1974; *The Unknown Orwell* by Peter Stansky and William Abrahams, London, Constable, and New York, Knopf, 1972, *Orwell: The Transformation* by Stansky, London, Constable, 1979, New York, Knopf, 1980, and *On Nineteen Eighty-Four* edited by Stansky, New York, Freeman, 1984; *A Reader's Guide to George Orwell,* London, Thames & Hudson, 1975, Totowa, New Jersey, Rowman & Littlefield, 1977, and *George Orwell: The Critical Heritage,* London, Routledge, 1975, both edited by Jeffrey Meyers; *George Orwell and the Origins of 1984* by William Steinhoff, Ann Arbor, University of Michigan Press, 1975, as *The Road to 1984,* London, Weidenfeld & Nicolson, 1975; *The Road to Miniluv: George Orwell, The State and God* by Christopher Small, London, Gollancz, 1975, Pittsburgh, University of Pittsburgh Press, 1976; *Primal Dream and Primal Scream: Orwell's Development as a Psychological Novelist* by Richard I. Smyer, Columbia, University of Missouri Press, 1979; *George Orwell: A Life* by Bernard Crick, London, Secker & Warburg, 1980, Boston, Little Brown, 1981, revised edition, Secker & Warburg, 1981, and *Orwell Remembered* by Crick and Audrey Coppard, London, BBC, and New York, Facts on File, 1984; *Approaching 1984* by Donald McCormick, Newton Abbot, Devon, David and Charles, 1980; *George Orwell: The Road to 1984* by Peter Lewis, London, Heinemann, 1981; *George Orwell: A Personal Memoir* by T.R. Fyvel, London, Weidenfeld & Nicolson, 1982; *A George Orwell Companion* by J.R. Hammond, London, Macmillan, and New York, St. Martin's Press, 1982; *George Orwell's Guide through Hell: A Psychological Study of 1984* by Robert Plank, San Bernardino, California, Borgo Press, 1984; *Orwell: The Road to Airstrip One* by Ian Slater, New York, Norton, 1985; *George Orwell and the Problem of Authentic Existence* by Michael Carter, London, and Dover, New Hampshire, Croom Helm, 1985; *Critical Essays on George Orwell* edited by Bernard Oldsey, Boston, Hall, 1986; *Reflections on America, 1984: An Orwell Symposium* edited by Robert Mulvihill, Athens, University of Georgia Press, 1986; *George Orwell: The Age's Adversary,* New York, Macmillan, 1986, and *Nineteen Eighty-four: Past, Present, and Future,* Boston, Twayne, 1989, both by Patrick Reilly; *A Preface to Orwell* by David Wykes, London, and New York, Longman, 1987; *The Diminished Self:*

Orwell and the Loss of Freedom by Mark Connelly, Pittsburgh Pennsylvania, Duquesne University Press, 1987; *George Orwell* edited by Courtney T. Wemyss and Alexej Ugrinsky, New York, Greenwood 1987; *George Orwell* by Averil Gardner, Boston, Twayne, 1987; *George Orwell: A Reassessment* edited by Peter Buitenhuis and I.B. Nadel, New York, Macmillan, 1988; *Orwell and the Politics of Despair: A Critical Study of the Writings of George Orwell* by Alok Rai, Cambridge, Cambridge University Press, 1988; *George Orwell* by Alok Rai, Cambridge, Cambridge University Press, 1988; *George Orwell* by Nigel Flynn, Hove, Wayland, 1989, Vero Beach, Florida, Rourke, 1990; *The Politics of Literary Reputation: The Making and Claiming of "St. George Orwell"* by John Rodden, Oxford, Oxford University Press, 1990.

*   *   *

Only George Orwell's last two novels have been much read by young adults, and these were, of course, the two that enjoyed the greatest fame and largest sales: *Animal Farm* and *1984.* Together they gave Orwell an international reputation. When concentrating on these works, it can't be ignored that some young readers have also enjoyed the earlier books, such as the nostalgic *Coming Up for Air;* the various documentaries and the vivid prose sketches, like "Shooting an Elephant"; and the autobiographical account of his schooldays, *Such, Such Were the Joys.*

Animal Farm is a brief, simple fable about the animals of Manor Farm who unite in rebellion against the cruelties and exploitation of the farmer, Mr. Jones, drive out him and his men, and set about running the farm themselves. Inspired by the example of Boxer, the hard-working horse, they survive difficulties and make the experiment in equality and cooperation prosper. However, as the years pass, the pigs, cleverest of the animals, gradually assume more and more power as a new elite under their leader Napoleon. The revolutionary ideals of equality are replaced by a new hierarchy, and the slogan "All animals are equal" is extended by the clause, often quoted since, "but some animals are more equal than others." At the end, the farm reverts to its original title, Napoleon restores relationships with the human farmers, and when the other creatures peep in the farmhouse windows they "looked from pig to man. . .but already it was impossible to say which was which." It is a pessimistic ending for a fable, and the nearest we get to a moral is the opinion of the choreic donkey, Benjamin, that "life would go on as it had always gone on—that is, badly." Particularly at its time of publication *Animal Farm* was seen by many readers as an anti-Communist tract, in which Snowball represented Trotsky and Napoleon was Stalin. Certainly this satirical fable about the nature of totalitarian societies was rooted in Orwell's experiences in Spain and his awareness of Bolshevik methods, but it can be read too simply as an allegory of the Russian revolution. Squealer represents any propagandist and, significantly, the book has been banned in countries of very different political persuasions. In *Animal Farm,* Orwell simplified the style he had used in earlier novels, writing in direct, concrete terms, largely avoiding metaphor, and using the vigorous language of speech. He himself said that it was the first book in which he had consciously tried "to fuse political purpose and artistic purpose in one whole."

Four years later came *1984* and the title has become a symbolic shorthand sign for totalitarian oppression. Written by a dying man and based on the work of the Russian author Zamyatin, it is a chilling picture of how the power of the state could come to dominate the lives of individuals through cultural conditioning. Perhaps the most powerful science fiction novel of this century, this apocalyptic Swiftian satire shows with grim conviction how Winston's individual personality is wiped out and how he is recreated in the Party's image, until he does not just obey but even loves Big Brother. There is an intense personal feeling throughout the novel and some critics have related Winston Smith's sufferings to those Orwell underwent at preparatory school, about which he wrote so passionately just before *1984*. Orwell said that the book was written with the explicit intention ''to alter other people's idea of the kind of society they should strive after.''

1984 is a dystopia, a negative utopia, in which a single, self-perpetuating elite has replaced all earlier forms of social and political hierarchy, ruling over a submissive slave class and maintaining a convenient warring balance between the three power blocks into which the world is divided. The monstrous O'Brien expresses the gospel of eternal power that Hitler had preached in extreme form. The opening is superbly economical. After the arresting first sentence (''It was a bright cold day in April, and the clocks were striking thirteen'') Orwell swiftly sketches in all the major themes of the book in scenes based on the shabby, rationed London of the post-war years but transmuted into a Kafkaesque nightmare in which War is Peace, Freedom is Slavery, Ignorance is Strength. Orwell's mistrust of empty political slogans is even more graphically conveyed in the linguistic destructiveness of the Ministry of Truth than in the changing proclamations of *Animal Farm*. One central theme is the idea that the destruction of language underlies all other destructive social changes, and that the real purpose of Newspeak was ''to make all other modes of thought impossible,'' to cancel the past. Winston's doomed love for Julia, expressed in terms of fleeting memories, eventually exposes the fallacy of her belief that ''they can't get inside you.''

Apart from arguments about the quality of his writing, there has been much debate about Orwell's last two major books. Are they simply negative, lacking any positive view? Is he a propagandist rather than a true novelist? Is his pessimism about the future justified or is he simply uttering a warning? Does he show a lack of belief in the qualities and the resistance of ordinary people, the proles? However we answer these questions, it is undeniable that his books have sharpened our awareness of the issues and that many of his words and ideas (Big Brother, more equal than others, double think) have become part of the way in which we ourselves think today.

—Robert Protherough

OWENS, Everett. *See* **THOMAS, Rob.**

P

PACKER, Vin. *See* **KERR, M.E.**

PAISLEY, Tom. *See* **BETHANCOURT, T. Ernesto.**

PARK, (Rosina) Ruth (Lucia)

Nationality: Australian. **Born:** Auckland, New Zealand. **Education:** St. Benedict's College; University of Auckland; New Zealand University. **Family:** Married the writer D'Arcy Niland in 1942 (died 1967); five children. **Career:** Proofreader and editor of children's page, Auckland *Star;* editor of children's page, *Zealandia,* Auckland; welfare worker in Auckland; reporter, *Sydney Mirror,* Australia, since 1941; scriptwriter, Twentieth Century-Fox, London, England; free-lance writer and journalist. **Awards:** *Sydney Morning Herald* prize, 1948, for *The Harp in the South;* runner-up in Australian Book of the Year award, 1975, for *Callie's Castle;* Miles Franklin award, for novel, 1978; Australian Children's Book Council Book of the Year award, 1981, *Boston Globe-Horn Book* award, 1982, runner-up, Guardian, 1982, IBBY honour list (author), 1982, and Parents' Choice, 1982, all for *Playing Beatie Bow;* Premier's award, 1981; Young Australian's Best Book award for picture story book, 1986, for *When the Wind Changed.* **Agent:** Curtis Brown, P.O. Box 19, Paddington, NSW 2021, Australia.

PUBLICATIONS FOR YOUNG ADULTS

Fiction

The Hole in the Hill, illustrated by Jennifer Murray. Sydney, Ure Smith, 1961; London, Macmillan, 1962; as *Secret of the Maori Cave,* New York, Doubleday, 1964.
The Ship's Cat, illustrated by Richard Kennedy. London, Macmillan, and New York, St. Martin's Press, 1961.
The Road to Christmas, illustrated by Noela Young. London, Macmillan, and New York, St. Martin's Press, 1962.
The Road under the Sea, illustrated by Jennifer Murray. Sydney; Ure Smith, 1962; London, Macmillan, 1963; New York, Doubleday, 1966.
The Shaky Island, illustrated by Iris Millington. London, Constable, and New York, McKay, 1962.

Uncle Matt's Mountain, illustrated by Laurence Broderick. London, Macmillan, and New York, St. Martin's Press, 1962.
Airlift for Grandee, illustrated by Sheila Hawkins. London, Macmillan, and New York, St. Martin's Press, 1964.
Ring for the Sorcerer, illustrated by William Stobbs. Sydney, Horwitz Martin, 1967.
The Sixpenny Island, illustrated by David Cox. Syndey, Ure Smith, and London, Macmillan, 1968; as *Ten-Cent Island,* illustrated by Robert Frankenberg, New York, Doubleday, 1968.
Nuki and the Sea Serpent: A Maori Story, illustrated by Zelma Blakely. London, Longman, 1969.
The Runaway Bus, illustrated by Peter Tierney. Sydney, Hodder & Stoughton, 1969.
Callie's Castle, illustrated by Kilmeny Niland. Sydney and London, Angus & Robertson, 1974.
The Gigantic Balloon, illustrated by Kilmeny and Deborah Niland. Sydney, Collins, 1975; London, Collins, and New York, Parents' Magazine Press, 1976.
Come Danger, Come Darkness. Sydney and London, Hodder & Stoughton, 1978.
Playing Beatie Bow. Melbourne, Nelson, 1980; London, Kestrel, 1981; New York, Atheneum, 1982.
When the Wind Changed, illustrated by Deborah Niland. Sydney, Collins, 1980; New York, Coward McCann, 1981.
The Big Brass Key, illustrated by Noela Young. Sydney, Hodder & Stoughton, 1983.
My Sister Sif. Ringwood, Victoria, Viking Kestrel, 1986; London, Viking Kestrel, 1987; New York, Viking, 1991.
Callie's Family, illustrated by Kilmeny Niland. Sydney, Angus & Robertson, 1988; Lodnon, Angus & Robertson, 1989.
James, illustrated by Deborah Niland. Ringwood, Victoria, Viking O'Neil, 1988.
Things in Corners (short stories). Ringwood, Victoria, and New York, Viking, 1989.
A Fence around the Cuckoo. Ringwood, Victoria, Viking, 1992.
Fishing in the Styx. Ringwood, Victoria, Viking, 1993.

PUBLICATIONS FOR CHILDREN

Fiction

The Muddle-Headed Wombat, illustrated by Noela Young. Sydney, Educational Press, 1962; London, Angus & Robertson, 1963.
The Muddle-Headed Wombat on Holiday, illustrated by Noela Young. Sydney, Educational Press, and London, Angus and Robertson, 1964.
The Muddle-Headed Wombat in the Treetops, illustrated by Noela Young. Sydney, Educational Press, and London, Angus & Robertson, 1965.
The Muddle-Headed Wombat at School, illustrated by Noela Young. Sydney, Educational Press, and London, Angus & Robertson, 1966.
The Muddle-Headed Wombat in the Snow, illustrated by Noela Young. Sydney, Educational Press, and London, Angus & Robertson, 1966.

The Muddle-Headed Wombat on a Rainy Day, illustrated by Noela Young. Sydney, Educational Press, 1969; London, Angus & Robertson, 1970.

The Muddle-Headed Wombat in the Springtime, illustrated by Noela Young. Sydney, Educational Press, and London, Angus & Robertson, 1970.

The Muddle-Headed Wombat on the River, illustrated by Noela Young. Sydney, Educational Press, and London, Angus & Robertson, 1971.

The Muddle-Headed Wombat and the Bush Band, illustrated by Noela Young. Sydney, Angus & Robertson, 1973.

The Muddle-Headed Wombat and the Invention, illustrated by Noela Young. London, Angus & Robertson, 1975.

The Muddle-Headed Wombat on Clean-Up Day, illustrated by Noela Young. Sydney and London, Angus & Robertson, 1976.

The Adventures of the Muddle-Headed Wombat, illustrated by Noela Young. Sydney, Angus & Robertson, 1979; London, Angus & Robertson, 1980.

The Muddle-Headed Wombat Is Very Bad, illustrated by Noela Young. Sydney, Angus & Robertson, 1981.

The Muddle-Headed Wombat Stays at Home, illustrated by Noela Young. Sydney, Angus & Robertson, 1982.

Plays

The Uninvited Guest. Sydney and London, Angus & Robertson, 1948.

Radio Play: *The Muddle-Headed Wombat* series.

Poetry

Roger Bandy, illustrated by Deborah and Kilmeny Niland. Adelaide, Rigby, 1977.

Other

Merchant Campbell, illustrated by Edwina Bell. Sydney, Collins, 1976.

PUBLICATIONS FOR ADULTS

Novels

The Harp in the South. Sydney, Angus & Robertson, London, Joseph, and Boston, Houghton Mifflin, 1948.

Poor Man's Orange. Sydney, Angus & Robertson, 1949; London, Joseph, 1950; as *12 1/2 Plymouth Street,* Boston, Houghton Mifflin, 1951.

The Witch's Thorn. Sydney, Angus & Robertson, 1951; London, Joseph, and Boston, Houghton Mifflin, 1952.

A Power of Roses. Sydney, Angus & Robertson, and London, Joseph, 1953.

Pink Flannel. Sydney, Angus & Robertson, 1955; as *Dear Hearts and Gentle People,* Ringwood, Victoria, Penguin, 1981.

One-a-Pecker, Two-a-pecker. Sydney, Angus & Robertson, 1957; London, Joseph, 1958; as *Frost and the Fire,* Boston, Houghton Mifflin, 1958; London, Pan, 1962.

The Good-Looking Women. Sydney, Angus & Robertson, 1961; London, Joseph, 1962.

Serpent's Delight. New York, Doubleday, 1962.

Swords and Crowns and Rings. Melbourne, Nelson, 1977; London, Joseph, and New York, St. Martin's Press, 1978.

Missus. Melbourne, Nelson, and London, Joseph, 1985; New York, St. Martin's Press, 1987.

Plays

The Harp in the South, with Leslie Rees, adaptation of the novel by Park (broadcast 1949). Montmorency, Victoria, Yackandandah, 1987.

Radio Play: *The Harp in the South,* with Leslie Rees, 1949.

Television Play: *No Decision,* with D'Arcy Niland, 1964.

Other

The Drums Go Bang (autobiographical), with D'Arcy Niland. Sydney, Angus & Roberston, 1956.

Tales of the South. London, Macmillan, 1961.

The Companion Guide to Sydney. Sydney and London, Collins, 1973; New York, Scribner, 1976.

Flights of Angels. Melbourne, Nelson, 1981.

Norfolk Island and Lord Howe Island. Dover Heights, New South Wales, Serendip, 1982.

The Sydney We Love, with Cedric Emmanuel. Melbourne, Nelson, 1983.

The Tasmania We Love. with Cedric Emmanuel. Melbourne, Nelson, 1987.

*   *   *

For a writer to be immensely popular and still receive critical acclaim is a difficult feat in Australia, where commercial success is sometimes viewed with suspicion, but Ruth Park is an exception. Her compelling narratives are so seductive they make readers gallop to the conclusion. With the exception of the family stories *Callie's Castle* and its sequel, her other writing is not easily pigeonholed, being variously a combination of history, fantasy, romance, and adventure. *My Sister Sif,* for example, is set in the future, features merpeople and underwater cities, has an ecological theme and a subplot about the sacrifices one makes for love.

Already famous for her adult novels and the "Muddle-Headed Wombat" series for children, Park achieved the special distinction of producing a classic in young adult fiction with the publication of *Playing Beatie Bow,* a time-slip novel set in The Rocks, an old harbourside Sydney suburb. *Playing Beatie Bow* is about the growing up of fourteen-year-old Abigail Kirk. When she was ten Abigail's father had left his wife and daughter for another woman but now wants the family back together again. Abigail is outraged that her mother could consider it, "He whistles and back she goes like a well-trained dog." In a mood of resentment and twisted pride Abigail, through the agency of a spooky children's game, Beatie Bow, finds herself in the hard, dangerous world of nineteenth-century Sydney. Here she sees life from a different perspective and experiences love. The extraordinarily vivid re-creation of colonial Sydney in this book is arguably the high-point of Park's writing.

Confronting change in oneself and those around you is the emotional core of Ruth Park's writing for young adult readers. The young heroines and heroes are usually puzzled and angered by adult perspectives on love or other relationships and through unsettling experiences of their own become more knowledgeable and therefore accepting of human foibles. In the short story "Where Freedom Is" from *Things in Corners* the troubled hero Gideon reflects, "It came to him then that when you're a small kid you don't realise much. You just are. But the time comes when you know what you're feeling, you can describe it, or take steps to change things." Facing hidden things is the major theme of the five stories in this fine collection of spooky tales. In the title story, illness prompts Theo to partly recall suppressed childhood memories of life with his mother before he was adopted. These memories take on the form of a frightening creature that inhabits lifts (elevators). That this is not a sombre tale of psychological disfunction but rather a wise, moving, and funny story says much for Park's storytelling ability.

Callie, the heroine of *Callie's Castle* and *Callie's Family,* needs solitude before she can understand why her once trouble-free life now seems tainted. She has fought with her best friend, is irritable with her mother, hates her once loved teacher, and is plagued by her younger siblings. Then Grandpa Cameron comes back into Callie's life and sees that she needs a place to herself, and so she gets the beautiful cupola—a feature of the family's new house—and gains a new perspective on change and relationships. Similarly Riko in *My Sister Sif* faces changes in the people she loves best. Riko and her sister, Sif, are part merpeople, part "landcrabs." Sif longs for the sea, but Riko is torn between two lifestyles. Linked to this is a strong message about environmental damage in the ocean.

Thirteen-year-old Otter Cannon, in the historical adventure novel *Come Danger, Come Darkness*, fights difficulties in others rather than within himself. He knows what he wants to be, a surgeon. However the Cannons are always soldiers and strict Uncle Daniel, Commandant of the penal colony Norfolk Island, is determined Otter will follow the family line. But apart from this battle, Otter is also planning the escape of a convict, Corny Stack, a childhood friend and retainer from the family estate in Ireland.

Park's first novel for older children, *The Hole in the Hill,* is an exciting adventure tale about two Australian children, Brownie and Dunk, who discover some extraordinary caves, the source of the terrifying noise heard on their dead uncle's New Zealand farm. The caves prove to be a special place for the Maoris. Although a particularly fine book of its type, it lacks the emotional depth of her more recent work. The fact that Park's first novel, *The Harp in the South,* has now been republished in a condensed version for younger readers, points to a change in what is thought acceptable adolescent reading and to the attraction of her adult novels for this readership.

—Kerry White

PASCAL, Francine

Nationality: American. **Born:** New York, New York, 13 May 1938. **Education:** New York University, B.A. 1958. **Family:** Married John Robert Pascal, 1965 (died 1981); three daughters. **Career:** Writer and lecturer. **Awards:** New York Public Library Books for the Teen Age citations, 1978-85; American Library Association Best Book for Young Adults citation, 1979; Dorothy Canfield Fisher Children's Book Award, Vermont Congress of Parents and Teachers, and *Publisher's Weekly* Literary Prize list, 1982; Bernard Versele Award, Brussels, 1988; Atlanta Public Library's Milner Award, 1988. **Agent:** Amy Berkower, Writers House, 21 West 26th St., New York, New York 10010, U.S.A.

PUBLICATIONS FOR YOUNG ADULTS

Fiction

Hangin' Out with Cici. New York, Viking, 1977.
My First Love and Other Disasters. New York, Viking, 1979.
The Hand-Me-Down Kid. New York, Viking, 1980.
Love and Betrayal and Hold the Mayo!. New York, Viking, 1985.

"Sweet Valley High" Series

Double Love. New York, Bantam, 1984.
Secrets. New York, Bantam, 1984.
Playing with Fire. New York, Bantam, 1984.
Power Play. New York, Bantam, 1984.
All Night Long. New York, Bantam, 1984.
Dangerous Love. New York, Bantam, 1984.
Dear Sister. New York, Bantam, 1984.
Heartbreaker. New York, Bantam, 1984.
Racing Hearts. New York, Bantam, 1984.
Wrong Kind of Girl. New York, Bantam, 1984.
Too Good to Be True. New York, Bantam, 1984.
When Love Dies. New York, Bantam, 1984.
Kidnapped!. New York, Bantam, 1984.
Deceptions. New York, Bantam, 1984.
Promises. New York, Bantam, 1985.
Rags to Riches. New York, Bantam, 1985.
Love Letters. New York, Bantam, 1985.
Head over Heels. New York, Bantam, 1985.
Showdown. New York, Bantam, 1985.
Crash Landing! New York, Bantam, 1985.
Runaway. New York, Bantam, 1985.
Too Much in Love. New York, Bantam, 1986.
Say Goodbye. New York, Bantam, 1986.
Memories. New York, Bantam, 1986.
Nowhere to Run. New York, Bantam, 1986.
Hostage! New York, Bantam, 1986.
Lovestruck. New York, Bantam, 1986.
Alone in the Crowd. New York, Bantam, 1986.
Bitter Rivals. New York, Bantam, 1986.
Jealous Lies. New York, Bantam, 1986.
Taking Sides. New York, Bantam, 1986.
The New Jessica. New York, Bantam, 1986.
Starting Over. New York, Bantam, 1987.
Forbidden Love. New York, Bantam, 1987.
Out of Control. New York, Bantam, 1987.
Last Chance. New York, Bantam, 1987.
Rumors. New York, Bantam, 1987.
Leaving Home. New York, Bantam, 1987.
Secret Admirer. New York, Bantam, 1987.
On the Edge. New York, Bantam, 1987.
Outcast. New York, Bantam, 1987.

Caught in the Middle. New York, Bantam, 1988.
Pretenses. New York, Bantam, 1988.
Hard Choices. New York, Bantam, 1988.
Family Secrets. New York, Bantam, 1988.
Decisions. New York, Bantam, 1988.
Slam Book Fever. New York, Bantam, 1988.
Playing for Keeps. New York, Bantam, 1988.
Troublemaker. New York, Bantam, 1988.
Out of Reach. New York, Bantam, 1988.
In Love Again. New York, Bantam, 1989.
Against the Odds. New York, Bantam, 1989.
Brokenhearted. New York, Bantam, 1989.
Teacher Crush. New York, Bantam, 1989.
Perfect Shot. New York, Bantam, 1989.
White Lies. New York, Bantam, 1989.
Two-Boy Weekend. New York, Bantam, 1989.
That Fatal Night. New York, Bantam, 1989.
Lost at Sea. New York, Bantam, 1989.
Second Chance. New York, Bantam, 1989.
Ms. Quarterback. New York, Bantam, 1990.
The New Elizabeth. New York, Bantam, 1990.
The Ghost of Tricia Martin. New York, Bantam, 1990.
Friend Against Friend. New York, Bantam, 1990.
Trouble at Home. New York, Bantam, 1990.
Who's to Blame. New York, Bantam, 1990.
The Parent Plot. New York, Bantam, 1990.
Boy Trouble. New York, Bantam, 1990.
Who's Who?. New York, Bantam, 1990.
The Love Bet. New York, Bantam, 1990.
Amy's True Love. New York, Bantam, 1991.
Miss Teen Sweet Valley. New York, Bantam, 1991.
The Perfect Girl. New York, Bantam, 1991.
Regina's Legacy. Bantam, 1991.
Rock Star's Girl. New York, Bantam, 1991.
Starring Jessica! New York, Bantam, 1991.
Cheating to Win. New York, Bantam, 1991.
The Dating Game. New York, Bantam, 1991.
The Long-Lost Brother. New York, Bantam, 1991.
The Girl They Both Loved. New York, Bantam, 1991.
Rosa's Lie. New York, Bantam, 1992.
Kidnapped by the Cult. New York, Bantam, 1992.
Steven's Bride. New York, Bantam, 1992.
The Stolen Diary. New York, Bantam, 1992.
Soap Star. New York, Bantam, 1992.
Jessica Against Bruce. New York, Bantam, 1992.
My Best Friend's Boyfriend. New York, Bantam, 1992.
Love Letters for Sale. New York, Bantam, 1992.
Elizabeth Betrayed. New York, Bantam, 1992.
Don't Go Home with John. New York, Bantam, 1993.
In Love with a Prince. New York, Bantam, 1993.
She's Not What She Seems. New York, Bantam, 1993.
Stepsisters. New York, Bantam, 1993.
Are We in Love? New York, Bantam, 1993.
The Morning After. New York, Bantam, 1993.
The Arrest. New York, Bantam, 1993.
The Verdict. New York, Bantam, 1993.
The Wedding. New York, Bantam, 1993.
Beware the Babysitter. New York, Bantam, 1993.
Almost Married. New York, Bantam, 1994.

The Boyfriend War. New York, Bantam, 1994.
A Date with a Werewolf. New York, Bantam, 1994.
Death Threat. New York, Bantam, 1994.
Double-Crossed. New York, Bantam, 1994.
Elizabeth's Secret Diary. New York, Bantam, 1994.
Jessica's Secret Love. New York, Bantam, 1994.
Left at the Altar. New York, Bantam, 1994.
Love and Death in London. New York, Bantam, 1994.
Operation Love Match. New York, Bantam, 1994.
College Weekend. New York, Bantam, 1995.
Crash Landing. New York, Bantam, 1995.
The Cousin War. New York, Bantam, 1995.
Jessica's Older Guy. New York, Bantam, 1995.
Jessica Quits the Squad. New York, Bantam, 1995.
Jessica the Genius. New York, Bantam, 1995.
Meet the Stars of Sweet Valley High. New York, Bantam, 1995.
The Morning After. New York, Bantam, 1995.
Nightmare in Death Valley. New York, Bantam, 1995.
The Pom-Pom Wars. New York, Bantam, 1995.
She's Not What She Seems. New York, Bantam, 1995.
"V" for Victory. New York, Bantam, 1995.
The Treasure of Death Valley. New York, Bantam, 1995.
When Loves Dies. New York, Bantam, 1995.
The Arrest. New York, Bantam, 1996.
Beware of the Babysitter. New York, Bantam, 1996.
Camp Killer. New York, Bantam, 1996.
Dance of Death. New York, Bantam, 1996.
Elizabeth's Rival. New York, Bantam, 1996.
Elizabeth's Secret Diary, No. 2. New York, Bantam, 1996.
The High School War. New York, Bantam, 1996.
In Love With the Enemy. New York, Bantam, 1996.
Jessica's Secret Diary, Vol 1. New York, Bantam, 1996.
Jessica's Secret Diary, Vol 2. New York, Bantam, 1996.
Kiss Before Dying. New York, Bantam, 1996.
Kiss of a Killer. New York, Bantam, 1996.
Left at the Alter. New York, Bantam, 1996.
Meet Me at Midnight. New York, Bantam, 1996.
Out of Control. New York, Bantam, 1996.
Tall, Dark, and Deadly. New York, Bantam, 1996.
Elizabeth's Secret Diary, Vol 3. New York, Bantam, 1997.
Fashion Victim. New York, Bantam, 1997.
Happily Ever After. New York, Bantam, 1997.
Jessica's Secret Diary, Vol 3. New York, Bantam, 1997.
Lila's New Flame. New York, Bantam, 1997.
Model Flirt. New York, Bantam, 1997.
Once Upon A Time. New York, Bantam, 1997.
To Catch a Thief. New York, Bantam, 1997.
Too Hot to Handle. New York, Bantam, 1997.
The Big Night. New York, Bantam, 1998.
Elizabeth Is Mine. New York, Bantam, 1998.
Fight Fire With Fire. New York, Bantam, 1998.
Picture Perfect Prom. New York, Bantam, 1998.
Please Forgive Me. New York, Bantam, 1998.
What Jessica Wants. New York, Bantam, 1998.

"Sweet Valley High" Super Editions

Perfect Summer. New York, Bantam, 1985.
Malibu Summer. New York, Bantam, 1986.

Special Christmas. New York, Bantam, 1986.
Spring Break. New York, Bantam, 1986.
Spring Fever. New York, Bantam, 1987.
Winter Carnival. New York, Bantam, 1987.
Murder in Paradise. New York, Bantam, 1995.
Return of the Evil Twin. New York, Bantam, 1995.
Falling for Lucas. New York, Bantam, 1996.
Cover Girls. New York, Bantam, 1997.
Jessica Takes Manhattan. New York, Bantam, 1997.
Mystery Date. New York, Bantam, 1997.
Last Wish. New York, Bantam, 1998.

"Sweet Valley High" Super Thriller Series

Double Jeopardy. New York, Bantam, 1987.
On the Run. New York, Bantam, 1988.
No Place to Hide. New York, Bantam, 1988.
Deadly Summer. New York, Bantam, 1989.
Murder on the Line. New York, Bantam, 1992.
Beware the Wolfman. New York, Bantam, 1994.
A Deadly Christmas. New York, Bantam, 1994.
Double Jeopardy. New York, Bantam, 1995.
A Killer on Board. New York, Bantam, 1995.
Murder in Paradise. New York, Bantam, 1995.
A Stranger in the House. New York, Bantam, 1995.
'R' for Revenge. New York, Bantam, 1997.

"Sweet Valley High" Super Star Series

Lila's Story. New York, Bantam, 1989.
Bruce's Story. New York, Bantam, 1990.
Enid's Story. New York, Bantam, 1990.
Olivia's Story. New York, Bantam, 1991.
Todd's Story. New York, Bantam, 1992.

"Sweet Valley" Magna Editions

The Wakefields of Sweet Valley. New York, Bantam, 1991.
The Wakefield Legacy: The Untold Story. New York, Bantam, 1992.
A Night to Remember. New York, Bantam, 1993.
The Evil Twin. New York, Bantam, 1993.
Elizabeth's Secret Diary. New York, Bantam, 1994.
Jessica's Secret Diary. New York, Bantam, 1994.

"Sweet Valley Twins" Series

Best Friends. New York, Bantam, 1986.
Teacher's Pet. New York, Bantam, 1986.
The Haunted House. New York, Bantam, 1986.
Choosing Sides. New York, Bantam, 1986.
Sneaking Out. New York, Bantam, 1987.
The New Girl. New York, Bantam, 1987.
Three's a Crowd. New York, Bantam, 1987.
First Place. New York, Bantam, 1987.
Against the Rules. New York, Bantam, 1987.
One of the Gang. New York, Bantam, 1987.
Buried Treasure. New York, Bantam, 1987.
Keeping Secrets. New York, Bantam, 1987.
Stretching the Truth. New York, Bantam, 1987.
Tug of War. New York, Bantam, 1987.

The Bully. New York, Bantam, 1988.
Playing Hooky. New York, Bantam, 1988.
Left Behind. New York, Bantam, 1988.
Claim to Fame. New York, Bantam, 1988.
Center of Attention. New York, Bantam, 1988.
Jumping to Conclusions. New York, Bantam, 1988.
Second Best. New York, Bantam, 1988.
The Older Boy. New York, Bantam, 1988.
Out of Place. New York, Bantam, 1988.
Elizabeth's New Hero. New York, Bantam, 1989.
Standing Out. New York, Bantam, 1989.
Jessica on Stage. Bantam, 1989.
Jessica the Rock Star. New York, Bantam, 1989.
Jessica's Bad Idea. New York, Bantam, 1989.
Taking Charge. New York, Bantam, 1989.
Big Camp Secret. New York, Bantam, 1989.
Jessica and the Brat Attack. New York, Bantam, 1989.
April Fool! New York, Bantam, 1989.
Princess Elizabeth. New York, Bantam, 1989.
Elizabeth's First Kiss. New York, Bantam, 1990.
War Between the Twins. New York, Bantam, 1990.
Summer Fun Book. New York, Bantam, 1990.
The Twins Get Caught. New York, Bantam, 1990.
Lois Strikes Back. New York, Bantam, 1990.
Mary Is Missing. New York, Bantam, 1990.
Jessica's Secret. New York, Bantam, 1990.
Jessica and the Money Mix-Up. New York, Bantam, 1990.
Danny Means Trouble. New York, Bantam, 1990.
Amy's Pen Pal. New York, Bantam, 1990.
Amy Moves In. New York, Bantam, 1991.
Jessica's New Look. New York, Bantam, 1991.
Lucky Takes the Reins. New York, Bantam, 1991.
Mademoiselle Jessica. New York, Bantam, 1991.
Mandy Miller Fights Back. New York, Bantam, 1991.
The Twins' Little Sister. New York, Bantam, 1991.
Booster Boycott. New York, Bantam, 1991.
Elizabeth the Impossible. New York, Bantam, 1991.
Jessica and the Secret Star. New York, Bantam, 1991.
The Slime That Ate Sweet Valley. New York, Bantam, 1991.
The Big Party Weekend. New York, Bantam, 1991.
Brooke and Her Rock-Star Mom. New York, Bantam, 1992.
The Wakefields Strike It Rich. New York, Bantam, 1992.
Big Brother's in Love! New York, Bantam, 1992.
Elizabeth and the Orphans. New York, Bantam, 1992.
Barnyard Battle. New York, Bantam, 1992.
Ciao, Sweet Valley. New York, Bantam, 1992.
Jessica the Nerd. New York, Bantam, 1992.
Sarah's Dad and Sophia's Mom. New York, Bantam, 1992.
Poor Lila! New York, Bantam, 1992.
The Charm School Mystery. New York, Bantam, 1992.
Patty's Last Dance. New York, Bantam, 1993.
The Great Boyfriend Switch. New York, Bantam, 1993.
Jessica the Thief. New York, Bantam, 1993.
The Middle School Gets Married. New York, Bantam, 1993.
Won't Someone Help Anna? New York, Bantam, 1993.
Psychic Sisters. New York, Bantam, 1993.
Jessica Saves the Trees. New York, Bantam, 1993.
The Love Potion. New York, Bantam, 1993.
Lila's Music Video. New York, Bantam, 1993.

Elizabeth the Hero. New York, Bantam, 1993.
Jessica and the Earthquake. New York, Bantam, 1994.
Yours for a Day. New York, Bantam, 1994.
Todd Runs Away. New York, Bantam, 1994.
Steven the Zombie. New York, Bantam, 1994.
Jessica's Blind Date. New York, Bantam, 1994.
The Gossip War. New York, Bantam, 1994.
Robbery at the Mall. New York, Bantam, 1994.
Steven's Enemy. New York, Bantam, 1994.
Amy's Secret Sister. New York, Bantam, 1994.
Choosing Sides. New York, Bantam, 1995.
Deadly Voyage. New York, Bantam, 1995.
Don't Go in the Basement. New York, Bantam, 1995.
Elizabeth the Seventh-Grader. New York, Bantam, 1995.
Escape from terror Island. New York, Bantam, 1995.
It Can't Happen Here. New York, Bantam, 1995.
Jessica's Cookie Disaster. New York, Bantam, 1995.
The Middle School Gets Married. New York, Bantam, 1995.
The Mother-Daughter Switch. New York, Bantam, 1995.
Romeo and Two Juliets. New York, Bantam, 1995.
Steven Gets Even. New York, Bantam, 1995.
The Battle of the Cheerleaders. New York, Bantam, 1996.
The Beast is Watching You. New York, Bantam, 1996.
The Beast Must Die. New York, Bantam, 1996.
Don't Talk to Brian. New York, Bantam, 1996.
Elizabeth the Spy. New York, Bantam, 1996.
Elizabeth's First Kiss. New York, Bantam, 1996.
The Incredible Madame Jessica. New York, Bantam, 1996.
The Mysterious Dr. Q. New York, Bantam, 1996.
Too Scared to Sleep. New York, Bantam, 1996.
Twins in Love. New York, Bantam, 1996.
Twins Little Sister. New York, Bantam, 1996.
Holiday Mischief. New York, Bantam, 1996.
If I Die Before I Wake. New York, Bantam, 1997.
Big Brother's in Love Again. New York, Bantam, 1997.
Breakfast of Enemies. New York, Bantam, 1997.
Cammi's Crush. New York, Bantam, 1997.
Elizabeth Solves It All. New York, Bantam, 1997.
Jessica's First Kiss. New York, Bantam, 1997.
Jessica's Lucky Millions. New York, Bantam, 1997.
Pumpkin Fever. New York, Bantam, 1997.
Sister's at War. New York, Bantam, 1997.
The Twins Hit Hollywood. New York, Bantam, 1997.
The Boyfriend Game. New York, Bantam, 1998.
The Boyfriend Mess. New York, Bantam, 1998.
Down With Queen Janet. New York, Bantam, 1998.
Happy Mother's Day, Lila. New York, Bantam, 1998.
If Looks Could Kill. New York, Bantam, 1998.
Jessica Takes Charge. New York, Bantam, 1998.

"Sweet Valley Twins" Super Series

Class Trip. New York, Bantam, 1988.
Holiday Mischief. New York, Bantam, 1988.
The Big Camp Secret. New York, Bantam, 1989.
The Unicorns Go Hawaiian. New York, Bantam, 1991.
Lila's Secret Valentine. New York, Bantam, 1994.
Jessica's Animal Instincts. New York, Bantam, 1996.
The Twins Go To College. New York, Bantam, 1997.

The Year Without Christmas. New York, Bantam, 1997.
Good-Bye Middle School. Countdown to Junior High, New York, Bantam, 1997.
Jessica's No Angel. New York, Bantam, 1998.

"Sweet Valley Twins" Super Chiller Series

The Christmas Ghost. New York, Bantam, 1989.
The Carnival Ghost. New York, Bantam, 1990.
The Ghost in the Graveyard. New York, Bantam, 1990.
The Ghost in the Bell Tower. New York, Bantam, 1992.
The Curse of the Ruby Necklace. New York, Bantam, 1993.
The Curse of the Golden Heart. New York, Bantam, 1994.
The Haunted Burial Ground. New York, Bantam, 1994.
The Secret of the Magic Pen. New York, Bantam, 1995.
Evil Elizabeth. New York, Bantam, 1995.
The Curse of the Ruby Necklace. New York, Bantam, 1995.

"Sweet Valley Twins" Magna Editions

The Magic Christmas. New York, Bantam, 1992.
A Christmas Without Elizabeth. New York, Bantam, 1993.
BIG for Christmas. New York, Bantam, 1994.

"Sweet Valley Kids" Series

Surprise! Surprise! New York, Bantam, 1989.
Runaway Hamster. New York, Bantam, 1989.
Teamwork. New York, Bantam, 1989.
Lila's Secret. New York, Bantam, 1990.
Elizabeth's Valentine. New York, Bantam, 1990.
Elizabeth's Super-Selling Lemonade. New York, Bantam, 1990.
Jessica's Big Mistake. New York, Bantam, 1990.
Jessica's Cat Trick. New York, Bantam, 1990.
Jessica's Zoo Adventure. New York, Bantam, 1990.
The Twins and the Wild West. New York, Bantam, 1990.
Starring Winston. New York, Bantam, 1990.
The Substitute Teacher. New York, Bantam, 1990.
Sweet Valley Trick or Treat. New York, Bantam, 1990.
Crybaby Lois. New York, Bantam, 1990.
Bossy Steven. New York, Bantam, 1991.
Carolyn's Mystery Dolls. New York, Bantam, 1991.
Fearless Elizabeth. New York, Bantam, 1991.
Jessica and Jumbo. New York, Bantam, 1991.
The Twins Go to the Hospital. New York, Bantam, 1991.
Jessica the Babysitter. New York, Bantam, 1991.
Jessica and the Spelling Bee Surprise. New York, Bantam, 1991.
Lila's Haunted House Party. New York, Bantam, 1991.
Sweet Valley Slumber Party. New York, Bantam, 1991.
Cousin Kelly's Family Secret. New York, Bantam, 1991.
Left-Out Elizabeth. New York, Bantam, 1992.
Jessica's Snobby Club. New York, Bantam, 1992.
The Sweet Valley Cleanup Team. New York, Bantam, 1992.
Elizabeth Meets Her Hero. New York, Bantam, 1992.
Andy and the Alien. New York, Bantam, 1992.
Jessica's Unburied Treasure. New York, Bantam, 1992.
Elizabeth and Jessica Run Away. New York, Bantam, 1992.
Left Back! New York, Bantam, 1992.

Caroline's Halloween Spell. New York, Bantam, 1992.
The Best Thanksgiving Ever. New York, Bantam, 1992.
Elizabeth's Broken Arm. New York, Bantam, 1993.
Elizabeth's Video Fever. New York, Bantam, 1993.
The Big Race. New York, Bantam, 1993.
Good-bye, Eva. New York, Bantam, 1993.
Ellen Is Home Alone. New York, Bantam, 1993.
Robin in the Middle. New York, Bantam, 1993.
The Missing Tea Set. New York, Bantam, 1993.
Jessica's Monster Nightmare. New York, Bantam, 1993.
Jessica Gets Spooked. New York, Bantam, 1993.
The Twins Big Pow-Wow. New York, Bantam, 1993.
Elizabeth's Piano Lessons. New York, Bantam, 1994.
Get the Teacher! New York, Bantam, 1994.
Elizabeth the Tattletale. New York, Bantam, 1994.
Lila's April Fool. New York, Bantam, 1994.
Jessica's Mermaid. New York, Bantam, 1994.
Steven's Twin. New York, Bantam, 1994.
Lois and the Sleepover. New York, Bantam, 1994.
Julie the Karate Kid. New York, Bantam, 1994.
The Magic Puppets. New York, Bantam, 1994.
Star of the Parade. New York, Bantam, 1994.
The Halloween War. New York, Bantam, 1995.
Jessica's Big Mistake. New York, Bantam, 1995.
The Jessica and Elizabeth Show. New York, Bantam, 1995.
Jessica + Jessica = Trouble. New York, Bantam, 1995.
Jessica Plays Cupid. New York, Bantam, 1995.
Lila's Birthday Bash. New York, Bantam, 1995.
Lila's Christmas Angel. New York, Bantam, 1995.
Lila's Secret. New York, Bantam, 1995.
Lila's Secret Valentine. New York, Bantam, 1995.
The Magic Puppets. New York, Bantam, 1995.
No Girls Allowed. New York, Bantam, 1995.
Scaredy-Cat Elizabeth. New York, Bantam, 1995.
The Amazing Jessica. New York, Bantam, 1996.
And the Winner Is . . . Jessica Wakefield! New York, Bantam, 1996.
Elizabeth's Horseback Adventure. New York, Bantam, 1996.
A Roller Coaster for the Twins! New York, Bantam, 1996.
The Secret of Fantasy Forest. New York, Bantam, 1996.
Steven's Big Crush. New York, Bantam, 1996.
Class Picture Day! New York, Bantam, 1997.
Good-Bye, Mrs. Otis. New York, Bantam, 1997.
Jessica's Secret Friend. New York, Bantam, 1997.
The MacAroni Mess. New York, Bantam, 1997.
The Witch in the Pumpkin Patch. New York, Bantam, 1997.
Danger: Twins at Work! New York, Bantam, 1998.
Little Drummer Girls. New York, Bantam, 1998.
Sweet Valley Blizzard! New York, Bantam, 1998.

"Sweet Valley Kids" Super Snooper Series

The Case of the Secret Santa. New York, Bantam, 1990.
The Case of the Magic Christmas Bell. New York, Bantam, 1991.
The Case of the Haunted Camp. New York, Bantam, 1992.
The Case of the Christmas Thief. New York, Bantam, 1992.
The Case of the Hidden Treasure. New York, Bantam, 1993.
The Case of the Million-Dollar Diamonds. New York, Bantam, 1993.
The Case of the Alien Princess. New York, Bantam, 1994.

"Sweet Valley Kids" Super Special Series

The Easter Bunny Battle. New York, Bantam, 1996.
Elizabeth Hatches an Egg. New York, Bantam, 1996
Jessica's Animal Instincts. New York, Bantam, 1996.

"Sweet Valley Kids" Hair Raiser Super Special Series

A Curse on Elizabeth. New York, Bantam, 1995.
Elizabeth Hatches an Egg. New York, Bantam, 1996.

"Sweet Valley University" Series

College Girls. New York, Bantam, 1993.
Love, Lies, and Jessica Wakefield. New York, Bantam, 1993.
What Your Parents Don't Know. . . . New York, Bantam, 1994.
Anything for Love. New York, Bantam, 1994.
A Married Woman. New York, Bantam, 1994.
The Love of Her Life. New York, Bantam, 1994.
Home for Christmas. New York, Bantam, 1994.
Behind Closed Doors. New York, Bantam, 1995.
College Cruise. New York, Bantam, 1995.
Deadly Attraction. New York, Bantam, 1995.
No Means No. New York, Bantam, 1995.
The Other Woman. New York, Bantam, 1995.
Shipboard Wedding. New York, Bantam, 1995.
Sorority Scandal. New York, Bantam, 1995.
S.S. Heartbreak. New York, Bantam, 1995.
Take Back the Night. New York, Bantam, 1995.
Billie's Secret. New York, Bantam, 1996.
Broken Promises, Shattered Dreams. New York, Bantam, 1996.
Busted. New York, Bantam, 1996.
Elizabeth's Summer Love. New York, Bantam, 1996.
For the Love of Ryan. New York, Bantam, 1996.
Here Comes the Bride. New York, Bantam, 1996.
His Secret Past. New York, Bantam, 1996.
Sweet Kiss of Summer. New York, Bantam, 1996.
The Trial of Jessica Wakefield. New York, Bantam, 1996.
Beauty and the Beach. New York, Bantam, 1997.
The Boys of Summer. New York, Bantam, 1997.
Elizabeth and Todd Forever. New York, Bantam, 1997.
Elizabeth's Heartbreak. New York, Bantam, 1997.
One Last Kiss. New York, Bantam, 1997.
Out of the Picture. New York, Bantam, 1997.
Spy Girl. New York, Bantam, 1997.
The Truth About Ryan. New York, Bantam, 1997.
Undercover Angels. New York, Bantam, 1997.
Breaking Away. New York, Bantam, 1998.
Channel X: Thriller Edition. New York, Bantam, 1998.
Elizabeth—New York. New York, Bantam, 1998.
Escape to New York. New York, Bantam, 1998.
Good-Bye, Elizabeth. New York, Bantam, 1998.
Have You Heard About Elizabeth? New York, Bantam, 1998.
Private Jessica. New York, Bantam, 1998.
Sneaking In. New York, Bantam, 1998.

"Sweet Valley University" Thriller Editions

Kiss of the Vampire. New York, Bantam, 1995.
Wanted for Murder. New York, Bantam, 1995.

He's Watching You. New York, Bantam, 1995.
He's Watching You, Vol 2. New York, Bantam, 1995.
The House of Death. New York, Bantam, 1996.
The Roommate. New York, Bantam, 1996.
Running for Her Life. New York, Bantam, 1996.
Dead Before Dawn. New York, Bantam, 1997.
Killer at Sea. New York, Bantam, 1997.
What Winston Saw. New York, Bantam, 1997.
Don't Answer the Phone. New York, Bantam, 1998.
Love and Murder. New York, Bantam, 1998.

"Unicorn Club" Series

Save the Unicorns. New York, Bantam, 1994.
Maria's Movie Comeback. New York, Bantam, 1994.
The Best Friend Game. New York, Bantam, 1994.
Lila's Little Sister. New York, Bantam, 1994.
Unicorns in Love. New York, Bantam, 1994.
Too Close for Comfort. New York, Bantam, 1995.
The Unicorns at War. New York, Bantam, 1995.
Unicorns in Love. New York, Bantam, 1995.
Ellen's Family. New York, Bantam, 1996.
Lila on the Loose. New York, Bantam, 1996.
Mandy in the Middle. New York, Bantam, 1996.
Five Girls and a Baby. New York, Bantam, 1996.
Who Will Be Miss Unicorn? New York, Bantam, 1996.
Bon Voyage, Unicorns. New York, Bantam, 1997.
Boyfriends for Everyone. New York, Bantam, 1997.
The Most Beautiful Girls in the World. New York, Bantam, 1997.
Rachel's In, Lila's Out. New York, Bantam, 1997.
Snow Bunnies. New York, Bantam, 1997.
In Love With Mandy. New York, Bantam, 1997
Jessica's Dream Date. New York, Bantam, 1998.
Trapped in the Mall. New York, Bantam, 1998.

"Unicorn Club" Super Editions

The Unicorns at War. New York, Bantam, 1995.
Angels Keep Out. New York, Bantam, 1996.

"Caitlin" Series

The Love Trilogy: Volume 1: Loving, Volume 2: Love Lost, Volume 3: True Love. New York, Bantam, 1986.
The Promise Trilogy: Volume 1: Tender Promises. New York, Bantam, 1986; *Volume 2: Promises Broken.* New York, Bantam, 1986; *Volume 3: A New Promise.* New York, Bantam, 1987.
The Forever Trilogy: Volume 1: Dreams of Forever, Volume 2: Forever and Always, Volume 3: Together Forever. New York, Bantam, 1987.

Publications for Adults

With J. Pascal, *The Strange Case of Patty Hearst.* New York, New American Library, 1974.
Save Johanna! (novel). New York, Morrow, 1981.
If Wishes Were Horses (novel). New York, Crown, 1994.

*

Critical Studies: Entry in *Authors and Artists for Young Adults,* Vol. 1, Detroit, Gale Research, 1989, 189-202; entry in *Children's Literature Review,* Vol. 25, Detroit, Gale Research, 1991, 175-182; entry in *Something About the Author,* Vol. 80, Detroit, Gale Research, 1992, 171-178; "Francine Pascal" in *Speaking for Ourselves, Too: More Autobiographical Sketches by Notable Authors of Books for Young Adults,* compiled and edited by Donald R. Gallo, Urbana, Illinois, National Council of Teachers of English, 1993, 154-155.

*   *   *

Francine Pascal is well regarded as an author of realistic fiction for young adolescent girls in which she addresses their concerns in humorous and sensitive ways. However she probably is best known for her "Sweet Valley High" series, paperback formula novels about teenagers who live in the middle-class suburb of Sweet Valley, California.

Pascal grew up reading the classics, adventure comics, and fairy tales since no young adult literature existed. She remembers loving a poem by Robert Louis Stevenson, "My Bed Is a Boat," and after hearing it she went to sleep pretending she was surrounded by the sea. She wrote poetry and plays at a very young age, and revealed in an interview with Marguerite Feitlowitz in *Authors and Artists for Young Adults,* "I have always had a very active imagination—my retreat when things don't go right. I realized early that this set me apart from most people. For example, it wasn't my habit to confide in others very much, particularly my parents. As far back as I can recall, I kept a diary. Important thoughts, imaginings, and events were recounted in my diaries, not people." As true of many adolescents, Pascal did not have the ideal high school experience. She believes that the feelings associated with adolescence are universal and that no matter when one goes to high school, it can be a pretty awful experience. She has added in the Feitlowitz interview that ". . . all of us think high school is wonderful for everyone else. The 'Sweet Valley' series come out of what I fantasized high school was like for everyone but me."

After college, she met her husband, a journalist, who Pascal felt was her mentor. He appreciated her ideas and encouraged her efforts. She began writing articles for magazines such as *True Confessions, Ladies' Home Journal,* and *Cosmopolitan.* With her husband she wrote for a soap opera, as well as collaborated on a musical and a book. She credits him with insisting that she immediately put in writing a potential plot she was pondering, a plot that became her first young adult novel, *Hangin' Out with Cici.* This story is about a young girl, Victoria, who while visiting her aunt was caught smoking a joint. On the train trip home, she imagines herself back in time where she meets a girl named Cici who shoplifts, sneaks cigarettes, and cheats on a test. Before waking from this dream Victoria realizes that Cici is her mother. Full of humor and realism, this intriguing time-travel fantasy focuses on the relationship of the daughter and mother and how understanding helped create a stronger relationship. Other early adolescent fiction included *My First Love and Other Disasters,* which uses a first-person narrative to add reality to the story, and

Hand Me Down Kid, one of her more popular books. The latter focuses on the meaning of self-respect and personal determination.

The first ideas for the ''Sweet Valley High'' series came to Pascal when she wanted to create a soap opera for teens. This idea didn't seem to interest producers, but someone suggested that she try a book series instead. Pascal planned that each book would have to be a complete story in itself but with a hook ending to lead you to the sequel. After she decided the main characters would be twins with opposite personalities, she wrote and submitted her proposal to Bantam and they immediately accepted it. Elizabeth and Jessica Wakefield became one of the most famous sets of twins in the world of young readers. Although they are identical, Elizabeth is friendly, outgoing, and sincere while Jessica is arrogant, superficial and conniving. The plot is designed around problems that are familiar to adolescent girls, such as relationships with boys, special events, or other personal situations. Adults are almost non-existent. Pascal calls it the ''essence of high school. . . It's that moment before reality hits, when you really do believe in the romantic values—sacrifice, love, loyalty, friendship—before you get jaded and slip off into adulthood.''

Although Pascal's fiction, as in the ''Caitlin Series,'' has been acclaimed for wit, precise use of dialogue and setting, understanding of characters and situations, and compelling plots, the ''Sweet Valley High'' series has received a strongly negative reaction from adult professionals. Many find these books problematic because of their simplistic plots, unbelievable characterizations, blatant morals, and facile writing as well as sexism and racism. Nevertheless, they continue to be very popular with young readers, even to the point of making publishing history when in 1985 *Perfect Summer* (Super Edition) became the first young adult novel to make the *New York Times* bestseller list.

Not everyone, however, disregards the significance of these books to many readers. Some recognize that the ''Sweet Valley High'' series, through high interest subjects and characters with whom readers identify, captures the attention of reluctant readers and nonreaders. Pascal herself says, ''Books encourage young people to read. 'Sweet Valley High' opened a market that simply didn't exist before. It is not that those millions of girls were not reading my books, they weren't reading any books. I have gotten many, many letters from kids saying that they never read before 'Sweet Valley High.' If nine out of ten of those girls go on to read Judith Krantz and Danielle Steel, so be it, they are still reading. . . . The reality is that not everyone is able, or wishes to read great literature. There should be books for all types of readers. Reading time is precious; it's a time for privacy, fantasy, learning, a time to live in our imaginations. No one should be denied that.''

The Sweet Valley High series prompted several spinoffs—''Sweet Valley Twins,'' in which Elizabeth and Jessica are in the sixth grade; ''Sweet Valley Kids,'' where they are six-year-olds; ''Sweet Valley'' super thriller series, which resembles adult mystery and horror stories; and ''The Wakefields of Sweet Valley,'' a novel that covers 100 years and five generations of Wakefield families originating in Sweden and England. In addition, they are translated in over 15 languages, have been adapted for a television series and films, and young fans themselves have created an Internet web site that focuses on the series and its characters.

The books are written by a stable of writers, because so many titles come out each month. Pascal has created all the plot outlines, character descriptions, time settings, plot twists and conflicts. She says she maintains artistic control over every aspect. Because of the universal characteristics of adolescence, Pascal said that the series could potentially could go on forever. The fact she has received over 1000 a month from young readers attests to the potential continuing popularity of this series.

—Janelle B. Mathis

PATERSON, Katherine (Womeldorf)

Nationality: American. **Born:** Qing Jiang, China, 31 October 1932; came to the United States, 1940. **Education:** King College, Bristol, Tennessee, 1950-54, A.B. (summa cum laude) 1954; Presbyterian School of Christian Education, Richmond, Virginia, 1955-57, M.A. 1957; Kobe School of Japanese Language, Japan, 1957-60; Union Theological Seminary, New York, 1961-62, M.R.E. 1962. **Family:** Married John Barstow Paterson in 1962; two sons and two adopted daughters. **Career:** Public school teacher, Lovettsville, Virginia, 1954-55; missionary, Presbyterian Church Board of World Missions, Nashville, Tennessee, and in Shikoku Island, Japan, 1957-62; teacher of Sacred Studies and English, Pennington School for Boys, Pennington, New Jersey, 1963-65; writer. **Awards:** American Library Association (ALA) Notable Children's Book award, 1974, for *Of Nightingales That Weep;* ALA Notable Children's Book award, 1976, National Book award for Children's Literature, 1977, runner-up for Edgar Allan Poe award (juvenile division) from Mystery Writers of America, 1977, and American Book award nomination, children's fiction paperback, 1982, all for *The Master Puppeteer;* ALA Notable Children's Book award, 1977, John Newbery Medal, 1978, Lewis Carroll Shelf award, 1978, and Division II runner-up, Michigan Young Reader's award, 1980, all for *Bridge to Terabithia;* Lit.D., King College, 1978; ALA Notable Children's Book award, 1978, National Book award for Children's Literature, 1979, Christopher award (ages 9-12), 1979, Newbery Honor Book, 1979, CRABbery (Children Raving About Books) Honor Book, 1979, American Book award nominee, children's paperback, 1980, William Allen White Children's Book award, 1981, Garden State Children's Book award, younger division, New Jersey Library Association, 1981, Georgia Children's Book award, 1981, Iowa Children's Choice award, 1981, Massachusetts Children's Book award (elementary), 1981, all for *The Great Gilly Hopkins;* D.H.L.: Otterbein College, Westerville, Ohio, 1980; U.S. nominee, Hans Christian Andersen award, 1980; *New York Times* Outstanding Book List, 1980, Newbery Medal, 1981, CRABbery Honor Book, 1981, American Book award nominee, children's hardcover, 1981, children's paperback, 1982, and Hans Christian Andersen award nominee, 1990, all for *Jacob Have I Loved; The Crane Wife* was named to the *New York Times* Outstanding Books and Best Illustrated Books lists, both 1981; Saint Mary-of-the-Woods College, Indiana, 1981; University of Maryland College Park, 1982; Washington and Lee University, Lexington, Virginia, 1982; Parent's Choice award, Parent's Choice Foundation, 1983, for *Rebels of the Heavenly Kingdom;* Irvin Kerlan award, 1983, ''in recognition of singular attainments in the creation of children's literature'';

University of Southern Mississippi School of Library Service Silver Medallion, 1983, for outstanding contributions to the field of children's literature; *New York Times* notable book citation and "Parent's Choice" citation, both 1985, for *Come Sing, Jimmy Jo;* nominee, Laura Ingalls Wilder award, 1986; Winchester, Virginia, 1986; Regina Medal award, Catholic Library Association, 1988, for demonstrating "the timeless standards and ideals for the writing of good literature for children"; *Boston Globe-Horn Book* award, 1991, for *The Tale of the Mandarin Ducks.* **Address:** c/o E. P. Dutton, 375 Hudson St., New York, New York 10014, U.S.A.

PUBLICATIONS FOR YOUNG ADULTS

Fiction

The Sign of the Chrysanthemum, illustrated by Peter Landa. New York, Crowell Junior Books, 1973; London, Kestrel, 1975.
Of Nightingales That Weep, illustrated by Haru Wells. New York, Crowell Junior Books, 1974; London, Kestrel, 1976.
The Master Puppeteer, illustrated by Haru Wells. New York, Crowell Junior Books, 1976.
Bridge to Terabithia, illustrated by Donna Diamond. New York, Crowell Junior Books, 1977; London, Gollancz, 1978.
The Great Gilly Hopkins. New York, Crowell Junior Books, 1978; London, Gollancz, 1979.
Jacob Have I Loved. New York, Crowell Junior Books, 1980; London, Gollancz, 1981.
Rebels of the Heavenly Kingdom. New York, Lodestar, 1983.
Come Sing, Jimmy Jo. New York, Lodestar, 1985; London, Gollancz, 1986.
Park's Quest. New York, Lodestar, 1988; London, Gollancz, 1989.
Lyddie. New York, Dutton, 1991.
Flip-flop Girl. New York, Dutton, 1994.
Celia and the Sweet, Sweet Water, illustrated by Vladimir Vagin. New York, Clarion Books, 1998.

Other

Who Am I?, illustrated by David Stone. Richmond, CLC Press, 1966.
Justice for All People. New York, Friendship, 1973.
To Make Men Free: Learning Center Box. Richmond, John Knox, 1973.
Translator, *The Crane Wife,* by Sumiko Yagawa, illustrated by Suekichi Akaba. New York, Morrow, 1981.
Consider the Lilies: Flowers of the Bible, with husband, John Paterson, illustrated by Anne Ophelia Dowden. New York, Crowell Junior Books, 1986.
Translator, *Tongue-Cut Sparrow* (Japanese folktale), retold by Momoko Ishii, illustrated by Suekichi Akaba. New York, Lodestar, 1987.
With Stephanie Tolan, *Bridge to Terabithia* (play), music by Steve Liebman. New York, S. French, 1992.
A Midnight Clear, Stories for the Christmas Season. New York, Lodestar Books, 1995.
Reteller, *The Angel and the Donkey,* illustrated by Alexander Koshkin. New York, Clarion Books, 1996.
With John Paterson, *Images of God: Views of the Invisible.* New York, Clarion Books, 1998.
Reteller, *Parzival: The Quest of the Grail Knight.* New York, Lodestar Books, 1998.

PUBLICATIONS FOR CHILDREN

Fiction

Angels and Other Strangers: Family Christmas Stories. New York, Crowell Junior Books, 1979; as *Star of Night: Stories for Christmas,* London, Gollancz, 1980.
The Smallest Cow in the World, illustrated by Jane Clark Brown. Burlington, Vermont Migrant Education Program, 1988.
The Tale of the Mandarin Ducks, illustrated by Leo and Diane Dillon. New York, Dutton, 1990.
The King's Equal, illustrated by Vladimir Vagin. New York, HarperCollins, 1992.
Editor, with Ann Durell and Jean Craighead George, *The Big Book for the Planet.* New York, Dutton, 1993.
Marvin's Best Christmas Present Ever, illustrated by Jane Clark Brown. New York, HarperCollins, 1997.

PUBLICATIONS FOR ADULTS

Other

Gates of Excellence: On Reading and Writing Books for Children. New York, Elsevier Nelson, 1981.
The Spying Heart: More Thoughts on Reading and Writing Books for Children. New York, Lodestar, 1989.
A Sense of Wonder: On Reading and Writing Books for Children (includes *Gates of Excellence* and *The Spying Heart*). New York, Plume, 1995.

*

Media Adaptations: "Bridge to Terabithia" (listening record or cassette; filmstrip with cassette), Miller-Brody, 1978, (filmstrip), Random House/Miller-Brody, 1980, (film), PBS-TV, 1985; *The Great Gilly Hopkins* (film), Hanna-Barbera, 1980, (listening record or cassette; filmstrip with cassette), Random House; "Angels and Other Strangers" (cassette), Random House; "Jacob Have I Loved" (listening cassette; filmstrip with cassette), Random House, 1982, (film) PBS-TV, 1990; "Getting Hooked on Books: Challenges" (filmstrip with cassette, with teacher's guide, contains "The Great Gilly Hopkins"), Guidance Associates, 1986.

Biography: Entry in *Fifth Book of Junior Authors and Illustrators,* Bronx, New York, Wilson, 1983; entry in *Dictionary of Literary Biography,* Volume 52: *American Writers for Children since 1960: Fiction,* Detroit, Gale, 1986, pp. 296-314; essay in *Authors and Artists for Young Adults,* Volume 1, Detroit, Gale, 1989; essay in *Speaking for Ourselves: Autobiographical Sketches by Notable Authors of Books for Young Adults,* Volume 1, compiled and edited by Donald R. Gallo, National Council of Teachers of English, 1990.

Manuscript Collections: Kerlan Collection, University of Minnesota, Minneapolis.

Critical Studies: Entry in *Children's Literature Review,* Volume 7, Detroit, Gale, 1984; entry in *Contemporary Literary Criticism,* Detroit, Gale, Volume 12, 1980; Volume 30, 1984.

Katherine Paterson comments:

I write as a way to struggle with the questions that life throws at me. I write for the young because we seem to be wrestling with the same questions.

*   *   *

In her own work on writing, *Gates of Excellence: On Reading and Writing Books for Children,* Paterson stresses the importance of writers "telling a story." And that, Katherine Paterson does very well. She did not set out to become a writer and was not particularly encouraged as a writer by her early teachers. Although she began writing seriously in 1964, she did not publish her first novel until 1973. In spite of her protest about not being a natural storyteller, she indeed is. Her books and speeches are laden with anecdotes about herself, family, and friends. Paterson's use of metaphors from country cooking, popular culture, nature, and the Bible brings life and poetic imagery to her characters and settings. Although she was born in China and spent her early childhood there, Paterson comes out of the southern tradition of writing. In a talk she gave at Simmons College, Paterson attributed three dominant influences to her development as a writer—her birth in China and later missionary years in Japan, her growing up in the American South, and her strong Biblical heritage.

Her fiction defies categorization as either intended for children or young adults. Her love and concern for children is demonstrated in her own life. She and her husband adopted one child and have taken in foster children. Paterson's passion for children is also evident in her speeches to various groups around the country.

Drawing on her knowledge of Japanese history and culture, Paterson's first three young adult novels are set in feudal Japan. *The Sign of the Chrysanthemum* takes place in twelfth-century Japan. Muna is a young orphan who sets out to find his samurai father and thus his identity. *Of Nightingales That Weep* and *The Master Puppeteer* are also set in medieval Japan. These novels are highly regarded for their accurate depiction of Japanese history and culture, particularly the features of the puppet theater in the latter. *The Master Puppeteer* received the Edgar Allan Poe Special Award from the Mystery Writers of American and the National Book Award in 1982. The sense of place and time is aptly conveyed by Paterson in all three novels, evident through her use of significant authentic details to set scene and atmosphere. Both *The Master Puppeteer* and *Of Nightingales that Weep* have also been praised by critics for their skillfully constructed plots, supported by strong characterizations.

Bridge to Terabithia, her fourth novel, is a shift from the historical fiction genre to a contemporary setting. It is the story of two fifth graders who become best friends and is based in part on the experience of Paterson's younger son whose best friend dies. Jesse and Leslie, the two main characters from very different backgrounds, spend much of their time together creating a fantasy world, Terabithia. The strength of *Bridge to Terabithia* lies in the convincing portrayal of the unusual relationship between Jesse and Leslie. But the novel presents an unromantic, realistic, and moving reaction to personal tragedy, demonstrating Paterson's skill in dealing with one of the most difficult topics in young adult literature — death. Jess and Leslie are effectively developed as characters that young readers might well recognize as classmates who sit next to them or ride on the same school bus. After the crushing blow of Leslie's death, rather than lingering on the lost friendship, Paterson allows Jesse to move toward maturity as he passes Terabithia on to his younger sister, May Belle. *Bridge to Terabithia* brought Paterson the literary and critical recognition that her earlier historical novels had not been able to do.

In 1978, *The Great Gilly Hopkins* was published, based on Paterson's personal experience as a foster mother, marking Paterson's entrance into the young adult social problem novel. Gilly, an eleven-year-old, like many of Paterson's earlier characters is in search of a parent, a common theme in her novels. Gilly has learned to survive the many foster homes in which she has been placed. She fights against any sign of love or care by lying and swearing, her defense from being emotionally hurt. Some critics felt the novel did not measure up to Paterson's previous *Bridge to Terabithia.* While the emotional impact of the novel is a very different one, Gilly does pull at the emotional strings of the reader. In spite of the critics' claims of shortcomings, the novel gained the attention of numerous awards and was named a Newbery Award Honor Book and earned Paterson a second National Book Award.

Jacob Have I Loved is set on the imaginary Chesapeake Island of Rass. The title of the novel refers to the Biblical story of the twins Jacob and Esau and is a story of the bitter jealousy of twin sisters, Louise and Caroline. The setting of the novel on an isolated Chesapeake Island contributes to and intensifies the theme of sibling rivalry between the twins. Unlike Paterson's earlier novels, it is written from the first person point of view, through Sarah Louise "Wheeze's" eyes. Some critics took Paterson to task on the first-person narrative suggesting that the first-person narrative loses some of its momentum as the main characters mature into adulthood. The voices of other reviewers and critics clearly praised the depth of characterization and the vitality and freshness in the writing style. *Jacob Have I Loved* garnered a second Newbery award for Paterson in 1980.

Returning to her historical fiction writing roots, Paterson in 1983 wrote *Rebels of the Heavenly Kingdom,* set in mid-nineteenth-century China. It is the story of Wang Lee who becomes an impassioned warrior of the Heavenly Kingdon, killing wantonly and bloodily, convinced that the cause of the kingdom is greater than individual human life. Paterson again faithfully demonstrates her knowledge of Oriental culture and history.

Paterson returns to the theme of the "quest for parents" in *Come Sing, Jimmy Jo* and *Park's Quest. Come Sing, Jimmy Jo* follows the musical achievements of shy, gifted mountain boy James Johnson, who later becomes "Jimmy Jo" in the world of country music. The novel did not receive the critical acclaim of Paterson's earlier works. *Park's Quest,* on the other hand, received wide acclaim with some reviewers calling it her best work. Park is the son of a pilot killed during the Vietnam war and his quest is to find out the kind of man his father was. The novel has been praised for its realistic portrayal of characters and sensitive treatment of a touchy event in our country's history.

Paterson's young adult novel, *Lyddie,* is a historical novel set in New England. The novel received glowing critical acclaim. Its riveting plot, engaging characters, and a New England setting make it a true grit story. The strength of the novel rests with its superb characterization. The spirited portrayal of Lyddie Worten serves as a model of hope for teenage readers.

Paterson's contribution to the field of young adult literature has been immeasurable. She not only knows how to "tell a good story" but does it in way that is challenging to her young adult audience. Paterson does not write about the trite; instead, she zeroes in on events and characters that ring true to life. She does not always choose to write about people and events that are uplifting, and the "happy ending" resolution so typical of many young adult novels cannot be applied to hers. It is this honesty that has gained her not only critical acclaim but the devoted following of young adult readers today.

—Donald J. Kenney

PATON WALSH, Jill

Nationality: British. **Born:** London, England, 29 April 1937. **Education:** St. Michael's Convent, North Finchley, London, 1943-55; St. Anne's College, Oxford, 1955-59, Dip. Ed. 1959, M.A. (honours) in English. **Family:** Married Antony Edmund Paton Walsh in 1961; one son and two daughters. **Career:** English teacher, Enfield Girls Grammar School, Middlesex, 1959-62; writer, since 1962. Whittall Lecturer, Library of Congress, Washington, D.C., 1978; visiting faculty member, Center for the Study of Children's Literature, Simmons College, Boston, 1978-86; founder, with John Rowe Townsend, *q.v.,* Green Bay Publishers, 1986. **Awards:** *Book World* Festival award, 1970, for *Fireweed*; Whitbread Prize (shared with Russell Hoban), 1974, for *The Emperor's Winding Sheet*; *Boston Globe-Horn Book* award, 1976, for *Unleaving*; Arts Council Creative Writing Fellowship, 1976-77, and 1977-78; Universe Prize, 1984, for *A Parcel of Patterns*; Smarties Prize Grand Prix, 1985, for *Gaffer Samson's Luck.* **Address:** c/o David Higham Associates, 5-8 Lower John St., Golden Square, London W1R 4HA, England.

PUBLICATIONS FOR YOUNG ADULTS

Fiction

Hengest's Tale, illustrated by Janet Margrie. London, Macmillan, and New York, St. Martin's Press, 1966.
The Dolphin Crossing. London, Macmillan, and New York, St. Martin's Press, 1967.
Fireweed. London, Macmillan, 1969; New York, Farrar Straus, 1970.
Goldengrove. London, Macmillan, and New York, Farrar Straus, 1972.
The Dawnstone, illustrated by Mary Dinsdale. London, Hamish Hamilton, 1973.
Toolmaker, illustrated by Jeroo Roy. London, Heinemann, 1973; New York, Seabury Press, 1974.
The Emperor's Winding Sheet. London, Macmillan, and New York, Farrar Straus, 1974.

The Butty Boy, illustrated by Juliette Palmer. London, Macmillan, 1975; as *The Huffler,* New York, Farrar Straus, 1975.
Unleaving. London, Macmillan, and New York, Farrar Straus, 1976.
Children of the Fox. New York, Farrar Straus, 1978.
Crossing to Salamis, illustrated by David Smee. London, Heinemann, 1977.
The Walls of Athens, illustrated by David Smee. London, Heinemann, 1977.
Persian Gold, illustrated by David Smee. London, Heinemann, 1978.
A Chance Child. London, Macmillan, and New York, Farrar Straus, 1978.
The Green Book, illustrated by Joanna Stubbs. London, Macmillan, 1981; illustrated by Lloyd Bloom, New York, Farrar Straus, 1982; as *Shine,* London, Macdonald, 1988.
Babylon, illustrated by Jenny Northway. London, Deutsch, 1982.
A Parcel of Patterns. London, Kestrel, and New York, Farrar Straus, 1983.
Gaffer Samson's Luck, illustrated by Brock Cole. New York, Farrar Straus, 1984; London, Viking Kestrel, 1985.
Torch. London, Viking Kestral, 1987; New York, Farrar Straus, 1988.
Grace. London and New York, Viking, 1991.

Other

Wordhoard: Anglo-Saxon Stories, with Kevin Crossley-Holland. London, Macmillan, and New York, Farrar Straus, 1969.
The Island Sunrise: Prehistoric Britain. London, Deutsch, 1975; as *The Island Sunrise: Prehistoric Culture in the British Isles,* New York, Seabury Press, 1976.

PUBLICATIONS FOR CHILDREN

Fiction

Lost and Found, illustrated by Mary Rayner. London, Deutsch, 1984.
Birdy and the Ghosties, illustrated by Alan Marks. London, Macdonald, 1989.
Can I Play Farmer, Farmer? London, Bodley Head, 1990.
When Grandma Came, illustrated by Sophie Williams. New York, Viking, 1992.
Matthew and the Seasingers. Hemel Hempstead, Simon & Schuster, 1992; New York, Farrar, Straus & Giroux, 1993.
Pepi and the Secret Names. New York, Lothrop, Lee & Shepard, 1994.
Connie Came to Play, illustrated by Stephen Lambert. London and New York, Viking, 1995.
The Dolphin Crossing, illustrated by Chris Molan. London, Puffin, 1995.
When I Was Little Like You, illustrated by Stephen Lambert. London, Viking, 1997.

PUBLICATIONS FOR ADULTS

Novels

Farewell, Great King. London, Macmillan, and New York, Coward McCann, 1972.
Lapsing. London, Weidenfeld & Nicolson, 1986; New York, St. Martin's, 1987.
A School for Lovers. Cambridge, Greenbay, and New York, Houghton Mifflin, 1989.

Knowledge of Angels. London, Weidenfeld & Nicolson, and Boston, Houghton Mifflin, 1994.
A Piece of Justice: An Imogen Quy Mystery. London, Hodder & Stoughton, and New York, St. Martin's Press, 1995.
The Serpentine Cave. London, Doubleday, 1997; New York, St. Martin's Press, 1997.

Short Stories

Five Tides. Cambridge, Green Bay, 1986.

*

Biography: Essay in *Something about the Author Autobiography Series,* Vol. 3, Detroit, Gale, 1987; essay in *Speaking for Ourselves: Autobiographical Sketches by Notable Authors of Books for Young Adults,* Vol. 1, compiled and edited by Donald R. Gallo, National Council of Teachers of English, 1990.

Manuscript Collections: Kerlan Collection, University of Minnesota, Minneapolis.

Critical Studies: Entry in *Children's Literature Review,* Vol. 2, Detroit, Gale, 1976; entry in *Contemporary Literary Criticism,* Vol. 35, Detroit, Gale, 1985.

Jill Paton Walsh comments:

Why am I a writer? It is the work that I find I can do.

I feel no need to justify being a writer for young readers. Children and adolescents are at once the most interesting characters to write about and the most important readers.

To those adults who do not see that what children read, what they come to think and feel is deeply important, I would say "Unless you die very soon you will soon learn better." With breathtaking speed, children become adults.

To young people who read my books I would say, "I hope you find food for thought here. I hope this story-telling will help you turn the unlimited possibilities ahead of you into lives full of achievement, kindness, and joy. Above all I hope you will read widely, life-long. Nothing empowers you more than a story you have taken to heart."

*   *   *

Throughout a long and prolific career, Jill Paton Walsh has presented young-adult readers with a great range and variety of novels. Although different in setting, genre, and style, they share an underlying seriousness and introduce young people to thought-provoking and often uncomfortable issues. Through strong and fully explored central characters, Paton Walsh draws young readers into a sensitive exploration of the difficulties of finding their own identities and making decisions for themselves. The most immediately attractive features of these novels, however, are their absorbing plots and believable settings.

Paton Walsh believes that historical fiction should portray people and events in a way that not only re-creates what is known but goes a step further and imagines characters' emotions and everyday experiences as well. She draws connections between the events of the past and those of the present, allowing her young reader to journey along with the protagonist through a society that is different and strange.

Hengest's Tale is about the mid-fifth-century ruler of Kent and one of the first of the successful Saxon invaders. As Hengest lies dying he tells the story of his youth, and his complex and ultimately tragic friendship with the king's son, Finn. Hengest has never recovered from killing Finn and confronts his feelings only at the point of death. The characters are three dimensional, but have enough differences in thought pattern and action to make them believable as people of the Dark Ages. At the same time they have enough similarities to modern people to be understandable. *Fireweed* and *The Dolphin Crossing* are set during the Second World War and explore the possibilities and dangers of a world in which young people are set free from the support or constraint of adults. Both of these stories look at the differences imposed by class structure. Pat Riley, an evacuee living in a derelict railway carriage, and John Aston, a boy from a wealthy family, meet and become partners in *The Dolphin Crossing.* In *Fireweed* we meet Bill, a lower class evacuee on his own for sometime, and Julie, a member of a wealthy family and a survivor from a torpedoed ship. In both of these novels, it is the war that brought the two pairs together.

The Emperor's Winding Sheet, set in Constantinople in the last days of the Byzantine Empire, gives an unflinching account of the siege and sacking of the city by the Turks. The events are seen through the eyes of Piers, and English youth who is found and adopted as mascot and servant by the new emperor, Constantine. Because Piers is so naive, everything has to be explained to him by his friend Stephanos, a technique that allows the reader to understand the background of the story and its characters, especially Emperor Constantine. Next Paton Walsh presents a trip down the nineteenth-century canals with *The Butty Boy.* A familiar plot is the poor little rich girl meeting two working-class children. Harry convinces fourteen-year-old Bess and eleven-year-old Ned that she is a mistreated servant girl and the two take her on as a "huffler" for the journey to the paper mill. Harry and the reader learn, as she travels down the canal, about the lives and the things she used daily. *A Parcel of Patterns* is drawn from records of the lives and deaths of the inhabitants of the Derbyshire Village of Eyam, recounting the effects of the plague brought to the community in 1665. The strong-willed Puritans are seen through the eyes of Mal Percival, a teenage girl whose faith and courage are tested with each new death. Though Mel has always behaved as a Puritan, near the end of the book she questions her faith in God because she does not understand him. Again, something familiar yet different for the youth of today to understand.

Paton Walsh returned to historical novels with *Grace,* a fictionalized account of a true story set in 1838. Grace and her father risk their lives to save the survivors of a wrecked ship. Through the eyes of Grace we see how uncomfortable she is being a heroine. She was disliked by the men who risked their lives, her motives for the rescue were questioned, and the aristocrats took over as her sponsor, demanding a different profile and lifestyle for Grace. As a working-class girl, Grace could not hope to marry a gentleman; yet, having acquired wealth above her station, she could not expect the poor fisherman who loved her to marry her and be known as a man who married for money. Grace is tormented and becomes obsessed with remembering what she was thinking of the morning of the wreck, to know whether she performed the rescue for reward. Grace becomes seriously ill but is haunted about her intentions that morning when she saved the shipwrecked survivors. She climbs to look at the rocks where the wreck took place; there she meets Mr. Tulloch, one of the survivors who tells her that it doesn't matter what her intention was; ''If you did it for rage and spite and greed, am I the less living for that?'' Grace's mind becomes free and she dies the next day.

Paton Walsh believes that ''if the novel has anything to say about history, it must say it through the story, through character and event, not merely through setting.'' Indeed, all of Paton Walsh's historical fiction has a young protagonist who thinks and acts differently than youth today. Walsh makes the past relevant through likable and credible characters: the protagonist in conflict with and alienated from the adult world is a universal and timeless subject.

Paton Walsh combines fantasy with a historical approach to child-labor practices in *A Chance Child.* This is a novel of time travel in which a young boy, locked away in a closet, neglected and unloved, escapes from his world to the past, where he finds children who are treated as badly as he. Because Creep is the only name he has ever known, that is the name he chooses on his journey aboard a boat from the twentieth-century to nineteenth-century England. His boat stops at a mine where he meets Tom, hurled against the wall and left to lie there groaning. Creep offers to help Tom and they take the boat into open waters where it runs by itself. The next time the boat stops they see Lucy: a little girl hanging on a sooty rope from a tree, blowing the fire of a furnace with a bellows. Lucy is called Blackie, because the whole side of her face is a black scar from an earlier fall into the fire. The three children run away to find employment. Conditions are appalling everywhere they go. If they do not work fast enough they get beaten by an overseer; the hours are extremely long; the work environment is dark, and either very cold or very hot. The realistic description and detail allow the young reader to experience what Creep and his friends are experiencing.

Paton Walsh uses the theme of a future world very differently in *The Green Book* and *Torch.* Both novels take place after man's destruction of the world. In *Torch,* the technological expertise and other forms of knowledge have been lost as a result of the nuclear war. The torch that the children carry symbolizes what is missing in the world. Togetherness, as in teamwork and in friendship, is the theme of *Torch.* The children are told that the downfall and destruction of the earlier people was that they stopped working together. The lesson is that people cannot survive along, that fragments of knowledge have to be shared to make a whole. In *The Green Book* the families who have to flee the earth are very sophisticated and literate; they have all of the modern technology and knowledge necessary to make themselves comfortable on a strange planet. The one common thread in both of these books is the death of literature. In *Torch* the children learn from the scholar that if people could read the world would be on its way back. It becomes apparent that the destruction of the world occurred because people stopped learning new ways to do things. In *The Green Book,* each selected person was allowed to bring one personal item. Very few thought to bring a book. ''The truth is, we didn't value that stuff when we had it, when we could just pick up a book any time. And now it's all dying out of our mind, and we must do without. . . .'' They find out that they no longer have ''the sort of goodness they needed to keep alive and well forever,'' and that ''it wasn't really hunger that was making us feel empty.'' The debates about literature and literacy will continue, but it is important that writers continue to impress upon children the importance of literature.

Goldengrove and *Unleaving* are perhaps this author's most ambitious and popular works. In *Goldengrove,* Paton Walsh sensitively and poignantly explores love between young people. On the verge of adulthood, Madge eagerly anticipates her annual holiday reunion in her grandmother's Cornwall house with Paul, the younger boy she knows as her cousin. When this September holiday disappoints their expectations, only the watching grandmother and the reader realize how Madge's growing up is unbalancing their relationship. The novel charts the changing feelings of the young people through the events of their visit until the climax, in which two revelations shatter Madge's expectations of the future and her faith in adults.

In *Unleaving,* the author returns to a slightly older Madge. The challenging structure of the novel intercuts scenes from her summer before university with others centering around an unnamed ''Gran.'' At the conclusion, the reader learns that Gran is the older Madge at last coming to an understanding of her own life. Through this extended portrait of Madge, Paton Walsh is able to show the development of a sensitive and intelligent girl into a young woman and also to suggest how ''growing up'' continues through old age.

Most recently Paton Walsh has written short fiction pieces for younger readers and three adult novels. The juvenile titles are *Matthew and the Sea Singers,* a folktale adaptation; *When Grandma Came,* a contemporary story; and *Pepi and the Secret Names,* set in Ancient Egypt. Her adult novels, *Knowledge of Angels* and *A Piece of Justice,* are mystery thrillers, and her newest novel, *The Serpentine Cave,* focusses on the search for one's identity, which hinges on the relationship of mother and child.

Jill Paton Walsh cannot be categorized. Although she clearly draws inspiration from well-researched historical periods, she is equally interested in the contemporary world and in ideas of a possible future. In her very different novels, she shows her understanding of her young readers' interests and concerns but pays them the tribute of neither patronizing nor sparing them.

—Judith Atkinson, updated by Rosanne Donahue

PAULSEN, Gary

Pseudonym: Paul Garrisen. **Nationality:** American. **Born:** Minneapolis, Minnesota, 17 May 1939. **Education:** Bemidji State University, Minnesota, 1957-58; University of Colorado, Boulder, 1976. **Military Service:** Served in the United States Army (sergeant), 1959-62. **Family:** Married Ruth Ellen Wright in 1971 (third marriage), one son; one son and one daughter from previous marriage. **Career:** Has worked as a teacher, electronics field engineer, editor, actor, director, farmer, rancher, truck driver, trapper, professional archer, migrant farm worker, singer, satellite tracker, musher, sculptor, and sailor. **Awards:** Central Missouri award for Children's Literature, 1976; New York Public Library's Books for the Teen Age, 1980, 1981 and 1982, for *The Green Recruit,* and 1982, for *Sailing: From Jibs to Jibbing*; ALA Best Books for Young Adults, 1983, for *Tiltawhirl John, The Foxman, The Night the White Deer Died, Popcorn Days and Buttermilk Nights,* and *Dancing Carl,* 1989, for *The Crossing* and *The Island,* 1990, for *The Voyage of the Frog* and *Canyons,* 1991, for *The Boy Who Owned the School, Woodsong, The Monument,* and *The Haymeadow,* 1993, for *Nightjohn* and *Harris and Me*; ALA Best

Book list, 1984, and Society of Midland Authors award, 1985, both for *Tracker*; Parents' Choice award for Literature, Parents' Choice Foundation, 1985, for *Dogsong*; Newbery Honor Book, 1986, for *Dogsong*, 1988, for *Hatchet,* and 1990, for *The Winter Room*; Child Study Association of America's Children's Books of the Year, 1986, for *Dogsong*; ALA Notable Children's Book, 1988, for *Hatchet,* 1990, for *The Voyage of the Frog,* and 1991, for *Woodsong*; Spur Award, Western Writers of America, 1993, for *Woodsong* and *The Haymeadow*; IRA-CBC Children's Choice, 1993, for *Nightjohn*; Children's Literature Award Finalist, PEN Center USA West, 1994, for *Sisters/Hermanas*; Margaret A. Edwards Award for lifetime achievement in writing for young adults, 1997; YALSA Best Books for Young Adults, 1998, for *The Schernoff Discoveries.* **Agent:** Jennifer Flannery, 34-40 28th Street #6, New York, New York 11106-3516, U.S.A.

PUBLICATIONS FOR YOUNG ADULTS

Fiction

Mr. Tucket, illustrated by Noel Sickles. New York, Funk and Wagnalls, 1969.

The C.B. Radio Caper, illustrated by John Asquith. Milwaukee, Raintree, 1977.

The Curse of the Cobra, illustrated by John Asquith. Milwaukee, Raintree, 1977.

The Foxman. Nashville, Nelson, 1977.

The Golden Stick, illustrated by Jerry Scott. Milwaukee, Raintree, 1977.

Tiltawhirl John. Nashville, Nelson, 1977.

Winterkill. Nashville, Nelson, and London, Abelard, 1977.

The Green Recruit, with Ray Peekner. Independence, Missouri, Independence Press, 1978.

Hope and a Hatchet. Nashville, Nelson, 1978.

The Night the White Deer Died. Nashville, Nelson, 1978.

The Spitball Gang. New York, Elsevier, 1980.

Dancing Carl. Scarsdale, New York, Bradbury Press, 1983.

Popcorn Days and Buttermilk Nights. New York, Dutton, 1983.

Tracker. New York, Bradbury Press, 1984.

Dogsong. New York, Bradbury Press, 1985.

Sentries. New York, Bradbury Press, 1986.

The Crossing. New York, Orchard, 1987.

Hatchett. New York, Bradbury Press, 1987; as *Hatchet,* London, Macmillan, 1989.

The Island. New York, Orchard, 1988.

Hatchet Rack Trim. New York, Puffin, 1989.

The Voyage of the Frog. New York, Orchard, 1989.

The Winter Room. New York, Orchard, 1989.

The Boy Who Owned the School. New York, Orchard, 1990.

Canyons. New York, Delacorte, 1990.

The Cookcamp. New York, Orchard, 1991.

The Monument. New York, Delacorte, 1991.

The River. New York, Doubleday, 1991.

A Christmas Sonata, illustrated by Leslie Bowman. New York, Delacorte, 1992.

Clabbered Dirt, Sweet Grass, illustrated by Ruth Wright Paulsen. Orlando, Florida, Harcourt, 1992.

Culpepper's Cannon. New York, Dell, 1992.

Dogteam, illustrated by Ruth Wright Paulsen. New York, Delacorte, 1992.

Dunc and the Flaming Ghost. New York, Dell, 1992.

Dunc Breaks the Record. New York, Dell, 1992.

Dunc's Doll. New York, Dell, 1992.

Dunc Gets Tweaked. New York, Dell, 1992.

Dunc's Halloween. New York, Dell, 1992.

The Haymeadow. New York, Doubleday, 1992.

Nightjohn. New York, Delacorte, 1993.

Amos Gets Famous. New York, Dell, 1993.

Dunc and Amos Hit the Big Top. New York, Dell, 1993.

Dunc and the Scam Artist. New York, Dell, 1993.

Dunc's Dump. New York, Dell, 1993.

Dunc and Amos and the Red Tattoos. New York, Dell, 1993.

Harris and Me. Orlando, Florida, Harcourt, 1993.

Dunc's Undercover Christmas. New York, Dell, 1993.

Sisters/Hermanas. Orlando, Florida, Harcourt, 1993.

Wild Culpepper Cruise. New York, Dell, 1993.

Dunc and the Haunted House. New York, Dell, 1993.

Dunc and the Flaming Ghost. New York, Dell, 1994.

Cowpokes and Desperados. New York, Dell, 1994.

Prince Amos. New York, Dell, 1994.

Coach Amos. New York, Dell, 1994.

Dunc Meets the Slasher. New York, Dell, 1994.

Amos and the Alien. New York, Dell, 1994.

Dunc and the Greased Sticks of Doom. New York, Dell, 1994.

Amos' Killer Concert Caper. New York, Dell, 1994.

The Legend of Red Horse Cavern. New York, Dell, 1994.

The Car. New York, Harcourt, 1994.

The Tent. New York, Harcourt, 1995.

The Rifle. New York, Harcourt, 1995.

Amos Goes Bananas. New York, Dell, 1995.

Amos Gets Married. New York, Dell, 1995.

The Rock Jockeys. New York, Dell, 1995.

Danger on Midnight River. New York, Dell, 1995.

Hook 'Em Snotty! New York, Dell, 1995.

Escape From Fire Mountain. New York, Dell, 1995.

Rodomonte's Revenge. New York, Dell, 1995.

The Gorgon Slayer. New York, Dell, 1995.

Dunc and Amos Go to the Dogs. New York, Dell, 1996.

Amos and the Vampire. New York, Dell, 1996.

Captive! New York, Dell, 1996.

Project: A Perfect World. New York, Dell, 1996.

Skydive! New York, Dell, 1996.

The Treasure of El Patron. New York, Dell, 1996.

Call Me Francis Tucket. New York, Delacorte, 1996.

Brian's Winter. New York, Delacorte, 1996.

The Seventh Crystal. New York, Dell, 1996.

Amos and the Chameleon Caper. New York, Dell, 1996.

Super Amos. New York, Dell, 1997.

Dunc and Amos on Thin Ice. New York, Dell, 1997.

Amos Binder, Secret Agent. New York, Dell, 1997.

Tucket's Ride. New York, Bantam Doubleday Dell, 1997.

Sarny: A Life Remembered. New York, Delacorte, 1997.

The Schernoff Discoveries. New York, Delacorte, 1997.

Worksong. San Diego, Harcourt, 1997.

The Creature of Black Water Lake. New York, Dell, 1997.

The Grizzly. New York, Dell, 1997.

Thunder Valley. New York, Dell, 1998.

Curse of the Ruins. New York, Dell, 1998.

Time Benders. New York, Dell, 1998.

Flight of the Hawk. New York, Dell, 1998.

Soldiers Heart: A Novel of the Civil War. New York, Delacorte, 1998.

The Transall Saga. New York, Delacorte, 1998.
Canoe Days. New York, Doubleday, 1998.

Other

Dribbling, Shooting, and Scoring Sometimes, photographs by Heinz Kluetmeier. Milwaukee, Raintree, 1976.
The Grass Eaters: Real Animals, illustrated by Kathy Goff, photographs by Wilford Miller. Milwaukee, Raintree, 1976.
Martin Luther King: The Man Who Climbed the Mountain, with Dan Theis. Milwaukee, Raintree, 1976.
The Small Ones, illustrated by Kathy Goff, photographs by Wilford Miller. Milwaukee, Raintree, 1976.
Careers in an Airport, photographs by Robert Nye. Milwaukee, Raintree, 1977.
Hitting, Pitching, and Running Maybe, photographs by Heinz Kluetmeier. Milwaukee, Raintree, 1977.
Riding, Roping, and Bulldogging—Almost, photographs by Heinz Kluetmeier. Milwaukee, Raintree, 1977.
Tackling, Running, and Kicking—Now and Again, photographs by Heinz Kluetmeier. Milwaukee, Raintree, 1977.
Forehanding and Backhanding—If You're Lucky, photographs by Heinz Kluetmeier. Chicago, Children's Press, 1978; revised edition, with Roger Barrett, as *Tennis,* Milwaukee and London, Macdonald, 1980.
Hiking and Backpacking, with John Morris, illustrated by Ruth Wright Paulsen. New York, Messner, 1978.
Running, Jumping, and Throwing—If You Can, photographs by Heinz Kluetmeier. Chicago, Children's Press, 1978; revised edition, with Roger Barrett, as *Athletics,* Milwaukee and London, Macdonald, 1980.
Canoeing, Kayaking, and Rafting, with John Morris, illustrated by John Peterson and Jack Storholm. New York, Messner, 1979.
Downhill, Hotdogging and Cross-Country—If the Snow Isn't Sticky, photographs by Heinz Kluetmeier and Willis Wood. Milwaukee, Raintree, 1979; revised edition, with Roger Barrett, as *Skiing,* Milwaukee and London, Macdonald, 1980.
Facing Off, Checking and Goaltending—Perhaps, photographs by Heinz Kluetmeier and Melchior DiGiacomo. Milwaukee, Raintree, 1979; revised edition, with Roger Barrett, as *Ice Hockey,* Milwaukee and London, Macdonald, 1980.
Going Very Fast in a Circle—If You Don't Run Out of Gas, photographs by Heinz Kluetmeier and Bob D'Olivo. Milwaukee, Raintree, 1979; revised edition, with Roger Barrett, as *Motor Racing,* Milwaukee and London, Macdonald, 1980.
Launching, Floating High and Landing—If Your Pilot Light Doesn't Go Out, photographs by Heinz Kluetmeier. Milwaukee, Raintree, 1979.
Pummeling, Falling and Getting Up—Sometimes, photographs by Heinz Kluetmeier and Joe DiMaggio. Milwaukee, Raintree, 1979.
Track, Enduro and Motocross—Unless You Fall Over, photographs by Heinz Kluetmeier. Milwaukee, Raintree, 1979; revised edition, with Roger Barrett, as *Motor-cycling,* Milwaukee and London, Macdonald, 1980.
TV and Movie Animals, with Art Browne, Jr. New York, Messner, 1980.
Sailing: From Jibs to Jibing, illustrated by Ruth Wright Paulsen. New York, Messner, 1981.
Woodsong, illustrated by Ruth Wright Paulsen. New York, Bradbury Press, 1990.

Full of Hot Air: Launching, Floating High, and Landing, photos by Ann Heltshe. New York, Delacorte, 1993.
Father Water, Mother Woods: Essays on Fishing and Hunting in the North Woods, illustrated by Ruth Wright Paulsen. New York, Delacorte, 1994.
Puppies, Dogs, and Blue Northers: Reflections on Being Raised by a Pack of Sled Dogs, paintings by Ruth Wright Paulsen. New York, Harcourt, 1996.
My Life in Dog Years, illustrated by Ruth Wright Paulsen. New York, Delacorte, 1998.

PUBLICATIONS FOR ADULTS

Novels

The Death Specialists. New York, Major, 1976.
The Implosion Effect. New York, Major, 1976.
C.B. Jockey. New York, Major, 1977.
The Sweeper. New York, Raven, 1980.
Meteorite-Track 291. New York, Pinnacle, 1981.
Survival Guide. New York, Pinnacle, 1981.
Compkill. New York, Pinnacle, 1981.
Clutterkill. New York, Raven, 1981.
The Meatgrinder. New York, Raven, 1984.
Murphy. New York, Walker, and London, Hale, 1987.
Murphy's Gold. New York, Walker, 1988.
Night Rituals. New York, Fine, 1989.
The Madonna Stories. Minneapolis, Van Bliet, 1989.
Murphy's Herd. New York, Walker, 1989.
Dirk's Run (as Paul Garrisen). New York, HarperWesterns, 1990.
Dirk's Revenge (as Paul Garrisen). New York, HarperWesterns, 1990.
Kill Fee. New York, Fine, 1990.
Murphy's War. New York, Walker, 1990.
The Case of the Dirty Bird. New York, Dell, 1992.
Murphy's Stand. New York, Walker, 1993.
Murphy's Ambush. New York, Walker, 1995.
Murphy's Trail. Maine, Thorndike Press, 1997.

Plays

Communications (produced New Mexico, 1974).
Together-Apart (produced in Denver, 1976).
A Cry in the Wind (screenplay; adaptation of *Hatchet*). Concorde-New Horizons, 1990.

Other

The Special War, with Raymond Friday Locke. Los Angeles, Sirkay, 1966.
Some Birds Don't Fly. Chicago, Rand McNally, 1968.
The Building a New, Buying an Old, Remodeling a Used, Comprehensive Home and Shelter How-to-Do-It Book. Englewood Cliffs, New Jersey, Prentice Hall, 1976.
Farm: A History and Celebration of the American Farmer. Englewood Cliffs, New Jersey, Prentice Hall, 1977.
Successful Home Repair. Farmington, Michigan, Structures, 1978.
Money-Saving Home Repair Guide. Milwaukee, Ideals, 1981.
Beat the System: A Survival Guide. New York, Pinnacle, 1983.
Eastern Sun, Winter Moon: An Autobiographical Odyssey. Orlando, Florida, Harcourt, 1993.

Winterdance: The Fine Madness of Running the Iditarod, with photographs by author. Orlando, Florida, Harcourt, 1994.
Pilgrimage on a Steelride: A Memoir about Men and Motorcycles. New York, Harcourt, 1997.

*

Media Adaptations: *Dogsong* (filmstrip with cassette), Random House/Miller-Brody, 1986; *Hatchet* (filmstrip with cassette), Random House, 1988.

Biography: Essay in *Authors and Artists for Young Adults,* Vol. 2, Detroit, Gale, 1989; essay in *Speaking for Ourselves: Autobiographical Sketches by Notable Authors of Books for Young Adults,* Vol. 1, compiled and edited by Donald R. Gallo, National Council of Teachers of English, 1990; "An Interview with Gary Paulsen" by Alice Edwards Handy, in *The Book Report,* May/June 1991, 28-31.

Critical Studies: Entry in *Children's Literature Review,* Volume 19, Detroit, Gale, 1990; *Presenting Gary Paulsen* by Gary M. Salvner, New York, Twayne, 1996.

Gary Paulsen comments:

I was a miserable student. I flunked the ninth grade and finally graduated from high school with probably a D- average. I had a miserable home life, and I would sell newspapers to the drunks at the local bars to make a little money. One night I went into a library to get warm and the librarian asked me if I wanted a library card. Then she started giving me books—Westerns and science fiction and every once in a while she'd slip in a Melville. It saved me, it really did. And now I tell kids to read like a wolf eats.

*   *   *

Gary Paulsen's books for young readers are largely coming-of-age stories in which protagonists are challenged to learn about themselves and life through the trials they encounter. Their survival stories may be quite literal, as with Russel in *Dogsong,* John in *Tracker,* and Brian in *Hatchett, River,* and *Brian's Winter* who emerge from the life-threatening wilderness with new knowledge of themselves and their world. Or the protagonists may come to terms with themselves through reflection rather than physical action, as with Wil in *The Island,* Janet in *The Night the White Deer Died,* and Brennan in *Canyons.* The literal and the introspective are combined by the fourteen-year-old protagonists in *The Haymeadow* and *The Car.* In *The Haymeadow,* John is forced by circumstance to spend summer alone in the mountains tending six thousand sheep, while Terry, in *The Car,* takes off alone to travel across the country. Both characters survive these experiences and in the process resolve their issues of identity.

In addition to his skill in crafting a good action adventure, Paulsen also commands respect for his poetic style. He writes in short, simple, energetic sentences, in sentence fragments, and in long, spiraling sentences that build on each other. It is the rhythm and pacing of the often repeated phrases that provide the poetry in this quote from *Dancing Carl:* "It's all movement—not a dance.

Everything in life is a movement, a swirl, a spin. And the movements have color. Like some swirls are red and some are green and some are blue like the ice and they all mix together and everything in life is a movement of color to music." His books have the same tense, compressed quality; some seem more like short stories than novels.

Occasionally his survival stories use a familiar setting, but one that is no less bewildering to the adolescent. Using school as the background, Paulsen combines comedy with a lighter theme. In *The Boy Who Owned the School,* an insecure teenage boy must make a place for himself while living in the shadow of his popular older sister, and in *The Schernoff Discoveries* two fourteen-year-old social outcasts survive junior high and the horrors of dating, bullies, sports, and cars. Paulsen has also begun two series for young readers. The "Culpepper Adventure Series" follows Duncan Culpepper and Amos Binder in now more than thirty titles as they solve one mystery after another. The "World of Adventure Series" numbers over a dozen books, with topics ranging from forest fires to genetic engineering. In each, the characters must solve a mystery, survive a danger, or save some aspect of civilization. Although brief, these novels conclude with survival guides that summarize the survival tips used in the stories that could translate to emergencies in the readers' lives.

From settings in the Canadian wilderness to the arid desert of New Mexico, Paulsen's stories include a strong acknowledgement of nature and a deep awareness of people's connection to it. Paulsen's writing reflects his recognition of what nature will teach you if you simply stop to observe. In *Woodsong,* a nonfiction account of his preparation for and running of the Iditarod—Alaska's grueling thousand-mile, dogsled race—he demonstrates the necessary interdependence of sledder and dogs during the ordeal. Also in *Woodsong* he explores the mysteries of the woods, just as Wil in *The Island* explores the mysteries of the island, and John in *Haymeadow* learns by watching the sheep.

Paulsen also weaves mystical elements into many of his novels. In *The Night the White Deer Died* Janet's dream of a young Indian warrior and the white deer foreshadows her experience with Billy Honcho, an old alcoholic Indian whose inner strength and beauty Janet comes to love. In *Canyons* Brennan finds a skull in a cave and connects with the skull's spirit. The spirit is Coyote Runs, an Apache boy murdered over one hundred years ago on his quest to manhood. Brennan agrees to return the skull to an ancient medicine place and this difficult challenge becomes his own rite of passage. Similarly, John Borne in *Tracker* makes a powerful connection when he touches the doe he has tracked to exhaustion. Her struggle to evade him through the woods gives him new understanding of her life, his own, and the approaching death of his ailing grandfather. When he touches her, he knows he must allow her to live. Paulsen conveys the intricate connections between life and death and the value of understanding fragile relationships across generations, cultures, and time.

Paulsen continues this fascination with connections in *Sisters/Hermanas,* a story told twice with English and Spanish versions bound back-to-back. In it, two fourteen-year-old girls, Traci who has everything and Rosa who has nothing, alternate in telling their stories until an unlikely coincidence causes their lives to intersect. Further pursuing the theme of chance meetings and connections are *The Tent* and *The Rifle. The Tent,* subtitled *A Parable in One Sitting,* looks at issues of religion and spirituality where Steven must choose between the material wealth of evangelism and doing the right thing. *The Rifle* traces the ownership of a black powder rifle and considers people's fascination with and casual dismissal of guns which lead to surprising and tragic consequences. All three of these short novels become parables leaving readers to reflect on their lessons.

Paulsen use of war associations in several books reflect his own background as the son of a career soldier and a former soldier himself. Carl Wenstrom, the eccentric veteran of *Dancing Carl,* harbors devastating memories of his war experiences, as does the old recluse of *The Foxman* who, disfigured by gas burns in World War I, befriends the teenager who discovers his simple shack. In *The Crossing,* Manny Bustros, a Mexican street child, and Sergeant Robert Locke, an alcoholic veteran of Vietnam, influence each other's lives after a coincidental meeting. In *The Monument,* the citizens of Bolton, Kansas, wish to erect their own Vietnam memorial. Rocky Turner is a racially mixed teen with a physical handicap whose monument project causes the people of Bolton to re-examine themselves. *The Car* also uses war associations. Terry Anders teams up with two Vietnam veterans who help him in his coming-of-age quest. Stories of war experiences are also significant plot elements in *Sentries,* a powerful reminder of the devastation of war.

Paulsen's early life provides him with a broad range of experiences to draw upon. In *Eastern Sun, Winter Moon: An Autobiographical Odyssey,* Paulsen recounts those early years when he and his mother remained in Chicago while his father served on Patton's staff in Europe during World War II, as well as the two years following the war they spent with his father in the Philippines. Paulsen's young adult novels often have characters with absent fathers. In some books (such as *Tiltawhirl John, The Crossing,* and *Tracker*) the father is deceased; in others the parents are divorced (*Hatchett* and *The Night the White Deer Died*), the father has deserted the family (*Canyons*), or he is away in the military (*The Cookcamp*). In *The Car,* Terry has been deserted by both of his parents, neither of which knows the other has left. In *Eastern Sun, Winter Moon,* although Paulsen describes his close relationship with his mother, he also resents her romantic relationships with other men. Paralleled in *Hatchett,* Brian's mother gives him the tool that becomes symbolic of his survival in the wilderness, but Brian also carries the burden of knowing that his mother was seeing another man before her divorce. After staying with his grandmother in northern Minnesota, the unnamed protagonist in *The Cookcamp* is anxious to return to his mother in Chicago but resents his mother's boyfriend. In *Harris and Me,* subtitled *A Summer Remembered,* an eleven-year-old city boy, because of abusive alcoholic parents, is sent to spend the summer with his nine-year-old cousin, Harris. The novel is outrageous, crude, hilarious, and charming, as the boy learns what life with a family could be and wishes that the summer could last forever.

Paulsen has made a strong entrance into the field of historic fiction with the appearance of *Nightjohn* and its sequel, *Sarny: A Life Remembered.* Narrated by Sarny, a young slave girl, *Nightjohn* tells the story of a slave who risks his life to teach her and others how to read and write. After escaping north to freedom, he returns to teach her more about what is important in life. In *Sarny,* the young slave girl finds herself a free woman after the Civil War and narrates her own story of family, friends, and learning until her death at the age of ninety-four. Also historic fiction but lighter in tone are *Call Me Francis Tucket* and *Tucket's Ride,* completing a trilogy staring with a much earlier *Mr. Tucket.* Both provide

enjoyable reads continuing the adventures of fourteen-year-old Francis Alphonse Tucket in the 1700s.

A heart attack forced Paulsen to give up dog sledding. The resulting changes in his life are reflected in his writing, more tempered and reflective, less centered on physical challenge. *Father Earth, Mother Sky* is a collection of sixteen essays on his own childhood experiences hunting, camping, and fishing. Poignantly told, they combine charm and comedy in describing the draw of nature and friendship. *Puppies, Dogs, and Blue Northers* is a tribute to his lead dog, Cookie. Beautifully illustrated in watercolor paintings by Ruth Wright Paulsen, it shares the antics of Cookie's last litter and the special relationship dog and owner shared until her death. *My Life in Dog Years* pays tribute to nine of Paulsen's favorite dogs over the course of his lifetime, each with its own chapter. It is clear from his narration how much of an impact these dogs made on his life.

Gary Paulsen's writing focuses on the complex and changing connections that we all have with our past, with nature, and with others. He is able to address such themes while introducing interesting, convincing characters and intriguing plots in a style that draws us in. As he ventures into new genres and explores new areas, Paulsen's readers still find the solid writing they have come to expect.

—Hugh Agee, updated by Susan Steffel

PEARSON, Kit

Nationality: Canadian. **Born:** Edmonton, Alberta, 30 April 1947. **Education:** University of Alberta, B.A., University of British Columbia, M.L.S., Simmons College Center for the Study of Children's Literature, M.A. **Career:** Worked as a children's librarian, teacher, and reviewer of juvenile literature. **Awards:** Canadian Library Association's Book-of-the-Year for Children Award, 1988, for *A Handful of Time;* Geoffrey Bilson Award for Historical Fiction for Young People, for *The Sky Is Falling* and *The Lights Go On Again;* Canadian Library Association Book of the Year for Children award, 1990, inaugural Mr. Christie Book Award, and runner-up Ruth Schwartz Award, all for *The Sky Is Falling;* Manitoba Young Reader's Choice Award, for *Looking At the Moon;* Violet Downey I.O.D.E. Award, for *The Lights Go On Again;* Ruth Schwartz Award and Governor-General's Award, for *Awake and Dreaming.* **Address:** 3888 West 15th Ave., Vancouver, British Columbia V6R 2Z9, Canada.

PUBLICATIONS FOR YOUNG ADULTS

Novels

The Daring Game. Markham, Ontario, Viking Kestrel, and New York, Viking Kestrel, 1986.
A Handful of Time. Markham, Ontario, Viking Kestrel, and New York, Viking Kestrel, 1987.
The Sky Is Falling. Markham, Ontario, Viking Kestrel, and New York, Viking Kestrel, 1987.
Looking at the Moon. Toronto, Viking, and New York, Viking, 1991.

The Lights Go On Again. Toronto, Viking, and New York, Viking, 1993.

Awake and Dreaming. Toronto, Viking, and New York, Viking, 1996.

Other

The Singing Basket, illustrated by Ann Blades. Toronto, Douglas & McIntyre, 1991.

''The Boggart'' in *The Witness And Other Short Stories,* selected by Barbara Greenwood. Toronto, Nelson Canada, 1993.

''Miss Kirkpatrick's Secret'' in *The Unseen: Scary Stories,* selected by Janet Lunn. Toronto, Lester, 1994.

Kit Pearson comments:

When I was young I was always pretending to be someone else, and that's why I write—to make up other worlds, to turn into other characters. These characters happen to be between ten and fourteen because those are the ages I most liked, and remember the clearest, from when I was young. All of my characters are uprooted from their former lives; I don't do this on purpose but, so far, each of my books has featured this theme. I like to emphasize Canadian settings because when I was young the only Canadian books I read were by L.M. Montgomery. I think my books are popular because I'm always on my protagonist's side; young people are often victims of adult society and I try to reflect this in my writing. Most of all, however, I write to tell a good story.

*   *   *

Kit Pearson is a writer with a long memory—one which stretches back to enable her to recreate with absolute conviction the intense feelings of longing, frustration, and occasional bliss which overpower all of us in youth but tend to fade in later life. The young girls who are the central characters in all her novels are wholly believable in their hesitations, insecurities, and aspirations; they grow and change in the course of the novels as each comes to some new point of understanding and acceptance of her place in the world through the action which has occurred. That action, like Pearson's writing as a whole, is quiet and undramatic but deeply grounded in felt experience. The novels conform to no particular fashion or current theory about what young women ought to feel or do but rise from honest recollection and observation, as well as a strong feeling for young people.

Although the tone and the fundamental concerns of each of her novels are somewhat similar, Pearson has written in the three quite different genres of the boarding school story, the time-slip fantasy, and the historical novel. In her first novel, *The Daring Game,* which was based to some extent upon her own experiences of being a boarder at a private girls' school in Vancouver, Pearson established her capacity for an intensely realistic evocation of the thoughts and feelings of her young protagonist and for writing convincingly about relationships between girls. Although the novel is episodic in structure, depicting both the pleasures and tensions of boarding-school life, a crisis builds as the shy eleven-year-old Eliza is increasingly drawn into friendship with the rebellious Helen, whose unhappy home life is reflected in her defiant and provocative attitude towards the school. Sympathizing with Helen and concerned for what will become of her if she is expelled, Eliza eventually has to make a choice between loyalty to the values of the school and loyalty to her friend. The ethical dilemma posed, and Eliza's eventual choice, give the novel a dimension beyond the usual ''larks and scrapes'' recounted in the genre. None of Pearson's subsequent novels present their protagonists with quite such an awkward decision, but at the climax of each of them some sort of choice or decision needs to be made which marks a significant point of emotional growth.

The relationships among the school girls in *The Daring Game* are created with a remarkably observant and unsentimental eye and ear; once established, however, they do not remain static as often happens in genre fiction where certain characters play the same roles continuously. Rather, Pearson shows the relationships within this little world as always in flux, with alliances forming and reforming in response to the pressures of school life and to the changing moods and preoccupations of the adolescent girls themselves. In Pearson's other novels, however, adults play a more significant role than do the teachers and house-mothers of *The Daring Game,* who are inevitably seen by the girls as alien authority figures to be appeased or outwitted.

A real mother cannot be so easily dealt with, and Pearson's second novel, *A Handful of Time,* concerns twelve-year-old Patricia's troubled feelings about her own mother. Slipping back and forth between her own time, where she is spending a lonely summer with unfriendly cousins at their lakeside cottage and the time of her mother's own girlhood spent at the same cottage, Patricia becomes an invisible but fascinated observer of crucial scenes from her mother's past life. She sees Ruth, her mother, treated differently from the boys of the family and denied the privileges they take for granted. She discovers how Ruth's mother, deprived of emotional fulfillment herself, slights her daughter's desire to be given the same educational opportunities as the boys in the family and wants her daughter to fit into a traditional feminine mold which Ruth rejects. Embittered by her own struggle to achieve and succeed on her own terms, Ruth has in turn neglected Patricia's emotional needs and tries to force her into a mold for which she is unsuited. Pearson has been criticized for having this daughter of the upwardly mobile Ruth say ''softly'' while discussing her own career plans that ''maybe I'll be a mother.'' In the context of the novel, however, this comment should be seen as marking Patricia's emotional growth away from the unhappiness and resentment which has blighted the relationships of three generations of women in her family. As Patricia learns to feel compassion rather than bitterness towards the emotional limitations of her own mother and grandmother, her interest in becoming a mother herself is a measure of the new security and capacity to love which she has found within herself. Through the three generations of women in this novel, Pearson shows the necessity for women, like men, to be free to find the balance between satisfaction in their work and emotional fulfillment. In her expression of interest in someday becoming a mother, Patricia is not denying but finding something of her full capacity as a human being.

The family, whether its members are present or absent, is shown to be of great importance in the lives of all of Pearson's protagonists; the experience of living away from home, however, is used to lead each of them to a greater self-reliance and self-acceptance. Norah, in the two published volumes of Pearson's projected trilogy set during World War II, and her younger brother Gavin, who is to be the protagonist of the third volume, are sent for safety to Canada from their English home and experience many problems adjusting to this displacement and to the domineering Mrs. Ogilvie who becomes their substitute parent. While both Eliza and Patricia were shown in the relatively confined worlds of boarding school and summer cottage, *The Sky Is Falling* has a larger canvas, showing Norah in England, in Canada, in relationships with her peers in and outside school, and with a number of adults as well as Mrs. Ogilvie. In the sequel, *Looking at the Moon,* Pearson returns to a single setting as she depicts a month spent by an older Norah at the Ogilvie's family cottage north of Toronto. Winner of a number of awards, *The Sky Is Falling* is a sensitive and absorbing account of Norah's transition between two very different lives. Norah is a sturdy, fiercely independent girl, who is completely at ease collecting newly-fallen shrapnel with her English schoolmates but unhappy in Mrs. Ogilvie's wealthy and strictly regulated home. Pearson's delicate but effective handling of symbol and her readiness to refer to other works of children's literature are both notable in this novel: Norah hears the folktale about Alenoushka's journey with her little brother, and the story becomes a metaphor for her own travails and for her eventual recognition of her bond with Gavin. The discovery of Arthur Ransome's novels is another important solace for Norah as she works through the difficult process of adjustment to life in Canada and with Mrs. Ogilvie. That adjustment takes on new dimensions in *Looking at the Moon* as the now thirteen-year-old Norah encounters the physical and emotional changes of adolescence, which are aggravated by the War and her long displacement from home. Norah falls painfully in love with a handsome, older Ogilvie cousin, who is himself tormented by the decision of whether or not to enlist. No easy solutions are offered although Norah is comforted by an eighty-three-year-old woman who points out that being thirteen doesn't last forever.

The young girl protagonists of Pearson's novels are all shown dealing with problems in their lives—problems of varying degrees of severity —but to call them ''problem novels'' would misrepresent them: the difficulties and dilemmas the girls encounter are treated as part of the fabric of life, and the world of each novel is larger than the immediate concerns of its protagonist. Although intensely aware of and empathetic with the feelings of her central characters, Pearson is also fair-minded in her portrayal of other people, even such antagonists as Patricia's grandmother and the formidable Mrs. Ogilvie. Not only are such characters given a past history which helps to explain their attitudes, they are also given the capacity to change and to surprise. Mrs. Ogilvie is not just a tyrant who undergoes a necessary change of heart: we come to see that she will always be tyrannical, and that those around her generally accept and even rely on that. Norah learns both to savor the pleasure of surreptitiously laughing at her with the other young cousins and to appreciate her matter-of-fact competence. This generous spirit and humane vision is an important but not altogether common quality in fiction for young adults, and it contributes to the reason that Kit Pearson is one of Canada's leading writers for young people.

—Gwyneth Evans

PECK, Richard (Wayne)

Nationality: American. **Born:** Decatur, Illinois, 5 April 1934. **Education:** University of Exeter, Devon, 1955-56; DePauw University, Greencastle, Indiana, B.A. 1956; Southern Illinois University, Carbondale, M.A. 1959; further graduate study at Washington University, St. Louis, 1960-61. **Military Service:** Served in the U.S. Army in Stuttgart, Germany, 1956-58. **Career:** English instructor, Southern Illinois University, Carbondale, 1958-60; high school English teacher, Glenbrook North High School, Northbrook, Illinois, 1961-63; textbook editor, Scott, Foresman Co., Chicago, 1963-65; instructor in English and education, Hunter College of the City University of New York and Hunter College High School, New York City, 1965-71; writer, since 1971. Assistant director, Council for Basic Education, Washington, D.C., 1969-70; English-Speaking Union fellow, Jesus College, Oxford University, England, 1973; lecturer. **Awards:** Child Study Association of America's Children's Book of the Year citations, 1970, for *Sounds and Silences,* 1971, for *Mindscapes,* and 1986, for *Blossom Culp and the Sleep of Death*; Writing award, National Council for the Advancement of Education, 1971; Edgar Allan Poe award runner-up, Mystery Writers of America, 1974, for *Dreamland Lake*; Best Books of the Year citations, American Library Association (ALA), 1974, for *Representing Super Doll,* 1976, for *Are You in the House Alone?,* and 1977, for *Ghosts I Have Been*; ALA Notable Book citations, 1975, for *The Ghost Belonged to Me,* and 1985, for *Remembering the Good Times*; Friends of American Writers award (older category), 1976, for *The Ghost Belonged to Me*; Edgar Allan Poe award for best juvenile mystery novel, 1977, and Author's award, New Jersey Institute of Technology, 1978, both for *Are You in the House Alone?*; *School Library Journal*'s Best Books of the Year citations, 1976, for *Are You in the House Alone?,* 1977, for *Ghosts I Have Been,* and 1985, for *Remembering the Good Times*; *New York Times* Outstanding Book of the Year citation, 1977, for *Ghosts I Have Been*; Illinois Writer of the Year citation, Illinois Association of Teachers of English, 1977; *School Library Journal*'s Best of the Best 1966-1978 citations, for *Dreamland Lake,* and *Father Figure*. New York Public Library Books for the Teen Age citations, 1980, for *Pictures That Storm inside My Head,* 1981, for *Ghosts I Have Been,* and 1982, for *Are You in the House Alone?* and *Close Enough to Touch*; ALA Best Books for Young Adults citations, 1981, for *Close Enough to Touch,* 1985, for *Remembering the Good Times,* 1987, for *Princess Ashley*; and 1996, *The Last Safe Place on Earth. School Library Journal*'s Best Books for Young Adults citations, 1981, for *Close Enough to Touch,* 1983, for *This Family of Women,* and 1985, for *Remembering the Good Times*; ALA's Young Adult Services Division's Best of the Best Books 1970-1983 citations, for *Are You in the House Alone?* and *Ghosts I Have Been*; ALA's Margaret Edwards Young Adult Author Achievement award, 1990; Empire Award, New York Library Association, 1997. **Agent:** Sheldon Fogelman, 155 East 72nd St., New York, New York 10021.

PUBLICATIONS FOR YOUNG ADULTS

Fiction

Don't Look and It Won't Hurt. New York, Holt, 1972.
Dreamland Lake. New York, Holt, 1973.
Through a Brief Darkness. New York, Viking, 1973; London, Collins, 1976.
Representing Super Doll. New York, Viking, 1974.

The Ghost Belonged to Me. New York, Viking, 1975; London, Collins, 1977.
Are You in the House Alone? New York, Viking, 1976; London, Pan, 1986.
Ghosts I Have Been. New York, Viking, 1977.
Father Figure. New York, Viking, 1978.
Secrets of the Shopping Mall. New York, Delacorte, 1979.
Close Enough to Touch. New York, Delacorte, 1981.
The Dreadful Future of Blossom Culp. New York, Delacorte, 1983.
Remembering the Good Times. New York, Delacorte, 1985.
Blossom Culp and the Sleep of Death. New York, Delacorte, 1986.
Princess Ashley. New York, Delacorte, 1987.
Those Summer Girls I Never Met. New York, Delacorte, 1988.
Voices after Midnight. New York, Delacorte, 1989.
Unfinished Portrait of Jessica. New York, Delacorte, 1991.
Bel-Air Bambi and the Mall Rats. New York, Delacorte, 1993.
The Last Safe Place on Earth. New York, Delacorte, 1994.
Lost in Cyberspace. New York, Dial, 1995.
The Great Interactive Dream Machine. New York, Dial, 1996.
Strays Like Us. New York, Dial, 1998.

Other

Contributor, *Sixteen: Short Stories by Outstanding Young Adult Writers,* edited by Donald R. Gallo. New York, Delacorte, 1984.
Contributor, *Visions: Nineteen Short Stories by Outstanding Writers for Young Adults,* edited by Donald R. Gallo. New York, Delacorte, 1987.
Contributor, *Connections: Short Stories by Outstanding Writers for Young Adults,* edited by Donald R. Gallo. New York, Delacorte, 1989.

PUBLICATIONS FOR CHILDREN

Fiction

Monster Night at Grandma's House, illustrated by Don Freeman. New York, Viking, 1977.

PUBLICATIONS FOR ADULTS

Novels

Amanda/Miranda. New York, Viking, and London, Gollancz, 1980.
New York Time. New York, Delacorte, and London, Gollancz, 1981.
This Family of Women. New York, Delacorte, and London, Gollancz, 1983.

Editor

Edge of Awareness: Twenty-five Contemporary Essays, with Ned E. Hoopes. New York, Dell, 1966.
Sounds and Silences: Poetry for Now. New York, Delacorte, 1970.
Mindscapes: Poems for the Real World. New York, Delacorte, 1971.
Leap into Reality: Essays for Now. New York, Dell, 1973.
Urban Studies: A Research Paper Casebook. New York, Random House, 1973.

Transitions: A Literary Paper Casebook. New York, Random House, 1974.
Pictures that Storm inside My Head. New York, Avon, 1976.

Other

Old Town, A Complete Guide: Strolling, Shopping, Supping, Sipping, with Norman Strasma, 2nd edition. Chicago, n.p., 1965.
A Consumer's Guide to Educational Innovations, with Mortimer Smith and George Weber. Washington, D.C., Council for Basic Education, 1972.
The Creative Word 2, with Stephen N. Judy. New York, Random House, 1974.
Housing and Local Government: A Research Guide for Policymakers and Planners. Massachusetts, Lexington Books, 1975.
Contributor, with Kenneth L. Donelson and Alleen Pace Nilsen, *Literature for Today's Young Adults.* Glenview, Illinois, Scott, Foresman, 1980.
Write a Tale of Terror. Book Lures, 1987.
"Love Is Not Enough," *Journal of Youth Services in Libraries.* (Chicago), Vol. 4. No. 1, 1990, 35-39.
Anonymously Yours. Englewood, New Jersey, Messner, 1991.
Handbook of Research on Curriculum: A Project of the American Educational Research Association, edited by Philip W. Jackson. New York, Macmillan, 1992.
"The Silver Anniversary of Young Adult Books," *Journal of Youth Services in Libraries,* (Chicago), Vol. 7, No. 1, 1993, 19-23.
Love and Death at the Mall: Teaching and Writing for the Literate Young. New York, Delacorte, 1994.
"From Strawberry Statement to Censorship," *School Library Journal,* (New York), Vol. 43, 1997, 28-29.

*

Media Adaptations: *The Ghost Belonged to Me* (audio cassette), Live Oak Media, 1976; *Don't Look and It Won't Hurt* (film with cassette), New York, Random House; *Remembering the Good Times* (cassette), Listening Library, 1987; *Are You in the House Alone?* (television movie), CBS, 1977; *Child of Glass* (television movie based on *The Ghost Belonged to Me*), Walt Disney Productions, 1979; *Father Figure* (television movie), Time-Life Productions, 1980; *Don't Look and It Won't Hurt* Spring 1983, (film), Cineville Production Company, 1991.

Biography: Essay in *Something about the Author Autobiography Series,* Vol. 2, Detroit, Gale, 1986; essay in *Speaking for Ourselves: Autobiographical Sketches by Notable Authors of Books for Young Adults,* Vol. 1, edited by Donald R. Gallo, National Council of Teachers of English, 1990.

Critical Studies: "The Death of the Mother, the Rebirth of the Son: *Millie's Boy* and *Father Figure*" by James T. Henke, in *Children's Literature in Education* (New York), Spring 1983, 21-34; "Blossom Culp and Her Ilk: The Independent Female in Richard Peck's YA Fiction" by Hilary Crew, in *Top of the News* (Chicago), Vol. 43, No. 3, 1987, 297-301; entry in *Children's*

Literature Review, Vol. 15, Detroit, Gale, 1988, 146-166; *Presenting Richard Peck* by Donald R. Gallo, Boston, Twayne, 1989.

*   *   *

Richard Peck's keen interest in young adults is shown through books whose themes touch young people closely: friendship, loneliness, and relationships with peers and with family. His work shows a concern that young people find a sense of belonging—that they should not feel alone at times when they must cope with problems that threaten to overwhelm them: the death of a friend or parent, rape, an unwanted pregnancy. At the same time, Peck's protagonists are young adults who are, or come to be, independent of the crowd, who learn to be responsible and to have respect for themselves and others. They "grow," Peck writes in his autobiography, *Anonymously Yours,* "by being backed into corners."

Peck incorporates mystery, melodrama, the supernatural, and humor into his novels—elements that appeal to teenage readers. He works to extend the horizons of his audience by featuring protagonists who venture out on journeys of independence into different locations of time and place. "Characters take trips into wider worlds," he explains in his biography, *Anonymously Yours.* In his books, adolescents meet a wealth of diverse characters ranging from perceptive and witty elderly people to lovesick teachers. Peck is adept at sketching a character in a few lines. Many of his secondary characters are parents: a father scarred by his Vietnam experience in *Princess Ashley,* parents who have opted out of the lives of their teenagers, and parents who are often themselves alone, trying single-handedly to understand and support their teenagers.

Peck writes sensitively about the emotions of boys and their relationships, especially those between father and son. When Jim Atwater's mother commits suicide in *Father Figure,* Jim is left fending off feelings of guilt, and describes his pent-up emotions and subsequent events in a glib tone, as if from a long distance. Left in the care of an elderly, sympathetic, though emotionally distant grandmother, Jim takes responsibility for his younger brother Byron. However, when it is arranged that he and Byron join their father, Jim finds that his buried resentment of his father's leaving the family eight years before causes him to feel anger and jealousy over the bond that grows between Byron and their father.

In *Remembering the Good Times* Buck adjusts to his parents' divorce and makes the decision to live with his father. Their easy-going relationship is contrasted by the distant relationship between Trav and his parents. Trav, driven by an inner despair, withdraws from his friends and his parents who do not realize the extent of his withdrawal and fail to read the warning signs of suicide. As Peck explains in *Love and Death at the Mall,* his treatment of topics such as suicide in this novel and acquaintance rape in *Are You in the House Alone?* are based on careful research. He offers no solution to the problem of teenage suicide; rather, he implies, it is an issue that concerns everyone. While Peck does write about the lack of communication and loss of roots in family life, he balances this with writing about love and friendship and moving forward with hope.

In *Close Enough to Touch* Matt's father is understanding and supportive when Matt is overwhelmed by grief after the death of his girlfriend Dory. Peck writes sensitively about Matt's emotions and growing love for Margaret, a girl who finally helps Matt free

himself from self-pity. In a lighter vein, Peck writes about the growing maturity of sixteen-year-old Drew in *Those Summer Days I Never Met.* Drew dreads the idea of a Baltic cruise with his sister Steph—a fourteen-year-old "pain"—and their unknown grandmother, when his plans had originally included a driving license and "maybe even girls." However, Drew's growing perceptiveness allows him to gauge the changes in Steph and himself that summer as they grow to love and respect their grandmother and the reason for their grandmother's invitation. Their grandmother, the "sweetheart of Swingtime," who is on the cruise for her last performance, is one of Peck's singular, clear-eyed elderly characters who seems to understand young people intuitively.

Peck blends humor and the supernatural in his four "Blossom Culp" books, which are set in Bluff City, U.S.A, during the years 1913-14. The incomparable, spunky Blossom Culp is described by Peck in *Love and Death At The Mall,* as having "more than a hint of Huckleberry Finn." Certainly she lives by her own rules and carefully distinguishes herself from the popular, beautiful, and wealthy people around her. First seen through the eyes of Alexander Armsworth in *The Ghost Belonged to Me,* Blossom and Alexander partake in a myriad of adventures, including a Blossom's psychic experience on the sinking *Titanic* in *Ghosts I Have Been.*

Blossom is one of several strong adolescent females in Peck's novels. He portrays intelligent, resourceful girls, who are willing and able to make their own decisions and take on responsibilities for themselves and others. In *Don't Look and It Won't Hurt,* Carol, the dependable middle sister, takes on the responsibility of visiting her sister and persuading her to give her baby up for adoption. Carol, in effect, takes her parents' place in showing love and care to both of her sisters. Similarly, Gail in *Are You in the House Alone?* also has a painful decision to make after she is raped. She is strong enough not to run away from the problem and thinks clearly through her options, realizing her responsibility in protecting others. Peck also touches upon the relationships between mothers and daughters in several novels. In *Representing Super Doll,* an overbearing snobby mother pushes her daughter toward being a "Super Doll." In *Princess Ashley,* Chelsea distances herself from her mother as much as possible until a tragic event occurs and she learns to value her mother's work as a guidance counselor. In *Unfinished Portrait of Jessica,* Jessica criticizes and blames her mother but idolizes her absent father. After a vacation with her father in Acapulco, however, she realizes his betrayal and returns to forge a new relationship with her mother whom she now feels she is meeting "for the first time."

Through displacements of time and place, Peck deftly weaves history in his novels. Young readers are introduced to an Egyptian princess and grave robberies in Ancient Egypt as well as the suffragette movement in Blossom's own time-frame in *Blossom Culp and the Sleep of Death.* An interest in local history sends seventh graders Flip and Brian looking for a roller coaster in an old amusement park in *Dreamland Lake,* where the discovery of a dead tramp leads to a real tragedy; a novel in which perhaps the real mystery is for Brian the different faces of death itself. In the suspenseful *Voices After Midnight,* Peck blends elements of history, the supernatural, and romance as Chad and his siblings travel between past and present in their New York rented house and its surroundings and become involved in the romantic lives of the

Dunlap family during the 1800's. Peck's ghost characters in this title, as in the Blossom Culp books, are not blurred spectral beings but distinct and memorable characters. The importance of family roots—another recurring theme in Peck's books—is central to this story as the Dunlaps prove to be long-lost cousins of Chad's family.

Peck's fascination with local and family history is also evident in two quasi science-fiction novels, *Lost in Cyberspace* and *The Great Interactive Dream Machine.* In the former novel, Josh and his friend, Aaron, a computer fanatic who has worked out a somewhat erratic means of traveling through cyberspace, become involved with the former inhabitants of the houses which now form part of the private school which they attend. In the latter, a similar formula propels the friends briefly into the future. Central to these novels, however, are stories of the past: the story of Phoebe, the governess of Cuthbert and Lysander Vanderwhitney in *Lost in Cyberspace*; and the romance between Lysander (now Josh and Aaron's elderly history teacher) and Miss Mather, which had been interrupted by the Second World War in *The Great Interactive Dream Machine.*

Peck uses his novels to write about what he sees as damaging about the culture and milieu in which young people live: the absence of parents and the concomitant influence of peer groups and gang culture that rule in their place. He conveys these concerns with humor and satire in *Secrets of the Shopping Mall* and *Bel-Air Bambi and the Mall Rats.* As Peck explains in *Love and Death at the Shopping Mall,* the mall "became a metaphor for coming of age, suburban, consumerist, and climate-controlled, the place to buy your disguises where no adult is truly in charge." The theme of *The Last Safe Place on Earth* is censorship—a subject which Peck has addressed in several of his articles. Censorship appears in the guise of Laurel Kellerman, who frightens tenth grader Todd Tobin's younger sister with warnings about witches and burning in hell. Laurel's family, struggling with an out-of-control son, is involved with a fundamentalist group who attempt to remove Robert Cormier's, *The Chocolate War* and Anne Frank's *The Diary of Anne Frank* from the school classrooms and library. Peck makes clear in the novel that censorship is about fear and control.

Drawing on his knowledge of young people gained through his years of teaching and speaking with them, Peck has created a cadre of work acknowledged by The Margaret Edwards Award. In his Acceptance Speech, "Love Is Not Enough," Peck reiterates what he sees as the "recurring theme" in his work addressed to young people: "you will never begin to grow up until you declare your independence from your peers."

—Hilary S. Crew

PECK, Robert Newton

Nationality: American. **Born:** Vermont, 17 February 1928. **Education:** Rollins College, Winter Park, Florida, A.B. 1953; studied law, Cornell University, Ithaca, New York. **Military Service:** Served in the U.S. Army, Infantry, 1945-47; served with 88th Division in Italy, Germany, and France; received commendation.

Family: Married Dorothy Anne Houston in 1958; one son and one daughter; married Sharon Ann Michael in 1995. **Career:** Writer and farmer. Formerly lumberjack, paper mill worker, hog butcher; advertising executive, New York City; owner of publishing company, Peck Press; teacher, and speaker at conferences; writer of songs and television commercials and jingles. **Awards:** American Library Association best book for young adults citation, Spring Book Festival award older honor, *Book World,* both 1973, *Media & Methods* Maxi Award, 1975, and Colorado Children's Book award, 1977, all for *A Day No Pigs Would Die; New York Times* outstanding book citation, 1973, for *Millie's Boy;* Child Study Association of America children's book of the year citations, 1973, for *Millie's Boy,* 1975, for *Bee Tree and Other Stuff,* 1976, for *Hamilton,* and 1987, for *Soup on Ice;* New York Public Library's books for the teen age citations, 1980 and 1981, for *A Day No Pigs Would Die,* 1980, 1981, and 1982, for *Hang for Treason,* and 1980 and 1982, for *Clunie;* Mark Twain award, Missouri Association of School Librarians, 1981, for *Soup for President;* Notable Children's Trade Book in the Field of Social Studies citations, National Council for Social Studies and the Children's Book Council, 1982, for *Justice Lion,* and 1986, for *Spanish Hoof;* Michigan Young Reader's award, Michigan Council of Teachers, 1984, for *Soup;* Bologna International Children's Book Fair, 1985, for *Spanish Hoof.* **Address:** 500 Sweetwater Club Circle, Longwood, Florida 32779, U.S.A.

PUBLICATIONS FOR YOUNG ADULTS

Fiction

A Day No Pigs Would Die. New York, Knopf, 1972; London, Hutchinson, 1973.
Millie's Boy. New York, Knopf, 1973.
Soup, illustrated by Charles Gehm. New York, Knopf, 1974.
Fawn. Boston, Little, Brown, 1975.
Soup and Me, illustrated by Charles Lilly. New York, Knopf, 1975.
Wild Cat, illustrated by Hal Frenck. New York, Holiday House, 1975.
Hamilton, illustrated by Laura Lydecker. Boston, Little, Brown, 1976.
Hang for Treason. New York, Doubleday, 1976.
King of Kazoo, illustrated by William Bryan Park. New York, Knopf, 1976.
Rabbits and Redcoats, illustrated by Laura Lydecker. New York, Walker & Co., 1976.
Last Sunday, illustrated by Ben Stahl. New York, Doubleday, 1977.
Patooie, illustrated by Ted Lewin. New York, Knopf, 1977.
Trig, illustrated by Pamela Johnson. Boston, Little, Brown, 1977.
Eagle Fur. New York, Knopf, 1978.
Soup for President, illustrated by Ted Lewin. New York, Knopf, 1978.
Trig Sees Red, illustrated by Pamela Johnson. Boston, Little, Brown, 1978.
Basket Case. New York, Doubleday, 1979.
Clunie. New York, Knopf, 1979.
Hub, illustrated by Ted Lewin. New York, Knopf, 1979.
Mr. Little, illustrated by Ben Stahl. New York, Doubleday, 1979.
Soup's Drum, illustrated by Charles Robinson. New York, Knopf, 1980.
Trig Goes Ape, illustrated by Pamela Johnson. Boston, Little, Brown, 1980.

Justice Lion. Boston, Little, Brown, 1981.

Kirk's Law. New York, Doubleday, 1981.

Soup on Wheels, illustrated by Charles Robinson. New York, Knopf, 1981.

Banjo, illustrated by Andrew Glass. New York, Knopf, 1982.

Trig or Treat, illustrated by Pamela Johnson. Boston, Little, Brown, 1982.

Soup in the Saddle, illustrated by Charles Robinson. New York, Knopf, 1983.

Dukes. Englewood, Florida, Pineapple Press, 1984.

Soup's Goat, illustrated by Charles Robinson. New York, Knopf, 1984.

Jo Silver. Englewood, Florida, Pineapple Press, 1985.

Soup on Ice, illustrated by Charles Robinson. New York, Knopf, 1985.

Spanish Hoof. New York, Knopf, 1985.

Soup on Fire, illustrated by Charles Robinson. New York, Delacorte, 1987.

Hallapoosa. New York, Walker & Co., 1988.

The Horse Hunters. New York, Random House, 1988.

Soup's Uncle, illustrated by Charles Robinson. New York, Delacorte, 1988.

Arly. New York, Walker & Co., 1989.

Higbee's Halloween. New York, Walker & Co., 1990.

Soup's Hoop, illustrated by Charles Robinson. New York, Delacorte, 1990.

Arly's Run. New York, Walker & Co., 1991.

Little Soup's Birthday. New York, Dell, 1991.

Little Soup's Hayride. New York, Dell, 1991.

FortDog July. New York, Walker & Co., 1992.

Little Soup's Turkey. New York, Dell, 1992.

Soup in Love, illustrated by Charles Robinson. New York, Delacorte, 1992.

Little Soup's Bunny, illustrated by Charles Robinson, New York, Dell, 1993.

A Part of the Sky. New York, Knopf, 1994.

Soup 1776, illustrations by Charles Robinson. New York, Knopf, 1995.

Soup Ahoy, illustrations by Charles Robinson. New York, Knopf, 1995.

Poetry

Bee Tree and Other Stuff, illustrated by Laura Lydecker. New York, Walker & Co., 1975.

My Vermont I. Englewood, Florida, Peck Press, 1985.

My Vermont II. Englewood, Florida, Peck Press, 1988.

Other

Path of Hunters: Animal Struggle in a Meadow, illustrated by Betty Fraser. New York, Knopf, 1973; London, Macdonald and Jane's, 1974.

Music and lyrics, *King of Kazoo* (play), illustrated by William Bryan Park. New York, Knopf, 1976.

PUBLICATIONS FOR ADULTS

Novels

The Happy Sadist. New York, Doubleday, 1962.

The King's Iron. Boston, Little, Brown, 1977.

The Seminole Seed. Englewood, Florida, Pineapple Press, 1983.

Other

Secrets of Successful Fiction. Cincinnati, Writer's Digest Books, 1980.

Fiction Is Folks: How to Create Unforgettable Characters. Cincinnati, Writer's Digest Books, 1983.

*

Media Adaptations: *Soup* (TV), ABC-TV, 1978; *A Day No Pigs Would Die* (cassette), Listening Library; *Soup and Me, Soup for President,* and *Mr. Little,* adapted for "Afterschool Specials," American Broadcasting Companies, Inc. (ABC-TV); *A Day No Pigs Would Die,* CBS-TV "Hallmark Hall of Fame" special, 1998.

Biography: Entry in *Fifth Book of Junior Authors and Illustrators,* Bronx, New York, H.W. Wilson, 1983; essay in *Something about the Author Autobiography Series,* Volume 1, Detroit, Gale, 1986; essay in *Speaking for Ourselves: Autobiographical Sketches by Notable Authors of Books for Young Adults,* Volume 1, compiled and edited by Donald R. Gallo, National Council of Teachers of English, 1990; entry in *Contemporary Authors, New Revision Series,* Detroit, Gale, 1990; entry in *Major Authors and Illustrators for Children and Young Adults,* Detroit, Gale, 1993.

Critical Studies: Entry in *Contemporary Literary Criticism,* Volume 17, Detroit, Gale, 1981.

*   *   *

Robert Newton Peck ranks among the more prolific contemporary authors of fiction for children and young adults. His autobiographical and highly successful first novel, *A Day No Pigs Would Die,* has become the critical touchstone for measuring the artistic merit of Peck's fiction. Unfortunately, few novels come close to achieving the warmth and intensity of this classic coming-of-age story. Set in rural Vermont, it is the story of thirteen-year-old Rob Peck, whose father makes his meager living slaughtering hogs. The fact that Haven Peck carries the smell of death foreshadows his own dying, which Rob must come to accept. The opening chapter in which Rob helps a neighbor's cow deliver its calf characterizes the realism that is a hallmark of this story. Rob's painful intervention in the birthing leads to his receiving a pig as a reward, and the pig becomes Rob's pet. Later when the pig proves to be barren, Rob learns that a poor family cannot afford the luxury of feeding a pet when food is scarce, so they must slaughter the pig. In this transition from childhood to the adult world, Rob builds a close, loving relationship with his father which equips him to deal with his father's death with greater maturity and responsibility.

Much of Peck's fiction is rooted in the past. *Eagle Fur, Fawn, Hang for Treason,* and *Rabbits and Redcoats* reach back to Colonial and Revolutionary War times for realistic stories that depict violent events in sometimes graphic detail. Father-son relationships continue to be a familiar Peck theme. In *Eagle Fur,* for instance, the protagonist, who comes to the new world as an indentured servant, not only develops a quasi father-son relationship with the fur trader to whom he is bound, but also falls in love with the Indian woman with whom he lives. Though *Eagle Fur* was not initially marketed as a young adult book, it has begun to appear in young adult collections in libraries. *Millie's Boy,* set in Vermont in the late 1890s, is the story of Titmouse Smith's search for his father after someone murders his mother. The close tie between Arly Poole and his father is central to the plot of *Arly,* which is set in rural Florida in 1927.

Peck's penchant for writing adventure stories for younger readers reflects the influence of Mark Twain's *The Adventures of Tom Sawyer* and is particularly evident in his Soup series. Also set in Vermont, these humorous tales trace the adventures of Rob and his pal, Soup (real name Luther Wesley Vinson) in slight and often predictable plots built around childhood escapades. Young readers are drawn to these books, which accounts for the long life of the series and, no doubt, the recent addition of Little Soup stories for beginning readers.

In keeping with his stated goal of writing four books a year, Peck began an adventure series for young female readers featuring Elizabeth Trigman, better known as Trig, but he retired his heroine and her genuine Marvin Purvis Official Junior G-Man Machine Gun after her fourth adventure. He has focused on female protagonists in other works of a more serious nature, such as *Clunie,* the story of a retarded girl, and *Spanish Hoof,* which deals with a mother and daughter struggling to manage during the Great Depression without a husband and father. Although these are hardly memorable books, they reflect Peck's efforts to address a range of social issues in his fiction.

Teachers are familiar supporting characters in a number of Peck's novels. Miss Kelly is the boys' favorite teacher in the Soup series, and in *Mr. Little,* Lester Little is the unexpected replacement for Miss Kellogg, the wonderful teacher Finley Streeter and his pal Stanley Dragavich had looked forward to having. Mr. Little weathers the series of pranks Finley and Drag play on him, but in the end his act of heroism ensures their respect and underscores a romantic if not sentimental bent in many books.

In *Arly* and *Arly's Run,* Peck has elevated the role of teacher to a dramatic high in the person of Miss Binnie Hoe, who, ironically, is brought to Jailtown by Miss Liddy Tant, daughter of the man who owns most of Jailtown and who has perpetuated the system that exists there. Miss Hoe offers education as an instrument of freedom to children and youth doomed to slave as farm laborers. Arly's father is in failing health, an added burden for an aging man attempting to meet the weekly rent for their dirt-floor shack. Like all the families on Shack Row, they are virtual prisoners, bound by continuing debt at the local store. As Dan Poole grows weaker, field boss Roscos Broda forces Arly and his friend Huff into service, which keeps them from attending Miss Hoe's new school. Miss Hoe realizes that Arly must leave Jailtown if he is to survive, and she and others make arrangements for his secret departure after his father's death. This sets the stage for the story's sequel, *Arly's Run,* in which Arly discovers that other forms of slavery exist beyond Jailtown and that freedom does have its price.

The Arly novels are refreshing in that they show what Peck can do with serious issues of social significance. These books still fall short of the excellence of *A Day No Pigs Would Die,* but Arly is a believable character that young adult readers can admire. Like Arly, readers will be angry that Huff's thirteen-year-old sister elects to go to work in Miss Angel Free's Lucky Leg Social Club rather than work in the fields; or that Brother Smith, who longs to

be able to read the Bible his wife has left him, would yield to community pressure and stop attending classes with the children, saying "School ain't no place for some old blacky like me." The novels reflect the importance of freedom in all its aspects—a freedom that Dodge Yardell in *The Horse Hunters* recognizes when young Ladd Bodeen urges him to join in capturing the wild stallion his own father had never been able to bring in.

Success along the lines of *A Day No Pigs Would Die* can be as much a curse as a blessing, and there is always pressure to top it. Perhaps the most dangerous way for an author to attempt to do so is with a sequel, but Peck did just that in 1994 with *A Part of the Sky.* The story begins just two weeks after the end of the first book, with Haven Peck dead and 13-year-old Rob forced to work at Ferguson's store to meet the payments on the farm. The sequel is certainly not as strong as its predecessor, but fans of the first book will enjoy it simply to learn what happens next.

There is no question that Peck is a capable storyteller. However, even *Arly* and *Arly's Run* continue his tendency to capture the folksy language of rural speakers with strained verbs and adjectives that smack of stereotyping. Nevertheless, his work also contains serious fiction that will go beyond mere entertainment and challenge readers to come to grips with the problems youth will always face.

—Hugh Agee, updated by Judson Knight

PETERSEN, P(eter) J(ames)

Nationality: American. **Born:** Santa Rosa, California, 23 October 1941. **Education:** Stanford University, California, A.B. 1962; San Francisco State College (now University), California, M.A. 1964; University of New Mexico, Albuquerque, Ph.D. 1972. **Family:** Married Marian Braun in 1963; two daughters. **Career:** Writer. English instructor, Shasta College, Redding, California, since 1964. **Awards:** National Endowment for the Humanities fellowship, 1976-77; *Would You Settle for Improbable?* and *Nobody Else Can Walk It for You* were named to the American Library Association's list of best books for young adults for 1982 and 1983, respectively. **Agent:** Ruth Cohen, Inc., P.O. Box 7626, Menlo Park, California 94025. **Address:** 1243 Pueblo Court, Redding, California 96001, U.S.A.

PUBLICATIONS FOR YOUNG ADULTS

Fiction

Would You Settle for Improbable? New York, Delacorte, 1981.
Nobody Else Can Walk It for You. New York, Delacorte, 1982.
The Boll Weevil Express. New York, Delacorte, 1983.
Here's to the Sophomores. New York, Delacorte, 1984.
Corky and the Brothers Cool. New York, Delacorte, 1985.
Going for the Big One. New York, Delacorte, 1986.
The Freshman Detective Blues. New York, Delacorte, 1987.
Good-bye to Good Ol' Charlie. New York, Delacorte, 1987.

How Can You Hijack a Cave? New York. Delacorte, 1988.
The Fireplug Is First Base. New York, Dutton, 1990.
I Hate Camping. New York, Dutton, 1991.
Liars. New York, Simon and Schuster, 1992.
The Sub. New York, Dutton, 1993.
I Want Answers and a Parachute. New York, Simon and Schuster, 1993.
The Amazing Magic Show, illustrated by Renee Williams-Andriani. New York, Simon and Schuster, 1994.
I Hate Company, illustrated by Betsy James. New York, Dutton, 1994.
Some Days, Other Days, illustrated by Diane deGroat. New York, Scribners, and Toronto, Maxwell Macmillan Canada, 1994.
Can You Keep a Secret?, illustrated by Meredith Johnson. New York, Dutton, 1997.
White Water. New York, Simon and Schuster, 1997.

*

Biography: Essay in *Speaking for Ourselves, Too* compiled and edited by Donald R. Gallo, National Council of Teachers of English, 1993.

P.J. Petersen comments:

Because I have tried to avoid repeating myself, my books vary enormously—from adventure novels to comedies to mysteries. The one similar element is in the approach to life taken by my most sympathetic characters: they keep trusting and hoping and caring, even though they're often hurt and disappointed.

*   *   *

P.J. Petersen writes novels with realistic characters, lively dialogue, vivid settings, in a simple briskly paced style easy to read and enjoy, placing him in the top bracket of twentieth century young adult authors.

Going for the Big One is a good example of dealing with problems. Thirteen-year-old Jefferson County Bates, his sister Annie, and his brother Dave have been abandoned by their stepmother who can't handle the job of raising this unwanted family by herself. Their truck-driving father is on the road somewhere in Alaska. After Dave has a run-in with the law for stealing a television, the kids escape to the mountains with camping gear and twenty dollars left by the stepmother, to face an eventful, frightening journey through the High Sierras. When a wounded cocaine dealer takes them hostage, they are faced with even more danger. A Literary Guild selection, this book is filled with excitement, including a fight with a bear, the struggle against starvation, besides facing a coke-crazed drug dealer. The three young people learn that together they can handle almost anything that comes along, even their father's shiftless ways. P.J. Petersen has written a colorfully portrayed, thrill-filled page-turner, filled with sibling love and loyalty.

Good-bye to Good Ol' Charlie is the funny story of a boy trying to be someone other than everyone's pal or a regular "good old boy." He tries on different roles and costumes, acting the parts of Chet the Mysterious, Chad the Poet, Chuck the Cowboy, and Chip

the Joe Cool. After he gets in a fight with the town bully, he decides to be just plain Charlie, having learned the world won't stop just because someone doesn't like him, and that his performances are only for somebody else's benefit. Mr. Petersen has written an amusing story of an adolescent coming to grips with reality, filled with humor and affection, frustrations and accomplishments, with the protagonist coming out where he should, just being himself.

The Freshman Detective Blues tells of two friends finding a skeleton weighted down by a boat motor in a lake. Jack is sure the skeleton is that of his father who has been missing for nine years. Jack's friend, Eddie, a freshman in high school, who is falling in love with a seemingly unattainable young beauty in his class, throws himself into trying to solve the mystery of the skeleton. Eddie not only solves the mystery, but solves the problem of being allowed by the parents of his girlfriend to spend time with her. Petersen builds up the suspense, throwing in humor with a little horror, to make a good mystery story with a surprise conclusion.

Liars is also a mystery, taking place in Alder Creek, California. Sam Thompson, whose mother was killed in a car accident a couple of years ago, lives with his forest ranger father in a little town in the mountains. Sam discovers he has the ability to dowse for water and also has the uncanny ability to detect if someone is lying to him. When Uncle Gene's house is burned down by someone searching for the man's map to his gold mine, Sam finds that even his own father is lying to him and things tend to get out of hand. Another exciting story, filled with laughter and family loyalty, this adventure also keeps the reader in suspense until the very end. The setting is memorable, the characters convincing, and the book is another of Petersen's thrillers.

A student teacher brings a juvenile offender into Michael Parker's English class in *Would You Settle for Improbable.* Arnold is not well-received by the class, but when he goes out on a limb to save a classmate from the wrath of the principal because of a prank, the class changes their attitudes. Then when he steals a car and runs away with the class money, another crisis is met and handled. A funny yet touching story with believable characters facing realistic problems, the story is fast-paced, dealing with the challenge of changing destructive behavior patterns, making for thought-provoking but fun reading for young adults.

Here's to the Sophomores is a sequel to *Would You Settle for Improbable* and involves the same characters, telling how they handle being sophomores in high school. The main character, Michael Parker, breaks his leg, gets expelled from school, and lands in a lunchroom brawl. He secretly finds himself in love but still has time for his friend, Warren, who is trying to cope with his parents getting a divorce. Young adults will enjoy reading this book about accepting differences and standing up for convictions.

The Boll Weevil Express is a story of runaways Lars and Doug, two young friends dissatisfied with their lives in general, who decide to run away to San Francisco. Doug's sister insists on going, too, so the three jump a railroad car. Thus ensues an adventure filled with trouble with the law, facing the dangers of San Francisco's Market Street, looking starvation in the eye with no money to buy food, concerning a trio of young people who face hurts and disappointments, trusting and hoping that things will get better, and who learn that life does go on regardless of frustrations and complexities that fill each day.

It is apparent that P.J. Petersen enjoys writing for young adults. He handles difficult ethical problems that young people confront with ease and intelligence. He doesn't preach, but subtly portrays possible solutions to problems encountered by young adults in their ever-changing .world. His realistic, exciting stories, filled with emotion, human relationships, the good and evil that fill the world of today, all deal with how young people can and do survive, as they seek and usually find the answers they need.

—Carol Doxey

PEYTON, Kathleen. *See* **PEYTON, K.M.**

PHIPSON, Joan (Margaret)

Nationality: Australian and British. **Born:** Warrawee, New South Wales, 16 November 1912. **Education:** Frensham School, Mittagong, New South Wales. **Family:** Married Colin Hardinge Fitzhardinge in 1944; one daughter and one son. **Career:** Secretary, London, 1935-37; librarian, Frensham School, 1937-39; copywriter, Radio 2-GB, Sydney, 1939-41; telegraphist, Women's Auxiliary Australian Air Force, 1941-44; author of children's books. **Awards:** Australian Children's Book award, 1953, for *Good Luck to the Rider;* Australian Children's Book Council Book of the Year award, 1963, for *The Family Conspiracy;* Boys' Clubs of America Junior Book award, 1963, for *The Boundary Riders;* New York Herald Tribune Children's Spring Book Festival award, 1964, for *The Family Conspiracy;* Elizabethan Silver Medal for *Peter and Butch;* Writers award, 1975, for *Helping Horse;* Australian Authors' award, 1975; Honour Book award from International Board on Books for Young People, 1985, for *The Watcher in the Garden.* **Agent:** A.P. Watt & Son, 20 John St., London WC1N 2DL. **Address:** Wongalon, Mandurama, NSW 2792, Australia.

PUBLICATIONS FOR YOUNG ADULTS

Fiction

Good Luck to the Rider, illustrated by Margaret Horder. Sydney and London, Angus & Robertson, 1953; New York, Harcourt Brace, 1968.
Six and Silver, illustrated by Margaret Horder. Sydney and London, Angus & Robertson, 1954; New York, Harcourt Brace, 1971.
It Happened One Summer, illustrated by Margaret Horder. Sydney, Angus & Robertson, 1957; New York, Harcourt Brace, 1964.
The Boundary Riders, illustrated by Margaret Horder. Sydney, Angus & Robertson, and London, Constable, 1962; New York, Harcourt Brace, 1963.
The Family Conspiracy, illustrated by Margaret Horder. Sydney, Angus & Robertson, and London, Constable, 1962; New York, Harcourt Brace, 1964.

Threat to the Barkers, illustrated by Margaret Horder. Sydney, Angus & Robertson, and London, Constable, 1963; New York, Harcourt Brace, 1965.
Birkin, illustrated by Margaret Horder. Melbourne, Lothian, and London, Constable, 1965; New York, Harcourt Brace, 1966.
A Lamb in the Family, illustrated by Lynette Hemmant. London, Hamish Hamilton, 1966.
The Crew of the ''Merlin,'' illustrated by Janet Duschesne. Sydney, Angus & Robertson, and London, Constable, 1966; as *Cross Currents,* New York, Harcourt Brace, 1967.
Peter and Butch. Melbourne and London, Longman, and New York, Harcourt Brace, 1969.
The Haunted Night. Melbourne, Macmillan, and New York, Harcourt Brace, 1970.
Bass and Billy Martin, illustrated by Ron Brooks. Melbourne and London, Macmillan, 1972.
The Way Home. London, Macmillan, and New York, Atheneum, 1973.
Polly's Tiger, illustrated by Gavin Rowe. London, Hamish Hamilton, 1973; illustrated by Erik Blegvad, New York, Dutton, 1974.
Helping Horse. London, Macmillan, 1974; as *Horse with Eight Hands,* New York, Atheneum, 1974.
The Cats. London, Macmillan, and New York, Atheneum, 1976.
Hide till Daytime, illustrated by Mary Dinsdale. London, Hamish Hamilton, 1977.
Fly into Danger. New York, Atheneum, 1978; as *The Bird Smugglers,* Sydney, Methuen, 1977; London, Methuen, 1980.
Keep Calm. London, Macmillan, 1978; as *When the City Stopped,* New York, Atheneum, 1978.
No Escape. London, Macmillan, 1979; as *Fly Free,* New York, Atheneum, 1979.
Mr. Pringle and the Prince, illustrated by Michael Charlton. London, Hamish Hamilton, 1979.
A Tide Flowing. Sydney and London, Methuen, and New York, Atheneum, 1981.
The Watcher in the Garden. Sydney, Methuen, and New York, Atheneum, 1982; London, Methuen, 1983.
Beryl the Rainmaker, illustrated by Laszlo Acs. London, Hamish Hamilton, 1984.
The Grannie Season, illustrated by Sally Holmes. London, Hamish Hamilton, 1985.
Dinko. Sydney, Methuen, 1985.
Hit and Run. New York, Atheneum, 1985; London, Methuen, 1986.
Bianca. London, Viking Kestrel, and New York, McElderry, 1988.
The Shadow. Nashville, Tennessee, Nelson, 1989.

Other

Christmas in the Sun, illustrated by Margaret Horder. Sydney and London, Angus & Robertson, 1951.
Bennelong, illustrated by Walter Stackpool. Sydney and London, Collins, 1975.

*

Media Adaptations: *The Boundary Riders, Fly into Danger, A Tide Flowing, Watcher in the Garden, Dinko,* and *Hit and Run* have been recorded on audio cassette. Most of Phipson's books appear in Braille editions, and have been published in foreign editions in seven different languages.

Manuscript Collection: Lu Rees Archives Collection, Canberra College of Advanced Education.

Biography: Essay in *Something about the Author Autobiography Series,* Volume 3, Detroit, Gale, 1987, pp. 205-219.

Critical Study: Entry in *Children's Literature Review,* Volume 5, Detroit, Gale, 1983.

*   *   *

Joan Phipson is not only one of the most prolific Australian writers for young people but one of the most diverse and versatile, and perhaps one of the least appreciated. Her early books were family adventure stories set in the rural Australia of the 1950s and 1960s.

As her own children grew up her characters became older, and Joan Phipson moved gradually, beginning with *The Crew of the "Merlin,"* toward a young adult audience. At the same time she continued to write for young developing readers. The implied readers of her young adult novels are not switched-on, trendy, sophisticated technocrats but thinking, perceptive—albeit imperfect—young people who are aware of their own limitations and shortcomings. They are prepared to learn about themselves and, through their interaction with others, grow in moral stature. But for whatever age group she is writing and whatever her subject—be it the menace of prowling feral cats *(The Cats),* the honors of bird trapping and smuggling *(Fly into Danger* and *Fly Free)* or the city of Sydney crippled by a general strike caused by the threat of building a nuclear reactor *(When the City Stopped)*—this author always tells a wonderfully graphic and suspenseful story.

In *The Haunted Night* four girls spend a night of horror in an old convict-built house, reputed to be haunted. More realistic and chilling is the tension in *Hit and Run* when Roland Fleming, having stolen a car and fearful that he has killed a baby, tries to elude his hunter, Constable Gordon Sutton. The two play a game of physical and psychological cat-and-mouse. Along with *Hit and Run,* inner tension mounts steadily, especially in *The Watcher in the Garden* and *Bianca.* In the former, both the physical landscape and the mind of Catherine, the protagonist, are in a "hushed tension of waiting" as the hoodlum, Terry, bides his time and plans the death of the blind Mr. Lovett who, of all the characters in the book, is in complete harmony with the environment. In *Bianca,* past terrors—her father's death and her mother's instinctual panic—intensify the present horror of a girl suffering from hysterical amnesia.

The power of the mind is a recurring theme in Phipson's writing. Twentieth-century Tom, the protagonist of *Dinko,* can not only see into the future but is a reincarnation of Dinko from Diocletian's time in history. This metaphysical element culminates in Catherine's psychic communication with Terry in *The Watcher in the Garden* and Bianca's refusing to admit her trauma to her conscious mind.

Bianca is at the end of a lengthy line of Phipson characters who have a deep longing for acceptance and a need to be understood. Because of this, they at times follow false gods and have to learn to evaluate what and whom they esteem. Young Charlie in *The Crew of the "Merlin"* unduly and misguidedly admires Jim, an undeserving older youth. The aggressive Butch Watson, who eschews his given name of Peter in *Peter and Butch,* has to learn the hard way that

self-satisfaction is not to be gained by associating with the criminal fringe. The basically solid Prue in *The Way Home* is blindly attracted to her urbane but shallow city cousin, Richard. In *No Escape* Wilfred's claustrophobic fears and sensitivity cause him great mental agony. But his less admirable friend, Johnny, a trapper of wild life, when caught in one of his own snares suffers both physically and psychologically. Both boys gain wisdom from a frightening ordeal.

Despite the number of hoodlums, layabouts, robbers, and delinquents among Phipson's characters, they are real, flesh-and-blood people who, although a menace to society, are not beyond redemption. Terry in *The Watcher in the Garden* is, perhaps, the supreme example. She is concerned, too, with social issues—conservation, delinquency, nuclear power, the possibility of another holocaust—but she never succumbs to slick social realism. She indicates that young people can be traumatised by perceived inner inadequacies but also by society and adult imperfection.

At the same time, many of her characters, although dreamers, are self-contained in that they possess rich inner resources, sometimes a metaphysical "gift." The most potent source of this personal strength comes from an affinity with the earth. This power as a life-force to be reckoned with is made explicit in an early historical novel, *Bass and Billy Martin.* In *The Way Home* it is a tangible presence. Peter who is in harmony with the earth and with water (water being another recurring positive image in Phipson's writing) is obviously one of the "elect," as opposed to the sauve, rational Richard. Water—the ocean—in *A Tide Flowing* obsesses Mark who has been driven, literally, almost to the edge by his mother's suicidal drowning. It is the sea and the redemptive death of his crippled friend, Connie, that bring healing and wholeness to Mark. Bianca, too, in her distress finds lake water "the last, safe, quiet refuge, the first mother." Mr. Lovett's garden is also an image of safety and regeneration. And as Mr. Lovett's life is being threatened by Terry, just beyond the border of the garden the earth slips into a landslide. So the land is not only stronger than people, it protects those who are in harmony with it, punishes those who reject it, but extends forgiveness and reconciliation to those who are open to its essence. A simple country girl, Margaret, in *The Bird Smugglers* and the seemingly slow-witted Willy in *The Cats* are just two of the diverse characters who attest Joan Phipson's passionate belief in the sanctity of the soil, in the firm reliability of the earth, "softened with the comfort of centuries of fallen leaves." *Dinko,* too, is a statement of faith in the perpetuation and renewal of life: an optimism badly needed by today's bewildered and often disillusioned youth.

—Maurice Saxby

PIERCE, Meredith Ann

Nationality: American. **Born:** Seattle, Washington, 5 July 1958. **Education:** University of Florida, B.A. 1978, M.A. 1980. **Career:** Writer. Teaching assistant, Office of Instructional Resources, 1978, and instructor of creative writing, 1984, Department of English, University of Florida; bookseller, Bookland, 1981, and Waldenbooks, 1981-87, both Gainesville, Florida; since 1987, library assistant, Alachua County Library District, Gainesville. **Awards:** First prize in junior division, *Scholastic/*Hallmark Cards creative writing contest, 1973, for short story "The Snail"; Best Books for Young Adults citation, American Library Association (ALA), Best of the Best Books 1970-1982 citation, ALA, *New York Times* Notable Children's Book citation, and Parents' Choice Award Superbook citation, all 1982, Children's Book Award, International Reading Association, 1983, California Young Reader Medal, 1986, and *Booklist* Best Books of the Decade (1980-89) list, all for *The Darkangel*; Jane Tinkham Broughton Fellow in writing for children, Bread Loaf Writers' Conference, 1984; Best Books for Young Adults semifinalist, ALA, 1985, for *A Gathering of Gargoyles*; Best Books for Young Adults citation, ALA, 1985, Parents' Choice Award for Literature citation, 1985, and New York Public Library Books for the Teen Age exhibit citation, 1986, all for *The Woman Who Loved Reindeer*; Individual Artist Fellowship Special Award for Children's Literature, Florida Department of State, Division of Cultural Affairs, 1987; Best Books for Young Adults citation, 1991, for *The Pearl of the Soul of the World*.

PUBLICATIONS FOR YOUNG ADULTS

Fiction

"Darkangel" trilogy

The Darkangel. Boston, Little, Brown, 1982; London, Collins, 1983.
A Gathering of Gargoyles. Boston, Little, Brown, 1984.
The Pearl of the Soul of the World. Boston, Little, Brown, 1990.

"Firebringer" series

Birth of the Firebringer. New York, Four Winds Press, and London, Macmillan, 1985.
Dark Moon. Boston, Little, Brown, 1992.
The Woman Who Loved Reindeer. Boston, Little, Brown, 1985; London, Hodder and Stoughton, 1987.
The Son of Summer Stars. Boston, Little, Brown, 1996.

Other

"Rampion," in *Four from the Witch World,* edited by Andre Norton. Tor Books, 1989.

PUBLICATIONS FOR CHILDREN

Where the Wild Geese Go (picturebook), illustrated by Jamichael Henterly. New York, Dutton, 1988.

*

Biography: Entry in *Sixth Book of Junior Authors and Illustrators,* New York, H.W. Wilson, 1989.

Critical Studies: Entry in *Children's Literature Review,* Vol. 20, Detroit, Gale, 1990.

*   *   *

The works of Meredith Pierce reflect the wellspring of myth and magic and religion that have influenced her and have taken new form in her interpretation. The well-read adolescent or adult can revel in both the story that Pierce tells and the search for connections to other stories in the body of fantasy literature.

The Darkangel and *A Gathering of Gargoyles* are the first two books of a trilogy. Ariel, the slave become heroine, had her beginning in a description of a patient's dream in Jung's autobiography. This stimulus-become-story is also influenced by the tales of Beauty and the Beast and Psyche and Eros. The resulting image, however, is Pierce's own. The books are a rich tapestry of love, devotion, faith, and courage; and like a tapestry, the weaving moves slowly but inexorably to its full realization. These are not quick reads for the casual reader, but are books to be savored and pondered. Ariel seeks to avenge her mistress who has been captured by a vampire and in the process first becomes his slave and then his savior. In her need to free Irrylath from his haunted past, Ariel follows a quest to find the missing lons who can become the steeds for Irrylath's brothers in the battle to free the land from the hold of the White Witch and her six vampire sons. The staunch love that Ariel extends to the creatures and beings with whom she comes in contact holds the key to the success of her mission.

The Pearl of the Soul of the World completes the trilogy, and it does so in dramatic fashion as the truth of the origin of Avaric is revealed. The Ancients from Oceanus had created a vibrant world on a lifeless planet, and when they were called back to their world because of a war, a few remained in their cities. Over centuries, entropy threatened the world with collapse into its original state. Ariel comes to Ravenna, the last of the Ancients, and learns that the White Witch is Ravenna's daughter, driven to madness by rage that she is not a true Ancient. There are two entwined plots, one is the doomed love story of Ariel and Irrylath and the other the relentless path that Ariel must take as she becomes a great sorceress who has the capacity to save her world. Pierce's writing is rich in metaphor, with clever turns of plot that keep the reader racing to the end. For those who have become involved with the characters, though this book completes the trilogy, it is obvious that there is more to come.

When Caribou is thirteen, her sister-in-law foists a bastard child onto her to raise. As the child grows, it is obvious that he is not fully human; indeed he is a trangl who can take both human and stag form. Caribou becomes the woman who loved reindeer in the story by the same name, though she is incapable of feeling human emotion until the end of the book. The elements of sacrifice, love, and devotion take many forms as Caribou becomes a leader and savior of her people as well as a woman who desires one she cannot have. There is a mythic quality to the story that is reminiscent of the tales of the Laplanders, though the setting is a two-mooned world. Pierce has told an adventurous tale, but at times the action seems overwrought.

It is obvious that Pierce is steeped in the mythology of our world, even when she chooses to create new worlds. The main characters in *Birth of the Firebringer* are unicorns who have been driven from their land by vicious wyverns and who inhabit a place that is threatened by deadly gryphons. The unicorns await a savior, the Firebringer, who will lead them back to their promised land. This is a tale of high adventure and of coming-of-age, the first of a proposed trilogy. Though it is a tale of good and evil, Pierce allows the reader to see that both good and evil are dependent on the perception of the viewer. As in life, there are no easy answers.

In *Dark Moon,* the second book of the trilogy, Jan, prince of the unicorns, is fated to be the Firebringer of his people. Separated from his tribe at the annual mating festival, Jan becomes a captive of humans who wish to use him as a sacrifice. Jan's discovery that different species can work together if they listen to each other has implications for the future. His return to the tribe and the birth of his two colts sets the stage for the last book of the trilogy. As with most high fantasy, there are several subplots working within the story, enriching the tale. The problem, in this case, is that the story drags in places and one wishes that it would move at a faster clip. The segment of Jan in captivity is overwritten and arch. That aside, those who have awaited this book will not be disappointed.

Pierce is a compelling storyteller, making use of the classic mythology that resonates with us and placing it within a new context. When she is at her best, the tales are rich and evocative, stirring the reader to question as well as absorb. There are times, however, that her tellings become too intricate, and the reader loses the thread of the tapestry.

—M. Jean Greenlaw

PIERCE, Tamora

Nationality: American. **Born:** Connellsville, Pennsylvania, 13 December 1954. **Education:** University of Pennsylvania, Philadelphia, B.A. 1977. Tax data collector, City of Kingston, New York, 1977-78; Tax clerk, Towns of Hardenburgh and Denning, New York, 1978; social worker and housemother, McAuley Home for Girls, Buhl, Idaho, 1978-79; Associate Editor of *OpenSpace,* 1978-79; assistant to literary agent, 1979-82, Harold Ober Associates, Inc., New York, 1979-82; creative director, ZPPR Productions, Inc. (radio producers), 1982-88; secretary, Chase Investment Bank, New York, 1985-89; freelance writer, since 1990. **Awards:** German Schüler-Express ZDF Preis der Leseratten (fantasy for German translation), 1985, and South Carolina Children's Book award nomination, 1985-86, both for *In the Hand of the Goddess; Lioness Rampant* was a City of Baltimore Enoch Pratt Free Library selection, 1989; Preconference on Genres of the Young Adult Services Division of the ALA Recommended Fantasy Author, 1991, for *Alanna: The First Adventure.* **Address:** c/o Random House Books for Young Readers, 201 East 50th St., New York, New York 10022, U.S.A.

PUBLICATIONS FOR YOUNG ADULTS

Novels

Alanna: The First Adventure. New York, Atheneum, 1983.
In the Hand of the Goddess. New York, Atheneum, 1984.
The Woman Who Rides Like A Man. New York, Atheneum, 1986.
Lioness Rampant. New York, Atheneum, 1988.
Wild Magic. New York, Atheneum, 1992.
Wolf-Speaker. New York, Atheneum, 1994.
Daja's Book. New York, Scholastic, 1998.
Tris's Book. New York, Scholastic, 1998.
The Realms of the Gods. New York, Atheneum, 1996.

Other

Contributor, *Digital Deli,* edited by Steve Ditlea. Workman Publishing, 1984.
Contributor, *Planetfall,* edited by Douglas Hill. New York, Oxford University Press, 1985.

*

Biography: Essay in *Speaking for Ourselves, Too* compiled and edited by Donald R. Gallo, National Council of Teachers of English, 1993.

Tamora Pierce comments:

Writing is something which I prefer to keep simple and direct, knowing that whenever I tackle the kind of Byzantine plot which I like to read about, I fall on my rump most painfully. Humor is always integral to my work: I relate best to those who don't take life too seriously. I want characters who are realistic, informal and down-to-earth, a reflection of the people I like and understand. My female and male protagonists try to deal equitably with one another, a reflection of my feeling that life is too hard to reject potential friends and allies on the grounds of sex. Most importantly, I try to work with misfits or outcasts who carve their own unique places in the world. It is my own experience, and in my books it seems to evoke a powerful response from readers.

In my mail I see things that *I* might have said, writing as a teenager to the writers who inspired me. That is a powerful bond, one I try hard to continue to foster. As a high school senior, I once asked a much-adored humanities teacher why she continued to work with high school students rather than college students who would be more committed to learning. She replied, ''Because I'm interested in beginnings, not endings.'' Fifteen years later, I discovered what she meant, and now I do my best to influence beginnings of my own.

*   *   *

Tamora Pierce's fantasy novels capture the attention of the adventurous young adult reader. In her novel, *Wild Magic,* which includes many of the characters found in her first four books, as in her other books, Pierce creates heroines that break through the sex role barriers in a medieval fantasy kingdom. Heroines of today, both real and fictional—such as women on the battle field, women as religious leaders, and women in roles of authority—are still trying to break through sex role barriers.

Alanna, the main character in the Song of the Lioness Quartet, is certainly not a damsel in distress. *Alanna: the First Adventure* begins with Alanna rebelling against the thought of living in a convent and her brother Thom against the rigorous training necessary to become a knight. Using their wits and Thom's ability to forge their father's signature, Alanna and her brother change identities. Disguising herself as a boy, Alanna begins the lengthy and grueling training toward knighthood. A willingness to stand up for oneself makes the slightly built Alanna/Alan a favorite friend of young Prince Jonathan. Alanna uses the healing power she has tried to hide to save Jonathan from a deadly sickness, one she suspects was magically conjured. While visiting the Bashir desert tribe Alanna and Jonathan ignore the warnings and enter the forbidden Black City and fight the immortals that lure and devour the Bashir young people. Alanna's true identity is exposed to Jonathan during the battle. The immortals taunt Jonathan: "How long do you think she will last?. . .She is a girl. She is weak." Though the same thoughts "taunted Alanna from within," she destroys her attackers with "a slender thread of violet fire." The first book of the Song of the Lioness Quartet concludes with Jonathan formally asking Alanna to be his squire, proving his acceptance of a female at his side in battle.

In the Hand of the Goddess, the second book, takes Alanna and Jonathan from the castle and into the streets as they become fast friends with George, the King of Thieves. Alanna and her magical sword Lightning battle Duke Roger, Jonathan's uncle, the most powerful sorcerer in the land. The sorcerer dies, but not before a too close swipe of his sword slices through Alanna's chest binding and the entire kingdom discovers her secret.

Having left Jonathan and her other friends behind, Alanna seeks new adventures and the time to accept her identity as a Lady Knight in *The Woman Who Rides Like a Man.* Returning to the desert, she is captured by Bashir tribesmen. Women have their place in this culture, and it certainly isn't upon a horse—thus her name—Woman Who Rides Like a Man. Alanna proves herself to the Bashir and becomes their first female shaman. She devotes her time to teaching magic to apprentices while her thoughts are torn between her love for the two men she has left behind—Prince Jonathan and George, the King of Thieves. She ponders whether love has a place in her life of freedom and adventure.

In *Lioness Rampant* Alanna comes face to face with yet another man after her heart, Liam Ironarm, the Shang Dragon. Alanna is on a quest for the Dominion Jewel, which in the right hands possesses limitless power for good. Thom, Alanna's twin brother and now a sorcerer, brings Duke Roger back from the dead. In the catacombs beneath the castle, Alanna again sends Roger to his death. Fate intervenes to solve her troubles of the heart. Liam, the Shang Dragon, dies in battle and Jonathan falls in love with the princess Thayet. The Song of the Lioness Quartet concludes with Alanna, still the King's champion, agreeing to marry George—on her terms of course.

While Alanna and George live happily at Pirate's Swoop, their seaside castle, Pierce was busy writing *Wild Magic.* The main character, Daine, is a lonely, frightened thirteen-year-old girl. She fears people as well as the power she has over animals before she meets Onua, a horse-mistress. Onua, sensing Daine's reluctance to share her past, allows the young girl to open up on her own terms. Onua soon learns that Daine has a unique relationship with the animal world. When the stormwings, immortal creatures that feast upon the dead, try to kill a hawk, Daine uses her "wild magic" to protect this hawk as well as to heal the other birds hurt in the fray. The hawk, in true form, is Numair, a mage who teaches Daine to better control her magic. Daine uses her "wild magic" to help save the kingdom. To do so she must let go of the fragile hold she has over the animals. Daine, fearing for their safety, puts a spell on them so they cannot aid the humans. Not until she realizes that they want to help defend their homes does she release them to help in any way they can. Daine, once alone in the world and afraid of her "wild magic," now finds herself surrounded by people and animals who love and accept her.

Adventure and fantasy readers will enjoy Pierce's books. Her characters are strong-willed, be they male or female. Although her main characters are all female, Prince Jonathan, George the King of Thieves, Liam the Shang Dragon, and the devious Duke Roger will attract the male fantasy or adventure reader as well. Pierce creates female heroines that a young adult reader can identify with: from Alanna and her desire to be something society does not find appropriate for a female, to Daine, a medieval animal-rights activist. Each title can be read alone, but for ultimate enjoyment and understanding, the Lioness Quartet should be read before *Wild Magic.*

Tamora Pierce has taken many issues facing adolescents today, especially young women, and addresses them in action packed, thought-provoking adventure fantasy novels.

—Ruth E. Dishnow

PIKE, Christopher

Nationality: American. **Career:** Writer. Worked as a computer programmer. **Agent:** Joe Rinaldi, St. Martin's Press Publicity Department, 175 Fifth Avenue, New York, New York 10010, U.S.A.

PUBLICATIONS FOR YOUNG ADULTS

Fiction

Slumber Party. New York, Scholastic, 1985.
Chain Letter. New York, Avon, 1986.
Weekend. New York, Scholastic, 1986.
Thrills, Chills, & Nightmares. New York, Scholastic, 1987.
Christopher Pike. New York, Pocket, 1989.
The Wicked Heart. New York, Pocket, 1993.
The Last Vampire. New York, Pocket, 1994.
The Last Vampire 2: Black Blood. New York, Pocket, 1994.
The Cold One. New York, TOR, 1995.
The Howling Ghost. New York, Pocket, 1995.
The Last Vampire 3: Red Dice. New York, Pocket, 1995.
The Lost Mind. New York, Pocket, 1995.
The Visitor. New York, Pocket, 1995.
The Last Vampire 6: Creatures of Forever. New York, Pocket, 1996.
The Starlight Crystal. New York, Pocket, 1996.

"Final Friends" series:

The Party. New York, Archway, 1989.
The Dance. New York, Archway, 1989.
The Graduation. New York, Archway, 1989.
Gimme A Kiss. New York, Archway, 1989.
Last Act. New York, Archway, 1989.
Remember Me. New York, Archway, 1989.
Scavenger Hunt. New York, Archway, 1989.
Spellbound. New York, Archway, 1989.
Fall Into Darkness. New York, Archway, 1990.
See You Later. New York, Simon & Schuster, 1990.
Witch. New York, Archway, 1990.
Bury Me Deep. New York, Pocket, 1991.
Die Softly. New York, Pocket, 1991.
Whisper of Death. New York, Pocket, 1991.

The Ancient Evil. New York, Pocket, 1992.
Master of Murder. New York, Pocket, 1992.
Monster. New York, Pocket, 1992.
The Season of Passage. New York, Doherty Associates, 1992.
The Eternal Enemy. New York, Pocket, 1993.
The Immortal. New York, Pocket, 1993.
Road to Nowhere. New York, Pocket, 1993.
Remember Me 2: The Return. New York, Pocket, 1994.
Remember Me 3: The Last Story. New York, Pocket, 1995.

PUBLICATIONS FOR ADULTS

Fiction

The Tachyon Web. New York, Bantam, 1987.
Sati. New York, St. Martin's, 1990.

*   *   *

Few authors can lay claim to inventing a genre, but Christopher Pike can. Although there had been mysteries for teens forever, Pike's *Slumber Party* broke the mold and created something new: the teen thriller. Bearing a slight resemblance to mysteries mixed with the horror shocks of movies likes *Friday the 13th,* teen thrillers took over the marketplace in the face of an exhausted romance genre. By 1992 the shelves of book stores and libraries clearly demonstrated the genre was the most popular and Pike its most popular writer, demonstrated by profiles in *Wall Street Journal* and *Entertainment Weekly.*

The reasons for Pike's huge popularity are varied. Like one of his influences, S.E. Hinton, Pike creates a world without adult characters or adult rules of conduct. His novels are filled with teens on their own, making decisions and suffering the consequences. Because of this, his audience is made up of both boys and girls spanning a large age range from high school down to fifth graders. Like another influence, Stephen King, Pike knows how to scare, shock and keep the pages flipping. His books are nothing if not readable; the complicated plot plays out through a series of nail-biting scenes. If his characters are sometimes no more than types, there are different types than stalk other young adult fiction: they aren't all "good kids," they are rarely innocent, some are sexually active, and most of them have a mean streak. And his characters feel intensely: Pike better than most "mainstream" young adult novelists captures the daily drama and roller coaster emotion of his teen characters ping ponging back and forth between emotions and conflicting desires. While he's not writing morality plays, he is writing stories where kids find themselves trapped between intense feelings of love/lust and hate/vengeance. Finally, unlike stupid slasher movies or many teen mysteries, Pike's plots are complex and clever, normally built around righting a past wrong or keeping a secret at all costs.

Slumber Party is textbook Pike: his first young adult novel contains the elements which would make his future work, and those of his many imitators, so successful. Pike takes his characters (six single girls) and puts them in a deserted setting (a snowed-in ski lodge). He lays out unexplained happenings (a snowman that melts), starts making characters disappear (all that's left of one is a ski), and adds a supernatural element (an Ouija board). The climax involves the girls about to be killed, not by some outside force, but

by one of their group. It seems the "new girl" of the group, Celeste, is really an old member of the group, Nicole. Nicole, of course, had been wronged by the others in the group. Eight years earlier she had been at another slumber party when a fire broke out which had "killed" Nicole. Now, it is eight years later and she wants revenge. This basic idea: group of kids, deserted setting, unexplained happenings, disappearing characters and supernatural elements would be the guts of *Weekend* and *Spellbound* and remain elements of just about everything else Pike would write.

New ideas were added with *Chain Letter* which lifted its plot from Lois Duncan's *I Know What You Did Last Summer.* Same set-up: a group of kids are out driving when they accidently kill someone. A letter comes telling the group they will be punished and then one by one each group member is terrorized. Yet, hanging from the same plot threads, Pike spins a different kind of tale adding two important elements to his character: the horror of humiliation and the gross out. The services the "caretaker" demands on the teens are not so much to punish them as to embarrass them: a straight A student is to fail a test, another is to "streak" through school, and another is to come to school dressed in a clown suit. When she refuses this humiliation, enter the gross out in the form of a bedroom floor covered with cockroaches. *Chain Letter* is easily one of Pike's best, inspiring a sequel *Chain Letter 2: The Ancient Evil. Last Act* and *The Final Friends* trilogy lost the deserted setting moving the action into the heart of high school life, but the rest of the elements remained. *Final Friends* reflects another of Pike's acknowledged influences, Agatha Christie, as he is working in more of a locked-room mystery than a thriller.

Pike's nastiest book, *Gimme A Kiss,* played heavily off the humiliation/revenge theme with its main character's diary being photocopied and passed around school. It also includes another Pike staple: the faked death. In an audacious act, Pike had a character in *Fall Into Darkness* use *Gimme A Kiss* as inspiration for her revenge plot. Despite this, *Fall Into Darkness* is great Pike and his first work translated to a book-on-tape format. The books concern two teenage girls (Ann and Sharon) who are friends yet intensely jealous of each other and with a shared secret in the past. Ann plots to destroy Sharon by faking her death so that Sharon will be tried for her "murder." Pike intercuts scenes from Sharon's trial with those in the past, building to the usual big, final "all is revealed and now you die" scene.

Remember Me was similar—another dead girl, but this one really is dead and telling the story as a ghost. While Pike often hints at the supernatural, *Remember Me* was the first full-blown "no logical explanation for this" novel. *Scavenger Hunt* followed and although not a really a good book, it is a pivotal one as Pike mixes his old stuff with more pronounced supernatural elements. There's also some heavy religious imagery which would show up in later works like *Witch. See You Later, Die Softly,* and *Bury Me Deep* are reworkings of past themes and even plots twists, plus all are fairly long. *Master of Murder* is a long inside joke: Pike's protagonist Marvin is a best selling author of teen fiction writing under a pen name (that sums up Pike himself) who is in fact a shy guy (Pike once wrote about himself that he was shy in high school). He gets a fan letter (ala thc chain letter) that says "I know who you are" (this is the plot of Stephen King's 1989 *The Dark Half*).

After getting this autobiographical novel out of his system, Pike switched gears. He had done a ghost story with *Remember Me* and an end of the world tale with *Whisper of Death,* but *Monster* is his first full-blown horror novel and a masterful one. It begins with a bang: a teen girl enters a party and shotguns away two classmates because they are monsters. The rest of the book is a rave-up: all red eyes and raw meat. It is outstanding horror, and fine young adult fiction. Pike followed with *Road to Nowhere,* a strange tale about good and evil, then *Eternal Enemy,* a *Terminator* style time travel piece. *The Immortal* was another time travel piece, this time back to ancient Greece as Pike continues to work outside of the thriller genre he created almost a decade ago.

In addition to selling a lot of books, Pike's influence has been considerable. Many other authors have imitated him yet none have come close to getting the right mix. Pike is also influencing young would-be teen writers much as he was influenced by S.E. Hinton. Like Hinton, Pike has sold film rights to his books and when those movies are made, his audience might grow even wider. The move to film is natural as Pike's writing is full of bang-bang scenes and characters in conflict. Finally, while known primarily as a thriller writer, Pike's books work with teens not just become of the chills, but also because they are good young adult fiction. While the characters might be broadly drawn, they are still recognizable to his readers. The problems, concerns and fears of his characters are those of his readers. His characters feel deeply and react strongly as they are trying to survive both Pike's mysterious killers and the horror of modern adolescence.

—Patrick Jones

PINKWATER, Daniel Manus

Pseudonym: Also writes as Manus Pinkwater. **Nationality:** American. **Born:** Memphis, Tennessee, 15 November 1941. **Education:** Bard College, Annandale-on-Hudson, New York, B.A. 1964. **Family:** Married Jill Miriam Schutz in 1969. **Career:** Art instructor, Children's Aid Society, 1967-69, Lower West Side Visual Arts Center, 1969, and Henry Street Settlement, 1969, all New York, and Bonnie Brae Farm for Boys, Millington, New Jersey, 1969; assistant project director, Inner City Summer Arts Program, Hoboken, New Jersey, 1970. Regular commentator, *All Things Considered,* National Public Radio, from 1987. Exhibitions: various small galleries and university shows. **Awards:** New Jersey Institute of Technology award, 1975, for *Fat Elliot and the Gorilla;* American Library Association Notable Book award, 1976, for *Lizard Music;* Junior Literary Guild selection, 1977, for *Fat Men from Space; New York Times* Outstanding Book, 1978, for *The Last Guru;* Children's Choice book award from the International Reading Association and the Children's Book Council, 1981, for *The Wuggie Norple Story;* Parents' Choice award, 1982, for *Roger's Umbrella.* **Address:** 111 Crum Elbow Rd., Hyde Park, New York 12538, U.S.A.

PUBLICATIONS FOR YOUNG ADULTS

Fiction

Lizard Music, illustrated by the author. New York, Dodd Mead, 1976.
The Last Guru, illustrated by the author. New York, Dodd Mead, 1978.
Alan Mendelsohn: The Boy from Mars. New York, Dutton, 1979.

Yobgorgle: Mystery Monster of Lake Ontario. New York, Clarion, 1979; revised edition, New York, Bantam, 1981.
Java Jack, with Luqman Keele. New York, Crowell, 1980.
The Worms of Kukumlima. New York, Dutton, 1981.
The Snarkout Boys and the Avocado of Death. New York, Lothrop, 1982.
Young Adult Novel. New York, Crowell, 1982.
Young Adults. New York, Tor, 1985.
Borgel. New York, Macmillan, 1990.
Chicago Days, Hoboken Nights. Reading, Massachusetts, Addison-Wesley, 1991.
Spaceburger. New York, Macmillan, 1993.
Five Novels (includes *Alan Mendelsohn: The Boy from Mars, Slaves of Spiegel, The Snarkout Boys and The Avocado of Death, The Last Guru,* and *Young Adult Novel*), foreword by Jules Feiffer. New York, Farrar Straus Giroux, 1997.
At the Hotel Larry, illustrated by Jill Pinkwater. New York, Marshall Cavendish, 1998.
Bongo Larry, illustrated by Jill Pinkwater. New York, Marshall Cavendish, 1998.
The Education of Robert Nifkin. New York, Farrar Straus Giroux, 1998.
Young Larry, illustrated by Jill Pinkwater. New York, Marshall Cavendish, 1998.

PUBLICATIONS FOR CHILDREN

Fiction

Wizard Crystal, illustrated by the author. New York, Dodd Mead, 1973.
Magic Camera, illustrated by the author. New York, Dodd Mead, 1974.
The Big Orange Splot, illustrated by the author. New York, Hastings House, 1977.
The Blue Thing, illustrated by the author. Englewood Cliffs, New Jersey, Prentice Hall, 1977.
Fat Men from Space, illustrated by the author. New York, Dodd Mead, 1977.
The Hoboken Chicken Emergency, illustrated by the author. Englewood Cliffs, New Jersey, Prentice Hall, 1977.
Pickle Creature, illustrated by the author. New York, Four Winds Press, 1979.
Return of the Moose, illustrated by the author. New York, Dodd Mead, 1979.
The Magic Moscow, illustrated by the author. New York, Four Winds Press, 1980.
The Wuggie Norple Story, illustrated by Tomie de Paola. New York, Four Winds Press, 1980.
Attila the Pun: A Magic Moscow Book, illustrated by the author. New York, Four Winds Press, 1981.
Tooth-Gnasher Superflash, illustrated by the author. New York, Four Winds Press, 1981.
Roger's Umbrella, illustrated by James Marshall. New York, Dutton, 1982.
Slaves of Spiegel: A Magic Moscow Story. New York, Four Winds Press, 1982.
I Was a Second Grade Werewolf, illustrated by the author. New York, Dutton, 1983.
Devil in the Drain, illustrated by the author. New York, Dutton, 1984.
Ducks!, illustrated by the author. Boston, Little Brown, 1984.

The Snarkout Boys and the Baconburg Horror. New York, Lothrop, 1984.

Jolly Roger, a Dog of Hoboken. New York, Lothrop, 1985.

The Frankenbagel Monster, illustrated by the author. New York, Dutton, 1986.

The Moosepire, illustrated by the author. Boston, Little Brown, 1986.

The Muffin Fiend, illustrated by the author. New York, Lothrop, 1986.

Aunt Lulu, illustrated by the author. New York, Macmillan, 1988.

Guys from Space, illustrated by the author. New York, Macmillan, 1989.

Uncle Melvin, illustrated by the author. New York, Macmillan, 1989.

Doodle Flute, illustrated by the author. New York, Macmillan, 1991.

Wempires. illustrated by the author. New York, Macmillan, 1991.

The Phantom of the Lunch Wagon, illustrated by the author. New York, Macmillan, 1992.

Author's Day, illustrated by the author. New York, Macmillan, 1993.

Ned Feldman: Space Pirate, illustrated by the author. New York, Macmillan and Toronto, Maxwell Macmillan Canada, 1994.

Mush: A Dog from Space, illustrated by the author. New York, Atheneum, 1995.

Wallpaper from Space, illustrated by Jill Pinkwater. New York, Atheneum, 1996.

Second Grade Ape, illustrated by Jill Pinkwater. New York, Scholastic, 1997.

Rainy Morning, illustrated by Jill Pinkwater. New York, Atheneum, 1998.

Wolf Christmas, illustrations by Jill Pinkwater. New York, Marshall Cavendish, 1998.

Fiction as Manus Pinkwater

The Terrible Roar. New York, Knopf, 1970.

Bear's Picture, illustrated by the author. New York, Holt Rinehart, 1972.

Fat Elliot and the Gorilla. New York, Four Winds Press, 1974.

Blue Moose, illustrated by the author. New York, Dodd Mead, 1975; London, Blackie, 1977.

Three Big Hogs. New York, Seabury Press, 1975.

Wingman, illustrated by the author. New York, Dodd Mead, 1975.

Around Fred's Bed, illustrated by Robert Mertens. Englewood Cliffs, New Jersey, Prentice Hall, 1976.

Other

Superpuppy: How to Choose, Raise, and Train the Best Possible Dog for You, with Jill Pinkwater, illustrated by Jill Pinkwater. New York, Seabury Press, 1977.

PUBLICATIONS FOR ADULTS

Fish Whistle: Commentaries, Uncommentaries, and Vulgar Excesses. Reading, Massachusetts, Addison-Wesley, 1989.

The Afterlife Diet. New York, Random House, 1995.

*

Media Adaptations: *Wingman* (cassette), Listening Library, 1981; *Blue Moose* (video cassette), Positive Images, 1982; *The Hoboken*

Chicken Emergency (television movie), Public Broadcasting System, 1984; *I Was a Second Grade Werewolf* (cassette), Live Oak Media, 1986.

Biography: Essay in *Something about the Author Autobiography Series,* Volume 3, Detroit, Gale, 1987; essay in *Authors and Artists for Young Adults,* Volume 1, Detroit, Gale, 1989.

Critical Studies: Marquardt, Dorothy A., and Martha E. Ward, *Authors of Books for Young People,* supplement to the 2nd edition, Scarecrow, 1975; entry in *Children's Literature Review,* Volume 4, Detroit, Gale, 1982; entry in *Contemporary Literary Criticism,* Volume 35, Detroit, Gale, 1985.

Daniel Manus Pinkwater comments:

I have done a great number of interesting and exciting things. Writing is more fun than any of them. If it were not for children's book editors, too many of whom are ignorant, tasteless, officious, and destructive, my life might be perfect, and the gods might be jealous of me. My work is not intended to teach or improve anybody. I think a great deal about how to make Art, but I don't believe it's a suitable topic for polite conversation—because it's apt to spoil the effect. Books purporting to explain how writing is done should be obtainable through the mail, and sent in plain brown wrappers. My books too.

*   *   *

Daniel Pinkwater's books for young adults crackle with antic energy. In a prose style marked by humor and a fondness for puns, he celebrates the eruption of the fantastic into everyday life. Although many of his books can be classified as science fiction or fantasy, his secondary worlds or alternate universes do not quite fit the standard paradigms for those genres because of the irreverent sensibility which informs them. One clue to that sensibility comes from the narrator of *Young Adult Novel,* Charles the Cat, a self-styled Dada artist. He says that the Dadaist expects that things will either go wrong or in an unexpected direction. Pinkwater's characters discover that something has gone wrong with the world or with their own lives, and that the remedy is to strike out in an unexpected direction. No matter how lighthearted, each of Pinkwater's books explore the rewards of being an individual in a society that urges conformity. This is the case even in *The Worms of Kukumlima* and *Yobgorgle: Mystery Monster of Lake Ontario,* books that aim simply at telling a good yarn. In both novels, the young protagonist is in the position of going along for the ride with older, and quite bizarre adults who are pursuing interests that might more accurately be termed "obsessions": in the first book, the search for extraordinarily intelligent, chess-playing earthworms; and the search for a Loch Ness-type beast in the second. Each search involves voyaging to interesting places—Africa or the depths of Lake Ontario—but more importantly, involves the protagonist's exposure to characters with a range of personal eccentricities, most of whom seem to revel in their respective enthusiasms. The reader is left with the impression that passionate interests are what make life worthwhile, so long as the interest does not become an obsession.

The Snarkout Boys and the Avocado of Death and The Snarkout Boys and the Baconburg Horror are more typical of Pinkwater's novels in that the young protagonists are themselves full-fledged nonconformists, complete with intense enthusiasms. ''Rat'' Bently Saunders, a fiercely independent young woman, and Winston Bongo and Walter Galt are movie buffs dedicated to sneaking out of the house in the late evening and making their way to the Snark Theater to see double bill showings of highly unusual foreign and domestic films. The plot of the films feature vampires, intelligent bagels from outer space, and the lives of German composers. Not surprisingly, in each Snarkout adventure the three young people soon find themselves in the middle of their own hybrid science fiction/horror movie/detective story plot. Like most of Pinkwater's fiction, the Snarkout books' frenetic energy is fueled by punning allusions and references to other books (some of them Pinkwater titles), to icons of both popular and high culture, and to food. This produces stories in which, for example, James Dean, Beethoven, The Sorrows of Young Werewolf, and a giant avocado capable of being modified into a thought-wave producing ''Alligatron'' all appear within the covers of the same book. The protagonists' madcap adventures serve as necessary antidotes to the boring routine of their days at Genghis Khan High School.

The disruption of boring routine is also the goal of the Wild Dada Ducks, five young men who attend Himmler High School in the short novel, Young Adult Novel. Their attempt to recruit a new member to their coterie backfires and they inadvertently create a demagogue who soon rules the high school and uses his power to get back at the Ducks who have disturbed his cherished routines and loner status. The narrator of the book claims that there is no moral to the story because it is a Dada story, but the book seems to have the intent of satirizing the plots and pat resolutions of some young adult ''problem'' novels. Similarly, The Last Guru pokes fun at attempting to solve life's dilemmas through adherence to the doctrines of fake gurus.

As funny as his satires can be, Pinkwater is at his best when his wit is tempered by his compassion for his characters' vulnerabilities. Lizard Music and Alan Mendelsohn, the Boy form Mars present intelligent and perceptive protagonists whose anxieties are resolved or made less threatening as a result of their fantastic adventures. Leonard Neeble finds friendship in an unexpected direction—from Alan Mendelsohn who claims that he is from Mars. At any rate, both he and Leonard, typical high school nerds, are treated as if they were Martians by the rest of the students and the faculty at the high school which they attend. Alan returns to Mars at the end of the novel, but Leonard returns to his high school better able to cope with its snobberies and ready to make friends with other students similarly written off by the snobs. Victor, of Lizard Music, is home alone because his parents have gone on a two-week vacation to try to resolve marital tensions, and Victor's shallow older sister has skipped out on keeping an eye on him. On the cusp of adolescence, Victor is concerned by what he sees as the plastic personalities of most of the people around him. By the end of his adventures with the talking lizards of Invisible Island, he has found friendship and a sense of community with the lizards and their other friends.

Chicago Days/Hoboken Nights, Pinkwater's collection of semi-autobiographical essays first read on public radio, suggests that there are many parallels between his protagonists' adventures and his own life. The parallels and correspondences are rarely one-to-one, however, because the storyteller's art always reshapes the incident from life—even in the autobiographical essays. By turns satiric and serious, Pinkwater's imagination is utopian at heart.

—Janice M. Alberghene

PLATH, Sylvia

Pseudonyms: Victoria Lucas. **Nationality:** American. **Born:** Boston, Massachusetts, 27 October 1932. **Education:** Harvard University, Cambridge, Massachusetts, summer, 1954; Smith College, Northampton, Massachusetts, B.A. (summa cum laude) in English 1955; Newnham College, Cambridge (Fulbright Scholar), 1955-57, M.A. 1957. **Family:** Married Ted Hughes in 1956 (separated, 1962), one daughter and one son. **Career:** Writer and poet. Worked as a volunteer art teacher at the People's Institute, Northampton, Massachusetts, while in college. Guest Editor, *Mademoiselle* magazine, New York, Summer 1953. Instructor in English, Smith College, 1957-58. **Awards:** *Mademoiselle* College Board contest award in fiction, 1953; Irene Glascock Poetry Prize, Mount Holyoke College, South Hadley, Massachusetts, 1955; Bess Hokin Award (*Poetry,* Chicago), 1957; Yaddo Fellowship, 1959; Cheltenham Festival award, 1961; Eugene F. Saxon Fellowship, 1961; Pulitzer Prize in poetry, 1982, for *Collected Poems.* **Died:** 11 February 1963.

PUBLICATIONS FOR ADULTS AND YOUNG ADULTS

Novel

The Bell Jar (as Victoria Lucas). London, Heinemann, 1963; as Sylvia Plath, London, Faber, 1966; with drawings, New York, Harper, 1971.

Poetry

A Winter Ship (published anonymously). Edinburgh, Tragara Press, 1960.
The Colossus and Other Poems. London, Heinemann, 1960; New York, Knopf, 1962; as *The Colossus,* London, Heinemann, 1967.
Ariel, edited by Ted Hughes and Alwyn Hughes. London, Faber, 1965; New York, Harper, 1966.
Uncollected Poems (booklet). London, Turret Books, 1965.
Wreath for a Bridal (limited edition). Frensham, Surrey, Sceptre Press, 1970.
Crossing the Water, edited by Ted Hughes. London, Faber, 1971; as *Crossing the Water: Transitional Poems,* New York, Harper, 1971.
Crystal Gazer and Other Poems (limited edition). London, Rainbow Press, 1971.
Fiesta Melons: Poems. Exeter, Devon, Rougemont Press, 1971.
Lyonnesse: Poems (limited edition). London, Rainbow Press, 1971.
Million Dollar Month (limited edition). Frensham, Surrey, Sceptre Press, 1971.
Winter Trees, edited by Ted Hughes. London, Faber, 1971; New York, Harper, 1972.
Collected Poems, edited by Ted Hughes. New York, Harper, 1981.
The Green Rock. Cambridge, Embers Handpress, 1982.

Stings (drafts). Northampton, Massachusetts, Smith College, 1983.
Sylvia Plath's Selected Poems, edited by Ted Hughes. London, Faber, 1985.

Plays

Three Women: A Monologue for Three Voices (broadcast, 1962; produced New York and London, 1973). London, Turret Books, 1968.

Radio Play: *Three Women,* 1962 (UK).

Short Stories

Penguin Modern Stories 2, with others. London, Penguin, 1969.

Other

Editor, *American Poetry Now: A Selection of the Best Poems by Modern American Writers.* London, Oxford University Press, 1961.
The Penguin Sylvia Plath. London, Penguin, 1975.
Letters Home: Correspondence, 1950-1963, edited by Aurelia Plath. New York, Harper, 1975.
Johnny Panic and the Bible of Dreams: Short Stories, Prose, and Diary Excerpts, edited by Ted Hughes. New York, Harper, 1979.
The Journals of Sylvia Plath, edited by Frances McCullough and Ted Hughes. New York, Ballantine, 1983.

PUBLICATIONS FOR CHILDREN

Poetry

The Bed Book. New York, Harper, 1976.

*

Media Adaptations: *The Bell Jar* (film), Avco-Embassy, 1978; *Letters Home* (play), by Rose Leiman Goldemberg, 1979.

Biography: *Sylvia Plath* by Eileen M. Aird, New York, Harper, 1973, Edinburgh, Oliver and Boyd, 1974; Entry in *Dictionary of Literary Biography,* Detroit, Gale, Volume 5, 1980, Volume 6, 1980; *Sylvia Plath: A Biography* by Linda Wagner-Martin, New York, Simon & Schuster, 1987; *Bitter Fame: The Undiscovered Life of Sylvia Plath* by Anne Stevenson, Boston, Massachusetts, Houghton, 1989.

Bibliography: By Mary Kinzie, Daniel Lynn Conrad, and Suzanne D. Kurman in *The Art of Sylvia Plath: A Symposium* edited by Charles Newman, Bloomington, Indiana University Press, and London, Faber, 1970; *A Chronological Checklist of the Periodical Publications of Sylvia Plath* by Eric Homberger, Exeter, Devon, University of Exeter American Arts Documentation Centre, 1970.

Critical Study: *The Art of Sylvia: A Symposium* edited by Charles Newman, Bloomington, Indiana University Press, and London, Faber, 1970; *A Closer Look at "Ariel": A Memory of Sylvia Plath* by Nancy Hunter Steiner, New York, Harpers Magazine Press, 1973, London, Faber, 1974; Entry in *Contemporary Literary*

Criticism, Detroit, Gale, Volume 1, 1973, Volume 2, 1974, Volume 3, 1975, Volume 5, 1976, Volume 9, 1978, Volume 11, 1979, Volume 14, 1980, Volume 17, 1981, Volume 50, 1988, Volume 51, 1989; *Sylvia Plath: Method and Madness* by Edward Butscher, New York, Seabury Press, 1975; *Sylvia Plath: A Dramatic Portrait* conceived and adapted from Plath's writing by Barry Kyle, London, Faber, 1976; *A Concordance to The Collected Poems of Sylvia Plath* edited by Richard M. Matovich, New York, Garland, 1986.

*   *   *

Since her suicide in 1963 at the age of thirty, Sylvia Plath especially has attracted the attention of Women's Studies enthusiasts, while at the same time she has become recognized as a preeminent American poet. Often categorized as "confessional," her poems are primarily inspired by actual events in her life, events that she transforms into probing psychoanalytical studies. For example, "The Mirror" captures the desperation of a young woman trying unsuccessfully to discern in her own slippery reflection the stable image of a valued, integrated person.

The mirror imagery that Plath uses so effectively in this poem pervades her one and only novel, *The Bell Jar,* a work that appeals to young adults because of its troubled young protagonist, Esther Greenwood. At a promotional event for *Mademoiselle* magazine, Esther, unable to smile on cue for the photographer, begins to cry. Gaining some control of herself, she fumbles in her purse for a gilt compact "with the side mirror. The face that peered back. . .seemed to be peering from the grating of a prison cell after a prolonged beating. It looked bruised and puffy and all the wrong colors." In the hospital later, after an unsuccessful suicide attempt, Esther insists "I want to see a mirror." The nurse reluctantly provides one, and faced with the unfamiliar reflection of her shaved head with the hair sprouting "in bristly chicken feather tufts" and her face with its "supernatural conglomeration of bright colors," Esther smiles.

Like Holden Caulfield in *The Catcher in the Rye,* with whom Esther has been compared, she experiences disillusionment with the compromised adult world, sexual curiosity and resultant guilt, and severe mental depression. Unlike Holden, Esther undergoes electroshock therapy following her suicide attempt.

Esther narrates her story in an eerily detached but precise manner that leads the reader to suspect that all is not well with her even before the undeniable signs of her breakdown (she cannot sleep, read, or write) become evident. In addition to Esther's cold, lucid "voice," there are other signs of her impending collapse. For example, she seems excessively disturbed by the upcoming execution of Julius and Esther Rosenberg, the couple accused and tried as Soviet spies in 1951. *The Bell Jar* opens in June 1953 when, after numerous appeals, the Rosenbergs were finally electrocuted: "It was a queer, sultry summer, the summer they electrocuted the Rosenbergs, and I didn't know what I was doing in New York." This opening reference to a notorious death by electrocution foreshadows numerous passages about death throughout the novel (most significantly Esther's father's death when she was nine) and Esther's own "electrocution" by shock therapy.

Paralleling the death images in the novel are references to difficult births, unwelcome children, and conflicting attitudes about sexual intercourse. All of these concerns might be considered typical for a young woman entering a stage when she might well be asked to choose between marriage and motherhood on one hand or a career on the other. Esther's reactions to these common dilemmas may seem excessive in an age when premarital sex and early sex education have become more the rule than the exception, and when a career does not necessarily preclude marriage and motherhood. However, fear of pregnancy was used as a way of ensuring the virginity of young unmarried women to much greater effect in the 1950s than it is today. Furthermore, in the 1950s, a gifted, intellectual woman like Esther had to make choices that might have contributed to the "splitting" of an already tenuous personality.

Esther is eventually rehabilitated, as Sylvia Plath was for a while, largely through the efforts of a supportive group of women including several friends of her own age, her mother, a literary patron, and her psychiatrist. In a period when teenage suicide rates are increasing, *The Bell Jar* is bound to be a controversial choice for young-adult reading. However, it is an important work by a major American writer, and surely there is as much to be gained from a candid approach to this autobiographical treatment of a young woman's suicide attempt as there is to studying such fictional suicidal antiheroines as Emma Bovary or Anna Karenina.

—Mary Lowe-Evans

POTOK, Chaim

Nationality: American. **Born:** Herman Harold Potok in the Bronx, New York, 17 February 1929. **Education:** Orthodox Jewish schools; Yeshiva University, New York, 1946-50, B.A. (summa cum laude) in English 1950; Jewish Theological Seminary, New York, 1950-54, M.H.L. and rabbinic ordination 1954; University of Pennsylvania, Philadelphia, 1959-65, Ph.D. in philosophy 1965. **Military Service:** Served as a chaplain in the United States Army in Korea, 1955-56: Lieutenant. **Family:** Married Adena Sara Mosevitsky in 1958; two daughters and one son. **Career:** National director of Leaders Training Fellowship, Jewish Theological Seminary, 1954-55; director, Camp Ramah, Ojai, California, 1957-59; Instructor, University of Judaism, Los Angeles, 1957-59; scholar-in-residence, Har Zion Temple, Philadelphia, 1959-63; member of the Teachers' Institute faculty, Jewish Theological Seminary, 1964-65; managing editor, *Conservative Judaism,* New York, 1964-65; associate editor, 1965, editor-in-chief, 1966-74, and since 1974 special projects editor, Jewish Publication Society, Philadelphia. Visiting Professor of Philosophy, University of Pennsylvania, 1983, and Bryn Mawr College, Pennsylvania, 1985. **Awards:** Edward Lewis Wallant award, 1968, and National Book award nomination, both for *The Chosen*; Athenaeum award for *The Promise.* **Address:** 20 Berwick Street, Merion, Pennsylvania 19131, U.S.A.

Publications for Young Adults

Novels

The Chosen. New York, Simon and Schuster, and London, Heinemann, 1967.
The Promise. New York, Knopf, 1969; London, Heinemann, 1970.
My Name Is Asher Lev. New York, Knopf, and London, Heinemann, 1972.

In the Beginning. New York, Knopf, 1975; London, Heinemann, 1976.
The Book of Lights. New York, Knopf, 1981; London, Heinemann, 1982.
Davita's Harp. New York, Knopf, 1985.
The Gift of Asher Lev. New York, Knopf, and London, Heinemann, 1990.
I Am the Clay. New York, Knopf, 1992.
The Tree of Here, illustrated by Tony Auth. New York, Knopf, 1993.
The Sky of Now, illustrated by Tony Auth. New York, Knopf, 1995.

Short Stories

"The Dark Place Inside," in *Dimensions in American Judaism* (New York), fall 1964.
"The Cats of 37 Alfasi Street," in *American Judaism* (New York), fall 1966.
"Miracles for a Broken Planet," in *McCall's* (New York), December 1972.
"The Fallen," in *Hadassah* (New York), December 1973.
"Reflections on a Bronx Street," in *May My Words Feed Others,* edited by Chayym Zeldis. Cranbury, New Jersey, A.S. Barnes, 1974.
"A Tale of Two Soldiers," in *Ladies Home Journal* (New York), December 1981.
"The Gifts of Andrea," in *Seventeen* (New York), October 1982.
"Long Distance," in *American Voice* (Louisville, Kentucky), fall 1986.
"Ghosts," in *Orim* (New Haven, Connecticut), spring 1987.
"The Seven of the Address," in *Winter's Tales,* edited by Robin Baird Smith. New York, St. Martin's Press, 1993.
Zebra and Other Stories. New York, Knopf, 1998.

Other

Jewish Ethics (pamphlet series). New York, Leaders Training Fellowship, 14 vols., 1964-69.
The Jew Confronts Himself in American Literature. Hales Corners, Wisconsin, Sacred Heart School of Theology, 1975.
Wanderings: Chaim Potok's History of the Jews. New York, Knopf, and London, Hutchinson, 1978.
Ethical Living for a Modern World. New York, Jewish Theological Seminary of America, 1985.
Contributor, *From the Corners of the Earth,* by Bill Aron. Philadelphia, Pennsylvania, Jewish Publication Society, 1985.
Theo Tobiasse: Artist in Exile. New York, Rizzoli, 1986.
Contributor, *The Jews in America,* edited by David Cohen. San Francisco, Collins Publishers, 1989.
Contributor, *Tales of the Hasidim,* edited by Martin Buber. New York, Pantheon, 1991.
"The Invisible Map of Meaning: A Writer's Confrontations" (essay), in *TriQuarterly 84,* spring/summer 1992.
Contributor, *Graven Images: Graphic Symbols of the Jewish Grave Stone,* edited by Arnold Schwartzman. New York, Abrams, 1993.
Contributor, *I Never Saw Another Butterfly: Children's Drawings and Poems from Terezin Concentration Camp 1942-1944,* edited by Hana Volavkova. New York, Pantheon, 1993.
Foreword, *As a Driven Leaf,* by Milton Steinberg. West Orange, New Jersey, Behrman House, 1996.
The Gates of November: Chronicles of the Slepak Family. New York, Knopf, 1996.

*

Media Adaptations: *The Chosen* (film), Landau Productions, distributed by Twentieth Century-Fox, 1981; *The Chosen* (musical, produced New York City, 1987).

Biography: Entry in *Dictionary of Literary Biography* by S. Lilliam Kremer, Vol. 28, Detroit, Gale, 1984; entry in *Dictionary of Literary Biography Yearbook: 1984,* Detroit, Gale, 1985; *Chaim Potok* by Edward A. Abramson, Boston, Twayne, 1986.

Critical Studies: Entry in *Contemporary Literary Criticism,* Detroit, Gale, Vol. 2, 1974, Vol. 7, 1977, Vol. 14, 1980, Vol. 26, 1983; entry in *Studies in American Jewish Literature,* edited by Daniel Walden, State University of New York, 1985.

Chaim Potok comments:

I've been writing about people and events that were of great concern to me as I grew up and began to make my way in this world. My hope has been that if I wrote about those people and events honestly enough, my world would open up and others would be caught up in it. I've been writing about the dreams, thoughts, and passions of individuals confronted by new ways of seeing and explaining the world; how they relate under such difficult and challenging circumstances to parents, friends, teachers, peers, and themselves.

I am deeply gladdened by the fact that young people all over the world read my books. I would like those young people to know James Joyce's response to someone who once asked him why he only wrote about Dublin: "For myself I always write about Dublin, because if I can get to the heart of Dublin I can get to the heart of all the cities of the world. In the particular is contained the universal."

On occasion someone will ask me: Why do you only write about Jews? (No longer quite true since *I Am the Clay.*) I answer that I have used Jews much as Joyce has used Irish, and Ibsen has used Norwegians. People will understand that in time. Many of my young readers understand it already.

*　　*　　*

Chaim Potok's richly detailed and descriptive novels about young American Jews dealing with the demands of traditional Judaism in a largely Christian and increasingly secular society have had a limited but very loyal following among young adult readers.

The Chosen and its more ambitious sequel *The Promise* focus on the intellectual, social, and religious conflicts between two groups of religiously observant American Jews: Hasidim who are anti-Zionist (some Hasidim are strongly Zionist) and whose lifestyle, clothing, and beliefs have changed little from their roots in eighteenth-century Europe; and "modern" Orthodox Jews deeply committed to the state of Israel who strictly observe biblical commandments and rabbinic law but base their beliefs and actions on a rational analysis of biblical text and Talmudic commentary. Metaphor and allegory play a large role in both novels, and the two young protagonists in each reflect the passions of and conflicts between the two groups—as well as the tensions with the larger world around them.

The Chosen begins with a baseball game in which the two protagonists face-off against one another. Reuven Malter, the son of a religiously observant Jewish scholar who argues on the basis of logic and reason rather than unexamined belief, is pitching for his yeshiva team. One of the batters on the opposing team is Danny Saunders, a child-genius son of a Hasidic "rebbe" (rabbi), who has inexplicably chosen to bring his son up in silence—except when study of the Torah or Talmud is concerned. With intensity and seeming purposefulness, Danny hits a line drive at Reuven and almost blinds him. However, as Reuven recovers, the two become close friends and involve themselves in each other's lives. Eventually, with the help of Reuven, Danny is freed from his father's self-imposed vow of silence and is permitted to leave the Hasidic community to become a psychiatrist, while Reuven studies to be a rabbi. The fact that the rigid world of Hasidism is unable to hold a genius like Danny while the more open environment of "modern" orthodox Judaism convinces Reuven to become a rabbi is meant by Potok to be more than a simple statement of irony. Although Potok respects the spiritual intensity of the Hasidim, he is very critical of their communal restrictions on the freedom of individuals within their communities and on the insularity of the communities.

The Promise, like *The Chosen,* begins with an allegory—a carnival where Reuven and a mentally-ill teen friend named Michael are cheated by an unscrupulous Hasid in charge of one of the carnival booths. This sets the stage for the involvement of Reuven—and eventually Danny—in helping Michael confront his illness. A parallel plot deals with Reuven's difficulties with his yeshiva's provincial and mean Talmud teacher, which gives Potok another vehicle for portraying the dichotomy between "enlightened" and "narrow-minded" Orthodox Judaism. The two novels are immersed in the details and the ambience of the study of Jewish texts and the observance of Jewish law. The problem is that the characters are rarely more than effective—and even sometimes dramatic—spokesmen for Potok's view of the Jewish world. Except for the action in the allegorical beginning chapter of the two books, the character changes are described rather than portrayed.

Potok, who grew up in a very strict orthodox Jewish community and was severely criticized by others in his religious community and by family members for the art work he did as a child, also wrote two novels about a fictional Hasidic Jewish artist named Asher Lev (*My Name Is Asher Lev* and *The Gift of Asher Lev*). In traditional Judaism, art has been discouraged because of the biblical injunction against idolatry (worshipping graven images). Feeling compelled and sometimes driven to express himself through his art, Asher has to contend with the deeply ingrained antagonism toward art in the Judaism he practiced and with the hostility within his religious community and even his own family (especially after he paints two pictures dealing with the crucifixion). Twenty years later, he and his family, who now live in France, return to New York for a funeral of a beloved uncle and once again encounter the harsh criticism that drove him to leave years before.

Potok's novel *In the Beginning* traverses similar territory but in a much broader setting, while *The Book of Lights, Davita's Harp,* and *I Am the Clay* range into different terrain altogether. For example, *Davita's Harp* focuses on a girl whose non-Jewish father and Jewish mother are committed to Communism. When her father is killed in the Spanish Civil War, her mother becomes an Orthodox Jew. Davita enrolls in an all-girls yeshiva and excels in her studies, but she is ultimately frustrated and disillusioned by the gender discrimination she encounters from the religious community. *The*

Book of Lights carries his Jewish protagonists to Japan and through the ravages of the Korean War and the memories of Hiroshima. *I Am the Clay* evokes Pearl Buck's *The Good Earth* and concerns Korean peasants trying to act humanely in war's aftermath.

Particularly interesting to teen readers is Potok's only book of nonfiction, *Wanderings: Chaim Potok's History of the Jews.* Like his fiction, this book is highly personalized and richly detailed. Surprisingly, it has perhaps even more appeal to teens than his fiction because history comes alive through Potok's narrative rather than being filtered through one-dimensional fictional characters.

Potok, who is an ordained Conservative Jewish rabbi, writes about what he has experienced in his life—the tensions between the traditional and the modern Jewish religious life; the dichotomy of the letter and spirit of Jewish law; and the mystical and the rational elements within Judaism. His fiction dealing with religious and social issues within a Jewish context touches on issues that most teens grapple with in different contexts, making his novels especially relevant and illuminating for young adult readers.

—Jack Forman

POWELL, Randy

Nationality: American. **Born:** Seattle, Washington, 1956. **Education:** University of Washington, B.A. in English, history, and communications 1981; M.A. in education 1984. **Family:** Married, two sons. **Career:** Teacher, alternative school for junior high and high school dropouts, 1984-88; technical writer/editor, The Boeing Company, Everett, Washington, from 1989. **Awards:** Starred selection, *School Library Journal,* for *My Underrated Year;* starred selection, *Booklist* and *School Library Journal,* American Library Association (ALA) Best Book for Young Adults, Pen West Award for Children's Literature, 1993, all for *Is Kissing a Girl Who Smokes Like Licking an Ashtray?*; ALA Best Book for Young Adults and ALA "Quick Pick" for Young Adults, for *Dean Duffy.* **Address:** c/o Farrar, Straus, & Giroux, 19 Union Square West, New York, New York 10003, U.S.A. **E-mail Address:** Randy.E.Powell@Boeing.com.

PUBLICATIONS FOR YOUNG ADULTS

Fiction

My Underrated Year. New York, Farrar, Strauss and Giroux, 1988.
Is Kissing a Girl Who Smokes Like Licking an Ashtray? New York, Farrar, Strauss and Giroux, 1992.
Dean Duffy. New York, Farrar, Strauss and Giroux, 1995.
The Whistling Toilets. New York, Farrar, Strauss and Giroux, 1996.

*

Randy Powell comments:

As a kid growing up in the Seattle area, I played a lot of sports, both organized and unorganized. My greatest moment of glory came when I was given the game ball after our team won the all-city championship football game. I was eleven years old. Our quarterback went on to play in the NFL. I didn't go on to play in the NFL. In fact, it was all downhill for me after that. In high school I concentrated on tennis, but I had many more disappointments than triumphs. Which is fortunate in a way. The disappointments make better stories. High school was also when I became interested in writing. I wrote short stories and typed them in the school typing room during lunch (no such thing as PCs or Macs in those days) and sent them to the New Yorker and the National Lampoon. They all got rejected of course, but I cherished the rejection slips because they began "Dear Author." They were calling me an author!

It's taken me a long time to learn to write honestly, about things I really care about. In fact I'm still learning. I don't try to target my books to a specific age group or audience. I'm not interested in novels that deal with sensational or trendy topics, or that teach lessons or preach sermons. I write to please myself. What pleases me most in fiction is voice, language, detail, feelings. But most of all people. Real people, struggling with themselves and undecided about life. My characters' experiences are a combination of my experiences, observation, and imagination. Their problems are pretty much the same problems people have been struggling with for years. I try to make them fresh through voice—through the unique voice and heart of the character.

I take my characters' problems seriously, but I try not to treat them in a pretentious or too-serious voice. The more real and human a character becomes to me, the more humor I find in him or her. It's true that teenagers take their problems very seriously, but I think they're basically pretty funny, and fun, people to be around. Just because a book has some humor and goofiness doesn't mean it's lightweight, or that its characters aren't complex and important and human and real. And worthy of our compassion.

*   *   *

In *My Underrated Year,* Roger Ottosen has it all going for him as he faces his sophomore year with confidence. He has a good chance of being one of the few sophomores to make the varsity football team and could rank as number one tennis player in the league. That is until the Mountain twins move to town. Paul Mountain threatens Roger's sure-fire success in football, and Paul's twin, Mary Jo, is an outstanding tennis player. When Roger fails to make varsity, he almost quits the j.v. team but with the help of his best friend fights his discouragement and reaches deep inside himself to persist. He finds himself more and more attracted to Mary Jo Mountain, his primary tennis rival, but confused by his feelings for her. While he wants nothing more than to beat her at tennis, he also realizes that he is falling in love with her. When he finally faces her in a friendly tennis match and loses, he is convinced that he is a failure. Pressured to attend the football awards dinner with his stepfather, Roger is surprised to receive the award for "Most Underrated." Bolstered by his increased confidence, he comes back determined to beat Mary Jo and maintain their friendship. Roger ends up finding his inner strength and realizing that he can make sense out of it all and keep going.

In *Is Kissing a Girl Who Smokes Like Licking an Ashtray?*, Biff Schmurr has a confidence problem. Half-way through his senior year, he is still working up the courage to ask Tommie Isaac, someone he has been in love with for the past two years, for a date. Then, Biff meets Heidi, the niece of his close family friends who has come to visit. Heidi is everything that Tommie is not. A thin, blond, smart-mouthed, fifteen-year-old who smokes, Heidi challenges his existence. Unable to dismiss her, Biff finds himself intrigued by Heidi and her life. They hang out, read, talk, and develop their friendship. Biff learns that Heidi's privileged life has its drawbacks. Her mother committed suicide, and her father has withdrawn from society. Heidi is shuffled back and forth between an aunt and a wealthy grandmother who wants to control her. With the help of her forthright approach to her difficulties, Biff learns to become an active participant in his own life, surprising himself at how much fun it can be. *Is Kissing a Girl* is a poignant story, weaving together two memorable characters as they form an unlikely friendship and help each other make some tough decisions.

Powell again focuses on the theme of coming of age in his third novel, *Dean Duffy*. Dean Duffy has been playing baseball since he was seven years old, but an arm injury forces him to give up pitching in his sophomore year. He focuses on batting during his junior and senior years and becomes an outstanding hitter. His peak comes during a game when he hits a 500-foot home run. He knows he hit it, but because the ball was not found, fans begin to doubt him, and Dean loses confidence in himself. He graduates, then moves north to a remote area with his parents to renovate an old farmhouse and run it as a bed and breakfast. Dean is relieved to move and welcomes the isolation. For him, dropping out of baseball is inevitable, and he insists that he doesn't care. Without the pressure of the sport, he thinks he will be able to enjoy life. His former coach has other ideas, however, and gradually encourages Dean to face the reality of his fears and take the risk again. Dean Duffy reconnects with his former coach, an ex-friend, and a former nemesis on his personal odyssey, learning that life is about living with and facing your fears. Ironically, Dean has already found the proof he needs to believe in himself again when he finds the concrete evidence of his legendary home run. Recognizing his own value, his talent, and his dream, Dean has to decide whether or not to return to baseball and college. The reader is left to predict his action, but whatever the decision, we know Dean Duffy is in control of his life once again.

In *The Whistling Toilets,* Ginny and Stan are childhood friends reunited after Ginny is brought back from tennis camp. Her tennis coach is concerned that she is losing her concentration, and brings her home to play less competitive matches in order to build her confidence. Stan is coaching beginning tennis at the community center and has the opportunity to become Ginny's temporary coach. He had been a rising tennis star once and wonders how his own life would have been different had he been driven to achieve. He questions whether the meaning of life is to pursue his passion or to simply accept himself and life as it comes. The two friends build each other's confidence, and in the process, Stan finds out what is really throwing off Ginny's game. Together, they begin to answer their own questions about life, realizing that it is important to continue to ask new ones. Both accept the direction their lives take them in, stronger than before and confident in their new maturity.

—Susan B. Steffel

PULLMAN, Philip

Nationality: British. **Born:** Norwich, England, 19 October 1946. **Education:** Oxford University, England, B.A. 1968. **Family:**

Married Judith Speller in 1970; two sons. **Career:** Teacher at Ivanhoe, Bishop Kirk, and Marston middle schools, Oxford, England, 1973-86; writer, since 1986. Lecturer at Westminster College, North Hinksey, Oxford. **Awards:** Lancashire County Libraries/National and Provincial Children's Book award and a Best Books for Young Adults listing from *School Library Journal,* both 1987, a Children's Book award from the International Reading Association and a Best Books for Young Adults listing from the American Library Association (ALA), both 1988, and a Preis der Leseratten from ZDF Television (Germany), for *The Ruby in the Smoke*; ALA Best Books for Young Adults listing, 1988, and Edgar Allan Poe award nomination, by the Mystery Writers of America. Inc., 1989, for *Shadow in the North*; Smarties Gold Award, 1996, for *The Firework Maker's Daughter*; Smarties Silver Award, 1997, for *Clockwork*; *Guardian* award co-winner, Carnegie Medal, and Children's Book of the Year, 1997, for *Northern Lights*; American Booksellers Association ABBY Honor Book, 1997, for *The Golden Compass*. **Agent:** Ellen Levine, 432 Park Ave. S., Suite 1205, New York, New York 10016, U.S.A. **Address:** 24 Templar Rd., Oxford OX2 8LT, England.

PUBLICATIONS FOR YOUNG ADULTS

Fiction

The Ruby in the Smoke. London, Oxford University Press, and New York, Knopf, 1985.

The Shadow in the Plate. London, Oxford University Press, 1987; as *The Shadow in the North,* New York, Knopf, 1988.

Spring-heeled Jack. illustrated by David Mostyn. London, Doubleday, 1989; New York, Knopf, 1991.

The Broken Bridge. London, Macmillan, 1990; New York, Knopf, 1992.

The Tiger in the Well. London, Viking, 1991; New York, Knopf, 1990.

The White Mercedes. London, Macmillan, 1993; New York, Knopf, 1993; as *The Butterfly Tattoo,* London, Macmillan, 1998.

The Tin Princess. London, Puffin, 1994; New York, Knopf, 1994.

Northern Lights (His Dark Materials Book 1). London, Scholastic, 1995; as *The Golden Compass,* New York, Knopf, 1996.

The Subtle Knife (His Dark Materials Book 2). London, Scholastic, 1997; New York, Knopf, 1997.

Plays

Frankenstein. London, Oxford University Press, 1990.

PUBLICATIONS FOR CHILDREN

Fiction

Ancient Civilizations. illustrated by G. Long. London, Wheaton, 1978.

Count Karlstein. London, Chatto & Windus, 1982; edition with illustrations by Patrice Aggs, London, Doubleday, 1991.

How to be Cool. London, Heinemann, 1987.

The Wonderful Story of Aladdin and the Enchanted Lamp. London, Andre Deutsch, 1993; as *Aladdin and the Enchanted Lamp,* London, Hippo, 1995.

Thunderbolt's Waxwork. London, Viking, 1994.

The Firework Maker's Daughter. London, Doubleday, 1995.
The Gas Fitter's Ball. London, Viking, 1995.
Clockwork. London, Doubleday, 1996; New York, Arthur A. Levine Books, 1998.

PUBLICATIONS FOR ADULTS

Novels

Galatea. London, Gollancz, 1978; New York, Dutton, 1979.

Also author of additional plays, including *The Adventure of the Sumarian Devil* and an adaptation of Alexandre Dumas's *The Three Musketeers.*

*

Media Adaptations: *How to be Cool* (TV), Granada, 1988.

Biography: Essay in *Speaking for Ourselves, Too,* compiled and edited by Donald R. Gallo, National Council of Teachers of English, 1993; essay in *Something About the Author, Autobiography Series,* Volume 17, Detroit, Gale, 1994.

Critical Studies: Entry in *Children's Literature Review,* Volume 20, Detroit, Gale, 1990.

*   *   *

Phillip Pullman writes in a variety of genres for a range of children. His work has gained in assurance in recent years so that he now writes with confidence and flair for all ages. His most acclaimed books, the fantasy sequence *His Dark Materials,* are also marketed for adult fans of fantasy.

His historical books are set in the London of the late nineteenth century. This atmosphere has been compared to that of Dickens, although one reviewer has suggested they have more in common with Wilkie Collins, and sometimes they do read like a pastiche of Victorian fiction. The protagonist in the first three books of the sequence is Sally Lockhart, a sixteen-year-old girl who finds herself alone in London. There is a mystery surrounding her father's death on board ship after he has sent Sally an enigmatic message, and she is being pursued by a powerful and ghastly woman, Mrs. Holland. Sally is helped by Frederick Garland, a photographer and detective, his actress sister, an office boy, and a slum child as the plot becomes more complex, involving a ruby which vanished when a maharajah was murdered during the Indian Mutiny. The villain of the piece is the evil Ah Ling, who is supposedly murdered at the end of the book, but whose body is not found.

The second book, *The Shadow in the Plate,* continues this relentless pace. This time the mystery involves the aristocracy, spiritualism, the music hall, high finance, and a conspiracy leading to the production of a Victorian "ultimate weapon": a steam-impelled machine gun to be deployed from railway carriages. Pullman defies all conventions at the end of this book by killing off Frederick, whom Sally has grown to love.

The Tiger in the Well touches on more serious concerns than the previous books. Sally is now a successful business tycoon, as well as an unmarried mother. Her world is thrown awry, however, when Mr. Parrish, a rent collector, claims she is his wife. The real man responsible for trying to destroy her turns out to be Tzaddik, otherwise known as Ah Ling. This book successfully and graphically demonstrates the much greater evil in the London slums where a vicious anti-Semitic campaign is opposed by active socialist groups. Sally's eyes are opened by Goldberg, a middle-aged, tough, and scruffy Jew, and the eccentric Dr. Turner and her compassion for the poor.

The Tin Princess, the fourth book in the sequence, concentrates on the Cockney waif, Adelaide, last seen escaping at the end of *The Ruby in the Smoke.* The setting is Ruritania, where a series of assassinations allow Adelaide to succeed to the throne, where she is aided by Jim Taylor from the previous novels and Becky, who is employed as an interpreter but who comes to admire Adelaide's character. Add to this mad princes, dramatic Spanish actresses, and a dashing hero who manages to escape from prison by using wool from his cardigan.

Pullman's two contemporary novels are the exciting and punchy *The Broken Bridge* and *The White Mercedes.* The first tells of sixteen-year-old Ginny's search for her true identity. She lives with her father in Wales and is one of only two blacks in her school. She discovers that she has a half brother, and tensions are provoked when he comes to live with them. This novel, named for its mysterious theme concerning a broken bridge, is packed with issues: race, fostering and adoption, sexuality and homosexuality, and voodooism. Possibly there is too much going on to be contained in the novel's structure.

The White Mercedes is more assured. Set in Oxford, where Pullman himself lives, it tells of seventeen-year-old Chris, who falls for the mysterious and more experienced Jenny. Her past has been hard, but she has emerged clear-headed and resourceful. This is in contrast to Chris, whose often naive reactions result in his becoming involved with the criminal past of his boss, ultimately leading to tragic consequences. Here, as with *The Shadow on the Plate,* Pullman plays with the rules of fiction as few young-adult writers attempt to do. Even after Jenny's tragic death, Chris remains as naive and innocent as he is at the beginning of the book. He totally misinterprets the situation, and one suspects he will continue to do so for the rest of his life.

Pullman's most astonishing achievement to date has been the fantasy trilogy, *His Dark Materials.* At the time of writing, the first two books have been published both to great critical acclaim and to a huge following among both children and adult fantasy fans. Both highly literary (the trilogy's title is taken from *Paradise Lost*) and hugely readable, the books take place in worlds similar to our own, worlds which are exact replicas and worlds which are total fantasy. The world of *Northern Lights* is a world of academia where all humans carry with them a daemon which changes shape according to its owner's mood and where a team of scientists is examining the dust which surrounds the bodies of the children who inhabit the world. The splendidly adventurous heroine, Lyra, finds herself drawn into the quest to discover why experiments are being performed to cut the children off from their daemons, all the time fighting the villainy of her mother. The second book, *The Subtle Knife,* is even more intricate, travelling as it does between three worlds. Much of it takes place in a recognisable contemporary setting as the resourceful Will tries to establish the truth of why he and his mother are being pursued by a group of people who are trying to eliminate what Will's father has discovered in the past. Will teams up with Lyra and a number of characters from the first book reappear in order to continue the struggle to confront the powers of tyranny. The book ends on a true cliff hanger which makes the publication of the third part of the trilogy a highly important event.

—Keith Barker

PYLE, Howard

Nationality: American. **Born:** Wilmington, Delaware, 5 March 1853. **Education:** Friends' School and Clark and Taylor's School, Wilmington; Mr. Van der Weilen's school, Philadelphia, 1868-72; Art Student's League, New York. **Family:** Married Anne Poole in 1881; seven children. **Career:** Author, artist, painter, teacher of illustration, and writer of children's stories. Illustrator for *Scribner's Monthly;* freelance illustrator for *St. Nicholas* magazine, *Harper's,* and *Harper's Young People;* taught illustration at Drexel Institute of Arts and Sciences, Philadelphia, 1894-1900, later established his own art school in Wilmington. **Died:** 9 November 1911.

PUBLICATIONS FOR YOUNG ADULTS (illustrated by the author)

Fiction

The Merry Adventures of Robin Hood of Great Renown in Nottinghamshire. New York, Scribner, 1883.
Pepper and Salt; or, Seasoning for Young Folk. New York, Harper, 1885.
Otto of the Silver Hand. New York, Scribner, 1888.
The Wonder Clock; or, Four and Twenty Marvellous Tales, Being One for Each Hour of the Day, with verses by sister, Katherine Pyle. New York, Harper, 1888.
The Rose of Paradise. New York, Harper, 1888.
Book of Pirates. New York, Harper, 1891; as *Howard Pyle's Book of Pirates,* edited by Merle Johnson. New York, Harper, 1921.
Men of Iron. New York, Harper, 1892.
A Modern Aladdin; or, The Wonderful Adventures of Oliver Munier. New York, Harper, 1892.
The Garden behind the Moon: A Real Story of the Moon Angel. New York, Scribner, 1895.
The Story of Jack Ballister's Fortunes. Century, 1895.
Twilight Land. New York, Harper, 1895.
The Price of Blood: An Extravaganza of New York Life in 1807. R. G. Badger, 1899.
The Story of King Arthur and His Knights. New York, Scribner, 1903; as *The Book of King Arthur,* Chicago. Children's Press, 1969.
The Story of the Champions of the Round Table. New York, Scribner, 1905.
The Story of Sir Launcelot and His Companions. New York, Scribner, 1907.
Strange Stories of the Revolution, with Winthrop Packard, Molly Elliot Seawell, and others. New York, Harper, 1907.
Adventures of Pirates and Sea-Rovers, with J. H. Upshur, Paul Hull, Reginald Gourlay, and others. New York, Harper, 1908.

The Ruby of Kishmoor. New York, Harper, 1908.
The Story of the Grail and the Passing of Arthur. New York, Scribner, 1910.

Other

Within the Capes. New York, Scribner, 1885.
Editor, *The Buccaneers and Marooners of America,* by Alexandre Olivier Exquemelin. New York, Macmillan, 1891.
School and Playground (stories). New York, D. Lothrop, 1891.
The Divinity of Labor (address). J. Rogers, 1898.
Rejected of Men: A Story of To-day. New York, Harper, 1903.
Contributor, *Shapes that Haunt the Dusk,* edited by Howells. New York, Harper, 1907.
Stolen Treasure (stories). New York, Harper, 1907.
Contributor, *The Book of Laughter,* edited by Katherine N. Birdsall and George Haven Putnam. New York, Putnam, 1911.
King Stork, illustrated by Trina Schart Hyman. Boston, Little, Brown, 1973.

*

Media Adaptations: *Wonder Clock Plays* (play by Sophie L. Goldsmith), Harper, 1925; *Robin Hood Plays Matchmaker* (one act play by Mary T. Pyle), Dramatists Play Service, 1939; *The Apple of Contentment* (one act play by Mary T. Pyle), Dramatists Play Service, 1939; *Three Strangers Come to Sherwood* (one act play by Mary T. Pyle), Dramatists Play Service, 1942; *The Men of Iron* (movie, *The Black Shield of Falworth,* starring Tony Curtis and Janet Leigh), Universal Pictures, 1954. Recording of *Tales of King Arthur and His Knights* (recording, read by Ian Richardson), Caedmon, 1975.

Biography: *Howard Pyle: A Chronicle* by Charles Abbot, Harper, 1923; *Howard Pyle* by Elizabeth Nesbitt, Walek, 1966; *Howard Pyle: Writer, Illustrator, Founder of the Brandywine School* by Henry C. Pitz, Clarkson N. Potter, 1975; entry in *Writers for Children* edited by Jane M. Bingham, Scribner, 1988; entry in *Dictionary of Literary Biography,* Vol. 42, Detroit, Gale, 1985.

Illustrator: *Yankee Doodle: An Old Friend in a New Dress,* 1881; *Lady of Shalott* by Alfred Lord Tennyson, 1881; *Old Times in the Colonies* by Charles Carleton Coffin, 1881; *Phaeton Rogers* by Rossiter Johnson, 1881; *The Chronicle of the Drum* by William Makepeace Thackeray, 1882; *Under Green Apple Boughs* by Helen Campbell, 1882; *Farm Ballads* by Will Carlton, 1882; *Story of Siegfried* by James Baldwin, 1882; *Building the Nation: Events in the History of the United States from the Revolution to the Beginning of the War between the States* by Charles Carleton Coffin, 1883; *A History of the United States of America Preceded by a Narrative of the Discovery and Settlement of North America and of the Events Which Led to the Independence of the Thirteen English Colonies for the Use of Schools and Academies* by Horace E. Scudder, 1884; *Illustrated Poems* by Oliver Wendell Holmes, 1885; *Indian History for Young Folks* by Francis S. Drake, 1885; *A History of New York,* two volumes by Driedrich Knickerbocker (pseudonym of Washington Irving), 1886; *A Larger History of the United States of America* by Thomas Wentworth Higginson, 1886; *City Ballads* by Will Carlton, 1886; *Story of the Golden Age* by

James Baldwin, 1887; *The Closing Scene* by Thomas Buchanan Read, 1887; *Storied Holidays: A Cycle of Historic Red-Letter Days* by Elbridge S. Brooks, 1887; *The Star Bearer* by Edmund Clarence Stedman, 1888; *Old Homestead Poems* by Wallace Bruce, 1888; *Youma: The Story of a West Indian Slave* by Lafcadio Hearn, 1890; *In the Valley* by Harold Frederic, 1890; *The Captain's Well* by John Greenleaf Whittier, 1890; *Flute and Violin, and Other Kentucky Tales and Romances* by James Lane Allen, 1891; *One Hoss Shay, with its Companion Poems* by Oliver Wendell Holmes, 1892; *Poetical Works of Oliver Wendell Holmes,* two volumes by Oliver Wendell Holmes, 1892; *Together with A Ballad of the Boston Tea Party and Grandmother's Story of the Bunker Hill Battle* by Dorothy Q. Holmes, 1893; *Autocrat of the Breakfast Table,* two volumes by Oliver Wendell Holmes, 1893; *A Tour around New York* and *My Summer Acre* by John Flavel Mines, 1893; *Abraham Lincoln* by Charles Carleton Coffin, 1893; *Giles Corey* by Mary E. Wilkens, 1893; *In Old New York* by Thomas A. Janvier, 1894; *Stops of Various Quills* by William Dean Howells, 1895; *Great Men's Shoes* by Elbridge S. Brooks, 1895; *The True Story of George Washington* by Elbridge S. Brooks, 1895; *The Parasite: A Story* by Arthur Conan Doyle, 1895; *The Novels and Tales of Robert Louis Stevenson,* three volumes by Robert Louis Stevenson, 1895; *Writings of Harriet Beecher Stowe,* two volumes by Harriet Beecher Stowe, 1896; *Hugh Wynne, Free Quaker* by Silas Weir Mitchell, 1896; *In Ole Virginia* by T.N. Page, 1896; *First Christmas Tree* by Henry Van Dyke, 1897; *George Washington* by Woodrow Wilson, 1897; *Works of Francis Parkman,* three volumes by Francis Parkman, 1897-98; *Odysseus, the Hero of Ithaca* (includes illustrations previously published in *Story of the Golden Age*) by Mary E. Burt, 1898; *Story of the Revolution* by Henry Cabot Lodge, 1898; *The Book of Oceans* by Ernest Ingersoll, 1898; *Silence, and Other Stories* by Mary E. Wilkens, 1898; *Old Chester Tales* by Margaret Deland, 1899; *A Story of the American Revolution,* two volumes by Paul Leicester Ford and Janice Meredith, 1899; *To Have and to Hold* by Mary Johnston, 1900; *The Man with the Hoe, and Other Poems* by Edwin Markham, 1900; *Modern Pen Drawings European and American* (includes illustrations previously published in *The Man with the Hoe*) edited by Charles Holmes, 1901; *Works of John Lothrop Motley* by John Lothrop Motley, 1900; *Complete Writings of Nathaniel Hawthorne* by Nathaniel Hawthorne, 1900; *Sir Christopher: A Romance of a Maryland Manor in 1644* by Maud Wilder Goodwin, 1901; *Captain Renshaw; or, The Maid of Cheapside: A Romance of Elizabethan London* by Robert Neilson, 1901; *A History of American Art* (includes illustrations previously published in *Captain Renshaw*) by Hartman, Sadakichi, 1901; *A History of the American People,* five volumes by Woodrow Wilson, 1902, published with additional illustrations in 1918; *Harper's Encyclopedia of United States History,* ten volumes, 1902; *The Poetical Works of James Russell Lowell,* five volumes by James Russell Lowell, 1904; *A History of the United States* by Wilbur F. Gordy, 1904; *The Island of Enchantment* by Justus Miles Forman, 1905; *The Line of Love* by J.B. Cabell, 1905; *Snow Bound: A Winter Idyl* by John Greenleaf Whittier, 1906; *Gallantry: An Eighteenth Century Dizain* by J.B. Cabell, 1907; *Dulcibel: A Tale of Old Salem* by Henry Peterson, 1907; *Chivalry* by J.B. Cabell, 1909; *Lincoln and the Sleeping Sentinel* by L.E. Chittenden, 1909; *Harper's Book of Little Plays* by Margaret Sutton Briscoe, John Kendrick Bangs, and others, 1910; *The Works of William Makepeace Thackeray* edited by Lady Ritchie, 1910; *On Hazardous Service: Scouts and Spies of the North and South* by William Gilmore Beymer, 1912; *The Buccaneers* by Don Seitz, 1912; *Founders of Our Country* by Fanny E. Coe, 1912; *The Soul of Melicent* by J.B. Cabell, 1913; *Etchings* by W.H.W. Bicknell, 1913; *Around Old Chester* by Margaret Deland, 1915; *Stories of Later American History* by Wilbur F. Gordy, 1915; *Saint Joan Of Arc* by Mark Twain, 1919; *Book of the American Spirit* edited by Francis J. Dowd, 1923; *Robin Hood* by Henry Gilbert, 1964.

*   *   *

Howard Pyle must be considered a giant in American literature for children. An innovative, vastly productive artist-writer-teacher, he was a modest man totally concerned with inspiring good artists and creating good books. But the term giant just might have appealed to him as a description, for his imagination was tuned in to the days of good knights and evil villains, heroes and dragons, magic stools and clever magicians, beautiful maidens and wicked queens, good boys, foolish men, and, surely among them, giants. And of course, King Arthur and Robin Hood.

In his fifty-eight years he accomplished an amazing amount of enduring work. His importance as an artist as well as writer must be mentioned here for several reasons. First, his work spanned a period of vital change in children's books. It began in an era when moralistic stories had themes of illness, suffering, and death, and were usually illustrated by inept saccharine pictures; standards for writing and illustrating were low. It ended with his work, both words and pictures, having produced the highest standards for others to follow. The author-artist Robert Lawson, writing in *Illustrators of Children's Books 1744-1945,* stated, "It is small wonder that the clean-cut, healthy, joyous work of Howard Pyle came to...children...like a fresh breeze flooding a fetid sick-room." Second, his illustration and stories intertwined and enhanced each other, growing equally from his concept of the subject undertaken, even though, to an extent rarely equalled by any other author-artist, each element is strong enough to stand alone. Third, any piece of artwork takes a great deal of time to produce. Thus to research, absorb, recreate, and retell the Robin Hood ballads and the vast lore of King Arthur was a gigantic, time-consuming task. He was a truly prodigious worker.

Although he could easily "see things in image-terms or in the continuity of words," as Henry C. Pitz describes his dual abilities, he was a deliberate craftsman. He actually experimented with various writing styles to achieve the effect of the archaic speech of Robin Hood's days and yet have it understandable to children. Reading it aloud today, now that we are even used to *you* taking the place of *thee-and-thou* in versions of the Bible, it sounds more unreal than ever to hear, "Now will I go too, for fain would I draw a string for the bright eyes of my lass, for so goodly a prize as that," or hear Pauline ask poor little Otto about his mother, "And didst thou never see her?" Such is his thoroughness in setting scene, delineating character, and sweeping all action forward in a dynamic plot—particularly in his own stories such as *Otto of the Silver Hand, Men of Iron* and his pirate tales—that one quickly accepts the language as another rich element of his writing skill.

Although *The Merry Adventures of Robin Hood* (1883) was his first book to be published, *Pepper and Salt* and *The Wonder Clock* contained stories and fables Pyle had written and illustrated for children's magazines. *Twilight Land* was more influenced by

Eastern folktales. While at first he borrowed and retold old tales in different guises (''The Salt of Life'' is the well-known Catskin motif of universal folklore), so steeped was he in folk and fairy lore that eventually he could turn his own rich imagination out into these forms to perfection, just as Andersen did. *The Garden behind the Moon,* a long allegorical fantasy, is less derivative than his short stories and it contains such strong beautiful prose that it makes him a classic writer of fantasy.

With the grim sad story of medieval revenge, *Otto of the Silver Hand,* and that of fifteenth-century adventure, *Men of Iron,* and in his tales of Robin Hood and King Arthur, Pyle achieved new heights in literature for young people: he gave them an immediate sense of their past, complete with authentic convincing details, replete with drama and pageantry, and taut with adventure.

Elizabeth Nesbitt, commenting on Pyle in *A Critical History of Children's Literature,* mentioned that the era in which Pyle developed his work has been called the Golden Age of children's literature and that ''it is difficult to do justice to his contribution to the shining quality of that era. The magnitude and diversity of his work elude definition.''

—Lee Kingman

Q-R

QUALEY, Marsha

Nationality: American. **Born:** Marsha Richardson in Austin, Minnesota, 27 May 1953. **Education:** Macalester College, St. Paul, Minnesota, 1971-72; University of Minnesota, Minneapolis, B.A. 1976. **Family:** Married David Qualey, 1976; three daughters, one son. **Career:** Homemaker and volunteer, 1979-1989; writer from 1990. **Awards:** Minnesota Book Award for Older Children, 1994, 1996; American Library Association Best Books for Young Adults list, 1994, 1995; Wisconsin Library Association Outstanding Achievement Award, 1995. **Address:** 11525 40th Avenue, North Plymouth, Minnesota 55441, U.S.A.

PUBLICATIONS FOR YOUNG ADULTS

Everybody's Daughter. Boston, Houghton Mifflin, 1991.
Revolutions of the Heart. Boston, Houghton Mifflin, 1993.
Come in from the Cold. Boston, Houghton Mifflin, 1994.
Hometown. Boston, Houghton Mifflin, 1995.
Thin Ice. New York, Delacorte, 1997.

*   *   *

Marsha Qualey explores the tensions young adults experience in establishing independent identities apart from their families. Despite their desire for autonomy, they frequently discover that the influences of others affect their lives deeply.

Three of Qualey's novels are interconnected, examining the impact of the Vietnam war on the generation of teenagers during that era and on their own teenage children years later. *Come in from the Cold* traces the paths of two Minnesotans who are 17 in 1969. Three years earlier, Maud Dougherty's older sister Lucy had dropped out of college and gone underground as a radical protester against the war. After Lucy dies in a bomb blast in a physics lab on the University of Minnesota campus, an apparent suicide, Maud tries to make sense of Lucy's actions by visiting the campus and talking with protesters. At the same time, Jeff Ramsey manages to persuade his student council in Red Cedar to pass a resolution condemning the war. His older brother Tom, a Marine who is home on leave, clashes with Jeff on almost every topic. Within six weeks of arriving in Vietnam, Tom is killed. Jeff's protest activities increase.

Maud's and Tim's stories converge at a protest march in Red Cedar. Slowly they share their common views and similar griefs. During a march in St. Paul, they meet a group of young people establishing a commune in northern Minnesota. After his best friend Gumbo leaves for Canada to avoid the draft, Jeff drops out of college to join the commune, away from "where the wars rage on, the government lies, and every summer another city goes up in flames." Maud marries him when both are 19.

Eighteen years later, the Woodlands commune has disbanded, but many former members still live in the area. In fact, they gather regularly at the bait shop run by Bob and Carolyn Flynn. *Everybody's Daughter* concentrates on the efforts of Merry Moonbeam

(Beamer) Flynn, the first child born in the commune, to deal with the ongoing influence of the Woodies on her life. Beamer characterizes the commune's disbandment after 12 years as failure. The Woodies see it as a successful experiment that resulted in a lasting support system. That system is put to the test when a former Woodie is involved in the accidental bombing death of a guard during a protest against nuclear power. That incident draws media attention to the group, and Beamer agrees to a newspaper interview about her childhood. Although her facts are accurate, the Woodies wish Beamer could have communicated their beliefs. She lashes out, "Whatever it is you pathetic old hippies had and whatever it is you think you've got now, I don't believe in it."

Her desire to detach from the Woodies makes her reluctant to care about anyone too deeply. Her boyfriend Andy patiently tries to nurture their relationship. She alternately draws closer and withdraws to test an attraction for Martin, a college student interest in casual, uncommitted encounters. When Beamer realizes Martin is only interested in her as material for a short story, she comes to appreciate loyalty and sustaining friendships. Maud and Jeff are among the Flynns' friends.

Jeff plays an offstage part in *Hometown*, in which Gumbo (Crosby) returns to Red Cedar with his teenage son, Border. Despite Jimmy Carter's pardon of draft dodgers, Crosby's father had never spoken to his son after he fled to Canada. However, Crosby decides to come back when he inherits his parents' home after their deaths. Border's views of events alternate with a third-person narration of his adjustment to small-town Minnesota. Working as a nurse at the hospital, Crosby fits into the community more easily than he had anticipated. Border, however, is taunted and beaten by those who know his father's past. Their hostility is intensified because of the patriotic fervor gripping the country as Operation Desert Shield develops into war against Iraq. Crosby still opposes war, and after he appears on a TV show about how war changes lives, the rift grows between father and son. Border joins a group to support servicemen. Crosby stays in touch with Jeff in phone conversations. Jeff's parents, who still live across the street from Crosby's home, play a large part in the story. Eventually Crosby and Border reconcile, and the town learns to accommodate different viewpoints on war.

Although each of the three novels stands alone, together they provide a complex study of characters and issues. Qualey's consideration of the cyclic pattern in generational distrust and conflict is thoughtful and unusual, especially in incorporating issues of war and social protest.

A divided town also forms the background of *Revolutions of the Heart*. Seventeen-year-old Cory Knutson lives in northern Wisconsin near reservations of American Indians. Most of the time informal segregation in her small town keeps whites and Native Americans apart, but clashes over fishing rights divide both the community and Cory's family. Her mother's friendship with a Native American reflects her tolerance, and Cory's stepfather Mike offers quiet support. However, her older brother Rob is a hotheaded demonstrator against the Indian spearing. Further complicating the issue is Cory's dating of Mac, a Native American, which makes her the object of harassment. Her mother's death before she can receive a heart transplant adds further stress to Cory's life, but with the support of her friends and stepfather, she remains undaunted in her relationship with Mac.

Seventeen-year-old Arden Munro can barely remember her parents because they were killed in a plane crash when she was six. Her brother Scott abandoned his plans for medical school to come home to raise her. *Thin Ice* is told by Arden as she tries to deal with her brother's disappearance in a snowmobile accident near their home in northern Wisconsin. For eleven years Scott had been reliable and responsible, earning a living as a mechanic. Rescued after going through thin ice on his new snowmobile, Scott seems unreasonably depressed and preoccupied with buying a new machine.

A second accident leaves his snowmobile at the bottom of a river and many unanswered questions. Small clues convince Arden that Scott staged the event. Her discovery that the woman he had been seeing is pregnant strengthens her conviction that he cannot face new responsibilities. The depiction of Arden's growing obsession with finding Scott at the cost of her academics, work, and friendships is taut and compelling. Qualey masterfully inserts just enough doubts to make readers waver between accepting Arden's theories and siding with the community anxious to help her through denial to grief. Unfortunately, the book's climax depends on an improbable chance meeting to resolve Arden's questions.

Although Qualey concentrates on the establishment of self-identity by her teenagers, she is equally successful at developing adult characters. Neither heroes nor villains, they struggle to live their own lives, often according to a set of principles that their children reject or emulate. Either way, Qualey reminds adolescent readers that their decisions occur within a context of family and society no matter how personal their struggles appear.

—Kathy Piehl

* * *

RAMPLING, Anne. *See* **RICE, Anne.**

* * *

RAND, Ayn

Nationality: American. **Born:** St. Petersburg, Russia, February 1905; emigrated to the United States in 1926; naturalized, 1931. **Education:** the University of Petrograd (now University of Leningrad); graduated with highest honors in history, 1924. **Family:** Married Charles Francis "Frank" O'Connor in 1929. **Career:** Worked as tour guide at Peter and Paul Fortress; Cecil B. DeMille Studio, Hollywood, California, movie extra and junior screenwriter, 1926-32, began as filing clerk, became office head in wardrobe department; worked as screenwriter for Universal Pictures, Paramount Pictures, and Metro-Goldwyn-Mayer, 1932-34; worked as free-lance script reader for RKO Pictures, then for Metro-Goldwyn-Mayer, both New York City, 1934-35; worked without pay as a typist for Eli Jacques Kahn, an architect in New York City, doing research work for *The Fountainhead,* 1937; Paramount Pictures,

New York City, script reader, 1941-43; Hal Wallis Productions, Hollywood, California, screenwriter (worked under special contract which committed her to work only six months of each year; during the other six months she pursued her own writing), 1944-49; full-time writer and lecturer, 1951-82. Visiting lecturer at Yale University, New Haven, Connecticut, 1960, Princeton University, New Jersey, 1960, Columbia University, New York, 1960 and 1962, University of Wisconsin, 1961, Johns Hopkins University, Baltimore, 1961, Harvard University, Cambridge, 1962, Massachusetts Institute of Technology, Cambridge, 1962. Presenter of annual Ford Hall Forum, Boston, Massachusetts, beginning 1963. Editor, *The Objectivist,* New York, 1962-71, and *The Ayn Rand Letter,* New York, 1971-82. D.H.L.: Lewis and Clark College, Portland, Oregon, 1963. **Awards:** Doctor of Humane Letters, Lewis and Clark College, 1963. **Died:** 6 March 1982.

PUBLICATIONS

Novels

We the Living. New York, Macmillan, and London, Cassell, 1936.
Anthem. London, Cassell, 1938; revised edition, Los Angeles, Pamphleteers, 1946.
The Fountainhead. Indianapolis, Bobbs Merrill, 1943; London, Cassell, 1947.
Atlas Shrugged. New York, Random House, 1957.

Short Stories

The Early Ayn Rand: A Selection from Her Unpublished Fiction, edited by Leonard Peikoff. New York, New American Library, 1984.

Plays

Night of January 16th (as *Woman on Trial,* produced Hollywood, 1934; New York, 1935; London, 1936; as *Penthouse Legend,* produced New York, 1973). New York, Longman, 1936; revised edition, New York, New American Library, 1987.
The Unconquered, adaptation of her own novel *We the Living* (produced New York, 1940).

Screenplays: *You Came Along,* with Robert Smith, 1945; *Love Letters,* 1945; *The Fountainhead,* 1949.

Other

Textbook of Americanism. New York, Branden Institute, 1946.
Notes on the History of American Free Enterprise. New York, Platen Press, 1959.
Faith and Force: The Destroyers of the Modern World. New York, Branden Institute, 1961.
For the New Intellectual: The Philosophy of Ayn Rand. New York, Random House, 1961.
The Objectivist Ethics. New York, Branden Institute, 1961.
America's Persecuted Minority: Big Business. New York, Branden Institute, 1962.
Conservatism: An Obituary (lecture). New York, Branden Institute, 1962.
The Fascist "New Frontier." New York, Branden Institute, 1963.

The Virtue of Selfishness: A New Concept of Egoism. New York, New American Library, 1964.
Capitalism: The Unknown Ideal, with others. New York, New American Library, 1966.
Introduction to Objectivist Epistemology. New York, Objectivist, 1967; revised edition by Leonard Peikoff and Harry Binswanger, New York, New American Library, 1990.
The Romantic Manifesto: A Philosophy of Literature. Cleveland, World Publishing, 1969.
The New Left: The Anti-Industrial Revolution. New York, New American Library, 1971.
Philosophy: Who Needs It? Indianapolis, Bobbs Merrill, 1982.
The Voice of Reason: Essays in Objectivist Thought. New York, New American Library, 1989.
The Ayn Rand Column: A Collection of Her Weekly Newspaper Articles. Oceanside, California, Second Renaissance Books, 1991.

*

Media Adaptations: *Night of January 16th* (film), Paramount, 1941; *We the Living* (film), Italy, 1942; *We the Living* (a revised and abridged version of the Italian film), United States, 1988.

Biography: Essay in *Authors and Artists for Young Adults,* Volume 10, Detroit, Gale, 1993, pp. 151-62.

Critical Studies: *The Philosophical Thought of Ayn Rand* edited by Douglas J. Den Uyl and Douglas B. Rasmussen, Urbana, University of Illinois Press, 1984; *The Ayn Rand Companion* by Mimi Reisel Gladstein, Westport, Connecticut, Greenwood Press, 1984; *The Passion of Ayn Rand: A Biography* by Barbara Branden, New York, Doubleday, 1986, London, W.H. Allen, 1987; *The Ayn Rand Lexicon: Objectivism from A to Z* edited by Harry Binswanger, New York, New American Library, 1986; entry in *Contemporary Literary Criticism,* Detroit, Gale, Volume 3, 1975, Volume 30, 1984, Volume 44, 1987; *Judgment Day; My Years with Ayn Rand* by Nathaniel Branden, New York, Houghton Mifflin, 1989.

*   *   *

Any discussion of the works of Ayn Rand must include a discussion of her philosophy; it is the essence of her work. Rand could not find a philosophy that reflected her beliefs, so she created her own. She called her philosophy "objectivism" because it is based on the premise that reality is an objective absolute; therefore, one's survival depends on one's ability to perceive and understand reality. Since one survives by reason, one's highest value should be one's own ability to reason—one's own mind. To place any concept or consideration above the mind is to act against one's own survival—to choose death instead of life.

Every book Rand wrote is an exploration of the philosophy of objectivism. This does not mean that her novels are dry tomes of academic discourse. The stories are interesting, dramatic, and well-written; and the philosophy is integral to the plot. Her words are not difficult to understand, and her ideas are not difficult to grasp. It

simply means that Rand cannot be read casually. The reader must pay attention, because every page is packed with ideas and meanings. Because of this, Rand's novels are not generally considered light reading.

For young adults, the most common introduction to Rand's work is either *Anthem* or *We the Living* because they have young adult protagonists and present a somewhat simplified version of her philosophy. Once exposed to Rand's philosophy, however, many young adults go on to read all her work, hungry for the message at its core: You must value yourself in order to survive.

The novella *Anthem* is Rand's simplest work, and explores objectivism only in terms of the value of the individual's mind. *Anthem* imagines a future society where collectivism has been taken to its extreme. It is a society where singular pronouns—I, me, he, she—are unknown. There is only "the great WE, One, indivisible and forever." Not only is an individual's mind not valued, it is considered a sin to even want to think thoughts that no others think. In fact, it is a sin to want to exist for any reason other than to serve the needs of the great WE.

What young adult whose identity has always been defined as a group—the "you're-not-important-you're-just-a-kid" group—would not share Equality 7-2521's joy in the discovery of the meaning and the value of the word "I"?

In *We the Living,* objectivism is explored in terms of a young Russian girl, Kira Argounova, entering adulthood just after the Communists came into power. In this, the story reflects Rand's life; she also began her adult life in Russia at the beginning of the Communist regime. Rand says in her forward that, *"We The Living* is as near to an autobiography as I will ever write. . .the specific events of Kira's life were not mine; her ideas, her convictions, her values were and are."

The title "We the Living" refers to both the character and the author's belief that living means consciously choosing life—by making one's own life one's highest value. When Kira heard the Communists claim that "man must live for the state," she believed that it was monstrous to ask anyone to think so little of his or her own life. Kira's one goal is to escape the monstrosity of communist ideology with the man she loves—to find a place where it is possible to choose life.

It is in *We the Living* that the moral code of objectivism is presented: If one's survival depends on one's own mind, then to claim another's mind is to claim another's life. The only moral course of action is to support one's own life by one's own mind—to live for one's own sake—and to allow others to do the same. Rand makes no distinction between those who seek to claim another's mind, and those who abdicate their own mind. Both are immoral: they act against their own survival; they choose death instead of life.

All young adults who remember the struggle to escape childhood restrictions, and reach the freedom of adulthood—where no one will tell them what to do, what to know, what to think, how to live—can appreciate Kira's struggle to live her own life, and her willingness to accept fully the consequences of fighting against those who would claim her life for their own use.

If these novels strike a responsive cord, the young adult reader will go on to read Rand's more comprehensive explorations of her philosophy, *The Fountainhead* and *Atlas Shrugged.* Both expand the scope of objectivist philosophy and explore the implications of the objectivist moral code in our society. In *The Fountainhead,* the focus is primarily on the objectivist individual's relationship to society; in *Atlas Shrugged,* the focus is on society's relationship to objectivist individuals.

The most striking implication of the objectivist moral code is the role of villains. Villains exist in all of Rand's novels, and their actions affect the protagonists, but they seem strangely irrelevant to the true story. The true story is the conflict between characters who draw different conclusions from the objectivist premise—not good against evil, but good against good-but-different. According to the objectivist moral code, villains are irrelevant. Their existence is granted to them by their victims; they can survive only as long as their victims permit them to survive. This theme is introduced in *The Fountainhead* and explored fully in *Atlas Shrugged.*

By any measure, *Atlas Shrugged* is Rand's masterwork. It superbly integrates a dramatic mystery story with a fully realized philosophy, achieving a scope and maturity of thought only suggested by her earlier works. But all her works deserve the attention of young adults—because growing up is about the quest for individual identity and self-esteem within adult society. Ayn Rand's works represent the epitome of that quest.

—Karen J. Gould

RASKIN, Ellen

Nationality: American. **Born:** Milwaukee, Wisconsin, 13 March 1928. **Education:** University of Wisconsin, Madison, 1945-49. **Family:** Married Dennis Flanagan in 1960; one daughter by a previous marriage. **Career:** From 1954 commercial illustrator and designer, New York City: group shows—50 Years of Graphic Arts in America, American Institute of Graphic Arts, 1966; Biennale of Illustrations, Bratislava, Czechoslovakia, 1969; Biennale of Applied Graphic Art, Brno, Czechoslovakia, 1972; author and illustrator of children's books, 1966-1984. Instructor in illustration at Pratt Institute, 1963, Syracuse University, 1976; guest lecturer at University of Berkeley, 1969, 1972, and 1977. Contemporary American Illustrators of Children's Books, 1974-75. **Awards:** Distinctive Merit award, 1958, Silver Medal, 1959, both from Art Directors Clubs; *New York Herald-Tribune* Spring Book Festival award (best picture book), 1966, for *Nothing Ever Happens on My Block; Songs of Innocence* was included in American Institute of Graphic Arts exhibit of 50 best books of the year, 1966; *Spectacles* was named one of the best illustrated children's books by *New York Times Book Review,* 1968; Children's Book Council chose *The Mysterious Disappearance of Leon (I Mean Noel),* 1972, *Who, Said Sue, Said Whoo?,* 1974, and *Figgs & Phantoms,* 1975, for the Children's Book Showcase; *Boston Globe-Horn Book* Honor, 1973, for *Who, Said Sue, Said Whoo?; Figgs & Phantoms* was chosen for the American Institute of Graphic Arts Children's Book Show, 1973-74, and as a Newbery honor book, 1975; Edgar Allan Poe Special award, Mystery Writers of America, 1975, for *The Tattooed Potato and Other Clues; Boston Globe-Horn Book* Best Fiction award, 1978, Newbery Medal, 1979, and American Book award nomination, all for *The Westing Game;* an Ellen Raskin Lecture Symposium has been established in Milwaukee. **Died:** 8 August 1984.

PUBLICATIONS FOR YOUNG ADULTS (illustrated by the author)

Fiction

The Mysterious Disappearance of Leon (I Mean Noel). New York, Dutton, 1972.
Figgs & Phantoms. New York, Dutton, 1974.
The Tattooed Potato and Other Clues. New York, Dutton, 1975; London, Macmillan, 1976.
The Westing Game. New York, Dutton, 1978; London, Macmillan, 1979.

Poetry

Silly Songs and Sad. New York, Crowell, 1967.
Who, Said Sue, Said Whoo? New York, Atheneum, 1973.

PUBLICATIONS FOR CHILDREN

Fiction

Nothing Ever Happens on My Block. New York, Atheneum, 1966.
Spectacles. New York, Atheneum, 1968.
And It Rained. New York, Atheneum, 1969.
Ghost in a Four-Room Apartment, illustrated by the author. New York, Atheneum, 1969.
A & THE; or, William T. C. Baumgarten Comes to Town. New York, Atheneum, 1970.
The World's Greatest Freak Show, illustrated by the author. New York, Atheneum, 1971.
Franklin Stein, illustrated by the author. New York, Atheneum, 1972.
Moe Q. McGlutch, He Smokes Too Much, illustrated by the author. New York, Parents Magazine Press, 1973.
Moose, Goose and Little Nobody. New York, Parents Magazine Press, 1974.
Twenty-two, Twenty-three. New York, Atheneum, 1976.

*

Manuscript Collection: Milwaukee Public Library, Wisconsin; Kerlan Collection, University of Minnesota, Minneapolis; Children's Cooperative Book Center, University of Wisconsin, Madison.

Biography: Entry in *Dictionary of Literary Biography,* Volume 52: *American Writers for Children since 1960: Fiction,* Detroit, Gale, 1986, pp. 314-325.

Critical Study: Entry in *Children's Literature Review,* Detroit, Gale, Volume 1, 1976, Volume 12, 1987.

Illustrator: *Happy Christmas: Tales for Boys and Girls* edited by Claire Huchet Bishop, 1956; *A Child's Christmas in Wales* by Dylan Thomas, 1959; *"Mama I Wish I Was Snow, Child" "You'd Be Very Cold"* by Ruth Krauss, 1962; *We Dickensons,* 1965, and *We Alcotts,* 1968, both by Aileen Fisher and Olive Rabe; *Poems of Edgar Allan Poe* edited by Dwight Macdonald, 1965; *The King of Men* by Olivia Coolidge, 1966; *Songs of Innocence* by William Blake, 2 vols., 1966; *The Jewish Sabbath* by Molly Cone, 1966; *The Paths of Poetry: Twenty-five Poets and Their Poems* edited by Louis Untermeyer, 1966; *D.H. Lawrence: Poems Selected for*

Young People edited by William Cole, 1967; *Ellen Grae,* 1967, and *Lady Ellen Grae,* 1968, both by Vera Cleaver and Bill Cleaver; *Poems of Robert Herrick* edited by Winfield Townley Scott, 1967; *Probability, The Science of Chance,* 1967, *This Is Four: The Idea of a Number,* 1967, *Symmetry,* 1968, *Three and the Shape of Three,* 1969, *Circles and Curves,* 1969, and *A Question of Accuracy,* 1969, all by Arthur G. Razzell and K.G. Watts; *Books: A Book to Begin On* by Susan Bartlett, 1968; *Inatuk's Friend* by Suzanne Stark Morrow, 1968; *A Paper Zoo: A Collection of Animal Poems by Modern American Poets* by Renée Weiss, 1968; *Piping Down the Valleys Wild: Poetry for the Young of All Ages* edited by Nancy Larrick, 1968; *Come Along!* by Rebecca Caudill, 1969; *Shrieks at Midnight: Macabre Poems, Eerie and Humorous* edited by Sara and John E. Brewton, 1969; *Goblin Market* by Christina Rossetti, 1970; *Elidor* by Alan Garner, 1970.

* * *

Ellen Raskin has written that she does not cater to arbitrary reading levels or age groups; instead her books are directed at readers who are curious enough to read slowly and carefully. Her four novels for young adults certainly reflect this philosophy. They tend to break the "rules" of young adult literature by employing literary allusions and puns that many young readers will miss and by using so many characters that one needs a score card to keep track of them. Alice Bach, one of Raskin's closest friends, has admitted that Raskin's work is unconventional and that writing mysteries full of subtle wordplay was a risk. All of Raskin's novels are thematically related, focusing on eccentric outsiders who learn to value their own unique qualities and move beyond the stereotypical roles that society has imposed on them. Generally, Raskin's characters are educated to see the world and themselves in new ways in the course of solving either a series of mysteries or puzzles.

The ability to break out of stereotypes and to look beyond surfaces is very important in Raskin's first novel, *The Mysterious Disappearance of Leon (I Mean Noel).* Its protagonist, Mrs. Carillon, a well-meaning soup heiress, lives her life according to her mistaken notions about her missing husband Noel's interests and preferences in case he reappears. It is not until the end of the novel that she realizes that she has drawn all of the wrong conclusions about her husband and sends her friends and family into shock when she discards the purple-flowered dresses she has worn in Noel's memory. Other characters in the novel are also entrapped by words and names. For example, Noel (Leon) feels that names define the individual, and he changes his twice—once to make himself sound more "genteel" and once to escape his marriage to Mrs. Carillon.

In the course of solving the mystery of Noel's disappearance, the characters learn not to be fooled by either language or appearances. It is Augie Kunkel, misleading other characters into thinking he is stupid because he stutters, who teaches Mrs. Carillon's adopted twins how to try new ways of thinking so they can finally solve the puzzle. It is also Kunkel who shows Mrs. Carillon that there is more to life than her search for Noel.

In many ways *Figgs & Phantoms,* a Newbery Honor book, reworks the ideas in *The Mysterious Disappearance of Leon (I Mean Noel).* The disjunction between surface appearances and reality is presented through Mona Lisa Figg Newton, a younger, more aggressive version of Mrs. Carillon. Like her Uncle Florence, Mona loves cataloging and collecting books. She has difficulty, however, discovering what is inside them. She has even more problems with the outward appearances of the people around her. She frequently projects onto the townspeople her insecurities about her eccentric family. Her family also has its own unusual religion which involves an afterlife in a place called "Capri."

At the end of the novel, however, Mona learns that she has misinterpreted most of the townspeople, whose true natures are revealed during a parade. But before this, Mona must journey to Capri where she realizes that trying to live someone else's dream is destructive. In fact, she gains no joy by finding her Uncle Florence. "Paradise" is not as she has envisioned it, partially because she has nothing to contribute to it. She must first develop her own imaginative faculties, getting beyond the covers of those books Uncle Florence leaves her.

The Tattooed Potato and Other Clues focuses on seventeen-year-old Dickory Dock who takes a job assisting an artist named Garson. In the course of the novel, Dickory and Garson solve a series of mysteries for Chief Quinn. Dickory soon discovers a number of other mysteries, however, which involve the true identities of almost everyone she meets. Through her association with Garson, she learns to observe people more carefully and develop a true artist's vision, one which helps her see the real person hidden behind masks and disguises.

As the case with all of Raskin's books, this novel features ample word play, including humorous names, such as those of a young art student named George Washington and gangsters named Manny Mallomar and Shrimp Marinara, as well as the aliases "Noserag" and "Kod" (Garson and Dock spelled backwards) which the main characters assume while solving mysteries. The novel is also filled with many artistic and literary allusions, including a character named Issac Bickerstaffe and Dickory's alias, "Christina Rossetti."

The Westing Game, which won the Newbery Prize, is Raskin's most well-known novel. Its many characters, representing a variety of ethnic and economic groups, are brought together to discover why paper magnate Sam Westing died. Like Raskin's other works, it also treats the problems of perception. None of the characters in this novel are what they seem. Indeed, part of the task the characters face is to determine who each other is. Mr. Westing, himself, has four different identities, the last of which is the solution to the mystery. Most of the sixteen "heirs" also have at least one "skeleton in the closet" (e.g. Angela is a bomber, her father is a bookie, Crowe is Westing's ex-wife, Grace has alcoholic tendencies). Each of the characters also exhibits a number of prejudices. Nevertheless, the game they play is designed to make them look past each other's superficial exteriors. In the end, each character changes and is provided with an appropriate happy ending which is connected to the ways they have changed.

Raskin's four novels have deservedly won a number of awards. In each of these works, the reader is constantly called upon to modify his or her own views of characters and events. Her books invite readers inside, asking them to leave behind their fixed notions about literature in order to experience some of what the novels' characters experience.

—Joel D. Chaston

RAWLINGS, Marjorie Kinnan

Nationality: American. **Born:** Washington, D.C., 8 August 1896.
Education: Western High School, Washington, D.C.; University
of Wisconsin, Madison, 1914-18, B.A. 1918 (Phi Beta Kappa).
Family: Married 1) Charles Rawlings in 1919 (divorced 1933); 2)
Norton Sanford Baskin in 1941. **Career:** Editor, YWCA National
Board, New York, 1918-19; assistant service editor, *Home Sector*
magazine, 1919; staff member, Louisville *Courier Journal,* Ken-
tucky, and Rochester *Journal,* Rochester, New York, 1920-28;
syndicated verse writer ("Songs of a Housewife"), United Fea-
tures, 1926-28; fulltime writer in Florida from 1928. **Awards:**
Second place, *McCall's* Child Authorship Contest, 1912, for short
story; second place, Scribner Prize Contest, 1931, for novella
Jacob's Ladder; O. Henry Memorial awards, 1933, for short story
"Gal Young Un," and 1946, for short story "Black Secret";
Pulitzer Prize for fiction, 1939, for *The Yearling;* Newbery Medal
Honor Book, 1956, for *The Secret River;* Lewis Carroll Shelf
award, 1963, for *The Yearling.* LL.D.: Rollins College, Winter
Park, Florida, 1939; L.H.D.: University of Florida, Gainesville,
1941; honorary degree, University of Tampa, Florida. **Died:** 14
December 1953.

PUBLICATIONS FOR YOUNG ADULTS

Fiction

South Moon Under. New York, Scribner, and London, Faber, 1933.
Golden Apples. New York, Scribner, 1935; London, Heinemann, 1939.
The Yearling, illustrated by Edward Shenton. New York, Scribner,
  and London, Heinemann, 1938.
Jacob's Ladder. Coral Gables, Florida, University of Miami
  Press, 1950.
The Sojourner. New York, Scribner, and London, Heinemann, 1953.
The Secret River, illustrated by Leonard Weisgard. New York,
  Scribner, 1955.

Short Stories

When the Whippoorwill. New York, Scribner, and London,
  Heinemann, 1940.

Other

Cross Creek. New York, Scribner, and London, Heinemann, 1942.
Cross Creek Cookery. New York, Scribner, 1942; as *The Marjorie
  Kinnan Rawlings Cookbook,* London, Hammond, 1961.
The Marjorie Kinnan Rawlings Reader, edited by Julia Scribner
  Bigham. New York, Scribner, 1956.
Selected Letters, edited by Gordon E. Bigelow and Laura V. Monti.
  Gainesville, University Presses of Florida, 1983.

*

Media Adaptations: *The Yearling* (film), MGM, 1946; *The Sun
Comes Up* (film based on several short stories), MGM, 1948; *The
Yearling* (musical, by Herbert E. Martin, Lore Noto, and Michael

Leonard), 1973; *Gal Young Un* (film), 1980; *Cross Creek* (film),
Universal, 1983; *The Yearling* (recording), Caedmon.

Biography: *Marjorie Kinnan Rawlings* by Samuel I. Bellman,
New York, Twayne, 1974; entry in *Dictionary of Literary Biography,* Detroit, Gale, Volume 9, 1981; Volume 22, 1983; Volume
102, 1991.

Manuscript Collection: University of Florida Libraries, Gainesville.

Critical Study: *Frontier Eden: The Literary Career of Marjorie
Kinnan Rawlings* by Gordon E. Bigelow, Gainesville, University
of Florida Press, 1966; Entry in *Twentieth Century Literary Criti-
cism,* Volume 4, Detroit, Gale, 1981; *Marjorie Kinnan Rawlings:
Sojourner at Cross Creek* by Elizabeth Silverthorne, New York,
Viking, 1988.

*   *   *

Marjorie Kinnan Rawlings is a regional writer. Her work is
inhabited by the simple people and natural settings of the Florida
backwoods which she adopted as her home. Often paramount in her
novels is the struggle against the vicissitudes of an uncertain
existence by the poor white—the Florida cracker—commonly
epitomized in an archetypical young protagonist with frontier
virtues. Her first three major novels and much of her short fiction
hold marked appeal for adolescent as well as adult readers.

South Moon Under depicts the difficulties of a hunter scratching
out a living as a moonshiner in the Florida scrub country. The novel
combines vividly descriptive scenes of rural existence with strong
characterizations and an eventful plot. *Golden Apples* recounts the
efforts of an orphaned and impoverished brother and sister to
survive in late nineteenth-century northern Florida. They "squat"
on the estate of an exiled and embittered young Englishman whom
they patiently regenerate. The resourceful protagonist is a more
convincing figure than the vaguely sketched Englishman in this
flawed but dramatically forceful novel. In the novella *Jacob's
Ladder* a rootless and destitute young couple encounter adversities
in luckless attempts to wrest a living from a bounteous but
treacherous environment. The pair's deep mutual reliance and
indomitable spirit are a poignant and emotionally powerful testament.

The author's internationally acclaimed novel *The Yearling*
represents her finest achievement. The hero is twelve-year-old
Jody Baxter, who lives with his parents in the Florida hammock
country of the 1870s. As his marginally existing family undergoes
severe setbacks, Jody tames a fawn which becomes his forest-
roaming companion. When, however, his pet cannot be restrained
from eating the precious crops, it must be killed. The anguished boy
feels betrayed by his father and severs their close relationship.
Eventually they are reconciled. Tragedy has made a man of him.
Throughout the story weave such themes as man's need to belong
to the land which, in turn, belongs to those who lovingly cultivate
it, and the inevitability of unfair and unexpected betrayal by man
and nature. Rawlings's compellingly truthful portrait of a boy and
his tender relationship is universally appealing. Her striking description of nature's elemental forces and the simple but significant
events in the lives of people close to the land enrich an absorbingly
ingenuous story. This distinguished novel stands as a classic of
adult and children's literature.

Intended primarily for young children is the posthumously published story *The Secret River*. Its heroine is a little girl who on her own helps her empty-handed father by finding in the forest a fish-filled secret river. After sharing her catch with forest animals, she returns home with enough fish to restore her father's modest prosperity which, consequently, restores that of his neighbors. When she looks for the river again it has vanished, since the need for it has gone. Charmingly illustrated, this woodland idyll with simple story and message offers enchantment for the young adult as well as the small child.

Rawlings is a pastoral writer of percipience and power all of whose stories—besides her memorable *The Yearling*—can be enjoyed by young people.

—Christian H. Moe

REAVER, Chap

Nationality: American. **Born:** Cincinnati, Ohio, 10 June 1935. **Education:** Palmer College of Chiropractic, D.C., 1957. **Military Service:** Served in the Air Force Reserve. **Family:** Married Dixie Reece in 1959; two children. **Career:** Private practice in chiropractic, Cincinnati, Ohio, 1957-80, Marietta, Georgia, since 1980; writer. Part-time writing instructor at Marietta Junior High School, in association with the Marietta Community School Program. **Awards:** Delacorte Press Prize for an Outstanding First Young Adult Novel, 1990, and Edgar Allan Poe award for best young adult mystery, Mystery Writers of America, 1991, both for *Mote*; Hugo award nomination for short story, World Science Fiction Society, 1992, for "Feel Good Stuff." **Address:** 1570 West Sandtown Rd., Marietta, Georgia 30064, U.S.A.

PUBLICATIONS FOR YOUNG ADULTS

Fiction

Mote. New York, Delacorte, 1990.
A Little Bit Dead. New York, Delacorte, 1992.

*   *   *

Chap Reaver's two young adult novels tackle important subjects with a marvelous sense of humor. His adolescent narrators are quick-witted and smart-alecky in their approach to serious situations. Even though his plots are somewhat contrived, Reaver captures the tone of adolescence with a realistic voice. His humor accompanies a firm sense of right and wrong, and his portrayals depict devoted friendships between adolescent males, as well as strong, though absent, adult male role models.

In Reaver's first young adult novel, *Mote,* sixteen-year-old Chris becomes involved with black detective Stienert when Chris's friend Mote is charged with murder. Through his well-honed sense of humor, Reaver shows the absurdity of stereotypical beliefs based on black dialect—as when Detective Stienert, talking in a verbless jargon, defends himself by saying, "Doing my part to preserve authentic Negro dialect. Else we all be sounding like Bryant Gumbel."

Reaver also shows the absurdity of racism when Chris attends an "Equal Rights for White Americans" meeting to try to learn who the murderer is. While there, he encounters people who are opposed to any race that is not white, and uses his repartee to make them look like fools.

Chris and his best friend, Billy, are both fatherless and have a close relationship, solidified at Billy's father's funeral. As Chris remembers, "Something happened to us as we watched each other crying across the open grave. Something that joined us in a special friendship." Though close, both boys miss the presence of their fathers, a role that is filled by Mote, a drifting Vietnam veteran who showed up shortly after both boys lost their fathers, and returns for a few weeks each year.

Although Mote is absent in most of the book, Chris and Billy recall conversations in which he has given them guidance and understanding they can't find elsewhere. At one point, Mote tells Chris about his feelings when his parents were divorced, and Chris later reveals how this has helped him: "You don't know this, Mote, but when you talked about the feelings you had when your parents got divorced, well, that helped me too. There were lots of times when you helped me like that." Reaver also uses Mote to speak to teens about growing up and accepting their parents, as when Chris remembers Mote's reflection that "you never really start to grow up until you can look at your parents objectively, see them as they really are."

In his second young adult novel, *A Little Bit Dead,* Reaver again tackles racism with a sharp-witted teen, though this time the setting is 1876. This novel employs some of Reaver's own background, as the main character is named Herbert Reece (but goes by Reece) and chiropractic skills are used to relieve arthritis pain. Like Chris and Billy, Reece and Shanti share a friendship born during a difficult time. Reece rescues Shanti, a Yahi Indian, from torture and hanging by bigoted, greedy men who want directions to the Yahi gold. One of the lynchers, Colby, has only one ear, and Reece shows his sarcastic wit when he first suggests that Colby grow his hair long on one side, then suggests that he do so on both sides: "If you just let one side grow long, people might think you're covering up something. Like maybe you don't have one of your ears or something."

Also like Chris, Reece has an absent father, but one whose memory is strong in Reece's mind, as he recalls much of his father's wisdom. Several times he remembers his father admonishing him to do what is right, and when he can't tell what's right, to trust his feelings. When Reece learns the location of the Yahi gold, he is tempted to take it, but then remembers his father's words and thinks to himself, "Shut up, Dad." His father's memory also serves to point out racism against the Yahi, as when Reece tells them what his father said about equality for everyone: "The white men say these words, but they do not hear them."

After rescuing Shanti, Reece is charged with the murder of one of the lynchers. At the trial, when the judge asks Reece if he'd like to question a witness, Reece can't resist another irreverent comment; instead of asking a question that might help his case, he says, "Do you know what happened to Colby's ear?"

In both of Chap Reaver's young adult novels, the main characters are savvy, witty teens with big hearts who do what is right even though doing so causes them problems. Reaver's humor and insight into adolescence prevent the books from becoming didactic, while conveying strong messages through enjoyable reading.

—Susanne L. Johnston

REISS, Johanna

Nationality: American. **Born:** Winterswijk, Holland, 1932; moved to America in the 1950s. **Education:** Educated in Holland as a teacher. **Family:** Formerly married; two daughters. **Career:** Taught school for several years in Holland; writer. **Awards:** Jewish Book Council's Charles and Bertie G. Schwartz Juvenile Award, 1972; Newbery Medal Honor Book, 1973; American Library Association Notable Book; Buxtehuder Bulle, 1976. **Address:** New York City.

PUBLICATIONS FOR YOUNG ADULTS

Autobiography

The Upstairs Room. New York, Crowell, 1972.
The Journey Back. New York, Crowell, 1976.

*

Critical Sources: "The Telling of the War" by Elie Wiesel, in *The New York Times Book Review,* November 5, 1972, 3, 22; review of *The Upstairs Room* by Diane Gersoni-Stavn, in *School Library Journal,* Vol. 19, No. 4, 1972, 62; review of *The Journey Back* by Margery Fisher, in *Growing Point,* Vol. 16, No. 2, 1977, 3134-40; *Our Family, Our Friends, Our World* by Lyn Miller-Lachmann, New Providence, New Jersey, R. R. Bowker, 1992; *Children's Literature in the Elementary School* by Charlotte Huck, Susan Hepler, Janet Hickman, and Barbara Z. Kiefer, Chicago, Brown & Benchmark, 1997.

*   *   *

Johanna Reiss has provided a significant contribution to the body of young adult literature dealing with World War II in Europe and the Nazi attempt to annihilate the Jewish people. In an intense autobiographical novel, *The Upstairs Room,* she has created an account of her childhood years spent hiding from the Nazis in Holland. Her postwar experiences are the focus of *The Journey Back.* Each book was well conceptualized to provide the reader with emotional and psychological insights as well as factual accounts. Autobiography can become too focused on the author, or in trying to avoid such, too focused on other significant people in the account. Johanna Reiss, however, has avoided a one-sided account by distancing herself, as Margery Fisher aptly stated in *Growing Point,* ". . .through reminiscence, ordered and selected in the manner of fiction and integrating personal feeling carefully with external event."

In *The Upstairs Room* the reader is introduced to the de Leeuws, a Jewish family living in Holland. Their family consisted of a father who was a cattle dealer, a mother who was frequently sick, and three daughters of which Annie was the youngest. When Annie de

Leeuw was eight, the Nazi terror began with decrees, Jew hunts, deportation, Jewish Stars, and overall terror. They had waited too late to attempt leaving for the United States because of the mother's illness, which soon led to her death. When the family was forced to split up, Annie and her sister Sini hid for two years with the Oostervelds, a Christian Dutch family. The story that follows is a moving account of Annie's memories of these years. Rich in characterization and realistic anecdotes, the reader becomes part of this family and the affection that grew despite the forced situation and the tragedy that was ongoing in the world beyond.

Three unique but caring individuals comprised the Oosterveld family: Johan, Dientje, and Opoe, Johan's mother. "Plain-folks values, salty language, and generosity. . ." characterize this rough farming couple who were proud of their efforts to protect the sisters in spite of the possible consequences for themselves, wrote the authors of *Children's Literature in the Elementary School.* Johanna Reiss conveyed the dispiriting feeling of confinement day after day, the resulting endless boredom, the need for fresh air and exercise, the realization of the fate of Jews in concentration camps, and over-stressed relationships. Occasional false hopes, surprise Nazi searches, and starving people hoping for a potato or other morsel of food occasionally interrupted the boredom. Tension among various individuals within the house was well described and manifested itself in disagreement and jealousy. Yet the reader is left reassured that the anger ultimately tightened the bond that grew among the two girls and the uncommonly brave family.

Young female readers of *The Upstairs Room* might identify with the personal situation of both preteen Annie and her sister, who was in her late teens. *School Library Journal* review Diane Gersoni-Stavn described the sisters as follows: "Sini, in her late teens, worried about her looks and desperately missed dating. Preteen Annie talked to imaginary playmates—e.g., a window—and her legs began to atrophy from disuse. She gradually became so withdrawn and passive that even after liberation she cringed from contact with strangers." However, they remained hopeful until the end. "The book is honest, graphic, and at times painful to read. It has the immediacy and authenticity of an autobiographical account. . . . It demands a certain maturity on the part of its readers," according to Lyn Miller-Lachmann in *Our Family, Our Friends, Our World.*

When the war was over Reiss movingly described the first chance to run and dance outside, as well as the moving return trip to their home of Winterswijk. The rich memories shared in *The Upstairs Room* help the reader connect the tragedies of the Nazi rage to real individuals. Johanna Reiss says in the brief forward to this book, "I have not tried to write a historical book, although it may have some historical value. What I did try to write was a simple, human book, in which my sister and I suffered and complained, and sometimes found fault with the Gentile family that took us in for a few years, in which the members of that family were not heroes but people, with strengths and weaknesses."

The *Journey Back* deals with the emotional aftermath as people try to reconstruct their lives and relationships. Regarding her writing of this book Johanna Reiss said:

There was still something I wanted to say, something that was as meaningful to me as the story I had told in the first book, the story of a war. "The fighting has stopped;" "Peace treaty signed," newspapers announce at the conclusion of every war. From a political point of view, the war is over, but in another sense it has not really ended. People are fragile. They are strong, too, but wars leave emotional scars that take a long time to heal, generations perhaps. I know this to be true of myself, and of others. And out of those feelings came *The Journey Back,* a story of the aftermath of the Second World War.

Annie and Sini endured many hardships during the years in hiding; however, the family taking care of them were quick to bestow their affection. In contrast, after returning to their home, Annie had to cope with the harshness and sharp words of a new step-mother in addition to the harsh conditions that accompanied the aftermath of war. A lack of food and other commodities and emotional scarring that is manifested in a variety of ways is not often considered by young readers or even adults as they contemplate the tragic effects of war. The difficult descriptions of real people in the peace following a war again helps the reader connect historical events to people like themselves.

The true stories told in both of these books for young people continues the horror of the Holocaust as told by other writings such as *The Diary of Anne Frank.* The characters become representative of ordinary people enduring a far from ordinary historical event. As with the body of Holocaust literature, these novels put hearts and souls with the statistics and sterile descriptions that often are found in the limited pages of history books. As Elie Wiesel wrote in *The New York Times Book Review* after *The Upstairs Room* was published: "[W]e are grateful to fate for having spared a child who can reminisce with neither hate nor bitterness but a kind of gentleness that leaves us with lumps in our throats."

—Janelle B. Mathis

RHUE, Morton. *See* **STRASSER, Todd.**

RICE, Anne

Original given name, Howard Allen; name changed c. 1947. **Pseudonyms:** Anne Rampling; A.N. Roquelaure. **Nationality:** American. **Born:** New Orleans, Louisiana, 4 October 1941. **Education:** Educated Texas Women's University, Denton, Texas, 1959-60; San Francisco State College (now University), California, B.A. 1964, M.A. 1971; graduate study at University of California, Berkeley, 1969-70. **Family:** Married Stan Rice in 1961; one daughter (deceased), and one son. **Career:** Writer. Held a variety of jobs, sometimes two at a time, including waitress, cook, theater usherette, and insurance claims examiner. **Awards:** Joseph Henry Jackson award honorable mention, 1970. **Agent:** Jacklyn Nesbit Associates, 598 Madison Ave., New York, New York 10022, U.S.A. **Address:** 1239 First St., New Orleans, Louisiana 70130, U.S.A.

PUBLICATIONS

Fiction

The Feast of All Saints. New York, Simon & Schuster, 1980.
Cry to Heaven. New York, Knopf, 1982.
The Mummy: Or Ramses the Damned. New York, Ballantine, 1989.
The Witching Hour. New York, Knopf, 1990.
Lasher. New York, Knopf, 1993.
Taltos. New York, Knopf, 1994.
The Servant of the Bones. New York, Knopf, 1996.
Violin. New York, Knopf, 1997.
Pandora: New Tales of the Vampires. New York, Knopf, 1998.

"Vampire Chronicles" Series

Interview with the Vampire. New York, Knopf, 1976.
The Vampire Lestat. New York, Ballantine, 1985.
The Queen of the Damned. New York, Knopf, 1988.
Vampire Chronicles (contains *Interview with the Vampire, The Vampire Lestat,* and *The Queen of the Damned*). New York, Ballantine, 1989.
The Tale of the Body Thief. New York, Knopf, 1992.
Memnoch the Devil. New York, Knopf, 1995.
The Vampire Armand. New York, Knopf, 1998.

Other

The Claiming of Sleeping Beauty, as A. N. Roquelaure. New York, Dutton, 1983.
Beauty's Punishment, as A.N. Roquelaure. New York, Dutton, 1984.
Beauty's Release, as A.N. Roquelaure. New York, Dutton, 1985.
Exit to Eden, as Anne Rampling. New York, Arbor House, 1985.
Belinda, as Anne Rampling. New York, Arbor House, 1986.
The Sleeping Beauty Novels (contains *The Claiming of Sleeping Beauty, Beauty's Punishment,* and *Beauty's Release*), as A.N. Roquelaure. New York, New American Library/Dutton, 1991.

*

Media Adaptations: Novels that have been recorded onto audio cassette and released by Random House AudioBooks include *Interview with the Vampire* (read by F. Murray Abraham), 1986, *The Queen of the Damned,* 1988, *The Vampire Lestat* (read by Michael York), 1989, and *The Mummy: Or Ramses the Damned* (read by York), 1990. *The Vampire Lestat* has been adapted into a graphic novel by Faye Perozich, painted by Daerick Gross, New York, Ballantine, 1991. The "Vampire Chronicles" have been optioned for film and stage productions; *Interview with the Vampire* (film), Geffen Pictures, 1994.

Critical Studies: Entry in *Contemporary Literary Criticism,* Vol. 41, Detroit, Gale, 1987; "Interview with Anne Rice" by W. Kenneth Holditch, in *Lear's,* Vol. 2, No. 7, October 1989; *The Witches' Companion: The Official Guide to Anne Rice's Lives of the Mayfair Witches* by Katherine M. Ramsland, New York, Ballantine Books, 1994; *The Vampire Companion: The Official Guide to Anne Rice's The Vampire Chronicles* by Katherine M. Ramsland, New York, Ballantine Books, 1995; *Conversations with*

Anne Rice, edited by Michael Riley, New York, Ballantine Books, 1996.

* * *

Though she writes in a variety of genres, Anne Rice is unmistakably a Southern writer in style and theme. The combined influences of Southern rhetorical syntax and Irish cadence make her language complex and ornate. Like her more traditional colleagues, Rice is also a writer firmly grounded in place—New Orleans' Irish Channel where she grew up and the physically near but spiritually remote Garden District where young Anne O'Brien wandered as an outsider.

The Southerner's interest in place is inextricably linked to a sense of the past; like Southern writers in general, Rice creates a mythic past, in her case based not upon tales of cavalier ancestors but on ancient and oft-repeated stories of ghosts and devils— stories which seem credible in the lush, semi-tropical atmosphere of New Orleans. Thus, like most Southern writers, Rice recreates the mythic past in multi-generational family epics. Clearly Maharet, the red-haired witch twin, speaks for Rice when she says the family is all-important, but Rice's families are matriarchal, differing markedly from conventional patriarchal families.

Though she rejects the limited, negative feminism of Akasha, queen of the damned, Rice considers herself part of the feminist literary tradition, influenced by writers as diverse as Jane Austen and Carson McCullers. She admires Eudora Welty's skill with language and Mary Renault's ability to involve her readers so deeply that they cannot bear for the novel to end. One of the most important influences, though, are the Brontë sisters; Rice's Garden District clearly is the New Orleans equivalent of Emily Brontë's moors.

In an interview transcribed in *Lear's* magazine, Rice describes her three voices. As Anne Rice, she writes in the "European-American" tradition, influenced primarily by the Brontës, Charles Dickens, and Leo Tolstoy. Anne Rampling, her "California voice," is influenced by Ernest Hemingway and Raymond Chandler. The A. N. Roquelaure novels, which Rice describes as "the Disneyland of S and M," are the type of pornography she considers legitimate—"literature intended to sexually arouse the reader."

The best known of the Anne Rice novels are the "Vampire Chronicles," begun shortly after her six-year-old daughter died of leukemia and written "out of the deep imagination, with echoes of vegetation gods, blood sacrifice, thousands of images that are more dreamed of than spoken" *(Lear's).* Unlike most vampire tales, which are written from the perspective of the victim, Rice's novels adopt the vampires' point of view. While writing *Interview with the Vampire,* the first of these novels, Rice found herself increasingly identifying with the vampire instead of the interviewer as she had originally intended. In the *Lear's* essay, she explains, "The vampire is a perfect metaphor for people who drain us dry, for our fear of the dead coming back, for the outsider who is in the midst of everything and yet feels monstrous and completely cut off. And I think most people feel that way at heart." Possessing the memory of being human, Rice's vampires enviously compare themselves to humans and often regard immortality as a kind of trap. Their concerns too are human ones: the past, their origin, individual identity and purpose.

Louis de Pointe du Lac, the protagonist of *Interview with the Vampire,* tells a young boy the story of his life in eighteenth-century New Orleans, the encounter with Lestat which resulted in his becoming a vampire, and his subsequent search for human blood. Rice acknowledges the autobiographical elements in the novel: "*Interview* is about grief, guilt, and the search for salvation even though one is, in the eyes of the world and one's own eyes, a total outcast. It's all autobiographical somehow, my story of growing up and losing illusions, losing faith, that sense of a world that has a beginning, a middle, and an end—and a top and bottom" *(Lear's).*

The "Vampire Chronicles" continue with *The Vampire Lestat,* as Lestat awakens from a long sleep to become a popular rock star. His songs and the autobiography he writes as a publicity stunt reveal legends and secrets of the vampires. In fact these constitute a history of vampires from ancient Egypt to modern time. As his popularity increases, the hostility of other vampires also grows, and they converge upon his concert, bent on destroying him.

In *The Queen of the Damned,* various vampire voices continue the story of Lestat's waking Akasha, the mother of all vampires and queen of the damned. As a result of his romance with Akasha, Lestat gains powers beyond those of most vampires and eventually seems prepared for a battle of wills with the Talamasca, who are studying vampires. Meanwhile, he discovers the meaning of his vision of the red-haired twins as Maharet explains the origin of vampires and Mekare fulfills her curse upon Akasha. Rice assures her readers that the "Vampire Chronicles" will continue in *The Tale of the Body Thief,* as Lestat confronts some of the author's moral concerns.

Rice's historical novels deal with social outcasts, many of whom are part of alternative societies. *The Feast of All Saints,* set in the New Orleans of the 1840s, is the story of *gens de couleur libre* (free people of color), especially the coming-of-age of copper-skinned, blue-eyed Marcel Ferronaire and his sister Marie, who appears white. *Cry to Heaven* portrays the life of the Italian *castrati* (male singers castrated before their voices change), as protagonist Tonio Treschi seeks both musical fame and revenge upon the brother who had him castrated and dispossessed.

Rice's continuing interest in the supernatural, especially as associated with ancient Egypt, is evident in *The Mummy: Or Ramses the Damned*; like Akasha, Ramses is a sleeping immortal who is awakened and brought into the modern world.

Rice's own antebellum mansion in New Orleans' Garden District serves as the setting for *The Witching Hour,* another multi-generational family epic. Like Lestat and his fellow vampires, the Mayfair family of witches are the subjects of investigation by the Talamasca. The twelfth of the Mayfair witches, Deidre, has been kept most of her life in a drug-induced catatonic state, attended by female relatives but occasionally accompanied by a mysterious young man who identifies himself as Lasher. Like Amel in *The Queen of the Damned,* Lasher seems to be absolute evil struggling to use Deidre's daughter Rowan to achieve human form. The struggle between Lasher and Rowan continues in the sequel, *Lasher.*

Influenced by Rice's California years, the Anne Rampling novels develop the themes of the conquering power of love and the positive value of sex. Lisa Kelly, the protagonist of *Exit to Eden,* resembles Rice: Lisa too was raised in an Irish-Catholic family but has lost her faith. Virtually obsessed with sadomasochistic fantasies, Lisa establishes the Club, a luxurious Caribbean resort where the guests' fantasies can be fulfilled; however, when she and Elliott fall in love, they decide their ultimate fantasy is to move to New Orleans and establish a conventional romantic relationship.

Belinda, a three-part novel, describes Jeremy Walker, an author and illustrator of children's books, who lives an isolated life in an old house until the teenage runaway Belinda moves in. Jeremy's lost sexuality is evoked by Belinda, a willing participant in his erotic fantasies. Criticized for his drawings of her, as Rice has been criticized for her erotic fiction, Jeremy disregards Belinda's warnings and pries into her past; so she runs away. Following a characteristic Rice pattern, the middle section of the novel relates Belinda's background, and the third part details Jeremy's search for her.

The A. N. Roquelaure novels are frankly erotic, but Rice claims they provide her with the same satisfaction as any of her other books: "setting out to create an illusion, something new, taking the reader someplace he or she has never been and then bringing him or her back" *(Lear's).* In *The Claiming of Sleeping Beauty, Beauty's Punishment,* and *Beauty's Release,* Rice's perspective is again unique, as she uses the traditional fairy tale to make explicit some of the erotic messages psychologists have long insisted are hidden within fairy tales.

Rice insists that there is "a strong moral overview" *(Lear's)* in everything she writes, and the conclusions of her novels reflect her overall optimism. Her protagonists generally have rejected conventional religious and societal values, but a strong sense of personal ethics and the enduring force of love result in lives based upon high principles.

—Charmaine Allmon Mosby

RICH, Robert. *See* **TRUMBO, Dalton.**

RICHTER, Conrad (Michael)

Nationality: American. **Born:** Pine Grove, Pennsylvania, 13 October 1890. **Education:** the Susquehanna Academy and Tremont High School, Pennsylvania, graduated 1906. **Family:** Married Harvena M. Achenbach in 1915; one daughter. **Career:** Teamster, farm laborer, bank clerk, and journalist, in Pennsylvania, 1906-08; editor, *Weekly Courier,* Patton, Pennsylvania, 1909-10; reporter, Johnstown *Leader,* Pennsylvania, and Pittsburgh *Dispatch,* 1910-11; private secretary in Cleveland, 1911-13; freelance writer in Pennsylvania, 1914-27; settled in New Mexico, 1928. **Awards:** National Book award nomination, 1937, for *The Sea of Grass;* Gold Medal for Literature from Society of Libraries of New York University, 1942, for *The Sea of Grass* and *The Trees;* Ohioana Library Medal, 1947; Pulitzer Prize for Fiction, 1951, for *The Town;* National Institute of Arts and Letters grant in literature, 1959; Maggie award, 1959, for *The Lady;* National Book award, 1960, for *The Waters of Kronos;* Litt.D., Susquehanna University,

Selinsgrove, Pennsylvania, 1944; University of New Mexico, Albuquerque, 1958; Lafayette College, Easton, Pennsylvania, 1966; LL.D., Temple University, Philadelphia, 1966; L.H.D., Lebanon Valley College, Annville, Pennsylvania, 1966. Member, American Academy. **Died:** 30 October 1968.

PUBLICATIONS

Novels

The Sea of Grass. New York, Knopf, and London, Constable, 1937.
The Trees (first book in the "The Awakening Land" trilogy). New York, Knopf, and London, Constable, 1940.
The Fields (second book in "The Awakening Land" trilogy). New York, Knopf, 1946; London, Corgi, 1958.
The Town (third book in "The Awakening Land" trilogy). New York, Knopf, 1950; London, Muller, 1951.
Tacey Cromwell. New York, Knopf, 1942; with *The Free Man,* London, Boardman, 1944.
The Free Man. New York, Knopf, 1943; with *Tacey Cromwell,* London, Boardman, 1944.
Always Young and Fair. New York, Knopf, 1947.
The Light in the Forest. New York, Knopf, 1953; London, Gollancz, 1954.
The Lady. New York, Knopf, and London, Gollancz, 1957.
Dona Ellen. Tübingen, Rauch, 1959.
The Waters of Kronos. New York, Knopf, and London, Gollancz, 1960.
A Simple, Honorable Man. New York, Knopf, and London, Gollancz, 1962.
The Grandfathers. New York, Knopf, 1964.
A Country of Strangers. New York, Knopf, and London, Gollancz, 1966.
The Awakening Land (trilogy). New York, Knopf, 1966.
The Aristocrat. New York, Knopf, 1968.

Short Stories

Brothers of No Kin and Other Stories. New York, Hinds, 1924.
Early Americana and Other Stories. New York, Knopf, 1936.
Smoke over the Prairie and Other Stories. London, Boardman, 1947.
The Rawhide Knot and Other Stories. New York, Knopf, 1978.

Other

Human Vibration: The Mechanics of Life and Mind. Harrisburg, Pennsylvania, Handy Book, 1925.
Principles in Bio-Physics: The Underlying Process Controlling Life Phenomena and Inner Evolution. Harrisburg, Pennsylvania, Good Books, 1927.
The Mountain on the Desert: A Philosophical Journey. New York, Knopf, 1955.
Over the Blue Mountain (for children). New York, Knopf, 1967.
Writing to Survive: The Private Notebooks of Conrad Richter, edited by Harvena Richter. Albuquerque, University of New Mexico Press, 1988.

*

Biography: Entry in *Dictionary of Literary Biography,* Volume 9: *American Novelists, 1910-1945,* Detroit, Gale, 1981.

Critical Studies: *Conrad Richter* by Edwin W. Gaston, Jr., New York, Twayne, 1965; *Conrad Richter* by Robert J. Barnes, Austin, Texas, Steck Vaughn, 1968; *Conrad Richter's Ohio Trilogy: Its Ideas, Themes, and Relationships to Literary Tradition* by Clifford Duane Edwards, Ann Arbor, University of Michigan Press, 1967; *Conrad Richter's America* by Marvin J. LaHood, The Hague, Mouton, 1975; entry in *Contemporary Literary Criticism,* Volume 30, Detroit, Gale, 1984.

*   *   *

Conrad Richter may be best known for his historical Ohio trilogy, *The Trees, The Fields,* and *The Town,* but it is his *Light in the Forest* which has attracted consistent attention in the public schools and has developed an acceptance among adolescent readers and teachers of adolescent literature. Because it is brief, challenging on several different levels of reading appreciation and because it addresses a timeless issue, the novel has continued to appear on many reading lists for adolescents; readers from seventh grade through senior high have enjoyed the story.

The novel has an omniscient author, follows a clear chronology, and provides a circular design. The plot follows the adventures of John Butler, a white boy who is captured and raised by the Delaware Indians and then recaptured by the whites when the boy is fourteen years old. The boy, who assumes the Indian name of True Son, leads an idyllic life with the Indians for ten years until he is forced to return to his natural parents as a result of an Indian treaty. Unable to adjust to his existence in the white world, True Son escapes and returns to the wilderness only to be forced into making a difficult decision that will shape the rest of his life. The Indians wish to use him as a decoy to lure white settlers into an ambush, but he ultimately refuses, leading to his expulsion from the tribe by his Indian father Cuyologa and leaving True Son fatherless and adrift between two worlds.

White men in the novel are not portrayed as the conventional heroes of encounters with Indians. Richter himself at an early age wanted to run away from home and live with the Indians. As an adult studying the lives of Indians, he found numerous accounts of white children who had been captured by Indians but who did not wish to return to their white world. In searching for an answer to why some of these children chose to remain with the Indians, Richter developed the background and the purpose for *Light in the Forest.* As he said about the novel, "I thought that perhaps if we understood how those First Americans felt toward us even then and toward our white way of life, we might better understand the adverse, if perverted, view of us by some African, European, and Asian peoples today."

The novel offers a valuable perspective on cultural differences. Although set in the American wilderness of the sixteenth century, the emphasis placed upon contrasting ways of life and the manner of thinking and the behaviors exhibited by both cultures dramatizes clearly the dilemma faced by people everywhere. Any individual who automatically accepts his or her culture as superior to others places restrictions on the ability to see good in others. The result is often the inability to see truth clearly and a reliance upon what one wants to believe, regardless of facts, to interpret the world. Through both the white men and the Indians in the story, Richter is able to show the prejudices that lead to misunderstanding and often

violence and the effect that can have on young people such as True Son.

True Son loves the freedom of the Indian way of life, primitive as it may be. Richter paints an appealing picture of this life:

They passed their days in a kind of primitive deliciousness. The past was buried. There was only the present and tomorrow. By day they lived as happy animals. Moonlight nights in the forest they saw what the deer saw. Swimming under water with open eyes, they knew now what the otter knew.

Juxtaposed to this way of life was the view of the white man's life from the Indian perspective and what might lie ahead for True Son if he returned:

Ahead of him ran the rutted road of the whites. It led, he knew, to where men of their own volition constrained themselves with heavy clothing, like harness, where men chose to be slaves to their own or another's property, and followed empty and desolate lives far from the wild beloved freedom of the Indian.

Deceptive in its brevity, the novel yields both a good adventure and a basis for serious discussion among adolescents. True Son, faced with difficult decisions, shows that he has principles for which he is willing to stand. He also discovers what for him is the "light in the forest"—the age of primitive deliciousness, the spiritual element which links all humans. Adolescent readers continue to respond strongly to True Son's dilemma and teachers, wishing to raise the awareness of their students about the original relationships between whites and Indians during the settling of America, find the book a valuable one.

—Charles R. Duke

RICHTER, Hans Peter

Nationality: German. **Born:** Cologne, Germany, 28 April 1925. **Education:** Universities of Cologne, Bonn, Mainz, and Tuebingen; Technical University Hanover, Dr. rer pol. 1968. **Military Service:** Served in the German Army, 1942-45; became lieutenant; wounded in action; received Iron Cross and other decorations. **Family:** Married Elfriede Feldmann in 1952, (died 1989); four children. **Career:** Independent social psychologist and writer, since 1954; radio and television broadcaster. Professor of scientific methods and sociology, Darmstadt, Germany, 1973. **Awards:** Jugendbuchpreis Sebaldus-Verlag, 1961, for *Damals war es Friedrich;* Cite Internationale des Arts (Paris) stipendiate, 1965-66; Woodward School Book award, 1971, and American Library

Association Mildred L. Batchelder award, 1972, Japanese book award, 1981, all for *Friedrich*. **Died:** 19 November 1993.

PUBLICATIONS FOR YOUNG ADULTS

Novels

Friedrich, translation by Edite Kroll. New York, Holt, 1970 (originally published as *Damals war es Friedrich,* Sebaldus, 1961).

I Was There, translation by Edite Kroll. New York, Holt, 1972 (originally published as *Wir waren dabei,* Freiburg, Herder, 1962).

The Time of the Young Soldiers. London, Kestrel, 1975 (originally published as *Die Zeit der jungen Soldaten,* Colmar, Alsatia, 1967).

Untranslated Nonfiction

Hoerermeinungsforschung auf einem Dorf. Archiv des Suedwestfunk, 1952.

Hausen vor der Hoehe: Eine Rundfunkuntersuchung. Two volumes, Archiv des Nordwestdeutschen Rundfunks, 1954.

Informationsbriefe fuer Fuehrungskraefte. Industrie-Verlag, 1955.

Geschichte und Quellensammlung zur Geschichte der Hoererforschung im deutschsprachigen Raum. Two volumes, Archiv der Historischen Kommission des deutschen Rundfunks, 1957.

Die Freizeit deines Kindes. Oeffentliches Leben, 1957.

Zwoelf Vorlesungen ueber Marktforschung und Werbung im Aussenhandel. Akademie fuer Welthandel, 1957.

Beitrag zu einer Phaenomenologie der Berufsunfaehigkeit, with Fritz W. Adam. Thieme, 1964.

Editor, *Der jungen Leser wegen.* Schwann, 1965.

Jagd auf Gereon. Styria, 1967.

Einfuehrungen zu Fernsehspielen und Spielfilmen. Archiv des Zweiten Deutschen Fernsehens, 1970.

Mohammed. Balve, Engelbert, 1974.

Saint-Just. Balve, Engelbert, 1975.

Gott—Was ist das? Stuttgart, Thienemanns, 1980.

Gut und boese. Stuttgart, Thienemanns, 1980.

Wissenschaft von der Wissenschaft. Stuttgart, Thienemanns, 1981.

Also author of more than a hundred radio and television scripts and of several book-length publications in journals, including "Einfuehrung in die Philosophie" in *Aufstieg,* 1955, and "Lehrgang der Philosophie," in *Geistesschulung,* 1956.

PUBLICATIONS FOR CHILDREN

Fiction, Translated into English

Uncle and His Merry-Go-Round. Berkeley, California, Bancroft & Co., 1959 (originally published as *Karussell und Luftballon,* Obpacher, 1958).

Hengist the Horse. Berkeley, California, Bancroft & Co., 1960 (originally published as *Das Pferd Max,* Obpacher, 1959).

Untranslated Fiction

Der Heilige Martin. Mainz, Grünewald, 1959.

Nikolaus der Gute (legends about St. Nicholas). Mainz, Grünewald, 1960.

Wie Heinz und Inge sich verlaufen haben. Dessart, 1960.

Hans Kauft ein. Scholz, 1961.

Immer ist etwas los! Bindlach, Loewes, 1961.

Das war eine Reise! Sebaldus, 1962.

Birgitta. Mainz, Grünewald, 1963.

Peter. Mainz, Grünewald, 1963.

Ein Reise um die Erde. Vienna, Ueberreuter, 1963.

Eine wahre Baerengeschichte. Vienna, Ueberreuter, 1964.

Nikolaus. Mainz, Grünewald, 1965.

Ich war kein braves Kind. Colmar, Alsatia, 1967.

Der Hundemord. Colmar, Alsatia, 1968.

Kunibert im Schlafanzug. Balve, Engelbert, 1972.

Katzen haben Vorfahrt. Balve, Engelbert, 1972.

Einschreiben vom Anwalt. Schaffstein, 1974.

Editor, Untranslated Works

Schriftsteller antworten jungen Menschen auf die Frage: Wozu leben wir? Colmar, Alsatia, 1968.

Schriftsteller erzaehlen von ihrer Mutter. Colmar, Alsatia, 1968.

Schriftsteller erzaehlen von der Gewalt. Colmar, Alsatia, 1970.

Harte Jugend. Steyler, 1970.

Schriftsteller erzaehlen aus aller Welt. Balve, Engelbert, 1973.

Schriftsteller erzaehlen von der Gerechtigkeit. Balve, Engelbert, 1977.

Biography: Essay in *Something about the Author Autobiography Series,* Volume 11, Detroit, Gale, 1991, pp. 275-287.

Critical Study: Entry in *Children's Literature Review,* Volume 21, Detroit, Gale Research, 1980, pp. 186-190.

*   *   *

Hans Peter Richter's three translated young adult books read better as autobiographical documentaries as opposed to fiction. The trilogy *Friedrich, I Was There,* and *The Time of the Young Soldiers* follows the progression of the narrator through different phases of World War II and Hitler's reign. In each story the unnamed narrator acts as a reporter, describing events in a straightforward and unbiased manner. The stories are first-person confessionals, intense in matter and delivery, conferring an immediate sense of the gravity of the time. The translations are merely satisfactory as they do not detract from the stories.

In *Friedrich,* a young boy describes his early childhood and his family's friendship with a Jewish family, the Schneiders. Friedrich and the narrator are good friends and both families share happy times together before Hitler assumes power. With the rise of Hitler comes the demise of the Schneider family; Frau Schneider is killed, Herr Schneider is sent to a concentration camp and Friedrich dies because none of the German families allow him to enter the air raid shelter during a bombing. Richter explores the effect of the imposed Nazi laws on both families and, without assigning blame, lets the honesty of the narrator and the facts of history speak for themselves. The narrator's ambivalence between being a Nazi or helping the Jews is frightening yet understandable. He feels a rush of excitement when he joins in the trashing of a place that means nothing to him, yet when he returns home and finds the Schneider's apartment destroyed, he feels sick to his stomach. Richter is perhaps most adept at describing what is necessary and allowing only pure unfabricated emotions to pervade. He ends *Friedrich* and *I Was There* by immersing the reader in the history of the novels, with an outline of events running concurrent to the stories.

I Was There continues the story of *Friedrich*'s narrator; Richter, however, shifts the focus from Friedrich, to the narrator and his two friends' initiation into the Hitler Youth. Richter then details the boys' impressions of the movement. The more involved the boys become, the deeper the emotions they feel; from nervousness, excitement, power, and fear to a disenchantment with war and finally, as they arrive at the front, a shattering of all the illusions they held as Nazi Youth. Richter brilliantly escapes melodrama by accurately portraying the characters of the boys. He allows their voices to flourish without superimposing his ideals or messages. Perhaps Richter is so skilled at telling their stories in simple, unadorned language because, as he states in the introduction, ''I was there, I was not merely an eyewitness. I believed—and I will never believe again.''

In *The Time of the Young Soldiers*, Richter focuses on a seventeen-year-old who volunteers for the army. The chapters are disjointed, each offering a different snapshot or vignette of war experience. The narrator sees his friends killed, his mother's suffering and extreme poverty, and endures the loss of his arm. Instead of portraying a young war hero, Richter realistically describes the intense experiences of a young and ignorant boy who is seemingly oblivious to Hitler's philosophies or the world outside his shell.

In the introduction to *The Time of the Young Soldiers*, Richter states, ''When the war broke out, I was fourteen years old; when it ended I was twenty. I was a soldier for three years. I thought the things I saw and the things I did were justified because no one spoke out openly against them.'' In all three novels, Richter explores why no one spoke out, why people believed in Hitler's policies and what motivated them to act in the ways they did.

In each of the novels, the narrator provides the reader with an honest, unapologetic behind-the-scenes look at what many Germans felt during the Nazi reign. There are no brilliant revelations or completed circles since these are real stories that don't depend on character development or surprise endings. What could be a series of depressing accounts of Nazi Germany are instead gripping and thought-provoking novels. The harsh and sincere tone of the three books will leave lasting impressions on any reader. Richter respects his young adult readers and neither gives in to melodrama or sentimentality; balancing sympathies between characters in each book and he refrains from covering up grim or embarrassing details.

—Kate Lentz

RIGG, Sharon. *See* **CREECH, Sharon.**

RINALDI, Ann

Nationality: American. **Born:** New York City, 27 August 1934. **Education:** a high school in New Brunswick, New Jersey. **Family:** Married Ronald P. Rinaldi in 1960; two children. **Career:** Writer; author of column, *Somerset Messenger Gazette,* Somerset, New Jersey, 1969-70; feature writer and author of column, *Trentonian,* Trenton, New Jersey, since 1970. Member of Brigade of the American Revolution. **Awards:** New Jersey Press awards from the New Jersey Press Association, first place, 1978, and several second place awards in subsequent years, all for newspaper columns; Notable Children's Trade Book in the Field of Social Studies by the joint committee of the National Council for Social Studies and the Children's Book Council, 1985, for *But in the Fall I'm Leaving;* one of American Library Association's Best Books for Young Adults, 1986, for *Time Enough for Drums.* **Address:** 302 Miller Ave., Somerville, New Jersey 08876, U.S.A.

PUBLICATIONS FOR YOUNG ADULTS

Fiction

Term Paper. New York, Walker & Co., 1980.
Promises Are for Keeping. New York, Walker & Co., 1982.
But in the Fall I'm Leaving. New York, Holiday House, 1985.
Time Enough for Drums. New York, Holiday House, 1986.
The Good Side of My Heart. New York, Holiday House, 1987.
The Last Silk Dress. New York, Holiday House, 1988.
A Ride into Morning: The Story of Tempe Wick. San Diego, Harcourt, 1991.
Wolf by the Ears. New York, Scholastic, 1991.
A Break with Charity: A Story about the Salem Witch Trials. San Diego, Harcourt, 1992.
In My Father's House. New York, Scholastic, 1992.
Hang a Thousand Trees with Ribbons: The Story of Phillis Wheatley. San Diego, Harcourt Brace, 1996.
The Blue Door. New York, Scholastic, 1996.
Keep Smiling Through. San Diego, Harcourt Brace, 1996.
Mine Eyes Have Seen. New York, Scholastic, 1997.
An Acquaintance with Darkness. San Diego, Harcourt Brace, 1997.
The Second Bend in the River. New York, Scholastic, 1997.
Cast Two Shadows. San Diego, Harcourt Brace, 1998.

*

Biography: Essay in *Speaking for Ourselves, Too* compiled and edited by Donald R. Gallo, National Council of Teachers of English, 1993.

* * *

In *Promises Are for Keeping,* Ann Rinaldi's protagonist, Nicki, remarks that Tony, her older brother, "always says I'm observant. He says I should be a writer. I get vibes about people." Rinaldi's readers quickly discover that she, like Nicki, does have good vibes about her characters and is observant of details, especially in her historical fiction. Rinaldi's mother, like Nicki's, died after she was born. For two happy years young Ann lived in the Brooklyn home of an aunt and uncle whose older children—not unlike Nicki's two older brothers—spoiled her, and then her father, a newspaper man, took her to New Jersey to live with her siblings and her new stepmother. While Nicki is more in control of her own future, young Ann's desire to write was subverted as she was steered instead toward secretarial work during and after high school. Her life took a significant turn in 1960; she married Ronald P. Rinaldi, and by 1964 they had a son and a daughter. In 1969 she began her journalism career as a columnist, first for the *Somerset Messenger Gazette* and then the *Trentonian* where she honed her skills and won awards for her writing. During this time she wrote several novels without any success until the publication in 1980 of *Term Paper,* followed by its sequel, *Promises,* in 1982, and *But in the Fall I'm Leaving* in 1985.

In Trenton, which some consider the crossroads of the American Revolution, Rinaldi covered stories of the American bicentennial which, with her son Ron's strong interest in military history, took the family to various Revolutionary War reenactments of encampments and battles. In the process Rinaldi not only learned much history from extensive reading, but she also gained a first-hand feel for lifestyles during these times. When Rinaldi decided to write a historical novel that centered on the War for Independence, her agent said no one would buy it or read it. Nonetheless she proceeded, and the result was *Time Enough for Drums.* Set in Trenton, this is the story of Jemima Emerson, a patriot whose older sister marries a British officer and whose older brother becomes an officer in the Continental army. Jem's parents also support the revolution in their special ways, but her grandfathers have divided loyalties. Jem is torn not only by her concern for her family and the hardships that befall them, but she also is in conflict with John Reid, her handsome Tory tutor who pushes her sternly toward emotional and intellectual maturity. Jem initially is decidedly spoiled and immature, but the realities of war, the death of her father, the support and wise counsel of the family's servant Lucy, and her discovery of Reid's real role in the war bring Jem to maturity and responsibility.

Time Enough for Drums set a new course for Ann Rinaldi, for in historical fiction she had found the vehicle for exploring her interests and developing more fully her talent as a writer. In *Time Enough for Drums* Rinaldi raised the issue of slavery which would figure prominently in several of her later novels. She has said that in the course of her research, Revolutionary War hero Henry "Light-Horse Harry" Lee and father of Robert E. Lee, took her by the hand and led her into the Civil War. From this journey came the novels *The Last Silk Dress* and *In My Father's House.* Set in Richmond during the Civil War, *The Last Silk Dress* traces the coming-of-age of fourteen-year-old Susan Chilmark who gives of her time and energy to support the Confederate cause by tending the wounded and sewing. The title of the book comes from the effort of Susan and her friend Connie to collect silk dresses from women in the city in order to make a balloon to spy on the Yankees who are besieging the city. Susan is burdened by the loss of her father, by the "half-mad" state of her mother who sometimes refers to Susan as a Yankee brat, and by the mysterious circumstances that have alienated her beloved brother Lucien from the family. In the course of the story Susan discovers many family secrets that involve slavery and adultery. She also learns that a devoted Southern woman can fall in love with a Yankee.

In *In My Father's House* Rinaldi builds her story of the Civil War around the fact that the first battle of the war began on property at Manassas owned by Will McLean and his family, and, ironically, ended in his parlor at Appomattox Court House with Lee's surrender to Grant. The narrator, Oscie Mason, begins her story in 1852 when Wilmer McLean begins to court her mother after her father's death. As the oldest child, Oscie is single-minded and resentful of McLean's intrusion. After the marriage McLean brings Miss Buttonworth from the North as the children's tutor. The conflict between Oscie and McLean is one of conflicting visions. Oscie resists change, while McLean is insistent that slavery as an institution cannot survive in the South. "Button," as the children call her, becomes a voice of reason and enlightenment, and even after she returns to the North when the war begins, she corresponds with the children. Oscie matures, accepts change as the war runs its course, and puts aside her infatuation with a dashing Southern officer who is already married in favor of a young man from Appomattox.

Rinaldi's historical research has also resulted in *A Ride into Morning: The Story of Tempe Wick* and *A Break with Charity: A Story about the Salem Witch Trials.* The Tempe Wick story, told by Wick's cousin Mary Cooper, is based on a legend that surrounds a mutiny of Continental troops encamped on the Wick farm. Rinaldi has researched the known facts about the event and has given her own fictional dimensions to the historical details. The dynamics of this story are not as arresting as those of *A Break with Charity.* The Salem Witch Trials are generally known to many literate Americans, yet the details are unfamiliar to most. Her choice of Susanna English as her narrator gives strength to the story, for she is an outsider in the eyes of the village girls who are caught up in playing a deadly game with the lives of innocent people, including Susanna's parents. The struggles within the Salem community make this a compelling story for contemporary American youth.

Wolf by the Ears could be Rinaldi's most creative book while possibly being her most controversial one as well. The title comes from Thomas Jefferson's statement about slavery: "As it is, we have the wolf by the ears, and we can neither hold him, nor safely let him go." The book is the journal of Harriet Hemmings, a Jefferson slave—although she is called a servant—with light skin, red hair, nice clothes, and a good education. Her mother, Sally, is Jefferson's personal servant, and there are rumors that Jefferson may be the father of Harriet and her brothers. The question of parentage continues to be debated among historians. Harriet professes to love the Master and knows that she and her brothers are promised their freedom when they reach twenty-one. She struggles with the notion of freedom, but she begins to consider the alternative of passing as a white woman after the master's son-in-law attempts to rape her. Some readers may raise issues of racism in Harriet's portrayal, in spite of Rinaldi's disclaimer that "I do not know what it felt like to be a slave, to be half black or three-quarters white. But I do know how it feels to be alienated, to wonder about part of one's background, and to be unable to get over the idea that one never quite belongs. These feelings are human, not exclusively belonging to blacks, whites, or anyone else...''.

Neither history nor historical fiction can always tell readers exactly what the past holds for the present, but good historical fiction will suggest connections, as *Wolf by the Ears* does in the area of race relations or as *In My Father's House* does, to a lesser degree, about feminist issues. Clearly, Ann Rinaldi has mastered the craft of storytelling, and she has found her niche as a writer of young adult historical fiction. She is an ardent researcher who offers readers background information and lucid explanations about the evolution of her books. Given the richness of American history, there are many stories still waiting for her inquisitive eye.

—Hugh Agee

ROBERTS, Willo Davis

Nationality: American. **Born:** Grand Rapids, Michigan, 28 May 1928. **Education:** Attended high school in Pontiac, Michigan, graduated 1946. **Family:** Married David W. Roberts in 1949; two daughters and two sons. **Career:** Writer. Worked in hospitals and doctors' offices, 1964-72; co-owner of dairy farm; has conducted writers' workshops in Granite Falls, Washington; consultant to executive board of Pacific Northwest Writers' Conference. Founder, Mystery Writers of America Seattle Chapter. **Awards:** Named a Notable Children's Trade Book by the National Council for the Social Studies and the Children's Book Council, 1977, for *Don't Hurt Laurie!;* Young Hoosier Book award, Association for Indiana Media Educators, 1980, West Australian Young Readers award, 1981, Georgia Children's Book award, University of Georgia, 1982, all for *Don't Hurt Laurie!;* Mark Twain award, Missouri Library Association and Missouri Association of School Librarians, 1983, and California Young Reader Medal, California Reading Association, 1986, all for *The Girl with the Silver Eyes;* named a West Virginia Children's Book award honor book, 1987, *Eddie and the Fairy Godpuppy;* Pacific Northwest Writers Conference Achievement award, 1986, for body of work; *Baby Sitting Is a Dangerous Job* received the Mark Twain award, the Young Hoosier award, the South Carolina Children's Book award, and the Nevada Young Reader's award; *Sugar Isn't Everything* was named an outstanding science trade book for children by the National Science Teachers Association and the Children's Book Council; Edgar Allan Poe award, 1989, for *Megan's Island,* 1995, for *The Absolutely True Story,* 1997, for *Twisted Summer*; Governor's award for contribution to the field of children's literature, Washington State, 1990, for body of work. **Agent:** Curtis Brown, 10 Astor Place, New York, New York 10019. **Address:** 12020 West Engebretsen Rd., Granite Falls, Washington 98252, U.S.A.

PUBLICATIONS FOR YOUNG ADULTS

Fiction

The View from the Cherry Tree. New York, Atheneum, 1975.
Don't Hurt Laurie!, illustrated by Ruth Sanderson. New York, Atheneum, 1977.
The Minden Curse, illustrated by Sherry Streeter. New York, Atheneum, 1978.

The Girl with the Silver Eyes. New York, Atheneum, 1980.
More Minden Curses, illustrated by Sherry Streeter. New York, Atheneum, 1980.
House of Fear. New York, Scholastic, 1983.
No Monsters in the Closet. New York, Atheneum, 1983.
The Pet-Sitting Peril. New York, Atheneum, 1983.
Caroline. New York, Scholastic, 1984.
Eddie and the Fairy Godpuppy, New York, Atheneum, 1984.
Elizabeth. New York, Scholastic, 1984.
Baby Sitting Is a Dangerous Job. New York, Atheneum, 1985.
Victoria. New York, Scholastic, 1985.
The Magic Book. New York, Atheneum, 1986.
Sugar Isn't Everything. New York, Atheneum, 1987.
Megan's Island. New York, Atheneum, 1988.
Nightmare. New York, Atheneum, 1989.
What Could Go Wrong? New York, Atheneum, 1989.
To Grandmother's House We Go. New York, Atheneum, 1990.
Dark Secrets. New York, Fawcett, 1991.
Scared Stiff. New York, Atheneum, 1991.
Jo and the Bandit. New York, Atheneum, 1992.
What Are We Going to Do about David? New York, Atheneum, 1993.
Caught! New York, Atheneum, 1995.
The Absolutely True Story: How I Visited Yellowstone Park with the Terrible Rupes. New York, Atheneum, 1995.
Twisted Summer. New York, Atheneum, 1996.
Secrets at Hidden Valley. New York, Atheneum, 1997.
The Kidnappers. New York, Atheneum, 1998.
Pawns. New York, Atheneum, 1998.

PUBLICATIONS FOR ADULTS

Novels

Murder at Grand Bay. New York, Arcadia House, 1955.
The Girl Who Wasn't There. New York, Arcadia House, 1957.
Murder Is So Easy. Fresno, California, Vega Books, 1961.
The Suspected Four. Fresno, California, Vega Books, 1962.
Nurse Kay's Conquest. New York, Ace Books, 1966.
Once a Nurse. New York, Ace Books, 1966.
Nurse at Mystery Villa. New York, Ace Books, 1967.
Return to Darkness. New York, Lancer Books, 1969.
Devil Boy. New York, New American Library, 1970; London, New English Library, 1971.
The House at Fern Canyon. New York, Lancer Books, 1970.
Invitation to Evil. New York, Lancer Books, 1970.
Shadow of a Past Love. New York, Lancer Books, 1970.
Shroud of Fog. New York, Ace Books, 1970.
The Tarot Spell. New York, Lancer Books, 1970.
The Waiting Darkness. New York, Lancer Books, 1970.
The Gates of Montrain. New York, Lancer Books, 1971.
The Ghosts of Harrel. New York, Lancer Books, 1971.
King's Pawn. New York, Lancer Books, 1971.
The Nurses. London, Pan, 1971; as *The Secret Lives of the Nurses,* New York, Ace Books, 1972.
The Terror Trap. New York, Lancer Books, 1971.
The Watchers. New York, Lancer Books, 1971.
Becca's Child. New York, Lancer Books, 1972.
Dangerous Legacy. New York, Lancer Books, 1972.
The Face of Danger. New York, Lancer Books, 1972.
Inherit the Darkness. New York, Lancer Books, 1972.

The M.D. New York, Lancer Books, 1972.
Nurse in Danger. New York, Ace Books, 1972.
Sing a Dark Song. New York, Lancer Books, 1972.
Sinister Gardens. New York, Lancer Books, 1972.
The Evil Children. New York, Lancer Books, 1973.
The Gods in Green. New York, Lancer Books, 1973.
Nurse Robin. New York, Lennox Hill, 1973.
Didn't Anybody Know My Wife? New York, Putnam, 1974.
Key Witness. New York, Putnam, 1975; London, Hale, 1978.
White Jade. New York, Doubleday, 1975.
Expendable. New York, Doubleday, 1976; London, Hale, 1979.
The Jaubert Ring. New York, Doubleday, 1976.
Act of Fear. New York, Doubleday, 1977; London, Hale, 1978.
Cape of Black Sands. New York, Popular Library, 1977.
The House of Imposters. New York, Popular Library, 1977.
Destiny's Women. New York, Popular Library, 1980.
The Search for Willie. New York, Popular Library, 1980.
The Face at the Window. Toronto, Harlequin, and New York, Raven Press, 1981; London, Hale, 1983.

"The Black Pearl" series:

The Dark Dowry. New York, Popular Library, 1978.
The Stuart Strain. New York, Popular Library, 1978.
The Cade Curse. New York, Popular Library, 1978.
The Devil's Double. New York, Popular Library, 1979.
The Radkin Revenge. New York, Popular Library, 1979.
The Hellfire Heritage. New York, Popular Library, 1979.
The Macomber Menace. New York, Popular Library, 1980.
The Gresham Ghost. New York, Popular Library, 1980.
The Gallant Spirit. New York, Popular Library, 1982.
A Long Time to Hate. New York, Avon, 1982.
Days of Valor. New York, Warner, 1983.
Keating's Landing. New York, Warner, 1984.
The Sniper. New York, Doubleday, 1984.
The Annalise Experiment. New York, Doubleday, 1985.
My Rebel, My Love. New York, Pocket Books, 1986.
To Share a Dream. Toronto, Worldwide, 1986.
Madawaska. Toronto, Worldwide, 1988.

*

Biography: Essay in *Something about the Author Autobiography Series,* Volume 8, Detroit, Gale, 1989; essay in *Speaking for Ourselves, Too* compiled and edited by Donald R. Gallo, National Council of Teachers of English, 1993.

Manuscript Collections: Bowling Green University, Ohio; (children's books): de Grummond Collection, University of Southern Mississippi, Hattiesburg; Central Missouri State University, Warrensburg.

Willo Davis Roberts comments:

All of my life, my favorite presents and possessions have been books. If there is one thing that I would like to pass on to all young people, it is a love for reading. My mother read to me when I was no more than an infant. I was telling stories by the time I was two years old. By the age of nine, I began to write them down, just for the fun of it. When I finally realized that other people got paid for the stores

that I loved to read, I got the exciting idea that maybe I, too, could make a living writing.

My advice to young writers is to practice every day. Write about a character who has a problem to solve or a goal to reach, and all the difficulties he or she encounters in doing that. Use emotion: make your readers laugh, or cry, or be scared, or angry. Make them keep turning that pages by cliff-hanger chapter endings. And never, never stop reading!

*   *   *

Willo Davis Roberts possesses the amazing ability to formulate plot after plot and then turn those plots into entertaining mysteries and adventure stories. She is a prolific writer who delivers delightful novels to the youngest of young adults. Besides having a talent for imaginative plots, Roberts also understands young people. She knows what problems young adults have and how they will react to them. Roberts portrays young adults sensitively and with empathy. Her modern realistic novels reflect several serious problems which young adults face. Ideas for her novels come from the young people she visits in schools and from her own children and grandchildren. When she needs some prompting to develop an idea, she does what many writers do to stimulate creativity. Roberts asks herself, "What if?" The answers to that question result in suspenseful plots for her readers and interesting situations for her characters.

Roberts's first novel for young adults, *The View from the Cherry Tree,* was originally written for adults, but her editor saw its potential for a younger audience. In this first mystery, Rob witnesses the murder of a nosy old lady next door. Rob is horrified by the old lady's death and tries to tell someone how she died, but Rob's sister is getting married and everyone is too busy to listen to him. Then someone shoots at Rob, and Rob realizes that the murderer knows he saw something and is trying to kill him.

In her mysteries, Roberts's characters could easily be the kids next door. They are ordinary young adults who find themselves in unusual situations. Her characters must draw on their own resources to be able to solve the mysteries they encounter. In *What Could Go Wrong?* three cousins set out on a flight from Seattle, Washington, to visit their Aunt Molly in San Francisco. It sounds simple enough; their parents will take them to the airport and Aunt Molly will pick them up at their destination. Once the cousins are on board the airplane, however, readers know that Roberts's "what if?" thinking has taken over. After an emergency landing in Portland, a bomb threat, a theft, and a chase through the airport, the cousins solve a mystery and survive their adventure.

Most of Roberts's main characters are eleven or twelve years old, but in *Nightmare* the main character, Nick, is a senior in high school. Nick's adventure begins when a man falls from an overpass just as Nick drives under it. The man's neck breaks when he hits the hood of Nick's old, blue Pinto. Nick consequently has nightmares about the accident. To get away from his policeman stepfather and his thoughts about the tragedy, Nick decides to drive the family motorhome to Texas to see his older brother. Instead of escaping his nightmares at home, Nick is drawn deeper into danger. Someone is following Nick, and he doesn't know who or why, but he guesses that it has to do with the dead man. Roberts tells a chilling story that keeps young adults reading until the suspenseful ending.

In her modern realistic novels, Roberts is an obvious advocate of young people. *Don't Hurt Laurie!* is the story of a young girl who is being physically abused by her mother. Laurie must get help or she won't survive her mother's anger. *Sugar Isn't Everything* is an informative story about an eleven-year-old girl who discovers that she has diabetes and must learn to adjust her life-style to survive. One of Roberts's most recent realistic novels centers on a theme that can also be found in some of her mysteries and adventure stories. Roberts writes about young adults who suffer because they have been abandoned by their parents. This abandonment may be unintentional, parents are kidnapped or die, but the results are the same. The adolescents feel insecure and unloved. In *What Are We Going to Do about David?* an eleven-year-old boy is sent to live with his grandmother while his mother goes to Hawaii on vacation for a month. David's father is too busy with work to take responsibility for his son. Through his parents' preoccupation with their own problems and concerns David is ignored and feels as if he has been abandoned.

In *Scared Stiff,* Roberts has created a suspenseful mystery about two boys who are abandoned by their parents. Their father leaves after an argument with their mother, then their mother disappears. The last time the boys saw her was when she was talking to some men in a car near a grocery store and they are sure that she has been kidnapped, but it's hard for them to convince anyone else of that. The thoughts and actions of the main characters realistically reflect typical behavior of two boys who are frightened and bewildered by their circumstances.

Although most of Roberts's novels take place in contemporary America, *Jo and the Bandit* is a departure from the contemporary setting. Here is a Western tale set in the late 1860s with plenty of details about daily living to satisfy fans of the Old West. Jo and her little brother Andrew are orphaned and must go out West to live with an uncle they have never met. On their way to Muddy Wells, Texas, their stagecoach is robbed, but Jo is able to draw sketches of some of the men who robbed them. Due to Jo's artistic talent and her bravery, she helps bring the bandits to justice. Roberts again shows her ability to write sympathetically about characters while she lets them meet and survive one heart-stopping challenge after another.

Roberts's knack for imaginative plots combined with her understanding and empathy for young adults result in stories that will entertain readers and leave them with messages of hope.

—Rosemary Chance

ROBERTSON, Keith (Carlton)

Pseudonym: Carlton Keith. **Nationality:** American. **Born:** Dows, Iowa, 9 May 1914. **Education:** the United States Naval Academy, Annapolis, Maryland, B.S. 1937. **Military Service:** Served in the United States Navy: radioman on a battleship, 1930-33; officer, on destroyers, 1941-45; Captain, United States Naval Reserve. **Family:** Married Elisabeth Hexter in 1946; two daughters, one son. **Career:** Refrigeration engineer, 1937-41; employee of publishing firm, 1945-47; free-lance writer, 1947-58; Bay Ridge Specialty Co., Inc. (ceramics manufacturer), Trenton, New Jersey, president, 1958-69; writer, 1969-91. Trustee, Hopewell Museum. **Awards:** Spring Book Festival award, 1956, for *The Pilgrim Goose;* William Allen White Award, 1961, for *Henry Reed, Inc.;* William Allen White award, 1969, Pacific Northwest Library Association's "Young

Reader's Choice" award, 1969, and Nene award, 1970, all for *Henry Reed's Baby-Sitting Service;* New Jersey Institute of Technology awards, both 1969, for *New Jersey* and *The Money Machine.* **Died:** 23 September 1991.

PUBLICATIONS FOR YOUNG ADULTS

Fiction

Ticktock and Jim, illustrated by Wesley Dennis. Philadelphia, Winston, 1948, as *Watch for a Pony,* London, Heinemann, 1949.
Ticktock and Jim, Deputy Sheriffs, illustrated by Everett Stahl. Philadelphia, Winston, 1949.
The Dog Next Door, illustrated by Morgan Dennis. New York, Viking, 1950.
The Missing Brother, illustrated by Rafaello Busoni. New York, Viking, 1950; London, Faber, 1952.
The Lonesome Sorrel, illustrated by Taylor Oughton. Philadelphia, Winston, 1952.
The Mystery of Burnt Hill, illustrated by Busoni. New York, Viking, 1952.
Mascot of the Melroy, illustrated by Jack Weaver. New York, Viking, 1953.
Outlaws of the Sourland, illustrated by Isami Kashiwagi. New York, Viking, 1953.
Three Stuffed Owls, illustrated by Weaver. New York, Viking, 1954.
Ice to India, illustrated by Weaver. New York, Viking, 1955.
The Phantom Rider, illustrated by Weaver. New York, Viking, 1955.
The Pilgrim Goose, illustrated by Erick Berry. New York, Viking, 1956.
The Pinto Deer, illustrated by Kashiwagi. New York, Viking, 1956.
The Crow and the Castle, illustrated by Robert Grenier. New York, Viking, 1957.
Henry Reed, Inc., illustrated by Robert McCloskey. New York, Viking, 1958.
If Wishes Were Horses, illustrated by Paul Kennedy. New York, Harper, 1958.
Henry Reed's Journey, illustrated by McCloskey. New York, Viking, 1963.
Henry Reed's Baby-Sitting Service, illustrated by McCloskey. New York, Viking, 1966.
The Year of the Jeep, illustrated by W. T. Mars. New York, Viking, 1968.
The Money Machine, illustrated by George Porter. New York, Viking, 1969.
Henry Reed's Big Show, illustrated by McCloskey. New York, Viking, 1970.
In Search of a Sandhill Crane, illustrated by Richard Cuffari. New York, Viking, 1973.
Tales of Myrtle the Turtle, illustrated by Peter Parnall. New York, Viking, 1974.
Henry Reed's Think Tank. New York, Viking Kestrel, 1986.

Other

The Wreck of the Saginaw, illustrated by Jack Weaver. New York, Viking, 1954.
The Navy: From Civilian to Sailor, illustrated by Charles Geer. New York, Viking, 1958.
New Jersey. New York, McCann, 1969.

PUBLICATIONS FOR ADULTS as Carlton Keith

Fiction

The Diamond-Studded Typewriter. New York, Macmillan, 1958;
    London, Heinemann, 1960; as *A Gem of a Murder,* New York,
    Dell, 1959.
Missing, Presumed Dead. New York, Doubleday, 1961.
Rich Uncle. New York, Doubleday, 1963; London, Hale, 1965.
The Hiding Place. New York, Doubleday, 1965; London, Hale, 1966.
The Crayfish Dinner. New York, Doubleday, 1966; as *The Elusive
    Epicure,* London, Hale, 1966.
A Taste of Sangria. New York, Doubleday, 1968, as *The Missing
    Book-Keeper,* London, Hale, 1969.

*

Biography: Entry in *More Junior Authors,* New York, H.W.
Wilson, 1963; essay in *Something about the Author Autobiography
Series,* Volume 15, Detroit, Gale, 1993.

Manuscript Collection: May Massee Collection, Emporia State
University, Kansas.

*   *   *

Keith Robertson's fiction portrays a cozy, 1950s world of
small-town America, where good-natured boys use ingenuity,
perseverance, and industry to triumph over external problems. If
his books have a common theme, it's that setting goals and working
toward them with determination and good cheer ensures success.

Animals figure prominently in many of Robertson's early
works. Frequently the protagonist has or wants to acquire a horse or
dog, but must spend considerable time working with it to demonstrate its worth. Robertson's first book told of Jim Meadows, who
trades a watch for a horse (Ticktock), carefully grooms and trains it,
then launches an all-purpose pony express service. In so doing, he
pays for Ticktock's upkeep and convinces his disapproving father
that Ticktock is a worthwhile investment. Other heroes follow a
similar pattern; their efforts are justified when the animal saves
lives, wins races, or otherwise shows its fine qualities. These books
often emphasize the bond between a pet and its owner, with the
animal languishing when separated from the boy, and the boy
anguishing when he believes his pet may die (one of the only times
Robertson's protagonists experience any deep emotional turmoil).
Ironically, Robertson revamped this plot for a later book, *The Year
of the Jeep,* but with a machine as the object of the boy's devotion.
Cloud Selby works as slavishly and loyally to restore an abandoned
jeep as any of his predecessors do for their pets, and is almost as
despondent when he thinks he may lose it.

Mysteries often provide a plot or subplot with a boy investigating strange happenings. Sometimes this combines with an animal
story, as in *The Phantom Rider,* where Tim Cottrell tries to catch a
mysterious morning rider said to be a ghost from the Revolutionary
War. In others, like the four Carson Street Detective agency books
(*The Mystery of Burnt Hill, The Crow and the Castle, Three Stuffed*

Owls, and *The Money Machine*), mysteries form the core of the
story. Here, teenaged amateur detectives Neil and Swede take on
minor problems—everything from a missing bicycle to photo-
graphing a rare chess set—only to discover their cases connect
with more serious crimes.

Robertson sets his books in small towns or rural areas. Earlier
stories take place in Iowa, later ones in New Jersey, near Princeton,
reflecting Robertson's own geographical shift. Nature and wildlife
serve as a backdrop, with characters regularly going on hikes or
camping out in the woods. The value and beauty of nature appear as
a theme as early as *The Pinto Deer,* in which a young boy resolves
to capture the title animal to earn money for college, developing a
deeper appreciation of wildlife in the process; a similar theme
occurs in the more recent *In Search of a Sandhill Crane.* These
natural settings also allow the protagonists their own special space,
and many have hideouts such as abandoned barns or secluded spots
in forests, where they can work or think undisturbed.

Several plot devices and character types recur in the books. One
is the value of the printed word or picture. Friendly booksellers or
professors with large libraries appear as secondary characters,
offering books with useful information (a tactic that also allows
Robertson to insert background material). Newspapers and reporters also play a part. In *Ticktock and Jim,* the local paper helps
promote Jim and Ticktock's pony express with free advertising; in
the sequel, Jim discovers the missing Ticktock through a news
photo, and in *The Crow and the Castle* another photo provides a
clue about an elusive chess piece.

The protagonists also team up with or receive assistance from
unlikely characters. Although it is never explicitly stated, an
underlying theme seems to be that good friends can be found in
unlikely guises and that kindness reaps rewards. Neil and Swede
are one of the few instances of two boys with similar backgrounds
working together. Instead, most characters meet an unattractive,
unsociable character—such as the irascible, unkempt hermit in
The Missing Brother—render aid, and thereby form a friendship
that benefits both parties. Robertson occasionally varies this by
teaming the male protagonist with a strong-minded female—such
as the angelic-looking, mischief-creating Wilhelmina (Billy)
Atkinson in *The Pinto Deer.* However, this pairing never involves
romance; the only objects that claim a Robertson hero's heart are
his pet, his car, or his hobbies.

Henry Reed is undoubtedly Robertson's most enduring—and
endearing—character, and the five Henry Reed books display
most of the above traits. Henry is the quintessential entrepreneur,
perpetually embarking on new schemes to test the free enterprise
system. His assorted businesses are housed in an unused barn
belonging to his mother, and he is aided by the unquenchable
Midge Glass, with occasional assistance from his dog Agony.
Although many of Robertson's other books incorporate humor, the
Henry Reed books are by far the funniest. Poor Henry doesn't try to
cause trouble; nonetheless, he has an unerring knack for attracting
it, equalled only by his ability to emerge unscathed from the
resulting chaos. It is typical of Henry that his stalled tractor (pulling
a cart, a bale of hay, a wagon, a bathtub, Midge Glass, and Agony)
causes a major traffic jam and delays a dozen distinguished
commuters, but also yields favorable publicity and increased
business for Henry's new research firm when a local reporter writes
about the incident. Although Henry doesn't solve mysteries, he
doesn't need to; he fills his days unwittingly creating—and calmly
resolving—myriad minor crises.

Robertson's protagonists seem far removed from many of today's more troubled heroes. Well-mannered, respectful, hard-working, and lighthearted—in a word, wholesome—they reflect an earlier time and offer readers a pleasant journey through a lighter, less complicated landscape.

—Deidre Johnson

ROBINSON, Spider

Nationality: American. **Born:** New York City, 24 November 1948. **Education:** State University of New York, Stony Brook, B.A. 1972; New York State University College, Plattsburgh; Le Moyne College, Memphis, Tennessee. **Family:** Married Jeanne Rubbicco in 1975; one daughter. **Career:** Realty editor, *Long Island Commercial Review,* Syosset, New York, 1972-73; science fiction writer, since 1973; Reviewer, *Galaxy,* 1974-77, *Destinies,* 1977-79, and *Analog,* 1978-80. Chairman of the Executive Council, Writers Federation of Nova Scotia, 1981-83. Instructor, Clarion SF Writers Workshop, Michigan State University, 1989. Chairmen of the board of directors, Dance Advance Association. **Awards:** John W. Campbell award, 1974, for short story "The Guy with the Eyes"; Hugo award, World Science Fiction Convention, 1977, for best novella, "By Any Other Name," 1978, for best novella, "Stardance," and 1983, for best short story, "Melancholy Elephants"; Skylark award, 1977; Nebula award, Science Fiction Writers of America, 1977, for best novella, "Stardance"; *Locus* (magazine) award, 1976, for best critic, and 1977, for best novella, "Stardance"; E.E. Smith Memorial award, 1977; Pat Terry Memorial award, 1977; Canada Council grant, 1983, and Senior Arts grant, 1984. **Agent:** Eleanor Wood, Spectrum Literary Agency, 111 Eighth Avenue, Suite 1503, New York, New York 19911, U.S.A.

PUBLICATIONS

Novels

Telempath. New York, Berkley, 1976; London, Macdonald and Jane's, 1978.
Stardance, with Jeanne Robinson. New York, Dial, and London, Sidgwick & Jackson, 1979.
Mindkiller. New York, Holt, 1982; London, Sphere, 1985.
Night of Power. New York, Baen, 1985.
Callahan and Company (Omnibus). West Bloomfield, Michigan, Phantasia Press, 1987.
Time Pressure. New York, Ace, 1987.
Callahan's Lady (Lady Sally's House). New York, Ace, 1989.
Copyright Violation (novella). Eugene, Oregon, Pulphouse, 1990.
Kill the Editor. Pulphouse, 1991.
Starseed (Stardance), with Jeanne Robinson. New York, Ace, 1991.
Lady Slings the Booze. New York, Ace, 1992.
The Callahan Touch. New York, Ace, 1993.
Off the Wall at Callahan's. New York, TOR, 1994.
Starmind, with Jeanne Robinson. New York, Ace Books, 1995.

Callahan's Legacy. New York, TOR, 1996.
The Callahan Chronicals (includes *Callahan's Crosstime Saloon, Time Travelers Strictly Cash,* and *Callahan's Secret*). New York, TOR, 1997.

Short Stories

Callahan's Crosstime Saloon. New York, Ace, 1977.
Antinomy. New York, Dell, 1980.
Time Travelers Strictly Cash. New York, Ace, 1981.
Melancholy Elephants. Toronto, Penguin, 1984; New York, Tor, 1985.
Callahan's Secret. New York, Ace, 1986.

Other

Contributor, *Chrysalis 4,* edited by Roy Torgeson. Kensington, 1979.
Contributor, *New Voices 2,* edited by George R.R. Martin. New York, Harcourt, 1979.
Editor, *The Best of All Possible Worlds.* New York, Ace, 1980.

*   *   *

Award-winning science fiction author Spider Robinson prefers crisp humor to lengthy prose to convey his message in his "Callahan's Place" series. Adamantly insisting that the three sequential books are absolutely not a trilogy, Robinson uses his short stories in book form to create a warm and wonderful Place for readers of all ages.

The first book, *Callahan's Crosstime Saloon,* introduces us to the characters who inhabit Callahan's Place, the bar where anything can happen, and usually does. Among the regular denizens of the Place are Jake, the pun-slinging guitar player narrator; Mike, the redheaded Irish barkeep; the Doc, a rotund sawbones who is a master of twisted language; and Fast Eddie, the monkey-faced piano man. During the course of *Callahan's Crosstime Saloon,* these characters interact with a man from outer space, a true time-traveller, two psychics, history's oldest woman, and a swindler, meanwhile saving the world and blowing up the parking lot.

The fictional Callahan's Place is special because only those who need it will find it. Those in pain—emotional, physical, or spiritual—are welcomed, given a drink, and invited to pour out their pain to people who genuinely *care*. The primary theme of these books is love, and Robinson has created a place in which people relate to one another simply as who they are and are accepted absolutely, no matter what their failings or past sins. His humor is alternately broad and sophisticated, with some jokes reserved for technical specialists, and others aimed at ten-year-olds. The characters never stop growing throughout the stories. They constantly change in a mirror of life.

The second Callahan book, *Time Travellers Strictly Cash,* is primarily a collection of Robinson's short stories and essays, including a celebration of the works of Robert A. Heinlein. The three Callahan short stories included in the book are excellent, among them the tale of a true talking dog, and most of the non-Callahan stories bear reading as well.

Callahan's Secret finishes up the plot line loosely begun in *Callahan's Crosstime Saloon.* During the course of the book, Jake falls in love with Callahan's blacksmith daughter, Mary, who eventually marries another man—an alien. Callahan and his family are revealed as not being quite of this world, and the final resolution is as gentle and humorous as the stories that precede it.

Callahan's Lady is for older readers, since the setting is an unusual brothel in Brooklyn. Lady Sally's House is run by Mike Callahan's wife, and their daughter Mary moonlights once in a while as a House "artist" in between blacksmithing and security work. The artists at Lady Sally's are all voluntary employees, well paid and happy with their jobs. When Maureen, a young street prostitute, is stabbed by her pimp, she finds the loving family that she has been searching for in Lady Sally's House. She also finds a husband after rescuing him from the clutches of a Mafia thug.

Like the characters in the Callahan series, the people of *Callahan's Lady* are vividly drawn, sophisticated, and funny. They can, and do, laugh at and with themselves and life, even when life is harsh. At times they lack the depth of characterization of the previous books, but generally the quality of writing in *Callahan's Lady* is high.

Stardance is a very different style, a high-tech science fiction novel. The characters are wooden and lifeless, far different from the vital people of the Callahan's universe. In *Stardance,* a group of performing artists take to space to create a new art form, one that is eventually used to communicate with a new alien life-form. During the course of the story, all of the characters find new goals and new lives, and when the entities from space change them, the stardancers become a new species.

Robinson's award-winning *Telempath* is the story of Isham, a young, black, inner-city assassin who is programmed to kill the man responsible for ending the world as we know it. When he fails to make the kill and then discovers that his father was the man who destroyed society, Isham snaps. Fleeing from his friends and murdering his father, Isham becomes the only human who can communicate with the telepathic "Muskies," gaseous creatures with whom the surviving humans are at war.

Telempath is crisply written, varying in styles and points of view between Isham, his father, friends, and assorted "works of history" to tell the story. Where *Stardance* bogs down in scientific justification, *Telempath* provides just enough to make clear the plot and reasons for action. Both are effective works of science fiction, and both are award winners, but neither has the warm humanity of Callahan's. Robinson's finest and best written works remain the Callahan series, and all ages will enjoy these funny and warm-spirited books.

—Melanie Belviso

ROGASKY, Barbara

Nationality: American. **Born:** Wilmington, Delaware, 9 April 1933. **Education:** University of Delaware, Newark, 1950-54. **Career:** Held various editorial positions for New York City publishers, including Macmillan Publishing Co., Pyramid Books, and Harcourt Brace Jovanovich, 1955-77; freelance editorial consultant, editor, and writer, since 1977. **Awards:** *Smoke and Ashes: The Story of the Holocaust* was named, in 1988, a notable children's book of the American Library Association, a best nonfiction book for young adults by *Publishers Weekly,* one of the best books of the year by *School Library Journal* and the Young Adult Services Division of the American Library Association, and

one of the best books of the year for teenagers by the New York Public Library; it also received the Present Tense/Joel H. Cavior award for children's literature from the American Jewish Committee. **Address:** Brick Hill Rd., Lyme, New Hampshire 03768, U.S.A.

PUBLICATIONS FOR YOUNG ADULTS

Nonfiction

Smoke and Ashes: The Story of the Holocaust. New York, Holiday House, 1988.

Other

Reteller, *Rapunzel.* New York, Holiday House, 1982.
Reteller, *The Water of Life.* New York, Holiday House, 1986.
Compiler, and editor, *Winter Poems,* illustrated by Trina Schart Hyman. New York, Scholastic, 1991.
Photographer, *Light & Shadow,* by Myra Cohn Livingston. New York, Holiday House, 1992.
Reteller, *The Golem: A Version,* illustrated by Trina Schart Hyman. New York, Holiday House, 1996.

*   *   *

Barbara Rogasky confronts her readers with the brutality of Hitler's war against the Jews in her documentary, *Smoke and Ashes: The Story of the Holocaust.* Accompanied by numerous photographs, Rogasky's text sketches the mistreatment of Jews from the dawn of Christianity to instances of anti-Semitism in the 1980s. However, the bulk of her book deals with the years 1933 to 1950.

Rogasky simplifies her account to the essentials, using short sentences and paragraphs to present her case. She includes many quotations from eyewitnesses to the events that transpired in the countries occupied by Nazi troops and in the camps where they sent their victims.

As she traces Hitler's rise to power, Rogasky explains how Jewish life grew increasingly circumscribed. She poses and answers questions such as why Jews did not flee Nazi-controlled countries. She describes the brutality of life in the ghettos, particularly in Warsaw, and notes the continual escalation of violence and death as German leaders moved toward their development of a "Final Solution" to the Jewish presence in Europe. Rogasky explains how the Jews resisted in overt and covert ways, even in concentration camps. She describes camp life, noting the intense desire to live that enabled at least some Jews to outlast their captors and testify against their brutality. She indicts the governments of other countries, particularly Great Britain and the United States, for failing to intervene to save those in the camps, even after the Nazis' murderous activities became widely known.

Some of the annotated lists, such as brief descriptions of people and governments that helped rescue Jews, or paragraphs noting the fate of Third Reich members judged by the War Crimes Commission, can grow tedious, and without accompanying analysis they may be easy for readers to skip. Yet, lists such as examples of those who fought back against the Nazis cumulate into a picture of resistance that stands without author commentary.

Rogasky acknowledges that her account is not objective. She presents the facts she has accumulated filtered through her underlying assumption that anti-Semitism dominated all governmental and individual decisions during the war. She devotes only four pages of text to other groups killed by the Nazis, including the incurably ill, Gypsies, Polish intellectuals, and Russian prisoners of war. She barely mentions others, such as homosexuals, singled out for persecution. In the introduction she notes that ''the war took millions of lives all over the world, not only Jews. Yet this is a story of their destruction, because only they were marked for extinction.''

Similarly, Rogasky dismisses other mass exterminations of populations in the recent past as being qualitatively different from the destruction of the Jews. Answering her question ''Is the Holocaust Unique?'' in the affirmative, Rogasky briefly summarizes such mass killings as the slaughter of the Armenians by the Turks in 1915 and the atrocities of Pol Pot's regime in Cambodia after 1975. Rogasky concludes that such examples do not measure up to the horror perpetrated against the Jews by Nazi Germany because the Holocaust represents the only instance in history when a government and its leaders adopted an avowed policy of murdering an entire group of people solely to exterminate them rather than to achieve some other end. That position might be debatable, particularly in the light of contemporary policies of ''ethnic cleansing'' aimed at a number of minority groups.

Rogasky's contention that world leaders did not intervene more quickly to save the victims of the Nazis because those victims were Jewish, not Catholic or Protestant, might also be questioned. Government reluctance to interfere in the ''internal affairs'' of another country seems part of the fabric of twentieth-century history, and the complexity of securing international cooperation on almost any matter has been demonstrated time and again.

Although Rogasky admits her book is not objective, one might still pose the question of its fairness, particularly in light of the fact that it is intended for an audience of young people who may have little knowledge of the topic. For the most part, Rogasky tries to lay out facts to support her contentions. However, in her chapter indicting other governments, she tells readers that presenting the facts is useless. She summarizes the 1943 Bermuda conference as follows: ''Several paragraphs could be spent describing the conference. But since from the very beginning the purpose was to lessen some of the public disapproval of both governments, it is wasted space to do so.'' She says that ''much has been left out of this chapter, including the attempts of people in government and elsewhere to change the attitudes and help the dying Jews. But since the result was always the same—little was done—only the most important points and responses seemed necessary to mention.''

Astute readers may recognize Rogasky's slant in her presentation, but others may simply absorb her tone of horror and disgrace, experiencing the shock and guilt stemming from the realization that people can be so systematically brutal and disgracefully indifferent.

Rogasky's major achievement lies in the sustained power of her book to indict anti-Semitism in any form. Although the final pages include examples of other recent instances of racism and oppression, she maintains her focus on examples that indicate that suspicion and persecution of Jews has not died. Through her book she tries to recruit a generation of readers to help prevent an escalation of violence that could result in atrocities such as those she graphically documents for them.

—Kathy Piehl

ROQUELAURE, A.N. *See* **RICE, Anne.**

ROSTKOWSKI, Margaret I.

Nationality: American. **Born:** Margaret I. Ellis in Little Rock, Arkansas, 12 January 1945. **Education:** Middlebury College, Vermont, B.A. 1967; University of Kansas, Lawrence, M.A.T. 1971. **Family:** Married Charles Anthony Rostkowski, 1970; one son. **Career:** Reading teacher, Washington Junior High School, Ogden, Utah, 1974-84; teacher of English and French, Mount Ogden Middle School, Utah, 1979-84; teacher of English and writing, Ogden High School, Utah, from 1984. **Awards:** Golden Kite Award, 1986; Best Books for Young Adults and Notable Children's Book lists, 1986; International Reading Association Children's Book Award, 1987; Jefferson Cup Award from the Virginia Library Association, 1987; honorable mention, Golden Spur Award, 1996, for *Moon Dancer*. **Agent:** Ruth Cohen, P.O. Box 7626, Menlo Park, California 94025. U.S.A. **Address:** 2830 Marilyn Drive, Ogden, Utah 84403, U.S.A.

PUBLICATIONS FOR YOUNG ADULTS

Fiction

After the Dancing Days. New York, Harper, 1986.
The Best of Friends. New York, Harper, 1989.
Moon Dancer. New York, Harcourt Brace, 1995.

*

Biography: Essay in *Speaking for Ourselves, Too,* compiled and edited by Donald R. Gallo, Urbana, Illinois, National Council of Teachers of English, 1993, 173-174.

Margaret I. Rostkowski comments:

My books begin with questions I have about people and how they live with one another and in situations where their lives change. *After the Dancing Days* began when I wondered what life could be for someone so badly mutilated that people turned away from him in horror. *The Best of Friends* began when I wanted to explore what happens when questions of conscience came in conflict with friendship. *Moon Dancer* follows two sisters as they explore the past in a canyon in southern Utah and also learn how to love each other and themselves as the grow older. I am currently working on a book with the working title of *Desert Dogs* that explores how two friends learn about an illness that has devastated them and their own community.

I love all of writing: the first excitement of falling in love with characters; the thrashing out of the plot; and the revision, the work of finding the exact feeling buried beneath the moment. I also am exhilarated by the pursuit of perfection, trying to get it just right, to tell the truth, the whole truth and nothing but the truth—usually impossible, but exciting to pursue.

In trying to write as well and as honestly as I can, I follow a few practices: I read writers whose work I admire; I listen to and play music as much as possible; I explore the land where I live by walking with my dogs in all weather; I am careful about the words I use in speaking and writing. And always, in my head, I write.

*   *   *

For Margaret Rostkowski's characters, familiar family conflicts inherent in adolescent's lives take place in a larger context. In her first two novels the background is war while in the third she includes parallels from an ancient civilization.

After the Dancing Days takes place in 1919, when 13-year-old Annie Metcalf waits for her father, Lawrence, to return with some wounded veterans he had cared for during the Great War. His decision to work at a medical facility for veterans rather than return to County Hospital in their town near Kansas City puzzles and upsets his wife and other community members.

Annie is torn between her desire for life to resume the routines of pre-war days and her growing knowledge that such an existence can never return. Katherine, Annie's mother, retains an absorption in music that has sustained her through past difficulties. She opposes Annie's visits to St. John's, where Lawrence works and where Annie's grandfather reads to a blind veteran he had known before the war. At first Annie is frightened by the condition of the men, particularly Andrew, who had suffered severe burns on his face and hands. Yet, she comes to appreciate Andrew and helps him reach out to others.

As the summer progresses, Annie decides that she must do what she believes is right and disobeys her mother's orders to stop visiting St. John's. Annie also explores the circumstances surrounding the last days of her mother's brother, Paul, who had died in France. With Andrew's help, she learns he had died of measles, not of war wounds. Annie's shock on learning her beloved uncle had not died heroically gradually recedes as she acknowledges the truth of Andrew's observation that how men died during the war matters less than that they had to die at all. Annie's confrontation with her mother over her visits causes Katherine to examine her own attitudes. Eventually, Katherine invites Andrew to dinner and agrees to play a concert for the patients.

Most townspeople, however, concentrate on putting the war behind them by erecting a memorial. When the monument is proposed at Independence Day, Annie anticipates seeing her uncle's name chiseled on the edifice. By its dedication on Armistice Day, she refuses to sing patriotic anthems, in part because the veterans at St. John's are not invited to the ceremony. Although Rostkowski does not minimize the horrible aspects of war, she does not categorize participants as villains. Andrew and Paul volunteered to fight, which upset their families. Annie's grandmother makes sense of her son's death by accepting the community's declarations about the nobility of the conflict. Annie realizes that the older woman could not cope with the facts.

Annie's first-person account of her changing view of war and its effects also chronicles an adolescent's growing realization that she must form independent opinions. Although she idolizes her father, Annie challenges his attempts to spare her emotional pain.

Yet, Annie too has trouble letting go as Andrew becomes more independent. Her reluctance to allow him to make decisions that will take him away parallels her parents' reluctance to have Annie enter adulthood.

From the post-World War I setting of *After the Dancing Days,* Rostkowski shifts to the war between the United States and Vietnam in *The Best of Friends.* Dan Ulvang and Will Spencer are about to graduate from high school. Dan's younger sister Sarah has been friends with both for years. However, their relationships undergo many changes, some of them precipitated by the escalating Vietnam conflict. Sarah's opposition to the war leads her to distribute anti-war materials on the community college campus where her father works as a janitor. Mr. Ulvang's devotion to discipline and duty extends to his service as head of the local draft board. Dan, a brilliant student who strives to meet his father's standards, has ignored the war because he is certain to receive a college deferment. Will, an indifferent student, has allowed Dan to help him through high school and make many decisions. Yet, Will refuses to be pushed by Dan into attending college to avoid the military. His enlistment severs their ties and calls into question his tentative romance with Sarah.

What is intriguing is the portrayal of young men's and women's decisions about participation in the Vietnam war. Although concern about politics is a factor, information about the war is scanty for Will, Dan, and Sarah. Will enlists before graduation, as much to prove to Dan he can make his own decisions as to serve his country. Sarah and Dan both react initially to Will's choice in terms of how he had rejected their influences. But Will's action motivates Dan to take a stand against the war and face his father, who sees Will only as a statistic in filling a monthly draft quota. By turning in his draft card, Dan contemplates a future as uncertain as Will's. At the novel's end Will and Dan face the consequences of the individual decisions they have made. Rostkowski not only leaves off a happy ending, she refuses to provide a conventional ending at all.

Rostkowski's third novel, *Moon Dancer,* is more predictable in structure. Told by fifteen-year-old Mira Galbraith, the story takes place in southern Utah during a four-day exploration of a canyon once inhabited by the Hisatsinom. Mira's cousin Emily has arranged the expedition as part of her women's studies senior project at the University of Utah. Emily is accompanied by Max, a college friend skilled in rock climbing. Mira and her older sister Jenny have joined the exploration at the urging of their mother, a photographer/scholar whose discovery of an old journal gave Emily the impetus to explore the area. One hundred years earlier Katie Weston had homesteaded alone, explored remote sites, and recorded Indian drawings in a sketchbook. Emily hopes to locate and photograph the drawings to document Katie's observations.

For Jenny, who relies on looks and charm to get what she wants, the primitive camping conditions fuel constant complaints. She clashes with the supremely organized Emily, whose chief concern is checking off the sites in Katie's journal. Mira, however, experiences an immediate affinity both for Katie's attraction to the sites and for the ancient people who had made the drawings. With almost mystical insights she constructs a narrative to provide connections among the various drawings. Because most hinge on mother-daughter relationships, the parallel need for her to resolve those issues in her own life seems obvious. Brief remembrances of her interactions with her own mother do not provide enough information for readers to understand the problematic relations between Jenny and Mira and their mother. The developing romance between Max and Mira surprises her since she has assumed all males will prefer the beautiful, flirtatious Jenny. Serious involvement is precluded by a climbing accident in which Mira injures her ankle, and the other three must cooperate in her rescue.

In *After the Dancing Days,* Rostkowski achieves a complex mingling of subplots and themes while creating an impressive set of major and supporting characters. Although her subsequent novels have not met that standard, they reveal her continued efforts to place questions of family relationships in larger societal and historical perspectives.

—Kathy Piehl

RUBINSTEIN, Gillian (Margaret)

Nationality: Australian. **Born:** Potten End, Hertfordshire, 29 August 1942. **Education:** Queen Anne's, Caversham, Berkshire, 1954-60; Lady Margaret Hall, Oxford, 1961-64, B.A. and M.A. (honors) in modern languages; Stockwell College, University of London, postgraduate diploma in education 1973. **Family:** Married Philip Rubinstein in 1973 (second marriage); one son and two daughters. **Career:** Research assistant, London School of Economics, 1964-65; administrative officer, Greater London Council, 1965-66; editor, Tom Stacey, publishers, London, 1969-72. Has also worked as a cook, cleaner, script assessor, part-time editor, journalist, and film critic; free-lance writer, since 1986. **Awards:** Children's Book Council of Australia honor book, 1987, Australian Children's Literature Peace prize, 1987, Australian National Children's Book award, 1988, and Young Australians Best Book award, 1990, all for *Space Demons*; Australian Council Literature Arts Board fellowship, 1988 and 1989-92; New South Wales Premier's award, 1988, and Children's Book Council of Australia honor book, 1989, both for *Answers to Brut*; Children's Book Council of Australia Book of the Year for Older Readers, 1989, and Adelaide Festival of Arts National Children's Book award, 1990, both for *Beyond the Labyrinth*; Children's Book Council of Australia honor book, 1989, and New South Wales Family Therapy Association Family award for Children's Books—Highly Recommended, 1989, both for *Melanie and the Night Animal*; Children's Book Council of Australia shortlist, 1990, for *Skymaze*; Children's Book Council of Australia honor book, 1993 and Victorian Premier's award Shortlist, 1993, for *Galax-Arena*; Parent's Choice Award for picture books, 1994, for *Dog In, Cat Out*; Australian Multicultural Children's Book Award, 1993, for *Mr. Plunkett's Pool*; Children's Book Council of Australia notable book, 1991, for *Flashback The Amazing Adventures of a Film Horse*, 1992, for *At Ardilla* and *Squawk and Screech* and *Dog In, Cat Out,* 1993, for *Mr. Plunkett's Pool,* 1994, for *The Giant's Tooth,* 1996, for *Jake and Pete,* 1997, for *Shinkei,* 1997 for *Sharon Keep Your Hair On*; Children's Book Council Book of the Year, 1995, for *Foxspell.* **Agent:** Jenny Darling, Australian Literary Management, 2-A Armstrong Street, Middle Park, Victoria 3206, Australia. **Address:** 29 Seaview Road, Lynton, South Australia 5062, Australia. **E-mail Address:** gillyru@ozemail.com.au.

PUBLICATIONS FOR YOUNG ADULTS

Fiction

Space Demons. Adelaide, Omnibus, 1986; New York, Dial Press, 1988.
Answers to Brut. Adelaide, Omnibus, 1988; London, Mammoth, 1991.
Beyond the Labyrinth. Melbourne, Hyland House, 1988; New York, Orchard Books and London, Mandarin, 1990.
Melanie and the Night Animal. Adelaide, Omnibus, 1988.
Skymaze. Adelaide, Omnibus, 1989; London, Mammoth, 1990; New York, Orchard Books, 1991.
Flashback: The Amazing Adventures of a Film Horse. Ringwood, Victoria, Penguin, 1990; London, Mammoth, 1991.
At Ardilla. Adelaide, Omnibus, 1991; London, Heinemann, 1991.
Galax-Arena. Melbourne, Hyland House, 1992; London Heinemann, 1993.
Foxspell. Melbourne, Hyland House, 1994; New York, Simon and Schuster, 1996.
Shinkei. Norwood, Omnibus, 1996.
Under the Cat's Eye. Sydney, Hodder Headline, 1997.

Other

Editor, *After Dark.* Adelaide, Omnibus, 1988.
Editor, *Before Dawn.* Adelaide, Omnibus, 1988.
Melanie and the Night Animal (play, for Patch Theatre Company, 1990).
Galax-Arena (play, produced by Patch Theatre and Adelaide Festival Centre Trust, Playhouse, 1995).
Witch Music (collected short stories). Melbourne, Hyland House, 1996.
Annie's Brother's Suit (collected short stories). Melbourne, Hyland House, 1996.

PUBLICATIONS FOR CHILDREN

Fiction

Squawk and Screech, illustrated by Craig Smith. Adelaide, Omnibus, 1991.
Keep Me Company, illustrated by Lorraine Hannay. Ringwood, Victoria, Viking, 1992.
Mr. Plunkett's Pool, illustrated by Terry Denton. Milson's Point, NSW, Random House, 1992.
Dog In, Cat Out, illustrated by Ann James. New York, Ticknor & Fields, and London, Hodder and Stoughton, 1993.
Giant's Tooth, illustrated by Craig Smith. Ringwood, Victoria, Viking, 1993.
Jake and Pete, illustrated by Terry Denton. Milson's Point, Random House, 1995.
Sharon Keep Your Hair On, illustrated by David Mackintosh. Milson's Point, Random House, 1996.
Jake and Pete and the Stray Dogs, illustrated by Terry Denton. Milson's Point, Random House, 1997.

Other

New Baby (play, for Magpie Theatre, 1989).
Alice in Wonderland (adaptation, for Magpie Theatre, 1989).
Paula (play, for Patch Theatre, 1992).

Wake Baby (play, for Out of the Box and Company Skylark, 1996).
Jake and Pete (adaptation, for Theatre of Image, 1997).
Each Beach (play, for Patch Theatre and AFCT, 1997).

*

Media Adaptations: *Space Demons* (by Robert Tulloch, Next Wave Festival, Melbourne, 1990) Sydney, Omnibus/Penguin, 1993; *Beyond the Labyrinth* (by Carolyn Burns, Patch Theatre Company, produced Space theatre, Adelaide Festival Centre, 1991); *The Giant's Tooth* (ABC-TV, 1995).

*   *   *

Gillian Rubinstein considers herself a writer for children, yet she is widely read and discussed by young adults and adults. Her status and popularity became instantly established with the publication of her first book, *Space Demons,* which also indicated her interests and concerns. Here, she places a group of children in front of a computer game which turns out to be fiendishly difficult and also fiendish in intent. To play the game fully, the children must be prepared to be physically drawn into it. Their life situations and emotional states influence their game-playing decisions and they must make sophisticated, complex, and moral choices which are eventually refined into "refusing to hate."

Rubinstein came to Australia as an adult from the United Kingdom. She speaks freely of having had an unhappy childhood and having felt totally powerless. These emotions inform and fuel her writing plus her constant interest in the outsider and in the patterns of family scapegoating. Like other writers for young people, Rubinstein is keenly aware of the impact of television, computer, and video games. She actively works towards structuring her books and engaging her readers by using similar strategies: multiple viewpoints, rapid "scene changes," and fast-paced, exciting adventure scenarios.

In *Skymaze,* a sequel to *Space Demons,* the same four children become involved in the hypergame "Skymaze," mysteriously sent to Andrew from Japan. Again a breathtaking, dangerous sequence is played out, and again the children's real life frustrations and anxieties are reflected in how they play and react to the game. Her books are avidly read by young people who admit they are not easily engaged by fiction.

Brenton, the protagonist of *Beyond the Labyrinth,* is an angry, bright, sensitive boy. He is obsessed with a role-playing game where life-determining decisions are made by the roll of a dice. He is also haunted by the threat of nuclear war. His mother is determined to maintain the illusion of a happy family, while his father bullies those around him, often with the help of alcohol and often using Brenton as a scapegoat.

Into their lives come the dark, alien anthropologist Cal and a phantom graffiti artist who daubs variations of the letters "dead end" everywhere. Set against an idyllic seaside landscape, the book questions our attitudes toward the environment, nuclear arms and war, other cultures, and children in the context of a powerful but pared down narrative. At the end of this complex, many faceted, shimmering contemporary tale, the reader is invited to roll the dice and choose alternative endings. Yet a careful reading and the relative placement of the two endings leave little doubt as to the author's view on which ending is the preferred one.

Rubinstein has written for the theatre and also a number of picture books and stories for younger readers. These are generally sunnier, though still devoted to looking at how families function and children see and respond to their world. Several of the stories look with sly humour at pompous power struggles and the human need to claim territory.

At Ardilla is also widely read beyond its implied readership. Rubinstein has frequently commented on the lack of acceptable and safe rite-of-passage activities for young people in western society. She believes this leads to many dangerous risk-taking activities such as experimenting with drugs and reckless driving. "Tense, moody, difficult Jen" is on the cusp of adolescence. Each summer her family moves to their beach house Ardilla, with one other family. This year Jen's father has invited a divorced friend and his children. This invasion is the last straw for Jen whose moodiness and resentment sour the holiday. What Jen is really fighting is change. She does not want to let go of the magic places and emblematic games of childhood. Like Jen's perceptions, the story hovers between a fully realised world of family activities, tensions, conversations, and the fantasy world of Jen's subconscious. After a cathartic near-drowning, Jen is able to "go forward, through the darkness." She is consoled and focused through her commitment to music and the support of her immediate family.

Families in Rubinstein's stories are not always supportive and she has produced a number of tough, unflattering portraits of adults. In *Galax-Arena* the one significant adult character is Hythe. All the images present him as an effective but unfeeling and manipulative animal trainer. Rubinstein is a great animal lover and here she draws possibly unwelcome parallels between methods of capturing, training, and subjugating animals with the way societies in different parts of the world treat children.

The "peb" are children captured after they have been in some way abandoned. Peter, Liane, and Joella are on their way to stay with an aunt because their mother has taken off and their much older father is feckless and erratic. As Joella, the narrator, observes, "People on journeys are easy to make disappear." Hythe has obviously been on the watch. He drugs them, kidnaps them, and takes to join the other children at the Galax-Arena. Here the children are isolated and rigorously trained to perform ever more daring acrobatic feats for the invisible Vexa. Those, like Joella, who do not have innate athletic ability or who cannot be cajoled or coerced into becoming single-mindedly competitive are, at worst, disposed of or, at best, placed in a "tank" as playthings for the Vexa.

The children develop an uneasy community and a "patwa" language (there is a glossary) to enable them to communicate.

Galax-Arena is brilliantly imagined and full of tension and menace. The scenes of training and performance are both exhilarating and terrifying, as is the sudden reversal of the plot halfway through. Eventually, the purpose of the Galax-Arena is revealed, and this in turn raises questions about the responsibilities of scientists and the purposes to which science and scarce resources are put.

Joella is an unlikely hero. As Rubinstein has said: "Joella's very ordinariness keeps her whole. . . . In my books. . .the boys set the action in motion. . . . They tend to be less well-adjusted, more vulnerable, more violent. . . . The girls end up having to put things right again" (*Magpies,* May 1993).

Rubinstein's vision may be bleak, but she shows young people as having the capacity to be compassionate, imaginative, and resourceful. Her tightly plotted narratives move seamlessly from reality to fantasy and, while they incorporate tough issues, they do so in ways that seem to both entertain and empower readers.

—Agnes Nieuwenhuizen

RUBY, Lois

Nationality: American. **Born:** San Francisco, California, 11 September 1942. **Education:** University of California, Berkeley, B.A. 1964; San Jose State College (now California State University), San Jose, M.A. 1968. **Family:** Married Thomas Ruby, a clinical psychologist, in 1965; three sons. **Career:** Young adult librarian, Dallas Public Library, Texas, 1965-67; art and music librarian, University of Missouri-Columbia, 1967-68; synagogue librarian, Temple Emanu-EL, Wichita, Kansas, since 1974; creative writing instructor, since 1985; youth group advisor, 1975-90; trustee, Wichita Public Library, since 1997. **Awards:** Best Books For Young Adults citation, American Library Association (ALA), 1977, for *Arriving at a Place You've Never Left*, and 1984, for *Miriam's Well*; Notable Children's Trade Book in the field of social studies citation, National Council for Social Studies and the Children's Book Council, 1982, for *Two Truths in My Pocket*, and 1995, for *Steal Away Home*; Fifty Notable Children's Books of Jewish Interest, 1980-84, for *Two Truths in My Pocket*; Books for the Teen Age, New York Public Library, 1994, for *Miriam's Well*, 1994, for *Skin Deep*, and 1996, for *Steal Away Home*; Sequoia Young Adult Award list, Oklahoma, 1995-96, for *Miriam's Well*; Young Adults' Choices, International Reading Association, 1996, for *Steal Away Home*; State reader's choice awards lists for *Steal Away Home* include: Charlotte Award, New York, 1996; California Young Reader's Medal, 1996-97; Sunshine State Award, Florida, 1996; William Allen White Award, Kansas, 1996-97; Heartland Award, Kansas, 1996; Tennessee Young Readers' Award, 1997; and Golden Sower Award, Nebraska, 1997-98; first prize, fiction category, Kansas Authors' Club, 1987, and honorable mention, *Writer's Digest* short story competition, 1991, for "Jubilee Year"; Professional Celebrate Literacy Award, Wichita Area Reading Council, 1996. **Agent:** William Reiss, John Hawkins and Associates, 71 West 23rd St., New York, New York 10010. **Address:** 9310 Shannon Woods Circle, Wichita, Kansas 67226, U.S.A. **E-mail Address:** ruby6200@aol.com.

PUBLICATIONS FOR YOUNG ADULTS

Fiction

Arriving at a Place You've Never Left. New York, Dial, 1977.
What Do You Do in Quicksand? New York, Viking, 1979.
Two Truths in My Pocket (short stories). New York, Viking, 1982.
This Old Man. Boston, Houghton, 1984.
Pig-Out Inn. Boston, Houghton, 1987.
Miriam's Well. New York, Scholastic, 1993.
Skin Deep. New York, Scholastic, 1994.
Steal Away Home. New York, Simon & Schuster, 1994.

*

Biography: Essay in *Speaking for Ourselves, Too*, compiled and edited by Donald R. Gallo, National Council of Teachers of English, 1993.

Lois Ruby comments:

At a recent school visit, kids asked me if I write mysteries; no. Science fiction? Fantasy? No, no. Animal stories? Ghost stories? Love stories? No, no, no. Just as I was beginning to feel like a useless worm with no business masquerading as a writer, one girl asked, "Well, what *do* you write?" Ah, a chance to redeem myself! "I write stories about typical young people," I said, "contemporary and historical people, who are plucked from their ordinary lives and dropped down into extraordinary situations." There, that explained it, didn't it?

The thing is, I'm not interested in fantasy and ghosts. Real life is spooky enough and endlessly fascinating—families, relationships, daily life-and-death decisions, school dilemmas, dislocations, broken hearts, love and loss, human rights, civil rights, and personal victories. Each of us is made for quiet heroism. So, for example, the fireman who storms into a burning building to rescue a child is far less interesting to me than the child who heroically survives the ordeal.

The only way I know to write is to begin with a character who comes to me, uninvited, who takes over my mind, taps me on the shoulder, and whispers, "I have a story. Ask me the right questions, and you may even have my story." So, I begin to interview that character until I see whether he or she interests me enough to probe still deeper. Once I know about the relationships and conflicts in that character's life, I file all these impressions away in my head and begin about two years of research to get the time, place, and technical or historical detail pinned down, because I don't believe you should write what you know. I believe you should write what you *want* to know, then go find out about it.

All right, the characters have been percolating and the research is well underway, and one day something amazing happens: the story begins chugging down a track, writing itself. Then all I have to do is chase it with a nice, flowing pen in my hand.

Sometimes people ask if I'm ever going to write a *real* book, as if writing about teenagers isn't respectable work. The fact is, teenagers are far more interesting and complex than most adults I know. Adults get stuck in place, but those characters rattling around in my head change day by day, minute to minute.

As long as they keep talking to me, I'll keep recording their stories. If the voices stop, I guess I'll go get a job at Wal-Mart.

* * *

Societal conventions do not inhibit Lois Ruby where writing is concerned. Her works deal with taboo subjects including prostitution, teenage pregnancy, child abuse, and interfaith relationships. The pull of modern society on such institutions as marriage and religion is explored from every angle. Ruby's skillful incorporation of these themes into detailed story lines results in compelling fiction that is relevant to today's young people.

Ruby's first book, *Arriving at a Place You've Never Left*, is a collection of seven short stories in which the very human characters fail to realize that their problems are universal. "Faces at a Dark Window" is a chillingly accurate portrayal of a mother's nervous breakdown, related by her daughter. When a teenager becomes an unwed mother, her boyfriend realizes that he has abandoned not only her but the baby in "Found by a Lost Child." Separation for the sake of finances intervenes in a love affair in "Heads You Go, Tails I Stay." "Justice" and fairness are at issue in the case of an adolescent boy who has killed his abusive father. "Spring" is about a terminally ill teenager coming to terms with his impending death. A boarding school plagued by a rash of thefts is the setting for "Like a Toy on the End of a String." "Arriving at a Place You've Never Left" deals with a Jewish girl whose family escaped the Holocaust only to have to flee a bigoted American town.

Ruby sketches the fine line between normalcy and mental illness in the novel *What Do You Do in Quicksand?* Matt Russell is only seventeen and already a father. Baby Barbara's mother does not want her, and Matt cannot stand the idea of someone else having her, so he accepts his responsibility. Leah McCauley Burke Aaronson, his next-door neighbor and a victim of sexual abuse, takes an instant attraction to Barbara, but things nearly get out of hand as Leah's unstable personality reveals itself. Not a model of perfection himself, Matt grows up in a hurry when he has to, and finally leaves with his baby to establish a life for the two of them.

Ruby returns to short fiction with *Two Truths in My Pocket,* in which each of the six stories has a Jewish theme. In "Inscriptions on Stone," a boy worries about not becoming a rabbi to follow in his father's footsteps, until his sister announces that she will carry on the tradition. A brain-damaged girl gets her wish for religious instruction in "Forgetting Me, Remembering Me." A young Jew falls in love with his English teacher in "Lighter Than Air." "Hasty Vows" deals with a girl's resurgence of faith during the Yom Kippur holiday. "Strangers in the Land of Egypt" is about the relationship of a Jewish couple who are of different races. The "Frail Bridge" of mortality is at issue as a young girl mourns her Bubbie that she never knew as a real person.

Sixteen-year-old Greta Janssen is the common link between two "old men"—one an ancient Chinese patriarch and the other a pimp—in the novel *This Old Man.* The daughter of a prostitute, Greta is living in a group home to escape going to work for the pimp when she meets Wing, a young Chinese-American who is caring for his Chinese-born grandfather. Greta has a love-hate relationship with both old men: the old grandfather resents her because she is not Chinese, and the pimp only sees her as a money-maker. In the end, she realizes that she can stand up to people and choose her own fate.

Dovie Chandler learns that other people's lives can be worse than her own in *Pig-Out Inn.* Dovie feels that her life is rootless because her mother is constantly on the move, but she realizes what real family problems are when a nine-year-old boy is left by his father at the Pig-Out Inn, Dovie's nickname for her mother's truck stop and latest business venture. Tag has been kidnapped from his mother, who has custody of him, and complications follow until a fair visitation schedule is arranged. Dovie's mother gives up the Pig-Out Inn, and the reader finds that a more mature Dovie is ready to face her uncertain future.

Miriam's Well treats both modern legal problems and ancient religious traditions. Seventeen-year-old Miriam Pelham is diagnosed with a treatable bone cancer, but she belongs to a strict religious sect which believes that only faith can cure illness. Her *pro bono* lawyer, Mr. Bergen, is determined to defend her First Amendment rights to refuse treatment. However, his son Adam is falling in love with Miriam and does not want to see her die. Eventually, under duress, Miriam receives some medical treatment (conventional and nonconventional) as well as faith healing. She does recover, but the cause of her remission cannot be determined. Even though "Miriam's well," she and Adam realize that their relationship cannot endure.

With *Skin Deep* and *Steal Away Home,* Ruby approached racial issues. The latter, its title from an old spiritual, takes place both in modern times and in the years before the Civil War, when Kansas was a tense battleground for the question of whether slavery should spread westward. In *Skin Deep,* the setting is thoroughly modern and timely: angered by various experiences, Dan turns to white supremacy as a way of trying to settle his personal problems on a political level. He drifts into a gang while his girlfriend Laurel (and the narrator herself) looks on in dismay. Critics questioned the "contrivance" evident in certain aspects of these stories—character making speeches about racism, for instance. Yet both books are unquestionably imbued with Ruby's good will toward her characters and her readers, and she skillfully manages difficult topics and difficult literary motifs.

While not everyone lives happily ever after in Ruby's books, answers are found that work—at least for the present—and these young adults are able to pick up the pieces and go on with their lives. In Ruby's tales, there is no lack of courage on the part of the characters or the writer.

—Sharon Clontz Bernstein, updated by Judson Knight

RYE, Anthony. *See* **CHRISTOPHER, John.**

RYLANT, Cynthia

Nationality: American. **Born:** Hopewell, Virginia, 6 June 1954. **Education:** Morris Harvey College (now University of Charleston), West Virginia, 1973-75, B.A. in English 1975; Marshall University, Huntington, West Virginia, 1975-76, M.A. in English 1976; Kent State University, Kent, Ohio, 1980-81, M.L.S. 1982. **Family:** Has one son. **Career:** Writer. Part-time English instructor, Marshall University, Huntington, West Virginia, 1979-80; children's librarian, Akron Public Library, Akron, Ohio, 1983; part-time English lecturer, University of Akron, Akron, 1983-84; part-time lecturer, Northeast Ohio Universities College of Medicine, Rootstown, Ohio, since 1991. **Awards:** Named a *Booklist* reviewer's choice, 1982, Caldecott Honor Book, American Library Association (ALA) notable book, and Reading Rainbow selection, all 1983, all for *When I Was Young in the Mountains;* American Book award nomination, 1983, and English Speaking Union Book-across-the-Sea Ambassador of Honor award, 1984, both for *When I Was Young in the Mountains;* named an ALA notable book, a *School Library Journal* best book of 1984, a National Council for Social Studies best book, 1984, and a Society of Midland Authors best children's book, 1985, all for *Waiting to Waltz: A Childhood;* named a *New York Times* best illustrated, a *Horn Book* honor book, a Child Study Association of America's children's book of the year, all 1985, and a Caldecott Honor Book, 1986, all for *The Relatives Came;* named a Child Study Association of America's children's book of the year, 1985, for *A Blue-eyed Daisy;* named a *School Library Journal* best book, 1985, for *Every Living Thing;* named a *Parents' Choice* selection, 1986, and a Newbery Honor Book, 1987, for *A Fine White Dust; Boston Globe/Horn Book* award for nonfiction, 1991, for *Appalachia: The Voices of Sleeping Birds;* Garden State Children's Book award, Children's Services Section of the New Jersey Library Association, 1992, for *Henry and Mudge Get the Cold Shivers; Boston Globe/Horn Book* award, 1992, Newbery medal, 1993, both for *Missing May.*

PUBLICATIONS FOR YOUNG ADULTS

Fiction

A Blue-eyed Daisy. New York, Bradbury, 1985; as *Some Year for Ellie,* illustrated by Kate Rogers, Viking Kestrel, 1986.
A Fine White Dust. New York, Bradbury, 1986.
A Kindness. New York, Orchard Books, 1989.
A Couple of Kooks: And Other Stories about Love. New York, Orchard Books, 1990.
Missing May. New York, Orchard Books, 1992.
I Had Seen Castles. San Diego, Harcourt Brace, 1993.
The Dreamer, illustrated by Barry Moser. New York, Blue Sky Press, 1993.

Poetry

Waiting to Waltz: A Childhood, illustrated by Stephen Gammell. New York, Bradbury, 1984.
Soda Jerk, illustrated by Peter Catalanotto. New York, Orchard Books, 1990.
Something Permanent, photographs by Walker Evans. San Diego, Harcourt Brace, 1994.

Other

But I'll Be Back Again: An Album. New York, Orchard Books, 1989.
Appalachia: The Voices of Sleeping Birds, illustrated by Barry Moser. New York, Harcourt, 1991.
Best Wishes, photographs by Carlo Ontal. New York, Owen, 1992.
Margaret, Frank, and Andy: Three Writers' Stories. San Diego, Harcourt Brace, 1996.

PUBLICATIONS FOR CHILDREN

Fiction

When I Was Young in the Mountains, illustrated by Diane Goode. New York, Dutton, 1982.
Miss Maggie, illustrated by Thomas DiGrazia. New York, Dutton. 1983.
This Year's Garden, illustrated by Mary Szilagyi. New York, Bradbury, 1984.
Every Living Thing (stories). New York, Bradbury, 1985.
The Relatives Came, illustrated by Stephen Gammell. New York, Bradbury, 1985.
Night in the Country, illustrated by Mary Szilagyi. New York, Bradbury, 1986.

Birthday Presents, illustrated by Sucie Stevenson. New York, Orchard Books, 1987.
Children of Christmas: Stories for the Season, illustrated by Stephen D. Schindler. New York, Orchard Books, 1987; as *Silver Packages and Other Stories,* London, Orchard Books, 1987; as *Silver Packages: An Appalachian Christmas Story,* illustrated by Chris K. Soentpiet. New York, Orchard Books, 1997.
All I See, illustrated by Peter Catalanotto. New York, Orchard Books, 1988.
Mr. Griggs' Work, illustrated by Julie Downing. New York, Orchard Books, 1989.
An Angel for Solomon Singer, illustrated by Peter Catalanotto. New York, Orchard Books, 1992.
The Everyday Books series: *The Everyday Children, The Everyday Garden, The Everyday House, The Everyday School, The Everyday Town, The Everyday Pets,* illustrated by the author. New York, Bradbury, 5 vols., 1993.
Mr. Putter and Tabby series: *Mr. Putter and Tabby Bake the Cake* [*Pour the Tea, Walk the Dog, Pick the Pears, Fly the Plane, Row the Boat, Take the Train, Toot the Horn*], illustrated by Arthur Howard. San Diego, Harcourt Brace, 8 vols., 1994-99; first vol. published San Diego, Harcourt Brace, 1994.
Dog Heaven, illustrated by the author. New York, Blue Sky Press, 1995.
Gooseberry Park, illustrated by Arthur Howard. San Diego, Harcourt Brace, 1995.
The Van Gogh Cafe. San Diego, Harcourt Brace, 1995.
The Old Woman Who Named Things, illustrated by Kathryn Brown. San Diego, Harcourt Brace, 1996.
The Bookshop Dog. New York, Blue Sky Press/Scholastic, 1996.
The Whales. New York, Blue Sky Press, 1996.
The Blue Hill Meadows, illustrated by Ellen Beier. San Diego, Harcourt Brace, 1997.
The Blue Hill Meadows and the Much-loved Dog, illustrated by Ellen Beier. San Diego, Harcourt Brace, 1997.
Cat Heaven, illustrated by the author. New York, Blue Sky Press, 1997.
Poppleton series: *Poppleton, Poppleton and Friends, Poppleton Everyday, Poppleton Forever, Poppleton in Spring,* illustrated by Mark Teague. New York, Blue Sky Press, 1997.
Scarecrow, illustrated by Lauren Stringer. San Diego, Harcourt Brace, 1997.
An Everyday Book. New York, Simon & Schuster Books, 1997.
Bear Day, illustrated by Jennifer Selby. San Diego, Harcourt Brace, 1998.
Bless Us All: A Child's Yearbook of Blessings, illustrated by the author. New York, Simon & Schuster, 1998.
The Bird House, illustrated by Barry Moser. New York, Blue Sky Press, 1998.
The Cobble Street Cousins series: *The Cobble Street Cousins: A Little Shopping,* [*In Aunt Lucy's Kitchen, Some Good News, Special Gifts*], illustrated by Wendy Anderson Halperin. New York, Simon & Schuster, 4 vols., 1998-99.
The Islander. New York, DK Ink, 1998.
Tulip Sees America, illustrated by Lisa Desimini. New York, Blue Sky Press, 1998.
The Cookie-store Cat. New York, Blue Sky Press, 1999.
Bunny Bungalow, illustrated by Nancy Hayashi. San Diego, Harcourt Brace, 1999.

In November, illustrated by Jill Kastner. San Diego, Harcourt Brace, 1999.
Thimbleberry Stories, illustrated by Maggie Kneen. San Diego, Harcourt Brace, 2000.
The Ticky-tacky Doll, illustrated by Harvey Stevenson. San Diego, Harcourt Brace, 2000.

Other (readers)

Henry and Mudge [*in Puddle Trouble, in the Green Time, under the Yellow Moon, in the Sparkle Days, and the Forever Sea, Get the Cold Shivers, and the Happy Cat, and the Bedtime Thumps, Take the Big Test, and the Long Weekend, and the Wild Wind, and the Careful Cousin, and the Best Day of All, in the Family Trees, and the Sneaky Crackers, and the Starry Night, and Annie's Good Move, and the Snowman Plan, and Annie's Perfect Pet, and the Funny Lunch, and the Tall Tree House, and Mrs. Hopper's house, and the Great Grandpas, a Very Special Merry Christmas, and the Wild Goose Chase, and the Big Sleepover, and the Tumbling Trip*], illustrated by Sucie Stevenson. New York, Bradbury Press, 28 vols., 1987-99; first vol. published London, Gollancz, 1989.

*

Media Adaptations: *When I Was Young in the Mountains* (filmstrip), Random House, 1983; *This Year's Garden* (filmstrip), Random House, 1983; *The Relatives Came* (filmstrip), Random House, 1986. Several of Rylant's books are available on film through American School Publishers.

Biography: Entry in *Sixth Book of Junior Authors,* New York, H.W. Wilson, 1989; essay in *Something about the Author Autobiography Series,* Volume 13, Detroit, Gale, 1991; essay in *Speaking for Ourselves, Too* compiled and edited by Donald R. Gallo, National Council of Teachers of English, 1993; essay in *Authors and Artists for Young Adults,* Volume 10, Detroit, Gale, 1993.

Manuscript Collections: Special Collections, Kent State University, Ohio.

Critical Studies: Entry in *Children's Literature Review,* Volume 15, Detroit, Gale, 1988, pp. 167-174.

*   *   *

Reflective, capable teens coping with life in rural or small town settings people the poems, short stories, and novels of Cynthia Rylant. Chip takes care of his single mom in *A Kindness;* Summer overcomes her own grief to encourage her uncle to keep living without his wife in *Missing May;* and the young man behind the fountain in *Soda Jerk* observes a universe of familiar stereotypes even though the drugstore owner thinks, "I've just been making sodas." Some critics question the believability of such perceptive teens, but Rylant respects her protagonists and unveils their individuality and vulnerability in tightly woven plots centering on everyday crises.

Rylant's *A Fine White Dust,* winner of a Newbery Honor Award, is a brave novel dealing with religion, a controversial topic for young-adult books. Peter becomes deeply religious and falls under the spell of the charismatic Preacher Man, who ultimately betrays him, leaving Peter to grapple with the betrayal and disillusionment. As he fingers the fine white dust of a broken ceramic cross he painted in bible school, before he became too cool to attend, he questions his blind faith in God.

It is Rylant's characters that the reader will remember, but she is adept at providing a sense of place within her writings. Small town life in the mountains of Virginia and West Virginia feels slow, almost claustrophobic, yet comfortable, a place the reader recognizes as safe. Summer's Uncle's beat-up house trailer on a hillside with whirligigs in the garden and Maywell's drugstore on Main Street become vivid images in the reader's mind. Rylant has lived in these places and stood elbow to elbow with the local people; she refers to places, characters, and events that turn up in her books in her autobiography, *But I'll Be Back Again: An Album.* Rylant chronicles her own coming of age in the 1960s in *Waiting to Waltz: A Childhood,* a series of autobiographical poems portraying the awkwardness of adolescence as well as the certainty of a young woman who has accomplished a goal. Readers will find themselves matching places from her autobiography and autobiographical poetry to the settings of her stories.

In interviews, Rylant has said she doesn't like neat, happy endings because life is much too complex. In *A Couple of Kooks: And Other Stories about Love,* two teens talk to their unborn baby about the things it should remember once it has been adopted, "And I'd keep you if I could but I truly can't, we don't have money or a place of our own." In another story, a grandfather watching the people and events at his granddaughter's wedding realizes he has missed passion: "I have not yet met anyone for whom I might wear strange hats or sing imbecilic songs or dance the limbo or completely flip-flop religions."

But Rylant's books are hopeful. The characters, although usually odd or different in some way, have humor and compassion. Their futures may not be certain, but they will meet the challenges with the help of the diverse families, friends, and acquaintances that people their tightly knit, rustic communities. In *Missing May,* Cletus, an absolute lunatic according to Summer, uses his collection of unusual photos to distract Uncle Ob from his grief; Chip's wisdom in *A Kindness* helps his mother's situation work out the best it possibly could; and Ernie from *A Couple of Kooks* grows flowers to brighten his days and the lives of the people who visit Stan's hardware store. In her autobiography, Rylant describes the pain of being left with grandparents at the age of four and the restorative power of families and communities: "I lay in my grandparents' bed and cried in agony as everyone stood in the driveway, saying goodbye to my mother as she got in the car. . . . Luckily, though, in that small white house lived those who could help me heal. I had two uncles and two aunts and two cousins and two grandparents. . .and they all loved me."

Rylant's books are a celebration of people and places. The picture book format of *Soda Jerk* and *But, I'll Be Back Again* may confuse some young adults, but their sophistication and emotional honesty engage readers of all ages. All of Rylant's stories, including her picture story books marketed for younger readers, create memorable characters and places and provide teens a window on the world. As the soda jerk says, ". . .and they leave behind / some secret with the jerk. / Tips are okay. / But the secrets are better."

—Hollis Lowery-Moore

S

SACHS, Marilyn (Stickle)

Nationality: American. **Born:** New York, New York, 18 December 1927. **Education:** Hunter College (now of the City University of New York), B.A. 1949; Columbia University, M.S. 1953. **Family:** Married Morris Sachs in 1947; one daughter, one son. **Career:** Librarian, Brooklyn Public Library, Brooklyn, New York, 1949-60, and San Francisco Public Library, 1961-67; writer. **Awards:** American Library Association (ALA) notable book citation, 1968, for *Veronica Ganz*, 1987, for *Fran Ellen's House*, and 1991, for *The Big Book for Peace*; *New York Times* outstanding book of the year awards, 1971, for *The Bears' House*, and 1973, for *A Pocket Full of Seeds*; *School Library Journal* best book of the year award, 1971, for *The Bears' House*, and 1973, for *The Truth about Mary Rose*; National Book award finalist, 1972, for *The Bears' House*; Jane Addams Children's Book Honor award, 1974, for *A Pocket Full of Seeds*; Silver Pencil award, Collective Propaganda van het Nederlandse Boek (Netherlands), 1974, for *The Truth about Mary Rose*, and 1977, for *Dorrie's Book*; Austrian Children's Book Prize, 1977, for *The Bears' House*; Garden State Children's Book award, 1978, for *Dorrie's Book*; *A Summer's Lease* was chosen one of *School Library Journal*'s best books for spring, 1979; *Fleet-Footed Florence* was selected as a children's choice by the International Reading Association, 1982; Association of Jewish Libraries award, 1983, for *Call Me Ruth*; *The Fat Girl* was chosen one of American Library Association's best books for young adults, 1984; Christopher award, 1986, for *Underdog*; Bay Area Book Reviewers Association award, 1988, for *Fran Ellen's House*, recognition of merit, George G. Stone Center for Children's Books, 1989, for *The Bear's House* and *Fran Ellen's House*; Jane Addams Children's Book award, 1990, for *The Big Book for Peace*. **Address:** 733 31st Ave., San Francisco, California 94121. U.S.A.

PUBLICATIONS FOR YOUNG ADULTS

Fiction

A Summer's Lease. New York, Dutton, 1979.
Bus Ride, illustrated by Amy Rowen. New York, Dutton, 1980.
Hello. . .Wrong Number, illustrated by Pamela Johnson. New York, Dutton, 1981.
Beach Towels, illustrated by Jim Spence. New York, Dutton, 1982.
Fourteen. New York, Dutton, 1983.
The Fat Girl. New York, Dutton, 1984; Oxford, Oxford University Press, 1985.
Thunderbird, illustrated by Jim Spence. New York, Dutton, 1985.
Baby Sister. New York, Dutton, 1986; Oxford, Oxford University Press, 1987.
Almost Fifteen. New York, Dutton, 1987; Oxford, Oxford University Press, 1988.
Fran Ellen's House. New York, Dutton, 1987.
Just Like a Friend. New York, Dutton, 1989.
At the Sound of the Beep. New York, Dutton, 1990.
Circles. New York, Dutton, 1991.

What My Sister Remembered. New York, Dutton, 1992.
Thirteen—Going on Seven. New York, Dutton, 1993.
Ghosts in the Family. New York, Dutton, 1995.
Another Day. New York, Dutton, 1997.

PUBLICATIONS FOR CHILDREN

Fiction

Amy Moves In, illustrated by Judith Gwyn Brown. New York, Doubleday, 1964.
Laura's Luck, illustrated by Ib Ohlsson. New York, Doubleday, 1965.
Amy and Laura, illustrated by Tracy Sugarman. New York, Doubleday, 1966.
Veronica Ganz, illustrated by Louis Glanzman. New York, Doubleday, 1968; London, Macdonald, 1969.
Peter and Veronica, illustrated by Louis Glanzman. New York, Doubleday, 1969; London, Macdonald, 1970.
Marv, illustrated by Louis Glanzman. New York, Doubleday, 1970.
The Bears' House, illustrated by Louis Glanzman. New York, Doubleday, 1971.
A Pocket Full of Seeds, illustrated by Ben Stahl. New York, Doubleday, 1973; London, Macdonald and Jane's, 1976.
The Truth about Mary Rose, illustrated by Glanzman. New York, Doubleday, and London, Macdonald, 1973.
Dorrie's Book, illustrated by Anne Sachs. New York, Doubleday, 1975; London, Macdonald and Jane's, 1976.
Matt's Mitt, illustrated by Hilary Knight. New York, Doubleday, 1975.
A December Tale. New York, Doubleday, 1976.
A Secret Friend. New York, Doubleday, 1978; London, Corgi, 1988.
Class Pictures. New York, Dutton, 1980.
Fleet-Footed Florence, illustrated by Charles Robinson. New York, Doubleday, 1981.
Call Me Ruth. New York, Doubleday, 1982.
Underdog. New York, Doubleday, 1985; Oxford, Oxford University Press, 1987.
Surprise Party. New York, Dutton, 1998.

Other

Reading between the Lines (play). New York, Children's Book Council, 1971.
Editor, with Ann Durell, *The Big Book for Peace,* illustrated by Thomas B. Allen. New York, Dutton, 1990.

*

Media Adaptations: *Veronica Ganz* (filmstrip), Insight Media Programs, 1975.

Biography: Entry in *Fourth Book of Junior Authors and Illustrators,* New York, H.W. Wilson, 1978; essay in *Something about the Author Autobiography Series,* Vol. 2, Detroit, Gale, 1986; essay in *Speaking for Ourselves: Autobiographical Sketches by Notable*

Authors of Books for Young Adults, Vol. 1, compiled and edited by Donald R. Gallo, National Council of Teachers of English, 1990.

Manuscript Collections: Kerlan Collection, University of Minnesota.

Critical Studies: Entry in *Children's Literature Review,* Vol. 2, Detroit, Gale, 1976; entry in *Contemporary Literary Criticism,* Vol. 35, Detroit, Gale, 1985.

Marilyn Sachs comments:

Books have always been a joy and comfort to me. They still are. Whenever the real world becomes too complicated, I can always retreat safely into some other world that books offer. Writing is nearly as great a pleasure as reading. And I feel proud that my books can offer young people another place to go safely.

*   *   *

A writer whose range includes fantasy, realism, history, tragedy, humor, love, and prejudice in a variety of realistic settings and eras, Marilyn Sachs has been one of the most popular writers for young adults for many years. She skillfully delves into the intricacies of family relationships, friendships of young people from entirely different backgrounds, and the horror facing Jewish families under the tyranny of the Nazi regime. She writes about romance, family catastrophes, feelings and fears of young people growing up; of death, social issues, and the need for kindness. It is clear that she is sympathetic to those more apt to lose than win, because many of her characters are young people who simply don't "fit in." She depicts them as struggling to find out who they are and where they are going.

Marv is a good example this type. He is a dreaming inventor, considered hopelessly stupid by most of his teachers and a failure by his older sister. He invents worthless objects unrecognizable for what he wants them to be, and usually leaves them unfinished, cluttering up the family's backyard. When Marv does invent something useful and cherished by his sister and also by all the little kids in the neighborhood, he wonders why his sister bursts into tears. A story about a dreamer, this is also a tale of a sister and brother loving each other in different ways, one showing love and the other not knowing how to receive it.

Being fourteen is tough enough, but having a mother writing books about her life in *Fourteen* makes Rebecca Jamison even more miserable. Sachs has combined humor and mystery in this story of a young girl encountering love for the first time with a boy from a somewhat shady family. This is a delightful story portraying an unusual romance of two young people, similar but different from that of Rebecca's mother when she first met Rebecca's father.

A heartrending story, *A Pocket Full of Seeds* tells of Nicole Nieman living in France during the Nazi occupation. Being Jewish, Nicole's family is taken away from their home by the Germans while Nicole is in school. When she finds them gone, Nicole wanders around aimlessly but ends up at her school where she decides to stay and wait for the end of the war, when she and her family will be reunited. Sachs has written a moving, lifelike story of a young Jewish girl facing the challenges of war and the bitter prejudice against the Jews. One can feel the terror and frustration as Nicole loses her family, and the doubt that Nicole will ever see them again. Sachs has dealt skillfully with the problem of fear that

people sometimes have when they are "different," which she does by showing Nicole maturing and becoming capable of facing life alone.

Almost Fifteen portrays Imogen Rogers, a young girl helping to supplement her family's income by babysitting. When she develops a crush on the father of the little boy for whom she babysits, she can think of nothing else but the young, handsome Adam Derman. Unfortunately, Mr. Derman does not return Imogen's feelings, and the girl is crestfallen. However, she snaps back to her vivacious self when she finds a new romance at her doctor's office. Sachs has created an amusing yet affecting story about an adolescent girl who deals with feelings that almost get out of hand. As she gets her romantic fantasies and dreams under control, however, she learns to become more responsible and dependable.

Dorrie's Book is a perceptive and cleverly written account of a young girl, always the center of attention in her family, who now faces the arrival of a new baby sibling. Dorrie's dialogue and feelings are amusing and not a little pitiable—especially when we discover that she has to deal with not just one new sister or brother, but screaming triplets.

Another poignant, comical, and thought-provoking book, *Class Pictures,* deals with the maturing of two very different best friends. The main character, dark, tall Pat Maddox, sees her friend Lolly Scheiner change over time from a fat wallflower to a beauty, and begins to feel left out of their friendship as Lolly's popularity increases. Pat turns to a former teacher for consolation, and finds herself in love with him, even though he is happily married and a father. Pat and Lolly's friendship becomes strained, but as the two girls mature, each facing problems at home, their friendship revives. Sachs has written sympathetically about a young girl facing facts: her mother will never grow up; her grandmother, who she has always considered her ally, is now happily married and living elsewhere; and her former teacher will always be part of her life—not as a lover, but as a beloved friend.

With *Ghosts in the Family* in 1995, Sachs opened herself up to criticism for her characters' didactic and "tidy" speeches on racism. Yet she makes an interesting and quite literal use of the image of a family ghost, not unlike the proverbial "skeleton in the closet." In this case the ghost serves as an symbol for the unpleasant secrets of Gabriella's family, not least of which is the bigotry of her father.

The recipient of many awards and honors, Marilyn Sachs rates high among young adult writers. A pioneer of contemporary realistic fiction, she deftly introduces appropriate social issues through characters with whom her readers can identify. Her more than thirty books, including those for younger readers, are always enlightening, unpredictable, and entertaining.

—Carol Doxey, updated by Judson Knight

SALINGER, J(erome) D(avid)

Nationality: American. **Born:** New York, New York, 1 January 1919. **Education:** McBurney School, New York, 1932-34; Valley Forge Military Academy, Pennsylvania (editor, *Crossed Sabres),* 1934-46; New York University, 1937; Ursinus College, Collegetown, Pennsylvania, 1938; Columbia University, New York, 1939. **Family:** Married 1) Sylvia Salinger in 1945 (divorced 1947); 2) Claire

Douglas in 1955 (divorced 1967), one daughter and one son. **Career:** Writer. Worked as an entertainer on the Swedish liner *M.S. Kungsholm* in the Caribbean, 1941. **Military Service:** Served in the 4th Infantry Division of the United States Army, 1942-45; staff sergeant, received five battle stars. **Agent:** Harold Ober Associates, Inc., 425 Madison Avenue, New York, New York 10017, U.S.A.

PUBLICATIONS

Novels

The Catcher in the Rye. Boston, Little, Brown, 1951; London, Hamish Hamilton, 1951.

Short Stories

Nine Stories. Boston, Little, Brown, 1953; as *For Esme—With Love and Squalor, and Other Stories,* London, Hamish Hamilton, 1953.
Franny and Zooey. Boston, Little, Brown, 1961; London, Heinemann, 1962.
Raise High the Roof Beam, Carpenters, and Seymour: An Introduction. Boston, Little, Brown, 1963; London, Heinemann, 1963.
Hapworth 16, 1924. Washington, Orchises, 1997.

*

Media Adaptations: *My Foolish Heart* (film adaptation of "Uncle Wiggily in Connecticut"), 1950.

Biography: Essay in *Authors and Artists for Young Adults,* Vol. 2, Detroit, Gale, 1989; entry in *Dictionary of Literary Biography,* Vol. 2, *American Novelists since World War II,* Detroit, Gale, 1978.

Bibliography: *J.D. Salinger: A Thirty Year Bibliography 1938-1968* by Kenneth Starosciak, privately printed, 1971; *J.D. Salinger: An Annotated Bibliography 1938-1981* by Jack R. Sublette, New York, Garland, 1984.

Critical Studies: *The Fiction of J.D. Salinger* by Frederick L. Gwynn and Joseph L. Blotner, Pittsburgh, University of Pittsburgh Press, 1958, London, Spearman, 1960; *Salinger: A Critical and Personal Portrait* edited by Henry Anatole Grunwald, New York, Harper, 1962, London, Owen, 1964; *J.D. Salinger and the Critics* edited by William F. Belcher and James W. Lee, Belmont, California, Wadsworth, 1962; *If You Really Want to Know: A Catcher Casebook* edited by Malcolm M. Marsden, Chicago, Scott, Foresman, 1963; *J.D. Salinger* by Warren French, New York, Twayne, 1963, revised edition, 1976, revised edition, as *J.D. Salinger Revisited,* 1988; *Studies in J.D. Salinger* edited by Marvin Laser and Norman Fruman, New York, Odyssey Press, 1963; *J.D. Salinger* by James E. Miller, Jr., Minneapolis, University of Minnesota Press, 1965; *J.D. Salinger: A Critical Essay* by Kenneth Hamilton, Grand Rapids, Michigan, Eerdmans, 1967; entries in *Contemporary Literary Criticism,* Detroit, Gale, Vol. 1, 1973; Vol. 3, 1975; Vol. 8, 1978; Vol. 12, 1980; Vol. 56, 1989; *Zen in the Art of J.D. Salinger* by Gerald Rosen, Berkeley, California, Creative Arts, 1977; *J.D.*

Salinger by James Lundquist, New York, Ungar, 1979; *Salinger's Glass Stories as a Composite Novel* by Eberhard Alsen, Troy, New York, Whitston, 1984; *J.D. Salinger: Modern Critical Views* edited by Harold Bloom, Pennsylvania, Chelsea House, 1987; *In Search of J.D. Salinger* by Ian Hamilton, London, Heinemann, and New York, Random House, 1988.

*   *   *

J. D. Salinger's single most popular work, *The Catcher in the Rye,* has been and probably always will be read by a majority of young adult readers. Part of its appeal lies in the long history of controversy this novel has accrued over its four-decade life. Perhaps, as most teachers know, the best way to ensure adolescents' reading a particular text is to censor or ban it from library access. *Catcher* has been more often removed from bookshelves than any other American young adult novel. Though its censors cite obscene language as the major cause for its removal, it is arguable that the smugly rebellious attitude of its narrator, Holden Caulfield, might be another hidden cause of disfavor. In Holden, Salinger created one of the first characters with whom young adults could identify, and thus influenced the thinking of an entire generation.

Holden's tale spans several days of wanderings in New York City during the late 1940s, after he has been expelled from his fourth private school. Holden views most people as either phonies or victims, whom he must avoid or else he becomes nauseous. Told exclusively from Holden's point of view, this search for authentic human contact and love turns out to be an often hilarious parody of the classical heroic odyssey. The hero separates from a previously intolerable existence, finds in himself new integrity and self-confidence, and returns to his homeland with the quality of leadership.

In the true parodic sense—and at the same time reflecting common adolescent behavior—Salinger arranges for Holden's initiatory wanderings to appear comically haphazard and purposeless most of the time. Holden seems only half conscious that he must find a special someone of substance to bond with in order to fulfill his heroic urge. Like many mythic heroes, Holden's ideal person is a female, making his quest a semi-humorous allegory to unify the masculine and the feminine elements of a complete spiritual entity.

Ultimately, it is his sister Phoebe who epitomizes for Holden the untainted feminine principle within the wasteland of adult hypocrisy, lust, and perversion. Almost pathetically, Holden projects upon Phoebe all that he seeks in others, even though she is only ten years old. At this point the young adult reader senses that Holden is in trouble because he so limits the realization of his ideal. Despite Phoebe's willingness, at novel's end, to accompany Holden on still another separation from intolerable life, he cannot draw her into his unresolved conflict. Young readers are drawn dramatically into an empathetic sharing of a troubled adolescent predicament, involving the withdrawal from family security to forge identity alone.

Again paralleling mythic-quest heroes, Holden seeks counsel from a Merlin-like male figure, Mr. Antolini—his former teacher and family friend—whose status and wisdom qualify him to provide answers to Holden's questions about the world. With a hint of androgynous homosexuality, Mr. Antolini "wakes" Holden by gently caressing his head, in the early morning after the boy spends the night under his protection. Unable to accept this unconventional affection, Holden flees in repulsion, thereby thwarting another rebirth after a descent into the underworld.

In the last chapter, when the young adult reader realizes that Holden has told his story from a West Coast mental institution several months later, he or she can comprehend the full impact of this cautionary tale. In the tradition of other great young adult novels, *Catcher in the Rye* offers its readers vicarious experience and value-clarifying scenarios within troubled lives that echo mythic struggles for identity. In an age of cynicism, the youthful idealist can glean from this novel the message that true heroism means not giving in to frustrations, but continuing to struggle for personal values.

Beyond *Catcher*, Salinger's reputation among young adult readers has been spread by his tales about the Glass family. A mostly northeastern mixture of urban, Catholic-Jewish values and attitudes, this disparate group provides unusual unity of interest and tone for youth. Told in *Nine Stories* (1953), *Franny and Zooey* (1961), and *Raise High the Roof Beam, Carpenter; and, Seymour: An Introduction* (1963), the Glass family portrait includes variable-length individual characterizations of each member. Though few families array the complex makeup of the Glasses', young readers can, once again, find vicarious experience in this imaginative extension of the tradition of the big family.

In the Glass family narratives, Salinger depicts the family members' respective searching for resolution after Seymour's suicide, related in the short story "A Perfect Day for Bananafish" from *Nine Stories*. Because this poetic mystic had mastered Zen and continually taught its truths, the several siblings attempt to grasp and apply his teachings to the smallest details of their own lives. All in all, Salinger's later work seems to balance the dysfunctional family and character of Holden against the spiritually questing Glass family. Arguably, Salinger's shift from hopelessness outside traditional values to a hopefulness and resolution in eastern mysticism mirrors not only a similar shift in his own personality but also a persuasive appeal to young readers to attempt the same. Though sometimes criticized for otherworldly elitism, Salinger's narratives give young adults a perspective for fashioning a spirituality in an age of anti-spiritual consumerism.

Though Salinger's body of work is limited, his books are widely praised for their universal relevance. As one of the first writers to examine and critique the world from the perspective of young characters, he captured the attention of a generation of readers seeking reassurance during the rough transition from childhood to adulthood.

—Ron Evans

SALISBURY, Graham

Nationality: American. **Born:** Philadelphia, Pennsylvania, 11 April 1944. **Education:** California State University, Northbridge, B.A. 1974; Vermont College of Norwich University, M.F.A. 1990. **Family:** Married second wife, Robyn Kay Cowan in 1988; three daughters and three sons. **Career:** Musician, teacher, graphic artist, commercial building manager, and author. **Awards:** Bank Street Child Study Award, Parents' Choice Book Award, Best Book of the Year, *School Library Journal,* American Library Association (ALA) Best Book for Young Adults, Judy Lopez Memorial Award, all 1992, and PEN/Norma Klein Award and Oregon Book Award, both 1993, all for *Blue Skin of the Sea*; Scott O'Dell Award for Historical Fiction, Oregon Book Award, ALA Best Book for Young Adults, all 1995, and Hawaii Nene Award, 1998, all for *Under the Blood Red Sun.* **Agent:** Emilie Jacobson, Curtis Brown Ltd., 10 Astor Place, New York, New York 10003.

PUBLICATIONS FOR YOUNG ADULTS

Blue Skin of the Sea. New York, Delacorte, 1992.
Under the Blood-Red Sun. New York, Delacorte, 1994.
Shark Bait. New York, Delacorte, 1997.
Jungle Dogs. Forthcoming.

Other

Contributor to periodicals, including *The ALAN Review, Bamboo Ridge, Chaminade Literary Review, Hawaii Pacific Review, Journal of Youth Services in Libraries, Manoa: A Journal of Pacific and International Writing, Northwest, Oregon Library Association Quarterly,* and *SIGNAL.*

*

Critical Studies: "'Writing My Way Home': An Interview with Graham Salisbury" by Janet Benton, in *The ALAN Review* (Urbana, Illinois), Vol. 24, No. 2, 1997, 6-10.

*   *   *

When Graham Salisbury sets his stories in Hawaii and creates the characters of his award-winning books, he writes about a place and people he loved as a boy growing up in the islands. The elements of his island childhood he considers idyllic show up in the way he depicts the beauty of the physical setting and the loyal friendships between boys; the less than idyllic elements of racial and class divisions often show up in the conflicts his young protagonists must face. The death of his father is another life experience that influences his writing; Salisbury was just a year old when his father died, an event which, by his own account, left some big holes in his life. As a result, he writes "a lot about relationships, especially family relationships." Salisbury typically writes about strong families in which the parents have provided strong support for the children they love; when children lack this influence, they suffer. Both parents are important, but the dynamic he explores most thoroughly in his novels is the on-going relationship between boys and their fathers; all of his young male protagonists are close to fathers who provide excellent role models and are fine mentors.

Despite the positive father-son connections in Salisbury's novels, the boys in each story must face and resolve conflicts and decisions both within and without the boundaries of that relationship. Most often those conflicts issue from what Salisbury in an interview with Janet Benton terms "the Silent Code of Conduct" that greatly influences the behavior of young males. This Code, which entangles boys in complex webs of peer pressure, loyalty to friends, and self-esteem, often causes characters in Salisbury's novels to behave in ways that go against their better judgment when they make decisions based on how they want others to perceive them rather than their own sense of what would be the better choice. While Salisbury never underplays the realistic situations adolescents face, ultimately, and largely because of the father's influence, the boys resolve the conflicts in ways that lead to greater maturity.

Salisbury's first novel, *Blue Skin of the Sea,* carries the subtitle *A Novel in Short Stories.* In eleven distinct but related stories taking place across the school years of his boyhood from 1953 to 1966, Sonny Mendoza tells about his life in a family of Hawaiian fishermen where he is the only one who fears the sea. Although Sonny lives his first years with his Aunty Pearl, Uncle Harley, and cousin Keo because of his mother's death, his father is a positive and constant, if somewhat silent, presence in the boy's life. Sonny most senses the absence of a mother when he wishes for someone to talk to about how his fears make him feel like an outsider even in a family which loves him or about other feelings that confuse him, especially feelings about girls and peer pressure. At one point Sonny laments, "I wasn't one of them. I didn't want to be different. But I was, that's all. I didn't have the guts to be one of them." Getting to the heart of his fear, the need for communication with his father, making decisions that set him a bit apart from his peers, and a hurtful first love comprise the conflicts that contribute to Sonny's maturation process. In the small world of his home town, friends, and family, Sonny's conflicts are so typical of adolescent experience as to seem unremarkable, but Salisbury creates a character whose voice makes readers care deeply about how he comes through these experiences—and admire him for insisting that even if each person is "always on his own" on the sea as a fisherman or in life in general, relationships with others and peace with one's self are two of life's greatest values.

Under the Blood-Red Sun, winner of the Scott O'Dell Award for Historical Fiction, takes place in Hawaii against the backdrop of World War II. Salisbury brings the world-wide political conflicts down to the scale of the individual by having the character of thirteen-year-old Tomakazu Nakajii narrate this story which takes place in the months just before and after the Japanese attack on Pearl Harbor on December 7, 1941. In the months leading up to the attack, the boy is aware of the war only as an event which occupies school discussion and home conversation. Until the day Tomi and his friend Billy witness the actual attack on Pearl Harbor, family, friends, and baseball occupy most of Tomi's energy. Tomi loves them all, but sees his grandfather as a source of embarrassment because of the old man's insistent need to validate himself as a Japanese person. He values his cultural traditions and wants Tomi to venerate as symbols of the family's heritage and honor the family *katana* (a samurai sword which has been in the family more than three hundred years) and the Japanese flag, which the grandfather displays far too freely for the place and time. As much as the old man insists he and his family are Japanese, Tomi, born in Hawaii and an American citizen, just as ardently insists he is an American. Tomi's fisherman father also values the Japanese heritage; from him Tomi learns the importance of honoring one's family by exercising self-control when his behavior might otherwise embarrass the family. Although the cultural conflict Tomi feels pulls him in another direction, the love and respect he feels for his father and grandfather underpin Tomi's resolve not to fight the prejudiced American neighbor boy who bullies him unmercifully; fighting would disgrace the family and Tomi is determined not to disappoint his father. Only when his father and grandfather are imprisoned after Pearl Harbor is attacked does Tomi come to draw strength from the traditions of his Japanese heritage.

In the aftermath of the attack on Pearl Harbor, Tomi's point of view makes clear the confusion felt by the Hawaiian Japanese about the conspiracy charges leveled against them. The unfairness of such wholesale condemnation is typified when shoppers in the grocery store turn away from Tomi and his mother. The boy and his mother are harmless; they pose no threat, nor do people like Tomi's father and grandfather. Tomi and his family do not understand why most Americans consider them dangerous, even if they look like other Japanese who do pose a very real threat. Later in the book, when Tomi's teacher, Mr. Ramos, is trying to help his class understand that wars are fought because some people want power over other people, he also helps readers understand the American fear of the Japanese which led to the internment of innocent people. Even as readers see the unfairness of this action, they see also that by locking up people they feared, Americans gained some sense of control over a situation which seemed out of control. Salisbury walks the fine line between explanation and condemnation of American actions during this difficult period of American history. What shines through the darkness of these days is Tomi's spirit and the spirit of the friends of various races who stand by each other, who see him and his family as *American* when others see them only as a personification of the Japanese threat.

In *Shark Bait,* readers meet another young boy who faces social conflict. Unlike the action of *Blue Skin of the Sea*—which unfolds over years—and *Under the Blood-Red Sun*—which traces several months—*Shark Bait* takes readers through about thirty crucial hours in the protagonist's life. Though he is only twelve, Eric "Mokes" Chock craves the excitement he knows will spark when rival gangs of "mountain guys and ocean guys" clash with each other and with sailors on leave in his small island village. Alcohol and violence attract this boy not so much because he likes drinking beer or fighting but because that's what his friends do, especially his hero, an older boy called Booley. This short book, narrated by Mokes in the patois of the island, captures the struggle between "the Silent Code of Conduct" and what the boy knows he should do rather than go along with his gang. Here there is a clear representation between responsible and irresponsible choices. Mokes's father is the Police Chief who by word and example tries to encourage his son's good choices; Booley, who has no parental guidance, offers bad choices. While Mokes loves and respects his father, it is Booley's power he finds attractive. His father calls him Eric, but it is Booley who made Eric into Mokes, who gave the new kid in town a place in the group and taught him that to survive he must stand by his friends, never rat on anyone, and always fight until he drops so that he will be respected even if he loses.

From the moment when his father makes Mokes promise to be home by six in the evening so he won't be around when the sailors come ashore, the boy's one purpose is to find a way to stay in town. He thinks about the trust he must break, but his desire to be in on the action overrides any compunction he feels. Salisbury paints Mokes's quandary in bold strokes that effectively capture the difficulties of making decisions between doing what is responsible and what is irresponsible, of going against a group or going along in order to fit in. In *Shark Bait,* Mokes's faces the quintessential adolescent dilemma, but the narrative makes clear that such choices are not easy choices. Salisbury has said in interviews that though he feels acutely the responsibility of presenting positive personal and social values, he has no intention of preaching to his young readers, but his intentions become perfectly transparent in the dedication of *Shark Bait*: "For the young people of Hawaii. Choose right. *Imua!*"

Readers will indeed come away from Salisbury's books well aware that succumbing to peer pressure against one's better judgement, racism, and the use of violence and alcohol represent wrong choices. One of the great appeals of Salisbury's work is that though his characters live in what would seem an exotic locale for most readers, the choices those characters must make look very familiar. Nor, even when the choices are difficult, does managing the conflict require extraordinarily heroic effort. Salisbury demonstrates in the most positive way that what his characters accomplish as they grow up can be managed also by his readers.

—Linda Benson

SALVATORE, R. A.

Nationality: American. **Born:** Leominster, Massachusetts, 1959. **Education:** Fitchburg State College, Massachusetts, B.S. 1981; B.A. in English 1989. **Family:** Married Diane; three children. **Address:** c/o Wizards of the Coast, P.O. Box 707, Renton, Washington 98057-0707, U.S.A.

PUBLICATIONS FOR YOUNG ADULTS

Science Fiction

The Crystal Shard (Icewind Dale trilogy). Lake Geneva, Wisconsin, TSR, 1988.
Streams of Silver (Icewind Dale trilogy). Lake Geneva, Wisconsin, TSR, 1989.
The Halfling's Gem (Icewind Dale trilogy). Lake Geneva, Wisconsin, TSR, 1990.
Homeland (Dark Elf trilogy). Lake Geneva, Wisconsin, TSR, 1990.
Exile (Dark Elf trilogy). Lake Geneva, Wisconsin, TSR, 1990.
Echos of the Fourth Magic. New American Library, 1990.
The Witch's Daughter. New American Library, 1991.
Sojourn (Dark Elf trilogy). Lake Geneva, Wisconsin, TSR, 1991.
Canticle (Cleric Quintet). Lake Geneva, Wisconsin, TSR, 1991.
Night Masks (Cleric Quintet). Lake Geneva, Wisconsin, TSR, 1992.
In Sylvan Shadows (Cleric Quintet). Lake Geneva, Wisconsin, TSR, 1992.
The Legacy. Lake Geneva, Wisconsin, TSR, 1992.
The Fallen Fortress (Cleric Quintet). Lake Geneva, Wisconsin, TSR, 1993.
Starless Night. Lake Geneva, Wisconsin, TSR, 1993.
The Woods Out Back (Spearwielders Tale). New York, Ace, 1993.
Siege of Darkness. Lake Geneva, Wisconsin, TSR, 1994.
The Chaos Curse (Cleric Quintet). Lake Geneva, Wisconsin, TSR, 1994.
Dragon's Dagger (Spearwielders Tale). New York, Ace, 1994.
The Sword of Bedwyr (Crimson Shadow). New York, Warner Books, 1995.
Dragonslayer's Return (Spearwielders Tale). New York, Ace, 1995.

Luthien's Gamble (Crimson Shadow). New York, Warner Books, 1996.
Passage to Dawn. Lake Geneva, Wisconsin, TSR, 1996.
The Dragon King (Crimson Shadow). New York, Warner Books, 1996.
The Dark Elf Omnibus. Lake Geneva, Wisconsin, TSR, 1996.
Tarzan: The Epic Adventures. New York, Ballantine, 1996.
The Demon Awakens. New York, Del Rey, 1997.
The Demon Spirit. New York, Ballantine, 1998.

*

R.A. Salvatore comments:

With all of the competition for a kid's time these days (Internet, computer games, etc.), I feel it is vital for teachers to have books to give to kids that they will *want* to read.

*   *   *

R. A. Salvatore is a popular fantasy author whose output has averaged nearly three novels per year. His stories focus on extraordinary characters caught up in inventive plots set in realms similar to those in role-playing games (RPG). Despite the RPG feel, his novels are not formulaic as is expected with RPG novels. Salvatore uses skillful description and heavy action, often involving stirring battle scenes. His characters, the most well-known being Drizzt of TSRs Forgotten Realms series, are well-developed over the course of the many novels in which they appear. Salvatore's popularity is evident in five novels that have made it to the *New York Times* bestseller list and his claim to more than three million books sold in North America alone.

Salvatore began his interest in fantasy fiction while a student at Fitchburg State College in Massachusetts. He was given a copy of J.R.R. Tolkein's *The Lord of the Rings* for Christmas and was so engrossed in the fantasy that he quickly changed his major from computer science to Communications and Media. His first successes as a writer came with the "Icewind Dale" and "Dark Elf" trilogies. The Dark Elf is Drizzt Do'Urden, a drow from the vast city of Menzoberranzan. Drizzt is a prince of the royal house but the drow society is unprincipled and as Drizzt grows to maturity he must decide if he can live among this race of dark elves who live underground and "whose sky is a ceiling of heartless stone and whose walls show the gray blandness of death in the torchlight of the foolish surface-dwellers that stumble here. This is not their world, not the world of light. Most who come here uninvited do not return." Young adult readers will find many qualities in Drizzit to identify with as the young hero struggles with moral and spiritual conflicts.

The "Spearwielders Tale," a trilogy, will also appeal to young adults, especially those who enjoy role-playing games. In *The Woods Out Back,* Gary Leger is tired of his dead-end job and seeks solace in the quiet woods behind his parents' home. He falls asleep and awakens to find he's been kidnapped by a leprechaun to the world of Faerie. He is reluctantly drafted to join in the quest of Kelsey, an elf bent on restoring the spear and armor of a legendary hero. The catch is that this armor will only fit Gary, and the spear must be reforged using the breath of the dragon Robert. Robert is helped in his ploy to stop the heroes by the evil witch, Ceridwin, who is magically imprisoned at the end of the first quest. In the next novel, *The Dragons Dagger,* Gary's wish to return to the world of Faerie is answered after five years, yet only one month has passed in Faerie. Because Gary has stolen a dagger from the dragon's lair at the end of his first quest, the dragon Robert has been released from his magical captivity. Gary, Kelsey, Mickey the leprechaun, and Geno the dwarf are on a quest to return the dagger, thus imprisoning Robert once more. Their moves are tracked by Ceridwin, who is able to see what they are up to using her crystal ball, and though trapped, still able to befuddle their plans using her pawns throughout the kingdom. The trilogy is concluded in *Dragonslayer's Return.* Gary is now married and again longs to return to Faerie. With Ceridwin sowing seeds of destruction, Gary's friends also wish he would return. As war looms in Faerie, the fate of the land once again rests in the dragonslayer's hands. The few female characters found in the trilogy, however, are not fully developed nor do they play any major role in the quest of the quartet of heroes, except for the evil witch Ceridwin.

The "Crimson Shadow" trilogy has a swashbuckling flavor reminiscent of the Robin Hood legends. The many battle scenes will especially entice the interest of male readers. The hero Luthien Bedwyr is in his early twenties, and carries the fate of his country on his shoulders. In *The Sword of Bedwyr,* Luthien is disappointed that his father, the Earl of Bedwyr, is powerless to stop the evil Wizard-King from dominating all the land. Luthien takes to the road to fight for justice and befriends Oliver, a halfling he meets on the highway, acquires a magical crimson cape with powers to make the wearer invisible, and gains the reputation of the legendary "Crimson Shadow" returned to save Eridaor from evil. The saga continues in *Luthien's Gamble,* where he is helped by the wizard Brind'Amour, the creator of the cape and the weapons Luthien uses. Among Luthien's allies are two women whom he both loves and admires for their courage and fighting skills. Siobahn is a half-elf, formerly enslaved by Greensparrow's ruling lords, and organizer of the rebellion. Katerin O'Hale is human, from Luthien's own land of Bedwyr, and a fierce warrior for justice. The resulting love triangle adds a subplot of conflict for the young hero, bringing depth to the storyline yet never turning into romantic triviality. The rebels are eventually able to drive the evil Greensparrow into submission and make Brind'Amour king. In *The Dragon King,* the conclusion to the trilogy, the struggle continues to keep all of Eriador out of the clutches of the evil wizard Greensparrow. Greensparrow's demon half has taken over in the form of a dragon that terrorizes the countryside. The action is nonstop since the battles are long and fierce, and Greensparrow's ultimate weapon is both terrifying and an inventive surprise in the plotline.

Salvatore's most recent trilogy takes place in Corona, a realm totally of his own creating, unlike previous novels. The first title, *The Demon Awakens,* has few new elements. Avid readers of Salvatore novels will see bits of previous stories rolled into this novel. The demon dactyl awakens and destroys the peaceful land of Corona. Two orphans find each other and using magical gems work together to destroy the demon. Criticized for having stock characters, predictable plot, and little drive behind the action of the heroes, it is still an enjoyable tale that fans of Salvatore will want to read. The triumphs of the young adult heroes will appeal to a young adult audience. If Salvatore can find the skill he was demonstrating with the Forgotten Realms series, and his development of the Drizzt character especially, he promises to be a leader within the genre. His previous work reaches beyond the traditions of the genre to establish new standards. As he continues to improve as a writer and stretch these barriers, he may well set the standards for the next generation writing within this genre. Readers continue to return to

Salvatore novels since he is known for strong, perceptive prose and entertaining stories that speak to the emotions and the senses.

—Lisa A. Wroble

SARGENT, Pamela

Nationality: American. **Born:** Ithaca, New York, 20 March 1948. **Education:** the State University of New York, Binghamton, B.A. in philosophy 1968, M.A. 1970. **Career:** Model and sales clerk, Monigsbaum's, 1965-66, solderer on assembly line, Endicott Coil Company, 1966, and sales clerk, Towne Distributors, 1966, all Albany, New York; typist in cataloguing department of Harpur College Library, University of New York at Binghamton, 1966-67; office worker and receptionist, Webster Paper Company, Albany, 1969; teaching assistant in philosophy, State University of New York, Binghamton, 1969-71. Managing editor, *Bulletin of the Science Fiction Writers of America,* 1970-73; assistant editor, 1973-75; market report editor, 1973-76; co-editor, *Bullentin of the Science Fiction Writers of America,* 1983-91. Writer, from 1969. **Awards:** Nebula award, 1992; Locus award, 1993. **Agent:** Joseph Elder Agency, 150 West 87th Street, Apartment 6-D, New York, New York 10024, U.S.A.

PUBLICATIONS FOR ADULTS AND YOUNG ADULTS

Fiction

Cloned Lives. New York, Fawcett, 1976; London, Fontana, 1981.
Starshadows (short stories). New York, Ace, 1977.
The Sudden Star. New York, Fawcett, 1979; as *The White Death,* London, Fontana, 1980.
The Golden Space. New York, Simon and Schuster, 1982.
The Alien Upstairs. New York, Doubleday, 1983.
Earthseed. New York, Harper, 1983; London, Collins, 1984.
The Mountain Cage, illustrated by Judy King-Rieniets. New Castle, Virginia, Cheap Street, 1983.
The Shore of Women. New York, Crown, 1986; London, Chatto and Windus, 1987.
Venus of Dreams. New York, Bantam, 1986; London, Bantam, 1989.
The Best of Pamela Sargent, edited by Martin H. Greenberg. Chicago, Academy, 1987.
Alien Child. New York, Harper, 1988.
Venus of Shadows. New York, Doubleday, 1988; London, Bantam, 1990.
Ruler of the Sky: A Novel of Genghis Khan. New York, Crown, 1993, London, Chatto and Windus, 1993.

"Earthminds" trilogy:

Watchstar. New York, Pocket Books, 1980.
Eye of the Comet. New York, Harper, 1984.
Homesmind. New York, Harper, 1984.

Other

Editor and contributor, *Women of Wonder: Science Fiction Stories by Women about Women.* New York, Random House, 1975; London, Penguin, 1978; as *Women of Wonder: The Classic Years, Science Fiction by Women from the 1940s to the 1970s.* San Diego, Harcourt Brace, 1995.

Editor and contributor, *Bio-Futures: Science Fiction Stories about Biological Metamorphosis.* New York, Random House, 1976.

Editor and contributor, *More Women of Wonder: Science Fiction Novelettes by Women about Women.* New York, Random House, 1976; London, Penguin, 1979.

Editor and contributor, *The New Women of Wonder: Recent Science Fiction Stories by Women about Women.* New York, Random House, 1978.

Editor, with Ian Watson, *Afterlives: Stories about Life after Death.* New York, Random House, 1986.

Editor, *Beneath the Red Star: Studies on International Science Fiction,* by George Zebrowski. San Bernardino, Borgo Press, 1996.

*

Biography: Entry in *Dictionary of Literary Biography,* Volume 8, Part 2: *Twentieth Century American Science-Fiction Writers,* Detroit, Gale, 1981; essay in *Contemporary Authors Autobiography Series,* Volume 18, Detroit, Gale, 1993; essay in *Speaking for Ourselves, Too* compiled and edited by Donald R. Gallo, National Council of Teachers of English, 1993.

Bibliography: *The Work of Pamela Sargent: An Annotated Bibliography and Guide* by Jeffrey M. Elliot. San Bernardino, California, Borgo Press, 1990.

Manuscript Collections: David Paskow Science Fiction Collection, Temple University, Philadelphia, Pennsylvania.

*   *   *

Pamela Sargent's work has done much to enhance and advance the role of women in science fiction. As an editor she has compiled three volumes, *Women of Wonder, More Women of Wonder,* and *The New Women of Wonder.* In the introductory essays to these volumes, Sargent addresses the position of women in science fiction. The collections bring together examples of short fiction of the genre by women.

In her own fiction, both for adults and young people, Sargent has created exemplary and exciting female characters who engage her readers. Adult readers find her works like *Venus of Dreams* and *The Shore of Women* to be entertaining and thought provoking. Sargent brings the same strengths to her novels for younger readers. In her introduction to *Women of Wonder* Sargent states: ''Science-fiction novels for young adults and children can also offer role models for younger readers. This has happened often enough in the past for boys. . .There is no reason why this cannot be true for girls as well. . .''

Sargent's ''Earthminds'' trilogy begins with *Watchstar.* On a transformed Earth, Daiya belongs to a society of telepaths, but she must undergo her rite of passage to join the mind Net of her village. The ordeal would not be an easy one; there were those who died in their quest and joined the Merged Ones. Daiya's journey takes on an added dimension when a glowing object falls from the sky. Rather than alerting the Village Net, she decides to explore alone. She finds an alien spacecraft and a young man. Reiho, the alien, is without telepathic powers but is connected to Homesmind, a cybernetic intelligence of his world, by an implant. The nature of Daiya's quest changes as she comes to learn more about Reiho, his world, and her own. What she learns makes her unable to rejoin the people of her village, and she accepts Reiho's invitation to visit his comet world. Daiya's powers of mind are lost to her in the comet world. She learns of the beauties and problems of that world, but does not feel at home there and returns to her village. She is rejected by the villagers, even by the young man she loved, for she has changed and become something new. When the comet world tries to connect with the village, there is fear and resentment and the villagers attack the aliens Etey and Reiho. Daiya's mother gives birth to a nontelepathic child, a solitary; but Daiya quickly gives her to Etey to take to the comet world, rather than see her killed. Daiya lives as an outcast of her village, but Homesmind promises to watch over her.

Eye of the Comet continues the saga with Lydee, the solitary sister Daiya rescued from infanticide. Once more Sargent creates a strong female character who must face a test. Lydee journeys to Earth where she was born to be a link between it and the comet world. Lydee is shocked by the primitive life on Earth and finds the ways of Earth's people alien to her. Unlike the action that marked Daiya's quest, Lydee's conflict is more philosophical and psychological. Sargent allows her character to become a sounding board for discussion of questions of death and afterlife, the existence of the soul, and powers of the mind. In *Eye of the Comet* Lydee meets Daiya, Reiho, and other characters from *Watchstar.* Although the cast of characters has grown and the setting is familiar to readers of the first novel, *Eye of the Comet* can stand alone as the story of a girl, searching for identity and love, who is caught in the clash of two cultures.

Homesmind concludes the trilogy and Sargent continues the story of conflict between telepathic earthlings and the comet dwellers whose advanced technology allows them to link minds. Anra, the Earthborn heroine. lacks the gift of telepathy and must use Homesmind technology to enter the Net of her people. Again Sargent explores the philosophical questions raised in the trilogy's previous volumes, as she tells of the conditions of life on Earth and the comet world. Once more, it is a young female character who must deal with portentous events, such as alien invasion and the dissolution of her society.

Sargent explores space colonization in *Earthseed.* A cybernetic spaceship carries genetic material for breeding Earth children through the universe. As the ship nears a habitable planet, the children are readied for the project. Zoheret, with all her adolescent insecurities and fears, must leave the ship and face an ordeal for survival with her peers. A complex examination of the motives for colonization provides part of the novel's conflict, and Sargent again focuses on the developing strengths of a young female character who finds herself in a rite of passage.

Sargent develops some of the same themes in *Alien Child.* Nita believes she is the only human being left on Earth as she lives her life in the Kwalung-Ibarra Institute with her alien guardian Lilpel. Nita's quest for knowledge of her origin leads to her discovery of Sven, a boy raised in the same fashion by Llare, Lilpel's companion. Nita and Sven leave the protection of the Institute to take up a quest to search for other human survivors. In a journey filled with hardship and wonder, they learn they are the only humans left on Earth. Lilpel and Llare are waiting for them at the end of the quest with a visitor from space. Raen is a human, one of those who left Earth in its decaying days, fearful of war, to wander the universe. Those in space have changed and adapted, linking minds telepathically. Nita and Sven are not like them. Yet, Nita and Sven are not alone; there are embryos to revive in the ''cold room.'' Nita and Sven will be their guardians until they can take their places on Earth or with Raen and his people in space.

Sargent's latest anthology explores a new area of interest to young adults. The collection *Afterlives,* which she co-edited with Ian Watson, contains short stories that deal directly with the concept of life after death. These stories, including one of her own ''If Ever I Should Leave You,'' presents a science fiction perspective on this theme. Young adults contemplating afterlife may find this collection to be thought provoking.

While Sargent is best known for her science fiction, she returned to the past in an epic-like novel *Ruler of the Sky.* This biographical novel explores the complex life of Ghengis Khan, the 13th Century warrior. The novel, replete with sex and violence, is told through the women who knew Ghengis Khan—His mother and his wives. This device allows Sargent to do what she does best, create women characters of intelligence and courage who cope with the conditions of their time and place. Sargent's historical fiction may be a departure from her futuristic novels, but her concern about women's roles and issues continues.

Apart from this latest foray into the past, Sargent's stories are filled with science fiction themes of space colonization, telepathy, aliens, and an Earth transformed. She provides the excitement of good storytelling and the intellectual speculations of quality science fiction. Sargent consistently provides strong female characters involved in arduous quest journeys who are the role models she stated girls needed to find. Her work contributes to the demise of the stereotype of women in the world of science fiction.

—Janice Antczak

* * *

SAUNDERS, Steven. *See* **JONES, Allan Frewin.**

* * *

SAVITZ, Harriet May

Nationality: American. **Born:** Newark, New Jersey, 19 May 1933. **Education:** Upsala College and Rutgers University. **Family:** Married Ephraim Savitz; one daughter, one son. **Career:** Writer. Teacher of writing, Philadelphia Writer's Conference; guest lecturer in English literature, University of Pennsylvania; holds workshops in novel-writing; helped organize workshop at Philadelphia's Free Library for the Blind to sensitize the media to the needs of the disabled; co-founder, Philadelphia Children's Reading Round Table. **Awards:** Dorothy Canfield Fisher Memorial Children's Book Award nomination, 1971, for *Fly, Wheels, Fly!*; *The Lionhearted* was listed in University of Iowa's Books for Young Adults, 1975-76, among the most popular books read by teenagers; Outstanding Author Award, Pennsylvania School Library Association, 1981; received recognition for *Wheelchair Champions,* 1981, from the President's Committee for the Handicapped in celebration of the International Year of Disabled Persons; California Young Reader Medal nomination, high school category, 1983-84, for *Run, Don't Walk.* **Agent:** Grace Morgan, 45 West 67th Street, Apt. 17A, New York, New York 10023. **Address:** 412 Park Place Ave., Bradley Beach, New Jersey 07720, U.S.A.

PUBLICATIONS FOR YOUNG ADULTS

Fiction

The Moon Is Mine with Maria Caporale Shecktor, (short stories), illustrated by Charles Robinson. New York, John Day, 1968.
Peter and Other Stories, with Maria Caporale Shecktor. New York, John Day, 1969.
Fly, Wheels, Fly! New York, John Day, 1970.
On the Move. New York, John Day, 1973.
The Lionhearted. New York, John Day, 1975.
Run, Don't Walk. New York, Watts, 1979.
Wait Until Tomorrow. New York, New American Library, 1981.
If You Can't Be the Sun, Be a Star. New York, New American Library, 1982.
Come Back, Mr. Magic. New York, New American Library, 1983.
Summer's End. New York, New American Library, 1984.
Swimmer. New York, Scholastic Inc., 1986.
The Cats Nobody Wanted. New York, Scholastic Inc., 1989.
With K. Michael Syring, *The Pail of Nails.* Illustrated by Charles Shaw. Nashville, Tennessee, Abingdon, 1989.
The Bullies and Me. New York, Scholastic Inc., 1991.
Firefighter. Germany, Bastei, 1992.
Remembering Jennifer. Gemany, Bastei, 1992.
A Girl's Best Friend. New York, Scholastic Inc., 1995.

Nonfiction

Consider—Understanding Disability as a Way of Life. Minneapolis, Minnesota, Sister Kenny Institute, 1975.
Wheelchair Champions: A History of Wheelchair Sports. New York, Crowell, 1978.
The Sweat and the Gold, illustrated by David C. Page. Norristown, Pennsylvania, VEEP, 1984.

PUBLICATIONS FOR ADULTS

Growing Up at 62. Atlantic Higlands, New Jersey, Little Treasure Publications, 1997.

*

Media Adaptations: *Run, Don't Walk,* Afterschool Special (television film), American Broadcasting Company.

Biography: Entry in *Fifth Book of Junior Authors and Illustrators,* New York, H.W. Wilson, 1983; essay in *Something about the Author Autobiography Series,* Vol. 9, Detroit, Gale, 1990.

Harriet May Savitz comments:

Writing is magic. What other explanation for words that appear without warning, paragraphs that form of their own will, and characters who come to life when yesterday they didn't exist. Only in front of the blank page do I feel a sense of power. Young people are magic and they possess power. Why would I want to write for anyone else? The answer to that question is—only when there is a message that must be shared—this time the message was for the adult world. Writing is a continuous adventure. I just follow the "brick road." It now takes me into the adult world.

*   *   *

Using some factual material, personal experiences, and feelings, Harriet May Savitz writes award-winning books about physically handicapped young people. It is apparent from her writings that she cares deeply about her characters and their disadvantages. She writes to make the public more aware of the disabled, and has published several books, both fiction and nonfiction, based on the lives of handicapped teenagers.

Listed among the most popular books read by teenagers, *The Lionhearted* tells of Rennie, who is resigned to spending her life in a wheelchair but finds friendship with pretty but overweight Bess and handsome, popular Lee. A touching story of a girl coping with being handicapped while finding love, Savitz has written an eye-opening, warm novel for young adults.

Award-winning *Fly, Wheels, Fly!* is a heartwarming story about Jeff Cobb, fourteen years old and confined not only to a wheelchair but to an orphanage where he has been since he was three. It is also the story of Chuck Robbins, an athletic high school senior who crashes through a banister on a stairway and breaks his back, confining himself to a wheelchair. Joe Johnson, born black with only three fingers on one deformed hand, dumped at the orphanage where he grew up, is now a recreation therapist in a county home for the handicapped and a coach for a wheelchair team representing the U.S. and headed for the Paralympics. Joe rounds up Jeff and Chuck and enters them in his rehabilitation program, pushing them to become wheelchair athletes and changing their lives. Chuck wins second place in the Paralympics in New York for javelin throwing, and Jeff wins the sixty-yard dash and triumphantly breaks all past wheelchair records. Savitz has written a story of awakening hope, not of two boys expecting to walk again, but to live again. She has also written of love and encouragement, of fighting and winning against staggering odds, of heartache and heartbreak, but of life going on and hope for others confined to wheelchairs.

Wheelchair Champions: A History of Wheelchair Sports depicts paraplegics, amputees, and quadriplegics, all who have been winners in sports, not only of awards and medals, but also of facing life once more in spite of their disabilities. Savitz has recorded the personal frustrations and successes of handicapped athletes, physically disabled men and women who have found sports, especially wheelchair sports, a method of learning to cope with their disadvantages and of relearning skills, establishing themselves as able and useful citizens. She shows that there is little danger involved in

wheelchair sports, but that the real danger is the physically handicapped person sitting at home, inactive, not trying to do anything at all, withdrawn and despondent. At the end of the book is a list of names and addresses of organizations where one can write for further information. A very informative book, young adults will learn a great deal about the physically disabled from reading it.

Nineteen-year-old Skip, bitter from losing a leg in a mine explosion in the Vietnam War two years earlier, is the center for the Zippers, a wheelchair basketball team in *On the Move.* Bennie Blue, another Zipper, is a black member of the team, also confined to a wheelchair after being stabbed in the back during high school. Twenty-one-year-old Carrie had polio when she was eight, leaving her crippled for life. She is dependent upon her family and her sister, Sandy, an energetic cheerleader at the local high school. Carrie and Sandy meet the Zippers and their coach, Glen Harris, and Carrie learns from her new friends how to take care of herself, even how to take a bath without the help of others, while Sandy strikes up a loving friendship with Skip. A poignant story filled with love, sharing, struggling, with many disappointments, but a constant determination to move onward, it is about a group of courageous young people who really aren't different from anyone else. They have the same dreams, hopes, and emotions as everyone, and their determination should be an inspiration to all.

Run, Don't Walk portrays a young girl returning to high school in a wheelchair after suffering a paralyzing diving accident. Samantha wants to be left alone, but another student at school, a disabled activist, wants and needs Samantha's help. When a marathon committee rejects her application because of her disability, she turns to him, and a friendship is sparked between them.

It is clear from her writings that Harriet May Savitz knows what she is writing about and has researched her material thoroughly. She portrays her characters realistically and vividly, filling her stories with humor while touching the reader's heart with the frustrations and heartaches of her protagonists, and finally conveying the joyful feelings of their accomplishments.

—Carol Doxey

SCOPPETTONE, Sandra

Pseudonym: Has also written as Jack Early. **Nationality:** American. **Born:** Morristown, New Jersey, 1 June 1936. **Career:** Writer. **Awards:** Eugene O'Neill award, 1972; Ludwig Wogelstein Foundation Grant, 1974; New Jersey Institute of Technology New Jersey Authors Award, 1976; California Reading Association Young Readers Medal, 1979; (as Jack Early) Shamus Award, Private Eye Writers of America, 1985; Edgar Allan Poe Award nomination, Mystery Writers of America, 1985 (as Jack Early), and 1986, for *Playing Murder.* **Address:** P.O. Box 1814, Southold, New York 11971, U.S.A.

PUBLICATIONS FOR YOUNG ADULTS

Novels

Trying Hard to Hear You. New York, Harper, 1974.
The Late Great Me. New York, Putnam, 1976.
Some Unknown Person. New York, Putnam, 1977.

Happy Endings Are All Alike. New York, Harper, 1978.
Such Nice People. New York, Putnam, 1980.
Long Time between Kisses. New York, Harper, 1982.
Innocent Bystanders. New York, New American Library, 1983.
Playing Murder. New York, Harper, 1985.

"Lauren Laurano" detective series:

Everything You Have Is Mine. Boston, Little, Brown, 1991.
I'll Be Leaving You Always. Boston, Little, Brown, 1993.
My Sweet Untraceable You. Boston, Little, Brown, 1994.
Let's Face the Music and Die. Boston, Little, Brown, 1996.

Novels as Jack Early

A Creative Kind of Killer. New York, F. Watts, 1984.
Razzamatazz. New York, F. Watts, 1985.
Donato and Daughter. New York, Dutton, 1988.

Plays

Three One-Act Plays (produced at Sheridan Square Playhouse, 1964).
One-Act Play (produced at Sheridan Square Playhouse, 1965).
Two One-Act Plays (produced at Cubiculo Theater, 1968).
Home Again, Home Again Jiggity Jig (produced at Cubiculo Theater, 1969).
Two One-Act Plays (produced at Assembly Theater, 1970).
Where the Heart Is, 1970.
Something for Kitty Genovese (performed by Valerie Bettis Repertory Company, 1971).
Love of Life, CBS-TV, 1972.
Stuck (produced at Eugene O'Neill Memorial Theater, Waterford, Connecticut, 1972).
Scarecrow in a Garden of Cucumbers (screenplay). Independent, 1972.
A Little Bit Like Murder, ABC-TV, 1973.
The Inspector of Stairs (short subject screenplay). Independent, 1975.

PUBLICATIONS FOR CHILDREN

Fiction

Suzuki Beane. New York, Doubleday, 1961.
Bang Bang You're Dead, with Louise Fitzhugh. New York, Harper, 1968.

*

Media Adaptations: *The Late Great Me* (film), Daniel Wilson Productions, 1982; *Donato and Daughter* (teleplay), CBS, 1993.

Manuscript Collections: Kerlan Collection, University of Minnesota.

Critical Studies: Essay in *Speaking for Ourselves: Autobiographical Sketches by Notable Authors of Books for Young Adults,* Vol. 1, compiled and edited by Donald R. Gallo, National Council of Teachers of English, 1990; "Murder, She Writes" by Michael Lassell, in *Advocate,* 2 July 1991, 93; entry in *Authors and Artists for Young Adults,* Vol. 11, Detroit, Gale, 1993; entry in *Gay and Lesbian Literature,* Vol. 1, Detroit, St. James, 2994.

*   *   *

Sandra Scoppettone's novels for young adults shock. An admitted lesbian and reformed alcoholic, Scoppettone peels the veneer off the lives of middle-class, suburban teenagers to show the emotional conflicts, physical addictions, and potential for violence that lurk near the surface of, and frequently explode into, their seemingly comfortable lives. Dysfunctional "problem" families are her stock in trade. Some may find the subject matter too distasteful to stomach; drunkenness, rape, and homophobia are not pleasant subjects. However, for many young readers she "tells it as it is."

Scoppettone frequently employs a brash but naive female narrator or a point-of-view character who gradually sees her own life or the lives of those she knows implode. In *Trying Hard to Hear You* Camilla Crawford recounts a summer in which a group of Long Island teenagers put on a musical comedy. For much of the novel Camilla recounts the tempestuous tantrums and crushes that occur among the group members. The tone turns serious when the group discovers that two popular males, Jeff Grathwohl and Phil Chrystie, are homosexual lovers. The consequences are tragic as ridicule and ostracism lead Phil to intentionally kill himself in a car accident. In *The Late Great Me* Geri Peters, another Long Island teenager, recounts her junior year in high school when a combination of parental conflicts and an emotional infatuation causes her to start drinking heavily and to be sexually active. Introduced to drinking by an attractive but enigmatic David Townsend, Geri's health deteriorates as she enters the world of drinking bouts and one-night stands. Only gradually through the intervention of a high-school teacher, herself a reforming alcoholic, do Geri and her family begin to mend. In *Happy Endings Are All Alike* Jaret Tyler, still another Long Island teenager, develops a lesbian relationship with Peggy Danziger. Another summer romance novel but with a twist, *Happy Endings* focuses on the deepening relationship between the two girls and the brutal consequences when a male teenager discovers their situation and rapes Jaret. Jaret refuses to be blackmailed and identifies and accuses her assailant. Her family supports her in her plight. In *Long Time between Kisses* Billie James, a teenager living in Greenwich Village and coping with difficult parents, tries to put her life together initially by bizarre behavior and, later, by learning to help others. Finally, in *Playing Murder* Anna Parker, a teenager transplanted from suburban New Jersey to seacoast Maine, finds that the bucolic village where she and her family have moved is the setting for the murder of a young man whose physical attractiveness has overwhelmed her. As she works to identify his killer, she learns secrets about the victim and the community that make her reassess her first impressions.

Chatty is the best way to describe Scoppettone's writing style. Her novels employ the slang and cliches characteristic of young adults. This can become annoying at times as the characters' blithely banter their way through episodes of increasing seriousness. However, Scoppettone's dialogue moves quickly and she does not bog readers down in detailed descriptions and narratives. More mature readers will frequently catch the ironies in the narrators' self-concepts. In some ways the very banality of the language often clearly reflects the shallowness of suburban, middle-class life.

In many ways Scoppettone's young adult novels are melodramas with a liberal, feminist twist. Geri receives considerable advice about the operations and philosophy of Alcoholics Anonymous from a female teacher. Jeff and Phil are dealt with sympathetically while their tormentors are attacked. Jared's rapist is depicted as a mean-spirited, vengeful, irrational boy who stalks his prey. Billie James learns to respect the disabled. Anna Parker comes to appreciate her abandoned, steady boyfriend's concern for her safety even though she no longer wants to date him. For some readers these "politically correct" resolutions may be too pat, although given the controversial nature of much of her material, Scoppettone may have had no alternative than to soften the endings.

Scoppettone's work is often quite violent. Since this violence evolves plausibly from the characters' personalities and circumstances most readers are willing to bear with it. However, for some the violence can become excessive, more like that encountered in Joyce Carol Oates or Stephen King. The most extreme case of this is *Such Nice People,* in which a deranged seventeen-year-old shoots, stabs, and butchers his family and others, and then he is killed. When descriptions of sodomy and masturbation are added, many readers will have had enough.

Scoppettone writes readable novels for young adults in which she bluntly and courageously explores areas of experience that many parents and teachers choose to ignore or deny. At times she deals with the material melodramatically or superficially, but her candor will please readers weary of adult cant. More sophisticated readers will want to explore the problems she deals with most knowledgeably—addiction and sexuality—in works of greater subtlety and complexity. Male readers may find her depictions of heterosexual men troublesome or antagonistic.

—Lawrence B. Fuller

SCOTT, Ann. *See* **FRITZ, Jean.**

SEBESTYEN, Ouida

Pseudonym: Igen Sebestyen. **Nationality:** American. **Born:** Ouida Dockery in Vernon, Texas, 13 February 1924. **Education:** University of Colorado, Boulder. **Family:** Married Adam Sebestyen in 1960 (divorced, 1966); one son. **Career:** Writer. Worked previously at a hamburger stand, repairing PT-19s during World War II, cleaning houses, and watching children in her home. **Awards:** *New York Times* outstanding book citation, *School Library Journal* best book citation, and American Library Association (ALA) best book for young adults and notable book citations, all 1979, International Reading Association Children's Book award, 1980, and American Book award, 1982, all for *Words by Heart;*

ALA best book for young adults citation, and *School Library Journal* best books of the year citation, both 1980, American Book award nomination, and Child Study Association recommended titles citation, both 1981, William Allen White Master List, 1982-83, and Zilveren Griffel (Silver Pencil) award, 1984, all for *Far from Home;* ALA best book for young adults citation, Library of Congress Children's Books, and National Council of Teachers of English Teacher's Choice-*Parents' Choice* remarkable book citation, all 1982, Child Study Children's Book Committee list, and Texas Institute of Letters Children's Book award, both 1983, and Mark Twain award list nominee, 1985, all for *IOU's; The Girl in the Box* was nominated for the Colorado Blue Spruce Young Adult award. **Address:** c/o Orchard Books, 95 Madison Ave., New York, New York 10016, U.S.A.

PUBLICATIONS FOR YOUNG ADULTS

Fiction

Words by Heart. Boston, Little, Brown, 1979; London, Hamish Hamilton, 1987.
Far from Home. Boston, Little, Brown, 1980.
IOU's. Boston, Little, Brown, 1982.
On Fire. New York, Atlantic, 1985.
The Girl in the Box. Boston, Little, Brown, 1988; London, Hamish Hamilton, 1989.
Out of Nowhere. New York, Orchard Books, 1994.

Also author of short stories under pseudonym Igen Sebestyen. Contributor to anthologies, including *Sixteen,* edited by Donald R. Gallo, Delacorte, 1984.

*

Media Adaptations: *Words by Heart* (television movie), PBS-Wonderworks, 1985.

Biography: Essay in *Something about the Author Autobiography Series,* Vol. 10, Detroit, Gale, 1990; essay in *Speaking for Ourselves: Autobiographical Sketches by Notable Authors of Books for Young Adults,* Vol. 1, compiled and edited by Donald R. Gallo, National Council of Teachers of English, 1990.

Manuscript Collections: Kerlan Collection, University of Minnesota, Minneapolis; de Grummond Collection, University of Southern Mississippi, Hattiesburg.

Critical Studies: Entry in *Children's Literature Review,* Vol. 17, Detroit, Gale, 1989; entry in *Contemporary Literary Criticism,* Vol. 30, Detroit, Gale, 1984; *Presenting Ouida Sebestyen,* by Virginia Monseau, Boston, Twayne.

Ouida Sebestyen comments:

I am instinctively, fiercely what is called a homebody. Most of my fiction has been set solidly in a home or a place someone longs to call home. These houses, or temporary rooms, or farms, or little towns where all sorts of people unite as families are rich, complex little worlds to write about while my dog snores and my garden grows. We all deserve to belong, safe within certain spaces, certain hearts, so I like sending out reminders that acceptance is worth fighting for, and something to cherish when we have it.

*   *   *

Ouida Sebestyen's first novel, *Words by Heart,* won numerous awards including the International Reading Association's Children's Book Award given to a promising new writer. Sebestyen was fifty-five at the time, but she had been writing since she was eighteen. She was a new writer only in the sense of being published. The promise is being fulfilled as Sebesteyn has produced five thought-provoking novels.

Sebestyen's novels are about family and love, but there is no easy love in any of her works. She writes of people struggling to understand and accept each other and about families trying to be. *Words by Heart* introduces Lena, a young black girl living in Texas in the early twentieth century. Lena has aspirations to succeed and her father tells her at one point "I want you not to know your place." But it seems that everyone in the community is striving to put the black family in a place of subservience. Papa accepts many slights and Lena struggles with her need for love and acceptance from her father and her anger at his forgiveness of others. The ultimate act of forgiveness comes when Papa saves the life of the boy who mortally wounds him, and asks Lena to forgive him as well. Lena acquiesces, but wonders who will come to fill her Papa's place in her life. The book is rich in detail and both major and minor characters are fully fleshed out. Each is seen with fears and hopes and the actions they use to mask their emotions. Just as one works up a real sense of spite toward a character, Sebestyen reveals an insight that makes the reader reassess. The strength of the book is in the careful rendering of character as well as the poignant story line.

On Fire is the sequel to *Words by Heart,* though it is Sebestyen's fourth novel and her least successful one. Tater Haney is the boy who killed Lena's father and this book picks up the Haney family after they have fled their home in Texas. The book is very disjointed in that it tries to explore the exploitation of mine workers in Colorado, the corruption of the leaders trying to form a union, and the emotions of various Haneys as well as a young woman that Sammy Haney hooks up with. There is little focus to the novel and one never gets emotionally involved as one does with *Words by Heart.*

A shabby boarding house and the emotionally wounded people inhabiting it provides a potent setting for an evocative novel about the tangled web of responsibilities and passions that underlies most human response. Each of the characters is *Far from Home* in the sense that each is lost and trying to make meaning out of a less than perfect life. Sebestyen allows the reader to see the loneliness and near despair of each character, but at the same time the hope that comes when people respond to each other and allow others to touch their lives. There are no easy answers and no happy ending, but the book is filled with the possibilities that hope brings.

None of Sebestyen's families is conventional and *IOU's* family consists of Annie, who is a single parent and determined to live life her way, and her thirteen-year-old son Stowe, who is stoical about their straitened circumstances but laments to himself that everything he wants belongs to someone else or is used. At one point, Annie tells Stowe that they have become pinched from hoarding little bits of money, but most especially from hoarding themselves. The novel is about enduring and about reaching out and building

bridges between those who have lost each other. As in most of her books, Sebestyen's characters are as real as the people you know.

The Girl in the Box is stylistically very different from Sebestyen's earlier works. Told through diary entries and notes, it is written in the voice of a teenage girl who has been kidnapped and thrown in a cellar of some kind by an unknown assailant. There is food and water in the room, but no light. Jackie uses the typewriter and paper that was in her backpack to record her fears and emotions, to question who the assailant might be, to write notes assuring her parents, and to write notes crying for help that she shoves through a crack in the door and that fall on uncaring ground. This is a frightening book in that this is a senseless crime with no motive and an ending that implies Jackie's death. It is at the same time a story of courage and resilience.

Sebestyen's works are provocative and thoughtful. They eschew the typical plot of the young adult novel and probe the inner recesses of human emotion. It took a long time for Sebestyen to find her voice, but it rings clearly.

—M. Jean Greenlaw

SERRAILLIER, Ian (Lucien)

Nationality: British. **Born:** London, 24 September 1912. **Education:** Brighton College, 1926-30; St. Edmund Hall, Oxford, 1931-35, M.A. 1935. **Family:** Married Anne Margaret Rogers in 1944; three daughters and one son. **Career:** Schoolmaster, Wycliffe College, Stonehouse, Gloucestershire, 1936-39, Dudley Grammar School, Worcestershire, 1940-46, and Midhurst Grammar School, Sussex, 1946-61. Since 1950 founder and general editor, with Anne Serraillier, New Windmill series (more than 400 books), Heinemann Educational Books, Oxford. **Awards:** *New York Times* Best Illustrated Book citation, 1953, for *Florina and the Wild Bird;* Carnegie Medal commendation, 1956, Spring Book Festival award, 1959, and Boys' Clubs of America Junior Book award, 1960, all for *The Silver Sword.* **Died:** 28 November 1994.

PUBLICATIONS FOR YOUNG ADULTS

Fiction

They Raced for Treasure, illustrated by C. Walter Hodges. London, Cape, 1946; abridged edition, as *Treasure Ahead,* London, Heinemann, 1954.

Flight to Adventure, illustrated by C. Walter Hodges. London, Cape, 1947; abridged edition, as *Mountain Rescue,* London, Heinemann, 1955.

Captain Bounsaboard and the Pirates, illustrated by Michael Bartlett and Arline Braybrooke. London, Cape, 1949.

There's No Escape, illustrated by C. Walter Hodges. London, Cape, 1950; New York, Scholastic, 1973.

Making Good, illustrated by Vera Jarman. London, Heinemann, 1955.

The Silver Sword, illustrated by C. Walter Hodges. London, Cape, 1956; New York, Criterion, 1959; as *Escape from Warsaw,* New York, Scholastic, 1963.

The Cave of Death, illustrated by Stuart Tresilian. London, Heinemann, 1965.

Fight for Freedom, illustrated by John S. Goodall. London, Heinemann, 1965.

Plays (in verse)

The Midnight Thief, music by Richard Rodney Bennett, illustrated by Tellosa. London, BBC Publications, 1963.

Ahmet the Woodseller, music by Gordon Crosse, illustrated by John Griffiths. London, BBC Publications, 1965.

The Turtle Drum, music by Malcolm Arnold, illustrated by Charles Pickard. London, BBC Publications, 1967.

A Pride of Lions, music by Phyllis Tate (produced Nottingham, 1970). London, Oxford University Press, 1971.

Poetry

The Weaver Birds, illustrated by the author. London, Macmillan, 1944; New York, Macmillan, 1945.

Thomas and the Sparrow, illustrated by Mark Severin. London, Oxford University Press, 1946.

The Tale of the Monster Horse, illustrated by Mark Severin. London, Oxford University Press, 1950.

The Ballad of Kon-Tiki and Other Verses, illustrated by Mark Severin. London, Oxford University Press, 1952.

Belinda and the Swans, illustrated by Pat Marriott. London, Cape, 1952.

Everest Climbed, illustrated by Leonard Rosoman. London, Oxford University Press, 1955.

Poems and Pictures. London, Heinemann, 1958.

A Puffin Quartet of Poets, with others, edited by Eleanor Graham, illustrated by Diana Bloomfield. London, Penguin, 1958.

The Windmill Book of Ballads, illustrated by Mark Severin and Leonard Rosoman. London, Heinemann, 1962.

Happily Ever After, illustrated by Brian Wildsmith. London, Oxford University Press, 1963.

The Challenge of the Green Knight, illustrated by Victor Ambrus. London, Oxford University Press, 1966; New York, Walck, 1967.

Robin in the Greenwood, illustrated by Victor Ambrus. London, Oxford University Press, 1967; New York, Walck, 1968.

Robin and His Merry Men, illustrated by Victor Ambrus. London, Oxford University Press, 1969; New York, Walck, 1970.

The Ballad of St. Simeon, illustrated by Simon Stern. London, Kaye and Ward, and New York, Watts, 1970.

The Tale of Three Landlubbers, illustrated by Raymond Briggs. London, Hamish Hamilton, 1970; New York, Coward McCann, 1971.

The Bishop and the Devil, illustrated by Simon Stern. London, Kaye and Ward, and New York, Warne, 1971.

Marko's Wedding, illustrated by Victor Ambrus. London, Deutsch, 1972.

Suppose You Met a Witch, illustrated by Ed Emberley. Boston, Little Brown, 1973.

I'll Tell You a Tale: A Collection of Poems and Ballads, illustrated by Charles Keeping and Renate Meyer. London, Longman, 1973; revised edition, London, Kestrel, 1976.

The Robin and the Wren, illustrated by Fritz Wegner. London, Kestrel, 1974.

How Happily She Laughs and Other Poems. London, Longman, 1976.

Songs

The Mouse in the Wainscot, music by Cyril Winn. J. Curwen & Sons, 1962; music by Dorothey Jenner, Chappell & Co., 1963; music by F. W. Wadely, Elkin & Co., 1965; illustrated by Giora Carmi, Chicago, Contemporary Books, 1988.

Two Rhymes, music by Neil Butterworth. Chappell & Co., 1962.

My Kitten, music by Cyril Winn. J. Curwen & Sons, 1963.

The Crooked Man, music by Felton Rapley. Chappel & Co., 1965.

Creatures, music by Elizabeth Machonchy. London, Wilhelm Hansen, 1980.

Other

Translator, with Anne Serraillier, *Florina and the Wild Bird,* by Selina Chönz, illustrated by Alois Carigiet. London, Oxford University Press, 1952.

Jungle Adventure (based on story by R.M. Ballantyne), illustrated by Vera Jarman. London, Heinemann, 1953.

Editor, with Ronald Ridout, *Wide Horizon Reading Scheme.* London, Heinemann, 4 vols., 1953-55.

The Adventures of Dick Varley (based on story by R.M. Ballantyne), illustrated by Vera Jarman. London, Heinemann, 1954.

Translator, *Beowulf the Warrior* (in verse), illustrated by Mark Severin. London, Oxford University Press, 1954; New York, Walck, 1961; Minto, North Dakota, Bethlehem Books, 1994.

Guns in the Wild (based on story by R.M. Ballantyne), illustrated by Shirley Hughes. London, Heinemann, 1956.

Katy at Home (based on story by Susan Coolidge), illustrated by Shirley Hughes. London, Heinemann, 1957.

Katy at School (based on story by Susan Coolidge), illustrated by Shirley Hughes. London, Heinemann, 1959.

The Ivory Horn: Retold from the Song of Roland, illustrated by William Stobbs. London, Oxford University Press, 1960.

The Gorgon's Head: The Story of Perseus, illustrated by William Stobbs. London, Oxford University Press, 1961; New York, Walck, 1962.

The Way of Danger: The Story of Theseus, illustrated by William Stobbs. London, Oxford University Press, 1962; New York, Walck, 1963.

The Clashing Rocks: The Story of Jason, illustrated by William Stobbs. London, Oxford University Press, 1963; New York, Walck, 1963.

The Enchanted Island: Stories from Shakespeare, illustrated by Peter Farmer. London, Oxford University Press, and New York, Walck, 1964; abridged edition, as *Murder at Dunsinane,* New York, Scholastic, 1967.

A Fall from the Sky: The Story of Daedalus, illustrated by William Stobbs. London, Nelson, and New York, Walck, 1966.

Chaucer and His World. London, Lutterworth Press, 1967; New York, Walck, 1968.

Havelok the Dane, illustrated by Elaine Raphael. New York, Walck, 1967; as *Havelok the Warrior,* London, Hamish Hamilton, 1968.

Heracles the Strong, illustrated by Rocco Negri. New York, Walck, 1970; London, Hamish Hamilton, 1971.

The Franklin's Tale, Retold, illustrated by Philip Gough. London, Kaye and Ward, and New York, Warne, 1972.

Have You Got Your Ticket? (reader), illustrated by Douglas Hall. London, Longman 1972.

Pop Festival (reader), illustrated by Douglas Hall. London, Longman, 1973.
The Sun Goes Free (reader). London, Longman, 1977.
The Road to Canterbury (tales from Chaucer retold), illustrated by John Lawrence. London, Kestrel, 1979.

PUBLICATIONS FOR ADULTS

Poetry

Three New Poets, with Roy McFadden and Alex Comfort. Billericay, Essex, Grey Walls Press, 1942.

Other

All Change at Singleton: For Charlton, Goodwood, East and West Dean (local history). London, Phillimore, 1979.
Goodwood Country in Old Photographs, with Richard Pailthorpe. Gloucester, Sutton, 1987.

*

Media Adaptations: *The Silver Sword* (television series), BBC-TV, 1957 and 1970, and dramatized as *The Play of the Silver Sword* by Stuart Henson, Heinemann Educational Books, 1982, first performed in Oldham, England, 1983.

Biography: Essay in *Something about the Author Autobiography Series,* Volume 3, Detroit, Gale, 1987; entry in *Third Book of Junior Authors,* New York, H.W. Wilson, 1972; entry in *Dictionary of Literary Biography,* Vol. 161, *British Children's Writers since 1960,* Detroit, Gale, 19??.

Critical Studies: Entry in *Children's Literature Review,* Volume 2, Detroit, Gale, 1976.

*   *   *

Ian Serraillier's love for words is evident. Whether reading his retellings of old ballads and legends, or one of his original works of prose, the text flows with a warmth and rhythm only a poet could impart.

Two of his better works include *Beowulf* and *The Silver Sword.* Both speak of heroes and perhaps this is the reason young adult readers often select these works to read. Infatuated with ballads, Serraillier captures their romance of courage, heroism, and survival in many of his works.

Beowulf is an excellent example of Serraillier's love for the legend and for the heroism it embraces. His success comes in foregoing translation and simply retelling the story in poetry that captures the essence of the original masterpiece. One of the most difficult of the ancient poems to translate, he superbly renders the tale in a style admissible by today's standards. The text rings with the clarity, rhythm, and emotion of the epic.

His introduction and description of Grendel is one example:

Misbegotten son of a foul mother,
Grendel his name, hating the sound of the harp,
The minstrel's song, the bold merriment of men

In whose distorted likeness he was shaped. . .

The character of Beowulf, with his royal breeding, unwavering composure, and heroic dissolution at the same time relates to ordinary emotions and ideals.

Serraillier also translated and wrote adaptions of many other legends, including tales from Greek mythology, the Bible, Shakespeare, about Robin Hood, and about King Arthur's knights. All attempt to authentically portray the scene and the aural appeal. With a rhythm meant to be spoken aloud, the words roll more easily off the tongue than the eyes can smoothly scan them in silence.

Like his poetry, Serraillier applies the same feeling for rhythm and inspiring word choice in his prose. *The Silver Sword,* written in 1956 and reprinted in 1963 as *Escape from Warsaw,* is undoubtedly his best original work. Because it is fiction based on fact and eyewitness accounts, Serraillier is able to treat it as a modern-day epic. The Balicki children, separated from their parents, struggle to survive in war-torn Poland. A silver sword, found by a scavenger boy, is the only link they have with their parents and provides hope for the family reuniting in Switzerland.

Allowing both the words and factual circumstances to convey the heroism of the characters in *The Silver Sword,* a reader has no choice but to reexamine his or her own personal world views. After all, the book may have fictitious characters but the events actually took place, and Serraillier succeeds in conveying the hope and endurance of both the characters and the Polish people in general. When the Russians begin to drive back the Nazis, the Resistance in Warsaw calls the Poles to arms: "At the same moment thousands of windows in the city were flung open, and a hail of bullets struck the passing Germans. All traffic ceased as the Polish Underground rushed to the attack. Starving people streamed out of the cellars and flung themselves upon the Nazis, with weapons if they had them, with their fists if they had nothing else."

The steadfast strength of the characters, whether modern-day or long-ago legend, offer hope that this endurance and courage lies within us all. We need only allow it to flourish.

—Lisa A. Wroble

SERVICE, Pamela

Nationality: American. **Born:** Berkeley, California, 8 October 1945. **Education:** University of California, Berkeley, B.A. 1967; University of London, M.A. 1969. **Family:** Married Robert Gifford Service in 1967; one daughter. **Career:** Publicist for Art Museum, Indiana University, Bloomington, 1970-72; curator, Monroe County Museum, Bloomington, 1978-95. Member of Bloomington City Council, since 1979. **Awards:** Society of Children's Book Writers Honor Book, 1988, for *The Reluctant God.* **Address:** 419 North Washington, Bloomington, Indiana 47408, U.S.A.

PUBLICATIONS FOR YOUNG ADULTS

Fiction

Winter of Magic's Return. New York, Atheneum, 1985.
A Question of Destiny. New York, Atheneum, 1986.
Tomorrow's Magic. New York, Atheneum, 1987.

When the Night Wind Howls. New York, Atheneum, 1987.
The Reluctant God. Athenaeum, 1988.
Stinker from Space. New York, Scribner, 1988.
Vision Quest. New York, Atheneum, 1989.
Under Alien Stars. New York, Atheneum, 1990.
Being of Two Minds. New York, Atheneum, 1991.
Weirdos of the Universe, Unite! New York, Atheneum, 1992.
Stinker's Return. New York, Scribner, 1993.
All's Faire. New York, Fawcett, 1993.
Phantom Victory. New York, Scribner, 1994.
Storm at the Edge of Time. New York, Walker, 1994.

Nonfiction

The Ancient African Kingdom of Kush. New York, Marshall
    Cavendish, 1997.
Mesopotamia. New York, Marshall Cavendish, 1998.
Great Britain. New York, Marshall Cavendish, forthcoming.

PUBLICATIONS FOR CHILDREN

Wizard of Wind & Rock (picture book), illustrated by Laura
    Marshall. New York, Atheneum, 1990.

*

Pamela Service comments:

I write science fiction and fantasy because that is the sort of
reading that stretches our minds and imaginations beyond the
everyday present world in which we normally live. And it is minds
expanded and enriched in this way that are often best equipped to
deal inventively and compassionately with that same real world. I
write for young people because theirs are the minds most open to
the joy and excitement of new ideas and to the wondrous possibilities of this world—or others.

*   *   *

If anyone is a master of genre fiction, it is Pamela F. Service—
she writes fantasy, science fiction, and mystery equally well. Many
of the fantasy novels deal with ancient civilizations, and her
archaeological background is readily apparent.

Winter of Magic's Return is both a retelling of the Arthurian
legend and a new twist on the theme of post-nuclear-holocaust
civilization. Five hundred years after most of the world has been
destroyed, nearsighted Wellington Jones and plain Heather McKenna
befriend amnesiac Earl Bedwas. Earl remembers that he is Merlin
the magician, who has been spellbound for 2,000 years. The three
set out on a quest to find King Arthur; they succeed and go forth to
save the world—the age of magic is returning to make up for the
lost age of science that ended so tragically. While convoluted
explanations are offered as to how magic works, the action is fast-
paced and suspenseful.

Tomorrow's Magic takes up two years after *Winter of Magic's
Return* left off. The fantasy continues, with King Arthur gradually
conquering England. Heather has begrudgingly come to realize
that she has magical talent; she also is falling in love with Merlin,
who is both respected and shunned for his magic. After Merlin

stages a vicarious re-creation of the nuclear disaster that ruined
civilization, he and Heather accept both their relationship and their
abilities in this new world. Their lives mirror the society as the
shortcomings of science are emphasized.

In *A Question of Destiny,* a science fiction work, Don Stratton is
just an average fourteen-year-old except that his father is a U.S.
senator. When his dad decides to run for president, Dan wants to
help with the campaign. He suspects that one of his father's top
aides, David Greer, is not what he claims to be. In a dramatic
confrontation, Dan discovers that Greer is not a Russian spy but an
alien. Greer enlists the help of Dan and Dan's friend Carla Brenner
to change the world's fate. Senator Stratton is running on an anti-
space exploration platform, believing that problems on earth are
more pressing. A top-secret experiment threatens to develop space
flight before humans are mature enough to move out into the
universe. The three manage to sabotage the research and solve the
''question of destiny.'' The theme of accepting others' differences
is treated honestly here: Greer's alienism is truly disconcerting to
the humans, yet they manage to overcome their discomfort. And
while the earth is saved from itself, the saviors must keep their feat
secret, the moral being that the best good deeds should remain
anonymous.

A supernatural mystery, *When the Night Wind Howls* portrays
Sid, a new member of a local acting troupe whose theater appears to
be haunted. Byron Vincenti, a handsome actor, is at the center of
the mystery. Along with her friend Joel, Sid investigates. Horror
plays a role as they discover a pact Vincenti has made with the
Devil in exchange for a successful career. Suspense builds as Joel
and Sid concoct a plot to redeem Vincenti's soul. Classic theories
of the occult are blended with theatrics to make an enthralling
narrative.

With her next novel, Service returns to fantasy. *The Reluctant
God* is Ameni, an ancient Egyptian prince. Placed in suspended
animation, he is set to guard two urns that are essential to the
preservation of Egypt, for their contents represent the eternal
afterlife. Four thousand years later, Lorna Padgett, the daughter of
an Egyptologist who is following in her father's footsteps, accidentally discovers Ameni's tomb; when one of the urns is then taken
from Egypt, Ameni awakens from his long sleep. By hook or by
crook, Lorna and Ameni recover the urn, and the gods intervene to
let them escape safely. But suddenly Ameni must sacrifice the urn
to save Lorna. He does so and is rewarded by the gods, who have
decided that life is more precious than objects. Ameni goes forth to
live in this modern world, understanding that eternity is found in
people. Although the story contains some weaknesses—money
and passports present no real problems for the teenagers—the
scientific and historical details add to the fantasy's appeal.

Archaeological mysteries are important in the next book too.
Vision Quest is set in Nevada, where Kate Elliot has just moved.
When she encounters a stolen charm stone, sacred to ancient Indian
shamans, she realizes she must return it to its rightful place. Wadat
and Hizu, two shamans of long ago, relate their tale of suffering:
through misfortune, both their charm stones were lost and not
buried properly. Kate then teams up with Jimmy Fong, an amateur
archaeologist, to solve the problem. They must find the petroglyphs
(rock paintings) that were created by the two shamans. After many
misadventures, the stones are properly buried at the petroglyphs, as
past and present fuse into one. Again, fantasy is blended with
authentic anthropology as Kate and Jimmy fulfill their own ''vision
quest.''

In *Under Alien Stars,* another science fiction work, Earth has become a Tsorian outpost and part of a galactic empire. Aryl is the daughter of Rogav Jy, the Tsorian commander of Earth. Jason Sikes, a young human, resents the invaders and thinks his mother is a collaborator because she works for Tsorian headquarters. It turns out, however, that Marilyn Sikes is a part of the organized resistance movement. Her group kidnaps Jy just as the Hykzoi—strange and vicious aliens—arrive. Jason and Aryl manage to rescue their parents from the Hykzoi and rendezvous with the Tsorian forces. The Tsorians defeat the Hykzoi, and Earth is upgraded from military outpost to colony status. In this book, enemies become friends when confronted with worse foes; the message is that technology must incorporate morality. Despite its lack of explanation regarding technical aspects, this is good science fiction.

Service's faculty for writing within multiple genres, coupled with her ability to make good use of her archaeological know-how, offers young adults a fine selection of books that both entertain and inform.

—Sharon Clontz Bernstein

SHANGE, Ntozake

Nationality: American. **Born:** Paulette Williams in Trenton, New Jersey, 18 October 1948; took name Ntozake Shange in 1971. **Education:** Attended schools in St. Louis and New Jersey; Barnard College, New York, 1966-70, B.A. (cum laude) in American studies 1970; University of Southern California, Los Angeles, 1971-73, M.A. in American studies 1973. **Family:** Married David Murray in 1977 (second marriage; divorced); one daughter. **Career:** Writer and performer. Faculty member in women's studies, humanities, and Afro-American studies at Sonoma State College, Rohnert Park, California, 1973-75, Mills College, Oakland, California, 1975, and the University of California Extension, 1972-75; artist-in-residence, Equinox Theatre, Houston, from 1981, and New Jersey State Council on the Arts. Creative writing instructor, City College, New York, 1975; currently Associate Professor of drama and creative writing, University of Houston, Texas. Lecturer at Douglass College, New Brunswick, New Jersey, 1978, and other institutions, including Yale University, Howard University, Detroit Institute of Arts, and New York University. Dancer with Third World Collective, Raymond Sawyer's Afro-American Dance Company, Sounds in Motion, West Coast Dance Works, and For Colored Girls Who Have Considered Suicide (her own dance company); has appeared in Broadway and Off-Broadway productions of her own plays, including *For Colored Girls Who Have Considered Suicide/When the Rainbow Is Enuf* and *Where the Mississippi Meets the Amazon.* Director of several productions, including *The Mighty Gents,* produced by the New York Shakespeare Festival's Mobile Theatre, 1979, *A Photograph: A Study in Cruelty,* produced at the Equinox Theatre, Houston, Texas, 1979, and June Jordan's *The Issue* and *The Spirit of Sojourner Truth,* 1979. Has given poetry readings. **Awards:** Obie award, Outer Critics Circle award, Audelco award, Mademoiselle award, and Antoinette Perry (Tony), Grammy, and Emmy award nominations, 1977, all for *For Colored Girls Who Have Considered Suicide/When the Rainbow Is Enuf*; Frank Silvera Writers' Workshop

award, 1978; *Los Angeles Times* Book Prize for Poetry, 1981, for *Three Pieces*; Guggenheim fellowship, 1981; Medal of Excellence, Columbia University, 1981; Obie award, 1981, for *Mother Courage and Her Children*; Pushcart Prize. **Address:** Department of Drama, University of Houston-University Park, 4800 Calhoun Rd., Houston, Texas 77004, U.S.A.

PUBLICATIONS

Poetry

Melissa and Smith. St. Paul, Bookslinger Editions, 1976.
Natural Disasters and Other Festive Occasions. San Francisco, Heirs, 1977.
Nappy Edges. New York, St. Martin's, 1978; London, Methuen, 1987.
Some Men. Privately printed, 1981.
A Daughter's Geography. New York, St. Martin's, 1983; London, Methuen, 1985.
From Okra to Greens. St. Paul, Coffee House Press, 1984.
Ridin' the Moon in Texas: Word Paintings. New York, St. Martin's, 1987.
The Love Space Demands: A Continuing Saga. New York, St. Martin's, 1991.

Plays

For Colored Girls Who Have Considered Suicide/When the Rainbow Is Enuf: A Choreopoem (produced New York, 1975, London, 1980). San Lorenzo, California, Shameless Hussy Press, 1976; revised version, New York, Macmillan, 1977; London, Eyre Methuen, 1978.
A Photograph: Lovers-in-Motion (as *A Photograph: A Still Life with Shadows, A Photograph: A Study of Cruelty* produced New York, 1977; revised version, as *A Photograph: Lovers-in-Motion,* also director: produced Houston, 1979). New York, French, 1981.
Where the Mississippi Meets the Amazon, with Thulani Nkabinda and Jessica Hagedorn (produced New York, 1977).
Black and White Two-Dimensional Planes (produced New York, 1979).
Spell #7: A Geechee Quick Magic Trance Manual (produced New York, 1979; London, 1985). Included in *Three Pieces,* 1981; published separately, London, Methuen, 1985.
Mother Courage and Her Children, adaptation of a play by Bertolt Brecht (produced New York, 1980).
Boogie Woogie Landscapes (produced on tour, 1980). Included in *Three Pieces,* 1981.
From Okra to Greens: A Different Kinda Love Story; A Play with Music & Dance (as *Mouths* produced New York, 1981; as *From Okra to Greens in Three for a Full Moon,* produced Los Angeles, 1982). New York, French, 1983.
Three Pieces: Spell #7, A Photograph: Lovers-in-Motion, Boogie Woogie Landscapes. New York, St. Martin's, 1981.
Educating Rita, adaptation of the play by Willy Russell (produced Atlanta, 1982).
Three for a Full Moon and Bocas (produced Los Angeles, 1982).
Three Views of Mt. Fuji (produced New York, 1987).

Author of introduction, *Plays: One* (collection). London, Methuen Drama, 1992.

Novels

Sassafrass. San Lorenzo, California, Shameless Hussy Press, 1976.
Sassafrass, Cypress & Indigo. New York, St. Martin's, 1982;
London, Methuen, 1983.
Betsey Brown. New York, St. Martin's, and London, Methuen, 1985.
Liliane: Resurrection of the Daughter. New York, St. Martin's
Press, 1994.
Whitewash, illustrated by Michael Sporn. New York, Walker &
Co., 1997.

Other

See No Evil: Prefaces, Essays, and Accounts, 1976-1983. San
Francisco, Momo's Press, 1984.
I Live in Music (recording). Watershed, 1984.
If I Can Cook/You Know God Can, with foreword by Vertamae
Grosvenor. Boston, Beacon Press, 1998.

Author of operetta, *Carrie,* produced 1981.

*

Theatrical Activities:

Director: **Plays**—*The Mighty Gents* by Richard Wesley, New
York, 1979; *A Photograph: Lovers-in-Motion,* Houston, 1979.

Actress: **Plays**—The Lady in Orange in *For Colored Girls Who
Have Considered Suicide When the Rainbow Is Enuf,* New York,
1976; in *Where the Mississippi Meets the Amazon,* New York,
1977; in *Mouths,* New York, 1981.

Media Adaptations: *Betsey Brown* (musical-operetta), produced
Off-Broadway, 1986.

Biography: Entry in *Dictionary of Literary Biography,* Volume
38: *Afro-American Writers after 1955: Dramatists and Prose
Writers,* Detroit, Gale, 1985.

Critical Studies: Entry in *Contemporary Literary Criticism,* De-
troit, Gale, Vol. 8, 1978; Vol. 25, 1983; Vol. 38, 1986; *Ntozake
Shange: A Critical Study of the Plays* by Neal A. Lester, New York,
Garland, 1995.

*   *   *

Ntozake Shange's poems, plays, and stories reveal the unique
voice of a strong African-American woman in contemporary
society. Her impassioned portrayals of both the joys and the
sorrows of women's lives touch on events and emotions, using
language that sometimes risks offending traditional western sensibilities. That language, however, is a perfect match for the emotions, and her unconventional spellings and punctuations reflect the
sounds of the human voice responding to the full range of lived
experiences. There is a musical beat in the language, and even the
placement of words on the page often gives the appearance of
letters and words dancing to that beat. There is also controlled rage

in many of Shange's works, calling attention to the violence,
violation, and oppression endured by her characters. This is both a
personal and political rage in response to international crises such
as apartheid as well as the daily indignities of everyday life. On the
other hand, in many of her works there is also the pure, exuberant
joy of a young child's playful spirit and her love for her mother.

*For Colored Girls Who Have Considered Suicide/When the
Rainbow Is Enuf,* probably Shange's best known work, is a
"choreopoem" in which seven women speak, dance, and sing of
the harsh realities of their lives. The beauty of the language of these
poems both releases and intensifies the power, the pain, and
especially the courage of women coping with the bitter experiences
of their lives. The pain in these women's lives was often inflicted
by men, and many black men objected to their portrayal in this
work. All women, not just women of color, however, recognized
themselves in Shange's poems and praised them as a celebration of
the oneness of women and the strength they draw from each other.

Betsey Brown is a novel of a young adolescent growing up in St.
Louis in the late 1950s during the beginning of school integration
and busing. Betsey was reluctant to leave the safety and comfort of
her middle-class black community to face the uncertainties and
stress of attending an integrated school. In her own home her
mother who is "almost white" is more concerned with fashion
than with civil rights, but her father begins every day with a black
history lesson. Distressed by teachers who devalue her culture and
by the fact that she is not welcome in the homes of her white
friends, Betsey runs away. She goes to Mrs. Maureen's beauty
parlor which she always considered a refuge for black women only
to find that it is a brothel where a young woman who had previously
cared for the Brown children awaits the birth of her child. Betsey
returns home, but before long Jane, her mother, also runs away on
her own search for self-discovery. Carrie is brought in to play the
role of the "other mother" in caring for the children, but she too is
proved unacceptable because she cuts someone and is jailed. Thus,
Betsey is repeatedly confronted with challenges to her comfortable
life and is forced to rethink her beliefs and her values.

Shange's *Sassafrass, Cypress & Indigo* tells the intergenerational
story of three daughters and their mother and explores their
individual and very personal points of view. Throughout this novel
there is a sense of oral language, of women sharing their lives
through music, poetry, dance, and dreams. Mama writes letters
which hold her daughters close at the same time that they venture
out to explore the choices available to black women in society.
Sassafrass is a weaver, a writer, and a dancer who, in her personal
vulnerability, cannot extricate herself from an abusive relationship
with a man. Cypress, on the other hand, exists in a feminist
community and resolves "to have no men." Indigo, the youngest
sister, creates large dolls which share her imaginative everyday
life. When she reluctantly puts those dolls away, she enters into
womanhood, keeping her imagination and her music alive. She also
devotes herself to perhaps the most creative of all female work, that
of midwifery. One of the most compelling aspects of this novel is
Shange's ability to transform the sometimes mundane work of
women such as cooking and weaving into artistic expressions and
celebrations of life.

Nappy Edges is a collection of hard-hitting, yet sensitive poems
which add to Shange's expressions of the fate of black women in
today's world. In "inquiry," we find an encapsulation of her vision
of poetry as "whatever runs out / whatever digs my guts / til
there's no space in myself." The poem "just as the del vikings

stole my heart'' exemplifies her ability to write politically devastating poems combined with imaginative visions that both provoke and sustain the reader. Shange is an intellectual as well as emotional poet who uses literary and socio-political references in her poetry. Readers need to bring both knowledge and caring to these poems to fully appreciate the richness within. The first poem in *A Daughter's Geography,* ''Mood Indigo,'' begins and ends with ''it hasnt always been this way / ellington was not a street.'' This, like many of her poems and stories, is taken from her own life experiences of growing up in an affluent black family, but, as always, she calls forth the universal from that which is unique and personal.

Ridin' the Moon in Texas presents a collection of poetry and prose based on the creations of visual artists. Shange writes in response to a selection of paintings, photographs, and artifacts as if she were seeking a verbal dialogue with each work of art. She perceives of the art as metaphor and writes in tandem with a selection of fifteen diverse images. ''Who Needs A Heart,'' her three-part dialogue with Linda Graetz's acrylic painting of the same title, is a poignant and heartrending account of a child and apartheid, letter writing, and in the jubilant segment ''Walk, Jump, Fly,'' a child speaking with her mommy. These word paintings that Shange presents are sometimes harsh and deeply sexual in nature. They scream with pain common to women, but they lift the spirit and provide a validation of women and life through these artistic dialogues.

—Kay E. Vandergrift

SHERBURNE, Zoa (Morin)

Nationality: American. **Born:** Seattle, Washington, 30 September 1912. **Education:** parochial schools in Seattle, Washington. **Family:** Married Herbert Newton Sherburne in 1935 (deceased); four daughters and four sons. **Career:** Writer. Teacher of short story writing, Cornish School of Allied Arts, Seattle, Washington, 1957; lecturer on writing. **Awards:** Woman of Achievement award, Theta Sigma Phi Matrix, 1950; Woman of the Year, Phi Delta Nu, 1951; Best Book for Young People award, Child Study Association, 1959, for *Jennifer*; Henry Broderick award, 1960; Governor's Writers' Day award, 1967. **Address:** 3711 164th St. SW, No. E19, Lynnwood, Washington 98037, U.S.A.

PUBLICATIONS FOR YOUNG ADULTS

Fiction

Almost April. New York, Morrow, 1956.
The High White Wall. New York, Morrow, 1957.
Princess in Denim. New York, Morrow, 1958.
Jennifer. New York, Morrow, 1959.
Evening Star. New York, Morrow, 1960.
Ballerina on Skates. New York, Morrow, 1961.
Girl in the Shadows. New York, Morrow, 1963.
Stranger in the House. New York, Morrow, 1963.
River at Her Feet. New York, Morrow, 1965.
Girl in the Mirror. New York, Morrow, 1966.
Too Bad about the Haines Girl. New York, Morrow, 1967.

The Girl Who Knew Tomorrow. New York, Morrow, 1970.
Leslie. New York, Morrow, 1972.
Why Have the Birds Stopped Singing? New York, Morrow, 1974.

Other

Shadow of a Star. London, Hurst & Blacklett, 1959.
Journey out of Darkness. London, Hurst & Blacklett, 1961.

*

Media Adaptations: *Memories Never Die* (television movie adaptation of *Stranger in the House*), Columbia Broadcast Service, Inc., 1982.

Biography: Essay in *Speaking for Ourselves: Autobiographical Sketches by Notable Authors of Books for Young Adults,* Volume 1, compiled and edited by Donald R. Gallo, National Council of Teachers of English, 1990.

*   *   *

Family life and romance have been strong themes for young adult novels. Louisa May Alcott's *Little Women,* one of the first works written specifically for this age group, described the joys and sorrows of the March sisters. Until the second half of the twentieth century, few books for teenaged readers dealt with life, love, and death as realistically as did Alcott. In 1956, a wife, mother, and writer for *Seventeen Magazine* came onto the literary scene—Zoa Sherburne.

Sherburne's books for young adults span three decades, from the 1950s to the 1970s. When her first books were published, Ike was president, hula hoops were the craze, and the move to suburbia was in full-swing. Elvis had just begun and pink poodle skirts were in fashion as were sock hops. ''Ozzie and Harriet'' were on television, and it seemed to be a black and white world with very few shades of grey. But for teenagers, the world wasn't quite this simple. While her initial stories portray first kisses and teenage crushes, Sherburne is best known for her contemporary novels which deal with problems real teenagers face in today's society. In a world which does not always have simple problems, her protagonists struggle with family divorce, illness, the death of loved ones, drug usage, being unpopular, and unwanted pregnancy.

Many of Sherburne's novels share the Pacific Northwest as their setting where she was born and raised. It is characteristic of her writing to portray the turbulence of youth in striking scenes of windswept beaches, stormy weather, and majestic snowcapped mountains. Adolescence is a time of considerable growth physically, but also mentally and emotionally. It is a time when young people need to learn to believe in themselves, to be confident, and to make intelligent decisions. Many teens today have never experienced a father and mother's love because of death or divorce. This emptiness can lead to self-doubt, sexual intimacy, alcohol, or drugs. The mother of eight children, Zoa Sherburne is primarily a realistic writer who shares her observations of contemporary teenagers, not through research, but from experience.

The themes of many of her books are based upon young people's desire for independence. Karen in *Almost April* travels to Oregon after the death of her mother to live with her father and his new wife. Since she has not seen her father for many years, Karen is bitter. But just as love, understanding, and time are healing the wounds, a romance with Nels develops and the division is reopened. Eighteen-year-old Leeann leaves her overcrowded home in *The High White Wall,* to take a summer job as a children's companion for a wealthy family in the exclusive Mountcastle area. She falls in love with Dick, the oldest son of the Kingsley family, and struggles with decisions about her future. Eden, the winner of the local Tulip Princess beauty pageant, learns that the Miss Washington contest is not fun, but a highly competitive and stressful experience. She returns home happy to be a *Princess in Denim.* Fourteen-year-old Nancy, a Native American living in the beautiful San Juan Islands of Puget Sound, also learns that happiness comes from within, in *Evening Star.*

Tragedy and its results upon the lives of all involved are also ingrained within many of Sherburne's plots. *Girl in the Mirror* is the story of a sixteen-year-old who has partially retreated from reality when her widowed father plans to remarry. Ruth Ann is very self-conscious of her problem with obesity. Her father's marriage to a young nurse and the tragic events that follow the honeymoon cause Ruth to re-examine life and to realize that the future holds promise. *Leslie* tells of a teen who has become self-sufficient in many ways as a result of living with her mother who has been embittered by divorce. But a party in which drugs were used is followed by a hit-and-run motor death and Leslie knows that she cannot deal with this problem alone. *Jennifer* is the poignant story of the effect of the death of Jennifer's twin sister upon the Martin family. Her mother's illness with alcoholism affects sixteen-year-old Jennifer who becomes withdrawn and unsocial. Sherburne skillfully considers her audience in this heartwarming story of family grief and adjustment. The characterization is superb, and the depth of the story is blended with humor, dances, conflicting romances, and Jennifer's newfound friend, Patsy. *Stranger in the House* examines the need for love and acceptance—by both youngsters and their parents. After nine years in a hospital where she was treated for mental illness, Kathy's mother returns home. Unfortunately, after such a long absence, she is considered a stranger by members of her own family. Finally, on the night of a party for members of a school play, Kathleen and her mother are able to communicate—and the barrier between them is gradually replaced with understanding and togetherness.

While considering problems that young adults face, Sherburne is also able to share in their fun. Both *Ballerina on Skates* and *River at Her Feet* are light reading and will appeal to young girls. The former tells of seventeen-year-old Karen's escapades as a professional ice-skater. The latter is the story of a teenage crush and its effects upon sixteen-year-old Elizabeth and her family.

Although neither a tragedy nor a comedy, *The Girl Who Knew Tomorrow* blends a little of each in the tale of a fifteen-year-old girl who has been able to see the shadows of events before their occurrence. Angie has ESP. In a conversation with her dying grandmother, Angie is encouraged to use her gift to help others. *Why Have the Birds Stopped Singing?* is a Gothic journey back in time. Sixteen-year-old Katie is epileptic. While on a school tour of Puget Sound, she forgets to take her medicine and falls. Upon awaking, she is in the nineteenth century and is thought to be her own great-great-great-grandmother Kathryn who was also epileptic. It is a historical novel of romance and suspense.

Critics consider *Too Bad about the Haines Girl* to be Sherburne's best work for young adult readers. Westwood High's popular

seniors, Lindy and Jeff, are very much in love. Zoa Sherburne has offered a straightforward account which is neither didactic nor conclusive, but instead is an honest discussion of premarital pregnancy and its effect upon many lives. The story ends with Lindy facing the fact that she needs to tell her parents and to receive their support. The final paragraph of the book expresses the change that has taken place in Lindy Haines' life. While listening to the radio, she hears a tune that Jeff and she had called their song. And she reminisces that they had danced to it many times last year, "when they were young."

From boy-next-door type of books for young girls to those dealing with serious problems and concerns that teens experience, Sherburne's work documents the changing scene of American life from the fifties to the seventies. Her characterizations are well written. Confident teenagers are shown as well as those who do not fit into the crowd; family, marriage and divorce, and birth and death are present; and lives in pain from drugs, alcohol, and other choices are vividly depicted. Sometimes her protagonists make mistakes and choices which they regret and sometimes not. There are happy times, sad times, bad times, and fun times. Youth is a time of transition—and Zoa Sherburne has documented the metamorphosis from childhood to adult. Life does not always have a Cinderella ending, but Sherburne's novels show that there is always hope for the future.

—Albert F. Spencer

SHOUP, Barbara

Nationality: American. **Born:** Barbara White in Hammond, Indiana, 4 May 1947. **Education:** Indiana University, Bloomington, Indiana, B.S. 1972, M.S. 1976. **Family:** Married attorney Steven V. Shoup in 1967; two daughters. **Career:** Community programs coordinator, Learning Unlimited, North Central High School, Indianapolis, Indiana, 1975-78; associate instructor in creative writing, Indiana University, Bloomington, Indiana, 1979; school programs coordinator, Indianapolis Museum of Art, Indianapolis, Indiana, 1980; writer in residence, Broad Ripple High School Center for the Humanities and Performing Arts, Indianapolis, Indiana, from 1982; coordinator, Prelude Academy, Indianapolis Children's Museum and Penrod Society, Indianapolis, Indiana, 1985-97. Contributing editor, *Arts Insight,* 1984, and *Other Voices,* from 1991; contributor to many periodicals, including *Mississippi Valley Review, Crazy Quilt,* and the *New York Times.* Member, Indiana Arts Commission on Grants Panels, 1983-86; fiction judge, Society of Midland Authors and National Society for Arts and Letters, 1988; member of the Authors Guild, Indiana Teachers of Writing, Indiana Writers' Center, and Midland Society of Writers. **Awards:** Association for Experiential Education Best Book in Field, 1980, for *Living and Learning for Credit;* Indiana Arts Commission and the National Endowment for the Arts Master Artists fellowship, 1990; Butler University Writers' Studio literary fellowship, 1990-91 and 1994; Pushcart Prize nomination, 1994; Bulletin for the Center of Children's Books Notable Young Adult Book citation, 1994, for *Wish You Were Here;* American Library Association Best Books for Young Adults citation, 1995, for *Wish You Were Here,* and 1997, for *Stranded in Harmony.* **Agent:** Mary Evans, Inc., 242 East 5th Street, New York, New York 10003,

U.S.A. **Address:** 6012 North Broadway, Indianapolis, Indiana 46220, U.S.A.

PUBLICATIONS FOR YOUNG ADULTS

Fiction

Wish You Were Here. New York, Hyperion Books for Children, 1994.
Stranded in Harmony. New York, Hyperion Books for Children, 1997.

PUBLICATIONS FOR ADULTS

Fiction

Nightwatch. New York, Corneha and Michael Bessie Books, Harper & Row, 1982.

Nonfiction

Living and Learning for Credit. Bloomington, Indiana, Phi Delta Kappa, 1978.
New Roles for Early Adolescents in Schools and Communities, with Joan G. Schine and Diane Harrington. Boston, Massachusetts, National Commission on Resources for Youth, 1981.
Learning Unlimited: A Model for Options Education, with Freddi Stevens-Jacobi. Indianapolis, Indiana, Washington Township Schools, 1981.

*

Critical Studies: "Problem Parents" by Joni Richards Bodart, in *The Book Report* (Worthington, Ohio), January/February 1995, 34; review of *Wish You Were Here* by Bonnie Morris, in *The Book Report* (Worthington, Ohio), March/April 1995, 40-41; entry in *Something about the Author,* Vol. 86, Detroit, Gale, 1996, 219-20; "Honesty, Relationship With Her Students Fuel Writer's Success" by Katie Tolle, Chelsea Hutton, and Aaron Carnahan, in *Children's Express,* http://www.ceindy.org/ce_feb97/feature/bshoup.html (4 May 1998).

Barbara Shoup comments:

I wanted to be a writer from the time I understood what a book was. As soon as I learned how to form the alphabet, I began to write stories in a special blue notebook. I was eleven when I attempted my first novel, the story of a black slave girl journeying north by Underground Railroad. Certainly fame and fortune were imminent—or so I thought until we got to the unit on the Civil War in Social Studies and I learned that the slave railroad was not a subway train than ran from Atlanta to New York City, as I'd imagined it to be. I was so mortified by my mistake, that I gave up writing for nearly twenty years.

When I began again, it was because one of my high school students asked me whether teaching was what I had always meant to do with my life.

"Oh, I used to want to be a writer," I said.

"Well—?," he replied

I knew exactly what he meant. You expect *me* to be what I dream, so why aren't you expecting it of yourself? I had to write, or risk losing his respect.

So I began to write.

Teaching has played an important part in my writing and in my sense of myself as a writer ever since. I am infinitely fascinated by the lives of my young writers, inspired by the earnestness and courage with which the best of them approach their work. Each of their lives is like a story to me, with wonderful details that cry out to be in books. But while my young adult novels reflect the lives of young people I know, no one life appears "factually" on the page. Each character is made of all sorts of details from various lives, plus completely made-up details. Each one seems completely real to me, a person in his or her own right

* * *

When Jackson Watt's best friend Brady suddenly takes off before their senior year, in Barbara Shoup's *Wish You Were Here,* all Jax wants is a postcard, letting him know that Brady is okay. Jackson and Brady had planned to rent an apartment together for their senior year—both sets of parents are divorced, the boys have felt that they're in the way living with their dating moms, and they've been looking forward to a free and easy year together before they leave for college. Jax looks up to Brady—"People think I'm good, but really, I'm just too scared to risk getting into trouble. Brady has the guts to do what he believes is right."—but as the days, the weeks, then the months go by, school's started, everyone's been worried about Brady, and Jax still hasn't heard from him, Jax starts to feel angry—"pissed," actually—at his best friend. Not even a postcard.

Jax finally gets a postcard from Brady, from Dubuque, Iowa: "Jax—Bulletin from the real world. Blew some weed in Strawberry Field, met up with some Deadheads there. We've been everywhere, it's a blast. Tell Oz the Dead live. There's nothing like the road, man. But I miss you. Kick ass—Brady." But Jackson's just got home from visiting his father, Oz, in the hospital where he's recuperating from a serious accident; his mother's remarried and he's got two sullen new little step-sisters; Jax has been working out at the gym and has fallen seriously in love with Amanda, a beautiful girl he's met on vacation in Jamaica; Halloween, Thanksgiving, and Christmas have come and gone. He is relieved to find that Brady is okay, but still angry that his best friend hasn't been there for him: "Then, almost instantaneously, I think, Do I need this? What's with Brady, anyway—sending me a postcard from Dubuque, Iowa, with no return address? He misses me? Ha. Bulletin from the real world? Give me a break. I pace around in my room, but in the end I'm too tired to work up a real, cleansing rage. The truth is, Brady couldn't help me now—even if I could find him. I'd tell him about Dad and he'd say, 'Jax, you ought to jet, like I did. Leave all this sorry shit behind you.' I'd tell him about Amanda and he'd say, 'Man, you blew it. All that time you could have been screwing your brains out.' That's when I get pissed. It's as if he actually did say those things to me, and I start pacing again, smacking my fist against my hand. 'You asshole,' I say. 'You complete and total asshole. You don't know jack shit about anything.'"

Brady finally shows up—at a Grateful Dead concert nearby—and Jax tracks him down. By now, Stephanie (both Brady and Jax's old girlfriend) has OD'd on drugs and died, Jax and the rest of

Brady's class have graduated, and Jax' father has married Brady's mother. Jax treats Brady to breakfast at Hardee's. Then both boys take off for Graceland, where Jax finally realizes that his image of his once-best friend is as phoney and stale as the images of Elvis that surround them. Jax has grown up—and Brady has grown out, far out. On his drive home to Indianapolis—alone—Jax turns on an R.E.M. tape, playing "It's the End of the World As We Know It (I Feel Fine)."

Lucas Cantrell, the hero of Barbara Shoup's next novel for young adults, *Stranded in Harmony*, seems to have everything going for him. He's the captain of his school's football team. His girlfriend Sara (who is also his sister Dawn's best friend) is a pretty cheerleader. His parents are happily married, and his father owns a successful car dealership in Harmony which he hopes Lucas will take over one day. But all of a sudden, toward the end of the summer before his senior year in high school, he starts thinking about the world outside of Harmony, the exotic places he'd read about as a young boy in issues of the National Geographic and always dreamt of travelling to one day: "When did I quit believing that there was a whole world out there, just waiting for me to step into it? When it happened, why didn't I notice? Suddenly . . . I started thinking about these questions all the time. I felt as if I'd just awakened from a long sleep. That dead-to-the-world kind of sleep, with no dreams. And I looked around and thought, This is what I've settled for? This is my life?" An offer of a full scholarship from a small Indiana college and a scare that he might have made Sara pregnant make him feel more trapped than ever in his predictable, small-town life. Then he meets Allie, a former Vietnam War protester who has spent some years in prison and has come to Harmony to be alone and get her life back together. Allie helps him with his term paper—on the 1960s—teaches him about taking responsibility for his actions, and helps him move on with his life, his "real life."

In a February 1997 interview for *Children's Express,* an electronic newspaper written by and for young people, Barbara Shoup, who teaches creative writing at an Indianapolis, Indiana, high school, spoke of the writing process: "When you're a writer of fiction, these people [the characters in your work] are very real to you and you don't want to sell them short. Just like when you're raising your children, you want to do it right. If you have a character in fiction, it's very important to make sure that you portray that person as close as the person is in your head. . . . What's more meaningful to me is when someone reads that book and they say to me something that tells me that I know I got the character right. I've done him right, I've stood by him. That's important to me." Barbara Shoup has stood by Jackson Watt and Lucas Cantrell, through all of their problems, growing pains, and dumb mistakes. She has portrayed them with honesty and realism, and patiently follows them through to the end, when they start on the course of the rest of their lives. She has got them right.

—Marcia Welsh

SILVER, Norman

Nationality: British. **Born:** Cape Town, South Africa, 3 March 1946. **Education:** Highlands North High School, Johannesburg, South Africa, 1958-62; University of the Witwatersrand, South Africa, 1964-67, B.A. in English and Philosophy, 1968-69, B.A. in Philosophy; University of Essex, Colchester, England, 1983-84, M.Sc. in I.K.B.S. **Family:** Married Evril Peltz in 1969; one daughter and one son. **Career:** Housefather in remand homes, London and Bristol, 1973-77; dealer in antique paintings, Bath, 1978-83; teacher of computer programming, Technology Centre, Ipswich, 1984-87; since 1987 full-time writer. **Awards:** Blue Cobra Award, Third World Children's Book Foundation, 1990. **Agent:** Laura Cecil, 17 Alwyne Villas, London N1 2HG, England.

PUBLICATIONS FOR YOUNG ADULTS

Fiction

No Tigers in Africa. London, Faber & Faber, 1990.
An Eye for Colour. London, Faber & Faber, 1991.
Python Dance. London, Faber & Faber, 1992.

Poetry

Words on a Faded T-Shirt. London, Faber & Faber, 1991.
The Comic Shop. London, Faber & Faber, 1992.
The Walkmen Have Landed. London, Faber & Faber, 1994.

PUBLICATIONS FOR CHILDREN

Cloud Nine. London, Bodley Head, 1995.
The Blue Horse. London, Faber & Faber, 1996.

*

Critical Studies: "The Alchemy of Silver" by James Carter, in *School Librarian,* Vol. 42, No. 4, November 1994.

Norman Silver comments:

A question I am often asked is: *Why do you only write for young readers?* My answer is *It is my privilege to write for young readers.* Perhaps these questioners feel I ought to graduate to the real stuff, writing for adults. But for me, writing for young readers *is* the real stuff. It is my pleasure.

There is a joy in writing for someone who is still fresh to the experience of reading, who is new to encountering the imaginary worlds of literature. I vividly recall my own experience of opening a book I had not come across before and embarking, with the author, on a voyage which would take me across wild oceans to exotic universes. Each book had its own feel, its own atmosphere, its own aroma.

How exciting it is to communicate with readers whose sense of possibility is so vast. The possibility of becoming anything! Of doing anything! And yet there's also something scary about those years, as innocence and spontaneity are supplanted by the burden of self-consciousness and responsibility.

I remember as an adolescent the word "adult" struck me with horror. For many years of my life it was a pejorative term, representing the end of growth, of openness, and the congealing of attitudes and ideas. If only we could all be as open to change and learning later in life as we are in the early years. To be able to experience things with that "for the first time" quality.

For me, writing is a continuing exploration of that magic and metamorphosis. In writing for young readers I feel privileged to explore those incredible moments of transition, of awakening. And perhaps, in the process, to express the most fascinating possibility: that a person might discover within themselves a common humanity with all people.

*   *   *

Norman Silver's young adult fiction reflects his adolescence in South Africa in the sixties, in that extremely beautiful country torn apart by apartheid. His narrators are Jewish, and this provides a family circle of customs and attitudes ordered by religion, within an urban and national framework of conflict over race and colour. His style is fluent, concise, and compelling to read.

Two quotes from *No Tigers in Africa* sum up Silver's humanitarian concerns in his fiction: "Sitting there with Rosalie, I began to feel the connections between all people and the stupidity of acting superior because of a skin colour or religion"; and "I wanted to live forever in the place where a human being shines like gold liquid, in the place where the poems are made, where all our roots come from." Selwyn Lewis, the fifteen-year-old narrator of this novel, moves with his family from Johannesburg, South Africa, to England because of his father's fears that the situation in South Africa will "explode any day." Selwyn is desperately unhappy about leaving his friends and the land he loves, he feels guilty over his involvement in the murder of a black boy back in Johannesburg. He hates his new school, and, while playing truant, sees his mother going into a house with a black man, and suspects her of having an affair. He believes himself to be against apartheid, but is conditioned by his upbringing and can't at first more liberal English attitudes. The novel is thus partly an exploration of the insidious nature of prejudice. Selwyn attempts suicide, and, as his parents' marriage founders, goes to live in a psychiatric unit for adolescents. His redemption comes about partly there, and partly through Rosalie, daughter of a liberal South African friend of his mother's, with whom he overcomes his earlier fear of white girls.

The forcefulness and driven energy of *No Tigers in Africa* are not matched in Silver's other South African fiction. *An Eye For Colour* is a collection of twelve linked stories narrated by teenage Basil Kushenovitz, mostly concerned in some way with issues of colour, and conveying a wonderful sense of the suburban neighborhood as experienced by children and adolescents, and a great understanding of adolescent behaviour and attitudes. Two stories involve Hester Conradie, who lives in a shabby house opposite Basil's. When she was young, she and Basil built dens in the thick hedge fronting her garden; now that she is older she has the local boys queuing up and paying one rand to see her naked. Later, the light-skinned Hester is reclassified by the government as coloured, which means that she must leave her officially white family and go to a coloured school. Basil still fancies her, but when they meet he finds the shocking experience has altered her. She tells him:

It's people that change. People like me and all the other coloureds at my school and throughout the Cape. We're all changing. You whites used to think you were superior to us, but that was all lies. We're sick of this white propaganda you give us. From now on we're equals whether you like it or lump it.

Set in Johannesburg, *Python Dance* describes the family and social life of sixteen-year-old Ruthie. Ruthie is extremely unhappy at home, living with her superstitious mother, her younger sister, and her hated stepfather. Her mother sacks John, the black garden boy, when Ruthie accuses him of staring in her bedroom window, and he takes his revenge by leaving on the mother's bed a bad spell which is—unintentionally—responsible for her death. Ruthie has a wide social circle and, in spite of her fear of physical and emotional involvement, a sequence of boyfriends. Her involvement with one such boyfriend leads Ruthie to start taking part in demonstrations: as she becomes drawn out of herself and into politics, so her extreme self-consciousness lessens and she becomes capable of love.

The heroes of Silver's fiction are primarily not agents, but observers to whom things happen. The energy and the structure of the earlier books ensure that this doesn't matter in terms of maintaining the reader's interest. *Python Dance* is longer and very complex, bubbling with serious ideas and issues with an exuberance that is sometimes raw and shocking, and that inevitably means that there isn't space for them all to be fully examined or resolved. There sometimes seems to be material for several novels here. Ruthie's mother's death, for example, coming right at the end of the novel, is surprising and disturbing to the reader, but Ruthie's feelings of guilt are glossed over in one line. Ruthie is for most of the book mixed-up and inconsistent, an adolescent muddle of emotions, sometimes funny, sometimes tragic, but she matures, most of all through her involvement with the student protests. Silver again expresses his humanitarian concerns, particularly about the nature of prejudice: "Prejudice is a strange thing. Mostly you don't know if you've got it or not, and if you think you have, then you probably haven't. But if you think you haven't, then most likely you do have it!"

In *No Tigers in Africa* the narrator Selwyn describes why he loves poetry: "Because poetry is written with a pen that's got gold ink in it." In the poem "From the Dark Forests," which appears in *The Walkmen Have Landed*, Silver describes how words

ache
to express
untamed feelings
which melt
on your tongue. . .

Silver's love of words is most evident, and his empathy with today's teenagers clearest, in his poetry. His poems are skillfully crafted with great sensitivity to language. They vary greatly in style and subject matter, ranging from the fantastic grotesque of *The Comic Shop*:

Emanations oozing from his apertures,
he manifests his anger in a spasm
of wrath, and points a skeletal finger
at a cop, who dissolves to ectoplasm.

to environmental concerns:

Use the sea as a garbage bin:
throw your dirty rubbish in

to adolescent humor:

> Always carry a condom in your holster
> in case your cowboy
> is involved in a shoot-out. . .

In such poems, Silver shows his appreciation of the beauty and the humor in ordinary experiences.

Since 1989 Silver has taught creative writing in mainstream and special schools, with able and disabled groups of children and teenagers, and been very effective in getting them to enjoy language and to esteem themselves and their own experiences of life. These concerns are reflected in his writing, which, above all, places value on human beings and their rights.

—Maggie Freeman

SINCLAIR, Upton (Beall)

Pseudonyms: Clarke Fitch; Frederick Garrison; Arthur Stirling. **Nationality:** American. **Born:** Baltimore, Maryland, 20 September 1878. **Education:** City College (now City College of the City University of New York), 1893-97, A.B. 1897; Columbia University, New York, 1897-1901. **Family:** Married 1) Meta H. Fuller in 1900 (divorced 1913), one son; 2) Mary Craig Kimbrough in 1913 (died 1961); 3) Mary Elizabeth Willis in 1961 (died 1967). **Career:** Writer from 1893; wrote nearly one hundred pseudonymous ''dime novels'' while attending graduate school; wrote Clif Faraday stories (as Ensign Clarke Fitch) and Mark Mallory stories (as Lieutenant Frederick Garrison) for various boys' weeklies, 1897-98; founded Intercollegiate Socialist Society (now League for Industrial Democracy), Helicon Home Colony, Englewood, New Jersey, 1906, and EPIC (End Poverty in California) League, 1934; assisted U.S. Government in investigation of Chicago stock yards, 1906; established theater company for performance of socialist plays, 1908. Socialist candidate for Congress, from New Jersey, 1906; settled in Pasadena, California, 1915; Socialist candidate for Congress, 1920, and for the United States Senate, 1922, and for Governor of California, 1926, 1930; moved to Buckeye, Arizona, 1953. Democratic candidate for governor of California, 1934. Occasional lecturer. **Awards:** Nobel Prize for literature nomination, 1932; Pulitzer Prize, 1943, for *Dragon's Teeth;* New York Newspaper Guild Page One award, 1962; United Auto Workers Social Justice award, 1962. **Died:** 25 November 1968.

PUBLICATIONS

Novels

Springtime and Harvest: A Romance. New York, Sinclair Press, 1901; as *King Midas,* New York and London, Funk, 1901.
The Journal of Arthur Stirling New York, Appleton, and London, Heinemann, 1903.
Prince Hagen: A Phantasy. Boston, Page, and London, Chatto & Windus, 1903.

Manassas: A Novel of the War. New York and London, Macmillan, 1904; as *Theirs Be the Guilt: A Novel of the War between the States,* New York, Twayne, 1959.
A Captain of Industry, Being the Story of a Civilized Man. Girard, Kansas, Appeal to Reason, and London, Heinemann, 1906.
The Jungle. New York, Doubleday, 1906; reprinted, Penguin, 1980; unabridged edition, New York, Doubleday, 1988.
The Metropolis. New York, Moffat, Yard, and London, Laurie, 1908.
The Moneychangers. New York, B.W. Dodge, and London, Long, 1908.
Samuel the Seeker. New York, B.W. Dodge, and London, Long, 1910.
Love's Pilgrimage. New York, M. Kennerley, 1911; London, Heinemann, 1912.
Damaged Goods. Philadelphia, Winston, 1913, and London, Hutchinson, 1913; as *Damaged Goods: A Novel about the Victims of Syphilis,* Girard, Kansas, Haldeman-Julius Publications, 1948.
Sylvia. Philadelphia, Winston, 1913; London, Long, 1914.
Sylvia's Marriage. Philadelphia, Winston, 1914; London, Laurie, 1915.
King Coal. New York, Macmillan, 1917, and London, Laurie, 1917.
Jimmie Higgins. London, Hutchinson, 1918; New York, Boni & Liveright, 1919.
The Spy. London, Laurie, 1919; as *100%: The Story of a Patriot,* privately printed, 1920; excerpt, as *Peter Gudge Becomes a Secret Agent,* Moscow, State Publishing House, 1930.
They Call Me Carpenter: A Tale of the Second Coming. New York, Boni & Liveright, and London, Laurie, 1922.
The Millennium: A Comedy of the Year 2000. Girard, Kansas, Haldeman Julius, 1924; London, Laurie, 1929.
Oil! New York, Boni, and London, Laurie, 1927.
Boston: A Documentary Novel of the Sacco-Vanzetti Case. New York, Boni, 1928; London, Laurie, 1929; abridged edition, as *August 22nd,* New York, Universal, 1965; Bath Chivers, 1971.
Mountain City. New York, Boni, and London, Laurie, 1930.
Roman Holiday. New York, Farrar & Rinehart, and London, Laurie, 1931.
The Wet Parade. New York, Farrar & Rinehart, and London, Laurie, 1931.
Co-op: A Novel of Living Together. New York, Farrar & Rinehart, and London, Laurie, 1936.
The Gnomobile: A Gnice Gnew Gnarrative with Gnonsense, but Gnothing Gnaughty (juvenile). New York, Farrar & Rinehart, and London, Laurie, 1936.
Little Steel. New York, Farrar & Rinehart, and London, Laurie, 1938.
Our Lady. Emmaus, Pennsylvania, Rodale Press, and London, Laurie, 1938.
Marie Antoinette. New York, Vanguard Press, and London, Laurie, 1939; as *Marie and Her Lover,* Girard, Kansas, Haldeman-Julius Publications, 1948.
World's End. New York, Viking, and London, Laurie, 1940.
Between Two Worlds. New York, Viking, and London, Laurie, 1941.
Dragon's Teeth. New York, Viking, and London, Laurie, 1942.
Wide Is the Gate. New York, Viking, and London, Laurie, 1943.
Presidential Agent. New York, Viking, 1944; London, Laurie, 1945.
Dragon Harvest. New York, Viking, and London, Laurie, 1945.

A World to Win, 1940-1942. New York, Viking, 1946; London, Laurie, 1947.

Presidential Mission. New York, Viking, 1947; London, Laurie, 1948.

One Clear Call. New York, Viking, 1948; London, Laurie, 1949.

O Shepherd, Speak. New York, Viking, 1949; London, Laurie, 1950.

Another Pamela; or, Virtue Still Rewarded. New York, Viking, and London, Laurie, 1950.

The Return of Lanny Budd. New York, Viking, and London, Laurie, 1953.

What Didymus Did. London, Wingate, 1954; as *It Happened to Didymus,* New York, Sagamore Press, 1958.

The Cup of Fury. Great Neck, New York, Channel Press, 1956; London, Arco, 1957.

Affectionately Eve. New York, Twayne, 1961.

The Coal War: A Sequel to King Coal, edited by John Graham. Boulder, Colorado Associated University Press, 1976.

Plays

Prince Hagen. adaptation of his own novel (produced San Francisco, 1909). Privately printed, 1909.

Plays of Protest (includes *Prince Hagen, The Naturewoman, The Machine, The Second-story Man*). New York, Kennerley, 1912.

Hell: A Verse Drama and Photo-play. Privately printed, 1923.

The Pot Boiler. Girard, Kansas, Haldeman, Julius, 1924.

Singing Jailbirds: A Drama in Four Acts (produced London, 1930). Privately printed, 1924.

Bill Porter: A Drama of O. Henry in Prison. Privately printed, 1925.

Wally for Queen! The Private Life of Royalty. Privately printed, 1936.

A Giant's Strength. Girard, Kansas, Haldeman-Julius, and London, Laurie, 1948.

The Enemy Had It Too. New York, Viking, 1950.

Three Plays (includes *The Second-Story Man, John D., The Indignant Subscriber*). Moscow, Progress, 1965.

Poetry

Songs of Our Nation (as Frederick Garrison). New York, Marks Music, 1941.

Other

Off for West Point; or, Mark Mallory's Struggle (as Frederick Garrison). New York, Street & Smith, 1903.

On Guard; or, Mark Mallory's Celebration (as Frederick Garrison). New York, Street & Smith, 1903.

The Toy and the Man. Westwood, Massachusetts, Ariel Press, 1904.

Our Bourgeois Literature. Chicago, Kerr, 1905.

Colony Customs. Englewood, New Jersey, Constitution, 1906.

The Helicon Home Colony. Englewood, New jersey, Constitution, 1906.

A Home Colony: A Prospectus. New York, Jungle, 1906.

What Life Means to Me. Girard, Kansas, Appeal to Reason, 1906.

The Overman. New York, Doubleday, and Boston, Page, 1907.

Good Health and How We Won It, with an Account of the New Hygiene, with Michael Williams. New York, F.A. Stokes, 1909; as *Strength and Health,* 1910; as *The Art of Health,* London, Health and Strength, 1909.

War: A Manifesto Against It. Girard, Kansas, Appeal to Reason, New York, Wilshire, and London, Clarion Press, 1909.

The Fasting Cure. New York, M. Kennerley, and London, Heinemann, 1911.

Four Letters About "Love's Pilgrimage." Privately printed, 1911.

The Sinclair-Astor Letters: Famous Correspondence Between Socialist and Millionaire. Girard, Kansas, Appeal to Reason, 1914.

Editor, *The Cry for Justice: An Anthology of the Literature of Social Protest.* Philadelphia, Winston, 1915.

Upton Sinclair: Biographical and Critical Opinions. Privately printed, 1917.

The Profits of Religion: An Essay in Economic Interpretation. Privately printed, 1918; New York, Vanguard, 1927; London, Laurie, 1936.

The Brass Check: A Study of American Journalism. London, Laurie, 1919; Pasadena, California, privately printed, 1920; excerpt, as *The Associated Press and Labor,* privately printed, 1920.

The High Cost of Living (address). Girard, Kansas, People's Press, 1919.

Russia: A Challenge. Girard, Kansas, Appeal to Reason, 1919.

Press-titution. Girard, Kansas, Appeal to Reason, 1920.

The Crimes of the "Times": A Test of Newspaper Decency. Privately printed, 1921.

The McNeal-Sinclair Debate on Socialism. Girard, Kansas, Haldeman Julius, 1921.

Mind and Body. New York, Macmillan, 1921; revised edition, Girard, Kansas, Halderman-Julius, 4 vols., 1950.

Biographical Letter and Critical Opinions. Privately printed, 1922.

The Book of Life. Pasadena, California, Sinclair Paine, 1922; London, Laurie, 1934.

The Goose-step: A Study of American Education. Privately printed, 1922; revised edition, n.d.; Girard, Kansas, Haldeman-Julius Publications, and London, Laurie, 1923.

Love and Society. Pasadena, California, Sinclair Paine, 1922; revised edition, Girard, Kansas, Haldeman-Julius, 4 vols., n.d.

The Goslings: A Study of the American Schools. Privately printed, 1924; London, Laurie, 1930; excerpt, as *The Schools of Los Angeles,* privately printed, 1924.

Mammonart: An Essay in Economic Interpretation. Privately printed, 1925; London, Laurie, 1934.

Letters to Judd, An American Workingman. Privately printed, 1926; revised edition as *This World of 1949 and What to Do about It: Revised Letters to a Workingman on the Economic and Political Situation,* Girard, Kansas, Haldeman-Julius, 1949.

The Spokesman's Secretary, Being the Letters of Mame to Mom. Privately printed, 1926.

Money Writes! New York, Boni, 1927; London, Laurie, 1931.

The Pulitzer Prize and "Special Pleading." Privately printed, 1929.

Mental Radio. New York, Boni, 1930; as *Mental Radio: Does It Work, and How?,* London, Laurie, 1930, revised edition, Springfield, Illinois, Thomas, 1962.

Socialism and Culture. Girard, Kansas, Haldeman-Julius, 1931.

Upton Sinclair on "Comrade" Kautsky. Moscow, Co-operative Publishing Society of Foreign Workers in the USSR, 1931.

American Outpost: A Book of Reminiscences. New York, Farrar & Rinehart, 1932; as *Candid Reminiscences: My First Thirty Years,* London, Laurie, 1932.

I, Governor of California, and How I Ended Poverty: A True Story of the Future. New York, Farrar & Rinehart, and London, Laurie, 1933.

Upton Sinclair Presents William Fox. Privately printed, 1933.

The Way Out: What Lies Ahead for America. New York, Farrar & Rinehart, and London, Laurie, 1933; revised edition, as *Limbo on the Loose: A Midsummer Night's Dream,* Girard, Kansas, Haldeman-Julius Publications, 1948.

The Book of Love. London, Laurie, 1934.

EPIC Answers: How to End Poverty in California. Los Angeles, End Poverty League, 1934.

The EPIC Plan for California. New York, Farrar & Rinehart, 1934.

The Lie Factory Starts. Los Angeles, End Poverty League, 1934.

An Upton Sinclair Anthology, edited by I.O. Evans. New York, Farrar & Rinehart, and London, Laurie, 1934; revised edition, Culver City, California, Murray & Gee, 1947.

Upton Sinclair's Last Will and Testament. Los Angeles, End Poverty League, 1934.

Depression Island. Pasadena, California, privately printed, and London, Laurie, 1935.

I, Candidate for Governor, and How I Got Licked. New York, Farrar & Rinehart, 1935; as *How I Got Licked and Why,* London, Laurie, 1935.

We, People of America, and How We Ended Poverty: A True Story of the Future. Pasadena, California, National EPIC League, 1935.

What God Means to Me: An Attempt at a Working Religion. New York, Farrar & Rinehart, and London, Laurie, 1936.

The Flivver King: A Story of Ford-America. Girard, Kansas, Haldeman-Julius Publications, 1937; as *The Flivver King: A Novel of Ford-America,* London, Laurie, 1938.

No Pasoran! (They Shall Not Pass): A Story of the Battle of Madrid. New York, Labor Press, and London, Laurie, 1937.

Terror in Russia?: Two Views, with Eugene Lyons. New York, Richard R. Smith, 1938.

Upton Sinclair on the Soviet Union. New York, Weekly Masses, 1938.

Expect No Peace! Girard, Kansas, Haldeman-Julius Publications, 1939.

Telling the World. London, Laurie, 1939.

What Can Be Done about America's Economic Troubles. Girard, Kansas, Haldeman-Julius, 1939.

Your Million Dollars. Privately printed, 1939; as *Letters to a Millionaire,* London, Laurie, 1939.

Is the American Form of Capitalism Essential to the American Form of Democracy? Girard, Kansas, Haldeman-Julius, 1940.

Peace or War in America? Girard, Kansas, Haldeman-Julius, 1940.

Index to the Lanny Budd Story, with others. New York, Viking Press, 1943.

To Solve the German Problem—A Free State? Privately printed, 1943.

A Personal Jesus: Portrait and Interpretation. New York, Evans, 1952; as *The Secret Life of Jesus,* Philadelphia, Mercury Books, 1962.

Radio Liberation Speech to the Peoples of the Soviet Union. New York, American Committee for Liberation from Bolshevism, 1955.

Cicero: A Tragedy of Ancient Rome. Privately printed, 1960.

My Lifetime in Letters. Columbia, University of Missouri Press, 1960.

The Autobiography of Upton Sinclair. New York, Harcourt, 1962; London, Allen & Unwin, 1963.

Upton Sinclair: Four Unpublished Letters. San Francisco, California, Artichoke Press, 1984.

Novels as Clarke Fitch

Courtmartialed. New York, Street & Smith, 1898.

Saved by the Enemy. New York, Street & Smith, 1898.

A Soldier Monk. New York, Street & Smith, 1899.

A Soldier's Pledge. New York, Street & Smith, 1899.

Wolves of the Navy; or, Clif Faraday's Search for a Traitor, New York, Street & Smith, 1899.

Clif, the Naval Cadet; or, Exciting Days at Annapolis. New York, Street & Smith, 1903.

The Cruise of the Training Ship; or, Clif Faraday's Pluck. New York, Street & Smith, 1903.

From Port to Port; or, Clif Faraday in Many Waters. New York, Street & Smith, 1903.

A Strange Cruise; or, Clif Faraday's Yacht Chase. New York, Street & Smith, 1903.

*

Media Adaptations: *The Adventurer* (film), U.S. Amusement Corp., 1917; *The Money Changers* (film), Pathe Exchange, 1920; *Marriage Forbidden* (film), Criterion, 1938; *The Gnome-Mobile* (film), Walt Disney Productions, 1967.

Biography: Entry in *Dictionary of Literary Biography,* Volume 9: *American Novelists, 1910-1945,* Detroit, Gale, 1981.

Bibliography: *Upton Sinclair: An Annotated Checklist* by Ronald Gottesman, Kent, Ohio, Kent State University Press, 1973.

Manuscript Collection: Lilly Library, Indiana University, Bloomington.

Critical Studies: *Upton Sinclair: A Study in Social Protest* by Floyd Dell, New York, Doubleday, 1927; *This Is Upton Sinclair* by James Harte Lambert, Emmaus, Pennsylvania, Rodale Press, 1938; *The Literary Manuscripts of Upton Sinclair* by Ronald Gottesman and Charles L.P. Silet, Columbus, Ohio State University Press, 1972; *Upton Sinclair* by John A. Yoder, New York, Ungar, 1975; *Upton Sinclair, American Rebel* by Leon Harris, New York, Crowell, 1975; *Critics on Upton Sinclair* edited by Abraham Blinderman, Coral Gables, Florida, University of Miami Press, 1975; *Upton Sinclair* by William A. Bloodworth, Boston, Twayne, 1977; entries in *Contemporary Literary Criticism,* Detroit, Gale, Volume 1, 1973; Volume 9, 1979; Volume 15, 1980.

*   *   *

Like a number of other writers, but with more zeal than most, Upton Sinclair dedicated himself to a cause—he once wrote that if his heart were cut in half after his death, the words inscribed there would be "Social Justice." This was his cause, and Sinclair supported it primarily in the form of devotion to the tenets of Socialism. The commitment began early; he joined the Socialist party in 1904. With an astounding production of books, articles, and letters, Sinclair attempted to advance Socialist principles, as he perceived them, all of his long life.

His very accessible fiction, most widely read of his works today, falls generally into two genres: the novel of social protest and the "historical" novel. Fame came early for Sinclair because of one of his social protest novels whose "cause" has largely vanished today but which is still assigned reading in many classrooms because of its realistic portrayal of the life and mistreatment of poor immigrants. His best-known title, *The Jungle* was never a great critical success, yet its fame was deserved: apart from presenting in great detail the grim events in the life of Jurgis Rudkus, a Lithuanian immigrant, and his family, Sinclair painted a naturalistic picture of the Chicago stockyards and the workings of that ghastly place which was so moving that it helped to cause the enactment of the Pure Food and Drug Act of 1906.

The Jungle reveals the strengths that were to mark Sinclair's work for the rest of his career. The ease and fluency with which Sinclair wrote tended to make him occasionally hasty and casual as to literary technique, but this easy-to-read style that lended itself to ready translation—into some forty-five languages in roughly forty countries—broadens Sinclair's appeal to young adults. Another strength of the novel lies in the painstaking research that went into it. Sinclair had an observing eye and strived tirelessly to determine facts; he even worked in a meatpacking plant for a time in order to observe details for himself.

The Jungle was followed by a long series of exposes of various immoral (and occasionally illegal) practices, usually by rich and unscrupulous capitalists. *King Coal* attempted to reveal the mistreatment of miners in Colorado, *Oil!* dealt with the Teapot Dome and other scandals involving the petroleum industry. The novel had considerable journalistic interest for contemporary readers, but it typically closes with a kind of sermon about "the black and cruel demon. . .an evil Power which roams the earth, crippling the bodies of men and women, and luring the nations to destruction by visions of unearned wealth, and the opportunity to enslave and exploit labor." A number of similar "message" novels followed. The long and comprehensive *Boston* delves into the injustices of the Sacco-Vanzetti case but also presents a sharp outline of Boston society with fine attention to detail. Another such work is Sinclair's vision of the immorality of a society that lives off great amounts of money—*The Metropolis,* in which New York is the central setting and in which, typically, the main character becomes sated with the life of easy wealth and luxury and rejects it.

Possessing a liveliness and spirit that appeals to many readers, Sinclair's historical novels are more pleasurable reading. Lanny Budd is the central character in a series of ten novels in which Sinclair covers leading world events, especially those from 1913 to 1950. Son of a munitions manufacturer and his socialite lady friend, Lanny is raised in Europe, where he begins as politically neutral, later learning to fear and hate the growing immorality which he finds in Nazi Germany. As Lanny grows older, he develops into a deeper and more rounded character, and becomes a secret agent for the president (a career founded on the real-life exploits of Cornelius Vanderbilt, Jr., according to Sinclair). A key aspect of these books, one that was typical of Sinclair himself, is Lanny's power of observation. He seems to overlook almost

nothing. While some of Lanny's meetings—with, for example, Joseph Goebbels, Adolf Hitler, Hermann Goering, and Franklin Roosevelt—seem improbable, this series has been highly praised for its accurate reflection of the sometimes calamitous events in the first half of this century. In his autobiography, Sinclair firmly asserted that no one had ever proved one of his "facts" to be in error.

While the series is strong in historical accuracy, one of the novels also found favor with the literary establishment: *Dragon's Teeth,* which deals with Germany's descent into Naziism during 1930 to 1934, won the Pulitzer Prize for fiction in 1943.

Very probably, Sinclair will be remembered best for *The Jungle;* however, his other works will repay the attention of young adults who desire to learn about social problems and important events in modern history in an easy and readable fashion.

—Fred McEwen

SINGER, Marilyn

Nationality: American. **Born:** New York City, 3 October 1948. **Education:** Attended University of Reading, 1967-68; Queens College of the City University of New York, B.A. (cum laude) 1969; New York University, M.A. 1979. **Family:** Married Steven Aronson in 1971. **Career:** Editor, Daniel S. Mead Literary Agency, 1967; assistant editor, *Where* (magazine), New York City, 1969; teacher of English and speech, New York City Public High Schools, 1969-74; writer, since 1974. **Awards:** Children's Choice Award, International Reading Association, 1977, for *The Dog Who Insisted He Wasn't,* 1979, for *It Can't Hurt Forever,* and 1988, for *Ghost Host;* Maud Hart Lovelace Award, Friends of the Minnesota Valley Regional Library (Mankato), 1983, for *It Can't Hurt Forever;* American Library Association (ALA) best book for young adults citation, 1983, for *The Course of True Love Never Did Run Smooth;* Parents' Choice Award, Parents' Choice Foundation, 1983, for *The Fido Frame-Up;* ALA best book for young adults nomination, 1988, for *Several Kinds of Silence;* New York Times best illustrated children's book citation, *Time* best children's book citation, both 1989, National Council of Teachers of English notable trade book in the language arts, 1990, and Texas Bluebonnet Award nomination, 1992, all for *Turtle in July.* **Address:** 42 Berkeley Pl., Brooklyn, New York 11217, U.S.A.

PUBLICATIONS FOR YOUNG ADULTS

Fiction

No Applause, Please. New York, Dutton, 1977.
The First Few Friends. New York, Harper, 1981.
The Course of True Love Never Did Run Smooth. New York, Harper, 1983.
Horsemaster. New York, Atheneum, 1985.
Ghost Host. New York, Harper, 1987.
Several Kinds of Silence. New York, Harper, 1988.
Storm Rising. New York, Scholastic, 1989.

Deal with a Ghost. New York, Holt, 1997.

Editor, *Stay True: Short Stories for Strong Girls* (short stories). New York, Scholastic Press, 1998.

PUBLICATIONS FOR CHILDREN

Picture Books

The Dog Who Insisted He Wasn't, illustrated by Kelly Oechsli. New York, Dutton, 1976.

The Pickle Plan, illustrated by Steven Kellogg. New York, Dutton, 1978.

Will You Take Me to Town on Strawberry Day?, illustrated by Trinka Hakes Noble. New York, Harper, 1981.

Archer Armadillo's Secret Room, illustrated by Beth Lee Weiner. New York, Macmillan, 1985.

Minnie's Yom Kippur Birthday, illustrated by Ruth Rosner. New York, Harper, 1989.

Turtle in July, illustrated by Jerry Pinkney. New York, Macmillan, 1989.

Nine O'Clock Lullaby, illustrated by Frane Lessac. New York, HarperCollins, 1991.

The Golden Heart of Winter, illustrated by Robert Rayevsky. New York, Morrow, 1991.

Out-of-Work Dog, illustrated by Cat Bowman Smith. New York, Holt, 1992.

In My Tent, illustrated by Emily Arnold McCully. New York, Macmillan, 1992.

Fiction

It Can't Hurt Forever, illustrated by Leigh Grant. New York, Harper, 1978.

Tarantulas on the Brain, illustrated by Leigh Grant. New York, Harper, 1982.

Lizzie Silver of Sherwood Forest (sequel to *Tarantulas on the Brain*), illustrated by Miriam Nerlove. New York, Harper, 1986.

The Lightey Club, illustrated by Kathryn Brown. New York, Four Winds, 1987.

Mitzi Meyer, Fearless Warrior Queen. New York, Scholastic, 1987.

Charmed. New York, Atheneum, 1990.

Twenty Ways to Lose Your Best Friend, illustrated by Jeffrey Lindberg. New York, Harper, 1990.

California Demon. New York, Hyperion, 1992.

Animal Greetings, illustrated by Normand Chartier. New York, Holt, 1996.

Bottoms Up, illustrations by Patrick O'Brien. New York, H. Holt, 1996.

Good Day, Good Night, illustrated by Ponder Goembel. New York, Marshall Cavendish, 1998.

"Sam and Dave" mystery series

Leroy Is Missing, illustrated by Judy Glasser. New York, Harper, 1984.

The Case of the Sabotaged School Play, illustrated by Judy Glasser. New York, Harper, 1984.

A Clue in Code, illustrated by Judy Glasser. New York,, Harper, 1985.

The Case of the Cackling Car, illustrated by Judy Glasser. New York, Harper, 1985.

The Case of the Fixed Election, illustrated by Richard Williams. New York, Harper, 1989.

The Hoax on You, illustrated by Richard Williams. New York, Harper, 1989.

"Samantha Spayed" mystery series:

The Fido Frame-Up, illustrated by Andrew Glass. New York, Warne, 1983.

A Nose for Trouble, illustrated by Andrew Glass, New York, Holt, 1985.

Where There's a Will, There's a Wag, illustrated by Andrew Glass. New York, Holt, 1986.

Nonfiction

Exotic Birds, illustrated by James Needham. New York, Doubleday, 1990.

Poetry

The Morgans' Dream, illustrations by Gary Drake. New York, H. Holt, 1995.

All We Needed to Say: Poems about School from Tanya and Sophie, photographs by Lorna Clark. New York, Atheneum Books for Young Readers, 1996.

PUBLICATIONS FOR ADULTS

Nonfiction

Editor and author of introduction, *A History of Avant-Garde Cinema.* American Federation of Arts, 1976.

Editor and contributor, *New American Filmmakers.* American Federation of Arts, 1976.

The Fanatic's Ecstatic, Aromatic Guide to Onions, Garlic, Shallots and Leeks, illustrated by Marian Perry. New York, Prentice-Hall, 1981.

Also author of several teacher's guides, catalogs, and program notes on films and filmstrips, including Jacob Bronowski's *The Ascent of Man* and David Attenborough's *The Tribal Eye.* Past curator of *SuperFilmShow!,* a series of avant-garde films selected for children. Writer of scripts for the children's television show *The Electric Company.* Contributor of short stories to books, including *Rooms of Our Own,* Holt, 1992.

*   *   *

Winner of numerous awards and honors, Marilyn Singer is a prolific writer of picture books, juvenile books, and young adult novels, which include mysteries and fantasies. Understanding the child in herself, she uses some of her own past experiences in writing for children and young adults because, as she says, she likes to.

Death can be very frightening when one is faced with it, but everyone has to confront it sooner or later. Ellie Simon is terrified that she is going to die in *It Can't Hurt Forever.* She has a patent ductus arteriosus, or heart defect, and must have an operation to repair it. This is a very informative story about Ellie's stay in the hospital, the various tests and diagnoses she has to go through before the operation, and it is also about hospitals and operations in general. Singer writes from experience, having had a similar operation when she was young, and she doesn't want anyone to face the terrifying unknown that she faced as a child. She tells of young people's fears and how ignorance of hospitals and surgery can lead to terror-filled misconceptions of the various medical procedures. Ellie fortunately has parents, doctors, and friends who take the time to tell her generally what she will be going through during her stay in the hospital. Unfortunately, everyone fails to inform her of the pain she must endure when she gets her cardiac catheterization. Her anger and frustration upset everyone, including herself, but she comes through her surgery like a champ, unhappy about the scar that begins in the middle of her chest and ends in the middle of her back, but knowing that she is going to live. Young people will appreciate reading this book, because it is written in a caring, descriptive, factual way, with a little humor woven among the explanations about hospitals and operations. It is simple to understand, and fears will vanish after reading it.

Horsemaster, a fantasy, is an example of Singer's varying genres. Jessica, the main character, is a fourteen-year-old rebellious girl, encouraged in her defiance against her domineering mother by Jessica's friend Jack, also a rebel. When the two young people go for a ride on a "borrowed" motorcycle, they stop at a deserted, ramshackle farmhouse where they find an ancient tapestry hanging on a wall. In the threads of the dusty material is woven the starred head of a horse named Gabdon that mysteriously appears before Jessica and Jack and carries them to another world, far away from Brown Dear, Wisconsin, where they live. In the new world Jessica learns to forgive her father for leaving his family, her mother for the sorrow and bitterness she has caused, and to forgive herself. Jack, too, overcomes his rebellious anger and restlessness, and the two young people realize they must change in order to get along in the real world, learning that there are other important people in their lives. An appropriate story for young adults in this seemingly uncaring contemporary world, readers will gain a new perspective on life after reading it.

Cited best book for young adults, *The Course of True Love Never Did Run Smooth* deals with the difficulties encountered by a gay couple, a rather touchy subject that is gaining more attention every day. Becky plays the part of Helena in the high school play *A Midsummer Night's Dream* and finds she has problems with her feelings toward Blake and her friend Nehemiah. The characters are unique, the dialogue humorously amorous at times, and a controversial topic is handled well, providing an interesting insight into the feelings of a gay couple who are finally admitting their true identities to others.

Ghost Host, another fantasy but more supernatural, portrays a poltergeist named Stryker and a friendly ghost named Millie who enter the lives of star quarterback Bart Hawkins, his girlfriend Lisa, captain of the cheerleading squad, and Arvie, a derisive classmate.

An amusing tale, Singer once more has written an appealing story for young adults.

Marilyn Singer's stories include such a variety of genres—mysteries, medical tales, romances, fantasies, as well as picture books for children—one doesn't know what she is going to write next. Every young adult knows, however, that whatever Singer writes for them will be enjoyable, entertaining reading.

—Carol Doxey

SLEATOR, William (Warner III)

Nationality: American. **Born:** Havre de Grace, Maryland, 13 February 1945. **Education:** Harvard University, Cambridge, Massachusetts, 1963-67, B.A. in English 1967; studied musical composition in London, England, 1967-68. **Career:** Accompanist for ballet classes, Royal Ballet School, London, 1967-68, and Rambert School, London, 1967-68; rehearsal pianist, Boston Ballet Company, Boston, Massachusetts, 1974-83; writer. **Awards:** Bread Loaf Writers' Conference fellowship, 1969; Caldecott Medal Honor Book, American Library Association (ALA), and *Boston Globe-Horn Book* award, both 1971, American Book award for Best Paperback Picture Book, 1981, ALA Notable Book citation, and *Horn Book* Honor List citation, all for *The Angry Moon;* Children's Book of the Year award, Child Study Association of America, 1972, and ALA Notable Book citation, both for *Blackbriar;* Best Books for Young Adults citations, ALA, 1974, for *House of Stairs,* 1984, for *Interstellar Pig,* 1985, for *Singularity,* and 1987, for *The Boy Who Reversed Himself,* Best of the Best for Young Adults citation, ALA Notable Book citation, *Horn Book* Honor List citation, and Junior Literary Guild selection, all for *Interstellar Pig;* Children's Choice award, International Reading Association and Children's Book Council, and Junior Literary Guild selection, both for *Into the Dream;* Best Book of the Year awards, *School Library Journal,* 1981, for *The Green Futures of Tycho,* 1983, for *Fingers,* and 1984, for *Interstellar Pig;* Junior Literary Guild selection, for *Singularity;* Golden Pen award, Spokane Washington Public Library, 1984 and 1985, both for "the author who gives the most reading pleasure." **Agent:** Sheldon Fogelman, 10 East Fortieth St., New York, New York 10016. **Address:** 77 Worcester St., Boston, Massachusetts 02118, U.S.A.

<small>PUBLICATIONS FOR YOUNG ADULTS</small>

Fiction

Run. New York, Dutton, 1973.
House of Stairs. New York, Dutton, 1974; London, Macdonald, 1988.
Among the Dolls, illustrated by Trina Schart Hyman. New York, Dutton, 1975.
Into the Dream, illustrated by Ruth Sanderson. New York, Dutton, 1979.
The Green Futures of Tycho. New York, Dutton, 1981; London, Macdonald, 1988.
Fingers. New York, Atheneum, 1983.

Interstellar Pig. New York, Dutton, 1984; London, Hodder and
   Stoughton, 1987.
Singularity. New York, Dutton, 1985; London, Macdonald, 1988.
The Boy Who Reversed Himself. New York, Dutton, 1986; London,
   Macdonald, 1988.
The Duplicate. New York, Dutton, 1988.
Strange Attractors. New York, Dutton, 1990.
The Spirit House. New York, Dutton, 1991.
Oddballs: Stories. New York, Dutton, 1993.
Others See Us. New York, Dutton, 1993.
Dangerous Wishes. New York, Dutton, 1995.
The Night the Heads Came. New York, Dutton, 1996.
The Beasties. New York, Dutton, 1997.
The Boxes. New York, Dutton, 1998.

PUBLICATIONS FOR CHILDREN

Fiction

Blackbriar, illustrated by Blair Lent. New York, Dutton, 1972.
Once, Said Darlene, illustrated by Steven Kellogg. New York,
   Dutton, 1979.
That's Silly, illustrated by Lawrence DiFiori. New York, Dutton, 1981.

Other

The Angry Moon (retelling), illustrated by Blair Lent. Boston,
   Little, Brown, 1970.

Composer of music for film *Why the Sun and Moon Live in the
Sky,* 1972.

PUBLICATIONS FOR ADULTS

Other

Take Charge: A Personal Guide to Behavior Modification, with
   William H. Redd. New York, Random House, 1976.

*

Media Adaptations: *The Angry Moon* (audiocassette), Read-
Along-House; *Interstellar Pig* (audiocassette), Listening Library, 1987.

Biography: Essay in *Speaking for Ourselves: Autobiographical
Sketches by Notable Authors of Books for Young Adults,* Vol. 1,
compiled and edited by Donald R. Gallo, National Council of
Teachers of English, 1990; essay in *Authors and Artists for Young
Adults,* Vol. 5, Detroit, Gale, 1991.

*   *   *

William Sleator's books for young adults present interesting
challenges for both the characters in the stories and readers alike. A
writer of mysteries initially, Sleator later branched out to create

works with science fictional elements—from technology and
experimentation gone awry to the capricious machinations of alien
beings to supernatural and occult forces. It has become his trademark to place seemingly ordinary young people in extraordinary
and often threatening situations involving at least one hidden
influence that changes the direction of the outcome. While his
novels tend to provide satisfactory endings, with most problems
solved and the future of the protagonist somewhat secure, Sleator
refuses to leave the reader feeling complacent. There is always the
hint that there is more to come, that maybe things aren't quite what
they seem, prompting the reader to use his or her own imagination
to consider the "what ifs" if the story were to continue.

In *House of Stairs,* six teenagers are placed in an unusual
environment, a building full of stairs leading nowhere—or everywhere—with no directions for survival. The teenagers learn to
cope by performing strange rituals before a machine that rewards
them with food and by forming relationships with others in the
group. Although they are not aware of it, the young people are part
of a scientific stimulus-response experiment enacted by the
government to induce behavior modification. Every reaction, movement, and even bodily function occurs under the watchful eyes of
the other young people and hidden observers. When two of the
young people refuse to perform the cruelty required to obtain food
and are close to starving, the scientists end the experiment. They
regard these two as symbols of hope for the survival of the human
spirit and its ability to fight against conformity and cruelty.

Other works by Sleator examine the possibility of time travel
both into the past and into the future, and the possible futures such
travel would bring about. In *The Green Futures of Tycho,* an egg-
like device dropped—planted—by aliens in prehistoric times is
found by eleven-year-old Tycho, who uses it to explore many
different futures, each more unpleasant than the last. Time travel
also occurs in *Singularity,* in an Illinois field, where time speeds up.
Overnight, a twin brother ages one year; he turns seventeen while
his twin remains sixteen. Characters in *The Boy Who Reversed
Himself* travel in both time and the fourth spatial dimension. In
Strange Attractors, time travel is made possible by a scientist who
inadvertently manages to clone himself and his daughter on one of
their trips.

Sibling rivalry is a theme in several of Sleator's books, including *Fingers, Singularity,* and *The Duplicate* in which sixteen-year-
old David finds a machine on the beach that can duplicate any
living thing. David duplicates himself so that he can spend time
with his girlfriend and have fun while his clone goes to school and
performs other unpleasant duties. However, the clone duplicates
itself, and David has to deal with his two other selves. In this
instance, sibling rivalry results in murder.

In *Interstellar Pig,* Barney is quite aware of the beauty and
sexuality of the mysterious Zena who lives next door. He is so
flattered by her attention that he acquires an acute sunburn to be in
her presence. However, since she is really an alien spider-like
creature, their relationship progresses no further. Although twins
Harry and Barry in *Singularity* are both attracted to Lucy, she
chooses Barry as a boyfriend. Jealousy is a major reason why Harry
decides to sleep overnight in the time-altering workshop, and when
he appears the next day one year older, taller, and more muscular
than Barry, Lucy's interest shifts to him. However, the relationship
between the brothers proves more important than their competition
over Lucy, when they reconcile and return home with their parents
at the end, she is left behind.

In *The Duplicate,* David and his clones are all enamored of Angela, one of David's classmates. While David is awkward, hesitant, and inept in his interactions with Angela, his clones are rough and insistent with her, to the point of near rape. Yet Angela realizes that she is not dealing with the real David and helps him destroy the two duplicates. By the end of the novel, she and David have established a good relationship.

Sexuality becomes more overt in some of Sleator's later novels, including *Strange Attractors* in which Max has a definite sexual encounter with Eve's evil clone. While Sleator does not try to shock the reader, as he does not go into detail about Max's experiences. For Max, sexual attraction for a girl who is evil represents one of those strange attractors that makes people do things they might not do otherwise. The reader is left with the hint that even though Max knows better, he will go back into the past to find Eve where he has safely trapped her.

Spirit House marks a change for Sleator in that he creates a female protagonist and uses his fascination with Thailand to supply the unusual twist. The family of fifteen-year-old Julie accepts an exchange student, Bia, from Thailand who turns out to be nothing like his pictures or letters. The Thai spirit house that her little brother builds in the back yard as a gift for Bia turns out to be more than anyone has bargained for. Mysteriously, Julie's health and looks begin to deteriorate until at last she appeases the spirit who inhabits the spirit house. Or does she? In his typical style, Sleator employs a quirky ending that sets the reader up for continuing the story in his or her imagination.

The protagonists in Sleator's fiction are primarily teenage males experiencing difficulties in their relationships with females, siblings, parents and even themselves. The appeal that such characters hold for young readers is that while they are encountering strange and often extraordinary forces and beings, they are also working out their own psychological issues and emerging with a stronger sense of self. Sleator challenges both his characters and his readers, whom he invites to take an active role in the stories by using their own imaginations. Regardless of the scenario, the reader is encouraged to do what Sleator himself does—create a new story.

—Hazel K. Davis

SLEPIAN, Jan(ice B.)

Nationality: American. **Born:** New York City, 2 January 1921. **Education:** Brooklyn College, B.A. 1942; University of Washington, M.A. (clinical psychology), 1947; New York University, M.A. (speech pathology), 1964; attended University of California—Berkeley, 1979. **Family:** Married 1) Urey Krasnopolsky in 1945 (divorced, 1948); 2) David Slepian in 1950, two sons and one daughter. **Career:** Language therapist, Massachusetts General Hospital, Boston, Massachusetts, 1947-49; private speech therapist, 1952-58; speech therapist, Easter Seal Clinic, Newton, New Jersey, 1953-55; speech therapist, Matheny School for Cerebral Palsy, Far Hills, New Jersey, 1955-57; writer. **Awards:** *The Alfred Summer* was named one of the best books of the year by *School Library Journal,* 1980, and was named a notable book by the

American Library Association (ALA); American Book Award finalist in children's fiction, and *Boston Globe/Horn Book* Honor for fiction, both 1981, for *The Alfred Summer;* Author's awards, New Jersey Institute of Technology, 1981, for *The Alfred Summer,* and 1983, for *The Night of the Bozos; Lester's Turn* was named one of the best books for children by the *New York Times,* and a notable children's book for older readers by *School Library Journal,* both 1981, a notable children's trade book in social studies by *Social Education,* and one of New York Public Library's books for the teen age, both 1982, and a notable book by the ALA; *The Night of the Bozos* was named one of the best books for young adults by the ALA, one of the children's books of the year by the Child Study Association of America, and one of the books of the year by the Library of Congress, all 1983; *Something beyond Paradise* was named one of the ten great books of the year for teens by *Redbook,* 1987; *The Broccoli Tapes* was named a notable book by the ALA, 1989; *Booklist* Editor's Choice, 1989, for *The Broccoli Tapes,* and 1990, for *Risk n' Roses; Risk n' Roses* was named one of New York Public Library's best books, 1990. **Agent:** Sheldon Fogelman, 10 East 40th St., New York, New York 10016. **Address:** 212 Summit Ave., Summit, New Jersey 07901, U.S.A.

PUBLICATIONS FOR YOUNG ADULTS

Fiction

The Alfred Summer. New York, Macmillan, 1980.
Lester's Turn (sequel to *The Alfred Summer*). New York, Macmillan, 1981.
The Night of the Bozos. New York, Dutton, 1983.
Getting On with It. New York, Four Winds, 1985.
Something beyond Paradise. New York, Philomel, 1987.
The Broccoli Tapes. New York, Philomel, 1989.
Risk n' Roses. New York, Philomel, 1990.
Back to Before. New York, Philomel, 1993.
Pinocchio's Sister. New York, Philomel, 1995.
The Mind Reader. New York, Philomel, 1997.

PUBLICATIONS FOR CHILDREN

"Listen-Hear" picture book series; all with Ann Seidler; all illustrated by Richard E. Martin:

Alphie and the Dream Machine. New York, Follett, 1964.
The Cock Who Couldn't Crow. New York, Follett, 1964.
Lester and the Sea Monster. New York, Follett, 1964.
Magic Arthur and the Giant. New York, Follett, 1964.
Mister Sipple and the Naughty Princess. New York, Follett, 1964.
The Roaring Dragon of Redrose. New York, Follett, 1964.

"Junior Listen-Hear" picture book series; all with Ann Seidler; all illustrated by Richard E. Martin:

Bendemolena. New York, Follett, 1967; as *The Cat Who Wore a Pot on Her Head,* New York, Scholastic, 1981.
Ding-Dong, Bing-Bong. New York, Follett, 1967.
An Ear Is to Hear. New York, Follett, 1967.

The Hungry Thing. New York, Follett, 1967.
The Silly Listening Book. New York, Follett, 1967.

With Ann Seidler

The Best Invention of All, illustrated by Joseph Veno. New York, Crowell-Collier, 1967.
The Hungry Thing Returns, illustrated by Richard E. Martin. New York, Scholastic, 1990.
The Hungry Thing Goes To a Restaurant, illustrated by Elroy Freem. New York, Scholastic, 1992.

Other

Building Foundations for Better Speech and Reading (teachers' training series and cassette tape program; with twelve tapes and discussion guide). Instructional Dynamics Inc., 1974.
Lost Moose (fiction). New York, Philomel, 1995.

*

Biography: Essay in *Something about the Author Autobiography Series,* Vol. 8, Detroit, Gale, 1989; essay in *Speaking for Ourselves, Too* compiled and edited by Donald R. Gallo, National Council of Teachers of English, 1993; *Major Authors and Illustrators for Children and Young Adults,* Detroit, Gale, 1993; *Something About the Author,* Vol. 85, Detroit, Gale, 1996.

Manuscript Collections: Kerlan Collection, University of Minnesota.

Jan Slepian comments:

I never thought of being a writer when I was growing up. The idea never occurred to me. It was on about the same unimaginable level as aiming to be the Pope or a horse. But always, always I was in love with words. I read myself silly, and to this day I get the greatest pleasure from the way words are arranged in a sentence. For me, in writing, the fun is in the way I say a thing.

*   *   *

Jan Slepian began writing picture books because of her work as a speech therapist. Later she wrote books for young adults, two of which were selected by Junior Literary Guild. Many of Slepian's characters are mentally, physically, or socially handicapped, but they learn about themselves and how to cope with their problems and the world around them.

The Alfred Summer, named *Boston Globe/Horn Book* Fiction Honor Book of 1980, portrays four outcasts. Lester has cerebral palsy, Myron is uncoordinated, Alfred Burt is mentally retarded, and skinny Claire dreams of becoming the world's fastest girl runner. Lester is smart—full of ideas, words and dreams—but can't express himself because of his handicap; besides, he is attached to his mother by invisible strings and feels he can't get along in life without her. Claire introduces the boys to her Aziff Theory, which is to act as if things don't really bother them when

they do, or that they are really happy when they aren't, or that they really have confidence when they don't. Slepian has written a very enlightening story about retardation and cerebral palsy, as well as the problems of a boy who is overweight and clumsy. She handles all these with delicacy and light humor, showing that the problems are not as big as they seem when faced with a positive attitude. Although the narrative shifts from the first person to the third unexpectedly, confusing the reader here and there, the story is moving, the reader can hear and smell Coney Island, and the wit of Lester is hilarious. Slepian has skillfully portrayed four admirable young people dealing with afflictions that cannot be changed, but can be accepted. Young adults will read this book and come away knowing they, too, can face problems using the Aziff Theory with success.

Lester's Turn continues the story of Alfred and Lester. Alfred's mother dies, and Alfred is placed in a hospital. Lester attempts to kidnap Alfred from the institution, but miserably fails. Eventually, Lester is allowed to take Alfred out of the building, but when Alfred becomes ill and dies of a burst appendix, even though Lester is devastated, he realizes he is now more able to face his own problems because of Alfred. Young people can learn that one's problems aren't as great as they seem when compared to those of others.

Death is a difficult subject to write about, but Slepian handles it forthrightly in *The Broccoli Tapes.* Sara Davidson and her family move to Hawaii for four months while Mr. Davidson teaches a biology class there. Sara records on cassette tapes events that happen in Hawaii for an oral history project for her social studies class back in Boston. Sara and her brother, Sam, find a cat caught in the rocks at the beach and rescue it. They sneak food to it, and are amazed to find the animal loves broccoli, so they name her for the vegetable. They are also amazed when Broccoli has kittens. Sara's grandmother, visiting them for a few weeks, is diagnosed with cancer and dies. The family members deal with her death in different ways: running away from it, holding it inside, or facing it head-on. Then Broccoli also dies and the young people reach their limit. Slepian has written a heartbreaking story of losing a loved person and a pet, but shows that the experience of love gives people the strength to handle loss. Cleverly written with the unique device of a tape machine recording happenings and revealing feelings, the book has the added advantage of its setting in beautiful Hawaii.

In *Something Beyond Paradise,* Slepian has written about several people who seem incapable of standing on their own two feet. Franny Simone, sixteen years old, lives with her single mother and somewhat senile grandmother in Hawaii. Franny's best friend, Akiko, joins a cult commune, The House of Regis, run by an overpowering man who seems to mesmerize his followers. Franny decides to leave home and move to New York and join a dance group. This is a disconcerting story, because sixteen seems young for a teenager to be making such an important decision without parental support. Moreover, the girl encourages her nineteen-year-old boyfriend to accompany her to New York, making the situation even more questionable. Although the reader is left not knowing if things are going to work out or not, the story is interesting and shows young people the dangers of becoming involved with cults.

Getting On with It, a Junior Literary Guild selection, portrays a young girl who is sent to stay with her grandmother for a month while her parents contemplate divorce. Berry Brice is faced with the death of a loved older friend, and the lopsided romance of a forty-year-old neighbor woman with a twenty-nine-year-old man, besides the frustration of her parents possibly splitting up. Quite a bit for a thirteen-year-old to manage, but somehow Berry does it, leaving the reader in awe at her and her creator.

Books such as *Lost Moose*—which is about exactly that—are for children, but Slepian continues to produce engaging stories for her young adult audience as well. In *Pinocchio's Sister,* she takes readers into the unfamiliar world of vaudeville around the turn of the century. Martha doesn't realize that her family is dysfunctional, since such a concept hardly existed at the time, but it is clear that her father's obsessive behavior is destructive to her self-esteem. Readers will be drawn in by the unusual setting, which Slepian paints in detail, and by the compelling story of Martha's ultimate triumph.

Jan Slepian is an intriguing writer, solving a variety of problems relating to the physically handicapped, death, divorce, and irrational behavior. She writes thought-provoking books, stimulating young adults to think for themselves and to strive to overcome problems that have seemed like mountains until, in the hands of Slepian's characters, they appear as speed bumps.

—Carol Doxey, updated by Judson Knight

SMITH, Doris Buchanan

Nationality: American. **Born:** Washington, D.C., 1 June 1934. **Education:** South Georgia College, Douglas. **Family:** Married 1) R. Caroll Smith in 1954 (divorced 1977), four sons and one daughter; 2) Bill Curtis, c. 1988. **Career:** Writer, since 1971. **Awards:** American Library Association Notable Book award and Child Study Association Book of the Year award, both 1973, Georgia Children's Book Author of the Year and Georgia General Author of the Year award, both from Dixie Council of Authors and Journalists, 1974, Georgia Children's Book award, 1975, and Sue Hafner award and Kinderbook award, both 1977, all for *A Taste of Blackberries*; Georgia Children's Book Author of the Year award, and Notable Children's Book award from National Council for Social Studies, both 1975, for *Kelly's Creek*; Breadloaf Writers Conference fellowship, 1975; Georgia Children's Book Author of the Year award, and Best Book of the Year award from *School Library Journal,* both 1982, for *Last Was Lloyd*; Parents' Choice Literature award, 1986, for *Return to Bitter Creek.*

PUBLICATIONS FOR YOUNG ADULTS

Fiction

A Taste of Blackberries, illustrated by Charles Robinson. New York, Crowell, 1973; London, Heinemann, 1975.
Kick a Stone Home. New York, Crowell, 1974.
Tough Chauncey, illustrated by Michael Eagle. New York, Morrow, 1974.
Kelly's Creek, illustrated by Alan Tiegreen. New York, Crowell, 1975.
Up and Over. New York, Morrow, 1976.
Dreams and Drummers. New York, Crowell, 1978.
Salted Lemons. New York, Four Winds Press, 1980.

Last Was Lloyd. New York, Viking Kestrel, 1981.
Moonshadow of Cherry Mountain. New York, Four Winds Press, 1982.
The First Hard Times. New York, Viking Kestrel, 1983.
Laura Upside-Down. New York, Viking Kestrel, 1984.
Return to Bitter Creek. New York, Viking Kestrel, 1986.
Karate Dancer. New York, Putnam, 1987.
Voyages. New York, Viking Kestrel, 1989.
The Pennywhistle Tree. New York, Putnam, 1991.
Best Girl. New York, Viking Kestrel, 1993.
Remember the Red-shouldered Hawk. New York, G.P. Putnam's Sons, 1994.

*

Biography: Essay in *Something about the Author Autobiography Series,* Vol. 10, Detroit, Gale.

Critical Studies: Entry in *Dictionary of Literary Biography,* Vol. 52, *American Writers for Children since 1960: Fiction,* Detroit, Gale, 1986.

*   *   *

Doris Buchanan Smith's seventeen novels, principally for young adult readers, describe teenager's daily lives, feelings, and problems with skill, sensitivity, and honesty. Her books have often broken new ground in realistic treatments of death, divorce, obesity, juvenile delinquency, unwed mothers, dyslexia, sexual drives, foster and stepparents, and child abuse. But they seldom focus on these problems. She begins with a character. Then, as she has said, the character has problems because people do in real life. Her books do not force neat solutions. Just as in life some problems cannot be solved but must be adjusted to or lived with.

Certainly Smith's experiences in raising five of her own children and numerous foster children gave insights into the nature of older children and their families. Her first published book, *A Taste of Blackberries,* brought critical success and several awards for her sensitivity to the internal life of a child. In dealing directly with the death of a child's playmate, it broke a taboo of twentieth-century American children's fiction. It focuses on the unnamed narrator's feelings of guilt and loss for his best friend Jamie, "a show-off and a clown," who dies from an allergic reaction to a bee sting.

Though her next books *Kick a Stone Home* and *Tough Chauncey* deal with alienation from family and friends, their main characters are very different. The protagonist of *Kick a Stone Home* is Sara Jane Chambers, a fifteen-year-old middle-class Atlanta girl, who has ordinary domestic problems: adjusting to her parents' divorce and moving to a new neighborhood. But Chauncey, a thirteen-year-old poor white, is illiterate, delinquent, belligerent, and disobedient to both parental and school authorities. He is beaten by his religiously fundamentalist grandfather and frequently abandoned by his immature mother, who drifts through life with a low-paying job and a series of rather worthless husbands and lovers. After Jack Levitt, a black boy from another broken home and his "best friend," frames him for the theft of a bike, he seriously injures himself while attempting to hitch a ride on a freight train. He soon realizes that a foster home promises him more of a chance than does his family. It is a powerful story, and well told.

Kelly's Creek deals with the social and educational problems of nine-year-old dyslexic Kelly O'Brian. Friendship with a college student who comes to do research in the tidal creek behind their coastal Georgia home helps Kelly to develop confidence and an interest in learning, which leads to success in biology class and a better relationship to his parents and old brother.

This simply written book with sparse yet accurate biological details was followed by *Up and Over,* which seems to crowd in everything remarkable about the 1960s: streaking, student protests, drug addiction, racial tension, teenage marriages or pregnancy, over-rigorous parenting, and mainstreaming of the handicapped. In the much simpler, much less traumatic story of *Dreams and Drummers,* fourteen-year-old Stephanie Stone's only problem is that she fails to agonize over the ordinary teenage woes of studies and dates.

Salted Lemons marked a return to more weighty issues. Set in the Atlanta of 1943 and drawing on details of Smith's youth, the book tells how ten-year-old Darby Bannister finds herself ostracized as a Yankee from Washington, D.C., and as a hick because she can not attend the city school as she lives just inside the county line. The novel focuses on the paradoxes of prejudice, alienation, and friendship, nicely symbolized by the salted lemons that Darby learns to share with Yoko, a Japanese-American girl whose family is subsequently interred in Florida during World War II spy hysteria. Religious extremes are represented by Darby's father's agnosticism; her mother's conventional Methodism; the Fundamentalism of Fancy Potter, a poor white girl and Darby's friend; and the millenarianism of Jeannine, another friend, whose family rents Yoko's empty house. Relating to these people teaches Darby the importance of tolerance.

In *Last Was Lloyd,* twelve-year-old Lloyd Albert, a mother-ridden and overweight sixth grader, is last in everything, especially school sports. As a result he is a bully and a glutton. Lloyd first picks on and then befriends another bright outsider, Ancil Witherspoon. She leads him into changing his behavior and establishing his independence from his over-protective mother.

The First Hard Times takes up where *Last Was Lloyd* left off. Ancil has to adjust to her mother's remarriage to Harvey Hutton and the family's subsequent move to the coastal Georgia town of Hanover. She clings to a futile hope that her real father Alexander will return, though he has been reported missing-in-action for eleven years. Her change from anger and grief to an acceptance of the new marriage is well handled.

Moonshadow of Cherry Mountain, a dog story set in the North Carolina mountains, where the author has a simple A-frame summer cabin, marked quite a departure in locale and main character. Moonshadow, a Labrador retriever, belongs to Greg, the fifteen-year-old son of school teachers Grant and Peg Riley. Just as the dog has to learn to adjust his territorial boundaries as the mountain lands are developed, so also people must adjust to families with different values who move in. And Greg has to adjust to the Riley's adoption of a daughter, who is allergic to, and frightened of, his beloved dog.

Laura Upside-Down attempts to explore severe religious intolerance and family conflicts. The central character, Laura Catherine or "Cat," is happiest seeing the world upside down,

hanging from a large tree. The novel deals with her attempts to see religious and family matters right side up. Her own family is agnostic. Her ten-year-old girlfriends Zipporah Greengold and Anna Banner come from an Orthodox Jewish family and a Fundamentalist Christian one. While researching the origins of Halloween, Thanksgiving, Hanukkah, and Christmas in preparation for seasonal parties, they learn tolerance for different views and persons. Unfortunately the messages and didacticism of the novel make for a very talky book, not one of action.

Much simpler and more believable is *Return to Bitter Creek.* Twelve-year-old Lacey Bittner, her mother Ann Campbell Bittner, and David Habib—her mother's lover of three years and a crafts blacksmith—return to the tiny mountain community of Bitter (i.e. Bittner) Creek, North Carolina, where Ann grew up, Lacey was born illegitimately, and from whence Ann fled when Lacey was two. An offer of a job for David at the local craft school brings the trio to Bitter Creek. Though it is another book about cultural, moral, and family differences, these concerns are embodied in the characters, who, major and minor, are strong and convincing. Smith's earlier books have been occasionally faulted for being too episodic or too crowded with peripheral details. This book has a nice unity; the final chapter echoes the opening with its title and action.

Karate Dancer features Smith's kind of paradoxical hero. Fourteen-year-old Troy Matthews, a karate enthusiast and political cartoonist for the local newspaper, is disappointed and resentful that his mother and father are not interested in his growing karate skills. In return he scorns their interests in music and photography. As the story develops, Troy and his family learn to meet each other halfway in their interests, while recognizing their differences. A romantic interest in Liesl Trunzo leads him to become her partner in the ballet *Coppelia.* His conflict with three karate students from a rival studio and his demonstration of karate skills to children with muscular dystrophy at a summer camp help him to redefine masculinity. Smith alludes skillfully to the developing sexuality of Troy and Liesl.

One of the most original current writers of young adult novels, Smith continues to surprise readers by the variety and depth of her books. In *Voyages,* fantasy adventures activate the story of twelve-year-old Janessa Kessel, forced to lie immobile in a hospital bed with a broken arm and back after being kidnapped and thrown from a car. The traumatized Janessa would prefer to isolate herself from parents, her brother and sister, the family dog, her friend Lynn, school, and the world by staying in her safe hospital bed. But when she unfolds a paper origami boat, it suddenly expands into the fabulous skin boat *Skidbladnir* piloted by the god Freyr. Through his help, her spiritual body is taken to the violent world of Norse myth, to such places as Asgard, Valhalla, and the caves of the Elves of Invaldi and to meet Odin, Thor, Loki, Sif, and fabulous animals. Her adventures in this fantasy world give her the courage at last to reject Asgard for Midgard and her life in this world.

The Pennywhistle Tree, a story of ordinary events in Hanover, Georgia, has a profound theme: how to relate to others vastly different in culture, economic class, and background without being either hostile or condescending. In late summer the large, poor white George family moves into a two-story rental Victorian house on the same block of Carr Street, where Jonathon Douglas, an only child, lives with his atypical upper-middle class family: his mother is a professional restorer of houses; his father stays at home and writes action novels. The invasion of the Georges and their seven children threatens Jonathon's relationship with his closest chums Alex, Benjy, and Craig. Twelve-year-old Sanders George and his six siblings soon take over the Douglas yard and even the large tree where the four boys have played together for years. Sanders makes a pest of himself to get Jonathon's attention in the neighborhood and at school. Jonathon's ambivalent feelings prevent more than half gestures of friendship: giving the illiterate but musically talented Sanders his pennywhistle and some easy readers before the George family suddenly moves away. Only then does he regret the opportunity for friendship that he missed.

Smith's book *Best Girl,* also set in Hanover, Georgia, uses a traumatic event in the author's life—the gutting of her home by an arsonist in 1984—as a catalyst in the life of imaginary heroine Nealy Compton. The author imagines Nealy to have had a secret hiding place beneath the house when it was burned. The story concerns her strained relationships in a modern alienated, divorced family. Docile Nealy is called her mother's ''best girl,'' while she drives her fourteen-year-old sister from the house and later calls the police to arrest her for breaking back in the home. Isolated by her mother's lack of affection, Nealy makes her hiding place under Mrs. Dees's house into a substitute home—keeping books, her drawings, and a butterfly collection there. When it burns, Nealy is forced into forming relationships with others and establishing a sense of community. The sensitive Nealy and her sexually mature sister Noel Anne are believable, but the reader never gets emotionally involved with the other characters or the plot.

In all of her varied books, Doris Smith excels best at describing the exterior details and the inner life of all of her protagonists, whether nine or seventeen, male or female. She writes assuredly and honestly about problems and situations that they confront. Awards continue to attest to the high respect of readers and critics of modern young adult novels for her work.

—Hugh T. Keenan

SNYDER, Zilpha Keatley

Nationality: American. **Born:** Lemoore, California, 11 May 1927. **Education:** Whittier College, California, 1944-48, B.A. 1948; University of California, Berkeley, summers 1958-60. **Family:** Married Larry Allan Snyder in 1950; one daughter, two sons. **Career:** Writer. Public elementary school teacher, Washington School, Berkeley, California, and in New York, Washington, and Alaska, 1948-62; master teacher and demonstrator for education classes, University of California, Berkeley, 1959-61; lecturer. **Awards:** George G. Stone Center for Children's Books award, 1973, Lewis Carroll Shelf award, Spring Book Festival first prize, both 1967, and Newbery honor book, 1968, all for *The Egypt Game*; Christopher Medal, 1971, for *The Changeling*; William Allen White award, Newbery honor book, Christopher Medal, all 1972, and Hans Christian Andersen International honor list of the International Board on Books for Young People, 1974, all for *The Headless Cupid*; *New York Times* Outstanding Book, 1972, National Book award finalist and Newbery honor book, both 1973, all for *The Witches of Worm*; *New York Times* Outstanding Book, 1981, for *A Fabulous Creature*; PEN Literary award, 1983, and

Parent's Choice award, both for *The Birds of Summer*; Bay Area Book Reviewers award, 1988, William Allen White Master Reading List, 1989-90, and Georgia Children's Book award Master List, 1990-91, all for *And Condors Danced*; New Mexico State award, 1989-90, and on the Notable Trade Books in the Language Arts list of the National Council of Teachers of English, both for *The Changing Maze*; *Season of Ponies, The Egypt Game, The Headless Cupid, The Witches of Worm,* and *A Fabulous Creature* were all named American Library Association Notable Books; *The Velvet Room* and *The Egypt Game* were named on the *Horn Book* honor list; *The Velvet Room, The Changeling, The Headless Cupid, Below the Root, Until the Celebration,* and *Blair's Nightmare* were all Junior Literary Guild selections; *Blair's Nightmare* was included on state awards master lists in Missouri, Texas, Nebraska, Pacific Northwest, and New Mexico; *Libby on Wednesday* was on the Virginia state award master list. **Address:** 52 Miller Ave., Mill Valley, California 94941, U.S.A.

PUBLICATIONS FOR YOUNG ADULTS

Fiction

Eyes in the Fishbowl, illustrated by Alton Raible. New York, Atheneum, 1968.

The Headless Cupid, illustrated by Alton Raible. New York, Atheneum, 1971; Guildford, Surrey, Lutterworth, 1973.

The Witches of Worm, illustrated by Alton Raible. New York, Atheneum, 1972.

Below the Root, illustrated by Alton Raible. New York, Atheneum, 1975.

A Fabulous Creature. New York, Atheneum, 1981.

The Birds of Summer. New York, Atheneum, 1983.

And Condors Danced. New York, Delacorte, 1987; London, Macmillan, 1989.

Libby on Wednesday. New York, Delacorte, 1990.

Song of the Gargoyle. New York, Delacorte, 1991.

Fool's Gold. New York, Delacorte, 1993.

Cat Running. New York, Delacorte Press, 1994.

The Gypsy Game. New York, Delacorte Press, 1997.

Gib Rides Home. New York, Delacorte Press, 1998.

PUBLICATIONS FOR CHILDREN

Fiction

Season of Ponies, illustrated by Alton Raible. New York, Atheneum, 1964.

The Velvet Room, illustrated by Alton Raible. New York, Atheneum, 1965.

Black and Blue Magic, illustrated by Gene Holtan. New York, Atheneum, 1966.

The Egypt Game, illustrated by Alton Raible. New York, Atheneum, 1967.

The Changeling, illustrated by Alton Raible. New York, Atheneum, 1970; Guildford, Surrey, Lutterworth, 1976.

The Princess and the Giants, illustrated by Beatrice Darwin. New York, Atheneum, 1973.

The Truth about Stone Hollow, illustrated by Alton Raible. New York, Atheneum, 1974; as *The Ghosts of Stone Hollow,* Guilford, Lutterworth, 1978.

And All Between, illustrated by Alton Raible. New York, Atheneum, 1976.

Until the Celebration, illustrated by Alton Raible. New York, Atheneum, 1977.

The Famous Stanley Kidnapping Case, illustrated by Alton Raible. New York, Atheneum, 1979.

Come On, Patsy, illustrated by Margot Zemach. New York, Atheneum, 1982.

Blair's Nightmare. New York, Atheneum, 1984.

The Changing Maze, illustrated by Charles Mikolaycak. New York, Macmillan, 1985.

The Three Men. New York, Harper, 1986.

Squeak Saves the Day and Other Tooley Tales, illustrated by Leslie Morrill. New York, Delacorte, 1988.

Janie's Private Eyes. New York, Delacorte, 1989.

Poetry

Today Is Saturday, photographs by John Arms. New York, Atheneum, 1969.

PUBLICATION FOR ADULTS

Novel

Heirs of Darkness. New York, Atheneum, 1978; London, Magnum, 1980.

*

Media Adaptations: *Black and Blue Magic* (filmstrip with tape), Pied Piper, 1975; *The Egypt Game* (recording and cassette), Miller-Brody, 1975; *The Headless Cupid* (from *Newbery Award Cassette* stories; recording and cassette), Miller-Brody, 1976, (filmstrip with tape) Pied Piper, 1980; *The Witches of Worm* (recording), Miller-Brody, 1978; *Below the Root* (computer game), Spinnaker Software's Windham Classics, 1985; *The Egypt Game* (filmstrip and tape), Piped Piper.

Biography: Essay in *Something about the Author Autobiography Series,* Vol. 2, Detroit, Gale, 1986; essay in *Speaking for Ourselves: Autobiographical Sketches by Notable Authors of Books for Young Adults,* Vol. 1, compiled and edited by Donald R. Gallo, National Council of Teachers of English, 1990.

Manuscript Collections: Kerlan Collection, University of Minnesota, Minneapolis.

Critical Studies: Entry in *Contemporary Literary Criticism,* Vol. 17, Detroit, Gale, 1981.

*   *   *

Zilpha Keatley Snyder decided to become a writer at age eight when she discovered that books were written by real people.

Snyder's books appeal to a wide range of readers from upper elementary to high school. Her topics are just as diverse, covering magic, ghosts, mystery, murder, integration, witchcraft, drugs, dysfunctional families, and environmental awareness. For inspiration Snyder draws on memories of her own childhood and the stories told to her then, her students, and from some mysterious source outside herself.

Most of Snyder's books have a young girl as the main character, but she did change that format with her first book for young adults, *A Fabulous Creature,* about fifteen-year-old James Fielding, a professor's son on vacation in the Sierra Nevada mountains. Lonely and bored, James discovers a magnificent stag in a hidden canyon whom he begins to visit and ply regularly with apples. Then, in his adolescent need to impress the daughter of a rich game hunter, he inadvertently betrays the deer and must confront the consequences.

Snyder's second and best-known young adult novel, *Birds of Summer,* is just as timely today as it was in 1983. Fifteen-year-old Summer must deal with her emerging sexuality; the irresponsibility of her mother, Oriole, who leaves the rearing of seven-year-old Sparrow to Summer; loneliness; drugs; and friendship. Summer handles these problems with understanding and sophistication. Set in California in the 1980s, Summer's family lives in a trailer on property owned by the Fishers, who have a son, Nicky, the same age as Summer. Oriole and the Fishers once lived in the same commune. Oriole tries to live as she did in those carefree days of the 70s, but now must depend on government welfare to do so. She has had many men in her life, but none ever stays long, including the fathers of her two daughters. Summer is especially bothered by the fact that she does not know her father, who left before he knew Oriole was pregnant.

The only stable adults in her life are Mr. Pardell, her English teacher, and the Olivers, a rich family who hire Summer to clean house for them. Each of them knows the problems Summer faces, but the solution offered by the Olivers is for Summer to come live with them, which she agrees to do if they will also take Sparrow. They agree since they want Summer to work for them and they too have come to love Sparrow. In the end Summer sends Sparrow to the Olivers, and she stays with her mother.

Snyder deals with Summer's emerging sexuality with sensitivity. Summer and a girlfriend discuss sex, but it is of minor importance to Summer, who must deal with the problems Oriole has managed to get the family into with her drug-raising boyfriend. Nicky had always been her best friend, but now, he, too, has discovered sex. She and Nicky realize that they are not ready for intimacy yet and join together in trying to extricate their parents from the difficulties they are in with the drug gang.

Snyder's "Green-sky" trilogy takes on the issues of violence as part of human nature, free access to knowledge, and the moral issues of governmental actions. Green-sky is a fantasy world of people living high above the forest floor in trees. The forest floor, a place of mystery and fear, is covered by impenetrable roots and below them are monsters trapped from entering the world of Green-sky. The falsification of history and governmental secrecy are a major motif as Raamo and Genaa, both thirteen, begin to find out the truth about the Pash-shan, the monsters who are below the roots.

Snyder is able to draw her readers into the worlds she creates, whether that is the fantasy world of Green-sky, or the real world of California or Nevada today. A versatile writer, Snyder has also written numerous books for younger children and one novel for adults.

—Hazel K. Davis

SOTO, Gary

Nationality: American. **Born:** Fresno, California, 12 April 1952. **Education:** California State University, Fresno, B.A. (magna cum laude) 1974; University of California, Irvine, M.F.A. 1976. **Family:** Married Carolyn Oda in 1975; one daughter. **Career:** Writer. **Awards:** Academy of American Poets Prize, 1975; award from *Nation,* 1975, for ''The Discovery''; United States award from International Poetry Forum, 1976, for *The Elements of San Joaquín*; Bess Hokin Prize from *Poetry,* 1978; Guggenheim fellowship, 1980; creative writing fellowship, National Endowment for the Arts, 1982 and 1991; Levinson award from *Poetry,* Chicago, 1984; American Book award, Before Columbus Foundation, 1985, for *Living up the Street*; California Arts Council fellowship, 1989; Andrew Carnegie Medal for video, 1993, with John Kelly, for *The Pool Party*; Tomas Rivera Prize, 1996. **Address:** 43 The Crescent, Berkeley, California 94708-1701, U.S.A.

PUBLICATIONS FOR YOUNG ADULTS

Poetry

The Elements of San Joaquín. Pittsburgh, University of Pittsburgh Press, 1977.
The Tale of Sunlight. Pittsburgh, University of Pittsburgh Press, 1978.
Where Sparrows Work Hard. Pittsburgh, University of Pittsburgh Press, 1981.
Black Hair. Pittsburgh, University of Pittsburgh Press, 1985.
A Fire in My Hands. New York, Scholastic, 1990.
Who Will Know Us? San Francisco, Chronicle, 1990.
Home Course in Religion. San Francisco, Chronicle, 1991.
Neighborhood Odes, illustrated by David Diaz. San Diego, Harcourt Brace, 1992.
Canto Familiar/Familiar Song San Diego, Harcourt Brace, 1994.
New and Selected Poems. San Francisco, Chronicle, 1995.
Junior College. San Francisco, Chronicle, 1997.

Fiction

Small Faces. Houston, Texas, Arte Publico, 1986.
Taking Sides. San Diego, Harcourt Brace, 1991.
Pacific Crossing. San Diego, Harcourt Brace, 1992.
The Pool Party, illustrated by Robert Casilla. New York, Delacorte, 1993.
Crazy Weekend. New York, Scholastic, 1994.
Jesse. San Diego, Harcourt Brace, 1994.
Buried Onions. San Diego, Harcourt Brace, 1997.

Short Stories

Baseball in April and Other Stories. San Diego, Harcourt Brace, 1990.
Local News. San Diego, Harcourt Brace, 1993.
Petty Crimes. San Diego, Harcourt Brace, 1998.

Other

Living up the Street: Narrative Recollections. San Francisco, Strawberry Hill Press, 1985.
Editor, *California Childhood: Recollections and Stories of the Golden State.* Berkeley, California, Creative Arts, 1988.
Lesser Evils: Ten Quartets (essays). Houston, Texas, Arte Publico, 1988.
A Summer Life (essays). Hanover, New Hampshire, University Press of New England, 1990.
Editor, *Pieces of the Heart: New Chicano Fiction.* San Francisco, Chronicle Books, 1993.
Novio Boy (play). San Diego, Harcourt Brace, 1997.

PUBLICATIONS FOR CHILDREN

Fiction

The Cat's Meow. San Francisco, Strawberry Hill Press, 1987.
Too Many Tamales, illustrated by Ed Martinez. New York, Putnam, 1993.
The Skirt, illustrated by Eric Velasquez. New York, Delacorte, 1992.
Chato's Kitchen. New York, G. P. Putnam's Sons, 1995.
Old Man and His Door. New York, G. P. Putnam's Sons, 1996.
Snap Shots from the Wedding. New York, G. P. Putnam's Sons, 1997.
Chato and the Party Animals. New York, G. P. Putnam's Sons, 1998.

*

Biography: Entry in *Dictionary of Literary Biography,* Vol. 82, *Chicano Writers, First Series,* Detroit, Gale, 1989; essay in *Speaking for Ourselves, Too,* compiled and edited by Donald R. Gallo, National Council of Teachers of English, 1993.

Critical Studies: Entry in *Contemporary Literary Criticism,* Vol. 32, Detroit, Gale, 1985.

Gary Soto comments:

For me, streets have always mattered. When I'm ready to write, ready to sit down, usually at our kitchen table, I conjure up inside my head an image of our old street in south Fresno, one that was torn down in the name of urban renewal at the beginning of the 1960s. It was, as one might imagine, a blighted area: a junk yard to the left of our house, Coleman Pickle across the street, a broom factory with its nightly *whack-whack* of straw taking shape and warehouses humming with machinery down the alley, and the almighty Sun-Maid Raisin factory in the distance. There were also weed-choked vacant lots where orange-colored cats wandered cautiously and gophers burrowed holes large enough to push a child's fist through. I did this a number of times and usually just came up with a fist of loose dirt and feathery seed.

These are pictures that I take into my work, both in poetry and prose, pictures that stir the past, which I constantly haunt with an inventory list. They muster up a power inside me, a delicious feeling of memory, imagination, and the willingness to care for the smallest of objects—shards of glass, taps on my shoes, a chicken claw that I worked like a lever, a bicycle part, and an inner tube I rolled from one end of the yard to the other. In short, all the raw and discarded elements of the world.

*   *   *

Gary Soto has been called "one of the finest natural talents to emerge" from among today's Chicano writers by Alan Cheuse in the *New York Times Book Review.* An award-winning author best known for his poetry, short stories, and novels for young adults, Soto brings the sights and sounds of the barrio, the urban Spanish-speaking neighborhood where he was raised, vividly to life within the pages of his books. The shrill whistle of a nearby factory piercing the gleeful screams of playing children, the coarse oaths of playground brawls, picking grapes in the fields beneath a harsh sun that turns the air to dust—the reader experiences an abundance of small details characteristic of growing up in a Mexican American tradition. Soto recreates telling, intimate vignettes from his own childhood and adolescence: he allows us to stand beside him in his mother's kitchen amid the aroma of warm butter and tortillas browning in a black, cast-iron pan and shares with us the strong sense of love and loyalty characteristic of his working-class Hispanic heritage.

Although his parents were both American-born, their Mexican heritage figured strongly in his upbringing. Like many Mexican Americans, both Soto's parents and his grandparents labored in the fields picking grapes, oranges, and cotton, worked in the packing houses of the Sun Maid Raisin Company, or found jobs as factory or warehouse workers; their lives were typical of the Mexican American employed in the areas around Fresno, the industrial center of the agriculture-based San Joaquin Valley.

Memories of a childhood spent in the barrio, including recollections of growing up in impoverished surroundings as his mother, step-father, and grandparents struggled to provide the children with a secure home, of neighbors and friends, and of the ethnic cultural traditions he experienced throughout his youth, serve as a basis for Soto's writing. In *Living up the Street,* a collection of narratives first published in 1985, he vividly recreates incidents of his youth.

Soto was greatly influenced by what he calls "very rambunctious, lively, irreverent writers" such as Gregory Corso, Edward Field, Kenneth Koch, and, later, Weldon Kees, Theodore Roethke, Gabriel Garcia Marquez, and W. S. Merwin, writers whom Soto considers more sophisticated. Another major influence on Soto was the noted poet Philip Levine, his instructor in creative writing from 1972 to 1973.

Living up the Street was followed by *Small Faces,* a selection of prose memoirs published in 1986, and *Lesser Evils: Ten Quartets,* a collection of autobiographical essays about growing up near Fresno, California, that Soto published in 1988. In each of these works, the element of youthful fantasy figures largely, and vivid details and Soto's obvious fondness for people and places from his youth effectively recreate his own childhood for the reader. As a *Publisher's Weekly* reviewer noted, Soto has an ability to make "the personal universal, and readers will feel privileged to share the vision of this man who finds life perplexing but a joy." His work may be imbued with his personal optimism and a sometimes poignant nostalgia, but it is poverty that serves as the thread binding the author, his friends, and his family together within Soto's narratives.

Soto has gone on to write several collections of short stories and novels specifically geared for youth. *Baseball in April, and Other Stories,* published in 1990, received both the American Library Association's "Best Book for Young Adults" designation and the

Beatty Award. A collection of eleven short stories about everyday events in a modern-day Mexican American neighborhood, *Baseball in April* is praised by a *Horn Book* reviewer as "an acute [observation] of the desires, fears, and foibles of children and teenagers going about the business of daily living." The ethnic flavor of the barrio setting is intensified by the Spanish vocabulary that Soto scatters throughout the text—many of his books contain a glossary of Spanish terms at the back to aid non-Spanish speaking readers. Soto focuses on a different young person as the subject of each of his stories. Alfonso wants to transform himself from an awkward young man to an Aztec warrior in "Broken Chain": "Last week he did fifty sit-ups a day, thinking that he would burn those already apparent ripples on his stomach to even deeper ripples, dark ones, so when he went swimming at the canal next summer, girls in cut-offs would notice. And the guys would think he was tough, someone who could take a punch and give it back." But Alfonso finds that the girl he likes accepts him just the way he is. In "Mother and Daughter," Yollie is looking forward to the eighth-grade dance, but has no dress to wear. Her mother dyes Yollie's white summer dress black, but the night of the school dance turns into a disaster when Yollie gets caught in a cloudburst and the rain causes the black dye to run.

Soto's depiction of the Americanization of a generation of Latino teenagers is one of the themes unifying his writing for young adults. Media pressures figure strongly in the lives of his characters: Alfonso wants his hair to look like that of the rock singer, Prince. Young Veronica covets a Barbie doll after watching numerous Barbie commercials, and a pretend one won't do. Fausto covets a guitar so that he can accomplish his mission in life: "to play guitar in his own band; to sweat out his songs and prance around the stage; to make money and dress weird." Unconscious of the threat of poverty weighing upon the shoulders of their parents—hard-working men and women trying to support their families as night watchmen, warehousemen, auto mechanics, and teacher's aides—the young people in Soto's stories are caught up in the commercialism aimed at a more affluent, primarily white culture.

While Soto's writing takes place in the ethnic neighborhoods that are familiar to him, the conflicts faced by his young protagonists are universal. One example is Soto's 1991 novel, *Taking Sides,* about an eighth-grade Mexican American boy named Lincoln Mendoza. One of the best basketball players on his school team, Lincoln's loyalties become divided after he and his mother move from the Mission District barrio in San Francisco, where he grew up, to the wealthier white suburb of Sycamore, California. Although he has problems fitting in at his new school, Lincoln joins the basketball team in his new junior high school. As a crucial basketball game between his old team and his new team approaches, Lincoln finds himself involved in confrontations with his coach and teammates, as well as with himself, as he wrestles with the fear that he is somehow a traitor to his old neighborhood. Soto's study of sportsmanship and loyalty ends on a positive note as the young man adapts to his circumstances in a mature way, makes peace with both his old and new friends, and learns a valuable lesson about maintaining his individuality and trusting in himself.

While much of his inspiration comes from the events of his Mexican American upbringing, Soto has expressed concern that limitations might be placed upon him because of his ethnic background. Rather than remain in a separate category and be judged solely against other Chicano writers, Soto wants his work to be considered on its own merits: ''One of the things I would like to do is make that leap from being a Chicano writer to being simply a writer,'' he told Jean W. Ross in an interview for *Contemporary Authors.*

Soto's ability to tell a story, to recreate moments of his own past in a manner that transcends the boundaries of race or age, to transport his reader to the world of his own childhood is felt within each of his written works. ''Soto's remembrances are as sharply defined and appealing as bright new coins,'' writes Alicia Fields in the *Bloomsbury Review.* ''His language is spare and simple yet vivid.'' But it is his joyful outlook, strong enough to transcend the poverty of the barrio, that makes his work so popular. The optimism with which he views his own life radiates from each of his young characters—Soto views life as a gift and his talent for expression is his gift to his readers.

—Pamela L. Shelton

SOUTHALL, Ivan (Francis)

Nationality: Australian. **Born:** Canterbury, Victoria, 8 June 1921. **Education:** Chatham State School; Mont Albert Central School; Box Hill Grammar School; Melbourne Technical College, 1937-41. **Military Service:** Served in the Australian Army, 1941, the Royal Australian Air Force, 1942-46, pilot, 1942-44, and war historian, 1945-46; became flight lieutenant; received Distinguished Flying Cross. **Family:** Married 1) Joyce Blackburn in 1945 (divorced), one son and three daughters; 2) Susan Stanton in 1976. **Career:** Engraver, Melbourne *Herald and Weekly Times,* 1936-41, 1947; freelance writer, since 1948. Whittall Lecturer, Library of Congress, Washington, D.C., 1973; May Hill Arbuthnot Honor Lecturer, University of Washington, Seattle, 1974; writer-in-residence, MacQuarie University, Sydney, 1978. Past president, Community Youth Organization, Victoria; foundation president, Knoxbrooke Training Centre for the Intellectually Handicapped, Victoria. **Awards:** Australian Children's Book Council Book of the Year award, 1966, for *Ash Road,* 1968, for *To the Wild Sky,* 1971, for *Bread and Honey,* and 1976, for *Fly West*; Australian picture book of the year award, 1969, for *Sly Old Wardrobe*; Japanese Government's Children's Welfare and Culture Encouragement award, 1969, for *Ash Road*; Carnegie Medal, British Library Association, 1971, for *Josh*; Zilver Griffel (Netherlands), 1972, for *To the Wild Sky*; Australian Writers award, 1974, for *Matt and Jo*; member, Order of Australia, 1981; National Children's Book award (Australia), 1986, for *The Long Night Watch.* **Address:** P.O. Box 25, Healesville, Victoria 3777, Australia.

PUBLICATIONS FOR YOUNG ADULTS

Fiction

Finn's Folly. Sydney and London, Angus & Robertson, and New York, St. Martin's, 1969.
Bread and Honey. Sydney and London, Angus & Robertson, 1970; as *Walk a Mile and Get Nowhere,* Englewood Cliffs, New Jersey, Bradbury, 1970.
Josh. Sydney and London, Angus & Robertson, 1971; New York, Macmillan, 1972.

Matt and Jo. Sydney, Angus & Robertson, and New York, Macmillan, 1973; London, Angus & Robertson, 1974.
What about Tomorrow? Sydney and London, Angus & Robertson, and New York, Macmillan, 1977.
King of the Sticks. Sydney, Collins, London, Methuen, and New York, Greenwillow, 1979.
The Golden Goose. London, Methuen, and New York, Greenwillow, 1981.
The Long Night Watch. London, Methuen, 1983; New York, Farrar, Straus, 1984.
A City out of Sight. Sydney, Angus & Robertson, 1984; London, Angus & Robertson, 1985.
Rachel. Sydney and London, Angus & Robertson, and New York, Farrar, Straus, 1986.
Blackbird. New York, Farrar, Straus, 1988; Melbourne, Heinemann, 1992.
The Mysterious World of Marcus Leadbeater. New York, Farrar, Straus, 1990; Melbourne, Heinemann, 1991.
Ziggurat. Melbourne, Viking, 1997; New York, Viking/Penguin, 1997.

Other

Seventeen Seconds. Sydney, Hodder & Stoughton, 1973; Leicester, Brockhampton, and New York, Macmillan, 1973.
Fly West (nonfiction). London, Angus & Robertson, 1974; New York, Macmillan, 1975.
Let the Balloon Go (screenplay), with others, 1976.

PUBLICATIONS FOR CHILDREN

Fiction

Meet Simon Black, illustrated by Frank Norton. Sydney and London, Angus & Robertson, 1950.
Simon Black in Peril [in Space, in Coastal Command, in China, and the Spaceman, in the Antarctic, Takes Over, at Sea], illustrated by I. Maher and Wal Stackpool. Sydney and London, Angus & Robertson, 1951-62.
Hills End, illustrated by Jim Phillips. Sydney and London, Angus & Robertson, 1962; New York, St. Martin's, 1963.
Ash Road, illustrated by Clem Seale. Sydney and London, Angus & Robertson, 1965, New York, St. Martin's, 1966.
The Fox Hole, illustrated by Ian Ribbons. Sydney, Hicks Smith, London, Methuen, and New York, St. Martin's, 1967.
To the Wild Sky, illustrated by Jennifer Tuckwell. Sydney and London, Angus & Robertson, and New York, St. Martin's 1967.
Let the Balloon Go, illustrated by Ian Ribbons. Sydney, Hicks Smith, London, Methuen, and New York, St. Martin's, 1968.
Sly Old Wardrobe, illustrated by Ted Greenwood. Melbourne, Cheshire, and London, Angus & Robertson, 1968; New York, St. Martin's, 1969.
Chinaman's Reef Is Ours. Sydney and London, Angus & Robertson, and New York, St. Martin's 1970.
Head in the Clouds, illustrated by Richard Kennedy. Sydney and London, Angus & Robertson, 1972; New York, Macmillan, 1973.
Over the Top, illustrated by Ian Ribbons. Sydney, Hicks Smith, and London, Methuen, 1972; as *Benson Boy,* illustrated by Ingrid Fetz, New York, Macmillan, 1972.

Three Novels (contains *The Fox Hole, Let the Balloon Go,* and *Over the Top*). London, Methuen, 1975.
What about Tomorrow? Sydney and London, Angus & Robertson, and New York, Macmillan, 1977.
Christmas in the Tree. Sydney, Hodder & Stoughton, 1985.

Other

Journey into Mystery: A Story of the Explorers Burke and Willis, illustrated by Robin Goodall. Melbourne, Lansdowne, 1961.
Lawrence Hargrave. Melbourne, Oxford University Press, 1964.
Rockets in the Desert: The Story of Woomera. Sydney, Angus & Robertson, 1964; London, Angus & Robertson, 1965.
Indonesian Journey. Melbourne, Lansdowne, 1965; London, Newnes, and Boston, Ginn, 1966.
The Sword of Esau: Bible Stories Retold, illustrated by Joan Kiddell-Monroe. Sydney, Angus and Robertson, 1967; New York, St. Martin's, 1968.
Bushfire!, illustrated by Julie Mattox. Sydney, Angus & Robertson, 1968.
The Curse of Cain: Bible Stories Retold, illustrated by Joan Kiddell-Monroe. Sydney, Angus & Robertson, and New York, St. Martin's, 1968.

PUBLICATIONS FOR ADULTS

Fiction

Out of the Dawn: Three Short Stories. Privately printed, 1942.
Flight to Gibraltar. Sydney, Horwitz, 1958; as *Terror Flight,* 1962.
Third Pilot. Sydney, Horwitz, 1958.
Mediterranean Black. Sydney, Horwitz, 1959.
Mission to Greece. Sydney, Horwitz, 1959.
Sortie in Cyrenaica. Sydney, Horwitz, 1959
Atlantic Pursuit. Sydney, Horwitz, 1960.

Other

The Weaver from Meltham (biography of Godfrey Hirst), illustrated by George Colville. Melbourne, Whitcombe & Tombs, 1950.
The Story of the Hermitage: The First Fifty Years of the Geelong Church of England Girls' Grammar School. Melbourne, Cheshire, 1956.
They Shall Not Pass Unseen. Sydney, Angus & Robertson, 1956.
A Tale of Box Hill: Day of the Forest. Box Hill, Victoria, Box Hill City Council, 1957.
Bluey Truscott: Squadron Leader Keith William Truscott, R.A.A.F., D.F.C. and Bar. Sydney, Angus & Robertson, 1958.
Softly Tread the Brave: A Triumph over Terror, Devilry, and Death by Mine Disposal Officers John Stuart Mould and Hugh Randall Syme. Sydney, Angus & Robertson, 1960.
Parson on the Track: Bush Brothers in the Australian Outback. Melbourne, Lansdowne, 1962.
Woomera. Sydney, Angus & Robertson, 1962.
Indonesia Face to Face. Melbourne, Lansdowne, 1964; London, Angus & Robertson, 1965.
Editor, *The Challenge—Is the Church Obsolete? An Australian Response to the Challenge of Modern Society* (essays). Melbourne, Lansdowne, 1966.
A Journey of Discovery: On Writing for Children. London, Kestrel, 1975; New York, Macmillan, 1976.

*

Biography: Essay 'A Product of Difficulty' in *The Early Dreaming: Australian Children's Authors on Childhood,* edited by Michael Dugan, Milton, Jacaranda Press, 1980; Essay in *Something about the Author Autobiography Series,* Volume 3, Detroit, Gale, 1987; essay in *Speaking for Ourselves, Too,* edited by Donald R. Gallo, Urbana, Illinois, National Council of Teachers of English, 1993.

Critical Studies: Entry in *Children's Literature Review,* Volume 2, Detroit, Gale, 1976.

Ivan Southall comments:

I wrote my first book for young people before the outbreak of the Second World War. It was published in 1950. Since then the world has changed. So have I. I played a part in the change that came upon the books that young people read, but few people of mature years can fail to observe that books and the world have gone on changing. I have become less and less concerned with the external adventure that once challenged me on paper and in life; more and more I'm concerned with the remarkable world that we inhabit internally. I have expressed this so much greater length than formerly in *Ziggurat.* I think of it as my "definitive" novel. It took bive years to write and has been stirring controversy since publication by Penguin Viking in 1997.

*   *   *

In forty years as a novelist Ivan Southall has lived through great changes in Australian children's literature. His range is dazzling—from entertainment to profound philosophical enquiry—and yet in another sense he has spent the whole of his writing life in an attempt to make sense of a single theme, which he describes as "the thrust for personal survival, whilst struggling with duty, discipline and the expectation of others." Southall writes powerful, challenging stories which dare to experiment with narrative and setting, confronting important themes such as mental retardation, cerebral palsy, religious intolerance, sexuality and passion, love and war: his protagonists are often introspective, agonised, confused, but also witty and extremely sensitive: *Let the Balloon Go* (like Gene Kemp's *The Turbulent Term of Tyke Tyler,* with its narrative secret), *Bread and Honey,* and *Josh* are amongst his best.

Southall began his career as a writer of children's fiction with the "Simon Black" series about a Royal Australian Air Force pilot who "possessed an incredible measure of virtue, honour, righteous anger, courage and inventiveness." In 1962 readers were startled and impressed by his new novel, *Hills End,* the story of a group of children who have to cope on their own when their town is cut off by floods, a book very different from Simon Black's formulaic adventures and from the holiday adventures of writers like Arthur Ransome, where middle-class children escape from parental restraints to go boating or camping without ever running into any real danger.

Indeed, Southall's next series of novels might better be described as survival stories than as adventure stories. In successive books during the next eight years, groups of children faced a bushfire in *Ash Road,* a fall into a mine shaft in *The Fox Hole,* being marooned on a deserted island in *To the Wild Sky,* a multiple-car crash in *Finn's Folly,* and a takeover of their town by a mining company in *Chinaman's Reef Is Ours.* In each book one of the boy characters faces a struggle with courage at a significant point in the novel, although this struggle never provides the central narrative impetus. The group itself, greater than the sum of its parts, is the true hero of the survival stories, and Southall's special achievement is the way he charts the fluctuations of the group mood.

During the 1970s, along with the majority of Australian children's writers, Southall began to pay more attention to notions of masculinity and femininity. However, where most writers concentrated on stretching the limits for their female characters, Southall zeroed in on the boys in his survival stories to construct a searching analysis of masculinity. This shift of focus, prefigured in *Let the Balloon Go,* becomes fully apparent in *Bread and Honey,* set around Australia's most masculine institution, Anzac Day, a commemoration of the Australian force's heroic stand at Gallipoli in World War I. Torn between the opposing philosophies of his scientist father and his story-telling grandmother, Michael Cameron is gradually forced to take his own semi-heroic stand against Bully Boy MacBaren in a novel where every word counts and every action raises simultaneous questions about the scientific and romantic perspectives of war, about civilization and violence.

By contrast, *Josh* is a more leisurely and expansive novel, giving full play to the characteristic Southall interior monologue with its carefully crafted rhythms that are sometimes biblical, sometimes Shakespearean, and always Australian. Josh Plowman goes to Ryan's Creek expecting to take a thoughtful look at his family history but instead finds himself staggering through a series of Chaplinesque accidents, mocked by the local children and lectured by his formidable Aunt Clara. However, the intensely normative pressures on Josh in fact make him more aware of his own choices, and while he looks back without anger at Ryan's Creek, he heads forward into a different kind of future: "Go away, crows. Find yourself a body that's had its day. I'm walking mine back to Melbourne town and living every mile."

After these substantial achievements came an interlude of playfulness with the mellow comedy of *Over the Top* and the romantic mood of *Matt and Jo.* Following two books based on his wartime experiences, there came a period described in the cover notes to *What about Tomorrow* as three years of personal anguish, during which Southall believed "his sun had set." An intriguing mixture of folklore patterns with an uncharacteristic abundance of realistic detail about the Depression, *What about Tomorrow* led directly into Southall's most purely celebratory novel, *King of the Sticks,* where the gold rush setting suitably distances a tale of forests and bandits and younger sons who start as simpletons but turn out to possess a special intuition. Its sequel, *The Golden Goose,* however, was completely overwhelmed by the riot of language, and Southall never finished the planned trilogy.

Instead he turned back to some of his earlier narrative modes. *The Long Night Watch* recalls the documentary fiction of his wartime books; *A City out of Sight,* the sequel to *To the Wild Sky,* is disturbingly similar in style to its predecessor, written seventeen years earlier; *Rachel,* Southall's only novel about a young woman, is basically another survival story, and interestingly, his girl character faces the same rites of passage as the boys.

But Southall is an expert at stepping back in order to leap forward. In *Blackbird,* set during World War II, he confronts Will Houghton with a classic choice between heroism and self-preservation, expanding on these choices in an inspired and surreal dialogue between Will and a vengeful blackbird whose fledgling has been killed by flying against the Houghtons' window. As Will explains consequences and responsibility to the bird, he begins to understand them for himself, turning from his war games to start clearing away the dangerous debris around his house. Will's decision carries the questioning of *Bread and Honey* and *Josh* to an authoritative conclusion—until Southall throws all the questions open again in his next novel.

The Mysterious World of Marcus Leadbeater is a wild book where dreams and metaphors have the validity of facts, and facts themselves are not to be relied on. Gramps, a charismatic wit and womanizer, impresses Marcus far more than does his steady and reliable father, but Marcus's identification with his grandfather's life carries over to an identification with his grandfather's death, and the powerful but enigmatic ending represents Southall's most strenuous testing of concepts of masculinity.

Virtually all Southall's books contemplate the inner experiences of heroism, and its alternate side, cowardice, with fear the linking emotion: from the child of an Air Force officer in *Hills End* hoping to live up to his hero-worshipping images of his father, through to the ambigous death-anxieties of the grandson of an RAAF Bomber Command pilot in *The Mysterious World of Marcus Leadbeater* and the fairwell to false-heroics and adoption of pacifism by the engineer colonel's youngest son in *Blackbird.*

Sometimes Southall is as difficult, inward, intense, as Alan Garner's masterpiece *Red Shift,* frequently using stream of consciousness, sometimes from several characters' viewpoints, gabbling to themselves in their heads, struggling to express themselves to others. Even *Rachel,* fictionalised childhood experiences of his mother, set on the late-nineteenth century gold fields of Victoria. Even the ecstatic teenage school-truant lovers in *Matt and Jo,* powerfully reworked in *Ziggurat.* His most recent novels, *Zigurrat, Blackbird,* and *The Mysterious World of Marcus Leadbeater,* are very intense, and, typically, rich, powerful, allusive, often dark.

—Jenny Pausacker, updated by John Gough

SPARK, Muriel (Sarah)

Nationality: British. **Born:** Edinburgh, Scotland, 1 February 1918. **Education:** James Gillespie's School for Girls and Heriot Watt College, both Edinburgh. **Family:** Married S. O. Spark in 1937 (divorced); one son. **Career:** Writer. Employed in the Political Intelligence Department of the British government's Foreign Office, 1944-45; affiliated with *Argentor* (jewelry trade magazine); general secretary, Poetry Society, 1947-49; founder, *Forum* (literary magazine), and editor of *Poetry Review,* London, 1949; part-time editor, Peter Owen Ltd. (publishing company). **Awards:** *Observer* short story prize, 1951, for "The Seraph and the Zambesi"; Prix Italia, 1962, for radio play adaptation of *The Ballad of Peckham Rye*; Fellow, Royal Society of Literature, 1963; Yorkshire Post Book of the Year award, 1965, and James Tait Black Memorial Prize, 1966, both for *The Mandelbaum Gate*; D.B.E. (Dame Commander of the Order of the British Empire), 1967; Honorary Member, American Academy, 1978; Booker McConnell Prize nomination, 1981, for *Loitering with Intent*; First Prize, F.N.A.C. La Meilleur Recueil des Nouvelles Etrangères, 1987, for the Editions Fayard translation of *The Stories of Muriel Spark*; Officier,

1988, and Commandeur, 1996, de l'Ordre des Arts et des Lettres, France, 1988; Bram Stoker award, 1988, for *Mary Shelley*; Royal Bank of Scotland—Saltire Society award, 1988, for *The Stories of Muriel Spark*; T. S. Eliot Award, The Ingersoll Foundation, 1992; David Cohen British Literature Prize, 1997. D.Litt., University of Strathclyde, Glasgow, 1971; University of Edinburgh, 1989; University of Aberdeen, 1995; D. Univ., Heriot Watt University, Edinburgh, 1995. **Agent:** Georges Borchardt, Inc., 136 E. 57th St., New York, New York 10022.

PUBLICATIONS

Novels

The Comforters. London, Macmillan, and Philadelphia, Lippincott, 1957.
Robinson. London, Macmillan, and Philadelphia, Lippincott, 1958.
Memento Mori. London, Macmillan, and Philadelphia, Lippincott, 1959.
The Bachelors. London, Macmillan, 1960; Philadelphia, Lippincott, 1961.
The Ballad of Peckham Rye. London, Macmillan, and Philadelphia, Lippincott, 1960.
The Prime of Miss Jean Brodie. London, Macmillan, 1961; Philadelphia, Lippincott, 1962.
The Girls of Slender Means. London, Macmillan, and New York, Knopf, 1963.
The Mandelbaum Gate. London, Macmillan, and New York, Knopf, 1965.
The Public Image. London, Macmillan, and New York, Knopf, 1968.
The Driver's Seat. London, Macmillan, and New York, Knopf, 1970.
Not to Disturb. London, Macmillan, 1971; Viking, 1972.
The Hothouse by the East River. London, Macmillan, and New York, Viking, 1973.
The Abbess of Crewe. London, Macmillan, and New York, Viking, 1974.
The Takeover. London, Macmillan, and New York, Viking, 1976.
Territorial Rights. London, Macmillan, and New York, Coward, 1979.
Loitering with Intent. London, Bodley Head, and New York, Coward, 1981.
The Only Problem. London, Bodley Head, and New York, Coward, 1984.
A Far Cry from Kensington. London, Constable, and Boston, Houghton, 1988.
Symposium. London, Constable, and Boston, Houghton, 1990.
Reality and Dreams. London, Constable, 1996; Boston, Houghton, 1997.

Short Stories

The Go-Away Bird and Other Stories. London, Macmillan, 1958; Philadelphia, Lippincott, 1960.
Voices at Play (includes the radio plays *The Party through the Wall, The Interview, The Dry River Bed, The Danger Zone*). London, Macmillan, 1961; Philadelphia, Lippincott, 1962.
Collected Stories I. London, Macmillan, 1967; New York, Knopf, 1968.
Bang-Bang You're Dead and Other Stories. London, Granada, 1982.

The Stories of Muriel Spark. New York, Dutton, 1985; London, Bodley Head, 1987.
Open to the Public: New & Collected Stories. New York, New Directions, 1997.

Poetry

The Fanfarlo and Other Verse. Aldington, Kent, Hand and Flower Press, 1952.
Collected Poems I. London, Macmillan, 1967; New York, Knopf, 1968.
Going Up to Sotheby's and Other Poems. London, Granada, 1982.

Plays

Doctors of Philosophy (produced London, 1962). London, Macmillan, 1963; New York, Knopf, 1966.

Radio Plays: *The Party through the Wall,* 1957; *The Interview,* 1958; *The Dry River Bed,* 1959; *The Ballad of Peckham Rye,* 1960; *The Danger Zone,* 1961.

Other

Co-editor, *Tribute to Wordsworth.* London, Wingate, 1950.
Child of Light: A Reassessment of Mary Wollstonecraft Shelley. London, Tower Bridge Publications, 1951; revised edition, as *Mary Shelley: A Biography,* New York, Dutton, 1987; London, Constable, 1988.
Editor, *A Selection of Poems,* by Emily Brontë. London, Grey Walls Press, 1952.
Emily Brontë: Her Life and Work, with Derek Stanford. London, Owen, 1953; New York, Coward McCann, 1960.
John Masefield. London, Nevill, 1953; revised, Macmillan, 1962, Hutchinson, 1992.
Co-editor, *My Best Mary: The Letters of Mary Shelley.* London, Wingate, 1953.
Editor, *The Brontë Letters.* London, Nevill, 1954; as *The Letters of the Brontës: A Selection,* Norman, University of Oklahoma Press, 1954.
Co-editor, *Letters of John Henry Newman.* London, Owen, 1957.
The Very Fine Clock (for children). New York, Knopf, 1968; London, Macmillan, 1969.
The French Window and the Small Telephone (for children). London, Constable, 1992.
Curriculum Vitae: Autobiography. Boston, Houghton, 1993.

*

Media Adaptations: Several of Muriel Spark's novels have been adapted for the stage, film, and television. *Memento Mori* (stage production), 1964, and BBC-TV, 1992; *The Prime of Miss Jean Brodie* staged at Wyndham's Theatre, London, 1967, and Broadway, 1968, filmed by Twentieth Century-Fox, 1968, and adapted in six parts for television in England in 1978 and in the United States in 1979; *The Driver's Seat* (film), 1972; *The Girls of Slender Means* (T.V.), 1974; *Nasty Habits* (film of *The Abbess of Crewe*), 1976.

Biography: Entry in *Dictionary of Literary Biography,* Vol. 15, *British Novelists, 1930-1959,* Detroit, Gale, 1983; *Muriel Spark* by Dorothea Walker, Boston, Twayne, 1988.

Bibliography: *Iris Murdoch and Muriel Spark: A Bibliography* by Thomas A. Tominaga and Wilma Schneidermeyer, Metuchen, New Jersey, Scarecrow Press, 1976.

Critical Studies: *Muriel Spark* by Karl Malkoff, New York, Columbia University Press, 1968; *Muriel Spark* by Patricia Stubbs, London, Longman, 1973; entry in *Contemporary Literary Criticism,* Detroit, Gale, Vol. 2, 1974; Vol. 3, 1975; Vol. 5, 1976; Vol. 8, 1978; Vol. 13, 1980; Vol. 18, 1981; Vol. 40, 1987; *Muriel Spark* by Peter Kemp, London, Elek, 1974, New York, Barnes & Noble, 1975; *Muriel Spark* by Allan Massie, Edinburgh, Ramsey Head Press, 1979; *The Faith and Fiction of Muriel Spark* by Ruth Whittaker, London, Macmillan, 1982, New York, St. Martin's Press, 1983; *Comedy and the Woman Writer: Woolf, Spark, and Feminism* by Judy Little, Lincoln, University of Nebraska Press, 1983; *Muriel Spark: An Odd Capacity for Vision* edited by Alan Bold, London, Vision Press, and New York, Barnes and Noble, 1984, and *Muriel Spark* by Bold, London, Methuen, 1986; *Muriel Spark* by Velma Bourgeois Richmond, New York, Ungar, 1984; *The Art of the Real: Muriel Spark's Novels* by Joseph Hynes, Rutherford, New Jersey, Fairleigh Dickinson University Press, 1988; *Irish Murdoch, Muriel Spark, and John Fowles: Didactic Demons in Modern Fiction* by Richard C. Kane, Rutherford, New Jersey, Fairleigh Dickinson University Press, 1988; *Vocation and Identity in the Fiction of Muriel Spark* by Rodney Stenning Edgecombe, Columbia, University of Missouri Press, 1990; *Critical Essays on Muriel Spark* edited by Joseph Hynes, New York, Maxwell Macmillan International, 1992; *The Women of Muriel Spark* by Judy Sproxton, New York, St. Martin's Press, 1992; *Reinventing Reality. Patterns and Characters in the Novels of Muriel Spark* by Mickey Pearlman, New York, P. Lang, 1996.

*   *   *

The Prime of Miss Jean Brodie, like all of Muriel Spark's books, is not a young adult novel in the sense that it was not written particularly for young adults. But because it is the story of six girls who come of age under the influence of an eccentric woman in the extremes of her prime, the book has "infiltrated" (a suitable word for a book written by someone as sly as Spark) the young adult shelves, and is therefore the Spark novel one is most likely to discover while in the young adult reading years. It's one of those little books that is not as little it as seems; the largeness of the matters at its heart—some of them rather dark—and the liberties taken with its form are disguised by wit, charm, and faultless craftsmanship. In that way, it's a deceptive kind of book, just as Muriel Spark is a deceptive kind of writer.

In many ways, she is a traditional novelist, as she goes about creating intellectual narratives with more or less complex plot schemes and patterns of events about people and their thoughts, feelings, and actions. At the same time, however, she takes the traditional conventions of the novel—things like point of view, climax, chronological progression—and does surprising, crafty things with them. The mysteries of religion and human behavior are at the core of all her work, and she very often makes use of bizarre, supernatural events that raise more questions than they answer. One gets the feeling that Spark would be a formidable chess opponent with her ability to see into space and then somehow create a pattern of calculated moves that bring her work to its desired conclusion. For Spark, creating forms seems to be just as important as creating fictions.

Miss Jean Brodie is a teacher in an Edinburgh school for girls who decides to devote her prime years to six chosen students whom she believes, under her tutelage, will become "the creme de la creme." An authoritarian who bucks authority, Miss Brodie follows her own progressive principles of education, schooling her girls in her favorite subjects—romance, art, and Italian politics—all the while keeping a sample math problem on the blackboard or instructing the girls to keep their history books in front of them in case her nemesis, the headmistress, should appear. The six soon become like "a body with Miss Brodie for the head." (The story is set in the 1930s, and the rise of fascism in Italy, where Miss Brodie spends her holidays, provides an obvious and interesting parallel to her methods.) However, beneath the surface along which the story does its amusing hops, skips, and jumps, larger motivational concerns are at the boil and begin to bubble up into the story. As the girls grow older, it becomes clear that Miss Brodie's intentions are not selfless ones. She has been grooming her girls so that she might vicariously experience through them the life and love that has been otherwise unattainable to her. She goes too far and one of the girls betrays her.

Spark tells us up front this is going to happen. She even tells us who will do it. These details come in unexpected bits and pieces as she moves back and forth in time in order to reveal what the Brodie girls will become later in life and what they will think about events that have yet to unfold. She doesn't bother much with the things her characters do so much as why they do them and what effects such motives have. This is characteristic of all Spark's fiction. She routinely gives away her endings, "spoils" what might have been climactic surprises, and moves back and forth with ease between past, present, and future. By doing this, she dispenses with the questions readers traditionally ask of plots (What will happen next? Who is responsible? When will we find out?) so that we might begin to ask deeper ones: Is Miss Brodie really leading out what is already in her students's souls, as she claims, or is she really thrusting in her own ideas, a method for which she criticizes traditional educators? At what point does nonconformity become conformity? Does one of Miss Brodie's girls betray her merely to stop her or is the motivation something deeper, something as much spiritual as it is personal? To what extent is loyalty a part of the betrayal? What is the truth of this novel? How, by thwarting, manipulating, and repatterning readers's expectations does the author make her fiction like life?

If Spark's fiction is sometimes steely and surgical and always lacking in the lifelike clutter of emotional response, it is because she seems to be dealing in carefully patterned parables; her fiction presents real life only to the extent that deeper truths about human nature, its good and its evil, can emerge. She leaves her readers in a Miss Brodie-like position to experience these truths vicariously through her fiction. Spark does this with the same instinct, insight, and economy of method that her characters admire and congratulate each other for. *The Prime of Miss Jean Brodie,* as it provides readers with a new way to experience and consider the novel, is a good introduction to Spark's other work as well as to further exploration of modern fiction.

—Tracy J. Sukraw

SPEARE, Elizabeth George

Nationality: American. **Born:** Melrose, Massachusetts, 21 November 1908. **Education:** Smith College, Northampton, Massachusetts, 1926-27; Boston University, Massachusetts, A.B. 1930, M.A. 1932. **Family:** Married Alden Speare, 26 September 1936; one daughter and one son. **Career:** English teacher, Rockland High School, Rockland, Massachusetts, 1932-35, and Auburn High School, Auburn, Massachusetts, 1935-36. Since 1955, writer. **Awards:** Society of Colonial Wars Award from the State of New York, and Newbery Medal from the American Library Association, both 1959, International Board on Books for Young People (IBBY) Honor List, and selected one of American Institute of Graphic Arts Children's Books, both 1960, and New England Round Table Children's Librarians Award, 1976, all for *The Witch of Blackbird Pond;* Newbery Medal, 1962, and IBBY Honor List, 1964, both for *The Bronze Bow;* one of American Library Association's Best Young Adult Books, Teachers' Choice from the National Council of Teachers of English, one of Child Study Association of America's Children's Book of the Year, one of *School Library Journal's* Best Books of the Year, a *Booklist* Children's Reviewers Choice, and one of *New York Times* Outstanding Books, all 1983, and Newbery Medal Honor Book, Scott O'Dell Award for Historical Fiction, and Christopher Award, all 1984, all for *The Sign of the Beaver;* Laura Ingalls Wilder Award, 1989, for a distinguished and enduring contribution to children's literature. **Died:** 1994.

PUBLICATIONS FOR YOUNG ADULTS

Novels

Calico Captive, illustrated by W.T. Mars. Boston, Houghton Mifflin, 1957; London, Gollancz, 1963.
The Witch of Blackbird Pond, illustrated by Nicholas Angelo. Boston, Houghton Mifflin, 1958; London, Gollancz, 1960.
The Bronze Bow. Boston, Houghton Mifflin, 1961; London, Gollancz, 1962.
The Sign of the Beaver, illustrated by Robert Andrew Parker. Boston, Houghton Mifflin, 1983; London, Gollancz, 1984.

Other

Child Life in New England, 1790-1840. Sturbridge, Massachusetts, Old Sturbridge Village, 1961.
Life in Colonial America. New York, Random House, 1963.

PUBLICATIONS FOR ADULTS

Novel

The Prospering. Boston, Houghton Mifflin, and London, Gollancz, 1967.

*

Media Adaptations: *Abby, Julia and the Cows* (television play; based on an article for *American Heritage),* Southern New England Telephone Company, 1958; *The Bronze Bow* (record, cassette, filmstrip with cassette), Random House; *The Witch of Blackbird Pond* (cassette), Random House; *The Sign of the Beaver* (cassette, filmstrip with cassette), Random House.

Manuscript Collections: Mugar Memorial Library, Boston University, Massachusetts.

Biography: *More Junior Authors,* New York, H.W. Wilson, 1963; *Elizabeth George Speare* by Marilyn Fain Apseloff, New York, Twayne, 1991; essay in *Speaking for Ourselves, Too* compiled and edited by Donald R. Gallo, National Council of Teachers of English, 1993.

Critical Studies: Entry in *Children's Literature Review,* Volume 8, Detroit, Gale.

*   *   *

Elizabeth George Speare's stories illuminate history through her well-defined characters and fascinating plots. Four out of five of her novels display a particular interest in North American life in the late seventeenth and early eighteenth centuries. Two are based on the lives of historically documented personages, while in the other two, the main characters are believable composites; all provide unique vision into their specific historical periods as well as underlining the universality of the themes presented. A fifth historical novel is set in Palestine at the time of Christ and is also linked to the others by common themes which transcend issues of race and culture.

The protagonists in Speare's work—two young men and three young women—range in age from thirteen to nineteen, and all struggle with issues of maturity and self-determination. Confronted with rigid legalism, bigotry, and injustice, these characters often find themselves acting outside of society's prescribed roles in order to follow their developing convictions. Although a strong moral tone pervades Speare's work, the vitality and ever present humanity of her characters excludes didacticism.

In her first novel, *Calico Captive* (1957), Speare spins a fast-moving tale, based on the real experience of Susanna Johnson, captured from her New England home in an Indian raid, forced to march north where she is caught up in the French and Indian War, and finally sold as a servant to a rich family in Montreal. The detailed descriptions and active use of dialogue create a compelling picture of both the geographical terrain and the colonial conflicts of the time; however Speare's depiction of the Abenaki Indian captors is stereotypical at best, and even her principal characters appear somewhat predictable and idealized.

This is not the case in her next work, *The Witch of Blackbird Pond* (1961), however, in which the sixteen-year-old Kit presents a strong and well-defined female protagonist. Kit arrives on a ship from Barbados to stay with her uncle's family at the colony of Wethersfield, Connecticut. With her "foreign" ways and boyish assertiveness, Kit is regarded suspiciously by the puritan community as she struggles to reconcile her own spontaneity with the rigid constrictions of that society. Defying convention, she befriends an isolated old woman and teaches a young girl to read, but in doing so brings upon herself hysterical accusations of witchcraft which eventually lead to a trial. In this captivating story, well worthy of its Newbery Medal, the adversity Kit faces serves to mature the strength and exuberance of her character as she works through disillusionment and alienation to understanding and compassion.

Speare introduces a male protagonist in her second Newbery Medal winner, *The Bronze Bow* (1961). Daniel, the nineteen-year-old Galilean patriot, is bent on revenging the brutal death of his parents and driving the occupying Romans out of Palestine. The relationships Daniel develops, like those of Kit, lead him into danger, growth, and the chance to resolve his bitterness. Carefully sketched characters such as a fellow Galilean, Joel, a group of outlaws and a black slave, Daniel's own mentally ill sister, a roman guard, and finally Jesus himself, provide the story with a rich interweaving of personalities and motivations. Although the novel could be criticized for imposing a western bias on a middle eastern setting, as well as for its unabashed presentation of this early period in the Christian religion, its predominant themes of hatred and forgiveness, coming of age, and war and peace are universal ones with relevance to any society and culture.

In contrast, *The Prospering* (1967) is less accessible to young adults because of its deep emphasis on religious division and fanaticism. The novel is based on the true story of the Williams family who left Boston in 1737 to take part in a social and religious experiment. This involved the establishment of the integrated community of Stockbridge in which Indians were to be taught the beliefs, the manners, and the livelihood compatible to the English way of life. The story is narrated in the first person by Elizabeth, another strong female protagonist whose inner depth and development is offset by her lack of outward beauty. Her story conveys a rich awareness of place as it details the growth of the small mission settlement through conflicts with the Indians, wars and revolution, to establishment as a town. However, its lengthy treatment of Elizabeth's religious and romantic fantasies detract from her genuine struggles to find a place of her own in the adult world.

The Sign of the Beaver (1988) has a younger protagonist who introduces themes of survival and interracial understanding. Thirteen-year-old Matt comes of age in the wilderness of eighteenth-century Maine. Left alone for several months to guard the family homestead, Matt learns to survive physically as well as discovering new strengths and resources in his inner person. Through an unexpected friendship with Attean, a Penobscot Indian, Matt becomes familiar with the woodland culture of this endangered race and develops a deep appreciation for their way of life. Speare's factual depiction of the Indians, so different from *Calico Captive*, shows both respect and sensitivity, and renders the book particularly relevant today.

Elizabeth George Speare's body of fictional work spans just five novels written over the course of thirty-one years. Her careful research, vivacious plots, and convincing characterization make it a selection of fine historical literary works which will continue to enlighten and encourage readers.

—Patricia Hill

SPENCE, Eleanor (Rachel)

Nationality: Australian. **Born:** Sydney, New South Wales, Australia, 21 October 1928. **Education:** Erina Primary School, 1935-40; Gosford High School, 1941-45; University of Sydney, 1946-48, B.A. 1949. **Family:** Married John A. Spence in 1952; two sons and one daughter. **Career:** Author of children's books. Teacher, Methodist Ladies' College, Burwood, New South Wales, 1949; librarian, Commonwealth Public Service Board, Canberra, Australia, 1950-52; children's librarian, Coventry City Libraries, Coventry, England, 1952-54; teaching assistant, 1974-75, and since 1976 teacher, Autistic Children's Association of New South Wales, Sydney, Australia. **Awards:** Australian Children's Book of the Year award, 1964, for *The Green Laurel,* and 1977, for *The October Child;* Facilities for Autistic Handicapped Winston Churchill fellow, 1978; Australian Literature Board writer's fellowship, 1980; Australian Children's Book Honor award, 1991, for *The Family Book of Mary Claire.* **Address:** 11 Handley Ave., Turramurra, NSW 2074, Australia.

PUBLICATIONS FOR YOUNG ADULTS

Fiction

Patterson's Track, illustrated by Alison Forbes. Melbourne, Oxford University Press, 1958; London, Angus & Robertson, 1959.

The Summer in Between, illustrated by Marcia Lane Foster. London, Oxford University Press, 1959.

Lillipilly Hill, illustrated by Susan Einzig. London, Oxford University Press, 1960; New York, Roy, 1963.

The Green Laurel, illustrated by Geraldine Spence. London, Oxford University Press, 1963; New York, Roy, 1965.

The Year of the Currawong, illustrated by Gareth Floyd. London, Oxford University Press, and New York, Roy, 1965.

The Switherby Pilgrims, illustrated by Corinna Gray. London, Oxford University Press, and New York, Roy, 1967.

Jamberoo Road, illustrated by Doreen Roberts. London, Oxford University Press, and New York, Roy, 1969.

The Nothing Place, illustrated by Geraldine Spence. London, Oxford University Press, 1972; New York, Harper, 1973.

Time to Go Home, illustrated by Fermin Rocker. London, Oxford University Press, 1973.

The Travels of Hermann, illustrated by Noela Young. Sydney, Collins, 1973.

The October Child, illustrated by Malcolm Green. London, Oxford University Press, 1976; as *The Devil Hole,* New York, Lothrop, 1977.

A Candle for St. Anthony. London, Oxford University Press, 1977; New York, Oxford University Press, 1979.

The Seventh Pebble, illustrated by Sisca Verwoert. Melbourne and London, Oxford University Press, 1980.

The Left Overs. Sydney, Methuen, 1982; London, Methuen, 1983.

Me and Jeshua. Melbourne, Dove, 1984.

Miranda Going Home. Melbourne, Dove, 1985.

Mary and Frances. Melbourne, Dove, 1986.

Deezle Boy. Melbourne, Dove, 1987.

Another Sparrow Singing. Melbourne, Dove, 1991; London, Oxford University Press, 1992.

The Family Book of Claire. Melbourne, Dove, 1991.

Other

A *Schoolmaster,* illustrated by Jane Walker. Melbourne, Oxford
University Press, 1969.
A *Cedar-Cutter,* illustrated by Barbara Taylor. Melbourne, Oxford
University Press, 1971.

PUBLICATIONS FOR ADULTS

Other

Another October Child: Recollections of Eleanor Spence. Melbourne, Dove, 1988.

*   *   *

Eleanor Spence has been publishing books for young people
since 1958, and her novels chart the changes that have occurred in
Australian children's fiction since that time. Spence began by
writing simple, outdoor family stories based on her own recollections of a happy childhood. The families in her early books were
largely conventional two-parent ones, where children followed the
patterns of behaviour set down by their elders. As the years went on
Spence recognised the changes in society and the family, and in the
late 1960s began weaving these threads into such novels as *The
Nothing Place* (1972) and *Time to Go Home* (1973), where she
takes special interest in characters who are disadvantaged in some
way. This process reached its peak with *The October Child* (1976),
a book largely written from her experience working with autistic
children. This interest in characters who are disadvantaged physically or socially remains the focus of her work. Spence's two
religious novels, centring upon the life of Jesus, are sometimes seen
as aberrations, but they deal directly with characters who are
different, displaced, or oppressed, and her interest in historical
settings and the nature of families is also apparent.

Spence's first novel, *Patterson's Track* (1958), is written within
the established tradition of its time. With their parents conveniently
out of the way, the children undertake a series of adventures, and
though danger is present, the outcome of their exploits is never in
any serious doubt. Karen Winter, the heroine—self-conscious,
untidy, poor at school work and sport—finds self-worth and self-
discovery at the end. Leadership qualities and the operation of
group dynamics play an important part in the workings of the story.
The impetus for the book is local history, as Karen decides to find
out the truth about an incident that happened in 1820, when she
believed a convict was treated unjustly.

An interest in history is an important feature of Spence's work.
Lillipilly Hill (1963) concentrates on developing relationships
among young people, but it is also a fine historical novel. Its
heroine, Harriet Wilmot, tries to convince her family to remain in
the Australia of the 1800s rather than return to a more comfortable
life in England. *Lillipilly Hill* is an absorbing book which is
carefully researched and crafted and expresses the need to belong
and to put roots down in permanent surroundings. *The Green
Laurel* (1963), for which Spence won her first Book of the Year
Award, expresses this idea too, as itinerant children long for
stability, though the book has a contemporary setting.

Spence wrote two novels of straight historical fiction in the
sixties, *The Switherby Pilgrims* (1967) and *Jamberoo Road* (1969).
The first begins the story of Arabella Braithwaite, who brings a
group of ten orphans to Australia to give them a better chance in
life, and its sequel continues her efforts to find careers for them.
The background of these stories is again well researched, and the
wealth of characters in each draws the reader into a rich family
saga. In the 1980s Spence published two more historical novels, *Me
and Jeshua* (1984) and *Miranda Going Home* (1985), which tell of
the extended family of Jeshua, whom readers come to realise is the
young Jesus when his family returned from Egypt and settled in
Nazareth. In the first story the events are seen through the eyes of
Jeshua's cousin Jude, who is a protector of Jeshua as he comes to
learn about his growing divinity. The second story stands in its own
right, as Miranda, living in Palestine at the time of the Roman
occupation, finds herself in a world of upheaval, racism, and the
aftermath of war. Nevertheless, its setting and the presence of
Jeshua and his family link it strongly to *Me and Jeshua.*

Spence's novel *The Family Book of Mary-Claire* (1991) is a
triumph of historical writing. It presents the history of one family in
New South Wales and reflects the changing society over time. The
story is told in three parts with a short epilogue and is built around
four young characters, each representing a generation. When each
character tells his or her own story, that character is aged between
ten and thirteen years. Each child makes an entry in the family
Bible and is curious about the lives of earlier family members. The
family provides a structure in time and is at the heart of the novel.
Through the generations the reader is able to see inherited traits and
talents being passed on. The documenting of nearly 100 years of
history in 300 large-print pages is masterly, as each child character
attempts to pass on the truth of the past that has created them. In
addition, the book records much social history.

In the 1970s Spence's focus began to shift from the happy
family to more specific and social problems centred within the
family. In *The Nothing Place,* Glen Calder is deaf and lacks the
support of his family. In *Time to Go Home,* Rowan Price comes
from a one-parent family and has to learn some difficult lessons
through hard experience. Rowan is irritable, deceitful, swears, and
steals, though he has another side which gains the reader's sympathy. Feeling he is useless at everything but football, Rowan hopes
to achieve there but loses his chance to play when he is beaten up by
his pot-smoking rival. Plots in Spence's later books, when
summarised, often appear sensational, but Spence is keenly aware
of what young people do and never sensationalises the issues.

Spence won her second Book of the Year Award for *The
October Child,* which explores the effect an autistic child has on a
family. Most of the responsibility for the autistic Carl falls on his
ten-year-old brother Douglas, who survives through his music and
the help of friends. There is a powerful scene at the end of the book
when Carl goes berserk and turns on Douglas, biting his arm and
publicly humiliating him. The frenzy drives Douglas to disown the
child, but he comes to terms with the situation at the end.

A Candle for St. Anthony (1977), one of Spence's most sensitively written novels, presents a situation new to Australian children's literature at the time. It deals with the adolescent friendship of
Justin and Rudi, two boys from different backgrounds and cultures.
Justin is Australian, affluent, middle-class, handsome, and macho,
while Rudi is European, poor, industrious, sensitive, and pretty.
Justin immediately dislikes Rudi for reasons he cannot understand,

but later the boys become firm friends. Eventually a mutual friend makes their friendship appear a homosexual one when he hears Rudi tell Justin he loves him, and the embarrassment this causes ends the friendship. But the novel is not about covert homosexuality. It is a compelling and involving book with haunting overtones at different levels. It is about the strong friendship of adolescence and the importance of finding someone who completely understands you. It is also about opposing lifestyles and the meeting of two cultures, and Spence implies that a combination of elements from both cultures would be a good thing.

The Seventh Pebble (1980) presents an authentic picture of religious and social prejudice in a small Australian town before World War II. Rachel Blackwood, the daughter of the highly respected town doctor, befriends Bridget Connell, a member of a large Irish Catholic family who are poor, and discovers for herself what it means to be different. *The Left Overs* (1982) is about four foster children whose home is being demolished to make way for a freeway and their attempt to find a home where they can still be together. Despite the seriousness of their themes, the books have many lighthearted moments.

As Spence's work progresses she moves from stories for the younger child to stories for the young adult; this probably goes hand in hand with the growth of her own three boys. But two later novels are again directed at a younger child, perhaps because Spence reached the grandmother stage. The hero of *Deezle Boy* (1987) has low self-esteem and is slow at working things out. He is adopted but then is kidnapped by his birth mother. Spence uses the situation to analyse parental custody, illiteracy, unemployment, and social change within the family. How family matters were handled in the past, the arrival of children out of wedlock, and the question of the elderly remaining part of the family are placed before the reader in a non-didactic, compassionate way, so once again readers are able to draw their own conclusions about issues. *Another Sparrow Singing* (1991) is a gentle and sympathetic book about children living in a caravan park after their father has deserted them. This novel brings together many of Spence's beliefs in the value of the human spirit, the need to belong, and the need for a peaceful place to resolve life's difficulties. Throughout her work readers are asked to avoid the insularity of life and become involved in useful and creative work.

Eleanor Spence's novels reflect the concerns of a complex Australian society over time. She has kept abreast of the times through observing the changing dress, habits, and language of young people. Although family structures may change, family relationships, peer group pressures, and school difficulties remain much the same. Though her work is often low-key, the more one comes to examine her novels, the more one comes to highly regard them. Their craftsmanship and literary worth is of a high order, and close rereading will often reveal new aspects and insights.

—Michael Stone

SPIEGELMAN, Art

Nationality: Swedish. **Born:** Stockholm, Sweden, 15 February 1948; immigrated to United States. Educated Harpur College (now State University of New York at Binghamton), 1965-68. **Family:** Married Francoise Mouly in 1977; one daughter and one son. **Career:** Freelance artist and writer, since 1965; creative consultant, artist, designer, editor, and writer for novelty packaging and bubble-gum cards and stickers, Topps Chewing Gum, Inc., Brooklyn, New York, 1966-88; editor, *Douglas Comix,* 1972; contributing editor with Bill Griffith, *Arcade, the Comics Revue,* 1975-76; founding editor with Francoise Mouly, *Raw,* since 1980. Instructor in studio class on comics at San Francisco Academy of Art, 1974-75, and in history and aesthetics of comics at New York School of Visual Arts, 1979-87. On advisory board of Swann Foundation. Art work featured in numerous exhibitions at galleries and museums in the United States and abroad, including the New York Cultural Center, the Institute of Contemporary Art in London, and the Seibu Gallery in Tokyo. Guest lecturer at universities throughout the United States. **Awards:** Annual *Playboy* Editorial award for best comic strip and Yellow Kid award (Italy) for best comic strip author, both 1982; Regional Design award from *Print* magazine, 1983, 1984, and 1985; Joel M. Cavior award for Jewish Writing, and National Book Critics Circle nomination, both 1986, both for *Maus;* Inkpot award from San Diego Comics Convention and Stripschappenning award (Netherlands) for best foreign comics album, both 1987; Pulitzer Prize and National Book Critics Circle Award nomination, both 1992, both for *Maus II;* Alpha Art Award, Angouleme, France, 1993; Jewish Culture Award, 1996; D.H.L.: S.U.N.Y. Binghamton, 1995. **Agent:** Wylie, Aitken & Stone, 250 West 57th St., Suite 2106, New York, New York 10107. **Office:** Raw Books and Graphics, 27 Greene St., New York, New York 10013, U.S.A.

PUBLICATIONS

Comics

The Complete Mr. Infinity. New York, S.F. Book Co., 1970.

The Viper Vicar of Vice, Villainy, and Vickedness. Privately printed by Spiegelman, 1972.

Zip-a-Tune and More Melodies. New York, S.F. Book Co., 1972.

Ace Hole, Midge Detective. New York, Apex Novelties, 1974.

Contributor, *The Apex Treasury of Underground Comics,* edited by Don Donahue and Susan Goodrich. New York, D. Links, 1974.

Language of Comics. State University of New York at Binghamton, 1974.

Breakdowns; From Maus to Now: An Anthology of Strips. New York, Belier Press, 1977.

Every Day Has Its Dog. New York, Raw Books, 1979.

Work and Turn. New York, Raw Books, 1979.

Two-Fisted Painters Action Adventure. New York, Raw Books, 1980.

Maus: A Survivor's Tale. New York, Pantheon, 1986.

Read Yourself Raw: Comix Anthology for Damned Intellectuals. with wife, Francoise Mouly. New York, Pantheon, 1987.

Jimbo: Adventures in Paradise, with Francoise Mouly. New York, Pantheon, 1988.

Raw. New York, Penguin, 1990.

Maus II: A Survivor's Tale; and Here My Troubles Began. New York, Pantheon, 1991.

Raw—Number Three: High Culture for Low Brows. New York, Viking, 1991.

Other

Compiling editor with Bob Schneider, *Whole Grains: A Book of Quotations.* New York, D. Links, 1972.

Contributor, *Drawn Together: Relationships Lampooned, Harpooned, and Cartooned,* edited by Nicole Hollander, Skip Morrow, and Ron Wolin. New York, Crown, 1983.

Contributor, *The Complete Color Polly & Her Pals, Vol. 1: The Surrealist Period, 1926-1927.* New York, Remco Worldservice Books, 1990.

Editor, with R. Sikoryak and Francoise Mouly, *Warts and All/ Drew Friedman and Josh Alan Friedman.* New York, Penguin, 1990.

Designer and author of introduction, *The Wild Party* by J. M. March. New York, Pantheon, 1994.

*

Illustrator: *Argonaut: Rediscovering American Resources* by Warren Hinckle, 1992; *The Wild Party* by J. M. March, 1994.

*   *   *

A father who is difficult to get along with, a mother who commits suicide, an only brother who is thought of as a perfect child, impossible to compete with because he is dead, are all issues for Art Spiegelman in his life and in his art. The Holocaust looms over all. Survivors of the Holocaust, Spiegelman's parents eventually relocated in the United States. Before his birth, his brother and most of Art Spiegelman's relatives had all been murdered as a result of the Holocaust.

Spiegelman created in comic-book form *Maus: A Survivor's Tale (Maus I)* and *Maus II: A Survivor's Tale II; and Here My Troubles Began, (Maus II)* to tell his father's story, his own story, and a universal story of the Holocaust. The action takes place on multiple levels, sometimes in the past and at other times in the present. The narration alternates between father, Vladek, and son, Artie.

Creator, artist, writer, and one of the two narrators of *Maus I* and *Maus II,* Spiegelman assumes the identity of the autobiographical character, Artie. Struggling to understand not only his father's past but the man his father has become, Spiegelman portrays the duality he sees in his father: the incredibly resistant and resourceful survivor of the Holocaust and the present-day cantankerous, stingy, fearful man. In coping with his own life, Art Spiegelman, the author and the character, is clearly a survivor as well.

Maus I and *Maus II* differ on many levels from what is most commonly thought of as traditional comics. Not flimsy in format or narration, nor frivolous in nature, *Maus I* and *Maus II* are substantial graphic novels, available as trade paperbacks. With a strong narrative voice, and a unique blend of words and illustrations, the overall effect of reading these books is similar to watching a riveting movie.

"The Jews are undoubtedly a race but they are not human." With this quote of Adolph Hitler, Art Spiegelman begins *Maus I.* The novel jumps in time and setting from pre-World War II Poland, near the border with Germany, to the trenches on the battlefields of the war, to prisoner of war camps, to a Jewish ghetto, and to the concentration camp Auschwitz. Not following strict chronological order, Spiegelman occasionally cuts away from his father's recollections of the past and moves to present-day events.

Just as Vladek recalls incidents of his past, Artie too has his memories. At ten years of age, Vladek tells Artie how to distinguish real friends. In his own particular manner of speaking English, Vladek says: "If you lock them together in a room with no food for a week, then you could see what it is friends." Vladek recalls how people act toward one another in situations far worse than in a locked room. Readers see both the heroic and the horrible.

Maus II continues the narrative begun in *Maus I.* Vladek remembers Auschwitz and Birkenau, the workshops, crematoriums with underground gas chambers, incineration rooms, ovens, and mass graves. He tells of forced marches, confinement on boxcars, and recounts the continued suffering after the official ending of the war. As in *Maus I,* interspersed with Vladek's narrative of the past is Artie's story of his father's difficult personality in the present. Spiegelman does not romanticize either story.

In *Maus II,* Artie reveals to his "shrink" the ambiguity he feels toward his father, and even readers who have lived without personal experience of the Holocaust may identify with this ambiguity. Artie discloses his mixed feelings about writing the *Maus* books. He says: "Some part of me doesn't want to draw or think about Auschwitz."

In both *Maus* books, Spiegelman uses animals to represent people. Jews are depicted as mice, Germans as cats, Poles as pigs, the British as fish, the French as frogs, Americans as dogs, the Swedes as reindeer, and gypsies as moths. Often not much beyond clothing differentiates characters.

The only scene in either book that depicts individuals as real people instead of animals is the self-contained comic strip, entitled "Prisoner on the Hell Planet." Located within *Maus I,* it tells of Artie's strong personal reaction to his mother's suicide. Drawn in an exaggerated, surrealistic manner, the change in the artistic style and character representation helps create a mood of heightened emotionalism. In contrast, the drawings that make up the rest of the books emphasize the factual, nonfictional aspects of the story.

Spiegelman worked hard to attain accuracy in recording even small details. He not only taped his father's recollections but traveled to his parents' house in Sosnowiec, to the concentration camps of Auschwitz and Birkenau, studied old family and archival photographs, read the accounts of other survivors, and looked at documentary film footage, drawings and paintings made by camp inmates.

Spiegelman uses only black-and-white drawings throughout *Maus I* and *Maus II.* Often the illustrations supply information not expressed in the narrative. Different sizes of cartoon frames co-exist on a single page, some traditionally rectangular or square, others round, and some without borders. Each frame fluidly moves the reader ahead in the narrative. Both *Maus* books contain some maps, charts, and diagrams to enhance visualization of places and events.

Maus I and *Maus II* have received wide critical acclaim. *Maus I* was nominated for the 1987 National Book Critics Circle Award and *Maus II* won a Pulitzer Prize. The animal metaphor, distilled language, and deliberately simple drawings create a powerful and moving story, accessible on many levels. Spiegelman's use of flashbacks and fast-forwards in both *Maus* books enhances multiple interpretations.

By dealing with the most serious of history in *Maus I* and *Maus II* and by telling his story eloquently, Art Spiegelman has done much to redefine the comic book. In so doing, he has shown that his chosen format need not be stereotyped as frivolous or trivial. Instead he has shown that graphic novels and comics can be multidimensional literature, capable of irony, emotional depth, and sophistication.

—Karen Ferris Morgan

SPINELLI, Jerry

Nationality: American. **Born:** Norristown, Pennsylvania, 1 February 1941. **Education:** Gettysburg College, Pennsylvania, A.B. 1963; Johns Hopkins University, Baltimore, Maryland, M.A. 1964; Temple University, Philadelphia, Pennsylvania, 1964. **Military Service:** Served in the U.S. Naval Air Reserve, 1966-72. **Family:** Married Eileen Mesi in 1977; four sons and two daughters. **Career:** Editor, Chilton Company (magazine publishers), Radnor, Pennsylvania, 1966-89; writer. **Awards:** Boston Globe/Horn Book award, 1990, and Newbery Medal, American Library Association, 1991, both for *Maniac Magee*; Carolyn Field award, 1991; Dorothy Canfield Fisher award, 1992; Indian Paintbrush award, Rhode Island Children's Book award, Flicker Tale award, Charlotte award, Mark Twain award, Nevada Young Readers' award, all 1992, William Allen White award, Pacific Northwest award, Massachusetts Children's Book award, Rebecca Caudill award, West Virginia Children's Book award, Buckeye Children's Book award, Land of Enchantment award, all 1993, all for *Maniac Magee*; South Carolina Children's book award, 1993, for *Fourth Grade Rats*; California Young Reader medal, 1993, for *There's a Girl in My Hammerlock*; American Library Association Best Book for Young Adults, 1996, and *School Library Journal* Best Book of the Year, 1996, both for *Crash*; Drexel University Children's Literature Citation, for body of work. **Agent:** Ray Lincoln Literary Agency, 7900 Old York Rd., Apt. 107-B, Elkins Park, Pennsylvania 19027, U.S.A.

PUBLICATIONS FOR YOUNG ADULTS

Fiction

Space Station Seventh Grade. Boston, Little, Brown, 1982.
Who Put That Hair in My Toothbrush? Boston, Little, Brown, 1984.
Night of the Whale. Boston, Little, Brown, 1985.
Jason and Marceline. Boston, Little, Brown, 1986.
Dump Days. Boston, Little, Brown, 1988.
The Bathwater Gang, illustrated by Meredith Johnson. Boston, Little, Brown, 1990.
Maniac Magee. Boston, Little, Brown, 1990.
Fourth Grade Rats. New York, Scholastic, 1991.
Report to the Principal's Office. New York, Scholastic 1991.

There's a Girl in My Hammerlock. New York, Simon & Schuster, 1991.
The Bathwater Gang Gets down to Business, illustrated by Meredith Johnson. Boston, Little, Brown, 1992.
Do the Funky Pickle. New York, Scholastic, 1992.
Who Ran My Underwear up the Flagpole? New York, Scholastic, 1992.
Picklemania. New York, Scholastic, 1993.
Tooter Pepperday. New York, Random House, 1995.
Crash. New York, Knopf, 1996.
The Library Card. New York, Scholastic, 1997.
Blue Ribbon Blues. New York, Random House, 1997.
Wringer. New York, HarperCollins, 1997.

Autobiography

In My Own Words. Old Tappan, New Jersey, Simon and Schuster, 1997.
Knots in My Yo-Yo String. New York, Knopf, 1998.

Other

Contributor to books, including *Our Roots Grow Deeper Than We Know: Pennsylvania Writers—Pennsylvania Life,* edited by Lee Gutkind, University of Pittsburgh Press, 1985, and *Noble Pursuits,* edited by Virginia A. Arnold and Carl B. Smith, Macmillan, 1988. Work represented in anthologies, including *Best Sports Stories of 1982,* Dutton, and *Connections: Short Stories by Outstanding Writers for Young Adults,* edited by Donald R. Gallo, Delacorte, 1989.

*

Media Adaptations: *Jerry and Eileen Spinelli* (video; interview moderated by Jaqueline Shacter Weiss), Norristown, Pennsylvania, J. S. Weiss, 1992; *Good Conversation! A Talk with Jerry Spinelli* (video; interview by Tim Podell), Bohemia, New York, Rainbow Educational Video, 1992; *Meet the Author: Jerry Spinelli* (video; interview by Jean Frey), Annandale, Virginia, Fairfax Network, 1996.

Biography: Essay in *Speaking for Ourselves: Autobiographical Sketches by Notable Authors of Books for Young Adults,* compiled and edited by Donald R. Gallo, Vol. 1, Urbana, Illinois, National Council of Teachers of English, 1990.

Jerry Spinelli comments:

Don't tell my English teachers, but not much planning goes into my novels. Oh, plenty of experience and imagination and hard work and such go into them, and I do jot down lots of notes, and I do have some idea where to start a story and maybe where to end it. But there's no outline telling me how to get from here to there, because I have found that there is no way to know what is inside the story until I am in there myself. In other words, for me, the product and the process are pretty much the same thing.

*   *   *

Jerry Spinelli creates realistic fiction with humorous dialogue and situations, but his stories go beyond humor: Spinelli's characters stumble and blunder through their lives until they emerge from the fog of adolescence guided by an optimistic light that readies them for their next challenge. While entertaining readers, Spinelli's young protagonists face social issues, such as racism and sex stereotyping, as well as ethical choices that sometimes put them at odds with their peers.

In his first book for young adults Spinelli introduces Jason Herkimer, a seventh grader entering junior high school. *Space Station Seventh Grade* chronicles the dilemmas and struggles through puberty that Jason and other young teens face. When Jason is suspended from school, Jason's mother is upset but Ham, Jason's stepfather, explains that the boy sprawled on the recliner is not the Jason they used to know. That Jason disappeared when Jason turned thirteen. Ham tells Jason's mother, ''The thirteen-year-old does not change from a worm to a butterfly, you know. It changes from a butterfly to a worm.'' Jason's humanism, as he suffers through his first pimple and his first crush, allows readers to identify personally with him. The slang words related to sexual activity used in the text may offend some readers, but Spinelli does not mince words when relating how teens act and speak. The book will be funny for adults who remember their own adolescence, while teens relate the story to their own strange feelings and alien urges.

Jason first discovers romance in the guise of the beautiful cheerleader, Debbie. But he realizes that she is interested in other boys, and not him. At the end of the book, Jason falls in love with Marceline McAllister, an affair which is detailed in *Jason and Marceline.* In this novel, Jason has more to learn about girls and relationships. According to his friends, the main reason to have a steady girlfriend is to make out. Marceline sets Jason straight right away. She refuses to let him give her hickeys as proof of his affection. Jason asks himself, ''Who ever heard of a girl like this?'' Through the ups and downs of their relationship, Spinelli treats readers to his sense of humor as Jason tries to drive down a romantic road filled with emotional potholes. Spinelli exaggerates conversations and situations enough to be witty without getting too far from reality. Young adults will sympathize with Jason and laugh when Marceline tells Jason at the end of the novel, ''There's one thing that hasn't changed, and isn't going to change. I hate to tell you. No hickeys!''

Spinelli claims that his ideas for his characters and plots come from the children in his house. The situations and people in *Who Put That Hair in My Toothbrush?* make this statement believable. Greg and Megin take turns narrating their individual lives over a background of sibling rivalry. Their hostilities toward each other lean toward slapstick humor as they jostle and grate against one another but, despite the insults and humor, Spinelli does provide readers with some sensitive moments: Greg's devotion to beautiful Jennifer Wade; Megin's grief over her friend Emily's death.

With *There's a Girl in My Hammerlock,* Spinelli shows readers his wittiest dialogue, his most focused social issue, and his uncanny ability to write from a girl's viewpoint. Maisie tries out for the wrestling team when she learns that the boy she's interested in, Eric Delong, is on the team. When she makes the team an uproar follows. The coach, the boys on the team, the kids at school, her best friend, her brother, Eric's girlfriend, and the townspeople all try to dissuade her from wrestling. But Maisie endures forfeits from

boys who will not wrestle with a girl and ridicule from all sides. At last she has Eric's attention, but his ungentlemanly advances are not her idea of romance. Maisie's independence and self-sufficiency serves as an inspiration to girls who have unconventional talents and want to develop them.

In 1991 Spinelli was awarded the Newbery Medal for *Maniac Magee.* This novel is a departure from Spinelli's other writing in the respect that it was written for younger readers and lacks his irreverent style of writing. Jeffrey Lionel Magee is not a mixed-up teenager. Instead, he represents the best in each of us: he's generous, sensitive, and lacks any inclinations for prejudice. At first, *Maniac Magee* appears to be another realistic novel. His parents are killed in a train wreck when he is three. An aunt and uncle take him into their loveless, divided home, where Jeffrey endures until he is eleven. Then he runs away. When he reaches Two Rivers, children there call him ''Maniac'' because of his amazing athletic feats and seemingly fearless behavior. Legends about this new boy quickly grow as readers learn that Maniac can dare more, run faster, jump higher, and untie knots quicker than anyone the kids of Twin Mills have ever seen. Even as Spinelli directs readers to consider how stories accumulate fantastic elements that distort the factual truth of hero tales and legends, he gives us Maniac McGee, a folk hero for modern times every bit as much as Johnny Appleseed or Paul Bunyan were for older times. But no matter how others perceive him, no matter what his public image, Maniac remains Jeffrey at heart, a homeless, orphaned boy whose search for a family and home ultimately changes the lives of many residents of Twin Mills.

Like Maniac Magee, John (Crash) Coogan is a super-athlete; unlike Maniac, the aptly named Crash is not sensitive to the feelings and needs of other people. In fact, for much of *Crash,* readers should find little to like about this seventh-grade boy with the monumental ego who readily bullies those smaller and more vulnerable than himself, who is competitive in every unhealthy way, even to having more expensive clothes and sneakers than his buddies, and who threatens the girl who wisely rejects him. Crash's only evident redeeming feature is his affection for his grandfather, but even that is tinged with sibling jealousy as he competes with his younger sister for the old man's affection. Written in the first person, *Crash* captures the bully's bravado in a way that fascinates the reader in the same way that turning over rocks or rotting logs to see what crawls out can be fascinating. It's repellant, but compelling. Not until his grandfather suffers a life-threatening stroke does Crash exhibit any sympathetic tendencies. Realizing for the first time that illness and death are forces he cannot beat back, Crash becomes aware of how much his grandfather's presence means to him. This awareness lifts him out of his egocentric self-absorption and allows him to make meaningful connections with other people, including his parents, his sister, and the boy he has tormented since they were both six-years old. Crash comes to understand that there are many ways of winning, and not all of them involve scoring the most touchdowns or always crossing the finish line first.

Moral choices lie at the center of *Wringer,* choices which push the almost ten-year-old Palmer LaRue close to a nervous breakdown. Palmer hates the idea of turning ten because it means he must take his place among the other boys who wring the necks of pigeons only wounded—''flutters,'' they're called—at the town's annual pigeon shoot. If he does not follow the tradition, he will be ostracized by his gang. Worse, if the gang finds out he secretly keeps Nipper, his pet pigeon, in his bedroom, he knows they will kill the bird. Although the protagonist is young, he must make a decision many much older people find difficult, one that young adult readers facing peer pressure will readily recognize: conform to behavior he at heart knows to be reprehensible, or stand up for what he believes to be right and become an outcast. Even with such momentous conflicts driving the narrative, *Wringer* manages to evidence Spinelli's trademark humor in the descriptions of the gang's initiation rite involving the town bully and a can of beans and the dead-on diction of the boys' conversations.

In view of the serious issues Spinelli's novels for young adults address, it seems odd to note that his specialty is his humorous view of adolescence. His readers know that he's laughing with them at the absurdities, even the difficulties, of growing up. It takes special talent to combine humor with sensitivity, but Spinelli manages this challenging combination well.

—Rosemary Chance, updated by Linda Benson

STAPLES, Suzanne Fisher

Nationality: American. **Born:** Philadelphia, Pennsylvania, 27 August 1945. **Education:** Cedar Crest College, Allentown, Pennsylvania, B.A. 1967. **Family:** Married 1) Nicholas Green in 1967 (divorced, 1976); 2) Eugene Staples in 1980. **Career:** Asian marketing director, Business International Corp., 1974-76; news editor and correspondent in New York, Washington, D.C., Hong Kong, and India, United Press International, Washington, D.C., 1975-83; part-time editor for foreign desk, *Washington Post,* 1983-85; consultant, U.S. Agency for International Development, 1986-87; fiction writer, since 1988. Lecturer on the status of women in the Islamic Republic of Pakistan. Citizens for a Better Eastern Shore, board member. **Awards:** Newbery Honor, American Library Association, 1990, and Ibby Honor List, 1992, both for *Shabanu: Daughter of the Wind.* **Agent:** Jeanne Drewsen, 250 Mercer, New York, New York 10012, U.S.A.

PUBLICATIONS FOR YOUNG ADULTS

Fiction

Shabanu: Daughter of the Wind. New York, Knopf, 1989.
Haveli. New York, Knopf, 1993.
Dangerous Skies. New York, Farrar, Straus, and Giroux, 1996.

*   *   *

Shabanu: Daughter of the Wind is a Newbery Honor book and a first offering by Suzanne Fisher Staples. It is the story of a spirited eleven-year-old girl, who lives with her nomad family in the Cholistan Desert of present-day Pakistan. Staples brings to us the experiences of a girl whose playfulness is not unlike an American girl her age. However, the carefree youth of a Pakistani girl is fleeting, for Muslim tradition in their country dictates that she marry young.

Phulan, her thirteen-year-old sister, is betrothed to Hamir. Their arranged marriage is planned for the summer monsoon rains. Shabanu (Shah-*bah*-noo) contentedly plays with her camel, Guluband, and plans to go to the great annual fair at Sibi with her father. However, as her family prepares for her sister's upcoming wedding, Shabanu realizes her own freedom will soon end, as it has been arranged that she will wed Murad, Hamir's brother.

Shabanu loves the camels and helps care for them. One day while tending to the herd, she sees the circling of vultures overhead. She runs to the side of a camel, who while giving birth has been bitten by a poisonous snake. Shabanu struggles to birth the young camel herself before its mother dies. She saves the baby and names him Mithoo, a name that means "sweet."

Leaving Mithoo behind with her sister and mother, Shabanu and her father begin the journey to Sibi where they hope to sell some of their camels, with the exception, she hopes, of Guluband. The money they make will be used for Phulan's wedding and dowry. On the way, they meet a band of men who are looking for one of their daughters. The young girl had eloped with a Marri tribesman. After they have left, Shabanu's father tells her that they will kill the young woman when they find her: a reminder that she must always do as she is told.

Shabanu loves the fair and when they arrive, they hurriedly set up camp so they can go to the carnival. Her father takes her on the rides. Little does she realize that it will be the last time she can be young and free.

They receive several offers for their fine camels. But Shabanu's greatest fear is realized when her father's outrageous asking price for the entire herd is met. They will now have enough for not only Phulan's wedding, but Shabanu's wedding as well. Her parents will no longer have to struggle, for they are now wealthy. Shabanu is numb, her beloved Guluband is gone. Her father has given her a puppy to replace her sorrow, but it doesn't help, for her childhood is now behind her. She must learn to sacrifice for the benefit of her family. This is only the beginning of her ascent into adulthood.

One day, Shabanu and her sister narrowly escape rape attempted by the hated landlord of Hamir's family property. In retaliation, the despised landowner takes the life of Hamir. To resolve the fury, the landowner has agreed to leave the families alone on one condition: Shabanu agrees to marry his wealthy brother, Rahim-*sahib*. The plans for the marriages are rearranged: Phulan will now marry Murad, Shabanu's intended; and Shabanu will wed Rahim-*sahib*. Her parents are very pleased as Shabanu's marriage will bring prestige to their family. However, Shabanu is not happy to wed an older man with three wives. She wonders whether these women will make her a slave. How will she survive?

"It isn't a matter of what she wants!" says her father. "She is intelligent and. . ." her mother tries to explain, "She'll find out where her intelligence will get her." Shabanu hasn't a choice according to her father. Shabanu calls upon the wise words of a respected elder: "No matter what happens—you have *you.*"

The story of *Shabanu* offers so much more than the tale of a young girl coming of age. From the colorful *chadr* draped over the head and shoulders of every woman in public view, to the making of *chapati,* a pan bread made of wheat flour and water, Staples takes you to another culture, teaches you another language, and makes you feel the pain and torment of a spirit struggling to survive when the rules of tradition seem destined to destroy it. It is a lesson for all who are determined to soar above that which seeks to keep them down.

This is a wonderful beginning for Suzanne Fisher Staples. In addition to being a Newbery Honor book, *Shabanu* was named an ALA Best Book for Young Adults, an ALA Notable Children's Book, and a New York Times Notable Book of the Year.

—Suzanne M. Valentic

STEINBECK, John (Ernst)

Nationality: American. **Born:** Salinas, California, 27 February 1902. **Education:** Stanford University, special student, 1919-25. **Family:** Married 1) Carol Henning in 1930 (divorced 1943); 2) Gwyn Conger in 1943 (divorced 1948), two sons; 3) Elaine Scott in 1950. **Career:** Variously employed as hod-carrier, fruit-picker, apprentice painter, laboratory assistant, caretaker, surveyor, and reporter; writer. Foreign correspondent in North Africa and Italy for *New York Herald Tribune,* 1943; correspondent in Vietnam for *Newsday,* 1966-67. Special writer for U.S. Army Air Forces, during World War II. **Awards:** General Literature Gold Medal, Commonwealth Club of California, 1936, for *Tortilla Flat,* 1937, for *Of Mice and Men,* and 1940, for *The Grapes of Wrath;* New York Drama Critics Circle award, 1938, for play, "Of Mice and Men"; Pulitzer Prize, 1940, for *The Grapes of Wrath;* Academy award nomination for best original story, Academy of Motion Picture Arts and Sciences, 1944, for "Lifeboat," and 1945, for "A Medal for Benny"; Nobel Prize for literature, 1962; Paperback of the Year award, Best Sellers, 1964, for *Travels with Charley: In Search of America.* **Died:** 20 December 1968.

PUBLICATIONS

Novels

Cup of Gold: A Life of Henry Morgan, Buccaneer. New York, Robert McBride, 1929.
The Pastures of Heaven. New York, Viking, 1932.
To a God Unknown. New York, Viking, 1933.
Tortilla Flat. New York, Viking, 1935.
In Dubious Battle. New York, Viking, 1936.
Of Mice and Men. New York, Viking, 1937.
The Red Pony. Covici, Friede, 1937.
The Grapes of Wrath. New York, Viking, 1939; revised edition, edited by Peter Lisca, New York, Viking, 1972.
The Forgotten Village. New York, Viking, 1941.
The Moon Is Down. New York, Viking, 1942.
Cannery Row. New York, Viking, 1945; new edition (includes manuscript, corrected typescript, corrected galleys, and first edition), Stanford Publications Service, 1975.
The Wayward Bus. New York, Viking, 1947.
The Pearl. New York, Viking, 1947.
Burning Bright: A Play in Story Form. New York, Viking, 1950.
East of Eden. New York, Viking, 1952.
Sweet Thursday. New York, Viking, 1954.
The Short Reign of Pippin IV: A Fabrication. New York, Viking, 1957.
The Winter of Our Discontent. New York, Viking, 1961.

Short Stories

Saint Katy the Virgin. Covici, Friede, 1936.
Nothing So Monstrous. Pynson Printers, 1936.
The Long Valley. New York, Viking, 1938; as *Thirteen Great Short Stories from the Long Valley,* New York, Avon, 1943; as *Fourteen Great Short Stories from the Long Valley,* New York, Avon, 1947.
How Edith McGillicuddy Met R.L.S. Cleveland, Ohio, Rowfant Club, 1943.
The Crapshooter. New York, Mercury Publications, 1957.

Plays

Of Mice and Men: A Play in Three Acts (produced Broadway, 1937), with George S. Kaufman. New York, Viking, 1937.
The Moon Is Down: Play in Two Parts (produced Broadway, 1942). New York, Dramatist's Play Service, 1942.
Burning Bright: Play in Three Acts (produced Broadway, 1950). New York, Dramatist's Play Service, 1951.

Screenplays: *Forgotten Village,* independently produced, 1939; *Lifeboat,* Twentieth Century-Fox, 1944; *A Medal for Benny,* Paramount, 1945, in *Best Film Plays—1945,* edited by John Gassner and Dudley Nichols, New York, Crown, 1946; *The Pearl,* RKO, 1948; *The Red Pony,* Republic, 1949; *Viva Zapata!,* Twentieth Century-Fox, 1952, edited by Robert E. Morsberger, New York, Viking, 1975.

Other

Their Blood Is Strong. Simon J. Lubin Society of California, 1938.
A Letter to the Friends of Democracy. Mountain Brook, Alabama, Overbrook Press, 1940.
Sea of Cortez, with Edward F. Ricketts. New York, Viking, 1941; as *Sea of Cortez: A Leisurely Journal of Travel,* Mount Vernon, New York, Appel, 1971; revised edition, as *The Log from the "Sea of Cortez": The Narrative Portion of the Book, "Sea of Cortez,"* New York, Viking, 1951.
Bombs Away: The Story of a Bomber Team. New York, Viking, 1942.
Steinbeck, edited by Pascal Covici. New York, Viking, 1943; expanded edition, as *The Portable Steinbeck,* 1946; as *Steinbeck Omnibus,* Australia, Oxford University Press, 1946; revised edition, New York, Viking, 1971.
A Russian Journal, photographs by Robert Capa. New York, Viking, 1948.
Short Novels: Tortilla Flat, The Red Pony, Of Mice and Men, The Moon Is Down, Cannery Row, The Pearl. New York, Viking, 1953; new edition, New York, Viking, 1963.
Once There Was a War. New York, Viking, 1958.
East of Eden and *The Wayward Bus.* New York, Viking, 1962.
Travels with Charley: In Search of America. New York, Viking, 1962.
The Red Pony, Part I: The Gift and *The Pearl.* Toronto, Macmillan, 1963.
Letters to Alicia (collection of newspaper columns written as a correspondent in Vietnam). Garden City, New Jersey, 1965.
The Pearl and *The Red Pony.* New York, Viking, 1967.

America and Americans. New York, Viking, 1969.

Cannery Row and *Sweet Thursday.* San Francisco, California, Heron Books, 1971.

To a God Unknown and *The Pearl.* San Francisco, California, Heron Books, 1971.

Of Mice and Men and *Cannery Row.* Harmondsworth, England, Penguin, 1973; New York, Penguin, 1978.

Steinbeck: A Life in Letters, edited by Elaine Steinbeck and Robert Wallsten. New York, Viking, 1975.

The Acts of King Arthur and His Noble Knights: From the Winchester Manuscripts of Thomas Malory and Other Sources, edited by Chase Horton. New York, Farrar, Straus, 1976.

The Collected Poems of Amnesia Glasscock (as Amnesia Glasscock) San Francisco, California, Manroot Books, 1976.

The Grapes of Wrath, The Moon Is Down, Cannery Row, East of Eden, and *Of Mice and Men.* North Pomfret, Vermont, Heinemann, 1976.

John Steinbeck, 1902-1968 (includes *Tortilla Flat, Of Mice and Men,* and *Cannery Row*). Franklin Center, Pennsylvania, Franklin Library, 1977.

Letters to Elizabeth: A Selection of Letters from John Steinbeck to Elizabeth Otis, edited by Florian J. Shasky and Susan F. Kiggs. San Francisco, California, Book Club of California, 1978.

Contributor, *Famous American Plays of the Nineteen Thirties,* edited by Harold Clurman. New York, Dell, 1980.

The Short Novels of John Steinbeck (includes *Tortilla Flat, The Red Pony, Of Mice and Men, The Moon Is Down, Cannery Row,* and *The Pearl*). New York, Viking, 1981.

The Harvest Gypsies: On the Road to the Grapes of Wrath. Berkeley, California, Heyday, 1988.

Working Days: The Journals of the Grapes of Wrath, edited by Robert DeMott. New York, Penguin, 1989.

*

Media Adaptations: *Of Mice and Men* (film), United Artists, 1939; (opera adapted by Carlisle Floyd), 1970; (teleplay by E. Nick Alexander); (film, starring Sherilyn Fenn), 1992; *The Grapes of Wrath* (film), Twentieth Century-Fox, 1940; *Tortilla Flat* (film), MGM, 1942; *The Moon Is Down* (film), Twentieth Century-Fox, in 1943; *The Red Pony* (film), Republic, 1949; *East of Eden* (film), Warner Bros., 1954; (musical, *Here's Where I Belong*), 1968; (television mini-series); *Pipe Dream* (musical, adapted by Oscar Hammerstein II, with music by Richard Rogers, based on *Sweet Thursday*), 1955; *The Wyaward Bus* (film), Twentieth Century-Fox, 1957; *America and Americans* (television movie), NBC-TV, 1967; *Travels with Charley* (television movie), NBC-TV, 1968; *The Harness* (television movie), 1971; *The Red Pony* (television movie), 1973; *Cannery Row* (film), MGM, 1982.

Biography: Entry in *Concise Dictionary of American Literary Biography: The Age of Maturity, 1929-1941,* Detroit, Gale, 1989; entry in *Dictionary of Literary Biography,* Detroit, Gale, Volume 7, 1981; Volume 9, 1981; entry in *Dictionary of Literary Biography Documentary Series,* Volume 2, Detroit, Gale, 1982; *John Steinbeck* by Warren French, Boston, Twayne, 1961.

Critical Studies: Entry in *Contemporary Literary Criticism,* Volume 1, Detroit, Gale, 1973; Volume 5, 1976; Volume 9, 1978; Volume 13, 1980; Volume 21, 1982; Volume 34, 1985; Volume 45, 1987; *Steinbeck: A Collection of Critical Essays* edited by Robert Murray Davis, Englewood Cliffs, New Jersey, Prentice-Hall, 1972; *John Steinbeck: An Introduction and Interpretation* by Joseph Fontenrose, New York, Barnes and Noble, 1963; *John Steinbeck: A Dictionary of His Fictional Characters* edited Tetsumaro Hayashi, Metuchen, New York, Scarecrow, 1976; *The Novels of John Steinbeck: A Critical Study* by Howard Levant, Columbia, University of Missouri Press, 1974; *The Wide World of John Steinbeck* by Peter Lisca, New Brunswick, New Jersey, Rutgers University Press, 1958; *Steinbeck: The Man and His Work* by Peter Lisca, Corvallis, Oregon State University Press, 1971; *John Steinbeck* by Paul McCarthy, Ungar, 1980; *The Novels of John Steinbeck: A First Critical Study* by Harry Thornton Moore, New York, Normandie House, 1939; *Steinbeck and His Critics: A Record of Twenty-Five Years* edited by E.W. Tedlock, Jr., and C.V. Wicker, Albuquerque, University of New Mexico Press, 1957; *John Steinbeck's Fiction: The Aesthetics of the Road Taken* by John H. Timmerman, Norman, University of Oklahoma Press, 1986; *John Steinbeck* by F.W. Watt, New York, Grove, 1962.

*   *   *

Justly renowned as one of America's classic modern writers, John Steinbeck is not an author for young adults in terms of his own intentions. He intended his fiction for a general audience, and, though he welcomed younger readers (as well as the use of his books in the schools), he wrote no important works specifically for young adults. However, his volumes of both fiction and nonfiction remain so readable and accessible for any audience that they have become favorites of both young adults and their teachers. Most of his novels would interest advanced readers at the secondary level, but his best stories for young adults are those which grow from his own childhood, adolescence, and young manhood.

The Depression had elicited a reevaluation of American culture, a reassessment of the American dream; a harsh realism of observation was balanced by a warm emphasis on human dignity. A writer of great talent, sensitivity, and imagination, John Steinbeck entered in the mood of the country in the late 1930s with an extraordinary responsiveness. Literature and the other arts joined social, economic, and political thought in contrasting traditional American ideals with the bleak reality of breadlines and shantytowns. Perhaps the major symbol of dislocation was the Dust Bowl, depicted in Steinbeck's classic *The Grapes of Wrath* (1939). The arts in the 1930s focused on these harsh images and tried to find in them the human dimensions which promised a new beginning.

The best of Steinbeck's works strikes this very balance. Although its attitude toward Hispanic Americans seems dated, Steinbeck's first successful novel, *Tortilla Flat* (1935), provides entertaining reading as do its sequels, *Cannery Row* (1945) and *Sweet Thursday* (1954). Several stories in *The Long Valley* are often collected in high school anthologies, most notably "Flight," (1938) a harsh story of a young Chicano boy's initiation into manhood. *Of Mice and Men* (1939) is also harsh and realistic, but its beautiful evocation of friendships and dreams makes it a timeless American classic. Another classic is Steinbeck's symbolic tale of a Mexican fisherman, *The Pearl* (1947). Although Steinbeck's epic *The Grapes of Wrath* is somewhat long and complex, the mature young person will enjoy and profit from reading it.

Steinbeck also wrote some fine works of nonfiction, such as *Log from the "Sea of Cortez"* (1941) and *Travels with Charley: In Search of America* (1962).

Steinbeck also has fared better at the hands of Hollywood than have most classic American writers. *Of Mice and Men* has received three fine film treatments (1939, 1973, 1993). Director John Ford's film version of *The Grapes of Wrath* (1940) remains as important a part of Americana as the novel. The Mexican film version of *The Pearl* (1947) is more than adequate. Steinbeck wrote the screenplay for the successful 1949 film treatment of *The Red Pony,* and Lewis Milestone produced and directed the film which starred Robert Mitchum and Peter Miles. A 1973 production of *The Red Pony,* directed by Robert Totten and starring Henry Fonda and Maureen O'Hara, received more favorable reviews. One of Steinbeck's best works of the postwar period was the script for the powerful film *Viva Zapata!* (1952), which was directed by Elia Kazan and starred Marlon Brando. Many of the films based on Steinbeck's work continue to appear on television, including the two versions of *East of Eden* (1955, 1981) and the 1982 adaptation of *Cannery Row.*

Perhaps Steinbeck's finest work for young adults is *The Red Pony.* The writer began *The Red Pony* fairly early in his career; his letters indicate he was working on a pony story in 1933, and the first two sections of the story sequence, "The Gift" and "The Great Mountains," were published in the *North American Review* in November and December of that year. The third section, "The Promise," did not appear in *Harpers* until 1937, and these three parts were published in a slim volume in 1937. "The Leader of the People," the final section, was not added until the publication of the fiction story collection *The Long Valley* in 1938. However, manuscript and textual evidence suggests that the later sections were written some time before their publication, not very long after the first two stories. The four sections are connected by common characters, settings, and themes, forming a clearly unified story sequence which was published separately as *The Red Pony* in 1945. A modestly successful movie version, for which Steinbeck wrote the screenplay, followed in 1949, and a television movie was even better received in 1973.

The Red Pony is among Steinbeck's finest works. This story sequence traces a young boy's initiation into adult life with both realism and sensitivity, a balance that Steinbeck did not always achieve. The vision of characters caught up in the harsh world of nature is balanced by their deep human concerns and commitments. The story takes place on the Tiflin ranch in the Salinas Valley, California. Steinbeck's evocation of the vital beauty of the ranch matches his fine work in *Of Mice and Men,* and his symbols grow naturally out of this setting. The setting stresses the end of the frontier and of the American dream; so in a sense Jody's maturation matches that of modern America. In its depiction of an American variation of a universal experience, *The Red Pony* deserves comparison with the finest of modern American fiction, especially initiation tales such as Williams Faulkner's *The Bear* (1942) or Ernest Hemingway's "Nick Adams" stories.

The literary qualities in *The Red Pony* typify the style that won Steinbeck immense popularity. Rising to prominence at the height of the Depression, Steinbeck seemed to reflect the mood of the era with his strong lines of simple prose. Yet Steinbeck derives his literary power from his use of symbolism for ironic effect. The symbolic images in the plot allow the reader to perceive the significance of an event on a much deeper level than do the characters. The pony in *The Red Pony,* for example, functions as a symbol of Jody's boyhood and innocence as well as a symbol of his maturation. When the pony dies, the reader experiences a sense of loss, because the pony's death represents Jody's loss of innocence. But while the reader understands that Jody's life has been dramatically altered by the death of the pony, Jody, ironically, grieves for his pony without the ability to fully see the death in a larger context.

During World War II, Steinbeck's development as a novelist faltered, and he never recovered his artistic momentum. Even *East of Eden,* the work he thought his masterpiece, proved a critical failure although it was a popular success. Since his death, Steinbeck's books have remained widely read, both in America and abroad. His critical reputation has enjoyed a modest revival, and will most likely continue to develop, for few writers have better celebrated the American dream or traced the dark shape of the American nightmare.

Although Steinbeck appeals to readers of all ages, much of his work is excellent fare for young adult readers. At least a dozen of his titles, along with the film versions made from them, prove excellent classroom reading. Perhaps the most accessible and readable of these are the narratives based on his own younger life. In particular *The Red Pony* remains a classic of young adult fiction, a sensitive yet realistic story of both personal and cultural maturation which becomes universal in its insights. For fiction like this, John Steinbeck will continue to be regarded as an important young adult author, despite the fact that he did not intend this aspect of his literary reputation.

—Joseph R. Millichap

STEVENSON, Robert Louis (Balfour)

Pseudonym: Captain George North. **Nationality:** British. **Born:** Edinburgh, 13 November 1850. **Education:** Edinburgh Academy; Edinburgh University, 1867-72; studied law in the office of Skene Edwards and Gordon, Edinburgh; called to the Scottish bar, 1875. **Family:** Married Fanny Van de Grift Osbourne in 1880; two stepsons, including Lloyd Osbourne. Contributor, *Cornhill Magazine,* London, 1876-82. **Career:** Novelist, poet, essayist, and writer of travel books. Called to the Scottish bar, 1875, but never practiced. Traveled widely in Europe, America, and the South Sea Islands, finally settling in Samoa in 1899. **Awards:** Silver medal, Royal Scottish Society of Arts, 1871, for a scientific essay on lighthouses. **Died:** 3 December 1894.

PUBLICATIONS

Novels

Treasure Island (first published serially under the pseudonym Captain George North in *Young Folks,* 1881-82). London, Cassell, 1883.
Prince Otto: A Romance. London, Chatto & Windus, 1885; Boston, Roberts Brothers, 1886.
Kidnapped. New York, Scribner, 1886.

The Strange Case of Dr. Jekyll and Mr. Hyde. New York, Scribner, 1886.

The Black Arrow: A Tale of the Two Roses. New York, Scribner, 1888.

The Master of Ballantrae: A Winter's Tale. New York, Scribner, 1889.

The Wrong Box, with Lloyd Osbourne. New York, Scribner, 1889.

The Wrecker, with Lloyd Osbourne, illustrated by William Hole and W.L. Metcalf. New York, Scribner, 1892.

David Balfour. New York, Scribner, 1893; as *Catriona: A Sequel to Kidnapped,* London, Cassell, 1893.

The Ebb-Tide: A Trio and a Quartette, with Lloyd Osbourne. Chicago, and Cambridge, Stone & Kimball, 1894.

Weir of Hermiston: An Unfinished Romance. New York, Scribner, 1896.

St. Ives; Being the Adventures of a French Prisoner in England (completed by Arthur T. Quiller-Couch). New York, Scribner, 1897.

Short Stories

New Arabian Nights. New York, Holt, 1882.

The Story of a Lie. Hayley & Jackson, 1882; as *The Story of a Lie and Other Tales,* Boston, Turner, 1904.

More New Arabian Nights: The Dynamiter, with Fanny Stevenson. New York, Holt, 1885.

The Merry Men and Other Tales and Fables. New York, Scribner, 1887.

The Misadventures of John Nicholson: A Christmas Story. New York, Lovell, 1887.

Island Nights' Entertainments: Consisting of The Beach of Falesa, The Bottle Imp, The Isle of Voices, illustrated by Gordon Browne. New York, Scribner, 1893.

The Body-Snatcher. Springfield, Merriam, 1895.

Fables. New York, Scribner, 1896.

Tales and Fantasies. London, Chatto & Windus, 1905.

The Waif Woman. London, Chatto & Windus, 1916.

When the Devil Well, edited by W.P. Trent. Boston, Bibliophile Society, 1921.

Two Mediaeval Tales, illustrated by C.B. Falls. New York, Limited Editions Club, 1929.

Tales and Essays, edited by G.B. Stern. Falcon, 1950.

The Complete Short Stories of Robert Louis Stevenson, edited by Charles Neider. New York, Doubleday, 1969.

Poetry

Not I, and Other Poems, illustrated by the author. Davos, S.L. Osbourne, 1881.

Moral Emblems, illustrated by the author. Davos, S.L. Osbourne, 1882.

A Child's Garden of Verses. New York, Scribner, 1885.

Underwoods. New York, Scribner, 1887.

Ballads. New York, Scribner, 1890.

The Poems and Ballads of Robert Louis Stevenson. New York, Scribner, 1896.

Songs of Travel and Other Verses, edited by Sidney Colvin. London, Chatto & Windus, 1896.

R. L. S. Teuila (fugitive lines and verses). Privately printed, 1899.

Poetical Fragments. Privately printed, 1915.

An Ode of Horace. Privately printed, 1916.

Poems Hitherto Unpublished, edited by G.S. Hellman. Two volumes, Boston, Bibliophile Society, 1916.

New Poems and Variant Readings. London, Chatto & Windus, 1918.

The Poems of Robert Louis Stevenson (the complete poems). New York, Gordon Press, 1974.

Plays

Deacon Brodie; or, The Double Life, with William E. Henley. Privately printed, 1880.

Admiral Guinea, with William E. Henley. Privately printed, 1884.

Beau Austin, with William E. Henley. Privately printed, 1884.

Macaire, with William E. Henley. Privately printed, 1885.

Three Plays: Deacon Brodie, Beau Austin, Admiral Guinea, with William E. Henley. New York, Scribner, 1892.

The Hanging Judge, with Fanny Stevenson, edited by Edmund Gosse. Privately printed, 1914.

Monmouth: A Tragedy, edited by C. Vale. New York, Rudge, 1928.

Travel Books

An Inland Voyage. Carmel, California, Kegan Paul, 1878; Boston, Roberts Brothers, 1883.

Edinburgh: Picturesque Notes, with Etchings. London, Seeley, Jackson & Halliday, 1879; London, Macmillan, 1889.

Travels with a Donkey in the Cevennes. Boston, Roberts Brothers, 1879.

The Silverado Squatters. London, Chatto & Windus, 1883; New York, Munro, 1884.

Across the Plains, with Other Memories and Essays. New York, Scribner, 1892.

The Amateur Emigrant from the Clyde to Sandy Hook. Chicago, Stone & Kimball, 1895.

In the South Seas. New York, Scribner, 1896.

A Mountain Town in France: A Fragment, illustrated by the author. New York, and London, J. Lane, 1896.

Essays of Travel. London, Chatto & Windus, 1905.

Silverado Journal, edited by John E. Jordan. San Francisco, Book Club of California, 1954.

From Scotland to Silverado, edited by James D. Hart. Cambridge, Massachussetts, Harvard University Press, 1966.

The Amateur Emigrant with Some First Impressions of America, edited by Roger G. Swearingen. Two volumes, Osborne, 1976-77.

Essays

The Pentland Rising. Privately printed, 1866.

An Appeal to the Clergy. Blackwood, 1875.

Virginibus Puerisque and Other Papers. New York, Collier, 1881.

Familiar Studies of Men and Books. London, Chatto & Windus, 1882; New York, Dodd, Mead, 1887.

Some College Memories. Edinburgh, University Union Committee, 1886; New York, Mansfield & Wessels, 1899.

Memoir of Fleeming Jenkin. New York, Longmans, Green, 1887.

Memories and Portraits. New York, Scribner, 1887.

Father Damien: An Open Letter to the Reverend Dr. Hyde of Honolulu. London, Chatto & Windus, 1890; Portland, Maine, Mosher, 1897.

A Footnote to History: Eight Years of Trouble in Samoa. New York, Scribner, 1892.

War in Samoa. Privately printed, 1893.

Essays and Criticisms. Boston, Turner, 1903.

Prayers Written at Vailima, with an Introduction by Mrs. Stevenson. New York, Scribner, 1904.

Essays in the Art of Writing. London, Chatto & Windus, 1905.

Essays, edited by W.L. Phelps. New York, Scribner, 1906.

Lay Morals and Other Papers. New York, Scribner, 1911.

Memoirs of Himself. Privately printed, 1912.

Records of a Family of Engineers. London, Chatto & Windus, 1912.

On the Choice of a Profession. London, Chatto & Windus, 1916.

Confessions of a Unionist: An Unpublished Talk on Things Current, Written in 1888, edited by F.V. Livingstone. Privately printed, 1921.

The Best Thing in Edinburgh: An Address to the Speculative Society of Edinburgh in March 1873, edited by K.D. Osbourne. New York, Howell, 1923.

Selected Essays, edited by H.G. Rawlinson. London, Oxford University Press, 1923.

The Manuscripts of Robert Louis Stevenson's "Records of a Family of Engineers": The Unfinished Chapters, edited by J. Christian Bay. Chicago, Hill, 1929.

The Essays of Robert Louis Stevenson, edited by M. Elwin. London, Macdonald, 1950.

Letter and Diaries

Vailima Letters: Robert Louis Stevenson to Sidney Colvin, 1890-1894. Chicago, Stone & Kimball, 1895.

The Letters of Robert Louis Stevenson to His Family and Friends, edited by S. Colvin. New York, Scribner, 1899.

Autograph Letters, Original Mss., Books, Portraits and Curios from the Library of the Late R.L. Stevenson (catalog of the Anderson Galleries sale of Stevenson's literary property). Three volumes, London, Brown, 1914-16.

Our Samoan Adventure, with Fanny Stevenson, edited by Charles Neider. New York, Harper, 1955.

R.L.S.: Stevenson's Letters to Charles Baxter, edited by De Lancey Ferguson and Marshall Waingrow. New Haven, Connecticut, Yale University Press, 1956.

Collections

The Works of R.L. Stevenson. Edinburgh edition, eighteen volumes, edited by S. Colvin. London, Chatto & Windus, 1894-98; Thistle edition, twenty-six volumes, New York, Scribner, 1902; Biographical edition, thirty-one volumes, New York, Scribner, 1905-39; Pentland edition, twenty volumes, edited by Edmund Gosse, London, Cassell, 1906-07; Swanston edition, twenty-five volumes, London, Chatto & Windus, 1911-12; Tusitala edition, thirty-five volumes, London, Heinemann, 1923-24; South Seas edition, thirty-two volumes, New York, Scribner, 1925.

Other

A Stevenson Medley, edited by S. Colvin. London, Chatto & Windus 1899.

Robert Louis Stevenson: Hitherto Unpublished Prose Writings, edited by H.H. Harper. Boston, Bibliophile Society, 1921.

Castaways of Soledad: A Manuscript by Stevenson Hitherto Unpublished, edited by G.S. Hellman. Privately printed, 1928.

The Charity Bazaar: An Allegorical Dialogue. Portland, Oregon, Georgian Press, 1929.

Salute to RLS, edited by F. Holland. Cousland, 1950.

A Newly Discovered Long Story "An Old Song" and a Previously Unpublished Short Story "Edifying Letters of the Rutherford Family," edited by Roger G. Swearingen. Hamden, Connecticut, Archon, 1982.

Robert Louis Stevenson and "The Beach of Falesa": A Study in Victorian Publishing with the Original Text, edited by Barry Menikoff. Palos Verdes Estates, California, Stanford University Press, 1984.

*

Manuscript Collections: Beinecke Rare Book and Manuscript Library, Yale University; the Pierpont Morgan Library, New York City; the Henry E. Huntington Library, San Marino, California; the Widener Library, Harvard University; the Edinburgh Public Library; the Silverado Museum, Saint Helena, California; and the Monterey State Historical Monument Stevenson House, Monterey, California.

Media Adaptations: *Robert Louis Stevenson's "Markheim"* (one-act play), Eldridge Publishing, 1963; *Robert Louis Stevenson's "The Suicide Club"* (one-act play), Eldridge Publishing, 1964; *The Bottle Imp* (film, starring Sessue Hayakawa), Jesse L. Lasky Feature Play Co., 1917; *Kidnapped* (film), Thomas A. Edison, Inc., 1917, Twentieth Century-Fox, starring Freddie Bartholomew and Warner Baxter, 1938, Teaching Film Custodians, 1947, Monogram Pictures, starring Roddy McDowall and Dan O'Herlihy, 1948, and Walt Disney, starring James MacArthur and Peter Finch, 1950; *Treasure Island* (film), Fox Film Corp., 1917, Famous Players-Lasky Corp., starring Lon Chaney, 1920, Metro-Goldwyn-Mayer, starring Jackie Cooper, Wallace Beery, and Lionel Barrymore, 1934, Teaching Film Custodians, 1945, Walt Disney Productions, starring Bobby Driscoll and Robert Newton, 1950, and Turner Network Television and Agamemnon Films, starring Charlton Heston, Christian Bale, and Oliver Reed, 1990; *Dr. Jekyll and Mr. Hyde* (film), Pioneer Film Corp., 1920, Famous Players-Lasky Corp., starring John Barrymore and Nita Naldi, 1920, Paramount Publix Corp., starring Fredric March and Miriam Hopkins, 1932, Metro-Goldwyn-Mayer, starring Spencer Tracy and Ingrid Bergman, 1941, and Sterling Educational Films, 1959; *The White Circle* (film adaptation of "The Pavilion on the Links," starring John Gilbert), Famous Players-Lasky Corp., 1920; *Ebb Tide* (film), Famous Players-Lasky Corp., starring Milton Sills, 1922, and Paramount Pictures, starring Ray Milland and Barry Fitzgerald, 1937; *Trouble for Two* (film adaptation of *The Suicide Club,* starring Robert Montgomery and Rosalind Russell), Metro-Goldwyn-Mayer, 1936; *The Body Snatcher* (film, starring Boris Karloff and Bela Lugosi), RKO Radio Pictures, 1945; *Adventure Island* (film adaptation of *Ebb Tide,* starring Rory Calhoun and Rhonda Fleming), Paramount Pictures, 1947; *Adventures in Silverado* (film adaptation of *The Silverado Squatters,* starring William Bishop and Forrest Tucker), Columbia Pictures, 1948; *The Black Arrow* (film, starring Louis Hayward and Janet Blair), Columbia Pictures, 1948, and Walt Disney, starring Oliver Reed and Stephan Chase; *Lodging for the Night* (film), Realm Television Productions, 1949; *Lord Maletroit's Door* (film), Realm Television Productions, 1949; *The Secret of St. Ives* (film, starring Richard Ney and Vanessa Brown), Columbia Pictures, 1949; *The Treasure of Franchard* (film), Realm Television Productions, 1949; *The Imp in the Bottle* (film), General Television Enterprises, 1950; *The Strange Door* (film adaptation of "The Sire de Maletroit's Door," starring Charles Laughton and Boris Karloff), Universal International Pictures, 1951; *The Treasure of Lost Cannon* (film adaptation of "The Treasure of Franchard"), Universal International Pictures, starring William Powell, 1951; *The Master of Ballantrae* (film, starring Errol Flynn), Warner Brothers, 1953, and six half-hour episodes by Time Life Television and BBC Enterprises, starring Julian Glover and Brian Cox; *Long John Silver* (film based on characters from *Treasure Island,* starring Robert Newton), Distributors Corp. of America, 1955; *The Wrong Box* (film, starring John Mills, Peter Sellers, Ralph Richardson, and Michael Caine), Columbia Pictures, 1966; *A Child's Garden of Verses* (film), Sterling Educational Films, 1967; McGraw-Hill, 1968, and University of California Extension Media Center, 1974; *Treasure Island* (adapted to films *Treasure Island Revisited* and *Treasure Island with Mr. Magoo*), both by Macmillan Films; *Treasure Island with Mr. Magoo* (thirty minute television series with Robert Newton); *Kidnapped* (filmstrip), Eye Gate House, 1958, Encyclopaedia Britannica Films, 1961, and Carman Educational Associates, 1966; *Treasure Island* (filmstrip), Encyclopaedia Britannica Films, 1960, Carman Educational Associates, 1966, Jam Handy School Service, 1968, Dufour Editions, 1969, Walt Disney Educational Materials, 1970, Universal Education and Visual Arts, 1971, Educational Record Sales, 1971, McGraw-Hill, 1972, and Teaching Resources Films, 1974; *The Owl and the Pussy-Cat [and] My Shadow* (filmstrips of the first poem by Edward Lear, the second by Stevenson), Cooper Films and Records, 1969; *Garden of Verses* (transparencies), Creative Visuals, 1970; *Highlights from Treasure Island* (filmstrips), Encyclopaedia Britannica Educational Corp., 1973; *Treasure Island* (record or cassette), read by Ian Richardson, Caedmon, Spoken Arts, 1971; *Treasury of Great Educational Records* (includes *Treasure Island*; twelve records), Miller-Brody Productions, also with *Robin Hood*, Columbia Special Products, 1977; *Adventure Library* (includes *Kidnapped* and *Treasure Island*; ten records or sixteen cassettes), Miller-Brody Productions; *Adventure Poets* (five cassettes), United Learning; *A Child's Garden of Verses* (two records), read by Nancy Wickwire and Basil Langton, Miller-Brody Productions, also read by Dame Judith Anderson, Caedmon; *Dr. Jekyll and Mr. Hyde* (three records or cassettes), read by Patrick Horgan, Miller-Brody Productions; *Kidnapped* (parts 1 and 2, cassettes only), read by John Franklyn, Alan MacDonald, Pamela Mant, David Thorndike, and Derek Young, Spoken Arts; *Markheim by Robert Louis Stevenson,* CMS Records; *Poetry in Song,* Crofut Productions; *The Strange Case of Dr. Jekyll and Mr. Hyde,* Caedmon, (parts 1 & 2, cassettes only), Spoken Arts.

Critical Studies: Entry in *Dictionary of Literary Biography,* Detroit, Gale, Volume 18: *Victorian Novelists after 1885,* 1983, Volume 57: *Victorian Prose Writers after 1867,* 1987.

*   *   *

Nearly all Robert Louis Stevenson's mature fiction, with the exception of *Dr. Jekyll,* takes the form of the historical romance. *Treasure Island, Kidnapped, Catriona, The Master of Ballantrae, St. Ives,* and *Weir of Hermiston* all fall into this category, with the action mainly taking place in eighteenth-century Scotland. The two exceptions are *The Black Arrow,* which is set in the Middle Ages, and *Treasure Island,* which has an English and exotic background.

The plots are nearly always concerned with long journeys, the search for treasure, or flight from capture, and they are usually fraught with great hazards—piracy, murder, intrigue—against which the hero, normally a young person of some resourcefulness, struggles to survive. But Stevenson does not merely use the ingredients of the historical romance for dramatic effects; he also tries to integrate them into a design by which they throw light on various aspects of the human situation as he saw it.

Many of the stories have not a single hero at the centre, but a pair. David and Alan in *Kidnapped,* Jim and Long John in *Treasure Island,* Dr. Jekyll and Mr. Hyde are the best known examples, and they seem to achieve a kind of complementarity as if each partner compensates for the defects of the other. Many of the books also deal with conflicts between clearly defined sides, such as pirates versus honest sailors, English versus Scots, or York versus Lancaster. But there is usually a good deal of changing sides between these antagonists. Long John Silver, for example, begins as an apparently honest sea cook, reveals himself as leader of the mutiny, then deserts the pirates, and finishes up by jumping Captain Smollett's ship. Dick Shelton in *The Black Arrow* switches his allegiance from Lancaster to York, while Alan Breck actually deserts King George at the Battle of Prestonpans. James in *The Master of Ballantrae* seems to have the best of both worlds, fighting for Bonnie Prince Charlie but spying for the other side. Finally, there is a good deal of intrigue and duplicity in the way Stevenson's characters behave, and physical disguises are frequently adopted. In *Catrion* the heroine pretends to be David's sister; in *The Black Arrow* Joanna passes herself off as a boy; and Dr. Jekyll's disguise is even more fundamental.

Stevenson's use of the dual hero, the changing of sides, and the adoption of disguises is not only appropriate to the kinds of stories he wrote, and adds to their dramatic effectiveness, but reveals his passionate concern with the problems of identity and morality. From Stevenson's biographers we know of the ambiguities of his own life, his troubled relations with his parents, whom he adored, and with Scotland, which he worshipped from afar. It may be that his literary interests developed there, but, from the evidence of the fiction, it is clear that Stevenson saw man's nature as constantly shifting, and therefore all the more difficult to define and come to terms with. Dr. Jekyll, who can transform himself physically into a murderous villain, and Deacon Brodie, the clergyman who becomes a robber by night, are simply extreme examples of such shifts. Long John Silver and Alan Breck are much more equivocal as their personalities and virtues fluctuate.

Long John, for example, is a pirate, thief, and murderer, and, as such, quite ruthless in pursuit of gold. But he is also cheerful, brave, witty, and above all kind to Jim, who has no father. In this way Stevenson is constantly challenging our responses. Who is good or bad? he seems to be saying. In your final judgment, do you find Long John sympathetic or not? Are these sorts of questions even relevant? David Balfour operates as a kind of moral censor of Alan Breck's behaviour in *Kidnapped,* but in the end, though he may be "right" in his quarrel with Alan in "The Flight in the Heather," he comes to see that their love complicates the whole matter of knowing who is right or wrong.

Stevenson's influence on later writers is less specific, more pervasive. The historical romance, first established by Scott at the beginning of the nineteenth century, and then adapted for children by such authors as Marryat and Henty, went from strength to strength, until it reached its Victorian peak with Stevenson himself. Though the quality of many early twentieth-century historical novels deteriorated, honourable exceptions can be found in the work of John Masefield and Geoffrey Trease, and since the 1950s the emergence of such writers as Leon Garfield, Cynthia Harnett, and Rosemary Sutcliff has sparked a renaissance of the form.

Though the influence of Stevenson on the specific narrative techniques of the adventure story is doubtful, the influence of his moral values issuing into literary attitudes is everywhere absolutely pervasive, even among those authors who would say they had never read him, and this for two reasons. First, he showed how it was possible to write books for young people that were both thrilling in the most fundamental sense, and yet at the same time deeply serious. The loss of innocence—for example, by Jim Hawkins—is as prevalent in Stevenson's work as in that of Henry James, and the friendship of the two writers was, of course, very significant. And second, in his treatment of the complexities of human behaviour, in his refusal to compartmentalise characters as either "good" or "bad," his writing revealed a maturity which the best children's writers of today can only hope to emulate but not excel. It is significant that a novelist like Leon Garfield, whose stories of the eighteenth century differ so much from Stevenson's, should return time and again to the equivocal nature of human relationships, and the difficulties of distinguishing appearance from reality in exciting books such as *Smith* and *Jack Holborn*. Without the achievement of Stevenson so much of today's best writing would never have appeared.

—Dennis Butts

STEWART, Mary (Florence Elinor)

Nationality: British. **Born:** Sunderland, County Durham, 17 September 1916. **Education:** Eden Hall, Penrith, Cumberland; Skellfield School, Ripon, Yorkshire; St. Hild's College, University of Durham, B.A. (honors) 1938, M.A. 1941. **Military Service:** Served in the Royal Observer Corps during World War II. **Family:** Married Sir Frederick Henry Stewart in 1945. **Career:** Lecturer in English, Durham University, 1941-45; part-time lecturer in English, St. Hild's Training College, Durham, and Durham University, 1948-56; writer, since 1954. **Awards:** Crime Writers Association Silver Dagger award, 1960, for *My Brother Michael*; Mystery Writers of America award, 1964, for *This Rough Magic*; Frederick Niven award, 1971, for *The Crystal Cave*; Scottish Arts Council award, 1974, for *Ludo and the Star Horse*. Fellow, Royal Society of Arts, 1968; fellow, Newnham College, Cambridge, 1986. **Agent:** c/o Hodder & Stoughton Ltd., Mill Road, Dunton Green, Sevenoaks, Kent TN13 2YA, England.

PUBLICATIONS FOR ADULTS AND YOUNG ADULTS

Novels

Madam, Will You Talk? London, Hodder & Stoughton, 1955; New York, Mill, 1956.
Wildfire at Midnight. London, Hodder & Stoughton, and New York, Appleton Century Crofts, 1956.

Thunder on the Right. London, Hodder & Stoughton, 1957; New York, Mill, 1958.
Nine Coaches Waiting. London, Hodder & Stoughton, 1958; New York, Mill, 1959.
My Brother Michael. London, Hodder & Stoughton, and New York, Mill, 1960.
The Ivy Tree. London, Hodder & Stoughton, and New York, Mill, 1961.
The Moon-Spinners. London, Hodder & Stoughton, 1962; New York, Mill, 1963.
This Rough Magic. London, Hodder & Stoughton, and New York, Mill, 1964.
Airs above the Ground. London, Hodder & Stoughton, and New York, Mill, 1965.
The Gabriel Hounds. London, Hodder & Stoughton, and New York, Mill, 1967.
The Wind Off the Small Isles. London, Hodder & Stoughton, 1968.
The Crystal Cave (first book in the "Merlin Trilogy"). London, Hodder & Stoughton, and New York, Morrow, 1970.
The Hollow Hills (second book in the "Merlin Trilogy"). London, Hodder & Stoughton, and New York, Morrow, 1973.
Touch Not the Cat. London, Hodder & Stoughton, and New York, Morrow, 1976.
The Last Enchantment (third book in the "Merlin Trilogy"). London, Hodder & Stoughton, and New York, Morrow, 1979.
Merlin Trilogy. New York, Morrow, 1980.
The Wicked Day. London, Hodder & Stoughton, and New York, Morrow, 1983.
Thornyhold. London, Hodder & Stoughton, and New York, Morrow, 1988.
The Stormy Petrel. London, Hodder & Stoughton, and New York, Morrow, 1991.
The Prince and the Pilgrim. London, Hodder & Stoughton, and New York, Morrow, 1995.
Rose Cottage. London, Hodder & Stoughton, and New York, Morrow, 1997.

Other

Frost on the Window (poetry). New York, Morrow, 1990.
Contributor, *Three Women Alone in the Woods.* West Liberty, Kentucky, Trillium, 1992.
Radio Plays: *Lift from a Stranger, Call Me at Ten-Thirty, The Crime of Mr. Merry,* and *The Lord of Langdale,* 1957-58.

PUBLICATIONS FOR CHILDREN

Fiction

The Little Broomstick. Leicester, Brockhampton Press, 1971; New York, Morrow, 1972.
Ludo and the Star Horse. Leicester, Brockhampton Press, 1974; New York, Morrow, 1975.
A Walk in Wolf Wood. London, Hodder & Stoughton, and New York, Morrow, 1980.
Yoga for Children. New York, Simon & Schuster, 1993.

*

Manuscript Collections: National Library of Scotland, Edinburgh.

Critical Studies: Entry in *Contemporary Literary Criticism,* Vol. 7, Detroit, Gale, 1977.

*   *   *

Mary Stewart's novels fall into two distinct categories. Her early books were all romantic thrillers, in which the spirited heroines invariably arrived at happy marriages after preparatory ordeals of involvement with violent crime, perplexing mystery, and serious personal danger. In the last few years she has added some gentler novels to her list—*Thornyhold* and *Stormy Petrel*—which are simple romances, still containing elements of mystery and wrongdoing but without the strong plotting and excitements of the early romantic adventures. Since settings are always important in Stewart's work, one can see the difference between her early and more recent romances by comparing *Stormy Petrel* with *Wildfire at Midnight,* both of which are set in the Scottish islands. *Stormy Petrel* is a pleasant low-key story, but it has nothing to compare with the psychotic menace which threatens the heroine of the earlier book.

In contrast to these romantic stories of the present day are Stewart's reworkings of the Arthurian legend. These are romances of an altogether different kind. Based on careful research into medieval sources, from the imaginative historian Geoffrey of Monmouth to Malory's *Morte d'Arthur,* these books transcribe the Matter of Britain into a modern idiom—not with the modernist ironic distance of T.H. White's *The Once and Future King* but with an eye to the realistic explanations and psychological plausibilities that might have underlain the more spectacular magic of the legend. These books offer to older readers the sensitive re-enactment of Arthurian romance in modern terms that Rosemary Sutcliff achieved for a younger audience in *The Lantern-Bearers.* Retaining the magic of the original tellings and respecting the essentials of the legend, Stewart's books nevertheless open up the psychology of romance and successfully reactivate the Arthurian story for a contemporary readership.

All Stewart's books were originally published for adults, but both categories of her work are popular with and have much to offer to an young adult audience. The romances, whether thrillers or not, will appeal predominantly to girls, because they have female protagonists, are written almost exclusively from a woman's viewpoint, and usually (the brilliant *Thunder on the Right* is an exception) are narrated in the first person. Male teenage readers free of prejudice against female narrators will find a great deal in these to enjoy. The Arthurian stories appeal equally to readers of both sexes, especially those who have previously enjoyed Arthurian re-tellings aimed at younger children.

For young adults the attraction of Stewart's romantic thrillers lies particularly in their use of a conventional romance framework to present a succession of intelligent and resourceful women who are fully equal to their male coadventurers in virtually every quality except brute muscular strength. Book after book ends with some impressive male chivalry, but one is often aware of a tongue-in-cheek quality in Stewart's depiction of these sexual partnerships, and when the story ends, as it invariably does, in the female protagonist's delighted surrender to protective marital union, the motive is clearly shown to be instinctive natural pleasure, not weakness or social necessity. The point is underlined by those stories—*The Gabriel Hounds* and *Touch Not the Cat*—in which

the lovers are also cousins, equalised in status by family relationships. As if to underscore the point still further, the lovers in *The Gabriel Hounds* have fathers who are identical twins, and those in *Touch Not the Cat* are linked by shared telepathic powers. Stewart is interested in isolated and hence self-reliant, independent heroines but also in closer than usual family bonding, and through permutations on these two extremes she subverts the clichés of dominant male and submissive female, presenting some formidable protagonists. They need to be formidable, too, because they inhabit excitingly treacherous worlds where appearances can never be trusted.

Although small period details have dated some of the books, their tone is remarkably modern and up-to-date. The exotic but accessible settings (Crete in *The Moon-Spinners,* Austria in *Airs above the Ground,* southern France in *Madam, Will You Talk?*) are vividly realised in authentic local detail and are Stewart's particular strength.

The Arthurian stories are likewise marked by their precise geographical locale and vivid sense of place and atmosphere. Above all, however, the power of the Arthurian stories lies in the humanising of a legend. The books comprise a trilogy (*Merlin of the Crystal Cave,* originally published as *The Crystal Cave, The Hollow Hills,* and *The Last Enchantment*) which forms the first-person story of the life of Merlin, the magician and seer who was King Arthur's guardian and teacher. *The Wicked Day* is a kind of coda to the trilogy, which is the third-person story of Arthur's bastard son Mordred. This last book is in many ways the most interesting and original of all. In the traditional legend Mordred is an evil figure, finally the cause of Arthur's ruin. He destroys Arthur in Stewart's story also, but against his will, and only as tragic proof that determined historical process is too powerful to be frustrated by the individual human will.

The Wicked Day has much to offer young adult readers and deserves to be widely known, but inevitably it is overshadowed by the Merlin trilogy. This is a fine piece of storytelling—immensely readable, full of action, incident, and suspense. It is extremely skilful in combining believable character, motive, and the actions of men in a stylised but intricate political world with the overarching sense of destiny and fatefulness which is true to the legend in all its classic forms. *The Last Enchantment,* which tells the story of Arthur's adult life at a time when the narrator Merlin was somewhat removed from it, is perhaps the least successful of the three, but the stories of Merlin's boyhood, in *Merlin of the Crystal Cave,* and of Arthur's, in *The Hollow Hills,* are triumphant narratives which take an honourable place in the literary history of Arthurian legend.

Following a minor vein in the Arthurian legend, *The Prince and the Pilgrim* follows the lives of a fatherless prince and a motherless pilgrim, whose lives converge when they meet and fall in love. When Alexander is still a babe his father is murdered and he and his mother are secreted away to safety during the night. Alexander, now a man, travels to Camelot to request revenge on his father's death but is sidetracked by Morgan LeFay into a quest for the holy grail. Alice, the daughter of a duke, has been on an extended pilgrimage to the Holy Land. During their return voyage they rescue a young French nobleman. He has salvaged from his family fortune a magical chalice with which he plans to buy his acceptance into a monastery. This chalice could be the mysterious holy grail which so many seek, including Prince Alexander. When Alice and Alexander meet at the monastery of St. Martin, Morgan's spell over

Alexander is broken and the two fall in love. Mary Stewart's work continues to represent popular romantic storytelling at its best, and both categories of her work deserve a large young adult readership.

—Peter Hollindale, updated by Lisa A. Wroble

STINE, R(obert) L(awrence)

Pseudonyms: Eric Affabee; Zachary Blue; Jovial Bob Stine. **Nationality:** American. **Born:** Columbus, Ohio, 8 October 1943. **Education:** Ohio State University, B.A. 1965; New York University, 1966-67. **Family:** Married Jane Waldhorn in 1969; one son. **Career:** Social Studies teacher at junior high schools in Columbus, Ohio, 1967-68; associate editor, *Junior Scholastic* (magazine), New York City, 1969-71; editor, *Search* (magazine), New York City, 1972-75; editor, *Bananas* (magazine), New York City, 1972-83; editor, *Maniac* (magazine), New York City, 1984-85; writer. **Address:** c/o Gareth Stevens, 1555 N. River Center Dr., Suite 201, Milwaukee, Wisconsin 53212.

PUBLICATIONS FOR YOUNG ADULTS

Fiction

The Time Raider, illustrated by David Febland. New York, Scholastic, 1982.
The Golden Sword of Dragonwalk, illustrated by David Febland. New York, Scholastic, 1983.
Horrors of the Haunted Museum. New York, Scholastic, 1984.
Indiana Jones and the Curse of Horror Island. New York, Ballantine, 1984.
Indiana Jones and the Giants of the Silver Tower. New York, Ballantine, 1984.
Instant Millionaire, illustrated by Jowill Woodman. New York, Scholastic, 1984.
Through the Forest of Twisted Dreams. New York, Avon, 1984.
The Badlands of Hark, illustrated by Bob Roper. New York, Scholastic, 1985.
Challenge of the Wolf Knight. New York, Avon, 1985.
Conquest of the Time Master. New York, Avon, 1985.
Demons of the Deep, illustrated by Fred Carrillo. New York, Golden Books, 1985.
Indiana Jones and the Cult of the Mummy's Crypt. New York, Ballantine, 1985.
The Invaders of Hark. New York, Scholastic, 1985.
Blind Date. New York, Scholastic, 1986.
Cavern of the Phantoms. New York, Avon, 1986.
Mystery of the Imposter. New York, Avon, 1986.
Operation: Deadly Decoy. New York, Ballantine, 1986.
Twisted. New York, Scholastic, 1986.
Jungle Raid. New York, Ballantine, 1988.
The Baby-Sitter. New York, Scholastic, 1989.
Beach Party. New York, Scholastic, 1990.
The Boyfriend. New York, Scholastic, 1990.
Curtains. New York, Pocket, 1990.
Fear Street: The Wrong Number. New York, Pocket, 1990.
Halloween Party. New York, Pocket, 1990.
How I Broke up with Ernie. New York, Pocket, 1990.

Missing. New York, Pocket, 1990.
Phone Calls. New York, Pocket, 1990.
The Stepsister. New York, Pocket, 1990.
The Surprise Party. New York, Pocket, 1990.
Baby-Sitter II. New York, Scholastic, 1991.
Broken Date. New York, Pocket, 1991.
Fear Street: Fire Game. New York, Pocket, 1991.
The Girlfriend. New York, Scholastic, 1991.
Haunted. New York, Pocket, 1991.
Jerks-In-Training. New York, Scholastic, 1991.
Lights Out. New York, Pocket, 1991.
Losers in Space. New York, Scholastic, 1991.
The New Girl. New York, Pocket, 1991.
The Overnight. New York, Pocket, 1991.
Party Summer. New York, Pocket, 1991.
The Secret Bedroom. New York, Pocket, 1991.
Silent Night. New York, Pocket, 1991.
Ski Weekend. New York, Pocket, 1991.
The Sleepwalker. New York, Pocket, 1991.
Snowman. New York, Scholastic, 1991.
Beach House. New York, Scholastic, 1992.
The Best Friend. New York, Pocket, 1992.
Bozos on Patrol. New York, Scholastic, 1992.
First Date. New York, Pocket, 1992.
The First Evil. New York, Pocket, 1992.
Goodnight Kiss. New York, Pocket, 1992.
The Knife. New York, Pocket, 1992.
Prom Queen. New York, Pocket, 1992.
The Second Evil. New York, Pocket, 1992.
Cheerleaders: The Third Evil. New York, Pocket Books, 1992.
Broken Hearts. New York, Pocket, 1993.
The Cheater. New York, Pocket, 1993.
Hitchhiker. New York, Scholastic, 1993.
Sunburn. New York, Pocket, 1993.
The Betrayal. New York, Pocket Books, 1993.
The Secret. New York, Pocket Books, 1993.
Silent Night 2. New York, Pocket Books, 1993.
The New Boy. New York, Pocket Books, 1994.
Superstitious. New York, Warner Books, 1995.
Beware of the Purple Peanut Butter. New York, Scholastic, 1996.

"Goosebumps" Series

Monster Blood. New York, Scholastic, 1992.
Welcome to the Deadhouse. New York, Scholastic, 1992.
Say Cheese and Die. New York, Scholastic, 1992.
The Haunted Mask. New York, Scholastic, 1993.
The Ghost Next Door. New York, Scholastic, Inc., 1993.
Be Careful What You Wish For. . . . New York, Scholastic, 1993.
The Curse of the Mummy's Tomb. New York, Scholastic, 1993.
Piano Lessons Can Be Murder. New York, Scholastic, 1993.
The Werewolf of Fever Swamp. New York, Scholastic, 1993.
Deep Trouble. New York, Scholastic, 1994.
The Scarecrow Walks at Midnight. New York, Scholastic, 1994.
Why I'm Afraid of Bees. New York, Scholastic, 1994.
One Day at HorrorLand. New York, Scholastic, 1994.
Welcome to Dead House. Milwaukee, Gareth Stevens, 1997.
Night of the Living Dummy. Milwaukee, Gareth Stevens, 1997.
Let's Get Invisible. Milwaukee, Gareth Stevens, 1997.
Welcome to Camp Nightmare. Milwaukee, Gareth Stevens, 1997.

Stay Out of the Basement. Milwaukee, Gareth Stevens, 1997.
The Girl Who Cried Monster. Milwaukee, Gareth Stevens, 1997.

As Jovial Bob Stine

The Absurdly Silly Encyclopedia and Flyswatter, illustrated by
    Bob Taylor. New York, Scholastic, 1978.
How to Be Funny: An Extremely Silly Guidebook, illustrated by
    Carol Nicklaus. New York, Dutton, 1978.
The Complete Book of Nerds, illustrated by Sam Viviano. New
    York, Scholastic, 1979.
The Dynamite Do-It-Yourself Pen Pal Kit, illustrated by Jared Lee.
    New York, Scholastic, 1980.
Dynamite's Funny Book of the Sad Facts of Life, illustrated by
    Jared Lee. New York, Scholastic, 1980.
Going Out! Going Steady! Going Bananas!, photographs by Dan
    Nelken. New York, Scholastic, 1980.
The Pigs' Book of World Records, illustrated by Peter Lippman.
    New York, Random House, 1980.
The Sick of Being Sick Book, with Jane Stine, edited by Ann
    Durrell, illustrated by Carol Nicklaus. New York, Dutton, 1980.
Bananas Looks at TV. New York, Scholastic, 1981.
The Beast Handbook, illustrated by Bob Taylor. New York,
    Scholastic, 1981.
The Cool Kids' Guide to Summer Camp, with Jane Stine, illustrated
    by Jerry Zimmerman. New York, Scholastic, 1981.
Gnasty Gnomes, illustrated by Peter Lippman. New York, Random
    House, 1981.
Don't Stand in the Soup, illustrated by Carol Nicklaus. New York,
    Bantam, 1982.
Bored with Being Bored!: How to Beat the Boredom Blahs, with
    Jane Stine, illustrated by Jerry Zimmerman. New York, Four
    Winds, 1982.
Blips!: The First Book of Video Game Funnies, illustrated by Bryan
    Hendrix. New York, Scholastic, 1983.
Everything You Need to Survive: Brothers and Sisters, with Jane
    Stine. New York, Random House, 1983.
Everything You Need to Survive: First Dates, with Jane Stine. New
    York, Random House, 1983.
Everything You Need to Survive: Homework, with Jane Stine. New
    York, Random House, 1983.
Everything You Need to Survive: Money Problems, with Jane Stine.
    New York, Random House, 1983.
Jovial Bob's Computer Joke Book. New York, Scholastic, 1985.
The Doggone Dog Joke Book. Dayton, Parachute Press, 1986.
Miami Mice, illustrated by Eric Gurney. New York, Scholas-
    tic, 1986.
One Hundred and One Silly Monster Jokes. New York, Scholas-
    tic, 1986.

As Eric Affabee

Attack on the King. New York, Avon, 1986.
G.I. Joe and the Everglades Swamp Terror. New York, Ballantine, 1986.

As Zachary Blue

The Jet Fighter Trap. New York, Scholastic, 1987.
The Petrova Twist. New York, Scholastic, 1987.

*

Biography: Essay in *Speaking for Ourselves, Too* compiled and
edited by Donald R. Gallo, National Council of Teachers of
English, 1993.

*   *   *

Robert L. Stine is a publisher's dream: a prolific writer who
turns out compact, marketable best sellers almost monthly. Between 1988 and 1993, Stine had over fifty books published under
his name, most of them in the teen thriller genre. His thriller series,
Fear Street, is among the most popular series in all YA fiction,
spinning off series like *The Cheerleaders, Fear Street Saga, Fear
Street Super Chillers,* and *Goosebumps.* Each one is unquestionably Stine: a collection of cliffhanging scenes creating a "safe
scare."

Stine's background in writing for humor magazines and
jokebooks shows in his thrillers. Unlike other writers in the genre,
Stine's books have a comic edge to them and are filled with
characters playing practical jokes which more than often backfire
or have unexpected tragic results. If writing jokes is about setting
up the joke then providing the punchline, Stine operates the same
way in a thriller as he sets up the situation then adds the punchline
in the form of a cliffhanger scene. In addition to humor, Stine also
wrote books in the *Find Your Fate, Wizards, Warriors & You* and
Twist-A-Plot series. The seeds of Stine's thriller are also here in
the multiple-ending adventure series titles as he builds the action,
gets to a cliffhanging sequences, then builds the action again.
Characters are secondary to the twisting "you'll never guess what
happens next" plots.

Blind Date and *Twisted* were Stine's first two novels and, along
with Christopher Pike's books, represented the beginning of the
teen thriller. *Blind Date* is an almost perfect thriller containing all
the elements of the mix: a teenage boy with a secret in his past,
some mysterious phone calls, lots of scenes set in school filled with
realistic teen dialogue and concerns, and a scene where Kerry
shows up for his date only to have the girl's mother tell him "she's
dead." The book then kicks along briskly as Kerry gets into more
trouble, there are more cliffhangers and red herrings, and finally the
big "saved just in the nick of time" finish where the killer's
identity is revealed. *Twisted* is more of the same including the
switched identity ending, but this time the setting is in a sorority
rather than a high school. *Broken Date* originally came out in the
Crosswinds romance series and is to form: the book begins with
blood (from a paper cut) and ends with a struggle involving a knife.

Then, Stine came upon *Fear Street.* Set in the town of Shadyside,
the *Fear Street* series is held together only by a common location
and all too familiar plots. Violence hangs in the air: almost every
book features the words "murder" or "kill" on the front cover
blurb, several covers feature knives, and every cover shows a
young woman or women in danger. Some, of course, are better than
others, but considering they are chucked out almost once a month,
the actual quality of them is quite surprisingly good. Rarely does
Stine fail to entertain and/or frighten. From the early creepiness of
The Surprise Party or *Missing* (a truly scary book), to the more
bared down stalking of *The Knife* or *The Cheater,* Stine loads every
book with false endings, "it was only a paper maché severed
hand" gross outs, and "so it was you!" endings, thus supplying his
audience, somewhat younger than that of Christopher Pike's crowd,
with their daily minimum requirement of chills. And while the

plots are fantastic, the characters are very real high school age kids. They worry a lot about grades, friends, dating, being popular and the like. That realistic backdrop of anxiety sets up wonderfully for high anxiety as Stine turns every day worries into outlandish thrillers. If being a teenager is about fitting in, then Stine writes books where "fitting in" is translated into being "singled out" for terror.

In addition to the *Fear Street* series, Stine also writes *Fear Street Super Chillers,* which are the same idea expanded by about fifty pages. His *Cheerleaders* series is also spun off from *Fear Street.* Choosing cheerleaders to be the victims *and* the villains shows Stine knows his audience, plus he adds even more supernatural mumbo jumbo than usual. The books in his *Baby Sitter* trilogy, which features the recurrent character of Jenny, the stalked baby sitter, read like movie ties to as-yet-unmade slasher films. Finally, *Goosebumps* contains many of the same tricks but rarely any real violence or body counts since they are aimed at younger readers. *Stay out of the Basement* is another reworking of an old horror staple—the mad scientist. The Stine angle is simple: what if that mad scientist was your father? Margaret and Casey's father is conducting experiments in the basement that get out of hand. Stine's style in *Goosebumps* is the same, yet even more compact: chapters are less than five pages and almost everyone has a cliffhanger. The scares are more cartoonish and the humor is also more evident.

Stine's non-*Fear Street* novels are both scarier yet less violent. This toning down might have something to do with the publisher, Scholastic, who market their YA novels through schools and therefore avoid controversial/violent novels. Unlike the "girls in trouble" covers of the *Fear Street,* Stine's Scholastic novels feature no such imagery, nor do the books as a rule rely as heavily on mayhem. In *The Boyfriend* Stine presents an evil character, Joanna, as the protagonist. Joanna feels no regret after causing the death of her boyfriend Dexter, only to feel fear when Dexter returns from the grave. Of course, he never really died and it was all part of a plan, but that is beside the point. In *The Girlfriend,* Stine works off a *Fatal Attraction* riff of the obsessed scorned woman, where in *Beach Party* and *Beach House* he has taken the thriller formula of a deserted exotic location, kids in trouble, and a stalking killer and applied it to great success. *Hit and Run* covers the same "they hit someone with a car now they have to pay" ground as Pike's *Slumber Party* and Lois Duncan's *I Know What You Did Last Summer,* yet is still enjoyable as Stine applies his bag-of-tricks to the formula. Even in a book like *Hitchhiker* which is not terribly original, with a stock premise (two girls pick up a mysterious hitchhiker) and writing that is not that special, Stine still manages to tell a good tale by pacing the novel so that chills happen at a regular interval and readers are kept guessing how it will all turn out.

Stine has broken from the thriller genre for the YA audience with *Phone Calls* and *How I Broke up with Ernie.* Both rely on situations similar to thrillers, but *Phone Calls* includes a slightly wacky revenge plot. *Phone Calls* fails because of the all dialogue gimmick, but *Ernie* works like a funny flipside to *The Girlfriend* about a person who just won't go away after a break-up. As always the story begins with a bang, with "I've decided to break up with Ernie," and ends with one; rather than getting a knife thrown at him Ernie gets a cake shoved in his face. But it is all done with enough character development to make the reader care about the fate of Ernie and the other characters.

That ability is what keeps Stine's audience waiting for his next book. While his characters are normally faceless suburban kids, they are so real to readers that when Stine puts them in jeopardy, over and over and over again, the readers care enough to read on. The plots are simpler than those in Pike's novels and the violence is more imagined than actual, thus keeping Stine popular with younger readers. Reading Stine is a lot like a roller coaster ride: the trip is quite short (most of his books are under 175 pages), the thrills plenty and smartly spaced, and after a while the fear is gone (because the experience ends) but the thrills are not.

—Patrick Jones

STIRLING, Arthur. *See* SINCLAIR, Upton (Beall).

STOLZ, Mary

Nationality: American. **Born:** Mary Slattery in Boston, Massachusetts, 24 March 1920. **Education:** Birch Wathen School, New York; Columbia University Teacher's College, New York, 1936-38; Katharine Gibbs School, New York, 1938-39. **Family:** Married 1) Stanley Burr Stolz in 1940 (divorced 1956); one son; 2) Thomas C. Jaleski in 1965. **Career:** Writer of books for children and young adults. Worked at R.H. Macy's, New York, and as secretary at Columbia University Teachers College. **Awards:** Notable Book citation, American Library Association (ALA), 1951, for *The Sea Gulls Woke Me*; Children's Book award, Child Study Children's Book Committee at Bank Street College, 1953, for *In a Mirror*; Spring Book Festival Older Honor award, *New York Herald Tribune,* 1953, for *Ready or Not,* 1956, for *The Day and the Way We Met,* and 1957, for *Because of Madeline*; ALA Notable Book citation, 1961, for *Belling the Tiger*; Newbery award Honor Book designation, 1962, for *Belling the Tiger,* and 1966, for *The Noonday Friends*; Junior Book award, Boys' Club of America, 1964, for *The Bully of Barkham Street*; Honor List citation, *Boston Globe/Horn Book* and National Book award finalist, Association of American Publishers, both 1975, for *The Edge of Next Year*; Recognition of Merit award, George G. Stone Center for Children's Books, 1982, for entire body of work; ALA Notable Book citation, 1985, for *Quentin Corn*; Children's Science Book Younger Honor award, New York Academy of Sciences, 1986, for *Night of Ghosts and Hermits: Nocturnal Life on the Seashore*; German Youth Festival award; ALA Notable Book citation, Notable Children's Trade Books in Social Studies, Children's Book Council, both 1988, and Teacher's Choice citation, International Reading Association, 1989, all for *Storm in the Night*; Kerlan award, 1993. **Agent:** Roslyn Targ Literary Agency, 105 West 13th St., Suite 15E, New York, New York 10011. **Address:** P.O. Box 82, Longboat Key, Florida 34228, U.S.A.

PUBLICATIONS FOR YOUNG ADULTS

Fiction

To Tell Your Love. New York, Harper, 1950.
The Organdy Cupcakes. New York, Harper, 1951.
The Sea Gulls Woke Me. New York, Harper, 1951.
In a Mirror. New York, Harper, 1953.
Ready or Not. New York, Harper, 1953; London, Heinemann, 1966.
Pray Love, Remember. New York, Harper, 1954.
Two by Two. Boston, Houghton, 1954; London, Hodder & Stoughton, 1955; revised version, as *A Love, or a Season,* New York, Harper, 1964.
Rosemary. New York, Harper, 1955.
The Day and the Way We Met. New York, Harper, 1956.
Hospital Zone. New York, Harper, 1956.
Because of Madeline. New York, Harper, 1957.
Good-by My Shadow. New York, Harper, 1957; London, Penguin, 1964.
And Love Replied. New York, Harper, 1958.
Second Nature. New York, Harper, 1958.
Some Merry-Go-Round Music. New York, Harper, 1959.
The Beautiful Friend and Other Stories. New York, Harper, 1960.
Wait for Me, Michael. New York, Harper, 1961.
Who Wants Music on Monday? New York, Harper, 1963.
By the Highway Home. New York, Harper, 1971.
Leap before You Look. New York, Harper, 1972.
The Edge of Next Year. New York, Harper, 1974.
Cat in the Mirror. New York, Harper, 1975.
Ferris Wheel. New York, Harper, 1977.
Cider Days. New York, Harper, 1978.
Go and Catch a Flying Fish. New York, Harper, 1979.
What Time of Night Is It? New York, Harper, 1981.
Ivy Larkin: A Novel. San Diego, Harcourt, 1986.
A Ballad of the Civil War, illustrated by Sergio Martinez. New York, HarperCollins, 1997.

PUBLICATIONS FOR CHILDREN

Fiction

The Leftover Elf, illustrated by Peggy Bacon. New York, Harper, 1952.
Emmett's Pig, illustrated by Garth Williams. New York, Harper, 1959; Kingswood, Surrey, World's Work, 1963.
A Dog on Barkham Street, illustrated by Leonard Shortall. New York, Harper, 1960.
Belling the Tiger, illustrated by Beni Montresor. New York, Harper, 1961.
The Great Rebellion, illustrated by Beni Montresor. New York, Harper, 1961.
Fredou, illustrated by Tomi Ungerer. New York, Harper, 1962.
Pigeon Flight, illustrated by Murray Tinkelman. New York, Harper, 1962.
The Bully of Barkham Street, illustrated by Leonard Shortall. New York, Harper, 1963.
Siri, the Conquistador, illustrated by Beni Montresor. New York, Harper, 1963.
The Mystery of the Woods, illustrated by Uri Shulevitz. New York, Harper, 1964.

The Noonday Friends, illustrated by Louis S. Glanzman. New York, Harper, 1965.
Maximilian's World, illustrated by Uri Shulevitz. New York, Harper, 1966.
A Wonderful, Terrible Time, illustrated by Louis S. Glanzman. New York, Harper, 1967.
Say Something, illustrated by Edward Frascino. New York, Harper, 1968; revised edition illustrated by Alexander Koshkin, 1993.
The Dragons of the Queen, illustrated by Edward Frascino. New York, Harper, 1969.
The Story of a Singular Hen and Her Peculiar Children, illustrated by Edward Frascino. New York, Harper, 1969.
Juan, illustrated by Louis Glanzman. New York, Harper, 1970.
Land's End, illustrated by Dennis Hermanson. New York, Harper, 1973.
Cat Walk, illustrated by Erik Blegvad. New York, Harper, 1983; London, Armada, 1985.
The Explorer of Barkham Street, illustrated by Emily Arnold McCully. New York, Harper, 1985.
Quentin Corn, illustrated by Pamela Johnson. Boston, David Godine, 1985.
The Cuckoo Clock, illustrated by Pamela Johnson. Boston, David Godine, 1986.
The Scarecrows and Their Child, illustrated by Amy Schwartz. New York, Harper, 1987.
Pangur Ban, illustrated by Pamela Johnson. New York, Harper, 1988.
Storm in the Night, illustrated by Pat Cummings. New York, Harper, 1988.
Zekmet, the Stone Carver: A Tale of Ancient Egypt, illustrated by Deborah Nourse Lattimore. San Diego, Harcourt, 1988.
Barkham Street Trilogy (contains *A Dog on Barkham Street, The Bully of Barkham Street,* and *The Explorer of Barkham Street*) New York, Harper, 1989.
Bartholomew Fair. New York, Greenwillow, 1990.
Tales at the Mousehole (contains revised versions of *The Great Rebellion, Maximilian's World,* and *Siri, the Conquistador*), illustrated by Pamela Johnson. Boston, David Godine, 1990.
Deputy Shep, illustrated by Pamela Johnson. New York, HarperCollins, 1991.
Go Fish, illustrated by Pat Cummings. New York, HarperCollins, 1991.
King Emmett the Second, illustrated by Garth Williams. New York, Greenwillow, 1991.
Stealing Home. New York, HarperCollins, 1992.
Say Something, illustrated by Alexander Koshkin. New York, HarperCollins, 1993.
Cezanne Pinto: A Memoir. New York, Knopf, 1994.
Coco Grimes. New York, HarperCollins, 1994.
The Weeds and the Weather. New York, Greenwillow, 1994.

Other

Night of Ghosts and Hermits: Nocturnal Life on the Seashore, illustrated by Susan Gallagher. San Diego, Harcourt, 1985.

PUBLICATIONS FOR ADULTS

Novel

Truth and Consequence. New York, Harper, 1953.

*

Media Adaptations: "Baby Blue Expression" (short story; first published in *McCall's*) adapted for television by Alfred Hitchcock; *The Noonday Friends* (recording), Miller-Brody, 1976.

Biography: Essay in *Something about the Author Autobiography Series,* Vol. 3, Detroit, Gale, 1986; essay in *Speaking for Ourselves: Autobiographical Sketches by Notable Authors of Books for Young Adults,* Vol. 1, compiled and edited by Donald R. Gallo, National Council of Teachers of English, 1990.

Manuscript Collections: Kerlan Collection, University of Minnesota, Minneapolis.

Critical Studies: Entry in *Contemporary Literary Criticism,* Vol. 12, Detroit, Gale, 1980.

*   *   *

Mary Stolz is a prolific writer who perceptively addresses the feelings and concerns of children and young adults. The themes of her early young adult works include coming of age and dealing with love. Her later books focus upon the interactions of family members who are coping with the stresses of modern life.

Stolz's work is particularly noteworthy for her strong characterization. Her characters are well-rounded and introspective. They observe and analyze their own behavior and feelings as well as the actions and emotions of family and friends.

One of Stolz's early works, *Because of Madeline,* is set in a posh private school. The main character is disdainful of her snobbish classmates and considerate of the scholarship students until Madeline arrives. Madeline, one of the girls accepted on scholarship, challenges the main character's egalitarian attitudes by her refusal to conform in any way to what others expect of her. Madeline's intellectual brilliance makes her schoolmates feel inferior and her nonchalance about her singing ability aggravates them. After reflecting about her relationship with Madeline, the protagonist recognizes and regrets her own hypocrisy. Despite the message about accepting others on their own merits without regard to appearances, this book's descriptions of prep schools and coming out parties has the haughty tone of a wealthy egocentric. For example, the main character considers herself thoughtful for not inviting her friend on a shopping trip to Bonwit's since, after all, she couldn't really afford to shop there.

The main characters in Stolz's recent books do not come from such privileged homes. Their conflicts do not center on acceptance of others but on the interactions of family members as they struggle to cope with some of the senseless suffering many people face.

By the Highway Home is the story of a family reeling from the tragic loss of a son in Vietnam. This loss is compounded by financial difficulties arising from the father's unemployment. Catty's outburst, decrying her family's unrelenting sadness and despair, helps to break the hold of grief upon their lives. As they

begin their lives in a new home they learn to feel joy with each other and with the memory of their dead child. The author's description of the effect that cold, empty silence can have on a child is reminiscent of *The Noonday Friends.*

The Edge of Next Year also addresses the difficulty of coping with death. In this story, Orin is given the responsibility of keeping house and caring for his younger brother after his mother is killed in an automobile accident. As Orin attempts to cope with his own sense of loss he is baffled by his brother's lack of grief and embittered by his father's gradual decline into alcoholism. Interestingly, Orin seems more troubled by his crushing domestic responsibilities than by the loss of his mother. Her importance, it would seem, was as a care-giver although Orin's recollections of his mother are riddled with conflict. He recalls her drinking and feels disdain; he remembers his inability to share her interest in ornithology; and he feels a mixture of frustration and admiration for the way she refused to adhere to conventional behavior.

The loss of a mother is anticipated throughout the book *Go and Catch a Flying Fish.* The mother in this story is also a nonconformist and her children seem rather troubled by her lack of interest in housekeeping. As the tensions between their parents rise, the children assume protective stances, attempting to defuse conflict between their parents. When their mother leaves they are hurt but display an understanding surprising for their years. The eldest child who collects fish for an aquarium uses the metaphor of a flying fish for his mother—if captured and contained, it would not be beautiful and may even die. *What Time of Night Is It?* continues the story as the family adjusts to life without a mother.

The plots of these stories are simple and revolve around the daily life of a family; eating, sleeping, and reacting to each other but remaining largely uninvolved with the outside world.

The setting of each story is fully described and becomes a backdrop for Stolz's love of nature. Each of her characters has a fascination for a type of animal. Catty, in *By the Highway Home,* loved wildlife and longed for a cat but her older brother was allergic to them. After the family accepts his death, Catty is given permission to have a cat. Orin's little brother, in *The Edge of Next Year,* is a budding herpetologist and convinces Orin to turn their attic into a life-scale vivarium. Taylor, in *Go and Catch a Flying Fish,* loves the birds of Florida and compiles an impressive lifetime list as her brother Jim collects fish for his aquarium. These interests provide another dimension for Stolz's characters who often seem too mature for their age. These children spend much of their time thinking about their parents' actions and emotions. They show striking perceptiveness about adult behavior, perhaps more than can be expected of adolescents.

Interaction between siblings is remarkably high and typifies the adolescent's tendency to settle differences in the face of stress. The closeness of the protagonists and their younger siblings is noteworthy and admirable if not entirely realistic.

In recent years, Stolz has discontinued writing for young adults because she does not wish to write about children involved with the drug scene. This is a pity because her books which deal with family stress are invaluable. These are not books for those seeking fast-paced adventure. They are, instead, for the reader who wants a reflective look at difficulties within the home and models for coping with them.

—Anne Drolett Creany

STRASSER, Todd

Pseudonym: Has also written as Morton Rhue. **Nationality:** American. **Born:** New York, New York, 5 May 1950. **Education:** Beloit College, B.A. 1974. **Family:** Married Pamela Older; one daughter, one son. **Career:** Public relations work for Beloit College, Beloit, Wisconsin, 1973-74; free-lance writer, since 1975; reporter, *Times Herald Record,* Middleton, New York; copywriter, Compton Advertising, New York City, 1976-77; researcher, *Esquire,* New York City; owner, Toggle, Inc. (fortune cookie company), New York City, 1978-89. **Awards:** American Library Association (ALA) Best Books for Young Adults citations, 1981, for *Friends Till the End,* and 1982, for *Rock 'n' Roll Nights*; New York Public Library's Books for the Teen Age citations, 1981, for *Angel Dust Blues,* 1982, for *The Wave* and *Friends to the End,* 1983, for *Rock 'n' Roll Nights,* and 1984, for *Workin' for Peanuts*; Notable Children's Trade Book in the Field of Social Studies, National Council for Social Studies, 1982, for *Friends Till the End*; Acton Public Library's CRABbery Award List, 1983, for *Rock 'n' Roll Nights*; Young Reader Medal nomination, California Reading Association, 1983, for *Friends Till the End*; Book Award, Federation of Children's Books (Great Britain), 1983, for *The Wave,* and 1984, for *Turn It Up!*; Outstanding Book Award, Iowa Books for Young Adult Program, 1985, for *Turn It Up!*; Colorado Blue Spruce Award nomination, 1987, for *Angel Dust Blues*; Edgar nomination, Mystery Writers of America, for *The Accident.*

PUBLICATIONS FOR YOUNG ADULTS

Fiction

Angel Dust Blues: A Novel. New York, Coward, MacCann, 1979.
Friends Till the End: A Novel. New York, Delacorte, 1981.
Rock 'n' Roll Nights: A Novel. New York, Delacorte, 1982.
Workin' for Peanuts. New York, Delacorte, 1982.
Turn It Up!: A Novel. New York, Delacorte, 1984.
A Very Touchy Subject. New York, Delacorte, 1984.
Rock It to the Top. New York, Delacorte, 1987.
Wildlife. New York, Delacorte, 1987.
The Accident. New York, Delacorte, 1988.
Beyond the Reef. New York, Delacorte, 1989.
Moving Target. New York, Ballantine, 1989.
The Diving Bell. New York, Scholastic, 1992.
Summer's End. New York, Scholastic, 1993.
Summer's Promise. New York, Scholastic, 1993.
How I Changed My Life. New York, Simon & Schuster, 1995.
The Boys in the Band. New York, HarperPaperbacks, 1996.
Girl Gives Birth to Own Prom Date. New York, Simon & Schuster, 1996.
Playing for Love. New York, HarperPaperbacks, 1996.
My Best Last Night on Earth. New York, Simon & Schuster, 1998.

Novelizations

The Wave, (as Morton Rhue). New York, Dell, 1981.
Ferris Bueller's Day Off: A Novel. New York, New American Library, 1986.
Cookie: A Novel. New York, New American Library, 1988.
Pink Cadillac: A Novel. New York, New American Library, 1989.
Home Alone: A Novelization. New York, Scholastic, 1990.

Home Alone 2: Lost in New York. New York, Scholastic, 1992.
Honey, I Blew Up the Kid. New York, Disney, 1992.
Addams Family Values: A Novel. New York, Pocket, 1993.
The Beverly Hillbillies: A Novelization. New York, HarperPaperbacks, 1993.
Free Willy. New York, Scholastic, 1993.
The Good Son. New York, Pocket, 1993.
Hocus Pocus. New York, Disney, 1993.
Rookie of the Year. New York, Trumpet Club, 1993.
Super Mario Bros.: A Novel. New York, Hyperion, 1993.
The Three Musketeers: A Novel. New York, Disney, 1993.
The Villains Collection. New York, Disney, 1993.
Disney's It's Magic: Stories from the Films. New York, Disney, 1994.
Miracle on 34th Street. New York, Scholastic, 1994.
The Pagemaster. New York, Puffin, 1994.
Richie Rich. New York, Scholastic, 1994.
Street Fighter. New York, Newmarket, 1994.
Tall Tale: The Unbelievable Adventures of Pecos Bill. New York, Disney, 1994.
3 Ninjas Kick Back. New York, Scholastic, 1994.
Walt Disney's Lady and the Tramp. New York, Disney, 1994.
Walt Disney's Peter Pan. New York, Disney, 1994.
Free Willy 2: The Adventure Home: A Novelization. New York, Scholastic, 1995.
Jumanji: A Novelization. New York, Scholastic, 1995.
Man of the House: A Novel. New York, Disney, 1995.
Home Alone 3: A Novelization. New York, Scholastic, 1997.

Short Fiction

''On the Bridge,'' in *Visions: Nineteen Short Stories by Outstanding Writers for Young Adults,* edited by Donald Gallo. New York, Delacorte, 1987.
''Bones,'' in *Ultimate Sports: Short Stories by Outstanding Writers for Young Adults,* edited by Donald Gallo. New York, Delacorte, 1995.

Other

Over the Limit (teleplay based on Strasser's *The Accident*). ABC Afterschool Special, ABC-TV, 1990.
The Kid's Book of Insults: How to Put Down, Dis, and Slam Your Best Friends. Mahwah, New Jersey, Troll, 1996.

PUBLICATIONS FOR CHILDREN

The Complete Computer Popularity Program. New York, Delacorte, 1984.
The Mall from Outer Space. New York, Scholastic, 1987.
Help! I'm Trapped in My Teacher's Body. New York, Scholastic, 1993.
Please Don't Be Mine, Julie Valentine. New York, Scholastic, 1994.
Help! I'm Trapped in the First Day of School. New York, Scholastic, 1994.
Abe Lincoln for Class President!. New York, Scholastic, 1995.
Help! I'm Trapped in Obedience School. New York, Scholastic, 1995.
Howl-a-ween. New York, Scholastic, 1995.

Wordsworth and the Cold Cut Catastrophe. New York, HarperPaperbacks, 1995.

Wordsworth and the Kibble Kidnaping. New York, HarperPaperbacks, 1995.

Wordsworth and the Mail-Order Meatloaf Mess. New York, HarperPaperbacks, 1995.

Wordsworth and the Roast Beef Romance. New York, HarperPaperbacks, 1995.

Hey, Dad, Get a Life! New York, Holiday House, 1996.

Help! I'm Trapped in My Gym Teacher's Body. New York, Scholastic, 1996.

Help! I'm Trapped in the President's Body. New York, Scholastic, 1996.

Wordsworth and the Tasty Treat Trick. New York, HarperPaperbacks, 1996.

Wordsworth and the Lip-Smacking Licorice Love Affair. New York, HarperPaperbacks, 1996.

Camp Run-a-Muck, #1: Greasy Grimy Gopher Guts. New York, Scholastic, 1997.

Camp Run-a-Muck, #2: Mutilated Monkey Meat. New York, Scholastic, 1997.

Camp Run-a-Muck, #3: Chopped-Up Birdy's Feet. New York, Scholastic, 1997.

Help! I'm Trapped in My Sister's Body. New York, Scholastic, 1997.

Help! I'm Trapped in Obedience School Again. New York, Scholastic, 1997.

Help! I'm Trapped in Santa's Body. New York, Scholastic, 1997.

Help! I'm Trapped in the First Day of Summer Camp. New York, Scholastic, 1997.

Kidnap Kids. New York, Putnam's, 1998.

Help! I'm Trapped in an Alien's Body. New York, Scholastic, 1998.

PUBLICATIONS FOR ADULTS

The Family Man. New York, St. Martin's, 1988.

*

Media Adaptations: *Workin' for Peanuts,* Home Box Office "Family Showcase," 1985; *Can a Guy Say No?* (based on *A Very Touchy Subject*), *ABC Afterschool Special,* ABC-TV, February 1986.

Biography: "I Was a Teenage Boy" by Todd Strasser, in *Media and Methods,* Vol. 19, No. 6, 1983, 10-12; *Behind the Covers: Interviews with Authors and Illustrators of Books for Children and Young Adults* by Jim Roginski, Libraries Unlimited, 1985; entry in *Speaking About Ourselves: Autobiographical Sketches by Notable Authors of Books for Young Adults,* edited by Donald Gallo, Urbana, Illinois, NCTE, 1990; "Nineteen Different Answers and One Black-Eye" by Todd Strasser, in *Authors' Insights: Turning Teenagers into Readers and Writers,* Boynton/Cook, 1992, 105-115; "For Best-Selling Author, What's in a Name?" by Kate Stone Lombardi, in *New York Times,* 12 October 1997.

Critical Studies: "The Music of Young Adult Literature" by Dick Abrahamson, Betty Carter, and Barbara Samuels, in *English Journal,* Vol. 71, No. 5, September 1982, 87-88; *Literature for Today's Young Adults* by Allen Pace Nilsen and Kenneth L. Donelson, 2nd ed., Scott, Foresman, 1985; "Stalking the Teen" by Todd Strasser, in *Horn Book,* March-April 1986, 236-39; "Author Profile: Todd Strasser" by Annette Thorson, in *Book Report,* November 1993, 30; "Beyond the Reef" by Reinhard Isenee, in *Beacham's Guide to Young Adult Literature,* edited by Kirk Beetz, Vol. 6, Beacham, 1994; "Workin' for Peanuts" by Joel D. Chaston, in *Beacham's Guide to Young Adult Literature,* edited by Kirk Beetz, Vol. 8, Beacham, 1994.

*   *   *

Todd Strasser is one of the most prolific and popular contemporary writers of fiction for young adults. His more than seventy novels for both children and young adults include critically-acclaimed realistic fiction, humorous romances, science fiction, historical fiction, and novelizations of motion pictures. Much of his work demonstrates Strasser's belief that writing for young readers should be entertaining and that teenage boys need books which reflect their own experiences and interests. In an early interview in *Media and Methods,* Strasser argued that he tries to "present *boyish* boys ... with emotions and sensitivities." For Strasser, books for young readers need to be both educational and entertaining. "If we give them books that they are not going to enjoy on a primary level," he explained, "that they're not going to be entertained by, we may be losing readers for life. I don't think we can afford to do that."

Strasser's books often reflect the anti-establishment feelings he embraced growing up in the 1960s and the gritty realism of young adult fiction of the 1970s and 1980s, as his characters search for self-identity through drugs, as in *Angel Dust Blues* (1979), and in rock and roll bands, like the protagonists of *Rock 'n' Roll Nights* (1982) and its sequels, *Turn It Up!* (1984) and *Wildlife* (1987). Strasser's early novels also straddle the fine line between comedy and tragedy as his protagonists move from innocence to experience through such events as terminal illness (*Friends Till the End,* 1981) and drunk driving (*The Accident,* 1988).

Strasser established himself as a major writer for young adults when he began writing comic teenage romances from the male point of view. In *Workin' for Peanuts* (1983), one of his fist efforts in the genre, Strasser explores the relationship between Jeff Mead, who works as a vendor in a baseball stadium, and Melissa Stotts, daughter of the stadium's owner. As in many of Strasser's novels, the romance between the main characters provides humorous action, exploring teenage prejudices and snobbery, and features a bittersweet ending, one in which the protagonist gains maturity and self-awareness.

Strasser has produced similar looks at teenage infatuation in such works as *A Very Touchy Subject* (1984), which focuses on seventeen-year-old Scott Tauscher's obsession with Paula, the fifteen-year-old girl next door; the *Rock 'n' Roll Summer* series (1996), two novels about aspiring young musicians and their romantic entanglements; and the widely-praised *How I Changed My Life* (1995) and its companion volume, *Girl Gives Birth to Own Prom Date* (1996). These last two books are among Strasser's best.

In the tradition of Paul Zindel's *The Pigman* (1968), these screwball comedies each feature both a male and female narrator who alternate telling the story from their point of view. In *How I Changed My Life,* overweight Bolita Vine and former football star Kyle Winthrop struggle to forge new identities as they work together on the school play. In *Girl Gives Birth to Own Prom Date,* popular Nicole Maris makes over her next-door neighbor, Chase Hammond, the grunge king, in order to make another boy jealous. Both books examine teenagers' obsessions with their images and the disjunction between reality and appearances. These themes are also present in *How I Spent My Last Night on Earth* (1998), in which Legs Hanover, spurred on by an Internet rumor that a giant asteroid is about to destroy Earth, determines to meet Andros Bliss, the boy of her dreams.

Over the years, Strasser has gained acclaim by trying his hand at a number of genres. He has produced novelizations of many popular television specials and motion pictures, including *The Wave* (1981), based on a frightening, but real, experiment in peer pressure in a California school, a story now known as much for Strasser's book as for the teleplay which was its source. Strasser has also tried his hand at writing adventure stories and historical fiction. *Beyond the Reef* (1989) is an adventure story about one family's obsession with sunken treasure in Florida, while *The Diving Bell* (1992) is historical fiction, set in the period after Cortés invaded Central America. This latter book, reminiscent of the work of Scott O'Dell, features Strasser's strongest female character, a young girl named Culca who attempts to rescue her brother and his friends when they are forced to dive for gold.

Strasser's most popular books, however, have been comic science fiction stories for middle grade readers, a form that allows broad slapstick humor and satirical jibes at contemporary life in the United States. Strasser's first venture in this genre, *The Mall from Outer Space* (1987), gently critiques the contemporary loss of culture created by shopping malls. Its protagonists, Erin and Dwight, must prevent a group of aliens transforming the earth into one gigantic shopping mall and all earthlings into mindless drones called "Betas." Their solution involves hooking the aliens on the game of baseball. A similar comic touch is present in Strasser's extremely popular "Help!" series about the misadventures of Jake Sherman. With Jake's first encounter with the mind-swapping machine invented by his science teacher, Mr. Dirksen in *Help! I'm Trapped in My Teacher's Body* (1993), Jake is plunged into a variety of strange adventures, which include trading bodies with his science teacher, gym teacher, sister, dog, the President of the United States, Santa Claus, and an alien. He is also forced to relive the first day of eighth grade and of summer camp over and over again. Other popular Strasser series revolve around the misadventures of a dog named Wordsworth, which include titles such as *Wordsworth and the Kibble Kidnaping* (1995) and *Wordsworth and the Lip-Smacking Licorice Love Affair* (1996), and life at a bizarre summer camp named "Camp Run-a-Muck." Strasser has suggested that even these light-weight, formulaic books have a serious side and often deal with such issues as respect, honesty, and self-acceptance.

A 1997 article in the *New York Times* suggests that Strasser "enjoys a curious kind of fame." Over 20 million copies of his books have been sold and his work has been translated into twelve languages, and yet his readers don't often recognize his name. Despite this lack of celebrity, Strasser has become a dominant force in the field of young adult literature, one whose work deserves the attention of scholars and teachers.

—Joel D. Chaston

SUTCLIFF, Rosemary

Nationality: British. **Born:** West Clanden, Surrey, 14 December 1920. Educated privately and at Bideford School of Art, 1935-39. **Career:** Writer, from 1945. **Awards:** Carnegie Medal commendation, 1955, and American Library Association (ALA) Notable Book, both for *The Eagle of the Ninth*; Carnegie Medal commendation and *New York Herald Tribune*'s Children's Spring Book Festival honor book, both 1957, and ALA Notable Book, all for *The Shield Ring*; Carnegie Medal commendation and *New York Herald Tribune*'s Children's Spring Book Festival honor book, both 1958, both for *The Silver Branch*; Carnegie Medal commendation and Hans Christian Andersen Award honor book, both 1959, International Board on Books for Young People honor list, 1960, Highly Commended Author, 1974, and ALA Notable Book, all for *Warrior Scarlet*; Carnegie Medal, 1960, and ALA Notable Book, both for *The Lantern Bearers*; ALA Notable Book, 1960, for *Knight's Fee*; *New York Herald Tribune*'s Children's Spring Book Festival Award, 1962, ALA Notable Book, and *Horn Book* honor list, all for *Dawn Wind*; ALA Notable Book and *Horn Book* honor list, both 1962, both for *Beowulf*; ALA Notable Book and *Horn Book* honor list, both 1963, both for *Hound of Ulster*; ALA Notable Book and *Horn Book* honor list, both 1965, and Children's Literature Association Phoenix Award, 1985, all for *The Mark of the Horse Lord*; *Horn Book* honor list, 1967, for *The High Deeds of Finn MacCool*; Lewis Carroll Shelf Award, 1971, ALA Notable Book, and *Horn Book* honor list, all for *The Witch's Brat*; *Boston Globe-Horn Book* Award for outstanding text and Carnegie Medal runner-up, both 1972, ALA Notable Book, and *Horn Book* honor list, all for *Tristan and Iseult*; *Heather, Oak, and Olive: Three Stories* was selected one of Child Study Association's "Children's Books of the Year," 1972, and *The Capricorn Bracelet* was selected, 1973; Officer, Order of the British Empire, 1975; *Boston Globe-Horn Book* honor book for fiction, 1977, and *Horn Book* honor list, both for *Blood Feud*; *Children's Book Bulletin* Other Award, 1978, for *Song for a Dark Queen*; *Horn Book* honor list, 1978, for *Sun Horse, Moon Horse*; Children's Rights Workshop Award, 1978; ALA Notable Book, 1982, for *The Road to Camlann: The Death of King Arthur*; Royal Society of Literature fellow, 1982; Commander, Order of the British Empire, 1992. **Died:** 23 July 1992.

PUBLICATIONS FOR YOUNG ADULTS

Fiction

The Armourer's House, illustrated by C. Walter Hodges. London and New York, Oxford University Press, 1951.
Brother Dusty-Feet, illustrated by Hodges. London, Oxford University Press, 1952.

Simon, illustrated by Richard Kennedy. London, Oxford University Press, 1953.

The Eagle of the Ninth, illustrated by Hodges. London, Oxford University Press, 1954; New York, Walck, 1961.

Outcast, illustrated by Kennedy. London, Oxford University Press; New York, Walck, 1955.

The Shield Ring, illustrated by Hodges. London, Oxford University Press; New York, Walck, 1956.

The Silver Branch, illustrated by Charles Keeping. London, Oxford University Press, 1957; New York, Walck, 1959.

Warrior Scarlet, illustrated by Charles Keeping. London, Oxford University Press; New York, Walck, 1958.

The Bridge-Builders. Oxford, Blackwell, 1959.

The Lantern Bearers, illustrated by Charles Keeping. London, Oxford University Press and New York, Walck, 1959.

Knight's Fee, illustrated by Charles Keeping. London, Oxford University Press and New York, Walck, 1960.

Dawn Wind, illustrated by Charles Keeping. London, Oxford University Press, 1961; New York, Walck, 1962.

The Mark of the Horse Lord, illustrated by Charles Keeping. London, Oxford University Press and New York, Walck, 1965.

The Chief's Daughter, illustrated by Ambrus. London, Hamish Hamilton, 1967.

A Circlet of Oak Leaves, illustrated by Ambrus. London, Hamish Hamilton, 1968.

The Witch's Brat, illustrated by Robert Micklewright, London, Oxford University Press, 1970; illustrated by Richard Lebenson, New York, Walck, 1970.

The Truce of the Games, illustrated by Ambrus. London, Hamish Hamilton, 1971.

Heather, Oak, and Olive: Three Stories (contains *The Chief's Daughter, A Circlet of Oak Leaves,* and *A Crown of Wild Olive*), illustrated by Ambrus, New York, Dutton, 1972.

The Capricorn Bracelet, illustrated by Charles Keeping, London, Oxford University Press, and New York, Walck, 1973.

The Changeling, illustrated by Ambrus. London, Hamish Hamilton, 1974.

We Lived in Drumfyvie, with Margaret Lyford-Pike. London, Blackie, 1975.

Blood Feud, illustrated by Charles Keeping. London, Oxford University Press, 1976, New York, Dutton, 1977.

Shifting Sands, illustrated by Laszlo Acs. London, Hamish Hamilton, 1977.

Sun Horse, Moon Horse, illustrated by Shirley Felts. London, Bodley Head, 1977; New York, Dutton, 1978.

Song for a Dark Queen. London, Pelham Books, 1978; Crowell, 1979.

Frontier Wolf. London, Oxford University Press, 1980; New York, Dutton, 1981.

Three Legions: A Trilogy (contains *The Eagle of the Ninth, The Silver Branch,* and *The Lantern Bearers*), London, Oxford University Press, 1980.

Eagle's Egg, illustrated by Ambrus. London, Hamish Hamilton, 1981.

Bonnie Dundee. London, Bodley Head, 1983; New York, Dutton, 1984.

Flame-Coloured Taffeta. London, Oxford University Press, 1985; New York, Farrar, Straus, 1986.

The Shining Company. New York, Farrar, Straus, 1990.

The Minstrel and the Dragon Pup, illustrated by Emma Chichester Clark. Boston, Candlewick, 1993.

Nonfiction

The Chronicles of Robin Hood, illustrated by C. Walter Hodges, London, Oxford University Press, 1950; New York, Walck, 1950.

The Queen Elizabeth Story, illustrated by Hodges. London, Oxford University Press, 1950; New York, Walck, 1950.

Houses and History, illustrated by William Stobbs. London, Batsford, 1960; New York, Putnam, 1965.

Beowulf, illustrated by Charles Keeping. London, Bodley Head, 1961; New York, Dutton, 1962; as *Dragon Slayer: The Story of Beowulf.* London, Penguin, 1966.

Hound of Ulster (Cuchulain Saga), illustrated by Victor Ambrus. London, Bodley Head, and New York, Dutton, 1963.

Heroes and History, illustrated by Charles Keeping. New York, Putnam, 1965.

A Saxon Settler, illustrated by John Lawrence. London, Oxford University Press, 1965.

The High Deeds of Finn MacCool, illustrated by Michael Charlton. New York, Dutton, 1967.

Tristan and Iseult, illustrated by Victor Ambrus. New York, Dutton, 1971.

Editor, *Is Anyone There?,* with Monica Dickens. New York, Penguin, 1978.

The Light beyond the Forest: The Quest for the Holy Grail, illustrated by Shirley Felts. London, Bodley Head, 1979; New York, Dutton, 1980.

The Sword and the Circle: King Arthur and the Knights of the Round Table, illustrated by Felts. New York, Dutton, 1981.

The Road to Camlann: The Death of King Arthur, illustrated by Felts. London, Bodley Head, 1981; New York, Dutton Children's Books, 1982.

Black Ships before Troy, illustrated by Alan Lee. New York, Delacorte, 1993.

PUBLICATIONS FOR CHILDREN

Fiction

The Roundabout Horse, illustrated by Alan Marks. London, Hamilton Children's, 1986.

A Little Dog Like You, illustrated by Jane Johnson. London, Orchard, 1987; New York, Simon and Schuster, 1990.

Little Hound Found, illustrated by Jo Davies. London, Hamish Hamilton, 1989.

PUBLICATIONS FOR ADULTS

Fiction

Lady in Waiting. London, Hodder and Stoughton, 1956; New York, Coward, 1957.

The Rider of the White Horse. London, Hodder and Stoughton, 1959, as *Rider on a White Horse.* New York, Coward, 1960.

Sword at Sunset, illustrated by John Vernon Lord. London, Hodder and Stoughton, 1963; New York, Coward, 1964.

The Flowers of Adonis. London, Hodder and Stoughton, 1969; New York, Coward, 1970.

Blood and Sand. London, Hodder and Stoughton, 1987.

Nonfiction

Rudyard Kipling. London, Bodley Head, 1960; New York, Walck, 1961, bound with *Arthur Ransome,* by Hugh Shelley, and *Walter de la Mare,* by Leonard Clark, Bodley Head, 1968.

Blue Remembered Hills: A Recollection (autobiography). London, Bodley Head, 1983; New York, Morrow, 1984.

Plays

Mary Bedell (produced Chichester, England, 1986).

Screenplay: *Ghost Story,* with Stephen Weeks). 1975.

*

Media Adaptations: *Song for a Dark Queen* was adapted for stage by Nigel Bryant, Heinemann, 1984; *Dragon Slayer: The Story of Beowulf* has been recorded onto audio cassette (read by Sean Barrett), G.K. Hall Audio, 1986.

Biography: Entry in *More Junior Authors,* New York, H.W. Wilson, 1963; essay in *Speaking for Ourselves: Autobiographical Sketches by Notable Authors of Books for Young Adults,* Volume 1, compiled and edited by Donald R. Gallo, National Council of Teachers of English, 1990.

Critical Studies: *Rosemary Sutcliff* by Margaret Meek, London, Bodley Head, and New York, Walck, 1962; entry in *Children's Literature Review,* Volume 1, Detroit, Gale, 1983; entry in *Contemporary Literary Criticism,* Volume 26, Detroit, Gale, 1983.

*　　*　　*

Rosemary Sutcliff is one of the most important authors of historical fiction for young people; from the late 1950's, her work set a new standard for historical fiction in both its depth of research and its imaginative power. She is best known for a number of novels which present the conflict between different ethnic groups, and within her characters themselves, in England before and shortly after the Roman occupation in the first four centuries A.D. Although her autobiographical *Blue Remembered Hills* is full of humour, her novels are on the whole serious, dealing as they do with warfare, colonisation, ethnic conflict, and the collapse of a civilization. Notwithstanding their emphasis upon struggle, suffering and difficult choices—or perhaps because of it, Sutcliff's novels are compellingly readable. She never "writes down" to her readers, but through dramatic action and depth of characterisation makes the life and concerns of a long-ago time exciting, convincing, and meaningful.

The underlying subject of most of Sutcliff's fiction is a conflict of loyalties, and the difficulties this poses for a young person who must make choices which involve betraying one group in order to support another. Sometimes the choice seems relatively easy, as in *Bonnie Dundee* when Hugh Herriot is forced to kill his cousin Alan in self-defence: although Hugh had previously hero-worshipped Alan, Alan had already proven himself a cold-blooded murderer, and Hugh's loyalty to his charismatic commander Claverhouse, "Bonnie Dundee," is a far stronger motive than any feeling for his

relatives, with their fanatical religious and political beliefs. In most cases, however, the decisions are harder, and made at greater cost to the hero. Owain in *Dawn Wind* voluntarily becomes a thrall, or slave, to a Saxon family in order to save the life of his young companion, while Lubrin in *Sun Horse, Moon Horse* gives up his life to purchase the freedom of his tribe. Almost every one of Sutcliff's protagonists has to make difficult choices, which are not so much ethical decisions as matters of commitment and responsibility, choosing where one's primary loyalties must lie. It is evident to the reader that the hero might have chosen, and acted, differently, but by his choice he helps to define his identity and his direction for the future. While most of Sutcliff's protagonists are male, her girl characters too must often make such difficult choices, as when Ness in *The Lantern Bearers* elects to stay with her husband rather than return to her own people, or when young Damaris in *Flame-Coloured Taffeta* deceives her father and runs some personal risk to help a wounded stranger.

Sutcliff is drawn to periods of history in which ethnic and political clashes make issues of loyalty particularly problematic: the struggles among Celts, Romans, Anglo-Saxons, Danes and Normans for control over Britain in the first milennium A.D. provide Sutcliff with a rich source of material. Although this turbulent era is scantily documented in comparison to later periods, Sutcliff's extensive research supplies her invented characters, as well as actual historical figures, with a richly-textured, convincing background. The research is so well incorporated into the action and issues of the novels that her books never feel like history lessons in disguise. Finely-noted details such as the difference in sound between the bronze wire strings of the Irish harp and the horse-hair strings of the harp played by the Northmen in *The Shield Ring* are not gratuitous bits of "authentic background" but play a significant role in the action of the novel. After some awkwardness with dialogue in her first few novels, Sutcliff developed a style in which subtle alterations in the phrasing and word order lend a certain feeling of dignity and distance to the writing, without falling into archaicism or an anachronistically modern tone.

Like her childhood favourite, Kipling, Sutcliff has a strong feeling for landscape—both for the details of soil, vegetation and atmosphere, and for the continuity of human habitation in one cherished place. In contrast to the scenes of battle, or arduous journeys through the wilds, are deeply felt scenes of homecoming, such as the one at the beginning of *The Lantern Bearers* when the soldier Aquila visits his father and sister at the family farm. Although farm and family are soon afterwards destroyed by invading Saxons, memories of that scene determine Aquila's choices and actions in the years to come. Writing of people who spend a large part of their lives outdoors, Sutcliff is generous in her descriptions, particularly of plants and trees, weather, and the sky. The amount of description in her novels, like their considerable length and the unfamiliar names of the characters, may deter some readers, but Sutcliff's descriptions merit a careful reading as they always enhance our understanding of the characters and the issues they are facing. Symbolism, particularly of light and darkness, and of flowering contrasted to barrenness, adds resonance to her novels, and expresses the emotion which her characters feel but seldom express in words. Symbolic elements may have a personal significance, like the "flame-coloured taffeta" petticoat which suggests the life-affirming exuberance of Damaris, or represent the identity and honour of a larger group, like the Eagle standard of the Ninth Legion, or the flawed emerald family ring which reappears in several novels, linking each new hero with his ancestors and descendants.

As well as historical novels, Sutcliff has also written distinguished retellings of traditional British and Irish hero tales, including stories of Beowulf, Finn MacCool, Cuchulain, Robin Hood, Tristan and Iseult, and a trilogy on the Arthurian legends (*The Light Beyond the Forest, The Sword and the Circle,* and *The Road to Camlann*). These retellings are of a piece with her historical fiction in their recreation of British settings in the Dark Ages, their tone of rather stern dignity, and their emphasis upon endurance and heroic struggle against great odds. Sutcliff herself demonstrated courage in suffering when as a young girl she developed a form of juvenile arthritis, which inflicted great pain and left her physically handicapped. Her childhood experiences are recounted, with humour and a complete lack of self-pity, in *Blue Remembered Hills,* a memoir which ends with the publication of her first book, when she was in her mid-twenties. Before discovering her gifts as a writer, Sutcliff had studied art and become an accomplished painter of miniatures; her training as an artist undoubtedly contributes to the vivid visual images in her writing, and her memorable use of colour. Some of her fictional heroes have artistic gifts which set them somewhat apart from their fellows. The process of artistic inspiration and creation is memorably evoked in *Sun Horse, Moon Horse,* as Lubrin imagines and brings into existence the great white horse carved into the chalk of the Downs near Uffington. Hugh Herriot of *Bonnie Dundee* neglects his calling as an artist to become a soldier, until a severe injury and resultant depression lead him to rediscover the joy of his painter's vision of the world. Sutcliff's best-known character, Marcus in *The Eagle of the Ninth,* also has a physical handicap resulting from a battle injury; the popularity of this novel rises in part from the skill and feeling which Sutcliff brings to her story of how Marcus comes to terms with his handicap and courageously takes on a new role in life.

While a few of Sutcliff's novels, such as the tragic *Song for a Dark Queen about Boadicea,* do have female protagonists, and there are always sympathetic girls in secondary roles, most of her central characters are male. Domestic roles, to which women were largely confined during the periods about which she chiefly writes, seem to have little interest for Sutcliff, whereas the world of combat, travel and adventure which attracts her is masculine. Mothers, too, play a relatively small part in her fiction, but the relationship between fathers and sons is an important, recurring subject. While many of the novels end with a marriage, romantic love is seldom evoked; more often, the lovers have been friends for a long time, and their relationship seems one of camaraderie rather than passion. Emotional ties between family members and friends are at the heart of the novels and their examination of conflicting loyalties.

There is little room for self-indulgence, emotional or physical, in the world of Sutcliff's fiction: it is a rigorous world, where the need to do one's duty and fulfil one's responsibilities has become an instinct as powerful as that of survival. To Aquila, the tormented Roman-British hero of *The Lantern Bearers,* King Ambrosius observes, "A strange and uncomfortable thing is honour." Each of Sutcliff's characters explores the strangeness and discomfort of the concept of honour—which might be linked now with the more fashionable term "self-esteem"—in his or her own way. While the ending for some is death, and most see their ideals and the world they believe in under attack, all of them do ultimately keep faith and retain their honour. Thus, whether the ending of the book is

ostensibly happy or sad, each book affirms the essential dignity of its main character, however scarred or maimed, and the value of honourable action in a world which seems to be crumbling into disorder and darkness.

—Gwyneth Evans

SWARTHOUT, Glendon (Fred)

Nationality: American. **Born:** Pinckney, Michigan, 8 April 1918. **Education:** University of Michigan, Ann Arbor, 1935-39, A.B. 1939, A.M. 1946; Michigan State University, East Lansing, 1952-55, Ph.D. 1955. **Military Service:** Served in the United States Army Infantry, 1943-45: Sergeant; awarded two battle stars. **Family:** Married Kathryn Blair Vaughn in 1940; one son. **Career:** Teaching fellow, University of Michigan, 1946-48; Instructor, University of Maryland, College Park, 1948-51; Associate Professor of English, Michigan State University, 1951-59; lecturer in English, Arizona State University, Tempe, 1959-62. Writer. **Awards:** Theatre Guild Playwriting award, 1947; Hopwood award in Fiction, 1948; O. Henry Prize Short Story, 1960; gold medal, National Society of Arts and Letters, 1972; Western Writers of America Spur award, 1975, 1988; Wrangler award, 1988; Owen Wister Lifetime Achievement award, Western Writers of America, 1991. **Died:** 23 September 1992.

PUBLICATIONS FOR YOUNG ADULTS

Fiction

Where the Boys Are. New York, Random House, and London, Heinemann, 1960.
Loveland. New York, Doubleday, 1968.
Bless the Beasts and Children. New York, Doubleday, and London, Secker & Warburg, 1970.
TV Thompson, with Kathryn Swarthout, illustrated by Barbara Ninde Byfield. New York, Doubleday, 1972.
Luck and Pluck. New York, Doubleday, and London, Secker & Warburg; 1973.
Whales to See The, with Kathryn Swarthout, illustrated by Paul Bacon. New York, Doubleday, 1975.
The Melodeon (autobiographical), illustrated by Richard Cuffari. New York, Doubleday, and London, Secker & Warburg, 1977; as *A Christmas Gift,* New York, St. Martin's, 1992.
Cadbury's Coffin. New York, Doubleday, 1982.

PUBLICATIONS FOR ADULTS

Fiction

Willow Run. New York, Crowell, 1943.
They Came to Cordura. New York, Random House, and London, Heinemann, 1958.
Welcome to Thebes. New York, Random House, 1962; London, Heinemann, 1963.
The Cadillac Cowboys. New York, Random House, 1964.
The Eagle and the Iron Cross. New York, New American Library, 1966; London, Heinemann, 1967.

The Tin Lizzie Troop. New York, Doubleday, and London, Secker & Warburg, 1972.

The Shootist. New York, Doubleday, and London, Secker & Warburg, 1975.

Skeletons. New York, Doubleday, and London, Secker & Warburg, 1979.

The Old Colts. New York, Fine, and London, Secker & Warburg, 1985.

The Homesman. New York, Weidenfeld and Nicolson, and London, Deutsch, 1988.

PUBLICATIONS FOR CHILDREN

Fiction

The Ghost and the Magic Saber, with wife, Kathryn Swarthout. New York, Random House, 1963.

Whichaway, with Kathryn Swarthout, drawings by Richard M. Powers. New York, Random House, 1966; London, Heinemann, 1967.

The Button Boat, with Kathryn Swarthout. New York, Doubleday, 1969; London, Heinemann, 1971.

*

Manuscript Collections: Hayden Memorial Library, Arizona State University, Tempe.

Media Adaptations: "Where the Boys Are," starring George Hamilton and Delores Hart, Metro-Goldwyn-Mayer, 1961.

*   *   *

Novelist, short story writer, and dramatist, Glendon Swarthout is a master storyteller who sets many of his novels in Michigan, where he was born and raised, or the Western part of the United States, where he lived during the latter part of his life. His most acclaimed and enduring work is unquestionably *Bless the Beasts and Children* (1970) which focuses on a collection of misfit adolescents sent to Box Canyon Camp in Arizona.

The camp, which boasts the motto: "Send us a boy. We'll send you a cowboy!" focuses on competition among the cabins in sports and crafts which in turn decides one's position in the camp. The group with the least points becomes known officially around the camp as the "Bedwetters." Formed by a process of elimination, they are composed of individuals driven out of other cabins into that of John Cotton, who establishes himself as their leader by accepting such immature behavior as thumb sucking, bedwetting, and teeth grinding. The camp director assures the campers that if a cabin really wants to be the top group in the camp but fails in the competition system (success in riflery, swimming, etc.), they could steal their way to the summit by raiding the leaders' cabins and making off with their trophy of an animal head. To avenge previous humiliation at the hands of the other campers, the misfits release the camp's horses and, as the entire camp rounds them up again, they successfully steal the trophies of every cabin.

Following the above success, the boys next persuade their counselor to allow them to visit a government holding area for buffalo. To their horror, they discover that the bison are being slaughtered by "hunters" who shoot rifles inaccurately from behind the safety of a fence. The display of unskilled brutality binds them together and delivers their only chance at making the summer meaningful: save the bison. The night escape from the camp to free the beasts is supremely suspenseful and tautly written, with the tension enhanced by prior incidents which elaborate and underscore lives full of unkept promises and self-doubt. Swarthout successfully cultivates the feeling of anxiety and excitement the boys feel as they break free of the camp.

In a novel with such simple characterization and plot, one might expect their mission to be accomplished with some effort and then conclude with a heroes' return to the camp to be welcomed and accepted by those who had once scorned them. This is not the case. On the contrary, once the boys get to the holding pens they realize they must overcome their own fears of the massive animals before they can act. Freeing the bison proves to be an undertaking which requires the ultimate sacrifice. The suspense finally breaks with the death of John Cotton when he goes over a rim in the "Judas truck" which has led the buffalo herd to freedom.

Although contemporary readers may find the references to films, music, and transistor radios to be somewhat dated, the urgent need these young men exhibit for acceptance and brotherhood holds a timeless appeal for young adults. The alienation of these losers from their parents, peers, and counselors is so great that comparisons to the more complex and subtle *Lord of the Flies* arise easily. Unlike Golding's characters, however, these boys band strongly together as nonhunters, preserving and supporting not only themselves but the mighty bison as well. Swarthout's description of the slaughter is horribly graphic and authentic, but anything less would leave the reader unsympathetic to the boys.

Swarthout's novels *The Shootist* and *The Homesman* are set in the "old West" and may be helpful to the young adult reader in challenging myths about life on the American frontier. *The Shootist* deals with the last days of a renowned gunfighter dying of cancer alone in a boarding house in El Paso. The year 1901 sees the passing of Queen Victoria and the era of the gunfighter. He discovers that somewhere between those who admire his skill with a gun and ability to survive and those who view him as a ruthless assassin, he is friendless. Those who come to visit him seek only to cash in on his former glory. The final scene in *The Shootist,* like the slaughter of the buffalo in *Bless the Beasts and Children,* is described in visceral detail, unlike a "clean" Hollywood death, slowing down the instantaneous destruction wrought by a gun.

The Homesman details the journey of a strong pioneer woman and a man of dubious character leading three women who have lost their minds as a result of the wrenching hardships of life on the American frontier. Unable to be cared for on the plains, these women are being shipped back east. As in Swarthout's other novels, the specifics of their ordeals are gruesome, but as they head east, the women seem to improve, and the real challenge emerges for the duo who lead them, avoiding eager pilgrims heading west who are fearful their own women will see what hardships may possibly lie ahead.

A number of Swarthout's books have been adapted for the screen. Among them are *Bless the Beasts and Children, The Shootist,* and *Where the Boys Are,* a story set in Ft. Lauderdale, Florida, during spring break. Swarthout has also collaborated with his wife, Kathryn Vaughn Swarthout, on books for children as well as young adults.

—Parish Lentz

SWINDELLS, Robert (Edward)

Nationality: British. **Born:** Bradford, Yorkshire, 20 March 1939. **Education:** Huddersfield Polytechnic, Yorkshire, 1969-72, teaching certificate, 1972; Bradford University, Yorkshire, 1986-87, M.A. in peace studies 1987. **Military Service:** Served in the Royal Air Force, 1957-60. **Family:** Married Brenda Marriott in 1982 (second marriage); two daughters (from first marriage). **Career:** Copyholder, 1954-57, advertising clerk, 1960-67, *Telegraph and Argus,* Bradford; engineer, Hepworth & Grandage (turbine manufacturer), Bradford, 1967-69; elementary school teacher, Undercliffe First, Bradford, 1972-77; part-time teacher, Southmere First, Bradford, 1977-80; full-time writer, since 1980. **Awards:** Child Study Association of America's Children's Books of the Year, 1975, for *When Darkness Comes*; National Book award nomination, children's category, Arts Council of Great Britain, 1980, for *The Moonpath and Other Stories*; Other award, 1984, Children's Book award, Federation of Children's Book Groups, and Carnegie Medal runner-up, British Library Association, both 1985, all for *Brother in the Land*; Children's Book award, 1990, for *Room 13*; Carnegie Award and Sheffield Children's Book Award, both 1994, and Segnalazione di Merito (Italy), all for *Stone Cold*; Earthworm Award and Young Telegraph Award shortlist, both 1995, both for *Timesnatch*; KJJ Preis (Netherlands), 1995, for *Secret of Weeping Wood*; Sheffield Children's Book Award, 1996, and Angus Book Award, 1998, both for *Unbeliever*; Sheffield Book Award shortlist, 1998, for *Smash!*; Children's Book Award shortlist, 1998, for *Nightmare Stairs*. **Agent:** Jennifer Luithlen, "The Rowans," 88 Holmfield Rd., Leicester LE2 1SB. **Address:** 4 Spring Row, Denholme Road, Oxenhope, Keighley, West Yorkshire BD22 9NR, England.

PUBLICATIONS FOR YOUNG ADULTS

Fiction

When Darkness Comes, illustrated by Charles Keeping. Leicester, Brockhampton Press, 1973; New York, Morrow, 1975.
A Candle in the Night. Newton Abbot, Devon, David & Charles, 1974; as *A Candle in the Dark,* Sevenoaks, Kent, Knight, 1983.
Voyage to Valhalla, illustrated by Victor Ambrus. London, Hodder & Stoughton, 1976; Portsmouth, New Hampshire, Heinemann Educational, 1977.
The Ice-Palace, illustrated by June Jackson. London, Hamish Hamilton, 1977.
The Very Special Baby, illustrated by Victor Ambrus. London, Hodder & Stoughton, 1977; Englewood Cliffs, New Jersey, Prentice-Hall, 1978.
Dragons Live Forever, illustrated by Petula Stone. London, Hodder & Stoughton, and Englewood Cliffs, New Jersey, Prentice-Hall, 1978.
The Moonpath and Other Stories. Exeter, Wheaton, 1979; as *The Moonpath and Other Tales of the Bizarre,* illustrated by Reg Sandland, Minneapolis, Carolrhoda Books, 1983.
Norah's Ark, illustrated by Avril Haynes. Exeter, Wheaton, 1979.
Norah's Shark, illustrated by Avril Haynes. Exeter, Wheaton, 1979.
The Weather-Clerk, illustrated by Petula Stone. London, Hodder & Stoughton, 1979.
Ghost Ship to Ganymede, illustrated by Jeff Burns. Exeter, Wheaton, 1980.

Norah and the Whale, illustrated by Avril Haynes. Exeter, Wheaton, 1981.
Norah to the Rescue, illustrated by Avril Haynes. Exeter, Wheaton, 1981.
World Eater. London, Hodder & Stoughton, 1981.
The Wheaton Book of Science Fiction Stories, illustrated by Gary Long. Exeter, Wheaton, 1982.
Brother in the Land. Oxford, Oxford University Press, 1984; New York, Holiday House, 1985.
The Thousand Eyes of Night. London, Hodder & Stoughton, 1985.
The Ghost Messengers. London, Hodder & Stoughton, 1986.
Staying Up. Oxford, Oxford University Press, 1986.
Mavis Davis. Oxford, Oxford University Press, 1988.
The Postbox Mystery, illustrated by Kate Rogers. London, Hodder & Stoughton, 1988.
A Serpent's Tooth. London, Hamish Hamilton, 1988; New York, Holiday House, 1989.
Follow a Shadow. London, Hamish Hamilton, 1989, New York, Holiday House, 1990.
Night School. Paperbird, 1989.
Room 13. New York, Doubleday, 1989.
Daz 4 Zoe. London, Hamish Hamilton, 1990.
Tim Kipper. London, Macmillan, 1990.
Dracula's Castle. New York, Doubleday, 1991.
Hydra. London, Doubleday, 1991.
Fallout. New York, Morrow, 1992.
Rolf and Rosie. Ann Arbor, Michigan, Andersen Press, 1992.
You Can't Say I'm Crazy. London, Hamish Hamilton, 1992.
Sam and Sue and Lavatory Lue. London, Simon & Schuster, 1993.
Stone Cold. London, Hamish Hamilton, 1993.
The Go-Ahead Gang. London, Puffin, 1994.
Inside the Worm. London, Doubleday, 1994.
The Siege of Frimly Prim. London, Mammoth, 1994.
Timesnatch, illustrated by Jon Riley. London, Doubleday, 1994.
Unbeliever. London, Hamish Hamilton, 1995.
Jacqueline Hyde. London, Doubleday, 1996.
Last Bus. London, Hamish Hamilton, 1996.
Hurricane Summer, illustrated by Kim Palmer. London, Mammoth, 1997.
Nightmare Stairs. London, Doubleday, 1997.
Smash! London, Hamish Hamilton, 1997.
Abomination. London, Doubleday, 1998.

"The Outfit" Series

Secret of Weeping Wood. London, Scholastic, 1993.
We Didn't Mean To, Honest. London, Scholastic, 1993.
Kidnap at Denton Farm. London, Scholastic, 1994.
The Ghosts of Givenham Keep. London, Scholastic, 1995.
Peril in the Mist. London, Scholastic, 1997.
The Strange Tale of Ragger Bill. London, Scholastic, 1998.

Other

Translator, *Alfie* series (*Alfie and His Secret Friend*; *Who'll Save Alfie Atkins?*; *Alfie and the Monster*; *You're a Sly One, Alfie Atkins!*), by Gunilla Bergström. Exeter, Wheaton, 4 vols., 1979.
Contributor, *The Methuen Book of Strange Tales,* edited by Jean Russell, London, Methuen, 1980.

*

Biography: Essay in *Something about the Author Autobiography Series,* Vol. 14, Detroit, Gale, 1992.

Robert Swindells comments:

Through my fiction I hope to hook young people on reading for pleasure, because I believe this is the single most important thing an adult can do for them. My childhood was circumscribed by a number of factors including an overcrowded home, relative poverty, and my failure at the age of eleven to pass the now discredited 11+ examination which would have give me access to education beyond the age of fifteen, and it was in books I found much needed places of temporary refuge and ultimately my escape route to a different life.

*   *   *

Robert Swindells lives in Yorkshire, England. His novels are usually set near the city of Bradford. However, in no sense can he be regarded purely as a regional novelist: the area and its people are what he knows best, but his narratives roam freely between past, present, and future, and his concerns are urgent and universal.

His stories exhibit sheer narrative energy to a high degree: common assent among readers is that few writers' pages are more compulsively turned over. Through an acute historical sense, profound understanding and unease about today's social conditions, and logical projection of them into convincing and disturbing dystopias, Swindells uses narrative to dramatise human failings and young adult possibility highly effectively.

Two among his earlier novels may serve to demonstrate important facets of his achievement. In *A Candle in the Night* (1974; later entitled *A Candle in the Dark*), we are in the Yorkshire coalfield at the time of Victorian child labour. Orphan Jimmy Booth is taken out of the workhouse to be a collier's apprentice. The apprentices are brutalised: the story chronicles a struggle between cruel ignorance and a possibility of better things. *World Eater* (1981) is an engaging science-fiction fantasy with a north-country background of pigeon racing: Orville loves his pigeons and is the only person to realize the errant planet threatening the entire solar system is a gigantic egg.

Swindells' best known novel, *Brother in the Land,* appeared in 1984. Few post-nuclear holocaust novels are as grim and uncompromising. Swindells himself wrote of other such novels: ". . . all shared a major flaw: they presented a picture of postcatastrophe which young readers might find attractive. . ." His novel, he says, shows ". . .no hope." Total desolation and a savage view of human nature in extremity present a Hobbesian future. In Danny and Kim, the young adult central characters, are vestiges of optimism: hope, the tenor of the narrative suggests, born to die. Swindells looks fearlessly at the overwhelming nature of his subject: a deserved award-winner, the novel has had great effect in schools and must rank at the top of its particular sub-genre.

Staying Up (1986) centres on Brian and Debbie. This severely contemporary novel revolves around the fictional town of Barfax and its third division football team whose fortunes mirror those of its people. Brian lives on a run-down estate; Debbie's parents aspire. Both are in a state of struggle, of finding out as the relationship develops—Brian between escape from his background and the attractions of "The Ointment" (a football hooligan gang), booze, and drugs, Debbie between Brian and her parents' restrictive views. All choices involve loss: the breakup of social and economic values in Barfax is typified by a serial killer—Debbie is nearly his last victim.

A Serpent's Tooth (1988) involves the supernatural. Lucy's parents—activist mother, careerist father—move to Yorkshire. Lucy is a pawn in their mutual animosities. The nearby Pitfield is to be used for nuclear dumping: Lucy's mother forms a noisy protest group (which becomes a women's camp similar to Greenham Common). But Lucy sees a strange, recurring vision—two shadowy figures wheeling a handcart. From the old recluse Alice Hazelborne she finds she has second sight. The Pitfield was a mass burial ground in the Black Death. The novel moves to a gripping climax, acutely observant about contemporary values.

In *Follow a Shadow* (1989) the themes of choice and loyalty in *Staying Up* and the supernatural as an image of continuity as in *A Serpent's Tooth* are combined. Tim South—small, unprepossessing, talented but dreamy—is torn between the gang values of the Barracloguhs and Janis Lee and the stability offered by Dilys, his girlfriend. The discovery of a sketch dated 1835 of a face like his, strange experiences of seeming taken out of place and time, conversation with his grandmother about family traditions, and a school trip to Howarth, home of the Brontes, convince him he is directly descended from Branwell Bronte. The contemporary narrative is handled surely: a shrewdly interspersed element involves nineteenth-century pastiche—Branwell's own diary chronicling his disastrous visit to London in 1835: opium, drink, failure to enter the Royal Academy, and a brief affair with a barmaid. Tim is not only descended from Branwell, he is a present-day version. In a brilliantly realised climax, the ghost of Branwell Bronte rescues Tim and the Barracloguhs from death from exposure on the moors. Tim makes resolutions about himself—starting with the confession of stealing from his grandmother's savings for the gang.

A Serpent's Tooth and *Follow a Shadow,* though pessimistic about much in modern life, have optimistic outcomes. *Daz 4 Zoe* (1990), like *Brother in the Land,* offers little hope except through its young main characters. Here is a different, no less frightening future: by extending present trends logically, Swindells depicts a society where the haves and have-nots—the "Subbies" and the "Chippies"—are institutionally separated. Zoe lives in a wealthy, protected suburb, Daz in an inner-city wasteland. Force and propaganda maintain this status-quo. Daz, till he meets Zoe and their irresistible Romeo and Juliet love begins, wants to join Dred, the Chippy terrorist gang.

The novel is formally and stylistically advanced. Two first-person narratives are intertwined, and that by Daz is eloquently illiterate. The power of this dystopia comes from its awful plausibility: Swindells is making a devastating critique of contemporary Western society. This novel is as much a warning for a new generation as *Brother in the Land.* With deepest irony, Swindells suggests that in the two centuries which separate *A Candle in the Night* and *Daz 4 Zoe* society will merely come back full circle to its old iniquitous barbarities. This pessimistic but consistent view has generated many fine novels.

Swindells has continued to develop several of the themes and issues raised in his earlier work, and to make use of stylistic devices such as dual narrators recounting alternating chapters, and short chapters which drive the narrative forward. His focus has shifted from stories set in the near future to books of social realism which highlight contemporary problems.

Stone Cold, with its hard-hitting description of life on London's streets for the young homeless, was a controversial winner of the Carnegie Medal for 1993. As in *Daz 4 Zoe* the narrative alternates between two first person accounts—one by a homeless teenage boy, the other giving chilling insight into the mind of a serial killer preying on young people like Link. Critics were divided about whether this was suitable subject matter for a prizewinning novel for young people. Swindells was prompted to write the book after hearing an insensitive remark by a politician about the homeless, and slept on the streets himself for several nights as part of his research.

Since *Stone Cold* he has written further novels which are thought-provoking and easy to read. *Unbeliever* and *Abomination* both deal with the theme of religious cults and the difficulties faced by young people whose parents insist on their participation and involvement.

Smash! is a fast moving story about the build up of racism in a northern English town using the lives of two young men, one Asian, one white. Cynical local businessmen are a destructive and corrupt force in this community, while the media in the shape of the editor and a reporter on a local newspaper are catalysts for the promotion of harmony. In Swindells' adventure series "The Outfit," which is for a younger age group, it is also a newspaper reporter who helps the young people to bring wrongdoers to justice.

Robert Swindells has maintained an interest in developing futuristic themes. In *Timesnatch,* an scientist in 2039 invents a machine which she uses to collect extinct species from the past and release them into the wild once more. However, once unscrupulous and irresponsible people find out about the invention, a number of ethical questions come into the frame.

In *Jacqueline Hyde* Swindells plays with the Robert Louis Stevenson classic in terms of both plot and the pun in the central character's name. Jacqueline is a "good girl" who feels neglected by her busy parents, until she gets a whiff of a liquid in Grandma's attic which turns her into "Jacqueline Bad." The first hint that this is not a straightforward story comes almost halfway through the book when Jacqueline suddenly deviates from her account to ask "What d'you keeping *writing* on that pad?" The narrative builds to a chilling climax as it gradually becomes apparent that Jacqueline is in a psychiatric hospital. Jacqueline has recurring nightmares about events from "Dr. Jekyll and Mr. Hyde," which she has not read. Swindells carries this motif of a recurring nightmare through to a subsequent novel, *Nightmare Stairs,* a thriller about a girl who believes she is the reincarnation of her grandmother.

In a recent interview with *Young Writer,* a magazine for children, Robert Swindells said: "I am constantly aware of the presence of injustice in the world, and try to point up various manifestations of injustice, structural violence and so forth which exist in our society, and their effects on victims. Sometimes I suggest possible solutions. I make no attempt to be even-handed in this: I write what I believe."

—Dennis Hamley, updated by Ann Lazim

T

TAN, Amy

Nationality: American. **Born:** Oakland, California, 19 February 1952. **Education:** San Jose State, California, B.A. 1973, M.A. 1974; postgraduate study at University of California, Berkeley, 1974-76. **Family:** Married Lou DeMattei in 1974. **Career:** Writer. Worked as language consultant to programs for disabled children, 1976-81, and as reporter, managing editor, and associate publisher for *Emergency Room Reports* (now *Emergency Medicine Reports*), 1981-83; free-lance technical writer, 1983-87. **Awards:** Commonwealth Club gold award for fiction, Bay Area Book Reviewers award for best fiction, American Library Association's best book for young adults citation, nomination for National Book Critics Circle award for best novel, and nomination for *Los Angeles Times* book award, all 1989, all for *The Joy Luck Club; The Kitchen God's Wife* was a 1991 *Booklist* editor's choice and was nominated for Bay Area Book Reviewers award. **Address:** c/o Putnam Berkley Group, 200 Madison Ave., New York, New York 10016, U.S.A.

PUBLICATIONS FOR ADULTS AND YOUNG ADULTS

Novels

The Joy Luck Club. New York, Putnam, 1989.
The Kitchen God's Wife. New York, Putnam, 1991.
The Chinese Siamese Cat, illustrated by Gretchen Schields. New York and Toronto, Macmillan, 1994.
The Hundred Secret Senses. New York, G.P. Putnam's Sons, 1995.

PUBLICATIONS FOR CHILDREN

Fiction

The Moon Lady. New York, Macmillan, 1992.

*

Media Adaptations: *The Joy Luck Club* (audiocassette); *The Kitchen God's Wife* (audiocassette), Dove, 1991.

Critical Studies: Entry in *Contemporary Literary Criticism,* Volume 59, Detroit, Gale, 1990, pp. 89-99.

*   *   *

Amy Tan would probably identify herself as a successful adult writer who also happens to enjoy a large young adult audience. Nevertheless, when the American Library Association added to the many awards already received by *The Joy Luck Club* by naming it a Best Book for Young Adults in 1990, Tan's reputation as a young adult writer was cemented. *The Kitchen God's Wife,* Tan's second novel, has only intensified her appeal to adolescent readers.

Because Tan is a relatively new writer it would seem ludicrous to generalize about such things as her "development" as a novelist or her "style." Two of her books are critically acclaimed: *The Joy Luck Club* and *The Kitchen God's Wife* tell different stories through markedly divergent structures. Still, the two novels share thematic concerns suggestive of reasons for Tan's popularity among young adults. Both are built around generational conflicts (specifically, the points of tension between mothers and their daughters) and the challenge of establishing personal identity. While such conflicts and challenges are circumscribed by a specific ethnic culture—the Chinese-American culture of northern California—they are universal in nature and significance. That the mothers in Tan's fiction are foreign-born Americans with American-born daughters is rarely off-putting to young readers outside the Chinese-American culture. Instead, Tan's novels stimulate ethnic appreciation while allowing readers to objectify their own situations, making connections between their own lives and the geographically/culturally distant lives of Tan's characters.

A reader's gender often determines the significance he or she assigns to Tan's work. While Tan's characters are often much older than themselves, young adult females find Tan to be a trustworthy guide to the challenges of adolescent identity crisis and familial conflicts, especially mother-daughter conflicts. Perhaps more than anything else, a young woman is moved by Tan's portrayals of a daughter's opposing desires concerning her mother: on one hand, the daughter wants to be like her mother, to be bound to her; on the other, she feels the unassailable need to separate herself from her mother, to establish a unique identity. The young adult male who is sufficiently mature and self-assured to read what are often perceived as "women's novels" will learn much about his own behavior towards women—and reasons for possibly changing his behavior. Few young men who read Tan's novels feel threatened by her. Instead, they are delighted by her humor and her life-affirming stance; they grow to respect her objectivity and fairness.

The Joy Luck Club is, in its most rudimentary form, a collection of related short stories told by four Chinese-American mothers and their four American-born daughters. (In actuality, one of the daughters is a voice for herself as well as her recently-deceased mother; she becomes a kind of "generational bridge" and the thematic focus of the novel.) While the novel is rather loosely plotted, its themes are wonderfully controlled: they are introduced, modified, and reprised with technical and aesthetic brilliance. The novel suggests that a woman's identity must be measured against her ethnic and cultural roots and that her mother is the most immediate embodiment of such roots. Accordingly, a central theme of the novel is that connections between daughters and their mothers are tenuous but priceless, the very key to selfhood.

The Kitchen God's Wife echoes the mother/daughter themes of *The Joy Luck Club* while also implying that male-centered social traditions subvert a woman's self-awareness and her relationships with other women. It also suggests that withholding one's "stories" (one's past experiences) from those one cares about is a kind of deception, a failure of trust which undermines mature and enduring relationships. The novel begins as the narrative of the American-born daughter of a Chinese-American mother; before the novel has progressed very far, however, the mother has wrested the narrator's responsibilities away from her daughter, recounting her own experiences to reveal her daughter's identity and potential. In the end, *The Kitchen God's Wife* is a profoundly moving, profoundly optimistic story of endurance, reconciliation, and love.

The Moon Lady is a picture book adaptation of a chapter by the same title in *The Joy Luck Club*. While *The Moon Lady* appeals to few teenage readers, and while it seems designed to be read aloud to young children, preteens nevertheless find it an accessible introduction to the style and themes of Tan's novels.

—Keith Lawrence

TAYLOR, Mildred D.

Nationality: American. **Born:** Jackson, Mississippi, 13 September 1943. **Education:** University of Toledo, B.Ed. 1965; University of Colorado, M.A. 1969. **Family:** Married Errol Zea-Daly in 1972 (divorced 1975). **Career:** Writer. English and history teacher with the Peace Corps, Tuba City, Arizona, 1965, and Yirgalem, Ethiopia, 1965-67, recruiter, 1967-68, instructor in Maine, 1968; study skills coordinator, University of Colorado, 1969-71; proofreader and editor in Los Angeles, California, 1971-73. **Awards:** First prize (African-American category), Council on Interracial Books for Children, 1973, outstanding book of the year citation, *New York Times*, 1975, and Jane Addams Honor citation, 1976, all for *Song of the Trees*; notable book citation, American Library Association, 1976, National Book Award (finalist), honor book citation, *Boston Globe-Horn Book*, Jane Addams Honor citation, and Newbery Medal, all 1977, and Buxtehuder Bulle Award, 1985, all for *Roll of Thunder, Hear My Cry*; outstanding book of the year citation, *New York Times*, 1981, Jane Addams Honor citation, 1982, American Book Award nomination, 1982, and Coretta Scott King Award, 1982, all for *Let the Circle Be Unbroken*; Coretta Scott King Award, and fiction award, *Boston Globe-Horn Book*, both 1988, both for *The Friendship*; notable book citation, *New York Times*, 1987, and Christopher Award, 1988, both for *The Gold Cadillac*; Coretta Scott King Award, 1990, for *The Road to Memphis*. **Address:** c/o Doubleday Publishers, 1540 Broadway, New York, New York 10036-4039, U.S.A.

PUBLICATIONS FOR YOUNG ADULTS

Fiction

Roll of Thunder, Hear My Cry. New York, Dial, 1976; London, Gollancz, 1977.
Let the Circle Be Unbroken. New York, Dial, 1981; London, Gollancz, 1982.
The Friendship, illustrated by Max Ginsburg. New York, Dial, 1987; London, Gollancz, 1989.
The Road to Memphis. New York, Dial, 1990.
The Well: David's Story. New York, Dial Books for Young Readers, 1995.

PUBLICATIONS FOR CHILDREN

Fiction

Song of the Trees, illustrated by Jerry Pinkney. New York, Dial, 1975.
The Gold Cadillac, illustrated by Michael Hays. New York, Dial, 1987.
Mississippi Bridge. New York, Dial, 1990.

*

Media Adaptations: *Roll of Thunder, Hear My Cry* was recorded by Newbery Awards Records, 1978, and adapted as a three-part television miniseries of the same title, American Broadcasting Companies, Inc. (ABC-TV), 1978.

Biography: Entry in *Dictionary of Literary Biography,* Vol. 52, *American Writers for Children since 1960: Fiction,* Detroit, Gale, 1986; essay in *Something about the Author Autobiography Series,* Vol. 5, Detroit, Gale, 1988; essay in *Authors and Artists for Young Adults,* Vol. 10, Detroit, Gale, 1993.

Critical Studies: *Contemporary Literary Criticism,* Vol. 21, Detroit, Gale, 1982; *Children's Literature Review,* Vol. 9, Detroit, Gale, 1985.

* * *

Upon examining the works of Mildred D. Taylor, one cannot fail to be inspired by her unusually cohesive and consistent approach to historical writing for young people. For each of her works to date Taylor has chosen an autobiographical base upon which to create stories of amazing power and spiritual ethos. Black experience of the 1930s through 1950 provides the framework for the stories. Taylor has selected various episodes both from her personal experience and from the stories related to her by her father, a powerful role model throughout her life.

The stories offer a moving and honest perspective on the perils and the joys of black family life, primarily in Mississippi. The strength of the black family as a unit is emphasized as is the successful potential for confronting and dealing with adversity, when one has spiritual and family resources upon which to call. Taylor's works would be welcome at any point in time, but particularly so during a period when the problems and/or dissolution of minority family life are stressed in the media. Taylor's writing communicates a natural and fluid style. The storylines are clear-cut, easy to follow but never simplistic. The reader is always left to muse and indeed wonder at human action, inaction, and the far-reaching effects these factors may have upon the lives of others.

The Logan family, consisting of David, Mary, Caroline (''Big Ma''), and the children—Stacey, Cassie, Christopher-John, and Little Man—are first introduced in *Song of the Trees,* a short novel. The basic story, told from Cassie's perspective, involves the threat to land owned by the Logan family posed by an unscrupulous white neighbor who wishes to exploit their property by cutting down and selling the trees. The land, passed down from David Logan's father, is symbolic of the fortitude and strength of the family. The conflict is a spiritual as well as physical one. The image of the trees and the land are dominant and almost mystical, almost placing the work within the category of a romance. Even before Cassie, the major protagonist, sights the men illegally marking the trees to be cut, she notes that the ''song of the trees'' (the sound made by the wind blowing through the branches), has stopped and senses that something is amiss. It is the return of Mr. Logan from his railroad job in Louisiana that halts the progress of the evil plan. Damage has been done, but total desecration has been avoided. The family has been shaken but strengthened through the experience.

Cassie Logan also figures prominently in *Roll of Thunder, Hear My Cry, Let the Circle Be Unbroken, The Friendship, The Road to Memphis,* and *Mississippi Bridge.* She is portrayed as a young woman whose feisty spirit becomes fully developed during the course of the works; an innocent with a far-seeing vision, questioning what others of her time fear to question. Knowingly and unknowingly, she risks both the futility and the danger of confrontation. Cassie is often shocked by what she learns, but in the true Logan tradition refuses to let her spirit be dominated or crushed.

Roll of Thunder, Hear My Cry traces the incidents in the lives of the Logan family over the period of about a year. The family continues its struggle to maintain balance and dignity in the face of Southern racism. Educational inequities are laid bare, and the terrifying visits of the night riders, who descend upon defenseless blacks, become a reality. The prosecution of the misguided teenager T.J. for a crime perpetrated by whites also shakes the family, but serves to bind them to each other even more tightly.

Let the Circle Be Unbroken is the powerful sequel in which Cassie continues the story of her family and its attempts to cope with the inequities of Southern justice. A foreshadowing of civil rights initiatives is seen in the actions of Mrs. Lee Annie, who at the age of sixty-five decides she is going to register to vote, a dangerous aspiration in the Mississippi of the 1930s.

The Gold Cadillac departs from the lives of the Logan family and introduces a new family and a new era—1950. Lois is the narrator of this story about a family of four who encounter the realities of racism when they travel from Ohio to Mississippi to visit relatives in a new gold Cadillac. Again, the protagonist begins as an innocent who must adjust to the injustices of contemporary society, but who does so with the support of a loving family.

In *The Friendship,* Taylor returns to the lives of the Logan family. This story focuses on the events of one day in the life of the Logan children who witness an incident in the local country store. Mr. Tom Bee, a neighbor who has appeared earlier in *Let the Circle Be Unbroken,* confronts John Wallace, owner of the store, in a test of wills. Tom Bee insists upon calling John Wallace by his first name, an ''offense'' not tolerated by white society of the 1930s. Bee is shot by Wallace for this ''infraction,'' but in a scene filled with pathos and courage, he crawls away from the store still refusing to acquiesce to the store owner's demands. This is a drama within drama; an incident involving Little Man in which he is insulted and threatened by Wallace's sons foreshadows the viciousness of the scene which follows. The reader is shown that the honesty of childhood and old age are treated with callous indifference by those who are steeped in racist philosophy. Yet the reader triumphs in the pride of both characters and (despite battles lost on the surface) in their continued strength.

While Taylor's later books *The Road to Memphis* and *Mississippi Bridge* continue the narrative of the Logan family and its associates, they add a new dimension to the author's work. The two books act as a duo; each appears designed to complement the other and makes a statement regarding all that has taken place before. Set in 1941, the riveting narrative of *The Road to Memphis* chronicles events surrounding a violent incident involving a young black man. Moe, a friend to the Logan family, is goaded by the evil taunts and actions of a group of young white men. He responds by hitting three of them with a crowbar, an incident which causes him to have to flee the town, aided by Cassie, Stacey, and a friend, Clarence. Taylor creates a spellbinding plot as the young people make their way through danger-filled Mississippi towards Memphis where Moe will be able to catch a train bound for Chicago—north and freedom. The desolation of black life here is shown as arguably more intense than in Taylor's other work, as incident upon incident serves to underscore the total disenfranchisement of the black populace in the 1940s.

Mississippi Bridge, while set years earlier, acts as biblical commentary upon the actions not only of those in *The Road to Memphis* but also of those in all other books which precede it. Told from the point of view of ten-year-old Jeremy Simms, the story involves the tragedy of a bus which goes over the side of a bridge in heavy fog, drowning all the passengers in the swirling waters below. All of the dead are white passengers—since blacks had been ordered off of the bus before it left town on its journey, in order to make space for white passengers. Ironically, it is a young black man, named Josias, previously ordered off of that very bus, who selflessly dives into the water in a fruitless attempt to save white lives. Taylor's irony seems less a contrivance of fate than a startling portrayal of Old Testament justice, enacting an event designed to exact payment for all of the injustices experienced in past stories, and in the past, collectively. Josias' desire to save human beings who represent the very race which constantly seeks his humiliation makes *Mississippi Bridge* at once a study in deific payment for wrongs and human kindness.

A poetic vision, the art of the storyteller, and the ability to recreate the past in a thoroughly convincing manner distinguish Mildred Taylor's work. She has provided us with important vignettes from an unforgettable era, which stand as classics in the genre of American historical fiction for young people.

—Karen Patricia Smith

TAYLOR, Theodore

Pseudonyms: T.T. Lang. **Nationality:** American. **Born:** Statesville, North Carolina, 23 June 1921. **Education:** Cradock High School, Virginia, 1934-1939; Fork Union Military Academy, Virginia, 1939-40; studied with American Theatre Wing, 1947-48. **Military Service:** Served in U.S. Merchant Marine, 1942-44; U.S. Naval Reserve, active duty, 1944-46, 1950-55; became lieutenant. **Family:** Married Gweneth Goodwin in 1946 (divorced 1977), children: (first marriage) two sons and one daughter; married Flora Gray Schoenleber in 1981. Cub reporter, *Portsmouth Star,* Portsmouth, Virginia, 1934-39, sports editor, 1941-42; copyboy, *Washington Daily News,* Washington, DC; sports writer, National Broadcasting Co. Radio, New York City, 1942; sports editor, *Sunset News,* Bluefield, West Virginia, 1946-47; assistant director of public relations, New York University, New York City, 1947-48; director of public relations, YMCA schools and colleges, New

York City, 1948-50; reporter, *Orlando Sentinel Star,* Orlando, Florida, 1949-50; publicist, Paramount Pictures, Hollywood, California, 1955-56; story editor, writer and associate producer, Perlberg-Seaton Productions, Hollywood, 1956-61; associate producer and free-lance press agent for Hollywood studios, 1961-68. Producer and director of documentary films. **Awards:** Commonwealth Club of California Silver Medal, 1969; Jane Addams Children's Book Award from Women's International League for Peace and Freedom (returned, 1975); Lewis Carroll Shelf Award, Southern California Council on Literature for Children and Young People Notable Book Award, Woodward Park School Annual Book Award, California Literature Medal Award, and Best Book Award from University of California, Irvine, all 1970, all for *The Cay; Battle in the Arctic Seas* was selected one of *New York Times* Outstanding Books of the Year, 1976; Spur Award for Best Western for Young People, Western Writers of America, and Commonwealth Club of California Silver Medal for the best juvenile book by a California author, both 1977, both for *A Shepherd Watches, a Shepherd Sings*; Southern California Council on Literature for Children and Young People Award, 1977, for distinguished contribution to the field of children's literature and body of work; George G. Stone Center for Children's Books Recognition of Merit Award, 1980, for body of work; Young Reader Medal from the California Reading Association, 1984, for *The Trouble with Tuck*; Jefferson Cup Honor Book, Virginia Library Association, 1987, for *Walking Up a Rainbow: Being the True Version of the Long and Hazardous Journey of Susan D. Carlisle, Mrs. Myrtle Dessery, Drover Bert Pettit, and Cowboy Clay Carmer and Others*; American Library Association Best Young Adult Book Award, 1989; Young Reader Medal Award, California Reading Association, 1992; Utah Young Adult Book Award, 1993, and Best Young Adult Book Award, Maryland Reading Association, 1995, for *Sniper*; American Library Association Best Young Adult Book Award, for *The Weirdo*; Edgar Allan Poe Award, 1993, Mystery Writers of America, for *The Weirdo*; Best Young Adult Book, ALA, 1995, for *The Bomb*; Scott O'Dell Award, for best historical fiction, 1996; Kerlan Award, for body of work, 1997. **Agent:** Gloria Loomis, Watkins Loomis Agency, Inc., 150 East 35th Street, Suite 530, New York, New York 10016. **Address:** 1856 Catalina Street, Laguna Beach, California 92651, U.S.A.

PUBLICATIONS FOR YOUNG ADULTS

Fiction

The Cay. New York, Doubleday, 1969; London, Bodley Head, 1970.
The Children's War. New York, Doubleday, 1971.
The Maldonado Miracle. New York, Doubleday, 1973.
Teetoncey, illustrated by Richard Cuffari. New York, Doubleday, 1974.
Teetoncey and Ben O'Neal, illustrated by R. Cuffari. New York, Doubleday, 1975.
The Odyssey of Ben O'Neal, illustrated by R. Cuffari. New York, Doubleday, 1977.
The Trouble with Tuck. New York, Doubleday, 1981.
Sweet Friday Island. New York, Scholastic Inc., 1984.
Walking Up a Rainbow: Being the True Version of the Long and Hazardous Journey of Susan D. Carlisle, Mrs. Myrtle Dessery, Drover Bert Pettit, and Cowboy Clay Carmer and Others. New York, Delacorte, 1986.

The Hostage, illustrated by Thomas McKeveny. New York, Delacorte, 1987.
Sniper. New York, Harcourt, 1989.
Tuck Triumphant. New York, Doubleday, 1991.
The Weirdo. New York, Harcourt, 1992.
Timothy of the Cay. New York, Harcourt, 1993.
Maria: A Christmas Story. New York, Harcourt, 1994.
The Bomb. New York, Harcourt, 1995.
Rogue Wave: and Other Red-Blooded Sea Stories. New York, Harcourt, 1996.
"The Grind of an Axe," in *Night Terrors: Stories of Shadow and Substance,* edited by Lois Duncan. New York, Aladdin, 1996.

Nonfiction

People Who Make Movies. New York, Doubleday, 1967.
Air Raid—Pearl Harbor! The Story of December 7, 1941, illustrated by W. T. Mars. New York, Crowell, 1971.
Rebellion Town: Williamsburg, 1776, illustrated by R. Cuffari. New York, Crowell, 1973.
Battle in the Arctic Seas: The Story of Convoy PQ 17, illustrated by Robert Andrew Parker. New York, Crowell, 1976.
A Shepherd Watches, a Shepherd Sings, with Louis Irigaray. New York, Doubleday, 1977.
The Battle off Midway Island, illustrated by Andrew Glass. New York, Avon, 1981.
H.M.S. Hood vs. Bismarck: The Battleship Battle, illustrated by A. Glass. New York, Avon, 1982.
Battle in the English Channel, illustrated by A. Glass. New York, Avon, 1983.
Rocket Island. New York, Avon, 1985.

Plays

Sunshine, the Whale (television play). 1974.
Threepersons (television play). 1962.

PUBLICATIONS FOR ADULTS

Fiction

The Body Trade. New York, Fawcett, 1968.
The Stalker. New York, D. I. Fine, 1987.
Monocolo. New York, D. I. Fine, 1989.
To Kill the Leopard, New York, Harcourt, 1993.

Nonfiction

The Magnificent Mitscher (biography), foreword by Arthur W. Radford. New York, Norton, 1954.
Fire on the Beaches. New York, Norton, 1958.
Special Unit Senator: The Investigation of the Assassination of Senator Robert F. Kennedy, with Robert A. Houghton. New York, Random House, 1970.
The Amazing World of Kreskin. New York, Random House, 1973.
Jule: The Story of Composer Jule Styne. New York, Random House, 1979.
The Cats of Shambala, with Tippi Hedren. New York, Simon & Schuster, 1985; London, Century Hutchinson, 1986.

Plays

Night without End (screenplay). 1959.
Tom Threepersons (television play). TV Mystery Theatre, 1964.
Showdown (screenplay). Universal, 1973.
The Girl Who Whistled the River Kwai (television play). 1980.
Diplomatic Immunity (screenplay). 1989.
The Hold-Up (screenplay).

Has also written seventeen documentaries.

*

Media Adaptations: *The Cay* was adapted as a movie by NBC-TV, 1974, and as a filmstrip by Pied Piper Productions, 1975. *The Trouble with Tuck* was adapted as a filmstrip by Pied Piper Productions, 1986.

Biography: Entry in *Authors of Books for Young People,* supplement to the 2nd edition, edited by Dorothy A. Marquardt and Martha E. Ward, Scarecrow, 1979; essay in *Something about the Author Autobiography Series,* Volume 4, Gale, 1987; essay in *Authors and Artists for Young Adults,* Volume 2, Gale, 1989; essay in *Speaking for Ourselves, Too* compiled and edited by Donald R. Gallo, National Council of Teachers of English, 1993; *Favorite Authors of Young Adult Fiction* by Diane Vick, illustrated by Jo Harden, Torrance, California, F. Schaffer, 1995; *Something about the Author,* Volume 83, Detroit, Gale, 1996; *Contemporary Authors New Revisions Series,* Volume 50, Detroit, Gale, 1996.

Manuscript Collections: Kerlan Collection, University of Minnesota.

Critical Studies: Bagnall, Norma, "Theodore Taylor: His Models of Self-reliance," *Language Arts,* January, 1980, 86-91; "Teachers at Work II: Two Novels in the Classroom" by Stephen Wicks, in *Children's Literature in Education,* New York, APS, Volume 11, No. 3, Fall 1980, 124-128; review of *Timothy of the Cay,* in *Publisher's Weekly,* 6 September 1993, 98; *A Literature Guide to The Cay: By Theodore Taylor* by Ellen and Pamela Reeves, Cambridge, Massachusetts, Book Wise, 1994.

*   *   *

Although Theodore Taylor's young adult novels touch current concerns of our society, they also include life-and-death adventures in which young people struggle to make decisions and/or solve mysteries that would challenge mature adults.

In these novels for young adults, *The Hostage, The Weirdo,* and *Sniper,* the theme of wildlife preservation is the background for tales of adventure and suspense. There's also a bit of romance. Each book portrays young characters risking their lives for a specific environmental issue. Also, the teenagers summon up previously unrecognized initiative and strength as they face up to their parents and other adults who sometimes seem insensitive to the issues involved.

In *The Hostage,* fourteen-year-old Jamie Tidd and his father capture a large killer whale for a marine park being established in California. The developers of the park offer $100,000 for the whale. This money would be a windfall which would permit Jamie's family to leave the isolated fishing camp in British Columbia and enjoy such benefits of town life as better schooling for their son. Jamie's mother dreams of taking a trip to Hawaii.

However, Angie, a girlfriend home for the summer, along with the television crew that comes to film the whale and other active environmentalists work to convince Jamie and his parents that to confine this large whale to an exhibit for humans would be cruel.

Interspersed with information about the Orca whale and the Tidd's conflict with environmentalists are such exciting episodes as the one in which Jamie saves Angie from drowning as she takes it upon herself to release the whale from the cove where it is held captive.

In *The Weirdo,* seventeen-year-old Chip Clewt, disfigured in a fiery airplane accident ten years ago and hiding from civilization in Powhatan Swamp in North Carolina, meets sixteen-year-old native Samantha (called "Sam") and an older graduate student from the state university who is doing research on the bear population of the swamp. The student (Tom) works with Chip and Sam to track bears and mark them for a project to help the government decide whether or not to allow bear hunting on the designated Natural Wildlife Refuge. Some hunters, feeling threatened, turn guns on the young people in their determination to win back their bear hunting privileges. Tom disappears. Chip and Samantha attempt to prove their belief that Tom has met with foul play from poachers.

Human relationships are important here as well as the action and the unusual setting. Chip comes to face up to the fact that physical scars need not cause him to continue to hide from people. Sam is torn between her feelings for Chip and her loyalty to her father who is a hunter.

Taylor is at his best in building suspense and creating action. As for the setting, Chip describes the swamp environment and the animals and birds who live there in short essays throughout the book. Although the essays tend to slow the action, they help you understand Chip and see the swamp through the eyes of someone who loves the area. Teenagers will want to finish this book once they start to read it.

A third novel for young adults, *Sniper,* provides even more suspense in the adventures of a youth, facing danger toward himself and the animals of a private zoological preserve. Ben Jepson ends up in charge of his family's Los Coyotes Preserve in Orange County, California. It's an area with compounds for lions, tigers, and other animals along with Ben's home and trailers for animal handlers.

Ben's parents are on assignment for a National Geographic piece about poaching and cannot be reached by telephone when someone attacks the animals and the boy at night with a gun equipped with a telescopic night vision lens. Alfredo, the man whom Ben's parents left in charge of the preserve during their absence, has met with a serious automobile accident. This leaves Ben, who's just turning fifteen, to make life and death decisions to protect the captive animals and the preserve itself. He does have the help of a resident veterinarian from Africa who is studying for the California veterinary exams and two Spanish-speaking handlers, Luis Vargas who also speaks English and Rafael Soto. Ben's girlfriend is his reliable confidant. This novel is so filled with suspense, action, and mystery that it seems like a good candidate for a screenplay, a type of writing with which Taylor has had much experience.

Over his long writing career, Mr. Taylor has also written historical fiction and nonfiction. *Walking up a Rainbow,* set on the American frontier in 1851 and 1852, is a young adult story of a fourteen-year-old orphan Susan and her guardian who attempt to drive sheep—which Susan has inherited—over the plains and deserts toward California. The first and third sections of the book are told by Susan and the middle section by her handsome cowboy Clay Carmer. The book has humor, characters who are lively, and an interesting historical setting.

The Bomb, set on Bikini atoll in the South Pacific during World War II, explores the relationship between powerful countries and those controlled by them. The Americans who liberate the islanders from Japanese occupation are initially seen as heroes. But then the United States, wanting to use Bikini as an atomic-bomb test site, forces the islanders to move to other, less hospitable islands, promising they may return a year later. Sixteen-year-old Sorry Rinamu doesn't believe the promise and tries to protest the testing, with disastrous results.

Taylor's best known novel for children, *The Cay,* is a survival tale about the boy Phillip who finds himself on a life raft in the Caribbean with only Timothy—an old West Indian man who is black—as a companion. Phillip is blinded as a result of the injuries to him in a torpedo attack on the freighter which was taking Phillip and his mother from a 1942 war zone to the United States.

In the biographical sketch about Taylor in *Something about the Author,* (Gale, 1986) Taylor says that he doesn't have a very good imagination. He writes from life experience. He lives in California which is the setting for *Sniper.* He has lived and worked around ocean ports and served in the Merchant Marines and the U.S. Navy. He grew up in North Carolina not far from the swampland in *The Weirdo.* He may use familiar locations for his settings, but his novels prove that he really does have a vivid imagination.

Timothy of the Cay is "more thoughtful than its well-loved antecedent," according to *Publisher's Weekly.* A sequel that picks up after Timothy's death and Phillip's rescue, it shows the boy's recovery and explains the irony of the German attack on such an insignificant-appearing ship. The novel is also a "prequel" that portrays Timothy's life from the age Phillip is now to the old man's boarding of the doomed freighter. In alternating chapters of narration, Taylor explores racism more fully than in *The Cay,* through presenting Timothy's experiences with prejudice and Phillip's attempt to explain his respect for a black man to his bigoted mother.

—Virginia L. Gleason, updated by Elbert R. Hill

TCHUDI, Stephen N.

Pseudonyms: Also writes as Stephen Judy; Stephen N. Judy. **Nationality:** American. **Born:** Waterbury, Connecticut, 31 January 1942. **Education:** Hamilton College, Clinton, New York, B.A. 1963; Northwestern University, Evanston, Illinois, M.A. 1964, Ph.D. 1967. **Family:** Married Susan Jane Schmidt in 1979; three sons and one daughter. **Career:** Assistant professor of English and education, Northwestern University, Evanston, Illinois, 1967-69; assistant professor, 1969-71, associate professor, 1971-76, professor of English, since 1976, and director of the Center for Literacy and Learning, since 1987, Michigan State University, East Lansing, Michigan. Visiting professor, University of British Columbia,

1975, Northeastern University, 1981, 1983, and University of Sydney, 1986; editor of *English Journal,* 1973-80. **Awards:** Eight awards from the Educational Press Association for excellence in educational journalism, for *English Journal*; Charles Carpenter Fries award from the Michigan Council of Teachers of English, 1978, for distinguished service to the profession of English teaching; *The Burg-O-Rama Man* was chosen as a Notable Children's Trade Book in the Field of Social Studies by the National Council for Social Studies and the Children's Book Council, 1985; *Soda Poppery* was selected one of Child Study Association of America's Children's Books of the Year, 1987. **Address:** 3735 Gibraltar Dr., Reno, Nevada 89509-5684, U.S.A.

PUBLICATIONS FOR YOUNG ADULTS

Fiction

The Burg-O-Rama Man. New York, Delacorte, 1984.
The Green Machine and the Frog Crusade. New York, Delacorte, 1987.

Nonfiction

With Susan J. Judy, *Gifts of Writing Creative Projects with Words and Art* (as Stephen Judy). New York, Scribner, 1980.
With Susan J. Judy, *Putting on a Play: A Guide to Writing and Producing Neighborhood Drama* (as Stephen Judy). New York, Scribner, 1982.
With Susan J. Tchudi, *The Young Writer's Handbook: A Practical Guide for the Beginner Who Is Serious about Writing.* New York, Scribner, 1984.
Soda Poppery: The History of Soft Drinks in America. New York, Scribner, 1986.
The Young Learner's Handbook: A Guide to Solving Problems, Mastering Skills, Thinking Creatively. New York, Scribner, 1987.
Lock and Key: The Secret of Locking Things Up, In, and Out. New York, Scribner, 1993.

PUBLICATIONS FOR ADULTS

Nonfiction

With Susan J. Tchudi, *Teaching Writing in the Content Areas: Elementary School.* Washington, D.C., National Education Association, 1983.
With Margie C. Huerta, *Teaching Writing in the Content Areas: Middle School/Junior High.* Washington, D.C., National Education Association, 1983.
With Joanne Yates, *Teaching Writing in the Content Areas: Senior High School.* Washington, D.C., National Education Association Professional Library, 1983.
Probing the Unknown: From Myth to Science. New York, Scribner, 1990.
With Susan J. Tchudi, *The English-Language Arts Handbook: Classroom Strategies for Teachers.* Portsmouth, New Hampshire, 1991.
Planning and Assessing the Curriculum in English Language Arts. Alexandria, Virginia, Association for Supervision and Curriculum Development, 1991.

Other

Editor, *Language, Schooling, and Society*. Portsmouth, New Hampshire, Boynton Cook, 1985.

Editor, *English Teachers at Work: Ideas and Strategies from Five Countries*. Portsmouth, New Hampshire, Boynton Cook, 1986.

Nonfiction as Stephen N. Judy

With others, *The Creative Word*. 6 vols., New York, Random House, 1973-74.

Explorations in the Teaching of Secondary English: A Source Book for Experimental Teaching. Palos Verdes, California, Dodd, 1974.

With James Edwin Miller, *Writing in Reality*. New York, Harper, 1978.

With Susan J. Judy, *The English Teacher's Handbook: Ideas and Resources for Teaching English*. Englewood Cliffs, New Jersey, Winthrop Publishers, 1979.

Editor, *Teaching English: Reflections on the State of the Art*. Rochelle Park, New Jersey, Hayden Book, 1979.

The ABCs of Literacy: A Guide for Parents and Educators. Oxford University Press, New York, 1980.

With Susan J. Judy, *An Introduction to the Teaching of Writing*. New York, Wiley, 1981.

Editor, *Publishing in English Education*. Portsmouth, New Hampshire, Boynton Cook, 1982.

*   *   *

For many teenagers, in fact as well as fiction, the high-school years constitute a wasteland journey. Excessive self-absorption, concern with trivia, uncaring adults, and a fragmented instructional curriculum stultify rather than stimulate the life of the young on their way to adulthood. Stephen Tchudi, obviously not unaware of that bleak scenario, undercuts it by creating characters who have brains, convictions, commitment, and courage as they confront issues that deal with the ecology of the body and the environment.

Karen Wexler in *The Burg-O-Rama Man* is editor of the school newspaper. She is gifted with a keen eye for the praiseworthy and the tawdry. And when a national fast food chain selects Crawford City High School as its source for a new series of TV commercials, that critical faculty gets plenty of exercise. She watches as the silver-tongued company rep, the Burg-O-Rama man, easily gains the enthusiastic cooperation of all, through the allure of fame and money; as the camera man invades the school, and students turn into junk food hucksters; as the school's most respected and principled educator turns out to be merely another opportunist when, for a hefty fee, he accepts a starring role in one of the commercials. When the Burg-O-Rama man finally selects Karen as the star for his last commercial, she refuses and thereby establishes the author's thematic intent.

There's plenty of stuff here for hard-hitting confrontations. But Tchudi tries hard for balance; perhaps too hard. Junk food may be bad for the body, but it's popular and it tastes good. Commercial exploitation of an educational institution may be questionable, but the money is much needed and can be put to good use. Sports fanatics may be bad for the game, but stars still emerge and feel good about their heroics. In that kind of context, Karen's lone act of ethical nonconformity signifies too little.

In *The Green Machine and the Frog Crusade*, Tchudi is less timid. Again the issue focuses on commercial versus personal values. Here the hero is sixteen-year-old David Morgan who becomes an environmental crusade leader when plans for a shopping mall threaten to turn his favorite swampland, with its unique wildlife, into concrete. The courage of his convictions impels him to oppose his father, city hall, and most of the town's leading citizens. With the help of a gadfly lawyer, his best friend, and his impetuous sister who rounds up half the school as coactivists, David is able to achieve a temporary victory. Yes, commercial interests predictably have the last word, but David's commitment has at least inspired the respect of his family, his town, his cute new girlfriend, as well as the reader. The last touch is too sentimental as David and girlfriend Sharon say good-bye to the doomed swamp: "I won't forget you. I'll never forget you." But the author has at least explored and pursued the main issue here in considerable depth.

However, Stephen Tchudi's most important contribution to literature for the young adult may rest not so much in his two novels, but in his nonfiction books that try to inspire the student's quest for knowledge and self-development. *Soda Poppery* not only traces the fascinating history of soft drinks in America but also educates the student through interesting side excursions in history, science, economics, and marketing. Deftly integrated ideas for experiments or further research appeal especially to the scientifically curious. Relevant stories, myths, and legends keep the tone light and the content consistently highly informative. And for readers eager to become do-it-yourselfers, the last section in the book offers them all the instructions they need.

The Young Writer's Handbook, a book cowritten by Susan Tchudi, is intended for the young writer but would serve well writers of any age who are still young in craft but have dreams of becoming accomplished. The title is unfortunate, with its connotations of rhetorical rules and grammar exercises. This book has none of that. Ironically, however, it accomplishes the aim of the typical handbook—the development of a better writer—far more effectively. It does so through an engaging, personal voice that motivates, advises, illustrates, guides, and inspires with a wide range of creative ideas for writing. As such, this book constitutes an ideal individualized program in writing instruction. But it needs updating; written at the dawn of the classroom computer age, the book still assumes the pen-and-paper writer.

The Young Learner's Handbook is less narrowly focused. It aims to reach and stimulate the young questing minds that are curious about much and perhaps in need of some method and guidance in their pursuits. The author introduces questing as a process, then goes on to discuss the art of questioning, the importance of data gathering, and the various information sources such as print, media, people, and places. An excellent guide to library literacy serves as an invaluable aid to the research-minded. Among the most important chapters are the last two in which young questers are challenged to apply and share what they learn through such activities as science fair projects, contests, exhibits, and videos. Again, a real strength of this handbook is the plethora of imaginative suggestions that are sure to incite the interest of readers. And now ComputerQuest sections are included as well for the computerphile.

Stephen Tchudi's pervasive aim in both his fiction and nonfiction is clearly to educate the middle and high-school age student. He does so in a personable voice that respects the student's intelligence and capacity for mature action. His fiction, so far, suffers at times from too heavy a theme or message orientation. The young reader would be served better by a spicier writing style that exudes more of the liveliness and excitement the author tries to engender in his audience. But it is refreshing to have a writer who can write entertainingly and offer a substantive learning experience.

—Henry J. Baron

TEMPLE, Frances (Nolting)

Nationality: American. **Born:** Washington, D.C., 15 August 1945. **Education:** Attended Wellesley College, 1963-1965; University of North Carolina, 1968-69, B.A. in English and African Studies 1969; University of Virginia, M.A. in Education 1976. **Family:** Married Charles Temple, 19 July 1969; three daughters. **Career:** Peace Corps volunteer in Sierra Leone, West Africa, 1965-67; VISTA volunteer in health services and low-income housing, central Virginia, 1970-74; taught pottery for children at the Open Door in Victoria, Texas, 1979-81; first and second grade teacher, Children's Hours School, Geneva, New York, 1983-95; professional potter, 1980s; played hammered dulcimer in the folk group "Apples in Winter", from 1983; taught theater classes for children, Magic Lantern Theater, Lyons, New York, 1985-1990; writer of teaching methodologies and author of books for young readers, 1990-95. **Awards:** Jane Addams Children's Book award, Hungry Minds Books of Distinction award, and National Council of Teachers of English recommended book citation, all 1993, all for *Taste of Salt*; American Library Association (ALA) Best Books for Young Adults citation, *School Library Journal* Best Books citation, and Children's Book Council's Notable Book in the Field of Social Studies citation, all 1993, all for *Grab Hands and Run*; ALA Best Books for Young Adults and Top of the List citations, *Booklist*'s Best of the Best Editors' Choice, New York Public Library's 100 Best Books of the Year, all 1994, all for *The Ramsay Scallop*; New York Public Library's 100 Best Books of the Year, 1994, for *Tiger Soup*; America's Award, Consortium of Latin American Studies Programs, 1996, for *Tonight, by Sea.* **Died:** Geneva, New York, 5 July 1995.

PUBLICATIONS FOR YOUNG ADULTS

A Taste of Salt: A Story of Modern Haiti. New York, Orchard Books, 1992.
Grab Hands and Run. New York, Orchard Books, 1993.
The Ramsay Scallop: A Novel. New York, Orchard Books, 1994.
Tonight, by Sea. New York, Orchard Books, 1995.
The Beduin's Gazelle. New York, Orchard Books, 1996.

PUBLICATIONS FOR CHILDREN

Adaptor and illustrator, *Tiger Soup: An Anansi Story from Jamaica* (picture book). New York, Orchard Books, 1994.

PUBLICATIONS FOR ADULTS

With Ruth Nathan et. al., *Classroom Strategies that Work: An Elementary Teacher's Guide to the Writing Process.* Portsmouth, New Hampshire, Heinemann, 1989.
With Ruth Nathan, Charles Temple, and Nancy Burris, *The Beginnings of Writing.* Needham Heights, Massachusetts, 1986; revised edition, 1992.
With Charles Temple and Ruth Nathan, *Writers in the Classroom,* edited by Ruth Nathan. Norwood, Massachusetts, Christopher Gordon, 1992.

Also contributor to *Writers in the Classroom* edited by Ruth Nathan, 1991, and to *Stories and Readers,* edited by Charles Temple and Patrick Collins, 1992.

*

Critical Studies: "Flying Starts" by Shannon Maughan, in *Publisher's Weekly,* 28 December 1992, 27-28; review of *The Ramsay Scallop* by Kathy Broderick, in *Book Links,* November 1994, 17-19; "Researching *The Ramsay Scallop*" by Frances Temple, in *Book Links,* November 1994, 18; entry in *Something about the Author,* Vol. 85, Detroit, Gale, 1995; "The Intelligent, the Witty, the Brave" by Anita Silvey, in *Horn Book,* September/October 1995, 518.

*   *   *

Frances Temple burst upon the world of children's literature with the publication of the much-honored *Taste of Salt: A Story of Modern Haiti* in 1992, followed in rapid succession by *Grab Hands and Run, The Ramsay Scallop,* and a picture book retelling of the Anansi tale *Tiger Soup* in 1994, and *Tonight by Sea,* 1995. Then, in July of 1995, just as many readers were discovering her work for the first time, word came of her untimely death on the day she had mailed the manuscript of her last book, *The Beduin's Gazelle,* to her editor, Richard Jackson, with whom she had a close working relationship. As her daughter Jessica Temple wrote in an obituary posted to the Childlit e-mail listserv on 27 September 1995, "Her books quickly gained attention for her ability to communicate with young people about moral and political questions that matter. They have been translated into Dutch, Danish, French, and German, and have won many awards."

A Taste of Salt is powerful and interesting in both subject and technique. Set in Jean Bertrand Aristide's Haiti in February 1991, the book opens as Djo, one of Aristide's young body guards, severely injured in a bombing and a beating, lies in his hospital bed, telling the story of his life to the beautiful young woman, Jeremie, whom Aristide has sent to interview him. As his gripping story unfolds, the focus shifts back and forth between the past and the present moment in the hospital. Djo's story ends abruptly as he slips into a coma at a crucial and painful moment in the telling, ending Part One of the book. Part Two consists of Jeremie's story, which she writes and then reads aloud to Djo, hoping that perhaps the sound of her voice will bring him back. Although less brutal than Djo's story, hers is equally compelling as she describes her life in the poorest slum in Port-au-Prince (built on-top of a garbage dump), her education by nuns which offers a possible way out of poverty, and her involvement with Aristide. In Part Three Djo regains consciousness and continues his story until the past meets the present. Jeremie and Djo, who have come to love each other, look forward to an uncertain future.

Grab Hands and Run, set in El Salvador and directed at a slightly younger audience, is another story of bravery in the face of oppression, disaster, and death. Jacinto, husband of Paloma and father of Felipe and Romy, is an architect who is also involved in political activities which put him at risk. He has told his family that if anything happens to him they should "Grab hands and run" all the way to Canada, where he will try to join them. Jacinto disappears, and when the family finds a note under the door warning, "Leave and Don't Come Back. If not, YOU die," they do "grab hands and run." In a story of heart-stopping suspense Paloma, Felipe, and Romy cross the border into Guatemala, then travel through Mexico, and finally illegally slip across the border into the United States. They travel in constant terror of being discovered and sent back to El Salvador or even killed.

The Ramsay Scallop was actually the first book that Temple had written, but her third to be published. A wonderfully realized historical novel set in the year 1300, the story manages to combine authentic details and what Temple characterized as the "steadfastly religious" thinking of the time with timeless concerns about tolerance, justice, and how best to live one's life in the world into which one is born. In "Researching *The Ramsay Scallop*," Temple wrote about the process of researching and imagining this story, from "walking cobbled paths and dusty trails of the Pilgrim Way in northern Spain, wading streams, kneeling in small stone chapels" to the "reach of feeling . . . the pilgrim's search for a cosmic compass" and her reading of over seventy books in English, French, medieval French, and Spanish. "Make believe, empathy, study, dreaming. These are what the author brings to a story, and these are also what each reader brings. Together author and reader transcend time to relive a story that we believe happened, 700 years ago."

Temple wrote that she first imagined Elenor, the heroine of *The Ramsay Scallop,* when she was a schoolgirl in France. As the daughter of Frederick Nolting, who was in the foreign service and later Kennedy's ambassador to Vietnam, Frances grew up in rural Virginia and in France and Vietnam. Her husband Charles recalled to contributor Linnea Hendrickson, "She took me to Ste. Chapelle once when we were in college, and described the priests blessing the pilgrims as they started off for Compostela, seven hundred years earlier." According to her husband, many of Temple's stories were gathered from people she talked to in her travels, to whom she listened with "keen intelligence" and "a wonderfully winning appreciation."

The structure of *The Ramsay Scallop* is the archetypal one of a journey, and in the tradition of Chaucer's *Canterbury Tales,* the adventures along the way, and the stories told by the travelers and those they encounter, are as important as the destination.

Teenagers Elenor of Ramsay and Thomas of Thornham, reluctantly betrothed to each other, are sent by the wise Father Gregory to travel as chaste companions on a pilgrimage from their home near Peterborough, England, through France to the shrine of Santiago de Compostela in northern Spain, carrying with them the sins of their village. In the process they experience hardships, adventures, and triumphs as they learn much about the world and about themselves, and eventually come to love each other.

Tonight, by Sea (1995) is set in Haiti in 1993, a hard time when many people were forced to try to escape from their island by boat in order to survive. Through the eyes of young Paulie, who does "the truest and hardest thing she could do," Temple movingly delineates the lives of the impoverished residents of Belle Fleuve, and reveals how warm family and community relationships and even life itself are gradually destroyed through fear, distrust, and the economic inequality imposed by the larger society.

Temple's last book, *The Beduin's Gazelle* (1996), is set in the Arab world of north Africa in the year 1303, and like *The Ramsay Scallop* and all of her books, hints of the storytelling traditions of the culture it portrays as the plot advances through stories told by the characters within the story as well as through the story Temple herself is telling. Etienne, the young French student of the *Ramsay Scallop,* has come to Fez to learn Arabic, originally with a goal of converting the Muslims, an idea he is beginning to question. He becomes fast friends with Atiyah, who loves Halima, but will not be united with her before each endures several Arabian Nights' worth of adventures. *The Beduin's Gazelle* was intended to be the second in a trilogy of books set in the years around 1300, with *The Ramsay Scallop* representing the European heritage, *The Beduin's Gazelle* the Muslim, and a future book to have been set in West Africa "before it was disrupted by the slave trade" to represent the African heritage, Temple told the interviewer in *Something About the Author.*

Temple also wrote and illustrated, with lively, colorful cut- and torn-paper collage, a traditional Jamaican Anansi tale, *Tiger Soup,* which includes, on the underside of the book jacket, the story in the form of a play script that children can perform.

Anita Silvey wrote in her *Horn Book* tribute, "Frances Temple epitomized the finest in new voices in the children's book field. Characterized by intelligence and conviction, her books challenge young readers to understand serious issues—but she never sacrificed characters or action or plot to do so. . . . we mourn not only the death of a unique individual, but also the books that might have been."

—Linnea Hendrickson

THIELE, Colin (Milton)

Nationality: Australian. **Born:** Eudunda, South Australia, 16 November 1920. **Education:** Adelaide Teachers College, South Australia, 1937-38; University of Adelaide, B.A. 1941, Dip.Ed. 1947, Dip.T. **Military Service:** Served in the Royal Australian Air Force, 1942-45. **Family:** Married Rhonda Gill in 1945; two daughters. **Career:** Teacher, Port Lincoln High School, South Australia, 1946-55, and Brighton High School, 1956; Lecturer, 1957-62, Senior Lecturer in English, 1962-63, Vice Principal, 1964, and Principal, 1965-72, Wattle Park Teachers College, Adelaide; Director, Murray Park College of Advanced Education, 1973; Principal, Wattle Park Teachers Centre, 1973-81. Formerly national book reviewer, Australian Broadcasting Commission; Commonwealth Literary Fund Lecturer in Australian Literature. Member, 1964-68, and since 1969 fellow, Australian College of Education; since 1967 council member, and president, 1987-89, Australian Society of Authors. **Awards:** W.J. Miles Memorial prize, for poetry, 1944; Commonwealth Jubilee prize, for radio play, 1951; South Australian winner, World Short Story Quest, 1952; Fulbright scholarship, 1959; Grace Leven prize, for poetry, 1961; Commonwealth Literary Fund fellowship, 1967; Hans Anderson award, 1972; Visual Arts Board award, 1972; Children's Literature prize (Austria), 1979, 1986; Australian Children's Book Council Book of the Year award, 1982; Silver Pencil award (Netherlands), 1986. Companion, Order of Australia, 1977. **Address:** Endeavour Lane, King Scrub, via Dayboro, Queensland 4521, Australia.

PUBLICATIONS FOR YOUNG ADULTS

Fiction

The Sun on the Stubble. Adelaide, Rigby, 1961; London, White Lion, 1974.

Storm Boy, illustrated by John Baily. Adelaide, Rigby, 1963; London, Angus & Robertson, 1964; Chicago, Rand McNally, 1966.

February Dragon. Adelaide, Rigby, 1965; London, Angus & Robertson, 1966; New York, Harper, 1976.

The Rim of the Morning: Six Stories. Adelaide, Rigby, 1966; as *Storm Boy and Other Stories,* 1986.

Blue Fin, illustrated by Roger Haldane. Adelaide, Rigby, 1969; New York, Harper, 1974; London, Collins, 1976.

Yellow-Jacket Jock, illustrated by Clifton Pugh. Melbourne, Cheshire, 1969.

Flash Flood, illustrated by Jean Elder. Adelaide, Rigby, 1970.

The Fire in the Stone. Adelaide, Rigby, 1973; New York, Harper, 1974; London, Penguin, 1981.

Albatross Two. Adelaide, Rigby, 1974; London, Collins, 1975; as *Fight against Albatross Two,* New York, Harper, 1976.

Magpie Island, illustrated by Roger Haldane. Adelaide, Rigby, 1974; London, Collins, 1975.

Uncle Gustav's Ghosts. Adelaide, Rigby, 1974.

The Hammerhead Light. Adelaide, Rigby, 1976; New York, Harper, 1977.

The Shadow on the Hills. Adelaide, Rigby, 1977; New York, Harper, 1978.

Chadwick's Chimney, illustrated by Robert Ingpen. Sydney, Methuen, 1979; London, Methuen, 1980.

River Murray Mary, illustrated by Robert Ingpen. Adelaide, Rigby, 1979.

The Best of Colin Thiele. Adelaide, Rigby, 1980.

Thiele Tales. Melbourne, Rigby, 1980.

The Valley Between. Adelaide, Rigby, 1981.

Patch Comes Home. Melbourne, Rigby, 1982.

The Undercover Secret. Adelaide, Rigby, 1982.

Pitch the Pony. Melbourne, Rigby, 1984.

Potch Goes down the Drain. Melbourne, Rigby, 1984.

Coorong Captive. Melbourne, Rigby, 1985.

Seashores and Shadows. Montville, Queensland, Walter McVitty, 1985; as *Shadow Shark,* New York, Harper, 1988; as *Sharks in the Shadows,* London, Dent, 1988.

Skipton's Landing; and River Murray Mary, illustrated by Robert Ingpen. Adelaide, Rigby, 1986.

Shatterbelt. Montville, Queensland, Walter McVitty, 1987.

Jodie's Journey. Montville, Queensland, Walter McVitty, 1988.

Klontarf. Melbourne, Rigby, 1988.

Stories Short and Tall. Melbourne, Rigby, 1988.

The Ab-Diver. Melbourne, Horwitz, Grahame, 1988.

Aftershock. Montville, Queensland, Walter McVitty, 1992.

Martin's Mountain. Adelaide, Lutheran Publishing House, 1993.

Gemma's Christmas Eve. Adelaide, Openbook Publishers, 1994.

High Valley. Montville, Queensland, Walter McVitty, 1994.

Other

The State of Our State. Adelaide, Rigby, 1952.

Editor, *Looking at Poetry.* London, Longman, 1960.

Editor, with Greg Branson, *One-Act Plays for Secondary Schools.* Adelaide, Rigby, 3 Vols., 1962-64; revised edition, as *Setting the Stage and The Living Stage,* 2 vols., 1969-70.

Editor, with Greg Branson, *Beginners, Please.* Adelaide, Rigby, 1964.

Editor, with Greg Branson, *Plays for Young Players.* Adelaide, Rigby, 1970.

PUBLICATIONS FOR CHILDREN

Fiction

Mrs. Munch and Puffing Billy, illustrated by Nyorie Bungey. Adelaide, Rigby, 1967.

Flip-Flop and the Tiger Snake, illustrated by Jean Elder. Adelaide, Rigby, 1970.

The Skunks, illustrated by Mary Milton. Adelaide, Rigby, 1977.

Ballander Boy, photographs by David Simpson. Adelaide, Rigby, 1979.

Tanya and Trixie, photographs by David Simpson. Adelaide, Rigby, 1980.

Little Tom Little, photographs by David Simpson. Adelaide, Rigby, 1981.

Pinquo, illustrated by Mary Milton. Melbourne, Rigby, 1983.

Farmer Schulz's Ducks. Montville, Queensland, Walter McVitty, 1986; New York, Harper, 1988.

Danny's Egg. London, Angus and Robinson, 1989; as *Rotten Egg Paterson to the Rescue,* illustrated by Karen Ritz. New York, Harper, 1991.

Emma Keppler. Montville, Queensland, Walter McVitty, 1991.

Speedy. Norwood, South Australia, Omnibus Books, 1991.

The Australian Mother Goose, illustrated by Wendy DePaauw. North Sydney, Weldon Kids, 1992.

The Australian ABC, illustrated by Wend DePaauw. North sydney, Weldon Kids, 1992.

Charlie Vet's Pet, illustrated by Michael Wright. south Melbourne, MacMillan Australia, 1992.

Timmy. Montville, Queensland, Walter McVitty, 1993.

The March of Mother Duck. Montville, Queensland, Walter McVitty, 1993.

Brahminy. Montville, Queensland, Walter McVitty, 1995.

Poetry

Gloop the Gloomy Bunyip, illustrated by John Baily. Brisbane, Jacaranda Press, 1962; revised version, in *Gloop the Bunyip,* 1970.

Gloop the Bunyip, illustrated by Helen Sallis. Adelaide, Rigby, 1970.

Songs for My Thongs, illustrated by Sandy Burrows. Adelaide, Rigby, 1982.

Poems in My Luggage. Norwood, South Australia, Omnibus Books, 1989.

Reckless Rhymes. Montville, Queensland, Walter McVitty, 1994.

With Max Fatchen and Craig Smith, *Tea for Three.* Adelaide, Moondrake, 1994.

PUBLICATIONS FOR ADULTS

Novels

Labourers in the Vineyard. Adelaide, Rigby, and London, Hale, 1970.
The Seed's Inheritance. Adelaide, Lutheran Publishing, 1986.

Plays

Burke and Wills (broadcast 1949). Included in *Selected Verse (1940-1970),* 1970.

Radio Plays: *Burke and Wills,* 1949; *Edge of Ice,* 1951; *The Shark Fishers,* 1953; *Edward John Eyre,* 1962.

Poetry

Progress to Denial. Adelaide, Jindyworobak, 1945.
Splinters and Shards. Adelaide, Jindyworobak, 1945.
The Golden Lightning. Adelaide, Jindyworobak, 1951.
Man in a Landscape. Adelaide, Rigby, 1960.
In Charcoal and Conte. Adelaide, Rigby, 1966.
Selected Verse (1940-1970). Adelaide, Rigby, 1970.

Other

Editor, *Jindyworobak Anthology.* Adelaide, Jindyworobak, 1953.
Editor, with Ian Mudie, *Australian Poets Speak.* Adelaide, Rigby, 1961.
Editor, *Favourite Australian Stories.* Adelaide, Rigby, 1963.
Editor, *Handbook to Favourite Australian Stories.* Adelaide, Rigby, 1964.
Barossa Valley Sketchbook. Adelaide, Rigby, 1968.
Heysen of Hahndorf (biography). Adelaide, Rigby, 1968, revised edition, 1974.
Coorong, photographs by Mike McKelvey. Adelaide, Rigby, and London, Hale, 1972.
Range without Man: The North Flinders, photographs by Mike McKelvey. Adelaide, Rigby, 1974.
Grains of Mustard Seed (on state education). Adelaide, South Australia Education Department, 1975.
The Little Desert, photographs by Jocclyn Burt. Adelaide, Rigby, 1975.
The Bight. Adelaide, Rigby, 1976.
Heysen's Early Hahndorf. Adelaide, Rigby, 1976.
Lincoln's Place, illustrated by Robert Ingpen. Adelaide, Rigby, 1978.
Maneater Man: The Story of Alf Dean, The World's Greatest Shark Hunter. Adelaide, Rigby, 1979.
The Adelaide Story. Nambour, Peacock, 1982.
Writing for Children: A Personal View (lecture). Dromkeen, Victoria, Oldmeadow, 1983.
Coorong, illustrated by Barbara Leslie. Adelaide, Wakefield Press, 1986.
Something to Crow About, illustrated by Rex Milstead. Adelaide, Commonwealth, 1986.
South Australia Revisited. Adelaide, Rigby, 1986.
A Welcome to Water. Adelaide, Wakefield Press, 1986.
Ranger's Territory: The Story of Frank Woerle. Sydney, Angus & Robertson, 1987.

*

Media Adaptations: *Storm Boy* (feature film), screenplay by Sonia Borg, South Australian Film Corporation, 1976; *Blue Fin* (feature film), South Australian Film Corporation, 1978; *The Fire in the Stone* (television film), screenplay by Graeme Koestveld, South Australian Film Corporation, 1983; *Danny's Egg* (television film), Channel Nine (Sydney), 1987; *The Water Trolley* (television film, adapted from the short story by the same name in *The Rim of the Morning),* Channel Nine, (Sydney), 1989; *The Sun on the Stubble, The Valley Between,* and *Uncle Gustav's Ghost* (television mini-series), Film Australia (ABC) and German producer Zweites Deutsches Fernsehen consortium, 1996.

Critical Studies: Entry in *Contemporary Literary Criticism,* Volume 17, Detroit, Gale, 1981; *Contemporary Authors, New Revision Series,* Volume 53, Detroit, Gale, 1997, pp. 463-466; *Children's Literature Review,* Volume 27, Detroit, Gale, 1992, pp. 192-212; *Something About the Author Autobiography Series,* Volume 2, Detroit, Gale, 1986, pp. 251-270; *Contemporary Literary Criticism,* Volume 17, Detroit, Gale, 1981, pp. 493-96; ''Colin Thiele: University in the Heart of Man'' by Walter McVitty, in *Innocence and Experience: Essays on Contemporary Australian Children's Writers,* South Melbourne, Thomas Nelson, 1981, pp. 197-232.

Colin Thiele comments:

Why do I write? The simple answer is that I can't help it. It's a kind of compulsion. I think most authors will say something like that.

More fundamentally, I like to explore human existence, past and present, and to search for meaning in the act of living. I like to wrestle with language and try to catch in words the fine nuances of human experience, even though it's usually an attempt to 'catch the uncatchable'. I'm interested in the value of solitude, and the importance of the natural environment, in morality and strength of character, and in the joy, sadness, hope, and despair of the world.

I'm not saying that I can achieve these aims, but I enjoy trying.

*   *   *

Colin Thiele is one of Australia's most admired writers, best known for the classic tale *Storm Boy* and another story of the sea, *Blue Fin.* Although very much a regional writer representing aspects of his home state South Australia in almost all his books, numerous translations point to his considerable international appeal. Many of his books such as *February Dragon, Chadwick's Chimney, Albatross Two, Coorong Captive,* and *Seashores and Shadows* feature breathtaking adventures but also reflect a love of, and concern for, the natural world. Adventure and slapstick humour are undoubtedly part of his appeal to readers the world over, but the special strength of Thiele's writing is its strong emotional core that recognises the joy and tragedy of ordinary lives. Thiele has written in Walter McVitty's *Authors and Illustrators of Australian Children's Books,* ''. . .My observation that the world and the people in it could be happy and sad, cruel and kindly, stupid and wise, all at the same time, and my belief that our daily experiences often educated us more profoundly than formal lessons. . .all these and more were part of the general background which I carried forward into my writing.''

Two major settings for his novels are the countryside—particularly the Barossa Valley, a general farming and wine making area settled by German immigrants north of Adelaide where Thiele was born and spent his youth—and the sea, based especially on his experiences as a teacher in the Eyre Peninsula region of South Australia. One of the ''Barossa'' novels, *The Valley Between* was Australian Book of the Year for 1982, the top award after earlier works achieved numerous commended listings. This is the fourth book set in the German community of a fictional town Gonunda. All the incidents involve a thirteen-year-old boy, Benno, who attracts trouble like sheep attract flies. The dramatic focus is on an ongoing feud between Jack Ryan, an easy going Irish farmer, and malicious Adolf Heinz who displays the worst characteristics of the dour Germans. The first in the series is *The Sun on the Stubble,* a humourous tale of an adolescent boy, Bruno Gunther, growing up in the Barossa Valley in the 1920s, and the pain he feels at leaving the farm when it is time to go to Adelaide to school. *The Sun on the Stubble* was initially published for a general readership with Thiele dedicating the book ''To the boys who were boys with me.'' Indeed the Barossa novels are still read with equal enjoyment by adults and children, not least of all the hilarious *Uncle Gustav's Ghosts,* where the hapless Uncle Gustav is plagued with ''Unseen Presences.'' The tin-kettling episode, a noisy and drunken ceremony that welcomes newlyweds to their new home, is one of the funniest in Australian literature.

There are boyish high jinks too in *The Shadow on the Hills* recounting the life of Bodo Schneider from birth to leaving school at Gonunda. Prominent is the special relationship between Bodo and old Ebenezer Blitz, a hermit who preaches from the hills each day accompanied by his dog Elijah. But as the sombre title suggests there are darker things. Ebenezer has supposedly been driven to madness by storekeeper Moses Mibus, whose greedy ways also bring financial ruin to Bodo's parents and other farmers. Eventually Moses is caught due to Bodo's testimony, but telling the truth brings unhappy consequences for Bodo and many changes, not least being the end of his childhood. But in Thiele's writing, change, however painful, brings hope of new beginnings. The title lines of the short story collection, *The Rim of the Morning,* reflects this conviction, ''The Boy and the Man went up the hill of the world together. But the Man grew old and stayed behind to rest. Then the Boy went on until he reached the rim of the morning, and there, in magic and pain and wonder, he looked out alone. . . .'' Bodo too is ''a dark figure silhouetted on the rim of the world'' and as unhappy Bruno of *The Sun on the Stubble* is being driven away to school, ''The car topped the rise and seemed to pause before moving down the other side.'' Similarly change, and a special relationship between young and old is the subject of the emotional story *The Hammerhead Light.*

Thiele's *Storm Boy,* first published as a short story in *The Rim of the Morning,* is a moving portrayal of a boy's transition from childhood to adulthood. Storm Boy and his father Hide-Away Tom live in a hut in the seashore wilderness known as the Coorong in South Australia. Their only friend is another solitary man, the Aboriginal Fingerbone Bill. Storm Boy loves his life by the sea and revels in its changing phases. One day he finds three orphaned pelicans and raises them. Mr. Percival is his special friend until the bird is cruelly killed by shooters, and the special happiness of Storm Boy's solitary life is altered forever. This story has been particularly popular since the 1976 film version. Also made into successful films are *Blue Fin* and *The Fire in the Stone,* both featuring boys with unsatisfactory fathers. Snook, in *Blue Fin,*

proves himself a hero after a series of adventures, but for Ernie Ryan in *The Fire in the Stone* life on the opal fields is harsh and eventually tragic.

Most of Thiele's books feature boys, but more recent novels have major girl characters. Emma in *Emma Keppler,* the fifth Barossa novel, decides to stand up for herself at a time when woman were meant to ''hold their tongues.'' She is a clever girl and her teacher wants her to go to high school, but her father thinks this is a joke. Like *Storm Boy, River Murray Mary* is an illustrated book that has much appeal for adolescents although the format might suggest a younger readership. These are delightful stories about the life of a resourceful young girl, Mary, whose father has a small farm on the banks of the Murray River. Two adventures also featuring resourceful heroines, *Jodie's Journey* and *Shatterbelt,* are set in the Adelaide Hills and are about real disasters in that part of Australia, bushfire and earthquakes. Jodie is a happy twelve-year-old girl but life changes dramatically for her when she is diagnosed as arthritic. This novel gives details of her treatment and also tells of a dramatic incident when Jodie and her horse are almost killed in the 1983 Ash Wednesday fires. In *Shatterbelt* Tracy starts to have dreams that forewarn her of disasters. Nobody believes her so she has to save the people of the Adelaide Hills from a mine collapse single-handedly. She has forebodings of an earthquake. The resolution of this exciting story is that the girl everyone, including her mother, thought peculiar gains the community's respect. A sequel, *Aftershock,* answers some questions left open in *Shatterbelt.*

Representative Thiele works written in the 1990s continued to reflect such characteristic themes as the increasingly threatening environment for nature's creatures—including man, and the phenomenon of young people discovering themselves and their self-worth by confronting the forces of nature, often becoming attached to endangered wild animals and gaining experience allowing them to arrive at a greater awareness of reality. *Timmy* concerns an orphan boy who takes into his care a baby hare. The author movingly parallels the development of the wild rabbit's assisted survival with the boy's own growth in self-assurance. *Brahminy* is an entertaining story of a boy in a remote Australian outback town who befriend and trains an abandoned eagle chick. Often Thiele's tales are played against the backdrop of a nature-threatening environment. *The March of Mother Duck* is the true account of a resourceful duck who raises her duckling brood in an ornamental pool outside an Australian city police station. Finding her present urban location intolerable, she gains the protection of the police as she marches her brood through the busy city to a hospitable lake in the park. Particularly appealing to young readers, the novel is both humorous and handsomely illustrated. In *High Valley,* an eleven-year-old boy and other people are devastated by the environmental changes caused by the building of a dam in a remote Australian farming community and are forced to abandon their property and move on. Most sadly accept the inevitable, and the few who do not create tragedy. Thiele compassionately and skillfully explores the issue of how people react to a heartbreaking situation, and how government faces a dilemma in providing adequate water supplies for the many at the expense of the suffering few.

Thiele's clarity and vigor as a skillful storyteller for the young has not diminished. His work continues to reflect a belief in the human spirit and in the peaceable coexistence of people and nature.

—Kerry White, updated by Christian H. Moe

THOMAS, Joyce Carol

Nationality: American. **Born:** Ponca City, Oklahoma, 25 May 1938. **Education:** San Francisco City College, California, 1957-58, and University of San Francisco, 1957-58; College of San Mateo, A.A. 1964; San Jose State College (now University), B.A. 1966; Stanford University, M.A. 1967. **Family:** Married 1) Gettis L. Withers, 31 May 1959 (divorced, 1968); 2) Roy T. Thomas, Jr., 7 September 1968 (divorced, 1979); one daughter and three sons. **Career:** Telephone operator, San Francisco, California, 1957-58; teacher of French and Spanish, Ravenwood School District, East Palo Alto, California, 1968-70; assistant professor of black studies, San Jose State College (now University), California, 1969-72; lecturer, English department, Contra Costa College, San Pablo, California, 1973-75; part-time lecturer of English, 1975-77, St. Mary's College, Moranga, California; reading program director, 1979-82, and associate professor of English, 1989-92, San Jose State University, San Jose; associate professor of English, School of Education, Pacific Islands Program, San Jose State University, summers 1982, 1983; since 1982, full-time writer; visiting associate professor of English at Purdue University, winter 1984; associate professor of English, 1989-92, full professor, 1992-95, University of Tennessee. Member of Berkeley Civic Arts Commission. **Awards:** Danforth Graduate Fellow, University of California at Berkeley, 1973-75; Stanford University scholar, 1979-80, and Djerassi Fellow, 1982 and 1983; *New York Times* outstanding book of the year citation, American Library Association (ALA) best book citation, and Before Columbus American Book Award, Before Columbus Foundation (Berkeley, California), all 1982, and the American Book Award for children's fiction (National Book Award), Association of American Publishers, 1983, all for *Marked by Fire*; Coretta Scott King Award, ALA, 1984, for *Bright Shadow*; named Outstanding Woman of the Twentieth Century, Sigma Gamma Rho, 1986; National Conference of Christians and Jews recommended title, 1991, for *A Gathering of Flowers*; Coretta Scott King Award, and Notable Children's Trade Book in the Field of Social Studies, National Council for Social Studies and Children's Book Council, and Notable Children's Book, National Council of Teachers of English, all 1994, all for *Brown Honey in Broomwheat Tea*; Poet Laureate for Life, University of Oklahoma Center for Poets and Writers, 1996. **Agent:** Mitch Douglas, International Creative Management, 40 West 57th St., New York, New York 10019, U.S.A.

PUBLICATIONS FOR YOUNG ADULTS

Novels

Marked by Fire. New York, Avon, 1982.
Bright Shadow (sequel to *Marked by Fire*). New York, Avon, 1983.
Water Girl. New York, Avon, 1986.
The Golden Pasture. New York, Scholastic, 1986.
Journey. New York, Scholastic, 1988.
When the Nightingale Sings. New York, HarperCollins, 1992.

Poetry

Bittersweet. San Jose, Firesign Press, 1973.
Crystal Breezes. San Jose, Firesign Press, 1974.
Blessing. Berkeley, Jocato Press, 1975.

Black Child, illustrated by Tom Feelings. Zamani Productions, 1981.
Inside the Rainbow. Zikawana Press, 1982.
Brown Honey in Broomwheat Tea, illustrated by Floyd Cooper. New York, HarperCollins, 1993.
Gingerbread Days, illustrated by Floyd Cooper. New York, HarperCollins, 1995.
The Blacker the Berry: Poems, illustrated by Brenda Joysmith. New York, HarperCollins, 1997.
Crowning Glory: Poems, illustrated by Brenda Joysmith. New York, HarperCollins, 1997.
I Have Heard of a Land, illustrated by Floyd Cooper. New York, HarperCollins, 1997.
Cherish Me, illustrated by Nneka Bennett. New York, HarperCollins, 1998.
You Are My Perfect Baby, illustrated by Nneka Bennett. New York, HarperCollins, 1998.

Plays

And producer, *A Song in the Sky* (two-act; produced San Francisco, 1976).
Look! What a Wonder! (two-act; produced Berkeley, 1976).
And producer, *Magnolia* (two-act; produced San Francisco, 1977).
And producer, *Ambrosia* (two-act; produced San Francisco, 1978).
Gospel Roots (two-act; produced Carson, California, 1981).
I Have Heard of a Land (produced Oklahoma City, Oklahoma, 1989).
When the Nightingale Sings (produced Knoxville, Tennessee, 1991).

Other

Editor, *A Gathering of Flowers: Stories about Being Young in America.* New York, HarperCollins, 1990.

*

Biography: *Dictionary of Literary Biography,* Vol. 33: *Afro-American Fiction Writers after 1955,* Detroit, Gale, 1984; essay in *Speaking for Ourselves: Autobiographical Sketches by Notable Authors of Books for Young Adults,* Vol. 1, compiled and edited by Donald R. Gallo, National Council of Teachers of English, 1990; interview in *Talks with America's Writing Women,* edited by Pearlman and Henderson, Kentucky, University of Kentucky Press, 1990; entry in *Something About the Author,* Vol. 78, Detroit, Gale, 1994; entry in *Authors and Artists for Young Adults,* Vol. 12, Detroit, Gale, 1994; "Evoking the Holy and the Horrible: Conversations with Joyce Carol Thomas," in *African American Review,* winter 1997.

Critical Studies: Entry in *Contemporary Literary Criticism,* Vol. 35, Detroit, Gale, 1985; entry in *Children's Literature Review,* Vol. 19, Detroit, Gale, 1990.

Joyce Carol Thomas comments:

As you already know, books can be wonderful places to visit. And there are many ways to visit books. In classrooms, in libraries, in bookstores, and now on the Web.

For me, writing is a wonderful adventure. On my writing journeys I meet characters who speak with colorful language. I hear rhythms that make me laugh. I feel a young girl's hope, a young boy's mischief, and a teenager's despair.

Reading, too, can be a splendid adventure. I hope my books will sometimes make you bounce with laughter, will often make you stop and think, and will open up many new pathways to joy.

*   *   *

Joyce Carol Thomas knows stories; she heard them from her mother, her aunts, and from the women of Ponca City, Oklahoma, where she lived until she was ten. She knows stories from the African American culture and from her own imagination. She has listened and recorded. Her novels are infused with the rich folklore of her people. She has written since she was a young girl, starting with poetry and eventually plays.

In 1982 Thomas wrote her first novel, and it won the American Book Award. *Marked by Fire* begins in 1951 with Patience Jackson working in the cotton fields of Oklahoma where she gives birth to Abyssinia. The child is marked by fire and water: the water for birthing and baptism and the fire which causes an ember to burst from a blaze and places a mark on her cheek. The child has many gifts: a keen and curious mind, the gift of singing, and the ability to tell stories, to love and care for others, and to solve problems. Abyssinia becomes an important member of her community. But life is not easy, and though a myriad of events scar Abyssinia emotionally, she learns how to heal.

Thomas's book *Journey* is a horror story in which Meggie Alexander discovers a horrible series of crimes and their perpetrator. This intriguing story begins when Meggie is a baby giggling in her crib while watching a tarantula above her head. As a result, she begins a kind of kinship with spiders, a unique relationship that works well for her when her life is later in danger.

A "Cinderella" story, *When the Nightingale Sings,* is about Marigold, who was found in a swamp and raised to do all of the work by a woman named Ruby and her twin daughters. Marigold has the gift of song, but she doesn't believe in her talent until she is discovered while attending the Great Gospel Convention.

Thomas's use of the language is exquisite; this craftsmanship provides words that are of music, voice, and song. Her characters are often musical, and the church—the gospel music, rhythm, movement, and harmony—provides not only a backdrop, but a language that expresses the spirit of the community. Proverbs, folk wisdom, scripture, and prophecy are liberally scattered among the voices of the characters.

In *Bright Shadow,* the sequel to *Marked by Fire,* Abyssinia is going to college and has fallen in love with Carl Lee Jefferson. Her father is not happy to see his daughter's love interest, and he discourages the relationship. In this story as in *Marked by Fire,* there is tragedy, brutality, and pain, but Abyssinia is once again able to see beauty, hope, and courage. The title suggests numerous symbols and images: the dark and light of human experience, the difficulty of knowing and seeing clearly, and, specifically, "Bright Shadow" is used to describe Carl Lee's mother, a Cherokee Indian, who spent her life in the woods and the shadows watching over her child from a distance. In *The Golden Pasture,* Thomas goes back to when Carl Lee was thirteen and spent most of his summers with his grandfather. He finds a beautiful horse and through the challenge of breaking him in, establishes a new relationship with his father.

California is the common setting for *Water Girl* and *Journey* although these two novels are quite different. *Water Girl* is a story of quest and self-discovery for Amber Wetbrook who is seeking to understand her place in a society that has allowed inhumanity such as the slave trade. Not only does the setting matter, but the physical elements also impact the fate of Thomas's characters. These elements shape and define events and sometimes destiny. Wind, rain, fire, hurricane, or tornado have the power to direct and change lives and sometimes they provide Thomas with metaphors for human emotions, behaviors, and experiences. The swamp, the fields, hills, flowers, heat and cold, insects, rocks, quicksand, grasses, all have color, texture, life and they frame the days of the characters.

Thomas has also edited *A Gathering of Flowers,* which features eleven stories representing different cultures in America. Her contribution is "Young Reverend Zelma Lee Moses," a short story about a gospel preacher and singer in a rural Oklahoma church. It pulsates with rhythm and energy, and the reader can almost feel the electricity and the swaying energy as Zelma attempts to fly.

Some of her characters reach for impossible notes and make them happen. Others reach for something else: a flight of the soul, a finding of the spirit, a knowing and understanding. They don't have money or the opportunity to go on a quest, so they look within. Their invisible flight is inside the human heart and soul wherein they reach incredible heights.

—Caroline S. McKinney

THOMAS, Rob

Has also written as Everett Owens. **Nationality:** American. **Born:** Sunnyside, Washington, 15 August 1965. **Education:** Attended Texas Christian University, Fort Worth, 1983; University of Texas, Austin, B.A. and teaching certificate 1987. **Career:** Journalism teacher, Reagan High School, Austin, Texas, 1991-93; advisor, University of Texas student magazine *UTmost,* 1991; administrative position, Channel One, Los Angeles television network for teenagers, 1993-1994; bass player for rock bands Hey Zeus and Public Bulletin; writer of screenplays for film projects and television show, "Dawson's Creek." **Awards:** Austin Writer's League Violet Crown Award for best fiction, 1996; American Library Association (ALA) Best Book for Young Adults, ALA Quick Pick for Reluctant Young Adult Readers, YALSA Top Ten Best Book, *School Library Journal* Best Book of the Year, and New York Public Library Book for the Teen Age, 1996-1997, all for *Rats Saw God*; ALA Quick Pick and Best Book, for *Doing Time*. **Address:** 1636 Courtney Ave., Los Angeles, California 90046-2708, U.S.A. **Website:** http://www.mediacomp.com/robt.

PUBLICATIONS FOR YOUNG ADULTS

Rats Saw God. New York, Simon & Schuster, 1996.
Doing Time: Notes from the Undergrad. New York, Simon & Schuster, 1997.
Slave Day. New York, Simon & Schuster, 1997.
Satellite Down. New York, Simon & Schuster, 1998.

Other

Author of lyrics for CDs *Call Your Mom* for band Hey Zeus, 1989, *Swimming Lessons* for Hey Zeus, 1991, and *Screen Door Kind,* Black Irish, 1993; ''Explode,'' episode of television show *Space Ghost: Coast To Coast,* February 1996; ''Cupid'' television series, ABC, forthcoming.

*

Critical Studies: ''Beginnings: New Voices, New Approaches'' by Teri S. Lesesne, in *Emergency Librarian* (Winnipeg), September/October 1997, 56-57; ''The New Classics of Young Adult Fiction'' by Laura Backes, in *Children's Book Insider* (Fairplay, Colorado), September 1997, 4-5; ''Rats Saw Rob: An Interview with Rob Thomas'' by Joel Shoemaker, in *Voice of Youth Advocates* (Washington, D.C.), 20 June 1997, 88-91; ''Teen Idol'' by Jason Cohen, in *Texas Monthly* (Austin), April 1997, 24.

*   *   *

Rob Thomas gives voice to jaded, cynical Generation X teenagers as they discover truths and become freed of psychological and social preconceptions. Protagonists survive in a high school culture tinged by drugs, sex, and profanity, and Thomas accurately captures the adolescent language they utter and philosophies they follow. His fiction contains popular culture references to such late twentieth-century figures as Yoda from ''Star Wars'' and Laura Ashley clothes, and Thomas incorporates technology, such as the internet and e-mail, to deliver dialogue and advance the plot, which at some time will date his work, but his themes will remain timelessly familiar to young adults. His characterization of alienated protagonists, functioning on the periphery of the adult and teenage spheres, have resulted in Thomas's works being compared to J.D. Salinger's *Catcher in the Rye.* As outsiders, his teens question societal values embraced by the mainstream, noting hypocrisy. They resent interference and desire autonomy. They seem subversive and self-defeating yet sometimes comical, expressing self-deprecating, adolescent humor, as they discover their identities through forced interactions with others. Thomas presents extremes of adolescent life, and his characters often seek escapism and rebellion to attempt conflict resolution.

Thomas's main characters are males who are striving to develop an identity while coping with the mass culture of high school. Often insecure and depressed, these protagonists are usually gifted in some way, whether creatively or intellectually. They deal with the subtle cruelties of narcissistic classmates and face issues common to teenagers. Most come from affluent communities and have attained a degree of sophistication but lack the power, status, and privileges of their peers. They indulge in high school rituals that many Americans consider a passage into adulthood, including the prom, spring break, and drinking games. Adults, for the most part, are absent, generally acting as irritants or mentors. And the protagonists encounter problems in experiencing adult emotions without sufficient knowledge or support to deal with them.

In Thomas's first novel, *Rats Saw God,* Steven York is a misunderstood underachiever. Through an autobiographical account he prepares to make up an English credit, he analyzes his high school years and reconciles with himself. The son of an Apollo astronaut, Steve is an articulate, intelligent student but unambitious. He angrily blames his father for his parents' divorce and communicates with him through notes taped on the refrigerator. Steve begins his text in California, where he has moved to live with his mother and sister. His drug addiction seems incongruent with him being named a National Merit finalist, and the school counselor, Jeff DeMouy, guides Steve's self analysis. This story within the story, framing the past in the present, is interwoven in the narrative and printed in bolder type to symbolize Steve remembering and admitting his rage at his father, friends, and himself.

Steve describes his life in a rich Houston suburb, including his first love with Dub (short for the ''W'' in Wanda) Varner, which is the catalyst for his traumatic transformation. With his best friend, Doug, Steve establishes the Grace Order of Dadaists so that Doug will have his photograph in the club section of the Grace High School yearbook to win a bet with his parents. Steve, a non-joiner, accepts the dadaists because they do not have to justify their actions or explain themselves (like he is later forced to do in his narrative). The group encourages Steve's apathy, aloofness, and attempt to be an anonymous nonconformist.

Steve's only goal seems to be to alienate his American hero father who is perfectionistic, rigid, controlling, and demands discipline. Steve resents his father's militaristic attitudes and wants to escape from his father's attempts to relive his youth through Steve. When asked to describe himself with one word in his creative writing class, Steve chooses ''Cynic.'' The class enables him to split away from his father because when he wins an essay contest he is identified simply as Steve York, not as the astronaut's son. He feels betrayed when he discovers that Dub and his mentor, the school's writing teacher Mr. Waters, known as Sky, have been having an affair, and Steve retreats from the infidelity to California where he numbs himself with drugs.

The dichotomy of his two identities as a National Merit finalist and drug user forces Steve to reevaluate his absolute opinions. Through his friendship with another gifted but tragic student, Allison Kimble, and an awareness of the truth behind his parents' relationship, Steve recognizes his creative potential and plans for the future and reconciliation with his father. He abandons his self loathing to realize that he lacks control over many facets of humanity and should be more flexible in his attitudes toward others. His metamorphosis into a mature, rational being seems almost too predictable, but like the swan in a picture his sister gives him, Steve is no longer an ugly duckling and has persevered to take flight and find his niche.

Eight points of view are revealed through alternating, first person narratives in *Slave Day.* Thomas examines one day at Robert E. Lee High School during which the student council holds a slave auction, selling students and faculty as temporary servants to raise money. Racial tensions exist in every layer Thomas creates, and stereotypes are debunked. Students and faculty are forced to redefine each other and redeem themselves. The book starts and ends with Keene Davenport, an African American student angered by the injustices that he is forced to encounter at school. Demanding that other students protest the event, Keene receives little support and instead purchases the first black student council president, Shawn Greeley. Other slave-master combinations include a jaded history teacher and his mediocre student, a cheerleader and her football-playing boyfriend, and the mayor's beautiful daughter and a computer geek.

Thomas quickly shows that school has little to do with education but rather focuses on athletics, relationships, and misunderstood traditions. As the pairs are forced to spend time together, they shift roles, realizing that nobody is precisely as they seem superficially and are actually complex. Slave Day provides teenagers a means to seek revenge and enact control over their temporary possessions. The students expect to have permission to dismiss and disrespect each other, but their judgments about each other are proven inaccurate. Keene tries to humiliate Shawn to emphasize his anger at the school's use of Confederate symbolism, but Shawn gracefully accepts his ridicule and accrues power among his classmates who form a more effective football boycott to protest racism on campus. Other duos develop dual identities, becoming empathetic with their partner and more tolerant of their realities. The pairs risk self-exposure to express feelings and explain misunderstood behaviors. They define themselves and attempt to shed identities ascribed to them by others. Their transformation is not as complete as Steve York's, but they initiate attempts at understanding their prejudices.

Community service is the connecting theme of *Doing Time: Notes From the Undergrad.* College student Randall examines the work done by volunteers from Robert E. Lee High School, exposing his own disillusionment because when he was younger a football player served as his "big brother" and abruptly abandoned him when his hours were completed. He cynically sees volunteers as being motivated only to graduate and pad their college applications with a suitable extracurricular activity. In the stories, though, characters learn to question their assumptions and stereotypes. A library volunteer in "Loss of Pet" judgmentally describes paradoxical social situations such as "women who come in here with blackeyes and check out romance novels" as "The Rot." She is shocked by a classmate's unexpected revelation and questions her antagonistic attitudes. Other characters undergo similar transitions as they face realities that force them to reconsider their beliefs and society.

In *Satellite Down,* high school student Patrick Sheridan is chosen for an internship with a school television network known as Classroom Direct in Los Angeles. He leaves his home, family, and girlfriend on the Texas prairie and is thrust into an erratic environment in which others do not value his devotion to journalistic integrity, ethics, and truth. Coping with sudden fame, he also faces secrets about his family and himself. Patrick flees to Ireland, home of his ancestors, but is unable to escape his problems. This dark satire is a window into the intense emotions of teenagers as they cope with maturity and the development of self-perception.

Irony permeates Thomas's profound fiction. Stylistically, his writing is of an intricate literary quality, based on an undercurrent of intimacy and emotional energy. His portrayals of late-twentieth century teenagers are accurate, honest, and respectful, and conflicts are not always happily resolved. Thomas's protagonists have imperfections and suffer from disillusionment yet become aware of the underlying truths of situations. They endure a teenage culture which is absurd and emotionally hostile and cruel, fostering racism, date rape, and callousness. Gifted in different ways, Thomas's characters learn who they and their peers truly are, enlightening the reader without ever resorting to didacticism.

—Elizabeth D. Schafer

TOLKIEN, J(ohn) R(onald) R(euel)

Nationality: British. **Born:** Bloemfontein, Orange Free State, South Africa, 3 January 1892; came to England, 1895. **Education:** King Edward's VI's School, Birmingham, 1900-02, 1903-11; St. Philip's School, Birmingham, 1902-03; Exeter College, Oxford (open classical exhibitioner; Skeat prize, 1914), 1911-15, B.A. (honours), 1915, M.A. 1919. **Military Service:** Served in the Lancashire Fusiliers, 1915-18: Lieutenant. **Family:** Married Edith Mary Bratt in 1916 (died 1971); three sons and one daughter. **Career:** Writer. Free-lance tutor, 1919. Assistant, Oxford English Dictionary, 1919-20; Reader in English, 1920-23, and Professor of the English Language, 1924-25, University of Leeds, Yorkshire; at Oxford University: Rawlinson and Bosworth Professor of Anglo-Saxon, 1925-45; Fellow, Pembroke College, 1926-45; Leverhulme Research Fellow, 1934-36; Merton Professor of English Language and Literature, 1945-59; Honorary Fellow, Exeter College, 1963; Emeritus Fellow, Merton College; Honorary resident fellow of Merton College, 1972-73. Sir Israel Gollancz Memorial Lecturer, British Academy, 1936; Andrew Lang Lecturer, University of St. Andrews, Fife, 1939; W.P. Ker Lecturer, University of Glasgow, 1953; O'Donnell Lecturer, Oxford University, 1955. Artist: individual show: Ashmolean Museum, Oxford, 1977. **Awards:** *New York Herald Tribune* Children's Spring Book Festival award, 1938, for *The Hobbit*; International Fantasy award, 1957, for *The Lord of the Rings*; Royal Society of Literature Benson Medal, 1966; Foreign Book prize (France), 1973; World Science Fiction Convention Gandalf award, 1974; Hugo award, 1978; *Locus* award for best fantasy novel, 1978, for *The Silmarillion.* D.Litt.: University College, Dublin, 1954; University of Nottingham, 1970; Oxford University, 1972; Dr. en Phil et Lettres: Liège, 1954; honorary degree: University of Edinburgh, 1973. Fellow, Royal Society of Literature, 1957. C.B.E. (Commander, Order of the British Empire), 1972. **Died:** 2 September 1973.

PUBLICATIONS FOR ADULTS AND YOUNG ADULTS

Novels

The Hobbit; or, There and Back Again, illustrated by the author. London, Allen and Unwin, 1937; Boston, Houghton Mifflin, 1938; revised edition, 1951; revised edition, 1966; *The Annotated Hobbit,* edited by Douglas A. Anderson, London, Unwin Hyman, and Boston, Houghton Mifflin, 1989.

The Silmarillion, edited by Christopher Tolkien. London, Allen and Unwin, and Boston, Houghton Mifflin, 1977.

"The Lord of the Rings" trilogy:

The Fellowship of the Ring. London, Allen and Unwin, and Boston, Houghton Mifflin, 1954; revised edition, Allen and Unwin, 1966; Houghton Mifflin, 1967.

The Two Towers. London, Allen and Unwin, 1954; Boston, Houghton Mifflin, 1955; revised edition, Allen and Unwin, 1966; Houghton Mifflin, 1967.

The Return of the King. London, Allen and Unwin, 1955; Boston, Houghton Mifflin, 1956; revised edition, Allen and Unwin, 1966; Houghton Mifflin, 1967.

Short Stories

Unfinished Tales of Númenór and Middle-Earth, edited by Christopher Tolkien. London, Allen and Unwin, and Boston, Houghton Mifflin, 1980.

Plays

The Homecoming of Beorhtnoth Beorhthelm's Son (broadcast, 1954). Included in *The Tolkien Reader,* 1966; in *Tree and Leaf, Smith of Wootton Major, The Homecoming of Beorhtnoth Beorhthelm's Son,* 1975.

Radio Play: *The Homecoming of Beorhtnoth Beorhthelm's Son,* 1954.

Poetry

Songs for the Philologists, with others. Privately printed, 1936.
The Road Goes Ever On: A Song Cycle, music by Donald Swann. Boston, Houghton Mifflin, 1967; London, Allen and Unwin, 1968; revised edition, Houghton Mifflin, 1978.
Poems and Stories. London, Allen and Unwin, 1980.

Other

A Middle English Vocabulary. Oxford, Clarendon Press, and New York, Oxford University Press, 1922.
Beowulf: The Monsters and the Critics. London, Oxford University Press, 1937.
Chaucer as a Philologist. London, Oxford University Press, 1943.
Tree and Leaf (includes short story "Leaf by Niggle" and essay "On Fairy-Stories"). London, Allen and Unwin, 1964; Boston, Houghton and Mifflin, 1965; revised edition, London, Unwin Hyman, 1975.
The Tolkien Reader. New York, Ballantine, 1966.
Smith of Wootton Major and Farmer Giles of Ham. New York, Ballantine, 1969.
Farmer Giles of Ham, The Adventures of Tom Bombadil. London, Allen and Unwin, 1975.
Tree and Leaf, Smith of Wootton Major, The Homecoming of Beorhtnoth Beorhthelm's Son. London, Allen and Unwin, 1975.
Pictures by J.R.R. Tolkien. London, Allen and Unwin, and Boston, Houghton Mifflin, 1979.
The Letters of J.R.R. Tolkien, edited by Humphrey Carpenter. London, Allen and Unwin, and Boston, Houghton Mifflin, 1981.
Finn and Hengest: The Fragment and the Episode, edited by Alan Bliss. London, Allen and Unwin, 1982; Boston, Houghton Mifflin, 1983.
The Monsters and the Critics and Other Essays, edited by Christopher Tolkien. London, Allen and Unwin, 1983; Boston, Houghton Mifflin, 1984.
The History of Middle-Earth (series), edited by Christopher Tolkien:
The Book of Lost Tales 1-2. London, Allen & Unwin, 2 vols., 1983-84; Boston, Houghton Mifflin, 2 vols., 1984.
The Lays of Beleriand. London, Allen and Unwin, and Boston, Houghton Mifflin, 1985.

The Shaping of Middle-Earth: The Quenta, the Ambarkanta, and the Annals. London, Allen and Unwin, and Boston, Houghton Mifflin, 1986.
The Lost Road and Other Writings: Language and Legend before The Lord of the Rings. London, Unwin Hyman, and Boston, Houghton Mifflin, 1987.
The Return of the Shadow: The History of The Lord of the Rings, Part 1. London, Unwin Hyman, 1988; Boston, Houghton Mifflin, 1989.
The Treason of Isengard: The History of The Lord of the Rings, Part 2. Boston, Houghton Mifflin, 1989.
The War of the Ring: The History of The Lord of the Rings, Part 3. Boston, Houghton Mifflin, 1990.
Sauron Defeated: The History of The Lord of the Rings, Part 4. Boston, Houghton Mifflin, 1992.
Morgoth's Ring. London, HarperCollins, 1993.
The War of the Jewels. London, HarperCollins, 1994.
The Peoples of Middle-earth. London, HarperCollins, 1996.
Editor, with C.L. Wiseman, *A Spring Harvest,* by Geoffrey Bache Smith. Erskine Macdonald, 1918.
Editor, with Eric V. Gordon, *Sir Gawain and the Green Knight.* Oxford, Clarendon Press, and New York, Oxford University Press, 1925; revised by Norman Davis, 1967.
Editor, *Ancrene Wisse: The English Text of the Ancrene Riwle.* London, Oxford University Press, 1962; New York, Oxford University Press, 1963.
Translator, *Sir Gawain and the Green Knight, Pearl, and Sir Orfeo,* edited by Christopher Tolkien. London, Allen and Unwin, and Boston, Houghton Mifflin, 1975.
Translator, *The Old English Exodus,* edited by Joan Turville-Petre. Oxford, Clarendon Press, 1981.
Contributor, *Oxford Poetry, 1915,* edited by G.D.H. Cole and T.W. Earp. B.H. Blackwell, 1915.
Contributor, *A Northern Venture: Verses by Members of the Leeds University English School Association.* Swan Press, 1923.
Contributor, *Realities: An Anthology of Verse,* edited by G.S. Tancred. Gay and Hancock, 1927.
Author of foreword, *A New Glossary of the Dialect of the Huddersfield District,* edited by Walter E. Haigh. London, Oxford University Press, 1928.
Contributor, *Report on the Excavation of the Prehistoric, Roman, and Post-Roman Sites in Lydney Park.* Gloucestershire, Reports of the Research Committee of the Society of Antiquaries of London, Oxford University Press, 1932.
Author of preface, *Beowulf and the Finnesburg Fragment: A Translation into Modern English Prose,* by John R. Clark Hall, edited by C.L. Wrenn. London, Allen and Unwin, 1940.
Contributor, *Essays Presented to Charles Williams.* London, Oxford University Press, 1947.
Author of preface, *The Ancrene Riwle,* translated by M. Salu. Burns and Oates, 1955.
Contributor, *Angles and Britons: O'Donnell Lectures.* University of Wales Press, 1963.
Contributor, *Winter's Tales for Children: 1,* edited by Caroline Hillier. New York, St. Martin's, 1965.
Contributor, *The Image of Man in C.S. Lewis,* by William Luther White. Nashville, Tennessee, Abingdon Press, 1969.
Contributor, *The Hamish Hamilton Book of Dragons,* by Roger Lancelyn Green. Hamish Hamilton, 1970.

Contributor, *A Tolkien Compass,* edited by Jared Lobdell. Chicago, Open Court, 1975.

Contributor, *J.R.R. Tolkien: Scholar and Storyteller,* by Mary Salu and Robert T. Farrell. Ithaca, New York, Cornell University Press, 1979.

PUBLICATIONS FOR CHILDREN

Fiction

Farmer Giles of Ham, illustrated by Pauline Baynes. London, Allen and Unwin, 1949; Boston, Houghton Mifflin, 1950.

Smith of Wootton Major, illustrated by Pauline Baynes. London, Allen & Unwin, and Boston, Houghton Mifflin, 1967.

The Father Christmas Letters, edited by Baillie Tolkien, illustrated by the author. London, Allen and Unwin, and Boston, Houghton Mifflin, 1976.

Mr. Bliss, illustrated by the author. London, Allen and Unwin, 1982; Boston, Houghton Mifflin, 1983.

Roverandom, illustrated by the author and edited by Christina Scull and Wayne G. Hammond. London, HarperCollins, 1998.

Poetry

The Adventures of Tom Bombadil and Other Verses from the Red Book, illustrated by Pauline Baynes. London, Allen and Unwin, 1962; Boston, Houghton Mifflin, 1963.

Bilbo's Last Song, illustrated by Pauline Baynes. London, Allen and Unwin, and Boston, Houghton Mifflin, 1974.

Oliphaunt, illustrated by Hank Hinton. Chicago, Contemporary Books, 1989.

Contributor of translations to *The Jerusalem Bible,* New York, Doubleday, 1966. Contributor to *The Year's Work in English Studies,* 1924 and 1925, *Transactions of the Philological Society,* 1934, *English Studies,* 1947, *Studia Neophilologica,* 1948, and *Essais de philologie moderne,* 1951.

*

Media Adaptations: *The Filmbook of J.R.R. Tolien's The Lord of the Rings,* Toronto, Methuen, 1978; Recordings of J.R.R. Tolkien reading from his own works, including "Poems and Songs of Middle-Earth," "The Hobbit and The Fellowship of the Ring," and "The Lord of the Rings," have all been released by New York, Caedmon; Christopher Tolkien reads "The Silmarillion: Of Beren and Luthien," also for Caedmon; Tolkien's illustrations from *Pictures by J.R.R. Tolkien* have been published in various editions of his books and have appeared on calendars, posters, and postcards; Rankin-Bass animated a version of *The Hobbit* for television, which aired in 1977; Ralph Bakshi directed a theater film based on *The Fellowship of the Ring* and bits and pieces of *The Two Towers,* which was released as *The Lord of the Rings* in 1978; A Bunraku-style puppet version of *The Hobbit* was produced in Los Angeles in 1984 by Theatre Sans Fil of Montreal.

Biography: *J.R.R. Tolkien* by Catherine Stimpson, New York, Columbia University Press, 1969; *J.R.R. Tolkien: A Biography* (includes bibliography) by Humphrey Carpenter, London, Allen and Unwin, and Boston, Houghton Mifflin, 1977; entry in *Dictionary of Literary Biography* by Augustus Kolich, Detroit, Gale, Volume 15, 1983.

Bibliography: *Tolkien Criticism: An Annotated Checklist* by Richard C. West, Kent, Ohio, Kent State University Press, 1970; revised edition, 1981.

Manuscript Collections: Marquette University, Milwaukee; Various of Tolkien's letters are in the collections of the BBC Written Archives, the Bodleian Library of Oxford University, the Oxford University Press and its Dictionary Department, the Humanities Research Center of the University of Texas at Austin, and the Marion E. Wade Collection of Wheaton College, Wheaton, Illinois.

Critical Studies: *Tolkien and the Critics* edited by Neil D. Harvey and Rose A. Zimbardo, Notre Dame, Indiana, University of Notre Dame Press, 1968; *The Tolkien Relation: A Personal Inquiry* by William B. Ready, Washington D.C., Regnery, 1968; *A Look behind The Lord of the Rings* by Lin Carter, Boston, Houghton Mifflin, 1969; *Good New from Tolkien's Middle-Earth: Two Essays on the Applicability of The Lord of the Rings* by Gracia F. Ellwood, Grand Rapids, Michigan, Eerdmans, 1970; *A Guide to Middle-Earth* by Robert Foster, Mirage Press, 1971, revised edition, *The Complete Guide to Middle-Earth,* New York, Del Rey, 1981; *Master of Middle-Earth: The Fiction of J.R.R. Tolkien* by Paul Kocher, Boston, Houghton Mifflin, 1972, London, Thames and Hudson, 1973; entries in *Contemporary Literary Criticism,* Detroit, Gale, Volume 1, 1973; Volume 2, 1974; Volume 3, 1975; Volume 8, 1978; Volume 12, 1980; Volume 38, 1986; *Lord of the Elves and Eldils: Fantasy and Philosophy in C.S. Lewis and J.R.R. Tolkien* by Richard L. Purtill, Grand Rapids, Michigan, Zondervan, 1974; *Myth, Allegory and Gospel: An Interpretation; J.R.R. Tolkien, C.S. Lewis, G.K. Chesterton, Charles Williams* by Edmund Fuller and others, Minneapolis Minnesota, Bethany Fellowship, 1974; *Tolkien's World,* London, Thames and Hudson, and Boston, Houghton Mifflin, 1974, and *Tolkien and the Silmarils,* Thames and Hudson, 1981, both by Randel Helms; *The Tolkien Companion* by J.E.A. Tyler, New York, St. Martin's Press, 1976; *The Mythology of Middle-Earth* by Ruth S. Noel, London, Thames and Hudson, and Boston, Houghton Mifflin, 1977; *The Complete Guide to Middle-Earth* by Robert Foster, London, Allen and Unwin, and New York, Ballantine, 1978; *A Hobbit's Journal* by Michael Green, Philadelphia, Running Press, 1979; *Tolkien's Art: A Mythology for England* by Jane C. Nitzche, London, Macmillan, 1979; *A Tolkien Bestiary* by David Day, New York, Ballantine, 1979; *The Languages of Tolkien's Middle-Earth* by Ruth S. Noel, Boston, Houghton Mifflin, 1980; *The Atlas of Middle-Earth* by Karen Wynn Fonstad, Boston, Houghton Mifflin, 1981; *Journeys of Frodo: An Atlas of J.R.R. Tolkien's The Lord of the Rings* by Barbara Strachey, New York, Ballantine, 1981; *Tolkien Criticism: An Annotated Checklist* compiled by Richard C. West, Kent, Ohio, Kent State University Press, 1970, revised edition, 1981; *Tolkien: New Critical Perspectives* edited by Neil D. Isaacs and Rose A. Zimbardo, Lexington, University Press of Kentucky, 1981; *The Road to Middle-Earth* by T.A. Shippey, London, Allen and Unwin, 1982, Boston, Houghton Mifflin, 1983; *J.R.R. Tolkien: This Far Land* edited by Robert Giddings, London, Vision, 1983; *The Song of Middle-Earth: J.R.R. Tolkien's Themes, Symbols, and Myths* by David Harvey, London, Allen and Unwin, 1985; *J.R.R.*

Tolkien: Six Decades of Criticism by Judith A. Johnson, Westport, Connecticut, Greenwood Press, 1986; *The Magical World of the Inklings: J.R.R. Tolkien, C.S. Lewis, Charles Williams, Owen Barfield* by Gareth Knight, Shaftesbury, Element, 1990; *A Tolkien Thesaurus* by Richard E. Blackwelder, New York, Garland, 1990.

*   *   *

The Lord of the Rings has become one of the key books which teachers and librarians recommend to young adults to lead them towards adult literature; but it was not always so. The making of the book was a series of accidents, and, once published, young people insisted on reading it despite the hostility of literary critics and some educationalists, and the sheer difficulty of obtaining all three instalments in the right order.

Professor J.R.R. Tolkien made up the story of *The Hobbit* for his children, without intending to publish it. While Tolkien was advising the publishers Allen and Unwin on a translation of the Old English poem *Beowulf,* an editor read *The Hobbit* in manuscript and recommended it for publication. Tolkien had not even written the final chapters! After *The Hobbit* was successfully published in 1937, Stanley Unwin, Tolkien's publisher, asked him for a sequel. After beginning a supposed companion piece for children, Tolkien's creativity led him on an unexpected journey.

Ever since he left his newly-wed wife to fight in World War I, Tolkien had been developing a mythology based on a series of invented languages, into which he had poured his feelings about religion, love, and war. This saga, later to be called *The Silmarillion,* told of the creation of the world of Middle-Earth, and how God's purpose was continually thwarted by Melkor, the Spirit of Evil, once one of His greatest angels or Valar, and how God still brought Good out of Evil. In this world, purporting to be ours at its earliest stage, Elves were created first, then Men, Dwarves, and Ents, while Melkor distorted creation to make Orcs, Trolls, and other creatures like Dragons and Balrogs. Elves and Men made war on Melkor, now named Morgoth, for the three magical Silmarils which he had stolen, and at the end of the First Age, with the aid of the Valar, Morgoth was permanently imprisoned. Morgoth's chief lieutenant, Sauron, remained on Middle-Earth to cause further trouble, especially the drowning of Numenor, the island given by the Valar as a reward to those Men who fought against Morgoth.

In composing *The Hobbit,* Tolkien drew on this mythology, setting the story in the same Secondary World of Middle-Earth in a later era; thus, as he developed the sequel, he began to make connections with *The Silmarillion.* He had already said that Bilbo's sword was made in Gondolin (an Elven city at war with Morgoth); now he discovered that Bilbo's magic ring had been made by Sauron, it was the Ruling Ring which governed all the others; and Sauron was also the Necromancer, the sorcerer whom Gandalf had defeated in *The Hobbit.*

Over twelve years *The Lord of the Rings* developed into a massive typescript, not the children's book his publishers had requested, and initially they rejected it, for Tolkien wanted *The Silmarillion* published as well. Several years later, owing to the enthusiasm of Stanley Unwin's son Rayner, Unwin and Tolkien reconsidered, and over 1954-55 *The Lord of the Rings* was published in three installments, with the cliff-hanger at the end of Volume Two causing tremendous frustration to many devoted readers.

Many critics, however, were hostile because the book did not fit current fashions of adult fiction: it was not a realistic contemporary novel, and in the words of Edmund Wilson, "It is essentially a children's book—a children's book which has somehow got out of hand." Such misunderstandings were anticipated by the three authors commissioned to write the jacket "blurb," who concentrated on genre and comparable authors: Malory, Ariosto, science fiction, "an heroic romance." As we now know, Tolkien re-awakened an appetite for fantasy literature among readers and inadvertently founded the genre of "adult fantasy." Since publication, those critics who enjoy Tolkien have striven to establish criteria by which Tolkien and other fantasists should be judged.

Among them was Elizabeth Cook, who wrote: "The inherent greatness of myth and fairy tale is a poetic greatness. Childhood reading of symbolic and fantastic tales contributes something irreplaceable to any later experience of literature. . .The whole world of epic, romance, and allegory is open to a reader who has always taken fantasy for granted, and the way into it may be hard for one who never heard fairy tales as a child." (*The Ordinary and the Fabulous,* Cambridge University Press, 1969, 1976).

Tolkien's reception in the USA was more whole-hearted. Independently of Tolkien, a popular style of heroic fantasy had developed, entitled "Sword-and-sorcery," usually written by science-fiction authors as recreation from stories of space-ships and aliens. Barbarians, sorcerers, seductive princesses, and treasure hoards were common features of yarns set amid a mix of fantasy cultures and periods, from Viking saga to the Arabian Nights. So, although Tolkien saw himself in a literary tradition running from the Volsung Saga and Celtic legend through Rider Haggard, William Morris, Dunsany, and Eddison, there was another "pulp" tradition from legend, Haggard, Dunsany, E.R. Burroughs, Cabell, H.E. Howard's Conan the Barbarian, Fritz Leiber and L. Sprague de Camp. Typical of this American style is an anti-heroic, tongue-in-cheek attitude to great deeds which invites the reader to bridge the gulf between "real life" and fantasy. Tolkien does employ this anachronistic approach in *The Hobbit,* in the person of Bilbo and in the authorial comments, but in *The Lord of the Rings* this self-consciousness disappears, replaced by a pervading down-to-earth quality in the four hobbits' response to the heroic world, to accustom readers to heroic attitudes and archaic language, without inviting ridicule.

After hardback publication of *The Lord of the Rings,* American SF fans put the word out that Tolkien was an essential read. Paperback reprints of the Conan stories popularised sword-and-sorcery in SF bookshops, and the market was prepared for paperback Tolkien, but there were more obstacles in the way. Tolkien disliked paperback editions and wanted to revise the text. In 1965 Ace Books forced his hand by publishing a legal but unauthorised paperback, with cover illustrations and blurb to appeal to fans of SF and fantasy, and *The Lord of the Rings* became a best-seller twice over: selling well in the Ace edition, and then as a controversial book when the story of the author's disapproval broke, and an authorised, revised edition came out months later. At last young people could afford to buy Tolkien for themselves: in England a one-volume paperback appeared in 1968.

Since then youngsters have continued to fall in love with the Middle-Earth sagas, overwhelmed by the suspense, joy, beauty, and poignancy of this unique reading experience. In fairness, Tolkien's work should be judged by the conventions of its genre, not by criteria devised for contemporary fiction. I will now propose reasons for asserting its literary value and attempt to counter some anti-Tolkien views.

First, the book's readability throughout its epic length helps novice readers to progress, giving them confidence and a sense of achievement so that they may tackle other long works. A series of cliff-hangers and surprise confrontations maintain the suspense, the whole epic being intricately patterned so that characters separate and reunite, and all tends towards the climaxes of Volume three, when the reader is thrilled by first, the arrival of the Riders of Rohan to relieve the Siege of Gondor, then Eowyn's challenge to the Lord of the Nazgul and his death, which fulfils the prophecy that "no man" would slay him, and finally Aragorn's arrival in the fleet of corsairs' ships.

Then the book is written by a master of language, ranging from plain English through archaisms to poetic prose in such scenes as Gandalf's defiance of the Lord of the Nazgul, and Aragorn's healing of Eowyn. Tolkien's use of epic diction has earned him much criticism: he responded that high deeds in a heroic setting needed that "ancient style," and he revelled in "the wealth of English which leaves us a choice of styles." Tom Shippey points out that Tolkien's success with millions of ordinary readers proved the critics wrong, and that Tolkien did the best he could to bring the heroic world close to the modern reader through the eyes of the hobbits.

In recalling features of myth and legend, *The Lord of the Rings* inspires its readers to search the past: Norse and Welsh legend, and Old English poetry. Teachers might encourage this, and also recommend fantasy authors who owe Tolkien a debt: he created the appetite for fantasy by which they have profited: published for children are C. S. Lewis, Alan Garner, Susan Cooper, Lloyd Alexander, and Ursula Le Guin; for adults and young adults, Jane Yolen, Robin Mckinley, David Eddings, Terry Pratchett, and Stephen Donaldson.

Tolkien has been criticised for flat characterisation: but in genre literature the reader must identify with the main character (or his partner, e.g. Dr. Watson), who must be an ordinary individual facing extraordinary pressures. Tolkien's main characters are drawn to three patterns: they have individual qualities; archetypal qualities; and they represent their species. All the main characters are well differentiated: the five hobbits, of course, and also the four heroes, Aragorn, Boromir, Eomer, and Faramir. Gimli and Legolas represent their races, and in the experiences of Gimli Tolkien includes a plea for racial tolerance. Wherever the Company goes, Gimli meets hostility because he is a Dwarf, but the Company stands by him and he wins the esteem of Elves and Men.

Tolkien's view of Evil has also been criticised. However, it is appropriate for supernatural genres to depict creatures of ultimate evil, like aliens and monsters, whereas fictions set in the real world cannot do this. So we need fantasy to experience the extremes of Good and Evil, testing real life against the fantasy. Sauron, in his desire to conquer and control the world, is not very different from a real-world dictator: it is his methods which count. Don't real-life soldiers deport and even massacre civilians? Consider the Nazi Holocaust of the Jews, taking place at the time when Tolkien wrote *The Lord of the Rings*. Issues in the real world may date: Shakespeare's play *Richard III* is a timeless portrait of a tyrant, but the real Richard III was probably not guilty of all the murders he commits or orders in the play.

Tolkien's orcs are not of course intended to stand for Germans or any other nation of the "real world"; they represent the worst aspect of humankind when engaged in indiscriminate violence. Tolkien does not show his orcs at their worst, in rape and massacre, and there is nothing observed or reported of the orcs which has not happened in our world. The human-like characters who choose evil, however—Denethor, Saruman, Wormtongue, and Gollum—are tempted, fall, and are given chances to repent. Moreover, throughout the epic Gollum's life is frequently spared: part of the essential patterning of the plot in order for Gollum to reach the Crack of Doom and save Frodo from the Ring.

Tolkien urges his readers to choose Good over Evil; but as a Roman Catholic believing the doctrine of original sin, he feared for the world's future. He was particularly concerned about ultimate war, which he predicted before the atom bomb was dropped on Hiroshima: "Shall there be two cities of Minas Morgul, grinning at each other across a dead land filled with rottenness?" In his hatred of industrial pollution and his portrayal of the Ents, he was also ahead of his time. Meanwhile the contemporary novel of personal relationships may ignore wider issues which Tolkien pondered throughout his life.

Of Tolkien's works, the YA library should have *The Hobbit, The Lord of the Rings* and *The Silmarillion,* and also *Unfinished Tales*—more material from *The Silmarillion* and an adult love story, "Aldarion and Erendis." Tolkien's son Christopher has edited Tolkien's early versions of *The Silmarillion* and *The Lord of the Rings:* under the overall title *The History of Middle-Earth* the series has reached ten volumes; the YA library could acquire these in paperback if there is demand, and also Tolkien's *Letters* and the *Biography*. Tolkien's work is not only enjoyable, but also relevant to contemporary life: we should recommend it to young people and rejoice when they become enthusiastic for tales of Middle-Earth.

—Jessica Yates

TOWNSEND, John Rowe

Nationality: British. **Born:** Leeds, England, 10 May 1922. **Education:** Leeds Grammar School, 1933-40; Emmanuel College, Cambridge, B.A. 1949, M.A. 1954. **Military Service:** Served in the Royal Air Force, 1942-46: Flight Sergeant. **Family:** Married Vera Lancaster in 1948 (died 1973); two daughters and one son. **Career:** Journalist, *Yorkshire Post,* Leeds, 1946, and *Evening Standard,* London, 1949; sub-editor, 1949-54, and art editor, 1954-55, Manchester *Guardian,* and editor of *Guardian Weekly,* 1955-69; part-time children's books editor, *Guardian,* Manchester and London, 1968-79, columnist, 1968-81; writer and lecturer, since 1969. Adjunct professor, Simmons College Center for the Study of Children's Literature, Boston, 1978-86; faculty member since 1987, member of adjunct board since 1990, Children's Literature New England; chairman of children's writers and illustrators group, British Society of Authors, 1977-78, 1990-91, member of management committee, 1982-85. Member of Harvard International Seminar, 1956. Visiting lecturer, University of Pennsylvania, Philadelphia, 1965, and University of Washington, Seattle, 1969, 1971; May Hill Arbuthnot Honor Lecturer, Atlanta, 1971; Anne Carroll Moore Lecturer, New York Public Library, 1971; Whittall Lecturer, Library of Congress, Washington, D.C., 1976. **Awards:** Carnegie Medal honors list, 1963, for *Hell's Edge;* Carnegie Medal honors list, 1969, Silver Pen award from English

Centre of International PEN, 1970, *Boston Globe-Horn Book* award, and 1971, Edgar Allan Poe award from Mystery Writers of America, all for *The Intruder;* Christopher award, 1982, for *The Islanders; Trouble in the Jungle, Good-bye to the Jungle, Pirate's Island, The Intruder, The Summer People, Noah's Castle,* and *Good-night, Prof, Dear* appeared on the American Library Association notable books list; *Trouble in the Jungle, The Intruder, The Islanders,* and *A Sense of Story* appeared on the *Horn Book* Honor List. **Address:** 72 Water Lane, Histon, Cambridge CB4 4LR, England.

PUBLICATIONS FOR YOUNG ADULTS

Fiction

Hell's Edge. London, Hutchinson, 1963; New York, Lothrop, 1969.
The Hallersage Sound. London, Hutchinson, 1966.
The Intruder, illustrated by Graham Humphreys. London, Oxford University Press, 1969; illustrated by Joseph A. Phelan, Philadelphia, Lippincott, 1970.
Good-night, Prof, Love, illustrated by Peter Farmer. London, Oxford University Press, 1970; as *Good-night, Prof, Dear,* Philadelphia, Lippincott, 1971; as *The Runaways,* edited by David Fickling, London, Oxford University Press, 1979.
The Summer People, illustrated by Robert Micklewright. London, Oxford University Press, and Philadelphia, Lippincott, 1972.
Forest of the Night, illustrated by Peter Farmer. London, Oxford University Press, 1974; illustrated by Beverly Brodsky McDermott, Philadelphia, Lippincott, 1975.
Noah's Castle. London, Oxford University Press, 1975; Philadelphia, Lippincott, 1976.
The Xanadu Manuscript, illustrated by Paul Ritchie. London, Oxford University Press, 1977; as *The Visitors,* Philadelphia, Lippincott, 1977.
King Creature, Come. Oxford, Oxford University Press, 1980; as *The Creatures,* New York, Lippincott, 1980.
The Islanders. Oxford, Oxford University Press, and New York, Lippincott, 1981.
A Foreign Affair. London, Kestrel Books, 1982; as *Kate and the Revolution,* New York, Lippincott, 1982.
Cloudy-bright. London, Viking Kestrel, and New York, Lippincott, 1984.
Downstream. New York, Lippincott, 1987; London, Walker, 1988.
The Golden Journey. London, Viking Kestrel, 1989; as *The Fortunate Isles,* New York, Lippincott, 1989.
The Invaders. Oxford, Oxford University Press, 1992.

PUBLICATIONS FOR CHILDREN

Fiction

Gumble's Yard, illustrated by Dick Hart. London, Hutchinson, 1961; as *Trouble in the Jungle,* illustrated by W. T. Mars, Philadelphia, Lippincott, 1969.
Pirate's Island, illustrated by Douglas Hall. London, Oxford University Press, and Philadelphia, Lippincott, 1968.
Widdershins Crescent. London, Hutchinson, 1965; as *Good-bye to the Jungle,* Philadelphia, Lippincott, 1967; as *Good-bye to Grumble's Yard,* London, Penguin, 1981.

Top of the World, illustrated by Nikki Jones. London, Oxford University Press, 1976; pictures by John Wallner, Philadelphia, Lippincott, 1977.
Dan Alone. London, Kestrel, and New York, Lippincott, 1983.
Tom Tiddler's Ground, illustrated by Mark Peppé. London, Viking Kestrel, 1985; New York, Lippincott, 1986; as *The Hidden Treasure,* New York, Scholastic, Inc., 1988.
The Persuading Stick. London, Viking Kestrel, and New York, Lothrop, 1986.
Rob's Place. London, Viking Kestrel, 1987; New York, Lothrop, 1988.

PUBLICATIONS FOR ADULTS

Fiction

Cranford Revisited, illustrated by Jane Langton. Cambridge, England, Green Bay Publications, 1989.

Nonfiction

Written for Children: An Outline of English Children's Literature. London, J. Garnet Miller, 1965; New York, Lothrop, 1967; revised edition, London, Kestrel, 1974 and Philadelphia, Lippincott, 1975; revised edition, London, Kestrel, and New York, Harper, 1983; revised edition, London, Penguin, 1987, and New York, Harper, 1988; 5th edition (25th anniversary edition), London, Bodley Head, 1990, and New York, HarperCollins, 1992; 6th edition, London, Bodley Head, 1995, and Lanham, Maryland, Scarecrow Press, 1996.
Editor, *Modern Poetry: A Selection for Young People.* London, Oxford University Press, 1971, with photographs by Barbara Pfeffer, Philadelphia, Lippincott, 1974.
A Sense of Story: Essays on Contemporary Writers for Children. London, Longman, and Philadelphia, Lippincott, 1971; revised edition, as *A Sounding of Storytellers: New and Revised Essays on Contemporary Writers for Children,* London, Kestrel, and New York, Lippincott, 1979.
Editor, *Twenty-five Years of British Children's Books.* London, National Book League, 1977.
Contributor, *The Openhearted Audience: Ten Authors Talk about Writing for Children,* edited by Virginia Haviland. Washington, D.C., Library of Congress, 1980.

*

Media Adaptations: *Gumble's Yard* (television); *The Intruder* (ITV television series), 1972; *Noah's Castle* (ITV television series), 1980.

Biography: Essay in *Something about the Author Autobiography Series,* Volume 2, Detroit, Gale, 1986; essay in *Speaking for Ourselves: Autobiographical Sketches by Notable Authors of Books for Young Adults,* Volume 1, compiled and edited by Donald R. Gallo, National Council of Teachers of English, 1990.

Manuscript Collections: Kerlan Collection, University of Minnesota, Minneapolis; International Youth Library, Munich.

Critical Studies: Entry in *Children's Literature Review,* Volume 2, Detroit, Gale, 1976.

John Rowe Townsend comments:

I wear two hats in connection with books for children and young people: as a writer of them and as a writer about them.

In the former capacity I began my career in the early 1960s with a sense that books dealing with the rougher side of real life, and with the problems and joys of growing up in contemporary society, were far too scarce in Britain. Hence *Gumble's Yard, Hell's Edge,* and *Widdershins Crescent.* Later, the feeling that these gaps were now being adequately filled, together with the continual urge to do something different, led me to broaden my fictional scope and to write on a variety of themes. I have always had a special interest in the intensely alive and active phase of life that a young person enters when moving out of childhood and this may be why my books have spanned both children's and young adult lists.

Under my other hat I have for many years written about children's books for various publications. I have also produced an historical survey of children's literature (*Written for Children*) and two sets of essays on contemporary children's writers (*A Sense of Story* and *A Sounding of Storytellers*). I tend to discuss children's books as literature rather than as influences in social, educational, or psychological development—but I hasten to add that literary criticism does not have to be narrowly aesthetic; it can and should take account of many aspects of a book. One thing I am certain of is that a good book for young readers must be a good book, period.

*   *   *

John Rowe Townsend—historian, critic, and author—is probably best known for his realistic portrayal of adolescents attempting to traverse the chasm which separates the child from the adult. Best known as a British realist, Townsend has directed his talents in a number of different directions: writing fantasies, pseudo-historical novels, science fiction, and a novel of teenage angst which gives dimensions to the internal quest for maturity (*Forest of the Night,* 1974). The result has been books of mixed quality, but the author remains true to his audience.

In his early works, *Trouble in the Jungle* (as *Gumble's Yard,* 1961), *Hell's Edge* (1963), *Good-bye to the Jungle* (as *Widdershins Crescent,* 1965), *The Hallersage Sound* (1966), and *Pirate's Island* (1968), Townsend frequently presents very young protagonists in bleak surroundings, allowing them to survive and even thrive without the help of, and often in spite of, the grown-ups in their lives. In the first of the "Jungle" books, Kevin (thirteen) and Sandra (twelve) are orphans being cared for by an alcoholic uncle; the two children must grow up before their time as they try to manage the family finances and protect their cousins Harold and Jean. While the surroundings are bleak and the situation nearly hopeless, Kevin, the narrator, manages to remain cheerful and hopeful.

What becomes clear as the reader examines Townsend's early work is that while he creates believable characters and settings, his plots often contain elements of the fantastic. The idea that Kevin and Sandra might be able to care for their cousins for a few days is believable, but when they find stolen diamonds and help stop an escaped convict, the story moves into the realm of fantasy. Most surprising, however, is the note of hope on which the novel ends.

The return of Uncle Walter in the first book leaves the young protagonists with a sense of contentment—their lives are not great, but at least they are back to normal. In the second book, Kevin, now fifteen, loses his own scholarship but takes pride in seeing young Harold receive honors, both in school and in the neighborhood.

In his later books, Townsend becomes less concerned about the teenager who is buffeted about by the winds of the adult world and focuses on the internal angst—particularly the tension caused by love and sexual experience—of his young protagonists. In *The Intruder* (1969), Townsend gives concrete form to the natural anxieties teenagers face in developing their own identities. Rather than wrestle with the abstract concept of identity, Townsend creates Arnold Haithwaite who is confronted by an evil man who claims that he is Arnold Haithwaite. The young boy must then discover who he is and ascertain his place in his world.

Several of Townsend's books struggle with the problems of love, many of them focusing on the trepidations brought on through early sexual encounters. *Good-night, Prof, Dear* (published as *Good-night, Prof, Love,* 1970) is a realistic novel in which a shy young Graham Hollis falls in love with a woman slightly older in age but years older in experience. The love affair is doomed almost from the start, but his sexual initiation is successful and his broken heart is soothed by the recognition that in her own way Lynn has loved him.

Downstream (1967) presents a darker version of young love and initiation. Alan Dollis also falls in love, and in lust, with an older woman, his tutor. Alan's own misdirected sexual energy and his discovery of his father's unfaithfulness add grim dimensions to the problems faced by young people as they are introduced to the adult world.

Perhaps the most haunting of Townsend's books on teenage initiation is his very difficult *Forest of the Night* (1974). It is unbelievable that this abstract journey through a symbolic sexual awakening can be intended for Townsend's usual young adult audience. The book is compelling as well as frightening. It must be sensed and becomes more difficult to put into perspective because of the structure which lies almost outside the scope of the analytical mind. The boy must, as all boys, face his monster or remain a child; in this book, the author invites others to share the experience, to become a guide or to be guided on the journey.

Another kind of tension the maturing teenager must face is the tension inherent in forming his or her own value system, especially if those values prove to be different than those of their parents. It is this belief that children can develop values which surpass their parent's which gives Townsend's works their spark of hope. In *Noah's Castle* (1975), Barry Mortimer must choose between his father's concern for the family's welfare and Barry's own desire to help his community. While Barry's father is not condemned by the author for hoarding food while others starve, his behavior is explained as a type of insanity, and it is Barry and other young people of England who offer the country hope in its darkest hour.

Townsend examines teenage problems and successes in many forms and genres. *The Summer People* (1972) is a realistic novel which examines a thwarted love over a period of twenty years. *The Visitors* (*The Xanadu Manuscript,* 1977), on the other hand, is a time travel fantasy which scrutinizes the same issue. *The Creatures* (*King Creature, Come,* 1980) is a science fiction story of young people changing their society, and *Kate and the Revolution* is nearly a satire on modern wars and intrigue, where change, though initiated by the young, is nearly meaningless.

Throughout his work Townsend emphasizes both the resilience of the young, and their ability to overcome the problems and the obstacles which block the path to maturity. Although he is a realist, it is hope not despair which crowds most of the pages of his novels. Generally, he acknowledges the pain, the fear, and the heartbreak of growing up, but he tells his audience that they can survive and that in surviving, they will gain hope for themselves and for the whole world.

—Judith Gero John

TOWNSEND, Sue

Nationality: British. **Born:** Leicester, Leicestershire, 2 April 1946. **Education:** Attended English secondary schools. **Career:** Worked in various capacities, including garage attendant, hot dog saleswoman, dress shop worker, factory worker, and trained community worker; full-time writer, since 1982. **Awards:** Thames Television Bursary, 1979, for *Womberang*. **Agent:** Giles Gordon, 43 Doughty Street, London WC1N 2LF, England.

PUBLICATIONS FOR YOUNG ADULTS

Fiction

The Secret Diary of Adrian Mole, Aged 13 3/4. London, Methuen, 1982.
The Growing Pains of Adrian Mole. London, Methuen, 1984.
Rebuilding Coventry: A Tale of Two Cities. London, Methuen, 1988
Mr. Bevan's Dream. North Pomfret, Vermont, Trafalgar Square, 1990.
True Confessions of Adrian Albert Mole, with Margaret Hilda Roberts. London, Teen, 1991.
Adrian Mole: From Minor to Major (collection). London, Methuen, 1991.
The Queen and I. London, Methuen, 1992; New York, Soho Press, 1993.
Adrian Mole: The Wilderness Years. London, Methuen, 1993.
Adrian Mole: The Lost Years. New York, Soho Press, 1994.
Ghost Children. New York, Soho Press, 1998.

Plays

Womberang (produced Leicester, England, 1979).
The Secret Diary of A. Mole (radio play). British Broadcasting Corporation Radio 4, 1982.
Groping for Words (produced London, 1983).
Bazaar and Rummage (television play). British Broadcasting Corporation, 1983.
Bazaar and Rummage, Groping for Words [and] Womberang (play collection). London, Methuen, 1984.
The Great Celestial Cow (produced Leicester, 1984).
The Secret Diary of Adrian Mole, Aged 13 3/4 (produced Leicester, 1984), with songs by Ken Howard and Alan Blaikley. London, Methuen, 1985.
Ear, Nose and Throat (produced Cambridge, England, 1989).
"Disneyland It Ain't," in *New Statesman and Society,* 29 June 1990.

Ten Tiny Fingers, Nine Tiny Toes. London, Heinemann, 1991.
The Queen and I: The Play with Songs, songs by Ian Dury and Mickey Gallagher. London, Methuen Drama in association with Royal Court Theatre, 1994.

*

Media Adaptations: *Secret Diary of A. Mole* (television series) Thames TV, first broadcast 1986.

*   *   *

Although she has been a fairly prolific stage and television dramatist and has written other novels, Sue Townsend's reputation and popularity have been founded on her creation of a spotty, self-absorbed and pretentious schoolboy called Adrian Mole. Mole's "growing pains," his rather halting progress through post-pubertal anxiety and secondary education, form the subject of his "secret diary," a document as rich in comic banality and inadvertent self-disclosure as its prototype, George and Weedon Grossmith's *Diary of a Nobody* (1892). Adrian's problems and preoccupations are the universal problems and preoccupations of moderately intelligent adolescent males. He is worried about his disfiguring acne, the unpredictable and uncontrollable behaviour of his sexual organs, the social embarrassments he is forced to suffer at his parents' hands, about whether or not he will pass his exams, and whether the beautiful Pandora (who sits next to him in geography) will ever return his love. He writes poems, reads voraciously and indiscriminately (at one point sprinting through *War and Peace* in the space of twenty-four hours), regards himself as politically radical, and adores the Royal Family. Beneath all of the teenage confusions and affectations, however, Adrian emerges as a genuinely sympathetic figure. His messily unsystematic reading, for example, suggests a real inquisitiveness which his school appears almost purposely designed to frustrate, and he becomes, albeit reluctantly, devoted to the cantankerous octogenarian Bert Baxter, whose care he is assigned in a community aid project.

The Mole books succeed partly because they credibly portray a character who is at the same time a target for comic irony and an object of affection. But Adrian is also very much the product of his time and place, and the books evoke, in sharply circumstantial detail, the England of the 1980s, a nation itself beset by "growing pains" as the conservative social and economic policies of Margaret Thatcher's successive governments take an increasing hold on people's lives. Adrian's father, for example, loses his job early on and remains unemployed apart from a brief stint as a Canal Bank Renovation Supervisor overseeing a reluctant group of similarly unemployed (and unemployable) school-leavers. The state education system is tottering towards terminal collapse: the school that Adrian attends is staffed by a succession of transient incompetents and presided over by an unstable autocrat who has a portrait of Mrs. Thatcher hanging in his office. Political opposition seems confined to the ineffectual gestures of Pandora's vaguely leftist parents and to the anachronistic Labour fundamentalism of Bert Baxter. Most of the diary's inhabitants, indeed, seem happy enough to be distracted from their immediate troubles by stirring displays of national grandeur like royal weddings ("We truly lead the world when it comes to pageantry!" notes Adrian approvingly) or the Falklands War ("Grandma has got a funny look in her eyes. My mother says it is called jingoism...''). Barry Kent, the school bully, proudly wears a Union Jack tee shirt while his family (his father is another of the book's many unemployed males) has to furnish his home with pickings from the local garbage-tip.

The confusions which beset Adrian as he gropes his way towards adulthood are, thus, not solely the result of patchy knowledge and immature judgment; rather, they reflect broader confusions within the society of which he is a part. He can be, simultaneously, buoyantly patriotic and dimly aware of a deepening social malaise; sometimes, he confesses, he thinks of Mrs Thatcher as a ''nice kind sort of woman'' but the next day discovers that ''she frightens me rigid.'' During the Falklands campaign he enthusiastically plots troop movements on a map, but he disgustedly throws the map away after seeing the official memorial service on television.

This account has perhaps made Adrian's fictional journals sound rather sombre. They are not, but their comic success is nevertheless based firmly on the sometimes satirical and always precise observation of an exactly defined social situation. Townsend is extremely adept at extracting humour from the specific detail of lower middle-class daily living in a Midlands town. Adrian's mother, for example, belatedly discovers feminism through reading Germaine Greer, but Adrian's hasty glance at *The Female Eunuch* results only in his first wet dream. Having been introduced at school to notions of dietary correctness, Adrian is dispatched to do the family shopping and proudly returns laden with a huge assortment of lentils, brown rice, and other nutritious comestibles, only to have his mother complain that he has forgotten the frozen black forest gateaux.

The first two Adrian Mole books, then, owe their deserved popularity to a shrewd combination of comic action with informed social observation. Some of Townsend's more recent work has suggested the difficulty of sustaining such a combination. The third Mole book (*True Confessions*) takes Adrian fully into adulthood but makes him over as a grotesque eccentric whose earlier curiosity has become undiluted pretension and whose kindliness has been largely replaced by egotism. Conversely, *Rebuilding Coventry,* a lightly feminized pilgrim's progress through the ''two nations'' of Margaret Thatcher's England, is too angry to be able to realize more than intermittently its comic purpose. Therefore, it seems probable that Townsend's durability as a writer will rest on her invention of the younger Adrian, a figure who manages to be representative both of his age-group and of English society at a particular moment in its evolution.

—Robert Dingley

TREASE, (Robert) Geoffrey

Nationality: British. **Born:** Nottingham, 11 August 1909. **Education:** Nottingham High School, 1920-28; Queen's College, Oxford (scholar), 1928-29. **Military Service:** Served in the British Army, 1942-46; infantry and educational corps, England and India. **Family:** Married Marian Haselden Granger Boyer in 1933 (died 1989); one daughter. Journalist and social worker, London, 1929-32; teacher, Clacton-on-Sea, Essex, 1932-33; full-time writer, since 1933. Lecturer on children's literature; Chairman, Children's Writers Group, 1962-63. Chairman, 1972-73, and since 1974 member of the Council, Society of Authors. Fellow, Royal Society of Literature, 1979. **Awards:** Welwyn Festival award (England), 1938, for *After the Tempest* (play); *New York Herald Tribune* Spring Book Festival award for Nonfiction, 1966, for *This Is Your Century.* **Agent:** David Higham Associates, 5-8 Lower John Street, Golden Square, London W1R 4HA, England. **Address:** 1 Yomede Park, Newbridge Rd., Bath, Avon BA1 3LS, England.

PUBLICATIONS FOR YOUNG ADULTS

Fiction

Bows against the Barons, illustrated by Michael Boland. London, Lawrence, and New York, International Publishers, 1934; revised edition, Leicester, Brockhampton Press, 1986; revised edition, illustrated by C. Walter Hodges, New York, Meredith Press, 1966.

Comrades for the Charter, illustrated by Michael Boland. London, Lawrence & Wishart, 1934; revised edition illustrated by Douglas Phillips, Leicester, Brockhampton Press, 1972.

The Call to Arms. London, Lawrence, and New York, International Publishers, 1935.

Missing from Home, illustrated by Scott. London, Lawrence & Wishart, 1936.

Red Comet, illustrated by Fred Ellis. Moscow, Co-operative Publishing Society of Foreign Workers, 1936; as *Red Comet: A Tale of Travel in the U.S.S.R.,* London, Lawrence & Wishart, 1937.

The Christmas Holiday Mystery, illustrated by Alfred Sindall. London, A. & C. Black, 1937; as *The Lakeland Mystery,* 1942.

Mystery on the Moors, illustrated by Alfred Sindall. London, A. & C. Black, 1937.

Detectives of the Dales, illustrated by A.C.H. Gorham. London, A. & C. Black, 1938.

In the Land of the Mogul: A Story of the East India Company's First Venture in India, illustrated by J.C.B. Knight. Oxford, Basil Blackwell, 1938.

North Sea Spy. London, Fore, 1939.

Cue for Treason, illustrated by Beatrice Goldsmith. Oxford, Basil Blackwell, 1940; illustrated by L.F. Grant, New York, Vanguard Press, 1941.

Running Deer, illustrated by W. Lindsay Cable. London, Harrap, 1941; as *The Running of the Deer,* illustrated by Maureen Bradley, London, Hamish Hamilton, 1982.

The Grey Adventurer, illustrated by Beatrice Goldsmith. Oxford, Basil Blackwell, 1942.

Black Night, Red Morning, illustrated by Donia Nachsen. Oxford, Basil Blackwell, 1944.

Army without Banners. London, Fore, 1945.

Trumpets in the West, illustrated by Alan Blyth. Oxford, Basil Blackwell, 1947; illustrated by Joe Krush, New York, Harcourt, 1947.

The Hills of Varna, illustrated by Treyer Evans. London, Macmillan, 1948; as *Shadow of the Hawk,* illustrated by Joe Krush, New York, Harcourt, 1949.

Silver Guard, illustrated by Alan Blyth. Oxford, Basil Blackwell, 1948.

The Mystery of Moorside Farm, illustrated by Alan Blyth. Oxford, Basil Blackwell, 1949.

No Boats on Bannermere, illustrated by Richard Kennedy. London, Heinemann, 1949; New York, Norton, 1965.

The Secret Fiord, illustrated by H.M. Brock. London, Macmillan, 1949; illustrated by Joe Krush, New York, Harcourt, 1950.

Under Black Banner, illustrated by Richard Kennedy. London, Heinemann, 1950.

The Barons' Hostage: A Story of Simon de Montfort, illustrated by Alan Jessett. London, Phoenix House, 1952; revised edition, Leicester, Brockhampton Press, 1973; Nashville, Thomas Nelson, 1975.

Black Banner Players, illustrated by Richard Kennedy. London, Heinemann, 1952.

The Crown of Violet, illustrated by C. Walter Hodges. London, Macmillan, 1952; as *Web of Traitors: An Adventure Story of Ancient Athens,* New York, Vanguard Press, 1952.

The New House at Hardale. London, Lutterworth, 1953.

The Silken Secret, illustrated by Alan Jessett. Oxford, Basil Blackwell, 1953; New York, Vanguard Press, 1954.

Black Banner Abroad. London, Heinemann, 1954; New York, Warne, 1955.

The Fair Flower of Danger. Oxford, Basil Blackwell, 1955.

Editor, *Six of the Best: Stories.* Oxford, Basil Blackwell, 1955.

The Gates of Bannerdale. London, Heinemann, 1956; New York, Warne, 1957.

Word to Caesar, illustrated by Geoffrey Whittam. London, Macmillan, 1956; as *Message to Hadrian,* New York, Vanguard Press, 1956.

Mist over Athelney, illustrated by R.S. Sherriffs and J.L. Stockle. London, Macmillan, 1958; as *Escape to King Alfred,* New York, Vanguard Press, 1958,

The Maythorn Story, illustrated by Robert Hodgson. London, Heinemann, 1960.

Thunder of Valmy, illustrated by John S. Goodall. London, Macmillan, 1960; as *Victory at Valmy,* New York, Vanguard Press, 1961.

Change at Maythorn, illustrated by Robert Hodgson. London, Heinemann, 1962.

Follow My Black Plume, illustrated by Brian Wildsmith. New York, Vanguard Press, 1963.

A Thousand for Sicily, illustrated by Brian Wildsmith. London, Macmillan, and New York, Vanguard Press, 1964.

Bent Is the Bow, illustrated by Charles Keeping. London, Thomas Nelson, 1965; New York, Nelson, 1967.

The Dutch Are Coming, illustrated by Lynette Hemmant. London, Hamish Hamilton, 1965.

The Red Towers of Granada, illustrated by Charles Keeping. London, Macmillan, 1966; New York, Vanguard Press, 1967.

The White Nights of St. Petersburg, illustrated by William Stobbs. London, Macmillan, and New York, Vanguard Press, 1967.

The Runaway Serf, illustrated by Mary Russon. London, Hamish Hamilton, 1968.

A Masque for the Queen, illustrated by Krystyna Turska. London, Hamish Hamilton, 1970.

Horsemen on the Hills. London, Macmillan, 1971.

A Ship to Rome, illustrated by Leslie Atkinson. London, Heinemann, 1972.

Popinjay Stairs: A Historical Adventure about Samuel Pepys. London, Macmillan, 1973; New York, Vanguard Press, 1982; as *The Popinjay Mystery,* London, Pan Macmillan, 1993.

A Voice in the Night, illustrated by Sara Silcock. London, Heinemann, 1973.

The Chocolate Boy, illustrated by David Walker. London, Heinemann, 1975.

The Iron Tsar. London, Macmillan, 1975.

The Seas of Morning, illustrated by David Smee. London, Penguin, 1976.

The Spy Catchers, illustrated by Geoffrey Bargery. London, Hamish Hamilton, 1976.

Violet for Bonaparte. London, Macmillan, 1976.

When the Drums Beat, illustrated by Janet Marsh. London, Heinemann, 1976; augmented edition, as *When the Drums Beat and Other Stories,* London, Pan Books, 1979.

The Claws of the Eagle, illustrated by Ionicus. London, Heinemann, 1977.

The Field of the Forty Footsteps. London, Macmillan, 1977.

Mandeville. London, Macmillan, 1980.

A Wood by Moonlight, and Other Stories. London, Chatto & Windus, 1981.

Saraband for Shadows. London, Macmillan, 1982.

The Cormorant Venture. London, Macmillan, 1984.

Tomorrow Is a Stranger. London, Heinemann, 1987.

The Arpino Assignment, illustrated by Paul Leith. London, Walker Books, 1988.

A Flight of Angels, illustrated by Eric Stemp. London, Macmillan, 1988; Minneapolis, Minnesota, Lerner Publications, 1989.

Hidden Treasure, illustrated by Chris Molan. London, Hamish Hamilton, 1989; New York, Lodestar, 1989.

Calabrian Quest. London, Walker Books, 1990.

Shadow under the Sea. London, Walker Books, 1990.

Aunt Augusta's Elephant, illustrated by Jean Foster. London, Macmillan, 1991.

Song for a Tattered Flag, London, Walker Books, 1992.

Fire on the Wind, London, Macmillan, 1993.

Bring out the Banners, London, Walker Book, 1994.

No Horn at Midnight. London, Macmillan, 1995.

Curse on the Seas. London, Hodder, 1996.

Cloak for a Spy. London, Macmillan, 1997

Danger in the Wings. London, Hodder, 1997.

Mission to Marathon. London, A and C Black, 1997.

Plays

The Dragon Who Was Different, and Other Plays (includes *The Mighty Mandarin, Fairyland Limited, The New Bird*). London, Muller, 1938.

The Shadow of Spain, and Other Plays (includes *The Unquiet Cloister* and *Letters of Gold*). Oxford, Basil Blackwell, 1953.

Popinjay Stairs (radio play), from his own story, 1973.

Other

Fortune, My Foe: The Story of Sir Walter Raleigh, illustrated by Norman Meredith. London, Methuen, 1949; as *Sir Walter Raleigh, Captain and Adventurer,* New York, Vanguard Press, 1950.

The Young Traveller in India and Pakistan [England and Wales, Greece]. London, Phoenix House, 3 Vols., 1949-56; New York, Dutton, 3 vols., 1953-56.

Enjoying Books. London, Phoenix House, 1951; revised edition, 1963.

Translator, *Companions of Fortune.* by René Guillot, illustrated by Pierre Collot. London, Oxford University Press, 1952.

The Seven Queens of England. London, Heinemann, and New York, Vanguard Press, 1953; revised version, Heinemann, 1968.

Translator, *The King's Corsair,* by René Guillot, illustrated by Pierre Rousseau. London, Oxford University Press, 1954.

Seven Kings of England, illustrated by Leslie Atkinson. London, Heinemann, and New York, Vanguard Press, 1955.

Edward Elgar: Maker of Music. London, Macmillan, 1959.

Wolfgang Mozart, The Young Composer. London, Macmillan, 1961; New York, St. Martin's, 1962.

The Young Writer: A Practical Handbook, illustrated by Carl Hollander. London, Thomas Nelson, 1961.

Seven Stages. London, Heinemann, 1964; New York, Vanguard Press, 1965.

This Is Your Century. London, Heinemann, and New York, Harcourt, 1965.

Seven Sovereign Queens. London, Heinemann, 1968; New York, Vanguard Press, 1968.

Byron: A Poet Dangerous to Know. London, Macmillan, and New York, Holt, 1969.

Days to Remember: A Garland of Historic Anniversaries, illustrated by Joanna Troughton. London, Heinemann, 1973.

D.H. Lawrence: The Phoenix and the Flame. London, Macmillan, 1973; as *The Phoenix and the Flame: D.H. Lawrence, A Biography,* New York, Viking, 1973.

Britain Yesterday, illustrated by Robert Hodgson. Oxford, Basil Blackwell, 1975.

Timechanges: The Evolution of Everyday Life. London, Kingfisher Books, 1985; New York, Watts, 1986.

Living through History: The Edwardian Era. London, Batsford, 1986.

Hidden Treasure, illustrated by Chris Molan. London, Hamish Hamilton, and New York, Lodestar, 1989.

King to Be: Henry VIII, illustrated by Pauline Hagelwood, Hove, England, Macdonald, 1995.

Page to Queen Jane, illustrated by Pauline Hagelwood, Hove, England, Macdonald, 1996.

Elizabeth, Princess in Peril, illustrated by Pauline Hagelwood, Hove, England, Macdonald, 1997.

PUBLICATIONS FOR ADULTS

Novels

Such Divinity. London, Chapman & Hall, 1939.

Only Natural. London, Chapman & Hall, 1940.

Snared Nightingale. London, Macmillan, 1957; New York, Vanguard Press, 1958.

So Wild the Heart. London, Macmillan, and New York, Vanguard Press, 1959.

Short Stories

The Unsleeping Sword. London, Lawrence, 1934.

Plays

After the Tempest (produced Welwyn, Hertfordshire, 1938; London, 1939). Published in *Best One-Act Plays of 1938,* edited by J.W. Marriott, London, Harrap, 1939; published separately, Boston, Baker, n.d.

Colony. (produced London, 1939).

Mr. Engels of Manchester Change (radio play). 1947.

Henry Irving (radio play). 1947.

Lady Anne (radio play). 1949.

The Real Mr. Ryecroft (radio play). 1949.

Time Out of Mind (televised, 1956; produced London, 1967).

Elgar of England (radio play). 1957.

Into Thin Air (television play). 1973.

Poetry

The Supreme Prize and Other Poems. London, Stockwell, 1926.

Nonfiction

Walking in England. Wisbech, Cambridge, Fenland, 1935.

Clem Voroshilov: The Red Marshal. London, Pilot Press, 1940.

Tales out of School: A Survey of Children's Fiction. London, Heinemann, 1949; revised edition, 1964.

The Italian Story: From the Earliest Times to 1946. London, Macmillan, 1963; *The Italian Story: From the Etruscans to Modern Times,* New York, Vanguard Press, 1963.

The Grand Tour. London, Heinemann, and New York, Holt, 1967.

Editor, *Matthew Todd's Journal: A Gentleman's Gentleman in Europe, 1814-1820.* London, Heinemann, 1968.

Nottingham: A Biography. London, Macmillan, 1970.

The Condottieri: Soldiers of Fortune. London, Thames & Hudson, 1970; New York, Holt, 1971.

A Whiff of Burnt Boats: An Early Autobiography. London, Macmillan, and New York, St. Martin's, 1971.

Samuel Pepys and His World. London, Thames & Hudson, and New York, Putnam, 1972.

Laughter at the Door: A Continued Autobiography. London, Macmillan, and New York, St. Martin's, 1974.

London: A Concise History. London, Thames & Hudson, and New York, Scribner, 1975.

Portrait of a Cavalier: William Cavendish, First Duke of Newcastle. London, Macmillan, and New York, Taplinger, 1979.

*

Media Adaptations: *Popinjay Stairs* (radio play), BBC, 1973; *Cue for Treason* (adapted for the stage by David Craig), produced by Toronto Young People's Theatre, Canada, 1986; *The Red Towers of Grenada* dramatized in a TV biographical film on Trease's life and work, London, Channel 4, 1992.

Biography: Essay in *Something about the Author Autobiography Series,* Volume 6, Detroit, Gale, 1988, pp. 237-256.

Manuscript Collections: Nottingham Central Library; Kerlan Collection, University of Minnesota, Minneapolis; University of Nottingham Library.

Critical Study: *Geoffrey Trease* by Margaret Meek, London, Bodley Head, 1960; New York, Walck, 1964.

Geoffrey Trease comments:

I have always disliked age-group classifications, though I can see why overworked adults demand them for timesaving reassurance. I despise the arrogant generalizations implied in "catering" for this group or that. At 88, with 113 books behind me, I have always written about what interested *me*, but am compelled by illness to call it a day. My work has appeared in twenty languages. How could I cater to the young Estonian or Brazilian, the Icelander or the Japanese? As for age-groups, the reader I am proudest to have roused to enthusiasm was the great historian G.M. Trevelyan, who, when old and going blind, told me what pleasure he had found in my adventure stories. Though I have written some shorter books with child characters, I was happiest with my ''junior novels,'' in which adult life is seen through the eyes of adolescents or the slightly older. Writing fiction was my absolute lifeline. There are still so many themes and so many backgrounds, crying out for treatment—and on the whole, so much more freedom of expression than in the strait-laced 1930s when I began. (Only the creeping censorship of political correctness worries me.) Though still loyal to my old favourite periods, such as Pepys's London, I have been drawn, in recent novels, to the dramas of my own century, from the women's struggle for the vote to post-Communist Russia and the Bucharest rising of 1989. I am only wistful that my recent physical weakness makes me powerless to tackle any more.

*   *   *

The excellence of modern English historical fiction for young people is in no small part due to the pioneering efforts and achievement of Geoffrey Trease. When his first novels were published in the early 1930s, realistic fiction for children in general, and historical fiction in particular, had few notable practitioners. The historical novels available for children tended to romanticize upper-class life, to ignore the poor, and to glorify warfare and picturesque, aristocratic lost causes. Trease was to change all this by writing historical fiction from the perspective of middle- or working-class children and from a position of support for liberal or radical and democratic movements in history. Although as a youth Trease won a scholarship to Oxford to study the classics, he left the university after one year, and his future studies in history were self-directed. Intensely aware of the social and economic distress throughout Britain as the Depression deepened, he first went to work with slum children in the east end of London, and then while employed as a teacher and journalist, he became a pacifist and adherent of the idealistic left-wing movement that flourished in Britain in the 1930s. Working with children, he was struck by the realization, as he noted in his later *Tales out of School*, that ''children's books were not reflecting the changed values of the age.'' Trease set about to remedy the situation with a novel about the age of Robin Hood, *Bows against the Barons*, whose very title reflects Trease's lifelong sympathy with the ordinary man and the underdog against the wealthy and powerful.

Partly inspired by the Soviet children's book *Moscow Has a Plan*, Trease's first novel presented Robin Hood as the people's hero, and had a fairly heavy political message which was toned down in a later edition. As well as its stirring presentation of the struggle of right against privileged wrong, *Bows against the Barons* revealed Trease's gift for telling an exciting story whose well-crafted incidents grip the reader's attention throughout the tale. As a child he had loved to read the adventure stories of writers like Henty and Ballantyne, and he proved able in his own writing to combine the dash of the adventure story with a serious view of the significance of historical events. While at this time even an innovative and relatively successful children's author received

little recognition or pecuniary reward, Trease continued to write and steadily gained command over his craft. Showing the relevance of history to the concerns of our own day has always been his aim although he admitted that *Comrades for the Charter,* his second novel, savoured more of the 1930s socialists than the 1830s Chartists who were its subject. Trease did, however, rapidly increase his own grasp of historical detail to add depth to his vision of the significance of historical movements, and learned to adapt contemporary speech patterns to characters in different historical settings.

The young characters of Trease's novels are almost always involved in important political events of their era as well as some aspect of its cultural and intellectual life. In one of the earliest and most popular of Trease's novels, *Cue for Treason,* two young people manage to foil a plot against the life of Queen Elizabeth I and to join Shakespeare's company and act in his plays. Apart from this exciting action, however, the novel is notable for its pairing of the fourteen-year-old narrator, Peter, with a spirited and resourceful heroine, Kit. Unlike the passive girls who had played largely decorative roles in most previous historical fiction which was aimed at young male readers, Kit is an active and interesting character who takes her fate into her own hands, runs away from a forced engagement disguised as a boy, and in that disguise has the opportunity to perform some of Shakespeare's great female roles. Trease was to retain through many of his novels this device of a paired hero and heroine who are fully equal as they travel and have adventures together. Sometimes they arrive at a mature appreciation of each other which is romantic but never cloying or sentimental and does not require the girl to give up the independence and self-assertion she has demonstrated throughout their adventures. Trease has received too little credit for his creation of these lively and strong-minded girls; while their disguises and successes may sometimes seem implausible in the historical context, they were a refreshing innovation to the genre and created at a time when the roles of young female characters were sadly limited.

While many of Trease's early novels were concerned with young people caught up in major events of English history (such as the Civil War, the Monmouth rebellion, and King Alfred's resistance against Danish invaders), later novels went further afield to deal with the Garibaldi uprising, the Russian Revolution, and the early years of the French Revolution. Yet others depict English characters travelling to far-off places, the link with the familiar being provided for his English readers by the age and English perspective of the central character. In *The Hills of Varna* a young English student of the early sixteenth century is sent by Erasmus to search in Italy and Dalmatia for a lost manuscript of a Greek play. Through all the ensuing dramatic adventures, Trease manages to evoke a real sense of the intellectual excitement of the rediscovery of Greek learning in the Renaissance, excitement shared not only by Alan and his fellow students but also by Angela, the clever and intrepid Italian girl who joins Alan in fulfilling the quest. Trease often gives a sense of historical development and perspective by linking elements from one novel to another: the manuscript sought by Alan and Angela reappears in *The Crown of Violet* as it is actually being written and then performed in the Theatre of Dionysus in fifth-century Athens. Athenian Alexis and Corinna, like many of Trease's paired young characters, are fascinated by the theatre, and Alexis writes the prizewinning comedy as well as engages in exciting maneuvers to foil a band of traitors who seek to undermine Athenian democracy.

Interestingly, when *The Crown of Violet* appeared in the U.S. at the height of the McCarthy era, it was given the title *Web of Traitors* and presented by its publishers as a kind of anticommunist allegory, with Alexis compared to an F.B.I. agent—a curious fate for an author of Trease's left-wing sympathies. Those sympathies were never rigidly doctrinaire, however; while writing from the Roundhead or Cromwellian point of view in his early Civil War novel *Silver Guard* and in the later *The Field of the Forty Footsteps,* he shows the harsh consequences resulting from the imposition of Puritan rule under Cromwell. But although he is willing and able to show two sides of a question and to grant that good people may be found on both sides, Trease always takes a stand on issues and directs his readers' support to defend popular and/or individual rights against assault by the privileged and powerful. Necessity, often rooted in social injustice, usually sends his young characters out on the road to adventure: farmer's son Peter in *Cue for Treason* has to leave home because he is in trouble for protesting against the enclosure of common land, sailor Denzil in *Popinjay Stairs* is penniless because the Navy can not afford to employ sailors through the winter, and Robin in *The Red Towers of Granada* is driven away from his home village because he is suspected of having leprosy; he is befriended by another medieval outcast, a Jew. Despite their breathtaking plots and the encounters with famous historical figures, Trease's historical novels are realistic in conveying a sense of the economic pressures and physical discomforts experienced by the characters, and Trease's conclusions rarely promise a simple solution to the problems—whether personal or political.

While best known for his historical fiction, Trease also writes about modern young people, and several recent novels such as *Song for a Tattered Flag,* about the Romanian uprising in 1989, find his characteristic young couple involved in the history-making events of our own day. The older novels of the Bannermere sequence, set in the English Lake District, depict the gradual maturing of a group of adolescent friends of both sexes; they rely less on dramatic events than do the historical novels and were both innovative and successful in depicting the school and home lives of ordinary young people at a time when the exclusive world of the boarding school stories dominated the field. The Maythorn novels of the 1960s present contemporary working-class characters and settings. In his 98th book, *A Flight of Angels,* Trease returned to his own background as the son of a wine merchant in Nottingham for a story of the discovery of long-lost sculptures in the cave-cellars of a Nottingham wine merchant. Directed at somewhat younger readers than usual, this novel gives an amusing depiction of how the children are lured into the pleasures and discipline of historical research; other recent novels such as *Calabrian Quest and Shadow Under the Sea* also center on archeological discovery, in such vividly-evoked surroundings as southern Italy and Yalta. In *Hidden Treasures* Trease skillfully presents factual background about such potential discoveries all over the world. Most of Trease's non-fiction, however, treats English history, and includes well regarded biographies of the writers Byron and D.H. Lawrence, both connected with Nottingham.

In his first autobiographical volume, *A Whiff of Burnt Boats,* Trease remarks that he is much more interested in older children than younger ones, and rather than encouraging them to cling to the magical world of childhood "my impulse was to beckon them on and shout: 'There is a wider view from the next bend.'" In well over half a century of writing for young people, Trease has

beckoned his readers around many bends in the river of human experience, and widened the view for all of them.

—Gwyneth Evans

TREMBATH, Don

Nationality: Canadian. **Born:** Donald James Trembath in Winnipeg, Manitoba, 22 May 1963. **Education:** Paul Kane High School, Morinville, Alberta, graduated 1981; Northern Alberta Institute of Technology, Diploma in Civil Engineering Technology, 1983; University of Alberta, 1984-88, B.A. 1988. **Family:** Married Lisa Murray in 1984; one son and one daughter. **Career:** Reporter/photographer/editor, *The Morinville Mirror* newspaper, Morinville, Alberta, 1988-90; freelance writer, from 1990. **Awards:** R. Ross Annett Juvenile Fiction Award, 1997. **Address:** 10011-104th St., Morinville, Alberta, T8R 1A5, Canada.

PUBLICATIONS FOR YOUNG ADULTS

The Tuesday Cafe. Victoria, British Columbia, Orca, 1996.
A Fly Named Alfred. Victoria, British Columbia, Orca, 1997.

*   *   *

Don Trembath is a relative newcomer to Canadian Young Adult literature, but the quality of the two titles he has produced suggests that he could become one of the nation's stronger voices in the YA field. *The Tuesday Cafe* is a fine character study which, over a one month period, convincingly explores the strained relationship which exists between loner Harper Winslow, 15, and his career-preoccupied parents. In their forties, Harper's mother, a clothing designer and store owner, and his father, a doctor and successful small town politician, had considered themselves nearing the end of their child rearing responsibilities when an unplanned pregnancy resulted in Harper. Because Harper's two siblings, now in their thirties, had left home when Harper was just four, Harper has been growing up essentially as an only child. Being parented via benign neglect and critical comparisons with his "perfect-but-absent" siblings has left Harper angry and confused. When Harper starts a fire in his school and is charged with arson, the judge, dripping sympathy for Harper's "wonderful" parents, imposes a sentence of community service and the writing of a 2000 word essay, "How I Plan to Turn My Life Around." To facilitate Harper's completing the essay, his mother enrolls him in "The Tuesday Cafe," an evening writing class in nearby Edmonton, Alberta. Unknown to her, the class is actually geared towards adults, either those learning disabled or needing upgrading. Via his weekly interactions with his six quite different adult classmates, Harper gradually gains the self-insight necessary to open a life-changing dialogue with his parents.

Readers who suspected that Harper's parents' transformation in *The Tuesday Cafe* came too easily to be permanent can have their suspicions confirmed or denied in *A Fly Named Alfred,* which continues Harper's story. Now in grade 11, Harper remains a social outcast, but his occasional writing for the school newspaper leads to new troubles. When "Alfred," the anonymous writer of a satirical column called "Fly on the Wall," mocks one of the school's most popular girls and her local hood boyfriend, Harper is pressured by Tommy Rowe, star football player and school bully, to use his newspaper connections to uncover the Fly's identity within the next month "or else." Harper's assignment is actually quite simple for he is the individual behind the pseudonym; however, the choices for Harper/the Fly are equally unpleasant— to be beaten up by Tommy as Harper or by the boyfriend as the Fly. Despite the seriousness of Harper's situation, the book is frequently very humorous, especially when Harper, attempting to dupe Tommy, involves Billy, one of the "intellectually challenged" adults from his writing group, the Tuesday Cafe. Would-be actor Billy, an avid movie fan and mystery/western reader, adopts, with hilarious results, the speech patterns of the characters whom he has most recently encountered. The plot arrives at a believable conclusion, and Harper learns that the reality of a person's life is often different than its surface appearance.

—Dave Jenkinson

TRUMBO, Dalton

Pseudonyms: Sam Jackson; Robert Rich. **Nationality:** American. **Born:** Montrose, Colorado, 9 December 1905. University of Colorado, 1924-25, Southern Branch, University of California (now University of California, Los Angeles), 1926, and University of Southern California, Los Angeles, 1928-30. **Military Service:** Served in the United States Army Air Forces as War correspondent, 1945. **Family:** Married Cleo Beth Fincher in 1939; two daughters and one son. **Career:** Screenwriter and novelist. Car washer; section hand; worked for nine years as a bread-wrapper and later as an estimator ont he night shift for Divis Perfection bakery, Los Angeles, California; reader at Warner Brothers. Served as national chairman of Writers for Roosevelt, 1944. **Awards:** National Book award, 1939, for *Johnny Got His Gun*; Academy award, 1957, for "The Brave One"; Teachers Union of New York annual award, 1960; Writers Guild Laurel award for achievement in screenwriting, 1970; Cannes Film Festival Special Jury Grand Prize, International Critics Prize, Interfilm Jury World Council of Churches Prize, Atlanta Film Festival Golden Dove Peace Prize, and Golden Phoenix for Best of Festival, all 1971, and Belgrade Film Festival Audience and Director's award and Japanese International Festival of the Arts Grand Prize, both 1972, all for *Johnny Got His Gun*. **Died:** 10 September 1976.

PUBLICATIONS

Novels

Eclipse. London, L. Dickson & Thompson, 1935.
Washington Jitters. New York, Knopf, 1936.
Johnny Got His Gun. Philadelphia, Lippincott, 1939.
The Remarkable Andrew. Philadelphia, Lippincott, 1941.
Night of the Aurochs, edited by Robert Kirsch. New York, Viking, 1979.

Plays

The Biggest Thief in Town (produced New York, 1949). New York, Dramatists Play Service, 1949.

Screenplays: *Jealousy,* 1934; *The Story of Isadore Bernstein,* 1936; *Love Begins at Twenty,* with Tom Reed, 1936; *Road Gang,* 1936; collaborator, *Devil's Playground,* 1937; *A Man to Remember* (based on Katharine Haviland-Taylor's short story *Failure,* 1938; *Fugitives for a Night,* 1938; *Sorority House,* 1939; *Career,* 1939; *Five Came Back,* with Nathanael West and Jerry Cady, 1939; *The Flying Irishman,* with Ernest Pagano, 1939; *Heaven with a Barbed Wire Fence,* 1939; *Half a Sinner,* 1940; *We Who Are Young,* 1940; *Kitty Foyle* (adaptation of the book by Christopher Morley), 1940; *A Bill of Divorcement,* 1940; *Curtain Call,* 1940; *The Remarkable Andrew,* 1942; *Tender Comrade,* 1943; *A Man Named Joe,* 1943; *Thirty Seconds Over Tokyo,* 1944; *Our Vines Have Tender Grapes* (adaptation of the book by George Victor Martin), 1945; *The Brave One,* as Robert Rich, King Brothers Production, 1957; *Exodus* (adaptation of the book by Leon Uris), 1960; *Spartacus* (based on the novel by Howard Fast), 1960; *The Last Sunset* (based on *Sundown at Crazy Horse* by Howard Rigsby), 1961; *Lonely Are the Brave* (based on *The Brave Cowboy* by Edward Abbey), 1962; *The Sandpiper,* 1965; *Hawaii* (adaptation of the book by James A. Michener, 1966; *The Fixer* (adaptation of the book by Bernard Malamud), 1968; *The Horsemen,* 1971; (and director) *Johnny Got His Gun,* 1971; *Papillon,* with Lorenzo Semple, Jr., 1973; *Executive Action* (based on a story by Donald Freed and Mark Lane), 1973.

Other

Harry Bridges (pamphlet). League of American Writers, 1941.
Additional Dialogue: Letters of Dalton Trumbo, 1942-1962, edited by Helen Manfull. New York, M. Evans, 1970.
The Time of the Toad: A Study of the Inquisition in American and Two Related Pamphlets (includes *The Time of the Toad, The Devil in the Book,* and *Honor Bright and All that Jazz*) New York, Harper, 1972.

*

Media Adaptations: *Washington Jitters* was dramatized by John Boruft and Walter Hart and produced at the Guild Theatre, New York, City, May 2, 1938. The films *The Kid from Kokomo,* Warner Brothers, 1939, *The Lone Wolf Strike,* Columbia, 1940, *Accent on Love,* Twentieth Century-Fox, 1941, and *You Belong to Me,* Columbia, 1941, refilmed as *Emergency Wedding,* Columbia, 1950, were based on Trumbo's stories. A novelization by Randall M. White of *A Man Named Joe* was published as *A Guy Named Joe,* Grossett, 1944. *The Biggest Thief in Town* was adapted for television and shown on the British Broadcasting Corp., 1957.

Critical Studies: Entry in *Contemporary Literary Criticism,* Volume 19, Detroit, Gale, 1981.

*   *   *

World War I killed more than people, it killed an age of innocence. When the fighting began, singing mothers and wives who expected to see their men home by Christmas sent young men away with fanfare to the battlefields of the "war to end all wars." That Christmas did not come until four years later, and many of the men never returned. Armed primarily with a sense of national pride, the desire to serve God and country, and an archaic albeit glorious notion of war, the young soldiers were faced with a brutal reality. Modern war with its machine guns, chemicals, grenades, and mines ravaged the European countryside and the armies along with it. Not until Vietnam would the United States experience such trauma again.

In fact, the worst of the trauma was never revealed. This is the story Dalton Trumbo tells in his sole completed novel, *Johnny Got His Gun.* His compelling yet chilling account, though published in 1939, still wrenches the soul of the reader. Trumbo, best known for his screenplays and political activities, relates in his novel the story of Joe Bonham, a young veteran who was wounded during the war. Bonham was not simply wounded, however, he was marred beyond recognition as a human being. His face was completely disfigured and all four of his limbs were lost. He was, in essence, a stump. His mental functions, however, were completely intact—and trapped inside a body that allowed him no expression. The story is told completely from Bonham's perspective, thus the reader becomes engaged in the character's struggle to figure out what has happened to him, create order in a new universe of which he is the only inhabitant, and establish contact with the outside world.

Part of Trumbo's success with *Johnny Got His Gun* was his use of cinematic techniques to keep his audience involved. Most of the novel takes place in Joe Bonham's head, but Trumbo kept the reader engaged in the stream of consciousness flow through the extensive use of flashbacks and even, on one occasion, a montage. The sensual detail of Bonham's flashbacks is exquisite. Often the character remembers the sights, sounds, smells, and tastes of his childhood. Trumbo describes these memories with such clarity and finesse that the reader lives these scenes along with the character. Not only are these flashbacks individually well-crafted, each of them is essential to the progression of the plot. Each flashback reveals new bits of information about Joe's present condition and together, they provide fascinating suggestions about how the human mind uses memory.

Although the book is a cogent and passionate argument for pacificism, it retains a vital significance even in times of peace. Because of Bonham's severe injuries, one of the central issues with which he must grapple is what gives life meaning? What makes one human? Clearly, Bonham is still human and keeps the reader engaged as such. Yet he is one over whom debate would rage on the outside world. Is his life worth continuing? To what lengths should society go to sustain him?

Trumbo also invites an examination of society in this book. Interestingly, Bonham becomes more of a problem to society once he regains access to it. When he was non-responsive, the outside world could more or less ignore him. Once he could make his wishes known, however, they knew he still was an alert and aware human being. The thought of that—the obligations that implied— were beyond society's ability to handle. He held an unkind mirror to society. The people within the system wanted to appear magnanimous as is evidenced by their bestowing Bonham with medals and offering him such extensive care for the rest of his life. But once Bonham could make his desires known, the system was revealed to be cruel, callous, and self-serving.

Perhaps this reflective aspect of the book is its most significant contribution to young adults. The pacifist argument is certainly an important one—war is not a glorious undertaking and should not be portrayed as such. Yet war is not always at issue. The more constant issue within society is the meaning and value of life. Teaching young people to ponder these issues and form conscious convictions about them is, perhaps, the more urgent matter at hand. Trumbo provides a vehicle through which both sets of issues can be addressed.

—Linda Ross

TUNIS, John R(oberts)

Nationality: American. **Born:** Boston, Massachusetts, 7 December 1889. **Education:** Harvard University, Cambridge, Massachusetts, A.B. 1911; Boston University Law School, 1916. **Military Service:** Served in the United States Army in France during World War I: Lieutenant. **Family:** Married Lucy Rogers in 1918. **Career:** Sportswriter, New York *Evening Post,* 1925-32, and Universal Service, New York, 1932-35; tennis commentator, NBC, New York, 1934-42. Regular contributor to *Harper's, Atlantic Monthly, Saturday Evening Post,* and other periodicals; sports columnist, the *New Yorker.* **Awards:** Spring Book Festival award, *New York Herald Tribune,* 1938, for *The Iron Duke,* 1940, for *The Kid from Tomkinsville,* 1948, for *Highpockets,* and 1949, for *Son of the Valley;* Child Study Children's Book award, 1943, for *Keystone Kids;* Junior Book award, Boys' Clubs of America, 1949, for *Highpockets.* **Died:** 4 February 1975.

PUBLICATIONS FOR YOUNG ADULTS

Fiction

Iron Duke, illustrated by Johan Bull. New York, Harcourt Brace, 1938.
The Duke Decides, illustrated by James MacDonald. New York, Harcourt Brace, 1939.
Champion's Choice, illustrated by Jay Hyde Barnum. New York, Harcourt Brace, 1940.
The Kid from Tomkinsville, illustrated by Jay Hyde Barnum. New York, Harcourt Brace, 1940.
World Series, illustrated by Jay Hyde Barnum. New York, Harcourt Brace, 1941.
All-American, illustrated by Hans Walleen. New York, Harcourt Brace, 1942.
Keystone Kids. New York, Harcourt Brace, 1943.
Rookie of the Year. New York, Harcourt Brace, 1944.
Yea! Wildcats! New York, Harcourt Brace, 1944.
A City for Lincoln. New York, Harcourt Brace, 1945.
The Kid Comes Back. New York, Morrow, 1946.
Highpockets. New York, Morrow, 1948.
Son of the Valley. New York, Morrow, 1949.
Young Razzle. New York, Morrow, 1949.
The Other Side of the Fence. New York, Morrow, 1953.
Go, Team, Go! New York, Morrow, 1954.
Buddy and the Old Pro, illustrated by Jay Hyde Barnum. New York, Morrow, 1955.

Schoolboy Johnson. New York, Morrow, 1958.
Silence over Dunkerque. New York, Morrow, 1962.
His Enemy, His Friend. New York, Morrow, 1967.
Grand National. New York, Morrow, 1973.

Other

$port$, Heroics, and Hysterics. New York, Day, 1928.
Was College Worth While? New York, Harcourt Brace, 1936.
Choosing a College. New York, Harcourt Brace, 1940.
Sport for the Fun of It. New York, A.S. Barnes, 1940; revised
    edition, 1950.
Democracy and Sport. New York, A.S. Barnes, 1941.
*This Writing Game: Selections from Twenty Years of Free-Lanc-
    ing.* New York, A.S. Barnes, 1941.
Million-Miler: The Story of an Air Pilot. New York, Messner, 1942.
Lawn Games. New York, A.S. Barnes, 1943.
The American Way of Sport. New York, Duell, 1958.

PUBLICATIONS FOR ADULTS

Novel

American Girl. New York, Brewer and Warren, 1930.

Other

A Measure of Independence (autobiography). New York,
    Atheneum, 1964.

*

Media Adaptations: *American Girl* (as film called *Hard, Fast and
Beautiful*), RKO.

Manuscript Collections: Mugar Memorial Library, Boston
University.

*   *   *

John R. Tunis was from early youth fascinated with sports. He
competed in high school; at Harvard he was active in tennis and
long-distance track. Following service in France during World
War I, he wrote sports articles for the New York *Evening Post* and
at the same time announced major sporting events. He wrote
literally thousands of articles on sports and education, about which
he felt keenly.

Most of his books for children are about college athletics or
professional sports. He covers equally well baseball, basketball,
football, and tennis. *All-American* was deemed by the New York
Herald Tribune as the best story offered to boys in 1942. *Keystone*

Kids was chosen by the Child Study Association as the most
challenging book of 1943 for young people. Tunis's plots are fast
moving, as are professional games; his dialogue is clipped and
colorful, as are radio and TV sportscasts. The drama of challenge
and skill set against competition and effort is the basis of the books.
In addition the books promulgate the ideal American sports values
of fair play and of consideration for individuals and for teams.
Tunis's concern with sportsmanship as well as sports is evident in
his focus on respect for others. Long before it was well understood,
Tunis discussed racial and religious discrimination in sports. *All-
American* focuses on a well-to-do boy who comes to an economically mixed high school and makes the football team. How this boy
learns to admire his fellow players and how he is able to help with
the special problems of one black player are realistically and
forcefully presented. Also clearly shown are the difficulties of
teamwork, of caring and looking out for one's fellow player.
Among Tunis's other first-rate sports stories are: *Champion's
Choice, The Kid from Tomkinsville, World Series, Rookie of the
Year, Young Razzle,* and *Go, Team, Go!*

In addition to his stories of American sports, Tunis also wrote
stories of politics—of American democracy (*A City for Lincoln*)
and of world war (*Silence over Dunkerque* and *His Enemy, His
Friend*). These works are more didactic, less exciting, and less
suspenseful than the sports stories. They express, though, Tunis's
deep concern for human beings and their interrelatedness.

—Mary Lystad

TWAIN, Mark

Pseudonym for Samuel Langhorne Clemens. **Nationality:** American. **Born:** Florida, Missouri, 30 November 1835; moved to
Hannibal, Missouri, 1839. **Family:** Married Olivia Langdon in
1870 (died 1904); one son and three daughters. **Career:** Printer's
apprentice and typesetter for Hannibal newspapers, 1847-50;
helped brother with Hannibal *Journal,* 1850-52; typesetter and
printer in St. Louis, New York, Philadelphia, for Keokuk *Saturday
Post,* Iowa, 1853-56, and in Cincinnati, 1857; apprentice river
pilot, on the Mississippi, 1857-58; licensed as pilot, 1859-60; went
to Nevada as secretary to his brother, then on the staff of the
Governor, and also worked as goldminer, 1861; staff member,
Virginia City *Territorial Enterprise,* Nevada, 1862-64 (first used
pseudonym Mark Twain, 1863); reporter, San Francisco *Morning
Call,* 1864; correspondent, Sacramento *Union,* 1866, and San
Francisco *Alta California,* 1866-69: visited Sandwich (i.e., Hawai-
ian) Islands, 1866, and France, Italy, and Palestine, 1867; lecturer
from 1867; editor, *Express,* Buffalo, New York, 1869-71; moved
to Hartford, Connecticut and became associated with Charles L.
Webster Publishing Company, 1884; invested in unsuccessful
Paige typesetter and went bankrupt, 1894 (last debts paid, 1898);
lived mainly in Europe, 1896-1900, New York, 1900-07, and
Redding, Connecticut, 1907-10. **Awards:** M.A.: Yale University,
New Haven, Connecticut, 1888; Litt.D.: Yale University, 1901;
Oxford University, 1907; LL.D.: University of Missouri, Colum-
bia, 1902. Member, American Academy, 1904. **Died:** 21 April 1910.

PUBLICATIONS

Novels

The Gilded Age: A Tale of Today, with Charles Dudley Warner, illustrated by Augustus Hoppin and others. Hartford, Connecticut, American Publishing, 1873; London, Routledge, 1874; Twain's portion published separately as *The Adventures of Colonel Sellers,* edited by Charles Nelder, New York, Doubleday, 1965.

The Adventures of Tom Sawyer, illustrated by True Williams. Hartford, Connecticut, American Publishing, and London, Chatto & Windus, 1876.

The Prince and the Pauper. London, Chatto & Windus, 1881; Boston, Osgood, 1882.

The Adventures of Huckleberry Finn, Tom Sawyer's Comrade, illustrated by Edward Windsor Kemble. London, Chatto & Windus, 1884; New York, Webster, 1885.

A Connecticut Yankee in King Arthur's Court, illustrated by Dan Beard. New York, Webster, 1889; as *A Yankee at the Court of King Arthur,* London, Chatto & Windus, 1889.

The American Claimant, adapted from the play by Twain and William Dean Howells. New York, Webster, and London, Chatto & Windus, 1892.

Tom Sawyer Abroad, by Huck Finn, illustrated by Dan Beard. New York, Webster, and London, Chatto & Windus, 1894.

Pudd'nhead Wilson: A Tale. London, Chatto & Windus, 1894; expanded as *The Tragedy of Pudd'nhead Wilson, and the Comedy of Those Extraordinary Twins,* Hartford, Connecticut, American Publishing, 1894.

Personal Recollections of Joan of Arc (under pseudonym Sieur Louis de Conte), illustrated by E. V. Du Mond, New York, Harper, and London, Chatto & Windus, 1896.

Extract from Captain Stormfield's Visit to Heaven. New York and London, Harper, 1909.

The Mysterious Stranger: A Romance, illustrated by N. C. Wyeth, edited by Albert Bigelow Paine and Frederick A. Duneka. New York and London, Harper, 1916; expanded as *The Mysterious Stranger and Other Stories,* New York and London, Harper, 1922.

Simon Wheeler: Detective (unfinished novel), edited by Franklin R. Rogers. New York, New York Public Library, 1963.

Short Stories

The Celebrated Jumping Frog of Calaveras County, and Other Sketches, edited by John Paul. New York, Webb, and London, Routledge, 1867.

Screamers: A Gathering of Scraps of Humour, Delicious Bits, and Short Stories. London, Hotten, 1871.

Eye Openers: Good Things, Immensely Funny Sayings, and Stories. London, Hotten, c. 1871.

A Curious Dream, and Other Sketches. London, Routledge, 1872.

Mark Twain's Sketches, illustrated by R. T. Sperry. New York, American News, 1874.

Mark Twain's Sketches: New and Old. Hartford, Connecticut, American Publishing, 1876.

Merry Tales. New York, Webster, 1892.

The 1,000,000 Pound Bank-Note, and Other New Stories. New York, Webster, 1893.

Tom Sawyer, Detective, as Told by Huck Finn, and Other Stories. London, Chatto & Windus, 1896.

The Man that Corrupted Hadleyburg, and Other Stories and Essays. New York and London, Harper, 1900; revised edition, London, Chatto & Windus, 1900.

A Double Barrelled Detective Story, illustrated by Lucius Hitchcock. New York and London, Harper, 1902.

A Dog's Tale, illustrated by W. T. Smedley. New York, Harper, 1904.

Extracts from Adam's Diary illustrated by F. Strothmann. New York and London, Harper, 1904.

Eve's Diary Translated from the Original Ms, illustrated by Lester Ralph. New York and London, Harper, 1906.

The $30,000 Bequest, and Other Stories. New York and London, Harper, 1906.

A Horse's Tale, illustrated by Lucius Hitchcock. New York and London, Harper, 1907.

The Curious Republic of Gondour, and Other Whimsical Sketches. New York, Boni & Liveright, 1919.

Sketches of the Sixties, with Bret Harte. San Francisco, Howell, 1926.

Short Stories of Mark Twain. New York, Funk & Wagnall, 1967.

Early Tales and Sketches, Volume 1: *1851-1864,* edited by Edgar M. Branch and Robert H. Hirst. Berkeley, University of California Press, 1979.

Plays

Colonel Sellers (five-act, produced New York, 1874).

Ah Sin, with Bret Harte (produced Washington, DC, 1877).

Travel Books

The Innocents Abroad; or, The New Pilgrims' Progress, illustrated by True Williams. Hartford, Connecticut, American Publishing, 1869; as Volume 1: *Innocents Abroad,* London, Hotten, 1870, Volume 2: *The New Pilgrims' Progress,* London, Hotten, 1870.

The Innocents at Home. London, Routledge, 1872.

Roughing It. London, Routledge, 1872; revised edition (includes *The Innocents at Home*), Hartford, Connecticut, American Publishing, 1872.

An Idle Excursion. Toronto, Rose-Belford, 1878; revised as *Punch, Brothers, Punch!, and Other Sketches,* New York, Slote, Woodman, 1878.

A Tramp Abroad, illustrated by Twain and others. Hartford, Connecticut, American Publishing, 1880.

Following the Equator: A Journey around the World. Hartford, Connecticut, American Publishing, 1897; as *More Tramps Abroad,* London, Chatto & Windus, 1897.

Europe and Elsewhere, edited by Albert Bigelow Paine. New York, Harper, 1923.

Traveling with the Innocents Abroad: Mark Twain's Original Reports from Europe and the Holy Land, edited by Daniel Morley McKelthan. Norman, University of Oklahoma Press, 1958.

Essays

How to Tell a Story, and Other Essays. New York, Harper, 1897.

English as She Is Taught. Mutual Book Co., 1900.

King Leopold's Soliloquy: A Defense of His Congo Rule. P. R. Warren, 1905.

Editorial Wild Oats. New York, Harper, 1905.

My Debut as a Literary Person, with Other Essays and Stories. Hartford, Connecticut, American Publishing, 1906.

What Is Man? (originally published anonymously). New York, De Vinne Press, 1906; revised as *What Is Man?, and Other Essays,* New York and London, Harper, 1917.

Christian Science, with Notes Containing Corrections to Date. New York and London, Harper, 1907.

Is Shakespeare Dead? New York and London, Harper, 1909.

In Defense of Harriet Shelley, and Other Essays. New York, Harper, 1918.

Concerning the Jews. New York, Harper, 1934.

Autobiographical Works

Old Times on the Mississippi. Toronto, Belford, 1876; reprinted as *The Mississippi Pilot,* London, Ward, Lock & Tyler, 1877; revised as *Life on the Mississippi,* Boston, Osgood, and London, Chatto and Windus, 1883.

Mark Twain's Autobiography (two volumes), edited by Albert Bigelow Paine. New York and London, Harper, 1924; edited as one volume by Charles Neider, New York, Harper, 1959.

Collected Journalism

Letters from the Sandwich Islands Written for the Sacramento Union, edited by G. Ezra Dane. San Francisco, Grabhorn, 1937.

The Washoe Giant in San Francisco, edited by Franklin Walker. San Francisco, Fields, 1938.

Mark Twain's Letters in the Muscatine Journal, edited by Edgar M. Branch. Mark Twain Association of America, 1942.

Mark Twain of the Enterprise: Newspaper Articles and Other Documents, 1862-1864, edited by Henry Nash Smith. Berkeley, University of California Press, 1957.

Contributions to the Galaxy, 1868-1871, edited by Bruce R. McElderry. Jr. Scholars' Facsimiles and Reprints, 1961.

Mark Twain's San Francisco, edited by Bernard Taper. New York, McGraw, 1963.

Clemens of the "Call": Mark Twain in San Francisco, edited by Edgar M. Branch. Berkeley, University of California Press, 1969.

Other

Mark Twain's (Burlesque) Autobiography and First Romance. New York, Sheldon, and London, Hotten, 1871.

Practical Jokes with Artemus Ward, with others. London, Hotten, 1872.

A True Story [and] *The Recent Carnival of Crime.* Boston, Osgood, 1877.

"1601"; or, Conversation as It Was by the Social Fireside in the Time of the Tudors. Published in Cleveland, 1880.

The Stolen White Elephant, Etc. Boston, Osgood, 1882; as *The Stolen White Elephant,* London, Chatto & Windus, 1882.

Editor, with William Dean Howells and others, *Mark Twain's Library of Humor,* illustrated by E.W. Kemble. New York, Webster, 1888.

Mark Twain's Speeches, edited by F.A. Nast. New York and London, Harper, 1910.

Mark Twain's Speeches (two volumes), edited by Albert Bigelow Paine. New York and London, Harper, 1924.

The Adventures of Thomas Jefferson Snodgrass (under pseudonym Thomas Jefferson Snodgrass), edited by Charles Honce. Chicago, Pascal Covici, 1928.

Mark Twain's Notebook, edited by Albert Bigelow Paine. New York and London, Harper, 1935.

Mark Twain's Travels with Mr. Brown, edited by Franklin Walker and G. Ezra Dane. New York, Knopf, 1940.

Mark Twain's First Story. Prairie Press, 1952.

Life as I Find It, edited by Charles Nelder. Hanover House, 1961.

Mark Twain's "Mysterious Stranger" Manuscripts, edited by William G. Gibson. Berkeley, University of California Press, 1969.

Mark Twain's Notebooks and Journals. Berkeley, University of California Press, Volume 1: *1855-1873,* edited by Frederick Anderson, Michael B. Frank, and Kenneth M. Sanderson, 1975, Volume 2: *1877-1883,* edited by Anderson, Lin Salamo, and Bernard L. Stein, Volume 3: *1883-1891,* edited by Robert Pack Browning, Frank, and Salamo, 1979.

*

Media Adaptations: *The Adventures of Huckleberry Finn* was adapted as a motion picture titled *Huckleberry Finn,* in 1931 by Paramount, in 1939 by Metro-Goldwyn-Mayer (MGM), and in 1974 by United Artists, and as a motion picture of the same title in 1960 by MGM; *The Adventures of Tom Sawyer* was adapted as *Tom Sawyer* in 1930 by Paramount, and as a motion picture of the same title in 1938 by Selznick International and in 1973 by United Artists; *The Adventures of Tom Sawyer* was adapted as the film *Tom Sawyer, Detective,* Paramount, 1939; *A Connecticut Yankee in King Arthur's Court* was adapted as the film *A Connecticut Yankee* in 1931 by Twentieth Century-Fox, and as *A Connecticut Yankee in King Arthur's Court* in 1949 by Paramount; *The Prince and the Pauper* was adapted as motion pictures of the same title in 1937 by Warner Brothers, and in 1969 by Childhood Productions; *The Prince and the Pauper* was adapted as a film titled *Crossed Swords* in 1978 by Warner Brothers; *A Double Barrelled Detective Story* was adapted as a film of the same title in 1965 by Saloon Productions; *The Celebrated Jumping Frog of Calaveras County, and Other Sketches* was adapted as a film titled *Best Man Wins* in 1948 by Columbia. Among the many stagings of Twain's works are *Tom Sawyer* and *Huckleberry Finn;* some of Twain's writings have also been adapted as radio plays; *Huckleberry Finn* has also been staged as a musical. Twain's own life inspired *The Adventures of Mark Twain,* filmed by Warner Brothers in 1944, and such stage productions as *Mark Twain Tonight!*

Biography: *Mark Twain: A Biography; the Personal and Literary Life of Samuel Langhorne Clemens* (four volumes) by Albert Bigelow Paine, Harper, 1912; *A Lifetime with Mark Twain* by Mary Lawton, Harcourt, 1925, reprinted, Haskell House, 1972; *Mark Twain: A Portrait* by Edgar Lee Masters, Scribner's, 1938; *Sam Clemens of Hannibal* by Dixon Wecter, Houghton, 1952; *Mark Twain Himself* by Milton Meltzer, Crowell, 1960; *Mr. Clemens and Mr. Twain* by Justin Kaplan, Simon & Schuster, 1966; *Mark Twain* by Charles Neider, Horizon, 1967; entries in *Dictionary of Literary Biography,* Gale, Volume 11: *American Humorists, 1800-1950,* 1982, pp. 526-55, Volume 12: *American Realists and Naturalists,* 1982, pp. 71-94, Volume 23: *American Newspaper Journalists, 1873-1900,* 1983, pp. 31-46, Volume 64: *American*

Literary Critics and Scholars, 1850-1880, 1988, pp. 34-47, Volume 74: *American Short-Story Writers before 1880,* 1988, pp. 54-83.

Critical Studies: *The Innocent Eye: Childhood in Mark Twain's Fiction* by Albert E. Stone, Yale University Press, 1961; *Mark Twain: A Collection of Critical Essays* edited by Henry Nash Smith, Prentice-Hall, 1963; *Plots and Characters in the Works of Mark Twain* (two volumes) by Robert L. Gale, Shoe String, 1973; *The Art of Mark Twain* by William H. Gibson, Oxford University Press, 1976; entries in *Twentieth-Century Literary Criticism,* Gale, Volume 6, 1982; Volume 12, 1984; *Mark Twain* by Robert Keith Miller, Ungar, 1983; essay by Michael Patrick Hearn in *Writers for Children,* edited by Jane Bingham, Scribner's, 1988.

*   *   *

Ernest Hemingway wrote, in *Green Hills of Africa,* "All modern American literature comes from one book by Mark Twain called *Huckleberry Finn...*it's the best book we've had. All American writing comes from that. There was nothing before. There has been nothing as good since."

As criticism, Hemingway's statement is admittedly overstated. Samuel Clemens, or Mark Twain, has always been an enigma for critics, many of whom have had great difficulty in analyzing his works, and others in psychoanalyzing him. Hemingway, however, was not speaking as a critic, but rather as a reader, as a devotee, as a writer who recognized his debt to one who came before him. In that role he is an apt and accurate spokesman for all of us who rejoice in listening to the voice of Mark Twain. Just as Lincoln remains the folk symbol of the American spirit, for many Twain remains the folk symbol of the American writer.

It is significant that Hemingway specifically referred to *The Adventures of Huckleberry Finn,* for it is in that work, along with *The Adventures of Tom Sawyer* and *Life on the Mississippi,* that Twain's narrative genius is self-evident. Today *Tom Sawyer* is usually categorized as a book for children, while *Huck Finn* is considered adult fiction. Nevertheless, in any discussion of Twain's influence on American authors of books for young people, both must be considered.

Oddly enough, when Twain wrote *Tom Sawyer* he did not have a young audience in mind. It wasn't until his friend William Dean Howells suggested that it was a story most appropriate for children that Twain "cleaned up" the manuscript and added a preface in which he said: "Although my book is intended mainly for the entertainment of boys and girls, I hope it will not be shunned by men and women on that account, for part of my plan has been to try to pleasantly remind adults of what they once were themselves, and of how they felt and thought and talked, and what queer enterprises they sometimes engaged in." That he did not consciously write it for children is perhaps the book's strongest attribute, though occasionally Twain as narrator speaks directly to the adult readers he originally had in mind. This is overwhelmingly outweighed by the absence of any condescension or moralizing. In fact at the time of its publication (1876) it came under attack as a children's book. The *New York Times* book review concluded: "In the books to be placed into children's hands for purposes of recreation, we have a preference for those of a milder type than *Tom Sawyer.*"

Tom Sawyer is much more than a grown man's reminiscences about the idyllic joys and pains of childhood. Twain stands high on the list of eminent writers like Stevenson, Dickens, and Saroyan who successfully depicted how young people "felt and thought and talked." Though they did not write specifically for children, they demonstrated for those who would how necessary it is to retain the heart of a child if your work is to have the ring of truth. Twain above all else sets out to entertain. One should not overlook the word "Adventures" in the titles of his "boy" books. He takes the blood and thunder stuff of the old-fashioned dime novels and the serial boy romances and makes it literature.

In *Huck Finn,* intended as a sequel to *Tom Sawyer,* Twain gets into the skin of Huck and tells the story through him, and by so doing he happens upon the narrative mode that is explicitly suited for his special talents. Huck, who could not possibly *write* a story, *tells* us the story. And that is how Twain himself would have it; as he says in his *Autobiography:* "With the pen in one's hand, narrative is a difficult art; narrative should flow as flows the brook down through the hills and leafy woodlands." This also was one of the reasons for Hemingway's acclaim, for he too, like many storytellers, was at heart a raconteur and a minstrel rather than a scribbler.

But there was even a more important reason. Hemingway recognized the straightforward honesty in *Huck Finn.* Twain possessed, as H.L. Mencken put it, "a truly amazing instinct for the truth." Today many writers of books for children and young adults have turned to first-person narrative, with only a meager few of them handling it successfully. They would do well to look closely at *Huckleberry Finn,* for there they will find Mark Twain's greatest legacy to them—his integrity. He doesn't use the first-person point of view as a literary device for simulating a peer relationship with young readers; but rather he turns over the complete narrative to Huck, allowing him to tell the story as only he can do it. Huck's understated and innocent "telling" is the primary reason that this story of a boy's adventure is, at the same time, a devastating denunciation of the society in which the tale takes place.

A final word of caution. Too often *Huck Finn* appears on children's reading book lists as a companion piece to *Tom Sawyer,* when in fact it is a work best suited for a more mature audience. Indeed, anyone who recommends *The Adventures of Huckleberry Finn* to a young reader must first consider whether that reader is capable or not of handling the intricacies of its ironic thrust.

—James E. Higgins

TWOHILL, Maggie. *See* **ANGELL, Judie.**

TYLER, Anne

Nationality: American. **Born:** Minneapolis, Minnesota, 25 October 1941. **Education:** Duke University, Durham, North Carolina,

1958-61, B.A. 1961; Columbia University, New York, 1961-62. **Family:** Married Taghi Modarressi in 1963; two daughters. **Career:** Writer. Russian bibliographer, Duke University Library, 1962-63; assistant to the librarian, McGill University Law Library, Montreal, 1964-65. **Awards:** *Mademoiselle* award for writing, 1966; award for Literature, American Academy and Institute of Arts and Letters, 1977; National Book Critics Circle fiction award nomination, 1980, Janet Heidinger Kafka prize, 1981, and American Book award nomination in paperback fiction, 1982, all for *Morgan's Passing*; National Book Critics Circle fiction award nomination, 1982, and American Book award nomination in fiction, P.E.N./Faulkner award for fiction, and Pulitzer Prize nomination for fiction, all 1983, all for *Dinner at the Homesick Restaurant*; National Book Critics Circle fiction award and Pulitzer Prize nomination for fiction, both 1985, both for *The Accidental Tourist*; Pulitzer Prize, 1989, *Breathing Lessons*. **Agent:** Russell & Volkening, 50 West 29th St., New York, New York 10001. **Address:** 222 Tunbridge Rd., Baltimore, Maryland 21212, U.S.A.

PUBLICATIONS

Novels

If Morning Ever Comes. New York, Knopf, 1964; London, Chatto & Windus, 1965.

The Tin Can Tree. New York, Knopf, 1965; London, Macmillan, 1966.

A Slipping-Down Life. New York, Knopf, 1970; London, Severn House, 1983.

The Clock Winder. New York, Knopf, 1972; London, Chatto & Windus, 1973.

Celestial Navigation. New York, Knopf, 1974; London, Chatto & Windus, 1975.

Searching for Caleb. New York, Knopf, and London, Chatto & Windus, 1976.

Earthly Possessions. New York, Knopf, and London, Chatto & Windus, 1977.

Morgan's Passing. New York, Knopf, and London, Chatto & Windus, 1980.

Dinner at the Homesick Restaurant. New York, Knopf, and London, Chatto & Windus, 1982.

The Accidental Tourist. New York, Knopf, and London, Chatto & Windus, 1985.

Breathing Lessons. New York, Knopf, 1988; London, Chatto & Windus, 1989.

Saint Maybe. New York, Knopf, and London, Chatto & Windus, 1991.

Tumble Tower, pictures by Mitra Modarressi. New York, Orchard, 1993.

Ladder of Years. New York, Knopf, 1995.

Other

Editor, with Shannon Ravenel, *The Best American Short Stories 1983.* Boston, Houghton, 1983; as *The Year's Best American Short Stories,* London, Severn House, 1984.

Anne Tyler: Three Complete Novels. New York, Wings Books, 1991.

Introduction, *Best of the South, from Ten Years of New Stories from the South,* edited by Shannon Ravenel. Chapel Hill, North Carolina, Algonquin Books, 1996.

A Patchwork Planet. New York, Random House Large Print, 1998.

*

Media Adaptation: *The Accidental Tourist* (film), Warner Brothers, 1988.

Biography: Entry in *Dictionary of Literary Biography,* Vol. 6; *Dictionary of Literary Biography, Yearbook: 1982,* Detroit, Gale, 1983.

Critical Studies: Entry in *Contemporary Literary Criticism,* Detroit, Gale, Vol. 7, 1977, Vol. 11, 1979, Vol. 18, 1981, Vol. 28, 1984, Vol. 44, 1987; *Art and the Accidental in Anne Tyler* by Joseph C. Voelker, Jackson, University Press of Mississippi, 1989; *The Temporal Horizon: A Study of the Theme of Time in Anne Tyler's Major Novels* by Karin Linton, Uppsala, Sweden, Studia Anglistica, 1989; *The Fiction of Anne Tyler* edited by C. Ralph Stephens, Jackson, University Press of Mississippi, 1990; *Understanding Anne Tyler* by Alice Hall Petry, Columbia, University of South Carolina Press, 1990.

*   *   *

Perhaps more forcefully than any other writer of her generation, Anne Tyler portrays disintegration of the traditional family structure and the resulting effect on the individual.

In her first novel, *If Morning Ever Comes,* Tyler shows the emptiness behind the facade of a conventional family: for several years Ben Joe Hawkes has known that his father has lived alternately with wife and mistress, dying at the mistress' home because, ironically, on the night of his death he forgot which was his current residence. Ben Joe also learns that his grandmother, actually in love with another man, married his grandfather as a matter of expediency. As with many of Tyler's protagonists, Ben Joe is lost until jolted out of his routine by a more forceful individual who demands commitment. Ben Joe resists any definite commitment regarding his possessions, his place of residence, or his relationship with his girlfriend until his ex-girlfriend demonstrates her love by her willingness to abandon the man she is supposed to marry.

Births and deaths upset the balance in several Tyler families. The Bedloes, another quasi-traditional, middle-class family in *Saint Maybe,* reluctantly adjust when thirty-year-old Danny marries opportunistic Lucy, a divorcee with two children. The supposedly premature birth of their child begins a chain of events which culminates in the deaths, probable suicides, of both Danny and Lucy, and radically changes the life of Ian, Danny's seventeen-year-old brother. Ian cannot forgive himself for his role in their deaths until years later when he marries Rita, originally hired to reorganize the house after his mother's death, who not only changes his life but shows him that change is a vital part of life.

The senseless murder of their son highlights the differences between Sarah and Macon Leary and leads to their separation in *The Accidental Tourist.* Macon, who writes travel guides for people like himself whose business forces them to travel but who hate to leave familiar surroundings, is lost and helpless until Muriel Pritchett not only trains his dog but shows him that accepting the unfamiliar makes him feel more alive.

There are few genuinely happy families in Tyler's novels. Pamela Emerson in *The ClockWinder* says the neighbors thought her family was happy, but she knew she had never really devoted her life to her seven children. Her husband dead and her children scattered, Pamela is alone until a new handyman appears and the family begins to draw together.

The most dysfunctional of Tyler's families is the Tulls in *Dinner at the Homesick Restaurant*. Having married to avoid the incompleteness of being alone, Pearl Cody Tull has three children when her husband leaves the family. Each child sees different facets of Pearl's personality: Cody remembers her as violently abusive, Ezra as nurturing, and Jenny as suspicious and accusative. Pearl's last request—that her entire family gather for dinner after her funeral—brings her husband and their children together at the Homesick Restaurant. Unlike previous attempts, this family meal concludes with everyone still together, suggesting that family bonds not only are inescapable but also can be healing.

Tyler vividly draws her characters, both major and minor. Morgan Gower, her most bizarre character, collects identities in the same way he collects hats and changes both with the same ease, posing as a glassblower, a tugboat captain, a lobster fisherman, a politician, a Mohawk Indian high-rise worker, and the only undefeated jockey in the history of Pimlico. Answering the appeal for a doctor to deliver the Meredith's baby, he becomes so involved with Emily and Leon that he assumes Leon's identity and eventually even his name. Other eccentrics include Morgan's sister Brindle, who marries her ''one true love'' only to feel the marriage threatened by her own high school photograph; Serena in *Breathing Lessons,* who attempts to reenact her wedding at her husband's

funeral; and the Peck family in *Searching for Caleb,* especially the ''genius,'' Duncan, who makes his own fertilizer by processing the household's organic garbage in a blender.

Most of Tyler's elderly characters possess a dignity which makes their memory lapses and erratic behavior seem endearing. *Breathing Lessons'* Daniel Otis is a stubborn and exasperating old man, but he manipulates the reader just as he manipulates his nephew and the Morans. Tyler also treats with sympathetic humor her emotionally disturbed characters, such as Dorrie Moran, who carries a department store suitbox filled with marshmallows wherever she goes, and Junie Moran, who can leave home only when she is disguised as someone else.

While there is much unhappiness in Tyler's works, her tone is essentially optimistic. Many of her characters achieve almost Joycean epiphanies and, at the very least, a kind of peaceful acceptance. Young-adult readers struggling with family problems may be able to relate to these characters and find, as Maggie found in *Breathing Lessons,* that life, like her husband's perpetual game of solitaire, is a series of narrowing options which one can only play with as much skill and judgment as possible.

—Charmaine Allmon Mosby

U-V

URE, Jean

Pseudonyms: Ann Colin; Jean Gregory; Sarah McCulloch. **Nationality:** British. **Born:** Surrey, England, 1 January 1943. **Education:** Croyden High School, Surrey, 1954-60; Webber-Douglas Academy of Dramatic Art, London, 1966-68. **Family:** Married Leonard Gregory in 1967. **Education:** Webber-Douglas Academy of Dramatic Art, 1965-67. Writer. Worked variously as a waitress, cook, washer-up, nursing assistant, newspaper seller, shop assistant, theatre usherette, temporary shorthand-typist, translator, secretary with NATO and UNESCO, and television production assistant. Since 1968, full-time writer. **Awards:** American Library Association best book for young adult citation, 1983, for *See You Thursday.* **Agent:** Maggie Noach, 21 Redan St., London W14 0AB, England. **Address:** 88 Southbridge Rd., Croydon, Surrey CR0 1AF, England.

PUBLICATIONS FOR YOUNG ADULTS

Novels

See You Thursday. London, Kestrel, 1981; New York, Delacorte, 1983.
A Proper Little Nooryeff. London, Bodley Head, 1982; as *What If They Saw Me Now?,* New York, Delacorte, 1982.
If It Weren't for Sebastian. London, Bodley Head, 1982; New York, Delacorte, 1985.
You Win Some, You Lose Some. London, Bodley Head, and New York, Delacorte, 1984.
After Thursday. London, Kestrel, and New York, Delacorte, 1985.
The Other Side of the Fence. London, Bodley Head, 1986; New York, Delacorte, 1988.
Trouble with Vanessa. London, Corgi, 1988.
One Green Leaf. London, Bodley Head, 1987; New York, Delacorte, 1989.
There's Always Danny. London, Corgi, 1988.
Say Goodbye, London, Corgi, 1989.
Tomorrow Is Also a Day. London, Methuen, 1989.
Plague 99. London, Methuen, 1990; as *Plague,* San Diego, Harcourt, 1991.
Play Nimrod for Him. London, Bodley Head, 1990.
Dreaming of Larry. New York, Doubleday, 1991.
After the Plague. London, Mammoth, 1992; as *Come Lucky April,* London, Mammoth, 1995.
Always Sebastian. London, Bodley Head, 1993; New York, Random House, 1996.
Seven for a Secret, London, Blackie, 1993; as *Who Says animals Don't Have Rights?,* London, Blackie, 1994.
Dance with Death. London, Scholastic, 1995.
Watchers at the Shrine Reed. London, Methuen/Mammoth, 1995.
Has Anyone Seen This Girl? New York, Random House, 1996.
With Leonard Gregory, *Great Safe Blag.* LondonHarperCollins, 1996.
Love Is for Ever. London, Orchard, 1996.
Place to Scream. London, Doubleday, 1996.
Sandy Simmons Superstar: Break a Leg. London, Orchard, 1998.

Echoes through Time. London, Walker, forthcoming.
Just Sixteen. London, Orchard, forthcoming.

PUBLICATIONS FOR CHILDREN

Fiction

Ballet Dance for Two. New York, Watts, 1960; as *Dance for Two,* illustrated by Richard Kennedy, London, Harrap, 1960.
Hi There, Supermouse!, illustrated by Martin White. London, Hutchinson, 1983; as *Supermouse,* illustrated by Ellen Eagle, New York, Morrow, 1984.
You Two, illustrated by Ellen Eagle. New York, Morrow, 1984; as *The You-Two,* illustrated by Martin White, London, Hutchinson, 1984.
Megastar. London, Blackie, 1985.
Nicola Mimosa, illustrated by Martin White. London, Hutchinson, 1985; as *The Most Important Thing,* illustrated by Ellen Eagle, New York, Morrow, 1986.
A Bottled Cherry Angel. London, Hutchinson, 1986.
Brenda the Bold, illustrated by Glenys Ambrus. London, Heinemann, 1986.
Swings and Roundabouts. London, Blackie, 1986.
The Fright, illustrated by Beverley Lees. London, Orchard, 1987.
Tea-Leaf on the Roof, illustrated by Val Sassoon. London, Blackie, 1987.
War with Old Mouldy!, illustrated by Alice Englander. London, Methuen, 1987.
Who's Talking?, illustrated by Beverley Lees. London, Orchard, 1987.
Frankie's Dad. London, Hutchinson, 1988.
Loud Mouth, illustrated by Lynne Willey. London, Orchard, 1988.
A Muddy Kind of Magic, illustrated by Michael Lewis. London, Blackie, 1988.
Soppy Birthday, illustrated by Michael Lewis. London, Orchard, 1988.
Two Men in a Boat, illustrated by Michael Lewis. London, Blackie, 1988.
King of Spuds. London, Orchard, 1989.
Who's for the Zoo? London, Orchard, 1989.
Cool Simon. London, Orchard, 1990.
Jo in the Middle. London, Hutchinson, 1990.
The Wizard in the Woods. LondonWalker, 1990.
Fat Lollipop. London, Hutchinson, 1991.
Spooky Cottage. London, Heinemann/Banana, 1991.
William in Love. London, Blackie, 1991.
Wizard in Wonderland. London, Walker, 1991.
Unknown Planet. London, Walker, 1992.
Captain Cranko and the Crybaby. London, Walker, 1993.
Ghost the Lived on the Hill. London, Reed, 1993.
Phantom Knicker Nicker. London, Blackie/Puffin, 1993.
Star Turn. New York, Random House, 1993.
A Dream Come True. New York, Random House, 1994.
Horrible Baby. Harlow, Longman, 1994.
Jug Ears. Harlow, Longman, 1994.

Night Fright. London, Blackie, 1994.
Poupette. Harlow, Longman, 1994.
Wizard and the Witch. LondonWalker, 1995.
Help It's Harriet! LondonHarperCollins, 1995.
Fandango! New York, Random House, 1996.
Girl in a Blue Tunic. New York, Scholastic, 1996.
The Gools. Aylesbury, Ginn, 1996.
Harriet Strikes Again! LondonHarperCollins, 1996.
Skinny Melon and Me. London, HarperCollins, 1996.
Whatever Happened to Katy Jane? LondonWalker, 1996.
Becky Bananas. London, HarperCollins, 1997.
Big Head. London, Walker, 1997.
Lucky. London, Orchard, 1997.
Whistle and I'll Come. New York, Scholastic, 1997.
Fruit and Nut Case. LondonHarperCollins, 1998.
Danny Dynamite. Transworld, forthcoming.

PUBLICATIONS FOR ADULTS

Novels

The Other Theatre. London, Corgi, 1966.
The Test of Love. London, Corgi, 1968.
Had We But World Enough and Time. London, Corgi, 1972.
If You Speak Love, London, Corgi, 1972.
The Farther off from England. London, Corgi, 1973.
Daybreak. London, Corgi, 1974.
All Thy Love. London, Corgi, 1975.
Marriage of True Minds. London, Corgi, 1975.
Hear No Evil. London, Corgi, 1976.
No Precious Time. London, Corgi, 1976.
All in a Summer Season. London, Corgi, 1977.
Dress Rehearsal. London, Corgi, 1977.
Early Stages. London, Corgi, 1977.
Bid Time Return, London, Corgi, 1978.
Curtain Fall, London, Corgi, 1978.
A Girl Like That, London, Corgi, 1979.
Masquerade, London, Corgi, 1979.
A Different Class of Doctor, as Ann Colin. London, Corgi, 1980.
Doctor Jamie, as Ann Colin. London, Corgi, 1980.
Love beyond Telling, as Jean Gregory. London, Corgi, 1986.

Novels as Sarah McCulloch

Not Quite a Lady. London, Corgi, 1980; New York, Fawcett, 1981.
A Lady for Ludovic. London, Corgi, 1981.
A Most Insistent Lady. London, Corgi, 1981.
Merely a Gentleman. London, Corgi, 1982.
A Perfect Gentleman. London, Corgi, 1982.

Other

Translator, *City of a Thousand Drums,* by Henri Vernes. London, Corgi, 1966.
Translator, *The Dinosaur Hunters,* by Henri Vernes. London, Corgi, 1966.
Translator, *The Yellow Shadow,* by Henri Vernes. London, Corgi, 1966.
Translator, *Cold Spell,* by Jean Bruce. London, Corgi, 1967.
Translator, *Top Secret,* by Jean Bruce. London, Corgi, 1967.

Translator, *Treasure of the Golcondas,* by Henri Vernes. London, Corgi, 1967.
Translator, *The White Gorilla,* by Henri Vernes. London, Corgi, 1967.
Translator, *Operation Parrot,* by Henri Vernes. London, Corgi, 1968.
Translator, *Strip Tease,* by Jean Bruce. London, Corgi, 1968.
Translator, *The Snare,* by Noel Calef. London, Souvenir Press, 1969.
Translator, *March Battalion,* by Sven Hassel. London, Corgi, 1970.
Translator, *Assignment Gestapo,* by Sven Hassel. London, Corgi, 1971.
Translator, *Hitler's Plot to Kill the Big Three,* by László Havas. London, Corgi, 1971.
Translator, *SS General,* by Sven Hassel. London, Corgi, 1972.
Translator, *Reign of Hell,* by Sven Hassel. London, Corgi, 1973.
Editor, *Collins Book of Ballet and Dance Stories.* London, Scholastic, 1994.

*

Biography: Essay in *Something about the Author Autobiography Series,* Volume 14, Detroit, Gale, 1992.

* * *

Jean Ure is a prolific author with whom children can progress from first readers to challenging young adult novels.

Increasingly, her teenage books have tackled serious themes, but even the lightest novels have convincing backgrounds. Two books which bring together teenagers from differing social settings are *A Proper Little Nooryeff,* published in the United States as *What If They Saw Me Now?,* dealing with the embarrassment of a boy pushed into taking part in a ballet, and *The Other Side of the Fence,* in which Richard rows with his affluent parents and teams up with Bonny, a streetwise, amoral, and chronic liar; each gains strength from the unlikely pairing.

Another early novel, *See You Thursday,* followed by *After Thursday* and *Tomorrow Is Also a Day,* rises above the usual boy-meets-girl story because of its subtle delineation of character. Marianne, initially a self-doubting sixteen-year old, befriends blind musician Abe, eight years her senior. The relationship—deepening into love—falters when Abe's musical career prospers, Marianne matures, and each wonders whether the other is being stifled. The trilogy involves the reader completely with its likeable, realistically fallible main characters.

Animal rights have always featured in Ure's novels, even when not a central issue. The subject takes centre stage in a trilogy beginning with *If It Weren't for Sebastian* and continuing eleven years later with *Always Sebastian* and *Seven for a Secret.* In the first novel, Maggie learns through Sebastian of the cruelties inflicted on animals in farms and laboratories. His disturbed, obsessive fear of violence has led to criticism of the novel for suggesting that only someone mentally unstable could be so sensitive; the possibility is left open, however, that Sebastian is perfectly sane, while the rest of the world is at fault.

In *Always Sebastian,* Ure moves on a generation, shifting the focus to Maggie's daughter, Martha, who hands out leaflets in the high street and argues with her science teacher about dissection. Sebastian, now Maggie's lover, is an animal rights activist; the dubious morality of using violence to make a point is questioned when a bomb is planted in a shopping centre. Unlike many current novels which have characters mouthing token protests about animal rights as if the issue is merely the trendiest bandwagon to be seen riding on, Ure treats the topic seriously, confronting her characters with realistic grey areas. Here, the younger daughter Sophie is a purist to the extent of being maddening to live with, and even tolerant Maggie experiences "compassion fatigue."

Career choices are often of crucial importance to Ure's characters, who frequently come to a decision after spurning the values of their parents, schools, peers, and the government. *A Place to Scream* shows a future Thatcher-like England sharply divided into haves and have-nots under a repressive, materialistic government with beggars on the streets and where old people are regarded as useless burdens. Gillian, sick of the undemanding job she is thought lucky to have, is tempted to escape abroad with Rick, an intelligent dropout who shares her humane values. The plan is abandoned when Gillian's ailing Grandfather needs her, and she finds fulfillment in nursing the elderly, even though it's a low-paid, squalid job. The serious theme is mediated by lightness of tone, although the warning note is unmistakable: Is this the sort of future we are heading for?

Plague 99 combines a survival story with a topical environmental theme. An accident with germ-warfare research releases a deadly plague virus; three teenagers, Fran, Harriet, and Shahid, join forces in an attempt to survive. The government and the passivity of citizens are blamed; Shahid comments: "We all thought it would be the Bomb or the ozone layer. We forgot all the nasty little bacterial messes they were cooking up behind their closed doors."

Although grim, *Plague 99* ends with a suggestion that Fran and Shahid will escape to Cornwall. The story is continued in *Come Lucky April*. Set a hundred years later, it brings together two societies with contradictory values. The main characters are descendants of those in *Plague 99;* April is living in Croydon in a society dominated by women, while Daniel comes from an isolated patriarchal community in Cornwall, and is shocked to discover that the Croydon group controls male aggression by castrating men. The balance between the need for harmony and communal safety on the one hand and individual freedom on the other is illustrated by April's choice: to go with Daniel to the male-dominated Cornwall society or stay with the eunuch, David, who has the courage to challenge the status quo.

Listing Ure's themes might suggest that her books are uniformly earnest, yet her lightness of touch makes this far from the case. *One Green Leaf,* about a teenager dying of cancer, could in other hands have been mawkish or morbid. Ure avoids this by giving the narrative to Robyn, whose friend Abbey is the victim's girlfriend. This enables Robyn to observe the effect of David's illness on both himself and Abbey, who has to put up with his frequent unkindness. Robyn's narrative gives humour to the story, and a skillfully-controlled ending shows the friends remembering David in a positive way after his death.

Some of Ure's strengths are also her weaknesses. Her crisp, easily-readable style lacks variety; conversations in a futuristic community of survivors are indistinguishable from exchanges in form room or ballet class. Ure admits that there is little sense of place in her writing, and certainly she does not achieve the easy, evocative scene-setting of, say, K. M. Peyton or Katherine Paterson. On the other hand, her novels are always expertly-paced, fast-moving without being rushed, and there is no doubt that she knows her readership. Ure has never produced the sort of book which librarians and award panels adore but which stay on the

shelves unread. She writes that one of her aims is "to make people think: to make them examine their motives and question their assumptions," and she unfailingly goes for topical and relevant issues on which to challenge her readers. The successful blend of provocation and entertainment ensures her continuing popularity.

—Linda Newbery

VINGE, Joan (Carol) D(ennison)

Nationality: American. **Education:** San Diego State University, California, B.A. in anthropology 1971. **Family:** Married 1) Vernor Vinge, in 1972 (divorced 1979); 2) James R. Frenkel in 1980. **Career:** Salvage archaeologist, San Diego County, 1971; writer since 1974. **Awards:** Hugo award for best novelette from World Science Fiction Convention, 1978, for "Eyes of Amber," and for best science fiction novel, 1981, for *The Snow Queen; Locus* award, 1981; North Dakota Children's Choice (older) award, 1984, for *Return of the Jedi: The Storybook.* **Agent:** Merrilee Heifetz, Writers House Inc., 21 West 26th Street, New York, New York 10010, U.S.A.

PUBLICATIONS FOR ADULTS and Young Adults

Novels

The Outcasts of Heaven Belt. New York, New American Library, 1978; London, Futura, 1981.
The Snow Queen. New York, Dial Press, and London, Sidgwick & Jackson, 1980.
Psion. New York, Delacorte Press, 1982; London, Futura, 1983.
World's End. New York, Bluejay, 1984; London, Futura, 1985.
Ladyhawke (novelization of screenplay). New York, New American Library, 1985; London, Piccolo, 1985.
Mad Max: Beyond the Thunderdome. New York, Warner, and London, W.H. Allen, 1985.
Return to Oz. New York, Ballantine, and London, Purnell, 1985.
Santa Claus. New York, Berkley, and London, Sphere, 1985.
Catspaw. New York, Warner, 1988; as *Cat's Paw,* London, Gollancz, 1989.
Willow (novelization of screenplay). New York, Random House, 1988.
Heaven Chronicles (includes "Legacy" and *The Outcasts of Heaven Belt*). New York, Warner, 1991.
The Summer Queen. New York, Warner, 1991.
Refuge. New York, Warner, 1993.
Dreamfall. New York, Warner Books, 1996.
Lost in Space. New York, HarperCollins, 1998.

Short Stories

Fireship. New York, Dell, 1978; as *Fireship, and Mother and Child,* London, Sidgwick & Jackson, 1981.
Eyes of Amber and Other Stories. New York, New American Library, 1979; London, Futura, 1981.
Phoenix in the Ashes. New York, Bluejay, 1985; London, Futura, 1986.

PUBLICATIONS FOR CHILDREN

Fiction

Return of the Jedi Storybook (novelization of screenplay). New York, Random House, and London, Futura, 1983.
Tarzan, King of Apes. New York, Random House, 1983.
The Dune Storybook (novelization of screenplay). New York, Putnam, 1984; London, Sphere, 1984.
The "Santa Claus—The Movie" Storybook. New York, Grosset & Dunlap, 1985.

*

Biography: Essay in *Speaking for Ourselves, Too* compiled and edited by Donald R. Gallo, National Council of Teachers of English, 1993.

Manuscript Collections: Elizabeth Charter Science Fiction Collection, San Diego University.

Critical Studies: *Suzy Charnas, Joan Vinge, and Octavia Butler* by Richard Law, with others, San Bernardino, California, Borgo Press, 1986.

*   *   *

This quote from *The Snow Queen* is the essence of Joan D. Vinge's work: "There is more to me, more to the universe, than I suspected. Room for all the dreams I ever had, and all the nightmares. . .Anything becomes possible after you find the courage to admit that nothing is certain. . .Life used to look like cut crystal to me—sharp and clear and perfect. But now those clean hard edges break up the light into rainbows, and everything gets soft and hazy." There are no simple characters in her work, no simple truths, and no simple answers—the conflict is not between good and evil, but between different facets of human nature; winning is sometimes indistinguishable from losing, success can sometimes feel like failure, and one person's dream is often someone else's nightmare.

While the societies Vinge creates for her stories are richly textured, they are primarily a device for exploring human nature. By taking humanity out of our own cultural context, Vinge can focus more clearly on universal human interactions—power, greed, honor, duty, love, justice—and on the human nature that is a part of those interactions.

Vinge's works are not specifically targeted to young adults. However, the "Snow Queen" series and the "Psion" novels have young adult protagonists, and deal with issues of interest to young adult readers.

The Snow Queen is a story of power—the validity of gaining it, keeping it, using it—and a story of the permutations of right and wrong. Its setting is Tiamat, a world where power ritually changes hands every 150 years. Arienrhod, the Snow Queen, is at the end of her rule, and "the Change" requires her death. She has one last scheme to carry out—a plan to save her world, not her life. But she does despicable things in pursuit of this worthy goal—is she right or wrong? Moon, Arienrhod's unknowing young pawn, is honorable and innocent, but her actions cause pain and suffering—is she

right or wrong? Vinge's answer is that they are both only human, with flaws and virtues which are ultimately the source of both their successes and their failures. All of the characters are quite sure they know what is right—and all of their certainties are turned upside down and inside out before the story ends.

World's End, the second book in the "Snow Queen" series, is only tangentially related to the events in *The Snow Queen;* it follows B.Z. Gundhalinu as he leaves Tiamat, and tries to fit his new worldview into the rigid structure of his old world. What he learns, however, plays a significant role in the final book of the series, the story of Moon's reign as Summer Queen.

In *The Summer Queen,* Vinge explores the interplay of the facets of human nature. All of her characters' flaws and virtues are heaped together like a precarious pile of pickup sticks, making unpredictable connections and supporting each other in unanticipated ways.

Psion focuses on the inner life of its protagonist, the half-human psion Cat, and his responses to the shifting circumstances of his life. Alone on the streets of Oldcity, Cat is a teenage pickpocket, prostitute, panhandler—whatever it takes to stay alive. His life disgusts him, and the price he must pay to keep it disgusts him. All of that changes when he's arrested, then released to participate in a psionic research project. For the first time in his memory, he's safe, well-fed, and cared about. But he soon learns that every kind of life has a price, and this life's price is to use the psionic ability he has suppressed to help the authorities he hates.

Catspaw takes the character Cat into the high-stakes world of the hereditary Combines—corporations so powerful that one member's flaws and virtues can affect the entire Interplanetary Human Federation. Cat is hired to use his psionic power to protect a woman of those Combines from enemies he doesn't know and whose power he can't even comprehend.

Vinge has also written a number of novellas and short stories published in magazines and anthologies. Some of these have been collected in *Phoenix in the Ashes, Fireship,* and the recently republished *Heaven Chronicles.* The brevity of the short story and novella formats require some simplification of detail, but her short-form work is no less thought-provoking than her novels are; the focus is still on the permutations of human nature within the society she creates.

To read Vinge is to have one's assumptions challenged; to see that faults can sometimes cause success, and virtues can sometimes cause failure; to understand that right and wrong do not exist in a vacuum. But life is not clear-cut, and blind assumptions should be challenged. Like B.Z. Gundhalinu, the young adult reader may discover through Vinge's works that, indeed, "There is more to me, more to the universe, than I suspected."

—Karen J. Gould

VINING, Elizabeth Gray

Pseudonyms: Elizabeth Janet Gray. **Nationality:** American. **Born:** Philadelphia, Pennsylvania, 6 October 1902. **Education:** Bryn Mawr College, A.B. 1923; Drexel Institute School of Library Science (now Drexel University), B.S. 1926. **Family:** Married Morgan F. Vining in 1929 (died 1933). **Career:** Tutor to Crown Prince Akihito of Japan, 1946-50; vice-president of board of trustees and vice-chairman of board of directors, Bryn Mawr

College, 1952-71; American Friends Service Committee staff member. Writer. **Awards:** American Women's Eminent Achievement Award; named Distinguished Daughter of Pennsylvania; Third Order of the Sacred Crown, Japan; Newbery Medal, 1943, for *Adam of the Road; Herald Tribune* Spring Festival Award, 1945, for *Sandy;* Constance Lindsay Skinner Award, Women's National Book Association, 1954; *Philadelphia Athenaeum* Literary Award, 1964, for *Take Heed of Loving Me,* and special award, 1980, for *Being Seventy.* Litt.D.: Drexel Institute of Technology (now Drexel University), 1951, Tufts College (now Tufts University), 1952, Douglas College, 1953, Women's Medical College, 1953, Lafayette College, 1956, and University of North Carolina at Greensboro, 1968; L.H.D., Russell Sage College, 1952, Haverford College, 1958, Western College for Women (now Western College), 1959, Cedar Crest College, 1959, Moravian College, 1961, Wilmington College, 1962, and International Christian University, 1966; D.Ed.: Rhode Island College of Education (now Rhode Island College), 1956. **Address:** 316 Kendal Drive, Kennett Square, Pennsylvania 19348, U.S.A.

PUBLICATIONS FOR YOUNG ADULTS AS ELIZABETH JANET GRAY

Fiction

Meredith's Ann, illustrated by G.B. Cutts. New York, Doubleday, 1927.
Tangle Garden, illustrated by G.B. Cutts. New York, Doubleday, 1928.
Tilly-Tod, illustrated by Mary Hamilton Frye. New York, Doubleday, 1929.
Meggy MacIntosh, illustrated by Marguerite de Angeli. New York, Doubleday, 1930.
Jane Hope. New York, Viking, 1933; London, Dickson, 1935.
Penny Marlowe of Charles Town, illustrated by Loren Barton. New York, Viking, 1936.
The Fair Adventure, illustrated by Alice K. Reischer. New York, Viking, 1940.
Adam of the Road, illustrated by Robert Lawson. New York, Viking, 1942; London, A. and C. Black, 1943.
Sandy. New York, Viking, 1945.
The Cheerful Heart, illustrated by Kazue Mizumura. New York, Viking, 1959; London, Macmillan, 1961.
I Will Adventure, illustrated by Corydon Bell. New York, Viking, 1962.
The Taken Girl (as Elizabeth Gray Vining). New York, Viking, 1972.

Other

Young Walter Scott. Viking, 1935; London, Nelson, 1937.
Penn, illustrated by George Whitney. New York, Viking, 1938.
Mr. Whittier (as Elizabeth Gray Vining). New York, Viking, 1974.

PUBLICATIONS FOR ADULTS

Fiction

The Virginia Exiles. Philadelphia, Lippincott, 1955.
Take Heed of Loving Me. Philadelphia, Lippincott, 1963.
I, Roberta. Philadelphia, Lippincott, 1967.

Other

The Contributions of the Quakers (as Elizabeth Janet Gray). Philadelphia, F. A. Davis, 1939.
Windows for the Crown Prince (autobiography). Philadelphia, Lippincott, 1952.
The World in Tune. Wallingford, Pennsylvania, Pendle Hill, 1952.
Friend of Life: The Biography of Rufus M. Jones. Philadelphia, Lippincott, 1958.
Return to Japan. Philadelphia, Lippincott, 1960.
Flora: A Biography. Philadelphia, Lippincott, 1966; as *Flora MacDonald: Her Life in the Highlands and America,* London, Bles, 1967.
William Penn, Mystic. Wallingford, Pennsylvania, Pendle Hill, 1969.
Quiet Pilgrimage (autobiography). Philadelphia, Lippincott, 1970.
The May Massee Collection: Creative Publishing for Children, with Annis Duff. Emporia, Kansas, William Allen White Library, 1972.
Being Seventy: The Measure of a Year. New York, Viking, 1978.
John Woolman, Quaker Saint. Philadelphia, Wider Quaker Fellowship, 1981.
A Quest There Is. Wallingford, Pennsylvania, Pendle Hill, 1982.

Editor as Elizabeth Janet Gray

Anthology with Comments. Wallingford, Pennsylvania, Pendle Hill, 1942.

*

Biography: Entry in *The Junior Book of Authors,* New York, H.W. Wilson, 1951.

Manuscript Collections: Quaker Collection, Haverford College Library, Pennsylvania.

*   *   *

Elizabeth Gray Vining will well be remembered for her historical novels and biographies for young people as well as the autobiographical account of her four years in Japan as tutor to the crown prince. Her books reflect her talents as a storyteller and careful historian, but also her belief in the worth and dignity of the individual, real or fictional.

Vining's storytelling skill lies in her ability to recreate a period in history and give it life and color through imagery and carefully chosen details. Although her attention to authenticity in her historical portrayal is evident, it is subordinated to the story she is telling, and her research is painlessly assimilated into the story. Vining uses a variety of narrative techniques to move her story along, but it is through the eyes and ears of her invariably delightful characters that the reader sees and hears the story unfold. Even her minor characters are thoughtfully and humanly portrayed, and the reader can readily identify with them.

Vining's best-known work, *Adam of the Road,* winner of the 1943 John Newbery Award, is a vivid recreation of the people and places of thirteenth-century England as seen through the eyes of a young boy. Historically accurate, medieval England comes to life with a diverse assortment of characters and settings. A series of incidents with relatively mild conflicts and few surprises for the reader comprises the story, but the book is ultimately satisfying because of the reader's immersion in time and place. All five senses are evoked in Vining's vivid descriptions, but most memorably in the sounds of minstrel songs and stories that are interwoven throughout the novel. It is through Adam's consciousness that the reader views this era of English history with the freshness and excitement with which a young person views life.

I Will Adventure is similar in setting and plot. Andrew, on the way to London, meets a traveling company of players which includes William Shakespeare. The reader encounters the noisy richness of Elizabethan England with inside glimpses of the theater through Andrew's consciousness.

Meggy MacIntosh, a historical romance, is based on the true accounts of Flora MacDonald and the Scottish immigrants who settled in North Carolina before the revolution. Meggy is an unspoiled, lovable heroine, and the book paints a vivid picture of the settlers.

The Taken Girl, set in the period before the Civil War, presents a picture of Quaker abolitionists in Philadelphia. Vining once more reflects her depth of knowledge and her compassionate understanding for the period and is especially effective in her portrayal of the poet Whittier. The story is quietly told except for a dramatic climax in the burning of the abolitionist hall.

Written for adults but accessible to mature teens, *Take Heed of Loving Me,* is based on the life of the English poet John Donne. Vining has again carefully researched her historical background and atmosphere in this very human, warmly felt story, but presents a debatable interpretation of Donne's poetry.

Vining's biographies for young adults include *Young Walter Scott, Penn,* and *Mr. Whittier.* The first is written with grace and understanding but in too romantic a vein to be good history. *Penn,* on the other hand, is most readable and authentic. William Penn comes alive as brilliant statesman, resolute defender of religious liberty, and uncompromising member of the Society of Friends (Quakers). *Mr. Whittier* is a quiet account of the abolitionist Quaker poet focusing on his involvement in political issues and the social ills of the nineteenth century. Vining reveals her deep attachment to literature as well in this portrait of a shy, sensitive, but determined man.

Perhaps Vining's most famous work is the adult *Windows for the Crown Prince,* an account of her four years as a tutor for Prince Akihito in Japan following World War II. Her story is simply and directly told with color and feeling for the cultural beauty of Japan and accurately depicts a people recovering from the devastation of war.

Always readable, Vining is the consummate storyteller despite a lack of exciting climaxes. Indeed, her books are worth returning to for the beauty of her language, especially her use of imagery.

—Mattie Jacks Mosley

VOIGT, Cynthia

Nationality: American. **Born:** Boston, Massachusetts, 25 February 1942. **Education:** Smith College, Northampton, Massachusetts, B.A. 1963; education courses at St. Michael's College (now College of Santa Fe), New Mexico. **Family:** Married Walter Voigt in 1974 (second marriage); one daughter and one son. **Career:** Secretary, J. Walter Thompson Advertising Agency, New York City, 1964; high school English teacher, Glen Burnie, Maryland, 1965-67; English teacher, 1968-69, department chair, 1971-79, and, 1981-1988, part-time teacher and department chair, Key School, Annapolis, Maryland; author of books for young readers, since 1981. **Awards:** Notable Children's Trade Book in the Field of Social Studies, National Council for Social Studies/Children's Book Council, *New York Times* Outstanding Books citation, and American Book award nomination, all 1981, all for *Homecoming*; American Library Association (ALA) Best Young Adult Books citation, 1982, for *Tell Me If the Lovers Are Losers,* and 1983, for *A Solitary Blue*; Newbery Medal, ALA, and *Boston Globe-Horn Book* Honor Book citation, both 1983, and ALA Notable Book citation, all for *Dicey's Song*; Parents' Choice award, 1983, Newbery Honor Book, and *Boston Globe-Horn Book* Honor Book citation, both 1984, all for *A Solitary Blue*; Edgar Allan Poe award for best juvenile mystery, Mystery Writers of America, 1984, for *The Callender Papers*; Child Study Association of America's Children's Books of the Year citation, 1987, for *Come a Stranger*; Silver Pencil award (Holland), 1988, and Deutscher Jugend Literatur Preis (Germany), 1989, both for *The Runner*; California Young Readers' Medal, 1990, for *Izzy, Willy-Nilly*; Margaret A. Edwards award, American Library Association, 1995; Anne V. Zanow award, Tulsa Library Trust, 1998. **Address:** c/o Scholastic, 555 Broadway, New York, NY 10012, U.S.A.

PUBLICATIONS FOR YOUNG ADULTS

Fiction

Homecoming. New York, Atheneum, 1981; London, Collins, 1983.
Dicey's Song. New York, Atheneum, 1982; London, Collins, 1984.
Tell Me If the Lovers Are Losers. New York, Atheneum, 1982.
The Callender Papers. New York, Atheneum, 1983.
A Solitary Blue. New York, Atheneum, 1983; London, Collins, 1985.
Building Blocks. New York, Atheneum, 1984; London, Fontana, 1988.
Jackaroo. New York, Atheneum, 1985; London, Collins, 1988.
The Runner. New York, Atheneum, 1985; London, Collins, 1986.
Come a Stranger. New York, Atheneum, 1986; London, Collins, 1987.
Izzy, Willy-Nilly. New York, Atheneum, 1986; London, Collins, 1987.
Stories about Rosie, illustrated by Dennis Kendrick. New York, Atheneum, 1986.
Sons from Afar. New York, Atheneum, 1987; London, Collins, 1988.
Tree by Leaf. New York, Atheneum, 1988; London, Collins, 1989.
Seventeen against the Dealer. New York, Atheneum, 1989.
On Fortune's Wheel. New York, Atheneum, 1990.
Tillerman Saga. New York, Fawcett, 1990.
The Vandemark Mummy. New York, Atheneum, 1991.
David and Jonathan. New York, Scholastic, 1992.
Orfe. New York, Atheneum, 1992.
The Wings of a Falcon. New York, Scholastic, 1993.
When She Hollers. New York, Scholastic, 1994.
Bad Girls. New York, Scholastic, 1996.
Bad, Badder, Baddest. New York, Scholastic, 1997.

Other

Editor, with David Bergman, *Shore Writers' Sampler II.* Easton, Maryland, Friendly Harbor Press, 1988.
Glass Mountain (for adults). New York, Harcourt, 1991.

*

Media Adaptations: *Dicey's Song* (filmstrip-cassette set), Guidance Associates, 1986; *Homecoming* (television film), 1996.

Biography: Essay in *Speaking for Ourselves: Autobiographical Sketches by Notable Authors of Books for Young Adults,* Vol. 1, compiled and edited by Donald R. Gallo, National Council of Teachers of English, 1990.

Critical Studies: Entry in *Contemporary Literary Criticism,* Vol. 30, Detroit, Gale, 1984; entry in *Children's Literature Review,* Vol. 13, Detroit, Gale, 1987.

*   *   *

Cynthia Voigt depicts adolescents with dignity and compassion in her impressive novels; her characters generally possess a streak of independence or self-reliance enabling them to succeed in tangible endeavors and in creating bonds of friendship and family ties despite serious hardships, such as the loss of one or both parents. The tragedy of dysfunctional families is usually overturned and triumphantly replaced by loving relationships in the earlier novels, but less often in the later ones. Voigt's characters, frequently outsiders initially, are fleshed out until they seem to breathe and ultimately belong in their settings. As a result, Voigt has won several literary prizes—a Newbery Medal for *Dicey's Song,* a Newbery Honor Award for *A Solitary Blue,* an Edgar Award for *The Callender Papers,* and the 1989 ALAN Award for her outstanding contribution to the young adult field.

Except for *Stories about Rosie,* an illustrated book for younger readers about a pet dog, and *Glass Mountain,* an adult novel, Voigt writes for young adults in genres that vary from fantasy (*Building Blocks*), to mystery (*The Callender Papers* and,*The Vandemark Mummy*), to realism set in the past (*Jackaroo, On Fortune's Wheel, The Wings of a Falcon,* and *Tree by Leaf*), to Voigt's forte, realistic contemporary (*Tell Me If the Lovers Are Losers, Izzy, Willy-Nilly, Orfe, David and Jonathan When She Hollers, Bad Girls, Bad, Badder, Baddest,* and the seven novels comprising the Tillerman family "saga"). The four Tillerman children of the second generation—Dicey, James, Maybeth, and Sammy—travel to Maryland from Connecticut in *Homecoming* and are adopted by their grandmother in *Dicey's Song.* James and Sammy search for their father in *Sons from Afar;* the children's uncle "Bullet" stars in *The Runner;* and friends of Dicey, Jeff Greene, and Mina Smiths become protagonists in *A Solitary Blue* and *Come a Stranger,* respectively. The final book of the saga, *Seventeen against the Dealer,* depicts the children as older teens and focuses on Dicey who attempts to realize her lifelong dream of becoming a boat builder.

Heroes and heroines, about equal in number, vary in age from six-year-old Sammy Tillerman to the college-age young women of *Tell Me If the Lovers Are Losers.* Voigt adeptly depicts blacks as well as whites; in *The Runner* she addresses the situation of the racially troubled 1960s without mincing words, focusing in part on the prejudicial attitude of a white boy against a black teammate. Advancing a step further in *Come a Stranger* with protagonist Mina Smiths, a black girl rejected from a dance camp by an all-white group whom she has tried to emulate and from whom she expected friendship, Voigt deftly and sensitively depicts Mina's awakening to the reality of racial prejudice.

When Voigt plots her novels around other contemporary dilemmas, usually familial ones, she evokes sympathy for the characters who may have lost parents or who may feel forced to separate from their families because of intolerable home situations. The younger Tillermans, for example, when deserted by their mother in a parking lot, initiate an odyssey that leads them to their "crazy" grandmother, Gram. That the group becomes a warm, loving family who grow individually by reaching out or communicating with others, even with those who do not reciprocate, is a measure of the journey's success in spite of its inauspicious origin.

The characters, although distinct individuals, possess many similar traits. Those who suffer from separation anxiety created by a missing or too reticent parent such as Professor Greene (*A Solitary Blue*), Mr. Thiel (*The Callender Papers*), or Mrs. Hall (*The Vandemark Mummy*), rely upon a surrogate. Dicey and then Gram provide for the younger Tillerman children; Patrice offers Bullet Tillerman work, food, and advice in *The Runner;* Brother Thomas, a close family friend, on occasion provides the affection that Jeff Greene lacks in *A Solitary Blue;* Aunt Constance cares for the "orphaned" Jean Wainwright in *The Callender Papers;* and news journalist O'Meara substitutes for Phineas Hall's absent mother in *The Vandemark Mummy.*

Voigt oversees the maturation of her youthful characters as they accept responsibility and plan future goals in the face of unsettling, often severe, obstacles, partially through her belief in the work ethic. Most learn self-reliance by assisting with family chores and by holding part-time jobs, such as working in a grocery, delivering papers, selling crabs, and baby-sitting. The children capitalize upon their own unique abilities whether they are a gift for music, a talent for academics or for organization, a deep spirituality, or an ability at sports. Maybeth Tillerman, though "slow" in school, excels in music. James, her brother, is the family's academic achiever. Jean Wainwright, although only twelve years old, sorts, organizes, and classifies the documents of the Callender family. Clothilde in *Tree by Leaf* relies on her strong religious faith; she believes that the voice she hears is God's, and she makes four requests of him. Although three are granted, they are not as she had imagined they would be. Other characters excel at sports, such as Bullet Tillerman at running or Hildegarde Koenig in *Tell Me If the Lovers Are Losers,* who so capably organizes and teaches a college freshman volleyball team about unity that they beat every opponent, even the seniors. The characters' participation in a variety of jobs and sports suggests that every child can find one he or she will enjoy and in pursuing it will become more well-rounded, less an outsider.

Voigt sets many novels in Crisfield, Maryland, just inland from Chesapeake Bay, where boating and crabbing provide sport, food, entertainment, and occasionally employment. Later novels, such as *The Vandemark Mummy* and *Tree by Leaf,* are set in Maine; the principal setting of *David and Jonathan* is Cape Cod. In all three settings a love of nature and the seashore appears side by side with a concern for protecting the environment. Even in a fantasy like *Building Blocks,* set primarily in Pennsylvania in 1939, pollution of the Ohio River prevents children from swimming. Brann Connell, a child in 1974 who travels backward in time and befriends his own father-to-be, Kevin Connell, is surprised to learn that pollution was a problem in the 1930s as well as the 1970s.

A thread of women's liberation or independence unites all of the novels, regardless of their time period. Two, although set in medieval times, depict their heroines in modern gender roles: *Jackaroo,* in which Gwyn is a type of precursor to Robin Hood but one who realizes that she must abide by society's rules, *On Fortune's Wheel,* in which Birle embarks on a dangerous journey reneging on her rash commitment to marry and is at one point a slave, but ultimately becomes an independent landowner, and the third book in the series, *The Wings of a Falcon* shows Oriel and Griff running away from the slavery of Damall's Island to become independent. The novels with more modern settings feature characters such as fearless Jean Wainwright, who solves the intriguing, exciting mystery in *The Callender Papers*; Althea Hall, who cleverly solves the mystery of the mummy's disappearance in the less exciting, but still provoking *Vandemark Mummy*; and high school sophomore Izzy who, with a leg amputated after an automobile accident caused by a drunk senior, subsequently learned independence and the meaning of true friendship in *Izzy, Willy-Nilly,* a book important for all high school students to read.

The theme of friendship appears in many guises: racist Bullet Tillerman learns to accept that his mentor is part black in *The Runner,* Burl dons the mark of Jackaroo to protect his friend Gwyn, Birle risks her life to save her friend's in *On Fortune's Wheel,* and Griff and Oriel are willing to dies for one another in *The Wings of a Falcon.* But perhaps the most extensive treatment of the theme of friendship occurs in Voigt's most sophisticated novel to date, *David and Jonathan,* when Henry Marr and his longtime Jewish friend, Jonathan Nafishe, try to adjust to David, a Holocaust survivor, who comes to live with his relatives, the Nafishes, and causes problems not only for Henry and Jonathan, but also for the entire Nafishe family. Set in both 1967 and some fifteen years earlier, *David and Jonathan,* explores themes of war, death, suicide, survival, and religion in addition to friendship.

Although Voigt adopts an appropriate vocabulary and style for the imaginary medieval kingdom in *Jackaroo, On Fortune's Wheel,* and *The Wings of a Falcon,* and accurately treats the settings (*The Callender Papers* in 1894, *Tree by Leaf* during World War I, and *Building Blocks* in 1939), her greatest strength lies in characterizing contemporary high school and college students and in depicting situations such as desertion and poverty which plague the modern family. Her characters learn middle-class values and other lessons without overt didacticism. For example, when one character tutors another in writing about a classic, the character and the reader derive a lesson and hopefully a greater appreciation for literature.

Voigt's novel *When She Hollers* is a serious and direct look at the victim of child abuse. When one of Trish's friends was found naked, six months pregnant, and hanging from a tree, Trish knew the truth. Randy was the victim of abuse from her father and there was no one to help her. Trish decides to take control of her own life: she threatens her father at breakfast with a butcher knife and tells him if he comes to her room at night, she will kill him. The reader follows Trish throughout the day and sees the victim scared to tell the truth and afraid to trust anyone. Trish hints to several teachers,

but they immediately stop her because she will cause trouble. The book ends on a positive note because an adult cared enough to believe her. The reader believes that Trish will be okay.

In *Bad Girls,* Mickey Elsinger and Margola Eppo enter the fifth grade at Washington Elementary School as new students. The girls sit beside each other because everything is arranged alphabetically, and they play off one another to cause havoc throughout the school year. Mickey and Margola are not predictable and neither of them wants to be nice. The major focus of *Bad Girls* is the fifth-grade classroom, where the bad girls get even with Louis, Rhonda, and anyone else who has bothered one of them. While Margola would look and act nice to woo many of her classmates, she was perhaps the more dangerous of the two girls because no one expected her to be mean. Though she was always thinking of ways to get even or cause trouble. Mickey, on the other hand, acted overtly mean and was very sarcastic. Both girls become good friends as they continue to complement each other in doing bad deeds. In *Bad, Badder, Baddest,* Mickey and Margola attempt to stop Mr. and Mrs. Elsinger from getting a divorce. The action moves away from the classroom as Mickey and Margola's attitude remains the same, but they are no longest the baddest because that Title now belongs to Gianette St. Etienne, a new girl in class. In order to stop her parents divorce, Mickey becomes the model child; despite her mother's excitement they go forward with divorce proceedings. When Mickey and Margola run away to scare the Elsingers, it's Gianette who foils the action. She blackmails the two girls to keep her quiet at the same time that she is providing information to Mickey's parents at a cost. Gianette disappeared before Mickey could get even; it turns out that she was part of a child-placement ring. Children are being sent to foster homes so that people could increase the money of their welfare checks. These people would pay money, get children sent to them and register them as dependents. The children stayed only long enough to be put on the welfare rolls; then they moved on, like Gianette. With Gianette gone, Mickey and Margola reign as the bad girls of the sixth grade.

Voigt often uses her knowledge of myth and legend, the classics, and the Bible to enhance her stories' plots or characters' names; for example, *Homecoming* features an odyssey of the Tillerman children; Bucephalus, the horse of Clothilde's father in *Tree by Leaf,* was named after Alexander the Great's horse; *David and Jonathan* depicts characters with Biblical names, including one who frequently refers to Biblical parables or creates his own; and *Orfe* retells the Orpheus and Eurydice myth with a reversal of the main characters' roles. Without knowledge of this myth, however, readers may be less satisfied with this book which focuses on Orfe, a singer and songwriter who tries without success to rescue her boyfriend, Yuri, from drug addiction.

A skilled craftsman, Voigt excels in creating characters who resonate in the reader's mind, particularly those in the Tillerman series; readers recognize with approbation the narrative links and repetitions of scenes, which aid in uniting the saga. For example, a scene in which Jeff Greene plays his guitar for Dicey is told from Dicey's point of view in *Dicey's Song,* but from Jeff's point of view in *A Solitary Blue.* The recognition of previously known characters and the déjà vu effect heighten the realism. Voigt's understanding of narrative techniques, power to create memorable characters, admirable but not goody-goody knowledge of the problems of youth, and desire to teach by transporting readers into the characters' inner lives usually result in reversing unpromising, perhaps even tragic, situations into positive, optimistic ones. Her novels make excellent reading.

—Sylvia Patterson Iskander, updated by Rosanne Donahue

VONNEGUT, Kurt, Jr

Nationality: American. **Born:** Indianapolis, Indiana, 11 November 1922. **Education:** Cornell University, Ithaca, New York, 1940-42; Carnegie Institute, Pittsburgh, 1943; University of Chicago, 1945-47. **Military Service:** Served in the United States Army Infantry, 1942-45; Purple Heart. **Family:** Married 1) Jane Marie Cox in 1945 (divorced 1979); one son and two daughters; 2) Jill Krementz in 1979; one daughter. **Career:** Police reporter, Chicago City News Bureau, 1946; worked in public relations for the General Electric Company, Schenectady, New York, 1947-50; writer, since 1950; teacher, Hopefield School, Sandwich, Massachusetts, beginning in 1965. Visiting lecturer, Writers Workshop, University of Iowa, Iowa City, 1965-67, and Harvard University, Cambridge, Massachusetts, 1970-71; visiting professor, City University of New York, 1973-74. Actor in several films, including *Between Time and Timbuktu,* 1972, *Back to School,* Orion, 1986, *Storytellers: PEN Celebration,* 1987, and *That Day in November,* 1988. Speaker, National Coalition against Censorship briefing for the Attorney General's Commission on Pornography hearing, 1986; one-man exhibition of drawings, 1980. **Awards:** Guggenheim Fellowship, 1967; American Academy grant, 1970; American Library Association's Best Books for Young Adults selection, 1975, for *Slaughterhouse Five,* and 1979, for *Jailbird*; New York Public Library's Books for the Teen Age selection, 1980, for *Jailbird,* and 1980, 1981, 1982, for *Slaughterhouse Five*; Literary Lion from the New York Public Library, 1981; Eugene V. Debs award, Eugene V. Debs Foundation, 1981, for public service; Freedom to Read award, Playboy Enterprises and the Friends of the Chicago Public Library, 1982, for his support against the suppression of books and his work to preserve First Amendment rights; Emmy award for Outstanding Children's Program, National Academy of Television Arts and Sciences, 1985, for *Displaced Person.* M.A.: University of Chicago, 1971; Litt. D.: Hobart and William Smith Colleges, Geneva, New York, 1974. **Agent:** Donald C. Farber, 1370 Avenue of the Americas, New York, New York 10019, U.S.A.

PUBLICATIONS

Novels

Player Piano. New York, Scribner, 1952; London, Macmillan, 1953; as *Utopia 14,* New York, Bantam, 1954.
The Sirens of Titan. New York, Dell, 1959; London, Gollancz, 1962.
Mother Night. New York, Fawcett, 1962; London, Cape, 1968.
Cat's Cradle. New York, Holt Rinehart, and London, Gollancz, 1963.
God Bless You, Mr. Rosewater; or, Pearls before Swine. New York, Holt Rinehart, and London, Cape, 1965.
Slaughterhouse Five; or, The Children's Crusade: A Duty-Dance with Death, by Kurt Vonnegut, Jr., a Fourth-Generation German-American Now Living in Easy Circumstances on Cape Cod (and Smoking Too Much) Who, as an American Infantry

Scout Hors de Combat, as a Prisoner of War, Witnessed the Fire-Bombing of Dresden, Germany, the Florence of the Elbe, a Long Time Ago, and Survived to Tell the Tale: This Is a Novel Somewhat in the Telegraphic Schizophrenic Manner of Tales of the Planet Tralfamadore, Where the Flying Saucers Come From. New York, Delacorte Press, 1969; London, Cape, 1970.
Breakfast of Champions; or, Goodbye Blue Monday. New York, Delacorte Press, and London, Cape, 1973.
Slapstick; or, Lonesome No More! New York, Delacorte Press, and London, Cape, 1976.
Jailbird. New York, Delacorte Press, and London, Cape, 1979.
Deadeye Dick. New York, Delacorte Press, 1982; London, Cape, 1983.
Galápagos: A Novel. New York, Delacorte Press, and London, Cape, 1985.
Bluebeard. New York, Delacorte Press, 1987; London, Cape, 1988.
Hocus Pocus; or, What's the Hurry, Son? New York, Putnam, and London, Cape, 1990.
Fates Worse than Death. New York, Putnam, 1991.
The Lie, edited by Vaughn McBride. Woodstock, Illinois, Dramatic Publishing Company, 1992.
Timequake. New York, Putnam, 1997.

Short Stories

Canary in a Cathouse. New York, Fawcett, 1961.
Welcome to the Monkey House: A Collection of Short Works. New York, Delacorte Press, 1968; London, Cape, 1969.
Who Am I This Time? For Romeos and Juliets, illustrated by Michael McCurdy. Minneapolis, Minnesota, Redpath Press, 1987.

Plays

Happy Birthday, Wanda June (as *Penelope,* produced Cape Cod, Massachusetts, 1960; revised version, as *Happy Birthday, Wanda June,* produced New York, 1970; London, 1977). New York, Delacorte Press, 1970; London, Cape, 1973.
The Very First Christmas Morning, in *Better Homes and Gardens* (Des Moines, Iowa), December 1962.
Between Time and Timbuktu; or, Prometheus-5: A Space Fantasy (televised, 1972; produced New York, 1976). New York, Delacorte Press, 1972; London, Panther, 1975.
Fortitude, in *Wampeters, Foma, and Granfalloons,* 1974.
Timesteps (produced Edinburgh, 1979).
God Bless You, Mr. Rosewater, adaptation of his own novel (produced New York, 1979).

Television Plays: "Auf Wiedersehen," with Valentine Davies, 1958; *Between Time and Timbuktu,* 1972.

Other

Wampeters, Foma, and Granfalloons: Opinions. New York, Delacorte Press, 1974; London, Cape, 1975.
Sun, Moon, Star (for young adults), with Ivan Chermayeff. New York, Harper, and London, Hutchinson, 1980.
Palm Sunday: An Autobiographical Collage. New York, Delacorte Press, and London, Cape, 1981.
Contributor, *Bob and Ray: A Retrospective, June 15-July 10, 1982.* Museum of Broadcasting, 1982.

Contributor, *Discrimination, Affirmative Action, and Equal Opportunity: An Economic and Social Perspective,* edited by W.E. Block and M.A. Walker. Vancouver, Canada, Fraser Institute, 1982.

Nothing Is Lost Save Honor: Two Essays. Jackson, Mississippi, Noveau Press, 1984.

Conversations with Kurt Vonnegut (interviews), edited by William Rodney Allen. Jackson, University of Mississippi Press, 1988.

Fates Worse Than Death: An Autobiographical Collage of the 1980's. New York, Putnam, 1991.

*

Media Adaptations: *Happy Birthday, Wanda June* (film), Red Lion, 1971; *Slaughterhouse Five* (film), Universal, 1972; *Who Am I This Time?* (film), Rubicon Films, 1982; *Slapstick of Another Kind* (film based on *Slapstick),* Paul-Serendipity, 1984; *Displaced Person* (film), Hemisphere, 1985; *Slaughterhouse Five* (cassette), Listening for Pleasure, 1985; *Jailbird* (cassette), Warner Audio Publishers, 1985; *Breakfast of Champions* (cassette), Caedmon; *Cat's Cradle* (cassette), Books on Tape, (abridged cassette), Caedmon; *Galapagos* (cassette), Simon and Schuster; *Slapstick* (cassette), Books on Tape; *The Sirens of Titan* (cassette), Books on Tape; *Welcome to the Monkey House* (cassette), Books on Tape; *Vonnegut Soundbook* (recording), Caedmon; *Kurt Vonnegut, Jr. Reads Slaughterhouse Five* (cassette), Caedmon; *Mother Night* (film), 1997.

Biography: Entry in *Dictionary of Literary Biography,* Detroit, Gale, Vol. 2, 1978; Vol. 8, 1981; *Kurt Vonnegut, Jr.* by Stanley Schatt, Boston, Twayne, 1976; entry in *Dictionary of Literary Biography Yearbook 1980,* Detroit, Gale, 1981; entry in *Dictionary of Literary Biography Documentary Series,* Detroit, Gale, Vol. 3, 1983.

Bibliography: *Kurt Vonnegut, Jr.: A Descriptive Bibliography and Annotated Secondary Checklist* Asa B. Pieratt, Jr., and Jerome Klinkowitz, Hamden, Connecticut, Shoe String Press, 1974; *Kurt Vonnegut: A Comprehensive Bibliography* by Asa B. Pieratt, Jr., Julie Huffman-Klinkowitz, and Jerome Klinkowitz, Hamden, Connecticut, Archon, 1987.

Critical Studies: *Kurt Vonnegut, Jr.: A Checklist* by Betty Lenhardt Hudgens, Detroit, Gale, 1972; *Kurt Vonnegut, Jr.* by Peter J. Reed, New York, Warner, 1972; *Kurt Vonnegut: Fantasist of Fire and Ice* by David H. Goldsmith, Bowling Green, Ohio, Popular Press, 1972; *The Vonnegut Statement* edited by Jerome Klinkowitz and John Somer, New York, Delacorte Press, 1973, London, Panther, 1975; *Vonnegut in America: An Introduction to the Life and Work of Kurt Vonnegut* edited by Jerome Klinkowitz and Donald L. Lawler, New York, Delacorte Press, 1977; *Kurt Vonnegut* by Jerome Klinkowitz, London, Methuen, 1982; entry in *Contemporary Literary Criticism,* Detroit, Gale, Vol. 1, 1973; Vol. 2, 1974; Vol. 3, 1975; Vol. 4, 1975; Vol. 5, 1976; Vol. 8, 1978; Vol. 12, 1980; Vol. 22, 1982; Vol. 40, 1986; *Vonnegut's Major Works* by Thomas R. Holland, Lincoln, Nebraska, Cliff's Notes, 1973; *Something to Believe In: Is Kurt Vonnegut Exorcist of Jesus Christ Superstar?* by Robert Short, New York, Harper, 1976; *Kurt Vonnegut* by James Lundquist, New York, Ungar, 1977; *Kurt Vonnegut: The*

Gospel from Outer Space by Clark Mayo, San Bernardino, California, Borgo Press, 1977; *Vonnegut: A Preface to His Novels* by Richard Giannone, Port Washington, New York, Kennikat Press, 1977; *Vonnegut Talks!* edited by Michael Chernuchin, Pylon, 1977; *Vonnegut's Duty-Dance with Death: Theme and Structure in Slaughterhouse-Five* by Monica Loeb, Umeå Studies in the Humanities, 1979; *Happy Birthday, Kurt Vonnegut: A Festschrift for Kurt Vonnegut on His Sixtieth Birthday* edited by Jill Krementz, New York, Delacorte Press, 1982.

*   *   *

Although Kurt Vonnegut, Jr., has not written any novels specifically for young adults, his works are broadly popular among students from late middle school through college. Certainly a part of this appeal derives from his clear, readable prose telling an interesting, though often puzzling story. Vonnegut informs young readers about the complexity of attitudes in modern life and delights them with a flippancy of tone which teenagers admire as a way of communicating early sophistication.

Many of Vonnegut's novels are tied together by recurring characters and settings such as the fumbling, failed science-fiction writer, Kilgore Trout, and the cerebral planet Tralfamadore. This continuity captures the fancy of young readers brought up on either print serials like Nancy Drew and the Hardy Boys or cartoons and television series. A comfortable Vonnegut ''family'' or literary style thus invites young readers back to familiar ground, even though the stories may be bizarre satires.

The majority of Vonnegut's novels span the years 1952 to 1990, a forty-year career beginning with *Player Piano* and recently culminating with *Timequake.* At first, he was labeled a ''science-fiction'' writer because of the futuristic settings and imaginative detailing of such early works as *Player Piano, Sirens of Titan,* and *Mother Night.* In the first of these, Paul Proteus, a brilliant, young executive with the megacorporate power industry of the future U.S.A., is stifled by the utopian perfection imposed by ''the company.'' He longs for the nostalgia of the old days, found in the player piano in a bar across the river in Homestead, where the workers live. To realize his longing, he becomes involved with the ''Ghost Shirt,'' society's revolution, in which he gains independent integrity though losing the struggle.

Like Proteus's mythic crossing of the water and descent into Homestead, Malachi Constant, hero of *Sirens of Titan,* descends into the caves of Mercury and passes a series of trials on Mars. He then returns heroically with the boon of being a messiah of the new Church of God the Utterly Indifferent, only to be scapegoated for its failure. Vonnegut's adapting of the mythic initiation theme bridges old and new narrative styles for young readers, again creating a more accessible route for reading.

In perhaps the best of his early novels for young adults, *Slaughterhouse Five,* subtitled *The Children's Crusade,* Vonnegut combines many of his narrative experiments. Child-like Billy Pilgrim narrates the entire tale of a young draftee's horrible experiences during World War II, his return to settled life with a family, his involuntary transportation to and secret life on Tralfamadore, and his assassination by a former antagonist in the German prison camp in Dresden. But this narration does not follow any linear, chronological plan. ''Unstuck in time,'' because of his all-knowing Tralfamadorian perspective, Billy's mind, along with the narrative, jump about between 1945 and 1968 with the disjointed abandon common to adolescent perspectives. In such juxtapositions of consciousness, the reader, together with Billy, knows all along about his death, the birth of his son on Tralfamadore by blue-movie queen Montana Wildhack, the firebombing of Dresden, the accidental death of his wife rushing to him after a foreknown plane crash, and the destruction of the universe by a Tralfamadorian accident. Although the book may be challenging at first, young readers find, after reading and discussing it, a dungeon-and-dragon-like confidence—awareness of all the variables and outcomes in Billy's life which brings to the forefront their powers of informed imagination.

The difficulty in understanding Vonnegut's works is offset by his direct simplicity of prose. Like the Tralfamadorian model of the novel, one may clearly read ''each clump of symbols'' all at once without there being any initial relationship among them, save that in retrospect one can see how the moment is structured in the whole image of life. Not unlike the notions of modern physics, this view offers a fascinating cross-disciplinary link between speculative science and literature.

By tracing symbolic links, the young reader can easily associate Billy with Christian in Bunyan's *Pilgrim's Progress* and find an updated initiation quest for moral vision and behavior. The modern version speaks as persuasively to its readers about finding the virtuous life as does its seventeenth-century counterpart, but in allegory more allusive and fitting our times. Bunyan's Mr. Wiseman and the lions are replaced by Vonnegut's Howard Campbell and a brutal humanity instrumental in the firebombing of Dresden. Ultimately, the quest for Christian love parallels Billy's quest for ''common, human decency.''

In all, Vonnegut's novels engage the young-adult reader who is seeking some transition between the accepting, unifying views of youth and the cynical, compartmentalizing frustration of the adult world. Bright readers will always be drawn to this writer because his work anticipates the future while speaking clearly to us in the present.

—Ron Evans

VOS, Ida

Nationality: Dutch. **Born:** Ida Gudema in Groningen, Netherlands, 13 December 1931. **Education:** Kweekschool Voorbereidend Ondervijs Training College, Netherlands, teaching certificates, 1950 and 1952. **Family:** Married Henk Vos in 1956; three children. **Career:** Writer; teacher in Den Haag, Rijswijk, Holland, Netherlands. Member of the Dutch Writers Association and Women's Club; contributor of articles and short stories to various periodicals. **Awards:** Has received numerous Dutch awards for writings. **Address:** Dr. Wibautlaan 69, 2285 xj Rijswijk, Holland, Netherlands.

PUBLICATIONS FOR YOUNG ADULTS

Fiction

Hide and Seek, translated by Terese Edelstein and Inez Smidt. Boston, Massachusetts, Houghton Mifflin, 1991.
Witte Zwanen Zwarte Zwanen. [Netherlands], 1992.

Anna Is Still Here, translated by Terese Edelstein and Inez Smidt. Boston, Massachusetts, Houghton Mifflin, 1993.
Dancing on the Bridge of Avignon, translated by Terese Edelstein and Inez Smidt. Boston, Massachusetts, Houghton Mifflin, 1995.
The Key Is Lost. New York, Morrow, 1998.

PUBLICATIONS FOR ADULTS

Poetry

Vijfendertig tranen. Netherlands, 1975.
Schiereiland. Netherlands, Nijgh and van Ditmar, 1979.
Miniaturen. Netherlands, Nijgh and van Ditmar, 1980.

Plays

De Bevrijding van Rosa Davidson (broadcast, 1984).

*

Critical Studies: *Something about the Author,* Detroit, Gale, 1992, Vol. 69, 200-202; review of *Anna Is Still Here* by Mary King, in *The Book Report* (Worthington, Ohio), September/October 1993, 49; review of *Dancing on the Bridge at Avignon* by Hanna B. Zeiger, in *Horn Book* Magazine (Boston, Massachusetts), January 1996, 75-76.

*   *   *

Ida Vos's novels for young adults—*Hide and Seek, Anna Is Still Here,* and *Dancing on the Bridge of Avignon*—are all based on her own experiences growing up in the Netherlands during the Holocaust. Raised in a traditional Jewish family, Ida was only eight years old when the Nazis bombed her home town of Rotterdam. After the bombing, Ida's family moved to the smaller city of Rijswijk, but by then Dutch Jews' lives were already being restricted—they had to wear prominent yellow stars of David inscribed ''Jew,'' they were unable to go to the library, public parks, the movies, or restaurants, children had to go to new, all-Jewish schools—and the Nazis were beginning to round up Jews (including Ida's grandparents) and take them to Polish concentration camps. Eventually, Ida's family went into hiding; they were together at first, then they had to separate, leaving Ida to look after her younger sister. Europe was liberated in 1943. Then came the task of trying to start a normal life again while grieving over the countless friends and relatives who had died and worrying over those still missing. Being a survivor took its toll. In 1973, Ida Vos suffered from a mental breakdown and was hospitalized. In the hospital, she suddenly found herself pouring out stories and poems about this terrible time. Finally able to express the horror, she felt able to endure life again.

''Come with me. Come with me to a small country in Western Europe. To the Netherlands, a land also known as Holland. Come with me, back to the year 1940.'' So begins the story of eight-year-old Rachel Hartog, the heroine of *Hide and Seek*. Like Ida Vos, Rachel must separate from her parents and go into hiding with her younger sister, Esther. But *Hide and Seek* is the story not only of Rachel's hiding, it is also the story of Rachel's search for a normal life after the Nazi occupation. ''Can you imagine how it feels when you find out that people you love are dead, all of a sudden? Imagine what it would be like not ever to go outside, year after year. . . . I know how difficult it is to imagine such things,'' Ida Vos tells the reader in her foreword to the American edition of the book, ''that is the reason I wrote *Hide and Seek.* To let you feel how terrible it is to be discriminated against, and to let you know how terrible it was to be a Jewish child in Holland during those years.''

Anna Markus, the thirteen-year-old heroine of *Anna Is Still Here,* has been in hiding during the Occupation and is now struggling to come to terms with the horrors that took place during that time. So many of her friends and relatives have died. Anna is still here, but having survived the horrors is not easy either. Anna's parents are unable to talk about the war. When she is befriended by the strange Mrs. Neumann, whose house she passes on her way to school each day, she is forced to listen to Mrs. Neumann's tragic story and, slowly she is able to tell her own story.

''Sur le pont d'Avignon/On y danse, on y danse. . . .'' *Dancing on the Bridge of Avignon* is the story of ten-year-old Rosa de Jong, whose Uncle Sander promises to help the family escape to unoccupied France. To Avignon. Everyone practices their French. But the Germans who come to get the de Jong family don't believe in Uncle Sander's papers and travel permits, and they haul everyone off to the police station anyway. A German officer is reminded of his own little daughter when he sees Rosa, though, and her brave, beautiful violin playing (the officer's daughter plays the violin, too, and he's noticed that Rosa has brought hers with her) moves him to let Rosa go. Down on the street, she encounters Uncle Sander, who escaped the Nazis, and after the liberation, Rosa comes to live with her uncle: ''They were a comfort to each other, and together they could mourn the loss of all their loved ones.''

Translated in a simple and direct style by Terese Edelstein and Inez Smith, the painfully realistic young adult novels of Ida Vos also exemplify—as Mary King said of Anna Markus in her review of *Anna Is Still Here* for the September/October 1993 issue of *The Book Report*—''the hope for the future that many readers have wished for after reading *The Diary of Anne Frank.*''

—Marcia Welsh

WALDEN, Amelia Elizabeth

Nationality: American. **Born:** New York, 1909. **Education:** Danbury State Teachers College (now Western Connecticut State College), Danbury, diploma (summa cum laude) 1928; Columbia University, New York, B.S. 1934; American Academy of Dramatic Arts, New York, certificate. **Family:** Married John William Harmon in 1946 (died 1950). **Career:** Teacher of English, speech, and drama, Benjamin Franklin School, Norwalk, Connecticut, 1935-45; novelist, since 1946. Playwright, producer, and director of several community theatre groups in Connecticut.

PUBLICATIONS FOR YOUNG ADULTS

Novels

Gateway. New York, Morrow, 1946.
Waverly. New York, Morrow, 1947.
Skymountain. New York, Morrow, 1948.
Sunnycove. New York, Morrow, 1948.
A Girl Called Hank. New York, Morrow, 1951.
Marsha on Stage. New York, Morrow, 1952.
Victory for Jill. New York, Morrow, 1953.
All My Love. New York, Morrow, 1954.
Daystar. Philadelphia, Westminster, 1955.
Three Loves Has Sandy. New York, McGraw, 1955.
I Found My Love. Philadelphia, Westminster, 1956.
My Sister Mike. New York, McGraw, 1956.
Palomino Girl. Philadelphia, Westminster, 1957.
Today Is Mine. Philadelphia, Westminster, 1958.
Queen of the Courts. Philadelphia, Westminster, 1959.
A Boy to Remember. Philadelphia, Westminster, 1960.
Where Is My Heart? Philadelphia, Westminster, 1960.
Shadow on Devil's Peak. Philadelphia, Westminster, 1961.
When Love Speaks. New York, McGraw, 1961.
How Bright the Dawn. Philadelphia, Westminster, 1962.
So Near the Heart. New York, McGraw, 1962.
My Dreams Ride High. Philadelphia, Westminster, 1963.
My World's the Stage. New York, McGraw, 1964.
To Catch a Spy. Philadelphia, Westminster, 1964.
Race the Wild Wind. Philadelphia, Westminster, 1965.
The Spy on Danger Island. Philadelphia, Westminster, 1965.
In Search of Ophelia. New York, McGraw, 1966.
The Spy with Five Faces. Philadelphia, Westminster, 1966.
A Name for Himself. Philadelphia, Lippincott, 1967.
A Spy Called Michel-E. Philadelphia, Westminster, 1967.
The Spy Who Talked Too Much. Philadelphia, Westminster, 1968.
Walk in a Tall Shadow. Philadelphia, Lippincott, 1968.
The Case of the Diamond Eye. Philadelphia, Westminster, 1969.
Same Scene, Different Place. Philadelphia, Lippincott, 1969.
A Spycase Built for Two. Philadelphia, Westminster, 1969.
Basketball Girl of the Year. New York, McGraw, 1970.
What Happened to Candy Carmichael? Philadelphia, Westminster, 1970.
Stay to Win. Philadelphia, Lippincott, 1971.

Valerie Valentine Is Missing. Philadelphia, Westminster, 1971.
Play Ball, McGill! Philadelphia, Westminster, 1972.
Where Was Everyone When Sabrina Screamed? Philadelphia, Westminster, 1973.
Go, Phillips, Go! Philadelphia, Westminster, 1974.
Heartbreak Tennis. Philadelphia, Westminster, 1977.

PUBLICATIONS FOR ADULTS

Novels

The Bradford Story. New York, Appleton, 1956.
Flight into Morning. New York, Appleton, 1957.
Escape on Skis. Philadelphia, Westminster, 1975.

*

Amelia Elizabeth Walden comments:

In the summer of 1945, I made one of the most momentous decisions of my life. I chose to give up the emotional, intellectual, and financial security of the teaching profession and cast my net into the unknown world outside the classroom. I was at that time writing short stories, which were returned from publishers as fast as I sent them out. Someone in the field told me I was writing in the wrong form and that I should try a novel.

The idea was challenging, and when a plot formed itself almost unbidden in my mind, the thought of writing for and about young people in a new and different way impelled me to start my first book. That Christmas Eve, I received a letter from William Morrow's new editor of young peoples' books saying they liked and would publish *Gateway.* I never deviated from my original idea of writing for young readers in an adult style, using an adult vocabulary.

I never had an agent and sold my forty-seven books by going personally into the top offices of the five publishers with whom I dealt. At that time, women were not thought to have the talent, strength, and staying power of men. I have been told that the curator of manuscripts at the university which will receive my collections made inquiries of my publishers and was told by all of them, "She's the best business person in the field."

*   *   *

If the success of any writer depends upon the number of times his or her books are taken out of the library to be read, Amelia Elizabeth Walden considers herself successful. She has written many books for young people, her first book, *Gateway,* being published in 1946. She considers herself to be the first to have written a genuine "young adult" novel, writing novels in the young adult language about young adult problems and interests.

One good example of Walden's young adult novels is *My Dreams Ride High,* portraying eighteen-year-old Jay Wyndham

Gilbert, daughter of the boss of Wyndham Engineering Company, a factory producing marine pumps and government projects (some secret). Jay prefers calculus to cooking and hates femininity, until she meets and falls in love with Shane Rogers, sent by the Navy to Wyndham Engineering to help develop a secret turbocraft. An exciting story about the perils of skin diving, sabotage, and a romance between two people of conflicting personalities, Walden has written a book that young adults will not put down until the end.

Ms. Walden's many novels of suspense and international intrigue include *To Catch a Spy* which features Sally Templeton, a young lady in her early twenties, who helps solve the mystery of an airplane crash in the Nigerian jungle, falls in love with one of two brothers raised by the infamous head of a spy ring, and keeps the reader guessing until the case is solved.

Ms. Walden has written many novels for young adults dealing with sports. *Race the Wild Wind* is about Marty Conover, senior in high school, who is following in the footsteps of famous ski champion, winner of Olympic medals, and beautiful older sister Glory Conover. Marty struggles to be herself while fighting the nightmare from the past of her only brother being killed on a ski slope while saving Marty's life. Marty flirts with danger on the ski slopes, plays the clown to gain the attention of others, and stuffs herself with food for consolation, adding a weight problem to her frustrations. Then she meets Garth Falkner, not at all her idea of Prince Charming, but a young man who helps her realize how she must change. Ms. Walden's keen knowledge of skiing and also of young people's feelings come through.

To Pat Palmer, tomboy and captain of Greenport's girl basketball team in *Basketball Girl of the Year,* life is mainly a rectangle with a hardwood floor, a ceiling overhead, with two backboards with metal hoops attached. Basketball is her life, until she meets Chris Landry who shows her there is more to life than winning the coveted Basketball Girl of the Year award. Because Pat learns to put her team first instead of herself, she loses the award but wins the Girl Athlete for All Seasons instead, and she wins it because she learns to grow up with the help of Chris Landry and a coach who teach her to open her eyes and see more around her than just her own little world.

Softball is the theme of *Play Ball, McGill!,* about Ginger McGill, a feisty senior in high school who has hot-rods, especially her souped-up Studebaker, and Snake Anderson, the handsome new boy on the block, all on her mind. Ginger is the best pitcher in her school, but she comes by it naturally, having two older brothers in the pros. When she hits a bad streak of luck playing ball, she turns to Snake and cars for consolation. Snake not only helps Ginger, he also helps her brother, Karl, when he too has a bad streak of luck at baseball and at love. Ms. Walden has written another knowledgeable book about sports, including auto racing and the building of cars themselves.

Walden writes vividly about the emotional upheavals and confusion that fill young adult lives because she has never forgotten her own adolescence. Her novels appeal not only to sports-minded young people, but to a larger teenage audience because she portrays situations that have appeal for her readers: romance, espionage, mysteries, and most of all, feelings. Her books are well-plotted with vivid backgrounds, whether on ski slopes, basketball courts, or in the ghetto.

—Carol Doxey

WALKER, Alice (Malsenior)

Nationality: American. **Born:** Eatonton, Georgia, 9 February 1944. **Education:** Spelman College, Atlanta, 1961-63; Sarah Lawrence College, Bronxville, New York, 1963-65; B.A. 1965. **Family:** Married Melvyn Rosenman Leventhal in 1967 (divorced 1976); one daughter. **Career:** Writer. Voter registration worker, Georgia; Head Start program worker, Mississippi, and with New York City Department of Welfare, mid-1960s; writer-in-residence and teacher of black studies at Jackson State College, 1968-69, and Tougaloo College, 1970-71, both Mississippi; lecturer in literature, Wellesley College, Massachusetts, 1972-73, and University of Massachusetts, Boston, 1972-73; associate professor of English, Yale University, New Haven, Connecticut, 1977; Distinguished Writer in Afro-American studies department, University of California, Berkeley, spring 1982; Fannie Hurst Professor of Literature, Brandeis University, Waltham, Massachusetts, fall 1982; co-founder and publisher, Wild Trees Press, Navarro, California, 1984-88. Lecturer and reader of own poetry at universities and conferences; member of board of trustees of Sarah Lawrence College; consultant on black history to Friends of the Children of Mississippi, 1967. **Awards:** Bread Loaf Writer's Conference scholarship, 1966; first prize, *American Scholar* essay contest, 1967; Merrill writing fellowship, 1967; MacDowell Colony fellowship, 1967, 1977-78; National Endowment for the Arts grant, 1969, 1977; Radcliffe Institute fellowship, 1971-73; National Book award nomination, and Lillian Smith award for poetry, Southern Regional Council, both 1973, both for *Revolutionary Petunias*; Richard and Hinda Rosenthal Foundation award, American Academy and Institute of Arts and Letters, 1974, for *In Love and Trouble*; Guggenheim award, 1977-78; National Book Critics Circle award nomination, 1982, Pulitzer Prize, 1983, and American Book award, 1983, all for *The Color Purple*; Ph.D.: Russell Sage College, Troy, New York, 1972; D.H.L.: University of Massachusetts, Amherst, 1983. **Address:** c/o The Wendy Weil Agency, Inc., 232 Madison Ave., Ste. 1300, New York, New York 10016, U.S.A.

PUBLICATIONS

Novels

The Third Life of Grange Copeland. New York, Harcourt, 1970; London, Women's Press, 1985.
Meridian. New York, Harcourt, and London, Deutsch, 1976.
The Color Purple. New York, Harcourt, 1982.
The Temple of My Familiar. San Diego, Harcourt, and London, Women's Press, 1989.
Possessing the Secret of Joy. New York, Harcourt, 1992.
By the Light of My Father's Smile. New York, Random House, 1998.

Poetry

Once. New York, Harcourt, 1968; London, Women's Press, 1986.
Five Poems. Detroit, Broadside Press, 1972.
Revolutionary Petunias and Other Poems. New York, Harcourt, 1973; London, Women's Press, 1988.
Goodnight, Willie Lee, I'll See You in the Morning. New York, Dial, 1979; London, Women's Press, 1987.

Horses Make a Landscape Look More Beautiful. New York, Harcourt, 1984; London, Women's Press, 1985.
Her Blue Body Everything We Know: Earthling Poems 1965-1990. San Diego, Harcourt, 1991.

Short Stories

In Love and Trouble: Stories of Black Women. New York, Harcourt, 1973; London, Women's Press, 1984.
You Can't Keep a Good Woman Down. New York, Harcourt, 1981; London, Women's Press, 1982.

Other

Langston Hughes: American Poet (children's biography). New York, Crowell, 1974.
Editor, *I Love Myself When I'm Laughing. . .and Then Again When I Am Looking Mean and Impressive: A Zora Neale Hurston Reader.* Old Westbury, New York, Feminist Press, 1979.
In Search of Our Mothers' Gardens: Womanist Prose. New York, Harcourt, 1983; London, Women's Press, 1984.
Living by the Word: Selected Writings, 1973-1987. San Diego, Harcourt, and London, Women's Press, 1988.
To Hell with Dying (for children), illustrated by Catherine Deeter. San Diego, Harcourt, and London, Hodder & Stoughton, 1988.
Finding the Green Stone, paintings by Catherine Deeter. San Diego, Harcourt, 1991.
With Pratibha Parmar, *Warrior Marks: Female Genital Mutilation and the Sexual Blinding of Women* (nonfiction). New York, Harcourt Brace Jovanovich, 1993; London, Random House, 1993.
Everyday Use, edited, and with an introduction by Barbara T. Christian. New Brunswick, New Jersey, Rutgers University Press, 1994.
Same River Twice: Honoring the Difficult: A Meditation on Life, Spirit, Art, and the Making of the Film, The Color Purple, Ten Years Later. New York, Scribner, 1996.
Alice Walker Banned (selections), with an introduction by Patricia Holt. San Francisco, Aunt Lute Books, 1996.
Anything We Love Can Be Saved: A Writer's Activism. New York, Random House, 1997.

*

Media Adaptations: *The Color Purple* (feature film directed by Steven Spielberg), Warner Brothers, 1985.

Bibliography: "Alice Walker: A Selected Bibliography, 1968-1988" by Keither Byerman and Erma Banks, in *Callaloo,* Vol. 12, No. 2, 1989, 162-163.

Biography: Entry in *Dictionary of Literary Biography,* Detroit, Gale, Vol. 6: *American Novelists since World War II, 2nd series,* 1980, Vol. 33: *Afro-American Fiction Writers after 1955,* 1984; *Alice Walker* by Donna Haisty Winchell, New York, Twayne, 1992.

Critical Studies: Entry in *Contemporary Literary Criticism,* Detroit, Gale, Vol. 5, 1976, Vol. 6, 1976, Vol. 9, 1978, Vol. 19, 1981, Vol. 27, 1984, Vol. 46, 1988; entry by Alyson R. Buckman, in *Gay and Lesbian Literature,* Vol. 2, edited by Tom and Sara Pendergast, Detroit, St. James Press, 1997.

*   *   *

Alice Walker is a novelist, short story writer, essayist, poet, and author of children's books. Of particular interest to young adults are her novels: powerful, strident stories principally set in America's rural and poor South. But Walker cannot be labeled as a southern writer, a black writer, a feminist writer. Her works speak of universal struggles for dignity and meaning and connectedness in life. She does view the African American woman as a symbol of hope for humanity, and stresses the importance of bonds between women in combatting racism and sexism, inequalities of any kind. Her prose is lyrical, and her skill at portraying grace and goodness in the lives of ordinary people is remarkable.

Walker's first novel, *The Third Life of Grange Copeland,* introduces themes she will use again and again, such as the domination of powerless women by equally powerless men. This work details the life of three generations of a black sharecropping family during the years between the depression and the beginning of the civil rights movement. The terrible effects of poverty and racism on the lives of the Copelands, resulting in suicide of a wife in the first generation, murder of a wife in the second generation, and murder of a son to provide freedom for the son's daughter in the third generation, are told with intensity and with clarity. Walker's message is that family members must not ignore family functioning and community relationships; if they do, they lose the major basis for understanding themselves.

Meridian, Walker's second novel, is a powerful story of black strength and perseverance. Also set in the rural South, it focuses on the civil rights movement. Meridian is a southerner who goes north to college and then returns to the South, committing her life to aiding southern blacks in gaining political and social equality. She joins a black militant group but is forced to leave when she refuses to agree to violence. Meridian continues her activist work, mostly alone, and becomes a legendary figure throughout the South. In order to align herself, though, with the larger social problems of blacks, she divests herself of immediate family relationships—her parents and her child. This rupture in family in the end allows Meridian to define herself. At the end of the novel, Meridian's self-identity is a collective identity, and Meridian becomes a model for others to take up the civil rights cause.

The Color Purple is Walker's most highly acclaimed book. It won both the Pulitzer Prize and the American Book Award for fiction, and became a well received movie. The novel describes thirty years in the life of Celie, a poor southern black woman who is subjected to physical and emotional abuse by her stepfather and her husband. The story begins when Celie is fourteen years old. She has been repeatedly raped by her stepfather, and the children she bore him were sold. She is then placed in a loveless marriage by her stepfather, with a widower who beats and ridicules her. The book is in the form of letters describing her ordeals to God and to her sister Nettie, who escapes a similar life by becoming a missionary in Africa. Celie finally finds comfort and love in her husband's mistress, Shug Avery, a flamboyant blues singer who treats her with dignity, provides her with love, and helps her leave her marriage. In the end Celie is reunited with her children and with Nettie. This is a rare and beautiful book, filled with characters who live and breathe. Its descriptions of adolescence as well as adulthood are moving, painful, and unforgettable.

The Temple of My Familiar continues Walker's fascination with African history in more detail. It attempts to record five hundred thousand years of human history, using multiple settings and narrative voices, shifting rapidly between past and present. It moves from the Americas, Europe, and Africa to nameless primal worlds. At center stage is Miss Lissie, an African goddess who has been incarnated hundreds of times—usually as a woman, sometimes as a man, once as a lion. Lissie enables Walker to go back in time to beginnings of (wo)man. This book, a mixture of fantasy and revisionary history, is more difficult to read and less eloquent than *The Color Purple.*

Alice Walker is a passionate writer. Her portrayals of young, poor, southern, black women are unsurpassed. These women may be uneducated and unappreciated, they may be abused, but they survive and they affirm themselves. All young people need to read *The Color Purple.* They will see in it their own doubts and fears, and they will see in it strength and staying power.

—Mary Lystad

WALLACE, Richard (Alan)

Nationality: American. **Born:** Hackensack, New Jersey, 29 January 1957. **Education:** Montclair State College, B.A. 1980. **Family:** Married (divorced, 1996); two sons. **Career:** Editorial assistant, 1978-79, sports reporter, 1979-82, *Herald News,* Passaic, New Jersey; sports editor, 1982-84, news editor, 1984-85, *Daily Advance,* Dover, New Jersey; copy editor, 1985-86, assistant city editor, 1986-87, *Trenton Times,* Trenton, New Jersey; copy editor, 1988-90, assistant editor, 1990-92, coordinating editor, from 1992, *Highlights for Children* magazine. **Awards:** American Library Association (ALA) Best Books for Young Adults selection, ALA Recommended Book for Reluctant Young Adult Readers, Pennsylvania Librarians' Association Best of the Best Books for Young Adults selection, all 1996, all for *Wrestling Sturbridge.* **Office:** *Highlights for Children,* 803 Church St., Honesdale, Pennsylvania 18431. **Address:** P.O. Box 698, Honesdale, Pennsylvania 18431, U.S.A.

PUBLICATIONS FOR YOUNG ADULTS

Fiction

Wrestling Sturbridge. New York, Knopf, 1996.
Shots on Goal. New York, Knopf, 1997.
Spit. New York, Knopf, forthcoming.

*

Media adaptations: *Wrestling Sturbridge* (recording), New York, Recorded Books, 1996; *Shots on Goal* (recording), New York, Recorded Books, 1998.

Richard Wallace comments:

Although I did read periodicals, I was among the most reluctant of "reluctant readers" of novels as a teenager. Instead, I found the world I was living in reflected, even celebrated in the work of songwriters like Bruce Springsteen, who was realistic, gritty, and

unflinchingly honest. I look for the universal in the very specific—the moment of self examination in the seconds before an athletic event, the painful truth in being rejected by a love interest, the sobering idea that a kid might be more mature than one of his parents. Young guys tend to keep these little discoveries to themselves. I've never been particularly verbal, but I do hope to share a few things I've learned by writing about them in my novels.

*   *   *

Sports have been central to Rich Wallace's life as far back as he remembers. "I majored in track and field in college," he told *St. James Guide to Young Adult Writers.* Now he runs almost daily, lifts weights, serves as president of the YMCA Board of Directors in Wayne County, Pennsylvania, and coaches youth sports teams of all sorts year-round. "If my kids are interested in it, I'm there."

Wallace grew up the middle of seven kids—all athletes—in Hasbrouck Heights, New Jersey, a suburb of New York City. His father, an executive in a large actuarial firm in New York City, commuted daily but managed to get to almost every sports event Rich Wallace was in. His mother kept track of all seven children and was involved in many community projects.

Wallace says, "I've been writing a long time," going back to what he calls his "intensive diaries" kept during his high school days which "helped me sort out my life." He occasionally returns to those diaries to help "relive a scene or an emotion I'm writing about." His editing consists of overseeing the content of *Highlights for Children,* which has the largest circulation of any kid's magazine.

After working as a sports writer when he was in college, Wallace later worked on a number of novels, some of which he says "showed promise but didn't go anyplace." One novel was rejected by Patricia Gauch at Philomel, but "she was kind enough to share in-house comments that were very useful." Tracy Gates at Philomel liked the book, and when *Wrestling Sturbridge* was completed Wallace found her at Knopf and asked her if she'd be interested in looking at the book. She was, and with her help *Wrestling Sturbridge* was published.

Wrestling Sturbridge was highly praised by reviewers with words rarely accorded a first time novelist. A *Publishers Weekly* reviewer called *Wrestling* a "finely wrought tale"; the *Los Angeles Times Book Review* said the novel was a "dignified, intelligent treatment . . . subtle, funny, cleanly drawn"; the *New Yorker* called the book "excellent, despondent . . . set in the Harry Angstrom country of failed-industrial Pennsylvania." *Seventeen* magazine may have come closest to the truth about the book when its reviewer said the main character was "sweet." Like other good writers, Wallace recognizes the importance of telling a story that involves readers—mostly boys, but also girls and women—who recognize that the book is about sports and much, much more. It is about young people who care about life and about keeping promises they've made to themselves and others. It is a rare sports story because there is no super-hero and no villains.

Ben is seventeen and the second best wrestler at 135 pounds in his school. Unfortunately, the best wrestler in the state at 135 pounds is Al, a friend of long standing in the same high school. Ben and Al have a love-hate relationship that is not surprising but is clumsy at school and on the wrestling mat. But Ben is wrestling with a lot more than just Al: he doesn't know why he's afraid of getting close to his intelligent and attractive girlfriend Kim, and he is confused about his moral relationships with his father and society. Sturbridge is a small town defined and limited by the cinder block plant and sports for young people (and the booster club for adults). Ben and Kim both know that they will not be held back by Sturbridge and what it represents to them, a claustrophobic way of life in a town that is going nowhere.

One of the more intriguing parts of the book is a series of Ben's comments that precedes each chapter. For example, chapter 19 opens with this list which makes clear Ben's passion for wrestling:

What happens before a match (in this order):
* diarrhea and mood swings
* a kind of prayer where you curse at God and beat yourself up, then tell God you're sorry and he says it's okay.
* a concentrated sense of focus
What doesn't:
* you don't joke around with anybody
* you don't resign yourself to losing
* you never say it doesn't matter what happens

Ben and Al get their chance to face off with each other in wrestling to find who's the best man, and while Ben comes close he loses 8-7. Ben, who often takes long walks after wrestling, goes off once more and the book ends with three brief paragraphs:

I look at the moon, and it's right where it should be, a quarter million miles away. I stop walking and shut my eyes in the cool, clear breeze, lifting my arms above my head and inhaling. The air smells piney, with just a hint of cows and of midnight.
Life is good. I have Kim
I am tired and warm and alive.

Shots on Goal is Wallace's more recent and somewhat lesser book. Barry ''Bones'' Austin is in his sophomore soccer season. As in *Wrestling Sturbridge* Bones' best friend, Joey, is the better player, ''always a half-step ahead of me in sports, but we've been on even ground in everything else,'' Bones says. But things are about to change for both Bones and Joey. Bones has had his eye on Shannon, but Joey cuts in on him, and once again Bones comes in second to his best friend. That carries over to the surprisingly successful Sturbridge soccer team as Bones and Joey vie to become the best player on the squad. Then as the season begins to go downward, Joey gets Bones fired from a job after Bones makes a pass at Shannon. Finally, reminiscent of *Wrestling Sturbridge,* the two friends square off in a fight which makes both aware how important their soccer team and their friendship are.

The book opens with a brief paragraph which sets the scene and establishes Bones's love of soccer.

You sweep it away with the outside of your foot, dodging quickly left, then right, and spurting past the defender. You're as tough as anybody out there, you keep telling yourself, racing now to keep up with the ball.

But even if *Shots* is about Sturbridge, readers will feel little of the smothering town that oppresses Ben and readers in *Wrestling.*

Partly it's the individuality of wrestling, the individual pitted against a foe and himself, as opposed to the team sport of soccer, which is less dramatic for Bones as an individual.

Wrestling Sturbridge is a brilliant start to a career. *Shots on Goal* advances Wallace's work just a bit. It's safe to say that many readers of both books await whatever Wallace has to offer. Whatever he writes next, the reviewer writing in the *Journal of Adolescent and Adult Literacy* was right to ''Welcome a new voice to the field of YA literature.''

—Ken Donelson

WALTER, Mildred Pitts

Nationality: American. **Born:** Sweetville, Louisiana, 9 September 1922. **Education:** Southern University, Louisiana, B.A. 1944; University of California, Los Angeles; California State College, 1950-52; University of Southern California, Los Angeles; Antioch College, Yellow Springs, Ohio, M.Ed. 1977. **Family:** Married Earl Lloyd Walter in 1947 (died 1965); two sons. **Career:** Shipwright helper in Vancouver, Washington, 1943-44; salesperson, City Dye Works, Los Angeles, California, 1944-48; personnel clerk, 1949-52, elementary schoolteacher, 1952-70, Los Angeles Public Schools; educational consultant and lecturer on cultural diversity for educational institutions, 1971-73. Civil rights activist for Congress of Racial Equality (CORE), during 1950s and 1960s. Northeast Women's Center, Denver, Colorado, cofounder and administrator, 1982-86. Delegate to Second World Black and African Festival of the Arts and Culture, Lagos, Nigeria, 1977. **Awards:** Runner-up for Irma Simonton Black award, 1981, for *Ty's One Man Band, Parents' Choice* awards, 1984, for *Because We Are,* and 1985, for *Brother to the Wind;* Coretta Scott King awards from Social Responsibility Round Table of American Library Association, honorable mention, 1984, for *Because We Are,* honorable mention, 1986, for *Trouble's Child,* winner 1987, for *Justin and the Best Biscuits in the World,* for *Mississippi Challenge,* Honor award 1993; Best Book Christopher award, for *Mississippi Challenge,* 1992; Carter G. Woodson Secondary Book award, for *Mississippi Challenge,* 1993; Jane Addams Honor Book award and Virginia Library Association Jefferson Cup Worthy of Special Note award, for *Second Daughter,* 1997.

PUBLICATIONS FOR YOUNG ADULTS

Fiction

Lillie of Watts: A Birthday Discovery, illustrated by Leonora E. Prince. Los Angeles, Ward Ritchie Press, 1969.
Lillie of Watts Takes a Giant Step, illustrated by Bonnie Helene Johnson. New York, Doubleday, 1971.
The Girl on the Outside. New York, Lothrop, 1982.
Because We Are. New York, Lothrop, 1983.
Trouble's Child. New York, Lothrop, 1985.
Mariah Loves Rock. New York, Bradbury Press, 1988.
Mariah Keeps Cool, illustrated by Pat Cummings. New York, Bradbury, 1990.
Second Daughter, New York, Scholastic, 1996.

Nonfiction

Mississippi Challenge. New York, Bradbury Press, 1992.

PUBLICATIONS FOR CHILDREN

Fiction

Ty's One-Man Band, illustrated by Margot Tomes. New York,
   Four Winds Press, 1980.
My Mama Needs Me, illustrated by Pat Cummings. New York,
   Lothrop, 1983.
Brother to the Wind, illustrated by Diane and Leo Dillon. New
   York, Lothrop, 1985.
Justin and the Best Biscuits in the World, illustrated by Catherine
   Stock. New York, Lothrop, 1986.
Have a Happy. . . , illustrated by Carole Byard. New York,
   Lothrop, 1989.
Two and Too Much, illustrated by Pat Cummings. New York,
   Bradbury, 1990.
Tiger Ride. New York, Macmillan, 1994.

*   *   *

In Mildred Pitts Walter's books for adolescents and young
adults, metamorphosis is a predominant theme. When Martha of
Trouble's Child realizes at the novel's end that "she was on the
threshold of searching, learning, knowing, of stretching her mind,"
her thoughts represent not only the growing recognition of her own
identity but the transformations that occur in all of Walter's black
characters. Walter writes with power, determination, and truth
about how young black people achieve self-awareness in diverse
social environments in the United States. She focuses on the
cultural defamation of black Americans and their struggle to face
the realities of their racial heritage and become fully integrated
human beings. While Walter writes about black Americans, her
books transcend that particular experience to speak movingly about
the connectedness of people despite differences in color, race, or
creed.

In *Lillie of Watts,* eleven-year-old Lillie must find meaning in a
world where racial differences parallel social and economic privileges. Advertisements bombard Lillie with the message that to be
white means to be valued by society while to be black means to be
overlooked. Over the course of the story, Lillie learns that "people
are more important than cats, sweaters, and cars." Her mother's
unconditional love helps Lillie appreciate and understand that pride
and a sense of self cannot be measured in material goods but by
how an individual conducts his or her life.

The setting for *Trouble's Child,* a young adult novel that was
named a Coretta Scott King Honor Book, is the lush Louisiana
bayou community of Blue Isle. In this coming-of-age story,
Martha, who dreams of finishing her high-school education, tries
to free herself from the binding ties of her small, isolated community and its expectation that she marry and follow in her grandmother's footsteps by becoming a midwife. Martha achieves her aspirations when she finds the courage to stand by her choices despite
community disapproval. Rich in detail and written in the soft
cadences of Louisiana speech, the book strongly but tenderly
portrays a universal adolescent experience.

The Girl on the Outside is a fictional re-creation of the
integration of Central High School in Little Rock, Arkansas, in
1957. Resonating with honesty and integrity, the novel focuses on
the experiences of two students: Sophie, a white girl who is caught
in a web of unconscious racism, and Eva, a black girl who
volunteers to be bused to the new school. *The Girl on the Outside*
takes a powerful and poignant look at the problems, fears, and
prejudices that must be faced during the process of accepting
integration.

Themes of racial pride and adolescent maturation also occur in
Because We Are, a recipient of the Coretta Scott King Award. A
misunderstanding between Emma Walsh, a black honor student,
and one of her teachers at a predominantly white high school results
in her transfer to an all-black high school. In dealing with the
discrimination against her, the African proverb "Because we are, I
am" resonates for Emma, who discovers strength in her community's collective racial heritage.

Mississippi Challenge, Walter's only nonfiction book to date
and a Coretta Scott King Honor Book, documents the struggles of
blacks in Mississippi from the pre-Civil War era through the
organization of the Mississippi Freedom Democratic Party (MFDP)
in the 1960s, and its role in changing the course of Mississippi
history. Using a reportorial style and aimed at a junior-high
audience, the book moves from recounting some of the dire
injustices committed against blacks during this time to detailing the
civil rights work of both the MFDP and the Student Nonviolent
Coordinating Committee (SNCC). Courage, choice, and change-
themes that are so integral to Walter's fiction—are also the
cornerstones of this probing examination of a dark period in
American history.

Integration of a different kind occurs in *Mariah Loves Rock,* in
which eleven-year-old Mariah must confront her feelings about
her father's daughter from his first marriage coming to live with
them. As she anticipates Denise's arrival, Mariah's concern that
she will lose her father's affections to this new family member
fosters jealousy and resentment. In the novel's sequel, *Mariah
Keeps Cool,* Mariah moves from viewing Denise as a rival to
accepting her as a sister. With keen insight into the psyche of the
family unit, Walter realistically and warmly chronicles Mariah's
transformation.

Walter's imbues her work with feeling and conviction of
purpose. Thematically complex yet stylistically accessible, her
writing addresses issues of race relations, family life, and adolescent maturation. It also celebrates change—at times frightening,
exhilarating, comforting, and perplexing—as an essential and
liberating force in coming to terms with oneself and society.
Wellsprings of hope, Walter's books embrace life even as they
acknowledge the sometimes seemingly insurmountable difficulties
of living.

—Carolyn Shute

WANGERIN, Walter, Jr

Nationality: American. **Born:** Portland, Oregon, 13 February
1944. **Education:** Concordia Senior College (now Concordia
Theological Seminary), Fort Wayne, Indiana, B.A. 1966; Miami
University, Oxford, Ohio, M.A. 1968; Christ Seminary, Seminex,

M.Div. 1976. **Family:** Married Ruthanne Bohlmann in 1968; two sons and two daughters. **Career:** Full-time writer. Worked at a variety of jobs, including migrant peapicker, lifeguard, and ghetto youth worker; producer and announcer, KFUO-Radiocomments, St. Louis, Montana, 1969-70; instructor in English literature, University of Evansville, Evansville, Indiana, 1970-74; ordained Lutheran minister, 1976; assistant pastor, Lutheran Church of Our Redeemer, Evansville, beginning 1974; assistant pastor, beginning 1974, senior pastor, 1977-85, Grace Lutheran Church, Evansville; Jockum Professor in English and Theology, Valparaiso University, Valparaiso, Indiana, beginning 1991. **Awards:** Best Children's Book of the Year, *School Library Journal* and *New York Times,* both 1978; National Religious Book award (children/youth category), 1980, American Book award for paperback science fiction, 1981, and American Library Association Notable Book citation, all for *The Book of the Dun Cow*; Best Book of 1983, School Library Journal, for *Thistle*; Best Fiction, Association of Logos Bookstores, 1986, for *The Book of Sorrows.* **Address:** Lives in Evansville, Indiana.

PUBLICATIONS FOR ADULTS and Young Adults

Fiction

The Book of the Dun Cow. New York, Harper, 1978.
The Book of Sorrows. New York, Harper, 1985.
The Orphean Passages: The Drama of Faith. New York, Harper, 1986.

Poetry

A Miniature Cathedral and Other Poems New York, Harper, 1986.

Other

Ragman and Other Cries of Faith. New York, Harper, 1984.
Miz Lil and the Chronicles of Grace. New York, Harper, 1988.
The Manger Is Empty. New York, Harper, 1989.
As for Me and My House: Crafting Your Marriage to Last. Nelson, 1987.
Mourning into Dancing. Grand Rapids, Michigan, Zondervan, 1992.
Reliving the Passion: Meditations on the Suffering, Death, and Resurrection of Jesus as Recorded in Mark. Grand Rapids, Michigan, Zondervan, 1992.

PUBLICATIONS FOR CHILDREN

Fiction

The Glory Story. Concordia, 1974.
God, I've Gotta Talk to You. Concordia, 1974.
A Penny Is Everything, with A. Jennings. Concordia, 1974.
The Baby God Promised. Concordia, 1976.
The Bible for Children. Rand McNally, 1981.
O Happy Day! Concordia, 1981.
My First Bible Book about Jesus, illustrated by Jim Cummins. Rand McNally, 1983.
Thistle, illustrated by Marcia Sewall. New York, Harper, 1983.
Potter, Come Fly to the First of the Earth, illustrated by Daniel San Souci. Cook, 1985.

In the Beginning There Was No Sky. Nelson, 1986.
The Bible for Children. Macmillan, 1987.
Elisabeth and the Water Troll. New York, Harper, 1991.
Branta and the Golden Stone, illustrated by Deborah Healey. New York, Simon & Schuster, 1993.

*   *   *

Walter Wangerin, Jr., is a master storyteller who is at his best in books in which he resurrects the fable and fairy tale, those age-old grandparents of storytelling forms, and fills them with rich, multilevel stories that are unique for their modern resonance and elusive use of symbols and religious parallels. Fables and fairy tales have always been a means of delivering stories to people of all ages, and Wangerin's are no exception. His first novel, *The Book of the Dun Cow,* and his more recent picture book, *Elisabeth and the Water-Troll,* deal with timeless themes—good versus evil, the nature of appearances and reality—and fall somewhere in between his books written specifically for children and his poetry, plays, and other adult books. *Elisabeth and the Water-Troll,* with folksy illustrations by Deborah Healy that incorporate the story's elements of wonder and adventure, is a "Beauty and the Beast" sort of fairy tale which, through its beautifully implied lessons of trust, loss, love, and inner beauty, invites older readers to enjoy it alongside children. *The Book of the Dun Cow* even more decidedly defies age appropriate categorization. Young readers and listeners are drawn to it for its lively and sometimes humorous animal characterization, lyrical language, and dramatic conflict that does not spare gruesome details. Full appreciation of these books, however, requires a more mature grasp of symbol and allusion and an ability to deal with questions for which there are no ultimate answers.

The Book of the Dun Cow is a beast fable, a story form that isolates, characterizes, and interprets human behavior by giving its unchanging aspects familiar animal forms—the industrious ant, the crafty fox, the prideful rooster. Other modern novels of appeal to young adults make powerful use of the form; George Orwell's *Animal Farm* and Richard Adams's *Watership Down* are examples. These give our virtues and vices names and faces and create a microcosm which helps us interpret the larger world. But what distinguishes *The Book of the Dun Cow* is that Wangerin works within the fable, demonstrating a working knowledge of medieval literature and a poetic facility with language that makes his tales sound old and familiar, stories that might have once been told aloud or sung, stories you would crowd up against others to hear. Additionally, in *The Book of the Dun Cow,* Wangerin goes beyond recreating the microcosmic barnyard or rabbit warren. His attempt is to take readers back to a time "when the animals could both speak and understand speech," "the earth was still fixed in the absolute center of the universe. . . . And the sun still traveled around the moored earth, so that days and nights belonged to the earth and to the creatures thereon, not to a ball of silent fire." The barnyard of his story is just one barnyard of many operating as one part of an infinitely larger scheme. Thus, he ambitiously creates an entire cosmology of the universe and the good and evil within it.

In *The Book of the Dun Cow,* the rooster Chaunticleer, a cocky, often cranky fellow, rules his roost and the land beyond with few cares beyond marking each part of the day with his crowing and trying to sleep, strut, and sun himself without too many interruptions from the egg-sucking Ebenezer Rat, the tattletale John Wesley Weasel or the mournful boot-nosed dog Mundo Cani, who arrives out of nowhere and stays. But unbeknownst to Chaunticleer and the other animals, evil embodied in a monstrous, putrescent snake called Wyrm is imprisoned within the earth and they are its keepers. When Wyrm's minion Cockatrice—an unnaturally born snake-like rooster—gets a foothold in a neighboring land and the death and destruction he brings to it begin to spread like a choking odor, Chaunticleer and his fellow creatures must wage war. Their efforts seem doomed from the start. For what is a ragtag band of God's creatures—representing good in all its meekness—against the insidious powers of evil? The animals admirably defeat an army of basilisks and Chaunticleer goes on to kill Cockatrice, but these make a weak victory won at the cost of too many animal lives and Chaunticleer's own faith, which is lost with the realization that "it is entirely possible to win against the enemy, it is possible even to kill the enemy, and still to be defeated by the battle." Wyrm is subdued for an indefinite time when Mundo Cani sacrifices himself for the others by throwing himself into the serpent's eye, armed with the horn of the mysterious Dun Cow.

The war in *The Book of the Dun Cow* is a Vietnam-like experience—how many battles make the war?—and is just one of the modern infusions Wangerin gives to his fable. What also lends to the modern resonance of Wangerin's work, and what makes it truly original, is his ability to deliver a tale about morality that contains no moralisms. The book is full of obvious biblical parallels: Chaunticleer, for instance, is Job-like as he rails at God over the loss of his children, Moses-like as he doubts his abilities to be the chosen leader, and Noah-like as he calls all creatures together against impending doom. But he never really becomes any of those characters, just as the dog Mundo Cani is Christ-like but is clearly not Christ. Readers are left to make what they will of Wangerin's changeable allusions and symbols, as well as his endings, which bring unsettling events to a conclusion but leave things far from settled.

—Tracy J. Sukraw

WARTSKI, Maureen (Ann) Crane

Has also written as M.A. Crane. **Nationality:** American. **Born:** Ashiya, Japan, 25 January 1940; naturalized U.S. citizen, 1962. **Education:** University of Redlands, 1958-59; Sophia University, B.A. 1962. **Family:** Married Maximilian Wartski in 1962; two sons. **Career:** Free-lance writer. Reporter, *English Mainichi,* Kobe, Japan, 1957-58; teacher at public schools in Sharon, Massachusetts, 1968-69; high school history teacher in Sharon, 1978-79. Has also taught creative writing, conducted workshops, and lectured on writing. **Awards:** Annual book award of the Child Study Committee at Bank Street College of Education, 1980, for *A Boat to Nowhere,* and honor book, 1980, for *A Long Way from Home*; Magazine Merit award, Society of Children's Book Writers, 1990, for "A Watcher in the Shadows." **Address:** c/o Fawcett Books, 201 East 50th St., New York, New York 10022, U.S.A.

PUBLICATIONS FOR YOUNG ADULTS

Fiction

My Brother Is Special. Philadelphia, Westminster, 1979.
A Boat to Nowhere, illustrated by Dick Teicher. Philadelphia, Westminster, 1980.
A Long Way from Home. Philadelphia, Westminster, 1980.
The Lake Is on Fire. Philadelphia, Westminster, 1981.
My Name is Nobody. New York, Walker, 1988.
Belonging. New York, Fawcett, 1993.
Dark Silence. New York, Fawcett, forthcoming.

*

Maureen Crane Wartski comments:

Writing for me is reflective communication. It means seizing the heartbeat of the moment and burnishing it with thought and experience. We all were young once, and we all experienced the exhilarating, sometimes painful, often wonderful world of the young. In my writing for young adults I try to renew these moments.

Writing also means responsibility. When I was younger, the book that most held my attention was one that took me into myself and beyond myself. Now I try to present readers with their world, the problems of their world, and the choices they themselves have as they interact with this world.

*   *   *

Maureen Crane Wartski, who has a knack for telling realistic stories, writes equally well about both children of other countries and American teenagers. Courage is the common theme of her fiction, in which believable characters must contend with difficult situations.

A Boat to Nowhere relates the adventures of Mai, an adolescent Vietnamese girl, her little brother Loc, and their grandfather Van Chi. The time is shortly after the Communist takeover of Vietnam; the setting, a remote Vietnamese fishing village. Mai, Loc, and their grandfather are forced to flee their homeland with Kien, a fourteen-year-old orphan who has come to live in their village. Wartski portrays their experiences through the eyes of children who do not understand why the world is so cruel and provides a bittersweet ending. Yet the ending is just a pause in the lives of the characters, for it is obvious there will be a sequel relating their new lives.

The sequel, *A Long Way from Home,* begins in a Hong Kong refugee camp, where the three children are awaiting word from Steve Olson, their American sponsor. Soon they are living in California. Kien, however, has trouble adjusting—he runs away to a fishing village where many Vietnamese refugees have settled, and finds himself mediating a dispute between the new arrivals and the American fishermen of the town. Even though he is a hero, he realizes that home is with the Olsons, and the book ends with his return to their house to take up the task of finding a place in American life. Wartski deals with prejudice directly in this story, making it clear that there are no easy answers.

Wartski's next two books deal with children who are physically rather than culturally different. In *My Brother Is Special,* Noni (Nora) Harlow is in the eighth grade, and her brother Kip is eight years old and mentally retarded; they have moved from California to Massachusetts, where the whole family is experiencing problems. Then Noni goes out for the track team and finds out about the Special Olympics, in which Kip eventually participates. Though Kip does not win the race, Noni learns that winning and popularity are not everything. Despite a few inconsistencies, such as Kip not being enrolled in school as legally required, the book treats the subject of families with handicapped children thoughtfully.

In *The Lake Is on Fire,* Ricky Talese, after being blinded in a freak accident, can only feel sorry for himself. When Ricky tries to commit suicide, some family friends take him to their mountain cabin. Though he used to love the cabin, nothing is the same since the accident that blinded him and killed his best friend. Moreover, Ricky now has to deal with King, a German shepherd, who dislikes people because a former owner mistreated him. Inadvertently, Ricky ends up alone in the cabin in the midst of a forest fire, with only King for company. He and the dog manage to survive by learning to trust each other, as Ricky risks his own life in order to rescue King and, through that action, regains his sense of competency. The depression often associated with sudden blindness is described very well here.

Holland, who has been abused by his alcoholic father, is the subject of *My Name Is Nobody,* in which the youth's severe emotional problems are profiled from his confused viewpoint. Abandoned by his father, Rob is taken in by Kurt Doyle, a retired policeman, after trying to kill himself. Under Kurt's tutelage, Rob learns how to sail a boat, and gradually develops some self-esteem. But he is continually beset by new problems, and once again suicide seems like the answer. Only when Kurt risks his own life intervening does Rob change his mind and, in a dramatic ending, save both of them. Again, the social commentary is gentle here, as Wartski shows societal institutions to be susceptible to human error.

Whether depicting youths confronting cultural, physical, or psychological problems, Wartski's young adult novels consistently evince both sensitivity and authenticity, and hold considerable appeal for contemporary adolescents struggling with issues of courage.

—Sharon Clontz Bernstein

WATSON, Sally (Lou)

Nationality: American. **Born:** Seattle, Washington, 28 January 1924. **Education:** Reed College, B.A. 1950. **Military Service:** Served in the United States Navy, 1944-46. **Career:** Area representative, Great Books Foundation, Los Angeles, California, 1953-56; executive secretary, writer, and artist, Listen and Learn With Phonics (basic reading instruction), Oakland, California, 1957-63. Member of juvenile panel, Pacific Northwest Writers Conference, Seattle, Washington, 1962; judo instructor, referee, and examiner, 1969-80. Copper enamelist, since 1976. **Awards:** Brooklyn Community Woodward School's annual book award, 1959, for *To Build a Land*; named to *Hornbook* honor list, 1963, for *Witch of the Glens.*

PUBLICATIONS FOR YOUNG ADULTS

Fiction

Highland Rebel. New York, Holt, 1954.
Mistress Malapert. New York, Holt, 1955.
To Build a Land. New York, Holt, 1957.
Poor Felicity. New York, Doubleday, 1961.
Witch of the Glens. New York, Viking, 1962.
Lark. New York, Holt, 1964.
Other Sandals. New York, Holt, 1966.
Hornet's Nest. New York, Holt, 1967.
The Mukhtar's Children. New York, Holt, 1968.
Jade. New York, Holt, 1969.
Magic at Wychwood. New York, Knopf, 1970.
Linnet. New York, Dutton, 1971.

*   *   *

The central theme of Sally Watson's fiction, from her historical novels to her stories about emergent Israel, is the difficulty that adolescents experience in adjusting to adult society, their peers, and even themselves. Her heroines and heroes struggle against political upheaval, exile from their homes, and cultural codes too rigid to contain them comfortably. But despite the daunting problems facing Watson's beleaguered teenagers, her novels not only trace the protagonists' attainment of the blend of wisdom, courage, and flexibility that will prepare them for happiness in the adult world, but suggest that these qualities also help young adults to change adult society to suit themselves. It is this respect for the good sense, emotional strength, and capability of her main characters (and, by implication, the reader who identifies with them), as much as the wit of the dialogue or the suspense of the plots, that makes Watson's works so engaging.

A major source of conflict in these novels is the practice of stereotyping. In the Middle Eastern fictions—*To Build a Land, Other Sandals,* and *The Mukhtar's Children*—the problems that stem from judging people in terms of their membership in a group instead of individually are most obvious in a religious context. The young refugees of *To Build a Land,* for instance, are survivors of Hitler's Europe whose attempts to turn the Israel of 1947 into a home are complicated by the violent resentments of some of their Arab neighbors. The narrative makes clear, however, that neither side can afford to condemn the other *en masse,* and that seeing an opponent's viewpoint is essential to national concord and even to inner peace. Similarly, *Other Sandals* (set in the mid-1960s) traces the parallel development of a city boy, Eytan, and a kibbutz girl, Devra, when they trade places for a summer: Eytan abandons his fear-based prejudice against belonging to a community, while Devra overcomes her hatred of Arabs. Meanwhile, *The Mukhtar's Children* provides a sympathetic look at a family on the other side of the Arab-Israeli conflict.

If xenophobia (ranging from Devra's pathological dislike of the culturally alien to Eytan's bitterness against anyone other than himself) is the major issue in Watson's Middle East novels, her historical works often focus on the frustrations felt by girls confronting the rigid rules that surround gender, class, or race. As the eponymous heroine of *Jade* puts it, few relish "being marked down as a sort of second-rate human just because of the body [they] happened to get born into." For many of Watson's heroines, the solution is to take on, at least temporarily, the attributes of another "body." Thus Valerie Leigh of *Mistress Malapert* and Lauren Cameron of *Highland Rebel* disguise themselves as boys, the one to go on the Elizabethan stage, the other to fight for Bonnie Prince Charlie. Lauchlin MacLeod trades her Scottish heritage for American citizenship in *The Hornet's Nest,* simultaneously learning to combine young ladyhood with revolutionary fervor; similarly, pioneer Felicity Dare moves from Virginia to Seattle and from invalid to capable tomboy in *Poor Felicity.* Kelpie in *Witch of the Glens* and Lark Lennox in *Lark* alternately adopt and shed Roundhead garb in their efforts to defeat the narrow-minded cruelty Puritanism represents in these novels. Finally, Jade Lennox, perhaps the most outspokenly rebellious of Watson's many feisty heroines, cuts her hair and puts on velvet breeches to sail with the cross-dressing pirates Anne Bonney and Mary Read, mounting her own crusade against hypocrisy, slavery, and boredom.

Each of these novels suggests that adolescence, and ultimately adulthood, is the state of becoming a new person. But if growing up holds out on the promise of sexual maturity (each heroine meets a male counterpart who appreciates her intelligence and spirit), it also threatens to enforce conformity and shatter idealism. The challenge for Watson's protagonists is to retain the virtues of childhood—resilience, honesty, impatience with convention—while developing the empathy and self-knowledge essential to wisdom. Her focus on the unjust social practices that disturb her central characters, such as slavery in Virginia or the Act of Proscription in Scotland, emphasizes that those in power all too often fail the moral tests that age imposes.

If these novels identify rigidity and lack of fellow feeling as the root of most evil, the solution to these flaws is implied in the structure of Watson's oeuvre. The Israeli tales trace the experiences of the "family" of Gan Shalom over two generations; the historical novels sketch a ten-generation pedigree within which each heroine is ultimately tied to the heroines of the other novels in the sequence, whether by birth or by marriage. (For instance, Valerie of *Mistress Malapert* is the ancestress of every protagonist save Kelpie, who eventually joins the bloodline when her grandson marries Valerie's great-great-great-granddaughter Jade.) This narrative strategy not only rewards the assiduous reader with glimpses at the later lives of favorite characters and makes plausible the strong likeness among all these young people, but suggests a sense of kinship as a remedy for the bigotry and lack of sympathy that darkens the historical picture the novels describe.

Watson's works clearly continue a tradition of American historical novels dealing with the maturation of a hoyden into a woman of character and competence (Carol Ryrie Brink's *Caddie Woodlawn* and Caroline Dale Snedeker's *Downright Dencey* are earlier examples). Equally clear in their emphasis on youthful idealism, freedom, and the rights of the oppressed, they reflect the concerns of the 1960s, the decade in which most of Watson's fiction was published. But because of the skill with which she mixes moralism with humor, adventure, and lively characterization in her most successful works—*Jade, The Hornet's Nest,* and *Witch of the Glens*—they are by no means dated. Although in the absence of reissues Watson's novels are increasingly difficult to find, they retain their appeal for young readers seeking strong heroines and vividly drawn settings.

—Claudia Nelson

WEAVER, Will

Nationality: American. **Born:** William Weller Weaver, Park Rapids, Minnesota, 19 January 1950. **Education:** Attended Saint Cloud State University, 1968-69; University of Minnesota, B.A. 1972; Stanford University, M.A. 1979. **Family:** Married Rosalie M. Nonnemacher (a teacher), 2 March 1975; two children. **Career:** Writer, educator, farmer, Park Rapids, Minnesota 1977-81; part-time writing instructor, 1979-81, associate professor 1981-90, professor of English, from 1990, Bemidji State University, Bemidji, Minnesota. Contributor to periodicals including *Loonfeather, Prairie Schooner, Hartford Courant, San Francisco Chronicle, Kansas City Star, Chicago Tribune, Minneapolis Tribune, Newsday, Northern Literary Quarterly, Library Journal* and *Minnesota Monthly.* **Awards:** Minnesota State Arts Board Fellowship for Fiction 1979, 1983; "Top Ten Stories" citation, PEN and the Library of Congress, 1984, for "Grandfather, Heart of the Fields," and 1985, for "Dispersal"; Bush Foundation fiction fellow, 1987-88; Friends of American Writers Award, 1989; Minnesota Book Award for Fiction, 1989; American Library Association Best Books for Young Adults, 1994, for *Striking Out.* **Agent:** Lazear Agency, 430 First Avenue N., Minneapolis, Minnesota 55401. **Address:** 1500 Birchmont Drive, Bemidji State University, Bemidji, Minnesota 56601.

PUBLICATIONS FOR YOUNG ADULTS

Striking Out (novel). New York, Harper Collins, 1993.
Farm Team (novel). New York, Harper Collins, 1995.
"Stealing for Girls" (short story), in *Ultimate Sports,* edited by Don Gallo. New York, Delacorte, 1995.
"The Photograph" short story, in *No Easy Answers,* edited by Don Gallo. New York, Delacorte, 1997.
Hard Ball (novel). New York, Harper Collins, 1998.

PUBLICATIONS FOR ADULTS

Fiction

Red Earth, White Earth (novel). New York, Simon & Schuster, 1986.
A Gravestone Made of Wheat (short stories). New York, Simon & Schuster, 1989.

Other

Snares, illustrated by Deborah M. Broad. Minneapolis, Minnesota Center for Book Arts, 1992.

*

Media Adaptations: *Red Earth, White Earth* adapted as television program, Columbia Broadcasting System, 1989.

Critical Studies: *Los Angeles Times Book Review,* 19 October 1986, 9, and 12 March 1989, 1, 13; *Washington Post Book World,* November 2, 1986, 8, and March 26, 1989, 11; *New York Times Book Review,* November 9, 1986, 33, and March 12, 1989, 22; review of *Striking Out,* in *Publisher's Weekly,* 30 August 1993; *School Library Journal,* October 1993; review of *Striking Out,* in

Kirkus Reviews, 15 November 1993; review of *Striking Out,* in *VOYA,* 1 December 1993; article on Weaver in *The ALA REview,* winter 1996; review of *Farm Team,* in Kirkus Reviews, 1 June 1995; *Minneapolis Tribune,* 3 September 1995; review of *No Easy Answers,* in *Kirkus Review,* 15 October 1997; review of *No Easy Answers,* in *VOYA,* October 1997; review of *Hard Ball,* in *Booklist,* 1 and 15 January 1998.

Will Weaver comments:

As a man in my forties, I still live a good deal in my past. Events of grade school, middle school and high school remain vivid and important to me. Some events, such as touching my tongue on a dare to a metal flag pole in winter—and getting it frozen there—are still almost physically painful; others, such as being kissed on the playground by Betty Branham, are still painfully embarrassing; others, such as running cross country races barefoot on the soft grass of the local golf course are dreamlike and wonderful.

I think our teenage years are the highs and lows of our life all squeezed into a short space. Teenage years are brutal and joyous and sad and great, their events all mixed together like crystals in a kaleidoscope. As an adult, I find myself looking back and writing about those days with the same joy and pain as when I went through them—as we all must.

School days, and then our teenage years, are probably the worst and the best of our lives. Our personalities are formed not by what we learn in the classroom, but by what goes down on the playground. Things get ''better'' when we reach adulthood (we get a job, and some money, and a new car), but adult life is hardly ever as exciting as when we were young. That's why I keep going back there in my fiction.

I don't mean to suggest that I'm sad to be an adult. No way. Every year older makes me wiser and gives me a better perspective on who I am and *why* I am that way. And I wouldn't want to go back and be a teenager again—except in my writing. One of the reasons I write for young adults is to show you how it was for me, for all of my fictional characters are some part of me. I hope you enjoy them.

* * *

Will Weaver had written two well received adult works—a novel and a collection of stories—before turning his attention to the young adult novel. He explains that since his own two children were teenagers at the time it seemed wise to concentrate on writing for this age group.

Striking Out, his first young adult novel, is the story of Billy Baggs, who lives with his parents on a dairy farm some twenty miles from the town of Flint in northern Minnesota. The family is poor and Billy is expected to work long hours on the farm to help his family maintain itself. His older brother, Robert, has been killed in a tractor accident some five years before. After Robert's death their father, Abner, has become increasingly bitter and reclusive. Billy is rarely allowed to go into town or to spend much time in play with others of his age. On one of the rare days when he is in town he walks past the baseball field and picks up a ball which has been hit over the fence. He throws it back to the catcher with impressive force and speed and the coach, Oswald Anderson, asks him to join the team. Billy very much enjoys baseball and enjoys being a team member. He becomes one of the star players. However, his father resents the amount of time practice requires and conflict arises between his desire to play baseball and his family's need for his help on the small dairy farm.

Billy Baggs story is continued in the sequel, *Farm Team.* At fourteen, Billy is a tall, skinny, blue-eyed, yellow-haired farm boy in patched blue jeans. Because his front teeth are crooked and protruding, he attempts to avoid smiling. Mavis, Billy's mother, has a full time job as a secretary in a medical clinic in Flint. The used car she purchased for transportation does not run, and the dealer refuses to make restitution. Appeals to the sheriff and local officials are of no avail. In his usual arbitrary and juvenile manner, Billy's father demolishes the vehicles in the used car lot and the office building of the used car dealer with his D-6 caterpillar tractor. Billy objects to this and warns his father that he will be jailed but he accompanies him. He is arrested and refuses to pay his bail. The reader cannot avoid concluding that Billy seems a great deal more mature and responsible as well as much more sensitive to how actions hurt members of the family than his father. The coach pays the bail and Billy quits the school baseball team because he knows his father will be in jail after the trial and he will have the farm to run.

Weaver offers detailed and accurate descriptions of the day-to-day farm work on a dairy farm. The descriptions Stretchy, Billy's favorite cow, Skinner, his black labrador retriever, and other animals are endearing. Billy, who reads his father's agricultural journals, increases milk production and he also whitewashes, cleans, and improves the appearance of the farm. His mother is concerned that he is working far too hard and having no fun. She suggests they make a baseball diamond in one of the farm fields and invite all the neighbors and others who wish to come to play or watch on Friday evenings for games. Mavis insists people will come. Billy says they will come mainly because they know Pa's not at home.

The farm team is an assorted group which Mavis is very successful at integrating into a functioning group. Billy makes new friends, becomes acquainted with persons of different backgrounds, and finds it a pleasant experience. The coach helps with the team and the Farm Team challenges the town team to a game. There are many baseball descriptions and a hilarious if not altogether believable ending. Throughout the book, Mavis provides a positive and tolerant image as an adult role model. The coach provides a desirable male image. The book is easy to read, unsentimental, and presents a variety of characters with humor and a talent for economy of description.

Billy has discovered when he pays the restitution to the car dealer—in dimes at Abner's insistence—that Abner actually has $20,000 hidden in a strong box on the farm. Billy thinks longingly of all the equipment and improvements this could provide for the dairy farm. Any real resolution of the father son conflict is left for some future account of the Bates family.

—Reba Pinney

WEIS, Margaret

Has also written as Margaret Baldwin. **Nationality:** American. **Born:** Independence, Missouri, 16 March 1948. **Family:** Married 1) Robert William Baldwin, 22 August 1970 (divorced 1982); one son, one daughter; 2) married Don Perrin in 1996. **Education:**

University of Missouri, B.A. 1970. **Career:** Director of advertising and of trade division, Independence Press, Independence, Missouri, 1976-82; editor of juvenile romances and other special product lines, TSR Hobbies, Inc., Lake Geneva, Wisconsin, 1983-87; freelance writer since 1987. **Agent:** Lazear Agency, 430 First Avenue, suite 416, Minneapolis, Minnesota 55401, U.S.A. **Address:** P.O. Box 1452, Williams Bay, Wisconsin 53191, U.S.A. **E-mail Address:** mweis@mag7.com; **Website:** www.mag7.com.

PUBLICATIONS FOR YOUNG ADULTS

Science Fiction

Curse of the Endless Catacombs (as Margaret Baldwin). Lake Geneva, Wisconsin, TSR, 1984.

With Tracy Hickman, *Dragons of Autumn Twilight* (DragonLance Chronicles). Lake Geneva, Wisconsin, TSR, 1984.

With Hickman, *Dragons of Winter Night* (DragonLance Chronicles). Lake Geneva, Wisconsin, TSR, 1984.

With Hickman, *Dragons of Spring Dawning* (DragonLance Chronicles). Lake Geneva, Wisconsin, TSR, 1985.

With Hickman, *Time of the Twins* (DragonLance Legends). Lake Geneva, Wisconsin, TSR, 1986.

With Hickman, *War of the Twins* (DragonLance Legends). Lake Geneva, Wisconsin, TSR, 1986.

With Hickman, *Love and War.* Lake Geneva, Wisconsin, TSR, 1987.

With Hickman, *DragonLance Adventures.* Lake Geneva, Wisconsin, TSR, 1987.

The Lost King. New York, Bantam, 1989.

With Hickman, *Dragon Wing* (Death Gate series). New York, Bantam, 1990.

With Hickman, *Elven Star* (Death Gate series). New York, Bantam, 1990.

King's Test. New York, Bantam, 1990.

With Hickman, *Fire Sea* (Death Gate series). New York, Bantam, 1991.

King's Sacrifice. New York, Bantam, 1991.

With Hickman, *Serpent Mage* (Death Gate series). New York, Bantam, 1992.

With Hickman, *The Hand of Chaos* (Death Gate series). New York, Bantam, 1993.

With Hickman, *Into the Labyrinth* (Death Gate series). New York, Bantam, 1993.

Ghost Legion. New York, Bantam, 1993.

With Hickman, *The Second Generation.* Lake Geneva, Wisconsin, TSR, 1994.

With Hickman, *The Seventh Gate* (Death Gate series). New York, Bantam, 1994.

With Don Perrin, *Knights of the Black Earth.* New York, ROC, 1995.

With Hickman, *DragonLance Saga: The Second Generation.* Lake Geneva, Wisconsin TSR, 1995.

With Hickman, *Dragons of Summer Flame* (DragonLance Chronicles). Lake Geneva, Wisconsin, TSR, 1995.

With Perrin, *The Doom Brigade.* Lake Geneva, Wisconsin, TSR, 1996.

With Hickman, *Starshield Sentinels.* New York, Ballantine, 1996.

With Perrin, *Robot Blues.* New York, ROC, 1996.

With Hickman, *Legacy of the Darksword.* New York, Bantam, 1997.

The Soul Forge. Lake Geneva, Wisconsin, TSR, 1997.

Nonfiction

With Pat O'Brien, *Wanted! Frank and Jesse James: The Real Story* (as Margaret Baldwin). New York, Messner, 1981.

Kisses of Death: A Great Escape Story of World War II (remedial reader; as Margaret Baldwin), illustrations by Norma Welliver. New York, Messner, 1983.

With Janet Pack, *Lost Childhood: Children of World War II.* New York, Messner, 1986.

PUBLICATIONS FOR CHILDREN

Nonfiction

Fortune-Telling (as Margaret Baldwin). New York, Messner, 1984.

My First Book of Computer Graphics (as Margaret Baldwin). New York, Franklin Watts, 1984.

The Boy Who Saved the Children (remedial reader; as Margaret Baldwin; based on autobiography *Growing Up in the Holocaust* by Ben Edelbaum). New York, Messner, 1981.

My First Book: Thanksgiving (as Margaret Baldwin). New York, Franklin Watts, 1983.

Other

Editor, *The Art of Dungeons and Dragons Fantasy Games.* Lake Geneva, Wisconsin, TSR, 1985.

Editor, with Tracy Hickman, *Leaves from the Inn of the Last Home: The Complete Krynn Source Book.* Lake Geneva, Wisconsin, TSR, 1987.

Editor, *The Art of the DragonLance Saga.* Lake Geneva, Wisconsin, TSR, 1987.

Contributor, *The DragonLance Saga,* edited by Roy Thomas. Lake Geneva, Wisconsin, TSR, 1987.

Contributor, and editor with Hickman, *The Dragons of Krynn.* Lake Geneva, Wisconsin, TSR, 1994.

Editor, with Hickman, *The History of DragonLance: Being the Notes, Journals, and Memorabilia of Krynn.* Lake Geneva, Wisconsin, TSR, 1995.

Editor, *Fantastic Alice.* New York, Ace, 1995.

Editor, *A Magic Lover's Treasury of the Fantastic.* New York, Warner Books, 1998.

*

Biography: Entry in *Something About the Author,* Detroit, Gale Research, Vol. 38, 1985, Vol. 92, 1997; entry in *Science Fiction & Fantasy Literature, 1975-1991* by Robert Reginald, Detroit, Gale Research 1992.

Margaret Weis comments:

My hope is that readers have as much fun reading my books as I have writing them!

*   *   *

Margaret Weis is a prolific author of fantasy science fiction who has written alone and in collaboration with several authors, including husband Don Perrin. Her most notable collaborations include the Death Gate Cycle, a series of seven novels, and the DragonLance saga created with Tracy Hickman.

Weis creates increasingly appealing and inventive worlds in which the action is fast-paced and the endings contain clever twists. Her short story "The Best" is such an example which additionally shows Weis's strength as a solo-author. In this short story the narrator seeks the help of the "best" in the land to pursue an especially troublesome dragon. They wish to seek revenge for the lives it has taken as well as reclaim the treasures it has stolen. The "best" are not the types to normally work together—a dwarf, a witch, a noble knight, and a thief—yet the taste for revenge and glory in beating the dragon allows them to work together to get into the dragon's lair. It is not until this point that the reader suspects the narrator is not who he claims to be. His true identity is a surprise, a thoroughly unexpected twist to a satisfying story that fits somewhere in the "ancient history" of the realm of Krynn.

All of Weis's novels contain clear writing using descriptive language that encourages a rapid and steady reading pace. Suspense and dialogue move the prose along, giving the feel of a quick read yet leaving the reader full and satisfied at the conclusion of the story. Most of her novels are pure fantasy. Many take place in the realm of Krynn, a fantasy world reminiscent of medieval or ancient Europe and Asia, with races of dwarves, elves, and humans living side by side but not always in harmony. Wizards, warriors, dragons, and magic play a role in the world and in determining the outcome of the sagas taking place in different time periods in the history of Krynn.

Perhaps her best known series is the Death Gate cycle of seven books written in collaboration with Tracy Hickman, whom she met while working as an editor at TSR, Inc. Hickman was then a developer of role-playing games, such as Dungeons and Dragons, TSR's best known role-playing game. The two first began collaborating in 1984 on the DragonLance saga set in Krynn.

The Death Gate cycle is fantasy science fiction. Two closely related races of demi-gods so fiercely feud that one race, the Sartan, sunders Earth into four separate worlds with a fifth serving as the prison for the other race of demi-gods, the Patryn. Haplo is one of this imprisoned race who has escaped the prison world and learns a magical ship can move between the separated worlds. His plan is to learn the condition of each world and set the stage for the Patryn to take over, eventually imprisoning the Sartan as his own people have been imprisoned.

Something has gone awry with the separated worlds, each unaware of the existence of the others or of the race of Sartan. Mensch—the lowly races of dwarves, elves, and humans—live on the worlds in secluded harmony. Haplo and his dog, in trying to stir up trouble to make it easier for the Patryn to take over each world, find the only surviving Sartan and befriend him despite Haplo's better judgment. Having only known the struggle to survive on his prison-home called the Labyrinth, Haplo learns about himself and about cooperation with the "lesser" races of humans, dwarves, and elves. Together Haplo and the Sartan, Alfred, unravel the mystery of the sundering of the Earth, the creation of the Labyrinth, and learn how all four of the worlds were to be dependent on each other in a tenuous link that has collapsed leaving each world to fend for itself while the Sartan have seemingly perished. Haplo and Alfred feel the weight of this incredible mistake created by their ancestors and struggle to fix the problems, each never fully trusting the other or their own self-worth. Their adventures take them to each of the four worlds, with a novel dedicated to each, before Alfred is

dropped into the Labyrinth in a fifth novel. Future novels deal with the trouble that Death's Gate, the link between the separated worlds, has created and its resolution when Haplo and Alfred team together despite the ancient hatred between their races.

The cycle is appealing to young adults for the action-packed saga and fast pace. The restrictions placed on Haplo's race by the Sartan and his methods for overcoming them is another identifying quality between the reader and the main character. Haplo and Alfred are also endearing to the reader for their many characteristics in common, which at first appear to be so opposite as to greatly separate them. One example, their magical abilities, which seem so opposite—Haplo's based on runes tattooed on his body and Alfred's based on the power of the spoken or chanted runes—draw them together as a complimentary team.

Whether set on Krynn or in the futuristic realm of linked worlds of fire, air, water, and earth, the novels are intricately woven and fully captivate the reader's attention. Just as in role-playing games, the reader is able to visit again and again, learning more about the realm as the adventure takes him into undiscovered territory with the goal of salvation of the "world" as it is known to the characters. Weis maintains an admirable level of quality in well-created characters having flaws, self-doubts, and personal problems that both adolescent and adult readers will relate to. As the main characters develop in their decision-making ability and realize their own self-worth, so too do the readers grow. The plot twists, details, and description so envelop the reader as to leave the feeling that a role-playing game has been concluded instead of the passive reading of a novel, no small feat in this world of multimedia sensory overload.

—Lisa A. Wroble

WELLS, H(erbert) G(eorge)

Nationality: British. **Born:** Bromley, Kent, 21 September 1866. **Education:** Mr. Morley's Bromley Academy until age 13; certificate in book-keeping; apprentice draper, Rodgers and Denyer, Windsor, 1880; pupil-teacher at a school in Wookey, Somerset, 1880; apprentice chemist in Midhurst, Sussex, 1880-81; apprentice draper, Hyde's Southsea Drapery Emporium, Hampshire, 1881-83; student/assistant, Midhurst Grammar School, 1883-84; studied at Normal School (now Imperial College) of Science, London (editor, *Science School Journal*) 1884-87; teacher, Holt Academy, Wrexham, Wales, 1887-88, and at Henley House School, Kilburn, London, 1889; B.Sc. (honours) in zoology 1890, and D.Sc. 1943, University of London. **Family:** Married 1) his cousin Isabel Mary Wells in 1891 (separated 1894; divorced 1895); 2) Amy Catherine Robbins in 1895 (died 1927), two sons; had one daughter by Amber Reeves, and one son by Rebecca West, the writer Anthony West. **Career:** Rodgers and Denyer, Windsor, England, apprentice draper, 1880; pupil-teacher at school in Wookey, England, 1880; apprentice pharmacist in Midhurst, England, 1880-81; Hyde's Southsea Drapery Emporium, Hampshire, England, apprentice draper, 1881-83; student-assistant at grammar school in Midhurst, 1883-84; teacher at schools in Wrexham, Wales, 1887-88, and London, 1889; Tutor, University Tutorial College, London, 1890-93; full-time writer from 1893; theatre critic, *Pall Mall Gazette*, London, 1895; member of the Fabian

Society, 1903-1908; Member of Research Committee for the League of Nations, 1917; affiliated with British Ministry of Information, 1918; director of Policy Committee for Propaganda in Enemy Countries, 1918; Labour candidate for Parliament, for the University of London, 1922, 1923; lived mainly in France, 1924-33. International president, PEN, 1934-46. **Awards:** D.Litt: Universtity of London, 1936. Honorary fellow, Imperial College of Science and Technology, London. **Died:** 13 August 1946.

PUBLICATIONS

Novels

The Time Machine: An Invention. London, Heinemann, and New York, Holt, 1895; as *The Definitive Time Machine: A Critical Edition,* edited by Harry M. Geduld, Bloomington, Indiana University Press, 1987.

The Wonderful Visit. London, Dent, and New York, Macmillan, 1895.

The Island of Doctor Moreau: A Possibility. London, Heinemann, and New York, Stone and Kimball, 1896.

The Wheels of Chance: A Holiday Adventure, illustrated by J. Ayton Symington. London, Dent, 1896; as *The Wheels of Chance: A Bicycling Idyll,* New York, Macmillan, 1896.

The Invisible Man: A Grotesque Romance. London, Pearson, and New York, Arnold, 1897; as *The Invisible Man: A Fantastic Sensation,* Cambridge, Massachusetts, Bentley, 1981.

The War of the Worlds. London, Heinemann, and New York, Harper, 1898.

When the Sleeper Wakes. London and New York, Harper, 1899; revised edition, as *The Sleeper Awakes,* London, Nelson, 1910.

Love and Mr. Lewisham: The Story of a Very Young Couple. London, Harper, and New York, Stokes, 1900.

The First Men in the Moon. London, Newnes, and Indianapolis, Bowen Merrill, 1901.

The Sea Lady: A Tissue of Moonshine. London, Methuen, 1902; as *The Sea Lady,* New York, Appleton, 1902.

The Food of the Gods, and How It Came to Earth. London, Macmillan, and New York, Scribner, 1904.

Kipps: A Monograph. London, Macmillan, and New York, Scribner, 1905; as *Kipps: The Story of a Simple Soul.* 1905.

A Modern Utopia, illustrated by E.J. Sullivan. London, Chapman and Hall, and New York, Scribner, 1905.

In the Days of the Comet. London, Macmillan, and New York, Century, 1906.

Tono-Bungay. New York, Duffield, 1908; London, Macmillan, 1909.

The War in the Air, and Particularly How Mr. Bert Smallways Fared While It Lasted. London, Bell, and New York, Macmillan, 1908.

Ann Veronica: A Modern Love Story. London, Unwin, and New York, Harper, 1909.

The History of Mr. Polly. London, Nelson, and New York, Duffield, 1910.

The New Machiavelli. London, Lane, and New York, Duffield, 1911.

Marriage. London, Macmillan, and New York, Duffield, 1912.

The Passionate Friends: A Novel. London, Macmillan, and New York, Harper, 1913.

The Wife of Sir Isaac Harman. London and New York, Macmillan, 1914.

The World Set Free: A Story of Mankind. London, Macmillan, and New York, Dutton, 1914.

Bealby: A Holiday. London, Methuen, and New York, Macmillan, 1915.

Boon, The Mind of the Race, The Wild Asses of the Devil, and The Last Trump: Being a First Selection From the Literary Remains of George Boon, Appropriate to the Times, Prepared for Publication by Reginald Bliss With an Ambiguous Introduction by H.G. Wells (as Reginald Bliss). London, Unwin, and New York, Doran, 1915; under name H.G. Wells, London, Unwin, 1920.

The Research Magnificent. London and New York, Macmillan, 1915.

Mr. Britling Sees It Through. London, Cassell, and New York, Macmillan, 1916.

The Soul of a Bishop: A Novel—With Just a Little Love in It—About Conscience and Religion and the Real Troubles of Life. London, Cassell, 1917; as *The Soul of a Bishop,* New York, Macmillan, 1917.

Joan and Peter: The Story of an Education. London, Cassell, and New York, Macmillan, 1918.

The Undying Fire: A Contemporary Novel. London, Cassell, and New York, Macmillan, 1919.

The Secret Places of the Heart. London, Cassell, and New York, Macmillan, 1922.

Men Like Gods: A Novel. London, Cassell, and New York, Macmillan, 1923.

The Dream: A Novel. London, Cape, and New York, Macmillan, 1924.

Christina Alberta's Father. London, Cape, and New York, Macmillan, 1925.

The World of William Clissold: A Novel at a New Angle. London, Benn, 3 vols., and New York, Doran, 2 vols., 1926.

Meanwhile: The Picture of a Lady. London, Benn, and New York, Doran, 1927.

Mr. Blettsworthy on Rampole Island. London, Benn, and New York, Doubleday, 1928.

The King Who Was a King: The Book of a Film. London, Benn, 1929; as *The King Who Was a King: An Unconventional Novel,* New York, Doubleday, 1929.

The Autocracy of Mr. Parham: His Remarkable Adventures in This Changing World. London, Heinemann, and New York, Doubleday, 1930.

The Bulpington of Blup: Adventures, Poses, Stresses, Conflicts, and Disaster in a Contemporary Brain. London, Hutchinson, 1932; New York, Macmillan, 1933.

The Shape of Things to Come: The Ultimate Revolution. London, Hutchinson, and New York, Macmillan, 1933; revised edition, as *Things to Come* (film story), London, Cresset Press, and New York, Macmillan, 1935.

The Croquet Player. London, Chatto and Windus, 1936; New York, Viking Press, 1937.

Brynhild. London, Methuen, 1937; as *Brynhild; or, The Show of Things,* New York, Scribner, 1937.

The Camford Visitation. London, Methuen, 1937.

Star Begotten: A Biological Fantasia. London, Chatto and Windus, and New York, Viking Press, 1937.

Apropos of Dolores. London, Cape, and New York, Scribner, 1938.

The Brothers: A Story. London, Chatto and Windus, and New York, Viking Press, 1938.

The Holy Terror. London, Joseph, and New York, Simon and Schuster, 1939.

All Aboard for Ararat. London, Secker and Warburg, 1940; New York, Alliance, 1941.

Babes in the Darkling Wood. London, Secker and Warburg, and New York, Alliance, 1940.

You Can't Be Too Careful: A Sample of Life, 1901-1951. London, Secker and Warburg, 1941; New York, Putnam, 1942.

The Wealth of Mr. Waddy: A Novel, edited with an introduction by Harris Wilson, preface by Harry T. Moore. Carbondale, Southern Illinois University Press, 1969.

A Story of the Days to Come. Corgi, 1976.

Short Stories

Select Conversations With an Uncle (Now Extinct) and Two Other Reminiscences. London, Lane, and New York, Merriam, 1895.

The Stolen Bacillus and Other Incidents. London, Methuen, 1895.

The Red Room. New York, Stone and Kimball, 1896.

The Plattner Story, and Others. London, Methuen, 1897.

Thirty Strange Stories. New York, Arnold, 1897.

A Cure for Love. New York, Scott, 1899.

Tales of Space and Time. London, Harper, and New York, Doubleday, 1899.

The Vacant Country. New York, Kent, 1899.

Twelve Stories and a Dream. London, Macmillan, 1903; New York, Scribner, 1905.

The Country of the Blind, and Other Stories. London, Nelson, 1911; revised edition of *The Country of the Blind,* London, Golden Cockerel Press, 1939.

The Door in the Wall, and Other Stories. New York, Kennerley, 1911; London, Richards, 1915.

The Star. Pitman, 1913.

Tales of the Unexpected [of Life and Adventure, of Wonder], edited by J.D. Beresford, introduction by Frank Wells. London, Collins, 3 vols., 1922-23.

The Short Stories of H.G. Wells. London, Benn, 1927; New York, Doubleday, 1929; as *The Complete Short Stories of H.G. Wells,* London, Benn, 1966, and New York, St. Martin's, 1970.

The Adventures of Tommy (for children), illustrated by the author. London, Harrap, and New York, Stokes, 1929.

The Stolen Body, and Other Tales of the Unexpected. London Book, 1931.

The Favorite Short Stories of H.G. Wells. New York, Doubleday, 1937; as *The Famous Short Stories of H.G. Wells,* Garden City Publishing, 1938.

Short Stories by H.G. Wells. London, Nelson, 1940.

The Empire of the Ants. Todd, 1943.

The Inexperienced Ghost. Todd, 1943.

The Land Ironclads. Todd, 1943.

The New Accelerator. Todd, 1943.

The Truth About Pyecraft, and Other Short Stories. Todd, 1943.

The Inexperienced Ghost and The New Accelerator. Vallancey Press, 1944.

Twenty-eight Science Fiction Stories. New York, Dover, 1952.

Seven Stories. New York, Oxford University Press, 1953.

The Desert Daisy (for children), introduction by Gordon N. Ray. Pittsburg, Pennsylvania, Beta Phi Mu, 1957.

Selected Short Stories. London, Penguin, 1958.

The Valley of Spiders. London, Collins, 1964.

The Cone. London, Collins, 1965.

The Inexperienced Ghost, and Nine Other Stories. New York, Bantam, 1965.

Best Science Fiction Stories of H.G. Wells. New York, Dover, 1966.

The Man With a Nose: And the Other Uncollected Short Stories of H.G. Wells, edited with an introduction by J.R. Hammond. London, Athlone Press, 1984.

The Complete Short Stories of H.G. Wells. London, Black, and New York, St. Martin's Press, 1987.

Plays

Kipps, with Rudolf Besier, adaptation of the novel by Wells (produced London, 1912).

The Wonderful Visit, with St. John Ervine, adaptation of the novel by Wells (produced London, 1921).

Things to Come: A Film Story Based on the Material Contained in His History of the Future "The Shape of Things to Come". New York, Macmillan, 1935.

The Man Who Could Work Miracles: A Film Story Based on the Material Contained in His Short Story "Man Who Could Work Miracles." London, Cresset Press, 1936; as *The Man Who Could Work Miracles: A Film by H.G. Wells, Based on the Short Story Entitled "The Man Who Could Work Miracles,"* New York, Macmillan, 1936.

Hoopdriver's Holiday, adaptation of his novel *The Wheels of Chance,* edited by Michael Timko. Lafayette, Indiana, Purdue University English Department, 1964.

Also author of *H.G. Wells Comedies (Bluebottle, The Tonic, Daydreams),* with Frank Wells, 1928.

Nonfiction

Text-Book of Biology, introduction by G.B. Howes. London, Clive, Volume 1, 1892; Volume 2, 1893; revised edition, as *Text-Book of Zoology* by A.M. Davies, 1898; revised edition, by J.T. Cunningham and W.H. Leigh-Sharpe, 1929.

Honours Physiography, with R.A. Gregory. London, Hughes, 1893.

Certain Personal Matters: A Collection of Material, Mainly Autobiographical. London, Lawrence and Bullen, 1897.

Anticipations of the Reaction of Mechanical and Scientific Progress Upon Human Life and Thought. London, Champman and Hall, 1901; New York, Harper, 1902.

The Discovery of the Future (lecture). London, Unwin, 1902; New York, Huebsch, 1913; revised edition, London, Cape, 1925.

Mankind in the Making. London, Chapman and Hall, 1903; New York, Scribner, 1904.

Faults of the Fabian (lecture). Privately printed, 1906.

The Future in America: A Search After Realities. London, Chapman and Hall, and New York, Harper, 1906.

Reconstruction of the Fabian Society. Privately printed, 1906.

Will Socialism Destroy the Home? London, Independent Labour Party, 1907.

First and Last Things: A Confession of Faith and a Rule of Life. London, Constable, and New York, Putnam, 1908; revised edition, London, Cassell, 1917; London, Watts, 1929.

New Worlds for Old. London, Constable, and New York, Macmillan, 1908; revised edition, London, Constable, 1914.

Floor Games (for children), illustrated by the author. London, Palmer, 1911; Boston, Small Maynard, 1912.

Editor with G.R.S. Taylor and Frances Evelyn Warwick, *The Great State: Essays in Construction*. London, Harper, 1912; as *Socialism and the Great State: Essays in Construction*, New York, Harper, 1914.

The Labour Unrest. London, Associated Newspapers, 1912.

Liberalism and Its Party. London, Good, 1913.

Little Wars: A Game for Boys From Twelve Years of Age to One Hundred and Fifty and for That More Intelligent Sort of Girls Who Like Boys' Games and Books With an Appendix on Kriegspiel (children's games). London, Palmer, and Boston, Small Maynard, 1913.

War and Common Sense. London, Associated Newspapers, 1913.

An Englishman Looks at the World: Being a Series of Unrestrained Remarks Upon Contemporary Matters. London, Cassell, 1914; as *Social Forces in England and America*, New York, Harper, 1914.

The War That Will End War. London, Palmer, and New York, Duffield, 1914; repirnted in part as *The War and Socialism*, London, Clarion Press, 1915.

The Peace of the World. London, Daily Chronicle, 1915.

The Elements of Reconstruction. London, Nisbet, 1916.

What Is Coming? A Forecast of Things After the War. London, Cassell, 1916; as *What Is Coming? A European Forecast*, New York, Macmillan, 1916.

God the Invisible King. London, Cassell, and New York, Macmillan, 1917.

Introduction to Nocturne. New York, Doran, 1917.

A Reasonable Man's Peace. London, Daily News, 1917.

War and the Future: Italy, France, and Britain at War. London, Cassell, 1917; as *Italy, France, and Britain at War*, New York, Macmillan, 1917.

British Nationalism and the League of Nations. London, League of Nations Union, 1918.

In the Fourth Year: Anticipations of a World Peace. London, Chatto and Windus, and New York, Macmillan, 1918; abridged edition, as *Anticipations of a World Peace*, London, Chatto and Windus, 1918.

History Is One. Boston, Ginn, 1919.

The Idea of a League of Nations: Prolegomena to the Study of World-Organisation, with Viscount Grey, Lionel Curtis, William Archer, H. Wickham Steed, A.E. Zimmern, J.A. Spender, Viscount Bryce, and Gilbert Murray. New York, Atlantic Monthly Press, 1919.

The Way to the League of Nations: A Brief Sketch of the Practical Steps Needed for the Formation of a League, with Viscount Grey, Gilbert Murray, J.A. Spender, A.E. Zimmern, H. Wickham Steed, Lionel Curtis, William Archer, Ernest Barker, G. Lowes Dickinson, John Hilton, and L.S. Woolf. New York, Oxford University Press, 1919.

Frank Swinnerton: Personal Sketches; Together With Notes and Comments on the Novels of Frank Swinnerton, with Arnold Bennett and Grant Overton. New York, Doran, 1920.

The Outline of History, Being a Plain History of Life and Mankind, with advice and editorial help of Ernest Barker, H.H. Johnston, E. Ray Lankester, and Gilbert Murray, illustrated by J.F. Horrabin. London, Newnes, 2 vols., and New York, Macmillan, 2 vols., 1920; as *The New and Revised Outline of History: Being a Plain History of Life and Mankind*, Garden City Publishing,

1931; as *The Enlarged and Revised Outline of History: Being a Plain History of Life and Mankind*, Kemp, Texas, Triangle Books, 1940; under original title revised and brought up to the end of World War II by Raymond Postgate, Garden City Publishing, 1949; as *The Outline of History: Being a Plain History of Life and Mankind From Primordial Life to Nineteen-sixty*, London, Cassell, 1961; under original title revised and brought up to date by Postgate and G.P. Wells, New York, Doubleday, 1971.

Russia in the Shadows. London, Hodder and Stoughton, 1920; New York, Doran, 1921.

The New Teaching of History, with a Reply to Some Recent Criticisms of "The Outline of History." London, Cassell, 1921.

The Salvaging of Civilization: The Probable Future of Mankind. London, Cassell, and New York, Macmillan, 1921.

A Short History of the World. London, Cassell, and New York, Macmillan, 1922; revised edition, London, Penguin, 1946.

Washington and the Hope of Peace. London, Collins, 1922; as *Washington and the Riddle of Peace*, New York, Macmillan, 1922.

The World, Its Debts, and the Rich Men. London, Finer, 1922.

Socialism and the Scientific Motive (lecture). Privately printed, 1923.

Contributor, *Thirty-one Stories by Thirty and One Authors*, edited by Ernest Rhys and C.A. Dawson Scott. Butterworth, 1923.

The P.R. Parliament. London, Proportional Representation Society, 1924.

The Story of a Great Schoolmaster: Being a Plain Account of the Life and Ideas of Sanderson of Oundle. London, Chatto and Windus, and New York, Macmillan, 1924.

Works (Atlantic edition). London, Unwin, and New York, Scribner, 28 vols., 1924.

A Year of Prophesying. London, Unwin, 1924; New York, Macmillan, 1925.

A Forecast of the World's Affairs. New York, Encyclopaedia Britannica, 1925.

A Short History of Mankind (adapted from *A Short History of the World* by E.H. Carter). New York, Macmillan, 1925.

Mr. Belloc Objects to "The Outline of History." London, Watts, 1926.

Works (Essex edition). London, Benn, 24 vols., 1926-27.

In Memory of Amy Catherine Wells. Privately printed, 1927.

Wells' Social Anticipations, edited by Harry W. Laidler. New York, Vanguard Press, 1927.

Editor and author of introduction, *The Book of Catherine Wells*. London, Chatto and Windus, 1928.

The Open Conspiracy: Blue Prints for a World Revolution. London, Gollancz, and New York, Doubleday, 1928; revised edition, as *The Open Conspiracy: Blue Prints for a World Revolution; a Second Version of This Faith of a Modern Man Made More Explicit and Plain*, London, Hogarth Press, 1930; revised edition, as *What Are We to Do With Our Lives?*, London, Heinemann, and New York, Doran, 1931; as *The Open Conspiracy*, New York, Gordon Press, 1979.

The Way the World Is Going: Guesses and Forecasts of the Years Ahead; Twenty-six Articles and a Lecture. London, Benn, 1928; New York, Doubleday, 1929.

The Common Sense of World Peace (lecture). London, Hogarth Press, 1929.

Imperialism and the Open Conspiracy. London, Faber, 1929.

Divorce as I See It, with Bertrand Russell, Fannie Hurst, Theodore Dreiser, Warwick Deeping, Rebecca West, Andre Maurois, and Lionel Feuchtwanger. Douglas, 1930.

Points of View: A Series of Broadcast Addresses, with G. Lowes Dickinson, Dean Inge, J.B.S. Haldane, Sir Oliver Lodge, and Sir Walford Davis. London, Unwin, 1930.

The Problem of the Troublesome Collaborator. Privately printed, 1930.

The Science of Life: A Summary of Contemporary Knowledge about Life and Its Possibilities, with Julian S. Huxley and G.P. Wells. London, Amalgamated Press, 3 vols., 1930; New York, Doubleday, 4 vols., 1931; revised edition, as ''The Science of Life'' series, New York, Doubleday, 1932; revised editon, as *Science of Life Series,* London, Cassell, 9 vols., 1934-37.

Settlement of the Trouble Between Mr. Thring and Mr. Wells: A Footnote to the Problem of the Troublesome Collaborator. Privately printed, 1930.

The Way to World Peace. London, Benn, 1930.

The New Russia: Eight Talks Broadcast, with H.R. Knickerbocker, Sir John Russell, Sir Bernard Pares, Margaret S. Miller, B. Mouat-Jones, Stafford Talbot, and Frank Owen. London, Faber, 1931.

Selections From the Early Prose Works of H.G. Wells. University of London Press, 1931.

The Work, Wealth, and Happiness of Mankind. New York, Doubleday, 2 vols., 1931; London, Heinemann, 1 vol., 1932; revised edition, Heinemann, 1934; as *The Outline of Man's Work and Wealth,* New York, Doubleday, 1936.

After Democracy: Addresses and Papers on the Present World Situation. London, Watts, 1932.

What Should Be Done—Now. New York, Day, 1932.

Experiment in Autobiography: Discoveries and Conclusions of a Very Ordinary Brain (since 1866), illustrated by the author. London, Gollancz-Cresset Press, 2 vols., and New York, Macmillan, 1 vol., 1934.

Stalin-Wells Talk: The Verbatim Record, and A Discussion, with others. London, New Statesman and Nation, 1934.

The New America: The New World. London, Cresset Press, and New York, Macmillan, 1935.

The Anatomy of Frustration: A Modern Synthesis. London, Cresset Press, and New York, Macmillan, 1936.

The Idea of a World Encyclopaedia. London, Hogarth Press, 1936.

World Brain. London, Methuen, and New York, Doubleday, 1938.

The Fate of Homo Sapiens: An Unemotional Statement of the Things That Are Happening to Him Now and of the Immediate Possibilities Confronting Him. London, Secker and Warburg, 1939; as *The Fate of Man: An Unemotional Statement of the Things That Are Happening to Him Now and of the Immediate Possibilities Confronting Him,* New York, Alliance, 1939.

Travels of a Republican Radical in Search of Hot Water. London, Penguin, 1939.

The Common Sense of War and Peace: World Revolution or War Unending? London, Penguin, 1940.

H.G. Wells, S. de Madariaga, J. Middleton Murry, C.E.M. Joad on the New World Order. National Peace Council, 1940.

The New World Order, Whether It Is Attainable, How It Can Be Attained, and What Sort of World a World at Peace Will Have to Be. London, Secker and Warburg, and New York, Knopf, 1940.

The Rights of Man; or, What Are We Fighting For? London, Penguin, 1940.

Guide to the New World: A Handbook of Constructive World Revolution. London, Gollancz, 1941.

The Pocket History of the World. New York, Pocket Books, 1941.

The Conquest of Time. London, Watts, 1942.

Modern Russian and English Revolutionaries: A Frank Exchange of Ideas Between Commander Lev Uspensky, Soviet Writer, and H.G. Wells. Privately printed, 1942.

The New Rights of Man. Girard, Kansas, Haldeman Julius, 1942.

The Outlook for Homo Sapiens: An Unemotional Statement of the Things That Are Happening to Him Now, and of the Immediate Possibilities Confronting Him (revised versions of *The Fate of Homo Sapiens* and *The New World Order*). London, Secker and Warburg, 1942.

Phoenix: A Summary of the Inescapable Conditions of World Reorganisation. London, Secker and Warburg, 1942; Girard, Kansas, Haldeman Julius, n.d.

Science and the World-Mind. London, New Europe, 1942.

A Thesis on the Quality of Illusion in the Continuity of Individual Life of the Higher Metazoa, with Particular Reference to the Species Homo Sapiens. Privately printed, 1942.

Crux Ansata: An Indictment of the Roman Catholic Church. London, Penguin, 1943; New York, Agora, 1944.

The Mosley Outrage. London, Daily Worker, 1943.

'42 to '44: A Contemporary Memoir Upon Human Behaviour During the Crisis of the World Revolution. London, Secker and Warburg, 1944.

Reshaping Man's Heritage: Biology in the Service of Man, with J.S. Huxley and J.B.S. Haldane. London, Unwin, 1944.

The Happy Turning: A Dream of Life. London, Heinemann, 1945.

Marxism vs. Liberalism: An Interview (interview with Joseph Stalin). New York, Century, 1945; as *H.G. Wells' Interview With J.V. Stalin (Marxism v. Liberalism),* Sydney, Australia, Current Book Distributors, 1950.

Mind at the End of Its Tether. London, Heinemann, 1945.

Mind at the End of Its Tether, and The Happy Turning. New York, Didier, 1945.

The Desert Daisy (for children), edited by Gordon N. Ray. Urbana, University of Illinois Press, 1957.

Henry James and H.G. Wells: A Record of Their Friendship, Their Debate on the Art of Fiction, and Their Quarrel, edited by Leon Edel and Gordon N. Ray. Urbana, University of Illinois Press, and London, Hart Davis, 1958.

Arnold Bennett and H.G. Wells: A Record of a Personal and a Literary Friendship, edited by Harris Wilson. London, Hart Davis, 1960.

George Gissing and H.G. Wells: Their Friendship and Correspondence, edited by Royal A. Gettmann. London, Hart Davis, 1961.

Journalism and Prophecy, 1893-1946: An Anthology, edited by W. Warren Wagar. Boston, Houghton Mifflin, 1964; revised edition, London, Bodley Head, 1965.

Contributor, *Masterpieces of Science Fiction,* edited by Sam Moskowitz. World Publishing, 1967.

H.G. Wells's Literary Criticism, edited by Patrick Parrinder and Robert M. Philmus. Brighton, Harvester Press, 1980.

H.G. Wells in Love: Postscript to an Experiment in Autobiography, edited by G.P. Wells. London, Faber, 1984.

Treasury of H.G. Wells. New York, Octopus Books, 1985.

Other

Socialism and the Family (pamphlet; contains "Socialism and the Middle Classes" and "Modern Socialism and the Family"). London, Fifield, 1906; Boston, Ball, 1908.

This Misery of Boots (pamphlet). London, Fabian Society, 1907; Boston, Ball, 1908.

The H.G. Wells Calendar: A Quotation From the Works of H.G. Wells for Every Day in the Year, selected by Rosamund Marriott Watson. London, Palmer, 1911.

Great Thoughts From H.G. Wells, selected by Rosamund Marriott Watson. Dodge, 1912.

Thoughts From H.G. Wells, selected by Elsie E. Morton. London, Harrap, 1913.

Democracy Under Revision: A Lecture Delivered at the Sorbonne, March 15th, 1927 (pamphlet). London, Hogarth Press, and New York, Doran, 1927.

The H.G. Wells Papers at the University of Illinois, edited by Gordon N. Ray. Urbana, University of Illinois Press, 1958.

H.G. Wells: Early Writings in Science and Science Fiction, edited by Robert M. Philmus and David Y. Hughes. Berkeley, University of California Press, 1975.

H.G. Wells Science Fiction Treasury. New York, Crown, 1987.

The Discovery of the Future, with The Common-Sense of World Peace and The Human Adventure, edited by Patrick Parrinder. London, PNL, 1989.

Also author of *Two Hemispheres or One World?,* 1940.

*

Media Adaptations: Numerous works by Wells have been adapted as comic books, films, plays, sound recordings, and radio and television productions, including *The Shape of Things to Come* (film), 1936; *The War of the Worlds* (radio broadcast), Columbia Broadcasting System, 1938.

Biography: *H.G. Wells: A Sketch for a Portrait* by Geoffrey H. West, Howe, 1930; *H.G. Wells: A Biography,* London, Longman, 1951; *H.G. Wells and His Family, As I Have Known Them* by Mathilde Marie Meyer, Chicago, Illinois, International Publishing, 1956; *The Life and Thought of H.G. Wells* by Julius Kagarlitsky (translated by Moura Budberg), London, Sidgwick and Jackson, 1966; *H.G. Wells* by Richard Hauer Costa, New York, Twayne, 1967, revised edition, 1985; *H.G. Wells: His Turbulent Life and Times* by Lovat Dickson, London, Macmillan, 1969; *I Told You So! A Life of H.G. Wells* by James Playsted Wood, New York, Pantheon, 1969; *Bertie: The Life After Death of H.G. Wells* by Elizabeth Hawley and Columbia Rossi, London, New English Library, 1973; Entry in *Dictionary of Literary Biography,* Volume 34, Detroit, Gale, 1985; Volume 70, 1988; *The Time Traveller: The Life of H.G. Wells* by Norman and Jeanne Mackenzie, London, Weidenfeld and Nicolson, 1973, as *H.G. Wells: A Biography,* New York, Simon and Schuster, 1973; *H.G. Wells: A Pictorial Biography* by Frank Wells, London, Jupiter, 1977; *H.G. Wells: Aspects of a Life* by Anthony West, London, Hutchinson, and New York, Random House, 1984; *H.G. Wells: Desperately Mortal: A Biography* by David C. Smith, New Haven, Connecticut, Yale University Press, 1986.

Bibliography: *The Works of H.G. Wells, 1887-1925: A Bibliography, Dictionary, and Subject-Index* by Geoffrey H. Wells, London, Routledge, 1926; *H.G. Wells: A Comprehensive Bibliography,* London, H.G. Wells Society, 1966, revised editions, 1968, 1972, 1986; *Herbert George Wells: An Annotated Bibliography of His Works* by J.R. Hammond, New York, Garland, 1977; *An H.G. Wells Companion: A Guide to the Novels, Romances, and Short Stories* by J.R. Hammond, New York, Macmillan, 1979.

Manuscript Collections: University of Illinois, Urbana.

Critical Studies (selection): *H.G. Wells* by John Davys Beresford, London, Nisbet, 1915, reprinted, Brooklyn, New York, Haskell House, 1972; *The World of H.G. Wells* by Van Wyck Brooks, New York, Mitchell Kennerley, and London, T. Fisher Unwin, 1915; *A Companion to Mr. Wells's "Outline of History,"* by Hilaire Belloc, Kansas City, Missouri, Sheed and Ward, 1926; *Mr. Belloc Still Objects* by Hilaire Belloc, Kansas City, Missouri, Sheed and Ward, 1926; *The Early H.G. Wells: A Study of the Scientific Romances* by Bernard Bergonzi, Manchester, Manchester University Press, 1961, and *H.G. Wells: A Collection of Critical Essays* edited by Bernard Bergonzi, Englewood Cliffs, New Jersey, Prentice Hall, 1976; *H.G. Wells: An Outline* by F.K. Chaplin, London, P.R. Macmillan, 1961; *H.G. Wells and the World State* by W. Warren Wagar, New Haven, Connecticut, Yale University Press, 1961; *H.G. Wells and His Critics* by Ingvald Raknem, London, Unwin, 1962; essay in *A Soviet Heretic* by Yevgeny Zamyatin (translated by Mirra Ginsburg), Chicago, University of Chicago Press, 1970; *H.G. Wells* by Patrick Parrinder, Edinburgh, Oliver and Boyd, 1970, New York, Capricorn, 1977, and *H.G. Wells: The Critical Heritage* edited by Patrick Parrinder, London, Routledge, 1972; *H.G. Wells: Critic of Progress* by Jack Williamson, Baltimore, Mirage Press, 1973; *H.G. Wells and Rebecca West* by Gordon N. Ray, New Haven, Connecticut, Yale University Press, and London, Macmillan, 1974; *The Scientific Romances of H.G. Wells* by Stephen Gill, Cornwall, Ontario, Vesta, 1975; *Anatomies of Egotism: A Reading of the Last Novels of H.G. Wells* by Robert Bloom, Lincoln, University of Nebraska Press, 1977; *H.G. Wells in the Cinema* by Alan Wykes, London, Jupiter, 1977; *H.G. Wells and Modern Science Fiction* edited by Darko Suvin and Robert M. Philmus, Lewisburg, Pennsylvania, Bucknell University Press, 1977; *The H.G. Wells Scrapbook* edited by Peter Haining, London, New English Library, 1978; *Who's Who in H.G. Wells* by Brian Ash, London, Elm Tree, 1979; *H.G. Wells, Discoverer of the Future: The Influence of Science on His Thought* by Roslynn D. Haynes, New York, New York University Press, and London, Macmillan, 1980; *H.G. Wells: Interviews and Recollections* edited by J.R. Hammond, London, Macmillan, 1980; *The Science Fiction of H.G. Wells: A Concise Guide* by P.H. Niles, Clifton Perk, New York, Auriga, 1980; *The Science Fiction of H.G. Wells* by Frank McConnell, New York, Oxford University Press, 1981; *H.G. Wells and the Culminating Ape: Biological Themes and Imaginative Obsessions* by Peter Kemp, London, Macmillan, and New York, St. Martin's Press, 1982; *The Logic of Fantasy: H.G. Wells and Science Fiction* by John Huntington, New York, Columbia University Press, 1982; *H.G. Wells* by Robert Crossley, Mercer Island, Washington, Starmont House, 1984; *H.G. Wells* by John Batchelor, London, Cambridge University Press, 1985; *H.G. Wells: Reality* *and Beyond* edited by Michael Mullin, Champaign, Illinois, Public Library, 1986; *The Prophetic Soul: A Reading of Things to Come* by Leon Stover, Jefferson, North Carolina, and London, McFarland, 1987; *H.G. Wells* by Michael Draper, London, Macmillan, and New York, St. Martin's Press, 1987; *Bennett, Wells, and Conrad: Narrative in Transition* by Linda R. Anderson, London, Macmillan, and New York, St. Martin's Press, 1988; *H.G. Wells* by Christopher Martin, Howe, Wayland, 1988; *H.G. Wells under Revision* edited by Patrick Parrinder and Christopher Rolfe, Selinsgrove, Pennsylvania, and London, Susquehanna University Presses, 1990; *H.G. Wells* by Brian Murray, New York, Continuum, 1990.

* * *

H.G. Wells, often considered the father of modern science fiction, helped popularize this genre and gave it a more solid foundation in science than it had ever enjoyed before. Wells was influenced by earlier writers—from Jonathan Swift to Jules Verne—but the prolific English author was better educated in science than any of them, and he developed a writing style that surpasses those of all but a few writers of science fiction.

Wells wrote over a hundred books, about fifty of them novels. His principal interest was the improvement of society—largely through the sensible application of scientific principles. While his nonfiction volumes contain some quite respectable titles, such as his *Outline of History* and *A Modern Utopia*, it is through his fiction that Wells became famous and is now still remembered and read. His novels generally fall into three categories—scientific romances, novels of personality and character, and novels of ideas—and Wells's reputation rests mainly upon the works of his early, "scientific" period. *The Time Machine, The Invisible Man,* and *The War of the Worlds.*

When *The Time Machine* was published, in 1895, it established Wells as a popular and influential writer. Some readers believe *The Time Machine* to be Wells's finest work, and several experts claim for it the distinction of being the best science fiction book ever written. Perhaps the most compelling feature of this novel is its realism, much of which is achieved by specific details and scientifically persuasive explanations that, if they do not supply absolute authenticity, do provide plausibility. When the Time Traveller (who is not named in the text) is explaining how his machine works, the details of his monologue contain materials regarding time as the fourth dimension that predate Einstein's theory by some years.

Wells's scientific novels gain much of their credibility from the fact that once the premise (as in this case, time travel) is accepted by the reader, the rest of the action seems quite believable. So, when the Time Traveller lands in the year 802701 and finds the Eloi (the weak little people who live above ground) and the Morlocks (the large, carnivorous creatures that live below ground), the situation may seem extreme, but not impossible, given the enormous amount of time that has passed. The book ends in a typically Wellsian fashion, with the Traveller lost somewhere in time.

One of Wells's most popular novels is *The Invisible Man,* which has been adapted for film, like several other of his books. The premise of invisibility is based on a known physical phenomenon: the refraction of light. The principal character, Griffin, is a scientist (as are many of Wells's protagonists) who has discovered this secret and has made himself invisible to all. The story is grim, owing something to the tradition of the Gothic novel, but it is replete with adventure as Griffin turns against everyone and finally meets his destruction by being beaten to death with shovels in the hands of irate citizens. The detailed and vivid style of Wells's writing in this novel is particularly effective, as when Griffin's dead body returns to visibility at the end: "his crushed chest. . .the dim outline of his drawn and battered features. . .there lay, naked and pitiful on the ground, the bruised and broken body of a young man about thirty."

Several critics have noted that Wells displayed, perhaps for the first time in English literature, a truly global view of the earth in *War of the Worlds.* This story of Martian invaders came at a time when readers were more interested in science than ever before and when there had been discovered on Mars indentations that resembled canals and thus which intensified speculation that there could be life on the Red Planet. The novel is a triumph of detail, even to the logical "fact" that the Martians have trouble moving about, since their planet, smaller than Earth, has less gravitational pull and therefore they feel much heavier here. Once more, the style is both realistic and expressive, as when one of the Martians is first seen leaving the spaceship: "A big greyish rounded bulk, the size, perhaps, of a bear, was rising slowly and painfully out of the cylinder. As it bulged up and caught the light, it glistened like wet leather." One of the most clever passages—a truly brilliant combination of a vivid imagination coupled with a sound knowledge of science—is the climax, where the Martians start to die off because they have no immunity to the bacteria of Earth. While the death rays they have used (not unlike the laser beams known today) and the poisonous gas (in a novel published well before the first such use, in World War I) employed are striking, the unexpected but quite believable ending is eminently satisfactory.

In this novel, Wells tried to do what he attempted in most of what he wrote: to help mankind attain a wiser, more informed attitude about the future of the human race. He wrote to a friend that perhaps such a catastrophe as a Martian invasion could bring the world's people to their senses and improve the state of society. Plenty of disasters have struck (many of them foretold by the insightful Englishman), and yet the problems remain. One can, though, give credit to H.G. Wells for a noble attempt to improve the future—his efforts in the scientific fiction novel remain among the most sensible and readable to be found anywhere.

—Fred McEwen

WELLS, Rosemary

Nationality: American. **Born:** New York City, 29 January 1943. **Education:** Red Bank High School, New Jersey; Museum School, Boston. **Family:** Married Thomas Moore Wells in 1963; two daughters. **Career:** Art editor, Allyn and Bacon, Inc., Boston, Massachusetts; art designer, Macmillan Publishing Co., Inc., New York City; free-lance author and illustrator, since 1968. **Awards:** Children's Book Showcase award, Children's Book Council, 1974, for *Noisy Nora*; Art Book for Children citation, Brooklyn Museum and Brooklyn Public Library, 1975, 1976, 1977, for *Benjamin and Tulip*; Irma Simonton Black award, for *Benjamin and Tulip,* and 1975, for *Morris's Disappearing Bag: A Christmas Story*; runner-up for Edgar Allan Poe award, Mystery Writers of America, for *Through the Hidden Door,* and 1981, for *When No One Was Looking*; *Hazel's Amazing Mother* was named one of the *New York Times* Best Illustrated Books, 1985; Washington Irving Children's Book Choice award, Westchester Library Association, 1986, for *Peabody,* and 1988, for *Max's Christmas*; *Boston Globe-Horn Book* award, 1989, for *Shy Charles*; *Noisy Nora, Morris's Disappearing Bag, Leave Well Enough Alone, Stanley and Rhoda, Max's Toys, Max's Breakfast, Max's Bedtime, Max's Bath, When No One Was Looking, Max's Christmas, Shy Charles,* and *Max's Chocolate Chicken* were named among the best books of the year by *School Library Journal*; American Library Association (ALA) Notable Book citations for *Noisy Nora, Benjamin and Tulip, Morris's Disappearing Bag, Max's Breakfast, Max's Christmas, Max's Chocolate Chicken,* and *Max's Dragon Shirt*; ALA Best Books for Young Adults citation for *Through the Hidden Door*; *Bulletin of the Center for Children's Books* Blue Ribbon for *The Little Lame Prince*; *American Bookseller* Pick of the Lists citations for *Abdul, Stanley and Rhoda, Goodnight Fred, Timothy Goes to School, A Lion for Lewis, Forest of Dreams,* and *Max's Chocolate Chicken*; *Booklist* Children's Editor's Choice citations for *Max's Toys, Timothy Goes to School,* and *Through the Hidden Door*; Child Study Association Children's Books of the Year citations for *Morris's Disappearing Bag* and *Don't Spill It Again, James*; *Horn Book* Fanfare citation and West Australian Young Readers' Book award, both for *When No One Was Looking*; Virginia Young Readers award and New York Public Library Books for Teenagers citation, both for *The Man in the Woods*; Parents' Choice award, Parents' Choice Foundation, for *Shy Charles*; Golden Kite award, Society of Children's Book Writers, and International Reading Association Teacher's Choices List, both for *Forest of Dreams*; International Reading Association Children's Choices citation for *Max's Chocolate Chicken*; International Reading Association/Children's Book Council Children's Choice citations for *Timothy Goes to School, A Lion for Lewis,* and *Peabody*; Cooperative Children's Book Center citation for *Max's Bedtime*. **Address:** c/o Doubleday and Co., 666 Fifth Ave., New York, New York 10103, U.S.A.

PUBLICATIONS FOR YOUNG ADULTS (illustrated by the author unless otherwise indicated)

Fiction

The Fog Comes on Little Pig Feet. New York, Dial, 1972.
None of the Above. New York, Dial, 1974.
Leave Well Enough Alone. New York, Dial, 1977.
When No One Was Looking. New York, Dial, 1980; London, Deutsch, 1984.
The Man in the Woods. New York, Dial, 1984; London, Deutsch, 1985.
Waiting for the Evening Star, paintings by Susan Jeffers. New York, Dial, 1993.
Mary on Horseback. New York, Dial, 1997.
Streets of Gold (based on Mary Antin's memoir, *The Promised Land*), illustrated by Dan Andreasen. New York, Dial, 1999.

PUBLICATIONS FOR CHILDREN

Fiction (illustrated by the author unless otherwise indicated)

John and the Rarey. New York, Funk & Wagnalls, 1969.
Michael and the Mitten Test. Englewood Cliffs, New Jersey, Bradbury, 1969.
The First Child. New York, Hawthorn, 1970.
Martha's Birthday. Englewood Cliffs, New Jersey, Bradbury, 1970.
Miranda's Pilgrims. Englewood Cliffs, New Jersey, Bradbury, 1970.
Unfortunately Harriet. New York, Dial, 1972.
Benjamin and Tulip. New York, Dial, 1973; London, Kestrel, 1977.
Abdul. New York, Dial, 1975.
Morris's Disappearing Bag: A Christmas Story. New York, Dial, 1975; London, Kestrel, 1977.
Stanley and Rhoda. New York, Dial, 1978; London, Kestrel, 1980.
Max's First Word [*New Suit, Ride, Toys, Bath, Bedtime, Breakfast, Birthday, Hooray for, Christmas, Chocolate Chicken, Dragon Shirt*]. New York, Dial, 12 vols., 1979-1991; London, Benn, 4 vols., 1980; London, Collins, 5 vols., 1985-86.
Good Night, Fred. New York, Dial, 1981; London, Macmillan, 1982.
Timothy Goes to School. New York, Dial, and London, Kestrel, 1981.
A Lion for Lewis. New York, Dial, and London, Macmillan, 1982.
Peabody. New York, Dial, 1983; London, Macmillan, 1984.
Hazel's Amazing Mother. New York, Dial, 1985; London, Collins, 1986.
Through the Hidden Door. New York, Dial, 1987.
Forest of Dreams, illustrated by Susan Jeffers. New York, Dial, and London, Collins, 1988.
Shy Charles. New York, Dial, and London, Collins, 1988.
The Little Lame Prince. New York, Dial, 1990.
Fritz and the Mess Fairy. New York, Dial, 1991.
Voyage to the Bunny Planet. New York, Dial Press, 1992.
First Tomato. New York, Dial, 1992.
The Island Light. New York, Dial, 1992.
Lucy's Come to Stay, pictures by Patricia Cullen-Clark. New York, Dial, 1992.
Moss Pillows. New York, Dial, 1992.
Max and Ruby's First Greek Myth: Pandora's Box. New York, Dial, 1993.
Reteller, *Lassie Come Home* by Eric Knight, illustrated by Susan Jeffers. New York, Holt, 1995.
Edward's Overwhelming Overnight. New York, Dial, 1995.
Edward in Deep Water. New York, Dial, 1995.
Edward Unready for School. New York, Dial, 1995.
The Language of Doves, illustrated by Greg Shed. New York, Dial, 1996.
Bunny Cakes. New York, Dial, 1997.
Bunny Money. New York, Dial, 1997.
McDuff and the Baby, illustrated by Susan Jeffers. New York, Hyperion, 1997.
Jack and the Beanstalk, illustrated by Norman Messenger. New York, Dorling Kindersley, 1997.
Max's Ride. New York, Dial, 1998.
Read to Your Bunny. New York, Scholastic, 1998.
Max's Breakfast. Rosemary Wells. New York, Dial, 1998.
McDuff's New Friend, illustrated by Susan Jeffers. New York, Hyperion, 1998.
Old MacDonald. New York, Scholastic, 1998.

The Bear Went Over the Mountain. New York, Scholastic, 1998.
Bingo. New York, Scholastic, 1998.
Itsy Bitsy Spider. New York, Scholastic, 1998.
Yoko. New York, Hyperion, 1998.
Rachel Field's Hitty: Her First Hundred Years with New Adventures, illustrated by Susan Jeffers. New York, Simon & Schuster, 1999.

Poetry

Noisy Nora. New York, Dial, 1973; London, Collins, 1976; with new illustrations by Rosemary Wells, New York, Dial, 1997.
Don't Spill It Again, James. New York, Dial, 1977.

Other

Contributor, *So I Shall Tell You a Story: The Magic World of Beatrix Potter.* New York, Warne, 1993.

PUBLICATIONS FOR ADULTS

Other

Cooking for Nitwits, with Joanna Hurley. New York, Dutton, 1989.

*

Media Adaptations: *Max's Christmas* and *Morris's Disappearing Bag* have been adapted as short films by Weston Woods.

Biography: Essay in *Something about the Author Autobiography Series,* Vol. 1, Detroit, Gale, 1986.

Critical Studies: Entry in *Children's Literature Review,* Vol. 16, Detroit, Gale, 1989; entry in *Contemporary Literary Criticism,* Vol. 12, Detroit, Gale, 1980.

Illustrator: *A Song to Sing, O!* (from *Yeoman of the Guard*), 1968, and *The Duke of Plaza Toro* (from *The Gondoliers*), 1969, both by Williams Schwenck Gilbert and Arthur Sullivan; *Hungry Fred* by Paula Fox, 1969; *Why You Look Like You Whereas I Tend to Look Like Me* by Charlotte Pomerantz, 1969; *The Shooting of Dan McGrew and The Cremation of Sam McGee* by Robert Service, 1969; *The Cat That Walked by Himself* by Rudyard Kipling, 1970; *Marvin's Manhole* by Winifred Rosen, 1970; *Impossible, Possum* by Ellen Conford, 1971; *A Hot Thirsty Day* by Marjorie Weinman Sharmat, 1971; *Two Sisters and Some Hornets* by Beryl Epstein and Dorrit Davis, 1972; *With a Deep-Sea Smile* edited by Virginia A. Tashjian, 1974; *Tell Me a Trudy* by Lore Segal, 1977; *The Christmas Mystery* by Jostein Gaarder (translated by Elizabeth Rokkan), 1996; *My Very First Mother Goose,* edited by Iona Opie, 1996.

*   *   *

Although Rosemary Wells is more famous for her picture books, like *Noisy Nora* and *Stanley and Rhoda* in which anthropomorphic animals explore typical family problems, she has also developed another area of creativity: thrillers written for a teenage audience. In *When No One Was Looking* Kathy is a tennis champion with a determination to win and a fierce temper. However, when one of her opponents is murdered, Kathy has to discover who has drowned the girl. This is a book which is intriguing in its detection and also shows insights into teenage friendships. More intricately plotted and suitably tense is *The Man in the Woods,* in which Helen discovers a mysterious man in the woods who is supposed to be throwing rocks at car windscreens, a discovery that leads Helen and her friend Pinky into a deeper mystery involving drug trafficking.

These thrillers help to demonstrate Wells's versatility. Whichever direction her talent leads her in future years, thousands of children will be grateful to her for her creations of Nora, Morris, and all those other characters with sibling problems.

—Keith Barker

WERSBA, Barbara

Nationality: American. **Born:** Chicago, Illinois, 19 August 1932. **Education:** Bard College, B.A. 1954; studied acting at Neighborhood Playhouse and at the Paul Mann Actors Workshop; studied dance with Martha Graham. **Career:** Actress in radio and television, summer stock, Off-Broadway, and touring companies, 1944-59; full-time writer, from 1960; publisher of own publishing company, The Bookman Press, from 1997. Summer lecturer at New York University; writing instructor at Rockland Center for the Arts. **Awards:** Deutscher Jugend Buchpreis, 1973, for *Run Softly, Go Fast;* American Library Association (ALA) Best Book for Young Adults and Notable Children's Book lists, both 1976, and National Book Award nomination, 1977, all for *Tunes for a Small Harmonica;* ALA Best Book for Young Adults, 1982, for *The Carnival in My Mind;* D.H.L. from Bard College, 1977. **Agent:** McIntosh and Otis, Inc., 310 Madison Ave., New York, New York 10017. **Address:** Box 1892, Sag Harbor, New York 11963, U.S.A.

PUBLICATIONS FOR YOUNG ADULTS

Fiction

The Dream Watcher also see below. New York, Atheneum, 1968; London, Bodley Head, 1988.
Run Softly, Go Fast. New York, Atheneum, 1970.
The Country of the Heart. New York, Atheneum, 1975.
Tunes for a Small Harmonica. New York, Harper, 1976; London, Bodley Head, 1979.
The Carnival in My Mind. New York, Harper, 1982.
Crazy Vanilla. New York, Harper, 1986; London, Bodley Head, 1987.
Fat: A Love Story. New York, Harper, and London, Bodley Head, 1987.
Love Is the Crooked Thing. New York, Harper, and London, 1987.
Beautiful Losers. New York, Harper, and London, Bodley Head, 1988.
Just Be Gorgeous. New York, Harper, 1988; London, Bodley Head, 1989.

Wonderful Me. New York, Harper, 1989.
The Farewell Kid. New York, Harper, 1990.
The Best Place to Live Is the Ceiling. New York, Harper, 1990.
You'll Never Guess the End. New York, Harper, 1992.
Life Is What Happens While You're Making Other Plans. London, Bodley Head, 1994.
Whistle Me Home. New York, H. Holt, 1997.

Play

The Dream Watcher (adaptation of her novel of the same title), first produced in Westport, Connecticut, 1975; Seattle Repertory Theater, 1977.

PUBLICATIONS FOR CHILDREN

Fiction

The Boy Who Loved the Sea, illustrated by Margot Tomes. New York, Coward, 1961.
The Brave Balloon of Benjamin Buckley, illustrated by Tomes, New York, Atheneum, 1963.
The Land of Forgotten Beasts, illustrated by Tomes. New York, Atheneum, 1964; London, Gollancz, 1965.
A Song for Clowns, illustrated by Mario Rivoli. New York, Atheneum, 1965; London, Gollancz, 1966.
Let Me Fall before I Fly. New York, Atheneum, 1971.
Amanda, Dreaming, illustrated by Mercer Mayer. New York, Atheneum, 1973.
The Crystal Child, illustrated by Donna Diamond. New York, Harper, 1982.

Poetry

Do Tigers Ever Bite Kings?, illustrated by Rivoli. New York, Atheneum, 1966.
Twenty-six Starlings Will Fly through Your Mind, illustrated by David Palladini. New York, Harper, 1980.

Other

Reteller, *The Wings of Courage,* by George Sand. Sag Harbor, New York, Bookman Press, 1998.

*

Biography: Entry in Martha E. Ward and Dorothy A. Marquardt's *Authors of Books for Young People,* 2nd edition, New York, Scarecrow Press, 1971; essay in *Something about the Author Autobiography Series,* Volume 2, Detroit, Gale, 1986, pp. 293-304.

Critical Studies: *Children's Literature Review,* Volume 3, Detroit, Gale, 1977. *Contemporary Literary Criticism,* Volume 30, Detroit, Gale, 1984; Kay E. Vandergrift, ''Barbara Wersba,'' *Dictionary of Literary Biography,* Volume 52, Detroit, Gale, 1986, pp. 374-380.

*   *   *

Barbara Wersba began writing for children and young adults only after a fifteen-year career as a professional actress. As she recuperated from hepatitis in a friend's house on Martha's Vineyard, she began to realize that her acting career was over. When the friend said to her, ''Barbara, why don't you write something?'' she decided to do just that, and a few weeks later had completed a children's fantasy called *The Boy Who Loved the Sea.* The book was accepted for publication, and a new career had begun for her. Over the next five years, she wrote three more well-received children's fantasies and a volume of children's poetry, but it was her first novel for young adults, *The Dream Watcher,* that launched her on the most successful area of her career.

The Dream Watcher is the story of Albert Scully, a teenager who just doesn't fit into the society in which he must live; he does not want to go to college, get a job, or be a success. Then he meets Mrs. Orpha Woodfin, an aged grande dame and former actress, and they become friends. Before Orpha dies, she has helped Albert to come to terms with his ''differentness'' and to be proud of it. The book so impressed actress Eva LeGallienne that she asked Wersba to turn it into a play in which LeGallienne would act the role of Orpha Woodfin. *The Dream Watcher* was followed by *Run Softly, Go Fast,* a conflict-of-generation story of life in the 1960s also featuring a young misfit, who survives that era's drug scene and comes to terms with both himself and his alienated father.

In *The Country of the Heart,* Wersba again presents a story of an alienated young person, who finds himself as an artist and as a man through his relationship with an older woman. Steven's brief love affair with Hadley Norman is told in the form of a memoir after Hadley's death from cancer; as Steven remembers, he realizes that Hadley has given him much more than love, and he is a far better person for it. *Country* was followed by one of Wersba's best novels, *Tunes for a Small Harmonica.* *Tunes* is the story of J. F. McAllister, a brash young New York woman who falls in love with her rather dim and pale poetry teacher, Harold Murth. Believing him to be too poor to return to Cambridge and finish his thesis, McAllister learns to play the harmonica so that she can earn enough money as a street performer to send him to England. As it turns out, however, Harold is neither poor nor single, and he has completed his thesis; devastated, McAllister decides on suicide but is saved only when her best friend gives her a brand-new Hohner Chromatic harmonica in the key of C. McAllister is a spunky character with a wonderful sense of humor who is at the same time, like so many of Wersba's other characters, vulnerable; the reader admires her pluck and determination and rejoices when she resolves her problems.

Wersba's next book, *The Carnival in My Mind,* is another story of a New York loner, Harvey Beaumont. Fourteen years old and only five feet tall, he is struggling to get along until he meets aspiring young actress Chandler Brown. While not as strong as *Tunes,* this is a charming, tender, and sad love story.

Wersba's next novel, *Crazy Vanilla,* is a book which does reach the level of *Tunes for a Small Harmonica.* A son of privilege, Tyler Woodruff is still not a happy young man, feeling stifled by the demands of his socialite parents and his ambivalent relationship with his older brother Cameron, who has been banished from the family because he is gay. Tyler's only salvation is in photography; this coupled with his interest in wildlife leads him to use his camera in shooting the fauna of Long Island, but it also leads him to further isolation. Then he meets Mitzi, an impoverished young waitress whose life with her unstable mother is as bleak as Tyler's. Miraculously, however, Mitzi is also a fine amateur wildlife photographer, and from this shared interest, a warm and loving bond is created which leads both Tyler and Mitzi to grow and mature in the face of very real obstacles in their lives.

Three of Wersba's more recent books were something of a departure for her. *Fat: A Love Story, Love Is the Crooked Thing,* and *Beautiful Losers* all tell the tale of Rita Formica, a fat, five-foot-three extrovert who is a compulsive eater. In *Fat,* Rita, who works in a cheesecake bakery run by an older man called Arnold Bromberg, meets the love of her life, gorgeous athlete Robert Swann. She resolves to become thin and svelte, as well as tone down her personality. However, Robert is interested only in Rita's friend Nicole, so despite Rita's best attempts Robert remains aloof. A series of very funny misadventures leads brokenhearted Rita into the arms of—of all people—Arnold Blomberg, and the two sequels chart the ups and downs of their very unconventional romance. Along the way, Rita goes from child to woman and from everybody's clown to a self-sufficient adult at peace with herself.

Another popular character in three of Wersba's books is Heidi Rosenbloom, a sixteen-year-old resident of Manhattan who feels unattractive, untalented, and misunderstood by her parents. In *Just Be Gorgeous* she meets a homeless street performer, Jeffrey, and falls in love. He is gay, and Heidi finally accepts this but not before Jeffrey has given Heidi some appreciation of her worth as a human being. In *Wonderful Me* we meet Heidi again, still a little weird and still not totally convinced that she is at all attractive. She has informed her parents that she is not going to college but is going to be a professional dog walker, when suddenly she begins to receive sensitive and passionate love letters from a secret admirer—who turns out to be her English teacher, Mr. Moss. In *The Farewell Kid,* Heidi is eighteen and emancipated from parents, college, and men (at least in her own mind). Her passion for dogs (canine ones) leads her to start a business (Dog Rescue, Inc.) to help the strays she finds in the city's streets, but she soon realizes that she needs a partner to handle the business end while she handles the dogs. She finds a partner—and not only a business partner—in Harvey, in a funny and tender love story.

All of Wersba's novels have as their protagonists young men or women who refuse to shape themselves to society's mold. They are often alienated from their families and loners among their peers; they face their problems alone until someone equally unconventional enters the picture, and together they learn to accept themselves and a world that will always have sharp corners. Critics have sometimes faulted her books for these "unrealistic" characters and situations, but Wersba's sensitivity and honesty in dealing with her characters have made her a favorite with a whole generation of young readers.

—Audrey Eaglen

WEST, (Mary) Jessamyn

Nationality: American. **Born:** Jennings County, Indiana, 18 July 1902. **Education:** Union High School, Fullerton, California, graduated 1919; Whittier College, California, 1919, 1921-23; A.B. in

English 1923; Fullerton Junior College, 1920-21; University of California, Berkeley, 1929-31; Oxford University, 1929. **Family:** Married Harry Maxwell McPherson in 1923; one adopted daughter. **Career:** Writer, 1935-84. Teacher and secretary, Hemet, California, 1924-29; taught at Bread Loaf Writers Conference, Vermont, Indiana University, Bloomington, University of Notre Dame, Indiana, University of Colorado, Squaw Valley University of Utah, Salt Lake City, University of Washington, Seattle, Stanford University, California, University of Montana, Portland University, University of Kentucky, and Loyola Marymount University. Visiting professor at Wellesley College, Massachusetts, University of California at Irvine, Mills College, and Whittier College. Visiting lecturer at numerous colleges. **Awards:** Indiana Authors' Day award, 1956, for *Love, Death, and the Ladies' Drill Team*; Thermod Monsen award, 1958, for *To See the Dream*; California Commonwealth Club award, 1970, and California Literature Medal, 1971, both for *Crimson Ramblers of the World, Farewell*; Janet Kafke prize for fiction, 1976; Indiana Arts Commission award for Literature, 1977, for body of work. Honorary doctorates from Whittier College; Mills College, Oakland, California; Swarthmore College, Pennsylvania; Indiana University; University of Indiana—Terre Haute, Western College for Women, Oxford, Ohio; Wheaton College, Juniata College, and Wilmington College. **Died:** 23 February 1984.

PUBLICATIONS

Novels

The Witch Diggers. New York, Harcourt, 1951; London, Heinemann, 1952.
Little Men, in *Star Short Novels,* edited by Frederik Pohl. New York, Ballantine, 1954; published separately, as *The Chile Kings,* 1967.
South of the Angels. New York, Harcourt, 1960; London, Hodder & Stoughton, 1961.
A Matter of Time. New York, Harcourt, 1966; London, Macmillan, 1967.
Leafy Rivers. New York, Harcourt, 1967; London, Macmillan, 1968.
The Massacre at Fall Creek. New York, Harcourt, and London, Macmillan, 1975.
The Life I Really Lived. New York, Harcourt, 1979.
The State of Stony Lonesome. New York, Harcourt, 1984.

Short Stories

The Friendly Persuasion. New York, Harcourt, 1945, reprinted, Buccaneer Books, 1982.
Cress Delahanty. New York, Harcourt, 1953; London, Hodder & Stoughton, 1954.
Love, Death, and the Ladies' Drill Team. New York, Harcourt, 1955; as *Learn To Say Goodbye,* London, Hodder & Stoughton, 1956.
Except for Me and Thee: A Companion to The Friendly Persuasion. New York, Harcourt, and London, Macmillan, 1969.
Crimson Ramblers of the World, Farewell. New York, Harcourt, 1970; London, Macmillan, 1971.
The Story of a Story and Three Stories. Berkeley, University of California, 1982.
The Collected Stories of Jessamyn West. San Diego, Harcourt, 1986.

Plays

A Mirror for the Sky, music by Gail Kubik (produced Eugene, Oregon, 1958). New York, Harcourt, 1948.

Screenplays: *Friendly Persuasion* (uncredited), with Michael Wilson, 1956; *The Big Country,* with others, 1958; *The Stolen Hours,* 1963.

Poetry

The Secret Look. New York, Harcourt, 1974.

Other

Contributor, *Cross Section 1948: A Collection of New American Writing.* New York, Simon & Schuster, 1948.
The Reading Public (address). New York, Harcourt Brace, 1952.
Friends and Violence. Philadelphia, Friends General Conference, n.d.
To See the Dream. New York, Harcourt, 1957; London, Hodder & Stoughton, 1958.
Love Is Not What You Think. New York, Harcourt, 1959; as *A Woman's Love,* London, Hodder & Stoughton, 1960.
Editor, *A Quaker Reader.* New York, Viking, 1962.
Hide and Seek: A Continuing Journey. New York, Harcourt, and London, Macmillan, 1973.
The Woman Said Yes: Encounters with Life and Death: Memoirs. New York, Harcourt, 1976; as *Encounters with Death and Life,* London, Gollancz, 1977.
Double Discovery: A Journey. New York, Harcourt, 1980.

*

Biography: Entry in *Dictionary of Literary Biography,* Volume 6: *American Novelists since World War II Second Series,* Detroit, Gale, 1980; entry in *Dictionary of Literary Biography Yearbook 1984,* Detroit, Gale, 1985.

Critical Studies: *Jessamyn West* by Alfred S. Shivers, New York, Twayne, 1972; entry in *Contemporary Literary Criticism,* Detroit, Gale, Volume 7, 1977, Volume 17, 1981; *Jessamyn West* by Ann Dahlstrom Farmer, Boise, Idaho, Boise State University, 1982.

Manuscript Collections: Whittier College, California.

*   *   *

During a writing career spanning more than forty years, Mary Jessamyn West wrote seventeen books, numerous short stories, several screenplays, an operetta (*A Mirror for the Sky*), and a collection of poetry (*The Secret Look*)—none of which, technically, is categorized as young adult literature. But for many years, certain of the "Cress Delahanty" stories were a staple of middle and junior high school literature anthologies. Motion picture versions of West's novels were popular among young audiences of the

1950s and 1960s. And with all her books, a large percentage of her readership has been comprised of young adult women (and some young adult men) who are attracted by her unadorned but powerful style and her knowing, memorable portraits of adolescent experience.

That West is often remembered as a warm, humanistic, and morally grounded Quaker writer (a perception which she is said to have struggled against as long as she lived) is the consequence of the immense popularity of her first book. Often referred to as a novel, *The Friendly Persuasion* is more accurately described as a collection of short stories about the Birdwells, a Quaker family in rural Indiana during the late 1800s. The mixture of humorous, serious, and nostalgic narratives follows a loose chronological structure; half the stories are about Jess Birdwell, while the other half tell about Jess's wife Eliza (a beautiful Quaker minister), two of their children, and one grandchild. The collection has no one emphatic recurring theme but is an implicit restatement of a guiding maxim about American transcendentalism: "The unexamined life is not worth living." A secondary theme is that religious morality, while vital to the continuance of society as we know it, must be tempered by humanity and common sense if it is to be an entirely positive force. *Except for Me and Thee,* another collection of short stories which constitutes a kind of prequel to *The Friendly Persuasion,* was published nearly twenty-five years after the first work; among other things, it recounts Jess's late adolescence, his and Eliza's courtship, and their early years of marriage. For the most part, it shares the tone and themes of the earlier collection.

West's first novel was *The Witch Diggers,* the tragicomic history of Cate Conboy, a highly individualistic but misguided eighteen-year-old who turns her back on the one fulfilling relationship of her life because she denies her sexual self. Set in the nondescript environs of a poor county farm, the novel relies upon a variety of unusual if not altogether bizarre secondary characters to underscore its themes of confusion, alienation, sexual repression, and futility. Critically acclaimed at its initial appearance, *The Witch Diggers* remains a tightly structured and highly readable work.

Among baby boomers, perhaps West's best-known work is her second collection of short stories, *Cress Delahanty,* whose title character seems based—at least in part—on West herself. In language that is often poetic but rarely sentimental or melodramatic, West shows carefully chosen moments in the gradual transformation of twelve-year-old awkwardness, promise, and wonder into the self-confident and newly-born womanhood of a sixteen-year-old. Many of the details of the stories are dated, as are certain of its cultural norms and social conflicts. Still, *Cress Delahanty* speaks to young readers who look past its surface to what it finally says about the responsibilities, challenges, and joys of being young.

Other works of fiction by West include *Love, Death, and the Ladies' Drill Team,* whose stories are now available in the *Collected Stories of Jessamyn West*; *South of the Angels,* an involved novel recounting the romantic and social history of the inhabitants of a small agricultural tract near Los Angeles in the early 1900s; *Leafy Rivers,* whose "formula plot" of adultery, guilt, and redemption has provoked more critical disfavor than any other West novel; *The Massacre at Fall Creek,* West's best-selling fictionalization of the 1824 execution of three Indiana whites for the brutal massacre of the women and children of a Seneca Indian encampment; and *The State of Stony Lonesome,* West's last novel (which was published posthumously), an intriguing but finally disturbing and dissatisfying account of a young woman's apparently innocent love for an uncle that the reader perceives as calculating, sexually aggressive, and at least potentially abusive.

For contemporary young readers, none of West's fiction can match the appeal of her autobiographical works, especially *Hide and Seek* and *The Woman Said Yes*. Sometimes compared to Thoreau's *Walden, Hide and Seek* is a highly introspective record of West's experiences with nature and with human "neighbors" during a period of encampment on the banks of the Colorado River. Included in her musings are memories of her childhood and her mother's hesitancy to discuss sex, muted observations on the significance of life and the worth of other people, and overt references to Thoreau and his philosophy. *The Woman Said Yes,* perhaps the most controversial of all West's books, is a somewhat discursive but emotionally gripping history of West's family, focusing on her mother and on West's sister, Carmen, who committed suicide five days before Halloween in 1963. In these two works, West's voice is immediate, insistent, real; young readers seem to find in them a haunting timelessness that often eluded her short stories and novels.

—Keith Lawrence

WEST, Owen. *See* KOONTZ, Dean R.

WESTALL, Robert (Atkinson)

Nationality: British. **Born:** Tynemouth, Northumberland, England, 7 October 1929. **Education:** Durham University, B.A. 1953; University of London, D.F.A. 1957. **Military Service:** Served in British Army, Royal Signals, 1953-55. **Family:** Married Jean Underhill in 1958 (divorced 1990), one son (deceased). **Career:** Art master, Erdington Hall Secondary Modern School, Birmingham, 1957-58, and Keighley Boys' Grammar School, Yorkshire, 1958-60; Head of Art, 1960-85, and Head of Careers, 1970-85, Sir John Deane's College, Northwich, Cheshire; antiques dealer, 1985-86. Writer, Whitehorn Press, Manchester, 1968-71; Northern art critic, *Guardian,* London, 1970, 1980; art critic, Chester *Chronicle,* 1962-1973. Director of Telephone Samaritans of Mid-Cheshire, 1965-75. **Awards:** Carnegie Medal from Library Association of Great Britain, 1976, for *The Machine-Gunners,* and 1982, for *The Scarecrows*; Boston *Globe/Horn Book* Honor Books citations, 1978, for *The Machine-Gunners,* 1982, for *The Scarecrows,* and 1983, for *Break of Dark; The Devil on the Road* was selected by the American Library Association as a best book for young adults, 1979; Carnegie Medal nomination, 1979, for *The Devil on the Road*; Leseratten Prize (Germany), 1988, for *The Machine-Gunners,* 1990, for *Futuretrack Five,* and 1991, for *The Promise*;

Children's Book prize nomination, 1988, for *Urn Burial*; Senior Smarties Prize, 1989, and Children's Book Award commendation, both for *Blitzcat*; Carnegie Award commendation, and Sheffield Children's Book Prize, both 1991, both for *The Promise*; *Guardian* Award and Carnegie Award runner-up, both 1991, both for *The Kingdom by the Sea*. **Died:** 22 April 1993.

PUBLICATIONS FOR YOUNG ADULTS

Fiction

The Machine-Gunners. London, Macmillan, 1975; New York, Greenwillow, 1976.

The Wind Eye. London, Macmillan, 1976; New York, Greenwillow, 1977.

The Watch House. London, Macmillan, 1977; New York, Greenwillow, 1978.

The Devil on the Road. London, Macmillan, 1978; New York, Greenwillow, 1979.

Fathom Five. London, Macmillan, 1979; New York, Greenwillow, 1980.

The Scarecrows. London, Chatto & Windus, and New York, Greenwillow, 1981.

Break of Dark. London, Chatto & Windus, and New York, Greenwillow, 1982.

The Haunting of Chas McGill and Other Stories. London, Macmillan, and New York, Greenwillow, 1983.

Futuretrack Five. London, Kestrel, 1983; New York, Greenwillow, 1984.

The Cats of Seroster. London, Macmillan, and New York, Greenwillow, 1984.

The Other: A Christmas Story. London, Macmillan, 1985.

The Witness. London, Macmillan, 1985.

Rachel and the Angel and Other Stories. London, Macmillan, 1986; New York, Greenwillow, 1987.

Rosalie. London, Macmillan, 1987.

Urn Burial. London, Viking Kestral, 1987; New York, Greenwillow, 1988.

The Creature in the Dark, illustrated by Liz Roberts. London, Blackie, 1988.

Ghosts and Journeys. London, Macmillan, 1988.

Ghost Abbey. London, Macmillan, 1988; New York, Scholastic, 1989.

Antique Dust: Ghost Stories. London, Viking Kestral, and New York, Viking, 1989.

Blitzcat. London, Macmillan, 1989; New York, Scholastic, 1990.

Old Man on a Horse. London, Blackie, 1989.

A Walk on the Wild Side. London, Methuen, 1989.

The Call, London, Viking Kestral, 1989.

Echoes of War. London, Viking Kestral, 1989.

Cat! London, Methuen, 1989.

The Kingdom by the Sea. London, Methuen, 1990; New York, Farrar, Straus, 1991.

Stormsearch. London, Blackie, 1990.

If Cats Could Fly. . . ? London, Methuen, 1990.

The Promise. New York, Scholastic, 1991.

The Christmas Cat. London, Methuen, 1991.

The Stones of Muncaster Cathedral. London, Kestral, 1991.

Yaxley's Cat. London, Macmillan, 1991; New York, Scholastic, 1992.
The Fearful Lovers. London, Macmillan, 1992.
Size Twelve. London, Heinemann, 1992.
The Ghost in the Tower. London, Methuen, 1992.
A Place for Me. London, Macmillan, 1993.
In Camera and Other Stories. New York. Scholastic, 1993.

Play

The Machine-Gunners (adapted from his own story). London, Macmillan, 1986.

PUBLICATIONS FOR ADULTS

Other

Editor, *Children of the Blitz: Memories of Wartime Childhood.* London, Viking, 1985.

*

Biography: Entry in *Fifth Book of Junior Authors and Illustrators,* New York, H.W. Wilson, 1983; essay in *Something about the Author Autobiography Series,* Volume 2, Detroit, Gale, 1986; essay in *Speaking for Ourselves, Too* compiled and edited by Donald R. Gallo, National Council of Teachers of English, 1993.

Critical Studies: *Children's Literature Review,* Volume 13, Detroit, Gale, 1987; *Contemporary Literary Criticism,* Volume 17, Detroit, Gale, 1981.

*   *   *

Robert Westall's first book, *The Machine Gunners* (winner of the Carnegie Medal), has been one of those rare novels that has proven equally popular with English teachers, seeking contemporary fiction for school use, and with young adult readers who have responded to this view of growing up during World War II. Twenty years later, it remains widely read as a vivid and authentic re-creation of that experience, and in *Fathom Five* Westall explored what might later have happened to some of the characters from the original novel. Westall occasionally returned to the wartime setting. In *The Kingdom by the Sea,* for example, he describes how Harry's home and family are destroyed by bombs, and how the boy sets out on a series of adventures in wartime Northumbria. A similar theme is more light-heartedly handled in *Blitzcat,* the story of a lost cat, Lord Gort, seeking his owners (an RAF pilot and his wife) through the chaos of bombed and rationed Britain, which entertainingly juxtaposes the cat's views of adults with theirs of him. Perhaps the best of the five stories in *Break of Dark* is "Blackham's Wimpie," about the experiences of a Wellington bomber crew, told in the characteristic tones of their wireless radio

operator. However, it would be a mistake to read these works simply as documentaries the past. *The Machine Gunners* is also an analysis of dual roles, relationships, moral issues, and choices, that remains relevant in the present.

Westall's later work generally consisted of tough stories, set firmly in contemporary times, where conventional patterns of marriage and family life are breaking up and where new fears and threats have replaced the wartime bombs, or in an even more chilling future. The young characters of the books are repeatedly faced by twin sets of problems: moral dilemmas springing from family tensions and pressures from usually evil or malevolent supernatural forces. What might seem a conventional theme, a family's boating holiday, is given a very different treatment in *The Wind Eye.* The recently married scientist and his wife quarrel endlessly and their children from previous marriages are caught up in a complex emotional web. These tensions are counterpointed with the forces unleashed when one of the characters deliberately challenges superstition by stepping on the tomb of St Cuthbert in Durham Cathedral. In *The Watch House,* Anne spends the summer at Garmouth because she has been deserted by her father and is unwanted by her mother. She becomes conscious of manifestations from the old Watch House with its relics of an ancient shipwreck, and her immediate anxieties are intercut with her growing understanding of the past.

Several of Westall's novels raise social issues in an accessible, if sometimes over-simplified, form. *Futuretrack 5* explores the nature of a future hierarchical society in an England run by a giant computer, where new state examinations are used to determine the future lives of the inhabitants. The most successful ("Ests") have a privileged life of sex and leisure; the less able are sent to the cities to fight and survive as best they can. Real power is in the hands of the "Techs," who programme the computer and are plotting to repopulate the country with artificially bred and conditioned citizens. *Urn Burial* also tackles major problems of goodness and human destructiveness, but the two sides of the book are awkwardly integrated. The Cumbrian setting is lively and convincing, with Ralph the young shepherd, his fearsome mother, his girlfriend Ruby working in the supermarket check-out, and country scenes like the sheep-dipping festival. Investigating a hill-top cairn, Ralph discovers a glass coffin wherein space warriors had buried two of their leaders, and so he unintentionally unleashes intergalactic forces. The ensuing "star wars" plot is rather predictable, with a last minute victory of good over evil and a heavily moralising view of Ralph as the "good shepherd," an embodiment of simple wisdom.

The central critical debate over Westall's novels has concerned his treatment of violence and destructive emotions, which has seemed over-intense or even disturbed to some readers. Westall made clear the influence of his son's death on a motorbike at the age of eighteen on emotionally powerful books like *The Devil on the Road,* in which John Webster narrates the strange biking experiences that lead him back into a world of witchcraft and the Civil War. Some reviewers were unhappy about what they saw as the obsessional feelings vividly realised in *The Scarecrows.* Simon still worships his father who was killed in Aden and bitterly resents his new stepfather. He eavesdrops on his mother making love with her new husband, and is filled with such ferocious anger that he awakens the spirits of three murderers, so that they will return from haunting the old mill in the form of threatening scarecrows and execute vengeance. What is at issue, here and elsewhere, is the extent to which the reader is encouraged to identify with emotions or to be detached and judge them.

Westall's sudden death meant the loss of a versatile and skilful writer who had drawn on his many years of teaching experience for books that might provide what he called "the survival equipment" needed by adolescents. He was strikingly successful in reaching reluctant male readers. Collections like *The Call* or *Fearful Lovers* demonstrate a range of short story skills: the use of different narrative voices, a physical sense of objects and surroundings, a lively sense of humour, and an ability to suggest strangeness by simple means. The novels have enormous narrative drive, impelling the reader to discover what happens next. There is little description or discussion to hold up the action, although there is always a strong sense of atmosphere. Westall was always a skilful and uncompromising storyteller, and his books thoroughly deserve the popularity they have achieved.

—Robert Protherough

WHELAN, Geraldine Valerie. *See* **MELLING, O. R.**

WHITE, Ellen E(merson)

Pseudonyms: Also writes as Zack Emerson. **Nationality:** American. **Address:** c/o Scholastic Inc., 555 Broadway, New York, New York 10012, U.S.A.

PUBLICATIONS FOR YOUNG ADULTS

Fiction

Romance Is a Wonderful Thing. New York, Avon, 1983.
Friends for Life. New York, Avon, 1983.
The President's Daughter. New York, Avon, 1984.
White House Autumn. New York, Avon, 1985.
Life without Friends. New York, Scholastic, 1987.
Long Live the Queen. New York, Scholastic, 1989.
All Emergencies, Ring Super. New York, St. Martin's Press, 1997.

"Echo Company" series, as Zack Emerson

Welcome to Vietnam. New York, Scholastic, 1991.
Hill 568. New York, Scholastic, 1991.

'Tis the Season. New York, Scholastic, 1991.
Stand Down. Scholastic, New York, 1992.
The Road Home. New York, Scholastic, 1995.

Nonfiction

Bo Jackson: Playing the Game. New York, Scholastic, 1990.
Jim Abbott against All Odds. New York, Scholastic, 1990.
Jennifer Capriati. New York, Scholastic, 1991.

*

Biography: Essay in *Speaking for Ourselves, Too,* compiled and edited by Donald R. Gallo, National Council of Teachers of English, 1993.

*   *   *

Ellen Emerson White was in college when she published her first novel, and she has been consistently putting out books ever since: seven young adult titles, three nonfiction books for younger readers, and four Vietnam novels for young adults under the name Zach Emerson. She is a versatile writer who enjoys researching her books thoroughly (for example, she likes to make each character a Red Sox fan so that she can attend the games!) She brings to her writing a kind of toughness and realism that young readers appreciate.

Her characters speak honestly with a sophisticated humor and sometimes a savvy cynicism. They are tough, but vulnerable, and often become victims of circumstances over which they have little control. They frequently find themselves becoming heroic and exhibiting an unexpected courage. Sometimes they have to assume leadership or demonstrate maturity when they feel unprepared. Emerson's characters often exist in an unkind world where friendship, loyalty, support, encouragement, and trust are sought and found after considerable efforts. They must be problem solvers, and they are forced to be independent.

Friends for Life, published in 1983, tells the story of Susan McAllister, who moves back to her childhood community and hopes to enjoy her senior year with her best friend. However, she becomes involved in a very dangerous mystery when her friend Colleen is found dead of a drug overdose. Only Susan believes that her friend was murdered, and in this page-turning suspense novel, she proves to be correct, but almost loses her own life in the process.

Emerson's first novel was quickly followed by *Romance Is a Wonderful Thing* which describes the relationship between Colin McNamara and Trish Masters. Trish is an honors student and Colin is a silly, fun-loving character who needs to grow up and find confidence in himself.

The next year the first of a very popular series, *The President's Daughter,* was published. The President is a woman, and her daughter, Meg, is completely unprepared for the tremendous changes in her life as her mother assumes the office. The sequel, *White House Autumn,* continues the story of Meg as she adjusts to the fish bowl life of the White House. Her mother survives an assassination attempt, and the family learns how to pull together and support each other through the extraordinary circumstances in which they find themselves.

The last of the series, *Long Live the Queen,* begins six months after the attempt on the President's life. Meg has managed to construct a social life of friends and activities in spite of the constant surveillance of the Secret Service. However, Meg is kidnapped by terrorists and undergoes a horrifying experience at the hands of her captors until she is able to free herself. Left with severe injuries, she strives to cope with coming to terms with the uncertainty about her future, her relationship with her family, and her anger about what happened to her. Chosen as an ALA Best Book for Young Adults, this story doesn't spare any words. Meg's experience is not glamorized or romanticized, and the violence of her kidnapping is told in vivid detail.

In *Life without Friends,* Emerson picks up part of the story from *Friends for Life* with Beverly, who had known about the murders and the person who had committed them but was unable to muster up the courage to tell. As a result, everyone judges her, believing that she failed to speak up and prevent the tragedies. Feeling the ostracism, Beverly pulls more and more into an isolated and lonely existence until she finally learns that there are some people she can trust to forgive her. This is a painful story depicting the enormous difficulty some young people have in communicating with both adults and peer groups.

The ''Echo Company'' series was written under the name Zach Emerson. This highly regarded series about Vietnam is brutal, violent, and realistic in its portrayal of war. Eighteen-year-old Michael Jennings is totally unprepared for the horrors of war, and the first novel, *Welcome to Vietnam,* describes in graphic detail Michael's experiences there. He is forced to grow up and gain confidence quickly as he lives through unmitigated misery. The second book, *Hill 568,* continues Michael's story and takes him into a leadership position. With somewhat less action than in the first book, *Hill 568* provides the reader with another side of the war experience; boredom. Sometimes the days are all exactly the same, and there is too much time to think, contemplate, and despair. However, when they battle for the hill, the description is so intense that it becomes excruciating.

The third book in the series, *'Tis the Season,* introduces a new character—Rebecca, an army nurse. She is seriously injured in a helicopter crash in the jungle. The story describes her terror and physical pain in raw detail and ends with her rescue. However, the reader is left not knowing the extent of her injuries or what happens next. With such a smart, tough, and courageous heroine, the reader is eager to move into the fourth book to find out if she lives.

Stand Down brings Rebecca and Michael together. Anxious to know how she survived after he found her in the jungle, he locates her still working as a nurse, even though she is recovering from serious injuries. He convinces her to spend an evening together, and they strike up a kind of instant romance, enjoying a brief respite from the realities of the war. Included in each book is a map and a glossary of terms providing definitions for the slang used by the military personnel. Many of these terms are medical, and the listing seems to highlight the grim and horrifying effects of war. *The Grateful Nation,* due to be published in fall of 1993, continues the Vietnam story.

Emerson's talent for creating interesting characters and spellbinding plots has earned her the status of an important writer for and about young adults. Her readers can count on her to find the

words to describe feelings and experiences that are often so difficult to explain. Although her characters find themselves in extreme situations, they are always survivors, though not without great effort and cost.

—Caroline S. McKinney

WHITE, Robb

Nationality: American. **Born:** Baguio, Luzon, the Philippines, 20 June 1909. **Education:** U.S. Naval Academy, Annapolis, Maryland, B.S. 1931. **Family:** Married 1) Rosalie Mason in 1937 (divorced 1964), one son, two daughters; 2) Ann C. Saunders in 1985. **Military Service:** Captain, U.S. Navy. **Awards:** Commonwealth Club medal for best juvenile book, for *No Man's Land.*

PUBLICATIONS FOR YOUNG ADULTS

Fiction

The Nub, illustrated by Andrew Wyeth. Boston, Little, Brown, 1935.
Smuggler's Sloop, illustrated by Andrew Wyeth. Boston, Little, Brown, 1937.
Midshipman Lee, illustrated by Anton Otto Fischer. Boston, Little, Brown, 1938.
Run Masked. New York, Knopf, 1938; as *Jungle Fury,* New York, Berkley Publishing, 1956.
In Privateer's Bay. New York, Harper, 1939.
Three against the Sea, illustrated by Aldren A. Watson. New York, Harper, 1940.
Sailor in the Sun, illustrated by Edward Shenton. New York, Harper, 1941.
The Lion's Paw, illustrated by Ralph Ray. Garden City, New York, Doubleday, 1946.
Secret Sea, illustrated by Jay Hyde Barnum. Garden City, New York, Doubleday, 1947.
Sail Away, illustrated by Dorothy Bayley Morse. Garden City, New York, Doubleday, 1948.
Candy, illustrated by Gertrude Howe. Garden City, New York, Doubleday, 1949.
The Haunted Hound, illustrated by Louis Glanzman. Garden City, New York, Doubleday, 1950.
Deep Danger. Garden City, New York, Doubleday, 1952.
Our Virgin Island. Garden City, New York, Doubleday, 1953.
Midshipman Lee of the Naval Academy. New York, Random House, 1954.
Up Periscope. Garden City, New York, Doubleday, 1956.
Flight Deck. Garden City, New York, Doubleday, 1961.
Torpedo Run. Garden City, New York, Doubleday, 1962.
The Survivor. Garden City, New York, Doubleday, 1964.
Surrender. Garden City, New York, Doubleday, 1966.
Silent Ship, Silent Sea. Garden City, New York, Doubleday, 1967.
No Man's Land. Garden City, New York, Doubleday, 1969.
Deathwatch. Garden City, New York, Doubleday, 1972.
The Frogmen. Garden City, New York, Doubleday, 1973.
The Long Way Down. Garden City, New York, Doubleday, 1977.

Fire Storm. Garden City, New York, Doubleday, 1979.
Two on the Isle: A Memory of Marina Cay. New York, W.W. Norton, 1985.

Screenplays

House on Haunted Hill. Allied Artists Pictures Corporation, 1958.
Macabre. Allied Artists Pictures Corporation, 1958.
The Tingler. Columbia Pictures Corporation, 1959.
Up Periscope. Warner Brothers Pictures, 1959.
13 Ghosts. William Castle Productions, 1960.
Homicidal. William Castle Productions, 1961.

*

Biography: Essay in *Something about the Author Autobiography Series,* Vol. 1, Detroit, Gale, 1986.

*   *   *

One of the most prolific young adult authors of the mid-century, Robb White has written more than two dozen novels, a half dozen screenplays, and three war/travel memoirs. Although most of these are not now in print, the well-worn (and still circulating) editions of White's works held by school and public libraries are testament to his appeal, to his capacity for spinning a good yarn.

More than half of White's novels are set wholly or in part in the islands and waterways of the Pacific Ocean during World War II. The majority of these novels, while dated, retain their ability to engage readers who possess enough historical interest in the Second World War to be willing to overlook recurrent similarities in characterization, plot, and viewpoint—and, unfortunately, to ignore the unedited and all-too-accurate portrayal of omnipresent American racism towards Japanese during the war. Though there are important exceptions, White's novels stress two important themes. The first, central to such novels as *Up Periscope, Flight Deck, Silent Ship, Silent Sea,* and *Deathwatch,* is the capacity of the underdog—through ingenuity and effort—to triumph over incredible odds; the second, best exemplified by *Torpedo Run, The Survivor,* and *The Frogmen,* is the all-too-human tendency to misjudge and alienate others. Several White novels explore both themes simultaneously.

The novels written during the first decade or so of White's career are stylistically uneven, beginning with *Run Masked* (ostensibly written as an "adult novel") and *Midshipman Lee,* and continuing through *The Haunted Hound,* a second-rate boy/dog story. While the early novels include passages of taut prose and absolutely convincing dialogue, there are also glaring instances of overwriting, of obvious cleverness, of melodrama. This is especially true of such novels as *The Lion's Paw* and *Secret Sea,* where primary characters are young adolescents. *The Lion's Paw,* the story of a fifteen-year-old boy who escapes from his uncle on a small boat, accompanied by two orphans who join in his search for a rare seashell (which becomes a metaphorical search for the boy's father, for parents and home), has been in print longer than any other White novel. The characters themselves are rather well drawn; their search for love and security, while superficial, is

nevertheless believable to preteens. But their dialogue repeatedly rings false to older readers: sometimes it is too childish, sometimes too wise, too "adult." Such readers will also find that emotional scenes involving the children quickly degenerate into melodrama. There are similar problems in *The Haunted Hound* as well as *Secret Sea,* the story of a former Navy commander who hires a fifteen-year-old renegade orphan to help him search for sunken treasure.

What might be called White's "middle period" stretches from the early 1950s to 1970. White wrote less quickly during this period than he had during the early years of his career, and the writing is much more careful, more mature. The World War II novels of this period are markedly influenced by White's increasingly objective and analytical view of the war: the plots are leaner; the characters more deftly drawn; the dialogue a sharper, wittier rendering of the serious exchanges and bantering of adult males. White's most famous war novels come from this period. They include *Up Periscope* (the screenplay of the popular movie was also written by White), whose protagonist is sent on a secret mission to locate a Japanese radar base and copy its codes; *Flight Deck,* the adventures of a Navy pilot who, after being grounded because of injuries, takes upon himself a covert reconnaissance operation on a small uninhabited island; *Torpedo Run,* where plot is encapsulated in the subtitle; and *Silent Ship, Silent Sea,* which tells how a boot-camp graduate and his Navy captain, the sole survivors of an air attack on their destroyer, attempt to torpedo the Japanese ship that has their damaged destroyer in tow. A somewhat unusual novel of this period is *The Survivor,* whose protagonist, a naval aviator assigned to a unit of Marines sent to explore a Japanese-inhabited island, dies after rescuing the companions that have never truly accepted him.

White's later period extends from 1971 to the mid-1980s. Works from this period include *Deathwatch,* White's best-selling novel pitting man against man in a struggle for survival; *The Frogmen,* the account of a World War II underwater demolition team commanded by a Japanese-American (White's largely unsuccessful effort, due to plotting difficulties and blurred characterizations, to redress the racism of his earlier World War II fiction); *The Long Way Down,* the story of a young woman who wants to become a trapeze artist and who falls in love with her trainer (one of only a few White novels with a female protagonist and perhaps the only one directed to a feminine audience); *Fire Storm,* a very short novel about two brothers caught in a forest fire; and *Memory of Marina Cay,* the best of White's war/travel memoirs, this with a Virgin Islands setting.

One novel from this later group merits additional comment, not simply because of its immense popularity but because of its aesthetic achievement. *Deathwatch,* the most unified and carefully plotted of all White's novels never out of print since its initial publication—is set in California's Mojave Desert, pitting a young loner against the wealthy and determined businessman/hunter who has hired him to track bighorn sheep. When the hunter mistakenly kills a grizzled desert prospector, the young man insists they take the body to the authorities. Angered, knowing that he cannot trust his guide not to turn him in, the hunter resolves to let the younger man die in the desert. The resulting conflict is an intensely gripping drama; it is also the stuff of myth, where spirited, ingenious and uncorrupted youth holds its own and eventually triumphs over the selfish, worldly-wise, and privileged ruthlessness of age. In cementing White's reputation as an intelligent writer with an exciting and significant story to tell, *Deathwatch* has attracted young readers to library holdings of other White fiction, fiction that remains an engrossing portrait of its era.

—Keith Lawrence

WHITE, T(erence) H(anbury)

Pseudonyms: Also wrote as James Aston. **Nationality:** British. **Born:** Bombay, India, 29 May 1906; brought to England, 1911. **Education:** Cheltenham College, 1920-24; Queens' College, Cambridge (exhibitioner), 1925-27, 1928-29, B.A. 1929. **Career:** Taught at a preparatory school, 1930-32; head of the English department, Stowe School, Buckinghamshire, 1932-36. **Died:** 17 January 1964.

PUBLICATIONS FOR YOUNG ADULTS

Fiction

The Sword in the Stone, illustrated by the author. London, Collins, 1938; New York, Putnam, 1939; revised edition, in *The Once and Future King,* 1958.

The Witch in the Wood, illustrated by the author. New York, Putnam, 1939; London, Collins, 1940; revised edition, as *The Queen of Air and Darkness,* in *The Once and Future King,* 1958.

The Ill-Made Knight, illustrated by the author. New York, Putnam, 1940; London, Collins, 1941; revised edition, in *The Once and Future King,* 1958.

Mistress Masham's Repose, illustrated by Fritz Eichenberg. New York, Putnam, 1946; London, Cape, 1947.

The Master: An Adventure Story. London, Cape, and New York, Putnam, 1957.

The Once and Future King. London, Collins, and New York, Putnam, 1958.

The Book of Merlyn: The Unpublished Conclusion to The Once and Future King, illustrated by Trevor Stubley. Austin, University of Texas Press, 1977; London, Collins, 1978.

PUBLICATIONS FOR ADULTS

Novels

Dead Mr. Nixon, with R. McNair Scott. London, Cassell, 1931.

Darkness at Pemberley. London, Gollancz, 1932; New York, Century, 1933.

First Lesson (as James Aston). London, Chatto and Windus, 1932; New York, Knopf, 1933.

They Winter Abroad (as James Aston). London, Chatto and Windus, and New York, Viking Press, 1932.

Farewell Victoria. London, Collins, 1933; New York, Smith and Haas, 1934.

Earth Stopped; or, Mr. Marx's Sporting Tour. London, Collins, 1934; New York, Putnam, 1935.

Gone to Ground. London, Collins, and New York, Putnam, 1935.

The Elephant and the Kangaroo. New York, Putnam, 1947; London, Cape, 1948.

Short Stories

The Maharajah and Other Stories, edited by Kurth Sprague. London, Macdonald, and New York, Putnam, 1981.

Poetry

The Green Bay Tree; or, The Wicked Man Touches Wood. Cambridge, Heffer, 1929.

Loved Helen and Other Poems. London, Chatto and Windus, and New York, Viking Press, 1929.

Verses. Privately printed, 1962.

A Joy Proposed. London, Rota, 1980; Athens, University of Georgia Press, 1983.

Other

England Have My Bones. London, Collins, and New York, Macmillan, 1936.

Burke's Steerage; or, The Amateur Gentleman's Introduction to Noble Sports and Pastimes. London, Collins, 1938; New York, Putnam, 1939.

The Age of Scandal: An Excursion Through a Minor Period. London, Cape, and New York, Putnam, 1950.

The Goshawk (on falconry). London, Cape, 1951; New York, Putnam, 1952.

The Scandalmonger (on English scandals). London, Cape, and New York, Putnam, 1952.

Editor and Translator, *The Book of Beasts, Being a Translation from a Latin Bestiary of the Twelfth Century.* London, Cape, 1954; New York, Putnam, 1955.

The Godstone and the Blackymor (on Ireland). London, Cape, and New York, Putnam, 1959.

America at Last: The American Journal of T.H. White. New York, Putnam, 1965.

The White/Garnett Letters, edited by David Garnett. London, Cape, and New York, Viking Press, 1968.

Letters to a Friend: The Correspondence Between T.H. White and L.J. Potts, edited by Franois Gallix. New York, Putnam, 1982; Gloucester, Sutton, 1984.

*

Bibliography: *T.H. White: An Annotated Bibliography* by Franois Gallix, New York, Garland, 1986.

Critical Studies: *T.H. White: A Biography* by Sylvia Townsend Warner, London, Cape-Chatto and Windus, 1967, New York, Viking Press, 1968; *T.H. White* by John K. Crane, New York, Twayne, 1974.

*   *   *

"T.H. White, 1906-1964, author who from a troubled heart delighted others, loving and praising this life" reads the inscription on his grave marker in Athens, Greece. It sums up well his life and work. Troubled by an abusive childhood and adolescence, a love-hate relationship with his mother, and the constant necessity of writing to support himself, he also had a passion for life, and a love of all sorts of animals—especially red setters—new experiences and skills, and voracious reading. His life and works are a series of paradoxes. While he loved to play various roles, he took equal delight in satirizing role-playing. His young adult books are both highly original and pastiches of the works of others.

His young adult books, a minor portion of his twenty-three books, are a major portion of his most memorable works. General readers best remember *The Once and Future King,* the book for the popular romantic 1960s musical *Camelot* and the subsequent film. *The Sword in the Stone* was the first book, and the most successful part, of that tetralogy. While it delighted children, its very learned and sophisticated content challenges and appeals to young adults. Exceedingly popular, *The Sword in the Stone* probably remains his best known story.

In a letter to L.J. Potts, his former Cambridge tutor, White describes *The Sword in the Stone* as a ''warm-hearted'' story ''mainly about bird and beasts'' and observes that it ''seems impossible to determine whether it is for grown-ups or children.''

The Sword in the Stone begins with a famous parody of medieval education reduced to a public school week schedule: ''On Mondays, Wednesdays and Fridays it was Court Hand and Summulae Logicales, while the rest of the week it was the Organon, Repetition and Astrology.'' Because Merlyn lives backwards, from the twentieth century to the fifteenth, White gets to satirize both contemporary and medieval culture. The book has several themes. The first is Sir Ector's search for a proper tutor for Arthur, called Wart. Another is Wart's discovery of his identity and fate. A general theme throughout the book is the pleasures of country life as expressed through accurate details of medieval farming, haymaking, and hunting.

When Wart finds Merlyn, his education begins. Following Rousseau's model for a teacher, a familiar pattern for many children's books, Merlyn waits for Wart to ask questions. Proclaiming that ''Education is experience,'' he transforms him into various animals for his learning. Wart learns about war, peace, and wisdom by becoming a fish, a hawk, a grass snake, an owl, and a badger. In the revised 1958 version, he also becomes an ant and a goose. The novel is full of autobiographical details: Merlyn's study, like White's, is messily full of books, animals, and insects; an owl Archimedes sits on Merlyn's head just as it did on White's. From his experience in the human world, Wart learns responsibility, courage, and the need for rules, humility, and honesty.

The novel gives explicit details about medieval life and compares it to contemporary country life; it also parodies medieval themes and situations such as the interminable quests and Merlyn's frequent ineptness as a magician. There are allusions to classic children's books. For example, Kay and Wart are invited to dine and are trapped by Madame Mim in her cottage in the forest, an episode which recalls Hansel and Gretel. The excessive sweets found at the castle of Queen Morgan burlesque the excessive food imagery of some children's and young adult books. As in many young people's books, friendly animals aid the hero to achieve a quest.

Sometimes the comedy is broad and modern. In the original version, a neon movie sign hangs over Morgan's door: ''The Queen of Air and Darkness, Now Showing'' and she is ''a very beautiful lady, wearing beach pajamas and smoked glasses.'' Quotations from and allusions to the classic literature abound, as well as silly rhymes and parodies of popular tunes.

There are realistic hunting scenes and a fantastic battle against griffins and wyverns. Wart and Kay talk and act like modern young teenaged boys, but the adults are mostly comic stereotypes. White's clever line drawings illustrate the book.

Drastically revised for *The Once and Future King,* the Arthurian story became a tetralogy about the futility of war, rather than a domestic tragedy of incest. As a result the revised version is more somber and lacks much of the playfulness and extravagance of the original as well as White's clever drawings.

Mistress Masham's Repose resulted from his infatuation for a thirteen-year-old farm girl and his interest in Jonathan Swift's *Gulliver's Travels.* Dedicated to Amaryllis Virginia Garnett, the daughter of David Garnett in whose rural cottage White stayed for a year upon returning from Ireland and before taking up permanent residence in Alderney, this comic children's novel with a complex plot owes something to White's earlier detective novels but much more to his experiences at the Stowe estate and his enthusiasm for Gulliver's visit to the Lilliputians.

The orphaned heroine of this book proves that White could write well about women, if they were young enough. Maria, ten years old, studious, bespectacled, but impulsive and adventurous, lives in Malplaquet, a nearly ruined eighteenth-century Northamptonshire mansion, four time longer than Buckingham Palace. Her enemies are Miss Brown, her governess and cousin; and Mr. Hater, the local clergyman and her guardian. Her only friends are Mrs. Noakes, the cook and only servant; and the impecunious Professor, who lives in a cottage on the grounds. This setting allows White to crowd in all sorts of allusions to persons, literature, events, and gossip of the eighteenth and nineteenth century, things that fill his eighteenth-century social histories, *The Age of Scandal: An Excursion through a Minor Period* and *The Scandalmonger.*

The story begins when Maria, playing pirate, invades an island in the midst of an ornamental lake and discovers that Mistress Masham's Repose, a classical summer pavillion, is home to five hundred descendants of Swift's Lilliputians.

The plot has two parts. One concerns the recovery of Maria's inheritance and the second concerns her rescue of the Lilliputians from Miss Brown and Mr. Hater, who wish to sell them as curiosities to the circus or the movies. Maria and the Professor join forces to prevent this.

This novel also has minute details of farming and hunting, along with a recreation of eighteenth-century British speech. Like Merlyn in *The Sword in the Stone,* the Professor acts as the patient Rousseau-like instructor of Maria. And like White, he is also an absentminded, scholarly pacifist, difficult to tear away from his scholarly researches and somewhat inept in practical matters.

The novel is filled with incongruous scenes such as the Professor's chopping wood with a sixpenny hatchet from Woolworth's beneath an eighteenth century marble monument to the theatre. The place names and those of the monuments on the grounds of the estate are often erudite jokes. The novel has obvious debts to both Swift's *Gulliver's Travels* and Lewis's *Alice in Wonderland.*

There are some flaws. Miss Brown's and Mr. Hater's plot to murder Maria does not ring true. The last chapter shifts in tone and perspective. Some of the language and allusions in the novel recall too closely White's eighteenth-century research notes. This is young people's literature only for the very bright. But its message of the difference between love and possession and how to become a true friend is very clear.

His publisher discovered his manuscript of *The Goshawk* after his move to Alderney and urged its publication. A fictionalized autobiographical account of how White trained a goshawk using seventeenth century methods and then lost it through carelessness, it has become a nature story for young people, at least in England, according to François Gallix. Many of the details of the three sections of this book, including the names of the goshawks Gos and Cully as well as their characterizations as insane and lunatic, appear earlier in *The Sword in the Stone.* It has an easy Attic style and is filled with exacting falconry details about jesses and swivels but also with a message about the harm in trying to own even an animal.

This book has some of the same concerns as his other books: the contrast between past and present, the inferiority of the present to the past, the evils of possession, the destruction of war, and the folly of mankind.

The Master: An Adventure Story, which continues some of the themes of his earlier books, is a curious failure. Dedicated to Robert Louis Stevenson and bearing a quotation from Shakespeare's *Tempest,* this formula adventure novel is set on the sterile island of Rockall, halfway between Russia and America. Conceived in 1941 out of White's concern for Hitler and World War II and abandoned in 1944, this story was taken up and recast in 1955 to reflect his current bêtes noires. Its situations and character types are flat, stereotyped, and dull. The story concerns the kidnapping of twelve-year-old twins, Nicky and Judy, by a 157-year-old scientist called the Master, who has invented a diabolical super vibrator to give him control of the world. The twins along with their dog Jokey are held prisoner in the caverns of Rockall by the megalomaniac but physically frail Master and his small staff of associates: a drunken Dr. Jones; weak-willed Squadron Leader Frinton; Pinkie, a tongueless black cook; Mr. Blenkinsop, a cultivated but villainous Chinaman; and a couple of anonymous mechanics. As the plot develops, the Master sets about educating Nicky to eventually rule the world that he plans to conquer and save it from the atomic bomb. The novel is full of topical references to the Cold War and political leaders, such as President Eisenhower, Sir Anthony Eden, and Premier Khrushchev. In this context, the characters' discussions over "Might is Right" and "Might for Right," vital in the Arthurian novels, sound only academic and petulant here. The Master is a perversion of White's voluble teacher figures such as Merlyn and the Professor.

White's delight in life and learning is evident in his fantasy novels. Because his works are so learned and unique in their points of view, they will probably remain sui generis in the history of young adult literature.

—Hugh T. Keenan

WHITNEY, Phyllis A(yame)

Nationality: American. **Born:** Yokohama, Japan, 9 September 1903. **Education:** Attended schools in Japan, China, the Philippines, California, and Texas; McKinley High School, Chicago, graduated 1924. **Family:** Married 1) George A. Garner in 1925 (divorced 1945), one daughter; 2) Lovell F. Jahnke in 1950 (died 1973). **Career:** Dance instructor, San Antonio, Texas, one year;

children's book editor, Chicago *Sun,* 1942-46, and Philadelphia *Inquirer,* 1947-48; instructor in juvenile fiction writing, Medill School of Journalism, Northwestern University, Chicago, Illinois, 1945, and New York University, 1947-58. Member, Board of Directors, 1959-62, and president, 1975, Mystery Writers of America. **Awards:** Edgar Allan Poe best juvenile award, Mystery Writers of America, 1961, for *Mystery of the Haunted Pool,* and 1964, for *Mystery of the Hidden Hand;* Edgar Allan Poe best juvenile nominations, 1962, for *The Secret of the Tiger's Eye,* 1971, for *Mystery of the Scowling Boy,* and 1974, for *The Secret of the Missing Footprint;* Sequoyah Children's Book award, 1963, for *Mystery of the Haunted Pool;* "Today's Woman" citation, Council of Cerebral Palsy Auxiliaries of Nassau County, 1983; Grandmaster award, Mystery Writers of America, 1988, for lifetime achievement; Malice Domestic award, 1989, for lifetime achievement; Lifetime Achievement award, Society of Midland Authors, 1995. **Agent:** c/o McIntosh and Otis Inc., 310 Madison Avenue, New York, New York 10017.

PUBLICATIONS FOR YOUNG ADULTS

Fiction

A Place for Ann, illustrated by Helen Blair. Boston, Houghton Mifflin, 1941.

A Star for Ginny, illustrated by Hilda Frommholz. Boston, Houghton Mifflin, 1942.

A Window for Julie, illustrated by Jean Anderson. Boston, Houghton Mifflin, 1943.

The Silver Inkwell, illustrated by Hilda Frommholz. Boston, Houghton Mifflin, 1945.

Willow Hill. New York, Reynal, 1947.

Ever After. Boston, Houghton Mifflin, 1948.

Mystery of the Gulls, illustrated by Janet Smalley. Philadelphia, Westminster Press, 1949.

Linda's Homecoming. Philadelphia, McKay, 1950.

The Island of Dark Woods, illustrated by Philip Wishnefsky. Philadelphia, Westminster Press, 1951; as *Mystery of the Strange Traveler,* 1967.

Love Me, Love Me Not. Boston, Houghton Mifflin, 1952.

Step to the Music. New York, Crowell, 1953.

A Long Time Coming. Philadelphia, McKay, 1954.

Mystery of the Black Diamonds, illustrated by John Gretzer. Philadelphia, Westminster Press, 1954; as *Black Diamonds,* Leicester, Brockhampton Press, 1957.

Mystery on the Isle of Skye, illustrated by Ezra Jack Keats. Philadelphia, Westminster Press, 1955.

The Fire and the Gold. New York, Crowell, 1956.

The Highest Dream. Philadelphia, McKay, 1956.

Mystery of the Green Cat, illustrated by Richard Horwitz. Philadelphia, Westminster Press, 1957.

Secret of the Samurai Sword. Philadelphia, Westminster Press, 1958.

Creole Holiday. Philadelphia, Westminster Press, 1959.

Mystery of the Haunted Pool, illustrated by H. Tom Hall. Philadelphia, Westminster Press, 1960.

Secret of the Tiger's Eye, illustrated by Richard Horwitz. Philadelphia, Westminster Press, 1961.

Mystery of the Golden Horn, illustrated by Georgeann Helms. Philadelphia, Westminster Press, 1962.

Mystery of the Hidden Hand, illustrated by H. Tom Hall. Philadelphia, Westminster Press, 1963.

Secret of the Emerald Star, illustrated by Alex Stein. Philadelphia, Westminster Press, 1964.

Mystery of the Angry Idol, illustrated by Al Fiorentino. Philadelphia, Westminster Press, 1965.

Secret of the Spotted Shell, illustrated by John Mecray. Philadelphia, Westminster Press, 1967.

Secret of Goblin Glen, illustrated by Al Fiorentino. Philadelphia, Westminster Press, 1968.

The Mystery of the Crimson Ghost. Philadelphia, Westminster Press, 1969.

Secret of the Missing Footprint, illustrated by Alex Stein. Philadelphia, Westminster Press, 1969.

The Vanishing Scarecrow. Philadelphia, Westminster Press, 1971.

Nobody Likes Trina. Philadelphia, Westminster Press, 1972.

Mystery of the Scowling Boy, illustrated by John Gretzer. Philadelphia, Westminster Press, 1973.

Secret of Haunted Mesa. Philadelphia, Westminster Press, 1975.

Secret of the Stone Face. Philadelphia, Westminster Press, 1977.

Star Flight. New York, Crown, 1993.

Daughter of the Stars. New York, Random House, 1994.

Amethyst Dreams. New York, Crown, 1997.

PUBLICATIONS FOR ADULTS

Novels

Red Is for Murder. Chicago, Ziff Davis, 1943; as *Red Carnelian,* New York, Paperback Library, 1968; London, Coronet, 1976.

The Quicksilver Pool. New York, Appleton Century Crofts, 1955; London, Coronet, 1973.

The Trembling Hills. New York, Appleton Century Crofts, 1956; London, Coronet, 1974.

Skye Cameron. New York, Appleton Century Crofts, 1957; London, Hurst and Blackett, 1959.

The Moonflower. New York, Appleton Century Crofts, 1958; as *The Mask and the Moonflower,* London, Hurst and Blackett, 1960.

Thunder Heights. New York, Appleton Century Crofts, 1960; London, Coronet, 1973.

Blue Fire. New York, Appleton Century Crofts, 1961; London, Hodder & Stoughton, 1962.

Window on the Square. New York, Appleton Century Crofts, 1962; London, Coronet, 1969.

Seven Tears for Apollo. New York, Appleton Century Crofts, 1963; London, Coronet, 1969.

Black Amber. New York, Appleton Century Crofts, 1964; London, Hale, 1965.

Sea Jade. New York, Appleton Century Crofts, 1965; London, Hale, 1966.

Columbella. New York, Doubleday, 1966; London, Hale, 1967.

Silverhill. New York, Doubleday, 1967; London, Heinemann, 1968.

Hunter's Green. New York, Doubleday, 1968; London, Heinemann, 1969.

The Winter People. New York, Doubleday, 1969; London, Heinemann, 1970.

Lost Island. New York, Doubleday, 1970; London, Heinemann, 1971.

Listen for the Whisperer. New York, Doubleday, and London, Heinemann, 1972.

Snowfire. New York, Doubleday, and London, Heinemann, 1973.

The Turquoise Mask. New York, Doubleday, 1974; London, Heinemann, 1975.

Spindrift. New York, Doubleday, and London, Heinemann, 1975.

The Golden Unicorn. New York, Doubleday, 1976; London, Heinemann, 1977.

The Stone Bull. New York, Doubleday, and London, Heinemann, 1977.

The Glass Flame. New York, Doubleday, 1978; London, Heinemann, 1979.

Domino. New York, Doubleday, 1979; London, Heinemann, 1980.

Poinciana. New York, Doubleday, 1980; London, Heinemann, 1981.

Vermilion. New York, Doubleday, 1981; London, Heinemann, 1982.

Emerald. New York, Doubleday, and London, Heinemann, 1983.

Rainsong. New York, Doubleday, and London, Heinemann, 1984.

Dream of Orchids. New York, Doubleday, and London, Hodder & Stoughton, 1985.

The Flaming Tree. New York, Doubleday, and London, Hodder & Stoughton, 1986.

Silversword. New York, Doubleday, and London, Hodder & Stoughton, 1987.

Feather on the Moon. New York, Doubleday, and London, Hodder & Stoughton, 1988.

Rainbow in the Mist. New York, Doubleday, and London, Hodder & Stoughton, 1989.

The Singing Stones. New York, Doubleday, and London, Hodder & Stoughton, 1990.

Woman without a Past. New York, Doubleday, 1991.

The Ebony Swan. New York, Doubleday, 1992.

Other

Writing Juvenile Fiction. Boston, The Writer, 1947, revised edition, 1960.

Writing Juvenile Stories and Novels: How to Write and Sell Fiction for Young People. Boston, The Writer, 1976.

Guide to Fiction Writing. Boston, The Writer, 1982; London, Poplar Press, 1984.

Writing to Win: Winning Essays Submitted to the Phyllis A. Whitney Writing Contest, 1983-1987. Patchogue. New York, Patchogue-Medford Library, 1988.

*

Manuscript Collections: Mugar Memorial Library, Boston University.

Biography: Elaine Budd, *Thirteen Mistresses of Murder,* New York, Ungar Publishing, 1986; entry in *The World Almanac Biographical Dictionary,* New York, World Almanac, 1990; entry in *Legends in Their Own Time,* New York, Prentice Hall, 1994.

Critical Studies: Entry in *Contemporary Literary Criticism,* Volume 42, Detroit, Gale, 1987, pp. 431-438; entry in *Critical Survey of Mystery and Detective Fiction,* Pasadena, California, Salem Press, 1988; entry in *Contemporary Authors, New Revision Series,* Volume 25, Detroit, Gale, 1989; entry in *Twentieth-Century*

Romance and Historical Writers, Chicago, St. James, 1990; entry in *Twentieth-Century Crime and Mystery Writers,* Chicago, St. James, 1991.

Phyllis A. Whitney comments:

Two elements from my early life have influenced me as a writer. When I was thirteen and living in Kobe, Japan, my mother, father and I spent many quiet winter evenings reading aloud. We read a number of mysteries of that period—and I was inoculated!

Since I grew up in beautiful, interesting places in Japan, China, and the Philippines, I developed an eye for settings. Now, for each new mystery novel that I write I look for a place that speaks to my imagination and excites my inventive faculties. This process has kept me writing for all these years—since new places can never grow stale.

*   *   *

In addition to her many adult novels, most of which can be classified as romance or mystery and which are enjoyed by young adult readers, Phyllis Whitney has written numerous young adult novels and mysteries. She is also the author of works about writing for juvenile audiences: *Writing Juvenile Fiction* and *Writing Juvenile Stories and Novels: How to Write and Sell Fiction for Young People.*

Many of her novels for young people, especially those published between 1941 and 1954, appeal to girls rather than boys, as indicated in the names of girls in the titles: *A Place for Ann* (1941), *A Star for Ginny* (1942), *A Window for Julie* (1943), *Linda's Homecoming* (1950), *Nobody Likes Trina* (1972). The novels are primarily didactic. With the exception of *The Vanishing Scarecrow,* published in 1971, all of Whitney's mysteries for young people have titles beginning with the word ''mystery'' or ''secret.'' These novels are characterized by strong adventure set against vivid backgrounds. *Secret of the Spotted Shell* is set in the Virgin Islands. Other novels are set in Turkey, Norway, Japan, Greece, South Africa, and many places in the United States.

Some of Whitney's adult fiction may also be enjoyed by female young adult readers. These novels deal with young women who try to make their own way in the world, who encounter a series of dangerous adventures, and who eventually marry their true loves. These novels include *The Quicksilver Pool,* set on Staten Island during the Civil War; *The Trembling Hills,* a love story set at the time of the San Francisco earthquake; *Skye Cameron,* set in nineteenth-century New Orleans; *The Moonflower,* with a background in modern Japan; *Thunder Heights,* about the nineteenth-century Hudson River Valley; *Blue Fire,* set in modern South Africa; and *Window on the Square,* set in Washington Square, New York, in the nineteenth century.

Other works written for older audiences may be appealing to younger female readers since they deal with relationships between mothers and daughters, female identity, and women trying to come to terms with their own pasts. Many of these women try to return to ancestral homes or reconcile with other women in their families. Phyllis Whitney's women are fallible, sometimes marrying the wrong man or misjudging character, but they see their wrongs and change. Novels with these themes include most notably *Columbella,*

Silverhill, Lost Island, Listen for the Whisperer, The Turquoise Mask, and *The Golden Unicorn.* Whitney's writing is eloquent and charming. Those of all ages susceptible to romance and mystery are drawn to the novels.

Whitney's first novel, *A Place for Ann,* brought her some success and allowed her to be self-sufficient. *Willow Hill,* published in 1947, was ahead of its time in dealing with a controversial subject: the story of a young white girl and her high school friends dealing with the integration of a housing project in their neighborhood.

Whitney's young adult mysteries are even more numerous. *The Mystery of the Gulls* involves Taffy Saunders and her adventure on Mackinac Island, in northern Michigan. Taffy's mother inherits a hotel, but someone keeps trying to scare them away from the island. Taffy decides she must be the one to solve the mystery of who is trying to close down the hotel. *The Island of Dark Woods,* later published as *Mystery of the Strange Traveller,* deals with a phantom stagecoach passenger who helps Laurie and her sister solve a mystery. *The Mystery of the Black Diamonds* involves a treasure map that an old prospector has given Angie and Mark, two youths who think the whole thing is a hoax. Their parents take them to a ghost town called Blossom, strange things start happening, and they then begin believing in and searching for the map's treasures. *The Mystery on the Isle of Skye* is about an orphan raised by her grandmother. When the grandmother falls ill, Cathy MacLeod is sent on a trip to the Isle of Skye with her uncle, aunt, and two cousins. A series of mysteries ensue and she and her cousins puzzle them out. *The Mystery of the Golden Horn* has Vicki, the young protagonist, being told by a young gypsy that a golden horn is the key to her fortune. Searching for the secret of this mysterious horn, Vicki faces many dangers.

Secret of The Emerald Star is about Robin Ward and a house with menacing stone lions and a high iron gate. This is Devery House, occupied by old Mrs. Devery, her daughter-in-law, and her blind granddaughter Stella. At first Robin feels sorry for Stella, but it soon becomes obvious to Robin that Stella's real problem is that her grandmother does not understand her. Robin is also troubled by Mr. Lemon, who is strange and menacing. The two girls play detective and become involved in a dangerous mystery.

The Mystery of the Angry Idol is about a summer of secrets. Jan Pendleton worries that her visit with her grandmother would be dull until she meets Neil, the boy next door, and the aloof Patrick. Soon comes the realization that a dark-bearded stranger is watching the house and watching over a fearsome-looking Chinese idol kept in great-grandmother Althea's room. The idol is stolen. Jan is not the only one trying to find out the idol's mysteries.

A family secret and another treasure map play prominent roles in *Secret of Goblin Glen.* In the town of Camberhills is the mystery of the great unsolved bank robbery. The thieves' hideout was Goblin Glen, but no one has ever been able to decipher the map and find the loot. Trina Lorey, grandniece of one of the robbers, tries her hand at finding the treasure. She has to work fast and quietly to solve the mystery and clear her family name.

Illness and other challenges created a lengthy gap in Whitney's publishing record, but in 1992 she was back with *Star Flight,* an intricately layered story about a young woman investigating the causes of her grandmother's suicide and her own husband's death. On the one hand, the book suffers from an abiding sense of disconnection from life in the 1990s, instead harkening back to the 1950s. On the other hand, this is one of its most appealing charms.

In 1997, at age 94, Whitney published her 76th book, *Amethyst Dreams*.

—Lesa Dill, updated by Judson Knight

WIELER, Diana

Nationality: Canadian. **Born:** Diana Jean Petrich in Winnipeg, Manitoba, 14 October 1961. **Education:** Lord Beaverbrook High School, Calgary, Alberta, 1976-79; Southern Alberta Institute of Technology, Calgary, Alberta, 1979-80. **Family:** Married Larry Wieler in 1981; one son. **Career:** Copywriter, CKXL Radio, Calgary, Alberta, 1981-82; copywriter, CJWW Radio, Saskatoon, Saskatchewan, 1982-84; advertising features writer, Star-Phoenix newspaper, Saskatoon, 1984-89. **Awards:** C.B.C. Literary Competition, 1984; Saskatchewan Writer's Guild Literary Award, 1985; Vicky Metcalf Short Story Award, 1986; Max and Greta Ebel Memorial Award for Children's Writing, 1987; Governor General's Literary Award, 1989; Ruth Schwartz Children's Book Award, 1990.; C.L.A. Young Adult Canadian Book Award, 1990; Mr. Christie's Book Award, 1994. **Agent:** Melanie Colbert, 17 West St., Holland Landing, Ontario L9N 1L4, Canada. **Address:** 133 Spruce Thicket Walk, Winnipeg, Manitoba R2 3Z1, Canada. **Website:** http://www.makersgallery.com/wieler/.

PUBLICATIONS FOR YOUNG ADULTS

Last Chance Summer. Saskatoon, Western Producer Prairie Books, 1986.
Bad Boy. Toronto, Groundwood, 1989.
Ran Van the Defender. Toronto, Groundwood, 1993.
Ran Van a Worthy Opponent. Toronto, Groundwood, 1995.
Ran Van Magic Nation. Toronto, Groundwood, 1997.

PUBLICATIONS FOR CHILDREN

A Dog on His Own. Winnipeg, Prairie Publishing, 1983.
To the Mountains by Morning, illustrations by Ange Zhang. Toronto, Groundwood, 1995.

*

Diana Wieler comments:

People often ask why most of my stories are about boys. The truth is that I grew up without a father or brothers and I found the male of the species fascinating from an early age. I would visit my friends' homes and watch their brothers as if they were alien creatures—which to me they were. I think this deep curiosity still fuels me as a writer. We are always told to "write what you know," but for me, I hunger to go places I've never been, look into experiences I will probably never have. As a woman, the most foreign and exciting landscape is the male perspective.

But how can you do this? young writers ask. For me, research is about watching and listening and asking questions. I find that almost everyone is interesting; my doctor, my mechanic, the person who sits beside me in art class. The world is full of fascinating

people who will share their stories if you are a good listener. I also draw on the experiences of my husband and son. Just living with them is an adventure of discovery.

I write about the teen years because that was a vivid, terrible, exhilarating time of my life. So much happens in a short space, and lives change forever. As a writer, that's the promise I make to my reader: someone's life is going to change forever. I can't think of any work more exciting than that.

*   *   *

It is not accidental that Diana Wieler's Young Adult novels all feature male central characters. "I was just fascinated with men from a very early age," explained Diana in an *EL* interview. "My father was sort of present until I was about six, but I really didn't know him that well, and he died when I was 13. When I would go to my girlfriends' houses and their fathers would be in the house, I would watch them like they were aliens." To date, Diana's ongoing "study" of the male specimen has provided adolescent males with five opportunities for new self-insights. Strong in characterization, Wieler's novels utilize both a variety of Canadian settings and types of troubled teens.

Awarded the 1987 Max and Greta Ebel Memorial Award for its promotion of understanding between two cultures, *Last Chance Summer* features Marl Silversides, a 12-year-old rebellious delinquent of mixed racial heritage, who has been shunted amongst foster homes and spent time in a provincial institution. Marl's social worker gives him a choice—succeed at the Jenner farm, a last chance group farm home for hard core juvenile troublemakers in the Alberta badlands, or face long-term incarceration in a reform school. Marl, who has fetal alcohol syndrome, encounters difficulties in dealing with the erratic, hostile behaviour of his nine fellow juvenile inmates, but he is ultimately able to rise above his own selfish inclinations and demonstrate concern for others.

Winner of three national awards, including the 1989 Governor-General's Literary Award for Children's Literature, *Bad Boy* is about friendship and sexual identity. Close friends A.J. Brandiosa, 16, and Tully Brown, 17, have achieved their goal of playing for the Moosejaw Cyclones, a Saskatchewan Triple A hockey team, but A.J. is devastated when he accidentally discovers that Tully is gay. His emotions run the gamut from feelings of betrayal over Tully's not sharing this most important fact with him to the fear that, should schoolmates learn of Tully's homosexuality, they might also think he is gay. Additionally, as A.J. still "likes" Tully, he is concerned that his continued affection might actually mean that he, too, is really gay. A.J.'s confused emotions eventually find expression in anger, and hockey becomes the outlet for his pent-up rage. With just scant encouragement from his coach, A.J. becomes the team's "goon" and his dirty style of play earns him a "Bad Boy" newspaper headline. As A.J.'s brand of hockey continues to match his nickname, Tully worries about his friend's negative transformation. Complicating the pair's relationship is A.J.'s romantic interest in Summer, Tully's younger sister. To "prove" to himself that he is straight, A.J. aggressively "romances" Summer and then must face an angry Tully who, in a climactic scene, forces A.J. to confront his sexuality demon. Not only was Wieler the first Canadian YA author to write about adolescent homosexuality, but she placed it within the most macho of Canadian sports, hockey. Despite having never played the game, Wieler creates authentic hockey scenes, both on ice and in the dressing room. By using alternating narrators, Wieler increases the story's emotional impact.

Wieler's most recent YA offering is a trilogy involving adolescent male self-discovery which begins with *RanVan the Defender,* winner of the Mr. Christie's Book Award. Rhan Van, a 15-year-old orphan living with his Gran in Vancouver, British Columbia, enjoys playing video games, especially one wherein he "becomes" an ill-equipped knight who fights his way into a castle against overwhelming odds to rescue a princess-in-distress. Under his video game moniker of RanVan, Rhan has accumulated the game's highest score, but his time spent before the video screen inadequately prepares him for the reality of rescuing a real "damsel-in-need." Rhan first encounters Thalie Ming, a 17-year-old Vietnamese immigrant, when she is apparently thrown from a parked car. Meeting her later in school, an idealistic and romantic Rhan quickly jumps to the conclusion that Thalie is being sexually abused by Garry, her mother's boyfriend, and has need of a contemporary knight to defend her honour, a role naive Rhan enthusiastically assumes. Thalie leads Rhan through a series of materially destructive episodes which culminate in Rhan's attempted arson of Garry's new home. There, as Rhan confronts the Dark Lord, aka Garry, he discovers the shocking truth about Thalie.

Rhan's odyssey continues in *RanVan a Worthy Opponent* as the 16-year-old and Gran relocate to Thunder Bay, Ontario. As in *The Defender,* Rhan's video game alter ego rashly leads him into more "knightly" pursuits, but this time, instead of trying to defend damsels, RanVan, in both the arcade and real life, confronts a worthy opponent, another video game player, Lee Dahl aka the Iceman. Again, Rhan eventually comes to discover that appearances are not reality for Lee's cool facade actually masks great emotional pain. Wieler balances the worsening conflict between RanVan and the seemingly imperturbable Iceman by means of Rhan's evolving romantic relationship with the vulnerable Kate Gervais.

In the trilogy's concluding volume, *RanVan Magic Nation,* Rhan, now 19, has moved to Calgary, Alberta, and enrolled in the demanding Cinema, Television, Stage and Radio program at the Southern Alberta Institute of Technology. As a child hearing the word, "imagination," Rhan had transmogrified it into "Magic Nation," a place of superheroes. Although the adult demands of Rhan's academic program and living independently have caused him to abandon his video game moniker, the larger game of life calls upon RanVan's knightly talents when he again encounters his "worthy opponent," Lee Dahl, now involved in a white supremacist group. In the book's climactic episode, Rhan Van's real world talents as a cameraman and RanVan's chivalric qualities ironically and tragically unite to produce what Rhan, at 15, had originally sought to be, RanVan the Defender. By removing Rhan from the "protected" adolescent world and placing him in the more adult setting of a postsecondary institution, Wieler again breaks new ground in Canadian YA literature.

—Dave Jenkinson

WIESEL, Elie(zer)

Nationality: American. **Born:** Sighet, Romania, 30 September 1928; immigrated to United States, 1956, naturalized citizen, 1963.

Education: Sorbonne, University of Paris, France, 1948-51. **Family:** Married Marion Erster Rose in 1969; one son and one stepdaughter. **Career:** Worked variously as foreign correspondent for *Yedioth Ah'oronoth,* Tel Aviv, Israel, *L'Arche,* Paris, France, and *Jewish Daily Forward,* New York City, 1949-68; writer and lecturer, since 1964; Distinguished Professor of Judaic Studies, City College of the City University of New York, New York City, 1972-76; Andrew W. Mellon Professor in the Humanities, since 1976, and University Professor of Philosophy and Religious Studies, since 1988, Boston University, Boston, Massachusetts. Visiting professor or lecturer at universities and conferences throughout the world; member, board member, advisor, and/or trustee of humanitarian organizations, congresses, and award juries throughout the world, including many dealing with Jewish or Holocaust-related causes; member of editorial and advisory boards, *Hadassah, International Journal of Holocaust and Genocide Studies* (Oxford), *Midstream, Passages* (France), *Religion and the Arts* (Boston College), *Religion and Literature* (University of Notre Dame), *Sh'ma: Journal of Jewish Responsibility.* **Selected Awards:** Herzl Literary award; David Ben-Gurion award; International Kaplun Foundation award from Hebrew University of Jerusalem; American-Israeli Friendship award; Prix Rivarol, 1963, and William and Janice Epstein Fiction award from Jewish Book Council, 1965, for *The Town beyond the Wall*; Ingram Merrill award, 1964; National Jewish Book awards, 1965, for *The Town beyond the Wall,* and 1973, for *Souls on Fire*; International Remembrance award from the World Federation of Bergen-Belsen Associations, 1965, for *The Town beyond the Wall* and all other writings; Jewish Heritage award, 1966, for excellence in literature; Prix Medicis (France), 1968, for *Le Mendiant de Jerusalem*; Prix Bordin from French Academy, 1972, and Frank and Ethel S. Cohen award from Jewish Book Council, 1973, both for *Souls on Fire*; Eleanor Roosevelt Memorial award, 1972; American Liberties Medallion from American Jewish Committee, 1972; Martin Luther King, Jr., Medallion from City College of the City University of New York, 1973; Jewish Heritage award from Haifa University, 1975; Spertus International award, 1976; King Solomon award, 1977; Joseph Prize for Human Rights from Anti-Defamation League of B'nai B'rith, 1978; Presidential Citation from New York University, 1979; Zalman Shazar award from the State of Israel, 1979; Prix Livre-International and Bourse Goncourt, both 1980, and Prix des Bibliothecaires, 1981, all for *Le Testament d'un poete juif assassine*; Jabotinsky Medal from State of Israel, 1980; Literary Lions award from New York Public Library, 1983; International Literary Prize for Peace from Royal Academy of Belgium, 1983; Le Grand Prix de la Litterature de la Ville de Paris, 1983, for *Le Cinquieme fils*; Le Grand Prix Litteraire de Festival International de Deauville, 1983; Anatoly Shcharansky Humanitarian award, 1983; Commander de la Legion d'Honneur, France, 1984, elevated to Grand Officier, 1990; Congressional Gold Medal of Achievement, 1984; Anne Frank award, 1985; International Holocaust Remembrance award from State of Israel Bonds, 1985; Voice of Conscience award from American Jewish Congress, 1985; Covenant of Peace award from Synagogue Council of America, 1985; Freedom of Worship Medal from Franklin D. Roosevelt Four Freedoms Foundation, 1985; Jacob Pat award from World Congress of Jewish Culture, 1985; Humanitarian award from International League of Human Rights, 1985; Nobel Peace Prize, 1986; Freedom Cup award from Women's League for Israel, 1986; Medal of Liberty award, 1986; Freedom award from International Rescue Committee, 1987; La

Grande Medaille de Vermeil de la Ville de Paris, 1987; Eitinger Prize from University of Oslo, 1987; Lifetime Achievement award from *Present Tense* magazine, 1987; special Christopher award, 1987; Profiles in Courage award from B'nai B'rith, 1987; Achievement award from State of Israel, 1987; Metcalf Cup and Prize for Excellence in Teaching from Boston University, 1987; Gra-Cruz da Ordem Nacional do Cruzeiro do Sul, Brazil, 1987; Golda Meir Senior Humanitarian award, 1987; Count Sforza Award in Philanthropy, American Hungarian Foundation, 1989; Lily Edelman Award for Excellence in Continuing Jewish Education, Commission on Continuing Jewish Education, B'nai B'rith International, 1989; International Brotherhood Award, Congress of Racial Equality, 1990; Award of Highest Honor, Soka University, 1991; Fifth Centennial Christopher Columbus Medal, City of Genoa, 1992; First International Primo Levi Award, 1992; Humanitarian of the Century, Council of Jewish Organizations, 1992; Golden Slipper Humanitarian Award, 1994; Freedom Award, National Civil Rights Museum, Memphis, Tennessee, 1995; Socio Honorario de la Sociedad Hebraica Argentina, 1995; Golden Plate Award, American Academy of Achievement, 1996; Guardian of Zion Prize, Rennert Center for Jerusalem Studies, Bar-Ilan University, 1997; approximately ninety-five honorary doctorates. **Agent:** Georges Borchardt, 136 East 57th St., New York, New York 10022. **Address:** University Professors, Boston University, 745 Commonwealth Ave., Boston, Massachusetts 02215, U.S.A.

PUBLICATIONS

Novels

L'Aube. Paris, Seuil, 1960; as *Dawn,* translated by Frances Frenaye, New York, Hill & Wang, 1961.

Le Jour. Paris, Seuil, 1961; as *The Accident,* translated by Anne Borchardt, New York, Hill & Wang, 1962.

La Ville de la chance. Paris, Seuil, 1962; as *The Town beyond the Wall,* translated by Stephen Becker, New York, Atheneum, 1964.

Les Portes de la foret. Paris, Seuil, 1964; as *The Gates of the Forest,* translated by Frances Frenaye, New York, Holt, 1966.

Le Mendiant de Jerusalem. Paris, Seuil, 1968; as *A Beggar in Jerusalem,* translated by the author and Lily Edelman, New York, Random House, 1970.

Le Serment de Kolvillag. Paris, Seuil, 1973; as *The Oath,* translated by Marion Wiesel, New York, Random House, 1973.

Le Testament d'un poete juif assassine. Paris, Seuil, 1980; as *The Testament,* translated by Marion Wiesel, New York, Simon & Schuster, 1981.

Le Cinquieme Fils. Paris, Grasset, 1983; as *The Fifth Son,* translated by Marion Wiesel, New York, Warner, 1985.

Le Crepuscule, au loin. Paris, Grasset et Fasquelle, 1987; as *Twilight,* translated by Marion Wiesel, New York, Summit, 1988.

Fiction

The Golem: The Story of a Legend as Told by Elie Wiesel, translated by Anne Borchardt. New York, Summit, 1983.

The Six Days of Destruction: Meditations toward Hope, with Albert H. Friedlander. Mahwah, New Jersey, Paulist Press, 1988.

Essays and Short Stories

Le Chant des morts. Paris, Seuil, 1966; as *Legends of Our Time,* translated by Steven Donadio, New York, Holt, 1968.

Entre deux soleils. Paris, Seuil, 1970; as *One Generation After,* translated by the author and Lily Edelman, New York, Random House, 1970.

Paroles d'etranger. Paris, Seuil, 1982.

Signes d'Exode. Paris, Grasset, 1985.

Against Silence: The Voice and Vision of Elie Wiesel, edited by Irving Abrahamson. Three volumes, New York, Holocaust Library, 1985.

Plays

Zalmen; ou, La Folie de Dieu. Paris, Seuil, 1968; as *Zalmen; or, The Madness of God,* translated by Lily Edelman and Nathan Edelman, New York, Holt, 1968.

Le proces de Shamgorod tel qu'il se deroula le 25 fevrier 1649: Piece en trois actes (first produced in Paris, 1981). Paris, Seuil, 1979; as *The Trial of God (as It Was Held on February 25, 1649, in Shamgorod): A Play in Three Acts,* translated by Marion Wiesel, New York, Random House, 1979.

Other

Un di velt hot geshvign (memoir; in Yiddish; title means ''And the World Has Remained Silent''). [Buenos Aires], 1956; as *La Nuit,* Paris, Minuit, 1958; as *Night,* translated by Stella Rodway, New York, Hill & Wang, 1960.

Les Juifs du silence (originally published in Hebrew as a series of articles for newspaper *Yedioth Ah'oronoth*). Paris, Seuil, 1966; as *The Jews of Silence: A Personal Report on Soviet Jewry,* translated by Neal Kozodoy, New York, Holt, 1966.

La Nuit, L'Aube, [and] Le Jour. Paris, Seuil, 1969; as *Night, Dawn, [and] The Accident: Three Tales,* New York, Hill & Wang, 1972.

Celebration hassidique: Portraits et legendes. Paris, Seuil, 1972; as *Souls on Fire: Portraits and Legends of Hasidic Masters,* translated by Marion Wiesel, New York, Random House, 1972.

Ani maamin: A Song Lost and Found Again (cantata; first performed at Carnegie Hall, 1973), translated by Marion Wiesel, with music by Darius Milhaud. New York, Random House, 1974.

Celebration biblique: Portraits et legendes. Paris, Seuil, 1975; as *Messengers of God: Biblical Portraits and Legends,* translated by Marion Wiesel, New York, Random House, 1976.

Conversations with Elie Wiesel by Harry James Cargas. Mahwah, New Jersey, Paulist Press, 1976.

Un Juif aujourd'hui: Recits, essais, dialogues. Paris, Seuil, 1977; as *A Jew Today,* translated by Marion Wiesel, New York, Random House, 1978.

Dimensions of the Holocaust, with others. Muskogee, Oklahoma, Indiana University Press, 1978.

Four Hasidic Masters and Their Struggle against Melancholy. Indiana, University of Notre Dame Press, 1978.

Images from the Bible, illustrated by Shalom of Safed. New York, Overlook Press, 1980.

Five Biblical Portraits. Indiana, University of Notre Dame Press, 1981.

The Haggadah (cantata), music by Elizabeth Swados. New York, S. French, 1982; *The Haggadah for Passover,* illustrated by Mark Podwal, New York, Simon & Schuster, 1993.

Somewhere a Master: Further Hasidic Portraits and Legends, translated by Marion Wiesel. New York, Simon & Schuster, 1982.

Job ou Dieu dans la Tempete, with Josy Eisenberg. Paris, Grasset et Fasquelle, 1986.

L'oublie. Paris, Seuil, 1989; as *The Forgotten,* translated by Stephen Becker, New York, Summit, in press.

Evil and Exile, with Philippe-Michael de Saint-Cheron, translated by Jon Rothschild. Indiana, University of Notre Dame Press, 1990.

From the Kingdom of Memory. New York, Summit, 1990.

A Journey of Faith: A Dialogue between Elie Wiesel and John Cardinal O'Connor, with John O'Connor. New York, Donald I. Fine, 1990.

In Dialogue and Dilemma with Elie Wiesel, interviewed by David Patterson. Wakefield, New Hampshire, Longwood Academic, 1991.

Sages and Dreamers: Biblical, Talmudic, and Hasidic Portraits and Legends. New York, Summit, 1991.

Nine and One-Half Mystics: The Kabbala Today. New York, Macmillan, 1992.

Author of commentaries, *A Passover Haggadah,* illustrated by Mark Podwal. New York, Simon & Schuster, 1993.

Tous les fleuves vont a la mer (memoirs). Paris, Editions du Seiul, 1994; as *All Rivers Run to the Sea,* New York, Schocken Books, 1996.

With François Mitterrand, *Memoire a deux voix.* Paris, O. Jacob, 1995; as *Memoir in Two Voices,* translated by Richard Seaver and Timothy Bent, New York, Arcade, 1996.

Et la mer n'est pas remplie (memoirs). 1996.

Ethics and Memory. New York and Berlin, W. de Gruyter, 1997.

*

Media Adaptations: *The Madness of God* (adapted for the stage by Marion Wiesel), Washington, D.C., 1974; *Night* (sound recording), New York, Caedmon, 1982.

Biography: *Elie Wiesel* by Ted L. Estess, New York, Ungar, 1980; essay in *Contemporary Authors Autobiography Series,* Detroit, Gale, Vol. 4, 1986, Vol. 40, 1991; entry in *Dictionary of Literary Biography,* Vol. 83, *French Novelists since 1960,* Detroit, Gale, 1989; *Elie Wiesel* by Caroline Lazo, New York, Dillon Press, 1994.

Critical Studies: *Elie Wiesel: A Bibliography* by Molly Abramowitz, Metuchen, New Jersey, Scarecrow, 1974; *Elie Wiesel: A Small Measure of Victory* by Gene Koppel and Henry Kaufmann, Tucson, University of Arizona, 1974; entry in *Contemporary Literary Criticism,* Detroit, Gale, Vol. 3, 1975, Vol. 5, 1976, Vol. 11, 1979, Vol. 37, 1986; *Confronting the Holocaust: The Impact of Elie Wiesel* edited by Alvin Rosenfeld and Irving Greenberg, Bloomington, Indiana University Press, 1979; *A Consuming Fire: Encounters with Elie Wiesel and the Holocaust* by John K. Roth, Louisville, Kentucky, Knox Press, 1979; *The Vision of the Void: Theological Reflections on the Works of Elie Wiesel* by Michael G. Berenbaum, Middletown, Connecticut, Wesleyan University Press, 1979; *Legacy of Night: The Literary Universe of Elie Wiesel* by Ellen S. Fine, Albany, State University of New York Press, 1982; *Elie Wiesel: Messenger to All Humanity* by Robert McAfee Brown, Indiana, University of Notre Dame Press, 1983; *Elie Wiesel: Messenger from the Holocaust* by Carol Greene, Chicago, Illinois,

Children's Press, 1987; *Elie Wiesel: Between Memory and Hope* by Carol Rittner, New York, New York University Press, 1990; *Elie Wiesel: Voice from the Holocaust* by Michael A. Schuman, Hillside, New Jersey, Enslow, 1994; *Elie Wiesel's Secretive Texts* by Colin Davis, Gainesville, University Press of Florida, 1994; *Elie Wiesel: Bearing Witness* by Michael Pariser, Brookfield, Connecticut, Millbrook Press, 1994; *Silence in the Novels of Elie Wiesel* by Simon P. Sibleman, New York, St. Martin's Press, 1995; *Cliffs Notes of Elie Wiesel's Night,* Lincoln, Nebraska, Cliffs Notes, 1996; *Elie Wiesel: A Voice for Humanity* by Ellen Norman Stern, Philadelphia, Jewish Publication Society, 1996.

*   *   *

"How can we imagine what is beyond imagination. . . . How can we retell what escapes language?" This is Elie Wiesel's response to the notion of Holocaust literature. Although he is considered by many to be the world's most eloquent and prolific author of this genre, Wiesel views *Un di velt hot geshvign,* published in 1956 (later edited and republished in English as *Night*) as his only work on the subject. His other novels, *Dawn, The Accident, The Town beyond the Wall, The Gates of the Forest, A Beggar in Jerusalem, The Oath,* and *The Testament* all take place either before or after the events of the Holocaust by design. "I try not to make it tolerable," Wiesel related to author Diane Cooper-Clark in *Interviews with Contemporary Novelists.* "When I see that it becomes tolerable, I don't speak about it. That's why I have written so little about the Holocaust."

Wiesel's silence is carefully executed. Although his works do not directly address the Holocaust, they are all informed by it and they introduce issues that force the reader to come to terms with humanity's capacity for degradation and God's seeming callousness in the midst of human suffering. Wiesel's simple writing style belies his ability to engage his audience in the grand conflict he has experienced as life. In this engagement, Wiesel displays his mastery by convincing even the most skeptical reader that life is an urgent act requiring each person to examine the significance of his existence.

Drawing on his early theological training to craft his works, Wiesel incorporates traditional Jewish approaches to understanding the human dilemma. In *By Words Alone,* Sidra DeKoven Ezrahi has identified the major influences of Jewish literature in Wiesel's works. The traditional Hebrew narratives, Ezrahi asserts, provided Wiesel with a model for the fusion of legend and real experience. In this respect, Wiesel also appeals to the Hasidic tradition that places more import on eyewitness testimony than accurate documentation to establish truth. This is of particular significance with the events of the Holocaust since official records of formal plans by the Germans to eradicate those they deemed "undesirable" do not exist. Wiesel establishes through his novel *Night* and his subsequent works that the Holocaust did happen and it continues to affect its perpetrators, victims, and all of humanity.

In *Dawn,* for example, Wiesel portrays a young Holocaust survivor, Elisha, who becomes involved in the fight for freedom in Palestine after the war. The roles are reversed for Elisha as he becomes the executioner of a British soldier who killed another young Israeli. Elisha is confronted with the bitter reality that those who just experienced humanity's most cruel act further brutalize themselves as they kill others to ensure the survival of their nation.

Elisha realizes in choosing to kill the British soldier, he has killed himself.

Another characteristic of Hebraic tradition is that the central conflict of the novel, which usually deals with the ramifications of God's involvement with human affairs, is left unresolved. Some have compared examples of traditional Jewish legends with what Ezrahi calls the "fragments of a violated theodicy" in Wiesel's works. Wiesel sets up the plot conflict by introducing situations that challenge the bond between God and humanity. Then, rather than neatly resolving the conflict, Wiesel leaves the reader with a myriad of unresolved questions about the essence of life and the nature of God.

The Accident clearly exemplifies Wiesel's use of this technique. After intense introspection, the protagonist realizes the "accident" that nearly killed him was really a suicide attempt—the ultimate act of rebellion against God. The act stemmed from the character's inability to resolve his concentration camp experience and the role of God in the Holocaust. Suicide became the most significant way in which the character could claim for himself what he had previously ascribed to God: the right to decide whether life is worth living. Through another round of agonizing self-examination, the character concludes that life's significance lies in questions rather than answers.

Wiesel's writings appeal to a wide range of readers from those just beginning to realize the questions of life to those well versed in the process of inquiry. The issues he addresses—identity, the breakdown of one's support network, the nature of God, human limitations, the construction of an orderly existence in the midst of chaos, man's inhumanity to man—are at the core of the human experience. To the young, Wiesel stands as a witness to the events of the Holocaust while he provides a framework for the questioning that inevitably occurs as people discover life is not as certain, concrete, and predictable as they once believed. The more experienced reader will find a challenge in the profound conflict hidden under Wiesel's deceptively simple writing style.

—Linda Ross

WIGHT, James Alfred. *See* **HERRIOT, James.**

WILKINSON, Brenda

Nationality: American. **Born:** Moultrie, Georgia, 1 January 1946. **Education:** Hunter College of the City University of New York. **Family:** Separated; two daughters. **Career:** Poet and author. Conducts poetry readings. **Awards:** National Book award nominee, 1976, for *Ludell*; *New York Times* outstanding children's books of the year and American Library Association best book for young adults, both 1977, for *Ludell and Willie*.

PUBLICATIONS FOR YOUNG ADULTS

Fiction

Ludell. New York, Harper, 1975.
Ludell and Willie. New York, Harper, 1976.
Ludell's New York Time. New York, Harper, 1980.
Not Separate, Not Equal. New York, Harper, 1987.
Definitely Cool. New York, Scholastic, 1993.

Nonfiction

Jesse Jackson: Still Fighting for the Dream. Morristown, New Jersey, Silver Burdett Press, 1990.

*

Biography: Essay in *Speaking for Ourselves, Too* compiled and edited by Donald R. Gallo, National Council of Teachers of English, 1993.

* * *

Brenda Wilkinson specializes in writing about African Americans growing up in the New South. Her first three books are autobiographical in nature while her fourth novel deals with more universal experiences. In every book there is a common theme of unity in the black community against the frighteningly cruel world of the whites.

Ludell, Ludell and Willie, and *Ludell's New York Time* tell the story of Ludell Wilson from age eleven to eighteen. Ludell is a fatherless child being raised by her grandmother in Waycross, Georgia, in the 1950s. *Ludell* deals mainly with her problems in a segregated school but also with her growing awareness of boys and the real world. The conversation is in authentic black dialect and the subjects discussed are those of concern to an eleven-year-old girl. Religion plays an important part. *Ludell and Willie* focuses on Ludell's growing attraction to Willie, the boy next door and the brother of her best friend, Ruthie Mae Johnson. They are truly in love but are bound to good behavior by the ironclad rules of Ludell's grandmother, Mama. Ludell matures quickly as she begins working for white people at very low wages and things come to a climax as Mama's health declines and Ludell nurses her through her final illness. Ludell's mother, Dessa, comes home from New York (where she has been living most of Ludell's life) to take care of business matters and she insists that Ludell return with her to New York, even though it means Ludell must leave high school just short of graduation. Even worse for Ludell is being separated from Willie. Reluctantly Ludell leaves Waycross for New York City. Upon her arrival in the North, *Ludell's New York Time* begins. She finishes high school and looks for work, experiencing prejudice in the North as her job search takes more time than expected. Eventually Ludell returns to Waycross and marries Willie.

Not Separate, Not Equal is the story of six African American students chosen to integrate the Pineridge, Georgia, white high school. Pineridge is a fictional town, but the real world of 1965 is portrayed accurately in the novel. Again, the heroine is a plucky teenager, in this case an orphan. Malene Freeman has been adopted by a well-to-do couple after the tragic death of her sharecropper parents. She is one of the six students picked to go to the formerly all-white Pineridge High. The usual demonstrations occur but Malene is personally targeted by a deranged white man. All six students fall victim to his scheming but are rescued in a bittersweet effort. The novel ends with the community moving toward desegregation: some black families leave town, some white families begin building a private school, yet none can escape the fact that the New South is here to stay.

Wilkinson has just the right level of sophistication in each book. *Ludell* is a rather simplistic book as it should be with an eleven-year-old heroine. Gradually the series becomes more complex as Ludell becomes more aware of the true rigors of life. She realizes that the easy-going nature of the blacks around her is an attempt to deal with the discrimination and outright hatred of the white world. However, she does not feel that her mother's escape to New York is the answer either. The forces of change have very little to do with Waycross except to make the local people more aware of their situation. Ludell has enough problems of her own; only when she moves up North does she begin to realize how the problems of all African Americans are her problems, too.

Although the "Ludell" series is more complex, *Not Separate, Not Equal* is an excellent attempt to deal with the issue of desegregation on its own. The social problems are more prominent in this book and there is not as much of the banter that makes the "Ludell" books so entertaining. *Not Separate, Not Equal* stands beside Ann Waldron's *The Integration of Mary-Larkin Thornhill* as a classic depiction of the school integration movement.

Brenda Wilkinson has done a good job altogether in capturing a recent time in American history as well as the personalities of some very believable teenagers. She also has a real feel for accurately depicting the backdrop of southern Georgia.

—Sharon Clontz Bernstein

WILLARD, Barbara (Mary)

Nationality: British. **Born:** Hove, Sussex, 12 March 1909. **Education:** Convent of La Sainte Union, Southampton. **Career:** Actress, novelist, and screenwriter. **Awards:** Guardian award for children's fiction, 1972, for *The Sprig of Broom,* 1973, for *A Cold Wind Blowing,* and 1974, for *The Iron Lily; The Iron Lily* was also named an American Library Association notable book; Whitbread award, 1984. **Died:** 1994.

PUBLICATIONS FOR YOUNG ADULTS

Fiction

Portrait of Philip (for adults), London, Macmillan, 1950; revised edition (for young adults), as *He Fought for His Queen,* London, Heinemann, and New York, Warne, 1954.
The House with Roots, illustrated by Robert Hodgson. London, Constable, 1959; New York, Watts, 1960.
Son of Charlemagne, illustrated by Emil Weiss. New York, Doubleday, 1959; London, Heinemann, 1960.
The Dippers and Jo, illustrated by Jean Harper. London, Hamish Hamilton, 1960.

Eight for a Secret, illustrated by Lewis Hart. London, Constable, 1960; New York, Watts, 1961.
The Penny Pony, illustrated by Juliette Palmer. London, Hamish Hamilton, 1961.
The Summer with Spike, illustrated by Anne Linton. London, Constable, 1961; New York, Watts, 1962.
If All the Swords in England, illustrated by Robert M. Sax. New York, Doubleday, and London, Burns Oates, 1961.
Stop the Train!, illustrated by Jean Harper. London, Hamish Hamilton, 1961.
Duck on a Pond, illustrated by Mary Rose Hardy. London, Constable, and New York, Watts, 1962.
Hetty, illustrated by Pamela Mara. London, Constable, 1962; New York, Harcourt, 1963.
Augustine Came to Kent, illustrated by Hans Guggenheim. New York, Doubleday, 1963; Kingswood, Surrey, World's Work, 1964.
The Battle of Wednesday Week, illustrated by Douglas Hall. London, Constable, 1963; as *Storm from the West,* New York, Harcourt, 1964.
The Dippers and the High-Flying Kite, illustrated by Maureen Eckersley. London, Hamish Hamilton, 1963.
The Suddenly Gang, illustrated by Lynette Hemmant. London, Hamish Hamilton, 1963.
A Dog and a Half, illustrated by Jane Paton. London, Hamish Hamilton, 1964; New York, Nelson, 1971.
The Pram Race, illustrated by Constance Marshall. London, Hamish Hamilton, 1964.
Three and One to Carry, illustrated by Douglas Hall. London, Constable, 1964; New York, Harcourt, 1965.
The Wild Idea, illustrated by Douglas Bissett. London, Hamish Hamilton, 1965.
Charity at Home, illustrated by Douglas Hall. London, Constable, 1965; New York, Harcourt, 1966.
Surprise Island, illustrated by Jane Paton. London, Hamish Hamilton, 1966; New York, Meredith Press, 1969.
The Richleighs of Tantamount, illustrated by C. Walter Hodges. London, Constable, 1966; New York, Harcourt, 1967.
The Grove of Green Holly, illustrated by Gareth Floyd. London, Constable, 1967; as *Flight to the Forest,* New York, Doubleday, 1967.
The Pet Club, illustrated by Lynette Hemmant. London, Hamish Hamilton, 1967.
To London! To London!, illustrated by Antony Maitland. London, Longman, and New York, Weybright & Talley, 1968.
Hurrah for Rosie!, illustrated by Gareth Floyd. London, Hutchinson, 1968.
Royal Rosie, illustrated by Gareth Floyd. London, Hutchinson, 1968.
The Family Tower. London, Constable, and New York, Harcourt, 1968.
The Toppling Towers. London, Longman, and New York, Harcourt, 1969.
The Pocket Mouse, illustrated by Mary Russon. London, Hamish Hamilton, and New York, Knopf, 1969; illustrated by M. Harford-Cross, London, MacRae, 1981.

"Mantlemass" series

The Lark and the Laurel, illustrated by Gareth Floyd. London, Longman, and New York, Harcourt, 1970.
The Sprig of Broom, illustrated by Paul Shardlow. London, Longman, 1971; New York, Dutton, 1972.

A Cold Wind Blowing. London, Longman, 1972; New York, Dutton, 1973.

The Iron Lily. London, Longman, 1973; New York, Dutton, 1974.

Harrow and Harvest. London, Kestrel, 1974; New York, Dutton, 1975.

The Miller's Boy, illustrated by Gareth Floyd. London, Kestrel, and New York, Dutton, 1976.

The Eldest Son. London, Kestrel, 1977.

A Flight of Swans. London, Kestrel, 1980.

The Keys of Mantlemass. London, Kestrel, 1981.

Priscilla Pentecost, illustrated by Doreen Roberts. London, Hamish Hamilton, 1970.

The Reindeer Slippers, illustrated by Tessa Jordan. London, Hamish Hamilton, 1970.

The Dragon Box, illustrated by Tessa Jordan. London, Hamish Hamilton, 1972.

Jubilee!, illustrated by Hilary Abrahams. London, Heinemann, 1973.

Bridesmaid, illustrated by Jane Paton. London, Hamish Hamilton, 1976.

The Country Maid. London, Hamish Hamilton, 1978; New York, Greenwillow, 1980.

The Gardener's Grandchildren. London, Kestrel, 1978; New York, McGraw, 1979.

Summer Season. London, MacRae, 1981.

Spell Me a Witch, illustrated by Phillida Gili. London, Hamish Hamilton, 1979; New York, Harcourt, 1981.

Famous Rowena Lamont. London, Hardy, 1983.

The Queen of the Pharisees' Children. London, MacRae, 1984.

Smiley Tiger, illustrated by Laszlo Acs. London, MacRae, 1984.

Ned Only. London, MacRae, 1985.

Other

Editor, *Hullabaloo! About Naughty Boys and Girls,* illustrated by Fritz Wegner. London, Hamish Hamilton, and New York, Meredith Press, 1969.

Junior Motorist: The Driver's Apprentice, with Frances Howell, illustrated by Ionicus. London, Collins, 1969.

Chichester and Lewes, illustrated by Graham Humphreys. London, Longman, 1970.

Editor, *Happy Families,* illustrated by Krystyna Turska. London, Hamish Hamilton, and New York, Macmillan, 1974.

Translator, *Convent Cat,* by Bunshu Iguchi, illustrated by Iguchi. London, Hamish Hamilton, 1975; New York, McGraw, 1976.

Editor, *Field and Forest,* illustrated by Faith Jaques. London, Kestrel, 1975.

Translator, *The Giants' Feast,* by Max Bollinger, illustrated by Monika Laimgruber. London, Hamish Hamilton, 1975.

PUBLICATIONS FOR ADULTS

Novels

Love in Ambush, with Elizabeth Helen Devas. London, Howe, 1930.

Ballerina. London, Howe, 1932.

Candle Flame. London, Howe, 1932.

Name of Gentleman. London, Howe, 1933.

Joy Befall Thee. London, Howe, 1934.

As Far as in Me Lies. London, Nelson, 1936.

Set Piece. London, Nelson, 1938.

Personal Effects. London, Macmillan, 1939.

The Dogs Do Bark. London, Macmillan, 1948.

Celia Scarfe. New York, Appleton-Century, 1951.

Proposed and Seconded. London, Macmillan, 1951.

Echo Answers. London, Macmillan, 1952.

Winter in Disguise. London, Joseph, 1958.

Plays

Brother Ass and Brother Lion, adaptation of the story of "St. Jerome, The Lion and the Donkey" by Helen J. Waddell. London, J. Garnet Miller, 1951.

One of the Twelve (one-act play). London, French, 1954.

Fit for a King. London, J. Garnet Miller, 1955.

Radio Play: *Duck on a Pond,* from her own book, 1962.

Television Play: *Merry Go Round,* 1965.

Other

Sussex. London, Batsford, 1965; New York, Hastings House, 1966.

Editor, *"I..."*: *An Anthology of Diarists.* London, Chatto & Windus, 1972.

*

Biography: Essay in *Something about the Author Autobiography Series,* Volume 5, Detroit, Gale, 1973, pp. 327-41; entry in *Fourth Book of Junior Authors and Illustrators* edited by Doris de Montreville and Elizabeth D. Crawford, New York, H.W. Wilson, 1978, pp. 350-52.

Critical Study: Entry in *Children's Literature Review,* Volume 2, Detroit, Gale, 1976.

*   *   *

After turning from adult fiction to novels for young readers, Barbara Willard continued to write regularly and enthusiastically for them for nearly thirty years. Although her works are enormously varied, Willard recognized, as do many of her readers, the particular success of the novels inspired by English history and the Wealden area of Sussex. Through absorbing stories of young people caught up in the effects of great historical events, Willard leads the reader to an understanding of the issues involved. At the same time, her fully realized and attractive characters face personal experiences which seem contemporary.

It was in the Wealden Forest novels that Willard "found her voice." Her descriptions of the forest create a world with which the reader grows familiar, learning to recognize how the landscape has evolved over centuries. A characteristic earlier book with a contemporary setting, *The Battle of Wednesday Week* is a competent, Arthur Ransome-style holiday story. Separated from adults, young people take risks, face dangers, and learn how to coexist with resented new members of an extended family. Willard pursues these themes in later novels, but here the plot which carries them seems contrived and the dialogue stilted.

By comparison, the historical books from *The Lark and the Laurel* onward show an author who is not only writing with confidence but also with enjoyment and commitment. This novel marks the beginning of the Mantlemass sequence, the series for which Willard will be best remembered. The eight novels share the setting of the forest and Mantlemass, the manor house in which generations of the Medley and Mallory families live, and the sequence stretches from the Wars of the Roses to the Civil War in the seventeenth century.

Although the periods and settings may seem alien to contemporary young adults, they are introduced through these novels to experiences and emotions with which they can readily identify: strong parents try to force children to live out their own dreams rather than enabling them to make choices for themselves, siblings compete for parents' attention and praise, large extended families create tensions as different generations and the children of different marriages try to live peacefully in the same house, and young people discover that intense love does not necessarily lead to happiness. In each of the novels, Willard returns to the problems girls face in finding satisfying lives for themselves. Some of the young women gain independence through circumstances and become respected equals with the men with whom they live and work. Others fight against society's expectations of women and succeed against the odds. These are strong, spirited characters developed over several novels.

As a historical novelist, Willard avoids the trap of didacticism by making her characters act out relevant situations so that the reader is drawn into complex issues through involvement in their experiences. Piers Medley in *A Cold Wind Blowing* is a powerless spectator as he watches his uncle, a monk, die for his beliefs and sees the local priory destroyed. His friend becomes one of the moving spirits in the Dissolution movement, and his young wife, Isabella, dies because she is unable to come to terms with breaking the vows she made as a novice nun. In one sense, the Mantlemass characters live a timeless life sheltered in the forest; in *The Sprig of Broom,* Richard Plantagenet, the illegitimate son of Richard III, lives in the forest undiscovered by the world outside for many years. Gradually, however, as the novels progress, the sanctuary of the forest is destroyed as woodland is cut down, industry begins to develop, and strangers move in. The central families become dispersed, and the divided loyalties of civil wars are acted out in Mantlemass itself. Above all, the historical settings provide the opportunity for plots in which action is important but always authentic. Willard is an accomplished storyteller.

Although each of the Mantlemass novels stands by itself, the reader gains additional pleasure from the cumulative effect of the whole sequence. Characters are further developed, mysteries are gradually solved, the long-term effects of important events can be traced, incidents are seen from different perspectives through the use of changing viewpoints, and there is the satisfaction of following the evolution of the forest and the central families. Throughout, the novels are linked by buildings and objects which become symbols of the past by the end of the sequence.

Willard's fascination with the forest continues into later novels, such as *Famous Rowena Lamont,* in which more recent events are set against the background, the people, and the dialect of the area. As she has written, "What happier fate for any author than to live in a setting that demands to be written about?" and it is for her novels inspired by the Sussex Weald for which Barbara Willard has won several awards and been rightly praised.

—Judith Atkinson

WILLEY, Margaret

Nationality: American. **Born:** Chicago, Illinois, 5 November 1950. **Education:** Grand Valley State College, Allendale, Michigan, B.Ph., B.A. 1975; Bowling Green State University, Ohio, M.F.A. 1979. **Family:** Married Richard Joanisse in 1980; one daughter. **Career:** Writer. **Awards:** Creative Artist Grant, Michigan Council of the Arts, 1984-85; American Library Association citations as one of the year's best books for young adults, 1983, for *The Bigger Book of Lydia,* 1986, for *Finding David Dolores,* 1988, for *If Not for You,* and 1990, for *Saving Lenny*; Creative Artist Grant, Michigan Arts Foundation, 1995; Paterson prize, ALA Quick Picks list, both 1997, both for *Facing the Music.* **Address:** 431 Grant, Grand Haven, Michigan 49417, U.S.A.

PUBLICATIONS FOR YOUNG ADULTS

Novels

The Bigger Book of Lydia. New York, Harper, 1983.
Finding David Dolores. New York, Harper, 1986.
If Not for You. New York, Harper, 1988.
Saving Lenny. New York, Bantam, 1990.
The Melinda Zone. New York, Bantam, 1993.
Facing the Music. New York, Delacorte, 1996.

Margaret Willey comments:

With each of the novels I have written for teenagers, I re-enter and relive a different aspect of the challenge to selfhood that adolescence represents. Whether it be the challenge of loneliness, or the challenge of a breaking-apart family, or the challenge to establish a healthy love relationship, or a healthy body image—all of these aspects of growing up need to be deeply felt in order to honor the courage and stamina of the real teenagers who experience them. This is the greatest challenge for me as a writer and a person—the task of re-claiming complicated childhood memories and crafting them into stories. The rewards are many. With each book I have discovered so much about the never-ending process of "growing up."

*   *   *

The success of Margaret Willey's books for young adults is due at least in part to her skill at presenting totally believable characters who must struggle to resolve their problems in her coming-of-age dilemmas. Hers are distinctly drawn personalities with a wide range of conflicts: problems with parents; troubles with boyfriends; breeches of loyalty between best friends; school woes; and particularly, always, the struggle to find and to be oneself. Diverse though the works and characters of this three-time ALA Best Book awardee certainly are, it is easy to recognize a common thread: the attempt of the protagonist to strike a balance in the chaotic blend of relationships that so often characterizes adolescence. It is precisely the efforts to reconcile their own needs and desires with the often urgent and sometimes demanding needs and expectations of those around them that form the central themes of Willey's writings.

The reconciliation of such competing forces has central focus in *The Melinda Zone,* a touching story which depicts the difficulties of a fifteen-year-old trying desperately to find herself while torn in an emotional tug-of-war between her parents. Caught between these two adults whose paths lead in drastically different directions, Melinda seeks to avoid having to choose between her mother and father by spending her summer instead with her aunt and uncle and the older cousin she has always idolized. The warm affectionate relationship between her caring Aunt Rita and carefree, witty Uncle Ted casts a telling shadow on the uneasy state of affairs between Melinda's own parents who have been divorced since Melinda was a baby. The problem with them, Melinda explains to her cousin, is that they spend all their time arguing ''over whose fault everything is.''

The only angry words in Melinda's summer home are those that pass between her cousin Sharon and Uncle Ted and Aunt Rita, but even those are not enough to prevent her from enjoying the uncustomary spirit of independence living with her uncle and aunt brings. It is to be a summer filled with—nothing, if that is what Melinda chooses. Sensing her niece's need to make her own decisions about how to spend her time, Aunt Rita allows the confused teen a season totally free of the usual pressures and demands her parents place on her.

Melinda's Michigan summer away from home and parents takes on added purpose with the growing conflict between Sharon and her own parents. Once again she is called upon to play the role she knows so well: peacemaker. But this time, someone else, not she, is at the center of the conflict. Strange, Melinda thinks, that this young woman, the one she always thought had it all, should be so unhappy, should get along so badly with clearly wonderful parents. Caught up in an unlucky relationship with a boyfriend who is much older than she, Sharon has her own ''finding'' of herself to do. The pain of their parent-child conflict mirrors somewhat the pain Melinda is causing by her own silence and reluctance to phone or write her mother or father.

And then there is Paul. One of Sharon's castaways, this sensitive, young boy-next-door has serious parent troubles of his own. But his perceptiveness and wit enable him to be what Melinda most needs at the moment—a friend. With Paul she can be totally at ease; with him she does not have to keep acting as if ''everything is fine, everything is wonderful. Even sometimes when it isn't.'' In turn, Melinda is there to help Paul discover whether there is life after Sharon, and perhaps more importantly, to listen with understanding as he reveals the fact that though he lives with his parents, he is separated from them by a barrier more unyielding and unreconcilable than any Melinda has ever known.

It is Paul to whom she confides her joy at being finally free ''from trying to be who my mother thinks I am when I'm with her and who my father thinks I am when I'm with him.'' Melinda returns to Milwaukee with many of her problems intact, but there is reason to believe she will not stray too far from the independence and self-identity she has found in that wonderful place, that place Paul dubbed ''The Melinda Zone.''

In another of Willey's works, Lydia's search for identity becomes somehow entangled in the tiny girl's obsession with size, with measurements, with detail, in *The Bigger Book of Lydia*. A confused and insecure Lydia has great difficulty in making friends and joining in activities that others relish; in a very real sense, her physical smallness does indeed make her fragile—not just physically but emotionally and socially as well. In spite of her considerable capability to help others in her family, Lydia can not help herself, at least not until Michelle arrives. Willey has created in Michelle one of her most truly unforgettable characters. The

troubled teenager's shocking physical condition reflects an inner chaos. She, too, needs assistance from Lydia, but this relationship is no one-way street. Together, the two girls seek the courage to deal with a world that previously has proven too much to bear.

In *Saving Lenny,* it is Jesse who does all the giving and Lenny who does all the taking in a misguided and painful relationship. Skillfully revealed through letters and passages written from the perspectives of the key players, this story deals with the conflicts which occur as a result of Jesse's blind devotion to a love which cannot survive. She must deal not only with the doomed relationship and with her own limitations at fulfilling Lenny's needs, but also with the chasm the relationship causes between Jesse and her parents and between Jesse and her best friend.

Loyalty between friends is also a central theme in *If Not for You.* A young girl becomes so engrossed in her friendship with her best friend's older sister that the two grow painfully distant, with Bonnie increasingly ensnared in a role she is unprepared to play. The process results in Bonnie's estrangement not only from her best friend, but also from her boyfriend and from her parents, and pulls her uncomfortably deep into an unnatural relationship with a young married couple. She must learn, as does Jesse in *Saving Lenny,* that a romanticized world gone sour can be the worst kind of nightmare. Her awakening is a difficult one.

Willey's books for young adults are marked by presentation of realistic dilemmas that are both timeless and contemporary, serious yet resolvable. By shaping her characters and crafting her plots with respect for reality she manages to produce satisfying outcomes without simplistic answers or sappy, happy endings. Through a blend of self-reliance and collaboration with others, her dynamic heroines come, if not to an absolute answer, then at least to an understanding of the problem that is life.

—Jan Tyler

WILLIAMS, Tad

Nationality: American. **Born:** Palo Alto, California, 1957. **Education:** Graduated from high school, 1974. **Family:** Married, wife's name Nancy. **Career:** Writer, since 1985; has worked selling shoes, singing in a band, managing a financial institution, designing military manuals; hosted a syndicated radio show, *One Step Beyond,* KFKC Radio; co-producer, *Valleyvision* television program; taught grade-school and college classes; technical writer, Knowledge Engineering Department, Apple Computer. **Address:** c/o DAW Books, 375 Hudson Street, New York, New York 10014, U.S.A.

PUBLICATIONS FOR YOUNG ADULTS

Fiction

Tailchaser's Song. New York, DAW Books, 1985.
The Dragonbone Chair. New York, DAW Books, 1988.
Stone of Farewell. New York, DAW Books, 1990.
To Green Angel Tower. New York, DAW Books, 1993.
Caliban's Hour. New York, HarperPrism, 1994.

Otherland: Volume 1, City of Golden Shadow. New York, DAW
    Books, 1996.
MirrorWorld: Rain. New York, BIG Entertainment, 1997.

PUBLICATIONS FOR CHILDREN

Fiction

With Nina Kiriki Hoffman, *Child of an Ancient City,* illustrated by
    Greg Hildebrandt. New York, Atheneum, and Toronto, Max-
    well Macmillan Canada, 1992.

                    *   *   *

Tad Williams is a popular author of epic-length fantasy and
science fiction whose love of folklore, literature, and history is
evident in his mesmerizing storytelling. Whether set in Osten Ard
or in a near future of technological turmoil, an element of magic or
the paranormal exists to heighten the drama and complicate the
quests of his main characters. Most appealing, especially to teen
readers, is the realization of the main characters that they need to
learn about themselves and find out who they are before they can
expect to change their world in any way.

His first novel, *Tailchaser's Song,* is told from the perspective
of a cat. Even in this cat-centered universe gods and fables and
history exist, beginning with how ''Meerclar Allmother came out
of the darkness to the cold earth.'' Tailchaser is a ginger tom cat on
a quest to rescue his friend Hushpad. Williams captures the
nuances of feline behavior to the delight of any reader who has truly
been ''allowed'' to live with a cat. Williams's subtle humor at
times pokes fun at the grand, drawn-out, magical quest novels of J.
R. R. Tolkien and, indeed, of Williams himself.

Only one other novel Williams wrote takes the perspective of a
wild, animal-like creature; *Caliban's Hour* tells the story of
Shakespeare's *The Tempest* covering the time before and after the
presence of Prospero and his daughter on the island of exile.
Caliban seeks out Miranda after several decades to seek revenge for
the loneliness he has suffered and the loss of his one great love—
Miranda. Intending to kill her father, Prospero, he finds him long
since deceased and so turns his vengeance toward Miranda. Before
he kills her, however, he insists on telling her what his life was like
before their coming, how Prospero enticed him to human ways,
how he fell in love with Miranda and was betrayed by them both.
Caliban's story is unique in that it is nearly a monologue yet holds
the attention of the reader with Williams's mesmerizing storytelling
and heightening suspense. Readers not familiar with *The Tempest*
may be drawn to read the play and garner better understanding of it,
since Williams's account fleshes out the missing pieces to the
incredible delight of those familiar with the play.

Williams is most well-known for his ''Memory, Sorrow, and
Thorn'' series taking place in his created realm of Osten Ard. Osten
Ard is a land once ruled by an elf-like race called the Sithi. In *The
Dragonbone Chair,* the undead Sithi ruler, the Storm King, driven
from his realm by humans long ago, plans his revenge as the human
high king lays dying. The Storm King unleashes his dormant evil
power, tearing the realm apart through a terrifying civil war
powered by dark sorcery, ancient hatreds, and immortal combat-
ants. Only a small group, known as the League of the Scroll, holds

knowledge of times past and hope for saving the dying land. Simon,
a young kitchen boy, is also an apprentice to a member of the
League. He learns he has magical powers, both good and evil, and
is chosen to seek the answer for the riddle of the long-lost swords.

The quest continues in *The Stone of Farewell,* with the human
army fleeing in search of a last sanctuary and a place to rally the
alliance of other races against the evil Sithi. The place they seek,
the Stone of Farewell, is shrouded in ancient mystery and sorrow.
The widely-scattered members of the League struggle to fulfill
their missions for the salvation of Osten Ard. The conclusion to the
monumental epic takes place in *To Green Angel Tower,* an impressively long volume which imparts some basic truths on the unfairness of life: revenge is eventually useless, some hurts never heal,
when life knocks us down the only thing left to do is get up again,
and even resisting hatred and revenge is no guarantee for personal
happiness. Young adult readers will especially identify with Simon, around whom the central action revolves. Though chosen as a
seer by the mystical beings seeking to aid the humans, Simon,
knighted by Prince Joshua, remains grounded. He is at times unsure
of himself, though the importance of his role and his ability to
complete his tasks is evident in the mystical beings. He is a superb
warrior yet hates killing, and he understands cosmic truths yet
thinks of himself as unlearned. The multiple plot lines unravel for
clear resolution, as the pieces of the ancient puzzle fit together. The
volume includes a synopsis of the first two volumes in the trilogy as
well as an appendix of names and places.

Williams's next work is a four-volume series titled *Otherland.*
This series switches gears to near-future science fiction involving
cybernetic virtual reality with a twist of sorcery that threatens to
deplete the Earth of its children to populate an alternate reality
known as ''Otherland.'' In the first volume, *City of Golden
Shadow,* Renie Sulaweyo, an African professor, is joined by a host
of other characters in her quest to discover what has made her
younger brother, and a multitude of other children, mysteriously ill.
Among her companions are her Bushman student, a World War I
soldier lost in time who also is seeking his true identity, a
physically frail role-playing gamer, and a mysterious old man,
Mister Sellars, a prisoner of both the government and his body, who
may be at the heart of the madness. As is always the case in
Williams's novels, the characters are well-drawn, credible, and
command the reader's loyalty. The plot is intricate, and promises to
become increasingly involved as future volumes appear. The
complete saga involves a wide range of characters, both human and
otherwise, who struggle to unravel the seemingly infinite connecting strands and side tangents to solve the mystery behind the
Earth's wealthiest and most ruthless power brokers, The Grail
Brotherhood.

Whether Williams is writing fantasy or science fiction, his
wonderfully intricate plots impart a philosophy and understanding
of life which are welcomed and absorbed by readers of all ages.

                                                —Lisa A. Wroble

WILLIAMS-GARCIA, Rita

Nationality: American. **Address:** c/o Viking Penguin, 375 Hudson St., New York, New York 10014, U.S.A.

Fiction

Blue Tights. New York, Dutton, 1988.
Fast Talk on a Slow Track. New York, Dutton, 1991.
Like Sisters on the Homefront. New York, Lodestar Books, 1995.

*   *   *

Focusing her attention on contemporary African American youth, Rita Williams-Garcia informs her fictional teenagers with her own experiences as student, as teacher, as dancer. Her two young adult novels concern black adolescents struggling for a sense of identity against the backdrop of inner city New York. In her 1988 *Blue Tights,* fifteen-year-old Joyce Collins is an outsider, desperate to belong in a school that derides her talent as a dancer and scoffs at her unballetic body. Seventeen-year-old Denzel Watson of the 1991 novel *Fast Talk on a Slow Track* is an insider, an urban success story as the valedictorian of his class on his way to his freshman year at Princeton. Both protagonists, brash and arrogant, hide behind masks. Challenged to ''show their face'' they adopt a bravado that poses real danger and threatens to undermine discovery of their best selves. Their self-absorption and cockiness—once the result of self-loathing; the other, of self-aggrandizing—belie the insecurity that define them. Williams-Garcia explores these two young people learning to trust themselves apart from the crowd and to develop strength of character ''alone and in touch.''

For Williams-Garcia this coming-of-age struggle involves confrontation with both one's family and one's peers. These two novels provide Williams-Garcia the opportunity to create dramatically different family constellations with whom the adolescents contend. Joyce has been reared mainly by her religiously fanatic aunt since her mother is often absent, herself a young teenager when Joyce was born. Williams-Garcia does not shy away from the harsh circumstances that define Joyce and her family. Aunt Em's severe treatment of Joyce stems from a horrific self-induced coat hanger abortion she suffered in her adolescence. Williams-Garcia provides less sensational, daily evidence of the grinding poverty that eats at this family. For them material possessions provide false security and love. Her mother Minnie atones to Joyce with the gift of a real leather coat. Williams-Garcia evinces that their desperation to be somebody too often gets confused with ownership of things. Minnie looks with both envy and disgust at the successful man who fathered Joyce, but now clothes his new wife and two young sons in real fur and leather. Joyce is similarly convinced that clothes serve as talisman to popularity.

No such difficulties surround Denzel's family. A product of an urban middle-class home, Denzel lives with both his parents and a younger sister in security and ease. Yet his home allows Williams-Garcia to present another model of familial interaction. More comfortable in the integrated school he attends and with the white friends he attracts, Denzel clashes with his Afrocentric father for whom black pride is the nucleus of all things. Denzel even rails against his given name Dinizulu.

With both novels, Williams-Garcia dramatizes with painful honesty the collision between class as well as race, not only in the home, but also among the teenagers at school and on the streets. Joyce ''didn't like the so-called better school or her honors classes.

The Jewish boys told jokes that the whole class laughed at, but that she never got at all.'' Once transferred out of those classes, Joyce finds ''someone else to cast are-they-for-real? glances to.'' Her discovery of an African American dance troupe refocuses the alternately angry and hurt Joyce on her talent as a dancer—she discovers brothers and sisters prideful of their culture who rejoice in movement that speaks to that culture. Here her crude and sexually explicit language has less relevance. Although written in the third person, Williams-Garcia creates an intimate voice for Joyce that rings true whether it is in its crassness or in its sweetness.

Denzel's first-person narrative also sizzles with believable black vernacular, especially in his conversations with the street-smart kids with whom he spends a summer selling candy door-to-door. Without flinching, Williams-Garcia places the cocky Denzel, recently back from a disastrous preparatory experience at Princeton, smack up against the illiterate Mello, a confident young salesman of the streets. The clash between their lives and their cultures forms the intense core of this novel and allows Williams-Garcia another arena to explore class differences. Each boy oversteps the code that defines his particular world, and choices and decisions flow from these transgressions.

Being responsible to and for oneself may be obvious rhetoric, but Williams-Garcia provides powerful resonance to this theme through her credible characters who speak in their own idiom with refreshing honesty and occasional humor. Williams-Garcia reminds readers that observing life from the wings may be safe but being onstage defines the real action—and the real character. Concluding her novels with her protagonists on stage (at her school's ballet class demonstrating a movement for the other students and back at Princeton signing the honor statement of an examination with his given name Dinizulu), Williams-Garcia indicates her characters' willingness to move on without guile and defense. Joyce looks in the dance mirror at herself ''as something wonderful opening up before her eyes'' while Denzel insists he has ''thrown down the mask and [is] ready to fly.''

—Susan P. Bloom

———

WILLIS, Charles. *See* **CLARKE, Arthur C(harles).**

———

WILSON, Budge

Nationality: Canadian. **Born:** Marjorie MacGregor Archibald in Halifax, Nova Scotia, 2 May 1927; name legally changed to Budge in 1987. **Education:** Dalhousie University, 1945-49, B.A. 1949; University of Toronto, 1949-51; Dalhousie University, Diploma in Education and Physical Education Certificate, 1952. **Family:** Married to Alan Wilson, 1953; two daughters. **Career:** Teacher, Halifax Ladies College, 1951-52; library assistant and artist, Boys & Girls House, Toronto Public Library, 1953-54; secretary/editor/artist, Institute of Child Study, University of Toronto, 1954-56,

1957-58; teacher, nursery school, Wolfville, Nova Scotia, 1956-57; self-employed photographer, c. 1960-1980; fitness instructor, Peterborough (Ontario) School Board and YWCA, 1968-88. **Awards:** First Prize for Short Fiction, CBC Literary Competition, 1981; First Prize for Short Fiction, Atlantic Writing Competition; City of Dartmouth Book Award, 1991; CLA Young Adult Canadian Book Award, 1991; CAA Marianna Dempster Award, 1992; Ann Connor Brimer Award, 1993. **Address:** 37 Southwest Cove Road, North West Cove, R.R. 1, Hubbards, Nova Scotia B0J 1T0, Canada.

PUBLICATIONS FOR YOUNG ADULTS

Breakdown. Richmond Hill, Ontario, Scholastic, 1988.
Thirteen Never Changes. Richmond Hill, Ontario, Scholastic, 1989.
The Leaving. Toronto, House of Anansi, 1990.
Lorinda's Diary. Toronto, General, 1991.
Oliver's Wars. Toronto, Stoddart, 1992.
Sharla. Toronto, Stoddart, 1997.

PUBLICATIONS FOR CHILDREN

The Best/Worst Christmas Present Ever. Richmond Hill, Ontario, Scholastic, 1984.
Mr. John Bertrand Nijinsky and Charlie. Halifax, Nova Scotia, Nimbus, 1986.
A House Far From Home. Richmond Hill, Ontario, Scholastic, 1986.
Mystery Lights at Blue Harbour. Richmond Hill, Ontario, Scholastic, 1987.
Going Bananas. Richmond Hill, Ontario, Scholastic, 1989.
Madame Belzile and Ramsay Hitherton Hobbs. Halifax, Nova Scotia, Nimbus, 1990.
Cassandra's Driftwood. Lawrencetown Beach, Nova Scotia, Pottersfield, 1994.
Harold and Harold. Lawrencetown Beach, Nova Scotia, Pottersfield, 1995.
Duff the Giant Killer. Halifax, Nova Scotia, Formac, 1997.
The Long Wait. Toronto, Stoddart Kids, 1997.

PUBLICATIONS FOR ADULTS

Cordelia Clark. Toronto, Stoddart, 1994.
The Courtship. Toronto, House of Anansi, 1994.
The Dandelion Garden. New York, Philomel, 1995.
Mothers and Other Strangers: Stories. New York, Harcourt Brace, 1996.

*

Budge Wilson comments:

People who write stories are often asked three questions:
—why do you write?
—where do your ideas come from?
—how do you write?

Here are a few answers.

I write because it's something I love to do. If I didn't love to do it, I'd probably find some other way to spend my time. I write because I always enjoy making something out of nothing: drawing a picture on a blank page; singing a song in a silent room; writing a story in an empty notebook. I also write because it's a way to express some of the things that I normally keep inside me—like fear, or anger, or a lot of noisy excitement. I can put those feelings into my characters instead of keeping them bottled up in my head. Sometimes I write because I can sense a story starting to tell itself inside my head; when that happens, I want to get it out there onto paper.

My ideas come from doing a lot of remembering and thinking and watching and listening. I remember my own past, and can pick little bits and pieces out of it and string them together into a new person and a new story. I think a lot about emotions (joy, jealousy, disappointment, anxiety) and how they affect people and their relationships. I watch people a lot—in restaurants, airports, and in the many schools I visit. I wonder about those things I see; and if you wonder hard enough, the wonderings can turn into a story. I also listen to people arguing, fooling around, expressing their grief, talking about what frightens them. There are stories in all of those experiences. And sometimes ideas just seem to fall out of the sky. I don't know where they come from.

Everyone writes differently, so all I can do is tell you how I do it. For a short story, I start with an idea or a character or sometimes a very sketchy plot. Then, trying not to think too hard, I start writing—very quickly. Believe it or not, the story then just simply begins to happen. If I'm writing a novel, I make a very rough plan (with maybe two sentences for each chapter). Then I treat every chapter like a short story—writing very quickly, and letting the story push me around. This is the swift part.

Later on, comes the slow part. I go through the story or book very carefully, line by line, word by word, smoothing out the rough spots, correcting my terrible spelling, working on the dialogue so that it sounds like real people speaking, making sure that I don't use one word six times in one paragraph. I like doing the quick first draft, but I also love doing the fine-tuning. But the process of one is very different from the way I do the other.

Anyone reading this book—no matter how young or old—can do all of these things I've mentioned. Everyone has stories to tell. Try it!

*   *   *

Although Budge Wilson was in her fifties when she began her writing career, she has been most prolific since and has written everything from picture storybooks to adult short story collections. Her novels for adolescents, which often incorporate diary entries, have been solidly rooted in the realities of Nova Scotia family life and, with one exception, have utilized female central characters.

Breakdown deals with a subject rarely addressed in fiction for juveniles, the emotional health of parents. Katie Collicut, 13, and her three younger brothers experience significant changes to family routine and cohesion when their father, Frank, has a nervous breakdown. With Frank hospitalized, Ethel, their mother, must go to work full time in order to support the family, a situation which threatens to change the children's plans.

Thirteen Never Changes is Wilson's fourth book about the Dauphinee family of Blue Harbour, Nova Scotia, the three previous titles being more suitable for a preteen audience. Although distance had kept Lorinda Dauphinee, 13, from getting to know her grandmother, Laura, Lorinda is still saddened when she learns about her paternal grandmother's death. Lorinda, however, is given a second chance to get to know this woman when she is given her grandmother's 21 diaries, written beginning in 1940 when Laura was 13 and living in Halifax. Although Laura writes about the "guest children" sent to Canada to escape the bombing in Great Britain and other aspects of the war, Lorinda comes to see that, although the world has changed in many ways since her grandmother's teen years, Laura's thoughts and emotions at 13 are very much like her own.

Lorinda's Diary, the fifth Dauphinee title, is told in diary form by Lorinda, now 14. Though the diary's entries span a brief period, three occurrences are central and to some degree intertwined. Lorinda's widower grandfather comes from Vancouver to live with the Blue Harbour family for six months. His constant whining and his complaining about his health get on everyone's nerves, but Lorinda eventually figures out why he behaves in this egocentric way. At a personal level, Lorinda's basketball team wins the provincial championship and is invited to a Winnipeg, Manitoba, tournament. And at an even more personal level, Lorinda realizes that her relationships with boys, one of whom has been her friend since playpen days, are changing in confusingly romantic ways.

Oliver's Wars finds Oliver Kovak, 12, outwardly calm and confident but inwardly in turmoil because his army father has to go to serve in the Persian Gulf War. Additionally, the remaining Kovak family members have moved from Moose Jaw, Saskatchewan, to stay with Oliver's maternal grandparents in Halifax. Besides the normal school adjustment problems, Oliver is a klutz in sports and believes that he is always being singled out by the physical education teacher. Oliver's situation is made worse by his having a twin brother, Jerry, to whom he is always being unfavourably compared, and a grandfather who always seems angry.

In *Sharla,* a job loss for the father of 15-year-old Sharla Dunfield has led to the family's move to the isolated community of Churchill in Northern Manitoba. There, an angry, resentful Sharla complains about everything, but especially her teachers and the wealthy southern tourists who come to visit the Polar Bear Capital of the world. She also develops a crush on Jake, a handsome "older man" and professional photographer from New York City who hires her to assist him with his photography shoots. In part because her parents are coping with their own financial problems, Sharla elects not to tell them about her job, but she also senses that what she is doing is somehow wrong. The climax occurs when Jake, in an attempt to lure a polar bear close enough for a photographic shoot by using a meat bait, succeeds too well, and the bear attacks their truck, an action which causes a Bear Patrol Officer to have to shoot it. A remorseful Sharla is relieved to learn later that the bear was just tranquilized, a reaction which confirms her emerging love for the North.

The Leaving, a collection of 11 short stories and the 1991 winner of the Canadian Young Adult Book of the Year, is a crossover book that would be equally at home in the adult section of a library or bookstore. Some of Wilson's other adult-labelled collections, such as *Cordelia Clark, The Courtship, The Dandelion Garden,* and *Mothers and Other Strangers: Stories,* have been marketed for young adults as well. *The Leaving*'s stories, all set in Nova Scotia, are united by a central theme—coming of age—which is explored through the experiences of adolescents or adults recalling those days.

—Dave Jenkinson

WINDLING, Terri

Has also written as Bellamy Bach. **Nationality:** American. **Born:** Fort Dix, New Jersey, 1958. **Career:** Editor, Ace Books, 1979-86; consulting editor, Tor Books, from 1986; author of "Folkroots" and "Gallery" columns, *Realms of Fantasy* magazine, from 1995; artist and author. **Awards:** World Fantasy Award winner (five times); Mythopoeic Society Award, Best Novel of the Year, 1997, for *The Wood Wife.* **Website:** The Endicott Studio Homepage, http://www.endicott.studio.com/index.html.

PUBLICATIONS FOR YOUNG ADULTS

Editor

With Mark Alan Arnold, *The Elsewhere Trilogy.* New York, Ace, 1982-84.
Faery. New York, Ace, 1984.
The Fairy Tale Series:
    The Sun, the Moon, and the Stars by Steven Brust. New York, Ace, 1986.
    Jack the Giant Killer by Charles de Lint. Ace, 1987.
    The Nightingale by Kara Dalkey. Ace, 1988.
    Snow White and Rose Red by Patricia Wrede. New York, Tor, 1989.
    Tam Lin by Pamela Dean. Tor, 1991.
    Briar Rose by Jane Yolen. Tor, 1992.
With Mark Alan Arnold, *The Borderland Series:*
    Borderland. New York, NAL, 1986.
    Bordertown. NAL, 1986.
    Life on the Border. Tor, 1991.
    Elsewhere by Will Shetterly. New York, Harcourt Brace, 1992.
    Nevernever by Will Shetterly. Harcourt, 1993.
    Finder by Emma Bull. Tor, 1994.
    With Delia Sherman, *The Essential Bordertown: A Traveler's Guide to the Edge of Faery.* Tor, 1998.
    Underhill. Tor, forthcoming.
With Ellen Datlow, *The Year's Best Fantasy and Horror* (annual anthology). New York, St. Martin's, from 1988.
With Ellen Datlow, *Snow White, Blood Red Series:*
    Snow White, Blood Red. New York, Avon, 1993.
    Black Thorn, White Rose. Avon, 1994.
    Ruby Slippers, Golden Tears. Avon, 1995.
    Black Swan, White Raven. Avon, 1997.
    Silver Birch, Blood Moon. Avon, 1998.
    Black Heart, Ivory Bones. Avon, forthcoming.
Brian Froud's Faerielands Series:
    The Wild Wood by Charles de Lint. New York, Bantam, 1994.
    Something Rich and Strange by Patricia McKillip. Bantam, 1994.

The Armless Maiden and Other Tales for Childhood's Survivors.
    Tor, 1995.
The Faces of Fantasy, photographs by Patti Perrit. Tor, 1996.
Good Faeries/Bad Faeries: The Art of Brian Froud. New York,
    Simon & Schuster, 1998.

Fiction

"Gray" (as Bellamy Bach) in *Borderland.* NAL, 1986.
"Exile" (as Bellamy Bach) in *Bordertown.* NAL, 1986.
With Ellen Kushner, "Mockery" (as Bellamy Bach) in *Bordertown.*
    NAL, 1986.
Changeling. New York, Random House, 1995.
The Wood Wife. Tor, 1996.
"The Color of Angels" in *The Horns of Elfland,* edited by Ellen
    Kushner, Donald G. Keller, and Delia Sherman. New York,
    Roc, 1997.
The Moon Wife. Tor, 1998.
With Wendy Froud, *A Day in the Life of a Faery.* Simon &
    Schuster, 1999.
With Iain McCraig, *The Sorcerer's Apprentice.* California, Ten
    Speed Press, forthcoming.

*

Terri Windling comments:

Like Joseph Campbell, David Abram, Lewis Hyde, and other
scholars of myth and folklore, I believe the oldest tales of humankind still have much to tell us about the world today—and so all of
my work (editing, writing, and painting) is based in some way on
the traditional, magical stories of our ancestors: the ones who came
from Europe and the ones Native to this American soil.

The other theme running through much of my work is a concern
for the plight of children in crisis situations, reflecting my own
experiences as a homeless teenager in the 1970s. The "Borderland" series for Young Adult readers, about runaway children in a
magical urban setting, grew out of these experiences—and a firm
belief that friendship, community and creativity are a powerful
kind of "magic," and can save your life.

In 1995, I edited The Armless Maiden, an anthology using old
fairy tale themes to tell new stories (for adults and older teens)
exploring the darker sides of childhood's passage. Just as the
symbolic figures in nightly dreams reflect the realities of waking
life, the symbols to be found in fairy tales and myths (which reflect
the collective dreams of entire cultures) provide useful metaphors
for grappling with the hard truths of our existence. These old tales
have much to say about heroism; about how one finds the courage
to fight and prevail against adversity. They are tales of children
abandoned in the woods; of daughters handed poisoned apples or
pressured to enter their fathers' beds; of sons thrown to the wolves,
sold to the devil or left by the roadside.

The old tales, which were often dark and brutal, were not
considered mere children's stories at all—not until our own
century, when the pendulum of adult literary fashion swung
sharply toward strict realism, and oral tales (associated with the
lower classes, and with women) were banished to the nursery. At
that point the tales (as set down in print by Victorian publishers)
were cleaned up, simplified, and watered down for children's ears,

so that many of the fairy tales we know today are but pale copies of
the older versions. It is significant to me that at a time when we
have dismissed the role these ancient stories might have in our
modern lives, we are also experiencing cultural confusion about the
role of the "hero". Actors and superstars of commercial sports are
whom we revere—not gifted teachers or tireless social activists.
Wealth and celebrity are our measures of stature; goodness, integrity, commitment are not. (Just listen to how old-fashioned those
three words sound today.)

Yet these later virtues are the qualities to be found in the heroes
of old fairy tales. They were not about passive Cinderellas and
Beauties and Little Mermaids who wait for a square-jawed prince
to save the day. In the older versions of fairy tales, many of the most
powerful stories tell variations on one archetypal theme: a young
woman or man beset by grave difficulties must set off through the
Dark Woods alone, armed only with quick wits, clear sight,
persistence, courage, and compassion. It is by these virtues that we
identify the heroes; it is with these tools that they make their way
through the woods and emerge on the other side. Without these
tools, no magic can save them. They are at the mercy of the wolf
and the wicked witch.

Recently, I have been distressed to hear that stories addressing
the subject of child abuse (or other difficult childhood subjects,
including death, divorce, physical and mental illness) have been
dismissed by some critics with the label "victim's art". "We're
bored with victims," the current cant goes; "we don't want to hear
about their problems anymore." I believe we've got the language
all wrong here. These aren't victims we're talking about, but
heroes. Victims (like the helpless modern Disney version of
Cinderella) are passive, powerless creatures. Heroes (like the
fiesty, clever, angry girl in the older Cinderella tales) are active,
purposeful agents of change—for themselves and the world
around them. To diminish such stories with the label "victim's
art" is to diminish the power of creation itself—our extraordinary
ability to turn light into darkness, pain into widsom, straw into
gold. Many of us have made the hero's journey through the Dark
Wood of a troubled past, and on to the brighter lands beyond. We
need never be ashamed of having travelled those roads, or of
drawing upon those transformative life experiences when it comes
time to make art—no matter what is labelled unfashionable.
Fashions change. And art remains.

We must also remember that the hero's journey is one that is
never really done. For all of us who have emerged from that dark
forest, there are times when we must turn around and head back
into the trees again—only now we've a different role to play. This
time we must be the Good Witch, the Fairy Godmother, or the
Animal Guide: the one who waits by the side of the road, ready to
light the way for those young heroes who struggle on behind us.

*   *   *

Terri Windling's main impact upon contemporary literature has
been in her creative vision as editor of various fantasy anthologies
and series. From her beginnings as a young associate editor with
Ace Books, Windling developed the careers of many of the best-
selling fantasy authors on the market today. In doing so, she helped
shape the shift in fantasy fiction away from blood-and-thunder
adventure books and quest stories and toward thoughtful, literary
works steeped in folklore and mythology. Thus she has been a

tremendous behind-the-scenes force in the publishing trends of the 1980s and 1990s towards urban fantasy, magical realism, and fairy-tale retellings. In conjunction with developing budding new writers with new visions, Windling also has had a hand in developing new artistic talent for fantasy fiction, artists who hearken back to the style of painting developed by the Victorian Pre-Raphaelites. She is responsible for furthering the careers of Tom Canty, Brian Froud, and other artists whose works are now seen on the covers of fantasy publications on a regular basis.

As an editor for Ace, she created the Magic Quest series of books for children, including works by such popular authors as Allison Uttley, Tanith Lee, Elizabeth Marie Pope, and Peter Dickinson. Also while at Ace, Windling began her ground-breaking Fairy Tale Series, novels for adults and young adults that purposely rework traditional fairy tales into new stories and forms. Several of the top-notch fantasy writers of today have made contributions to this series; the most recent, Jane Yolen's *Briar Rose,* won the 1992 Nebula Award. The cover art for each of the books in this series is designed by fantasy artist Tom Canty. Windling's first anthology of short stories that recast fairy tales into new forms was *Faery,* published in 1984. Her Elsewhere Trilogy, begun in 1982 with co-editor Mark Alan Arnold, however, was her first editorial venture into crossing genre boundaries, with its mix of mainstream and genre stories by both known and unknown writers for adults. This series won Windling her first of five World Fantasy Awards.

In 1986 Windling moved to Tor Books, where she still works as a Consulting Editor as well as an author in her own right. While at Tor, Windling helped create the cult classic Borderland series, a collection of both stories and novels aimed at the young adult audience, with whom the mix of rock-and-roll music and funky storylines was an immediate success. The Borderland books are set in a mythical town on the border between Fairyland and the ordinary world. A magical barrier between the two worlds (the "border" of the series' title) prevents interaction between the Elves and humans except at certain times.

One of Windling's most personal editorial works was *The Armless Maiden,* a collection of stories and poems for an adult audience about child abuse. This collection grew out of a successful exhibit in Boston of original art by Windling which was also based on the theme of child abuse. Each of the stories or poems in the anthology retells a classic fairy tale with this theme in mind. Windling wrote the central essay that ties the anthology together, "Surviving Childhood," revealing her own history of growing up in an abusive family and providing a powerful testimonial to survivors of childhood's darker side. Windling is an on-going advocate of children's rights; proceeds from this collection go to organizations that work with children in crisis, and Windling's website has a link that advocates helping such organizations.

Windling's first published work of her own creation was a novella for middle readers, *Changeling,* in which twelve-year-old Charlie is convinced that his sister Polly's soul has been taken by evil fairies and replaced by that of a mountain fairy. With an obvious nod to traditional folktales, Charlie must fiddle all night for the fairies in order to free his sister and himself from the grip of the fairy folk.

The Wood Wife is an adult novel in the magical realism tradition. Set in the Sonoran desert on the edge of Tucson, Arizona (Windling's real-life part-time home), the novel tells the story of Maggie Black, a poet who finds herself face-to-face with the spirits who inhabit the Rincon Mountains. Maggie has come to the Rincons to find the reason for the mysterious death of her mentor. In doing so, she enlists the aid of her neighbors and also comes to a deeper understanding of her own creative instincts. *The Wood Wife* is reminiscent of the popular Carlos Casteneda books, which are also set in the Sonoran desert, in that it draws on such various folkloric themes as animism, archetypes, and the interactions between the spirit world and the ordinary world. The sense of place, and the impact the desert has on those who choose to live in its harsh environment, is particularly well done in this novel.

As a painter, Windling has had several successful exhibitions in various galleries across the United States and Europe, but perhaps her most influential contribution to this artistic field was again as a stimulant for others' artistic energies, when she established Endicott Studio in Boston in 1987. The studio's purpose is to serve as a creative center for modern mythic art, both visual and literary. Endicott Studio has since been moved to the dual locations of Devon, England, and Tucson, Arizona, where it continues to influence various visual and literary artists whose works are grounded in mythology and folklore.

—Martha P. Hixon

WINDSOR, Patricia (Frances)

Pseudonyms: Colin Daniel, Katonah Summertree. **Nationality:** American. **Born:** New York City, 21 September 1938. **Education:** Bennington College, and Westchester Community College; New York University, associate's degree. **Family:** Married 1) Laurence Charles Windsor, Jr., in 1959 (divorced 1978), one daughter and one son; 2) Stephen E. Altman in 1986 (divorced 1988). **Career:** Writer. Vice-president, Windsor-Morehead Associates, New York, 1960-63; teacher of creative writing, Westchester, New York, 1975-78; member of faculty, Institute of Children's Literature, Redding Ridge, Connecticut, 1976-96; editor-in-chief, *Easterner,* American Telephone and Telegraph, Washington, D.C., 1979-81; instructor, University of Maryland Writers Institute, 1981-83, and OPEN University, Washington, D.C.; instructor, Long Ridge Writers Group, since 1995, and Armstrong Atlantic State University, since 1996. Member, Citizens' Committee on Employment, Chicago, 1963-64; assistant director of central inquiries, 1972-73, counselor, 1974-75, Family Planning Associations, London, England; correspondent, National Council of Social Service, London, since 1974; active in YWCA and North Westchester Association for Retarded Children; columnist, *The Blood Review,* and (as Katonah Summertree) contributing editor, *Savannah Parent* and *Coastal Senior.* **Awards:** *Chicago Tribune Book World* Honor Book award, 1973, Best Books for Young Adults award, American Library Association, 1973, Austrian State award for Books for Children and Youth, 1981, all for *The Summer Before*; *Diving for Roses* was named a notable book of 1976 by the *New York Times*; Edgar Allan Poe award, Mystery Writers of America, 1985, for *The Sandman's Eyes*; Edgar Allan Poe award nomination, 1991, for *The Christmas Killer*; YALSA Quick Pick, 1996, for *The Blooding.* **Agent:** Amy Berkower, Writers House, Incorporated, 21 West 26th Street, New York, New York 10010, U.S.A.

PUBLICATIONS FOR YOUNG ADULTS

Novels

The Summer Before. New York, Harper, 1973.
Something's Waiting for You, Baker D. New York, Harper, 1974.
Home Is Where Your Feet Are Standing. New York, Harper, 1975.
Diving for Roses. New York, Harper, 1976.
Mad Martin. New York, Harper, 1976.
Killing Time. New York, Harper, 1980.
The Sandman's Eyes. New York, Delacorte, 1985.
How a Weirdo and a Ghost Can Change Your Entire Life, illustrated by Jacqueline Rogers. New York, Delacorte, 1986.
The Hero. New York, Delacorte, 1988.
Just Like the Movies. London, Macmillan, 1990.
The Christmas Killer. New York, Scholastic, 1991.
Two Weirdos and a Ghost. New York, Dell, 1991.
Very Weird and Moogly Christmas. New York, Dell, 1991.
The Blooding. New York, Scholastic, 1996.
The House of Death. London, Macmillan, 1996.

Novels as Colin Daniel

Demon Tree. New York, Dell, 1983.

Short Stories

Old Coat's Cat. Macmillan, 1974.
The Girl with the Click Click Eyes. London, Heinemann, 1977.
"Toad in the Hole," in *On the Edge.* London, Macmillan, 1990.
"Teeth," in *Short Circuits.* New York, Delacorte, 1991.
"A Little Taste of Death," in *Thirteen.* New York, Scholastic, 1992.
"Moonkill," in *Night Terrors.* New York, Simon & Schuster, 1995.

Also contributor of short stories to *Scholastic Scope, Self,* and *Seventeen.*

*   *   *

Patricia Windsor was born in The Bronx, started college in Vermont, has worked in Maryland, and has lived in New Jersey and Georgia. But the time she spent as a counselor at a social services agency in England, a job which brought her into direct contact with troubled youngsters, may have been the seminal influence behind her successful string of novels, books which deal centrally with problems confronted by today's adolescents. Her discovery of Paul Zindel's *My Darling, My Hamburger* provided Windsor with a useful model: Zindel's novel convinced her that literature for young adults need not be the treacly, escapist fare of her own youth, but could deal authentically with the dilemmas of real life. Windsor's frequently dark, brooding novels reflect her early appreciation for the science fiction and fantasy writings of Isaac Asimov and Theodore Sturgeon. Nonetheless, she consistently avoids mere escapism, seeking rather to portray the real struggles and conflicts of young protagonists who, for a variety of reasons, find themselves simultaneously isolated from and in bitter conflict with the society around them.

The Summer Before (1973), her first and most widely read novel, details young Alexandra Appleton's emotional breakdown following the death of her eccentric, life-loving boyfriend Bradley—a death for which she partially blames herself. Typical of Windsor's protagonists, Alexandra feels isolated—in this case, from her parents, who fail to understand both the nature of her attachment to Bradley and the depth of her wrenching grief following his death. Ultimately, the passage of time, the intervention of a sympathetic psychiatrist, and the promise of new personal attachments combine to nudge Alexandra in the direction of health, self-forgiveness, and the possibility of happiness.

Diving for Roses (1976) describes a similar odyssey toward personal wholeness, although Jean, that novel's young narrator, faces distinctly different challenges: the awakening of her own sexuality, a broken home, an out-of-wedlock pregnancy, and an alcoholic mother. In Jean's instance, her sense of isolation is quite justified: the small community where she lives is well aware of her mother's sickness, and the townspeople routinely shun both mother and daughter, who are caught up in an unhealthy cycle of mutual dependency. Jean has long assumed that her mother is merely "crazy," mentally deranged, but she ultimately learns the true nature of her problem from young Doctor Curtin, a man with whom the girl entertains a brief flirtation. Jean confronts her mother, who sets out on the road toward health by joining Alcoholics Anonymous. Having become comfortable with the role of caretaker, however, Jean is puzzled by the fact that she cannot wholeheartedly celebrate her mother's recovery. But when Jean becomes pregnant by her predatory boyfriend, she herself seeks help from peers at ALANON (Alcoholics Anonymous Family Groups). Finally, an infinitely more self-sufficient Jean is able to join her mother in severing the cords of shared victimization which had bound them together for so long.

In *The Hero* (1988), the specific problem faced by teenager Dale O. Fither is, ironically, a gift: he is a psychic and can foresee threats to the lives of children around him. His courageous interventions on behalf of these children win Dale (or, rather, his alter ego "Joe Dean") the reputation of a hero—an isolating, differentiating mantle which Dale desperately wants to cast off. Dale's distant, mercenary father, however, sees in Dale's abilities the potential for family fame and fortune. Soon Dale is an unwilling resident of a rural Virginia institute presided over by the sinister Dr. Airman, who, for twisted reasons of his own, has surrounded himself with a cadre of psychic youngsters. Even as he seeks to uncover the true nature of Airman's evil designs, Dale struggles to come to terms with the burdensome aspects of his own makeup which set him apart from others.

The Hero reflects many characteristics of the traditional detective story, and indeed Windsor has embraced the mystery genre with notable success. For example, in *The Sandman's Eyes* (1985), eighteen-year-old Mike Thorn returns to his small hometown after two years in a reformatory, determined to clear his name from the suspicion that he was involved in the murder of a woman whose body he had discovered. Toward that end, he must track down the real killer, but his quest leads him along unexpected paths—lost and found parents, old and new loves. And in one of Windsor's later novels, *The Christmas Killer* (1991), Rose Potter is visited by the ghost of a murdered girl who shows her the resting places of other victims of a maniacal serial killer. Rose's twin brother is supportive and sympathetic, and her mother is able to provide the answer as to why Rose has been singled out for these macabre visitations. But no one can spare Rose from her own ultimate confrontation with the crazed murderer, that ''other'' with whom she shares a terrifying psychic bond.

Windsor's novels for young adults have been critically well-received. For example, *The Summer Before* was cited in 1973 as a Best Book for Young Adults by the American Library Association, and, in 1981, its German translation was honored with the Austrian State Award for Books for Youth; similarly, *The Sandman's Eyes* won the Edgar Allan Poe Award from the Mystery Writers of America in 1986 for the best juvenile mystery. And her dozen books, especially *The Summer Before,* have enjoyed the allegiance of a host of young readers, who may well identify with Windsor's tortured protagonists.

It is true that these same protagonists, especially to an adult audience, might often seem overly precocious, self-pitying, rebellious, and resolutely solipsistic. Indeed, Windsor emerges as an implicit apologist for her self-absorbed protagonists, sharing their mistrust of and reaction against such authority figures as parents, mental health professionals, the police, and organized religion. For example, in Windsor's novels (*The Christmas Killer* is a notable exception), parents are repeatedly portrayed as weak, distant, deceptive, or ineffective, and her characters frequently invent their own religious systems, having found only aridity in the established church.

Still, these twin strains of concern with the self and rebellion against authority have clearly struck resonant chords among Windsor's young readership. And *any* reader—adult or juvenile—can find much to admire in Windsor's taut, exciting plots and in the lyrical beauty of her prose style.

—William Ryland Drennan

WINFIELD, Julia. *See* **ARMSTRONG, Jennifer.**

WOJCIECHOWSKA, Maia (Teresa)

Also writes as Maia Rodman. **Nationality:** American. **Born:** Warsaw, Poland, 7 August 1927; immigrated to the United States, 1942; became citizen, 1950. **Education:** Sacred Heart Academy, Los Angeles; Immaculate Heart College, Hollywood, 1945-46. **Family:** Married 1) Selden Rodman in 1950 (divorced 1957), two daughters; 2) Richard Larkin in 1972 (divorced 1981). **Career:** Poet, translator, and writer of children's fiction. Translator for Radio Free Europe, 1949-51; assistant editor, *Retail Wholesale and Department Store Union Record,* New York City, 1953-55; copy girl, *Newsweek,* New York City, 1956; assistant editor, *RWDSU Record* (labor newspaper), New York City, 1957; assistant editor, *American Hairdresser* (trade publication), New York City, 1958-60; agent and editor, Kurt Hellmer, New York City, 1960-61; independent literary agent, 1960-61; publicity manager, Hawthorn Books, Inc., New York City, 1961-65. Professional tennis player and instructor, 1949—. Founder and president of

Maia Productions, Inc., Independent Books, 1975—, and ENOUGH!!!, 1986—; Councilwoman, Township of Bergen, New Jersey, 1992-95. **Awards:** *New York Herald Tribune* Children's Spring Book Festival Awards honor book, 1964, and John Newbery Medal, 1965, both for *Shadow of a Bull;* awarded Deutscher Jugendbuchpries, 1968; named to New Jersey Literary Hall of Fame, 1985. **Agent:** George M. Nicholson, Sterling Lord, 65 Bleeker St., New York, New York 10012, U.S.A. **Address:** 659 Valley Road, Oakland, New Jersey 07436, U.S.A.

PUBLICATIONS FOR YOUNG ADULTS (as Maia Wojciechowska in the United States and as Maia Rodman in the United Kingdom)

Fiction

Shadow of a Bull, illustrated by Alvin Smith. New York, Atheneum, and London, Hamish Hamilton, 1964.
A Kingdom in a Horse. New York, Harper, 1966.
The Hollywood Kid. New York, Harper, 1967.
A Single Light. New York, Harper, 1968.
Tuned Out. New York, Harper, 1968; London, Macmillan, 1976.
Hey, What's Wrong with This One?, illustrated by Joan Sandin. New York, Harper, 1969.
Don't Play Dead Before You Have To. New York, Harper, 1970.
The Rotten Years. New York, Doubleday, 1971.
The Life and Death of a Brave Bull, illustrated by John Groth. New York, Harcourt, 1972.
Through the Broken Mirror with Alice. New York, Harcourt, 1972.
How God Got Christian into Trouble. Philadelphia, Westminster/ John Knox, 1984.
Dreams of [Golf, Soccer, the Superbowl]. Pebble Beach, California, Pebble Beach Press Ltd., n.d.

Other

Odyssey of Courage: The Adventure of Alvar Nunez Cabeza de Vaca, illustrated by Alvin Smith. New York, Atheneum, 1965; London, Burns Oates, 1967.
Till the Break of Day: Memories, 1939-1942 (autobiographical). New York, Harcourt, 1973.
Winter Tales from Poland, illustrated by Laszlo Kubinyi. New York, Doubleday, 1973.

PUBLICATIONS FOR CHILDREN

Fiction

Market Day for Ti Andre, illustrated by Wilson Bigaud. New York, Viking, 1952.

PUBLICATIONS FOR ADULTS

Fiction

The People in His Life. New York, Stein and Day, 1980.

Play

All at Sea, adaptation of a work by Slawomir Mrozek, produced in New York, 1968.

Other

The Loved Look: International Hairstyling Guide. New York, American Hairdresser, 1960.

Translator, *The Bridge to the Other Side,* by Monika Kotowska. New York, Doubleday, 1970.

*

Media Adaptations: *Tuned Out* was adapted for film and released as *Stoned: An Anti-Drug Film* by Learning Corp. of America, 1981; *A Single Light* was adapted for film and released by Learning Corp. of America, 1986; the movie rights to *The People in His Life* and *Shadow of a Bull* have been optioned.

Biography: Entry in *Third Book of Junior Authors,* New York, H.W. Wilson, 1972; entry in *More Books by More People* edited by Lee Bennet Hopkins, Citation, 1974; essay in *Something about the Author Autobiography Series,* Volume 1, Detroit, Gale, 1986.

Manuscript Collections: Kerlan Collection, University of Minnesota; De Grummond Collection, University of Mississippi.

Critical Studies: Entry in *Children's Literature Review,* Volume 1, Detroit, Gale, 1976; *Contemporary Literary Criticism,* Volume 26, Detroit, Gale, 1983.

Maia Wojciechowska comments:

It's sort of funny because I always thought that the whole business of living is to make sure that, as you get older, you get wiser. In my case I have, slowly but surely, come to the conclusion that since the beginning, when God created the universe, there had been an enemy present among His people. Every age sees the enemy differently. Like the flavor of the month, enemies come and go while we keep forgetting that from the beginning of time, and until the ends of time, we've had but one: sin. The only thing that conquers sin is *truth.*

The funny thing is that ever since I pinpointed the enemy and the enemy's foe, it's been hard for me to find an agent or a publisher. Maybe they think I am crazy? Do you? Let me know if you don't (If you do, don't bother). Because I've written some books for you, and will be writing one, *The Golden Calf Gang,* about how it was for a couple of kids during the time of Christ. But the adults are not interested in what I write nowadays. And while they're not, I can't reach you.

*   *   *

Well-known as poet, translator, and author of young people's fiction, Maia Wojciechowska has been popular since the early 1960s, mainly because she portrays her protagonists struggling to assert themselves, something that all young people long to accomplish.

Winner of the Newbery Medal in 1965 for *Shadow of a Bull,* Wojciechowska makes it apparent that she once fought a bull. With the knowledge she gleaned from studying bullfighting in the arena and from books, she makes the story of Manolo Olivar an exciting, danger-filled drama. Manolo is expected by the whole town of Arcangel in Spain to become a famous, fearless bullfighter like his father who died as he killed the bull in his greatest of all bull fights. But, as in most of Wojciechowska's novels, the protagonist needs to become his own true self and refuses to become what others wish him to be. In this case, Manolo wishes to be a doctor and not a bullfighter. But he also knows he must not disgrace his family and his father's name. The reader cannot help feeling the agonies, the loneliness, the frustrations of Manolo as he gathers his courage to face not only his first bull, but also to admit to himself and to the city of Arcangel that he wants to help and heal instead of maiming and killing.

Wojciechowska eloquently writes of individuals struggling to conquer fear, to belong, and to acquire knowledge of themselves. She makes the reader feel like he or she is part of the story and inside the main character, no matter what the setting. Her settings are vivid, whether in Spain or in New York's East Village. The characters are realistic, and her dialogue generally rings true.

A story containing a variety of lonely, lost people who are brought together by a miraculous discovery, *A Single Light* portrays a deaf-and-dumb girl in Spain who grows up with no one to love and no one loving her. Her mother died when she was just a baby and her father rejects her because he feels she is punishment for his sins. The girl is eventually taken in by a priest, and it is at his church that the girl discovers a beautiful, white marble statue of the Christ Child hidden behind the altar. The girl is happy because she has found something to love, until a Renaissance art expert from America, so obsessed with finding the lost statue that he has no time for love or friendship in his life, happens upon the little village and discovers the lost statue. Everything is changed in the village. Greed becomes the overwhelming conqueror of all except the girl. The story changes from sadness to happiness as Wojciechowska cleverly weaves this simple tale of love and understanding around a poor, unfortunate girl with no name. It is a moving story of regeneration, one of longing and hope for the future, of love and understanding, themes easily recognized and remembered by readers.

Drugs will always be a social issue that confronts young people. *Tuned Out* takes place during the sixties, when LSD made its ruinous entrance into so many young lives. The story portrays sixteen-year-old Jim looking forward to his older brother Kevin coming home from college. Jim's happiness is short-lived, because he discovers that Kevin is not only smoking marijuana, but is using LSD as well. This is a typical "bad-trip from drugs" story, including laid-back hippies and the "hey, man, cool" talk, but the message is still important today. Wojciechowska tells the story so vividly and realistically, the reader experiences the pain and frustration that each of the boys feels as they learn the consequences of using drugs. One feels the anguished misery and glimpses the road leading to nowhere when drugs are involved in one's life. Even though the story takes place in the sixties, it will never be outdated so long as the drug scene never changes, and death waits around the corner for the users. Wojciechowska clearly portrays her knowledge of human nature, the weaknesses and frustrations, the doubts and needs, giving young adults something to think about as they face temptations.

The Hollywood Kid is about another troubled young person. Bryan, who has a glamorous mother, a stepfather who is a director, and a father he scarcely knows who is a teacher and a poet, attends a school in the East, out of the way of his movie actress mother. He loses his stepfather to death as the book begins, and throughout the novel he struggles with anxieties and confusion, unhappy in the world of movie stars and famous celebrities. Through the need and search for love, Wojciechowska once again conveys to young adults that even though adults are what they are and may sometimes lean on their own children for support, the realities of life must be faced and one can go on, learning from the shortcomings of others.

Everyone longs for a better world and a happier environment, and everyone has problems, especially preteens and teenagers, who not only have to deal with changing bodies and feelings but face the overwhelming prospect of soon becoming responsible adults. Wojciechowska effectively articulates the doubts and fears, the awkwardness and frustrations, the struggles and temptations of her characters. Sometimes her monologues tend to drag a little and the pace slows somewhat, but the appeal of her books for teenagers remains strong as they deal with the universal themes of self-realization and the need for love.

—Carol Doxey

WOLFF, Virginia Euwer

Nationality: American. **Born:** Portland, Oregon, 25 August 1937. **Education:** Smith College, Northampton, Massachusetts, A.B. 1959; Long Island University, New York, 1974-75; Warren Wilson College, Swannanoa, North Carolina. **Family:** Married Art Wolff in 1959 (divorced, 1976); one son and one daughter. **Career:** English teacher at junior high school in the Bronx, 1959-60; elementary teacher at the Micquon School, Philadelphia, 1968-72; the Fiedel School, Glen Cove, New York, 1972-75; English teacher at Hood River Valley High School, Oregon, 1976-1986; Mt. Hood Academy, Government Camp, Oregon, from 1986. Violinist, Mid-Columbia Sinfonietta, Hood River, Oregon, from 1976; Oregon Sinfonietta, Portland, from 1988; Quartet con brio, Portland, Oregon, from 1989; Parnassius Quartet, Portland, Oregon, from 1996. **Awards:** International Reading Association Children's Book Award, 1989; PEN-West Book Award, 1989; Best Books for Young Adults list, 1992 and 1994; Children's Book Award from Child Study Children's Book Committee at Bank Street College, 1993; Oregon Book Award, 1994; Golden Kite Award, 1994. **Agent:** Marilyn E. Marlow, Curtis Brown, Ltd., 10 Astor Place, New York, New York 10003-6935, U.S.A.

PUBLICATIONS FOR YOUNG ADULTS

Probably Still Nick Swansen. New York, Holt, 1988.
The Mozart Season. New York, Holt, 1991.
Make Lemonade. New York, Holt, 1993.

PUBLICATIONS FOR ADULTS

Rated PG. New York, St. Martin's, 1980.

*

Biography: Essay in *Speaking for Ourselves, Too,* compiled and edited by Donald R. Gallo, Urbana, Illinois, National Council of Teachers of English, 1993, 228-229; ''The Booklist Interview: Virginia Euwer Wolff'' by Stephanie Zvirin, *Booklist,* (Chicago), Vol. 90, No. 13, 1994, 1250-1251.

*   *   *

Virginia Euwer Wolff introduces young adult readers to worlds of adolescence they may have never considered. Whether learning disabled or precocious, affluent or poor, her protagonists must learn to fit into a world that frequently lacks accommodations for those who are atypical.

In *Probably Still Nick Swansen,* Wolff's central character, sixteen-year-old Nick, attends high school in Room 19, a special class for students with learning problems. Although Wolff never supplies a precise diagnosis of Nick's condition, Shana, who had attended Room 19 before ''Going Up'' categorizes both of them as suffering from ''minimal brain dysfunction.'' The label is unnecessary for readers because Wolff creates Nick's world through language. She includes notes he tries to decipher that leave out crucial words; she reveals his hesitation about asking questions for fear of looking stupid; she documents the shame and despair he experiences when he overhears adults characterize students in Room 19 as ''droolers,'' even though Nick possesses an encyclopedic knowledge of amphibians and the uncanny ability to remember complex scientific data about them.

Nick faces two major crises during the novel. The first involves the immediate problems connected with inviting Shana to the prom, making necessary arrangements, and dealing with the embarrassment of having her stand him up the night of the dance. The second source of turmoil comes from a recurring nightmare based on the drowning of his older sister nine years before. Although he had loved and idolized Dianne, he had not been able to save her and cannot free himself from guilt for her death. His inarticulate memories of trying to force her back to life wrench the readers into his world of pain.

As Wolff provides Nick's perspective on events, she might easily have turned Shana into a villain for snubbing him. But the explanation is not so simple. Despite her move ''Up'' from Room 19, Shana must cope with a world that often proves too complex and parents that label her stupid. She tells Nick that she has learned where ''Up'' is: '''It's where you flunk tests all the time, and everybody wants you to be so smart all the time, it's so much faster. . . .''' By the novel's end, Nick's growing acceptance of life's ambiguities brings a measure of peace.

Because much of the story is told from Nick's viewpoint, although not in first person, the novel is sometimes difficult to read. However, Nick shares many concerns with all adolescents, including the problem of handling well-meaning but misguided teachers and parents who offer unsolicited advice.

Suggestions from family, friends, and teacher almost overwhelm Allegra Shapiro in Wolff's second novel, *The Mozart Season.* An extraordinary violinist, twelve-year-old Allegra, is the youngest musician chosen as a contestant in the Ernest Bloch Competition held in her hometown of Portland, Oregon. Her summer is devoted to extended rehearsals of the required Mozart concerto and to the intense struggle required to fuse her own interpretation of the music with the composer's original vision.

Allegra's childhood has been dominated by music. Both her parents are professional musicians who perform in numerous concerts and give lessons. Only Allegra's older brother does not play a musical instrument, turning instead to art. Most acquaintances of Allegra's parents are also musicians. Allegra's own best friends are beautiful and talented achievers, one determined to be an architect, the other a dancer. The world of concerts, practice, lessons, and musical interpretation rarely appears in such detail as that provided by Wolff. Talented young adults might appreciate finding fellow artists in the pages of a novel, but the appeal seems limited.

In *Make Lemonade* Wolff takes readers to a world of poverty, where survival sometimes requires a person's total energy. The novel is told by fourteen-year-old LaVaughan, who takes an after-school babysitting job to earn money for college. Seventeen-year-old Jolly needs someone to care for two-year-old Jeremy and baby Jilly while she works at a factory.

The relationship between LaVaughan and Jolly is complex. LaVaughan is horrified by the filth and cockroaches in Jolly's apartment but admires her determination to support her children. Jolly rebuffs LaVaughan's advice to seek help, fearful that her children will be taken from her. Then she is fired for refusing her boss's sexual advances. Unsuccessful in finding another job, Jolly finally agrees to enter a program that provides day care while she completes high school.

LaVaughan's own life is far from affluent. She lives in a housing project, where no one has gone to college. However, she has an asset Jolly lacks: Mom. Not only does Mom monitor LaVaughan's activities, she serves as captain of the Tenant Council, organizing political action and local programs to improve life in public housing. LaVaughan also recalls images of her dead father, who was gunned down by gang members intending to shoot someone else. Sometimes she is almost convinced she glimpses him on the street. In contrast, Jolly has had no adult support since her foster mother died.

Mom worries that Jolly will have a negative influence and that LaVaughan's grades will suffer. Yet, she recognizes the importance of LaVaughan to Jeremy and Jilly and their mutual affection. In some ways, LaVaughan's experiences strengthen her resolve to attend college. She recognizes the irony of taking money from Jolly so that she can save enough to have a chance for a different life than Jolly has. Yet, there is laughter even in the squalid surroundings. As Jolly puts her life together through the school program, she stops calling LaVaughan, who muses, "I been broken off, like part of her bad past."

The narrative style meshes well with the story. Short lines give a look of poetry to the pages, and the cadences of spoken language provide a sense of immediacy. Simple sentences and brief chapters offer an additional sense of change and movement. Wolff's empathy with her characters and her willingness to take risks in viewpoint and style serve her well here, as in her earlier books. She has helped expand the range of experiences available to readers of young adult novels.

—Kathy Piehl

WOLITZER, Hilma

Nationality: American. **Born:** Brooklyn, New York, 25 January 1930. **Education:** Brooklyn Museum Art School, Brooklyn College of the City University of New York, and New School for Social Research, New York. **Family:** Married Morton Wolitzer in 1952; two daughters. **Career:** Writer and teacher of writing workshops; has also worked as nursery school teacher and portrait artist at a resort. Bread Loaf Writers Conference, staff assistant, 1975 and 1976, staff member, 1977-78 and 1980-92; visiting lecturer in writing at University of Iowa, 1978-79 and 1983, Columbia University, 1979-80, New York University, 1984, and Swarthmore College, 1985. **Awards:** Bread Loaf Writers Conference scholarship, 1970; fellowships from Bread Loaf Writers Conference, 1974, Guggenheim Foundation, 1976-77, and National Endowment for the Arts, 1978; Great Lakes College Association award, 1974-75, for *Ending*; New York State English Council Excellence in Letters award, 1980; American Academy and Institute of Arts and Letters award (literature), 1981; Janet Heidinger Kafka Prize (honorable mention), University of Rochester, 1981, for *Hearts*. **Agent:** Amanda Urban, ICM, 40 West 57th St., New York, New York 10019. **Address:** 500 East 85th St., Apt. 18H, New York, New York 10028, U.S.A.

PUBLICATIONS FOR YOUNG ADULTS

Novels

Ending. New York, Morrow, 1974.
In the Flesh. New York, Morrow, 1977.
Hearts. New York, Farrar, Straus, 1980.
In the Palomar Arms. New York, Farrar, Straus, 1983.
Silver. New York, Farrar, Straus, 1988.
Introducing Shirley Braverman. New York, Farrar, Straus, 1975.
Out of Love. New York, Farrar, Straus, 1976.
Toby Lived Here. New York, Farrar, Straus, 1978.
Wish You Were Here. New York, Farrar, Straus, 1985.
Tunnel of Love. New York, HarperCollins Publishers, 1994.

Other

Contributor, *From Pop to Culture.* New York, Holt, 1970.
Contributor, *The Secret Life of Our Time,* edited by Gordon Lish. New York, Doubleday, 1973.
Contributor, *Bitches and Sad Ladies,* edited by Pat Rotter. New York, Harper Magazine Press, 1975.
Contributor, *The Bread Loaf Anthology of Contemporary Short Stories,* edited by Robert Pack and Jay Parini. Middlebury, Vermont, Bread Loaf, 1987.
Contributor, *The Bread Loaf Anthology of Contemporary American Essays,* edited by Robert Pack and Jay Parini. Middlebury, Vermont, Bread Loaf, 1989.
Contributor, *Vital Lines,* edited by John Mukand, M.D. New York, St. Martin's Press, 1990.

Screenplays: *In the Flesh* and *Ending,* an episode from the series *Family,* ABC-TV, three shows for PBS-TV, and *Single Women, Married Men* (teleplay), CBS-TV.

*

Media Adaptations: *Ending, In the Flesh,* and *Hearts* have been optioned for motion picture production.

Biography: Essay in *Speaking for Ourselves, Too,* compiled and edited by Donald R. Gallo, National Council of Teachers of English, 1993.

* * *

Hilma Wolitzer writes with a realism that invokes both emotion and a correlation to one's own life. The autobiographical quality makes it easier for the reader to identify with the characters, the pace of the stories are brisk yet the plots are complex enough to keep the reader interested and concerned about the outcome, and an overall theme in her young adult novels is taking control of one's life for growth. A prominent story line includes a recent death in the family with which the main character is coming to terms. The end result of working through the grief process is emotional development and maturity in the main character.

In *Wish You Were Here,* Bernie Segel struggles with accepting his father's death and his mother's remarriage. The main focus is Bernie's obsession to secretly earn enough money for a plane ticket so he can go live with his paternal grandfather in Florida. Torn between missing his father and feeling guilty when he doesn't, Bernie stumbles through a series of typical adolescent problems involving relationships: strong feelings for a girl, bickering with an older sister, resentment toward his future stepfather, and clinging to memories of his relationship with his grandfather.

Bernie is strong willed. As he learns to work through the problems in his various family relationships, he reminds himself he won't be around later to enjoy the fruits of his labor and that he will actually miss each of these people he is so anxious to get away from. He realizes he must keep his plan in focus if he is to succeed.

When his plan is botched by the surprise visit of his grandfather, he is disappointed but eventually realizes running away would have solved nothing. Because his grandfather looks much older than he remembered and admits to Bernie that he, too, misses his father, Bernie realizes he is only afraid of forgetting his father altogether. He solves this new problem by deciding to follow an old Jewish custom for remembering the dead. In this way, a piece of his father can always be with him, even if the family situation must change. Since Bernie discovers the way to solve his problem and in doing so comes to understand why he came up with his original "solution" to his dilemma, the resolution of the story is not only very realistic but satisfying.

A similar novel focuses on a female protagonist who struggles to accept not only the sudden death of her father, but to overcome the embarrassment of her present situation. In *Toby Lived Here,* twelve-year-old Toby and her six-year-old sister Anne find themselves in a foster home. Their mother has suffered an emotional breakdown after the death of their father. While worrying that such an illness may be hereditary, Toby is deceptive about the circumstances that brought the girls into foster care. Wolitzer again employs an involved plot and ardent realism to elicit empathy for Toby and to establish an understanding in the reader for emotional and mental disorders.

Though *Hearts* was written for an adult audience, it will appeal to young people because they will be able to relate to the emotionally immature main character and her thirteen-year-old stepdaughter. Linda Reismann is a twenty-six-year-old widow. Her husband dies after only six weeks of marriage, and Linda sets off across the country to deposit the malcontent Robin with relatives she's never met.

Robin resents her stepmother, and the hostility that surrounds their relationship intensifies as they travel from New Jersey to Iowa and then to California. Arrangements had been made for Robin to live with her grandfather, but when they arrive in Iowa they find he's had a stroke and will soon be placed into a nursing home. Linda, unclear of her own goals, makes an attempt to find Robin's mother. As they travel, the ice in their relationship at times melts, but at other times it begins to freeze again. Their cross-country quest becomes a learning experience as their lives converge with an array of people they meet at stops along the way. As the cloak of naivete falls from Linda's shoulders, she realizes the anger Robin displays to both Linda and her real mother is a mask for feeling abandoned. Linda realizes, too, that Robin is her only link to her deceased husband, her only family. "It was because she could not say aloud that she was *bound* to Robin, that you can become a family by the grace of accident and will, that we have a duty to console one another as best we can."

Like the other protagonists in Wolitzer's novels, Linda—and to an extent Robin—have journeyed to a closing of one part of their lives and the opening of a new part. They've both grown emotionally by accepting the death of husband and father, while at the same time they've learned to gain more control over their lives.

—Lisa A. Wroble

WOODSON, Jacqueline

Nationality: American. **Born:** Columbus, Ohio, 12 February 1963; grew up in Greenville, South Carolina, and Brooklyn, New York. **Education:** Adelphi University, B.A. in English 1985; studied creative writing at the New School for Social Research. **Career:** Has held a variety of jobs including editorial assistant and drama therapist with runaway and homeless young adults in East Harlem; teacher of writing, Eugene Lang College, 1994, and Goddard College, 1993-95; freelance writer, from 1987; writer-in-residence, National Book Foundation, 1995 and 1996. Contributor to periodicals, including *American Voice, American Identities: Contemporary Multi-Cultural Voices, Common Lives Quarterly, Conditions, Essence, Horn Book, Kenyon Review,* and *Out/Look;* editorial board, Portable Lower East Side/*Queer City.* **Awards:** MacDowell Colony fellowship, 1990, 1994; Fine Arts Works Center fellowship, Provincetown, 1991-92; Best Book Award, American Library Association, 1994; Editor's Choice Award, *Booklist,* 1994; Best Book Award, *Publisher's Weekly,* 1994; Jane Addams Children's Book Award, 1995, 1996; Coretta Scott King Honor Book Award, 1995, 1996; Kenyon Review Award, for Literary Excellence in Fiction, 1996; *Granta* Fifty Best American Authors under 40 Award, 1996; Lambda Literary Award, for Best Fiction and for Best Children's Fiction, 1996; American Film Institute Award. **Agent:** Charlotte Sheedy, Literary Agency, 65 Bleeker Street, New York, New York 10012, U.S.A.

*

Critical Studies: "A World without Childhood" by Catherine
Bush, in *New York Times Book Review,* 26 February 1995, 14.

*   *   *

The novels of talented young author Jacqueline Woodson are
uniformly notable for their thematic richness, strong female characters, and convincing demonstration of friendship's power to
breech the walls society erects between people of different race and
economic condition.

In *The Dear One,* for example, 12-year-old Feni's life is
changed when her mother invites Rebecca, the unwed, pregnant
daughter of an old college friend, to stay with them in their affluent
suburban home. Coming from an economically disadvantaged
household in Harlem, 15-year-old Rebecca is at first suspicious of
her new surroundings and openly hostile to Feni. The younger girl,
who has not recovered from the death of her grandmother, whom
she considered her best friend, is equally resentful of this unwelcome visitor. But gradually and believably, with the patient support
of Feni's mother and a lesbian couple who are longstanding family
friends, the two girls begin to develop mutual trust and, finally, a
redemptive friendship. Feni, whose name means "The Dear One"
in Swahili, is able to let go of her attachment to her grandmother—
and when Rebecca names her baby "Feni," the reader understands
that whole new generations of "Dear Ones" will inevitably grow
up to help each other through times of crisis with loving and
enduring support.

The capacity of friendship to survive separation and personal
growth is explored in Woodson's trilogy about best friends Margaret and Maizon. In *Last Summer With Maizon,* the two are eleven-
year-olds who, living a scant block apart in Brooklyn, are so alike
as to be "almost twins—could be cousins". However, when
Margaret's father dies and Maizon is awarded an academic scholarship to Blue Hill, a private school in Connecticut, the two begin to
grow apart. Left to herself, Margaret discovers a talent for writing
and wins a citywide poetry competition. Meanwhile, as readers
learn in *Maizon at Blue Hill,* her friend—though academically
successful—is miserably unhappy at a school populated by
affluent white girls who are afraid of her because she's black and,
thus, different. To make matters worse, the handful of upperclass
African-American students simultaneously patronize her and warn
her, for her own "protection," not to socialize with the white
students. Feeling increasingly alienated, Maizon decides to leave
Blue Hill to find a place where "smart black girls from Brooklyn
could feel like they belonged".

Ironically, when she returns home in *Between Madison and
Palmetto,* she finds both her old neighborhood and her friend
Margaret changed. The construction of new apartment buildings
has brought an influx of white residents to the neighborhood, while
Margaret has become increasingly self-sufficient and solitary. A
growing interest in boys and a dissatisfaction with her changing
body have also caused Margaret to become bulimic, a condition
which further isolates her. For her part, Maizon is challenged by the
sudden return of her father, who had abandoned her when she was
an infant, and is surprised to discover a new friendship with a white
girl who has moved to the neighborhood. If Woodson's work has a
flaw, it is that it sometimes tries to support too many issues and
themes, as it does here, without the space necessary to resolve
them. Lacking the focus and richly developed characterization of
her earlier novels, *Between Madison and Palmetto* comes perilously close to being a standard "problem" novel. And though ultimately Margaret's and Maizon's friendship survives, it happens
more through the manipulation of the author than through the
efforts of the characters.

Woodson juggled many issues and themes in *Autobiography of
a Family Photo* but this time with a new writing style. In a series of
artfully crafted vignettes, Woodson explores the impact of the
Vietnam War on many areas of African American life: on family,
community, and national relations; on sexual abuse; and on
homophobia. Her vivid imagery contrasts the stereotypical white
families seen on television with a dysfunctional African American
family. Woodson ties her themes to a story that follows the coming
of age of the unnamed narrator as she deals with a sexually abusive
brother and stepfather and the families mourning after the death of
their homosexual brother in the war. Catherine Bush noted in the
New York Times Book Review that *Autobiography of a Family
Photo* "is the best kind of survival guide: clear-eyed, gut-true."

Woodson's talent, intelligence, and compassionate understanding of her characters find their finest expression in her novel, *I
Hadn't Meant to Tell You This.* Set, like *The Dear One,* in an
affluent black suburb, this novel explores the problems which
plague two teenage girls—an affluent African-American and a
poor white—when they defy social convention, peer pressure, and
parental opposition to become friends. The relationship is further
tested when it is revealed that the white girl, Lena, is the victim of
incest. The strength which Lena finds in her friendship with Marie
helps her endure, though it does not guarantee a traditional happy

ending. Indeed, Woodson's refusal to impose a facile resolution on this heartbreaking dilemma is one of her singular strengths as a writer.

"Every character I write about," Woodson notes, "is in some way outside of the mainstream—black, working-class poor white, a pregnant teen, gay." Virtually all of her characters are also female and almost all derive from fractured families, broken by death, divorce, or parental abandonment. It is the redeeming power of friendship and the loving support of powerful adult women which helps these young characters to pull together the fragments of their lives and emerge as whole and complete persons with viable futures and an understanding that, as Woodson herself concludes, "there are only positive things to come from being different."

—Michael Cart, updated by Sara Pendergast

WREDE, Patricia C(ollins)

Nationality: American. **Born:** Chicago, Illinois, 27 March 1953. **Education:** Carleton College, Northfield, Minnesota, A.B. 1974; University of Minnesota, M.B.A. 1977. **Family:** Married James M. Wrede in 1976 (divorced, 1992). **Career:** Rate review analyst, Minnesota Hospital Association, Minneapolis, Minnesota, 1977-78; financial analyst, B. Dalton Bookseller, Minneapolis, Minnesota, 1978-80; financial analyst, 1980-81, senior financial analyst, 1981-83, senior accountant, 1983-85, Dayton-Hudson Corporation, Minneapolis, Minnesota; full-time writer, from 1985. **Member:** Science Fiction Writers of America. **Awards:** "Books for Young Adults" Recommended Reading List citation, 1984, for *Daughter of Witches,* and 1985, for *The Seven Towers*; Minnesota Book Award for Fantasy and Science Fiction, 1991, and American Library Association (ALA) "Best Book for Young Adults" citation, for *Dealing With Dragons*; *Booklist*'s Editor's Choice, 1989, for *Snow White and Rose Red*; ALA "Best Books" 1992, for *Searching for Dragons*; ALA "Notable Books for Young Adults" 1993, for *Calling on Dragons.* **Agent:** Valerie Smith, 1746 Route 44-55, Mondena, New York 12548, U.S.A. **Address:** 4900 West 60th Street, Edina, Minnesota 55424-1709, U.S.A.

PUBLICATIONS FOR YOUNG ADULTS

Fiction

Shadow Magic. New York, Ace, 1982.
Daughter of Witches. New York, Ace, 1983.
The Seven Towers. New York, Ace, 1984.
The Harp of Imach Thyssel. New York, Ace, 1985.
Talking to Dragons. Tempo/MagicQuest Books, 1985.
Caught in Crystal. New York, Ace, 1987.
With Caroline Stevenmer, *Sorcery and Cecelia.* New York, Ace, 1988.
Snow White and Rose Red. New York, Tor, 1989.
Dealing with Dragons. San Diego, Harcourt, 1990.
Mairelon the Magician. New York, Tor, 1991.
Searching for Dragons. San Diego, Harcourt, 1991.
Calling on Dragons. San Diego, Jane Yolen Books, 1993.

The Raven Ring. New York, Tor, 1994.
Magician's Ward. New York, Tor, 1997.
Book of Enchantments. San Diego, Jane Yolen Books, 1996.

Other

Contributor, *Liavek,* edited by Will Shetterly and Emma Bull. New York: Ace, 1985.
Contributor, *Liavek: The Players of Luck,* edited by Will Shetterly and Emma Bull. New York, Ace, 1986.
Contributor, *Spaceships and Spells,* edited by Jane Yolen. New York, Harper & Row, 1987.
Contributor, *Liavek: Spells of Binding,* edited by Will Shetterly and Emma Bull. New York, Ace, 1988.
Contributor, *The Unicorn Treasury,* edited by Bruce Coville. New York, Doubleday, 1988.
Contributor, *Liavek: Festival Week,* edited by Will Shetterly and Emma Bull. New York, Ace, 1990.
Contributor, *Tales of the Witch World 3,* edited by Andre Norton. New York, Tor, 1990.

*

Critical Studies: "Patricia C. Wrede," in *Authors and Artists for Young Adults,* Vol. 8, Detroit, Gale, 1992; "Wrede, Patricia C(ollins)," in *St. James Guide to Fantasy Writers,* edited by David Pringle, New York, Gale, 1996.

*   *   *

Two trademarks of Patricia Wrede's fantasy fiction are humor and light romance, two elements sure to appeal to the young adult audience that has made her works so popular. Wrede (pronounced "Reedy") is perhaps best known for two sets of fantasy novels, the Enchanted Forest Chronicles and the cycle of novels set in a secondary world called Lyra.

In the Enchanted Forest Chronicles humor predominates as Wrede plays with fairy-tale convention, turning the familiar motifs upside down and inside out. The first novel in the series, *Dealing with Dragons,* recounts the adventures of Cimorene, an unconventional princess who chooses to become the servant of a dragon rather than submit to boring court life and marriage to good-looking but very conventional Prince Therandil. The villains in the Enchanted Forest Chronicles are the wizards, and in this novel Cimorene helps the dragons thwart the wizards' scheme for taking control of the dragon colony. The action of this story takes place primarily in the Mountains of Morning, where the dragons reside, but many of the main characters of the series are first introduced here: Kazul, Cimorene's dragon mistress, Morwen, a witch, and the bumbling yet definitely sinister wizards, who stop at no destruction in their search for magical power.

The second novel, *Searching for Dragons,* has Cimorene falling in league and in love with Mendanbar, the young King of the Enchanted Forest, as together they unravel the next magic-stealing plot of the wizards. Mendanbar is as unconventional a fairy-tale hero as Cimorene is a fairy-tale princess, and much of the humor in this book results from his practical, down-to-earth attitude and his aversion to the pomp his manservant Willin would inject into the kingly duties. Mendanbar, who at first considers all princesses to be beautiful airheads, is pleasantly surprised at Cimorene, and predictably, the book ends with a royal marriage.

In the third novel, *Calling on Dragons,* the wizards again attack the Enchanted Forest, and this novel ends on a surprising somber note: the wizards succeed in taking over Mendanbar's castle and in trapping the king in a dimensional warp; Cimorene and the other denizens of the Enchanted Forest must wait for the newborn prince to grow up and wield the king's magic sword in order to free Mendanbar and the castle. This ending sets up the plot of the fourth book, *Talking to Dragons,* in which Prince Daystar comes into his power and conquers the wizards once and for all.

The appeal of the Enchanted Forest Chronicles lies in its play with traditional fairy-tale conventions and in its strongly delineated characters. Wrede's typical female character is strong-minded and practical, good-looking (though never beautiful), courageous, and able to think on her feet. The three dominant female characters in the Enchanted Forest Chronicles, Cimorene, Kazul, and Morwen, are especially well done.

Wrede's fiction, however, is not as ardently feminist as some reviewers would like to imply, nor does she truly defy the overall conventions of fairy-tale fantasy. Her heroines, while not beautiful and feminine, are also never old or ugly, the plots include a marriage or at least a spice of romance, and good and evil are clearly delineated. In Wrede's stories, the good guys escape serious harm and eventually win in the end, despite a few mishaps along the way. In fact, her strong-minded heroines are themselves a now-established convention in fantasy fiction, in part through Wrede's contributions to the genre. The fun of the Enchanted Forest Chronicles results from the offbeat mix of the ordinary and everyday with magic and fairy tale. the Enchanted Forest is peopled not only with talking animals and wicked wizards but also with traveling shoe salesmen (who stock seven-league boots and ruby slippers in addition to ordinary footwear), plumbers, and an unlimited supply of questing princes and damsels in distress.

The plots that make up the four Lyra novels are not sequential like the Enchanted Forest Chronicles, but rather are connected by a similar sense of place. Lyra is a magical world dominated by two moons and inhabited by a variety of sentient beings: humans of various tribes and cultures, the fairy-folk Shee, forest cat-people known as the Wyrd, and the evil Shadowborn, spirits who inhabit human bodies. Claiming that one of her complaints about secondary worlds in fantasy fiction is that the worlds are limited in scope, Wrede consciously develops different aspects of Lyra in these novels, adding new details with each novel to the diversity of the world she has created. *Shadow Magic* recounts the history of Lyra and concerns the reuniting of the four races of one of its countries, Alkyra. Alethia, the daughter of a noble house of Alkyra, is of mixed blood and must learn to use her magical heritage to defeat the Shadowborn and save her country. *Daughter of Witches* takes place in a totally different culture and time period on Lyra. The plot concerns how Ranira, like Alethia before her, is ultimately forced to come to terms with her magical heritage and use her hidden powers in a fight against evil. *The Harp of Imach Thyssel,* one of the few Wrede novels with a male main character, and *The Raven Ring* comprise the rest of the Lyra cycle at this point.

Wrede also has written novels in the historical fantasy vein: *Snow White and Rose Red* is set in Renaissance England, while *Sorcery and Cecelia, Mairelon the Magician,* and *Magician's Ward* take place in an alternate Regency England where magic is a part of real life. *Snow White and Rose Red,* Wrede's contribution to

Terri Windling's Fairy Tale Series, is a retelling of the familiar Grimms' folktale of two sisters whose goodness and mercy are able to free an enchanted bear from the curse of an evil gnome. Wrede remains faithful to the basic plot of the fairy tale while fleshing it out into a full-length romantic fantasy novel. *Mairelon the Magician* and its sequel, *Magician's Ward,* recount the adventures of Kim, a street orphan, and the young magician who takes her under his wing.

Although she prefers to write novel-length fantasies, Wrede has also produced many fine short fantasy stories, several of which have been collected in the *Book of Enchantments.* Other of her short works appeared in the five Liavek anthologies, edited by Will Shetterley and Emma Bull, which are collections of stories that are all set in the shared world of Liavek, a large trading city on the edge of the Sea of Luck.

Wrede's strengths as a writer are characterization and a strong sense of plot, humor, and romance. Her fantasies are rather conventional, but her gentle style of romantic fantasy appeals to a large audience and a wide age range. The Enchanted Forest Chronicles reveal her inventiveness and sense of fun, the Lyra books reveal her ability to establish a strong sense of place, and the historical fantasies demonstrate an ability to evoke a believable, recognizable time period.

—Martha P. Hixon

WRIGHT, Richard (Nathaniel)

Nationality: American. **Born:** near Natchez, Mississippi, 4 September 1908. **Education:** a junior high school in Jackson, Mississippi. **Family:** Married 1) Rose Dhima Meadman in 1938 (marriage ended); 2) Ellen Poplar in 1941, two daughters. **Career:** Novelist, short story writer, poet and essayist. Worked for the Federal Writers Project, and the Federal Negro Theatre Project; clerk at U.S. Post Office in Chicago, Illinois, during 1920s. Communist Party member, 1932-44; Harlem Editor, *Daily Worker,* New York. **Awards:** Prize from *Story* magazine, 1938, for *Uncle Tom's Children*; Guggenheim fellowship, 1939; Spingarn Medal from National Association for the Advancement of Colored People, 1940, for *Native Son.* **Died:** 28 November 1960, in Paris, France.

PUBLICATIONS

Novels

Native Son. New York, Harper, and London, Gollancz, 1940.
The Outsider. New York, Harper, 1953; London, Angus & Robertson, 1954.
Savage Holiday. New York, Avon, 1954.
The Long Dream. New York, Doubleday, 1958; London, Angus & Robertson, 1960.
Lawd Today. New York, Walker, 1963; London, Blond, 1965.
The Man Who Lived Underground. Paris, Aubier-Flammarion, 1971.

Short Stories

Uncle Tom's Children: Four Novellas. New York, Harper, 1938; London, Gollancz, 1939; augmented edition; as *Uncle Tom's Children: Five Long Stories,* New York, Harper, 1940.
Eight Men. Cleveland, World, 1961.
Quintet. San Diego, California, Pyramid Books, 1961.
Farthing's Fortunes. New York, Atheneum, 1976.

Plays

Native Son (The Biography of a Young American), with Paul Green (produced New York, 1941; London, 1948). New York and London, Harper, 1941.
Daddy Goodness, adaptation of a play by Louis Sapin (produced New York, 1968).

Screenplay: *Native Son,* 1951.

Other

How Bigger Was Born: The Story of "Native Son," One of the Most Significant Novels of Our Time and How It Came to Be Written. New York, Harper, 1940.
The Negro and Parkway Community House. Chicago, privately printed, 1941.
Twelve Million Black Voices: A Folk History of the Negro in the United States. New York, Viking Press, 1941; London, Londsay Drummond, 1947.
Black Boy: A Record of Childhood and Youth. New York, Harper, and London, Gollancz, 1945.
Black Power: A Record of Reactions in a Land of Pathos. New York, Harper, 1954; London, Dobson, 1956.
Bandoeng: 1.500.000.000 hommes, translated by Helene Claireau. Paris, Calman-Levy, 1955; as *The Color Curtain: A Report on the Bandung Conference,* Cleveland, World, and London, Dobson, 1956.
Pagan Spain. New York, Harper, 1956; London, Bodley Head, 1960.
White Man, Listen! New York, Doubleday, 1957.
Letters to Joe C. Brown, edited by Thomas Knipp. Kent, Ohio, Kent State University Libraries, 1968.
What the Negro Wants. Japan, Kaitakusha, 1972.
American Hunger (autobiography). New York, Harper, 1977.
The Richard Wright Reader, edited by Ellen Wright and Michel Fabre. New York, Harper, 1978.
The Life and Work of Richard Wright, edited by David Ray and Robert M. Farnsworth. Columbia, Montana, University of Missouri, 1979.
New Essays on Native Son, edited by Keneth Kinnamon. New York, Cambridge University Press, 1990.
Works. New York, Viking, 1991.

*

Bibliographies: "A Bibliography of Richard Wright's Words" by Michael Fabre and Edward Margolies, in *New Letters 38* (Kansas City, Missouri), Winter 1971; "Richard Wright: An Essay in Bibliography" by John M. Reilly in *Resources for American Literary Study* (College Park, Maryland), Autumn 1971.

Critical Studies: *Richard Wright* by Constance Webb, New York, Putnam, 1968; *Richard Wright* by Robert Bone, Minneapolis, University of Minnesota Press, 1969; *The Art of Richard Wright* by Edward Margolies, Carbondale, Southern Illinois University Press, 1969; *The Example of Richard Wright* by Dan McCall, New York, Harcourt Brace, 1969; *Richard Wright: An Introduction to the Man and His Work* by Carl Brignano, Pittsburgh, University of Pittsburgh Press, 1970; *The Emergence of Richard Wright: A Study in Literature and Society* by Kenneth Kinnamon, Urbana, University of Illinois Press, 1972; *Twentieth Century Interpretations of "Native Son,"* edited by H.A. Baker, Englewood Cliffs, New Jersey, Prentice Hall, 1972; entry in *Contemporary Literary Criticism,* Detroit, Gale, Volume 1, 1973, Volume 3, 1975, Volume 4, 1975, Volume 9, 1978, Volume 14, 1980, Volume 21, 1982; *Richard Wright* by David Bakish, New York, Ungar, 1973; *The Unfinished Quest of Richard Wright* by Michel Fabre, translated by Isabel Barzun, New York, Morrow, 1973; *Richard Wright Impressions and Perspectives,* edited by David Ray and R.M. Farnsworth, Ann Arbor, University of Michigan Press, 1973.

*   *   *

Richard Wright's novels, autobiographies, essays, dramatic scripts, poetry, and other nonfiction draw on the poverty and segregation of his childhood in the South and early adulthood in Chicago. A politically oriented writer, Wright focuses clearly and forcefully on the brutal and dehumanizing effects of racism on the black person. His first published work, *Uncle Tom's Children,* is a collection of novellas dealing with confrontations of blacks and whites, emphasizing the dignity of man and the oppression of a black underclass. His first novel, *Lawd Today,* was not published until after his death. In a bold, naturalistic style it centers around the life of Jake Jackson, a violent, untutored man from Chicago whose mean environment offers little opportunity and little hope.

Of more interest to the young adult is Wright's powerful protest novel, *Native Son,* which introduces us to Bigger Thomas, a poor, young, black man of twenty years who accidentally murders a rich, young, white woman. A prominent theme in this book is that blacks become criminals because of their environment. Bigger's crime, though, has two effects on him—that of giving him an identity and that of consuming him with fear and guilt so that he rapidly brings about his own destruction. By the end of the story, Bigger, imprisoned and sentenced to death, realizes that his life does have meaning and that the black man is no less human than the white man. The birth of Bigger, Wright has written, occurred in his own childhood, and there was not just one Bigger, but many. This novel is a powerful indictment of racism, an indictment of the white man as the oppressor, of the black man as submissive to the oppressor. *Native Son* was the first novel by a Black American writer to achieve critical acclaim and popular success. It was later made into a stage play and twice was adapted on film.

Wright's most salient work for the young adult, and regarded by many as his masterpiece, is his autobiography, *Black Boy,* the highly readable, poignant account of Wright's childhood in the South. The book begins as he accidentally burns his house down lighting broom straws in the fireplace. Readers learn how he became a drunkard in his sixth year, when older drunks gave him drinks in the saloon; how begging for drinks became his obsession; how the older drunks paid him nickels for repeating obscenities to women. Wright's father was a night porter but left home when Wright was still of preschool age. His mother worked as a cook. Throughout the book the descriptions of his hunger, of his fantasies about food, occur over and over. By eighth grade, despite all his troubles and tragedies, Wright had a clear goal of going to the North, where everything was possible—he had read the Horatio Alger books—and becoming a writer. By the time he left the South, however, seventeen-year-old Wright knew that he was not really leaving, because his feelings already had been formed there. He was taking a part of the South to transplant in different soil, to see if it could grow differently and bloom. Wright felt if that miracle happened, he would know that the South, too, could overcome despair and violence. He headed north with the hope that life could be lived with dignity, that other persons need not be violated.

Black Boy is a violent book, describing how Wright's mother and grandmother beat him, so hard sometimes that he lost consciousness. For a time he was in an orphan home, again with too little to eat. From a religious family, Wright eventually was sent to a Seventh-day Adventist school where his teacher, also his aunt, beat him. He had several stints in public school, but his primary concern there was to prove himself, as a newcomer, by fighting fellow students. As he grew older and taller, Wright spent more time with older boys and with them developed a sense of camaraderie, strengthened by their fear and loathing of white boys. There are violent expressions of hate and hostility involving real and bloody battles. Wright describes throwing rocks, cinders, coal, sticks, and broken bottles, all the while longing for deadlier weapons. Although set in the 1920s, readers will make comparisons with the gang warfare among big-city poor of the 1990s.

The posthumously published *American Hunger* is a sequel to *Black Boy,* tracing Wright's migration to and his early years as a writer in Chicago. Wright gradually became disillusioned with race relations in the United States and moved to France, where he wrote several other lesser novels, short stories, and strident political essays.

It is *Black Boy* that most eloquently presents Wright's message of the destructive power of racism. The book is an American classic, a powerful, sad, and hopeful story of growing up in this country, as important today as when first published almost fifty years ago.

—Mary Lystad

WRIGHTSON, (Alice) Patricia

Nationality: Australian. **Born:** Lismore, New South Wales, 21 June 1921. **Education:** State Correspondence School, 1933-34; St. Catherine's College, Stanthorpe, Queensland, 1932. **Family:** Married in 1943 (divorced 1953); one daughter and one son. **Career:** Secretary and administrator, Bonalbo District Hospital, 1946-60, and Sydney District Nursing Association, 1960-64; assistant editor, 1964-70, and editor, 1970-75, *School Magazine,* Sydney; writer. **Awards:** Australian Children's Book Council Book of the Year award, 1956, for *The Crooked Snake;* American Library Association Notable Book, 1963, for *The Feather Star;* Book of the Year award runner-up, Children's Book Council of Australia, and Children's Spring Book Festival award from *Book*

World, both 1968, and Hans Christian Andersen Honors List award of the International Board on Books for Young People (IBBY), 1970, all for *A Racecourse for Andy;* Book of the Year Honour List award, Children's Book Council of Australia, 1974, IBBY's Honor List for text award, 1976, *Voice of Youth Advocate's* Annual Selection of Best Science Fiction and Fantasy Titles for Young Adults, 1988, and Hans Christian Andersen Medal, all for *The Nargun and the Stars;* O.B.E. (Officer, Order of the British Empire), 1978; Book of the Year award from Children's Book Council of Australia, and *Guardian* award commendation, both 1978, IBBY's Books for Young People Honor List award, and Hans Christian Andersen Honors List award, both 1979, all for *The Ice Is Coming;* New South Wales Premier's award for Ethnic Writing, and selection as one of the Children's Books of the Year by Child Study Association of America, both 1979, both for *The Dark Bright Water;* Book of the Year award high commendation, Children's Book Council of Australia, 1982, for *Behind the Wind;* Carnegie Medal Commendation, 1983, Book of the Year award, Children's Book Council of Australia, *Boston Globe/Horn Book* award for Fiction, Hans Christian Andersen Medal, and *Observer* Teenage Fiction Prize, all 1984, all for *A Little Fear;* Dromkeen Children's Literature Foundation Medal, 1984, for "a significant contribution to the appreciation and development of children's literature in Australia"; chosen to deliver sixteenth annual Arbuthnot Lecture, 1985; Golden Cat award, Sjoestrands Forlag AB, 1986, for "a contribution to children's and young adult literature"; Hans Christian Andersen Medal, 1986, for *Moon Dark;* Lady Cutler award, 1986; New South Wales Premier's Special Occasional award, 1988. **Address:** Lohic, P.O. Box 91, Maclean, NSW 2463, Australia.

PUBLICATIONS FOR YOUNG ADULTS

Fiction

The Crooked Snake, illustrated by Margaret Horder. Sydney and London, Angus and Robertson, 1955.
The Bunyip Hole, illustrated by Margaret Horder. Sydney and London, Angus and Robertson, 1958.
The Rocks of Honey, illustrated by Margaret Horder. Sydney, Angus and Robertson, 1960; London, Angus and Robertson, 1961.
The Feather Star, illustrated by Noela Young. London, Hutchinson, 1962; New York, Harcourt Brace, 1963.
Down to Earth, illustrated by Margaret Horder. New York, Harcourt Brace, and London, Hutchinson, 1965.
I Own the Racecourse!, illustrated by Margaret Horder. London, Hutchinson, 1968; as *A Racecourse for Andy,* New York, Harcourt Brace, 1968.
An Older Kind of Magic, illustrated by Noela Young. London, Hutchinson, and New York, Harcourt Brace, 1972.
The Nargun and the Stars. London, Hutchinson, 1973; New York, Atheneum, 1974.
The Ice Is Coming. Richmond, Victoria, and London, Hutchinson, and New York, Atheneum, 1977.
The Dark Bright Water. Richmond, Victoria, and London, Hutchinson, and New York, Atheneum, 1979.
Night Outside, illustrated by Beth Peck. Melbourne, Rigby, 1979; New York, Atheneum, 1985.
Behind the Wind. Richmond, Victoria, and London, Hutchinson, 1981; as *Journey Behind the Wind,* New York, Atheneum, 1981.

A Little Fear. Richmond, Victoria, and London, Hutchinson, and New York, McElderry, 1983.

Moon-Dark, illustrated by Noela Young. Richmond, Victoria, Hutchinson, 1987; New York, McElderry, 1988.

The Song of Wirrun. Richmond, Victoria, Century Hutchinson, 1987.

Balyet. Richmond, Victoria, and London, Hutchinson, and New York, McElderry, 1989.

The Sugar-Gum Tree, illustrated by David Cox. Ringwood, Victoria, Australia, and New York, Viking, 1991.

Shadows of Time. Milsons Point, N.S.W., Random House Australia, 1994.

Rattler's Place, illustrated by David Cox. Ringwood, Victoria, Penguin, 1997.

Other

Editor, *Beneath the Sun: An Australian Collection for Children.* Sydney, Collins, 1972; London, Collins, 1973.

Editor, *Emu Stew: An Illustrated Collection of Stories and Poems for Children.* Melbourne and London, Kestrel, 1976.

The Haunted Rivers. Maclean, New South Wales, Eighth State Press, 1983.

*

Media Adaptations: *The Nargun and the Stars* (television series), ABC-TV, 1977; *I Own the Racecourse* (film), Barron Films, 1985.

Biography: Essay in *Something about the Author Autobiography Series,* Vol. 4, Detroit, Gale, 1987, pp. 335-46; essay in *Authors and Artists for Young Adults,* Vol. 5, Detroit, Gale, 1990, pp. 236-237.

Critical Studies: Entry in *Children's Literature Review,* Detroit, Gale, Vol. 4, 1982, Vol. 14, 1988; entry in *Fourth Book of Junior Authors and Illustrators,* New York, H.W. Wilson, 1978.

Manuscript Collections: Lu Rees Archives, Canberra College of Advanced Education Library, Australia; Kerlan Collection, University of Minnesota.

*   *   *

Few authors have changed the literature of their country, but Patricia Wrightson is one of them. Publication of *The Nargun and the Stars* in 1972 marked the beginning of an authentic Australian fantasy based upon the folklore of Australia's indigenous people rather than that of its European inhabitants and upon Wrightson's skill at rendering the country's ancient, distinctive landscapes. After publishing two fairly conventional holiday adventure stories, she found her own voice in *The Rocks of Honey,* a realistic novel that deals with themes she develops in her later fantasy: of the deep and long-standing attachment of Australia's Aboriginal people to their land, of the possibility of understanding between Aboriginal and European Australians based upon respect for Aboriginal culture and attachment to the land itself, and of the healing power of nature.

Wrightson's novel *The Feather Star* depicts the awakening of a fifteen-year-old girl to a sense of time and mortality. Lindy Martin realizes that she has grown beyond unreflective childhood and can choose between finding self-realization in human fellowship and in enjoyment of the natural world, and a doctrine of sin and retribution in an after-life preached by a loveless old religious crank who rails at Lindy and her friends. Wrightson also uses the symbols of a regenerating feather starfish and of the stars themselves to carry an idea central to her later work: that of the continuity of life on earth and its relationship with the life of a self-sufficient universe.

In *The Nargun and the Stars* Wrightson's discovery of the creatures of Aboriginal folklore enables her to create the fantasy she had long wished to write by allowing magic to enter believably into the Australian bushland. Further, the spirits of the land constitute a specifically Australian link between humankind and nature and provide the cause for a fantastic hero-journey and the means by which it is conducted. The huge stone figure of the Nargun is simultaneously an adversary of great power and an embodiment of the land and of an aspect of the hero's psyche; the tale of Simon Brent's learning to understand the Nargun and helping to deal with it is also a tale of his healing through acceptance of his angry loneliness after his parents' death. In the remote setting of Wongadilla, a sheep station among the ridges of the Great Dividing Range, Simon learns to trust the shrewd simplicity of two middle-aged cousins who see themselves as stewards rather than owners of the land and to feel, in moments of unity with the natural world, the transience of human life that is part of that world. Again Wrightson rejects belief in sin and retribution; the land and its ancient spirits are neither good nor evil, and Simon's symbolic experience of rebirth helps him to appreciate the isolation and mortality of all human beings and to find, in love and responsibility for others and in patient endurance, a creed by which to live.

The Song of Wirrun, a fantasy trilogy consisting of *The Ice is Coming, The Dark Bright Water,* and *Behind the Wind,* further develops the theme of self-realization through the hero-tale of Wirrun, a young Aboriginal Australian whose story encompasses an entire life in the setting of the whole continent. Wirrun journeys from late adolescence to fully initiated adulthood. He accepts his special calling as a hero, and comes to understand the darker side of his own nature in the person of his friend Ularra; he accepts the contrasexual part of himself in the person of the spirit-wife, the Yunggamurra, and endures the pain of losing her; he achieves final apotheosis after facing the figure of Wulgaru, who embodies the man-made but tormenting belief in sin and purgation. Wirrun overcomes his apparent annihilation by asserting his self-hood, and achieves the status of a culture-hero, present throughout the country, living on "behind the wind." Most of Wrightson's human characters, especially in the second and third volume of the trilogy, are Aboriginal Australians; the remainder are the Aboriginal spirits of the land. She is scrupulously careful to remain faithful to her sources and to the strongly localized nature of Aboriginal folklore, yet she seamlessly incorporates both into a narrative of high fantasy unprecedented in Australian literature for young adults, and unmatched in length, scope, and moral seriousness.

A Little Fear extends Wrightson's examination of individuation to encompass old age. Agnes Tucker has run away from the constraint of a home for the elderly to the independence of her dead brother's farm, certain that in its pastoral setting she will find peace and fulfilment. Wrightson undercuts the conventions of pastoral, however; this land has defeated settlers in the past, and in the person of the Njimbin, a small but truculent spirit, will defeat Mrs. Tucker also. The dog Hector understands the unsentimental reality of the land better than Mrs. Tucker does, and knows that the seemingly inexplicable events that she fears are symptoms of senile dementia are actually the work of the Njimbin and the creatures he controls. Mrs. Tucker's courage seems sufficient to save her, but in the suffocating storm of midges that brings the narrative to a climax she realizes that, unlike the Njimbin, she is a mortal part of a larger reality that she cannot ignore. She accepts the limitations of age, but her restored assertiveness enables her to bargain for a future that retains the greatest possible independence.

In *Moon-Dark* the dog of *A Little Fear* develops into Blue, the central character in an exploration of the effects of ecological imbalance among the animal communities in the Clarence River estuary. Wrightson uses the local Aboriginal figure of Keeting, the moon, to resolve the problem, but not without requiring self-help and co-operation among the animals. *Balyet,* the most recent of Wrightson's novels for young adults, uses an Aboriginal story of the echo to explore the theme of an adolescent girl's growth through testing social rules and the authority of elders. The ancient story and its modern re-enactment show that the old should learn that the wisest rules must change with changing circumstances, and the young that self-absorption is incompatible with maturity.

—John Murray

YATES, Elizabeth

Nationality: American. **Born:** Buffalo, New York, 6 December 1905. **Education:** Franklin School, Buffalo; Oaksmere, Mamaroneck, New York. **Family:** Married William McGreal in 1929 (died 1963). Writer, lecturer. Staff member at writers conferences at University of New Hampshire, University of Connecticut, and Indiana University, beginning 1956; instructor at Christian Writers and Editors conferences, Green Lake, Wisconsin, beginning 1962; trustee, Peterborough Town Library. **Awards:** *New York Herald Tribune* Spring Book Festival juvenile award, 1943, for *Patterns on the Wall;* Newbery honor book, 1944, for *Mountain Born;* Spring Book Festival older honor, 1950, John Newbery Medal, 1951, William Allen White Children's Book Award, 1953, all for *Amos Fortune, Free Man;* Boys' Clubs of America Gold Medal, 1953, for *A Place for Peter;* Jane Addams Children's Book Award from U.S. section of Women's International League for Peace and Freedom, 1955, for *Rainbow 'round the World: A Story of UNICEF;* Sara Josepha Hale Award, 1970; New Hampshire's Governor's Award of Distinction, 1982; Boys' Club of America Junior Book Award, 1994, for *A Place for Peter;* Charles H. Pettee bronze medal, 1994. Honorary degrees: Litt.D. from Aurora College, 1965, Eastern Baptist College, 1966, University of New Hampshire, 1967, Ripon College, 1970, New England College, 1972, Rivier College, 1979, and Franklin Pierce College, 1981. **Address:** 149 Eastside Dr., Concord, New Hampshire 03301, U.S.A.

PUBLICATIONS FOR YOUNG ADULTS

Fiction

Patterns on the Wall, illustrated by Warren Chappell. New York, Knopf, 1943; as *The Journeyman,* Greenville, South Carolina, Bob Jones University Press, 1990.
A Place for Peter, illustrated by N.S. Unwin. New York, Coward, 1953.

Other

Amos Fortune, Free Man, illustrated by N.S. Unwin. New York, Aladdin, 1950.
David Livingstone. Evanston, Illinois, Row Peterson, 1952.
Prudence Crandall, Woman of Courage, illustrated by N.S. Unwin. New York, Aladdin, 1955.
Someday You'll Write. New York, Dutton, 1962.
New Hampshire. New York, Coward, 1969.

Autobiographical trilogy

My Diary—My World. Philadelphia, Westminster, 1981.
My Widening World. Philadelphia, Westminster, 1983.
One Writer's Way. Philadelphia, Westminster, 1984.

PUBLICATIONS FOR CHILDREN

Fiction

High Holiday. London, A. & C. Black, 1938.
Hans and Frieda in the Swiss Mountains, illustrated by Nora S. Unwin. New York and London, Nelson, 1939.
Climbing Higher. London, A. & C. Black, 1939; as *Quest in the Northland,* New York, Knopf, 1940.
Haven for the Brave. New York, Knopf, 1941.
Under the Little Fir and Other Stories, illustrated by N.S. Unwin. New York, Coward, 1942.
Around the Year in Iceland, illustrated by Jon Nielsen. Boston, Heath, 1942.
Mountain Born, illustrated by N.S. Unwin. New York, Coward, 1943.
Once in the Year, illustrated by N.S. Unwin. New York, Coward, 1947.
Sam's Secret Journal, illustrated by Allan Eitzen. New York, Friendship, 1964.
Carolina's Courage, illustrated by N.S. Unwin. New York, Dutton, 1964, as *Carolina and the Indian Doll,* London, Methuen, 1965.
An Easter Story, illustrated by N.S. Unwin. New York, Dutton, 1967.
With Pipe, Paddle and Song: A Story of the French-Canadian Voyageurs, illustrated by N.S. Unwin. New York, Dutton, 1968.
Sarah Whitcher's Story, illustrated by N.S. Unwin. New York, Dutton, 1971.
We, the People, illustrated by N.S. Unwin. Taftsville, Vermont, Countryman Press, 1975.
The Seventh One, illustrated by Diana Charles. New York, Walker, 1978.
Silver Lining, illustrated by A.L. Morris. Canaan, New Hampshire, Phoenix, 1981.

Other

Joseph (Bible story), illustrated by N.S. Unwin. New York, Knopf, 1947.
The Young Traveller in the U.S.A. London, Phoenix House, 1948.
The Christmas Story, illustrated by N.S. Unwin. New York, Aladdin, 1949.
Children of the Bible, illustrated by N.S. Unwin. New York, Aladdin, 1950; London, Meiklejohn, 1951.
Rainbow 'round the World: A Story of UNICEF, illustrated by Betty Alden and Dirk Gringhuis. Indianapolis, Bobbs-Merrill, 1954.
Gifts of True Love: Based on the Old Carol ''The Twelve Days of Christmas,'' illustrated by N.S. Unwin. Wallingford, Pennsylvania, Pendle Hill, 1958.
Skeezer, Dog with a Mission, illustrated by Joan Drescher. New York, Harvey House, 1973.

Editor

Piskey Folk: A Book of Cornish Legends, by Enys Tregarthen, photographs by husband, William McGreal. New York, John Day, 1940.

The Doll Who Came Alive, by E. Tregarthen, illustrated by N.S. Unwin. New York, John Day, 1942; London, Faber, 1944.

The White Ring, illustrated by N.S. Unwin. New York, Harcourt, 1949.

Sir Gibbie, by George MacDonald. New York, Dutton, 1963; London, Blackie, 1967.

The Lost Princess; or, The Wise Woman, by G. MacDonald. New York, Dutton, 1965.

PUBLICATIONS FOR ADULTS

Fiction

Wind of Spring. New York, Coward, 1945; London, Cassell, 1948.

Nearby. New York, Coward, 1947; London, Cassell, 1950.

Beloved Bondage. New York, Coward, 1948.

Guardian Heart. New York, Coward, 1950; London, Museum Press, 1952.

Brave Interval. New York, Coward, 1952; London, Bakers, 1953.

Hue and Cry. New York, Coward, 1953.

The Carey Girl. New York, Coward, 1956.

The Next Fine Day. New York, John Day, 1962; London, Dent, 1964.

On That Night. New York, Dutton, 1969.

Other

Pebble in a Pool: The Widening Circles of Dorothy Canfield Fisher's Life. New York, Dutton, 1958, as *The Lady from Vermont: Dorothy Canfield Fisher's Life and World.* Brattleboro, Vermont, Greene, 1971.

The Lighted Heart. New York, Dutton, 1960.

Howard Thurman: Portrait of a Practical Dreamer. New York, John Day, 1964.

Up the Golden Stair: An Approach to a Deeper Understanding of Life through Personal Sorrow. New York, Dutton, 1966.

Is There a Doctor in the Barn?: A Day in the Life of Forrest F. Tenney, D.V.M. New York, Dutton, 1966.

The Road through Sandwich Notch. Brattleboro, Vermont, Stephen Greene, 1972.

A Book of Hours. Norton, Connecticut, Vineyard Books, 1976.

Call It Zest: The Vital Ingredient after Seventy. Brattleboro, Vermont, Stephen Greene, 1977; London, Prior, 1978.

Sound Friendships: The Story of Willa and Her Hearing Ear Dog. Woodstock, Vermont, Countryman Press, 1987.

Editor

Gathered Grace: A Short Selection of George MacDonald's Poems. Cambridge, Heffer, 1938.

Your Prayers and Mine. Boston, Houghton, 1954.

*

Media Adaptations: *Amos Fortune, Free Man* was adapted as a filmstrip and record by Miller-Brody, 1969. *Skeezer, Dog with a Mission* was adapted as a television film by National Broadcasting

Company (NBC), 1981. *Mountain Born* was adapted as a film by Disney Films.

Biography: Entry in *The Junior Book of Authors,* New York, H.W. Wilson, 1951; essay in *Something about the Author Autobiography Series,* Volume 6, Detroit, Gale, 1988.

Bibliography: *A Bio-Bibliography of Elizabeth Yates* by Sister Margaret L. Trudell, Nashua, New Hampshire, Rivier College, unpublished thesis, 1970.

Manuscript Collections: Special Collections, Mugar Memorial Library, Boston University.

Elizabeth Yates comments:

It was a startling question, and it came from a fourth grader in a small group of children who had come to talk with me about writing. ''Has aging improved your writing?'' I had to think for a moment. The other questions had been fairly routine: How long does it take to write a book? What can I do when I get stuck in the middle? Where do I get an idea? But this was one directed at me, where I am now, even before that, the years of apprenticeship and the long years of work with their richness and their agony, even up to this very moment. Thinking back I found my answer, and it was unequivocal: ''Yes, because life is a learning process, and the longer we live, the more we become aware of this.''

I wanted to give these children an instance, so I told them of the time when an idea had come to me with such insistency that I had to act on it. It could not be shelved, or put away in a notebook. It was when I was standing by the stone that marked the grave of Amos Fortune in the old cemetery in Jaffrey, New Hamshire. Reading the eloquent though brief words about a man whose life spanned from Africa in 1715, to America in 1801 I wanted to know more, to find the story within those lines. The idea took hold of me, or I of it, and I knew that nothing must keep me from following it. A line of William Blake's came to mind, ''He who kisses the joy as it flies/ Lives in Eternity's sunrise.'' Months of research were before me, months of work, the writing and then the careful revision, but finally when the words looked up at me from the page, I felt right about them. So, more than ever, I want to take hold of the idea that grips me, not because time may be running out on me, but because of the marvelous freshness. (Excerpted from *The Writer Magazine,* March 1998, with permission of the author.)

*   *   *

Although Elizabeth Yates has written numerous books for adult audiences, her most abiding interest has been her young adult readers, to whom her work has introduced a range of topics from biographies and folktales to travel and writing techniques. Her books have retained their appeal to a second and third generation of these young readers; for example, forty years after its initial publication, *Amos Fortune, Free Man* continues to sell more than three thousand copies annually. Well into her eighties, Yates has continued to discuss books and writing with school groups, often driving a considerable distance to do so. In addition, when a young girl asked for advice on becoming a writer, Yates's answer was the book *Someday You'll Write,* in which she describes writing as a craft requiring patience, discipline, and hard work. She further describes her own development as a writer in her memoirs (*The Lighted Heart*) and her published diaries (*My Diary—My World, My Widening World,* and *One Writer's Way*).

Influenced by Thomas Hardy and George Eliot, Yates chronicles the lives of actual and fictional individuals whose characters determine their destiny. She has written biographies of people of strong convictions like Dorothy Canfield Fisher (*Pebble in a Pool*), David Livingston, Howard Thurman (subtitled *Portrait of a Practical Dreamer*), Amos Fortune, and Prudence Crandall, who challenged the laws of Connecticut when, in 1833, she began a private girls' school which admitted black and white students on an equal basis.

Elizabeth Yates is best known, of course, for *Amos Fortune, Free Man,* winner of the 1951 Newbery Award and Herald Tribune Spring Festival Prize, as well as the 1953 William Allen White Children's Book Award. Yates's approach to this subject is typical of her method in writing. Seeing Amos Fortune's grave in a Jaffrey (New Hampshire) cemetery, she was intrigued by the inscription and began a thorough search of the historical records. When she knew everything that the records could tell her about Amos's life and about the slave trade, her knowledge of New England history and her artist's eye for understanding and portraying people helped her fill in the gaps. As a result, the reader shares not only Amos's hopes and triumphs, but also his fears, frustrations, and errors in judgment; Amos Fortune is a complex and credible character whose actions are completely plausible.

Amos possesses the character traits Yates admires. For instance, he feels a strong sense of responsibility to lead and care for others. When he and his fellow At-mun-shi are captured by the slavers, he tries unsuccessfully to organize resistance. Equally futile is his lengthy search for his sister, but when he cannot find her and buy her freedom, he tries instead to give other helpless women at least a few last days of dignity and freedom. Repeatedly he emphasizes to younger slaves and freedmen alike, the overwhelming importance of the freedom and respect earned through developing a skill. Amos's will further demonstrates his belief in the importance of education, as he leaves a substantial bequest to the local schools.

Amos's self-respect comes from his pride in craftsmanship and his well-developed sense of honor. He will not accept manumission until he also possesses skills sufficient to earn a living for himself and his family. He therefore masters two trades, weaving and tanning, and when finally he is freed, it is because he has bought his freedom and so has fulfilled his commitment to help provide for his master's widow. A skilled weaver and tanner, he prospers because he and his wife are industrious and thrifty.

Even though Amos was a prince among the At-mun-shi, more important to him is his identity as a simple Christian. Thus he consistently displays fortitude, humility, charity, and consideration for the feelings of others. He patiently endures setbacks in gaining his long-delayed freedom, and, despite his skills and his growing wealth, he makes no retort to the infrequent instances of overt racism, nor to the many small slights and the pervasive atmosphere of insensitivity. Also, whether in the lush forests of Africa or in the hilly New England countryside, Amos retains his attitude of humble awe toward the natural world. To him, Mount Monadnock speaks a language of signs that allows him to anticipate and prepare for storms, and though he eventually forgets all At-mun-shi words except his own name, Amos continues the tribal custom of reverently kissing the earth.

Likewise, even while he is busily engaged in establishing his own home and his business, Amos continues to show concern for the welfare of others. A notable example is the Burdoo family, whose improvidence makes them foils for Amos and his family. Moses Burdoo was, like Amos, a skilled craftsman, but even when he was alive, the town frequently was called upon to help support his family, and his death has reduced his children to a kind of indentured servitude. When Amos in effect adopts Polly Burdoo and sets her brothers on the path to learning trades, he offers a kind of charity that allows the family to regain their dignity.

Several of Yates's fictional characters share Amos Fortune's attributes. For example, Peter of *Mountain Born* and *A Place for Peter* is, like Amos, a youth who grows toward maturity in a pastoral setting which instills in him an appreciation of the changing seasons and—through his caring for his pet ewe—a love for animals. Moreover, when the farmhand Benj explains to Peter that he kills the rattlesnakes only to protect the humans and the sheep and thus he asks the rattlesnakes' forgiveness before killing them, he demonstrates a reverence for nature similar to that of the At-mun-shi, who also kill only out of necessity and then burn the entrails in expiation to the spirits of their animal victims.

In *Carolina's Courage,* inspired by a century-old Indian doll given to her by a friend, Yates relates the story of young Carolina Putnam and her treasured doll Lydia-Lou. The Putnam family must leave behind most of their possessions when they leave their New Hampshire home to become homesteaders in Nebraska. The delicately beautiful china and sawdust doll is the one personal possession Carolina's father allows her to take, a major source of consolation for her during the trying journey. Just short of their destination, however, as the wagon train is delayed by the threat of hostile Indians, Carolina wanders to the banks of a nearby stream, where she meets an Indian girl with a crude doll made of buffalo hide. After playing together for a while, the two girls part, but the Indian girl insists that they exchange dolls. Remembering that she has been taught to share, Carolina reluctantly agrees and so, without being aware of it, ensures the safety of the entire party as they travel through Indian territory.

Like the Indian doll, the stencil wall designs discovered during the renovation of her home Shieling (named for a type of shelter used by shepherds on the Isle of Skye) led Yates to write the novel *Patterns on the Wall*. Fascinated by the art of stenciling, she combined her research on the subject with historical facts about the dreadful New Hampshire winter of 1816, to tell the story of Jared Austin, an artist whose talent makes him suspect among his fellow New Englanders. Blamed for the snowfalls that occur in every month that year, Jared is accused of being a devil, and he becomes an outcast, losing everything but the consolation he derives from his art. With a fortitude akin to that of Amos Fortune, however, Jared considers his troubles part of a divine plan to remind him of God's power and providential care.

Throughout her career, Yates's books have reflected her interests and her values. She has written about *Children of the Bible* and children affected by the work of UNICEF (*Rainbow 'round the World*), about those who work with animals (*Is There a Doctor in the Barn?*) and those who train animals to assist the hearing-impaired (*Sound Friendships* and *Skeezer, Dog with a Mission*). *The Lighted Heart* is an inspirational account of the modifications Yates and her husband, William McGreal, made in their lives as—with courage and fortitude worthy of her most heroic characters—they adapted to his increasing loss of sight. In *Call It Zest: The Vital*

Ingredient after Seventy, Elizabeth Yates explains a lifestyle that includes service on the Boards of the New Hampshire Association for the Blind, Hearing Ear Dog Program, and White Pines College, as well as volunteer work at three nursing homes, the community hospital, and the town library. Obviously she, like Amos Fortune, has discovered that hard work for the benefit of others is the secret to a long and vigorous life.

—Charmaine Allmon Mosby

YEP, Laurence (Michael)

Nationality: American. **Born:** San Francisco, California, 14 June 1948. **Education:** Marquette University, Milwaukee, 1966-68; University of California, Santa Cruz, B.A. 1970; State University of New York at Buffalo, 1970-75, Ph.D. 1975. **Career:** Writer. Part-time instructor of English, Foothill College, Mountain View, California, 1975, and San Jose City College, California, 1975-76; visiting lecturer in Asian American studies, University of California, Berkeley, 1987-1989, writer-in-residence, 1990. **Awards:** Book-of-the-Month-Club Writing Fellowship, 1970; *New York Times* Outstanding Books of the Year selection, 1975, Newbery Medal Honor Book, American Library Association (ALA), Children's Book Award, International Reading Association, Jane Addams Children's Book Award Honor Book, Jane Addams Peace Association, and Carter G. Woodson Book Award, National Council for Social Studies, all 1976, *Boston Globe-Horn Book* Award Honor Book, 1977, Lewis Carroll Shelf Award, University of Wisconsin, 1979, selected as one of New York Public Library's Books for the Teen Age, 1980, 1981, and 1982, and Friends of Children and Literature Award, 1984, all for *Dragonwings*; *School Library Journal*'s Best Books for Spring selection, and *New York Times* Outstanding Books of the Year selection, both 1977, both for *Child of the Owl*; *Boston Globe-Horn Book* Award for fiction, 1977, and Jane Addams Children's Book Award, 1978, both for *Child of the Owl*; Commonwealth Club of California Silver Medal, 1979, for *Sea Glass*; Child Study Association of America's Children's Books of the Year selection, 1986, for *Dragon Steel*; *Boston Globe-Horn Book* Honor Award, 1989, for *The Rainbow People*. **Agent:** Maureen Walters, Curtis Brown Agency, 10 Astor Place, New York, New York 10003. **Address:** 921 Populus Place, Sunnyvale, California 94086, U.S.A.

PUBLICATIONS FOR YOUNG ADULTS

Fiction

Sweetwater, illustrated by Julia Noonan. New York, Harper, 1973; London, Faber, 1976.
Dragonwings. New York, Harper, 1975.
Child of the Owl. New York, Harper, 1977.
Sea Glass. New York, Harper, 1979.
Dragon of the Lost Sea. New York, Harper, 1982.
Kind Hearts and Gentle Monsters. New York, Harper, 1982.
The Mark Twain Murders. New York, Four Winds Press, 1982.
Liar, Liar. New York, Morrow, 1983.
The Serpent's Children. New York, Harper, 1984.

The Tom Sawyer Fires. New York, Morrow, 1984.
Dragon Steel. New York, Harper, 1985.
Mountain Light (sequel to *The Serpent's Children*). New York, Harper, 1985.
Shadow Lord. New York, Harper, 1985; Bath, Chivers, 1987.
The Curse of the Squirrel, illustrated by Dirk Zimmer. New York, Random House, 1987.
Dragon Cauldron. New York, HarperCollins, 1991.
The Star Fisher. New York, Morrow, 1991.
Tongues of Jade. New York, HarperCollins, 1991.
Dragon War. New York, HarperCollins, 1992.
The City of Dragons, illustrated by Jean and Mou-Sien Tseng. New York, Scholastic, 1995.
Thief of Hearts. New York, HarperCollins, 1995.
Ribbons. New York, G.P. Putnam's Sons, 1996.
The Case of the Goblin Pearls. New York, HarperCollins, 1997.
The Case of the Lion Dance. New York, HarperCollins, 1998.
The Cook's Family. New York, Putnam, 1998.
The Imp that Ate My Homework, illustrated by Benrei Huang. New York, HarperCollins, 1998.

Other

Age of Wonders (play; produced by Asian American Theater Company, 1987).
Pay the Chinaman, and Fairy Bones (play; produced in San Francisco, 1987).
Reteller, *The Rainbow People* (collection of Chinese-American folk tales), illustrated by David Wiesner. New York, Harper, 1989.
A Lesson Plan Book for Dragonwings. Jefferson City. Missouri, 1990.
Lost Garden (autiobiography). Englewood Cliffs, New Jersey, Silver Burdett Press, 1990.
When the Bomb Dropped: The Story of Hiroshima. New York, Random House, 1990.
Editor, *American Dragons: A Collection of Asian American Voices.* New York, HarperCollins, 1993.
Reteller, *The Shell Woman and the King,* illustrated by Yang Ming-Yi. New York, Dial, 1993.
Reteller, *Foxfire,* illustrated by Jean and Mou-sien Tseng. New York, Scholastic, 1994.
Dragonwings (play). New York, Dramatist Play Service, 1993.
Reteller, *The Khan's Daughter: A Mongolian Folktale,* illustrated by Jean and Mou-Sien Tseng. New York, Scholastic, 1997.
Reteller, *Dragon Prince: A Chinese Beauty & the Beast Tale,* illustrated by Kam Mak. New York, HarperCollins, 1997.

PUBLICATIONS FOR ADULTS

Fiction

Seademons. New York, Harper, 1977.
Monster Makers, Inc. New York, Arbor House, 1986.

*

Media Adaptations: *Dragonwings* (filmstrip with record or cassette), Miller-Brody, 1979; *The Curse of the Squirrel* (cassette),

Random House, 1989; *Sweetwater* is available in braille and on cassette.

Biography: Entry in *Dictionary of Literary Biography,* Vol. 52, *American Writers for Children since 1960: Fiction,* Detroit, Gale, 1986, 392-98; essay in *Authors and Artists for Young Adults,* Vol. 5, Detroit, Gale, 1990; essay in *Speaking for Ourselves: Autobiographical Sketches by Notable Authors of Books for Young Adults,* Vol. 1, compiled and edited by Donald R. Gallo, Urbana, Illinois, National Council of Teachers of English, 1990.

Critical Studies: Entry in *Children's Literature Review,* Vol. 3, 1978; Vol. 17, 1989, Detroit, Gale; entry in *Contemporary Literary Criticism,* Vol. 35, Detroit, Gale, 1985.

*   *   *

Laurence Yep is a literary bridge builder. Some of his bridges connect his readers with Chinese-American and Chinese traditions, folklore, history, thought, and experiences. Since he began publishing in 1969, Yep has authored works of folklore, science fiction, fantasy, short stories, essays, plays, realistic fiction, historical fiction, and picture books.

Employing universal themes in his work, Yep touches concerns that affect all people; finding personal and cultural identity, separating from parents, becoming independent, and coming to terms with a changing body are all masterfully handled in Yep's books for young people. He bridges the gap between the concerns of young people and their resolution by his characters. As Yep straddles the line between children's and young adult literature, his books are links between the reading of elementary school and the reading of middle, junior high school, and early high school years.

Yep frequently deals with a multidimensional, multicultural world. Explaining in his autobiography, *Lost Garden,* that he was brought up in an urban neighborhood of mixed ethnicity, where, as the neighborhood changed, he felt like an outsider in a place wherein he once felt most at home. "At a time when so many children are now proud of their ethnic heritages, I'm ashamed to say that when I was a child, I didn't want to be Chinese. It took me years to realize that I was Chinese whether I wanted to be or not. And it was something I had to learn to accept: to know it's strengths and weaknesses. It's something that is a part of me from the deepest levels of my soul to my most every day actions."

Yep utilizes Chinese-American and Chinese characters in many of his books. Moon Shadow, the young protagonist in *Dragonwings,* who was born in China, sees the United States with fresh eyes when he joins the father and the Tang men who comprise the Chinese bachelor society in San Francisco in the early 1900s. While exploring the theme of a man fulfilling a dream, Yep shows the beauty and strengths of Chinese culture, the racism and bigotry against the Chinese as it existed at the time of the story, and the strong bonds of friendships that can develop between people of different races.

Both China and the United States are used as the settings for *Serpent's Children* and *Mountain Light.* Yep begins each novel by painting a vivid portrait of the life of the rural poor from Kwangtung province in the mid-1800s. The commitment to the cause of eliminating British and Manchu rule plays a major role in shaping

many characters. Seen through the eyes of Cassia, the female narrator, and Squeaky Lau, the male narrator, the novel deals with issues of tradition: foot binding, the role of women in society, belonging and acceptance, etc. Taking a stand and sacrificing for beliefs are sensitively handled in these books as well. Both books contrast life in China with the life of some characters in the United States.

In contrast to Yep's historical fiction, *Child of the Owl, Sea Glass,* and *Star Fisher* have a modern American setting and feature Chinese-American protagonists, between twelve and fifteen, who undertake personal journeys to discover their individuality. To some degree autobiographical, two of the these novels feature strong female voices. *American Dragons* is also set in contemporary America, but instead of a single voice, it contains many. Consisting of a variety of poems, short stories, and an excerpt from a play, gathered by Yep but written by a variety of authors with Asian roots, this timely collection of personal and often moving narratives examines questions of personal, cultural, and sexual identity, and looks at intergenerational and cultural problems.

The Rainbow People and *Tongues of Jade* supply readers with two additional collections of stories. With a single black-and-white illustration by David Wiesner at the beginning of each story, both books consist of simple yet powerful folktales with roots in the traditional folklore of China's Kwangtung province. The author used old Chinese myths as background material when he wrote *Dragon of the Lost Sea, Dragon Steel, Dragon Cauldron,* and *Dragon War,* interconnected fantasy novels that trace the adventures of Shimmer, the dragon princess, who forges friendships and interdependencies as she tries to restore her lost home.

Yep writes for outsiders, or those who don't fit in. For Yep this can mean being overweight, not being athletic, not being the perfect child—dilemmas faced by many young adults or at least ones they can relate to. Streetwise Casey, in *Child of the Owl,* begrudgingly leaves behind the only life she has ever known, living on the edge with her father, a compulsive gambler who is suddenly hospitalized, until she goes to live with her elderly grandmother. Casey learns, changes, and grows as she discovers more about her heritage. Overweight Craig in *Sea Glass* feels as if he is a constant disappointment to his athletic parents, but through experiences and the friendship he develops with his uncle, he gains the strength and wisdom to accept who he is. Craig learns that his "Chineseness" separates him because of the bigotry of some, but his humanity and inner strengths connect him with others. Joan Lee and her family in *Star Fisher* encounter both bigotry and kindness in West Virginia. They adapt to new traditions like baking apple pies and find the courage to begin again, blending the new with the old.

In *Sweetwater,* Yep uses the genre of science fiction to explore differences between groups sharing the same planet with indigenous people. Thirteen-year-old Tyree's love of music enables him to form a strong bond with the aliens and discover his family roots as well. Yep contrasts the inhabitants of another future civilization and how its people deal with differences in *Seademons.* On still another planet, Yep uses a somewhat older protagonist seeking to find his place in his own society in *Shadow Lord,* the twenty-second novel of the "Star Trek" series.

Yep sensitively develops complex characters who wrestle with self-understanding, and struggle to develop new relationships with family members and peers. All share concerns about where they fit into society. Charley and Chris, two teens who on the surface are vastly different, come to care for each after an initial confrontation in *Kind Hearts and Gentle Monsters. Liar, Liar* generates excitement and tension when a fatal car crash occurs and questions of murder begin to be asked. Suspense builds as Sean, the sixteen-year-old protagonist, confronts the killer and overcomes his panic to save himself.

In *The Mark Twain Murders* and *The Tom Sawyer Fires,* Yep mixes fact and fiction to re-create San Francisco in the late Civil War years when Samuel Clemens, a.k.a. Mark Twain, worked as a newspaper reporter and when Tom Sawyer, an actual city firefighter, became a local hero. A fifteen year old, the Duke of Baywater, narrates both books. After his mother's death and the murder of his brutal stepfather, the teen maintains his illusions regarding the royal identity of his real father as he helps to solve crimes and thwart confederate plots. The teen discovers that heroic actions matter even when they are kept secret and a title attached to a name does little to establish identity, taking action means much more.

Yep's books ask questions about growing up. In *Sea Glass,* the father queries, "So it doesn't matter to you if you win or lose?" Craig, the son, replies with the question, "How do you measure success anyway?" His characters offer advice on living. Cassia in *Mountain Light* says, "Stand tall when you go home. Don't let anyone shrink to a clown." By including both young and old people with much to learn, young and old who feel they already know it all, elders as mentors, Yep gives a sense of authenticity to his multi-dimensional characters.

Writing fiction, folklore, and his autobiography, Yep illustrates that there is no stereotypical Chinese-American, Chinese, or Asian family and/or character. Rather than appealing to one specific group, his work has qualities that have universal appeal. The insights Yep gained as an outsider flavor his writings. Bridging different cultures, readers are able to enjoy the stories Yep weaves, while looking through a window to greater understandings of the worlds of differences and similarities that co-exist in life. Vivid images, complex characters, and well-plotted action linger on the pages of Yep's novels.

—Karen Ferris Morgan

YOLEN, Jane (Hyatt)

Nationality: American. **Born:** New York City, 11 February 1939. **Education:** Staples High School, Westport, Connecticut, graduated 1956; Smith College, Northampton, Massachusetts, B.A. 1960; New School for Social Research, New York; University of Massachusetts, Amherst, 1975-76, M.Ed. 1976. **Family:** Married David W. Stemple in 1962; one daughter and two sons. **Career:** Staff member, *This Week* magazine and *Saturday Review,* New York, 1960-61; assistant editor, Gold Medal Books, New York, 1961-62; associate editor, Rutledge Books, New York, 1962-63; assistant editor, Alfred A. Knopf Juvenile Books, New York, 1963-65; Lecturer in Education, Smith College, 1979-84. Columnist (*Children's Bookfare*), *Daily Hampshire Gazette,* Northampton, Massachusetts, 1972-80. Massachusetts delegate, Democratic National Convention, Miami, 1972. Member of the Board of Directors, Society of Children's Book Writers since 1974, and Children's

Literature Association, 1977-79; President, Science-Fiction Writers of America, 1986-88. Editor in chief, Jane Yolen Books, imprint of Harcourt Brace, since 1988. **Awards:** Boys' Club of America Junior Book award, 1968, for *The Minstrel and the Mountain*; Lewis Carroll Shelf award, 1968, for *The Emperor and the Kite,* and 1973, for *The Girl Who Loved the Wind*; *The Emperor and the Kite* was selected one of the *New York Times*'s Best Books of the Year and as a Caldecott Honor Book, both 1968; *World on a String: The Story of Kites* was named an ALA Notable Book, 1968; Chandler Book Talk Reward of Merit, 1970; Children's Book Showcase of the Children's Book Council, 1973, for *The Girl Who Loved the Wind,* and 1976, for *The Little Spotted Fish*; Society of Children's Book Writers Golden Kite award, 1974, ALA Notable Book and National Book award nomination, both 1975, all for *The Girl Who Cried Flowers and Other Tales*; Golden Kite Honor Book, 1975, for *The Transfigured Hart,* and 1976, for *The Moon Ribbon and Other Tales*; Christopher Medal, 1978, for *The Seeing Stick*; Children's Choice from the International Reading Association and the Children's Book Council, 1980, for *Mice on Ice,* and 1983, for *Dragon's Blood*; Parents' Choice award from the Parents' Choice Foundation, 1982, for *Dragon's Blood,* 1984, for *The Stone Silenus,* and 1989, for *Piggins* and *The Three Bears Rhyme Book*; *The Gift of Sarah Barker* was selected one of *School Library Journal*'s Best Books for Young Adults, 1982, and *Heart's Blood,* 1985; Garden State Children's Book award from the New Jersey Library Association, 1983, for *Commander Toad in Space*; CRABerry award from Acton Public Library, Maryland, 1983, for *Dragon's Blood*; *Heart's Blood* was selected one of ALA's Best Books for Young Adults, 1984; Daedelus award, 1986, for "a body of work—fantasy and short fiction"; *The Lullaby Songbook* and *The Sleeping Beauty* were each selected one of Child Study Association of America's Children's Books of the Year, 1987; Caldecott Medal, 1988, for *Owl Moon*; World Fantasy award, 1988, for *Favorite Folktales from around the World*; Kerlan award for "singular achievements in the creation of children's literature," 1988; Parents' Choice Silver Seal award, Jewish Book Council award, and Association of Jewish Libraries award, all 1988, Judy Lopez Honor Book and Nebula award finalist, both 1989, all for *The Devil's Arithmetic*; Golden Sower award from the Nebraska Library Association, 1989, and Charlotte award, New York State Reading Council, 1991, both for *Piggins*; Regina Medal, Catholic Library Association, 1992, for body of work; Smith College Medal, 1992; Distinguished Alumna Mythopoeic Society award, 1993, for *Briar Rose*; Rhysling award, for best science fiction/fantasy poem, 1993, for *Will*; thirteen of Yolen's books have been selected by the Junior Literary Guild. LL.D.: College of Our Lady of the Elms, Chicopee, Massachusetts, 1980. **Agent:** Marilyn Marlow, Curtis Brown, 10 Astor Place, New York, New York 10003. **Address:** 31 School Street, Box 27, Hatfield, Massachusetts 01038, U.S.A.

PUBLICATIONS FOR YOUNG ADULTS

Fiction

Simple Gifts: The Story of the Shakers, illustrated by Betty Fraser. New York, Viking Press, 1976.
The Gift of Sarah Barker. New York, Viking Press, 1981.
Dragon's Blood. New York, Delacorte Press, 1982; London, MacRae, 1983.

Neptune Rising: Songs and Tales of the Undersea Folk, illustrated by David Wiesner. New York, Philomel, 1982.

Children of the Wolf. New York, Viking Kestrel, 1984.

Heart's Blood. New York, Delacorte Press, and London, MacRae, 1984.

The Stone Silenus. New York, Philomel, 1984.

A Sending of Dragons, illustrated by Tom McKeveny. New York, Delacorte Press, and London, MacRae, 1987.

The Devil's Arithmetic. New York, Viking Kestrel, 1988.

Vampires. New York, Harper, 1991.

Briar Rose. New York, Tor, 1992.

Here There Be Dragons, illustrated by David Wilgus. San Diego, Harcourt Brace, 1993.

Here There Be Unicorns, illustrated by David Wilgus. San Diego, Harcourt Brace, 1994.

Here There Be Witches, illustrated by David Wilgus. San Diego, Harcourt Brace, 1995.

Water Music, photographs by Jason Stemple. Honesdale, Pennsylvania, Boyds Mills Press, 1995.

Dragon's Blood. New York, Magic Carpet Books, 1996.

Here There Be Angels, illustrated by David Wilgus. San Diego, Harcourt Brace, 1996.

Passager. San Diego, Harcourt Brace, 1996.

Hobby. San Diego, Harcourt Brace, 1996.

Merlin. San Diego, Harcourt Brace, 1997.

Twelve Impossible Things Before Breakfast: Stories. San Diego, Harcourt Brace, 1997.

The Wild Hunt, illustrated by Francisco Mora. New York, Scholastic, 1997.

Armageddon Summer, with Bruce Coville. San Diego, Harcourt Brace, 1998.

Other

The Faery Flag: Stories and Poems of Fantasy and the Supernatural. New York, Orchard, 1989.

A Letter from Phoenix Farm, photographs by Jason Stemple. Katonah, New York, Owen, 1992.

Milk and Honey: A Year of Jewish Holidays, music arranged by Adam Stemple, illustrated by Louise August. New York, Putnam, 1996.

Editor, *Zoo 2000: Twelve Stories of Science Fiction and Fantasy Beasts.* New York, Seabury Press, 1973; London, Gollancz, 1975.

Editor, *Shape Shifters: Fantasy and Science Fiction Tales about Humans Who Can Change Their Shapes.* New York, Seabury Press, 1978.

Editor, with Martin H. Greenberg and Charles G. Waugh, *Dragons and Dreams: A Collection of New Fantasy and Science Fiction Stories.* New York, Harper, 1986.

Editor, with Martin H. Greenberg and Charles G. Waugh, *Spaceships and Spells.* New York, Harper, 1987.

Editor, with Martin H. Greenberg, *Werewolves.* New York, Harper, 1988.

Editor, with Martin H. Greenberg, *Things That Go Bump in the Night.* New York, Harper, 1989.

Editor, *2040 A.D.* New York, Delacorte, 1990.

Editor, *Camelot: A Collection of Original Arthurian Stories,* illustrated by Winslow Pels. New York, Philomel, 1995.

Editor, with Martin H. Greenberg, *The Haunted House,* illustrated by Doron Ben-Ami. New York, HarperCollins, 1995.

PUBLICATIONS FOR CHILDREN

Fiction

The Witch Who Wasn't, illustrated by Arnold Roth. New York, Macmillan, and London, Collier Macmillan, 1964.

Gwinellen, The Princess Who Could Not Sleep, illustrated by Ed Renfro. New York, Macmillan, 1965.

Trust a City Kid, with Anne Huston, illustrated by J.C. Kocsis. New York, Lothrop, 1966; London, Dent, 1967.

Isabel's Noel, illustrated by Arnold Roth. New York, Funk and Wagnalls, 1967.

The Emperor and the Kite, illustrated by Ed Young. Cleveland, World, 1967; London, Macdonald, 1969.

The Minstrel and the Mountain, illustrated by Anne Rockwell. Cleveland, World, and Edinburgh, Oliver and Boyd, 1968.

Greyling: A Picture Story from the Islands of Shetland, illustrated by William Stobbs. Cleveland, World, 1968; London, Bodley Head, 1969.

The Longest Name on the Block, illustrated by Peter Madden. New York, Funk and Wagnalls, 1968.

The Wizard of Washington Square, illustrated by Ray Cruz. New York, World, 1969.

The Inway Investigators; or, The Mystery at McCracken's Place, illustrated by Allan Eitzen. New York, Seabury Press, 1969.

The Seventh Mandarin, illustrated by Ed Young. New York, Seabury Press, and London, Macmillan, 1970.

Hobo Toad and the Motorcycle Gang, illustrated by Emily McCully. New York, World, 1970.

The Bird of Time, illustrated by Mercer Mayer. New York, Crowell, 1971.

The Girl Who Loved the Wind, illustrated by Ed Young. New York, Crowell, 1972; London, Collins, 1973.

The Girl Who Cried Flowers and Other Tales, illustrated by David Palladini. New York, Crowell, 1974.

Rainbow Rider, illustrated by Michael Foreman. New York, Crowell, 1974; London, Collins, 1975.

The Adventures of Eeka Mouse, illustrated by Myra Gibson McKee. Middletown, Connecticut, Xerox, 1974.

The Boy Who Had Wings, illustrated by Helga Aichinger. New York, Crowell, 1974.

The Magic Three of Solatia, illustrated by Julia Noonan. New York, Crowell, 1974.

The Little Spotted Fish, illustrated by Friso Henstra. New York, Seabury Press, 1975.

The Transfigured Hart, illustrated by Donna Diamond. New York, Crowell, 1975.

The Moon Ribbon and Other Tales, illustrated by David Palladini. New York, Crowell, 1976; London, Dent, 1977.

Milkweed Days, photographs by Gabriel Amadeus Cooney. New York, Crowell, 1976.

The Sultan's Perfect Tree, illustrated by Barbara Garrison. New York, Parents' Magazine Press, 1977.

The Seeing Stick, illustrated by Remy Charlip and Demetra Marsalis. New York, Crowell, 1977.

The Hundredth Dove and Other Tales, illustrated by David Palladini. New York, Crowell, 1977; London, Dent, 1979.

The Giants' Farm, illustrated by Tomie de Paola. New York, Seabury Press, 1977.

Hannah Dreaming, photographs by Alan Epstein. Springfield, Massachusetts, Springfield Museum of Fine Arts, 1977.

The Mermaid's Three Wisdoms, illustrated by Laura Rader. New York, Collins World, 1978.

No Bath Tonight, illustrated by Nancy Winslow Parker. New York, Crowell, 1978.

The Simple Prince, illustrated by Jack Kent. New York, Parents' Magazine Press, 1978.

Spider Jane, illustrated by Stefen Bernath. New York, Coward McCann, 1978.

Dream Weaver and Other Tales, illustrated by Michael Hague. New York, Collins, 1979.

The Giants Go Camping, illustrated by Tomie de Paola. New York, Seabury Press, 1979.

Spider Jane on the Move, illustrated by Stefen Bernath. New York, Coward McCann, 1980.

Mice on Ice, illustrated by Lawrence Di Fiori. New York, Dutton, 1980.

Commander Toad in Space, illustrated by Bruce Degen. New York, Coward McCann, 1980.

The Robot and Rebecca: The Mystery of the Code-Carrying Kids, illustrated by Catherine Deeter. New York, Random House, 1980.

Shirlick Holmes and the Case of the Wandering Wardrobe, illustrated by Anthony Rao. New York, Coward McCann, 1981.

Uncle Lemon's Spring, illustrated by Glen Rounds. New York, Dutton, 1981.

The Boy Who Spoke Chimp, illustrated by David Wiesner. New York, Knopf, 1981.

Brothers of the Wind, illustrated by Barbara Berger. New York, Philomel, 1981.

The Acorn Quest, illustrated by Susanna Natti. New York, Crowell, 1981.

The Robot and Rebecca and the Missing Owser, illustrated by Lady McCrady. New York, Knopf, 1981.

Sleeping Ugly, illustrated by Diane Stanley. New York, Coward McCann, 1981.

Commander Toad and the Planet of the Grapes, illustrated by Bruce Degen. New York, Coward McCann, 1982.

Commander Toad and the Big Black Hole, illustrated by Bruce Degen. New York, Coward McCann, 1983.

Commander Toad and the Dis-Asteroid, illustrated by Bruce Degen. New York, Coward McCann, 1985.

Commander Toad and the Intergalactic Spy, illustrated by Bruce Degen. New York, Coward McCann, 1986.

Piggins, illustrated by Jane Dyer. San Diego, Harcourt Brace, 1987; London, Piccadilly Press, 1988.

Owl Moon, illustrated by John Schoenherr. New York, Philomel, 1987.

Commander Toad and the Space Pirates, illustrated by Bruce Degen. New York, Putnam, 1987.

Picnic with Piggins, illustrated by Jane Dyer. San Diego, Harcourt Brace, 1988.

Piggins and the Royal Wedding. San Diego, Harcourt Brace, 1989.

Dove Isabeau. San Diego, Harcourt Brace, 1989.

Dream Weaver. New York, Putnam, 1989.

Baby Bear's Bedtime Book, illustrated by Jane Dyer. San Diego, Harcourt Brace, 1990.

Sky Dogs, illustrated by Barry Moser. San Diego, Harcourt Brace, 1990.

Tam Lin, illustrated by Charles Mikolaycak. San Diego, Harcourt Brace, 1990.

The Dragon's Boy. New York, Harper, 1990.

Elfabet: An ABC of Elves. Boston, Little Brown, 1990.

Letting Swift River Go. Boston, Little Brown, 1990.

All Those Secrets of the World, illustrated by Leslie Baker. Boston, Little Brown, 1991.

Wizard's Hall. San Diego, Harcourt Brace, 1991.

Eeny, Meeny, Miney Mole, illustrated by Kathryn Brown. San Diego, Harcourt Brace, 1992.

Encounter, illustrated by David Shannon. San Diego, Harcourt Brace, 1992.

Honkers, illustrated by Leslie Baker. Boston, Little Brown, 1993.

Mouse's Birthday, illustrated by Bruce Degen. New York, Putnam, 1993.

The Girl in the Golden Bower, illustrated by Jane Dyer. Boston, Little Brown, 1994.

Beneath the Ghost Moon, illustrated by Laurel Molk. Boston, Little Brown, 1994.

Grandad Bill's Song, illustrated by Melissa Bay Mathis. New York, Philomel, 1994.

The Ballad of the Pirate Queens, illustrated by David Shannon. San Diego, Harcourt Brace, 1995.

Before the Storm, illustrated by Georgia Pugh. Honesdale, Pennsylvania, Boyds Mill Press, 1995.

A Sip of Aesop, illustrated by Karen Barbour. New York, Blue Sky Press, 1995.

Merlin and the Dragons, illustrated by Li Ming. New York, Cobblehill Books, 1995.

With Heidi E. Y. Stemple, *Meet the Monsters,* illustrated by Patricia Ludlow. New York, Walker, 1996.

Little Mouse and Elephant: A Tale from Turkey (retelling), illustrated by John Segal. New York, Harper, 1996.

The Musicians of Bremen: A Tale from Germany (retelling), illustrated by John Segal. New York, Harper, 1996.

Child of Faerie, Child of Earth, illustrated by Jane Dyer. New York, Little, Brown, 1997.

Nocturne, illustrated by Anne Hunter. San Diego, Harcourt Brace, 1997.

Once Upon a Bedtime Story (retelling), illustrated by Ruth Tietjen Councell. Honesdale, Pennsylvania, Boyds Mills Press, 1997.

Miz Berlin Walks, illustrated by Floyd Cooper. New York, Philomel, 1997.

A Sending of Dragons. San Diego, Harcourt Brace, 1997.

The Traveler's Rose, illustrated by Leo and Diane Dillon. New York, Philomel, forthcoming.

Poetry

See This Little Line?, illustrated by Kathleen Elgin. New York, McKay, 1963.

It All Depends, illustrated by Don Bolognese. New York, Funk and Wagnalls, 1969.

An Invitation to the Butterfly Ball: A Counting Rhyme, illustrated by Jane Breskin Zalben. New York, Parents' Magazine Press, 1976; Kingswood, Surrey, World's Work, 1978.

All in the Woodland Early: An ABC Book, music by the author, illustrated by Jane Breskin Zalben. Cleveland, Collins, 1979.

How Beastly! A Menagerie of Nonsense Poems, illustrated by James Marshall. New York, Collins, 1980.

Dragon Night and Other Lullabies, illustrated by Demi. New York, Methuen, 1980; London, Methuen, 1981.

Ring of Earth: A Child's Book of Seasons, illustrated by John Wallner. San Diego, Harcourt Brace, 1986.

The Three Bears Rhyme Book, illustrated by Jane Dyer. San Diego, Harcourt Brace, 1987.

Best Witches. New York, Putnam, 1989.

Bird Watch, illustrated by Ted Lewin. New York, Philomel, 1990.

Dinosaur Dances, illustrated by Bruce Degen. New York, Putnam, 1990.

Raining Cats and Dogs, illustrated by Janet Street. San Diego, Harcourt Brace, 1993.

What Rhymes With Moon?, illustrated by Ruth Tietjen Councell. New York, Philomel, 1993.

With Nancy Willard, *Among Angels: Poems,* illustrated by S. Saelig Gallagher. San Diego, Harcourt Brace, 1995.

The Three Bears Holiday Rhyme Book. San Diego, Harcourt Brace, 1995.

O Jerusalem, illustrated by John Thompson. New York, Scholastic, 1996.

Sacred Places, illustrated by David Shannon. San Diego, Harcourt Brace, 1996.

Sea Watch: A Book of Poetry, illustrated by Ted Lewin. New York, Philomel, 1996.

Other

Pirates in Petticoats, illustrated by Leonard Vosburgh. New York, McKay, 1963.

Robin Hood (play; music by Barbara Green; produced Boston, 1967).

World on a String: The Story of Kites. Cleveland, World, 1968.

Editor, *The Fireside Song Book of Birds and Beasts,* music by Barbara Green, illustrated by Peter Parnall. New York, Simon and Schuster, 1972.

Friend: The Story of George Fox and the Quakers. New York, Seabury Press, 1972.

The Wizard Islands, illustrated by Robert Quackenbush. New York, Crowell, 1973.

Ring Out! A Book of Bells, illustrated by Richard Cuffari. New York, Seabury Press, 1974; London, Evans, 1978.

Editor, *Rounds about Rounds,* music by Barbara Green, illustrated by Gail Gibbons. New York, Watts, 1977; London, Watts, 1978.

Editor, *The Lullaby Songbook,* music arranged by Adam Stemple, illustrated by Charles Mikolaycak. San Diego, Harcourt Brace, 1986.

The Sleeping Beauty (retelling), illustrated by Ruth Sanderson. New York, Knopf, 1986.

The Lap-Time Song and Play Book, musical arrangements by Adam Stemple, illustrated by Margot Tomes. San Diego, Harcourt Brace, 1989.

Publisher, *Appleblossom.* San Diego, Harcourt Brace, 1991.

Hark!, A Christmas Sampler, original music and arrangements by Adam Stemple, illustrated by Tomie de Paola. New York, Putnam, 1991.

Publisher, *The Jewel of Life.* San Diego, Harcourt Brace, 1991.

Publisher, *The Patchwork Lady.* San Diego, Harcourt Brace, 1991.

Publisher, *The Red Ball.* San Diego, Harcourt Brace, 1991.

Editor, *Street Rhymes around the World,* illustrated by seventeen international artists. Honesdale, Pennsylvania, Wordsong, 1992.

Welcome to the Greenhouse: A Story of the Tropical Rainforest, illustrated by Laura Regan. New York, Putnam, 1993.

Jane Yolen's Songs of Summer, music arranged by Adam Stemple, illustrated by Cyd Moore. Honesdale, Pennsylvania, Boyds Mills press, 1993.

Editor, *Sleep Rhymes Around the World.* Honesdale, Pennsylvania, Woodsong, 1994.

Editor, *Alphabestiary: Animal Poems From A to Z,* illustrated by Allen Eitzen. Honesdale, Pennsylvania, Wordsong, 1995.

Editor, *Sky Scrape/City Scape: Poems of City Life,* illustrated by Ken Condon. Honesdale, Pennsylvania, Wordsong, 1996.

Editor, *Mother Earth, Father Sky: Poems of Our Planet,* illustrated by Jennifer Hewitson. Honesdale, Pennsylvania, Wordsong, 1996.

Welcome to the Sea of Sand, illustrated by Laura Regan. New York, Putnam, 1996.

Editor, *Once Upon Ice and Other Frozen Poems,* illustrated with photographs by Jason Stemple. Honesdale, Pennsylvania, Wordsong/Boyds Mills Press, 1997.

PUBLICATIONS FOR ADULTS

Fiction

The Lady and the Merman, illustrated by Barry Moser. Easthampton, Massachusetts, Pennyroyal Press, 1977.

Cards of Grief. New York, Ace, 1984; London, Futura, 1986.

Sister Light, Sister Dark. New York, Tor, 1988.

White Jenna. New York, Tor, 1989.

The Books of Great Alta. New York, Tor, 1996.

Short Stories

Tales of Wonder. New York, Schocken, 1983; London, Futura, 1987

Dragonfield and Other Stories. New York, Ace, 1985.

Merlin's Booke. New York, Steeldragon Press, 1986.

Nonfiction

Writing Books for Children. Boston, The Writer, 1973; revised edition, 1983.

Touch Magic: Fantasy, Faerie, and Folklore in the Literature of Childhood. New York, Philomel, 1981.

Guide to Writing for Children. Boston, The Writer, 1989.

Other

Contributor, *Dragons of Light,* edited by Orson Scott Card. New York, Ace, 1981.

Contributor, *Elsewhere,* edited by Terri Windling and Mark Alan Arnold. New York, Ace, 2 vols., 1981-82.

Contributor, *Hecate's Cauldron,* edited by Susan Schwartz. New York, DAW, 1982.

Contributor, *Heroic Visions,* edited by Jessica Amanda Salmonson. New York, Ace, 1983.

Contributor, *Faery!,* edited by Terri Windling. New York, Ace, 1985.

Contributor, *Liavek,* edited by Will Shetterly and Emma Bull. New York, Ace, 1985.

Contributor, *Moonsinger's Friends,* edited by Schwartz. Bluejay, 1985.

Contributor, *Imaginary Lands,* edited by Robin McKinley. New York, Greenwillow, 1985.

Contributor, *Don't Bet on the Prince: Contemporary Feminist Fairy Tales in North America and England,* by Jack Zipes. New York, Methuen, 1986.

Editor, *Favorite Folktales from around the World.* New York, Pantheon, 1986.

Contributor, *Liavek: Players of Luck,* edited by Will Shetterly and Emma Bull. New York, Ace, 1986.

Contributor, *Liavek: Wizard's Row,* edited by Will Shetterly and Emma Bull. New York, Ace, 1987.

Contributor, *Visions,* by Donald R. Gallo. New York, Delacorte, 1987.

Contributor, *Liavek: Spells of Binding,* edited by Will Shetterly and Emma Bull. New York, Ace, 1988.

Contributor, *Invitation to Camelot,* by Parke Godwin. New York, Ace, 1988.

Contributor, *The Unicorn Treasury,* by Bruce Coville. New York, Doubleday, 1988.

Editor, with Martin H. Greenberg. *Xanadu.* New York, Tor, 1993.

Editor, with Martin H. Greenberg. *Xanadu Two.* New York, Tor, 1994.

Editor, with Martin H. Greenberg. *Xanadu Three.* New York, Tor, 1995.

With Nancy Willard, *Among Angels,* illustrated by S. Saelig Gallagher. San Diego, Harcourt Brace, 1995.

*

Media Adaptations: *The Seventh Mandarin* (film), Xerox Films, 1973; *The Emperor and the Kite* (filmstrip with cassette), Listening Library, 1976; *The Bird of Time* (play, produced Northampton, Massachusetts, 1982); *The Girl Who Cried Flowers and Other Tales* (cassette), Weston Woods, 1983; *Dragon's Blood* (television movie), CBS Storybreak, 1985; *Commander Toad in Space* (cassette), Listening Library, 1986; *Touch Magic. . .Pass It On* (cassette), Weston Woods, 1987; *Owl Moon* (filmstrip with cassette), Weston Woods, 1988; *Piggins and Picnic with Piggins* (cassette), Caedmon, 1988; *Commander Toad* (half hour movie), Churchill Films, 1993; *Commander Toad in Space* (videocassette), 1993; *Briar Rose* (cassette), Recorded Books, 1996; *The Devil's Arithmetic* (cassette), Recorded Books, 1996.

Biography: Entry in *Dictionary of Literary Biography,* Vol. 52, Detroit, Gale, 1986; essay in *Something about the Author Autobiography Series,* Vol. 4, Detroit, Gale, 1987; essay in *Speaking for Ourselves: Autobiographical Sketches by Notable Authors of Books for Young Adults,* Vol. 1, compiled and edited by Donald R. Gallo, National Council of Teachers of English, 1990.

Manuscript Collections: Kerlan Collection, University of Minnesota, Minneapolis.

Critical Studies: Entry in *Children's Literature Review,* Volume 4, Detroit, Gale, 1982; "An Empress of Thieves" by Jane Yolen, in *Horn Book* (Boston), November/December 1994, 702-706; entry in The Internet Public Library, http://www.ipl.org, updated 5 July 1995; "An Interview With . . . Jane Yolen" by John Koch, in *The Writer* (Boston), 1 March 1997, 20-21; "All in the Family" by Jane Yolen, in *Book Links* (New York), September 1997, 47-50.

Jane Yolen comments:

I am a storyteller. I never feel more alive than when I am sitting at my desk in front of my typewriter and stories simply leak out of my fingertips onto the keyboard. I don't know where they come from, but once the first draft is out there, the hard work really begins: the shaping, pounding, kneading, pummeling the thing into shape.

Of course the story is never quite as wonderful at the end as one hopes at the beginning. As Edith Wharton said: "I dream of an eagle, I give birth to a hummingbird." That's why we writers keep on writing, looking for that great soaring eagle, forgetting that the hummingbird is also beautiful. And it flies.

*   *   *

Jane Yolen is the author of over one hundred and fifty books in a variety of genres. Best known for her books of fantasy, written in the style of folk and fairy tales, her books have won major state and national awards and have been translated into ten languages. Because of her versatility, imagination, and use of language, she is a perfect author for young adults.

Several of Yolen's books in the fairy tale genre are meant for older readers. Although her books are inspired by folk literature, they are generally not retellings but her own creations. Young adult readers learn that fairy tales and fantasy can teach them about themselves, the nature of love, and their place in the world. *Neptune Rising: Songs and Tales of the Undersea Folk* contains original stories and poems about "sea folks." The stories, centered around the multifarious relationships that might arise between sea folk and humans, teach that there is pain and danger in seeking out and loving those belonging in a different element. In *The Mermaid's Three Wisdoms,* Melusina (who as a mermaid cannot speak), breaks the code of the merfolk by showing herself to humans and is banished from her home beneath the sea to live on earth. There she is found by Jess, a twelve-year-old deaf girl. The deaf and the dumb form a unique and touching friendship. Gradually, the impulsive Jess learns from Melusina the wisdom of the merfolk: have patience, like the sea; move with the rhythm of life around you; and know that all things touch all others, as all life touches the sea.

"If you ask me 'What was the greatest story ever told?'" Jane Yolen said in an interview for *The Writer,* "I'd say 'King Arthur—with a little more emphasis on the girls.'" *The Dragon's Boy* is Yolen's imaginative retelling of King Arthur's boyhood, *Camelot* is a lively collection of "original Arthurian stories" by herself and others, and in "The Young Merlin Trilogy" (*Passager, Hobby,* and *Merlin*), Yolen retells—and freshly reimagines—the life and adventures of the young Merlin. (Given her rich imagination and her prolificacy, one assumes she'll get around to some Arthurian girls one day soon!)

The pit dragon trilogy, *Dragon's Blood, Heart's Blood,* and *A Sending of Dragons,* are three fantasy novels set on the distant planet Austar. In this series, the reader watches the psychological, moral, and spiritual development of Jakkin as he moves from slavery to freedom, from boyhood to manhood, and from responsibility only for himself to taking on responsibility for others. In *Dragon's Blood,* Jakkin works as a bond servant in the nursery for fighting dragons. To attain his freedom, he steals a dragon hatchling. In the next two titles in the series, Jakkin rescues Akki, the girl he loves, first from a dangerous group of rebels and then from a society in which robot-like people live underground and sacrifice dragons to remain alive. The planet Austar is a complete fantasy world. In it Yolen develops a complete life cycle for dragons, making them familiar animals to the reader. The many fans of this series will be happy to learn that Yolen is thinking of writing a fourth volume in it.

Dragons, unicorns, witches, angels—these are the inhabitants of fantasy, and these are the subjects of Yolen's four collections of her own poetry, stories, and other imaginings for older children and young adults: *Here There Be Dragons, Here There Be Unicorns, Here There Be Witches,* and *Here There Be Angels.*

Jane Yolen has written about her own Jewish heritage in three notable books. In *The Devil's Arithmetic,* Hannah is magically transported in time and place from her safe home in New York to a small Jewish village in Poland, where she is captured by the Nazis and sent to a concentration camp. She dies there, heroically. When she returns to the living present, she understands the importance of keeping the past alive. In *Briar Rose,* the death of her grandmother leads Becca to seek information about her grandmother's past. This search ends at the site of an internment camp in Poland, where Becca begins to understand her grandmother's unique life. The elements of the fairy tale ''Sleeping Beauty'' are metaphorically intertwined with Becca's grandmother's experiences: briars are barbed wire; sleep is an endless ride in a death truck; and, the prince's kiss is the cardiopulmonary resuscitation! Most recently, Yolen has written a wonderful book of Jewish lore, song, and ritual as she explains to young people the meaning and background of Jewish holidays and festivals (*Milk and Honey: A Year of Jewish Holidays*).

The Gift of Sarah Barker and *Children of the Wolf* are two novels of historical fiction. Set in a Shaker Community during the middle 1800s, *The Gift of Sarah Barker* tells the story of the growing love between two adolescents. Because the Shakers profess celibacy, the two try to keep their relationship a secret. Again, characteristics of fairy tales infuse themselves within the story. The two adolescents are young innocents, the girl's mother represents the ''cruel'' parent, while the kind and supporting mother of the sect is comparable to a godmother. *Children of the Wolf,* based on actual newspaper accounts, is an imaginative recreation of the attempt of a missionary to raise two children who have lived with wolves. Although it would seem, that the two feral children should be the center to the story, the story is told from the point of view of the missionary, Mohandas, who comes to understand his own gift for love, compassion, and ability to care for others.

In an essay for the *Horn Book* magazine, Jane Yolen wrote, ''The book speaks to individuals in an individual voice. But then it is taken into the reader's life and re-created, re-invigorated, re-visioned. That is what literature is all about.'' And that is certainly what Jane Yolen's fine literature for older children and young adults is all about.

—Etta Miller, updated by Marcia Welsh

YOUD, Christopher Samuel. *See* CHRISTOPHER, John.

ZALBEN, Jane Breskin

Nationality: American. **Born:** New York City, 21 April 1950. **Education:** Queens College of the City University of New York, B.A. 1971; Pratt Institute Graphic Center, graduate study in lithography, 1971-72. **Family:** Married Steven Zalben in 1969; two sons. **Career:** Painter, etcher, lithographer, and illustrator; designer and author of children's books. Assistant to art director of children's book department, Dial Press, New York, 1971-72; book designer, Holt, Rinehart & Winston, Inc., New York, 1973-74; Thomas Y. Crowell Co., New York, 1974-75; art director, Charles Scribner's, 1975-76; instructor, School of Visual Arts, Manhattan, 1976-1993. **Awards:** AIGA award 1978, 1979; *American Bookseller* Pick of the Lists, 1988; *Parents* magazine award, 1993; IRA Teachers' Choice award, 1993. **Agent:** Marilyn Marlow, Curtis Brown Ltd., 10 Astor Place, New York, New York 10003, U.S.A. **Address:** 70 South Road, Sands Point, New York 11050, U.S.A.

PUBLICATIONS FOR YOUNG ADULTS

Fiction

Maybe It Will Rain Tomorrow. New York, Farrar, Straus, 1982.
Here's Looking at You, Kid, New York, Farrar, Straus, 1984.
Water from the Moon. New York, Farrar, Straus, 1987.
Earth to Andrew O. Blechman, illustrated by the author. New York, Farrar, Straus, 1989.
The Fortuneteller in 5B. New York, Holt, 1991.
Unfinished Dreams. New York, Simon & Schuster, 1996.

PUBLICATIONS FOR CHILDREN

Fiction (illustrated by the author unless otherwise noted)

Cecilia's Older Brother. New York, Macmillan, 1973.
Lyle and Humus. New York, Macmillan, 1974.
Basil and Hillary. New York, Macmillan, 1975.
Penny and the Captain. New York, Philomel Books, 1978.
Norton's Nighttime. New York, Collins, 1979.
Will You Count the Stars without Me? New York, Farrar, Straus, 1979.
Oliver's and Alison's Week, illustrated by Emily Arnold McCully. New York, Farrar, Straus, 1980.
A Perfect Nose for Ralph, illustrated by John Wallner. New York, Philomel, 1980.
Oh, Simple! New York, Farrar, Straus, 1981.
Porcupine's Christmas Blues. New York, Philomel Books, 1982.
Beni's First Chanukah. New York, Holt, 1988.
Happy Passover, Rosie. New York, Holt, 1990.
Leo & Blossom's Sukkah. New York, Holt, 1990.

Beni's Little Library. New York, Holt, 1991.
Goldie's Purim. New York, Holt, 1991.
Buster Gets Braces. New York, Holt, 1992.
Happy New Year, Beni. New York, Holt, 1993.
Papa's Latkes. New York, Holt, 1994.
Miss Violet's Shining Day. Honesdale, Pennsylvania, Boyds Mill
    Press, 1995.
Pearl Plants a Tree. New York, Simon & Schuster, 1995.
Pearl's Marigolds for Grandpa. New York: Simon & Schuster, 1997.
Beni's First Wedding. New York, Holt, 1998.
Pearl's Eight Days of Chanukah. New York, Simon & Schuster, 1998.

Other

Beni's Family Cookbook for the Jewish Holidays. New York,
    Holt, 1996.

Illustrator: *Jeremiah Knucklebones* by Jan Wahl, 1974; *An Invitation to the Butterfly Ball,* 1976, and *All in the Woodland Early: An ABC Book,* 1979, both by Jane H. Yolen, 1976; *Jabberwocky,* 1977, and *The Walrus and the Carpenter,* 1986, both by Lewis Carroll; *Starlight & Moonshine: Poetry of the Supernatural* by William Shakespeare, 1987; *Inner Chimes: Poems on Poetry,* edited by Bobbye S. Goldstein, 1992.

*   *   *

Jane Breskin Zalben sets her first-person narratives for young adults in the complex, sprawling world of New York City and its suburbs. The urban environment provides her middle-class characters with ready access to such pleasures as art museums, Chinese food, music lessons, and foreign films. Within this setting, however, they must learn to cope with the same misunderstandings and misinterpretations in relations with family and friends common to adolescents in any surroundings.

Just as New York City provides a context for Zalben's writing, so do the observances and traditions related to Judaism form strands in her novels. While *The Fortuneteller in 5B* includes the strongest Jewish elements, Jewish backgrounds of her characters are apparent elsewhere. *Earth to Andrew O. Blechman* includes preparations for a bar mitzvah. Nicole's family exchanges Hanukkah gifts in *Water from the Moon.* Jason Glass and others carpool to and attend Hebrew School in *Unfinished Dreams.*

In many ways her first novel, *Maybe it will Rain Tomorrow,* remains her most powerful for older readers. Sixteen-year-old Beth Corey must come to terms with her mother's suicide. Confused and abandoned, she moves in with her father, his second wife Linda, and their baby daughter. However, Beth has never reconciled herself to her father's seeking a divorce and blames him and Linda for her mother's death. At the same time she feels guilty and angry with herself for not preventing the suicide. Feeling like an intruder in her new home, she clashes with Linda in particular. Beth's search for a new relationship leads to involvement with Jonathan, a handsome, talented flute player in her music theory class. Beth joins his informal musical group that performs sidewalk concerts in New York City.

Like all Zalben's adolescents, Beth is frankly interested in sex and places a high value on physical attractiveness. Her sexual involvement with Jonathan is handled matter-of-factly. Yet, when

he tells her he plans to spend the summer working at a resort in the Catskills to earn money for music lessons, Beth feels betrayed again. "'I slept with you because I trusted you,'" she tells him. A tentative reconciliation through letters ends after Beth visits the resort and realizes that Jonathan's involvement had been more casual than she realized. By the novel's end, Beth starts to recognize the aspects of her mother's life and personality that made her decide to commit suicide and makes initial efforts to fit in with her new family.

While Zalben tells *Maybe It Will Rain Tomorrow* through Beth's voice, in *Here's Looking at You Kid,* the narrator is a young man. Seventeen-year-old Eric Fine must find his place in the Long Island neighborhood to which his family has moved recently. His first friendship develops after he meets Enid Tannenbaum at a Bergman film. Sharing a love for movies, they plan to collaborate on a screenplay. But Eric is diverted by gorgeous Kimberley Wright, who dates him while her boyfriend is gone during spring vacation. Even though Eric suspects that Kimberley is using him and realizes his attraction to her hurts Enid, Eric cannot resist.

Zalben returns to a female narrator in *Water from the Moon,* Nicole Bernstein has successful, happily married parents, a supportive best friend, and economic security. Her longing for romance leads her to magnify the interest Joshua Brent, an intern in her father's advertising company, expresses in her. She convinces herself that the five-year age gap between her and Joshua makes no difference then is hurt when she discovers his interest in a woman his own age.

Nicole's longing for adventure leads to a friendship with Tanya Rubano, a fellow art student. Nicole's efforts to secure promises of abiding friendship are rebuffed by Tanya, who refuses to make strong emotional attachments because her hippie mother moves from city to city in search of old friends and new experiences. Nicole's extreme disappointment over Joshua's and Tanya's unwillingness to make commitments to her seems strange, especially when contrasted with the losses suffered by Beth in Zalben's first novel. In sum, *Water from the Moon* represents a less substantial and emotionally involving novel than its predecessors.

Zalben's latest novels are directed at readers in a lower age range. In *Earth to Andrew O. Blechman,* Andrew agrees to help tutor Lou Pearlstein, his upstairs neighbor, in preparation for a long-delayed bar mitzvah. In return, Lou, a vaudeville veteran, teaches aspiring comedian Andrew some of his jokes. Andrew's grandmother lives in the basement of the same brownstone, and her developing romance with Lou culminates in an engagement announcement at Lou's bar mitzvah.

In *The Fortuneteller in 5B,* a sequel of sorts, Madame Van Dam has moved into the brownstone. She occupies the apartment vacated by Lou, who has moved in with Andrew's grandmother after their wedding. Alexandria Pilaf tells about her discovery of Van Dam's past. The speculations by Alexandria and her friend Jenny that the elderly woman is a vampire are replaced with the truth: Van Dam's parents and sister, along with many other Gypsies, had died in Nazi concentration camps. The knowledge that Madame Van Dam has survived such horror helps Alexandria work through her loss of her father, who died of cancer. Readers will be moved by the author's note about the concentration camp at Terezin, where thousands of children were sent during World War II. Most died in Auschwitz. Zalben notes that hundreds of Christians, such as Van Dam's relatives, died along with Jews at the hands of Nazis.

Zalben captures a wide range of emotions in *Unfinished Dreams.* Sixth grader Jason Glass tells about a year in which he deals with many sorrows, including his pet rabbit's death, his solo competition loss, and his best friend's move. But the overarching loss is the illness and death of his principal, Mr. Carr.

Mr. Carr's offbeat humor and creative approaches to education had enriched the lives of all Sherman Elementary School students for years. He had tried to make every student feel special. But in particular, he had encouraged young musicians like Jason, a gifted violinist. The news that Mr. Carr is dying of AIDS divides the community. One group of parents condemns him as morally unfit and tries to discontinue his insurance and pension. Others, including Jason's parents, argue for compassion and fairness. Jason's letters to Mr. Carr inform him about Jason's musical progress and life at school. He also reveals his emotional devastation after vandals maliciously destroy his violin, an extension of himself. Jason's family cannot afford to replace the valuable instrument immediately. Jason flirts with revenge, taking the baseball mitt of the boy he suspects, but he cannot bring himself to slash the glove. One of Jason's comments expresses the book's theme: "'It takes more courage to be different than the same.'" Zalben's prefatory comments indicate that some of the plot is based on incidents from her son's life. Perhaps the personal involvement contributes to the emotional intensity of this fine novel.

—Kathy Piehl

ZINDEL, Paul

Nationality: American. **Born:** Staten Island, New York, 15 May 1936. **Education:** Port Richmond High School, Staten Island; Wagner College, New York, B.S. in chemistry 1958, M.Sc. 1959. **Family:** Married Bonnie Hildebrand in 1973; one son, one daughter. **Career:** Technical writer, Allied Chemical, New York, 1958-59; chemistry teacher, Tottenville High School, Staten Island, New York, 1959-69; playwright and author of children's books, since 1969. Playwright-in-residence, Alley Theatre, Houston, Texas, 1967. **Awards:** Ford Foundation grant, 1967, for drama; Children's Book of the Year, Child Study Association of America, 1968, and *Boston Globe-Horn Book* award for text, 1969, both for *The Pigman*; *New York Times* Outstanding Children's Book of the Year citations for *My Darling, My Hamburger,* 1969, *I Never Loved Your Mind,* 1970, *Pardon Me, You're Stepping on My Eyeball!,* 1976, *The Undertaker's Gone Bananas,* 1978 and *The Pigman's Legacy,* 1980; *Village Voice* Obie award for the Best American Play, the New York Drama Critics Vernon Rice Drama Desk award for the Most Promising Playwright, and New York Drama Critics Circle award for Best American Play of the Year, all 1970; Pulitzer Prize in Drama and New York Critics award, both 1971, for *The Effect of Gamma Rays on Man-in-the-Moon Marigolds*; American Library Association's Best Young Adult Books citations, for *The Effect of Gamma Rays on Man-in-the-Moon Marigolds,* 1971, *Pigman,* 1975, *Pardon Me, You're Stepping on My Eyeball!,* 1976, *Confessions of a Teenage Baboon,* 1977, *The Pigman's Legacy,* 1980, and *To Take a Dare,* 1982; *Media & Methods* Maxi award, 1973, for *The Pigman*; New York Public Library "books for the teen age" citations for *Confessions of a Teenage Baboon,*

1980, *The Effect of Gamma Rays on Man-in-the-Moon Marigolds,* 1980, 1981 and 1982, *A Star for the Latecomer,* 1981 and *The Pigman's Legacy,* 1981 and 1982; Honorary Doctorate of Humanities from Wagner College, 1971. **Agent:** Curtis Brown, Ltd., 10 Astor Place, New York, New York 10003, U.S.A.

PUBLICATIONS FOR YOUNG ADULTS

Fiction

The Pigman. New York, Harper, 1968; London, Bodley Head, 1969.
My Darling, My Hamburger. New York, Harper, 1969; London, Bodley Head, 1970.
I Never Loved Your Mind. New York, Harper, 1970; London, Bodley Head, 1971.
The Effect of Gamma Rays on Man-in-the-Moon Marigolds, illustrated by Dong Kingman. New York, Harper, 1971.
Pardon Me, You're Stepping on My Eyeball! New York, Harper, and London, Bodley Head, 1976.
Confessions of a Teenage Baboon. New York, Harper, 1977; London, Bodley Head, 1978.
The Undertaker's Gone Bananas. New York, Harper, 1978; London, Bodley Head, 1979.
The Pigman's Legacy. Mew York, Harper, and London, Bodley Head, 1980.
With Bonnie Zindel, *A Star for the Latecomer.* New York, Harper, and London, Bodley Head, 1980.
The Girl Who Wanted a Boy. New York, Harper, and London, Bodley Head, 1981.
With Crescent Dragonwagon, *To Take a Dare.* New York, Harper, 1982.
Harry and Hortense at Hormone High. New York, Harper, 1984; London, Bodley Head, 1985.
The Amazing and Death-Defying Diary of Eugene Dingman. New York, Harper, and London, Bodley Head, 1987.
A Begonia for Miss Applebaum. New York, Harper, and London, Bodley Head, 1989.
The Pigman & Me. New York, HarperCollins, 1992.
David & Della. New York, HarperCollins, 1993.
Fifth Grade Safari, illustrated by Jeff Mangiat. New York, Bantam Books, 1993.
Attack of the Killer Fishsticks. New York, Bantam Books, 1993.
Fright Party, illustrated by Jeff Mangiat. New York, Bantam Books, 1993.
Loch. New York, HarperCollins, 1994.
The 100% Laugh Riot, illustrated by Jeff Mangiat. New York, Bantam Books, 1994.
The Doom Stone. New York, HarperCollins, 1995.
Raptor. New York, Hyperion, 1998.
Reef of Death. New York, HarperCollins, 1998.

PUBLICATIONS FOR CHILDREN

Fiction

I Love My Mother, illustrated by John Melo. New York, Harper, 1975.

PUBLICATIONS FOR ADULTS

Fiction

When Darkness Falls. New York, Bantam, 1984.

Plays

Dimensions of Peacocks (produced New York, 1959).
Euthanasia and the Endless Hearts (produced New York, 1960).
A Dream of Swallows (produced Off-Broadway, 1962).
And Miss Reardon Drinks a Little (produced Los Angeles, 1967; produced on Broadway, 1971). New York, Dramatists Play Service, 1971.
The Secret Affairs of Mildred Wild (produced New York City, 1972). New York, Dramatists Play Service, 1973.
Let Me Hear You Whisper. New York, Dramatists Play Service, 1973; illustrated by Stephen Gammell, New York, Harper, 1974.
The Ladies Should Be in Bed (produced New York, 1978). With *Let Me Hear You Whisper,* New York, Dramatists Play Service, 1973.
Ladies at the Alamo (also director; produced New York, 1975). New York, Dramatists Play Service, 1977.
A Destiny on Half Moon Street (produced Coconut Grove, Florida, 1985).
Amulets against the Dragon Forces. New York, Circle Repertory Company, 1989.

Screenplays: *Up the Sandbox,* 1972; *Mame,* 1974; *Maria's Lovers,* with others, 1984; *Runaway Train,* with Djordje Milicevic and Edward Bunker, 1985.

Television Plays: *Let Me Hear You Whisper,* 1966; *The Effect of Gamma Rays on Man-in-the-Moon Marigolds,* 1966; *Alice in Wonderland,* 1985; *Babes in Toyland,* with Leslie Briscusse, 1986.

*

Theatrical Activities: Director, *Ladies at the Alamo,* New York, 1975.

Media Adaptations: *The Effect of Gamma Rays on Man-in-the-Moon Marigolds* (play), produced in Houston, Texas, at Alley Theatre, 1964, produced Off-Broadway at Mercer-O'Casey Theatre, April 7, 1970; *Let Me Hear You Whisper* (television movie), NET-TV, 1966; *The Pigman* (cassette; filmstrip with cassette), Miller-Brody/Random House, 1978; *My Darling, My Hamburger* (cassette; filmstrip with cassette), Current Affairs and Mark Twain Media, 1978.

Manuscript Collections: Boston University.

Biography: Essay in *The Marble in the Water: Essays on Contemporary Writers of Fiction for Children and Young Adults* by David Rees, Boston, Massachusetts, Horn Book, 1980; entry in *Dictionary of Literary Biography,* Vol. 7, *Twentieth-Century American Dramatists,* Detroit, Gale, 1981; *Fifth Book of Junior Authors and Illustrators,* New York, Wilson, 1983; essay in *Speaking for Ourselves: Autobiographical Sketches by Notable Authors of Books*

for Young Adults, Vol. 1, compiled and edited by Donald R. Gallo, National Council of Teachers of English, 1990.

Critical Studies: Entry in *Children's Literature Review,* Vol. 3, Detroit, Gale, 1978; *Presenting Paul Zindel* by Jack Jacob Forman, Boston, Twayne, 1988.

*   *   *

The first thing one remembers about Paul Zindel's young adult novels are the incongruous, often nonsensical titles—*My Darling, My Hamburger; Pardon Me, You're Stepping on My Eyeball; The Undertaker's Gone Bananas.* Then there are the bizarre-sounding names of even more bizarre characters—Paranoid Pete; Schizoid Susie; Edna Shinglebox; Chris Phlegm; Joan Hybred. The stories with these strange titles and odd characters are an amalgam of usually mixed-up, well-meaning teenagers interacting with one another to resolve personal problems in a world peopled with irresponsible single parents, foolish teachers, cruel cops, and other adults of whom the most sane and least destructive could be characterized as innocuous. Zindel's novels are made to order for young adults because they confirm and flesh out two of the most widely-held beliefs of adolescents: that they are superior to adults and live more honest lives than adults do. It's not that Zindel himself shares these beliefs, but because he thinks that many teenagers do, he creates a world of exaggeration and caricature that appeals to the young adult sensibility.

Most of Zindel's young adult fiction is narrated by teen protagonists whose literary voices are snappy and colloquial ("My mother and father never touch each other, which makes me wonder how on earth I was ever born."); the teen characters often communicate using what Zindel refers to as "transitional pictures"—letters written in cursive, graffiti, lists, and doodling. Even in his autobiographical portrait *The Pigman and Me,* Zindel writes messages to his readers in cursive to gain their attention. The plots put parents in the background, who then seem to emerge only to harass or stifle the teen heroes and heroines. The interpersonal relationships of Zindel's fictional teenagers are largely of three kinds: boy-girl; teenager-senior adult; and son/daughter-single parent.

Above all, Zindel's fiction is written to teach lessons to his readers—lessons that Zindel himself and his protagonists have learned. The most important lesson for Zindel is self-worth. Before one can reach out to relate to and help others, one must have a sense of one's own worth. It is a lesson that Zindel didn't learn until he was an adult. His father left home for another woman when Zindel was two years old, and his itinerant nurse-mother dragged him and his older sister from one dwelling to another, often moving every year. When he was fifteen, he spent a lonely year-and-a-half in a sanitorium recovering from tuberculosis. Only after he won the Pulitzer Prize in 1971 for the autobiographical play *The Effect of Gamma Rays on Man-in-the-Moon Marigolds* did Zindel feel comfortable with his own sense of self-worth.

Zindel's first young adult novel, *The Pigman,* which many feel is his best work, was a ground-breaking event because—along with S.E. Hinton's *The Outsiders*—it transformed what had been called the teen "junior novel" from a predictable, stereotyped story about high school sports and dances to one about complex teenage protagonists dealing with real concerns: broken families, peer pressure, drug use, sexuality, runaways, and ethnic and racial differences. *The Pigman* and *The Pigman's Legacy* (the sequel written thirteen years later) feature John and Lorraine, two teenagers alienated from their parents and school who learn the twin lessons of self-worth and taking responsibility for their actions. In the first book, the two young teens meet and grow close to Mr. Pignati (they call him The Pigman because of his treasured collection of marble pigs), an old man who has not accepted his wife's death. They also gain a sense of self-worth and grow fond of one another because of their genuine friendship with the old man. But in a rash moment, they betray his trust by throwing a party in his house while he is recovering in the hospital from a heart attack. The party gets out of hand, and the collection of marble pigs is destroyed. Broken by this breach of trust, The Pigman suffers a fatal heart attack soon after—and John and Lorraine are left questioning their complicity in his death. In the sequel, the two teenagers—still guilty about their friend's death two years later—go to the abandoned house and find a homeless and sick old man living there. Plagued by the memories of their experience with The Pigman, they bring the tramp food and just before his death go on a gambling spree with him to Atlantic City.

In one way or another Zindel's other novels are concerned with building self-confidence. *My Darling, My Hamburger* focuses on the contrast between two sets of boyfriend-girlfriend relationships and how the attitudes and actions of parents affect the sexual responsibility of these teens; the boy and girl whose parents show love, tolerance, and understanding act responsibly while the other pair, afflicted by low self-esteem and alienated from their parents, act irresponsibly. *Pardon Me, You're Stepping on My Eyeball* is about fifteen-year-old Marsh Mellow, who can't accept his father's death and can't cope with his mother's alcoholism and emotional abuse of him. In a special education class, he meets Edna Shinglebox whose parents pull her in two directions: she's pushed into doing things she doesn't want to do and is overprotected from doing what she wants to do. Together, these two misfits face an even crazier world. After surviving a series of wild and unbelievable events, they eventually confront the reality of their lives and earn hard-won esteem. Similarly, in *The Confessions of a Teenage Baboon,* a teenager overcomes his mother's mental abuse to forge a positive self-identity and declare independence from her emotional control.

Zindel also would like his readers to appreciate life by learning how to cope with death. He portrays teen protagonists who deal with death directly in the two "Pigman" books, *Confessions of a Teenage Baboon, Harry and Hortense at Hormone High,* and *A Begonia for Miss Applebaum,* in which two of the science teacher's students celebrate life with Miss Applebaum as she is dying of cancer. In these stories—and especially in the lighter novel *The Undertaker's Gone Bananas*—Zindel looks at death "not as a foe, but as an inevitable adventure." It is a part of life which should be accepted and not feared.

Zindel's humor permeates even the most serious of his novels. His humor is exaggerated, farcical, mocking, and sometimes slapstick. In *Harry and Hortense at Hormone High,* Harry says of his mother: "When my mother prepares meat loaf, she looks like a woman trying to beat an abalone." Marsh Mellow in *Pardon Me* says the food in the school cafeteria is served on a plate "that looked like it was the final resting place for a stuffed rodent." The humor is not subtle, and adults may think it is juvenile and derogatory, but that's precisely why teen readers like it and why Zindel uses it.

Zindel's later writing *(The Girl Who Wanted a Boy, The Amazing and Death-Defying Diary of Eugene Dingman, Harry and Hortense at Hormone High* especially) is more contrived than his earlier work, although *A Begonia for Miss Applebaum* is genuinely touching in places. More recent yet is a memoir entitled *The Pigman and Me* that describes the real people on whom he modelled many of his fictional characters throughout his career. Because his characters are drawn from his life and because his stories are driven by lessons he has learned from his life, it is not surprising that many of his novels are derivative of one another. Yet Zindel feels that his books have something to teach his readers. "If you haven't croaked before finishing the book," Zindel writes to his teen readers in *The Pigman and Me,* "then you'll understand how I survived being a teenager and you'll know this important secret." How Zindel survived his adolescence is how his characters survive; the author hopes that "this important secret" will help his readers deal with their own lives.

—Jack Forman

NATIONALITY INDEX

Below is the list of entrants divided by nationality. The nationalities were chosen largely from information supplied by the entrants. It should be noted that "British" was used for all English entrants and for any other British entrant who chose that designation over a more specific one, such as "Scottish."

American

C. S. Adler
Louisa May Alcott
Lloyd Alexander
Margaret Jean Anderson
V. C. Andrews
Judie Angell
Maya Angelou
Piers Anthony
Jennifer Armstrong
William H. Armstrong
Brent Ashabranner
Sandy Asher
Isaac Asimov
Avi
Alice Bach
Thomas Baird
Tom A. Barron
Marion Dane Bauer
Peter S. Beagle
Patricia Beatty
Harry Behn
Nathaniel Benchley
Jay Bennett
T. Ernesto Bethancourt
Richard Allen Blessing
Francesca Lia Block
Joan W. Blos
Judy Blume
Janet Bode
Nancy Bond
Frank Bonham
Malcolm Joseph Bosse
Ray Bradbury
Marion Zimmer Bradley
Robin F. Brancato
Robbie Branscum
Sue Ellen Bridgers
Bruce Brooks
Terry Brooks
Eve Bunting
Robert J. Burch
Olive Ann Burns
Edgar Rice Burroughs
Octavia E. Butler
Betsy Byars
Michael Cadnum
Patricia Calvert
Eleanor Cameron
Philip Caputo
Orson Scott Card
Alden R. Carter
Sylvia Cassedy
Rebecca Caudill
Betty Cavanna
C. J. Cherryh
Alice Childress
Marchette Chute

Sandra Cisneros
Patricia Clapp
Mary Higgins Clark
Eldridge Cleaver
Vera and Bill Cleaver
Bruce Clements
Elizabeth Coatsworth
Brock Cole
Christopher and James Lincoln Collier
Hila Colman
Ellen Conford
Jane Leslie Conly
Pam Conrad
Caroline B. Cooney
Robert Cormier
Sharon Creech
Linda Crew
Michael Crichton
Chris Crutcher
Christopher Paul Curtis
Karen Cushman
Richie Tankersley Cusick
Maureen Daly
Edwidge Danticat
Paula Danziger
Jenny Davis
Terry Davis
Julie Reece Deaver
Carl Deuker
John Donovan
Michael Anthony Dorris
Sharon Mills Draper
Diane Duane
Lois Duncan
David Eddings
Clyde Edgerton
Amy Ehrlich
Ralph Ellison
Sylvia Engdahl
Jeannette Hyde Eyerly
Walter Farley
Nancy Farmer
Howard Fast
Tom Feelings
Jean Ferris
Paul Fleischman
June Foley
Esther Forbes
James D. Forman
Paula Fox
Russell Freedman
Jean Fritz
Ernest J. Gaines
Nancy Garden
Jean Craighead George
William Gibson
Nikki Giovanni
Fred Gipson

Mel Glenn
Lorenz Graham
Cynthia D. Grant
Joanne Greenberg
Bette Greene
Sheila Greenwald
Rosa Guy
Barbara Hall
Lynn Hall
Virginia Hamilton
James S. Haskins
Esther Hautzig
Ann Head
Robert A. Heinlein
Joseph Heller
Nat Hentoff
Frank Herbert
Patricia Hermes
Karen Hesse
Tony Hillerman
S. E. Hinton
Will Hobbs
Felice Holman
H. M. Hoover
Gloria Houston
Langston Hughes
Dean Hughes
Irene Hunt
Kristin Hunter
Zora Neale Hurston
Johanna Hurwitz
Hadley Irwin
Paul B. Janeczko
Annabel and Edgar Johnson
June Jordan
Norton Juster
Harold Keith
Carol Kendall
M. E. Kerr
Ken Kesey
Jamaica Kincaid
Stephen King
David Klass
Sheila Solomon Klass
Annette Curtis Klause
Norma Klein
John Knowles
R. R. Knudson
Ron Koertge
E. L. Konigsburg
Dean R. Koontz
William Kotzwinkle
Trudy Krisher
Joseph Krumgold
Madeleine L'Engle
Mercedes R. Lackey
Jane Langton
Kathryn Lasky
Jean Lee Latham
Ursula K. Le Guin
Harper Lee

Mildred Lee
Julius Lester
Steven Levenkron
Sonia Levitin
Myron Levoy
Elizabeth Foreman Lewis
Robert Lipsyte
Jack London
Lois Lowry
Katie Letcher Lyle
Chris Lynch
R. A. Macavoy
Victor Martinez
Bobbie Ann Mason
Mark Mathabane
Sharon Bell Mathis
Harry Mazer
Norma Fox Mazer
Carson McCullers
Eloise Jarvis McGraw
Vonda N. McIntyre
Patricia A. McKillip
Robin McKinley
Terry McMillan
Florence Crannell Means
Cornelia Lynde Meigs
Milton Meltzer
Eve Merriam
Carolyn Meyer
Gloria D. Miklowitz
Betty Miles
Frances A. Miller
Jim Wayne Miller
Margaret Mitchell
Louise Moeri
Nicholasa Mohr
N. Scott Momaday
Toni Morrison
Jess Mowry
Shirley Rousseau Murphy
Walter Dean Myers
Donna Jo Napoli
Phyllis Reynolds Naylor
Theresa Nelson
John Neufeld
Emily Cheney Neville
Joan Lowery Nixon
Han Nolan
Sterling North
Andre Norton
Robert C. O'brien
Scott O'Dell
Jean Davies Okimoto
Zibby Oneal
Doris Orgel
Francine Pascal
Katherine Paterson
Gary Paulsen
Richard Peck
Robert Newton Peck
P. J. Petersen

Meredith Ann Pierce
Tamora Pierce
Christopher Pike
Daniel Manus Pinkwater
Sylvia Plath
Chaim Potok
Randy Powell
Howard Pyle
Marsha Qualey
Ayn Rand
Ellen Raskin
Marjorie Kinnan Rawlings
Chap Reaver
Johanna Reiss
Anne Rice
Conrad Richter
Ann Rinaldi
Willo Davis Roberts
Keith Robertson
Spider Robinson
Barbara Rogasky
Margaret I. Rostkowski
Lois Ruby
Cynthia Rylant
Marilyn Sachs
J. D. Salinger
Graham Salisbury
R. A. Salvatore
Pamela Sargent
Harriet May Savitz
Sandra Scoppettone
Ouida Sebestyen
Pamela Service
Ntozake Shange
Zoa Sherburne
Barbara Shoup
Upton Sinclair
Marilyn Singer
William Sleator
Jan Slepian
Doris Buchanan Smith
Zilpha Keatley Snyder
Gary Soto
Elizabeth George Speare
Jerry Spinelli
Suzanne Fisher Staples
John Steinbeck
R. L. Stine
Mary Stolz
Todd Strasser
Glendon Swarthout
Amy Tan
Mildred D. Taylor
Theodore Taylor
Stephen N. Tchudi
Frances Temple
Joyce Carol Thomas
Rob Thomas
Dalton Trumbo
John R. Tunis
Mark Twain

Anne Tyler
Joan D. Vinge
Elizabeth Gray Vining
Cynthia Voigt
Kurt Vonnegut, Jr.
Amelia Elizabeth Walden
Alice Walker
Richard Wallace
Mildred Pitts Walter
Walter Wangerin, Jr.
Maureen Crane Wartski
Sally Watson
Will Weaver
Margaret Weis
Rosemary Wells
Barbara Wersba
Jessamyn West
Ellen E. White
Robb White
Phyllis A. Whitney
Elie Wiesel
Brenda Wilkinson
Margaret Willey
Tad Williams
Rita Williams-Garcia
Terri Windling
Patricia Windsor
Maia Wojciechowska
Virginia Euwer Wolff
Hilma Wolitzer
Jacqueline Woodson
Patricia C. Wrede
Richard Wright
Elizabeth Yates
Laurence Yep
Jane Yolen
Jane Breskin Zalben
Paul Zindel

Australian
James Aldridge
Gary Crew
Ursula Dubosarsky
Simon French
Sonya Hartnett
Catherine Jinks
Robin Klein
John Marsden
James Moloney
Garth Nix
Judith O'Neill
Ruth Park
Joan Phipson
Gillian Rubinstein
Ivan Southall
Eleanor Spence
Colin Thiele
Patricia Wrightson

Austrian
Christine Nöstlinger

British

Richard Adams
Joan Aiken
Vivien Alcock
Bernard Ashley
Lynne Reid Banks
Nina Mary Bawden
L. M. Boston
Anthony Burgess
Hester Burton
Aidan Chambers
Grace Chetwin
Agatha Christie
John Christopher
Arthur C. Clarke
Susan Cooper
Gillian Cross
Kevin Crossley-Holland
Roald Dahl
Peter Dickinson
Berlie Doherty
Arthur Conan Doyle
Eileen Dunlop
Penelope Farmer
Nicholas Fisk
Ian Fleming
Monica Furlong
Jane Gardam
Leon Garfield
Alan Garner
Eve Garnett
Adèle Geras
William Golding
Ann Halam
Cynthia Harnett
James Herriot
Janni Howker
Linda Hoy
Ted Hughes
Aldous Huxley
Brian Jacques
Allan Frewin Jones
Diana Wynne Jones
Josephine Kamm
Victor Kelleher
Louise Lawrence
Tanith Lee
Robert Leeson
C. S. Lewis
Kenneth Lillington
Joan Lingard
Michelle Magorian
Jan Mark
William Mayne
Geraldine McCaughrean
Michael Morpurgo
Patricia Moyes
Beverley Naidoo
Jan Needle
George Orwell
Jill Paton Walsh
K. M. Peyton

Philip Pullman
Ian Serraillier
Norman Silver
Muriel Spark
Robert Louis Stevenson
Mary Stewart
Rosemary Sutcliff
Robert Swindells
J. R. R. Tolkien
John Rowe Townsend
Sue Townsend
Geoffrey Trease
Jean Ure
H. G. Wells
Robert Westall
T. H. White
Barbara Willard

Burmese

Minfong Ho

Canadian

Margaret Atwood
William Bell
Karleen Bradford
Martha Brooks
Lesley Choyce
Charles de Lint
Brian Doyle
Sarah Ellis
Marilyn Halvorson
Douglas Hill
Linda Holeman
James A. Houston
Monica Hughes
Julie Johnston
Welwyn Katz
Paul Kropp
Jean Little
Alison Lohans
Kevin Major
Carol Matas
O. R. Melling
Farley Mowat
Kit Pearson
Don Trembath
Diana Wieler
Budge Wilson

Chinese

Lensey Namioka

Danish

Anne Holm

Dutch

Ida Vos

French

Janine Boissard

German

Anne Frank
Hans Peter Richter

Haitian
Edwidge Danticat

Indian
Farrukh Dhondy

Irish
Eilis Dillon
Anne McCaffrey
O. R. Melling

Japanese
Kyoko Mori

New Zealander
Tessa Duder
Margaret Mahy

Polish
Uri Orlev

Puerto Rican
Judith Ortiz Cofer

Scottish
Allan Baillie
Mollie Hunter

South African
Nadine Gordimer
Mark Mathabane

Swedish
Art Spiegelman

TITLE INDEX

The following list includes the titles of all fiction, drama, poetry, and selected nonfiction and other works for young adults. Titles of series listed in the main entries are included, along with the date of the earliest published title in the series. The name in parentheses is meant to direct the reader to the appropriate entry where fuller information is given.

13 Clues for Miss Marple (short story; Christie), 1966
13 for Luck! (short story; Christie), 1961
18th Emergency (Byars), 1973
100% Laugh Riot (Zindel), 1994
100%: The Story of a Patriot (Sinclair), 1920
1984 (Orwell), 1949
1984: Spring: A Choice of Futures (Clarke), 1984
1985 (Burgess), 1978
1,000,000 Pound Bank-Note (short story; Twain), 1893
21st Century Sub (Herbert), 1956
290 (O'Dell), 1976
2001: A Space Odyssey (Clarke), 1968
2010: Odyssey Two (Clarke), 1982
2061: Odyssey Three (Clarke), 1988
3 Ninjas Kick Back (Strasser), 1994
3-7-11 (play; Ashley), 1994
3001: The Final Odyssey (Clarke), 1997
$30,000 Bequest (short story; Twain), 1906
4:50 from Paddington (Christie), 1957
40000 in Gehenna (Cherryh), 1983
555 Pointers for Beginning Actors and Directors (Latham), 1935

A, My Name Is Ami (Mazer, N.), 1986
A.B.C. Murders (Christie), 1936
ABC's of Ecology (Asimov), 1972
ABC's of Space (Asimov), 1969
ABC's of the Earth (Asimov), 1971
ABC's of the Ocean (Asimov), 1970
A.D. (play; Burgess), 1985
Ab-Diver (Thiele), 1988
Abba Abba (Burgess), 1977
Abbess of Crewe (Spark), 1974
Abby, My Love (Irwin), 1985
Abomination (Swindells), 1998
About Michael Jackson (Haskins), 1985
About the B'nai Bagels (Konigsburg), 1969
Absent in the Spring (Christie, as Westmacott), 1944
Absolutely Invincible (Bell), 1991
Absolutely Normal Chaos (Creech), 1990
Absolutely True Story: How I Visited Yellowstone Park with the Terrible Rupes (Roberts), 1995
Absurdly Silly Encyclopedia and Flyswatter (Stine), 1978
Abysmal Brute (London), 1913
Abyss (Card), 1989
Accent on April (Cavanna), 1960
Acceptable Time (L'Engle), 1988
Access Denied (Jones, A. F., as Coleman), 1997
Accident (Colman), 1980
Accident (Strasser), 1988
Accident (Wiesel), 1962
Accidental Tourist (Tyler), 1985
Ace Hole, Midge Detective (Spiegelman), 1974

Achingly Alice (Naylor), 1997
Acorn Pancakes, Dandelion Salad and 38 Other Wild Recipes (George), 1995
Acorn-Planter: A California Forest Play... (play; London), 1916
Acorna: The Unicorn Girl (McCaffrey), 1997
Acorna's People (McCaffrey), 1997
Acquaintance with Darkness (Rinaldi), 1997
Across Five Aprils (Hunt), 1964
Across Five Summers (play; Card), 1971
Across the Barricades (Lingard), 1972
Across the Fruited Plain (Means), 1940
Across the Grain (Ferris), 1990
Across the Plains: The Journey of the Palace Wagon Family (play; Asher), 1997
Acts of Love (Daly), 1986
Adam and Eve and Pinch-Me (Johnston), 1994
Adam Clayton Powell: Portrait of a Marching Black (Haskins), 1974
Adam of the Road (Vining), 1942
Adam's War (Levitin), 1994
Addams Family Values: A Novel (Strasser), 1993
Adelaide Ghost (Garfield), 1977
Adella Mary in Old New Mexico (Means), 1939
Admiral Guinea (play; Stevenson), 1884
Adrian Mole series (Townsend, S.), from 1991
Adrift (Baillie), 1983
Adulthood Rites (Butler), 1988
Adventure (London), 1911
Adventure in Granada (Myers), 1985
Adventure of Sherlock Holmes (short story; Doyle), 1892
Adventure of the Christmas Pudding (short story; Christie), 1960
Adventure of the Solitary Cyclist (short story; Doyle), 1991
Adventures and Brave Deeds of the Ship's Cat on the Spanish Maine (poetry; Adams), 1977
Adventures of Ali Baba Bernstein (Hurwitz), 1985
Adventures of Captain Grief (short story; London), 1954
Adventures of Colonel Sellers (Twain), 1965
Adventures of Gerard (short story; Doyle), 1903
Adventures of Huckleberry Finn, Tom Sawyer's Comrade (Twain), 1884
Adventures of Johnny May (Branscum), 1984
Adventures of Pirates and Sea-Rovers (Pyle), 1908
Adventures of the Speckled Band (short story; Doyle), 1991
Adventures of Tom Sawyer (Twain), 1876
Adventures of Tommy (short story; Wells, H. G.), 1929
Affectionately Eve (Sinclair), 1961
African American Entrepreneurs (Haskins), 1998
African American Military Heroes (Haskins), 1998
African Beginnings (Haskins), 1998
African Treasury: Articles, Essays, Stories, Poems by Black Africans (Hughes, L., ed.), 1960
African Women: Three Generations (Mathabane), 1994
After Many a Summer Dies the Swan (Huxley), 1939

Alvin Webster's Sure Fire Plan for Success and How It Failed (Greenwald), 1987

Always and Forever Friends (Adler), 1988

Always in August (Head), 1961

Always Movin' On: The Life of Langston Hughes (Haskins), 1976

Always Sebastian (Ure), 1993

Always to Remember: The Story of the Vietnam Veterans Memorial (Ashabranner), 1988

Always Young and Fair (Richter, C.), 1947

Am I Blue? Coming out from the Silence (Bauer, ed.), 1996

Amazing and Death-Defying Diary of Eugene Dingman (Zindel), 1987

Amazing Jessica (Pascal), 1996

Amazing Journey of Jazz O'Neill (play; Doherty), 1984

Amazing Magic Show (Petersen), 1994

Amazing Miss Laura (Colman), 1976

Amazing Potato (Meltzer), 1992

Amber Brown series (Danziger), from 1994

Ambrosia (play; Thomas, J.), 1978

Ambush in the Amazon (Myers), 1986

Amen, Moses Gardenia (Ferris), 1983

America (poetry; Bradbury), 1983

American: A Middle Western Legend (Fast), 1946

American Adventures 1620-1945 (Coatsworth), 1968

American Claimant (Twain), 1892

American Heroes: In and Out of School (Hentoff), 1987

American Politics: How It Really Works (Meltzer), 1989

American Promise: Voices of a Changing Nation, 1945-Present (Meltzer), 1990

American Revolution, 1763-1783 (Collier), 1998

American Revolution series (Carter), from 1988

American Revolutionaries: A History in Their Own Words, 1750-1800 (Meltzer), 1987

American Sports Poems (poetry; Knudson, ed.), 1988

Amethyst Dreams (Whitney), 1997

Amethyst Ring (O'Dell), 1983

Amish Family (Naylor), 1974

Amish People: Plain Living in a Complex World (Meyer), 1976

Amistad: A Long Road To Freedom (Myers), 1998

Among Friends (Cooney), 1987

Among the Dolls (Sleator), 1975

Amos series (Paulsen), from 1993

Amy Elizabeth Explores Bloomingdale's (Konigsburg), 1992

Amy series (Pascal), from 1990

Amy's Wish (Kropp), 1984

Anarchism: Political Innocence or Social Violence? (Forman), 1975

Anastasia series (Lowry), from 1979

Anastasia Syndrome (short story; Clark), 1989

Anchor's Aweigh: The Story of David Glasgow Farragut (Latham), 1968

Ancient African Kingdom of Kush (Service), 1997

Ancient Child (Momaday), 1989

Ancient Evil (Pike), 1992

Ancient Forests: Discovering Nature (Anderson), 1995

Ancient Heritage: The Arab-American Minority (Ashabranner), 1991

Ancient One (Barron), 1992

And All Our Wounds Forgiven (Lester), 1994

And Both Were Young (L'Engle), 1949

And Condors Danced (Snyder), 1987

And Eternity (Anthony), 1990

And I Heard a Bird Sing (Guy), 1987

And Love Replied (Stolz), 1958

And Never Again (Mayne), 1992

...And Now Miguel (Krumgold), 1953

And One for All (Nelson), 1989

And Pigs Might Fly! (Morpurgo), 1990

And Still I Rise (play; Angelou), 1976

And the Winner Is ... Jessica Wakefield! (Pascal), 1996

And Then There Were None (Christie), 1940

And Then What Happened? (play; Latham), 1937

And This Is Laura (Conford), 1977

Andra (Lawrence), 1971

Andrew Jackson and His America (Meltzer), 1993

Andrew Jackson's America, 1821-1850 (Collier), 1998

Andrew Young: Man with a Mission (Haskins), 1979

Android at Arms (Norton), 1971

Andromeda Strain (Crichton), 1969

Andy and the Alien (Pascal), 1992

Andy's Landmark House (Colman), 1969

Angel Baker, Thief (Eyerly), 1984

Angel Death (Moyes), 1980

Angel Dust Blues: A Novel (Strasser), 1979

Angel Face (Klein, N.), 1984

Angel on Skis (Cavanna), 1957

Angel Park All-Stars series (Hughes, D.), from 1990

Angel Park Football Stars series (Hughes, D.), from 1994

Angel Park Hoop Stars series (Hughes, D.), from 1992

Angel Park Karate Stars series (Hughes, D.), from 1994

Angel Park Soccer Stars series (Hughes, D.), from 1991

Angel Square (Doyle), 1984

Angel with the Sword (Cherryh), 1985

Angela (Moloney), 1995

Angel's Gate (Crew, G.), 1993

Angels Keep Out (Pascal), 1996

Angle of Geese (poetry; Momaday), 1974

Animal Architects (Freedman), 1971

Animal Farm: A Fairy Story (Orwell), 1945

Animal Fathers (Freedman), 1976

Animal Games (Freedman), 1976

Animal Instincts (Freedman), 1970

Animal Library (Mayne), 1986-87

Animal Stories: Tame and Wild (Herriot), 1985

Animal Superstars: Biggest, Strongest, Fastest, Smartest (Freedman), 1981

Animal, the Vegetable, and John D. Jones (Byars), 1982

Animals Can Do Anything (George), 1972

Animals in That Country (poetry; Atwood), 1968

Animals Tame and Wild (Herriot), 1979

Ann of the Wild Rose Inn (Armstrong, J.), 1994

Ann Veronica: A Modern Love Story (Wells, H. G.), 1909

Anna Is Still Here (Vos), 1993

Anne Frank: The Diary of a Young Girl (Frank), 1952

Anne Frank's Tales from the Secret Annex (Frank), 1959

Annerton Pit (Dickinson), 1977

Annie, Gwen, Lily, Pam, and Tulip (short story; Kincaid), 1986

Annie John (Kincaid), 1985

Annie on My Mind (Garden), 1982

Annie's Promise (Levitin), 1993

Another Day (Sachs), 1997

Another Fine Mess (Needle), 1982

Another Heaven, Another Earth (Hoover), 1981

Axe-Age, Wolf-Age: A Selection from the Norse Myths (Crossley-Holland), 1985

B, My Name Is Bunny (Mazer, N.), 1987
Babe Didrikson: Athlete of the Century (Knudson), 1985
Babe Ruth and Hank Aaron: The Home Run Kings (Haskins), 1974
Babes in the Darkling Wood (Wells, H. G.), 1940
Baby, Baby (Kropp), 1982
Baby Be-Bop (Block), 1995
Baby Blues (Kropp), 1989
Baby Project (Ellis), 1986
Baby Sister (Sachs), 1986
Baby-Sitter (Stine), 1989
Baby-Sitter II (Stine), 1991
Baby Sitting Is a Dangerous Job (Roberts), 1985
Babyface (Mazer, N.), 1990
Babylon (Paton Walsh), 1982
Babylon Boyz (Mowry), 1997
Bachelors (Spark), 1960
Back Home (Magorian), 1984
Back of Beyond (Ellis), 1996
Back to Before (Slepian), 1993
Back to Class (poetry; Glenn), 1988
Back to the Stone Age (Burroughs), 1937
Backlash (Fisk), 1988
Backup Goalie (Hughes, D.), 1992
Backup Soccer Star (Hughes, D.), 1995
Back-yard War (Fisk), 1990
Bad (Ferris), 1998
Bad and the Beautiful (Cooney), 1985
Bad, Badder, Baddest (Voigt), 1997
Bad Bell of San Salvador (Beatty), 1973
Bad Blood (Ashley), 1988
Bad Boy (Jones, A. F.), 1996
Bad Boy (Wieler), 1989
Bad Boys (poetry; Cisneros), 1980
Bad Girls (Voigt), 1996
Bad Guys (Baillie), 1993
Bad Penny (Jones, A. F.), 1990
Bad Place (Koontz), 1990
Badger on the Barge (Howker), 1984
Badger on the Barge (play; Howker), 1987
Badlands of Hark (Stine), 1985
Baily's Bones (Kelleher), 1988
Baker Street Dozen (short story; Doyle), 1989
Baker's Dozen (Garfield, ed.), 1973
Ballad For Hogskin Hill (Forman), 1979
Ballad of Kon-Tiki (poetry; Serraillier), 1952
Ballad of Lucy Whipple (Cushman), 1996
Ballad of Peckham Rye (Spark), 1960
Ballad of St. Simeon (poetry; Serraillier), 1970
Ballad of the Civil War (Stolz), 1997
Ballad of the Sad Cafe: The Novels and Stories of Carson McCullers (McCullers), 1951
Ballad of Two Who Flew (play; Asher), 1976
Ballerina on Skates (Sherburne), 1961
Ballet Fever (Cavanna), 1978
Ballet One series (Asher), from 1989
Balook (Anthony), 1990
Balyet (Wrightson), 1989
Bananas Looks at TV (Stine), 1981

Bandit of Hell's Bend (Burroughs), 1925
Bang-Bang You're Dead (short story; Spark), 1982
Banjo (Peck, Robert Newton), 1982
Banjo, the Puppy (Harnett), 1938
Banner Year (Cavanna), 1987
Barbara Jordan (Haskins), 1977
Barbary (McIntyre), 1986
Bardic Voices: The Lark & the Wren (Lackey), 1992
Barn (Avi), 1994
Barney the Beard (Bunting), 1975
Barnyard Battle (Pascal), 1992
Barons' Hostage: A Story of Simon de Montfort (Trease), 1952
Barracuda Gang (Bosse), 1983
Barrie and Daughter (Caudill), 1943
Baseball Fever (Hurwitz), 1981
Baseball in April (short story; Soto), 1990
Basket Case (Peck, Robert Newton), 1979
Basketball Girl of the Year (Walden), 1970
Bass and Billy Martin (Phipson), 1972
Bathwater Gang (Spinelli), 1990
Bathwater Gang Gets down to Business (Spinelli), 1992
Batterpool Business (play; Jones, D. W.), 1967
Battle in the Arctic Seas: The Story of Convoy PQ 17 (Taylor, T.), 1976
Battle in the English Channel (Taylor, T.), 1983
Battle of Gettysburg (Carter), 1990
Battle of the Cheerleaders (Pascal), 1996
Battle of the Ironclads: The Monitor and the Merrimack (Carter), 1993
Battle of Wednesday Week (Willard), 1963
Battle off Midway Island (Taylor, T.), 1981
Battlefield (Mayne), 1967
Battleground: The United States Army in World War II (Collier), 1965
Bawshou Rescues the Sun: A Han Folktale (Baillie), 1991
Bayard Rustin (Haskins), 1997
Bazaar and Rummage (play; Townsend, S.), 1983
Be Careful What You Wish For... (Stine), 1993
Be Ever Hopeful, Hannalee (Beatty), 1988
Be Still My Heart (Hermes), 1989
Beach House (Stine), 1992
Beach Party (Stine), 1990
Beach Towels (Sachs), 1982
Bealby: A Holiday (Wells, H. G.), 1915
Bearcat (Johnson, A. and E.), 1960
Beardance (Hobbs), 1993
Beardream (Hobbs), 1997
Beard's Roman Women (Burgess), 1976
Bearing an Hourglass (Anthony), 1984
Bearstone (Hobbs), 1989
Beast Handbook (Stine), 1981
Beast is Watching You (Pascal), 1996
Beast Master (Norton), 1959
Beast Must Die (Pascal), 1996
Beast of Darkness (Orlev), 1976
Beastchild (Koontz), 1970
Beasties (Sleator), 1997
Beastly Inventions: A Surprising Investigation into How Smart Animals Really Are (George), 1970
Beasts of Tarzan (Burroughs), 1916
Beating the Odds: Stories of Unexpected Achievers (Bode), 1991

Big Base Hit (Hughes, D.), 1990
Big Brass Key (Park), 1983
Big Brother (Orlev), 1983
Big Brother Barges In (Latham, as Lee), 1940
Big Brother's in Love! (Pascal), 1992
Big Brother's in Love Again (Pascal), 1997
Big Burn (Choyce), 1995
Big Camp Secret (Pascal), 1989
Big Cheese (Bunting), 1977
Big Egg (Mayne), 1967
Big Find (Bunting), 1978
BIG for Christmas (Pascal), 1994
Big Four (Christie), 1927
Big Green Umbrella (Coatsworth), 1944
Big Head (Ure), 1997
Big-Little Girl (Orlev), 1977
Big Night (Pascal), 1998
Big Party Weekend (Pascal), 1991
Big Race (Pascal), 1993
Big Red Barn (Bunting), 1979
Big Rock Candy (Johnson, A. and E.), 1957
Big Sea (Hughes, L.), 1940
Big Splash (Kendall), 1960
Big Step (Colman), 1957
Big Time (Grant), 1982
Big Wander (Hobbs), 1992
Big Wheel and the Little Wheel (Mayne), 1965
Bigger (Calvert), 1994
Bigger Book of Lydia (Willey), 1983
Biggest Thief in Town (play; Trumbo), 1949
Bigmouth (Angell, as Twohill), 1986
Bike Repairman (poetry; Bradbury), 1978
Bilgewater (Gardam), 1976
Bill of Rights: How We Got It and What It Means (Meltzer), 1990
Bill Porter: A Drama of O. Henry in Prison (play; Sinclair), 1925
Billie's Secret (Pascal), 1996
Billy Bedamned, Long Gone By (Beatty), 1977
Billy the Great (Guy), 1992
Binary (Crichton, as Lange), 1972
Binding Ties (Adler), 1983
Bingo Brown series (Byars), from 1989
Bird at My Window (Guy), 1966
Bird of Paradise (Furlong), 1995
Bird Smugglers (Phipson), 1977
Bird, The Frog, and the Light (Avi), 1994
Birds of Summer (Snyder), 1983
Birkin (Phipson), 1965
Birth of the Firebringer (Pierce, M.), 1985
Birth of the Republic (Carter), 1988
Birthday Murder (Bennett), 1977
Bishop and the Devil (poetry; Serraillier), 1971
Bitter Rivals (Pascal), 1986
Bittersweet (poetry; Thomas, J.), 1973
Bittersweet Temptation (Donovan), 1979
Bizarre Insects (Anderson), 1996
Bizou (Klein, N.), 1983
Black Americans: A History in Their Own Words, 1619-1983 (Meltzer), 1984
Black and White Two-Dimensional Planes (play; Shange), 1979
Black Arrow: A Tale of the Two Roses (Stevenson), 1888
Black Banner Abroad (Trease), 1954

Black Banner Players (Trease), 1952
Black, Blue, and Gray (Haskins), 1998
Black Cauldron (Alexander), 1965
Black Child (poetry; Thomas, J.), 1981
Black Cloud (Orlev), 1979
Black Coffee (play; Christie), 1930
Black Diamonds (Whitney), 1957
Black Diamonds: A Search for Arctic Treasure (Houston, J.), 1982
Black Doctor (short story; Doyle), 1925
Black Eagles (Haskins), 1995
Black-Eyed Susan (Armstrong, J.), 1995
Black Feeling, Black Talk (poetry; Giovanni), 1968
Black Foxes (Hartnett), 1996
Black Girl, White Girl (Moyes), 1989
Black Gryphon (Lackey), 1994
Black Hair (poetry; Soto), 1985
Black Hearts in Battersea (Aiken), 1964
Black Hearts in Battersea (play; Aiken), 1996
Black Horses for the King (McCaffrey), 1996
Black Jack (Garfield), 1968
Black Judgement (poetry; Giovanni), 1968
Black Magic: A Pictorial History of the Negro in American Entertainment (Hughes, L.), 1967
Black Maria (Jones, D. W.), 1991
Black Misery (Hughes, L.), 1969
Black Music in America: A History through Its People (Haskins), 1987
Black Night, Red Morning (Trease), 1944
Black Pearl (O'Dell), 1967
Black Pearl and the Ghost: or, One Mystery After Another (Myers), 1980
Black Pilgrimage (Feelings), 1972
Black Sails, White Sails (Dubosarsky), 1997
Black Ships before Troy (Sutcliff), 1993
Black Spaniel Mystery (Cavanna), 1945
Black Stallion series (Farley), from 1947
Black Star, Bright Dawn (O'Dell), 1988
Black Swan (Dhondy), 1992
Black Symbol (Johnson, A. and E.), 1959
Black Theatre in America (Haskins), 1982
Black Unicorn (Brooks, T.), 1987
Black Unicorn (Lee, T.), 1991
Black Widower (Moyes), 1975
Blackbird (Southall), 1988
Blackbird Singing (Bunting), 1980
Blacker the Berry: Poems (poetry; Thomas, J.), 1997
Blackmail! (Jones, A. F., as Kelly), 1996
Blacksmith at Blueridge (Bunting), 1976
Blade of the Poisoner (Hill), 1987
Blaine's Way (Hughes, M.), 1986
Blemyahs (Mayne), 1987
Bless the Beasts and Children (Swarthout), 1970
Blessing (poetry; Thomas, J.), 1975
Blessing Way (Hillerman), 1970
Blewcoat Boy (Garfield), 1988
Blind Ally (Jones, A. F.), 1989
Blind Date (Stine), 1986
Blind Dating (play; Asher), 1992
Blinded by the Light (Brancato), 1978
Blips!: The First Book of Video Game Funnies (Stine), 1983
Blissful Joy and the SATs (Greenwald), 1982

Cowboys Don't Quit (Halvorson), 1994
Cowboys of the Wild West (Freedman), 1985
Cowpokes and Desperados (Paulsen), 1994
Coyote in Manhattan (George), 1968
Coyote Waits (Hillerman), 1990
Crab the Roan (Peyton, as Hereld), 1953
Crabbe (Bell), 1986
Crabbe's Journey (Bell), 1987
Cracker Jackson (Byars), 1985
Cradle (Clarke), 1988
Cradle Will Fall (Clark), 1980
Cradlefasts (Mayne), 1995
Crapshooter (short story; Steinbeck), 1957
Crash (Spinelli), 1996
Crash Landing! (Pascal), 1985
Crazy about German Shepherds (Ashabranner), 1990
Crazy Fish (Mazer, N.), 1998
Crazy Horse Electric Game (Crutcher), 1987
Crazy Lady! (Conly), 1993
Crazy Vanilla (Wersba), 1986
Crazy Weekend (poetry; Soto), 1994
Creating the Constitution, 1787 (Collier), 1998
Creative Kind of Killer (Scoppettone, as Early), 1984
Creative Romance (Bunting), 1978
Creative Science Fiction (Bunting), 1978
Creature (Baillie), 1987
Creature in the Dark (Westall), 1988
Creature of Black Water Lake (Paulsen), 1997
Creatures (Townsend, J.), 1980
Creatures of the Claw (Hill), 1998
Credit-Card Carole (Klass, S. S.), 1987
Creep Street (Marsden), 1997
Creepy Company: Ten Tales of Terror (Aiken), 1995
Creole Holiday (Whitney), 1959
Creoles of Color of New Orleans (Haskins), 1975
Cress Delahanty (short story; West), 1953
Crew of the "Merlin," (Phipson), 1966
Crewel Lye: A Caustic Yarn (Anthony), 1985
Cricket and the Emperor's Son (Coatsworth), 1932
Crickets and Bullfrogs and Whispers of Thunder (poetry; Behn), 1984
Crime in America (Meltzer), 1990
Crime in Cabin 66 (short story; Christie), 1944
Crimes of Conscience (short story; Gordimer), 1991
Crimson Ramblers of the World, Farewell (short story; West), 1970
Crimson Witch (Koontz), 1971
Crinoline and Candlelight (play; Latham), 1931
Cripples' Club (Bell), 1988
Crisis on Conshelf Ten (Hughes, M.), 1992
Crisis on Doona (McCaffrey), 1992
Crome Yellow (Huxley), 1921
Crooked Apple Tree (Meigs), 1929
Crooked House (Christie), 1949
Crooked Snake (Wrightson), 1955
Croquet Player (Wells, H. G.), 1936
Cross Currents (Phipson), 1967
Crossed Line (Jones, A. F., as Kelly), 1994
Crossfire (Moloney), 1992
Crossing (play; Fast), 1962
Crossing (Fast), 1971
Crossing (Paulsen), 1987

Crossing the Water (poetry; Plath), 1971
Crossing to Salamis (Paton Walsh), 1977
Crossroads of Time (Norton), 1956
Crosstime Agent (Norton), 1975
Crow and the Castle (Robertson), 1957
Crown Diamond (play; Doyle), 1921
Crown Fire (McGraw), 1951
Crown for Gina (Colman), 1958
Crown of Dalemark (Jones, D. W.), 1993
Crown of Violet (Trease), 1952
Crowning Glory: Poems (poetry; Thomas, J.), 1997
Crows of Pearblossom (short story; Huxley), 1967
Croxley Master (short story; Doyle), 1925
Cruel Miracles (short story; Card), 1992
Cruise of the Dazzler (London), 1902
Cruise of the Santa Maria (Dillon), 1967
Cry Havoc (Forman), 1988
Cry in the Night (Clark), 1982
Cry of the Crow (George), 1980
Cry to Heaven (Rice), 1982
Crybaby Lois (Pascal), 1990
Crying in the Dark (Halam), 1998
Crystal (Myers), 1987
Crystal Breezes (poetry; Thomas, J.), 1974
Crystal Cave (Stewart), 1970
Crystal Drop (Hughes, M.), 1992
Crystal Gazer (poetry; Plath), 1971
Crystal Gryphon (Norton), 1972
Crystal Image (Janeczko, ed.), 1977
Crystal Line (McCaffrey), 1992
Crystal Shard (Salvatore), 1988
Crystal Singer (McCaffrey), 1982
Crystal Stair (Chetwin), 1988
Crystal Star (McIntyre), 1994
Cuckoo in the Nest (Magorian), 1994
Cuckoo Sister (Alcock), 1985
Cuckoo Tree (Aiken), 1971
Cuckoo's Egg (Cherryh), 1985
Cuddy (Mayne), 1994
Cue for Treason (Trease), 1940
Cujo (King), 1981
Culpepper's Cannon (Paulsen), 1992
Cup of Fury (Sinclair), 1956
Cup of Gold: A Life of Henry Morgan, Buccaneer (Steinbeck), 1929
Cure (Levitin), 1978
Cure for Love (short story; Wells, H. G.), 1899
Curious Affair of the Third Dog (Moyes), 1973
Curious Dream (short story; Twain), 1872
Curious Fragments (short story; London), 1975
Curious Republic of Gondour (short story; Twain), 1919
Curley Tale (play; Clapp), 1958
Curse of the Cobra (Paulsen), 1977
Curse of the Endless Catacombs (Weis, as Baldwin), 1984
Curse of the Golden Heart (Pascal), 1994
Curse of the Mummy's Tomb (Stine), 1993
Curse of the Ruby Necklace (Pascal), 1993
Curse of the Ruins (Paulsen), 1998
Curse of the Squirrel (Yep), 1987
Curse on Elizabeth (Pascal), 1995
Curse on the Seas (Trease), 1996
Curtain Fall (Ure), 1978

Curtain: Hercule Poirot's Last Case (Christie), 1975
Curtains (Stine), 1990
Cutting Loose (Miller, F.), 1991
Cybil War (Byars), 1981
Cycle of the Werewolf (King), 1983
Cygnet and the Firebird (McKillip), 1993
Cyrano de Bergerac (play; Burgess), 1971
Cyteen (Cherryh), 1988

D, My Name Is Danita (Mazer, N.), 1991
D. J.'s Worst Enemy (Burch), 1965
Daddy Goodness (play; Wright), 1968
Daddy's Climbing Tree (Adler), 1993
Dagmar Schultz series (Hall, L.), from 1988
Daisy (Coatsworth), 1973
Daja's Book (Pierce, T.), 1998
Dalemark series (Jones, D. W.), from 1975
Damaged Goods (Sinclair), 1913
Damia (McCaffrey), 1991
Damia's Children (McCaffrey), 1993
Damiano (MacAvoy), 1984
Damiano's Lute (MacAvoy), 1984
Damned (Hoy), 1983
Dance (Pike), 1989
Dance for Two (Ure), 1960
Dance Hall of the Dead (Hillerman), 1973
Dance of Death (Pascal), 1996
Dance on My Grave: A Life and Death in Four Parts (Chambers), 1982
Dance with Death (Ure), 1995
Dance with the Devil (Koontz, as Dwyer), 1973
Dancing Bear (Dickinson), 1972
Dancing Bear (Morpurgo), 1994
Dancing Carl (Paulsen), 1983
Dancing Girls (short story; Atwood), 1977
Dancing on Dark Water (Carter), 1993
Dancing on the Bridge of Avignon (Vos), 1995
Dancing on the Edge (Nolan), 1997
Dancing Tom (Coatsworth), 1938
Dancing with Strangers (play; Asher), 1993
Dandelion Wine (Bradbury), 1957
Dandelion Wine (play; Bradbury), 1967
Dandelions (Bunting), 1995
Danger! (short story; Doyle), 1918
Danger Dog (Hall, L.), 1986
Danger in the Wings (Trease), 1997
Danger on Midnight River (Paulsen), 1995
Danger Quotient (Johnson, A. and E.), 1984
Danger: Twins at Work! (Pascal), 1998
Danger Zone (Klass, D.), 1995
Dangerous Angels: The Weetzie Bat Books (Block), 1998
Dangerous Love (Pascal), 1984
Dangerous Promise (Nixon), 1994
Dangerous Skies (Staples), 1996
Dangerous Summer (Colman), 1966
Dangerous Tricks (Jones, A. F., as Kelly), 1993
Dangerous Wishes (Sleator), 1995
Dangling Witness (Bennett), 1974
Daniel's Story (Matas), 1993
Danny and the Kings (Cooper), 1993
Danny Dynamite (Ure), 1966

Danny Goes to the Hospital (Collier), 1970
Danny Means Trouble (Pascal), 1990
Danny: The Champion of the World (Dahl), 1975
Danza! (Hall, L.), 1981
Darcy (Cormier), 1990
Dare (Halvorson), 1988
Daring Game (Pearson), 1986
Dark and Deadly Pool (Nixon), 1987
Dark Angel (Andrews), 1986
Dark Behind the Curtain (Cross), 1982
Dark Bright Water (Wrightson), 1979
Dark but Full of Diamonds (Lyle), 1981
Dark Canoe (O'Dell), 1968
Dark Card (Ehrlich), 1991
Dark Carnival (short story; Bradbury), 1947
Dark Corridor (Bennett), 1990
Dark Dance (Lee, T.), 1992
Dark Elf Omnibus (Salvatore), 1996
Dark End of Dream Street (Choyce), 1994
Dark Half (King), 1989
Dark Harvest: Migrant Farmworkers in America (Ashabranner), 1985
Dark Intruder (short story; Bradley), 1964
Dark Is Rising (Cooper), 1973
Dark Is Rising series (Cooper), from 1965
Dark Mirror (Duane), 1993
Dark Moon (Pierce, M.), 1992
Dark of Summer (Koontz, as Dwyer), 1972
Dark of the Tunnel (Naylor), 1985
Dark of the Woods (Koontz), 1970
Dark Piper (Norton), 1968
Dark Rivers of the Heart (Koontz), 1994
Dark Secrets (Roberts), 1991
Dark Side of the Moon (short story; Naylor), 1969
Dark Silence (Wartski), forthcoming
Dark Stairs : A Herculeah Jones Mystery (Byars), 1994
Dark Streets of Kimballs Green (play; Aiken), 1976
Dark Sun, Bright Sun (Fisk), 1986
Dark Symphony (Koontz), 1970
Dark Tower: The Gunslinger (King), 1982
Dark Wind (Hillerman), 1982
Darkangel trilogy, from 1982
Darkest Hour (Andrews), 1993
Darkest Hours (Carter), 1988
Darkfall (Koontz), 1984
Darkling (Peyton), 1989
Darkness, Be My Friend (Marsden), 1996
Darkness Comes (Koontz), 1984
Darkness in My Soul (Koontz), 1972
Darkness Visible (Golding), 1979
Darkover (Bradley), 1993
Darkover Landfall (Bradley), 1972
Darkover series (Bradley), from 1962
Date for Diane (Cavanna, as Headley), 1946
Date with a Werewolf (Pascal), 1994
Dateline: Troy (Fleischman), 1996
Dating Game (Pascal), 1991
Daughter of Discontent (Colman), 1971
Daughter of Don Saturnino (O'Dell), 1979
Daughter of the Sea (Doherty), 1996
Daughter of the Snows (London), 1902

Dog Stories (Hall, L.), 1972
Dog's Tale (short story; Twain), 1904
Doggone Dog Joke Book (Stine), 1986
Dogs Think That Every Day Is Christmas (poetry; Bradbury), 1997
Dogsbody (Jones, D. W.), 1975
Dogsong (Paulsen), 1985
Dogteam (Paulsen), 1992
Dogwolf (Carter), 1994
Doing Time: Notes from the Undergrad (Thomas, R.), 1997
Doings of Raffle Haw (Doyle), 1892
Dollar for Luck (Coatsworth), 1951
Dollar Man (Mazer, H.), 1974
Dolores Claiborne (King), 1992
Dolphin Crossing (Paton Walsh), 1967
Dolphins of Pern (McCaffrey), 1994
Dom and Va (Christopher), 1973
Domes of Fire (Eddings), 1993
Don't Answer the Phone (Pascal), 1998
Don't Blame the Music (Cooney), 1986
Don't Forget to Fly: A Cycle of Modern Poems (Janeczko, ed.), 1981
Don't Go Home with John (Pascal), 1993
Don't Go in the Basement (Pascal), 1995
Don't Hurt Laurie! (Roberts), 1977
Don't Look and It Won't Hurt (Peck, Richard), 1972
Don't Look Behind You (Duncan), 1989
Don't Play Dead Before You Have To (Wojciechowska), 1970
Don't Rent My Room! (Angell), 1990
Don't Scream (Nixon), 1996
Don't Sit under the Apple Tree (Brancato), 1975
Don't Stand in the Soup (Stine), 1982
Don't Talk to Brian (Pascal), 1996
Don't Tell Me That You Love Me (Colman), 1983
Don't Think Twice (Lohans), 1997
Dona Ellen (Richter, C.), 1959
Donato and Daughter (Scoppettone, as Early), 1988
Donkey for the King (Beatty), 1966
Donna Summer (Haskins), 1983
Doodle and the Go-Cart (Burch), 1972
Doom Brigade (Weis), 1996
Doom Stone (Zindel), 1995
Doomsday Plus Twelve (Forman), 1984
Doomwater (Leeson), 1997
Door Between (Garden), 1987
Door in the Hedge (McKinley), 1981
Door in the Wall (short story; Wells, H. G.), 1911
Door Through Space (Bradley), 1961
Door to December (Koontz, as Paige), 1985
Door to the North: A Saga of Fourteenth Century America (Coatsworth), 1950
Doors of the Universe (Engdahl), 1981
Dope Deal (Kropp), 1979
Doris Fein, Dead Heat at Long Beach (Bethancourt), 1983
Doris Fein, Deadly Aphrodite (Bethancourt), 1983
Doris Fein, Legacy of Terror (Bethancourt), 1984
Doris Fein, Murder Is No Joke (Bethancourt), 1982
Doris Fein, Quartz Boyar (Bethancourt), 1980
Doris Fein, Superspy (Bethancourt), 1980
Doris Fein, The Mad Samurai (Bethancourt), 1981
Doris Fein, Phantom of the Casino (Bethancourt), 1981
Dormouse Tales (Mayne, as Molin), 1966

Dorothea Lange: Life through the Camera (Meltzer), 1985
Dosadi Experiment (Herbert), 1977
Dot and the Line: A Romance in Lower Mathematics (Juster), 1963
Double Barrelled Detective Story (short story; Twain), 1902
Double Bucky Shanghai (Bach), 1987
Double-Crossed (Pascal), 1994
Double Dutch (Haskins), 1986
Double Jeopardy (Pascal), 1995
Double Life of Angela Jones (Colman), 1988
Double Life of Pocahontas (Fritz), 1983
Double Life: Newly Discovered Thrillers of Louisa May Alcott (short story; Alcott), 1988
Double Love (Pascal), 1984
Double Persephone (poetry; Atwood), 1961
Double Sin (short story; Christie), 1961
Double Trouble Squared (Lasky), 1991
Dougy (Moloney), 1993
Dove and Sword: A Novel of Joan of Arc (Garden), 1995
Dover's Domain (play; Asher), 1980
Down & Up Fall (Hurwitz), 1996
Down a Dark Hall (Duncan), 1974
Down among the Dead Men (Moyes), 1961
Down by the River (Adler), 1981
Down in the World (Dillon), 1983
Down to Earth (Wrightson), 1965
Down Tumbledown Mountain (Coatsworth), 1958
Down With Queen Janet (Pascal), 1998
Downbelow Station (Cherryh), 1981
Downriver (Hobbs), 1991
Downstream (Townsend, J.), 1987
Downtown (Mazer, N.), 1984
Downwind (Moeri), 1984
Dr. Doom, Superstar (Bethancourt), 1978
Dr. Elizabeth: The Story of the First Woman Doctor (Clapp), 1974
Dr. J: A Biography of Julius Irving (Haskins), 1975
Dr. Martin Luther King, Jr. (Miklowitz), 1977
Drac and the Gremlin (Baillie), 1989
Drackenberg Adventure (Alexander), 1988
Dracula's Castle (Swindells), 1991
Dragon (Bradbury), 1988
Dragon Box (Willard), 1972
Dragon Cauldron (Yep), 1991
Dragon Charmer (Hill), 1997
Dragon Dance (Christopher), 1986
Dragon Defiant (Hall, L.), 1977
Dragon Harvest (Sinclair), 1945
Dragon Hoard (Lee, T.), 1971
Dragon in the Ghetto Caper (Konigsburg), 1974
Dragon in the Sea (Herbert), 1956
Dragon King (Salvatore), 1996
Dragon Magic (Norton), 1972
Dragon of the Lost Sea (Yep), 1982
Dragon on a Pedestal (Anthony), 1983
Dragon Slayer: The Story of Beowulf (Sutcliff), 1966
Dragon Steel (Yep), 1985
Dragon Tears (Koontz), 1993
Dragon War (Yep), 1992
Dragon Who Was Different (play; Trease), 1938
Dragon Wing (Weis), 1990
Dragon's Blood (Yolen), 1996
Dragon's Crown (Orlev), 1985

Face at the Edge of the World (Bunting), 1985
Face of Abraham Candle (Clements), 1969
Face of Fear (Koontz, as Coffey), 1977
Face on the Milk Carton (Cooney), 1990
Face to Face (Bauer), 1991
Face to Face (short story; Gordimer), 1949
Faces in the Water (Naylor), 1981
Faces of Fantasy (Windling, ed.), 1996
Faces of Fear (Hughes, M.), 1997
Facing the Enemy (Hughes, D.), 1982
Facing the Music (Willey), 1996
Facing Up (Brancato), 1984
facts speak for themselves (Cole), 1997
Fade (Cormier), 1988
Faded Banners: A Treasury of Nineteenth Century Civil War Fiction (Alcott), 1986
Faded Sun Trilogy (Cherryh), 1987
Faery (Windling, ed.), 1984
Fahrenheit 451 (Bradbury), 1953
Fair Adventure (Vining), 1940
Fair American (Coatsworth), 1940
Fair Day, and Another Step Begun (Lyle), 1974
Fair Flower of Danger (Trease), 1955
Fair Maiden (Hall, L.), 1990
Fair Play (Kropp), 1980
Fair Wind to Virginia (Meigs), 1955
Fair With Rain (Head), 1957
Fair's Fair (Garfield), 1981
Fairy Tale series (Windling, ed.), 1986
Faith Fox: A Nativity (Gardam), 1996
Faith of Men (short story; London), 1904
Faith of Tarot (Anthony), 1980
Faithless Lollybird (Aiken), 1977
Falcon Bow: An Arctic Legend (Houston, J.), 1986
Falcons of Narabedla (Bradley), 1964
Fall Into Darkness (Pike), 1990
Fall of Atlantis (Bradley), 1987
Fall of Moondust (Clarke), 1961
Fall of the Dream Machine (Koontz), 1969
Fallen Angels (Myers), 1988
Fallen Fortress (Salvatore), 1993
Fallen Hearts (Andrews), 1988
Fallen Man (Hillerman), 1996
Falling Angel (Peyton), 1983
Falling for Lucas (Pascal), 1996
Falling in Love Is No Snap (Foley), 1986
Falling Star (Moyes), 1964
Falling Through the Cracks (Choyce), 1996
Falling Upward (play; Bradbury), 1988
Fallout (Swindells), 1992
False Face (Katz), 1987
Family and the Fugitive (Colman), 1972
Family (Donovan), 1976
Family Apart (Nixon), 1987
Family Book of Claire (Spence), 1991
Family Circle (poetry; Merriam), 1946
Family Conspiracy (Phipson), 1962
Family from One End Street and Some of Their Adventures (Garnett), 1937
Family of Foxes (Dillon), 1964
Family Picture (Hughes, D.), 1990

Family Pose (Hughes, D.), 1989
Family Project (Ellis), 1988
Family Reunion (Cooney), 1989
Family Secrets (Klein, N.), 1985
Family Secrets (Pascal), 1988
Family Tower (Willard), 1968
Family Trap (Colman), 1982
Famous Animals (George), 1994
Famous Rowena Lamont (Willard), 1983
Fancy Free (Cavanna), 1961
Fandango! (Ure), 1996
Fanfarlo (poetry; Spark), 1952
Fantastic Mr. Fox (Dahl), 1970
Fantastico (Fisk), 1994
Fantasy Stories (Jones, D. W.), 1994
Fantasy Worlds of Peter S. Beagle (Beagle), 1978
Far Cry from Kensington (Spark), 1988
Far Forests: Tales of Romance, Fantasy, and Suspense (Aiken), 1977
Far from Home (Sebestyen), 1980
Far from Shore (Major), 1980
Far North (Hobbs), 1996
Far-Off Land (Caudill), 1964
Far Side of Evil (Engdahl), 1971
Far Side of Victory (Greenberg), 1983
Far Voyager: The Story of James Cook (Latham), 1970
Faraway Lurs (Behn), 1963
Faraway Summer (Hurwitz), 1998
Farewell Kid (Wersba), 1990
Farm Babies (Freedman), 1981
Farm Team (Weaver), 1995
Farm that Ran Out of Names (Mayne), 1989
Farmer in the Sky (Heinlein), 1950
Farther off from England (Ure), 1973
Farthest Shore (Le Guin), 1972
Farthing's Fortunes (short story; Wright), 1976
Fascism: The Meaning and Experience of Reactionary Revolution (Forman), 1974
Fashion Victim (Pascal), 1997
Fast and Furious (play; Hurston), 1931
Fast Green Car (Fisk), 1965
Fast Sam, Cool Clyde, and Stuff (Myers), 1975
Fast Talk on a Slow Track (Williams-Garcia), 1991
Fat: A Love Story (Wersba), 1987
Fat Girl (Sachs), 1984
Fat Lollipop (Ure), 1991
Fatal Secrets (Cusick), 1992
Fates Worse than Death (Vonnegut), 1991
Father Every Few Years (Bach), 1977
Father Figure (Peck, Richard), 1978
Father, Mother, Mother, and Mom (play; Card), 1974
Father Poems (poetry; Koertge), 1974
Father's Arcane Daughter (Konigsburg), 1976
Fathom Five (Westall), 1979
Fawn (Peck, Robert Newton), 1975
Fear Man (Halam), 1995
Fear Nothing (Koontz), 1998
Fear Place (Naylor), 1994
Fear Street: Fire Game (Stine), 1991
Fear Street: The Wrong Number (Stine), 1990
Fear That Man (Koontz), 1969
Fearful Lovers (Westall), 1992

Feast of All Saints (Rice), 1980
Feather Crowns (Mason), 1993
Feather Star (Wrightson), 1962
Feathered Serpent (O'Dell), 1981
February Dragon (Thiele), 1965
Feet (short story; Mark), 1983
Felicia, the Critic (Conford), 1973
Felita (Mohr), 1979
Fell (Kerr), 1987
Fell Back (Kerr), 1989
Fell Down (Kerr), 1989
Fellowship of the Ring (Tolkien), 1954
Fence around the Cuckoo (Park), 1992
Ferlie (Hunter, M.), 1968
Ferris Bueller's Day Off (Strasser), 1986
Ferris Wheel (Stolz), 1977
Festival Moon (short story; Cherryh), 1987
Feud at Spanish Ford (play; Bonham), 1954
Fever Dreams (short story; Bradbury), 1970
Few Fair Days (Gardam), 1971
Ffangs the Vampire Bat and the Kiss of Truth (Hughes, T.), 1986
Fiancé for Fanny (Latham, as Lee), 1931
Fiddlers Three (play; Christie), 1971
Field Bazaar (short story; Doyle), 1934
Field of the Forty Footsteps (Trease), 1977
Fields (Richter, C.), 1946
Fields of Wonder (poetry; Hughes, L.), 1947
Fiesta Melons: Poems (poetry; Plath), 1971
Fifteenth Century Wool Merchant (Harnett), 1962
Fifth Grade Safari (Zindel), 1993
Fifth Son (Wiesel), 1985
Figgs & Phantoms (Raskin), 1974
Fight against Albatross Two (Thiele), 1976
Fight Fire With Fire (Pascal), 1998
Fight for Freedom (Serraillier), 1965
Fight for Freedom: The Story of the NAACP (Hughes, L.), 1962
Fighting Back: How to Cope with the Medical, Emotional and Legal Consequences of Rape (Bode), 1978
Fighting Ground (Avi), 1984
Fighting Man of Mars (Burroughs), 1931
Fighting Shirley Chisholm (Haskins), 1975
Figure in Grey (Christopher, as Ford), 1973
Figure of Speech (Mazer, N.), 1973
File on Fraulein Berg (Lingard), 1980
Filthy Beast (Garfield), 1978
Final Adventures of Sherlock Holmes (short story; Doyle), 1981
Final Friends series (Pike), from 1989
Find a Stranger, Say Goodbye (Lowry), 1978
Find the Power (Hughes, D.), 1994
Finders, Keepers (Johnson, A. and E.), 1981
Finders, Losers (short story; Mark), 1990
Finders Weepers (Lyle), 1982
Finding (Bawden), 1985
Finding a Poem (poetry; Merriam), 1970
Finding David Dolores (Willey), 1986
Finding Fever (Baird), 1982
Finding Moon (Hillerman), 1995
Finding Providence (Avi), 1997
Fine and Private Place (Beagle), 1960
Fine Clothes to the Jew (poetry; Hughes, L.), 1927
Fine, Soft Day (Forman), 1978

Fine Summer Knight (Mark), 1995
Fine White Dust (Rylant), 1986
Fingers (Sleator), 1983
Finn's Folly (Southall), 1969
Finn's Island (Dunlop), 1991
Finn's Roman Fort (Dunlop), 1994
Finn's Search (Dunlop), 1994
Fire (Cooney), 1990
Fire and Hemlock (Jones, D. W.), 1984
Fire and the Gold (Whitney), 1956
Fire Bug Connection: An Ecological Mystery (George), 1993
Fire Down Below (Golding), 1989
Fire in My Hands (poetry; Soto), 1990
Fire in the Stone (Thiele), 1973
Fire on the Wind (Crew, L.), 1995
Fire on the Wind (Trease), 1993
Fire Rose (Lackey), 1995
Fire Sea (Weis), 1991
Fire Storm (White, R.), 1979
Fire-Brother (Crossley-Holland), 1975
Fireball (Christopher), 1981
Firebird (Lackey), 1996
Firebringer series (Pierce, M.), from 1985
Firefighter (Savitz), 1992
Fireflood (short story; McIntyre), 1979
Firelings (Kendall), 1981
Fireplug Is First Base (Petersen), 1990
Fires of Azeroth (Cherryh), 1979
Fires of Fate: A Modern Morality (play; Doyle), 1909
Fires of Merlin (Barron), 1998
Fireship (short story; Vinge), 1978
Fireship, and Mother and Child (short story; Vinge), 1981
Firestarter (King), 1980
Fireweed (Paton Walsh), 1969
Firm of Girdlestone (Doyle), 1890
First a Dream (Daly), 1990
First Adventure (Coatsworth), 1950
First Book of Samuel (Dubosarsky), 1995
First Date (Stine), 1992
First Days of Life (Freedman), 1974
First Evil (Stine), 1992
First Few Friends (Singer), 1981
First Five Fathoms: A Guide to Underwater Adventure (Clarke), 1960
First Hard Times (Smith), 1983
First Job (Kamm), 1969
First King of Shannara (Brooks, T.), 1996
First Men in the Moon (Wells, H. G.), 1901
First on the Moon (Clarke), 1970
First Place (Pascal), 1987
First Thanksgiving (George), 1993
First the Egg (Moeri), 1982
First, the Good News (Angell), 1983
First Two Lives of Lukas-Kasha (Alexander), 1978
First Wedding, Once Removed (Deaver), 1990
Fisherman and the Bird (Levitin), 1982
Fishing in the Styx (Park), 1993
Fishing Party (Mayne), 1960
Fit of Shivers: Tales for Late at Night (Aiken), 1990
Five August Days (Burton), 1981
Five Autumn Songs for Children's Voices (poetry; Hughes, T.), 1969

Five Bushel Farm (Coatsworth), 1939
Five Days of the Ghost (Bell), 1989
Five Fates (short story; Herbert), 1970
Five Girls and a Baby (Pascal), 1996
Five Hundred (Dillon), 1972
Five Little Pigs (Christie), 1942
Five Patients: The Hospital Explained (Crichton), 1970
Five Were Missing (Duncan), 1972
Flagship Hope: Aaron Lopez (Alexander), 1960
Flambards series (Peyton), from 1967
Flame-Coloured Taffeta (Sutcliff), 1985
Flamers (Fisk), 1979
Flash Fire (Cooney), 1995
Flash Flood (Thiele), 1970
Flashback: The Amazing Adventures of a Film Horse (Rubinstein), 1990
Fledgling (Langton), 1980
Flesh in the Furnace (Koontz), 1972
Flight #116 Is Down (Cooney), 1992
Flight Deck (White, R.), 1961
Flight of Angels (Trease), 1988
Flight of Swans (Willard), 1980
Flight of the Hawk (Paulsen), 1998
Flight of the Kingfisher (Furlong), 1996
Flight to Adventure (Serraillier), 1947
Flight to the Forest (Willard), 1967
Flip-flop Girl (Paterson), 1994
Floating Admiral (Christie), 1931
Floatplane Notebooks (Edgerton), 1988
Flood at Reedsmere (Burton), 1968
Flower Fables (short story; Alcott), 1855
Flower Garden (Bunting), 1994
Flowers in the Attic (Andrews), 1979
Flowers of Anger (Hall, L.), 1976
Flute in Mayferry Street (Dunlop), 1976
Flux (short story; Card), 1992
Fly Away Home (Bunting), 1991
Fly Away Home (Hermes), 1996
Fly Away Home (Nöstlinger), 1975
Fly-by-Night (Peyton), 1968
Fly Free (Adler), 1984
Fly Free (Phipson), 1979
Fly into Danger (Phipson), 1978
Fly Named Alfred (Trembath), 1997
Fly on the Wall (Hillerman), 1971
Fly, Wheels, Fly! (Savitz), 1970
Flyaway (Hall, L.), 1987
Flying 19 (Aldridge), 1966
Flying Changes (Hall, L.), 1991
Flying Machine (play; Bradbury), 1986
Fog (Cooney), 1989
Fog (Lee, M.), 1972
Fog Comes on Little Pig Feet (Wells, R.), 1972
Fog Hounds, Wind Cat, Sea Mice (Aiken), 1984
Fogarty (Neville), 1969
Foghorn (play; Bradbury), 1977
Foghorn Passage (Lohans), 1992
Folk of the Air (Beagle), 1987
Folk of the Fringe (short story; Card), 1989
Follow a Shadow (Swindells), 1989
Follow My Black Plume (Trease), 1963

Follow My Leader (Harnett), 1949
Follow the Drum (Norton), 1942
Follow the Footprints (Mayne), 1953
Follow the River (Forman), 1975
Food Chains: The Unending Cycle (Anderson), 1991
Food Fight: A Guide to Eating Disorders for Preteens and Their Parents (Bode), 1997
Food Is Love (play; Asher), 1979
Food of the Gods, and How It Came to Earth (Wells, H. G.), 1904
Fool (Garfield), 1977
Fool's Gold (Snyder), 1993
Fool's Hill (Hall, B.), 1992
Foot in the Grave (Aiken), 1990
Footprints at the Window (Naylor), 1981
Footsteps (Garfield), 1980
Footsteps on the Stairs (Adler), 1982
For Ami (Mazer, N.), 1988
For Colored Girls Who Have Considered Suicide... (play; Shange), 1975
For Esme—With Love and Squalor (short story; Salinger), 1953
For Love of Evil (Anthony), 1988
For Love of Jody (Branscum), 1979
For the Love of Ryan (Pascal), 1996
For Your Eyes Only: Five Secret Exploits of James Bond (short story; Fleming), 1960
Forbidden (Cooney), 1993
Forbidden City (Bell), 1990
Forbidden Fountain of Oz (McGraw), 1980
Forbidden Love (Pascal), 1987
Forbidden Paths of Thual (Kelleher), 1979
Forbidden Tower (Bradley), 1977
Foreign Affair (Townsend, J.), 1982
Foreign Policy (play; Doyle), 1893
Foreigner: A Novel of First Contact (Cherryh), 1994
Forerunner Foray (Norton), 1973
Forest House (Bradley), 1994
Forest of the Night (Townsend, J.), 1974
Forever (Blume), 1975
Forever Amber Brown (Danziger), 1996
Forever and the Earth (play, poetry; Bradbury), 1984
Forever Formula (Bonham), 1979
Forever Trilogy (Pascal), 1987
Forever X (McCaughrean), 1997
Forged by Fire (Draper), 1997
Forgotten Beasts of Eld (McKillip), 1974
Forgotten Girl (Colman), 1990
Forgotten Island (Coatsworth), 1942
Forgotten Village (Steinbeck), 1941
Formal Feeling (Oneal), 1982
Fort Hogan (play; Bonham), 1980
Fort of Gold (Dillon), 1961
FortDog July (Peck, Robert Newton), 1992
Fortress in the Eye of Time (Cherryh), 1995
Fortress of Eagles (Cherryh), 1998
Fortress of Frost & Fire: The Bard's Tale II (Lackey), 1993
Fortunate Isles (Townsend, J.), 1989
Fortuneteller in 5B (Zalben), 1991
Forty-third War (Moeri), 1989
Foster Child (Bauer), 1977
Founder's Praise (Greenberg), 1976
Fountainhead (Rand), 1943

Garden of Broken Glass (Neville), 1975
Garden of Rama (Clarke), 1991
Garden of Shadows (Andrews), 1987
Gardener's Grandchildren (Willard), 1978
Garland for Girls (Alcott), 1887
Gate of Ivrel (Cherryh), 1976
Gates of Bannerdale (Trease), 1956
Gates of Hell (Cherryh), 1986
Gates of Paradise (Andrews), 1989
Gates of the Forest (Wiesel), 1966
Gateway (Walden), 1946
Gather Together in My Name (Angelou), 1974
Gathering (Hamilton), 1981
Gathering of Days: A New England Girl's Journal, 1830-32 (Blos), 1979
Gathering of Gargoyles (Pierce, M.), 1984
Gathering of Old Men (Gaines), 1983
Gavriel and Jemal: Two Boys of Jerusalem (Ashabranner), 1984
Gemma's Christmas Eve (Thiele), 1994
General Zapped an Angel (short story; Fast), 1970
Generation Warriors (McCaffrey), 1991
Genie on the Loose (Leeson), 1984
Genie with the Light Blue Hair (Conford), 1989
Genius and the Goddess (Huxley), 1955
Gentlehands (Kerr), 1978
Gently Touch the Milkweed (Hall, L.), 1970
George and Red (Coatsworth), 1969
George McGinnis: Basketball Superstar (Haskins), 1978
George W. Goethals: Panama Canal Engineer (Latham), 1965
George Washington and the Birth of Our Nation (Meltzer), 1986
George Washington and the Water Witch (play; Fast), 1956
George's Marvellous Medicine (Dahl), 1981
Georgia, Georgia (play; Angelou), 1972
Gerald's Game (King), 1992
Get Lost (Klein, R.; Kropp), 1987
Get Lost, Little Brother (Adler), 1983
Get off the Unicorn (short story; McCaffrey), 1977
Get on out of Here, Philip Hall (Greene), 1981
Get the Teacher! (Pascal), 1994
Getting Born (Freedman), 1978
Getting Even (Kropp), 1986
Getting On with It (Slepian), 1985
Ghost Abbey (Westall), 1988
Ghost Behind Me (Bunting), 1984
Ghost Belonged to Me (Peck, Richard), 1975
Ghost Brother (Adler), 1990
Ghost by the Sea (Dunlop), 1997
Ghost Canoe (Hobbs), 1997
Ghost Carnival: Stories of Ghosts in Their Haunts (Chambers), 1977
Ghost Children (Bunting), 1989
Ghost Children (Townsend, S.), 1998
Ghost Dance Caper (Hughes, M.), 1978
Ghost Downstairs (Garfield), 1972
Ghost Eye (Bauer), 1992
Ghost-Fish (Morpurgo), 1979
Ghost from the Grand Banks (Clarke), 1990
Ghost Front (Bonham), 1968
Ghost Host (Singer), 1987
Ghost in the Bell Tower (Pascal), 1992
Ghost in the Graveyard (Pascal), 1990
Ghost in the Tower (Westall), 1992

Ghost Inside the Monitor (Anderson), 1990
Ghost Legion (Weis), 1993
Ghost Messengers (Swindells), 1986
Ghost Next Door (Stine), 1993
Ghost of a Chance (play; Clapp), 1958
Ghost of Ballyhooly (Cavanna), 1971
Ghost of Grania O'Malley (Morpurgo), 1996
Ghost of Lone Cabin (Latham, as Lee), 1940
Ghost of Rhodes Manor (play; Latham), 1939
Ghost of Summer (Bunting), 1977
Ghost of the Great River Inn (Hall, L.), 1981
Ghost of Tricia Martin (Pascal), 1990
Ghost of Uncle Arvie (Creech), 1996
Ghost Paddle: A Northwest Coast Indian Tale (Houston, J.), 1972
Ghost Ship to Ganymede (Swindells), 1980
Ghost that Lived on the Hill (Ure), 1993
Ghost Wore White (Cavanna, as Allen), 1950
Ghostlight (Bradley), 1995
Ghostly Companions (Alcock), 1984
Ghosts (play; Chambers), 1980
Ghosts and Journeys (Westall), 1988
Ghost's Hour, Spook's Hour (Bunting), 1987
Ghosts I Have Been (Peck, Richard), 1977
Ghosts in the Family (Sachs), 1995
Ghosts of Departure Point (Bunting), 1982
Ghosts of Forever (poetry; Bradbury), 1981
Ghosts of Givenham Keep (Swindells), 1995
Ghosts of Glencoe (Hunter, M.), 1966
Ghosts of Now (Nixon), 1984
Ghostway (Hillerman), 1985
Ghoul Keepers (short story; Bradbury), 1961
Giant and the Biscuits (play; Latham), 1934
Giant Bones (Beagle), 1997
Giant Golden Book of Cat Stories (Coatsworth), 1953
Giant Golden Book of Dog Stories (Coatsworth), 1953
Giant Golden Books of Dogs, Cats, and Horses (Coatsworth), 1957
Giant's Bread (Christie, as Westmacott), 1930
Giant's Strength (play; Sinclair), 1948
Gib Rides Home (Snyder), 1998
Gideon Ahoy! (Mayne), 1987
Gideon's People (Meyer), 1996
Gift (Dickinson), 1973
Gift for Lonny (Bunting), 1973
Gift of Asher Lev (Potok), 1990
Gift of Magic (Duncan), 1971
Gift of Sarah Barker (Yolen), 1981
Gifts of Writing Creative Projects with Words and Art (Tchudi, as Judy), 1980
Gigantic Balloon (Park), 1975
G.I. Joe and the Everglades Swamp Terror (Stine, as Affabee), 1986
Gilded Age (Twain), 1873
Gilded Six-Bits (Hurston), 1986
Gillian's Choice (Meyer), 1991
Gimme A Kiss (Pike), 1989
Gimme an H, Gimme an E, Gimme an L, Gimme a P (Bonham), 1980
Gingerbread Days (poetry; Thomas, J.), 1995
Ginn Science Program (Asimov), 1972-73
Gioconda Smile (short story, play; Huxley), 1938
Giraffe and the Pelly and Me (Dahl), 1985
Giraffe Trouble (George), 1998

Horse-Tamer (Farley), 1958
Hospital Sketches (short story; Alcott), 1863
Hospital Sketches [and] Camp and Fireside Stories (short story; Alcott), 1869
Hospital Zone (Stolz), 1956
Hostage (Holm), 1980
Hostage! (Jones, A. F., as Kelly), 1996
Hostage! (Pascal), 1986
Hostage (Taylor, T.), 1987
Hostages to Fortune (Lingard), 1976
Hot and Cold Summer (Hurwitz), 1984
Hot Cars (Kropp), 1979
Hot Day (Greenwald), 1972
Hot Sleep (Card), 1978
Hothouse by the East River (Spark), 1973
Hound-Dog Man (Gipson), 1949
Hound of Death (short story; Christie), 1933
Hound of the Baskervilles (Doyle), 1902
Hound of Ulster (Sutcliff), 1963
Hour of the Wolf (Calvert), 1983
House between the Worlds (Bradley), 1980
House beyond the Meadow (poetry; Behn), 1955
House Gun (Gordimer), 1998
House Like a Lotus (L'Engle), 1984
House Made of Dawn (Momaday), 1968
House of Death (Pascal; Windsor), 1996
House of Dies Drear (Hamilton), 1968
House of Fear (Roberts), 1983
House of Pride (short story; London), 1912
House of Secrets (Bawden), 1964
House of Shadows (Norton), 1984
House of Stairs (Sleator), 1974
House of Temperley (play; Doyle), 1910
House of the Fifers (Caudill), 1954
House of the Swan (Coatsworth), 1948
House of Thunder (Koontz, as Nichols), 1982
House of Tomorrow (Crew, G.), 1988
House of Wings (Byars), 1972
House on Fairmont (Mayne), 1968
House on Mango Street (short story; Cisneros), 1983
House on Mayferry Street (Dunlop), 1977
House on Parchment Street (McKillip), 1973
House on the Hill (Dunlop), 1987
House on the River Terrace (Moloney), 1995
House on the Shore (Dillon), 1955
House under the Hill (Means), 1949
House with Roots (Willard), 1959
House You Pass on the Way (Woodson), 1997
Houseboat Summer (Coatsworth), 1942
Houses and History (Sutcliff), 1960
How a Weirdo and a Ghost Can Change Your Entire Life (Windsor), 1986
How Animals Defend Their Young (Freedman), 1978
How Animals Learn (Freedman), 1969
How Birds Fly (Freedman), 1977
How Bright the Dawn (Walden), 1962
How Can You Hijack a Cave? (Petersen), 1988
How Edith McGillicuddy Met R.L.S (short story; Steinbeck), 1943
How God Got Christian into Trouble (Wojciechowska), 1984
How Green You Are! (Doherty), 1982
How Happily She Laughs (poetry; Serraillier), 1976

How I Broke up with Ernie (Stine), 1990
How I Changed My Life (Strasser), 1995
How I Nearly Changed the World, but Didn't (play; Asher), 1977
How Many Days to America? A Thanksgiving Story (Bunting), 1988
How Many Miles to Sundown (Beatty), 1974
How Mr. Cork Made the Brain Work (Orlev), 1979
How Stella Got Her Groove Back (McMillan), 1996
How the Whale Became (Hughes, T.), 1963
How to Be Funny: An Extremely Silly Guidebook (Stine), 1978
How to Find Your Wonderful Someone (poetry; Naylor), 1972
How to Live on Five Dollars a Day (poetry; Koertge), 1976
Howard Fast Reader (Fast), 1960
Howard Pyle's Book of Pirates (Pyle), 1921
Howard's Field (play; Doherty), 1980
Howling Ghost (Pike), 1995
Howling Hill (Hobbs), 1998
Howl's Moving Castle (Jones, D. W.), 1986
Hub (Peck, Robert Newton), 1979
Huffler (Paton Walsh), 1975
Human Drift (short story; London), 1917
Human Rights Book (Meltzer), 1979
Humbug (Bawden), 1992
Hundred Secret Senses (Tan), 1995
Hungry Lizards (Choyce), 1990
Hunted Like a Wolf: The Story of the Seminole War (Meltzer), 1972
Hunter & Moon series (Jones, A. F.), from 1997
Hunter and the Trap (Fast), 1967
Hunter in the Dark (Hughes, M.), 1982
Hunter of Worlds (Cherryh), 1976
Hunter's Moon (Melling), 1993
Hunters of the Red Moon (Bradley), 1973
Hunting of Shadroth (Kelleher), 1981
Huntsman (Hill), 1982
Hurrah for Rosie! (Willard), 1968
Hurray for Ali Baba Bernstein (Hurwitz), 1989
Hurricane Elaine (Hurwitz), 1986
Hurricane Hazel (short story; Atwood), 1986
Hurricane Summer (Swindells), 1997
Hut School and the Wartime Home-Front Heroes (Burch), 1974
Hydra (Swindells), 1991

I am Rosa Parks (Haskins), 1997
I Am a Barbarian (Burroughs), 1967
I Am a Man: Ode to Martin Luther King, Jr. (poetry; Merriam), 1971
I Am David (Holm), 1965
I Am Leaper (Johnson, A. and E.), 1990
I Am Phoenix: Poems for Two Voices (poetry; Fleischman), 1985
I Am Somebody! A Biography of Jesse Jackson (Haskins), 1992
I Am the Cheese (Cormier), 1977
I Am the Clay (Potok), 1992
I Am the Mummy Heb-Nefert (Bunting), 1997
I Be Somebody (Irwin), 1984
I Don't Want to Go to Camp (Bunting), 1996
I Feel a Little Jumpy Around You (Janeczko, ed.), 1996
I Found My Love (Walden), 1956
I Had Seen Castles (Rylant), 1993
I Hate Being Gifted (Hermes), 1990
I Hate Camping (Petersen), 1991
I Have Heard of a Land (play, poetry; Thomas, J.), 1989
I Hear You Smiling (poetry; Holman), 1973
I Know What You Did Last Summer (Duncan), 1973

Little Lady of the Big House (London), 1916
Little Little (Kerr), 1981
Little Love (Hamilton), 1984
Little Love, a Little Learning (Bawden), 1965
Little Love Song (Magorian), 1991
Little Lower than the Angels (McCaughrean), 1987
Little Men (Alcott), 1871
Little Men (West), 1954
Little Mexican (short story; Huxley), 1924
Little Monster (Baillie), 1991
Little Old Ladies in Tennis Shoes (play; Asher), 1985
Little Orange Book (Donovan), 1961
Little Red Hen (Garner), 1997
Little Sister series (Jones, A. F.), from 1995
Little Soup series (Peck, Robert Newton), from 1991
Little Steel (Sinclair), 1938
Little Treasury of Dinosaurs (Asimov), 1989
Little Women (Alcott), 1868
Littlejim (Houston, G.), 1990
Littlejim's Dreams (Houston, G.), 1997
Littlest House (Coatsworth), 1940
Live and Let Die (Fleming), 1954
Live Coal in the Sea (L'Engle), 1996
Lives of Christopher Chant (Jones, D. W.), 1988
Living Fire (short story; Fisk), 1987
Livingstone's Companions (short story; Gordimer), 1971
Lizard Music (Pinkwater), 1976
Lizzie's Leaving (Lingard), 1995
Llama in the Family (Hurwitz), 1994
Llana of Gathol (short story; Burroughs), 1948
Load of Unicorn (Harnett), 1959
Loads of Codes and Secret Ciphers (Janeczko, ed.), 1981
Local News (short story; Soto), 1993
Loch (Zindel), 1994
Lock and Key (Tchudi), 1993
Locked in Time (Duncan), 1985
Locker (Cusick), 1994
Log Jam (Hughes, M.), 1987
Logan's Choice (play; Bonham), 1964
Lois & Clark (Cherryh), 1996
Lois and the Sleepover (Pascal), 1994
Lois Strikes Back (Pascal), 1990
Loitering with Intent (Spark), 1981
Lonely Hearts Club (Klein, R.), 1987
Lonely Maria (Coatsworth), 1960
Loners (Garden), 1972
Lonesome Sorrel (Robertson), 1952
Long after Ecclesiates (poetry; Bradbury), 1985
Long after Midnight (short story; Bradbury), 1976
Long Black Coat (Bennett), 1973
Long Claws: An Arctic Adventure (Houston, J.), 1981
Long Day Wanes (Burgess), 1965
Long Dream (Wright), 1958
Long Journey Home: Stories from Black History (Lester), 1972
Long Live the Queen (White, E.), 1989
Long-Lost Brother (Pascal), 1991
Long Night (Mayne), 1957
Long Night Watch (Southall), 1983
Long, Short and Tall Stories (play; Chambers), 1980-81
Long Sleep (Koontz, as Hill), 1975
Long Time between Kisses (Scoppettone), 1982

Long Time Coming (Whitney), 1954
Long Time Passing (Crew, L.), 1997
Long Tom and the Dead Hand (Crossley-Holland), 1992
Long Valley (short story; Steinbeck), 1938
Long Walk (King, as Bachman), 1979
Long Way Down (White, R.), 1977
Long Way from Home (Wartski), 1980
Long Way from Verona (Gardam), 1971
Long Way Home (Morpurgo), 1996
Long Way to Whiskey Creek (Beatty), 197 1
Look through My Window (Little), 1970
Look to the North: A Wolf Pup Diary (George), 1997
Look! What a Wonder! (play; Thomas, J.), 1976
Looking at the Moon (Pearson), 1991
Looking for Home (Ferris), 1989
Looking for Trouble (Marsden), 1993
Looking for Your Name (Janeczko, ed.), 1993
Looking On (Miles), 1978
Loose Woman (poetry; Cisneros), 1994
Lord Baden-Powell of the Boy Scouts (Fast), 1941
Lord Edgware Dies (Christie), 1933
Lord God Made Them All (Herriot), 1981
Lord of the Flies (Golding), 1954
Lord of the Rings trilogy, from 1954
Lord of Thunder (Norton), 1962
Lorinda's Diary (Wilson), 1991
Losers and Winners (Miller, F.), 1986
Losers in Space (Stine), 1991
Losers Weepers (Needle), 1981
Lost and Found (Garnett), 1974
Lost at Sea (Pascal), 1989
Lost Boy (Fox), 1988
Lost Boys (Card), 1992
Lost Childhood: Children of World War II (Weis), 1986
Lost Continent (short story; Burroughs), 1963
Lost Face (short story; London), 1910
Lost in Cyberspace (Peck, Richard), 1995
Lost in Space (Vinge), 1998
Lost Island (Dillon), 1952
Lost King (Weis), 1989
Lost Mind (Pike), 1995
Lost on Venus (Burroughs), 1935
Lost Star (Hoover), 1979
Lost World (Crichton), 1995
Lost World (Doyle), 1912
Lost Worlds of 2001 (Clarke), 1972
Lost Years of Merlin (Barron), 1996
Lothian Run (Hunter, M.), 1970
Lots and Lots of Candy (Meyer), 1976
Lottery Rose (Hunt), 1976
Lottery Winner (Clark), 1994
Lotus Caves (Christopher), 1969
Lou in the Limelight (Hunter, K.), 1981
Loud Mouth (Ure), 1988
Loud, Resounding Sea (Bonham), 1963
Louis Armstrong: An American Success Story (Collier), 1985
Louis Farrakhan and the Nation of Islam (Haskins), 1996
Louisa's Wonder Book: An Unknown Alcott Juvenile (Alcott), 1975
Love Affair (poetry; Bradbury), 1983
Love Among the Walnuts (Ferris), 1998
Love and Betrayal and Hold the Mayo! (Pascal), 1985

Malcolm X: By Any Means Necessary (Myers), 1993
Maldonado Miracle (Taylor, T.), 1973
Malibu Summer (Pascal), 1986
Mall (Cusick), 1992
Mama (McMillan), 1987
Mama, Let's Dance (Hermes), 1991
Mama's Going to Buy You a Mockingbird (Little), 1984
Man Called Hughes (Lillington), 1962
Man Dead? Then God Is Slain! (poetry; Bradbury), 1977
Man from Archangel (short story; Doyle), 1898
Man from Mundania (Anthony), 1989
Man from the North Pole (Mayne), 1963
Man from the Other Side (Orlev), 1988
Man in Motion (Mark), 1989
Man in the Brown Suit (Christie), 1924
Man in the Woods (Wells, R.), 1984
Man of Nazareth (Burgess), 1979
Man of the House: A Novel (Strasser), 1995
Man of the Monitor: The Story of John Ericsson (Latham), 1962
Man of Two Worlds (Herbert), 1986
Man that Corrupted Hadleyburg (short story; Twain), 1900
Man Who Could Call Down Owls (Bunting), 1984
Man Who Kept His Heart in a Bucket (Levitin), 1991
Man Who Lived Underground (Wright), 1971
Man Who Was Poe (Avi), 1989
Man with the Golden Gun (Fleming), 1965
Man With a Nose (short story; Wells, H. G.), 1984
Man without a Soul (short story; Burroughs), 1921-22
Man-Eater (short story; Burroughs), 1955
Manassas: A Novel of the War (Sinclair), 1904
Mandelbaum Gate (Spark), 1965
Mandeville (Trease), 1980
Mandrake (Peyton, as Hereld), 1949
Mandy in the Middle (Pascal), 1996
Maniac Magee (Spinelli), 1990
Mansy Miller Fights Back (Pascal), 1991
Mantlemass series (Willard), from 1970
Many Deadly Returns (Moyes), 1970
Many Waters (L'Engle), 1986
Map of Nowhere (Cross), 1986
Maplin Bird (Peyton), 1964
Maps in a Mirror series (Card), from 1990
Mara, Daughter of the Nile (McGraw), 1953
Maracot Deep (short story; Doyle), 1929
Marble Crusher (Morpurgo), 1980
March on Washington (Haskins), 1993
Margaret Sanger: Pioneer of Birth Control (Meltzer), 1969
Margin of Error (Choyce), 1992
Maria: A Christmas Story (Taylor, T.), 1994
Maria's Mountain (Garden), 1981
Maria's Movie Comeback (Pascal), 1994
Mariah Delany Author of the Month Club (Greenwald), 1990
Mariah Delany Lending Library Disaster (Greenwald), 1977
Mariah Keeps Cool (Walter), 1990
Mariah Loves Rock (Walter), 1988
Marie and Her Lover (Sinclair), 1948
Marie Antoinette (Sinclair), 1939
Mariel of Redwall (Jacques), 1991
Marion's Angels (Peyton), 1979
Mariposa Blues (Koertge), 1991
Mark of Conte (Levitin), 1976

Mark of Merlin (McCaffrey), 1971
Mark of the Horse Lord (Sutcliff), 1965
Mark Twain: A Writer's Life (Meltzer), 1985
Mark Twain Murders (Yep), 1982
Marked by Fire (Thomas, J.), 1982
Market Day (Bunting), 1996
Marko's Wedding (poetry; Serraillier), 1972
Marra's World (Coatsworth), 1975
Marriage (Wells, H. G.), 1912
Marriage of True Minds (Ure), 1975
Married Woman (Pascal), 1994
Marrying Off Mother (Nöstlinger), 1978
Mars (Asimov), 1967
Mars, the Red Planet (Asimov), 1977
Marsh Hawk (poetry; Atwood), 1977
Marsha on Stage (Walden), 1952
Martha Graham, A Dancer's Life (Freedman), 1997
Martian Chronicles (Bradbury), 1950
Martian Chronicles (play; Bradbury), 1977
Martians at Mudpuddle Farm (Morpurgo), 1991
Martin Eden (London), 1909
Martin the Warrior (Jacques), 1993
Martina Navratilova: Tennis Power (Knudson), 1987
Martin's Mountain (Thiele), 1993
Marvellous Mongolian (Aldridge), 1974
Marvelous Misadventures of Sebastian (Alexander), 1970
Mary and Frances (Spence), 1986
Mary, Bloody Mary (Meyer), 1969
Mary-in-the-Middle (Asher), 1990
Mary Is Missing (Pascal), 1990
Mary McLeod Bethune: Voice of Black Hope (Meltzer), 1987
Mary Mehan Awake (Armstrong, J.), 1997
Mary on Horseback (Wells, R.), 1997
Mary Wolf (Grant), 1995
Mascot of the Melroy (Robertson), 1953
Mask (Koontz, as West), 1981
Mask Magic (Meyer), 1978
Masked Prowler: The Story of a Raccoon (George), 1950
Masks: A Love Story (Bennett), 1972
Masque for the Queen (Trease), 1970
Masquerade (Ure), 1979
Massacre at Fall Creek (West), 1975
Master: An Adventure Story (White, T. H.), 1957
Master Cornhill (McGraw), 1973
Master Mind of Mars (Burroughs), 1928
Master of Ballantrae (Stevenson), 1889
Master of Fiends (Hill), 1987
Master of Murder (Pike), 1992
Master of Space (Clarke), 1961
Master of the Grove (Kelleher), 1982
Master Puppeteer (Paterson), 1976
Master Rosalind (Beatty), 1974
Master Simon's Garden (Meigs), 1916
Masterharper of Pern (McCaffrey), 1998
Mat Pit and the Tunnel Tenants (Greenwald), 1972
Mates (Baillie), 1989
Matilda (Dahl), 1988
Matt and Jo (Southall), 1973
Matter of Feeling (Boissard), 1980
Matter of Time (West), 1966
Mattimeo (Jacques), 1991

Poppy (Avi), 1995
Poppy & Rye (Avi), 1998
Port Eternity (Cherryh), 1982
Portrait of Ivan (Fox), 1969
Possessed (short story; Clarke), n.d.
Possessing the Secret of Joy (Walker), 1992
Postbox Mystery (Swindells), 1988
Postcard Poems (Janeczko, ed.), 1979
Postern of Fate (Christie), 1973
Postmarked the Stars (Norton), 1969
Pot Boiler (play; Sinclair), 1924
Pot of Caviare (play; Doyle), 1910
Potch Goes down the Drain (Thiele), 1984
Potter Thompson (play; Garner), 1975
Poupette (Ure), 1994
Poverty in America (Meltzer), 1986
Power (Fast), 1962
Power Lines (McCaffrey), 1994
Power of Stars (Lawrence), 1972
Power of Three (Jones, D. W.), 1976
Power Play (McCaffrey), 1995
Power Play (Pascal), 1984
Power Politics (poetry; Atwood), 1971
Power to the People (Haskins), 1997
Powerhouse (Halam), 1997
Powers That Be (McCaffrey), 1992
Practical Music Theory (Collier), 1970
Prairie Songs (Conrad), 1985
Prairie Visions (Conrad), 1991
Pram Race (Willard), 1964
Prank (Lasky), 1984
Pray Love, Remember (Stolz), 1954
Predator! (Brooks, B.), 1991
Prelude (L'Engle), 1968
Prelude to Space (Clarke), 1951
Premonitions (Bonham), 1984
Prentice Alvin (Card), 1989
Preposterous: Poems of Youth (Janeczko, ed.), 1991
Present Takers (Chambers), 1983
Presenting Chris Crutcher (Davis, T.), 1997
President's Daughter (White, E.), 1984
Presidential Agent (Sinclair), 1944
Presidential Mission (Sinclair), 1947
Pressure Play (Hughes, D.), 1990
Pretend You Don't See Her (Clark), 1997
Pretender (Anthony), 1979
Pretenses (Pascal), 1988
Price of a Bride (play; Hughes, T.), 1966
Price of Blood (Pyle), 1899
Pride of Chanur (Cherryh), 1982
Pride of Lions (play; Serraillier), 1970
Priests of Psi (short story; Herbert), 1980
Prime of Miss Jean Brodie (Spark), 1961
Primrose Path (Matas), 1995
Prince (Brooks, B.), 1998
Prince Alexis and the Silver Saucer (play; Asher), 1987
Prince Amos (Paulsen), 1994
Prince and the Patters (play; Latham), 1934
Prince and the Pauper (Twain), 1881
Prince and the Pilgrim (Stewart), 1995
Prince Caspian: The Return to Narnia (Lewis, C. S.), 1951

Prince Charlie's Year (Forman), 1991
Prince Commands (Norton), 1934
Prince Hagen (play; Sinclair), 1909
Prince Hagen: A Phantasy (Sinclair), 1903
Prince in Waiting (Christopher), 1970
Prince of the Pond; Otherwise Known as De Fawg Pin (Napoli), 1992
Prince on a White Horse (Lee, T.), 1982
Prince Otto: A Romance (Stevenson), 1885
Princes (Hartnett), 1997
Princess Alice (Bawden), 1985
Princess Ashley (Peck, Richard), 1987
Princess Elizabeth (Pascal), 1989
Princess Hynchatti and Some Other Surprises (Lee, T.), 1972
Princess in Denim (Sherburne), 1958
Princess of Mars (Burroughs), 1917
Priscilla Pentecost (Willard), 1970
Prison of Ice (Koontz, as Axton), 1976
Prison Window, Jerusalem Blue (Clements), 1977
Prisoner of Psi (Johnson, A. and E.), 1985
Prisoner of Vampires (Garden), 1984
Prisoners of September (Garfield), 1975
Prisoners of Time (Cooney), 1998
Private Eyes (Armstrong, J., as Winfield), 1989
Private I (short story; Naylor), 1969
Private Jessica (Pascal), 1998
Private Life of Axie Reed (Knowles), 1986
Private Worlds of Julia Redfern (Cameron), 1988
Probably Still Nick Swansen (Wolff), 1988
Problem at Pollensa Bay (short story; Christie), 1943
Problem with Sidney (Meyer), 1990
Procedures for Underground (poetry; Atwood), 1970
Professor Challenger Stories (short story; Doyle), 1952
Profiles in Black Power (Haskins), 1972
Profiles of the Future (Clarke), 1962
Project: A Perfect World (Paulsen), 1996
Project 40 (Herbert), 1973
Prom Queen (Stine), 1992
Promise (Hughes, M.), 1989
Promise (Potok), 1969
Promise (Westall), 1991
Promise for Joyce (Duncan, as Kerry), 1959
Promise of Space (Clarke), 1968
Promise Song (Holeman), 1997
Promise Trilogy (Pascal), 1986-87
Promises (Pascal), 1985
Promises Are for Keeping (Rinaldi), 1982
Proper Little Nooryeff (Ure), 1982
Proper Place (Lingard), 1975
Prophecy of Tau Ridoo (Katz), 1982
Prostho Plus (Anthony), 1971
Proud and the Free (Fast), 1950
Proud Taste for Scarlet and Miniver (Konigsburg), 1973
Prove Yourself a Hero (Peyton), 1977
Prydain series (Alexander), 1964-68
P.S. Longer Letter Later (Danziger), 1998
Psion (Vinge), 1982
Psyche's Art (Alcott), 1868
Psyched! (Hughes, D.), 1992
Psychic Sisters (Pascal), 1993
Public Image (Spark), 1968

Ride When You're Ready (Bunting, as Bolton), 1974
Rider at the Gate (Cherryh), 1995
Riders of the Storm (Burton), 1972
Ridin' the Moon in Texas: Word Paintings (poetry; Shange), 1987
Riding the Whales (Kelleher), 1995
Riff Remember (Hall, L.), 1973
Rifle (Paulsen), 1995
Rifles for Watie (Keith), 1957
Right to an Answer (Burgess), 1960
Right to Remain Silent (Meltzer), 1972
Righteous Revenge of Artemis Bonner (Myers), 1992
Right-Hand Man (Peyton), 1977
Rim of the Morning: Six Stories (Thiele), 1966
Rimrunners (Cherryh), 1989
Rinehart series (Knudson), from 1980
Ring (Anthony), 1968
Ring for the Sorcerer (Park), 1967
Ring of Death (Hoy), 1990
Ring of Endless Light (L'Engle), 1980
Ring of Fear (McCaffrey), 1971
Ring of Fire (Murphy), 1977
Ring Out, Bow Bells! (Harnett), 1953
Ring the Judas Bell (Forman), 1968
Ring-Rise, Ring-Set (Hughes, M.), 1992
Rings of Ice (Anthony), 1974
Rings on Her Fingers (Mayne), 1991
Rio Grande Stories (Meyer), 1994
Riot on the Street (Kropp), 1993
Rip-Roaring Russell (Hurwitz), 1983
Rising Sun (Crichton), 1992
Risk 'n' Roses (Slepian), 1990
Risking Love (Orgel), 1985
Rita Hayworth and Shawshank Redemption: A Story from "Different Seasons." (short story; King), 1983
Rita the Weekend Rat (Levitin), 1971
Rites of Passage (Golding), 1980
Rites of Passage (short story; Greenberg), 1971
Rivan Codex (Eddings), 1998
River (Paulsen), 1991
River at Green Knowe (Boston), 1959
River at Her Feet (Sherburne), 1965
River Murray Mary (Thiele), 1979
River Rats, Inc. (George), 1979
River Runners: A Tale of Hardship and Bravery (Houston, J.), 1979
River Thunder (Hobbs), 1997
Riverman (Baillie), 1986
Road Ahead (Lowry), 1988
Road Goes Ever On: A Song Cycle (poetry; Tolkien), 1967
Road Home (White, E., as Emerson), 1995
Road of Dreams (poetry; Christie), 1925
Road to Camlann: The Death of King Arthur (Sutcliff), 1981
Road to Christmas (Park), 1962
Road to Damietta (O'Dell), 1985
Road to Dunmore (Dillon), 1966
Road to Irriyan (Lawrence), 1996
Road to Memphis (Taylor, M.), 1990
Road to Nowhere (Pike), 1993
Road under the Sea (Park), 1962
Roadside Valentine (Adler), 1983
Roadwork (King, as Bachman), 1981
Roanoke: A Novel of the Lost Colony (Levitin), 1973

Robber Bride (Atwood), 1993
Robbers (Bawden), 1979
Robbery at the Mall (Pascal), 1994
Robbie and the Leap Year Blues (Klein, N.), 1981
Robin & the Kestrel (Lackey), 1993
Robin in the Middle (Pascal), 1993
Robin of Sherwood (Morpurgo), 1996
Robin series (poetry; Serraillier), from 1967
Robin's Country (Furlong), 1995
Robinsheugh (Dunlop), 1975
Robinson (Spark), 1958
Robodad (Carter), 1990
Robot Adept (Anthony), 1988
Robot Birthday (Bunting), 1980
Robot Blues (Weis), 1996
Robot Revolt (Fisk), 1981
Rock (Kropp), 1989
Rock and the Willow (Lee, M.), 1963
Rock Band: Big Men in a Great Big Town (Meyer), 1980
Rock It to the Top (Strasser), 1987
Rock Jockeys (Paulsen), 1995
Rock 'n' Roll Is Here to Stay (play; Doherty), 1984
Rock 'n' Roll Nights: A Novel (Strasser), 1982
Rock Star (Collier), 1970
Rock Star's Girl (Pascal), 1991
Rock Tumbling: From Stones to Gems to Jewelry (Meyer), 1975
Rocket Island (Taylor, T.), 1985
Rocket Ship Galileo (Heinlein), 1947
Rocks of Honey (Wrightson), 1960
Rodney Stone (Doyle), 1896
Rodomonte's Revenge (Paulsen), 1995
Rodrigo Poems (poetry; Cisneros), 1985
Rogue Wave: and Other Red-Blooded Sea Stories (Taylor, T.), 1996
Rolf and Rosie (Swindells), 1992
Roll of Thunder, Hear My Cry (Taylor, M.), 1976
Roller Coaster for the Twins! (Pascal), 1996
Roller Madonnas (Ashley), 1997
Roller Skating (Miklowitz), 1979
Rolling Season (Mayne), 1960
Rolling Stones (Heinlein), 1952
Roman Holiday (Sinclair), 1931
Romance Is a Wonderful Thing (White, E.), 1983
Romance on Trial (Cavanna), 1984
Romeo and Two Juliets (Pascal), 1995
Romulan Way (Duane), 1987
Ronnie and Rosey (Angell), 1977
Ronnie and the Chief's Son (Coatsworth), 1962
Rooftops (Mayne), 1966
Rookie of the Year (Strasser), 1993
Rookie of the Year (Tunis), 1944
Rookie Star (Hughes, D.), 1990
Room Made of Windows (Cameron), 1971
Room 13 (Swindells), 1989
Roommate (Pascal), 1996
Rosalie (Westall), 1987
Rosa's Lie (Pascal), 1992
Roscoe's Leap (Cross), 1987
Rose and the Yew Tree (Christie, as Westmacott), 1948
Rose Cottage (Stewart), 1997
Rose Daughter (McKinley), 1997
Rose Family: A Fairy Tale (Alcott), 1864

Rose in Bloom (Alcott), 1876
Rose Madder (King), 1995
Rose of Paradise (Pyle), 1888
Rose of Puddle Fratrum (play; Aiken), 1978
Rosemary (Stolz), 1955
Rosie and Mr. William Star (Bunting), 1981
Rosy Cole series (Greenwald), from 1985
Rosy Starling (Garfield), 1977
Rosy's Romance (Greenwald), 1989
Rotten Years (Wojciechowska), 1971
Round and Round with Kahlil Gibran (poetry; Miller, J.), 1990
Round Dozen: Stories (short story; Alcott), 1963
Round the Fire Stories (short story; Doyle), 1908
Round the Red Lamp, Being Facts and Fancies of Medical Life (short story; Doyle), 1894
Rowan (McCaffrey), 1990
Royal Dirk (Beatty), 1966
Royal Harry (Mayne), 1971
Royal Pain (Conford), 1986
Royal Rosie (Willard), 1968
Roz and Ozzie (Hurwitz), 1992
RT, Margaret and the Rats of NIMH (Conly), 1990
Ruby (Guy), 1976
Ruby in the Smoke (Pullman), 1985
Ruby Knight (Eddings), 1990
Ruby of Kishmoor (Pyle), 1908
Ruffles and Drums (Cavanna), 1975
Rufus, Red Rufus (Beatty), 1975
Ruins of Isis (Bradley), 1978
Rule of Three (play; Christie), 1962
Ruler of the Sky: A Novel of Genghis Khan (Sargent), 1993
Rumble Fish (Hinton), 1975
Rumor of War (Caputo), 1977
Rumors (Cooney), 1985
Rumors (Pascal), 1987
Run (Sleator), 1973
Run, Don't Walk (Savitz), 1979
Run Masked (White, R.), 1938
Run Softly, Go Fast (Wersba), 1970
Runaway (Graham), 1972
Runaway (Kropp), 1979
Runaway (Miklowitz), 1977
Runaway (Pascal), 1985
Runaway Bus (Park), 1969
Runaway Hamster (Pascal), 1989
Runaway Serf (Trease), 1968
Runaway Summer (Bawden), 1969
Runaway Voyage (Cavanna), 1978
Runaways (Kamm), 1978
Runaways (Townsend, J.), 1979
Runner (Voigt), 1985
Running Deer (Trease), 1941
Running for Her Life (Pascal), 1996
Running Girl: The Diary of Ebonee Rose (Mathis), 1997
Running Loose (Crutcher), 1983
Running Man (King, as Bachman), 1982
Running of the Deer (Trease), 1982
Running on Ice (Doherty), 1997
Running Scared (Ashley), 1986
Running Scared (play; Ashley), 1986
Running with the Demon (Brooks, T.), 1997

Runt of Rogers School (Keith), 1971
Rusalka (Cherryh), 1989
Russell and Elisa (Hurwitz), 1989
Russell Rides Again (Hurwitz), 1985
Russell Sprouts (Hurwitz), 1987

Sabre, the Horse from the Sea (Peyton, as Hereld), 1948
Sabre-tooth Sandwich (Garfield), 1994
Sabriel (Nix), 1995
Sacred Clowns (Hillerman), 1993
Sacred Cows . . . and Other Edibles (poetry; Giovanni), 1988
Sacred Ground (Lackey), 1994
Sad Cypress (Christie), 1940
Safe as the Grave (Cooney), 1979
Safe at First (Hughes, D.), 1991
Sail Away (White, R.), 1948
Sailing Hatrack (Coatsworth), 1972
Sailor in the Sun (White, R.), 1941
Sailor Song (Kesey), 1992
St. Ives; Being the Adventures of a French Prisoner in England (Stevenson), 1897
Saint Katy the Virgin (short story; Steinbeck), 1936
Saint Maybe (Tyler), 1991
St. Patrick's Day in the Morning (Bunting), 1980
Saints (Card), 1988
Salamandastron (Jacques), 1992
'Salem's Lot (King), 1975
Salt: From a Russian Folktale (Langton), 1992
Salt River Times (Mayne), 1980
Salted Lemons (Smith), 1980
Sam and Sue and Lavatory Lue (Swindells), 1993
Sam Houston: Hero of Texas (Latham), 1965
Same Scene, Different Place (Walden), 1969
Sam's Duck (Morpurgo), 1996
Samuel F.B. Morse: Artist-Inventor (Latham), 1961
Samuel the Seeker (Sinclair), 1910
Samuel Todd series (Konigsburg), from 1990
Samurai and the Long-Nosed Devils (Namioka), 1976
Samurai, Inc. (Klass, D.), 1992
San Sebastian (Dillon), 1953
Sanctified Church (Hurston), 1983
Sand (Mayne), 1964
Sand Hoppers (Harnett), 1946
Sandgame (Orlev), 1996
Sandman and the Turtles (Morpurgo), 1991
Sandman's Eyes (Windsor), 1985
Sands of Mars (Clarke), 1951
Sandwriter (Hughes, M.), 1984
Sandy (Vining), 1945
Sandy Simmons Superstar: Break a Leg (Ure), 1998
Sang Spell (Naylor), 1998
Santa Claus (Vinge), 1985
Santaroga Barrier (Herbert), 1968
Sapphire Rose (Eddings), 1991
Sara Will (Bridgers), 1985
Saraband for Shadows (Trease), 1982
Saracen Maid (Garfield), 1991
Sarah and After: The Matriarchs (Banks), 1975
Sarah and Me and the Lady from the Sea (Beatty), 1989
Sarah Bishop (O'Dell), 1980
Sarah with an H (Irwin), 1996

Shadows Offstage (Bennett), 1974
Shadows on a Sword (Bradford), 1996
Shadows on Little Reef Bay (Adler), 1985
Shadows on the Wall (Naylor), 1980
Shadrach's Crossing (Avi), 1983
Shake Up (Hughes, D.), 1993
Shaker, Why Don't You Sing? (poetry; Angelou), 1983
Shakespeare in Harlem (poetry; Hughes, L.), 1942
Shaky Island (Park), 1962
Shampoo on Tuesdays (Orlev), 1986
Shape of Things to Come (Wells, H. G.), 1933
Shardik (Adams), 1974
Sharelle (Neufeld), 1983
Sharing Susan (Bunting), 1991
Shark (Brooks, B.), 1998
Shark Bait (Salisbury), 1997
Shark beneath the Reef (George), 1989
Sharks (Freedman), 1985
Sharks in the Shadows (Thiele), 1988
Sharla (Wilson), 1997
Sharra's Exile (Bradley), 1981
Shatterbelt (Thiele), 1987
Shattered (Koontz, as Dwyer), 1973
Shattered Chain (Bradley), 1976
Sheila's Dying (Carter), 1987
Shell Lady's Daughter (Adler), 1983
Shelter from the Wind (Bauer), 1976
Shelter on Blue Barns Road (Adler), 1981
Shepherd Moon: A Novel of the Future (Hoover), 1984
Shepherd Watches, a Shepherd Sings (Taylor, T.), 1977
Sherlock Holmes (play; Doyle), 1899
Sherlock Holmes: Two Complete Adventures (short story; Doyle), 1989
She's My Girl! (Cavanna, as Headley), 1949
She's Not What She Seems (Pascal), 1995
Shield of Achilles (Forman), 1966
Shield Ring (Sutcliff), 1956
Shifting Sands (Sutcliff), 1977
Shiloh (short story; Mason), 1982
Shine (Paton Walsh), 1988
Shining (King), 1977
Shining (Lester), 1997
Shining Company (Sutcliff), 1990
Shining Ones (Eddings), 1993
Shinkei (Rubinstein), 1996
Ship to Rome (Trease), 1972
Ship Who Sang (McCaffrey), 1969
Ship Who Searched (Lackey), 1993
Ship Who Searched (McCaffrey), 1992
Ship Who Won (McCaffrey), 1994
Shipboard Wedding (Pascal), 1995
Ship's Cat (Park), 1961
Ships in the Night (short story; Naylor), 1970
Ships of Earth (Card), 1994
Shirley Temple Black: Actress to Ambassador (Haskins), 1988
Shizuko's Daughter (Mori), 1993
Shoemaker's Boy (Aiken), 1994
Shon the Taken (Lee, T.), 1979
Shooting Star: A Novel About Annie Oakley (Klass, S. S.), 1996
Shore of Women (Sargent), 1986
Short! A Book of Very Short Stories (Crossley-Holland), 1998

Short Reign of Pippin IV: A Fabrication (Steinbeck), 1957
Shoshoni (Carter), 1989
Shotgun Shaw: A Baseball Story (Keith), 1949
Shots on Goal (Wallace), 1997
Showdown (Pascal), 1985
Shuttered Windows (Means), 1938
Shy Ones (Hall, L.), 1967
Siamina (Orlev), 1979
Sick of Being Sick Book (Stine), 1980
Siege of Babylon (Dhondy), 1978
Siege of Darkness (Salvatore), 1994
Siege of Frimly Prim (Swindells), 1994
Siege of Silent Henry (Hall, L.), 1972
Sighting (Mark), 1997
Sign of the Beaver (Speare), 1983
Sign of the Chrysanthemum (Paterson), 1973
Sign of the Four (Doyle), 1890
Sign of the Green Falcon (Harnett), 1984
Signs of Life (Ferris), 1995
Silas Timberman (Fast), 1954
Silence over Dunkerque (Tunis), 1962
Silent Dancing: A Partial Remembrance of a Puerto Rican Childhood (Cofer), 1990
Silent Night (Stine), 1991
Silent Night: A Novel (Clark), 1995
Silent Night 2 (Stine), 1993
Silent Ship, Silent Sea (White, R.), 1967
Silent Stalker (Cusick), 1993
Silken Secret (Trease), 1953
Silly Songs and Sad (poetry; Raskin), 1967
Silmarillion (Tolkien), 1977
Silver (Mazer, N.; Wolitzer), 1988
Silver Branch (Sutcliff), 1957
Silver Chair (Lewis, C. S.), 1953
Silver Coach (Adler), 1979
Silver Crown (O'Brien), 1968
Silver Days (Levitin), 1989
Silver Fleece (Means), 1950
Silver Gryphon (Lackey), 1996
Silver Guard (Trease), 1948
Silver Inkwell (Whitney), 1945
Silver Kiss (Klause), 1990
Silver Locusts (Bradbury), 1951
Silver on the Tree (Cooper), 1977
Silver Pitchers [and] Independence, a Centennial Love Story (short story; Alcott), 1876
Silver Secret (Cavanna, as Allen), 1956
Silver Sword (Serraillier), 1956
Silver Woven in My Hair (Murphy), 1977
Silver's Revenge (Leeson), 1978
Simon (Sutcliff), 1953
Simon and the Game of Chance (Burch), 1970
Simon Wheeler: Detective (Twain), 1963
Simple Gifts (Greenberg), 1986
Simple Gifts: The Story of the Shakers (Yolen), 1976
Simple, Honorable Man (Richter, C.), 1962
Simple series (short story; Hughes, L.), from 1950
Sing a Song of Ambush (Peyton), 1964
Sing and Scatter Daisies (Lawrence), 1977
Sing Down the Moon (O'Dell), 1970
Sing Me a Death Song (Bennett), 1990

Sorceress of Darshiva (Eddings), 1989
Sorcery and Cecelia (Wrede), 1988
Sorority Scandal (Pascal), 1995
Sos the Rope (Anthony), 1968
SOS Titanic (Bunting), 1996
Soul Brothers and Sister Lou (Hunter, K.), 1968
Soul Catcher (Herbert), 1972
Soul Forge (Weis), 1997
Soul Looks Back in Wonder (poetry; Angelou; Feelings, 1993
Soul of a Bishop (Wells, H. G.), 1917
Soul of the City (Cherryh), 1986
Soul of the Silver Dog (Hall, L.), 1992
Soul on Fire (Cleaver, E.), 1978
Soul on Ice (Cleaver, E.), 1968
Sound of Chariots (Hunter, M.), 1972
Sound of Coaches (Garfield), 1974
Sound of Gunfire (play; Bonham), 1959
Sound of Strings (Keith), 1992
Sound to Remember (Levitin), 1979
Sounder (Armstrong, W.), 1969
Soup series (Peck, Robert Newton), from 1974
Sour Land (Armstrong, W.), 1971
Source of Magic (Anthony), 1979
South Moon Under (Rawlings), 1933
South of the Angels (West), 1960
South Sea Tales (short story; London), 1911
South Town (Graham), 1958
Space Cadet (Heinlein), 1948
Space Demons (Rubinstein), 1986
Space Dictionary (Asimov), 1970
Space Dreamers (Clarke), 1969
Space Family Stone (Heinlein), 1969
Space Hostages (Fisk), 1967
Space Station Seventh Grade (Spinelli), 1982
Space Trap (Hughes, M.), 1983
Spaceburger (Pinkwater), 1993
Spain and Peace (Fast), 1952
Spanish Hoof (Peck, Robert Newton), 1985
Spanish Letters (Hunter, M.), 1964
Spanish Roundabout (Daly), 1960
Spanish Smile (O'Dell), 1982
Spanish-American War: Imperial Ambitions (Carter), 1992
Sparkle and Nightflower (Hartnett), 1986
Sparkles for Bright Eyes (Alcott), 1879
Sparkling Cyanide (Christie), 1945
Sparrows Work Hard (poetry; Soto), 1981
Spartacus (Fast), 1951
Speak to the Earth (Bell), 1994
Speaker for the Dead (Card), 1986
Special Christmas (Pascal), 1986
Specially Wonderful Day (play; Clapp), 1972
Speckled Band: An Adventure of Sherlock Holmes (play; Doyle), 1910
Spectre (Nixon), 1982
Speeches for Doctor Frankenstein (poetry; Atwood), 1966
Speed (Knudson), 1983
Speedway Contender (Bonham), 1964
Spell #7: A Geechee Quick Magic Trance Manual (play; Shange), 1979
Spell for Chameleon (Anthony), 1977
Spell Is Cast (Cameron), 1964

Spell Me a Witch (Willard), 1979
Spell Sword (Bradley), 1974
Spellbound (Pike), 1989
Spellcoats (Jones, D. W.), 1979
Spellhorn (Doherty), 1989
Spence + Lila (Mason), 1988
Sphere (Crichton), 1987
Spice Island Mystery (Cavanna), 1969
Spider's Web (play; Christie), 1954
Spike Lee (Haskins), 1997
Spindle River (O'Neill), 1998
Spinning-Wheel Stories (short story; Alcott), 1884
Spiral Stair (Aiken), 1979
Spire (Golding), 1964
Spirit House (Sleator), 1991
Spirit River (Hughes, M.), 1988
Spirit Seekers (Nixon), 1995
Spit (Wallace), forthcoming
Spitball Gang (Paulsen), 1980
Spite Fences (Krisher), 1994
Split Infinity (Anthony), 1980
Split Sisters (Adler), 1986
Split Up (Kropp), 1989
Spock's World (Duane), 1988
Spook Birds (Bunting), 1981
Spooky Cottage (Ure), 1991
Sport of Nature (Gordimer), 1987
Sports and Games (Keith), 1941
Sports Great Magic Johnson (Haskins), 1989
Sports Poetry (Knudson), 1971
Spreading Fires (Knowles), 1974
Sprig of Broom (Willard), 1971
Spring Begins in March (Little), 1966
Spring Break (Hurwitz), 1997
Spring Break (Pascal), 1986
Spring Comes Riding (Cavanna), 1950
Spring Comes to the Ocean (George), 1966
Spring Fever (Pascal), 1987
Spring, Summer, Autumn, Winter (poetry; Hughes, T.), 1974
Springboard to Summer (Bunting), 1975
Spring-heeled Jack (Pullman), 1989
Springtime and Harvest: A Romance (Sinclair), 1901
Spud Sweetgrass (Doyle), 1992
Spud Tackett and the Angel of Doom (Branscum), 1983
Spunk: The Selected Stories of Zora Neale Hurston (Hurston), 1985
Spurs for Suzanna (Cavanna), 1947
Spy (Sinclair), 1919
Spy Called Michel-E (Walden), 1967
Spy Catchers (Trease), 1976
Spy Girl (Pascal), 1997
Spy on Danger Island (Walden), 1965
Spy Who Loved Me (Fleming), 1962
Spy Who Talked Too Much (Walden), 1968
Spy with Five Faces (Walden), 1966
Spycase Built for Two (Walden), 1969
Spy-catchers (Jones, A. F., as Kelly), 1995
Spying on Miss Muller (Bunting), 1995
Square Root of Wonderful (play; McCullers), 1957
Squaw Dog (Beatty), 1965
Squib (Bawden), 1971
S.S. Heartbreak (Pascal), 1995

Thanksgiving Programs for the Lower Grades (Latham, as Lee), 1937

That Bloody Bozeman Trail-Stagecoach West (play; Bonham), 1990

That Fatal Night (Pascal), 1989

That Ghost, That Bride of Time (play; Bradbury), 1976

That Girl Andy (Means), 1962

That Horse Whiskey (Adler), 1994

That Julia Redfern (Cameron), 1982

That Mad Game: War and the Chances for Peace (Forman), 1980

That Son of Richard III: A Birth Announcement (poetry; Bradbury), 1974

That Sweet Diamond: Baseball Poems (poetry; Janeczko), 1998

That Was Then, This Is Now (Hinton), 1971

Thatcher Jones (Morpurgo), 1975

That's How (Morpurgo), 1979

That's My Baby (Klein, N.), 1988

That's One Ornery Orphan (Beatty), 1980

That's the Way It Is, Amigo (Colman), 1975

Theft: A Play in Four Acts (play; London), 1910

Their Eyes Were Watching God (Hurston), 1937

Theirs Be the Guilt: A Novel of the War between the States (Sinclair), 1959

Them That Glitter and Them That Don't (Greene), 1983

Then Again, Maybe I Won't (Blume), 1971

Then Is All Love? It Is, It Is! (poetry; Bradbury), 1981

Thendara House (Bradley), 1983

Theo Zephyr (Hughes, D.), 1987

Theodore Roosevelt and His America (Meltzer), 1994

There Is a Tide... (Christie), 1948

There Will Be Wolves (Bradford), 1992

There's a Bat in Bunk Five (Danziger), 1980

There's a Girl in My Hammerlock (Spinelli), 1991

There's Always Danny (Ure), 1988

There's an End of May (play; Lillington), 1975

There's an Owl in the Shower (George), 1995

There's No Escape (Serraillier), 1950

There's Something on the Roof! (Fisk), 1966

They Call Me Carpenter: A Tale of the Second Coming (Sinclair), 1922

They Came to Baghdad (Christie), 1951

They Do It with Mirrors (Christie), 1952

They Do Things Differently There (short story; Mark), 1994

They Lived with the Dinosaurs (Freedman), 1980

They Never Came Home (Duncan), 1969

They Raced for Treasure (Serraillier), 1946

They Walk in the Night (Coatsworth), 1969

They'll Never Make a Movie Starring Me (Bach), 1973

Thicker Than Water (Farmer, P.), 1989

Thief (Needle), 1989

Thief Island (Coatsworth), 1943

Thief of Hearts (Yep), 1995

Thief of Time (Hillerman), 1988

Thiele Tales (Thiele), 1980

Thin Ice (Qualey), 1997

Things Are Seldom What They Seem (Asher), 1983

Things I Did for Love (Conford), 1987

Things in Corners (Park), 1989

Things to Come (Wells, H. G.), 1935

Think about Space: Where Have We Been and Where Are We Going (Asimov), 1989

Thinner (King, as Bachman), 1984

Third Class Genie (Leeson), 1975

Third Day, the Frost (Marsden), 1996

Third Eagle: Lessons Along a Minor String (MacAvoy), 1989

Third Eye (Duncan), 1984

Third Eye (Hunter, M.), 1979

Third Girl (Christie), 1966

Third Life of Grange Copeland (Walker), 1970

Third Magic (Katz), 1988

Thirteen at Dinner (Christie), 1933

Thirteen—Going on Seven (Sachs), 1993

Thirteen Great Short Stories from the Long Valley (short story; Steinbeck), 1943

Thirteen Moons series (George), from 1976

Thirteen Never Changes (Wilson), 1989

Thirteen O'Clock (Mayne), 1960

Thirteen Problems (short story; Christie), 1932

Thirteenth Child (Bradford), 1994

Thirteenth Member: A Story of Suspense (Hunter, M.), 1971

Thirty Pieces of Silver (play; Fast), 1951

Thirty Strange Stories (short story; Wells, H. G.), 1897

Thirty-six Exposures (Major), 1984

This Attic Where the Meadow Greens (poetry; Bradbury), 1980

This Dear-Bought Land (Latham), 1957

This Delicious Day: 65 Poems (Janeczko, ed.), 1987

This Old Man (Ruby), 1984

This Place Has No Atmosphere (Danziger), 1986

This Rough Magic (Stewart), 1964

This School Is Driving Me Crazy (Hentoff), 1976

This Star Shall Abide (Engdahl), 1972

This Strange New Feeling (Lester), 1982

This Time of Darkness (Hoover), 1980

This Way Out (Jinks), 1991

Thomas (Burton), 1969

Thomas Alva Edison (Freedman), 1966

Thomas and the Sparrow (poetry; Serraillier), 1946

Thomas and the Warlock (Hunter, M.), 1967

Thomas Jefferson: The Revolutionary Aristocrat (Meltzer), 1991

Thornyhold (Stewart), 1988

Thoroughly Modern Millie (Colman), 1966

Those Barren Leaves (Huxley), 1925

Those Other People (Childress), 1989

Those Summer Girls I Never Met (Peck, Richard), 1988

Those Who Ride the Night Winds (poetry; Giovanni), 1983

Thousand Eyes of Night (Swindells), 1985

Thousand for Sicily (Trease), 1964

Thousandstar (Anthony), 1980

Threat to the Barkers (Phipson), 1963

Three Act Tragedy (Christie), 1935

Three against the Sea (White, R.), 1940

Three and One to Carry (Willard), 1964

Three Blind Mice, (short story; Christie), 1950

Three Buckets of Daylight (Branscum), 1978

Three for a Full Moon and Bocas (play; Shange), 1982

Three Friends (Levoy), 1984

Three Loves Has Sandy (Walden), 1955

Three Musketeers: A Novel (Strasser), 1993

Three on the Run (Bawden), 1965

Three Sisters (Mazer, N.), 1986

Three Stuffed Owls (Robertson), 1954

Three Views of Mt. Fuji (play; Shange), 1987

Three Wars of Billy Joe Treat (Branscum), 1975

Twisted Summer (Roberts), 1996
Twisted Trinity (poetry; McCullers), 1946
Twisted Window (Duncan), 1987
Twisting the Rope: Casadh and t'Sugain (MacAvoy), 1986
Twits (Dahl), 1980
Two against the Tide (Clements), 1967
Two and a Bit (Harnett), 1948
Two Arrows (Meigs), 1949
Two by Two (Stolz), 1954
Two Deaths of Christopher Martin (Golding), 1957
Two Faces of Adam (Meyer), 1991
Two Love Stories (Lester), 1972
Two Mediaeval Tales (short story; Stevenson), 1929
Two Men in a Boat (Ure), 1988
Two Moons in August (Brooks, M.), 1991
Two on the Isle: A Memory of Marina Cay (White, R.), 1985
Two or Three Graces (short story; Huxley), 1926
Two Stories: The Road to Dunmore and The Key (Dillon), 1968
Two That Were Tough (Burch), 1976
Two Thousand Years of Space Travel (Freedman), 1963
Two to Conquer (Bradley), 1980
Two Towers (Tolkien), 1954
Two Truths in My Pocket (Ruby), 1982
Two Valleys (Fast), 1933
Two Weirdos and a Ghost (Windsor), 1991
Two-Boy Weekend (Pascal), 1989
Two-Fisted Painters Action Adventure (Spiegelman), 1980
Two-Headed Poems (poetry; Atwood), 1978
Two's Company (Cavanna), 1951
Two-Thousand-Pound Goldfish (Byars), 1982
Tyger Voyage (poetry; Adams), 1976
Tyler, Wilkin, and Skee (Burch), 1963

Ugliest Boy (Branscum), 1978
Unaccompanied Sonata (short story; Card), 1981
Unbeliever (Swindells), 1995
Uncharted Stars (Norton), 1969
Un-Civil War (Klass, S. S.), 1997
Uncle Bernac: A Memory of Empire (Doyle), 1897
Uncle Daniel and the Raccoon (Hunter, K.), 1972
Uncle Gustav's Ghosts (Thiele), 1974
Uncle in the Attic (Needle), 1987
Uncle Matt's Mountain (Park), 1962
Uncle Ronald (Doyle), 1996
Uncle Tom's Children: Five Long Stories (short story; Wright), 1940
Uncle Tom's Children: Four Novellas (short story; Wright), 1938
Uncle Vampire (Grant), 1993
Unconquered (play; Rand), 1940
Under Alien Stars (Service), 1990
Under Black Banner (Trease), 1950
Under Cover (Kropp), 1987
Under Dog, (short story; Christie), 1929
Under Pressure (Herbert), 1974
Under the Autumn Garden (Mark), 1977
Under the Blood-Red Sun (Salisbury), 1994
Under the Cat's Eye (Rubinstein), 1997
Under the Lilacs (Alcott), 1878
Under the North Star (poetry; Hughes, T.), 1981
Under the Orange Grove (Dillon), 1968
Under the Same Stars (Hughes, D.), 1979
Under the Sun and Over the Moon (Crossley-Holland), 1989

Undercover Angels (Pascal), 1997
Undercover Secret (Thiele), 1982
Underground Alley (Mayne), 1958
Underground Creatures (Mayne), 1983
Underground Man (Meltzer), 1972
Understanding the Floatplane (Edgerton), 1987
Undertaker's Gone Bananas (Zindel), 1978
Underwoods (poetry; Stevenson), 1887
Undying Fire: A Contemporary Novel (Wells, H. G.), 1919
Unearthing Suite (short story; Atwood), 1983
Uneasy Money (Brancato), 1986
Unexpected Guest (play; Christie), 1958
Unfinished Dreams (Zalben), 1996
Unfinished Portrait (Christie, as Westmacott), 1934
Unfinished Portrait of Jessica (Peck, Richard), 1991
Unfinished Tales of Númenór and Middle-Earth (short story; Tolkien), 1980
Unforgettable (Cooney), 1994
Unicorn Club series (Pascal), from 1994
Unicorn Point (Anthony), 1989
Unicorn Sonata (Beagle), 1996
Unicorns series (Pascal), from 1991
Unknown Planet (Ure), 1992
Unleaving (Paton Walsh), 1976
Unquiet Spirits (Peyton), 1997
Unseen: Scary Stories (Hughes, M.), 1994
Unvanquished (Fast), 1942
Unwed Mother (Miklowitz), 1977
Up a Road Slowly (Hunt), 1966
Up and Down Spring (Hurwitz), 1993
Up and Over (Smith), 1976
Up Country (Carter), 1989
Up from Jericho Tel (Konigsburg), 1986
Up Hill and Down: Stories (Coatsworth), 1947
Up in Seth's Room (Mazer, N.), 1979
Up Periscope (White, R.), 1956
Up the Chimney Down (Aiken), 1984
Up to Bat (Hughes, D.), 1991
Up to Low (Doyle), 1982
Uphill All the Way (Hall, L.), 1984
Ups and Downs of Carl Davis III (Guy), 1989
Upstairs Room (Reiss), 1972
Urn Burial (Westall), 1987
Us and Uncle Fraud (Lowry), 1984
Us Maltbys (Means), 1966
Utopia 14 (Vonnegut), 1954

"V" for Victory (Pascal), 1995
Vacant Country (short story; Wells, H. G.), 1899
Vagabundos (Bonham), 1969
Vale of the Vole (Anthony), 1987
Valentine (Garfield), 1977
Valentine Bears (Bunting), 1983
Valentine Frankenstein (Angell, as Twohill), 1991
Valentine Rosy (Greenwald), 1984
Valerie Valentine Is Missing (Walden), 1971
Valley Between (Thiele), 1981
Valley of Broken Cherry Trees (Namioka), 1980
Valley of Deer (Dunlop), 1989
Valley of Fear (Doyle), 1914
Valley of Spiders (short story; Wells, H. G.), 1964

Walk Out a Brother (Baird), 1983
Walk Two Moons (Creech), 1994
Walk with a Wolf (Howker), 1998
Walking across Egypt (Edgerton), 1987
Walking Stones: A Story of Suspense (Hunter, M.), 1970
Walking through the Dark (Naylor), 1976
Walking Up a Rainbow (Taylor, T.), 1986
Walkmen Have Landed (poetry; Silver), 1994
Wall (Bunting), 1990
Wall of Masks (Koontz, as Coffey), 1975
Walls of Athens (Paton Walsh), 1977
Wally for Queen! The Private Life of Royalty (play; Sinclair), 1936
Walt Disney's Lady and the Tramp (Strasser), 1994
Walt Disney's Peter Pan (Strasser), 1994
Wanderers (Coatsworth), 1972
Wandering Family (Orlev), 1997
Wanted (Cooney), 1997
Wanted: A Girl for the Horses (Cavanna), 1984
Wanted for Murder (Pascal), 1995
Wanted! Frank and Jesse James: The Real Story (Weis, as Baldwin), 1981
Wanted...Mud Blossom (Byars), 1991
Wanting Seed (Burgess), 1962
War and Peace: Observations on Our Times (Fast), 1993
War and the Protest: Vietnam (Haskins), 1971
War beneath the Sea (Bonham), 1962
War between the Classes (Miklowitz), 1985
War Between the Twins (Pascal), 1990
War Chief (Burroughs), 1927
War Comes to Willy Freeman (Collier), 1983
War Horse (Morpurgo), 1982
War in the Air, and Particularly How Mr. Bert Smallways Fared While It Lasted (Wells, H. G.), 1908
War of 1812: Second Fight for Independence (Carter), 1992
War of Jenkins' Ear (Morpurgo), 1993
War of the Twins (Weis), 1986
War of the Worlds (Wells, H. G.), 1898
War of the Worms (Needle), 1992
War on Villa Street (Mazer, H.), 1978
War with Old Mouldy! (Ure), 1987
War Work (Oneal), 1971
Warding of Witch World (Norton), 1996
Warlock (Koontz), 1972
Warlock at the Wheel (Jones, D. W.), 1984
Warlord of Mars (Burroughs), 1919
Warrior Scarlet (Sutcliff), 1958
Warrior Woman (Bradley), 1985
Warriors of Taan (Lawrence), 1986
Warriors of the Wasteland (Hill), 1983
Wart, Son of Toad (Carter), 1985
Washington for All (Latham, as Lee), 1931
Washington Jitters (Trumbo), 1936
Waste Lands (King), 1991
Watch for a Pony (Robertson), 1949
Watch House (Westall), 1977
Watch That Watch (Colman), 1962
Watcher in the Garden (Phipson), 1982
Watchers (Koontz), 1987
Watchers at the Shrine Reed (Ure), 1995
Watching the Roses (Geras), 1992
Watchstar (Sargent), 1980

Water Boatman (Mayne), 1964
Water Cresses (Alcott), 1879
Water from the Moon (Zalben), 1987
Water Girl (Thomas, J.), 1986
Water in the Air (Halam, as Jones), 1977
Water Music (Yolen), 1995
Water Sky (George), 1987
Waterloo (play; Doyle), 1899
Waterpower Workout (Knudson), 1986
Waters of Kronos (Richter, C.), 1960
Watership Down (Adams), 1972
Watersmeet (Garden), 1983
Watsons Go to Birmingham-1963 (Curtis), 1995
Wave (Strasser), 1981
Wave Watch (Choyce), 1990
Wave without a Shore (Cherryh), 1981
Waverly (Walden), 1947
Way Home (Phipson), 1973
Way in the Middle of the Air (play; Bradbury), 1962
Way Past Cool: A Novel (Mowry), 1992
Ways of White Folks (short story; Hughes, L.), 1934
Wayward Bus (Steinbeck), 1947
We All Fall Down (Cormier), 1991
We Are Mesquakie, We Are One (Irwin), 1980
We Bombed in New Haven (play; Heller), 1967
We Both Have Scars (Kropp), 1990
We Didn't Mean To, Honest (Swindells), 1993
We Had a Picnic This Sunday Last (Woodson), 1997
We Interrupt This Semester for an Important Bulletin (Conford), 1979
We Lived in Drumfyvie (Sutcliff), 1975
We Need a Bigger Zoo! (Bunting), 1974
We the Living (Rand), 1936
Wealth of Mr. Waddy: A Novel (Wells, H. G.), 1969
Weary Blues (poetry; Hughes, L.), 1926
Weather the Storm (Ferris), 1996
Weather-Clerk (Swindells), 1979
Weathermonger (Dickinson), 1968
Weaver Birds (poetry; Serraillier), 1944
Web of Darkness (Bradley), 1984
Web of Dreams (Andrews), 1990
Web of Light (Bradley), 1982
Web of Traitors: An Adventure Story of Ancient Athens (Trease), 1952
Websters' Leap (Dunlop), 1995
Wedding (Pascal), 1993
Wedding Ghost (Garfield), 1985
Wednesday Surprise (Bunting), 1989
Weekend (Pike), 1986
Weekend Sisters (Colman), 1985
Weekend Was Murder! (Nixon), 1992
Weep No More, My Lady (Clark), 1987
Weetzie Bat (Block), 1989
Weight Training for Young Athletes (Knudson), 1979
Weir of Hermiston: An Unfinished Romance (Stevenson), 1896
Weird Disappearance of Jordan Hall (Angell), 1987
Weird Eyes File (Jones, A. F.), 1997
Weirdo (Taylor, T.), 1992
Weirdos of the Universe, Unite! (Service), 1992
Weirdstone of Brisingamen: A Tale of Alderley (Garner), 1960
Welcome to Camp Nightmare (Stine), 1997

Whipping Star (Herbert), 1970
Whisper in the Night: Stories of Horror, Suspense, and Fantasy (Aiken), 1982
Whisper of Death (Pike), 1991
Whisper of Glocken (Kendall), 1965
Whisper of Lace (Cross), 1981
Whispered Horse (Hall, L.), 1979
Whispering Girl (Means), 1941
Whispering Mountain (Aiken), 1968
Whispers (Koontz), 1980
Whispers from Beyond (short story; Bradbury), 1972
Whispers from the Dead (Nixon), 1989
Whistle and I'll Come (Ure), 1997
Whistle Me Home (Wersba), 1997
Whistling Rufus (Mayne), 1964
Whistling Toilets (Powell), 1996
White Archer: An Eskimo Legend (Houston, J.), 1967
White Company (Doyle), 1891
White Crow (Forman), 1976
White Death (Sargent), 1980
White Dragon (McCaffrey), 1978
White Fang (London), 1906
White Gryphon (Lackey), 1995
White Guinea-Pig (Dubosarsky), 1994
White Horse (Coatsworth), 1942
White Horse (Grant), 1998
White Horse (Leeson), 1977
White Horse Gang (Bawden), 1966
White Horse of Morocco (Coatsworth), 1973
White Horse of Zennor (Morpurgo), 1982
White House Autumn (White, E.), 1985
White Lies (Pascal), 1989
White Lilacs (Meyer), 1993
White Mercedes (Pullman), 1993
White Mountains (Christopher), 1967
White Nights of St. Petersburg (Trease), 1967
White Peak Farm (Doherty), 1984
White Plague (Herbert), 1982
White Romance (Hamilton), 1987
White Serpent Castle (Namioka), 1976
White Water (Petersen), 1997
Whiteout (Houston, J.), 1988
Whitewash (Shange), 1997
Whitman Kick (Burch), 1977
Who Am I This Time? For Romeos and Juliets (short story; Vonnegut), 1987
Who Are the Handicapped? (Haskins), 1978
Who Cares About Karen? (Lohans), 1983
Who Comes to King's Mountain? (Beatty), 1975
Who Comes with Cannons? (Beatty), 1992
Who Did It, Jenny Lake? (Okimoto), 1983
Who Has the Lucky Duck in Class 4-B? (Angell, as Twohill), 1984
Who Is Carrie? (Collier), 1984
Who Is Eddie Leonard? (Mazer, H.), 1993
Who Is Simon Warwick? (Moyes), 1978
Who Killed Mr. Chippendale?: A Mystery in Poems (poetry; Glenn), 1996
Who Look at Me? (Jordan), 1969
Who Owns the Moon? (Levitin), 1973
Who Put That Hair in My Toothbrush? (Spinelli), 1984
Who Ran My Underwear up the Flagpole? (Spinelli), 1992

Who Really Killed Cock Robin? An Ecological Mystery (George), 1971
Who, Said Sue, Said Whoo? (poetry; Raskin), 1973
Who Saw Her Die? (Moyes), 1970
Who Says animals Don't Have Rights? (Ure), 1994
Who Wants Music on Monday? (Stolz), 1963
Who Was in the Garden (poetry; Atwood), 1969
"Who Was That Masked Man, Anyway?" (Avi), 1992
Who Will Be Miss Unicorn? (Pascal), 1996
Who Will Know Us? (poetry; Soto), 1990
Who Will Take Care of Me? (Hermes), 1983
Who's for the Zoo? (Ure), 1989
Who's Going to Take Care of Me? (Magorian), 1990
Who's Hu? (Namioka), 1981
Who's Talking? (Ure), 1987
Who's to Blame (Pascal), 1990
Who's Who? (Pascal), 1990
Whose Town? (Graham), 1969
Why Didn't They Ask Evans? (Christie), 1934
Why Does Everybody Think I'm Nutty? (Collier), 1971
Why Have the Birds Stopped Singing? (Sherburne), 1974
Why Haven't You Written?; Selected Stories, 1950-1972 (short story; Gordimer), 1992
Why I'm Afraid of Bees (Stine), 1994
Why Me? (Conford), 1985
Why the Whales Came (Morpurgo), 1985
Whys and Wherefores of Littabelle Lee (Cleaver, V. and B.), 1973
Wicked Day (Stewart), 1983
Wicked Heart (Pike), 1993
Wicked One: A Story of Suspense (Hunter, M.), 1977
Wide Is the Gate (Sinclair), 1943
Wielding a Red Sword (Anthony), 1986
Wife of Sir Isaac Harman (Wells, H. G.), 1914
Wild Breed (short story; Bonham), 1955
Wild Cat (Peck, Robert Newton), 1975
Wild Children (Holman), 1983
Wild Culpepper Cruise (Paulsen), 1993
Wild Geese Flying (Meigs), 1957
Wild Horses (Bunting, as Bolton), 1974
Wild Hunt (Yolen), 1997
Wild Idea (Willard), 1965
Wild in the World (Donovan), 1971
Wild Jack (Christopher), 1974
Wild Little House (Dillon), 1955
Wild Magic (Pierce, T.), 1992
Wild Mustang (Hall, L.), 1976
Wild One (Bunting), 1974
Wild One (Kropp), 1982
Wild Rover (Meyer), 1989
Wild Seed (Butler), 1980
Wild, Wild Cookbook: A Guide for Young Wild-Food Foragers (George), 1982
Wilderness Bride (Johnson, A. and E.), 1962
Wilderness Tips (short story; Atwood), 1991
Wildfire at Midnight (Stewart), 1956
Wildlife (Strasser), 1987
Wildman (Crossley-Holland), 1976
Wilful Blue (Hartnett), 1994
Wilkin's Ghost (Burch), 1978
Will and Testament: A Fragment of Biography (short story; Burgess), 1977

READING LIST

The following selected list includes critical works dealing in whole or in part with English-language creative writing for young adults in the modern era. Studies of individual writers are cited in the appropriate entries.

Adamson, Lynda G. *Recreating the Past: A Guide to American and World Historical Fiction for Children and Young Adults.* Westport, Connecticut, Greenwood Press, 1994.

Alano, Becky. *Teaching the Novel,* edited by Mary Morgan. Bloomington, Indiana, ERIC Clearinghouse on Reading and Communication Skills, 1989.

Bodart, Joni Richards. *100 World-class Thin Books; or, What to Read When Your Book Report Is Due Tomorrow.* Englewood, Colorado, Libraries Unlimited, 1993.

Breedlove, Wanda G. *Contemporary Trends in Children's and Young Adults' Literature: Research Perspectives.* South Carolina State Council of the International Reading Association, 1990.

Brown, Jean E., and Elaine C. Stephens. *Teaching Young Adult Literature: Sharing the Connection.* Belmont, California, Wadsworth Publishing, 1995.

Burress, Lee. *Battle of the Books: Literary Censorship in the Public Schools, 1950-1985.* Metuchen, New Jersey, Scarecrow Press, 1989.

Bushman, John H., and Kay Parks Bushman. *Using Young Adult Literature in the English Classroom.* Upper Saddle River, New Jersey, Merrill, 1997.

Calvert, Stephen, editor. *Best Books for Young Adult Readers.* New Providence, New Jersey, R.R. Bowker, 1997.

Carruth, Gorton. *The Young Reader's Companion.* New Providence, New Jersey, R. R. Bowker, 1993.

Carter, Betty, and Richard F. Abrahamson. *Nonfiction for Young Adults: From Delight to Wisdom.* Phoenix, Arizona, Oryx Press, 1990.
Carter, Betty. *Best Books for Young Adults: The Selections, the History, the Romance.* Chicago, American Library Association, 1994.

Chambers, Aidan. *Reluctant Reader.* London, Pergamon Press, 1969.

Christenbury, Leila, editor. *Books for You: An Annotated Booklist for Senior High Students.* Urbana, Illinois, The Council, 1995.

Copeland, Jeffrey S., and Earl D. Lomax, editors. *Contemporary Issues in Young Adult Literature.* Needham Heights, Massachusetts, Ginn Press, 1992.

Cuseo, Allan A. *Homosexual Characters in YA Novels: A Literary Analysis, 1969-1982.* Metuchen, New Jersey, Scarecrow Press, 1992.
Day, Frances Ann. *Latina and Latino Voices in Literature for Children and Teenagers.* Portsmouth, New Hampshire, Heinemann, 1997.

Donelson, Kenneth L., and Alleen Pace Nilsen. *Literature for Today's Young Adults.* 5th edition, New York, Longman, 1997.

Drew, Bernard A. *The 100 Most Popular Young Adult Authors: Biographical Sketches and Bibliographies.* Englewood, Colorado, Libraries Unlimited, 1997.

Drotner, Kirsten. *English Children and Their Magazines, 1751-1945.* New Haven, Yale University Press, 1988.

Egoff, Sheila A. *Thursday's Child: Trends and Patterns in Contemporary Children's Literature.* Chicago, American Library Association, 1981.

Eiss, Harry Edwin, compiler. *Literature for Young People on War and Peace: An Annotated Bibliography.* New York, Greenwood Press, 1989.

Feehan, Patricia E., and Pamela Petrick Barron, editors. *Writers on Writing for Young Adults: Exploring the Authors, the Genre, the Readers, the Issues, and the Critics of Young-adult Literature, Together with Checklists of the Featured Writers.* Detroit, Michigan, Omnigraphics, 1991.

Gallagher, Mary E. *Young Adult Literature: Issues and Perspectives.* Haverford, Pennsylvania, Catholic Library Association, 1988.

Gallo, Donald R., compiler and editor. *Speaking for Ourselves: Autobiographical Sketches by Notable Authors of Books for Young Adults.* Urbana, Illinois, National Council of Teachers of English, 1990.

Gallo, Donald R., compiler and editor. *Speaking for Ourselves, Too: More Autobiographical Sketches by Notable Authors of Books for Young Adults.* Urbana, Illinois, National Council of Teachers of English, 1993.

Gillespie, John Thomas, and Ralph J. Folcarelli. *Guides to Collection Development for Children and Young Adults.* Englewood, Colorado, Libraries Unlimited, 1998.

Gillespie, John Thomas, editor. *Best Books for Senior High Readers.* New Providence, New Jersey, Bowker, 1991.

Gillespie, John Thomas. *Characters in Young Adult Literature,* compiled by John T. Gillespie and Corinne J. Naden. Detroit, Gale Research, 1997.

Harrison, Barbara, and Gregory Maguire, editors. *Innocence and Experience: Essays and Conversations on Children's Literature.* New York, Lathrop, Lee, and Shepard, 1987.

Hearne, Betsy, and Marilyn Kaye, editors. *Celebrating Children's Books: Essays on Children's Literature in Honor of Zena Sutherland.* New York, Lothrop, Lee, and Shepard, 1981.

Herald, Diana Tixier. *Teen Genreflecting.* Englewood, Colorado, Libraries Unlimited, 1997.

Herz, Sarah K., with Donald R. Gallo. *From Hinton to Hamlet: Building Bridges between Young Adult Literature and the Classics.* Westport, Connecticut, Greenwood Press, 1996.

Hipple, Ted, editor. *Writers for Young Adults.* New York, Charles Scribner's Sons, 1997.

Hunt, Gladys M., and Barbara Hampton. *Read for Your Life: Turning Teens into Readers.* Grand Rapids, Michigan, Zondervan, 1992.

Immell, Myra, general editor. *The Young Adult Reader's Adviser.* New Providence, New Jersey, Bowker, 1992.

Johnson-Feelings, Dianne. *Telling Tales: The Pedagogy and Promise of African American Literature for Youth.* New York, Greenwood Press, 1990.

Jones, Patrick. *Connecting Young Adults and Libraries: A How-to-do-it Manual.* New York, Neal-Schuman Publishers, 1992.

Kaywell, Joan F., editor. *Using Literature to Help Troubled Teenagers Cope with Family Issues.* Westport, Connecticut, Greenwood Press, 1998.

Kaywell, Joan F. *Adolescents at Risk: A Guide to Fiction and Nonfiction for Young Adults, Parents, and Professionals.* Westport, Connecticut, Greenwood Press, 1993.

Khorana, Meena. *Africa in Literature for Children and Young Adults: An Annotated Bibliography of English-language Books.* Westport, Connecticut, Greenwood Press, 1994.

Kuta, Katherine Wiesolek. *What a Novel Idea!: Projects and Activities for Young Adult Literature.* Englewood, Colorado, Teacher Ideas Press, 1997.

Lenz, Millicent, and Mary Meacham. *Young Adult Literature and Nonprint Materials: Resources for Selection.* Metuchen, New Jersey, Scarecrow Press, 1994.

Lenz, Millicent, and Ramona M. Mahood, editors. *Young Adult Literature: Background and Criticism.* Chicago, American Library Association, 1980.

Lenz, Millicent. *Nuclear Age Literature for Youth: The Quest for a Life-affirming Ethic.* Chicago, American Library Association, 1990.

Lindgren, Merri V., editor. *The Multicolored Mirror: Cultural Substance in Literature for Children and Young Adults.* Fort Atkinson, Wisconsin, Highsmith Press, 1991.

Lives and Works: Young Adult Authors. Danbury, Connecticut, Grolier Educational, 1998.

Lukens, Rebecca J., and Ruth K.J. Cline. *A Critical Handbook of Literature for Young Adults.* New York, HarperCollins, 1995.

Lynn, Ruth Nadelman. *Fantasy Literature for Children and Young Adults: An Annotated Bibliography.* New Providence, New Jersey, Bowker, 1995.

MacCann, Donnarae, and Gloria Woodward, editors. *The Black American in Books for Children: Readings on Racism.* Metuchen, New Jersey, Scarecrow Press, 1972.

Maddy, Yulisa Amadu, with Donnarae MacCann. *African Images in Juvenile Literature: Commentaries on Neocolonialist Fiction.* Jefferson, North Carolina, McFarland, 1996.

Manning, M. Lee, and Leroy G. Baruth. *Appreciating and Teaching Young Adult Literature.* Upper Saddle River, New Jersey, Merrill, 1999.

Maxwell, Rhoda J. *Images of Mothers in Literature for Young Adults.* New York, P. Lang, 1994.

McCaffery, Laura Hibbets. *Building an ESL Collection for Young Adults: A Bibliography of Recommended Fiction and Nonfiction for Schools and Public Libraries.* Westport, Connecticut, Greenwood Press, 1998.

McVitty, Walter. *Innocence and Experience: Essays on Contemporary Australian Children's Writers.* Melbourne, Nelson, 1982.

Miller-Lachmann, Lyn. *Our Family, Our Friends, Our World: An Annotated Guide to Significant Multicultural Books for Children and Teenagers.* New Providence, New Jersey, R.R. Bowker, 1992.

Monseau, Virginia R. *Responding to Young Adult Literature.* Portsmouth, New Hampshire, Boynton/Cook Publishers, 1996.

Moore Kruse, Ginny, and Kathleen T. Horning, with Merri V. Lindgren and Katherine Odahowski. *Multicultural Literature for Children and Young Adults: A Selected Listing of Books, 1980-1990, by and about People of Color.* Madison, Wisconsin, Cooperative Children's Book Center, University of Wisconsin-Madison, Wisconsin Dept. of Public Instruction, 1991.

More Teens' Favorite Books: Young Adults' Choices, 1993-1995. Newark, Delaware, International Reading Association, 1996.

Moss, Joyce, and George Wilson, editors. *From Page to Screen: Children's and Young Adult Books on Film and Video.* Detroit, Gale Research, 1992.

Nakamura, Joyce, editor. *High-interest Books for Teens: A Guide to Book Reviews and Biographical Sources.* Detroit, Gale Research Co., 1988.

Osa, Osayimwense, editor. *The All-white World of Children's Books and African American Children's Literature.* Trenton, New Jersey, Africa World Press, 1995.

Povsic, Frances F., compiler. *The Soviet Union in Literature for Children and Young Adults: An Annotated Bibliography of English-language Books.* New York, Greenwood Press, 1991.

Reed, Arthea J. S. *Comics to Classics: A Guide to Books for Teens and Preteens.* New York, Penguin Books, 1994.

Reed, Arthea J. S. *Reaching Adolescents: The Young Adult Book and the School.* New York, Merrill, and Toronto, Maxwell Macmillan Canada, 1994.

Rees, David. *The Marble in the Water: Essays on Contemporary Writers of Fiction for Children and Young People.* Boston, Horn Book, 1980.

Roginski, Jim. *Behind the Covers: Interviews with Authors and Illustrators of Books for Children and Young Adults*. Littleton, Colorado, Libraries Unlimited, 1985.

Rosenberg, Judith K., with C. Allen Nichols. *Young People's Books in Series: Fiction and Non-fiction, 1975-1991*. Englewood, Colorado, Libraries Unlimited, 1992.

Samuels, Barbara G., and G. Kylene Beers, editors. *Your Reading: An Annotated Booklist for Middle School and Junior High*. Urbana, Illinois, National Council of Teachers of English, 1996.

Shapiro, Lillian L., editor. *Fiction for Youth: A Guide to Recommended Books*. New York, Neal-Schuman, 1980.

Sherman, Gale W., and Bette D. Ammon. *Rip-roaring Reads for Reluctant Teen Readers*. Englewood, Colorado, Libraries Unlimited, 1993.

Smith, Karen Patricia, editor. *African-American Voices in Young Adult Literature: Tradition, Transition, Transformation*. Metuchen, New Jersey, Scarecrow Press, 1994.

Snodgrass, Mary E. *Characters from Young Adult Literature*. Littleton, Colorado, Libraries Unlimited, 1991.

Stanford, Barbara Dodds, and Karima Amin, editors. *Black Literature for High School Students*. Urbana, Illinois, National Council of Teachers of English, 1978.

Stover, Lois T., and Stephanie F. Zenker, editors. *Books for You: An Annotated Booklist for Senior High, Covering Books Published from 1994-96*. Urbana, Illinois, The Council, 1997.

Stover, Lois T. *Young Adult Literature: The Heart of the Middle School Curriculum*. Portsmouth, New Hampshire, Boynton/Cook Publishers, 1996.

Stringer, Sharon A. *Conflict and Connection: The Psychology of Young Adult Literature*. Portsmouth, New Hampshire, Boynton/Cook Publishers, 1997.

Sullivan, C.W., III, editor. *Science Fiction for Young Readers*. Westport, Connecticut, Greenwood Press, 1993.

Teens' Favorite Books: Young Adults' Choices, 1987-1992. Newark, Delaware, International Reading Association, 1992.

Varlejs, Jhana, editor. *Young Adult Literature in the Seventies: A Selection of Readings*. Metuchen, New Jersey, Scarecrow Press, 1982.

Walker, Elinor, compiler. *Book Bait: Detailed Notes on Adult Books Popular with Young People*. Chicago, American Library Association, 1988.

Williams, Helen E. *Books by African-American Authors and Illustrators for Children and Young Adults*. Chicago, American Library Association, 1991.

NOTES ON
ADVISERS AND CONTRIBUTORS

AGEE, Hugh. Professor of English Education, University of Georgia, Athens; Past President of the Assembly on Literature for Adolescents (ALAN) of NCTE. Contributor of articles and reviews to *ALAN Review* and other publications. **Essays:** Robbie Branscum; Robert Burch; Gary Paulsen; Robert Newton Pcck; Ann Rinaldi.

ALBERGHENE, Janice M. Associate Professor of English, Fitchburg State College, Massachusetts. Author of numerous articles on children's literature, including "Moralists, But with No Pretense," 1988, "Humor in Children's Literature," 1988, and "Artful Memory: Jean Fritz, Autobiography and the Child Reader," 1989. Past President of the Children's Literature Association. **Essays:** M.E. Kerr; Daniel Manus Pinkwater.

ANTCZAK, Janice. Professor of Literature, Brookdale Community College, Lincroft, New Jersey. Author of *Science Fiction: The Mythos of a New Romance*; contributor to *School Library Journal, Children's Literature Quarterly,* and other journals. **Essay:** Thomas Baird; Jay Bennett; Pamela Sargent.

APSELOFF, Marilyn. Associate Professor of English, Kent State University, Kent, Ohio. Author of *Virginia Hamilton: Ohio Explorer in the World of Imagination,* 1978, *Nonsense Literature for Children: From Aesop to Seuss* (with Celia Catlett Anderson), and 1989, *They Wrote for Children Too: An Annotated Bibliography of Children's Literature in Education.* **Essays:** Joan Blos; Louise Lawrence.

ATKINSON, Judith. Head of English Department, Wolfreton School. Author of numerous articles on English teaching, including contributions to *Developing Response to Fiction,* 1983, and *Teaching Literature for Examinations,* 1986. **Essays:** Jill Paton Walsh; Barbara Willard.

BARKER, Keith. Resources development manager, Westhill College, Birmingham; review editor, *School Librarian.* Author, *In the Realms of Gold,* 1986; editor, *Information Books for Children,* 1995; contributor to *The Routledge International Companion Encyclopedia of Children's Literature,* 1996, and *Children's Book Publishing in Britain since 1945,* 1998. **Essays:** Farrukh Dhondy; Monica Furlong; Christine Nostlinger; Philip Pullman; Rosemary Wells.

BARON, Henry J. Department of English, Calvin College, Grand Rapids, Michigan. **Essays:** Lorenz Graham; Stephen Tchudi.

BARROW, Craig W. Instructor, Department of English, University of Tennessee at Chattanooga. Author of articles about science fiction, contemporary fiction, drama in performance, and issues in humanities; author of *Montage in James Joyce's Ulysses.* Contributor to *Beacham's Guide to Literature for Young Adults.* **Essays:** Ernest J. Gaines; William Golding.

BELVISO, Melanie. Freelance writer. **Essays:** Lynn Hall; R.R. Knudson; Anne McCaffrey; Spider Robinson.

BENSON, Linda. Instructor in English, Southwest Missouri State University. **Essays:** Octavia Butler; Arthur C. Clarke; Sharon Creech; Vonda N. McIntyre; Graham Salisbury; Jerry Spinelli.

BERNSTEIN, Sharon Clontz. Librarian for the Blind and Physically Handicapped, South Georgia Regional Library, Valdosta, Georgia. **Essays:** Kristin Hunter; Lois Ruby; Pamela F. Service; Maureen Crane Wartski; Brenda Wilkinson.

BLOOM, Susan P. Director and Assistant Professor, Center for the Study of Children's Literature, Simmons College, Boston. **Essays:** Russell Freedman; Milton Meltzer, Rita Williams-Garcia.

BRADLEY, Patricia L. Instructor in English, Western Kentucky University, Bowling Green. **Essays:** Paula Danziger; Irene Hunt.

BUCHANAN, Bill. Librarian, Clarion University. **Essay:** Margaret Mahy; Jean Davies Okimoto; Theresa Nelson.

BUTTS, Dennis. Freelance writer and critic; editor, *Henty Society Bulletin.* Former Principal Lecturer in English, Bulmershe College of Higher Education, Reading, Berkshire. Author of *Living Words* (with John Merrick), 1966, and *R.L Stevenson,* 1966. Editor of *Pergamon Poets 8,* 1970, *Good Writers for Young Readers: Critical Essays,* 1977, and *The Secret Garden,* 1987. **Essay:** Robert Louis Stevenson.

CART, Michael. Former director of California Public Library, Beverly Hills; now full-time writer and critic of young adult literature. **Essays:** Bruce Brooks; John Donovan; Jacqueline Woodson.

CHANCE, Rosemary. Middle school librarian; instructor of children's and young adult literature, Department of Library Science, Sam Houston State University, Texas; member of Young Adult Library Services Association of the American Library Association. **Essays:** Willo Davis Roberts; Jerry Spinelli

CHAPMAN, Edgar L. Ph.D. in English literature; author of numerous articles on science fiction including an essay on T.H. White for *Twentieth-Century Science Fiction Writers*; contributor to *Beacham's Guide to Literature for Young Adults.* **Essays:** Edgar Rice Burroughs; Aldous Huxley.

CHASTON, Joel. Associate Professor of English, Southwest Missouri State University. Author of *Lois Lowry,* 1997, co-author of *Theme Exploration: A Voyage of Discovery,* 1993, and author of many articles on literature for the young. **Essays:** Carl Deuker; S.E. Hinton; Mollie Hunter; Ellen Raskin; Todd Strasser.

CHAUVETTE, Cathy. Reviewer, *School Library Journal,* "Adult Books for YAs"; coauthor "Easy Talking;" contributor to "Up for Discussion," "How Do You Manage," and *Twentieth-Century Science Fiction Writers.* **Essays:** Marion Zimmer Bradley; R.A. MacAvoy.

CLINE Ruth K.J. Coauthor of a column in the *ALAN Review*; author of *Focus on Families,* 1990, a resource book for young adults; currently revising a text on young adult literature with Bill McBride. **Essay:** Will Hobbs.

COLLINS, Carol Jones. Librarian, Montclair Kimberley Academy, New Jersey; author of article "A Tool for Change: Young Adult Literature in the Lives of Young Adult African Americans," in *Library Trends.* **Essay:** Jim Haskins.

CREANY, Anne Drolett. Associate Professor of Education, Clarion University, Clarion, Pennsylvania. Author of articles on censorship, environmental children's literature and gender issues in picture books; storyteller, specializing in multicultural folktales. **Essays:** Marion Dane Bauer; Walter Farley; Jean Craighead George; Virginia Hamilton; Mary Stolz.

CREW, Hillary S. Assistant Professor, Kean University, Union, New Jersey. Contributor to *African American Voices: Tradition, Transition, Transformation, Mosaics of Meaning: Enhancing the Intellectual Life of Young People through Story,* and *Writers of Multicultural Fiction for Young Adults: A Bio-Critical Sourcebook.* **Essays:** Robin McKinley; Kyoko Mori; Richard Peck.

DAVIS, Hazel K. Instructor, Ohio University, Athens; Past President of ALAN. Author of essays in *Beacham's Guide to Literature for Young Adults* and teaching guides for Bantam on *Animal Farm* and *A Midsummer Night's Dream.* **Essays:** Jenny Davis; William Sleator; Zilpha Keatley Snyder.

DAVIS, J. Madison. Professor of Journalism and head of the professional writing program at the University of Oklahoma. Author of *The Murder of Frau Schutz,* and *Red Knight;* author of numerous works of nonfiction. **Essays:** Ralph Ellison; Harold Keith.

DILL, Lesa. Assistant Professor of English, Western Kentucky University, Bowling Green; Ph.D. in English and linguistics. **Essays:** Richard Adams; V.C. Andrews; Piers Anthony; Isaac Asimov; Peter Beagle; Phyllis A. Whitney.

DINGLEY, Robert. Senior Lecturer in English, University of New England, Australia. Contributor to *Dictionary of Literary Biography Series, The Victorian Fantasists, Makers of Nineteenth-Century Culture,* and other reference guides. **Essays:** Agatha Christie; Sue Townsend.

DISHNOW, Ruth E. District librarian, School District of Rib Lake, Wisconsin; President, Wisconsin Association of School Librarians. **Essay:** Tamora Pierce.

DONAHUE, Rosanne. Assistant to the Vice Chancellor for Academic Affairs, University of Massachusetts, Boston. Author of "New Realism in the Twentieth Century," in *Masterworks of Children's Literature,* 1986, and "A Solitary Blue," in *Beacham's Guide to Literature and Biography for Young Adults,* 1989. **Essays:** Virginia Hamilton; Cynthia Voigt; Jill Paton Walsh.

DONELSON, Ken. Professor of English, Arizona State University, Tempe. Co-author of *Literature for Today's Young Adults,* 5th edition, 1997. **Essays:** Rich Wallace.

DOXEY, Carol. Librarian, South Georgia Regional Library, Valdosta. Former librarian, Estherville Public Library, Iowa. **Essays:** C.S. Adler, Sandy Asher; June Foley; Betty Miles; P.J. Petersen; Marilyn Sachs; Harriet May Savitz; Marilyn Singer, Jan Slepian; Amelia Elizabeth Walden; Maia Wojciechowska.

DRENNAN, William Ryland. Associate Professor of English, University of Wisconsin Center-Baraboo/Sauk County. Contributor to *Beacham's Guide to Literature for Young Adults.* **Essay:** Patricia Windsor.

DUKE, Charles R. Dean, College of Education and Human Services, Clarion University, Pennsylvania; reviewer, *ALAN Review;* coeditor of *Poets' Perspectives;* editor of *Exercise Exchange;* director of Penn Rivers Writing Project, an affiliate of the National Writing Project. **Essays:** Maureen Daly; Conrad Richter.

DUNLOP, Eileen. Writer of novels for children and young adults, including *The Maze Stone, Clementina, The House on the Hill, The Valley of Deer, Finn's Island,* and *Green Willow's Secret.* Former headmistress, Preparatory School of Dollar Academy. **Essays:** Josephine Kamm; Joan Lingard; Geraldine McCaughrean.

EAGLEN, Audrey. Order Department Manager, Cuyahoga County Public Library, Cleveland; Assistant Professor, Kent State University, Kent, Ohio; contributing editor, *Collection Building;* columnist, *School Library Journal;* reviewer, *New York Times Book Review* and other journals. Author of *Buying Books: A Practical Guide for Librarians,* 1989. **Essays:** Anonymous (*Go Ask Alice*); Francesca Lia Block; Judy Blume; Lois Duncan; Norma Klein; Barbara Wersba.

EDWARDS, Edna Earl. Instructor, West Georgia College, Carrollton; reviewer, *ALAN Review;* author of two young adult biographies for Salem Press. **Essays:** Robin F. Brancato; Gloria Miklowitz.

ELLEMAN, Barbara. Distinguished Scholar of Children's Books, Marquette University, Milwaukee; creator and editor-in-chief, *Book Links: Connecting Books, Libraries, and Classrooms;* former editor, Children's Books Section, American Library Association's *Booklist,* Chicago. Author of *Tomie dePaola, His Art and His Stories,* 1999. **Essay:** Nancy Bond.

ENO, Laurie Ann. Graduate student, Center for the Study of Children's Literature, Simmons College. **Essay:** Rosa Guy.

ERICSON, Bonnie O. Associate Professor of English Education, California State University, Northridge. Former high school teacher; reviewer, *ALAN Review;* wrote a column in *California English* for five years. **Essays:** Christopher Crutcher; Hadley Irwin.

ESSELMAN, Mary D. Instructor and coordinator of writing program, Georgetown University, Washington, D.C. Contributor, *Beacham's Guide to Literature for Young Adults.* **Essays:** Sandra Cisneros; Terry McMillan.

EVANS, Gwyneth. Instructor, Malaspina University College, Vancouver Island, British Columbia. Contributor to *Canadian Children's Literature, Canadian Children's Literature,* and *The Lion and the Unicorn.* **Essays:** John Christopher; Kit Pearson; K.M. Peyton; Rosemary Sutcliff; Geoffrey Trease.

EVANS, Ron. Professor of English and former Dean of Arts and Sciences, University of West Florida, Pensacola: author of three monographs, numerous journal articles, and three books. **Essays:** Ken Kesey; J.D. Salinger; Kurt Vonnegut.

FORMAN, Jack. Reference/bibliographic services librarian, Mesa College Library, San Diego; book reviewer for *Library Journal, School Library Journal,* and *Journal of Youth Services in Libraries.* Author of *Presenting Paul Zindel,* 1988, and of several articles on children's literature. **Essays:** Anne Frank; Robert Lipsyte; Nicholasa Mohr; Walter Dean Myers; Chaim Potok; Paul Zindel.

FREEMAN, Maggie. Freelance writer and tutor in community education, Essex. Former regular contributor of Y.A. book reviews to *The Sunday Times.* **Essay:** Norman Silver.

FULLER, Lawrence B. Instructor, Bloomsburg University, Pennsylvania; contributor, *Beacham's Guide to Literature for Young Adults.* **Essays:** Phil Caputo; Sandra Scoppetone.

GARRETT, Linda. High school librarian; Ph.D. candidate, Texas Woman's University, Denton; author of two articles for *Masterplots* series and a book of media center skills for Neal-Schuman Press. **Essays:** Jean Fritz; Kathryn Lasky.

GIBSON, Lois Rauch. Professor of English and Chair of the Department of Language and Literature at Coker College, Hartsville, South Carolina. **Essay:** Mark Mathabane.

GLEASON, Virginia L. Children's librarian, Springfield-Greene County Public Library, Missouri. Author of a children's book review column for ten years for Gannett Press's Pennywhistle Press. **Essays:** James Houston; Theodore Taylor.

GOULD, Karen J. Freelance writer. **Essays:** C.J. Cherryh; Ayn Rand; Joan D. Vinge.

GOUGH, John. Lecturer in Mathematics Education, Victoria College, Malvern, Victoria. Author of several articles on children's literature, including "The Dark is Rising: An Assessment" in *English in Education,* 1985, and "Reconsidering Judy Blume's Young Adult Novel *Forever*" in *Use of English,* 1985. **Essays:** John Marsden; Ivan Southall.

GREENLAW, M. Jean. Regents Professor, University of North Texas, Denton. Author of *Ranch Dressing: The Story of Western Wear,* 1993, and *Welcome to the Stock Show,* 1997. **Essays:** John Christopher; H. M. Hoover; Kathryn Lasky; Carolyn Meyer; Zibby Oneal; Meredith Ann Pierce; Ouida Sebestyen.

GRONER, Marlene San Miguel. Department of Humanities, State University of New York, College at Farmingdale. Co-author, *A Blueprint for Writers,* 1992; contributor, *Beacham's Guide to Literature for Young Adults.* **Essay:** Robert Heinlein.

GUTTENBERG, Laurie Schwartz. Instructor, State University of New York, College at Farmingdale and College at Old Westbury. **Essays:** Jeannette Eyerly; Howard Fast; Joanne Greenberg; Betty Cavanna.

HAGEN, Lyman B. Professor of English, Arkansas State University; author of books and articles on a wide range of American writers; contributor, *Beacham's Guide to Literature for Young Adults.* **Essay:** Maya Angelou.

HAMLEY, Dennis. University instructor, Hertfordshire; school librarian; reviewer, *The School Librarian* and *Times Educational Supplement*; organizes the *Lending Our Minds Out* residential creative writing courses for children. Author of children's books, including *Hare's Choice, Badger's Fate, Tigger and Friends,* and *The War and Freddy.* **Essays:** Nicholas Fisk; Robert Leeson; Robert Swindells.

HANNIGAN, Jane Anne. Professor Emerita, Columbia University, New York; editor, *The Best of Library Literature.* Author and editor of numerous articles and books. **Essays:** Annette Curtis Klause; Sonia Levitin.

HEBLEY, Diane. Freelance writer and part-time teacher. Regular columnist on children's books for *New Zealand Listener,* 1985-88. Author of the bibliography *Off the Shelf: Twenty-One Years of New Zealand Books for Children,* 1980, and of the children's books *A Is for Albatross,* 1981, *High on a Hilltop,* 1984, *The Gully That Gabriel Found,* 1985, *Jack Mackenzie and His Dog,* 1986, and *The Ballad of Young Nick: How He Sailed with Captain Cook,* 1987, and of articles in *Landfall* and other periodicals. **Essays:** Tessa Duder.

HELLER, Terry. Department of English, Coe College, Cedar Rapids, Iowa. Contributor, *Beacham's Guide to Literature for Young Adults, Dictionary of Literary Biography,* and Salem Press publications; author of *The Turn of the Screw: Bewildered Vision.* **Essays:** Orson Scott Card; Frank Herbert.

HENDRICKSON, Linnea. Part-time teacher, College of Education, University of New Mexico. Author of *Children's Literature: A Guide to the Criticism,* 1987, and of numerous articles on children's literature. **Essays:** Mel Glenn; Minfong Ho; Francis Temple.

HIGGINS, James E. Professor of Education, Queens College, City University of New York. Author of *Beyond Words: Mystical Fancy in Children's Literature,* 1970. **Essay:** Mark Twain.

HILL, Elbert R. Professor of children's and adolescent literature, Southeastern Oklahoma State University, Durant. Contributor, *Beacham's Guide to Literature for Young Adults*; author of "A Hero for the Movies," in *Children's Novels and the Movies.* **Essays:** Sue Ellen Bridgers; Leon Garfield; Monica Hughes; Theodore Taylor.

HILL, Patricia. Elementary school teacher, Vancouver, British Columbia; graduate student, Children's Literature, Center for the Study of Children's Literature, Simmons College, Boston; intern for the managing editor, *Horn Book* Magazine; member, Children's Literature Roundtable, Vancouver, and Canadian Children's Book Center. **Essays:** Brian Doyle; Sarah Ellis; Elizabeth George Speare.

HIMMEL, Maryclare O'Donnell. Graduate, Center for the Study of Children's Literature, Simmons College, Boston. Contributor *Sixth Book of Junior Authors and Illustrators* and *A Reader's Companion to Twentieth Century Children's Literature*; editor for children's books, *Boston Globe.* **Essays:** Eve Bunting; Sheila Greenwald.

HIXON, Martha. Ph.D. in English, University of Southwestern Louisiana, 1997. **Essay:** Charles de Lint; Donna Napoli; Terri Windling; Patricia Wrede.

HOLLINDALE, Peter. Instructor in English, York University, England; author of *Choosing Books for Children,* 1974, *Ideology* *and the Children's Book,* 1988, and several articles on children's literature and drama. **Essays:** Jan Needle; Mary Stewart.

HUNT, Caroline C. Department of English, College of Charleston, South Carolina. Contributor of numerous articles to various publications, including *Beacham's Guide to Literature for Young Adults* and *Dictionary of Literary Biography.* **Essays:** Vivien Alcock; Cynthia Harnett; Robert Leeson; Michelle Magorian; Jan Mark.

ISKANDER, Sylvia Patterson. Professor of English, University of Southwestern Louisiana, Lafayette; guest editor, *Children's Literature Quarterly,* 1989. Author of *Rousseau's Emile and Early Children's Literature,* 1971, and of the entry on Isaac Bashevis Singer in *Dictionary of Literary Biography,* and other articles on children's literature, including "Arabic Adventurers and American Investigators: Cultural Values in Adolescent Detective Fiction" for *Children's Literature.* **Essay:** Robert Cormier; Cynthia Voigt.

JENKINSON, David H. Associate Dean, Faculty of Education, University of Manitoba, Winnipeg. Author of essays in *Profiles* and *Meeting the Challenge,* and contributor to *The Junior Encyclopedia of Canada* and *Twentieth-Century Children's Writers;* editor of electronic reviewing journal *CM.* **Essays:** William Bell; Karleen Bradford; Martha Brooks; Lesley Choyce; Marilyn Halvorson; Linda Holeman; Julie Johnston; Paul Kropp; Alison Lohans; Kevin Major; Carol Matas; O. R. Melling; Don Trembath; Diana Wieler; Budge Wilson.

JOHN, Judith Gero. Assistant Professor of Literature, Southwest Missouri State University, Springfield. Author of several articles; contributor, *Dictionary of Literary Biography.* **Essays:** Dean Hughes; John Rowe Townsend.

JOHNSON, Deidre. Assistant Professor, West Chester University, Pennsylvania. Editor of *Stratemeyer Pseudonyms and Series Books: An Annotated Bibliography of Stratemeyer and Stratemeyer Syndicate Publications,* 1983; author of numerous essays on series books and children's literature. **Essays:** Ellen Conford; Keith Robertson.

JOHNSTON, Susanne L. Former lecturer in English, University of Wisconsin, Stout, Menominee, Wisconsin. Reviewer, *ALAN Review;* co-author (with Elizabeth Poe) of *Focus on Relationships.* **Essays:** Jean Craighead George; Chap Reaver.

JONES, Patrick. Manager, Tecumseh Branch, Allen County Public Library, Fort Wayne, Indiana. **Essays:** Christopher Pike; R.L. Stine.

KAYWELL, Joan F. Instructor, University of South Florida, Tampa. Former teacher of high school English, Kathleen High School, Lakeland, Florida; Executive Secretary for the Florida Council of Teachers of English (FCTE); contributor to numerous journals, including *ALAN Review;* author, *Adolescent Literature as a Complement to the Classics* and *Adolescents At Risk: Fiction and Nonfiction for Young Adults, Parents, and Professionals.* **Essay:** Bette Greene.

KEENAN, Hugh T. Professor of English, Georgia State University, Atlanta. Author of articles on Old English, Middle English, and medieval literature; essays on James Marshall, Doris B. Smith,

Molesworth, Robert Burch, and Joel Chandler Harris. Editor of *Papers by Medievalists,* 1971, *Narrative Theory and Children's Literature, Typology and English Medieval Literature,* 1992, "Narrative Theory and Children's Literature" issue of *Studies in the Literary Imagination,* 1985, and *Joel Chandler Harris: The Author in His Time and Ours,* 1986. **Essays:** Shirley Rousseau Murphy; Doris Buchanan Smith; T.H. White.

KENNEY, Donald J. Academic Librarian, Assistant to the University Librarian, Virginia Polytechnic Institute and State University; former middle school librarian; co-editor, American Library Association's *Journal of Youth Services in Libraries* (JOY); editor, "Library Connection" column, *ALAN Review;* former co-editor of the "Young Adult Literature" column in the *English Journal.* Contributor of articles on young adult literature, library literacy, and reference service to various journals. **Essays:** Frank Bonham; Katherine Paterson.

KIES, Cosette. Chair and Professor, Department of Library and Information Studies, Northern Illinois University. Author of numerous articles and books, including *Supernatural Fiction for Teens,* 1992, *Presenting Young Adult Horror Fiction,* 1992, and *Presenting Lois Duncan,* 1994. **Essay:** Richie Tankersley Cusick.

KINGMAN, Lee. Director, *Horn Book,* Boston; former assistant and juvenile editor, Houghton Mifflin, Boston; book editor, poster and calendar designer. Author of numerous books for children and adults. **Essays:** Esther Forbes; Florence Crannell Means; Howard Pyle.

KNIGHT, Judson. Freelance writer, Atlanta, Georgia. **Essays:** Maya Angelou; Eve Bunting; Sheila Greenwald; Joan Lingard; Mark Mathabane; Geraldine McCaughrean; Phyllis Reynolds Naylor; Uri Orlev; Robert Newton Peck; Lois F. Ruby; Marilyn Sachs; Jan Slepian; Phyllis A. Whitney.

LAFFERTY, Fiona. Freelance editor and writer. Former editor of *British Book News Children's Books;* children's books editor of *The Daily Telegraph;* advisor to *Good Book Guide* and compiler of the annual *Good Book Guide to Children's Books.* **Essays:** Kenneth Lillington; Judith O'Neill.

LAWRENCE, Keith. Associate Professor, American Literature, Brigham Young University, Provo, Utah. Author of articles on early American narratives and contemporary Asian American literature. **Essays:** Eloise Jarvis McGraw; Toni Morrison; Farley Mowat; Lensey Namioka; Amy Tan; Jessamyn West; Robb White.

LAZIM, Anne. Librarian, Centre for Language in Primary Education, London. Chair of the British Section of the International Board on Books for Young People (IBBY). **Essays:** Robert Swindells.

LENTZ, Kate. Graduate student, Center for the Study of Children's Literature, Simmons College, Boston. **Essays:** Ann Head; Linda Hoy; Hans Peter Richter.

LENTZ, Parish. Middle school teacher, Providence Country Day School, Rhode Island. **Essay:** Glendon Swarthout.

LESESNE, Teri S. University instructor of children's and young adult literature. Contributor of reviews to various journals. **Essays:** Terry Davis; Mel Glenn.

LEWIS, Leon. Professor of English, Appalachian State University, Boone. Author of *Henry Miller: The Major Writings*, 1986; contributor to the *Dictionary of Literary Biography*; regular contributor to *Magill's Cinema Journal*. **Essays:** Langston Hughes; June Jordan; William Kotzwinkle; Chris Lynch.

LIVINGSTON, Myra Cohn. Senior Extension Instructor, University of California, Los Angeles; lecturer on poetry; former creative writing instructor for children, Dallas Public Library; instructor, Los Angeles County Museum of Art, Beverly Hills Public Library, and University of California Elementary School, Los Angeles; former instructor and poet-in-residence, Beverly Hills Unified School District. Author of fiction and poetry for children and adults. **Essays:** Arnold Adoff; Harry Behn; Paul Janeczko; Eve Merriam.

LOWE-EVANS, Mary. Instructor, University of West Florida, Pensacola. Author of *Crimes against Fecundity: Joyce and Population Control*, 1989, and *Frankenstein: Mary Shelley 's Wedding Guest*, 1993. **Essays:** Margaret Atwood; Anthony Burgess; Eilis Dillon; Nadine Gordimer; Sylvia Plath.

LOWERY-MOORE, Hollis. Chair of Language, Literacy, and Special Populations, Sam Houston State University, Huntsville; teacher of middle and secondary school reading. Contributor to several journals, including *Exercise Exchange* and the *ALAN Review*. **Essays:** Janet Bode; Madeleine L'Engle; Louise Moeri; Cynthia Rylant.

LYSTAD, Mary. Former research sociologist, National Institute of Mental Health, Washington, D.C. Author of *A Child's World*, 1974, *From Dr. Mather to Dr. Seuss: 200 Years of American Books for Children*, 1980, *At Home in America*, 1982, and several books for children. **Essays:** Joan Aiken; William Armstrong; Olive Ann Burns; Betsy C. Byars; Eleanor Cameron; Rebecca Caudill; Bill and Vera Cleaver; Bruce Clements; Hila Colman; Clyde Edgerton; Nikki Giovanni; E.L. Konigsburg; Elizabeth Foreman Lewis; Sharon Bell Mathis; Harry Mazer, Norma Fox Mazer; Emily Neville; Joan Lowery Nixon; Scott O'Dell; John Tunis; Alice Walker; Richard Wright.

MacLENNAN, Alexandra. Freelance writer, Toronto, Canada; former professor, Seneca College of A.A. & T. **Essays:** Nina Bawden.

MacRAE, Cathi Dunn. Young adult specialist in Maryland and Colorado libraries for nineteen years. Editor of *Voice of Youth Advocates* (*VOYA*). Author of "The Young Adult Perplex" review column for *Wilson Library Bulletin*, 1988-1995; winner of the 1995 Econo-Clad/ALA/YALSA Award for Outstanding Achievement in the Development of a Literature Program for Young Adults. Author of *Presenting Young Adult Fantasy Fiction*, 1998.

MAPPIN, Alf. Editor of three Australian journals about children's literature: *Magpies, The Literature Base*, and *Papers: Explorations into Children's Literature*. **Essay:** Allan Baillie.

MATHIS, Janelle. Professor of English, University of North Texas, Denton. **Essays:** Tom A. Barron; Malcolm Bosse; Tom Feelings; James Forman; Francine Pascal; Johanna Reiss.

McEWEN, Fred. Professor of English, Waynesburg College, Pennsylvania. Author of numerous articles; contributor, *Beacham's Guide to Literature for Young Adults*. **Essays:** John Knowles; Jack London; Upton Sinclair; H.G. Wells.

McKINNEY, Caroline S. High school teacher. Contributor of articles on young adult literature to *English Journal, ALAN Review, Beacham's Guide to Literature for Young Adults*, and Instructor's *Middle Years*. **Essays:** Pam Conrad; Frances A. Miller; Joyce Carol Thomas; Ellen Emerson White.

MERCIER, Cathryn M. Associate Director and Assistant Professor, Center for the Study of Children's Literature, Simmons College, Boston; former Chair, *Boston Globe-Horn Book* Award and member, 1994 Caldecott Committee. Author of *Presenting Zibby Oneal* (with Susan Bloom) and reviews for *Five Oak*. **Essays:** Brock Cole; Amy Ehrlich; Paula Fox; Cynthia D. Grant.

MILLER, Etta. Instructor, Curriculum & Instruction, Texas Christian University, Fort Worth; developed drama strategies for helping students respond to literature. Contributor, *Beacham's Guide to Literature for Young Adults*. **Essays:** Jean Little; Jane Yolen.

MILLICHAP, Joseph R. Professor of English, Western Kentucky University, Bowling Green. Author of four books and more than fifty articles on American literature; contributor, *Beacham's Guide to Literature for Young Adults*. **Essays:** Carson McCullers; Margaret Mitchell; John Steinbeck.

MOE, Christian H. Professor of Theatre, Southern Illinois University, Carbondale; director of Playwrights' Program, Association for Theater in Higher Education. Author of *Creating Historical Drama* (with George McCalmon), 1965, and of an essay on D.H. Lawrence as playwright, and, with Cameron Garbutt, of several plays for children. Joint editor of *The William and Mary Theatre: A Chronicle*, 1968, "Bibliography of Theatrical Craftsmanship" (published annually in several journals), 1971-80, and *Six New Plays for Children*, 1971. **Essays:** Nathaniel Benchley; Marjorie Kinnan Rawlings; Colin Thiele.

MORGAN, Kareo Ferris. Ph.D. candidate; freelance writer. **Essays:** Michael Dorris; Jamaica Kincaid; Art Spiegelman; Laurence Yep.

MORTON, Gerald W. Department of English, Auburn University, Montgomery. Contributor, *Beacham's Guide to Literature for Young Adults*. **Essays:** James Herriot; Sterling North.

MOSBY, Charmaine Allmon. Professor of English, Western Kentucky University, Bowling Green. Contributor, *Beacham's Guide to Literature for Young Adults*. **Essays:** Monica Hughes; Bobbie Ann Mason; N. Scott Momaday; Patricia Moyes; Anne Rice; Anne Tyler; Elizabeth Yates.

MOSLEY, Mattie J. Associate Professor of Library Science, Louisiana State University, Shreveport. Contributor, *Beacham's Guide to Literature for Young Adults, Masterplots 11*, and *Louisiana Library Bulletin*. **Essay:** Elizabeth Gray Vining.

MURRAY, John. English Department Head, Australian Catholic University, Strathfield. Author of articles on Patricia Wrightson and Rudyard Kipling; reviewer of Australian children's literature. **Essays:** John Marsden; Patricia Wrightson.

NELSON, Claudia. Assistant Professor of English, Southwest Texas State University. Author of *Boys Will Be Girls: The Feminine Ethic and British Children's Fiction, 1857-1917* and of assorted articles on children's literature. **Essays:** Sylvia Louise Engdahl; Sally Watson.

NELSON, Harold. Professor of English and Literature, Minot State University, North Dakota; director of the Northern Plains Writing Project, and North Dakota State coordinator for the National Writing Project. Contributor, *Beacham's Guide to Literature for Young Adults* and *Masterplots*. **Essays:** Stephen King; Julius Lester.

NEWBERY, Linda. English teacher; reviewer, *School Librarian* and *Books for Keeps*. Author of young adult fiction, including *Run with the Hare, Hard and Fast*, and a trilogy set during World War I and in Ireland: *Some Other War, The Rind Ghosts*, and *The Weaving of the Green*. **Essays:** K. M. Peyton; Jean Ure.

NIEUWENHUIZEN, Agnes. Freelance writer. **Essay:** Gillian Rubinstein.

NILSEN, Alleen Pace. Professor of English and assistant vice president of Academic Affairs, Arizona State University, Tempe. Author of *Presenting M.E. Kerr*, 1986, and *Literature for Today's Young Adults* (with Ken Donelson), 5th edition, 1997, and of numerous articles in *School Library Journal, College English, English Journal*, and *Language Arts*. **Essay:** Alice Childress.

O'NEAL, Michael J. Freelance writer and editor; former college teacher; holds a Ph.D. from Bowling Green State University. **Essays:** Judie Angell.

PATON WALSH, Jill. English teacher, Enfield Girls Grammar School, Middlesex; Whittall lecturer, Library of Congress, Washington, D.C. Author of several books for children and adults. **Essays:** Nina Bawden; L.M. Boston; Penelope Farmer; Ursula K. Le Guin.

PAUL, Lissa. Professor of English, University of New Brunswick, Fredericton. Author of *Growing with Books*, 1988. **Essays:** Aidan Chambers; Ted Hughes.

PAUSACKER, Jenny. Freelance writer of plays, educational kits, short stories, and novels. Author of two novels for young adults, *What Are Ya?* and *Can You Keep a Secret?*, and a junior novel, *Fast Forward*. **Essay:** Ivan Southall.

PEARSON, Kit. Author of children's books, including *The Daring Game*, 1986, *A Handful of Time*, 1987, *The Sky Is Falling*, 1989, *The Singing Basket*, 1990, *Looking at the Moon*, 1991, and *The Lights Go on Again*, 1993. **Essay:** Sylvia Cassedy.

PFLIEGER, Pat. Assistant Professor of English, West Chester University, Pennsylvania. Author of *A Reference Guide to Modern Fantasy for Children*, 1984, and *Beverly Cleary*, 1991. **Essay:** Jane Langton.

PIEHL, Kathy. Assistant Professor and Reference Librarian, Mankato State University, Minnesota. Contributor of articles on children's and young adult books in *Children's Literature in Education, New Advocate, Children's Literature Association Quarterly, English Journal, Journal of Youth Services in Libraries, Voice of Youth Advocates*, and other journals. **Essays:** Patricia Calvert; Gillian Cross; Julie Reece Deaver; Jan Mark; Marsha Qualey; Barbara Rogasky; Margaret Rostkowski; Virginia Euwer Wolff; Jane Breskin Zalben.

PINNEY, Reba. Professor of Education, Ohio University, Athens. Author of various journal articles and reviews. **Essays:** Marchette Chute; Esther Hautzig; Anne Holm; David Klass; William Weaver.

POE, Elizabeth A. Associate Professor of English, Radford University, Virginia. Editor, *Signal*; past President, Assembly on Literature for Adolescents of NCTE (ALAN); former book review editor, *ALAN Review*; former chair, Colorado Blue Spruce Young Adult Book Award Committee. Author of *Focus on Sexuality, Focus on Relationships*, and journal articles. **Essay:** Alden R. Carter.

PRICE, Catherine. Associate Professor, Department of Secondary Education, Valdosta State College, Georgia; former school media specialist. **Essay:** Patricia Beatty; Paul Fleischman.

PROTHEROUGH, Robert. Formerly senior lecturer in English in Education, Hull University. Author of seven books for teachers and lecturers, numerous articles; editor, *English in Education*; reviewer for many journals, including *Times Educational Supplement* and *School Librarian*. **Essays:** Bernard Ashley; Aidan Chambers; Peter Dickinson; Alan Garner; William Mayne; George Orwell; Robert Westall.

RANSON, Nicholas. Associate Professor of English, University of Akron; published poet and regular contributor to the *Henry Society Bulletin*; co-editor, *Ideological Approaches to Shakespeare*, 1992. **Essays:** Arthur Conan Doyle; Eve Garnett; Ted Hughes.

RAY, Sheila. Editor, *School Librarian*; retired librarian and library school lecturer in literature and librarianship for young people. Author of *Children's Fiction: A Handbook for Librarians*, 1972; *The Blyton Phenomenon*, 1982; and *Library Service to Schools*, 3rd edition, 1982; contributor of reviews and articles to several periodicals, including *Children's Literature Abstracts*. **Essays:** Eileen Dunlop; Adele Geras.

REED, Arthea J.S. Professor and Chair, Educational Department, University of North Carolina, Asheville; reviewer, *ALAN Review*. Author of *Reaching Adolescents: The Young Adult Book and the School*, 1985; *Comics to Classics: A Parent's Guide to Books for Teens and Preteens, Teacher's Guides to the Signet Classic Steinbeck Novellas*, and numerous articles in the field of young adult literature. **Essay:** Christopher and James Lincoln Collier.

REISS, John. Instructor, Department of English, Western Kentucky University, Bowling Green. **Essay:** Jim Wayne Miller.

RICH, Susan. Graduate student, Center of the Study of Children's Literature, Simmons College, Boston. Intern, *Horn Book*. **Essays:** Nancy Garden; Norton Juster.

ROBERTS, Garyn G. Assistant Professor, Department of American Thought and Language, Michigan State University. Author and editor of several books on American literary and cultural topics, including *Dick Tracy and American Culture: Morality and Mythology, Text and Context*; author of "Humor and the Apocalypse: Jack London's *The Scarlet Plague*" in *THALIA: A Journal of Literary Humor*. **Essay:** Ray Bradbury.

ROSS, Linda. Freelance writer. **Essays:** Tanith Lee; Stephen Levenkron; C.S. Lewis; Dalton Trumbo; Elie Wiesel.

RUTHERFORD, Leonie Margaret. Instructor, Department of English and Communication Studies, University of New England, Australia. Contributor, *Dictionary of Literary Biography*; wrote articles about eighteenth-century British literature, Australian literature, historical and textual bibliography, and children's literature. **Essays:** Jane Gardam; Robin Klein.

RUTLEDGE, Walker. Instructor in English, Western Kentucky University, Bowling Green; Director, English Honors Program. **Essays:** Eldridge Cleaver; Roald Dahl; Joseph Heller.

SAULSBURY, Rebecca. Graduate student in American Studies, Purdue University. **Essays:** Francesca Lia Block; Richie Tankersley Cusick; Ron Koertge; Jane Langton; Lensey Namioka.

SAXBY, Maurice. Former English department head, lecturer, and teacher, Kuring-gai College, now University of Technology, Sydney, Australia; developed Australia's first master's program in children's literature; first national president and lifetime member of the Children's Book Council of Australia. Served as judge for the Hans Christian Andersen awards and the Australian Children's Book of the Year awards. Author of several reference works on Australian young people's literature, including *A History of Australian Children's Literature, 1841-1941*, *A History of Australian Children's Literature, 1941-1970*, and *The Proof of the Puddin': Australian Children's Literature, 1970-1990*. Contributor to various journals and reference works. **Essays:** Gary Crew; Simon French; Joan Phipson.

SCHAFER, Elizabeth D. Independent scholar; Ph.D. in American History, Auburn University. Co-author of *Women Who Made a Difference in Alabama*, 1995, and contributor of article to *African American Review*. **Essays:** Margaret Anderson; Sharon Draper; Jean Ferris; Carolyn Meyer; Rob Thomas.

SCHMIDT, Gary D. Chairman, Department of English, Calvin College, Grand Rapids, Michigan. Reviewer for *ALANReview*. Author of *Robert McCloskey*, 1989, *Hugh Lofting*, 1992, and *Katherine Paterson*, forthcoming. Co-editor of *The Voice of the Narrator in Children's Literature*, 1988, and *Sitting at the Feet of the Past: Retelling the North American Folktale*, 1992. **Essays:** Patricia Clapp; Minfong Ho; Felice Holman; Jean Lee Latham; Myron Levoy; Beverly Naidoo; Uri Orlev.

SEITER, Richard D. Associate Professor of English, Central Michigan University, Mount Pleasant. Author of articles on Eleanor Cameron, Roald Dahl, Ezra I. Keats, Robert C. O'Brien, and Henry Treece. **Essays:** Jane Leslie Conly; Caroline B. Cooney; Robert C. O'Brien.

SHELTON, Pamela L. Columnist and freelance writer. **Essay:** Gary Soto.

SHUTE, Carolyn. Graduate, Center of the Study of Children's Literature, Simmons College, Boston; Content Research Editor, Houghton Mifflin. Instructor in children's literature, University of Prince Edward Island, Charlottetown, and Northern Essex Community College, Massachusetts; reviewer, *Horn Book* Guide; contributor, "Bookviews." **Essays:** Berlie Doherty; Ron Koertge; Mildred Pitts Walter.

SMITH, Karen Patricia. Assistant Professor, Graduate School of Library and Information Studies, Queens College, Flushing; board member, Children's Literature Association. Author of *The English Psychological Fantasy Novel: A Bequest of Time*, 1985, and *Claiming a Place in the University: The Portrayal of Minorities in Seven Works by Andre Norton*, 1986; editor, with Rod McGillis, of *Special Section on Black Children's Literature* in *Children's Literature Association Quarterly*, 1988; contributor of articles and essays to several journals, including *Children's Literature Association Quarterly, Wilson Library Bulletin, School Library Journal, Journal of Youth Services in Libraries*, and *Library Trends*. **Essays:** Susan Cooper; Mildred D. Taylor.

SNYDER, Mary. Graduate student in Library and Information Science, Texas Woman's University. Director of Texas Women's University Children's Library. Instructor in Children's Literature. Teacher at the elementary and secondary levels and secondary school librarian. **Essay:** Brent Ashabranner.

SPENCER, Albert F. Assistant Professor of Education, University of Nevada, Las Vegas. Author of articles on education and book reviewer for the *Library Journal*. **Essays:** Nat Hentoff; Zoa Sherburne.

STAHL, John D. Associate Professor of English, Virginia Tech, Blacksburg, Virginia. Author of *Mark Twain, Culture and Gender* (Georgia, 1994) and of articles about children's literature in *Children's Literature, The Lion and the Unicorn*, and other journals. **Essays:** Katie Letcher Lyle; Phyllis Reynolds Naylor; Doris Orgel.

STEFFEL, Susan B. Associate Professor of English, Central Michigan University, Mount Pleasant, Michigan; former high school teacher; contributor of articles and reviews to journals; co-author, *Fantasy Literature for Children and Young Adults*. **Essays:** Linda Crew, Han Nolan, Gary Paulsen, Randy Powell.

STERN, Madeleine B. Freelance writer; partner in Leona Rostenberg and Madeleine Stern Rare Books, New York. Author and editor of numerous books on 19th-century literature. **Essay:** Louisa May Alcott.

STONE, Michael. Senior lecturer in English, University of Wallongong, Australia. Contributor to children's literature journals, including *Children's Literature in Education, Reading Time, Viewpoint,* and *Orana*. **Essays:** James Aldridge; Sonya Hartnett; James Moloney; Eleanor Spence.

STRICKLAND, Robbie W. Associate Professor of Secondary

Education, Valdosta State College, Georgia; coordinator of conference on young adult literature. Contributor, *ALAN Review*. **Essays:** Avi; Sue Ellen Bridgers.

SUKRAW, Tracy J. Freelance writer; reviewer of books for children and young adults; author of articles for *Episcopal Times*. **Essays:** Janine Boissard; William Gibson; Fred Gipson; Barbara Hall; Lynne Reid Banks; Muriel Spark; Walter Wangerin, Jr.

SUTHERLAND, Zena. Professor Emerita, University of Chicago Graduate Library School; associate editor, *Bulletin of the Center for Children's Books*. Author of *History in Children's Books*, 1967, *The Best in Children's Books*, 1973 (revised 1980, 1986), *Burning Bright*, 1979, *Close to the Sun*, 1979, *Barnboken i USA* (with Fred Erisman), 1986, and, with M. Cunningham, *Across the World, From Sea to Shining Sea, Over the Moon, Promises to Keep, Slide Down the Sky, Arbuthnot Anthology* (with May Hill Arbuthnot), 4th edition 1976, *The Arbuthnot Lectures 1970-1979*, 1980, *Children in Libraries*, 1981, and *The Scott Foresman Anthology of Children's Literature* (with Myra Cohn Livingston), 1984. **Essay:** Cornelia Lynne Meigs.

TARBOX, Gwen Athene. Assistant Professor of American Literature, Children's Literature, and Ethnic Studies, California State University, Hayward. **Essays:** Michael Cadnum; Judith Ortiz Cofer; Christopher Paul Curtis; Victor Martinez; Jess Mowry.

TAYLOR, Jennifer. Freelance writer, reviewer, and editor; contributor to *Bookseller* and *School Librarian*. **Essay:** Michael Morpurgo.

THOMAS, Gillian. Associate Professor of English, Saint Mary's University, Halifax, Nova Scotia. Author of *Harriet Martineau*, 1985, and of numerous articles and reviews on 19th-century fiction and children's literature. **Essay:** Joseph Krumgold.

TODOROVICH, Divna. Staff member, Children's Literature Section, Subject Cataloging Division, Library of Congress, Washington, D.C. **Essay:** Welwyn Katz.

TOWNSEND, John Rowe. Part-time children's books editor, *Guardian*, Manchester and London; visiting lecturer, University of Pennsylvania, Philadelphia, and University of Washington, Seattle; May Hill Arbuthnot lecturer, Atlanta; Anne Carroll Moore lecturer, New York Public Library; Whittall lecturer, Library of Congress, Washington, D.C.; faculty member, Simmons College, Boston. Author of books for children and adults. **Essay:** Janni Howker.

TROTMAN, Felicity. Freelance editor and writer; fiction editor, Puffin, 1971-79, and Macmillan, 1980-82; co-founder, Signpost Books; has written on animals in the movies. **Essays:** Adèle Geras; Ann Halam.

TYE, Margaret M. College librarian, North Cheshire College, Warrington. **Essay:** Berlie Doherty.

TYLER, Jan. Instructor of English and German, Black River Technical College, Pocahontas, Arkansas; freelance writer of feature articles; President, Pocahontas School Board, Arkansas. Author of children's book, *Holly Lolly*; author of booklet of original skits used by and for teens in drug awareness/self esteem programs. **Essay:** Margaret Willey.

TYRKUS, Michael J. Freelance writer and filmmaker. Graduate student in English, University of Toledo, Ohio; assistant editor, Gale Research Inc., Detroit. **Essays:** Arthur C. Clarke; Michael Crichton.

VALENTIC, Suzanne M. Freelance writer and critic. **Essays:** James Baldwin; Linda Crew; Zora Neale Hurston; Suzanne Fisher Staples.

VANDERGRIFT, Kay E. Associate Professor, School of Communication, Information and Library Studies, Rutgers University, New Brunswick, New Jersey; children's book reviewer for *School Library Journal*. Author of *Child and Story: The Literary Connection*, 1980, and *Children's Literature: Theory, Research and Teaching*, 1989. **Essay:** Ntozake Shange.

WALSH, Karen E. Graduate student, Center for the Study of Children's Literature, Simmons College, Boston. Intern, *Horn Book* magazine. **Essays:** Ian Fleming; Patricia Hermes.

WELSH, Marcia. Reference librarian and cataloguer, Guilford Free Library, Connecticut. Reviewer for *Library Journal*. **Essays:** Jennifer Armstrong; Ernesto Bethancourt; Richard Blessing; Edwidge Danticat; Nancy Farmer; Karen Hesse; Sheila Solomon Klass; Trudy Krisher; Barbara Shoup; Ida Vos.

WHITE, Donna R. Assistant Professor of English, Clemson University, South Carolina Editor of *Books for Children*, a review service of Clemson University English Department. Member, Modern Language Association Children's Division and Children's Literature Association. **Essays:** Lloyd Alexander; Grace Chetwin; Kevin Crossley-Holland; Carol Kendall; Patricia McKillip; Andre Norton.

WHITE, Kerry. Freelance writer and bibliographer. Author of *Australian Children's Books: A Bibliography*, 1992, *Australian Children's Fiction: The Subject Guide*, 1993, and numerous articles and reviews on Australian writing. **Essays:** Ursula Dubosarsky; Catherine Jinks; Victor Kelleher; David Metzenthen; Garth Nix; Ruth Park; Colin Thiele.

WHITEHEAD, Frank. Reader in English and Education, University of Sheffield, 1973-81; editor, *Use of English*, 1969-75. Author of *The Disappearing Dais*, 1966, *Creative Experiment*, 1970, and *Children and Their Books* (with others), 1977. **Essays:** Hester Burton; A.E. Johnson.

WHITEHEAD, Winifred. Former senior lecturer in English literature and curriculum studies, Sheffield City Polytechnic. Author of *Different Faces: Growing Up with Books in a Multicultural Society*, 1988, *Old Lies Revisited: Young Readers and the Literature of War and Violence*, 1991, and many articles on children's writers. **Essay:** Lynne Reid Banks.

WIGAN, Angela. Freelance writer. Co-author of *A Short and Remarkable History of New York City*; has written for *Time* and the Museum of Modern Art, New York City. **Essay:** Elizabeth Coatsworth.

WILSON, Linda. Co-editor of *Journal of Youth Services in Libraries (JOY)*. Contributing annotator *to Books for* You, a publication of the National Council of Teachers of English. **Essays:** Alice Bach; Mildred Lee.

WINTERS, Louise J. Freelance writer. **Essays:** Terry Brooks; Tony Hillerman; Brian Jacques; Mercedes Lackey; Patricia Wrede.

WROBLE, Lisa A. Freelance writer and author of fiction and non-fiction for children and nonfiction for adults. Contributor to *Dictionary of Literary Biography*. **Essays:** Terry Brooks; Mary Higgins Clark; Karen Cushman; Lois Duncan; David Eddings; Jean Fritz; Johanna Hurwitz; Robin Klein; Dean R. Koontz; Anne McCaffrey; John Neufeld; R. A. Salvatore; Ian Serraillier; Mary Stewart; Margaret Weis; Tad Williams; Hilma Wolitzer.

YATES, Jessica. Former librarian, the School of St. David and St. Katharine, Homsey, London. Freelance writer; reviewer for *School Librarian, Times Educational Supplement,* the British Science Fiction Association, and the Tolkien Society. Author of *Tudors and Stuarts: An Annotated Bibliography of Children's Fiction,* 1977, the text for *A Middle-earth Album,* 1979, *Teenager to Young Adult: Recent Paperback Fiction for 13 to 19 Years,* 1986, and editor of *Dragons and Warrior Daughters: Fantasy Stories by Women Writers,* 1989. Author of articles on children's literature and librarianship in *Children's Literature in Education, Children's Book Bulletin, Books for Keeps, Times Educational Supplement,* and *School Librarian.* **Essays:** Diane Duane; Ann Halam; Douglas Hill; Allan Frewin Jones; Diana Wynne Jones; Louise Lawrence; J.R.R. Tolkien.

ZAIDMAN, Laura M. Professor of English, University of South Carolina, Sumter. Contributor to *Dictionary of Literary Biography,* and of articles in other journals. Editor of *British Children's Writers, 1880-1914,* Vol. 141 of the *Dictionary of Literary Biography.* Guest co-editor, with Lois Rauch Gibson, of *Children's Literature Association Quarterly,* winter 1991 issue. **Essays:** Harper Lee; Lois Lowry; Eleanora Tate.